The Concise Routledge Encyclopedia of the Documentary Film

The Concise Routledge Encyclopedia of the Documentary Film is a fully international reference work on the history of the documentary film from the Lumière brothers' Workers Leaving the Lumière Factory (1885) to Michael Moore's Fahrenheit 9/11 (2004).

Documentary film dates back to the last decades of the nineteenth century and has been practiced since then in every region of the world. This Encyclopedia provides a resource that critically analyzes that history in all its aspects. Entries examine individual films and the careers of individual filmmakers, but also include overview articles of national and regional documentary film history.

Previously published in three volumes, entries have been edited for the new, concise edition and two new entries have been added, on India and China.

The Concise Routledge Encyclopedia of the Documentary Film:

- discusses individual films, bringing together all aspects of documentary film.
- introduces filmmakers, including lesser-known filmmakers from countries such as India, Bosnia, China, and others.
- examines the documentary filmmaking traditions within nations and regions, including places such as Iran, Brazil, Portugal, and Japan.
- explores themes, issues, and representations in regard to specific documentary films, including human rights, modernism, homosexuality, and World War I, as well as types of documentary film such as newsreels and educational films.

This accessible concise edition provides an invaluable resource for both scholars and students. With stills from key films, this resource provides the decisive entry point into the history of an art form.

Ian Aitken is Professor, in the Department of Cinema and TV, Hong Kong Baptist University. He is the author of *Film and Reform: John Grierson and the British Documentary Film Movement* (Routledge, 1990, 1992), *The Documentary Film Movement: An Anthology* (Edinburgh University Press, 1998), *The Cinema of Alberto Cavalcanti: Realism, Surrealism and National Cinemas* (Flicks Books, 2000) and *The Encyclopedia of the Documentary Film*, three-volume set (Routledge, 2006).

The Concise Routledge Encyclopedia of the Documentary Film

Edited by
Ian Aitken

Routledge
Taylor & Francis Group
LONDON AND NEW YORK

First published as *The Encyclopedia of the Documentary Film* in 2006
This concise edition published 2013
by Routledge
2 Park Square, Milton Park, Abingdon, Oxon OX14 4RN

Simultaneously published in the USA and Canada
by Routledge
711 Third Avenue, New York, NY 10017

Routledge is an imprint of the Taylor & Francis Group, an informa business

British Library Cataloguing in Publication Data
A catalogue record for this book is available from the British Library

Library of Congress Cataloging in Publication Data
The concise Routledge encyclopedia of the documentary film / ed. by Ian Aitken.
p. cm.
Includes bibliographical references and index.
1. Documentary films–Encyclopedias. I. Aitken, Ian.
PN1995.9.D6C545 2011
070.1′8–dc23
2011024554

ISBN: 978-0-415-59642-8 (hbk)

Typeset in Baskerville
by Taylor & Francis Group

Printed and bound by CPI Group (UK) Ltd, Croydon, CR0 4YY

Contents

List of stills

Board of advisers

List of contributors

Ian Aitken
Hong Kong Baptist University

D. Jae Alexander
University of Southern Mississippi

Samara L. Allsop
Independent scholar

Joshua Amberg
University of California, Los Angeles

Carolyn Anderson
University of Massachusetts, Amherst

Kevin Taylor Anderson
University of Massachusetts, Amherst

Richard Armstrong
British Film Institute

Isabel Arredondo
State University of New York, Plattsburgh

Michael B. Baker
Independent scholar

Kees Bakker
Independent producer of documentaries

Charles Bane
Louisiana State University

Ilisa Barbash
Harvard University

Elke Bartel
Middle Tennessee State University

Stefano Baschiera
National University of Ireland, Cork

Gerd Bayer
University of Wisconsin, Whitewater

Phillip Bell
University of New South Wales, Australia

Nitzan Ben-Shaul
Tel-Aviv University

Jeff Bergin
Independent producer

Robert Beveridge
Napier University

Mira Binford
Quinnipiac University

Brett Bowles
Iowa State University

Melissa Bromley
British Film Institute National Film and Television Archive

John Burgan
Documentary filmmaker

Marina Burke
University College Dublin

Alan Burton
De Montfort University

Andreas Busche
Film critic and film archivist

Lou Buttino
University of North Carolina, Wilmington

José Cabeza San Deogracias
Complutense University, Madrid

María Elena de las Carreras-Kuntz
University of California, Los Angeles, and California State University, Northridge

Michael S. Casey
Graceland University

Catalina Ceron
Independent director and producer of documentaries

Michael Chanan
University of the West of England

David Chapman
University of East London

Thomas Cohen
Rhodes College

John Cook
Glasgow Caledonian University

Pat A. Cook
Brunel University

Sarah Cooper
University of Cambridge

Kirwan Cox
Concordia University, Canada

Sean Cubitt
University of Waikato, New Zealand

Jacobia Dahm
Johannes Gutenberg-University, Germany, and Columbia University

Fergus Daly
University College Dublin

Amy L. Darnell
Southern Illinois University, Carbondale

Jonathan Dawson
Griffith University

Annette Deeken
University of Trier, Germany

David Scott Diffrient
University of California, Los Angeles

Dean Duncan
Brigham Young University

Camille Deprez
Hong Kong Baptist University

Sarah Easen
British Universities Film and Video Council

Suzanne Eisenhut
San Francisco State University

Jack C. Ellis
Northwestern University (emeritus)

Robert A. Emmons, Jr
Rutgers University, Camden

Leo Enticknap
University of Teesside, Middlesbrough

Rafael de España
University of Barcelona

Dino Everett
UCLA Film and Television Archive

Kirsty Fairclough
University of Salford

Tamara L. Falicov
University of Kansas

Seth Feldman
York University, Canada

Ramona Fotiade
University of Glasgow

Steven R. Foxon
Independent scholar

Hugo Frey
University College, Chichester

Oliver Gaycken
University of Chicago

Jeffrey Geiger
University of Essex

Aaron Gerow
Yale University

Hal Gladfelder
University of Rochester

Marcy Goldberg
University of Zurich

Ian Goode
University of Glasgow

Barry Keith Grant
Brock University, Canada

Leger Grindon
Middlebury College

Tom Grochowski
Queens College, City University of New York

Sapna Gupta
University of Calgary

Roger Hallas
Syracuse University

Benjamin Halligan
York St John College, University of Leeds

Martin Halliwell
University of Leicester

Britta Hartmann
Universität der Künste Berlin

Vinzenz Hediger
Ruhr University, Bochum, Germany

Gillian Helfield
York University, Toronto, Canada

Walter Hess
Independent scholar

Jeremy Hicks
Queen Mary College, University of London

Christine Marie Hilger
University of Texas at Dallas

Jim Hillier
University of Reading

Roger Hillman
Australian National University

Lisa Hinrichsen
Boston University

Kay Hoffmann
Haus des Dokumentarfilms, Germany

Bert Hogenkamp
Netherlands Institute for Sound and Vision, and Utrecht University

Bruce Horsfield
University of Southern Queensland

Kerr Houston
Maryland Institute College of Art

Amanda Howell
Griffith University

Robert Hunt
Webster University

Michael Ingham
Lingnan University

Dina Iordanova
University of Leicester

Jeffrey Isaacs
University of Chicago

Gunnar Iversen
Trondheim University, Norway

D.B. Jones
Drexel University

Chris Jordan
Pennsylvania State University

Verónica Jordana
Independent scholar

Uli Jung
University of Trier, Germany

Brett Kashmere
Concordia University, Canada

Alexander L. Kaufman
Purdue University

Tammy A. Kinsey
University of Toledo

Michael Kogge
Fulbright Scholar in Iceland, 2000–1

Yves Laberge
Film historian and Series Editor, *Cinéma et Société*, Les Presses de l'Université Laval

Suzanne Langlois
York University, Canada

Maximilian le Cain
Independent filmmaker and writer

Charles Lee
St Martin's College

Neil Lerner
Davidson College

C. Melinda Levin
University of North Texas

Jean-Luc Lioult
Université de Provence

Derek Loh

André Loiselle
Carleton University

Alice Lovejoy
Yale University

David M. Lugowski
Manhattanville College

Catherine Lupton
Roehampton University of Surrey

Theresa C. Lynch
University of New Hampshire

Susan McFarlane-Alvarez
Georgia State University

Heather McIntosh
Pennsylvania State University

Luke McKernan
British Universities Film and Video Council

Misha MacLaird
Writer and editorial contractor

Joshua Malitsky
Northwestern University

Starr Marcello
Independent scholar

Gina Marchetti
University of Hong Kong

Harriet Margolis
Victoria University of Wellington, New Zealand

Christopher Meir
Concordia University, Canada

Paul Miller
Davidson College

Ángel Miquel
Universidad Autónoma del Estado de Morelos, Mexico

Julio Montero
Complutense University, Madrid

Patrick Murphy
Independent scholar, and York St John College, University of Leeds (emeritus)

Justine Nagan
University of Chicago

Caryn E. Neumann
Ohio State University

Abé Markus Nornes
University of Michigan

Harvey O'Brien
University College Dublin

Jules Odendahl-James
Southwestern Missouri State University

Dina Oirdanova
University of St Andrews

Tony Osborne
Gonzaga University

Derek Paget
University of Reading

Andreas Pagoulatos
Independent scholar

Silke Panse
University of Kent

María Antonia Paz Rebollo
Complutense University, Madrid

Judith Pernin
Ecole des Hautes Etudes in Science Sociales

Geraldene Peters
University of Auckland, New Zealand

Rod Phillips
Michigan State University, James Madison College

Shira Pinson
London Film School

Carl R. Plantinga
Calvin College

Reza Poudeh
Texas Southern University

Jason Price
New York University

Paula Rabinowitz
University of Minnesota, Twin Cities

Fernão Pessoa Ramos
Universidade de São Paulo

Laura Rascaroli
National University of Ireland, Cork

Richard Raskin
University of Aarhus, Denmark

Ramon Reichert
University of Art and Industrial Design, Linz, Austria

Robert C. Reimer
University of North Carolina, Charlotte

John Riley
British Universities Film and Video Council

Churchill Roberts
University of Florida

Michael D. Robinson
Doc Films, Chicago

Jane Roscoe
Griffith University

Tom Ruffles
National Extension College, Cambridge

Theresa Scandiffio
University of Chicago

Frank Scheide
University of Arkansas

Ralf Schenk
Film historian

Jesse Schlotterbeck
University of Iowa

Alexandra Schneider
Freie Universität, Berlin

Steven Jay Schneider
New York University

Danielle Schwartz
McGill University

Rada Sesic
International Documentary Film Festival Amsterdam, and International Film Festival Rotterdam

Jamie Sexton
University of Wales, Aberystwyth

Sharon Shelton-Colangelo
Northwest Vista College

Kevin Sherman
San Francisco State University

Philip L. Simpson
Brevard Community College, Palm Bay Campus

James M. Skinner
University of Victoria, Canada

Belinda Smaill
Monash University

Jean-Luc Smith

Ryan Smith
Clatsop Community College, Oregon

Beretta E. Smith-Shomade
University of Arizona

Gustavo Soranz
Independent scholar

Pierre Sorlin
University of Paris, Sorbonne

Nikos Stabakis
Independent scholar

Eva Maria Stadler
Fordham University

Sunny Stalter
Rutgers University

Cecile Starr
Film reviewer and film critic

D. Bruno Starrs
University of Melbourne

Tracy Stephenson Shaffer
Louisiana State University

Julianne Stewart
University of Southern Queensland

Martin Stollery
Southampton Institute

Dan Streible
University of South Carolina

Thomas Stubblefield
University of Illinois, Chicago

Catherine Summerhayes
Australian National University

Yvan Tardy
De Montfort University

Thomas Tode
Independent scholar

Peter Urquhart
University of Nottingham

Trudi Van Dyke
William Paterson University, and Rutgers

Cristina Vatulescu
Society of Fellows, Harvard University

Joe Wagner
University of North Carolina, Greensboro

Alistair Wardill
Harrow College

Charles Warren
Harvard University and Boston University

Mark Westmoreland
University of Texas, Austin

Catherine Wheatley
St John's College, University of Oxford

Helen Wheatley
University of Reading

Diane R. Wiener
University of Arizona

Danielle Williams
Auburn University

Deane Williams
Monash University

Gordon Williams
University of Wales, Lampeter

Keith Williams
University of Dundee

Ronald Wilson
University of Kansas

Sheena Wilson
University of Alberta, Canada

J. Emmett Winn
Auburn University

Charles C. Wolfe
University of California, Santa Barbara

Alan Wright
University of Canterbury, New Zealand

John Young
University of Nottingham

List of entries A–Z

H

I

J

K

L

Thematic list of entries

Films

Abel Gance: Yesterday and Tomorrow
Act of God
Adolescents, The (aka That Tender Age)
American Family, An
Anais Nin Observed
Angela: Portrait of a Revolutionary
Ark, The
Ascent of Man, The
Aubervilliers
Back of Beyond, The
Basic Training
Bataille du rail, La
Battle for Our Soviet Ukraine, The
Battle of Chile, The
Battle of China, The
Battle of Midway, The
Battle of Russia, The
Battle of San Pietro, The
Battle of the Somme, The
BBC: The Voice of Britain
Berlin: The Symphony of a Great City
Beruf: Neonazi
Black Box BRD
Blue Eyed
Bridge, The
Bronx Morning, A
Burden of Dreams
Burma Victory
Camera Natura
Canada Carries On
Cane Toads: An Unnatural History
Chair, The
Chang: A Drama of the Wilderness
Children at School
China!
Chronique d'un été
Chulas Fronteras
Churchill's Island
City, The
City of Gold
Close-Up
Coal Face
Contact
Cuba Sí!
Dead Birds
Death of a Princess
December 7
Del Mero Corazón
Desert Victory
Diary for Timothy, A
Dinner Party, The
Divided World, A
Divine Horsemen
Dockers
Dont Look Back
Drifters
Eiffel Tower, The
Enough to Eat?
Enthusiasm
Eternity
Être et avoir
Every Day Except Christmas
Exile and the Kingdom
Fall of the Romanov Dynasty, The
Family Portrait
Far from Vietnam
Finding Christa
Fires Were Started
First Love
For Love or Money
Forest of Bliss
400 Million, The
Frantz Fanon: Black Skin, White Mask
Georgia O'Keeffe
Gertrude Stein: When This You See, Remember Me
Gimme Shelter
Glass

Individuals: directors and producers

Production companies, organizations, festivals, and institutions

Countries and regions

Documentary film: an introduction

Ian Aitken

It is with great pleasure that I acknowledge the invitation to write this new Introduction to the *Concise Routledge Encyclopedia of the Documentary Film*. The original three-volume, hardback edition of *The Encyclopedia of the Documentary Film* appeared in 2006, and met with considerable acclaim. For example, the Encyclopedia was awarded the prestigious Dartmouth Medal by the American Library Association in 2006 for the 'outstanding work of reference of the year'. Unfortunately, the single-volume *Concise Routledge Encyclopedia of the Documentary Film* is unable to accommodate all that appeared in the original hardback edition of the Encyclopedia and, as a consequence, many entries have, necessarily, had to be excluded from the present edition. Readers interested in these entries are referred to the 2006 edition, which is widely available. The entries appearing in the Concise edition have, after some deliberation, been limited to those concerning films, filmmakers, and national traditions. Two new entries on India and China have also been added to the national traditions covered in the original work.

Given the necessary abridgement involved here, it might be assumed that the task of a new Introduction would be to provide an overview of the contents of the new work. However, this is not my intention, as I do not believe that such a summary would be especially enlightening, or useful. Instead, I intend to take the opportunity presented to me here to do something perhaps more trying: to think about the documentary film in general, and to reflect upon the nature, character, structure, purpose and role of the documentary film. In doing so, I also draw on my own theoretical interests, as set out in my trilogy of books on cinematic realism: *European Film Theory and Cinema* (2001), *Realist Film Theory and Cinema* (2006), and *Lukácsian Film Theory and Cinema* (2011). Rather than an overview, therefore, I intend to use this Introduction to reflect more generally on the documentary film, and I also hope that this modest contribution will play some role in initiating and escalating further debate on what I regard to be one of the most important of contemporary aesthetic media: the documentary film.

I The likeness of everyday occurrence

Documentary film is the founding genre of the cinema and, like still photography before it, the original imperative of that genre was to record existing human, social, physical and natural reality. Documentary film is thus, always was, and ever will be, intrinsically related to issues of realism and realistic representation, and this affiliation has certainly influenced the development of the medium up to the present day. The earliest films, shot by the Lumière brothers and others towards the end of the nineteenth century, were, as a consequence of this orientation, chiefly concerned to represent aspects of everyday life—the ephemeral life of the street—and, in doing so, these films also carried on some of the central traditions of nineteenth-century realist art, traditions that were deliberately concentrated upon the representation of the quotidian and low, rather than the elevated and eminent. In carrying through this intrinsically democratic-realist mission, these films also passed on one of the principal—perhaps *the* principal—aesthetics and representational accomplishments of photography: the preservation and perpetuation of moments of everyday life which would otherwise be doomed to fade into darkness within the ever-changing flux of perceptual experience.

For early spectators, therefore, the chief initial fascination with these films lay in the fact that those spectators were now not only able to see moments of everyday life approximately as they appeared within perceptual experience, but were also able to spend time reflecting on and considering those moments. For the first time, the rich, concrete tapestry of commonplace lived experience, with all its peculiar, surprising, evolving and information-rich particularities, had now been made lastingly visible, and the *actual* perceptible reality, within which all people are necessarily domiciled, had been made tellingly and unbrokenly manifest. 'So that is what that street corner really looks like', would have been the exclamation arising from spectators who may have passed by that same street corner in 'real life' a hundred times before. Here, what also distinguishes film from photography, of course—the crucial element that film adds to still photography—is the portrayal of the experience of temporal duration. Film now becomes much more like perceptual experience than the stationary images of photography: images that simply lack the humanity which the moving image is able to both invoke and evoke, by virtue of its ability to secure the human perceptual experience of duration. Of course, still photographs are also able to evoke a powerful sense of human essence, when observed by a spectator. However, the crucial difference here is that film is able to create a simulacrum of how human beings exist within perceptual experience—of how human beings experience life—and this simulacrum is also, essentially, *documentary* in essence. One provisional definition of the documentary film, therefore, might be that it is the type of film that embodies most fully a simulacrum of the perceptual experience of human existence, although, of course, not all documentary films can be accommodated within this definition, and some much more so than others.

The crucial and momentous ability that the documentary film possesses to portray the evolving material complexities of everyday life—what phenomenologists frequently refer to as the *Lebenswelt*, or 'lifeworld'—was also to eventually come to fascinate both of the two major theorists of classical cinematic realism: André Bazin and Siegfried Kracauer. Bazin's influential essay 'The Morphology of the Photographic Image', written shortly after the atrocities and carnage of World War II had become more conspicuously and chillingly apparent to the European consciousness, is permeated by the idea, one also shared with the larger terrain of post-war French existentialist thought, that contemporary man is increasingly alienated from the ever more cold-blooded contemporary world that surrounds him: the 'machine world' that was also portrayed so effectively in the art of the Weimar New Objectivity movement. However, the essay is also characterised by the idea that all men—from the beginning of time until the present—are also deleteriously affected by a human condition in which man is inexorably caught up within the flow of temporality, and is, unfortunately, unable to stand outside of that flow and arrest its relentless passage towards finitude. What Bazin referred to as the 'corrupting' effect of temporality, therefore, refers, in part, to an existential inability to hold on to phenomenological experience, and to genuinely and meaningfully encounter the 'complex fabric of the objective world' (Bazin 1967: 15).

For Bazin, the human experience of temporality is 'corrupting' in two ways. First, it is corrupting in that existence within temporal duration eventually leads to decline and death. Second, it is corrupting because we cannot ever really, as the saying goes, 'grasp the moment', but must always be predestined to observe that moment fall away from us. Bazin argues that there is little we can do about the first of these consequences of temporal corruption and decline. However, he does argue that film can do something about the second, and that the filmed sequence of images is able to portray and secure the perceptual experience of temporal duration, and thus allow us to encounter the 'complex fabric of the objective world' as it is experienced through time. As Bazin argues, in film a span of temporal duration is captured as 'change mummified', and the flowing of the present out of and into the past can be observed time after time, as a section of the once-having-been-present that has now become the past completely (what we see in the film sequence is something that has already happened, and is now *in* the past); this can, therefore, also be said to amount to a more consequential experience of totality than is ever available through a perceptual experience which is always characterised by ephemerality and fragmentation. In this sense, film can be said to compensate for that which is missing from perceptual experience—permanency—almost as though, as Bazin hints, the medium was brought into existence in order to fulfil this existential requirement and so advance the capacities of the human condition in an auspicious evolutionary manner. Such compensation is also *documentary* in essence, as Bazin insists that the filmed sequence should remain as close as possible to what he refers to as the 'physiology of existence': in other words, to our perceptual experience of reality (Bazin 1967: 133).

Taking the above into account, it can also be argued that the film sequence functions in an analogous way to human memory, which similarly links past and present into a unified whole. However, the act of memory—like the moment of perceptual experience—cannot, of course, be held on to for very long and, as argued above, such debility must again be distinguished from the immutability which characterises the film sequence. Despite this, it is possible to argue that there is a similarity in another sense between the act of remembering and the act of viewing the film sequence. For example, the act of remembering must also, and always, remain necessarily part of the present—that is, of present experience—because we can only remember from the site of the present moment; in a similar manner, the act of viewing the film sequence also remains located as part of the present, because we can only watch a film sequence from the site of the present moment. However, despite this similarity, a key difference must also be recognised here. In the act of memory, the person remembering is remembering his or her own past, whereas in viewing a film the spectator watches a picture of the past that is not part of his or her own past (unless we are talking about the untypical case of home movies). Film, therefore, broadens out beyond the individual in a way that memory cannot, and the act of viewing the film takes the individual *out* of his or her own individuality, rather than further *into* that individuality, and in so doing both possesses the capacity to challenge the preconceptions upon which such an individuality is founded and directs that individuality into the domain of social experience.

However, while such a challenge clearly has benefits, this process of raising up the spectator out of his or her own individuality, and of positioning the spectator within a more trans-individual context, is also problematic because it means that, unlike the act of memory, the spectator is not the sole protagonist involved in the experience of spectatorship, but must share that experience with something that already persists in itself and, in addition, as a totality: the material, fabricated film sequence. In memory there is only one totality involved, one which consists of the person remembering, and that which he/she remembers. However, in the act of spectatorship two totalities are involved, the first of which consists of the film sequence, which is complete unto itself, and the second of the union of film sequence and spectator in the act of spectatorship. The loss of creative sovereignty involved here, and concomitant propensity for manipulation entailed by a possible subordination of the latter of these two totalities to the first, has exercised many who have thought about the documentary film, and particularly so when such a film is perceived to be connected to an economic, industrial and ideological apparatus, as is the case with many documentary films made yesterday and today (the 'official' film, propaganda, the public relations film, etc.).

However, a more propitious outcome can also be envisioned here, and one that takes us back to an important similarity between the acts of spectatorship and of memory. The act of memory is surely an enlightening one, which is not only about remembering for its own sake, but is also meant to illuminate the present circumstances of the person who remembers, and to perhaps show the way forward. Given this, it can also be argued that the act of watching the documentary film has an analogous effect. The act of *watching* (rather than remembering) the past illuminates the present circumstances of the person who is watching, because the past world that is presented to us in the documentary film is *different* from our own, and is, therefore, capable of making us view our present world in a different light: as mutable and open to the prospect of change, rather than as unchallengeable and inevitable. Here the comparison with memory throws up something quite important: by virtue of this ability to show a realistic world which yet differs from the one within which we are domiciled, the act of watching a documentary film always has the potential to expand the critical insight and reflective powers of the spectator, or at the least shake that spectator up a little. Of course, the fiction film is also able to establish a 'world'. However, and as the philosopher Georg Lukács argues in other contexts and respects, the photographic foundation of the documentary film confers a certain 'authenticity' on the world established within the medium (Lukács 1987: 473).

In addition to this ability to show a different world to the one which we inhabit, the notion that film, and particularly, by implication, documentary film, is able to recover a transient or even lost world of human experience and then redirect our attention to that world, is also echoed in the writings of Siegfried Kracauer, who, like Bazin, also believed that the ordinary everyday life of the street was the proper domain of the film. In his *Theory of Film* (1960), for example, Kracauer argues that the way to escape from the abstract character of the modern condition is to experience the world in all its phenomenological richness: to return to the concrete and intermediate labyrinth of the *Lebenswelt.* As he puts it: 'there is no substitute for the direct perception of the concrete achievement of a thing in its actuality' (Kracauer 1997: 296). When discussing Paul Rotha's 1953 documentary film World Without End, Kracauer also echoes Bazin when he argues that the 'substance of the images' in a documentary film should exhibit the 'continuum of physical reality' (Kracauer 1997: 212), while the leading argument of Kracauer's *Theory of Film* is based on the notion that film is able to redeem the material world for us through its ability to replicate and portray perceptual experience.

In his writings on the cinema—writings that still remain relatively little known in the English-speaking world because they are written in German—the Hungarian philosopher and literary critic Georg Lukács also argued that film's 'closeness to life' (*Lebensnähe*) determined the aesthetic specificity of the medium. For Lukács, film possessed a 'photographic basis' which must be respected and, clearly, this amounts to a documentary-naturalist form of film theory. However, all three of these theorists also went beyond arguing that film could reveal reality, to argue that film also possessed the ability to render the ordinary as beautiful, mysterious, enchanting and resonant with human meaning. In a disenchanted world, characterised by alienation and manipulation, film—especially film of a documentary-realist character—could, therefore, become a medium of necessary enchantment; at the heart of such enchantment lies an ability to return man to the reality of concrete, phenomenological, *actual* existence—to what Kracauer calls 'physical reality', and Lukács the 'outside world', or *Aussenwelt.*

II The art of record

If documentary film is a medium that is able to show the reality of transient, empirical experience, and then 'embalm'—to use Bazin's term—such experience, it is also able to embalm experience that took place in the distant past, and is thus able to produce a long-standing *record* of times past. However, it also seems that, because of this predilection for the transient, in the long run what we find embalmed in the documentary film *in a consequential manner* is not the big issue, the historic event, but the miscellaneous elements of quotidian experience: what, for example, Kracauer referred to when discussing the documentary films of Louis Lumière, as the apparently *inconsequential* 'jumble of transient, forever dissolving patterns accessible only to the camera [...] the ripple of leaves in the wind [... these are subjects which film appears] predestined (and eager) to exhibit' (Kracauer 1997: 82–3). For Kracauer, such a predestination to demonstrate the impermanent is far from unimportant, and his conception of 'ante-room historiography', as set out in his posthumously published work *History: The Last Things Before the Last,* is also premised on the conviction that film should not show the 'last things'—the big issues and events—but the 'last things before the last'—the concrete, intermediate and apparently unimportant things which 'lie in the hollows between the lands we know'. Here, the importance of the documentary film lies in the ability of the medium to render-record that which 'lies in the hollows' that lie below that which we know, or what we are told to know: that which cannot be recovered through, or is generally disregarded by, other media bent on the portrayal of more evidently consequential matters.

The Battle of the Somme (Charles Urban 1916) was designed as a propaganda film, aimed at raising morale amongst the British people during a period in which many family members were being routinely slaughtered in the inhuman carnage of World War I. Admittedly, the film is a rather understated example of film propaganda, far removed from other, more jingoistic efforts that appeared at the time, such as the aggressively patriotic Our Empire's Fight for Freedom (1918). Nevertheless, and even taking this aspect of the film into account, The Battle of the Somme is not ultimately significant because of this propagandistic imperative—this 'last thing'—but because the film reveals aspects of human experience that may, in other quarters, be regarded as incidental, and which may also have faded from our knowledge had they not been represented in this film. What we observe here, in The Battle of the Somme, are images of real people, but in soldiers' uniforms, living within a milieu of trenches and violently disfigured landscape. We see how these individuals move about. We observe their dress and body language. We notice how they interact with each other, and with the physical environment of trenches, mud and bomb-destroyed landscapes. We monitor the subsistence of a living, though bygone, gestural idiom. These soldiers seem to smile a lot (though this may be induced by the unfamiliar presence of the then bulky camera apparatus), and what in fact is most moving and touching in these scenes of now long-dead men are these instances of commonplace, easy-going companionship and comradeship, and it is this ordinary world of value, rather than any rhetoric of war valour or instrumentality of purpose, which renders the film so important and still eminently watchable. In his book on World War II, the British historian Angus Calder referred to that conflict as the 'people's war', and his ground-breaking study focused on the experience of ordinary people in the conflict, rather than the activities of government and the high command. However, documentary film is, in a sense, always really a record of the people, rather than the elite and, while documentary film has, historically, always presented us with records of leaders and monarchs, these portrayals seem to matter far less in the end than the portrayal of an ordinariness which, in its captivating involvedness, never ceases to beguile. Countless examples could be given, but think only of the scene in Listen to Britain (Humphrey Jennings 1942) in which workers congregate in a staff canteen awaiting the performance of a song. What pulls you forwards here is the dishevelled temperament of their demeanour as they loiter aimlessly, occasionally spitting tobacco-tainted phlegm onto the muddled floor.

Extracts from the wartime films of the British documentary film movement are often used to illustrate expositions carried out in more contemporary films or television programmes that take as their subject World War II. Here, these extracts function both as a putative testimony to what happened, and as corroboration of the explanatory theses being deployed within the commentary and narrative, almost as though these extracts were somehow umbilically linked to both the place and time that they depict, and the diegesis of the later film within which they appear. However, of course, this is not the case and, correspondingly, these extracts cannot therefore be presumed to be either a testimony to historical real-world events or a substantiation of whatever is said and appears in the later film. Instead, these extracts must be conceived of as portraying events and aspects taking place at a particular place and time in relation to the representational imperatives and purposes of the *original* film, where that film was also premeditated as a unitary, purposive whole and not as a concoction of extracts, or source of primary data for unspecified future filmmaking. In addition, when that original film was made, it, and all within it, represented the *present*, not the *past*; this is a point that has important consequences for the documentary film, and which, therefore, will be returned to later.

The sort of 'insertion-as-testimony-and-substantiation' being discussed here sometimes happens, for example, in a television documentary film series on World War II such as The World at War (1973–74), where extracts from a film such as Britain Can Take It (1940) may be used to back up a construal of the London Blitz informed, at least surely in part, by an historical perception projecting backwards from the world view of the 1970s. At any rate, this documentary film series itself was definitely *produced* in the 1970s, not the 1940s, and for reasons, and with an agenda, that are quite different from the reasons and agenda that influenced Britain Can Take It. What we have here, therefore, at least at a philosophical level, is what might be described as an abstract disarticulation from the original film, in that these sequences are lifted entirely out of historical and filmic context, rather like pearls plucked from the ocean bed or diamonds cut out of the rock face. In addition, a different *role* has now been grafted onto these sequences-become-extracts. In Britain Can Take It, these sequences play the role of indeterminate descriptive portrayal, evoking the general atmosphere of the period, and do not really substantiate any particular point being made in the narrative or commentary. However, in some sections of The World at War, these *extracts* are more straightforwardly related to narrative and commentary, and this, in turn, means that they come to play a role in what is a primarily *intellectual* exercise; this is, as argued, not the role that they play within Britain Can Take It, where these sequences form part of a more organic whole, like diamonds embedded still in their native terrain. This problem becomes particularly evident in the first episode of The World at War, 'A New Germany 1933–39', in which an exposition on Hitler's brutal rise to power is embellished with extracts taken from Leni Riefensthal's Olympia (1936) and Triumph of the Will (1935), giving the impression almost that these extracts are sections of newsreel footage.

This is not to say that there is anything axiomatically wrong with the modus operandi utilised by The World at War, which is, arguably, one of the finest achievements of the documentary film, and anyway, as will be argued later, The World at War also uses extracts from other kinds of filmed material in different and more fruitful ways. Clearly, it depends on how the modus operandi is utilised. However, this is to say that the practice certainly invites reflection upon its consequences, because there is a conceptual difficulty involved here, in that a sequence is not the same as an extract and the two should not be confused, and there is also, perhaps, an ethical quandary, in that a degree of instrumental disingenuousness is involved. One answer to both of these problems, and one which will also be discussed later in relation to The World at War, when the issue of the *structure* of the documentary film is discussed, is to retain as much as possible of the sequence *as sequence*, rather than as extract—in other words to retain more of the sense of the sequence as something relatively autonomous and also, in some cases, as part of something much more extensive than the host film. In terms of the latter, this, for example, is something that The World at War manages to achieve when the historical footage used in the film is *archival* footage, rather than footage taken from a specific, autonomous work.

It can also be argued that the primary value of a film such as Britain Can Take It—and also the principal value of the film *as record*—lies not in the capacity of its sequences to be used either as testimony, or in order to substantiate one intellectual-interpretative point or another about the past made in a later film. Instead, at least in respect of the discussion here, the principal value of the film lies in its ability to portray elements of a particular and then currently *present* time and place within a constructed whole, so that what we see emanating from the diegesis of the film is the whole 'world' that then surrounded the film's filmmakers and related agents. Britain Can Take It, like Triumph of the Will, allows us as modern-day spectators to intuit that 'world', and it is in this more indeterminate sense that the film constitutes a 'record' of the past. If the documentary film is an art of record, therefore, it is a form of record far removed from objectivist premises and imperatives, and it may even be possible to argue that the documentary film can never 'prove' anything at all.

What is also so revelatory about these sequences, from films such as Britain Can Take It, or, for example, from Humphrey Jennings' Spare Time (1939), is how intrinsically *humane* the worlds that they capture appear to be; how genuinely humanitarian people appear to be within their everyday relations with each other and their environment; and it is also this underlying kindness that these films record. It is possible to believe that human society is a competitive jungle, characterised by a constant struggle to attain power and advantage and weaken rivals (anyone who works in a university will recognise *this* picture), but these documentary films seem to disclose something quite different to this: that whilst the pursuit of such calculating self-interest may indeed exist, underlying it is something far more extensive and prevailing. People shown running to catch a bus, as in Britain Can Take It, do not contend with each other, but are almost light-hearted and co-operative in their actions. Here, the documentary film seems to shows us evidence of, and, in a sense, record, an actually existing reality, and may also, therefore, be used to contest a vision of human life based in a belief in the necessity of antagonism, manipulation, exploitation, trickery and deceit. Happy eighteenth-century Enlightenment philosophers such as Marie Jean-Antoine Condorcet once believed that all men were endowed with 'an active and enlightened benevolence [and] a decorous and generous sensibility', and the documentary film sometimes seems to show that this might be the case (Aitken 2006: 10). Of course, the documentary film can also reveal the calculating duplicity that exists in human beings, but such duplicity may not be as widespread as has been thought.

As a form of record, therefore, the documentary film seems to be imbued with a humanist imperative, and is even able to make demagogues appear defective, apprehensive and tentative: in other words, human. Look closely, for example, at the shots of Adolf Hitler in Riefensthal's Triumph of the Will, a film that was meant to venerate the Nietzschean authority of the Führer and his party. What we actually see, though, is what Krakauer referred to in other respects as a 'man of skin and hair'—a man with a comical moustache, a stumbling gait, shifty eyes, and a coat that appears to be far too big and heavy for him—and this seeps out into the film, between those darkly lit episodes that attempt to extol a rhetoric of high xenophobia and chauvinism (oddly this undermining is also augmented by the choice of music used in the opening sections of the film: extracts from Richard Wagner's *The Mastersingers of Nuremberg*, which is, of course, a *comedy*). Of course, one of the ideological projects of the film was to make the Nazis appear congenial; however, this project is not always carried through and often fades into the portrayal of idiosyncrasy. The documentary film, therefore, seems able to excavate such frailties and incongruities almost as a matter of course, and although such a humanist imperative is much more noticeable when documentary film turns to the portrayal of the lower orders, and the suffering and destitute, it also seems to be intrinsic to the documentary film in general.

Of course, Hitler was an ogre, but his monstrous nature is something that is *internal*, rather than, for the most part, able to be displayed externally, and the documentary film chiefly shows what is *external*. Hitler does not particularly *look* like a monster in this documentary film, even though he may have been one in real life, and the portrayal of 'monstrousness', or evil, or, for that matter, epic adamant leadership, is not easily accomplished within the documentary film without, for example, the accompaniment of a detailed supporting commentary, which an important film such as Triumph of the Will does not possess. In many documentary films there is often a contradiction to be found between the images used and the narrative/commentary/plot that is employed, and whatever degree of bombast is being articulated in the commentary, the images remain essentially descriptive-empirical in character. This is not to say that Triumph of the Will intentionally seeks to subvert the Hitler myth, but it is to say that this does appear to happen at certain points in the film.

What this also amounts to is a point concerning the value of *naturalism*. As record, the documentary film seems most valuable in its indeterminate portrayal of the empirical and intermediate details of times past and present, and less valuable when such details are connected up to an over-dominant and controlling intellectual diegesis. Even when the subject matter involved is weighty—for example, the rise of Hitler and Nazism—the documentary film is better employed showing a whole 'world' in all its empirical detail, rather than placing emphasis on consequential, concept-laden subject matter. This is what Riefensthal achieves in Triumph of the Will, and also in her Olympia. It does not matter here if such portrayals are of things, nature or people, because, ultimately, everything is filtered through a human sensibility: we cannot escape the fact that every conception of reality is filtered through our human perspective. So, for example, in Joris Ivens' Regen (1929), shots of reflections in a river, or of raindrops falling into a pool of water, appear emotionally moving not because they are so in themselves, but because we relate these images to our emotional and visceral experience of reality. The poetry involved here is partly invoked by the fact that when we see this film, and these images, we realise that our general experience of reality is, as Kracauer argues, 'abstract', and that we have consequently failed to recognise qualities such as those captured in Regen. What we have in the documentary film, therefore, is an intensified empiricism in which the rich and complex detail that we would normally fail to notice in daily life is held up for our pleasure and scrutiny. At its best, therefore, and also as a type of 'record', the documentary film appears to be characterised by a form of indeterminate, empirical and intermediary naturalism, which attempts to show us a 'whole world', and invites us to intuit a whole world.

III The structures of the documentary film

The quandary for the documentary film begins when the simulacrum of perceptual experience constituted by the film sequence must be inserted into a narrative structure of some sort. However, this is also, quite obviously, the point at which the film—as film—comes into existence. So, the documentary film is a necessarily and inherently problematical medium in that what lies at its essential centre—the representation of perceptual reality—loses its primacy once such representation become inserted into mechanistic narrative configurations drawn from other sources, whether those sources lie in the arts or the social and natural sciences. There is, therefore, ground present for a potential antithetical conflict here between the deployment of empirical sequences that preserve the continuum of human perceptual experience and a concomitant deployment of intermediary and abstract structures that negate that continuum; this antithesis between an unadulterated, unmediated model of the documentary film, and one that employs mediation to a greater or lesser extent, has driven many of the debates and controversies that have arisen around the development of the medium. In fact, it could even be argued that the question of which type of structure to adopt in a documentary film, and the issue of the impact of such implementation upon the simulacrum of perceptual experience which the film mobilises, has dominated documentary film studies since the earliest days. Should, for example, the documentary film be structured like a work of art, or like a scientific enquiry? Should the documentary film be highly structured, or structured as little as possible? Should the film disclose its principles of structuration, or is this not necessary? These questions related to structure have, historically, also dominated discussion of the documentary film within the field of film theory, often to the detriment of a contemplation of documentary film in terms of questions relating to the first two categories considered in this Introduction: the documentary film as simulacrum of the experience of perceptual reality; and the documentary film as record. Of course, these two areas are inevitably caught up in debates over how the documentary film should be structured, but the prevailing and widespread focus on structure often leads to a situation in which they are not addressed directly, nor sufficiently.

The question of what structure to adopt in the documentary film is also frequently, even perhaps at all times, raised in relation to the *purpose* of the documentary film: what is the documentary film *for*; what is/should be the *objective* in making a documentary film; and, related to this, what purpose can/should a documentary film be said to possess, irrespective of film-making intentionality? Some documentary films are made for entirely aesthetic purposes and, here, purpose and structure are primarily related to interactions within and the evolution of the aesthetic sphere. Films such as Walter Ruttmann's Berlin: Symphony of a Great City (1927), a combination of observed documentary and experimental filmmaking, have been characterised—and also sometimes criticised—as formalist-modernist films because of the emphasis they place on questions of aesthetic form and substance. However, the phrase 'formalist-modernism' is a contentious one, and modernism has both supporters and detractors. For the former an absolute engagement with the aesthetic could, as Theodor Adorno and others before him have argued, constitute a standpoint of rejection against the instrumentality and degradation of contemporary human existence. Even though Ruttmann (a former painter) himself may have had only or mainly formalist aesthetic intentions when making Berlin, this does not mean that other forms of meaning and significance cannot be attributed to the film, which, it could be argued, stands today as an example of Adorno's 'autonomous art': art that stands against the 'machine world'. Much the same can also be said about later so-called 'structuralist' experimental documentaries such as Larry Gottheim's Fog Line (1970), Malcolm Le Grice's Little Dog for Roger (1967), or Michael Snow's influential Wavelength (1967)—films that have also been disparaged for their alleged lack of social-political substance. Such films constitute an aesthetic practice founded upon freedom, creativity and the importance of art in a materialistic society.

A considerable number of documentary films produced today are, however, not examples of 'autonomous art', but are largely generic products, produced within the commercial or other marketplace, and largely destined for the various purpose of entertainment. The rapid expansion of cable and satellite television—not to mention the internet and various other forms of new information technology—has spawned a huge increase in such films, and a number of channels have also appeared that are dedicated to their dissemination. Many of these films do not so much challenge or critically analyse the status quo, as reinforce it. For example, many natural history films convey a rhetoric of life as a competitive jungle, marked by the survival of the fittest, which conforms without difficulty with the ideology and needs of contemporary globalising capitalism. One thinks of a Discovery Channel series such as Predators here, and this and similar series of documentary films also draw upon a familiar range of stock conventions drawn from the standard (and often sub-standard) Hollywood film and various other entertainment genres. However, this is not the full picture, at least in relation to natural history documentary films, and series such as Life on Earth use the highest standards of filmmaking to paint a more enlightening portrait of animal communities which habitually engage in forms of social and familial cooperation and support. In such series the metaphor of the survival of the fittest is still evident, but is mediated by more providential and genuinely educational themes.

At their best, documentary film series such as Life on Earth convey knowledge to us about the opulence and wonder of the natural world. Their purpose is to educate, enlighten and enthral, and also, sometimes, to make us become more environmentally aware and active. The same is also true, for example, of Arne Sückdorff's The Great Adventure (1954), and the undersea photography in Jacques Cousteau's The Silent World (1956) and World Without Sun (1964). These films also show us another 'world'—the animal world—which often seems to contain the sort of absolute values that we would seek to emulate, values such as lifelong companionship and dedication to the care of the young. Other series of films also attempt something of the same in relation to the structures of the physical world, and also the story of human history. Carl Sagan's Cosmos, and Kenneth Clarke's Civilization come to mind here. Such primarily 'educational' series also show us a past 'world', the intricacies of which exist beyond our present knowledge, and make us aware of how little we know of things.

Such films as these may have no overt political or ideological agenda, but they usually always have covert ones. In addition, they sometimes do very much have overt ones, and one thinks here of Joseph Bronowski's The Ascent of Man, in which Bronowski declares that the thought of Hegel led directly and inevitably to Nazism. Bronowski's remarks here reveal the sort of dislike of 'continental' European philosophy, which one also finds elsewhere in the Anglo-American tradition and in 'educational' television documentary series such as The Ascent of Man. In addition to such epic 'grand narrative' series as Civilization, other documentary film series seek in contrast to tackle more circumscribed historical events or periods. Outstanding examples here might be The Nazis: A Lesson from History, and the landmark achievement of The World at War. Here, in one of the undoubted masterpieces of the documentary film, an episode such as 'Red Star', which portrays the defence of Leningrad, reaches great heights of emotional and rhetoric power. Here, the emotions provoked are absolute ones, related to matters of extreme heroism and refusal to accept defeat in the face of overwhelming odds.

In addition to such films, which have a primarily—though by no means exclusively—educative or academic orientation, other documentary films have a much more direct political and ideological agenda, and in these films the desire to have an impact on the world and effect change is also inevitably much stronger. Some of these adopt the hybrid form of the documentary drama, and important examples here would be Cathy Come Home (Ken Loach, Tony Garnett, 1966), Culloden (Peter Watkins, 1964), Death of a Princess (Anthony Thomas, 1980) and Who Bombed Birmingham (Granada Television, 1990). It seems, though, that the documentary drama is not so effective in dealing with situations that occur at the nationwide level, perhaps because the extent of reconstruction required tends to turn the work into more of a feature film than a documentary: they become feature-drama documentaries. Consequently, those documentary films that have more effectively turned to address national-political situations have tended to be far more obviously and classically documentary in format. Examples here would be The Battle of Chile (Patricio Guzman, 1975–7), the highly committed Cuba Sí! (Chris Marker, 1961), and the remorselessly committed The Battle of Algiers (Gilo Pontecorvo, 1966). The primary purpose of these and similar films is to speak up and out on behalf of the weak and defenceless, the dispossessed and the oppressed, and, in doing so, these films exhibit one of the central principled charges of the documentary film.

At one level, the documentary film of genuine substance must seek to inform, educate and, possibly, also entertain (though 'entertainment' does not seem to be medium-specific to the documentary film), but the documentary film is often, at its best, also endowed with an ethical imperative to defend and seek redress for those who are treated unjustly, to bring such unwarranted conduct to the attention of the local, national and international community, or, at the least, to raise up the disadvantaged into the sphere of representation. It was this latter objective, for example, which characterised the films of the British documentary film movement, in films such as Drifters (John Grierson, 1929), Housing Problems (Arthur Elton and Edgar Anstey 1935), and Coal Face (Alberto Cavalcanti, Basil Wright and others 1935). In this mission, documentary film can also be compared with the best investigative journalism, although, of course, unlike such journalism, the documentary film is also an *aesthetic* medium. Like the best investigative journalism, documentary film is also rarely particularly effective when used as an instrument of the ruling powers. Eventually, all documentary films that function as propaganda on behalf of one dominant group or another come to seem ridiculous and an object of scorn.

This ethical purpose of the documentary film also returns us to the matter of structure and to the question of what form and structure it would be best to adopt in order to realise this purpose, which also takes us into the realm of documentary film theory and practice. One of the unquestionable masterpieces of the documentary film is Dziga Vertov's The Man with a Movie Camera (1929). Vertov's film is, of course, far less important for its ideologically affirmative portrayal of the newborn Soviet Union than it is for its affectionate evocation of the lives of ordinary Russian people as they go about their various businesses during the course of a single day. Vertov wishes to present a panoramic view of everyday life in his film, and in order to achieve this he adopts a form of lateral, rather than linear editing, which allows him to portray a great many people and activities. Of course, Vertov's mission to raise up the image of the masses was, in theory, concomitant with the then dominant ideology within the Soviet Union. However, Vertov's modernist hierarchy-less, warts-and-all populism went too far, as far as the authorities were concerned, and propelled him into exile in the Russian outback.

The Man with a Movie Camera carries on the documentary film's representational mission to portray the lower classes, and the same can be said of the films of the British documentary film movement, some of which have already been mentioned. A film such as Spare Time (Humphrey Jennings, 1939), for example, adopts a similar lateral style as Vertov's film, though on a much smaller scale and without the formalist montage editing that characterises The Man with a Movie Camera. Instead, an impressionistic, observational style is employed, drawn from Jennings' involvement in the Mass Observation movement of the 1930s, and a paradoxical style is also employed, drawn from the filmmaker's familiarity with surrealist art. Other films made by the documentary film movement adopt a variety of styles, including the symbolic Soviet montage-inspired style of Drifters, the lyrical poetic naturalism of Song of Ceylon (Basil Wright 1934), and the social realism of Fires Were Started (Jennings 1943). However, whatever the style employed, the same underlying intention to portray the lower classes is always evident within these films, and virtually all the films of the British documentary film movement. Much the same can also be said of the committed Marxist filmmaker Joris Ivens, who combines montage editing, documentary naturalism and a socialist-realist style in films spread as far apart as The Spanish Earth (1937) and How Yukong Moved the Mountains (1976).

From the 1960s onwards debates then taking place within film studies began to spill over into the area of the documentary film. One consequence of this is that various influences, including that of Soviet montage theory, the work of Bertolt Brecht, and 'screen theory', led to the production of documentary films that sought to intentionally foreground their technical structures and ideological imperatives. From that point on, the 'reflexive' documentary film then became an important filament in the history of the documentary film. One of the earliest, and also most historically important, of these films was Jean Rouch and Edgar Morin's Chronique d'un été/Chronicle of a Summer (1961), in which Rouch sets out how his film was conceived and made, and then invites the subjects he has filmed to pass their opinion on the finished article. Various filmmakers have since followed this and similar reflexive approaches, including Nicholas Broomfield in his The Leader, the Driver and the Leader's Wife (1991), Michael Moore in his Fahrenheit 9/11 (2004), and others. However, the reflexive documentary, and the related 'performative' documentary, has always (and probably always will) remained a minority genre, perhaps because of the extent to which reflexivity inevitably disrupts the coherent diegesis of the film. As argued earlier, it is the evocation of a complete 'world' which is often important in the documentary film, and reflexivity is *sometimes* inimical to this.

Another approach to documentary filmmaking which developed in the late 1950s and 1960s, in many respects contrary to the reflexive approach, was based on the conviction that the documentary film should not only attempt to mask, rather than reveal, its structures, but also possess as little structuration as feasibly possible. Here, the underlying presumption was that a more 'objective' account of a situation could be achieved if whatever had been filmed had not been affected at all by the process of filmmaking, and if it could be verified that the same situation would have occurred exactly as it had whether the camera had been present or not. In order to achieve this degree of detachment the documentary film would not so much attempt to *portray* as *record* a situation. Underlying this notion of filmmaking is an inductive-empiricist theory of knowledge based on two principal premises: first, that a more 'objective' interpretation of a particular phenomenon can be achieved if no a priori pre-existing suppositions are imposed upon that phenomenon; and second, that only limited, rather than general or abstract, extrapolations should be derived from the observation of that phenomenon. According to this model, methods must be devised through which the subjectivity and mindset of the interpreter of the phenomenon are constrained to play only a minor role in that interpretation and, when this occurs, that interpretation will possess a higher epistemic value than that which is produced as a consequence of bringing more complex and abstract levels of supposition to bear.

When this empiricist model of knowledge was transplanted into the realm of the documentary film a new kind of 'observational', or 'direct', film appeared in which, or so its practitioners argued, the filmmaker's intrusion into events was reduced to a minimum, the events filmed appeared as they would have had the camera not been present, and the final edited structure of the films arose from the inner logic of the events and situations themselves. In order to facilitate this, a new mode of film shooting and editing was also employed, in which the filmmaker embedded himself or herself within the shooting location for extended periods of time, to the point at which, it was believed, the filmmaker ceased to have any influence on circumstances. Around this period (the late 1950s) new, more portable filmmaking equipment had also appeared, which enabled the filmmaker to interact more closely with the subjects and events being filmed, and also additionally enhanced the possibility that the filmmaker would be able to avoid influencing events less than had been the case when earlier, more bulky equipment had to be employed. After shooting, the film would then be edited in such a way that the narrative structure that emerged conformed as closely as possible to the linear development of the events that had taken place, so that the film reflected the essential structures of those events.

The American 'direct cinema' films of the 1950s and 1960s sometimes went to extreme lengths in carrying out this empiricist project, as, for example, in Andy Warhol's deliberately experimental Sleep (1963), a film of a man sleeping, in which there is no editing, hardly any camera movement, and in which commentary, plot, story and even titles are completely absent. Warhol's film also emerges from a context of post-war 'conceptual art', in which the artist followed intellectual premises regarding the formation of the art object to their logical conclusions. However, in the main, the bulk of films that constituted American direct cinema were not closely associated with the movement of conceptual art, and did employ the various cinematic devices eschewed by Sleep, although because of the predominance of their empiricist orientation, these films tended to give a lesser priority to such devices than observation of the events portrayed. That empiricist approach also led these films to excel at rendering detailed and intimate—and often surprisingly revelatory—portrayals of individuals and their immediate reactions with each other and their environments. For example, Primary (Don Pennebacker and others, 1960) followed closely the Wisconsin primary contest between Hubert Humphrey and John F. Kennedy, showing the often contradictory and chaotic relations and events that took place during the primary. Here, the primary appears not so much as an integral component of the democratic process, as an almost tribal affair with its own internal—and highly animated—protocols. Similarly, The Chair (Robert Drew and Richard Leecock 1963) explores the dramatic and tense interactions and uncertainties evident within a cast of characters—real people—who are caught up in one way or another with the execution—of a real man—to be carried out by electrocution. The films of Frederick Wiseman also fall into this category, although Wiseman eschews the dramatic events favoured by Pennebacker, Drew and Leacock in favour of portraying the micro-complexities of the everyday and mundane, as for example in his Law and Order (1969), which centres on some of the more idiosyncratic aspects of routine police work.

However, just as a pure empiricist theory of knowledge is untenable, so also is a pure empiricist conception of the documentary film. As virtually all philosophers would avow, it is not possible to transcend subjectivity in order to reach the 'truth', just as we are unable to step outside of our conceptual schemes in order to encounter reality directly. In practice, therefore, the films of direct cinema were all influenced, in one way or another, by the presuppositions of the filmmakers involved, as well as by background ideological formations, and were unable to encounter reality in an unmediated fashion. These films also drew on a whole host of narrative and other conventions in developing their structures, and this, in turn, meant that those structures could not replicate the structures of the real-world events taking place in front of the camera. Real-world events do not *and cannot* possess a definite structure: they are part of the indeterminate generality of the lifeworld, or *Lebenswelt*. In this sense one can also say that, philosophically speaking, Warhol was perhaps on the right track with Sleep. Warhol apart, though, the danger that lies here, within the ideological orientation of direct cinema, and one which makes that cinema both problematical and controversial as a mode of documentary filmmaking, is both twofold and important. First, by focusing on immediate interactions, these films tend to reduce context to a minimum and, while the documentary film is well suited to portray immediate interactions, the presentation of context is also central to the medium's role. Second, by attempting to transcend the subjective inclinations and ideology of the filmmaker, they also disguise, or leave aside, the extent to which intentionality and subjectivity play a necessary and determining role in any form of filmmaking, including the documentary film. The gate is now open for premeditated manipulation

In terms of the epistemic and moral mission of the documentary film outlined earlier, both of these factors constitute clear and present danger. However, arguing that the underlying theoretical model of direct cinema is untenable is not the same as arguing that this form of filmmaking itself is disreputable, and, as has been argued earlier, the empirical focus of the direct cinema model is both fundamental and indispensable to the documentary film. What is of most value in this approach also takes us back to the classical theories of cinematic realism, in Bazin, Kracauer and others. What this type of direct cinema can do is preserve moments and sections of everyday life which would otherwise be doomed to fade into non-existence within the ever-changing flux of perceptual experience. This 'mummified'—to use Bazin's phrase—*naturalism*, which allows us to see and be amazed—or appalled—by aspects of experience to which we would otherwise not have access, or would not have noticed in any meaningful way or contemplative manner, is an essential ingredient of the documentary film and lies at the heart of some of the greatest achievements of the medium. What, therefore, seems to be of primary importance here is that these films can present us with information that goes beyond our pre-existing, often stereotypical understanding of a particular subject, and in doing so these films expand our understanding and make us more knowledgeable about the world around us. As Frederick Wiseman put it:

> You start off with a little bromide or stereotype about how prison guards are supposed to behave or what cops are really like. You find that they don't match up to that image, that they are a lot more complicated. And the point of each film is to make that discovery.
>
> (Bordwell and Thompson 1994: 695)

Wiseman's hoped for 'discovery' points to what can be, in certain circumstances, genuinely illuminating about the documentary film, though, of course, the character of the 'complications' he discovers will always be influenced to a certain extent by his own pre-existing bromidic-stereotypical understandings, whether he believes that to be the case or not. In addition, his portrayal of individual complicated cops will not necessarily tell us much about the institution of the American police force as a whole. Bearing these difficulties in mind, it is worth returning to the argument made earlier, that the truly, or even predominantly, naturalist documentary film potentially possesses the two foreseeable dangers referred to previously: that of disguising ideological positions, and limiting the representation of context. This is also why in its attempt to overcome both of these dangers, while retaining an effective naturalist emphasis and adding to our understanding of the culture and people it portrays, Chronique d'un été remains one of the classic films of the documentary cinema.

In many respects the reflexive documentary and the observational documentary represent the Alpha and Omega of the documentary film. However, in addition to these two paradigms of the documentary film, neither of which can be realised in a pure form in any particular film anyway, a number of identifiable genres can also be discerned within the field of the documentary film, and perhaps the most historically important of these is the 'interview film', which often, though not always, also uses archival materials alongside the interviews it displays. In these films interviewees are allowed to have their significant say and the interviewer or narrator does not overly govern proceedings. The objective here, for many of these films, is to break with the omniscient—and conventionally prevailing—'expositionary' 'voice-of-God' narrative, in which an account or interpretation is given from a singular—and often officially sanctioned—perspective, or in which two or more accounts are given and then are brought into cohesion through a 'balancing' commentary and narration. In both cases here an *order* is imposed upon the subject and, inevitably, the disposition of such order will reflect institutional authority and dominant ideology, especially so in the age of the television documentary film.

Many of the interview-based documentary films that appeared from the 1970s onwards, after the worldwide advance of television, attempted to dispense with such an overall 'order' and, instead, present a more indeterminate understanding of their subjects. Many of these were also influenced by the New History movement, which also came to prominence during the 1970s. Here, historians attempted to develop histories of everyday life, rather than of high events and noble persons. It is, perhaps, because of this historiographic influence that many of these interview films also link past, present and memory using historical archival footage of the everyday past; in these films the testimonies of commonplace, individual people are linked to a past, and also largely *elapsed*, and indeterminate world of the everyday.

There is also a crucial distinction to be made here between these interview-based films and other types of documentary films which also use filmed extracts to illustrate their exposition. In such latter films, and as also argued earlier, a sequence is taken from a pre-existing film—which has a particular logic and coherence of its own—and is then inserted into the body of the host film in order to illustrate the exposition being mobilised by that film. However, as previously maintained, this is in fact a disingenuous and misleading type of illustration because the original footage was both intended and structured to illustrate another and completely different exposition, and may even not have directly illustrated any exposition at all but, rather, had the purpose of accompanying or even contradicting that exposition (if the original film even had an overall exposition). On the other hand, the footage used in the interview films being discussed here is largely *archival*: part of a huge, indeterminate body of filmed sequences which were originally shot as record, or in the case of war footage, with, at least initially, only vaguely formulated propaganda intentions in mind, or for no particular purpose of any consequence at all. Most of this footage was, therefore, never part of any pre-existing filmic-compositional totality. In addition, in these interview-based films the archival footage is not generally used in an illustrative manner but mainly exists partly in its own right and character, as an extract from a corpus—a sampling taken from the indeterminate historical materials record of filmed everyday life.

The most important of these interview-based films may, as argued earlier, be The World at War (Thames Television 1973–6), a film of twenty-six episodes and thirty-two hours in length. A breakthrough in British documentary film's attempt to represent World War II, the film adopts the perspective of the New History movement in consisting to a substantial extent of interviews given by commonplace people, rather than major political figures, and also employs an extensive range of archival footage, including home movies, instructional footage and captured enemy footage, as well as—as previously discussed—extracts from films such as Britain Can Take It, Triumph of the Will, and others. In a similar way, another landmark film, Marcel Ophuls' The Sorrow and the Pity: Chronicle of a French City Under the Occupation, also consists largely of interviews, and although some of these interviews are of dignitaries, the film largely consists of interviews with the man and woman in the street and focuses on everyday relationships to the Occupation. As the title suggests, The Sorrow and the Pity is an emotionally charged film, which forces participants to confront the sorrow and the pity of collaboration and betrayal. In both this film and The World at War, interviews and archival materials work together to show a sometimes emotionally overwhelming human-social reality of heroism and fearfulness, anguish and achievement, order and confusion.

It could be argued that these archival-interview films correspond more closely to the epistemic and moral imperative of the documentary film than perhaps almost any other kind of documentary film, and it is perhaps no accident that it is here that some of the most powerful examples of the medium have emerged. It has been argued earlier that the documentary film is most suited to explore the interstices of everyday human, animal and natural life. Clearly, the interview film which focuses on the everyday and the ordinary lends itself to this mission and supposed aesthetic specificity. The archival-interview film can bring Kracauer's 'terra incognita' into view, and present the voices of the oppressed and those treated unfairly. At their best, interview-based documentaries also do not seek some mythical 'balance' but display their preferences openly. The humanist-ethical stance of The World at War, The Sorrow and the Pity, and, another landmark achievement, Claude Lanzmann's twelve-hour long Shoah (1985), is, for example, openly evident. However, the interview film is not restricted to a humanist paradigm, and films such as Harlan County, USA (Barbara Kopple, 1976) and The Life and Times of Rosie the Riveter (Connie Field, 1980) reveal a clear social class and feminist agenda, respectively. In all of these films the interface between interviews and archival footage is, of course, handled in different ways. For example, in The World at War there is an overall commentary and the witnesses who appear are not normally cross-examined in any way. In Shoah, on the other hand, the director, Lanzmann, is often present, challenging as well as guiding his interviewees. Despite these distinctions, however, all these films can be linked together into a format which places indeterminate interview materials in conjunction with indeterminate archival materials, and which is also driven by a strong sense of purpose.

In addition to the three types of documentary film that have been discussed in the present section of this Introduction—the reflexive, direct and archival-interview film—other sub-genres of the documentary film are, of course, also identifiable, but can, unfortunately, only be referred to in passing here, given limitations of wordage. These would include the compilation film, such as Fredric Rossif's To Die in Madrid (1963), and many of the films of the British documentary film movement. They would also include the documentary film of primarily personal expression, which may be found in the work of the British Free Cinema movement and in the work of filmmakers as diverse as Chris Marker, Alain Resnais, Georges Franju, Werner Herzog and many others. It is not possible to cover the work of these and other filmmakers here, and readers are referred, instead, to the various entries within this Encyclopedia. Instead, it may be more appropriate to conclude this brief Introduction with a conjecture concerning the present and future role of the documentary film.

IV In conclusion: the role of the documentary film

The documentary film, today and tomorrow, has, and will continue to have, many roles to play. Many of these relate to the spheres of entertainment, commerce and uncomplicated gratification, and these are certainly significant domains. Beyond this, though, what are and will be the most imperative of these roles? The contemporary dominance of television from the 1960s onwards means that most documentary films are commissioned by, produced by, or shown on some form of television outlet. Often, these outlets are controlled by nation-states, capitalist corporations or a combination of both. Where the controllers of these outlets are *enlightened*, say—and to take a by no means unequivocal example—in the public broadcasting services of advanced, capitalist, liberal-democratic nations, the ideal role of documentary film should be to stay close to the mission of the documentary film as set out earlier: that is, to challenge the abuse of power, struggle to overcome injustice, defend the weak and powerless, and communicate information in a sophisticated, disinterested and impartial manner, taking into account the existence and authentic needs of a wide spectrum of types of persons, in terms of race, social class, ethnicity, gender, belief and other factors. However, even in such supposedly advanced nations, dominant relations of power and influence work against the realisation of such a mission, and, in these circumstances, where inequality and injustice is still ubiquitous, the documentary film will have to maintain a forcefully independent character and not shy away from the articulation of uncomfortable avowals.

In other countries, authoritarian and repressive nations of various sorts, which control their media and make that media work in the interests of the powerful, the mission of the documentary film may only be fulfilled by taking on the role of a covert fifth column or by going underground to a substantial degree. Today, documentary film is an important and essential vehicle for social and political change and protest in many countries around the world, where filmmakers often take great risks in order to stand up for the various victims of the current world order. New technology has also made it much easier—and much safer—for independent, underground networks of documentary filmmaking to persist. For example, in China an important movement of independent documentary filmmaking exists which challenges the blanket control that the Communist Party imposes upon the Chinese media and, ultimately, the Chinese people. This form of activity involving the documentary film is being repeated in many parts of the world today and needs to be encouraged. In this sense, the documentary film could become crucially important in the near future as an instrument for progress. The rulers of the contemporary world order will do whatever they can to maintain their power and authority and keep uncomfortable ideas that challenge that power and authority out of the public sphere. The German philosopher and heir to the German philosophical critique of modernity, Jürgen Habermas, has argued that Enlightenment values such as universal freedom and communicative rationalism are the instruments best able to deconstruct the forms of instrumental rationality which dominate and characterise contemporary experience; if this is so, then the documentary film must be part of that process. The documentary film must be both communicative and activist, in relation to the personal, social and globalised spheres.

Apart from this crucial role, documentary film also has a phenomenological and existential role to play in bringing us back to the material world. Siegfried Krakauer argued that the modern individual's experience of her/himself was an *abstract* one and, as has been argued earlier here, all the major theorists of cinematic realism comment on this abstract nature of the human condition. All of them, in one way or another, also emphasise the importance of film in bringing us back to the one thing that really exists: the present moment, in all its richness and reality. The documentary film is the aesthetic medium par excellence best suited to achieve this outcome, and here the documentary film takes on a utopic dimension. This is not to argue that the documentary film should be prescribed, like a medicinal drug, to persons suffering from various psychological disorders. It may never happen that 'documentary film therapy', like taking-a-holiday therapy, becomes established as a form of curative treatment; however, it is to argue that there is something essentially beneficial about watching a documentary film because, for once, one is faced with the rich and fascinating tapestry of the real world as we actually experience it. The world and our experience of it ceases to become abstract or manipulative, and the world in which we actually persist reveals itself as essentially purposeless and unmanipulative, and as consisting of a plethora of things available for our pleasure and enlightenment. As Georg Lukács put it in his *The Specificity of the Aesthetic* (1963), film is able to bring the *Aussenwelt* (outside world) up to the level of the human world so that we are better able to understand our authentic existential condition. If that is true of film in general, it is even more true of the documentary film. The documentary film also has an *aesthetic* role to play. In his ground-breaking 1913 article, 'Thoughts Toward an Aesthetic of the Cinema', Lukács asserts that film can show us a poetic aesthetic vision of reality. Let the last word be his:

> The livingness of nature here acquires artistic form for the first time: the rushing of water, the wind in the trees, the stillness of the sunset and the roar of the storm, as natural processes, are here transformed into art [...] Those achievements of modern technology that are irrelevant to every great art will also become powerfully fantastic and poetic here. For the first time, in the 'cinema'—to give but one example—a car can become poetic, as in a romantic and thrilling pursuit involving other cars. In this way also the common bustle in the street and in the market place acquires a powerful humor and an elementally forceful poetry.
>
> (Lukács 1913)

Further reading

Aitken, Ian, *European Film Theory and Cinema*, Edinburgh: Edinburgh University Press, 2001.

——(ed.) *The Encyclopedia of the Documentary Film*, Abingdon and New York: Routledge, 2006.

——*Realist Film Theory and Cinema: The Nineteenth-Century Lukácsian and Intuitionist Realist Traditions*, Manchester: Manchester University Press, 2006.

——*Lukácsian Film Theory and Cinema*, Manchester: Manchester University Press, 2012.

Bazin, André, *What is Cinema? Volume I*, Berkeley, CA and London: University of California Press, 1967.

Bordwell, David and Thompson, Kristin, *Film History: An Introduction*, New York: McGraw Hill, 1994.

Kracauer, Siegfried, *History: The Last Things Before the Last*, Princeton, NJ: Markus Wiener Publishers, 1995.

——*Theory of Film: The Redemption of Physical Reality*, Princeton, NJ: Princeton University Press, 1997.

Lukács, Georg, 'Gedanken zu einer Ästhetik des Kino' [Thoughts Towards an Aesthetic of the Cinema], Frankfurter Zeitung und Handelsblatt, 1913.

——*Die Eigenart des Ästhetischen/The Specificity of the Aesthetic*, Berlin and Weimar: Aufbau-Verlag, 1987.

Abel Gance: Yesterday and Tomorrow

(France, Kaplan, 1962)

Abel Gance: Yesterday and Tomorrow is the dubbed version of Abel Gance, hier et demain, produced by the Office de Documentation par le Film and directed by Nelly Kaplan.

In the 1960s the motion picture rose to prominence as a key medium of expression. A newly focused and invigorated interest in the movies manifested itself both in new styles of filmmaking and the study of cinema's history. This generation questioned current cinematic conventions, watched old motion pictures, and identified with forgotten filmmakers and cinematic icons. An important outcome of this renaissance was a new appreciation for the art of the silent cinema. This audience was particularly receptive to Abel Gance: Yesterday and Tomorrow, which championed a rediscovered genius and his neglected silent masterpieces.

Nelly Kaplan, the director of Abel Gance, was in the vanguard of this new generation of film enthusiasts. Born in Buenos Aires in 1934, Kaplan abandoned her studies in economics at the University of Buenos Aires because of her fascination with film. She went to Paris as a representative of the Argentine Film Archive, and found employment as a film journalist writing for Argentine newspapers.

Shortly thereafter, in 1954, the 20-year-old met Abel Gance and worked as an actor, assistant director, and collaborator on a number of his film projects. A second unit camera operator on Gance's feature film, Cyrano et d'Artagnan (1963), Kaplan used footage of the 74-year-old filmmaker taken on the set to frame the flashback of his life and career in Abel Gance: Yesterday and Tomorrow, which was made that same year.

In this dubbed version of Abel Gance, hier et demain, an English speaker provides a first-person account of the filmmaker's story. Recognized as a great technical innovator as well as an artist, Gance tells us that he invented prototypes of Cinerama and stereophonic sound. As his cinematic achievements are identified, film clips support his claims. We see examples of Gance's use of montage in his La Roue (1921). Yet, despite the quality of his cinematic innovations, Gance claims that the studios were initially reluctant to support his style of filmmaking. With the advent of sound in film, the director was no longer encouraged to make silent films, which he preferred to make. When asked to work for Adolph Hitler during the war, he fled to Spain. Gance did not make another film for over ten years.

Abel Gance: Yesterday and Tomorrow ends with Gance discussing his later work as a director, his disappointment with the current cinema, and his dreams of once again making sensational motion pictures in the future.

Abel Gance: Yesterday and Tomorrow presents its subject as a living treasure still capable of great work, one of the cinema's great innovators. Although her motives are understandable, Nelly Kaplan's narrowly focused concern that Gance be recognized as a hero of the cinema has its drawbacks. The constant emphasis on Gance's cinematic accomplishments to the exclusion of everything else hinders us from knowing him as a person. The limiting effect of offscreen narration, which could have been relieved by having Gance occasionally speak on camera, particularly accentuates our feeling of being distanced from the subject and prevents us from experiencing some sense of intimacy with Gance as a human being.

One way in which the interested viewer can get a better sense of Abel Gance as a person is to watch the other important documentary on the filmmaker from this period. Kevin Brownlow's 1968 production of Abel Gance: The Charm of Dynamite centers on a trip that Gance made to England in 1965. This documentary uses extensive interviews with the filmmaker to underscore the importance of his films. Abel Gance: The Charm of Dynamite also documents the beginning of Kevin Brownlow's lifelong pursuit of reconstructing Napoleon, a quest that confirmed Napoleon as one of the major accomplishments of the silent cinema.

Both Abel Gance: Yesterday and Tomorrow and Abel Gance: The Charm of Dynamite capture a 1960s cineaste's excitement in recognizing the art of a neglected major silent filmmaker. These documentaries also put Abel Gance in the select company of such maverick geniuses of the motion picture as D.W. Griffith, Erich von Stroheim, Sergei Eisenstein, and Orson Welles. Lauded today for his innovative cinematic achievements, Gance ultimately was denied the freedom to make motion pictures the way he wished, as his iconoclastic vision could not be supported by the film industry.

FRANK SCHEIDE

Abel Gance, hier et demain/Abel Gance: Yesterday and Tomorrow (France, 1962, 30 mins). Directed by Nelly Kaplan.

Further reading

n.a., 'Abel Gance, hier et demain', review, *Factual Films* 20, no. 241, 1966: 626.

n.a., 'Abel Gance, hier et demain', review in 'Current Non-Fiction and Short Films', *Monthly Film Bulletin* 34, no. 402, 1967: 411.

Daria, Sophie, *Abel Gance, hier et demain*, Paris: La Palatine, 1959.

Holmund, Chris, 'The Eyes of Nelly Kaplan', *Screen* 37, no. 4, 1996: 351–67.

Kaplan, Nelly, *Napoléon*, London: BFI Publishing, 1994.

Act of God

(UK, Greenaway, 1980)

One of the most controversial and innovative filmmakers of the British film renaissance of the 1980s, Peter Greenaway is a director of fiction films, documentaries, and TV programmes; a painter; and an author of essays and novels. His very distinctive poetic universe is characterized by a proliferation of details and references, and is driven by an encyclopaedic ambition. Fiction features such as The Belly of an Architect (1986), Drowning by Numbers (1988), and The Pillow Book (1996) alternate in his filmography with documentaries that, for their utter originality, are situated at the limits of the genre. He often employs the form of the documentary either to represent something true but futile, as in Dear Phone (1977), or Water Wrackets (1975), to tell a fictional story through absolutely neutral images of a series of rivers and ponds. As Jorge Luis Borges does, Greenaway applies a scientific language to nonscientific topics, considering the language of science itself as articulated in essay writing, in Darwin's books, and in mathematical formulae as a form of narration.

Act of God is a twenty-six-minute film made for Thames TV as part of a series produced by Udi Eichler. It consists of an investigation into the elusive nature of the phenomenon of lightning, through a series of filmed interviews with people who, from 1966 to 1980, were struck by lightning in various European locations. Act of God was presented at several international festivals, including Edinburgh, Chicago, and New York, and won prizes as Best Documentary at the festivals of Melbourne and Sidney. Made with his regular collaborator, musician Michael Nyman, Act of God is a documentary that, for its subject matter and aesthetic characteristics, is perfectly consistent with the filmmaker's artistic world and, in particular, with the obsessive cataloguing effort, which has always been at the core of his project. Act of God, in fact, confirms Greenaway's passion for taxonomy and categorization, which previously emerged, for instance, in the documentary The Falls (1980), the result of lengthy research carried out in the attempt at producing a sort of encyclopaedia of humanity, a gargantuan effort evocative of Borges.

In Act of God, Greenaway tries to classify and understand the most unclassifiable and unpredictable event on the face of the Earth. Always looking for the point in which all the lines of the world converge and everything happens simultaneously, he searches for a mathematical formula for lightning, which he tries to extract from the numbers that recur in the different accidents, keeping into account the site, the date, and the precise time when the lightning struck, the weight and shoe size of the victim, and anything the subject was carrying or wearing at the time. Greenaway makes a list of all the numbers and objects, but also includes advice deriving from popular belief, thus ironically mixing and granting the same importance to science and to folklore, in tune with his postmodern stance.

Act of God is composed of thirteen interviews with victims of lightning who are asked to describe in detail their experiences and the circumstances that preceded and followed the accident. Searching for a manifestation of God in the discovery of the presence of coherence even in the most absolutely indeterminate event, Greenaway is particularly interested in finding out whether and how intensely the victims believed that their accident had a religious meaning and saw it as a divine punishment. Finding that they did not, Greenaway suggests how these extraordinary instances have happened to ordinary people, who failed to interpret them as exceptional events, and tries to offer through the editing a sort of metaphorical interpretation of the stories told. These direct testimonies are intertwined with ten apocryphal stories also related to lightning, narrated in voice-over, in which the focus is always on the site and date of the accident, the victim, and the objects that she or he was carrying. Greenaway consistently highlights the accidental nature of the events narrated in the made-up stories, and intertwines with them a series of references to literary and music works that refer to lightning, drawing attention to the recurrence of this natural phenomenon in Shakespeare's oeuvre.

The interviews of Act of God are shot in a way that is utterly unique for a documentary. Every frame is composed by the filmmaker as if it were a painting, displaying a profound attention for location and background, and an obsessive research for symmetry between the body of the interviewee and the space that surrounds it. In some cases, Greenaway creates a game of shadows behind the interviewee's body; in other cases, he constructs an impressive depth of field through open doors and windows. In one interview held over the phone, Greenaway invents a shot with a strange perspective: a telephone handle in close-up looks unnaturally big, and from a window in the background the tops of some trees and a threatening sky are visible. Interviews are conducted both in interiors and in exteriors; when they are set outside, they are generally shot in gardens, always with an emphasis on the element of water (for instance, the rain is falling and the interviewee is under an umbrella, or water sprays out of a watering can, filling in the space between the camera lens and the interviewee). It must be noted that water is a recurrent presence in Greenaway's work, an ambivalent element, which is the object of innumerable associations and contradictions, loved by the director for its photogenic quality as well as for being a component of the human body that links us to the world. In Act of God, Greenaway suggests in fact the idea of the liquefaction of the body hit by lightning, in a sort of 'water to water' (rather than 'ashes to ashes') cycle.

The composition of the shots, the subject matter, and the music by Nyman make Act of God a product that is closer to video art than to traditional documentary. As always with Greenaway, the documentary is a language among other languages, to be deconstructed and reconstructed at will. Although the starting point is a real issue, the structure and visual quality of his documentary invite the spectator to doubt the reality of the testimonies, immersed as they are in an aesthetic surplus.

STEFANO BASCHIERA

Act of God (UK, Thames TV, 1980, 25 mins). Distributed by Thames Television—British Film Institute. Produced by Udi Eichler for Thames Television. Directed and written by Peter Greenaway. Music by Michael Nyman. Cinematography by Peter George. Edited by Andy Watmore. Filmed in Devon, London, Lincolnshire, Germany, Surrey, Cardiganshire, Lancashire, Norway, Oxfordshire, Italy, Westmorland, Gwent.

Further reading

Ciecko, Anne T., 'Peter Greenaway's Alpha-Bestiary Ut Pictura Poesis: A Zed and Two Noughts', *Post Script* 12, no. 1, 1992: 37–48.

Hacker, Jonathan and Price, David, 'Peter Greenaway', in *Take Ten: Contemporary British Film*

Directors, New York: Oxford University Press, 1991: 188–227.

Lawrence, Amy, *The Films of Peter Greenaway*, Cambridge: Cambridge University Press, 1997.

Pally, Marcia, 'Order vs. Chaos: The Films of Peter Greenaway', *Cineaste* 18, no. 3, 1991: 3–8.

Steinmetz, Leon and Greenaway, Peter, *The World of Peter Greenaway*, Boston, MA: Journey Editions, 1995.

Adolescents, The (aka That Tender Age)

(France, Baldi, Brault, Rouch, Teshigahara, 1964)

In 1964, at the height of the omnibus film phenomenon sweeping throughout Europe and parts of Asia, a four-part docudrama about the travails of the teenage years was jointly produced by Cinematografica, Les Films de la Pléiade, the National Film Board of Canada, and Ninjin Club. Released that year in Italy under the title Le adolescenti, in France and Canada as La fleur de l'âge, and in Japan as Shishunki, The Adolescents (as it eventually came to be known in the United States and Great Britain after a belated 1967 release) is a curious quartet, its many national affiliations and linguistically differentiated incarnations a product of the polyglot sensibilities of that era. With each of its four episodes helmed by a different director (Gian Vittorio Baldi, Michel Brault, Jean Rouch, and Hiroshi Teshigahara—all of whom had gained international notoriety by that time for their ability to wed documentary and fiction filmmaking), The Adolescents is, as its title implies, a plural text, one that deploys ruptures and discontinuities across a broad, indeed global, spectrum so as to point out similarities as well as differences between people based on national, cultural, racial, and ethnic backgrounds. Moreover, like other multidirector coproductions of the early 1960s, such as L'Amour à vingt ans/Love at Twenty (1962), Boccaccio '70 (1962), and RoGoPaG (1962), the film calls into question our critical dependency on the perhaps outmoded notions attending 'auteurist cinema' (in particular, the idea that a single director puts his or her personal stamp on a film), even as its trumpets the individual talents of the contributing filmmakers. Perhaps more importantly, however, it is plural insofar as it combines fiction and nonfiction aesthetics, thus collapsing distinctions between dramatic artifice and documentary verisimilitude, between narrative construct and unmediated reality.

The Adolescents is differentiated from the above mentioned and other omnibus films—besides its reliance on nonscripted action—by its overriding focus on youth. Although certainly not the first episode film to tap into the existential uncertainties and emotional problems faced by teenagers (Michelangelo Antonioni mined this rich thematic material as early as 1953, when he made I vinti/The Vanquished, a three-episode study of the moral bankruptcy and dehumanized behavior of Europe's postwar youth), The Adolescents provides a timely reminder of the generational and cultural schisms of the 1960s.

The only scripted episode is that of Gian Vittorio Baldi, who also served as one of the six producers of the film. His tale, 'Fiammetta', concerns a fourteen-year-old Florentine girl (played by Micaela Esdra) whose father has recently passed away. Left to reminisce in her widowed mother's sprawling estate, Fiammetta spends her days moping about the tourist-filled mansion. Eventually, her sexual curiosity and growing awareness of her developing breasts are deflected onto her jealousy for her attractive mother, who is forced to give up her new lover and live a quiescent life alone with her demanding daughter. These interwoven themes of sexual curiosity and jealousy reemerge in the second episode, Canadian director Michel Brault's 'Geneviève'. The titular teen in this slim story is actually one-half of a female duo whose friendship is tested in a moment of indiscretion and dishonesty. Both Geneviève (Geneviève Bujold) and her companion Louise (Louise Marleau) are seventeen years old, and their simultaneous sexual awakenings spark a silent rivalry during a winter carnival in Montreal. Having met a young man named Bernard (Bernard Arcand) the day before, Louise oversleeps and misses her early morning date to see him again. Geneviève steps in and takes her place, spending the day with Bernard while her friend remains blissfully unaware. Later, at the end of the date, Louise discovers the truth when she spies the two kissing—an impulsive yet tentative act on Geneviève's part and one that she steadfastly refuses to admit. Although the plot may sound trite, what energizes it is Brault's deft handling of space, and his judicious use of the wide-angle lens and mobile framing, which extends the social milieu of the two teens to include a panorama of 'real' people doing 'real' things.

The third story, Jean Rouch's contribution to The Adolescents, similarly revolves around the exploits of two girls. Titled 'Marie-France et Véronique', this miniature psycho-drama—starring sixteen-year-olds Marie-France de Chabaneix and Véronique Duval—could be said to have paved the way for Eric Rohmer's 4 Aventures de Reinette et Mirabelle/4 Adventures of Reinette and Mirabelle, another episodic, fragmented film whose main characters' emotional restlessness and perambulatory predispositions provide spectators with numerous opportunities to catch glimpses of Paris—a city that has been fetishized throughout the history of cinema, yet in Rouch's (and Rohmer's) work is portrayed in a subtle way. In 'Marie-France et Véronique' Paris is an expressive backdrop against which this diametrically opposed duo make difficult choices in life and love before ultimately going their separate ways.

Followers of Rouch—a socially engaged anthropologist-documentarian sympathetic to the plight of marginalized dock workers, lumbermen, day laborers, vagabonds, and other fringe-dwellers populating postcolonial Africa—may be taken aback by his decision to focus neither on the dispossessed nor the diasporic, but instead on two well-to-do Parisians whose affluence affords them the luxury of grappling with such seemingly trivial issues as the need to escape boredom, family expectations, and marriages of convenience. However, in delving into the everyday details of contemporary adolescence, the filmmaker gestures back to his first feature-length film, Moi, un noir/I, a Black (1958). That film focuses on three young men as they go about their daily routines in Treichville, a suburb of Abidjan in the Ivory Coast. Having emigrated from Niger to this so-called New York of West Africa, these laborers could effectively communicate a sense of rootlessness in improvised scenes that invite the spectator to ruminate on the effects of proletarianization and cultural imperialism. By the time he made his contribution to The Adolescents, Rouch had mastered not only the technical aspects of fiction and nonfiction filmmaking but also the thematic motif central to that film, which called for spontaneity on the young performers' parts as well as diegetic participation on the director's part.

The Adolescents is an important historical artifact capturing a decisive moment in the careers of all four directors, when 'straight' documentary was giving way to fictional forms of cinematic discourse. For instance, Baldi, who drew on his training at the venerable Centro Sperimentale di Cinematografia in Rome when making such pro-proletariat documentaries as Il pianto delle zitelle (for which he took home the Venice Film Festival's Golden Lion in 1959), had begun segueing into short fiction during the early 1960s, when he contributed episodes to the omnibus films Le italiane e l'amore/Latin Lovers (1961) and The Adolescents. Although he continued to nurture his documentary roots and—as the organizer and director of the Istituto Italiano del Documentario—became close friends with Joris Ivens and John Grierson (with whom he cofounded the Associazione Internazionale del Film Cortometraggio e del Documentario), Baldi became increasingly ensconced in the world of fiction once he began overseeing the production of works by Pier Paolo Pasolini and Robert Bresson in the late 1960s.

Similarly, the multitasking Brault, one of the innovators behind the 1950s' 'Candid Eye movement' in Canadian documentary, who stepped behind the lens on such groundbreaking productions as Les raquetteurs (1958), La lutte (1961), Golden Gloves (1961), and Pour la suite du monde (1963), began to feel that fiction did not lie because it did not pretend to be the truth. Rouch was so deeply impressed by Brault's technical expertise and belief that the imagination was a necessary tool for penetrating reality that he proclaimed the Canadian to be the basis for French breakthroughs in cinéma vérité. Significantly, The Adolescents—released just one year before Brault left the National Film Board to found Nanouk Films—was made just a few months after his collaboration with friend Claude Jutra on the nondocumentary A tout prendre (1963), a film that suggests that Brault had indeed begun to question the ethical dimensions of documentary and shift into fictional modes of filmic discourse.

Like the other contributors to The Adolescents, Hiroshi Teshigahara had begun to feel that dramatic truth was as viable as documentary reportage, something to which the Japanese director's many films about artists and designers (such as Hokusai (1953), 12 Photographers (1955), and Ikebana (1956)) only faintly attest. Made a few months before his haunting depiction of moral descent, Suna no onna/

Woman in the Dunes (1964), Teshigahara's 'Ako' (sometimes referred to as 'White Morning') is the fourth and final episode of The Adolescents, although it was cut from US prints due to time constraints and has since been shown on its own as a short film in retrospectives.

DAVID SCOTT DIFFRIENT

See also: Brault, Michel; Rouch, Jean

Further reading

Betz, Mark, 'Film History, Film Genre, and Their Discontents: The Case of the Omnibus Film', *The Moving Image: Journal of the Association of Moving Image Archivists* 2, 2001a: 56–87.

——'The Name Above the (Sub)Title: Internationalism, Coproduction, and Polyglot European Art Cinema', in *Camera Obscura* no. 46, 2001b: 1–44.

MacDougall, David (ed.), *Transcultural Cinema*, Princeton, NJ: Princeton University Press, 1998.

Rouch, Jean, *Cine-Ethnography*, trans. Steven Feld, Minneapolis, MN: University of Minnesota Press, 2003.

Ruby, Jay (ed.), *The Cinema of Jean Rouch*, London: Harwood Academic Publishers, 1989.

Agee, James

The American writer James Agee was one of the most significant contributors to the development of the documentary form in the United States in the mid-twentieth century. He offered no systematized theory of documentary film, and he was only peripherally involved in the industry—first as a reviewer in the 1940s, and then as a screenwriter for such films as The African Queen (1951) and The Night of the Hunter (1955). However, the publication of *Let Us Now Praise Famous Men* in 1941 and his collected writings in *Agee on Film* in 1958 are evidence of his importance to the history of the documentary. Agee argued that many documentaries in the 1930s and 1940s were as removed from reality as Hollywood movies, with the filmmaker often adopting a didactic and polemical approach to the subject. Agee's solution was to develop a hybrid form, or semi-documentary, which he believed would offer a truer record of experience than the 'flat' presentation of life then presented in documentary films. He argued that propagandists had corrupted the documentary form in Germany and in the Soviet Union by degrading the film craft of Dziga Vertov and Sergei Eisenstein (arguing that by the 1940s it had become 'posterish, opportunistic, and anti-human'), but he believed the form still held great promise in the United Kingdom and the United States.

Agee wrote extensively on British World War II films and newsreels in the early 1940s, applauding them for capturing the bravery of servicemen and offering a cathartic encounter with reality (calling them 'the finest "escapes" available'). He also praised poetic documentaries such as Robert Flaherty's Nanook of the North (1922), recommending it for its 'beautiful simplicity', and Man of Aran (1934), which manages to convey the drama and nuances of human behavior in its portrayal of the daily struggle of Aran fishermen. He particularly liked the use of nonactors, which imparted a naturalness that would have been lacking, he believed, in actors' performances. Agee considered documentary no less a creative experience than fiction. As a modernist thinker, Agee was interested in the 'musical coherence' of documentary film and wrote about the 'real poetic energy' of its better exponents throughout his reviews for *The Nation* and *Time*, written between 1941 and 1948. This kind of poetic realism, which cuts across generic boundaries, was popular among other American cultural producers such as Tennessee Williams, who developed a plastic form of theater in his dramatic work in the 1940s and 1950s, and later, the New Journalists, who attempted to blend factuality and fiction in their prose.

Agee's major work, *Let Us Now Praise Famous Men*, was derived from a feature article commissioned in 1936 by *Fortune* magazine, for which he was asked to document the lives of white tenant farmers in the South (the article never appeared in the magazine). His research was conducted in Hale County, Alabama. Agee wanted to interfere as little as possible in the lives of his subjects. He relied heavily on montage in the book, with Walker Evans's sixty photographs, literary and biblical allusions, poetic meditation, autobiographical reflection, newspaper reportage, and domestic anecdotes, creating a fragmented text that invites the reader to recognize the artifice involved in producing documentary. The result is a text that shuttles between detailed observation and a broader statement about poverty, deprivation, and human need that cuts across different modes of inquiry—a technique that accords with Agee's claim that he and Walker did not position themselves 'as journalists, sociologists, politicians, entertainers, humanitarians, priests, or artists, but seriously'. His radical documentary technique challenged the flat realist documentaries of the 1930s, as well as the conservative ideology of the southern agrarians, with their emphasis on past glories at the expense of engaging with the present.

In light of Agee's disdain for certain modes of documentary technique, *Let Us Now Praise Famous Men* can be read as an attempt to create not only a semidocumentary but, as T.V. Reed (1988) argues, an 'anti-documentary', marked by complexity and an apparent lack of structure. Because it is so difficult to classify, the book can be interpreted as a serious modernist intervention into the verbal and visual language of documentary, or even a playful postmodern pastiche of styles. In fact, its hybridity stems from Agee's interest in the same kind of affinity between documentary and art that is evident in his film criticism. Agee was more comfortable with photographic images than language in capturing 'truth', arguing that words tend to be slippery, ambiguous, and often inaccurate. He describes the camera as belonging to an 'absolute' realm: 'an ice-cold, some ways limited, some ways more capable, eye, it is, like the phonograph record and like scientific instruments and unlike any other leverage of art, incapable of recording anything but absolute, dry truth'. This emphasis on the absolute objectivity of photography echoes the American visual artist Paul Strand's statement in 1917 that 'objectivity is the very essence of photography, its contribution and at the same time its limitation'. For Agee, if handled 'cleanly', photography could provide a documentary record unsurpassed in other media. However, he was aware that the artist's tendency to interfere with the subject, or to make aesthetic choices in terms of framing, would distort the truth of the moment or transform it into something else. In *Let Us Now Praise Famous Men* Agee displays his modernist colors by insisting that 'truth' lies in the photographic image, but he also goes beyond conventional documentary form by juxtaposing a range of texts and opening an interpretative space that encourages the reader to engage with the processes of composition.

MARTIN HALLIWELL

See also: Flaherty, Robert; Man of Aran; Nanook of the North; Vertov, Dziga

Biography

James Agee was born in 1909 in Knoxville, Tennessee. He was raised in the Cumberland mountain region and used the topography of his childhood as the basis for his two autobiographical novels, *The Morning Watch* (1951) and the unfinished *A Death in the Family* (1957), for which he was posthumously awarded the Pulitzer Prize in 1958. Graduating from Harvard University, Agee became a feature writer for *Fortune* magazine. The research for one feature on sharecroppers in Alabama led to the publication of *Let Us Now Praise Famous Men* (1941) with the photographer Walker Evans. Agee published his first collection of poetry, *Permit Me Voyage*, in 1934 and spent the 1940s as a film reviewer working for *Time* and *The Nation*. In 1948 he worked as a scriptwriter in Hollywood, producing scripts for The African Queen (1951) and The Night of the Hunter (1955). Agee died in 1955 at the age of forty-five.

Selected films

1949 The Quiet One: scriptwriter
1951 The African Queen: scriptwriter
1952 Crin-Blanc (Fr)/White Mane (US): commentary
1952 Face to Face: scriptwriter and actor
1955 The Night of the Hunter: scriptwriter

Further reading

Agee, James, *Agee on Film: Criticism and Comment on the Movies*, introduction by David Denby, New York: Modern Library, 2000.

Agee, James and Evans, Walker, *Let Us Now Praise Famous Men*, introduction by John Hersey, Boston, MA: Houghton Mifflin, 1988.

Böger, Astrid, *Documenting Lives: James Agee's and Walker Evans's Let Us Now Praise Famous Men*, Frankfurt: Peter Lang, 1994.

Coles, Robert, *Doing Documentary Work*, New York: Oxford University Press, 1997.

Reed, T.V. 'Unimagined Existence and the Fiction of the Real: Postmodern Realism in Let Us Now Praise Famous Men', *Representations* 24, 1988: 156–75.

Rufus, James, *Agee on Film: Five Film Scripts by James Agee*, Boston, MA: Beacon, 1964.

Snyder, John J., *James Agee: A Study of his Film Criticism*, New York: Arno, 1977.

Stange, Maren, *Symbols of Ideal Life: Social Documentary Photography in America, 1890–1950*, New York: Cambridge University Press, 1989.
Stott, William, *Documentary Expression and Thirties America*, New York: Oxford University Press, 1973.
Ward, J.A. *American Silences: The Realism of James Agee, Walker Evans, and Edward Hopper*, Baton Rouge, LA: Louisiana State University Press, 1985.

Agland, Phil

Phil Agland is known to be an unusual film-maker in the landscape of television documentaries. Agland's theory and techniques are often compared to those of a careful and detailed painter or a patient hunter. His films are often referred to as poetical and epical accounts of life.

Agland's first film, Korup—An African Rain Forest, was a five-year enterprise. Agland, a wildlife enthusiast concerned about the plight of the endangered species in the rainforests, had ventured to make the documentary in an attempt to raise awareness of the problem. Despite having no cinematography experience and with a very small budget, he went into the depths of the rainforest in spells of three months over a period of five years. This endeavour resulted in a poetic film containing images never seen on screen before and in an award-winning documentary.

Since that time, Agland has turned his focus on people. He returned to Cameroon's rain-forest to spend two years living among the Baka people with a small crew of two, filming Baka—The People of the Rain Forest. In the Western world, the Baka people are considered pygmies. Yet, Agland's impression was that this was in no way how the Baka perceived themselves. Agland's feelings were that the Baka's perception should be reflected in his camera work. Had he kept the camera on his shoulder, he would be filming the Baka from up high, giving cause to view them as pygmies. It was in the attempt to be truthful to the Baka's own image of their height that Agland developed what became his unique camera technique. Instead of perching the camera on the shoulder, Agland cradled the camera at waist height. This technique enabled him to film the Baka people from below their eye-level for a more intimate and nonpatronising viewpoint. Later on, Agland kept to this technique, claiming that by avoiding direct eye contact and by avoiding pointing the camera lens directly at his subject, he can minimise the presence of the camera.

Agland's theory is that in order to achieve genuine and intimate moments, the camera and crew should be as invisible as possible. He uses a radio microphone technique that enables the sound recordist to be at a fair distance and away from the scene. This radio microphone technique not only enables removal of the sound recordist from the scene but it also eliminates the presence of a third and sometimes a fourth person holding a somewhat intimidating boom pole, minimising the crew to two members or sometimes even one. The invisibility, claims Agland, is crucial in this observant, unobtrusive type of documentary-making, allowing the people in front of the camera to become oblivious to its presence.

Agland believes in observant documentaries rather than interview-based ones. His theory is that genuine stories or emotions will not emerge during an interview but rather in the small, sometimes insignificant and usually unpredictable moments in life, when the subjects are unaware of the camera and, hence, do not feel obliged to deliver or to satisfy. Agland also believe that the audience should feel part of the scene yet not in the middle of it. The centre of attention should be the story, the moment and the feelings within it rather than the camera or the audience. Agland therefore minimises his camera movements and often favours static camera shots.

Allowing for time and film stock is also a crucial aspect in Agland's careful work of portrayal. He avoids setting up situations and prefers to wait for moments and stories to emerge. Spending time with his characters allows them to get used to the presence of the camera and enables Agland to explore and capture rare and intimate moments in their lives. The structure and story are revealed throughout the filming process and during the editing period rather than in the scripting stage.

In his documentaries Agland creates scenes that follow the grammatical rules and language of a fiction film rather than adopting a documentary style of filming. Using a considerable coverage and carefully thought out editing ideas, both during and after filming, Agland creates rich and round scenes, covered with wide shots, close-ups and details and, hence, creating an illusion of fiction-style, multi-angled scenes.

Though his films appear not to be focusing on a specific place or a certain subject matter, Agland's passion and curiosity lie in people and in the small matters of life. Despite some views that would claim that Agland has an anthropologist's eye, Agland himself claims the very opposite. His aim is to emphasise the similarities between humans wherever they may live or come from, regardless of religion, cultural background or life circumstances. Agland strives to show the audience the familiar in the stranger on the screen.

Agland, therefore, comes back to the common subjects—family structure, sibling jealousy, parents' concern for their children, and the mutual need for attention and love. He deals with questions of age, health, and death as well as love, friendship, and community life. In Baka—The People of the Rain Forest, the focus of the film is four-year-old Ali and his family, his father's concern preparing him for life, his parents' relationship, and Ali's reaction to the newborn baby. Through these themes Agland explores the issues common to all humans and paints a portrait of what life is about, beyond the backdrop of place and time.

In China: Beyond the Clouds, set in Lijang, a small rural town located in the southwestern region of China, it seems that Agland furthers his attempt to paint a rich and full portrayal of life. He creates an epic about the small, familiar details of life. Agland interlaces different stories: a loss of a child alongside a lifetime friendship, a juvenile crime in a small town alongside a young mother's struggle to heal her child who suffers from cerebral palsy. Maintaining a fine balance between the tragic and the comic in life, Agland offers a complex and multilayered picture.

In his only fiction film so far, The Woodlanders, which is based on a nineteenth-century novel by Thomas Hardy, Agland challenges his audience to the same themes of finding the similarities beyond the differences by taking the audience on a journey to a different time, rather than to a faraway place.

SHIRA PINSON

Biography

Born in Weymouth, England in 1950. Read Geography at Hull University, Yorkshire, England. 1982 Completed his first documentary film, Korup—An African Rain Forest. 1982–6 coproduced and codirected a six-hour series, Fragile Earth, associated with Michael Rosenberg of Partridge Films. 1987 completed Baka—The People of the Rain Forest. 1992 Executive Producer of Turmid Hed—Sound Stuff, produced by Agland's company, River Films. 1994 completed a seven-hour series, China: Beyond the Clouds, produced by River Films for Channel 4. 1997 completed his first fiction feature, The Woodlanders, based on a novel by Thomas Hardy. 1999 completed Shanghai Vice, a seven-hour documentary produced by River Films for Channel 4 and Discovery Communications. 2003 completed a three-hour series, A French Affair, produced by River Films for Channel 4.

Further reading

Articles in:
Broadcast, July 30, 1999: 6.
Sight & Sound, June 1999: 28.
Music from Movies, Spring 1999: 28.
Radio Times, February 27, 1999: 11.
Broadcast, February 26, 1999: 34.
Sight & Sound, September 1998: 58.
Broadcast, September 11, 1998: 19.
Television, August/September 1998: 12–13.
New-Zealand Film Music Bulletin, May 1998: 19.
Empire, March 1998: 48.
Neon, February 1998: 86.
Sight & Sound, February 1998: 56.
Independent Eye, February 6, 1998: 4–5.
Times, January 30, 1998: 33.
Variety, September 1, 1996: 28.
Variety, October 3, 1994: 54.
Financial Times, November 4, 1987: 25.
Listener, November 2, 1987: 42.
TV Times, October 31, 1987: 18–19, 21.
Listener, October 29, 1987: 35.
Broadcast, October 19, 1984: 12.
Guardian, November 11, 1982: 12.
Broadcast, November 8, 1982: 12.
TV Times, November 6, 1982: 26–7.

Akerman, Chantal

Like Pasolini, members of the French New Wave, Sembène, Kiarostami, and others, Akerman has found her own way to push the boundaries of film realism. She has made a number of creative observational films, or documentaries. Yet the fiction films, for which she is best known, repeatedly allow in, or call forth, a documented reality that turns the film inside out, or makes the viewer ask: Where is it really grounded, in imagination or in fact? In the third and final episode of Je tu il elle (1974), two young women make love in a bed, rendered in three long takes with three different fixed camera positions. Are the women acting? Can they be? In a way, it seems that the earlier part of the film—a woman at home writing and thinking, and then a road journey through the night—is brought to earth by this ultimate dose of reality. Everything must be judged by the standard set here. Everything previous seems, in retrospect, fanciful. In another way, the first part of the film seems an ordinary experience, tied to reality, waiting for the sexual and emotional explosion that goes beyond imagination. In Akerman's most acclaimed film, Jeanne Dielman, 23 quai du Commerce, 1080 Bruxelles (1975), Delphine Seyrig gives a consummate, highly poised performance as the housewife, mother, and prostitute of the title. However, the film has her assemble a meatloaf from scratch, or peel all the potatoes necessary for a meal, or wash all the dinner dishes, each action filling one extraordinarily long take with a fixed camera. The pure act, documented as such, takes over the film. Les Rendez-vous d'Anna (1978) begins with a long-running fixed shot of a railway platform, where a train arrives, a crowd of people leave it, and a woman enters a phone booth fairly far away from us, makes a call, and then leaves the area. Akerman is fond of the long-distant look at a place, where the visual and aural environment seems to absorb people and their particular stories. Throughout this film, memories of 1930s and 1940s history, as well as personal problems of the present, struggle to find voice against the all-but-overwhelming documentation of Europe's cities, trains, train stations, and hotel rooms. In Toute une nuit (1982) the many characters, whose lives we see bits of in and around Brussels through a hot summer night, are never named, and their dialogue is largely inaudible; they are parts of the city and the atmosphere.

Akerman has said that she does not believe in the distinction between documentary and fiction. A film is made to project feelings and understanding, and the film may use an invented story and characters to do this, or it may take the world more or less as found, arranging a meeting of facts with what the filmmaker knows in her soul. Akerman's films without story and characters are perhaps best regarded in light of this denial of special documentary status, as personal, poetic works, which of course have the potential to reveal the world, to be true. Hotel Monterey (1972) is a silent film, giving us mostly fixed, long-held shots of the lobby area, elevator, hallways, and guest rooms of a modest old New York hotel, perhaps a residence for pensioners. People come and go in the shots, mysterious, ordinary, seemingly defined by their 1950s-ish attire and by the once stylish, now a bit desolate, clean atmosphere of this place they inhabit. The camera finds an abstract fascination in details of architecture or in the changing lights on an elevator call panel, suggesting forces that shape people's lives, which may not usually be acknowledged, and which may not even be fully understandable. The silence adds to this sense of incomprehensible power in some things we see. Late in the film the camera begins moving forward and back in a hallway, peering out a window at the end, as if curious and seeking escape. In the film's final moments the camera is up on the roof, panning across the New York skyline and Hudson River. The outdoors, the daylight, and the vistas accentuate by contrast the lurid light, the hothouse quality, something even gothic about the hotel interior. The film becomes a comment on the in-bred comforting worlds people make for themselves, or allow themselves, to live in.

Varied nonfictional work followed, including portraits of artists (choreographer Pina Bausch, pianist Alfred Brendel) and in Aujourd'hui, dis-moi (1982) a forum for older women to talk about their grandmothers and the Polish Jewish community that was obliterated or displaced by the Holocaust. Two of Akerman's most interesting observational films of the 1970s and 1980s show a great contrast in style. News from Home (1976) is a New York film akin to Hotel Monterey, this time with sound, giving us a succession of color shots of lonely alleys, streets busy with traffic and pedestrians, subway stations, subway cars with the camera inside among people, and a nearly empty diner at night. From time to time Akerman in voice-over reads letters from her mother in Brussels, at moments drowned out by the sounds of the city. The letters may be made up—but why be sceptical, or what difference does it make? With the reading there is a wonderful tension created between the pull of family ties, something going on in the head and heart, and what we otherwise see and hear in the film, evidence of the daughter artist confronting a multifarious new urban world, huge and forbidding, but where she can find an uncanny beauty. Les Années 80 (1983) is about preparation for the making of Akerman's romantic musical Golden Eighties (1986). We see auditions and rehearsals, with Akerman's voice giving instruction from off screen. At one point the director appears in a recording booth to do her own version of one of the film's songs. We see acting and filmmaking prepared and executed, and the series of Golden Eighties fragments of scenes, some rough and very much in preparation, others perfected, takes us more and more into the world of the fiction film to come. The documentary, with its consciousness about performance, is another version of the fiction's exploration of the psychology of love and the moods of loss.

With D'Est (1993) Akerman's documentary work takes a serious turn into history and geography. This is her most impressive film in the observational mode and one of her very best films altogether, a grand two-hour study of Eastern Europe and, mainly, Moscow, just watching and listening, offering no commentary and registering no one's words. Here, as a traveler, Akerman seems to find material she has always deeply known and understood, with which her filmmaking connects powerfully. The film opens with images of space—empty roads and intersections, and flat fields—and one never gets over the impression that human life in this East is lived against a background of emptiness. We see people sitting in their apartments, seeming to have agreed to pose for a portrait, exposing their somberness. Some eat a meal alone. There are long mobile shots—one a full ten minutes—as if looking at an endless world, moving through the streets of Moscow taking in crowds waiting for buses, or moving through railway stations where crowds sit quietly on benches, bundled up in the cold, as if displaced from home and waiting forever. Much of the film is shot at night, with all its beauty and uncertainty, and mostly in winter, where the physical world weighs heavily. It is a picture of life lived against the void, of a sameness with little sign of change. The many faces are intriguing, but do not show much; they acknowledge the camera, but only obliquely. People seem experienced and complex, but closed off. At the end of the film we are at a concert and hear a full solo cello piece by Boris Tchaikovsky, which is greeted with a strong ovation. This old-fashioned, soulful music, with some painful modernist twists, one feels could be playing inside the heads of all the people we see in the film.

Akerman's more recent films continue to look at places and the cultures associated with them. Sud (1999) journeys across the American South, staring at the lush vegetation and the air's heat waves that surround all activity, and listens to people talk about poor lives and racial problems. The journey comes to an uneasy rest in Jasper, Texas, gathering information on the then recent murder by dragging of James Byrd, a black man, at the hands of whites. Twice the camera, looking back at the road, travels over the route the man was dragged behind a truck. It is a simple, unnerving gesture, confronting the event in a way only film could do. De l'autre côté (2002) centers on the Mexican/US border in the Sonoran desert/southern Arizona region. The problems of economically desperate Mexicans trying to cross into the United States come into the film in interviews and monologues, as do the attitudes of fearful white Americans. However, the film mostly contemplates the place, the beautiful and threatening desert spaces, the skies in various light, the ugly, endless border wall, the ramshackle buildings that have grown up in the region and, viewed at night, the fence lights and search lights, roads or desert paths traversed by the camera like a migrant or the pursuer of migrants, barely revealing what is there, and finally the view through the night-vision device of an airborne surveillance mechanism or weapon. Human pressures have made this place what it is, yet the place takes on a life of its own, as if it is a destiny that has drawn people into it. As always in Akerman, film registers an inhuman power of place and things, which, paradoxically, is all too human.

CHARLES WARREN

Biography

Born in Brussels on June 6, 1950, Akerman was inspired to take up filmmaking after seeing Godard's Pierrot le fou. She studied for several months at the Belgian film school INSAS in 1967, completed her first film, Saute ma ville, in 1968, and won recognition when this was shown at the Oberhausen Short Film Festival in 1971. From 1971–3 Akerman spent time in New York doing odd jobs, seeing avant-garde films, and making films. She won international acclaim for Jeanne Dielman, 23 quai du Commerce, 1080 Bruxelles in 1975, and was given a retrospective at the Venice Film Festival that year. With Aujourd'hui, dis-moi (1980), she began making films for television, which would sponsor much of her future documentary work. With Hall de nuit (1991), she began writing plays, several of which were produced over the next decade. In 1995 her D'Est traveled to several museums in the United States and Europe. Two years later, she was given a retrospective at the Pesaro Festival in 1997. Akerman then taught filmmaking at Harvard University from 1997 to 1998. In 1998 she published *Une famille à Bruxelles*, a memoir/fiction centering on her mother, 1998. She used De l'autre côté for an installation at Documenta 11 in 2002.

Selected films

1968 Saute ma ville (Blow Up My Town)
1971 L'Enfant aimé ou je joue à être une femme mariée (The Beloved Child, or I Play at Being a Married Woman)
1972 Hotel Monterey; La Chambre 1 (The Room, 1); La Chambre 2 (The Room, 2)
1973 Le 15/8; Hanging Out Yonkers 1973
1974 Je tu il elle (I You He She)
1975 Jeanne Dielman, 23 Quai du Commerce, 1080 Bruxelles
1976 News from Home
1978 Les Rendez-vous d'Anna (Meetings with Anna)
1980 Dis-moi (Tell Me)
1982 Toute une nuit (All Night Long)
1983 Les Années 80 (The Eighties); Un jour Pina m'a demandé (One Day Pina Asked Me); L'Homme à la valise (The Man with the Suitcase)
1984 Lettre d'un cinéaste (Letter from a Filmmaker)
1986 Golden Eighties/Window Shopping; La Paresse (Sloth); Le Marteau (The Hammer); Letters Home; Mallet-Stevens
1989 Histoires d'Amérique (American Stories/ Food, Family, and Philosophy); Les Trois dernières sonates de Franz Schubert (The Last Three Sonatas of Franz Schubert); Trois strophes sur le nom de Sacher ('Three Stanzas on the Name Sacher' by Henri Dutilleux)
1991 Nuit et jour (Night and Day)
1992 Le Déménagement (Moving In); Contre l'oubli (Against Forgetting)
1993 D'Est (From the East); Portrait d'une jeune fille de la fin des années 60 à Bruxelles (Portrait of a Young Girl at the End of the 1960s in Brussels)
1996 Un Divan à New York (A Couch in New York); Chantal Akerman par Chantal Akerman (Chantal Akerman by Chantal Akerman)
1999 Sud (South)
2000 La Captive (The Captive)
2002 De l'autre côté (From the Other Side)
2004 Demain, on déménage (Tomorrow We Move)

Further reading

Foster, Gwendolyn Audrey (ed.), *Identity and Memory: The Films of Chantal Akerman*, Trowbridge: Flicks Books, 1999.

Halbreich, Kathy and Jenkins, Bruce, *Bordering on Fiction: Chantal Akerman's D'Est*, Minneapolis, MN: Walker Art Center, 1995.

Indiana, Gary, 'Getting Ready for the Golden Eighties: An Interview with Chantal Akerman', *Artforum* 21, no. 10, 1983: 55–61.

Margulies, Yvonne, *Nothing Happens: Chantal Akerman's Hyperrealist Everyday*, Durham, NC and London: Duke University Press, 1996.

Akomfrah, John

John Akomfrah was one of the founders of the Black Audio Film Collective in 1982, a group that went on to produce Handsworth Songs (1986). As a member of this cooperative, Akomfrah performed the role of director and writer alongside other writers and producers within a cooperative mode of production. The group's audiovisual practice was marked by a preference for discursive interrogation and recontextualization of archival documentary sources over documentary realism. After Black Audio ceased working as a collective in 1995, Akomfrah set up production of a company called Smoking Dogs with former members of Black Audio Lina Gopaul and David Lawson. The company produced television documentaries such as Goldie: When Saturn Returnz (1998) and Riot (1999) for the United Kingdom's Channel 4, and The Wonderful World of Louis Armstrong as part of the Omnibus season for the BBC.

Akomfrah has frequently favored the documentary form as a means of formal innovation, while also making feature-length films that invoke the relation between drama and documentary. The resources of drama and archival documentary are called on as a means of articulating the diasporic experience in Testament (1988), whereas in Who Needs a Heart (1991) the combination is used to highlight the cultural politics of the 1960s and a figure rather overlooked by history in the form of Michael X. The style of documentary demonstrated in Handsworth Songs involves a nonlinear structure, modernist techniques of juxtaposition and layering, and, in collaboration with Trevor Mathison, a dissonant and contrapuntal relation between sound and image. The interrogation of the relation between narrative, the poetic expression of diasporic memory, and the documentation of history in Handsworth Songs is recast via a female dramatic protagonist to Ghana in Testament. As a result, the referent for Akomfrah's filmmaking is not only black experience but also an ongoing exploration of form that looks into the problematic form of the bounded categories of fiction and nonfiction and simultaneously raises recurring questions concerning historiography. The concern with materializing history through documentary is underlined in The Cheese and the Worm (1996), featuring the historian Carlo Ginsberg and addressing Christianity, heresy, and witchcraft in Italy during the sixteenth century.

Akomfrah documents the diasporic experience of black British subjects in Touch of the Tarbrush (1991), which revisits J.B. Priestley's *English Journey* of 1933 as a starting point from which to enquire how the mixed-race community of Liverpool describes its own routes to a hybrid identity. Here, Akomfrah fuses his personal and remembered history as a black English subject with the memories of some members of the mixed-race community that is 'rooted and located in Liverpool'.

The expositional documentary and the tradition of surveying the condition of a particular place and time through history is annexed by Akomfrah in order to represent 'the lives and histories that represent the hope for another England'.

Akomfrah has produced work focused on significant cultural and political figures such as Malcolm X, Michael X, and Louis Armstrong. Who Needs a Heart, commissioned by Channel 4 in the United Kingdom, combines archival footage of the life of Michael X with a dramatic portrayal centered on a group of black people and white people who are caught up in the politics of black power and the culture of the 1960s. The dramatic element of the docudrama is supported by reportage. Diegetic sound and dialogue are frequently muted into silence and replaced by fragments of official voices denouncing the compromised life of Michael X. Who Needs a Heart emphasizes the problem of history as narrative and an approach to documenting a relatively undocumented political figure, where the outcome of historical knowledge and truth is rendered less secure and cannot be guaranteed.

Seven Songs for Malcolm X (1993) was produced for and broadcast by Channel 4 in the UK at the same time as the release in the UK of Spike Lee's film Malcolm X (1992). This documentary takes the form of a tableau, in which various black personalities and members of his family present a range of perspectives on Malcolm X. It comprises a combination of expositional testimonies, eyewitness accounts, archival footage, and dramatic reenactments. Sound is again used as a mechanism for drawing the viewer's attention to the relation between the different elements that constitute the documentary, and the different manifestations of Malcolm X within African American culture.

In The Mothership Connection (1995), Akomfrah attempts to understand the African diasporic experience of displacement through the vehicle of science fiction and new technology. Connections are suggested between the musical sources of George Clinton and Sun Ra, the history of the blues, and science-fiction narratives of abduction and transportation. The Mothership Connection questions the boundaries that separate the history of the African diaspora from the scenarios of narrative fiction.

Akomfrah's documentary output spans both television and film. Productions for Black Audio, such as Testament (1988) and Seven Songs for Malcolm X (1993), were exhibited and awarded prizes at international film festivals—for example at the African Film Festival of Perugia, where Testament received the Special Jury Prize in 1989. In the UK his films are generally either broadcast on television or receive a limited cinematic release. As a result, the critical context for Akomfrah's filmmaking is, somewhat problematically, a combination of the documentary tradition and European Art Cinema rather than the black communities in Britain (Gilroy 1989).

Throughout the 1980s and 1990s Akomfrah extended his reach beyond the context of black British experience, emphasizing the internationalism of the African diaspora. Testament (1988), The Mothership Connection (1995), and the African Political Broadcasts (1995) together represent a documenting of pan-African experience. Akomfrah's contribution to documentary represents both a formal interrogation of the materials and limits of documenting, and a significant contribution to the cultural representation of the black diaspora. Akomfrah, in collaboration with the members of the Black Audio Film Collective, opens up and places in doubt the language of documentary, while simultaneously exposing the gaps, silences, and blind spots of official, recorded history.

IAN GOODE

See also: Handsworth Songs

Biography

Born in Ghana in 1957 to parents who had met in England and who had returned to Ghana, where Akomfrah's father was a member of the government under President Kwame Nkrumah. Raised in London. Attended Portsmouth Polytechnic, where he met some of the future members of Black Audio Film Collective. Returned to London and helped to establish Black Audio Film Collective in 1982. Formed Smoking Dogs production company in 1995 with Lina Gopaul and David Lawson. Member of PACT Cultural Diversity Panel (The Producers' Alliance for Cinema and Television). Appointed governor on the board of the British Film Institute in October 2001.

Selected films

1986 Handsworth Songs: director
1988 Testament: director
1991 Who Needs a Heart: director, writer
1993 Seven Songs for Malcolm X: director, writer
1996 The Cheese and the Worm: director

Further reading

Auguiste, Reece and Black Audio Film Collective, 'Black Independents and Third Cinema: The British Context', in Jim Pines and Paul Willemen (eds), *Questions of Third Cinema*, London: British Film Institute, 1989.

Diawara, Manthia, 'The "I" Narrator in Black Diaspora Documentary', in Phyllis Klotman and Janet Cutler (eds), *Struggles for Representation. African American Documentary Film and Video*, Bloomington and Indianapolis: Indiana University Press, 1999.

Gilroy, Paul, 'Cruciality and the Frog's Perspective: An Agenda of Difficulties for the Black Arts Movement in Britain', *Third Text* 5, 1989.

Marks, Laura, 'Ghosts of Stories. Black Audio Film Collective's Who Needs a Heart', *Cineaction* 36, February 1995.

Mercer, Kobena (ed.), *Black Film/British Cinema*, London: ICA, 1988.

——*Welcome to the Jungle*, London: Routledge, 1994.

Alexander, Donald

Donald Alexander was a typical representative of the 1930s generation, which—shocked as it was by the human waste caused by the Depression—welcomed the social changes begun during the war and ending in the British Labour government's welfare programme. After graduating from the University of Cambridge, he gained his first film experience in the South Wales coal fields in 1935. Using a borrowed 16mm camera, he and his companion filmed such typical sights as miners looking for coal high upon the slagheaps. Once the film was finished it was shown to Paul Rotha. He invited Alexander to be his assistant at Strand Films—an offer that was immediately accepted.

Rotha ensured that Alexander learned all the tricks of the trade by having him work with the company's more experienced staff. For Today We Live, commissioned by the National Council for Social Service, Alexander, acting as assistant to director Ralph Bond, personally reshot on 35mm stock the sequence from his novice film on the Tylorstown slagheap. The footage would be incorporated in countless historical documentaries.

In 1937 Alexander was ready for his first directorial assignment: Eastern Valley, about a substance farm for unemployed miners in Cwmavon, run by the Order of Friends. In his last prewar film, about the city of Dundee, he made use of the more complex narrative structure that would become so characteristic of his 1940s documentaries. The frame story for Dundee is provided by a group of people meeting by chance on the ferry crossing the Tay; each character is used to impart factual information to, and derive empathy from, the spectator.

In December 1940 Alexander was asked by Paul Rotha to return to London. In response to the plans of former Shell publicity officer, Jack Beddington (now head of Films Division at the Ministry of Information (MOI)), to involve outside units in the production program, Rotha had the idea of setting up a new unit. Its aim was making 'films of social importance with an eye to the future' (Alexander), in line with the 'war aims' presented in the very first issue of Documentary Newsletter (1940), which demanded that 'the Educational system, Public Health Services, Child Welfare, the Housing Problem' be reviewed and reformed.

In 1941 Alexander was first introduced to Bridget (Budge) Cooper, who would soon become his (second) wife and close companion in film production. While working at Paul Rotha Productions (PRP), they tackled several social and health topics in films about day nurseries, rural local government, rehabilitation, female agricultural labor, and the contributions of West Indians to the war effort. However, it was Cooper's Children of the City (1944), analyzing the social roots of child delinquency, that epitomized PRP's social approach to documentary. Alexander acted as the film's producer, but it was Rotha who got the credit. It was out of resentment against this and similar incidents that Alexander, Cooper, and eight others decided in 1944 to break away from PRP. They formed Documentary Technicians Alliance (DATA), a cooperative recognized by the Co-operative Productive Federation. Until his departure in 1950, Alexander was annually elected as chairman by the DATA shareholder-employees.

To a large extent, the new unit was dependent on the MOI. When Labour won the 1945 general election by a significant majority, DATA felt proud in having contributed to this beginning of a new era through their films. However, Labour showed little concern for the documentary. It disbanded the MOI, replacing it with a common service department, the Central Office of Information. This remained the biggest sponsor of DATA, but its nongovernmental status proved a growing source of friction. By 1948 DATA, now employing more than forty technicians, had changed its direction by looking for other sponsors such as the National Coal Board (NCB, for which it produced the monthly Mining Review) and the Steel Company of Wales.

In 1950 Alexander left DATA. The following year he was asked to take over the one-day-a-week job of Films Adviser at the NCB. He discovered that there was a great need for technical, training, and safety films, and argued for the setting up of an in-house technical film unit; in 1953 the unit was operative. Over the years, the volume of its work increased and Alexander, whose NCB job gradually became a full-time one, had to hire more employees. It was his policy not only to give young people the chance to learn the trade but also to make sure that there would always be a place for those who had already 'paid their dues' in documentary.

After a twelve-year stint at the NCB, Alexander decided to step down. He continued working for the Coal Board, and made several films, including The 4 M's, a film that NCB Chairman Alf Robens personally used in his presentations. In 1969 Alexander became Director of Audiovisual Aids at the University of Dundee. Being back in his beloved Scotland offered him the chance to get involved in the (second) Films of Scotland Committee. In 1979 he retired from the University of Dundee. Donald Alexander died July 20, 1993.

BERT HOGENKAMP

Biography

Born in London, August 26, 1913. Graduated from St John's College, Cambridge, reading classics, and later modern and medieval languages, in 1935. Joined Strand Films in 1936 as an assistant. Joined Film Centre in 1939. Director at Paul Rotha Productions, 1941–4. Founding member and first chairman of the film production cooperative Documentary Technicians Alliance (DATA), 1944–50. Secretary of British Documentary, 1947–9. Films Adviser to the Steel Company of Wales, 1950–1. Films Adviser to the National Coal Board and later head of the NCB Film Unit, 1951–63. Director of Audiovisual Aids at the University of Dundee, 1969–79. Died near Inverness, Scotland, July 20, 1993.

Selected films

1936	Rhondda: director, photographer
1937	Today We Live (Bond, Ruby Grierson): assistant director
1937	Eastern Valley: director
1938	Wealth of a Nation: director
1939	Dundee: director
1944	Children of the City (Budge Cooper): producer
1948	Here's Health: director
1958–62	Experiment: Workstudy Experiment at Nafodynyrys Colliery: producer, director, editor
1966	The 4 M's: director
1974	Tayside: treatment, written commentary

Allégret, Marc

Although often remembered as the long-time companion and protégé of eminent French novelist André Gide, Marc Allégret was also among the most prolific directors of his generation. Between 1927 and 1970 he made nearly eighty films, including fifteen documentaries clustered at the beginning and end of his career. His only two feature-length offerings were his most important: Voyage au Congo/Travels in the Congo (1927), a portrait of life in central Africa that played a seminal role in the emergence of cinematic ethnography; and Avec André Gide/With André Gide (1952), an affectionate retrospective of the writer's life and work.

In July 1925 Allégret and Gide embarked on a ten-month expedition across French Equatorial Africa. Allégret was in charge of all the logistical details, foremost among which was crafting a written, photographic, and cinematic record of the journey. He had no formal training as a photographer or filmmaker, but he practised extensively prior to the trip under the guidance of the renowned surrealist artist Man Ray. In contrast to both Robert Flaherty's influential Nanook of the North (1922) and Léon Poirier's hit La Croisière noire/The Black Journey (1926), Allégret wanted his film to be an objective record of African cultures that informed and explained rather than entertaining through adventure and exoticism. To that end, the first-time director deliberately excluded references to the trip itself, the many technical challenges he faced, his own presence behind the camera, and grotesque elements of African culture, such as the large wooden discs worn in the lips of Massa women.

Voyage au Congo presents scenes of daily life among eight distinct ethnic groups, focusing on agricultural practices, hunting and fishing techniques, architectural styles, and key collective rituals, all of which are carefully contextualized with didactic intertitles (over one hundred and fifty in the eighty-minute montage that survives today) and detailed maps (ten in all). In so doing, Allégret rejected the sensationalism and racial stereotyping that had long characterized newsreel and documentary representations of so-called primitive cultures. Instead, the film promoted intercultural understanding by appealing to spectators' intellect and steeping them in knowledge. This approach, which reflects Gide's biting assertion that 'the less intelligent the white man is, the dumber he perceives Blacks to be' was nothing short of revolutionary, for it revealed the potential of cinema as a legitimate ethnographic tool.

Perhaps most importantly, Allégret realized the impossibility of ever achieving total objectivity because of the inherently unequal power dynamic that exists between the filmmaker and his or her subjects. His travel diary, which first appeared in 1987 under the title *Carnets du Congo/Notebooks from the Congo*, charts the emergence of a precocious self-reflexivity that would inform the later work of anthropologists such as Michel Leiris, Jean Rouch, and Claude Lévi-Strauss. In order to minimize the contaminating impact of his presence, Allégret shot much of the film with a long-range telephoto lens and whenever possible accustomed his subjects to the camera through repeated pantomime before taking any actual footage.

Whereas Gide's written accounts of the trip, *Voyage au Congo/Travels in the Congo* and *Retour du Tchad/Return from Chad*, sparked a national debate over colonial policy by exposing forced labour, crushing taxes, starvation, and insufficient medical care throughout central Africa, Allégret's film was more subtle in its politics, eschewing invective in favour of a primitivist aesthetic that celebrated African physical beauty, vitality, and moral purity. This brand of primitivism—which had its origins in the Enlightenment philosophers' critique of modern civilization and idealization of 'natural man'—had a significant influence on French art (particularly sculpture and painting) throughout the

1920s as concerns about European decadence and the need for cultural rejuvenation intensified in the wake of World War I.

In this regard, Allégret's footage of athletic competitions and dances is particularly striking. His long, graceful shots of contracting backs, arms, legs, and breasts create living, neo-classical sculptures reminiscent of the Renaissance. From today's perspective such scenes are disturbingly objectifying and voyeuristic, yet as an exercise in visual aesthetics and eroticism their appeal remains undeniable. Moreover, in the context of the late 1920s they constituted a powerful, if at root equally stereotypical, corrective to the widely held European prejudice that blacks were ugly, brutish, and unworthy of artistic attention.

The film's potentially incompatible aesthetic and ethnographic dimensions in fact complement each other, culminating in a sixteen-minute segment that dramatized courtship and marriage customs among the Sara people near Lake Chad. Although the practices represented on screen are sociologically accurate, the story of a young couple who meet by the river, fall in love, and struggle to satisfy their families' demands is entirely fictional. As Allégret's *Carnets* reveal, he carefully managed all aspects of the production, from scouting picturesque locations and choosing his actors among the local population, to directing their movements on camera and writing the explanatory intertitles. The result is a primitivist melodrama disguised as a documentary that uses the universal theme of love to inform European viewers about African cultural differences.

Although Voyage au Congo did not enjoy commercial success or have a substantial impact on popular mentalities, it received praise from critics and it launched Allégret's career as a filmmaker. During the following year he made short documentaries about native culture in Djerba, a small island off the coast of Tunisia, life in the region surrounding Tripoli, and a publicity film for the Belgian National Railroad Company. He then embarked on a successful career as a fiction film director, returning to documentary over twenty years later with Avec André Gide.

Released in early 1952 during a series of official ceremonies commemorating the first anniversary of Gide's death, the film was the first feature-length cinematic biography of a French writer. Its first two parts provide a historically contextualized overview of Gide's life and work through a smoothly edited montage of newsreel footage, photos, and voice-over narration. The narrative is accurate but highly selective and at times superficial, omitting major novels such as *Les Faux-Monnayeurs/The Counterfeiters* and *Les Caves du Vatican/Lafcadio's Adventures*, as well as allusions to Gide's homosexuality and its crucial place in his work.

The third and final section, shot in Gide's small Paris apartment during the last months of his life, is an intimate portrait that awkwardly attempts to humanize the Nobel Prize winner and to ensure his legacy for posterity. Rather than conveying nonchalance and spontaneity—as Allégret clearly intended by filming Gide reading aloud from his works in slippers and robe, playing with his grandchildren, and smoking at the kitchen table while reflecting on his career—this part of the film comes off as pretentious, transparently disguised hagiography. It is obvious that many scenes have been scripted, rehearsed, and edited in order to paint Gide as both the quintessential French intellectual whose genius enlightens the world and, quite inaccurately, as a devoted family man with whom everyone can identify. The film ends pointedly on that note as Gide paraphrases the final lines of *Thésée/Theseus*: 'I have built my city, which is to say my writing. Through it my thought will live eternally.'

In 1952 the film bitterly divided critics as Gide's work always had, eliciting lavish praise and sarcastic denunciation. Despite its obvious flaws, in retrospect Avec André Gide can be appreciated as the innovative forerunner of a film genre that is now a standard part of television programming. Also, despite its flaws, on a meta-textual level the film exemplifies Gide's penchant for self-reinvention and the growing role that cinema would play in shaping celebrity and public memory during the last half of the twentieth century. Allégret gave up fiction film in 1963 under the influence of the New Wave, whose exponents heavily criticized his traditional style. However, several years later he returned to directing with a series of well-crafted television documentaries based on the Lumière newsreel archives from the late nineteenth and early twentieth centuries.

In the end, Allégret's contribution to the development of documentary film is quantitatively modest but qualitatively significant for his pioneering experimentation with form and genre. Though Avec André Gide was an ambitious failure, Voyage au Congo stands as a masterpiece of early ethnographic cinema and the most influential film of Allégret's entire career.

BRETT BOWLES

See also: Voyage au Congo

Biography

Born in Basel, Switzerland, December 23, 1900, son of a French Protestant pastor. Trip to England and beginning of lifelong relationship with André Gide, 1917–18. Organized short-lived performing arts festival known as Les Soirées de Paris, 1924. Graduated from the prestigious Ecole des Sciences Politiques with a concentration in diplomacy, 1925. Travelled through central Africa with Gide, 1925–6. Release of Voyage au Congo and emergence as a director, 1927–39. Continued making fiction films in Nice during World War II, 1940–5. Pursued various film projects in Switzerland and England, 1946–50. Returned to France to make Avec André Gide, 1950–1. Joined Cannes Film Festival Jury and received Chevalier de l'Ordre des Arts et des Lettres award, 1960. Named President of the Cinémathèque Française, 1966. Died in Paris, November 3, 1973.

Selected films

1927 Voyage au Congo/Travels in the Congo: director
1927 En Tripolitaine/Around Tripoli: director
1928 L'Ile de Djerba/The Island of Djerba: director
1928 Les Chemins de fer belges/The Belgian Railroad System: director
1952 Avec André Gide/With André Gide: director
1952 Occultisme et magie/Occultism and Magic: director
1967 Exposition 1900/The 1900 World's Fair: director
1967 Lumière (Lumière, part 1): director
1968 Lumière (Lumière, part 2): director
1968 Début de siècle/Beginning of the Century: director
1968 Jeunesse de France/French Youth: director
1968 La Grande Bretagne et les Etats-Unis de 1896 à 1900/Great Britain and the United States from 1896 to 1900: director
1969 L'Europe continentale avant 1900/Continental Europe before 1900: director
1969 L'Europe méridionale au temps des rois/Southern Europe in the Time of the Kings: director

Further reading

Allégret, Marc, 'Voyage au Congo: Explications sur le film', *Les Cahiers de Belgique*, 4 May 1928: 138–43.

——*Carnets du Congo: Voyage avec André Gide*, Daniel Durosay (ed.), Paris: CNRS Editions, 1993.

Durosay, Daniel, 'Les images du Voyage au Congo: L'oeil d'Allégret', *Bulletin des amis d'André Gide* 73, 1987: 57–79.

——'Images et imaginaire dans le Voyage au Congo: Un film et deux auteurs', *Bulletin des amis d'André Gide* 80, 1988: 9–30.

——'Le document contesté: Avec André Gide, sa réception hier et aujourd'hui', *Bulletin des amis d'André Gide* 98, 1993: 287–92.

——'Analyse synoptique du Voyage au Congo de Marc Allégret avec l'intégralité des inter-titres', *Bulletin des amis d'André Gide* 101, 1994: 71–85.

Geiger, Jeffrey, 'Sightseeing: Voyage au Congo and the Ethnographic Spectacle', in Tom Connor (ed.), *André Gide's Politics: Rebellion and Ambivalence*, New York: Palgrave Macmillan, 2000: 111–30.

Gide, André, *Voyage au Congo, suivi du Retour du Tchad*, Paris: Gallimard, 1929.

Houssiau, Bernard, *Marc Allégret: Découvreur de stars*, Paris: Editions Cabédita, 1994.

Leprohon, Pierre, *L'Exotisme au cinéma: les chasseurs d'images à la conquête du monde*, Paris: J. Susse, 1945.

Putnam, Walter, 'Writing the Wrongs of French Colonial Africa: Voyage au Congo and Le Retour du Tchad', in Tom Connor (ed.), *André Gide's Politics: Rebellion and Ambivalence*, New York: Palgrave Macmillan, 2000: 89–110.

Alvarez, Santiago

Santiago Alvarez was not only the man who put Cuban documentary on the world map but he was also one of the most powerful and innovative documentarians in the history of cinema. Politically a supporter of Fidel Castro (he was once described as Castro's poet laureate for his loving film portrayals of the Cuban leader), his aesthetics were anything but conventional. Not only did Alvarez become a master of agitprop, whom many have compared with the Russian Dziga Vertov (although Alvarez himself knew nothing of Vertov's work until later), but he also extended the art of documentary in several directions. He did this through a highly personal style with huge visual impact, in which a rough-hewn lyricism was carried along by montage work that was often satirical or ironic, frequently using animated titles in place of commentary, and backed by the iconic use of music. In the 1950s Alvarez worked as a record librarian in a television station, and he developed a keen sense of the possibilities of matching—and mismatching—music and images.

One of the founder members of the Cuban film institute ICAIC (Instituto Cubano de Arte e Industria Cinematográficas), which was set up in 1959 during the first year of the Revolution, Alvarez was already forty years old when he was put in charge of the newsreel section and made his first short films. He once called himself a product of 'accelerated underdevelopment' and was always grateful to the Cuban Revolution for making him a filmmaker and enabling him to fulfill his youthful dreams. Born in the working-class district of Colonial Old Havana, he was the son of immigrant parents from Spain. When he was five years old, his shopkeeper father was arrested for anarchist activities and spent two years in prison, while the young family struggled to survive on their own. Alvarez started working at the age of fifteen as a compositor's apprentice, became active in the union of graphic arts workers, went to night school, and set up a students' association.

At the end of the 1930s he went to the United States, working as a coal miner in Pennsylvania and as a dishwasher in New York. Back in Cuba in 1942, he joined the Communist Party and got a job in radio, and later in television. He also attended a film club in Havana run by the Young Communists, which became a recruiting ground for the new film institute. At ICAIC, he was put in charge of newsreels and quickly proceeded to turn them into a veritable art form, as well as a training ground for several generations of young filmmakers in how to make films quickly, cheaply, and using whatever materials were at hand. Perhaps it was his anarchist susceptibilities that gave his aesthetics their particular slant: a healthy disapproval of schools, conventions, and orthodoxy, together with a penchant for the deployment of pithy, intelligent, didactic montage. These susceptibilities rapidly induced him to discard the conventional language of the newsreel, and turn the format inside out. Instead of an arbitrary sequence of disconnected items, Alvarez combined them into a political argument, or turned them into single-topic documentaries. He used this technique in the first of his films to win international awards, Ciclón/Hurricane in 1963, and Now (1965), a denunciation of racial discrimination in the United States.

The newsreel job gave Alvarez the chance to film abroad, and here too he took a radical approach. In 1966 he accompanied Cuban athletes to the Pan-American Games in Puerto Rico, using the opportunity to turn out his longest film yet (thirty-four minutes), a biting satire of US imperialism named after the ship that took them there, Cerro Pelado. ICAIC was still at this time filming newsreels on mute, handheld 35mm cameras, but Alvarez was already at the height of his creative powers and using only a few intertitles to convey basic information, eschewing a verbal voice-over and instead using music to narrate the events. At one point in Cerro Pelado, shots of a training center for Cuban counterrevolutionaries (as a caption describes it) are juxtaposed with a band arrangement of Rossini's 'William Tell Overture', which naturally recalls the use of the same piece as the title music of the television series The Lone Ranger; thus Alvarez presents the counterrevolutionaries as imitation cowboys, an image both satiric and deflating. In 1967 came Hanoi Martes 13/Hanoi, Tuesday 13th, a lyrical and wordless forty-minute portrayal of what daily life was like in war-torn North Vietnam (Tuesday the 13th is the Spanish equivalent of Friday the 13th in English). Here, the music was an original score by Leo Brouwer, who was emerging as Cuba's most original film composer.

The same experimental approach produces both LBJ (1968), a stunning satire on US political assassinations, and 79 Primaveras/79 Springtimes of Ho Chi Minh (1969), a deeply poetic tribute to the Vietnamese leader Ho Chi Minh. LBJ uses the three letters of President Johnson's initials to stand for Luther, Bob, and John—Martin Luther King and the two Kennedys—in a bold play on the strange coincidence that the corpses of these three men littered Johnson's ascent. Visually, the core of the satire is the image culled from a North American newspaper cartoon of Johnson as the incarnation of the Texan cowboy on his bronco. Alvarez doubles this up with Johnson as a medieval knight in armor astride his mount, reinforced with clips from two classic Hollywood genres—Westerns and the historical adventure—which appear distorted. (They came from wide-screen films that had been copied directly without using the appropriate lens to unsqueeze them.) The film is thus as much a deconstruction of the imagery of the mass media as of US politics, in which assassination became an almost accustomed weapon that remained veiled in misinformation and mystery. Except for some linking animation and a few shots in the sequence on Martin Luther King, almost everything in this twenty-minute film is found material. As Alvarez put it himself, it was the US blockade of Cuba that prompted this approach by denying Cuba access to new live material, so instead he raided the archives and used cuttings from newspapers and magazines.

One of his best-known films of these years, Hasta la victoria siempre/Always Until Victory (1967), was made in only forty-eight hours so that it could be shown in the Plaza de la Revolución in Havana before Castro delivered his eulogy for Che Guevara. Less well known abroad are the films that Alvarez made on internal politics, including the forty-minute Despegue a las 18:30/Take-off at 18:30 (1969), which confronted the failures of the Cuban economy, although it was made in a Guevara-like spirit of moral exhortation rather than as criticism. Even here, Alvarez eschews conventional narration in a long opening sequence that portrays the lines of potential customers at the food shops and the despondency of 'No hay!' ('there isn't any!').

A series of longer films in the 1970s brought Alvarez's style back toward reportage. In Piedra sobre piedra/Stone Upon Stone (1970), Alvarez goes to Peru to report on the radical military regime that had just restored diplomatic relations with Cuba, and is interrupted by a major earthquake, from which he draws a metaphor: an equation between the sixty seconds of the earthquake, the effects of which he films, and the earthquake of underdevelopment that lasted for three hundred and sixty-five days a year. Then came three films that chronicled Castro's foreign tours of the 1970s (to Chile in 1971, Africa and Eastern Europe in 1972, and Africa again in 1977), where Alvarez developed a unique style of informal, observational filming that evidently took the Cuban leader's fancy. (Castro gave Alvarez a Russian Lada car for his sixtieth birthday.) De América soy hijo/Born of the Americas (1972), the film of Fidel's visit to Chile, is by far the longest—one hundred and ninety-five minutes in the full version. The length is justified by taking the cue from Castro's oratory: Alvarez used Castro's speeches as entry points to sequences analyzing aspects of Latin American history and the Cuban experience, which Castro explained to his Chilean audiences, and a similar technique was used for Y el cielo fue tomado por asalto/And Heaven was Taken by Storm, which covers Castro's 1972 tour of ten different countries in just over two hours, except that here the interpolated sequences concerned the histories of the countries visited. As one commentator put it after a retrospective of Alvarez's work in London in 1980, these lengthy films have an easy pace and 'a certain discursive quality which can be deceptively innocent'—especially De América soy hijo, which is 'loose-jointed but powerful in its cumulative effect and its insistent contextualization of the Chilean situation' (Hood 1980). At the same time, these films offer a rich collection of glimpses of Fidel Castro in a large variety of circumstances, both formal and informal. There is no denying that Castro greeting crowds and crowds greeting Castro can become repetitive, but such images are frequently offset by moments of individual interaction, such as an exchange he has with a working woman at a rally in Chile, or by the habit Alvarez has of leaving in the scenes that many editors would wish to leave on the cutting room floor (Castro fidgeting with the microphones on the podium in front of him, for instance).

Alvarez himself was a man of unflagging energy, until he was slowed by the onset of Parkinson's disease. His filmography is enormous. In the 1970s alone, important titles included two more films on Chile, ¿Cómo, por qué y para qué se asesina un general?/How, Why and for What is a General Assassinated (1971), and El tigre saltó y mató, pero morirá … morirá/The Tiger Leapt and Killed but it Will Die … it Will Die (1973), which are both rapid responses to events using a montage of library and archive images. Other notable achievements include the two-hour portrait of Vietnam, Abril de Vietnam en el año del gato/April in Vietnam in the Year of the Cat, commissioned by the Vietnamese to celebrate the thirtieth anniversary of the founding of the Democratic Republic, and Mi hermano Fidel/My Brother Fidel (1977), an intimate portrait in which Castro meets a man aged ninety-three who had met the Cuban patriot José Martí when he was eleven years old, shortly before Martí was killed in battle.

Elected to the Cuban national assembly for the Havana district where he lived, Alvarez remained a significant figure at ICAIC and in 1991 was one of the signatories of the unprecedented letter of protest with which ICAIC's film directors greeted the suppression of the controversial film Alicia en el pueblo de Maravillas/Alice in Wondertown, and the threat, later withdrawn, to merge ICAIC with Cuban television.

MICHAEL CHANAN

See also: LBJ; Now; 79 Springtimes of Ho Chi Minh

Biography

Born in 1919. Died May 20, 1998, in Havana, Cuba.

Further reading

Chanan, Michael, *The Cuban Image*, London: BFI, 1984.

Hood, Stuart, 'Murder on the Way', *New Statesman* April 18, 1980.

American Family, An

(US, Gilbert, 1973)

The twelve-part 1973 PBS series An American Family marked the culmination of the direct cinema movement in the United States. Producer Craig Gilbert's decision to move his crew into the home, positioning living cinema in the living room of middle-class suburbia, and then broadcasting it into the living rooms of America, erased the divide between public and private, a recurrent dream of cinéma vérité. Instead of revealing the private moments of public figures as the Drew Associates had in Primary (1960), Alan and Susan Raymond reversed the logic, making public the very private rituals of bourgeois family life as found at 35 Wood Dale Lane, Santa Barbara, California, thus acknowledging it to be an institution as open to surveillance as that of welfare recipients. Joining direct cinema documentary methods with television sitcom format, An American Family created a hybrid that fascinated its viewers.

In Pat and Bill Loud, Gilbert found a family defined, because of their cultural, economic, and political centrality, by their lack of definition. Seemingly raceless and classless, they were nevertheless marked by changing sexual mores, divorce, and homosexuality. The serial exposure of the Loud family on television revealed the suburban home as a central institution of postwar, middle-class experience. Filmed over seven months, the saga of the Louds, 'not the American family, but an American family', in the introductory words of Gilbert, begins with only the sketchiest background about the family prior to the moment of filming; the show, like all living cinema, features present-time experience shorn of sociological or historical context. The opening credits focus the series: first the house appears, then, in succession, Bill, Pat, and each of the children frozen in the middle of doing some typical activity. Their portraits surround the house, which dominates the frame. The sun-drenched family home becomes a spectacle, a source of envy in a consumer culture. Incredibly successful, Bill has built his own business forging replacement parts for heavy-mining equipment, marketing his products worldwide. Thus his home is linked to a global economy that makes possible the expansive ranch house with a pool and ocean view and the comfortable lives of his wife and children, who pursue their interests, secure in the knowledge that he will foot the bill for dancing lessons, apartments in New York City, musical instruments, and a horse and stable.

Yet, for all his economic centrality, Bill is not the center of the home. Rather, Pat, his wife and mother of his five children, dominates and maintains the family, and the footage. In her early forties, she is always perfectly made-up, her hair neatly done, wearing matching outfits and strands of gold around her neck and wrists. During the first episode, which includes both the end of the marriage (surrounded by friends, Pat tells Bill she is seeking a divorce, in the midst of drunken party at a restaurant) and the first day of filming, Pat is up at 6:30, poaching eggs and pouring mugs of coffee for her large family; however, the substance of the film is the emotional labor Pat expends in caring for her children. With the exception of the voluble and 'flamboyant' Lance, her oldest son, the Loud children are barely articulate teenagers.

They mumble about Michelle's horse, Delilah's tap dancing, Grant's band, Kevin's movies, and Lance's acting career.

The close monitoring that goes on in the Loud home (everyone checks in with the others about the day's activities, Lance calls long-distance from New York frequently, parents discuss problems relating to their children) reflects the scrutiny of Alan and Susan Raymond's camera and microphone. It also typifies the emotional intensity of the postwar middle-class family. During the first episode, as the camera follows Lance unpacking after his move into New York's Chelsea Hotel, he describes his siblings. Kevin is 'humane, the only one to buy presents for the others' birthdays'. Delilah 'lives a very Tammy existence, like Trisha Nixon with spice'. Michelle is selfish and bratty, 'made in the image of me', and Grant is 'talented but arrogant'. Summing up what will become clear over the course of the next eleven weeks, Lance's astute eye has been trained by gauging the emotional timbre of the home in which he was raised. The community he finds at the Chelsea Hotel, and continues to make in Copenhagen and Paris, becomes yet another form of this intimate social world.

This televised family saga codified a new political grammar, the rhetoric of celebrity. Both Lance and Pat launched careers from the series: Pat got her own talk show, and Lance became a minor star at Warhol's factory. HIV-positive since 1983, he died of complications from hepatitis C in December 2001, as the Raymonds were filming his last days in a Los Angeles hospice.

PAULA RABINOWITZ

See also: Primary

An American Family (US WNET/13, 1973, 720 mins). Produced by Craig Gilbert; co-ordinating producer: Jacqueline Donnet; associate producer: Susan Lester. Director: Craig Gilbert. Camera: Alan Raymond; additional camera, Joan Churchill and John Terry. Sound: Susan Raymond; assistant sound, Tom Goodwin; additional sound, Peter Pilafian and Alber Mecklinberg. Editor: Eleanor Hamerow (episode one); David Hanser, Pat Cook, and Ken Werner (episodes two to twelve).

Further reading

Goulet, Ron (ed.), *An American Family*, New York: Warner Paperback Library, 1973.

Rabinowitz, Paula, *They Must Be Represented: The Politics of Documentary*, London: Verso, 1994.

Ruoff, Jeffrey, *An American Family: A Televised Life*, Minneapolis, MN: University of Minnesota Press, 2002.

Anais Nin Observed

(France, Snyder, 1974)

Released in 1974, Anais Nin Observed is one of a number of films directed by Robert Snyder that takes an intimate look at the lives and personalities of celebrated artists. Snyder describes his films as 'voyages of discovery', and openly admits that he knew very little about Nin's life or works before he began the film. He was introduced to her in 1968, when filming The Henry Miller Odyssey (1974), and after a prolonged period of acquaintance she agreed to let him film her for a separate documentary, of which she would be the focus. The two films make up a kind of unofficial diptych: Nin not only features in the work on Miller, as he later would in the Nin documentary, but she also helped Snyder to edit the film, providing encouragement and advice, just as Miller spent a long time with Snyder editing Anais Nin Observed.

Snyder's film follows Nin through her daily life, as she takes tea, swims in her pool, works on her journal, and chats with friends. The vast body of the documentary consists of her conversations with Snyder, as well as with friends such as Frances Steloff and students from University of California, Los Angeles (UCLA). Although frequently categorised as biography, Anais Nin Observed, like the majority of Snyder's works, makes no attempt to give a comprehensive historical account of Nin's life and works. The film is aimed rather at providing accessibility to the writer for an interested audience without the barriers of experts. It does not delve into her personal life, but is rather a mouthpiece for her musings on art, literature, and her own life. This is Anais Nin in her own words. She is, as the title states, observed.

To this end, the film sets out to reflect qualities of Nin's personality and work within its form. Snyder's signature as a documentary director, paradoxically, tends to consist of a deferral to the artistic stamp of the documentary's subject, with whom he works very closely. In this regard he calls to mind the many female critics of Anais Nin who have adopted her prose style, writing about her as she wrote about herself. The film echoes the quality in Nin's writings that the literary critic Edmund Wilson describes as 'half … story, half dream', and recreates the 'special world, a world of feminine perception and fancy' that is the circumscribed universe that Nin's characters inhabit. His success in this area is due in no small part to the work of the film's director of photography, Baylis Glascock, who uses soft focus and filters to recreate the aura of mystery that surrounds Nin. Repeated shots of light catching on glasses and water create a lilting quality that echoes that of Nin's writing. The film is edited in slow rhythms; conversations are conserved in their actuality rather than edited for highlights, so that, for example, when Nin finishes a thought, and gazes off into the distance before beginning her next conversation, the pause resonates with Nin's careful, well-thought out intellect.

Snyder's film mirrors Nin's diary in other ways—a fact he comments on in his notes on the film. At the time of filming, Nin was editing her journals for publication. The editing of the film echoes the process by which Nin selects material from her books: 'We could always pick up new material in the future and—together with material of our current film—make another one … that's how diaries work!' Nin refers to the diaries constantly within the film: They are, she says, her 'cultural landscape', and she dips back into them daily. Snyder's film echoes this dialectic between past and present, opening with the contemporary Nin, before moving backwards to look at her past life and then forwards again into the present (Snyder 1976).

While Anais Nin Observed is unmistakably part of Snyder's oeuvre, at the same time we might consider it to be coauthored by Nin. The film is by no means an academic or historical study made about the subject, but is rather an experience of her: the director's authorship is in many ways secondary to Nin's, both in form and in content. In keeping with Miller's request for Snyder to 'mythologise' her, the director gives a very positive portrayal of Nin that might not be as objective as a more conventional biography, such as Coky Giedroyc's Spy in the House of Love—Anais Nin, shown as part of the UK's Channel 4 Arthouse series on in the late 1990s. Snyder's film is certainly a lot more flattering, portraying Nin as gracious, unpretentious, and intelligent. Unlike Giedroyc's film and the numerous written biographies of Nin, there is little mention of her infamous sex life, and a great deal more emphasis is placed on her intellect and artistic merit. It is perhaps no coincidence that Nin agreed to the documentary at approximately the same time as Miller, Sherwood Anderson, and a group of other intellectuals were campaigning to have Nin nominated for the Nobel Prize for Literature. Until 1963 Nin was relatively unheard of as an author in the United States and had been very frustrated by it. In many ways, the film provides her with the artistic recognition that had so long eluded her.

As an objective history, Snyder's film certainly leaves gaps. Nin's husband, Rupert Pole, for example, who was sharing the house in which Nin was filmed (unbeknownst to her other husband, Hugo Guiler), is omitted from the film altogether, as if he never existed (probably for Guiler's sake!). However, as a portrait of Anais Nin as she saw herself, or more importantly as she wanted others to see her, Snyder's film complements content with form elegantly. Through the film, Anais continues the constant process of seduction that has characterised her life and writing, reaching out to new audiences through the screen. In this respect, Snyder's documentary is an almost perfect replica of the diaries in intent and content. Even before the editing process begins, a great deal has been cut out, leaving us as mystified as to who the real Anais Nin is as she has always wanted the world to be.

HELEN WHEATLEY

Selected films

Anais Nin Observed (US, Masters & Masterworks Productions, 1973, 60 mins). Distributed by The Grove Press. Produced by Robert Snyder. Directed by Robert Snyder; Associate Director: R.A. Fitzgerald, Jr. Cinematography by Baylis Glascock. Edited by R.A. Fitzgerald and Tom Schiller. Sound recorded by John Glascock and Leslie Shatz. Re-recorded by George Porter, Ryder Sound Services Inc. Colour by DeLuxe.

1974 The Henry Miller Odyssey (dir. Robert Snyder)
1990 Henry and June (dir. Paul Kaufman)
1998 Anais Nin: A Spy in the House of Love (dir. Coky Giedroyc)

Further reading

n.a., *Hollywood Reporter* 234, no. 17, December 1974: 4.

Snyder, Robert, *This is Henry, Henry Miller from Brooklyn*, book to accompany The Henry Miller Odyssey, incorporating photo stills and transcripts of interviews, some featured within the films and some not, along with Snyder's descriptions of the filming and musings on the subject, Chicago, IL: Swallow Press Incorporated, 1975.

——*Anais Nin Observed*, book to accompany Anais Nin Observed, incorporating photo stills and transcripts of interviews, some featured within the films and some not, along with Snyder's descriptions of the filming and musings on the subject, Chicago, IL: Swallow Press Incorporated, 1976.

Anderson, Lindsay

Lindsay Gordon Anderson, a Scottish director, critic, and cofounder of the Free Cinema movement, played a seminal role in postwar British filmmaking. When Anderson entered the film world in 1947, British filmmakers had largely forsaken art for propaganda because of the utilitarian demands created by World War II. Accustomed to making movies that served a national purpose, British directors churned out works that, to Anderson's eyes, lacked aesthetic appeal. Preferring romanticism to realism, he urged documentarians to abandon the studios, abstain from sophisticated technology, and rediscover the freedom found in the harmony of expression and substance. His search for high art led him to direct low-budget documentaries in the 1940s and 1950s and to create the Free Cinema movement, which encouraged other filmmakers to slip out of their political and social chains. The naturalistic look at the working classes promoted by Anderson would culminate in the British New Wave.

As an editor with the influential film magazine *Sequence* in the late 1940s and early 1950s, Anderson championed film as art and the director as the master of the medium. He argued that only the director was in a position to determine cinematic expression. On the basis of his reputation, he received a commission to make a series of industrial films for a Yorkshire conveyor belt company, Richard Sutcliffe Ltd. He accepted the offer because he wanted to learn how to make films and he believed that documentaries offered an avenue to larger projects. Anderson's first documentary, Meet the Pioneers (1948), focused on the firm's underground conveyor system that brought coal from the mines to the pithead in Yorkshire. This series of films shares a characteristic common to Anderson documentaries, in that the subject is work itself, with the director focusing on how things are made and how processes are set in motion.

Anderson's first nonindustrial film, the thirty-minute Wakefield Express (1952), was commissioned to celebrate the one hundredth anniversary of the newspaper. Shot as usual with 16mm film, the documentary begins in typical Anderson fashion—not with background information, but with people. Although the history of the paper is provided, the director focuses on the work of producing an edition. Aiming to capture the dignity of ordinary Britons, Anderson follows a reporter as he interviews local people in search of stories, shows communal activities such as children playing, and has a final sequence of the paper going to press. Anderson was an admirer of Humphrey Jennings, and this film reflects Jennings's influence in its poetic style and focus on common subjects. By showing a reporter interviewing a ninety-five-year-old woman, Anderson imitates Jennings's manner of linking person to person to show the relationship of the past to the present. Nothing about the film is impartial—another Anderson trait. The subjects frequently play to the camera, while the director does not attempt to hide his affection, respect, and occasional exasperation for the Wakefield community.

For his next film, Anderson collaborated with Guy Brenton, an Oxford acquaintance, to direct Thursday's Children (1953), about the Royal School for Deaf Children in Margate, UK. Named after the old nursery rhyme in which 'Thursday's child has far to go', the twenty-minute documentary follows Anderson's adage that to make a film, one must create a world. Immersing the viewer fully in the lives of the children, he shows them in their boarding school as they receive lessons and explains how they came to live away from their families. Without informing the filmmakers, the British Office of Information in New York submitted the film to the Motion Picture Academy and it won an Oscar for best short subject.

Not far from the deaf school was the most popular working-class amusement park in the south of England, called 'Dreamland'. Anderson paid it a visit, and was fascinated by exhibits such as 'Torture Through the Ages' and 'Famous Executions'. He reacted harshly to the passivity of the audience in the face of the unimaginative diversions, sad exhibitions, and pitifully caged animals. It is his anger at the undemanding aesthetic criteria of the crowd that makes this documentary an aggressive criticism rather than the positive affirmation found in his other films. The thirteen-minute O Dreamland (1953) was the first film that Anderson directed with no other impetus other than his own wish to make it.

Every Day Except Christmas (1957) is a forty-minute portrait of the workers who sold fruit, flowers, and vegetables three hundred and sixty-four days a year in London's Covent Garden market. The bustling workers, who occasionally mug for the camera, were generally filmed in long shot or close-up to show both their coordinated physical activity and their unique personalities.

Once Anderson had developed a mastery of filmmaking, his impatience with the mediocrity and prescriptive narrative style of most British films of the era increased. To encourage social realist films and freedom for the filmmaker, Anderson helped to develop the small Free Cinema movement. This British group presented six programs of films at the National Film Theatre from 1956 to 1959, including O Dreamland in 1956, Wakefield Express in 1957, and Every Day Except Christmas also in 1957. In the broadest sense, Free Cinema had two objectives: to show what it valued in the cinema, with the emphasis on the work of the young contemporary filmmakers, and to show films to encourage other similar films to be made. Anderson coined the phrase 'Free Cinema', wrote most of the movement's propaganda, and directed the greatest percentage of documentaries in the programs.

Anderson always refused to give his definition of a documentary, arguing that the term limited discussion of the film in question. He cherished freedom, and his films both reflect and examine this concept. In all of his works, Anderson explores the ways in which subjects interact, and the ultimate impossibility of being subjective. Poetic and lacking technological tricks, his documentaries are unvarnished portrayals of British life during the mid-twentieth century.

CARYN E. NEUMANN

See also: Every Day Except Christmas; Jennings, Humphrey

Biography

Born in Bangalore, India, to a South African mother and Scottish father in the Royal Engineers, April 17, 1923. Parents separated in 1926; moved to England with his mother. Graduated from Wadham College, University of Oxford, reading classical studies, in 1942. Drafted into the Army, serving with the King's Royal Rifles as a clerk in India, 1943–5. Graduated from Oxford with a Master of Arts in English, 1948. Cofounder and editor of *Sequence*, 1949–51. Directed industrial films for Richard Sutcliffe Ltd, the National Society for the Prevention of Cruelty to Children, the National Industrial Fuel Efficiency Service, and the Central Office of Information for the Ministry of Agriculture, Fisheries and Food, 1948–55. Wrote *Making a Film: The Story of 'Secret People'* in 1952. Directed and acted in feature films and television commercials, 1963–87. Wrote *About John Ford* in 1981. Died of a heart attack in Angoulême, Charente, Poitou-Charentes, France, August 20, 1994.

Selected films

1948 Meet the Pioneers: director, editor, commentator
1949 Idlers That Work: director, commentator
1952 Three Installations: director, commentator
1952 Trunk Conveyor: director, commentator
1952 Wakefield Express: director
1953 Thursday's Children: codirector
1953 O Dreamland: director
1955 Green and Pleasant Land: director and scriptwriter
1955 Henry: director and scriptwriter
1955 The Children Upstairs: director and scriptwriter
1955 A Hundred Thousand Children: director and scriptwriter
1955 £20 a Ton: director
1955 Energy First: director

1955 Foot and Mouth: director and scriptwriter
1957 Every Day Except Christmas: director

Further reading

Graham, Allison, *Lindsay Anderson*, Boston, MA: Twayne, 1981.
Hedling, Erik, *Lindsay Anderson: Maverick Film-Maker*, London: Cassell, 1998.
Lambert, Gavin, *Mainly About Lindsay Anderson*, New York: Alfred A. Knopf, 2000.
Lovell, Alan and Hillier, Jim, *Studies in Documentary*, New York: Viking Press, 1972.

Angela: Portrait of a Revolutionary

(US, du Luart, 1971)

Angela: Portrait of a Revolutionary paints a picture of the educator Angela Davis from the point of view of one of her students at the University of California in Los Angeles in 1971. It explores the challenges that Davis faced because of her political activism, and shows the consequences of her being a communist. Shot entirely in black and white, this low-budget, student-produced documentary film is nonetheless ambitious. It tries to capture the essence of Angela Davis, lending a multidimensional view to the person behind the picture on the Federal Bureau of Investigation (FBI) 'Ten Most Wanted' poster. Yolande du Luart, the film's director, takes a sympathetic view of Davis, while at the same time presents the story from a number of different perspectives. The film is du Luart's attempt to legitimize Angela Davis personally, politically, and professionally.

Angela: Portrait of a Revolutionary begins with sound images of police car sirens combined with footage of Angela Davis's arrest in New York for her alleged involvement in the failed attempt to free Black Panther George Jackson, who was on trial for allegedly killing a prison guard at Soledad Prison in California. This scene is followed by a sound image of a cell door crashing shut against a totally dark screen. The camera then focuses on the Women's House of Detention on December 5, 1970, with a voice-over by Angela Davis stating that she is 'now being held captive'. Next, the camera focuses on still shots of her supporters rallying outside the Women's House of Detention, carrying posters saying, 'Free Our Sisters in the House of D' and 'Free Angela Davis'. Angela Davis is thus painted as a political prisoner, not a common criminal.

The film then flashes back in time to the autumn of 1969. The viewer is given an insider's look at Angela Davis, the academic, who is preparing for and then teaching a class in the philosophy department at University of California, Los Angeles (UCLA). This scene is followed by one of two interviews with the Chairperson, Professor Donald Kalish, who is filmed in the middle of the screen behind his desk in his office, thus presenting an authoritative image. He discusses in a measured way why and how Professor Davis was hired, and he is quick to point out that her appointment was based on her outstanding academic credentials and the needs of the department.

Later in the film, Professor Kalish explains why the Board of Regents fired Professor Davis, and he concludes that it was because of her membership in the Communist Party. The film also includes a voice-over by Max Rafferty, a member of the Board of Regents, giving his rationale for her dismissal (Professor Davis had yet to earn her doctorate). It is important to note that the film uses more than one voice to tell the story. This use of multiple points of view ultimately gives credibility to Professor Kalish's account. He explains how Max Rafferty is misinformed about higher education, since a completed doctorate is not a requirement for the job of Assistant Professor in the early 1970s at UCLA. In addition, toward the end of the film, Angela Davis herself tells the story of her dismissal. This scene gives Davis ownership of her story. In sum, by illustrating her academic credentials and demonstrating the reasons for her dismissal, the film invites its audience to look at the politics behind the Board of Regents' decision.

Angela: Portrait of a Revolutionary also illustrates Davis's core beliefs. In it, Davis tries to spell out the difficulty of not only organizing a movement for social change and equality but also struggling to maintain that movement. The film seeks to merge the political with the personal, with a series of carefully spliced scenes that move between private spaces that Davis occupies in her home and study, for example, and public spaces where she teaches, lectures, and gives political speeches. These scenes do justice to the idea that the personal and political cannot be separated. Finally, the film demonstrates how repression comes in many forms by linking the killing of two students at Jackson State College, the war in Vietnam, the killing of four white students at Kent State University, the trial in Connecticut of Bobby Seale, and the Soledad Brothers facing the gas chamber.

Other techniques include the use of sound images to remind viewers of what is not visually present (e.g. police car sirens with gunshots ringing in the background while pictures of the bloody police raid on the Black Panther Party Office in South Central Los Angeles on December 8, 1969, are shown in still shots). This series of still shots serves to imprint police brutality of African Americans on the viewer's mind, especially since it is quickly juxtaposed with still shots of posters declaring 'Feed Hungry Children' and 'Free Breakfast for School Children', representing a Black Panther Party humanitarian initiative for inner-city poor children. By juxtaposing images of mainstream atrocities and Black Panther activism, not only are Davis's political views illustrated but also the notion that Jonathan and George Jackson and other Black Panthers are simple thugs who should be locked up, is challenged.

Angela: Portrait of a Revolutionary was little noted nor long remembered. Angela Davis herself, now a Professor of Social Consciousness at the University of California in Santa Cruz, neither owns a copy of it nor has she stayed in touch with its filmmaker, Yolande du Luart, who is now translating mysteries from French to English. Yet, to use a 1960s term, Angela: Portrait of a Revolutionary seems 'relevant' to those interested in experiencing a pivotal moment in the life and work of the controversial and iconic Angela Davis, and in the production of student documentary films rooted in the political milieu of the early 1970s. Not only is the film Davis's story of struggle but it is also a political act in and of itself. In the end, it powerfully demonstrates the means and methods by which Angela Davis dedicated her life to the struggle against fascism and racism.

THERESA C. LYNCH

Angela: Portrait of a Revolutionary (US, New Yorker Films Release, 1971, 60 mins). Distributed by New Yorker Films. Produced by Mae Mercer. Directed by Yolande du Luart. Cinematography by Roger Andrieux and Lynn Merrick. Music by Yolande du Luart. Edited by Jacqueline Mappel. Sound direction by Nancy Dowd. Filmed in New York and California.

Further reading

Davis, Angela, *If They Come in the Morning: And Other Political Prisoners*, New York: The Third Press, 1971.

——*Angela Davis: An Autobiography*, New York: Random House, 1974.

——*Women, Race and Class*, New York: Random House, 1981.

——*Women, Culture, and Politics*, New York: Random House, 1984.

——*Blues Legacies and Black Feminism: Gertrude 'Ma' Rainey, Bessie Smith, and Billie Holiday*, New York: Pantheon Books, 1988.

Anstey, Edgar

Edgar Harold Macfarlane Anstey OBE, a documentary film director, producer, and critic, was perhaps one of the most versatile documentary filmmakers of the twentieth century, moving easily between the aesthetics of his time and its science.

Living in the shadow of John Grierson's desire to reshape society with ideals of social and ethical cohesion, Anstey was the only member of the Empire Marketing Board with technical and scientific training, and he urgently felt a need to make technological processes comprehensible. Anstey instantly recognized the value of the informational film for the purpose of training and educating. He sought an opportunity to follow through this conception of the informational film, and worked on the report that brought into being the Shell Film Unit. He produced Shell's first film, Airport (Roy Lockwood, UK, 1934), an observation of a day at Croydon Airport and the systematic examination and refurbishment of an aeroplane engine.

The film lasted only seventeen minutes, but nothing could quite compare with aircraft, and everything associated with them, for excitement. Many people had never seen an aeroplane, yet everyone recognised the exotic glamour of flight. Airport informed, entertained and educated while simultaneously indicating Shell's own position in the vanguard of modernity (Howarth 1997).

Anstey shared John Grierson's view that documentary must both criticize the agents of state and represent the interests of the exploited worker. He became frustrated and unhappy with the rate of progress at Shell and resigned to pursue his ideology.

Anstey found his opportunity with the Gas, Light and Coke Company, and (along with Arthur Elton) brought to the screen Housing Problems (1935), which focused on the plight of a Stepney (in London's East End) slum dweller. In doing so, he sparked a new approach to documentary filmmaking. Housing Problems marked the beginning of Anstey's long commitment to social change. The film was well received, although Joris Ivens, a fellow documentary filmmaker, commented in hindsight:

> There have been cases in the history of documentary when photographers became so fascinated by dirt that the result was the dirt looked interesting and strange, not something repellent to the audience. In my opinion [...] Housing Problems, fell into this error of exotic dirt. You could not smell these London slums.
> (Ivens, 1969)

However, John Betjemen, film critic of the *Evening Standard*, praised this new style of filmmaking and in 1935 wrote movingly of these 'films without sex'. Betjemen came later to admire Anstey's perceptive gifts as a critic with the BBC and *The Spectator*.

Grierson, too, later praised Housing Problems, and noted that both Anstey and Elton had taken 'the documentary film into the field of social problems, and keyed it to the task of describing not only industrial and commercial spectacle, but social truth as well' (Grierson, 1966: 215).

Housing Problems convinced Anstey of the power of documentary, and he followed it with Enough to Eat? (1936), an examination of the problem of malnutrition. Pushing for social change, Anstey claimed that the film was a contribution to ongoing national research on nutrition and nutritional issues. Its success can be attributed to the media coverage it received, rather than the quality of the filmmaking displayed. *The Catholic Herald*, for example, wrote:

> The film does not show the terrible ravages that undernourishment has created in England. Director Edgar Anstey has chosen the better method of revealing the tragedy of poverty and the consequent semi-starvation which is the result of a cheap diet chosen more for its filling qualities than for its nutritive value.
> (*The Catholic Herald*, October 10, 1936)

Like Grierson, Anstey believed that documentary could act as an effective medium of communication between the government and the working classes. During World War II, while at Film Centre, he made an abundance of films for the Ministry of Information to encourage more intensive cultivation of urban gardens and mixed farms throughout Great Britain.

It was during this time that the Scientific Film Association was formed. Anstey and Arthur Elton were convinced that film had a singular power to impart information. Anstey believed passionately that the scientist and the technologist shared the imagination and insight of the artist, and after the war he and Elton created the International Scientific Film Association to disseminate a wider corroboration of their outlook.

Anstey, like Grierson, had established himself at the forefront of documentary production. From the early 1940s he largely settled into the role of producer. His appointment as Films Officer and Producer in Charge to the British Transport Commission in 1949 allowed him to use his gifts and abilities to satisfy his vision for documentary film.

STEVEN R. FOXON

See also: Elton, Arthur; Enough to Eat?; Granton Trawler; Housing Problems; Industrial Britain; March of Time

Biography

Born February 16, 1907, in Watford, England. Educated at Watford Grammar School and Birkbeck College, University of London. Married Daphne Lilly (Canadian documentary filmmaker NFBC) in 1949. Joined Grierson's Empire Marketing Board Film Unit after answering to an advertisement in *The Times* in 1931. Started the Shell Film Unit in 1934. Joined the March of Time Film Unit, initially as London Director of Productions, later Foreign Editor in New York from 1936 to 1938. Member of the Board and Producer at Film Centre (UK), 1940–8. Regular member of BBC radio programme 'The Critics', from 1949 to 1966. Organized and acted as producer-in-charge of British Transport Films (BTF) from 1949 to 1974. In 1956 and in 1967 served as Chairman of the British Film Academy. President of the International Scientific Film Association from 1961 to 1963. Won an Academy Award for Wild Wings (1965) in 1966. Chairman, British Industrial & Scientific Film Association from 1969 to 1970. Board of Governors at the British Film Institute from 1974 to 1975. Chairman of Children's Film Foundation Production Committee from 1981 to 1983. Died September 25, 1987, in London, England.

Selected films

1931 Industrial Britain: editor
1934 Granton Trawler: editor
1935 Housing Problems: director/producer (with A. Elton)
1936 Enough to Eat?: director
1943 Crown of the Year (Ministry of Information): associate producer
1947 Caller Herrin' (Scottish Home Dept): producer
1950 Berth 24 (BTF): producer
1954 Elizabethan Express (BTF): producer
1957 Journey into Spring (BTF): producer
1961 Terminus (BTF): producer
1965 Wild Wings (BTF): producer
1970 Site in the Sea (BTF): producer
1975 Age of Invention (BTF): producer

Further reading

Gordon, Douglas, *Shell Films: The First Sixty Years*, London: Balding and Mansell, 1994.
Grierson, John, *Grierson on Documentary*, Berkeley, CA: University of California Press, 1966.
Hardy, Forsyth, *John Grierson: A Documentary Biography*, London: Faber, 1979.
Howarth, Stephen, *A Century in Oil: The Shell Transport and Trading Company 1897–1997*, London, 1997.
Ivens, Joris, *The Camera and I*, Berlin: Seven Seas, 1969.
Roth, Paul, *Documentary Diary*, London: Secker and Warburg, and New York: Hill and Wang, 1973.
Sussex, Elizabeth, *The Rise and Fall of British Documentary*, Berkeley, CA: University of California Press, 1975.
Tallents, Sir Stephen, *The Projection of Britain*, London: Faber, 1932.

Antonio, Emile de

Emile de Antonio is best known for his innovations in the approach to documentary filmmaking. His works engage viewers in pointed political discourse through the clever arrangement of images, historical footage, interviews, text, sound, and other elements compiled to create a story without the use of a narrator. Although he came to filmmaking in his forties and made relatively few major films, de Antonio is a significant figure in the history of documentary. Nearly all of his films are explorations of the Cold War, its legacies, and its effects on US culture and values systems.

Perhaps the most fascinating thing about de Antonio's work is his challenge to the idea of truth being told about historical events. De Antonio is quite willing to accept that any story may have as many explanations and meanings given as it does witnesses. The notion of direct address of the witness championed by de Antonio is a simple principle with extremely complex implications for the understanding of history. This concept was well illustrated by his pioneering use of found footage. Television images are used to strengthen the inherent arguments about power and human nature that surface in his work.

De Antonio's first film was formulated in this way. Point of Order (1964) used historical footage of the McCarthy hearings to illustrate the trajectory of the tale. De Antonio employed distinctive editing techniques to create meaningful juxtapositions. He continued to explore the recontextualization of previously filmed material for the next few films, honing his skills in the compilation images. Although this is interesting as a formal technique, it is even more intriguing when the content is considered as well. The films of Emile de Antonio are largely about sociopolitical concerns, and this is well supported by the use of the televised image as a storytelling device. In a 1971 interview de Antonio spoke of his impetus for creating the film:

> The Army-McCarthy hearings were a peak in American political theater. And there were lessons derived from it [...]

> You get something like the Army-McCarthy hearings on television—in all its body, all of it—and something is revealed about the nature of our governmental structure, our society, where the real power is [...] because the whole thing about American politics is that it's a game, a game whereby you hide what's really happening from the American people while its happening. And that's part of what the film is all about, to show that game.
>
> (Weiner 1971: 9)

This concept continued to propel de Antonio's work throughout the 1960s and 1970s.

Among de Antonio's best-known works is 1968's In the Year of the Pig, a film comprising found footage from many diverse sources designed to illustrate the high-level confusion of the Vietnam War. De Antonio skillfully organized images to raise difficult questions about the nature of US involvement in the war. Composed of his own interviews and new footage—combined with material gleaned from a detailed study of footage shot by the National Liberation Front, the Democratic Republic of Vietnam, the French Army, the American Broadcasting Company, and the BBC—In the Year of the Pig examines a complex issue from many angles. At the time of the 1971 *Film Quarterly* interview, de Antonio spoke of the impact of the news media and the war that was still underway.

> There is nothing as bad that's happened concerning the war as the networks' coverage of it, because it seems as if they're covering the war whereas in fact, they're not. The networks have made the American people, in a final way, comfortable with the war—because it appears between commercials, every day; it's become part of our quotidian existence, like armpit commercials. There's never the question asked, 'Why are we doing this? What is this war about?' It's never suggested by anything that occurs on television that we should even be interested in that type of question. Television is a way of avoiding coming to terms with the fact that we're in this war.
>
> (Weiner 1971: 7)

It is intriguing that this statement has continued relevance today.

Perhaps the most unique of de Antonio's films is Painters Painting (1972), in that it is unlike any of his other work. This exploration of several artists' thoughts and concerns in their working environments is still compelling today for its direct approach to the artists and their processes. His first film in 35mm, this work sought to create a synthesis of form and content as it used this collage style of filmmaking to look at several artists who worked in collage painting. De Antonio stated:

> This is a film about the System of the art world in the words of the people in that world: [Willem] de Kooning, [Robert] Motherwell, Jasper Johns, Andy Warhol, Robert Rauschenberg, Frank Stella, Barney Newman [...] and so on. Most of these are people I've known and who are friends of mine, but the film also includes the collectors, the manipulators, and the museum people and how an art market is created.
>
> (Weiner 1971: 14)

The film is entertaining and insightful, like other de Antonio works, but its political inquiry is less overt than in the rest of his catalog.

Emile de Antonio remains an important figure in documentary filmmaking. In recent memory, his works have taken on a renewed sense of social poignancy and verve. As documentary film has become more mass produced and widely screened throughout the world, the significance of de Antonio is heightened.

TAMMY A. KINSEY

See also: In the Year of the Pig

Biography

Born 1919. Studied history at Harvard University. Figure in New York art scene. Began making films aged forty. Pioneered use of found television footage as documentary filmmaking tool. Died 1989.

Selected films

1964 That's Where the Action Is
1965 Rush to Judgment
1968 In the Year of the Pig
1969 America is Hard to See

1970 Millhouse: A White Comedy
1976 Underground
1989 Mr Hoover and I

Further reading

Kellner, Douglas and Dan Streible (eds), *Emile de Antonio: A Reader*, Minneapolis, MN: University of Minnesota Press, 2000.

Lewis, Randolph, *Emile de Antonio: Radical Filmmaker in Cold War America*, Madison: University of Wisconsin Press, 2000.

Weiner, Bernard, 'Radical Scavenging: An Interview with Emile de Antonio', *Film Quarterly* XXV, no. 1, fall 1971.

Apted, Michael

Michael Apted has been involved in documentary filmmaking since the early 1960s. He has long been known for his patient, probing interviews and the simple truths revealed through them. Apted is perhaps best known for his Up series, a remarkable continuation of a project he worked on as a researcher in 1963. Directed by Paul Almond for Granada TV, this film (Seven Up) was the start of an idea that is clearly and uniquely Apted. Fourteen British boys and girls were interviewed for this work, and the thoughts and hopes of seven-year-olds were revealed. Apted endeavored to continue this notion in 1970, when he interviewed the same set of youngsters (now fourteen years old) in his Seven Plus Seven. At seven-year intervals, Apted has interviewed these same people, producing 21 Up (1977), 28 Up (1985), 35 Up (1991), 42: Forty-Two Up (1998) and 49 Up (2005). This is unlike any other cinematic endeavor on record, and although a few of the original fourteen have dropped out of the project, those who remain have become very close to Apted and to each other. This careful study of human life, its simplicity, joys and sorrows, is indeed an epic documentary project.

Amid the years of this ongoing cinematic task, Apted has worked as a director for both independent and Hollywood features as well as continuing his documentary work. In 1985 he released Bring on the Night, a document of musician Sting and his tour experience, both backstage and in concert.

Apted's interest in political and social issues is evident in much of his work. His 1992 documentary, Incident at Oglala, explores the controversial case of two murdered Federal Bureau of Investigation (FBI) agents on the reservation at Pine Ridge, South Dakota, USA and the incarceration of Native American Leonard Peltier for these crimes. The film painstakingly investigates witnesses' accounts of the events of July 1975, showing testimonials from the legal proceedings, surveying evidence, and interviewing various players. Apted ultimately provides a study not only of the events themselves but also of the way in which people respond to the pressures of accusation, the role that race plays in such a case, and the notion of justice itself. Apted's 1994 film Moving the Mountain continues with this political framework as it explores the Tiananmen Square student demonstrations of June 1989 in Beijing, China. The 1997 project Inspirations is not overtly political, yet it investigates ideas themselves in a very critical manner, a kind of creative activism at play in the film. Apted interviewed artists about the specifics of their process in art-making, with attention paid to the exercise of problem solving. Musician David Bowie, pop art painter Roy Lichtenstein, glass artist Dale Chihuly, dancer Edouard Locke, actress Louise LeCavalier, architect Tadao Ando, and ceramicist and poet Nora Noranjo-Morse answer questions regarding the nature of their creativity and the origins of their ideas. In an interview with Pamela Klaffke, Apted explained his views on filmmaking and art:

> You have to have a vision. That was why I was so interested in having an architect [in the film]. I felt a real sense of camaraderie with him because I felt both of our jobs are very public jobs, very collaborative, very man-management, very political jobs. It's a form of art, but not what I would call pure art of the blank page, the oil, the clay, the glass or whatever. It is a sort of art, but a wider view of art being a film director than being a composer, poet, painter or sculptor—because there are so many hands on your work.
>
> (Klaffke 1998)

Apted continues this tack of social and political observation in his new serial documentary, Married in America. A production of A&E Television Networks, this 2002 work represents the second time Apted has used the notion of returning to a subject as a method of storytelling. Married in America explores the lives of nine diverse couples, including racially mixed pairs, those who were previously married or of different religions, and a lesbian couple. All of these couples live in or near Los Angeles, New York, or Birmingham, Alabama. Surely this regional specificity will allow for closer examination of the social issues at hand in these places and the things they create in these relationships. Apted intends to visit the couples, whether they remain together or not, to see what has transpired in their lives. Of interest to him is the question of 'family values' rhetoric in a society filled with divorce and single-parent households. Do age and class differences, past relationships, and family pressures complicate these unions in similar ways? (Chocano 2002). The institution of marriage itself is examined here. Are there things that make a marriage work in today's world? Can the success of a union be predicted from the interactions between the people involved? Are the struggles of the early years always beneath the surface as the relationship continues? Apted is intrigued by these simple human dramas that shape society's attitudes. The second series was made in 2006.

TAMMY A. KINSEY

Biography

Born February 10, 1941, in Aylesbury, Buckinghamshire, England. Worked as a researcher for Granada TV. Member of the Directors Guild of America since 1978. Received the International Documentary Association (IDA) Award for 28 Up in 1985. Vancouver International Film Festival Best Documentary Feature Award, 1994, for Moving the Mountain. In 1998, 42: Forty-Two Up received the Flaherty Documentary Award. Awarded the Doubletake Documentary Film Festival's Career Award in 1998. International Documentary Association's Career Achievement Award, 1999. Special Jury Award, Florida Film Festival, 2000, for Me and Issac Newton. President of the Directors Guild of America, 2003–9.

Selected filmography

1963 7 Up
1970 7+7 (14 Up)
1977 21 Up
1985 28 Up
1985 Bring On the Night
1991 35 Up
1992 Incident at Oglala
1994 Moving the Mountain
1997 Inspirations
1998 42: Forty-Two Up
2002 Married in America (TV)
2005 49 Up
2006 Married in America 2 (TV)

Further reading

Chocano, Carina, 'Who Wants to Marry a Regular Person?' 2002, www.salon.com/ent/tv/diary/2002/06/15/married/print.html

Klaffke, Pamela, 'Up and Away with Michael Apted', *Moviemaker*, April 1998.

Robinson, Julie, 'Michael Apted's 7 Up Series', *DGA Magazine* 27, no. 3, September 2002.

Arcand, Denys

Denys Arcand made his first film, A l'est d'Eaton/East of Eaton (1959), with Stéphane Venne when he was eighteen years old. A few years later, while studying history at the Université de Montréal, he codirected Seul ou avec d'autres/Alone or with Others (1962) with Stéphane Venne and Denis Héroux. Seul ou avec d'autres was a docudrama on the life of university students. Although Arcand did not intend to pursue a career as a filmmaker at that time, he applied for a summer job at the National Film Board of Canada (NFB) and was hired to research and write a screenplay for a documentary on the founder of Québec City, Samuel de Champlain. He was eventually hired to direct the short film Champlain (1964) and two other shorts on the history of New France, Les Montréalistes/Ville-Marie (1965) and La route de l'ouest/The Westward Road (1965). After working on a few generic shorts in the late 1960s, such as Volleyball (1966), he made his first feature-length documentary, On est au coton/Cotton Mill, Treadmill (1970), an examination of the textile industry in Québec. The film was deemed subversive by NFB commissionaire Sydney Newman, and banned from distribution until 1976.

The controversy surrounding On est au coton brought attention to Arcand, and he was given the opportunity to direct three fiction films in the private sector: La maudite galette/The Damed Dough (1971), Réjeanne Padovani (1973), and Gina (1975). The latter offers an intriguing commentary on the then censored On est au coton by presenting a fictionalized account of the shooting of the documentary.

Before leaving the NFB to work in the private sector, Arcand had shot a film on the provincial electoral campaign of 1970. Released in 1972, Québec: Duplessis et après .../Québec: Duplessis and After ..., argues that the right-wing ideology of Maurice Duplessis, who dominated the Québec political scene from 1936 until his death in 1959, was still present in the political discourse of 1970, even in the supposedly left-wing platform of the separatist Parti Québécois. With this film, Arcand managed to attract criticism from both sides of the political spectrum. He returned to the NFB in the late 1970s to make his last documentary, Le confort et l'indifférence/Comfort and Indifference (1981), on the failure of the 1980 referendum on Québec's independence (sixty percent voted against Québec's sovereignty). Arguing that pro-sovereignty Premier René Lévesque (in power from 1976 to 1985) misread the population's seeming enthusiasm for separation from Canada, Arcand was reproached by nationalists for his claim that residents of Québec were more interested in personal gratification than social and political issues.

Since the 1980s, Arcand has worked exclusively in fictional film. Le déclin de l'empire américain/ Decline of the American Empire (1986) and Jésus de Montréal/Jesus of Montreal (1989) enjoyed tremendous success both in Canada and abroad.

From Champlain to his latest fiction film, The Age of Ignorance (2007), Arcand has consistently adopted a dialogic approach to his material, always articulating at least two discourses simultaneously as a means of 'problematizing' any simplistic reading of his subject matter. For instance, although On est au coton carries out a Marxist examination of working conditions in textile mills, it also undermines Marxist teleology by demonstrating the proletariat's inability to improve its circumstances. Similarly, in Le confort et l'indifférence, he exposes the weaknesses of both the separatist project and the federalist status quo. Arcand rarely provides solutions in his films, but never fails to make his audience think.

ANDRÉ LOISELLE

Biography

Born 1941. Studied history at the Université de Montréal. Directed several documentaries before turning exclusively to narrative/fictional film, 1980s.

Selected films

1964 Champlain: director, screenwriter
1965 Les montréalsites/Ville-Marie: director, screenwriter
1965 La route de l'ouest/The Westward Road: director, screenwriter
1965 Montréal un jour d'été/Montréal on a Summer Day: director, editor
1966 Volleyball: director, editor
1967 Parcs atlantiques/Atlantic Parks: director, editor
1970 On est au coton/Cotton Mill, Treadmill: director
1972 Québec: Duplessis et après ... /Québec: Duplessis and After ... : director, editor
1976 La lutte des travialleurs d'hôpitaux/The Struggle of Hospital Workers: director
1981 Le confort et l'indifférence/Comfort and Indifference: director

Further reading

Coulombe, Michel, *Denys Arcand: la vraie nature du cinéaste*, Montréal: Boréal, 1993.
Loiselle, André and McIlroy, Brian (eds), *Auteur/ Provacateur: The Films of Denys Arcand*, Trowbridge: Flicks Books, 1995.

Ark, The

(UK, Dineen, 1993)

The Ark of the title refers to the Regent's Park Zoo in London. Shot over the course of a year, Molly Dineen's four-part series won a BAFTA for its portrayal of the zoo as it struggled to find both financial security and a resolution to the often conflicting demands of being both a center of scientific research and a popular visitor attraction.

As producer, photographer, and director, Dineen is central to all aspects of the film. As in her previous work, Dineen uses a minimal contextualizing voice-over and develops an informal, dialogic relationship with her subjects. Dineen's direct interjections are also fairly minimal and used only where necessary to draw out further revelations. These are often interspersed with long observational sequences that reveal the workings of the zoo, and interactions between the staff and between keepers and animals. However, Dineen's presence is clearly announced. The 'performance', both in terms of her own interventions and direction, as well as her subjects' response to her and the camera, provides the dynamic on which she builds her narratives (Bruzzi 2000). By creating such clearly authored films, Dineen makes transparent the constructed nature of documentary filmmaking and, to a certain extent, avoids the more extravagant claims for objectivity that normally accompany observational approaches. Rather than an attempt to disguise her presence, the films are a record of the developing and fairly informal relationship between Dineen and her subjects.

Episode one, Survival of the Fittest, establishes the basic financial crisis facing the zoo. The second episode, Natural Selection, illustrates the logistical problems facing the zoo after a round of layoffs, and the next phase of cost cutting—the reduction and dispersal of the animal collection. The Political Animal covers the complex negotiations surrounding the arrival of two giant pandas and establishes the growing struggle over the future of the zoo, underscored by the open challenge to management by a dissident group of keepers and the Fellows of the Royal Zoological Society. The last episode, Tooth and Claw, shows the final confrontation between the reform group and management, which leads to the departure of David Jones, the zoo's director.

The role and fate of public and cultural institutions in the face of neo-liberal economic theory was a central theme in the political discourse of the 1980s and 1990s. The Ark creates an intriguing picture of the internal workings of a venerable and seemingly unshakeable organization under threat in the shifting economic sands of the period. However, the wider issue of the place of zoos in relation to contemporary cultural mores and environmental concerns go unexamined in The Ark. Dineen's focus here, as in her other work, is primarily on character. As she states, 'Through focusing on the human drama and trying to tell a story through character[...], you can portray more of life's transparent complexities and contradictions' (MacDonald and Cousins 1998: 365). In the crisis that overtakes the zoo, Dineen's sympathy appears to lie with the keepers, due mainly to their clear dedication to their work and attachment to the animals. Yet, they are presented either as relatively passive in their acceptance of layoffs, or—in the case of those who organize to oust management—inappropriately conspiratorial. The dedication of the keepers is most dramatically revealed in the twenty-four-hour battle to save a sick koala bear. This emergency is contrasted with the ruthless politicking of senior management and the reform group of keepers and Fellows. However, David Jones, the zoo's director, who oversaw the cuts to the staff and collection, becomes a figure who, in turn, is treated with increasing sympathy as his own job is threatened. The eventual death of the koala is tellingly juxtaposed with news of Jones's redundancy.

Dineen's expressed determination to treat all sides with equanimity and to avoid stereotyping makes her appear uncomfortable at times with the very real conflicts made manifest as the crisis develops. Her frequent reappearance in the final episode to seek the views of the world-weary, apolitical Senior Keeper of Birds, David Robinson, is perhaps indicative of the need to find expression for her own neutral stance to the situation (Bruzzi 2000). Much of Dineen's work, such as Home from the Hill (BBC2, 1985) and In the Company of Men (BBC2, 1995), is overtly constructed around her relationship with male characters. This is also apparent in The Ark. Although the female staff members are approached, these interactions tend to be relatively formal in tone and lack the more familiar, even flirtatious, manner of her dealings with some of the central male figures. Her sympathetic treatment of Jones is perhaps symptomatic of the 'glorifying and exonerating of masculinity' (Bruzzi 2000: 169), which, it could be argued, is an underlying tendency in much of her earlier work. The final shots show the zoo's disused Bear Mountain, portrayed as a desolate wasteland. Shot in this way, this highly symbolic indicator of the zoo's wellbeing appears to reflect Dineen's own uncertainty about the situation, after the status quo has been disrupted by Jones's dismissal.

If Dineen's approach consciously glosses over the details and wider implications of the zoo's crisis, her ability to develop close relationships with her subjects, and to entreat them to speak openly about themselves before the camera, allows for a revealing glimpse of the zoo to be communicated. The Ark is also memorable for the finely observed relationships between the keepers and their animals, providing moments of real affection and humor.

DAVID CHAPMAN

The Ark (UK, RTO Pictures for BBC2, 1993, four episodes of 59 mins). Photographed, produced, and directed by Molly Dineen. Executive producer, Edward Mirzoeff. Associate producer, Margaret Young. Sound by Phil Streather. Edited by Edwards Roberts with Heather Morley. Graphics by Christine Büttner. Music by John Keane.

Further reading

Billen, Andrew, 'Where's Molly', *Observer Review*, December 10, 1995: 9.

Bruzzi, Stella, *New Documentary: A Critical Introduction*, London: Routledge, 2000.

Lawson, Mark, 'High Flyer on the Wall', *The Guardian*, October 10, 1995: 10–11.

MacDonald, Kevin and Cousins, Mark, *Imagining Reality*, London: Faber & Faber, 1998.

Ascent of Man, The

(UK, 1973)

The Ascent of Man (1973), BBC TV's critically acclaimed major television documentary series of thirteen fifty-minute parts, is a television history of scientific ideas from prehistory to the late twentieth century. Its central organising metaphor is the optimism of the 'long childhood' of the growth of human intelligence. The BBC saw the series as the scientific counterpart of Civilisation, its impressive series on Western art and architecture. The Ascent of Man was written and narrated to camera by the late Dr Jacob Bronowski, a scientific humanist whose aim throughout was to portray science as an historically contextualized human achievement and progress, made possible by evolving human biology and intelligence, and not as a dry, abstract, and depersonalised array of scientific theories and facts. For example, in Part Five, 'The Music of the Spheres', Bronowski humanises mathematics: 'Calculation was an endless delight to Moorish scholars. They loved problems.' Similarly, in Part Six, 'The Starry Messenger', he observes: 'There are good Renaissance reasons—emotional, rather than intellectual—that made [Copernicus] choose the golden sun' as the centre of the universe. Late in life, Bronowski wrote: 'All that I have written […] turns on the same centre: the uniqueness of man that grows out of his struggle (and his gift) to understand both nature and himself' (O'Conner and Robertson 2003).

Although remembered mainly as a scientist and mathematician, Bronowski was also an accomplished writer and poet. His first book, *The Poet's Defence* (1939), examined the relationship between scientific and poetic or human truth. Bronowski's integration of biology and physics is the central motif of The Ascent of Man. In the final chapter of the book of The Ascent of Man series, Bronowski states that he moved from physics to biology when it occurred to him that 'justice is part of the biological equipment of man', that we are 'ethical creatures' and that 'knowledge is not a loose-leaf notebook of facts'. In his *Science and Human Values* (1956, revised 1965), Bronowski addressed the two-culture debate between science and humanism. He believed that through science the human mind has always sought to find unity in the chaos of nature. Bronowski's instinct for presenting his ideas as strong, interesting narratives is central to his desire to make abstract and normally difficult notions lucid, and to facilitate narrativity he organised the vast amount of content thematically. Sir David Attenborough, Director of Programmes for the BBC when the series was made, commented, 'Bronowski was nothing short of inspired [… He] understood that one of the secrets of programme-making is great story telling'.

Permeating Bronowski's script is his rejection of the subject-object dualism that characterised scientific rationality up to the nineteenth century and that was discarded in the twentieth century with the revolution in philosophy towards a relational reality. In The Ascent of Man he states, 'Physics becomes […] the greatest collective work of art of the twentieth century.' In Part Eleven, 'Knowledge or Certainty', Bronowski prioritises humanity over scientific preoccupation in an unforgettable sequence where, as he wades into the ashes pond at Auschwitz death camp, he says to the camera, 'We have to cure ourselves of the itch for absolute knowledge and power. We have to close the distance between the push-button order and the human act. We have to touch people.' He then reaches into the water and pulls up a handful of mud in a sequence of stop-motion shots. The effect, in context, is a sudden, emotionally charged move from cognition to emotion. Another example from Part Eleven is when Bronowski states to the camera, 'There is no absolute knowledge. And those who claim it, whether scientists or dogmatists, open the door to tragedy. All information is imperfect. We have to treat it with humility. That is the human condition; and that is what quantum physics says. I mean that quite literally.' His statement is followed by actual images of what the world would look like if seen successively through each band of the electromagnetic spectrum, not only from infrared to ultraviolet but also through the radio waves of radar, X-rays, and the electron microscope. He concludes that, in seeking the ultimate image of reality, there is no ideal wavelength: 'Even the hardest electrons do not give a hard outline. The perfect image is still as remote as the distant stars.'

Responses to the series also reflect the old tension between Education and Media Studies over assumptions that television is so constrained that it can say nothing that is not intrinsically superficial. This is part of the continuing contest for cultural authority between conceptual knowledge derivable from the printed word and the kind of knowledge of actuality derivable from pictures. Prior to making The Ascent of Man, Bronowski had shown considerable ability in both writing and broadcasting for television and radio and he believed that the written word had advantages over the audiovisual medium in the amount of detail of data that can be presented. However, as both poet and scientist, Bronowski was interested in successfully reconciling abstraction and actuality: previously in the BBC's Insight he had won a reputation for being able to express abstract and difficult ideas in science (e.g. entropy), mathematics (e.g. probability), human intelligence, and philosophy. He similarly approached The Ascent of Man with a strong sense of the need for television to acquit itself as a medium capable of effectively representing abstract ideas. The title of the series is ironic: the work of male scientists abounds but the contribution of women to the history and philosophy of science is lacking.

Critically, The Ascent of Man is still regarded as a tour de force among television documentaries. Christopher Dunkley of the *Financial Times* wrote that it was the 'most colossal concept I have ever come across in television', and the *Daily Telegraph* described its form as 'splendid'. Another observed that The Ascent of Man is a series 'looked up to by every producer of factual, educational programmes', and that it is made 'in a style much copied since'.

BRUCE HORSFIELD

The Ascent of Man (UK, BBC TV, 1973, thirteen episodes of 50 mins).

Further reading

Bronowski, Jacob, *The Ascent of Man*, Boston: Little, Brown, 1974.

O'Connor, J.J. and Robertson, E.F., *Jacob Bronowski, School of Mathematics and Statistics*, University of St Andrews, Scotland, 2003, www-history.mcs.st-and.ac.uk/Mathematicians/Bronowski.html (accessed 26 August 2011).

Aubervilliers

(France, Lotar, 1945)

Aubervilliers was made early in the post-World War II period by the director Eli Lotar. The French provisional government under Charles de Gaulle had some communist representatives, and the Fourth Republic, the Marshall Plan, and the prosperity and baby boom of the late 1940s and 1950s were yet to come. In the film, the narrator asserts that the ruins of Aubervilliers, a suburb of Paris, 'are not the brand new ruins of the war', but rather 'ancient, commonplace ruins, the mere ruins of workers' misery'.

Appearing ten years after Anstey and Elton's Housing Problems, Aubervilliers embraces the documentary forms of its time. Shot with no synchronous sound, it relies on commentary and music to maintain its discursive function. The narrative is driven by both the commentary and a song performed by Germaine Montero, both written by Jacques Prévert. The essentially denunciative intention intertwines with nostalgia, irony, humanism, and optimism. This approach recalls the feature films of French poetic realism. Lotar had previously worked as a cameraperson with Jean Renoir (Une Partie de campagne), Pierre Prévert (L'Affaire est dans le sac), Luis Buñuel (Las Hurdes), and Joris Ivens (Zuiderzee).

In a firm demonstration, sustained by striking and often shocking images, the film rises up in protest before misery, siding with workers and paying tribute to their strength and dignity. The commentary, as well as the song, salute repeatedly the 'good children of Aubervilliers, good children of proletarians, good children of misery, good children of the whole world'. At the end, the voice-over states, 'It is once again the simple, rude hand of the worker that will shake up this stiff and depressed world, this world that badly needs to change, that will finally change some day.'

The documentary strategy employed by Aubervilliers is threefold. An unconcealed camera presents shots and scenes that depict the general mood of the time. Short sequences are obviously reenacted, such as one of a girl walking to a water fountain. More specifically, persons working at home are filmed frontally, as if posing for a photographer, in a collaborative relationship. Their words, failing to be recorded, are reformulated off screen.

Aubervilliers is the major work of a minor filmmaker.

JEAN-LUC LIOULT

See also: Housing Problems; Ivens, Joris

Aubervilliers (France, Lotar, 1945, 24 mins). Directed by Eli Lotar. Codirected by Jacques Prévert and Joseph Kosma. Narrated by Jacques Prévert. Filmed in Aubervilliers, France.

Further reading

Collas, Gérald, 'D'Aubervilliers (1945) à La Courneuve (1967), Correspondances', *Images Documentaires* 20, 1995: 23–32.

Australia

From the very birth of cinema, successive Australian governments had observed and developed strategies to explore and use the possibilities of film as a means of national projection. Before 1912 the Commonwealth government contracted private production companies to film official events and produce short nonfiction films for theatrical release. Following the appointment of an official cinematographer in 1912, the Cinema and Photographic Branch was established on a temporary basis with the brief 'to film anything of interest'.

On 27 May 1913 the Department of External Affairs sent a letter to cinematographer Bert Ives: 'Sir: in confirmation of my telegrams of yesterday's date I have the honour to inform you that the Minister has approved of your appointment as cinematographer and photographer in this department at the rate of pounds five per week.' Ives was now the official cameraman to the nation (he remained in the position until 1939), with the more specific brief to make films promoting Australia abroad and to record major events.

The new department developed along predictable lines. During the 1920s and 1930s the Melbourne Cinema Division increased its staff and produced newsreels and short features, much as the Empire Marketing Board under John Grierson would a decade later in Britain. Wheat, beef, and tobacco were featured in a series, 'Know Your Country', using a simplistic flat-on film style and using the mantra of Australia—'the vast and rich land'.

From 1915 to 1930 approximately one reel of film per week was produced by the Branch for theatrical release. During the 1930s sound films were released less regularly. There are several of these in the National Film and Sound Archive Collection, including This is Australia, Mineral Wealth, and Australian Sugar. Such films were typically overburdened with long-winded commentaries that were still the official mode of address until the war years when there was something to be portentous about. The stereotypes of the nation thus projected were directly in line with the views of national character advanced by historians such as C.E.W. Bean and film studios (Efftee and Cinesound) producing epic and pastoral features or rural comedies like Dad and Dave (1932).

Documentary features were also intermittently produced, notably featuring the location cinematography of pioneering documentary-maker Captain Frank Hurley. Hurley was celebrated for his sweeping romantic nature still photography and film work in the heroic style of colonial painters like John Glover. Hurley established an early international fame with his Antarctic films Home of the Blizzard (1913) and In the Grip of the Polar Pack-Ice (1917), which contained much sensationalisation of 'cannibal attacks', but was a huge touring success in England and the United States, as well as later tropical adventures documented in Pearls and Savages (1921).

The now-developed tradition of filming in exotic or dangerous locations would, sixty years later, be a feature of the political documentaries of Gil Scrine and David Bradbury (Chile: Hasta Cuando?, Front Line). During World War II it saw the rise of a generation of war correspondents. Damien Parer won the Academy Award for Best Documentary in 1942 for his coverage of Pacific action in World War II in Kokoda Front Line (Cinesound Review, 1942). Following an invitation by the Australian government, John Grierson visited Australia in 1940 to report on the setting up of a more responsive and creative film production arm of government along the lines of the Crown Film Unit.

Grierson strongly recommended the non-theatrical use of 16mm film for general purposes. The Commonwealth Government established the ANFB (Australian National Film Board) in 1945 with the principal task of overseeing the production and distribution of documentary films and the importation of overseas documentaries. The National Library, in collaboration with the state libraries, became the national distributor of 16mm films for nontheatrical, educational use.

Instead of being set up as an independent statutory authority along the lines of the Canadian National Film Board, the ANFB in Australia soon came under the direct control of the Department of Information. In 1946 Stanley Hawes was appointed to the new position of Producer-in-Chief, a position he held until his retirement in 1970. Hawes was effectively a Grierson appointment, having worked with the General Post Office (GPO) Film Unit in London and later with Grierson in Ottawa before accepting the new post in Australia.

The key films produced by the Film Division in this period were Native Earth (John Heyer, 1946), Journey of a Nation (John Heyer, 1947), School in the Mail-Box (Stanley Hawes, 1947), Born in the Sun (John Heyer, 1947), The Cane Cutters (Hugh McInnes, 1948), The Valley is Ours (John E. Seyer, 1948), Goldtown (R. Maslyn Williams, 1949), Mike and Stefani (R. Maslyn Williams, 1951), and Outback Patrol (Lee Robinson, 1952). All of the films of this period were very much in the GPO Film Unit mold, but featured mobile and fluid camera work (influenced by the successful Cinesound and Movietone newsreels) and a keen sense of a plastic landscape moulded by heat and time to very different forms and vistas than the familiar European models. Cities might look much alike the world over but the documentary filmmakers of this period were concerned, in line with nationalist literary movements, to express the difference of the Australian landscape and its unique challenges. Thus, School in a Mail-Box (1947) dealt with the unique outback correspondence school systems developed to serve far-flung rural communities, and the oeuvre of the filmmakers taken as a collective expressed a coherent vision of Australia as a country where highly urbanised cities clung to the rim of a harsh and unrelenting (the favourite adjectives of voice-over) inland.

The outstanding filmmaker of this period was to be John Heyer, whose best work was with the ANFB and whose most iconic and successful work was Back of Beyond (Shell, 1954), a lyrical film about the overland delivery run of the mail and provisions truck driver, shot entirely on location often in the most difficult circumstances—a decision rewarded with some of the finest location cinematography of the period and an outstanding film dealing with a vanished outback world that still has resonance today.

The aims and styles of the ANFB production slate changed little throughout the 1950s and 1960s. The 1964 film From the Tropics to the Snow, however, dealt in a self-reflexive way with the efforts of a team of ANFB producers to showcase Australia's tourist attractions. It provided a humorous insight into the production system and it introduced many of the key figures of the postwar period. The film is now considered an essential research aid for any film historian rather than a great piece of documentary work, indicating an institution more interested in self-perpetuation than breaking new ground—or the rules.

Public broadcasting and documentary practice

The national broadcaster ABC (Australian Broadcasting Commission to 1983, the Australian Broadcasting Corporation thereafter) provided both the training and the showcase for more innovative documentary practice from the introduction of television in 1956.

The tradition of Australia's Public Broadcaster as major producer of documentaries, inherited from the BBC in the early 1960s, continues today in diminished form. In the 1960s outstanding documentary filmmakers like director Bill Fitzwater (Boom Radio 1967) and Geoff Barnes (formerly head of documentary at the ABC) all shot their early films with the national broadcaster. Oscar-winning cinematographers Dean Semmler (Dances with Wolves) and John Seale (The English Patient) both trained as news and documentary cameramen at the ABC.

The best work of salaried ABC directors and crew was often to be seen in cinéma vérité documentary series such as Chequerboard (1968–72). Other series that used documentary techniques and often tackled major subjects were A Big Country (1968 until the early 1990s) and Four Corners (1961 and continuing), based on the BBC Panorama series, which on occasion continues with its one-hour format to produce and break major investigative stories, beginning with a controversial feature documentary on the Returned Services League (RSL) in 1963 and continuing to disturb the status quo to this day. As a documentary forum, Four Corners has consistently produced programmes that have effected more social and political change than any comparable series in the media history of the nation.

Outside the public broadcasters: independent documentary and dramatised documentary

Today, the market and creative development systems are now dominated by a near monopoly on larger budget film funding by the (Australian) Film Finance Corporation. Some documentaries continue to be produced by both the ABC and the multicultural broadcaster, SBS, under various banners (The View from Here, ABC) through the late 1990s, and some fine documentaries are still being produced in-house—notably and most regularly, the short weekly documentary series Australian Story (1996 and continuing).

Former ABC producers such as Jenny Brockie continue to contribute personal evocations of the Australian (mainly suburban) zeitgeist with series like Our Street (2000–1). Here, personal style and involvement painted a striking series of portraits of Australia in cinéma vérité style, focusing on lives as far apart as those of the middle class in the larger coastal cities to the wilder eccentricities of hot and coastal Darwin.

The most influential free-to-air filmmakers of the period work outside the main channels as freelancers and include the writer Ian David, whose research and obsession led to the making of two dramatised documentaries of great influence, politically as well as aesthetically. The first was Police State (Chris Noonan, 1989), which mixed transcripts and newsclips to project a detailed and powerful vision of Queensland as a police state under the long-surviving rightist government of Joh Bjelke-Petersen. David writes dramatised documentary films that stylistically and thematically have much in common with Errol Morris's Thin Blue Line (1988) in their handling of suppressed materials and silenced witnesses. Blue Murder (Michael Jenkins, 1995) moved from a collagist approach to a more dramatised and character-driven style, documenting corruption within the New South Wales police force that had major legal repercussions and was partly responsible for the establishment of a Royal Commission. Few writers, however, have been as influential as David, and his writer-director (auteurist) mode of work remains the norm as well as the most likely to be funded under the rubric of 'director's vision' obsessively employed by all the major bodies (both Federal and State).

SBS and its independent production arm, SBSi, have also become key players in factual film production from experimental and arts programming to documentaries commissioned to reflect the multicultural remit of the channel. Arguably the most successful and important initiatives from SBS came with a season of documentaries on Aboriginal dispossession (Unfinished Business, 2000) from which grew the outstanding films Stolen Generations by Tom Zubrycki and Sally Browning, and Cry from the Heart by Jeni Kendall. Both films examined the disastrous effects of the policies of forced removal of Aboriginal children, which had been the subject of a national inquiry (published as *Bringing Them Home*, released in 1997). These and similar films on Aboriginality and cultural identity have been produced and screened by SBS at a steady rate and seem set to continue as a core activity for the broadcaster as long as it survives under its current charter.

The independent sector up to the present

The most consistently interesting and provocative documentary-makers of the last two decades have been those filmmakers who engaged with the margins of political and social themes.

David Bradbury's documentary oeuvre has proved paradigmatic of many Australian filmmakers' fascination with international political trouble spots and the exotic. Works echoed the much earlier work of Frank Hurley and Damien Parer and the more recent outstanding work of frontline war zone cinematographers like Neil Davis, who was himself the subject of a film by Bradbury.

'Keep the camera rolling, no matter what', was Neil Davis's motto, and in 1985 he literally filmed his own death. Bradbury's powerful tribute, Front Line, was an account of the Vietnam War as seen through the camera of Neil Davis, and is a fine record, full of astonishing action footage of a life lived on the edge—Davis's own death and legend echoing Damien Parer's death while filming in a war zone forty years before. The more political films of Bradbury include Public Enemy Number One (1980), an examination of controversial Australian journalist Wilfred Burchett who chose to report from the 'other side' in the Vietnam War and whose unorthodox views and activities caused him to be labeled a traitor by many. Burchett was the first Western journalist to report on the devastating aftereffects of the atomic bomb dropped on Hiroshima.

Nicaragua—No Pasarán (Bradbury 1984) tracks from 1978 the postrevolutionary Sandinista movement and the past, present, and future of this small Central American nation—another strongly personal portrait of a brutal military dictatorship made during a three-month visit to Chile. The footage reveals a country torn with civil strife and political unrest, military intimidation of the population, and indiscriminate arrests, murder, torture, and disappearances. Bradbury's personal involvement in his subjects and his sharp sense of irony are nowhere more apparent than in the opening scenes showing a wealthy right-wing couple in their Santiago mansion pontificating uninterrupted on the excellence of Augusto Pinochet's attitude to and actions against dissenters (especially young students). Bradbury often narrates his own work, diary-style, and his work overall has a spare quality that makes overt political comment unnecessary. South of the Border (1988) examines how the political and economic struggle in Central America is expressed through the music of the people south of the US border. Bradbury later turned to more local Australian themes with films such as State of Shock (1989), which deals with a notorious court case involving the dispossessed semi-tribal Aborigines.

Tom Zubrycki is widely respected as one of Australia's leading documentary filmmakers. He has worked consistently over the last decades as director of a series of films with strong social and political themes. Waterloo (1981), Kemira: A Diary of a Strike (1984), and Friends and Enemies (1987) were all shot in an offhand style. The subjects were allowed free expressive rein and thus remained valuable documents of Australian union and class struggle in confrontations in what were primarily heavy industry and inner-urban settings. Lord of the Bush (1989), Amongst Equals (1990), Homelands (1993), and Billal (1996) continued Zubrycki's role as diarist of social upheaval and issues-based filmmaking. Later he was to become equally influential as a producer of equally edgy films ranging from the migrant experience, as relived through the filmmaker's return to a war-shattered former Yugoslavia in Exile in Sarajevo (1997, International Emmy 1998), as well as more quirky local subjects like Dr Jazz (1998), and social documents such as Whiteys Like Us (1999) and Stolen Generations (2000).

Arguably Zubrycki's own most 'international' film was also his most internationally successful: The Diplomat (2000) follows East Timor's freedom fighter and Nobel Peace Prize winner José Ramos Horta in the final tumultuous year of his campaign to secure independence for his country. This feature-length film takes up Ramos Horta's story in the final dramatic stages of his long journey—the fall of Indonesia's President Suharto, the referendum to determine East Timor's future, the overwhelming vote for independence, the devastating carnage that ensued, the intervention of United Nations peacekeepers, and Ramos Horta's final triumphant return to his homeland.

Dennis O'Rourke, the most internationally recognised of recent Australian independent documentary filmmakers began his career with two films dealing with the early days of Papua New Guinea (Niugini) independence: Yumi Yet (1976) and Ileksen (1978), featuring striking handheld cinematography by Dick Marks. The films are distinguished by unusual access to key figures of power, such as the first Prime Minister of Niugini, Michael Somare.

O'Rourke had now attracted international funding as well as critical acclaim. His next film, Yap … How Did You Know We'd Like TV? (1980), dealt with the total corruption of local Solomon Islands culture by a wholesale bombardment of American daily television (flown in daily from Los Angeles). The film revealed a sardonic streak in O'Rourke's later projects that became a recognisable trait in all his work as he moved into edgier territories with The Shark Callers of Kontu (1982), Couldn't Be Fairer (1984), and the fine Half Life: A Parable for the Nuclear Age (1985), which established O'Rourke as a world filmmaker whose filmmaking and sociological interests were now outrunning the Pacific Rim.

Nevertheless, O'Rourke returned to Niugini with Cannibal Tours (1988), a witty examination of European tourists juxtaposed with the 'authentic' lives of the Niuginians held up for their entertainment.

With (again government funded) The Good Woman of Bangkok (1991) O'Rourke became the centre of an international controversy as the film documented his relationship with a Thai prostitute, Aoi. The resulting outcries circled the globe through every means, both at academic conferences and at professional associations, and raised issues of gender, sexism, third-world politique, and exploitation.

O'Rourke's work continues to provoke and attract audiences and his film Cunnamulla (2000) played to a wide art house audience in Australia and garnered interest and acclaim internationally. Although it deals for the first time with O'Rourke's own very personal 'backyard'—the people who live in the fast-failing outback town of Cunnamulla—the film, with all the irony and quiet savagery, is O'Rourke's best work.

Bob Connolly was another filmmaker to have developed his skills at the ABC (1964–78), first as a foreign correspondent and later as a documentary filmmaker. He and Robin Anderson (as cameraman-director and sound recorder, respectively) worked from a base of strict social observation and deep research, using on location a remarkable degree of ability to relax and literally live with their filmic subjects. Anderson also had worked at the ABC, as a researcher, and both he and Connolly left to begin work as independent filmmakers with the masterful interweaving of themes of colonialism and kinship with First Contact (1983). The film was an anthropological study of the impact of the pioneering Leahy brothers in the New Guinea Highlands in the 1930s, leading to a consideration of both the cultural impact of their visit and the effects produced on Old Joe Leahy's scarcely acknowledged son, Joe, the child of a liaison with a tribal woman. This subject and associated themes developed further in three years of filming that produced Joe Leahy's Neighbours (1989) and the richly ironic and ultimately tragicomic Black Harvest (1992). These films, like the earlier part of the trilogy, won many international and local awards and enjoyed successful cinema releases, setting a pattern that has now become quite common for at least two or three major documentaries a year—creating a broad audience where none had really existed outside the academy since the 1950s. Anderson and Connolly have become the exemplars of the nonpurist anthropological style that has helped raise both public appreciation and, in association with independent cinema owners, much broader cinema screenings and good box office returns for most of their films in the commercial film market. Their success has also interacted with that of other equally accessible filmmakers' works, notably those of Dennis O'Rourke, in being able to guarantee good audiences by strength of reputation alone.

Rats in the Ranks (1996) was also the product of Connolly and Anderson's ability to win the trust of their subjects. This film, also running for a long season in cinemas before becoming a bestselling video, deals with the machinations and power struggles in an inner-city municipal council led by a Machiavellian mayor who will do anything to stay in power. The extraordinary access to all parties to the back-room death struggles leading up to an internal party schism and the next election are as powerful and revealing as Pennebaker and Hegedus' War Room (1992) (which, along with Rats in the Ranks, makes a perfect Australian political primer).

Equally successful and also the result of nearly a year of filming is Facing the Music (2001), another multiple award winner that also penetrated the independent cinema market, indicating that Connolly and Anderson now had a steady following and a 'brand name' among audiences. Shot inside Sydney University's Music Department and focusing on the travails of Department Head Professor Anne Boyd (herself also a noted Australian composer), this film actually treads deeper waters of unconscious irony than even the filmmakers may have realised. Their portrait of a threatened university department reveals a group of apparently self-serving academics—and, in one shocking scene, a young woman composer is both verbally and artistically assaulted by a teacher. However, the positioning of the film seems to be on the side of the 'threatened' teachers. What are perceived by the filmmakers as the strengths of the focus of the film, the professor and the role of the music department, are never interrogated.

The subsequent selling of the film by the filmmakers as unproblematic suggests that Australian documentary or its audiences are not necessarily possessed of a wide range of analytical or comparative tools. If shot and screened in Europe, for example, this film might well have been pitched as a satire on academic self-absorption and the dysfunctional approach taken by so many teachers working in 'creative' departments to their very raison d'être, the hapless students. For these reasons, of course, Facing the Music is the most tantalising and intriguing work yet from Australia's leading cinéma vérité team.

Few documentaries have dealt in detail with the supposed Australian national obsessions of sport and drink. Remarkably, only one major documentary has penetrated the mystique of a sporting club, but Michael Cordell's Year of the Dogs (1997) manages to sum up an Australian ambivalence to sporting heroes with cinéma vérité filming and a laconic and undercutting editorial style. As with the work of Connolly and Anderson's and Dennis O'Rourke's later projects, Year of the Dogs proved a success at cinemas. Audiences were composed in roughly equal parts of sports enthusiasts and those in search of the more complex pleasures of the well-made cinéma vérité film in a society where subjects are often surprisingly candid and articulate about their obsessions.

Although the supposed wry, self-deprecating defining characteristics of Australians are not always in evidence in documentary (feature films have appropriated that territory), two films have become small national treasures by stressing the darker aspects of living in contemporary Australia: David Caesar's Bodywork (1989) and Mark Lewis's Cane Toads (1987).

Bodywork is a cool and subtle gaze at the undertaking profession and Australian attitudes to death and what follows, shot in a Candide-like (wide angles) shooting style. The international success of the film is in part due to Caesar's great directorial control over the carefully composed 'look' of the film. Caesar uses the interviewees as dramatis personae and often interviews two or more at a time to increase the sardonic effect. This documentary, still very influential as a model for film students of the full possibilities of the carefully constructed documentary, led Caesar directly into a career as a maker of sharp and satirical feature films.

Cane Toads, too, was a success and won numerous awards. It took a bleak view of the disastrous attempts of overly optimistic scientists to solve ecological problems. The film is about the introduction in the 1930s of the *Bufo Marinus* (Cane Toad) to Queensland (in semi-tropical northern Australia) to control small insects annoying the crops. Toads multiply and then assume a horrific and unending advance from the northern Australia slowly throughout the nation. Bleak, yet very funny, Cane Toads remains influential and indicates a road down which Australian documentary may profitably stray.

JONATHAN DAWSON

See also: Cane Toads; Good Woman of Bangkok, The; Heyer, John; O'Rourke, Dennis

Further reading

n.a., *The Big Picture: Documentary Filmmaking in Australia*, Papers from the Second Australian Documentary Conference, Clayton Monash University, 1991.

Bean, C.E.W., *The Story of Anzac*, Sydney: Angus & Robertson, 1921.

Berry, C., Hamilton, H. and Jayamanne, L. (eds), *The Filmmaker and the Prostitute*, Sydney: Power Institute, 1997.

Bertrand, Ina, *Government and Film in Australia*, Sydney: Currency Press, 1981.

Blonski, A., Creed, B. and Freiburg, F. (eds), *Don't Shoot Darling: Women's Independent Filmmaking in Australia*, Sydney: Greenhouse, 1987.

Commonwealth Government, *Bringing Them Home: The Report of the National Inquiry into the Separation of*

Aboriginal and Torres Strait Islander Children from their Families, Canberra: Commonwealth of Australia, 1997.
Cunningham, Stuart and Turner, Graeme, *The Media in Australia: Industries, Audiences*, Sydney: Allen and Unwin, 1993.
Dawson, Jonathan and Molloy, Bruce, *Queensland Images*, Brisbane: University of Queensland Press, 1990.
Dimond, Peter, *Writing Documentary Script and Narration*, Sydney: Australian Film and Television School, 1980.
FitzSimons, Trish, Laughren, Pat and Williams, Dugald, 'Towards a Contemporary History of Australian Documentary', *Metro* 123, 2000: 62–73.
Hartley, John, *Popular Reality: Journalism, Modernity, Popular Culture*, London: Arnold, 1996.
Inglis, Ken, *This is the ABC*, Melbourne: Melbourne University Press, 1983.
Lansell, Ross and Beilby, Peter, *The Documentary Film in Australia*, Melbourne: Cinema Papers, 1982.
Moran, Albert, *The Projection of Australia*, Sydney: Currency, 1991.
Moran, Albert and O'Regan, Tom (eds), *Australian Film Reader*, Sydney: Currency Press, 1985.
Turner, Graeme, *National Fictions*, Sydney: Allen & Unwin, 1986.

Austria

The origins: 1895 to 1918

In the summer of 1895, a moving pictures machine was installed for the first time in Prater, an amusement quarter that continues to exist in Vienna today. Five machines were placed in a 'Kinetoscope Hall', where documentary pictures from American Thomas Alva Edison and his assistants were exhibited (Fritz 1980). The Viennese Prater was one of the first sites of the Habsburg monarchy Austria-Hungary where moving pictures were projected, and Prater was a popular film location during the beginnings of film history. On March 26, 1896 Eugene Dupont, collaborator of the firm Lumière, organized the first public performance in Austria: documentary films about Vienna were shown in the building located at Kärtnerstraße 45 (later in the contiguous building number 39). The work of Charles Moisson, principal operator of Lumière, was presented there. In the exhibition programme were the films Feuerwehr-Centrale am Hof, Kärtnerstraßs Le Ring, and Freudenau, Sattelraum nach dem Pisek-Rennen. Pictures of Prater—such as Der Volksprater, Der Prater, and Die Hauptalle (Main Avenue)—were among the scenes that Alexander Promio and his assistant and interpreter Alexander Werschinger were shooting in Vienna on behalf of Lumière in mid-April 1896. These pictures belong to the earliest examples of Austrian cinematography. The company Pathé Frères produced in 1908 two documentary films: Blumenkorso in Mai/Flower Parade in May, and In der Prater Hauptallee/In Prater's Main Avenue (Büttner and Dewald 2002: 22).

Pioneering documentary films, which have been referred to in this way only since 1926, joined images together without tying them into a story. Different film types, such as newsreels, scientific films, and educational and cultural films, were later developed from this technique. At the beginning, the camera viewer played the role of a passive observer; later, the camera viewer was converted into a tourist or researcher (Büttner and Dewald 2002). The camera reflected the world exactly as it was: the Viennese locations filmed between 1896 and 1910 by Lumière, Pathé, and other directors staged representation rooms for the Viennese bourgeoisie. The Opera House, the 'Ring', the 'Trabrennplatz', and the 'Burgmusik' staged theatrical rooms in the film Wien um 1908/ Vienna around 1908 (Pathé Frères) within the frame of related patterns between time and behavior. The early documentary film showed principally the large city and the bulk as admiring spectacles in themselves. In this sense, in the film presented in 1896 by Lumière (Kärtnerstraße 45), Verkehr bei dem Cinematographen/Traffic in the Cinematographer, the spectators convert themselves into their own performers. 'Open to the public' is an understood political, institutional kind of openness that serves only to create a specific audience (around 1900, only four percent of the inhabitants were elective). The early (documentary) film created a carefully selected image of the city and therefore did not show only a sensory real picture in which the spectacle is based. At the turn of the century these early film pioneers were followed by other filmmakers who produced 'scientific films'. As examples we can cite the ethnologist and anthropologist Rudolf Pöch (1870–1921) and the Viennese teacher Alto Arche. The first attempts took place from 1904 to 1908. The beginnings of 'racial research' in Austria are associated with the ethnographic film pioneer, the Viennese doctor, and Pöch. The central themes of Pöch's first film about the so-called

Buschmaenner der Kalahari/Kalahari Bushmen, produced between 1908 and 1909, were technical aspects of specific works, such as culling and trampling on grass and bulbs, fabricating ropes, and/or sparking a fire. The external characteristics of the people created by Pöch's camera categorized him as a specific 'people classificator'.

In 1909 the first Austrian full-length documentary film was shown as an independent film in Viennese movie theaters: Die Kaisermanoever in Maehren/The King's Manoeuvre in Moravia. The film Se, Majestaet Kaiser Franz Josef I auf der Gemsjagd/His Majesty Kaiser Franz Josef I at the Gem Hunt was shown in the Viennese Prater in the cinematographic exhibition 'International Hunt Exhibition Vienna 1910' (Pathé Frères 1909). Besides feature films, film pioneers such as Anton and Luise Kolm (Der Faschingzug in Ober-St Veit/The Carnival Train at Ober St Veit, and Der Trauerzug Sr Exzellenz des Buergermeisters Dr Karl Jueger/The Funeral Procession Sr Exzellenz of Mayor Dr Karl Jueger (1910)), regularly produced documentary films. In 1910 Graf Alexander 'Sascha' Kolowrat—who later founded Sascha Film—also began to produce documentary films (Die Gewinnung des Erzes am steirischen Erzberg in Eisenerz/Ore Extraction at the Ore Mountain of Iron Ore (1912)). Hans Theyer shot cultural films about glassblowers, painters, and carpenters; his works led to the creation of the 'Central Office for Scientific and Educational Cinematography'.

This function of the documentary film had also been used to give pictures another conscious meaning, which was deliberately created, particularly during wartime. In August 1914 the war department commissioned film producers Sascha-Filmfabrik, Wiener Kunstfilmindustrie-Gesellschaft, and Österreichisch-Ungarische Kinoindustrie-Gesellschaft, to produce war film propaganda based on war archives. The first series of the Kriegs-Journal/War Journal produced by Wiener Kunstfilm appeared in September. At the end of 1914 Sascha-Film in cooperation with Philipp und Pressburger and the Österreichisch-Ungarische Kinoindustrie-Gesellschaft presented a war newsreeler titled Österreichischer Kino-Wochenbericht vom nördlichen und suedlichen Kriegsschauplatz/Austrian Weekly Report from Northern and Southern War Theater. Until 1918 field cinema was limited to showing the world upstanding images and frontline experience could no longer find visual expression.

In 1918 the UFA (Universumfilm Aktiengesellschaft) started production on documentaries in Berlin with a popular scientific content. This concept was imitated in Austria by Kurt Köfinger in his tourist films of the 1920s and later in the controlled propaganda documentary films of the Wien-Film (1938–45). The newsreels combined the characteristics of newscast and chronicle documentaries in their thematic mixture of politics, sports, and culture, which were sometimes presented in newsreel cinemas (from 1936 as nonstop cinemas in Vienna and also in Linz, Salzburg, and Innsbruck). The Viennese documentary film was presented as a 'war journal' for the first time in 1914, followed in 1930–3 by Sascha-Messter-Wochenschau/The Sascha Messter Newsreel, an international newsreel production based on the Austrian 'Selenophon' technique (Selenophon, together with Gustav-Mayer-Film, produced a newsreel from 1930 to 1932), and from 1934 to 1938 by Oesterreich in Bild und Ton/Austria in Vision and Sound.

Austro-Fascism/The Third Reich: 1933–45

In 1927 cameraman Rudi Mayer shot a three-piece documentary about the burning of the palace of justice in Vienna. The ten-minute documentary, titled Die Schreckenstage in Wien/Time of Horror in Vienna, shows objectivity: the destruction of a national institution is in the foreground, and the film compares the national values (order, security) with the crowd's bestiality (disorder, chaos).

On a traumatically staged world picture, the burning of the palace of justice represents a sign of imminent danger of civil war and collapse of the government's power and control. From this historic event of 1927, documentary practices and styles were invaded by Austro-Fascist propaganda concepts, which eventually became the rigorous standard-type for newsreels and documentary films (Achenbach and Moser 2002). Documentary films had to be systematically concerned with increasing the credibility and authenticity of the government's image. Just three weeks after the parliament's release, the Dollfuss-Regime deliberated on a central organization for film propaganda. One of the most important productions of this propaganda machine was the Austro-Fascist newsreel

Oesterreich in Bild und Ton (OEBUT)/Austria in Vision and Sound. It was created through the initiative of the federal chancellor, Engelbert Dollfuss, and was produced between June 1933 and March 1938 by the Vaterländischen Tonfilmgesellschaft of the film company Selenophon Licht- und Tonfilm Ltd. OEBUT worked principally on the establishment of the authoritarian regime's legitimacy, with its principal objectives being to spread Catholic values, reinforce Austrian identity, and counteract annexation to the German Reich.

Beginning in November 1934 all movie theaters had to show a 'cultural movie' in their preliminary programs. These were sometimes art and nature documentaries but often they were also propaganda movies about racial doctrine, political parties, and military matters. The newsreel became the most important propaganda instrument during wartime and its screening became mandatory every night at every showing of a film. The centerpoint of these educational and advertising short films was always Austria—its cultural, scientific, and political autonomy, together with its tradition and historical legacy.

Marshall Plan movie and 'documentary films' 1945–65

During the first two decades of the postwar period, documentary productions were characterized principally by the creation of cultural and propaganda films that were produced either for the Wiener ECA-Mission (Economic Cooperation Administration), the local office for the distribution and translation of the European Recovery Program (ERP), better known as the Marshall Plan, or for important cultural performances (screen adaptation of operas and plays).

The Österreichische Produktivitätszentrum (OEPZ, Austrian Center for Productivity), founded in the spring of 1950, is a direct outcome of the American reconstruction program. The OEPZ 'film office' section was established in 1951 on the initiative of the US administration, in line with the 'technical assistance' to effectively disseminate the pedagogy of 'productive managing and working' among the Austrian population. The 'Marshall Films', distributed by the OEPZ, promulgated a capitalistic Europe befriended by America (Reichert 2000: 83).

The Information Officer of the European film unit commissioned diverse documentary filmmakers to produce regional documentary films aimed at building consensus on specific local and regional needs. Austrian Georg Tressler, film officer of the ECA-Mission, was one of the most relevant documentary film producers of that time (Buchschwenter 2003). The films Gute Ernte/Good Crop (1950), Hansl und die 200,000 Küchen/Hansl and the 200,000 Kitchens (1952), Traudls neuer Gemüsegarten/Traudl's new Vegetable Garden (1952), Ertagreicher Kartoffelanbau/Fruitful Potato Cultivation (1952, exhibited at the Documentary Film Festival in Venice), Wie die Jungen Sungen/How the Boys Sang (1954), and Rund um die Milchwirtschaft/On the Dairy Farm (1954), followed the same objectives as the Marshall Plan films from Tressler, focusing on educating the public about effective management techniques, promoting identification with the concept of 'productivity improvement', and propagating the extension of US economic aid to broader population spheres.

An old-fashioned, pedagogical film type dominated so-called cultural films until the 1960s. This type of film is still produced today, mainly for government-commissioned TV productions such as tourist promotional films and Austrian historical reportage. These films were dependent on subsidies because they were not commercially viable.

About 680 cultural films were produced during the period from 1945 to 1961. Most of them fell more in line with the style of the National Socialist (NS) cultural films than with the artistic evolution of international documentary films. Tourism promotion was the principal motivation for regional and federal supporters. In this sense, Hans Pebahl produced the popular documentary film Und neues Leben blüht aus den Ruinen/And New Life Blooms in the Ruins in 1953. In this film, as in other postwar films, the reconstruction of the old cultural monuments was overvalued. This overvaluation was based on restorative cultural meaning, which simultaneously devalued contemporary culture. In award-winning films such as Wege in die Zukunft/Roads to the Future (Erich Pochlatko, 1959) and Die andere Seite/The Other Side (Bruno Loetsch, 1958), a gentle voice-over commented on pleasant pictures which ritualized the NS suppression.

In 1955 prizes for documentary films were awarded for the first time. The films were divided into two categories: the first comprised those films that bore representation of existing subjects; the second category consisted of the documentary films that went beyond the central theme, looking for creative, imaginary or artistic interpretation (Reichert 2000: 84). Most movie theaters had to close at the beginning of the 1960s because of low demand caused by the introduction of television—'culture for the masses'. Documentary films experienced a decline in the market too. With a high value placed on civic education from the projection of cultural images, the National Funding Policy for Documentary Production was dedicated exclusively to the screen adaptation (in the studio) of diverse performances presented at the Viennese Burg Theater between 1955 and 1965.

The New Documentary Film

At the end of the 1960s and the beginning of the 1970s there was little structure to the production and commercialization of independent documentary films in Austria. From the 1970s a tendency to produce films called 'New Documentary Films' was identified, but they had only marginal importance in film evolution. Most of these films were produced in private studios by individuals who financed the productions with their own money earned through work in another field (Blümlinger 1986). In this way Michael Pilz, who worked for three years on his five-hour film essay, Himmel und Erde/Sky and Earth (1979–82), and lived for one year of that time with the miners whom he filmed, could perform a project of this kind as an independent producer. The controversial film Bonjour Capitaliste (1982) from Werner Grusch, which deals with the colonization of white tourists in black Africa, was also financed by private resources.

The Film Advisory Board of the Board of Education, founded in the 1970s, could implement a policy for the promotion of documentary films only until the creation of the Oesterreichischen Filmförderungsfonds (OEFF, Austrian Film Promotion Fund). The cultural film thereby faded into the background. In the early 1970s Ferry Radax, who had been involved with documentary film production since the 1950s, created some outstanding artist portrayals. Through great exertion, he achieved the outstanding formal depiction of the painter Hundertwasser (1965), for which he was awarded with the Austrian State Prize. Other films include Konrad Bayer (1969), Thomas Bernhard (1970), Ludwig Wittgenstein (1975), and Japan oder die Suche nach dem verlorenen Reis/Japan or the Search for the Lost Rice (1981/82).

At the end of the 1970s the Filmladen (film store) and the Medienwerkstatt (media workshop) were founded and a longer-term structure for independent documentary film and video work finally could be created. Ruth Beckermann was cofounder of the rental business 'film store', which began in 1977 with an appropriate structure for commercialization and public distribution of documentary films beyond Austrian television. At the beginning of the film rental business, a series of so-called 'Flugblattfilme' (flight sheet films) about sociopolitical and work-political themes came into existence. In this sense, the film from Josek Aichholzer and Ruth Beckermann, Auf amol a Streik/Amol on Strike (1978), expounded the problems of a more than three-week-long strike in Semperit in Traiskirchen. The film was presented at numerous union meetings and was enthusiastically received. The fight for the former Viennese slaughterhouse Sankt Marx was documented in 1977 by 'Video Group Arena' in the film Arena besetzt/Arena Occupied. The same year saw the start of the collective work Wir kommen wieder/We Come Back from Syndikat der Filschaffenden, about the Austrian movement against atomic power plants. From many Medienwerkstatt productions emerged important experimental and sociopolitical video work. From 1983 to 1984 Niki List filmed—without any public financial support—on 16mm/SW Mama Lustig, a sociocritical documentary about the daily life of a disabled young person, which caused a sensation across Austria.

Margarethe Heinrichs' films, called 'solidarity films', were devoted to production conditions in the revolutionary Latin American countries, unlike the ethnographic-oriented films about black Africa from director Grusch. The 16mm film Traum des Sandino/Sandino's Dream (1981) and the television reportage No Pasarán/They Won't Get Through (1984), both subsidized by the government, describe without any formal experiments the literacy campaign in Nicaragua and the exploitative conditions in the so-called Third World. The development of new documentary films has a connection with sociopolitical tendencies—essentially in the 'Neue Linken' environment. They were involved with daily life, the world of workers, and emancipation projects. The primordial objective for the film organization for documentary production was that the values of socially and politically segregated people, which were already faded out by the mass media, became visible.

Historical archaeology in the present context

In the 1980s the infrastructure of political groups (peace movement, Third World, antinuclear power, anti-racism) and the search for opposing ideas gradually broke down. Since then, a new trend in content and form has emerged: an orientation toward contemporary issues, but also toward ordinary life and subjective themes. Since the early 1980s, the Austrian film has practiced historical archaeology, which has been so meaningful that it revived the film category and the past started to open up to the present (Beckermann and Blümlinger 1996). 'Wien Retour—Franz West 1924–34' (1983) was the first Austrian documentary film to deal with contemporary history. The film Erzschmerz/Ore Pain (1983), produced by Bernhard Frankfurter on behalf of ORF, tried for the first time to expose the lengthy repression of fascism through some miners' experiences.

Axel Corti, motivated by the taboos of historical development during the NS period, produced films such as Die Verweigerung/The Refusal (1971), Der Fall Jaegerstätter/Fighter's Fall (1972), and An uns glaubt Gott nicht mehr/God Does Not Believe in Us Anymore (1985) with documentary film elements. Some techniques were the provision to the spectator of information about date and place; newsreel material insertions, which gave the film a realistic note; and the use of black and white, which provided a more authentic reference. This mixture of fiction and reality may serve to remind the audience that the time portrayed was real and did not exist only in films. In the 1980s other documentary producers besides the remarkable Corti, such as Josef Aichholzer, Ruth Beckermann, Karin Berger, Karin Brandauer, Eduard Erne, Bernhard Frankfurter, Andreas Gruber, Johanna Heer, Margareta Heinrich, Egon Humer, Wilma Kiener, Dieter Matzka, and Werner Schmiedel, undertook a memorial documentary work that the Austrian feature film was not capable of accomplishing because of melodramatic fictionalization. In 1997 Ruth Beckermann received the Bibliotheque prize at the Festival Cinema du Reel in Paris for the documentary film Jenseits des Krieges/Beyond War (1996), which became very popular at the Armed Forces Exhibition.

In the film produced by the multimedia performer Andre Heller and the documentary producer Othmar Schmiederer, Im toten Winkel/On the Dead Angle (2002), the eighty-one-year-old Traudl Junge recounts the time when she was working as private secretary to Adolf Hitler. The film was presented in February 2002 at the Berlin Film Festival, garnering a great reception by the media and was distinguished with the 'Audience Prize'.

In the 1980s 'oral history' projects, which relied on the presence of primary witnesses and on the authenticity of the on-camera effect, became more popular within the documentary field. Angela Summereder used a radically different semidocumentary technique for relating an historical court case. The case was staged in the film Zechmeister/Carousing Master (1981). The film does not reconstruct a 'case' per se, but recreates the history of a patriarchal law dominated by male representatives. The film Zur Lage/To the Circumstance (2002), filmed by four directors (Barbara Albert, Michael Glawogger, Ulrich Seidl, and Michael Sturminger), is an ethnological study of the conservative and reactionary thinking that emerged in Austria after the change of government.

The globalization of documentaries

Numerous documentary productions of the last decade led filmmakers out of the country: Megacities (1998) by Michael Glawogger was the most successful Austrian documentary of the 1990s. Glawogger links his observations to portrayals of individual inhabitants in the film, which was shot in four 'megacities'—Bombay, New York, Mexico City, and Moscow. Megacities refuses to relate the social condition of individual persons to complex structures.

One of the most successful contemporary documentaries is Hundstage/Dog Days (2002), produced in Austria by Ulrich Seidl. Dog Days consists of five independent stories of Viennese suburbs that are arranged and interwoven. It is a feature film that cleverly makes use of the documentary style of reality TV. Dog Days was awarded the Grand Jury Prize at the Vienna

Film Festival. Ulrich Seidl became famous for his provocative documentaries in which he exposed the unpleasant side of the Austrian soul. In his second film, Der Ball/The Prom (1982), he staged the preparation for a high school prom and thereby exposed the class conceit, smugness, narrow-mindedness, and prudish behavior of a town. In Good News (1990), he documented the living conditions of foreign newspaper salesmen. Die letzten Männer/The Last Men (1994) is a TV drama about men with no self-confidence who look for a mail order Thai bride. In Tierische Liebe/Animal Love (1995) Seidl examines the intimate relationship of Austrian pet owners with their pets, while Models (1999) tells of the daily degradation of a photo model's life.

During the last decade of the twentieth century, Nikolaus Geyrhalter's films found a significant cinema audience. The film Pripyat (1999), awarded numerous international prizes, tells the story of survival in the dead zone around the former atomic power plant Chernobyl, evacuated in 1986. Elsewhere (2000), Geyrhalter's magnum opus, compress twelve twenty-minute episodes, one for every month of the year 2000, filmed at a remote, supposedly untouched, place on the globe. It is intended to show that there may not be a single place on Earth that is unaffected by tragedy. 'Phantom rides' was the name given to those films (like rollercoaster rides, railway journeys) that created a subjective experience by installing the camera onto a moving object. Martin Bruch created in his film Handbikemovie (2003) a phantom ride of a special kind: the audience 'sits' on the handlebars of the tricycle on which the film producer, suffering from multiple sclerosis, moves himself around.

It could be concluded that the sensibility for symbolic images and the interest in different political cultures were developed during the second half of the 1970s, when the 'newer' documentary film, which displaced the antiquated 'cultural film' of the 1950s and 1960s, made its appearance. Since the 1980s countercultural references to established cultures and societies have been gradually expanded. During the last decade of the twentieth century, a clear rejection of subjective-essayistic documentary productions emerged. In this sense, in the era of medium format reality TV, Austrian documentary film production was characterized by the need to visualize 'reality'.

RAMON REICHERT

Further reading

Achenbach, Michael and Moser, Karin (eds), *Osterreich in Bild und Ton. Die Filmwochenschau des austrofaschistischen Ständestaates*, Wien: Filmarchiv Austria, 2002.

Aichholzer, Josef (ed.), *Dokumentarfilmschaffen in Osterreich*, Wien: Filmladen, 1986.

Beckermann, Ruth and Blümlinger, Christa, *Ohne Untertitel: Fragmente einer Geschichte des österreichischen Kinos*, Wien: Sonderzahl, 1996.

Blümlinger, Christa, *Verdrängte Bilder in Osterreich. Möglichkeiten des Dokumentarfilms in der II. Republik*, Salzburg: university dissertation, 1986.

Buchschwenter, Robert (ed.), *Georg Tressler: Zwischen Auftrag und Autor*, Wien: Filmarchiv, 2003.

Büttner, Elisabeth and Dewald, Christian, *Das tägliche Brennen, Eine Geschichte des österreichischen Films von 1945 bis zur Gegenwart*, Salzburg: Residenz, 2002.

Fritz, Walter, *Dokumentarfilme aus Osterreich 1909–14*, Wien: Filmarchiv, 1980.

Reichert, Ramón, 'Die Popularisierung der Produktivität: Die Filme des Osterreichischen Produktivitätszen trums 1950–87: Ein Beitrag zur Diskussion um den Film als historische Quelle', *Osterreichische Akädemie der Wissenschaften*, Relation 2, 7, 2000: 69–128.

B

Back of Beyond, The
(John Heyer, 1954)

One of the most successful documentary films ever made in Australia, The Back of Beyond was also one of the most significant productions of the Shell Film Unit during the 1950s. A dramatized documentary in the tradition of Night Mail and Fires Were Started, it won critical acclaim at international film festivals and was the most widely seen Australian film of the era, due to extensive nontheatrical distribution at home and overseas.

The Back of Beyond was produced, written, and directed by Tasmanian-born John Heyer, who had left the Australian National Film Board in 1948 to lead the newly formed Australian Shell Film Unit. Given a brief to make a 'prestige' documentary that would capture the essence of the country, he undertook an extended three-month trip into the Outback, traveling through the Central Australian desert before returning to Sydney to prepare a detailed shooting script with the assistance of his wife, Janet, and writer Roland Robinson. Narration and dialogues were written in collaboration with the poet and playwright Douglas Stewart.

The Back of Beyond follows mailman Tom Kruse along the three hundred miles of the Birdsville Track between Marree, South Australia, and Birdsville, in southwest Queensland. His two-week journey in a 1936 Leyland truck takes him across hazardous terrain to deliver the post and supplies to remote outposts, crossing sand dunes, flooded creeks, and featureless plains. Dramatized scenes with locals playing themselves alternate with fictional reenactments, such as the story of two girls losing their way in the desert following the death of their mother on an isolated farm. The narration alternates between the commentary, spoken by Kevin Brennan and a chorus of voices—the mailman, women chatting on two-way radio, and an Aboriginal man reflecting on the abandoned Lutheran mission where he grew up—and the Birdsville policeman's laconic diary entry. The poetic, multilayered quality of the soundtrack is matched by the music of John Kay and complemented by the strong picture composition of cinematographer Ross Wood.

The Outback, the ostensible subject of The Back of Beyond, is seen in both a realistic and romanticized light. Beyond the obvious themes of communication (the mail run) and the battle against the elements, the film touches on some of the complexities of Australian identity, including not only indigenous people but also characters such as one of the very last Afghan camel-drivers in Marree. Heyer has a touch for comedy, a feel for evocative locations, and an eye for surreal details and recurring leitmotifs. Although some elements, such as the dubbed dialogues, might now seem somewhat wooden, the achievement of the film is the subtle interweaving of disparate story elements into a satisfying whole. Regarded as a minor classic of the genre, it was awarded the Grand Prix at the 1954 Venice Film Festival before being screened across Australia in theatrettes, town halls, schools, and traveling vans.

JOHN BURGAN

See also: Australia; Heyer, John

Back of Beyond (Australia, Shell Film Unit, 1954, 66 mins). Distributed by National Film and Sound Archive, Australia. Produced and directed by John Heyer. Script by John Heyer, Janet Heyer and Roland Robinson. Cinematography by Ross Wood. Music by Sydney John Kay. Edited by John Heyer. Sound by Mervyn Murphy and John Heath. Commentary and dialogues by Douglas Stewart and John Heyer. Narrated by Kevin Brennan. Cast: Tom Kruse, William Buttler, Jack the Dogger, Old Joe the Rainmaker, the Oldfields of Ettadina, Bejah, Malcolm Arkaringa, the people of the Birdsville Track. Filmed on the Birdsville Track between Marree, South Australia, and Birdsville, Queensland.

Further reading

Else, Eric, *The Back of Beyond: A Compilation by Eric Else for Use in Studying John Heyer's Film of Inland Australia*, London: Longman, 1968.

Pike, Andrew and Cooper, Ross, *Australian Film 1900–977*, Melbourne: Oxford University Press, 1980.

Bang Carlsen, Jon

Best known for his radical approach to the staging of documentaries, Jon Bang Carlsen has played a prominent role on the Danish film scene since about 1980, and remains one of Denmark's most innovative documentarists, with a number of feature films behind him as well.

Bang Carlsen's documentaries often focus on the daily lives and rituals of people whom viewers would consider either ordinary or marginal. Often living outside his native Denmark, Carlsen is drawn to other cultures and landscapes, and a number of his documentaries were shot in other countries—in the United States (Hotel of the Stars (1981) and Phoenix Bird (1986)), Germany (Ich bin auch ein Berliner (1990)), Ireland (It's Now or Never (1996), My Irish Diary (1996), and How to Invent Reality (1997)), and South Africa (Addicted to Solitude (1999), My African Diary (2000), and Portrait of God (2001)). Each of his films forcefully evokes a sense of place as an integral part of its storytelling, and Carlsen often uses long takes, dwelling on faces and settings as part of a highly controlled visual style.

Carlsen's unconventional views on the staging of documentaries date from the very start of his career and were given their fullest expression in his film essay How to Invent Reality in which he outlines his method and explains its underlying logic. Casting as his actors people who essentially play themselves on screen, but speak the lines he has written for them, Carlsen deliberately blurs the boundaries between documentary and fiction, uninhibitedly transforming the data other documentarists might prefer to record unchanged. He argues: 'I don't want to be a hostage to life's coincidences in my work. I allow myself to rearrange reality in order to express the inner life of my characters' (How to Invent Reality, 1997). However, these transformations are not gratuitous. The lines of dialogue he writes are tailor-made to suit the people speaking them, so that their words come across as natural and unrehearsed expressions of their own experience. At the same time, this staging of reality is an act whereby the filmmaker becomes a part of—and illuminates—what he films. As Carlsen puts it, 'My films are not the truth. They are how I sense the world. Nothing more' (How to Invent Reality, 1997).

In some cases, the viewer is entirely unaware of the degree to which the action has been staged and the dialogue written by the director. This is true, for example, of Before the Guests Arrive (1986), in which a woman who runs a small seaside hotel and her only employee are shown preparing the place for the approaching season. The viewer has every reason to believe that the two women are spontaneously expressing their own thoughts during their dialogue. On the other hand, with It's Now or Never, about an ageing Irish bachelor who is searching for a bride, the observant viewer will notice the rapidly changing camera positions and realize that the action must have been carefully orchestrated as a series of shots, just as if the film were a work of pure fiction.

In Jon Bang Carlsen's own words:

> Whether you work with fiction or documentaries, you're telling stories because that is the only way we can approach the world: to fantasize about this mutual stage of ours as it reinvents itself in the sphere between the actual physical world and the way your soul reflects it back onto the world. For me documentaries are no more real than fiction films and fiction films no more invented than documentaries.
>
> (Bang Carlsen 2003)

His most recent works depart somewhat from the staged documentaries in that his interviewees do in fact tell their own stories—for example, inmates in a South African prison describe how they imagine God in Portrait of God (2001). However, the director is just as present here as in his earlier works, in that he tells of his own life in a voice-over, speaking in the first person:

> When I was a boy I often lay for hours staring up into the summer sky for a hole into heaven or a lazy angel daydreaming on a cloud who'd forgotten old God's strict orders never to be seen by us people from down on this earth.
>
> In middle age my search for God had taken me all the way to southern Africa, but his trail was as fleeting as the banks of mist that rolled in from the Atlantic to mist up my windowpane as I tried to create a portrait of a person, who might only be a rumour.
>
> (Portrait of God, 2001)

In one way or another in all of Jon Bang Carlsen's work the subjective experience of the filmmaker is deliberately made a central part of the film, and the director's own doubts and ongoing, tentative explorations are as much the subject of the documentary as are the people whose stories unfold before the camera.

RICHARD RASKIN

Biography

Born September 28, 1950, in Vedbæk, Denmark. Worked in theatre, then entered the National Film School of Denmark, from which he graduated in 1976. Published books of essays and poetry and has lectured extensively at film schools and universities throughout Europe. Won numerous national and international awards for his films. Lives in both Denmark and Ireland with his wife and four children.

Selected films

1979 A Rich Man
1981 Hotel of the Stars
1984 The Phoenix Bird
1986 Before the Guests Arrive
1990 Ich bin auch ein Berliner
1996 It's Now or Never
1997 How to Invent Reality
1999 Addicted to Solitude
2001 Portrait of God
2002 Zuma the Puma
2004 Confessions of an Old Teddy

Further reading

Bang Carlsen, Jon, 'How to Invent Reality: Extracts from a Forthcoming Book', *A Danish Journal of Film Studies*, 16, December 2003, imv.au.dk/publikationer/pov/Issue_16/section_1/artc10A.html

——*Locations: Essays*, Copenhagen: Tiderne Skifter, 2002 (in Danish).

Hjorth, Mette and Bondebjerg, Ib (eds), *The Danish Directors: Dialogues on a Contemporary National Cinema*, Bristol: Intellect Books, 2001: 195–207.

Madsen, Mette, 'Art versus McBurger Dramaturgy: An Interview with Jon Bang Carlsen', *A Danish Journal of Film Studies*, 12, December 2001, imv.au.dk/publikationer/pov/Issue_12/section_1/artc1A.html

Nielsen, Allan Berg, 'A Modern, Humanist Profession of Faith', *Film*, November 2001, www.dfi.dk/sitemod/moduler/index_english.asp?pid=8170

Barclay, Barry

Barry Barclay established his unique place in the history of New Zealand culture during 1973 to 1974, when a six-part documentary series called Tangata Whenua aired on New Zealand television. Since then he has enhanced his significance with completion of the first feature film directed by a Maori male (Ngati, 1987), a book on issues associated with indigenous representation (*Our Own Image*, 1990), social activism (resulting in increased New Zealand on-air funding for Maori-produced and -targeted film material for local broadcast television), and The Feathers of Peace (2000), a mixture of documentary and drama that carries local history studies into controversial terrain.

What unites Barclay's filmmaking, writing, and activism is his respect for community and his advocacy for the integrity of indigenous communities. Early in his career he began working for John O'Shea's Pacific Films, a breeding ground for filmmakers inclined toward an independent point of view. Along with the trade films and television commercials that were Pacific Films' primary source of income, Barclay made documentaries and feature films with O'Shea's backing from the 1970s until Te Rua (1991), when the director and the producer had a falling out. With the appearance of The

Feathers of Peace, Barclay's public profile has again increased; out of the limelight, he has also been involved in further efforts supporting Maori training and filmmaking.

Despite funding and policy obstacles, Barclay has creatively developed filming strategies designed to accommodate cultural sensitivities. Chief among these has been a set of practices designed to make documentary subjects feel comfortable throughout the filming process, from the extensive use of lenses to keep cameras as far as possible away from subjects while they are speaking, to the synching of sound and image via the clapperboard at the end, rather than the beginning, of takes. He also argues that the Western medium can accommodate indigenous narrative strategies. Taking Ngati as an example, he speaks of its emphasis on the community rather than the individual, with a narrative structure that avoids single heroic figures in favor of group interaction. From Te Rua, he cites moments involving Maori oral practice and traditions that would be clear to an audience familiar with them, but which could not be read in the same way by most non-Maori audiences. In the docudrama The Feathers of Peace, using text from legal testimony of the day as well as other historical documents, he gives nineteenth-century characters the opportunity to speak, following the example of marae practice.

For Barclay, the heart of a movie is its metaphor; until he has his metaphor, he says, the film cannot be made. Simultaneous with making the Tangata Whenua series, Barclay was a member of Nga Tamatoa, a group of young Maori organized around undermining social institutions that prevented Tino Rangatiratanga (self-determination) at every level. Although Barclay is modest about the extent of his involvement in a left-wing group that critiqued the television establishment that allowed Barclay to make his films, Barclay agreed with Nga Tamatoa's ideological premises. He was among the earliest members of Te Manu Aute, a group that, like Nga Tamatoa, focused on media control.

Our Own Image, the most important published statement of his philosophy so far, is in part a gift to Native Americans and First Peoples, made after Barclay attended a film festival of indigenous people's work. Among Barclay's most interesting points in this short book is the distinction between 'talking in' and 'talking out'. The latter could refer to an indigenous group trying to speak to a dominant culture, but 'talking in' refers to the opportunity for a group within the nondominant culture to speak in its own terms rather than in those of the dominant culture, without regard for whether the dominant culture understands (Barclay 1990: 75).

Not a speaker of Maori himself, Barclay has said that he thinks 'a Maori filmmaker is someone Maori who identifies as Maori and is proud to use the camera as a Maori for Maori purposes, at least some of the time', adding that 'it's good fun to do other things as well' (Read 2000–1: 3). To be Maori is to have a strong awareness of the spiritual; to be a filmmaker is to be aware of film's 'access to [...] visceral communal icons' (ibid.: 4).

As Barclay moved away from television toward feature filmmaking, he also turned away from lobbying for political change. In the late 1990s, however, Barclay returned to political activism in a spectacular way. He picketed one of Aotearoa's (New Zealand) funding bodies, camping out on the median in the boulevard in front of their office building. His private campaign gained widespread public attention. Barclay himself benefited through funding for The Feathers of Peace. At least one Maori filmmaker acknowledges Barclay as a force behind funding and other policy changes that have increased opportunities for Maori filmmaking, along with exhibition possibilities encompassing mainstream audiences.

Throughout his career, Barclay has mentored other filmmakers, particularly young Maori who have trained with him. Along with Merata Mita, he has called for and tutored in workshops to train Maori, as well as internships and apprenticeships. Like Mita, he and his work have been well received in Hawaii, and he has used his speaking opportunities there to discuss indigenous filmmaking as he perceives of it. For example, in 2001, he gave a keynote address in which he developed his concept of 'indigenous cinema', or 'fourth cinema'. Unlike 'Hollywood, arthouse, and Third World cinema' (Read 2000–1: 1), fourth cinema should be committed to using its viscerally persuasive powers to raise consciousness of ethical issues, particularly through giving indigenous peoples their own voice (Turner 2002: 11).

Barclay has developed and articulated his philosophy regarding the representation of indigenous groups through his own films, in interviews and talks, and in his own published work. He has influenced archival protocol, government funding, and public opinion through his work and action. Barclay's oeuvre is at least as well appreciated overseas as it is in his home country, where he has often raised issues that others wish to forget.

HARRIET MARGOLIS

See also: Australia

Biography

Born 1944 in the Wairarapa, an agrarian area near Wellington, New Zealand, of Ngati Apa, Scottish, and French descent. Trained in Australia to be a Roman Catholic priest (1960–7). After making the Tangata Whenua series lived and worked in Sri Lanka, England, France, and the Netherlands, before returning to Aotearoa, (New Zealand), and making Ngati. Media Peace Award, 2000. 'FirstLegacyAppreciation Award', Hawaii Film Festival, 2001.

Further reading

Barclay, Barry, 'A Way of Talking', in Jonathan Dennis and Sergio Toffetti (eds), *Te Ao Marama*, Turin: Le Nuove Muse, 1989: 117–20.

——*Our Own Image*, Auckland: Longman Paul, 1990.

——'Amongst Landscapes', in Jonathan Dennis and Jan Bieringa (eds), *Film in Aotearoa New Zealand*, Wellington: Victoria University Press, 1992: 116–29.

——'Alistair in the Dreaming: A Personal Reflection on Maori Image Sovereignty', in Margo Fry (ed.), *A Century of Film in New Zealand: Papers from the Conference 'Cinema, Film & Society'*, Wellington: Stout Research Centre (Victoria University of Wellington), 1998: 13–16.

Blythe, Martin, *Naming the Other: Images of the Maori in New Zealand Film and Television*, Metuchen, NJ: Scarecrow, 1994.

Dalzell, Julie, 'The Independents of Our Film Industry', *Designscape* 70, June 1975: 23–6.

Fox, Derek Tini, 'Honouring the Treaty: Indigenous Television in Aotearoa', in T. Dowmunt (ed.), *Channels of Resistance: Global Television and Local Empowerment*, London: BFI, 1993: 126–37.

King, Michael, *Being Pakeha: An Encounter with New Zealand and the Maori Renaissance*, Auckland: Hodder and Stoughton, 1985.

May, Sue, 'No More White-Wash', *On Film*, February 1984: 13–15.

Quennell, Megan, 'Te Manu Aute', *Illusions* 5, 1987: 4–5.

Read, Lynette, 'Interview', *Illusions* 31, 2000–1: 2–6.

Turner, Stephen, 'Cinema of Justice: The Feathers of Peace', *Illusions* 33, 2002: 11.

Basic Training

(US, Wiseman, 1971)

The first of three films about the United States Armed Forces made by American documentary filmmaker Frederick Wiseman, Basic Training documents the standard eight-week training for new army inductees and enlistees at Fort Polk, Kentucky, before being shipped out to Vietnam. The processes of institutional indoctrination and maintenance of power, primary aspects of institutional functioning explored in Wiseman's other films, are emphasized in the film's vision of the military machine. As commanding officer Lt Hoffman puts it bluntly in his welcoming speech to the men early in the film, 'The best way to go through basic training is to do what you're told, as you're told, and there'll be no problems.'

In the brief montage sequence that opens the film, the new inductees are immediately stripped of their individuality. The opening shot is of the men arriving on a bus, from which they walk unhurriedly to the barracks, dressed in a variety of civilian clothes. In the second shot they are assigned bunks by number. In the third shot they are measured for uniforms, the tailor calling out measurements. Next come three shots of men having their hair cut short, all the same, a recurrent Wiseman image signifying loss of individuality and absorption into an institutional system. Then there is one quick shot each of fingerprinting, ID photos being taken, and one man, in answer to an interview question, giving his social security number, his identity now only a statistic. At the end of this opening sequence, the men are in uniform, a striking contrast to their varied appearance just a few moments before.

The music in the film further emphasizes the loss of individuality within the larger group. The function of music is established early on in Basic Training, when the commanding officer and his entourage smartly march into a room to welcome the trainees accompanied by the musical fanfare of 'The Caissons Go Rolling Along'. The entire film is punctuated with shots of the men drilling, keeping time to marching tunes. In these shots the camera frequently tilts down to isolate in close-up the legs and feet of the men, showing that no one is allowed to march to the beat of a different drum.

When Lt Hoffman tells a black private that 'the Army's not just one man, it's millions of people', and that he must work with the group, he echoes the social message of virtually every classic Hollywood war movie, but with a crucial difference, for while the classic war films depict the compromise of individualism as a noble sacrifice necessary for the war effort, Wiseman views the military as unacceptably dehumanizing. In one particularly striking shot in Basic Training, the soldiers march in the foreground as if 'beneath' a large American flag waving in the background. Here, Wiseman finds a visual expression of the extent to which the individual is subject to the state—a point ominously reiterated in the image of the soldiers entering a transport plane shot from a position within or under it, the dark, jagged edges of the plane's bay doors suggesting a giant maw about to consume the men.

Basic Training also offers a disturbing view of masculinity in its suggestion that violence is innate in men and easily nurtured by the process of basic military training. The men readily cheer each other on ('get him from behind', 'hit him in the head') as they fight in pairs. Even after the whistle blows, signaling that the combatants should stop, we see one pair continue on, their potential for violence now fully aroused. In the toothbrushing scene, several of the men are shown, in effect, foaming at the mouth, and in the scenes of bayonet practice, the men seem reduced to animals, 'grunts' abandoning language for screams of violence. Several scenes make the connection between firearms and the phallus. On the firing range, a demonstrator fires his weapon from his crotch, accompanied by a crude joke from the instructing sergeant, and one trainee is visited by his family, who concentrate their attention and conversation on his rifle, 'fetishizing' it and investing it with unmistakable phallic implications.

Much screen time is devoted to the hapless Private Hickman, a trainee who has trouble with everything from executing the to-the-rear march, to making his bed. Attempting to learn something as simple as reversing his direction while marching, behind him we see the other men drilling with increasing uniformity and competence. Just as they tend to march in the opposite direction from Hickman within the frame, so the lack of ability by this one individual in the foreground sets him up as a foil to the many in the background, all of whom are quickly becoming professional soldiers. (Their growing proficiency also provides Wiseman with a visual way of 'marking time' in the film.)

For Wiseman, Hickman is emblematic of the misfit literally out of step with society, scorned by his comrades as a result. The weakest link, he is threatened with a 'blanket party', a military hazing ritual in which a blanket is thrown over the victim before he is beaten, thus rendering him unable to name his attackers. Hickman's response, we discover, is to attempt to overdose on drugs. Finally, Hickman evolves from a comic figure to a tragic one, for he represents that spark of human imperfection that is all but ruthlessly eliminated as the men become trained soldiers.

BARRY KEITH GRANT

See also: Wiseman, Frederick

Basic Training (US, 1971, 89 mins). Distributed by Zipporah Films. Produced, edited, and directed by Frederick Wiseman. Cinematography by William Brayne. Sound recorded by Frederick Wiseman.

Further reading

Atkins, Thomas R. (ed.), *Frederick Wiseman*, New York: Monarch Press, 1976.

Benson, Thomas W. and Anderson, Caroline, *Reality Fictions: The Films of Frederick Wiseman*, Carbondale, IL: Southern Illinois University Press, 1989.

Grant, Barry Keith, *Voyages of Discovery: The Cinema of Frederick Wiseman*, Urbana and Chicago: University of Illinois Press, 1992.

Mamber, Stephen, *Cinéma Vérité in America: Studies in Uncontrolled Documentary*, Cambridge, MA: MIT Press, 1974.

Nichols, Bill, *Ideology and the Image*, Bloomington, IN: Indiana University Press, 1981.

Basse, Wilfried

Wilfried Basse's oeuvre bridged the gap between German avant-garde filmmaking of the Weimar Republic and the conventional educational filmmaking propagated during the Nazi period. When he started out in 1929, he counted prominent avant-garde artists such as Kurt Schwitters and other members of the Kestner Society as his friends. He dissociated himself from the Bauhaus aesthetic.

Basse's main filmic interest was people in their everyday surroundings, whom he observed from a short distance. His first film, Baumblütenzeit in Werder (1929), about a crude spring fair near Berlin, was noted for the satirical tone it employed with regard to human foibles and inadequacies. The film garnered comparisons to George Grosz and Heinrich Zille for Basse.

Basse used a small, handheld camera that allowed for great immediacy and intimacy in shooting. This was illustrated by Market in Berlin (1929), which depicts the hustle and bustle of a Berlin peasants' market. The film's style was praised by many reviewers; others, Siegfried Kracauer among them, criticized it for its lack of an overt political message. The same could not be said of Das Rote Sprachrohr (1931), a portrait of a communist agitprop company. Inspired by Russian formalism, this film was Basse's experiment with a specified screenplay and indoor shooting with studio lighting.

Basse's primary work was Deutschland—zwischen gestern und heute (1932–4), which demonstrated how historical developments determine the present. While Basse was editing the film, the Nazis came into power. Reviewers criticized the lack of Nazi ideology in the film, while audiences seemed to avoid the film exactly because they expected Nazi propaganda. Nevertheless, it was awarded a gold medal at the Venice Film Festival in 1935.

Suspected of communist sympathies, Basse and his production company faced numerous obstacles. For the rest of his career he worked with the Reichsanstalt für den Unterrichtsfilm (RfdU, Reich Institute for Educational Films), for which he shot nearly forty films. Since these films were not publicly shown, they were not censored. In fact, the RdfU worked independently, free of Nazi control. During this time, Basse's films focused on topics relating to handicrafts and sports. In 1940 he was commissioned to make a film about genetic diseases—Erbkrank–Erbgesund—Basse's only overt concession to the Nazi regime.

ULI JUNG

Biography

Born on August 17, 1899, the son of a banker. After several failed attempts at various professions, turned to filmmaking due to the influence of the films of Hans Cürlis. Formed his own production company in 1929. The Nazis' takeover brought about political difficulties, which led him to the Reichsanstalt für den Unterrichtsfilm, to which he was one of the most prolific contributors. Assigned to oversee the slow-motion photography for Leni Riefenstahl's film, Olympia, 1936. Died June 6, 1946.

Selected films

1929 Baumblütenzeit in Werder
1929 Market in Berlin
1929 Wochenmarkt auf dem Wittenbergplatz
1930 Der wirtschaftliche Baubetrieb
1931 Mit Optik 1,4—Kamerastudien von Wilfried Basse
1931 Das Rote Sprachrohr
1930–32 Abbruch und Aufbau
1932–34 Deutschland—zwischen gestern und heute
1934 Glückliche Heimat
1934–35 Bunter Alltag
1935 Der Böttcher baut einen Zober
1935 Der Kohlenmeiler
1936 Roggenernte
1936 Hausbau
1936 Dachschiefer
1936 Der Schuhmacher/Wie ein Schuh entsteht
1936 Tabakbau in der Uckermark
1936 Handweberei
1936 Wie ein Ziegelstein entsteht
1936 Wie ein Pflasterstein entsteht
1936 Ein Brief wird befördert
1936 Braunkohle-Tagebau
1936 Ein Kohlenschleppzug auf dem Mittelrhein
1936–40 Erbkrank–Erbgesund
1937 Kugelstoßen
1937 Schwälmer Bäuerin am Spinnrad
1937 Perspektivisches Sehen
1937 Städtische Feuerwehr
1937 Dämmen einer Schornsteingruppe
1937 Kurzstreckenlauf
1937 Weitsprung
1937 Schwimmen
1937–40 Vom Korn zum Brot
1938 Junge Löwen im Zoologischen Garten
1938 Junge Paviane im Zoologischen Garten
1938 Junge Bären im Zoologischen Garten

1938	Das Anlernen junger Pferde zum Zuge
1938	Schwäbische Kunde
1939	Ein Tag auf einer fränkischen Dorfstraße
1939	Deutschland—gastliches Land
1939	D-Zug fertig zur Fahrt
1939–40	Der Jockey

Further reading

Avril, Frank, *Avantgardisten des deutschen Film: II. Wilfried Basse, Der deutsche Film* No. 8, February 1937.

Basse, Wilfried, *Notizen zu einem fast vergessenen Klassiker des deutschen Dokumentarfilms*, in Kraft Wetzel and Peter A. Hagemann (eds), *Liebe, Tod und Technik: Kino des Phantastischen, 1933–45*, Berlin, 1977: 75–97.

Freier, Rolf, 'Linksbürgerliche Filmaktivitäten am Beispiel Ella Bergmann—Michels und Wilfried Basses', *Der eingeschränkte Blick und die Fenster zur Welt: Zur politischen Ästhetik visueller Medien*, Marburg, 1984: 96–111.

Bataille du rail, La

(France, Clément, 1946)

La Bataille du rail (The Battle of the Rails) began as Résistance fer, a short film relating the contribution of the cheminots, the French railway workers, to the struggle against German occupation. This documentary, among a series of projects commissioned in 1945 to celebrate the Résistance by the Comité de Libération du Cinéma Français, made such a strong impression on the producers that they asked the director, René Clément, to turn it into a feature-length film. Professional and amateur actors were hired, stories of resistance in the railways were collated by the writer, Colette Audry, and German prisoners of war were brought in. La Bataille du rail was released in 1946 and gained instant acclaim as the most moving account of the Résistance.

La Bataille du rail is a rather disjointed film, half-documentary and half-fiction, where its transformation from a court-métrage to a ninety-minute, full-length feature is quite apparent. It is rather chaotic in its loose structure and confusing in its script. The odd juxtaposition of fiction to a documentary is nevertheless what makes La Bataille du rail so special. As a docudrama, it acquires unique qualities of being a detailed and dramatic account of the plight of railway men trying desperately to derive all sorts of obstacles to prevent the movement of trains through sabotage, diversion, and cooperation with the Maquis, the armed resistance to German occupation.

The film spans the four years of the war and can be divided into two sections. The first part is a documentary using actors; it explains the resistance to German occupation in the railways during these years, in particular its effect on the movement of trains between the occupied zone in the north and the 'free zone' in the south of France. The considerable risks taken by the workers of the SNCF, the nationalized French railways, are described in detail, almost in a didactic manner: the sabotage of the rolling stock, the meticulous deception of the German army officers, and the ensuing reprisals are narrated with an acute sense of patriotic duty and drama.

The second part of the film is set in the aftermath of D-Day and describes the attempts by the cheminots, allied with the Maquis, to stop a heavily armored train taking German reinforcements to the front line, ending with its dramatic derailment. The film becomes much closer to a work of fiction than a documentary. It finishes with scenes of triumph, greeting the arrival of the first train in a liberated France, the ultimate symbol of a nation freed by the sacrifice of its railway workers.

La Bataille du rail received the award for best film at the 1946 Cannes festival, and René Clément received the award for best director. It is still considered to be the first film that managed to capture the spirit of the Résistance, the heroism of a nation, and the dangers involved in resisting German occupation. Undoubtedly the circumstances of its release explain its success, among a public desperately looking for a film that would capture the emotional intensity of such acts of bravery. It is also a fine and rare example of French neorealism, not unlike the Italian postwar films, in its unique blend of reality and fiction and in its attempts to reach humanity in the most inhumane circumstances of war against an occupying army.

René Clément envisages acts of resistance in the SNCF as a patriotic epic and relies quite heavily on the 'feel-good' factor that prevailed after the war, hence its considerable success. The film does not, however, demonize German occupation—there is even some sympathy for the German soldiers relaxing on the side of the tracks where their military convoy is stranded, a sharp contrast with the violence unleashed in the attack that follows.

La Bataille du rail portrays a collective struggle, where there is no hero, where the fight for survival from both sides is described with a sense of the unavoidable. It ignores the real divisions that existed during these years among the French population. There is also little reference to the involvement of Allied troops or of the Gaullist resistance. Patriotism is mixed with socialist undertones: these acts of bravery are those of the cheminots, who symbolize the working class as the driving force in resisting German occupation.

The style of Clément is a cold assessment as well as a tense account of resistance by railway workers: there is some of Eisenstein's sense of drama in the languishing whistling of a steam engine during the summary execution of cheminots suspected of sabotage, and in the accordion rolling down the side of the track after the spectacular derailment of the German convoy. The photography of Henri Alekan contributes greatly to the dramatic effect of the film, and La Bataille du rail will establish him as one of the greatest photographers in black and white for the cinema. He had already collaborated on Beauty and the Beast with Jean Cocteau and worked with Wim Wenders in 1983 on The State of Things and on Wings of Desire in 1987.

La Bataille du rail transformed the career of René Clément from that of a minor documentary filmmaker to one of the prominent directors of his generation. Born in 1913, he made short documentary films during the 1930s and 1940s, in particular Ceux du rail in 1942, which gave him an insight into the railway industry that would be useful when filming La Bataille du rail. Until the late 1950s Clément confirmed his stature as a world-class director, receiving an Oscar for Au-delà des grilles in 1948 and Jeux interdits in 1952.

Clément belongs to the generation of directors left behind by the desire for change demanded by the La nouvelle vague advocates, who criticized his filming technique for its lack of subjectivity and its detachment from reality. His last noticeable success, Plein soleil, released in 1960, inaugurated a slow decline in a career that had been prolific and successful, until his last film, Jeune fille libre le soir, which came out in 1975, the year before his death. La Bataille du rail remains the film for which he is best known.

YVAN TARDY

La Bataille du rail/The Battle of the Rails (France, 1946, 85 mins). Distributed by L.C.J. Editions et Productions, 2002. Produced by La Coopérative générale du cinéma Français, 1946. Directed by René Clément. Script by René Clément. Photography by Henri Alekan. Music by Yves Baudrier. Dialogues by Colette Audry. Filmed in black and white. With Jean Clarieux (Lampin), Jean Daurand (Cheminot), Jacques Desagneaux (Athos), François Joux (Cheminot), Latour (Cheminot), Tony Laurent (Camargue), and French railway workers.

Further reading

Barrot, Jean-Pierre, *L'Ecran Français*, 27 February 1946.

Bertin-Maghit, J.-P., 'La Bataille du rail: de l'authenticité à la chanson de geste', *Reue d'histoire Moderne et Contemporaine* 33, April–June 1986: 280–300.

O'Shaughnessy, Martin, 'Bataille du rail: Unconventional form, conventional image?' in R. Wood and N. Wood (eds), *The Liberation of France*, Oxford: Berg, 1995.

Totaro, Donate, 'La Bataille du rail', *Hors Champ*, September 1997.

Battle for Our Soviet Ukraine, The

(USSR, Dovzhenko, 1942–3)

The Battle for Our Soviet Ukraine (Bitva za nashu Sovetskuiu Ukrainu) is an account of the German Army Group South's invasion of the Ukraine and its repulsion in the Great Patriotic War. Produced for the Central and Ukrainian Newsreel Studios, the film was begun in early May 1943, completed on October 6, and released on October 25, 1943. Often attributed to Alexander Dovzhenko, the nominal directors were his wife, Julia Solntseva, and Jacob Ovdeyenko. However, although credited only as 'supervisor', bucolic sections link to Dovzhenko's earlier feature films, particularly Earth. The contrast between these lyrical scenes showing, in an idealized manner, what life was like before the invasion, and the starkness of the war footage, gives the images of destruction much of their impact.

Dovzhenko, with a number of other documentarists, remained in Moscow when the bulk of film production, along with much of industry that stood in the path of the invading forces, was evacuated to the east. He also spent time in liberated areas of the Ukraine, so he saw firsthand more of the effects of war than many of his colleagues. The authenticity that Dovzhenko's team managed to convey is remarkable. The film is put together with a freedom from the bureaucratic interference that filmmakers working on fiction production experienced, allowing Dovzhenko greater latitude than if he had gone to Alma Ata with the others.

Dovzhenko's feelings about the invasion are summed up in a letter to his wife dated June 4, 1942 (Marshall 1983: 152), in which he wrote that although Hitler would be defeated, the Ukraine had been ruined. Despite this pessimism, he and his team made another documentary, Victory in Right-Bank Ukraine and the Expulsion of the German Aggressors from the Boundaries of the Ukrainian Soviet Earth (released in May 1945), which contained material on reconstruction. Of the two films, The Battle for Our Soviet Ukraine is more harrowing, with many shots of dead bodies, including children, and the devastation in the reconquered areas is brought home vividly.

This graphic depiction of despoliation and despair runs contrary to Graham Roberts's (1999: 136) characterization of wartime Soviet documentary as 'a mirror image of reality', projecting confidence in a time of tragedy. Dovzhenko's diary indicates that before its release he was skeptical about the film's likely official reception, as it ran counter to the positive portrayals depicted in the bulk of Soviet films. He feared that it might be banned altogether, or marred 'by cutting the difficult and unheroic scenes'. His more subtle conception of the complexity of war—'the grandiose woe of retreat and the incomplete joy of advance' (Dovzhenko 1973: 91)—was at odds with the simplistic official ideology.

The original title was Ukraine in Battle, but the addition of the word Soviet served to lessen the nationalistic interpretation by stressing the common struggle of all the Soviet peoples. The political message was that the Ukraine was still part of the Soviet Union. The sensitivity of the nationalism issue can be gauged by the fact that while working on The Battle for Our Soviet Ukraine, Dovzhenko also wrote the script for Ukraine in Flames (not to be confused with The Battle for Our Soviet Ukraine's US release title). It had a similar theme to The Battle for Our Soviet Ukraine, but its perceived nationalism blocked its realization and blighted Dovzhenko's career.

Many contemporary reviewers claimed that there were twenty-four camera operators, although in fact twenty-nine are credited on The Battle for Our Soviet Ukraine and twenty-five on Victory in Right-Bank Ukraine. Both films feature footage taken by German forces that was later captured, providing a more rounded depiction of the conflict. There was enough material to allow adherence to the one-hundred-and-eighty-degree rule, with Germans usually attacking from left to right and the Soviet forces from right to left. Interspersed are speeches from party and army leaders, including Nikita Kruschev, head of the Ukrainian Communist Party, and direct-to-camera witness accounts from ordinary people with harrowing stories to tell. Considering the disparate origins of its elements, The Battle for Our Soviet Ukraine displays a remarkable coherence. Jay Leyda (1983: 377) proclaimed it 'an inspiration to every artist who works in the documentary film'.

Dovzhenko was dismayed by the indifferent reception that the film received in the United States when it was released there in the spring of 1944. He noted in his diary entry for April 8, 1944: 'She [the United States] didn't even want to look at the blood she is buying with her canned bacon' (Dovzhenko 1973: 105). This was a sentiment that echoed his government's demand for the opening of a second front, and the feeling that the Soviet Union was being asked to make enormous sacrifices while its allies stood by.

Critical opinion in the United States was indeed lukewarm. While acknowledging the unvarnished presentation and the effectiveness of the battle sequences, many of the reviews were carping, with negative comments on the clarity of the photography, the quality of the translated commentary, and the tendency of the pictures of devastation to have a certain sameness. These blasé assessments of the film's lack of technical polish ignored the far from ideal circumstances of production.

The British *Kinematograph Weekly*, by contrast, while noting the 'family resemblance' of films depicting the effects of occupation, could still concede that The Battle for Our Soviet Ukraine was 'a vivid indictment of German brutality', and highlight its depiction of suffering and the realism of the battle sequences. Similarly, *Monthly Film Bulletin* considered that of the many documentaries originating from the Soviet front, few had 'been so vivid or poignant as this'. The difference in tone perhaps reflected the relative complacency of a country that had not experienced invasion, compared to one whose civilian population had itself suffered from direct attacks, and thus could empathize with the misery of those subjected directly to the German war machine.

TOM RUFFLES

See also: Russia/Soviet Union

Further reading

n.a., 'The Battle for the Ukraine', *Kinematograph Weekly*, 16 March 1944: 33.
n.a. 'The Battle for the Ukraine', *Monthly Film Bulletin* 11, no. 125, 31 May 1944: 61.
n.a. 'Ukraine in Flames', a compilation of reviews from New York newspapers published in April 1944, *Motion Picture Critics' Reviews*, 22 January 1945: 419–21.
n.a. 'Ukraine in Flames', *Motion Picture Herald*, 15 April 1944: 1845.
Dovzhenko, Alexander, *The Poet as Filmmaker: Selected Writings*, Cambridge, MA: MIT Press, 1973.
Kenez, Peter, *Cinema and Soviet Society: From the Revolution to the Death of Stalin*, London: I.B. Tauris, 2001.
Leyda, Jay, *Kino: A History of the Russian and Soviet Film*, third edn, London: George Allen and Unwin, 1983.
Marshall, Herbert, *Masters of the Soviet Cinema: Crippled Creative Biographies*, London: Routledge and Kegan Paul, 1983.
Roberts, Graham, *Forward Soviet: History and Non-Fiction Film in the USSR*, London: I.B. Tauris, 1999.

Battle of Chile, The

(Cuba, Guzmán, 1975–7)

Patricio Guzmán's The Battle of Chile marks the end of a brief but intense period of revolutionary filmmaking in his native country. In the late 1960s and early 1970s Chilean feature and documentary filmmakers joined together in support of Popular Unity, a coalition of left-wing parties, producing work that protested the endemic poverty in their country. Guzmán's film covers the political upheaval of 1973 from the election of Salvador Allende in February to the coup in September that overthrew the political changes effected by the Popular Unity and forced Guzmán and his colleagues to work in exile.

The Battle of Chile is composed of three parts, 'The Bourgeois Insurrection' (1975), 'The Coup d'État' (1977), and 'Popular Power' (1979). Part One covers the election of Allende and the ensuing middle-class revolt. Part Two covers popular demonstrations in support and opposition to Allende. It also treats strategic debates within the left. Part Three focuses on later mass organization efforts. The film opens with some of the last footage shot by Guzmán and his crew: Allende is killed in the bombing of the La Moneda Palace and the Popular Unity party is effectively overthrown by the military coup supported by the middle class. With the denouement established at the outset, The Battle of Chile is set up to be studied more than experienced as a surprising narrative. Guzmán intended the film, while polemical, to be more analytic than propagandistic: 'From the very beginning, our idea was to make an analytical film, not an agitation alone' (Burton 1986: 51). After this opening shot, the film moves back to February, when the crew began filming, shortly before the narrow election of Allende.

Led by cinematographer Jorge Müller Silva, The Battle of Chile was shot with a team of handheld cameras by Guzmán and his team of collaborators, called El Equipo Tercer Año (The Third Year Group). The group participated in extended technical and theoretical discussions before filming began, defining five 'fronts of struggle' to focus the project (Pick 1980: 46–9). This allowed the cameramen to focus on capturing certain events effectively rather than worry over which events to record or neglect. From Guzmán's account, the more polished shots of the film were the result of his collaboration with Müller, where he would survey ongoing events while relaying specific filming strategies to Müller: 'Since I tried to anticipate for him what was about to happen, I could tell him to pan, to lower the camera, to raise it, instructing him to make certain movements that are much more readily identified with fictional than with documentary filmmaking' (Burton 1986: 57).

Even with this preplanning and improvised direction, the nature of the subject meant that the group had a limited amount of control over what they were able to film or, in some cases, found themselves filming. The filmmakers often captured planned events, such as governmental meetings, protests, and funerals, but as frequently taped unexpected developments.

Distinct scenes are often bridged by voice-over commentary, but the majority of analysis is provided by interviewed subjects. This one camera, one soundman style of filmmaking is most commonly known as direct or observational cinema. Here, the cameramen aim more to record as much of what unfolds before them than to produce polished shots. The editors of The Battle of Chile seem to have selected which scenes to include based on their impact or historical significance much more than their technical perfection. Shots with a shaky axis or blurring pans are often left in the film. In one scene, amidst unrest in the streets, the camera sweeps past the marquee of a movie theater. It announces that Violent City, starring Charles Bronson, is showing in Metrocolor. This brief reference to mainstream feature filmmaking reminds the spectator of the rhetorical, stylistic, and substantive differences between the type of cinema exemplified by The Battle of Chile versus this American feature. Moving past the marquee, the camera reveals an urban landscape lit with fire, running crowds, and the sounds of an ambulance. The fact that Violent City is showing in a truly riven, violent city jolts the spectator into recognition that, though certainly not shot in 35mm or Metrocolor, The Battle of Chile is a real document not to be conflated with Hollywood filmmaking. A more insistent reminder of this comes later.

In the most famous scene of the film, which closes Part One and opens Part Two, Argentine cameraman Leonardo Henricksen is shot and killed by a Chilean Army officer during the aborted coup in June. Here, the camera focuses on an officer who looks directly at the camera and fires; the image loses its balance and turns black.

Although the observational method of filmmaking employed in The Battle of Chile frequently produces objective shots that neither explicity support nor oppose Allende, the left-wing political interest that was the impetus behind the project is more forcefully present in certain scenes, sometimes even in the shooting style. While the filmmakers begin by covering both sides of the electorate prior to Allende's election, often interviewing families at home in addition to mass demonstrations, afterwards the filmmakers appear more frequently and more intimately with Allende's sympathizers. Guzmán and his colleagues frequently film amidst leftist demonstrations, interviewing participants in the middle of crowds. They also travel with and interview workers on truck beds en route to union meetings. The right wing is shown in more formal settings or, if on the streets, from a greater distance. At a meeting of the American Institute for Free Trade Unionism (a group funded indirectly by the CIA, which encourages managers in the transportation sector to oppose Allende's policies), an unidentified speaker is shot in a low-angle close-up. His face monstrously fills the screen, with deep black nostrils flaring and a gaping mouth. Words that may already displease the viewer are colored even more insidiously by this stylistic choice.

In an interview, Guzmán states that the film was made to support Popular Unity, but none of its constitutive parties, mostly notably the Communists and Socialists, in particular. This was typical of Chilean documentary in this period, which was galvanized by a manifesto by Miguel Littín, another filmmaker and head of Chile Films, the national film production company. Littín called for the development of a leftist cinema that would valorize the workers and labor leaders who fought for Allende's reforms. Although Guzmán follows the principles that Littín outlines, The Battle of Chile was made without the help of Chile Films, which was too unstable to support the project.

The Battle of Chile, while shot by Chileans, received a great deal of international support in terms of production. French documentary filmmaker Chris Marker provided the film stock with which the picture was shot. After shooting was complete, fearing the destruction of his footage, Guzmán smuggled his film to Cuba following Allende's assassination. The Battle of Chile was edited in Cuba at the Cuban Institute of Film Art and Industry (ICAIC). With the help of solidarity campaigns, the film was distributed around the world and became the most prominent testament of the coup. Guzmán and other Chilean filmmakers went on to produce a startling amount of work in exile (one hundred and seventy-six films, fifty-six of which were features between 1973 and 1983), becoming the most successful Latin American 'cinema of exile' in this period.

JESSE SCHLOTTERBECK

See also: Guzmán, Patricio

The Battle of Chile/La Batalla de Chile (Chile, El Equipo Tercer Año/ICAIC, 1975–9, 315 mins). Directed by Patricio Guzmán. Produced by Chris Marker. Cinematography by Jorge Müller Silva. Edited by Pedro Chaskel.

Further reading

Burton, Julianne (ed.), 'Patricio Guzmán: Chile, Politics and the Documentary in People's Chile', in *Cinema and Social Change in Latin America: Conversations with Filmmakers*, Austin, TX: University of Texas Press, 1986.

Gupta, Udayan and journal staff, 'An Interview with Patricio Guzmán, director of The Battle of Chile', *Film Library Quarterly* 11, no. 4, 1978: 16–20.

King, John, *Magical Reels: A History of Cinema in Latin America*, New York: Verso, 2000.

Lopez, Ana M., 'The Battle of Chile: Documentary, Political Process, and Representation', in Julianne Burton (ed.), *The Social Documentary in Latin America*, Pittsburgh, PA: University of Pittsburgh Press, 1990: 267–88.

Martin, Michael T. (ed.), *New Latin American Cinema*, Detroit, MI: Wayne State University Press, 1997.

Pick, Zuzana M., 'Chile: The Cinema of Resistance, 1973–79', 'Interview with Patricio Guzmán: La Batalla de Chile', 'Letter from Guzmán to Chris Marker', 'Reflections Previous to the Filming of The Battle of Chile', 'The Battle of Chile: A Schematic Shooting Script', part of a special section on Chilean cinema, *Ciné-Tracts* no. 9, vol. 3, no. 1, 1980: 18–49.

Schumann, Peter B., *Historia del cine latinoamericano*, Buenos Aires: Editorial Legasa, 1987.

Battle of China, The

(US, Capra, 1944)

Sixth in the 'Why We Fight' series produced by the US Army during World War II, The Battle of China builds on The Nazis Strike (1943), Divide and Conquer (1943), and The Battle of Russia (1944) through collaboration among Hollywood's top hands. Frank Capra, one of America's premier theatrical filmmakers, directed the film, stamping it with his recognizable personal style. Anatole Litvak, another influential Hollywood figure, codirected and oversaw production, without credit in both cases. Julius Epstein handled writing, William Hornbeck edited, Dimitri Tiomkin composed original music, and Anthony Veiller narrated. All worked together on the earlier documentaries.

Lacking Germany's propaganda machinery, Japan offered meager film footage for Capra to exploit for propaganda purposes. While some scenes in The Battle of China originated in Japan, Capra turned to stock Hollywood theatrical footage to help offset the deficit. The film states, 'Certain non-combat stock scenes were used from historical pictures', but never identifies theatrical footage. Where documentary film ends and Hollywood stock begins is deliberately indistinct.

The Battle of China appropriates and makes use of several stock patriotic symbols and images. Visual and auditory cues, such as the 'V for Victory' symbol superimposed on a ringing Liberty Bell, solicit predictable audience response. A rousing bugle call summons the troops, over an image of a road sign pointing to Tokyo. Thematic elements emphasize similarities, real and imaginary, between China and the United States. Confucius represents the Golden Rule and Sun Yat Sen becomes China's George Washington. While General Chiang Kai-Shek marches, Patton-like, across the screen, Madame Chiang addresses Congress. 'China's war is our war' is the resounding theme.

The Battle of China permits neither balance nor misinterpretation. The Chinese, with 'indestructible spirit', proceed on their 'Homeric journey to freedom', while their 'courage never faltered'. Through simplistic graphics, Chinese military disasters become 'trading space for time', while 'feverish' or 'blood-crazed' Japanese soldiers 'outdid themselves in barbarism', perpetrating a 'nightmare of cruelty'. The 'oldest and youngest of the world's great nations', filmgoers are assured, fight 'side-by-side', 'civilization against barbarism', 'good against evil'. In the process, this film demonstrates effective propaganda. In 2000 The Battle of China won the National Film Registry award of the National Film Preservation Board.

MICHAEL S. CASEY

See also: Battle of Russia, The; Capra, Frank; Litvak, Anatole

The Battle of China (US, Army Signal Corps, 1944, 65 mins, black and white). Produced by War Department. Directed by Frank Capra and Anatole Litvak (uncredited). Music composed by Dimitri Tiomkin (uncredited), performed by

Army Air Force Orchestra. Edited by William W. Hornbeck (uncredited). Narrated by Anthony Veiller.

Further reading

Capra, Frank, *The Name Above the Title: An Autobiography*, New York: Da Capo Press, 1997.

——(ed.), *The Men Who Made the Movies*, Chicago, IL: Ivan R. Dee, 2001.

Jeavons, Clyde, *A Pictorial History of War Films*, Seacaucus, NJ: Citadel Press, 1974.

Battle of Midway, The

(US, Ford, 1942)

The first US combat documentary to receive wide commercial distribution during World War II, The Battle of Midway, was a project largely without precedent. As might be expected of a work sanctioned by the US Navy and President Franklin Roosevelt, the film commemorates the heroism of American forces in battle and illustrates the vital link between home front and war front at an early stage of US involvement in the war. Director John Ford, who was on leave from Hollywood as head of the Field Photographic branch of the Office of the Coordinator of Information (later the OSS), also experiments with formal elements and incorporates themes of importance to his work as a fiction filmmaker. In this regard, The Battle of Midway seems no less deeply personal a work for the political calculations that shaped its making.

Ford had previously supervised the production of training films for new recruits and reconnaissance films for the high command, but the three-day battle at the Pacific Ocean atoll of Midway, 1,100 miles northwest of Pearl Harbor, in early June 1942 provided Ford with an opportunity to extend his wartime work in a new direction. Accepting an assignment to photograph the defense of the US Naval Air Station at Midway, Ford navigated the shoals of military, governmental, and studio bureaucracies to retain control over the footage, shifting post-production from Washington to Los Angeles on the Twentieth Century Fox lot. Speculations about the distribution of Ford's new documentary was a topic of much comment in the Hollywood trade press in late summer, leading up to the release of The Battle of Midway by the War Activities Committee and Fox in September. Seven first-run houses in New York ran the film, as did six in Los Angeles; eventually five hundred prints were circulated nationwide. The following March, The Battle of Midway was among four films named Best Documentary by the Academy of Motion Picture Arts and Sciences.

Remarkably, The Battle of Midway devotes little of its eighteen minutes to explaining the wider causes and significance of the battle, a turning point in the Pacific campaign. We learn nothing about the arrangement of naval and air forces on the eve of battle or the tactical maneuvering on either side, including the crucial decoding of cables that alerted US officials to a feint of Japanese forces toward the Aleutians and the pending Midway air attack. Instead, the film offers a series of impressions of the Midway outpost and its occupants before, during, and after the battle, emphasizing the natural beauty and serenity of the islands and surrounding waters, the ominous stillness of an evening watch as silhouetted soldiers stand guard before a setting sun, the perceptual disorientation and confusion produced by the bombing and strafing of the islands, and the resilience and determination of the American marines tested by the attack.

Ford's account of the battle, moreover, does not shy away from images of destruction—billowing black smoke against a cobalt sky; gutted buildings; twisted metal, wreckage, and rubble; the injured and the dead—and a concluding account of burial at sea functions as an elegiac counterpoint to a more aggressively martial coda in which victory is asserted and the costs to the enemy are enumerated. Alfred Newman's musical score, incorporating familiar military and national anthems and hymns, is crucial to the overall rhythmic effects. In this regard, The Battle of Midway seems less journalistic than musical in design, indebted, as Tag Gallagher has suggested, to nineteenth-century battle compositions, with different musical markers signaling striking shifts in tone.

Contemporaneous reviewers found The Battle of Midway's combat footage—shot in 16mm Technicolor by Ford and Jack MacKenzie, his twenty-year-old first mate, from their post on Midway's Eastern Island—particularly compelling. (Additional air and sea photography was provided by Kenneth M. Pier, who accompanied pilots off the USS *Hornet*, and brief footage of an 'Ohio family' at home was supplied by cinematographer Gregg Toland.) The footage was assembled by editor Robert Parrish in two extended battle passages marked by freehand camerawork and expressively disjointed cutting, with the descent of planes and multiple explosions interspersed with the reactions of marines returning anti-aircraft fire. At times, the image track seems to slip its sprockets, as a visible frame line optically registers the force of the concussion, and a sense of geography is lost amid the smoke and floating debris. Early in the assault Ford was knocked unconscious by one such explosion and received a flesh wound, for which he was awarded the Purple Heart. Reports of this, circulated by the press, only served to enhance the perceived authenticity of the film as a photographic document.

Ford's experiments with vocal commentary proved more controversial. Soliciting scripts from screenwriter Dudley Nichols and MGM executive James Kevin McGuinness, based on personal notes, Ford supervised the reading of the commentary by four actors—Donald Crisp, Irving Pichel, Henry Fonda, and James Darwell—the last two of whom were currently at work on The Ox Bow Incident on the Fox lot. Above and beyond conventional scene-setting, the commentary dramatizes, and works to bridge, the gap between depicted events and their presentation to the viewer, a function most conspicuously evident when Darwell, speaking as if an American mother watching the Midway footage, expresses urgent concern for the well-being of the young pilots far from home.

Some critics at the time found the commentary overly intrusive or sentimental; Darwell's dialogue, in particular, was thought an unwarranted Hollywood touch. Ford, however, who claimed to have wanted to make the film for 'the mothers of America', never expressed regret about these choices, and Parrish recalls that audiences at Radio City Music Hall were audibly moved by it. Certainly the selection of this particular quartet of voices was not gratuitous; Fonda and Darwell evoke the poignant leave-taking scene from Ford's film version of The Grapes of Wrath (1940); Crisp and Pichel likewise use Ford's adaptation of How Green Was My Valley (1941), with its wistful memorial view of a Welsh mining family. Strands of 'Red River Valley', lifted from the soundtrack to The Grapes of Wrath for the evening watch in The Battle of Midway, reinforce these associations. Trading in heightened emotion, certain moments on the soundtrack thus demonstrate possible points of intersection between combat narratives and domestic melodrama, genres then sharing the screen of movie houses. They also serve a wider project of reimagining community ties between home front and battle front under the pressure of a global war.

CHARLES C. WOLFE

The Battle of Midway (US, United States Navy, 1942, 18 mins). Distributed by Reel Media International, Twentieth Century Fox Film Corp., and the War Activities Committee. Directed by John Ford. Written by John Ford, Dudley Nichols, and James Kevin McGuiness (as James K. McGuiness). Produced by John Ford. Original music by Alfred Newman. Cinematography by John Ford, Jack MacKenzie, and Kenneth M. Pier. Edited by John Ford and Robert Parrish.

Further reading

Doherty, Thomas, *Projections of War: Hollywood, American Culture and World War II*, New York: Columbia University Press, 1993.

Ford, Dan, *Pappy: The Life of John Ford*, New York: DaCapo, 1998.

Gallagher, Tag, 'John Ford: Midway, The War Documentaries', *Film Comment*, September–October 1975: 40–46.

——*John Ford: The Man and His Films*, Berkeley, CA: University of California Press, 1986.

McBride, Joseph, *Searching for John Ford: A Life*, New York: St Martin's Press, 2001.

Murphy, William T., 'John Ford and the Wartime Documentary', *Films & History*, February 1976.

Parrish, Robert, *Growing Up in Hollywood*, New York: Harcourt Brace Janovich, 1976.

Wolfe, Charles, 'Historicizing the "Voice of God": The Place of Vocal Narration in Classical Documentary', *Film History* 9, no. 2, 1997: 149–67.

Battle of Russia, The

(US, Litvak, 1944)

The Battle of Russia was the fifth installment in the group of American World War II propaganda films known as the Why We Fight series. The films in the series, a total of seven, fall into two major groups: those that provided historical background for the events in Europe and Asia

(Prelude to War (1943), The Nazis Strike (1943), Divide and Conquer (1943), and War Comes to America (1945)), and those that detailed specific campaigns of the war and the respective allies involved in those campaigns. The Battle of Russia, along with The Battle of Britain (1943) and The Battle of China (1944), form the latter group. The Battle of Russia, like the other films in this subgroup, was intended to educate the audience about a nation and ally to which most Americans were traditionally adverse. The resulting film is one of the only pro-Soviet films ever produced by the US government.

Although most of the credit for the Why We Fight series has traditionally, and justifiably, been given to Frank Capra, these films were collaborative projects, and thus it is important to recognize all of those involved in the production of The Battle of Russia. Capra received producer credit for the film and, by all accounts, worked closely and intensively with director Anatole Litvak to give the film its shape and orientation. Eric Knight, who headed a team of seven screenwriters, is largely responsible for the film's verbose scripted narration, which was spoken by Walter Huston. The score for the film was done by Hollywood veteran Dmitri Tomkin and drew heavily on Tchaikovsky as well as traditional Russian folk songs and ballads. Although collaboration was obviously important to the genesis of The Battle of Russia, it is important to reiterate the important role that Litvak and Capra played in combining the elements of the film into a cohesive whole. As a compilation film, The Battle of Russia's footage is derived from various sources, including newsreels, amateur filming, and fiction films. From these disparate sources Litvak and Capra, along with veteran editor Walter Hornbeck, created a cogent report on the Russian people and their battle against Hitler's army.

The film itself consists of two parts, the first dealing with a history of the Russian people up to and including the peak of the Nazi invasions of Russia (December 1941). The second part of the film begins with winter falling on the Nazi invaders and goes on to detail the heroic Russian counterattack launched during that winter, which not only drove the Germans back, but also, as the film's narrator pointedly reminds us, 'shattered the myth of Nazi invincibility', and thus boosted the Allied hopes for an eventual defeat of Hitler and his forces. To illustrate all of this, the second part focuses especially on two decisive battles: that at Leningrad and that at Stalingrad.

Formally, The Battle of Russia is the epitome of the compilation film. Shots and sounds are recontextualized in such a way as to present the images as supportive of the film's argument, without a questioning of the image itself; thus, viewers take footage from Alexander Nevsky (Eisenstein, 1938) as representation of historical fact. This phenomenon is achieved in The Battle of Russia not only through skillful montage but also through the employment of a unifying voice-over that dominates the film's soundtrack. Thomas Bohn points out that voice-over narration is present in seventy-five percent of the film, well above contemporary theoretical protocol, which called for no more than two-thirds of the visual track to be accompanied by narration. Nonetheless, the narration in The Battle of Russia is not excessive. The material presented was both complex and obscure to the film's audience, and at no point does the film's propagandistic tone break down into obvious repetition. Besides the prominent narration, the film's informative mode demanded an abundance of animated effects to illustrate tactical concepts such as 'wedge and trap' and 'defense in depth', as well as troop movements and other military maneuvers.

Thematically, the film falls in line with the messages presented throughout the Why We Fight series: Germany's invasion of Russia represents an encroachment of the 'slave world' into the 'free world' of Russia, with a fascist army threatening a peace-loving, pious, and proud people. The depravity of the Germans is reiterated throughout the film with constant reminders that German soldiers were literally raping and pillaging their way through the Russian countryside. However, as the film's most famous line, 'Generals may win campaigns, but people win wars', indicates, the film is concerned with showing how the spirit of a people can defeat even the mightiest army. The film's concluding shots, showing the Russian army along with the armies of all of the Allies marching off to presumable victory, underscore the idea that the United States and Russia are 'in this together', and thus point to the film's true goal, that of propagandizing unity with the heretofore (and afterwards as well) adversarial Russians.

The success of the film in achieving this goal is illustrated by the film's popularity, which extended beyond the military audience for which it was initially intended. The Battle of Russia was the second of the Why We Fight films to receive an Academy Award nomination for Best Documentary feature. The film was also popular abroad, with Stalin ordering hundreds of prints to be shown in Russian theaters. Like all propaganda films, though, The Battle of Russia served its historical purpose and was quickly dated as an artifact of government policy. The necessary propagandistic elisions that the film presents (not mentioning the word communist once, the avoidance of any mention of the Stalin–Hitler nonaggression pact, and the praise for the piety of an officially atheist state), made the film unsuitable for postwar policies. The film was too good at sympathetically portraying Stalin and Russia, and was withdrawn from circulation during the Cold War, making it one of the most ironically effective propaganda pieces in documentary history.

CHRISTOPHER MEIR

See also: The Battle of China; Capra, Frank; Litvak, Anatole

The Battle of Russia (US, 1944, 80 mins). Distributed by Twentieth Century Fox Film Corporation, Questar Pictures, and the War Activities Committee of the Motion Pictures Industry. Produced by Frank Capra. Directed by Frank Capra and Anatole Litvak. Written by Julius J. Epstein, Philip G. Epstein, Rober Heller, Anatole Litvak, and Anthony Veiller. Edited by William Hornbeck. Original music by Dimitri Tiomkin. Non-original music by Pyotr Ilyich Tchaikovsky. Commentary by Walter Huston.

Further reading

Barsam, Richard, 'Why We Fight', in Richard Glatzer and John Raeburn (eds), *Frank Capra: The Man and his Films*, Ann Arbor, MI: University of Michigan Press, 1975: 149–54.

Bohn, Thomas, *An Historical and Descriptive Analysis of the 'Why We Fight' Series*, New York: Arno Press, 1977.

Culbert, David, *Film and Propaganda in America: A Documentary History Vols. II–IV*, New York: Greenwood Press, 1990.

Maland, Charles J., *Frank Capra*, Boston, MA: Twayne Publishers, 1980.

Rollins, Peter C., 'Frank Capra's Why We Fight Series and Our American Dream', *Journal of American Culture* 19, no. 4, 1996: 81–6.

Battle of San Pietro, The

(US, Huston, 1945)

The Battle of San Pietro, a documentary about one battle in Italy in the Allied campaign in World War II, is the most critically acclaimed wartime documentary ever produced under the auspices of the US War Department. The film makes use of maps, charts, and voice-over narration to provide an account of this battle. The more lasting contribution of The Battle of San Pietro, however, emerges from its meditation on the experience of the infantryman, and its larger insights into the destructiveness of war and the resilience of the human spirit.

The Battle of San Pietro bears the unmistakable stamp of its director, writer, and voice-over narrator, the Hollywood filmmaker John Huston. Before the war, Huston had been primarily known as a screenwriter, but his talents as a director were proven after the release of The Maltese Falcon (1941). Along with Frank Capra, William Wyler, John Ford, and others, Huston was one of several prominent filmmakers enlisted in the American war effort. Huston made three war documentaries for the US Army Pictorial Service: Report from the Aleutians (1943), The Battle of San Pietro, and Let There Be Light (1945). The latter film, about veterans under treatment for various mental problems resulting from combat, was suppressed by the War Department until 1980 (Simmon 2000: 58).

Huston was sent to Italy in 1943 to document the triumphant entry of American forces into Rome, but the ground offensive met stiff resistance from the Germans and slowed to a halt north of Naples. Huston was reassigned to make a film 'that would explain to American audiences why U.S. forces in Italy were no longer advancing' (Huston 1980: 109). American forces had moved into position at the foot of the Liri Valley, through which meandered the main road to Rome. The German defenses had taken position in and around the little village of San Pietro, and were about to offer some deadly resistance to Allied advances.

The film begins with a two-minute introduction by General Mark Clark, who led the US Fifth Army into the Liri Valley, explaining that San Pietro was key to the region and that in light of the importance of the objective, casualties were 'not excessive'. It is widely assumed that Clark's introductory words were designed and tacked on by the War Department to counter the film's implication that casualties were excessive. According to William Nolan, however, Huston wrote the opening narration for Clark, thinking that Clark would have it reworked for his own purposes. Huston was surprised when Clark used the speech unaltered: 'Now, there was this four-star general repeating, word for word, the strategy of the campaign as I saw it [...] and me just a dogface in it! I guess he didn't know any more about what was going on than I did' (Nolan 1965: 51).

In part the film chronicles the progress of, and military strategy employed in, Allied attempts to take San Pietro and the surrounding hills. The film's finest points are to be found elsewhere, however. Huston's film unit, with its 35mm handheld Eyemo newsreel cameras (Haskew 2000: 82), was attached to the 143rd Infantry Regiment of the 36th Texas Infantry Division. The Battle of San Pietro manages to convey the men's experience through footage that captures the violence of battle, including numerous close-ups of men's faces, shots of the many casualties as they lie on the battlefield or are wrapped in shrouds, and narrated accounts of the extreme danger of the infantry attacks. The 143rd Regiment alone required 1,100 replacements after the Battle of San Pietro (Huston 1980: 115). Huston has said that he made the film to express admiration for the courage and fortitude of the common foot soldier.

Where Frank Capra's wartime documentaries are highly propagandistic, Huston was unable or unwilling to hide his strong misgivings about the war. The Battle of San Pietro archly and subtly demonstrates the war's effect on the townspeople, on the town, on San Pietro's artistic and cultural treasures, and on nature itself. It does so in part through what has been called 'one of the most memorable voice-over narrations in film—both in script and delivery' (Simmon 2000: 59). After shots of the broken town of San Pietro, we see a pock-marked statue of St Peter as well as the ruined church of St Peter's, its dome missing to reveal the sky above. In voice-over Huston intones something apparently taken from a tourist guidebook: 'Patron Saint, Peter, point of interest, St Peter's, 1438, note interesting treatment of chancel'. Toward the film's end, Huston sums up with shots of men digging graves and slow pans across the faces of the survivors:

> The lives lost were precious lives—to their country, to their loved ones, and to the men themselves [...] many among these you see alive here have since joined the ranks of their brothers at arms, who fell at San Pietro. For ahead lay San Battore, and the Rapido River, and Cassino, and beyond Cassino more rivers, and more mountains, and more towns, more San Pietros, greater or lesser, a thousand more.
>
> (The Battle of San Pietro, 1945)

Toward the film's end we see a montage of images of children emerging from the rubble, some smiling, some obviously frightened but too curious to remain in hiding. James Agee objected to the 'emotional sales pressure' of the music of the Mormon Tabernacle Choir here. Nonetheless, he called the scene 'radiant with illimitable suggestions of meaning and mystery' and 'the first great passage of war poetry that has got on the screen' (Agee 1945). We see shots of the people of the village returning to their daily routines, carrying water, plowing, and sowing seeds. Huston's narration tells us that although the prime military aim had been to defeat the enemy, the people looked upon the Americans as their deliverers. We see a religious procession, and the voice-over narration ends the film: 'And the people pray to their patron saint to intercede with God on behalf of those who came to deliver them [...] and passed on to the North with the passing battle.'

Upon finishing the film, Huston showed it to a group of officers, who pronounced the film 'antiwar' and decided to withhold distribution. Huston told the officers that if he ever made a picture that was pro-war, he 'hoped someone would take me out and shoot me' (Huston 1980: 120). The Battle of San Pietro presented the battle not as a strategic victory, but as a small battle in a costly and continuing campaign. General George C. Marshall asked to see the film, and later pronounced that all army trainees should see it to become better prepared for the shock of battle. Huston was promoted to major. The Battle of San Pietro was released in 1945, however, after the Allied victory, and having been cut from five to three reels. Although it did not fulfill its original military objective, it remains one of the most humane and artful war documentaries ever made. As James Agee wrote in 1945, 'it is in every way as good a war film as I have seen; in some ways it is the best'.

CARL R. PLANTINGA

See also: Huston, John

The Battle of San Pietro (US, John Huston, 1945, 33 mins). Produced by the US Army Pictorial Service. Directed, written, and narrated by John Huston. Cinematography by Jules Buck, John Huston, and other Signal Corps cameramen. Music by Dmitri Tiomkin, performed by the Army Air Force Orchestra, the Mormon Tabernacle Choir, and St Brendan's Boys Choir.

Further reading

Agee, James, 'Review of San Pietro', *The Nation* 160, May 1945: 608.

Haskew, Michael E., 'San Pietro: Capturing the Face of War', *Military History* 17, December 2000: 50–9.

Huston, John, *John Huston: An Open Book*, New York: Alfred A. Knopf, 1980.

Nolan, William F., *John Huston: King Rebel*, Los Angeles, CA: Sherbourne Press, 1965.

Simmon, Scott, 'The Battle of San Pietro', in *Treasures from the American Film Archives*, National Film Preservation Foundation, 2000: 58–61.

Battle of the Somme, The

(UK, Urban, 1916)

Of the various documentaries made under official auspices during World War I, The Battle of the Somme has rightly assumed a key place. It broke all box office records, as thousands were turned away in the first week despite its having opened simultaneously at over thirty London cinemas. More than one theatre was exhibiting it to ten thousand people a day, and the Finsbury Park Cinema attracted over fifty thousand people in that first week. Thereafter, one hundred prints were distributed around the provinces, and within two months hiring fees had been scaled down from £40 a week to £8 for three nights, bringing it within reach of the smallest cinemas. Bioscope complained of unfair competition when music halls hired it instead of limiting themselves to shorts, but it drew many into the cinema for the first time. Still more important, it provided a huge stimulus for the idea of a British film archive. Langford Reed noted that in 1913 both Copenhagen's Royal Library and the Louvre had established film sections, similar archives existing in the Vatican, Madrid, and New York. Meanwhile, the British Museum resisted because film was combustible and impermanent. However, the press considered it unthinkable that Somme prints should not be preserved for posterity.

The film covers the first phase of the Somme offensive, which was to last about four months, with an advance of some thousand yards at the expense of more than half a million British casualties. This opening phase, and the huge preparations that had been necessary, generated footage enough for a feature-length propaganda film, although disjointedness betrays its opportunist origins. Both the Germans and French produced their own Somme films, the former claimed by *The Times* to be technically superb. It focused on the devastation wrought on French towns by Allied guns, and German care for enemy wounded. The two German attacks were obvious fakes. The film allegedly 'followed the British model as closely as possible', and certainly the French version did so. This began with preparations: 'long files of marching soldiers and vast stores of ammunition', then trenches 'full of soldiers ready to leap out', the attack, and numerous Germans surrendering.

French troops, who had bled too freely at Verdun to be able to make their expected contribution on the Somme, have little place in the British film, but there is an image of enduring French peasant women, toiling within view of a military camp that proclaims the ever-present hazards of war. The film is especially distinguished by the amount of attention given to casualties. Topicals, no longer free from censorship, were shorn of 'realistic horrors of war' by either civil censor or service departments, leaving *Cinema*'s reviewer unprepared for the Somme film's images of 'war, rich with death'. These same images continue to shape people's understanding of the war, because the 'over the top' sequence has been used repeatedly as television producers' shorthand. Indeed, it was passed off, in the official compilation America Goes Over (1927), as US Signal Corps' filming of the Doughboys' 'Jump-off' at St Mihielin in September 1918. A contemporary letter to *The Nation* quoted the *Manchester Guardian*: 'Two years ago the public exhibition of horrors like this would have been condemned as an indecency.' Its writer, wondering what could have happened in the course of those two years, resented the soldiers' suffering being turned into entertainment. Others, notably the Dean of Durham in a letter to *The Times*, protested 'against an entertainment which wounds the heart and violates the very sanctities of bereavement'. However, the *Daily News* gloated that the provinces were devouring it 'with an eagerness which must be not a little disturbing to the Dean of Durham', and bereaved *Times* readers found his objections 'squeamish and sentimental'.

John Raphael, *Era*'s Paris correspondent, focuses on those 'over the top' scenes, the core of the film since without them people would have been unconvinced by the remainder. Apparently an officer friend gave him an eyewitness account of their filming, when the cameraman 'was actually crouching in that foremost trench, protected by nothing but a few sandbags, and operating through a hole'. These scenes were almost certainly staged, though his remarks may result from confusion rather than a desire to tell a good story or offset rumors of faking. Faked or not, they worked powerfully on many people. 'My God, they're dead', cried one woman; at another cinema 'two men fainted, but not a single woman'. Elsewhere 'a woman felt faint, but after a sip of water outside insisted on returning to the theatre and seeing the film through'. On the whole, audiences seem to have been awe-stricken at feeling themselves witness to youthful vitality extinguished by unseen forces; however, one evening-gowned flapper complained: 'It is rather too sad. They ought to cut out the gruesome bits.'

That 'gruesome bits' were included at all was doubtless due to the need to make some acknowledgment of the appalling casualty lists, and of public resentment that official films had revealed so little. Thus, this film purports to let people in on war's grim secrets while still keeping them from the truth. Malins knew how mild it was. Even so, he had feared 'that some of the dead scenes' might offend. Graves's 'certain cure for lust of blood' had to be avoided if the film was not to provoke demand for an end to the carnage. At the same time thrills were needed to draw the public; the trick was to offer glimpses of war's grimness before sending them home, cheered with the prospect of victory. Malins discovered that editing involved 'discretion, diplomacy and tact' with so many interests to be served and 'so much [...] at stake'. The central ploy was to translate death to willing and glorious sacrifice. This was the rhetoric used in Lloyd George's statement that accompanied the film, canny enough to infect responses from some of the bereaved: 'I never understood their sacrifice until I had seen this film.' It was blazoned on countless happily smiling faces of men marching up the line, earnest in their belief in what they were doing. The authorities, far more skilled in mass psychology than in handling world affairs, understood that people wanted to be persuaded: it was so much easier to cope with loss if the bereaved could believe in the cause and its leaders. However, the justness of a cause is not sufficient to maintain people's commitment to it; they must believe that it will prevail. Raphael was one among many who found the film worked wonderfully in this respect. Although he had never doubted final victory, the film made him feel safer and more confident than ever: 'Look at the German prisoners as they pass on the film and you can see that Germany knows that she is fighting a losing fight.' To his selective eye, personal shabbiness proclaims their loss of morale, whereas there is not 'a dirty or unshaven man' among the British (the German film showed Germans brushing their uniforms). British citizens smile while Germans cringe, and the 'poor fellow whose own leg is badly smashed, giving up the corner he has found to rest it in to a fainting German prisoner', typifies the chivalry of troops assured of their own superiority.

Another resource for victory on display was British hardware—guns of many calibers being shown in action. Here is the neat evasion used in TV coverage of the Gulf War. Audiences marvel at the technology, losing sight of end results: people blown to pieces or shredded by shrapnel. There was also targeting of the many munition workers seeking relief in the cinema. Pre-battle sequences include great stacks of shells that not only acknowledge the logistics of conflict but also the hard work being done at home to sustain the army in the field. This is both a pat on the back and an exhortation to continued effort. The aim is to balance humanity with technology. As 'Blanche' says in the *Bystander*, the horror of modern war is that people become cogs in a destructive machine. Naturally, it is the Hun who has robbed war of its romance, and a main objective of the struggle is to reeducate him. This shows on screen when, 'a German prisoner, sitting dazed among his enemies, is offered a cigarette by a British soldier'. In a moment, as someone put it, 'his face is beautifully lit—lit with the sudden glory of the truth that men are men, and in their humanity triumphant over any process that would make them less than men'.

There were complaints that the film was sometimes screened in incongruous company, even farce, but it was often slotted at short notice into existing programs. Whatever the circumstances, it is clear that the film was never viewed passively, although there is evidence that audiences had generally lost their old demonstrativeness. People shouted excitedly when they recognized someone on screen. At the Maida Vale Palace one interruption came from 'a wounded Gordon [who] saw himself being medically attended at Minden Post'. There were also more formal commentaries: Lieutenant F.R. Holmes, later to accompany one of the cinemotors touring the country, lectured at the Scala in 'a breezy, pleasant, chatty manner'. At Norwich and elsewhere parties of wounded were taken to see the film, and many of them would have had no trouble in filling out the gaps left by editorial reticence. One wounded soldier in a Shaftesbury Avenue cinema broke down when he saw 'the dead Devons lying on the battlefield, with the battery of artillery moving forward. He sobbed like a child and a nurse led him out of the theatre'. *Cinema*'s reviewer noted how dozens of wheels passed the bodies without any desecrating them, but perhaps the wounded soldier was an artilleryman, who knew that gun teams could hardly avoid sprawled bodies as they careered along corduroy tracks. Besides, the fastidiousness of men and horses (who prefer not to trample on bloodied corpses) succumbs to the terrors of shellfire.

There are various other moments when frontline experience would have taken viewers behind the film's glib narrative. Even scenes of soldiers' ablutions, reassuring to mothers with soldier-sons still young enough to forget to wash behind their ears, would remind the trench soldier of the scarcity of clean water up the line. If he had been in any large attack, he would probably imagine General de Lisle's pep talk on the eve of battle not in the clichéd terms recorded by Malins, but more like Brigadier-General Tuxford's distortions about German war on the wounded, which had fighting mad troops screaming 'Remember the Llandovery Castle!'

Some deconstruction of the film's narrative has been undertaken by Smithers, who points to a dozen questionable episodes. Most striking is the July 1 mine explosion at Hawthorn Redoubt, which is followed by a shot of what purports to be the resulting crater. It probably represents the aftermath of a July 5 explosion, and its later repetition smacks of editorial carelessness. What was probably editorial calculation was the inclusion of that moment of irritation as 'one of the English "Tommies" gives a German prisoner a dig in the ribs'. The American trade paper *Variety*, seeing the film as a potential 'gold mine', proposed the omission of this moment of 'actual feeling' and some rearrangement. American audiences demanded a stronger narrative, and Charles Urban, handling British official documentaries in America, achieved this by splicing in sections of Britain Prepared and shots of an American Field Ambulance (interest was apt to lapse without an American presence). Titles were rewritten, 'eliminating what we should call British patriotism', and the resultant seven-episode serial proved highly successful with American audiences. It was shown in sixteen thousand theatres in twelve thousand towns from coast to coast, and by the end of 1917 some sixty-five million people had paid to see it.

GORDON WILLIAMS

The Battle of the Somme (UK, British Topical Committee for War Films sponsored by War Office, 1916, 79 mins). Produced by William Jury. Cinematography by J.B. McDowell and Geoffrey Malins. Edited by Charles Urban and Geoffrey Malins. Filmed in France.

Further reading

Badsey, Stephen 'Battle of the Somme, British War-Propaganda', *Historical Journal of Film, Radio and Television* 3, 1983: 99–115.

Brownlow, Kevin, *The War, the West and the Wilderness*, London: Secker and Warburg, 1979.

Culbert, David, 'The Imperial War Museum: World War I Film Catalogue and "The Battle of the Somme" (video)', *Historical Journal of Film, Radio and Television* 15, 1995: 575–80.

Hiley, Nicholas, 'The British Cinema Auditorium', in Karel Dibbets and Bert Hogenkamp (eds), *Film and the First World War*, Amsterdam: Amsterdam University Press, 1995: 160–70.

Reeves, Nicholas, 'Cinema, Spectatorship and Propaganda: Battle of the Somme (1916) and its

Contemporary Audience', *Historical Journal of Film, Radio and Television* 17, 1997: 5–29.

——*Official British Film Propaganda During the First World War*, London: Croom Helm, 1986.

Rother, Rainer, '"Bei unseren Helden an der Somme" (1917): The Creation of a "Social Event"', *Historical Journal of Film, Radio and Television* 15, 1995: 525–42.

Smither, Roger (ed.), *The Battles of the Somme and Ancre*, London: Imperial War Museum/DD Video, 1993.

Smither, Roger, '"A Wonderful Idea of the Fighting": The Question of Fakes in The Battle of the Somme', *Historical Journal of Film, Radio and Television* 13, 1993: 149–68.

BBC: The Voice of Britain

(UK, Legg, 1934–5)

BBC: The Voice of Britain was the first General Post Office (GPO) Film Unit film to use synchronized sound. It featured appearances by H.G. Wells, J.B. Priestley, G.K. Chesterton, George Bernard Shaw, and even a brief showing by the young filmmaker Humphrey Jennings (as a witch in Macbeth).

As early as 1932, the Empire Marketing Board (EMB) was approached by the BBC to produce a film advertising and celebrating the new national broadcaster. 'They informed the EMB that, after an examination of the field, they were satisfied that Mr Grierson and his EMB Film Unit were best qualified to make the particular type of film they desired' (Post Office memorandum to the Select Committee, undated 1932, in Rotha 1973: 128).

In many ways BBC: The Voice of Britain was the first film internationally to make clear the power of any major broadcasting institution, as well as spelling out the Reithian ideals that informed her public face. The irony of yet another government body making such a project is invisible in the film itself. Nevertheless, the film gives some clues as to why Legg, in his subsequent career, was to be so favoured by large institutional backers including, after the war, that ultimate global player, the United Nations. Grierson biographer Forsyth Hardy commented: 'The GPO film is admittedly diverse, but not only is there a plan behind the diversity but an individual approach is established and maintained. The film dramatises its material but humanises it as well' (Hardy in *Cinema Quarterly* vol. 3, no. 4, 1935).

The plan of the film is a straightforward, now classic, one for the 'behind the scenes' film: the film diary of a day's broadcasting activity at the BBC, itself less than ten years old at the time of the shoot.

The set-up of the film is equally normative. The popular cinematic trope of the sleeping (British) countryside is used to convey a land whose natural voice the BBC had, in the mind of the literary and intellectual world, rapidly become. An early morning service conducted by the Reverend Dick Sheppard is the first of the BBC programmes (that day) to 'gently wake the land'. This lyrical and elegiac mode, later often referred to as the 'ecclesiastical', using musical and poetic thematics and images quite unselfconsciously, was to be more fully worked out in later films such as Coal Face (1935) and Night Mail (1936). In these films the words of poet W.H. Auden and the music of Benjamin Britten were woven into the visual montage in what was to become the paradigm of early British public documentary (the GPO and the Crown Film Unit) style and the bedrock of the BBC's own characteristic (and schooled) Documentary House Style for the next fifty or more years.

Paul Rotha saw no particular signs of personal style in the film, however. Writing of a group of films made in the mid-1930s, he stated: 'None of them had any individual characteristics of direction. Any of these three directors [Evelyn Spice, Stuart Legg, and Edgar Anstey] could have made any of the three films' (Rotha 1933).

Apparently, there were many periods of funding crisis in the making of the film. This might have been expected in Arthur Elton's first (public) filmmaking intersection with the perpetually beleaguered world of public broadcasting. Elizabeth Sussex reported that according to *World Film News*, in May 1936, the actual cost of the shoot through to the final release print was between £7,000 and £8,000.

JONATHAN DAWSON

See also: Legg, Stuart

BBC: The Voice of Britain (UK, GPO Film Unit, 1934–5) 56 mins, black and white). Directed, scripted, and edited by Stuart Legg.

Further reading

Barnouw, Erik, *Documentary: A History of the Non-Fiction Film*, Oxford: Oxford University Press, 1977.

Hardy, Forsyth, *Grierson on Documentary*, revised. edn, London: Collins, 1966.

Rotha, Paul, *Documentary Film*, London: Faber, 1933 (revised edn 1952).

——*Documentary Diary*, New York: Hill and Wang, 1973.

Sussex, Elizabeth, *The Rise and Fall of British Documentary*, London: Faber and Faber, 1976.

Benoit-Lévy, Jean

Jean Benoit-Lévy was a filmmaker, screenwriter, and one of the most important producers of French educational and scientific films before World War II. Deprived of his professional position by the anti-Jewish statutes promulgated by the Vichy government in 1940, he sought refuge in the United States in 1941. There, by refocusing and redefining his contribution to educational films, he became a teacher, an author, and an executive officer for the United Nations. He continued his dedication to the importance of film in mass education.

His vision of film is based on his strong family values and the late nineteenth century's scientific outlook, imbued with positivism. He began his career as assistant filmmaker just before World War I, a time when Europeans were adjusting to the political, social, and educational challenges of mass society. Benoit-Lévy was introduced to the promising new technology by his uncle, Edmond Benoit-Lévy, a lawyer and pioneer of French cinema. The family shared a commitment to the republican ideals of equality, rationality, modern teaching, social reform, and progress.

Benoit-Lévy perceived film as both an art and formidable educational tool. His films testify to his preoccupation with applied scientific knowledge—particularly in medicine, hygiene, and engineering—to improve the living conditions of ordinary people, especially children. He believed that everyone had the right to live a healthy and rewarding life. His films on professional training and craftsmanship are tributes to technical skills and beauty.

He was well acquainted with the small group of talented avant-garde filmmakers of the late 1920s who connected formal research and social documentary. In 1945–6 Jean Benoit-Lévy would consult this group, which included John Grierson, Alberto Cavalcanti, Paul Rotha, and others, when he reflected on the role and the orientation of future film production for the United Nations Film Board.

In his work during the 1920s and 1930s Benoit-Lévy's position was reformist, opposed to the revolutionary and authoritarian solutions that flourished during his lifetime. He was attached to traditional values, a strong work ethic, and individual freedom. Nevertheless, he believed that state intervention was necessary to ensure adequate ongoing funding for educational film production, as well as to create a centralized institution dedicated to documentary film exchanges. Furthermore, he was convinced that France had an international cultural influence in this field that should be maintained and strengthened. He was well known in France, a person of stature among the cultural elite of the interwar period, and well acquainted with government officials. The war completely disrupted his personal and professional life. The deprivation he suffered and his exile contributed to his being almost forgotten.

Benoit-Lévy made more than three hundred films, many commissioned by institutions and ministries. As an educational film expert, he wrote articles and reports. His proposal to further the use of film in the school system was ambitious: the development of a new pedagogy (pédagogie cinégraphique) that would involve a connection between filmmaker, teacher, and student. Moreover, different kinds of educational and social films were required, because learning was not restricted to the classroom. In accord with several documentary filmmakers of his time, Benoit-Lévy believed that film audiences should be educated to appreciate different genres. His friend, Germaine Dulac, called this éducation cinégraphique. His films were shown in both nontheatrical and theatrical networks. For the latter, he used the category 'films éducatifs spectaculaires', which included such films as Pasteur (1922).

He referred to films de vie (films of life) to describe more precisely what documentary films should be. Films of life were 'documents of life'; they not only express human activities but 'transfer life itself to the screen'. They had a profound social function. During the interwar period he focused on educational and scientific films but also made eleven feature films. For many of those, he worked with Marie Epstein as a writer-director team. The most well known, La Maternelle (1933) and La Mort du cygne (Ballerina, 1937), follow his film of life (documentary) approach. The truth and reality of social issues could be addressed through a free creative process.

In 1941 Benoit-Lévy and his family came to New York with the help of the Rockefeller Foundation. Unwilling to compromise his vision of film to participate in the American commercial film industry, he taught film studies at the New School for Social Research alongside many refugee scholars. It was during his teaching tenure that he wrote *Les Grandes Missions du cinéma*, published in 1945. Film was an autonomous art with its own laws, technique, and means of expression. He believed that logic and visual and intellectual clarity were indispensable to filmmaking. The aesthetics and the editing—beauty and drama—contributed to the idée-force, the main idea, which must always be immediately accessible.

He was also convinced that cinema had a social and civic mission. This idea was not new, but it was forcefully repeated as the war was ending and social concern predominated. Then Benoit-Lévy insisted on freedom more than in his prewar writings. Film was a most powerful medium for the diffusion of human thought. After World War II the discourse was about film bringing people closer together to learn, to discover, and to understand the world.

SUZANNE LANGLOIS

Biography

Born in Paris in 1888, to a middle-class family originally from Alsace. Trained at the Laboratoires Pathé and Gaumont, then began his career as an assistant in 1910. In 1922 founded his company, the Édition française cinématographique, dedicated to producing educational films. In 1945 named Director of the Film and Visual Information Division of the United Nations Department of Public Information. Appointed director of the United Nations Film Board in January 1947. Left the UN in 1949 but maintained a lifetime commitment to the ideals of international cooperation and mass education. In 1958 the International Council for Film and Television (ICFT) was founded under the patronage of UN Educational, Scientific and Cultural Organization (UNESCO), and he was elected its first delegate-general. Died in Paris in 1959.

Selected films

1915	Les Vainqueurs de la Marne: director
1920	Le Travail du potier: director
1922	Pasteur: producer (Jean Epstein, director)
1925–30	L'École départementale primaire et professionnelle de Vitry-sur-Seine: director, producer
1933	La Maternelle: codirector, cowriter, producer
1935	La haute fréquence médicale: director, writer, producer
1935	Le Maroc terre de contrastes: director, producer
1937	La Mort du cygne/Ballerina: codirector, cowriter
1948	La Charte des peuples/The People's Charter: director
1955	Ballets de France: director

Further reading

Andrew, Dudley, *Mists of Regret. Culture and Sensibility in Classic French Film*, Princeton, NJ: Princeton University Press, 1995.

Benoit-Lévy, Jean, *L'Instruction visuelle aux États-Unis*, Paris: Editions du Cinéopse, 1936.

——*Les Grandes Missions du cinéma* [The Art of the Motion Picture], New York: Coward-McCann, [1945]1946.

Borde, Raymond and Perrin, Charles, *Les Offices du cinéma éducateur et la survivance du muet 1925–40*, Lyon: Presses universitaires de Lyon, 1992.

Albera, François and Gili, Jean A. (eds), 'Dictionnaire du cinéma français des années vingt', *1895 Revue de l'Association française de recherche sur l'histoire du cinéma* 33, June 2001.

Eck, Hélène, 'Notes et documents sur l'oeuvre et les activités pédagogiques de Jean Benoit-Lévy de 1922 à 1934', *Revue internationale d'histoire du cinéma*, May 28, 1978, microfiche: 91.

Gauthier, Guy, *Le Documentaire. Un autre cinéma*, Paris: Nathan/VUEF, 2003.

Vignaux, Valérie, 'Jean Benoit-Lévy, l'ignorance est une maladie contagieuse', in Thierry Lefebvre, Jacques Malthête and Laurent Mannoni (eds), *Sur les pas de Marey*, Paris: L'Harmattan, 2004.

Berlin: The Symphony of a Great City

(Germany, Ruttmann, 1927)

One of the internationally best known and most influential German documentaries of the 1920s was Walter Ruttmann's Berlin: Die Sinfonie der Großstadt (1927, Berlin: The Symphony of a Great City). With Alberto Cavalcanti's famous Rien que les heures (1926) on Paris, the film started the tradition of the city-films of that period. Walter Ruttmann and his two co-authors, Karl Freund and Carl Meyer, planned to show Berlin in a course of one day from sunrise to around midnight. The latter two wanted to report simply on the daily life in the metropolis, but Ruttmann prefered to create a visual symphony with his material. His tool was the montage of formal symbols and abstract structure, which was obviously influenced by his abstract animation films before. The form and movement became more important than the content. 'During editing it became clear how difficult it was to visualize the symphonic curve that I had before my eyes. Many of the most beautiful shots couldn't be used, because it is not a nice picture book that should be created, but something like a construction of a complex machine, which can only run when even the smallest parts fit into each other with precision,' as Ruttmann stated in an article shortly after the premiere on September 23, 1927.

Ruttmann succeeded, as the first images demonstrate, when waves of water changed into graphic structures. These abstract images then dissolve into a train crossing; a fast-moving train comes, which is heading in the direction of Berlin. The landscape is rushing past the window. The detailed rhythmic montage again builds up a close intensity. The spectator is already reaching Berlin with high expectations. What will happen next? After this hectic start, a calm moment follows. At five o'clock in the morning life on the streets begins slowly. The previous night's revellers head home exhausted, and the first workers start to rush to the factories. Now the streets and subway fill up. The machines start to run. The montage develops a growing speed and Ruttmann sometimes experiments with ironic comparisons, for example when a close-up of the walking feet of the laborers is followed by the feet of cows on their way to the slaughterhouse, which is then followed by marching soldiers. The second act shows pupils on the way to school, employees go to their offices, a group is riding in the park. The shops are opening, city life is awakening. An important element of the film is the traffic of cars, railways, trams, subway, and even airplanes, which symbolizes the rhythm of the modern metropolis. The lunch break at noon follows the different classes with their specific meals and behavior. Even the animals in the zoo get something to eat. After a short nap, life goes on. The suicide of a woman attracts onlookers. When work is over, leisure time with different kinds of sport begins. The last part shows the nightlife of the roaring twenties with theater, cabaret, variety, dance, and drinking. Berlin is illuminated by neon light. The traffic is still heavy. The film ends with fireworks. The next day is waiting in the wings.

In Berlin: Die Sinfonie der Großstadt the metropolis is the main actor. The people often appear in a group, or they are anonymous elements and only part of a mass. There are no individuals with whom to identify, and Ruttmann shows different classes without bias. He often contrasts the rich and the poor, but he also shows the wealthy middle class or simple workers. The film was, as a result, criticized by many from Siegfried Kracauser to Jerzy Toeplitz to Klaus Wildenhahn. They claimed that the film showed only the surface and that Ruttmann did not analyze the society deeply enough. They also claimed that he did not take a political position. These criticisms miss the point. Ruttmann was most interested not in a sociological study, but in creating a special symphony of Berlin. 'The strict rhythmic style of editing indicates that Berlin doesn't wait or pause for anything, and that the rythm of the city, of which the activities of the masses function as a part, is the very essence of the city itself' (Chapman 1979: 39). Ruttmann aimed to show this as well as the modernity of Berlin. The broad range of impressions and images in their formalistic structure of editing become a dynamic flow and spectators were attracted by that rhythm, which shows typical life without any heroes. The Hungarian film theorist Béla Balázs experienced Berlin as 'optical music'. It was also discussed as an example of an 'absolute film', where the structure and visual impression is more important than the story. The avant-garde worked on this new form of abstract film, and Ruttmann had been one of the leaders of that group since 1922. The concept of new realism was best represented in this film, which became the model for many documentaries. Sequences of his Berlin film are still used in historical television programs to symbolize city life in the Weimar Republic. Ruttmann's symphony shows the city in a new way and was one of the first documentaries in the 1920s in Germany that attained the status of a classic.

The film was later often adapted and quoted in other films. Between 1936 and 1943 Leo de Laforgue shot another Berlin film. The theatrical release was in 1950 under the title Symphonie einer Weltstadt (Berlin wie es war) (1950, Symphony of the Metropolis (Berlin as it was)), and it showed Berlin before the destruction resulting from World War II and tried to imitate Ruttmann, but he was not successful. The most recent adaption was Thomas Schadt's Berlin: Sinfonie einer Großstadt (2002, Berlin: Symphony of a City). He was inspired by Ruttmann's classic film. The 2002 film is shot in black and white and follows a day in modern Berlin, but the new film also reflects the history of the metropolis in the last century and thus develops its own quality. The film is accompanied by modern, abstract music, which gives the film a rhythm of its own. This proved the actuality that Ruttmann's Berlin film still has today.

KAY HOFFMANN

Berlin: Die Sinfonie der Großstadt (Berlin: The Symphony of a Great City) (Germany, Deutsche Vereins-Film, 1927, 65 mins). Directed by Walter Ruttmann. Written by Karl Freund, Carl Mayer, and Walter Ruttmann. Original music by Timothy Brock and Edmund Meisel. Cinematography by Robert Baberske, Karl Freund, Reimar Kuntze, and László Schäffer. Edited by Walter Ruttmann. Art direction by Erich Kettelhut.

Further reading

Chapman, Jay, 'Two Aspects of the City: Cavalcanti and Ruttmann', in Lewis Jacobs (ed.), *The Documentary Tradition*, second edn, New York and London: Norton & Co., 1979.

Goergen, Jeanpaul and Ruttmann, Walter, *Eine Dokumentation*, Berlin: Freunde der Kinemathek, 1989.

Möbius, Hanno and Vogt, Guntram, *Drehort Stadt: Das Thema 'Großstadt' im deutschen Film*, Marburg: Hitzeroth, 1990.

Prümm, Karl, 'Symphonie contra Rhythmus. Widersprüche und Ambivalenzen in Walter Ruttmanns Berlin-Film', in Klaus Kreimeier, Antje Ehmann and Jeanpaul Goergen (eds), *Geschichte des dokumentarischen Films in Deutschland, Bd. 2 Weimarer Republik (1918–33)*, Stuttgart: Reclam, 2005.

Ruttmann, Walter, 'Lichtbild-Bühne, 8.10.1927', in Uta Berg-Ganschow (ed.), *Berlin Aussen und Innen*, Berlin: Stiftung Deutsche Kinemathek, 1984.

Schadt, Thomas, *Berlin: Sinfonie einer Großstadt*, Berlin: Nicolai, 2002.

Toeplitz, Jerzy, *Geschichte des Films, Bd.1 1895–1928*, Berlin: Henschel, 1979.

Berliner, Alan

Alan Berliner has been delving into the intricacies of family life in his documentary film work for many years. His style is at once one of meticulous research and down-to-earth story-swapping as he skillfully blends the personal and the universal. While Berliner's early work was essentially avant-garde or experimental in form and content, he gravitated toward documentary filmmaking largely out of a love for genealogy, family collections of home movies, and an interest in discovering his place in the world through an investigation of his own heritage. This is reflected in the various subjects he has taken for his work, both in form and content.

Berliner's early work explored notions of the avant-garde as well as documentary. Short films made in 1975–85 are compiled from found footage and use scraps to create new narrative tales. His move into the style of his later, better-known work came in 1987 with Family Album. Again, this film used found footage, but the 'bricolage' here (as Berliner calls it) was culled from estate sales. This led to a film reminiscent of Edward Steichen's Family of Man photographic project of the 1950s. Berliner constructed this experimental work from personal home movies from the 1920s through the 1950s, moving from birth to death in its progression. Footage celebrating new babies, graduations, birthdays and weddings are juxtaposed with images of life's more sorrowful passages. The film was screened at over twenty major festivals, including the 33rd Robert Flaherty Film Seminar (1987), the Sundance Film Festival (1988), and the Munich International Film Festival (1987). The work was featured in the 1987 Whitney Museum of American Art Biennial Exhibition.

Berliner's next work was Intimate Stranger. The 1991 film takes as its subject Berliner's maternal grandfather, Joseph Cassuto, a Palestinian Jew who worked as a merchant for the Japanese in the cotton industry in Egypt in the years prior to World War II. His break from his family during the war and the reunion in New York following it give a context for this study of a man admired in his professional life yet unpopular in his own family. Cassuto was unhappy in the United States and ultimately left his wife and children for most of the year to live in his beloved Japan to pursue business interests. Berliner finds means of constructing an elaborate portrait of his grandfather in a way that gives credence to the man's two distinct lives. The multifaceted approach to the discovery of this man's humanity brings dynamism to this complex investigation. This film was accepted into nearly forty international festivals upon its release, including the Margaret Mead Film Festival, Sundance, and Cinéma du Réel in Paris (where it garnered a Special Jury Award in 1992). Berliner was honored with the Distinguished Achievement Award from the International Documentary Association in 1993.

Following a pattern of increasingly personal approaches to his particular style of exploring family and history, Berliner revealed Nobody's Business in 1996. This film investigates his father, Oscar Berliner, a self-professed 'ordinary guy'. Berliner's reclusive father is initially in no way interested in being a willing participant in his son's investigation. The film is delightful in its depiction of the conflict between the two men, one endeavoring to learn more about his father's life, the other deeply concerned with his own privacy and seclusion. Nobody's Business takes its title from Oscar's relentless insistence that no one needs to know anything about him. It is not their business, it is not interesting, and he is not interested in making these things known to anyone. Slowly, though, the events of his life are discovered, as Berliner presses his father for clues and explanations. He shows his father old photographs and asks personal questions about their contexts. Stock footage is also employed, most notably the repetition of an image of boxers sparring, seen whenever the discussion between father and son becomes heated. Berliner's research took him to the massive archive run by the Church of Jesus Christ of Latter-Day Saints in Salt Lake City, and he shows the magnitude of this genealogical project alongside the microcosm of records relating to his father. This work was an enormous success in its ability to unite the personal tale of one man with the universal story of all mankind.

The film was shown as the first installment in the tenth season of PBS' POV (point of view) series, where it created a massive level of viewer response. This prompted the combined efforts of several agencies, including the National Archives, to encourage people to explore their own genealogies. The film was screened at over fifty festivals, including a place in the 'Frames of Reference' show at the Guggenheim Museum. It won an Emmy in 1998 from the Academy of Motion Picture Arts and Sciences, and received major awards from several international festivals.

The 2001 release of The Sweetest Sound, Berliner's film exploring the meaning of our names, takes him to Holocaust Memorials, the Vietnam Wall, the NAMES project, AIDS quilt, and other great repositories of memory. He finds that he shares a name with many other Alan Berliners in the world, including another filmmaker, Belgian Alain Berliner. He deals with the concept of 'Same Name Syndrome', visiting the Jim Smith Society and the National Linda Convention, before finally deciding to invite the Alan Berliners of the world over to his house for dinner. The study again shows the exquisite communion shared by all humans, even in the face of so much difference. Again a large success, this film was screened by over fifty festivals throughout the world and in such venues as the Hirshhorn Museum in Washington, DC. Berliner won the Storyteller Award at the Taos Talking Picture Film Festival in 2001, and has had retrospectives of his work at the Museum of Modern Art as well as the International Center for Photography in New York City. He continues to explore documentary forms, and is also very active as an installation artist working with found sound and audio environments.

TAMMY A. KINSEY

Biography

Born New York, 1963. Attended SUNY—Binghamton and the University of Oklahoma. Early film work explored notions of the avant-garde and documentary. Film Family Album featured in 1987 Whitney Museum of American Art Bienniel. Recipient of grants from National

Endowment for the Arts, New York State Council for the Arts, New York Foundation for the Arts, Rockefeller Foundation Fellowship. Guggenheim Foundation Fellowship. Distinguished Achievement Award from the International Documentary Association, 1993, for Intimate Stranger. Berlin International Film Festival, Caligari Film Award, 1997. Nyon Visions du Réel, Switzerland, Grand Prix Award, 1997. Retrospective show at the International Center for Photography, New York. Storyteller Award, Taos Talking Picture Film Festival, 2001. Family Album, Intimate Stranger, and Nobody's Business all screened on PBS series, POV. Artist-in-residence at Walker Center for Art, Minneapolis, Minnesota.

Selected films

1986 Family Album
1991 Intimate Stranger
1996 Nobody's Business
2001 The Sweetest Sound

Further reading

Albert, Mitch, 'A Family Affair: The Films of Alan Berliner. When is Personal Documentary Nobody's Business?' *The Independent Film and Video Monthly* 20, 1997.

Cuevas, Efren and Muguiro, Carlos (eds), *The Man Without the Movie Camera: The Cinema of Alan Berliner*, Ediciones Internacionales Universitarias, 2002.

MacDonald, Scott, *A Critical Cinema 4: Interviews with Independent Filmmakers*, Berkeley, CA University of California Press, 2004.

Beruf: Neonazi

(Germany, Bonengel, 1993)

Beruf: Neonazi (Profession: Neo-Nazi) sparked a controversy on its release in June 1993, leading to its temporary ban in several regions of Germany. Later it served as evidence in the trial of the main protagonist, who was convicted on grounds of comments he made in the documentary, pre-eminently those in which he denied that the Holocaust took place. In Germany the 'Auschwitz-lie' is a crime that has been punishable in law since 1985 and 1994 (Long 2002). The intense reaction to the film also has to be seen against the backdrop of growing right-wing violence in Germany during the early 1990s.

The post-vérité documentary was criticized for its sympathetic treatment of the hero, Ewald Althans, whose neo-Nazi views, it was argued, the film presented without taking a stance against them. Althans was not merely a private person, a social actor, observed by the documentary, but an experienced agitator. Beruf: Neonazi made the limitations of observational documentary apparent and raised questions as to whether observation is an appropriate method to 'expose' a political performer, or whether it merely provides a neo-Nazi demagogue with a platform. The director, Winfried Bonengel, argued that only observation could penetrate the slick veneer of Althans, who would unmask himself involuntarily in moments in which his expressions manifested his doubts. Challenging Althans verbally would not lead anywhere, because he was such a rhetorically articulate operator who would dismiss any opposition as merely defensive. Instead of countering his views in a direct verbal debate, the film, Bonengel claimed, visually parodied the convictions of its protagonist through low camera angles that depicted his poses as pompous, like an exaggeration of the elevated angles in Leni Riefenstahl's Triumph of the Will (1935). The director and the cameraman saw Althans as 'a robot with a tiny little ball for a head' (Niroumand 1993). The film's critics, on the other hand, contested the claim that the images provided a parody or critique and found that the camera's positioning merely depicts Althans as superior and enhances his appeal. The cameraman had no choice other than to make images from a low angle, it was suggested, because he was short and his subject was tall (Donner 1993).

In the documentary's most controversial scene—the one that ultimately led to Althans's conviction—he talks a visibly shocked young American into the ground with his rhetoric that no one could have been gassed in Auschwitz. Instead, Althans manages to label him as rude and leaves the debate as a victor. Whether the close-up of his face when he is not speaking arrests it in a telescopic prison, as the cameraman Johann Feindt argued (Niroumand 1993) and reveals a 'rare loss of composure' (Bathrick 1996), or not, is down to interpretation. In fact, that none of the other Auschwitz visitors objects strongly to Althans's provocations might also be due to the fact that they were intimidated because he was accompanied by a film team rather than by his rhetorical skills. After this scene, the camera, arguably, takes Althans's side when it shows him walking away, and not the young tourist, whose political views the filmmaker and most of the film's audience share: Bonengel 'shows Althans from behind as with upright stride he moves away from the camera toward the exit. Like a cowboy who has just brushed off the dust from his pants or like a gladiator leaving the arena' (Wienert 1994).

The director's argument against using direct verbal challenge does not preclude an expository commentary. Bonengel rejected authoritative voice-over because it would be patronising and block an allegedly less educated audience from judging for themselves. The dangers of the attraction of fascism needed be experienced in order to be properly rejected, and not be contained by a pedagogic narration, one newspaper agreed (Niroumand 1993). Similarly, the German Studies scholar David Bathrick finds that the reception in Germany expressed 'an immense fear of any visual ambiguity' rooted in a 'legitimating notion of antifascism, that comes to function so successfully in the service of Bilderverbot (censoring of images)' (Bathrick 1996).

Beruf: Neonazi was also criticized for showing a right-wing extremist who was attractive, eloquent, and young (born 1966) rather than repellent, repetitive, and old as were the usual exponents of National Socialism in Germany at the time. These were much easier to dismiss. The 'Nazi-Yuppie' constituted an unwelcome reminder that beauty does not preclude fascism and earned the documentary the reproach of glamorizing fascism. Althans himself proclaimed elsewhere: 'I am a National Socialist and I am socially acceptable. And National Socialism is then only dangerous, when it becomes socially acceptable' (from Eckerle, Hohmann, 'Sein Kampf, mein Sieg', in *Münchner*, 1992, cited in Long 2002: 4). However, in another of the paradoxes that make out Beruf: Neonazi's history of reception, Althans was regarded as dangerous only by the media and the courts, which in turn boosted his visibility. This was in contrast to his much lower standing in the Holocaust-denial movement itself, especially after he was outed as gay. The 'revisionist international' did not want another closeted gay leader after the neo-Nazi Michael Kühnen had died of AIDS in prison (Long 2002: 76).

At the end of November 1993 the Hessian state parliament banned Beruf: Neonazi and confiscated copies because the film did not counter the neo-Nazi statements with its own commentary, and it rather seduced young viewers to Althans's position. The Frankfurt court ruled that the documentary 'circulated national socialist propaganda without providing commentary, incited the masses, insulted and disparaged the memory of the dead, and maintained that Auschwitz was a lie' ('Die Deutschen sind noch nicht reif dafür', in *Berliner Zeitung* 11 December 1993, cited in Bathrick 1996). Rallies were held against screenings of the film, it was demanded that the director pay back the film's grant money, and the distributors withdrew. At the end of December 1993, by contrast, the public prosecutor's office in Berlin pronounced that Beruf: Neonazi could be screened in that region, since it was a 'critical and realistic representation of actual neo-Nazi activities' and 'maintains distance to its protagonist [...] through artistic means, through the presentation of counter-positions and externally through the choice of its title' (Donner 1993).

In a typical succession of contradictory moves for the sake of generating publicity, the German magazine *Der Spiegel* initially attacked the film as neo-Nazi propaganda paid for by taxes in November 1993 (*Der Spiegel*, 15 November 1993). Three months later, however, Spiegel-TV wanted to broadcast the whole film, but was forced to drop this on account of the strong protest of prominent German public figures (Wienert 1994). Instead, it screened a discursive programme with the title 'Show It, Don't Censor It' about the film, including interviews with the director and the protagonist, and a thirty-minute excerpt of the eighty-three-minute film (Bathrick 1996). Bonengel objected to the broadcast of his film. While he defended a screening in the cinemas, arguing that the public space of the movie theatre would foster a debate among an audience, a broadcast to individuals at home would diminish their ability to be critically distanced and make the solitary viewer more susceptible to Althans's views. Had the film not originated in Germany—or indeed had it been neo-Nazi propaganda rather than a production by a serious filmmaker—it would probably not have evoked such a heated debate.

In September 1994 the same State Court of Berlin that previously had allowed the screening of Beruf: Neonazi arraigned Althans on grounds of his utterances in the film, which again effected a temporary ban on the documentary. Ironically, the screening of the film resulted in a court case against its main protagonist, which eventually resulted in his conviction after he previously had been acquitted due to lack of evidence for his right-wing activism. The former documentary subject represented himself in the trial, claiming that he had merely re-enacted his previous neo-Nazi persona for the documentary. He further maintained that with his statement in the documentary, 'What is going on here is a massive hoax', he meant the film itself and not the gas chambers of Auschwitz, in which he stood at the time. In a sense, Althans claimed to have taken the same position toward his own comments as the filmmaker did: he 'only wanted to make a neutral statement, as to what an orthodox neo-Nazi would be' (Associated Press, 13 June 1995). Furthermore, he argued that he played up to the image of a neo-Nazi because he did not want to alienate anyone. While conducting his own defense, Althans was sometimes moved to tears by his own depictions of his life, bearing witness to the director's suggestion that his subject became the victim of his own narcissism. The film team was enlisted in court as witnesses that their subject was authentic in the documentary. The cameraman testified that Althans's behavior in the documentary was genuine; that is, he was not acting when making his right-wing comments (Associated Press, 13 June 1995). The courts accepted his utterances as evidence, and in 1994 and 1995 Althans was sentenced to three-and-a-half years altogether, six months longer than asked for by the prosecution, for denial of the Holocaust, glorification of Nazism, defaming the memory of the dead, and incitement to hatred.

SILKE PANSE

Further reading

Bathrick, David, 'Anti-Neonazism as Cinematic Practice: Winfried Bonegel's Documentary Film Beruf Neonazi', *New German Critique* 67, 1996: 33–46.

Davidson, John E., '"In der Führer's Face": Undermining Reflections in and on Beruf: Neonazi', *Arachne: An Interdisciplinary Journal of the Humanities* 3, 1996: 67–96.

Donner, Wolf, 'Draufhalten is nicht genug', *Frankfurter Allgemeine Zeitung* 27, 1993: 11.

Long, Anthony, 'Forgetting the Führer: the Recent History of the Holocaust Denial Movement in Germany', *Australian Journal of Politics and History* 48, 2002: 72–84.

Niroumand, Mariam, 'Vorsicht Bissiger Hund' and 'Nimm die Sonnenbrille ab. Zwischen Golem und Robocop: Gespräch mit Johann Feindt, dem Kameramann von Beruf Neonazi', *Die Tageszeitung* 18, 1993: 12.

Wienert, Klaus, 'Proteste kippen Filmausstrahlung. Spiegel-TV sendet Beruf: Neonazi nur in Ausschnitten', *Frankfurter Rundschau* 18, 1994.

Bitomsky, Hartmut

In his essay 'The Documentary World', the German documentary filmmaker Hartmut Bitomsky advanced the idea of the documentary film image as ready-made. Like the artist, the filmmaker takes an object out of its original environment into a new context (Bitomsky 2003: 206). Taking this idea further, it is not only that he treats images as objects but that his images are also of objects: the Autobahn, the Beetle, the B-52 bomber. Arguing against the current focus in documentary film on the depiction of lives as individual or bizarre cases, Bitomsky is interested in the socioeconomic and planned effects of these functional objects of transport and war (Bitomsky 2003: 275). Tellingly, Bitomsky did the voice-over narration on the experimental documentary Four Corners (1997) by James Benning, another filmmaker who prefers the filming of streets, machinery, and landscape to that of individuals (Benning also did the sound on B-52).

The 'object' of Bitomsky's films, however, is not a closed entity. For Bitomsky, the dialogue with the images is imperative. The images are not merely 'objective' material untouched by the viewing process. Playback (1995), for example, follows the articulated thoughts of workshop participants at the Amsterdam Film museum as they closely analyze early silent film footage. In Playback the filmmaker narrates: 'There are not new films and old films, there are only films one has seen and films one has not seen.' It is the relation between both the visible, on the one hand, and the imagination of the filmmaker and the viewer, on the other, that produces a new entity. His documentaries do not merely depict an empirical, visible surface, but they make it visible (Bitomsky 1972). Bitomsky is interested in not only creating original images but in producing new images through the viewer's interaction with existing ones. His films examine the processes of production and trace the path of its material in the way they are made, as well as in what they depict. Der VW-Komplex begins the way B-52 ends, with the dismantling of its object on a scrapheap. The discarded machinery makes for new images, though. Bitomsky's 'recycling' of images is economic.

In many of his documentaries Bitomsky finds 'reality' in photos and footage stored in archives. In his examination of cinema through the medium's own means, the fragment retains its quality in itself and is not subsumed under a new whole. Bitomsky's 'interest starts after reality and event has already been formed into story' (Pirschat 1992: 5). The fragment can be a part of a machine or a section of a moving image. Exposing the found footage as fragments that are not integrated allows the viewer to examine their construction without being drawn in. In Bitomsky's films the viewer is always made aware of the viewing process. This is achieved by making the image itself into an object by, for example, framing it. Bitomsky follows Levi-Strauss's dictum that to understand images better, one must resist experiencing them, and this is realized by making them smaller (Kubitz 1992). In Die UFA, for example, the camera films several monitors at the same time, each showing different footage. Another way Bitomsky distances the viewer is to show photographs instead of moving images with the hand of the filmmaker moving his material and turning the pages of books full of images, rather than having the image fill the whole of the screen. This gives viewers the space to detach themselves from the image, but it also depicts the filmmaker as a manual worker given that the still images are propelled forward by manual labor.

Work has an aesthetic and aesthetics are work. Both impact on one another. At the beginning of Reichsautobahn the filmmaker narrates: 'The Autobahn is the biggest German edifice. At its inauguration Hitler said: "We'll make sure that the work does not become separated from those who built it".' Bitomsky argues that it was the aestheticisation of the Autobahn—it it was made for sight—which was a means for work placement, rather than its functionality. His documentaries reflect the reciprocal influencing of ideology, industry, and images, as well as the interlacing of the civilian and the military, and of culture and war (Bitomsky 2003). Bitomsky's interest in the functional aspects of the aesthetic is consonant with Brecht, who wrote that 'less than ever does a simple reproduction of reality tell us anything about reality. A photograph of Krupps or the AEG yields hardly anything about those industries. True reality has taken refuge in the functional' (Brecht 1967: 161). The subject matter of his documentaries often is industrial and technological (roads, cars, fighter planes) and, as such, decidedly masculine. The image engineer Bitomsky, however, is interested in the unplanned malfunctions of these grand designs of modern technology: the disintegration of the pompous, totalitarian plans of Hitler's Autobahn in Reichsautobahn, or the many accidents in the power weapons of the Cold War in B-52. In Die UFA, another example, Bitomsky points out that the Nazi propaganda minister Joseph Goebbels had to prohibit the anti-communist propaganda films that initially they had commissioned. Even though the Nazis used communist footage against the Soviet's original intent, this inspired people to see the original films. This does not happen with Bitomsky's documentaries using found footage, however, as they examine and work through the originals and do not just reject them. In Germany, showing Nazi propaganda footage within a film has to be indexed by commentary, subtitles, or intertitles. The German film scholar Klaus Kreimeier argued that announcing the Nazi footage as propaganda precludes any experience of the images as anything other than propaganda (Kreimeier 1992: 16). In contrast to television reports or other German documentary filmmakers such as Erwin Leiser and Joachim C. Fest, who use Nazi footage as evidence, Bitomsky's documentaries do not use the markers of authenticity such as speech in sync-sound technology as proof. Rather, his films show Hitler before he talks and then paraphrase the content. Moreover, unlike for instance Emile de Antonio's narration in his compilation films, Bitomsky's is not merely contrapunctual against the original footage of, for example, Nazi images. Instead, Bitomsky carves out their inherent contradictions. Even though Bitomsky's documentaries address the concrete consequences of an ideology, they are not directly political. His films delineate the conflicts between the concepts of ideology and the causes and effects of industry not only in terms of his subject matter but also with respect to the film industry, which his documentaries are in the least possible way part of.

Since 1974 Bitomsky has published, edited, and contributed to the influential German film journal, *Filmkritik* (1957–85), amongst others with his friend the documentary filmmaker Harun Farocki. With his fellow Anglo-American and French film semioticians at the time, the documentary filmmaker shared an enthusiasm for American fiction film such as those by Samuel Fuller or John Ford. The latter features Das Kino von John Ford (1979) in Bitomsky's portrait. Although his earlier reviews in *Filmkritik* and his book *Die Röte des Rots von Technicolor* (1972) were influenced by semiotics, they are written like an instruction manual. Bitomsky approached semiotics like the Volkswagen in Der VW-Komplex. His style of writing is similar to that of his film narrations: profound and—untypical for analytic texts in German—constructed in short sentences. Bitomsky does not only analyze found images in his documentaries, but unusual for a documentary filmmaker, he has published texts about his films. The visual 'quoting' of found images in Bitomsky's films can perhaps be seen as a continuation of his frequent citing of texts in his early film reviews. In writing about the reception of his documentaries that already reflect production processes of other objects of modernity, Bitomsky constructs a circular trajectory in which he engages in a similar process with his writing about his films as he does in his filming about found images and objects.

Before Bitomsky left Germany his documentaries could broadly be divided into two groups: films that reflect on their medium such as the videofilms about the cinema, Das Kino und der Tod (1988), Kino Flächen Bunker (1991), and Das Kino und der Wind und die Photographie (1991), and films about images of Germany such as Deutschlandbilder (1983), Reichsautobahn (1986), and Der VW-Komplex (1989) (Pirschat 1992). Die UFA (1993), about the national-socialist image politics with respect to the German cinema studios, combined both. With B-52 (2001), invented by the Germans in the World War II and further developed by the Americans for the Cold War, the focus shifted to his chosen home country. Hartmut Bitomsky has produced more than forty documentaries.

SILKE PANSE

Biography

Born in Bremen, Germany, 1942. Read German literary studies, theater studies, and journalism at the Freie Universität Berlin, 1962–6. Changed to the then new German Film and Television Academy Berlin, 1966–8. Expelled for political activism during the student revolts. Worked for West German Television (WDR) from 1973. Published, edited, and wrote for the film journal *Filmkritik*, 1974–85. Visiting Lecturer at the Academy for Film and Television in Munich, the Freie Universität Berlin and the German Film and Television Academy Berlin after 1975. Dean of the School of Film and Video at the California Institute of the Arts in Los Angeles, 1993–2002. Still teaches there. Fellow of the Rockefeller Foundation.

Selected films

1970	Die Teilung aller Tage
1971	Eine Sache, die sich versteht
1976	Humphrey Jennings. Bericht über einen englischen Filmemacher
1976	Das Kino von John Ford
1980–1	Highway 40 West—Reise in Amerika
1983	Deutschlandbilder (with Heiner Mühlenbrock)
1985–6	Reichsautobahn
1988	Das Kino und der Tod
1988–9	Der VW-Komplex
1991	Kino Flächen Bunker
1991	Das Kino und der Wind und die Photographie
1993	Die UFA
1995	Playback
1999–2001	B-52

Further reading

Bitomsky, Hartmut (ed.), 'Introduction', in *Béla Balázs der Geist des Films*, Frankfurt/Main: Makol Verlag, 1972.

——*Die Röte des Rots von Technicolor. Kinorealität und Produktionswirklichkeit*, Neuwied und Darmstadt: Sammlung Luchterhand, 1972.

——reviews in *Filmkritik*, 1974–85.

——(ed.), *André Bazin. Was ist Kino? Bausteine zur Theorie des Films*, introduction by Eric Rohmer, Cologne: DuMont Schauberg, 1975.

——'Die Dokumentarische Welt' [The Documentary World], in Ilka Schaarschmidt (ed.), *Kinowahrheit*, Berlin: Verlag Vorwerk, 2003: 8.

Brecht, Bertold, 'Der Dreigroschenprozess, ein soziologisches Experiment', *Gesammelte Werke in 20 Bänden*, Band 18, Frankfurt-am-Main: Suhrkamp Verlag, 1967.
Kreimeier, Klaus, 'Deutschlandbilder: Ein imaginärer Indizienprozess', in Jutta Pirschat (ed.), *Die Wirklichkeit der Bilder. Der Filmemacher Hartmut Bitomsky*, Essen: Edition Filmwerkstatt, 1992.
Kubitz, Peter Paul, 'Man muß die Dinge verkleinern, damit sie verstanden werden', *Süddeutsche Zeitung* 10, 1992: 9.
Pirschat, Jutta, 'Die Wirklichkeit der Bilder', in Jutta Pirschat (ed.), *Die Wirklichkeit der Bilder. Der Filmemacher Hartmut Bitomsky*, Essen: Edition Filmwerkstatt, 1992.

Black Box BRD

(Germany, Veiel, 2001)

Germany's long and painful struggle to overcome the legacy of the Nazi regime reached a cataclysmic peak during the terrorist siege to which the Rote Armee Fraktion (RAF, Red Army Faction) subjected the nation and its government in the late 1960s and 1970s. The terrible violence during the fall of 1977 was portrayed by Rainer Werner Fassbinder, Volker Schlöndorf, and a team of other directors in their joint film Deutschland im Herbst/ Germany in Autumn (1978). The following decades saw a decrease in the number of terrorist assaults, but the attacks on representatives of industry and government continued into the 1990s and ended only when the RAF eventually announced its own dissolution on April 20, 1998.

In his much-acclaimed film, Black Box BRD, which won both a German and a European Film Award, Andres Veiel follows the lives of two people directly connected to this conflict, Alfred Herrhausen and Wolfgang Grams. In the film, they represent the two opposing sides, although both died a violent death. Herrhausen was senior manager of Deutsche Bank when he was killed by an RAF bomb on November 30, 1989 while driving to work in his car. Grams, a leader of the third generation of the RAF, had been living underground since 1984. He died on June 27, 1993 during an exchange of fire with police officers attempting to arrest him. Investigations into the exact circumstances of his death have failed to provide conclusive answers.

Veiel approaches his difficult topic in a manner that is personal, yet remains distant from a narrative point of view. At no point in his film does the filmmaker comment directly on the events portrayed. The film ends with a few lines of text that do not attempt to answer the many questions raised by the film, but simply provide specific historical data on Herrhausen's and Grams's deaths. The text states that it is 'unclear' whether and to what extent Grams was involved in the attack on Herrhausen, causing hesitation on the part of the viewer who may be attempting to create a direct connection between the two stories.

The personal atmosphere of the film is a result of the many private memories shared by family members, as well as former friends and colleagues of the two main characters. These interviews are the main sources of information from which the film draws. In addition to these interviews, which make up the overwhelming majority of the film's running time, Veiel incorporates archival footage from private home movies which strengthen the personal tone of his biographical film. To provide the audience with some context, Black Box BRD also includes scenes from original news programs, thereby providing not only necessary historical information for a contemporary audience, but also a sense of the urgency and drama that surrounded the political conflicts during the decades when Germany was finally taking a closer look at its historical legacy.

It becomes increasingly apparent throughout Black Box BRD that the unconstrained idealism with which both segments of society were pursuing their political and societal goals still prevents many people, years and decades later, from analyzing the incidents with any degree of objectivity. The issues that initially stirred the student demonstrations, and then escalated into the RAF's terrorism might have been overcome had those issues been dealt with appropriately during the conflict. One of the great and sad ironies of Herrhausen's murder is that it occurred at a time when he was already starting to steer Deutsche Bank away from the hard-line capitalist ideology of the postwar boom years. After a meeting with Mexico's president, he proposed to the bank's board that they take greater account of the social consequences of their operations. Although his intentions alienated many of his senior colleagues, Herrhausen's plans might have found much support in the public debate about the social role and responsibilities of corporations.

Black Box BRD is aptly named after a technological device, the workings of which most of its users do not comprehend. The film is structured like a mosaic or puzzle and thus also presents itself as a mysterious object. Its manifold pieces, mostly brief segments smoothly cut from longer interviews, resist the temptation of presenting a conclusive or linear narrative. The film moves back and forth between the lives of its two main subjects, following their biographies in more or less chronological order. Beyond the interviews, Veiel filmed very little additional material: staged footage of the fateful auto convoy, neighborhoods, Deutsche Bank, and prison buildings. Veiel clearly refused to follow the current trend of producing a docudrama, in which historical and archival material is edited in a way that it becomes almost indistinguishable from reenacted scenes. The additional (fictitious) footage that Veiel included is helpful, however, as it often provides subtle clues whenever the film's narrative moves from one of its main characters to the other. Because there is no voice-over narrator in Black Box BRD, these transitions perform a crucial function. In general, however, the film's almost detached relationship to its topic is noticeable. The camera remains mostly immobile, and sound is natural, with only the theme song occasionally providing some distraction from the tense statements of the people on the screen.

As did his earlier film about German youth in the 1970s, Die Überlebenden/The Survivors (1996), Veiel's Black Box BRD refuses to judge the two people it portrays so intimately. It presents them as complex individuals who have, on occasion, questioned their own ideologies and principles. As a rule, the interviewees are not questioned while on camera. The film instead presents testimonials, memories, and the lasting pain deriving from the search for answers by the friends and relatives of Herrhausen and Grams, who represent all those who did not survive the dark terrorist phase of Germany's postwar history. Black Box BRD is not afraid of silence, as when family members are overcome by emotion and unable to continue. Yet, the film's very existence provides an outspoken and powerful reminder that the absence of clear answers does not have to mean that the past can be forgotten, thereby providing a valuable counterweight to cultural and political amnesia.

GERD BAYER

Selected films

Black Box BRD (Germany, X Verleih/Zero Film, 2001, 102 mins). Distributed by Warner Home Video. Produced by Thomas Kufus. Directed by Andres Veiel. Shooting script by Andres Veiel. Cinematography by Jörg Jeshel. Assistant direction by Andreas Teuchert. Music by Jan Tilman Schade. Edited by Katja Dringenberg. Sound direction by Paul Oberle.

1991–2 Winternachtstraum: director, writer
1993 Balagan: director, writer
1995–6 Die Überlebenden: director, writer
2003 Die Spielwütigen: director, writer

Further reading

Becker, Jillian, *Hitler's Children: The Story of the Baader-Meinhof Terrorist Gang*, third edn, London: Pickwick, 1989.

Varon, Jeremy, *Bringing the War Home: The Weather Underground, the Red Army Faction, and the Revolutionary Violence in the Sixties and Seventies*, Berkeley, CA: University of California Press, 2004.

Veiel, Andres, *Black Box BRD: Alfred Herrhausen, die Deutsche Bank, die RAF und Wolfgang Grams*, Stuttgart: Deutsche Verlags-Anstalt, 2002.

Blank, Les

An independent documentary filmmaker from the United States, Les Blank is considered a maverick for his lush films on food, regional music styles, and communities on the fringes of mainstream American society. The founder of Flower Films in El Cerrito, California, Blank has directed and/or produced approximately thirty-three documentary films since 1960. In addition, he has served as crew member on approximately seven other films, including additional photography on Little Dieter Needs to Fly (1997, Werner Herzog) and uncredited second camera on Easy Rider (1969).

Les Blank studied in the PhD film program at the University of Southern California and worked as a freelance industrial and commercial filmmaker in Los Angeles before directing his own independent documentary films. Blank initially financed these films by continuing to make promotional films for such companies as Holly Farms Poultry, Archway Cookies, and the National Wildlife Federation. His work has since been funded by such entities as the National

Endowment for the Arts, the American Film Institute, the National Endowment for the Humanities, the Ford Foundation, the Guggenheim Foundation, PBS, and the BBC.

Major retrospectives of his work have been mounted worldwide, and feature articles have appeared in such publications as *Film Quarterly*, *The New York Times*, *The Los Angeles Times*, *Mother Jones*, *Rolling Stone*, and *The Village Voice*. Blank was awarded the American Film Institute's Maya Deren Award for outstanding lifetime achievement as an independent filmmaker in 1990, and his documentaries have been internationally recognized with awards, including the British Academy Award, the Grand Prize at the Melbourne Film Festival, the Special Jury Award at the Sundance Film Festival, the Grand Award at the Houston Film Festival, the Golden Jugo at the Chicago Film Festival, and the Best of Festival Award at the San Francisco Film Festival.

His documentary films are praised for the intimate and privileged glimpses they provide into artistic and culinary subcultures in the United States and are particularly recognized for capturing and visually/aurally preserving aspects of American culture that have now faded or disappeared altogether. He incorporates an organic and sensual shooting style that allows the viewer privileged views of artists, food lovers, and others who are committed to living life to the fullest. Possibly best characterized as artistic visual ethnographies, most of Blank's films invite the viewer to a better appreciation of common folk who have dedicated their lives to community around a common interest. These interests include garlic; late 1960s flower children; Serbian-American, Hawaiian, Afro-Cuban, Louisiana-French and Tejano music; bluegrass fiddling; German filmmaker Werner Herzog; women with gaps between their front teeth; beer; and Cajun and Creole cooking. Music is often an important cinematic element in his films, and close-up shots of steaming pots of sauce, pigs suckling, women dancing, people laughing and enjoying whatever it is that gives them pleasure and their lives meaning, are delicately paced to weave a tapestry of experience for the audience. Often presented as tight vignettes or segments, Blank's films unfold to gradually allow the viewer more information on the subject and people at hand. The subject matter, often quirky and outside of mainstream American experiences, are engaging and gratifying to observe. Blank uses a delicate hand to unfold stories of commitment to craft and community, often intercutting snatches of informal conversations, relaxed interviews, imbedded and privileged observational footage, and occasional hand-lettered explanations and subtitles. As a filmmaker, Les Blank appears to be at ease in every situation he documents and with every person he engages. He allows them to demonstrate and discuss their cultural nuances with dedication and passion, rarely seeming sentimental or patronizing. His shooting and editorial styles are as earthy and dedicated as the subjects he explores, and his films are noted for their devotion to vision and independence.

C. MELINDA LEVIN

See also: Del Mero Corazón

Biography

Born November 27, 1935, in Tampa, Florida. Received a BA in English literature and an MFA in theater from Tulane University. Studied in the PhD film program at the University of Southern California. Awarded the American Film Institute's Maya Deren Award for outstanding lifetime achievement as an independent filmmaker in 1990.

Selected films

1960 Running Around like a Chicken with its Head Cut Off
1965 Dizzie Gillespie
1968 God Respects us when we Work, but Loves us when we Dance
1969 The Sun's Gonna Shine
1969 The Blues Accordin' to Lightnin' Hopkins
1970 Chicken Real
1971 A Well Spent Life
1971 Spend it All
1973 Dry Wood
1973 Hot Pepper
1976 Chulas Fronteras
1978 Always for Pleasure
1979 Del mero corazon
1980 Werner Herzog Eats his Shoe
1980 Garlic is as Good as Ten Mothers
1982 Burden of Dreams
1983 Sprout Wings and Fly

1984 In Heaven there is No Beer?
1985 Cigarette Blues
1986 Huey Lewis and the News: Be-FORE!
1987 Ziveli! Medicine for the Heart
1987 Gap-Toothed Women
1988 Ry Cooder and the Moula Banda Rhythm Aces: Let's Have a Ball
1989 J'ai ete au bal
1990 Yum, Yum, Yum! A Taste of Cajun and Creole Cooking
1991 Christopher Tree
1991 Julie: Old Time Tales of the Blue Ridge
1991 Marc and Ann
1991 Puamana
1995 Sworn to the Drum: A Tribute to Francisco Aguabella
1995 Maestro: King of the Cowboy Artists
1995 My Old Fiddle: A Visit with Tommy Jarrell in the Blue Ridge

Blue Eyed

(Germany, Verhaag, 1996)

Blue Eyed was selected as one of the outstanding documentaries of 1996 by the Academy of Motion Pictures. The film is centered on Jane Elliot, who has committed herself to fighting prejudice, ignorance, and racism in society after the assassination of Martin Luther King in 1968. Elliot, a former teacher, offers a special training course, in which she divides people on the basis of two arbitrary physical properties: blue or brown eyes. She declares the latter to be better and more intelligent and grants them privileges that she denies to the blue-eyed, who are deemed to be inferior and less intelligent. When she started this workshop in her school, all the members of her family were aggressively attacked by their white fellow citizens and their restaurant had to close.

At the beginning of the experiment, the blue-eyed people are marked with a green collar around their necks. These seventeen candidates are sent to a small, overheated room with only three seats. They have to wait a long time for their appearance in the workshop and do not really know what will happen. The brown-eyed participants are encouraged to consider themselves special, and to treat the blue-eyed contemptuously. For the first time, many white people become acquainted with the feeling of belonging to a condemned group that can never win. They experience the feeling of being discriminated against, in the same way that society today discriminates against women, people of a different color, homosexuals, or the disabled.

The film documents this workshop with three observing cameras. They keep close to the protagonists, creating a sense of discomfort and tension for the viewer. There are only short breaks with typical images from America, beautiful shots that are accompanied by a jazz sound track, giving an impression of the atmosphere of the American middle class. The film was shot with a budget of $200,000, and the crew shot seventy hours of Digi-Beta material. The final film was than transferred to 35mm. The director, Bertram Verhaag, shows how the group dynamics work and why nobody among the blue-eyed can resist the mechanisms of suppression. The film shows the core of racism: power and its use against the weak or disenfranchised.

As film critic Thomas Klingenmaier wrote: 'It won't help much to be prepared to face Jane Elliot. This elderly woman will tear down any shield. Even we, the spectators of Blue Eyed, can't get rid of this feeling of uneasiness, embarrassment, anxiety and utterly helpless hatred when she starts putting people down, humiliating them, deriding them, incapacitating them. No doubt about this: for three quarters of the time in this documentation Jane Elliot is the meanest, the lowest, the most detestable, the most hypocritical human being hell has ever spit back on Earth. But she should be an example for all of us.'

KAY HOFFMANN

Blue Eyed (Germany, 1996, 90 mins). Directed by Bertram Verhaag, in cooperation with Jane Elliot. Produced by Denkmalfilm Ltd, in coproduction with: WDR, 3SAT, BR. Production Manager: Alon Gilk. Director of Photography: Waldemar Hauschild. Additional cameras: Hans-Albrecht Lusznat and Glenn Eddins. Camera Assistant: Christina Schultz. Edited by Uwe Klimmeck. Music by Wolfgang Neumann. Sound by Zoltan Ravasz, with Bopp King and Joe Thoennes.

Further reading

Kleber, Reinhard, 'Wenn er läuft, dann schlägt er ein', in *Filmecho/Filmwoche*, 1997: 34.

Klingenmaier, Thomas, 'Blaue Augen, weiche Hirne', in *Stuttgarter Zeitung* 16, 1997: 1.
Platthaus, Andreas, 'Blaue Augen, schwarze Hände', in *Frankfurter Allgemeine Zeitung* 6, 1997: 6.
Weidinger, Birgit, 'Blauäugige sind blöd', in *Süddeutsche Zeitung* 29–30, 1997: 11.
Wolf, Fritz, 'Denn ich bin eine Weiße', in *Epd Medien* 18 January 1997.

Bond, Ralph

Ralph Bond's talent as a filmmaker was limited, but his political activism and organisational abilities have clearly left a mark on British documentary. Having worked in the insurance business, Bond, a young communist, started a career in politics in 1927 as the secretary of the National Left Wing Movement. In 1929 the new communist political line favouring the development of an independent proletarian culture offered Bond the chance of organising the cinema side of it. Following the examples of Germany (Volksfilmverband) and France (Les Amis de Spartacus), he set out to establish a workers' film movement to give working-class audiences access to Soviet and other films of artistic and political merit. Like its 'bourgeois' counterpart, the Film Society, and its political rival, the Masses Stage and Film Guild (controlled by the Independent Labour Party), the workers' film movement used the legal and organisational form of the private society to get around censorship measures. The London Workers' Film Society, the flagship of the UK-wide Federation of Workers' Film Societies (FOWFS), was the first to start its activities in November 1929. Writing in periodicals as far apart as the cinephile *Close-Up*, the Communist Party-controlled *Daily Worker* and the movement's own *Workers' Cinema*, Bond acted as a tireless propagandist for the cause.

As a manager of the Atlas Film Co., which imported films from Germany and the Soviet Union for FOWFS member societies, he also embarked on an ambitious production programme.

With limited means, Atlas produced three issues of the newsreel Workers' Topical News (1930–1), a compilation film Glimpses of Modern Russia (1930) and a twenty-minute film to support the Workers' Charter Campaign, entitled The Charter Film (1931). By the end of that year, however, the supply of new Soviet films dried up as a result of the coming of sound, and Atlas was on the verge of bankruptcy. Bond was happy to accept an invitation from John Grierson, who had occasionally helped out Atlas, to join his Empire Marketing Board (EMB) Film Unit.

Working as production and studio manager at the EMB Film Unit, Bond earned the respect of his colleagues for his knowledge of Marxism, which in the eyes of many in the documentary movement offered the only viable political alternative to the crisis-ridden capitalist system. Bond, on the other hand, completely endorsed the social realism of the documentary movement, 'the drama of the doorstep' as he coined it later, and respected Grierson as 'a man of extraordinary talent'. Bond had the chance to direct a few documentaries at the General Post Office (GPO) Film Unit, successor to the EMB Film Unit, and then moved on to Strand Films. In Today we Live (1937) he was able to show his views on the plight of the unemployed. Commissioned by the National Council for Social Service, the film was codirected by John Grierson's sister, Ruby. Her location was a seemingly picturesque Cotswold village, but Bond chose the bleak coal mining village of Pentre in South Wales. This visit resulted among others in the archetypical depression years sequence of unemployed miners looking for coal on the Tylorstown slagheap, shot by Bond's assistant, Donald Alexander. From 1938 Bond was given the chance to make a series of short films demonstrating the virtues of cooperation, as part of a 'five-year plan' of the big London Cooperative Societies. The first, Advance, Democracy! (1938) was directed by Bond himself, with a musical score by Benjamin Britten. It showed how a London crane driver and his wife, a staunch member of the Women's Co-operative Guild, start taking an interest in the political situation and join the May Day demonstration. Like most of his colleagues, Bond was busy making documentaries for the Ministry of Information during the war.

A committed trade unionist (he was an active member of the Association of Cinematograph and Allied Technicians (ACT) from 1935 onwards, serving as vice-president from 1942 to 1974), Bond welcomed the fact that at the end of the war some unions were finally showing an interest in having their own films. For the Amalgamated Engineering Union (AEU), he directed Unity is Strength (1945), and he acted as producer for A Power in the Land (1946), commissioned by the Electrical Trades Union. In 1950 the ACT started its own production company, ACT Films Ltd, with Bond serving as its general manager. With the financial support of the National Film Finance Corporation, ACT Films managed in the 1950s and 1960s to produce more than a dozen feature films, thus helping film technicians who were out of work with temporary employment. To Bond's personal regret, however, it was not until 1970 that a trade union—once more the AEU—would commission ACT Films to make a film. Bond, by now retired as general manager from ACT Films, acted as production controller for what was a rather disappointing documentary directed by Robert Kitts, We are the Engineers.

As a delegate of the ACT (from 1958 ACTT, when an extra T for Television was added), Bond attended the annual Trades Union Congress (TUC) without fail. In 1960 he successfully moved a resolution that called for 'a greater participation by the Trade Union movement in all cultural activities'. It prompted playwright Arnold Wesker to establish Centre 42 (referring to the number of the resolution), which, for lack of financial support, did not become the success that Bond had envisaged. Likewise the recommendations of a TUC Working Party on the Arts (1975–6), of which Bond was a prominent member, failed to make an impact.

In the 1970s Bond became Documentary Course Director and Lecturer at the London International Film School, enabling him to pass on his experiences to a younger generation. Bond witnessed the reemergence of a left-wing film culture in Britain in the same decade with a certain detachment, always willing to share his recollections, but unrelenting when it came down to what he considered basic trade union principles.

BERT HOGENKAMP

Biography

Born in London, December 5, 1906. Educated at the Tottenham Grammar School. Secretary of the National Left Wing Movement, 1927–9. Manager of Atlas Film Co., 1929–31. Joined the EMB Film Unit in 1931. Joined Strand Films in 1936 and Realist Film Unit 1938. Member of the Association of Cinematograph and Allied Technicians 1935, elected to the ACT Executive Committee in 1936, vice-president of the ACT 1942–74. Founding member of the World Union of Documentary, Brussels 1947. Founding director of ACT Films Ltd, 1950. Director of Bond Films, 1951–c. 1954. Moved Resolution 42 at the 1960 Trades Union Congress. Documentary Course Director and Lecturer at the London International Film School. Died in Torbay, May 29, 1989.

Selected films

1930–1	Workers' Topical News nos. 1–3: director
1931	The Charter Film: director
1937	Today We Live: director (with Ruby Grierson)
1938	Advance, Democracy!: director
1939	People with a Purpose: director
1940	Neighbours under Fire: director
1945	Unity is Strength: director
1945	Today and Tomorrow: producer
1946	A Power in the Land: producer
1970	We are the Engineers: production controller

Further reading

Bond, Ralph, 'Cinema in the Thirties: Documentary Film and the Labour Movement', in Jon Clark, Margot Heinemann and Carole Snee (eds), *Culture and Crisis in Britain in the Thirties*, London: Lawrence and Wishart, 1979.

Hogenkamp, Bert, *Deadly Parallels. Film and the Left in Britain, 1929–39*, London: Lawrence and Wishart, 1986.

——'Today We Live: The Making of a Documentary in a Welsh Mining Valley', *Llafur. Journal of Welsh Labour History* 5, 1, 1988: 45–52.

——*Film, Television and the Left in Britain, 1950–70*, London: Lawrence and Wishart, 2000.

MacPherson, Don (ed.), *Traditions of Independence. British Cinema in the Thirties*, London: BFI, 1980.

Orbanz, Eva, *Journey to a Legend and Back*, Berlin: Edition Volker Spiess, 1977.

Bossak, Jerzy

Jerzy Bossak, a teacher, filmmaker, and journalist, was one of the most important and influential figures in post-World War II Polish cinema. He has often been called, in fact, the 'father' of Polish documentary filmmaking. He was instrumental in organizing the film company Start, a company founded on the following philosophy of cinematography: filmmaking should be as free as possible from commercial constraints and corporate demands, and filmmakers should understand their work not only as art, but as useful art. This pragmatic notion of usefulness went hand-in-hand with the notion of action: Bossak argued that film, documentary film in particular, should work to raise its viewers' social consciousness and inspire them to act, to make changes in their society. Such thinking was at the center of Bossak's philosophy of documentary filmmaking. He was critical of the film industry before the war, observing that, 'In prewar Poland there were no good films, not just because there was no difference between the maker of films and the maker of artificial jewelry, but also because we did not know how to make films and look at them[...] Today we have to create conditions in which Polish film can flourish' (Haltof 2002). Bossak's company, Start, was successful in altering the industry and in many ways instituting his fresh philosophy of cinematography.

Bossak's theory of documentary filmmaking is derived in part from the Aristotelian approach to persuasion, which involves the three rhetorical appeals of logos (logical argument, an appeal to reason), pathos (pathetic argument, an appeal to the emotions), and ethos (the way in which writers, or director, situate their characters and present their work). Bossak felt that, for the most part, English and American documentary film focused far too much (or even entirely) on logical or reasoned presentations, on attempting to present just the 'facts'. Together with logical appeals, Bossak also played to his audiences' 'heart strings', or to their emotions, in an attempt to move them to action; both reasoned persuasion and emotional appeal, he espoused, were necessary. Also necessary in this equation was the way in which the filmmaker presented, organized, and interpreted the material. The 'authors' of any film presented themselves through the film by the way in which the chosen material was arranged. That is, the way in which logical and emotional footage were arranged by the filmmaker (the way the filmmaker set out his ethos) went a long way to whether an audience might be persuaded to act.

Underlying much of Bossak's work was an interest not only in war but in the tenuous relationship that existed between the government and the general population. He attempted to break away from the typical nationalistic propaganda films that both dominated the industry and disseminated what Bossak saw as untrue messages operating to pacify the masses. Warszawa 1956, by many accounts one of his best films, is a good example of his attempt to critique the government. Completed in 1956, this film juxtaposes modern, towering, clean government buildings with the run-down, filthy tenement buildings in which the masses were forced to live. Warszawa 1956 was one of the first films of the 'Black Series' of documentary film, a term attributed to the cinematography of Kazimierz Karabasz, which depicted the stark, everyday harsh realities of living under a socialist state. As part of such a cinematic approach, Bossak chose to focus on single, simple events, or on specific people and their individual realities to try and extract some fundamental, universal truths that apply to all humans. Such an inductive move—moving from a specific premise (or focus) to a more general conclusion—can be seen in many of his films, particularly Deluge (an award-winning film from 1947 depicting the catastrophic flooding of the Wistula river) and Requiem for 500,000 (an award-winning film from 1963 depicting a montage of German propaganda footage from the Warsaw ghetto).

In working from specific events to more universal conclusions, Bossak's films often took on an epic aura; in fact, Bossak saw himself in some regard as an epic historian. It was this epic element of his filmmaking, however, that drew some criticism of his work. Several critics noted that the political and human issues he attempted to address were so large that the specific person or place from which he started often got lost (in asserting such a claim, critics have pointed, for instance, to Bossak's film 273 Degrees below Zero). In the same vein, others have argued that the overarching conclusions he attempted to reach necessarily dictated that he oversimplify the issues at hand. Such criticism notwithstanding, however, Jerzy Bossak remains one of the most respected and influential filmmakers in the history of Polish cinematography.

JOE WAGNER

See also: Poland

Biography

Born in Rostow in 1910. Studied law and philosophy at Warsaw University. Worked as a film critic for several newspapers and was instrumental in forming the film companies Start and Kamera. Fought as an officer during World War II in the Soviet Union and returned to Poland to serve as the senior editor of *Polish Film Chronicles* and programme director of Polish Film from 1944–9. Served as the dean of the department of film directing in Lodz from 1956 to 1968, and then from 1987 to 1989. Received numerous awards for his filmmaking, including at Cannes, and several lifetime achievement awards including one from the Ministry of Art and Culture in 1978. Died in Warsaw, 1989.

Selected films

1944 Majdenek: Cemetery of Europe
1947 Deluge
1954 Return to Old Town
1956 Warszawa
1963 Requiem for 500,000
1967 Document of War
1985 Impressario

Further reading

Avisar, Ilan, *Screening the Holocaust: Cinema's Images of the Unimaginable*, Bloomington, IN: Indiana University Press, 1988.

Bren, Frank, *World Cinema 1: Poland, London*, Flicks Books, 1986.

Fuksiewicz, Jacek, *Film and Television in Poland*, Warsaw: Interpress, 1976.

Haltof, Marek, *Polish National Cinema*, New York: Berghahn Books, 2002.

——'Film Theory in Poland Before World War II', *Canadian Slavonic Papers* 40, 1–2, 1998: 67–78.

Sobanski, Oskar, *Polish Feature Films: A Reference Guide 1945–85*, West Cornwall, CT: Locust Hill P, 1987.

Whyte, Alistair, *New Cinema in Eastern Europe*, New York: Dutton, 1971.

Böttcher, Jürgen

Jürgen Böttcher is a documentary film director from eastern Germany. Initially a painter, Böttcher turned to film, regarding it as a medium more in keeping with reality: 'documentary film, the way I understand it, is one of the most magic forms of art, the invocation of the entire and indeed real' (Böttcher 1989: 5). The influence of the filmmaker's background in painting is clear. In his films, Böttcher has repeatedly examined artists and their work. Moreover, he attempts to mimic the compositional methods and attributes of visual art in his films. He constructs precise and atmospheric settings, mostly in black and white, shot on 35mm film. Böttcher belongs to 'GDR's true avant-garde' (Roth 1984), a paradox in a political system that did not tolerate subversive artistic expression.

From 1961 until its dissolution in 1991, Böttcher was a documentary director at the state's DEFA-Studio, shooting short films for the cinema program. His first film for DEFA, Three of Many (1961), is an homage to three friends, all workers and artists. Böttcher shows the young men in their spare time, painting or relaxing. In their shabby apartments, they do not act as exemplary representatives of their class. Three of Many was censored by the government and had its first public screening only in 1988, at the Edinburgh Film Festival.

With Furnace Builders (1962), about an ironworks factory, Böttcher found his subject. The primary focus of his work thereafter was the lives of the working class. Furnace Builders follows workers as they attempt to move a fifty-six meter-high, two thousand-ton furnace roughly eighteen miles. The film depicts the precise mechanics of the work and conveys a belief in the power of the workers to achieve their goal, while assiduously avoiding sentimentality.

In Stars (1963), which follows a group of women working in a Berlin lightbulb factory, Böttcher attempted for the first time to record synchronous dialogue. The filmmaker was unable to procure a low-noise camera for shooting the film, as none were available in Berlin at the time. Therefore, the cameraman wrapped covers around the Arriflex to soften the sound it made while in operation. The words of the women themselves form the heart of the film, although they were impeded by both the poor sound technology and censorship.

Böttcher again focused on the plight of working women in Washerwomen (1972). The film follows apprentice washerwomen at a large laundry. Although their work is dull, Böttcher does not look at them condescendingly. Instead, he allows these young women to articulate their work and their lives, and they appear honest and confident.

Böttcher eventually pared down narration and dialogue in his films, protesting at 'the inflation of language'. The highlight of this evolution is Rangierer (1984), a lyrical black-and-white movie, shot in winter in the freight depot in Dresden. The switchers at the depot carry out their difficult and dangerous work, focused and silent. The low sounds of the ghostly rolling wagons, the screech of the shocks, the hollow loudspeaker announcements, and the few words the workers speak to one another make up the aural aspect of the film.

In Georgia (1987), Böttcher's first full-length feature motion picture, marks the first occasion on which he was allowed to direct in a foreign country. The film is a document of a trip through a land with an ancient culture and living traditions.

Böttcher directed The Wall (1990) in November and December of 1989 near the Brandenburg Gate, Berlin. It documents without commentary, making use of long, silent shots, the activities of people at the Berlin Wall in the days after its opening. The director sees the Berlin Wall, the symbol of the German division, as a document on which history has written itself. Historical images of the Brandenburg Gate are projected on a huge, painted area, including scenes of Prussian military parades, Nazi torch processions, Hitler in an open car, soldiers of the Red Army raising the Soviet flag, men starving during wartime, and the construction of the wall.

Böttcher stopped making films for ten years, instead working as a visual artist. In 2001 he returned to filmmaking with Konzert im Freien/A Place in Berlin. In this experimental documentary, Böttcher examines the shifting meanings of the Marx-Engels-Forum in Berlin, a large monument of the East German era. He presents footage of the monument's construction, which he shot in the 1980s, in new and unexpected ways.

BRITTA HARTMANN

Biography

Born July 8, 1931 in Frankenberg/Sachsen (Germany) and raised in the small village of Strawahlde in Oberlausitz. Studied at the Academy of Formative Arts in Dresden (GDR), 1949–53. From 1953 until 1955 self-employed artist and lecturer at the Volkshochschule. In 1965 took a directing course at the newly opened German College for Cinematic Art (today College for Film and Television 'Konrad Wolf') in Potsdam-Babelsberg, which ended 1960. Worked from 1961 to 1991 as a director of documentaries for DEFA. In 1989 became a member of the Academy of Arts Berlin (West). After the reunification of the two German states in 1990 and the dissolution of DEFA in 1991, worked as an artist. Works were shown in exhibitions in Berlin, Paris, Salzburg, Toronto, Brussels, Toulouse, Chicago, and New York, and retrospectives of his films could be seen in Paris, Edinburgh, Frankfurt am Main, Munich, Berlin, Bologna, and Leipzig. Received the European Award for Film for The Wall. The Festival for Documentary and Animation Film from Leipzig awarded him the 'Goldenen Taube' (The Golden Pigeon) in 2000. Lives in Berlin.

Selected films

1960	Notwendige Lehrjahre/Necessary Years of Apprenticeship (25 mins, Diploma film): writer, director
1961/1988	Drei von vielen/Three of Many (33 mins, forbidden, staged 1988): writer, director
1962	Im Pergamonmuseum/In the Pergamon Museum (19 mins): writer, director
1962	Ofenbauer/Furnace Builders (15 mins): writer, director
1963	Stars (20 mins): writer, director
1964	Barfuß und ohne Hut/Barefoot and without a Hat (26 mins): writer, director
1966/1990	Jahrgang 45/Born in '45 (94 mins, fiction, forbidden; made available and first performed 1990): cowriter, director
1967	Der Sekretär/The Secretary (29 mins): writer, director
1968	Ein Vertrauensmann/A Shop Steward (19 mins): writer, director
1969	Arbeiterfamilie/A Working-class Family (31 mins): writer, director
1970	Dialog mit Lenin/Dialogue with Lenin (32 mins): writer, director
1971	Song International (45 mins): writer, director
1972	Wäscherinnen/Washerwomen (23 mins): cowriter, director
1974	Erinnere dich mit Liebe und Haß/ Remember with Love and Hate (40 mins): cowriter, codirector

1977 Ein Weimarfilm/A Weimar Film (69 mins): writer, director
Im Lohmgrund/In the Loamy Soil (27 mins): writer, director
1978 Martha (56 mins/abridged version 46 mins): writer, director
1981 Experimental film—Triptychon: Potters Stier, Venus nach Giorgione, Frau am Klavichord/Experimental Film—Triptych: Potter's Bull, Venus According to Giorgione, Woman at the Clavichord (16 mins, 21 mins, 17 mins): writer, director
1983 Drei Lieder/Three Songs (28 mins): writer, director
1984 Rangierer/Shunters (22 mins; reconstructed long version, first performed 2000: 45 mins): cowriter, director
1985 Kurzer Besuch bei Hermann Glöckner/Short Visit to Hermann Glöckner (32 mins): writer, director
1986 Die Küche/The Kitchen (42 mins): cowriter, director
1987 In Georgien/In Georgia (107 mins): writer, director
1990 Die Mauer/The Wall (99 mins): cowriter, director
2001 Konzert im Freien/A Place in Berlin (88 mins): writer, director

Further reading

Böttcher, Jürgen, 'Zu meinem Film Stars', in Hermann Herlinghaus (ed.), *Dokumentaristen der Welt in den Kämpfen unserer Zeit. Selbstzeugnisse aus zwei Jahrzehnten (1960–81)*, Berlin: Henschelverlag Kunst und Gesellschaft, 1982: 408–16.

——'Die Wahrheit des Märchens ist unerhört gültig', in Akademie der Künste Berlin (ed.), *Abenteuer Wirklichkeit. Dokumentarfilmer in Deutschland*, Abteilung Film und Medienkunst und Aktuelle Presse ZDF/3sat. Berlin, 1989: 5.

Brinckmann, Christine Noll, 'Experimentalfilm, 1920–90', in Wolfgang Jacobsen, Anton Kaes and Hans Helmut Prinzler (eds), *Geschichte des deutschen Films*, Stuttgart and Weimar: Metzler, 1993: 417–50.

Jordan, Günter, 'Schatten vergangener Ahnen. Bilder aus der Arbeitswelt: die 60er und 70er Jahre', in Peter Zimmermann and Gebhard Moldenhauer (eds), *Der geteilte Himmel. Arbeit, Alltag und Geschichte im ost und westdeutschen Film*, Konstanz: UVK Medien, 2000: 103–31.

Kilborn, Richard, 'The Documentary Work of Jürgen Böttcher: A Retrospective', in Seán Allan and John Sandford (eds), *DEFA. East German Cinema, 1946–92*, New York and Oxford: Berghahn Books, 1999: 267–82.

n.a., 'Filme von Jürgen Böttcher: Die Küche (1986), Im Lohmgrund (1976), Frau am Klavichord (1980/81)', 17, 1979.

n.a., *Internationales Forum des Jungen Films*, programme notes and transcripts of interviews, Berlin 1987.

Schwarzweiß und Farbe (ed.), *Filmuseum Potsdam*, DEFA-Dokumentarfilme, 1946–92.

n.a., *Red, Günter Jordan and Ralf Schenk*, Berlin and Potsdam: Jovis/Filmmuseum Potsdam, 1996.

n.a., *Strawalde (Jürgen Böttcher)—Maler und Filmregisseur*, Berlin: Berliner Festspiele, 1990.

n.a., *Wenn die Begegnung das Ereignis ist … Filme von Jürgen Böttcher*, Bundesarchiv-Filmarchiv Berlin (ed.), *Programmheft zur Retrospektive des Bundesarchiv-Filmarchivs während des 43. Internationalen Leipziger Festivals für Dokumentar-und Animations-film*, 2000.

Prinzler, Hans Helmut, 'Babelsberger Elegie. Frank Beyer, Jürgen Böttcher und Erika Richter im Gespräch mit Hans Helmut Prinzler', *Filmgeschichte*, Nr. 16, 17, 2002: 57–64.

Progress Film-Verleih (ed.), *Dokumentaristen der DEFA und ihre Filme*, Berlin (GDR), o.J. 1979: 4–13.

Richter, Rolf, ' … vom Leben der Arbeiter Bericht geben', interview, *Film und Fernsehen*, Nr. 11, November 1974: 20–7.

Roth, Wilhelm, 'Jürgen Böttcher—Dokumentarfilmregisseur', Hans-Michael Bock (ed.), *Cinegraph: Lexikon zum deutschsprachigen Film*, München: Text und Kritik, 1984, Lieferung, 17.

Schenk, Ralf, 'Erinnere dich mit Liebe und Hass. Zum 70. Geburtstag des Dokumentaristen Jürgen Böttcher', *Film-Dienst* 54,14, 2001: 8–11.

Voss, Gabriele (ed.), *Dokumentarisch arbeiten. Jürgen Böttcher […] im Gespräch mit Christoph Hübner*, Berlin: Vorwerk 8, 1996: 10–27.

Wetzel, Kraft, 'Jürgen Böttcher: Eine Karriere im Arbeiterund Bauern-Staat', in Akademie der Künste Berlin (ed.), *Abenteuer Wirklichkeit. Dokumentarfilmer in Deutschland*, Abteilung Film- und Medienkunst und Aktuelle Presse ZDF/3sat. Berlin, 1989: 6–18.

——(ed.), *Jürgen Böttcher. Films/Filme. 1957–2001*, (German/English), Berlin: Nirwana Edition, 2000.

Boulting, John and Roy

The Boulting brothers were one of the great partnerships in British film. As independent producer-directors, they made a substantial contribution to the national cinema between the 1930s and 1970s, principally with intelligently made commercial feature films. They came to prominence with the wartime Pastor Hall (1940), a thought-provoking and controversial drama about Nazi persecution. Their work in documentary was largely confined to the wartime period, and they participated in a number of important and ambitious productions of the service film units.

Before enlistment, the Boultings produced Dawn Guard (1941) for the Ministry of Information, a short propaganda feature of immense significance. It features two members of the Home Guard on sentry duty discussing peace aims and reconstruction, cut against contrasting images of slums and new housebuilding, dole queues and busy factories, and playgrounds swarming with jolly children. The film stands out as the first cinematic expression of 'New Jerusalemism' and the desire for a better post-war world, and was an early indication of the filmmakers' social views.

For a brief period the brothers served conventionally in the armed forces, Roy as a trooper in the Royal Armoured Corps, and John as a flight mechanic in the RAF. Eventually Roy was redirected to the Army Film and Photographic Unit (AFPU), where he reached the rank of captain, and John to the RAF Film Unit, in time becoming a flight lieutenant. The service film units had been established early in the war to produce record and training films but gradually progressed to more substantial documentaries suitable for commercial release. This was the only sustained period when the brothers worked apart, and in fact they were each given a special period of leave to make the propaganda feature Thunder Rock (1942). With its pronounced interventionist theme, it was deemed an important film to help develop the Anglo-American entente.

Roy was the more prolific of the brothers. With the AFPU based at Pinewood, he contributed to a number of shorts such as Via Persia (1942), Minefield! (1944), and REME (1944). Of much greater consequence was his involvement in the trilogy of Victory documentaries, feature-length records of significant Allied campaigns. These began with Desert Victory (1943), which dealt with the war in the Western Desert and the British breakthrough at El Alamein. The film was compiled from footage shot by service cameramen and augmented by some material staged at Pinewood. Major David MacDonald was in charge of production, but the creative work of editing and direction was the responsibility of Roy Boulting. The production enjoyed support at the highest levels of government, where it was deemed crucial to publicize Britain's first significant success in the field. Released in February 1943, it won great praise and popular acclaim. In America it was surprisingly granted an Academy Award as 'the Most Distinctive Documentary of 1943' and was generally held up as among the best achievements of wartime documentary. The film's distinctive imagery and treatment of the Desert campaign clearly influenced later reconstructions, notably The Way Ahead (1944), Sea of Sand (1958), and The Desert Fox (1951), with the latter film relying heavily on documentary footage taken uncredited from Desert Victory.

Tunisian Victory (1944) and Burma Victory (1945) were similar campaign records, this time detailing the Anglo-American liberations of North Africa and Southeast Asia, respectively. The Tunisian film eventually emerged as a coproduction between the AFPU and the official American filmmaker Frank Capra, who assumed dominance over the production. The collaboration was troubled by tension and rivalry, and Tunisian Victory has fared the least well with critics. The final Victory film was much more securely in the hands of the AFPU and Roy Boulting, as the British and Americans had wisely decided on separate documentaries covering the theatre of operations. The war in Southeast Asia was somewhat secondary to events in Europe, and hence Burma Victory was an important document to publicize and memorialize the conflict. The film effectively brings out the hardships and unpleasantness of the experience, with troops enduring rain, mud, exhaustion, dysentery, and malaria, as well as confronting a fanatical enemy. Each of the Victory films relied heavily on the striking images secured by combat cameramen. They brought an immediacy to war never previously experienced by a cinema-going public, and this has been their considerable legacy. Acclaimed American documentaries of the later war years, such as John Ford's The Battle of Midway (1944), were clearly in their debt.

The RAF Film Unit had been established in 1942 and was also based at Pinewood, meaning that the twins could remain in close contact. John similarly contributed to the routine training and informational films of the unit, such as the short Between Friends (1943). Throughout 1944, however, he was engaged as director on the RAF's principal film production of the war years, Journey Together (1945), a realistic but scripted depiction of pilot trainees. A small role was played by Hollywood star Edward G. Robinson, with the principal British characters being played by the up-and-coming actors Richard Attenborough and Jack Watling. Journey Together used much location shooting, including scenes in the United States, and the film propagandized British-American collaboration. The film was a significant example of the wartime trend in British documentary that blended fictional and factual styles. Each of the Victory films had incorporated small but significant staged scenes shot at Pinewood under the guidance of Roy, and John substantially developed this approach into what was essentially a feature-length treatment. John declared that he was after a 'straightforward public entertainment', and in this sense Journey Together was more in line with developments in realism taking place at commercial studios like Ealing, with such productions as Nine Men (1943), rather than the more austere experiments in documentary fiction being conducted at the Crown Film Unit, especially in the celebrated Western Approaches (1944).

ALAN BURTON

See also: Burma Victory; Desert Victory

Biography

Born identical twins at Bray, Berkshire, England, November 21, 1913. Educated at Reading School, where they formed one of the first film societies in a public school. John joined a small film distribution company in 1933; Roy gained some film experience in Canada. Early in 1937 John volunteered for the Republican forces in the Spanish Civil War. Later in November 1937 the twins formed Charter Films and produced modest films for quota distribution. During World War II, Roy served with the Army Film and Photographic Unit and John with the RAF Film Unit. For three decades after the war the Boultings were important independent producer-directors in British commercial films. John died on June 17, 1985 in Sunningdale, Berkshire, and Roy at his Oxfordshire home on November 5, 2001.

Further reading

Burton, A., O'Sullivan, T. and Wells, P. (eds), *The Family Way: The Boulting Brothers and British Film Culture*, Trowbridge: Flicks Books, 2000.

Chapman, James, *The British At War: Cinema, State and Propaganda, 1939–45*, London: I.B. Tauris, 1998.

Coultass, Clive, *Images for Battle: British Film and the Second World War, 1939–45*, London, AUP, 1989.

Brakhage, Stan

Stan Brakhage, one of the most influential American avant-garde filmmakers of the twentieth century, is not strictly considered a documentary filmmaker. However, his 'lyrical' films, often shot from a first-person perspective, are part of an American artistic culture interested in documenting individual perception and defamiliarizing everyday life (Sitney 1974). For Brakhage, perception is radically subjective; reality is comprehensible only through the implied point of view of the camera. Documentary, then, has an anti-traditional or anti-normative purpose. Instead of using conventional narratives or assuming objectivity, it should take nothing for granted, showing the world as it is experienced from a specific place.

Brakhage's position as an artist who rejects conventional forms to depict his own view of reality comes out of a long tradition of American individualism and rejection of tradition (Elder 1998). During the postwar era existentialist philosophers and abstract expressionist painters also rejected traditional notions of self and tradition, believing that fixed definitions were forms of commodification. For them (and for Brakhage) the only way of relating to the world was through action. The rapid cuts in early films such as Cat's Cradle (1959) and Mothlight (1963) were influenced by Sergei Eisenstein's theories of montage as a tool that documented reality while it created ideas. In Cat's Cradle, for example, the rapid movement between shots of a cat's head, a man and a woman, and the flowers on their bedspread and wallpaper blur the line between man and animal, nature and artifice. The quick cutting also prevents the films from fetishizing the images they present, focusing instead on the movement of vision and ideas.

The dynamic quality and shifting perspective seen in these films are central to his early documentaries. Brakhage was the cameraman for two early documentaries shot under the direction of American surrealist Joseph Cornell. The first film on which they collaborated, The Wonder Ring (1955), was a documentary of Manhattan's last elevated train, shot just before the city closed it down. Rather than an objective presentation of the El's history, Brakhage offers a silent and mobile first-person depiction of a typical ride on the train. The film starts with squares of light falling through the El tracks to the pavement below and an ascent to the El platform that repeats the abstract rectangular patterns. Throughout the film, the city flows past, occasionally focusing on a picturesque sight in a dialectic that echoes the train's stopping and going. People are on the train with our stand-in viewer, but they are mostly seen reflected in windows, glimpsed through the door into the next car, or framed off-center. The focus of this film is vision itself, as epitomized by the film's last shot. The focus on what's seen through a train window becomes more and more blurry until the focus is on the dusty and scratched glass itself.

The idea of defamiliarization is important to early twentieth-century avant-garde artists like Marcel Duchamp and Phillip Glass, who took everyday objects and sounds out of context to transform them into art and music. Like The Wonder Ring, most of Brakhage's films contain many close-ups that defamiliarize the objects being shown in order to explore how vision makes sense of the world when it is not mediated by language or convention. Language was social and, he believed, eliminated the personal perceptions of the world; Brakhage felt that the raw experience of the physical unmediated by structure is the only authentic way to know the world. In his early manifesto, *Metaphors on Vision*, he asks his readers to 'Imagine [...] an eye which does not respond to the name of everything but which must know each object encountered in life through an adventure of perception. How many colors are there in a field of grass to the crawling baby unaware of "Green"?' (Brakhage 1976).

The final, and perhaps most important, influence on Stan Brakhage is Gertrude Stein. Stein shares this use naive perspective of reality as a means of redefining it; her book *Tender Buttons* repeats simple words and phrases from daily life in various permutations that do not have conventional linguistic meaning but instead offer a combination of sound and intuitive sense. Brakhage uses repetition in a similar way in his films, both to imbue the images with new meaning in each context and to rid them of their conventional metaphorical associations. In Window Water Baby Moving (1962), his first film depicting his wife's pregnancy and childbirth, Brakhage repeats shots of his wife's pregnant stomach as seen in the film's first scene, where she sits in the bathtub kissing and embracing him. When this scene repeats in the middle of a sequence graphically depicting her giving birth, it serves both as a flashback to more peaceful times and an assertion that both states of being depict the body as sexual and natural.

Brakhage's interest in the body is another way in which he attempted to document the prelinguistic experience of reality. The struggles of humanity against the natural world are most evident in his quasi-mythic epic film cycle called Dog Man Star, but he also attempted to connect the mythic with documenting everyday physical reality in his work. One grant proposal described a project he wished to pursue, which he called a 'dailiness film'; through this film, he wished to document his and his family's daily life as it allegorically represented principles of creation in the natural world:

> our coming to life in the morning would also be visualized as the creation of the world; that sun which streaks our room with light still being the explosive source of life, drying our eyes (or rather the photography through rippled glass) as we emerge from the waters of sleep. The very sheets we push away from us in arising would photographically relate to the thaw of the glaciers.
>
> (Brakhage 1976)

With the films of his wife in childbirth and this unproduced mythical documentary, Brakhage moved beyond depiction of the subjective and into universal realities. In his lyrical and mythical work Brakhage uses the documentary form to alter people's perceptions of reality by defamiliarizing either sight itself or the context in which the sight makes sense. Later films take this even further, moving into the abstraction of hand-painted colors and swirls of light.

SUNNY STALTER

Biography

Born in Kansas City, Missouri, January 14, 1933. Attended Dartmouth College in 1951, dropped out, and attended the Institute of Fine Arts in San Francisco in 1953. Met Joseph Cornell in 1955 and shot several films with him. Married Jane Collom in 1957 and had five children with her. Taught at the School of the Art

Institute of Chicago in the 1970s, later at the University of Colorado, Boulder. Received American Film Institute award for independent film and video in 1986. Divorced Jane Collum in 1987. Married Marilyn Jull in 1989 and had two children with her. Died March 9, 2003.

Selected filmography

1955 The Wonder Ring: cinematographer
1955 Centuries of June: cinematographer
1959 Cat's Cradle: director
1962 Window Water Baby Moving: director
1963 Mothlight: director
1968 Lovemaking: director

Further reading

Barrett, Gerald R., *Stan Brakhage: A Guide to References and Resources*, Boston, MA: G.K. Hall, 1983.

Brakhage, Stan, *Essential Brakhage: Selected Writings on Filmmaking*, ed. Bruce R. McPherson, Kingston, NY: Documentext/McPherson, 2001.

——*Metaphors on Vision*, ed. P. Adams Sitney, Film Culture, 1976.

Elder, R. Bruce, *The Films of Stan Brakhage in the American Tradition of Ezra Pound, Gertrude Stein, and Charles Olson*, Waterloo, Ontario: Wilfrid Laurier University Press, 1998.

Keller, Marjorie, *The Untutored Eye: Childhood in the Films of Cocteau, Cornell, and Brakhage*, Rutherford, NJ: Fairleigh Dickinson University Press, 1986.

Sitney, P. Adams, *Visionary Film: The American Avant-Garde*, New York: Oxford University Press, 1974.

Brault, Michel

Although Michel Brault has directed a number of important documentaries, his first passion was photography, and it is as a cinematographer rather than as a film director per se that he has had the most influence on Québec cinema. His achievements as director of photography greatly influenced the look of both documentary and narrative cinema in Québec in the 1960s and 1970s, as he shot some of the most significant works of the period, from his own and Pierre Perrault's Pour la suite du monde (1963), Claude Jutra's A tout prendre (1963), Mon oncle Antoine (1971), and Kamouraska (1973), to Anne Claire Poirier's Mourir à tue-tête (1979) and Francis Mankiewicz's Le temps d'une chasse (1972) and Les bons débarras (1980). His contribution to the imaging of 'la Nation québécoise' on screen has been crucial.

In 1957–8 he worked on the Candid Eye series, developed by the Anglophone filmmakers of the National Film Board of Canada's (NFB's) renowned Unit B, which used recently developed lighter film equipment to capture people in everyday situations with spontaneity and free from judgmental commentary. After shooting the milestone Candid Eye film The Days Before Christmas (1958, Terence Macartney-Filgate, Stanley Jackson and Wolf Koenig), Brault codirected with Gilles Groulx Les raquetteurs/The Snowshoers (1958), about a congress of snowshoeing clubs in Sherbrooke (Québec). Both in its form and its content, this film marked a turning point in Québec documentary. Unlike the Candid Eye films, which sought to observe everyday activities from a distance, Les Raquetteurs attempted to show the event from within. The film's innovative visual style resulted from Brault's use of a handheld camera equipped with a wide-angle lens to shoot the subjects up close. He walked among the 'snowshoers' and their entourage, capturing with immediacy their conversations and interactions.

On the eve of the Quiet Revolution—the period of liberalization and modernization that began in 1960 and saw the emergence of Québec's separatist movement—Les Raquetteurs was hailed as a sort of manifesto for cinéma direct, a home-grown film practice that could depict real people and their everyday concerns. Brault has always insisted that Les Raquetteurs itself is not actually an instance of cinéma direct, but it did trigger the movement, as subsequent NFB documentaries tried to reproduce its style and nationalist purpose in, for example, La lutte/ Wrestling (1961, Brault, Marcel Carrière, Claude Fournier, and Claude Jutra) and Québec-USA ou l'invasion pacifique/Visit to a Foreign Country (1962, Brault, Jutra). Les raquetteurs also had an impact beyond the frontiers of Québec. A screening at the Flaherty Seminar in 1959 inspired Jean Rouch to develop his conception of cinéma vérité and led him to invite Brault to film Chronique d'un été/ Chronicle of a Summer (1961) and La Punition/ Punishment (1963) in France.

While Brault and Groulx's Les Raquetteurs announced the emergence of cinéma direct, Brault's first feature-length documentary, Pour la suite du monde/For the Continuation of the

World (1963), which he codirected with Pierre Perrault, marked the culmination of the movement. In this film, Brault and Perrault follow the habitants of a small island in the St Lawrence River, Île-aux-Coudres, as they attempted to revive the traditional hunt of the beluga whale. Acclaimed both in Canada and abroad, especially in France, Pour la suite du monde owes its success to two fundamental aspects of direct cinema. First, Brault's cinematography, which is equally sensitive to the beauty of the island's landscape as to the weathered faces of old fishermen and the bewildered expressions of the young people who have no knowledge of the practice that their parents are trying to rediscover, and second, a profound respect for the subjects, based on a trusting relationship established before filming.

Brault transposed this documentary practice to fiction, first in Entre la mer et l'eau douce/Drifting Upstream (1967), a fictionalized depiction of the life and career of the film's main actor, Claude Gauthier (the title of this film actually comes from a quote in Pour la suite du monde taken from Jacques Cartier's diaries), and later in Les ordres/The Orders (1974), on the effects of the War Measures Act decreed during the hostage crisis of October 1970. Brault interviewed dozens of innocent people incarcerated as a result of the sweeping powers that the Act gave the police and created fictional characters to reenact the humiliating experiences of those imprisoned. Brault's ability to put the techniques of direct cinema at the service of narrative film earned him the best director award at the Cannes Film Festival in 1975. He remains the only Canadian cineaste to have received this honor.

From 1974 to 1980 Brault produced and directed, with André Gladu, an ambitious series of documentaries entitled Le son des français d'Amérique devoted to the various manifestations of francophone cultures throughout North America. He had already examined the question of French Canadian culture outside Québec in L'Acadie, l'Acadie?!?/Acadia, Acadia?!? (1971), codirected with Pierre Perrault and Éloge du chiac/Praise 'chiac' (1969). He also directed a series of documentaries on René Lévesque (three shorts in 1969, 1972, and 1976), a docudrama on domestic violence, L'Emprise (1988, with Suzanne Guy), and a portrait of a little-known Québec painter, Ozéas Leduc … comme l'espace et le temps/Ozéas Leduc … like space and time (1996). Since the 1980s he has made a handful of fiction features, the best of which is Les Noces de papier/Paper Wedding (1989) with Geneviève Bujold. His most recent fiction is Quand je serai parti … vous vivrez encore (1999), an historical epic on the rebellion of French Canadian patriots against British forces in 1837–1938.

ANDRÉ LOISELLE

Biography

Born in 1928. Began making amateur films in the late 1940s with Claude Jutra. Directed a short film, Matin; worked briefly at the National Film Board of Canada, 1950. Assistant director on La petite Aurore l'enfant martyre, the most commercially successful French Canadian feature film of the 1950s, 1950–1. Worked on a number of short films for the Canadian Broadcasting Corporation (CBC) television series, 'Petites médisances', 1953. Began his career as a filmmaker in earnest after the NFB moved from Ottawa (Ontario) to Montréal (Québec), 1956.

Selected films

1958 Les Raquetteurs: director of photography, editor
1961 La Lutte: director of photography
1962 Pour la suite du monde: director of photography
1962 Québec-U.S.A. ou l'Invasion pacifique: director of photography
1962 Les Enfants du silence: director of photography
1964 Le Temps perdu: director of photography
1968 Le Beau Plaisir: director
1969 Éloge du chiac: director of photography
1969 René Lévesque vous parle: les 6 millards: director of photography
1971 L'Acadie, l'Acadie?!?: director of photography
1972 René Lévesque pour le vrai: director of photography
1974–80 Le son des français d'Amérique (series of 27 short films)
1976 René Lévesque, un vrai chef: director of photography
1985 Freedom to Move: director

Further reading

Loiselle, André, 'Michel Brault's Les Ordres: Documenting the Reality of Experience and the Fiction of History', in Gene Walz (ed.), *Canada's Best Features: Critical Essays on Fifteen Great Canadian Films*, Amsterdam and New York: Rodopi, 2002.
Marsolais, Gilles, *Michel Brault, Montréal: Conseil québécois pour la diffusion du cinéma*, 1972.
n.a., 'Montréal: Cinémathèque québécoise', special issue on Michel Brault, *Copie Zéro 5*, 1980.

Brazil

Documentary film production stretches back to the origins of film in Brazil. In 1896 film first arrived in Brazil, brought by European immigrants. Early documentary films from this time focus on the natural landscape, as well as habits and traditions of the different regions of Brazil. These remained the primary focus of early Brazilian documentary. Afonso Segreto and Pascoal Segreto dominated the production of Brazilian documentary through its first decade.

Early ethnographic documentaries exposed urban Brazilians to images of an immense and unknown country, while emphasizing national integration and an idealized image of an Indian still savage. Major Luiz Thomas Reis made several films for the Comissão de Linhas Telegráficas e Estratégicas do Mato Grosso ao Amazonas (Commission of Telegraphic and Strategic Lines of Mato Grosso to Amazonas), known as Comissão Rondon (Rondon Comission). His Rituais e Festas Bororó/Bororo's rituals and parties (1917) was considered by film critics as an early example of skillful film editing, while also being an important early anthropological film.

The classics of the silent period include Rudolf Rex Lustig and Adalberto Kemeny's São Paulo, A Sinfonia da Metrópole/São Paulo, the Symphony of the Metropolis (1929), which portrays the continuing urbanization of the city; and Lampião, Rei do Cangaço/Lampião, King of the Cangaço (1936), directed by Benjamim Abrahão. This film is a study of the Lampião group, in the northeastern interior.

In 1936 the federal government created the Instituto Nacional do Cinema Educativo (INCE, National Institute of Educational Movies), with the goal of bringing intellectually stimulating works to the working classes. For thirty years the direction of INCE was the responsibility of film director Humberto Mauro, who completed three hundred and fifty-four short educational films in the period. Despite the official and didactic nature of the produced material, the INCE was able to stamp a personal aesthetic on most of its work. Approximately fifty directors had their films financed by the INCE.

In the 1960s the prevalent theme of an exoticized forest and rural milieu gave way to a focus on national underdevelopment and social inequality, advancing aesthetic subjects of the cinema novo (new cinema) movement. Paulo César Saraceni and Mário Carneiro directed Arraial do cabo/Village of the Cable (1959), and Linduarte Noronha directed Aruanda (1960), two films that display the influence of this trend. Brazilian documentaries increasingly focused on issues relating to culture, economy, and popular religiosity, but without the overtly educational and didactic tone of INCE films.

In 1962 the Swedish director Arne Sucksdorff held a film seminar in Rio de Janeiro. As a result, the techniques of cinéma vérité films spread throughout Brazil. Leon Hirszman's Maioria Absoluta/Absolute Majority (1964), Paulo César Saraceni's Integração Racial/Racial Integration (1964) and Arnaldo Jabor's O Circo/The Circus (1965) are films influenced by this trend early on.

Brazilian documentary was also influenced by the work of Chilean filmmakers. In São Paulo a group formed by Vladimir Herzog, João Batista de Andrade, Maurice Capovilla, Sérgio Muniz, and Renato Tapajós maintained contact with Argentina's documentary filmmakers, through Fernando Birri, an initiate in practice of the cinéma vérité.

Between 1964 and 1965 the producer Thomas Farkas produced four documentaries: Geraldo Sarno's Viramundo (1965), Paulo Gil Soares' Memória do Cangaço/Memory of Cangaço (1965), Manuel Horácio Gimenez's Nossa Escola de Samba/Our Samba School (1965), and Maurice Capovilla's Subterrãneos do Futebol/Underground of Soccer (1965). These filmmakers formed the Caravana Farkas, and they collectively documented popular culture. The group produced nineteen documentaries of short films between 1969 and 1971 under the series title A Condição Brasileira/The Brazilian Condition, all influenced by cinéma vérité.

From the 1960s Brazilian film was censored by the military dictatorship in power. Eduardo

Coutinho's Cabra Marcado para Morrer/Guy Marked to Die (1964–84), João Batista de Andrade's Liberdade de Imprensa/Freedom of the Press (1966), and Vladimir Carvalho's País de São Saruê/São Saruê's Country (1970) were all censored.

In 1972 the public television station of São Paulo began airing A Hora da Notícia/Hour of the News to show the real Brazil, as opposed to the official, sanitized images propagated by the military government. Film director João Batista de Andrade was called on to create small-scale documentaries directly in the streets. After a period of political persecution, the show was cancelled in 1974. Batista de Andrade was invited by Paulo Gil Soares to assume management of the team of special reporters for TV Globo of São Paulo. Eduardo Coutinho, Maurice Capovilla, Hermano Penna, and Walter Lima Jr were a part of the group. Thus the Globo Repórter was born.

Composed of a series of ten documentaries called Globo Shell Especial/Shell Globe Specials, the Globo Repórter was enthusiastically supported by the film directors and displayed accomplished cinematographic and authorial style. A few films in particular stand out from the series: João Batista de Andrade's Wilsinho Galiléia (1978), Eduardo Coutinho's Teodorico, o imperador do sertão/Teodorico, the emperor of the interior (1978), and Maurice Capovilla's O Último dia de Lampião/The Last Day of Lampião (1975). Although the nation was taking steps toward democracy at the time, the program suffered several occasions of forced internal censorship.

The boundary between fiction and documentary was explored in 1975 by Jorge Bodansky and Orlando Senna in Iracema, uma transa amazônica/Iracema, an Amazonian Affair. Bodansky continued as a documentary filmmaker for German television, in partnership with Wolf Gauer.

A number of filmmakers who have focused on documentary film stand out: Vladimir Carvalho of Conterrâneos velhos de Guerra/Old Fellow Citizens of War (1990), Sylvio Back, Revolução de 30/Revolution of 30 (1980), Sílvio Tendler, director of Os anos JK, uma trajetória política/The years JK, a political path (1976–80), which was a popular success, and Eduardo Coutinho, who eventually focused on making films in video that were later enlarged for 35mm film, such as Santo Forte/Strong Saint (1999).

In the 1980s two Brazilian documentary filmmakers in particular stood out. Sérgio Bianchi's Mato Eles?/Did I kill them? (1982), and Jorge Furtado's Ilha das Flores/Island of the flowers (1989) are both marked by an innovative narrative style and resonant visual references.

The Associação Brasileira de Vídeo Popular (ABVP, Brazilian Association of Popular Video) was founded in the early 1980s. Its aim was to popularize a cohesive production model for filmmakers across the country, while encouraging popular participation in documentary filmmaking. One of the founders of the ABVP, Luiz Fernando Santoro, was also the first member of the Comitê de Cineastas da América Latina (Committee of Film Directors of Latin America), which emphasized the value of works done on video, as much of the recent history of Latin America had been documented in this format.

The Centro de Trabalho Indigenista (CIT, Center of Indigenous Work) encourages debate and discussion of the documentary use of video, while also encouraging reflection on the identity of indigenous people and their place in the contemporary world.

In the mid-1990s television became increasingly involved in the production and screening of documentary film. Several film directors made works for television. Nelson Pereira directed Casa Grande e Senzala/Big House and Slave Quarter (2000), a film in four episodes on the work of the anthropologist Gilberto Freire.

Documentary film assumed a central place in Brazilian media in the late 1990s. Paulo Sacramento's O Prisioneiro da Grade de Ferro/The Prisoner of the Iron Grating (2003), made inside the prison of Carandiru, was filmed in digital video with the assistance of the prisoners. Brazilian video documentaries continue to push the boundaries of documentary film, questioning the relationship between the documentary and the reality it purports to represent.

GUSTAVO SORANZ

See also: Coutinho, Eduardo

Further reading

Andrade, Joaquim Batista de, *João Batista de Andrade por ele mesmo!*, revista de estudos avançados da USP, no. 16, São Paulo: Edusp, 2002.

——*O povo fala*, São Paulo: Senac, 2002.

Bernardet, Jean-Claude, *Cineastas e imagens do povo*, São Paulo: Brasiliense, 1985.
——*Cinema brasileiro: propostas para uma história*, Rio de Janeiro: Paz e Terra, 1979.
——*Brasil em tempo de cinema: ensaios sobre o cinema brasileiro*, Rio de Janeiro: Paz e Terra, 1978.
Carvalho, Vladimir, *O país de São Saruê, Brasília/ Distrito Federal*, Ed. Universidade de Brasília, 1986.
France, Claudine de, *Do Filme Etnográfico à Antropologia Fílmica*, Campinas: Ed. Unicamp, 2000.
Gomes, Paulo Emilio Salles, *Cinema: trajetória no subdesenvolvimento*, São Paulo: Paz e Terra, 2001.
Lins, Consuelo, *O Documentário de Eduardo Coutinho—televisão, cinema e vídeo*, São Paulo: Jorge Zahar, 2004.
Ramos, Fernão and Miranda, Luiz Felipe, *Enciclopédia do cinema brasileiro*, São Paulo: Senac, 2000.
Santoro, Luiz Fernando, *A imagem nas mãos: o vídeo popular no Brasil*, São Paulo: Summus, 1989.
Teixeira, Francisco Elinaldo, *Documentário no Brasil: tradição e transformação*, São Paulo: Summus, 2004.
Xavier, Ismail, *Ocinema brasileiro moderno*, São Paulo: Paz e Terra, 2001.

Bridge, The

(Holland, Ivens, 1928)

De Brug (The Bridge) can be considered as the first notable work of Joris Ivens's film career, although initially it was for him nothing more than an experiment and a film study. As manager of the Amsterdam branch of his father's photo business, Ivens's career was already determined. However, this did not stop him from using the available equipment for some film experiments and other projects. By 1927 Ivens had become increasingly involved in film. As one of the cofounders of the Dutch Film League, he participated in the projection and discussion of artistic films. He thoroughly analyzed films such as Pudowkin's The Mother and Eisenstein's Potemkin, and he himself was experimenting with camera work and editing. De Brug was for Ivens no more than a study in movement, made by an amateur in order to learn about camera movements, composition and editing. Upon its first projection at a Film League screening, however, the film was received with much acclaim, and it put Dutch film on the map of European avant-garde filmmaking.

While he was working on some films for Leiden University, Ivens took long lunch breaks to go to Rotterdam to film the lift bridge. He used a simple handheld Kinamo camera, normally used by amateur filmmakers. The use of this handheld camera allows the transformation of the huge static steel object into a dynamic filmed sequence.

The structure of De Brug is simple, composed entirely of the opening and closing of a rail road lift bridge. Though technically imperfect, the careful construction of the film, the composition of the images, the camera movements and the editing still encourage the consideration of this film as an avant-garde masterpiece. The film starts with two long shots of the bridge, to show its place and function. Spanning the water, it allows trains to cross the river and ships to pass underneath. Next there is a beautiful sequence of shots and camera movements that depict the massive steel bridge, emphasizing its vertical, horizontal, and diagonal lines and the shadows it casts on the water and the pillars. Ivens shows the interplay between these lines by carefully composing the images and following them with camera movements.

The static structure of the bridge is contrasted with the speed and dynamics of the approaching train, which has to stop when the signal is urging it to halt. With the train gradually coming to a standstill the bridge slowly begins to move. Ivens repeats the first sequence, but now with many parts of the bridge in movement: the big wheels turning, the contrasting movements of the bridge going upwards and the counterweights going down, the ships passing slowly underneath, and the train impatiently waiting and steaming. Ivens carefully composes the vertical, horizontal and diagonal lines and plays with the movements within the frame. He adds to the dynamics of this moment with several camera movements, before the scene reassembles itself, and we see a closed bridge and trains crossing the river. The result is an almost abstract composition of lines and movements. The bridge is no longer operative, but is now an industrial monument in Rotterdam.

KEES BAKKER

See also: Ivens, Joris

De Brug/The Bridge (the Netherlands, CAPI Amsterdam, 1928, silent, 11 mins). Produced, directed, and edited by Joris Ivens. Cinematography by Joris Ivens.

Further reading

Bakker, Kees (ed.), *Joris Ivens and the Documentary Context*, Amsterdam: Amsterdam University Press, 1999.
Delmar, Rosalind, *Joris Ivens, 50 Years of Film-making*, London: British Film Institute, 1979.
Ivens, Joris, *The Camera and I*, Berlin: Seven Seas Books, 1969.
Ivens, Joris and Destanque, Robert, *Joris Ivens ou la mémoire d'un regard*, Paris: Editions BFB, 1982.
Schoots, Hans, *Dangerous Life. A Biography of Joris Ivens*, Amsterdam: Amsterdam University Press, 2000.
Waugh, Thomas, *Joris Ivens and the Evolution of the Radical Documentary 1926–46*, New York: Columbia University, 1981.

Bronx Morning, A

(US, Leyda, 1931)

A Bronx Morning was photographer-turned-filmmaker Jay Leyda's first film and the only solo effort in his filmmaking practice. Leyda is best known for his translations of Sergei Eisenstein's film theories, and for his own books on film analysis and history ranging from Soviet and Chinese cinema to the compilation documentary. However, Leyda's actual work in film is an essential part of his wide-ranging career as an artist-scholar, and this eleven-minute experimental documentary is significant on several fronts. It is, first, a highly creative and accomplished film that explores many tropes of film style and renders a memorable impression of New York City early in the Depression years. Among those who admired the film in its day were no less than Eisenstein and Dziga Vertov: this was the film that gained Leyda admission to the Moscow Film School in 1933, and both Soviet artists were pleased to claim that they saw their influence upon Leyda. (Surely the numerous shots of the baby carriage in one sequence show Leyda referencing the Odessa Steps massacre in Potemkin.) Thus, this film enabled to some degree Leyda's seminal years studying and working in Moscow and all the later books and translations of Eisenstein and others that Leyda brought to English-language readers, filmmakers, and cinema studies in general. In some sense, then, this effort also matters because it indirectly had a huge impact on generations of scholarship and production. Third, in more recent years A Bronx Morning has proved to be a key film in the historiographic reevaluation of American avant-garde cinema. For years a great variety of film made in the 1920s and 1930s was understudied and undervalued. Now, however, the days are gone when Maya Deren's undeniable landmark Meshes of the Afternoon (1943) was somehow seen as giving birth singlehandedly to experimental film in the US. Finally, Leyda's film makes an interesting and significant contribution to the city symphony, a documentary subgenre more often studied in the light of a handful of earlier European classics. Indeed, city films such as this one point to a time when distinctions between documentary and the avant-garde had not become fully established (Uricchio 1995).

An impressionistic portrait of New York's northernmost borough in the early days of the Great Depression, A Bronx Morning does not follow the chronological 'day in the life' structure of many city symphonies of the period. Rather, the film has a sense of formal play that heralds a new filmmaker, a student emulating but not merely copying his teachers. One finds awnings and sacks used as wipes; a graphic match from two pumpkins to the O's in the 'LOOK' on a sandwich man's placard; and even an example of the Kuleshov effect, when shots of cats are followed by ones of birds scattering, as if in fear of the felines. The use of the 'LOOK' is but one of many highly reflexive tropes active in the film, starting with its disorienting opening as the camera rides along an elevated train. The train enables not only a vivid and self-conscious tracking shot, but also an interplay with light and dark patches evocative of the filmstrip itself, and also later reflected images in the train windows and distancing created by grating in the foreground. Leyda's work in still photography and his apprenticeship with Ralph Steiner appear too, in the film's fascination with objects and the care with composition, photographically centripetal yet cinematically centrifugal, as the film transcends traditional, premodernist ideas of framing. Even the focus upon feet hints at the still photographer traipsing about to set up his next shot (Lugowski 1999).

Historians have aptly linked the film with Ruttmann (Uricchio 1995) and have also read the film as a tribute to Eugene Atget, one of Leyda's favorite photographers (Horak 1993). Images of objects in deserted streets, before they are filled with pedestrians and cars, delay anything resembling an establishing shot until twenty-five shots into the film, and have a surrealistic touch like Atget. Leyda himself, though, admitted a far wider range of influence, from art cinema and documentary he saw when he moved to New York, to many films that he had only seen via stills in camera magazines he collected as a youth in Ohio (Cavalcanti's Rien que les heures, Man Ray's L'Etoile de mer, Dudley Murphy and Fernand Leger's Ballet Mecanique).

In later years, Leyda tended to downplay his first film, complaining that it was too 'formalistic' and not sufficiently political. Yet critics have argued that the city symphony, in moving experimental film away from abstraction and frequently either documenting the plight of the poor, or criticizing urban institutions, was actually a politicized, experimental play with realism. One certainly finds such commentary in Leyda's sardonic use of three intertitles. 'The Bronx does business … ' is followed by shots of businesses that have lost their leases. A second title, 'And the Bronx lives … ', while followed by shots of tenements that denotatively represent living quarters, nonetheless heralds a series of shots devoid of any people, as if to highlight the difficulties of living in such crowded, impoverished conditions. Finally, the third title, ' … on the street' continues the ongoing trope of irony, as we see garbage trucks and a possibly homeless woman's legs sprawled on the pavement. This shot of the legs is but part of a larger fragmentation of the body seen throughout the film, combined with decentered framings and a prominent use of empty spaces. Horak (1993) notes that the film displays an essentially 'feminine perspective' in its world of children, pets and cleaning, unlike those city symphonies that emphasize men at work. Others have argued that a gender politics is in play here, that the absence of agency speaks to the 'crisis in masculinity' brought about by the socioeconomic conditions of the Depression (Lugowski 1999). However read, the film has belatedly come into its own for film scholars and cultural historians.

DAVID M. LUGOWSKI

See also: Leyda, Jay

A Bronx Morning (US, 1931–2, 11 mins, silent). Directed, photographed, and edited by Jay Leyda.

Further reading

Horak, Jan-Christopher, 'Avant-Garde Film', in Tino Balio (ed.), *Grand Design: Hollywood as a Modern Business Enterprise, 1930–39*, New York: Charles Scribner's Sons, 1993.

Kirstein, Lincoln, 'Experimental Films', *Arts Weekly* vol. 1, March 25, 1932: 52, 62.

Leyda, Jay, 'A Note on A Bronx Morning', Lausanne, Switzerland: FIAF Symposium, 1979, in clippings file on Jay Leyda, Museum of Modern Art, New York.

Lugowski, David M., *Queering the (New) Deal: Lesbian, Gay and Queer Representation in U.S. Cinema of the Great Depression, 1929–41*, PhD dissertation, NYU, 1999.

Uricchio, William, 'The City Viewed: The Films of Leyda, Browning and Weinberg', in Jan-Christopher Horak (ed.), *Lovers of Cinema: The First American Avant-Garde, 1919–45*, Madison, WI: University of Wisconsin Press, 1995: 287–314.

Wolfe, Charles, 'Straight Shots and Crooked Plots: Social Documentary and the Avant-Garde in the 1930s', in Jan-Christopher Horak (ed.), *Lovers of Cinema: The First American Avant-Garde, 1919–45*, Madison, WI: University of Wisconsin Press, 1995: 234–66.

Burch, Noël

Although Noël Burch was schooled as a filmmaker in France in the early 1950s, his career as a director did not become fully realized until much later in life. From the time he graduated from L'IDHEC (translated roughly as the Institute for High Cinematographic Studies) now known as la FEMIS (the National Film School of France) until the mid-1980s, Burch gained recognition as a film theorist, teacher, and critic, engaging in landmark studies of formal film analysis, Japanese cinema, and early, silent cinema.

Throughout his life, Burch was never far from the camera. In the 1950s he assisted directors Preston Sturges and Michel Fano. Soon afterward, while becoming a respected film critic and theorist, Burch honed his filmmaking skills by making several short films. These included Et sur cette Pierre … (1963), Noviciat (1964), Tout est ecrit (1970), Correction, Please or How We Got into Pictures (1979), The Year of the Bodyguard (1981), The Impersonation (1983), and Not Distant Observers (1985). As Burch himself admits, however, before 1986, he 'was not really going anywhere' as a filmmaker.

In 1986 he made a series of six documentaries for England's Channel 4 television, titled together, What Do Those Old Films Mean? As his subject, Burch chose an often neglected period of film history: early cinema. In each of the six segments, Burch investigated how cinema developed after the turn of the century in a different part of the world. The six volumes are divided as follows: volume one examines English cinema from 1900 to 1912; volume two examines French cinema from 1904 to 1912; volume three examines American cinema from 1902 to 1914; volume four examines Soviet cinema from 1926 to 1930; volume five examines Danish cinema from 1910 to 1912; and volume six examines German cinema from 1926 to 1932.

That Burch chose to highlight the cinematic art in those particular countries during those specific time frames comes as no surprise. In his first book, *Theory of Film Practice* (1967), Burch had analyzed the work of key filmmakers who fit into those parameters, extolling, for example, the editing technique of Soviet filmmaker Sergei Eisenstein, and the structure of the gags in the films of American slapstick performer Buster Keaton.

As a self-proclaimed communist and expatriate, strongly influenced by the radicalism of the student movement in France in May 1968, it is not surprising that Burch was deeply critical of US politics. This criticism, along with his ongoing dedication to cinema, became the basis for Burch's most acclaimed documentary, Red Hollywood (1995). Although Burch had explored the subject of American dissidents in his 1994 film, Voyage Sentimental, he and codirector Thom Anderson's investigation into the blacklisted filmmakers of 1950s Hollywood brought him greater recognition as a documentarian than any of his previous films. Red Hollywood examines the forgotten works of several blacklisted filmmakers who fled to France rather than struggle within the US film industry. Burch and Anderson's subjects included Dalton Trumbo, Michael Wilson, John Berry, and Jules Dassin. Using fifty-three clips from their films, Red Hollywood explores the ways in which these political leftists were able to infuse communist ideas into their work. The documentary received a great deal of praise from critics in the United States.

Early in his career as a film theorist, Burch defined himself as a formalist, calling attention to a film's mise-en-scène over its narrative in his writing and teaching. Burch analogized cinema to music, arguing in *Theory of Film Practice* that film form could be conceived of in terms of 'atonal' formal elements, in which no single element consistently dominates. In that sense, in any given film narrative is just another element, not inherently more important than sound, editing structure, or a different aesthetic component. Burch demonstrates his thesis using a wide range of films and filmmakers, including Fritz Lang's M and Jacques Tati's Play Time.

Burch opposes what he calls mainstream cinema's institutional mode of production (IMP), which uses invisible editing, framing, and mise-en-scène to call the spectator's attention to the narrative, rather than the aesthetics of the film. Burch holds that the rise of the IMP in the early days of the medium was linked to the film industry's economic interest in attracting a bourgeois demographic. Toward that end, the industry wanted to create films with which the audience could identify psychologically, films that created the effect of reality. Burch preferred modernist and avant-garde films that stressed formal properties such as offscreen space and spatial framing. He praised the films of Antonioni and Resnais, in particular, for their elaborate orchestration and use of offscreen space.

In his seminal book on Japanese cinema, *To the Distant Observer*, Burch argues that Japanese film is inherently critical of the Hollywood realist cinema of the 1930s and 1940s. Burch points to the directors Ozu Yasujiro and Mizoguchi Kenji as two stylistically different filmmakers whose works both illustrate the difference between the realism of Hollywood and modernism of Japanese cinema. Whereas Hollywood privileges a continuous, coherent, character-driven narrative above other formal elements in film, Japanese cinema uses long shots, frontality, and, in the case of Ozu, a narrative in which nothing seems to be happening. For Burch, this is a deliberate and intentional stylistic indifference to the codified mode of filmmaking manufactured by Hollywood.

Although Burch has continued teaching, writing, and theorizing about film, publishing several books during the 1990s and beyond, *Theory of Film Practice* and *To the Distant Observer* remain his most influential and ground-breaking achievements. His attention to film form and overall concern for the medium became the subjects of his filmmaking ventures. His most successful documentaries, What Do Those Old Films Mean? and Red Hollywood both encourage a reevaluation of film outside the narrative-driven conventions of American cinema. As both a scholar and a filmmaker, Burch continues to be a powerful influence on the field of film studies.

STARR MARCELLO

Biography

Born in San Francisco, 1932. Emigrated to France to attend film school in 1951. Graduated from L'IDEC (now called La FEMIS) in 1954. Worked as an assistant to Preston Sturges and Michel Fano in the 1950s. Began teaching and making short films in the 1960s. Joined the Communist Party. Published *Theory of Film Practice* in 1967, and participated in the radical student movement in Paris in May 1968. Moved to Japan in the mid-1970s to study Japanese film. Published *To the Distant Observer* in 1979. Returned to Europe and agreed in 1986 to direct the six-part series on early cinema, What Do Those Old Films Mean? for the UK's Channel 4 television. Published his third book, *Life to Those Shadows* in 1990. Continued writing on film theory and practice. Directed the critically acclaimed Red Hollywood with Thom Anderson in 1995.

Further reading

Bordwell, David, 'The Musical Analogy', *Yale French Studies* 60, Cinema/Sound 1980: 141–56.

Burch, Noël, *Theory of Film Practice*, trans. Helen R. Lane, New York: Praeger Publishers, 1973.

——*To the Distant Observer: Form and Meaning in the Japanese Cinema*, ed. Annette Michaelson, Berkeley, CA: University of California Press, 1979.

——*Life to Those Shadows*, trans. and ed. Ben Brewster, Berkeley, CA: University of California Press, 1990.

——*In and Out of Sync: The Awakening of a Cine-Dreamer*, trans. and ed. Ben Brewster, London: Scolar Press, 1991.

——*Loin de Paris, cinémas et sociétés: textes et contexts*, ed. Laurence Allard, Paris: Harmattan, 2001.

Burch, Noël and Sellier, Geneviève, *La drôle de guerre des sexes du cinéma français: 1930–56*, Paris: Nathan, 1996.

Elsaesser, Thomas and Barker, Adam (eds), *Early Cinema: Space, Frame, Narrative*, London: BFI Publishing, 1990.

Rosen, Philip (ed.), *Narrative, Apparatus, Ideology: A Film Theory Reader*, New York: Columbia University Press, 1986.

Burden of Dreams

(Germany, Blank, 1982)

Regarded as one of the finest films ever made about movie-making, Burden of Dreams is also the most widely seen work by prolific documentarian Les Blank. In October 1979 and again in April–June 1981, director Werner Herzog brought in Blank and Maureen Gosling to document the production of his feature Fitzcarraldo (1982), being shot in Peru. Herzog eventually completed his quixotic jungle venture, but Blank's portrait of the director running amok in the Amazon emerged as the superior film. Burden of Dreams combines a 'making-of' chronicle with Les Blank's characteristic humor, keen eye for detail, and ethnographic sensitivity, creating a compelling portrait of the notoriously eccentric German filmmaker.

Burden of Dreams begins with a sequence both beautiful and cheeky. To the sounds of a Vivaldi chorale, aerial shots display the Peruvian Amazon. Unlike Hitler's arrival through the clouds in Triumph of the Will (1935), Herzog's shaky landing in a small plane signals his lack of command over this place. Blank then cuts to the director sitting in a small boat, explaining his film's 'Sisyphus-like story', which he based on an historical character. Fitzcarraldo, an Irish rubber merchant, dreams of bringing Enrico Caruso to sing at a new opera house in the Amazon. To finance his venture, he accesses untapped rubber trees by transporting a steamship over a mountainous isthmus. As we learn, although the actual Carlos Fitzcarraldo disassembled his boat, Herzog insists on having his hauled in one piece, even though it is ten times heavier. Blank builds his documentary's narrative around this literal and metaphorical feat.

The film next takes us back to November 1979, when shooting commenced. A narrator's detached voice condenses the production history throughout, emphasizing the complicated negotiations between the European crew and the divergent groups of people living in these remote parts of the Amazon. We see Aguaruna Indians working at the Fitzcarraldo encampment while one explains the political tensions and violence that force the production to flee. Cut to the city of Iquitos, Peru, where shooting resumed in January 1981, only to be suspended when the star Jason Robards fell ill. We see outtakes of Robards with co-star Mick Jagger, as Herzog relates: 'If I abandon this project, I would be a man without dreams.' In April, actor Klaus Kinski arrives to take the title role, as he had for Herzog's earlier tale of madness, Aguirre, der Zorn Gottes/Aguirre, the Wrath of God (1972), also filmed in the rainforests of Peru.

The remainder of Burden of Dreams chronicles three months of shooting from a second camp, one thousand five hundred miles to the south of Iquitos. Blank records moments of danger and the tedium of numerous delays. An understated voice-over narrator relates that, in fact, the crew must work with three ships, all representing Fitzcarraldo's one. In addition to the three hundred-ton steamer to be forced over a hill, a similar vessel stays in Iquitos for principal photography, and a third goes down a river for shooting on the 'Rapids of Death'. Alternating with vérité sequences of the production are interviews with Herzog, which become articulate but mad monologues on the 'curse' on his production, the 'authentic natives' in his cast, and the 'collective murder' and 'obscenity of all this jungle'. Blank concludes with a qualified fulfillment of the director's quest. We hear that, after several hazardous attempts, Herzog wins 'a painful victory' by getting his ship to the mountaintop with bulldozers. This climax, however, falls between despondent soliloquies. First, asked by Blank what he will do after the movie has wrapped, Herzog grimaces as he jokes that he 'shouldn't make movies anymore'. Even if Fitzcarraldo gets done, he says, 'Nobody on this Earth will convince me to be happy about all that'. Finally, Blank concludes his portrait of the artist on a note of bittersweet redemption, with Herzog saying: 'I make films because [...] it is my duty. Because this might be the inner chronicle of what we are, and we have to articulate ourselves.'

As a commissioned documentary, Burden of Dreams gives Werner Herzog the first and last word, but the film far from lionizes him. With characteristic aplomb, Les Blank reveals the beauty of the Amazon and the people who live in this place that Herzog finds both irresistible and horrible. His portrait is sympathetic to Herzog's artistry but revelatory of its cruel excesses. We see, for example, the filmmaker playing football with local Indians, only to find that when the Machiguengas engage in their traditional sport of arrow catching, he urges them to shoot harder, and at one another's heads. Blank intercuts this with footage of Herzog first explaining that a hostile tribe has attacked three of his camp members, then smiling as he says he will give his son the gruesome arrow that went through a man's throat.

Burden of Dreams was only one of several documentaries of the time that centered on the German filmmaker's eccentricities and droll lunacy. Erwin Keusch's Was ich bin, sind meine Filme/I Am My Films (1979) shows the director during the making of Stroszek (1977). It reveals a less assured cineaste, but one who declares that films are more important than life itself, hence Herzog's predilection for dangerous locales and outlandish actions. Shortly before embarking on Fitzcarraldo, he also participated in Werner Herzog Eats his Shoe (1980), Blank's whimsical short about his comrade's appearance at the premiere of Errol Morris's Gates of Heaven (1978). Herzog had encouraged the fledgling filmmaker to make this peculiar nonfiction feature about pet cemeteries, claiming he would eat his shoe if Morris succeeded. In filming the literal cooking of leather boots at Chez Panisse, Blank not only paved the way for his 1980 film Garlic is as Good as Ten Mothers (in which Herzog briefly appears), but he also established the character rendered full-scale in Burden of Dreams—Herzog, the cinema-obsessed extremist who wants to save the world from banality by pursuing cinematic visions.

Although movies routinely commission documentaries about their making, Blank's work began a subgenre about troubled productions, often with their own directors going half mad in isolated locations. Most notably, Hearts of Darkness (1991) chronicles Francis Ford Coppola's trials and tribulations in directing Apocalypse Now (1979). The former, incidentally, includes footage shot by Les Blank, whom Coppola hired to film the Apocalypse wrap party. Mika Kaurismäki's Tigrero: A Film That Was Never Made (1994) records Sam Fuller's return to the Brazilian locales of a movie he abandoned forty years prior, and Terry Gilliam's failure to complete The Man Who Killed Don Quixote is recorded in Lost in La Mancha (2002). Arguably, the subgenre evolved beyond parody with a twisted homage to Burden of Dreams. In Zak Penn's presumed mockumentary, Incident at Loch Ness (2004), a crew sets out to film a documentary about Werner Herzog, who is himself directing a documentary about the Loch Ness monster.

Whatever the strengths of these kindred films, only Burden of Dreams goes beyond its commission. Rather than simply presenting a portrait of a filmmaker lost in an alien environment, Blank also respectfully documents the people who live in the place that Herzog can only see as 'unfinished' and 'prehistorical'. As in his many films celebrating American subcultures, Blank delights in presenting people via their music and food. Although we see Klaus Kinski disgusted by the fermented masato that the Campas Indians offer to Fitzcarraldo, Blank counters with a long sequence documenting the communal process of making this staple food and ritual drink, even recording a zesty Campas song about the subject. After giving Herzog the last word, he tellingly gives Peruvians the final image. Burden of Dreams ends with the visiting German filmmaker having his portrait taken by an itinerant photographer, who frames the black-and-white photo in a heart, trimmed with drawings of flowers, vines, and songbirds, an artful domestication of the jungle to which Herzog could only surrender.

DAN STREIBLE

See also: Blank, Les; Herzog, Werner

Burden of Dreams (US/Germany, Flower Films, 1982, 94 mins). Produced, directed and photographed by Les Blank. Edited and sound recorded by Maureen Gosling. Written by Michael Goodwin. Narrated by Candace Laughlin. Interpreting, interviewing, and camera assistance by Bruce 'Pacho' Lane. Cast: Werner Herzog, Klaus Kinski, Claudia Cardinale, Jason Robards, Mick Jagger, Huerequeque Bohorquez, José Lewgoy, Walter Saxer, Thomas Mauch, Paul Hittscher, Evaristo Nunkuag Ikanan, Nelson de Rio Cenepa, Carmen Correa, Elia de Rio Ene, Alfredo de Rio Tambo, Miguel Angel Fuentes, Laplace Martins, David Pérez Espinosa, Angela Reina, Jorge Vignati, Father Mariano Gagnon. Music: Vivaldi's 'Dixit Dominus', performed by Vienna Kammerchor; 'Uchpagallo', 'Mi Selva Obscura', 'Madrugador', performed by Corazón de la Selva; 'Vamos a Belén', performed by Los Solteritos; 'M'Appari', 'Demeure, Chaste e Puro', 'Pagliacci', 'Chi mi Frena in tal Moment', recordings of Enrico Caruso; chorale music by Popul Vuh. Filmed in Peru. Robert Flaherty Documentary Award (1983), British Academy of Film and Television Arts. Alternate version: US broadcast, for the series Non-Fiction Television (PBS, 58 mins).

Further reading

Blank, Les and James Bogan (eds), *Burden of Dreams: Screenplay, Journals, Reviews, Photographs*, Berkeley: North Atlantic Books, 1984.

Corliss, Richard, 'Burden of Dreams', *Time*, October 25, 1982: 77–8.

Durgnat, Raymond, 'Burden of Dreams', *Films*, November 1982: 29–30.

Goodwin, Michael, 'Herzog the God of Wrath', *American Film*, June 1982: 36–51, 72–3.

Margolis, Janet, 'Burden of Dreams', *Cineaste* 12, 4, 1983: 54.

Rouyer, Philippe and Bordes, Sophie, 'Jubilation de la caméra: sur le cinéma de Les Blank', *Positif*, March 1988: 19–25.

Burma Victory

(UK, Boulting, 1945)

Burma Victory was the final film in a wartime series of documentaries dealing with significant Allied campaigns. The previous 'victory' films, Desert Victory (1943) and Tunisian Victory (1944), had addressed the war in North Africa, whereas Burma Victory was an account of the arduous fighting in Southeast Asia. The feature-length documentaries were compiled from footage taken by the service film units and Tunisian Victory and The True Glory (1945), about the liberation of northern Europe, were notable, if troubled collaborations between the British and Americans. The films were widely screened, both theatrically and nontheatrically, and were considered principal achievements in the war documentary.

Britain's main contribution to the war in the East was the struggle to recover Burma. It was a long, hard-fought, and unpleasant campaign, yet it was secondary to the events in Europe. The Fourteenth Army that operated there was awarded the epithet of 'the forgotten army' and its commander, Admiral Lord Mountbatten, aimed to get the recognition that the Allied forces were due. One way to achieve this goal was an ambitious campaign film such as Tunisian Victory, and early in 1944 he was encouraged London and Washington into a further Anglo-American documentary film. In the event, and very much a consequence of the previous difficulties of coproduction, it was decided in May 1945 to make separate British and American records of the Burma campaign.

Burma Victory begins with a series of bleak images depicting the hostility of the terrain and the ravages attendant on the monsoon. After early setbacks at the hands of the Japanese, a firmer resolve is brought to the Fourteenth Army by its new commander Mountbatten, who is seen addressing groups of servicemen and demanding no further retreats. The Allied campaign of 1944–5, including the successful defense of Imphal and Kohima, the system of supply by air operated by the Americans, the daring behind the enemy lines mission of the 'chindits', Stilwell's Chinese Expeditionary Force advancing from the northwest, the crossing of the Chindwin and Irrawaddy rivers, the long, hard-fought march to Mandalay, and the relief of Rangoon, is presented through a combination of combat and documentary footage, reenactments, models, and diagrams. The war ends with the Japanese surrender in September 1945, after the dropping of atomic bombs on Nagasaki and Hiroshima.

David MacDonald of the Army Film and Photographic Unit (AFPU) had arrived in the region late in 1944 to commence work on a film. He was able to draw on and coordinate the activities of the Southeast Asia Command (SEAC) Film Unit, which was led by Derek Knight. After his work on the previous 'victory' films, Roy Boulting was again assigned to direct and edit the project, and everyone was required to work quickly, as the war was concluding. Burma Victory understandably bears much similarity to its predecessors. In a few respects, though, it develops techniques introduced in the earlier titles and gives them a new prominence. Boulting had staged a small but vitally effective scene in Desert Victory to provide some dramatic impact to the commencement of the Battle of El Alamein. Here, he opens the film with a studio-staged scene featuring two British Tommies in a tent, one of whom is reading aloud from a guidebook to Burma. Dispirited at its idealized vision, he tosses the book into the previously concealed rain and mud outside, now brought into view with a panning shot. A further, more developed reenactment occurs in the middle of the film. It is a nighttime scene and Boulting effectively uses sound, performance, and lighting to evoke the eerie atmosphere of the jungle. These scenes were shot at Pinewood Studios, the home base of the AFPU. Although examples of the wartime trend in blending fiction and documentary, such reenactments are of a quite different order to those being developed within the documentary film movement at the Crown Film Unit, such as Pat Jackson's work on Western Approaches (1944). Boulting was primarily a commercial filmmaker and intended such scenes to help dramatize the material and make the film more palatable at the box office. In a similar vein, the film makes use of the narrative device of a diarist, thus individualizing and humanizing the events depicted.

Burma Victory also includes restaged briefings of the Allied commanders. These scenes would have been shot on location by the SEAC Film Unit and, although extremely stilted, perform the vital democratic function of information and explanation. The 'victory' documentaries have been credited with promoting the ideals of a people's war, and access to the military leaders and strategists is seen as a fulfillment of this. The notions of a democratic leadership and citizen army, strongly present in Desert Victory, are further stamped into the Burma film. On reflection, however, these qualities are compromised by Britain's imperial role in the region, the aristocratic credentials of the Supreme Commander, and the over-prominence of the British Tommy in the film. After all, the brunt of the action was borne by Empire troops, especially the highly tenacious Indians who were fighting to keep the Japanese out of their homeland.

Burma Victory differed from its two predecessors in one important respect: they had carefully established the connection between the war front and the home front—that the former relied on the material produced by the latter. This was a central articulation of people's war ideology. The geographic remoteness and sideshow status of the Southeast Asia theatre seemingly precluded such a presentation and, besides, virtually all of the heavy equipment on view—tanks, planes, bulldozers—was of American origin. Perhaps a growing rivalry at that stage in the war prompted the British filmmakers to leave unmentioned such factors. In addition, the British were still smarting from Hollywood's astonishingly insensitive treatment of the war in the region, Objective Burma (1945), which depicted Errol Flynn and a few American troops dispatching the Japanese singlehandedly.

Despite the intense effort, the film was not completed until October 1945. It attracted excellent reviews and was praised in the *Monthly Film Bulletin* as a 'masterly survey of a vast and complex campaign, presented with vivid realism'. It clearly went some way to providing recognition to the struggle in the East, and was the last great documentary to emerge from the wartime service film units.

ALAN BURTON

See also: Boulting, John and Roy; Desert Victory; Tunisian Victory

Burma Victory (UK, British Army Film Unit, 1945, 62 mins). In charge of Production, Lt. Col David MacDonald. Director and supervising editor, Capt. Roy Boulting. Commentary written by Capt. Frank Harvey, Capt. Roy Boulting. Commentary spoken by David King-Wood, Ivan Brandt, Norman Claridge. Music by Alan Rawsthorne.

Further reading

Chapman, James, *The British at War. Cinema, State and Propaganda, 1939–45*, London: I.B. Tauris, 1998.

Coultass, Clive, *Images for Battle. British Film and the Second World War, 1939–45*, London: AUP, 1989.

Jarvie, Ian, 'The Burma Campaign on Film: "Objective Burma" (1945), "The Stilwell Road" (1945) and "Burma Victory" (1945)', *Historical Journal of Film, Radio and Television* 8, 1, 1988: 55–73.

Paris, Michael, 'Filming the People's War: The Dawn Guard, Desert Victory, Tunisian Victory and Burma Victory', in A. Burton, T. O'Sullivan and P. Wells (eds), *The Family Way. The Boulting Brothers and British Film Culture*, Trowbridge: Flicks Books, 2000.

Burns, Ken

Ken Burns is the documentary phenomenon of the last decade of the twentieth century. From The Civil War (1990) through Jazz (2001), Burns has produced and directed nine documentaries with a total running time of more than sixty hours for the Public Broadcasting System (PBS) in the United States. More than seventy million viewers have seen The Civil War and more than fifty million have seen Baseball (1994). Budgets for the Burns projects range from more than $3 million for The Civil War to $14 million for Jazz. (The sales of The Civil War on video had exceeded a million copies by 1993.) Public schools and libraries across America present this documentary to children and make it readily available to the public. The Civil War can stand with The Birth of a Nation (1915) and Gone with the Wind (1939) as landmarks in the politics of historical representation and of popular culture in twentieth-century America. Burns himself is a media celebrity, featuring widely on television, radio, and in the press (he was invited to the White House by both George H. Bush and Bill Clinton). Few would contest Gary Edgerton's observation that this documentary filmmaker is 'arguably the most recognizable and influential historian of his generation'. With the financial backing of PBS and the General Motors Corporation, and an experienced team of collaborators, at mid-career Burns appears likely to continue production at a remarkable pace.

Burns's project is to grapple with the national identity by exploring American history. His belief that the Civil War, baseball, and jazz are central to our culture motivated his grand documentary trilogy. So too, his conviction that individuals shape our historical destiny underlies his parallel series of American profiles. His respect for American institutions and his biographies of 'great' men and women testify to an allegiance to traditional values; yet his projects regularly portray reformers and even revolutionary figures, such as Frank Lloyd Wright, Susan B. Anthony, and Thomas Jefferson. Burns claims that America's racial heritage is the thread connecting all his work. (African Americans are obviously central to The Civil War and Jazz, and the prominence given the Negro leagues and Jackie Robinson's integration of the sport in Baseball offers more compelling evidence of the centrality of race to the Burns understanding of the United States.) A liberal, progressive sensibility guides the Burns exploration of what it means to be an American, and a fundamental allegiance to the national heritage unites the work.

The Ken Burns style helps to account for his enormous productivity. His historical documentaries have a fixed vocabulary of elements that offer flexibility within a well-established formula. Central to the method is the animation of still materials: photographs, paintings, and periodicals. With editing, moving camera, or zooming lens, Burns constructs a scene out of a single image. He wants his viewer to inhabit the picture as he brings it to life. The volume of this material can be enormous. The Civil War is reported to have used sixteen thousand photographs. In counterpoint, the filmmaker takes filmed footage, unpopulated landscapes, or empty buildings associated with an era and uses a stable, balanced composition to invest the image with stillness, allowing the shot to evoke a frozen past. A range of archival moving pictures fills out his compilation. Of course, the animation of still images in documentary goes back to Michelangelo (1940) and was used with eloquence by Alain Resnais in his documentaries from the 1950s. Burns himself acknowledges the influence of films such as City of Gold (1957) and The Real West (1961). The Burns visual style is derivative, but in his best work, outstanding.

The images from the past are further brought to life with the accompanying soundtracks. Various characters (such as Elijah Hunt Rhodes, Mary Chestnut, or Frederick Douglas among many others from The Civil War) constitute a 'chorus of voices' whose letters, diaries, speeches, and so forth are read by a distinguished actor, cultivating a highly personalized vocal delivery as the basis for each characterization. The documentaries establish and return to the cast of historical characters, allowing them to assume the intimacy and depth of figures from fiction. At their best, this chorus establishes contending characters animating dramatic conflict, as well as a sense of the variable forces propelling change. The soundtrack further evokes the past with folk tunes, period music, or other sounds associated with the era. These voices from the past are integrated with a general narrator and contemporary authorities (such as Gary Giddens, Gerald Early, or Wynton Marsalis in Jazz), who offer commentary and analysis culled from interviews. However, the authorities speak directly to the camera and address the viewer in the absence of any prompting or presence from the filmmaker. Rather than appearing as interviewees, these on-camera storytellers appear to be speaking directly to the viewer.

Finally, Burns segments his episodes into short sections of approximately ten to fifteen minutes, each one introduced by a simple title framed in black. The sections allow for a shift in subject or emphasis from a narrative description to an affecting personal tale, a flash forward or backward in time, or a montage of contending opinions. Episodes typically begin with an evocative introduction setting the tone before the general subject of the installment is announced with the credits.

In 1981 Burns's first film, The Brooklyn Bridge, appeared to have a fresh and engaging approach to the historical documentary. By the turn of the century, his style had become so widely imitated that television programming on the History or the Discovery Channel seems to have transformed it into an institutional practice. A challenge facing Burns at this point in his career is to develop his style, lest his work become undistinguishable from a movement he is largely responsible for inspiring.

The historical documentaries of Ken Burns have excited a new interest in history among the general public. Historians have greeted the phenomenon with mixed feelings. Though gratified by the attention, scholars are concerned because the films glide past controversy over evidence, method and interpretation that characterizes the discipline of history. Nonetheless, Ken Burns's documentaries address serious questions about what it means to be an American and explore a range of answers for an audience that is eager for more.

LEGER GRINDON

Biography

Born July 29, 1953 in Brooklyn, New York to Robert Kyle Burns, an anthropologist, and Lyla Smith (Tupper) Burns. Grew up in Newark, Delaware, and Ann Arbor, Michigan, where his father held positions as a university professor. Graduated from Hampshire College in 1975, majoring in film studies and design under the direction of Jerome Liebling and Elaine Mayes. Founded Florentine Films in 1975 with former classmates Buddy Squires and Roger Sherman. Beginning with The Brooklyn Bridge (1981) through Horatio's Drive: America's First Road Trip (2003), has worked as the producer and director, and frequently cinematographer and cowriter, on documentaries focusing on various aspects of American history and culture. Many of these works are multiple episode programs running between ten and twenty hours, most notably The Civil War (1990), Baseball (1994), and Jazz (2001). Has coauthored illustrated books that have accompanied his documentaries. Recipient of many awards including the Television Critics' Association Awards

(1991, 1995, 2001), Peabody Awards (1990, 1999, 2000), Emmy Awards (1991, 1994), and the Erik Barnouw Prize.

Selected films

1981 Brooklyn Bridge
1985 The Statue of Liberty
1990 Lindbergh
1990 The Civil War
1991 Empire of the Air: The Men Who Made Radio
1994 Baseball
1996 The West
1997 Lewis & Clark: The Journey of the Corps of Discovery
1998 Frank Lloyd Wright
1999 Not for Ourselves Alone: The Story of Elizabeth Cady Stanton & Susan B. Anthony
2001 Jazz
2001 Mark Twain
2003 Horatio's Drive: America's First Road Trip

Further reading

Blight, David W., 'Homer with a Camera, Our "Iliad" without the Aftermath: Ken Burns's Dialogue with Historians', *Reviews in American History* 25, 2, 1997: 351–9.

Burns, Ken 'In Search of the Painful, Essential Images of War', *The New York Times*, 27 January 1991: sec. 2:1.

Cripps, Thomas, 'Historical Truth: An Interview with Ken Burns', *American Historical Review* 100, 3, 1995: 741–64.

Edgerton, Gary R., 'Ken Burns: A Conversation with Public Television's Resident Historian', *Journal of American Culture* 18, 1, 1995: 1–12.

——*Ken Burns's America*, New York: Palgrave Macmillan, 2001.

Hackney, Sheldon. 'A Conversation with Ken Burns on Baseball', *Humanities* 15, 1994: 4–7, 48–53.

Henderson, Brian, 'The Civil War: "Did It Not Seem Real?"', *Film Quarterly* 44, 3, 1991: 2–14.

Lancioni, Judith, 'The Rhetoric of the Frame: Revisioning Archival Photographs in The Civil War', *Western Journal of Communication* 60, 1996: 397–414.

——'Ken Burns: The Art of the Artifact', in David Marc and Robert J. Thompson (eds), *Prime Time, Prime Movers: From I Love Lucy to L.A Law—America's Greatest TV Shows and the People Who Created Them*, Boston: Little, Brown, 1992.

McPherson, Tara, 'Both Kinds of Arms: Remembering The Civil War', *Velvet Light Trap* 35 1995: 3–18.

Thelen, David, 'The Movie Maker as Historian: Conversations with Ken Burns', *Journal of American History* 81, 3, 1994: 1031–50.

Tibbetts, John C., 'The Incredible Stillness of Being: Motionless Pictures in the Films of Ken Burns', *American Studies* 37, 1, 1996: 117–33.

Toplin, Robert B. (ed.), *Ken Burns's The Civil War: Historians Respond*, New York: Oxford, 1996.

C

Camera Natura

(Australia, Gibson, 1984)

Camera Natura uses an essay mode to deconstruct the discourses around the nonaboriginal imaging of the landscape. The film had its origins in director/writer Ross Gibson's writings, in particular his essays 'Camera Natura: Landscape in Australian Feature Films' and 'Geography and Gender', which appear in rewritten form in his book South of the West (1992). Gibson used images from films such as The Sons of Matthew (1949), Gallipoli (1981), Picnic at Hanging Rock (1975), and Mad Max II (1981) in Camera Natura to answer the question he set for himself in the initial article: 'What can the preoccupation [with the landscape] tell us about Australian culture, cinematic and general?' Gibson's essaying in this film involved the same elliptical image-voice relationship that is evident in the seminal role model for this mode—Chris Marker's Sunless (1983)—except that Camera Natura exhibits a critical poesy informed by a postcolonial and deconstructionist examination of Australian film culture evident in several independent films of the early to mid-1980s. These include Helen Grace's Serious Undertakings (1983) and Tracey Moffatt's Nice Coloured Girls (1987).

Although Camera Natura involves a bricolage of images, voices, and sounds, it contained a distinct line of argument, which is that the dominance of landscape images in Australian feature films of the 1970s and early 1980s can be linked to a reemergent nationalism at the time, and the landscape was seen as a delimited, manageable source of 'Australianness'. In this respect, Camera Natura could be called an 'essay in futility', bolstered by the inclusion of such images as the girls entering the rock from Picnic at Hanging Rock, footage of Donald Campbell's failed attempt at the world land speed record, and of Jack Thompson crashing his car from Sunday Too Far Away (1975). The idea of nonproductivity that these images denote implies that Australian film culture was exhausting itself and creating few future opportunities for itself.

Formally, Camera Natura is an adventurous departure from traditional documentary practices, including poetic and evocative voice-overs, drawing on the 'personal' style associated with a lineage of writing that can be traced back to the writing of the sixteenth-century essayist Michel de Montaigne. The film is also partly a compilation film, drawing on a host of images and sounds from Australian feature films to reconfigure these images and sounds in relation to the contemporary Australian social imaginary. In this regard the critical aspect of Camera Natura is related to the kind of postcolonial critique operating in a host of Australian films, all of which are concerned with examining white settler culture's inherited discursive patterns.

DEANE WILLIAMS

Camera Natura (Australia, 1984, 32 mins). Distributed by Ronin Films. Directed and written by Ross Gibson. Produced by John Cruthers. Cinematography by Ray Argall. Edited by Ian Allen. Sound by John Cruthers. Commentary by Vivienne Garrett, Alan Becher, Susan Dermody and Steve Bisley.

Further reading

Gibson, Ross, *The Diminishing Paradise: Changing Literary Perceptions of Australia*, Sydney: Sirius-Angus and Robertson, 1984.

——*South of the West: Postcolonialism and the Narrative Construction of Australia*, Bloomington, IN: Indiana University Press, 1992.

Martin, Adrian and Kaufman, Tina, 'Bushed: An Interview with Ross Gibson', *Filmnews* 16, 1986: 9–10.

Williams, Deane, 'From Camera Natura to Dead to the World', *Metro* 86, 1991: 27–31.

——*Mapping the Imaginary: Ross Gibson's Camera Natura*, Melbourne: Australian Film Institute/Australian Teachers of Media, 1996.

Canada

If documentary is the 'creative treatment of actuality', as John Grierson said, then in the beginning there was a lot more actuality then creative treatment. However, the actuality was not Canadian and the pattern that prevailed throughout the twentieth century was established. Moving pictures shown in Canadian theatres were rarely Canadian.

Lumière Bros representatives, Messieurs Minier and Pupier, brought moving pictures to Canada with a cinematographe screening in Montreal on June 27, 1896, at 78 Boulevard St Laurent. Among the early Lumière films shown that night were a train arriving at a station, a cavalry charge, waves breaking against rocks at the seashore, a card game between Lumière and friends in a garden, and a wall being torn down.

Three weeks later, on July 21, 1896, the rival Edison Vitascope was shown to an outdoor audience in Ottawa at the West End Park. Organized by Andrew and George Holland, the evening included live tricks on stage by pioneer exhibitor John C. Green, then known as Belsaz the Magician. The audience saw May Irwin, Canadian actress from Whitby, Ontario, kiss John Rice, as well as a train, a bathing scene at Atlantic City, four 'coloured boys' eating watermelons, and LoLo Fuller's serpentine dance.

Itinerant cameramen, such as Felix Mesguich and W.K.L. Dickson, began arriving in 1897 to shoot 'scenics' of the Canadian landscape. They usually headed for Niagara Falls, which was added time and again to the exotic sights seen by film viewers around the world. Robert Bonine went further afield to shoot footage of the Klondike Gold Rush.

James D. Freer, a Manitoba farmer and cinema hobbyist, was probably Canada's first filmmaker. He shot local scenes in 1897 and then was hired by the Canadian Pacific Railway (CPR) to tour Britain, showing his films and promoting immigration to Canada's 'golden west'. The CPR ensured that winter scenes were not on the program. Thus began a long tradition of sponsored films by the CPR, which led to the creation of a production company, Associated Screen News. Massey-Harris, which made farm equipment, and other companies also began sponsoring films.

The battle for Canadian screens

Leo-Ernest Ouimet, who established Canada's first luxury movie theatre in Montreal in 1906, soon began showing his own newsreels. After World War I he started the twice-weekly British Canadian Pathé News (1919–22), which combined Canadian and British newsreel items. Though popular, it could not compete with better-funded and -distributed American newsreels.

In fact, led by Adolph Zukor's Paramount, the major American companies were vertically integrating into exhibition, distribution, and production by the end of the war. This 'Hollywood studio system' left little room for an independent film industry in the United States or Canada. By 1922 Allen's, the largest Canadian exhibitor and one of the largest theatre chains in the world, went bankrupt competing against Famous Players, Paramount's Canadian theatre chain.

Private Canadian producers such as Ouimet or Ernest Shipman, whose most successful film was the feature drama Back to God's Country (1919), could no longer access the first-run Canadian theatre screens if they were outside the Hollywood system. They had to leave Canada and move to Los Angeles or New York if they wanted their films to be seen in Canada, or anywhere else.

The Canadian public did not seem concerned that their movie theatres showed mostly American films until the United States entered World War I. Then Canadians were outraged by patriotic war movies awash in American flags, which ignored the sacrifices of the French, British, and Canadians on the Western Front. Led by the Ontario Government, and soon followed by the federal government, public production bureaus were established to make Canadian nonfiction films.

State production of films in Canada began in 1917 with the establishment of the Ontario Government Motion Picture Bureau (1917–1934). The Ontario Bureau produced educational films, often on agricultural subjects, until it was closed down during the Depression. It was soon followed by the Canadian Government Motion Picture Bureau, which was absorbed by the National Film Board during World War II (see below). Thus, the National Film Board and its predecessors is probably the oldest continuously operating public film producer in the world (1918–).

Besides direct production through the public sector, the Canadian Government Motion Picture Bureau, and the Ontario Bureau to the NFB, the most important impetus to the production of Canadian nonfiction films was the Ontario 'talking newsreel' quota. This provincial screen-time quota was established in 1930 and continued until the end of theatrical newsreels in the 1950s. It required that each newsreel had to have forty percent 'British Empire' content, including twenty-five percent Canadian content. This created a theatrical market for Canadian newsreel items. Some private newsreel producers, such as Associated Screen News, then expanded into related documentary production.

Later, with the arrival of television, similar measures were tried, and Canadian programming was assured through the production of the public broadcaster and Canadian content quotas for all broadcasters.

Documentary explorers

Explorers increasingly used film to record their work and help raise funds for their explorations. From 1913 to 1916 George H. Wilkins filmed Canadian explorer Vilhjalmur Stefanssons's expedition in the Arctic. Richard S. Finnie shot many films about the North and directed the first Canadian feature documentary for the Canadian Government Motion Picture Bureau, In the Shadow of the Pole (1928), which recorded Canada's 1928 Arctic expedition.

Explorers like Robert Flaherty in northern Quebec, or Varick Frissell in Labrador, used film to document their work. Then, following the lead of Edward Curtis, they began to record the life of the people they knew and respected before their way of life was gone.

American photographer Edward S. Curtis had begun a lifelong project to record the American Indians before they disappeared. In 1914 he extended this work to create a 'documentary drama' using Kwakiutl natives of British Columbia as actors. His film, In the Land of the War Canoes (1914), however, is more fiction than nonfiction, more drama than documentary.

Varick Frissell was an American who had been drawn to the work of the Grenfell Mission in northern Newfoundland and went on to explore the interior of Labrador. By 1930 Frissell had raised enough money to produce a feature based on his own experiences of the seal hunt. At the insistence of the distributor, Paramount Pictures, The Viking (1931) had a romantic story and drama sequences directed by George Melford. Frissell directed the incredible documentary sequences in the film. These cost him his life when his ship blew up while he was filming.

Robert Flaherty, another American who grew up in Canadian mining camps and had spent most of his life in Canada, explored and prospected along Hudson's Bay for the Canadian Northern Railway. His employer, Sir William Mackenzie, encouraged Flaherty to record the life of the Inuit on film. In 1913 Flaherty began taking camera gear on his prospecting trips. His first film on Inuit life caught fire while being edited in Toronto. Undeterred, Flaherty returned to Hudson's Bay with the support of France's Revillon Frères fur traders. His second film was also produced with the help of Inuit, from developing film to suggesting ideas to shoot. Nanook of the North (1922) was about survival in the Arctic, and its dramatic footage was real, or seemed real. It was a hit around the world.

Robert Flaherty created a new film form by successfully marrying nonfiction, or apparent nonfiction, with a narrative storyline. Flaherty wanted a film showing the Inuit before their use of firearms, so his work is not an accurate record of the period. Yet Nanook seems true in its whole if not its parts, and it is usually considered the first Canadian documentary and indeed the first documentary ever made. Flaherty's work was an inspiration to the young John Grierson who developed a close, and often contentious, relationship with Flaherty.

Associated Screen News

The most important early Canadian production company was Associated Screen News (ASN), which was organized in 1920 in Montreal by the Canadian Pacific Railway. Ben Norrish moved from the public sector to run this company until it was sold in the 1950s. ASN produced sponsored films, newsreel segments, and theatrical shorts. It also depended on release print laboratory work from Hollywood companies.

A series of monthly nonfiction theatrical shorts called Canadian Cameos (1932–54) was produced by Gordon Sparling for ASN. One of the best of these is Rhapsody in Two Languages (1934), which Sparling directed in the 'city symphony' style with imaginative special effects. It is about a day in the life of Montreal and is one of the first Canadian sound films to have an original music score (by Howard Fogg).

Sparling directed Royal Banners Over Ottawa (1939), a record of the Royal visit to Canada's capitol. This was the first Canadian documentary shot in colour. Sparling also ran the Army Film and Photo Unit during the war and, after ASN's production department was closed down in 1957, he joined the National Film Board.

Crawley Films

The Canadian Film Awards was organized in 1949 and was Canada's first competitive film festival. Its first 'Film of the Year Award' went to a short documentary on Indian masks titled The Loon's Necklace (1948) by F.R. (Budge) Crawley and his wife Judith. Budge Crawley produced Newfoundland Scene (1952), which also won the Canadian Film Awards' 'Film of the Year'. Budge and Judy Crawley set up their film company in Ottawa during the war, but it came to national attention after winning these awards. Crawley Films grew, depending primarily on sponsored production, and became the largest private film production house in Canada from the 1950s to the 1970s. Towards the end of his career, Budge Crawley risked his company by making feature films, and Crawley films had to be sold owing to indebtedness in 1982.

Canadian Government Motion Picture Bureau

In response to requests for films on Canada's resources and industry, the Canadian government established a film production unit in 1918 under Ben Norrish, who moved on to ASN. This Publicity and Exhibits Bureau produced a successful series of theatrical shorts, Seeing Canada (1919–39), to encourage tourism and foreign investment.

Under Raymond Peck the Publicity and Exhibits Bureau was renamed the Canadian Government Motion Picture Bureau in 1923. The Bureau's most ambitious project was the feature documentary Lest We Forget (1935), produced and directed by Frank Badgley, who was also head of the Bureau. This film was a compilation documentary using newsreels, graphics, and reenacted scenes to tell the story of Canada's involvement in World War I.

NFB and John Grierson

Under the leadership of John Grierson, the work of the British Documentary Movement in the 1930s impressed Ross McLean, a member of the Canadian High Commission in London. By contrast, the films of the Canadian Government Motion Picture Bureau seemed dull and uninspired. Ross McLean believed that Grierson could do something about that.

In 1938 the Canadian Government invited Grierson to report on the work of the Bureau, and how it might be improved. Grierson quickly wrote a report that recommended a new organization be established to centralize all government film production. The National Film Board of Canada (NFB) was established in Ottawa in 1939 under its first Government Film Commissioner and CEO, John Grierson (1939–45). The Canadian Government Motion Picture Bureau was absorbed by the NFB in 1941.

The war provided a propaganda focus for the NFB, which quickly grew under Grierson's energetic leadership. Grierson invited veteran documentary filmmakers, such as Boris Kaufman and Joris Ivens, to work at the Ottawa offices of the Board, which were located in an old sawmill. Members of the British Documentary Movement, such as Stanley Hawes, Stuart Legg, Raymond Spottiswoode, and Norman McLaren, arrived to teach documentary and animation to their young staff.

Canadians hired by Grierson included Tom Daly, Sydney Newman, Louis Applebaum, Jim McKay, Vincent Paquette, Margaret Ann Adamson, George Dunning, Lorne Greene, Donald Buchanan, Grant McLean, Jim Beveridge, Jane Marsh Beveridge, Julian Roffman, Evelyn Spice Cherry, Lawrence Cherry, Guy Glover, and many more. At the end of the war the NFB had a staff of more than seven hundred employees.

The Case of Charlie Gordon (1939), directed by Stuart Legg, was the first film distributed by the NFB. The NFB went on to produce hundreds of films during the war but was best known for its two theatrical series of one- or two-reel shorts. The Canada Carries On (1940–59) series was produced by Stuart Legg and began with the release of his Atlantic Patrol (1940).

The World in Action (1942–5) series took a more international slant and began with a re-release of Warclouds in the Pacific (1941) by Stuart Legg. It warned of a possible Japanese attack on the American Pacific fleet. As a result of this timely film, the NFB got a contract to show this series in six thousand American theatres. This series was also produced by Stuart Legg with the assistance of Tom Daly, using a great deal of compilation footage from all the combatants.

Other important titles included Inside Fighting Russia (1942), Our Northern Neighbour (1943), The War for Men's Minds (1943), and Balkan Powder Keg (1944).

The NFB won the first Oscar for documentary in 1941 with Legg's Churchill's Island (1941). It showed English resolve to resist an anticipated German invasion, and was narrated by Lorne Greene, who became known as 'the voice of doom'.

The Canadian Army Film and Photo Unit was created in 1943 to provide newsreel footage shot by Army cameramen. It included ASN's Gordon Sparling and future Canadian Film Development Corporation head Michael Spencer. However, Grierson was unsuccessful in his attempt to incorporate this unit into the NFB's operations.

The Canada Carries On theatrical series continued until 1959, as did the Eye Witness/ Coup d'oeil (1947–59) series, which replaced The World in Action series. However, Grierson often said that there were more seats in community halls than in theatres.

In 1942 Donald Buchanan, cofounder of the National Film Society in 1935, was hired by the NFB to organize nontheatrical film circuits. Itinerant NFB projectionists took films to rural, industrial, and union audiences. In 1943 the Volunteer Projection Service was established to encourage film distribution to urban community groups not covered by the industrial or trade union circuits. More than six hundred libraries distributed NFB films under contract by the end of the war. After the war the film circuits continued as Film Councils, which numbered nearly five hundred in 1955.

John Grierson resigned as Government Film Commissioner in November 1945 and was replaced by his deputy, Ross McLean (1945–50). Now at the peak of his influence, Grierson became one of the first victims of the Cold War 'red scare'. Cipher clerk Igor Gouzenko defected from the Soviet Embassy in Ottawa with documents proving that the Soviets ran a spy ring in Canada during the war. One ambivalent reference to Grierson cast suspicion on him. As the red scare deepened, the staff of the NFB came under growing suspicion. The new Film Commissioner, Arthur Irwin (1950–3), let some staff go to satisfy the Board's political critics.

NFB's Unit B

After World War II NFB filmmakers wanted their work identified with screen credits, which Grierson had discouraged to avoid undermining anonymous 'public service' values. When the NFB was reorganized into four production units in 1948, the 'unGriersonian' idea that 'public service' filmmakers should be recognized as artists took hold and screen credits were initiated.

Unit B was responsible for scientific, cultural, and animated films. Under executive producer Tom Daly, Unit B became known for its groundbreaking work that won numerous awards and gave the NFB an international reputation for quality and innovation. The core of Unit B included Roman Kroitor, Wolf Koenig, Terry Macartney-Filgate, Stanley Jackson, Colin Low, Bob Verrall, Bill Greaves, Don Owen, Gerald Potterton, Arthur Lipsett, as well as the veteran animator Norman McLaren.

Neighbours (1952), a live-action pixilation film by the NFB's Norman McLaren, won the Oscar for Best Documentary Short. This was a surprise because his film is not a documentary, but rather an animated drama. It also has a strong anti-war message, which one would not expect the American Academy to appreciate since it was at that time fighting the Cold War and losing soldiers in Korea.

One of the first films directed by Colin Low, and shot by Wolf Koenig, was Corral (1954), about a cowboy breaking a wild horse on a ranch in Alberta. Breaking with traditional Griersonian voice-over narration, Eldon Rathburn's guitar score is the only sound in the film. Another important NFB production was Paul Tomkowicz: Street-railway Switchman (1954), directed by Roman Kroitor. It is a melancholy 'film noir' short about an immigrant who keeps the trolleys running through Winnipeg's severe winter.

American ex-patriot Bill Greaves joined Unit B as an editor. When he directed the NFB documentary Putting It Straight (1957), he became Canada's first black filmmaker. Encouraged by the Civil Rights movement, Greaves returned to New York and continued his film career.

Using an animation stand modified by Roman Kroitor, Wolf Koenig and Colin Low successfully combined historical photos and new footage in City of Gold (1957). A new kind of photo-documentary, their evocative film about the Klondike Gold Rush was narrated by Yukon native Pierre Berton.

NFB and cinéma vérité

The NFB was a key innovator in the worldwide race to produce location sync-sound films, better known as cinéma vérité or direct cinema. The Board's staff worked on many technical innovations to make its 16mm sync-sound production equipment much lighter and more portable. The key to the NFB's early handheld shooting was the 'Sprocketape' portable magnetic sound recorder invented by Ches Beachell in 1955.

Influenced by the work of French photographer Henri Cartier-Bresson, Unit B experimented with cinéma vérité sequences in the Candid Eye (1958–9) TV series. Days Before Christmas (1958), directed by Terry Macartney-Filgate, Stanley Jackson, and Wolf Koenig, is a pastiche of events preceding 1957's Christmas in Montreal, and includes some of the first handheld sync-sound location shooting. Terry Macartney-Filgate's The Back-breaking Leaf (1959), about migrant tobacco workers in Ontario, used more extensive sync-sound location shooting.

The Candid Eye films, together with NFB French-language productions such as Michel Brault and Gilles Groulx's Les Raquetteurs (1958), as well as the work of Robert Drew Associates in New York, Jean Rouch in Paris, and the Free Cinema filmmakers in England, began the cinéma vérité documentary movement.

Perhaps the most important cinéma vérité film made at this time was Lonely Boy (1961), directed by Wolf Koenig and Roman Kroitor and shot by Koenig. It is a portrait of Canadian teenage pop singer Paul Anka. This film experiments with sound as well as image and 'reflexively' puts the filmmakers into the story.

Although not a Unit B alumnus, ex-journalist Don Brittain becomes one of the NFB's foremost documentary fillmmakers with a cinéma vérité portrait of Canada's greatest living poet in Ladies and Gentleman … Mr Leonard Cohen (1965), codirected with Don Owen. Brittain then codirected and wrote Memorandum (1965) with cinematographer John Spotton. This film blends archival and cinéma vérité footage to create a moving testament to the Holocaust. Later in his career Brittain increasingly turned to drama documentary and TV drama in a series of CBC-NFB coproductions.

NFB's Labyrinth

The Montreal World's Fair, Expo '67, was a showcase for film experimentation and prestige multiscreen or large-screen projects. Two notable Canadian contributions were antecedents of IMAX. One was A Place to Stand (1967) by Chris Chapman, a multi-image short projected in 70mm on a large screen at the Ontario Pavilion. The other was the NFB's most ambitious project, its Labyrinth pavilion for Expo '67, created by Hugh O'Connor, Roman Kroitor, and Colin Low. They invented a cruciform, multi-image screen as well as a display on two screens at a ninety-degree angle from each other. The $4.5 million pavilion was a stunning success with more than 1.3 million visitors.

Kroitor, Graeme Ferguson, and Robert Kerr formed the Multiscreen Corporation to bring the new IMAX format to the Osaka World's Fair. Their first IMAX film was Tiger Child (1970), directed by Don Brittain. Graeme Ferguson directed North of Superior (1971), which opened the first dedicated IMAX theatre, the Cinesphere in Toronto. IMAX films are also projected in three hundred and sixty-degree dome theatres called OMNIMAX. The first 3-D IMAX film, Transitions (1986), by Colin Low and Tony Ianzelo, was produced by the NFB for Vancouver's Expo '86.

NFB's Challenge for Change

The Things I Cannot Change (1966), directed by Tanya Ballantyne, shot by Paul Leach, and produced by John Kemeny, is a cinéma vérité film about a poor Montreal family. Unfortunately, the family was ridiculed after the film was broadcast, and they decided to leave their neighbourhood. However, the film was a critical success and sparked the groundbreaking Challenge for Change (1967–80) programme of social action filmmaking developed by John Kemeny, Colin Low, and George C. Stoney.

A French counterpart, Société nouvelle, was established under producer Léonard Forest. Challenge for Change/Société nouvelle experimented with half-inch video technology as early as 1967. VTR St-Jacques (1969) by Bonnie Sherr Klein and Dorothy Henaut was produced entirely on videotape. Despite the occasional controversy, this innovative programme produced about one hundred and forty films, which encouraged communication between the disenfranchised and the decision-makers. It was renewed until 1980.

NFB and aboriginal production

Challenge for Change changed the way in which the NFB, and perhaps the country, looked at native issues when it brought together natives from across the country to learning filmmaking skills. The most significant result was The Ballad of Crowfoot (1968) by Willie Dunn, a compilation documentary of photos and old footage about the white man's broken promises. The soundtrack is a bitter ballad written and sung by Dunn.

Other important Challenge for Change films on native issues include You Are on Indian Land (1969) by Mort Ransen, which showed natives demonstrating at a Mohawk reserve on the St Lawrence River. Cree Hunters of Mistassini (1974) by Boyce Richardson and Tony Ianzelo follows Cree families at a winter camp and shows the ecological principles that guide their way of life.

The best-known aboriginal filmmaker in Canada is the NFB's Alanis Obomsawin. Her work has documented social and political problems, often providing historical context. Obomsawin made Kanehsatake: 270 Years of Resistance (1993) and Rocks at Whiskey Trench (2000) about the confrontation between natives and the military at a Mohawk reserve near Montreal.

NFB's Studio D

In 1974 Challenge for Change producer Kathleen Shannon (Working Mothers series, 1974) succeeded in setting up a feminist production studio to 'make films by, for, and about women'. Studio D was known for innovative non-theatrical distribution and controversial films. It also won more Oscars than any other NFB studio, often for content more than filmmaking style. Oscar winners are I'll Find a Way (1977) by Beverly Shaffer, who interviewed a child with spina bifida; If You Love This Planet (1983) by Terre Nash, an antinuclear war speech by Dr Helen Caldicott; and Flamenco at 5:15 (1984) by Cynthia Scott, which gives an impressionistic view of a flamenco class at the National Ballet School of Canada.

Among the studio's more controversial and popular films were Not a Love Story: A Film About Pornography (1981), by Bonnie Sherr Klein and Dorothy Henaut, and Forbidden Love: The Unashamed Stories of Lesbian Lives (1993), by Margaret Pettigrew, Aerlyn Weissman, and Lynne Fernie about the portrayal of the lesbian subculture of the 1950s and 1960s. Studio D was closed down as the NFB faced growing financial pressures in the mid-1990s.

NFB decentralization

The NFB moved its headquarters from the Ottawa sawmill to a new building in Montreal. This move had a large impact on the use of French at the Board, and the balance of relations between the linguistic groups. Guy Roberge (1957–66), former Liberal member of the Quebec National Assembly, replaced Albert Trueman (1953–7) as Government Film Commissioner and Chief Executive Officer (CEO) of the NFB. He was the first francophone Film

Commissioner and, arguably, his tenure marked the creative peak of the Board.

The NFB set up an autonomous French Production unit under Fernand Dansereau in 1962. In 1964 Pierre Juneau was appointed director of French Production and Grant McLean headed English Production. McLean dismantled the producer-run unit system in favour of the 'pool' system, which gave greater autonomy to directors through a programme committee, and decentralized program planning.

The 1965 Sheppard Report, commissioned by the government from filmmaker Gordon Sheppard, recommended that the NFB 'gradually cease to staff-produce most of its films and instead have the majority of them made by private Canadian producers and freelancers on contract' (in 'A Special Report on the Cultural Policy and Activities of the Government of Canada, 1965–66'). Partly in response to the Sheppard Report, the NFB took the first steps toward regionalization of English production by setting up an office in Vancouver under Peter Jones in 1965. Eventually, most English production was produced by regional offices from Vancouver to Halifax. Over time, regionalization and privatization had a radical impact on the NFB and Canadian filmmaking.

'Make or buy?'

The Canadian government had responded to the problems of a small and linguistically fragmented market by establishing public sector production organizations such as the NFB and CBC. The private sector producers then complained about the resources going to the public sector and successfully lobbied to have public funding schemes created to finance private or independent production such as the Canadian Film Development Corporation in 1967 (now Telefilm Canada) or the Canadian Broadcast Program Development Fund in 1983 (now the Canadian Television Fund).

This production funding was aimed at independent producers but also supported private commercial broadcasters. As a result, direct funding for vertically integrated public producers or broadcasters, such as the NFB and CBC, has declined. The government has shifted its emphasis from 'make' in the public sector to 'buy' in the private sector. Now it is often difficult to tell whether a documentary is an 'NFB film', a 'CBC film', or 'independent'.

Decline of the NFB

NFB budgets declined beginning in 1968 when the federal government announced austerity measures that reduced NFB revenues. In addition, the filmmakers and technicians organized a union and negotiated a collective agreement that increased the Board's costs. Hugo McPherson, the new Film Commissioner (1967–70), was forced to dismiss recently hired staff. Caught between ongoing financial cuts and filmmaker discontent, McPherson resigned in 1970.

French and English tensions increased during the tenure of Sydney Newman (1970–5). He was a unilingual NFB wartime producer who had worked extensively in British television drama. Despite the appointment of francophone producer André Lamy as his deputy, Newman had ongoing problems with Quebec nationalist filmmakers. André Lamy (1975–9) succeeded Newman as Film Commissioner.

In 1980 the Federal Cultural Policy Review Committee was created and chaired by Louis Applebaum and Jacques Hebert. Its 'Applebert' report suggested that the NFB had outlived its usefulness, and that all of its production should be in the private sector. The report recommended that the NFB should be scaled back to a research and training facility. NFB head James Domville (1979–84) forcefully rejected this recommendation, but the report influenced government policy.

In 1984 Minister of Communications Francis Fox released his 'National Film and Video Policy', which significantly reduced the responsibilities and size of the NFB. The Board lost control of government-sponsored films, the still photo unit, film certification, and most of its foreign offices.

The new Film Commissioner, François Macerola (1984–8), was forced to initiate more cutbacks, and he then faced a major controversy. The docudrama The Kid Who Couldn't Miss (1982) by Paul Cowan claimed that Canada's most famous World War I flying ace, Billy Bishop, had lied about the number of enemy planes he had shot down. Veterans' groups were outraged, though they could not disprove the thesis of the film. A Senate subcommittee requested that the NFB withdraw the film, but Film Commissioner Macerola refused. A compromise was reached and a credit was added to the film that it was interpretive and dramatic in nature.

After Macerola, Joan Pennefather (1989–94) became the first woman to head the NFB, and celebrated its fiftieth anniversary in 1989. Sandra MacDonald (1995–2001) replaced her and faced the most severe of many funding cutbacks in 1995 and 1996. MacDonald cut one hundred and eighty jobs, closed the Board's film laboratory, and rented out the soundstage. Jacques Bensimon served as Film Commissioner from 2001 to 2006, when in constant dollars, the budget of the NFB was about twenty-five percent of its budget in 1966. Nearly all of its productions now require some outside financing and are made by freelance filmmakers. Tom Perlmutter took over as Film Commissioner in 2007.

Canadian Broadcasting Corporation

In 1952 Canadian Broadcasting Corporation Chair and CEO Davidson Dunton launched Canadian television in Toronto and Montreal. The American television networks wanted the CBC to become their affiliate and launched a programme boycott that lasted for three months. Dunton overcame the boycott, and the CBC won the battle for control of television in Canada. TV soon became the primary distribution outlet for documentaries.

CBC public affairs series

The line between CBC documentaries and public affairs programmes has not always been clear. The development of CBC public affairs programs began with Tabloid (1953–63) and Close-Up (1957–63), which were produced by Ross McLean (no relation to the NFB's Ross McLean) and his protégées, Douglas Leiterman and Patrick Watson.

Leiterman and Watson, influenced by the cinéma vérité movement and the British programme, This Was the Week That Was (1962–3), developed the hugely popular and controversial This Hour Has Seven Days (1964–6). This programme was cancelled by the CBC in a clash between senior management and the producers over control of the programme's content and its increasingly dramatic, even theatrical, approach to journalism.

Douglas Leiterman and Patrick Watson left Canada after the programme was cancelled and worked for some years in New York. There Leiterman was involved in the development of CBS's 60 Minutes public affairs series, while Patrick Watson hosted WNET's public affairs programme The Fifty-First State. He later produced the series The Struggle for Democracy (1989–90) with Ted Remerowski, Nancy Button, and Michael Levine, which was broadcast by CBC.

Following Seven Days, the flagship CBC public affairs series has been the fifth estate (1974–). Its best-known documentary was Just Another Missing Kid (1982) by Ian Parker and John Zaritsky, which won the 1983 Academy Award. The Trouble with Evan (1994), by Neil Docherty, recorded a troubled young boy's home life using cameras attached to ceilings in his family's apartment. There was no camera crew for much of the film.

The CBC moved the twenty-two-minute national news from 11 pm to 10 pm and added a public affairs segment called The Journal (1982–92) for the balance of the hour. This new programme was produced by Mark Starowicz and proved a popular success.

The longest running public affairs series has been the science programme, The Nature of Things (1961–), first produced by James Murray. It is currently hosted by David Suzuki and called The Nature of Things with David Suzuki (1980–). This programme has been a powerful voice, and Suzuki a popular advocate for environmental issues.

CBC documentary series

As early as 1953 the CBC established a film unit in Vancouver under Stan Fox. It became a training ground for Allan King, Ron Kelly, Daryl Duke, Gene Lawrence, Arla Saare, and many others. Memorable among these early CBC documentaries was Skid Row (1956) by Allan King.

The Document (1962–9) series was also produced by Douglas Leiterman and Patrick Watson and later Richard Nielsen. It often ran cinéma vérité documentaries. Among the most powerful were The Seven Hundred Million (1964) by Patrick Watson, about China; Summer in Mississippi (1964) by Beryl Fox, about the Civil Rights movement in the US South; and Mills of the Gods: Vietnam (1965) directed by Beryl Fox, shot by Erik Durschmeid, and edited by Don Haig. This was one of the earliest films critical of the Vietnam War and it is considered by some to be the best Canadian documentary of all time.

After the demise of Document, the centre of documentary gravity in the CBC moved from Toronto to Ottawa. Cameron Graham produced a number of important series such as The Tenth Decade (1971) about Canada from 1957 to 1967; First Person Singular (1973 and 1975), with Munroe Scott, the memoirs of former Prime Minister Lester Pearson; The Days Before Yesterday (1973), with Brian Nolan, Scott, and Ed Reid, about Canadian history in the first half of the twentieth century; and The Canadian Establishment (1980–1) with Marrin Canell, Ted Remerowski, and Peter Pearson and based on Peter C. Newman's book. James Murray produced the extremely popular The National Dream (1974) narrated by Pierre Berton and based on his history of the Canadian Pacific Railway.

Besides The Journal, Mark Starowicz produced an hour-long anthology documentary series called Witness (1982–2003). This was the major venue for one-off prime-time documentaries on the English network and included documentaries from Canada and around the world.

The most ambitious documentary series the CBC ever attempted was the international coproduction Canada: A People's History (2000). This seventeen-part series included dramatic sequences in both languages and was the brainchild of Mark Starowicz. It became a popular event attracting as many as 2.3 million English-speaking viewers.

Controversial CBC documentaries

As a public broadcaster, controversial subjects often generate a great deal of criticism for the CBC. Therefore, management has sometimes been hesitant to broadcast a documentary that it feared would cause controversy. More recently, the nature of the criticism, and the CBC's reaction to it, has changed.

The CBC refused to broadcast Mr Pearson (1964) by Dick Ballentine and shot by Donn Pennebaker. This cinéma vérité portrait showed the Prime Minister in a sometimes unflattering light and was not broadcast until 1969, after Alphonse Ouimet had stepped down as president of the CBC.

The cinéma vérité classic Warrendale (1967), by Allan King, is about a controversial home for disturbed kids. It was never broadcast by the CBC because the children in the film used profanity. King then made the cinéma vérité A Married Couple (1969), shot by Richard Leiterman, about a disintegrating marriage. Gradually, he moved into dramatic films.

Perhaps the most influential CBC documentary was Air of Death (1967) by Larry Gosnell. This film raised questions about air pollution in a small Ontario town and helped start the environmental movement in Canada. It was attacked by the Ontario government and the industries in question. The federal regulator (CRTC) held a major hearing in 1969 to review the criticisms. The CBC stood by the programme and said that a democratic society needed to see minority, or controversial, opinions. The CRTC agreed.

The Valour and the Horror (1992) was a brilliant series of three feature documentaries with dramatic segments. The series was a CBC, NFB, and Gala-film coproduction directed by Brian McKenna with Terrence McKenna and produced by Arnie Gelbart, André Lamy, Darce Fardy, Adam Symansky, and D'Arcy O'Connor. Particularly controversial was the episode Death by Moonlight (1992), which maintained that the bombing campaign against Germany was deliberately planned by Air Marshall Athur Harris to maximize civilian casualties. Veterans' organizations were outraged, though they couldn't dispute the facts cited, and Senator Jack Marshall investigated. The CBC seemed to indicate that it would be more careful in the future, especially with dramatic reenactments in documentaries. Together with the NFB's The Kid Who Couldn't Miss, it would seem that revisionist military history is the most sensitive subject on Canadian television.

Theatrical feature documentaries

The subjects of Canadian feature documentaries have evolved over the decades, from royal visits, wildlife, and shipwrecks to more controversial subjects. As the economics of the industry changed, feature documentaries also moved from NFB productions to NFB coproductions and independent films.

Theatrical dramas have also been influenced by Canadian documentary style, particularly in the 1960s and 1970s. Examples include the NFB's Nobody Waved Goodbye (1964) by Don Owen and the independent Goin' Down the Road (1970) by Don Shebib.

The NFB's The Royal Journey (1951), directed by David Bairstow, Gudrun Parker, and Roger Blais, recorded the visit of Princess Elizabeth and Prince Philip to Canada and the United States. It was shot in the new Eastman color negative stock. In three months, more than two million people saw The Royal Journey in theatres, and it became Canada's most successful theatrical documentary feature.

Naturalist Bill Mason's NFB feature documentary about raising wolves, Cry of the Wild (1972), became a surprise hit, opening in five hundred American theatres. It grossed $4.5 million in North America.

Budge Crawley had built the largest private film company in Canada on sponsored films, but he always had larger ambitions and wanted to produce features. Janis (1974), produced by Crawley and directed by Howard Alk and Seaton Findlay, is a compilation documentary on the life of singer Janis Joplin before her untimely death in 1970. The Man Who Skied Down Everest (1975) was produced and directed by Crawley from footage he acquired of Japanese skier Yuichiro Miura attempting to ski down Everest. It won the Oscar for best feature documentary.

Peter Wintonick and Mark Achbar coproduced with the NFB a magnum opus on Noam Chomsky titled Manufacturing Consent: Noam Chomsky and the Media (1992). This film found clever visual metaphors to demonstrate Chomsky's ideas about the media, as well as his life as a public intellectual. Despite its length and subject, it grossed about $1 million in theatres worldwide.

Titanica (1992) was produced by Stephen Low and Pietro Serapiglia and directed by Stephen Low. It is a feature IMAX documentary about the exploration of the wreck of the Titanic. It has been one of the highest-grossing Canadian films.

Independent filmmaker Ron Mann has explored a range of marginal cultures through his feature documentaries. These include Poetry in Motion (1982), Comic Book Confidential (1988), and Grass (2000), which is about marijuana.

A Place Called Chiapas (1999) by Vancouver filmmaker Nettie Wild, was produced with Kirk Tougas and Betsy Carson. It is a cinéma vérité look at the Zapatista uprising in Mexico that takes a strong political position.

Another independent Vancouver production, The Corporation (2003), directed by Mark Achbar and Jennifer Abbott, written by Joel Bakan, and produced by Bart Simpson, takes a critical look at capitalism by psychoanalysing the corporation. It has grossed nearly $5 million in theatres worldwide.

At present, the audience for theatrical feature-length documentaries has never been greater or more interested in seeing a uncompromising point of view, as The Corporation and Michael Moore's Fahrenheit 9/11 have shown.

Television explosion: the best of times and the worst of times

Between 1952 and the arrival of commercial television in 1960, the CBC was the only television outlet for documentaries. As a public broadcaster, it accepted its responsibility to broadcast public affairs and documentaries. In general, the commercial channels were not interested in documentaries and preferred scheduling dramas, usually from the United States, which could attract larger audiences.

In 1970 the first provincial educational channel was set up in Ontario, TVOntario, and this was followed by a similar educational channel in Quebec in 1974, Télé-Québec. These, and other provincial channels that followed, increased the market for documentaries, but they could not pay as much as national broadcasters.

Three fundamental changes occurred in the broadcasting landscape in the 1980s and 1990s that increased the demand for, and supply of, Canadian documentaries. First, in 1983 the federal government set up the Canadian Broadcast Program Development Fund (now called the Canadian Television Fund) with $35 million to support independent television production. Some of this money, as well as tax benefits, was available for documentaries. The creation of these funds shifted the balance of financial power from public broadcasters and the NFB, which faced ongoing cutbacks, to commercial broadcasters. This trend to private broadcasters also increased the industrialization of documentary production and commercialization of subjects, including 'reality TV'.

Second, in 1984 the federal broadcast regulator (CRTC), began licensing 'specialty channels', which were distributed by satellite and cable. In 1987 the CBC's second channel, Newsworld, was licensed, along with Vision TV, a multi-faith channel. These were followed by other specialty channels that depended heavily on documentaries such as Discovery Channel (1994), Bravo (1994), and the History Channel (1996). In 2000 the NFB and CBC became minority partners with a private broadcaster in The Documentary Channel, a specialty digital cable network. Although these channels increased the demand for documentaries, this market fragmentation lowered the average fees paid to documentary producers.

Third, documentary production was revolutionized by videotape and digital technology. These technological changes reduced the cost of production compared to film. Yet the supply of new funding, through a complicated network of tax credits and production funds, could not keep pace with demand created by a cascade of new specialty channels. As a result of these technological and market changes the average budget for Canadian documentaries fell rapidly in the last few decades of the twentieth century, while audiences for documentaries increased both on television and in theatres.

Faced with deteriorating budgets and working conditions, independent documentary filmmakers started an organization in Toronto in 1983 to lobby on their behalf. Called the Canadian Independent Film Caucus (CIFC), it created Point of View magazine in 1991 and the Hot Docs film festival in 1993. The CIFC expanded nationally in 1995 and changed its name in 2003 to the Documentary Organization of Canada.

KIRWAN COX

See also: Janis; Obomsawin, Alanis

Further reading

Bidd, Donald F., *The NFB Film Guide: The Productions of the National Film Board of Canada from 1939 to 1989*, Ottawa: NFB, 1991.

Evans, Gary, *John Grierson and the National Film Board: The Politics of Wartime Propaganda*, Toronto: University of Toronto Press, 1984.

——*In the National Interest: A Chronicle of the National Film Board of Canada from 1949 to 1989*, Toronto: University of Toronto Press, 1991.

Leach, Jim, *Candid Eyes: Essays on Canadian Documentaries*, ed. Jeanette Sloniowski, Toronto: University of Toronto Press, 2003.

Morris, Peter, *Embattled Shadows: A History of Canadian Cinema 1895–1939*, Montreal: McGill-Queen's University Press, 1978.

Steven, Peter, *Brink of Reality: New Canadian Documentary Film and Video*, Toronto: Between the Lines Press, 1993.

Veronneau, Pierre, *Self Portrait: Essays on the Canadian and Quebec Cinemas*, ed. Piers Handling, Ottawa: Canadian Film Institute, 1980.

Wise, Wyndam, *Take One's Essential Guide to Canadian Film*, Toronto: University of Toronto Press, 2001.

Canada Carries On

(1940–51)

Canada Carries On is the title given to the first major program of films undertaken by the National Film Board of Canada (NFB). The brainchild of NFB founder and Commissioner John Grierson and his chief lieutenant, Stuart Legg, it was initiated immediately after Canada's entry into World War II and continued long afterward. Sixty-two films were made for the series during the war, and one hundred and thirty-six after the war. The wartime phase of the series is its most significant.

Grierson put Legg in charge of the series. Legg directed, edited, and wrote the early entries, and throughout the war the series reflected Legg's approach to filmmaking. The films' style was inspired by the American March of Time series. They were compilation films, made from a combination of original footage, Allied combat footage, captured enemy footage, and other material that poured into the Film Board's vaults during the war. The first film in the series, Atlantic Patrol (1940), used some original footage but mostly stock footage from the Canadian Navy. The next two films, Letter from Aldershot (1940) and The Home Front (1940), used mostly original footage but some stock material. Whatever the particular mix of footage, the films were fast-paced and ranged from ten to twenty-two minutes long. They contained little or no dialogue and were narrated somewhat bombastically by Lorne Greene. Structurally they aimed to capture the audience's full attention early on, then rising in intensity, leading to a climactic ending. They were essentially filmed lectures, but the rich variety of footage, deft editing, solid writing, and other production values, such as original music, rendered them highly watchable.

The original aim of the series was to build and sustain Canadian morale by dramatizing Canada's war effort. Although the series emphasized Canada, however, it portrayed Canada's war efforts in relation to the world, and a few of the films had little or no Canadian content. The films displayed an intellectual boldness that often led to controversy for the NFB. When they were criticized for acknowledging the military strength of the Axis powers, Grierson countered that to deny the strength of the enemy would undermine the films' credibility. Occasionally, the perceived ideology of the films upset politicians and government officials.

Churchill's Island (1941), about the defense of Britain, made use of British material and footage from captured Germans. It presents the Germans as a ferocious enemy, but the British as determined and able to repel them. It was regarded at the time as innovative in its treatment of its subject a whole, and it won a special Academy Award in 1942. Geopolitik: Hitler's Plan for Empire (1942) also shows Germany as a formidable enemy while exemplifying the broader view that Grierson and Legg wanted the series to project, and it probably stands up even today as reliable history. The Gates of Italy (1943) was alleged to be soft on fascism because it lauds Italian culture and history and treats the Italian people warmly, praising them for honesty and lamenting their suffering. The film quotes contemptuous remarks about Hitler by Mussolini, but it also portrays Mussolini as a fool. Other films provoked charges of communist sympathies.

The analytical caliber of the series, as well as its creative energy, was exemplified in War Clouds in the Pacific (1941). Compiled from stock footage, the film predicted, against prevailing expert opinion, a Japanese attack on North America. Ten days after the film's release in late November, the Japanese attacked Pearl Harbor. Suddenly the film was in demand in the United States. The NFB released the film there under a new series title, The World in Action, which became a free-standing series in its own right for the duration of the war. The new series closely resembled Canada Carries On, the main difference being that while the original series emphasized Canada in relation to the world, the new series emphasized the world in relation to Canada; however, it is sometimes difficult to tell from the film itself to which series it belonged.

Legg took over The World in Action, and Canada Carries On was turned over to Canadian filmmakers Sydney Newman and Guy Glover. They employed a range of Canadian directors, put more Canadian content into the films, and loosened them up stylistically. Lorne Greene was dropped as the narrator. Post-synchronized sound effects began to be used, as in Ordeal by Ice (1945). After the war the series continued, but grew increasingly parochial and dull. By the late 1950s it had become somewhat eclectic. Some outstanding films, such as Corral (1954), although not initiated by the series, were appropriated for it and distributed under its title, as were various animation films such as The Romance of Transportation in Canada (1953).

D.B. JONES

See also: Churchill's Island; Grierson, John; Legg, Stuart; March of Time; World in Action, The

Further reading

Beveridge, James, *John Grierson: Film Master*, London: Macmillan, 1979.

Ellis, Jack, 'John Grierson's Relation with British Documentary During World War Two', in *John Grierson and the NFB*, The John Grierson McGill University Project, ECW Press, 1984.

Evans, Gary, *John Grierson and the National Film Board*, Toronto: University of Toronto Press, 1986.

Fielding, Raymond, *The March of Time, 1935–1951*, New York: Oxford University Press, 1978.

Jones, D.B., *Movies and Memoranda*, Ottawa: Deneau, 1982.

——*The Best Butler in the Business: Tom Daly of the National Film Board of Canada*, Toronto: University of Toronto Press, 1996.

Leyda, Jay, *Films Beget Films: A Study of the Compilation Film*, London: George Allen & Unwin, 1964.

Nelson, Joyce, *The Colonized Eye: Rethinking the Grierson Legend*, Toronto: Between the Lines, 1988.

Rotha, Paul, *Documentary Film*, third edn, London: Faber & Faber, 1952.

Canada, French

The history of documentary film practice in French Canada is closely related to the history of the National Film Board of Canada (NFB). Although the NFB, from its inception in 1939 to the mid-1950s, focused almost exclusively on

English-language productions, the relocation of its headquarters from Ottawa (Ontario) to Montréal (Québec) in 1956 had a profound impact on francophone documentary filmmaking. In fact, the move to Montréal could be seen as marking the beginning of the documentary in Québec. Undoubtedly, the period immediately after the 1956 move represents something of a 'golden age' in the history of French-language cinema in Canada. However, a documentary practice in Québec can be traced back to at least the 1930s, and the foundations laid during the early years of the sound film had a lasting influence on the documentaries made by the NFB's équipe française starting in the late 1950s.

The three most important figures of the 'pre-NFB' era in French Canada are Maurice Proulx (1902–88), Paul Provencher (1902–81), and Albert Tessier (1895–1976), all of whom made their first documentaries in the 1930s. The former, a priest educated at Université Laval and Cornell University, is primarily associated with the conservative Union National government of Maurice Duplessis (Premier of Québec from 1936 to 1959, with a brief interruption during World War II). Proulx was often commissioned by governmental agencies to make films on agricultural, religious, and touristic topics. His most famous work, En pays neufs/In New Lands (1937), the first feature-length sound documentary made in Canada, glorifies the life and work of settlers in the developing Abitibi region of northwest Québec. Although the voice-over commentary comes across as little more than a conservative propagandist lecture on the virtues of rural traditions and Catholic faith, the images of Abitibi evoke a strong sense of place and belonging that influenced later filmmakers. Bernard Devlin's (1923–83) Les brûlés/The Promised Land (1958), one of the first significant films made by the NFB after the move to Montréal, was directly inspired by En pays neufs in its depiction of settlers in Abitibi; and in the mid-1970s, Pierre Perrault (1927–99), one of the central figures of the francophone documentary after 1960, borrowed images from Proulx's film for his Le retour à la terre/Back to the Land (1976) about the failure of the Abitibi developments of the 1930s.

Other NFB films by Perrault also bear witness to the influence of the ethnographic tradition established by Paul Provencher in the 1930s. A forestry expert by trade, Provencher spent thirty-five years making films on nature and Native people. His Les Montagnais/The Montagnais (1935) and Les scènes montagnaises/Montagnais scenes (1936) were perhaps the first attempts by a French-Canadian filmmaker to produce authentic documents on the customs and rituals of Amerindians. Perrault's Le goût de la farine/The Taste of Flour (1977), with Bernard Gosselin (1934–2006) and Le pays de la terre sans arbre ou le Mouchouânipi/The Land without trees, or Mouchouanipi (1980), Arthur Lamothe's (b. 1928) series of documentaries Chronique des Indiens du Nord-Est du Québec/Chronicle of North-Eastern Quebec Indians (1973–83), as well as the films of Native cineaste Alanis Obomsawin (b. 1932) follow in the footsteps of Provencher, whom Jean-Claude Labrecque (b.1938) nicknamed Le dernier coureur des bois in his 1979 film portrait of the documentary pioneer.

Albert Tessier shared Provencher's interest in nature and the relationship between people and their natural environment, but Tessier's interest was less ethnographic than poetic. Tessier wanted to celebrate the beauty of his country to arouse in his audience an emotional connection to the ancestral land, the terroir. Many of his films, such as Hommage à notre paysannerie/A Tribute to Our Peasantry (1938), show images of simple Québec folk, working on the farm or sharing a meal. Tessier was a priest like Proulx, but his documentary practice was quite different. He was never commissioned to make films and was less didactic than his contemporary, preferring the panegyric to the lecture. He made amateur films that he distributed himself. The visual style of his work is perhaps best described as rustic. He never used a tripod, artificial lighting or preconceived scenarios and always preferred spontaneity to classical aesthetics. As such, he has been recognized by Québec film historians such as Yves Lever (Histoire générale du cinéma au Québec), as the precursor of cinéma direct, the most important documentary movement to occur after the move of the NFB to Montréal. Perhaps not surprisingly, some shots from Tessier's early films bear an uncanny resemblance to images from landmark works of cinéma direct, such as Perrault and Michel Brault's (b. 1928) Pour la suite du monde/The Moontrap (1963). Tessier's films of the 1930s and 1940s had shown with candor a way of life that was prevalent in Québec until the end of World War II but that had become obsolete by the 1960s. In Pour la suite du monde, Brault and Perrault sought both to recapture this disappearing tradition—here the tradition of beluga whale hunting formerly practiced by the inhabitants of Île-aux-Coudres—and to reproduce the qualities of spontaneity, intimacy, and respectfulness that Tessier had displayed twenty-five years earlier.

Michel Brault was among the new generation of francophone filmmakers who joined the NFB in 1956, and he quickly emerged as the leading cinematographer of cinéma direct. In 1957–8 Brault worked on the Candid Eye series developed by the anglophone filmmakers of the NFB's renowned Unit B, who used recently developed, lighter film equipment to capture people in everyday situations with spontaneity and free from judgmental commentary. After shooting the milestone Candid Eye film The Days Before Christmas (1958, Terence Macartney-Filgate (b. 1924), Stanley Jackson (1914–81), and Wolf Koenig (b. 1927)), Brault codirected with Gilles Groulx (1931–94) Les Raquetteurs/The Snowshoers (1958), about a congress of snowshoeing clubs in Sherbrooke (Québec).

In both its form and its content, this film marked a turning point in Québec documentary. Unlike the Candid Eye films, which sought to observe everyday activities from a distance, Les Raquetteurs attempted to show the event from within. The film's innovative visual style resulted from Brault's use of a handheld camera equipped with a wide-angle lens to shoot the subjects from up close. He walked amongst the snowshoers and their entourage, capturing with immediacy their conversations and interactions. Breaking with the Griersonian rules of expository documentary, replacing rhetorical narrative and authoritative composition with a sense of picaresque spontaneity, Brault and Groulx made a film that endeavored to evince the customs and rituals of French Canadians as a gesture of national affirmation.

On the eve of the Quiet Revolution—the period of liberalization and modernization that followed the fall of the Duplessis regime in 1960 and marked the beginning of Québec's separatist movement—Les Raquetteurs was hailed as a sort of manifesto for a home-grown film practice that could show real people (vrai monde) and contribute to their emancipation. Until the 1980s the nationalist aspirations introduced by Groulx and Brault would remain the unofficial mandate of most French-speaking filmmakers working at the NFB. Immediately after Les Raquetteurs numerous NFB documentaries tried to reproduce, to various degrees, its style and nationalist purpose. La Lutte/Wrestling (1961, Brault, Marcel Carrière (b. 1935), Claude Fournier (b. 1931), and Claude Jutra (1930–86)), Golden Gloves (1961, Groulx), and Québec-USA ou l'invasion pacifique/Visit to a Foreign Country (1962, Brault, Jutra) are but a few examples of films that took as their subject matter the mundane but important communal practices of French Canadians to assert, more or less explicitly, the distinct culture of Québec. Les raquetteurs also had an impact beyond the frontiers of Québec. A screening at the Flaherty Seminar in 1959 inspired Jean Rouch to develop his conception of cinéma vérité and led him to invite Brault to film Chronique d'un été/Chronicle of a Summer (1961) in France. For the first time in the history of Québec cinema, French Canadian filmmakers were at the vanguard of an international movement that included such significant filmmakers as Rouch, D.A. Pennebaker, Richard Leacock, Robert Drew, and the Maysles brothers.

The year 1963 marked the culmination of cinéma direct. First, the term itself was officially adopted at the MIPE TV (Marché International des Programmes et Équipements) in Lyon to clarify the confusion surrounding the term cinéma vérité. Furthermore, the NFB's first feature-length cinéma direct documentary, Pour la suite du monde, was released and presented at the Cannes Film Festival. With this film, Perrault became one of the few Québec filmmakers to find a place within the high-brow discourse of French film theory through the work of writers such as Gilles Deleuze and Jean-Louis Comolli. Finally cinéma direct took a turn toward fiction with Claude Jutra's New Wave-inspired feature, A tout prendre/Take It All (1963), one of the few productions of the early 1960s made outside the NFB. Jutra used techniques of direct cinema to tell the convoluted love story of a young French Canadian bourgeois repressing his homosexuality, and his girlfriend who claims to be from Haiti. The next year, Groulx made Le chat dans le sac/The Cat in the Bag (1964), an even more explicit hybrid of direct cinema and fiction. Groulx actually used funds allocated by the NFB for the production of a short documentary on how young people spend their time during the winter to make his feature-length drama on the nationalist awaking of a Québécois intellectual and the disintegration of his relationship with an English-speaking Jewish woman. These two films are often acknowledged as marking the beginning of modern Québec fiction cinema. Starting in the mid-1960s, many cinéastes left documentary practice and followed Groulx's and Jutra's lead to produce fictions that adopted cinéma direct's visual style. To this day, much of Québec's narrative cinema still exhibits a degree of documentary realism.

Those who continued to make documentaries used direct cinema techniques to create increasingly political films, thus shedding any claim to objectivity that earlier productions might have harbored. Furthermore, the observatory mode of direct cinema started being replaced by a more interactive and self-reflexive approach, with the filmmakers' involvement with their subjects becoming more explicitly acknowledged. Tanya Ballantyne's (b. 1944) English-language The Things I Cannot Change (1966) is worth mentioning here as a precursor for two important developments. On the one hand, this film about a poverty-stricken family in Montréal did not only observe but denounced the unbearable conditions in which these people live. Such proactive use of documentary eventually became the official mandate of the NFB's program Société nouvelle/Challenge for Change, established in 1969 to foster social improvement. This program, which lasted until 1979, sponsored film and video productions in French and English Canada that dealt with everything from the disenfranchisement of immigrants and terminal illness, to child abuse and the struggle of French-speaking Acadians in the largely anglophone Maritime provinces east of Québec. The Société nouvelle films often encouraged the full participation of the public, even at the level of production.

On the other hand, as the first feature-length documentary directed by a woman in Canada, The Things I Cannot Change paved the way for the emergence of a feminist voice at the NFB. A year after Ballantyne's film, Anne Claire Poirier (b. 1932) directed the feature De mère en fille/ Mother-to-Be (1967), which dealt with the issue of pregnancy and maternity and is generally recognized as the first French-Canadian feminist documentary. Poirier consolidated her position as the leading figure of feminist cinema in Québec by producing the six-film series En tant que femme, sponsored by Société nouvelle from 1972 to 1975, which laid solid foundations upon which women's cinema could grow in French Canada. Poirier's most famous film is Mourir à tue-tête/Scream from Silence (1979), a powerful and controversial docudrama on the tragic effects of rape.

Controversy often accompanied the more politically radical documentaries of the late 1960s and 1970s. Some films, such as Jacques Leduc's (b. 1941) Cap d'espoir/Cape Hope (1969), Denys Arcand's (b. 1941) On est au coton/Cotton Mill, Treadmill (1970) and Groulx's 24 heures ou plus … /24 hours or more … (1973) were literally banned from circulation for a few years by NFB commissionaire Sydney Newman because of their putative Marxist critique of Canadian society. In fact, Arcand's defeatist perspective on the textile workers' struggle in On est au coton undermines any Marxist agenda that the film might have had, but it doubtlessly remains a caustic condemnation of capitalism in Québec. Arcand was equally caustic in his documentary on Québec politics, Québec: Duplessis et après … / Quebec: Duplessis and After … (1972), which argues that the right-wing ideology of Maurice Duplessis was still present in the post-Quiet Revolution 1970s, even in the supposedly left-wing platform of the separatist Parti Québécois. With this film Arcand managed to attract criticism from both sides of the political spectrum. Arcand's Le confort et l'indifférence/Comfort and Indifference (1981) was also controversial in its commentary on the failure of the 1980 referendum on Québec's independence (sixty percent voted against Québec's sovereignty). Arguing that sovereignist Premier René Lévesque (in power from 1976 to 1985) misread the population's seeming enthusiasm for separation, Arcand was reproached by nationalists for his claim that Quebeckers were more interested in personal gratification than social and political issues, a point he reasserted in his fiction film Le déclin de l'empire américain/Decline of the American Empire (1986). In 1992 Jacques Godbout (b. 1933) came to a similar acknowledgment of political apathy in his documentary Le mouton noir/The Black Sheep, on the 1990 failure of the Meech Lake Accord, which proposed to grant special status to Québec in the Canadian federation.

Whether Arcand's analysis of the failure of the first referendum is accurate remains debatable, but the 1980s and 1990s were certainly characterized by a pull away from Québec politics on the part of documentarians and an increased interest either in private questions or international issues. In a number of documentaries, individual experiences became more important than the collective condition of the people of Québec. Jean Beaudry (b. 1947), François Bouvier (b. 1948), and Marcel Simard's (b. 1945) Une classe sans école/A Class Without a School (1980) on high school dropouts, Guy Simoneau (b. 1953) and Suzanne Guy's (b. 1956) On n'est pas des anges/We're No Angels (1981), on the sexual life of handicapped people, Michel Audy's (b. 1957) Crever à 20 ans/Dead at 20 (1984) on male prostitution, and Gilles Blais's (b. 1941) Les adeptes/The Followers (1981), on the initiation of three young people in the Krishna religious sect, are all early signs of this shift toward the personal experience of marginalized characters. Bernard Emond's (b. 1951) Ceux qui ont le pas léger meurent sans laisser de trace/ Those with a Light Step Go Without a Trace (1992), about an anonymous man in an urban wasteland, and Andrée Cazabon's Enfer et contre tous/No Quick Fix (2000), which documents the struggle of drug addicts and their parents, are more recent examples of this interest in individuals on the margins of society. Marginalised celebrities, if such an oxymoron can be used, also became the focus of several films, such as in Jacques Leduc's Albédo/ Albedo (1982) about a little-known photographer, Serge Giguère's (b. 1946) Oscar Thiffault (1987) about a folk singer, and Le roi du drum/King of Drums (1991) about an eccentric jazz musician, as well as in Pierre Falardeau (b. 1946) and Manon Leriche's Le steak/The Steak (1992) about an aging professional boxer. Introspection started to appear in several films, as in Marilú Mallet's (b. 1944) Journal inachevé/ Unfinished Diary (1982) a film diary, Michka Saäl's L'arbre qui dort rêve à ses racines/A Sleeping Tree Dreams of its Roots (1992) about the personal experiences of cultural displacement, Esther Valiquette's Le singe bleu/The Measure of Your Passage (1992) about the personal journey of a woman diagnosed with AIDS, and Anne Claire Poirier's Tu as crié LET ME GO/You Screamed: LET ME GO (1997), a moving reflection on the violent death of the filmmaker's daughter in a drug-related dispute. These films often have little in common with the cinéma direct tradition. Le singe bleu, for instance, is much closer to experimental film aesthetics than to Les Raquetteurs.

At the opposite end of the spectrum, but equally far from the nationalist politics of pre-1980 productions, documentaries on international or global issues have emerged in large numbers during the last twenty years. Although the NFB has long produced films on international subjects, including Jutra's Niger, jeune république/Niger—Young Republic (1961) and Louis Portugais's (1932–82) Alger 1962—chronique d'un conflit/Algeria 1962—Chronicle of a Conflict (1962), such topics became increasingly common after 1980. Films such as Diane Beaudry's (b. 1946) L'autre muraille/The Great Wall of Tradition (1986) about the condition of Chinese women, Laurette Deschamps's (b. 1936) La fin d'un long silence/No longer Silent (1986) about women in India, and Louise Carré's (b. 1936) Mon coeur est témoin … au pays des femmes des mondes musulmans/My Heart is My Witness (1996) have extended feminist discourses far beyond the frontiers of Canada. Political documentaries have also focused their criticism on the broken promises of free trade agreements and the threat of globalization on marginal cultures. From Godbout's Un monologue Nord-Sud/A North-South Monologue (1982) to Magnus Isacsson's (b. 1948) Le nouvel habit de l'empereur/The Emperor's New Clothes (1995) and Vue du sommet/View from the Summit (2001), a large portion of engagé documentaries are now used as symbolic weapons in the struggle against globalization.

There are obviously a few relatively recent documentaries that still deal with specifically French-Canadian questions. These films, however, often adopt the disillusioned perspective of Jean-François Mercier's Disparaître/Vanishing (1989), a veritable requiem for French-Canadian culture. Georges Payrastre's Parlons franc/ Frankly Speaking (1992), Stéphane Drolet's Référendum—prise 2/take 2/Referendum—Take 2/Prise 2 (1996), and Marie-Claire Dugas's L'Eternité? ou la disparition d'une culture/Eternity? Or the Disappearance of a Culture (2000) all express strong doubts regarding the ability of francophone cultures to survive in an overwhelmingly English-speaking North America.

ANDRÉ LOISELLE

See also: Arcand, Denys; Brault, Michel; Perrault, Pierre

Further reading

Coulombe, Michel and Jean, Marcel, *Le Dictionnaire du cinéma québécois*, Montreal: Boreal, 1999.

Evans, Gary, *In the National Interest: A Chronicle of the National Film Board of Canada from 1949 to 1989*, Toronto: University of Toronto Press, 1991.

Lever, Yves, *Histoire générale du cinéma au Québec*, Montreal: Boreal, 1995.

Marshall, Bill, *Québec National Cinema*, Montreal and Kingston: McGill-Queen's University Press, 2001.

Marsolais, Gilles, *L'aventure du cinéma direct revisitée*, Laval: Les 400 coups, 1997.

Veronneau, Pierre (ed.), *Les Cinémas canadiens*, Montreal: Cinemathèque quebecoise; Paris: Pierre Lhermier Editeur, 1978.

Cane Toads: An Unnatural History

(Australia, Lewis, 1988)

Cane Toads: An Unnatural History was Mark Lewis's first 'feature' documentary, and probably the most commercially successful Australian documentary film ever released. It has been screened at film festivals and has enjoyed significant worldwide television and video sales. From its inception as a television documentary, Cane Toads was pitched at a commercial audience, with all the attendant marketing considerations taken into account (Stott 1990: 103).

The Bufo marinus, introduced to Queensland from Hawaii to combat pests attacking the sugar cane crop, is a real threat to the environment of northern Australia. With the release of Lewis's film, the cane toad also entered the Australian and international imagination as fictional kitsch symbol, emblematic of everything from colonization and regional identity to environmental neglect and tourism. Former journalist Lewis worked closely with Glenys Rowe, a publicist with Film Australia, in a collaborative venture that emphasized the marketing potential of such a film. They flew in Betty, a live cane toad, to accompany Lewis on a day-time variety show. They sent one hundred stuffed cane toads to journalists who were to attend the media previews and had T-shirts, badges, and radio advertisements, replete with cane toad noises, produced to facilitate publicity (Stott 1990: 104).

Like the films of Errol Morris, Cane Toads uses the rhetorical devices of a range of fiction and nonfiction films to render a multiperspective account of this environmental and social phenomenon. In this regard, Lewis is as interested in the broader cane toad 'culture' that can be ascertained only through interviews with so-called expert interviewees and the rendering of this (un)natural being as it stands within the cultural world. While the film constantly oscillates between a topic that is a serious and major threat to the environment and rhetoric that fictionalizes and diminishes any such threat, Cane Toads successfully enlarges the issues at hand to appeal to a wide range of audiences.

Self-conscious in its form, Cane Toads teeters on the brink of 'mockumentary' without the hollowness of topic that is featured in the likes of This is Spinal Tap, melding formal satire with savage social critique in the manner of films such as Roger & Me and The Thin Blue Line. Because of its scope, the film has been used in environmental studies, Australian history, documentary film theory and criticism, biology, and cultural studies, successfully negotiating the borders these disciplines have attempted to erect for themselves. In keeping with the multidisciplinary applications of the film, Cane Toads exists in a space between independent film and commercial, mainstream television documentary and therefore extends both the Griersonian traditions of social imperative and those of commercial entertainment (McMurchy 1994: 198).

DEANE WILLIAMS

See also: Morris, Errol; Roger & Me; Thin Blue Line, The

Cane Toads: An Unnatural History (Australia, 1988, 48 mins). Distributed by Film Australia. Written and directed by Mark Lewis. Executive producer: Tristram Miall. Camera: Jim Frazier, Wayne Taylor. Editor: Lindsay Frazer. Sound: Rodnet Simmons. Sound Mix: George Hart. Music mix: Michael Stavrou. Original music: Martin Armiger, Tim Finn, Don Spencer and Allan Caswell. Graphics: David Johnson. Voice-overs: Stephanie Lewis, Paul Johnstone. Production Manager: Ian Adkins.

Further reading

Gibson, Ross, 'A Marriage Made in Heaven', *Filmnews* (Australia), February, 1988: 7.

McMurchy, Megan, 'The Documentary', in Scott Murray (ed.), *Australian Cinema*, Sydney: Allen and Unwin/Australian Film Commission, 1994.

Moran, Albert, 'Multiculturalism, Ecology and the Invasion of the Body Snatchers', in Jonathan Dawson and Bruce Molloy (eds), *Queensland Images in Film and Television*, Brisbane: University of Queensland Press, 1990.
Stott, Jennifer, 'Case Study: Cane Toads', in John Cruthers (ed.), *Taking Care of Business: A Practical Guide to Independent Film and Video Production*, Australian Film, Television and Radio School/Australian Film Commission, 1990.

Canudo, Ricciotto

An Italian expatriate who settled in Paris in 1901 and a friend of artists such as Apollinaire and Gabriele D'Annunzio, Marcel L'Herbier, and Jean Cocteau, Ricciotto Canudo was a multitalented intellectual. He was a poet and a novelist; a prolific critic of art, literature, music, and cinema; a theorist; a trendsetter; and a vivacious cultural mover. Canudo is, with Boleslaw Matuszewski, one of the first intellectuals to acknowledge the artistic quality of the cinema and to attempt a definition of the specificity of its language. He is particularly well known for having coined the fortunate expression 'seventh art' (and, as some claim, photogénie), and for his pioneering vision of cinema as the total art that presents characteristics of all the other arts, and that merges the arts of 'space' (architecture, painting, sculpture) and those of 'time' (music, dance, poetry), synthesizing and superseding them (Canudo 1995: 161–4).

Canudo is probably the first theorist to have pointed to the necessity of distinguishing between types of films and to have attempted a classification of the genres—a classification in which he gave particular relevance to the documentary (Canudo 1995: 334–5). It is opportune to read his contribution on two levels: against the backdrop of the theorization on modernist documentary filmmaking in France in the 1920s and against the backdrop of Canudo's own theoretical framework, which is split between the idea of a 'pure cinema', the ultimate purpose of which is the representation of inner life through the creation of a high aesthetic and poetic emotion, and the conception of cinema as the perfect expression of the dynamism, speed, and scientism of modern life.

French modernist documentary filmmaking, which produced films such as Alberto Cavalcanti's Rien que les heures/Nothing but the Hours (1926) and Jean Vigo's A propos de Nice/On Nice (1930), was influenced by poetic impressionism and by naturalism. These influences are evident in the use of terminology and in the ideas that informed the articles and reviews of critics of the time, such as Hubert Revol and André Sauvage. Canudo was no exception; he saw the documentary as particularly suited for representing nature. Its mission was to show the relationship of humans with their environment (Canudo 1995: 303–5). 'Such a mission clearly draws on the French naturalist and realist tradition, and illustrates the extent to which these documentaries constituted a bridge between impressionist modernism and naturalist pictorialism' (Aitken 2001: 73).

In particular, Canudo's conception of the documentary is partly 'poetic' and partly 'historical'. He defined the documentary as both the true art film (Canudo 1995: 222) and—abhorring the melodramatic style of costume dramas at that time—as the true historical film (Canudo 1995: 183). In a review of W.G. Barker's London by Night (1913), Canudo noticed that the best documentaries are able to reconcile the 'commercial instinct of the cinema with a vast and exact expression of life' (Canudo 1995: 259). He repeatedly praised the documentary for its ability to elicit emotion and even attain the tragic. Rather than being confined to the lower status of intermission filler, as was the practice in Canudo's time, the documentary must inspire 'new dramas' (Canudo 1995: 222, 237). In an article about some documentaries of the early 1920s, including Flaherty's Nanook of the North (1922), he praised them for having reached a level of expression far superior to that of contemporary fiction films: 'more moving, more "direct" than all the most pathetic plot complications that the poets have ever imagined' (Canudo 1979: 20). He singled out the 'prodigious' Nanook, in which he admired the depiction of the struggle between humans and the elements, and which he compared to Aeschylus's tragedies, but then extended his praise to all travel and mountaineering documentaries: 'The voyages around the world, the "documentaries" of the well-known lakes and famous sites[...] have acquired a personality and are loved by all audiences. They attain the dimension of tragedies' (Canudo 1995: 222). Canudo's idea of the tragic quality of documentaries reflects his belief that these should 'transcend the limitations of the photographic reportage and transfigure the contingency of the observed phenomenon, communicating to the spectator universal meanings' (Boschi 1988: 149), as is true for Nanook, in which 'the Everyday Tragedy of polar man spreads out into the emotion of the entire world' (Canudo 1979: 20), as well as for the minor A l'assaut du mont Everest/The Assault on Mount Everest (1922), which shows 'the tragedy of the struggling man, only armed of the weapon of his courage, against the formidable power of nature' (Canudo 1995: 222).

With the documentary format, Canudo distinguished the biographical film, the war documentary, the propaganda film, and the scientific film. A biographical film (or 'retrospective documentary', as he also called it) that has been reviewed by Canudo is Jean Epstein's Pasteur (1922), which for the author showed how this type of film is, once again, 'a drama of the struggle of man against the hostility of evil' (Canudo 1995: 216). War documentaries are particularly valued by the author and are seen as being in between contemporary epic and novel journalism, with the camera operator depicted as the heroic witness of the human tragedy of the war (Canudo 1995: 229–31). The propaganda film, instead, a sort of biased subgenre of the war documentary, is for the author the cinematographic equivalent of the newspaper article. The cinema is destined to replace the printed newspaper with a product that will be suitable for 'unintelligent and utterly illiterate people' (Canudo 1995: 229). In line with the 'fascination with the science film [that] since the mid-1920s French avant-garde film circles had developed' (Barnard 2000: 14), as well as with his own conception of the cinema as educational art, Canudo also pointed to the importance of the use of film in popularizing great discoveries and scientific advancements (Canudo 1995: 167–8), as well as in the diffusion of visual knowledge of other peoples (Canudo 1995: 325).

LAURA RASCAROLI

See also: Cavalcanti, Alberto; Flaherty, Robert; France; Nanook of the North; Rien que les heures; Sauvage, André

Biography

Born in Gioia del Colle, Bari (Italy), January 2, 1877. Moved to Florence to study oriental languages, 1898, and then to Rome, 1899. Wrote for magazines under the pseudonym of Kàrola Olga Edina. Published his first volumes of poetry, 1898. Moved to Paris, 1901. Founded the journal *Montjoie!*, 1913. Fought with the French army in World War I. Published the manifesto of a movement called Art Cerebriste, 1914. Founded *Le Gazette de sept arts*, 1920. Founded the world's first film club, the Club des amis du septieme art, 1920. Died in Paris, November 10, 1923.

Further reading

Aitken, Ian, *European Film Theory and Cinema. A Critical Introduction*, Edinburgh: Edinburgh University Press, 2001.

Barnard, Timothy, 'From Impressionism to Communism: Leon Moussinac's Technics of the Cinema, 1921–1933', *Framework* 42, (summer), 2000, www.frameworkonline.com/42tb.htm

Boschi, Alberto, *Teorie del cinema. Il periodo classico 1915–1945*, Rome: Carocci, 1988.

Canudo, Ricciotto, *L'Usine aux images*, Paris: Seguier, 1995.

——'Another View of Nanook', in Lewis Jacobs (ed.), Harold J. Salemson (trans.), *The Documentary Tradition*, New York: W.W. Norton & Co., 1979.

Dotoli, Giovanni, *Ricciotto Canudo ou le cinéma comme art*, Bari-Paris: Schena and Didier Erudition, 1999.

Capra, Frank

Initially known for his Hollywood features, Frank Capra became recognized as a documentary filmmaker through his famous Why We Fight series, which he made between 1942 and 1945. Capra also produced and directed a series of military informational films entitled Know Your Ally/Know Your Enemy during the war, but these motion pictures were not as critically acclaimed. His wartime documentaries differed substantially from those made by other Hollywood directors in the military at this time. Filmmakers John Ford, William Wellman, and John Huston shot their footage in actual combat zones, thereby capturing the immediacy of the war, but Frank Capra's films were produced from behind the lines. The Why We Fight pictures were compilation documentaries that used 'found footage' to inform new soldiers as to why they were being asked to fight.

Frank Capra was commissioned as a major in the US Army Signal Corps in 1942, where General George Marshall assigned him the task of making informational films for the war effort.

Never having made documentaries, Capra educated himself on the subject by looking at propaganda films produced by the enemy. He was particularly affected by Leni Riefenstahl's classic Nazi propaganda film, Triumph of the Will (1935). Capra was both impressed with how Riefenstahl artfully conveyed her message through film and appalled at the way she used the medium to promote Adolph Hitler and the Nazi party.

Although Frank Capra had no qualms about attacking Riefenstahl's dogma, he was concerned about his method for rebuttal. Unlike Riefenstahl, Capra did not have the unlimited resources of his government to produce propaganda. He also felt challenged by the fact that while the enemy could tell lies, his documentaries had a moral obligation to uphold the truths of a free society.

Capra justified becoming a propagandist by taking a position similar to that of John Grierson. He envisioned himself as an educator who was using propaganda to teach. Instead of staging expensive sequences for the camera, Capra became a spin doctor who reedited found footage taken from enemy propaganda films to promote his own ideological views. The seven Why We Fight films were presented as a series of history lessons in which Capra contrasted the negative philosophy and behavior of the Axis powers with the positive alternative of the Allies. Originally intended to be used solely as instructional films for raw recruits, these documentaries were so effective in delivering their message that they were shown to civilian audiences in the United States and to millions of viewers overseas.

Although Frank Capra claimed to have had qualms about making propaganda films during World War II, he is considered one of the most ideological Hollywood directors of the 1930s and 1940s. Mr Deeds Goes to Town (1936), Mr Smith Goes to Washington (1939), Meet John Doe (1941), and It's A Wonderful Life (1946) are particularly overt in expressing Capra's populist philosophy. Starring either Gary Cooper or James Stewart, these films feature a heroic 'common man' whose deeply rooted values challenge the corruption fostered by dishonest government officials and big business interests. This type of message film fell out of favor after the war. By the 1970s Capra's most famous pictures were criticized for being overly sentimental and labeled 'Capracorn'. Despite Capra's condemnation of Adolph Hitler in the Why We Fight series, some detractors even accused his films of being fascist.

Other critics have suggested that Capra's populist motion pictures are not so easily pigeonholed. His most famous work clearly champions a heroic common man, but the existence of corrupt government officials and angry mobs in his movies can also be interpreted as revealing a darker and less idealistic side to this director's view of humanity. Frank Capra clearly believed that the individual hero can prove a moral point. How much more the Capra hero is capable of doing relative to combating corruption, controlling a mob, or formulating governmental policy is questionable given the information provided in his films.

Capra went into semiretirement when his postwar Hollywood movies failed to be popular at the box office. The government was now torn between involving Capra in various projects and questioning his loyalty. The depiction of corrupt American politicians in Capra's 1948 feature State of the Union, for example, was viewed as a controversial theme during this period of McCarthyism, and questions about Frank Capra's politics affected his career. Capra was able to exercise some creative expression using the film medium by returning to the documentary. He wrote, produced, and directed a series of educational documentaries for Bell Systems entitled Our Mr Sun (1955), Hemo the Magnificent (1957), The Strange Case of Cosmic Rays (1957), and The Unchained Goddess (1958).

Frank Capra pursued the role of being an educator in the 1970s by visiting universities and speaking to film students. During this time the American television producer Bill Moyers hosted a PBS broadcast for which Capra was invited to compare his philosophy of documentary filmmaking with that of the young filmmaker Barbara Kopple, who was receiving recognition for her feature Harlan County, USA (1976). In a taped review made after their conversation, Moyers noted that Capra had felt compelled to use this occasion to claim that his production of the Why We Fight series was justified because of Hitler's misuse of power. Moyers saw Capra's defense of the series as an indication that the filmmaker was uncomfortable with having made propaganda, justifiable though it may have been. If Bill Moyers's interpretation is true, Frank Capra, like some of his critics, was still finding it difficult to reconcile ideological contradictions in his work decades after it was produced.

FRANK SCHEIDE

See also: Grierson, John; Triumph of the Will; Why We Fight

Biography

Born Bisaquino, Sicily, May 18, 1897. Emigrated with his family to the United States in May 1903, and settled in Los Angeles. Attended Throop College of Technology (Caltech) in 1915, where he discovered poetry and began writing. Enlisted in the army in 1917 when the United States entered World War I, discharged in 1918 after he contracted Spanish influenza, graduated from Throop College with a bachelors degree that same year. Involved in various aspects of filmmaking, 1919–24. Achieved success as a gag writer for Mack Sennett in 1924 when he worked on a series of short comedies with Harry Langdon. Followed Langdon to First National in 1925 and directed the comedian's feature-length picture, The Strong Man, in 1926. Employed as a director at Columbia in 1927, a very modest studio at the time. Popularity of his films between 1927 and 1941 transformed Columbia into a major studio. President of Academy of Motion Picture Arts and Sciences, 1935–41. Commissioned as a major in US Army Signal Corps in 1942, and produced the Why We Fight series, 1942–5. Formed Liberty Films in 1946, which proved unsuccessful, and career went into decline. Recipient of the Distinguished Service Medal and American Film Institute Lifetime Achievement Award. Winner of three Best Director Oscars. Died September 3, 1991, in La Quinta, California.

Selected films

1915 Our Wonderful Schools (Wagner): uncredited editor
1943 Prelude to War: uncredited codirector, uncredited coproducer
1943 The Battle of Russia: codirector, producer
1943 The Nazis Strike: codirector, producer
1943 Divide and Conquer: codirector, uncredited producer
1943 The Battle of Britain: codirector, producer
1944 Tunisian Victory: codirector, producer
1944 The Battle of China: codirector
1944 The Negro Soldier (Heisler): producer
1944 Attack! Battle of New Britain: producer
1945 San Pietro (Huston): uncredited co-supervising producer
1945 Two Down and One to Go: director, producer
1945 War Comes to America: codirector, producer
1945 Your Job in Germany: director
1945 Know Your Enemy: Japan: codirector, producer, cowriter
1956 Our Mr Sun: codirector, producer, writer
1957 Hemo the Magnificent: codirector, coproducer, writer
1957 The Strange Case of the Cosmic Rays: codirector, coproducer, writer
1958 The Unchained Goddess: codirector, coproducer
1964 Rendezvous in Space: director

Further reading

Capra, Frank, *The Name Above the Title*, New York: Macmillan, 1971.
Carney, Raymond, *American Vision: The Films of Frank Capra*, Cambridge: Cambridge University Press, 1986.
Gehring, Wes D., *Populism and the Capra Legacy*, Westport, CT: Greenwood Press, 1995.
McBride, Joseph, *Frank Capra: The Catastrophe of Success*, London: Faber, 1992.
Maland, Charles J., *Frank Capra*, New York: Twayne Publishers, 1995.
Poague, Leland, *Another Frank Capra*, Cambridge: Cambridge University Press, 1995.

Cavalcanti, Alberto

Alberto de Almeida Cavalcanti was born in Rio de Janeiro on February 6, 1897. His father, Manoel, was originally of Italian extraction, while his mother came from the north of Brazil. It was his mother, Doña Aña, who was to have the greater influence on Alberto, and when he left for England in 1934 he lived with his mother until her death in 1945. In 1923 Alberto began work in Paris for the impressionist film director Marcel L'Herbier, as a set designer and assistant producer, but his first significant nondirectorial involvement in filmmaking came as an editor, with his participation in Voyage au Congo (1927), a documentary directed by Marc Allégret, with the participation of the novelist André Gide. Between 1926 and 1934, when he left France for England, Cavalcanti directed a number of films, but the most important of these were Rien que les heures and En Rade. Both films exhibit the influence of the French avant-garde cinema of the 1920s. Rien que les heures, in particular, can be described as a work of high modernism, although Cavalcanti was to make few other films in this mode during his career.

The coming of the sound film in 1927 had a terminal impact on the French cinematic avant-garde, the aesthetic of which was based on the silent film. As opportunities for filmmaking dried up and to support his family (his father had died in 1922, and Alberto was forced to support his mother, his brother, and a maid), Alberto accepted employment in the Paris studios of Paramount Studios. He had wanted to work in sound film since 1927, but between 1928 and 1930 ended up working on a number of undistinguished, commercial sound film projects. The exceptions here were his more experimental short sound films: La P'tite Lilie and Little Red Riding Hood. Between 1930 and 1931 Cavalcanti made a number of sound films for Paramount, but his involvement was mainly that of making foreign-language remakes of popular Hollywood films. Between 1930 and 1934 Cavalcanti continued to be involved in a number of undistinguished projects, and this led him to eventually take up an offer of employment to work for John Grierson's documentary film movement in England. When he left France, in 1934, the major influences on him were French realism and cinematic impressionism, and a tendency toward popular melodrama. However, life in England was to be very different from France.

By 1934, then, Cavalcanti's filmmaking remained grounded in the French realist tradition, and also exhibited a use of modernist features, melodramatic and sentimental formats, and comic, musical or folkloric elements. This complex and uneven set of stylistic characteristics did not add up to a systematic or coherent aesthetic position, although had Cavalcanti not been thrown off course by his involvement in the commercial film industry, it might well have eventually done so. Cavalcanti left France in 1934 because he had become increasingly frustrated by the lack of opportunity available to him within the French film industry. It is debatable, however, whether this was the right thing to do. Had he remained, he may well have emerged as one of the most important French directors of the 1930s, and one can imagine that his style may have evolved into something like that of Jean Vigo, the filmmaker whom he most admired, and to whom he devoted his Filme e Realidade (1952).

In England Cavalcanti made decisive contributions to both the British documentary film movement and Ealing Studios. However, his approach to filmmaking at both organisations was often at odds with those who employed him. Consequently, although Cavalcanti made some important films between 1934 and 1946, he was often unable to make the sorts of films that he would, ideally, have liked to make. In fact, it was only with For Them That Trespass (1949), and after a gap of some twenty years, that he was able to return to the French poetic realist tradition, in which he was most at home. However, even that film was the product of compromise, and it was not really until O Canto do Mar/The Song of the Sea that he was able to effect a full return to poetic realism. Unfortunately, however, what some Brazilian critics described as the 'unjustified gloom and futility' of the film was not what the film industry and film critics in Brazil wanted either.

Cavalcanti's contribution to the documentary film was made in England, both at the General Post Office (GPO) Film Unit, and at Ealing Studios. At the GPO, Cavalcanti brought a command of filmmaking technique to the young filmmakers employed by John Grierson. In particular, he brought expertise in the creative treatment of sound to a production unit that had only just acquired sound facilities. The first fruits of his involvement came with one of the most important documentaries to be produced during the 1930s. Basil Wright's The Song of Ceylon (1934) is particularly impressive in its use of impressionistic, nonsynchronous sound technique, a technique that was brought into the documentary film movement by Cavalcanti. The same use of modernist technique can be found in Cavalcanti's first directed film for the documentary film movement, Pett and Pott (1934). However, this surrealist fantasy was at odds with the intentions of John Grierson, and the film was criticised elsewhere within the movement, for example by Paul Rotha.

The problem over Pett and Pott was to illustrate a more general problem. Cavalcanti and Grierson were very different people, with very different sensibilities. Grierson was a dogmatic, obsessive Scot; Cavalcanti was an expressive, cultured man, and a homosexual. Grierson's distrust of Cavalcanti resulted in the latter directing few films between 1934 and 1936. However, he did make important contributions to a number of the GPO Film Movement's most important films over this period, most notably Coal Face (1935) and Night Mail (1936). These two films, with their use of music by Benjamin Britten and poetry by W.H. Auden, also exhibit Cavalcanti's knowledge of the creative use of sound and modernist technique.

Grierson left the GPO Film Unit in 1936, after which Cavalcanti was promoted to production leader. He remained in charge of the Unit until 1940, when it became integrated into the war effort as the Crown Film Unit. Between 1936 and 1940 Cavalcanti's major involvement was again as a producer. In particular, he formed a close relationship over this period with Humphrey Jennings. Jennings's Spare Time (1939) again exhibits Cavalcanti's concern for indeterminate, evocative forms of filmmaking and for associative editing. The section in the film showing a Welsh male choir is a remarkably affecting piece of filmmaking. Another important documentary in which Cavalcanti played a major role was Men of the Lightship (1940). Cavalcanti's influence is apparent here in the pictorial quality of some of the images and in one edited sequence which employs the kind of subjective camerawork characteristic of the French impressionist movement of the 1920s and which Cavalcanti first employed in Rien que les heures and En Rade.

In 1940 Cavalcanti left the GPO Film Unit, shortly to become the Crown Film Unit, to work for Michael Balcon at Ealing Studios. Cavalcanti really wanted to get back to the feature film, and this was the major influence on his move; however, during his first year at Ealing he continued to make documentaries. The most important of these films were Yellow Caesar, a parodic send-up of Mussolini, in which Cavalcanti again uses the forms of caricature he used in some of his French films, and Pett and Pott. However, Cavalcanti soon switched to feature film direction and production, and he brought to Ealing films a complicating sensibility that often elevated the films out of the mundane. This is apparent, for example, in the highly caricatured The Big Blockade, and in the montage edited sequences of The Foreman Went to France. A concern for forms of documentary realism is also apparent in Champagne Charlie and in Cavalcanti's first post-Ealing film: They Made Me a Fugitive. The same concern for documentary realism also surfaces in Cavalcanti's Brazilian films, particularly Caiçara, O Canto do Mar, Terraé sempre Terra, and Volta Redonda, a documentary about steelmaking in Brazil. During the 1950s Cavalcanti also made a documentary in East Germany with Joris Ivens. Die Windrose was made as part of East Germany's attempt to build a cultural reputation for itself. Made to celebrate International Woman's Day, the film does not particularly display Cavalcanti's influence, and is now little known. Later, in the 1960s, Cavalcanti made Thus Spoke Theodore Herzl, a film made in Israel, celebrating the Israeli leader. The fact that Cavalcanti could make such a film, however, after making the pro-communist Die Windrose/The Windrose, and his 1955 adaptation of Brecht's Herr Puntila und sein Knecht Matti/Mr. Puntilla and his servant Matti, speaks volumes for Cavalcanti's lack of political nous. His involvement with East Germany, for example, was to lead Michael Balcon, at Ealing Studios, to blacklist Cavalcanti from any future work at Ealing.

One final documentary that must be mentioned here was Cavalcanti's 1942 film, Film and Reality, a compilation documentary which attempted to put together the high points of achievement in the documentary film up to that date. In his film Cavalcanti emphasised the aesthetic achievement of the documentary. However, this had the effect of enraging Grierson and his associates, who believed that the prime purpose of the documentary film should be a social one. The fuss over Film and Reality was to rumble on for a long time, and it significantly affected Cavalcanti's relationship with Grierson. The film is not remarkable in itself, and the controversy it engendered says much more about the sorts of conflicts that Cavalcanti tended to get involved in with all his employers than about the film itself.

Cavalcanti's most important films can be divided into three groups. First are those that attempt to subvert dominant mores or positions. This group includes the avant-garde Rien que les heures, and, in England, the films Pett and Pott, Went the Day Well?, and Dead of Night. However, although these films are important, they do not fully represent Cavalcanti's core filmmaking concerns. The second major group of films consists of transitional films such as Champagne Charlie, They Made Me a Fugitive, and One-Eyed Simon. Although these films also critique dominant mores, they are also more positive in approach to their subjects. This shift from critique to a more affirmative approach, for example, differentiates a film such as Champagne Charlie from one like Went the Day Well? Finally, there are those films that come closest to realising and embodying Cavalcanti's core aspirations for his own filmmaking. These include En Rade, For Them That Trespass, and O Canto do Mar. These films are all made within the French poetic realist tradition.

Cavalcanti's major contribution to film culture was made in England, not as a director but as a producer, and his production work at both the GPO Film Unit and Ealing Studios had a considerable impact on two of the most important institutions within British film culture. In fact, Cavalcanti was not really a documentary filmmaker, and he made few documentaries after leaving the documentary film movement. In France in the 1920s he was also mainly active within the feature film industry, and even Rien que les heures is better described as an avant-garde modernist film than a documentary. Within the domain of documentary, however, his greatest achievements came in England, with the GPO Film Unit, where he was able to inject a poetic sensibility into films such as The Song of Ceylon, Coal Face, Night Mail, and Spare Time.

IAN AITKEN

See also: Coal Face; Line to Tcherva Hut; Night Mail; Rien que les heures; Song of Ceylon, The; We Live in Two Worlds

Biography

Alberto de Almeida Cavalcanti, born Rio de Janeiro, February 6, 1897. Son of Manoel and Doña Aña de Almeida Cavalcanti. Educated in Brazil, France, and Switzerland. Directed more than fifty films between 1926 and 1976, and produced many more. Died, Paris, 1982.

Selected films

1926 Rien que les heures
1927 En Rade
1927 La P'tite Lilie
1931 Au Pays du scalp
1934 Pett and Pott
1934 The Song of Ceylon
1934 The Voice of Britain
1935 Coal Face
1936 Night Mail
1936 Line to Tcherva Hut
1937 We Live in Two Worlds
1938 North Sea
1939 Spare Time
1939 The First Days
1940 Men of the Lightship
1941 Yellow Caesar
1942 The Big Blockade
1942 The Foreman Went to France
1942 Film and Reality
1944 Champagne Charlie
1945 Dead of Night
1947 They Made Me a Fugitive
1949 For Them That Trespass
1952 Volta Redonda
1953 O Canto do Mar
1955 Herr Puntila und sein Knech Matti
1956 Die Windrose
1967 Thus Spoke Theodore Herzl
1976 Un Homem e o Cinema

Further reading

Abel, Richard, *French Cinema: The First Wave, 1915–1929*, Princeton, NJ: Princeton University Press, 1984.

Aitken, Ian, *Alberto Cavalcanti, Realism, Surealism and National Cinemas*, London: Flicks Books, 2001.

——*The Documentary Film Movement, An Anthology*, Edinburgh: Edinburgh University Press, 1998.

——*Film and Reform*, London: Routledge, 1990.

Audra, Mario, *Cinematográfica Maristela: Memórias d um produtor*, São Paulo: Silver Hawk, 1997.

Cavalcanti, Alberto, *Filme e Realidade*, Rio de Janeiro: Editora Artenova, in collaboration with Empresa Brasiliera de Filmes—Embrafilme, 1977.

Danischewsky, Monja, *White Russian—Red Face*, London: Victor Gollancz, 1966.

Ghali, Noureddine, *L'Avant-Garde Cinématographique en France dans les Anées Vingt*, Paris: Editions Paris Experimental, 1995.

Ivens, Joris, *The Camera and I*, Berlin: Seven Seas Publishers, 1969.

Low, Rachel, *The History of the British Film 1929–1939: Documentary and Educational Films of the 1930s*, London: George Allen & Unwin, 1979.

Orbanz, Eva, *Journey to a Legend and Back: The British Realistic Film*, Berlin: Volker Speiss, 1977.

Pellizari, Lorenzo and Valentinetti, Claudio M. (eds), *Alberto Cavalcanti*, Locarno: Editions du Festival international du films de Locarno, 1988.

Sussex, Elizabeth, 'Cavalcanti in England', *Sight and Sound* 44, no. 4, autumn, 1975.
——*The Rise and Fall of British Documentary: The Story of the Film Movement Founded by John Grierson*, Berkeley, CA: University of California Press, 1975.
Swann, Paul, *The British Documentary Film Movement, 1926–1946*, Cambridge: Cambridge University Press, 1989.
Watt, Harry, *Don't Look at the Camera*, London: Paul Elek, 1974.

Chair, The

(US, Shuker, 1963)

One of the most important films produced in the 1960s by Drew Associates, and certainly the most widely known of The Living Camera series, The Chair remains grounded in many of the stylistic conventions of cinéma vérité while telling a compelling and tense narrative. Originally titled Paul, following the practice of naming the films in a series after the main subject of each film (it was the last produced in the series), the film has since been referred to as The Chair, that central, inanimate object that plays so crucial a role in the documentary. Filmed in July 1962, The Chair recounts a crisis in Chicago, that in five days' time Paul Crump is sentenced to die in Cook County Jail's electric chair for a murder he committed nine years ago. His lawyers, the young Donald Page Moore and the experienced Louis Nizer, must convince the Illinois State Parole Board that their client has been rehabilitated (a line of argumentation that in the United States had yet to be successful in the overturning of a death sentence), and that Governor Kerner should commute Crump's sentence.

As with the more than forty films produced by Drew Associates in the 1960s, The Chair is really a collaborative effort between executive producer Robert Drew, his chief filmmaker Gregory Shuker, the two additional filmmakers, Richard Leacock and D.A. Pennebaker, and his team of correspondents: Shuker, Drew, John MacDonald, and Sam Adams. Drew assigned the ideas of the film and oversaw production, the filmmakers photographed and planned the shoots, and the correspondents often acted as soundmen and journalists. The role each associate played often changed from film to film. Having first worked with Drew Associates as a correspondent in On the Pole (1960), Shuker was soon assigned the role of filmmaker. The Chair and Crisis: Behind a Presidential Commitment (1963) are his two most acknowledged accomplishments with Drew Associates.

As with Crisis, The Chair involves just that, a crisis. In The Chair, the resolution of the crisis may end with a man being executed. Shuker and his filmmakers were able to achieve a dramatic unity within the film by initially introducing us to the principal characters, Crump being the first. At the start of the film, narrator James Lipscomb states gravely, 'It's Sunday, less than five days before the condemned man, Paul Crump, is scheduled to die in the chair'. The phrase 'the chair' is repeated several times in the opening few minutes, and the direness in which Lipscomb repeats it only heightens the urgency of the crisis situation.

One of the more significant scenes of The Chair that builds on this crisis involves the introduction of Warden Jack Johnson. In charge of executions at the jail, Johnson is seen, ironically enough, as the man who will execute Crump (he is Crump's best friend, and the convict asked the Warden to perform the execution) and also as one of many who will testify on Crump's behalf. Through a series of following shots, we journey with the Warden from his office down endless hallways lit with eerie florescent lighting. We hear the sound of Johnson's echoing footsteps, down a dark elevator, through the bowels of the jail that are lit by a single window (producing wide-cast and attached shadows), into the chapel, and then finally into the sealed room that houses the chair. The handheld camera continues to follow Johnson as he circles the chair and then pans from the chair to the Warden's sullen face, and then back to the chair to end the scene. The long takes in this scene show the effectiveness at hiding the presence of the camera so as to allow the true emotions of the Warden, especially in his office, to be brought forth.

Some believe that the stylistic differences between the two camera crews (Pennebaker and Shuker; Leacock and Drew) coupled with the sudden alternation between one filmed subject and another, with little regard for temporality, created an oversimplified crisis situation that resembled a fictional story rather than a realistic one. Thus, at times The Chair appears to drift away from the stylistic and creative precepts of cinéma vérité, namely that of filming real people in real and uncontrolled situations. Nizer, and particularly Moore, often resemble characters from a play or a novel; they are teeming with emotions, and one could argue they are overacting. Some of Moore's performances, particularly his phone conversation filmed in a very long take with Church officials who will make a statement on Crump's behalf, in which the lawyer weeps openly (later in the scene, they decide not to release their statement), do not appear genuine. Yet in another apparent disregard for filming in the cinéma vérité style, portions of the film were shot well after Crump's sentence had been commuted. Jean-Luc Godard who, with his fellow directors from the French New Wave influenced the cinéma vérité movement, was highly critical of The Chair, calling it a melodrama full of stereotypical images and simplified, one-dimensional characters.

Members of Drew Associates admit that there are problems with the film. Pennebaker believes that the real story was too complex. Drew, who made the final edit, acknowledges his error in simplifying the story in exchange for hype and suspense. Yet, despite these apparent drawbacks, the film succeeds in placing a human face on a condemned man. Although Paul Crump does not appear as often in The Chair as other title characters in The Living Camera series, most notably the exceptionally strong film David (1961), Crump's brief time on camera, as well as his brevity and humility of speech (as opposed to Moore's), allows him to be viewed sympathetically. While Crump's sentence is commuted by Governor Kerner (he will serve one hundred and ninety-nine years with no parole), the final shot, that of the doors of Crump's dim cell being shut and his cell backlit by a small window, creating high contrast between light and dark, underscores Crump's future as one of confinement and isolation.

ALEXANDER L. KAUFMAN

See also: Pennebaker, D.A.; Shuker, Gregory

The Chair (US, Drew Associates, 1963, 58 mins). Distributor (since 1980): Drew Associates in Brooklyn, New York. Executive Producer: Robert Drew. Coproducers: Time-Life Broadcast and Drew Associates. Filmmaker: Gregory Shuker. Additional filmmakers: Richard Leacock and D.A. Pennebaker. Correspondents: Gregory Shuker, Robert Drew, John MacDonald, and Sam Adams. Editing by Ellen Huxley, Joyce Chopra, Patricia Powell, and Richard Leacock. Assistants: Gary Youngman, Sylvia Gilmour and Nicholas Proferes. Narrated by James Lipscomb. Filmed in Chicago and Springfield, Illinois. Winner of the Special Jury Prize at the 1962 Cannes Film Festival; Invited Participant at the 1963 New York Film Festival.

Challenge for Change/Société Nouvelle

The National Film Board of Canada's (NFB) Challenge for Change and its francophone component, Société Nouvelle, were designed to use documentary filmmaking to address social, cultural, and economic disenfranchisement in Canadian society. Between 1967 and 1980 the initiative produced approximately one hundred and fifty films in the areas of community organization, native issues, labor, welfare and poverty, and women's issues. The most conventional were mass audience social documentaries, typified by their prototype film, Tanya Ballantyne's The Things I Cannot Change. The program produced films such as the series on the American community organizer, Saul Alinsky, meant to train social activists.

Most emblematic of Challenge for Change/Société Nouvelle were the films and videotapes generated by the disenfranchised themselves. The first example produced were Colin Low's twenty-eight films shot in the remote Newfoundland fishing community of Fogo Island. The Fogo residents, threatened with the failure of their fishery and a forced relocation, spoke uninterrupted, directly to the camera and were given the opportunity to edit the footage before its release.

Portable videotape recorders and community access cable television facilitated the use of the Fogo model as a tool for community organization. Challenge for Change/Société Nouvelle sponsored individual community video projects (and the documentation of those projects in films such as VTR St Jacques, VTR Rosedale), as well as the establishment of ongoing community video centers.

Challenge for Change/Société Nouvelle generated considerable discussion as to the role of the documentary filmmaker. Was it not disingenuous in an institution like the NFB, known for its documentary auteurs, to now claim a complete disinterest in style? Was it possible? John Grierson, while offering an equivocal approval of Challenge for Change/Société Nouvelle, found that 'the old unsatisfactory note of faraway liberal concern for humanity-in-general creeps in, in spite of these real excursions into the local realities' (Grierson 1977: 134).

A second critique of Challenge for Change/ Société Nouvelle was the mandate itself. As Jones points out, 'A film could criticize practices, policies or situations that tended to bar certain groups from equitable participation in the mainstream of Canadian life [...] But films which criticized something fundamental about society were not encouraged and rarely permitted' (Jones 1981: 171). Even when focusing on the needs of their constituencies, the seven federal ministries cosponsoring the program could be put off by issues hostile to their own agendas. Indian Affairs, for example, attempted to block production of Cree Hunters of the Mistassini, a film that countered the Trudeau government's refusal to negotiate land claim treaties with native bands.

By the late 1970s all but two of the sponsoring federal ministries had left the program, making its collapse inevitable. The legacy of Challenge for Change/Société Nouvelle, however, remains in its raising of fundamental issues of public sponsorship of political filmmaking, the role of the documentary filmmaker in such work, and the uses of video and other ostensibly democratizing media. The program also served as a training ground, most notably for the women who were to become the founders of the National Film Board of Canada's women's unit, Studio D.

SETH FELDMAN

See also: Canada; Grierson, John; Low, Colin

Selected films

1966 The Things I Cannot Change: Tanya Ballantyne, director
1967 Fogo Island Films: Colin Low, director
1967 Encounter with Saul Alinsky, Pts I and II: Peter Pearson, director
1968 Saul Alinsky Went to War: Peter Pearson and Donald Brittain, directors
1968 Challenge for Change: Bill Reid, director
1969 Up Against the System: Terrence Macartney-Filgate, director
1969 You Are on Indian Land: Mort Ransen, director
1969 VTR St Jacques: Bonnie Sherr Klein, director
1974 Cree Hunters of the Mistassini: Boyce Richardson, Tony Ianzelo, directors
1974 VTR Rosedale: Len Chatwin, director
1974 Luckily I Need Little Sleep: Kathleen Shannon, director
1974 Urba 2000 series: Michel Régnier, director
1980 Unemployment: Voices from the Line: Pierre Lasry, director

Further reading

Fourteen issues of *Challenge for Change Newletter* (aka *Challenge for Change/Société Nouvelle Newsletter* and *Access: Challenge for Change/Société Nouvelle*) were published by the National Film Board of Canada between spring, 1968 and spring, 1975.

Bodolai, Joe and Isobel, Harry, 'Decentralization of the Means of Visual Production', *Artscanada* 30, no. 4, October, 1973: 66–72.

Burnett, Ron, 'Video: The Politics of Culture and Community', in *Resolutions: Contemporary Video Practices*, Minneapolis, MN: University of Minnesota Press, 1966: 282–303.

——'Video/Film: From Communication to Community', in Alain Ambrosi and Nancy Thede (eds), *Video, the Changing World*, Montreal: Black Rose Books, 1991.

Cox, Kirwan. 'Videographe', *Cinema Canada* 4, October–November, 1972: 16–19.

Dansereau, Fernand, 'Saint-Jerôme: The Experience of a Filmmaker as Social Animator', in Seth Feldman and Joyce Nelson (eds), *Canadian Film Reader*, Toronto: Peter Martin Associates, 1977: 128–31.

Friedlander, Madeline S., 'Challenge for Change: An American View', *Film Library Quarterly* 2, no. 4, fall, 1969: 48–52.

Grierson, John, 'Memo to Michelle About Decentralizing the Means of Production', in Seth Feldman and Joyce Nelson (eds), *Canadian Film Reader*, Toronto: Peter Martin Associates, 1977: 132–6.

Henaut, Dorothy Todd, 'Film as an Instrument for Social Change', *Artscanada* 26, no. 1, February, 1969: 34–5.

——'Implicating People in the Process of Change: Canada's New King of Film Making', *Film Library Quarterly* 2, no. 4, fall, 1969: 44–7.

——'Films for Social Change: The Hammer and the Mirror', in Gertrude J. Robinson and Donald Theall (eds), *Studies in Canadian Communication*, Montreal: McGill University Press, 1975: 175–88.

——'The Challenge for Change/Société Nouvelle Experience', in Alain Ambrosi and Nancy Thede (eds), *Video, the Changing World*, Montreal: Black Rose Books, 1991: 48–53.

Jones, D.B., *Movies and Memoranda: An Interpretative History of the National Film Board of Canada*, Ottawa: Canadian Film Institute, 1981: 157–75.

Kurchak, Marie, 'What Challenge? What Change?' in Seth Feldman and Joyce Nelson (eds), *Canadian Film Reader*, Toronto: Peter Martin Associates, 1977: 120–8.

Low, Colin, 'Grierson and Challenge for Change', in *John Grierson and the NFB*, Toronto: ECW Press, 1981: 103.

Mackenzie, Scott, 'Societe nouvelle: The Challenge for Change in the Alternative Public Sphere', *Canadian Journal of Film Studies* 5, no. 2, fall, 1996: 67–83.

Marchessult, Janine, 'Amateur Video and the Challenge for Change', in *Mirror Machine: Video and Identity*, Toronto: YYZ Books, 1995: 13–25.

——'Reflections on the Dispossessed: Video and the "Challenge for Change" Experiment', *Screen* 36, no. 2, summer, 1995: 131–46.

Summers, Bob, 'Challenge for Change', *Cineaste* 3, no. 4, spring, 1970: 16–18.

Watson, Patrick, 'Challenge for Change', in Seth Feldman and Joyce Nelson (eds), *Canadian Film Reader*, Toronto: Peter Martin Associates, 1977: 112–19.

Weisner, Peter K., 'Media for the People: The Canadian Experiments with Film and Video in Community Development', *American Review of Canadian Studies* 22, no. 1, spring, 1992: 65–99.

Chan, Evans

Although best known as a transnational fiction filmmaker based in New York City and Hong Kong, Evans Chan has a considerable body of documentary work to his credit. Before making his debut feature, To Liv(e), in 1990, Chan had spent much of his professional life as a journalist and media arts commentator in Asia and within the Chinese-language press in America. His interest in political affairs, current events, social trends, and the broad spectrum of personalities that make up the contemporary arts scene from Hong Kong to New York underpins all of his films—both fiction and nonfiction. Influenced by Bertolt Brecht's epic theater and Jean-Luc Godard's counter-cinema, Chan breaks the illusion of a seamless fiction in his dramatic features by including interviews with political figures, snippets of stage performances, and documentary inserts of life on the street. Like Godard and Marker, Chan works within the tradition of the film essayist. He uses fiction and nonfiction, as Georg Lukacs says of the essay form, as a 'springboard' (Lukacs 1974: 16) to engage the critical events of the day with the commitment of an activist.

The shockwaves that went through the global Chinese community after the Tiananmen Square incident of June 4, 1989 can be felt throughout Chan's entire oeuvre, and the impact that the events in Beijing in 1989 had on Hong Kong in 1997 and Macau in 1999, when those two colonies returned to Chinese rule, plays a major role in Chan's film dramas as well as his documentary work. To date, Chan has made four feature-length documentaries: Journey to Beijing (1998), Adeus Macau (1999), The Life and Times of Wu Zhong-Xian (2003, based on the play The Life and Times of Ng Chung Yin), and Sorceress of the New Piano (2004).

Journey to Beijing and Adeus Macau

These two documentaries constitute a filmic diptych with the umbrella title of China Decolonized. They deal with the transfer of sovereignty of Hong Kong in 1997 and Macau in 1999 to China. While neither film adopts an alarmist or negative perspective on the respective handovers, each expresses the aspiration for the retention of unique local characteristics, some of which represent the inevitable legacy of a long period of colonial influence. The thorny issue of political self-determination is raised in both films, and Chan's documentary approach is to allow his subjects to speak for themselves, unencumbered by intrusive voice-over.

Journey to Beijing, which brought Chan's documentary making to international critical attention at festivals in 1998, follows the trail of an assorted, Canterbury Tales-like group of Hong Kong 'pilgrims' on a charity walkathon from Hong Kong to Beijing under the auspices of Sowers' Action Group, which collects funds through sponsorship and other activities to develop schooling facilities in poorer regions of China. At the literal level the film charts the progress of the unlikely band of walkers toward their destination, with their arrival timed to coincide with the handover of Hong Kong, thus ensuring maximum publicity. At the metaphorical and symbolic level, however, the journey is presented as a microcosm of the complex process of reunification and mutual understanding.

Although Chan does not use a 'walk' as a metaphor for Macau's return to Chinese sovereignty in 1999, he does look broadly at the cultural landscape of Macau, the response of artists and intellectuals to the transfer of power, the distinct Portuguese colonial history of Macau, and some of the misunderstandings and failed hopes that accompanied the handover there. The film unfolds through a series of interviews and visual observations of the cityscape of Macau, including the handover ceremony and demonstrations/street theater by artists critical of the event. Law Kar, who was born in Macau and who has been involved in Hong Kong film culture through the Hong Kong Film Festival and Hong Kong Film Archive for many years, talks about making an experimental film in Macau during the late 1960s, when riots inspired by China's Cultural Revolution spilled across the border: 'We felt compelled to express our disorientation—dangling between the ruthless rioters and the repressive imperialists. Setting the film in Macau seemed safer, more disarming.' Although not as long or elaborate as Journey to Beijing, Adeus Macau may, indeed, be a more 'disarming' view of the end of European colonialism in the Pearl River Delta.

The Life and Times of Wu Zhong-Xian and Sorceress of the New Piano

In Sorceress of the New Piano, Evans Chan's camera literally gets inside the piano with Tan, actively engaging her as a creative force during her performances and bringing to the screen the excitement of seeing how musical experimentation opens new avenues for aesthetic expression. As in others of his documentary and fiction films, Chan highlights the role that women artists and intellectuals play in the international avant-garde. Just as Tan opens up this world to new audiences by playing Beatles tunes on toy pianos, Chan's film brings Tan's music to those who have never considered the importance of Asians, Asian Americans, and women within the musical avant-garde.

The 2002 film adaptation, The Life and Times of Wu Zhong Zian, is based on a play by Asian People's Theatre Festival Society about the Hong Kong-born democracy activist, Ng Chung Ying, who is strongly associated with Hong Kong's emergent political awareness in the 1970s. Chan's film title reflects the film's appeal to a broader audience in using the Mandarin Chinese version of his name. Chan assisted actor and director, Mok Chiu Yiu (who also appears in Adeus Macau) in the New York English stage adaptation. His decision to base the film version primarily, but not exclusively, on a filmed performance of the piece at Club 64 in Hong Kong's Lan Kwai Fong, testifies to his keen understanding and empathy with the aims of the original dramatic project.

Chan does an effective job of giving a film audience a clearer idea of the egregious character of Ng than would be possible in a purely filmed recording of the live performance. His blend of the respective media works well in giving a rounded portrait of Ng's passionately committed but inevitably frustrated idealism. To understand the derivation of popular activism in Hong Kong in the response to the Tiananmen Square massacre, and more recently the July 1 demonstrations against planned anti-subversion legislation emanating from Beijing, Ng Chung Ying's role and legacy are of crucial significance. The documentary is compelling for its typically dialectical quest for a balanced, if at times ironic and bitter, truth instead of mere hagiography.

Lukacs observes about the essay, 'the value-determining thing about it is not the verdict […] but the process of judging' (Lukacs 1974: 18). Chan's film essays are very much about this process of judging, thereby opening up trans-national conversations about contemporary Hong Kong, Chinese, and global politics through his documentaries.

MICHAEL INGHAM AND GINA MARCHETTI

Biography

Evans Yiu Shing Chan was born in China and raised in Hong Kong. Staff film critic for *The Hong Kong Standard*, 1981–4. Founded his production company, 1990. Has lived in both New York and Hong Kong since 1984.

Selected films

1998 Journey to Beijing
1999 Adeus Macau
2003 The Life and Times of Wu Zhong-Xian
2004 Sorceress of the New Piano

Further reading

Lukacs, Georg, 'On the Nature and Form of the Essay', in Anna Bostock (trans.), *Soul and Form*, London: Merlin Press, 1974.

Chang: A Drama of the Wilderness

(US, Cooper and Schoedsack, 1927)

In part because of its considerable craftsmanship, Merian Cooper and Ernest Schoedsack's Chang is a vivid record of its time and setting, or at least an engineered perception of the time and setting in question. If its commercial motivations and narrative contrivances ultimately reduce its strictly documentary value and status, then it remains of great interest and importance in the history of both the documentary and the commercial fiction film.

Grass (1925) and Chang, which Cooper and Schoedsack referred to as their 'natural dramas', were created at a time when the parameters and ethics of the documentary form were being debated and established. Robert Flaherty's early work in this period, in both its exemplary and problematical aspects, would have the most influence on this defining process.

Chang was shot and set in Siam (modern-day Thailand). It tells the story of a family of Lao tribesmen homesteading on the outskirts of a Siamese settlement, trying to eke out a living in the harsh jungle environment. The plot of the film was substantially formed in Cooper's head ever before he reached Siam, and its central aim was to entertain while taking advantage of a novel and exotic setting. On-set preparations were devoted to embodying the producers' preconceptions.

The filming of Chang was marked by an atmosphere of improvisation and openness, even of collaboration, in keeping with Cooper and Shoedsack's production method. As a result, the film's primarily fictional representations are embellished with documentary details. The film provides a brief but vivid representation of the fictional family's domestic arrangements and agricultural practices, for example. There were also incidents (such as when the mother elephant pulls the house down in the process of rescuing her baby) that occurred spontaneously during preparation for filming and were subsequently reenacted for the camera. The details of the film's many hunting sequences, such as the traps and dummies used, reflect authentic processes and methods.

Chang has been criticized for its perceived insensitivities and cultural missteps. At times, Cooper and Schoedsack subjected their actors (including children) to dangerous situations for the sake of the narrative. A modern audience may also be struck by the amount of violence against animals in the film. It is clear that a number of beasts were rather indiscriminately harmed during the picture's production.

Although Chang was well received at the time of its release, even contemporary reviews took consistent exception to the film's alternatively stilted and facetious titles: 'The very last grain of rice is husked, O very small daughter', says the noble native, and 'Give him hell, boys!' says the ribald-talking gibbon.

Chang reflects and implicitly supports the subservience and oppression that characterize colonial relations. Such attitudes are evident in the treatment of animals during the filming and in the film. The animals, which are domesticated and often killed, might be seen as having a metonymic relation to the Siamese themselves. Nevertheless, it is necessary to remember that Chang is a product of its time, and that much of common intercultural practices we now take for granted cannot fairly be expected of its producers. The film, for good and ill, reflects the enthusiasms and insensitivities of its time. The influence and continued presence of these incomplete, essential sensibilities should not be underestimated.

It is clear that Cooper and Schoedsack were motivated by more than just commercial or financial considerations. They encountered numerous technical challenges during the production of the film, and their recollections suggest that much of their motivation and satisfaction stemmed from finding successful solutions to these difficulties. The problems they faced included determining how to trap wild cats without killing them, inciting a tiger to attack, filming said attack without endangering the cameraman, protecting film stock from mildew, and incorporating the wide-screen magnascope process.

As they would again later with King Kong, Cooper and Schoedsack demonstrated remarkable ingenuity and aplomb in solving each of these problems. As was the case with Robert Flaherty and Werner Herzog, the adventures encountered during production were at least as important as the adventures portrayed in the production. With few exceptions, the serious, groundbreaking, critically validated documentary film would not follow in Chang's manic steps. Nevertheless it has many descendants, and its good-natured absurdity and superb sleights of hand are echoed in a great many diverse places. The influence of Chang is present in Jean Painlev's surreal scientific films. They prefigure, as Kevin Brownlow has observed, Walt Disney's True Life Adventures and in some ways the films of Arne Sucksdorff as well. Its influence is discernible in any number of large-format nature films that couch cinematic spectacle in appreciation of the natural.

Contemporary audiences seem to have taken Chang at face value for the most part. Chang is emblematic of a great deal of commercial cinema; although there is much in it to criticize, we may finally find it difficult, and too delightful, to dismiss.

DEAN DUNCAN

See also: Flaherty, Robert; Grass

Chang (US, Paramount Famous Lasky Corp., 1927, 69 mins). Presented by Adolph Zukor and Jesse Lasky. Produced by Merian Cooper and Ernest Schoedsack. Directed by Merian Cooper and Ernest Schoedsack. Intertitles by Achmed Abdullah (with uncredited work by Schoedsack and Cooper). Cinematography by Ernest Schoedsack. Edited by Merian Cooper and Ernest Schoedsack. Starring Kru and Chantui as the pioneers, Nah and Ladah as their children.

Further reading

Behlmer, Rudy, 'Merian C. Cooper', *Films in Review* 17, no. 1, January 1966: 17–35.

——'The Adventures of Merian Cooper', in James V. D'Arc (ed.), *Register to the Merian C. Cooper Papers*, Provo: Department of Special Collections/College of Fine Arts and Communications, 2000.

Brownlow, Kevin, *The War, the West, and the Wilderness*, New York: Alfred A. Knopf, 1979.

Cooper, Merian C., *Grass*, New York: Putnam, 1925.

——'Mr. Crooked', *Asia Magazine* 27, no. 6, June 1927: 477–81, 504–16.

——'The Warfare of the Jungle Folk: Campaigning Against Tigers, Elephants, and Other Wild Animals in Northern Siam', *National Geographic* 53, no. 2, February, 1928: 233–68.

Mould, D.H. and Veeder, G., 'The Photographer-Adventurers: Forgotten Heroes of the Silent Screen', *Journal of Popular Film and Television*, 16, no. 3, Washington, DC, fall, 1988.

Turner, George (ed.), *The Cinema of Adventure, Romance and Terror*, Hollywood: The ASC Press, 1989.

Children at School

(UK, Wright, 1937)

The National Film Archive summarizes the content of Children at School with the following: 'Deals with the physical conditions of schools in which many children are educated'. The accompanying shot list is as follows: Democratic education compared with that in a dictatorship; the organization of education in England—nursery, infant, junior, senior and secondary schools progressing to technical schools and universities. Scenes from life in the progressive schools follow. Nursery schools: free activity, air and sunlight, meal times and rest periods; training in hygiene and social habits; a trained nurse supervises the children's health. Infant schools; teaching of a sense of rhythm, reading by acting, confidence through verbal expression, creative play, provision of mid-morning milk. Reading aloud; regular supervision of health by school doctor—parents' help encouraged. Post-primary schools: encouragement of freedom, self-reliance. School scenes show gymnastics, woodwork, geography, chemistry, etc.; the use of films in teaching. Provision of nutritious meals.

In contrast there are many 'blacklist' schools, insanitary, unsafe, out of date. Great difficulties experienced by teachers in out-of-date buildings not yet scheduled for destruction—inadequate light, overcrowded classes, outside noises.

Mr Fred Mander, Secretary of the National Union of Teachers (NUT), campaigns for better working conditions. We see a meeting of the Council for the ten-year plan for children at which Lady Astor speaks. Student teachers discuss large classes. A meeting of headmaster and staff of his school. The question remains 'Can democracies afford to fall behind?'

Children at School was the first production arranged through Film Centre, which had been established in 1937. Realist Film Unit had been established in the same year by Basil Wright, after his departure from the General Post Office (GPO) Film Unit. The commentator, Wilson Harris, was editor of the *Spectator*, which published a good deal of writing on the documentary film. It is a continuation of the series sponsored by the gas industry, which had included Housing Problems (1935) and Enough to Eat? (1936). Through reportage and argument these films called public attention to pressing problems faced by the nation, insisted that they needed to be solved, and suggested their causes and possible solutions. By making use of stock shots and newsreel footage plus interviews, they were given coherence and rhetorical effectiveness through editing and voice-over commentary. Heavily influenced by the American The March of Time series, they represent the beginnings of what would become standard format for subsequent television documentaries.

Though competent in technique and hard-hitting as exposé, in its impersonality Children at School might have been directed by any number of documentarians. It represents Wright's deep and genuine social concern arrived at intellectually rather than the emotional core of his being out of which his most personal and best work came. The journalistic style of this film and the lyricism of The Song of Ceylon is frequently contrasted.

JACK C. ELLIS

See also: Enough to Eat?; Grierson, John; Housing Problems; Song of Ceylon, The; Wright, Basil

China

For historical reasons, documentary film in China has long been more valued for its ability to articulate political or moral discourses than for its cinematic qualities. Documentary film production, and especially newsreels, started in China around 1900. Expatriates living in Shanghai, or foreigners sent by overseas film companies such as Pathé and Edison, were the first to shoot and show fiction and documentary films. In 1905 Ren Qingtai, a former Chinese overseas student in Japan, owner of a photographic shop in Beijing, made his first film: The Battle of Dingjunshan. This documentary recording of a Beijing opera performance is the first film shot by a Chinese national and the starting point of Chinese film production. However, the economical and political situation of early twentieth-century China made film production an activity largely placed in the hands of foreigners. One of the first Shanghai-based companies was The Asia Film Company, founded by American Benjamin Brodsky, in which a team of foreigners and Chinese shot newsreels and fiction films.

After two decades of watching foreign images about China, the importance of themselves filming the reality of their country became more and more crucial to Chinese intellectuals and entrepreneurs during the 1920s. At that time, intellectuals were already commenting on the selectivity of the documentary filmmaking process and criticising the negative image of China conveyed by biased foreign newsreels and fiction films. Instead, they emphasised the power of documentary as an educational and moral media, potentially able to contribute to save the country from war, domination and disunity. In 1918 the Commercial Press of Shanghai was the first to open an image department, and it soon started to shoot newsreels and other documentary films, such as travelogues, educational films and opera recordings. A number of other Chinese film production companies were then soon established in Shanghai and throughout the country, reaching by 1925 over one hundred and seventy-nine registered companies. Aiming at educating the audience and competing with foreign documentaries, these films depicted landscapes and Chinese customs, and reported news about the current political situation. Other companies became famous for their involvement with documentary filmmaking. Li Minwei, known as the father of Hong Kong cinema with the fiction film Zhuangzi Tests his Wife (1913), cofounded the Mingxin (Star) Film Company in 1923 with his brothers Li Beihai and Li Haishan. Considering documentary film as a means to save the country, the revolutionary Li Minwei, an early member of the Nationalist Party (Guomindang, GMD hereafter), considered documentary film as a means to voice patriotic concerns by recording China's current political situation. His company produced twenty newsreels in the 1920s, half of which reported on miscellaneous events such as sports competitions in Guangdong or Shanghai, and opera performances in Beijing. Ten documented the political activities and discourses of Sun Yat-Sen, whom Li Minwei followed during his travels. In 1927 Li Minwei gathered this footage and reedited it as a documentary film on Sun Yat-sen's life and actions, released as late as 1941, under the name A Page of History.

Commercial companies such as the Mingxing Film Company, focused more on fiction films, but also used documentary film in a very innovative way, in productions blending documentary footage and fictionalised narration.

As early as 1928 Zhang Shichuan and Hong Shen directed the romance Classmates (aka Kick), in part a recording of a real football game and in part a fictional love story between modern, athletic young people. Cheng Bugao's Raging Torrents (1932) also combined recordings of an actual flood in Hubei province with staged shots, to emphasise the impact of the natural disaster on different social classes, and criticise the gap between the lives of peasants and rich people.

From 1931 to 1945 documentary films became even more political, torn between the antagonism of Nationalists and communists; however, China's biggest threat was Japanese invasion. While fighting on the battlefield, the three forces were also struggling in the realm of images through film production. Documentary films from that era can roughly be divided into three categories: short newsreels reporting on various events without necessarily bearing a political discourse and educational films with a visible didactic purpose; those dealing with scientific or historical subjects, which used staged scenes as well as documentary shots to educate the audience with or without delivering a political message; and finally, long war documentaries, depicting battles and army leaders for the purposes of propaganda, incorporating both genuine recordings and staged scenes.

At the beginning of the 1930s the newsreel and documentary film departments of private companies such as the Lianhua Film Company and the Mingxing Film Company continued to record current political events, but also actors' and celebrities' lives such as Mei Lanfang and Hu Die; travelogues or local sports competitions. Fearing the influence of a growing number of 'left-wing' authors working for private film companies, however, the GMD government asserted its authority on the industry by establishing film administrations, placed under the leadership of the Propaganda Committee. The Script Censorship Committee and the Film Censorship Commission, both founded in 1933, aimed to control the content of the films produced by private companies, while the government-ruled Central Film Studio, established in 1934, produced pro-GMD films, newsreels (News of China), anti-communist films, as well as military educational documentaries. In 1937, when the Chinese Communist Party (CCP) and the GMD joined forces against Japan, the Central Film Studio stopped the production of anti-communist films and launched a series of newsreels called Record of the Opposition to the Japanese.

Sun Mingjing was a prominent figure of the 1930s educational films. A former student of sciences and electronic engineering at Jinling University (Nanjing University), he worked on over one hundred educational films financed by the Nationalist government. When the university founded in 1936 a Department of Educational Cinematography (DEC), Sun Mingjing became its head and, until 1948, he supervised the production of one hundred and twelve films, mainly travelogues (Scenes of the Capital City, 1936) and educational films on national defence, education, agriculture, industrial production (Coal Mining, 1937) and science (Solar Eclipse, 1936, the first Chinese colour film). Half of them were directed or edited by Sun Mingjing. Some, like The Front Line of Democracy (1946)—the first Chinese sound movie in colour—reflected the current situation of China. However, Sun Mingjing's films also illustrated his fascination for science and technology. To him, documentaries were first a tool to educate the people, before being an artistic or political medium. Sun Mingjing also published in 1942 the magazine *Film and Radio Monthly*, in which he wrote important articles on documentaries and translated some of John Grierson's articles too. His Peasants' Spring (1935), a script-based educational film on the everyday life of a family in the countryside, was screened at Brussels' World Expo, and was the first Chinese film to win a prize at an international competition.

When the second Sino–Japanese war broke out in July 1937, the Chinese film industry underwent a series of major changes. While most of the Shanghai film production houses moved to Hong Kong temporarily or permanently to escape Japanese invasion, the China Film Studio had to relocate to Chongqing at the end of 1938, along with the other governing bodies. Zheng Junli, a former actor and leftist filmmaker, who advocated the use of documentary in a fictionalised way, was the head of the newsreel department of the Guomindang film production house. He supervised the shooting of a feature-length documentary film depicting the heroism of Chinese ethnic minorities from northwest and southwest China in their fight against the Japanese. This film combines on-the-spot shooting and staged scenes, showing the traditions of Mongol, Tibetan, Miao and

Hui minorities, and was released in 1942 as Long Live the Nation.

In Hong Kong, the 1930s were a period of prolific newsreel production, both by former Shanghai-based companies (such as Lianhua and Tianyi) and local ones. The War Effort in Guangzhou, for instance, was released in 1937 by Grandview Film Company and testified to the resistance of Guangzhou's residents against the Japanese. In 1938 the Youth Photographic Unit, a group of Hong Kong-based filmmakers (Lam Tsong and Tsui Tin-tseong among them), went to Yan'an to shoot Scenes of Yan'an, a documentary on the communist base.

Until 1938 the communists, although influential in some of the private film companies, had no financial means to produce documentary films themselves. When Edgar Snow, an American journalist, visited the Yan'an communist base in 1936, it was the first time that someone had recorded everyday life in this remote area. Soon after, however, Yuan Muzhi—the famous director of the fiction film Street Angels (1937)—saw Snow's film in Beiping (Beijing), and decided to follow his steps in documentary filmmaking. After a meeting arranged by Zhou Enlai between Yuan Muzhi and Joris Ivens—then in China for the shooting of The 400 Million (1939)—he received a 35mm camera from the Dutchman. In 1938 Yuan Muzhi and Wu Yinxian brought cameras and film equipment to Yan'an and established the Yan'an Film Group. From then on, they shot newsreels about the political life of the base and worked on two long documentaries (Yan'an and the Eighth Route Army, unfinished, and Production and Fighting Combine: Nanni Bay, shot by Xu Xiaobing and Wu Yinxian).

The occupying forces of imperial Japan also had their own film production company in Manchuria. The Manchukuo Film Association (Man-ei) founded in 1937, produced until the Liberation a fairly large number of fiction films (one hundred and twenty) and newsreels (three hundred, called Man-ei News and News of Manchuria). Aiming to enlighten the people, the Japanese documentaries were labelled *Kulturfilme*, as a reference to the German concept of educational films. All of them, as well as the films produced in Shanghai for the Japanese government, took the occupant's standpoint to describe the war and exalt their efforts in China (education, industrial production, etc.). After the defeat of Japan in 1945, the relationship between Nationalists and communists remained officially peaceful until June 1946. During this time, the Changchun-based Manchukuo Film Association—back in Chinese hands and renamed the Northeast Film Company—produced newsreels about the war and the liberating troops of USSR, China and North Korea. The communist workers insisted on translating and helping to distribute Soviet and North Korean films. However, at the outbreak of the civil war, communist and Nationalist armies fought to keep control of the film studio. Eventually, the communist film workers had to flee to Heilongjiang province, where they established the Northeast Film Studio in Xingshan, on October 1, 1946. From two hundred members in 1946, they reached nine hundred and eighty-three workers in 1949—including Yuan Muzhi, Wu Yinxian and Chen Bo'er. This film studio aimed to produce art films, newsreels, scientific educational films, and long documentaries (Three Years of Liberation War in the Northeast, 1949). To promote exchanges and mutual help between communist film teams, the Yan'an Film Studio, founded in 1946, sent a mobile film group across the country to develop film production in communist-ruled areas. They also brought to the Northeast Film Studio the footage of the archive documentary Protect Yan'an, Protect Shaanxi, Gansu and Ningxia (1947) in order to complete the postproduction work there. Shot in Yan'an during the war, this film introduced to the audience the main communist leaders Mao Zedong and Zhou Enlai and explained the politics undertaken by the communists, such as agrarian reform.

As the communists became stronger and progressively took back the major northern cities, they established film production and administrative structures even before the founding of the People's Republic of China. In spring 1949 communist film workers gathered in Beiping and founded the Beiping Film Studio (renamed Beijing Film Studio on October 1, 1949). Along with the Shanghai and the Northeast film studios, this structure's main task was to keep a record of the final stages of the civil war. The newsreels, closely monitored by CCP leaders, and especially by Zhou Enlai, were the first production priority, ahead of fiction films. The Central Film Management Bureau was also set up, with Yuan Muzhi at its head. In July a meeting officially announced the missions for the arts: unite the people and contribute in the cultural, educational and economic construction of the New China. Cinema was the only art with a central administration, indicating its prominence over the other cultural fields.

After the founding of the People's Republic of China on October 1, 1949, the film studios continued to record the liberation and the end of civil war. In 1950 the Beijing Film Studio sent a team to Tibet to shoot Marching to Liberate Tibet. The Korean war was filmed by a group led by Xu Xiaobing in the long documentary Resist America and Support North Korea (1951). The documentaries also reported on the new leaders' actions and the measures they implemented, such as the agrarian reform in The Great Land Reform (1954). On July 7, 1953 the Central Newsreel and Documentary Studio (CNDS) was established, remaining until the 1980s China's main production house for documentary films and newsreels, a task it later shared with the Shanghai Science Education Film Studio (founded in 1953), the China Agricultural Film Studio (1954), and the Beijing Science Education Film Studio (1960). A centralised body, the CNDS put together shooting teams, usually formed by members of the film crews previously working in different communist armies. The shooting teams were sent across the country to film the newsreels News Document Exhibit (ten minutes) and Global Sights and Sounds, screened before feature films in cinemas.

Post-1949 documentary aesthetics gradually took shape under the influence of Soviet films. In 1950 USSR filmmakers Serguei Gerasimov and Leonid Varlamov came to China to shoot, respectively, Liberated China and Victory of the Chinese People upon an invitation of the Beijing Film Studio. Many theory books from the USSR were translated and contributed to the great aesthetical homogeneity of Chinese documentary films: the shots were short and clear; the voice-over commentaries simplified events to make sure that the audience understood the meaning of the images and their underlying political discourse. Music was a mandatory accompaniment and, as in fiction films, it served to highlight the emotional significance of the events or people on screen. Understood as a visual political discourse aiming at constructing a new China, documentary films followed the eventful flow of Chinese politics, clearly articulating the communist ideology.

Before the start of the Cultural Revolution in 1966, a number of ethnographic documentaries on China's national minorities had already emerged. The first films of this kind were shot between 1927 and 1935 by a group of scientists led by Swedish geographer Sven Anders Hegin in the northwestern provinces. From then on, films dedicated to social sciences gave way to war and ideological documentaries, which became a priority. At the end of the 1950s Chinese ethnographic films depicting the traditions of non-Han populations started to develop (The Wa, 1958; The Naxi's Culture and Art from Lijiang, 1960). These films were usually the result of cooperation between cinema operators and social scientists from the Chinese Academy of Science or provincial universities, and were based on the scientists' research. The shootings consisted of immersing the filmmakers in the communities to record not only local traditions, but also the changes brought about by communism and the supposedly positive evolution of the group under the new leadership. Soon the universities in Yunnan established themselves as great contributors to this field, starting a long tradition of anthropological documentary that continues today.

The Cultural Revolution (1966–76), however, brought these projects to a halt, and created tremendous changes in documentary production. The film studios and TV stations—the first of which, Beijing TV, was launched as early as 1958—were controlled even more tightly than before, and the content of each film was closely scrutinised, while many film workers were deprived of their positions and publicly criticised. Production dropped drastically and the names of team workers disappeared from the credits, to underline the importance of the group over individual contributions. On Beijing TV and provincial TV channels the only programmes broadcast at the beginning of the Cultural Revolution were reports on Mao Zedong swimming across the Yangzi, live transmissions of struggle sessions, or Tiananmen Square's Red Guards meetings. During this period documentary film was supposed to follow even more closely than before the slogan 'truthfulness has to serve politics', as in Educated Youth in the Countryside (1973), in which the audience is brought to a village where young people from the city experience working and living with peasants. Careful framing of the students shows them building irrigation systems or collecting rubber from the trees. The voice-over commentary names each young worker and describes their actions, backgrounds, and even their thoughts, with all expressing irreproachable communist feelings. During this troubled era only two foreign filmmakers, communist sympathisers themselves, were allowed to shoot documentaries in China: Joris Ivens and Michelangelo Antonioni (How Yukong Moved the Mountains, 1976, and China, 1972 respectively).

At the very end of the 1970s, after a decade of turmoil and as the country started the Reform and Opening Policy under Deng Xiaoping's rule, the development of television began to seriously affect the position of the Central Newsreel and Documentary Studio as the main provider of documentary films. TV news programmes and the beginning of reform in the audiovisual sector reconfigured the modes of production and dissemination of documentary films. The reforms aimed to implement economic autonomy in the cinematographic sector—distribution, screening and production—and allow coproduction with private companies. The position of documentaries weakened in the film industry—they were less lucrative than feature films for newly economically responsible cinema theatres—but their presence increased on television networks. In 1993 the Central Newsreel and Documentary Studio was placed under the supervision of China Central Television (CCTV), its main task being to supply documentary programmes for television channels. Being drawn away from the realm of cinema, documentary films became television products, which secured them as a prominent educational media, but also made them more economically constrained. At first, television documentaries maintained most of the characteristics inherited from the Central Newsreel and Documentary Studio, but soon the growing influence of the market demanded more diversity and brought new opportunities for filmmakers to experiment with their medium. Yesteryear's 'mouthpiece of the Party', television started to be considered a tool of information and entertainment, trying to attract audiences with new types of programmes and thus new forms of documentaries. During the mid-1980s movement of 'cultural fever', and among great debates about the course of reforms, an important television documentary generated a heated controversy. This eight-part series called River's Elegy, broadcast twice in 1988 on CCTV, was a joint production of CCTV and external collaborators. Though it became a great audience success, River's Elegy was also very controversial. Supported by then Party General Secretary Zhao Ziyang and the reformist faction of the CCP, its narrative conflicted with the conservatives' views on reform, and would later be denounced as one of the causes of the Tiananmen incidents in 1989. Its main authors, Xia Jun, Su Xiaokang and Wang Luxiang, used the cycles of the Yellow River as a symbol of the eternal return of political disasters in Chinese history. Depicting Chinese culture in a negative manner expressed a wish for changes and reforms, and articulated a criticism of the conservatism in the CCP, the current Chinese political system being compared to older forms of despotism. Visually, this series draws close to becoming a travelogue, and the tone of the half poetic, half messianic voice-over commentary is similar to the all-knowing voice of god of 'traditional' documentaries. However, the novelty of River's Elegy lies in its political content, also carried by 'real' interviews, notably of a prominent philosopher of the 1980s, Jin Guantao.

The Tiananmen Square massacre of 1989 froze the relative freedom of criticism and cultural opening up of the 1980s, but not the course of economic reform in terms of the mode of production of TV programmes. After a certain period of stagnation, and even repression, documentary films were then reinvented both inside and outside of the official structures, owing to innovative television programmes and a growing movement of independent filmmakers recording China's present and past in a more personal way. While some important documentary projects were cancelled after the events, and while political control over broadcasting increased, television channels were still experimenting with new forms of (noncontroversial) documentary programmes, and some individuals also started to shoot their own personal documentary projects. Shi Jian's Tiananmen, an eight-part documentary series, each episode fifty minutes long, is an example of the U-turn taken by television channels. Although it received the approval of the network at the start of filming in 1988, this documentary showing various people living around the famous square was then forbidden to be broadcast after completion in 1991.

The new documentary forms appearing on television during the 1990s belonged to a genre called 'entertainment documentary programmes'. These TV documentaries tried to get closer to ordinary people and reflect their personal lives. Life Space, created in 1993, was a short documentary programme (eight to ten minutes long) that appeared among other 'infotainment' subjects in the programme Oriental Time. Its purpose was to 'let ordinary people tell their own stories', and this proximity to individual concerns was the reason for its success. Similar documentaries multiplied on other TV channels, all of them quite successful in focusing on ordinary people instead of the grand themed narratives found in earlier television documentaries. Later, this trend generated into other TV programmes using a participatory filmmaking process: Ordinary People's Lives created in early 2000 had ordinary people filming their own personal lives. Professionals monitored the editing and the narrative construction, but this pioneering programme still allowed normal citizens to participate in the making of images and to express their personal concerns on national television.

Most of these novelty programmes came, in fact, from filmmakers who, besides working for television networks, also had their personal projects and were using the channel's equipment (cameras and editing rooms) to complete their own films. With or without the agreement of their employers, and not necessarily with the prospect of broadcasting the final product, they started to film reality in a more personal way. Jiang Yue, for instance, who contributed to Life Space, and also worked for Tibetan TV, filmed The Other Bank (1995), a recording of Mou Sen's creation of Gao Xingjian's play. Duan Jinchuan, employed by Tibetan TV, became internationally famous for his independent project No. 16 Barkhor South Street in 1997. Wu Wenguang, formerly employed by Kunming TV, started to film his artist friends from 1988 to 1991, and finally established himself as an 'independent' director.

A certain number of common points are shared by these 'independent' filmmakers and are manifest in these films: a rejection of television documentary conventions such as explanatory voice-over commentary and a certain influence of direct cinema embodied in the frequent use of observational camera. No. 16 Barkhor South Street, for instance, showed the daily tasks of a neighbourhood committee in Lhasa without the intervention of the filmmaker, who focused instead on depicting the protagonists, their aspirations, difficulties and personal stories, without imposing judgment on the audience. In Bumming in Beijing the precarious lives of five wishful artists, all friends of the director Wu Wenguang, are shown through discussions between the filmmaker and the protagonists, and shots depicting their everyday lives. Through this film, Wu Wenguang drew a portrait of a generation of young, marginal artists struggling to find means, and meaning, in their lives.

By the end of the 1990s the commercialisation of small digital cameras and editing software for personal computers brought new possibilities for filmmakers. In China a growing number of amateurs or professionals started to record reality and express themselves with this new technology. As more films and directors appeared throughout the country, the tiny group of independent documentary filmmakers grew into a 'movement' and attracted worldwide attention for the subjects they dealt with and the aesthetics they proposed. The films' circulation, restricted in the past to very small circles of friends or film festivals abroad, started to reach in the 2000s a limited but growing national audience, thanks to independent film festivals, screenings and archive collections in newly established alternative film structures.

Ranging from humble amateur recordings to acclaimed masterpieces, the diversity of the films encompassed in this movement seems quite broad, as much as the differences between the filmmakers themselves. Through investigation of historical issues (Hu Jie), social activism (Ai Xiaoming), memory seeking (Wang Bing) or formal experiments (Huang Weikai), the common practices of the filmmakers ensure for this movement a coherence by focusing on China's social transformations, while their differences make possible a plurality never seen before in Chinese documentary films.

The 'New Documentary Film' movement has contributed greatly to renewing the documentary style and expanding the range of topics filmed in China. However, it still has to find an economically viable way to survive among other more appealing film productions, and to secure a legitimate position vis-à-vis the Chinese audiovisual institutions. Its role within society and its growing position on the international stage will, it is hoped, help the filmmakers to continue their work and push the boundaries of Chinese documentary films.

JUDITH PERNIN

Further reading

Berry, Chris, Lu Xinyu and Lisa Rofel, *The New Chinese Documentary Film Movement: For the Public Record*, Hong Kong: Hong Kong University Press, 2010.

Chu Yingchi, *Chinese Documentaries: From Dogma to Polyphony*, New York: Routledge, 2007.

Fang Fang, *Zhongguo jilupian fazhan shi*, Beijing: Zhongguo xiju chubanshe, 2003.

Lü Xinyu, *Ji Lu Zhongguo: Dang Dai Zhongguo Xin Ji Lu Yun Dong*, Beijing: San lian shudian, 2003.

Mei Bing, Zhu Jingjiang, *Zhongguo Duli Jilu Pian Dang'an*, Xi'an: Shaanxi Shifan Daxue chubanshe, 2004

Shan Wanli, *Zhongguo Jilu Dianying Shi*, Beijing: Zhongguo dianying chubanshe, 2005.

Wang Yiman, 'The Amateur's Lightning Rod: DV Documentary in Postsocialist China', *Film Quarterly* 58, no. 4, summer, 2005: 16–26.

Ying Zhu and Tongdao Zhang, 'Sun Mingjing and John Grierson, a comparative study of early Chinese and British Documentary Film Movements', *Asian Cinema* 17, no.1 (spring/summer) 2006: 230–45.

Zhang Xianmin, *Kanbu jian de yingxiang*, Shanghai: Shanghai sanlian shudian, 2001.

Zhang Yingjin, *Cinema, Space, and Polylocality in a Globalizing China*, Honolulu: University of Hawaii Press, 2009.

China!

(US, Greene, 1965)

A socially and politically important film when first released, China! remains a striking and powerful document of Felix Greene's desire to show the West, for the first time, just how vibrant and progressive life was for the majority of Chinese since the Communist Revolution. The film is not as complete as some of Greene's other documentaries on China, such as One Man's China (1972), or as focused, as in Freedom Railway (1974), but China! can be seen as an early representation of Greene's guerrilla filmmaking style, which is more fully realized in Inside North Vietnam (1973), and of his artistic skill of using color, montage, sound, and a highly controlled narrative structure so as to inform, but also persuade, the viewer that the West has been misinformed as to the quality of life in communist China.

In 1963 Greene did not set out to make a documentary when he visited China. His goal was to study the nation so as to gather material for another book. After filming for four months and traveling fifteen thousand miles, Greene and his photographer, Hsu Chih-Chiang, had more than twelve hours of film. The resulting film was produced and written by Felix Greene and edited by John Jeremy. Greene recorded the music, mostly of Chinese songs played on traditional instruments. Narrator Alexander Scourby's minimal contribution of informative voice-overs allows the viewer to focus on the images and the actions of the people. However, the US Justice Department attempted to prevent the exhibition of China! on the grounds that, since the film stock was exposed in China, bringing the film into the United States would make it an import that would require a special license, which they would not grant. Senator Fulbright intervened on Greene's behalf and convinced Secretary of State Rusk and members of the White House that the film should be released. This controversy did not hurt, for China! proved to be a success, earning favorable reviews from *The New York Times*, running for sixteen weeks at Carnegie Hall Cinema, and showing in one hundred and sixty-five American cities.

China! is organized into two distinct sections. The first, a prologue narrated by Greene, serves as a preview of representative images to come (of schoolchildren, or parades, for example), while also establishing the central theme of the film—that Greene's own perceptions of China, and therefore possibly our own, have been incorrect. As Greene comments in the prologue, 'I know very well how personal feelings and evaluations can influence any kind of reporting, whether it's in newspapers or on film. So you will see China as I saw it'. There are two montage sequences in China!, and both exhibit a distinct stylistic difference from the rest of the film. The first comes soon after Greene's statement. Here, a series of quick shots of life in China, the first being a dramatic point-of-view parachute drop, followed by parades, workers, dancers, and other archetypal images that are repeated throughout China!, are cut together to the rhythm of the song 'Socialism is Good', sung by the Shanghai Workers' Cultural Palace. It is a sequence and song that, despite Greene's previous statement regarding the inclusion of one's own beliefs in a movie, lies at the heart of the film's argument that the Marxist Revolution helped to bring China from a destitute nation rife with poverty, disease, and class warfare, to a civilization that was ready to enter into the modern world and succeed.

The prologue sets the argument in place, but it is with the remainder of the film that Greene attempts to support his ideological convictions. Communist China is first contextualized by Greene in a series of archival images of the 1931 Japanese invasion and the subsequent civil war between the factions of Mao Tse-tung and Chiang Kai-shek. The final black-and-white newsreel shot, that of an infant wailing in the arms of its mother while their village lies in ruins, fades, and suddenly we are witness to a sea of red flags at the annual celebration of the Revolution.

This use of graphic discontinuity serves to bring the audience into modern China; it is a country that is alive with striking colors—the orange molten metal used to make trucks, the green rice fields, the white snow in the northern regions. This sudden graphic transition also supports the film's sense of historical progression, that through surviving the horrors of the first half of the twentieth century, China has established a system of government that treats all citizens as integral persons who will help bring about positive moral and industrial change.

The citizens of Shanghai are better off because of the sweeping economic and social reforms that transformed the city from a criminal and moral cesspool into a leading economy and a sober example of socialism at work. This may be one of the more serious drawbacks of Greene's film: at times it borders on propaganda. Although there were areas of China that were off-limits to Greene and Hsu, Greene did not attempt to broach the subject of human rights abuses in the nation, or of the countless millions who were executed in political purges. Instead, there are short segments on different aspects of Chinese life: school, entertainment, manufacturing, family, art, farming, advancements in medicine, life in a typical rural village, and the building of a causeway from the mainland to the island of Amoy. Each segment follows the same general style of framing: a series of extreme long shots to introduce the topic, of terraced farming, for example, followed by a series of medium and close-up shots of the people at work. Life in China! does not seem very different from life in the Western world, and although that may be Greene's implicit belief in this far left-leaning film, the unanswered questions regarding the past and current state of human rights in China remain highly problematic.

ALEXANDER L. KAUFMAN

See also: Greene, Felix

China! (US, 1965, 60 mins). Distributor (since 1984): Contemporary Films, Great Britain. Produced by Felix Greene. Written by Felix Greene. Associate producer: L.M. Cole. Photography: Felix Greene and Hsu Chih-Chiang. Edited by John Jeremy. Sound edited by Walter Storey. Music recorded in China by Felix Greene. Music by The Peking Symphony Orchestra, conducted by Li The-Lun, piano by Yin Cheng-Tsung. Opening chorus 'Socialism is Good' sung by members of the Shanghai Workers' Cultural Palace. Narrated by Alexander Scourby. Filmed throughout China, including Shanghai, Peking, the Sinkiang region, Inner Mongolia, Kweichow Province, and Amoy. Winner of the first prize at the Melbourne International Film Festival and received the Award of Merit at the Edinburgh Film Festival.

Chronique d'un été

(France, Rouch and Morin, 1961)

From its opening sequence, Chronique d'un été/Chronicle of a Summer self-consciously proclaimed its novelty: 'this film was not played by actors, but lived by men and women who have given a few moments of their lives to a new experiment in cinéma vérité'. The film has since been celebrated as a turning point in the history of the documentary film.

A joint project of sociologist Edgar Morin and filmmaker Jean Rouch, Chronique d'un été was conceived as a query into how Parisians lived their lives. Taking advantage of a newly portable sync-sound technology that made it possible to film people speaking spontaneously, the filmmakers took to the street, stopping Parisians with the question: 'Are you happy?' The film gradually comes to focus on a handful of characters: a worker, two immigrants, and a concentration camp survivor. Following them through the summer of 1960, the film achieved an unforgettable portrait of its times and breached a new way of filmmaking—cinéma vérité. Despite the confusion generated by this term, Chronique d'un été did not make simplistic claims to truthfulness. A self-reflexive film if ever there was one, it articulated the question of what truth means in the cinema, with unprecedented force and sophistication.

This experiment certainly did not arise in a void. The name cinéma vérité, a translation of the Russian Kino-Pravda (film truth), was meant to honour a predecessor, Dziga Vertov, who had done away with actors and gone out into the city in an attempt 'to catch life unawares' in the 1920s. Another often-mentioned predecessor was Robert Flaherty's Nanook of the North. The last scenes of Chronique d'un été directly mirrored Flaherty's practice of showing the film subjects rough cuts and recording their reactions.

The experiment was also deeply rooted in its own times. For those documentary filmmakers who were becoming weary of 'showing life in its Sunday best' (Morin 1985: 4), the new portable sync-sound equipment opened the way to unprecedented explorations of the everyday. In its attempt to go beyond 'the official and the ritualised', the cinéma vérité introduced by Chronique d'un été shared many affinities with its American contemporary, direct cinema (Rothman 1997: 87).

The classic distinction between cinéma vérité and kindred experiments like direct cinema is that 'cinéma vérité provokes and participates, whereas direct cinema observes' (Rothman 1997: 87). In Erik Barnouw's memorable formulation, the filmmaker acts as a 'catalyst' for the action of its subjects (Barnouw 1993: 253). Rouch insisted that 'he did not film reality as it was but reality as it was provoked in the act of filmmaking. It is this new reality, which would not exist apart from the making of the film, that the filming 'documents' revealing a new truth, a cinema truth' (Rothman 1997: 87). Insofar as his subjects were concerned, Rouch did not try to play down or disguise the presence of the camera. Assuming 'the disjunction caused by the very presence of the camera', he expected 'that people will act, will lie, will be uncomfortable', and regarded 'this manifestation of this side of themselves as the most profound revelation that anything a "candid" camera or "living cinema" could reveal' (Eaton 1979: 51). In other words, cinéma vérité is based on the premise that the masks that people choose for themselves, and the way they wear them on screen, can be more telling than a soul-baring confession.

The truth that cinéma vérité hopes to reveal is thus akin to 'psychoanalytic truth, that is, precisely that which is hidden or repressed comes to the surface in these roles' that people play in front of the camera (Morin 1985: 5). From the very beginning, Morin envisioned replacing the interviews and dialogue of traditional documentary film with a 'psychodrama carried out collectively among authors and characters' (Morin 1985: 6). He believed that this intersection between psychoanalysis and film was 'one of the richest and least exploited universes of cinematographic expression' (ibid.). The response of the characters to this psychoanalytic side of the cinéma vérité experiment varied widely. These differences are polemically articulated in the last scene of the film, as the participants openly discuss their impressions of the rough cut. They are largely divided into two camps that reproach each other for having been either 'too real', or 'not real enough'. This polemic crystallizes around the two women protagonists, Marceline and Marilou. Marilou argues that 'to have a tiny spark of truth the character has to be [...] alone and on the verge of a nervous breakdown' (Feld 1985: 68). This is, of course, exactly how she is throughout the film, baring her soul in tete-à-tete with Morin. In her confession she attempts to communicate her extreme alienation from the world and from herself. Her success in communicating her alienation, that is, her inability to communicate to Morin and, through the camera, to the world would have de facto cured her alienation, but this talking cinema cure fails and Marilou falls helplessly, desperately silent in front of the camera in a gesture that Rothman interprets as an onstage suicide (Rothman 1997: 77–8). Unable to express and thus vanquish her alienation, Marilou is condemned to poignantly reenact it in front of the camera.

While Marilou's confessions are considered by some of the characters/viewers to be the most moving part of the film, other characters openly attack them as 'indecent and exhibitionistic'. The starkest critic is Marceline, who opposes Marilou's confessional mode with a careful direction of her own stage persona. Marceline revisits her most intimate and traumatic memories in front of the camera—memories of her time in the concentration camps, her relationship to her father who was also deported, and to the family she had left behind. However, Marceline insists that the heartrending scene of her walking alone through a deserted Paris and reminiscing about her past was a thoroughly controlled and crafted performance that she had carefully planned in advance. What we see in the film, Marceline claims, is just one of many possible 'characters of Marceline' that she created for the medium of film (Morin and Rouch 1985: 77). Marceline's self-creation testifies to her sophisticated understanding of film as a specific medium with certain expressive possibilities and limitations. (Marceline also notes that during her performance she consciously thought of Hiroshima Mon Amour and also of Michelangelo Antonioni's films.) Marceline's insistence on her acting is also a reminder of the existence of a part of her that is not on display in the film, a part of her that is not public and not accessible through this particular medium. While exposing a most vulnerable part of herself, Marceline also lays claim to her ability to control that exposure, not only by acting but also by directing her performance. (Thus her displeasure when the directors of the film override her self-direction and manipulate her character (ibid.).) Of all the characters, Marceline appears most aware of the politics and power dynamics of the film, and most invested in controlling her own representation.

The debate between Marceline and Marilou's modes of self-presentation throws new light on the initial psychoanalytic ambitions of the film. In the course of the filming, it is clear that Morin's idea of a communal psychodrama openly played between actors and authors remains utopian. The direction of the psychoanalytic exploration is marked by strong power dynamics. There is no psychoanalyzing of the directors by the characters. Among the characters, it is the women who are the choice subjects of analysis. Marceline accepts the premise of the game, that is, that the roles that one plays in front of the camera may reveal a deep part of oneself, but she is intent on carefully directing what gets revealed. In carefully constructing a persona or mask that expresses her, she guards herself against those privileged moments in cinéma vérité where the director and spectator see, through the cracks and slippages of hasty masks, parts of the character of which she is unaware or would rather repress. Unlike Marilou, who has little control over her persona and helplessly lays herself bare in front of the camera, Marceline usurps the position of power that the cinéma vérité director, spectator, and the psychoanalyst traditionally share.

If Chronique d'un été uses a psychoanalytic lens to approach some of its characters, its overall scope is much wider. In Edgar Morin's words, the film was conceived as an ethnographic study 'in the strong sense of the term: it studie[d] humanity' (Morin 1985: 6). The film was to participate in forging a new direction in ethnographic filmmaking 'by emphasizing kinship rather than exotic foreignness' (Morin 1985: 5). Having made his name directing ethnographic films in Africa, Rouch intended to turn his ethnographic lens toward 'his own tribe'. One of the most interesting aspects of this ethnographic project is contributed by Laundry, a student from Côte d'Ivoire. The film's casting of Laundry in the role of 'African explorer of a France on vacation' (Morin 1985: 13) attempts to reverse the traditional ethnographic relationship between white observer and colonized subject. Laundry catalyzes some of the most revelatory discussions of the film, revealing a rich spectrum of contemporary French attitudes towards colonization, race, and racism. At the same time, this casting of Laundry in the role of explorer is limiting. The film is interested in Laundry in as much as he can shed light on French society, and less in him as a new member of that society. For example, as Laundry remarked, in the discussion on interracial marriage the film gave airtime only to the white women's attitudes toward marrying blacks, while excluding his and other black students' ideas about marrying whites.

Chronique d'un été's ethnographic project was planned as a survey of contemporary France taken 'at three levels: the level of private life, internal and subjective; the level of work and social relations; and finally the level of present history, dominated by the war in Algeria' (Morin 1985: 10). The two directors disagreed, however, on the method of bringing this project into being. Rouch was interested in organizing the film chronologically and focusing it tightly on just a few characters (Morin 1985: 24). Morin wished for a less individualized, 'mosaic-like montage of sequences' sustained by the question 'How do you live?' (ibid.). As a result, the film often vacillates between these two main approaches, sometimes further divided by the diverging approaches of the characters. Nowhere is this more evident than in the representation of the worker's plight in contemporary France. The film starts by formally interviewing a group of workers who sharply express their dissatisfaction with the conditions of their work. Then, in one of its most innovative moves, the film focuses on one worker, Angelou, following him from the moment his eyes open in the morning throughout his work day and leisure hours to bedtime. This sequence suggestively shows the alienation that the workers had openly articulated in the previous scenes. Once again changing registers, the camera descends into the factory where it films people at work. This factory scene briefly flirts with another movie genre, what a worker calls 'a film about work in the twentieth century', a film that Angelou wishes would record life in the factory, with an emphasis on relationships among workers, unions, and management (Morin and Rouch 1985: 76–7). This oscillation between different cinematic registers is representative of the experimental, searching quality of the film. At times this experimentation might threaten the unity of the film, but it also allows for a plurality of approaches to the workers' problem to coexist.

As Edgar Morin modestly put it: 'The film is a hybrid, and this hybridness is as much the cause of its infirmity as of its interrogative virtue' (Morin 1985: 26). Chronique d'un été relinquished the authority of the traditional voice-over and instead allowed its subjects to speak spontaneously. As the debate between Marceline and Marilou shows, the ensuing dialogue was not always free of tension or of problematic power dynamics. Furthermore, allowing a plurality of voices to be heard assumed the risk of creating a cacophony. Still, this imperfect plurality is one of the path-breaking achievements of the film. It gave the film its experimental novelty and complexity, which has made Chronique d'un été an inspiration for the upcoming documentary and nouvelle vague cinema.

CRISTINA VATULESCU

See also: Morin, Edgar; Rouch, Jean

Chronique d'un été/Chronicle of a Summer (France, 1961, 90 mins). Directed by Jean Rouch and Edgar Morin. Production: Argos Film (Anatole Dauman and Philippe Lifchitz). Production Director: Andre Heinrich. Production Secretary: Annette Blamont. Photography by Roger Morillère, Raoul Coutard, Jean-Jacques Tarbes, Michel Brault. Assistants: Claude Beausoleil and Louis Bocher. Lighting by Moineau and Cretaux. Sound by Guy Rophe, Michel Fano, Barthelemy. Edited by Jean Ravel, Nina Baratier, Francoise Colin. Filmed in Paris and Saint Tropez.

Further reading

Barnouw, Erik, 'Catalyst', in *Documentary: A History of the Non-Fiction Film*, New York: Oxford University Press, 1993.

Dornfeld, Barry, 'Chronicle of a Summer and the Editing of Cinema Verite', *Visual Anthropology* 2, 1989: 3–4.

Eaton, Mick, *Anthropology—Reality—Cinema: The Films of Jean Rouch*, London: British Film Institute, 1979.

Feld, Steven (ed.), 'Chronicle of a Summer', special issue of *Studies in Visual Communication* 1, 1985: 38–71 (an abridged translation of Jean Rouch and Edgar Morin, Chronique d'un été).

——'Themes in the Cinema of Jean Rouch', *Visual Anthropology* 2, 1989: 223–47.

Freyer, Ellen, 'Chronicle of a Summer—Ten Years After', in Lewis Jacobs (ed.), *The Documentary Tradition*, New York: W.W. Norton, 1979.

Gauthier, Guy, 'Jean Rouch, gourou nouvelle vague', *CinémAction* 104, 2002: 70–5.

Georgakas, Dan Uayan Gupta and Janda, Judi, 'Politics of Visual Anthropology, an Interview with Jean Rouch', *Cineaste* 8, 4, 1978: 22.

Morin, Edgar, 'Chronicle of a Film', *Studies in Visual Communication* 1, 1985: no. 4–29.

Morin, Edgar and Rouch, Jean, 'The Point of View of the "Characters"', *Studies in Visual Communication* 1, 1985: 71–78.

Rothman, William, 'Eternal Verites', in Charles Warren (ed.), *Beyond Document: Essays on Non-Fiction Film*, Hanover: Wesleyan University Press, 1996.

——'Chronicle of a Summer', in *Documentary Film Classics*, Cambridge: Cambridge University Press, 1997.

Rouch, Jean, 'The Cinema of the Future?' *Studies in Visual Communication* 1, 1985: 30–8.

Rouch, Jean and Fulchignoni, Enrico, 'Conversation Between Jean Rouch and Professor Enrico Fulchignoni', *Visual Anthropology* 2, 1989: 265–301.

Rouch, Jean and Morin, Edgar, *Chronique d'un été, Domaine Cinema 1*, Paris: Interspectacles, 1962.

Stroller, Paul, *The Cinematic Griot: The Ethnography of Jean Rouch*, Chicago, IL: University of Chicago Press, 1992.

Wintonick, Peter and National Film Board of Canada, *Cinéma Vérité: Defining the Moment*, Montreal: NFB, 1999.

Chulas Fronteras

(US, Blank, 1976)

Les Blank's Chulas Fronteras holds a prominent place in this documentary director's notable body of work, many of his films dealing with the folk music of communities on the fringes of mainstream America or with the specific delights of particular foods. It is a loving ode to the conjunto music of the Texas–Mexico frontier. (A conjunto is a small group including an accordion, a twelve-string guitar, a bass, and drums.) The solid research was provided by producer and writer Chris Strachwitz, founder of Arhoolie Records. When Chulas Fronteras was made (in 1976), the music was little known outside the Chicano world, but Blank's film contributed to its wider dissemination and was to inspire later, enthusiastically appreciative documentary treatments. The title means 'Beautiful Borderlands' and it suggests the considerable strengths but also the limits of Chulas Fronteras. It is above all a presentation and celebration through music of a simplified, occasionally sentimentalized version of Tex-Mex life (in general outside the big cities) and only 'a selective' exploration of the more complex experience, emotions, and society behind the music.

The Rio Grande (for Mexicans the Rio Bravo) passes behind the credits as water and a blue curve on the map along with a song of yearning for the Mexico left behind. The beauty of Texas-Mexican women is sung and soon after, the camera roams through a barbecue and later, in the kitchen of singer Lydia Mendoza, another mouth-watering abundance of food as she and other women prepare tamales. We hear Mendoza's rendition of Mal Hombre, about a woman enchanted and deceived in her youth by an unfaithful man. The song plus the food (and other songs about women performed by male conjunto singers) add up to a traditional depiction of the role of the woman in an essentially conservative and seemingly static society. There is no presentation of the extended impact of machismo or of possibly more independent roles for women in a society of immigrants. Even for its time, the film tends toward a nostalgic vision rooted in the past. It also ignores the darker, more stoically tragic side of the northern Mexican sensibility in general. There are no songs (common in norteño music) about the defense of honor or a man's reckless or heroic embracing of death.

The social dilemma of the Mexican immigrant (or illegal 'wetback') of the time does appear strongly, taking up the middle third of the film. Blank uses a mixture of expressively cut footage from the present, moments of interview and photos of workers (and some of their oppressors), many from decades earlier. The photos are seen through an orange-tinted filter as we hear a corrido (ballad) sung about a strike in the melon fields, with the footage full of oranges and carrots and the laborers who pick them. A story of anti-Mexican prejudice and an organizing song for Cesar Chavez's Farmworkers' Union led up to the high point of the sequence, the blessing of the vehicles, suddenly without music, as a priest sprinkles rows of cars and trucks with holy water and blesses them in Spanish. The camera panning across vehicles and faces, together with the rare absence of music, turns the blessing of the vehicles into the most solemn moment of Chulas Fronteras. Most of these vehicles will carry Mexican farm laborers northward in search of more crops, often with adolescents taken out of school to help feed the families.

The extended cadenza on social issues ends with a fairly long interview sequence, at least for this film, which skims along elegantly and boisterously to the swift, dance-beat of the conjuntos. A tractor driver working near the border comments on the need for schooling, for youngsters to have the time to learn how to better themselves, and on the hardships of the wandering life, which he has earlier described as the pattern of his own childhood, a constant moving from state to state and crop to crop through a long year of harvesting. More securely employed as he is now, he is grateful that he need not travel 'north'.

This sense of enforced travel, a necessary but difficult roaming away from home, is the primary serious underpinning of Chulas Fronteras, like a bass note below all the visible and audible vocals and accordions and guitars. It marks the present-day Mexican Diaspora, too, with its much greater numbers and its dispersion across the entire United States into numerous different lines of hard work. However, it is still a Diaspora that retains close links to its spatial origins—practical (in the importance of the money sent back home) and emotional (in the will to return). From this angle, the tone of the film still rings true about important aspects of the Chicano and emigrant Mexican experience.

The concluding movement, as it should be, is all musicians and music, with one performer, El Flaco ('Skinny') Jiménez, embodying continuity in time. He performs, he teaches the accordion to his young son, and we also see his father playing the same instrument and telling us he learned from his father, who was 'one of the best accordionists of his time' and whom we know only through a photo. Then quickly, with a sound cut to another voice repeating the word padre, another photo of a musician father appears and another description of musical skill passed down as inheritance, to yet another accordionist, Eugenio Abrego of the group Los Alegres de Terán. The elegant sequence deserves its critical placement, because the rapid runs of the accordions dominate the instrumental sound of the film while, for most of the many songs, clever lyrics soar with a sense of music as pure pleasure. It is from the beautifully recorded music and the inventive images mirroring its notes—from animals skittering at a zoo to dancers to farm laborers to a bouncing, swaying low-rider automobile—that Chulas Fronteras derives its verve and its lasting value.

MIRA BINFORD

See also: Blank, Les

Chulas Fronteras (US, 1976, 58 mins). Production Company, Brazos Films. Language: English and subtitled Spanish. In color. Directed by Les Blank. Conceived, produced, and sound-recorded by Chris Strachwitz. Cinematography by Les Blank. Film Edited by Les Blank. Assistant editor Maureen Gosling. Assistant Camera and Interpreter: Pacho Lane. Consultant: Guillermo Hernandez. Performers: Lydia Mendoza, Flaco Jiménez, Narciso Martínez, Los Alegres de Terán, Rumel Fuentes, Don Santiago Jiménez, Los Pingüinos del Norte, Ramiro Cavazos (Canción Mixteca), and others. Filmed in Texas and Mexico.

Further reading

Acosta, Belinda, 'Roots of Tex-Mex Music', *Austin Chronicle*, May 20, 2003.

Goodwin, M.A., 'Tex-Mex Masterpiece', *Village Voice*, January 3, 1977.

Scruggs, T.M., 'Chulas Fronteras, Del Mero Corazon', *Journal of the Society for Ethnomusicology* 43, no. 3, fall 1999: 572.

Wald, Elijah, 'Various Roots of Tex-Mex Music', *Sing Out! The Folk Song Magazine*, Winter, 2004.

Churchill's Island

(Canada, Legg, 1941)

Churchill's Island is primarily remembered as the first film of the National Film Board of Canada to win an Academy Award (best documentary, 1941). However, it is not so much its acceptance by the commercial mainstream, as its departure from that mainstream's conventions and institutional presuppositions, that makes the film historically significant and of some continuing interest. Churchill's Island marks the visible beginning of a Canadian film alternative to industrial Hollywood and an extension and elaboration of the documentary idea to new national circumstances and possibilities.

In the early years of its existence, the Board's founder and first commissioner, John Grierson, discovered that much of his time was occupied by administrative and political duties. As a result, much of the responsibility for day-to-day producing and mentoring fell to Stuart Legg, a Grierson recruit from the days of the Empire Marketing Board. Legg was particularly noted for his subtle grasp of public, political, and—as he would increasingly demonstrate—geopolitical issues. As head of production he would explore these topics through the Board's flagship wartime series, Canada Carries On (of which Churchill's Island was an early entry) and The World in Action.

The March of Time was an acknowledged influence on the Canadian series. Legg was impressed by the quality of its reporting, its concision, and its cinematic craft; however, Legg and his collaborators began immediately to move beyond the entertaining reportage so often characteristic of the existing newsreels. Propaganda played a role in this decision. The United States was still officially neutral with regard to the European conflict, and so the Board series had a great gap to fill in informing and motivating its domestic audiences.

Churchill's Island is a vivid response to this challenge. The film, which recounts the details of Britain's defense of itself against the Nazis, is completely compiled from the Board's extensive stock library. Future Board stalwart Tom Daly was largely responsible for maintaining this library. His seemingly complete recall of its holdings would make him increasingly central to the compilation films that would make up a good portion of the Board's early output. Daly has ascribed much of their motivational success to Legg's principle of 'waves', which was that sequences were to rise to a climax and then diminish, before the next sequence came along and increased the intensity. The emotional results are still clear in Churchill's Island, in which the high stakes, the national peril, and the national opportunity are quite palpable.

Although there were motivational (and manipulative) imperatives, Legg also intended to move his films toward the depth and breadth of the best investigative journalism. In Churchill's Island this deepening process is visibly well underway. There is a conceptual, and even dialectical, element to the film that was emblematic of the innovations and elaborations that Legg and his newsreel collaborators would develop throughout the war period. In addition to emotional appeal, there is a constant illumination of causal chains, a setting forth of the tactical and strategic elements of the conflict.

Legg introduces us to the main participants and the key processes, ensuring not only sympathetic identification, but also understanding. The exposition discusses varying threats of invasion, the defensive responses thereto, and the courage of Britain's army. These three elements recur through what are essentially the film's three acts. The first gives an account of the Blitz, during which Legg takes a characteristic retrospective turn, reviewing the causes and conditions of the German action to that point, ensuring that the audience member remains historically oriented. Next we witness the Royal Air Force's defense of Britain's skies and, from the Nazi perspective, the German blockade that was devised in response. During this second act, there is a clear discussion of the tactics of the U-boats and a frank admission of the great cost of their activities. There is also a clear message, quite common in this period (cf. London Can Take It, Foreign Correspondent), to the neutral United States. With the rising toll of sinkings, the ever more bold encroachments toward North American soil, it is intimated that no one is safe, and no one can remain neutral.

In keeping with Grierson's instruction that these films be 'truthful, but not defeatist', the warnings give way to an expression of gratitude for help rendered, and confidence for the future. The U-boats are on the run, and even as the third act outlines, and then just slightly glosses over, the possibilities of and preparations against a possible land invasion, the film moves toward a stirring climax. As the last wave crashes we hear narrator Lorne Greene's mighty challenge to the Nazis to 'come if you dare!' This justifiably famous conclusion remains extraordinarily powerful.

Churchill's Island was a great success. Along with the practically prophetic War Clouds in the Pacific (November 1941), it facilitated the remarkable access that Board newsreels would have not only to Canadian audiences but to screens in the United States as well. Although that access would continue, the tone of the newsreels would be altered. Wartime propaganda under Legg would further shift from the emotional and the partisan—however justifiable such approaches may have been at the time—to a more global, humanitarian approach. In this endeavor, Legg's sensibilities coincided with one of Grierson's most important convictions, which was that wartime films were also a preparation for peacetime, and that an awareness and anticipation of the needs of peacetime were essential to their successful execution. The Board's activities strongly prefigured the international role that Canada, and Canada's documentary films, would assume in the decades after the war.

DEAN DUNCAN

See also: Canada Carries On; Grierson, John; Legg, Stuart; March of Time; World in Action, The

Churchill's Island (Canada, National Film Board, 1941, 21 mins). Produced, directed, and edited by Stuart Legg. Commentary by Stuart Legg. Narrated by Lorne Greene. Music by Lucio Agostini. Sound by Walter Darling. Research by Tom Daly.

Further reading

Aitken, Ian, *Film and Reform*, London: Routledge, 1990.

——*The Documentary Film Movement: An Anthology*, Edinburgh: Edinburgh University Press, 1998.
Ellis, Jack C., *John Grierson*, Carbondale, IL: Southern Illinois University Press, 2000.
Evans, Gary, *John Grierson, and the National Film Board*, Toronto: University of Toronto Press, 1986.
——*In the National Interest: A Chronicle of the National Film Board of Canada from 1949 to 1989*, Toronto: University of Toronto Press, 1991.
Grierson, John, *Grierson on Documentary*, ed. Forsyth Hardy, London: Collins, 1946 (also New York: Harcourt Brace, 1947; revised edn London: Faber, 1966, New York: Praeger, 1971; abridged edn Faber, 1979).
Hardy, Forsyth, *John Grierson: A Documentary Biography*, London: Faber, 1979.
James, C. Rodney, *Film as a National Art: The NFB of Canada and the Film Board Idea*, New York: Arno Press, 1977.
Jones, D.B., *The Best Butler in the Business: Tom Daly of the National Film Board of Canada*, Toronto: University of Toronto Press, 1996.
Rotha, Paul, *Documentary Diary*, London: Secker and Warburg, and New York: Hill and Wang, 1973.
Sussex, Elizabeth, *The Rise and Fall of British Documentary*, Berkeley, CA: University of California Press, 1975.

City, The

(US, Steiner, 1939)

A brief history of the American city and a call for better civic planning, made at the behest of the American Institute of Planners, The City was one of the most celebrated and widely viewed documentary films of the 1930s and 1940s in the United States. The production benefited from financial backing from the Carnegie Corporation, which awarded $50,000 to the project, and from close collaboration among a group of gifted artists brought together to make the film. The City also had the advantage of a well-publicized debut at the New York World's Fair in May 1939, where it was screened in the Science and Education Pavillion four times daily for the next eighteen months, aptly placed among an array of fairground exhibitions devoted to the theme of 'The World of Tomorrow'. Subsequent distribution through various channels boosted The City's reputation further, although not always in ways that were in keeping with the sponsor's intentions.

Key figures in the making of The City included director-photographers Ralph Steiner and Willard Van Dyke, who formed American Documentary Films in 1938 to handle sponsored films of this kind; associate producer Henwar Rodakiewicz, who assisted at various points with the writing, directing, and editing; and composer Aaron Copland, who participated during the editing stage to create an integrated score, his first for film. Pare Lorentz, mentor to both Steiner and Van Dyke, contributed an outline that shaped the film's tone and structure. Urban critic Lewis Mumford wrote the narration, which was spoken by Morris Charnovsky of the Group Theater. The assembled talent alone ensured that critical attention would be given to this particular documentary.

For the American Institute of Planners, The City was intended to promote not simply the idea of thoughtful planning but a specific development project: 'garden' or 'green' cities, suburban centers built into the countryside, ringed by trees and hillsides and equipped with efficiently designed modern housing and hospitable spaces for work and play. In the past, the planners argued, unregulated industrial development had fractured community relations and led to incalculable environmental and human waste. 'Green' cities were the remedy. Inhabitants of these planned communities would regain the sociability and breathing space of the nineteenth-century village, while also enjoying the advantages of modern engineering, a combination made possible by the emergence of what Mumford labeled a 'neotechnic' age.

The assignment presented to the filmmakers thus involved a problem-solving narrative and images of nature and industry common to many American social documentaries of the previous decade, including those of Lorentz. In its finished form, The City organizes this material into five loosely bracketed sequences: a New England village idyll; an industrial city marked by smoke, slagheaps, and decay; a modern metropolis where the work day is automated and congested; a weekend traffic jam on a suburban highway; and a 'green' community of the kind the planners sought to promote.

Stylistic differences underscore social distinctions among the five segments. Compositions in the New England section, for example, favor horizontal framing, leisurely and lateral movement, and a balanced arrangement of people and structures, whereas the modern metropolis is defined through spatial constriction, sharp angles, and diagonal lines. Commentary, gentle and poetic in the village sequence, becomes clipped and sardonic in the industrial section that follows. Copland's innovative score establishes motifs for each section while also linking passages, as when a melodic line accompanying scenes of the New England village is recast in an elegiac key during bleaker parts of the industrial and metropolis segments, or a series of dissonant brass chords at the beginning of the industrial segment are converted into a harmonious closing at the film's end. Select stylistic devices exemplify the power of technological change, as when smokestacks multiply through superimpositions, or editing rhythms accelerate in coordination with the pace and mechanized movement of metropolitan life. A picture of the 'green' town—composited from footage of working prototypes filmed in Maryland, New Jersey, Wisconsin, and Ohio—includes aerial views of buildings set amid foliage and curved streets and roadways that thread their way to and through the community in patterns that are seemingly organic yet dynamic, conforming to topographical features. In this fashion, The City itself constituted a form of spatial planning and design.

Yet if such strategies lent emotive or expressive force to the planners' arguments, the filmmakers also clashed with the sponsors over key details, leading to telling compromises on both sides. The automated movement, rapid cutting, and sprightly music of parts of the metropolis sequence, for example, had a humorous, playful aspect that the sponsors believed undercut their sober critique. Steiner prevailed on this point, and the passage was singled out for discussion by critics, pro and con. Moreover, a contentious offscreen debate among a quartet of voices, scripted for the final segment by Rodakiewicz, was vetoed outright by the sponsors, who also demanded that the filmmakers extend the ending and spell out the advantages of the 'green' community in detail.

The City also circulated in ways that emphasized values that fell outside, and even ran counter to, the sponsor's promotional aims. The teaming of the film on a double bill with the French film La Principessa Tarakanovz/ Betrayal at New York's Little Carnegie Theater in the fall of 1939, and the inclusion of The City in major documentary retrospectives mounted by the Museum of Modern Art (MoMA) in the winter of 1939–40 and again in 1946, foregrounded the aesthetic accomplishment of the film over the planners' argument. (MoMA's curator, Iris Barry, in 1946 declared the The City a 'three-quarter masterpiece on town-planning', alluding to the aesthetic weakness of the sponsor-imposed ending.) Non-theatrical distributors, including MoMA, also circulated 16mm prints to educational groups, where the historical claims of the film were more closely scrutinized. The American Association for Adult Education, for example, published a movie study guide for community groups that asked discussants to assess the political adequacy of The City's history of urban development, opening up the topic to the kind of controversy that the planning association wanted the filmmakers to avoid. During the 1940s excerpted passages from The City also were recycled in montage sequences of urban life in a variety of different films, including War Comes to America (1945), a US Army documentary; Humoresque (1947), a Warner Bros. urban melodrama; and Mr Blandings Builds his Dream House (1948), an RKO urban-suburban comedy. From this angle, the durability of The City seems in part a function of the varied kinds of attention it attracted and a stylistic virtuosity that permitted individual sequences to take on an identity apart from the whole.

CHARLES C. WOLFE

The City (US, American Documentary Films, Inc., 1939, 43 mins). Distributed by Civic Films. Directed by Ralph Steiner and Willard Van Dyke. Written by Pare Lorentz and Lewis Mumford. Cinematography by Ralph Steiner and Willard Van Dyke.

Further reading

Alexander, William, *Film on the Left: American Documentary Film from 1931 to 1942*, Princeton, NJ: Princeton University Press, 1981.

Barry, Iris, 'Challenge of the Documentary Film', *The New York Times*, January 6, 1946: SM9.

Gillette, Howard, Jr, 'Film as Artifact: The City (1939)', *American Studies*, fall, 1977: 71–85.

Griffith, Richard, 'Films at the Fair', *Films* 1, no. 1, 1939: 61–75.

Keil, Charlie, 'American Documentary Finds Its Voice: Persuasion and Expression in The Plow That Broke the Plains and The City', in Barry Keith Grant and Jeannette Sloniowski (eds), *Documenting the Documentary: Close Readings of Documentary Film and Video*, Detroit, MI: Wayne State University Press, 1998.

Mumford, Lewis, *The Culture of Cities*, New York: Harcourt, Brace & World, 1938.

Rodakiewicz, Henwar, 'Treatment of Sound in The City', in Lewis Jacobs (ed.), *The Movies as a Medium*, New York: Farrar, Straus and Giroux, 1970.

Wolfe, Charles, 'The Poetics and Politics of Nonfiction: Documentary Film', in Tino Balio (ed.), *Grand Design: Hollywood as a Modern Business*, New York: Charles Scribner's Sons, 1993.

City of Gold

(Canada, Koenig and Low, 1957)

The National Film Board of Canada's City of Gold (1957) is one of the most celebrated short films ever produced and is one of the most decorated. Its numerous international awards, as well as its influence on the historical documentary and on noted contemporary filmmakers, testify to its merit and innovation.

City of Gold relates the history of the 1898 Klondike Gold Rush. The origins of the film lie in the 1949 discovery of several hundred Klondike-era photographs in Dawson City, of the Yukon Territories. These images, preserved on 8 x 10 glass-plate negatives, had been stored and forgotten in a sod-roof cabin and were found only by chance just before its demolition. They were largely the work of A.E. Hegg, an American photojournalist and entrepreneur, who captured the ferment of the Gold Rush with extraordinary vividness.

In ensuing years, through numerous means, these remarkable images attained wide circulation. In 1955 board director and animator Colin Low saw them at Ottawa's National Archive. He had been working on a Gold Rush project and quickly saw that these photographs might provide his film's centre. The challenge for Low and his collaborators was determining how to render this windfall of static imagery in some kind of dynamic cinematic fashion.

The solution came in the form of a mechanism devised by Roman Kroitor and Brian Salt, which enabled Low and codirector Wolf Koenig to plot and execute the most minute camera movements with complete precision and to explore their fixed images with unprecedented flexibility and fluidity. It is for this innovation that City of Gold is most cited today, but the film would probably remain a mere technical footnote were it not for the material that the technology served and the sensibilities that informed the arrangement and presentation.

City of Gold was a collaboration. In its production there was a democratization of roles and relationships and a neutralization of film elements, resulting in an impressively integrated work of art and information. These characteristics and qualities were strongly associated with the board's legendary Unit B, of which City of Gold is perhaps the most well-known product. In the ideal Unit B production, the ego of individualism was subordinated to the needs and values of the creative community and, as behooved a publicly funded institution, of the larger community the creators served. The idea and actuality of Unit B at the Film Board was not without contradiction and controversy. Nevertheless, with this film and with many others besides, the ideal and the real seem to have been substantially correlated.

City of Gold is notable for being very well made. There is a telling tension between the stasis of present-day Dawson, as illustrated by the film's live-action prologue and epilogue, and the dynamism of the still photographs that preserve the vivid past. The contrast is emphasized by the exquisite transitions between the two periods. Much of the credit for this seamless assembly goes to editor, and Unit B head, Tom Daly.

Daly pointed out that the edges of the photographs were never shown, leaving audiences with the illusion of extended offscreen spaces. This quality had been integral to realist filmmaking for some time, but what was remarkable was how that space operated in a photographed context. As Erik Barnouw observed, it was not only space that was expanded in City of Gold, but time as well. The vividness of the images and the superb coordination of their rendering opened up the documentary film to times and events that predated it.

Some of the credit for this must also go to Eldon Rathburn's superb score. The immediacy of the historical is also aided by the film's narration, cowritten and delivered by Pierre Berton, a Dawson native who was on the brink of becoming Canada's most prolific and popular historian. The voice that he presents combines the scholar's rigor with the citizen's affection and commitment. This combination communicates a concrete sense of past realities, as well as a clear sense of their relevance to the present.

Low and Koenig's film appeared at an important juncture in the development of the North, and the Canadian identity. Dire notions of the inhospitable and the impossible had long pervaded northern representations. Inevitably these pictures had affected the perceptions and self-concept of the nation as a whole; however, competing voices had also spoken for the necessity, even the inevitability, of successful community in this savage environment. In the light of more recent events (the Leduc oil strike of 1947, the subsequent establishment of the Canadian pipeline system, the dissemination of native cultural ideas and aspirations), this idea had assumed even greater importance. For the sake of the region's own economic and social development, there was a need for a more nuanced, more optimistic view of the region.

City of Gold filled a number of present needs, and it continues to resonate in more contemporary contexts. In parallel to the organization that produced it, the film recalls how individual pursuit within a strong community led to great prosperity in the midst of environmental and geographical obstacles. It presents a model for peaceful relations between Americans and Canadians, in which the values of both sides are defended and combined to greatest mutual advantage. It affirms the importance of history's obscure, for whom difficulties are assured, but whose flexibility and decency in the face of inevitable frustration presents a worthy model for living, and for representing life.

DEAN DUNCAN

See also: Koenig, Wolf; Low, Colin

City of Gold (Canada, National Film Board, Unit B, 1957, 22 mins). Produced by Tom Daly. Directed by Wolf Koenig and Colin Low. Commentary by Pierre Berton and Stanley Jackson. Narration by Pierre Berton. Location camera by Wolf Koenig and Colin Low. Animation camera by Douglas Roberts. Music by Eldon Rathburn. Edited Tom Daly. Sound by George Croll. Filmed in Dawson City, Yukon Territories.

Further reading

Berton, Pierre, *The Mysterious North*, Toronto: McLelland & Stewart, 1954.

——*Klondike*, Toronto: McLelland & Stuart, 1958.

Evans, Gary, *In the National Interest: A Chronicle of the National Film Board of Canada from 1949 to 1989*, Toronto: University of Toronto Press, 1991.

Grey Owl, *Tales of an Empty Cabin*, Toronto: Key Porter Books, 1998.

Houston, James, *Confessions of an Igloo Dweller*, Toronto: McLelland & Stewart, 1995.

James, C. Rodney, *Film as a National Art: NFB of Canada and the Film Board Idea*, New York: Arno Press, 1977.

Jones, D.B., *Movie and Memoranda: An Interpretive History of the National Film Board of Canada*, Ottawa: Canadian Film Institute, 1981.

——*The Best Butler in the Business: Tom Daly of the National Film Board of Canada*, Toronto: University of Toronto Press, 1996.

London, Jack, *Klondike Tales*, New York: Modern Library, 2001.

Service, Robert, *The Shooting of Dan McGrew and Other Poems*, New York: Dover, 1993.

Clair, René

René Clair was a French filmmaker whose films spanned forty years and represented a wide variety of genres, from experimental shorts to musicals to Hollywood studio dramas. His contribution to theories of documentary film was chiefly as a writer who championed the power of the film image as a nonnarrative form of communication, the importance of film rhythm and movement, and the independence of film as an art form. Condensing the thinking of several different French avant-garde intellectual traditions in the late 1910s and 1920s with his practical experience in the French studio system, Clair valued films whenever their fantastic or documentary powers circumvented, or offered alternatives to, traditional fictional narratives. As a practitioner of documentary and documentary-influenced film, he was interested in conveying the realities of the city (in his case, Paris) through on-location shooting. He was not a believer in the absolute truth conveyed by the image itself. His experiences with Dada, the iconoclastic post-World War I art movement, led in part to his films playing with an image's absolute truth through contrapuntal sound or camera work. In theory and in practice, Clair always foregrounded the process of filmmaking as it created reality rather than simply reproducing it on film; in addition, he always emphasized the power of film in general (and documentary film in particular) as a visceral experience with its own unconscious communicative power unrelated to that of other arts.

Clair first participated in the film industry as a newspaper writer and actor. His writing entered into the 'great debates' in French film magazines during the 1920s, where film critics and practitioners argued over the purpose and direction cinema should take (Abel 1988). Poetic documentaries—epitomized by Nanook of the North (1922)—flourished in this period, and Clair used these documentaries as examples of what film could achieve as an independent art form. In his opinion, the documentary was the only genre that could communicate its message in a wholly new way because it was the only one not parasitically dependent on earlier art forms. While the French films d'art of the 1920s seemed dependent on theater and literature as models, Clair believed that the documentary made it possible to communicate ideas, emotions, and intellectual arguments purely through the visual experience. In an essay on the Abel Gance film La Roue, he rejects the literary and theatrical aspirations of the 'cinema of ideas' in favor of a cinema that creates ideas in the mind of the viewer through image and movement alone:

> Oh, if M. Abel Gance would only give up making locomotives say yes and no, lending a railroad engineer the thoughts of antiquity, and quoting his favorite authors! If he were willing to create a pure documentary, since he knows how to give life to a machine part, a hand, a branch, a wisp of smoke! If only he were willing to contribute in that way to the creation of the Film that can barely be glimpsed today! Oh, if he were willing to give up literature and place his trust in the cinema!
>
> (quoted in Abel 1988)

Here, Abel Gance is made to stand in for all filmmakers who lazily use conventions for earlier art forms instead of using film to communicate in a new way. Gance's films are both metaphorical and descriptive, but Clair believed that 'pure documentary' could show instead of telling. Through lighting, shot framing, and the like film invested an object with meaning and life that could be interpreted or intuited by the viewer on an unconscious level. This idea is similar to that of other theorists of 'photogenie', a belief that the skill of an auteur and the power of film as a medium could articulate previously unseen truths about objects, faces, and places (such as the 'life' Gance imbues in hands, branches, and smoke). This understanding of the image is similar to that expressed in cinematic impressionism, a French movement that used pure and often not referential film images to convey a subjective, poetic emotion. Clair's ideas about the power of the documentary image are not purely impressionist, however, as they focus on the power of the image and the film as both subinfluence, but Clair's understanding of the power of documentary film belongs to a larger tradition of European modernism. This movement held, among other things, that old narrative forms could no longer adequately communicate the realities of the newly mechanized world (particularly after World War I), and instead it turned to forms that worked through fragmentation, collage, juxtaposition, and unconscious association. For Clair, this meant that 'pure cinema' untainted by commercial concerns could never truly exist, but the filmmaker could create fragments of purely visual story that communicated emotion unconsciously and helped the audience arrive at a new understanding of reality. Clair is best known as a filmmaker shaped by Dada and surrealism, and those art movements shared with cinematic impressionism a belief in the dreamlike power of images. Clair also took from Dada in particular a sense of film's power, through montage, to thwart conventional understanding. He believed that the logical culmination of the poetic documentaries of the 1920s would be a chain of images held together by 'no definable link but united by a secret harmony' (Clair 1972) like that which unified his seemingly nonsensical Dadaist film, Entr'acte. Clair thought that a film with a sense that was structural rather than narrative would hold a viewer's attention in the same way that a symphony does. Although Clair was initially opposed to sound film (chiefly because he thought it would return film to the status of theater), he later believed it had the same power to shock through juxtaposition with the image. His musicals in the 1930s and his later writing used sound to counterpoint, ironize, or call into question the unmediated reality the image presents, a technique important to many documentarians, and to those who use found footage in particular.

As an actor in Louis Feuillade's troupe, Clair was exposed to an important early French film tradition, one that had the most concrete influence on his experiences as a documentary filmmaker. This movement, described by critics as 'pictorialist naturalism' was influenced by the theories of nineteenth- and twentieth-century writer Emile Zola, whose novels of lower-class life explored the effect environment has on character (Aitken 2001). In practice, this meant that the films used on-location shooting and nonprofessional actors in an attempt to represent objective, unmediated, and unaestheticized reality. Even in his serials like Les Vampires, a fantastic crime thriller that the surrealists loved for its bizarre plots and imagery, Feuillade still shot on-location to document the reality of Paris at night, a reality that he believed could not be realized on a constructed set.

Clair shot on location for La Tour/The Eiffel Tower (1928), his only documentary, as well as the street scenes in his science fiction film, Paris qui dort/The Crazy Ray (1925). These films emphasize film's rhythmic qualities and the emotional and intellectual resonance of an image's movement and duration. For Clair, movement was the most important and effective technique for unconsciously conveying the film's meaning to the viewer: 'I don't mean the movement recorded in the shot itself, but the movement of the shots in relation to one another. Movement, the primary base of cinematic lyricism, whose mysterious rules become clearer every day' (Dale 1986). He used this concept to think about the basic elements of montage, such as shot length, action, and the visual field, in a musical way, taking into account the feelings of shock and connection that arise from each shot's place in the larger composition.

Through both his on-location shooting and his musical techniques of composition in La Tour and Paris qui dort, Clair can be understood as part of a larger tradition of European modernist documentary films of the 1920s and 1930s, and in particular the 'city symphony films' such as Rien que les heures/Nothing but the Hours (1926), Chelovek s kinoapparatom/Man with the Movie Camera (1929), and Berlin: Die Symphonie der Grosßstadt/Berlin: The Symphony of a Great City (1927). Neither of Clair's films aspires to the kind of epic totality in its presentation of the rhythms of urban life seen in those films. The city scenes in Paris qui dort are part of a larger narrative and La Tour is about one landmark rather than Paris as a whole. Clair does share with Vertov the interest in paralleling the rhythms of city life with those of film itself, in particular by calling attention to materiality and construction of the film. In Paris qui dort, a mad scientist uses a ray to stop all motion in Paris, and the few residents who are not immobilized ransack the city, eating in fine restaurants and stealing from stores. Because of the scientist's actions, documentary footage of Paris pauses, fast forwards, and rewinds, showing the city while calling attention to how the city gets shown. Here, Clair is using film techniques such as stop-motion to undercut the intrinsic, unquestioned reality of the city in the same way that he later uses sound to undercut the intrinsic truth of the image.

La Tour uses rhythm and movement to redefine the viewer's understanding of the most clichéd of Paris landmarks, the Eiffel Tower. This film is an articulation of all Clair's theories of the poetic documentary, as it unites film's ability to show the world in a fantastic or impossible way and its ability to communicate the concrete details of reality. Clair starts the film with a conventional postcard view of the Eiffel Tower, then splits this whole image into rapidly changing impressions of different pieces of the tower coming together and moving apart. This section's composition owes much to Cubist painting, particularly its method of presenting disparate views of an object as a way of both emphasizing the subjective nature of perception and presenting a more complete picture than a 'whole' view of the Eiffel Tower would give. Clair transcends the techniques of the canvas, however, by constantly showing these different fragments in motion. As with Paris qui dort, Clair uses techniques such as fast motion and superimposition as a way of defamiliarizing a familiar place and calling into question precisely how we perceive it. Clair is somewhat interested in the tower's history. He shows a picture of Georges Eiffel and some blueprints and then mimics the construction of the Tower through matching dissolves of still images. The film then returns to the subject of perception through a first-person focus on the experience of ascending to the top of the tower; once the top has been reached, a shot multiplies this experience, looking down on a lower platform where a man looks down on even lower spectators. Throughout the film, shots where the camera moves upward mimic the structure of the tower and the first-person experience of moving to the top. After a rapid descent, the film ends with the same establishing shot of the Eiffel Tower, invested with new meaning through the firsthand experience of it.

The interplay of poetic fantasy and prosaic reality is important both to Clair's entire filmography and to the genre of poetic documentary that was shaped during his most productive and influential period as a writer in the 1920s. Clair's experience working on a variety of film projects, from the most independent and experimental to studio-funded adaptations of classic French plays, led to a more balanced view on the possibilities of documentary film than other film theorists and practitioners of the period. He agreed that film should attempt to communicate through visual effects, but this never descended into a purely subjective vision of the cinema. Perhaps his most important contribution to documentary film was the idea that images and their movement on screen, no matter how fantastic, could always intervene into reality and alter the audience's perception of it.

SUNNY STALTER

See also: Eiffel Tower, The; Man with the Movie Camera; Rien que les heures

Biography

Born René Chomette, November 11, 1898. In ambulance corps on the front lines during World War I, 1917–18. Wrote newspaper articles and appeared in films, 1919–22. Worked as an assistant director, 1922. Involved with Paris Dada/surrealist group throughout the 1920s. First novel, *Adams*, published in 1926. Made films in Paris in the early 1930s, London in the late 1930s, and the United States during World War II. Returned to Paris after World War II. Directed stage and radio plays throughout the 1950s. Elected to the Académie Française in 1960. Died in 1981.

Selected films

1924 Entr'acte: director
1925 Paris qui dort/The Crazy Ray: director
1928 La Tour/The Eiffel Tower: director

Further reading

Abel, Richard, *French Film Theory and Criticism: A History/Anthology 1907–1939*, vol. 1, Princeton, NJ: Princeton University Press, 1988.

Aitken, Ian, *European Film Theory and Cinema: A Critical Introduction*, Edinburgh: Edinburgh University Press, 2001.

Amengual, Barthelemy, *René Clair*, Paris: Seghers, 1969.

Clair, René, *Cinema, Yesterday and Today*, trans. Stanley Applebaum, ed. R.C. Dale, New York: Dover Publications, 1972.

Dale, R.C., *The Films of René Clair*, Metuchen, NJ: Scarecrow Press, 1986.

De La Roche, Catherine, *René Clair, an Index*, London: British Film Institute, 1958.

McGerr, Celia, *The Films of René Clair*, Boston, MA: Twayne Publishers, 1980.

Close-Up

(Iran, Kiarostami, 1990)

Like certain films of Buñuel, Chris Marker, and others, Close-Up puts into question what it is we are prepared to call reality, or documented reality, on film. Despite all its words and reasoning, its modernity and sophistication, Close-Up brings us at last to the issue of faith. What is to be feared in faith? What can faith bring?

Without title, credits, or any announcement, the film begins with a fifteen-minute sequence in which a journalist travels with two policemen in a taxi to a Tehran residential district to arrest an impostor. He has been taking advantage of a well-off family, pretending to be the famous film director Mohsen Makhmalbaf. The sequence feels like fiction, a careful staging with precise timing of lines and the camera set up where the car's dashboard or windshield would be. Once the arrest is made, the film's title and credits appear, informing us of a 'screenplay' by Kiarostami 'based on true events', and listing the names of the persons of the film, who 'appear as themselves'. The titles are superimposed over the image of a press printing newspapers, which suggests that the film understands its status as something like that of a newspaper, hardly a transparent medium, yet a medium of mass communication to which one turns for information and, presumably, truthful and accurate information.

The film proceeds to present four scenes that, by all accounts, are directly filmed, first-encounter interviews with individuals involved in the story. The first interview, with policemen outside the jail where the arrested man is being held, gives Kiarostami his first information about the arrest. Therefore, the opening sequence, showing the arrest at the time it happened, is certifiably a reenactment, as Kiarostami did not know about the arrest at the time it occurred and thus could not have been present at the actual event.

The film moves on to an interview with the victimized family, the Ahankhahs, in their well-appointed home. They address Kiarostami by name, bringing him more explicitly into the film. The interview seems a first encounter simply because the family so frankly expresses its concern not to be depicted as credulous in what appears now to be a film project in which they have agreed to participate. The family makes clear its interest in film. The unemployed son, Mehrdad, writes screenplays as an escape from bourgeois boredom and disappointment. Interest in film drew the family in with the impostor, and it now draws them in with Kiarostami.

Next, in a prison interview, we meet the impostor, one Hossein Sabzian, the figure on whom the whole film hinges. Here we actually see Kiarostami for the first and only time, although only from the back. It is the filmmaker pressing forward to confront his subject, the source that generates the film. Kiarostami's cameraman frames the prison office where the interview takes place, staying, presumably as required by prison rules, on the near side of a glass partition with columns, beyond which sit Kiarostami and Sabzian. A lens is used gradually to penetrate the barrier and come close to Sabzian's face as he speaks. The situation here illustrates documentary's perennial task and desire, to overcome barriers, to look closely, to let its attention be drawn by what is interesting. Here that interest is the face of this complex, emotional, working-class man possessed, he tells us, by cinema, and drawn by this possession into committing his crime. 'Make a film about my suffering', he entreats.

Kiarostami speaks with a court official and then the judge who presides over Sabzian's trial, securing permission to film the trial and getting the court date moved forward. Film's power to intervene in the justice system is impressive and, at the end of the interview, two of the filmmakers pass in silhouette across the foreground, spectral figures, suggestive of angels. The judge, a small man with large eyes, dressed as a cleric, wants to participate in the film.

A filmmaker's chalkboard announces the trial scene, which will take up the lengthy middle portion of Close-Up, at once a crucial public event and a film. The first words are the judge's, 'In the name of God', picking up on the suggestion of angels, reiterating the issue of faith, and opening the dimensions of film's power and source wider than the film has done so far.

If this is God's court, it is very much a film director's court, or film's court. The episode appears to be shot on videotape or some lower grade of material than the rest of Close-Up, perhaps out of necessity in the courtroom setting, or perhaps to set this material apart formally. Are we watching the actual trial or a reenactment, perhaps with changes? Does it matter if we trust Kiarostami? Here Sabzian and the Ahankhahs are allowed to explain fully their motives and actions in all that has transpired.

Kiarostami asks questions and guides the proceedings to a degree, directing them. He explains to Sabzian that he will use a 'close-up lens' to allow Sabzian to express himself fully. Pans across the room reveal Kiarostami's lighting man, making it clear that the filmmakers suggestively put Sabzian's face half in strong light, half in deep shadow. The long trial scene involves two flashback reenactment scenes, suggesting that what is being talked about builds a pressure that requires staged scenes to make things clear, to let things be fully what they are. There is argument about whether Sabzian is still performing, now as a repentant, which raises the question of whether performance can be avoided. Sabzian says that he speaks from the heart and quotes Tolstoy to the effect that the sincere sharing of feeling is art. Close-Up is at once sincere and artful, if we accept it. At the judge's behest, the Ahankhah family forgives Sabzian.

Close-Up concludes with a sequence in which, seen at a distance, Mohsen Makhmalbaf appears on the street and meets a weeping Sabzian, and the two ride across Tehran on Makhmalbaf's motorbike to call on the Ahankhahs and offer them flowers. Kiarostami and crew follow in another vehicle, filming. Makhmalbaf's lapel microphone appears to fail, and Kiarostami and an associate appear to make on-the-spot comments about the progress of the scene, such as 'we can't retake this'. From its opening (that first journey across town to the Ahankhahs), Close-Up has established a pattern of confinement breaking out into the open. The trial scene breaks out into flashbacks. The whole film seems a preparation to break out into the highly mobile final sequence, a complicated artistic trick or a case of film doing all it can to keep up with events not under its control. The film ends on a freeze frame of Sabzian's face, his head bowed in repentance, tears having flowed, a subtle smile starting to take over.

CHARLES WARREN

See also: Kiarostami, Abbas

Close-Up (Nama-y Nazdik, Iran, 1990, 90 mins). Produced by A.R. Zarin. Directed and edited by Abbas Kiarostami. Screenplay by A. Kiarostami based on a true story, with the persons concerned appearing as themselves. Photographed by A.R. Zarindast. Filmed in Tehran.

Further reading

Dabashi, Hamid, *Close Up: Iranian Cinema, Past, Present and Future*, London and New York: Verso, 2001.
Perez, Gilberto, *The Material Ghost: Films and Their Medium*, Baltimore, MD and London: Johns Hopkins University Press, 1998.
Saeed-Vafa, Mehrnaz and Rosenbaum, Jonathan, *Abbas Kiarostami*, University of Illinois Press, 2003.

Coal Face

(UK, Cavalcanti, 1935)

The National Film Archive summarizes the content of the film Coal Face as: 'The work of the British miner and its importance.' The shot list is as follows: Shots of pitheads. Overhead transporters dump slag onto slagheaps. Mechanized washing and grading of coal at a pithead. The location and size of the main coalfields are indicated on a map of Britain. Miners walk along a shaft to the Coal Face for the night shift. Horses pulling wagons. A miner working at the face. A Davey safety lamp in operation. A naked flame lamp in a gasless Scottish pit. Miners working at the face. A sandwich break. An electric coal cutter in operation. Coal is shovelled into trucks which are hauled off—commentary gives statistics of accidents in the mine. The winding machinery brings the men to the surface in the morning. They check out. The miners make their way home, rows of terraced houses owned by the company. Pithead chimneys. A tree. A miner walks under a line of washing. Slagheaps. Tree blowing in the wind. Ruined building. Trees and sky. A railway marshalling yard. A train moves off with coal. Shunting coal wagons—a signalman operates points. Horse-drawn coal carts distribute coal locally. Commentary gives statistics of coal used by the major industries: the electricity industry—shots of pylons, worker in a power station; railways: coal is loaded into a tender, the locomotive moves off; express trains. Shipping: dockers loading coal into a ship. A mechanical grab hoists a load of coal and empties it. Industrial landscapes. Pitheads. Miner walking along a street. Pithead at evening.

Coal Face was presented at the [London] Film Society as an experiment in sound. The commentary provides factual information—data, processes, by-products—overpoetic images of coal mines. The commentator's voice is unconventional and nonprofessional sounding (even the maps are abstract at first). The music is modern, cacophonous, discordant piano with percussion are prominent. As miners walk into the mine, choral speech and drumbeat begin. The choruses are of male and female voices, separate and combined. The commentator is objective, the chorus subjective. We hear snatches of miners' talk, individual men's voices, whistling, choir in a kind of keen. The poem sung by the female voices on the return of the miners to the surface was written for the film by W.H. Auden:

> O lurcher loving collier black as night,
> Follow your love across the smokeless hill.
> Your lamp is out and all your cages still.
> Course for her heart and do not miss
> And Kate fly not so fast,
> For Sunday soon is past,
> And Monday comes when none may kiss.
> Be marble to his soot and to his black be
> white.

Coal Face continued the formal experimentation with sound in relation to sight so strongly evident in The Song of Ceylon (1934), though this time as an exalted tribute to the lives of British miners. It was the editing of sound in relation to image that was the strongest and most original line of formal invention in the British documentary of the 1930s (and on into the 1940s). It is generally agreed that Cavalcanti, much more than Grierson, was responsible for that rich and innovative use of sound, ahead of anything being attempted in feature fiction filmmaking at the time. Of course it was Grierson who brought Cavalcanti, with his background in the avant-garde and work in early sound features, from France to the General Post Office (GPO) Film Unit for that purpose. (Though it was also suggested, given the youthfulness of the GPO Unit filmmakers, that Grierson may have invited Cavalcanti to have someone of his age with whom to talk.) In any case, the films they worked on together maintain their interest as artistic experiments. Coal Face won a medal of honour at the International Film Festival in Brussels in 1935.

Cavalcanti, while assisting on most of the GPO Unit's productions, had films for which he was mainly responsible. Coal Face was the second and perhaps most important of these (Pett and Pott, in 1934, was the first). It was, wrote Roger Manvell, 'an oratorio of mining'. He added that 'oratorios are not popular with film-goers. The visuals were good but not exceptional,' in Manvell's opinion. 'What mattered was the sound' (Manvell 1946: 362). Part of the problem may well have been that the recording quality of this soundtrack is substandard. Because of government regulations, the GPO Film Unit was at first required to purchase British sound equipment (Visatone-Marconi) for its Blackheath Studio. RCA equipment was purchased later.

In addition to Grierson and Cavalcanti the poet W.H. Auden and the composer Benjamin Britten were part of the film crew. They worked together and separately on subsequent documentaries (most notably Night Mail, 1936). In 1935 Britten would have been twenty-three years old and at the beginning of his career. Edgar Anstey suggested that Coal Face anticipated Britten's later operatic work, in Peter Grimes, for example (Anstey 1966). It also anticipated and may even have been a source of inspiration for Willard Van Dyke's Valley Town (US, 1940), with its daring use of sung soliloquy. However, the mixing of stylized song and actuality footage was not actively pursued in documentary.

Even in Coal Face, along with the experimentation and poetry, the drabness and hardship of the miners' lives, including their resilience, courage, and dignity, are made prominent. Although the last images we see are of an individual miner walking against a background of mining village and pithead at evening, the commentary ends with the assertion that 'Coal mining is the basic industry of Britain.'

JACK C. ELLIS

See also: Cavalcanti, Alberto; Grierson, John

Coal Face (UK, GPO Film Unit, 1935, 11 mins). Distributed by Associated British Film Distributors. Produced by John Grierson. Direction and script by Alberto Cavalcanti. Commentary by W.H. Auden and Montagu Slater. Music by Benjamin Britten. Sound supervision by Cavalcanti, Stuart Legg, Benjamin Britten. Sound recorded by E.A. Pawley. Edited by William Coldstream.

Further reading

Anstey, Edgar, *The Sound-track in British Documentary*, UNESCO, 1966.
Manvell, Roger, *Film*, Harmondsworth, Middlesex: Penguin, 1946.

Contact

(UK, Rotha, 1933)

Contact was Paul Rotha's directorial debut. It was released when the British documentary film movement was being critically hailed within intellectual circles. Rotha had already established himself as a film critic with his large history/theory of the cinema, *The Film Till Now* (1929), and had then gone on to briefly work for John Grierson at the Empire Marketing Board (EMB) film unit. Although clashes with Grierson led to Rotha leaving the EMB film unit, Contact can be placed firmly within the more aesthetic school of filmmaking at the EMB and subsequently at the General Postal Office Film Unit (a school that also includes, most significantly, Drifters).

Contact was made to advertise Imperial Railways at a time when the company was facing stiff competition from new air companies, after its civic aviation monopoly came to an end in 1930. The film was originally shot by British Instructional Film (BIF) cameraman Horace Wheddon, who was replaced by another BIF employee, Frank Goodliffe, as a result of illness mid-way through shooting. During the making of the film, Rotha and crew traveled thirty-five thousand miles around the world to shoot footage in different countries. As the camera could not be mounted on the airplane used because of insurance restrictions, aerial shots were obtained by shooting through a small sliding window in the cockpit.

The film dramatizes the evolution of transport and also constructs air travel as something at which to marvel, aestheticizing the flight of the aircraft. It can roughly be divided into two parts, the first being much shorter than the second. The first part looks at the evolution of travel and the background of air flight; the second concentrates on aerial vision. The film begins with a fast montage of different transportation vehicles from a variety of angles. Titles then announce that the plane is the next wonder of transport and a montage of airplanes and views from the plane follow briefly. We then see workers involved in constructing the airplane and people boarding a plane. The film then enters a more relaxed, leisurely mode, as the plane in midair is contrasted with the many images that can be seen from the plane: deserts, seas, mountains, and famous landmarks from places such as Nairobi, Athens, and Cairo. The second part of the film settles into a romantic, picturesque view of distant lands. It provides a kind of symphony of air travel, an impression bolstered by its musical score by Clarence Reybould, who mostly adapted music by Mozart, Rossini, and Tchaikovsky.

Contact can be considered alongside the early travel films that were a staple of cinema's first decade. Early travel films used transportation (especially trains) to provide mobile views of distant, exotic lands for audiences who would not have been able to experience such views first hand. Many early railroad films also provided covert advertising, as did Contact. Contact is, in one sense at least, an updating of these early travel films, with the plane now replacing the wonders of the railway. At the time the film was made, only a small fraction of economically advantaged people could afford to travel by air, so Contact provided a simulated virtual reality of an aerial journey.

The film also tackles a theme that was prevalent within the more modernist films of the documentary film movement: the dialectic between nature and industry. Both Drifters (1929) and The Song of Ceylon (1933–4), in different ways, portray links between nature, humankind, and technology. In both of these films industrial progress is largely seen in a positive light (despite elements of criticism), and a benign process of evolution is posited in which industry develops in a manner that also respects and preserves nature. Likewise, Contact extols the wonders of industrial progress in creating new modes of transport and, at the same time, admires at the wonders of nature. Technology and nature are thus seen as interdependent in this film: technological progress has enabled new ways of perceiving natural beauty.

Contact is ultimately less successful than both Drifters and The Song of Ceylon, as it does not attain the level of formal sophistication of either of those films. It begins interestingly, but its dominant mode of aerial views, although beautifully photographed, is rather repetitive and uninspired. It feels, for the most part, like a straightforward travelog, which was exactly the type of filmmaking that both Grierson and Rotha attacked. They thought that travelogs were nothing more than an agglomeration of pretty pictures, lacking both aesthetically and sociologically. Aesthetically, they were not structured in an imaginative or 'artistic' manner; sociologically, they did not reveal anything about the structure of the modern world.

The beginning of Contact does, to an extent, integrate Rotha's aesthetic and sociological agenda. The film uses highly stylized montage, with images and titles interwoven at a rhythmic pace, displaying a modernist approach to filmic organization. The evolutionary sketch of technological progress, although promotional, builds a sense of industrial purpose. The film also shows a number of materials needed to construct an airplane and shows workers involved in construction, thus moving beyond the superficial details of the flight to the complex assemblage involved in its constitution.

Yet the main pictorial sequences of the film dominate Contact, and these are more one-dimensional than the earlier scenes. The industrial interconnections at the beginning of the film become overshadowed by a more romantic portrayal of travel cinematography. The film does share with Drifters and The Song of Ceylon an evolutionary purview that nevertheless stresses the importance of nature, but it also tends to provide a somewhat more ruthless, simplistic view of progress in comparison to those two films. Rotha does not quite manage to negotiate the rather complicated mixture of aesthetic expression, sociological investigation, and promotional message in a successful manner. Instead, the promotional origins of the film become all too evident.

JAMIE SEXTON

See also: Drifters; Song of Ceylon, The

Contact (UK, 1933, 42 mins). Produced by British Instructional Films and Imperial Airways. Directed by Paul Rotha. Camera work by Frank Goodliffe. Sponsored by British Petroleum and Shell-Mex.

Further reading

Aitken, Ian (ed.), *The Documentary Film Movement: An Anthology*, Edinburgh: Edinburgh University Press, 1998.

Aldcroft, Derek H., *British Transport Since 1914: An Economic History*, Newton Abbot: John Sherratt & Sons, 1975.

Kirby, Lynne, *Parallel Tracks: The Railroad and Silent Cinema*, Exeter: Exeter University Press, 1997.

Musser, Charles, 'The Travel Genre in 1903–1904: Moving Towards a Fictional Narrative', in Thomas Elsaesser and Adam Barker (eds), *Early Cinema: Space, Frame, Narrative*, London: BFI, 1990.

Petrie, Duncan and Kruger, Robert (eds), *A Paul Rotha Reader*, Exeter: University of Exeter Press, 1999.

Rotha, Paul, *Documentary Film*, London: Faber and Faber, 1952 [1935].

——*The Film Till Now*, London: Vision Press, [1930] 1963.

——*Documentary Diary*, London: Secker and Warburg, 1973.

Sussex, Elizabeth, *The Rise and Fall of the British Documentary Movement*, Berkeley, CA: University of California Press, 1978.

Swann, Paul, *The British Documentary Film Movement 1926–1946*, Cambridge: Cambridge University Press, 1989.

Cooper, Merian C.

Merian C. Cooper—best known in cinema history for his role as coproducer, cowriter, and codirector of the 1933 classic film King Kong—began his filmmaking career in documentaries. In partnership with Ernest B. Schoedsack, Cooper made expeditionary documentaries such as Grass (1925) and Chang (1927). These films (especially Chang) are part travelog, part adventure tale. Even King Kong was originally conceived as a semidocumentary project to be shot on location and feature a real gorilla enlarged through trick photography. As has often been pointed out by critics, the fictional filmmaker Carl Denham, the adventurous protagonist of King Kong who is willing to travel far and risk his own life as well as the lives of others for the most exciting film possible, could very well stand in for Cooper himself. Like Denham, Cooper was a natural showman intent on thrilling his audience through cinema's ability to place the spectator in the midst of the action.

Cooper and Schoedsack's first completed documentary together, in close collaboration with foreign journalist Marguerite Harrison, was entitled Grass: A Nation's Battle for Life. The team traveled to the Persian Gulf to chronicle with two cameras the forty-eight-day annual migration of a nomadic Iranian tribe called the Bakhtiari over hundreds of miles in search of suitable grazing land. The film follows in the documentary tradition established by Robert Flaherty's classic film about the North American Inuits, Nanook of the North (1922). Cooper originally intended to screen Grass on the college lecture circuit. However, a Paramount executive named Jesse Lasky, who had distributed Nanook, saw the film by chance at a private dinner and later obtained Grass for theatrical distribution. Intertitles were inserted into the action to provide the film with some kind of conventional structure for mainstream audiences. In its final form, Grass begins with scenes of Harrison interacting with the tribespeople. Then the tribe embarks on its quest in a huge caravan, a scene evocative for American audiences of mythic pioneer migration westward (lest the point is missed, the film's intertitles frequently refer to covered wagons). The tens of thousands of Bakhtiari, including their hundreds of thousands of cattle and goats, journey through an impressive range of hazardous terrain, including desert and mountain and raging water, to reach the grasslands. Frequently, against this epic backdrop, the film foregrounds the chief of the tribe and his son, perhaps in an effort to provide a narrative focus for audience identification among the mass of humanity. As a Hollywood feature film, Grass proved exciting in its visual spectacle of the Bakhtiari mass migration. Also, the film was exotic enough in subject matter to appeal to the American imagination, yet close enough to American pioneer myths to seem familiar to domestic audiences.

Most important for the future direction of Cooper's career, the film was profitable. Cooper and Schoedsack promptly began planning other films.

The pair's next film was Chang: A Drama of the Wilderness. In some ways, Chang anticipates the contemporary craze for 'reality programming' in combining elements of live action shot in Siam (Thailand today) into a preconceived storyline for maximum dramatic effect. The result is a hybrid film that is fictional but partially constructed from spontaneous, real-life events. Cooper and Schoedsack captured the wild animals that appear in the film and shot the action sequences themselves, including the famous shot where a tiger leaps up a tree toward the camera. After fourteen months of often hazardous location shooting, Cooper and Schoedsack returned to the United States to complete postproduction at Paramount. The completed film centers on a Siamese family. The central characters are played by local people, not professional Hollywood actors. The patriarch of the family is Kru (Cooper and Schoedsack's interpreter in real life). His wife is Chantui, their son is Nah, and their daughter is Landah. They have livestock and a pet white gibbon. The family attempts to establish a rice-farming homestead in the jungle while threatened by tigers, leopards, snakes, elephants (the 'chang' of the title), and about every other menace the filmmakers could coerce into action for the cameras. The plot is set in motion by predators' attacks on the family's animals. Kru successfully fights back by organizing his pioneer neighbors into hunting parties. The jungle's threat to domesticity escalates, however, when a rampaging 'chang' herd destroys Kru's home and a nearby village. Kru has to organize another hunting party that eventually captures the elephants. The primal natural force represented by the elephants is finally conquered when the elephants are domesticated to work for Kru. Victorious, Kru and his family rebuild their home. Continuing his usual flair for showmanship at the film's New York premiere, Cooper had installed a special projector lens (or 'magnascope') that enlarged the screen to three times its normal size during the film's intense action scenes, such as an elephant charge that levels a village. In addition to garnering favorable critical reviews, Chang was nominated for an Academy Award for Unique and Artistic Production on the occasion of the first Academy Awards ceremony in 1929—the only year this award was presented.

Cooper's work in the documentary and semi-documentary genre paved the way for his next and greatest success. While in Africa with Schoedsack to shoot location footage for the fictional film Four Feathers, Cooper photographed many apes and began thinking of a story about a giant gorilla captured and taken to the urban jungle of Manhattan. In Cooper's scenario, the gorilla would escape and eventually climb to the top of the Empire State Building before being killed by fighter planes. The publication of a friend's book about the fearsome monitor lizards or 'dragons' of Komodo Island inspired Cooper to incorporate a fight scene between the giant gorilla and the giant lizard into his proposed film. Cooper then took the name for 'gorilla' from the language of an East Indies tribe and entitled his proposed film Kong, or as it came to be known, King Kong. The film production ultimately eschewed location shooting and live animal photography for the special-effects work of animator Willis O'Brien, but Cooper applied all of the lessons he had learned from Grass and Chang to King Kong. The phenomenal success of King Kong, starring Four Feathers veteran Fay Wray as the giant gorilla's 'love interest', enshrined Cooper as one of the industry's legends. Over the years he was twice a studio vice-president and a producer. After more military service during World War II, he formed a production company named Argosy Film Pictures with famous director John Ford in 1941. He served as producer for many classic films, including Rio Grande in 1950, The Quiet Man in 1952, and The Searchers in 1956. For all of his contributions, Cooper was given a special Academy Award in 1952. He died in 1973.

PHILIP L. SIMPSON

See also: Chang; Grass

Biography

Born in Jacksonville, Florida, on October 24, 1893. Attended the United States Naval Academy in Annapolis, Maryland, 1911–15. Resigning from Annapolis, became a military aviator who saw combat in France in 1918, was a prisoner of war on two separate occasions, and aided the Polish in their struggle against the newly formed Communist government of

Russia. In Poland, met a combat photographer, Ernest B. Schoedsack, who would later become his business partner. During the 1920s gave up military flying, worked as a reporter for *The New York Times* and the *New York Daily News*, published an anonymous autobiography entitled *Things Men Die For*, and sought adventure as a traveler on a world cruise led by explorer Edward A. Salisbury. Served as producer for many classic films, including Rio Grande in 1950, The Quiet Man in 1952, and The Searchers in 1956. Honored with a special Academy Award in 1952. Died in 1973.

Selected films

1925 Grass: director
1927 Chang: director

Further reading

Brownlow, Kevin, *The War, the West, and the Wilderness*, New York: Alfred A. Knopf, 1978.
Cooper, Merian C., *Grass*, New York: G.P. Putnam and Sons, 1925.
Goldner, Orville and Turner, George E., *The Making of King Kong*, Cranbury, NJ: A.S. Barnes and Company, 1975.
Steinbrunner, Chris and Goldblatt, Burt, *Cinema of the Fantastic*, New York: Galahad Books, 1972.
Vertlieb, Steve, 'The Man Who Saved King Kong', in Ronald Gottesman and Harry Geduld (eds), *The Girl in the Hairy Paw: King Kong as Myth, Movie, and Monster*, New York: Avon Books, 1976.

Cousteau, Jacques-Yves

Jacques-Yves Cousteau, a prolific author, environmental activist, explorer, inventor, and filmmaker, has long been regarded as a respected pioneer of the documentary film genre for his innovative efforts to record the undersea environment. Cousteau is often considered to be the creator of the underwater documentary, not only because of his novel approach to documentary filmmaking but also because he was, along with French engineer Emile Gagnan, the cocreator of the first underwater diving apparatus, the aqualung, or scuba (McGill 2000). Cousteau's underwater breathing invention, coupled with his creation of a waterproof enclosure for movie cameras, made it possible for divers, scientists, and film crews to explore and document the undersea world as they never could before (Kempke 2002). By using these new inventions, Cousteau, who had previous experience producing, directing, and acting in feature films, began to make his unprecedented documentaries about the sea, its vegetation, animal inhabitants, and sunken vessels. For many members of the audience, Cousteau's documentaries heralded the actual viewing of entities and environs that once could be conjured only in the imagination.

Although Cousteau had made several short documentaries in the 1940s during the German occupation of France, it was his feature-length documentary films and television programmes that gained him worldwide recognition. Cousteau's film Le Monde du silence/The Silent World (1956), his first feature-length documentary film, which was codirected by Louis Malle, won the Grand Prize at the Cannes Film Festival in 1956 (McGill 2000). A 1956 review of The Silent World in *The New York Times* lauded the film for its ability to leave the audience not only in awe but also wishing to participate in the deep-sea dives themselves, owing to the unique way in which the film contrasted the images of undersea explorers with the ocean creatures being investigated (Crowther 1971).

After the success of The Silent World, Cousteau continued to make feature-length documentaries for the cinema chronicling marine life and its environs, including Histoire d'un poisson rouge/The Golden Fish (1959) and Le Monde sans soleil/World Without Sun (1964).

In the late 1960s and the 1970s Cousteau's documentaries began to reach audiences differently. Instead of feature-length films for the cinema, Cousteau's documentaries became the subject of several critically acclaimed television series and specials, including his most famous, The Undersea World of Jacques Cousteau, which ran from 1968 to 1976. Each episode of The Undersea World of Jacques Cousteau was the result of a minor feat of filmmaking and would not have been possible without an extraordinary amount of editing. Extra footage was a requirement for Cousteau's documentaries, because undersea creatures are not often cooperative with the filmmakers, and because of the temperamental nature of the ocean itself. For approximately fifty-one minutes of air time, one thousand seven hundred and fifty feet of picture edit was necessary, and it often took the production staff more than ten weeks to prepare (Shaheen 1987). In addition to the remarkable images, another factor that made the series well received among critics and viewers alike was its innovative narration. With conarration responsibilities divided between Cousteau and Rod Serling (widely recognized for his work on the television series The Twilight Zone), the audience was presented with two very distinct tones of voice and narration styles, which helped to ward off monotony (Shaheen 1987).

Perhaps the most enlightening element of these later documentaries, however, was the intensification of Cousteau's environmental activism, which ultimately became his greatest passion when his undersea explorations revealed to him the destruction the sea and its inhabitants were enduring at the hands of humankind. As a consequence of his environmental concerns, Cousteau founded several nonprofit organizations to help spread awareness about the endangered ecology, including the most famous one, which is still in existence, the aptly named Cousteau Society (McGill 2000).

In a June 1985 interview in the Cousteau Society's membership publication, the *Calypso Log*, Cousteau mused about the significance of film in his own personal life. Cousteau asserted that he considered the cinema so 'important' because it encompasses other forms of art, including literature and music. Cousteau also declared that because cinema is an art form that uses the element of time, film is akin to 'a flower, [created] to bloom and die'. Apparently, for Cousteau, the ephemeral nature of film is preferable to art forms that are 'here for eternity' and represent a 'challenge to death'; thus, for Cousteau, film was ostensibly analogous to humanity itself, a living and breathing entity (Cousteau 1985).

TRUDI VAN DYKE

See also: Silent World, The

Biography

Born in St André-de-Cubzac, France, on June 11, 1910. After high school, served in the French navy. Also a prolific author and staunch environmentalist. Died of heart failure June 25, 1997 in Paris.

Selected films

1956 Le Monde du silence/The Silent World: director, writer, cinematographer

1959 Histoire d'un poisson rouge/The Golden Fish: producer

1964 Le Monde sans soleil/World Without Sun: producer, director

1968–76 The Undersea World of Jacques Cousteau: executive producer, actor

Further reading

Cousteau, Jacques, 'Interview', *Calypso Log*, n.p., 1985.

Crowther, Bosley, 'Cousteau's The Silent World', in Lewis Jacobs (ed.), *The Documentary Tradition: From Nanook to Woodstock*, New York: Hopkinson and Blake Publishers, 1971.

Kempcke, K., 'Jacques Cousteau', in *St James Encyclopedia of Popular Culture*, Gale Group, 2002, articles. findarticles.com/p/articles/mi_g1epc/is_bio/ai_2419200261

McGill, Sara Ann, 'Jacques Cousteau', *History Remembers Scientists of the 20th Century*, 2000.

Shaheen, Jack G., 'The Documentary of Art: "The Undersea World of Jacques Cousteau"', *Journal of Popular Culture* 21, no. 1, 1987: 93–101.

Coutinho, Eduardo

Coutinho played an important role in the first generation of Brazil's Cinema Novo. He began his career in 1962 as the production manager of the feature-length fiction Cinco Vezes Favela/Five Times Shantytown, produced by the National Student Union (União Nacional dos Estudantes, UNE). In the same year, he filmed the travels of the so-called UNE-on-the-Move. UNE's idea was to make a documentary about the cities that the student union leaders were visiting in 1962 and 1963. They filmed in Manaus, Paraíba, Maranhão, Belo Horizonte, and other places, but the material was never assembled into a documentary. Through UNE-on-the-Move, Coutinho met Elizabeth Teixeira, the widow of João Pedro Teixeira, a peasant leader who was murdered in 1962. When he returned to Rio de Janeiro, Coutinho made a new proposal to the UNE through their cultural centers (CPCs). He wanted to make a film about the life of João Pedro Teixeira in which the same peasants who had experienced the tragedy would participate as actors. In February 1964

Coutinho began to film the never-to-be-completed first version of Cabra Marcado Para Morrer/Marked for Death, a docudrama that reconstructs the life of João Pedro Teixeira. It was filmed at the Galiléia Plantation in the city of Vitória de Santo Antão of Pernambuco state, and Elizabeth Teixeira played the role of herself as a widow. The film was interrupted by the military coup of March 31, 1964, and the production team was dispersed. Elizabeth Teixeira changed her name and spent seventeen years hiding in the interior of the northeastern state of Rio Grande do Norte.

Coutinho returned to Rio and developed a career in fiction films as a screenwriter and director. He encountered documentary film during the second half of the 1970s when he began to work for Globo Repórter, a program of Rede Globo, Brazil's major television broadcaster. He directed several editions of the program, some in a true vérité documentary style. The remake of the unfinished Cabra Marcado Para Morrer (also known as Twenty Years Later) marks the beginning of Coutinho's authorial career. Based on his experience in television, Coutinho incorporated the flexible techniques of the new documentary, including a nervous moving camera, direct sound, and the intense use of interviews. Coutinho began to see the possibility of a second version of Cabra in 1979, when amnesty was decreed and it became possible for him to safely contact Elizabeth Teixeira. The idea for this documentary was to search for the same peasants who had participated, as actors, in the docudrama that had been interrupted in 1964 and to film their daily life in 1981. Coutinho had secretly kept the negatives of the first Cabra for twenty years, and he used them in his new film. The main part of the documentary was filmed in March 1981, in the state of Rio Grande do Norte, interviewing the same peasants of 1964. Back in Rio de Janeiro, during 1982 and 1983, Coutinho finished filming interviews with Elizabeth's sons and daughters, with whom she had lost contact for twenty years. The film was released in 1984, generating a strong response from the public and the media. By portraying the fragmentation of Elizabeth Teixeira's family, Twenty Years Later presented a portrait of a country that, after a twenty-year military dictatorship, was also finding itself.

In 1986 Coutinho directed Santa Marta—2 Semanas no Morro/Santa Marta—Two Weeks in a Slum at the Santa Marta favela (Brazilian hillside slum) in the middle of Rio's wealthy and chic southern region. The film was produced by the Superior Institute of Religious Studies (ISER, a nongovernmental institution) and is the first documentary work that Coutinho made in a Rio favela. Coutinho's career as a documentary filmmaker became more firmly established in the 1990s. In 1992 he rediscovered the strongest stylistic vein of his work in a vérité-form documentary, Boca do Lixo/The Scavengers. It was filmed in video and takes place in a large garbage dump in the city of São Gonçalo, close to Rio de Janeiro. Through interviews, marked by Coutinho's active participation, the film manages to discover unique characters with strong and impressive personalities. This search for 'types' can be defined as the core of Coutinho's style, based on interviews or testimonies that his subjects deliver directly to the camera. During the 1990s the interview scenes of Coutinho's documentaries became more and more static, resembling a series of identity card photos with intense facial expressions.

It is through this kind of minimalist method that Coutinho affirmed his distinctive style throughout the 1990s and even today. In 1998–9 he filmed Santo Forte/The Mighty Spirit, which depicts the everyday religiosity of the people of Vila Parque da Cidade favelas in Rio de Janeiro. The narrative portrays the common people of Brazil by using religious experience and trance as motifs. Santo Forte is a landmark of Coutinho's work, where his style takes the shape we will find in his three next feature-length documentaries (Babilônia 2000, Edificio Master/Master a Building in Copacabana, and Peões/Workers). Babilônia 2000 was made during the celebration of the new millennium in the hillside of Babilônia, where the Chapéu Mangueira and Babilônia favelas are located, with an extraordinary view of Rio de Janeiro's most famous beaches. Most of the documentary was shot on December 31, 1999.

After his 'trilogy' about favelas (Santa Marta, Santo Forte and Babilônia 2000), Coutinho continued to use this characteristic 'portrait' style but switched social classes and filmed in a typical petit bourgeois building in the Copacabana beach neighborhood. Through Coutinho's static interview method, Master, a Building in Copacabana, reveals astonishing personalities living in the small apartment rooms. Coutinho's 2004 film, Peões/Workers, is a project made together with João Salles, a new figure in Brazilian contemporary documentary. They planned to make two feature-length films together (Peões/Workers directed by Coutinho and Entreatos/Entr'acts by Salles) about the life of the poor northeastern migrant who became Brazil's current president. Loyal to his distinctive method, Coutinho went to the factories and the neighborhood where Lula used to work and live and interviewed the anonymous metallurgical workers who once met him. Through a series of personal testimonies, Peões unveils the diverse personalities and life stories of Brazilian industrial workers.

FERNÃO PESSOA RAMOS

Biography

Born in São Paulo, 1933, and lives and works in Rio de Janeiro. Studied at the Institut de Hautes Etudes Cinematographiques (IDHEC) before starting his career as the production manager of 5 Vezes Favela. Films the unfinished Cabra Marcado para Morrer in 1954, which would later be transformed into 20 Years Later (1981–4). During the 1960s and 1970s worked with fiction films, mostly as screenwriter (Garota de Ipanema/The Girl from Ipanema (1967), Dona Flor e Seus Dois Maridos/Dona Flor and her Two Husbands (1976); Lição de Amor/A Lesson in Love (1975); A Falecida/The Death (1963)); and also as director of one episode from ABC do Amor/The ABC of Love (1966), O Pacto/The Agreement and the features O Homem que Comprou o Mundo/The Man Who Bought the World (1968) and Faustão (1970). In 1970s films for television, in Globo Networks, making programs for the Globo Repórter series. In 1980s starts an authorial career, working exclusively in documentary. Next four features (Santo Forte, 1999; Babilônia, 2000; Edifício Master, 2002; and Peões, 2004) were shown widely in cinemas.

Selected films (as director)

1964 Cabra Marcado Para Morrer/Marked for Death (unfinished)
1976 Seis Dias de Ouricuri/Six Days of Ouricuri (TV–Globo Repórter)
1977 O Pistoleiro da Serra Talhada/The Pistoleer of the Carved Mountains (TV–Globo Repórter)
1978 Theodorico, o Imperador do Sertão/Theodorico—The Emperor of the Backlands (TV–Globo Repórter)
1979 Exu, uma Tragédia Sertaneja/Exu, a Tragedy in the Back Country (TV–Globo Repórter)
1980 Portinari, o Menino de Brodósqui/Portinari, Brodosqui's Little Boy (TV–Globo Repórter)
1981–84 Cabra Marcado Para Morrer/Twenty Years Later (feature)
1987 Santa Marta: Duas Semanas no Morro/ Santa Marta: Two Weeks in the Hillside Slums (mid-length)
1989 Volta Redonda, Memorial da Greve/Volta Redonda: Memorial of a Strike (mid-length, codirected with Sérgio Goldenberg)
1989 O Jogo da Dívida/The Debt Game (mid-length)
1991 O Fio da Memória/The Strand of Memory (feature)
1992 Boca do Lixo/The Scavengers (mid-length)
1994 Mulheres no Front/Women in the Front (mid-length)
1999 Santo Forte/The Mighty Spirit (feature)
2000 Babilônia 2000 (feature)
2002 Edifício Master/Master, a Building in Copacabana (feature)
2004 Peões/Workers (feature)

Further reading

Bernardet, Jean-Claude, *Le Documentaire,in Le Cinema Brésilien*, edited by Paulo Antonio Paranagua, Paris: Centre Georges Pompidou, 1987.

——'Vitória Sobre a Lata de Lixo da História', in Jean-Claude Bernardet (ed.), *Cineastas e Imagens do Povo*, São Paulo: Companhia das Letras, 2003.

Lins, Consuelo, *O Documentário de Eduardo Coutinho: televisão, cinema e vídeo*, Rio de Janeiro: Zahar, 2004.

Mattos, Carlos Alberto, *Eduardo Coutinho: O Homem que Caiu na Real*, Portugal: Festival de Cinema Luso-Brasileiro de Santa Maria da Feira, 2004.

Ramos, Fernão and Miranda, Luis Felipe (eds), *Enciclopédia do Cinema Brasileiro*, São Paulo: Senac, 2000.

Schwarz, Roberto, 'O Fio da Meada', in Roberto Schwarz (ed.), *Que Horas São?* São Paulo: Companhia das Letras, 1987.

Xavier, Ismail, *Indagações em Torno de Eduardo Coutinho*, *Cinemais* 36, 2003: 221–36.

Craigie, Jill

Although frequently referred to as the first female film director in Britain, several directors preceded Jill Craigie in the silent period. Nonetheless, Craigie's contribution to British film culture is important. Her directorial career was relatively brief, spanning seven years, but two of her films stand out because of their innovative approach to documentary filmmaking and because of Craigie's feminist and socialist political beliefs.

Craigie entered the film industry in 1937 as an actress but made only one film. When war broke out she began writing short documentary scripts for the British Council, as well as cowriting the script for the Two Cities production The Flemish Farm (1943) with her then husband, Jeffrey Dell. This inspired her to direct her first short film, Out of Chaos (1944), a documentary about how to appreciate modern art, using the work of British war artists as examples.

After the war, Craigie's interest in the postwar reconstruction of Britain's bomb-damaged cities and, in particular, the need to consult with the citizens living there, led to the making of The Way We Live (1946), a docudrama outlining plans for the rebuilding of Plymouth. The socialist leanings of the film did not deter the conservative J. Arthur Rank from backing the film, and it was funded by the Rank subsidiary, Two Cities Film, which distributed Out of Chaos. The Way We Live combines an orthodox documentary style of straight visual exposition with a dramatic narrative featuring a cast drawn almost entirely from the local community. Seen predominantly from the female characters' viewpoint, the plight of a bombed-out family living in temporary accommodation provides the framework for a social and political examination of town planning procedures. During the making of this film Craigie met her third husband, the Labour MP Michael Foot.

Craigie next directed a short documentary for the United Nations Educational, Scientific and Cultural Organization (UNESCO) about efforts to improve the living conditions of children displaced by two world wars. She followed this with Blue Scar (1949), which, like The Way We Live, blurred the boundaries between fiction and documentary. Set in a South Wales mining village, Blue Scar is a feature-length docudrama about poverty and conflict in a South Wales mining village, partly scripted by the villagers themselves. Made by Outlook Films, the production company Craigie formed with William MacQuitty in 1948, the film also featured several cast members drawn from the local population. She then directed a documentary short for Outlook, To Be a Woman (1951), arguing the case for equal pay for women.

Frustrated by the feature industry's obstructive attitude to women directors, Craigie gave up directing and returned to scriptwriting before retiring from the film business. Her political fervour did not diminish with age, however, and in 1994, appalled by what was happening in war-torn Yugoslavia, she financed and directed a documentary about the ravaged city and people of Dubrovnik. Two Hours from London (1994) was shown on BBC television in 1995 and was her final film.

SARAH EASEN

Biography

Born in London, March 7, 1914. Educated at various boarding schools in Britain and Europe. Journalist on teen magazine, *Betty's Paper*, 1932. Journalist and writer, 1933–7. Actress, 1937. Documentary scriptwriter, British Council 1940–2. Scriptwriter and director, Two Cities Film 1943–6. Director, Crown Film Unit. 1948. Director, Outlook Films 1948–51. Scriptwriter, Group Film Productions, 1952–3. Scriptwriter, Rank Film Productions, 1957. Director, independent production, 1994. Died in London, December 13, 1999.

Selected films

1944 Out of Chaos: director, writer
1946 The Way We Live: director, producer, writer
1948 Children of the Ruins: director
1949 Blue Scar: director, writer
1951 To Be a Woman: director, producer, writer
1994 Two Hours from London: director, coproducer

Further reading

Haggith, Toby, *Castles in the Air: British Films and the Reconstruction of the Built Environment 1939–1951*, London: I.B. Tauris, 2003.

Cuba Sí!

(France, Marker, 1961)

Of the many filmmakers drawn to Cuba by the Revolution of 1959, it was Chris Marker who made what Cubans regarded as the best documentary on the Revolution at the time. According to Marker, in his preface to the published version of the script, the film was shot rapidly in January 1961, 'during the first alert period (you know, at the time when the majority of French papers were hooting over Fidel's paranoia in imagining himself threatened with invasion)', and it 'aims at communicating, if not the experience, at least the vibrations, the rhythm of a revolution that will one day perhaps be held to be the decisive moment of a whole era of contemporary history' (Marker 1961: preface).

Marker's sense of solidarity is announced by the title, one half of the slogan that was one of the Revolution's mottos: ¡Cuba Sí! ¡Yanqui No! Marker's method is interrogative, inclusive, and visually ironic. Filming the crowds in the streets or at a baseball match (baseball and tourist posters remind the viewer that the United States is less than an hour away by plane), he picks out faces who look at the camera directly and unaggressively, as people enjoying their newfound right to take full possession of public space. The effect is to ask the viewer to consider before judging. These scenes give way to newsreel of the guerrillas in the mountains, with shots of Fidel Castro, Che Guevara, and Camilo Cienfuegos, through which the events and motivations of the Revolution are recounted, including the hostile responses of the US administration. The interpellation of shots of a printing press and an open-air film projection speak of the necessary supplement to guerrilla struggle and victory: the battle of the media at home and abroad. The headline of a Miami newspaper reads 'Fidel Hurls New Barbs at US'. A moment later, we hear shots of execution by a firing squad followed by crowds at a boxing match, and then a French newspaper headline appears that reads, 'The State Department accuses Fidel Castro of having betrayed the Cuban Revolution'.

Marker eschews the conventional solidarity film and instead uses montage to raise the question of how the events he chronicles are to be represented. Hence the comparison he makes between Fidel and Robin Hood. As the commentary puts it: 'Perhaps he is Robin Hood [...] Only in this century taking from the rich to give to the poor does not necessarily mean attacking stage-coaches. And when Robin Hood has read Marx, when, up in the mountains he is preparing the laws and reforms of the future republic, some parts of the world realize painfully that they too are one Robin Hood late.' There is a song about revolutionary decrees on agrarian reform and rent, and the commentary concludes, 'So legends die. The myth of Robin Hood is shattered. In its place a Revolution.'

The film was banned in France for three reasons according to the Minister of Information: it was not a documentary but 'an apologia for the Castro regime'; no film 'which is ideological propaganda can be authorized if only because of the risks this type of production entails for public order'; and the Cuban press frequently attacks the administrations of Martinique and Guadeloupe, and it therefore 'does not seem suitable to offer a cinematographic hearing to Cuba's leaders' (Marker 1962). Marker got round the ban by providing a new commentary full of the touristic clichés of a travelog, which enabled him to get an export visa, then sending the film to Belgium with the original commentary restored.

If the ban tells us of French government nervousness about its Caribbean territories in the year that Paris finally acceded to Algerian independence, it is doubtless Fidel Castro's analysis of democracy, which he gives in an interview in the film, that the government wished to keep as inaccessible to the public as possible. For sixty years, he says, Cuba had to put up with the farce of a pseudo-democracy, and:

> the French ought to be the first to understand: the French have an election almost every year: municipal [...] national [...] for a president, for an MP [...] perhaps no other country in the world has had more elections than France in the last six decades. And even so the French are not content [...] they can perfectly understand that political factions [and] electoralism have not solved a single one of France's fundamental problems.

In sum, Cuba Sí! is a political travelog that never collapses into mere rhetoric. If Marker now regards it as more a pamphlet than a film, edited in a hurry as an urgent response to events

(Marker 2003), it exemplifies, nevertheless, something of what the Argentine filmmakers Fernando Solanas and Octavio Getino would define at the end of the same decade as one of the aims of what they called 'third cinema', the political film feared and rejected by the political mainstream.

MICHAEL CHANAN

See also: Marker, Chris

Cuba Sí! (France, 1961, 50 mins). Directed and written by Chris Marker. Cinematography by Chris Marker.

Further reading

Marker, Chris, 'Cuba Sí!', *L'avant scène du cinéma* 6, 1961.
——'Cuba Sí!, Censor No!', trans. Garry Broughton, *Movie 3*, 1962: 15–21.
——Personal communication, 2003.

Czech Republic/Slovakia

The evolution of documentary film in both the Czech Republic and Slovakia can be traced back to the 1900s, when the two separate states were intermingled into one: Czechoslovakia. After its formation into an independent republic in 1918, Czechoslovakia faced grave economic insecurity. Although Czechoslovak documentaries were gaining popularity owing to their emphasis on patriotism, producers struggled to compete with foreign imports in order to realize success. Until the early 1920s technical standards were hampered by the lack of properly equipped studios. In 1921 the A-B company was converted into a film studio and technical standards began to ameliorate. In 1933 the A-B Company built the Barrandov Film Studios in Prague. Being the heart of the majority of prewar and postwar developments, the establishment of these film studios led to an increase in domestic film production. Czechoslovak films gained early international success in the late 1940s, when the Venice Grand Prix was awarded to Karel Stekly's locally produced film Sirena/The Stroke (1947). As Czechoslovak films continued winning film prizes including Academy Awards, critics around the world became more and more familiar with Czechoslovak cinema.

After World War II a newly established democracy in Czechoslovakia lasted less than three years before a new communist rule was established in 1948. With the communist rule came the nationalization of the film industry, which led producers to focus their films on politically significant themes (Hames 1985: 37). During this time all documentary films were expected to portray reality and its revolutionary transition as accurately as possible. Jiri Weiss's film Uloupena Hranice/The Stolen Frontier (1947) is one such film in which Munich and the crisis in the Sudetenland is depicted. This film was an immediate success because the Munich problem was a massive ordeal that especially affected those growing up in Weiss's generation. In making Uloupena Hranice, Weiss takes advantage of his experience with British documentaries, in which amateur actors and nonprofessionals are videotaped with the use of a hidden camera.

Similarly, Otakar Vavra makes use of the expectation of shorts to capture reality and the transition that individuals were undergoing in Czechoslovakia. Vavra's film Nema Barikada/Silent Barricade (1948) documents the Prague uprising against the Nazis before the arrival of the Red army. His film, although extremely nationalistic, manages to document the struggle of the Czechoslovak people in a time of war.

After World War II 'the theory of lack of conflict' emerged. This theory introduced the concept of positive heroes, also known as protagonists, triumphing over negative characters, also known as antagonists. This theory quickly became the foundation for films and gave rise to a standardized plot in which a happy ending was inevitable. Producers would continue documenting reality, while illustrating conflicts between heroes and villains, but ensuring that their films would always end in the expected, optimistic light.

The years 1947 and 1948 marked the beginning of the Cold War. Despite the war, the radical youth went on believing that the revolution went hand in hand with art and expression.

During the 1950s Czechoslovak shorts mainly served to illustrate socialist-realist dogma and historical events. In 1956, with the denunciation of Stalinism, Czechoslovakia experienced a scene of cultural 'thaw' followed by reaction (Hames 1985: 44).

In the 1960s there were two main types of documentary films. As Anton Navratil, Czech historian of documentary film, put it: 'Ways of Lies, Ways of Truth'. 'The ways of lies' were those films produced using an ideological filter that supported what the communist authorities preached, regardless of how much this would distort reality. The filmmakers exploring 'the ways of truth' were those who produced short films that were highly creative, and risky. Living in a communist nation, it was difficult to openly express one's opinions. Producers of truth documentaries went out on a limb on many occasions and found ways to express concepts and opinions that would otherwise be impossible to state verbally and openly. This approach gave audiences a glimpse into what communism really was, without the authority's filter of distortion and propaganda.

In 1956, once 'de-Stalinization' was under way, an enormous hunger developed for the flourishing of ideas, the sphere of culture, and the need for freedom of expression. By the 1960s a new film movement had emerged, also known as the Czechoslovak New Wave. By 1963 the first wave of the Czechoslovak New Wave was underway. The first wave is defined as 'that group of directors who prepared the way for the developments of the 1960s through thematic or formal breaks with the conventions of Socialist Realism' (Hames 1985: 35).

Czechoslovakia's film movement, the Czechoslovak New Wave, can be traced back to the years after World War II. During this movement, film producers looked for ways to portray society in a new light by 'combining criticism of the status quo with the rejection of traditional narrative' (Hames 1985: 92). Filmmakers desired the ability to portray society in a nonstereotyped fashion, without the integration of propaganda, or communist standards and expectations. The focus of shorts revolved around the everyday life, of the everyday individual, less emphasis on protagonists and antagonists, and more on just the average individual going about daily life. The need to have to end the film with a happy ending diminished, as filmmakers continued ensuring that their films would record and expose everyday reality.

Milos Forman, a scriptwriter and director, is one of many who has produced a number of films that follow the trend of recording and exposing the everyday. This standard procedure, known as the realist/documentary tradition, reflects an Italian neorealism and cinéma vérité approach. Both approaches strongly influenced the Czechoslovak film industry. The use of the two approaches helped audiences and filmmakers to deal with social reality and its connection with the individual. Film producers relied on these techniques to tie together the world of the subjective with that of the objective. Cinéma vérité can best be described as 'the act of filming real people in uncontrolled situations. Uncontrolled means that the filmmaker does not function as a director nor, for that matter, as a screenwriter [...] no one is told what to say or how to act' (Hames 1985: 120).

Most scholars, when referring to the Czechoslovak New Wave, are aware that the majority of the films produced during this time were concerned with both the individual and society. For example, two of Forman's films, Cerny Petr/ Black Peter (1963) and Lasky Jedne Plavovlasky/Loves of a Blonde (1965), take on a boy-meets-girl theme, which is deemed acceptable by socialist-realist cinema audiences. By integrating elements of cinéma vérité and classical film comedy into their work, Forman carefully describes the life of two young children and the society in which they live. The importance of personal life is juxtaposed next to the struggle of everyday life. The result in both films is one of the most profound analyses of Czechoslovak society yet to be illustrated.

Because short films would often stimulate one's mind, individuals turned to them as a means to stimulate change in reality. Documentaries represented a factor of real life; in fact, they changed real life. As the presence of creative ideas increased in documentaries, ideas on economics, politics, literature, and the arts also increased. It was not long before all these ideas led to the development of the Czechoslovak Reform Movement, which led to the fall of the Novotny regime. In 1968 Alexander Dubček, the first secretary of communist Czechoslovakia, implemented a variety of democratic, political, and economic reforms known as the Prague Spring. A Socialist democracy was underway in Czechoslovakia. The Soviet Union, alarmed at what appeared to be the collapse of communism in Czechoslovakia, invaded the republic in August 1968 in hopes of crushing the Prague Spring. The invasion was successful in abolishing any continuation of democratic reforms, and Czechoslovakia was forced into 'normalization' back into a communist state. For the brief period that the Czechoslovaks had a taste of a Western-style democracy, the level of filmmaking surpassed any level known before. As Pryl argues, 'these remarkable achievements were not merely works born during the spell of freedom [...] they were quite conscious demonstrations of a refusal to give in' (Hames 1985: 257).

Although the republic had again been taken over by a communist authority, the government did not actually reorganize the film industry until the latter part of 1969. Many films were forced to cease production, one of which was Helge's Jak Se U Nas Pece Chleba/How Bread is Made (1969). By 1973 a number of films that were perceived as segregating society, as oppose to strengthening it, were banned, including Forman's Hori, Ma Panenko/The Fireman's Ball (1967).

In the 1970s, rather than producing films based on aesthetic value, conviction, ideas, and risks, the majority of filmmakers centered their work around the theme of the world wars and Czechoslovakia's struggle. One of the most popular films produced during this time was Vladmir Cech's Klic/The Key (1971), a film illustrating the life of a communist official during World War II. 'The unifying characteristic of nearly all the films made in the seventies was a lack of ideas at the script level—a fear of ideological nonconformity that resulted in films being about almost nothing at all' (Hames 1985: 261). Kachyna's Laska/Love (1973), Hubacek's Znamost Sestry Aleny/Sister Alena's Boy (1973), and Jires' Lide Z Metra/People of the Metro (1974) are three of the many films that fell into the standard category of 1970s empty films.

As a result of the declining economy and the reorganization of the film industry between 1968 and 1970, many of Czechoslovakia's best-known film directors emigrated to different parts of the world to continue producing successful films. Forman and Passer took their talents to North America; Stanislav Barabas and Jan Němec moved to West Germany. The majority of film producers who did choose to stay in Czechoslovakia faced unemployment.

The mid-1970s marked the return of a number of skilled and talented directors and actors who were eager to rejuvenate the Czechoslovak film industry. The number of films produced slowly improved. Although there was not much room to deviate from the status quo and the communist authority beliefs, scholars were optimistic that with the continuance of this 'thaw', brought about by the post-1969 regime, film achievements would again parallel those brought about during the New Wave. Scholars were hopeful that as political pressure lifted, a critical and aesthetic diversity would surface, as it did amidst the New Wave.

On March 11, 1985 Mikhail Gorbachev was made the general secretary of the Communist party of the Soviet Union. Gorbachev introduced perestroika (restructuring) and glasnost (openness) to the communist regime, and these two practices posed unexpected challenges to the status quo.

By the 1990s, the years after the time known as the Velvet Revolution, voices in favor of Slovakia's independence grew stronger. Finally, the prime ministers of both republics were left with no choice but to divide the country into two parts. On January 1, 1993 Czechoslovakia was broken up into Slovakia and the Czech Republic.

Today, many look at Czech cinema as being on the verge of experiencing a New Wave in the film industry, just as Czechoslovakia did in the 1960s. Since 1993 Czech films have been winning countless prizes and awards. In 1997 Jan Svěrák's short Kolya/Kolja (1996) won an Oscar, and many have cited this event as marking the beginning of a resurgence of the film industry in the Czech Republic. With a number of Czech films, such as Petr Zelenka's Knoflikari/Buttoners (1997), gaining praise all across the world, it is no wonder that the Czech film industry is so admired. As Hames states, 'Since 1993 no fewer than 30 directors have made feature debuts, most of them graduates of the documentary and screenwriting departments of the Prague Film School' (Hames 1985: 32).

The majority of Czech documentaries that are produced today juxtapose everyday life with the politics prevalent in society. Czech shorts depict individuals' means of adapting, conforming, and changing according not only to their surroundings but to historical experiences as well. Filmmakers are careful to integrate the critical, the personal, and the historical into their documentary masterpieces. One of the many documentaries produced during the 1990s that hit the box office top ten lists was Jan Hřebejk's Pelisky/Cosy Dens (1999). This short illustrates family relations during the Prague Spring. By taking on their own personal approach to filmmaking, Czech directors are producing critically acclaimed masterpieces.

By contrast, since its 1993 separation from the Czech Republic, Slovakia's film industry has been struggling to survive. Having only produced two or three movies per year on average, the Slovak film industry is far behind compared to its neighbors. The lack of technical progress and financial security is the biggest impediment of both the quantitative and qualitative growth of Slovak cinema. The majority of filmmaking equipment has to be imported, while a great deal of production is being completed abroad (Karpaty 2002: 1). Because of the underdeveloped film industry, many Slovak film producers are emigrating to neighboring countries.

Although Slovakia still faces great challenges before realizing a healthy film industry, critics comment that the industry has improved greatly since 1998, when Mikuláš Dzurinda became head of the government. New means of support are being established to make the gaining of funds for film production a lot easier. Initiatives such as the founding of the European Community's Media Plus Program and the establishment of an advisory Media Desk office are helping to ensure that the Slovak film industry will see vast improvement in coming years.

Despite all the social, political, and economic changes of the past, documentary film in both the Czech Republic and Slovakia has survived and continues to evolve and develop in both regions. Shorts are realizing higher levels of success in the Czech Republic than in Slovakia, but scholars are convinced that, in time, Slovakia will catch up to its neighbor, just as the two regions' documentary film industries once paralleled each other's success.

SAPNA GUPTA

Further reading

Broz, Jaroslav, *The Path of Fame of the Czechoslovak Film*, Prague: Edmunds Inc, 1967.

Dwyer, Ruth and Petrie, Graham (eds), *Before the Wall Came Down*, Lanham, MD: University Press of America, 1990.

Forbes, Jill and Street, Sarah, *European Cinema: An Introduction*, New York: Palgrave, Macmillan, 2000.

Hames, Peter, *The Czechoslovak New Wave*, Berkeley, CA: University of California Press, 1985.

——'Czechs on the Rebound', *Sight and Sound* 10, no. 7, 2000: 32–34.

Karpaty, Miroslav, 'Slovak Cinema Shows Signs of Life', *The Slovak Spectator* 8, 47, December 9–15, 2002, www.slovakspectator.sk/clanok-11301.html

Liehm, J. Antonin, *Closely Watched Films: The Czechoslovak Experience*, New York: International Arts and Sciences Press Inc, 1974.

Zalman, Jan, *Films and Filmmakers in Czechoslovakia*, Prague: Orbis, 1968.

D

Davis, Peter

Director, producer, writer, and cinematographer Peter Davis challenged political and public institutions with his documentary television and film works in the 1970s, courting controversy in the process. He began working on documentaries for CBS television in 1965. Davis served as an associate producer and writer for Hunger in America (1968), which won a Writer's Guild Award. For CBS Reports he served as a writer and producer of both Heritage of Slavery (1968) and The Battle of East St Louis (1968).

This training prepared Davis well for taking on US politics and institutions during the social unrest of the Vietnam War. In The Selling of the Pentagon (1971), writer and producer Davis explores how the public relations arm of the Department of Defense manipulated public opinion about the war through propaganda. The film questions how the department spent large amounts of tax money by scrutinizing its films, speakers' bureau, and corporate contracts. The film also looks at how the Pentagon controlled news about the military: daily briefings did present information, but the news media could not verify the information, given that much of it was classified.

The Selling of the Pentagon aired on February 23, 1971. Its controversial subject matter led to a House Special Subcommittee investigation into the film's production. The subcommittee subpoenaed outtakes and other production-related materials, but CBS refused to turn them over, citing the First Amendment. Congress eventually threw out its own subpoena, resulting in a win for CBS. The Selling of the Pentagon went on to win an Emmy award.

Davis took a leave of absence from CBS in 1972 to pursue his next project, Hearts and Minds (1974). He wanted to explore three questions about the Vietnam War and its impact: 'Why did we go to Vietnam? What precisely did we do there? And, what did doing this do, in turn, to all of us?' (Berman 1975). Davis interviews US political leaders, US military members, Vietnamese leaders, and Vietnamese civilians. Following the direct cinema tradition, Davis remains offscreen. In an interview with famed economist Walt Rostow, Davis, offscreen, asks, 'Why do they [the Vietnamese] need us?' Stuttering in surprise, Rostow first replies, 'Because they were subject to, uh, military attack from the outside', and after more stuttering, he asks, 'Are you really asking me this goddamn silly question?' Unlike other documentaries about the Vietnam War, Hearts and Minds features interviews with Vietnamese individuals. Vu Duc Vinh lost both his son and his daughter in a bombing mission. He demands to know, 'What have I done to Nixon so that he comes here to bomb my country?' Another unidentified Vietnamese person observes, 'Look, they're focusing on us now. First, they bomb as much as they please, then they film'. Hearts and Minds also incorporates archival footage, including some now-famous images that capture the horror of the Vietnam War. At the age of nine, Kim Phuc was immortalized in a famous photograph as she ran away from her bombed village, her clothes burned off her body from a napalm blast. Another famous archival piece shows a Vietnamese prisoner shot in the head by a passing military officer. All of these elements combine to create a hard-hitting look at an unpopular war.

Hearts and Minds, like The Selling of the Pentagon, generated controversy. Rostow filed an injunction against the film, claiming his reputation was compromised, and the lawsuit provided Columbia Pictures with an excuse to withhold the film from distribution for six months. A California court dismissed the case in January 1975, but Columbia's monetary problems became another obstacle to distribution, until Warner Brothers eventually distributed the film. Hearts and Minds won the Oscar for Best Documentary Feature.

The next major project for Davis was Middletown (1982), a documentary series about life in Muncie, Indiana. He served as executive producer for the six-episode series, which included The Campaign, The Big Game, Community of Praise, Family Business, Second Time Around, and Seventeen. The series again followed the direct cinema style Davis preferred, and it aired March 24 to April 21, 1982. As with The Selling of the Pentagon and Hearts and Minds, the series was controversial, especially the episode titled Seventeen. An examination of the life of a high school student, the episode includes scenes of pot smoking, interracial dating, drinking, and teen pregnancy. Excessive swearing punctuates the dialogue in the episode. Seventeen was never broadcast, partially because of its subject matter and foul language. Because of the episode, sponsor Xerox also withdrew its funding in late January 1982, leaving Davis to scramble for additional funds. Some groups began to campaign for certain cuts, but preferring to leave Seventeen intact, he pulled it from the air.

Davis continues exploration of sociopolitical subjects through writing. He is the author of several books, including *Hometown* (1982), *Where is Nicaragua?* (1987), and *If You Came This Way: A Journey through the Lives of the Underclass* (1995). He has contributed articles to *The Nation*, *Esquire*, *The New York Times Magazine*, *New York Woman*, *The Boston Globe*, and *The Los Angeles Times*.

HEATHER MCINTOSH

See also: Hearts and Minds; Selling of the Pentagon, The

Biography

Born in 1937 in Los Angeles to a family of screenwriters. Father, Frank Davis, and mother, Tess Slesinger, did script work on such films as A Tree Grows in Brooklyn (Elia Kazan, 1945), The Train (John Frankenheimer, 1964), and The Good Earth (Sidney Franklin, 1937). In 1957 graduated magna cum laude with an English degree from Harvard University. After college, worked as an editorial assistant for *The New York Times*. Drafted by the army in 1959, and during his time in the service he worked as a public relations officer. Following discharge, returned to New York to work as an interviewer, researcher, and writer for Sextant Productions. Worked for WNET-TV. Did film work for WNBC-TV.

Selected films

1971 The Selling of the Pentagon: director
1974 Hearts and Minds: director
1982 Middletown: producer

Further reading

Berman, Bruce, 'The Making of Hearts and Minds: An Interview with Director Peter Davis', *Filmmakers Newsletter* 8, April 1975: 20–4.

Davis, Peter, *Hometown*, New York: Simon and Schuster, 1982.

——*If You Came This Way: A Journey through the Lives of the Underclass*, New York: John Wiley & Sons, 1995.

——*Where is Nicaragua?* New York: Simon and Schuster, 1987.

Handleman, Janet, 'The Selling of the Pentagon', in Lewis Jacobs (ed.), *The Documentary Tradition*, New York: W.W. Norton, 1979: 518–20.

Hoover, Dwight W., *Middletown: The Making of a Documentary Film Series*, Philadelphia: Harwood, 1992.

Vander Hill, Warren, 'The Middletown Film Project: Reflections of an "Academic Humanist"', *Journal of Popular Film and Television* 10.2, summer 1982: 48–65.

Dead Birds

(US, Gardner, 1963)

Dead Birds is a landmark film by Robert Gardner, about both ritual warfare and cultural conceptions of humanity, as refracted through symbolism of mortality, among the Dugum Dani of Irian Jaya, Indonesia (formerly Netherlands New Guinea). Dead Birds marks an extraordinary achievement in both nonfiction filmmaking and in collaborative anthropological research. It is the result of the three-year 1961–3

Harvard-Peabody New Guinea Expedition. Under the auspices of the Harvard Film Study Center, the Expedition's members included the initiator and filmmaker Robert Gardner; anthropologist Karl Heider as assistant cinematographer; anthropologist Jan Broekhuijse as interpreter; Michael Rockefeller as sound recordist and still photographer; and naturalist and writer Peter Matthiessen.

Although the Dani had already encountered the Western world and industrial modernity before the Harvard-Peabody expedition arrived, many were still using stone axes and conducting warfare with spears and bows and arrows. Gardner has written that:

> [my] job was made much easier because no one knew what I was doing. My camera was no more or less interesting or threatening than my belt buckle or sunglasses. It was part of the strange costume which I always wore and that it made a noise was a matter of complete indifference. I might have been holding a large insect which occasionally murmured as I put it to my eye. Such innocence worked, of course, to my advantage, and I kept as strictly as possible to the rule that no photographs be shown to anyone.
>
> (Gardner 1972: 2–34)

This interest in nonacted behavior, unprovoked by the presence of a camera, continues to characterize the core of ethnographic filmmaking today, unlike mainstream documentary, which has become in recent decades increasingly performative and, in certain respects, fictional.

Gardner has explained that the intention of the expedition was 'to make a comprehensive study of a single community of Neolithic warrior farmers [… and to] document verbally and visually the whole social and cultural fabric of this community' (Gardner and Heider 1968: xv). Thus, in addition to the feature-length Dead Birds, Mattheissen published the ecological essay *Under the Mountain Wall: A Chronicle of Two Seasons in Stone Age New Guinea* (1962), Heider completed his PhD dissertation, *The Dugum Dani* (1970), Broekhuijse authored *De Wiligiman-Dani* (1967), and Gardner and Heider together composed the remarkable photographic essay, Gardens of War: Life and Death in the New Guinea Stone Age (1968). With affinities to both the Griaule-Leiris Mission Dakar-Djibouti of 1931–3 and the Marshall family expedition of 1952–3, this collaborative Harvard-Peabody expedition has been essentially without sequel in both the social sciences and the visual arts. Although the aspiration to complete a 'comprehensive' verbal and visual documentation of the 'whole social and cultural fabric' of the Dani might be thought to imply a yearning after a totalizing holism that has since been abandoned by anthropology, the multidisciplinary, multi-authored, multimedia, and multigenre nature of the expedition and its publications in certain regards prefigured experimental, reflexive anthropology by almost half a century. In Heider's words in *The Dani of West Irian*, a study guide designed to complement the film, the intention was to produce a multitude of image-based and textual materials 'from different points of view, and give somewhat different pictures of the Dugum Dani […] which has important implications for anthropological methodology' (Heider 1972: 2–3).

The film is perhaps best known for its extraordinary sequences of actual, unstaged warfare between different Dani alliances. These were produced, it must be remembered, during the Vietnam War, at a time when the ethics of US military involvement in Southeast Asia were on the minds of filmmakers and spectators alike. Although the battle scenes in Dead Birds would later be criticized for their synthetic nature—they were composed of shots taken from various battles in various locations—they were no less astonishing for that. As anthropologist Margaret Mead wrote, invoking the contrast between a filmic depiction of people's actual, lived experience, and interview testimony commenting on that experience, 'There is a great difference between hearing from the lips of people to whom warfare had been forbidden what war was once like […] and on the other hand, having a visual record of how such warriors really confront each other across a traditional battlefield' (Gardner and Heider 1968: viii). Moreover, any cut between shots necessarily entails a rupture in time and/or space, and for the most part written ethnography is also synthetic in similar ways to film. Dead Birds was also notable for its innovations with technical limitations of the time, especially with the recording of location sound. Produced on the eve of portable synchronous equipment, much of the audio in Dead Birds, and even some (unsubtitled) dialogue, was postsynchronized in the editing studio.

Dead Birds follows a classic narrative structure, akin to those of fiction films. It reveals social patterns through the actions of two main characters: Weyak, a warrior, and Pua, a child swineherd who functions as a surrogate son of Weyak. Both stand apart from their peers. Weyak is characterized as unusually vigilant, and also responsible. Pua, on the other hand, is slower, frailer, and weaker than his friends. As the film progresses various tensions and contrasts are developed within the narrative. There is the large-scale conflict of Weyak and Pua's alliance against a neighboring one. There are the visual and thematic contrasts between the labor of women and the labor of men. There are the pitfalls that little Pua encounters as he struggles to take care of his pigs. There is the larger symbolic contest that humans wage, however vainly, with death. Indeed, the film's climax comes when Wejakhe, a young tribe member, is found dying by the Aikhe River. The film's denouement occurs after his funeral, as Weyak and the others ponder their roles in the boy's death and contemplate revenge, and in turn the audience is implicitly prompted to reflect on its own mortality.

Significantly, much of Gardner's work draws from symbolism and world mythology. Dead Birds is no exception. The very title, Dead Birds, is a translation of the Dani term for weapons and other ornaments captured during warfare (Gardner 1972: 2–35). The image of birds as a symbol for war, death, and mortality is prevalent throughout the film. Bird plumage is the desired battle attire, as the otherwise almost unclothed Dani adorn themselves with feathered headdresses. After Wejakhe is killed, Pua finds and eats a small dead bird, bedecking himself with its feathers 'like a warrior'. The recurring, ominous image portending Wejakhe's fate is one of ducks swimming on the Aikhe River. These birds, we are told early on, are avoided at all costs because of the debilitating magic they contain. They ascend with piercing squawks as the narrator announces Wejakhe's death. It is later revealed to be the very place where Wejakhe ('wrong path') is killed.

In addition to presenting its disparate images of battles as a pastiche of a single battle, Dead Birds has been criticized on various counts. The apparently affectless narration, voiced in the third-person passive by Robert Gardner himself, has been taken to task for its omniscience of its characters' actions and thoughts, at times resulting in a literal one-to-one correspondence between picture and soundtrack. However, anthropologist Karl Heider has contended that the thoughts and sensations attributed to individual Dani in the film are, to his mind, entirely credible. Moreover, as with that in John Marshall's The Hunters, it is also possible to understand the narration as an experimental exercise in mythopoetic representation, obliquely evoking the inner lives of its subjects through narratively constructed poetic symbolism, rather than as purporting to convey a comprehensive, objective account of their thought processes in toto.

Additionally, the film has been criticized in contemporary classrooms for its inattention to the lives of Dani women. Although the bulk of women's activities are shown in a subordinate light to those of men, this criticism is not entirely correct. We are introduced to Weyak's wife, Lakha, and follow her and other women as they process salt (even if the salt-making is intercut, as parallel action, with the more visually arresting scenes from the battlefield). Later in the film, after Wejakhe's death, women and girls figure prominently—as funeral mourners and as instruments of religious sacrifice. Indeed, one of the most unsparing sequences of the film shows tiny girls whose fingers have been partially chopped off by the Dani in order to placate the ghosts of the deceased. For all its containment within the symbolic logic of the film, the realism and violence of this sequence in many ways resists metalinguistic translation, making it both 'cruel', in Antonin Artaud's sense, and 'obtuse', in Roland Barthes's sense.

Finally, some anthropologists have taken Gardner to task for being a universalist, with insufficient interest in and knowledge of the cultural particularities of the subjects he has chosen for his films. However, this line of criticism is arguably more revealing about the trajectory of late twentieth-century cultural anthropology, with its increasing and arguably disproportionate attention to cultural difference in the face of widespread global homogenization, than it is a shortcoming of the films themselves. As Gardner himself has spoken of Dead Birds:

> I seized the opportunity of speaking to certain fundamental issues in human life. The Dani were then less important to me than those issues [...] I saw the Dani

> people, feathered and fluttering men and women, as enjoying the fate of all men and women. They dressed their lives with plumage, but faced as certain death as the rest of us drabber souls. The film attempts to say something about how we all, as humans, meet our animal fate.
>
> (Gardner 1972: 2–34)

In 1989 Gardner returned to the Baliem Valley to work on a sequel film, called Roads End. While there he located both Pua and Weyak, who were working in the tourist industry. Although a video cassette copy of Dead Birds had made its way to the local Protestant Mission, it had not been seen by its subjects. Gardner consequently arranged (and documented on film) a screening of Dead Birds for them. Afterwards, Gardner wrote:

> It was not long before I realized that it hardly mattered what they saw that day. Their pleasure was not in the shape but in the content of what they watched. The film could have begun in the middle or gone backwards or forwards or have been composed of any of the thousands of scene that had been left out when I edited the film so scrupulously more than twenty-five years ago.
>
> (Gardner 1996: 65)

ILISA BARBASH

See also: Gardner, Robert

Dead Birds (USA, Harvard Film Study Center, 1963, 85 mins). Produced by the Film Study Center of the Peabody Museum with help from the former Netherlands Guinea Government and the National Science Foundation. Directed, photographed, edited, writen by Robert Gardner. Sound recording by Michael C. Rockefeller. Sound edited by Jarius Lincoln and Joyce Chopra. Photographic assistant, Karl G. Heider. Titles by Peter Chermayeff. Advisors, Jan Broekhuisje and Peter Matthiessen. Filmed in Irian Jaya, Indonesia.

Further reading

Barbash, Ilisa, 'Out of Words: The Aesthesodic Cine-Eye of Robert Gardner: An Exegesis and Interview', *Visual Anthropology* 14, no. 4, 2001.

Cooper, Thomas W., *Natural Rhythms: The Indigenous World of Robert Gardner*, New York: Anthology Film Archives, 1995.

Gardner, Robert, 'On the Making of Dead Birds', in Karl Heider (ed.), *The Dani of West Irian: An Ethnographic Companion to the Film Dead Birds*, Warner Modular Publications, Module 2, 1972.

——'The Impulse to Preserve', in Charles Warren (ed.), *Beyond Document: Essays on Non-Fiction Film*, Hanover, NH: University Press of New England, 1996.

Gardner, Robert and Heider, Karl G., *Gardens of War: Life and Death in the New Guinea Stone Age*, New York: Random House, 1968.

Heider, Karl G., *The Dugum Dani: A Papuan Culture in the Highlands of West New Guinea*, New York: Wenner-Gren Foundation for Anthropological Research, Inc, 1970.

——*The Dani of West Irian: An Ethnographic Companion to the Film Dead Birds*, Warner Modular Publications, Module 2, 1972.

——*Ethnographic Film*, Austin, TX: University of Texas Press, 1976.

Mattheissen, Peter, *Under the Mountain Wall: A Chronicle of Two Seasons in the Stone Age*, New York: The Viking Press, 1962.

Mead, Margaret, 'Introduction', in *Gardens of War: Life and Death in the New Guinea Stone Age*, New York: Random House, 1968.

Ruby, Jay, *Picturing Culture*, Chicago: University of Chicago Press, 2000.

Death of a Princess

(UK, Thomas, 1980)

Death of a Princess was one of the most controversial documentary dramas ever screened on British television. Filmed in the style of the investigative documentary for which British television had achieved a justified reputation in the postwar period, it depicts a journalist's attempt to discover the truth behind the public executions of a member of the Saudi royal family and her lover. London's *Daily Express* had reported the incident in 1977, using the account of a British contract construction worker who had witnessed and taken photographs of the executions. Antony Thomas, a South African-born documentary filmmaker, researched this story of royal adultery and its punishment under Islamic law in both the UK and the Middle East between July and November 1978. He was struck by the stark contrasts in interpretation among the various Western and Arab witnesses and authorities he met.

The film caused a diplomatic furore before and after its screening in 1980. Between April (just before the film was transmitted) and July, diplomatic relations between Saudi Arabia and Britain were directly affected. The Saudis at one point asked ATV to withdraw the film; at another time they demanded cuts to be made. King Khalid's planned State Visit to Britain was then cancelled, and finally Lord Carrington, the British foreign minister, felt constrained to offer what amounted to an apology. Only then could relations be normalized and lucrative contracts for British industry restored. In the United States, too, there was pressure on the PBS network from both government and programme sponsors (Mobil Oil) to withdraw the film. It was, however, transmitted in the UK, Europe, Australasia, and the United States.

The controversial subject caused additional questions to be asked about the form and function of the film. Writer/producer Thomas chose to dramatize his own real quest for truth about this historical incident via a fiction structured like a documentary. He did this, he claimed, because he was especially concerned about protecting his Arab sources. He also felt that the very excess evident in the opinions and prejudices the incident generated meant that fictional analogy held out greater possibilities than pure documentary. Thomas's intention was to interrogate the difficulty of establishing truth through the documentary form in a fraught situation where cultures were clashing. Ironically, he succeeded in making the East–West situation even more fraught, as well as raising questions about the legitimacy of the documentary drama. Death of a Princess was accused of blurring the boundaries between fiction and nonfiction, and it intensified the debate about what was permissible in mixing modes on broadcast television.

The film illustrates the truth of the proposition that it is never the form of a documentary drama that causes controversy in the wider political world beyond media representation. Thomas's angle on the comprehension gap between Western and Middle Eastern societies was certainly sophisticated; the film's self-conscious attempt to meditate on the wider ramifications of the act of representation makes it into one of the first 'metadocumentary dramas'. The film's main protagonist, standing for Thomas himself, is journalist Christopher Ryder (played by Paul Freeman). Identification with this character situates the audience in the subject position of 'seeker after truth'. Ryder takes a literal and metaphorical 'journey to the East' as a kind of cultural explorer (clearly evident in a central sequence of the film in which shots of religious chanting and calls to prayer are juxtaposed with his difficulties in making headway with Saudi officials).

In Ryder's gathering bafflement can be discerned a critique of the documentary claim of authenticity as well as a measurement of the East–West divide. By 1980 documentary no longer had an unproblematical claim on truth, with its essentially constructed nature being increasingly seen by academics as based on a questionable belief in the representational power of the camera and the quasi-legal authority of the witness. In the narrative structure of Death of a Princess can also be seen the fictional template of an international thriller. This genre-hybridizing tendency was to become a major feature of late twentieth-century British and American docudrama.

The form, then, was more conscious, more knowing, in 1980 than ever it had been before, but it did not protect this film from blatantly aberrant readings in the public sphere. Its coproducer, Martin McKeand, once remarked that it became a film about which everybody had an opinion—even if they had not actually seen it. The controversy was primarily generated by the sensitive nature of US/European relations with the Middle East at this point in history. Formal experimentation was no guarantee against the film becoming a media event, and part of a wider 'moral panic'. The film's fascination for a Western audience was increased by the portrait it offered of a sexually active Arab woman making choices in a quasi-Western way. (Allegedly, Saudi princesses regularly procured men for casual sex.) Ten years after the beginning of the women's movement, this aspect played provocatively to Western audiences, going against the stereotype of the submissive Arab woman hidden behind a veil. The punishment suffered by the Arab princess was all the more shocking when seen from this angle. Thus, not only was the Saudi government infuriated but also postcolonial cultural commentators such as Edward Said (in his *Covering Islam*, 1981) felt that the film shamelessly used the Arab as 'Other' and was more interested in debating

Western social and political issues than in understanding Middle Eastern culture and values.

The documentary drama achieves a kind of formal maturity in films like Death of a Princess, even more so than in the other 'foreign policy' films of the same era. Many of these dealt with the struggle toward political liberalization in Iron Curtain satellite states (e.g. Granada's 1980 Invasion). Because they had a European cultural and political focus, and human rights credentials, these films were seen as campaigning against the worst abuses of a discredited political system. Death of a Princess, by contrast, mobilized a much more complex set of issues. Issues of form, function, and reception have continued to reverberate around the documentary drama.

DEREK PAGET

See also: Thomas, Antony

Death of a Princess (tx. 1980, 120 mins). Coproduction UK (ATV), USA (WGBH, Boston), Netherlands (Telepictures), Australia (Seven Network), New Zealand (Eastern Media). Produced by Antony Thomas and Martin McKeand. Directed by Antony Thomas. Scripted by Antony Thomas and Sala Jaheen.

December 7

(US, Ford/Toland, 1942)

December 7 deals with the surprise attack on US military installations in Hawaii by the Japanese in 1941. Two versions exist. The first, an eighty-three-minute docudrama, was never released to the public. The other, comprising thirty-four minutes of footage drawn entirely from this original, was exhibited widely, winning an Oscar for Best Short Subject in 1943. Footage from December 7 has since been used extensively in World War II documentaries, yet almost all of it is bogus, having been created in a Hollywood studio. Through constant repetition, its spurious images have become the accepted record of the 'Day of Infamy'.

The US government, in consultation with John Ford, chose Gregg Toland (photographer of Citizen Kane) to direct. In Hawaii Toland discovered that less than six minutes of indifferent quality footage of the actual raids existed. On his return to Hollywood, he proceeded to restage events using miniatures, rear screen, and matte projection. US aircraft were painted with Japanese insignia and military personnel were pressed into service as extras. The dramatic leads were played by Walter Huston, Charles Davenport, and Dana Andrews.

A weary Uncle Sam (Huston) is convalescing in Hawaii on December 6 after a year of international crises that have sorely tried his endurance. His conscience (Davenport), whose geniality masks a racism no less chilling for being charmingly delivered, materialises to cast doubt on America's trust in the loyalty of the one hundred and fifty-seven thousand Japanese-Americans on the islands. A series of vignettes would seem to prove that a proliferation of spies exists. Also bemoaned is the ostrich-like behaviour of Washington's politicians faced with evidence of Japanese militarism in the Far East. Following the simulated raids and massive reconstruction effort, the film concludes in Arlington National Cemetery with a ghostly sailor (Andrews) insisting to a skeptical fellow-phantom from the Great War that the United States will not return to its isolationist shell when this conflict ends.

Official reaction was almost unanimously negative. The major flaw was seen as the picture's fence-sitting equivocation. Effective screen propaganda must be factually selective, allowing no room for doubt or compassion. Those aims are not achieved by providing a forum for reasoned debate. Given December 7's intended audience, the need was for a work that would elicit a negative response to all things Japanese as well as pride in the accomplishments of those who had literally salvaged much from the débâcle that was Pearl Harbor. The print remained locked away until 1943, when Ford suggested the government could obtain some recompense for its $80,000 investment. The result was the abbreviated version, shorn of all but the attacks and reconstruction footage.

December 7 in either format is not a negligible achievement. It provides an excitement and immediacy that few World War II documentaries surpass. Continued recourse to its images by filmmakers over the past half-century bears testimony to its lasting impact and, specifically, to the visual and dramatic flair of Gregg Toland, its discredited director.

JAMES M. SKINNER

December 7 (US, Field Photographic Unit, 1942–3, 83 mins and 34 mins). Produced by John Ford. Directed by Gregg Toland and John Ford. Shooting script by Sam Engel. Edited by Robert Parrish. Music by Alfred Newman.

Further reading

Gallagher, Tag, *John Ford: The Man and His Films*, Berkeley, CA: University of California Press, 1986.

Koppes, Clayton R. and Black, Gregory D., *Hollywood Goes to War: How Politics and Profits Shaped World War II Movies*, New York: The Free Press, 1987.

Murphy, William T., 'John Ford and the Wartime Documentary', *Film and History* 4, February 1986.

n.a., *Eye of the Eagle: December 7*, documentary hosted by Richard Schickel, Britannica Learning Materials, Cambridge, Ontario, Canada.

Rollins, Peter C. (ed.), *Hollywood as Historian: American Film in a Cultural Context*, Lexington, KY: University of Kentucky Press, 1983.

Skinner, James M., 'December 7: Filmic Myth Masquerading as Historical Fact', *Journal of Military History* 55, no. 4, October 1991: 507–16.

Del Mero Corazón

(US, Blank, 1979)

According to its collaborators, director Les Blank's Del Mero Corazón: Love Songs of the Southwest (1980) was an attempt to preserve some of the cutting-room leftovers from their previous venture into the world of Tejano and Norteña music, Chulas Fronteras/Beautiful Borders (1975). In the process of making the first film, the scope of the subject matter grew from an investigation of a regional music tradition into a poetic commentary on the lifestyles and hardships of the musicians and the communities that support them. Producer and sound recorder Chris Strachwitz worried that, despite the cinematic accomplishment of Chulas, many of the songs that initially sparked his interested in the subject—the heart-wrenching love ballads—were not given enough depth. A DVD released by Strachwitz's Arhoolie Records in 2003 puts both films together, with an abundance of commentary and outtakes from the entire project.

Watching the films in chronological order, Del Mero Corazón's stylistic and thematic inspiration can be seen in two of Chula's most poignant moments: in an interview the legendary Lydia Mendoza explains that with every song she performs, she experiences emotionally what the lyrics detail; later, the camera fixates on a taut barbed wire, pulls its focus to a spiny cactus paddle, continues to the plant's bursting yellow blossoms, all while the lead vocalist of Los Alegres de Terán bitter-sweetly contemplates long-distance love. The latter sequence illustrates the overlay of lyrical poetry and symbolically relevant images that serves as the staple of Del Mero Corazón's montage structure. The result is an audiovisual poem stripped of narrative interpretation, which allows the viewer—like Mendoza—to live rather than listen to each song on the soundtrack.

The film's opening sequence shows a hand chopping chiles, barbecue festivities, several close-ups of flames and glowing embers, and a crimson crepuscular sky. As each shot burns red, the lyrics of Ricardo Mejía and Rubén Valdez's 'Seis pies abajo' (six feet under) weeps of unrequited love and bleeding hearts. At same time, the bouncing accordion and rhythmic clapping align the mood with the general revelry of the banquet, pointing out that tragic lyrics and celebratory music are not mutually exclusive in the culture under scrutiny.

The film's primary concern is a consistent matching of visual, musical, and emotional passions in a variety of settings. In nearly all of the twelve sequences a unique musical track is performed, while the visuals build a bricolage of voyage and place icons, from trains and eighteen-wheeler trucks, to the landscape they traverse and the towns and truck stops they approach. Spliced together five years after Chulas was released, Del Mero Corazón makes a point to 'travel' beyond its predecessor's border theme. The footage is taken primarily from filming done in San Antonio, Texas, and Monterrey, Nuevo León; it also includes performances in California, showing that the Tejano music's audience is geographically broader than its name implies. Much like Chulas, it brings the political issues of migratory work and travel (in particular with regard to the toll distance takes on romantic relationships) into a film that at first glance simply celebrates the southwestern traditions of music and dance, food, and beer. One fictitious heroine's story pervades various lyrics in both films with Homeric tribulations, as Zenaida's laments are interpreted in corridos by Los Madrugadores and later by Andrés Berlanga.

In two sequences late in the film, the interview and performances of accordionist Chavela Ortiz break up the masculine voices and gazes, bring an inspirational air of political evolution to this musical field heavy with history and tradition. Ortiz tells of her beginnings performing with her mother and sister, but that neither chose to continue due to the pressure and resentment shown by many male colleagues, romantic partners, and audience members. Ortiz persisted and succeeded despite the same struggle until her untimely death after the production of the film (mentioned by the filmmakers in the 2003 DVD commentary). This documentation of her music and insight augments Del Mero Corazón's value as a cultural-historical artifact.

Rich in color, the film uses fuchsia stucco buildings and aqua wedding attire to underscore the musical excitement. Hand-painted graphics on the façades of Mexican and Texan businesses, along with California murals, show how the vibrant rural landscape infuses artistic and artisanal sensibilities. The desire to capture the chromatic intensity can be seen carried over into editor Maureen Gosling's later directorial work, Blossoms of Fire (2000), about the matriarchal Zapotec culture of Mexico. Gosling considers this project with Blank and Strachwitz to have informed much of her later work on Latin American cultures. At other points in the film, the colorful exteriors are left behind in order to show the true home of the music: inside the bars, cantinas, and dance halls. Les Blank films an energetic performance by Leo Garza's conjunto, with shots from a shadowy stage behind the two vocalists. The camerawork creates the aura of their sweat-drenched profiles with the moisture reflecting a makeshift lighting set-up attached to the rafters of an otherwise dark locale. The film ends by studying the details of a Chicano Power mural in California while the ballad 'Las Nubes' (The Clouds), updated to a 1970s sound and style with electronic keyboards and infusion of English callouts, is performed by Little Joe y la familia. The vocalist contemplates a life journey of political struggle, and much as in Chulas, the theme of love is pushed beyond romance, to cultural pride, passion, and self-empowerment.

The few small segments of narration in the film, read by María Antonia Contreras, are recent. Historical lyrical texts chosen by professor of Hispanic literature Guillermo Hernández to underscore the Mexican American culture's extensive tradition of emotive expression through lyrical verse. The film is seamlessly subtitled for both Spanish- and English-speaking audiences, thanks to a government grant awarded to the filmmakers shortly after the production of Blank's Burden of Dreams (1982), allowing several of the director's films to be screened throughout Latin America.

MISHA MACLAIRD

See also: Blank, Les; Chulas Fronteras

Del Mero Corazón (US, Blank, 1979, 29 mins). Directed and written by Les Blank. Produced by Les Blank and Chris Strachwitz. Edited by Maureen Gosling.

Depardon, Raymond

Raymond Depardon began his professional life as a photographic journalist. Having worked for press agencies and cofounded the agency Gamma in 1966, his subsequent move into filmmaking in 1969—with his first film, Ian Pallach—owes a great deal to his initial training. Although the trajectory of his career has gradually taken him away from the more journalistic reportage style of the earlier work, his filming and his photography remain inextricably linked. Known mainly for his documentaries, Depardon also explores the border between fact and fiction, straying into the latter domain almost entirely in some films (e.g. Empty Quarter) and revisiting documentary subjects to test the limits of fictional representation in others (e.g. Tchad (2) et (3) and La Captive du désert). From the outset, he has traveled the world to work in settings as varied as Prague, Yemen, Chad, India, and New York, to name but a few, but returning periodically yet repeatedly to film French-based subjects in Parisian and, most recently, rural settings.

Depardon became interested in filmmaking at a time when the direct cinema of Leacock, Pennebaker, and the Maysles brothers was prominent. When he eventually began making his own films, they turned out to be more influenced by this US tradition than by that of the French cinéma vérité of Rouch. Depardon's filming is not participatory in the Rouchian sense in that he does not intervene or communicate with his subjects, nor does he explicitly interrogate his own relationship to them. Although the filmed subjects of his documentaries may acknowledge the presence of the camera, neither Depardon nor any of his assistants stage this encounter in order to turn the camera on the observer(s).

This activity is saved for his more autobiographical, self-reflective works. Another crucial connection to the direct cinema tradition is via the work of Wiseman. Like Wiseman in the United States, Depardon has filmed institutions crucial to the French establishment, notably in the three films Faits divers, Urgences, and Délits flagrants, all set in Paris, which deal respectively with law and order, psychiatric health care, and justice. In contrast to the filming of Wiseman, however, Depardon films the institutions concerned in order to focus on the people who allow them to function and not on a critique of the institutions in themselves.

Although infinitely varied in approach to his subjects and adopting a correspondingly appropriate style, Depardon's films have traits that recall the influence of still photography in his work. The photograph features literally in Les Années Déclic, as does discussion of the profession of photographer in Reporters and in his section of the collaboratively made Contacts. Yet, even when there is no place afforded to the photographic still, Depardon's filming is characterized by a patient, motionless focus that is reminiscent of this other medium. This is particularly apparent in the Paris-based Urgences and Délits flagrants, for example, where the psychiatric emergencies of the Hôtel Dieu and the interviews of offenders at the Palais de Justice are stationary encounters. Even within the films that deploy this fixed framing technique most frequently, the camera becomes more mobile when necessary. However, when he uses the long static shot, Depardon does not steer the viewer's gaze to certain aspects of a given scene but keeps a steady focus on the space of the encounter, allowing people to enter or leave it without following them.

Depardon waits for his subjects to come into the space of his enclosure rather than moving into theirs, even though he is conscious of being located in the space of the other as soon as he begins filming. He keeps his distance, an ethical one in some respects, but he is fully aware that approaching any of his subjects with a camera is a form of violence. He comments specifically on the violence of the filming encounter when making San Clemente, set in the Italian asylum. His contribution to Contacts focuses on the photographer as a professional voyeur, distance here becoming ultimately more damaging than respectful. Continuing from his desire not to disturb the scene he is filming, this does not, however, prevent him from focusing on himself in other ways. Indeed, consideration of the filming self becomes an important ethical concern. The presence of what he terms 'le regard mixte' or 'la caméra mixte' in the fiction Empty Quarter is an attempt to negotiate a point of view for the camera that is somewhere between the gaze of the filmmaker and that of the fictive male subject of the film. Without turning the camera on himself in Contacts, he sees himself being totally implicated in the pain he views such that the greatest violence is done toward the filming self. The most complete turn toward the filming self, however, has been in the more autobiographical mode of Les Années Déclic.

Numéros zéro and Reporters focus on linked aspects to his profession but Les Années Déclic, in contrast, features photographs that tell the tale of his life up until that point while featuring extracts from some of the films he had made thus far. One film in particular, 50.81 pour cent, was banned by Giscard d'Estaing at the time, since he did not like its portrayal of his electoral campaign (the film is now distributed as 1974: Une partie de campagne). Les Années Déclic is a film with a difference, since Depardon sits in front of a projector with the light shining in his eyes, looking down at the still images on which he then comments. These images are brought to life occasionally by the films to which they relate. He dedicated this quasi-autobiography to his parents. He makes touching reference to his father, who died when Depardon was on location making another film; his mother died during the making of this particular film. Rather than having gone round the world, he states that he should perhaps have spent more time getting to know his father, whom he loved a great deal.

Although this is now impossible, the return to film a French rural community in his 2001 work, Profils paysans: l'approche (Chapter one in an evolving series), seems in some way to represent the displacement of this desire to return home.

SARAH COOPER

See also: Leacock, Richard; Maysles, Albert; Pennebaker, D.A.

Biography

Born in Villefranche-sur-Saône, July 6, 1942, into a farming family. Left home for Paris in 1958 to work alongside Louis Foucherand, his first contact with the profession of photographic journalist. Became attached to the Dalmas agency, via Foucherand, in 1959. Left for the Sahara at the request of Louis Dalmas, then subsequently to Algeria for his first trip to Africa, 1960. Employed on return by Dalmas, part of a team of photographers who worked with papers such as *Samedi-Soir*, *France-Dimanche*. Called to military service in March 1962, Dalmas agency insisted that he be photographer for *Bled 5-5*, the journal for the armed forces, and was subsequently transferred to Paris. Cofounded the Gamma agency with Hubert Henrotte and Gilles Caron, 1966. A special report on Chile earned him and two other Gamma photographers a Robert Capa Gold Medal Award. In 1977 he received a Pulitzer Prize for his work in Chad. Among his prestigious film accolades to date, he was awarded the Prix Georges Sadoul for Numéros zéro and Césars for best documentary for Reporters, Délits flagrants and for the documentary short, New York, NY.

Selected films

1969	Ian Pallach
1974	50.81 pour cent
1975–6	Tchad (2) et (3)
1977	Numéros zéro
1980	Reporters
1982	San Clemente
1983	Faits divers
1984–5	Empty Quarter
1984	Les Années Déclic
1986	New York, NY
1987	Urgences
1989	La Captive du désert
1990	Contacts
1994	Délits flagrants
1996	Afriques: comment a va avec la douleur?
2001	Profils paysans: l'approche

Further reading

Depardon, Raymond, *Tchad*, Paris: Gamma, 1978.

——*Correspondance new-yorkaise*, Paris: Libération/ Editions de l'Etoile, 1983.

——*San Clemente*, Paris: Centre National de la Photographie, 1984.

——*Errance*, Paris: Seuil, 2000.

Depardon, Raymond and Sabouraud, Frédéric, *Depardon/Cinéma*, Paris: Cahiers du cinéma, 1993.

Gauthier, Guy, *Le Documentaire, un autre cinéma*, Paris: Nathan, 1995.

Guerrin, Michel, *Raymond Depardon*, Paris: Centre National de la Photographie, 1999.

n.a., *Confrontations avec Raymond Depardon, Daniel Humair, Emir Kusturica, Artazvad Pelechica, Claude Regy, Alain Rocca, Martin Scorsese*, Paris: Femis, 1993.

Deren, Maya

Maya Deren (née Eleanora Derenkowsky), one of the most prolific advocates for experimental and independent film practice in the United States, helped to establish a paradigm (based on a unified front of institutional patronage and collective social action by art cinema's practitioners) for the funding, circulation, and presentation of avant-garde films. Her labors as both a filmmaker and proponent of 'non-industrial' film work were a result of her interest in sustaining a countersystem to that of the distribution circuit of America's popular commercial cinema, and include a range of activities that enriched the fields of independent film manufacturing, distribution, exhibition, and promotion following World War II.

Although Deren's contributions to the language of indigenous art cinema in the United States have been characterized by some critics and historians within formalist categories and as autoethnography, the broad language of her work, including the corpus of critical texts she produced in order to frame her films' reception, suggests otherwise. Her awareness and concern with the acts of historical classification and collective modes of interpretation were as much a part of the working methodology of her artistic practice (thus eluding or making complex the subsequent linear categorization of her work) as the construction and circulation of the art-object she produced.

During World War II, the state of experimental or avant-garde film production in the United States was limited by a lack of material resources and exhibition venues. Further restricting potential attempts at filmic experimentation or production outside of the commercial center of film manufacturing in Los Angeles was the high cost of 35mm film production, with its large and cumbersome equipment, and the lack of funding bodies engaged to support nonindustrial film work.

The conclusion of the war helped to rectify these conditions as new and used portable 16mm equipment and a surplus of 16mm stock produced by Eastman Kodak for use by the US military prompted a consumer market to be developed in order to expend the surplus film resources that were now available domestically. In New York the end of the war brought with it a great number of import films that were available for commercial use and an art house exhibition circuit that quickly expanded in order to serve this market.

During this period Deren had completed work on her first film, Meshes in the Afternoon (1943), in collaboration with her husband, filmmaker Alexander Hammid, in Los Angeles. By 1946 she had her first opportunity to screen her films 'outside of the law of industrial production' in a rented theater in Greenwich Village. It was her first few initial experiences with self-distribution and production that exposed Deren to the difficulties of operating outside of the commercial mainstream. However, through her ability to sustain a market for her work from the support of screenings held at educational institutions, museums, and film societies, a viable model for alternative praxis was developed. This model was held together primarily through Deren's own advocacy, taking the form of public lecture presentations, numerous published articles, and seeking the support of organizations offering fellowship support or financing for the plastic arts, which led to her being awarded the first Guggenheim Fellowship granted for 'creative work in the field of motion pictures' in 1946. By 1954, unable to obtain consistent financial backing, Deren focused her efforts on establishing the Creative Film Foundation (CFF), a nonprofit organization that was to offer grants for the 'development of motion pictures as a creative fine art form'. She expanded the CFF's activities in 1956 with the Creative Film Awards, which promoted the work of a select group of experimental filmmakers. Although limited funds would end up being distributed through the CFF, the organization helped to aid the dissemination of avant-garde film work in the United States and provided a formal platform for the broad dissemination of experimental filmic praxis.

In 1946 Deren was invited to collect her writing on film by Alicat Press publisher Oscar Baradinsky. For Deren this was an opportunity to make available for the first time the range of her theories on film and film art in one concise volume that could then subsequently be made available through her distribution company, Maya Deren Films, and aid her in the management of her financial difficulties. This text, published as *Anagram of Ideas on Art, Form and Film* (1946), is an exploration of numerous topics, including an analysis of the field of documentary film and documentary realism. In *Anagram*, Deren posits that the 'real value' of the documentary mode is found in its ability to make material an 'otherwise obscure or remote reality', but cautions that its status as art must result not from its pursuit of narrative or poetic realism but by its particular affinity to film form. She criticizes the successes of documentaries produced during the 1930s and 1940s as misguided, and asserts that the integrity, or by her own term 'validity', that these films found was a false celebration of the medium's capabilities. Of the documentaries that she praises in *Anagram* for producing an 'art reality [...] independent of the reality by which it was inspired', she includes The Song of Ceylon (1934) and the early work of Dziga Vertov (aka Denis Arkadyevich Kaufman).

A year after the publication of *Anagram*, Deren had the opportunity to perform within the field of documentary through ethnographic field work while in Haiti, where she began to film secular dance and voudoun possession rituals with the financial backing of her 1946 Guggenheim Fellowship. By 1953, having made multiple trips to Haiti in order to gather footage for her voudoun project, Deren was still in pursuit of financing, but had been able to publish the monograph, *Divine Horsemen: The Living Gods of Haiti*, an observational analysis and history of Haitian voudoun culture. Although she was never able to complete work on her documentary film project, she continued to look for financing until her death in the early 1960s. In 1977 Deren's Haitian footage and audio recordings were collected and edited together by Teiji Ito, her third husband, and Cherel Winett Ito and released under the same title as her monograph.

JOSHUA AMBERG

See also: Divine Horsemen

Biography

Born in Kiev, Ukraine, 20 April 1917. In 1922 arrived with parents at Ellis Island in the United States. Attended the League of Nations International School in Geneva, Switzerland, 1930–3. Received BA degree from New York University in 1936. Participated in activities with the socialist movement and the Young People's Socialist League, 1934–7. In 1938–42 worked as a freelance secretary and editorial assistant, including a period in which Deren held a position with the Dunham Dance Company during 1941–2. Earned a Master's degree in English Literature from Smith College in 1939. Married filmmaker Alexander Hammid in 1942. Production of Meshes in the Afternoon in 1943. In 1945 began to self-distribute and promote films, arrange speaking engagements, and publish written work about film. In 1946 received Guggenheim Fellowship and published *Anagram of Ideas on Art, Form and Film.* Awarded the 'Grand Prix International for 16mm Film, Experimental Class' at Cannes for Meshes in the Afternoon, 1947. From 1947 to 1955 toured the Caribbean and studied secular and ritualistic dance and culture focusing on Haitian voudoun. In 1954 founded the Creative Film Foundation and in 1956 established the Creative Film Awards. Married composer Teiji Ito in 1960. Died October 13, 1961 in New York.

Selected films

1934 The Song of Ceylon (Basil Wright)
1943 Meshes of the Afternoon: director, writer
1944 Witch's Cradle: director
1944 At Land: director
1945 A Study in Choreography for Camera: director
1946 Ritual in Transfigured Time: director
1948 Meditation on Violence: director, writer
1958 The Very Eye of Night: director, writer
1977 Divine Horsemen: The Living Gods of Haiti (Teiji Ito and Cherel Winett Ito)

Further reading

Clark, Veve A., Hodson, Millicent and Neiman, Catrina, *The Legend of Maya Deren: A Documentary Biography and Collected Works: Volume One, Part One—Signatures (1917–42)*, New York: Anthology Film Archives, 1984.

——*The Legend of Maya Deren: A Documentary Biography and Collected Works: Volume One, Part Two—Chambers (1942–47)*, New York: Anthology Film Archives, 1988.

Deren, Maya, *An Anagram of Ideas on Art, Form and Film*, Yonkers: Alicat Book Shop Press, 1946.

——*Divine Horsemen: The Living Gods of Haiti*, New York: Thames and Hudson, 1953.

Jackson, Renata, *The Modernist Poetics and Experimental Film Practice of Maya Deren (1917–61)*, Lewiston: Edwin Mellen Press, 2002.

Nichols, Bill (ed.), *Maya Deren and the American Avant-garde*, Berkeley, CA: University of California Press, 2001.

Rabinovitz, Lauren, 'Maya Deren and an American Avant-garde Cinema', in *Points of Resistance: Women, Power & Politics in the New York Avant-garde, 1943–71*, second edn, Chicago: University of Illinois Press, 2003, pp.49–91.

Desert Victory

(UK, Boulting, Macdonald, 1943)

Desert Victory is a documentary record of the British Eighth Army's campaign in North Africa against German and Italian forces under the command of Field Marshall Erwin Rommel. It consists almost entirely of footage shot by combat cameramen, including some captured German film. In this kind of filmmaking, two creative problems are uppermost for the filmmakers working with miles of actuality material: first, to give clarity to the mass of confusing, technical detail; and second, to give it dramatic form.

In Desert Victory, the first problem was solved by the use of animated maps to establish the overall patterns and movement of the campaign, and by a carefully planned narration. As for the second, all of the nonartistic material with the randomness and irregularity of history inherent in it was given a beginning, middle, and end—like the chronicle plays of Shakespeare. (Henry V gives considerable attention to an English army at war on foreign soil, and Laurence Olivier's film version of it (1944) fitted into the patriotic spirit of the time.) To organize these events so that they would appear both clear and dramatic, the filmmakers contrived an alternation of cause and effect. To personalize the mass action and to gain empathy, a number of close-ups of individual soldiers were inserted. (Some of them were obviously recreated; for those, actuality footage was augmented with brief scenes shot at Pinewood Studios.) Generals Alexander, Montgomery, and Wavell, and Prime Minister

Churchill are introduced as well. In addition, the irrelevancies of the sponsor's requirements—to show each branch of the armed forces, the civilian workers, the presence of US aid, and so on—were fitted into the whole without warping it out of shape.

Desert Victory starts at the lowest point of the campaign, in the summer of 1942. The British, who had retreated across the Sahara, pursued by the seemingly invincible Afrika Korps, are halted just sixty miles from Alexandria, deep inside Egypt. Then, in October, there is the fierce battle at El Alamein, with the British emerging victorious. From there the film follows the triumphant one thousand three hundred-mile pursuit of the German and Italian armies to the final victory at Tripoli.

In comparison with the British indoctrinational semi-documentaries (Target for Tonight, 1941; Fires Were Started, 1943; Western Approaches (The Raider in the United States), 1944), which tended to make the violence of war part of a job of work to be done, Desert Victory is singularly bloodthirsty. Perhaps these filmmakers weren't inclined to conceal their elation over this first major British victory following the battering that Britain had received in the previous desert fighting and from the air Blitz of Britain itself.

Desert Victory was an enormous critical and popular success. Apparently its sincerity and feeling of authenticity were most responsible for this. In Britain it became the most successful of all official films at the box office up to that point. *The Times* (of London) wrote of it that it was not only a valuable document but that it also succeeded in being good 'cinema' as well (March 4, 1943). In the United States two respected reviewers (tough-minded realists) praised it highly. Manny Farber wrote that it was a pleasure and an excitement: 'It is a real documentary, not a newsreel assembly [...] This is the first time a movie has been the original source for the clearest account of an event. The filmmakers of the British government were obviously as well prepared [...] as was the Eighth Army under Montgomery' (*New Republic*, April 12, 1943). James Agee thought that 'Desert Victory is the first completely admirable combat film, and if only film makers and their bosses can learn the simple lessons it so vigorously teaches, its service to the immediate future and to history will be incalculably great' (*The Nation*, May 1, 1943). It received an Academy Award as the year's most distinctive achievement in documentary features.

Its success prompted a series of large-scale, feature-length 'victory' films. Tunisian Victory (1944), a British-American coproduction, also directed by Roy Boulting, carried the North African story from the US landings in November 1942 to the annihilation of the German forces at Cape Bon. Burma Victory (1945), also directed by Boulting, may have been prompted in part by a Hollywood feature, Objective Burma (1945, directed by Raoul Walsh), which annoyed the British. In it Errol Flynn, as a US paratrooper, pretty much single-handedly mops up the Japanese enemy. The True Glory (1945), the final film in the series, was produced jointly by the British Ministry of Information and the US Office of War Information. It was codirected by Englishman Carol Reed and American Garson Kanin, fiction film directors of considerable distinction. It covers the period from the preparation for the D-Day landings in Normandy, through the fall of Berlin, to the establishing of contact between the Western Allies and Soviet troops at the Elbe River. Desert Victory may also have been a model for the highly successful and influential American television series Victory at Sea (1952–3).

JACK C. ELLIS

See also: Boulting, John and Roy; Fires Were Started; Tunisian Victory

Desert Victory (UK, Army Film and Photographic Unit and the Royal Air Force Film Production Unit, 1943, 60 mins). Distributed by Ministry of Information. Produced by David Macdonald. Directed by Roy Boulting; assistant direction by Patrick M. Jenkins. Cinematography by British Service Film Units. Music by William Alwyn. Edited by Richard Best and Frank Clarke. Screenplay and commentary spoken by James Lansdal Hodson.

Diary for Timothy, A

(UK, Jennings, 1945)

The last of Humphrey Jennings's artime documentaries, A Diary for Timothy looks to the end of war with a disturbing, perhaps disturbed, ambivalence. Following his attempt to integrate

Figure 1 Desert Victory, 1943. The British Eighth Army Routs Rommel in Africa (Courtesy of the Everett Collection)

documentary materials with rather conventional, heavily fictionalized narrative structures in Fires Were Started and two subsequent short films (The Deserted Village and The True Story of Lilli Marlene), Jennings returned in A Diary for Timothy to what Jim Hillier has called the 'distinctively associative and non-narrative style' of such earlier short films as Listen to Britain (Hillier 1972). The result was arguably the most aesthetically accomplished of Jennings's films, with regard to both the graphic quality and compression of its individual images (photographed by Fred Gamage) and the sophistication and complexity of its montage. At the same time, Jennings's own ideological uncertainties as to the significance, for Britain, of the imminent end of World War II are embodied in the film's formal irresolution, the impression it conveys of a filmmaker straining against both the Griersonian model of documentary and his own aesthetic of synthesis. It is precisely this sense of strain that gives A Diary for Timothy a poignancy and tension missing from Jennings's earlier films, and that makes it a more interesting work than either its partisans or its antagonists have allowed.

Jennings began work on A Diary for Timothy in the summer of 1944 and began location work in the autumn; filming continued into the following spring, and the war was over by the time the film was released. Although it documents some setbacks for the Allied side (notably the Arnhem campaign of late 1944), the whole film is shaped by the certainty of the war's end, and all its images of sacrifice, loss, and mortality are set in relation to the filmmaker's—and the viewer's—confidence in a happy ending (one of the narrative conventions Jennings both adopts and worries over). The voice-over commentary was written by E.M. Forster, but clearly he worked to Jennings's design; indeed, some phrases from Jennings's working notes turn up more or less intact in the final version. While the film was certainly affected by the unfolding of public, historical events, the essential structure was in place early on in the filming.

A Diary for Timothy presents itself as an account, addressed to the protagonist, Timothy James Jenkins, of the first six months of his life. Jennings weaves together scenes from the child's life (homecoming, baptism, first Christmas) with episodes from the lives of four other 'typical' characters: Goronwy, the Welsh coal miner; Alan, the gentleman farmer; Bill, the London engine driver; and Peter Roper (the only one of these characters with a surname), an injured fighter pilot recovering in a hospital. Intercut with these continually interrupted and deliberately inconclusive narrative strands are scenes of landmines being cleared from the British coastline (as fears of invasion recede); children playing amidst the wreckage of bomb sites; people standing in line for coal on the street; Myra Hess performing Beethoven at an afternoon concert; John Gielgud playing Hamlet; rescue workers looking for survivors of a V-2 attack; a woman unable to sleep in an underground shelter; young people at a dance hall; and, running through the whole film, within and around all these other strands, scenes of people listening to the radio for news of the war. The familiar voices of the radio newsreaders connect the listeners in their separate rooms, but what we see is the separation; the montage isolates what it joins.

Jennings's scenario in A Diary for Timothy, with its simple stock characters identified by their work, has certain qualities reminiscent of a children's story. This makes sense in a film addressed to an infant, but that device itself may have the effect, as Andrew Britton contends, of infantilizing the spectator. There is some truth to this observation, although it oversimplifies the multiple levels on which the film actually addresses its audience, and its multiplicity of voices. Jennings constructs representative rather than individualized characters in order to convey a sense of social totality: a Griersonian strategy, but adapted by Jennings to more critical and less obvious ends. Here, the sense of totality is a product of total war. 'You were part of the war, even before you were born,' the commentary runs. 'Everyone was in it; it was everywhere; not only on the battlefields but in the valleys, where Goronwy, the coal miner, carries his own weapons to his own battlefront.' Such language might be taken to affirm a patriotic sense of connectedness and common purpose, but equally it articulates a feeling of inescapability, of history as nightmare—and not only in wartime, as the film's recurrent references to the unchangingly terrible conditions in the mines make clear.

A Diary for Timothy celebrates the Allied advances of early 1945, but it also pushes its audience to think more critically about war and its 'sides'. In a 1948 essay Jennings named a 'propensity for endless aggressive war' as one of the defining traits of the English, and wrote that 'some of the English achievements in the late war, notably the burning of Hamburg, make the blood run cold'. So, in a late sequence in the film, when we see a series of shots of London being rebuilt while on the soundtrack a radio announcer describes massive Allied bombing raids on Berlin, the juxtaposition should complicate our response to the good news from the front, as should a later sequence intercutting images of bombing with Timothy crying in his small white cot. Timothy's comfortable whiteness is contrasted throughout the film with the hellish darkness in which Goronwy works, and it is Goronwy's voice we hear in a sequence just after the Berlin air raids: 'I was sitting thinking about the past: the last war, the unemployed, broken homes, scattered families. And then I thought, has all this really got to happen again?' The apprehension that runs through A Diary for Timothy as to what comes after the war's end is not rooted in a hollow nostalgia for 'the war as golden age' (Britton 1989), but in a disenchanted historical memory of the economic and social conditions—not just 'there', but 'here'—that brought the war into being.

HAL GLADFELDER

See also: Fires Were Started; Grierson, John; Jennings, Humphrey; Listen to Britain

A Diary for Timothy (UK, Crown Film Unit, 1945, 38 mins). Produced by Basil Wright. Written and directed by Humphrey Jennings. Commentary by E.M. Forster, read by Michael Redgrave. Cinematography by Fred Gamage. Edited by Jenny Hutt and Alan Osbiston. Music by Richard Adinsell. Sound by Ken Cameron and Jock May.

Further reading

Aitken, Ian, *The Documentary Film Movement: An Anthology*, Edinburgh: Edinburgh University Press, 1998.

Anderson, Lindsay, 'Only Connect: Some Aspects of the Work of Humphrey Jennings', in Richard Meran Barsam (ed.), *Nonfiction Film Theory and Criticism*, New York: Dutton, 1976: 263–70.

Britton, Andrew, 'Their Finest Hour: Humphrey Jennings and the British Imperial Myth of World War II', *CineAction!* 18 (1989): 37–44.

Drazin, Charles, *The Finest Years: British Cinema of the 1940s*, London: André Deutsch, 1998.

Hillier, Jim, 'Humphrey Jennings', in Alan Lovell and Jim Hillier (eds), *Studies in Documentary*, New York: Viking, 1972: 62–132.

Jennings, Humphrey, '"The English", and working notes for *A Diary for Timothy*', in Kevin Jackson (ed.), *The Humphrey Jennings Film Reader*, Manchester: Carcanet, 1993.

Dindo, Richard

Richard Dindo is the best-known documentary filmmaker to emerge from Switzerland, and one of the country's most prolific. Active since the early 1970s, he has made more than twenty-five films, most of which are documentaries. Within Switzerland, Dindo's reputation is based primarily on his rereadings of key episodes of twentieth-century Swiss history. Several of his films—such as the 1975 The Execution of the Traitor Ernst S., on Swiss collaboration with the Nazis, and Dani, Michi, Renato & Max (1987), on police brutality against the youth movement—raised controversy when they were first released but are now considered definitive accounts of the period in question. Grüninger's Case (1998) took a critical look at Swiss refugee policy during World War II through the case of a police chief who was dismissed in disgrace for helping Jewish refugees to enter the country at a time when the borders were officially closed to Jews.

Internationally, Dindo is known mainly for his critical biographies of literary as well as artistic and political figures, such as Arthur Rimbaud, Jean Genet, Max Frisch, Charlotte Salomon, and Che Guevara. In nearly every case, Dindo has based his film on documents and/or art works created by the protagonists themselves, and the films are thus often filmic adaptations of their subjects' own autobiographical accounts.

Throughout his career, Dindo has continually returned to a handful of major themes: the process of artistic creation; the potentially political role of the artist in society; oppositional social movements and the often tragic outcome for their participants; and the way in which accounts of such movements and individuals have been suppressed or distorted by official history. In his 2003 Ni olvido ni perdón (Neither Forget Nor Forgive) Dindo combines all these themes in his analysis of the 1968 student movement in Mexico, which was brutally crushed by the government but continues to live on in the films, plays, monuments, and songs created to try to come to terms with the tragedy.

Dindo's body of work is distinctive not only in the consistency of his themes and choice of subjects but also in his signature filmmaking approach, which has remained remarkably constant over the years. Dindo has often referred to himself as 'a documentarist of the past', more interested in rereading past events than in chronicling the present as it unfolds. In most cases his protagonists are long dead, forming a central absence around which the films are structured. Dindo's aim is to reconstruct past events so that they may be reexamined by contemporary viewers. In doing so he makes little use of standard methods such as archival footage or docudrama. Instead, he relies on a range of other devices that suggest fragmentary links with past events, rather than directly reproducing them.

A main element in Dindo's films is always testimony, both written and spoken, whether in the form of his protagonists' autobiographical writings or the memories of surviving witnesses. Letters, photos, paintings, excerpts from fiction films, old newspaper coverage, and other historical materials are also cited for their ability to partially recall the past. A recurring motif in nearly every Dindo film is the return to the location of a key event, where the very absence of any traces testifies to the difficulty of bridging the gap between then and now. To emphasize this juxtaposition of past and the present, Dindo will often contrast a writer's description of a place with newly shot views of the location. In other cases, eyewitnesses visit the scene of the events they are describing and may comment on what is missing in the present time.

If Dindo does use staging, it is usually partial or indirect: introducing a catalyst into a situation but not determining its outcome. The return to an historical location may provoke an eyewitness reaction, but the reaction itself is clearly unrehearsed. In some cases Dindo has had actors follow the path of his dead subjects, retracing their steps as described in their writings. Only rarely has he used actors to literally restage scenes from a protagonist's life. In his Arthur Rimbaud, a Biography (1990) Dindo explicitly addresses the boundary between documentary and fiction by having actors playing Rimbaud's friends and having relatives read authentic texts from the poet's life, such as diaries and letters, in the original locations. In his 1983 portrait of actor and film director Max Haufler, he films scenes from a project that Haufler himself was unable to shoot, with Haufler's actress daughter playing the role her father had intended for himself (Max Haufler, 'The Mute').

In talking about his work (see for instance the chapter-length interview in Hübner 1996), Dindo has often expressed a fundamental mistrust in the ability of the film image alone to adequately represent a documentary situation. For Dindo the true power of documentary film as an analytical tool resides in the juxtaposition of, or the dialectical relationship between, image and text. Thus, an idyllic landscape gains new significance when we are told by a witness that the film's hero died there, and a scene read out loud from a protagonist's diary becomes truly moving when it is accompanied by contemporary footage of the place it describes.

Moving the spectator and inspiring the viewer's imagination—these play a fundamental part in Dindo's declared documentary goal of restoring contact with his absent protagonists. Dindo has cited Marcel Proust's *In Search of Lost Time* novel cycle as his biggest artistic influence. In Dindo's own attempt to temporarily conjure up an otherwise irrecoverable past, he depends on the viewer's willingness to take an active role. In his 2000 essay, 'Ich erzähle die Erzählung des anderen' (which can be loosely translated as 'I Am the Teller of Others' Stories') Dindo writes: 'My viewers must also perform the work of memory by participating in the construction of the film [as] they watch it, shot by shot and sentence by sentence'. Through the artifice of his films' construction, Dindo invites the viewer to engage in authentic dialogue with historical figures and events.

MARCY GOLDBERG

See also: Switzerland

Biography

Born in Zurich on June 5, 1944, as the grandson of Italian immigrants, left school at the age of fifteen, working at a series of odd jobs and traveling widely before moving to Paris in 1966. The encounter with French culture—literary and cinematic—would have a lasting influence on his work. As a self-taught filmmaker with no formal training, he considers the hundreds of books and films he encountered in those years as his filmic education. In 1970 returned to Switzerland to make his first film, and has divided his time between Zurich and Paris ever since. Has made over twenty-five documentaries and fiction films.

Selected films

1972 Naive Maler in der Ostschweiz/Naive Painters in Eastern Switzerland
1973 Die Schweizer im Spanischen Bürgerkrieg/The Swiss in the Spanish Civil War
1975 Die Erschiessung des Landesverräters Ernst S./The Execution of the Traitor Ernst S. (with Niklaus Meienberg)
1977 Hans Staub, Fotoreporter/Hans Staub, Photojournalist
1981 Max Frisch, Journal I–III
1983 Max Haufler, 'Der Stumme'/Max Haufler, 'The Mute'
1987 Dani, Michi, Renato & Max
1990 Arthur Rimbaud, une biographie/Arthur Rimbaud, a Biography
1992 Charlotte, 'Leben oder Theater?'/Charlotte, 'Life or Theatre?'
1994 Ernesto 'Che' Guevara, le journal de Bolivie/Ernesto 'Che' Guevara, the Bolivian Diary
1998 Grüningers Fall/Grüninger's Case
2000 Genet à Chatila/Genet in Chatila
2002 La Maladie de la mémoire/The Illness of Memory
2003 Aragon, le roman de Matisse/Aragon, the Novel of Matisse
2003 Ni olvido, ni perdón/Neither Forget Nor Forgive
2005 Wer war Kafka?/Who was Kafka?

Further reading

A booklet on Richard Dindo and his entire filmography is available in English or German from the Swiss Films foundation, www.swissfilms.ch

Dindo, Richard, 'Ich erzähle die Erzählung des andern', *Neue Zürcher Zeitung*, 14 January 2000: F11.
Goldberg, Marcy, 'Hier ist es geschehen: Dindos Landschaften der Erinnerung', *CINEMA* 47, Zurich: Chronos Verlag, 2002: 84–94.
——'Performances of the Act of Remembering', in Frances Guerin and Roger Hallas (eds), *The Image and the Witness*, Wallflower Press, 2007.
Hübner, Christoph, 'Richard Dindo: Alles ist Erinnerung', in *Dokumentarisch Arbeiten*, Berlin: Verlag Vorwerk 8, 1996.
Lachat, Pierre, Goldberg, Marcy and Dindo, Richard, 'Werkschau Richard Dindo', *Filmbulletin* 4.03, n.d.: 41–51.
Perret, Jean, 'The Archives of Richard Dindo', *DOX Documentary Magazine*, winter 1994: 30–2.

Dinner Party, The

(UK, Watson, 1997)

While not his most well-known work, Paul Watson's The Dinner Party (1997) exemplifies the British filmmaker's 'fly on the wall' documentary style, his socially introspective slant and biting tone. Watson's methodology and cinematic aim are prevalent as the camera turns a critical and often satirical eye on society to reveal all of the quirks, warts and banalities of everyday people in a particular class or social situation.

Like the majority of his other works, the film was created for and broadcast on television, allowing it to reach a expansive spectrum of society in their own homes.

Paul Watson has made a career of creating powerful and award-winning documentaries for UK television entities including the BBC, ITV, Granada and Channel 4. Watson's earlier works, the ground-breaking The Family (1974), The Fishing Party (1985) and Sylvania Waters (1993), were striking in their then innovative portraits of working- and middle-class British and Australian life on camera.

The Dinner Party focuses on a wealthy group of British Conservatives gathered for dinner preceding the Labour Party's election victory. The film's release caused great controversy due to both the dramatic interactions unfolding in the work on-screen and the resulting accusations by the dinner party guests offscreen. The bold, bigoted views, largely centring around race and sexual orientation, expressed by the participants in the film predictably shocked many viewers. These same film participants then maintained that Watson distorted their conversations and attitudes following the public outcry. The discussion about truth and representation in the media that developed brought the film to light again, and served to both re-establish Watson as a progressive and non-orthodox documentary filmmaker and fit The Dinner Party sturdily into his socially critical 'docusoap' oeuvre.

Paul Watson, known for his years at the BBC, as Governor of the Bournemouth Film and Television School in England and then at Granada TV, is part of a 'new generation' of British documentary directors. While earlier British documentary works were renowned for their concern with greater societal issues, the films of Watson and his contemporaries present a more focused, personal view of the world. Watson's first major foray into this style that gained critical and audience attention was The Family (1974) for the BBC. This film became part of a genre of so-called 'docusoaps', a grouping that Watson credited with founding, but tries to separate himself from as they developed into reality television trends. These controversial films use the power of the documentary form to entertain instead of educate. They also often feature a biased narrator and seemingly bizarre individual everyday lives rather than large societal issues that effect a collective. The Dinner Party fits into the later part of the docusoaps' reign with British audiences as popular interest began to wane toward the end of the century. Watson tries to distance his career from this heading and maintains his films' serious intent over entertainment.

However, it cannot be overlooked that the primary themes in his body of work, over three hundred films in total, resound with the style and popularity of the docusoap genre. It is significant that The Dinner Party, made nearly twenty-five years following Watson's initial success with The Family, employs similar cinematic styles to corresponding rhetorical aims.

JUSTINE NAGAN

The Dinner Party (UK, 1997). Produced and directed by Paul Watson.

Further reading

Bruzzi, Stella, *New Documentary: A Critical Introduction*, London and New York: Routledge, 2000.

Ogle, Tina, 'Lord of the fly-on-the-walls', *The Observer*, January 27, 2002.

Divided World, A

(Sweden, Sucksdorff, 1948)

While not the most acclaimed of Arne Sucksdorff's shorts at the time of its premiere, En kluven varld/A Divided World stands now as one of his best-known films and one of his masterworks. The film's 'story' is simple and, unlike a number of Sucksdorff's other nature shorts, has no voice-over narration. After opening shots of water and the dark Swedish forest in winter, we see a church and graveyard as the music of Bach's 'Fantasia', continuing from the credits, swells. A white weasel stops munching its food and hides in the snow from a wolf. The wolf eats the rest of what the weasel had started. We next see a white rabbit eating from the branches of a tree. Similarly spooked, it dashes across the snow. A pair of flashing eyes indicate, however, that the wolf is near. The weasel and an owl watch and listen as the wolf captures and kills the rabbit. The owl then swoops down next to the wolf, successfully battling the larger animal and flying off with the rabbit. Later, however, we see the wolf licking at another piece of food. The film ends with shots of a house, separated from the forest by a modest fence.

Seemingly highly Darwinian, the film nonetheless posits that the world of humans is strongly divided from that of animals. One way to read Sucksdorff's film, in fact, is as a response to those who were inclined to anthropomorphize the motivations of the animals in his work. Early on, the reflections of trees bent over the water appear on its surface, separated from the actual trees, giving the film's first signifiers of division. We see shots of a graveyard, a repository for when people die. When animals die, they receive no burial but rather are eaten by their predators or by scavengers. That said, there is no sense of judgment in the framing, camera movement, or editing; this very lack is also part of what gives the film its remarkable suspense. No reason is given for a world in which cute bunnies die, lucky weasels hide, and an owl can defeat a wolf. The film thus combines the almost childlike, observational innocence that is one of Sucksdorff's greatest strengths as a filmmaker with a maturity resigned to the harsh beauty of the ways of nature.

Sound plays a crucial role in the film. The opening sound of water bubbles calls attention to the precision and intensity of sounds that pierce the winter silence. The expressionistic use of sound critics find in other Sucksdorff films is in evidence here, especially in the howling wind, highlighted in stunning shots of moonlight through trees, that seems to warn the animals of impending danger. Sound is especially important

Figure 2 A Divided World, 1948 (Courtesy of the British Film Institute)

in telling Sucksdorff's highly arranged narrative. We only hear the rabbit's death as the camera dwells on what we read as the reactions of the weasel and the owl. Later, we see the owl land next to the wolf but are not privy to their battle for the rabbit. Only the weasel is seen as, with another use of somewhat amplified sound, the scuffle between the owl and the wolf takes place, ending with the surprising sound of the wolf's whimper. Thus, neither of the film's moments of violence is actually shown. Either Sucksdorff was unable to fully capture the battle, or it did not turn out as scripted, and what we see later is either a different owl or the same one carrying a different carcass. What is equally likely is that Sucksdorff was uninterested in the gore attendant upon the kill and the battle. Such scenes would have disrupted the austere beauty, or worse, they would have encouraged viewers to pass judgment on the animals. In Sucksdorff's vision there are no villains. The sound proves that he does not exploit the savagery, but neither does he find it contemptible or unnecessary.

The use of Bach works on several levels. Given that it is heard most clearly during shots that show, or appear to be near, the world of humans, this music represents civilization, the separation from the world of animals. This latter world has its own music, one of rustling trees, burbling water, roaring winds, scampering animals and, of course, the fierce, isolated cries of attack and the agonized death screams of the rabbit. At the same time the music suggests the stylized nature of the entire enterprise, one well aware of the ominous tones in Bach's deep chords. For all the appeal of the animals, this film is no Disney Fantasia: winsome animals kill, or they die painfully.

Critics have complained about the fakery in shots of the church and graveyard, but such criticism is essentially beside the point, for this fakery only emphasizes the larger theme of a divided world. The same might apply to those shots where the wolf's eyes flash and suddenly disappear. Since one continuous shot pans and tracks from the frightened rabbit to the lupine eyes, one might wonder whether Sucksdorff staged two flashes of light to suggest the moonlight momentarily capturing the animal's glassy eyes. An earlier flash of the wolf's eyes appears where one of the film's buildings appears in the distance; this, too, raises the question of staging in order to contrast the world of humans with that of animals. Elsewhere, concerns about staging arise simply because some shots seem too amazing to be 'true'. Was the wolf's tail that close to the hiding weasel, or did Sucksdorff place a fake tail near the hole and film the weasel's emergence? One might similarly wonder how he managed to track the owl flying off with the rabbit's carcass, or if it battled the wolf at all. It is in the framing and the editing that, while the observational strength of individual long takes gives the film its persuasiveness, Sucksdorff's film states its themes in an overtly essayistic manner.

The tendency of critics to read this film allegorically also stems from its structure of repetition and variation. When the wolf appears, the weasel responds by hiding, and it survives. When the rabbit senses the wolf, it runs, but is caught and killed. Finally, when the owl sees that the wolf has food, it attacks and successfully seizes the carcass. To hide, to flee, to confront—these choices, the film suggests, cover the range of options in the animal world. For all the timeless quality of this film, given that it was made just after World War II and the Holocaust, hiding, fleeing, and attacking must have summed up for many the choices that people made. The fence that separates the cozy cottage from the forest in the film's final shot, while demarcating a divided world, nonetheless appears jagged and rickety.

DAVID M. LUGOWSKI

A Divided World/En kluven varld (Sweden, Svenska Filmindustri, 1948, 8.5 mins). Direction, scenario, and cinematography by Arne Sucksdorff. Music: 'Fantasia' by J.S. Bach, played by Erik Johnsson.

Further reading

Cowie, Peter, *Swedish Cinema, from Ingeborg Holm to Fanny and Alexander*, Stockholm: Swedish Institute, 1985.

——*Scandinavian Cinema*, London: Tantivy Press, 1992.

Hardy, Forsyth, *Scandinavian Film*, London: Falcon Press, 1952.

Soila, Tytti, Soderbergh Widding, Astrid and Iversen, Gunnar, *Nordic National Cinemas*, London and New York: Routledge, 1998.

Wakeman, John (ed.), 'Arne Sucksdorff', in *World Film Directors, Vol. One, 1890–1945*, New York: H.W. Wilson, 1987.

Divine Horsemen

(US, Deren, 1977)

Maya Deren's Divine Horsemen: The Living Gods of Haiti is a visually rich, ethnographic study of the rituals of the Haitian religion of voudoun and its dance rituals. Unable to edit her own footage during her lifetime, Deren instead wrote a book with the same title, which, although she had no formal training in anthropology, became an authoritative work on Haitian voudoun—more commonly known by its colloquial name 'voodoo'—for many decades to come.

Divine Horsemen is Deren's last film, and probably also her most mystical piece of work, not least due to its subject matter. Teiji Ito, who had composed the music for Deren's Meshes of the Afternoon and who became her third husband, produced the film after Deren's death, together with his later wife, Cherel, using Deren's twenty thousand feet of film and her music recordings. The film had its first screening in 1978.

Having worked as an assistant to Katherine Dunham, a choreographer and anthropological researcher of Caribbean dance, Deren had seen Dunham's dance footage from the West Indies and was inspired to write essays on religious possession and dancing. In 1946 Deren received a grant of $3,000, the first given out by the Guggenheim Foundation for filmmaking. Deren had originally proposed a film that would contrast the ritual of children's games with ritual ceremonies of traditional societies in Bali and Haiti, but once in Haiti she changed her mind, feeling, according to her own account, 'defeated in her original intentions' (Deren 1953: 7). Over the period of four years Deren took three trips to Haiti and spent a total of eighteen months on the island, mostly staying with a community outside Port-au-Prince.

Divine Horsemen, shot in black and white, is divided into two parts. The first part—consisting of seven of the film's eight chapters—explores Haitian religious dance ceremonies and the various gods for whom these are performed. The last chapter shows footage from carnival festivities in Port-au-Prince. The individual chapters begin with a black screen and the vever, the sacred symbol of the god, drawn with flour onto dust. The film follows the ceremonies in the order they are performed for the gods. Hence, the first chapter shows a dance for the loa Legba, the gatekeeper between the visible and mortal and the invisible and immortal world. There follow dance ceremonies for Agwe, the loa of wisdom, Erzulie, the goddess of love, Ogoun, the loa of might and power, Ghede, the loa of life and death, Azacca, the god of agriculture, and last, a presentation of the fast rhythmic music of the Kongo tribe.

Maya Deren was highly suspicious of an alleged scholarly detachment from the subject matter as a means to understand the 'object', and instead regarded subjectivity as the characteristic approach of the artist (Deren 1953: 8–9). She particularly avoided learning anything about the dances and their meaning beforehand, in order to respond purely to the direct impacts that they would have on her.

In recording the energetic dances, Deren's camera focuses on the individual and collective bodies of the dancers and, in particular, their arms and legs. The camera is unusually close to the action, at times immersed, and yet the dancers and bystanders hardly ever seem distracted by the camera. The fast music and the numerous close shots of moving limbs, rather than the focus on the faces of the dancers, pull the viewer into the action and by doing so almost make it difficult to treat the dancers as exotic objects. The result is the intimate perspective of a camera that is very close but never intrusive. Also, the recorded 'possessions'—the visible manifestations of the gods—are not artificially dramatized or exoticized. Were it not for the voice-over the viewer might hardly notice them. Voudoun, 'a religion of rare poetic vision and artistic expression' (Deren 1953: 15), is depicted as a complex social ritual and a source of communal enjoyment and strength rather than as an unfathomable primitive cult.

Divine Horsemen is also a study in movement. Although Deren made only seven films, she is often considered the first dance filmmaker. Her interest is not so much in documenting facts as in representing the diverse aesthetic forms that reality takes, as is made clear in her use of slow motion and freeze-frames. They also reveal Deren's interest in these ceremonies as aesthetic, sensory experiences.

The impression of an immersed rather than a 'prying and staring' (Deren 1953: 7) spectator is further reinforced by the voice-over. Although Deren's other films usually do not use language, Divine Horsemen uses a male and a female voice-over to elaborate on the ceremonies. The voice-over narration is also used to move the film outside the purely aesthetic and visual spheres, as it links the religious dances of the Petro rites to the political history of Haiti, and to its successful fight for independence in 1804. The Petro loa incorporates 'the rage against the evil fate which the African suffered, the brutality of his displacement and his enslavement' (Deren 1953: 62), and eventually gives the slaves the moral force to pursue independence. Throughout, these descriptions—themselves excerpts from Deren's book—are given in the language of an insider who very benevolently explains the facts of this society to an outsider.

Although superficially the film does not have much resemblance to Deren's earlier films—partly because Divine Horsemen is her only documentary film—there are important themes that link the film with her broader work. Like the majority of her films, Divine Horsemen is concerned with dance and body movement as an aesthetic form of communication. The film also focuses on an aspect of a theme that is core to Deren's other work: transformation of identities. It seems that all these concerns amalgamate in Divine Horsemen in a way unforeseen by Deren herself. The inclusion of voudoun in her life stands as an experience that transformed her personally and as an artist. Deren herself read her inability to edit her material as a sign of the power of voudoun: 'I had begun as an artist [...] I end by recording, as humbly and accurately as I can, the logics of a reality which had forced me to recognize its integrity, and to abandon my manipulations' (Deren 1953: 6).

JACOBIA DAHM

See also: Deren, Maya

Divine Horsemen: The Living Gods of Haiti, (US, 1947–51/1977, 52 mins). Directed by Maya Deren. Cinematography by Maya Deren. Sound recorded by Maya Deren. Film editor: Cherel Ito. Sound editor: Teiji Ito. Narrators: John Genke and Joan Pape. Titles and animation: Yudel Kyler. The narration was adapted from Deren's book *Divine Horsemen: The Living Gods of Haiti* (1953).

Further reading

Arnheim, Rudolf, 'To Maya Deren', in P. Adams Sitney (ed.), *Film Culture Reader*, New York: Praeger, 1970: 84–6.

Brakhage, Stan, *Film at Wit's End. Eight Avant-Garde Filmmakers*, New York: McPherson & Company, 1989.

Clark, Veve Amasasa, Hodson, Millicent, Neiman, Catrina and Bailey, Francine, *The Legend of Maya Deren: A Documentary Biography and Collected Works, Volume I, Part I: Signatures, Part II: Chambers (1942–47)*, New York: Anthology Film Archives, 1984–88.

Deren, Maya, *Divine Horsemen: The Living Gods of Haiti*, Foreword by Joseph Campbell, London: Thames and Hudson, 1953.

Epple, George M., 'Divine Horsemen: The Living Gods of Haiti', film review, *American Anthropologist* 84, no. 4, December 1982: 979–80.

Nichols, Bill (ed.), *Maya Deren and the American Avant-Garde*, Berkeley, CA: University of California Press, 2001.

O'Pray, Michael, *Avant-Garde Film: Forms, Themes and Passions*, London: Wallflower Press, 2003.

Ruby, Rich B., *Chick Flicks: Theories and Memories of the Feminist Film Movement*, Durham, NC: Duke University Press, 1998.

Sitney, P. Adams, *Visionary Film: The American Avant-Garde*, Oxford: Oxford University Press, 1979.

Sullivan, Moira, 'Maya Deren's Ethnographic Representation of Ritual and Myth in Haiti', in Bill Nichols (ed.), *Maya Deren and the American Avant-Garde*, Berkeley, CA: University of California Press, 2001: 207–34.

Warren, Charles (ed.), *Beyond Document. Essays on Nonfiction Film*, Hanover, NM: University Press of New England, 1996.

Wilcken, Lois, 'Divine Horsemen: The Living Gods of Haiti', review of film, book, and audio recordings, *Ethnomusicology* vol. 30, no. 2 (spring–summer) 1986: 313–18.

Dockers

(UK, Anderson, 1999)

Dockers stands at the ambiguous intersection between feature and documentary film. It tells the story of a fictitious family's involvement in an historical event: the industrial dispute at Liverpool Docks from 1995 to 1998. What is unique about the film, though, is that it has been written, acted, produced, and televised, in part, by participants of the dispute, with the intention of documenting their experiences during this dispute.

In September 1995 Mersey Docks sacked five hundred Liverpool dockers for refusing to cross the picket line raised by fellow dockers over a labour rights dispute. Dockers narrates the events of the strike from the dockers' point of view. It focuses in particular on the life of one family, the Waltons, in which both father and son are caught up in the strike. The story's starting point is the days immediately before the strike—the miserable working conditions on the dockside—and it continues up to the workers' defeat twenty-eight months later, when three hundred dockers were paid off with £28,000 each.

Dockers was written as a three-part television drama and televised in the summer of 1999. In Dockers the fact-fiction boundary is an intricate one. The sacked dockers and their wives themselves—in workshops run by the Workers' Educational Association (WEA)—wrote the screenplay and successively signed a contract for the screenplay to be televised. Moreover, even though the film uses professional actors in many key roles, some of the dockers who wrote the script also acted in the film, although they do not play themselves. Actors play alongside nonactors and together they reconstruct a dramatized version of reality. All this makes Dockers a drama that could be described as a 'creative treatment of actuality' (Rotha 1952: 70).

As is the nature of a television drama, Dockers focuses more on the individual and private repercussions of the strike than on the collective and political ones. It uses the development of these personal narratives to move from one dramatic sequence to the next. The drama of the film is heightened by a focus on two brothers, one who supports the strike, and dies as a result of the hardship of the strike, and the other, who, to support his family, turns 'scab' and crosses the picket line, losing the friendship and support of all around him. The music—for the most part a highly dramatic refrain carried by multiple violins and intended to draw in the audience emotionally—complements the dramatic structure and adds to the tension of the story.

Dockers continues a long tradition of the representation of working-class lives in British film. It works by juxtaposing the public and the private aspects of the conflict into a tightly woven tableau of interrelations, where the fight of the dockers and their families touches all spheres of life and all is political. Despite the focus on the personal experience of fictitious characters, the film follows a tight script, aimed at conveying as much historical information about the politics of the strike as possible. Alongside a representation of the daily struggles of the working class is a more bitter critique of the unions that failed the dockers—despite huge international support for their actions—and ultimately of the new left Labour government of Tony Blair.

JACOBIA DAHM

Selected films

Dockers (UK, 1999, 90 mins). Directed by Bill Anderson. Script by Jimmy McGovern, Irvine Welsh, and the Dockers of the Writers' Workshop. Produced for Channel 4 by Parallax Pictures and The Initiative Factory. Cinematography by Cinders Forshaw. Edited by Kristina Hetherington. Music by Nick Bicât. Filmed in Liverpool, London, and Dublin.

1999 Writing the Wrongs (Planet Wild)

Further reading

Bruzzi, Stella, *New Documentary: A Critical Introduction*, New York: Routledge, 2000.

Gibbons, Fiachra, 'Union Leader is Traitor in Strikers' Film', *The Guardian*, 2 July 1999, www.guardian.co.uk/uk_news/story/0,293276,00.html

Lawson, Mark, 'Work Experience', *The Guardian* 5 July 1999, www.guardian.co.uk/tv_and_radio/story/0,290518,00.html

Lay, Samantha, *British Social Realism: From Documentary to Brit Grit*, (Short Cuts 15), London: Wallflower Press, 2002.

Rotha, Paul, *The Documentary Film*, second edn, London: Faber & Faber, [1935] 1952.

Rowbotham, Sheila and Beynon, Huw (eds), *Looking at Class: Film, Television and the Working Class in Britain*, London: Rivers Oram Press, 2001.

Dont Look Back

(US, Pennebaker, Leacock, 1967)

Donn Alan Pennebaker's Dont Look Back [sic] is the prototypical rock performance/tour movie, a genre that promises an all-access pass to the onstage, backstage, and offstage arenas of the life of a public figure. Reveling in direct cinema's ability to provide unprecedented access to its subject, Dont Look Back goes well beyond simply documenting Bob Dylan's 1965 concert tour of England, by criticizing attempts by more traditional media to label the young singer-songwriter, by turns, a precocious teen idol, an anarchist, and a poet. Dylan's propensity for 'playing' these roles for the camera while offstage raises the question of whether or not the singer-songwriter participates in this packaging process as he negotiates the swirl of adulation generated by his breakneck accomplishments as an emerging young artist.

As a performance-based observational documentary, Dont Look Back depends on Bob Dylan's ease before the camera. The brash and opinionated young Dylan's effusive willingness to speak for himself during press conferences, onstage performances, and offstage critiques of news reports about him makes him the perfect subject for a documentary that celebrates direct cinema's superiority to older forms of journalistic reportage such as print and radio. However, Dont Look Back also revels in the paradox inherent in its ostensibly objective presentation of a subject with an established public persona.

A shot during which Pennebaker follows Dylan as he strolls from a dressing room, down a dark passageway, and out onto a brightly lit stage to deafening applause exemplifies direct cinema's greatest advantage over radio and print media: its ability 'to go into a situation and simply film what you see there, what happens there, what goes on, and let everybody decide whether it tells them' about an event of public significance (Levin 1971: 235). Incumbent in this goal is a journalistic philosophy of filmmaking that insists that objectivity can be achieved by simply documenting an event and allowing the audience to decide for itself its newsworthy implications. In foregrounding the role of the journalist, direct cinema afforded Pennebaker the ability to mount a critique of other more traditional newsgathering practices on the basis of a realist style that characterizes photography, television news, radio interviews, and newspaper reports as inferior because of their subjective dependence on an intermediary to select and organize facts and details into a story.

For this reason, Pennebaker resisted attempts by critics to elicit an admission that Dont Look Back also harbors a hidden agenda of organizing details into a subjective construction of 'Bob Dylan'. On one hand, the director described Dylan as a 'guy acting out his life' and gleefully noted that someone had performed part of Dont Look Back onstage. On the other hand, Pennebaker insisted that 'you couldn't fake it in a hundred years' and that 'if there's any artistry in what I do, it is deciding who to turn this fearsome machine on' (Levin 1971: 241, 261).

Dont Look Back delights in revealing the constructed nature of press images and words. By allowing Dylan to speak for himself, the film launches both direct and indirect criticisms of print journalism. During a seven-minute retort to a *Time* magazine reporter, Dylan notes the potential for human error in newsgathering ('You might hear the wrong words' and 'You have to weed it out—I can't teach you to weed it out'); the impossibility of objectivity in print journalism ('There's no ideas in *Time* magazine, there's just these facts'); and print's implicit use of social and cultural guidelines to 'frame' the meaning of a news event ('I mean, it's a certain class of people that take the magazine seriously'). To be sure, Dylan simultaneously effaces direct cinema's own subjectivity by defining the truth as 'just a plain picture', evading in the process any recognition of documentary's construction of truth through its juxtaposition of strips of celluloid frames. For example, Pennebaker contrasts Dylan's assertion to a reporter that he doesn't compose music or write lyrics while on the road with a scene of the songwriter hunching over a typewriter in his hotel room. While it is impossible to tell if Dylan is composing a song, the indisputable evidence provided by Pennebaker's 'picture logic' suggests that the interviewer who relies on Dylan's 'word logic' is more likely to get it wrong (Hall 1998: 232).

In a similar condemnation of radio as a newsgathering technique, Pennebaker abruptly cuts short an interview that begins with a BBC reporter asking, 'How did it all begin for you, Bob? How did you get started?' As Dylan organizes a reply, Pennebaker suddenly cuts to even earlier footage of the singer accompanying himself on acoustic guitar and singing before a group of black men, apparently farm workers, in a rural setting. The timing of the cut again implies that if a picture is worth a thousand words then radio simply cannot convey the truth as vividly as direct cinema. That the director chose to include the pre-interview segment at all is perhaps best understood on the basis of how it upholds the film's agenda of flaunting its own ostensible verisimilitude. That Pennebaker shows the radio interviewer submitting his four questions to his subject for prior approval suggests that the director is once again criticizing the false spontaneity of the interview and the contrived nature of Dylan's pre-formulated responses.

In Dont Look Back's final scene, Pennebaker and his subject launch one last fusillade at the mainstream media. Responding to another printed attempt to label him, Dylan sighs, 'Give the "anarchist" a cigarette. A singer such as I. It probably took them a while to think of that name.' While the comment on one level offers a conclusive critique of the press's propensity for packaging Dylan, on another plane it stakes out direct cinema's position as a decidedly liberal rather than revolutionary reportage style. In the tradition of the press's role as provocateur of public discussion, Dont Look Back offers the deceptively simple claim that detached observation can yield objective truth while masking its own implicit—albeit inspired—construction of reality.

CHARLES LEE

See also: Pennebaker, D.A.

Dont Look Back (US, 1967, 60 mins). Distributed by LPI. Produced by Albert Grossman and John Cort. Directed by Donn Alan Pennebaker. Cinematography by Howard Alk and Jones Alk. Edited by Donn Alan Pennebaker. Sound directed by Bob Van Dyke and Jones Alk.

Further reading

Allen, Robert C. and Gomery, Douglas, *Film History: Theory and Practice*, New York: Knopf, 1985.

Bernard, Jami, 'Review of Dont Look Back', *New York Post*, September 4, 1992: 92.

Gilliatt, Penelope, 'The Current Cinema: Under Thirty', *New Yorker*, September 9, 1967: 109–16.

Hall, Jeanne, '"Don't You Ever Just Watch?": American Cinéma Vérité and Dont Look Back', in Barry Keith Grant and Jeannette Sloniowski (eds), *Documenting the Documentary: Close Readings of Documentary Film and Video*, Detroit: Wayne State University Press, 1998.

Issari, Mohammad Ali, *Cinema Verite*, East Lansing, MI: Michigan State University Press, 1971.

Levin, G. Roy, 'D.A. Pennebaker', in *Documentary Explorations: 15 Interviews with Film-makers*, Garden City, NY: Doubleday, 1971.

Mamber, Stephen, *Cinéma Vérité in America: Studies in Uncontrolled Documentary*, Cambridge, MA: MIT Press, 1974.

Maslin, Janet, 'Bob Dylan', in Jim Miller (ed.), *The Rolling Stone Illustrated History of Rock and Roll*, New York: Random House/Rolling Stone Press, 1980.

Rosenthal, Alan, *The New Documentary in Action: A Case-book in Film Making*, Berkeley, CA: University of California Press, 1971.

Drew, Robert

Aided and inspired as much by the programming opportunities in the still-developing medium of television as by technological improvements that added to a filmmaker's mobility, Robert Drew shares a reputation with his collaborator Richard Leacock as the father of 'direct cinema'. Drew Associates, the company they founded in the 1950s, produced seminal films that shaped what would become known as cinéma vérité and offered a new, intimate way of looking at news events.

As a photographer for the weekly magazine *Life*, Drew became interested in moving documentary film away from the authoritarian model of John Grierson and others and toward the 'candid' viewpoint offered by photojournalism. After a year's fellowship at Harvard exploring his theories, Drew made an unsuccessful effort to develop a news show for NBC, but the results were unaired. Convinced that television remained the best vehicle for the films he envisioned, and inspired by the similarly minded Leacock, Drew obtained sponsorship from his former publisher, Time-Life, which owned a few television stations and was interested in developing programming for them. Drew and Leacock formed Drew Associates in 1957 and began to explore the methods that would eventually become the standard techniques of direct cinema: multiple camera crews using lightweight, portable equipment and synchronized sound recording, combined with an objective approach to the subject which allowed no outside, authoritative narrative voice molding the viewers' perceptions.

After three years of producing short films designed to coincide with stories in *Life*, Drew and his team filmed what is commonly regarded as the first important work to come from Drew Associates. For Primary, Drew and Leacock, aided by D.A. Pennebaker and Albert Maysles, among others, spent five days covering the simultaneous efforts of two US Senators, John F. Kennedy and Hubert Humphrey, as they campaigned in the Wisconsin primary for the

Democratic presidential nomination. With its close, intimate focus on the campaigners, the film caught not only the details of a political campaign but also the historical moment in which style and image came to dominate the political process; Kennedy and his glamorous wife mesmerize their audience through sheer movie star charm, making Humphrey's earnest but old-fashioned baby-kissing and hand-shaking style seem quaintly archaic by comparison.

Drew's narrative approach to documentary can be summed up by the title of one of his most recognized films, Crisis: Behind a Presidential Commitment. For the 1963 film showing the behind-the-scenes reaction from the White House as the first black students prepared their court-ordered integration of the University of Alabama, Drew benefited from his previous access to Kennedy, who understood the importance of the media. Crisis, however, is also the implicit subject of many of the Drew Associates films of that period, which tend to focus on a group or an individual as they face a major decision within a set period of time: a young heroin addict faces a week without drugs (David), Jane Fonda rehearses a short-lived Broadway play (Jane), attorneys try to have a death sentence overturned in the week before the scheduled execution (The Chair).

Working in a challenging period while US media was changing rapidly, the Drew films set many of the standard operational methods for documentary filmmaking, but the interest and support of the television broadcasting companies proved to be unreliable. While Leacock, Pennabaker, the Maysles brothers, and other filmmakers who worked for Drew continued to develop his model of an intimate and immediate form of film journalism, they turned to theatrical distribution to counter the indifference and interference of network television.

ROBERT HUNT

Biography

Born Toledo, Ohio, US, February 15, 1924.

Selected films

1960 Primary
1960 Yanki No!
1961 Adventures on the New Frontier
1961 Football (Mooney vs. Fowle)
1962 The Chair
1963 Crisis: Behind a Presidential Commitment
1966 Storm Signal
1974 On the Road with Duke Ellington

Further reading

Mamber, Stephen, *Cinéma Vérité in America: Studies in Uncontrolled Documentary*, Cambridge, MA: MIT Press, 1974.

Monaco, James, 'American Documentary Since 1960', in Richard Roud (ed.), *Cinema: A Critical Dictionary, Volume One*, New York: Viking Press, 1980.

Musser, Charles, 'Extending the Boundaries: Cinema-Verite and the New Documentary', in Geoffrey Nowell-Smith (ed.), *The Oxford History of World Cinema*, Oxford: Oxford University Press, 1996.

Drifters

(UK, Grierson, 1929)

Drifters (1929) encapsulates many of the paradoxes of the British documentary film movement, both in itself and in terms of how it is perceived. Sandwiched ideologically and aesthetically between the cinema of Robert Flaherty and the agitprop of the Soviet Union, John Grierson's directorial debut was both the annunciation of a new type of cinema for the United Kingdom and an attestation of its potential failings. Nominally a record of the working lives of herring fishermen working off the coast of Britain, the film charts the activities of an industrial flotilla of fishing boats and the role of their crew in bringing 'the harvest of the sea' to the market of the world. It is divided into four parts, beginning with the departure of the men, proceeding through their casting of their nets before bedding down for the night, reaching a climax with the retrieval of the loaded nets in anticipation of a storm, and concluding with the cargo being brought to port, where it is bartered and packaged for delivery to the market.

Drifters was made with the avowed aim of documenting the hithertofore largely unrepresented life of the British working class and exploring the role their labour played in the physical and psychic fabric of the age of steam and steel. Representation of this section of society to date had mostly consisted of comic burlesques in fiction films in which actual labour played no part. Grierson's determination to change this came both as part of a general move toward realism to counter the increasing illusionism proffered by fiction film and as part of a more specific attempt to 'open, for Britain, a new vista of film reference' (Grierson 1938) by establishing reality-based filmmaking as an instrument of propaganda and education. Inspired by the political ideals of Soviet cinema, Grierson envisioned factual film as a conduit via which the experience of life need not be bound by geography or economic circumstance, but could be expanded through cinematic interconnection that showed one section of society how the others actually lived and worked.

The film went into production in the summer of 1928 with the New Era Film Company, known mostly for promotional shorts. Drifters was originally to be one of four films produced by the Empire Marketing Board that year as part of a package of educational/promotional material. It is said that the selection of this subject was partly an attempt to curry favour with the Treasury, the Financial Secretary of which was among the country's leading authorities on the fishing industry. The film would eventually cost just short of £3,000. It was shot silently, with Grierson serving as both director and editor, assisted by cinematographer Basil Emmott, then known as one of Britain's most accomplished cameramen. Grierson himself had almost no practical experience of filmmaking, although he had been observing and writing about it since the early 1920s. At the time, he wrote, 'What I know of cinema I have learned partly from the Russians, partly from the American westerns, and partly from Flaherty' (Grierson 1966: 136).

Superficially, Drifters demonstrates the influence of Flaherty most plainly. Its photographic style and narrative structure follow patterns of observation and visual storytelling used by Flaherty on Nanook of the North (1922) and Moana: A Romance of the South Seas (1926). Although less explicit in its use of character, it concentrates on observing real people in a mixture of real and recreated environments in the course of routine tasks that supposedly make up their everyday lives. It collects the action into an overall 'story', then segments this story into broad narrative movements that are illustrated with anecdotal and illustrative detail. Its opening scenes portray fishermen departing their village and use repeated images of waves crashing against the shore. The combination of imagery prefigures Flaherty's Man of Aran (1934), while its sentimental intertitles signal an attempt to distance the film from Flaherty by hesitantly suggesting that it will document a moment in which the traditions of the past are giving way to technological and industrial progress.

The film is fraught with formal tensions, as if, regardless of its polemical objectives, it is uncertain as to whether or not the exaltation of the labours of the working man within the industrial infrastructure is enough in itself to sustain an emotional connection with the audience. Grierson responds by taking a Flahertyesque turn to the poetic, although he avoids the excesses of romanticism because of the continued presence of technological imagery and because of the subject's stated direct connection with contemporary social reality.

Drifters departs from Flaherty and moves toward the Soviets in its attempts to integrate its observation of the rhythms of man and the sea with industrial imagery. It establishes a dialectical relationship between the surface and the underneath through a form of montage that, although less pronounced than that employed by Eisenstein, nonetheless betrays his influence. Grierson had garnered experience as an editor by working on the print of Battleship Potemkin (Eisenstein, 1925) being prepared for exhibition in the United Kingdom. According to Basil Wright (1976), 'to work with him at the editing bench was a liberal education'. As such, it is in its editing that Drifters assumed a more radical aspect. Shots of boats forging their way through the waves are intercut with images of pistons and engines, and the sight of a man shovelling coal into the furnace below decks informs our perception of the operations above where a sea captain barks silent orders at his crew. Emblemetic imagery of scavenging dogfish stealing herring from the nets at night and ragged seagulls pecking and squabbling over the catch while men in suits barter for the payload indicate ideological awareness.

The film is organized around a series of physical conflicts: between land and sea, sea and boats, men and boats, fish and men, men and nets, nets and fish. It illustrates these tensions with close observation of the energies involved, be they expended preparing the boats for launch, fuelling and driving them at sea, letting out the nets, catching fish, or preparing them for market. It also uses conflict, or the expectation of conflict, to supply the climax: the fishermen suit up in rain gear and prepare to haul in the nets as the storm moves in. Although Flahertyesque in one sense, these contests are portrayed within an overall rhythmic structure that demonstrates some attempt to create imagistic and intellectual collision reminiscent of the work of the Soviets. The film is also, like Eisenstein's, driven by a sense of movement, not only in terms of the overall story, but within individual frames and sequences where images are rarely static. Almost every shot is filled with objects or elements in constant motion, and many are filmed from the deck of actual ships being tossed on the waves. The rise and fall of the horizon makes for an onomatopoeic representation of the experience of being on board one of the boats. Imagistic and ideological conflict coupled with a sense of visual and social movement are cornerstones of montage, yet the film still seems to lean more towards Flaherty than Eisenstein. There is an underlying sense that the rhythms of the fishermen's lives are congruent with those of the sea, not quite to the point of the neo-Rousseauianism of Flaherty's work, but still demonstrating what Ian Aitken terms a 'pantheistic humanism' (Aitken 1998) not too far from it. Meanwhile, the relationship between labour and production is not framed so much by an overarching dialectic of society or economy as by a simpler, more mechanical attempt to illustrate the process of production (fishing) in an informative, expositional, and educational way.

The film is of questionable value as a social document insofar as the term implies an engagement with society that extends beyond the specific instance of social reality that it represents. The section of the film that has come in for most criticism in this regard is the final one, which undertakes to contextualise the activities of the fishermen by suggesting that they are part of a larger economic and social infrastructure. A series of uncomfortable juxtapositions attempt to link imagery of the fish being prepared for shipping with white-collar commerce and trade. Images are quite literally blended together by superimposition, clumsily forcing connections between them in an attempt to convince the audience of a breadth of social analysis that is simply not present. The film concludes with faintly elegiac intertitles suggesting that what has been seen is merely the first link in a great chain of commerce and enterprise, but it does not in itself attempt to chart it.

Brian Winston, citing David Schrire, has referred to this as a 'flight from social meaning' (Winston 1995), a deliberate avoidance of the issues raised by social representation by recourse to the poetic. Winston sees this failure as symptomatic of the British documentary film movement on the whole. The recourse to the poetic is, he argues, endemic to the methodology of Grierson's 'creative treatment of actuality', which, as he says, 'depends on an assumption of a particular naivety in the audience. Without such naivety, the audience could not believe that anything of the real would survive "creative treatment".' Harry Alan Potamkin, writing on the film's original release, went deeper into its structural weaknesses by observing that Grierson had failed to understand that true power of montage cinema was cumulative. Though Potamkin recognised the qualities that Grierson had brought to individual scenes, he noted that the scenes were separated from one another on a level of deeper meaning. This prevented the film on the whole from achieving results at the measure of the political aesthetics of the Soviets. 'This was a film intended to show labor. If Mr. Grierson thought to extend it to inferences beyond the facts of toil, to the total economy of exploitation, his attempts at inter-reference between sea and market, fisher and broker, were certainly too inadequate' (Potamkin 1979).

In spite of its flaws, Drifters had enormous impact. It was famously premiered at the London Film Society on November 10, 1929 in a double-bill with Grierson's edit of Battleship Potemkin, and drew largely favourable notices. Its portrayal of the working class was seen as a triumph for the common man, and Grierson's direction was singled out for praise by many contemporary commentators. Many observers saw the film as a preferable alternative to Potemkin. Its humanism was more easily subsumed into a socially democratic conception of state-sponsored cinema. The film subsequently received screenings at a number of commercial venues, and was also shown at the House of Commons by special request. A year after its release Drifters had recouped its production costs. Its success cemented the Empire Marketing Board's commitment to documentary film as a component of its publicity and promotional activities. The EMB Film Unit was officially established in 1930, by which time Grierson had already begun to gather talented young amateur filmmakers of similar mind to himself to make more of the same. As Erik Barnouw observed, 'After Drifters, they flocked to the Grierson banner' (Barnouw 1993).

HARVEY O'BRIEN

Drifters (UK, New Era Film Company, 1929, 49 mins). Produced and distributed by the Empire Marketing Board. Directed, written, and edited by John Grierson. Photography by Basil Emmott.

Further reading

Aitken, Ian, 'Introduction', in Ian Aitken (ed.), *The Documentary Film Movement: An Anthology*, Edinburgh: Edinburgh University Press, 1998.

Barnouw, Erik, *Documentary: A History of the Non-Fiction Film*, second edn, New York: Oxford University Press, 1993.

Grierson, John, 'The Course of Realism', in Charles Davy (ed.), *Footnotes to the Film*, London: Readers' Union, 1938.

——*Grierson on Documentary*, Berkeley, CA: University of California Press, 1966.

——'Drifters', in Ian Aitken (ed.), *The Documentary Film Movement: An Anthology*, Edinburgh: Edinburgh University Press, 1998.

Potamkin, Harry Alan, 'Grierson's Drifters', in Lewis Jacobs (ed.), *The Documentary Tradition*, second edn, New York: Norton, 1979.

Swann, Paul, *The British Documentary Film Movement, 1926–46*, Cambridge: Cambridge University Press, 1989.

Winston, Brian, *Claiming the Real: The Documentary Film Revisited*, London: BFI, 1995.

Wright, Basil, *The Long View: An International History of Cinema*, Herts: Paladin, 1976.

Dyke, Willard Van

Willard Van Dyke, originally a photographer, joined the world of film as one of three cinematographers on Pare Lorentz's The River (1937). Along with a number of writers, playwrights, filmmakers, and others prominent in the arts at the time, he became associated with the left-wing organization Nykino, which metamorphosed into Frontier Films in 1937. When Van Dyke and Ralph Steiner left Frontier Films on ideological grounds, a large-scale sponsored project left with them (creating tension among some of those involved in Frontier Films which was never assuaged).

The film became The City (1939), produced for the American Institute of Planners. It promotes the concept of planned greenbelt communities detached from urban centers. Codirected and cophotographed by Steiner and Van Dyke, it was a notable success, and was well received at the New York World's Fair of 1939.

Van Dyke followed The City with Valley Town (1940). Throughout his life he considered those two films to be his best. Sponsored by the Sloan Foundation, Valley Town concerns the problem of technological unemployment. Directed by Van Dyke, the cinematography was by Roger Barlow and Bob Churchill, and the editing by Irving Lerner; the score was composed by Mark Blitzstein.

A dark view of a depressed US industrial community, Valley Town offers a partial solution to the bitter problem it examines. However, as with many American documentaries of this era, the hopeful ending seems tacked on to meet the sponsor's requirements without much conviction on the part of the film's makers. The impression that remains after viewing it is of an impersonal and vast economic system that serves few well.

Aesthetically and technically, Valley Town is remarkable in several ways. The extraordinary force and effectiveness of its images is striking. Its use of soliloquy, including some sung soliloquy, is daring.

Following the US entry into World War II, Van Dyke (with Ben Maddow) made a film for the Coordinator of Inter-American Affairs, The Bridge (1944). It is about the economies of South America and the importance of air transport in connecting its countries with each other and with North America. For the Office of War Information he made Pacific Northwest (1944), which describes and interprets the northwestern states, rarely settings for Hollywood entertainment (or other documentaries, for that matter).

After the war Van Dyke made films for industrial sponsors, such as American Frontier (1953), produced for the American Petroleum Institute. Although he retained some of the themes and style of his earlier work, a prevailing blandness replaced his originality and conviction. He also made a film about his former teacher, Edward Weston, for the United States Information Agency, entitled The Photographer (1948). He made films for television when that possibility became available, including a number for the Twentieth Century series: Ireland: The Tear and the Smile (1961), Sweden (1961), and So That Men Are Free (1962). From 1965 to 1973 he was director of the film department of the Museum of Modern Art, where he distinguished himself by being particularly interested in and supportive of emerging and young experimental and documentary filmmakers. In his retirement, he returned to his first love, still photography.

JACK C. ELLIS

See also: City, The; River, The

Biography

Born in Denver, December 5, 1906. Attended University of California, Berkeley. Photographer on government Works Progress Administration (WPA) Art Project in San Francisco, 1934; photographer for *Harper's Bazaar* magazine, 1935; cinematographer on The River, 1936–7; co-directed first film (with Ralph Steiner), The City, 1939; producer for Office of War Information's Motion Picture Bureau, 1941–5; made films for a variety of sponsors and for television, 1945–65; director of film department, Museum of Modern Art (New York City), 1965–73; vice-president, International Federation of Film Archives. Died January 23, 1986, in Jackson, Tennessee.

E

Eiffel Tower, The

(France, Clair, 1928)

René Clair's short film La Tour (The Eiffel Tower), with a running time of fifteen minutes, is a paean to the French icon of modernity—the Eiffel Tower. The film is constructed as a cinematic postcard using rhythmical montage and editing as its poetic means of expression. Similar to the 'city symphonies', many of which were being made at the same time, Clair's film straddles the margins between documentary and experimental film in its treatment of subject matter. Traveling up and down the monument, Clair's camera emphasizes the 'iron lass' itself and the materials used to create it: the iron girders, the elevators, the cages. Clair constructs his film with sequences of varying lengths and speed, which make up a visual poem. As a hybrid genre it represents, as do many of Clair's short films, an attempt at 'pure cinema', a film that is totally free of narrative restraints, and whose subject is realized completely through the creative use of the film medium.

The Eiffel Tower was made after René Clair had completed Une Chapeau de paille d'Italie/ The Italian Straw Hat in 1927. Clair had used the French landmark as an important setting in his film, Paris qui dort (1924), and felt that he had not used it enough because of the requirements of the scenario. The director wanted to make a film ('une documentaire lyrique') expressing his adoration of the Eiffel Tower. He discussed the idea with his production company, Albatros-Kamenka, which in turn provided him with a camera and film for the project. The short film was shot on location at the Eiffel Tower during the spring of 1928, and editing was completed in the autumn of that year.

The Eiffel Tower begins with a postcard-like image of the tower standing against a cloud-filled sky. This pictorial stasis is soon broken by a rapid montage of images of portions of the tower. Clair then returns to the opening shot and fades out. The director then uses a series of short sequences, interconnected by dissolves, showing the history of the construction of the monument. Beginning with a portrait of Gustave Eiffel and architectural blueprints, the sequence progresses through the birth of the tower. The final shot of this sequence shows the completed tower with a title card that reads '1889'. Clair then uses a slow tilt all the way up the tower that fades to black. The camera then enters the structure and begins an upward ascent to the various observation decks. Clair's camera movements progress upward from shot to shot, either by tilting the camera or with 'crane shots' taken from the tower elevator. At each level Clair pauses the camera to inspect the surroundings before progressing to another upward tilt to the next platform. When Clair's camera reaches the top, it briefly looks down to observe a man below looking down on the crowd below him. The camera then begins to descend much more quickly until it reaches ground level. Clair then returns to a close shot of the top of the tower. The end of the film returns to its opening postcard-like image of the Eiffel Tower amid a cloud-filled skyline.

The Eiffel Tower can be placed in the category of the 'city symphony' in that it is concerned solely with a particular monument associated with the city of Paris. According to Richard M. Barsam, the city symphonies 'present brief and realistic views of city life, united within a larger rhythmic structure—a symphony—by the recurrence of images, motifs, and themes that provide continuity and progression of ideas' (Barsam 1992). Two of the most famous city symphonies, Alberto Cavalcanti's Rien que les heures (1926) and Walther Ruttmann's Berlin: The Symphony of a Great City (1927), attempted to express the life of a city on film through rhythmic and associational editing. The synaesthetic montage portrait is a key element of these films. Clair uses tilts, pans, crane shots, fades, and dissolves to provide a rhythmic movement to a stationary object. Clair's technique was created in the editing room in an attempt to produce a purely cinematic portrait of the French monument. In this approach, he was probably influenced by the ideas of his brother, Henri Chomette (1896–1941), whose short film, Cinq Minutes de cinéma pur/Five Minutes of Pure Cinema, was made in 1926. Chomette had been promoting the idea of 'pure cinema' as an avant-garde form, even collaborating on a film with the artist Man Ray. The Eiffel Tower in many ways is, because of its editing technique, a realization of 'pure cinema' in that it lets the camera create an impressionistic viewpoint. When a friend suggested that his film should be accompanied by a Bach fugue, Clair made sure that was suggested to theater musicians wherever the film was shown. The mathematical precision of the fugue is the perfect accompaniment to the rhythmical cadence of Clair's editing technique.

RONALD WILSON

See also: Clair, René

The Eiffel Tower/La Tour (France, Films Albatros-Kamenka, 1928, 15 mins). Produced by Films Albatros-Kamenka. Directed by René Clair. Assistant director Georges Lacombe. Cinematography by Georges Perinal and Nicolas Roudakoff. Edited by René Clair. Filmed in Paris at the Eiffel Tower. Released by Film Albatros on December 15, 1928.

Further reading

Barsam, Richard M., *Non-Fiction Film: A Critical History*, Bloomington: Indiana University Press, 1992.

Dale, R.C., *The Films of René Clair*, Metuchen, NJ: Scarecrow Press, 1986.

Greene, Naomi, *René Clair: A Guide to References and Resources*, Boston: G.K. Hall, 1985.

Loyrette, Henri, *Gustave Eiffel*, New York: Rizzoli, 1985.

McGerr, Celia, *René Clair*, Boston: Twayne Publishers, 1980.

Elton, Arthur

The career of Arthur Elton is an exemplar of John Grierson's approach to appointing and developing young, traditionally trained university graduates into documentary filmmakers throughout the 1930s in Britain and thereafter in Canada and Australia. Stuart Legg, Humphrey Jennings, and Basil Wright were Elton's contemporaries at Cambridge University. As an undergraduate in English Literature and Psychology, as well as *Granta*'s film critic, Elton embodied the qualities sought by Grierson and joined the screenwriting department at Gainsborough in 1927 under Michael Balcon.

While at Gainsborough, Elton was encouraged by Ian Dalrymple to script and shoot a documentary about London, a film never finished. When the studios burned down, Elton immediately applied for a job at the Empire Marketing Board (EMB) under Grierson. Of the remit of the EMB and its successor under Grierson, the General Post Office (GPO) Film Unit, Grierson was later to state in part: 'When it came to making industry not ugly for people, but a matter of beauty, so that people would accept their industrial selves [...] who initiated the finding of beauty in industry?' (Hardy 1966: 91).

Arthur Elton's earliest works with the GPO Film Unit exactly matched this ideal. In speaking of his young directors, Grierson also noted that: 'In the three years that followed (the founding of the GPO Film Unit in 1930) we gathered and, in a sense, created Basil Wright, Arthur Elton [...] Wright was the best lyrical director in the country, Elton the best industrial [director] ' (Hardy 1966: 167).

Elton's Aero-Engine (1933, silent), however, is elegantly photographed in black and white and is an intricate and richly detailed observation of every step in the making of an aircraft engine. Narrative is subordinated to the internal visual rhythms of the industrial flow, and the film lies almost more in the tradition of films like Berlin: The Symphony of a Great City (Ruttmann, 1927) than in the realist propaganda mode so often espoused by Rotha and Grierson.

> I was asked to make a film on British craftsmanship, particularly in the aeroplane industry, so I made Aero-Engine, which took me at once into engineering [...] I became fascinated with the processes and the people.
>
> (Elton in Sussex 1976: 32)

Elton's fascination with craft and manufacturing set this work apart from the more formal artistic experimentations of Ruttmann or Richter. His eye was always on the actual work, the design flowing into the final metal stamping. He was, in that sense, close to a director of drama in following the action and then cutting in the editing suite to make the narrative clearer.

Elton's Voice of the World (1932) also revealed elements of stylistic experimentation. Paul Rotha was later to reflect that the film was the first documentary: 'at any rate in Britain which used sound at all imaginatively' (Rotha 1973: 162).

Just as with Aero-Engine, Elton had experimented with the formal flows of industrial process. When he came to make Housing Problems, Elton (with Edgar Anstey) tried out new ways of using the soundtrack in a documentary film. Directed for the British Commercial Gas Association by Elton and Edgar Anstey, the film used no omniscient narrator, but rather a linked series of slum dwellers on location (in freezing kitchens, hallways) talking directly to the camera and offering a sound montage on the failures of modern housing policy.

One of the narrators, a woman detailing heroic struggles with a rat, offers a direct way into the experience, for all the 'amateur' delivery of her words. Arthur Elton had also used direct address or spontaneous and unrehearsed speech in an earlier GPO film, Workers and Jobs (1935), but Housing Problems used the more tentative experiments of the earlier film to more powerful effect—foreshadowing the effects of British television documentary makers of the 1960s (notably Loach and Watkins) and beyond. John Grierson was to comment:

> Housing Problems is not so well made nor so brilliant in technical excitements but something speaks within it that touches the conscience. These other films 'uplift', Housing Problems transforms and will not let you forget.
>
> (Grierson in Hardy 1966: 216)

As Production Chief of the Films Division of the Ministry of Information during the War, Elton presided over the making of some superb footage, but also continued the running battle forever run by filmmakers on matters of both budget and policy. Immediately after the war Elton revealed a Griersonian ability to be influential everywhere, from acting as Film Adviser to the Film Department in the British Zone of Germany to, later, on invitation, producing a group of films on 'Social Denmark' to which many outstanding filmmakers including Carl Dreyer contributed.

As he had in the GPO and Gas Association years, Elton became a leading filmmaker for industrial sponsors, taking over the prewar Shell Film Unit from Edgar Anstey and acting as its 'able guiding spirit' (Barnouw 1977: 214) as he moved to widen the remit and scope of the unit's work after the war, producing films as ambitious and successful as Louisiana Story (Robert Flaherty, 1948) and, in Australia, Back of Beyond (John Heyer, 1954).

Elton's work at Shell cannot be judged in any traditional sense as advertising work; indeed, the company policy excluded references to any Shell product or to the company itself in the film. In the 1950s, however, films like Grand Prix (1949) and 21st Monte Carlo Car Rally (1951) were palpably 'Shell products'.

JONATHAN DAWSON

See also: Anstey, Edgar; Grierson, John; Housing Problems

Biography

Attended Cambridge University, studied English literature and psychology. Joined the screenwriting department at Gainsborough in 1927 under Michael Balcon. Made documentaries at Shell and Film Centre. Worked as a freelancer before his death on January 1, 1973.

Selected films

1932 Voice of the World: director
1933 Aero-Engine (silent): director
1935 Workers and Jobs: director
1935 Housing Problems: director
1939 The Obedient Flame (McLaren): producer
1940 Transfer of Skill (Bell): producer

1948 Louisiana Story (Flaherty): producer
1954 Back of Beyond (Heyer): producer

Further reading

Balcon, Michael, *A Lifetime of Films*, London: Hutchinson, 1969.

Barnouw, Erik, *Documentary: A History of the Non-Fiction Film*, Oxford: Oxford University Press, 1977.

Dawson, Jonathan, 'A Brief History of the Documentary: The 1930s', in Ross Lansell and Peter Beilby (eds), *The Documentary Film in Australia*, Melbourne: Cinema Papers, 1984.

Hardy, Forsyth, *Grierson on Documentary*, London: Collins (revised edn), 1966.

Rotha, Paul, *Documentary Film*, London: Faber, 1933 (revised 1952).

——*Documentary Diary*, New York: Hill and Wang, 1973.

Sussex, Elizabeth, *The Rise and Fall of British Documentary*, London: Faber & Faber, 1976.

Emigholz, Heinz

Heinz Emigholz is highly regarded as an experimental filmmaker, but his body of work owes much to the aesthetics of documentary film in combination with a variety of ideas derived from the tradition of early film theory. Coming from a background as a plastic artist, Emigholz adopted early the notion that not only the film stock, but also time itself, captured onto the emulsion of the film base, is a material of its own and therefore can be shaped by filmmakers in any way they want. The premise of this thinking was the conviction that in the age of recording technology, time had become such an abstract concept that the cinematic representation of time can be analyzed based on its technical and physical occurrence. As a consequence, Emigholz suggests that any filmmaker should always take into account the constructiveness of the technically reproduced motion (in opposition to the real-life motion).

With his first experiments, the short film cycle Schenec-Tady I–III (1972–5), Arrowplane (1973–4), and Tide (1974), Emigholz examined the process of cinematic motion and also established some key issues for his later films: (1) the parameters of time, architecture/landscapes, and memory; (2) the interaction of time and space in the continuity of the moving image; and (3) the moving image as an 'imaginary architecture within time' (Emigholz 1991). The method used in these early experiments was rather simple: Emigholz dismantled the linear motion of pan shots of landscapes into their smallest units, frames of a 1/24th second, which he then 'reanimated' according to a complicated mathematical scheme, comparable to a musical score. The results were complex visual compositions, 'artificially generated with cinematic time and real-life motion' (Emigholz). With his long-time project Photography and Beyond (1999–), Emigholz later returned to the principal ideas of his early work; however, at that time he had developed a less theoretical form of representation of time and space that would manifest within the aesthetical framework of documentary film.

With his examination of the process of technically reproduced motion, Emigholz indirectly referred to Roland Barthes's notion that the 'filmic image', removed from a chronological continuity, reveals a 'third sense': a disruption of its immediate significance as part of a pictorial sequence. The nature of film, according to Barthes, lies beyond the film itself. Emigholz picked up Barthes's conception of the single frame, applying the idea of its outer-filmic reality onto the motion picture. He considered the technicity of the medium as the key to this 'other', metaphysical reality; however, metaphysics was never his concern. Emigholz's theories did not drift into areas of irrationality, although the common use of image/sound asynchronicity and experimental printing techniques indeed projected a ghostly aura onto his 1980s films.

Throughout the 1970s, Emigholz had pursued a personal project of long-term observations titled Eine kleine Enzyklopädie des Alltags: Wohnen, Essen, Schlafen, Räume, Straßen, Verkehr/A Little Encyclopaedia of the Everyday: Living, Eating, Sleeping, Space, Streets, Traffic, which would mark a link to his narrative films of the 1980s. Sequences of this project, randomly shot on 16mm footage, were included in his first feature film, Normalsatz (1982). Normalsatz was Emigholz's departure from a strictly formalist method toward a less structured, narrative-based essay form. The fact that Emigholz introduced actors into one of his films for the first time was a deliberate step, as he stated, to free the experimental film from its stigma as being solely self-referential. Emigholz had always rejected the label 'structuralist film' for his own work. At that time it seemed he had lost interest in documentary film aesthetics, but Emigholz's 1980s oeuvre essentially refined the ideas of his earlier experiments and paved the ground for his later 'film-photographic' work. The angular compositions of his cinematic space were traceable back to his formalist short films, the shooting locations reflected Emigholz's fascination with extravagant architectural designs and the direction expressed a formal reference to photography, a discipline that would gain new importance in his work in the late 1990s. Emigholz's disapproval of any authoritative narrative concept had finally resulted in a open form of narrative film that he, as in his formalist short films, considered rather as 'text' than as the product of an author. His conviction that the meaning of a cultural object is brought by the audience instead of residing in the object itself, refers again to Barthes and his concept of intertextuality. The form of a narrative feature film allowed Emigholz to work with 'text' on a more literal level.

In the late 1990s Emigholz returned to a more formal approach with his still ongoing film cycle Photografie und Jenseits/Photography and Beyond. The project is conceived as a system of twenty-five freely combinable 'modules', each documenting a cultural artefact, and structured into topical groups as buildings, sculptures, paintings, photos, or historical documents. According to Emigholz, Photographie und Jenseits is intended to recall the origins of cinema and its ability to depict space and objects in a 'preconditioned' state. As a consequence of this premise Emigholz dismissed the idea of montage in order to present these artefacts in a deliberately 'undramatic' way. It is his pivotal concern to document the spatial relations of these artefacts as realistically as possible. Every film is shot on 35mm stock to guarantee that the viewer's experience will not be affected by the technical limitations of electronic recording systems.

Goff in der Wüste/Goff in the Desert (2003), the seventh film in the cycle, is the most elaborate example of Emigholz's 'film-photographic' films so far. It documents twenty-six buildings by the American architect Bruce Goff, each in a series of long, motionless shots of exterior and interior parts of the architectural design. Emigholz's decision to suspend all editorial comments from the soundtrack reflects his conviction that every space can create a specific 'awareness'—apart from its external dramatization and functionalization. As another consequence, Emigholz worked only with the diegetic sound to preserve the initial experience of Goff's architecture.

This concept of 'immediate' representation within a technical-reproductive framework might seem an utterly naive approach, but it really is the essence of a thoroughly evolved, interdisciplinary art theory that Emigholz has developed during the last twenty-five years. Emigholz's film theory, in the cycle Photography and Beyond applied on documentary film aesthetics, takes into account his own experience as an artist, as well as the 'institutionalized' circumstances of the spectator-object relationship. He described his films as an empowering act against the 'passive look'. In his mission statement for Photography and Beyond, Emigholz called for a new reception of the arts: 'Seeing as an expression, not an impression'. By 'reversing the process of seeing' (Emigholz 1991), his films aspire to mediate between the viewer and his environment.

ANDREAS BUSCHE

Biography

Born 1948 near Bremen, Germany. Trained as an artist, later studied at the University Hamburg. Since 1973 has been active in various artistic disciplines, working as an independent filmmaker, director of photography, plastic artist, actor, publisher, and producer. In 1974 started to work on an encyclopedic series of documentary films titled Die Basis des Make Up. Founded his own production company Pym Films, in 1978. In 1984 finished the short film The Basis of Make-Up I, which later was recognized by Emigholz as the starting point for his film cycle Photographie und Jenseits. In the same year, published a journal that accompanied the release of The Basis of Make-Up I. His books *Krieg der Augen, Kreuz der Sinne* (1991), and *Seit Freud gesagt hat, der Künstler heile seine Neurosen selbst, heilen die Künstler ihre Neurosen selbst* (1993) served as a first introduction to Emigholz's theories of the 'arts as science'. Since 1993 Professor for Experimental Film Design at the Akademie der Künste in Berlin. In 1999 started to conceive his film cycle Photographie und Jenseits, which is still a work in progress. In 2003 he released the seventh part about the American architect Bruce Goff. There are eighteen parts still to come.

Selected films

1972–5	Schenec-Tady I–III
1973–4	Arrowplane
1974	Tide
1982	Normalsatz (Ordinary Sentence)
1999	Photografie und Jenseits (Photography and Beyond)
2003	Goff in der Wüste (Goff in the Desert)

Further reading

Emigholz, Heinz, *Krieg der Augen, Kreuz der Sinne*, Kassel: Martin Schmitz Verlag, 1991.

——*Seit Freud gesagt hat, der Künstler heile seine Neurosen selbst, heilen die Künstler ihre Neurosen selbst*, Kassel: Martin Schmitz Verlag, 1991.

——(ed.), *Normalsatz–Siebzehn Filme*, Kassel: Martin Schmitz Verlag, 2003.

——*Das schwarze Schamquadrat*, Kassel: Martin Schmitz Verlag, 2003.

Enough to Eat?

(UK, Anstey, 1936)

Enough to Eat? (The Nutrition Film) was one of the celebrated films of social enquiry produced within the British documentary film movement in the latter half of the 1930s and on which its reputation for social progressiveness rests. The films investigated contemporary social issues such as slum housing (Housing Problems, 1935), nutrition (Enough to Eat?), education (Children at School, 1937), and public health (The Smoke Menace, 1938), and attracted unprecedented popular discussion. Arthur Elton's Workers and Jobs, made at the General Post Office (GPO) Film Unit in 1935, influenced this group of films. This film had used location shooting in a Labour Exchange and direct sound recording to capture spontaneous, unscripted interviews with unemployed workers.

John Grierson had sought to widen the corporate sponsorship of documentary production, and an important success was the commission for a programme of five films from the British Commercial Gas Association in the mid-1930s. Arthur Elton and Edgar Anstey were responsible for the productions and, significantly, were allowed to collaborate on the choice of subject. Enough to Eat? was the second film in the series, following Housing Problems (1935), and the general approach to the series was more direct and expositional than the classic Griersonian model that combined montage with social reportage. In the absence of a suitable independent documentary film production unit, Elton and Anstey simply hired the necessary studio facilities to realise the first two films. The latter titles in the series were produced by the Realist Film Unit, which had been formed in 1937 to handle exactly this kind of commission.

Enough to Eat? is an examination into the problem of malnutrition among the working classes in Britain. The eminent scientist Julian Huxley, who occasionally speaks to the camera while seated at a desk, provides a commentary. The recent research of Sir John Orr is described and illustrated, and the results of contrasting diets are presented across various animal groups and humans. In a notable example, well-built Christ's Hospital schoolboys are compared with ill-fed, working-class boys. The principles of good nutrition are explained and, with the use of diagrams and graphs, the link between income and dietary deficiency is established. Three working-class mothers give direct-to-camera interviews about their difficulties (in the style of the pioneering Housing Problems). The methods used to deal with the problem are outlined: the provision of cheap milk in schools, free school dinners, the distribution of free meals, education in nutrition to poor mothers, and so forth. At intervals, authorities and experts give their views, including Dr G. C. M. M'Gonigle, Herbert Morrison (on the work of the London County Council), and Viscount Astor (on the work of the League of Nations).

During the interwar period, the general health of the nation was improving. Nevertheless, social investigators consistently revealed the persistence of poverty, which was condemning a significant proportion of the population to ill health. Knowledge of nutritional science was increasing and many medical conditions were being recognised as 'deficiency diseases', the result being a greater emphasis on diet as an agent of improving health. The most influential study into nutrition was Food, Health and Income (1936), conducted by John Boyd Orr. According to his findings, one-tenth of the population were chronically ill-nourished; the figure was higher for children, at one-fifth, and one-half of the population had a deficient diet in some respect. The study was severely criticised in some quarters; however, other surveys, such as Dr M'Gonigle's in the northeast, confirmed the link between poor diet, ill health, and low income.

In terms of theme and style, two aspects stand out in relation to Enough to Eat? The first concerns the role and influence of sponsorship in these documentaries of social enquiry, and the view that the filmmakers were essentially compromised in their critical intentions by the nature of corporate funding. This criticism has been strongly levelled against Housing Problems, and holds for the later Kensal House (1936) and The Smoke Menace (1937), where the Gas, Light and Coke Company clearly had a stake in slum clearance and house building. In matters of nutrition, though, there is no such obvious narrow self-interest, and the film seems to conform to the Griersonian ideal of disinterested corporate sponsorship, where documentary filmmakers were left free to tackle important social questions of the day. In the broader sense, though, the sponsored documentaries were only part of a larger public relations strategy to improve the standing of the gas industry, especially in relation to the electricity industry and its clean, smart, and modern image.

Although the social purpose of the film was widely applauded, there was a more mixed response to its method of construction. For some reviewers there was a clutter of detail, a tendency for the film to drag through repetition, and a basic simplicity to the solutions offered. There was particular praise, however, for the interviews with the mothers as assessed by the reviewer at *Sight and Sound* as 'straight-forward, undramatized, infinitely revealing and shocking'. Also, a sequence comparing the fate of two rats fed on contrasting diets had a noticeable impact.

Enough to Eat? was the cause of considerable press debate on the issue of nutrition, and brought much attention onto the documentary film movement. Its style of presentation through diagrams and graphs, although attracting some criticism at the time, was ultimately influential and was developed with great finesse by Paul Rotha in his wartime documentaries such as World of Plenty (1943). More immediately, the film led Anstey to the March of Time, which appreciated this didactic approach, and where he was invited to reprise his work for the documentary news series.

ALAN BURTON

See also: Anstey, Edgar; Grierson, John

Enough to Eat? (UK, 1936, 23 mins). Produced and distributed by the Gas, Light and Coke Company. Directed by Edgar Anstey, assisted by Frank Sainsbury. Cinematography by Walter Blakeley and Arthur Fisher. Sound by Charles Poulton. Commentary by Julian S. Huxley.

Further reading

Aitken, Ian, *Film and Reform*, London: Routledge, 1990.
The Arts Enquiry, *The Factual Film*, London: PEP, 1947.
Monthly Film Bulletin, November, 1936: 187–8.
Sight and Sound, Autumn, 1936: 88–9.
Stevenson, John, *British Society 1914–45*, Harmondsworth: Penguin, 1984.
Sussex, Elizabeth, *The Rise and Fall of British Documentary*, Berkeley: University of California Press, 1975.
Swann, Paul, *The British Documentary Film Movement, 1926–46*, Cambridge: Cambridge University Press, 1989.

Enthusiasm

(USSR, Vertov, 1930)

On completion, Enthusiasm (also known as Symphony of the Don Basin), Dziga Vertov's 1930 film on coal mining in the Don Basin region of the Soviet Union, was criticized for its unconventional use of sound and visual style. The film was produced a few years after Soviet cinema had gained recognition on an international scale. Produced when films with simple and didactic narratives were endorsed by the Soviet state, this documentary was charged as being too abstract and belonging to the much maligned art movement of Formalism. Made during the Five Year Plan, Enthusiasm is an important documentary, as it is an experiment on Vertov's theories of the kino-eye and the radio-ear. It is one of the first full production sound films in the Soviet Union and illustrates how Vertov tackled the issue of sound at its advent in the cinema.

Vertov was the main creative force in all stages of the film's production. He developed the script in two stages. Beginning in 1929, Vertov conceived of an idea for the film in terms of its sound components. One year later, he came up with a plan outlining the film's visual shots. It was at this time that he gave the film its two titles, Enthusiasm and Symphony of the Don Basin; Vertov preferred the former title. Vertov wanted the speech and natural sounds of the film to be recorded as clearly and precisely as its musical score composed by N. Timofeyev and D. Shostakovich. However, in 1929 sound systems by inventors such as A.F. Shorin and P.G. Tager were only beginning to be produced and tested. By being the first film to use an innovative sound system created by Shorin, Enthusiasm pioneers the practice of producing high-quality, on-location sound as a means to further his approach of Kino-Pravda or film truth. This documentary was thus able to use the natural sounds from the coal mines, rather than rely on simulating industrial soundscapes during postproduction.

Enthusiasm is a documentary celebrating the coal mine laborers of the Don Basin community as they work toward realizing the agricultural and industrial goals established in their country's Five Year Plan. The film is not structured in chronological order but rather sets up and contrasts a series of themes surrounding the lives of the Don Basin coal miners at work and play. The first section of the film is about Russia of time past and its reliance on the Tsar and religion. The spell of religion leaves the people disoriented and drunk with idleness. The film then shifts its attention to the destruction of the church and its icons to signify the society waking up. The next section of the film focuses on the motivated laborers of the coal mine as they help move their country toward greater industrialization. Numerous shots of the workers mining coal and producing steel celebrate the hard-working Soviet people of the present and future. The final section of the film focuses on the agricultural sector of labor as people work alongside machinery to tend to the harvest and reap its benefits. Enthusiasm is one of many first Soviet sound films of the early 1930s to deal with workers and their role in constructing the Cultural Revolution. Others include Abram Room's The Five Year Plan (The Plan for Great Works), Alexander Macheret's Deeds and People, and Yuli Raizman's The Earth Thirsts. In this context Vertov's film can be seen as having a very clear political agenda. However, the means through which he used the new technology of sound distinguishes Enthusiasm from these other films.

Consistent with Vertov's theories concerning documentary film, Enthusiasm was made to demystify the process of making a sound film for the spectator. In this film Vertov combines his kino-eye with his radio-ear. Throughout the film sound and aural reality is not used as a supplement of visual reality, but rather helps to heighten the spectator's ability to register Kino-Pravda. Like the image of the cinematographer in Vertov's Man with the Movie Camera (1929), images of sound technicians and composers appear in Enthusiasm. This is illustrated at the beginning of the film with a shot of a woman actually dispatching radio sounds onto a radiotelegraph. After recording these natural and ambient sounds as they unfold, Vertov then experimented at the postproduction stage to create complex dynamics between the sound and image tracks. Such innovation is found in the seemingly infinite ways the film works to disorient the spectator's sense of the sound in relation to the cinematic space. Vertov reveals sonic and visual realities through a number of techniques, some of which are the alteration of the speed of the sounds and visuals (acceleration/deceleration), mismatching and rupture of natural sounds from its image, and use of fragmented as well as disjointed sound/visual collages alongside severe tonal and distortion contrasts. Vertov's desire for the spectator to be aware of the technology was reinforced during the film's exhibition. Vertov would often alter the level of volume of the film at individual screenings. Such techniques are meant to make the spectator see and hear what the human eye and ear on its own cannot.

Vertov's approach to sound in Enthusiasm works in direct opposition to the often cited 'Statement on Sound' by Eisenstein, Pudovkin, and Aleksandrov, which limits sound in cinema to strictly contrapunctal uses. In the journal *Kino-Front* Vertov states that cinema should not be divided by categorizing films as talkies, noisies, or sound films; rather the distinction should rest on whether the film is a documentary or is staged. More specifically, the filmmaker should be concerned with whether sound was produced through real or artificial means. Made at a time when recording sound on-location was repudiated, Vertov used Enthusiasm as a means to disprove sound critic Ippolit Sokolov's widely accepted caterwauling theory, which claimed that nature was photogenic but not sonogenic. Vertov did not believe that the future of sound cinema resided in artistic simulacra of natural sounds in soundproof studios. Such a process was not conducive to Vertov's emphasis on cinema as producing a new world unmediated and freed from the limitations of human perception.

In what Vertov refers to as his 'symphony of noises', Enthusiasm allows the spectator to not only see but also hear the new world created and freed by cinema. Techniques inaugurated in this film, such as the use of on-location sound, revolutionized how documentary film movements such as direct cinema and cinéma vérité construct sound/image relations. A restored version of Enthusiasm by Peter Kubelka offers filmmakers, scholars, and cinéphiles insight into Vertov's perception of visual and aural (cinematic) truth.

THERESA SCANDIFFIO

See also: Vertov, Dziga

Enthusiasm (Soviet Union, VUFKU, 1930, 69 mins). Produced by Aleksandr Nemirovskii. Directed by Dziga Vertov. Assistant Director Elizaveta Svilova. Scenario by Dziga Vertov. Photography by B. Tsteitlin and K. Kuyalev. Sound Director Petr Shtro. Sound Assistants N. Timarzev and K. Chybiosov. Composed by Timofeyev and Shostakovich. Additional Music by Dziga Vertov. Filmed in Don Basin region in the Soviet Union. Restored by Peter Kubelka.

Further reading

Dickinson, Thorold and Roche, Catherine de la, *Soviet Cinema*, London: Falcon Press, 1948.

Eisenstein, S., Pudovkin, V.I. and Alexandrov, G.V., 'A Statement on the Sound Film', in Jay Leya (ed.), *Eisenstein, Sergei Film Form*, New York: Harcourt, 1977.

Fischer, Lucy, 'Enthusiasm: From Kino-Eye to Radio-Eye', *Film Quarterly* 31, 1977–8: 25–36.

Herring, Robert, *Enthusiasm?*, *Close Up* 9, 1932: 20–4.

Koster, Simon, 'Dziga Vertoff', *Experimental Cinema* l, 1934: 27–8.

Leyda, Jay, *Kino: A History of Russian and Soviet Film*, New York: Macmillan, 1960.

Taylor, Richard (ed. and trans.), with Ian Christie (coed.), *The Film Factory: Russian and Soviet Cinema in Documents*, Cambridge, MA: Harvard University Press, 1988.

Taylor, Richard and Christie, Ian (eds), *Inside the Film Factory: New Approaches to Russian and Soviet Cinema*, New York: Routledge, 1991.

Vertov, Dziga, *Kino-Eye: The Writings of Dziga Vertov*, edited by Annette Michelson, trans. Kevin O'Brien, Berkeley, CA: University of California Press, 1984.

Epstein, Jean

From his debut in 1922, director, writer, and philosopher Jean Epstein produced a number of films and theoretical texts that are essential to an understanding of the evolution of the cinema, both from a technical and an aesthetic perspective. Epstein's filmography comprises numerous avant-garde films, documentaries, and semi-documentaries, which are the product and consequence of his conception of the cinema as a machine that is able to produce an objective and novel form of vision, distinct from the human gaze. In 1926 he broke his contract with Pathé and founded his own production company, Les Films Jean Epstein, with which he made films such as La glace à trois faces/The Mirror with Three Faces (1927) and La chute de la Maison Rouge/The Fall of the Red House (1928). In 1929, after the collapse of his production company, he began to dedicate writings and films to Brittany, to its locations, inhabitants, folklore and traditions, and in particular to the relationship between the fisherman and the sea, seen as an emblem of the struggle between life and death. Even in his commercial films he always tried to use nonprofessional actors and local inhabitants, thus revealing an anthropological attitude. He often accompanied his films with writings about the shooting locations or with actual documentaries that he made alongside the fiction films.

Especially in the first phase of his career, Epstein shared the avant-garde spirit of renovation, a position that makes him akin to theoreticians/filmmakers such as Vertov and Canudo. He took part in the discussions on the artistic value of the cinema, which characterized the intellectual debate in 1920s France. In Le Cinématographe vu de l'Etna/Filming around Etna (1926, an account of his experiences in Sicily during the shooting of the lost documentary on Mount Etna, La Montagne infidèle/The Unfaithful Mountain, 1923), taking inspiration from the writings of Delluc, Epstein presents his opinion on the notion of photogénie. Epstein defines photogénie as the opposite of literariness and immobility: the founding characteristic of the cinema, photogénie belongs to any mobile element of the world, the moral quality of which is increased by being reproduced cinematically. The close-up has the power to annul the distinction between subjectivity and objectivity. For Epstein, the camera lens first produces an objective gaze, originated by the mechanical apparatus; thus the world as it is represented on screen is independent of human consciousness. Subjectivity comes into play only subsequently. These ideas push him in the direction of a type of animism similar to that of his contemporary Ricciotto Canudo. The cinema for Epstein allows the uncovering of a universe in which each object is endowed with its own life. Epstein has full confidence in the technical possibilities of the cinema to empower human sight, freeing it from its physical and psychic impediments. In this light, the introduction of sound is useful for Epstein only if it allows an increment of our knowledge of the noises and sounds of the world. The cinema must also become a source of phonogénie. This idea urged him to experiment on the slow motion of sound in his last fiction film, Le Tempestaire (1947).

Epstein made his debut in 1922 with the semi-documentary Pasteur, which was commissioned to celebrate the centenary of the birth of the famous scientist, and which attracted the attention and praise of contemporary French documentarists and, in particular, of Canudo, who defined it as 'the first biographical film'. In 1924 the lost documentary Photogénies marks the end of the first phase of Epstein's career. Made for a specific occasion, the lecture 'A New Avant-Garde', which Epstein read at the Théatre Raymond Duncan on April 11, 1924, Photogénies was afterward disassembled. It consisted of a series of sequences that were meant to represent the idea of photogénie.

In fiction features such as La chute de la maison Usher/The Fall of the house of Usher (1928) and Mauprat (1926), exterior settings are often the only object of the exploratory and documentary gaze of the camera, which produces panoramic views of castles, landscapes, and trees shaken by the wind. Superimpositions and mobility of the camera are the main characteristics of Epstein's style. In the same locations of the exteriors of Mauprat Epstein shot the lost documentary Au pays de George Sand/In the Country of George Sand (1926), dedicated to the valley of the Creuse, North of the Massif Céntral. With Finnis Terrae/End of the World (1929), Epstein moves to Brittany and starts to shoot without actors and sets, somehow anticipating Italian neorealism and cinéma vérité. He focuses on the inhabitants of the Ouessant Archipelago and theorizes for the first time a cinema in which the work of the director is to try to endow an existing reality with the characters of fiction. Epstein defined Finnis Terrae as 'a psychological documentary, the portrayal of a brief drama in episodes that really took place, of authentic people and things' (Epstein 1974–5). By portraying the truth of places and people, the cinema is the witness of a reality that the director reconstructs in dramatic form.

Epstein insists on his anthropological interests with the subsequent Mor Vran (La mer des corbeaux)/The Sea of the Crows (1930), a semi-documentary about the inhabitants of the Island of Seine, which tells the story of a shipwreck, making use of authentic characters and settings. The film opens with a map of the island—a prologue that is already a declaration of the scientific aim of the film and of its anthropological value. Epstein here analyses Brittany's traditions, myths, and folklore and produces an accurate documentation of life in the Ouessant Archipelago, in relation to the idea that the sea brings both life and death, and in light of the always impending danger of a storm (a danger of which Epstein was a direct witness, having escaped a shipwreck).

Epstein returned to Brittany in 1931, to the isle of Hoedik, to shoot L'Or des mers (1932), once again using locals for actors. He chose to live in close contact with them, sharing their relationship with the sea. During an era in which the cinema withdrew to the studios, Epstein continued to shoot on location, often in extreme conditions. He returned to Brittany once again to make the film in the Breton language Chanson d'Armor/Song of Armor (1934) and the short documentary Une visite à l'Ouest-Eclair (La vie d'un grand journal)/A Visit to West-Éclair (The Life of a Great News paper) (1934), particularly interesting for the focus on Brittany's modern aspects. He then shot two documentaries intended for the promotion of the region: La Bretagne/Brittany (1937) and La Bourgogne/Burgandy (1937), both for the Exposition Internationale des Arts et Techniques in Paris.

STEFANO BASCHIERA

Biography

Born in Warsaw, 1897, left Poland as a child to study in Switzerland. Moved to France and studied medicine in Lyon, a scientific formation that influenced his work. Interested in the arts, befriended Auguste Lumière. Established the avant-garde magazine *Le Promenoir*, 1920, which had contributors such as Auguste Lumière and Fernand Léger. Moved to Paris to work at the Editions de la Sirène and as an assistant to Louis Delluc for Le Tonnerre. Published La Lyrosophie and his first essay on the cinema, *Bonjour cinéma*, 1922. Made first film, Pasteur, 1922; established production company, Les Films Jean Epstein, 1926. Moved to Brittany, 1929. Professorship of Aesthetics at the Istitute des Hautes Etudes Cinématographiques, Paris (1945). Wrote his two major essays on the cinema, *L'intelligence d'une machine* (1946) and *Le Cinéma du diable* (1947). Died 1953 after a long illness.

Selected films

1922 Pasteur: director
1924 Photogénies: editor
1926 Au pays de George Sand: producer, director
1929 Finis Terrae: writer, director
1930 Mor Vran (La mer des corbeaux): writer, director
1931 Notre Dame de Paris: director
1934 Une visite à l'Ouest-Eclair (La vie d'un grand journal): director
1937 La Bretagne: director
1937 La Bourgogne: director
1948 Le feux de la mer: director

Further reading

Aumont, Jacques (ed.), *Jean Epstein: Cinéaste, poète, philosophe*, Paris: Cinémathèque Française, 1998.
Canudo, Ricciotto, *L'Usine aux images (1927)*, Paris: Séguier/Arte édition, 1995.
Deleuze, Gilles, *L'image-mouvement*, Paris: Editions de Minuit, 1983 (English-language edn as *Cinema 1: The Movement Image*, London: Athlone, 2002).
Epstein, Jean, *Ecrits sur le cinéma*, two vols, Paris: Seghers, 1974–5.
Leprohon, Pierre, *Jean Epstein*, Paris: Seghers, 1964.
Vichi, Laura, *Jean Epstein*, Milano: Il Castoro, 2003.

Ertel, Dieter

The concept of a new form of documentary in West German television was much influenced by Dieter Ertel. Having gained his first experience in the production of newsreels and as writer at the weekly magazine *Der Spiegel*, he had learned how powerful words could be and how important it was to search for facts and information. Ertel participated actively in the discussions about a new style at the Süddeutscher Rundfunk (SDR) in Stuttgart in the 1950s. His film Ein Großkampftag/Boxing Day (1957) became the model for the documentary serial Zeichen der Zeit/Signs of the Time, which was regularly produced until 1973. It brought a critical analysis of German society in a dynamic visual style and with ironic commentaries into private homes and was not appreciated by all viewers. However, this style, referred to as 'Stuttgarter Schule', was influential for documentary production in German television and was an alternative to the documentary films from Hamburg, which were more oriented to Anglo-American reportage style. Ertel was quite aware that a documentary could not be an objective representation of reality and grasped the opportunity to make subjective statements.

His concept was to produce films that do not just present finished results but instead try to motivate the viewers to make up their own minds. Ertel did not trust the official versions of a story, but tried to look behind the scenes and searched for other perspectives. Although today his commentaries seem to dominate his films, for him the image was more important. His style was influenced by Ed Murrow and Richard Leacock, and, together with his cameramen, he looked for specific details that could be edited in a visual rhythm and as ironic as his commentaries. He was more interested in specific qualities and developments of the times and less in the daily business of politics. Over time he produced 'something like filmic behavioural research about humanness' (Netenjakob 1968). One of his main topics was classical music and portraits of conductors, but his masterpieces are on sports; these films are self-reflexive commentaries on media and bourgeois conformism, in which growing commercialisation was criticized. Good examples are Ein Großkampftag about boxing fights and Tortour de France (1960), where he followed the Tour de France and tried to show the machinery behind the event. A portrait of a rifle club and its yearly meeting (Schützenfest, 1961) provoked massive protest because he interviewed drunken riflemen, asking them what importance guns have for them or why they shoot again after the experience of World War II; he got very open answers. In Der totale Urlaub/The Total Holiday (1967) he visited a holiday camp on the south coast of England, in which the whole day was strictly organized. After becoming responsible for the documentary department of the SDR, Ertel did not make many more films and ran into conflict with the station because he tried to retain a privileged position for documentary film. He then went on to become manager of various public stations in Germany. He is one of the founders of the Haus des Dokumentarfilms in Stuttgart.

KAY HOFFMANN

Biography

Born in Hamburg, Germany, February 2, 1927. Studied German and English literature at Hamburg University 1947–50. 1950–3 trainee, and editor at the German newsreel (Neue Deutsche Wochenschau). 1954–5 sports editor at the news magazine *Der Spiegel*. From October 1955 to 1968, editor in the documentary department of Süddeutscher Rundfunk (SDR). 1968–73 head of the documentary department of SDR. 1974–9 head of TV programming at Radio Bremen. 1979–81 head of Program III (television movies, film, entertainment, and family) at Westdeutscher Rundfunk (WDR), Cologne. 1981–9, head of programming at Südwestrundfunk (SWF) in Baden-Baden. 1991–4 chairman of the Documentary Film Center Stuttgart.

Selected films

1957 Ein Großkampftag: director, writer
1958 Der große Cannes-Cannes: Beobachtungen am Rande der Filmfestspiele: director, writer
1959 Neubauwunderlichkeiten: director, writer
1960 Tortur de France: Bericht über eine Radrundfahrt: director, writer (together with Hans Blickensdörfer)
1963 Fernsehfieber: Bemerkungen über das Massenmedium und sein Publikum: director, writer (together with Georg Friedel)
1967 Der totale Urlaub: Beobachtungen in einem englischen Ferienparadies: director, writer
1974 Richard Wagner: director, writer

Further reading

Ertel, Dieter, 'Rückblick auf meine Stuttgarter Jahr', *Stuttgarter Zeitung* 16, no. 1, 1974: 29.
Gmelin, Otto, *Philosophie des Fernsehens*, Pfullingen: Gmelin, 1967: 143–52.
Harms, Michael, 'Dieter Ertel', *SWF Journal* 2, 1992: 12–13.
Hattendorf, Manfred, *Dokumentarfilm und Authentizität*, Ästhetik und Pragmatik einer Gattung, Konstanz: Ölschläger, 1994.
Hoffmann, Kay, *Zeichen der Zeit: Zur Geschichte der, 'Stuttgarter Schule'*, Munich: TR-Verlagsunion, 1996.
Netenjakob, Egon, 'Schöner Zwang zur Wirklichkeit. Die zeitkritische Sendereihe, Zeichen der Zeit und Dieter Ertel', *Funk-Korrespondenz* 19, 1968: 1–5.
Steinmetz, Rüdiger and Spitra, Helmut (eds), *Dokumentarfilm als 'Zeichen der Zeit'. Vom Ansehen der Wirklichkeit im Fernsehen*, Munich: Ölschläger, 1989.

Eternity

(Australia, Lawrence Johnston, 1994)

Eternity is significant as an Australian documentary that makes use of a nonrealist documentary aesthetic to create a portrait of a well-known and enigmatic character who holds a unique place in the national consciousness. Directed by Lawrence Johnston, Eternity traces the life and work of Arthur Stace. Known as 'Mr Eternity', Stace spent forty years of his life writing the word Eternity in chalk on Sydney's city streets. The narrative moves from Stace's struggle with alcoholism following his experiences as a stretcher bearer in World War I, through his conversion to Christianity in 1930 and his death in 1967. Motivated by his religious beliefs, an essentially illiterate Stace roamed the inner city and wrote Eternity an estimated five hundred thousand times in perfect copperplate on pavements around Sydney. Stace's identity, however, was not revealed until 1956, twenty years after the first inscription had appeared.

As a biography, Eternity is remarkable in the way that it not only charts the life of Stace but also attempts to situate him culturally and spatially. The narrative of Stace's life is constructed through a voice-of-God commentary and interviews with a number of people who knew him. These accounts offer an intimate access to specific formative events in this enigmatic character's life. The film also draws on interviews with cultural commentators such as writers, artists, broadcasters, and journalists. The differing perspectives provided by these personalities reinforce the enigma that Stace has become while also suggesting the ways in which he has influenced Sydney's artistic community and cultural psyche.

Eternity is a highly stylized documentary that uses modes of reflexivity not only to question the production of meaning but also to express the multiple personal and cultural dimensions that contribute to the symbolism that Lawrence believes Stace represents. Each of the interviews is shot against a colorful back-projected image, which include landscapes, flowers, and the word 'eternity' itself. This is a device through which Lawrence offers added insight into the experience and character of the interviewee. This device complements the move away from realist representation that characterizes the images that dominate the rest of the film, which construct a collage of archival or found footage and black-and-white recreations of Stace and his wanderings. The Sydney cityscape features prominently in these images. The noir-like scenes evoke a sense of the historical city in which the haunting figure of Stace and the myth that surrounds him can be located. The music of Ross Edwards's 'Symphony Da Pacem Domine' accentuates this ghostly quality.

Eternity stands as one of the most internationally renowned Australian documentaries of the decade. Not only did it win the prize for the best documentary at the 1995 Sydney Film Festival, but also the Golden Gate award at the San Francisco International Film Festival and the 1995 Los Angeles International Documentary Association Award for Best Documentary, among others.

BELINDA SMAILL

See also: Australia

Eternity (Australia, Vivid Pictures, 1994, 56 mins). Distributed by Ronin Films. Produced by Susan MacKinnon. Directed and written by Lawrence Johnston. Cinematography by Dion Beebe. Edited by Annette Davey. Sound by Liam Egan and Paul Finlay. Music composed by Ross Edwards.

Further reading

Deacon, Kathy, 'Eternity Directed by Lawrence Johnston/Is That All There Is Directed by Lindsay Anderson', *The Village Voice*, May 16, 1995: 40, 20, 60.

Hughes, Peter, Lindsay, Andrew and Slavin, John, 'M99—Documentaries at the Melbourne and Sydney Film Festivals', *Metro Magazine* 99, 1994: 55–61.

Levy, Emanuel, 'Eternity Directed by Lawrence Johnston', *Variety*, New York, October 3, 1994: 356, 10, 64.

Être et avoir

(France, Philibert, 2002)

One of the most celebrated feature-length documentaries of 2002, Nicholas Philibert's Être et avoir/To Be and To Have, can in some ways be seen as the polar opposite of the other big documentary of that year, Michael Moore's Bowling for Columbine.

Where Moore opts for bombast, Philibert strives for gentle tranquility. Where Moore's 'argument' about the state of the world he is examining utterly dominates his film, Philibert offers no 'argument' at all.

Not interested in making documentaries that are 'about' a subject, Philibert prefers to construct his films, as he says, 'with' subjects and locations. Être et avoir examines a one-room school in Auvergne in France, where the dozen students, who range from four to ten years old, are all taught by one teacher, M. Georges Lopez. The film takes place over the course of six months, beginning in a blustery snowstorm and ending in the bright breezes of summer. Adopting an almost entirely observational approach (with the exception of the interview sequence with Monsieur Lopez, the teacher, in which he explains why he is a schoolteacher), the film negotiates an intermediate space between those observational films that present a world as if it had not been recorded on camera and those that foreground the existence of the mediating existence of the cinematographic apparatus. Thus, there are scenes in which the teacher and pupils appear completely at ease and nonchalant in front of the camera, and others in which they seem acutely aware of it.

Philibert has expressed his deep conviction—echoing Cesare Zavattini's call for films about the poetry of everyday life—in the cinematic potential of the quotidian aspects of life. Situating his camera in a milieu in which the everyday struggles of children are, for these young humans, monumental ones—mastering basics of numeracy and literacy, not to mention the vital lessons of sociability and communication—Philibert has found ideal locations and conditions for allowing the poetry of everyday life to expose itself on film. The selection of a small school, with so few pupils and of such wide-ranging ages, allows for heightened connection with the characters. This is possible because their number and diversity allow us to know them as individuals to a greater degree than would have been the case had we been situated in a more traditional classroom—one grade level with twenty to thirty students.

As much as the film relies on audiences' willingness and ability to pay careful attention to the children, the film is centred on the quiet authority of Monsieur Lopez, the teacher. His commanding presence is felt (again to contrast with Moore's bombastic performance in Bowling for Columbine) in his gentleness and his quietness. He is one of those figures who, because he speaks so softly, demands our (and the children's) attention because he forces us to lean into what he is saying. In his dealings with the wee ones, he is a model of firm patience; with the older children, of guidance and certainty; and with the parents, of understanding and empathy.

While much of what we see takes place in the classroom, the film emphasizes that which surrounds it. We are treated not only to pretty, natural images of the local seasons but also to the farms where some of the children live, a school outing to a library, bus rides, and, significantly, the decamping of instruction from the classroom to the school's playground, tables, chairs, and all, once the warm summer breezes start blowing. The metaphor represented by this venue change by the teacher Lopez, and its inclusion in the film by Philibert, is perfectly representative of the film's expansive aspirations.

Formally, the film makes some powerfully affective choices. The first sounds and images of the film, though they contain no children and no teacher, suggestively set the tone for what follows: a blustery snowstorm, with cattle being guided through the pasture followed by a cut to a high-angle shot of the classroom floor, where gradually, leisurely, a turtle, and then another, ambles into the frame. These juxtapositions of chaotic nature with measured control illuminate the central tensions at the heart of the film—those between the individual and society, between teacher and pupil, between humankind and nature.

Phillipe Hersant's tender and calming score is used only for scenes outside the classroom; in the classroom we have only direct sound. The images of rural life that surround the village school, gorgeously photographed as the seasons turn, place the developmental milestones of the children in a natural order in which snowstorms, rainstorms, summer breezes, and dappling sunlight all converge in a sensation of the small universalities of the human experience. We were all once children and had to learn how to grow up and make our way in the world.

The title, which translates as To Be and To Have, refers on the surface to a conjugation exercise that normally comes early in a French-language education, that is, at a moment in language-learning where we find these schoolchildren. However, the film's expansion outwards from the classroom, into the rural countryside that surrounds it and further still into the universal experiences of childhood, lends this title a much weightier significance. The film's reach, then, ultimately strives to consider questions of existence in this world (being) and acquiring the means as children to navigate through it (having).

Produced partly with the participation of various French state bodies, Être et avoir was a modestly budgeted film that attracted huge audiences in France (becoming the highest grossing documentary in that country's history), as well as attracting significant critical attention around the world, winning both prestigious prizes and large audiences. Named best documentary of the year by both the European Film Awards and the National Society of Film Critics in the United States, the film was also nominated for (or won) major film prizes in Britain, France, and Spain.

PETER URQUHART

Every Day Except Christmas

(UK, Anderson, 1957)

Every Day Except Christmas was shown in the third Free Cinema programme, 'Look at

Britain', at the National Film Theatre, London, in May 1957 (along with Alain Tanner and Claude Goretta's Nice Time (1957), and two earlier short films, Anderson's own Wakefield Express, and Nigel McIsaac's The Singing Street, both made in 1952). Like other Free Cinema films, all victims of the distribution difficulties of documentaries since the advent of television, even the best of the Free Cinema documentaries are not as well known or respected as they should be outside (and to some extent even inside) Britain.

The structure of the film is relatively simple, beginning with the loading of mushrooms in Sussex for transportation to Covent Garden market in central London, following the van through its late night journey—through the suburbs to the strains of the national anthem, signalling the end of radio broadcasting for the day. At the market, work is just beginning and the film follows the night's activities—laying out the produce, taking an early morning break, returning to the market for the arrival of the buyers, and ending mid-morning as the market winds down.

Free Cinema was a product of its time—John Osborne's play Look Back in Anger (1956) and the stir and storm it caused in British theatre (which also engaged Anderson's talents), and the emergence of the New Left. Anderson's 1957 manifesto for Free Cinema argued that their aim was to 'say something about our society today [...] to look at Britain, with honesty and affection'. Every Day Except Christmas and We Are the Lambeth Boys, the two 'Look at Britain' films sponsored by Ford, are probably the best examples.

Anderson's manifesto's 'if we are to interpret ... ' invokes Grierson's creative interpretation of actuality, and in many ways we should see Every Day Except Christmas in a direct line from 1930s (and World War II) British documentary. In a revealing interview comment many years later, Anderson accused his interviewers of being too taken with direct cinema and having a narrow view of documentary. In his film, he says, 'even the bits that have natural sound are all composed [... direct cinema is] just an excuse for not being creative'. Though several sequences seem to want to persuade us that we are hearing what we can see, more recall the finale of Housing Problems, with conversational voices, as well as other sounds, over image, created at the editing stage. Anderson observed in a later interview that institutions like the BBC would not 'understand the creative effort or the poetic quality' of a film like Every Day Except Christmas. Certainly, the film uses sound and image in 'creative ways' much like earlier documentaries. Anderson likes to contrast busy scenes with quiet, still ones, and jaunty with slow, lyrical music. One central, striking sequence, for example, juxtaposes the bustle of Albert's café with the deserted market alleys, a stray cat, slow panning, and tracking shots over the laid-out flowers, with, first, silence and then poetic music.

One of the films shown in the second Free Cinema programme (September 1956) was Georges Franju's Le Sang des bêtes/Blood of the Beast (1949), and Anderson's creative methods are sometimes reminiscent of Franju's evocative use of music and camera (though without the characteristic Franju 'bite'). In the Free Cinema manifesto, Anderson's 'if we are to interpret ... ' is followed by 'we must have an attitude, we must have values and beliefs', which he seems to see as distinguishing Free Cinema from the 'social propaganda' aspect of 1930s documentary. What are the 'values and beliefs' in Every Day Except Christmas?

Although Anderson is interested in the different kinds of activities in the market, this is not a conventionally 'polemical' film, hence, perhaps, the omission (as Basil Wright pointed out) of those podding peas in the market's dark basement. Anderson is clearly more interested in communicating what he saw as the dignity and importance of ordinary people as they go about their work, and enjoys observing the faces and simple skills of working men (particularly in relation to flowers, not without some hints of homoeroticism—compare the openly gay character in the café). The film's credentials at the class level are sustained by the voice-over commentary, spoken by Alun Owen, a prolific working-class radio and television (and later theatre) dramatist during the 1950s and 1960s, with more than a suggestion of working-class Welsh, but with a soft lilt. As the commentary concludes, things change 'but work will still be with us, one way or another, and we all depend on each other's work as well as our own, on Alice, and George, and Bill [...] and all the others who keep us going'.

At the same time, as in the Humphrey Jennings films, which Anderson so admired, there is an attachment—akin, perhaps, to Flaherty's in

Industrial Britain, but more personalised—to history and tradition, and the present threat to their survival. There is a real sense of regret and loss, for example, when the film talks about the disappearance of women flower porters ('Alice has been on the job for thirty-five years, and when she goes, that's the end of it'), and the aged women flower sellers who come round as the market closes down. Of course, in fifteen years or so the markets had been removed to the concrete wastes of Nine Elms in Vauxhall, where there was precious little poetry to be had.

JIM HILLIER

See also: Anderson, Lindsay; Franju, Georges; Grierson, John; Jennings, Humphrey; We Are the Lambeth Boys

Every Day Except Christmas (UK, Graphic Films for the Ford Motor Company Ltd, 1957, 47 mins) (first film in series Look at Britain). Distributed by the British Film Institute. Produced by Leon Clore and Karel Reisz. Directed and scripted by Lindsay Anderson. Cinematography by Walter Lassally. Music by Daniel Paris. Editing and sound by John Fletcher. Commentary spoken by Alun Owen. Assistants Alex Jacobs, Brian Probyn, and Maurice Ammar. Filmed in London.

Further reading

Anderson, Lindsay, 'Free Cinema', *Universities and Left Review*, no. 2, Summer 1957 (reprinted in Barsam, Richard Meran (ed.), *Nonfiction Film Theory and Criticism*, New York: E.P. Dutton, 1976).

Ellis, Jack, *The Documentary Idea*, Englewood Cliffs, NJ and London: E.P. Dutton, 1989.

Graham, Alison, *Lindsay Anderson*, Boston: E.P. Dutton, 1981.

Hedling, Erik, *Lindsay Anderson: Maverick Film-Maker*, London and Washington, DC: E.P. Dutton, 1998.

Higson, Andrew, 'Britain's Outstanding Contribution to the Film: The Documentary-Realist Tradition', in Charles Barr (ed.), *All Our Yesterdays: 90 Years of British Cinema*, London: E.P. Dutton, 1986.

Jacobs, Lewis (ed.), *The Documentary Tradition*, New York: E.P. Dutton, 1974.

Lambert, Gavin, 'Free Cinema', *Sight and Sound* 25, spring, 1956.

Levin, G. Roy (ed.), *Documentary Explorations*, Garden City, NY: E.P. Dutton, 1971.

Lovell, Alan and Hillier, Jim, *Studies in Documentary*, London: E.P. Dutton, 1972.

Orbanz, Eva, Tuchtenhagen, Gisela and Wildenhahn, Klaus, *Journey to a Legend and Back: The British Realistic Film*, Berlin: E.P. Dutton, 1977.

Silet, Charles L.P., *Lindsay Anderson: A Guide to References and Resources*, Boston: E.P. Dutton, 1978.

Sussex, Elizabeth, *Lindsay Anderson*, London: E.P. Dutton, 1969 (also New York: Praeger, 1970).

Exile and the Kingdom

(Australia, Frank Rijavec, 1993)

Exile and the Kingdom is a unique and comprehensive historical account of a group of Aboriginal peoples from ancient times to the present. It continues a mode of collaborative or consultative filmmaking between indigenous and nonindigenous Australians that was initiated in the 1970s. Frank Rijavec directed Exile and the Kingdom and also cowrote the film in conjunction with Roger Solomon of the Injibarndi and Ngarluma tribes. As an on-screen narrator, Solomon also plays a central role in the finished film.

Exile and the Kingdom focuses on an area in the north of Western Australia around the Fortescue River and the town of Roebourne. Elders of the Injibarndi, Ngarluma, Kurama, and Bandjima tribes of this area were involved with developing the different approaches that the film used. Exile and the Kingdom begins by outlining a number of the traditional ceremonies that have been integral to the Injibarndi and Ngarluma cultures of the area since times well before colonisation. Themes that are reiterated throughout the documentary are the importance of ancestral lands, and sacred sites in particular, and the codes of respect and discipline that compose Aboriginal law. Exile and the Kingdom goes on to chart a history of colonisation that includes forced labor, the dispossession of lands, wars against colonists or 'squatters', and an eventual massacre of Aboriginal people. This history extends into the present, with an account of the detrimental impact of alcohol, the iron ore mining boom of the 1960s and 1970s, and the ghettoization of these tribes in government reserves. Exile and the Kingdom persuasively argues for the recognition of land rights and an emphasis on Aboriginal law and spirituality as a means of restoring indigenous communities.

In addition to Solomon's narration, the film is structured around interviews with a diverse range of Aboriginal people about the history of the area, their experiences, and tribal knowledge. Written accounts by British colonists are also recited in the earlier part of the film. Exile and the Kingdom is a feature-length documentary that is divided into two fifty-five-minute parts to facilitate television screening. In contrast with another significant indigenous/nonindigenous collaborative documentary, Two Laws (1981), Exile and the Kingdom was produced for viewing by a mainstream Australian television audience.

The importance of this collaborative mode as a means of self-representation to a broader national audience can be understood in the context of a history of Australian cinema. For the past century a huge archive of film has been produced that situates Aboriginal people as ethnographic subjects, or, to a lesser extent, melodramatic stereotypes. Projects in the 1970s, such as Martha Ansara's collaboration with Essie Coffey on the landmark documentary My Survival as an Aboriginal (1979), led the way for more indigenous people to take up a position on the other side of the camera in order to represent alternative aesthetic and political strategies. This collaborative documentary mode of which Exile and the Kingdom is a part was carried on in the 1990s by indigenous directors working in a more autonomous way, such as Rachel Perkins, Tracey Moffatt, Darlene Johnson, and Ivan Sen.

BELINDA SMAILL

See also: Australia

Exile and the Kingdom (Australia, Ngurin Aboriginal Corporation/Frank Rijavec/Noelene Harrison, 1993, 110 mins). Distributed by Film Australia. Produced by Frank Rijavec and Noelene Harrison. Directed by Frank Rijavec. Written by Frank Rijavec and Roger Solomon. Cinematography by Frank Rijavec and Peter Kordyl. Edited by Liz Goldfinch. Sound by Lawrie Silvestrin and Roslyn Silvestrin.

Further reading

Bryson, Ian, Burns, Margaret and Langton, Marcia, 'Painting with Light: Australian Indigenous Cinema', in Sylvia Kleinert and Margo Neale (eds), *The Oxford Companion to Aboriginal Art and Culture*, Melbourne: Oxford University Press, 2000: 297–305.

Langton, Marcia, *'Well I heard it on the Radio and I saw it on the Television … ', An Essay for the Australian Film Commission on the politics and aesthetics of filmmaking by and about Aboriginal people and things*, Sydney: Australian Film Commission, 1993.

O'Regan, Tom, *Australian National Cinema*, London: Routledge, 1996.

F

Fall of the Romanov Dynasty, The

(USSR, Shub, 1927)

Assembled in 1927, Esfir Shub's The Fall of the Romanov Dynasty was the first compilation documentary ever produced. The film was the first of three compilation films she made during 1927–8 (the other two being The Great Way, 1927, and Lev Tolstoy and the Russia of Nicholas II, 1928), which introduced this new genre of documentary. Shub's creation of a documentary film out of newsreel material not only establishes her as a pioneer of compilation and radical documentary but also emphasizes her position as one of the most significant women filmmakers of the first half of the twentieth century.

After assisting Sergei Eisenstein on scripts and editing newsreels with Dziga Vertov from 1924–5, Shub saw a new direction for her work. She wrote, 'it is clear that work in newsreel must begin with artistic labor. Newsreel apart from this must begin with history, profoundly with the party chronicle of our epoch.' At the end of 1926, she received a commission from Sovkino to make an historical film for the tenth anniversary of the Bolshevik Revolution.

Shub researched the film at the Museum of the Revolution in Leningrad, where for two months she pored over sixty thousand meters of film. Her major difficulties were locating and organizing existing film material. Much of the footage had been taken out of the country, sold to foreign producers, or destroyed by terrible archive conditions. She persuaded the government to buy two thousand feet of negative film about the February Revolution (including famous shots of Lenin) from the United States. Eventually, however, she had to shoot one thousand of the total six thousand feet of the film. Her other major challenge was organizing footage with different styles, film formats, and emulsion qualities into a coherent artistic and ideological whole. In The Fall of the Romanov Dynasty Shub aims to convey in essay style her own ideological attitude without distorting the filmic documents. Her innovative method and editing skill enabled these potential problems to become the film's strengths.

From 1912 to 1917 The Fall of the Romanov Dynasty is divided into four sections: prewar Russia, international preparation for the war, the war, and the Revolution. The first part presents images of a doomed regime, opening with the title 'Tsarist Russia in the Years of the Black Reaction'. The slow, even pace recalls the rural atmosphere, whereas the images of State Duma politicians casually conversing and wealthy landowners enjoying leisure time contrast sharply with shots of industrial workers and peasants laboring in the fields. Shub's use of titles and editing patterns functions ironically to juxtapose the two social and economic spheres. The first part concludes with images of the Romanovs and other Russian nobility parading above a crowd. Whereas this procession is initially contrasted with the marching of needy peasants to prison, the parade scenes also function in contradistinction to the forthcoming images of the Bolsheviks. While the images of the nobility emphasize a static quality and distance from the crowd, shots of the Revolution articulate dynamism and an organic connection with the people, one of the central themes of the film.

In the second section Shub illustrates the Marxist argument that the war was between imperial powers and contends that, instead, Russia should be fighting imperialism itself. 'Europe at the time' is illustrated by capitalists, banks, and gold, and European leaders are visually matched with the tsar. In preparation for the war, new destructive technology is manufactured and military training becomes intense. Shub's attitude is made clear in the title 'Tsarist Russia Marched in Step with the Other Imperialist Powers'. Dramatic and violent combat footage of land and sea follows, in one stretch, uninterrupted by titles for seven minutes. The slow, even pacing of the beginning of the film has become more rapid, heightening the drama and tension. The section concludes with the most powerful intertitle in the film: 'Killed, Wounded, and Maimed in the World War—35 Million People'. The devastating impact of the war on Russians is made apparent and leads to the final section of the film.

The title '1917' opens the extensive coverage of the uprising in which Alexander Kerensky seizes power. Shub's attitude toward the subject is unambiguous. Kerensky is a member of the 'bourgeoisie, striving to use the revolution for its own purposes'. Kerensky and the Mensheviks are visually and thematically equated with the tsarists. Like Nicholas II, he is shown advocating war, and like the previous Duma, the Mensheviks are seen disengaged from the people. In contrast, Lenin is shown speaking to huge crowds while the mass demonstrations are edited together with pages of *Pravda* calling for 'Peace, Land, and Bread', the Bolshevik party slogan. Shub's film concludes as it must—with images of Lenin greeting and shaking hands with members of the crowd.

The Fall of the Romanov Dynasty presents the inevitability and the energy of the Revolution. The dynamism of the Bolshevik Revolution and the Party's connection with the people contrasts sharply with the pomp and circumstance of the tsarists and their distance from the people. Shub's editing and titling skill is apparent. Her montage is intuitive and associative rather than metrical or mathematical (terms often used to describe Vertov's method). She bitingly juxtaposes images and, in an innovative way, uses slogans found on flags and signs as titles. Yet while Shub's cinematic essay may be highly agitational and propagandistic, she, like Vertov, is devoted to maintaining the ontological authenticity of the filmic documents. She writes: 'authentic material is something that gives life to a documentary film, regardless of the fact that it might be composed of archival footage or shot by the filmmaker'. Shub's goal was to achieve a delicate balance between commenting on events by means of a juxtaposition of images and preserving the authenticity of each image, a goal resonating today with many compilation documentarists. Her exceptional skill and innovative method are both formidable and instructive.

JOSHUA MALITSKY

The Fall of the Romanov Dynasty (The Soviet Union, Sovkino, 1927, 90 mins; restored Gosfilmofund, USSR, 1991). Distributed by Kino Video. Directed and edited by Esfir Shub. In Russian with English subtitles.

Further reading

Leyda, Jay, *Kino*, New York: Collier Books, 1960.

Petric, Vlada, 'Vertov, Lenin and Perestroika: The Cinematic Transposition of Reality', *Historical Journal of Film, Radio, and Television* 15, no. 1, 1995: 3–17.

——'Esfir Shub: Film as Historical Discourse', in Thomas Waugh (ed.), *'Show Us Life': Towards a History and Aesthetics of the Committed Documentary*, Metuchen, NJ: Scarecrow Press, 1984: 21–46.

Roberts, Graham, *Forward Soviet: History and Non-Fiction Film in the USSR*, London: I.B. Tauris, 1999.

Taylor, Richard, *The Politics of Soviet Cinema 1917–29*, Cambridge: Cambridge University Press, 1979.

Taylor, Richard and Christie, Ian (eds), *The Film Factory: Russian and Soviet Cinema in Documents 1896–1939*, Cambridge, MA: Harvard University Press, 1988.

Family Portrait

(UK, Jennings, 1951)

Family Portrait, Humphrey Jennings's final film, was made for the 1951 Festival of Britain. Film was an integral part of the Festival's celebration of Britain's achievements in the arts, industry, and science, so a cinema was built at the London South Bank Exhibition site for the screening of the specially commissioned Festival films. More than twenty films were made for exhibition at the Telekinema, but Family Portrait most reflects the Festival's aims of celebrating the past and heralding a bright new future. Unfortunately, these aims proved more of a limitation than an inspiration, resulting in one of Jennings's least imaginative films.

The film is constructed around the opening and closing shots of a photograph album featuring images of family holidays, a christening, and a picnic. It proceeds to showcase British artistic achievement (the plays of William Shakespeare), science (Charles Darwin and Britain's records of exploration), and industry (Stephenson's Rocket and James Watt), echoing the displays of the Festival exhibitions. Jennings regards these 'heroes' of British life with warmth and refers to them as 'local lads who used their wits and had a good laugh, and then, like Shakespeare and Newton and Watt started something at home that went right around the globe'. Ultimately this is a quietly patriotic film that acknowledges the contradictions of the British character: an admiration for invention versus a love of tradition, eccentricity versus practicality, domesticity versus pageantry, agriculture versus industry.

Family Portrait is a rather literal film. Although the sentiments expressed in the voice-over and through the narrative structure of the film are poetic, the visual execution of these sentiments is lacklustre. All too often the images are simply a literal translation of the narrator's words; for example, the evolution of British tradition, particularly democracy, is discussed over bland images of the field at Runnymede, clichéd shots of the Houses of Parliament, and council committee meetings. The images are frequently overwhelmed by the richness of the narration.

Nevertheless, Family Portrait was well received by the critical press and Jennings's fellow documentarists. In retrospect, however, it is difficult to say just how much of this praise was a result of Jennings's accidental death at the end of 1950. Many of the film's contemporary notices read like eulogies. Edgar Anstey pronounced it the most important documentary film made since the war. *Monthly Film Bulletin* thought it perhaps the most polished in style of all Jennings's films and *Today's Cinema* recommended it 'as a yardstick for contemporary documentary'. Three years later Lindsay Anderson noted that Family Portrait could stand beside Jennings's wartime films but that it lacked the passion. In a 1981 reevaluation, however, Anderson decided that the film should be dismissed as 'sentimental fiction'. He berated Jennings for his 'fantasy of the Empire' and his use of the past as a refuge' (Jennings and Anderson 1982). Although the film's patriotism is very much of its time and Jennings closes the film by recognising the impact of Britain's imperial past, he also realises that Britain's future will depend on wider global alliances.

SARAH EASEN

See also: Jennings, Humphrey

Family Portrait (UK, Wessex Film Productions, 1951, 24 mins). Executive produced by Ian Dalrymple. Written and directed by Humphrey Jennings. Assistant direction by Harley Usill. Unit management by R.L.M. Davidson. Film edited by Stewart McAllister. Sound by Ken Cameron. Photography by Martin Curtis. Music directed and conducted by Muir Mathison. Music composed and arranged by John Greenwood. Commentary spoken by Michael Goodliffe.

Further reading

Jennings, Mary-Lou and Anderson, Lindsay (eds), *Humphrey Jennings: Film-Maker/Painter/Poet*, London: British Film Institute, 1982.

Fanck, Arnold

Arnold Fanck's name is closely linked with the filmic image of the Alpine mountains. He is primarily known for his feature films, which he mostly shot on location in the Alps. In his documentary films he glorified the experience of sports and nature, notably in 4628 Meterhoch auf Skiern. Besteigung des Monte Rosa (1913), Im Kampf mit dem Berge (1921), and the two-part Das Wunder des Schneeschuhs (1919–20; 1922). Moreover, Fanck's production company took charge of other sports subjects such as jiu-jitsu, boxing, sailing, soccer, and rowing. Likewise exotic subjects became relevant in a number of travelogs, notably Tibet, Africa, and especially Asia. On the occasion of the shooting of his feature film, Die Tochter des Samurai (1938), Fanck produced six short documentaries that he shot in Japan, China, and Manchuria. These films dealt with the history, traditions, and culture of the Japanese people. They took on a political undertone, for example, when they legitimized, under the guise of a *Kulturfilm*, the Japanese occupation of southern Manchuria in Winterreise durch Südmandschurien (1938). Kaiserbauten in Fernost (1938) deals with the Chinese wall with the same emphasis as does Atlantik-Wall (1944) with the German bulwark along the coast of the North Sea.

Fanck was often accused of a certain proximity to the aesthetics of fascist film art. Although he was never a grassroots Nazi, he must be considered a protagonist of the reactionary avant-garde, as he advocated an ideology of virile strength. Still, because his feature films signified a certain lethargy vis-à-vis nature (where heroism was called for), the Nazis neutralized Fanck in 1940 and banned him from feature filmmaking. Leni Riefenstahl assigned him a documentary film on the New Berlin, a project aborted after years of work. Fanck's late short documentaries do not carry his personal style.

ULI JUNG

See also: Riefenstahl, Leni

Biography

Born on March 6, 1889 in Frankenthal, the son of an industrialist. A frail child who, after recovering from tuberculosis, turned to skiing and mountain climbing. After studying geology (he earned a PhD in 1915), founded his own production company, Berg und Sportfilm GmbH Freiburg, which produced feature and documentary films made by Fanck and other directors. Fanck specialized in mountain films. Der Berg des Schicksals (1924) and Der heilige Berg (1926) marked his breakthrough. Together with Luis Trenker and Leni Riefenstahl, more or less single-handedly created the genre of the German mountain film. His success afforded him bigger budgets but greater dependencies. While the location shots of his feature films were still superb, the shallow storylines of his features failed to convince audiences. Der ewige Traum (1934) was the last feature he could accomplish in Germany (there followed two films shot in Japan and Chile). Concentrated on documentaries regardless of their impersonal styles, from which he made his living until the end of World War II. Postwar efforts to resume work in the film industry faltered. Died on September 28, 1974 in Freiburg.

Selected films

1913 4628 Meter hoch auf Skiern. Besteigung des Monte Rosa/Up 4628 Meters in the Sky. Climbing the Monte Rosa
1920–2 Das Wunder des Schneeschuhs/The Wonders of Skis
1924 Das Wolkenphänomen in Maloja/Clouds over the Malaja Pass
1928 Das weißse Stadion/The White Stadium
1931–5 Höchstleistungen im Skilauf/Record Achievements in Ski Training
1931–5 Zum Skifilmen/How to Film on Skis
1936–8 Kaiserbauten in Fernost/Imperial Buildings in the Far East
1943 Josef Thorak, Werkstatt und Werk/Josef Thorak, Studio and Oeuvre
1944 Arno Breker
1944 Atlantik-Wall/Atlantic Bulwark

Further reading

Arnold Fanck, Special issue of *Filmhefte*, summer, 1976, no. 2.

Cosandey, Roland, '4628 Meter hoch auf Skiern: Mit Ski und Filmkamera 1913 auf dem Monte Rosa', *Neue Zürcher Zeitung*, 22 September, 2000.

Fanck, Arnold, *Er führte Regie mit Gletschern, Stürmen und Lawinen: Ein Filmpionier erzählt*, Munich: Nymphenburger, 1973.

Horak, Jan-Christopher (ed.), *Berge, Licht und Traum: Dr Arnold Fanck und der deutsche Bergfilm*, Munich: Bruckmann, 1997.

Kiefer, Bernd, 'Eroberer des Nutzlosen: Abenteuer und Abenteurer bei Arnold Fanck', in Thomas Koebner (ed.), *Idole des deutschen Films*, Munich: edition text + kritik, 1997.

Kreimeier, Klaus (ed.), *Fanck—Trenker—Riefenstahl: Der deutsche Bergfilm und seine Folgen*, Berlin/West: SDK, 1972.

n.a., 'Revisited: Der Fall Dr. Fanck—Die Entdeckung der Natur im deutschen Bergfilm', special issue of *Film und Kritik*, no. 1, June 1992.

Far from Vietnam

(France, Resnais and others, 1967)

Far from Vietnam/Loin du Vietnam is an anthology film made by a collective of French filmmakers 'to assert in the exercise of their profession, their solidarity with the people of Vietnam in their resistance to aggression' (n.a. 1968). Like other protest films made during the war by Newsreel collectives and others, its purpose is clearly polemical, underpinned by Che Guevara's manifesto of 1960s radical politics: 'one, two, many Vietnams', whereby social, national, and racial differences, likewise geographical distance, are bridged by a common cause. However, as its title suggests, while the film endorses the cause of solidarity with the Vietnamese fighting America, it tempers the easy identification and 'romantic populism' (Renov 1990) characteristic of many other anti-war films produced in the period through its reflexive formal strategies.

The film was produced by the Société pour le Lancement des Oeuvres Nouvelles (SLON, Society for the Launching of New Works), a Marxist arts collective begun by Chris Marker in 1966 specifically for the film. (Later, Marker would revive SLON and the collective would continue production into the 1970s.) In 1967 Joris Ivens and Marcelline Loridan went to Vietnam to work on what would become 17e Parallèle/The 17th Parallel. Marker persuaded them to participate in the collective and they sent back from Hanoi footage showing daily life under bombardment. Others who joined Marker and Ivens included New Wave film-makers Alain Resnais, Agnès Varda, Jean-Luc Godard, as well as American photographer William Klein. Marker edited Far from Vietnam, which, like his previous film, Lettre de Sebérie/Letter from Siberia (1957), plays on conventions and viewer expectations of non-fiction film.

The film begins in a manner similar to other antiwar films of the period, as it compares the 'rich man's war' to a 'poor man's war', with images of high-tech warfare—the aircraft carrier, Kitty Hawk, loading bombs in the Gulf of Tonkin—contrasted to a bucolic image of rural Vietnam. However, it quickly undermines the simplicity of that opposition. What appears at first to be an empty field waiting to be torn apart by bombs is not empty at all; it comes alive when concealed soldiers emerge, advance, and then recede into the land. A simple but powerful image of guerilla warfare, it consolidates metaphorically a point addressed in various ways throughout the film—the difficulty for Europeans and Americans to understand, to clearly see the war in Vietnam. It is a point made a few years later by Frances Fitzgerald in her analysis of the war, *Fire in the Lake*: 'American soldiers had […] walked over the political and economic design of the Vietnamese revolution. They had looked at it, but they could not see it, for it was doubly invisible: invisible within the ground and then again invisible within their own perspective as Americans' (Fitzgerald 1972).

The segments that follow are strikingly varied in style and quality, including vérité images of demonstrations in France and the United States in 'A Parade is a Parade', footage of a musical comedy performance by a travelling North Vietnamese theatre group in 'Johnson Cries', a monologue by a fictitious contemporary Parisian author in 'Claude Ridder', distorted and manipulated television images in 'Why We Fight', a collage of vérité images, advertisements, store window displays, American icons, and cartoons in 'Vertigo'. Surveying in this way the formal options available to the political film-maker, the discursive range of this anthology film works to forestall any possibility of the war's authoritative representation.

The best known of these segments and the most succinct in its discussion of the problem of representing the war from a Western perspective is Jean-Luc Godard's Camera Eye. Despite the allusion to Dziga Vertov, Godard's comments on the difficulty of conceptualising Vietnam for film qualify the accessibility of what Vertov called Kino-Pravda (film truth) while maintaining its political necessity as a goal. The segment begins with a close-up of Godard addressing the camera to say what he might film in Vietnam were he a cameraman for a newsreel or television network. However, he is neither of those things and is still in Paris, having been refused entrance by officials in Hanoi. Reframed to a medium shot we see that Godard is seated behind a Mitchell camera, which functions in the sequence as a technological metonym for Hollywood and the United States. He then speaks of the difficulty of conceptualizing Vietnam for film, despite a shared struggle against the United States—his against cultural imperialism and theirs against military aggression. Godard concludes that there's really no understanding Vietnam until such time as 'we can let Vietnam invade us […] and find out what part it plays in our everyday lives'. Such are the limits and ideals of political filmmaking, that only complete identification could close the gap between Godard and his subject. Moreover, he continues to observe that the breach between himself and the Vietnamese is the same one as that which exists between himself and the French working class, for whom he also makes films and with whom he also claims solidarity, even though they never see his films. These are the conditions of the making of protest films like

Far from Vietnam, in which ultimately all he and other filmmakers can do is 'listen and [...] relay all the screams that we possibly can'.

Like Godard in Camera Eye, the SLON collective makes its political alliance with North Vietnam clear, but Far from Vietnam focuses overall on the difficulty of representing the war, the difficulty of responding adequately to it on film, and of claiming identification as a European or American filmmaker with the struggle of the Vietnamese. In this way it is a film about the war in Vietnam but it is also about the conditions of political and nonfiction filmmaking more generally.

AMANDA HOWELL

Loin du Vietnam/Far from Vietnam (France, SLON, 1967, 115 mins). Distributed by New Yorker Films (US). Directed by Alain Resnais, William Klein, Joris Ivens, Agnès Varda, Claude Lelouch, Jean-Luc Godard. Principal collaborators: Michèle Ray, Roger Pic, K.S. Karol, Marceline Loridan, François Maspero, Chris Marker, Jacques Sternberg, Jean Lacouture, Willy Kurant, Jean Boffety, Kieu Tham, Denis Clairval, Ghislain Cloquet, Bernard Zitztermann, Alain Levent, and Théo Robichet.

Further reading

Ellis, John, *The Documentary Idea, A Critical History of English-Language Documentary Film and Video*, Englewood Cliffs, NJ: Prentice-Hall, 1989.

Fitzgerald, Frances, *Fire in the Lake: The Vietnamese and the Americans in Vietnam*, New York: Vintage Books, 1972.

James, David E., 'Film and the War: Representing Vietnam', in *Allegories of Cinema: American Film in the Sixties*, Princeton, NJ: Princeton University Press, 1989: 195–213.

n.a., 'Far from Vietnam', *Variety*, October 4, 1967, 12.

n.a., 'Loin du Viet-Nam (Far from Vietnam)', *Monthly Film Bulletin* 35, no. 409, 1968: 29.

Plantinga, Carl, *Rhetoric and Representation in Nonfiction Film*, Cambridge: Cambridge University Press, 1997.

Renov, Michael, 'Imaging the Other: Representations of Vietnam in Sixties Political Documentary', in *From Hanoi to Hollywood: The Vietnam War in American Film*, New Brunswick, NJ: Rutgers University Press, 1990: 255–68.

Sarris, Andrew, 'The New York Film Festival (1967)', in *Confessions of a Cultist: On the Cinema 1955–69*, New York: Simon and Schuster, 1970: 317–18.

Field, Mary

Surprisingly, for someone with such a prolific career in educational film, little has been written about Mary Field in histories of documentary film. No doubt this is because educational film in the 1930s existed on the fringes of the documentary movement, regarded by Grierson and his followers as little more than lecture films unlikely to make a contribution to the fuller art of the documentary (Grierson 1966). However, the natural history films made by Field and her colleagues are the forerunners of the popular wildlife television programmes of today and should not be dismissed because they did not fit Grierson's definition of documentary.

Field started her career as a teacher and historian. She was an authority on seventeenth-century fishing in the West Atlantic, and it was with this specialist knowledge that she entered the film industry. Visiting Bruce Woolfe's British Instructional studios in late 1925 to advise them on the historical accuracy of one of their films, she was offered a post as Education Manager. Within a year she had became a member of the production staff, learning editing, continuity, scriptwriting, and direction while working on educational, documentary, and feature films. By 1927 she was directing for the famous pioneering biological and wildlife series, the Secrets of Nature, started by Bruce Woolfe in 1919. Working with the cinematographer Percy Smith, an expert in time lapse and macro-photography, Field helped to create a series covering many aspects of the natural world including insects, plants, animals, and sea life. Compared with the sophisticated technology available to wildlife filmmakers today, the equipment used by Field and Smith was cumbersome and noisy; the lenses were so long and heavy that braces were used to fix them to the camera and tripod. This makes the results they achieved all the more remarkable. In 1929 Field became the Secrets of Nature series editor, as well as the director of more than fifty films for the series in the next four years. Other films directed during this period include the hygiene film Deferred Payment (1929) and the comedy feature Strictly Business (1932). She also edited the World War I drama, Tell England (1931).

When British Instructional was taken over in 1933, Field worked briefly for Woolfe's new company before joining Gaumont-British Films' recently formed educational unit,

Gaumont-British Instructional. When Woolfe joined her they continued to make nature films under a new moniker, Secrets of Life. Field also diversified her subject matter and began directing films for geography, history, language, physical education, and hygiene syllabi in schools. Invited on to the Board of Gaumont-British Instructional, Field exercised a decisive influence in both policy matters and in the making of the films themselves. She began experimenting with the use of animated diagrams for classroom films as is seen in two of her films, The Expansion of Germany (1936) and Changes in the Franchise (1937). She was also active in promoting the pedagogical use of film in the wider world and sat on various committees, notably the British Film Institute Panels. Her early years in teaching meant that she understood the importance of tailoring educational films to the requirements of the classroom, and the knowledge she acquired from teachers on these committees was more often than not successfully translated to the screen.

During the war, along with other documentary and educational filmmakers, Field's skills were used in making government films for the war effort. Drawing on the images of the nature series she had edited and directed, Field humorously adapted the wildlife genre to the human and political concerns of rationing, agricultural production, and the use of pigeons as messengers by the army. These home front propaganda films demonstrate a clarity of thought and assured direction that had become Field's hallmark in more than fifteen years of educational filmmaking.

In 1944 J. Arthur Rank set up the Children's Entertainment Division of the Rank Organisation to produce entertainment films for his Saturday morning Odeon and Gaumont Children's Cinema Clubs. With her background in the production of classroom films and an increasing interest in the need for children's entertainment films, Field was the logical choice to head the new division. Her initial attempts to provide stimulating entertainment for children were not well received by the industry or critics, and she was accused of not knowing what children wanted by a technician at the 1946 Association of Cinematograph Technicians' conference. Nevertheless, Field is a figure who stands out in an era when cinema was often attacked as a morally degenerative influence on children; her motivation was to broaden the experiences of children through entertaining but informative filmmaking, and this legacy remains with us today in public sector children's television programming such as Blue Peter. When financial cutbacks closed the Children's Entertainment Division, Field spent a year at the British Board of Film Classification before taking up the post of executive officer at the newly created Children's Film Foundation.

In 1954 Field was awarded an OBE for her work in educational and children's entertainment film. In 1955 she was made a fellow of both the Royal Photographic Society and the British Kinematograph Society. Two years later the British Film Academy awarded her the same status. Her final years were spent doing consultancy work for children's television programming, as well as founding an International Centre of Films for Children, of which she became honorary president until her death in 1968.

SARAH EASEN

Biography

Born in Wimbledon, London February 24, 1896. Graduated with an MA in history and became a teacher. Married Gerald Hankin in 1944. Fellow of the Royal Photographic Society, the British Kinematograph Society, and the British Film Academy; Order of the British Empire 1951. Education manager, British Instructional, 1926. Production assistant, continuity, editor, scriptwriter, director, British Instructional Films, 1927–9. Director, producer, series editor: Secrets of Nature, British Instructional Films, 1929–33. Production manager, British Independent Pictures, 1933. Series editor: Secrets of Life; director, producer, board member, Gaumont-British Instructional, 1934–44. Chief officer, Children's Entertainment Division of the Rank Organisation, 1944–50. Examiner, British Board of Film Classification, 1950. Chief executive officer, Children's Film Foundation, 1951–5. Chair/honorary president, International Centre of Films for Children (Brussels) 1957–68. Children's programme consultant, ATV/ABC Television, 1959–63. Died in Worthing December 23, 1968.

Selected films

1933	Secrets of Nature (natural history series): series editor and director
1933–42	Secrets of Life (natural history series): series editor and director
1934	Farming in Suffolk series: director
1934–9	Farming in East Anglia series: director
1935	Face of Britain: This Was England: director
1939	They Made the Land: director
1940	Wisdom of the Wild: director
1941	Winged Messengers: director
1943	Development of an English Town: director

Further reading

Field, Mary and Smith, Percy, *Secrets of Nature*, London: The Scientific Book Club, 1939.

Field, Mary, *Good Company: The Story of the Children's Entertainment Film Movement in Great Britain, 1943–50*, London: Longmans Green, 1952.

Grierson, John, *Grierson on Documentary*, ed. Forsyth Hardy, revised edn, London: Faber, 1966.

Low, Rachael, *Documentary and Educational Films of the 1930s*, London: George Allen and Unwin, 1979.

MacNab, Geoffrey, *J. Arthur Rank and the British Film Industry*, London and New York: Routledge, 1993.

Thorpe, Frances and Pronay, Nicholas, with Clive Coultass, *British Official Films in the Second World War: A Descriptive Catalogue*, Oxford: Clio Press, 1980.

Finding Christa

(US, Billops and Hatch, 1991)

Finding Christa is an autobiographical account of filmmaker Camille Billops's 1961 decision to put her then four-year-old daughter, Christa, up for adoption. The film formalizes its episodic narrative beneath a backdrop of both conventional documentary aesthetics and lightly avant-garde subjectivity. The resulting film both challenges and conforms to its subject matter. Finding Christa successfully manages to question multiple ideologies while offering up far more questions than it answers, thereby challenging the viewer.

Finding Christa is the third in an ongoing series of collaborative projects from the husband and wife team of James Hatch and Camille Billops, including Suzanne Suzanne (1982) and Older Women and Love (1987), and shared a 1992 Grand Jury prize at Sundance. The series of films are not expressly related, yet there are various thematic threads coupled with the use of similar formal techniques. Although the couple seems to share in the production roles of their films, Billops usually takes on a more visual role. The films relay a definite female authorial voice. Even Hatch's screen role within Finding Christa is more that of supporting player to the complex dynamics of Billops and daughter Christa Victoria. The mother and daughter are not only presented in conventional dramatic installments, but multiple artistic sequences as well. Many of the formative passages also become vehicles for the participants, including numerous musical installments from both Christa and her adopted mother, Margaret Liebig.

The premise of Finding Christa, as the title implies, takes the viewer to the reunion whereby mother and child in essence find each other again after a twenty-year separation. Although the film does manage to keep the reunion as its predominant dramaturgical device, the overall focus is often that of Billops's life, displayed through moments of autobiographical reflections. The film addresses not only the complexities of the relationship between the reunited mother and daughter, but other interfamily relationships as experienced by Billops in response to her 1961 decision. Through a series of interviews with sometimes critical family members and ongoing personal commentaries (some in the form of rebuttals to her family's testimonials), Billops attempts to explain, and come to terms with, the choice to put her child up for adoption. This comes across as not being so much for herself, or even as justification of the act, but what seems to be more a type of education into the decision for the interviewees and viewers. Billops seems as secure in her decision at the end of the film as she was in 1961; it is only those around her who perhaps have changed their minds.

The title of Finding Christa reveals the complexities of the film. Among other meanings, it refers to the mother finding a child she left behind, the child finding herself through the mother, the viewer finding the child, and even the artist once again finding the mother. All of the relationships in the film seem to exist in a harmony that is anything but harmonious. This point seems to be one of the underlying currents of the narrative's questions of reality and its versions of such views. None of her family's reflections of the 1961 episode seem to be sufficient to answer the question of why Billops did what she did; yet the film and Billops herself seem content with that question remaining unanswered, instead positing the response of why is it necessary for others to feel content with something she needed to do.

One of the film's underscored revelations is found in Billops's old family home movies. Shot by her mother and father, the clips present a middle-class counterpoint to the usual iconographic imagery of 1950s and 1960s black America, as well as the same era's portrayal of the unwed mother. The film uses such footage to call all such ideologies into question including those of the middle class, for it is the breakdown of middle-class ideologies that is at the heart of Finding Christa. Just as the title questions its linguistic interpretations, the film questions those of the roles of mother, woman, child, and others in the eye of such. Such a breakdown is not one of destruction so much as of analysis, as the film is not one for answers, merely one that questions, which is one of the ways in which it engages the viewer.

The narrative structure in Finding Christa is separated into four episodes, each with its own introductory intertitle. Besides providing a means for directional switches of the narrative, they serve as effective ways to voice that of the film's subjects, while maintaining the film's ongoing dialectical conflict. The first title is that of Christa, yet the segment is about Billops. Billops voices the next two and they end with the ambiguity of the closing, 'Almost Home', title. This final title, which in essence not only reflects both subjects' voices, but exerts a certain surface level (previously exhibited in the subjective visualizations) of reflexive humor, because the film is almost over. In some ways, it is this final title that gives the viewer the most insight, being that it is the first and only title not posed in question form, allowing it to stand as more of a statement. Yet it reminds the viewer of an ambiguity that runs much deeper, as it provides no resolution, instead suggesting that the subjects never quite did get home. What this title and the subsequent scenes that follow reveal is not only that they did not reach home, but that the mere notion of such a possibility might reside only in the ideological implications that the film sets itself up to question.

Multiple interpretations of this film are inevitable, especially of Billops herself. Her demeanor throughout the film regarding the adoption is one that some might even find troubling, but that is all part of the intrigue that the film invokes. There are no easy answers to the questions addressed within Finding Christa, but that is part of the message being delivered, that of diversity and the complexities involved with such diversity.

DINO EVERETT

Finding Christa (US, Hatch-Billops Productions, 1991, 55 mins). Distributed by Third World Newsreel. Produced by Camille Billops and James Hatch. Directed by Camille Billops and James Hatch. Written by Camille Billops and James Hatch. Cinematography by Dion Hatch. Archival footage by Alma and Walter Dotson. Edited by Paula Heredia. Sound edited by Ray McCutcheon. Original music by Christa Victoria. Filmed in Oakland, New York.

Further reading

Goffman, Erving, *The Presentation of Self in Everyday Life*, Woodstock, NY: The Overlook Press, 1973.

Haskell, Molly, *From Reverence to Rape*, second edition, Chicago: University of Chicago Press, 1987.

Lane, Jim, 'Black Autobiographical Documentary', *Jump Cut* 40, 1996: 38–46.

Lekatsas, Barbara, 'Encounters: The Film Odyssey of Camille Billops', *Black American Literature Forum* 25, no. 2, 1991: 395–408.

May, Elaine Tyler, *Homeward Bound: American Families in the Cold War Era*, New York, Basic Books, 1988.

Nichols, Bill, *Representing Reality: Issues and Concepts in Documentary*, Bloomington, IL: Indiana University Press, 1991.

Smith, Valerie, 'Telling Secrets: Narrative and Ideology, in Suzanne, Suzanne by Camille Billups and James V. Hatch', in Diane Carson, Linda Dittmar and Janice Welsch (eds), *Multiple Voices in Feminist Film Criticism*, Minneapolis, MN: University of Minnesota Press, 1994.

White, Hayden, *Narrative Discourse and Historical Representation*, Baltimore, MD: John Hopkins University Press, 1987.

Fires Were Started

(UK, Jennings, 1943)

Fires Were Started (1943) is considered the pre-eminent film about Britain at war. It was made by the highly acclaimed film director, Humphrey Jennings. Fires Were Started uses powerfully poetic visuals to offer a dramatic reconstruction of events associated with the Blitz on London, while at the same time offering a high degree of emotional realism in characterisation. The film has had a powerful influence on succeeding generations of British filmmakers. Leading filmmakers Lindsay Anderson and Karl Reisz, prominent figures in the experimental British Free Cinema Movement (1955–9), have singled out Fires Were Started as a unique film that had a significant influence on their approach to filmmaking. In an article on Jennings's work for *Sight and Sound* (April–June 1954), Anderson refers to the poetic power of Jennings's film style and argued that, 'In fact it might reasonably be contended that Humphrey Jennings is the only real poet the British Cinema has yet produced' (Jacobs 1979: 236). Reisz acknowledged the influence of Jennings's work and cited Fires Were Started as, 'the source film for Free Cinema' (Orbanz 1977: 57).

Fires Were Started was one of several films made by Humphrey Jennings under the auspices of the General Post Office (GPO) Film Unit and the Crown Film Unit. This collection of films addressed the various ways in which the British civilian population were involved and affected by the war. London Can Take It (1940), codirected by Harry Watt, represented the effects of the Blitz. Listen to Britain (1942) portrayed in a positive way the mood of the nation through descriptive sound, with scenes of high-spirited female factory workers collectively singing popular songs as they made their contribution to Britain's war effort. A Diary for Timothy (1944–5) was a more poignant film, and commented on the uncertain effects of five years of a world at war.

Fires Were Started was made in cooperation with the Home Office Ministry of Home Security and the National Fire Service, and was part of a propaganda drive to maintain high morale within civil defence organisations and the civilian population that they served. Brian Winston, in his book *Fires Were Started* (1999), comments on the propagandist function of the film while acknowledging the acute observation and impressive formal qualities deployed in Jennings's poetic realist style. He argues that, 'Fires Were Started, not (say) Triumph des Willens, is the real propaganda masterwork of the BFI list' (Winston 1999: 38).

Ostensibly, Fires Were Started is in the genre of documentary drama, in the sense that it is a dramatic reenactment of the type of events that the fire service encountered. Its documentary authority, however, rests more with the way in which the film communicated accurate information about how the fire service was coordinated during wartime. A variety of scenes accurately represented the levels of organisation involved in civilian defence, the functions of the chain of command, and the ways in which information was communicated to best use available resources. It offered a reassuring account of the way in which the organisations that served and protected the civilian population operated in times of crisis.

The narrative of Fires Were Started recounts twenty-four hours in the lives of the firemen of the Auxiliary Fire Service, from the time they leave home for work, through the routines of their job and everyday interaction with colleagues, to the telephone call that summons the firemen to fight a dangerous warehouse fire at the docks, which threatens to spread to a heavily laden munitions ship. The narrative culminates in the death of one of the firemen, a popular Cockney character called Jacko who is much valued by his colleagues. The film ends with scenes of Jacko's funeral intercut with shots of the ship sailing out of dock with its vital munitions cargo intact.

The film graphically depicted that although there may be a high cost in human terms to maintain Britain's war effort, the men and women on the home front were fulfilling their duties with an unquestioning bravery. This aspect of the film, a representation of the national spirit of Britain during the war, is perhaps more solidly anchored in the director's earlier interests. Jennings's friend and contemporary at Cambridge, the poet Kathleen Raines, commented that, 'What counted for Humphrey was the expression, by certain people, of the ever-growing spirit of man, in particular, of the spirit of England' (Jacobs 1979: 239). As a young man Jennings had cofounded the Mass Observation movement in 1937. The Mass Observation movement recruited a team of observers and a panel of volunteer writers who focused on British public life, attending public gatherings such as sporting events, open-air meetings, and entertainment venues.

The power of Jennings's representation of the men and women of the fire service in Fires Were Started lies in the dramatic tension created by a constant foregrounding of the ordinariness of the firefighters, which is contrasted with the unpredictable and heroic acts that the task of fire fighting requires. Winston (1999) argued that Jennings used masterly sociological or 'indirect' propaganda in the way he tapped into the mythic qualities that already circulated around the men and women of the fire service in London, who were acclaimed for their part in tackling blazing infernos and for rescuing many people from heavily bombed areas during the Blitz.

Although the basic narrative structure of Fires Were Started is unremarkable, the characterisation, as well as the visually exciting representation of dramatic firefights, have attracted much praise. Actual firemen from the Auxiliary Fire Service played the fictional characters in the film, and throughout the film Jennings maintains the sense that he is telling real people's stories. The film clearly underscores the essential ordinariness of the characters and their daily routines, in the everyday scenes of men saying goodbye to their families as they leave for work, to scenes of friendly banter with colleagues at the station house. These scenes, which foreground the unexceptional in life and the ordinariness of the characters, however, are later contrasted with visually dramatic scenes of a raging inferno at the warehouse, and acts of firefighting that necessitate extraordinary human courage as the fire spreads towards the munitions ship moored in the dock. Nevertheless, in these latter highly dramatic scenes, Jennings refrained from representing the firefighters as infallible heroes and managed to retain a sense of authentic ordinariness in the characterisation of the firemen. The firemen are shown making mistakes and having to deal with unpredictable situations as they arise in an often imperfect manner. This sense of ordinary men being called on to deal with superhuman events enables the narrative to play in the space between the mythic and the real.

The film achieves a more powerful emotional address by avoiding the depiction of the firefighters in action as invincible heroes, and instead by striving for a more authentic representation of the firefighters as ordinary men who risk their lives, and in the case of Jacko, die in the service of others. Lindsay Anderson (1954) cogently argued, 'In outline it is the simplest of pictures; in treatment it is of the greatest subtlety, richly poetic in feeling, intense with tenderness and admiration for the unassuming heroes whom it honours.' Anderson (1954) further argued that it was an exceptional film that had managed to capture an essential truth about the nature of the men and women it represented: 'No other British film made during the war, documentary or feature, achieved such a continuous and poignant truthfulness, or treated the subject of men at war with such a sense of its incidental glories and its essential tragedy' (Jacobs 1979: 241).

Jennings's film career was cut short, as he died at the age of forty-three in an accident on the Greek island of Poros, while researching locations for a film. Fires Were Started is arguably his greatest film legacy and continues to be considered a classic film of the period.

PAT A. COOK

See also: Anderson, Lindsay; Diary for Timothy, A; Jennings, Humphrey; Listen to Britain; London Can Take It; Reisz, Karel

Fires Were Started (UK, Crown Film Unit, 1943, 80 mins). Produced by Ian Dalrymple. Directed by Humphrey Jennings. Written by Humphrey Jennings. Cinematography by C. Pennington-Richards. Original music by William Alwyn. Musical direction by Muir Mathieson. Edited by Stewart McAllister. Sound recorded by Ken Cameron and Jock May. Production management by Dora Wright.

Further reading

Anderson, Lindsay, 'Some Aspects of the Work of Humphrey Jennings', *Sight and Sound* (London), April–June 1954.

Jackson, Kevin (ed.), *The Humphrey Jennings Film Reader*, Manchester: Carcanet Press, 1995.

Jacobs, Lewis, *The Documentary Tradition*, Toronto: George J. McLeod Ltd, 1979.

Lovell, Allan and Hillier, Jim, *Studies in Documentary*, London: Secker and Warburg, 1972.

Orbanz, Eva, *Journey to a Legend and Back: The British Realistic Film*, Berlin: Verlag Volker Spiess, 1977.

Winston, Brian, *BFI Film Classics: 'Fires Were Started'*, London: BFI, 1999.

First Love

(Poland, Kieślowski, 1974)

One in a loose series of Krzysztof Kieślowski documentaries concerning ordinary people and places made across the 1970s, First Love (Pierwsza Miłość) follows a young couple as they marry and, within months, become parents. Despite the odds stacked against Romek and Jadźka—she is pregnant aged seventeen, and both are ill-prepared for their impending responsibilities and disoriented by the bureaucracy they face in terms of setting up a family home—they are resolute and determined. With severity, and just the occasional glimpse of sympathy, authority figures intervene in their lives but fail to detract from the couple's shared, unarticulated sense of joy and trepidation as they journey from 'first love' to adulthood and parenthood. Jadźka's façade only cracks after the wedding (an austere and functional ceremony that begins with the paying of a fee); she weeps silently as she receives advice and best wishes from her family. Such scenes, and Romek's fumbling phone call to his mother from the hospital announcing the birth of their daughter, suggest emotional pain equal to the pain of the actual birth, which is also recorded.

Kieślowski does not flinch in the face of these intimate and private scenes and yet, shortly afterwards, was to declare himself a trespasser on forbidden territory. Not only were such events inappropriate to film, but the act of filming itself blocked that which Kieślowski seems to have perceived as a greater, phenomenological 'truth'. From a Bazinian perspective, reality ultimately refuses to yield up such a truth for the camera. Žižek posits the resultant shift from documentary to feature films—indicative of a structural failure of documentary realism in the face of the all-too-real, something only encountered at the very limits of experience—as central to his reading of Kieślowski: 'a fidelity to the Real' is only possible via the mask of fiction (Žižek 2001). Such a tension is detectable in First Love's reconstructed scenes (Jadźka learning of her pregnancy, for example) and the lack of a methodological objective rigour. At one point, Kieślowski presents an actual and precise point-of-view shot (Jadźka absent-mindedly gazes through the glass panes of a phone booth at mothers and their children outside). Such a shot is impossible within the conceptual framework of an observational documentary.

Thus, by the 1980s Kieślowski had virtually abandoned the documentary. For contemporary viewers primarily familiar with Kieślowski as one of the most celebrated European auteurs of the late twentieth century, First Love engenders a kind of ahistorical déjà vu. The intimacy and obsessiveness with which Kieślowski frames the female 'recalls' Trois Couleurs: Bleu/Three Colours: Blue (1993); the series of events that irrevocably alter the course of a protagonist's life 'recalls' Przypadek/Blind Chance (1981); and the figure of the lone male, calling up to his partner in a high window 'recalls' the moment that closes Trois Couleurs: Blanc/Three Colours: White (1994). In such ways, Kieślowski mapped the real onto the fictional.

With none of the savvy of their aspirational reality television successors, Romek and Jadźka seem mostly oblivious to the documentary makers (a minimal crew, shooting in 16mm for thirty to forty days over the course of a year). Kieślowski favours long takes, allowing the characters to dictate the rhythm of the sequences. Nevertheless, a measure of direct manipulation is apparent, as well as one self-confessed 'clear provocation' (Stok 1993), in an engineered visit by a policeman. Kieślowski surrounds Romek and Jadźka with friends and family, creating the situation in which they would behave freely and naturally. This is achieved to the extent that the occasional glance at the camera by Kieślowski's subjects and the intrusion of the microphone into the frame serves to remind the viewer of the documentary nature of the film. Discreet jump cuts work in the same way, as do reestablishing shots from semi-hidden positions, denoting the essentially voyeuristic nature of the film.

Despite the seemingly dour subject matter, and with Kieślowski's taste for the oppressive Polish cityscape much in evidence, the aesthetic choices allow no pessimism. The colours are bright and vibrant and speak of the joie de vivre of the time and place; sunny overexposures for externals blur colour and form, joyously reimagining the Woodstock-esque cast of adolescent supporting characters with a kind of saturated pictorialism. Indeed, these characters are the benefactors of 1960s liberalism. Jadźka is met with acceptance rather than ostracism, support rather than disdain (with the sole exception of the board of school teachers, who downgrade her for lack of sexual morals). Such subject matter, only a decade before, made for some of the bleakest expressions of postwar European realism, particularly in British Northern Realism.

The defining and dominant characteristic of Kieślowski's method is his use of the tightly framed medium close-up, even with the (mostly) handheld camera. Even during the wedding ceremony and the birth, Kieślowski deftly holds the faces, rendering such events as steps on the emotional journey of the protagonists, catching fleeting and sometimes contradictory expressions as they sweep across their faces. This is the vantage point, intimates Kieślowski, from which the sociopolitical order must be examined. After all, if there is no hope for such a couple, and no sense in which their tribulations, however commonplace, can be understood to be both gracious and noble, then what hope is there for society? This could be read as a strategy of subversion in relation to the historical prerequisite of a socialist perspective (or 'optimistic facts', as Kieślowski jokingly referred to it (Stok 1993)). Kieślowski relocates the idea of socialist perspective, from the clichés of Socialist Realism (abundant farms, happy toiling workers, youths bright-eyed with ideology) to the everyman hopes of a contemporary young couple.

BENJAMIN HALLIGAN

See also: Kieślowski, Krzysztof

First Love (Poland, Pierwsza Miłość, 1974, 52 mins; a thirty-minute 'short film' cut was subsequently prepared). Produced for Polish Television. Directed by Krzysztof Kieślowski. Cinematography by Jacek Petrycki. Edited by Lidia Zonn. Sound by Magorzata Jaworska, and Michae Zarnecki. Filmed in Warsaw. Grand Prize, 1974 National Short Film Festival, Kraków. Special Jury Award, 1974 International Short Film Festival, Kraków.

Further reading

Coates, Paul (ed.), *Lucid Dreams: The Films of Krzysztof Kieślowski*, London: Flicks Books, 1999.

Haltof, Marek, *The Cinema of Krzysztof Kieślowski: Variations on Destiny and Chance*, London and New York: Wallflower Press, 2004.

Insdorf, Annette, *Double Lives, Second Chances: The Cinema of Krzysztof Kieslowski*, New York: Talk Miramax Books, 1999.

Stok, Danusia (ed. and trans.), *Kieslowski on Kieslowski*, London and Boston: Faber & Faber, 1993.

Žižek, Slavoj, *The Fright of Real Tears: Krzysztof Kieślowski between Theory and Post-Theory*, London: British Film Institute, 2001.

Flaherty, Robert

Robert J. Flaherty is a legendary figure in film history and often called the 'father' of American documentary, with a reputation that rests primarily on four feature-length works: Nanook of the North (1922), Moana (1926), Man of Aran (1934), and Louisiana Story (1948). Nanook was the first documentary feature to achieve mainstream box office success and is still considered by many as an exemplary piece of ethnographic filmmaking. Yet in recent years, Flaherty's films—and the more general construction of what has come to be known as the Flaherty myth—have been intensely scrutinized by scholars and critics. The problems most frequently found in Flaherty's work lie in two primary areas. The first relates to the question of documentary authenticity and, more specifically, to Flaherty's common practice of staging scenes and reconstructing 'primitive' life in his films. The second area of inquiry examines the extent to which Flaherty might have reproduced imperial hierarchies in his representations of racial and cultural difference. This latter issue becomes particularly difficult to ignore given the director's early career as an explorer, surveyor, and prospector in the Hudson Bay region for the industrialist and financier Sir William Mackenzie, whom Flaherty once referred to as 'the Cecil Rhodes of Canada' (Rotha 1983).

The story of Flaherty's early life as an explorer forms the backdrop to his career directing films in a mode that John Grierson and Paul Rotha would define as the naturalist tradition of documentary. Born in Michigan, Flaherty began by closely following the career path of his father, a mining engineer who often took his teenage son on prospecting expeditions to the remote regions of northern Ontario. The young Flaherty had little patience for academics, and a brief attempt to study mineralogy at the Michigan College of Mines, where he met his future wife and collaborator Frances Hubbard, ended in dismissal. In 1910, after returning to prospecting, Flaherty encountered Mackenzie, who engaged him to explore for iron ore along the sub-Arctic coast of

Hudson Bay. In 1913, at Mackenzie's suggestion, Flaherty purchased a Bell and Howell camera, which he took with him on a major expedition to the Belcher Islands. One important innovation during these early attempts to film in the frozen north was Flaherty's decision to develop the negative on site and then screen the rushes to local Inuits, so that they could see the results of his efforts and work together with him 'as partners' (Rotha 1983). The practice led Flaherty to be seen as a pioneer of the collaborative feedback method, later adopted by Jean Rouch for such films as Moi, un Noir (1958) and Chronique d'un été (1961). By 1916, after several journeys and numerous failed attempts at filming in extreme conditions, Flaherty compiled seventy thousand feet of exposed negative. Editing it in Toronto, he accidentally, though some have thought intentionally, dropped a cigarette on the film and it instantly went up in flames. He was left with a single positive print (now lost), which is sometimes called the Harvard Print after his intention to screen it at the university.

The survival of the Harvard Print had at least two significant effects on Flaherty's development as a filmmaker. The first involved aesthetics and narrative: viewing it after the fire, he determined it to be an inferior piece of work, lacking dynamic visuals and a coherent storyline. The second was material, as he was able to screen the print in subsequent years in an effort to secure financing for his 'Eskimo film'. In the meantime he concentrated on writing and collaborating with Frances, and he edited the journals of his numerous northern journeys, released in 1924 as *My Eskimo Friends*. It was not until 1920 that another filming opportunity arose, when the French fur-trading firm Revillon Frères agreed to sponsor a trek north to their trading post in Cape Dufferin, Ungava. The relationship with Revillon Frères has since disturbed critics as it raises unsettling questions about the commercial and imperial forces behind the film. This is further compounded by the evident product placement of Revillon's furs in scenes at the trading post and inside Nanook's igloo (Rony 1996). After sixteen months of shooting in difficult climatic conditions, followed by months of editing and securing a distributor, the film was released by Pathé in 1922. With a total production and postproduction cost of $53,000, the film was a relative bargain for a feature, and it is estimated that it grossed $251,000 by September of the year of its release (Murphy 1978).

Flaherty had tapped into a growing public demand for films that not only documented travel to foreign places but also highlighted and investigated racial and cultural difference, a collective desire already partially in evidence in the ongoing success of shorter and more simply structured film travelogues. Nanook of the North's commercial success also paved the way for a range of expeditionary films, such as Osa and Martin Johnson's Simba: The King of the Beasts (1928) and Cooper and Schoedsack's Grass (1925) and Chang (1927). Though still held in higher critical esteem than these expeditionary adventures, Flaherty's film was arguably similar in relying on staged sequences and skillful editing to produce a seamless illusion of documentary reality. This practice of staging certain sequences while also filming candid scenes and events, then cutting the footage together to form a coherent episodic narrative, was to become a Flaherty trademark, evident in most of his major films. The key to appreciating Flaherty's style lies not in seeking out the strands of documentary or ethnographic authenticity, but in recognizing his skill in bridging the gap between on-site improvisation and narrative continuity on the screen. This improvisational skill is in evidence in Nanook near the end of the seal hunting sequence, where Flaherty's slight pans and tilts capture the raging sled dogs with the same fullness and immediacy as the more carefully produced moments earlier in the film, such as the dramatically staged opening shot of the walrus hunt.

Flaherty's next film, Moana, was shot in western Samoa, where he lived and worked with Frances and their children for nearly two years. The Flahertys were determined to recreate Nanook's heroic survival tale while relocating the story to a tropical climate. Nanook had defined the major themes that would dominate Flaherty's other work: the visual power of natural settings, the importance of familial bonds, nostalgia for ways of life presumed to be dead or dying, and the human struggle against nature. However, Samoan life failed to produce the latter key dramatic element, and the film that resulted was arguably the first feature-length documentary to focus to such an extent on the details of everyday life. Moana is reputed to have inspired the first written use of the term 'documentary' (Grierson 1979), though the claim has more recently been disputed (Winston 1988). Some of the film's most lasting contributions were aesthetic. Flaherty experimented with long focus lenses while in Samoa, finding that a greater distance between the camera and observed subjects helped to capture performances that appeared less controlled and self-conscious. He also rejected the standard use of orthochromatic film stock in favour of more sensitive panchromatic film, resulting in resonant images that helped to influence a shift in Hollywood practice. Perhaps even more than his other films, Moana reflects Flaherty's alignment with a modernist primitivism that arrived with the emergence of American cultural relativism, embodying Western longings for an untouched and timeless native world where one might escape from the routines of an increasingly industrialized and mechanized society.

To fund Moana, Flaherty had been offered a 'blank check' by Jesse Lasky of Famous Players–Lasky, but the film's lacklustre box office receipts meant that his honeymoon period with Hollywood was effectively over. Flaherty had, in any case, already gained a reputation for faithfully working in exotic locations with native peoples just at a moment when Hollywood was pioneering the large-scale location shoot and banking on the popularity of expeditionary films. After two smaller projects, The Potterymaker (1925) and the elegant Manhattan 'city symphony', Twenty-four Dollar Island (1926), Flaherty entered a difficult period during which he contributed to a number of mainstream projects. Having provided a poetic image of the South Pacific as a lost paradise in Moana, he was determined to make a film that would reveal the effects of colonial exploitation upon the region. In 1927 he went to Tahiti to codirect the MGM adaptation of Frederick O'Brien's best-seller, *White Shadows in the South Seas*, but his slow and extravagant shooting methods fell foul of the more commercial expectations of his codirector, W.S. Van Dyke. Another opportunity in the Pacific came in 1929, when his brother David helped to cement a partnership between Flaherty and the German expressionist director, F.W. Murnau. The film was completed as the South Seas fantasy Tabu (1931), though Flaherty was also to abandon this project; he contributed to the screenplay and to the photography until aesthetic and financial disagreements led him to sell his share in the film. This episode ended what is sometimes called the first American phase of his career (Murphy 1978).

Many have argued that Flaherty's next phase, working for the head of the film unit of the Empire Marketing Board, John Grierson, marked a subtle shift in his directing style. Certainly his trust in his own visual instincts was in full force when he decided to spurn a preconceived script while shooting Industrial Britain for Grierson. The relationship between Grierson and Flaherty during this period suggests their differing approaches to the documentary form. Grierson insisted on a script, which Flaherty refused to produce, and while Grierson admired Flaherty's powers of observation, he ultimately enlisted Basil Wright and Arthur Elton to finish the photography, while Grierson himself completed the editing (Murphy 1978).

In many respects, Man of Aran widened the rift developing between Flaherty and the purveyors of the British social documentary movement. Sponsored by Gaumont, it marked a return to studio financing arrangements, which also meant that Flaherty was able to draw on the long-term filming methods, high shooting ratio, and eye for ethnographic detail he had developed while making Nanook and Moana. However, the finished product also brought to a head debates about Flaherty's escapism and his penchant for reconstructing worlds from bygone eras. Many critics saw Flaherty's 'evasive documentary' as a product of romantic idealism and even fascism (an argument exacerbated when it won the Mussolini Cup at the Venice Film Festival) (Murphy 1978). Returning to the dramatic 'man against nature' theme of Nanook, sequences such as the shark hunt episode hid the fact that such practices had ceased to exist nearly a hundred years before. Rotha would argue that the film failed to achieve the paramount objective of documentary practice: the careful examination and analysis of contemporary social problems. Grierson, however, defended Flaherty's unquestionable influence on a generation of filmmakers, noting his gift for natural observation and his highly personal style.

Critics continued to ask whether Flaherty's contributions to the documentary form were primarily aesthetic. He appeared unable or unwilling to address the political and social demands of the 1930s documentary film movement. However, his next nonfiction project, The Land, went some distance toward lessening, if not completely suppressing, these doubts. After working for Alexander Korda on Elephant Boy in India, he returned to the United States to make The Land for Pare Lorentz, who had recently become head of the United States Film Service. The Land takes as its subject the use and abuse of land, but also dwells on the themes of journey and displacement, perhaps revealing Flaherty's own preoccupations more than it examines the social and political contexts of its subject, an impression somewhat underscored by Flaherty's voice-over narration. Still, according to Rotha and Wright, this was the one film in which Flaherty had faced up to contemporary sociological and technological problems (Murphy 1978).

'Sometimes you have to lie', Flaherty once stated; 'one often has to distort the thing to catch its true spirit' (Calder-Marshall 1963). Flaherty's final documentary was the Standard Oil-financed Louisiana Story, which was clearly made in the spirit of this quote, for it is a highly stylized work that, at the same time, draws on the moods, rhythms, and ambience of its bayou setting in an effort to capture the essence of Cajun life. It followed another aborted effort working for a larger film unit during the war, Frank Capra's Army orientation unit. Like many of Flaherty's efforts, this ended in a falling out. Louisiana Story was generously financed and thus provided the more relaxed conditions under which Flaherty thrived. Working with the team of Richard Leacock on camera, Helen van Dongen as on-site editor, and Frances, Flaherty produced what many have considered his finest achievement.

As Richard Barsam suggests, Louisiana Story perhaps best illustrates the ways in which Flaherty's films defy classification within traditional notions of the nonfiction genre, suggesting that Flaherty's work is best understood as that of a realist filmmaker (Orbanz 1988). Flaherty tended to avoid densely critical or philosophical assessments of his work, but it can be said that those elements most often criticized in the films—narrative distortion, romantic escapism, and nostalgia—might have been the preconditions that made possible a distinctive documentary aesthetic, and they provide the grounds for reading Flaherty as a documentary auteur.

JEFFREY GEIGER

See also: Capra, Frank; Grierson, John; Industrial Britain; Leacock, Richard; Lorentz, Pare; Louisiana Story; Man of Aran; Moana; Nanook of the North; Wright, Basil

Biography

Born in Iron Mountain, Michigan, February 16, 1884. Attended Michigan College of Mines. Worked as prospector and explorer for Canadian industrialist Sir William Mackenzie 1910–16. Released his first feature, Nanook of the North, in 1922. Lived in Safune, Western Samoa, 1923–5, while making the Famous Players–Lasky-financed Moana, released in 1926. Worked on White Shadows in the South Seas for Irving Thalberg and MGM in 1927; worked with F.W. Murnau on Tabu in 1929. Worked for the Empire Marketing Board making Industrial Britain, 1931. Lived in Ireland while making Man of Aran, 1932–3. Won best foreign film, Venice Film Festival and National Board of Review, 1934. Returned to the United States for The Land, 1939–41, and worked for Frank Capra and the Army orientation film unit, 1942. Lived in Abbeville, Louisiana, working on Louisiana Story, 1946–7, released in 1948. Nominated for best writing Academy Award (with Frances Flaherty), 1949. Died in Brattleboro, Vermont, July 23, 1951.

Selected films

1922 Nanook of the North: producer, director, writer, photographer, editor
1925 The Potterymaker: director, photographer, writer
1926 Moana (Moana: A Romance of the Golden Age; Moana: The Love Life of a South Sea Siren): coproducer, director, photographer, writer, coeditor
1926 The Twenty-Four Dollar Island: director, photographer, writer
1931 Industrial Britain: codirector, cophotographer
1934 Man of Aran: director, photographer, writer
1942 The Land: director, cophotographer, writer, narrator
1948 Louisiana Story: producer, director, cophotographer, cowriter

Further reading

Barsam, Richard Meran (ed.), *Nonfiction Film Theory and Criticism*, New York: E.P. Dutton, 1976.

Calder-Marshall, Arthur, *The Innocent Eye: The Life of Robert J. Flaherty*, London: W.H. Allen and Co., 1963.
Danzker, Jo-Anne Birnie (ed.), *Robert Flaherty Photographer/Filmmaker: The Inuit 1910–22*, Vancouver: Vancouver Art Gallery, 1980.
Grierson, John, 'Flaherty's Poetic Moana', in Lewis Jacobs (ed.), *The Documentary Tradition*, New York: W.W. Norton, 1979.
Griffith, Richard, *The World of Robert Flaherty*, Boston: Little, Brown, and Co., 1953.
Murphy, William T., *Robert Flaherty: A Guide to References and Resources*, Boston: G.K. Hall and Co., 1978.
Orbanz, Eva (ed.), *Filming Robert Flaherty's Louisiana Story: The Helen van Dongen Diary*, New York: The Museum of Modern Art, 1988.
Rony, Fatimah Tobing, *The Third Eye: Race, Cinema, and the Ethnographic Spectacle*, Durham, NC: Duke University Press, 1996.
Rotha, Paul, *Robert J. Flaherty: A Biography*, ed. Jay Ruby, Philadelphia, PA: University of Pennsylvania Press, 1983.
Winston, Brian, 'Before Grierson, Before Flaherty: The Documentary Film in 1914', *Sight and Sound* 57, autumn, 1988: 277–9.

For Love or Money

(Australia, McMurchy, 1983)

For Love or Money is a feature-length documentary that was produced over a five-year period, from 1979 to 1983, which endeavors to comprehensively document the working lives of Australian women since colonial times. The scope of the documentary is impressive as it ranges from the exploitation of convict women and Aboriginal workers to the equal pay debates of the 1960s and 1970s.

The film was made collaboratively by Megan McMurchy, Margot Nash, Margot Oliver, and Jeni Thornley. Three of the filmmakers, McMurchy, Oliver, and Thornley, also produced a book that draws on and extends the central themes addressed by the film. For Love or Money is constructed around four sections that divide the documentary into distinct historical periods. These periods are represented through a collage of extracts from other texts such as still photographs, newspaper archives, newsreels, feature films, and documentaries. Interviews with women from diverse social backgrounds are also interspersed between this collage. For Love or Money had its genesis in the late 1970s, and the final product is concerned with the feminist issues that dominated the movement at that time. It addresses the underrepresentation of women's experience and their contribution to the world of work. For Love or Money endeavors to 'make visible', or 'recover' that which has been consistently ignored and undervalued (Moore 1987).

The voice-over is also compiled from a variety of sources drawing on testimonials, quotations, and a voice-of-God narration that was scripted specifically for the film. The juxtapositions and bricolage of sound and images lends the documentary a poetic quality that marks the film as the product of a creative authorship rather than a transparent historical record. This approach values the first person, subjective address as a legitimate form of historical knowledge, and this element again locates the film in relation to the strategies of feminist theory that developed through the 1970s and into the 1980s. However, For Love or Money also embodies the shifts and contradictions in theory and politics that were increasingly debated at this time. While many aspects of the film seek a subjective retelling of history, it also draws on an authoritative address and an objective historiography to represent the 'truth' of women's exploitation and experience. When the film was finally released, as a result of this inherent ambivalence it was afforded a mixed reception (Curthoys and Dermody 1987).

For Love or Money is not only a painstaking account of women and work throughout Australian history, but, because of what Curthoys and Dermody call an 'asynchrony' of theoretical paradigms, it also bears all the traces of the intellectual shifts of the time. It preceded a number of films produced in the 1980s that went on to use traditional modes of documentary representation such as the use of archival material and interviews, while also attempting to subvert this convention in different ways. Notable examples include Red Matildas (1985), Snakes and Ladders (1987), and A Singular Woman (1985). This fusion of formal elements became a hallmark of feminist filmmaking in Australia at this time (Blonski and Freiberg 1989).

BELINDA SMAILL

For Love or Money (Australia, Flashback Films, 1983, 109 mins). Distributed by Ronin Films and Women Make Movies. Produced and written by Megan McMurchy, Margot Oliver, and Jeni Thornley. Directed by Megan McMurchy and Jeni Thornley. Cinematography by Erika Addis. Edited by Margot Nash. Sound by Cliff Pugsley.

Further reading

Blonski, Annette and Freiberg, Freda, 'Double Trouble: Women's Films', in Albert Moran and Tom O'Regan (eds), *The Australian Screen*, Melbourne: Penguin Books, 1989.

Curthoys, Ann and Dermody, Susan, 'For Love or Money: A Work of Loving', in Annette Blonski, Barbara Creed and Freda Freiberg (eds), *Don't Shoot Darling!: Women's Independent Filmmaking in Australia*, Melbourne: Greenhouse, 1987.

Dermody, Susan, 'Not Necessarily a Lead Dress: Thinking Beyond "Redress" in Women's Films', in Megan McMurchy and Jennifer Stott (eds), *Signs of Independents: Ten Years of the Creative Development Fund*, Sydney: Australian Film Commission, 1988.

McMurchy, Megan, Oliver, Margot and Thornley, Jeni, *For Love or Money: A Pictorial History of Women and Work in Australia*, ed. Irina Dunn, Melbourne: Penguin Books, 1983.

Moore, Catriona, '"Woman": For Love or Money and We Aim to Please', in Annette Blonski, Barbara Creed and Freda Freiberg (eds), *Don't Shoot Darling!: Women's Independent Filmmaking in Australia*, Melbourne: Greenhouse, 1987.

O'Regan, Tom, *Australian National Cinema*, London: Routledge, 1996.

Forest of Bliss

(US, Gardner, 1986)

Forest of Bliss is a poetic nonfiction film by Robert Gardner about death and regeneration. Set in Benares, India, the film is at once highly specific to its setting, on the ghats (stone steps leading directly into the water) of the Ganges River, and universal in its resonance. The film has been much lauded for its revitalization of the genre of the city symphony, and for the almost sublime beauty of its unsparing yet evidently reverent images. Its detractors have been primarily anthropologists, who have highlighted as the film's shortcoming precisely that quality most acclaimed by film critics and historians—its absence of verbal explication in any form. There is no voice-over narration, nor subtitling of speech, nor any direct-address interviews with the film's subjects. However, the film's largely nonverbal engagement with its subject displays a critical acumen and perceptual acuity rare in ethnographic film, which conveys respect at once for its subject (Benares and its inhabitants) and for its viewers, who are trusted to navigate through the images without any voice-over direction. Forest of Bliss resolutely refuses to condescend to the viewer after the fashion of the canonical ethnographic film, travelog, or liberal documentary. In retreating from language, Gardner is renouncing the dominant expository modality of documentary, and seeking instead to impart a more corporeal, intersubjective engagement with his subject, the willful ambiguity and open-endedness of which seeks to mirror that of human existence itself.

Forest of Bliss is also the apogée of Gardner's own oeuvre to date (which includes Blunden Harbor (1951), Dead Birds (1963), The Nuer (with Hilary Harris, 1971), Rivers of Sand (1974), Deep Hearts (1981), Ika Hands, and Passenger (1998)), in that it is his most consummate experimentation with nonrealist montage. The film moves back and forth between a number of protonarrative strands (or 'slight narratives', in Paul Rotha's memorable phrase), but tells no story and develops no character in any conventional sense. Although Forest of Bliss contains three distinct main characters, Gardner is concerned more with situating them within the larger ecology of Benares, than establishing them as individuals. This is an ecology of water, fire, marigolds, dogs, cows, boats, bamboo, sand, stone, and wood, all elements with a significance, use, and interrelatedness that we grasp only gradually through the course of the film. It is an ecology of life and death, of dirt and purification, of the sacred and the profane. Death, no less than life, is marked by a limitless series of rituals, both individual and collective. Yet at the same time, death is the local industry; Benares, as the holiest Hindu city, has for millennia been the pilgrimage site of a vast mortuary migration. If Forest of Bliss is about the ecology of Benares, it is also about the economy of death. The 'slight narratives' of the film—the sorting of the golden marigolds, the assembling of the bamboo funerary litters, the transporting of the sand, the weighing of the firewood, the caring and cleansing of the recently departed, the baptizing of a new boat—all coalesce on the Burning Ground of the sacred ghats on the banks of the Ganges.

The film is driven by a sense of constant motion, conveyed as much by the elaborate, polyphonic soundtrack as the interwoven images. The city of Benares bustles and rings with the collective activities of individuals. Gardner's gaze is simultaneously wandering and unwavering, as countless people, animals, and objects ascend and descend the extensive and elaborate flights of stairs that attach the city to its river—and life to death. Whereas the city streets resound with near collisions of vehicles and cargo, beggars and dogs, cows and children, and pilgrims and priests, the chorus of the Ganges is one of amplified splashes, squeaking boat oars, and chirping birds. The business of death is conducted both inside and outside, with each space evoking the other through sound. Early in the film a priest is making offerings in a sheltered altar. His solitude and concentration are emphasized by the sounds of his labored breathing. At the same time we hear a chorus of children's voices playing nearby; adult men talking, coughing, hammering; birds singing—all unseen, but present nonetheless. Almost all of the nonverbal or ambient sounds in the film seem amplified, while the few verbal communications appear—unlike the more guttural exclamations—to be muted somewhat. The effect is to reflect an intention on the part of the filmmaker to divert us from attending to the denotative meaning of what is being said, and to evoke in us instead a synaesthetic response to the full realm of connotations in all that we see and hear.

Forest of Bliss is arguably without parallel in nonfiction cinema in its exploration of the polyvalence of (aural and visual) imagery, almost unmediated by any verbal exegesis, diegetic or extra-diegetic, circumscribing their meaning. The one verbal element the significance of which the film, as it unfolds, repeatedly invites us to ponder is the opening epigraph from Yeats, itself a translation from the Upanishads: 'Everything in the world is eater or eaten, the seed is food and the fire is eater'. In its refusal of conventional notions of linearity and realism, its experimentation with montage, and its polyphonic, non-narrative soundtrack, Forest of Bliss explores the reciprocal provocations of ethnographic and avant-garde filmmaking in a fashion that had largely been neglected since the work of Maya Deren, but in a manner altogether more sensuous. Although the film was initially disavowed by anthropologists, it is now recognized as having taken ethnographic film to unequalled aesthetic and sensory heights.

Since its original release on 16mm and 35mm film in 1986, Forest of Bliss has been released on DVD as an accompaniment to a detailed exegesis of the film by Robert Gardner and his coproducer, Ákos Östör, *Making Forest of Bliss: Intention, Circumstance, and Chance in the Non-Fiction Film* (Harvard University Press, 2001).

ILISA BARBASH

See also: Gardner, Robert

Forest of Bliss. A film by Robert Gardner. Produced for the Film Study Center, Harvard University by Robert Gardner and Ákos Östör. Cinematography and editing by Robert Gardner. Sound recorded by Ned Johnston. Sound edited by Michael Chalufour. Production associates Baidyanath Saraswati, Om Prakash Sharma, and R.L. Maurya. Post-production assistant Maria Sendra. Second camera Ned Johnston.

Further reading

Chopra, Radikha, 'Robert Gardner's *Forest of Bliss*: A Review', *SVA Newsletter*, spring 1989: 2–3.

Coover, Roderick, 'Worldmaking, Metaphors and Montage in the Representation of Cultures: Cross-Cultural Filmmaking and the Poetics of Robert Gardner's *Forest of Bliss*', *Visual Anthropology* 14, no. 4, 2001: 415–33.

Eck, Diana, *Banaras, City of Light*, London: Routledge, 1983.

Östör, Ákos, '*Forest of Bliss*: Film and Anthropology', *East-West Film Journal* 8, no. 2, 1994: 70–104.

Östör, Ákos and Gardner, Robert, *Making Forest of Bliss: Intention, Circumstance, and Chance in the Non-Fiction Film*, Cambridge, MA: Harvard University Press, 2001.

Forgács, Péter

An independent media artist working in Budapest since the 1970s, Péter Forgács emerged in the 1990s as an important creative force in the shaping of documentary style. He revitalized the art of compilation filmmaking by incorporating poetic, stylistic touches more often found in the experimental sphere. As an archivist and researcher, Forgács helped to bring attention to amateur films as documentary materials to be mobilized in revising the historiography of the twentieth century, particularly that of Europe in the 1930s and 1940s.

Much of Forgács's early work was not in documentary film per se, but in eclectic parts of the fine arts: video installation, theater, and musical performance. In 1988, after five years of archiving home movie collections, he received his first commission from Hungarian television. Establishing a specialization in the revivification of amateur films, he turned to work that was more obviously, though not conventionally, documentary. He classified several of his feature-length pieces as 'video operas', for the ways in which they shape actuality footage into musical and rhythmic arrangements. The mesmeric scores of his musical collaborator, Tibor Szemzö, are key to holding the patchwork visuals together. Although Forgács clearly retains the influence of experimental art movements, he has created a body of work dedicated to historical narrative and individuals living within the sweep of historical forces.

Forgács is often characterized as a 'found-footage' filmmaker, but this is misleading in two ways. He tracks down small-gauge, amateur films (8, Super 8, 9.5, and 16mm footage), but does not treat them as anonymous, mysterious 'found' objects. Rather, he does research about the owners, makers, and subjects of these home movies and other amateur productions. His short Wittgenstein Tractatus (1992), a collage of unidentified imagery and philosophical aphorisms, is the exception to his usual method of scrupulously identifying and historicizing such films. Although Forgács uses small-gauge celluloid as source material, his own production is video-based. His authorial signature is indebted to the postproduction tools available in digital video. Without overwhelming the film artifact, his work uses a full palette of layered embellishments: color graphics, freeze-frames, slow motion, tinting, superimpositions, and stylized text.

Since 1988 Forgács has produced more than a dozen hour-long documentaries in his 'Private Hungary' series. Beginning with A Bartos család/The Bartos Family, these contemplative works examine the daily life of Europeans at the time of World War II by reanimating home movies. Because amateur cinematography was an expensive hobby, the films principally record the households of privileged and bourgeois families. In addition to the expected birthdays, weddings, and holiday scenes, there are often artful, constructed passages done by filmmakers who edited, directed, and titled their silent footage. In the most remarkable episodes, such as Az örvény/Free Fall (1996), Forgács suggests a radical rereading of the history of documentary. His film reveals the process by which sophisticated amateur cineastes, such György Petö, photographed private, domestic moments. In so doing they also created documents of the social spheres in which their lives were shaped.

Forgács sparingly uses conventional archival materials, such as newsreels, in these compilations. When he does, it is to situate 'private' films in public space and history. The contrasts between the private view and 'official' documentation are dramatic, but left open and contradictory. In De Maalstroom/The Maelstrom (1997) home movies of the Jewish Peereboom family (taken in Holland, 1933–42) take on a tragic irony that is heightened by the intercutting of films shot at home by a Nazi commissar, who oversaw their deportation to a concentration camp. At other times, amateur footage takes on a heroic, public dimension. In Angelos' Film (2000), we see footage of the Nazi occupation of Greece, which aristocrat Angelos Papanasstassiou clandestinely recorded with a hidden camera: swastikas hung on the Acropolis, public hangings, and other events never shot by the official newsreels.

The legacy of Forgács's work is in both these finished tapes and the Private Film and Photo Archive that he established to save these alternate histories. The collection is housed at the Central European University and includes more than five hundred hours of amateur films (1910–85) from Hungary and elsewhere, as well as three hundred hours of audio interviews with the filmmakers' families.

DAN STREIBLE

Biography

Born in Hungary, September 10, 1950. Studied at Academy of Fine Arts, Budapest, 1971–2, 1974–7. Began work at Béla Balázs Film Studio, 1978. Collaboration with the minimalist music ensemble, Group 180, including composer Tibor Szemzö, from 1978 on. Established Private Film and Photo Archives Foundation, 1983. Researcher at Hungarian Sociological Institute of the Academy of Sciences, 1987. Documentary series 'Conversations on Psychoanalysis', for

Hungarian television, 1988–93. Taught for University of California Berkeley's Central European studies program in Budapest, 1990–1. Visiting artist, Arizona State University, 1993. Fellow at the Getty Research Institute, Los Angeles, 2000–1.

Selected films

1988 A Bartos család/The Bartos Family
1989 Dusi és Jenô/Dusi and Jeno
1991 Photographed by László Dudás
1992 Wittgenstein Tractatus
1992 Bourgeois Dictionary
1994 Egy úrinô notesza/Notes of a Lady
1995 Miközben valahol/Meanwhile Somewhere
1996 Az örvény/Free Fall
1997 Class Lot
1997 De Maalstroom/The Maelstrom: A Family Chronicle
1998 A dunai exodus/The Danube Exodus
2000 Angelos' Film
2002 Bibó breviarium/Istvan Bibo's Fragments

Further reading

Bikacsy, G., 'Privat Magyarorszag' (Private Hungary), *New Hungarian Quarterly* winter, 1991: 159–61.

Boyle, Deirdre, 'Meanwhile Somewhere: A Conversation with Péter Forgács', *Millennium Film Journal* 37, 2001: 53–66.

Forgács, Péter, 'Filmic Memories', *Film Quarterly* 52, no. 1, 1998: 60–1.

Portugues, Catherine, 'Home Movies, Found Images, and "Amateur Film" as a Witness to History: Péter Forgács's Private Hungary', *The Moving Image* 1, no. 2, 2001.

Waller, Marguerite R., 'Notes of a Lady (Private Hungary 8)', *American Historical Review* 99, 1994: 1252–6.

400 Million, The

(Holland, Ivens, 1939)

The Dutch filmmaker Joris Ivens used his camera in his roles as both political activist and humanitarian filmmaker. Ivens is noted for having produced social and political documentaries that go beyond depictions of nature and scientific feats. He had a prolific career, directing his camera toward monumental events and helping to assert the role motion pictures can play in the recording of history. The 400 Million reflects this commitment to historical documentation.

The film was shot over four months during the spring of 1939 and documents China's struggle against invading Japanese forces. Ivens admitted that his recent experience shooting a film during the Spanish Civil War (The Spanish Earth) taught him the difficulties of documenting military conflicts; however, the experience also bolstered his commitment to giving voice to the courageous efforts being made against fascism. Production of The 400 Million forced Ivens to negotiate his way around multiple obstacles placed in his way by Chiang Kai-shek's government, testing his nerve and his commitment to the project. He was initially restricted by the Chinese military commanders from going to the forefront of the conflict, but as he has stated, he drew courage and strength from the spirit and confidence displayed by the Chinese soldiers who surrounded him, who unfailingly continued in their roles as soldiers. Ivens mirrored this commitment as a filmmaker, unwilling to let surveillance, curfews, or personality differences prevent him from carrying out his goals in filming this important moment in history. During production, Ivens moved between guerilla units, Communist Party members, and the nationalist army (under Chiang Kai-shek), much to the dismay and suspicion of each faction. Even though they were fighting the common enemy of Japan, these groups held opposing sociopolitical views; however, Ivens's film depicts these factions as comrades united by a common cause.

After six weeks of frustrating delay, Ivens and his crew were finally allowed access to the frontlines of the war. Nonetheless, once they arrived, the general in command changed his mind and told them that they could go no further. Angry and determined, Ivens declared that he and his crew had come to China to film battles as they unfolded, informing the general that the crew was going to push on, with or without him. Ultimately, the general conceded to Ivens's demands. Such encounters continued to limit the crew's access to the battles. Ivens was constantly frustrated with such restrictions, but at the same time was sensitive to the fact that military personnel struggled to comprehend why someone would risk his life on the battlefield for no visible reward. Ivens had hoped that the film would not only garner support for the Chinese struggle but also serve in the fight against fascism and totalitarian regimes in Europe.

Ivens's critical talent for composing sequences of visual poeticism and his skillful editing to create engrossing and rhythmic sequences elevate this film above typical newsreel footage and most other early twentieth-century war documentaries. Such techniques are used to elicit sympathy for the Chinese people. The rich visuals and montage are aurally linked to commentary spoken by actor Frederic March, shifting between a subjective voice (adopting the perspective and sentiment of Chinese soldiers and civilians) and that of an authoritative, though impassioned, observer. Although the visuals are dramatic, moving, and at times horrific, the footage lacks continuity; therefore, because of the restraints placed on Ivens and his crew, the film relies heavily on the spoken word both to carry the story forward and to evoke a sense of the subjectivity and nuances of life in a nation under siege. Even Ivens himself admitted that the commentary was rather extensive. Considering the limitations that tormented Ivens and his crew, the heavy reliance on voice-over appears somewhat justified, if not consistent with most documentaries of that age. The soundtrack is artfully and illustratively textured, complementing the visuals with a quasi-polyvocal narration, Chinese folk music, the raucous sounds of war, and excerpts (in Mandarin) from military officials and youth leaders, which are accompanied by their English translations and spoken by American actors.

The film begins with a jarring image sequence of the aftereffects of Japanese bombings in northeastern China, blatantly referring to the atrocities as acts of unprovoked military aggression. The next section characterizes China as a nation with a long history whose cultural contributions have benefited the world since the time of Marco Polo. China's link with the West is hinted at as a further narrative means to stir interest and concern from Europe and North America. This section concludes by reasserting the value and import of Chinese culture on an historical and humanitarian level, while emphasizing that although it is a nation of four hundred million (one-fifth of the world's population at that time), its people are united in defending their vast and diverse homeland. The film then shows a China on the road to modernization after deposing its emperor, its emerging civil infrastructure and transportation system, and the development of modern technology and industry. These efforts at modernization, as the film suggests, may have provoked Japan's aggression, which saw China as an immense landscape of untapped natural resources.

This provocation is addressed in the next section of the film, in which Japan's history of military aggression toward eastern Asia is recounted. It is also noted that the United States was still exporting iron and steel to Imperial Japan, placing the United States in a position of complacency, if not accountability, in regard to the atrocities afflicted on the Chinese people. Ivens's own political sentiments are apparent through the film's privileging of commoners and China's former Red Army. In tribute to the hurriedly trained commoners of China, brave farmers are shown using guerilla war tactics, which were an invaluable component to China's defense strategy. Ivens suggests that the most heroic military efforts are those of the Eighth Route Army, a unit from China's former Red Army.

None of this detracts from Ivens's overall effort to create a film that emphasizes, at least temporarily, the unity of China's various political factions. One of the final sequences of the film circumvents intra-China political differences to recount and emphasize the importance of China obtaining even the smallest of victories against Japanese forces (the recapture of Tai'erzhuang, for example). The overriding message of this final sequence is that one small victory is not only the essential first step toward reestablishing a free and stable China, but one that will, ideally, help to elicit support from the West.

On completion of The 400 Million, Ivens donated his film camera to a representative of the Chinese Communist Party. Little did he know that his camera was to become the first motion picture camera owned by the Yan'an Film Group, preserved today at the Museum of Chinese Revolutionary History. Portions of Ivens's film were later used by American director Frank Capra as part of his World War II propaganda film series, Why We Fight.

KEVIN TAYLOR ANDERSON

See also: Ivens, Joris; Why We Fight

The 400 Million (US, black and white, sound, 35mm, 1939, 52 mins). Directed by Joris Ivens; story by Ivens and John Ferno; photography by

Ferno and Robert Capa; music by Hanns Eisler; commentary spoken by Frederic March. The film is also known as China in 1938, released in 1939.

France

From the famous film show of December 1895 to 1940, documentaries were considered uninteresting productions that were fine for amateurs but not worth being shown in movie theatres. Such contempt is all the more surprising, as during this initial period, theoreticians and filmmakers defined, on paper and in actual practice, the four main traits that have characterized the French documentary tradition up to the present: (1) the observation films aimed at recording what is significant in an object or a procedure; (2) the explanatory films intended not only to describe but also to comment; (3) the critical films that explored the unseen side of actions or events; and (4) the formal movies that question the nature and purpose of documentaries. The respective importance of these groups varied according to the main concerns of any period and to spectators' reactions. In a second epoch, roughly from 1940 to 1968, documentaries became fashionable. At a time when their country was in decline the French were anxious to obtain information about the world and about the new techniques coming from the United States. Film directors no longer looked down on 'factual' films. During the last decades of the twentieth century, those involved in the film industry were obliged to work for television. There was a division between the channels that made instructive movies and a handful of independent filmmakers eager to experiment with new formulae.

The Lumière brothers, authors of the first French movies, were manufacturers of cinematic equipment and raw film. Their 'views' were aimed only at showing the quality of their products. However, some of their operators, instead of merely recording ephemeral happenings, filmed relevant aspects of the current social life. The first French documentary was shot in July 1886 by an unknown operator who went to Carmaux, a then important coal mining area. He filmed the coke coming out of the oven and, more importantly, the women sorting and carrying big coal blocks. His was a typical observer's attitude. He adopted, in both cases, a unique position. His presence cannot be spotted; the workers, absorbed in their job, never look at the camera. Only a small minority of the more than 1,400 'views' shot for the Lumières are of such quality. The firm soon ceased production.

The Lumières had dispatched operators throughout the world to advertise their material. A wealthy financier, Albert Kahn, thought he could carry out the same operation to constitute a vast picture library, the Planet's Archives. Instructed to film the customs, living conditions, and resources of the countries they visited, the cameramen sent to Europe, the Middle East, Asia, and Africa from 1908 to 1931 brought back hundreds of documents that were roughly edited for people to consult. Wars, Kahn believed, are caused by reciprocal ignorance; a better knowledge of 'the other' would help the progress of universal peace. Few were interested. Later, in the 1960s, this prodigious collection became famous and was used extensively by television.

Documentaries did not appeal to French spectators during the first decades of the century. The eight thousand movies that Pathé, the main producer, diffused before 1920 were comedies or melodramas. Made in studio, they did not cost much and Pathé did not want his crew to work outside. One of his directors, Alfred Machin, personally shot, during his holidays, the pictures edited in 1913 for Pathé's only feature-length (fifty-five-minute) documentary Voyages et grandes chasses en Afrique/Journeys and Big Hunts in Africa.

Documentaries developed away from commercial circuits, thanks to various forms of sponsorship. Instead of merely recording aspects of the world, they were meant to reveal and explain precise, well-defined processes. A minority of scientists understood early on the importance of moving pictures. Subsidized by Pathé and then Albert Kahn, Dr Jean Commandon made a series of instructional movies on the functioning of the human body and on chirurgical operations. Accurate, surgical and detailed, his films were too difficult for the common people to follow. Another doctor, Jean Painlevé (1902–89), was less demanding and won an excellent reputation; his La chirurgie correctrice/Corrective Surgery (1926) or L'étude du sang/The Study of Blood (1935) introduced the topic clearly, displayed long shots with much contrast, and commented extensively on every image. Sometimes Painlevé proved fanciful: he treated animals—Les oursins/Sea Urchins (1925), Les crevettes/Shrimps (1930)—like humans, attributing them intention and siding with them against their enemies. Backed by the authorities, he was able to reach a wide audience of pupils and students.

Having lost their foreign clients during the World War I, French producers were obliged to turn towards the domestic market. The state and various public offices provided them with a new outlet. Gaumont launched a 'Série enseignement' (educational series) and Pathé a 'Pathé revue', both comprising shorts (ten to fifteen minutes) dealing with a highly specific topic such as the making and functioning of an engine, the strength of various types of sewing threads, and the best way of using a particular tool. More than one thousand of these items found in the Gaumont or Pathé archive have been restored and are now available for consultation at the Paris Bibliothèque Nationale. Less interested in cinema than the state, industrial firms financed few publicity films. The case of car factories is typical. The Ford Company produced more than five thousand cinematic documents from 1914 onward; Fiat and Volkswagen made extensive use of films to advertise their vehicles. In France Citroën was content to sponsor prestige operations: a film crew followed long-distance trips shooting La croisière noire/The Black Cruise (1926) and La croisière jaune/The Yellow Cruise (1933) in praise of Citroën cars' reliability. Renault, the main French manufacturer, ordered only four pictures between the world wars. The longest (fifty-seven minutes), Automobiles de France, shot by Pathé-Natan in 1934, is a good example of average publicity documentaries. A journalist calls Renault and asks to visit the factory. He is first informed about steel production and about the components of a car. He is then taken through the plant, with much emphasis on the building of the bodywork and on the assembly line. The director, Jean Loubignac, used clever tricks, for instance making a reverse tracking-shot from the end to starting point of the the assembly line to compensate for its slowness and apparently doubled its speed. Not accurate enough for a specialist but too long and complicated for the lay spectator, this movie illustrates the imperfections of most French documentaries—while not aimed at a large public, they were often of poor quality.

Oddly enough it was among these films that the first and possibly most challenging documentary theory was developed. France boasts a wealth of film experts who have never held a camera. Such was not the case of Jean Epstein (1897–1953), director of a series of fiction films and documentaries and author of several books, notably *Bonjour cinéma* (Good Morning Cinema, 1921). By playing with time and space, Epstein contended, by jumping from one point to another and by accelerating or slowing down, the cinema drastically alters our relationship to the world and suggests that other connections are possible. Its aim is neither to become a mechanical eye used to observe things nor to comment, but rather to go beyond appearances. Documentaries must not inform; they have to disclose a yet unknown universe. Epstein was not a loner but rather the spokesman of a small group of intellectuals hastily labelled 'avant-gardists', although no army followed them. Avant-gardists loathed informative movies and wanted cinema to break with the humdrum of daily activities. They were divided into two groups: the critics and the formalists.

The critics reacted against the smooth, alternately sentimental and comforting vision offered by fiction films. With La Zone/The Slum Belt (1928), Georges Lacombe, leaving Paris's animated centre, explored the most derelict sectors of urban periphery. Banking on surprise and disorientation, he mapped out no itinerary and wrote practically no commentary. This 'zone' was a non-city, a no-man's-land close by affluent districts but totally neglected. Refuting in advance Africa's pleasant aspect filmed by the Citroën crew, Marc Allégret (1900–73), travelling with André Gide, evoked in Voyage au Congo/Voyage to the Congo (1925) a country threatened by malnutrition and illness. While denouncing another form of destitution, the absolute poverty of Extremaduran country people in Las Hurdes, also known as Terre sans pain/Land without Bread (shot in 1932, released in 1937), Luis Buñuel (1900–83) took another course. After travelling to the village of Alberca, he lined up a series of appalling pictures: children and pigs wallowing in the only fountain, a little girl about to die, brain-damaged boys smiling at the camera, and men and women sleeping together in tiny dark sheds. In contrast to these images, Brahms's Fourth Symphony and a pompous, dry voice-over was meant to disturb the audience and make it apprehend the artificial character of documentaries shot by foreigners and projected to far-away, indifferent spectators. Jean Vigo's A propos de Nice/On the Subject of Nice (1930), played also on oppositions between rich and poor, leisure and work, life and death. Swift motions, unpredictable views, and aburd transformations (a man turned into a lobster) made up for the banality of the comparisons; the movie mocked simultaneously modish resorts and the pseudo-objectivity of documentaries.

Less satirical, other avant-gardistes were intent on exploring the potential of cinema. Alberto Cavalcanti's Rien que les heures/Only the Hours (1926) brought into fashion the city symphonies, movies attempting to visually document the frantic agitation of a big metropolis. Cavalcanti (1897–1982) fancied a 'typical' Parisian day: bizarre linkings, frozen pictures coming after accelerated motions, wipes hinted at an engulfing of time by the whimsical rythm of urban life. Many drew their inspiration from this model in European capitals, so Marcel Carné chose to invert it. His Nogent, Eldorado du dimanche/Nogent, Sunday's Eldorado (1929) stretched the Sunday hours by accompanying in slow panning shots the idle city dwellers who had left the town centre to rest by a river. Far away, at the very end of Brittany, Jean Epstein evoked nature's timelessness in Finis Terrae (1930). The same waves assaulted in vain the same rocks; the same sky lingered over an infinite heath.

Avant-garde films have been revalued by critics, but at the time they were as despised as any other documentary. Financing them was problematic; it was only thanks to their friends' help that Buñuel or Vigo were able to work. Businessmen did not believe in cinematic advertising. Public offices gave money for didactic movies provided that they were mere illustrated lessons. French documentaries seemed not to have a future.

The year 1940, the year of France's most mortifying defeat, was a watershed for documentaries. In October the Vichy government imposed the screening of a short during any film show. Nazi Germany and Fascist Italy had made extensive use of informative movies for propaganda; the Vichy authorities thought that imitating them would accelerate France's recovery. The Republic regulated these films and decided that only those with professional qualifications could work in studios. The result was twofold: producers were no longer reluctant to finance documentaries likely to yield a profit; and the young who wanted to become qualified had no choice but to make shorts. In liberated France, the Americans organized free film shows to illustrate their way of life and later to promote the Marshall Plan. French audiences realized that documentaries were not necessarily boring by-products.

There was a rising flood of documentaries, from four hundred during the German occupation to four thousand between 1945 and 1955. There were a great deal of quota shorts and among the good ones many were factual films. The big firms—Renault, Esso-France, the Electricity Company—funded instructional movies adapted to the needs of their potential clients. Technically, their products were of excellent quality, with sharp pictures, perfect lighting, and a didactic voice-over. They were all aimed at showing how progress, symbolized by cars, tractors, fertilizers, and electricity, could improve daily life. Ministerial bodies, especially the Foreign Office and the Ministery of Agriculture, subsidized a significant number of shorts, but their funds were limited, which resulted in an uncomfortable mixture of awkardness and pretentiousness. Paysans d'hier et d'aujourd'hui/Countrymen of Yesterday and Today (1946) is a typical example. While encoutering modern farmers, backwards countrymen suddenly understand their ignorance. The film unveils a touch of scorn: the backwards men never wash their hands, and marvel at the use of electricity.

In addition to professional life, much attention was devoted to cultural activities, tourism first but also sport, mountain climbing, theatre, and architecture. One-tenth of the movies focused on animals, nature, and landscapes. The same percentage dealt with the colonial empire. Except for Indochina, nothing was said about nationalism; the commentary stressed the mutual interest of France and African countries and the necessity of assimilation. Consider Kalla, produced as late as 1955: a black student (in fact an actor) confronts his former life in Cameroon and his present life in Paris, but if the camera follows him he is not allowed to speak—it is a French voice-over that tells what he is supposed to think.

Until 1964 there was one television channel in France, which transmitted five hours a day in black and white. The programmes were also influenced by cinema because what was not broadcast live from a studio was shot on film.

The ascendancy of cinema is apparent in the choice of themes and stylistic practice. Elie Lotar's Aubervilliers (1945), a stern description of slum life in the north of Paris, and a series of documentaries made by Jean Dewever, La crise du logement/The Housing Shortage (1995) and Des logis et des hommes/On Abodes and Men (1956) revealed how archaic housing conditions were in suburbs and had a strong impact on public opinion. Television followed suit with a documentary series, A la découverte des Français/In Search of the French (1957–8); fourteen programmes explored various regions, visited families, and invited their members to talk. These documentaries were more detailed than Lotar's or Dewever's, but did not introduce data they had not already tackled. The most popular television series were La vie des animaux/Animal Life (1952–76) and Les Médicales/Concerned with Medicine (1956–84). The former adopted a cinematic approach with extensive panning shots on beautiful landscapes, animals shot at long distance, and surprising jumps from a distantce to a close frame. The latter was built like a serial, a fight between human beings and illness in which every item opened with a problem (how to cure it?) and closed with a happy ending. Television was initially unable to give new life to audiovisual expression; however, it offered jobs to young filmmakers and helped to acquaint spectators with documentary films.

Hurriedly interviewing derelict families was not likely to introduce new approaches to the documentary formulae. Documentaries changed when filmmakers adopted other methods. Georges Rouquier (1909–89) was a printer. Fond of films, he succeeded in convincing a producer that it would be a good idea to make a full-length picture about a rural family that had been living for a long time in an isolated farm in Aveyron. Rouquier settled in at the farm, watched carefully, and wrote a script. A small crew of technicians then joined him, and shooting began in the autumn of 1944. Filming took a whole year. The editing process was rather painful and the film was not released until the spring of 1947. It is as stunning today as it was in its time. After the credits, the nine members of the family and their neighbours are introduced. An establishing sequence, the longest in the film, describes a day in autumn, the emphasis being on the children who have to walk several miles to the village school, care for the animals, and make bread. During the winter, long evenings allow the grandfather to tell the story of the family and its farm. In the spring, the mother gives birth to a child and the female livestock breed; the farm is furnished with electricity. The summer, as the most important season, is divided into three parts. The first section shows haymaking. The portrayal of a typical Sunday introduces important topics such as the relationship of the family with the village, the church, the café, and collective entertainment. The summer ends with harvesting and threshing. In autumn we see glimpses of vintage and tree cutting, but another topic, the division of the property between the children, is dealt with at length.

Superficial though it is, this summary gives an idea of the richness of a picture that is both clever and subtle. In 1947 audiences approved. This was the real thing, more credible than the fanciful farms of fictions. The film still appeals to contemporary spectators. They see precisely how oxen are harnessed, how they draw the plough and how people learn to build a haystack. More importantly, the film gives them a glimpse of the lifestyle, based on sociability and fairness, that brought the agricultural workers together. The relationships between the members of the family, the family and the neighbours, and the family and the village are vividly portrayed. The conflicts underlying the common life of three generations living under the same roof are not hidden but are subtly exposed throughout the movie.

Rouquier was an amateur who filmed to please himself, not to captivate an audience. In contrast, Jean Rouch, born in 1917, was a trained ethnographer. While investigating black Africa's traditions, he used a camera to record local ceremonies. He settled in a village and while they were unaware he filmed the villagers' actions and attitudes. Some Africans condemned this practice as typically colonialist; others said he had captured a trace of customs that were soon to disappear. Rouch's Les maîtres fous/The Manic Priests (1955) gave rise to much controversy. Accompanying villagers who had moved into a town, the short showed how the rituals they attempted to maintain had been distorted by contact with white people. Moi un noir/I, a Black (1958), a feature-length documentary, was discussed for other reasons. Rouch reconstructed several days in the life of three Africans in Abidjan (Côte d'Ivoire).

They were authentic workers but played their own character according to a screenplay written by the filmmaker. Moreover, the voice-over alternated between two commentaries, one by the director and the other by one of the Africans.

While breaking with the optimistic vision of mainstream colonial documentaries, Rouch denounced neither the anarchic urbanization of African towns nor the French authorities' responsibility. The tradition of critical documentaries was not lost at the time, but in a difficult period marked by the German occupation, the Cold War, decolonization, and the Algerian conflict, criticism became mostly political. Its main exponents, Alain Resnais and Frédéric Rossif, both born in 1922, had witnessed war, resistance, and the opening of the concentration camps. The memory of such dramas weighed heavily on their movies. Resnais's Nuit et brouillard/Night and Fog (1955) and Rossif's Le temps du ghetto/The Ghetto Time (1961) were shot while French public opinion tried to forget war horrors, and Rossif's Mourir à Madrid/To Die in Madrid (1963) was shot during the worst period of the Algerian war. Resnais flashed back and forth between past and present; archival footage of the camps was interspersed with clips of postwar trials and pictures taken for the film. Rossif stuck to chronology. Both raised serious questions about moral responsibility and the possibility of other mass murders. To Die in Madrid was a lampoon against Franco shot against the background of de Gaulle's authoritarian rule. Instead of merely narrating the Spanish civil war, Rossif attempted to evoke the atmosphere of a domestic conflict and to document its everyday nature by stressing civilians' suffering, their fear of aerial bombings, and their anxious wait of a predictable issue. The editing was extremely clever. Describing the defence of Madrid, the director emphasized the deep involvement of an entire population. He showed the men digging trenches, the children and women passing on stones, all social groups taking part in a common action, without leaders and without any military presence. Rossif had slanted his message to appeal to those who opposed Gaullism, but even those who blamed its bias found his account gripping.

There was something new in Resnais's and Rossif's movies. They were keen on editing their own images and underlined the importance of 'montage', which is not a mere linking of pictures but an association of correlated images. In the second epoch of French documentaries, the difference between critical films and formal films, with regard to investigating the nature and function of the cinematic language, was less and less visible.

Resnais's Les statues meurent aussi/Statues also Die (1951) wanted to make spectators think about their relationship with images but also to criticize the presence of African statues in French museums. The film opened with a pan shot of visitors looking at a museum showcase: 'Are you sure that African objects do not observe you like strange animals?' Such mixing of upsetting queries was stronger in the works of Chris Marker (born in 1921). His Lettre de Sibérie/Letter from Siberia (1957) invited viewers to become aware of the deceptive influence of commentaries by showing the same visual footage three separate times with three different soundtracks: one full of enthusiasm for the Soviet achievements, one strongly disapproving, and one purely factual. His Le Joli Mai/The Lovely May (1963) attempted to deal with happiness in a France emerging from the Algerian war. A few people gave their opinion about that idea as in any banal public opinion poll, but once the viewer is confronted with violent, appalling, or thought-provoking images and challenged by other interviews, such answers looked vague and irrelevant. Ingenious and amusing, the film brought to the fore a gap between individuals' simple desires of happiness and the larger problems surrounding them. At the same time it expressed doubts about the reliability of documentaries; the way of organizing one's images can radically transform a message.

Marker's works were often given as examples of 'cinéma vérité', or 'film truth'. This strange expression did not mean that cinema must copy life. On the contrary, it signified that truth, being never directly accessible, must be transcribed to become apparent. Any cinematic operation—framing, moving the camera, editing—is a manipulation. It is the filmmaker's duty to make spectators apprehend the manipulations and understand that what they see is partial and biased. Cinéma vérité was no more than a slogan, but most directors mentioned in this section, without forming a group, let alone a school, were convinced that they had to introduce in their films a flux of meanings and forms.

Audiences were sometimes disconcerted but never repelled. The success of documentaries in the 1950s and 1960s resulted, to a large extent, from their ability to raise challenging questions.

With the end of the state monopoly on television (1982), the number of networks increased dramatically. All channels needed factual films to include in their schedules, and some even specialized in the broadcasting of documentaries. The avaibility of light cameras gave political and professional organizations an incentive to produce and circulate their own documentaries. Industrial and financial corporations anxious to diversify their clientele sponsored informative movies. Filmmakers were offered several opportunities to make shorts, but these proposals, coming mostly from private companies, modified the conception and structure of documentaries. Television channels wanted the films to fit either cinema or television; they provided little money and instructed their technicians to work as fast as possible and to leave space for advertisements.

In the wake of the 1968 student revolt and factory occupations, films were considered weapons for the class struggle. Cooperatives such as Slon and Cinélutte and Dziga Vertov Group, developed a 'counter-cinema' informed by revolutionary ideologies. A few contended that by giving the most destitute the power of speech, cinema would disclose the misery of the human condition under capitalism. Militant filmmakers went to factories to ask the workers to depict their problems and demands. One of the most famous 'ciné-tract' ('cinematic pamphlet') was La rentrée des usines Wonder/The Reopening of the Wonder Factories (1968). Following a big strike a female worker does not want to return to work. In front of the factory her co-workers, the foreman, and unionists try to persuade her that the main objectives of the walk-out have been achieved. In only ten minutes and one take, this short summarizes the worker-management-union relationship in May–June 1968. The method looked so convincing that it was used by Jean-Luc Godard, already well known as a major exponent of the New Wave. In Vent d'Est/Wind from the East (1970) and Louison (1976), Godard let an individual speak at length with few cuts and no editing.

A question soon arose: Is it possible for people urged to talk in front of a camera to avoid perpetuating stereotypes? The interviewees seemed to play their role to perfection and said what they were expected to say, making the film look like a fiction. Most directors prefered 'cinéma d'intervention', a cinema that is part of an event; it does not observe it from without but intervenes and takes part in it. Marker led the way by filming a strike at the Rhodiaceta factory in A bientôt j'espère/See You Soon, I Hope (1968). Among the numerous 'intervention films' that followed, a few deserve mention. During the 1972 strike at the Penaroya factory in Lyons Penaroya, a short denouncing scandalous labour conditions, had such an impact on public opinion that the management gave in, provided that the film was no longer distributed. Other movies made by workers under the direction of a professional popularized social conflicts in Besançon (Puisqu'on vous dit que c'est possible/As you are told that it is possible, 1974) and Sochaux (Le lion, sa cage et ses ailes/The Lion, its Cage and its Wings, 1976). The economic crisis of the mid-1970s put an end to mass demonstrations and strikes. The last militant film, Lorraine coeur d'acier/Lorraine Steel Heart (1981) showed how internal dissension ruined a radio station founded by steel workers. Critical films abandoned the subject of social unrest to focus on more general concerns such as politics, education, and health.

Documentaries played a crucial part in staining politicians' reputation. Seen in retrospect, the evolution is striking. Jean-Louis Comolli's Les deux Marseillaises/The Two Marseillaises (1969) presented the June 1968 election in the light of an ideological confrontation between Gaullism and the left. Raymond Depardon's 1974, En campagne avec Giscard/1974, On the Campaign Trail with Giscard disclosed the mechanisms of a presidential election but showed much respect for President Giscard. Portraying the March 1986 election that marked the defeat of the left, Serge Moati's Chroniques de mars/Chronicles of March (1987) proved extremely ironic. Spectators could only laugh at the outgoing socialist minister's joking unnaturally and singing the Marseillaise nervously. Claude Otzenberger's La conquête de Clichy/The Conquest of Clichy (1994) was so devastating that public television postponed its broadcast for three years. In it a cynical manipulator manifested that he had no political beliefs and was only interested in winning a seat in an affluent constituency.

Political scepticism led to historical revisionism regarding the most dramatic periods of the twentieth century, the German occupation and the Algerian war. The Gaullist myth that all France had supported the Resistance was shaken by Marcel Ophüls's Le chagrin et la pitié/The Sorrow and the Pity (1971). Some believe that the film was censored. In fact, the commercial company that had produced it offered it to public television, which did not respond. It was first screened in movie theatres and broadcast in 1981. Previously historical films were compilations with a well-structured commentary. Mixing archival material and provocative interviews, Ophüls adopted a colloquial, dispassionate tone. Evoking, for instance, the German invasion, the film showed French and German audiences watching the May 1940 newsreels in 1970. The former were grief-stricken by images that they had tried to forget; the latter were satisfied but embarrassed to manifest their contentment in front of the French. Confronted with traces of their past, individuals acknowledged that for most, the main preoccupation had been to survive, not to fight. 'Official' Resistance, either Gaullist or communist, had shadowed other forms of struggle. Mosco's Terroristes à la retraite/Retired Terrorists (1983) explained how foreigners working in France, who were forced to go underground, increased the bomb attacks against the Germans but who were never called 'patriots'.

The most impressive documentary about the war was a six-hour film, Claude Lanzman's Shoah (1985). In their works on the mass murder of Jews, Resnais and Rossif had used old pictures and testimonies. Lanzman objected that such documents, taken either by the Germans or by the Allies at the end of the war, could not recreate the reality of the death camps. In his view all that had survived was the memory of both victims and executioners. Most did not want to remember, but they would soon die and it was urgent to make them talk. Taking witnesses to the former camps, now empty, plaguing them with questions, the filmmaker provoked painful reactions. People, often on the verge of crying, related what they had endured or seen. Such remembrance was not triggered by an historical account of the Nazi policy; it was stimulated by impressions coming back from the past, a walk in the forest where the prisoners worked, a song heard in the camp, an object that belonged to a companion in suffering. It was not the representation of torture and death but the unbearable sorrow of those who had remained alive that obliged spectators to feel sorrow for the annihilation of European Jews.

Documentaries on the Algerian war underwent a similar evolution. Yves Courrière's La guerre d'Algérie (1972) was a chronological account of the main events illustrated by well-chosen archival pictures. Using testimonies of fifty-year-old men mobilized during the conflict, Bertrand Tavernier's La guerre sans nom/The Nameless War (1991) exposed the doubts of a generation involved in dangerous, often brutal, and eventually ineffective operations. It was only in 2002 that Patrick Rotman's L'ennemi intime/The Close Enemy confronted Algerians and Frenchmen, posed harrowing, contentious questions such as the recourse to torture in both camps, underlined the abdication of French authorities, and attempted to evaluate the impact of the war on both countries.

The Close Enemy was broadcast to celebrate the fortieth anniversary of Algerian independence. Documentaries in the last decades of the twentieth century were often shot on the occasion of important events or to meet some general concern. While Parliament was debating abortion rights, Charles Belmont's Histoire d'A/A's Story (1973), following an anonymous person, A, disclosed the complication and dangers of illegal abortion, thereby elaborating a real dialectic of responsibility between those involved in the enforcement of a prohibitive law. For more than a decade, feminism and birth control education became ubiquitous topics. Contrasting the lives and concerns of eight women, Coline Serreau's Mais qu'est-ce qu'elles veulent?/What Do They Want? (1978) summarized the changes occurring in women's lives. In Alertez les bébés/Alert Babies (1978) and Votre enfant m'intéresse/I Am Interested in Your Child (1981), Jean-Michel Carré dealt with medical care in delivery and with primary education. Exploring the foods that make up a meal, Luc Moulet's Genèse d'un repas/Genesis of a Meal (1978) expanded on food hygiene and on the changes that take place from the producer to the consumer.

Owing to the continuing economic crisis, new anxieties surfaced in the 1990s that affected mainstream documentaries. Immigration, unemployment, mixed blood, and fear of downward mobility appeared daily on television. Continuing a tradition already present in other eras, Denis Gheerbrandt explored Marseilles' periphery in Et la vie/Life Also (1991), but instead of lingering on abandoned industrial areas and impoverished houses, he concentrated on faces. People's behaviour, their willingness or their reluctance to talk, revealed social attitudes and reactions to a depressing situation.

Filmmakers focused less on misery than on another deep preoccupation of the late twentieth century: police and policing. After spending two months in a police station where he had filmed overtly, without trying to conceal either his presence or his possible influence on questioning, Raymond Depardon produced Délits flagrants/ Caught Red-handed (1994). Ignoring the spoils, fights, or aggression that had caused the arrests, he attempted to recreate the nocturnal atmosphere of the station and to interpret the relationship, half-hostile, half-conniving, that developed between the police and the offenders. In the same way, Renaud Victor's De jour comme de nuit/Day and Night (1991), the result of several months spent in the prison of Beaumettes in Marseilles, focused neither on the prisoners nor on their vision of punishment, but rather on the tricks they use to survive without prospects for the future.

Many documentaries released between 1980 and 2000 were mere series of talking heads. The best tried to go beyond appearances and to suggest something that was not said but that was conveyed only visually. Yet most filmmakers were anxious to find a fashionable, up-to-date topic likely to seduce a producer and then to attract a large audience.

Once screened or broadcast, their works were left for tomorrow's historians to reedit in historical programmes. What was almost totally lost was the formalist inheritance. Not surprisingly, only well-known directors could find the funds to shoot documentaries dealing with the cinematic language itself, not with modish objects or events. Wandering through Marseilles, René Allio contrived in L'heure exquise/The Delightful Hour (1981) an unlikely but possible city where past and present mingle harmoniously. Strolling around Los Angeles, Agnès Varda photographed hundreds of advertisements. Her Murs, murs/Walls, Walls (1981) was a curious, often disturbing succession of lines, shapes, and colours linked by visual similarities. Varda also closed the century with Les glaneurs et la glaneuse/The Gleaners and the She-gleaner (2000). Gleaners were often represented in late nineteenth century paintings as emblems of rural France. Varda used the figure of the gleaner to denounce archaisms in contemporary France but also to mock the modern tendency to buy short-lived consumer goods. Change occurs so fast that no time has been left for gleaning.

Varda's film could be taken as a symbol of the fate of French documentaries. During the first decades of cinema, the public paid little attention to informative movies. They were considered mere documents to be picked up when necessary and then discarded; audiences used to 'glean' them. The 1950s and 1960s were the heyday of cinema. Being interested in all sorts of pictures, spectators stopped despising documentaries. Instead of 'gleaning' they began to take these works seriously. With the expansion of television at the end of the twentieth century, the supply of factual programmes boomed. Audiences saw documentaries daily but seldom noticed them; the wealth of information made 'gleaning' useless.

PIERRE SORLIN

See also: Cavalcanti, Alberto; Land Without Bread; Lanzmann, Claude; Lumière Brothers, The; Ophüls, Marcel; Rien que les heures; Rouch, Jean; Shoah; Sorrow and the Pity, The; Voyage au Congo

Further reading

Breton, Emile, and Vigo, Luce (eds), *Filmer le réel. La production documentaire en France*, Paris: La Bande à Lumière, 1987.

Coleyn, Jean-Paul, *Le Regard documentaire*, Paris: Centre Pompidou, 1993.

Epstein, Jean, *Ecrits sur le cinéma*, two vols, Paris: Seghers, 1974–5.

Gauthier, Guy, *Le Documentaire. Un autre cinéma*, Paris: Nathan, 1995.

Huret, Marcel, *Ciné actualités. Histoire de la presse filmée, 1895–1980*, Paris: Henri Veyrier, 1984.

Jacquinot, Geneviève, *Image et pédagogie*, Paris: PUF, 1977.

Leblanc, Gérard, *Quand l'entreprise fait son cinéma*, Saint-Denis, PUV, 1983.

Lyant, Jean-Charles and Odin, Roger (eds), *Cinéma et réalités*, Saint Etienne: Cierec, 1984.

Meusy, Jean-Jacques (ed.), *La Science à l'écran*, Paris: Cerf, 1986.

Odin, Roger (ed.), *L'âge d'or du documentaire*, two vols, Paris: L'Harmattan, 1998.

Pessis, Georges, *Entreprise et cinéma*, Paris: La Documentation française, 1997.

Prédal, René (ed.), *Le Documentaire français*, Paris: Cerf, 1987.

——*Cinquante ans de cinéma français, 1945–95*, Paris: Nathan, 1996.

Sicsic, Josette, *Quand l'automobile fait du cinéma*, Paris: Editions France-Empire, 1986.

Franju, Georges

In the films of Georges Franju, the line between documentary and fiction, never all that clear in any case, seems continually on the verge of dissolution. Although his career as a filmmaker is usually described as falling into two parts—'the early period of documentary shorts, and a subsequent period of fictional features' (Wood 1991)—the continuities between these two periods are more significant than the differences, and Franju himself, in his films as well as in interviews and other writings, undermined any straightforward opposition between artifice and reality.

For Franju, cinematic artifice is a device for making realities visible that we have not seen, or refuse to see: slaughterhouses secreted away on the outskirts of cities (Le Sang des bêtes/Blood of the Beasts), the desolation and pain hidden behind historical myths of national honour (Hôtel des Invalides), the invisible by-products of industrialization that destroy the workers (Les Poussières/The Dust Particles). These three are among the most clearly 'documentary' of Franju's films and could even be said to belong to such familiar subgenres as the industrial short (Le Sang des bêtes, Les Poussières) or travelog (Hôtel des Invalides). However, what is one to make of the 'surrealist overture' (Vialle 1968) of Blood of the Beasts, with its young lovers in the midst of an antique bazaar in a featureless wasteland, or the horror film visual style and music of Hôtel des Invalides, or the ghostly shadow of the worker's hand seen through a white porcelain plate in Les Poussières, which allegorically figures the silicosis in his lungs? According to Franju, 'we strove in our film [Le Sang des bêtes] to give back to documentary reality its artificial appearance and to natural settings their look of stage sets' (Leblanc 1992). More broadly, he argued that 'Dreams, poetry, the fantastic must emerge from reality itself. Every film is a documentary, even the most poetic' (Durgnat 1967). The claim is deliberately provocative, but Franju meant it literally. Of his own unquestionably fictional feature Thérèse Desqueyroux, adapted from the novel by François Mauriac, Franju asserted that 'the film is a documentary about a character in a novel' (Brown 1983).

Nevertheless, if he rejected any strict differentiation between documentary and fiction, Franju recognized that there was a practical distinction, and it is the short films of the first half of his career that have earned him a significant place in the history of documentary cinema, in part because they are unlike the works of anyone else. The distinctiveness of Franju's documentaries is rooted in the specifics of his own intellectual and aesthetic development, which was far removed from the worlds of the university, journalism, politics, or colonialism, the preoccupations and professional discourses of which have determined many of the conventions of mainstream documentary film. Franju, born in 1912, belonged to that first generation of filmmakers whose sensibilities were shaped within and by the history of cinema itself, and although his own career as a director only began after World War II, in 1949, Franju's greatest affinities were with the work of an earlier generation: the surrealism of Buñuel, the expressionism of Lang and Murnau, and the Popular Front-influenced poetic realism of Carné and Renoir.

Franju, born in Brittany, had a conventional provincial-religious education, which fostered his anarchism, atheism, and anti-clericalism. After leaving school he evidently went to Paris, for he later wrote that 'at the age of fifteen, I educated myself in the Bois de Vincennes with the following readings: Fantômas, Freud, and the Marquis de Sade' (Buache 1996). Fantômas was the 'Master of Terror' whose exploits are narrated in a thirty-two-volume serial by Souvestre and Allain. Franju later observed that 'the enthralling power of the novels lies precisely in their sadistic invention, the teeming violence, the spectacularly extreme cruelty' (Milne 1975). These qualities endeared Fantômas to the surrealists, and Franju explicitly evoked Fantômas in his last feature film, L'Homme sans visage/The Man without a Face. After military service in Algeria from 1928 to 1932, Franju returned to Paris to work as a theatre set decorator. During this period he met Henri Langlois, a fellow cinephile with whom he made an experimental short film, Le Métro (1934)—later disowned by Franju—and, more significantly, with whom he founded a film club (the Cercle du Cinéma, 1935), a film journal (*Cinématographe*, 1937), and, in 1937, a film archive, the Cinémathèque Française.

The Cinémathèque, of which Langlois remained director until his death in 1977, was among the first and most important film archives in the world, and Franju's founding role attests not only to his centrality to the emergence of film culture from the 1930s on, but also to the formative role of older styles of filmmaking in his own aesthetic development. The clearest instance of this is his fourth short film, Le Grand Méliès, a semi-fictional or reconstructed documentary on the career of the filmmaker-magician-toyshop proprietor Georges Méliès, inventor of such fantastic story-films as A Voyage to the Moon (1902). Franju reconstructs Méliès's workshop, revisiting, in effect, the origins of fiction film itself, and particularly of that strain of the fantastic that runs through much of Franju's own work. What is the periscope in Hôtel des Invalides, for example, in which the museum visitor can impossibly 'see' scenes of trench warfare from World War I, if not a magic projector such as Méliès himself might have devised?

If Le Grand Méliès is Franju's tribute to early cinema, it is also an elegy for the individual Méliès, for 'the vanished, pre-1914 world' (Durgnat 1967), even, in a sense, for cinema itself. In 1937 Franju and Langlois had come up with an idea for a film, Le Métro fantôme, to be based on a 'fantastic and poetic' script by Jacques Prévert (screenwriter for Renoir and Carné, and later for Franju's Mon chien/My Dog). They asked Méliès, who had been forced out of the movie business through bankruptcy twenty-five years earlier, to design the sets and special effects. Méliès declined, writing to Franju that he found the story 'funereal', but when Franju went to visit him some months later, he saw that Méliès had actually made sketches for sequences set in Père-Lachaise cemetery, and that he 'was looking forward merrily to animating […] the funerary monuments of the well-known dead' (Brumagne 1977). However, Méliès, who had been in poor health, soon grew worse, and died a few weeks later; Franju and Langlois actually called the doctor who attended Méliès during his last days.

This personal connection between the two filmmakers is not presented in Le Grand Méliès, but it seems to underlie the film's elegiac mood. Opening with a series of shots of the home where Franju had visited Méliès just before his death, Franju's documentary ends with Méliès's widow emerging from a Métro station to take a bouquet of violets to her husband's grave in Père-Lachaise. One does not need to recognize the personal associations (Franju's visits, the Métro, Père-Lachaise) to grasp that Le Grand Méliès is a film of mourning, but the private iconography of grief is characteristic of Franju, who in both his short and feature-length films—as such critics as Wood, Durgnat, Milne, and Leblanc have demonstrated—returns again and again, almost obsessively, to certain images or motifs: dead landscapes, November skies, doves, the Paris Métro, windows, and World War I. His films, for all their black humor and 'elements of rage and protest' (Wood 1991), are filled with a sense of irretrievable loss. What Durgnat has called the archaism and nostalgia of Franju's work is the opposite of sentimental, however; he does not invoke the past as a golden age but as a repository of images charged with emotion. World War I, for example, recurs in Franju's films from Hôtel des Invalides through the features Judex (1963) and Thomas l'imposteur/Thomas the Imposter (1965), not because the years preceding it were necessarily happier but because for Franju, who had grown up in its wake, it stood, simply, as the clearest embodiment of all that's most terrible, in every period, about our civilization.

Similarly, Franju's affinity for the films of the 1920s and 1930s has little to do with critical evaluation or his own intentions as a filmmaker, but testifies to the indelibility of the impression they had made on him, being, as they were, the films of his movie-mad youth. In an essay on 'Realism and Surrealism', Franju wrote, 'I've often been asked whose films—as far as my own tastes are concerned, not as to any influence they might have had on me—are the most poetic of all, and I named Buñuel; the most beautiful works of horror, and I named Murnau; the most visually expressive, and I named Lang' (Vialle 1968). Franju's essay on 'The Style of Fritz Lang', which appeared in the first issue of his and Langlois's Cinématographe in 1937, was arguably the first critical analysis of a director's whole body of work in terms of visual style and mise-en-scène, and anticipated auteur criticism by almost twenty years. However, it is most important in terms of Franju's own career for what it reveals of his overriding interest in the image, rather than in narrative or ideas in the abstract. 'I can retell the stories of movies that have bored me', Franju stated in an interview; 'of those that have captivated me, I retain images without stories' (Brumagne 1977).

Franju's own films are nothing like those of Lang, Murnau, Buñuel, or Méliès; what he developed through immersion in their work was a way of seeing, a sensitivity to the poetic density and concentration of certain images. These might be images constructed in a studio—Franju had watched Renoir and Carné at work during the filming of, respectively, Régles du jeu/Rules of the Game and Point du jour/Daybreak—but equally they could be documentary images. In the same essay in which he invoked Lang, Murnau, and Buñuel, Franju ended with a rhapsodic account of a medical documentary: Dr Thierry de Martel's Trépanation pour une crise d'épilepsie, which recorded a particularly gruesome procedure of brain surgery. 'That was an authentic horror film', Franju later recalled; 'twenty people were out flat, I've never seen anything so drastic. It was an atrocious film, but a beautiful and poetic one, because it was also realistic' (Durgnat 1967). Franju would never go so far in his own work, even in showing, for instance, the slaughterhouses of Blood of the Beasts, not out of timidity, but to keep us just this side of being knocked 'out flat', which would excuse us from seeing.

Not long after the founding of the Cinémathèque, Franju and Langlois went their separate ways. In 1938 Franju became executive secretary of the International Federation of Film Archives and, in 1945, secretary general of the Institute of Scientific Cinematography, directed by Jean Painlevé. In 1946, together with his wife, Dominique Johansen, Franju founded the Académie du Cinéma. This immersion in the films of others, especially from the domains of scientific, avant-garde, and early cinema, meant that Franju's aesthetic was fully formed before he wrote and directed his first film, Le Sang des bêtes/Blood of the Beasts, in 1949. There was no period of apprenticeship, but also, as Robin Wood has noted, no real development in Franju's own approach, even when he shifted from documentaries to fiction, and from short films to features, in 1958 (Wood 1973). In his many interviews Franju never expressed any interest in films made after his debut, other than his own—a symptom not of self-regard or an old-fashioned aesthetic (he worked with such modernist writers as Jean Genet and Marguerite Duras), but of a need to preserve a certain creative isolation, and an indifference to both controversy and fashion.

The consistency of Franju's work results in part from some sustained collaborations with the assistant director Michel Worms, the composer Maurice Jarre, and the cinematographer Marcel Fradetal. Fradetal had worked on Carl Dreyer's Vampyr in 1932, and his elegantly composed medium and long shots, unhurried camera movements, and mastery of the full tonal range of greys available on black-and-white film gave Franju's works their singular atmosphere, what he himself called their 'sense of baleful, ceremonial ritual' (Milne 1975). There is an inexorable quality to the unfolding of Franju's films, and an apprehension of mortality, even when the subject matter seems banal: travelogues on Notre Dame or the Lorraine province, for example (Notre-Dame, cathédrale de Paris; En passant par la Lorraine), or an instructional film on the wearing of safety masks (Les Poussières). The films' mood of dread is linked to certain recurrent themes: hellish factories (the slaughterhouses of Blood of the Beasts, the steel mills of En passant par la Lorraine, the porcelain works of Les Poussières), dead faiths (Catholicism in Notre-Dame, military glory in Hôtel des Invalides), and the propensity for violence and cruelty barely concealed by the veneer of conventionality.

Franju's method in his documentaries is to strip objects of their familiar associations. As Durgnat writes, 'he removes the ordinary to reveal the tragic'. However, such stripping away of the visible surface is itself a form of artifice, no less than the cinematic and theatrical illusionism that Franju celebrates in his films on Méliès and the Théâtre Nationale Populaire (TNP). The filmmaker does not just turn on the camera and wait for reality to appear; instead, as he told G.R. Levin, 'you must re-create reality because reality runs away [...] you illuminate the subject, go beyond the subject—and that's documentary'.

HAL GLADFELDER

See also: Hôtel des Invalides; Sang des bêtes, Le

Biography

Born in Fougères, Brittany, France, April 12, 1912. Educated at religious school in Fougères. Military service in Algeria, 1928–32. Worked as theatre set decorator, Paris, 1932–3. Co-directed (with Henri Langlois) Le Métro, 1934; cofounded (with Langlois) the Cercle du Cinéma, 1935; cofounded (with Langlois)

Cinématographe (journal) and the Cinémathèque Française (film archive), 1937. Executive secretary of the International Federation of Film Archives (FIAF), 1938–45. Secretary general of the Institute for Scientific Cinematography, 1945–54. Cofounded (with Dominique Johansen) the Académie du Cinéma, 1946. Directed first documentary short film, 1949; directed first feature-length fiction film, 1958. Director for French TV, 1965–76. Died November 5, 1987.

Selected films

1949 Le Sang des bêtes/Blood of the Beasts: director, writer
1950 En passant par la Lorraine: director, writer
1951 Hôtel des Invalides: director, writer
1952 Le Grand Méliès: director, writer
1953 Monsieur et Madame Curie: director, writer
1954 Les Poussières/Dust: director, writer
1955 A propos d'une rivière (Le Saumon Atlantique) About a River: director, writer
1955 Mon chien/My Dog: director, writer
1956 Le Théâtre National Populaire (Le TNP): director, writer
1956 Sur le pont d'Avignon/On the Avignon Bridge: director, writer
1957 Notre-Dame, cathédrale de Paris/Notre Dame, A Parisian Cathedral: director, writer

Further reading

Brown, Robert, 'Georges Franju: Behind Closed Windows', interview, *Sight and Sound* 52, no. 4, 1983: 266–71.
Brumagne, Marie-Magdeleine, *Georges Franju: impressions et aveux*, Editions l'Age d'Homme, 1977.
Buache, Freddy, *Georges Franju: poésie et vérité*, Paris: Cinémathèque Française, 1996.
Durgnat, Raymond, *Franju*, London: Studio Vista, 1967.
Leblanc, Gérard, *Georges Franju: une esthétique de la déstabilisation*, Paris: Maison de la Villette, 1992.
Leblanc, Gérard, Gaudin, Pierre and Morier, Françoise (eds), *Georges Franju: cinéaste*, Paris: Maison de la Villette, 1992.
Levin, G. Roy, *Documentary Explorations*, New York: Doubleday and Co., 1971.
Martini, Andrea (ed.), *Georges Franju*, Milan: Il Castoro, 1999.
Milne, Tom, 'Georges Franju: The Haunted Void', interview, *Sight and Sound* 44, no. 2, 1975: 68–72.
——'Georges Franju', in Richard Roud (ed.), *Cinema: A Critical Dictionary*, New York: Viking, 1980: 387–93.
Vialle, Gabriel, Georges Franju, Paris: Editions Seghers, 1968.
Wood, Robin, 'Terrible Buildings: The World of Georges Franju', *Film Comment* 9, no. 6, 1973: 43–6.
——'Franju, Georges', in Nicholas Thompson (ed.), *International Dictionary of Films and Filmmakers, vol. 2: Directors*, second edn, Chicago: St James Press, 1991.

Frantz Fanon: Black Skin, White Mask

(UK, Julien, 1996)

Isaac Julien's 1996 documentary, Frantz Fanon: Black Skin, White Mask, explores the life of West Indian psychoanalyst Frantz Fanon, a key theorist in the decolonization movement of the 1960s. The documentary investigates the significance, as well as the more problematic aspects of Fanon's writings and especially of his most influential book, *An Essay for the Dis-alienation of Blacks*, later called *Black Skin, White Masks*. Published in 1952, the book was a milestone insofar as it provided the first study of the psychological impact of racism on colonized and colonizer and of the more sexualized aspects of racism.

Frantz Fanon was born in 1925 in French-ruled Martinique. Brought up within an assimilationist environment, he fought for France in World War II and later studied medicine in France, specializing in psychiatry. In 1953 he was appointed head of the psychiatric department of the government hospital in Algeria, where he arrived to find the non-French patients kept in appalling conditions. Drawn into Algeria's struggle for independence and increasingly demoralized by his work with victims of both sides of the violence, Fanon eventually dedicated his time fully to the Algerian uprising against France. In 1960 he became ambassador to Ghana for the Algerian provisional government. In the following year he published his second book, *The Wretched of the Earth*, which concludes with the necessity of armed struggle to break the ties of dependency between colonizer and colonized. Fanon died of leukaemia in the United States in 1961.

One of the most significant features of Isaac Julien's documentary, Frantz Fanon: Black Skin, White Mask, is its remarkable mixture of fictional and nonfictional material. Julien draws as much on excerpts from fictional material, such as staged imagery, films, and dramatic recreations of Fanon's life, as he does on classic documentary material, such as interviews and contemporary and historical footage.

The opening scenes introduce the usage of fictional material. In the first shot the camera passes through two wooden window shutters and out onto a yard, and is accompanied by the beautiful singing of a female opera voice. The next scene shows the shadow of a man in a cell, and a male voice-over is heard nervously uttering words in Arabic. The subsequent frame discloses the frightened, sweating face of an imprisoned man. Suggestively staged scenes such as these help situate the documentary contextually, but they also set an unsettling tone, mixing anguish and reflection, that continues throughout the film.

Later, such scenes, explicitly fictional, as signaled by the lighting, staging, and camera angles, combine with so-called tableau vivants, painterly staged scenes, that depict Fanon's life. Remarkably, not a single still or moving image of the historical Fanon is used. Instead, largely as a result of the lack of historical film footage of Fanon, the film reconstructs scenes from Fanon's life. Some of these scenes center on the more problematical aspects of Fanon's thinking, such as his support of the Algerian woman's veil as a means to support the rebellion (an argument welcomed by the Algerian conservatives) and also his denial of the existence of homosexuality in Martinique. In one dramatic mixing of archival material and staged imagery, the images of French war photographer Marc Garanger are projected onto veiled Algerian women; in a similarly staged scene, we see Fanon in the foreground and two men kissing in the background who turn their heads to look at Fanon as if in challenge.

The film moves effortlessly, and at times indistinctively, between historical and fictional material. A brief scene from Gillo Pontecorvo's La Battaglia di Algeri/The Battle of Algiers (1965) mixes black-and-white and color archival and contemporary footage of Martinique, Algeria, and the Algerian War of Independence to recreate the historical background of Fanon's work. The more conventional documentary material consists of interviews with Fanon's family and friends, contemporaries, and critics of Fanon, who describe his complexities and contradictions.

The collage style of Black Skin, White Mask continues on the level of language, sound, and music. The film features English, French, and Arabic, as well as different music genres—classical opera music, jazz tunes, and drums. This constant juxtapositioning of different elements produces a Brechtian alienation effect, one likely to reinforce the audience's act of intellectual participation with the subject matter.

The British actor Colin Salmon, who plays Fanon, recites excerpts from Fanon's writings throughout the film. His highly stylized, demonstrative performance is accompanied by uncanny, high-contrast, chiaroscuro lighting from below, which gives Fanon an isolated position within the frame.

British filmmaker Isaac Julien, who was shortlisted for the Turner Prize in 2001, has long been concerned with questions of race and gender and their importance within the politics of looking. He takes up these themes on multiple occasions in the film. In one scene, Julien reconstructs one of Fanon's epiphanies: his encounter with a little girl on the streets of Paris. The girl, seeing Fanon, exclaims: 'Look, a Negro! Look, a Negro! Look, a Negro! Mum, look at the Negro, I'm frightened!' The scene, in the film recounted, not staged, by Colin Salmon, triggered in Fanon a close examination of his blackness and his self-image in which he recognized the workings of an unequal, colonial relationship: Black Skin, White Mask.

Throughout, this multilayered film does not simply eulogize Fanon but examines the complexity of the historical figure and of the themes with which he dealt. Tensions between his thinking and his actions are emphasized throughout, and highlighted particularly through a series of candid interviews. Hence, Fanon's explanation for why black women fall in love with white men is implicitly critiqued in the interviews through references to Fanon's failure to examine the implications of his logic for his own decision to marry a white woman.

Frantz Fanon: Black Skin, White Mask responds to a recent rediscovery of Fanon's social and psychological theories by psychologists and critical thinkers. The skillful fusion of fictional with nonfictional material creates a stimulating and informative work of art full of intertextual references. Fanon becomes the ghostlike narrator of his own life and his urgent and direct addresses of the camera transport his ideas and their relevance directly into the present. In the final image of the film, the fictional Frantz Fanon looks straight into the camera, presenting an undeviating gaze that challenges the viewer to grapple with the themes that the historical Fanon raised more than a half century ago and that are still unresolved today.

JACOBIA DAHM

See also: Julien, Isaac

Frantz Fanon: Black Skin, White Mask (UK, 1996, 73 mins). Directed by Isaac Julien, written by Isaac Julien and Mark Nash, produced by Mark Nash for BBC and the Arts Council of England in assistance with Illuminations. Assistant directors: Catrin Strong, Carwyn Jones. Cinematography by Nina Kellgren. Camera assistants: Lorraine Luke, Nick Wheeler. Gaffer: Ashly Palin. Key grip: Phil Murray. Makeup artist: Sharon Martin. Production managers: Grischa Duncker, Craig Paull. Sound recordists: Michel Hildéral, Trevor Mathison, Olivier de Neste. Online editor: Gary Brown. Costume design: Annie Curtis-Jones. Art director: Mick Hurd. Dubbing mixer: Katja Sehgal. Music composed by Paul Gladstone, Reid Tunde Jegede. Avid editor: Nick Thompson and Robert Hargreaves. Frantz Fanon played by Colin Salmon. Musicians: Lynette Eaton, Dominic Glover, Tracey McSween, C. Wellington, Paul Weymont, Seddik Zebiri. Archive research: Nicole Fernandez Ferrer. Consultants: David Bailry, Ilisa Barbach, Homi Bhabha, Steve Farrer, Dora Bouchoucha Fourati, Paul Gilroy, Lucien Taylor. Archive film: ECPA, INA, Pathé. Archive stills: Bureau du Patrimonie Martinique, Oliver Fanon, Loïs Hayor, Martinique. Photographs: John Riddy. Film extracts: Battle of Algiers, Algerie en flamme, J'ai huit ans, Dr Pinel délivrant les aliénés à la Salpêtrière en 1795. Extracts from Frantz Fanon's *Black Skin, White Masks*, *Studies in a Dying Colonialism*, *Toward the African Revolution*, *The Wretched of the Earth*, extracts from 'Force of Circumstance' by Simone de Beauvoir.

Further reading

Alessandrini, Anthony (ed.), *Frantz Fanon: Critical Perspectives*, London and New York: Routledge, 1999.

Allon, Yoram, Cullen, Del and Patterson, Hannah (eds), *Contemporary British and Irish Film Directors*, A Wallflower Critical Guide, London: Wallflower Press, 2001.

Baker, Houston A., Jr, Diawara, Manthia and Lindeborg, Ruth H. (eds), *Black British Cultural Studies: A Reader*, Chicago: University of Chicago Press, 1996.

Fanon, Frantz, *The Wretched of the Earth* (translated from the French), preface by Jean-Paul Sartre, New York, Grove Press, 1963 (original: *Les damnés de la terre*, préface de Jean Paul Sartre, Paris: F. Maspero, 1961).

——*Black Skin, White Masks* (translated from the French), New York: Grove Press, 1967 (original: Peau noire, masques blancs, Paris, Editions du Seuil, 1952).

——*Studies in a Dying Colonialism* (translated from the French), New York: Monthly Review Press, 1965 (original: L'an cinq de la revolution algerienne, Paris, 1959).

Gordon, Lewis R., Sharpley-Whiting, T. Denean and White, Renée T. (eds), *Fanon: A Critical Reader*, London: Blackwell, 1996.

Haddour, Azzedine (ed.), *The Fanon Reader*, London: Pluto, 2003.

ICA, *Black Film. British Cinema*, ICA Documents No. 7, Institute of Contemporary Arts: London, 1988.

Julien, Isaac, 'Black Is, Black Ain't: Notes on De-essentializing Black Identities', in Gina Dent (ed.), *Black Popular Culture*, Dia Center for the Arts, Discussions in Contemporary Culture No. 8, Seattle, WA: Bay Press, 1992.

——*The Film Art of Isaac Julien*, New York: Bard College (Center for Curatorial Studies), 2000.

Memmi, Albert, 'The Impossible Life of Frantz Fanon', *Massachusetts Review*, winter, 1973: 9–39.

Mercer, Kobena, *Isaac Julien*, with essays by Kobena Mercer and Chris Darke, London: Ellipsis, 2001.

Read, Alan (ed.), *The Fact of Blackness: Frantz Fanon and Visual Representation*, Seattle, WA and London: Bay Press and ICA, 1996.

Stam, Robert, 'Fanon, Algeria, and the Cinema: The Politics of Idenification', in Ella Shohat and Robert Stam (eds), *Multiculturalism, Postcoloniality, and Transnational Media*, New Brunswick, NJ and London: Rutgers University Press, 2003.

Freyer, Ellen

Ellen Freyer, an independent producer of award-winning family films, has also produced and directed three documentary films that address social and political issues affecting women and children. Girls' Sports: On the Right Track (1975) and Marathon Woman: Miki Gorman (1980) concern changing attitudes and opportunities for women in sports, and The Splendors of Terror (2003) reveals the culture of hatred and violence that is being taught to children in the West Bank and Gaza.

Girls' Sports: On the Right Track dispels myths and explores new opportunities in girls' sports as a result of Title IX. The seventeen-minute educational film, which includes archival footage of track stars 'Babe' Didricksen and Wilma Rudolph, provides a short history of track and field, and contrasts the limited experiences of Didricksen and Rudolph with the expanded opportunities available to three contemporary high school girls. Marathon Woman: Miki Gorman, which premiered at the Lincoln Center Film Festival in New York, is an award-winning, twenty-minute film that profiles a champion Japanese/American marathon runner whose tiny size did not deter her ambition. The film was broadcast on PBS and distributed internationally. The Splendors of Terror is a fourteen-minute program that includes footage produced by the Palestinian Authority and broadcast on Palestinian television that has never been broadcast in the United States. It shows generations of Arab children being educated to hate and kill (even themselves) in order to murder Jews.

Freyer's fiction films, The Whipping Boy (1994), The Secret Garden (1995), The Summer of the Monkeys (1998), and Anatole (1998), have all been based on award-winning children's books. The Whipping Boy, winner of the National Education and Cable Ace awards, was based on the Newberry Award-winning children's novel by Sid Fleischman. Produced for the Disney Channel and starring George C. Scott, the film follows the adventures of an orphaned street urchin who supports himself and his sister as a 'rat catcher' until he is suddenly kidnapped to become the 'whipping boy' for a spoiled, rich prince. The Secret Garden is an animated musical version of Frances Hodgson Burnett's classic children's story. Produced for ABC and distributed by Paramount Home Video, the film stars the voices of Sir Derek Jacobi, Honor Blackman, and Glynis Johns, and was a Humanitas Award finalist. Summer of the Monkeys, based on the novel by Wilson Rawls (the author of the children's classic Where the Red Fern Grows), is a coming-of-age drama. Set on the western plains in the 1880s, it follows the adventures of a young boy who dreams of getting enough money to buy his own horse. Produced in Canada and distributed by Walt Disney, the film, which stars Michael Ontkean and Wilford Brimley, won the National Education Award, the Best of Festival at the Children's Film at the Breckeridge Festival, the Crystal Heart Award at the Heartland Film Festival, and the Audience Award, Best Feature Drama, at the Marco Island Film Festival. Anatole, an animated series about the adventures of a French mouse who is a 'cheese taster', his wife, and their three sets of twins, was based on the Caldecott-winning children's books written by Eve Titus and illustrated by Paul Galdone. The series was produced in Canada and was broadcast internationally, in the United States on CBS.

Before working as an independent producer Freyer was a television production executive and part of the original PBS team that created Wonderworks, a weekly family movie series. Produced for a PBS consortium under the leadership of WQED Pittsburgh, Wonderworks was described by *TV Guide* as the 'Best Family Drama Series', and by the TV Critics' Association as the 'Best Children's Programming'. From 1984 to 1992 Freyer supervised development, initiated and packaged programs from domestic and foreign producers, and traveled in the United States and abroad to supervise various productions. Included among the fifty productions that won an aggregate of one hundred and twenty-five awards were the international coproductions of The Little Princess and The Lion, the Witch and the Wardrobe (UK), both three-hour mini-series based on the classic children's books; The Haunting (NZ), based on the award-winning book by Margaret Mahey; and Clowning Around (AU), an original mini-series produced in Perth, Australia. The domestic productions that Freyer developed and supervised were Jacob Have I Loved, starring Bridget Fonda; Sweet 15, starring Tony Plana, Jenny Gago, and Jerry Stiller; and Necessary Parties, starring Alan Arkin, Julie Hagerty, and Mark Paul Gosselaar. The most well-known and -loved production that Freyer supervised was the four-hour Canadian coproduction of Anne of Green Gables. Directed by Kevin Sullivan and starring Megan Follows, Colleen Dewhurst, and Richard Farnesworth, the program won more than fifteen awards including the Peabody, Emmy, and Prix Jeunesse.

Freyer has written numerous articles and reviews about experimental, documentary, and children's films. She has been awarded grants from the National Endowment for the

Humanities, the NYS Council on the Arts, the NY Foundation for the Arts, the Women's Fund-Joint Foundation Support, the Hoso Bunka Foundation (Japan), and Mitsubishi International.

Freyer's projects have included films based on Karen Cushman's Newberry Award-winning young adult book *Catherine, Called Birdy*, and Mrs Piggle Wiggle, based on Betty McDonald's classic children's book series.

SUZANNE EISENHUT

Biography

Born in Hollywood, California. Father, Lewis Jacobs, was a pioneer filmmaker, critic, and historian, and the author of the 1939 seminal work *The Rise of the American Film: A Critical History*. Education: Barnard College, BA (Art History), New York University, MA (Cinema Studies). Taught art at elementary and intermediate schools in New York City and Madison, Wisconsin, before receiving her masters degree; taught Cinema Studies at St Peter's College (established St Peter's College Film Society), Syracuse University, and Hunter College; freelance assistant editor, post-production supervisor, and segment producer for independent documentary and educational films; award-winning documentary filmmaker; PBS production executive and member of the original team that created Wonderworks, coordinating producer and project manager on fifty productions and coproductions for Wonderworks 1984–92; independent producer of children's and family entertainment. Juror/consultant: American Film Festival, ACE Awards, Emmy Awards, International Festival of Films by Women, New York Film Festival, San Sebastian Film Festival (Spain), Student Academy Awards, Notable American Women.

Selected films

1976 Girls' Sports: On the Right Track: producer, director
1981 Marathon Woman: Miki Gorman: producer, director
1994 The Secret Garden (TV): producer
1995 The Whipping Boy (TV): producer
1998 Summer of the Monkeys (TV): executive producer
1998 Anatole (TV): executive producer
2003 The Splendors of Terror: producer, director

Further reading

Freyer, Ellen, *Chronicle of a Summer—Ten Years After, The Documentary Tradition: From Nanook to Woodstock*, New York: Hopkinson and Blake, 1971.

——'The New York Underground', *Craft Horizons Magazine*, 1973.

——'Formalist Cinema: Artistic Suicide in the Avant-Garde', in *Velvet Light Trap*, Madison, WI: University of Wisconsin, 1974.

——'Three Women's Films at the Whitney', *Craft Horizons Magazine*, 1974.

——'Women's Experimental and Personal Film Festival', *Feminist Art Journal*, 1977.

——'Profile of Nell Cox, Feminist Filmmaker', *Feminist Art Journal*, 1977.

——'Adapting Children's Literature to Film', in *The Lion and the Unicorn*, Baltimore, MD: Johns Hopkins University Press, 1987.

G

Galan, Hector

Hector Galan is a prolific independent filmmaker, notable for his insightful and comprehensive documentation of the Latino experience in America. He has produced and directed more than thirty documentaries, most under the banner of the Austin, Texas-based Galan Productions Inc. Galan founded the company in 1984, in large part to fill a void in media representation of Mexican American culture, politics, and history. Since then Galan has won numerous national and international awards for exploring such diverse topics as illegal immigration, race relations in the military, HIV/AIDS prevention, college athletics, and women in ranching culture. His productions appear regularly on national PBS television. He has produced or directed eleven episodes of the provocative Frontline series, as well as two programs for the acclaimed The American Experience series. Galan's seminal four-part series, Chicano! History of the Mexican American Civil Rights Movement, was screened at the White House for President Bill Clinton. In 1998 a retrospective of his work was shown at the Smithsonian.

Taken as a whole, Galan's substantial body of work represents a compelling and multifaceted visual record of the Latino experience in America.

Mexican American himself, Galan must be noted as one of a growing number of indigenous filmmakers who are using media to recover and reappropriate images and ethnic identities across diverse mediascapes. Yet Galan is unique among indigenous filmmakers for two important reasons: his productions achieve a thoughtful, objective distance despite the intimacy he shares with his subjects; and national public television has offered his productions a relatively large, mainstream audience. This is a credit to Galan, whose task is particularly challenging, for his films are made both for and about his audiences, for insiders and outsiders. They intend to both salvage and incite, to reflect and to inform. Yet, in speaking to different audiences with different needs, Galan's films rarely presume too much or too little. Instead, they achieve a delicate balance that faithfully serves both audiences with equal effect.

Galan's style reflects his tendency to produce for public television. His work is understated, balanced, thoughtful, informative, and objective, even though much of it borders on the controversial or macabre. He regularly relies on archival footage, photography, and voice-over narration to complement original footage and interviews. When he has opted for vérité, as in his acclaimed production on border shantytowns, Las Colonias, his films still retain an unlikely reticence and stoicism. This subtlety is intentional. It serves his overarching goal—'to bring stories to the public that were not being told'—and modest ambition—'that a television show isn't going to change the world, but it can give you a glimpse, an insider's glimpse, that is very important'. These reticent, unyielding 'glimpses' into forgotten Latino worlds have established Galan as an important documentarian and an invaluable advocate, historian, spokesperson, and ethnographer for the Mexican American community en masse.

Many of Galan's productions have explored some of the most desperate places in contemporary American society. Examples include maximum-security prisons, shantytowns, copper mines, the foster care system, illegal immigration, life on the Mexican-American border, racism, HIV/AIDS infection, and the agrarian industrial complex and drug addiction. Galan has called these productions studies of the 'invisible', those communities whose worlds have been disenfranchised by political and cultural systems beyond their control and whose plight has been swept beneath the carpet of national attention. Frontline's Shakedown in Santa Fe is an excellent example. The documentary examines the conditions of a New Mexico maximum security penitentiary eight years after one of the most violent riots in American penal history. Twelve prison guards were beaten, stabbed, and raped, and dozens of inmates were tortured to death by their peers. Despite its wretched details and violent imagery, the documentary is delivered with a sobriety that lacks moral judgment or sentimentality. By developing complex characters, exploring the culture of prison life, initiating questions about the criminal justice system, and inviting abstract questioning regarding the nature of punishment and reconciliation, Galan creates a multidimensional production that engages its audience on a variety of levels.

Galan is as equally concerned with making visible the many attributes of Latino culture and history as with exposing the inequalities and injustice that have plagued so much of the Mexican American population. Galan appears particularly enamored by Latino musical culture. Los Lonely Boys, Accordion Dreams, I Love My Freedom, I Love My Texas, Songs of the Homeland, and The Tejano Music Awards Selena Tribute document the production, distribution, and reception of contemporary Latino musical forms. Yet they also explore how tradition has shaped and affected current trends in artistic expression. This is not extraordinary for Galan who regularly favors historicity in his work. Accordion Dreams, Power, Politics and Latinos, La Mujer en el Rancho, and Vaquero: The Forgotten Cowboy trace ideas or subjects over time. Two of Galan's most renowned productions, The Hunt for Pancho Villa and Chicano! History of the Mexican-American Civil Rights Movement, are historical reconstructions. Galan's magnum opus (when it comes to explicating Latino ethnic heritage) is the six-part series Visiones: Latino Art and Culture. It provides a definitive visual history of Latino artistic achievement and includes theater, music, dance, and visual art, as well as its relations to history, ethnic identity, and social change. The series premiered in the fall of 2004 and took four years to complete.

The films of Hector Galan shed light on forgotten worlds rich in culture and history and beset by human suffering and degradation. They explore the systems and mechanisms of oppression and refuse to deny the resiliency of cultural tradition and the fact of individual complexity. They are remarkably sober and lacking in self-consciousness, less innovative, and original as they are thorough and comprehensive. They successfully appeal to a variety of audiences as evidenced by their success on national PBS television. With Latino populations in the United States ballooning at unprecedented rates, Galan's body of work as a documentarian of the Latino experience in America will undoubtedly prove to be an important resource.

JASON PRICE

Biography

Born in San Angelo, Texas, September 12, 1953. Received his BA in Telecommunications in 1977 from Texas Tech University in Lubbock. In 1980 became a senior producer for the Southwest Center for Educational Television in Austin. Produced Checking it Out, a twenty-six-part PBS magazine series for Hispanic teenagers. In 1982 became a producer for Warner-Amex in Dallas. His work in Texas won him a job as a staff producer/writer/director for WGBH-TV in Boston, Massachusetts. Began to produce long-form documentaries for the PBS news and public affairs series Frontline. In 1984 founded his own production company, Galan Productions Inc. in Austin. The company specializes in long-form news, cultural and public affairs documentaries for national broadcast. It has won numerous national and international awards.

Selected films

1988 Shakedown in Santa Fe: producer, director, writer, film editor
1990 New Harvest, Old Shame: producer, director, writer, film editor
1993 The Hunt for Pancho Villa: producer, director
1996 Chicano! History of the Mexican-American Civil Rights Movement: series producer
2004 Visiones: Latino Art and Culture: series coproducer

Further reading

Berg, Charles Ramreg, *Latino Images in Film: Stereotypes, Subversion and Resistance*, Austin: University of Texas Press, 2002.

Davila, Arlene M., *Latinos, Inc.: The Marketing and Making of a People*, Berkeley, CA: University of California Press, 2001.

Flores, William V., *Hispanic Cultural Citizenship*, Boston, MA: Beacon Press 1998.

Fox, Geoffery, *Hispanic Nation: Culture, Politics and the Construction of Identity*, Tucson, AZ: University of Arizona Press, 1997.

Noriega, Chan A., *Shot in America: Television, the State, and the Rise of Chicano Cinema*, Minneapolis, MN: University of Minnesota Press, 2000.

Rodriquez, Clara, *Latin Looks: Images of Latinas and Latinos in the U.S. Media*, Boulder, CO: Westview Press, 1997.

Ruiz, Vicki L., *From Out of the Shadows: Mexican Women in Twentieth Century America*, Oxford: Clarendon Press, 1999.

Suoro, Roberto, *Strangers Among Us: Latinos' Lives in a Changing America*, New York: Vintage, 1999.

Gardner, Robert

The films of Robert Gardner represent the conjunction of science and art. Gardner has said he would choose a large measure of Tarkovsky in making up an ideal cinematic genetic inheritance for himself. We should remember that Tarkovsky argues strenuously in his manifesto, Sculpting in Time, for film as a means to knowledge. All the art and technique of film is to be brought to bear for the sake of understanding the world, as only film can understand it, and to convey understanding to audiences.

Trained as an anthropologist, Gardner has made his largest and best-known films about Native Americans, New Guineans, and African peoples living very traditional ways of life, or about an India where people withdraw, as it seems, from the country's modernity to focus attention on and to live out traditional rituals or life processes. A smaller body of films looks at artists at work: painters Mark Tobey and Sean Scully, printmaker Michael Mazur, filmmaker Miklós Janscó, all notably resembling the many craftsmen seen at work in the films about traditional cultures. In all these films there is a deliberate shooting style that probes for meaning, alert to the symbolic and the coincidental, and a deliberate sound and image editing that draws attention to certain things, makes connections, and fashions small stories within the larger study. In most cases there is a reflective, even poetic, voice-over commentary. Gardner seeks understanding and calls on all of film's creative powers to engage with the world, to render complex experience, and to move viewers in more than rational ways.

At the beginning of his first film, Blunden Harbor (1951), made using footage shot by William Heick and Pierre Jaquemin, the camera moves on a boat across a forested bay on the coast of Vancouver Island. A voice-over relates the story of how the Kwakiutls original godlike chief came here to establish a home, 'become a real man', and begin the way of life of these people that we observe throughout the twenty-minute film. The film approaches its subject; the first few shots take us naturally from the water to the dwellings and workplaces of the people who live along its edge and draw food from it. In the movement of the camera and in our awareness of its uncanny power to find out and to create, we sense something like the coming of the god. In the beautiful black-and-white images of the water surface reflecting various light and the surrounding forest, we have a figure for the realm of imagination and the numinous, so important to these people's life and way of understanding themselves. In the water surface we have even a figure for the film screen and the power of the medium of film. Film converges with the larger imagination here. Blunden Harbour goes on from its opening to give many images of people at work, focusing, characteristically of Gardner, on hands and their activity, as if the hand needs discovery and attention, or matters more, or means more, than the face. Also characteristic of Gardner is the voice-over's reminder, midway through the film, of the fact of death, the great counterforce to all the life and work and use of imagination that we see. The film draws to a close accumulating images and sounds of mask-making and then ceremonial dancing, as if, on the part of the filmmaker as well as the Kwakiutl themselves, to fight off oblivion.

After Mark Tobey (1952) and collaborative work with John Marshall on The Hunters (1957), Gardner made his best-known and most discussed film, Dead Birds (1963). This contemplation of the warring Dani of central New Guinea stands as the first of four major feature-length studies of the human condition, followed by Rivers of Sand (1974) and Deep Hearts (1981), both shot in Africa, and then Forest of

Bliss (1986), shot in India. These films function as a tetralogy of research and meditation, or a large-scale four-movement symphony, each film with its own mood and way of tapping into layers of subrational experience. Ika Hands (1988), about a vanishing priestly culture in the high mountains of Colombia, serves as a coda to all this.

Dead Birds is a film of grandeur, in color like all the subsequent Gardner films discussed here, with wide shots of the lush valley setting, large-scale battle sequences between enemy tribes, and a homeric alternation of direct war material with the civic and domestic life that backs up the war, proceeding always in war's shadow. Here Gardner focuses on the day-to-day concerns of a few individuals whom we get to know by name. The film presents the beauty of life, great expense of energy, romantic images of human endeavor fitting into the patterns of nature, while the voice-over speaks of the grim and absurd conditions under which the Dani live, committed to immemorial war, dominated by ghosts. Overall the film is very interested in these people and is hopeful and excited about life, despite the consciousness of death and of the cultural traps people fashion for themselves. Gardner's fast, tense spoken commentary, providing names and much detailed information, seems just a partial view of a larger and richer life the film senses and registers, but knows it cannot encompass. Like Blunden Harbor this film ends with ongoing chant and dance, a lyrical outpouring that seems to transcend its cause and definition, in this case at first a grief ceremony for an assassinated child, which then turns into celebration on the news of the death of an enemy.

Rivers of Sand, about the Hamar of southwestern Ethiopa, is Gardner's darkest film, and more than Dead Birds it stresses its own fragmentariness. Various means are used: a sparse voice-over commentary, a Hamar woman's recurrent address to the camera, shots of diverse and sometimes baffling activities of the Hamar, symbolism such as the dry riverbeds these people live among and look to with hope, or the perpetual grinding of sorghum that mirrors the grinding of women's spirits. The film has the feel of making one kind of attempt after another to look into a life that cannot be comprehended, in part because it is a forbidding horror. These beautifully formed and beautifully dressed people live a life of male oppression, vanity, and ineffectiveness, and female hard labor, whippings, decorative scarring where we see the blood flow, and cutting out of teeth to please the male eye. It is a world of hunger and thirst, hunger above all on the part of men and women to be liberated, and not daring to think of taking the first step. Yet through all of this, people maintain a perverse merriment.

Gardner's handheld camera moves restlessly over distances with people and domestic animals, seeking meaning, as if seeking escape. The camera's quieter attention is drawn, as always, to the work of hands, of women at work at home, or men casting the 'sandal oracle' to see how things will go with their ostrich hunt. The vistas are of dust and sand, the desolate background to these people's lives, or of an evening thunderstorm that seems to threaten destruction. With the film's editing, animals and their sounds, mostly cattle and goats, are made present, as if a chaotic animal nature is the energy feeding human life, or as if the animal world cries out at its mistreatment by humans (there is marked contrast with The Nuer, made collaboratively a few years earlier with Hilary Harris and George Breidenbach, where the cattle seem both loved and loving, and there is an ecstatic blurring of a gentle human nature with a gentle animal nature). The film's mood of social critique, focused in the conscious and explicit feminism of the woman who talks to the camera, resonates with much thinking worldwide in the later 1960s and the 1970s, but the sense of a disturbing mystery that cannot be fathomed is more like a Faulkner novel than a confident political analysis.

Working with experimental filmmaker Robert Fulton, Gardner made in Deep Hearts, his most lighthearted film, the scherzo of the sequence one might say. The subject is the annual male beauty contest of the nomadic Bororo Fulani of central Niger, in the southern Sahara (the same subject is taken up seven years later, after devastating changes in Bororo life, by Werner Herzog in Herdsmen of the Sun). The words 'deep hearts' suggest an Iago-like concealment of feeling, and we learn that the Bororo, in fact, value a deep heart and the hiding of desire and envy behind a sunny exterior. Further, Gardner's spoken commentary, even sparser here than in Rivers of Sand, refers to the hard life of the Bororo outside these few days of festival in the brief rainy season, while the images and sounds of the film give us a world of joy and good humor, a façade, it might seem.

The power of film seems to yield to, and to be taken over by, the preparation of make-up and coiffure and costumes, the lines of men dancing and singing for days, the spectators, the everyday chores of maintaining a camp for this special period. Slow motion, freeze frames, swish pans, and altered sound all help film and viewer to get into the spirit of this prolonged lyrical outpouring that sublimates who knows what harsh experience or compromised feeling. The film brings us right into a particular event, without much distance or perspective, and yet the film works virtually on an abstract level, making the point that a great gulf lies between festival and art on the one hand, and on the other the matter of life we know must be resting there, but that festival and art transmogrify or obscure. In this film we live for a time in the pure ecstatic world.

Deep Hearts is about men who dress and behave as women, with the aim that one of the men be chosen as exemplar by a woman, who may be acting at the behest of still other men. Central to the festival is a freeing of gender identity and the camera itself enters a zone of gender ambiguity, just as it lets go of the perspectives of psychological and sociological analysis. Midway through the film Gardner's voice-over tells us that the Bororo are worried about consumption by others' eyes, and this reference makes us think of the camera, because nothing else in the film evokes such worry; we do not see it in the interpersonal relations of the people on view. The issue of the camera is raised, and a few minutes later, still in the same sequence alternating views of performers and spectators, the camera identifies itself with a woman, in a striking prolonged shot where we see a watching woman in sharp focus in the foreground, and the performing men an out-of-focus blur in the background, their visibility, their existence, as if subject to the watching woman's whim. The camera in Deep Hearts lets go in many ways, and transforms the film's subject matter overall into a dreamlike experience, perhaps a woman's experience, for the sake of getting close to, of getting to know, a certain reality.

With a complete withdrawal of voice-over commentary and subtitled translation of people's words, Forest of Bliss becomes a pure encounter of film's aural and visual sensitivities within a complex world, in this case Benares, India, and its business of care for the dying and disposal of the dead. Gardner has worked in India several times, collaborating on films about the perpetuation of ancient rituals: Altar of Fire (1976), Sons of Shiva (1985), and others. With Forest of Bliss, old and specifically Indian customs surrounding death come into play, but the film opens itself to something larger, the involvement of human activity in the metamorphoses and cycles of water and earth, feeding and excrement, wood and fire, light and dark, noise and silence. The film yields itself up to what is to be seen and heard in Benares, and to the suggestions everything makes of analogy to something else, human beings to scavenging dogs, marigolds, or the spirit vaguely sensed in kites, sails, and air. The film yields itself up, but at the same time the camera is probing and active, and the editing very deliberate, every cut seeming to start a new sentence. Some sounds are heightened, just as the camera finds visual close-ups in a larger perspective. One lives in the hospices and temples of Benares, in the lanes, along the ghats, and out on the broad Ganges. At times human faces and feeling, or the amazing funeral pyres, take over all consciousness. Yet one is aware throughout of an artist fashioning a film.

Gardner has always, and especially with Forest of Bliss, met with criticism from anthropologists who do not want to let go of words and rational understanding, and who look to film as properly a transparent medium to furnish illustration or proof for what words can comprehend. Gardner's work is impelled by belief in film as an unaccountable powerful force, which, if negotiated by an artist, will lead into areas of understanding that words cannot anticipate or be adequate to. The proof for any viewer is in the particular film, Forest of Bliss or another, opening oneself to it, reflecting, being willing to think in a new way.

In Ika Hands, Gardner confronts his way of doing things, and a race of people and way of life so strange and elusive as almost to defy filming; it is the filmmaker's ultimate interesting, important, difficult subject. The film begins with the image of Gardner talking with anthropologist Gerardo Reichel-Dolmatoff, whose writings have led Gardner to want to film the Ika. Thus these people begin as an idea for him, something on paper and imagined. Reichel-Dolmatoff's voice comes back again and again in the film, juxtaposed with what we see of the Ika and their high mountain world. Also, brief intertitles occur to name or explain actions. All of this comes to seem only a partial help to comprehend what is larger than our faculties.

The camera follows these aristocratic, long-haired, essentially pre-Colombian beings as they walk ridges, sing, meditate, and see visions; we seem to be in another time dimension, or not on this Earth. The many images of hands at work seem to want to ground the film, but there is a humanity or spirituality here widely distant from the hands, constantly seeming to take off and fly out of reach. The film takes us somewhere remarkable and makes us aware that we can never fully be there.

CHARLES WARREN

See also: Dead Birds; Forest of Bliss

Biography

Born in Brookline, Massachusetts, November 5, 1925. Graduated from Harvard University in 1948. Taught history and made and produced films in the state of Washington and on Vancouver Island, 1949–52. Studied anthropology at the graduate level at Harvard, 1952–6. Established the Film Study Center at Harvard's Peabody Museum of Archaeology and Ethnology in 1956, which continues to the present as an independent entity at Harvard for research and film production. Led the Harvard research team to the Grand Valley of the Baliem in Netherlands, New Guinea, 1960–1, out of which grew Dead Birds (1963), which won the Flaherty Award and the Florence Film Festival Grand Prize and established Gardner's international reputation. Helped found Harvard's Carpenter Center for the Visual Arts in 1962, an exhibition space and teaching facility for the creative arts. Taught filmmaking and film study in Harvard's Visual and Environmental Studies Department, 1962–98. Inducted into the American Academy of Arts and Sciences, 1964. Co-authored Gardens of War with Karl Heider, 1969, about the Dani of West Irian, New Guinea. Hosted Screening Room, a Boston television series of interviews and screenings with documentary and experimental filmmakers, 1973–80. Won the Florence Film Festival Grand Prize for Forest of Bliss in 1985. Given retrospectives at the Film Forum Freiburg in 1989, the Oesterreichisches Filmmuseum in 1991, the Whitney Museum of American Art in 1992, Anthology Film Archives in 1995, the Zürich Völkerkunde Museum in 1997, and the Beeld voor Beeld Amsterdam in 1998.

Further reading

Barbash, Ilisa, 'An Interview with Robert Gardner', *Visual Anthropology* 14, no. 4, 2001.

Cooper, Thomas, *Natural Rhythms: The Indigenous World of Robert Gardner*, New York: Anthology Film Archives, 1995.

Gardner, Robert, 'The More Things Change ... ', *Transition* 58, 1992.

——'The Impulse to Preserve', in Charles Warren (ed.), *Beyond Document: Essays on Nonfiction Film*, Hanover, NH: Wesleyan University Press/University Press of New England, 1996.

Gardner, Robert and Ákos Östör, *Making Forest of Bliss: Intention, Circumstance, and Chance in Nonfiction Film*, Cambridge, MA: Harvard Film Archive/Harvard University Press, 2001.

Loizos, Peter, *Innovation in Ethnographic Film: From Innocence to Self-Consciousness, 1956–85*, Manchester: Manchester University Press and Chicago: University of Chicago Press, 1993.

Paz, Octavio, 'The Feather and the Grindstone', *Harvard Magazine*, October 1974: 44–53.

Weinberger, Eliot, 'The Camera People', in Charles Warren (ed.), *Beyond Document: Essays on Nonfiction Film*, Hanover, NH: Wesleyan University Press/University Press of New England, 1996.

Georgia O'Keeffe

(US, Miller, 1977)

Produced by WNET/THIRTEEN for the series Women in Art, Perry Miller Adato's portrait of the artist as an older woman was timed to coincide with the publication of the Viking Press edition of Georgia O'Keeffe's prints, selected by her and her assistant Juan Hamilton. Together, the film and the book relaunched O'Keeffe's career, turning her into a feminist icon of endurance, feistiness, and creativity. In the film, O'Keeffe wanders through her beloved New Mexico landscape dressed in her signature black chemise and long coat, her hair pulled severely off her face in a tight bun. She describes her life before coming to New Mexico, how she came to meet her husband Alfred Stieglitz, and how she became attached to the Southwest. Especially when she sits in her studio inspecting the negatives of the prints for the book, O'Keeffe's brief comments about her life and art resemble, almost verbatim, its text. Declaring simply, 'I tried to paint what I saw ... I can see shapes,' she explains her recurrent organic forms, her simple lines and bold colors.

Using the extensive archive of photographs made of O'Keeffe primarily by Stieglitz (she was

Figure 3 Georgia O'Keeffe, 1977 (Courtesy of the British Film Institute)

known as the most photographed woman in the world) and pictures made by members of his circle, close-up scrutiny of the paintings, interviews with O'Keeffe, as well as commentary by leading art curators and critics Barbara Rose and Daniel Catton Rich, the film breaks no new ground cinematically. Its sixty-minute PBS format is designed to bring high culture into the living rooms of middle-brow America by emphasizing a one-to-one correspondence between objects or places and the paintings of them. Moreover, coming at a moment when feminism had been mainstreamed, and every woman was searching for foremothers who rebelled and excelled, O'Keeffe's insistence throughout the film that 'I've taken hold of anything I wanted' not only brought the artist and her art into every woman's home (a gesture repeated in the posters, calendars, and postcards hanging in college dormitories and gynecologists' offices), but offered an inspiring example of how to be a homey, independent, creative woman. O'Keeffe's ecstatic claims to landscape and space, 'When I got to New Mexico, that was mine,' provided viewers with a model of female desire to the territorial rights to one's vision, to ownership of one's desires. Later, she describes why she pursued her ten-year struggle to purchase her Abiquiu home from the Catholic Church: 'I thought that door [subject of many of her paintings] was something I had to have.'

Nothing in this film would suggest the strategic way in which O'Keeffe and Stieglitz crafted her career, or the fortuitous convergence of film and book, which seems serendipitous. However, O'Keeffe learned from Stieglitz how to market one's art and one's artistic self. Thus the picture of the spry, pixie-like O'Keeffe who just happens to have been 'lucky' masks a more complicated story of self-promotion. Barbara Rose comments that 'when Stieglitz married O'Keeffe, he not only married a woman, he married America'. This emphasis on O'Keeffe's American roots, from her birth in Sun Prairie, Wisconsin, to her early years in Texas and South Carolina, to the mistaken attribution of her name as 'Virginia' rather than 'Georgia' when Stieglitz hung her first show of charcoal drawings, to her final merger with the New Mexico landscape, is part of the original myth of O'Keeffe that this film and the book supposedly subverted through their candid revelations. In effect, the film is merely the most recent version of O'Keeffe's public persona, profiled in *Life* magazine in the 1930s and *Time* magazine in the 1940s. Early in the film, while telling about how her interest in bones led to her skull paintings, she mocks 'the great American everything' that obsessed her generation of playwrights, poets, and novelists. The stark white cow skull, suspended amid a field of blue, needed something to complete it; she shrewdly added two red stripes as borders, her sardonic commentary on the New York City men's lack of knowledge about the vastness of the country she had actually traversed and inhabited.

It is rare that film captures the full depths of paintings: usually the color is off, the texture invisible, the scale deceptive. O'Keeffe's paintings look exceptionally good in this documentary. In part, as she comments to Juan Hamilton apropos the prints for the book: 'It doesn't really matter if the color isn't absolutely right, if it feels right when you finish the print.' However, there is more to it. O'Keeffe's early training at the Art Institute of Chicago, barely glanced over except to say she was a gifted, prize-winning student there and at the Art Students League in New York, stressed magazine illustration and design. She was extremely aware, through her close working relationship with Stieglitz, of presentation. Her work reproduces well because of its monochromatic colors, its Dow-inspired properties to 'fill up space in a beautiful way', its rigorous lines, its recurrent shapes. Both she and her work were supremely suited to television: her wry, laconic affect, coupled with her determination to control the interview, disclosing only what she wants known, makes her an engaging, enigmatic figure. She appears to undo the legend surrounding her as she produces a new one for a new generation of fans. Her paintings repeat imagery with variations, much as television series depend on familiarity with a difference. As Rich comments, for O'Keeffe landscape and still life are essentially the same; they are exercises in the serial investigation of forms and color, not psychological examinations typical of portraiture.

In this, the 'portrait of an artist' made for the PBS series 'Women in Art', is also more of a study in comforting repetitive shapes, colors and forms—returning to a few key paintings, such as the New Mexico cross, the yellow and red pelvis, the red poppy, and a few melodic lines for flute—rather than a revelatory inspection of the woman. Despite the series' claims to 'interweave the artists' works and their lives', O'Keeffe manages to subvert the filmmaker's push to learn her inner workings. She remains as implacable as the 'dark place' she visits on foot and on canvas. By appearing to reveal herself—she speaks always in the first person, claiming over and over an identity: 'I was busy'—she weaves the myth of O'Keeffe that has lasted for decades. In this, O'Keeffe once again demonstrates her savvy understanding of the terms and procedures of the art market, disclosing only what she deems apt, undercutting any efforts by others to read themselves into her. As she remarks of the critics who read all sorts of sexual symbolism into her gigantic flowers: 'They were speaking of themselves, not me.'

PAULA RABINOWITZ

Georgia O'Keeffe (US, WNET/THIRTEEN, 1977, 60 mins). Produced by WNET/THIRTEEN for Women in Art. Produced and directed by Perry Miller Adato. Associate Producer, Catherine Tatge. Music by John Morris.

Further reading

Cowart, Jack and Hamilton, Juan, with Sarah Greenough, *Georgia O'Keeffe: Art and Letters*, Washington, DC: National Gallery of Art, 1987.

Merrill, Christopher and Bradbury, Ellen (eds), *From the Faraway Nearby: Georgia O'Keeffe as Icon*, Albuquerque: University of New Mexico Press, 1998.

O'Keeffe, Georgia, *Georgia O'Keeffe*, New York: The Viking Press, 1976.

German Democratic Republic

On May 17, 1946, the Soviet Military Administration (SMAD) handed a license over to German filmmakers for the production of new films. With it, the German Film Inc. (DEFA, Deutsche Film-Aktiengesellschaft) was created as the first German film enterprise after World War II. Four months earlier, in mid-January 1946, on behalf of 'DEFA in Formation', Kurt Maetzig had already begun shooting the newsreel Der Augenzeuge/The Eye-Witness. Its first edition consisted of ten copies that where released to Berlin cinemas on February 19. Two more sequels had appeared from March to July, before The Eye-Witness turned into the actual 'newsreel' in August 1946. This periodic film program continued until December 1980, when it was suspended.

During the course of its existence, DEFA produced five thousand two hundred documentaries and popular scientific films for the cinema, including The Eye-Witness and other periodic programs (for example, a monthly cultural newsreel and a monthly sports newsreel). In 1975 the former DEFA Studio for Newsreel and Documentary Films Berlin and DEFA Studio for Popular-Scientific Films Potsdam-Babelsberg merged and became DEFA Studio for Documentary Films. Here hundreds of commissioned films were produced for the German Democratic Republic (GDR) television until the end of the GDR. As in the case of feature films, DEFA almost had a monopoly in the production of documentary films in the GDR. Documentary productions from students of the German University for Cinematographic Art (later the University for Film and Television) Potsdam-Babelsberg, soon followed to the screen.

Besides the newsreel The Eye-Witness, the first original DEFA documentary film was also created in 1946. On behalf of the Kommunistische Partei Deutschlands (KPD, German Communist Party), Director Kurt Maetzig filmed the documentary Einheit SPD-KPD/SPD-KPD Unity (premiere, May 1, 1946), which to a large extent was an objective reportage about the unity of the two German labor parties, KPD and SPD, in the Soviet zone. The films Berlin im Aufbau/Berlin under Construction (director: Kurt Maetzig), Potsdam baut auf/The Rebuilding of Potsdam (director: Joop Huisken), Dresden (director: Richard Groschopp), and Halle/Halle (Director: Red Braun) appeared in the same year, showing the same objectivity and redeemed pathos. They chose the new beginning as the central theme, and at the same time they referred to the root of the destruction: German militarism and imperialism. Likewise in 1946, Richard Brandt directed the film Todeslager Sachsenhausen/Death Camp in Saxony about a concentration camp at the gates of Berlin.

The SED (Sozialistische Einheitspartei Deutschlands), other political parties, the Soviet Military Administration, the Metal Industrial Union, the Union of the Persecuted by the Nazi Regime (VVN, Vereinigung der Verfolgten des Naziregimes), and the Red Cross were among the early clients of DEFA's documentary films. Enterprises and authorities commissioned cinematographic documents. DEFA developed self-help reportages and productions about injured war homecomings, industrial safety, energy savings, and women's rights.

In 1948–9, after a period of relative freedom, the DEFA documentary films suffered from stronger political oppression. The cinema produced in the GDR, which was created in October 1949, had the main objective of convincing society to switch to socialism, thereby creating 'new individuals'. At the beginning of 1950 the SED's leaders took the decision of tying DEFA documentary film production closely to the party. From then on the SED guided and controlled the ideology. The SED demanded vehemently and exclusively the 'political documentary film' that supported their objectives. Besides short films, movie theaters presented feature-length film productions, whose main objective was to provide a chronicle of successes: Immer Bereit/Always Ready (1950) directed by Kurt Maetzig and Feodor Pappe, a reportage about the Free German Youth (FDJ, Freie Deutsche Jugend) meeting in Germany, and DEFA's first color documentary film, Der Weg nach oben/The Way Forward (1950) and

Wilhelm Pieck—Das Leben unser Praesidenten/Our President's Life (1952) by director Andrew Thorndike. These films present neither doubts about the course of things nor questionable nuances of the social development in Soviet occupation zones and the GDR. They modeled German history and its current situation exclusively after the official propaganda format. The SED made sure that tickets were distributed throughout enterprises, schools, and institutions and that hundreds of thousands of spectators formed the impression that attending the film shows was a compulsory activity. The documentary film had become a political tool.

It was not until the mid-1950s, after Stalin's death and the institution of a 'new course', that the studio production became more polymorphic. Joop Huisken reverted to filming simple humans instead of 'heroes' in the film Turbine I (1953), in which he observed a specific working process in an electrical power station. His assistant, Karl Gass, and other directors dabbled with the production of film feuilletons Im Paradies der Ruderer/The O Paradise (1953), Vom Alex zum Eismeer/From Alex to the Polar Sea (1954). Max Jaap produced feature-length films about the life of several artists such as Ludwig van Beethoven (1954) and Friedrich Schiller (1956). Hugo Hermann, a native Austrian, let children and workers talk directly into the camera about their hopes, desires, and concerns in Träumt für Morgen/Dream for Tomorrow (1956) and Stahl und Menschen/Steel and People (1957).

The commitment of the Dutch director Joris Ivens, who produced the international full-length film Lied der Ströeme/Song of Streams (1954) and Die Windrose/The Wind Rose (1957) among others on behalf of DEFA, brought a new impulse to the world of documentary films. Andrew and Annelie Thorndike were dedicated to producing international material. They produced several compilation films based on international archive material, which highlighted the course of German history during the twentieth century, the emergence of the two world wars and the career of former Nazis in the Federal Republic. For the creation of the film Du und mancher Kamerad/You and Some Comrades (1956), the Thorndikes had to sift through more than six million meters of film, and the film's final version cites approximately seven hundred different films and newsreels. Der Fall Harzmann und andere/The Case of Harzmann and Others (1957) is a critic of former Nazi judges taking total control of the West German law system; Urlaub auf Sylt/Vacation on Sylt (1957) is based on the biography of former SS officer Reinefahrt, who was involved in the abatement of the Warsaw rebellion in 1944 and afterwards became mayor of Sylt; Unternehmen Teutonenschwert/Enterprise Teutonenschwert (1958) described the role of a North Atlantic Treaty Organization (NATO) General named Speidel in World War II and Speidel's career after 1945. The impressive assembly of these films sometimes helped to obscure the fact that the Thorndikes were not always moving on safe ground. They usually showed irrefutable facts but also suggested that simple presumptions were the truth and constantly affirmed that the West German state and its political leaders, Adenauer and Schuhmacher, were as bellicose as fascists.

On August 13, 1962, one year after the construction of the Berlin Wall, DEFA brought to the big screen the film Schaut auf diese Stadt/Look at this City (director: Karl Gass), which marked the end of the documentary film productions of the 1950s. On the one hand this film displays abhorrence toward Western development, but on the other hand it provides certainty about the historical superiority of the GDR and the socialist system. Gass merely depicted West Berlin as a simple concentration area of war mongers, old Nazis, saboteurs, and agents, like a 'stake in the flesh of the GDR'. Look at this City soon became an enthusiastic 'high song' of the GDR and its new borders; in this film there was no room for the tears and sorrow that the Wall brought to people on one or the other side of the razor wire.

The separation of the GDR raised DEFA's documentary film producers' and coworkers' hope of finally being able to operate more openly and critically, without any Western influence. A young generation of directors educated at the Babelsberg University for Cinematographic Art and interested in their own country's life and reality, started working at DEFA's studio. Karl Gass became the spiritual rector of many of these young people mainly after the presentation of his film Feierabend/Spare Time (1946), a spectacular survey that critically analyzes workers and shows them drinking and celebrating for the first time. Gass, who was temporal director of the documentary film class at the university and from 1961 was head of its own artistic working group for documentary film at DEFA, encouraged Winfried Junge to produce a film series about children from the village of Golzow, which lies on the GDR frontier with Poland. In Wenn ich erst zur Schule geh … /When I Go To School … (1961) Junge narrates about a first school day; in Nach einem Jahr/After a Year (1962), he takes a balanced look after one year; in Elf Jahre Alt/Eleven Years Old (1966) he shows a group representation in which the children talk about their experiences and dreams. Up to the end of the GDR Junge produced five more 'Golzow films', which, according to the original plan, should have reflected the growing up of the 'first communist generation' until the year 2000.

The films actually emancipated themselves from this theoretical image and showed instead historical time-related and social insights. As a result of this perspective change, Junge could continue with the production of the Golzow series even after the end of the GDR and the end of DEFA. Thus far, the longest full-length international documentary series comprises almost twenty films from which the compilation of Lebensläufe/Personal Records (1980) and Drehbuch: Die Zeiten/Screenplay: The Times (1992) most attracted the attention of an international audience. In Screenplay: The Times Junge meditates on the special conditions for making films in the GDR and on censorship and self-censorship.

Like Junge, other important directors of his generation were also interested in contributing to the democratization of the community of the GDR by showing the lifestyles and hopes of people, in this way touching people's sensitivity. Outstanding films were shot from the mid-1960s by Jürgen Böttcher, Gitta Nickel, Richard Cohn-Vossen, Karlheinz Mund, Kurt Tetzlaff, and Volker Koepp. The French cinéma vérité and particularly the film by Chris Maker, Le Joli Mai (1963), which had received an award at the Documentary Film Week in Leipzig, became of enormous importance to these film producers. Juergen Böttcher was mainly tied to productions such as Barfuss Und Ohne Hut/Barefoot and Without a Hat (1965), about young people spending their summer vacations in the Baltic Sea, Der Sekretaer/The Secretary (1967) about an unorthodox party secretary, and Wäscherinnen/Laundresses (1972). In 1978 he produced the film Martha, a subtle portrayal of a sixty-eight-year-old Berlin 'rubble woman', who removes stones to pay the rent, lives a modest life, and is not interested in politics. This type of 'heroine' had hardly been seen in the GDR's documentary film until that time.

Gitta Nickel produced Heuwetter/Hay Weather (1972), which narrates a one-decade period at an agricultural production cooperative. The film begins with unpublished images from 1963, which deal with several issues such as sloppiness, alcohol addiction, and irresponsibility, until the village chronicle reaches the present day. Thus the social development is confirmed and fractioned by a countrywoman's personal memories. Volker Koepp lets young women talk directly into the camera in Mädchen in Wittstock/Girls in Wittstock (1975), his first film about female personnel in a new knitwear factory. Reflections about work, free time, and dreams integrate with a picture that shows the lack of democracy in a 'large socialist enterprise'. This Wittstock enterprise became a cinematographic research object for Koepp more or less in the same way as Golzow village had been for Winfried Junge. Until 1996 he returned to Wittstock again and again, always following the lives of three women, observing the transformation of the place and its inhabitants in the free market economy. Koepps's films are considered the best DEFA productions: the peace and tenderness of their expression, the confidence acquired through closeness, the sensitivity for landscape motifs, which also often represent the spiritual condition. The quality of the best DEFA documentary films was principally the result of the exceptional DEFA cameramen: Christian Lehmann, Thomas Plenert, Wolfgang Dietzel, and Hans Eberhard Leupold, among others, who always worked masterfully and sensitively.

Walter Heynowski and Gerhard Scheumann gained a privileged position in the documentary film business of East Germany. Between 1969 and 1982 they managed their still existing 'Studio H&S', which was financed by the State but was officially independent of DEFA. The studio was considered an independent artistic workshop in the spirit of Dziga Vertov, and provided principally 'anti-imperialistic enlightenment'. Many H&S films, principally those in which the central theme is the war and peace cycles in Vietnam, the putsch in Chile, or the genocide in Kampuchea, attracted international attention during the 1970s and early 1980s.

Retrospectives from Heynowsky and Scheumann were presented in more than forty cities all over the world.

Both directors owned their own studio principally as a result of the film Des Lachende Mann/The Laughing Man (1966), for which they put a West German major in front of the camera, who narrated his life as a mercenary in Africa. Under the influence of alcohol and unaware of the filmmaker's identity and the purposes of the film, the anti-hero chatted frankly about his war adventures. For H&S, this meant the exposure of the system in which they grew up—'West German imperialism'. As a result of this film, as well as others such as Piloten In Pijama/Pilots in Pyjamas (1968) about US pilots killed in Vietnam, Heynowski and Scheumann were considered star political directors, who enjoyed financial and material success. To aid the fight against worldwide class conflict they shot a film cycle about Chile, which began in 1974 with Der Krieg der Mumien/The War of the Mummies and continued with analytical work such as Ich war, ich bin, ich werde sein/I Was, I Am, I Will Be (1974) and Der Weißse Putsch/The White Putsch (1975), as well as some sharply pointed short films. In their films H&S analyzed the mechanisms that led to the fall of Salvador Allende's government and outlined the role of the Chilean bourgeoisie and the military. However, the films omitted, to a large extent, any objections against the left-wing movement.

For the production of Die Teufelsinsel/The Devil's Island (1976), Der erste Reis danach/The First Rice Thereafter (1977), and others, H&S returned to Vietnam immediately after the end of war to search for traces of crimes, resistance, and a new life. They analyzed in the feature-length documentary films Kampuchea—Sterben und Auferstehen/Kampuchea—Death and Resurrection (1980) and Die Angkar/The Angkar (1981) the terror regime of Pol Pot and the consequences for Kampuchea. However, neither director was interested in the GDR's contemporary life; Heynowski and Scheumann returned to their country only when they started the production of Die Dritte Haut/The Third Skin (1989), a beautifully colored homage to Erich Honecker's housing policy.

The denaturalization of the political songwriter Wolf Biermanns by the SED leaders began in autumn 1976, and this event, together with the government's attempt to discipline the GDR's artists, also left deep marks on the documentary film studio. One of the most important directors, Richard Cohn-Vossen, who produced the fascinating biography of composer Paul Dessau (1976) among other films and critically questioned the practice of socialist democracy in films like Monika (1975) and Abgeordnete in Rostock/Deputy in Rostock (1976), left the GDR and migrated to the Federal Republic of Germany. His colleagues Jürgen Böttcher, Werner Kohlert, and Heinz Brinkmann, who protested against Biermanns's denaturalization, experienced massive political pressure. During the 1980s DEFA documentary producers as a whole showed the reality of the GDR in a more critical way and staged productions that displayed taboo subjects (often despite the resistance of the State), which were financed by DEFA.

The film Erinnerung an eine Landschaft—für Manuela/Memory of a Landscape—for Manuela (1983) by Kurt Tetzlaff, a full-length survey about a village in central Germany that had to succumb to the opening of a brown coal mine, Jugendwerkhof/Industrial School (1982) by Roland Steiner about subjugated young people, Abhängig/Dependent (1983) and Rückfäellig/Recidivist (1988) by Eduard Schreiber about alcoholics, Berlin—Auguststraße/Berlin—August Street (1981) by Günter Jordan about young people in East Berlin, as well as some films from Karlheinz Mund, Gunther Scholz, and Konrad Weiss about mentally and physically disabled persons are among the most outstanding films of the last decade of the GDR.

The documentary films from Jürgen Böttcher, Rangierer/Switchman (1984) and Die Küche/The Kitchen (1987), which show intense black-and-white pictures, reflected the end time mood: symbols of hard work in an imaginary room, in which shadowy movements seemed to be produced, but no real motive is given. Jochen Krausser approached the country's condition in a grotesque way: Leuchtkraft Der Ziege—Eine Naturerscheinung/The Goat's Luminance—A Natural Phenomenon (1988) was the first surrealistic contribution of DEFA's documentary film studio. The rock film Flüstern & SCHREIEN/Whispering and Shouting (1989, directors: Dieter Schumann and Jochen Wisotzki) showed for the first time sections of the GDR's subversive music scene and put a piece of counterculture on the public cultural map. … Und Freitag in die grüne Hoelle/… And Friday in the Green Hell (1989, director: Ernst Cantzler) portrayed football fans and trouble-makers in East Berlin, while Unsere Kinder/Our Children (1988, Roland Steiner) brought punks, old gits, skinheads, and young neo-Nazis in front of the camera. In Unsere alten Tage/Our Old Times (1989), Petra Tschoertner illustrated the treatment of the elderly in the GDR, which was not always humane. All these productions are valiant films and the same can be said of Karl Gass's historic precise compilation Das Jahr 45/In the Year 45 (1985), about existential confusion in the history of the German people.

Helke Misselwitz had great success with a production that covered a complex description of the GDR's condition and the mood of its inhabitants at the end of the 1980s. She undertook a cinematographic journey across the country for the production of the documentary Winter Ade/Goodbye Winter (1987), and she outlined experiences of women of different ages and diverse social positions. Goodbye Winter became the most significant and emotional film at the end of the GDR.

The film diary Leipzig im Herbst/Leipzig in Fall from Andreas Voigt and Gerd Kroske, a reportage about demonstrators and policemen, oppositionists and functionaries, opened DEFA's last chapter. After the collapse of the prevailing state party and the fall of the Wall, there was no longer the need to say or show the facts between lines or images. Movies such as Imbiss Spezial/Special Snack (1990, director: Thomas Heise), Kehraus/Last Dance (1990: director: Gerd Kroske), Sperrmül/Bulk Waste (1990, director: Helke Misselwitz), Wind sei stark/Wind is Strong (1990, director: Jochen Kraußer), Im Durchgang/On the Pathway (1990, director: Kurt Tetzlaff), Letztes Jahr Titanic/Last Year Titanic (1991, director: Andreas Voigt), Eisenzeit/Iron Age (1991, director: Thomas Heise), and Kein Abschied—Nur Fort/No Farewells—Just Go (1991, director: Joachim Tschirner, Lew Hohmann) described the mood of the GDR citizens as both agonized and optimistic and described the new difficulties that were a result of German unification. Heinz Brinkmann and Jochen Wisotzki produced the film Komm in den Garten/Come into the Garden (1990) about three friends in the Berlin municipality Prenzlauer Berg, which was in fact an homage to outsiders, who DEFA had considered before as 'cinematically unworthy'. In the film Östliche Landschaft/Eastern Landscape (1990), which was filmed entirely at a garbage site, Eduard Schreiber pleaded with viewers not to sacrifice one's own roots exclusively for a new reality.

Directors and authors also worked on the history of the GDR and the history of real socialism besides the contemporary reportages and essays. In the film Walter Janka—Aufstehen und Wiedersetzen/To Rise and Resist (1990), Karlheinz Mund depicted a publisher who had been under political arrest for many years. In Christa Wolf—Zeitschleifen/Time Warps (1991), Mund became known to the East German writer, who had become a positive role model for many countrymen due to her disturbed critical attitude towards politics. Konrad Herrmann revealed the biography of the GDR's first minister of culture and former expressionist poet Johannes R. Becher in Die Angst und die Macht/Fear and Power (1991). Director Sybille Schoenemann, who was arrested in the mid-1980s owing to 'subversive activities' and deported to the West, showed in her autobiographical film Verriegelte Zeit/Barred Times (1991) the role that DEFA's assistants had in the GDR political system. She outlined her own spying, arrest, and denaturalization experiences.

Jüergen Böttcher performed a special farewell to the GDR. His film Die Mauer/The Wall (1990), developed between paintings and film scenes, silently showed the slow disappearance of the Berlin Wall through long contemplative settings. One can see and hear, for example, bird swarms concentrated over the still-deserted city center, the closed underground station at Potsdamer Platz, or the multicolored graffitis, people and propaganda noise, sounds of excavators, fireworks on New Year's Eve 1989–90, and the wooden crosses for those who sacrificed their lives at the border. The director projected additional historical film passages onto the wall: from Emperor Wilhelm's ride through the Brandenburg Gate, completely lit by Nazi torches, a picture of a policeman who jumped to the West in 1961, until the day of the collapse of the Wall.

On July 1, 1990, the day of the monetary union between GDR and the Federal Republic of Germany and of the introduction of the D-mark as the unique legal currency, the DEFA documentary film studio was transformed into a limited corporation and was put up for sale by the privatization agency. To comply with the privatization conditions, the studio laid off most of its employees until mid-1991. Nearly all were directors, cameramen, and dramaturges. The rest of DEFA, mostly service providers, were in charge of TV program production and they made technology available and assisted in coproductions. The quality of the DEFA documentary films survived the new productions of the East German directors. Even though many former directors, authors, and cameramen retired, lost their jobs, or changed professions, the work of Volker Koepp, Thomas Heise, Eduard Schreiber, Peter Voigt, Andreas Voigt, Jochen Krausser, Heinz Brinkmann, and Winfried Junge are still associated with the most exhilarating German documentaries.

Jürgen Böttcher, internationally the best-known DEFA director, returned to the screen in 2001. In his film Konzert im Freien/Outdoor Concert, he assembled new pictures with old, previously unpublished DEFA material about the construction of the Marx-Engels-Forum in East Berlin, which was conceived as a monument and public park. The outcome of this work was an essay about hopes and errors, utopias and tragedies of the twentieth century.

RALF SCHENK

See also: Böttcher, Jürgen

Further reading

Jordan, Günther and Schenk, Ralf (eds), *Schwarzweiß und Farbe. DEFA-Dokumentarfilme 1946–92*, Berlin: Jovis Verlag, 1996.

Kersten, Heinz, *Das Filmwesen in der Sowjetischen Besatzungszone Deutschlands*, Bonn/Berlin: Bundesministerium für Gesamtdeutsche Fragen, 1963.

Liebmann, Rolf, Matschke, Evelyn and Salow, Friedrich (eds), *Filmdokumentaristen der DDR*, Berlin (DDR): Henschelverlag, 1969.

Moldenhauer, Gebhard and Steinkopff, Volker (eds), *Einblicke in die Lebenswirklichkeit der DDR durch dokumentare Filme der DEFA*, Oldenburg: Bibliotheks-und Informationssystem der Universität Oldenburg, 2001.

Mückenberger, Christiane and Jordan, Günter, *'Sie sehen selbst, Sie hören selbst … ', Die DEFA von ihren Anfängen bis 1949*, Marburg: Hitzeroth, 1994.

Opgenoorth, Ernst, *Volksdemokratie im Kino. Propagandistische Selbstdarstellung der SED im DEFA-Dokumentarfilm 1946–57*, Köln: Verlag Wissenschaft und Politik, 1984.

Pflaum, Hans Günther and Prinzler, Hans Helmut, *Film in der Bundesrepublik Deutschland*, second edn, München/Wien: Carl Hanser Verlag, 1992.

Pusch, Steffi, *Exemplarisch DDR-Geschichte leben. Ostberliner Dokumentarfilme 1989/90*, Frankfurt/Main: Peter Lang Europäischer Verlag der Wissenschaften, 2000.

Roth, Wilhelm, *Der Dokumentarfilm seit 1960*, München/Luzern: Verlag C.J. Bucher, 1982.

Zimmermann, Peter (ed.), *Deutschlandbilder Ost. Dokumentarfilme der DEFA von der Nachkriegszeit bis zur Wiedervereinigung*, Konstanz: UVK-Medien/Verlag Olschläger, 1995.

Zimmermann, Peter and Moldenhauer, Gebhard (eds), *Der geteilte Himmel: Arbeit, Alltag und Geschichte im ost- und westdeutschen Film*, Konstanz: UVK-Medien, 2000.

Germany

The production of nonfiction films in Germany is comparable to other European or North American countries. From 1895 on, short local views of cities and small towns were often shot by foreign film companies, such as Lumière, Pathé, Gaumont, and Raleigh & Robert, which worked on an international level. The content of the images is quite universal in this early period and follows a similar aesthetic direction. Besides views of marketplaces, streets, and important buildings in a particular city, the official visits of emperors, kings, dukes, and tzars became regular subjects for films, as did military parades and festive processions. The German emperor, Wilhelm II, was open to the new medium and thus became one of the early movie stars. Natural disasters and sports were attractive subjects, along with exotic places and folkloristic traditions.

In November 1911, the first German newsreel, Der Tag im Film, was produced by Express Films in Freiburg. Oskar Messter, one of the most important German pioneers of film technology, had shot nonfiction films since 1897. He founded his Messter-Woche newsreel in October 1914, shortly after the beginning of World War I. With the Eiko-Woche it became the most important newsreel during the war. During World War I the important role of film for propaganda became clear, so around 1916 the state, the military, and heavy industry became interested in bringing film production companies under their control. On December 18, 1917, the Universumfilm Aktiengesellschaft (UFA) was founded by the merger of the three most successful film production companies (Nordisk, Messter, and PAGU) and with the German state as the most influential shareholder.

In June 1918 the UFA also opened a cultural department, which first produced educational films and *Kulturfilme*, the German term for documentaries in that period. This department was intended to produce and distribute scientific, educational, and entertaining films that which would be edifying and serve the educational system. One main activity was to produce medical training films and in the first five years, approximately one hundred and thirty-five of these films were produced for a medical film archive. In 1920 the department visited universities to promote the concept of using film for educational purposes and to get suggestions for new topics. The idea was to produce films for the huge market of universities and especially the sixty thousand schools. Some cities started or supported noncommercial film activities to create an alternative to the commercial, sensational fiction film.

However, the UFA discovered that there was no market in the educational field, because universities and schools had no budgets for film, and the costs for projectors and film rentals were quite high. The UFA changed its strategy and started to produce ten- to twenty-minute cultural films that were screened with the newsreels before the feature film. Most of these films were given good ratings for their high quality, and created a tax reduction for the whole screening. Every year, a few long nonfiction films were also produced. Examples are Arnold Fanck's Das Wunder des Schneeschuhs/The Wonder of the Snowshoe (1920–2) on skiing, Der Rhein in Vergangenheit und Gegenwart/The Rhine River in Past and Present (1922), and Wilhelm Prager's Wege zu Kraft und Schönheit/Ways to Strength and Beauty (1925) on modern body culture and sports. The *Kulturfilmbuch* (book on cultural film), published by Edgar Beyfuss und Alexander Kossowsky in 1924, helped to make the public aware of the broad spectrum of film production. It is a comprehensive study on the practical and theoretical state-of-the-art of nonfiction film in Germany and the subgenres that had already been developed (e.g. films on art, cities, biology, animals, geography, medicine, industry, promotion, animation, sports). The German *Kulturfilm* used and tested new technologies such as cameras, lenses, and film emulsions and experimented with new effects, such as slow motion, stop motion, fast motion, and dissolves. It gained an international reputation and the films were exported to various countries. In Russia the term *Kulturfilm* was even taken up. Besides the UFA, there were many other production companies such as Deulig, Nationalfilm, Emelka, and Dafu that concentrated on nonfiction films. Some directors also founded their own production companies. Hans Cürlis and his Kulturinstitut produced portraits of artists from the 1920s to the 1960s; such continuity despite all the political changes is more typical than the exception.

In the second half of the 1920s avant-garde directors such as Walter Ruttmann, Wilfried Basse, and Hans Richter produced the first so-called documentaries including Berlin: Die Sinfonie der Großtadt/Berlin: The Symphony of a Great City (1927), Markt in Berlin/Street Markets in Berlin (1929), and Deutschland—zwischen gestern und heute/Germany Yesterday and Today (1933). They were cross-section or montage films, which were influenced by the international avant-garde movement, especially French films and the Russian montage of Vertov and Eisenstein. In the second half of the 1920s the filmmakers knew each other and exchanged and discussed their films. Associations were founded to present new styles and modern films in the United Kingdom, the Netherlands, France, the United States, and other countries. There was an active international exchange and it is hard to discuss these films as specifically national cinematography. In 1929 there was a meeting of the film avant-gardists at La Sarraz Castle in Switzerland. Now the rhythm of the montage, the modern aesthetic of extreme camera positions and unconventional use of sound and music developed a new style, which became very influential.

In 1933 the National Socialists came to power and started to control film production through the Ministry of Enlightenment and Propaganda of Joseph Goebbels. The films of Leni Riefenstahl are the best known internationally, although she directed only seven films, as well as some propaganda films from that period. Between 1933 and 1945 approximately twelve thousand nonfiction films, mainly industrial films and commercials, approximately one thousand educational films, a few thousand cultural films, and eight hundred and fifty longer films of more than one thousand meters long (thirty-six minutes). There is a strong continuity in the style of nonfiction films and the people involved in making them, and few directors and producers were forbidden to work after 1933. Even former communist filmmakers, such as Carl Junghans, were able to make films such as Jugend der Welt/Youth of the World (1936) on the Winter Olympics in Garmisch-Partenkirchen. The visual style with the dominance of perfect images and modern montage was declared to be the new German camera style by official Nazi papers. The films of Leni Riefenstahl on the NSDAP party rallies in 1933 and 1934 and her two films on the Olympic Games were declared models for the new documentary. After 1945 the nonfiction production of the period was viewed as pure propaganda and nobody was interested in the films. Only recently have there been attempts to analyze these films again and to differentiate them more closely. Comparable to the fictional film production in Nazi Germany, where only approximately fifteen percent of the films were regarded as propagandistic, in the nonfiction production the majority cannot seriously be discussed as propaganda. Of course, the National Socialist propaganda films became famous and have been analyzed in detail. Central examples are Riefenstahl's Triumph des Willens/Triumph of the Will (1935), Fritz Hippler's Feldzug in Polen/Campaign in Poland (1940) or his demagogic Der ewige Jude/The Eternal Jew (1940), Hans Bertram's Feuertaufe/Baptism of Fire (1940), and Sieg im Westen/Victory in the West (1941) by Svend Noldan and Fritz Brunch.

However, these famous National Socialist propaganda films were not typical nonfiction productions. Of course, the state wanted to be presented in the best possible way, and in cultural films you will also find aesthetic styles very typical for the Nazi period; for example, the swastika flag is omnipresent. The flag, though, was also part of the German reality at that time and cannot be discussed only as a symptom of propagandistic purpose. The nonfiction production covers the same broad range of subgenres described for the Weimar Republic period and reflects a high technical standard. Often the films tested new possibilities of micro- and macrophotography and even X-ray films with sound were produced. Directors Walter Ruttmann, Martin Rikli, Ulrich K.T. Schulz, Svend Noldan, Willy Zielke, and others tried to break aesthetic limits and to push modern visual styles. Typical of this attempt is a mixture of real sequences, staged scenes, animation, effects and text, which now would be called hybrid forms. This form also has to do with the technical conditions. Generally the cameras were heavy and needed a tripod, and there were only a few minutes in the magazine. The speed of the film material was not very high, so it was only possible to shoot using the sun or with artificial light. Therefore, the shots had to be planned extremely carefully.

The four previously existing German sound newsreels (UFA, Deulig, Tobis, and Fox) were merged into Die Deutsche Wochenschau during World War II. Newsreel screenings were obligatory for all five thousand four hundred and ninety-two theaters in Germany from 1938 on. The number of prints was increased from about four hundred in 1939 to two thousand four hundred in 1943. So it was only during the war that newsreels were screened close to their production date, which was very professional. Special propaganda companies were formed, which were integrated in the military structure and which made it possible to shoot realistic images from the front lines. The silent shots were selected centrally in Berlin and combined with sound, an aggressive commentary, and a dynamic music score. 'Nazi newsreel music makes the motor nerves vibrate; it works directly upon the bodily feelings,' as Siegfried Kracauer analyzed as early as 1943. The Ministry of Propaganda viewed the newsreels as a perfect tool to influence the German public, but they worked well only in times of victory; from 1943 on they lost their credibility. Images from Nazi newsreels are regularly used in historical TV programs on the Third Reich; thus they still contribute to the image that we have of that time.

The years after 1945 are again characterized by continuity. Most of the people involved in the production of nonfiction film in the Third Reich were able to work again after the end of the war. Members of the propaganda companies became pioneers of German postwar television and of the various newsreels in East and West Germany. The film Michelangelo: Das Leben eines Titanen (1940) by Curt Oertel was reedited by Robert Flaherty for the American version as The Titan: The Story of Michelangelo (1950) and won an Academy Award for Best Feature Documentary in 1951. In East Germany the DEFA studio was founded in 1946 with a special documentary department. They developed their own style and regularly shot in

35mm black-and-white film. In West Germany, mostly small production companies continued to shoot the whole spectrum of nonfiction films.

Bernhard Grizmek was successful in the theaters with Kein Platz für wilde Tiere/No Place for Wild Animals (1956), on African wildlife, which also won a Golden Bear at the Berlin International Film Festival. Hans Domnick was also popular with Traumstraßen der Welt/ Dream Roads of the World (1958), depicting travel through North and South America from Alaska to Chile.

In the 1950s television was established in Germany, and it became the primary source for financing documentary films. Peter von Zahn established a more reportage-like style for the NWDR in Hamburg; in 1959 Klaus Wildenhahn started at the NDR and developed a special style of an observing camera, not disturbing reality too much. In the southwest the SDR founded a documentary department, which became known as the Stuttgart School. Its films were intended to be something different from the Nazi newsreels and the more pedagogic Kulturfilm tradition. They produced very critical and ironic commentaries on West German society, which were masterpieces of montage. In the 1960s directors such as Dieter Ertel, Wilhelm Bittdorf, and Roman Brodmann were highly influenced by the direct cinema movement. During the student protest movement political documentaries were shot at the film school in Berlin, which was founded in 1966, and at the film school in Ulm, which was headed by Alexander Kluge und Edgar Reitz, and at the new film school in Munich. Most of the young directors then developed an interest in daily life in Germany and wanted to shoot films on political issues such as ecology, the socially underprivileged, or minorities including handicapped people. The declared goal of the video movement, which was very active in the 1970s, was to give such groups a voice, as well as to change society with the help of documentaries. Political content became more important than aesthetic quality and the documentaries got the reputation of being boring. In 1980 the German Documentary Association (AG Dok) was created at the Duisburg Festival. With more than seven hundred members, it has now developed into the most important pressure group for documentary filmmakers.

The documentary changed fundamentally in the 1990s, experiencing a renaissance in theatrical release and on TV. From 1990 on, the documentary film in Germany developed a whole range of different styles and narrational forms and abandoned the notion that a documentary has to be educational and boring. Often the films present subjective positions or follow a more essayistic style. The multiplicity is of course only one reason for the attraction of the genre. Also important are technical developments such as digital DV and HD cameras or digital editing, as well as because the commercial TV market, which was not introduced in Germany until 1984, is pushing new popular formats like docusoap, docudrama, or even reality TV. To be successful, a director has to develop a personal style and has to decide what she or he is willing to deliver to which system. Electronic editing as well as computer graphics and animation have an aesthetic influence and the digitization of production and postproduction enables a director to get exactly the images he or she wants. Questions of narration and storytelling become more relevant for documentaries. Sometimes these changes raise ethical questions about how far a documentary filmmaker can and should go, but these discussions have made the documentary so vivid and extraordinarily interesting and have furthered its new popularity.

KAY HOFFMANN

See also: Basse, Wilfried; Ertel, Dieter; Fanck, Arnold; Junghans, Carl; Kluge, Alexander; Riefenstahl, Leni; Zielke, Willy

Further reading

Bartels, Ulrike, *Die Wochenschau im Dritten Reich*, Frankfurt: Peter Lang 2004.

Beyfuss, Edgar and Kossowsky, Alexander, *Das Kulturfilmbuch*, Berlin: Chryselius & Schulz 1924.

Bolesch, Cornelia (ed.), *Dokumentarisches Fernsehen: Ein Werkstattbericht in 48 Portraits*, Munich, Leipzig: List 1990

Drewniak, Boguslaw, *Der deutsche Film 1938–45*, Düsseldorf: Droste, 1987.

Hoffmann, Hilmar, *'Und die Fahne führt uns in die Ewigkeit'. Propaganda im NS-Film*, Frankfurt: Fischer, 1988.

Hoffmann, Kay, *Zeichen der Zeit: Zur Geschichte der 'Stuttgarter Schule'*, Munich: TR-Verlagsunion, 1996.

——'Propagandistic Problems of German Newsreels in World War II', *Historical Journal of Film, Radio and Television* 24, no. 1, 2004: 133–42.

Jacobs, Lewis, *The Documentary Tradition*, second edn, New York, London: Norton, 1979.
Jung, Uli and Loiperdinger, Martin (eds), *Geschichte des dokumentarischen Films in Deutschland. Band 1: Kaiserreich (1895–1918)*, Stuttgart: Reclam, 2005.
Kalbus, Oskar, *Pioniere des Kulturfilms*, Karlsruhe: Neue Verlags-Gesellschaft, 1956.
Keitz, Ursula von and Hoffmann, Kay (eds), *Die Einübung des dokumentarischen Blicks*, Marburg: Schüren, 2001.
Kessler, Frank, Lenk, Sabine and Loiperdinger, Martin (eds), *KINtop Band 1: Früher Film in Deutschland*, Frankfurt: Stroemfeld, 1992.
——(eds), *KINtop Band 4: Anfänge des dokumentarischen Films*, Frankfurt: Stroemfeld, 1995.
Kreimeier, Klaus, Ehmann, Antje and Goergen, Jeanpaul (eds), *Geschichte des dokumentarischen Films in Deutschland. Band 2: Weimarer Republik (1918–33)*, Stuttgart: Reclam, 2005.
Roth, Wilhelm, *Der Dokumentarfilm seit 1960*, Munich, Lucerne: Bucher, 1982.
Segeberg, Harro (ed.), *Mediale Mobildmachung I. Das Dritte Reich und der Film*, Munich: Wilhelm Fink, 2004.
Ziegler, Reiner, *Kunst und Architektur im Kulturfilm 1919–45*, Konstanz: UVK, 2003.
Zimmermann, Peter, 'Geschichte von Dokumentarfilm und Reportage von der Adenauer-Ära bis zur Gegenwart', in Peter Ludes, Heidemarie Schuhmacher and Peter Zimmermann (eds), *Geschichte des Fernsehens in der Bundesrepublik Deutschland Band 3: Informations-und Dokumentarsendungen*, Munich: Wilhelm Fink Verlag, 1994.
Zimmermann, Peter and Hoffmann, Kay (eds), *Triumph der Bilder. Kultur- und Dokumentarfilme vor 1945 im internationalen Vergleich*, Konstanz: UVK, 2003.
——(eds), *Geschichte des dokumentarischen Films in Deutschland. Band 3: 'Drittes Reich (1933–45)'*, Stuttgart: Reclam, 2005.

Gertrude Stein: When This You See, Remember Me

(US, Miller Adato, 1971)

Perry Miller Adato's Gertrude Stein: When This You See, Remember Me was initially conceived as a documentary about the Paris art scene of the 1920s and 1930s, the working title of which was Paris, the Luminous Years. When the concept was rejected by various networks as being too broad in scope, Miller Adato decided to focus on one person whose life, she believed, symbolised and encompassed the period, and to tell the story of the age through that person. True to Miller Adato's original idea, France, as it progresses from the early twentieth century through two world wars, is the film's leitmotif. One senses throughout Miller Adato's film the profound truth of Stein's observation that, 'It was not what France gave you, but what it did not take away that was important.'

There is much evidence of Miller Adato's original, broader focus in the finished film. The film includes numerous talking head-style interviews, with such notables as Virgil Thomson, Jaques Lipschitz, Sherwood Anderson, Janet Flanner, Daniel-Henri Kahnweiler, Pierre Balmain, and Bennett Cerf. Different people knew Stein at different times in her life: Kahnweiler knew both Stein and Picasso and touches on the early 1904 period; Janet Flanner knew her in the 1920s, and Virgil Thomson in the 1920s and 1930s. An interview with a Mrs Bradley, wife of Stein's literary agent and acquaintance of Hemingway and Alice B. Toklas, discusses the later years of Stein's time in Paris, and a Mrs Chapman, who brought Stein to America, covers the American period, along with Stein's publisher Bennett Cerf. In addition to these interviews are animation stills, film footage, segments of plays by Stein, and a great number of photographs and transparencies of paintings. Approximately one thousand photographs and seventy transparencies were reduced to four hundred, and fifty, respectively, for the final edit. The film is remarkably fast-paced for a documentary, incorporating a vast amount of material into ninety minutes, and features twice as many cuts as a standard Hollywood feature film.

In editing the phases of Stein's life, Alan Pesetsky does admirable work, for despite the diverse material on which Miller Adato draws, there is little sense of fragmentation. Miller Adato counterbalances her reconstruction of the times with a tight focus on Stein herself. It is as if we see the entire period through Stein's eyes. The director works in a style consistent with Gertrude Stein's own artistic perception: the rhythm of repetition and the equalizing of elements. Repetition is a particularly important quality to the film just as it was to Stein herself, as anyone familiar with her famous rose poem could confirm. One beautiful sequence takes a single, realistic image and gradually multiplies it. A prism lens was used to fragment, multiply, and distort the shapes of the photographed images to visualise the Cubist tendencies pioneered by Braque and Picasso and reflected in Gertrude's abstract writings. A Picasso drawing of Leo Stein is animated to show him walking rapidly first in one direction, then in the other, to portray the shifting paths of his involvement.

The camera also makes use of zooms, pans, and dissolves to keep the images constantly moving and to create dynamic visual equivalencies to the sensitive narration culled from the writings by or about Gertrude Stein. Visualising Stein's 'A Valentine to Sherwood Anderson', for example, the camera dissolves from an old-fashioned valentine, resplendent with hearts, angels, and flowers, to a picture of Anderson nestled in its centre. To bring to life the section of *The Autobiography of Alice B. Toklas*, which describes how Alice and Gertrude found the house they would live in, Miller Adato and her crew went to Bilignin and shot a twenty-nine-second zoom, beginning with a long shot and ending with a close-up of the house. The timing and positioning of this shot accurately recreates the description of the incident in the book.

Miller Adato not only reflects Stein's work through the form of her film, but also incorporates actual segments of Stein's various literary pieces into the film. These include a sequence from Al Carmine's musical In Circles, based on Stein's play of the same name, which serves as evidence that Stein could still inspire something as contemporary as Carmine's work, and excerpts from Four Saints in Three Acts, on which she and Virgil Thomson collaborated. There is no narration, per se, for the spoken text, outside of the interviews with her friends and colleagues and quotes from people who knew her well, is composed entirely of Stein's writings. *The Autobiography of Alice B. Toklas*, Stein's own biographical work, is the most heavily referenced work, but there are segments and quotations from *Tender Buttons*, *Lucy Church Amiably*, and *The Making of Americans* amongst other works.

The film presents us with an intimate portrait of Gertrude's day-to-day life and in particular her relationship with Alice B. Toklas. Some remember Alice's exquisitely tasty cakes; others recall that in their household Gertrude never bothered to do any chores, while Alice managed things deftly and smoothly. Gertrude, the woman, is contrasted with Stein, the writer, thinker, art collector, and genius, so as to bring a touch of humanity to what might otherwise be a documentary overwhelmingly populated with historical, literary, and artistic figures about whom so much is written and filmed that they cease to have any real meaning for us. Within Miller Adato's film Stein's life and career incorporates the story of Paris in the early twentieth century as the director intended, but Gertrude never ceases to be the focus of the film as both artist and as a person. As the director herself puts it, Gertrude Stein: When This You See, Remember Me is basically, 'the story of a woman and an artist who happened to live in the right place at the right time'.

Gertrude Stein: When This You See, Remember Me received two Emmy nominations. The film has been shown numerous times on American TV, and has become WNET's most widely shown film in 16mm distribution to museums, universities, libraries, adult groups, and for film festivals.

HELEN WHEATLEY

See also: Miller Adato, Perry

Selected films

Gertrude Stein: When This You See, Remember Me (US, WNET, 1971, 89 mins). Distributed by Contemporary/McGraw-Hill. Produced by Perry Miller Adato, Mariana Norris, and Alan Pesetsky. Directed by Perry Miller Adato. Shooting Script by Mariana Norris. Cinematography by Francis Lee. Additional cinematography by Bert Gerard. Edited by Alan Pesetsky and Aveva Slesin. Voice-over by Barbara Chason (Gertrude), Betty Henritze (Alice), and William Redfield (male voices).

1987 Waiting for the Moon: director, Jill Godmilov
2003 Hubby Wifey: director, Todd Hughes

Further reading

Gerard, Lillian, 'When This You See, Remember Me—Review', *Film Library Quarterly* 5, no. 1, 1971–72: 54–7.

Rogers, William Garland, *When This You See, Remember Me: Gertrude Stein in Person*, London: Greenwood Press, 1948.

Schutzer, Anne, 'Interview with Perry Miller Adato', *Filmmakers' Newsletter* 5, no. 5, 1972: 20–5.

Gimme Shelter

(US, Maysles, 1970)

Gimme Shelter depicts the intersection of 1960s rock music, the counterculture movement, and the cinéma vérité documentary. The film began as an agreement between the Rolling Stones and filmmakers Albert Maysles, David Maysles, and Charlotte Zwerin to document the band's 1969 Madison Square Garden concert in New York City. Following their instincts and using their own finances, the filmmakers traveled with the tour for about five days, and in the process they turned what began as a standard assignment into a landmark contribution to American documentary cinema.

In balancing the tensions between representing personality and representing social issues, Gimme Shelter functions structurally on two concurrent levels. On one level it features cinéma vérité concert film conventions: behind-the-scenes telephone calls and negotiations, press conferences, stage and equipment setup, the band's travel, and the fans' arrival. It also includes footage of the New York City performance and of the free concert at Altamont Speedway in California. In another technique, members of the Rolling Stones join the filmmakers in the editing room, reviewing footage and commenting on it.

This technique offers an additional form of commentary otherwise unavailable to the filmmakers, who practiced a purer variety of what Albert Maysles called 'direct cinema'. They eschewed both narration and formal interview segments; the press conference footage provides the closest substitute. By following both song performances and other instances with the bandmates' reactions, the film offers a more intimate form of insight. During 'Wild Horses', the camera cuts to band members' solemn faces. Charlie Watts, the drummer, looks directly into the camera that zooms in and frames him in close-up, breaking its fly-on-the-wall invisibility. He almost challenges the camera's presence before turning away and ignoring it.

The events at the Altamont Speedway provide the notoriety for which Gimme Shelter is well known. Approximately three hundred thousand fans attended the free concert, dubbed 'Woodstock West' in the spirit of the several peace-and-love rock festivals also held in 1969. Comparisons to Woodstock occurred, but peace was not the dominant atmosphere in the crowd that day. Instead, a certain restlessness prevailed, and performers such as The Flying Burrito Brothers and Jefferson Airplane dealt with fans rushing the stage, climbing scaffolding, and fighting among themselves. The Hell's Angels were hired to provide security and crowd control, but their sense of maintaining order involved fighting back, a tactic that at one point led to Jefferson Airplane singer Marty Balin being knocked unconscious when he attempted to intervene in a dispute. By the time the Rolling Stones took the stage behind an escort of Harley Davidson motorcycles parting the masses, tensions were running high and the crowd was agitated.

The film's structure and cinematography highlight just how deep those tensions ran and just how keenly the Angels' presence was felt. Concert footage from Madison Square Garden focuses primarily on Mick Jagger's stage presence. As he sings 'Jumpin' Jack Flash', 'Satisfaction', and other songs, Jagger prances and struts freely around the stage, and shots of the audience show adoring fans gazing back and mouthing the words along with him. At Altamont the tone changes completely. The band constantly stops its performance so that Jagger can issue pleas to the audience to settle down. The Hell's Angels dominate the scene. One shot frames Jagger singing on the left, while one Angel stares straight at the camera on the right. Another shot situates the scene from behind the band, with Jagger closest, a wall of Angels (and their logo jackets) between Jagger and the crowd, and then the obscured crowd behind them. The Angels also bodily remove anyone who sets foot on the stage.

A shot on the commotion in the crowd reveals another scuffle, and it shows a girl in a crocheted dress moving out of the way, a man in a green suit running past her, and a group of Angels crowding around someone. The distance and poor lighting make it difficult to discern what actually is happening. When Jagger in the studio asks, 'Can you roll back on that, David?', the scene cuts back to the editing room, and David Maysles rewinds the tape and plays it again in slow motion. A question about a gun is raised, and Maysles freezes the shot that shows a gun's outline against the girl's dress. At this point the events become clearer, but other than, 'It's so horrible', the film offers no commentary on them. Subsequent wrap-up scenes provide more explanation but little closure for the concert.

A bystander explains how he saw events, explaining that the Hell's Angels saw the gun, took it away from a man, and then began to beat and stab him. The man, eighteen-year-old Meredith Hunter, dies from his injuries, and the Stones are airlifted out of the fray. The Stones exit the studio, and the fans leave.

Many American cinéma vérité films use a crisis structure, wherein the crisis, or emotional high point, becomes the organizational system (see Mamber 1974). In Gimme Shelter the filmmakers document a potential moment with Hunter's murder, but they face a choice in focusing either on the crisis situation or on the personalities of the Rolling Stones. Earlier Maysles films such as Salesman (particularly in the case of Bible salesman Paul Brennan) center almost exclusively on character, and members of the Stones certainly offer much material with which to work. However, the murder brings to light the question of the filmmaker's social obligation in representing it. Gimme Shelter also raises the question of the murder's exploitation as a form of publicity for the Rolling Stones. The film did, after all, begin as a promotional film of a concert, but whether the band should be held responsible for the incidents that occurred is a debatable issue. In the end Maysles and Zwerin leave the issue open to interpretation.

In direct cinema tradition, they offer no excuses or conclusions.

HEATHER MCINTOSH

See also: Maysles, Albert; Salesman

Gimme Shelter (US, Maysles, 1970, 91 mins). Distributed by Twentieth Century Fox and the Criterion Collection. Directed by Albert Maysles, David Maysles, and Charlotte Zwerin. Produced by Richard Schneider. Cinematography by Ron Dorfman, George Lucas, Albert Maysles, and David Maysles. Edited by Joanna Burke, Ellen Giffard, and Kent McKinney. Sound by Walter Murch and Susumu Tokunow. Original music by Mick Jagger, Keith Richards, and the Rolling Stones.

Further reading

'The Criterion Collection: Gimme Shelter', www.criterionco.com/asp/release.asp?id=99

Maysles Films, Inc., www.mayslesfilms.com

Kael, Pauline, 'Gimme Shelter', in Kevin Macdonald and Mark Cousins (eds), *Imagining Reality: The Faber Book of Documentary*, London: Faber & Faber, 1996.

Mamber, Stephen, 'Cinema Verite and Social Concerns', *Film Comment* 9, 1973: 8–15.

——*Cinema Verite in America: Studies in Uncontrolled Documentary*, Cambridge, MA: MIT Press, 1974.

Maysles, Albert, Maysles, David and Zwerin, Charlotte, 'A Response to Pauline Kael', in Kevin Macdonald and Mark Cousins (eds), *Imagining Reality: The Faber Book of Documentary*, London: Faber & Faber, 1996.

Glass

(Holland, Haanstra, 1958)

Dutch film director Bert Haanstra was born May 31, 1916 in Holten, Overijssel, Netherlands, and died October 23, 1997 in Hilversum, Noord-Holland, Netherlands. He started his career in painting and photography, and eventually moved into documentary film directing in 1949.

Glass/Glas, produced in 1958, is one of the best-known films from Bern Haanstra's body of work, which includes forty-one documentary and fiction films produced between 1948 and 1988. Haanstra is considered one of the most original documentary film directors from Holland and won dozens of international awards for his films, including the Grand Prix at the Cannes Film Festival for Mirror of Holland, and the 1959 Academy Award and approximately twenty other awards for Glass.

Glass is a lyrical process documentary that examines the simple act of manufacturing glass bottles and the people who craft them. Taking place entirely in a glassmaking plant in the Netherlands, the camera observes the equipment and raw materials coming together. The film weaves a story of machine-made glass versus handmade glass and makes superb use of various filmic elements, including color, sound, camera and subject movement, musical score, and editing.

Glass is often shown in filmmaking/cinematography classes as a classic example of proper exposure and color representation, complex shooting in terms of location lighting sources, and wide variety of camera angles and distances. The editing is poetic and finely paced, with wide shots, close-ups and extreme close-up shots weaving seamlessly together in a vivid representation of human beings, machine, and raw material. Although this topic may seem somewhat pedestrian, it is the lack of guiding voice-over narration that thrusts this film out of the realm of simple 'how to' or 'educational' documentary into the domain of a truly artistic visual essay that is part film ethnography and part nostalgic, sensitive vision of a dying artform.

C. MELINDA LEVIN

Glass/Glas (Holland, 1958, 11 mins). Directed by Bert Haanstra.

Godard, Jean-Luc

Operation Béton/Operation Concrete (1954) is Godard's first film and his only documentary proper in his fifty-year career. The construction of the Grande Dixence dam, shot ambitiously in 35mm, is in fact his only conventional film, with only the odd nod to Russian cinema and a seeming fascination with machinery and structure testifying to his future preoccupations as a filmmaker. Although his most famous feature films, made in the early to mid-1960s, are works of fiction, all featured documentary elements (A bout de souffle/Breathless, 1960, famously filmed its actors on the streets of Paris during Eisenhower's visit), and Godard always maintained that they were never fictional works in the standard sense: 'reportage is interesting only when placed in a fictional context, but fiction is interesting only if it is validated by a documentary context'. From the outset Godard considered himself as a creator of film essays, finding audiovisual means (with particular attention given to montage) to extend his work as a *Cahiers du Cinéma* critic.

As the dozen or so features he made between A bout de souffle and Deux ou trois choses que je sais d'elle/Two or Three Things I Know About Her (1966) became progressively more political in terms of content, Godard began to seek new formal means to film his essays politically. Caméra-oeil/Camera Eye (1967), his contribution to the collective film Loin du Vietnam/Far from Vietnam (1967) proved a major step towards the unmistakable shape his essays would later take and provided the experimental groundwork he would continue to build on right up to the great masterpieces of the 1980s and 1990s. Caméra-oeil, a film about filming Vietnam far from the war, features Godard himself with his camera (the first of his films in which authorial intervention becomes a structuring element), the machinic nature of the camera pegged to images of the war machine. The fifteen-minute essay contains archive footage, shots from the films of other filmmakers as well as from his own work, and material specially shot for the film, thereby proving a trial run for most of the elements by which his later essays will come to be defined.

Godard's finest commentator, Alain Bergala, points out how Fernand Braudel's distinction between histoire événementielle, the chronicling of events as they happen, and attention to the slower development of events over time (la longue durée) can be profitably applied to the changes Godard's essay film has undergone in the last thirty-five years.

The political films that Godard made in the decade after Caméra-oeil, either alone, as part of the Dziga Vertov Group, or with Anne-Marie Mieville, are concerned with the short term and with topical events, and are addressed to the present and to an audience of the already or soon-to-be converted. These works, which have acquired a reputation for tediousness in the extreme, are not simply Maoist tracts but explorations of the medium as alternately oppressive and liberating, of desire and the gaze, of workers' and women's exploitation and of the (im)possibility of any form of representation or semiotic activity ever communicating with the 'real', in short products of the post-1968 climate of disappointment and a generalized phobia of all forms of power. However, Godard's return to fiction in the 1980s (with Sauve qui peut (La Vie)/Slow Motion in 1979) is accompanied by a major shift in the preoccupations of his essay work. Politics (in the sense of active militancy) is superseded by history as the focus moves to la longue durée as the devastating history of the twentieth century is tied to Godard's personal take on the death of cinema, not to mention his middle-aged preoccupation with the landscape of his childhood around Lac Léman. At this point it is the dead who become the primary addressees of this cinema of anamnesis seeking 'to defend the dead against the living'. The title of the Amnesty International film to which Godard contributed, Contre l'oubli/Against Forgetting (1991), could be said to exemplify this turn in Godard's work.

Godard had begun to experiment with video during his militant period but quickly discovered the aesthetic possibilities of the new medium. Beginning with France/Tour/Détour/Deux/Enfants/France/Tour/Detour/Two/Children (1978), the essays begin to display a range of techniques such as superimposition, rapid flashing, staccato slow motion, images that seem to be born from other images, and the electronic and computerized treatment of colour—in short, those formal features that have become a trademark of Godard's video works, elements retained from his militant experiments and often also incorporated into the feature films he continues to make.

However, it is with his true masterwork Histoire(s) du cinéma/History/ies of Cinema (1988–98) that his mastery of video technologies is stretched to breaking point by the vast subject-matter: no less than the history of the twentieth century conceived as a series of parallel histories: of war and the concentration camps, of cinema, of literature, philosophy, and music. In eight episodes varying in length from twenty-six to fifty-one minutes, Histoire(s) du cinéma offers an extended montage of images and sounds full of startling and often very moving juxtapositions guided by the idea borrowed from Pierre Reverdy: 'The image is a pure creation of the mind, it cannot be born from a comparison, but comes from the bringing together of two distant realities [...] An image is not powerful because it is brutal and fantastic, but because the association of ideas is distant and true.' This might appear to give Godard carte blanche to bring together arbitrarily any images he pleases, but what is incredible in Histoire(s) is that the effect of Godard's image/sound clusters need bear no obvious relation to his conscious intentions, and therefore accusations of hermeticism or solipsism completely miss the mark. For example (and I choose one that has deliberately courted controversy), an image of Elizabeth Taylor cradling Montgomery Clift in her arms in George Stevens' A Place in the Sun (1951) finds an overwhelming poignancy (one completely independent of the individual images themselves) when superimposed on images of a pile of concentration camp corpses, as well as being autonomous of Godard's explanation. It refers to the fact that George Stevens had previously filmed the camps, and this is precisely why his close-up of Taylor could 'radiate a kind of shadowed happiness'. The effect is not one of tragedy plus sentiment (since the camp images of necessity need no embellishment in order to devastate us) but a new type of hybrid affect, of emotion plus thought, and patently a result of the very incongruity of these 'distant realities'. We can see that in fact the juxtaposition of images here (as so often in Histoires) involves the images in a process of mutual interpretation, but, in this case, the viewer need not know about Stevens's experience at the camps to feel the multilayered mystery of their coexistence.

The extraordinary novelty of Godard's essay films has yet to be widely appreciated, especially in the English-speaking world. His most recent features, Eloge de l'amour/In Praise of Love (2001) and Notre musique/Our Music (2004) have continued to develop further those formal elements discovered by him in the essays, for example the second part of the former film being shot on Digital Video and its colour treated to resemble Fauvist painting. Fictional essays or documentary fictions? As Godard said on the release of Eloge de l'amour: 'They say my film is a documentary but I don't even know the meaning of the word documentary.'

FERGUS DALY

Biography

Born in Paris, December 3, 1930, to Protestant parents, his father was a doctor, his mother from a wealthy banking family. Studied anthropology briefly before devoting himself first to film criticism and from 1954 to filmmaking. Contributed to *Cahiers du Cinéma* on and off for many years before and during the development of his filmmaking career from the first shorts (beginning with Operation béton/Operation Concrete in 1954) to the success of his first feature A bout de souffle/Breathless (1960). Twenty-odd features and shorts later Godard turned his back on auteurist filmmaking and dissolved his identity in the work of the Dziga Vertov Group, which produced a series of politically militant films between 1969 and 1972. Following a serious motorcycle accident in 1972, Godard moved to Grenoble with Anne-Marie Mieville where they set up a small independent studio experiment with film/video relations before leaving France altogether in 1976 to settle in Switzerland. Godard returned to the commercial cinema in 1979 with Sauve qui peut (la vie)/Slow Motion. In 1988 he undertook a major video project

Histoire(s) du cinéma/History/ies of Cinema, completed in 1998. Continues to alternate between feature films and essay films largely shot on video.

Selected films

1954	Operation béton
1966	Deux ou trois choses que je sais d'elle
1967	Caméra-oeil
1972	Letter to Jane (as part of Dziga Vertov collective)
1975	Numéro deux (with A.-M. Mieville)
1978	France/Tour/Détour/Deux/Enfants (with Mieville)
1982	Scénario du Film Passion
1988–98	Histoire(s) du cinéma
1991	Contre l'oubli (with Mieville)
1994	JLG/JLG: Autoportrait de Décembre

Further reading

Bergala, Alain (ed.), *Jean-Luc Godard par Jean-Luc Godard*, two vols, Paris: Cahiers du Cinéma, 1998.

——*Nul Mieux que Godard*, Paris: Cahiers du Cinéma, 1999.

Godard, Jean-Luc, *Histoire(s) du Cinéma*, four vols, Paris: Gallimard-Gaumont, 1998.

n.a., 'Le Siecle de Jean-Luc Godard', *Art Press* (Special Journal Issue), November 1998.

Temple, Michael and Williams, James S., *The Cinema Alone: Essays on the Work of Jean-Luc Godard 1985–2000*, Amsterdam: U.P., 2000.

Godmilow, Jill

Jill Godmilow's films straddle the boundaries between narrative and documentary, often deploying reenactment and thematizing performance. They are at once theoretically informed and visually engrossing. Beginning in 1973, her collaboration with Judy Collins on Antonia: A Portrait of the Woman brought to light the life story of an amazing, but relatively unknown, creative woman; the tale told a typical story of a lone woman struggling to make it in a sexist profession. What distinguished Antonia from many feminist films of the era was the emphasis on performance as a visual metaphor for lived experience, a theme continued in her film Nevelson in Process.

It was Far from Poland (1984) that cemented her reputation as a theoretical practitioner of documentary. Invoking virtually all the postmodern debates about realism and the reality effect, about gender and romance, about ideology and truth, about politics and representation, about socialism and democracy circulating within the cultural left during the mid-1980s, it calls attention to theoretical developments in film studies' deconstructive concerns with the apparatus, narrative, and image by foregrounding the constructedness of (among other things) 'location' shooting. 'On location' has always signified access to the real, to the true scene, against the stagy atmosphere of the studio; yet locations themselves are carefully chosen to stage meanings. When Poland became unavailable to Godmilow, location's essentialist truth was called into question, as were virtually all the shibboleths of 1960s New Left politics under Ronald Reagan's regime. The film is a stunning achievement: at once offering detailed information on the Gdansk Strike and Solidarity, as well as undercutting its form of transmission—documentary—and all done with a wry, disarming sense of humor.

Working with reenacted texts performed by actors such as Ruth Maleczech, Godmilow evolved a form of feminist 'speculative fiction' to tell the story of Gertrude Stein and Alice B. Toklas in the feature-length 1987 bioflick Waiting for the Moon, produced for PBS's 'American Playhouse', which won First Prize at the Sundance Film Festival. A crucial element of Far from Poland was the staged interviews of the striking crane operator Anna Walentynowicz and government censor K62. During these long segments, the camera reveals an intense identification between actors and their roles to the point of noting that Maleczech, who plays Anna, is crying when she concludes her life story. The concentration on performing extends as well to the interludes between Jill and Mark, directed by Maleczech as mini-soap operas. In Waiting for the Moon, the camera lingers over the faces and gestures of Linda Bassett (as Stein) and Linda Hunt (as Alice) in a series of brief sequences staged to foreground the verbal exchanges between these two difficult women. The repartee and the sets where they occur—a room, a car, a garden, a hillside—are designed to mimic Steinian poetics as they repeat with a difference the same scene visually and linguistically. These awkward moments highlight the subtleties of performing for the camera, as the tiniest facial tic magnifies mood and emotion.

Roy Cohn/Jack Smith (1994), the film interpretation of Ron Vawter's theater performance, displays another aspect of her deconstructive documentary technique. The sheer tour-de-force performance by Vawter is matched by the uncanny way in which Godmilow reassembles a piece of theater into a film. Translating stage to celluloid, Godmilow queers the record by daringly cutting up the two performance pieces about two notorious gay men, one very out, the other very closeted, who both died of AIDS in 1989. This montage is then intercut with video footage from rehearsals and of Vawter, himself HIV positive, his body covered with lesions, making up in the dressing room. In challenging the sacred unity of the performance, she also mixes media, emphasizing the differences between film and video. The film dwells on the careful collaboration between Godmilow and Vawter—the way Godmilow's editing adds a third term, Vawter himself—to the dyad Roy/Jack to enrich our understanding of performance as a process of impersonation and identification even when the figure(s) are radically other than the self.

This theoretical interest in the place of the body and identity—gendered, sexual, ethnic, and political—in performance and of the tense relationship between filmic and theatrical performing animates the project Godmilow developed in collaboration with Mabou Mines' Lear '87 Archive (2001). Working again with Vawter and Maleczech, the six-hour DVD condensed archive of workshops to develop a fully gender-reversed production of Shakespeare's King Lear celebrates the labor of the actor and of the theater company. Recording the workshop process of the experimental and radical group through close, sometimes repetitive, dissections of how movements, intonations, and gestures are calculated to evoke emotions and thus create meanings for the viewer, the two (sometimes three) different video cameras also stress the differential meanings incurred through camera position, lighting, and format. Her continuing interest in the process of reenactment led to her 1998 remake of Harun Farocki's 1969 Inextinguishable Fire. What Farocki Taught contains a perfect replica of his black-and-white German documentary, itself made with actors reconstructing documents from Dow Chemical Company, as well as Farocki's self-inflicted cigarette burn demonstrating how Dow researched and tested Napalm B for use in Vietnam, in color and in English. This deconstructive work explores documentary technologies to represent history as/through representation. In restaging the already staged piece of documentary history that has never been shown in the United States, Godmilow engages debates about film preservation, cultural memory, and the historical archive. Once again, her political engagement with the form demands that she both trumpet anti-war sentiments and analyze how war itself is synonymous with the fabric of American life, including life as an oppositional filmmaker or her audience.

Nothing simply happens in Godmilow's work; just as history becomes a staged event and actors perform other lives with their bodies, viewers are required to produce meaning through the holes left by the filmmaker. This collaboration demonstrates an extraordinary commitment to furthering awareness of our culture's investments in the visual regime. Her films ask about the conditions of their own possibility. Documentary filmmakers may seek to change the world, but their efforts are premised on technologies and desires—machinery and voyeurism—that perpetuate it. Insisting that theatricality and presence are central to the documentary project, Godmilow traverses borders between liveness and projection, truth and memory; she claims responsibility.

PAULA RABINOWITZ

Biography

Born in Philadelphia in 1943 to a Jewish dentist and a Jewish truant officer. Studied Russian literature at the University of Wisconsin, Madison; never took a film course because there weren't any back then. Made her first film, La Nueva Vida, a feature-length romp in Spanish, with her Puerto Rican boyfriend in 1968, and then her first documentary, Tales, in 1971 with an all-women crew in New York City. Recipient of two Rockefeller Fellowships and a Guggenheim Fellowship, as well as grants from the National Endowment for the Arts. Work has been featured at numerous film festivals and museums around the world, including the 2000 Whitney Museum of American Art Biennial Exhibition. Film Antonia was nominated for an Academy Award and received the Independent New York

Film Critics Award for Best Documentary. Professor of Film, Theater and Television at Notre Dame University. Lives in New York.

Selected films

1971 Tales
1973 Antonia: A Portrait of the Woman: director
Nevelson in Process
1977 The Popovich Brothers of South Chicago: director
1984 Far from Poland: director
1987 Waiting for the Moon: director
1988 The Odyssey Tapes: director, producer
1994 Roy Cohn/Jack Smith: director
1998 What Farocki Taught: director, producer
1999 The Loft Tapes: producer

Further reading

Godmilow, Jill, in conversation with Ann-Louise Shapiro 'How Real is the Reality in Documentary Films?' *History and Theory* 36, no. 4, 1997.

——'What's Wrong with the Liberal Documentary?' *Peace Review*, March, 1999.

Miller, Lynn C., '(Un)documenting History: An Interview with Filmmaker Jill Godmilow', *Text Performance Quarterly* 7, no. 3, 1997.

Rabinowitz, Paula, *They Must Be Represented: The Politics of Documentary*, London: Verso, 1994.

Gold, Jack

Jack Gold was a director of both screen and stage works, having made twelve feature films, more than forty films for television, and hundreds of short films for television. He worked in radio as a trainee studio manager, moving to television in 1955 as a trainee assistant film editor for the BBC. He eventually became the film editor on school programmes and topical interview-based investigative documentaries and news reports such as Tonight. He found directing work on the latter, producing from three to five short items a week working mainly with reporters. He left the BBC in 1964 and became a freelance documentary filmmaker, directing television dramas such as The Lump (1967), a Tony Garnett production, and his first fiction film, The Bofors Gun (1968).

Gold had a notable ability to construct a story with a filmic approach, exploiting and showing locations, and interweaving pertinent commentary and music to create film stories, while exploiting the major technological revolution that transformed the documentary—the development of the 16mm camera and the transistorised sound recorder. This made him very much part of the British Realist Tradition that followed Free Cinema.

Journalistic techniques developed during his directing of reportage programmes and documentary essays between 1960 and 1964 for Tonight permeated into the documentaries he made, enabling him to analyse and comment on subjects in observational documentary, while using different forms of counterpoint to enforce his point of view.

His documentaries found another layer of illumination and revelation beyond observation, merging varied aspects to present another synthesis.

Gold explored different documentary techniques including reportage, impressionistic tendencies, analytical vérité and docudrama. Feeling that he was in the hands of his subjects and wanting to have more control in filmmaking, he moved into drama, having already had some experience with the style with The Visit (1959). In recreating real situations in drama, Gold used his experiences from documentary filmmaking regarding technology, location, and subject behaviour. He had experience of reconstruction with docudramas such as Ninety Days (1966) a reconstruction using the protagonist as subject. Before that experience, he had used actors in other reconstructions.

His documentary films were often impressionistic, for example, Wall Street (1966), Famine (1967), and The Schlemiel, the Schlemozzel, and the Doppess (1990). They often had neither shape nor structure initially—that coming later in the cutting room—and the resulting film was always more than observational as Gold looked for ways to shape or comment on his subject using counterpoint, with a mix of different footage or between picture and sound.

In others, however, he organised and orchestrated his shoots to be shot in a way that meant he attained detailed coverage of a situation scripted and controlled rather than shaped in the cutting room. His move to the single drama resulted in features strong in character and storytelling with a naturalistic base.

ALISTAIR WARDILL

Biography

Born in London, June 28, 1930. Graduated from the University of North London (London Polytechnic), reading economics, in 1950, and University College London, reading law, in 1953, where he worked on amateur films for the College Film Society. In 1954 joined BBC Radio Department as trainee studio manager, where he worked on variety shows. Moved to British television in 1955, first editing then directing factual programmes including current affairs programme Tonight. Moved to feature filmmaking, forging a career that has spanned decades. Has taught at the London International Film School, the Royal College of Art, and the National Film and Television School. Affiliated with Screen South, and the Directors Guild, chairing the status committee. Alongside film-making Gold has directed stage plays including Council of Love (1972), The Devil's Disciple (1976), Tribute to Lili Lamont (1978), and Crossing Jerusalem (2003). Recipient of the following awards (selected): BAFTA: Best Documentary: Death in the Morning, 1964. Best Drama: Stocker's Copper, 1973. Lew Grade/ Radio Times award: Goodnight Mr Tom, 1998. Lew Grade/Radio Times award: The Remorseful Day, 1987. Evening News Best Film Award: Aces High, 1976. Evening News Best Comedy Award: The National Health, 1973. International: Emmy: The Naked Civil Servant, 1975. Prix Italia, Barcelona, Chicago, San Remo; The Naked Civil Servant, 1975. Peabody Award: Catholics, 1973. Christopher Award: Little Lord Fauntleroy, 1980. Christopher Award: She Stood Alone, 1991. Golden Globe: Escape from Sobibor, 1987. ACE Award: Murrow, 1986. ACE Award: Sakharov, 1984. Martin Luther King Award: The Sailor's Return, 1978.

Selected films

1959 Happy as Can Be (BBC): director
1959 The Visit (BFI): director
1960 Living Jazz (BFI): director
1963 The Model Millionairess (Tonight, BBC): director
1963 The Solitary Billionaire (BBC): director
1963 West Indians (BBC): director
1964 Death in the Morning (Tonight, BBC): director
1965 Ladies and Gentlemen It Is My Pleasure (BBC): director
1966 Ninety Days (BBC): director
1966 On Top of the World (BBC): director
1966 Wall Street (ATV): director
1967 Dispute (2X 60 Minutes, BBC): director
1967 Famine (Rediffusion): director
1967 The Lump (Wednesday Play, BBC): director
1967 World of Coppard (Omnibus, BBC): director
1968 Black Campus (BBC): director
1968 The Bofors Gun: director
1969 The Reckoning: director
1971 Dowager in Hot Pants (Thames): director
1972 Stockers Copper: director
1973 Arturo Ui: director
1973 Catholics: director
1973 The National Health (Columbia Pictures Corporation): director
1973 Who?: director
1975 Man Friday: director
1975 The Naked Civil Servant: director
1976 Aces High: director
1978 Thank You, Comrades (BBC): director
1978 The Medusa Touch: director
1978 The Sailor's Return: director
1980 Little Lord Fauntleroy: director
1983 Red Monarch: director
1984 Sakharov: director
1984 The Chain: director
1986 Murrow: director
1987 Escape from Sobibor: director
1988 Jack Gold on the Battle of Algiers: Movie Masterclass (Peter West, Third Eye Productions): writer
1990 The Schlemiel, the Schlemozzel, and the Doppess (Bookmark, BBC): director
1991 She Stood Alone: director
1998 Goodnight Mister Tom: director
2002 The John Thaw Story: director

Further reading

Falk, Quentin, 'All That Glisters is Jack, "National Health"', *CinemaTV Today* 10060, December 1, 1973: 10–11.

Gold, Jack and Brownlow, Kevin, 'The Pressures of Opportunity and Frustration', *Vision* 1 March 1976: 12–14.

Griffin, Sue, 'Horror's Tough Going for Gold', *Broadcast*, May 8, 1987: 21.
Harris, Ian, 'Names and Faces', *Listener* 106, 2726, September 10, 1981: 270.
Littlefield, Joan, '"Capture Reality, Not Create It", Says Jack Gold', *Film World* 5, no. 1, January/March 1969: 71–72.
McPherson, Don, '"Muffin" Gives Euston Films Another Big Boost', *Screen International* 197, July 7, 1979: 9.
Madden, Paul and Wilson, David, 'Getting in Close. An Interview with Jack Gold', *Sight and Sound* 43, no. 3, 1974: 134–7.
n.a., 'The Difference between TV and Film is That in TV You've Got to Compromise', *Television Today*, April 1979: 17–19.
n.a., 'A Director Without a Script is Most Limited of All Vision', *Television Today* December 31, 1975: 10, 4, 1.
n.a., 'Jack Gold: An Interview', *Framework* 9, Winter, 1978–9: 38–42.
Pascal, Julia, 'Dying to Strauss', *City Limits* 292, May 7, 1987: 21.
Spiers, David, 'Interview with Jack Gold', *Screen* 10, nos. 4/5, July/October 1969: 115–28.
Summers, Sue, 'Jack Gold', *CinemaTV Today*, 10135, May 24, 1975: 18.
Sussex, Elizabeth, *The Rise and Fall of British Documentary*, Berkeley, CA: University of California Press, 1975.

Goldovskaya, Marina

Marina Goldovskaya, a prominent Russian documentary filmmaker, gained recognition in the 1970s, 1980s, and 1990s for a series of landmark works documenting Soviet life and history, the collapse of communism, and its turbulent aftermath. Her father, Yevsei Goldovsky, was a cofounder in 1924 of VGIK, the renowned Moscow Film Institute, and a leading Soviet expert in film technology. Goldovskaya graduated from VGIK in 1964 with a degree in cinematography and directing. She spent the first twenty years of her professional life as a newsreel camerawoman and filmmaker for Gosteleradio, the USSR Central Television agency.

Having found a niche in news documentaries and directed more than twenty-five films, besides working on countless others, Goldovskaya developed a style of documentary portrait using techniques similar to those favored by cinéma vérité and direct cinema in the 1960s: 16mm handheld camera, synch sound, and fly-on-the-wall approach to the material. At this time she had written accounts only of Western documentary pioneers D.A. Pennebaker, Richard Leacock, and Robert Drew.

In her 1981 book, *Chelovek krupnim planom/* Close-up, Goldovskaya described her method of observation, noting her preference for people obsessed with their professions. She tried this method first in 1968, as a cinematographer in Tkachihi/Weavers, a television documentary about seven alienated female textile workers. The hopelessness of their lives was made visible by this method of filming, which avoided narration or any authorial intervention. The film ran afoul of the censors and was banned. In her directorial debut, Raisa Nemchinskaya, artistka zirka/Raisa Nemchinskaya, Artist of the Circus (1970), about an old acrobat who does not want to give up the circus, Goldovskaya had the essentials of her method in place. 'My films used to be mostly portraits; I was interested in how to grasp a character, how to reveal it, how to uncover an individual's obsessions, motives and moral principles', she wrote in a 1991 article for *Iskusstvo Kino*.

This strategy allowed the filmmaker to find drama outside of politics, thus minimizing clashes with the censors. Her first documentary with a clear political subject was Vosmoj Director/Eighth Director (1981), the profile of a factory manager who fights the system. It was shown on prime-time television, and caused a storm in the press.

The filmmaker's reputation as the leading documentarian of Soviet Russia was secured during perestroika. She took up Premier Mikhail Gorbachev's call for reform and transparency in two polemic works: Archangelsky Mujik/The Peasant from Archangelsk (1986) and Vlast' Solovetskaya/Solovki Power (1988). Both documentaries tackled with honesty and candor—and at the time, considerable personal risk—the failure of Soviet economic methods and the Leninist origins of the Gulag concentration camp system.

Archangelsky Mujik profiled a farmer, Nikolai Sivkov, who fights to take charge of sixty cows on his own farm. He speaks to the camera, extolling the virtues of private property and deploring the inefficiency of the collective farming system. 'In "the land where socialism has triumphed" it was a truly heroic deed,' Goldovskaya wrote in the *Iskusstvo Kino* article. Banned after its first broadcast, the documentary was later reaired under the policy of glasnost.

In 1988 it won the top national prize for best documentary.

The film was a turning point in the filmmaker's career because it showed her ability to turn a simple character into a political metaphor about larger issues. This interweaving of the personal with the political, and the historical, a trademark of the director's work since the 1980s, would reach a higher degree of artistry and complexity in Solovki Power.

A 35mm feature-length documentary produced by Mosfilm, the Moscow State studio, Solovki Power turns the double meaning of its title, Solovki as Soviet might, into a political metaphor: this medieval monastery on a remote island in the White Sea, operating as a concentration camp between 1923 and 1939, becomes a symbol of the regime's destruction of dissidence. The film skillfully combines the testimonies of survivors and prison guards, with present-day color footage of the location, and a 1927 government propaganda short about the 'reeducation' of Soviet citizens in this 'model' camp. The soundtrack counterpoints the sober voice of a narrator with heartbreaking readings from letters found in the camp and the haunting recollections of former prisoners.

Solovki Power became one of the filmic landmark events of glasnost. Initially banned, it was later released and won several top awards at the national and international film festivals. This success led to European and American funding of Goldovskaya's 1990s projects. Dom s rizariami/The House on Arbat Street (1993), for example, is another remarkable instance of her ability to capture Soviet history through individual stories. The documentary profiles the Filatov House, a luxurious apartment building of the Romanov era located in Moscow's central Arbat district. With imaginatively edited interviews, old photos, propaganda, and entertainment films, seventy years of the Soviet experiment in communism emerge. These intimate portraits, laced with vivid recollections, depict a human fresco marked by suffering and loss.

Compelled to record the seismic changes brought about by the breakup of the Soviet Union, Goldovskaya made a series of journals, in video and film, chronicling the first post-Soviet times as they affected herself, her friends in the intelligentsia, and ordinary Muscovites. The emphasis is not on the fall of the Soviet regime per se, but on the portrait of individuals caught in the collapse of the system. These video diaries marry the techniques of a vérité style with an openly subjective involvement in the subject: Goldovskaya and her ubiquitous camera become an integral part of the films. Vkus svobodi/A Taste of Freedom 1991, Oskolki zerkala/The Shattered Mirror—A Diary of a Time of Trouble (1992), Povezlo roditsia v Rossii/Lucky to be Born in Russia (1994), and The Prince is Back (1999) cover a decade from the perspective of a passionate observer, who is also a cautious optimist. A Taste of Freedom and The Prince is Back profile a television journalist and an engineer of aristocratic origins obsessed with achieving goals such as truth in the news and the restoration of an ancestral palace; these efforts become, once more, a rich metaphor of the times.

Naum Kleiman, director of the Film Museum in Moscow, remarked in 1998 that Goldovskaya's work 'presents small individual lives in the larger context of history. In our cinema, we traditionally showed the larger view, with a few figures inside. Her reverse angle is very important. It's as if she's painting a fresco; you can examine each figure by itself, but together they form a panorama of the entire country.'

Now living in the United States, Goldovskaya combines a teaching career at UCLA with work on two ambitious projects: an oral history of the documentary cinema and Russian Chronicles: Diary of Change, a portrait of her generation, for which she has amassed more than four hundred hours of footage.

The artistic and historical significance of Marina Goldovskaya's body of work makes it an indispensable document to examine the life and times of twentieth-century Russia.

MARÍA ELENA DE LAS CARRERAS-KUNTZ

See also: Russia/Soviet Union

Biography

Born in Moscow, Soviet Union, July 15, 1941. Graduated from State Moscow Film Institute (VGIK), with degrees in cinematography and direction in 1964, and a doctorate in Fine Arts in 1987. Worked for USSR Central Television (Gosteleradio), as director, scriptwriter, and cameramen in more than fifty films, 1964–88. Professor in the Department of TV Journalism, Moscow State University, 1968–95. Chief Executive, Department of Video Technology, in the Moscow Research Institute of Film Art, 1988–96. Since 1990, professor and lecturer of film in several European and American universities. Author of several books in Russian on the art and technique of documentary filmmaking. Her documentaries chronicling the demise of the Soviet system and its aftermath have been awarded many national and international prizes. Interviewed by Chris Marker about directors of the Soviet cinema in his television documentary Le Tombeau d'Alexandre/ The Last Bolshevik (1992). Head of the documentary program at the UCLA Department of Film and Television, where she created its Documentary Salon series and organizes workshops with documentary filmmakers. Board member of the International Documentary Association. Member of the Russian Academy of Television. Based in Los Angeles, California, Goldovskaya continues to make films about her native country and the art scene of the United States.

Selected films

1972 Valentina Tereshkova: director, writer, cinematographer
1973 Eto nasha professia/This is Our Profession: director, writer, cinematographer
1975 Arkadi Rajkin: director, writer, cinematographer
1978 Ispitanije/The Experiment: director, writer, cinematographer
1981 Posle zatvi/After the Harvest: director, writer, cinematographer
1985 Zdravstvujte, eto Bedulia govorit/Hello, It Is Beduliya Speaking: director, writer, cinematographer
1986 Archangelsky Mujik/The Peasant from Archangelsk: director, cinematographer
1987 Chtobi bil teatr/For the Theater to Be: director, writer, cinematographer
1988 Tumbalalaika v Amerike/Tumbalalaika in America: director, cinematographer
1988 Vlast' Solovetskaya/Solovki Power: director, writer, cinematographer
1989 Mne 90 let, esche legka pohodka/I Am 90. My Steps are Light: director, cowriter, cinematographer
1989 Vishe, chem Liubov/More Than Love: director, writer, cinematographer
1991 Iz Bezdni/Aus dem Abgrund/From the Abyss—Part 1: Liudi Blokadi/The Siege of Leningrad; Part 2: Liudi I vojna/ People and War: director, cowriter, cinematographer
1991 Vkus svobodi/A Taste of Freedom: director, cinematographer
1992 Oskolki zerkala/The Shattered Mirror—The Diary of a Time of Trouble: director, writer, editor, cinematographer
1992 Dom s rizariami/The House on Arbat Street: director, writer, editor, cinematographer
1994 Povezlo roditsia v Rossii/Lucky to be Born in Russia: director, writer, editor, cinematographer
1995 Etot sotriasajuschijsia mir/This Shaking World: director, editor, writer, cinematographer
1997 Deti Ivana Kuzmicha/L'Ecole pas comme les autres/The Children of Ivan Kuzmich: director, editor, writer, cinematographer
1997 A Poet on the Lower East Side: A Docu-Diary on Allen Ginsberg: cinematographer
1997 The Prince is Back: director, writer, editor, cinematographer
2002 Peter Sellars: Art as Moral Action (in progress): director, writer, editor, cinematographer

Further reading

Dyomin, Victor, 'Marina Goldovskaya: Close-Up', *Soviet Life*, May 1988: 5, 380.
Goldovskaya, Marina, *Chelovek krupnim planom* (Closeup), Moscow, 1981.
——*Tvorchestvoi technika* (Creativity and Technology), Moscow, 1986.
——'Zenshchina s kinoapparatom', *Iskusstvo Kino* 6, 1991.
Jennings, Peter and Brewster, Todd, *The Century*, New York: Doubleday, 1998: 506–7.
Menashe, Louis, 'Woman with the Movie Camera: The Films of Marina Goldovskaya', *Cineaste* xxiv, 2–3, 1999.
Ramsey, Nancy, 'A Filmmaker's Duty: To Document her Homeland', *The New York Times*, December 6, 1998.
Taubman, Jane, 'The Art of Marina Goldovskaia', *Slavic Review* 54, no. 4, 1995: 1010–15.

Goldson, Annie

Annie Goldson's career offers telling evidence of the predicament of the politically concerned documentary filmmaker in a millennial culture of globalisation, electronic media, and multinational capitalism. Her work mobilises the force of factual information, personal testimony, social commentary against the oppressive realities of social injustice, and human rights abuse. It often mounts a critique of the recording and reporting techniques of the media, thus revealing the ideological basis of their claim to objectivity and truth. From this perspective, documentary provides the means for promoting an awareness of the cultural politics of image production. It gives voice and visibility to the stories of those whose freedom of speech, political beliefs, or legal status is not recognised within the dominant system of representation.

Yet despite affirming the values of difference and self-determination, Goldson's dependence on a liberal-democratic understanding of documentary's function within the public sphere—as social and moral conscience, arbiter of justice, confessor, advocate, accuser—reinstalls the procedures of address and authority that guaranteed an earlier paternalistic and moderately progressive tradition of documentary filmmaking. Such a position fails to acknowledge the degree to which it participates in the maintenance and revision of those discursive and institutional structures that facilitate the circulation of power and knowledge in a globalised economy of information and media imagery. The inauguration of a postcolonial model of documentary practice, to which Annie Goldson's work contributes, must equally interrogate the vestiges of imperial and instrumental reason that govern its own method and message.

Goldson's development as a documentary filmmaker roughly coincides with New Zealand's steady integration and assumption of the values of a 'knowledge-based society'. Her films provide an interesting example of the role of documentary in negotiating the transition from ideological state apparatus to the conceptual hegemony of communication as a world system. They also reflect an unresolved conflict between a documentary practice that serves the interests of a local/national community and a global/multinational constituency. In Framing the Panthers (black and white, 1991), Counter-Terror: The North of Ireland (1990), and Punitive Damage (1999), Goldson takes an oppositional position against the processes of global imperialism and media (dis)information, whereas Wake (1994), Seeing Red (1995), and Georgie Girl (2001) establish a range of strategic alliances with the production of a national image and identity that is more in keeping with the restructuring of New Zealand society as a postmodern, postindustrial culture.

Between 1990 and 1993, Goldson produced and directed a number of videos that expose the practices of racism and colonialism in Puerto Rico, Northern Ireland, and the United States. These pieces possess a philosophy of social criticism, political education, and media activism. They provide an alternative source of information, interpretation, and expression for communities and causes that are ghettoised or suppressed, and supply the method and materials for a counteranalysis of historical events and current affairs. Goldson's political agenda also includes a reflexive critique of the media. To this end, she clearly shows how the act of representation is ideologically motivated. For instance, African American high school students admit their lack of knowledge about the Panthers in strictly staged interviews, the construction of news clips is analysed to reveal how the British authorities 'frame' the story of 'terrorist' incidents in Northern Ireland.

On returning to New Zealand, Goldson abandoned a direct activist stance. Rather, she assumes a critically reflexive attitude towards personal and public history. The emphasis shifts from issues to ideas, from content to concept. The language of film theory and cultural studies increasingly informs her films. Wake examines the conditions of visuality that permit a colonialist politics of looking and naming. The paintings of the early settlers and her father's home movies illustrate the immigrant's reinscription of landscape and community as markers of a displaced identity. Stylistically, the film foregrounds the codes of documentary representation with its use of narrative voice, fictional reconstruction, found footage from the family album, and popular film.

Goldson perfects these techniques of formal and theoretical reflection in Seeing Red, a film about the scandal that erupted in 1949 around Cecil Holmes, a young filmmaker with Communist sympathies. Subject matter and cinematic style thoroughly reinforce the critical project of reimagining the tradition of New Zealand documentary and redefining its place in the present. Goldson composes an historical narrative that locates her own work in a political and artistic context. The story of Cecil Holmes acts as a myth for the institution of a new chapter in the development of a national film culture. Seeing Red constitutes its subject as a means of authorising its own discourse. Its recuperation of a forgotten cinematic legend parallels the successful effort of the New Zealand Film Archive in recovering and restoring the nation's moving picture heritage. Goldson brilliantly uses archival footage, particularly from The Coaster, a film that Holmes made for the National Film Unit (NFU), to support her reading of documentary history. The NFU, established with John Grierson's advice, promoted the interests of social and national unity. Goldson accommodates for the demise of such an institutional and ideological framework by endorsing the discourse of the academy and the archive. The university and the arts sector lend credibility to the rebranding of New Zealand's past for consumption as a contemporary commodity. In the process, a state-sponsored, civically sanctioned ideal of documentary as a public service is recast as a professionally accredited enterprise in managing and marketing the national imaginary.

Punitive Damage and Georgie Girl complete the cycle of legitimation for documentary as a homegrown form of social discourse. They successfully present stories of local interest—a mother's fight for justice after the death of her son in an East Timor massacre, the life and times of the world's first transsexual, Maori MP—according to an international standard of value. An official round of film festivals, conferences, awards and prizes, funding panels, press releases, public talks, and interviews guarantee the quality of the film's documentary veracity. The global resurgence of documentary as a form of serious entertainment fosters an audience and artist with a shared set of moral and political reflexes: cultural tolerance, emotional empathy, and human understanding. Annie Goldson fits the bill well.

ALAN WRIGHT

Biography

Filmmaker and Associate Professor in the Department of Film, Television and Media Studies at the University of Auckland, New Zealand. Has been producing and directing award-winning documentaries for fifteen years in the United States and New Zealand. Published extensively on a variety of topics such as the documentary, feminism, and experimental video.

Selected films

1990 Counterterror: The North of Ireland: coproducer, codirector
1991 Framing the Panthers (black and white): coproducer, codirector
1993 Death Row Notebooks: coproducer, director
1993 A Small War: The United States in Puerto Rico: director
1994 Taonga: director
1994 Wake: director
1995 Seeing Red: producer, director
1999 Punitive Damage: director (produced with Gaylene Preston)
2001 Georgie Girl: codirector with Peter Wells, producer

Good Woman of Bangkok, The

(Australia, O'Rourke, 1991)

The Good Woman of Bangkok is a controversial account of the Australian documentary filmmaker Dennis O'Rourke's nine-month involvement with a Thai prostitute named Yaiwalak Conchanakun, called Aoi. Modeled after Bertolt Brecht's The Good Woman of Szechuan, which uses the central figure of a prostitute to examine the possibility of living a good life in a corrupt world, O'Rourke's film explores the conjunctions of sex and money in the East-meets-West world of Bangkok and examines the ethical complexity of his multiple roles as client, lover, and director in relation to Aoi. Although O'Rourke remains an off-camera voice throughout the film, his work is centrally concerned with his intercession into and interrogation of Aoi's life, which culminates in his offer to rescue her from prostitution by buying her and her family a rice farm. O'Rourke provocatively positions his very personal film as 'documentary fiction', an antithesis of the objective documentary that rearranges chronology for dramatic effect and self-consciously examines the voyeuristic nature of filmmaking. Although the film centers on the life of Aoi, it indicates the elusive edges of a larger story about the intercultural, interracial, and economic complexity of postcolonial capitalism.

Figure 4 The Good Woman of Bangkok, 1991 (Courtesy of the British Film Institute)

The film begins after the collapse of O'Rourke's marriage, when he travels to the notorious Patpong region of Bangkok to explore the nature of love and sexual desire. The forty-three-year-old O'Rourke hires the twenty-five-year-old Aoi for her sexual services and begins to film her as she tells a life story full of victimization and exploitation. The film traces the trajectory of Aoi's life: her birth into a poor peasant family, her parenting by an alcoholic father, and her pain from an untreated birth defect that has left her blind in one eye. She spent her adolescence in servitude before making a bad marriage to a man who deserted her when she was two months' pregnant. Aoi eventually moved to Bangkok at the urging of her mother and worked in the Patpong area to support her family and pay off their debts. The camera unblinkingly follows Aoi as she plies her trade at night, tells her story during the day, and performs the intimate acts of eating, sleeping, and tending to her dead father's shrine. Aoi eventually moves to the rice farm that O'Rourke has promised to buy her and her family. The Good Woman of Bangkok concludes with an epilogue that reveals Aoi's return to the sex trade underworld, from which O'Rourke attempted to rescue her. The reason for her return to Bangkok is never revealed, suggesting that there is much that O'Rourke does not know and perhaps cannot know about Aoi, bound as he is by cultural, economic, and sexual lines that frame Aoi as an ever-elusive subject.

LISA HINRICHSEN

The Good Woman of Bangkok (Australia, 1991, 82 mins). Produced by Dennis O'Rourke and Glenys Rowe. Directed by Dennis O'Rourke. Cinematography by Dennis O'Rourke. Edited by Tim Litchfield. Filmed in Bangkok.

Further reading

Berry, Chris, *The Filmmaker and the Prostitute: Dennis O'Rourke's 'The Good Woman of Bangkok'*, Sydney: Power Institute Press, 1997.

Stones, Rob, 'Social Theory, Documentary Film and Distant Others: Simplicity and Subversion in The Good Woman of Bangkok', *European Journal of Cultural Studies*, 2003.

Gorin, Jean-Pierre

Jean-Pierre Gorin was initially known for his collaboration with Jean-Luc Godard in the late 1960s and early 1970s. Working collectively under the banner of the Dziga Vertov Group, the New Left activist, who later said 'I'm a Nietzschean-Marxist … certainly more Nietzschean than Marxist' (Walsh 1976), codirected a series of formally experimental films strongly influenced by the theoretical debates of the time, questioning bourgeois notions of representation and ideology and exploring alternatives in works such as Wind from the East (1969), Struggle in Italy (1970), Tout va bien (1972), and Letter to Jane (1972). Godard, while ultimately sharing coauthorship for these works, maintains that the majority of the initial concepts came from his younger collaborator. Gorin for his part has insisted that the creative relationship was based on a 'constant exchange of ideas'.

Poto and Cabengo (1978), his first film after leaving Paris for California in 1975, was a documentary portrait of seven-year-old identical twins, Virginia and Grace Kennedy, who had apparently developed their own private language. Stylistically a departure from the rigours of the earlier work, the project was as much an essay on language and communication as a wry outsider's commentary on the underside of the American dream as reflected in the isolated social circumstances of the German-American family. The second of the Southern California trilogy, Routine Pleasures (1986) juxtaposes the singularly unspectacular activities of a club of model train enthusiasts with an exploration of the creative process of carpenter, film critic, and artist Manny Farber (who had originally invited Gorin to the University of California at San Diego). The miniature train sets of the middle-aged men (' … in [a] hangar on Jimmy Durante Boulevard across from the Bing Crosby Hall') seem to preserve America in a nostalgic microcosm, mirrored by and in contrast to the epic landscapes and movie myths of Farber's paintings. Switching between black and white and colour, the film is a celebration of 'Flaubertian dullness', undoubtedly inspired by Farber's dictum on filmmaking that Gorin summarised thus: 'I make films in my backyard […] the way I define my subject matter is by planting myself on the ground, whirling around my own axis, extending my two arms, and within that square foot radius, defining where my subjects are' (Seidenberg 1992).

My Crasy Life (1992), which was awarded the Special Jury Prize at Sundance in 1992, looks at the everyday lives of Samoan gangs in Los Angeles. Gorin and his producer Dan Marks wrote the film in close collaboration with the gang members, scripting scenes that were then acted out by the gangsters themselves. The formal compositions of cinematographer Babette Mangolte (who shot Routine Pleasures), as well as fictional elements such as a quasi-human talking computer in a patrol car, distance the film strongly from vérité and hark back to earlier experimentation with genres.

Although his output has been limited in quantity over the past decade, Gorin's playful exploration of the no-man's-land between documentary, fiction, and the essay form mark him as an influential innovator, one who can no longer be regarded as wholly European or American but perhaps both.

JOHN BURGAN

See also: Blank, Les; Marker, Chris; Vertov, Dziga

Biography

Born in Paris, France, April 7, 1943, and graduated in philosophy from the Sorbonne in 1964. Collaborated on Les Cahiers Marxistes-Léninistes and Les Cahiers pour l'analyse, also worked as literary critic at *Le Monde* (1965–8). Advisor on Jean-Luc Godard's La Chinoise (1967) before cofounding the Dziga Vertov Group with him (1968–72). Moved to California in 1975 to join the Cinema Department of the University of San Diego.

Selected films

1972 Tout va bien: codirector (with J.L. Godard)
1972 Letter to Jane: codirector (with J.L. Godard)
1978 Poto and Cabengo: writer, director
1986 Routine Pleasures: director, cowriter (with Patrick Amos)
1991 My Crasy Life: writer, director
1992 Letter to Peter: writer, director

Further reading

Farber, Manny, *Negative Space*, New York: Da Capo, 1998.
Harvey, Sylvia, *May '68 and Film Culture*, London: British Film Institute, 1980.

MacCabe, Colin, *Godard, Images, Sounds, Politics*, London: British Film Institute, 1998.

Schafaff, Jörn, 'Routine Pleasures or All About Eve or A Point in the Landscape', in Jörn Schafaff and Barbara Steiner (eds), *Jorge Pardo Ostfildern-Ruit*, Hatje Cantz Verlag, 2000: 45–60.

Seidenberg, Steven, 'In Search of the Feature Documentary', London: BBC, 1992.

Sobchack, Vivian, '16 Ways to Pronounce Potato: Authority and Authorship in Poto and Cabengo', *The Journal of Film and Video*, XXXVI, fall, 1984.

Ullman, Erik, 'Jean-Pierre Gorin', www.sensesofcinema.com/contents/directors/03/gorin.html, n.d.

Walsh, Martin, 'Godard and Me: Jean-Pierre Gorin Talks', *Take One* 5, no. 1, 1976 (reprinted in *The Brechtian Aspect of Radical Cinema*, London: BFI, 1981).

Wollen, Peter, *Readings and Writings: Semiotic Counter-Strategies*, London: New Left Books, 1982.

Grabe, Hans-Dieter

Hans-Dieter Grabe has had a long and varied career in documentary film, as a director, writer, cinematographer, and producer. From 1963 to 2002, Grabe worked at the ZDF (Zweiten Deutschen Fernsehen), the second national German television network, making more than fifty television documentaries during his tenure.

By the beginning of the 1970s Grabe had found his own style of documentary editing. He produces dialogue-based films, which focus on drawing out the memories and life experiences of the filmed subjects. The film's titles are frequently based on a headline drawn from the news. Grabe looks for and focuses on the real people behind the event, shunning sensationalism.

Grabe has a wide spectrum of themes. He has produced films about the Berlin Trümmerfrauen (1968), about a former prisoner at a concentration camp (1972), a Varietekünstler, who lets people shoot themselves (1972), about the wife of a child murderer (1977), the survivors of a mine disaster (1979), a German resistance fighter (1983), a Turkish worker who has killed her daughter (1986), a ZDF colleague diagnosed with cancer (1987), about the parents of a child with multiple disabilities (1990) and about the victims of war. The films are connected by their focus on the themes of responsibility, guilt, misery, and fear as they stem from individual personal experiences. 'Better more than less': with these words, Grabe summarizes his guiding principle as documentary film director (Voss 2000: 13).

An historical image is usually projected at the beginning of a Grabe film, and a brief commentary provides the necessary background information. Grabe then withdraws the explanatory information, limits the use of voice-over narration, and relies primarily on his principal characters to convey what is essential.

Grabe has worked with the same camera crew repeatedly, including Horst Bendel, Fritz Adam, Per Mustelin, and Carl Franz Hutterer, and with the same editor, Elfi Kreiter. They all refrain from making use of any sensationalistic effects. Camera movements are subtle and limited, and pacing is generally slow and consistent.

Grabe's conversation with his film subjects is a necessary step that directly impacts the outcome of the film. After a lengthy preliminary conversation, he interviews his subjects on-camera, attempting to be friendly while maintaining some degree of distance, which he calls 'positive distance'. The filmed exchange mimics a therapeutic session, in which people who have repressed their emotional reactions to past events gradually reveal their emotional wounds. Grabe creates spaces full of silence, in which he focuses on the faces of his subjects, to convey the full impact of the words previously spoken. The intense conversation slowly approaches the point at which the emotional cocoon breaks and tears run; it is a cathartic moment.

Grabe achieved the most consequential effect of this emotional close-up in the film Mendel Schainfelds zweite Reise nach Deutschland/ Mendel Szajnfeld's Second Journey to Germany (1972). The film was shot exclusively on a train. Grabe documented the journey of former Polish forced laborer Szajnfeld from Oslo, where he had lived since his release from camp, to Munich, where he wants to obtain a medical certificate that will allow him to receive a higher pension based on his inability to work, which is a long-term consequence of his time in camp. During this journey, Szajnfeld slowly opens up, until he speaks of a particularly traumatic event: desperately taking a piece of bread from a deceased person. He admits that this memory still tortures him and says 'perhaps somebody would have needed it more than me'.

Grabe's films expose both psychological and physical wounds. Shots of the film Nur leichte

Kämpfe im Raum Da Nang/Only Light Skirmishes in the Da Nang Area (1970), were taken in 1970 in the German hospital-ship Helgoland. The title comes from a short press report about the Vietnam War, which had been already almost forgotten in Europe. The film shows the effects of 'light skirmishes' on the so-called 'civil population'. It is a pitiless film that is difficult to watch. Grabe shows, in precise detail, bodies destroyed by gunshots, lacerated by mines, and burned by napalm, and lets a doctor explain each of the wounds. By forcing us to look, he gives the victims their dignity back: 'we had to show the devastation of the body in precise detail—we owed it to those broken people. They offered us their bodies to film them and therefore we felt this was a way to contribute to the ending of war' (Goldsmith 2003: 50).

Hiroshima, Nagasaki—Atombombenopfer sagen aus/Hiroshima, Nagasaki—Atom Bomb Victims Speak Out (1985), Grabe's first long documentary film, was made to commemorate the fortieth anniversary of the nuclear bombing of Japan by the United States. The central section of the film is a mute sequence, which initially shows parts of American archive material. For example, doctors bend over a boy, whose back is a single bloody and purulent wound, in which they sink their cotton swabs. These images are followed by pictures of the same man in front of Grabe's camera. He shows his deformed body and explains that the skin on his back is dead, he is cold even during the summer because he has no more fatty tissue, and he may never eat until he is full because by doing so, the skin stretches intolerably.

Grabe's interest in his subjects occasionally extends past a single film. For example, Grabe met Do Sanh, a severely wounded Vietnamese boy, while shooting Nur leichte Kämpfe im Raum Da Nang. He made five films about Do Sahn over a period of twenty-eight years. Do Sanh—Der letzte Film/Do Sanh—The Last Film (1998) was completed after Sanh's death, which resulted from the long-term consequences of his wartime injuries.

Grabe viewed television as the appropriate medium for his political films because it is such a universal and populist vehicle.

BRITTA HARTMANN

Biography

Born March 6, 1937 in Dresden, Germany. In February 1945, after the destruction of Dresden, relocated to Cottbus with his family, where he attended school until 1955. From 1955 to 1959 Grabe studied film direction, specializing in documentary film, at the Deutschen Hochschule für Filmkunst (German University for Cinematic Art, today University for Film and Television 'Konrad Wolf') in Potsdam-Babelsberg. From the beginning of 1960 to the end of 1962 worked as a freelancer at Bavarian Television. From the end of 1962 until his retirement in March 2002, worked as an editor with the Zweiten Deutschen Fernsehen (ZDF, Second Channel of German Television) in Mainz. As author and director has contributed to several magazines and made over fifty full-length documentary films. Has been awarded the Special Prize of the Union of Asiatic Broadcast and TV Organizations, the Special Prize of the Film and Television Federation, the Robert Geisendörfer Prize (twice), the Eduard Rhein Prize (twice), the Adolf Grimme Prize (three times), the ARTE-Documentary Film Prize, the Peace Film Prize of the International Film Festival of Berlin, as well as the Grand Prix of all Categories at the Festival of the Independent Film in Brussels, among others. In 2002, received the Federal Cross of Merit.

Selected films

1966 Hoffnung—fünfmal am Tag, Beobachtungen auf einem Zonengrenzbahnhof/Hope, Five Times a Day (30 mins): writer, director

1966 Die Helgoland in Vietnam (28 mins): writer, director

1968 Die Trümmerfrauen von Berlin/The Women Who Cleared Away the Ruins of Berlin (40 mins): writer, director

1970 20 Meilen vor Saigon/20 Miles to Saigon (44 mins): writer, director

1970 Nur leichte Kämpfe im Raum Da Nang/Only Light Skirmishes in the Da Nang Area (44 mins): writer, director

1972 Mendel Schainfelds zweite Reise nach Deutschland/Mendel Szajnfeld's Second Journey to Germany (43 mins): writer, director

1972 Wer schießt auf Ralf Bialla? Warum läßt Herr Bialla auf sich schießen? (43 mins): writer, director
1975 Sanh und seine Freunde (44 mins): writer, director
1977 Mehmet Turan oder Nioch ein Jahr, noch ein Jahr (44 mins): writer, director
1977 Gisela Bartsch oder Warum haben Sie den Mörder geheiratet? (45 mins): writer, director
1978 Simon Wiesenthal oder Ich jagte Eichmann (46 mins): writer, director
1979 Das Wunder von Lengede oder Ich wünsch' keinem, was wir mitgemacht haben (44 mins): writer, director
1981 Bernauer Straße 1–50 oder als uns die Haustür zugenagelt wurde (72 mins): writer, director
1982 Fritz Teufel oder warum haben Sie nicht geschossen? (53 mins): writer, director
1983 Ludwig Gehm—ein deutscher Widerstandskämpfer (55 mins): writer, director
1984 Dr. med. Alfred Jahn, Kinderchirurg in Landshut (59 mins): writer, director
1985 Hiroshima, Nagasaki—Atombombenopfer sagen aus (90 mins): writer, director
1986 Abdullah Yakupoglu: Warum habe ich meine Tochter getötet? (45 mins): writer, director
1987 Gudrun Pehlke—Statistisch gesehen sind Sie tot (61 mins): writer, director
1990 Jens und seine Eltern (80 mins): writer, director
1990 Dien, Chinh, Chung und Tung—Lebensversuche in Vietnam (59 mins): writer, director
1991 Do Sanh (56 mins): writer, director
1994 Tage mit Sanh (34 mins): writer, director
1994 Er nannte sich Hohenstein—Aus dem Tagebuch eines deutschen Amtskommissars im besetzten Polen 1940 bis 42 (89 mins): writer, director
1995 Drei Frauen aus Poddembice (36 mins): writer, director
1995 Letzte Stunden in Poddembice—Jakob Rosenkranz und Abraham Ziegler (72 mins): writer, director
1996 Frau Siebert und ihre Schüler (118 mins): writer, director, camera
1998 Do Sanh—der letzte Film/Do Sanh—The Last Film (99 mins): writer, director, camera
1999 Mendel lebt (99 mins): writer, director, camera
2002 Diese Bilder verfolgen mich—Dr. med. Alfred Jahn/These Pictures Haunt Me—Alfred Jahn, MD (100 mins): writer, director, camera

Further reading

Erlewein, Christian, 'Annä hern, nicht anbiedern. Hans-Dieter Grabe über die behutsame Methode seiner Dokumentarfilme im Gespräch mit Christian Erlewein', *Medium* 2, 1992: 42–6.

Goldsmith, David A., *The Documentary Makers. Interviews with 15 of the Best in the Business*, Mies (CH)/Hove, East Sussex (GB): Roto Vision, 2003: 46–53.

Grabe, Hans-Dieter, 'Der sprechende Mensch. Mein Weg zum Gesprächsfilm', *Medium* 3, 1992: 20–6.

Roth, Wilhelm, *Der Dokumentarfilm seit 1960*, München/Luzern: Bucher, 1982: 151–3.

——'Mit Fragen einen Prozeß auslösen', *Süddeutsche Zeitung* (München), 23 January 1986.

Rothschild, Thomas, 'Zur Dramaturgie des Dokumentarfilms. Do Sanh—Der letzte Film von Hans-Dieter Grabe', *Filmbulletin* 41, no. 2, 1999: 12–17.

Voss, Gabriele (ed.), *Ins Offene … Dokumentarisch Arbeiten* 2. Christoph Hübner im Gespräch mit Hans-Dieter Grabe … , *Berlin: Vorwerk* 8, 2000: 12–59.

Wetzel, Kraft, 'Hans-Dieter Grabe: Oral History als Offenbarung', in Akademie der Künste Berlin (ed.), *Abenteuer Wirklichkeit. Dokumentarfilmer in Deutschland*, Berlin: Abteilung Film- und Medienkunst und Aktuelle Presse ZDF/3sat, 1989: 19–28.

Graef, Roger

Roger Graef is a highly acclaimed observational documentary filmmaker renowned for working in 'a very austere' direct cinema mode (Winston 1995: 207). Graef and his long-term film crew, which included cinematographer Charles Stewart, developed a series of work practices through which they hoped to minimise the intervention of the film crew and gain the trust of those being filmed. Their code of practice included no use of scoops, a firm agreement to film only what was previously agreed upon, and an agreement to offer a degree of confidentiality on material that the crew might come across during filming, careful consideration of camera angles, no lights, no staging of events, no interviews, but rather observation of events.

Graef's major work included the television series The Space Between Words (1972) about interpersonal and public communication; Decisions (1975–6), which observed the decision-making process and workings of powerful institutions, such as The British Steel Corporation and Occidental Petroleum, as well as Hammersmith Council; and, State of the Nation (1973–5), which included two programmes filmed inside the headquarters of the Common Market, in Brussels, and the Department of Industry.

One of Graef's later television programmes made for the BBC in 1981 was to prove controversial and was at the centre of a public outcry on police procedures. A Complaint of Rape, an episode from his series Police (1981), showed the insensitive handling of a rape victim by three Thames Valley police officers and provoked change in the way that the police deal with rape cases. Twenty years later Graef returned to make another film about the Thames Valley Police, Police 2001, which proved to be less contentious and, in a departure from previous practice, Graef appeared on screen.

Graef's documentary films set out to demystify the power brokers in society and, in doing so, made an informed contribution to the democratic process. Through the use of classic observational filming conventions, audiences were offered insight into the decision-making processes that affect ordinary people's lives.

PAT A. COOK

Biography

Born in New York in 1936. Studied law at Harvard University before moving to England in 1962. Initially worked in theatre before developing a distinguished career as an acclaimed documentary filmmaker. Appointed as a governor of the British Film Institute in the mid-1970s and was a founding member of Channel 4 in the United Kingdom. Awards include The British Academy Award, The Television Critics Award, and The European TV Critics Awards at Cannes. Has lectured at universities throughout Europe and the United States, and in January 2000 was appointed as News International Visiting Professor of Broadcast Media at Oxford University. Has written for a number of English newspapers and is the author of several books on law and order, which include, *Talking Blues: Police in Their Own Words* (1999), *Living Dangerously: Young Offenders Talking in Their Own Words* (1993).

Further reading

n.a., *Sight and Sound* 41, no. 4, autumn 1972: 190–1.
n.a., *Sight and Sound* 45, no. 1, winter 1975–76: 2–7.
n.a., *Vision* 1, spring 1962: 10–12.
Rosenthal, Alan, *New Challenges for Documentary*, Berkeley, CA: University of California Press, 1988.
Winston, Brian, *Claiming the Real: The Documentary Film Revisited*, London: BFI, 1995.

Granton Trawler

(UK, Cavalcanti, 1934)

The shot list of the National Film Archive for Granton Trawler is as follows: 'The work of a trawler on the Viking Bank in the North Sea [...] The trawler *Isabella Greig* moored at Granton. She sets off. On the outward journey the crew check and prepare the nets. On arrival at the fishing grounds the trawl is lowered. A storm blows up and the trawler has to ride out the rough seas. The seagulls circle the ship. When calm returns the nets are hauled in by the crew and the catch hoisted on board, as the seagulls flock round. The fish are tipped out on the deck. The crew gut the fish and throw them into baskets. The trawler on the homeward run, the pilot at the wheel, sunset over the sea.'

Granton Trawler can be thought of as a shorter version of Drifters, lyric rather than epic in its intentions and form. Grierson himself shot it on a busman's holiday in the North Sea. Edgar Anstey edited it under his supervision (as he had Industrial Britain). Though shot during the Empire Marketing Board (EMB) period, it was finished after the unit had been transferred to the General Post Office (GPO). Cavalcanti added the sound, one of his first creative acts after arriving at the GPO Film Unit. The soundtrack is made up of the rhythmic thumping of the ship's engine, the creaking of its rigging, the cries of gulls, the harsh metallic sound of a winch playing out cable, muffled shouts of the men as they pull the nets, a repeated fragment of a plaintive tune played on an accordion and another whistled, and random and mostly unintelligible comments from members of the crew. There is no commentary. The sounds were all post-recorded, simulated in the studio (one of the 'fishermen's' voices is Grierson's).

The sounds are laid over a succession of impressionistic views of parts of the ship, the fishermen's activities, and the shifting horizon, which becomes vertiginous in high seas. It is as if the makers of the film, and therefore the viewers, were standing on the trawler looking about as their eyes are led to one thing or another while their ears register certain sounds. Simple as it is, the track is a remarkably strong component of the picture. This montage of seemingly natural sounds arbitrarily modified and arranged is what would come to be called musique concrète. Not only was it an aesthetic experiment ahead of its time, but it represents the kind of poetry that can be achieved by a stylized rendering of reality completely controlled by the creator(s). It has not dated and is still in active nontheatrical distribution.

JACK C. ELLIS

See also: Anstey, Edgar; Cavalcanti, Alberto; Grierson, John

Granton Trawler (UK, New Era Films for Empire Marketing Board (silent version; sound version completed at GPO Film Unit), 1934, 11 mins). Distributed by New Era Films. Produced and photographed by John Grierson. Edited by Edgar Anstey. Sound direction by Alberto Cavalcanti; sound recorded by E.A. Pawley.

Grass

(US, Schoedsack, Cooper, Harrison, 1925)

Along with Robert Flaherty's Nanook of the North (1922), Ernest B. Schoedsack, Merian Cooper, and Marguerite Harrison's Grass (1925) helped to define the explorer-as-documentarist tradition in nonfiction film. Filmed under dire circumstances, as well as financial difficulties, Grass, nevertheless, is a unique example of an attempt, in the words of the filmmakers themselves, to 'dramatize exploration'. That it is not as well known as Flaherty's ethnographic film can be attributed to its filmmakers' hardships in compiling their footage into a cohesive narrative framework. The subject of human beings living and surviving in conflict with their natural surroundings is the primary attraction of these films. In the case of Grass, that subject is not an individual, as in the titular hero of Flaherty's film, but a nomadic tribe.

Ernest B. Schoedsack and Merian C. Cooper first formulated the idea of making an epic film set in some little-known region of the world in London. The original plan was to film a nomadic tribe during their annual migration for survival. The Kurdistans were the people of choice for their initial film project. Schoedsack had served as a second assistant cameraman for Mack Sennett at Keystone studios and also as a news photographer in Europe during and after World War I. Cooper was a decorated pilot during the war, as well as a worker for the American Relief Association after the war. After a brief stint as a reporter for the *Daily News* and *The New York Times*, Cooper signed on as first officer on the schooner Wisdom II. The purpose of the voyage was to collect information on little-known areas of the world for a book, magazine articles, and motion picture films. When the expedition's cameraman left, Cooper contacted Schoedsack, whom he had met on several occasions in Europe. When the expedition ended after the Wisdom II was disabled during a storm, Cooper and Schoedsack began making plans for their own epic film.

With a financial capital of $10,000, the two explorer-photographers, now accompanied by Marguerite Harrison, a journalist, made their way to Ankara, Turkey. The plan was to cross Anatolia to Turkestan and join with the Kurds to accompany their migratory route. The Turks, who had recently driven both the French and German forces out of Anatolia, were highly suspicious of all foreigners and delayed the intended expedition for several weeks. By the time they had crossed the border into French-occupied Syria, the only nomadic tribe they encountered were the Beduins. A British official, Sir Arnold Wilson, told Cooper about the Bakhtiari tribe in southern Persia. These nomadic people made an annual trek through mountainous terrain in search of green pastureland. Cooper, Schoedsack, and Harrison met with the khans at Shustar, the capital of Arabistan, and were given permission to join one of their tribes on its annual migration. The Great Trek of the Bakhtiari, accompanied for the first time by foreigners, began on April 17, 1924. The migration involved thirty thousand men, women, and children, with herds totaling approximately two hundred and fifty thousand animals including sheep, goats, cattle, horses, asses, and camels.

The people traveled along five separate routes; about one-sixth of this number was represented by the Baba Ahmedi tribe, which Cooper, Schoedsack, and Harrison elected to accompany because their route was the most difficult. Grass was the filmed record of that expedition.

Grass is the account of the annual migration of the Bakhtiari people in what is now Iran. The film begins with an opening shot of a camel caravan traveling east. A map of the region denotes Constantinople, Persia, and Arabia. The caravan encounters several natural obstacles including a sandstorm and mountains before meeting up with the 'Forgotten People', the Bakhtiari and their tribal leader, Haidar Khan, and his son, Lufta. The Bakhtiari are preparing to migrate to the east for more fertile lands. They first encounter the river Karun, which the Bakhtiari cross by constructing rafts supported by inflated goat skins. They also cross through several mountainous terrains and finally come to the dreaded Zardeh Kuh, described by the filmmakers as 'twelve thousand feet of defiance in rock and snow and ice'. The ascent is accomplished when the Bakhtiari dig a path through the snow and ice, and climb barefoot, because shoes were as 'useless as bedroom slippers in a blizzard'. The final descent from the mountain top into the fertile valley below ends the epic trek and the film.

The lack of a specific subject for their 'natural drama' cost the explorer-filmmakers both time and footage. When Cooper, Schoedsack, and Harrison met up with the Bakhtiari, the tribe were making preparations for their journey, and the filmmakers had used a considerable amount of film while they were delayed in Ankara. Much of the footage that was shot of the trek had to be taken during a short time span, as the tribe slept during the hot hours of the day and traveled at night. When the migration ended after the crossing of Zardeh Kuh, Schoedsack had only eighty feet of film left and quickly shot an ending for the film. When the filmmakers were in Paris, they realized that it was far from a finished product. Cooper and Schoedsack decided that one of them would return to the Bakhtiari to record additional footage, while the other would try to raise more money by writing articles about their expedition. The additional footage would focus more clearly on the tribal chief, Haidar, his two wives, and his son. This film footage was never shot and consequently, the resulting film, according to many critics (as well as the filmmakers themselves), lacks a central human focus.

The economic market for travel films (which necessitated that the filmmakers shoot whatever they thought would make an interesting subject) initiated a hasty and disjointed filmmaking process. Travel films, particularly of exotic places and peoples, were extremely popular in the 1920s. Travelogs or 'scenics' were popularized by Burton Holmes, whose short films usually situated a Western adventurer in exotic settings.

Robert Flaherty, with the success of Nanook of the North (1922), proved that the personalization of a subject for a documentary could be as exciting as a fiction film. Although it does have some footage of Hadair and his son, Lufta, Grass, out of necessity, concentrates on the Bakhtiari tribe itself, primarily in long shots of the migration. These are dramatic, particularly the crossing of both the river Karun and the mountain Zardeh Kuh, but the overall effect is weakened by the lack of human interest.

Once the film was bought for distribution by Jesse Lasky at Paramount Studios, additional footage (of the filmmakers themselves) and intertitles were added. Though the film was not a huge box office success, it did allow Schoedsack and Cooper to finance and eventually produce other projects of a more fictive nature, primarily Chang (1927), The Four Feathers (1929), The Most Dangerous Game/The Hounds of Zaroff (1932), and a film in which they lampooned themselves, as well as appearing as biplane pilots in the climatic sequence, King Kong (1933). Grass, nevertheless, still remains a good example of the early romanticist documentary style, which offered its audiences a glimpse into another culture and its epic struggle for survival.

RONALD WILSON

See also: Anstey, Edgar; Cavalcanti, Alberto; Grierson, John

Grass: A Nation's Battle for Life (aka Grass: The Epic of a Lost Tribe) (US, Famous Players Lasky, 1925, 69 mins). Distributed by Paramount Pictures. Presented by Adolph Zukor and Jesse Lasky. Produced and directed by Merian C. Cooper, and Ernest B. Schoedsack, and Marguerite Harrison. Photography by Ernest B. Schoedsack and Merian C. Cooper.

Music arranged by Hugo Riesenfeld. Edited by Merian C. Cooper. Titles by Terry Ramsaye. Filmed in New York, Turkey, Arabia, Iran. New York premiere at the Paramount Theatre, March 30, 1925.

Further reading

Barnouw, Eric, *Documentary: A History of the Non-Fiction Film*, New York: Oxford University Press, 1993.

Barsam, Richard M., *Non-Fiction Film: A Critical History*, Bloomington, IN: Indiana University Press, 1992.

Brownlow, Kevin, *The War, the West and the Wilderness*, New York: Alfred A. Knopf, 1979.

Cooper, Merian C., *Grass*, New York: Putnam's, 1925.

Goldner, Orville and Turner, George, *The Making of King Kong*, New York: A.S. Barnes & Company, 1975.

Mould, D.H. and Veeder, G., 'The Photographer-Adventurers: Forgotten Heroes of the Silent Screen', *Journal of Popular Film and Television* 16, no. 3, Fall, 1988.

Schoedsack, Ernest B., 'Grass: The Making of an Epic', *American Cinematographer* 64, no. 2, February, 1983.

Great Adventure, The

(Sweden, Sucksdorff, 1953–5)

Arne Sucksdorff's feature-length debut, his best-known effort, and almost certainly his greatest, most influential achievement, Det stora aven-tyret/The Great Adventure occupies an important yet troublesome spot in documentary history, because it seems like one of his least documentarian films. It has been claimed that it founded 'the style that stretches the definition of a documentary to its absolute limits. It is held together by a continuous narrative where the images illustrate the voice's narration, and creates a closed world that is built on assumptions about the state of things rather than their reality' (Soila, Soderberg Widding and Iversen 1998). The film strikes many as a break in Sucksdorff's work, given its fictional framing story, narrated by an adult voice as the movingly poetic memory of the elder of two brothers. Sucksdorff, acting for the only time in his films, plays a small role as the father of two boys, Anders and the younger Kjell (played by Sucksdorff's own son Kjell), who capture an otter and secretly try to raise it as a pet. Others, however, productively read the film as the summation of Sucksdorff's work up to this point, imposing a slight narrative framework and themes consistent with his oeuvre upon footage essentially documentarian in its shooting, style, and spirit.

The film is justly noted for many individual shots and sequences. Sucksdorff's penchant for water imagery is evident from the early shots of water beads on reeds to those on a spider's web, to later shots of icicles and water ripples evoking nature's vibrant delicacy. The work and the world of humans can be beautiful, too, as with shots of a threshing machine. Most famous, however, are the animal scenes, often presented without narration; the film does not show a human until seven minutes in, and the story of the boys and their otter does not commence until the film is half over. The mating of the wood grouse combines fascinating footage with the careful, foregrounded use of sound typical of Sucksdorff. His legendary patience in seeking shots, many in close-up, shows in shots of an owl swooping down to catch a dormouse, a fox cub tugging at a sibling's corpse, or in the best-known example of a lynx waiting in a tree. One is left to wonder if the boys were indeed close to a lynx as one swish pan seems to indicate. Such effects blend seamlessly into those created by editing, or the stylized montage of spring's return.

The film succeeds remarkably at balancing its documentary and fictional aspects. The extended nature scenes, so rewarding in themselves, never make the story of the boys seem perfunctory or forgotten, while the 'adventure' of the boys never imposes itself so strongly as to make one feel that this is not a nature documentary. Given that the division between the world of choice-making humans and that of instinctual animal nature is so important to Sucksdorff (viz., A Divided World), perhaps this is why he had such insight into children, those creatures who most closely span the divide, driven more by base desires and impulses. When the boys slide down a snowy hill, we then hilariously see 'Ottie' belly-wop as well. At the same time, the interaction between humans and animals is at the heart of his work, whether in the story of the boys and their pet, the nuisance and economic threat the fox presents to farmers, or even a shot of an owl appearing to watch airplanes skywriting. Sucksdorff's flair for simulating point-of-view shots from animal as well as human perspective is on display, lending credence to the nonjudgmental claims he made: 'I try to show an acceptance of life and other human beings. After all, one of the main human rights is the right to make mistakes!' (quoted in Cowie 1985).

That said, mistakes by animals or humans can prove fatal, and Sucksdorff, in typical form, never flinches from the cruelty of circumstance, the constraints that humanity places on animals, and the harsh ironies of the wild. The most piercing example occurs as the fox escapes with its takings from the henhouse. The dog pulls away from his post and dashes after the fox, who seems doomed, given his size and the burden he carries. Ironically, the dog's dangling chain gets caught on a branch, trapping the dog, who soon falls prey to a lynx. Linking the animals with humans, the film reminds us of the lynx when Anders is startled by suddenly falling snow clumps. The parallels, however, are even richer, for Nature appears to give its replacements. By February 'Ottie' is tame enough to know his own name and to follow the boys around like a dog. Still, the otter and the foxes responsible for the dog's death play together, and Ottie, too, pilfering food, becomes a menace to the fishermen. The boys' toughest realization of that lingering division, though, comes near the end. For all of Ottie's apparent bonding with them, he is also content to simply run off and return to the wild. The powers of recovery in nature, however, be they human or animal, are considerable. Kjell's blabbing to others about Ottie's existence is forgiven, and it only takes a flock of cranes on the wing to enchant the boys once again. The gentle narration, highlighting the theme of 'life as a great adventure', is not as sentimental as it might first seem: 'No happiness of ours exists without heartache [...] no love without anxiety[...] In the forest so little time for grief, and joy is short-lived too.'

DAVID M. LUGOWSKI

The Great Adventure/Det stora aventyret (Sweden, Svenska Filmindustri, 1953, 77 mins). Direction, production, scenario, cinematography and editing by Arne Sucksdorff. Original music by Lars-Erik Larsson.

Further reading

Cowie, Peter, *Swedish Cinema, from Ingeborg Holm to Fanny and Alexander*, Stockholm: Swedish Institute, 1985.

——*Scandinavian Cinema*, London: Tantivy Press, 1992.

Hardy, Forsyth, *Scandinavian Film*, London: Falcon Press, 1952.

Kwiatkowski, Aleksander, *Swedish Film Classics*, Stockholm: Swedish Film Institute and New York: Dover, 1983.

Soila, Tytti, Soderbergh Widding, Astrid and Iversen, Gunnar, *Nordic National Cinemas*, London and New York: Routledge, 1998.

Wakeman, John (ed.), 'Arne Sucksdorff', in *World Film Directors, Vol. One, 1890–1945*, New York: H.W. Wilson, 1987.

Great Day in Harlem, A

(US, Bach, 1994)

A celebration of the famous photograph of nearly sixty jazz luminaries posing in front of a Harlem brownstone apartment block, taken by Art Kane for *Esquire* magazine in 1958, A Great Day in Harlem has some striking parallels with Jazz on a Summer's Day (1959). Kane had been a magazine art director hitherto, this being his first photographic assignment; Bert Stern had been an advertising stills photographer before directing his first (and only) film. The photograph was another instance of the interface, in the late 1950s, between commercial art and jazz iconography. Where it differs, however, is in the kinds of iconography deployed. The bustling inner-city backdrop captured in pristine monochrome contrasts sharply with Stern's boldly coloured juxtaposition of old money and youthful exuberance.

A Great Day in Harlem pays tribute to as many of the musicians featured in the photograph as can be crammed into its sixty minutes, ranging from veteran stride pianist Willie 'The Lion' Smith to then-younger musicians on the rise, including Sonny Rollins and Horace Silver. That it avoids feeling repetitive can be attributed to skilful pacing. It can also be attributed to the different kinds of footage utilised. Jean Bach, the director, conducted contemporary interviews with surviving participants on their reminiscences of the day and of the other musicians featured in the photograph. A sometime journalist in Chicago, later a radio and television producer, Bach had a long-standing acquaintance with many of her interviewees. The ensuing mutual respect resulted in a series of engaging interviews, by turns moving, elegiac, hilarious, with musicians whose experiences, in most cases, made them reluctant to talk expansively with the uninitiated.

The somewhat visually bland interview footage is combined with home movie photography, in colour, shot on the day by veteran swing bassist, Milt Hinton, or his wife, Mona. The vibrancy of this material is, again, reminiscent of the quality of immediacy in the cinematography of Jazz on a Summer's Day. This, in turn, is interposed with black-and-white archive footage of the musicians being discussed, mostly from 1950s television, characterised by low-key lighting and grainy film stock.

In these ways, the effect is of cumulative layers of an artfully constructed authenticity: in the iconography of the photograph, in the other contemporaneous photography capturing the event, and in the direct testimony of those who were there. Hearing the music on the sound track, of which improvisation was an important component, alongside the awareness of the intervention of several decades since its recording, is analogous to the film overall, in its chronological distance from Kane's photograph, and in its fusion of the here and now and the elegiac. Once an artefact of glossy contemporaneity, the photograph now acts as a springboard to a multifaceted oral history. As such, the film is not only an invaluable resource for those wishing to know more about jazz; it is also a nuanced meditation on the nature of time and memory.

JOHN YOUNG

A Great Day in Harlem (US, Flo-Bert/Jean Bach/New York Foundation for the Arts, 1994, 60 mins). Distributed by Castle Hill Productions. Produced by Stuart Samuels and Matthew Seig. Directed by Jean Bach. Shooting script by Jean Bach, Susan Peehl, and Matthew Seig. Cinematography by Steve Petropoulos, Del Hall, Milt Hinton, and Mona Hinton. Animation camera by Ralph Pitre. Title animations by Michael Bianchi. Edited by Susan Peehl. Interviews by Jean Bach. Narrated by Quincy Jones. Interviews with Robert Altschuler, Robert Benton, Art Blakey, Scoville Browne, Buck Clayton, Art Farmer, Steve Frankfurt, Bud Freeman, Dizzy Gillespie, Benny Golson, Johnny Griffin, Nat Hentoff, Milt Hinton, Mona Hinton, Chubby Jackson, Hank Jones, Taft Jordan, Jr, Max Kaminsky, Mike Lipskin, Eddie Locke, Elaine Lorillard, Marian McPartland, Felix Maxwell, Paula Morris, Gerry Mulligan, Everard Powell, Sonny Rollins, Horace Silver, and Ernie Wilkins. Archive footage of Henry 'Red' Allen, Count Basie, Vic Dickenson, Roy Eldridge, Sonny Greer, Coleman Hawkins, Jo Jones, Gene Krupa, Charles Mingus, Thelonious Monk, Jimmy Rushing, Pee Wee Russell, Zutty Singleton, Stuff Smith, Willie 'The Lion' Smith, Rex Stewart, Maxine Sullivan, Mary Lou Williams, and Lester Young.

Further reading

Bruzzi, Stella, *New Documentary: A Critical Introduction*, London: Routledge, 2000.

Clark, Andrew (ed.), *Riffs and Choruses: A New Jazz Anthology*, London and New York: Continuum, 2001: 448–9.

DeVeaux, Scott, 'Constructing the Jazz Tradition: Jazz Historiography', *Black American Literature Forum* 25, no. 3, fall 1991: 525–60.

Gilroy, Paul, *The Black Atlantic: Modernity and Double Consciousness*, Cambridge, MA: Harvard University Press, 1993: 72–110.

Harlos, Christopher, 'Jazz Autobiography: Theory, Practice, Politics', in Krin Gabbard (eds), *Representing Jazz*, Durham, NC: Duke University Press, 1995: 131–66.

Levine, Lawrence W., 'Jazz and American Culture', *Journal of American Folklore* 102, no. 403, January–March 1989: 6–22.

Shapiro, Nat and Hentoff, Nat (eds), *Hear Me Talkin' to Ya: The Story of Jazz as Told by the Men Who Made It*, Harmondsworth: Penguin, 1963.

Stowe, David W., *Swing Changes: Big Band Jazz in New Deal America*, Cambridge, MA: Harvard University Press, 1994.

Walser, Robert (ed.), *Keeping Time: Readings in Jazz History*, New York: Oxford University Press, 1999.

Great White Silence, The

(UK, Ponting, 1924)

The Great White Silence was the first feature documentary version of the footage shot by the photographer and cinematographer Herbert Ponting (1870–1935) during the failed attempt to reach the South Pole on foot by a team lead by the naval officer and explorer Robert Falcon Scott in 1910–12.

Scott was the best known of a group of polar explorers who mounted expeditions on foot across the Arctic and Antarctic continents during the late Victorian and early Edwardian period. The 1910–12 expedition—his last, as it would turn out—followed a previous unsuccessful attempt to reach the Pole in 1901–4, and voyages by others including his arch-rival Ernest Shackleton and the Australian Sir Douglas Mawson. Their work coincided with the rapid growth of still photography as a mass medium and of cinema as industrialised entertainment, hence the reason both Scott and Shackleton enlisted the services of cameramen on their later journeys. Fundraising was always a problem, and advance sales of the distribution rights for both still and moving images provided much-needed income (it took Scott more than a year to raise the £40,000 needed to finance his attempt on the Pole).

Scott's second voyage was an unmitigated disaster. His colleagues were largely inexperienced, and the party relied heavily on untested motorised sledges, all of which broke down at an early stage in the expedition. Scott and his party of five colleagues had to manually haul their supplies almost eight hundred miles from Ross Island to the South Pole. They achieved this on January 18, 1912, only to discover that Scott's rival, the Norwegian Roald Amundsen, had got there first. As a result of a combination of exhaustion and unusually bad weather on the return trip, Scott's party became stranded and all eventually died.

Despite the expedition not only having been a failure, but one that could have been easily foreseen and prevented (as demonstrated by Amundsen's having reached the Pole with relatively little difficulty), Scott was celebrated as a national hero when news of the expedition's outcome reached Britain in February 1913. A memorial service held the following month characterised Scott's attempt as a 'heroic failure', rhetoric that would characterise the commercial exploitation of Ponting's footage over the next two decades.

Herbert Ponting was born in Salisbury in 1870 and emigrated to California in the early 1890s. Within a decade he had gained a formidable reputation as a documentary photographer, largely as a result of his visits to Japan in 1902–5. It was on the strength of this reputation that he persuaded Scott to hire him to photograph and film the 1910–12 expedition. Ponting was not among the group of five who died on the return march from the South Pole, and on his return to London he devoted the rest of his life to publicising the work of Scott through the medium of his photographs and films. He presented more than a thousand lectures during the following years, illustrated by both slides and film, and in 1921 published *The Great White South*, the first of many illustrated books documenting Scott's final expedition.

The Great White Silence, released in 1924, was the first of three stand-alone feature versions of Ponting's edited film footage. The continuity is clumsy and relies heavily on intertitles, and the film was not shown widely (nor is it readily available for viewing today). The second version, 90° South (1933), featured recorded music and a synchronised commentary by Ponting. It is far more fluently edited and uses animated diagrams to recount the details of Scott's final march (on which, given that Ponting did not take part, no actual footage was shot). A shortened version was released in 1936 as The Story of Captain Scott, shortly after Ponting's death the previous year.

The two decades that Ponting spent in tirelessly promoting his Scott footage undoubtedly established the 'heroic failure' genre as a mainstay franchise in British documentary and realist cinema, especially in depicting military conflicts with negative outcomes. Its influence can be seen in settings as diverse as the politically controversial account of Edith Cavell's execution in Dawn (UK, 1927, director Herbert Wilcox) and the Arnhem landings in Brian Desmond Hurst's reconstruction, Theirs is the Glory (1946).

The image of Scott as the gallant loser was further cemented in a highly budgeted and publicised biopic (shot in Technicolor and featuring music by Ralph Vaughan-Williams), Scott of the Antarctic (UK, 1948, director Charles Frend). Though a fictionally re-created account of Scott's last expedition the film appears to have been based heavily on Ponting's work, including staged versions of some of the more memorable scenes in both The Great White Silence and 90° South. With this film Scott's final expedition took its place alongside the Charge of the Light Brigade or the battles of Trafalgar and The Somme as a distinct strand in the British cultural memory, which the historian Jeffrey Richards argues is characterised by an emphasis on self-belief and on trying rather than succeeding. It is perhaps for this reason that Scott of the Antarctic was a box office failure in the United States. Interestingly, the Ealing version does explicitly note a number of key errors made by Scott as having contributed to the eventual disaster (most notably the decision to rely on motorised sledges); the Ponting films give a more simplistic impression of a visionary battling elements beyond his control.

In this respect, therefore, both The Great White Silence and 90° South have been seen as overtly propagandist in the context of Ponting's largely unproblematic and sycophantic depiction (at times bordering on worship) of his protagonist, and the hindsight of what we now know to be a number of serious errors on Scott's part. That having been said, it must be borne in mind that Ponting (and, for that matter, his counterpart on the 1914–16 Shackleton expedition, Frank Hurley) was primarily a photographic ethnographer by trade, and did not approach filmmaking with the same institutional and cultural baggage as Grierson's generation of documentary-makers and the 'social realist' tradition of British filmmaking that followed.

LEO ENTICKNAP

See also: South

Great White Silence, The (UK, Ponting, 1924). Distributed by New Era Films. Produced and directed by Herbert G. Ponting.

Further reading

Arnold, H.J.P., *Photographer of the World: The Biography of Herbert Ponting*, London: Hutchinson, 1969.

Ponting, Herbert, *The Great White South*, London: Gerald Duckworth & Co., 1921.

——*With Scott to the Pole*, second edn, London: Bloomsbury, 2004.

Richards, Jeffrey, *Films and British National Identity*, Manchester: Manchester University Press, 1997.

Savours, Ann (ed.), *Scott's Last Voyage: Through the Antarctic Camera of Herbert Ponting*, New York: Praeger, 1975.

Greece

In the early decades of the twentieth century, the practice of documentary was hardly thought of as an important aspect of Greece's cinematic output (relatively slim, at any rate). The considerable value that has since been attached to the many newsreels produced in that era is attributable to the country's tumultuous history, the political and military events of which are evoked in those documentaries. These documentaries were made beyond any notion of adherence to the various evolving international theories and practices of 'addressing the real', and being (for the most part) uninformed by formal concerns of an aesthetic or diegetic order.

Nevertheless, Greek cinema actually begins with documentary, arguably via the pioneering work of the Manakias brothers, Greek Vlachs, who inaugurated Balkan cinematography in May 1905 with Yfantres/The Weavers, featuring their one-hundred-and-sixteen-year-old grandmother in their native Macedonian village. This was the first of sixty-seven films of mainly ethnographic interest. It should be pointed out, however, that the Manakias's output did not belong to the Greek 'national cinematography' to start with, given that their work coincides historically with the upheavals that resulted in the formation of Greek Macedonia. The Manakias brothers' story has become familiar to the international viewing public mostly by way of its recent incorporation into the plot of Theo Angelopoulos's 1995 fiction film To Vlemma tou Odyssea/Ulysses' Gaze.

Also worthy of mention is the work of Dimitris Meravidis, a Greek based in Istanbul, Turkey, whose earliest (1903) newsreels actually predated those of the more celebrated brothers, but were neither produced nor exhibited on the Greek mainland. From 1905 onward Meravidis produced several such films, which he sent to the Gaumont and Pathé companies in Paris for exhibition. Later he became the first important Greek director of photography, and, in 1928, he filmed Prometheas Desmotis/Prometheus in Chains in Delphi, capturing the attempted revival (by the poet Angelos Sikelianos and his wife Eva) of Delphic Mysteries. That document, funded by a French company for the promotion of ancient drama, was coupled with a later (1930) performance of Prometheus, this time in Athens, a pairing that remains of great historical interest, insofar as it constitutes the first full-length film on Greek tragedy.

Particularly notable are the 1917 film I Katastrofi tis Thessalonikis/The Destruction of Thessaloniki by an unnamed director (a work that, in ten minutes and thirty-five seconds, captured by purely cinematic means the fire that ravaged a part of Thessaloniki) and M. Dorizas's Meteora, of uncertain date. These films are of special value, insofar as they are among the few of that period that have survived integrally.

Of the important early makers of Greek newsreels, the Hungarian Joseph Hepp merits mentioning, as do Costas Theodoridis, the Gaziadis brothers (Dimitris and Michail), and especially the painter Yorgos Prokopiou, with his remarkable films on the campaign to Asia Minor and the 1922 catastrophe that followed, resulting in the expulsion of the Greek community (approximately one-and-a-half million refugees). Many of the episodes captured by Prokopiou reveal a coherence and singularity of purpose that lends them a diegetic quality with strong humanist overtones.

Before World War II, those Greek documentaries that did not fall under the 'newsreels' label aimed at capturing the singularities of the indigenous landscape. This continued after the war, notably via the shorts made by Prodromos Meravidis (Dimitris's son), photographed, edited, and produced by himself. Other directors who worked in this field include Elias Paraskeuas and Gavriil Loggos, whose films also registered the spectacle of countryside, by now wounded by the recent wartime experience. It is precisely this factor, as well as the tendency evident in the works of such filmmakers, to focus on the unexpected as opposed to the typical, that often differentiated their work from a facilely picturesque and folkloric treatment of the natural spectacle. The latter ideologically charged option, aiming from the outset at the passive acceptance, consumption, and tourist exploitation of the said spectacle, contrasts sharply with the surprising or disturbing aspects revealed by highlighting the peculiarities of the Greek landscape.

The aforementioned recent experience, of course, included not only the Nazi occupation of Greece, but also the events immediately following its liberation. The country's allegiance to the Western bloc, and the consequent defeat of the Left in the catastrophic 1945–9 civil war (a matter the complexity of which is beyond the scope of this essay), meant that by the end of the 1940s Greece was at once politically divided and materially devastated. At the same time, the conservative political powers that, under various guises, ruled almost uninterruptedly until the advent of the 1967–74 colonels' junta, imposed, among other things, a Cold War policy regarding freedom of expression.

This overview illustrates the evolution of Greek cinematography, as well as the problems faced by documentary makers in the first decades after the war. Although a number of developing companies produced innumerable generic fiction films, thereby giving rise to a 'tradition' with a popular following, albeit lacking the foundations of a film industry proper (hence the tradition's gradual demise on the advent of television in the late 1960s), the documentary mode was plagued by limitations, both on the level of expression and on production, distribution, and exhibition.

Put simply, the 'short' format was deemed non-lucrative by commercial producers and cinema owners alike and useless save for special cases funded for propagandist purposes by the state itself (ministries and public companies). This was a sector in which directors such as Yannis Panagiotopoulos produced some notable work in the early postwar period. This resulted in the majority of documentaries being self-funded and made with few prospects regarding consumption. A Law on Cinematography, which passed in 1961, imposed on all film theatres the obligation of projecting at least four indigenous short films per month, but was never put to practice.

A potential outlet for documentary work appeared in 1960, with the inauguration of the Thessaloniki Film Festival. Yet this type of exhibition (which was much later systematized via the shorts-only annual festival held in the town of Drama) did not guarantee an actual career. Certain directors thus resorted to projects designed for propaganda purposes, such as those promoting Greek tourism. Television's appearance, as well as the 1970 inauguration of the Greek Film Center (EKK), entailed further possibilities that will be addressed later.

One of the earliest important documentaries that appeared after the civil war was Daphni (1952) by the art historian Angelos Prokopiou (son of the aforementioned Yorgos), a film unrelated to the country's recent history, albeit of special interest, as it was the first documentary on Greek art. The film explored the mosaics of an eleventh-century Byzantine church near Athens, with an English commentary (translated from Prokopiou's text by Aldous Huxley) and a voice-over featuring Ethel Barrymore and Maurice Evans. It inaugurated a long line of documentaries that dealt with the indigenous cultural heritage and that proliferated in the following decades, notably via several works made especially for TV, from the 1970s onward.

Roussos Koundouros became the first Greek filmmaker exclusively occupied with the documentary mode. In 1953 he founded the Institute for Educative and Scientific Cinematography and went on to produce a multitude of films, many of which corresponded precisely to the 'educative' principle, insofar as they dealt with matters of medical and scientific information. Others explored the countryside-centered themes of previous filmmakers. His 1965 film Aluminio tis Ellados (Greek Aluminum), however, was a formally experimental documentary, focusing on an industrial topic and funded by the aluminum factory, the construction and function of which it captured. The film adopted an aesthetic attitude toward its topic by stressing the symmetry of the machines' geometrical shapes beyond any sentimental or social rhetoric and replacing commentary with atonal music. This formal treatment, which suppressed work conditions in favor of abstraction and highlighted a quasi-metaphysical transformation of the machinery into a kind of enigmatic sculpture, coupled an apparent lack of social concerns with a bold experimental tendency, foreign to the history of Greek documentary and actually reminiscent of the Soviet constructivist films of the 1920s.

Leon Loisios directed certain documentaries in 1959–61, addressing the everyday activities of islanders: Psarades kai Psaremata/Fishers and Fishing, I Zoi sti Mytilini/Life in Mytilene, and Lesbos. These films, which purported to readdress the familiar theme of 'provincial life', while rejecting the option of folklore, were produced and distributed by Loisios's own documentary company and later represented Greece in international festivals. Following John Grierson's dictum on documentary as a 'creative treatment of actuality', the films contained prewritten commentaries, albeit informed by experience and thereby aspiring toward a synthesis of aesthetic construction and factual authenticity.

In the early 1960s Loisios collaborated with Koundouros's institute, which at the time made certain state-funded films. By 1964–5, however, Loisios also attempted a series of political newsreels on behalf of EDA, Greece's major left-wing party at the time. That series, named Elliniki Zoi (Greek Life) and otherwise known as Ta Epikaira tis EDA (EDA's Newsreels), was not completed, but the surviving documentaries are of prime historical importance, given the era's political upheavals, which would soon culminate in the abolition of the parliamentary system by the junta. Loisios would reemerge in the 1980s via TV work, the series Panorama tou Aiona/Panorama of the Century (1982–6), an historical project based on old Greek newsreels.

The long-standing tradition of documentaries focusing on the Greek landscape and provincial life informs part of Vassilis Maros's work as well. This exceptionally important director, however, has also touched on urban themes, as in his first two documentaries, Uranoxystes/Skyscrapers and Rock and Roll stin Athina/Rock and Roll in Athens, both made in 1957. The second of these films in particular attempted a social approach of the rock and roll phenomenon and its early reception in Greece, while predating the first films of the nouvelle vague, which it largely resembled stylistically, while its semifictional, diegetic character presaged a tendency developed by later filmmakers, as we shall see.

Maros has expressed his debt to the modernist documentaries of the Dutch filmmaker Joris Ivens and to certain works of the British (Griersonian) school. These influences may illuminate his simultaneously social and lyrical tendencies. The latter are mostly apparent in his films of ethnographic aspirations, such as Hydra (1958), Kalymnos, to Nisi ton Sfouggaradon/Kalymnos, the Island of Sponge-fishers (1963), Pascha sto Agio Oros/Easter on the Holy Mount (1966), Sina: Enas Theos, Treis Prophites/Sina: One God, Three Prophets (1968), Criti kai Neoellines Poietes/Crete and Modern Greek Poets (1978), and Meteora, oi Katakomves tou Ouranou/Meteora, the Sky's Catacombs (1992). Maros has also directed numerous portraits of painters, actors, and other public personalities.

Yet Maros's most important work is probably the diptych I Tragodia tou Aigaiou/The Tragedy of the Aegean (1961) and I Ellada xoris Kolones/Greece without Columns (1964). The former consisted of early newsreels capturing important moments of Greece's history between 1912 and 1945, which Maros synthesized into a seventy-five-minute narrative presenting the tumultuous fate of a small, war-torn, and manipulated country. The commentary used in the film was written by Angelos Prokopiou, the original material having been largely supplied via the archive of Prokopiou's father, Yorgos, whose films on the Asia Minor campaign have been previously mentioned. This montage of historical fragments was highly acclaimed, gaining prizes in various world festivals and later being transmitted by the BBC, NBC, and other international TV channels. The film's political aspects, however, resulted in its Greek release being almost jeopardized by state censorship because of its implicitly critical attitude toward the treatment of Greece by those world powers on whose side the country had been firmly placed after the Nazi occupation and the Left's defeat in the civil war.

Greece Without Columns (the title of which may as well be cited in English, given that it was a BBC production, not projected in Greece until 1995) was in its way a sequel to the earlier film, albeit with a crucial difference. Rather than a montage of preexisting material, this was an original work of social observation, free of the limitations imposed by censorship and addressing in a pioneering mode several crucial problems of contemporary Greece, such as poverty and unemployment and its side effects, forcibly felt in the 1960s (movement toward the urban centers, bureaucracy, and mass immigration). The film used a kind of poetic irony in its critical treatment of the topic, whereby an impeccably thought out, quasi-musical editing expressed the rhythms of a troubled social body. Here, as elsewhere, Maros displayed a directorial clarity of purpose, partly obtained via his long previous experience (as a maker of newsreels) vis-à-vis the treatment of immediate reality, yet also involving a technical and formal sophistication in addressing the inner, perhaps hidden, side of this same reality. Maros's method was thus a combination of the aleatory and the preplanned, in the sense that his abstract principles preclude any resort to facile spectacle, while allowing the registration of unpredicted factors occurring in the course of the filmmaking process.

The first female director of Greek documentary was Lila Kourkoulakou, who, having first appeared in the late 1950s with fiction features, went on to direct a number of works on historical themes. Her documentary debut, Eleutherios Venizelos (1965), was a portrait of perhaps the single most important Greek political figure of the early twentieth century, based on newsreels from that era. Made in a period of great political instability, Kourkoulakou's film involved an underlying stance in favor of the challenged (and soon to be abolished) parliamentary democracy. In 1973 Kourkoulakou made another documentary, Dionysios Solomos, on the most celebrated poet of modern Greece and later went on to produce TV work.

Starting with Takis Canellopoulos's 1960 film Makedonikos Gamos/Macedonian Wedding, an innovative and experimental approach would mark the work of several young filmmakers, who made their first appearances in the course of that crucial decade. One could even speak of a clearly modernist tendency, echoing the situation brought about in poetry and the plastic arts by the 1930s generation. Thematically, nevertheless, documentary would continue to verge toward a twofold preexistent tradition, namely, the recording of ritualistic movement within a rural context. There was still a kind of hesitation on behalf of Greek filmmakers toward the complexity of the urban landscape, although the popular districts of cities were filmed with considerably greater ease, albeit seen as metaphors-cum-transformations of village life. Given that such areas, populated by the more destitute portion of the new urban crowd, were themselves gradually transformed by the struggles of their inhabitants, however, these films are situated at a crucial position regarding the documentation of the struggles in their successive stages.

The problem nevertheless remains as to the reasons for which this emphatic preference for rural themes continued to be apparent, as much in the choices of certain documentary makers whose works may be said to promote both research and experimentation, as in those of others, who seem more academic and unquestioning in their approaches. One possible reason is the evocation, through the medium of documentary, of the 'Greek-ness' issue, an ideological factor that has marred many discussions of the aforementioned 1930s generation (whose modernist elements are often interpreted in tandem with the 'ethnocentric' inclinations of some of its representatives).

At the same time, the survival of ancient, ritualistic forms of collective behavior in the context of agricultural production was open to study, entailing as it did the individual's harmonic incorporation into its particular society, thereby determining (up to a point, as we shall see) the actual character and function of the said society. Herein lies the value of certain ethnographic films by Yorgos Zervoulakos and Nestoras Matsas.

Another factor that may account for Greek filmmakers' reluctance vis-à-vis urban themes is the nature of the Greek urban landscape itself. Rather than being at once an emblem of the industrial revolution and a token of high modernity, thereby encouraging a treatment analogous to that adopted in numerous classic Western European documentaries (but also in Soviet films, such as Dziga Vertov's Man with the Movie Camera), the Greek city is a chaotic, arbitrarily structured space, in the context of which those revolutionary developments that shaped modernity are late imports rather than organically evolved features. At the same time, Greece's 'modernization' has tended to destroy or obscure the available evidence of the urban centers' historical past.

Takis Canellopoulos, on the other hand, had stressed the survival of the ritual in his debut, Makedonikos Gamos. By capturing the ancient wedding customs of a Macedonian village, a process of initiation whereby the newlyweds are accepted into the adult world, but also a reaffirmation of the community in its collective and circular function, Canellopoulos internalized in the very filmic form the depersonalized nature of social myth. The role of commentary was assumed by folksong, and the recording of the events evaded all intellectualization by its extreme concision and literalness. At the same time, the processes of production (the ritualistic preparation of the wedding banquet) were seen to attain a religious-cum-magical character via their incorporation into an organic whole, whereby myth and social life seemed inextricably linked. This line of documentary would find an echo in the work of another director, Takis Hatzopoulos, who made films such as Prespes (1966) and Gynaikokratia/Women's Rule (1969), which recaptured the theme of the Macedonian landscape and of the customs surviving therein.

In Apostolos Kryonas's 1973 documentary Itan Mera Giortis/It Was a Feast Day, a film thematically similar to Makedonikos Gamos, the viewer faces a countryside that has suffered the devastation effected in the course of the 1960s by its population's move toward the cities and the gradual abandonment of the local landscape and architecture to decay. Here, too, the 'feast' ritual was seen to survive, albeit this time in spite of the factors that challenge a no longer self-evident community. Kryonas (who, like Hatzopoulos, served his apprenticeship as an assistant of Canellopoulos) also directed the lyrical Anemoi/Winds (1967), as well as Entos ton Teihon/Within Walls (1977), a film that dealt boldly with the custom of circumcision as celebrated by the Muslim minority of Didymoteicho, the town closest to the Greco–Turkish northern border.

Another example of a countryside-set documentary, also made in the midst of the junta, which registers this change in the organic experience of the ritual, while being radically innovative in form, is O Thiraikos Orthros/The Matins of Thera (1968) by Costas Sfikas and Stauros Tornes. Focusing on the island of Santorini, the film presented a traditional community alienated by tourism, industrial production, and the exploitation of crops. Here, the ritualistic life of an agricultural society disappeared in the maddening rhythm of sounds and images, wholly deprived of commentary. The form, at once elliptic and dynamic, attained the precision of an essay.

Among the earliest examples of urban documentaries made in the 1960s by younger filmmakers, one may single out those testifying to specific sociopolitical problems of the era such as Ekato Ores tou Mai/One Hundred Hours in May (1963) by Dimos Theos and Fotos Lambrinos. This film deals with the recent assassination of Grigoris Lambrakis, an EDA MP (an event that would later inspire Costa-Gavras' semi-fictional French feature Z). Gramma apo to Charleroi/Letter from Charleroi (1965) by Lambros Liaropoulos dealt with mass immigration, describing the personal lives of Greek coal miners in Belgium. The same overall topic was addressed by Mily Giannakaki's Achilleas (1965), describing immigrants in France, and in Alexis Grivas's 750000 (1965), set in Germany. These three filmmakers were the first to produce, almost concurrently, films on this burning issue, while maintaining a modernist attitude in their treatments. On an even more experimental level, Theodoros Adamopoulos' almost surrealistic I Roda/The Wheel (1964) focused on bizarre aspects of urban reality, with a tone of sarcastic, rather cynical humor, regarding the city's decay following a wheel's revolutions.

Also of note is Gazi/Gas (1967) by Dimitris Stavrakas, a film on the life of workers in a gas factory, with special emphasis on their visible alienation vis-à-vis the production procedures. In total contrast both to Koundouros's Aluminio tis Ellados (in which the industrial functions were subjected to an aesthetic/abstract treatment) and to Maros and Loisios's ethnographic films on island life (where the community was seen to participate in the double ritual of life's cycle and the work process), Stavrakas's documentary at once pointed out the human factor involved in industrial production and implied the transgression of ritualistic integration (as a mythic notion that had here ceased to function) in favor of class solidarity, apparently the sole potential token of community in the context of modern work relations.

A tendency to recapture Greek history in tandem with its contemporary repercussions was evident in two documentaries by Lakis Papastathis. Periptoseis tou Ochi/Instances of 'No' (1965), a montage of photographs, drawings, and comments from the World War II era, made in collaboration with Dimitris Augerinos, was complemented by Papastathis's 1972 film Grammata apo tin Ameriki/Letters from America, wherein the same method was used to address the first wave of Greek immigration to the United States in the early years of the twentieth century. Apart from the innovative technique of construction used in these films, Papastathis also adopted a semi-fictional approach, harking back to Maros' Rock and Roll stin Athina, but also apparent in Liaropoulos' Gramma apo to Charleroi. He incorporated documentary evidence into a loose diegetic context by framing the nonfictional aspect within an elementary fictional 'story'. This tendency, the continuation of which may be detected in such recent films as O Dromos pros ti Dysi/The Way West, also incorporated documentary footage into essentially fictional films, an example of which is the film made by Papastathis in collaboration with Avgerinos, Odos Ermou 28/28 Ermou Street (1968).

Finally, with regard to the documentary makers who made their early appearances in the early 1960s let us also mention the work supervised by Roviros Manthoulis in collaboration with Fotis Mesthenaios and Heraklis Papadakis. Between 1958 and 1965, this group made a number of films, either state-funded or in collaboration with Koundouros's institute such as Acropolis ton Athinon/Acropolis of Athens, Leukada, to Nisi ton Poieton/Leukada, the Poets' Island, Prassino Chryssafi/Green Gold, and Anthropoi kai Theoi/Men and Gods, mostly involving a highly aesthetic treatment of the Greek landscape, with particular emphasis on classical monuments. Manthoulis, also a notable director of fiction features, went into self-exile in France after the colonels' coup d'état, and went on to produce some important documentary work there.

In the course of the seven-year junta, a great deal of material regarding social struggle was filmed clandestinely by certain filmmakers of the younger generation, such as Pantelis Voulgaris and Costas Zirinis. These documents were used after the reinstatement of the parliamentary system in the production of politically engaged works. The latter current, a predictable development given the circumstances, gave rise to numerous films, some of which were even projected commercially as features in the years that followed. These dealt with the regime's rise and fall, its consequences and the experience of its victims, including footage from that period and from its direct aftermath, as well as interviews, filmed extracts from the colonels' trial, and related forms of evidence.

Of particular note are Martyries/Testaments (1975) by Nikos Kavoukidis, Ellas Ellinon Christianon/Greece of Greek Christians (1976) by Diagoras Chronopoulos, Megara (1974) by Yorgos Tsemberopoulos, and the collective work Agonas/Struggle (1975), a politically engaged montage of filmed events by a group of six filmmakers. Meanwhile, the almost four-hour-long film Parastasi gia ena Rolo/Performance for a Role (1978) by Dionysis Grigoratos was an experiment in historical documentary that used newsreels footage to address Greece's recent history within the wider context of the country's positioning vis-à-vis the international events of the twentieth century and its function within the geopolitical developments of the period.

Otherwise, the general thematic tendencies apparent in the first post-1974 efforts of Greek documentary may be roughly divided into the following main categories, with several overlaps and variants: first, a number of films that attempted to extend geographically the ethnographic aspirations of earlier works and second, an increasing presence of social and political issues within a spatial and thematic framework that also acknowledged and developed that of the pioneering works made in the 1960s. Of prime (tone-setting) importance in this context were the documentaries of Dimitris Maurikios and Lefteris Xanthopoulos.

Maurikios made his first appearance with Polemonta (1975), a feature-length film on the surviving Greek-speaking community of South Italy. The film depicted the harsh realities of their agricultural life, which transcend ethnic boundaries, as well as their cultural and linguistic suspension between a fading if ancient tradition and their problematic integration into the specificities of time and place. An underlying problem on the meaning of 'Greek-ness', as implied by the survival of rituals and challenged by historical change and geographic diversity, echoes the concerns of the earlier ethnographic films addressed previously. The film created a sensation at the Thessaloniki Film Festival, but was never projected commercially.

Maurikios went on to make a number of documentaries, including some important work for the national TV network (ERT)—the latter having evolved into the most prominent factor in matters of documentary production and exhibition after the watershed year of 1974. Amongst the films that Maurikios directed for TV in the 1980s and 1990s, it is worth mentioning Oi Gefyres tou Ioniou/The Bridges of the Ionian Sea, a series of documentaries made in the early 1980s dealing with the correspondence exchanged between Greece and South Italy. Also worth noting is Mesogeiako Triptycho gia ta Pathi/ Mediterranean Triptych on the Passion (1986), a comparative study of the rituals pertaining to the Holy Passion in Spain, Italy, and Greece. Finally, Aenigma Est (1990) was a feature-length portrait of the Greek-born Italian painter Giorgio de Chirico that was even exhibited on the commercial circuit.

This last film captured de Chirico's cosmopolitanism along with the enigma of his work's and thought's origins, a theme that remained indirectly related to the persistent questioning of Greece's social/cultural past and present, vis-à-vis an increasing acknowledgment of 'global' concerns.

Lefteris Xanthopoulos first made his mark with a trilogy of films on the Greek diaspora, the first of which was funded by the community of immigrants whose everyday lives and testimonies it addressed. These films were Elliniki Koinotita Haidelbergis/Greek Community of Heidelberg (1976), O Yorgos apo ta Sotirianika/Yorgos from Sotirianika (1978), and Tourkovounia (1982). The films focused on both the living conditions of immigrant Greeks and the situation of the abandoned provinces that they had left behind (and, rarely, came back to). They also attempted to examine the reasons and consequences of immigration. The persistence and indeed flourishing of these themes attests to the long-term effects of the mass immigration first evoked in documentaries made in the 1960s. Xanthopoulos, also a director of fictional features on related topics, has since worked widely on TV. The 1970s documentary works of filmmakers such as Yorgos Antonopoulos and Yorgos Karypidis have moved along similar thematic lines.

Of the other documentary makers who appeared in that period, Takis Papayannidis has produced films that testify to a special sensibility, starting with Yorti sti Drapetsona/Feast in Drapetsona (1977), whereby a local feast was used as a pretext for an attempt to capture the history of a marginal urban district. Papayannidis's feature-length I Ilikia tis Thalassas/The Sea's Age (1978) developed this tendency by using the marine element (so obviously pertinent to various notions of 'Greek-ness') as a catalyst between myth and historical experience via the evocation of the major events that had shaped modern Greece in the course of past decades.

Of the filmmakers touching on urban themes, with a social-centered perspective, albeit deprived of a political stance or a standardized formal approach, Gaye Aggeli made two original works, the idiosyncratically structured and purposely fragmentary Monastiraki (1976) and the direct and precise in its rough material and perspective Thessaloniki 6.5 Richter (1976). With Karvouniarides/Coalmen (1977), Alinda Dimitriou created a plain-styled and convincing social portrait. Let us also mention the historical, essayistic in scope, documentaries of Yorgos Dizikirikis, such as Ellines Laikoi Zografoi/ Greek Folk Painters (1974).

Tasos Psarras, a politically minded filmmaker who has also directed several fiction features, made a number of documentary shorts in the 1970s, notably Mellele (1972), a film on the life of a gypsy community. Using methods of pointed immediacy, such as a handheld camera (not a common practice at the time) and interviews, Psarras provided a prototype for much of his later work in which the ethnographic or biographic perspective contained a latent political element in the shape of detectable social factors and processes. Psarras has worked extensively for TV from the early 1980s onward, and his documentaries touch on topics as diverse as the Greek communities of the former Soviet Union and the lives of celebrated Greek writers, albeit maintaining a consistency in their attempts to register and illuminate the underlying presence of the historical conditions framing the primary subject matter.

The first urban Greek documentary that had the country's capital as its sole topic, while attempting to address it in all its complexity, was made by Theo Angelopoulos, best known in Greece and abroad for his fiction features. Athena/Athens (1982), a made-for-TV work, was informed by a tendency, apparent in the early 1980s, toward an increasingly idiosyncratic type of documentary, touching on a set of specialized topics, whose treatment registered an emphatically structural and formal approach. This current, essayistic in scope, addressed reality in its elusive or chaotic aspects, abandoning the certainties of a granted common 'mythology', and thereby perhaps also signaling a move away from earlier 'rural' and 'ritualistic' themes. Thus, Angelopoulos's film had no precedent in its wandering, labyrinthine structure. The various contrasting layers of history (from archeological findings to architectural remnants bearing testament to stages in the development of modern Athens) captured a complex 'whole', whose ultimate meaning was suspended over a void, as evidenced by the absence of people and hence of indices regarding historical continuity and meaning.

A short while before Athena was released, Costas Vrettakos had finished his important documentary Stroma tis Katastrofis/Layer of Destruction (1980), which had been three years in the making. Here, the provincial setting entailed an approach somewhat similar in principle, if not in form, to that of Angelopoulos. The film's topic was the archeological search for an ancient town under a village, a town revealed but momentarily, before sinking into the waters of an artificial lake. Again, archeology was used at once as a link with the historical past and as a sign of temporal divergence underlying spatial contiguity.

Other directors have used the documentary mode in the last three decades, with notable results. Of the older names, Fotos Lambrinos (former collaborator of Dimos Theos) has made several interesting films, and Lakis Papastathis, having started with documentary, has continued to incorporate elements of that mode in his fictional works. Yannis Smaragdis's TV series Ide Polis elalisen/Thus Spoke the City (1990) revealed a new genre—a cinema deprived of fictional intrigue, rather in the form of an essay. Menelaos Karamaggiolis, with the feature-length Rom (1989), marks a search for new aesthetic principles, while addressing the topic of national definition, identity, and otherness, its focus being the relations between ethnic and religious minorities in Greece. This question is touched on in certain previous documentaries, as we have seen, albeit one that will become increasingly crucial in the 1990s and beyond.

Significant work has also been produced by filmmakers such as Eleni Alexandraki, Popi Alkouli, Nikos Anagnostopoulos, Soula Drakopoulou, Yannis Ekonomidis, Kleoni Flessa, Stauros Ioannou, Stavros Kaplanidis, Marios Karamanis, Despoina Karvela, Stathis Katsaros, Yannis Lambrou, Pandora Mouriki, Olga Panagopoulou, Antonis Papadopoulos, Maria Papaliou, Thanassis Rentzis, Yorgos Sifianos, Memi Spyratou, Eva Stefani, Minas Tatalidis, Stella Theodoraki, Yanna Triantafylli, Antonis Voyazos, Dimitris Yatzoutzakis, Layia Yourgou, and others.

Meanwhile, the problems of funding, distribution, and exhibition have never ceased plaguing Greek documentary, albeit not without significant improvements, reflecting the country's political situation and the increasing respectability film culture has attained from the viewpoint of official cultural institutions. The catalytic role played by national TV has already been mentioned. Yet while providing a solution in terms of funding, that institution's policy regarding the mode of production (given that from the early 1990s onward, recording on film has been replaced by video) all but precludes the works' consumption beyond the medium of TV, that is, their commercial exhibition and participation in international festivals. The Greek Film Center also evolved into a seminal funding source, albeit at a relatively late stage. However, the actual consumption of films not made specifically for TV transmission has remained an unsolved issue. So has the question of adjusting documentary to the demands of a commercially exploitable venture, given the prevalent (after the combined influences of TV production and age-old tradition) tendency to associate that filmic mode with the 'short' format.

After the inauguration, in 1978, of the aforementioned Shorts festival in the town of Drama (originated by the local film club, but now an international event sponsored by the Ministry of Culture, as well as by the European Community project Media, and involving a wider if brief distribution of prize-winning films), there has been a proliferation of fiction and nonfiction works alike, of which documentaries form a substantial and constantly increasing minority. To this there must be added the Athens festival, 'Cinema and Reality', which has been operating for the past twenty-seven years, and the Thessaloniki Documentary Festival, 'Images of the 21st Century', which started in 1999.

In recent years a few feature-length documentaries have been screened commercially with a considerable degree of success. Most notable in this respect was Agelastos Petra/ Mourning Stone (2001) by Filippos Koutsaftis, already a director of documentary shorts. The film, widely praised as an aesthetic achievement, was actually informed by several precedents in the history of Greek documentary, but was still original in its approach. It focused on Eleusis (a district universally known because of the Eleusinian mysteries) by juxtaposing the still-enigmatic remnants of antiquity with views of contemporary life, thereby revisiting the earlier themes of landscape and the problematic relation of modern Greek society with ancient ritualistic traditions.

Another documentary that met with warm public reception was Stelios Haralambopoulos' Yorgos Seferis—Imerologia Katastromatos/ Yorgos Seferis—Logbooks (2003), a film on the poet, diplomat, and Nobel Laureate Seferis, addressing its subject's relation both to the landscape and poetic tradition of Greece and to the political events that shaped the country's history in the past century. Finally, let us mention a feature film that may be classified as a semi-documentary, and that is also notable for touching on a topic peculiar to the past decade. Kyriakos Katzourakis's O Dromos Pros ti Dysi/ The Way West (2003) deals with the problems of illegal immigrants (a community created after the collapse of the Eastern bloc and the mass immigration to Greece from the early 1990s onward), focusing in particular on the female experience and mixing fictional representation with real-life documentation. All these films were either produced or coproduced by the Greek Film Center; whether their success will mean the beginning of a new era for Greek documentary, perhaps entailing a degree of involvement on the part of private producers remains, of course, to be proven.

Greek documentary has registered in various (and still evolving) ways the country's history over the course of the past century, as well as its collective or contrasting concerns regarding self-definition and relations to international processes. The discernible themes, practices, and aesthetic and ideological attitudes reflect a wider network of discourses operating parallel to cinematic production. The open question is the films' international potential—a question pertaining to a combination of the country's geopolitical situation and the extent to which the situation (and/or its images and representations) affects the forms and perspectives of works.

ANDREAS PAGOULATOS AND NIKOS STABAKIS

Further reading

Dimitriou, Alinda, *Lexiko Ellinikon Tainion Mikrou Mikous 1939–92* (Dictionary of Greek Short Films 1939–92), Athens: Kastaniotis, 1993.

Mitropoulou, Aglaia, *Ellinikos Kinimatografos* (Greek Cinema), Athens, private publication, 1980.

n.a., *Praktika B⁰ Synantisis gia to Documentaire, Drama 13–15 Maiou 1994* (Minutes of the B⁰ Conference on Documentary, Drama 13–15 May 1994), Drama: Ekdosi tou Festival Tainion Mikrou Mikous Dramas kai tou *Dimou Dramas* (The Drama Festival of Short Films and by the Municipality of Drama), 1994.

Pagoulatos, Andreas, 'Regards sur le Documentaire Grec', in Michel Dimopoulos (ed.), *Le Cinéma Grec*, Paris: Cinéma Pluriel (Centre Georges Pompidou), 1995.

Pagoulatos, Andreas and Kontogeorgi, Eleni, *Praktika A⁰ Synantisis gia to Documentaire, Drama 2–4 Apriliou 1993* (Minutes of the A⁰ Conference on Documentary, Drama 2–4 April 1993) Drama: Ekdosi tou Fetival Tainion Mikrou Mikous Dramas kai tou Dimou Dramas (The Drama Festival of Short Films and the Municipality of Drama), 1993.

Pagoulatos, Andreas and Spiliopoulos, Vassilis, 'Astiko kai Ypaithrio Topio sto Elliniko Documentaire' (Urban and Rural Landscape in Greek Documentary), *Utopia* 47, November–December 2001: 45–53.

Soldatos, Yannis, *Istoria tou Ellinikou Kinimatografou/ History of Greek Cinema*, Athens: Aigokeros, 1982.

Greene, Felix

Felix Greene, filmmaker, journalist, and author, played a crucial role in opening the tightly closed doors of Asian society to Western eyes. As a filmmaker he sought to expose and publicize the realities of life found within the Communist world. Seeing himself as a counterbalance between the prevailing assumptions he believed were often deliberately engendered by Western governments, Greene sought to ease the Western fear of Communism through the documentation of not the Communist government, but the people beneath the governmental shroud.

The driving catalyst of Greene's documentary films formed during his first visit to China in 1957. Armed with Western misapprehensions common to the era, Greene began his Communist venture prepared to see a vast expanse of squalor, disease, and impoverishment, and although those conditions did exist in varying degrees, he did not find a nation of embittered people broken by the rigid coercions of a police state. Instead, he found a buoyancy in the people, an optimism, a tangible vitality that directly opposed the brutalized peasant/ oppressive militant binary nurtured within the Western press.

Having walked among, spoken to, and dined with the people of China, Greene found himself bewildered at the contradiction his China experience suggested of his cultural conditioning. His films depict this tension through his continued commitment to focus not on the negatives to be found within a Communist-ruled country, but on the universality of humanity. Armed with a crew of three—himself as photographer, his wife Elena as sound technician, and his daughter Ann as production assistant—Greene departed with films that allowed Western audiences to view their political enemy completing the simple tasks of daily life during a time in history when Chinese imports did not exist. His universality in presenting the Chinese to the West pioneered new views on old preconceptions that aided the eventual modification of both general and official attitudes toward China culminating in the 1970s with President Nixon's dramatic reversal of his own anti-China policies, as well as his historic visit to China.

Greene's first visit to China, moreover, awakened an awareness in the filmmaker that China was on the cusp of a momentous social and industrial explosion that was being ignored by the West. Granted, mutual mistrust existed between the Western nations (primarily America and England) and China, but the tragic outcome resulting in a virtual breakdown in communications would only serve to further hinder what he viewed to be a desperate situation. To Greene, this Communist country did not simply encapsulate one-fourth of the world's population; it contained the most relevant story in the world, one he was determined to report despite bureaucratic tangles or Western criticism.

Although Greene's concept of documentary film envisaged the role that documentary would play in providing a medium of communication between two states with vastly contrasting political ideologies, he found hardship both in the making of his documentaries and in bringing them to the American public. In China, authorities tried to dictate the subjects and scenes depicted within his films, and government 'chaperones' accompanied Greene during filming, often exposing film to the sunlight to destroy the images that might reach Western viewers. In the West, Greene reached an impasse when authorities refused to grant him a license to show the film China in Carnegie Hall, which he had rented at his own expense. The legal maneuvering that followed resulted in a remarkable sixteen-week run for the documentary. American audiences filled the theater seven times a day eager for a glimpse into a world previously banned for reasons of national security and found, as Greene did, an enemy with the same basic needs, wants, and joys that combated the same basic struggles. By putting a face to Communism through documentary, Greene humanized political difference.

Although Greene used the documentary as a tool to mediate two diverse cultures, critics charge that his writings, all of which hold sociopolitical themes, served only to further his anticapitalism beliefs. The Enemy: What Every American Should Know About Imperialism, written in 1970, reads as a sharp polemic. Following a lucid and well-documented critique of imperialism, Greene explains how imperialism distorts our thinking, and why—unless the people revolt against it—imperialism will destroy all that is best in humanity and society. Critics assailed the anti-American implications of the book, yet Greene's self-appointed role as apologist for modern China provided him with a 'voice' in the Western world. He discovered in the Vietnam War a new plight needing public exposure. His films and writing, however contrary to the American ideology of the time, acted as seeds sown for the emerging peace movement that was to sweep the country. Again, the eyes of the American people were opened to a view beyond the 'good propaganda' generated by the government's war machine, and again, the documentary medium served to awaken debate.

CHRISTINE MARIE HILGER

See also: China!

Biography

Born in Berkhamsted, England on May 21, 1909. Graduated from Sidcot School and attended the University of Cambridge for two years. 1931–3 served the office of the Prime Minister doing political work. 1932–40 senior official in London and in United States for the BBC. 1940–78 freelance filmmaker, radio and television writer, and lecturer on international affairs. Died June 15, 1985.

Selected films

1963 China!: director, producer
1967 Inside North Vietnam: director, producer
1968 Cuba Va!: director, producer
1972 One Man's China: director, producer
1977 Tibet: director, producer

Further reading

Aiken, Ian, *Film and Reform*, London: Routledge, 1990.

——*The Documentary Film Movement: An Anthology*, Edinburgh: Edinburgh University Press, 1998.

Barnouw, Erik, *Documentary: A History of the Non-fiction Film*, New York: Oxford University Press, 1983.

Corner, John, *Documentary and the Mass Media*, London: Arnold, 1986.

Greene, Felix, *Awakened China*, New York: Doubleday, 1961.

——*A Curtain of Ignorance*, New York: Doubleday, 1964.

——*Vietnam! Vietnam!*, Palo Alto, CA: Fulton Publishing Co., 1966.

——*The Enemy: What Every American Should Know About Imperialism*, New York: Vintage, 1970.

Rotha, Paul, *Documentary Diary*, New York: Hill and Wang, 1973.

Grierson, John

John Grierson, the founder of the British documentary film movement, played a pivotal role in the development of British film culture during the 1930s and 1940s. Grierson's theory of documentary film was fashioned against the backdrop of World War I, economic recession, and the build-up to war during the 1930s, and his ideas were closely linked to the events and intellectual terrain of the inter-war period. During this time conservative political convictions on the value of laissez-faire free enterprise and limited state intervention in the economy dominated social and political discourse within Great Britain. From 1931 to 1939, however, various strands of intellectual opinion gradually converged to form an emergent social democratic consensus, which eventually achieved political ascendancy in 1945 with the formation of the first postwar Labour government. It is this configuration of political and cultural discourse, designated by its champions as a 'middle way' between unfettered capitalism and a nationalizing state socialism with which the documentary film movement, and Grierson in particular, must be associated, and Grierson is best understood as a social-democratic, corporatist reformist, rather than a socialist, or proto-Marxist thinker.

Grierson's theory of documentary film was conceived against a dual context of national and international instability and the growth of social-democratic corporatist thought, and was premised on the belief that the documentary film could both play a vital role in preserving social stability and act as an effective medium of communication between the state and the public. Grierson's social democratic corporatist ideology, however, was also influenced by neo-Hegelian ideas, derived from philosophers such as F.H. Bradley and T.H. Green, which asserted the importance of the state and corporate institutions within national life. This influence led Grierson to the conviction that the needs of the individual must be subordinated to the requirements of corporate institutions and structures that possessed an intrinsic historical legitimacy and that guaranteed the unity and progress of society.

The origins of Grierson's conception of 'good totalitarianism', whereby the principal role of the documentary film was to promote an understanding of the essentially unified and interdependent character of society, rather than the transient, idiosyncratic conceits of individual filmmakers, can be located in this neo-Hegelian model of the corporate state (Aitken 1998). Similarly, and closely associated with this, is Grierson's conviction that the documentary filmmaker must be constrained by the 'degree of general sanction': the consensual ideological and ethical framework that 'imposes a clear limit upon the creative artist' (Aitken 1990). Such a formulation appears to rule out any fundamental criticism of the status quo. However, in a key distinction—again drawn from Bradley—that he drew between the agents and institutions of state, Grierson argued that, during the 1930s, the agents of state (the government and ruling class) had turned against the needs of the people and had subverted the institutions of state to promote sectional interest (Aitken 1990). This led Grierson to argue that the documentary film must both criticize the agents of state and represent the interests of the exploited working classes. Grierson's theory of documentary film, therefore, was motivated by a desire to reshape British society in closer accord with an ideal of ethical social cohesion and unity and was derived from the Hegelian ideas of the 'Absolute', and 'universal will'.

Grierson's theory of documentary film envisaged that documentary would play a role in providing a medium of communication between the state and the people. Although Grierson acknowledged that ideally this should be a two-way process, however, he paid little attention to the means by which the views of the people were to influence the actions of the state. As a consequence, Grierson's theory of documentary film implicitly endorses a hierarchical practice of social ideology production, in which social communication is passed down from a bureaucratic elite, via the documentary film, to the public. Similarly, and despite his belief that democratic representation was the principal means through which the agents of state were to be prevented from recasting a liberal corporate society into 'something else' (that is, totalitarianism), Grierson's conception of a society managed by mandarins and public relations experts can only be characterized as 'democratic' with some difficulty (Aitken 1990).

Although Grierson's theory of documentary film was concerned to a considerable extent with the issue of the civic and social purposiveness of film, it was also centrally preoccupied with questions of aesthetic technique and judgment, and many of his ideas can be traced back to aesthetic theories that have their origins within the idealist philosophy of Kant, Hegel, Bradley, and others. Grierson's first systematic elaboration of his theory of documentary film appeared in a memorandum he prepared for his then employers, the Empire Marketing Board (EMB), in 1927. In the second part of this memorandum, 'English Cinema Production and the Naturalistic Tradition', Grierson postulated two different categories of film production, one consisting of films between seven and nine reels long, the other of films four reels long. The first of these categories was based on the theory of 'epic cinema', which Grierson had elaborated in America in the mid-1920s. Here, in addition to their usual preoccupation with matters of individual characterization and psychological motivation, commercial feature films would also contain representations of national social and political institutions and would demonstrate how individuals were indissolubly connected to such institutions within an overarching social totality.

Grierson initially developed his theory of epic cinema in response to a number of right-wing, anti-democratic theories that he encountered during the 1920s. In 1924 Grierson was awarded a Rockefeller scholarship to study the impact of immigration on the United States. When he arrived in the United States he came into contact with theorists who argued that restrictions should be placed on immigration, and that the voting franchise should be limited to members of the professional classes. Grierson rejected the disavowals of democracy then being promoted by figures such as Harold Lasswell and Walter Lippmann, however, and argued, instead, that film could be used to sustain democracy by providing the public with crucial social information.

Grierson's ambitious model of epic cinema, however, bore little relation to the limited budget and resources available to the EMB and, in the second part of his 1927 memorandum, he suggested the development of a form of cinema more appropriate to such circumstances. This second category of film production would consist of shorter films, the principal objective of which would be to represent social interconnection in both primitive cultures and modern industrial society. Grierson believed that these films would mark a 'new phase' in cinema production, and that, in them, the visual features of often prosaic, everyday subject matter would be orchestrated into expressive cinematic sequences through the sophisticated use of montage editing and visual composition (Aitken 1998). Such an approach would necessarily involve the abandonment of rudimentary documentary naturalism, and many of the processes of narrative construction common to the commercial feature film, as well as the adoption of more modernist stylistic techniques.

Although this original model of the Griersonian documentary emphasized modernist, formative editing technique, the actuality content of the documentary image also remained an important factor for Grierson. This is well illustrated by a key distinction that he drew between the 'real' and the 'actual'. Writing about Drifters shortly after it was premiered, Grierson argued that the empirical content (the actual) of the film's documentary images was organized so as to express general truths (the real) that existed at a level of abstraction beyond the empirical, and that could not, therefore, be directly represented (Aitken 1990). Grierson's definition of the real is not fully theorized, but was essentially derived from the Hegelian notion of Zeitgeist, or 'spirit of the age'. From this Grierson arrived at a conception of the real that consisted of those general determining factors and predispositions specific to a particular historical stage in the development of human society, and argued that documentary imagery should be so organized as to express this underlying reality. Grierson's first definition of documentary film, therefore, was based on the revelation of the real through the manipulation of documentary footage by formative editing techniques.

Although Grierson believed that the principal objective of the documentary film was to represent the 'real', he also argued that the documentary image was able to signify that underlying reality more profoundly than the image produced within the artificial environment of the film studio because it transcribed the 'phenomenological surface of reality', and because, for Grierson, an existential relationship existed between the phenomenal world (the actual) and the real (Aitken 1998). The origin of Grierson's conceptualization of the relationship between the empirical image of reality and underlying, more abstract realities can be traced back to his influence by Kantian aesthetics. However, it can also be related to models of film theory that emerged in Europe during the 1920s and 1930s, and, in particular, to the ideas of the Hungarian Marxist theorist Béla Balázs.

Grierson's early theory of documentary film consisted of three principal elements: (1) a concern with the content and expressive richness of the actuality image; (2) a concern with the interpretive potential of editing; and (3) a concern with the representation of social relationships. All of these can be found in his early film theory and in his first and perhaps only film as a director: Drifters (1929). Drifters reveals the influence of idealist aesthetics in its elevation of symbolic expression over more rudimentary forms of naturalistic representation and is replete with impressionistic imagery of natural forces and phenomena. Here, Grierson uses symbolic expression to depict the 'real' through the 'actual', and to imply the existence of an underlying unity (the real), which bonds the labour of fishermen to a surrounding natural order. Later in the film this concern with the depiction of wholeness is also extended to include representations of commercial and technological forces within a filmic 'Absolute'. The underlying idealist imperative within Drifters led to a prioritization of essence over appearance, and Grierson spoke of 'exalting' each sequence in the film and 'attaching splendour' to the film as a whole (Aitken 1990). One consequence of this stance is that Drifters makes extensive use of metaphor, allegory, and impressionistic suggestion. Drifters can best be defined (as Grierson himself did in 1932) as an 'imagist' film, influenced by the formalist imperatives of avant-garde film theory and by the philosophical idealist distinction between the real and the phenomenal (Hardy 1979). Drifters was to be Grierson's only major film as a director, however, and, after 1930 he put his energies into the role of producer, rather than director. Nevertheless, the 'imagist' approach embodied in Drifters can be observed in a number of important films made by the documentary movement between 1929 and 1936, including The Song of Ceylon (Wright, 1934), Granton Trawler (Grierson and others, 1934), Coal Face (Cavalcanti and others, 1935), and Night Mail (Wright, Watt, Cavalcanti, and others, 1936).

After 1936 the poetic montage style of films such as Drifters and The Song of Ceylon gradually gave way to a more didactic, journalistic style, and the earlier concern with philosophical aesthetics gave way to a discourse grounded in issues of propaganda and civic education. The preoccupations and concerns of this later period are most clearly expressed in *Grierson on Documentary*, the collection of Grierson's essays first published by his official biographer, H. Forsyth Hardy, in 1946. In 'The Documentary Idea: 1942', the essay within this collection that embodies Grierson's later position on the documentary film most uncompromisingly, he argues that the documentary film movement was an 'anti-aesthetic movement', and that what was now required was instrumental filmmaking that would abandon depictions of the 'beautiful' and that would play a more directive role in processes of social persuasion (Hardy 1979). Between 1939 and 1945 Grierson was employed as the first Film Commissioner of the National Film Board of Canada and was in charge of the production of documentary series such as The World in Action and Canada Carries On. At the National Film Board he took every opportunity to champion the more didactic, instrumental style adopted by such films; in 'The Documentary Idea: 1942' and elsewhere he criticized the more 'aesthetic' work of earlier colleagues such as Alberto Cavalcanti and Humphrey Jennings.

It is arguable that not only the 1942 essay, but most of Grierson's writings of the war period should be considered as uncharacteristic of his true position, and as a temporary and strategic response to the pressing demands of the time. Such an argument is, however, undermined by the fact that what is particularly striking about Grierson is that his general ideology remained largely unchanged from the 1920s to the 1970s. This unusual degree of continuity makes it unlikely that any sort of epistemological shift occurred during the war period and demonstrates the importance of understanding the ideological continuity that underlay Grierson's pre- and post-1936 positions on the relationship between the aesthetic and the sociological.

The radical change of emphasis in Grierson's ideas from the pre- to the post-1936 period was influenced by the increasing emphasis he gave to authoritarian tendencies that were always implicit in his ideology, but that before 1936 were dialectically linked with more progressive tendencies. This change of emphasis can also be explained in terms of a shift from a concern with the phenomenological naturalism of the image to a more directive stance always implicit in Grierson's notion of the creative interpretation of reality. In the later period this more directive approach became increasingly allied to the cardinal objective of representing unified social relationships, while the earlier aesthetic of the image was increasingly discarded.

There is evidence to suggest, however, that towards the end of his life Grierson returned to his earlier concerns and increasingly emphasized the importance of the aesthetic within documentary. In I Remember, I Remember, the film he made for BBC TV in 1970, he described documentary almost entirely in terms of its artistic qualities and abandoned the instrumental discourse that characterized his middle period. This indicates that the dialectical tension between the aesthetic and the sociological, a tension always implicit in his ideology and one that was skewed decisively in one direction during the 1937–67 period, had reverted once again to the kind of balance that had characterized the 1929–36 period.

IAN AITKEN

See also: BBC: The Voice of Britain; Cavalcanti, Alberto; Coal Face, Drifters; Granton Trawler; Housing Problems; Industrial Britain; Jackson, Pat; Jennings, Humphrey; Night Mail; Song of Ceylon, The; Taylor, John; Wright, Basil

Biography

Born near Stirling, Scotland, April 26, 1898. Graduated from Glasgow University, reading literature and philosophy, in 1923. Served in the naval minesweeping service during World War I. Awarded a Laura Spellman Rockefeller scholarship to study the impact of immigration on the United States, 1924–7. Assistant Films Officer at the Empire Marketing Board, 1927–33. Film Officer at the GPO, 1934–6. Established Film Centre and other independent documentary film production units 1936–9. First Film Commissioner of the National Film Board of Canada, 1939–45. Appointed Head of Information at UNESCO, 1946. Controller, Film, at the Central Office of Information, 1948–50. Joint head of Group 3, a production arm of the National Film Finance Corporation, 1951–5. Presented the Scottish Television Programme This Wonderful World, 1957–67. Died in Bath, February 19, 1972.

Selected films

1929 Drifters: director, writer
1931 The Country Comes to Town (Wright): producer
1931 Industrial Britain (Flaherty): producer, coeditor
1933 Cargo from Jamaica (Wright): producer
1933 Windmill in Barbados (Wright): producer

1934 Granton Trawler: codirector, producer, photographer
1934 Pett and Pott (Cavalcanti): producer
1934 The Song of Ceylon (Wright): producer, cowriter
1936 Night Mail (Wright, Watt, Cavalcanti and others): producer, cowriter
1938 The Face of Scotland (Wright): producer

Further reading

Aitken, Ian, *Film and Reform*, London: Routledge, 1990.

——*The Documentary Film Movement: An Anthology*, Edinburgh: Edinburgh University Press, 1998.

——*Alberto Cavalcanti: Realism, Surrealism and National Cinemas*, London: Flicks, 2000.

——*European Film Theory and Cinema: A Critical Introduction*, Edinburgh: Edinburgh University Press, 2001.

Beveridge, James, *John Grierson: Film Master*, London: Macmillan, 1979.

Ellis, Jack C., *John Grierson*, Carbondale, IL: Southern Illinois University Press, 2000.

Evans, Gary, *John Grierson and the National Film Board*, Toronto: University of Toronto Press, 1986.

Grierson, John, *Grierson on Documentary*, ed. Forsyth Hardy, London: Collins, 1946 (revised edn, London: Faber, 1966; abridged edn, Faber, 1979).

——*Grierson on the Movies*, ed. Forsyth Hardy, London: Faber, 1981.

Hardy, Forsyth, *John Grierson: A Documentary Biography*, London: Faber, 1979.

Rotha, Paul, *Documentary Diary*, London: Secker and Warburg, and New York: Hill and Wang, 1973.

Sussex, Elizabeth, *The Rise and Fall of British Documentary*, Berkeley, CA: University of California Press, 1975.

Swann, Paul, *The British Documentary Film Movement*, Cambridge: Cambridge University Press, 1989.

Grigsby, Michael

Michael Grigsby is an important figure in British documentary, having ploughed a doggedly individual path over the last forty years. Grigsby has worked almost exclusively within television and has managed to retain his commitment to serious documentary work despite the increased commercial restrictions that have come to characterise television during the 1990s. Grigsby's ability to sustain an individual voice over so many years within television can be likened to figures such as Roger Graef and Denis Mitchell. In a sense, Grigsby is a figure who straddles the approaches of these two figures: Graef's rigorous vérité style is evident in some of Grigsby's work, while Mitchell's attempts to poeticise the margins of everyday life is also apparent in many films he has made.

Although Grigsby's work is not at all homogeneous and does vary in style, it is marked by a number of recurring themes and stylistic approaches. The most striking of these, and the one that Grigsby himself would stress, is his dedication to documenting the working classes and other voices that are usually denied access to the media. He thinks that it is important to give the 'voiceless' a voice and to allow the working- and under-classes a chance to speak on their own terms, rather than have another class speak for them.

Grigsby joined Granada as a trainee cameraman after leaving school, a post he found unsatisfactory because it was studio-based. In his spare time, with friends, he formed a filmmaking group, Unit Five Seven. After purchasing a Bolex camera, they managed to shoot Enginemen (1959), a documentary about the transition from steam to diesel on the railways. The film was shot over two years in spare time and was eventually finished after Lindsay Anderson and Karel Reisz saw rushes and managed to secure money from the British Film Institute (BFI) Experimental Film Fund to complete the film. A romantic documentary, the film was very much in the tradition of the more poetic films made within the British Documentary Film Movement. It was actually shown on the final Free Cinema programme at the National Film Theatre on March 22, 1959.

Grigsby made one more film with Unit Five Seven, Tomorrow's Saturday (1962), before the group disbanded. He then began to make a name for himself within television. At Granada he directed the Inside series (1965), which examined prison life. Grigsby was still unhappy with his lack of freedom, however, and at this point managed to persuade Granda Chairman Denis Forman to allow him to make a film on his own terms. The result was Deckie Learner (1965), another film about rail workers, which was nominated for a British Film Academy Award. Grigsby argues that this was his first 'proper' television excursion because it was conceived as a film, rather than a piece of television journalism. Grigsby's connection to the cinematic documentary school is betrayed in such comments; while his work is investigative, he criticises many television documentaries because they tell stories with words and are too journalistic. For Grigsby, films must tell stories with images; whilst this does not mean that the soundtrack is of no importance, it does mean that the selection and composition of images should be carefully thought out.

Grigsby's approach to documentary filmmaking is rather different from that of American direct cinema, although he started to make television films when the influence of that style was becoming marked. His methods are not totally removed from such an approach. His dedication to filming on location, his tendency to shoot using only available light, and his belief in an image-driven form of documentary are similar to methods associated with direct cinema. Yet, there are two major areas where Grigsby diverts from such filmmakers. First, he does not claim any position of 'objectivity' within his films. He believes films must be made from a specific viewpoint, his being 'marginal' interventions within the dominant power structures. Second, he thinks that the form of a documentary should be carefully planned out, so that methods 'appropriate' to the subject matter at hand are deployed.

Grigsby's commitment to allowing 'marginal' figures to speak runs through his work. A Life Apart (1973) and A Life Underground (1974) expose the isolation of trawlers and miners, respectively. They examine the fragmentation of industrial communities by unlocking the thoughts of community members and, alternately, focusing on their work. The Silent War (1990) uncovers the fear and resentment of communities in Belfast living with sectarian violence and the continual presence of the British army. In Lockerbie—A Night Remembered (1998), he looks at the effects of the Lockerbie plane crash of 1988 on the community, revealing how the lives of its residents were turned upside down.

The formal methods that Grigsby used are not so consistent as his themes, but two main approaches mark his work. The first is a rather minimal approach, in which careful, long, static takes of communities predominate. This formal approach can be found in films such as A Life Apart and Eskimos of Pond Inlet (1976, part of the Disappearing World series), the latter depicting the life of an Eskimo community whose traditions have been disrupted by growing consumerism. The second main approach evident in Grigsby's work is a more poetic, montage-based aesthetic. Probably the most impressive example of this style can be found in Living on the Edge (1986), an ambitious, collage-style film that cuts between historical moments and uses archive footage to build up a rich, intertextual picture of lost hope. The film is undoubtedly inspired by Humphrey Jennings, even pictorially 'quoting' Listen to Britain (1942) in one sequence. Jennings' depictions of national unity are replaced, however, with a more pessimistic portrait of social fragmentation. These two approaches certainly do not exhaust Grigsby's formal palette, and he has occasionally worked outside of them, as with the documentary-drama SS Lusitania (1967). Yet much of his work can be seen to fall somewhere between the two extremes already outlined.

Grigsby has been criticised in some quarters; his obsession with troubled communities, for instance, has been seen as nostalgic. This nostalgic tendency is not offset by his formal approach, which refuses to supply easy answers to the problems depicted (Grigsby steers clear of using 'objective' narration). Grigsby claims that this would be an arrogant manoeuvre. Whether or not one agrees with him on this issue, it cannot be denied that his body of work is impressive and consistent, and is welcome in that he continually airs the views of those who are often left unheard, thus adding a different dimension to events often covered very differently (or not at all) in media journalism.

JAMIE SEXTON

See also: Graef, Roger; Listen to Britain; Mitchell, Denis

Biography

Born in Reading, 1937. Educated at Abingdon school. Trained as cameraman at Granada after leaving University. Set up Unit Five Seven in 1957. From 1956 freelance producer and director with Granada. Later works for a number of other television production companies.

Selected films

1959 Enginemen: producer
1962 Tomorrow's Saturday: director
1965 Inside (Granada, series): director
1965 Deckie Learner (Granada): director

1967 Death by Misadvenure: SS Lusitania (Granada): director
1969 Deep South (Granada): producer
1970 I Was a Soldier (Granada): director
1973 World in Action: Working the Land (Granada): producer
1973 A Life Apart (Granada): producer
1974 A Life Underground (Granada): producer
1976 Disappearing World: Eskimo's of Pond Inlet (Granada): director
1979 Before the Monsoon (ATV, series): producer
1990 True Stories: Silent War (Central): director
1994 Fine Cut: Time of Our Lives (BBC): director
1994 Sound on Film: Pictures on the Piano (BBC): director
1995 Fine Cut: Hidden Voices (BBC): director
1996 Witness: Living with the Enemy (Channel 4): director
1998 Lockerbie—A Night Remembered (Channel 4): director
1999 Sound on Film: The Score (BBC): director
2001 Lost at Sea: Solway Harvester (BBC): director

Further reading

Butler, David, '"Progressive" Television Documentary and Northern Ireland—The Films of Michael Grigsby in a "Postcolonial Context"', in Mike Wayne (ed.), *Dissident Voices: The Politics of Television and Cultural Change*, London and Sterling, Virginia: Pluto Press, 1998.

Corner, John, *The Art of Record: A Critical Introduction to Documentary*, Manchester: Manchester University Press, 1996.

Grigsby, Michael and McLintock, Nicolas, 'The State We're In', *DOX: Documentary Film Quarterly* 6, summer 1995.

Macdonald, Kevin and Cousins, Mark (eds), *Imagining Reality: The Faber Book of Documentary*, London: Faber and Faber, 1996.

Orbanz, Eva, *Journey to a Legend and Back: The British Realistic Film*, Berlin: Edition Volker Spiess, 1977.

Petley, Julian, 'Living on the Edge', *Monthly Film Bulletin* 54, no. 640, 1987.

Groulx, Gilles

Born into a large working-class family in Montreal, Gilles Groulx worked his way up to the middle class by obtaining an office job. Unhappy in the corporate milieu, he turned his back on the mainstream (a choice to which he remained true all his life) and started moving in artistic and intellectual circles, including Paul-Émile Borduas's radical Automatist group.

He tried his hand at poetry and painting, made a short experimental documentary in 1954, Les héritiers/Heirs (released 1998), and worked as a film editor for the CBC television news service. He was hired as an editor at the National Film Board of Canada (NFB) after its move from Ottawa to Montreal in 1956. In 1958 he made his directorial debut at the NFB, with his documentary, Les Raquetteurs/Snowshoers, which he codirected with Michel Brault. This seemingly simple reportage on a congress of snowshoeing clubs became a landmark in the evolution of direct cinema. The visual style of the film (owing primarily to Brault's camera work and use of a wide-angle lens) and its ironic structure (owing primarily to Groulx's editing) made it a film that revealed a side of French-Canadian culture that had rarely been acknowledged: the mundane but important rituals and customs that make Québec unique.

During the few years after the release of Les Raquetteurs, Groulx directed a handful of shorts in the direct cinema style, the best of which are Golden Gloves (1961) on an unemployed aspiring boxer; Voir Miami … /To See Miami (1963), which analyzes the Quebecker's fascination with, and resistance against, American culture; and Un jeu si simple/Such a Simple Game (1964), on hockey.

Late in 1963 Groulx was commissioned by the NFB to direct a documentary on how young people spend their time during the winter. Groulx used the budget for this project to make Le chat dans le sac/The Cat in the Bag (1964), a feature-length fiction film on the nationalist awakening of a twenty-something French-Canadian and the disintegration of his relationship with an English-speaking Jewish woman. Blending a documentary look with New Wave self-referentiality, and examining contemporary issues such as nationalism, feminism, and Marxism, Le chat dans le sac became a model for subsequent engagé features and is often acknowledged as marking the beginning of modern fiction film in Québec (Harcourt 1980).

Groulx moved again from documentary to fiction in Où êtes-vous donc?/Where Are You? (1968), an experimental narrative on the evils of consumerism. A similar theme is explored in another experimental fiction, Entre tu et vous/ Between 'tu' and 'vous' (1969).

Groulx returned to a more 'traditional' mode of documentary with 24 Hours or More (1973) a passionate study of Québec politics and society in the early 1970s. The film was deemed subversive by the NFB's conservative commissioner, Sydney Newman, and was banned from circulation until 1976. After making a commissioned documentary on education, Place de l'équation/The Place of the Equation (1973), he directed a coproduction with Mexico in 1977, Première question sur le bonheur/Primera pregunta sobre la felicidad/The First Question on Happiness, on the struggle of Mexican farmers against bourgeois landowners.

In all of his films Groulx remained critical of capitalist society and of the inability of Quebeckers to escape a culture saturated with vacuous images and useless products. As he was finishing his surrealist fiction on a selfish businessman, Au pays de Zom/In the Land of Zom (1982), Groulx was involved in a serious accident that put an end to his career. Richard Brouillette made the documentary Trop c'est assez/Too Much is Enough (1995) on Groulx's life.

ANDRÉ LOISELLE

Biography

Born May 30, 1931, Montreal, Québec, Canada. Made a short experimental documentary, Les héritiers/Heirs (released 1998), 1954. Worked as a film editor for the CBC television news service. Hired as an editor at the NFB after its move from Ottawa to Montreal in 1956. In 1958 made his directorial debut at the NFB, with his documentary, Les Raquetteurs/ Snowshoers, which he codirected with Michel Brault. While finishing Au pays de Zom/In the Land of Zom (1982), involved in a serious accident that put an end to his career. Died August 22, 1994.

Selected films

1958 Les Raquetteurs/Snowshoers: director, editor
1959 Normétal/Normétal: director, script
1961 La France sur un caillou/France on a Rock: director, editor
1961 Golden Gloves: director, photographer, editor
1962 Voir Miami … /To See Miami: director, editor
1964 Un jeu si simple/Such a Simple Game: director, editor
1973 24 heures ou plus/24 Hours or More: director, editor
1973 Place de l'équation/The Place of the Equation: director, script, editor
1977 Première question sur le bonheur/The First Question on Happiness: director, editor

Further reading

Groulx, Gilles, *Montréal: Conseil québécois pour la diffusion du cinéma*, 1969.
Harcourt, Peter, '1964: The Beginning of a Beginning', in Pierre Véronneau and Piers Handling (eds), *Self-Portrait: Essays on the Canadian and Quebec Cinema*, Ottawa: Canadian Film Institute, 1980: 64–76.

Guzmán, Patricio

Chilean Patricio Guzmán is one of the foremost directors of Latin American and worldwide political documentary cinema. During his ongoing and internationally acclaimed career he has directed more than fifteen award-winning documentary feature films and has successfully combined his political militancy as a committed Marxist with his concept of the filmmaker's role. His primary contribution has been to document certain aspects of Chile's political history from 1970 forward, including the country's socialist revolution, Salvador Allende's three-year presidency, the violent coup d'état by General Augusto Pinochet's army in 1973, Pinochet's seventeen-year reign of terror as a military dictator, eventual exile in 1992, and the legal proceedings that led to his arrest in London in 1998.

Guzmán has made six films documenting this turbulent period in Chile's history: Primer año/ The First Year (1971), La Respuesta de octubre/ The October Answer (1972), La batalla de Chile, Parts I, II, and II/The Battle of Chile (1975–80), Chile, la memoria obstinada/Chile, Obstinate Memory (1998), El Caso Pinochet/ The Pinochet Case (2001), and Salvador Allende (2004).

In 1971, after making several shorts, Guzmán directed and wrote his first documentary feature, Primer año, which covers the first year of Allende's presidency. The film includes topics ranging from land reform to the nationalization of various industries, to the empowerment of workers and peasants, to the state visit of Fidel Castro. In 1972 Guzmán directed and wrote La Respuesta de octubre, a film about the first management strike against Allende's government. Although neither film was circulated widely outside of Allende's Chile, they were well received by working-class audiences.

In 1973, using stock footage donated by Marker, Guzmán began coproducing (with Marker), directing, and writing La batalla de Chile Parts I, II, and III, an epic trilogy that documents Allende's final period, the violent right-wing counterrevolution against his government, and the accession of Pinochet's military junta. Using just one 16mm Eclair camera and one Nagra tape recorder, Guzmán, aided by five associates, filmed events during ten weeks immediately before, during, and after the military coup. On the first day of the coup, Guzmán was imprisoned in the National Stadium and filming was halted. After his release fifteen days later, he left for Europe and began to live in exile. One by one, four of the other five filmmakers escaped the country, and the film was smuggled safely out to Europe and then Cuba. The last filmmaker, Jorge Muller, was seized by the secret police in 1974 and was never heard of again. Over a period of four years, Guzmán completed the film in Cuba with funding and support from the Instituto cubano del arte y industria cinematográficos, the Cuban national film institute. The three parts were released in 1975, 1977 and 1979, and established and secured Guzmán's international reputation as a documentary filmmaker.

In the trilogy Guzmán found and developed his distinctive documentary style. He uses a rich mixture of direct cinema observation and investigative reporting. Deciding to use actuality footage rather than archival footage and the compilation method, he was able to obtain extraordinary footage by skillfully combining his rigorous and disciplined production techniques with his ability to understand, foresee, and immerse himself in the flow of political events. Guzmán frequently uses the sequence shot, a cinematic device that allows viewers to see events unfold without breaks in the flow of the images. The four-hour film, a poignant work of historical testimony, conveys both a sweeping drama of the historic events portrayed and an emotional texture that gives the footage multiple dimensions. While the film strongly favors Allende's efforts and does not pretend to be objective, it does present and convey a high level of information in a balanced manner and is not uncritical of the Left.

Part I, La insurrección de la borguesia/The Uprising of the Bourgeoisie (1975) documents the final days of Allende's presidency through the first day of the military coup. Part II, El golpe de estado/The Coup d'État (1977) documents the 'Popular Unity' period of Allende's government, the tumultuous events leading up to the coup, and Allende's controversial death (some believe he committed suicide and others that he was murdered by Pinochet's henchmen). Part III, El poder popular/The Power of the People (1979) documents the thousands of local groups of 'Popular Power' that were created during Allende's presidency by ordinary workers and peasants to perform various services in the country. Guzmán, following the Marxist concept that views classes as the protagonists of history and conflict as an inherent dimension of class societies, frames events in terms of class conflict. Parts I and II track the military's drift to the right and the anti-Allende activities of the legislature, and Part III centers on workers organizing as a class so that they can achieve emancipation from, and the transformation of, the bourgeoisie-dominated world.

The trilogy is considered by most international critics, Marxist and non-Marxist alike, to be one of the major political documentaries of the period, and, by some, to be one of the most important political documentaries ever made. The film has been screened internationally in more than eight countries, has been shown commercially in more than thirty-five countries, has won seven Grand Prizes in Europe and Latin America, has been distributed in more than twenty countries, and has been televised in more than ten countries.

In 1998, twenty-eight years after the death of Allende, Guzmán returned to Chile for the first time and screened La Batalla de Chile to students and to those who actually witnessed and/or participated in the battle. Their reactions formed the subject of his next documentary, Chile, la memoria obstinada/Chile, Obstinate Memory, which he directed, wrote, and narrated. Guzmán's premise is that the memory of those times and events that were captured in the trilogy was largely barred from the collective consciousness of the Chilean people, and the film investigates this political amnesia and the reawakening of memory in the Chilean people.

In 2001 Guzmán coproduced, directed, and wrote El Caso Pinochet, a film that examines the landmark legal case brought against Pinochet in Spain, both before and after his arrest in London in 1998. In 2004 Guzmán directed and wrote Salvador Allende, a film that documents the political career of the fallen leader by exploring both his rise to the presidency and the forces that collaborated against him to remove him from office.

Guzmán also has made a number of other types of documentaries, including several that have focused on Chilean and Latin American historical and religious concerns. In 1983 he directed and cowrote La Rosa de los vientos/ The Compass Rose, a mythological fable about Latin America. In 1985 he directed and wrote Precolombian Mexico, a Spanish television series about the ancient times of the Mayan and Aztec cultures. In 1987 he produced, directed, and wrote En nombre de Dios/In the Name of God, a film about the Catholic Church's fight for human rights in Chile under the Pinochet regime. In 1988 he directed and wrote El proyecto aclarado de Carlos III/The Enlightened Project of Carlos III, a Spanish television series about the age of Enlightenment in Spain and the United States.

In 1992 he produced, directed, and wrote La Cruz del Sur/The Southern Cross, a Spanish television series about the discovery of America and the popular religions in Latin America. In 1995 Guzmán directed and wrote Las barreras de la soledad/The Barriers of Loneliness, a film about history and memory in a Mexican village. In 1999 he directed and wrote Isla de Robinson Crusoe/Robinson Crusoe Island, a film about Daniel Defoe's novel, and the remote island with the same name that lies off the Chilean coast. In 2001 he codirected and wrote Invocación/ Invocation, and in 2002 he directed and wrote Madrid, a film that explores Spain's capital.

Guzmán is also a cinematographer, writer, and actor. In addition to working as a cinematographer on several films in the 1960s, he has published four books, several short stories, and numerous articles, and has acted in three films: Vivir al día/To Live a Day (1996), El Cobrador/The Collector (1994), and Moon Over Parador (1988). He also worked as the cinematographer on 11'09'01/September 11, 2001 (2002) and Salvador Allende (2004).

SUZANNE EISENHUT

See also: Battle of Chile, The

Biography

Born Patricio Guzmán Lozanes in Santiago, Chile, August 11, 1941. Attended the University of Chile from 1960 to 1965; the Theater School (1960), the Faculty of History (1961), and the Faculty of Philosophy (1962–5). Attended the Film Institute at the Catholic University of Chile (1963–5). Attended the Official Cinematographic School of Madrid (1966–9), where he received a Director-Producer degree (1970). Joined Chile-Films (Chile's national film production company) and headed the Documentary Films Workshops (1970). Formed Grupo del tercer año (Group of the Third Year) to produce The Battle of Chile. Presented at numerous conferences and cinema seminars in Canada, Chile, Cuba, Mexico, Spain, and the United States (since 1978). Served as a member of the jury for the documentary sections of many acclaimed film festivals, including those in Brazil, France, Germany, India, Italy, Mexico, and the United States (since 1993). Received a Scholarship from the John Simon Guggenheim Memorial Foundation (1993). Served as the Director of the International Documentary Film Festival in Santiago (1997–9), and as the Malaga Director of the Documentary Section in Spain (1998–9). Employed as a professor of documentary film at various schools in Europe and Latin America. Currently resides in Paris with Renate Sachse, who also collaborates on the scripts for his films. Father of two daughters, Andrea and Camila, who are also filmmakers and often work on his projects. Production company: Patricio Guzmán Producciones, S.L.

Selected films

1971 Primer año/The First Year: director, writer
1972 La Respuesta de octubre/The October Answer: director, writer
1975 Part I: La insurrección de la borguesia/ The Uprising of the Bourgeoisie

1975–80 La Batalla de Chile/The Battle of Chile: coproducer, director, writer
1977 Part II: El golpe de estado/The Coup d'état
1978–83 La Rosa de los vientos/The Compass Rose: director, cowriter
1979 Part III: El poder popular/The Power of the People
1985 Precolombian Mexico: director, writer
1987 En el nombre de Dios/In the Name of God: producer, director, writer
1988 El proyecto aclarado de Carlos III/The Enlightened Project of Carlos III: director, writer
1988 Moon Over Parador: actor
1992 La Cruz del Sur/The Southern Cross: producer, director, writer, production designer
1994 El Cobrador/The Collector: actor
1994 Vivir al día/To Live a Day: actor
1995 Las barreras de la soledad/The Barriers of Loneliness: director, writer
1997 Chile, la memoria obstinada/Chile, the Obstinate Memory: director, writer, narrator
1999 Isla de Robinson Crusoe/Robinson Crusoe Island: director, writer
2001 El Caso Pinochet/The Pinochet Case: coproducer, director, writer
2001 Invocación/Invocation: codirector
2002 Madrid: director, writer
2002–3 11'09'01/September 11, 2001 (2002): cinematographer
2004 Salvador Allende: director, writer, cinematographer

Further reading

Angry Arts Group, 'Battle of Chile in Context', *Jump Cut* (Chicago), November, 1979.

'La Batalla de Chile Section', *Cine Cubano*, March 1978.

Delmas, Jean, 'La Batalla de Chile, deuxieme partie: La Coup d'etat', *Jeune Cinema*, February 1977.

Gauthier, Guy, 'Chile: la premiere annee', *Image et Son*, March 1973.

——'La Bataille du Chile, premiere partie: L'Insurrection de la bourgeoisie', *Image et Son*, January 1976.

Guzmán, Patricio, *Cansancio en la Tierra* (Exhaustion in the Land), 1961.

——*Juegos de Verdad*, ed. Luis Rivano, Santiago, 1962.

'Le Cinéma dans la politique de l'Unite Populaire', *Jeune Cinema*, January 1974.

——*La insurección del la burgesia*, ed. Racinante, Caracas, 1975.

——*El cine contra el fascismo*, with P. Sempere, ed. by Fernando Torres, Valencia, 1977.

——*La batalla de Chile: La lucha de un pueblo sin armas*, Madrid: Colección Libros Hiperion, 1977.

'"La Bataille du Chile II", interview with Marcel Martin', *Ecran*, 1977.

'Politics and the Documentary in People's Chile', interview with Julianne Burton, *Socialist Review*, October 1977.

'"La Batalla de Chile", interview with Carlos Galiano', *Cine Cubano*, 1978: 91–2.

——'"Chile" 3: Guzmán', and 'Chile', *Framework*, spring and autumn, 1979.

'Interview with Z.M. Pick', *Cine-Tracts*, Winter 1980.

Mouesca, J., 'El cine chileno en el exilio (1973–82)', *Cine Cubano*, 109, 1984.

n.a., *Interview with Patricio Guzmán, 'El Cine Contra el Fascismo'* (Cinema Against Fascism), 1971.

Niogret, Hubert, 'La Batalla de Chile: el golpe de estado', *Positif*, July/August 1976.

Wallis, V., 'Battle of Chile: Struggle of People without Arms', *Jump Cut* (Chicago), November 1979.

West, Dennis, 'The Battle of Chile', *Cineaste*, 11, no. 2, 1978.

——'Documenting the End of the Chilean Road to Socialism: La Batalla de Chile', *The American Hispanist*, February 1978.

Guzzetti, Alfred

American filmmaker Alfred Guzzetti has been a central figure in the documentary film culture of the United States from the 1970s to the present day. Since the early 1970s he has examined how the realm of the subjective and the role of personal reflection were perceived as challenging obstacles to established models of documentary form. Guzzetti's interest in the nuances of personal experience has resulted in a long career of simultaneously building on as well as dismantling the general understanding of the roles of filmmaker and audience of nonfiction film. His body of work spans four decades and is often divided into three distinct yet interwoven types of nonfiction form: personal documentary, political documentary, and experimental film and video.

For Guzzetti, the subject and the realm of the subjective complicate rather than challenge the potency of the indexical nature of documentary. His emergence into documentary filmmaking began at a moment when he saw both American culture and artistic practices meld aspects of the personal with the political. The political and social issues of the 1960s such as the Vietnam War, as well as the civil rights and the women's movements helped mark a shift on what had previously been considered private or personal topics into the political arena. This fusion of the personal and political also took hold in many arts. Much of Guzzetti's earlier work and ideas were influenced by well-known photographers such as Henri Cartier-Bresson and Henry Callahan, as well as revolutionary and experimental filmmakers such as Jean-Luc Godard, Peter Kubelka, and Jean Rouch.

In the 1970s and 1980s Guzzetti made a cycle of autobiographical documentaries that included private moments filmed by and about his family. Although it was not commonplace for filmmakers to combine 8mm archival footage and 16mm contemporary images from their personal lives in their documentaries, Guzzetti was not alone in this practice. In his catalogue essay for the 1993 Cinéma du Réel, 'The Documentary Gets Personal', he proposes that the personal documentary is not the practice of a single filmmaker but rather a mode that spans decades, social classes, genders, and continents. By evoking examples from a broad range of filmmakers such as the Lumière brothers, Martin Scorsese, Robb Moss, Maya Deren, Ross McElwee, Ed Pincus, and Su Friedrich, Guzzetti demonstrates how private images, although present in nonfiction films, often remain unsung in criticism on documentary film history. This essay provides a much needed historical mapping of the legacy behind the personal and autobiographical cinema.

His model of personal documentary filmmaking challenged filmmakers, not only to interact and observe their subjects but to use their own experiences and relationships with them to guide the filmmaking process. For instance, the second film of Guzzetti's autobiographical cycle, Scenes from Childhood (1977–80), was inspired by a staple of cinéma vérité film, Jean Rouch's and Edgar Morin's Chronique d'un été (1961). Guzzetti chose to use conventions of direct cinema such as synchronized sound, as well as an avoidance of interviews and voice-over narration to convey the intimacy of his personal relationship with the film's subjects, his child and his child's playmates. In this sense Guzzetti's personal documentaries can be seen as both a continuation of and a radical response to what are often considered more social and public issue-oriented modes of nonfiction filmmaking such as direct cinema and cinéma vérité.

By the late 1980s, Guzzetti became involved in a series of collaborative political film projects. In the 1990s he also worked on two anthropological projects with Lina Fruzzetti, Ákos Östör, and Ned Johnston: Seed and Earth (1994) and Khalfan and Zanzibar (2000). Such collaborations reflect the interests and skills of their coauthors, but strong connections can be made between these documentaries and Guzzetti's other nonfiction projects. Many of Guzzetti's sensibilities and preoccupations resurface in his second collaboration with Susan Meiselas and Richard Rogers, Pictures from a Revolution (1991), a film that combines cine and still photography to convey the social unrest in postrevolutionary Nicaragua. This film, as in his earlier autobiographical film, Family Portrait Sittings (1971–5) and in many of his later experimental films and videos, uses many formal devices and motifs found in much of Guzzetti's works: the role of the filmmaker and subject as eyewitness, the employment of various techniques that destabilize common assertions about the medium of photography while refusing to flatten out its power as artistic beauty or relativize its use as historical record, fragmenting and mismatching sound from its image to complicate the audience's sense of temporal order, and a preoccupation with the passage of time.

Guzzetti's writing on documentary positions fiction film as working, in part, to compensate and distract the spectator from the 'disruptive forces' of the cinematic medium. In his 1996 critical essay, 'Notes on Representation and the Nonfiction Film', Guzzetti asks: 'Might it not also be true that it was only through fiction that styles could have been evolved capable of managing the disruptive forces that Lumière let loose? Was fiction among other things a defense erected against all that is disquieting and problematical in the moving image?' This concern for tackling 'all that is disquieting and problematical in the moving image' is found not only in his personal and political documentaries but also in Guzzetti's more experimental nonfiction films and videos such as A Tropical Story (1998) and The Tower of Industrial Life (2000). He posits his later more experimental films and videos as a species of nonfiction consistent with his earlier approach to documentary. He began to use first Hi8 and later digital video formats to convey, in his words, 'the daily experience of contemporary life, its assaults on us in public places, in television, our ineffectual refuge in the private and the distant'.

Guzzetti's consistent personal vision and diverse approaches to nonfiction form provide insightful ways for individuals concerned with the 'disruptive forces' of documentary film to mobilize questions of medium specificity (how cinema represents) alongside questions of identity politics (who gets represented and in what manner). His critical and filmic explorations offer historical records for not only how we lived but what in our lives we choose to document and archive. In his words: 'For when future generations try to understand our civilization, it will be films such as these that provide the most vivid record of who we were and how we lived.' Such a democratization of history-making places Guzzetti's past and current projects alongside contemporary scholars and filmmakers dedicated to revealing personal experiences seldom told or heard in nonfiction works.

THERESA SCANDIFFIO

Biography

Born in Philadelphia, PA in 1942. Graduated from Harvard College with Bachelor of Arts degree in 1964. Graduated from Harvard University with a doctorate in English literature in 1968. Professor at Harvard University 1968 to present. Received numerous National Endowment of the Arts grants, Artists Foundation fellowships and film festival prizes for many of his nonfiction film and video projects. He is a member of numerous panels and groups such as the Academy of Motion Picture Arts and Sciences. He continues to produce and discuss his film and video works at museums, galleries, cinematheques and film festivals around the world. He is the Osgood Professor of Visual Arts at Harvard University.

Selected films

1970–1 Air
1971–5 Family Portrait Sittings
1977–80 Scenes from Childhood
1981–6 Beginning Pieces
1984–5 Living at Risk: The Story of a Nicaraguan Family: codirector
1988–94 Seed and Earth: codirector
1989–91 Pictures from a Revolution: codirector
1997 Under the Rain
1998 A Tropical Story
1999 Khalfan and Zanzibar: codirector
2000 The Tower of Industrial Life
2002 Down from the Mountains
2003 Calcutta Intersection

Further reading

Askew, Kelly, 'Khalfan and Zanzibar', *American Anthropologist* 103, March 2001: 189–90.

Canby, Vincent, 'Pictures from a Revolution', *The New York Times*, November 19, 1992: C26–9.

Charlip, Julie A. and Bloomquist, Charly, 'Pictures from a Revolution', *The American Historical Review* 97, October 1992: 1166–8.

Guzzetti, Alfred, *Two or Three Things I Know About Her: Analysis of A Film By Godard*, Cambridge: Harvard University Press, 1981.

——'The Documentary Gets Personal/Le documentaire la première personne', catalogue essay for Cinéma du réel, Paris, March, 1993: 90–1 (French translation, 88–9).

——'Notes on Representation and the Nonfiction Film', *New Literary History* XXVII, spring, 1996: 263–70.

Kopkind, Andrew, 'Living at Risk: Witness to War', *The Nation* 241, 15, November 9, 1985: 484–5.

Leighton, Tanya, 'Places of Images, Plus Sounds: Alfred Guzzetti's Films and Videotapes', www.location1.org/artists/guzzetti/files/text.html, n.d.

Rothman, William, 'Alfred Guzzetti's Family Portrait Sittings', *The Quarterly Review of Film Studies* 2, no. 1, 1977: 96–113.

Sutherland, Allan T., 'Family Portrait', *Sight and Sound* 48, no. 1, winter 1978–9: 29–30.

Handsworth Songs

(UK, Akomfrah, 1986)

The importance of Handsworth Songs can be located within the politics and aesthetics of its form, but also within the specific context of Britain in the 1980s. The formation of the Black Audio Film Collective in 1982, and its subsequent membership in the workshop movement, resulted in a genuinely collective filmmaking practice that emphasised formal experimentation, but also tried to anchor it in some kind of cultural and political address (Petley 1989). Handsworth Songs represents a documentary that investigates the inner-city riots that occurred in the Handsworth area of Birmingham and in other British cities during 1985 and the period of the Conservative government of Margaret Thatcher.

One of the repeated motifs of Handsworth Songs is that 'there are no stories in the riots, only the ghosts of other stories'. The ghosts of other stories are voices and experiences of the black population that arrived at the shores of the mother country from the Caribbean colonies in the 1950s.

An excavation of archival sources that ranges from British movietone news, to Birmingham Central Library and Yorkshire television documents this historical moment and the official response to it. A series of poetic ruminations on this journey to the heart of Empire reflexively inscribes a diasporic subjectivity onto this footage.

Through an aesthetic of assemblage and juxtaposition Handsworth Songs discursively exposes the gaps and silences in the response of politicians to the riots and the media reporting of the riots. For example, there is a sequence that brings together the newspaper headlines such as 'this bleeding heart of England' with a number of versions of the song 'Jerusalem'. The combination of dub reggae together with a brass band extract of 'Jerusalem' set against the images of newspaper extracts unfixes and hybridizes the language of English. The assembly of audio and visual sources in Handsworth Songs constructs a document with a syncretic dynamic (Kobena 1994) that fuses issues of race and ethnicity with the cultural tradition of the English working class so that black experience is articulated through the documentary form as an experience of England (Kobena 1988).

The structure of Handsworth Songs combines sources from the archival past and the present context of the riots and refuses a linear narrative trajectory. One of the recurring motifs is a black bus conductor in a museum gazing at the rotating wheels, axles, and cranks of machinery from the Industrial Revolution. The use of recurring imagery, the returning to the present context of the riots, and the use of oral songs lend the documentary a circular structure. Underlying this is a movement across the archival sources that represent black experience of England. Ambient and asynchronous sound that functions as counterpoint to the image denaturalizes the footage and accentuates the reflexivity of construction.

Handsworth Songs also generates a resonance between the archival footage and the coverage of the riots through interweaving a number of poetic and unauthored songs. The voice-over of the songs express a diasporic subjectivity that combines a feeling of displacement with an innocent faith in the mother country. Overlaying archival film describing a moment of arrival, they replace the voice-of-god commentary that might be expected from such footage. This strategy is reflexive and reflects a collective desire to find a structure and a form to deconstruct the hegemonic voices of British television newsreels. This not only corrects the blind spots of the archive but also lends a degree of subjectivity to part of the population who have not been granted access to this mode of expression within the history of British documentary. Handsworth Songs is a reflexive documentary where the consequences of reflexivity are rooted in the particular context of black British experience where the power relation that underpins the subject of knowledge assumed by documentary becomes part of the process of documentary (Nichols 1991; Trinh 1990).

The reception of Handsworth Songs generated a critical debate about the relationship between the film and its representational constituency between Salman Rushdie and Stuart Hall (Kobena 1988). The legacy of this debate is an ongoing opposition between the struggle to find a new language of documentary and the imperative to represent sufficiently the black population (Malik 1996). Rushdie highlights the successive generation of subjectivities and Asian subjectivities that are not represented by the film, while others have questioned the relevance of the aesthetics of Handsworth Songs and other workshop films (Kobena 1988; Lovell 1990).

Handsworth Songs and the work of the Black Audio Film Collective question the assumption that there exists a singular and correct mode of articulating black experience. The problem of being seen to only address an elite audience is not only a recurring issue within British film culture but also an issue of how documentary films such as Handsworth Songs are distributed and viewed. Black Audio succeeded in producing a documentary that places black British filmmaking within an international context and at the same time eludes the discourse of auteurism that characterises European art cinema (Pines and Willemen 1989).

Handsworth Songs revisits one of the central traditions of British cinema—the documentary. In its refusal to serve as a realist riot film, Handsworth Songs poses the question of whether a concern with form and with modernist and avant-garde techniques can be legitimately claimed by black filmmakers during a period of assumed postmodernity (Kobena 1988).

IAN GOODE

See also: Akomfrah, John

Handsworth Songs (UK, Black Audio Film Collective, 1986, 61 mins). Produced by Lina Gopaul. Directed by John Akomfrah. Cinematography by Sebastian Shah.

Further reading

Corner, John, *The Art of Record*, Manchester: Manchester University Press, 1996.

Kobena, Mercer (ed.), *Black Film/British Cinema*, London: ICA, 1988.

——*Welcome to the Jungle*, London: Routledge, 1994.

Lovell, Alan, 'That Was the Workshop That Was', *Screen* 31, no. 1 spring 1990: 102–8.

Malik, Sarita, 'Beyond "The Cinema of Duty?" The Pleasures of Hybridity: Black British Films of the 1980s and 1990s', in Andrew Higson (ed.), *Dissolving Views. Key Writings on British Cinema*, London: Cassell, 1996.

Nichols, Bill, *Representing Reality*, Bloomington, IN: Indiana University Press, 1991.

Petley, Julian, 'Possessed by Memory', *Monthly Film Bulletin* 56, no. 668, 1989: 260–1.

Pines, Jim and Willemen, Paul, *Questions of Third Cinema*, London: BFI, 1989.

Trinh, T. Minh-ha, 'Documentary Is/Not a Name', *October* 52, spring 1990: 76–100.

Happy Mother's Day, A

(US, Leacock, 1963)

A Happy Mother's Day is the first film that Richard Leacock made after leaving Drew Associates. He was assigned by the *Saturday Evening Post* to make a film about the Fisher quintuplets, the first surviving quintuplets born in the United States. Leacock and Joyce Chopra filmed the family and the events surrounding the publicity of the births in Aberdeen, South Dakota. The *Post* was not pleased with the finished product, and eventually ABC acquired the rights to Leacock's footage and created its own film, Quint City, U.S.A., which is significantly different from Leacock and Chopra's—a funny, yet disturbing, report on the mass media's obsession with, and crass commercialization of, a remarkable event.

The film opens with news footage of Mrs Fisher leaving the hospital after the births (taken before Leacock and Chopra's arrival). She is then seen two weeks later, attending a 'Gypsy Day' parade. The aerial shots of Aberdeen and of the parade work to establish a 'typical', small-town American scene, and the folksy tone of the film continues as we are shown the Fisher home: shots of Mr Fisher tending his cows and of the older children playing affectionately with newborn kittens. The mood begins to shift here, as a *Ladies Home Journal* reporter arrives, along with a *Post* photographer, who will arrange a picture of all the gifts that the family has received. Although Mrs Fisher insists that her children will never be on display, the second half of the film clearly shows us that the local leaders have every intention of exploiting this event; the official reaction to the births becomes the focus of the film.

Businessmen meet to discuss the influx of tourists to Aberdeen. At a meeting of the Chamber of Commerce, the sales of quintuplet souvenirs are discussed, although the idea of running newspaper ads for them is deemed by some as 'too commercial'. It is suggested that the ads could indicate that proceeds will go to the Fisher Foundation, but someone points out that there is no such foundation. The wife of the Chamber of Commerce leader takes Mrs Fisher clothes shopping, where, seeming embarrassed, she tries on a mink coat. Later, a women's club member makes suggestions to Mrs Fisher as to what she should wear at the upcoming luncheon being held in her honor. The film finishes with the celebration of the quintuplets' first month: the Fisher family poses for pictures, and the mayor of Aberdeen delivers an 'extraordinarily inflated speech' (Mamber 1975). A woman then sings a terrible song; the parade begins but abruptly ends when it starts to rain. The Fishers, along with everyone else, run for cover. 'It was a typical celebration in Aberdeen, South Dakota, USA,' the narrator concludes.

A Happy Mother's Day gives pleasure to the spectator yet makes one feel uncomfortable at the spectacle. We are shown the foolishness and excessive attention being given to this event, yet in viewing this, we are also contributing to the spectacle. Implicitly we contrast Leacock's desire to objectively report what he sees, consciously refusing to ask the Fishers to do anything for the camera, with the way others in the community and the news media direct them. Leacock's sensitivity to detail is impressive. As the *Post* photographer directs the Fishers and their older children in the family Model T Ford, making sure he can see everyone, Leacock frames three geese in the foreground and even follows the animals as the photographer speaks to the family. A press review of the parade is held before the actual one (to facilitate the reporters' deadlines, the narrator says), and amid the insistent directions given to the family, who pose with a local official and an Indian chief, Leacock films a nun taking a picture.

The tension the city leaders feel between commercializing the quintuplets and giving them privacy is reflected in the tension the spectator feels between laughing at the hypocrisy and feeling inappropriately superior to it. A question arises as to whether or not the film judges those who seek to exploit the births, rather than merely reports their actions. The businessmen come off as well-meaning, but nonetheless willing to exploit the commercial possibilities surrounding the infants. The mayor is represented as a pompous fool. The narrator's tone is especially sarcastic throughout, adding to the sense of mockery.

The central contrast that makes the film work is between the town and the Fishers themselves, especially Mrs Fisher. She is clearly a modest woman, not comfortable in the spotlight but willing to endure it, at least briefly. She is at times embarrassed at the attention, as when she is trying on the fur coat. When the head of the ladies' club asks her if she has a favorite color, Mrs Fisher shrugs and says no—she has clearly never thought about such matters. Finally, at the luncheon, during the awful song, Leacock pans through the crowd, and Mrs Fisher, noticing him, smirks, conveying her understanding of the absurdity of all this attention lavished on her.

It is obvious why the *Post* and ABC could not really accept Leacock and Chopra's cut of the film. It too accusingly points the fingers at all institutions seeking to exploit the quintuplets' births, including the news media. ABC constructed a different film, sponsored by a baby food manufacturer, and broadcast what 'looks like a half-hour baby food commercial' (Mamber 1975). All references to commercialism are qualified, minimizing the effect in Leacock's film. ABC uses more baby footage, including material not shot by Leacock. Long scenes in Leacock are cut, also distorting the effects of the original. Studying both films offers interesting insights into the difference between a filmmaker working in the Flaherty tradition of nonpreconception and a commercial network whose motive, like the businessmen in Aberdeen, is profit.

TOM GROCHOWSKI

See also: Leacock, Richard

A Happy Mother's Day (US, Leacock Pennebaker Films, 1963, 26 mins). Distributed by Pennebaker Hegedus Films. Filmmakers: Richard Leacock and Joyce Chopra, with Nancy Sen. Narrator: Ed McCurdy. Filmed in Aberdeen, South Dakota.

Further reading

Barnouw, Erik, *Documentary: A History of the Nonfiction Film*, New York: Oxford University Press, 1993.

Barsam, Richard M., *Nonfiction Film: A Critical History*, Bloomington, IN: Indiana University Press, 1992.

Issari, M. Ali and Paul, Doris A., *What is Cinema Verite?*, London: Scarecrow Press, 1979.

Jaffe, Patricia, 'Editing Cinema Verite', *Film Comment* 3, 1965: 43–7.

Mamber, Stephen, *Cinema Verite in America: Studies in Uncontrolled Documentary*, Cambridge, MA: MIT Press, 1975.

Heart of Spain

(US, Kline, Karpathi, 1937)

Heart of Spain was one of the major contributions of Frontier Films, based in New York, to the Republican cause during the Spanish Civil War. The history of Frontier Films (sometimes referred to as the New York Documentary School) is generally associated with a type of film that went beyond any box office gains and added a social counterbalance to Hollywood's way of filmmaking. Until 1941, when the group disbanded as a result of World War II, Frontier Films imitated Russian film, which had a great impact on left-wing circles worldwide, to narrate the American reality emotionally by including the audience in the filmmaking experience.

Herbert Kline, a writer who was involved in theatre, and the photographer Geza Karpathi had the idea to make a documentary in Spain and eventually found a topic for their film. Norman Bethune had left his comfortable position at a Montreal hospital to assist the Republican cause by setting up a blood bank in Madrid to supply the front-line hospitals with blood. In New York, Paul Strand and Leo Hurtwitz remade the first cut of Heart of Spain with the help of John Howard Lawson, who did not appear in the credits, and Ben Maddow, who was featured as David Wolff. In the final cut, some newsreels were added to enhance the expressiveness of the final product. The topic had to be health-related to justify the $5,000 that the North American Committee to Aid Spanish Democracy granted to produce the documentary. Heart of Spain, however, went beyond the original central idea and, applying the theory of emotional impact of Frontier Films, constructed a defence of the need for American military intervention in favour of the Republican cause.

Heart of Spain renders an epic description of the people of Madrid, who bravely endure the siege of the city, during which normal life is impossible. Madrid is a front line of the war, and its inhabitants carry conventional weapons to defend themselves. They also carry symbolic weapons, however, such as solidarity and sacrifice. The film starts with scenes of Madrid as a city in ruins, devastated by the bombardments that, as a leitmotif, are omnipresent throughout the documentary. Facing the physical destruction of the city, its people rise up in arms as a collective hero who defends the freedom of all; Madrid is not just the scene of a specific war, but of an all-out, universal war. A banner expresses the underlying statement of the entire documentary: 'Our cause is the cause of the whole of civilized and progressive mankind.'

In Heart of Spain the Spanish enemy does not exist. It does not contain a single reference to the fraternal standoff between the Spanish and renders a Manichaean representation of the war between the forces of good (the Republicans) and evil (the Fascists). The objective is clear: to show an unequal war in order to stir the international conscience. The Republican militia has its power base among bakers, carpenters, or those forced to go to war: the 'people's army' helped by men from all over the world, including Italy and Germany, to fight for democracy. The enemy is a dehumanized antagonist. Through their actions, the fascists resemble villains in a feature film: their cruelty shows through the mutilation and death caused by their bombs. Even Red Cross vehicles are perfect war targets and must go about camouflaged to elude any attacks.

The climax of the documentary's political argument, which criticizes the international hypocritical attitude of neutrality, is summed up in the scene where a black nurse takes off the bandage from the stump of the arm of a militia member, mutilated by an Italian grenade.

The commentator anticipates the feeling of repulsion that such a harsh image provokes in the audience by directly addressing the viewers, asking them not to turn away at the sight of this and see for themselves the effects that the policy of nonintervention, 'the Italian way', causes.

Heart of Spain wishes to batter the viewer emotionally, encouraging him or her to take action for the cause. To this end, the story of the defence of Madrid is centred on the most defenceless, the protagonists from whom the maximum emotional effect can be obtained: the women and children. A woman weeping while helping recover bodies is a metaphor for the grief of all Republicans. Children are constantly used to enhance the cruelty of the situation: children crying and dying in the bombardments, children playing war games, children helping to put up barricades, and so on.

Heart of Spain was never released in Spain, unlike The Spanish Earth by Joris Ivens, which did make it to the Spanish cinemas. In 1937 it was shown in the Playhouse, in New York, for seven weeks. Garrison Film distributed the documentary and took care of the distribution of another Frontier Films production, Return of Life (1938), which broaches the subject of hospital life during the defence of Madrid. Kline and Karpathi's film, which attracted approximately two million American viewers during the war, has gone down in documentary history as a paradigm of the exploitation of emotions for propaganda purposes.

JOSÉ CABEZA SAN DEOGRACIAS

See also: Kline, Herbert

Heart of Spain (US, Frontier Films/Canadian Committee to Aid Spain/American Bureau to Aid Spanish Democracy, 1937, 30 mins). Distributed by Garrison Film. Produced by Herbert Kline. Directed by Herbert Kline and Geza Karpathi. Shooting script by Herbert Kline. Photography by Geza Karpathi. Material scenarized and edited by Paul Strand and Leo Hurwitz. Commentary by David Wolf and Herbert Kline. Narrated by John O'Shaughnessy. Music arranged by Alex North. Filmed in Madrid, Spain.

Further reading

Alexander, William, 'Frontier Films 1936–41: The Aesthetics of Impact', *Cinema Journal*, XV, no. 1, autumn 1975.

Amo, Alfonso del, *Catálogo general del cine de la Guerra Civil*, Madrid: Cátedra-Filmoteca Española, 1996.

Coma, Javier, *La brigada de Hollywood: guerra española y cine americano*, Barcelona: Flor del Viento Ediciones, 2002.

Gubern, Roman, *La guerra de España en la pantalla. De la propaganda a la historia*, Madrid: Filmoteca Española, 1986.

Jacobs, Lewis (ed.), *The Documentary Tradition: From Nanook to Woodstock*, New York: Hopkinson and Blake, 1971.

Hearts and Minds

(US, Davis, 1974)

Released the year after peace agreements ending the Vietnam War were signed in Paris, Hearts and Minds is particularly significant in an American context, as its production and reception history mark shifts in popular attitudes toward the war by its end. During the war most anti-war documentaries made in the United States were low-budget films with limited exhibition, and most anti-war documentaries made outside the United States were never seen by Americans. By contrast, Hearts and Minds had a budget of $900,000 from Columbia Pictures, was released theatrically to a relatively large, mainstream audience and won the Academy Award for Documentary in 1974. A cultural landmark in these terms, Hearts and Minds still divides critics in their assessment of its efforts to show the devastating effects of war on the Vietnamese, to expose the corrupt origins of the war in American culture, and to communicate the moral and emotional fervour of the anti-war movement to mainstream America.

Hearts and Minds was produced by Bert Schneider whose previous projects with his company BBS (an affiliate of Columbia Pictures) had included anti-establishment fiction films Easy Rider (1969) and Five Easy Pieces (1970), as well as The Monkees television show (1967–69). Interested in making an anti-Vietnam War film, Schneider chose Davis to direct on the strength of his 1971 CBS documentary The Selling of the Pentagon. Broadcast in primetime, The Selling of the

Pentagon marked a departure in US television from its previously held stance of uncritical support for government policy, as Davis exposed the methods by which the US Department of Defense promoted military intervention in Vietnam. Before Hearts and Minds the Hollywood industry had largely ignored Vietnam, preferring to leave the representation of this problematic and unpopular war to television. Thus it was not too surprising when Columbia Pictures dropped Hearts and Minds before its release because of the bad publicity it garnered for the studio.

Hearts and Minds is a compilation film that combines archival material of various kinds—horrific combat footage, segments from Hollywood films, domestic scenes from the United States and Vietnam, clips of political speeches—with interviews of American and Vietnamese politicians, veterans, civilian leaders, Vietnamese victims of American bombs, and ordinary Americans at home. There is no voice-over narration, but Davis's perspective on the Vietnam War as the product of American racism and militarism is made clear. To the end of exciting emotional responses in the viewer against the war and against those who promoted and supported it, Hearts and Minds is organized thematically in patterns of binary opposition and ironic juxtaposition: daily life in the Vietnamese countryside juxtaposed with images of American military technology at work; interviews with US pilots who praise advancements in war technology followed by images of destruction caused by US bombing raids; the Saigon office and industrial holdings of a self-proclaimed war profiteer compared to a small business that fits prosthetic limbs on injured veterans. It saves its most devastating juxtaposition for its conclusion. In one of its best-known and most effective sequences, General Westmoreland's explanation of the difference between American and Vietnamese attitudes towards death ('the Oriental doesn't put the same high price on life as does the Westerner') is intercut with images of bereaved families in a South Vietnamese cemetery in intimate moments of grief. Key interviews with veterans and other expert witnesses opposed to the war, such as Daniel Ellsberg, are likewise edited to build to a climax by the end of the film, when terrible physical injuries and emotional scars from the war are revealed and mourned.

The film has been justly praised for its ability to generate sympathy for both Vietnamese victims and US veterans who opposed the war through such striking juxtapositions and carefully paced revelations, but its strengths are inextricably bound to its weaknesses as a documentary account of the war. Because the film privileges affect over analysis and works largely by personifying war's origins and effects through its witness-participant interviews, it does little to address social, political, and economic contexts. For instance, owing perhaps to its objective to reach as broad an audience as possible in the United States where anti-communist sentiment still ran high or perhaps to Davis's stated interest in psychological rather than political origins of the war, the film fails to recognise the political and military organization of communist forces in Vietnam. Instead, the Vietnamese in Hearts and Minds are movingly depicted as passive victims, powerless and largely apolitical, the embodiment of pure human suffering, an oversimplification that ultimately reverses but does not actually correct the racist stereotypes (of the Oriental-as-in-human-menace) familiar from government propaganda and Hollywood film. Likewise, Davis's representations of those Americans who supported the war and the nature of US war culture that informed their actions offer little insight into the war's causes. For instance, Davis draws no distinction between those politicians who led the country into war and those veterans who were conscripted and persuaded, and remained persuaded, of its justice. Davis appears to imply, in fact, that war's violence is somehow natural to, and emerges from, blue-collar and small-town America, as demonstrated in the sequences that compare a high school football game in Ohio to combat in Vietnam. This assumption likewise underpins the film's representation of Lt Coker, a prisoner of war who returns from Vietnam to his working-class neighbourhood in Linden, NJ after six years of imprisonment with a message of gratitude and patriotism for his neighbours. Coker appears a brutal buffoon, particularly when placed in opposition to the more sophisticated and articulate anti-war veterans. For Davis to simply demonize, rather than attempt to understand, a veteran like Coker and the community who welcomed him home is a significant failing in a film whose stated purpose was to explore the psychological basis of the war in American society. It also effectively demonstrates both the power and limitations of Davis's preferred formal strategies in representing the Vietnam War and its causes and effects.

AMANDA HOWELL

Hearts and Minds (US, Touchstone-Audjeff-BBS Production, 1974, 112 mins). A Warner Bros/Columbia Presentation. Distributed by Nelson Entertainment. Produced by Bert Schneider and Peter Davis. Directed by Peter Davis. Script by Peter Davis. Cinematography by Richard Pearce. Edited by Lynzee Klingmann.

Further reading

Anderegg, Michael (ed.), *Inventing Vietnam: The War in Film and Television*, Philadelphia, PA: Temple University Press, 1991.

Barnow, Eric, *Documentary: A History of the Non-Fiction Film*, second edn, Oxford: Oxford University Press, 1993.

Barsam, Richard M., *Nonfiction Film: A Critical History*, Bloomington, IN: Indiana University Press, 1992.

Biskind, Peter, 'Hearts and Minds', *Cineaste* 7, 1975: 31–2.

Grosser, David, '"We aren't on the wrong side, we are the wrong side": Peter Davis Targets (American) Hearts and Minds', in *From Hanoi to Hollywood: The Vietnam War in American Film*, New Brunswick, NJ: Rutgers University Press, 1990: 269–85.

Landau, Saul, '"Hearts and Minds": An American Film Trial', *Jump Cut* 8, 1975: 3–5.

Rosenthal, Alan, *The Documentary Conscience: A Casebook in Film Making*, Berkeley, CA: University of California Press, 1980.

Ryan, Michael and Kellner, Douglas, *Camera Politica: The Politics and Ideology of Contemporary Hollywood Film*, Bloomington, IN: Indiana University Press, 1990.

Hearts of Darkness: A Filmmaker's Apocalypse

(US, Bahr, Hickenlooper, Coppola, 1991)

During the two hundred and thirty-eight days that it took for Francis Ford Coppola and company to finish principal shooting of Apocalypse Now in the Philippines (chosen as a location for its physical resemblance to Vietnam), Coppola's wife Eleanor documented on camera and in writing the nightmarish trials experienced by the film's cast, crew and, perhaps most profoundly (certainly on the most levels: physical, psychological, economic, spiritual), its renowned director. The astounding commercial and critical success of Apocalypse Now after its eventual release in 1979—a share of the Palm D'Or at Cannes, three Golden Globes, two Academy Awards, more than $150 million at box offices worldwide—resulted in its attaining almost immediately the status of a contemporary American classic. Contributing mightily to the legend is Hearts of Darkness: A Filmmaker's Apocalypse (1991), directed by Fax Bahr with George Hickenlooper, which chronicles and reflects on the turbulent making of Coppola's film. Hearts of Darkness seamlessly blends together the on- and off-set footage shot by Eleanor (as well as private conversations between her and her husband that Coppola was unaware at the time were being taped) with more standard 'talking head' interviews with numerous people involved in the production (conducted by Bahr more than ten years later). Also punctuating the documentary are outtakes and scenes left on the cutting-room floor, as well as brief but effective aural snippets of Orson Welles narrating Joseph Conrad's 1901 novel *Heart of Darkness* (on which the Apocalypse Now screenplay was loosely based) for the Mercury Theater radio programme in 1938.

Hearts of Darkness is widely considered to be among the very best entries in the subgenre loosely known as 'making-of' documentaries, in large part because of its creators' access to primary source materials that would normally be extremely difficult to obtain, much less receive permission to use. These were among the highlights (lowlights for those involved): interruptions on set by the Filipino military; increasingly grim confessions of insecurity and despair by the director, whose artistic/commercial reputation and financial well-being were very much on the line, to his wife; a serious heart attack suffered by the film's main actor, Martin Sheen, during the middle of shooting; and heated discussions between Coppola and two of his key cast members, Dennis Hopper (seemingly stoned the entire time and incapable of remembering his lines) and Marlon Brando (who showed up on-set grossly overweight, without having read Conrad's source novel and costing the already way over-budget production a cool million dollars a week). Add to all this the sacking of the originally contracted lead, Harvey Keitel; a massive typhoon that destroyed numerous sets; Coppola's endless dissatisfaction with his film's

Figure 5 Hearts of Darkness: A Filmmaker's Apocalypse, 1979; documentary released 1991 (Courtesy of the Everett Collection)

conclusion; and the fact that a project originally scheduled for sixteen weeks of shooting ended up taking more than three years to complete (Bahr and Hickenlooper insert shots of trade paper headlines at the time snidely asking, 'Apocalypse When?'), and one has to figure that the creators of Hearts of Darkness must have known they had a 'making-of' goldmine on their hands.

Reviewers such as Roger Ebert have gushed of Hearts of Darkness that 'the making of a film has never been documented with more penetration and truth'. A running joke (not without a hint of seriousness) even has it that Bahr and Hickenlooper's documentary is more cogent and entertaining than the film it is about. For all its much-deserved credit, however, Hearts of Darkness is actually highly atypical for a 'making-of' documentary and, in fact, bears a problematic relationship with this species of nonfiction filmmaking. Because the principal shooter had so much personally at stake in her subject—she was, after all, married to the larger-than-life auteur in charge of the entire production/circus she was covering—any aspiration on her part to provide an objective recording of events would of necessity be compromised from the start. As Eleanor wrote at the time in her subsequently published *Notes on the Making of Apocalypse Now*, 'I was watching from the point of view of the observer, not realising that I was on the journey too.' The viewer of Hearts of Darkness may well wonder why, despite all of the amazing behind-the-scenes footage that Eleanor managed to obtain, there is nothing of Harvey Keitel and very little by way of explanation for Coppola's decision to fire his well-known star; why there is hardly any indication of Coppola's notoriously bad temper on set; or why the seriously strained relationship between Eleanor and her husband goes unnoted. (By way of contrast, in *Notes* Eleanor writes of Coppola's numerous affairs during the shoot, his general lack of interest in her, and their discussion near the end of production as to whether or not to get a divorce.) As an online analysis of Bahr and Hickenlooper's documentary astutely puts the point, 'despite the fact that Hearts of Darkness is not Eleanor's documentary, Hearts of Darkness is still very much the "official Coppola family" version of events'.

Not addressed in previous writing on Hearts of Darkness, but one of the documentary's most fascinating aspects, is the way it effectively (though almost certainly unintentionally) reveals the paradoxical nature of auteurism as a critical concept in film scholarship, as well as in popular thinking about Coppola's career as a maverick director with a unique and uncompromising artistic vision. On the one hand, and as the documentary labours to make clear beyond the shadow of a doubt, Apocalypse Now could only have been a Coppola picture (we learn from Eleanor's voice-over narration that Orson Welles, another genius auteur, from a different era, failed in his efforts to adapt Conrad's novel for his directorial debut, so he made Citizen Kane (1941) instead). On the other hand, it is just as clear that Apocalypse Now could never have been anything near the masterpiece it turned out to be had Coppola not received such magnificent contributions from his cast and crew—not to mention from Eleanor, who, if Hearts of Darkness is at all to be trusted, had much more faith in her husband than he had in himself.

STEVEN JAY SCHNEIDER

Hearts of Darkness: A Filmmaker's Apocalypse (US, American Zoetrope, 1991, 96 mins). Distributed by Showtime Networks Inc. and Triton Pictures. Produced by Doug Claybourne, Les Mayfield, Fred Roos, and George Zaloom. Directed by Fax Bahr, George Hickenlooper, and Eleanor Coppola (additional footage). Written by Fax Bahr and George Hickenlooper. Cinematography by Larry Carney, Igor Meglic, and Steven Wacks. Edited by Michael Gree and Jay Miracle. Original music by Todd Boekelheide. Non-original music by Carmine Coppola, Francis Ford Coppola, and Mickey Hart. Sound by Craig M. Otte and Brian Risner.

Further reading

Anon, 'Real 2 Reel: Hearts of Darkness: A Filmmaker's Apocalypse', Film Education website: www.filmeducation.org/secondary/s_archive/documentary/heartsofdarkness (accessed April 15, 2002).

Biskind, Peter, *Easy Riders, Raging Bulls*, London: Bloomsbury, 1998.

Coppola, Eleanor, *Notes on the Making of Apocalypse Now*, London: Faber & Faber, 1979.

Cowie, Peter, *The Apocalypse Now Book*, London: Faber & Faber, 2000.

——*Coppola*, London: Faber & Faber, 1989.

Ebert, Roger, 'Hearts of Darkness: A Filmmaker's Apocalypse', *Chicago Sun-Times*, January 17, 1992, www.suntimes.com/ebert/ebertreviews/1992/01/736538_html

Haber, Darren, 'Deconstructing Francis: Apocalypse Now and the End of the '70s', *Images: A Journal of Film and Popular Culture* 9, January 2000, www.imagesjournal.com/issue09/features/coppola/default-yes.htm (accessed April 15, 2002).

Hegedus, Chris

Chris Hegedus has been actively engaged in the direct cinema style of filmmaking since the mid-1970s. Her work as half of the well-respected team of Pennebaker-Hegedus has brought much to the discussion of documentary style and technique. Hegedus began her personal and professional relationship with D.A. Pennebaker in 1976, first as an editorial assistant and later as a codirector, editor, and sound technician.

The filmmakers were married in the 1980s. Hegedus embraced notions of documentary form championed by Pennebaker and his colleagues Richard Leacock and David and Albert Maysles.

The Energy War, released in 1978, was the first major work of the Pennebaker-Hegedus team. The three-part PBS series explores the eighteen-month battle over the National Energy Plan put forth by the Carter administration (Thompson 1993). During this time Hegedus had also begun work editing the raw material Pennebaker had shot in 1971 of the historic debate between Norman Mailer and such feminist activists as Germaine Greer, Jill Johnston, Susan Sontag, and Jaqueline Ceballos (president of the National Organization for Women at the time). The filmed footage had been shelved for years, and Hegedus saw the potential within the reels for an exciting work. Her editing, according to Pennebaker, gave the film a life: 'Chris did a really good job of editing. It's pretty ratty, probably as badly shot as anything I've ever done. Chris edited it for content, and content always wins over form. Nobody ever pays attention after the worst five minutes of the most horribly shot movie you can imagine, even if it's about something interesting' (Gordon 2001). Hegedus found that the material lent itself to the aesthetic cultivated by the Direct Cinema movement. 'In some ways [...] it was appropriate that it took place in Town Hall. Everyone was participating, screaming and yelling back, and they were as much a part of the event as those on stage. I felt when I edited it, it was important to keep that feeling of excitement. Those swing pans were helpful for knowing this person made that comment or look' (Gordon 2001). This film, like others in the Pennebaker-Hegedus oeuvre, creates an environment in which viewers feel very much a part of the action. There are no questions asked of the subjects, no canned responses from press release-style preparations, and the actions that occur are filmed as they happen. Little interaction exists between the filmmaker and the subject in the area of content.

The team received an Oscar nomination for their 1993 documentary work The War Room. This film began as an invitation to create a work about the presidential election of 1992 but quickly evolved into a more specific investigation of the public relations machine behind the Clinton candidacy. Pennebaker and Hegedus were not allowed to directly follow or constantly film the presidential hopeful, but they were allowed unlimited access to the activities of George Stephanopolis, the communications director, and James Carville, chief political strategist for the campaign. The film gives the viewer an intimate look at the process behind the candidate, the frustrations and triumphs within the daily activities, and the very human elements of the political landscape. Hegedus said, 'I never understand why people let us film them, because I hate to be filmed so much. But people do see some reason for showing this, for people to see this process' (Thompson 1993).

These stylistic concerns are apparent in the various works done by the filmmaking team, as well as in works directed by Hegedus herself. Startup.com is a work codirected by Hegedus and Jehane Noujaim. The work, released in 2001, chronicles the 'spectacularly speedy rise and fall of an internet company called govWorks.com. Conceived and developed by Kaleil Isaza Tuzman and Tom Herman, friends since childhood, govWorks was designed to facilitate interaction between local government, citizens, and businesses and began during the dotcom boom' (Fuchs 2001). Noujaim was the roommate of Tuzman at the time the film was conceived, so the filmmakers had, again, an amazing level of access to the subjects. Hegedus explains her approach to contemporary documentary filmmaking: 'We're always looking for a story where we can follow some person through something in their life that is important to them, that has some kind of risk and built-in dramatic structure, so that we can make a film in a style that is as similar to a fictional feature as possible, and gives the viewer the sense that he's dropped in that world and gets to experience it. That's what has always been interesting to me in filmmaking, and quite often you can't do that, you don't get the dramatic arc or a character that is interesting' (Fuchs 2001). The concept is solidified in the approach to production: 'We don't do much interviewing along the way' because the subjects 'start seeing themselves as actors in their own lives'. The relationship that is created between the filmmakers and the subjects by the constant presence of the camera is one in which trust is a necessary by-product. Hegedus says, 'You don't deny that you're there. But if you are there enough, you really are part of their life and they can't be bothered with you after a while.' The piece was shot entirely on a small DV camera, thus adding to the ability to work in an unobtrusive fashion to capture the story. Says Hegedus, 'I am striving for films that give me the same excitement that the first cinéma vérité films gave me. Those were films where I felt I was inside this world getting a peak at it, the primal voyeurism that we all have that early vérité films gave, with a story as dramatic as any story can be' (Gordon 2001). Hegedus's works since include 2002's Only the Strong Survive, which features performances by Wilson Pickett, Issac Hayes, and other soul artists, and her 2003 work Elaine Stritch at Liberty, which documents a theatrical performance.

TAMMY A. KINSEY

See also: War Room, The

Biography

Born 1952. Early interest in the arts, photography, and minimalist filmmaking. Attended Hartford Art School, then Nova Scotia School of Art and Design. Worked at University of Michigan Hospital filming surgical procedures. Moved to New York City, 1975. Camera work on Lizzie Borden's feminist feature Born in Flames. Begins collaboration with D.A. Pennebaker, 1976. Served as editor for Town Bloody Hall material left untouched since 1971. Oscar nomination for The War Room, 1993. DoubleTake Documentary Film Festival Career Award (shared with D.A. Pennebaker), 2000. DoubleTake Documentary Film Festival MTV News Documentary Prize (shared with Jehane Noujaim) for Startup.com, 2001. Philadelphia Film Festival Jury Award, Best Documentary for Startup.com (shared with Jehane Noujaim), 2001. Awarded International Documentary Association (IDA) Award for Feature Documentary for Startup.com (shared with Jehane Noujaim), 2001. Directors' Guild of America Award for Outstanding Directorial Achievement in a Documentary (shared with Jehane Noujaim), 2002. Munich Film Festival Bavarian Documentary Honorary Award (shared with D.A. Pennebaker), 2002. CINE Trailblazer Award (shared with D.A. Pennebaker), 2004.

Selected films

1977 Energy War
1979 Town Bloody Hall
1981 DeLorean
1986 Jimi Plays Monterey
1993 The War Room
1997 Moon over Broadway
1999 Searching for Jimi Hendrix
2000 Down from the Mountain
2001 Startup.com
2002 Only the Strong Survive
2003 Elaine Stritch at Liberty

Further reading

Fuchs, Cynthia, 'It Is Kind of a Dance: An Interview with Jehane Noujaim and Chris Hegedus', www.nitrateonline.com/2001/fstartup.html, 2001.

Gordon, Rachel, 'Documenting Life: A Conversation with D.A. Pennebaker and Chris Hegedus', filmcritic.com/misc/emporium.nsf/84dbbfa4d710144986256c290016f76e/f452990a995db11988256afe008326aa?OpenDocument&Highlight=0,pennebaker, 2001.

The Music and Film Network, 'Visionary Documentary Filmmakers D.A. Pennebaker and Chris Hegedus: What Makes It Art Anyway?' The Music and Film Network Inc., 2002, www.musicandfilmnetwork.com/penneheg.htm.

Stubbs, Liz, *Documentary Filmmakers Speak*, New York: Allworth Press, 2002.

Thompson, Patricia, 'Inside the Clinton Campaign War Room with Chris Hegedus and D.A. Pennebaker', *The Independent* 16, no. 1, January/February 1993: 30–5, New York: Foundation for Independent Film and Video, Inc.

Heidi Fleiss: Hollywood Madam

(UK, Broomfield, 1995)

Nick Broomfield's progress as a documentary filmmaker has in many ways mirrored wider aesthetic, political, and production/distribution trends in the genre. Early films such as Behind the Rent Strike (1974) and Juvenile Liaison (1975) (both codirected with Joan Churchill) are good examples of a direct cinema or vérité style of polemical filmmaking; middle-period films such as Tattooed Tears (1978) and Soldier Girls (1981) (still with Churchill) are more like—though not quite like—Frederick Wiseman-type observational films; the sole directed films since the late 1980s, with Broomfield playing a large on-screen role, might be called self-reflexive or postmodern. There is a sense that in them he established a persona and found a distinctive personal style (so much so that this persona—Broomfield with headphones and microphone, asking awkward questions and casting conspiratorial looks at the camera—featured in a series of 1999 Volkswagen commercials).

Clearly, Broomfield belongs among those documentary filmmakers, including Errol Morris, who are reacting against claims that documentary may have made in the past to objectivity and the capacity to capture the real. Instead, viewers experience the encounter and negotiation between the filmmaker (whether on-screen or, like Morris, not), the camera, and the subject. This echoes the cinéma vérité tradition associated with Jean Rouch and Edgar Morin's Chronique d'un été, in which Rouch and Morin are frequently seen and heard on camera setting situations up, orchestrating encounters to be filmed, and discussing what they are doing. Several commentators, including Stella Bruzzi, have called this mode the 'performative documentary'.

Like Michael Moore, whose films also feature an on-screen persona whose relationship to any 'real' Michael Moore is essentially unknowable, Broomfield's commercial success (or perhaps we should say his ability to continue making films) seems to have depended on the combination of controversial subjects—serial killers, rock star suicides, fascist leaders, sexual fetishists—all of which seem to lure him, whether from perversity or for purely commercial reasons and humour. Certainly in Heidi Fleiss Broomfield demonstrates a fascinated, prurient interest in the Los Angeles/Hollywood underworld of pornography, drugs, call girls, and crime.

Two insistent motifs recur. First are the images that open the film—shaky, slowed-down television footage of Fleiss, smiling, at her first court appearance, which are linked with the film's quest to discover who is/was the real Heidi and why she did what she did. Second are the images of that quest, through Broomfield's car window, driving forward, to the sound of expectant music (reminiscent of Morris's Thin Blue Line) and Broomfield's voice explaining what leads are being followed; however, the impression of investigative journalism is misleading. Even quite early on, bereft of ideas and leads, Broomfield, introducing a sequence of random meetings with street prostitutes, comments that 'in desperation, we drove down Sunset Boulevard looking for clues'.

As this implies, the film relies quite heavily on irony and understatement. At another point, his lead collapsing, Broomfield concedes that he 'could tell things weren't going so well'. Later, he asks a thug, over the telephone, sweetly and reasonably, 'I just wanted to ask you if you put the bullet holes in Ivan's ceiling'. Much humour derives from the tension between Broomfield's polite, ingratiating English manner, verging on the disinterested and smug, and the more brash, vulgar style of his subjects; it is striking that most of Broomfield's recent subjects have been American.

One way to think about Broomfield's films, and Heidi Fleiss in particular, is as documenting the preparatory processes for documentary filmmaking before actually shooting the film—researching, interviewing, trying to find an appropriate structure. Broomfield goes out of his way, for example, to show the cash transactions that underpin the interviews. These preliminaries, which we would not normally see, provide the substance for the film. Most filmmakers, after the 'research' process we witness, would have reached the conclusion that there was not really a film here—that not enough had been, or could be, discovered—and abandoned it. With Broomfield, reaching this conclusion is the film. Early on, Alex, former madam and FBI informer, comments that 'Hollywood doesn't want to be revealed', nor is it. Thus, though the film starts as 'investigative journalism', it discovers very little (although, obliquely, we begin to guess a good deal about Heidi, Alex, and Ivan Nagy and the milieu in which they operate). Indeed, the film leaves us with precious few means to make much sense of the sound-over conversation between Heidi and Ivan as the end credits play out.

Bruzzi highlights the question of directorial or authorial 'control' in our responses to Heidi Fleiss. To a certain extent, we feel initially that Broomfield is in control—following leads, connecting, revealing. By the end, however, the film is clearly going nowhere investigatively, and Broomfield, or his persona, is lost. Still trying to follow up pointless leads, he is told by Alex that he is a 'greedy pig', by Ivan that he is a 'fool' and 'rube', 'flogging a dead horse' and 'there is nothing to understand'. Heidi ends with 'You're missing something, Nick [...] It's so funny, you're way off', and walks out on him.

How we should read this apparent floundering remains uncertain. Is this an invitation to ironic reflection on the filmmaker's incompetence? Is it a conceit, a carefully engineered descent into confusion and chaos? Is it innocent evidence of Broomfield's defeat and loss of control? The pattern of failing to achieve objectives is so familiar from other Broomfield films that we must take it as willed here, too. Either way, Broomfield succeeds—fascinatingly and entertainingly—in reminding us of the artificial nature of the documentary enterprise and its inherent contradictions.

JIM HILLIER

Heidi Fleiss: Hollywood Madam (UK, A Lafayette Film Production for the BBC, produced in association with IN Pictures, the Canadian Broadcasting Corporation, Cinemax and Westdeustcher Rundfunk, Koln, 1995, 107 mins). Produced and directed by Nick Broomfield. Coproduced by Kahane Coru, and Jamie Ader-Brown. Director of photography: Paul Kloss. Sound by Dirk Farner. Music by David Bergeaud. Edited by S.J. Bloom. Post supervision by Joan Churchill.

Further reading

Broomfield, Nick, 'The Burning Question', in Kevin Macdonald and Mark Cousins (eds), *Imagining Reality*, London and Boston: Faber & Faber, 1996.

Bruzzi, Stella, *New Documentary: A Critical Introduction*, London and New York: Routledge, 2000.

Macdonald, Kevin and Cousins, Mark (eds), *Imagining Reality*, London and Boston: Faber & Faber, 1996.

Pearson, Allison, 'Nick Broomfield: The Fly in the Ointment', in Kevin Macdonald and Mark Cousins (eds), *Imagining Reality*, London and Boston: Faber & Faber, 1996.

Hell Unlimited

(UK, McLaren, 1936)

Hell Unlimited was made by Norman McLaren and Helen Biggar to protest against profits in armaments during a period when fascism was growing throughout Europe. McLaren had already made a few artistic experiments on film that were largely formalist in nature and would become a renowned abstract filmmaker, undertaking the majority of his work at the National Film Board of Canada. Biggar was a sculptress and an active member of the British Communist Party, and went on to make Challenge to Fascism in the following year. Though McLaren is not generally known as a political filmmaker, this was a period when many international avant-garde artists became more socially aware, and when documentary filmmaking and the avant-garde film became somewhat intertwined. McLaren briefly became involved in overtly political films and had also been the cameraman on Ivor Montagu's Defence of Madrid (1936), which documented Franco's attack on the city.

Made with help from students and tutors at the Glasgow School of Art, Hell Unlimited is one of the most interesting films to merge avant-garde formalism and direct political protest in the interwar period. In the 1930s there was a rise in political workers' film movements, and a number of exhibiting outlets, distribution units, and production bases arose, such as Kino and the Workers Film and Photo League. While the primary activity of this movement was to distribute and exhibit films of a left-wing, political nature, a number of films were also produced in this milieu. For the most part, these were 'alternative' newsreels: documents of left-wing activities. There were, however, a few films made that were more ambitious in nature, such as Bread (1934), which used experimental montage sequences to comment on class inequalities. While Hell Unlimited was not made directly under the auspices of the workers' film movement, it was indirectly relate to this movement. It should also be seen as part of the more modernist, experimental activities occurring in Britain at the time, activities that can be traced back to the formation of the Film Society (in 1925) and the existence of the journals Close Up (1927–33) and Film Art (1933–7).

Hell Unlimited is both extremely experimental in nature and highly didactic in tone. It uses a mixture of animation, stock shots, and rapid montage to protest against profits made from armaments and implores citizens to do everything that they can to protest the war. It begins with a chart reflecting spending on health, education, and armaments over the years. As the years peel away into the 1930s, the armaments bar gets higher and higher, eventually bursting out of the chart. The situation is explicitly linked to World War I, and a depiction of events that took place in 1915 follows. Titles such as 'die' and 'to make a world safe for democracy' are flashed across the screen, followed by scenes of dead bodies, intercut with a stop-motion sequence of money piling high, eventually rising out of the screen, and titles declaring the statistical costs of war (both monetary and human). The titles reflect the contradictory ideology that is bandied about by governments in times of crisis, while the graphics and footage attempt to portray the chasm between rhetoric and actuality.

The film continues to attack the government for its links with capitalist concerns and for placing profits above human concerns. It relentlessly mocks the 'official' truth propagated by governments, as well as by the mainstream media, by using dialectical montage and animation. For example, at one stage in the film a title reads 'Prosperity is returning'. This is followed by headlines reporting an economic revival, with a chart showing a rise in financial prosperity. Shots of factories are then shown, whilst a government official shouts (via titles): 'we have reduced the absolute limit whilst other countries have been rearming'. This sequence, though, is a parody of 'official truth'. The next sequence shows a man listening to the speech through his radio, followed by a cut to models in his room watering plants that sprout monstrous growths, such as grenades and fighter planes. Here, pixillation methods reveal a deeper truth than official newsreels and question the often-accepted veracity of such newsreels (and, by extension, of naturalistic/actuality aesthetics). Animation and 'tricks'—by conventional methods connected to illusion (while actual footage was connected to reality)—are associated with a deeper, unspoken 'truth'.

Although Hell Unlimited may seem slightly naïve in its politics, in that it fails to address the issue of what would happen if nobody confronted fascism, it does address serious issues, such as the undemocratic operations of supposedly democratic governments and the underhand ways in which they go about business. It does not shy away from attacking particular targets, and although it may be dogmatic and propagandistic, it also questions any 'innocent' or 'transparent' representation, placing doubt on the ability of images to be equated with 'truth'. It may be dogmatic and propagandistic in one sense, but its use of animation to reveal deeper truths behind newsreel images opens up room for scepticism toward any form of 'transparent' representation.

Although arguments that aesthetics and politics did not merge within British culture during this period have most definitely been overstated (because of a simplistic appreciation of what is 'political'), there was hostility in some areas between 'bohemian' formalism and direct political agitation. Hell Unlimited brings together such areas, probably because, as Marris has pointed out, the film emerged from the 'intersection of two apparatuses (filmmakers with Communist Party connections in an art school context)'. Apart from the two films that I have mentioned, as well as Peace and Plenty (Montagu/Kino, 1939), there is little evidence that workers' film groups adopted aesthetic formalism on many occasions.

JAMIE SEXTON

Hell Unlimited (UK, Glasgow Kino and Kino, 1936, 16mm, black and white, 14 mins). Directed, produced, and edited by Norman McLaren and Helen Biggar. Camera work by Norman McLaren, made with the support and assistance of the Glasgow School of Art.

Further reading

Collins, Maynard, *Norman McLaren*, Ottawa: Canadian Film Institute, 1976.

Curtis, David, *Norman McLaren*, Edinburgh: Scottish Arts Council Catalogue, 1977.

Dobson, Terrence, 'The Film Work of Norman McLaren', PhD thesis: University of Canterbury, New Zealand, 1994.

Dusinberre, Deke, 'The Avant-Garde Attitude in the Thirties', in Don Macpherson (ed.), *Traditions of Independence: British Cinema in the Thirties*, London: BFI, 1980.

Hogenkamp, Bert, 'Film and the Workers' Movement in Britain, 1929–39', *Sight and Sound* 45, no. 2, spring 1976.

——*Deadly Parallels: Film and the Left in Britain, 1929–39*, London: Lawrence and Wishart, 1986.

Marris, Paul, 'Politics and "Independent" Film in the Decade of Defeat', in Don Macpherson (ed.), *Traditions of Independence: British Cinema in the Thirties*, London: BFI, 1980.

O'Pray, Michael (ed.), *The British Avant-Garde Film 1926–95*, Luton: University of Luton Press, 1996.

Richard, Valliere T., *Norman McLaren: Manipulator of Movement*, East Brunswick, NJ: Associated University Presses, Inc., 1982.

Heller, Peter

To locate the world in the personal, immediate reality, to use the micro to explain the macro—these are central strategies adopted in the films of Peter Heller. This filmmaker concentrates on the developing world, and the media images from that region that are made available to the rest of the world. Heller's work also focuses on the underprivileged in German society. For Heller, as a political filmmaker in the tradition of the student movement, these seemingly disparate realities are related, and he continually draws attention to similarities among seemingly different societies. He is convinced that Europeans are not able to teach other societies anything, but should respect the culture and knowledge of those other societies. He considers it a privilege of his professsion, that he is allowed to search out these similarities in regions around the world, and report on what he finds via film.

A commitment to in-depth research is the backbone of his work; often, the shoot itself is the shortest portion of the overall filmmaking project. In his films, Heller often challenges cliché images of poor Africans decimated by famine and war, which dominate mainstream news. He wants to propagate other images that convey the dignity of African lifestyles, although he sometimes faces challenges, as in the making of the film Adalil (1991). In this film, his protagonist, a strong woman he wants to show as independent, reneged on the film contact in objection to the hectic pace of filmmaking, as he disclosed in articles that he later wrote.

Beside his numerous films on Africa and Latin America, one of his strongest pieces is a film series on a poor family with eight children in Cologne, whom he filmed for a number of years starting in 1976. It is an intimate chronicle of poverty in Germany and a testament to the strength needed to maintain a cohesive family unit in the face of such circumstances. Peter Heller visited the family without the camera as well, and essentially became a part of the family. It is an ethnographic view on an aspect of German reality that is not often of interest to filmmakers.

In his first film on the family, Arm würd' ich nicht sagen (1977), he had to transfer the small apartment into a studio with lights and other film equipment. It was followed by … arm würd' ich nicht sagen oder die Kunst zu leben (1986) and Mama General (1997). The use of additional cameras in the later films made it possible to follow the daily life of the family much more closely and intimately. After the death of the mother, the family fell apart, as depicted in Mutter Jahre (2004).

KAY HOFFMANN

Biography

Born in Prague (CSSR) on December 12, 1946. Moved to Germany in 1960. 1967–9 apprenticeship as photographer. 1969–72 studied at the film school in Munich. Practical courses at TV stations in Europe, Latin America, and Asia. 1973–4 freelancer at German and Swiss stations; worked as a cameraman for different productions while producing own films. Conducted many film seminars for the Goethe Insitute and German universities. Published regularly on problems associated with media in the developing world. A founding member of the German media advisory council for political development, the international film network 'Zebra', and the EDI/dfi in Mühlheim. Founding member and chairman of the Association Documentary Film (AG, DOK). Received many international prizes, awards, and recognition and films were shown in retrospectives in Amsterdam, Munich, Atlanta, Chicago, and Washington.

Selected films

1973 Heile Welt und Dritte Welt/Nice World and Third World: director, scriptwriter
1973 Mama und Papa/Mum and Dad: director, scriptwriter
1975 Das Geschäft mit der Party/The Business with the Party: director, scriptwriter
1976 Herren im eigenen Land/Masters in Their Land: director, scriptwriter
1977 Sklaven im eigenen Land/Slaves in Their Land: director, scriptwriter
1977 arm würd' ich nicht sagen/I Wouldn't Say/Poor: director, scriptwriter
1978 Die Liebe zum Imperium/Love of the Empire: director, script, camera
1980 Usambara: director, scriptwriter
1980 Mbogos Ernte oder die Teilung der Welt/Mbogos Harvest: director, scriptwriter
1982 Der vergessene Führer/The Forgotten Führer: director, scriptwriter
1983 Wie andere Neger auch/The Same as All Negroes: director, scriptwriter

1985 Dschungelburger-Hackfleischordnung international/Jungleburgers: director, scriptwriter
1987 Das Brot des Siegers/Winner's Bread: director, scriptwriter
1991 Hungersnot zum Abendbrot/Famine at Supper: director, scriptwriter
1991 Adalil-Herrin der Zelte/Adalil—The Mistress of the Tents: director, script with Sylvie Banuls
1993 Sieg im Osten/Victory in the East: director, scriptwriter
1996 Die Grille mit dem Maulkorb/The Cricket with the Muzzle: director, scriptwriter
1997 Mama General/General Mama: director, script (both with Silvie Banuls)
1999 Tam Tam zur Tagesschau/Tam Tam at the News: director, scriptwriter
2003 Rauchopfer/Smoke Sacrifice: director, scriptwriter
2004 Mutter Jahre/Mother for Life: director, script (both with Sylvie Banuls)

Further reading

Banuks, Sylvie and Heller, Peter, 'Fremde Nähe—Vertraute Distanz', in Julia Bayer, Andrea Engl and Melanie Liebheit (eds), *Strategien der Annäherung. Darsellungen des Fremden im deutschen Fernsehen*, Bad Honnef, 2004: 40–61.

Petermann, Werner, *Peter Heller Werk-Schau*, München, 1985.

Roth, Wilhelm, *Der Dokumentarfilm seit 1960*, München, Luzern, 1982.

Herzog, Werner

Along with Wim Wenders and Rainer Werner Fassbinder, Werner Herzog was the most internationally prominent member of the New German Cinema. He is popularly associated with a remarkable series of fictional narrative films from the 1970s and early 1980s that won him the reputation of being the movement's 'romantic visionary'. Yet even in that period of his career he was as active in documentary as in fiction. With his fiction output decreasing in quantity and consistently failing to match the standards or attract the acclaim of his earlier work, the 1990s and 2000s saw him concentrate increasingly on the documentary with often happier results.

Both strands of his oeuvre are thematically linked by a preoccupation with 'visionary' characters whose perceptions of the world leave them alienated from mainstream society and often existing at the limits of human (in)communication. Grandiose dreamers, madmen, dwarves, vampires, the physically and mentally handicapped, and survivors like Dieter Dengler in Flucht aus Laos/Little Dieter Needs to Fly (1997) and Juliane Köpcke in Julianes Sturz in den Dschungel/Wings of Hope (1999) whose traumatic experiences have in some way set them apart, are representative of the characters from whose extreme modes of being Herzog has posited an expanded vision of existence consistently challenging to the perceived spiritual blindness of societal norms. His major trope in creating images of these characters' subjective existences is his Romanticist use of landscapes, which while real, take on the attributes of 'landscapes that exist only in our dreams [...] inner landscapes' (Cronin 2002). Such documentaries as Fata Morgana (1970) and Lektionen in Finsternis/Lessons in Darkness (1992) even dispense with a central human focus altogether in favour of 'dreaming' pre- and post-human desertscapes through existing locations. Crucial to the process of endowing his landscapes with oneiric qualities is Herzog's careful selection of accompanying music track. Whether opera in a jungle, Leonard Cohen in an African desert or the formerly ubiquitous sounds of Florian Fricke's group Popol Vuh, the music often supplies a decisively enriching contrast to the image. La Soufrière (1977) marks Herzog's most lucid and self-reflexive exploration of his work with apocalyptically inflected landscape. Accompanied by two cameramen, he visits the evacuated island of La Soufrière, which is on the verge of an apparently inevitable volcanic disaster. The volcano's eventual nonexplosion frustrates the confessedly embarrassed filmmaker's desire to record the island's destruction. The landscape has for once rejected his 'dream' of it, even as it appeared as appropriately unworldly. This leaves comically transparent the manipulative dynamic involved between artist and landscape even in an ostensible documentary.

Yet Herzog is clear in his refusal to view his documentary output as distinct from his other work, and he has profitably explored fiction/documentary interfaces to the benefit of both forms. He sees no harm in, for example, falsely claiming in voice-over that firemen are reigniting recently extinguished oil wells out of madness, in order to have something to put out again, in Lessons in Darkness, or in hiring local drunks to play pilgrims in Glocken aus der Tiefe/Bells from the Deep (1993). His poetic conception of the 'truth' of a situation takes precedence over its factual details. In filming Herz Aus Glas/Heart of Glass (1976), a fiction film, with the entire cast under hypnosis or in starring ex-asylum inmate Bruno S. in two other nondocumentaries that both, to varying degrees, draw on his troubled character, Herzog takes risks that are arguably more appropriate to the more flexible documentary format. Yet it is possible that the psychodrama of Bruno S.'s performance in Jeder für sich und Gott gegen alle/The Enigma of Kaspar Hauser (1974) foreshadows Herzog's leading Vietnam survivor Dieter Dengler to recreate the circumstances of his captivity while blindfolded in the documentary Little Dieter Learns to Fly. The desire to surmount the incommunicability of his protagonists' experiences is clear in both cases, but the presence of Herzog as interacting interviewer/narrator in the latter film personalises his wish to empathetically engage with his 'characters'. This process of identification, although not common to all his film portraits, is most pronounced in Die Grosse Ekstase des Bildschnitzers Steiner/The Great Ecstasy of Woodcarver Steiner (1973) in which Herzog, ski-jumper manqué, possessively hounds his taciturn ski-jumper hero even in his most stressful moments. Communication with (and among) the alienated becomes the explicit theme of Land des Schweigens und der Dunkelheit/Land of Silence and Darkness (1971), his moving study of deaf and blind woman Fini Straubinger and some of her fellow sufferers.

Aesthetically, the documentary has aided fiction in Herzog. For example, it has been more than once noted that the jungle adventures Aguirre, der Zorn Gottes/Aguirre, the Wrath of God (1972) and Fitzcarraldo (1982) draw much of their power from documenting their own gruelling and hazardous shoots; a vérité edge that endows the fiction with an effective textural vividness. Equally, the artistic failure of Invincible (2001) can be largely attributed to his adoption of a slicker style that sits awkwardly with his fundamentally raw approach to filming people and spaces. Yet he has theorised against the ethics of cinéma vérité as a documentary practice, denouncing the approach as superficial, 'the truth of accountants', and has used scenes of overt visual stylisation in his nonfiction work such as the famous extreme slow motion images of Woodcarver Steiner ski-flying. It is, beyond a doubt, the sometimes paradoxical dialectic between documentary and fiction inherent in Herzog's style that dynamises his entire filmmaking.

MAXIMILIAN LE CAIN

Biography

Born Werner Stipetic in Munich, Germany, 1942. Grew up in the remote mountain village of Sachrang. Travelled widely, making his first journey at the age of fourteen. While still at school, financed his first film by working nights at a steel factory. Founded Werner Herzog Filmproduktion which went on to produce the vast majority of his films. Made his first feature, Lebenszeichen/Signs of Life in 1968. In spite of accusations of fascism from the left, mainly centred around his 1970 film Auch Zwerge haben klein angefangen/Even Dwarfs Started Small, rose to prominence as part of the New German Cinema of the 1970s. Best known for his five-film collaboration with the actor Klaus Kinski.

Selected films

1970 Fata Morgana: director, writer, producer
1971 Land des Schweigens und der Dunkelheit/Land of Silence and Darkness: director, producer
1973 Die Grosse Ekstase des Bildschnitzers Steiner/The Ecstasy of Woodcarver Steiner: director, producer
1976 How Much Wood Would a Woodchuck Chuck: director, producer
1977 La Soufrière: director, producer
1980 God's Angry Man: director, producer
1980 Huie's Sermon: director, producer
1984 Ballade vom kleinen Soldaten/Ballad of the Little Soldier: director
1984 Gasherbrum—Der leuchtende Berg/The Dark Glow of the Mountains: director
1992 Lektionen in Finsternis/Lessons in Darkness: director, writer
1993 Glocken aus der Tiefe/Bells from the Deep: director
1995 Gesualdo—Tod für fünf Stimmen/Death for Five Voices: director, writer

1997 Flucht aus Laos/Little Dieter Learns to Fly: director, writer
1999 Julianes Sturz in den Dschungel/Wings of Hope: director, writer
1999 Mein liebster Feind/My Best Fiend: director, writer
2001 Pilgrimage: director, writer

Further reading

Blank, L. and Bogan, J. (eds), *Burden of Dreams: Screenplay, Journals, Photographs*, Berkeley, CA: North Atlantic Books, 1984.

Carrère, E., *Werner Herzog, Cinegraphique Series*, Paris: Edilig, 1982.

Corrigan, T., (ed.), *The Films of Werner Herzog: Between Mirage and History*, New York and London: Methuen, 1986.

Cronin, P. (ed.), *Herzog on Herzog*, London: Faber & Faber, 2002.

Pflaum, H.G., Prinzler, H.H., Theobaldy, J. and Wetzel, K. (eds), *Werner Herzog, Reihe Film 22*, München: Hanser, 1979.

Sirianni, P., *Il Cinema di Werner Herzog*, Firenze: La Nuova Italia, 1980.

Heyer, John

In recent times, amongst the talk of 'global cinema' John Heyer is a salient reminder of how, from its earliest days, Australian documentary film was an international medium.

Like many others of his generation, Heyer established his connection to the international documentary community in the 1930s and 1940s through the cinema publications he read.

He read journals such as *Close Up*, *Cinema Quarterly*, *Experimental Cinema*, and corresponded with the State Film School in Moscow, with British documentary filmmakers, and with counterparts in the United States. Heyer also watched imported films such as the Soviet classics that were at this time becoming available through the cultural arms of embassies.

John Grierson and Robert Flaherty provided, respectively, lasting models for Heyer's agitation for documentary film sponsorship and a poetic vision for his documentary films. Heyer began his career as a factotum on a range of Australian features in the late 1930s. During this period he also made advertising films as well as his first documentary film, New Pastures (1940), for the New South Wales Milk Marketing Board. This documentary saw the emergence in Australia of the sponsored documentary that looked to nationalist concerns tempered with an aesthetic framework.

Like many documentary filmmakers internationally, World War II provided the focus on propaganda that realist filmmaking could provide. During the war Heyer was appointed producer for the Allied Works Council and member of the Prime Minister's Propaganda and Morale Committee. In 1944 he worked as second unit director and shooting script collaborator with Harry Watt on the Ealing production The Overlanders. Heyer was given the difficult task of following an authentic cattle drive across the Australian outback to provide the documentary footage that was to be interspersed with the footage of Chips Rafferty, John Nugent, and Daphne Campbell in the dramatic sequences.

After the war Heyer took on another significant role for the documentary community: that of the promulgation of the film society movement. Heyer was appointed president of the Australian Society of Film Societies and of the Sydney Film Society. The work of these organisations culminated in the establishment of the Sydney and Melbourne Film Festivals. Heyer's passion for cinema included both producing and making available little-seen films from around the globe. Following Grierson, he also understood film to have an educative purpose, lobbying through his 1940 appointment to the Documentary Films Committee of New South Wales for the use of films in schools and universities and for the development of a national movement such as Britain's of the 1930s and 1940s. Heyer's participation in this agitation for government involvement in film production in no small way contributed to the formation of the Australian National Film Board (ANFB, later the Commonwealth Film Unit) in 1945 to which he was appointed its first senior producer and director.

For the Film Board Heyer was to produce the institution's international award-winning Native Earth (1945), Journey of a Nation (1946), The Cane-cutters and Men and Mobs (1947), and The Valley is Ours (1948), through which he gained international renown, leaving the ANFB to head the Shell Film Unit (Australia).

Heyer's Shell appointment led to the production in 1954 of one of Australia's sentimental favourites, The Back of Beyond, one of the most important films to be made in Australia since the war. The film, a documentary about a weekly mail-truck run along the Birdsville Track, follows its driver, Tom Kruse, through the numerous stations and natural obstacles along the way in a poetic rendering of the relationship between the people and the place they inhabit. Seen by an estimated seven hundred and fifty thousand Australians in the first two years of its release and with subsequent television and film festival retrospectives and tertiary education screenings, it is familiar to generations of Australians. Internationally, the film has led another life. In its year of release the film won the Grand Prix Assoluto at the Venice Biennale Film Festival in competition with Flaherty's Louisiana Story. The Back of Beyond continued to work its way around the globe, with hundreds of prints being distributed by Shell to countries as far away as Finland, Hong Kong, Venezuela, Canada, and the Philippines.

In 1956 Heyer was appointed executive producer, Films and Television, Shell International, London. During the 1950s and 1960s Heyer produced or directed more than sixty films for Shell, all of which were promotional vehicles. Having left Shell, he set up the John Heyer Film Company in 1967 and he produced and directed a series of documentaries including a series on the technological achievements of the government in Dubai and The Reef (1978) for the Australian Conservation Foundation.

In 1970 Heyer was awarded the Order of the British Empire for achievements in cinema, in 1986 he became a member of the European Academy of Arts, Sciences and Humanities, and in 1997 he was awarded an Order of Australia.

John Heyer had an enormous influence on Australian documentary film culture, not only through his film production but through his advocacy of and support for film societies, festivals, and film schools that support the international film culture in which Australia participates.

DEANE WILLIAMS

See also: Back of Beyond, The; Australia

Biography

Born in Devonport, Tasmania, September 14, 1916. Producer for the Allied Works Council (Australia) and member of the Prime Minister's Propaganda and Morale Committee, 1944. President of the Australian Federation of Film Societies and of the Sydney Film Society. Documentary Films Committee of New South Wales. Senior producer and director of the Australian National Film Board, 1945–8. Head of Shell Film Unit Australia, 1949–56. Executive producer, Films and Television, Shell International, London, 1956–67. John Heyer Film Company, 1967–2001. Died June 19, 2001, in London.

Further reading

Gibson, Ross, 'Yarning', in *South of the West: Postcolonialism and the Narrative Construction of Australia*, Bloomington, IN: Indiana University Press, 1992: 135–57.

Heyer, John, 'John Heyer: Documentary Filmmaker', *Cinema Papers* 10, 1976: 120–2, 190.

Moran, Albert, *Projecting Australia: Government Film Since 1945*, Sydney: Currency Press, 1991.

Williams, Deane, 'Crossing the Cattle Drive', in John Izod and Richard Kilborn with Matthew Hibberd (eds), *From Grierson to Docu-Soap: Breaking the Boundaries*, London: University of Luton Press, 2000: 35–45.

——'John Heyer: International Documentary Filmmaker', *Metro* 129/130, spring 2001: 248–53.

High School

(US, Wiseman, 1968)

Frederick Wiseman's High School is a direct cinema account of life in a Philadelphia public school that exemplifies a theme that pervades the filmmaker's work: the way power is exercised and manipulated by institutions. High School provides a compelling study of the public education system's role in molding free-thinking adolescents into blindly obedient adults during an era of generational revolt against prevailing economic, political, and social institutions. Enough documentaries had been made about the problems of inner-city schools, the filmmaker argued. To choose one would have led to heavy-handed caricature and one-sided condemnation of the public school system. Instead, Wiseman chose Northeast High because its reputation as one of the best schools in the city provided him with an opportunity to explore the values being taught in a highly touted educational setting.

High School opens with the camera riding in a car, on the way to school in the morning, as Otis Redding's 'Dock of the Bay' provides one of the film's few instances of nondiegetic commentary on the discrepancy between the myth and the reality of the American dream of freedom from conformity. With its fenced-in perimeter, jutting smokestacks, and boxlike shape, the school bears a striking resemblance to a General Motors plant. Inside, students take their places in classrooms as the day begins with announcements and a regimented schedule of activities, including lunch. The camera remains indoors until a scene late in the movie during which a soldier home on leave talks with the gym coach. The movement from exterior to interior suggests that the film will penetrate the institution and analyze its inner workings rather than observe it from an outer perimeter.

Wiseman's hunt for the places where power is exercised in the school leads to a focus on the contrast between the values of openness, democracy, and sensitivity the school espouses and its actual operating practices, which are strikingly authoritarian. During a classroom discussion, one of the few students of color in the school praises its facilities as first-rate but denounces its pedagogy as morally and socially archaic. Thus, High School indicts the public school as a factory that strips students of individuality through an assembly-line process of ideological indoctrination under the rationale of grooming them into responsible, middle-class adults.

Style and authorship sometimes receive short shrift in direct cinema criticism because the form is perceived as a recording of profilmic reality that subordinates the filmmaker's 'vision' to an ethical obligation of relating experience as truthfully as possible. High School's stylistic choices underscore Wiseman's subjective fascination with bureaucracy's ruthless efficiency in socializing willful adolescents into docile adults. The relationship between generic form and directorial vision constitutes an additional aspect of the film's subjectivity. Acknowledging that his movies play against the clichés of Hollywood genres, Wiseman evokes the coming-of-age movie by focusing on the generational politics involved in the rite of passage from adolescence to adulthood.

This opposition forms a structural logic that alternates between the didactic 'school as factory' theme and a roughly chronological 'day in the life' approach. Wiseman skillfully explores the tension between these perceptions by using shot selection, editing, and sound to construct a series of striking dialectical contrasts within such routine activities as classes, student/teacher interactions, sports activities, and a variety show. The director frequently isolates the wagging fingers, menacingly large mouths, and droopy-eyed faces of teachers (almost exclusively) in close-ups. When shot in close-up, faces of silent students suggest passivity because they are accompanied by a voice-over of a counselor barking 'don't you talk and you just listen!' or a Spanish teacher reciting a phrase for a class that dutifully repeats it.

A lunchtime conversation in the teacher's cafeteria lapses into garbled noise under the clamor of dishes and other distractions. Wiseman's inclusion of the ambient sounds surrounding the teachers' conversation implies that their talk is so much noise, void of significance during peer discussions as it is in the classroom. A shot of a music teacher keeping the beat during a percussion lesson by repetitively conducting a group of students forcefully conveys the idea that there is no place in the public school for those who challenge the norms of this assembly-line system of education that teaches one to obey rather than question the status quo.

Lessons in sexual difference complement this exploration of the contradiction between American values of individualism and conformity incumbent in the school's force-fed ideology. During a variety show in which boys dress as buxom cheerleaders, the obviousness of the costumes reminds the students of the intractability of sexual difference and condones sexist caricatures of women as both humorous and socially acceptable. A boys' health class during which a gynecologist draws laughs by using his thrusting pointed finger as a sexual metaphor is followed by an assembly of girls being lectured about the importance of remembering that 'you can't always have what you want when you want it'. Boys learn to objectify women in physical terms while girls learn to think of themselves as passive recipients of male attention.

The final scene, which equates high school education with the military, makes painfully evident the inherent contradictions in a system that conflates learning with unquestioning conformity to a prescribed role. A female principal reads to a teacher assembly a letter from an ex-student in Vietnam about to go to the demilitarized zone. The graduate urges teachers and students not to worry because 'I am not worth it. I am only a body doing a job'. The irony in the teacher's response ('When you get a letter like this, to me it means that we are very successful at Northeast High School. I think you will agree with me') underscores the human costs of a system that conflates achievement with unthinking conformity to bureaucratic norms. According to Wiseman, a film that begins by showing a factory process of institutional indoctrination ends with a view of the perfect product (Rosenthal 1971).

CHRIS JORDAN

See also: Wiseman, Frederick

High School (US, 1968, 75 mins). Distributed by Zipporah Films. Produced, directed, and edited by Frederick Wiseman. Photographed by Richard Leiterman. Filmed in Philadelphia, PA.

Further reading

Benson, Thomas W., *Reality Fictions: The Films of Frederick Wiseman*, Carbondale, IL: Southern Illinois University Press, 1989.

Bordwell, David and Thompson, Kristin, *Film Art: An Introduction*, New York: McGraw-Hill, 1997.

Grant, Barry Keith, *Voyages of Discovery: The Cinema of Frederick Wiseman*, Urbana, IL: University of Illinois Press, 1992.

Rosenthal, Alan, *The New Documentary in Action: A Case-book in Film Making*, Berkeley, CA: University of California Press, 1971.

Wiseman, Frederick, 'Interview with Frederick Wiseman by G. Roy Levin', in *Documentary Explorations: 15 Interviews with Film-makers*, Garden City, NY: Doubleday, 1971: 313–28.

Hiroshima-Nagasaki, August 1945

(US, Barnouw, 1970)

Hiroshima-Nagasaki, August 1945 is a documentary chronicle of the destruction and suffering wrought by the atomic bombings of the Japanese cities of Hiroshima and Nagasaki at the close of World War II. A black-and-white film short on running time (sixteen minutes) but long on visceral impact, it was produced by preeminent filmmaker, author, and media critic Erik Barnouw, who in turn carefully assembled it from hours of footage shot by a Japanese film crew within days of the bombings. The film depicts not only the devastated wasteland that used to be two thriving urban centers but also the bombing victims, including many who are showing the effects of advanced radiation sickness. As an advocate of activist documentary, producer Barnouw, who died in 2001, lived to see his own documentary acclaimed by media critics as one of the most influential anti-war statements ever committed to film.

As the producer of this understated but powerful anti-war documentary, Barnouw had already ensured his place in media history by 1970. He was born in 1908 in The Hague, Netherlands, and emigrated with his family to the United States in 1919. Educated at Princeton University and the University of Vienna, he then began a career in the media as a program director and advertising writer. By the early 1940s Barnouw advanced to writing and editorial positions with CBS and NBC. In 1943 he became an overseas commentator and worked for the US War Department and the Armed Forces Radio Service. He began accumulating the first of his many prestigious media awards when his NBC radio series Words at War garnered the George Foster Peabody Award for Achievement in Radio or Television. After World War II he became a faculty member of Columbia University in New York City, founding the department of film, radio, and television. He was a professor of dramatic arts by the time of Hiroshima-Nagasaki's release.

The documentary is a compilation of images taken primarily from footage shot by film producer Akira Iwasaki in August of 1945. Iwasaki had been imprisoned by the Japanese government during the war for his anti-war stance. At war's end, at the behest of a Japanese research council, he took a film crew with him to the ruins of Hiroshima and Nagasaki. With the permission of the American military authorities in charge of the area, Iwasaki shot three hours of silent, black-and-white footage. Then, on October 17, 1945 the American military suddenly arrested one of the cameramen and confiscated Iwasaki's film. A US Strategic Bombing Survey lieutenant named Daniel McGovern persuaded the American government to allow Iwasaki to continue filming. The finished footage was edited together into a three-hour documentary entitled The Effects of the Atomic Bombs against Hiroshima and Nagasaki. Once the film came to the United States in May of 1946, however, the American government classified the documentary and held it in secrecy for the next twenty-five years.

In 1968, in response to an official Japanese request, the United States sent a copy of the film to Japan. As recounted in his book *Media Marathon*, Erik Barnouw read about the film's existence and requested a screening from the Pentagon. He then obtained a copy of the film for Columbia University. In collaboration over a year with writer and editor Paul Ronder, Barnouw selected the most gripping of the images and placed them within a scripted framework that opens with images of city rubble and builds toward the revelation of the men, women, and children gruesomely but stoically dying from radiation sickness. A New York screening attracted wide attention and many colleges and libraries placed orders for the film. Television networks were reluctant to air the documentary, however, most likely because of the graphic images of bomb victims. Only National Education Television broadcast the film to high ratings in August 1970 on the twenty-fifth anniversary of the Hiroshima bombing. Some controversy centered on the question of whether the documentary in its exclusive focus on the Japanese as victims failed to provide historical context for the decision to drop the bombs. For his part, Barnouw believed (and at least one 1972 study of audience reaction to the film tended to bear out his belief) that if the film had been available for public viewing in the past twenty-five years, it would have been much more difficult for the US government to find the support and funding for nuclear weapons. Finally, producer Iwasaki was able to see at least some of his film released to the public through Barnouw's version. His response is quoted in *Media Marathon*: 'I was [...] deeply moved by this film [...] I was speechless.'

Barnouw's documentary, as the distilled essence of Iwasaki's footage, confronts the spectator with a brutal succession of images of destroyed buildings and human beings dying in hospitals. As Patty Zimmerman writes in *States of Emergency*, 'Like Night and Fog (Alain Resnais' 1955 Holocaust documentary), Hiroshima-Nagasaki emphasizes details that chart the senses, in an attempt to reposition the dropping of the bomb from the ground'. The graphic nature of the images is foreshadowed in the film's opening title card, which reads: 'The Scenes of Hiroshima and Nagasaki which you are about to see were withheld from the public for more than 20 years'. The title credits are superimposed over brief images of idyllic, pre-bombing Hiroshima. The film's narrator (Paul Ronder) ironically notes that from overhead, the bombing crew about to destroy Hiroshima could see flowers in the gardens below. Archival footage of the American bombing mission (including a glimpse of the iconic mushroom cloud rising over the city) quickly gives way to various images of the destruction from the ground, recorded by Iwasaki's crew. The narrator lists a series of grim statistics about the bomb: it weighed nine thousand pounds, its explosive force was equivalent to twelve and a half thousand tons of TNT, it created a fireball eighteen thousand feet across with a center temperature as hot as the sun, and it generated a cloud of smoke forty thousand feet high and black raindrops the size of marbles. Then, against a series of panoramic vistas of the devastated cityscape, a female survivor in voice-over describes losing her friend in the smoke and dark as people died all around. She says, 'I think if I knew hell, it is like this.' The film next shows the shadows of leaves, flowers, ladders, and a human being burnt by the bomb blast onto wood and stone surfaces. As the film then begins to show for the first time, the human victims transported to hospitals, the narrator observes that there was no panic in Hiroshima that day and in the days that followed, only silence—including an official silence that prevented the citizens from learning the true nature of the weapon that had destroyed their city.

The film moves on to the destruction of Nagasaki three days later, in which fifty thousand people initially died. The narrator's voice catalogues what the camera silently records: statues at a cathedral burned black six hundred yards from the bomb's epicenter, a destroyed Mitsubishi factory at which six thousand two hundred men were killed or injured nine hundred yards from the epicenter, a collapsed medical center six hundred yards from the epicenter, and burnt trolley cars and a field of human skeletons six hundred and fifty yards from the epicenter. The film's climactic focus on the human body tortured by atomic radiation begins with images of kimono patterns burnt onto women's backs. Within twelve to fourteen days after the bombings, burns and other wounds that had begun to heal opened back up, and people otherwise unaffected began to vomit, bleed from the gums, and slough off portions of their skin. These 'special victims of the atomic bomb', in the narrator's words, are shown one by one. The narrator observes that vegetation was paradoxically hyperstimulated by this same radiation: 'As people died of radiation sickness, the cities were blanketed with flowers'. This section of the film concludes with two unforgettable images: a living child's face partially eaten to the skull and jawbone by radiation, and a woman's staring dead eye exposed as her lids are pulled back by forceps. The film ends with stock footage of atomic explosions and the famous quote from Robert Oppenheimer (one of the bomb's creators) in voice-over: 'I am become death, the destroyer of worlds.' The narrator leaves the viewer with the unsettling fact that single nuclear weapons are being tested that are as powerful as two thousand five hundred of the first atomic bomb, a single blast equivalent to thirty-one million tons of TNT.

After the release of Hiroshima-Nagasaki, the versatile Barnouw continued to work in various media and write numerous classic works in the field of communications studies. In his capacity as critic and curator, he earned the praise and recognition of filmmakers and academics around the world. His documentary about the effects of the atomic bombings became a fixture in film classrooms, seminars, and conferences around the world. He died at the age of ninety-three in July 2001. His legacy, in addition to his written scholarship, is a film that briefly but eloquently reminds the world of exactly what horror befell the citizens of Hiroshima and Nagasaki that August in 1945.

PHILIP L. SIMPSON

Hiroshima-Nagasaki, August 1945 (US, 1970, 16 mins). Distributed by The Video Project. Produced by Erik Barnouw. Script by Geof Bartz and Paul Ronder. Cinematography by Akira Iwasaki. Music by Lina Johnson and Terrill Schukraft. Edited by Geof Bartz and Paul Ronder. Narrated by Kazuko Oshima and Paul Ronder.

Further reading

Barnouw, Erik, 'Hiroshima-Nagasaki: The Case of the A-Bomb Footage', in Alan Rosenthal (ed.), *New Challenges for Documentary*, Berkeley, CA: University of California Press, 1988: 581–91.

——'The Hiroshima-Nagasaki Footage: A Report', *Historical Journal of Film, Radio, and Television* 2, 1982: 91–100.

——*Documentary: A History of the Non-Fiction Film*, second revised edn, New York: Oxford University Press, 1993.

——*Media Marathon: A Twentieth-Century Memoir*, Durham, NC: Duke University Press, 1996.

Lifton, Robert Jay and Mitchell, Greg, *Hiroshima in America: Fifty Years of Denial*, New York: Grosset/Putnam, 1995.

Zimmerman, Patricia R., *States of Emergency: Documentaries, Wars, Democracies*, Minneapolis, MN: University of Minnesota Press, 2000.

Honigmann, Heddy

Heddy Honigmann gained Dutch nationality in 1978 and lives in Amsterdam. Her internationality is reflected in her cinematic work. Her status as an inhabitant of different countries seems to enable her to connect with people of different traditions, cultures, and life circumstances. In most of her work, Honigmann emphasizes the common emotional responses of people in varied situations and locations, be they poor inhabitants of Brazilian suburbs (O Amor Natural), Bosnian women whose sons and husbands were killed in war (Good Husband, Dear Son), or soldiers facing the horrors and difficulties of military life (Crazy). In most of her films, the audience hears Honigmann's voice asking questions off camera or sees the filmed subject addressing her by name and talking to her in an intimate matter.

In Metal and Melancholy (1993), her first internationally acclaimed film, Honigmann returned to her birthplace of Lima twenty years after she left. The film depicts a society marked by a disappearing middle class, in which people struggle to live on meager wages. Metal and Melancholy is shot mostly from the inside of taxi cabs, and focuses on the taxi drivers of Lima.

In O Amor Natural (1996) Honigmann continues her examination of everyday life in Latin America. The film's foundation is the erotic poetry of Carlos Drumond de Andrade (1902–87). Starting from his work, the filmmaker challenges people to open up and comment on human sexuality, love, and erotic fantasy. The film is humorous, but also bold in its depiction of sensual—but also macho—Brazilian culture.

Honigmann's recent documentaries are about migration and global exchange. The Underground Orchestra (1997) is about the flow of refugees and economic migrants to the West. By conquering the tunnels of the Paris Métro, musicians (mostly highly educated) seek shelter from the political and economical misery of their homelands of Mali, Yugoslavia, Algeria, and Romania.

In Crazy (1999) Honigmann depicts Westerners working in developing nations ravaged by war. This memorable documentary allows, for example, the Dutch Blue Helmet soldiers to express their hidden fears and frustration. Honigmann addresses the topic of violence, but the violence itself is not shown in the film; however, its impact is still conveyed by the soldiers. During long conversations Honigmann succeeds in drawing out the deeply felt emotions each soldier has contained within himself.

Although Honigmann often uses the interview format, she moves beyond the traditional limitations of this approach and establishes a real and open conversation with her subjects. She manages to create a personal, deep bond with her film subjects. Honigmann's editing technique sets a calm rhythm that emphasizes the focus on the inner lives of the subjects. By keeping the camera on an individual's face, Honigmann reveals the inner emotional state. For example, in Good Husband, Dear Son (2001), she depicts wives and mothers who have survived the massacre in central Bosnia. In this moving documentary on war, the enemy is almost not mentioned. No archive material or news footage of war events are shown, but the horror of what happened is nevertheless painfully present. The agony of loss is especially vivid when wives speak about their sensual and sexual experiences with their husbands who have died in the war.

Honigmann's movies address human tragedy while avoiding pathos. She communicates via ordinary human conversations and records the subtle changes on people's faces as they speak. Her films display an almost ethnographic precision in their portrayal of people of specific traditions and cultures.

Honigmann has directed two fictional feature films. Her work has been screened worldwide, and she has had several retrospectives at film festivals. She recently started to work as a producer at the company Appel & Honigmann, which she runs with Dutch filmmaker John Appel.

RADA SESIC

Biography

Born in 1951 in the Peruvian capital Lima, where she lived until 1973. After studying biology and literature at the University of Lima, she studied film at the Centro Sperimentale di Cinematografia in Rome. Gained Dutch nationality in 1978 and currently lives in Amsterdam. She has had several retrospectives, including the Videothèque of Paris/Festival du Cinéma de Paris; the Robert Flaherty Seminar, New York City; in the film museums of Barcelona, Valencia, and Madrid, Spain; in Berlin (Cinema Arsenal in cooperation with the Berlin Film Forum); the Walker Art Center, Minneapolis; the Museum of Modern Art, New York; the Pacific Film Archive, San Francisco; and in Toronto and Chicago.

Selected films

1986–7 Mind Shadows (Hersenshimmen)
1988–9 Your Opinion Please
1992–3 Metal and Melancholy
1995 Au Revoir
1996 O Amor Natural
1997 The Underground Orchestra
1998 2 Minutes Silence, Please
1999 Crazy
2001 Good Husband, Dear Son
2003 Dame la Mano

Hoop Dreams

(US, James, 1994)

Hoop Dreams follows two aspiring African American basketball players, Arthur Agee and William Gates, from their 'discovery' on the playground and then their next four years of high school, as they set upon the statistically improbable venture of using a career in professional basketball as a way to transport themselves and their families out of their low-income world in Chicago's inner city. What was first planned in 1986 as a thirty-minute documentary on the 'street basketball' culture of urban playgrounds became a multi-year epic as the filmmakers met fourteen-year-old Agee and Gates, both then in the eighth grade and recruited by a private suburban high school (Saint Joseph High School). Six days of shooting became one hundred and sixty, and then it required several years of editing to shape the two hundred and fifty hours of footage. The commercial release and consequent media flurry of Hoop Dreams came at a moment where categories of 'fiction' and 'documentary' filmmaking were encountering particular scrutiny in mainstream media culture, as films like Schindler's List and Forrest Gump exploited the shrewd blending of real and fictional on their way to critical and commercial successes. Hoop Dreams, snubbed by the Academy during the nomination process, may have garnered even more publicity because of its omission from the Best Film and Best Documentary categories. It enjoyed a healthy life as a commercial product, grossing close to $8 million in ticket sales and generating spin-offs (such as novelizations, music recordings, and a 'fictional sequel' in the form of Spike Lee's He Got Game) typical of a new Hollywood blockbuster.

The film has a complicated generic status: it invokes the expectations of both cinéma vérité documentary and melodramatic sports movies such as Hoosiers. William and Arthur's pursuit of their NBA dream provided a compelling narrative for the filmmakers, full of surprises and reversals. Arthur does not develop as quickly as William as a basketball player, and midway through his sophomore year of high school, Saint Joseph High School drops him from their team, revokes his scholarship, and refuses to release his transcript until his tuition debts are repaid. He transfers to the public Marshall High School in Chicago and gradually regains his self-confidence. William, on the other hand, enjoys early successes in his young athletic career. Some saw him as the next Isiah Thomas, who was earlier 'produced' by the same Saint Thomas program, but he finds his trajectory toward professional basketball stymied by a serious knee injury. By their senior years, William has signed an early letter of intent to receive a scholarship and play basketball at Marquette University, but his high school team loses early in the postseason tournaments. Arthur's team enjoys a surprising and deep run toward the state title. The dialectical editing, the continual crosscutting between William and Arthur, accounts for many of the film's judgments. While William spends the summer before his senior year playing at prestigious all-star camps (where one scout grins at what he calls the 'fresh meat'), enjoying pizza at night in his dorm room, Arthur occupies his summer earning minimum wage at a pizza shop. Most jarring may be the contrast between the Agee family's darkened apartment, after electricity bills have gone unpaid, and William's MRI procedure, which required considerable electricity and money provided by athletic boosters. Except for a rare handful of moments where a filmmaker will ask a question off camera, the filmmakers chose to assume a fly-on-the-wall perspective on the lives of William and Arthur. The novelization of the film goes one step further and tells their story while completely writing out the fact that for nearly five years these two African Americans were followed around the housing projects by a white camera crew. Later interviews and presentations by the filmmakers contained tantalizing revelations about these interactions, such as the filmmakers' decision to aid the Agees with their own money when they discovered that the family's electricity had been discontinued.

The film has been criticized for participating in the same culture of commodified marginality that it purportedly exposes. For instance, to what extent is nonphysical education presented as a viable method of escape from the ghetto? Sheila Agee's successes in a nurse's aid program are offered up, and her graduation scene marks one of the emotional highpoints of the film, but both Arthur and William struggle in the classroom, and Arthur's decision to attend Mineral Junior College seems to represent a change more in the size, not the nature, of his marginalization (at Mineral he lives with six of the seven black students at the entire college in an isolated house set apart from the rest of the campus). However, while William may have figured out that he is being treated well by coaches and schools simply for the entertainment value of his body (at the end of the film he explains that 'playing' basketball has become more like a job than a game for him), the filmmakers seem hesitant to cast too harsh an eye toward the NBA and the wildly improbable carrot it dangles. Indeed, the film seems to suggest that William's disillusionment with the dream of playing professional basketball represents a kind of failure next to Arthur's continuing belief in the lottery system of the NBA. Some writers argue that the film undermines any attempted critique of the basketball/entertainment industry by valorizing Arthur's successes and particularly by profiting from a voyeurist glimpse into a lower-income world. (Some of the financial profit from the film was eventually disbursed to William, Arthur, and even the high schools, the latter after a lawsuit from Saint Joseph.) Still, coming from a country where politicians sometimes ridicule welfare recipients as 'lazy' and 'entitled', Hoop Dreams allowed the rare opportunity for someone like Sheila Agee to respond, as she does directly to the camera after Arthur's eighteenth birthday and the automatic revocation of a hundred dollars from her family's monthly budget, even though he was still in school: 'Do you all wonder sometime "how am I livin'?" or "how do my children survive", or "how they living?" It's enough to make people really wanna go out there and just lash out and hurt somebody.'

NEIL LERNER

Hoop Dreams (US, standard EBR scan from videotape to 35mm color; stereo sound; Kartemquin Film, KCTATV; 1994; 170 mins). Released October 14, 1994 (US). Distributed by Fine Line Features. Filmed in Illinois, Wisconsin, Missouri, and New Jersey. Produced by Peter Gilbert, Steve James, and Frederick Marx. Directed by Steve James. Cinematography: Peter Gilbert. Edited by Fred Marx, Steve James, and Bill Haugse. Sound: Adam Singer, Tom Yore. Music supervision and scoring by Ben Sidran. Budget estimated at $700,000. Awards include: Audience Award for Best Documentary, Sundance Film Festival, 1994; Best Edited Documentary, American Cinema Editors, 1995; Best Documentary, Boston Society of Film Critics Award, 1994; Best Film, Chicago Film Critics Association Award, 1995; Best Documentary, Los Angeles Film Critics Association Awards, 1994; Outstanding Directorial Achievement in Documentary/Actuality, Directors Guild of America, 1995; Best New Filmmaker (Steve James), MTV Movie Awards, 1995; Best Documentary, National Board of Review (US), 1994; Best Documentary, National Society of Film Critics Awards (US), 1995; Best Documentary, New York Film Critics Circle Award, 1994; Best Film Editing, Academy Awards, 1995.

Further reading

Arthur, Paul and Cutler, Janet, 'On the Rebound: Hoop Dreams and its Discontents', *Cineaste* 21, no. 3, 1995: 22–4.

Boruszkowski, Lilly, 'Film Dreams: Steve James & Frederick Marx', *Creative Screenwriting* 2, no. 2, summer 1995: 7–14.

Hooks, Bell, 'Dreams of Conquest', *Sight and Sound* 5, no. 4, April 1995: 22–5.

James, Steve, 'Full Court Press Against Cineaste Critics', *Cineaste* 21, no. 4, 1995: 4–5.

Jones, Lee, 'Hoop Dreams/Hoop Realities', *Jump Cut* 40, March 1996: 8–14.

Joravsky, Ben, *Hoop Dreams: A True Story of Hardship and Triumph*, Atlanta, CA: Turner Publishing, 1995.

Sandell, Jillian, 'Out of the Ghetto and Into the Marketplace: Hoop Dreams and the Commodification of Marginality', *Socialist Review* 25, no. 2, spring 1995: 57–82.

Sperber, Murray, 'Hoop Dreams/Hollywood Dreams', *Jump Cut* 40, March 1996: 3–7.

Hospital

(US, Wiseman, 1970)

Hospital, the fourth film by American filmmaker Frederick Wiseman, takes as its subject the emergency room of New York City's Metropolitan Hospital. The film shows a constant stream of patients suffering from a variety of physical and emotional ailments crowding into the emergency room (ER), and the hospital staff trying desperately to deal with them.

Wiseman does exploratory surgery on his subject, and the malignancies he finds in the hospital's ER are seen as symptomatic of more general social ills. The remark by the doctor giving a lecture on musculature to a group of interns, that 'Man is not born with disease. He acquires these disorders when he tries to adapt to a certain level of civilization,' addresses the film's concern with viewing Metropolitan Hospital as a social microcosm.

Wiseman has said that he is interested in revealing the gaps between an institution's mandate and how it works in practice. The biggest gap revealed in Hospital, however, is not between the ideology of the institution and its practice, but rather between the rich and poor. Hospital was filmed in a large, overburdened public health facility located near Harlem and Spanish Harlem. Many of the patients seen in the film suffer from drug-related problems, injuries received in fights, or from family or social neglect, problems of course not restricted to a particular class, but certainly more prevalent among the economically underprivileged.

Economic issues are therefore inevitably foregrounded in the film, as these patients are obtaining medical service at Metropolitan not by choice but because of economic necessity.

Towards the beginning of Hospital, Dr Schwartz telephones another hospital that had authorized the transfer of a patient, to complain about the sloppiness of the procedure. The patient seems to have been regarded as so much baggage, a situation that is apparently all too common. With stoic resignation, Dr Schwartz says, 'This is the sort of thing that we see all the time, and whenever it happens, I make it a habit of calling the administrator and voicing my complaint.' Near the end of the film, similarly, an ambulance driver and a policeman discuss the case of a woman just brought into the hospital. The driver had searched for several hours without success for a hospital to admit her. He says repeatedly that 'It don't make sense', but the policeman diagnoses the problem as an economic one: 'I guess that's what happens when you don't have no money at all. You have to take what comes.' These two sequences bracket most of the medical procedures in the film, lending them all a sense of economic determinism.

Perhaps the film's most visually striking instance of this theme is the sequence of the psychiatrist's interview with the young, gay, black man. Throughout the interview the man is seated against a wall, on which hangs above him a picture of then mayor of New York, the dapper John V. Lindsay. The gay man and the image of Lindsay within the film's image offer a striking contrast: one is black, the other white; one is poor, 'freakish', and disempowered, unable to obtain welfare assistance and rejected even by his mother; the other is wealthy, glamorous, and politically influential. The stark contrast between them is amplified by the fact that the gay man's body, arm, and head are arranged in a manner almost identical to Lindsay's pose in the photograph. The patient can never attain the cultural ideal literally hanging over his head in this scene, because of his skin colour, economic status, and sexual orientation.

The film extends its social criticism to the viewer as well, particularly in the conclusion, one of the most powerful moments in all of Wiseman's work. This last sequence shows patients praying in the hospital's chapel, followed by a cut to a long shot of the hospital taken from a nearby highway. The hospital seems to recede with the slow reverse zoom of the camera, while cars travelling on the highway enter the frame in the foreground, zipping by. The voices of the patients singing a hymn in the chapel can still be heard, but they gradually diminish in volume and are replaced by the rush of the automobiles driving past the camera. In the peripatetic rush of daily experience, the film suggests, we tend to forget spiritual values, just as when we are healthy we prefer not to think about illness. The end of Hospital reminds us of our common social responsibility: that no matter how busy we may be, we remain responsible for the health and welfare of the body politic.

From Hospital's very first image—a high-angle shot of an anaesthetized patient—Wiseman seeks to wake up his viewers to the dire social problems evident at Metropolitan Hospital. In one scene a psychiatrist tries desperately to get welfare assistance for a psychologically disturbed patient, only to get the run-around on the telephone from an aloof administrator at the welfare office named, appropriately, Miss Hightower. In exasperation the psychiatrist seemingly appeals to the camera (actually he speaks to a resident in the room with him, but kept entirely out of frame and thus invisible to the viewer), a moment that directly connects the viewer to the film.

Hospital is a clear example of what Bill Nichols has called Wiseman's 'tactlessness', for some viewers might well find such scenes as the one of the young man who had taken mescaline and vomits profusely to be deliberate violations of 'good taste'. Yet, despite the many unpleasant sights in the film, Hospital generally avoids a sensationalistic approach. Most important, the film does not condemn the staff of Metropolitan Hospital by showing them brutalizing patients or being indifferent to their plights.

BARRY KEITH GRANT

See also: Wiseman, Frederick

Hospital (US, 1970, 84 mins). Distributed by Zipporah Films. Produced, edited and directed by Frederick Wiseman. Cinematography by William Brayne. Sound recorded by Frederick Wiseman.

Further reading

Atkins, Thomas R. (ed.), *Frederick Wiseman*, New York: Monarch Press, 1976.

Benson, Thomas W. and Anderson, Caroline, *Reality Fictions: The Films of Frederick Wiseman*, Carbondale, IL: Southern Illinois University Press, 1989.
Grant, Barry Keith, *Voyages of Discovery: The Cinema of Frederick Wiseman*, Urbana, IL and Chicago: University of Illinois Press, 1992.
Mamber, Stephen, *Cinema Verite in America: Studies in Uncontrolled Documentary*, Cambridge, MA: MIT Press, 1974.
Nichols, Bill, *Ideology and the Image*, Bloomington, IN: Indiana University Press, 1981.

Hôtel des Invalides

(France, Franju, 1951)

The third of Georges Franju's documentaries, Hôtel des Invalides, is at once an apparently conventional guided tour of the French Musée de l'Armée and the most implacable of horror films. Indeed, for Franju the horror lies coiled within conventionality itself. Like the surgeon-antihero of his later (fictional) feature Eyes Without a Face, the filmmaker uses his own instruments to peel back the surface of the visible and expose the gruesome, painfully vulnerable reality that conventions of visibility exist to mask. In the case of Hôtel des Invalides, the conventions of the guided tour, drawing the viewer's or visitor's attention to a carefully selected set of venerated objects—Napoleon's tomb, the armour of Louis XIV, and the like—are strictly maintained even as they are undermined by Franju's almost surgical deployment of lighting, framing, camera movement, editing, and sound to construct an anti-militarist way of responding to such objects. By juxtaposing, at certain key moments of the film, the two functions of the Hôtel des Invalides, army museum and veterans' hospital, Franju ensures that 'every object in the museum becomes an emblem of pain, mutilation, or cruelty' (Wood 1973). All the same, he is under no illusions as to the efficacy of his representations. Just as the museum visitors within the film fail (with perhaps one exception) to see what's right in front of their eyes, so, Franju seems to imply, the film's viewers may fail to make the connection between this visual spectacle or entertainment and the self-destructive veneration of warfare and aggression that still prevails in our own culture.

The film's structure is simple. Hôtel des Invalides begins with a prologue (read by the actor Michel Simon, best known at the time as the anarchist-tramp of Renoir's Boudu Saved from Drowning) locating the Hôtel among the monuments of Paris and narrating its history. The prologue continues, but abruptly changes tone: 'Legend has its heroes; war has its victims', Simon recites, as the camera pans from a low-angle view of a statue of Napoleon to a long shot of a wounded veteran being pushed along in a wheelchair, followed by a close-up of his stricken, paralyzed face. The commentary informs us that the Hôtel houses not only these human wrecks but the army museum, and we see a series of shots of cannon, one of which, oddly, is being laughed at by two young lovers (a similar couple appeared in the prologue of Franju's Le Sang des bêtes/Blood of the Beasts, and these two will reappear, equally incongruously, at two later moments in Hôtel des Invalides). Their laughter provokes the prologue's final voice-over: 'Some of these engines of war may, by their strange appearance, amuse the visitor; but when one considers the dangerous growth of an industry that is pushing up like a poisonous mushroom'—here Franju wipes from a close-up of the woman laughing to a newsreel shot of a mushroom cloud—'one must recognize that there's really nothing to laugh about' (Franju 1964). Another wipe shifts us to an interior, a closed door: the door opens, and the tour of the museum, the main body of the film, begins. The voice-over from this point consists almost entirely of the actual commentary of two museum guides, both wounded veterans of World War I.

According to Franju, the idea for the film came to him accidentally, in the office of Henri Claudel, director of the film branch of the Ministry of Foreign Affairs. When Claudel asked if he had an idea for a short film, Franju looked out the window, saw the dome of the Hôtel, and said, 'That!' As Franju later reflected, 'I didn't know the Hôtel des Invalides and it's probable I'd never have thought of making a film about it if, at the moment Claudel asked his question, I hadn't seen it framed in his window' (Brumagne 1977: 26). This story, which Franju told many times, may seem suspect, but the film's opening image is an iris shot of the dome, and certainly one of Franju's concerns is the contrast between the Hôtel's status as monument—an instantly recognizable, tourist attraction and attractive part of the Parisian skyline—and the realities of war it memorializes. The fortuitous framing of the Hôtel's dome may have given Franju his subject, but only insofar as this resonated with already-rooted moral and political convictions. 'I told [Claudel] I wanted to make a pacifist film' (Leblanc 1992: 81), Franju recalled; as he later elaborated, the film laid bare 'my horror of war, the pathetic and senseless beauty of its ruins, its tattered remnants, its weapons, the wounds of its victims. It laid bare, above all, the terrible evidence of death without meaning' (Brumagne 1977: 26–7).

For Franju, such evidence, some five years after the end of World War II, was everywhere; however, in his films, from Hôtel des Invalides through such later features as Thomas the Imposter and Judex, his primary historical point of reference is the 1914–18 war. The casualties we encounter—the veteran in his wheelchair, the two museum guides, the broken-down, shattered congregation in the hospital chapel—all came out of that conflict, and the climax of the museum tour is the '14–18 Room', where, weirdly, the detritus of war is transformed into a cinematic device. A young woman, the same whose earlier laughter either ignited or was annihilated by the atom bomb, picks up a trench periscope, and after looking at her own image in one of its mirrors, readjusts it so that we now see, as if framed by the periscope, jerky newsreel footage of trench warfare. Over shots of explosions and 'soldiers running like cockroaches', statistical titles are superimposed: 'French war casualties, 1914–18. Wounded: 3,594,889. Disappeared: 314,000. Dead: 1,071,000 … ' (Franju 1964). For Franju, this war, the scale of violence of which was unprecedented, defined the modern world. It is telling that the two artistic movements the influence on Franju's work of which is most apparent—German expressionism, traceable in the dreamlike slow tracking shots and heightened contrasts of shadow and light of his cinematographer, Marcel Fradetal; and surrealism, with its strategies of disorientation and juxtaposition underlying the periscope/newsreel and other sequences—both emerged in the wake of that war as responses to the breakdown of cultural confidence it signaled. In the eerily peaceful confines of the army museum Franju's disruptive and paradoxically anti-realist documentary cinema, in the shape of a trench periscope, can make the terrible reality of war visible; however, within the film neither the young lovers nor any of the other visitors ever see this reality, any more than they ever see the crippled or shell-shocked war casualties kept isolated from the public space of the museum. With one possible exception, as I suggested earlier, a little girl in the 14–18 Room, who stops in front of a soldier's statue, is frightened, and flees. Flight, as exemplified also by the crazily wheeling doves of the film's final shot, is perhaps not a sufficient response to the horrors adumbrated in Hôtel des Invalides, but it is at least an acknowledgment of them, and thus a beginning.

HAL GLADFELDER

See also: Franju, Georges; Sang des bêtes, Le

Hôtel des Invalides (France, 1951, 28 mins). Directed by Georges Franju. Assistant directed by Roland Coste and Michel Worms. Script by Georges Franju. Cinematography by Marcel Fradetal, assisted by Henri Champion. Edited by Roland Coste. Commentary read by Michel Simon and the museum guides, Brigadier Bordaene and Adjudant Ruse. Sound by Pierre Vuillemin. Music by Maurice Jarre. Produced by Paul Legros for Forces et Voix de France.

Further reading

Brumagne, Marie-Magdeleine, *Georges Franju: impressions et aveux*, Paris: Editions l'Age d'Homme, 1977.

Franju, Georges, Hôtel des Invalides, (script), *L'Avant-scène du cinéma* 38, 1964 : 45–8.

Leblanc, Gérard, *Georges Franju: Une esthétique de la déstabilisation*, Paris: Maison de la Villette, 1992.

Vaughan, Dai, 'Arms and the Absent' in *For Documentary: Twelve Essays*, Berkeley, CA: University of California Press, 1999: 29–53.

Wood, Robin, 'Franju, Georges', in Nicholas Thomas (ed.), *International Dictionary of Films and Filmmakers*, second edn, Chicago: St James Press, 1991.

——'Terrible Buildings: The World of Georges Franju', *Film Comment*, 9, no. 6, 1973: 43–6.

Hour of the Furnaces, The

(Argentina, Solanas, 1968)

The Hour of the Furnaces/La Hora de los Hornos was one of the most influential 1960s films, a three- (or four-) part documentary about the politics and history of Argentina, Latin America, and the 'Third World' in general. Its major parts are: (1) 'Violence and Liberation: Notes on Neocolonialism', itself broken down into thirteen sections (ninety-five minutes); and (2) 'Act for the Revolution', subdivided into 'A Chronicle of Peronism' (twenty minutes), concerned with the 1945–55 period of Juan Perón's period in power, and 'The Resistance' (one hundred minutes), an account of the period from 1955 to the time of the film's making (1966–68). The broader final section, 'Violence and Liberation' (forty-five minutes) includes interviews and letters and looks at liberation struggles more generally, including those in Africa.

Much in part two (such as interviews with Peronist activists) is particular to Argentina and of less interest to non-Argentine and non-Latin American audiences. Part one, more concerned with general issues of underdevelopment, has been most widely seen and is the main focus here. If the film's analysis of Argentine history is unashamedly Peronist in orientation, this seems to be less a matter of political ideology than of practical politics; Peronism is seen as offering Argentina the best practical chance of social and political change.

As Getino later recognised, Hour of the Furnaces makes proper sense only in the context of its time, when real change in the world order seemed not only possible but imminent (with African states achieving independence, the United States struggling in Vietnam and, vitally for this film, the Cuban revolution in 1959), and when cinema seemed in the vanguard of change, with a transformative role. Emblematically, the film is dedicated to Ernesto Che Guevara, the Argentine-born, Cuban revolutionary leader who also fought for independence in the Congo and died fighting with revolutionaries in Bolivia. In Cuba documentary film became a privileged revolutionary form, and Cuban filmmakers looked to earlier examples of revolutionary film practice, not least the Soviet filmmakers, to adopt and adapt. In some respects, The Hour of the Furnaces borrows ideas from Cuban work, notably that of Santiago Alvarez.

It is difficult to consider The Hour of the Furnaces without also considering the influential manifesto, *Towards a Third Cinema*, published by Solanas and Getino shortly after the film's appearance—a sort of theorisation and justification for the form(s) the film takes, and a very useful framework for thinking about it. Much of the film was made either in secret or under the guise of a different kind of film, and both the making and the initial screenings of the film fulfilled one of the objectives of the manifesto, functioning as a pretext for bringing disparate progressive forces together. It was, as 'Towards a Third Cinema' puts it, a time of 'hypothesis, rather than of thesis, a time of works in process—unfinished, unordered, violent works made with the camera in one hand and a rock in the other'.

The film's title is taken from the cooking fires seen by the first explorers of the continent, taken up in the 1960s as an anti-imperialist war cry by Guevara: 'Now is the hour of the furnaces: let them see nothing but the light of the flames.' This idea, linking the European 'discovery' of Latin America with contemporary struggles, strongly informs the film's prologue, which combines black screen with often violent and/or confusing flares or flashes of action and captions from anti-colonialist thinkers and fighters such as José Marti and Frantz Fanon—'Colonised man frees himself through violence'—while a drumbeat, rhythmic soundtrack increases in volume. This is in some ways a very didactic opening, but at the same time one trying to find the images, words, and sounds appropriate for representing the need for revolutionary change.

Having risen to a crescendo, the film calmly proceeds into the first section, 'History', which is an account—via voice-over commentary and both historical and contemporary images—of the neocolonialist relationships between Europe/North America and Argentina/Latin America. Here, as elsewhere, as in the prologue, The Hour of the Furnaces is primarily a film of montage, both within sections and as a whole, a montage requiring spectators to make connections. Pauline Kael found the contrast between the voice-over historical commentary and the contemporary images of the leisured classes playing golf 'risible', but this is simply the dynamic, complex juxtaposition of history and its consequences in the present. Section two, 'The Country', adopts a very different radical strategy. While the camera tracks through landscapes and zooms in on isolated inhabitants, a voice-over reads out statistics, including a long list of the European countries that would all fit into Argentina, a 'making strange' designed to shake up the perceptions of both Argentine and European spectators.

There are many other examples of striking juxtapositions: images of factory workers accompanied by the sounds of sirens and 'gunfire' that turns out to be the (distorted) sound of clocking-in machines (Section three: 'Daily

Violence'); images of police rounding-up demonstrators while an elite voice-over speaks of ethics and cultural values (Section five: 'The Oligarchy'); images of a national military parade while a voice-over speaks of the difficulty, unlike the Vietnamese, of recognising an enemy 'disguised as an Argentine' (Section six: 'The System').

Two final examples within the same section demonstrate the radically experimental range of the film. Section nine: 'Dependence' begins with a high three hundred and sixty-degree pan around the city, which, as Brecht said of a photograph of the Krupp works, tells us nothing, accompanied by voice-over information about US, British, and Spanish control of the economy. This is followed by perhaps the most conventional, yet powerful, example of montage in the film: images of cattle and sheep being slaughtered in an abattoir juxtaposed with US-style advertising for a modern, 'cool' lifestyle—soft drinks, cars, and 'cool' music. The debt to the final images of Eisenstein's Strike—the slaughter of the workers cut against cattle being slaughtered—is clear, but all the more telling here, for an economy so dependent on the export of meat products and other raw materials to finance a bourgeois lifestyle—for a few, at least.

Though primarily a montage film, other sequences depend on quite different documentary strategies. Section eight, 'Neo-racism', for example, exploits the intrusive potential of cinéma vérité-type camera work to give a sense of the abused and embattled situation of the Indians. Most striking of all, perhaps, is the official photograph of Che Guevara's face in death, which concludes part one. Guevara was killed while the film was being made. Audaciously, the filmmakers hold this still image on screen for more than three minutes, during which time the spectator's response and relationship to it undergoes several changes. Though we know it is an image of Guevara in death, a death mask that was circulated as evidence of his death, the image seems to take on life, become alive, as the accompanying drumbeat from the prologue increases in volume. We are reminded that if the film's confusing, fragmented prologue were searching for an image for revolution, then its end has found it in this image of Guevara in death/life.

JIM HILLIER

La Hora de los Hornos/The Hour of the Furnaces (Argentina, a Grupo Cine Liberación production, completed with the assistance of Arger Film, Rome, 1968, 260 mins). Produced and directed by Fernando Ezequiel Solanas. Script by Octavio Getino and Fernando Ezequiel Solanas.

Further reading

Fusco, Coco (ed.), *Reviewing Histories: Selections from New Latin American Cinema*, New York: Hallwalls Contemporary Arts Center, 1987.

Getino, Octavio, 'Some Notes on the Concept of a Third Cinema', in Barry Grant and Jeannette Sloniowski (eds), *Documenting the Documentary: Close Readings of Documentary Film and Video*, Detroit, MI: Wayne State University Press, 1998.

King, John, *Magical Reels: A History of Cinema in Latin America*, London and New York: Verso, 1990.

MacBean, James Roy, *Film and Revolution*, Bloomington, IN and London: Indiana University Press, 1975.

Nichols, Bill (ed.), *Movies and Methods, Vol. 1*, Berkeley, CA and London: University of California Press, 1976.

Solanas, Fernando and Getino, Octavio, 'Towards a Third Cinema', *Tricontinental*, no. 13, October 1969 (reprinted in *Twenty Five Years of the New Latin American Cinema*, ed. Michael Chanan, London: Channel 4/British Film Institute, 1983).

Stam, Robert, 'The Hour of the Furnaces and the Two Avant-Gardes', *Millennium Film Journal* 7–9, fall–winter 1980–1 (reprinted in *Reviewing Histories: Selections from New Latin American Cinema*, edited by Coco Fusco, New York: Hallwalls Contemporary Arts Center, 1987).

Stam, Robert and Miller, Toby (eds), *Film and Theory: An Anthology*, Malden, MA and Oxford: Blackwell, 2000.

Housing Problems

(UK, Anstey, Elton, 1935)

In the mid-1930s the British gas industry was persuaded to sponsor socially purposive projects like Housing Problems, even though gas supply is only briefly mentioned when designs for new housing are represented in the film's second section. The primary focus of this film, directed by British documentary movement filmmakers Edgar Anstey and Arthur Elton, is the issue of slums and slum clearance. Given the equipment available then, shooting and particularly location sound recording posed considerable difficulties for the filmmakers (Sussex 1975). They rose to the challenge, and Housing Problems achieves its impact through an austerity of means: utilitarian rather than elegant cinematography and editing, and an absence of music. Clear and direct in its address to the viewer, the film nevertheless has quite a sophisticated rhetorical structure.

Housing Problems' historical significance is considerable. Its identification and discussion of a social problem and its victims can be seen as a precursor to the investigative documentary that later became a staple of television production (Winston 1995; Corner 1996). In its time Housing Problems combined social extensiveness with innovative application of film technique. Its inclusion of direct-to-camera testimony from slum dwellers can be seen as a distant ancestor of public access television and video diary formats. Responses to the film now encompass continuing recognition of the immediacy of these personal testimonies and a critical stance towards the social reformist discourse informing its rhetorical structure.

The film's basic structure defines a problem and points toward a solution. Its first section is a visual record of dilapidated exteriors and four domestic spaces in which slum dwellers deliver their testimonies. The second section shows model designs for new housing. The absence of working-class voices in this section demarcates the solution as entirely a matter for design and planning experts. The third section is a visual record of some of these new exteriors and includes positive testimony from tenants located within two of the new interiors. Closing images remind viewers of current conditions in some slums. Speech in the film operates on three levels: a briskly authoritative, southern, English, white male middle-class voice-over narration that introduces and helps to structure the film; a subsidiary voice-over from Councillor Lauder, Chairman of Stepney Housing Committee, which provides more specific detail about slums and slum clearance; and the testimonies of slum dwellers.

The speech of the slum dwellers is best described as testimony rather than interview, because it resembles public speaking addressed directly to the viewer rather than responses to an interviewer's questions. For several of the speakers the novelty of this situation manifests itself in a certain awkwardness of delivery; however, this can be seen as underwriting the integrity of their speech insofar as it suggests relatively minimal coaching by the filmmakers (Corner 1996). The testimonies supply a compellingly subjective dimension but the anonymous voice-over introducing the film, regulating transitions between shots and sequences, and defining the problem in its most general terms, provides an authoritative position from which to comprehend the social issues that Housing Problems raises (Higson 1986). Councillor Lauder's voice-over provides more localised expertise that mediates between these subjective and apparently objective dimensions.

The interplay of different levels of speech enables Housing Problems to elaborate a multilayered yet tightly integrated argument: that is, that slums are a temporary rather than endemic problem, which can be solved only by enlightened local authorities planning and building new housing. Issues such as land ownership, the relationship between capital and labour, the culpability of slum landlords, and the option of tenants' action groups do not form part of Housing Problems' agenda. The logic of the film's argument requires slum dwellers to be defined primarily as victims of conditions beyond their control or resistance, compliant with local authority plans, and deserving of the efforts made on their behalf (Winston 1995). The testimonies selected for inclusion in the first section are largely confined to statements about the immediate environment: overcrowding, unhygienic living conditions, and lack or dilapidation of basic amenities. The authoritative and expert voice-overs outline the preferred solution to this and also provide reassurance that the new housing will be kept clean and orderly by the rehabilitated slum dwellers.

To a certain extent representations of slum dwellers in Housing Problems relate to a tradition originated by Victorian middle-class social explorers venturing into degraded environments and using data recorded there to make a case for improved conditions for the deserving poor (Harvey 1986). The only hint of an alternative, more confrontational socialist perspective is provided by Mr Burner, whose testimony is strategically placed at the end of the first section just before the preferred solution is outlined. His more assertive self-description is as a 'working-class man' and he challenges Stepney Council to 'liven their ideas up'.

The rich vernacular of the testimonies in Housing Problems bears traces of other ways of understanding and responding to the experiences described (Cowie 2001). Overwhelmingly, however, the testimonies are deftly integrated into the central thrust of the film's reformist argument. The affective power of slum dwellers' speech is reasserted and recuperated at the end of the film in a sound montage of their comments about present conditions. The final words spoken over the end credits are of an unidentified female slum dweller's voice, strategically placed there to elicit an implicitly middle-class outsider's sympathy. Describing the fact that some children go to school infested with vermin, she states: 'it's no fault of ours, but still, they don't always look at that, do they?'

Recent discussions of voice-over narration have emphasised how, in many cases, it can be a complex and shifting rather than reductive or didactic mode of address (Bruzzi 2000). Although it assumes a certain authority over them, the anonymous voice-over in Housing Problems introduces slum dwellers as 'Mr' or 'Mrs', people potentially able to attain middle-class respectability. The film replicates the dominant 'regenerative' perspective of 1930s literature on the slums. This writing emphasised how the health and progress of the nation depended on the elimination of 'abnormal' environments so that even former slum dwellers could perpetuate middle-class ideals of 'normal' family life (Crothall 1999).

Housing Problems endorses this perspective by recording images of women and children susceptible to degeneration or rescued from this threat. A significant number of the film's exterior shots record children playing in the street. That four of the six slum dwellers who give testimony are women and four of the five voices in the closing sound montage are female must in part be due to Ruby Grierson's contribution to selecting and preparing people for inclusion in the film (Cowie 2001). At the same time, this selection also fits neatly within the 'regenerative' discourse. The danger that slums pose to domestic respectability in the first section, contrasted with its attainment in the final section, is highlighted through wide shots of women, associating them with interiors. For example in the final section, Mrs Reddington sits in wide shot in her living room praising her new flat. At the end of the first section, Mrs Burner stands holding a young child, while Mr Burner comments on how hard slum conditions are for his wife in particular.

MARTIN STOLLERY

See also: Anstey, Edgar; Elton, Arthur

Housing Problems (UK, British Commercial Gas Association, 1935). Directed by Edgar Anstey and Arthur Elton. Cinematography by John Taylor. Sound recorded by York Scarlett. Assisted by Ruby Grierson. Filmed in Stepney, London.

Further reading

Bruzzi, Stella, *New Documentary: A Critical Introduction*, London: Routledge, 2000.
Corner, John, *The Art of Record*, Manchester: Manchester University Press, 1996.
Cowie, Elizabeth, 'Giving Voice to the Ordinary: Mass Observation and the Documentary Film', *New Formations* 44, autumn 2001: 100–9.
Crothall, Geoffrey, 'Images of Regeneration: Film Propaganda and the British Slum Clearance Campaign 1933–38', *Historical Journal of Film, Radio and Television* 19, no. 3, August 1999: 339–58.
Harvey, Sylvia, 'Who Wants to Know What and Why?' *Ten* 8, no. 23, 1986: 26–31.
Higson, Andrew, 'Britain's Outstanding Contribution to the Film: The Documentary-Realist Tradition', in Charles Barr (ed.), *All Our Yesterdays*, London: BFI, 1986: 72–97.
Sussex, Elizabeth, *The Rise and Fall of British Documentary*, Berkeley, CA: University of California Press, 1975.
Swann, Paul, *The British Documentary Film Movement 1926–46*, Cambridge: Cambridge University Press, 1989.
Winston, Brian, *Claiming the Real*, London: BFI, 1995.

Hughes, John

John Hughes has directed and written documentaries on a broad range of subjects. From 1998 to 2001 he was commissioning editor, Documentary, for Australia's Special Broadcasting Service (SBS) commissioning agency. His films are 'committed' political studies in the ethics of representation both at the level of governance and of textual practice. During the 1980s he made a number of 'sponsored' short documentaries in the context of the trade union movement, and Moments Like These (1989), which examines race relations between Aboriginal and nonindigenous Australians through the representation of aboriginality in Australian cinema. His independent filmmaking continues his exploration into ways in which power is manipulated in society; using a wide array of filmic and narrative devices, his films consistently confront their audiences with an abiding awareness that a film's content is inextricably concerned with filmic form.

Hughes's work is concerned with 'the production of meaning and of knowledge [...] the problematic nature of the text audience relation [...] the fluidity of the boundaries between fiction and nonfiction' (Hughes 1993: 48). These concerns manifest through a Brechtian sense of performance that combines several textual modes: music, song, symbolic image, the polemic force of direct address to audience and various other devices of distanciation. The two most arresting of these devices are: (1) his interweaving of 'fictional' narrative drama with 'nonfictional' footage of social actors and historical events; and (2) the use of 'found' footage. Hughes's use of 'found' footage extends beyond the conventional documentary technique of well-sutured compilation. It confronts an audience with several, often conflicting, representations of a particular social issue. For example, in After Mabo (1997), Hughes uses footage from the fiction film Bitter Springs (Ralph Smart, 1950). His quotation of conversations between a 'frontier' pastoralist (Chips Rafferty) and a policeman (Michael Pate) describes two opposing but passionately held positions on Aboriginal land rights (or dispossession) from the nineteenth century, positions that Hughes's documentary shows as continuing to be locked in unresolved conflict. The early 'fiction' film not only resonates with contemporary politics, it vibrates with illuminating relevance. It simultaneously calls into question the notion that 'history' only speaks to the 'past' and the place of fictional drama in documentary practice.

The idea that history also speaks to the future is explicitly taken up in All That is Solid (1988), as people are asked to speculate on the future through free association with a number of small objects from the 'present' and 'past': a bullet, an angel snow dome, a globe, and a plastic wedding cake decoration. Hughes's films do not 'blur' fiction and nonfiction; they offer a narrative montage that aligns both forms within a single documentary text. They progress through polyphonic montage, Sergei Eisenstein's idea of 'a simultaneous advance of a multiple series of lines', which, although compositionally independent of each other, contribute to the overall composition of a sequence. Hughes's combining of fictional drama with observational footage performs a sense of immediacy, of copresence between viewer and events depicted, which brings to mind Jane Gaines's note that 'the "creative treatment of actuality" describes fiction as well as nonfiction film' (Gaines 1999: 84) and her understanding of 'political mimesis' in documentary film: a film is 'radical' when it 'derives its power (magically) from the political events that it depicts' (Gaines 1999: 95). In this sense, Hughes's films are radical.

In Traps (1985), the fictional story thread is overwhelmed by footage of political events and the musings of senior journalists and politicians about their role in representing such events to the general public. All That is Solid whimsically locates feminism, the anti-nuclear debate, consumerism and religious fundamentalism via dramatic vignettes and an array of socially prominent 'talking heads' whose testimony is embedded within a politicised matrix of Karl Marx's philosophy and the lyric contradictions of David Byrnes's song 'In the Future'. Film Work (1981) archives political documentary filmmaking sponsored by the Australian Waterside Workers' Federation (1953–8). One Way Street draws its radical (Benjaminian) 'aura' from the persecution of Jews in Nazi Europe during and before World War II. After Mabo presents an unequivocal documentation of Australia's dramatic debates about Native Title during the years 1992–97. In River of Dreams, Hughes writes and directs a powerful polemic that argues against the damning of the Fitzroy River in northwestern Australia for the purposes of cotton farming. These last two films are cross-cultural in the sense that they argue from a subjective position of aboriginality. They evoke an Aboriginal perspective whilst including testimony (often conflicting, sometimes contradictory) from both indigenous and non-indigenous people. The Bakhtinian concept of dialogical communication well describes the ways in which Hughes's work textually interrogates multiple 'speaking positions'. The political coherence that nevertheless pervades all his films both indicates his own political and ethical position that all textual practice produces the overall performance of a particular point of view, even when a film's overall textual address is one of inquiry.

The many 'voices' that are represented in his four later films, however, certainly offer a complex range of meanings, and they open out his texts into sites for speculation and further inquiry. His format of split screen, masking, freeze frame, and visual (and audio) overlay in After Mabo and River of Dreams strongly suggest interactive websites. Hughes acknowledges that his frozen frames could 'work as "action images" providing access to a kind of annotation beyond the frame' (personal communication, May 22, 2002). These two films perform complex layers of information across a constantly moving narrative stream. The inclusion in After Mabo of news broadcasts and segmented reportage of meetings between frustrated indigenous committees and beguiling politicians rather suggest 'more information to come' rather than a closed, completed view of the world. This sense of speculation and excessive information can also be sourced to Hughes's explicit fascination with the work of Walter Benjamin, whose own poetic, speculative writings in the 1930s on the rising prominence of visual over written forms of communication have strongly influenced many contemporary theories of representational practice. Benjamin's words first appear in Film Work and they become the central focus of One Way Street (1992). This film is a documentary study in and tribute to the jouissance of Benjamin's texts; it performs Benjamin's vividness of thought and his generous, simultaneously optimistic and pessimistic, commentary on the turbulent time and place in which he lived. All of Hughes's films locate broad debates and complex philosophies at the level of individuals who are striving to understand their own participation in historical events. His localisation of complex social issues transforms historical situations from disempowering stories to accessible sites for understanding. Hughes's filmmaking does not offer an observational or expository 'window on the world'. His eclectic use of documentary and dramatic filmmaking modes, however, does provide access to many 'windows' for reflection and further inquiry.

CATHERINE SUMMERHAYES

Biography

Born in Coburg, Melbourne, Australia in 1948. Left school early and worked in a wide variety of casual labouring jobs culminating with work as cinecamera operator in the 1970s for the Australian Broadcasting Association. During this period worked as a media activist, developing public 'video access' sites. While working out of the Trades Hall in Melbourne during the mid-1980s, made films for Australian trade unions, established a Trade Union Video Unit and made a number of experimental works for art gallery installations. Completed his MA in Critical Theory and Cultural Studies at Monash University in 1992 and lectured in Film Theory, Documentary and Television Studies for the Visual Arts Department at Monash University 1990–3. In 1996 first narrative drama, What I Have Written, was released in Competition in Berlin. Consultancies include feature film and documentary script assessment for the Australian Film Commission and script consultancy with the Australian Screen Directors' Association (ASDA) 1996–8. In 1998 was a board member of ASDA, and 1998–2001 commissioning editor, Documentary SBS Independent (television).

Selected films

1981 Film Work: producer, director, writer
1985 Traps: producer, director, writer
1988 All That is Solid: producer, director, writer
1989 Moments Like These: director, writer
1992 One Way Street: producer, director, writer
1997 After Mabo: coproducer, director, writer
1998 River of Dreams: coproducer, director, writer

Further reading

Gaines, Jane M., 'Political Mimesis', in Jane M. Gaines and Michael Renov (eds), *Collecting Visible Evidence*, Minneapolis, MN, London: University of Minnesota Press, 1999.

Gibson, Ross, 'Life as a Project of Montage', *Filmnews*, November 1992.

Hughes, Peter, 'A Way of Being Engaged with the World: The Films of John Hughes', *Metro*, 93, September 1993: 46–55.

McMurchy, M., *Signs of Independence*, Sydney: Australian Film Commission, 1988.

Moran, A., *The Australian Screen*, Melbourne, Australia: Penguin 1989.

n.a., *The Films of John Hughes*, Melbourne: Australian Film Institute, 1987.

O'Regan, Tom, *Australian National Cinema*, London and New York: Routledge, 1996.

Slavin, John, 'Firth Column: The Hole in the Doughnut', *The Age Monthly Review*, May 1988.

Stratton, David, *The Avocado Plantation*, Melbourne: Macmillan, 1990.

Tiley, D., 'Interview with John Hughes', *Film Views* 127, autumn 1986.

Human, Too Human

(France, Malle, 1972)

About the manufacturing and selling of automobiles, Human, Too Human/Humain, Trop humain is organized in thirds, with seamless transitions among them. The first third deals with the overall process of manufacture. The second focuses on promotion and selling at a large auto show. The third, back at the factory, concentrates on the workers and the nature of the work they do. So, most of the time is spent in the factory observing the making of automobiles.

The machines, materials, and processes are curiously handsome. The workers are attractive, sophisticated-looking for the most part, and predominantly young. We see them through their machines; they seem dominated by them. However, then they also appear to be beautifully in control of their tools and materials, athletic and energetic. They have the ability to make splendid things, strong, complicated things. They engage in a kind of ensemble performance; the camera becomes part of the choreography.

This film does not permit one to compute the pros and cons of its attitude about this work and these workers into an inarguable sum. Are we seeing exploited laborers in an inhumane economy that destroys them physically through mindless repetition of a single mechanical task? Or are we seeing members of a new race who somehow have learned to soar above routine and repetition of their tasks to make them into a graceful and soothing ballet of a sort?

The reality offered is being mediated, to be sure. The images are selectively chosen and strikingly composed. The artistry of the hand-held cinematography is exceptional. The light, the color, and the fluid grace are lovely; the sensitivity in response to the workers' motions goes beyond mere skill. There is lots of camera movement (with constant alteration of frame and focus) including a number of long tracking shots.

The sound is all source sound and recorded synchronously with the image, it seems, even when it need not have been. There is no commentary; the only words we hear are bits of conversation at the auto show, mostly between company representatives and potential customers. In the factory we hear no conversation and see very little of it taking place.

When presented in this way, actuality becomes strangely opaque and unrevealing or ambiguous. The effect may not stem from an ambivalence on Malle's part; his approach is seemingly one of openness, of unemotional response to what he is observing. However, whereas most Anglo-American documentarians attempt to answer the question of what a film is about so clearly and emphatically that the question will never be raised, Malle presents audiences with seemingly insurmountable difficulties in arriving at the essential meaning of Human, Too Human. In this respect, it is rather more like the 'difficult' fiction films of Malle's New Wave contemporaries like Jean-Luc Godard or Jacques Rivette. In spite of its apparent 'reality', Human, Too Human is ultimately sensuous and abstract.

JACK C. ELLIS

See also: Malle, Louis

Human, Too Human/Humain, trop humain (France, Louis Malle and NEF, 1972, 77 mins). Distributed by New Yorker Films (in the United States). Produced and directed by Louis Malle. Cinematography by Etienne Becker. Edited by Suzanne Baron, Reine Wechstein, and Jocelyne Riviere. Filmed at the Citroën plant at Rennes, in northeast France, and at the Salon de l'Auto in Paris.

Hunters, The

(US, Marshall, 1957)

An early classic in ethnographic film, The Hunters is the first of a number of films made by John Marshall among the !Kung Ju/'hoansi in the Kalahari desert of southern Africa. At the time Marshall began filming, in 1952, the !Kung were one of the few surviving peoples who lived largely, if not entirely, as nomadic hunter-gatherers. Marshall's subsequent work, in particular the film !Nai: The Story of A !Kung Woman (1980), follows the !Kung through the transition from hunting and gathering, through agriculture, to their problematic incorporation into the capitalist economies of modern-day South Africa, Namibia, and Botswana. In addition to The Hunters and !Nai, Marshall has made more than twenty shorter films about the !Kung, many exemplifying an editing technique he and fellow ethnographic filmmaker Timothy Asch developed called 'sequence filmmaking'. These were short, single-event films designed for teaching key anthropological concepts such as a 'joking relationship' or 'reciprocity'. In 2002 Marshall completed a five-part, six-hour documentary series, A Kalahari Family, which includes footage shot over 1951–94, and follows the drastic changes in the lives of the !Kung over the second half of the twentieth century. In addition to his filmmaking, Marshall and Claire Ritchie have been advocates for the !Kung, setting up a private development agency called the Ju/wa (Bushman) Development Foundation.

Marshall's longstanding relationship with the !Kung began with a series of family expeditions. The first one was undertaken with his father, Laurence, who had made a fortune during World War II as a founder of Raytheon Corporation, developing radar and other defense technologies. In 1949 the two set off 'to find the Lost City of The Kalahari'. Before departing, they consulted the director of the Harvard Peabody Museum who advised them 'to look for "Wild Bushmen"' (John Marshall 1993: 136), conceived, in what by now are anachronistic evolutionist terms, as a 'window onto the Pleistocene'. They reached the eastern edge of Nyae Nyae and met two Ju/'hoansi who lived by hunting and gathering. All were sufficiently impressed with each other that they made arrangements for the entire Marshall family, as well as a number of scientists, to return in 1951.

Filmmaking was just one of a number of ethnographic projects on the !Kung undertaken by the Marshall family over the following years. Although none of them had had formal training in anthropology, their work is regarded as important in the field. Lorna, John's mother, conducted extensive ethnography on kinship, writing *The !Kung of Nyae Nyae* in 1976. John's sister Elizabeth, who would later become an accomplished nonfiction writer, also undertook written ethnography, publishing the classic *The Harmless People* in 1959. John himself took thousands of photographs, and learned how to film motion pictures. Laurence asked John to provide a film record of !Kung technology and equipped him with Kodachrome film, a wind-up Bell and Howell 16mm camera, and the 1929 edition of *Notes and Queries in Anthropology* by way of a script. As John has written, 'For two years my shooting in Nyae Nyae was stiff and distant, like old snapshots. I followed the rules in the Eastman Kodak *How to make a Movie* guide with which the company encouraged aspiring filmmakers in those days. The instructions said: "First take an establishing shot; then a middle shot; then a close up"'. Marshall admits that the results of this were somewhat stilted, saying, 'it is often hard to see people's expression in the miles of hardy Kodachrome. Major events are covered with a middle shot or missed. It is almost impossible to meet anyone as a person in the early record of Nyae Nyae' (Marshall 1993: 35). After many reels dispassionately depicting !Kung technology, however, John had what filmmaker-critic David MacDougall has described as a 'kind of epiphany'. While John was filming a man making a carrying net, a !Kung woman he knew took off for the bush (to relieve herself, he assumed). Instead, she gave birth to a baby, and returned with it. From this point on, John's interest turned away from technology to informal moments of interaction, and a concern to depict their subjective, emotional lives.

The structure of The Hunters follows the classic narrative of a hero's journey, a fight for survival against 'Nature'. Food is scarce and they have been without meat for a month. Women, and babies especially, will suffer. Four valiant !Kung men, Ao, Toma, Qui, and Xao—dubbed by film critic Bill Nichols the Headman, the Beautiful, the Shaman, and the Clown, for their allegorical identities—embark on foot on a long and arduous giraffe hunt, armed only with spears, bows, and arrows. The climax of the film occurs when after days of skillful tracking, they confront their prey. The giraffe looms over the men as they battle to take her. Finally she falls. The men then return to their families, as heroes, having gotten enough food to sustain them for quite some time. The giraffe is cut up and distributed carefully among the !Kung. The story of this hunt is recounted and passes into legend, both for the !Kung and for viewers of the film.

The film is striking because of its sincere efforts, just before the invention of portable synchronous sound, to evoke the subjectivity and humanity of its Fourth World subjects. !Kung men are depicted equally as highly skilled hunters and devoted fathers, tenderly kissing their babies goodbye as they set off to find food. While many ethnographic films of that era presented their subjects as an anonymous, primitive mass, Marshall took great pains to depict the !Kung as individuals, with at least somewhat nuanced and culturally inflected subjectivities. To this end, Marshall used a third-person voice-over narration that has since been criticized for its godly omniscience. The narration not only recounted the characters' sentiments, but even anthropomorphically imputed thoughts to the giraffe, with such lines as 'She no longer had her predicament clearly in mind.'

More important, the film's ethnography has also been criticized because it foregrounded (male) hunting rather than (largely female) gathering. At the time the !Kung subsisted much more on gathering than on hunting and were not as short of food as the film implies. In addition, the realism of the film has also been called into question, as Marshall now freely admits that what the film presents as a single hunt is actually a synthetic compilation of shots from numerous hunts. Marshall himself has remarked, 'The reality of what I was seeing while the men were hunting was far less important to me than the way in which I was shooting and interpreting the reality to reflect my own perceptions [...] If I had used the rules of filming I use today, The Hunters would have appeared as a slowly expanding series of events rather than a narrow story' (Marshall 1993: 36). However, at an angle to this directorial mea culpa, filmmaker-critic David MacDougall has contended that: 'The film is notable for presenting itself implicitly as a cinematic version of a San hunter's tale, of a sort that might well be repeated and poetically embroidered around a campfire. In this respect, its form and semi-fictionalized construction, although later dismissed by Marshall as a Western overlay, may not necessarily be greatly at odds with San narrative practice' (MacDougall 1998: 108).

ILISA BARBASH

See also: Marshall, John

The Hunters, from the !Kung Series by John Marshall (US, color, 72 mins, 1957). Cinematography by John Marshall. Sound by Daniel Blitz. Edited by John Marshall and Robert Gardner. Produced by Film Study Center, Peabody Museum, Harvard University. Shooting dates 1952–3. Release date 1957.

Further reading

Biesele, Megan (with Robert Gordon and Richard Lee), *The Past and Future of !Kung Ethnography: Critical Reflections and Symbolic Perspectives. Essays in Honour of Lorna Marshall*, Hamburg: H. Buske, 1986.

Heider, Karl, *Ethnographic Film*, Bloomington, IN: Indiana University Press, 1976.

Lee, Richard, *The Dobe Ju/Hoansi*, third edn, South Melbourne, Australia: Wadsworth Thomson Learning, 2003.

Loizos, Peter, *Innovation in Ethnographic Film: From Innocence to Self-Consciousness, 1955–85*, Chicago: University of Chicago Press, 1993.

MacDougall, David, *Transcultural Cinema*, Princeton, NJ: Princeton University Press, 1998.

Marshall, John, 'Filming and Learning', in Jay Ruby (ed.), *The Cinema of John Marshall*, Switzerland: Harwood Academic Publishers, 1993.

Marshall, Lorna, *The !Kung of Nyae Nyae*, Cambridge, MA: Harvard University Press, 1976.

Ruby, Jay (ed.), *The Cinema of John Marshall*, Switzerland: Harwood Academic Publishers, 1993.

Shostak, Marjorie, *Nisa: The Life and Words of a !Kung Woman*, New York: Vintage Books, 1981.

Thomas, Elizabeth Marshall, *The Harmless People*, New York: Vintage Books, 1959.

Hurley, Frank

In the silent era of cinema Frank Hurley was one of the best-known Australian documentary filmmakers and the only Australian producer to achieve commercial and international success. Hurley ran away from home at the age of thirteen to avoid a bullying schoolteacher and became absorbed in photography. Self-taught, he travelled six times to the Antarctic where he documented the expeditions of the Australian explorer, Sir Douglas Mawson (Home of the Blizzard, 1913, and Siege of the South, 1931), and the British explorer, Sir Ernest Shackleton (In the Grip of the Polar Ice, 1917, and Endurance, 1933). Hurley described this period as the 'Homeric age of Antarctic exploration'. He travelled to Australia's remote north to produce Into the Unknown in 1914, and was an official photographer with the Australian armed forces in both World Wars. In 1919 he filmed the exploits of pioneer aviator Ross Smith (The Ross Smith Flights, 1920) and in the 1920s, eschewing the deep polar chill, focused on tropical British New Guinea in the successful travelogue Pearls and Savages 1921 (screened in America as The Lost Tribe and expanded in 1923 as With the Headhunters in Papua). 'Hurley's arrival with movie cameras and two sea-planes and his brilliantly shot footage make Pearls and Savages memorable[... T]he film was widely seen in the

United States and Britain (Baxter 1970: 34). Pearls and Savages was also praised at home for maximizing audiences by appealing to both educationally middle-brow and working-class people, as dramatic spectacle (Tulloch 1982: 33).

Later Hurley combined documentary footage with fiction to produce two commercially successful feature films: The Hound of the Deep (1926), shot on Thursday Island, and The Jungle Woman (1926), filmed in what was Dutch New Guinea. In Australia in the 1930s the best-recognized documentaries were those of Frank Hurley. 'Several, like Fire Guardian (1931) and Treasures of Katoomba (1936) give intriguing glimpses into the period's parochialism' (Shirley and Adams 1983: 129). Hurley's output for most of the decade consisted largely of travelogues (Jewel of the Pacific, Oasis, Here is Paradise) and industrials (Pageant of Power, Brown Coal to Briquettes) (ibid.). Also in the 1930s, Hurley shot feature films for the Australian production company Cinesound, and was a documentary maker for the British Ministry of Information.

Hurley was 'a visual perfectionist' (Bertrand 1989: 72) and an artist. He said in 1910 at the age of twenty-five, 'Your camera is only a piece of apparatus. To copy nature, as seen in the viewfinder, has nothing to do with pictorial art' (*Snow, Sand and Savages*). Hurley was always a showman. In making his feature film Jungle Woman, Hurley stressed dramatic realism. His actress Grace Severi 'had to be actually bitten by a snake' (Tulloch 1981: 289). During World War I, Hurley was strongly attacked by C.E.W. Bean, the respected official Australian war historian, who described Hurley's composite photographs of battle action, with their superimposed 'transcendental' or 'divine' clouds and sunbeams breaking through, not as 'truer images' but as 'fakes', but Hurley remained convinced that representation should also capture the feeling of the action, even if artistry had to be applied. Perhaps the consensual view is that Hurley's 'composite pictures fail as realist representations; they mean little to soldiers who were at the Front' (Legg and Hurley 1966: 12).

Tulloch observes that 'Hurley's early documentaries [...] were, for all their "factual" quality, direct descendants of popular melodrama as it had developed from the nineteenth century stage to the twentieth century picture show', characterized by a highly romantic, eventful adventure in tension with a pictorial 'realism' of setting (Tulloch 1981: 288). In Southward Ho! With Mawson, documenting Mawson's 1929–30 expedition to the Antarctic, Hurley added sounds to the images to increase the 'realism' of the story. For a fight between sea lions, with flocks of watching penguins, Hurley rang bells rendering it like a prize fight (Bertrand 1989: 157).

However, Hurley's Antarctic achievements as a hardy explorer stand apart from his successful Antarctic documentary films and photographs. In 1911, on his first expedition, Mawson sent Hurley and two others on a six-hundred-mile dash to locate the South Magnetic Pole. During a ferocious blizzard, Mawson lost two companions to exposure and later described Hurley's surviving party as 'supermen'. Hurley filmed in blizzards in appalling conditions. Blown off his feet by the subzero wind, he built a wind break of ice for outdoor filming. The resulting Hurley film, Home of the Blizzard, did well financially in London. A film rights offer of £20,000, on condition that Hurley did the filming, helped to finance the next polar expedition with Shackleton. On this trip their ship, the *Endurance*, was crushed in the pack ice and Hurley shot its destruction in minus seventy degrees, lighting the scene with flares. The subsequent survival of Shackleton's party is a famous epic of exploration and resulted in Hurley's epic film, In the Grip of the Polar Ice.

Hurley's work exemplified the spirit of high modernism of the British Empire. He was 'certainly in the David Livingstone and Richard Burton school of adventure' (Thomas 1990: 15). In his 1938 documentary, A Nation is Built, Hurley described Australia as 'the natural setting for the new Anglo-Saxon Empire under the Southern Cross', and 'a white settlement [with a] national destiny provided by God' (Thomas 1990: 17). Pearls and Savages is 'boys' own adventure stuff [...] composed in adventurous, bombastic style' (Thomas 1990: 14). Thomas sees Hurley's films as a showman's adventure serial where he constructed himself commercially as an adventurous explorer within the heroic convention popular in 'Australia and the West' (Thomas 1990: 7). In his films 'there are no people coming close to the filmmaker [...] and, in a sense, codirecting the film' (Thomas 1990: 15). Hurley 'wanted glory and he wanted to make money' (Thomas 1990: 15). Hurley's trips to Antarctica were made possible by a combination of imperial rivalry, scientific interest, and the huge popularity and profitability of Antarctic photography (Thomas 1990: 7). While Thomas's judgements are perhaps overly severe, Hurley's style did go 'out of fashion in his own lifetime' (*Snow, Sand and Savages*). In the 1930s Hurley's images, with their hard, flat lighting, became outmoded when Hollywood moved to composing detailed psychological characterizations through varying light and shade, the mode of representation of bourgeois art, especially based on the Rembrandtian code of painting (Tulloch 1982: 156).

However, 'Hurley is important because, in a sense, he delivered some of the most beautiful pictures of our early years [… H]e really had an eye for composition […] His work deserves to be seen; it's artistic—he is salvaged only for that reason' (Calvert 1997: 13–15).

BRUCE HORSFIELD

Biography

Born in 1885. OBE, Silver Polar Medal, Bronze Polar Medal, MID. Died 1962.

Further reading

Baxter, John, *The Australian Cinema*, Sydney: Angus and Robertson, 1970.

Bertrand, Ina (ed.), *Cinema in Australia: A Documentary History*, Sydney: University of Queensland Press, 1989.

Bickel, Lennard, *In Search of Frank Hurley*, Sydney: Macmillan, 1980.

Calvert, Frances, *Frances Calvert on Frank Hurley*, *Metro* 112, 1997: 13–15.

Legg, Frank and Hurley, Toni, *Once More on My Adventure*, Sydney: Ure Smith, 1966.

n.a., *Snow, Sand and Savages*, videorecording, Sydney: Screensound Australia, n.d.

Reade, Eric, *History and Heartburn: The Saga of Australian Film 1896–1978*, Sydney: Harper and Row, 1979.

——*The Australian Screen*, Melbourne: Landsdowne, 1975.

Shirley, Graham and Adams, Brian, *Australian Cinema: The First Eighty Years*, Sydney: Angus and Robertson, 1983.

Thomas, Julian, *Showman: the Photography of Frank Hurley*, Canberra: The National Library of Australia, 1990.

Thompson, John, *Hurley's Australia: Myth, Dream, Reality*, Canberra: The National Library of Australia, 1999.

Tulloch, John, *Australian Cinema: Industry, Narrative, Meaning*, Sydney: George Allen and Unwin, 1982.

——*Legends on the Screen: The Narrative Film in Australia 1919–29*, Sydney: Currency Press and the Australian Film Institute, 1981.

Huston, John

In April 1942 John Huston left Hollywood to volunteer for military service in World War II, accepting a commission as a lieutenant in the US Signal Corps. He was one of many to do so, including such heralded directors as Frank Capra, John Ford, and William Wyler. The shift to nonfiction had an impact on these craftsmen, especially Huston, who joined the army at a formative moment in his career. Though he had a decade of experience as a screenwriter, he had only just completed production in September 1941, on The Maltese Falcon, his first film as a director.

In the Signal Corps Huston completed three documentaries. Report from the Aleutians (1943, forty-seven minutes) chronicled the building of a base in the northern Pacific and an air attack against the Japanese; The Battle of San Pietro (shot in fall–winter 1943–4, released in 1945, thirty minutes) portrayed the assault on a town in the Italian campaign; and Let There Be Light (1946, release delayed until 1980, fifty-nine minutes) observed the rehabilitation of mentally disabled veterans. In addition, Huston worked on another production, Tunisian Victory (1943), which was under the general supervision of Frank Capra. As John McCarty and David Desser have pointed out, the three Huston films fall into a trilogy focusing on the preparation for combat, combat itself, and the consequences of combat.

The reputation of Huston's documentaries rests on The Battle of San Pietro. Report from the Aleutians has been dismissed as competent but conventional war propaganda. Let There Be Light was withheld from public exhibition for thirty-four years by the military, so its impact was limited. The Battle of San Pietro was touted on release in May 1945 as a remarkable film, most conspicuously by James Agee. Over the years it has continued to garner attention and praise.

No war documentary, Agee declared, has been so attentive to the grim cost of battle in terms of the men who were actually fighting and the people and place caught in the line of fire. Gary Edgerton called San Pietro 'unique in that the winning is constantly underplayed while the suffering and sacrifice is accorded tantamount attention'. The narration, spoken by Huston himself, begins with shaded irony as he introduces the Liri Valley; his camera presents fields pockmarked with shell holes, orchards torn by rifle fire, and a Renaissance church destroyed by bombs. Once the assault begins, the voice-over assumes a dispassionate tone as we see the stalled infantry assaults, thwarted flanking maneuvers, and tanks destroyed by enemy fire. 'Volunteer patrols made desperate attempts to reach enemy positions and reduce strong points,' the narrator intones. 'Not a single member of any such patrol ever came back alive.' The footage recorded by Huston's camera crews rings with authenticity. The soldiers pinned down in an olive grove under fire, or the infantry lounging after the battle portray episodes distinct from the drive toward victory, but invests the film with conviction. Finally, after a week of fighting, Allied troops dislodge the enemy from a key defense position, and the Germans withdraw. One regiment alone required more than one thousand one hundred replacements, Huston reports, as the graves are dug. In spite of the carnage, the film testifies to the courage, discipline, and self-sacrifice of the soldiers without hyperbole. Heroism appears ordinary and widespread. A generous humanity arises in counterpoint to the destruction. The expression of dignity, respect, and affection extends to the Italian civilians returning to their village after the fighting. The shots of women, children, and the old emerging from hiding after their homes have been destroyed invest this film with an abiding compassion for all people victimized by war. Agee describes the wordless images of children as 'the first great passage of war poetry that has got on the screen'. At the same time, the film never retreats from the necessity of the campaign, even as it acknowledges that the cost is dear.

Let There Be Light portrays a unit of mentally traumatized troops moving from arrival at a military hospital through diagnosis and therapy toward rehabilitation. Huston's camera watches soldiers struggling to describe their mental anguish and undergoing various therapies, including hypnosis and drug treatments. Compassion arises from the simple observation of suffering. At times the transformations—one soldier regains his ability to speak, another overcomes paralysis—are astonishing. Though the valorization of the military doctors smacks of propaganda, the portraits of agony and hope are genuinely moving. Huston's strength as a documentarian lies in understatement, to trust his camera and allow the extraordinary sights of battle or psychic turmoil to make themselves known. (This requires the resources necessary to be patient; Let There Be Light is reported to have had a shooting ratio of 72:1.) Huston's war documentaries are characterized by attention to the humanity of the common soldier. In Let There Be Light he finds fortitude and determination even in men broken by the trauma of combat.

The relationship between Huston's films and the military was troubled. Commanding officers walked out of the initial screening of San Pietro and blocked its release. The combat was too harrowing and the movie was described as 'anti-war'. Eventually the controversy attracted the attention of General of the Army George Marshall, who requested a screening. He applauded the picture as an excellent means of training soldiers for combat, but asked, and gained Huston's consent, to cut a number of the most disturbing sequences. With that, praise followed and Huston was promoted to major. The filmmaker wasn't as lucky with Let There Be Light. The Army refused to allow the film to be released, and even blocked a screening personally arranged by Huston at the Museum of Modern Art in New York. Public exhibition was delayed until 1980.

Back at Warner Brothers in 1947 John Huston insisted that The Treasure of the Sierra Madre be shot on location in Mexico. There he made what many believe to be his most successful film. After his military service, Huston was eager to work outside the studio and no doubt incorporated into his work other aspects of human fortitude and suffering that he had encountered during the war.

LEGER GRINDON

Biography

Born August 5, 1906. Son of actor Walter Huston and Rhea Gore, a journalist. First stage appearance at three years of age. Little formal education. Had a distinguished record as an amateur welterweight boxer (1921–3) and served briefly in the Mexican cavalry (1926). Worked as a journalist, playwright, and short-story writer before rising as a Hollywood screenwriter during the 1930s, most notably at Warner Brothers where his credits included Jezebel (1938), Juarez (1939), and High Sierra (1941). The Maltese Falcon (1941) was his first film as a director. Served in US Signal Corps 1942–5, where he directed three documentaries, was promoted to Major, and was awarded the Legion of Merit. Formed Committee for the First Amendment in1947 to counteract the House on UnAmerican Activities Committee investigations. Academy Award for Best Director and Best Screenplay for The Treasure of the Sierra Madre (1948). Moved to Ireland in 1952, to Mexico in 1972, but remained active in Hollywood. Other noteworthy productions include The Asphalt Jungle (1950), The African Queen (1951), The Man Who Would Be King (1975) and Prizzi's Honor (1985). Father of Anjelica Huston. American Film Institute Life Achievement Award (1983) among many others. Died August 28, 1987 in Middletown, Rhode Island.

Selected films

1943 Report from the Aleutians: director, screenwriter, narrator
1945 The Battle of San Pietro: director, screenwriter, narrator
1946 Let There Be Light: director, co-screenwriter, cophotographer, narrator

Further reading

Agee, James, 'San Pietro', in *Agee on Film*, Boston: Beacon Press, 1966: 162–4 (originally appeared in *The Nation*, May 26, 1945).

Bertelsen, L., 'San Pietro and the "Art" of War', *Southwest Review* 74, spring 1989: 230–56.

Cohen, Allen and Lawton, Harry (eds), *John Huston: A Guide to References and Resources*, New York: G.K. Hall, 1997.

Desser, David, 'The Wartime Films of John Huston: Film Noir and the Emergence of the Therapeutic', in Gaylyn Studlar and David Desser (eds), *Reflections in the Male Eye*, Washington, DC: Smithsonian Institution Press, 1993.

Edgerton, Gary, 'Revisiting the Records of Wars Past: Remembering the Documentary Trilogy of John Huston', in Gaylyn Studlar and David Desser (eds), *Reflections in the Male Eye*, Washington, DC: Smithsonian Institution Press, 1993.

Garrett, Greg, 'Let There Be Light and Huston's Film Noir', *Proteus*, fall, 1990: 30–3.

——'John Huston's "The Battle of San Pietro"', *War, Literature, and the Arts* 5, no. 1, 1993: 1–12.

Hughes, Robert (ed.), 'The Courage of Men: An Interview with John Huston', in *Film Book 2, Films of Peace and War*, New York: Grove Press, 1962: 22–35.

Huston, John, *An Open Book*, New York: Alfred A. Knopf, 1980 (especially chapters 8–10).

Jameson, Richard T., 'John Huston', *Film Comment* 16, no. 3, May–June 1980: 25–56.

MacCann, Richard Dyer, *The People's Films: A Political History of U.S. Government Motion Pictures*, New York: Hastings House, 1973.

I

I Do Not Know What It Is I Am Like

(US, Viola, 1986)

Since the early 1970s, Bill Viola (born in the United States in 1951) has been a pioneering figure in the development of video as a medium within fine art practice. In both his installation and tape-based work he has readily engaged with innovations in media technology to explore themes of sensory perception and the body as the locus of consciousness and spiritual discovery.

I Do Not Know What It Is I Am Like is one of Viola's most ambitious and significant tape-based works. Created for the Contemporary Art Television Fund, with support from a number of other agencies, it was broadcast in 1987 by WGBH Boston as part of their 'New Television' season. It was made from footage gathered over a period of several years, during part of which Viola was artist in residence at San Diego Zoo. During this time he also visited and recorded religious festivals in Fiji and spent many weeks following a herd of bison in Wind Cave National Park, South Dakota. The title is taken from the Sanskrit text Rig Veda, which reflects Viola's long-term interest in Eastern religions. The work is a highly personal meditation on the cycles of life and death, animal consciousness and the human condition, with humanity being considered as bound to the natural world, yet also striving to understand and transcend this reality thorough art, technology, and spiritual quest.

I Do Not Know What It Is I Am Like is structured thematically in five chapters: 'Il corpo scuro (The Dark Body)', 'The Language of the Birds', The Night of the Senses', 'Stunned by the Drum', and 'The Living Flame'. It commences with the camera sliding slowly beneath the surface of a mountain lake, suggesting the submersed body and drowning imagery, which is a familiar visual theme in Viola's work. This sense of slippage into another realm is compounded as the camera explores the underground world of a cave system, followed by a series of close-ups of a flyblown animal carcass and a sequence of long, mainly static, shots of a bison herd in a wilderness landscape. The second chapter, 'The Language of the Birds', comprises a series of close-up shots of the eyes of a variety of captive birds, the section closing with an emblematic image of the artist reflected in the eye of an owl. This self-reflexive imagery is developed in the following chapter, 'Night of the Senses'. In a play of reflections and direct shots, Viola is seen working at a desk at night where he studies various books, views footage of birds on a video monitor, and eats an elaborately arranged meal.

The work shifts in form throughout the chapters. The long durational shots and naturalistic sound of the early chapters convey both a strong sense of time unfolding in the present as well as the timelessness of natural cycles. This meditative pace is violently disrupted in 'Stunned by the Drum'. Here, a rapid-fire succession of images of news footage, natural disasters, urban scenes, landscapes, and reprises of previous imagery is cut to a thumping drumbeat, and culminates in a pulsing black and white screen. There is a further shift in the final chapter, 'The Living Flame', which documents a Hindu religious festival where devotees mortify their flesh with skewers and walk on hot coals. This dramatic visualization of the transcendent power of ritual and spirituality is enhanced by the use of slow-motion images and ceremonial music. Viola's willingness to use a range of techniques and effects to develop his themes is further demonstrated by the time-lapse sequence that concludes I Do Not Know What It Is I Am Like. Here, a dead fish is shown being slowly devoured by animals and decaying away until no trace remains.

Situating I Do Not Know What iIt Is I Am Like as a documentary practice raises a number of interesting questions. Meaning is generated through a highly evolved personal lexicon of symbols and the observation, or organization, of events which in themselves have a strong metaphorical resonance. In this way, the work perhaps evokes comparisons with earlier generations of 'poetic' documentarists, such as Joris Ivens and Jean Vigo. The numerous reflexive strategies seen here, which highlight the functioning of the medium and the subjectivity of the artist as a central organizing element, also indicate the evolution of Viola's work from the overtly conceptual approach of US experimental filmmakers of the 1960s, such as Stan Brakhage.

In documentary terms, bereft of an obvious expository strategy or organizing narrative device (such as voice-over or personal testimony), the work is open to criticism as obscurantist. If a large percentage of the footage is more clearly documentary in nature, much is also meticulously constructed. Viola's work here is a useful illustration of the collapsing distinctions between seemingly discrete areas of cultural practice. As artists increasingly use electronic media and make use of the same distribution and exhibition systems, there is perhaps an inevitable merging, or at least overlaying, of traditions, understandings, and methods between individuals working within the differing institutional practices of fine art, television, and cinema. In many ways this work can be seen as prescient of recent shifts in documentary practice, which now appears much more open to the use fictional construction as part of its constituent elements.

Viola has stated his desire for audiences to engage with his work in a total bodily or sensory manner and this is perhaps served less well by this tape-based work. Images and techniques, which may be affecting in the more determined environment of a gallery installation, or site-specific work, may prove less so when viewed on a television monitor. However, I Do Not Know What It Is I Am Like is a significant piece of work that demonstrates Viola's ability to engage convincingly with a wide range of audiovisual technologies and forms. Through images of great beauty and mystery, Viola creates here a highly challenging, provocative, and often moving meditation on the fundamentals of existence.

DAVID CHAPMAN

See also: Brakhage, Stan; Ivens, Joris

I Do Not Know What It Is I Am Like (US, 1986, 89 mins). Produced by Bill Viola. Additional camera and production manager, Kira Perov. Produced in association with the American Film Institute, Los Angeles; The Contemporary Art Television Fund, a project of WGBH New Television Workshop; the Institute of Contemporary Art, Boston; and ZDF, Mainz, Germany. Shot in San Diego Zoo, Wind Cave National Park, South Dakota, Fiji, and the Canadian Rocky Mountains.

Further reading

London, Barbara (ed.), *Bill Viola: Installations and Videotapes*, New York: Museum of Modern Art, 1987.

Pühringer, Alexander (ed.), *Bill Viola*, Klagerfurt, Austria: Ritter Klagenfurt, 1994.

Ross, David A. and Sellars, Peter (eds), *Bill Viola*, New York: Whitney Museum of American Art, and Paris: Flammarion, 1997.

Rush, Michael, *New Media in Late 20th Century Art*, London: Thames and Hudson, 1999.

Syring, Marie Luise (ed.), *Bill Viola: Unseen Images*, Düsseldorf: R. Meyer, 1992.

Iceland/Greenland

Alone at the top of the world, both Iceland and Greenland have shared a common history as Danish colonies and are the common parent for their national cinemas: the Danish film industry. Danish filmmaker Peter Elfelt represented Greenland first in his short, Kørsel med grønlandske hunde/Trip with Greenlandic Dogs (1897), in which the island's most populous inhabitants, a pack of sled dogs, drove a sled around a Copenhagen park. Nine years later another Dane, Alfred Lind, brought his camera to the North and shot the earliest known motion picture footage of Iceland. Although P. Petersen projected his own amateur movies in his Reykjavík cinema, it took almost twenty years for the first Icelandic feature-length film to be made, the documentary Ísland ílifandi myndum/Iceland in Moving Pictures (dir. Loftur Guðmundsson, 1925). Greenlanders, however, remained mostly in front of the camera as subjects for foreign anthropologists until the 1990s. With no access to filmmaking equipment or training, they seldom had any say in their cinematic representation.

The ethnographic 'Eskimo film', a genre popular with Europeans that depicted how these exotic Northern people lived, began with the three-part Grønland 1914, a collection of research and photographs obtained by the Copenhagen linguistics professor William Thalbitzer. Robert Flaherty's documentary on the Hudson Bay Inuit, Nanook of the North (1922), soon became the cornerstone of these ethnographic films, although critics pointed out that Flaherty had staged traditional Inuit rituals of hunting, sealing, and fishing. A 1934 docudrama, The Wedding of Palo (1934, dir. Friedrich Dalshiem), produced by the famed half-Danish, half-Greenlandic explorer Knud Rasmussen, was a rare exception to the other Eskimo films in that he allowed the Inuit to make most of the creative decisions. Rasmussen had nonprofessional Greenlandic actors improvise a scenario based on one of their classic oral stories about rivals for the same girl.

In the 1930s and 1940s a steady diet of American and Scandinavian films prompted more Icelanders to experiment with the medium. Óskar Gíslason, considered the father of modern Icelandic film, began his career shooting events like the establishment of the Icelandic Republic in 1944. For his acclaimed documentary Björgunarafrekið við Látrabjag/The Great Látrabjag Sea-Rescue (1948), he scaled the treacherous Látrabjag cliffs with his 16mm Bolex to capture the fishermen and farmers who saved the lives of shipwrecked British sailors. He combined dramatic and documentary scenes in Iceland's first sync-sound feature, Nýtt hlutverk hlutverk/New Role (1954), which looked at the lonely life of a retired harbor worker.

The Danish government prohibited most filmmakers and journalists from traveling to Greenland up until the 1940s, fearing a public outcry at its perceived treatment of the Inuit. Instead, newsreels of the Arctic expeditions of Robert Peary, Eigil Knuth, and other explorers sated audiences' interest in Greenland. Films became the main method of publicizing and verifying expeditions to the extent that 16mm cameramen accompanied explorers. In Med Leo Hansen på Østgrønland/With Leo Hansen in Greenland (1935), cartographer and producer Lauge Koch compiled the footage that cinematographer Leo Hansen shot on his travels across the polar north with Knud Rasmussen and Peter Freuchen. Other film crews flew over the vast mountains and glaciers to capture the impassable terrain. The 1931 British Air Route tours under H.G. Watkins filmed Greenland from above for their English-language dispatch, Northern Lights. Charles Lindbergh's flight over Greenland in 1933 provided aerial footage for Pan American Airlines.

The Danish government's fears proved accurate when it permitted journalists' entry into Greenland in 1946. Newspapers ignited a widespread debate concerning the poor living conditions and commercial exploitation of the Inuit. Nevertheless, films continued to legitimize Danish control over Greenland, particularly in a documentary about preparations of the Pearyland expedition, Vejen med Nord/The Way Towards the North (directed by Hagen Hasselbach, 1948). Hasselbach portrayed the Danish explorers as if they were heroes from the sagas, undertaking a dangerous journey in the north. Greenland itself was referred to as one of Denmark's 'possessions', while the Inuit population received only the barest mention in excavation of an ancient 'Eskimo' house. An anomaly to these expedition films was Paul Hansen's portrait of Greenlandic musician Andreas Hendriksen in Grønland i Sommer og Sol/Greenland in Summer and Sun (1942). Hagen Hasselbach used the music from Hansen's film eight years later in Grønland i sol/Greenland in the Sun (1950).

Around the same time, Ósvaldur Knudsen started to chronicle Iceland's volcanoes. His work established a genre that dominated Iceland's international releases for much of 1950s and 1960s. In 1947 Ósvaldur covered the eruption at Mount Hekla, followed Askja's activity in 1961, recorded the birth of the Surtsey volcanic island in his prizewinning Surtur fer Sunnan/Birth of an Island (1963), and returned to another Hekla eruption in 1970. His most well known documentary was a thirty-minute short he made with his son, Vihjálmur. Elduri Heimæy/Fire of Heimæy (1974) detailed the unforeseen 1973 eruption in the Westmann Islands, which buried a town in ash and forced an immediate evacuation. Their film and a similar short about the Heimæy disaster, Eldeyjan/Days of Destruction (produced by Kvík Co., 1973), reached the height of the volcano genre's success. Both of the Heimæy shorts garnished numerous awards at film festivals in Hollywood, Poland, and Atlanta.

Barring the volcano films, Icelandic documentaries received little international attention during the 1960s. The silence concealed the stirrings of a new generation. One of Iceland's first foreign film school graduates, þorgeir þorgeirsson, returned to his homeland to make many shorts, among them Maður og verksmið ja/Man and Factory, and Róður/Rowing. A national training opportunity for motion picture production arose with the debut of Icelandic television in 1966. The station devoted much of its programming to noncontroversial films about Iceland's natural history, such as Magnús Jóhannsson and Magnús Magnússon's documentaries on Icelandic birdlife, although occasionally it commissioned programs of a more radical bent such as Reynir Oddsson's epic two-part docudrama about the US military in Iceland, Hernámsárin/Iceland under Occupation (1967 and 1968).

The escalation of the Cold War also informed documentaries about Greenland. The US Army Signal Corps produced the twenty-four-minute Operation Blue Jay (1952), which recorded the building of the US military base in Thule. It argued that the US presence in Greenland was necessary to protect the West and curb the influence of the Soviet Union. The film was nominated for an Academy Award in 1953, but lost in the short subject category to another film about the far north, Walt Disney's The Alaskan Eskimo. Fifty years passed before the other side of the story was told on film. Ulrik Holmstrup and Jørgen Pedersen's Hingitaq/The Outcasts (2003) showed how the Danish and US governments pressured the native Inuit to leave their home in the Thule mountains so that the US military base could be built.

Although Frank Wenzel made shorts about Greenland's natural beauty, Moskusoksen/The Musk Ox (1967) and Ved bræens rand/By the Edge of the Glacier (1969), most filmmakers in Greenland concentrated on the political controversy that saw Danish commercial interests abusing the indigent Inuit population. To soften the criticism, a governmental committee, Danish Kulturfilm, hired the husband and wife team of Bjarne and Astrid Henning-Jensen in 1955 to shoot two documentaries that would present Greenland in a more positive light. Astrid Henning-Jensen's nostalgic short, En sælfangsti Nordgrønland/A Sealing in North Greenland (1955) documented the vanishing Inuit tradition of harpoon hunting that the rifle had replaced. Her husband's featurette was much more politically overt. Hvor bjergene sejler/Where the Mountains are Sailing (1955) highlighted the benefits of Danish involvement in the life of a Greenlandic boy, Mikisoq. Doctors at a Danish-built hospital cured Mikisoq from the deadly tuberculosis epidemic that had killed his mother, while Danish authorities provided a new house for his family, and gave his father, an unemployed seal hunter, a more reliable job as a fisherman.

The optimism found in Henning-Jensen's film about Greenland's future did not last. Ten years later, Christian Kryger's breakthrough television series investigated Danish policy toward Greenlanders and caused another storm in the press. The Danish Foreign Ministry again called on filmmakers to rectify the situation. Among them was Carl Th. Dreyer's former cinematographer, Jørgen Roos, who would become one of Greenland's most prolific documentarians. Along with experimental biographical shorts of Hans Christian Andersen and Tristan Tzara, Roos had made Fiskere på Grønland/The Fishermen of Greenland (1950) and Knud, an award-winning 1965 portrait of arctic explorer Knud Rasmussen. However, his resulting film, Sisimiut (1966), which focused on the difficulties of Greenlandic family living in a subsidized Danish town, did not impress the Foreign Ministry.

Roos heeded the Ministry's requests the second time and combined old material with new in a bland, uncritical 17 minutters Grønland/17 Minutes Greenland (1967). He continued to refrain from judgment in En fangerfamilie i Thuledistriktet/A Hunting Family in the Thule District (1967), although his subsequent effort, Ultima Thule (1968), condemned the American presence that had brought tourists and had crashed an H-bomb plane in the district of Thule. In 1970 Roos dissected his hometown, Copenhagen, to look at the lives of young city-dwelling Greenlanders in Kalâliuvit?/Are You a Greenlander?, one of the first films primarily in Greenlandic. Roos made three short documentaries in 1972: To mændi ødemarken/Two Men in the Wilderness retold the 1909 expedition to the northeast of Greenland;

Udflytterne/The Settlers looked at a group of Greenlanders who left their village and returned to hunting; and Ulrik fortæller en historie/ Ulrik Tells a Story recorded one of the last Greenlandic storytellers.

The establishment of the Icelandic Film Fund (Kvikmyndasjóður) in 1979 broke new ground in the financing and development of Icelandic cinema. Nevertheless, documentary filmmakers still found themselves in the same quandary. The Film Fund supported feature fiction films almost exclusively at the expense of the documentary. One of the few documentaries that received a grant, Mörg eru dags augu/The Day has Many Eyes (dirs Gudmunður P. Ólfasson and Óli Örn Andreassen, 1980), was a five-year photographic project that questioned why inhabitants left the once-bustling isles of Breiðafjörður. Otherwise, outside of shooting nature programs for Icelandic television, Icelandic filmmakers continued to make documentary shorts rather than full-length features because of the financial demands.

Some filmmakers turned to industry to bankroll their films, while others preferred to use loans and second mortgages to make personal, political films. The Icelandic Freezing Plants Corporation hired Sigurdur Sverrir Pálsson to shoot industrial shorts that illustrated the stages of fish processing, from catching to packaging to marketing and distribution (Fagur fiskur úr sjó/From the Ice-cold Deep, 1981, and Med kvedgau frá Íslandi/With Compliments from Iceland, 1982). Heiðar Matreinsson stayed on board for Humarveiðar/Lobster Fishing (1978) and detailed a three-man crew trawling the waters of the Westmann islands for lobster. Jón Hernansson and þrándur Thoroddsen's Will There Be Salmon Tomorrow? (1982) examined salmon-catching at a government farm and in two Icelandic rivers.

German filmmaker Wim Wenders served on the jury of the first Reykjavík Film Festival in 1978, which awarded its top prize to a half-hour documentary short, Bóndi/Farmer (directed by þorsteinn Jónsson, 1975), about a lone farmer in an isolated northern fjord who refused to abandon his traditional methods. A similar theme inspired director Friðrik þór Friðriksson's short about an eighty-year-old blacksmith who crafted the first multigear bicycle (Eldsmiðurinn/The Blacksmith, 1981). For his film about a Danish officer's trek through the rocky center of Iceland in the nineteenth century, Águst Guðmundsson used his talents as a feature director to re-create historical scenes in his picturesque Yfir Kjöl/ Across the Interior of Iceland (1982). Jón Björgvinsson ventured out to Iceland's other great frontier, the ocean, where he filmed a modern expedition of Icelandic sailors collecting Siberian driftwood (Fast þeir sóttu rekann/From Siberia with Love, 1981).

The mid-1970s saw a surge of documentaries about Greenland, a few produced in the political battle between competing Danish sponsors, KGH (The Royal Greenland Trade Department) and SFC (Statens Filmcentral). KGH wanted to promote a better image of Greenland to the trade community, whereas SFC sought to balance their commercial agenda. Sune Lund-Sørensen's two KGH shorts, Emilie fra Sarqaq/ Emilie from Sarqaq (1972) and Havet ved Grønland/The Sea around Greenland (1972), showed young Greenlanders, a prawn peeler and a fisherman, upbeat about their future in the Greenland-Danish economy. The SFC feature-length documentary, Nâlaqkersuissut oqarput tássagôq/Da myndighederne sagde stop!/The Authorities Said Stop! (1972), took the opposite angle. Directed by Arqaluq Lynge and the Danish painter, Per Kirkeby, the provocative film denounced Danish policy in Greenland more than any previous film had. Native women voiced their complaints about the low wages and working conditions of a KGH prawn factory in Lene Aidt and Merte Borker's Arbejderkvinder i Grønland/Working Women in Greenland (1975). On the other hand, Umá naq 75 (directed by Jeppe Mendel and Jørn Kjer Nielsen, 1975) showed Greenlanders grappling with the decision of how to spend an influx of money that the new local mine had generated. An interesting footnote in this battle over Greenland's image was the Icelandair production, They Shouldn't Call Iceland, Iceland (1977), which described Greenland as a 'primitive' island and promoted Iceland as the green country of happy vacations.

Iceland's biggest splash on the international documentary scene happened in 1982 with Rokk í Reykjavík/Rock in Reykjavík, Friðrik þór Friðriksson's gritty feature-length music collage that strung together church basement performances from nineteen Icelandic rock groups. It offered the rest of the world a peek at Icelanders who did not think of themselves as removed from global popular culture, drugs, and punk rock. A fourteen-year-old singer named Björk, and her band, Tappi Tíkarrass, stole the film's spotlight in one of her first recorded concerts. Friðrik followed up on his success with another documentary, Kúrekar norðursinns/Icelandic Cowboys (1984), which covered the first and only Icelandic country music festival held in a northern Icelandic village.

Documentaries boomed in the early millennium, particularly in Iceland. The affordability of digital video technology attracted young filmmakers and produced countless shorts and videos about Iceland's renowned music scene. Directors scavenged the Reykjavík streets to trail a petty criminal (Lalli Johns, directed by Þorfinnur Gudnason, 2001), explored the World War II barracks left by the British army (Barracks, directed by Ólafur Jóhannesson, 2001), found a new frontier in Europe Vardi Goes Europe (directed by Grímur Hákonarson, 2002), and took stock of alcoholics at the Hlemmur city bus station (Last Stop, directed by Ólafur Sveinsson, 2003). Erlendur Sveinsson turned his camera on his ailing father in Passio—A Painter's Psalm of Colors (2002) and blurred the lines between reality and creation. One documentary was even banned by the Icelandic Supreme Court. The court considered Hrönn Sveinnsdóttir's video diary of her journey in the 2000 Miss Iceland competition, I skóm drekans/In the Shoes of the Dragon (2002), a violation of the other contestants' privacy.

Greenland continued to be a spectacular stage for science documentaries such as the IMAX film, Journey into Amazing Caves (directed by Stephen Judson and Greg MacGillivray, 2001). The genre of the 'Eskimo film', however, had changed considerably since Flaherty's Nanook. Jorgen Roos and other directors of the 1960s and 1970s gave Greenlanders the chance to express their own views about themselves and their nation in their own language, and both foreign and Greenlandic filmmakers continued this approach into the 1990s. Ivar Silis's 1996 film, Greenland on its Way—Home Rule Since 1979, analyzed how semi-independence from Denmark changed and challenged the lives of ordinary Greenlanders. Silis's son, Inuk Silis Høegh, broke stereotypes about the Eskimo people in his 2002 film, Eskimo Weekend, which followed a young rock band enjoying their weekend like other Western youths.

Not all filmmakers presented a glossy view of Greenlandic life. Danish director Morten Hartkorn called attention to the problems of alcohol, suicide, and violence among the East Greenlanders in Den sidste koloni/The Last Colony (1997). Sasha Snow illustrated similar dilemmas in Arctic Crime and Punishment (2002), which many Greenlanders considered too harsh.

The turn of the millennium saw more women making documentaries about Greenlandic issues. Director Karen Littauer interviewed fourteen elderly Inuit storytellers who vividly relate a Greenland that the camera cannot capture for her film, Jeg husker … Fortællinger fra Grønland/I Remember … Tales from Greenland (2003). Ulla Boye Rasmussen focused on a single Inuit woman in Dage of Katrine/Days with Katrine. The first Greenlandic female director, Laila Hansen, attempted a sequel of sorts to Jørgen Roos's Are You a Greenlander? with Inuk Woman City Blues (2002), which probed the dislocation of Greenlandic women in Copenhagen.

Documentary production is poised to prosper in the twenty-first century as video becomes more accessible. Iceland has already experienced a national renaissance; perhaps the most interesting work will happen in Greenland, as the emphasis on the exotic declines in favor of an original, personal cinema produced by native artists.

MICHAEL KOGGE

Further reading

Cowie, Peter, *Scandinavian Cinema*, London: Tantivy Press, 1992.

Fledelius, Karsten, *et al.*, 'Danish Official Mass Communication on Films about Greenland', in *History and the Audio-visual Media*, Copenhagen: Eventus, 1979.

Icelandic Films, *Reykjavík: Icelandic Film Fund*, 1996.

Kardish, Lawrence, 'New Cinema from Iceland', *Film Comment*, September–October 1980: 6–8.

Neergaard, Ebbe, *The Story of Danish Film*, trans. Elsa Gress, Copenhagen: The Danish Institute, 1963.

Nørrested, Carl, 'Blandt eskimoer, eventyrere og enthografer: Film dokumentarisme om Grønland (Among Eskimos, Adventurers, and Ethnographers: Documentaries about Greenland), *Kosmorama* 232, winter 2003: 68–98.

Soila, Tytti, *Astrid Soderbergh Widding, and Gunnar Iversen, Nordic National Cinemas*, London: Routledge, 1998.

Sveinsson, Erlendur, *Icelandic Films 1980–83*, Reykjavík: Icelandic Film Fund, 1983.

Torfason, Olafur, 'Iceland', in Peter Cowie (ed.), *Variety International Film Guide 2002*, London, 2002.

——'Iceland', in Peter Cowie (ed.), *Variety International Film Guide 2003*, London, 2003.

Ichikawa, Kon

Although Kon Ichikawa's documentary films are minimal, compared to his nondocumentary feature film output, they nonetheless reveal visual aesthetics and thematic motifs present throughout his work. A significant contributor to the sports documentary, Ichikawa's Tokyo Orinpikku/Tokyo Olympiad (1965), Youth (1968), and his segment on the one-hundred-meter dash in the omnibus film Visions of Eight (1973) emphasize a humanist approach to this documentary form. The primary focus for Ichikawa is on the athletic event itself and the athlete's endurance of pain and suffering in order to test both the human body and spirit. Stylistically, Ichikawa's camera movements and editing contribute to the reinforcement of this humanism. Movement and the breaking up into individual shots of a particular action are predominant in this style—a reflection of his early film career as a manga cartoonist. Similarly, Ichikawa's nonsports-related documentaries, Kyoto (1969) and Japan and the Japanese (1970), follow the form of the 'city symphony' with subtle additions of the director's irony.

Ichikawa's first documentary film, Tokyo Olympiad/Kiroku chusein eiga (1965) presented a one-hundred-and-seventy-minute, formally innovative record of the 1964 Olympic Games in Tokyo. Unlike the television coverage of the event, Ichikawa's technical staff of five hundred and sixty-six, including one hundred and sixty-four cameramen, focused more on the human element of the games—most often the losers of some athletic events, as well as the spectators themselves. Their barrage of techniques, including the use of telephoto lenses (even at some points a 1600mm ultra-telephoto lens), widescreen (Italian Techniscope), and slow-motion photography contribute to a depiction of the effects of physical toil and suffering to the human body. The film is also a paean to the new Japan—a Japan that was to experience an economic upsurge in the 1960s and 1970s. This upsurge is indicated in the opening scenes when buildings are laid waste to make way for the Olympic Games. Ichikawa's focus on the spectacle of parades and the crowds of spectators hints at Japan's own restoration as a national identity following the end of World War II. Since Japan itself lost the war, it seems clear that Ichikawa's focus on several losers of athletic events stresses the fact that there is more than simply winning. When the film does focus on an athletic victory, such as that of Abebe Bikila (1932–73), the Ethiopian marathon runner, it is masterful in its technical artistry. Ichikawa's film is a tribute to the pain and suffering that athletes endure simply from competing with one another and themselves. Following the success of Tokyo Olympiad at the Cannes Film Festival, Ichikawa became typecast as a maker of 'official' documentaries. What followed was a brief period of short documentary films, after which the director returned to narrative features and television.

Both Seishun/Youth (1968) and Vision of Eight (1973), the director's other sport-related documentaries, utilize similar approaches to the genre. Youth is concerned with the Japan High School All-Star Baseball Series. The prologue shows the empty Koshien Stadium. Ichikawa then cuts to a history of the series from its beginnings in 1914, through 1924, when Koshien Stadium was built, to 1968 when the fiftieth game in the series was played. The training of the participants is shown, as well as the local contests in which the field is narrowed to forty-eight participants, one for each prefecture and one for Okinawa. The finale of the fiftieth game concludes the short documentary. Ichikawa' slow-motion segment of the one hundred-meter dash for the film Visions of Eight, titled 'The Fastest', a feature-length documentary on the 1972 Munich Olympics, expanded on his previous treatment of the event at Tokyo Olympiad. Both utilized slow-motion photography in order to stress the physicality of the event itself and the depiction of the human form in motion. In order to slow down the ten seconds of the event to six minutes of screen time, twenty thousand feet of film was used. Ichikawa utilized thirty-five cameras to cover the ten-second race, all concentrating on different details, such as a leg or thigh movement. The color footage was shot at high speed while the black-and-white footage, representing real time, was shot at twenty-four frames per second.

Both Kyoto (1969) and Nihon to Nihonjin/Japan and the Japanese (1970) offer impressionistic views of the country and its culture. Kyoto, commissioned by the Olivetti typewriter company, is segmented into six sections, revolving around the ancient city and its customs and people. The first section of the thirty-minute documentary focuses on the rock garden of Ryoanji. Ichikawa's camera emphasizes the texture of the rocks themselves. The film also shows

Zen Buddhist priests in training, the moss garden at Saihoji, an apprentice geisha being dressed, the empty Imperial Villa Katsura, and the celebration of the Gion Festival. The conclusion of the film shows the Japanese islands in the distance with a setting sun. Japan and the Japanese, made for the Osaka '70 Exposition, similarly creates an impressionistic depiction of the land and its people.

Kon Ichikawa is often viewed as a link in the postwar 'golden age' of Japanese cinema and the emerging New Wave directors of the 1960s. In much the same way, particularly in regard to Tokyo Olympiad, Ichikawa's documentary films illustrate an attempt to show the new postwar Japan reentering the world scene as a competitor and an equal.

RONALD WILSON

See also: Tokyo Orinpikku, Visions of Eight

Biography

Born in Ise, Mie Prefecture, November 20, 1915. Attended Ichioka Commercial School in Osaka. He worked as a cartoonist in the animation department of J.O. Studios in Kyoto from 1933. He worked as an assistant director on the feature filmmaking staff there in the late 1930s. In the early 1940s he was transferred to Tokyo when J.O. Studios became part of the Toho Company. In 1946 the Toho Company split and Ichikawa and others formed Shin (new) Toho. He was promoted to director in 1948. He married the scriptwriter Natto Wada in 1948. From 1948 to 1956 he collaborated on scripts with his wife. After 1956 Ichikawa worked primarily for Daie. Writer and director for Japanese television from 1958 to 1975. In 1983 Ichikawa's wife and long-time collaborator, Natto Wada died. Ichikawa himself died February 13, 2008.

Further reading

Allyn, John, *Kon Ichikawa: A Guide to References and Resources*, Boston: G.K. Hall & Company, 1985.

Corman, Cyd, 'Tokyo Olympiad', *Film Comment* 3, no. 3, summer 1965: 38–40.

Milne, Tom, 'The Skull Beneath the Skin', *Sight and Sound* 38, no. 4, autumn 1966: 185–9.

Plimpton, George, 'Olympic Visions of Eight', *Sports Illustrated* 39, no. 27 August 1973: 30–5.

Quandt, James (ed.), *Kon Ichikawa*, Toronto: Cinematheque Ontario Monographs, 2001.

Richie, Donald, 'The Several Sides of Kon Ichikawa', *Sight and Sound* 35, no. 2, spring 1966: 84–6.

In the Company of Men

(UK, Dineen, 1995)

This three-part television documentary about the Prince of Wales Company within the the Welsh Guards regiment, an elite regiment of the British Army, was made for the BBC in 1995 by Molly Dineen. In the Company of Men continues Dineen's preferred method of documentary filmmaking based on a close and sustained observation of, and interaction with, her chosen subject matter that was previously demonstrated in Heart of the Angel (1989) and The Ark (1993). Dineen occupies a position behind the camera and works with a single sound recordist in accumulating a large amount of raw footage. The final three-hour cut of In the Company of Men was formed from eighty-five hours of footage and a sustained editing process.

Dineen combines expositional background to the functions of the company with observational and interactive exchanges between herself, the officers, and the guardsmen who form the exclusively male company. The regiment was formed at the height of World War I by King George V, who expressed the wish to recruit the Welsh as a part of his household troops. This colonial demarcation of power is replicated in the organization of the regiment, where it is soon apparent that most of the officers are white, middle-class English men and educated at institutions such as Harrow School and Cambridge University, and the Guardsmen are mostly working-class men from Wales. Dineen films the regiment at various locations in Northern Ireland where the company guards a police station and patrols farmlands on the border. Dineen summarises the role of the regiment as one where 'twenty five years in Northern Ireland has taught the British Army to fight a war in which it was supposed not to take sides'. While questions of Empire, colonialism, and the reasons for the British military presence in Northern Ireland are implied by the documentary, it is also clear that these wider political and historical questions will not determine the argument of the documentary. Dineen's documentaries are constructed out of the relationship that she forms with her subjects and, in the case of In the Company of Men, over the course of the eighteen-month period spent with the regiment. The first two parts of the documentary—The Commander and The Novice—reveal the roles of Major Crispin Black and the less experienced Second Lieutenant Bruce MacInnes, who has recently completed his officer training at Sandhurst. Their differing responses to Dineen's presence and to her questioning not only reveal how Dineen's scrutinizing proximity to her subjects generates familiarity and informality but also how the presence of the camera affects the behaviour of men whose working lives involve a degree of public display. The assurance and measured candour of Black is contrasted with the naivety, inexperience, and hesitation of MacInnes and the alienation of some of the Guardsmen. Because Dineen does not conceal the nature of the interaction between the filmmaker and the subject, her documentaries have been located within the performative mode (Nichols 1994; Bruzzi 2000). The degree of performativity in In the Company of Men is mitigated by the strong elements of observation and interaction as well as the expository factor of Dineen and her sound recordists' presence as women making a documentary within the operational military context of Northern Ireland.

The implications for the spectator of Dineen's documentaries is that there is less a sense of a rhetoric of telling and argument than a process of revealing the nature of the interaction between the filmmaker and her subjects and its implications. The imbalance between the unseen presence of Dineen and the voice of her questions and the responses and answers of her subjects draws attention to the apparatus of inaction and observation and the level of trust that has to be acquired for this mode of documentary. Through the combination of interaction and observation, Dineen occupies—in her own particular style—a mediating space between the public perception of an institution such as the Welsh Guards and the much less public beliefs, hopes, and personalities of the individual role players that form that institution and the values and rituals that define the company and its functions. The role of the British Army in Northern Ireland does not form part of Dineen's questioning but it nevertheless implicitly emerges from the documentary along with the hierarchy of social class within the structure of the regiment. As a result of privileging interaction and observation, Dineen is open to the accusation of vindicating a masculine institution and masculine behaviour (Bruzzi 2000). In this way, In the Company of Men is symptomatic of that trend in British television documentary in the late 1990s that problematizes the value of the knowledge that the documentary form is traditionally assumed to disseminate (Corner 1999; Dovey 2000). However, in contrast to the serial production of the docusoaps, Dineen's documentaries are single productions and are also legitimized by the discourse of authorship.

In the Company of Men continues Dineen's propensity for investigating and interacting with masculine subjectivities as well as confirming her inclination to confound any assumption that she will assume a preexisting political stance in relation to her subject matter. This concentration on the combination of the personal and the public continues to inform Dineen's documentaries while simultaneously exercising the tenets of documentary criticism.

IAN GOODE

Further reading

Bruzzi, Stella, *New Documentary: A Critical Introduction*, London, Routledge, 2000.

Corner, John, 'Documentary. The Transformation of a Social Aesthetic', in Jostein Gripsrud (ed.), *Television and Common Knowledge*, London: Routledge, 1999.

Dovey, Jon, *Freakshow: First Person Media and Factual Television*, London, Pluto Press, 2000.

Nichols, Bill, *Blurred Boundaries: Questions of Meaning in Contemporary Culture*, Bloomington, IN: Indiana University Press, 1994.

In the Year of the Pig

(US, de Antonio, 1969)

Emile de Antonio established the genre of collage or compilation documentary, developing it specifically as a form of historical reconstruction and politically charged historiographic inquiry. Following Point of Order (1963)—a documentary comprising footage from the Army-McCarthy hearings that was rejected from the New York Film Festival because it was 'not a film'—and Rush to Judgement (1966), In the

Figure 6 In the Year of the Pig, 1969 (Courtesy of the British Film Institute)

Year of the Pig was de Antonio's third compilation film, and the point at which he refined the form. In this intricately wrought film, de Antonio combines lengthy interviews with experts together with archival materials and stock footage. Despite the fact that he is neither seen nor heard in the film, his perspective on the history of Vietnam and its struggle for independence, and his belief in the heroism of Ho Chi Minh and the culpability of the United States and its leaders is made clear. On its release in the United States, it was well received, although many critics called the film propaganda. This was a term that de Antonio accepted as praise rather than censure, observing that 'you cannot edit film without indicating prejudice' (Rosenthal 1980).

Despite de Antonio's views as an admirer of Ho Chi Minh being made clear in the film, In the Year of the Pig is not polemical in the same manner as many other protest films made during the Vietnam War. Instead, it appears by contrast coolly analytical in achieving its political and aesthetic objectives, making an appeal to the intellect of the audience. Notable for the depth and breadth of its coverage of Vietnamese history, it offered what no film or television coverage of the war had offered previously. While contemporary historians would undoubtedly contest aspects of de Antonio's scholarship, it remains today as one of the most thorough critical accounts of the background and historical context of the conflict put on screen.

In the Year of the Pig, like many other de Antonio films, was funded by various wealthy, high-profile liberals in the United States, and along with Point of Order and Painters Painting (1973), it was one of de Antonio's commercial successes. Much of the footage used in In the Year of the Pig had never been seen before by US audiences, as de Antonio collected (or 'scavenged') it from a variety of sources worldwide, including the NLF offices in Prague as well as Hanoi, the ABC and BBC television networks, and the French Army. Deeply critical throughout his career of cinéma vérité as being inappropriate to a filmmaker with political convictions, de Antonio credited the idea of working with 'dead footage' or 'collage junk' (Rosenthal 1980) to the contemporary artists and painters with whom he socialized in the 1950s and 1960s, such as Robert Rauchenberg and Jasper Johns.

De Antonio's collage method and his reliance on lengthy interviews with a variety of experts and witnesses—including journalists and academics, as well as politicians and military leaders—along with his suppression of conventional didactic features such as voice-over narration, support his political and aesthetic ideal of 'democratic didacticism' (Waugh 1985). De Antonio's complex use of archival materials on both the sound and image tracks in In the Year of the Pig not only asserts the film's historical authority, but likewise moves the film into the realm of historiographic inquiry, as the viewer is encouraged to engage in interpretation and critical thought. De Antonio's perspective on historical events is always clear through the choice and arrangement of materials, but these yield not so much a singular truth baldly stated as an image of history as a series of competing discourses that demand analysis.

Organized overall as a chronological account of the build-up to and escalation of the Vietnam War beginning with Vietnam's colonial history and Ho Chi Minh's family background, In the Year of the Pig is not strictly linear in its structure, but instead organises itself as a series of debates over key historical events, concepts, and personalities, such as the battle of Dien Bien Phu, the domino theory, Ngo Dinh Diem, Ho Chi Minh, and the bombing of North Vietnam. Addressed particularly to an audience whose understanding of the world is dependent on, and circumscribed by, television news, these debates are not only between and among those experts interviewed for the film but also between and among archival sources of various kinds. To this end, de Antonio often layers sound or voice-over with disparate images, to force critical reevaluation of what otherwise might be considered reliable sources of historical truth, in such a way that the authority of news media in particular is placed into question. For instance, Hubert Humphrey's statement to the press that prisoners are not being mistreated is intercut with and used as a voice-over for an image of a Vietnamese being beaten and kicked; this is followed by an interview with a US soldier who recalls orders to execute prisoners. Thus, at the same time that de Antonio carefully outlines trajectories of cause and effect, he also effectively undermines institutionalized versions of history, particularly those limited historical accounts, those authoritative statements by political and military figures that circulated as justification for the American entry into Vietnam and the escalation of its military presence.

AMANDA HOWELL

In the Year of the Pig (US, Cinetree, 1969, 101 mins). Produced and directed by Emile de Antonio. Edited by Lyn Zee Klingman, with Hannah Moreinis and Helen Levitt. Assistant director, Albert Maher. Cinematography by John F. Newman. Cinematography in Paris by Jean Jacques Rochut. Sound by Jeffry Weinstock. Sound in Paris by Harold Maury. Music by Steve Addiss.

Further reading

Barsam, Richard M., *Nonfiction Film: A Critical History*, Bloomington, IN: Indiana University Press, 1992.

Bruzzi, Stella, *New Documentary: A Critical Introduction*, New York: Routledge, 2000.

Crowdus, Gary and Georgakas, George, 'History is the Theme of All My Films: An Interview with Emile de Antonio', in Alan Rosenthal (ed.), *New Challenges for Documentary*, Berkeley, CA: University of California Press, 1988.

James, David E., 'Film and the War: Representing Vietnam', in *Allegories of Cinema: American Film in the Sixties*, Princeton, NJ: Princeton University Press, 1989: 195–213.

Morgenstern, Joseph, 'History Right in the Face', in Lewis Jacobs (ed.), *The Documentary Tradition from Nanook to Woodstock*, New York: Hopkinson and Blake, 1971.

Nichols, Bill, *Representing Reality: Issues and Concepts in Documentary*, Bloomington, IN: Indiana University Press, 1991.
Rosenthal, Alan, *The Documentary Conscience: A Casebook in Film Making*, Berkeley, CA: University of California Press, 1980.
Rowe, John Carlos, 'Eyewitness: Documentary Styles in the American Representations of Vietnam', in John Carlos Rowe and Rick Berg (eds), *The Vietnam War and American Culture*, New York: Columbia University Press, 1991: 148–74.
Waugh, Thomas, 'Beyond Vérité: Emile de Antonio and the New Documentary of the Seventies', in Bill Nichols (ed.), *Movies and Methods (vol. 2)*, Berkeley, CA: University of California Press, 1985.
Weiner, Bernard, 'Radical Scavenging: An Interview with Emile de Antonio', *Film Quarterly* 25, 1971: 3–15.

India

Colonized India discovered cinema as early as 1896, when Marius Sestier, one of the Lumière brothers' operators, organized a show in a Bombay hotel. These pioneering short films, including The Arrival of a Train at a Station, tried to capture and record contemporary events in a detailed and vivid manner. Although this session was exclusively organized for a European audience, Indian interest in the invention was immediate. Harishchandra Sakharam Bhatavdekar purchased a movie camera in 1899 and shot his first newsreels, each a series of real events recorded on a single reel. His film The Wrestlers, shot in 1899 during a wrestling match in Bombay, can be considered the first documentary ever made by an Indian filmmaker. However, these factual films were not only made in Bombay. Other cities like Madras and Calcutta, the then capital of the British colony, also became active film production centres. Very early on, Hiralal Sen shot street life in his hometown, or rituals along the local river. Life in India, made in Bengal in 1906 with the help of a Pathé crew, showed a moving tramway, the ghats (stone steps leading directly into the water) where Hindus perform ablutions, and cremation sites. From 1906 on, Madan, an entrepreneur who worked with his son in Calcutta, played an important role in producing regular newsreels, capturing local industry, religion, and daily life. Initially, nonfiction films mainly displayed dazzling images of the colonial Empire, or Raj, to Indian and British audiences. These included the coronation ceremonies, or Delhi Durbar, of Kings Edward VII in 1903 (Delhi Durbar) and George V in 1911 (With Our King and Queen Through India). These projects were filmed by British crews, who travelled to India for the occasion.

The colonial authorities promptly understood that this new medium could serve as a powerful propaganda tool. During World War I, they circulated images of the war effort in India, as the country supplied men and raw materials essential to victory. In 1918, facing a growing independence movement, the local government passed the Cinematograph Act to control the content of the films, using censors' boards based in Calcutta, Bombay, Madras and Lahore, composed of members devoted to the Empire's interests. Newsreels were thus produced locally, but in a biased manner, so that any dissent amongst the Indian population would always present the British in a favourable light. While the Empire's political unity prevailed over local production, the nonviolent resistance movement led by the Mahatma Gandhi captivated independent foreign newsreels agencies, such as the French Gaumont Graphic or the American Universal Newsreel. In 1930 his march against the British salt tax became the subject of unprecedented media coverage. As moving images of Gandhi defying the British Crown travelled around the globe, Indian films on the subject (Mahatma Gandhi's March to Freedom, Mahatma Gandhi's March, and Mahatma's Historic March) were immediately censored and kept from public view, leaving the Indian audience deprived of these historic images. Although the introduction of sound in 1931 increased the documentary's power of persuasion, the accurate representation of the local social life was set back by both censorship and film industry's growing focus on entertainment and commercial profitability. After living for a few years in France, P.V. Pathy returned to his homeland in 1935 with a new approach to documentary cinema. He made commissioned films for British Paramount and Universal News, and travelled across the country, unswerving in his dedication to detailed and instructional reportage on subjects as diverse as political events, social matters, and natural disasters. However, his approach was rare: most documentary film production in the 1930s remained patronizing and out of touch with local living conditions.

In 1939 the Bombay film industry organized a meeting to discuss the importance of documentaries and newsreels, which until then had been neglected by both politicians and exhibitors alike. Being left in the hands of the colonial ruler, these images of India were invariably limited to exotic or backward ways of life, or luxurious fauna and flora, and reinforced arguments for the British occupation. That same year, Great Britain entered World War II, dragging India with it. The Ministry of Information in London once again used newsreels for propaganda purposes, either to support the war effort or the so-called progressive British colonial policy in India. Keeping this objective in mind, in 1940 the Raj created the Film Advisory Board (FAB), the first state documentary production and distribution company in India. At that time, most of the films were sent from Great Britain or made in India by British crews, before being dubbed in Hindi or other regional languages. The Indian participants were trained by the FAB only to be assistants to foreign filmmakers. In 1943 London, determined to maintain control over this powerful medium, unilaterally dismantled the FAB. It imposed the showing of one government newsreel program prior to any feature-film screening, and restricted reel quotas to authorized Indian films. The FAB was replaced by a new organisation based in Bombay, which soon also included members from Calcutta, Madras and Lahore. It became a tripartite, pan-Indian body, overseeing Information Films of India (IFI), Indian News Parade (INP) and the Army Film Centre (AFC). Under the INP, the Indian newsreels agency, a team established India Today, a series of six films projecting images of India grappling with modernity and eager to compete with developed countries (The Changing Face of India, in 1941, The Grand Trunk Road, The Dak, Four Hundred Million People, Women of India, and Youth of India in 1942). In the meantime, the AFC, based in Bombay, produced around one hundred films in support of the war effort.

These three institutions finally realized that their productions were having little impact and started to develop projects made by Indian people for Indian audiences, such as Ezra Mir's films on local health, industry, agriculture, communications, but also on arts and architecture. Films on Indian traditional art forms, like Tribal Dances (1944), demonstrated unprecedented ethnographic interest in entire sections of Indian society, which were usually ignored by the media. However, controversial films, especially those dealing with the rise of nationalism in India, were systematically censored and never reached their audience. These seized films are now lost, and were most likely destroyed by the authorities. Between 1941 and 1945 the FAB and IFI produced around one hundred and seventy films, mainly for the war effort, and for the first time about social and economic issues. Exploring new themes was futile, though, due to the reluctance of the local film industry to be associated with a colonial institution, but also in view of the mass audience, more and more supportive of pro-independence ideas. After World War II, the British Empire was in decline in India and decided to close down its local documentary production units, depriving the population of a record of Independence for posterity. British newsreels focused on the protocol related to the passing of powers, ignored Jawaharlal Nehru's first speeches to his free people, but emphasized bloody images of the Partition or of Mahatma Gandhi's assassination, presenting them as tragic consequences of the British leaving the country, and justification for their colonial policy.

The Films Division, founded in 1948, rose from the ashes of the IFI and INP to lead the production and distribution of information films, enlisting documentary cinema for the larger project of nation-building and integration. Its first task was to gain the acceptance of both audiences and exhibitors, who were still required to show newsreels before each feature film. They planned to produce as many films as possible at reduced prices, to reach a wide, heterogeneous audience, urban and rural, educated and illiterate, speaking various regional languages. These films favored themes related to the development of India (hygiene, family planning, agricultural productivity), and promoting patriotic feelings. While getting rid of the cultural influence of the West, they never really dealt with the yet unsolved challenges of the country (poverty, illiteracy, communalism). The main idea was to glorify the government's policies towards its people. Although the Films Division pioneered the ethnographic documentary genre (The Adivasis of Madhya Pradesh in 1948, Our Original Inhabitants in 1953), its objective was to include diverse ethnic groups within the restrictive limits set by the Indian nation-building project. Film crews knew very little about regional customs and habits in their own country, and did not hesitate to stage tribes' daily lives, so that they fitted neatly into the national project of unity, modernization and development. These documentaries can be criticized as exotic voyeurism, but they remain some of the first images reporting the sociocultural diversity of India. During the 1950s the Films Division produced about one hundred and fifty documentaries per year, as well as a weekly newsreels programme in thirteen languages. It also did so in bureaucratic fashion, earning the nickname 'Files Division'. During this period documentary films were produced by self-taught individuals, without any profound and reflective thoughts on the medium, and without any substantial contact with world cinema. Independent documentarists struggled to find a place of their own in this very limited environment. The German director Paul Zils took some major initiatives to encourage Indian documentary cinema: he created the *Indian Documentary* magazine in 1949, the Indian Documentary Producers' Association in 1956, which founded the first Indian documentary film festival in several cities in 1958. These were the first signs of interest in independent films, made outside the Films Division circuit, but still in its shadow. The films of Roberto Rossellini (L'India vista da Rossellini, 1957, which combined a documentary approach with fictional elements) and Louis Malle (L'Inde fantôme, 1969, which added Malle's explanatory voice-over to observational images), or the international programmes selected by film societies (membership film clubs), exposed Indian directors to new working methods and invited them to rethink the documentary genre. During the prolific 1950s many films were also financed by foreign agencies, such as the United States Information Service, the American Technical Cooperation Mission, the Shell Film Unit or industrial companies like Tata and Dunlop. With this support, complacent images of human, industrial, and agricultural development were again brought to the foreground.

Bureaucratic slowness prevented the Films Division from capturing the fast-changing society of the 1960s. The reforms recommended by the Chanda Committee in 1966—aimed at solving the situation—failed to turn into action, despite the introduction of lighter equipment and new technologies, such as synchronized sound techniques, that allowed filmmakers to get closer to their subjects and reach out for more spontaneity. Under the European influence of cinéma vérité and direct cinema, some documentarists opted for an observational approach and strove to give viewers sensations of immediacy and intimacy. These innovative directors included Fali Bilimoria, with films like The House that Ananda Built (1967), which recounts a peasant's daily life in Orissa and the generational divide between a man and his sons after migrating to the big city, or Sukhdev and his eclectic films, such as India 67, about the complex negotiation between tradition and modernity in contemporary India, told through details gleaned at the four corners of the country. S.N.S. Sastry, in his unique I Am Twenty (1968), discussed with Indian youths the subjects that mattered to them (their love stories, dreams, visions of the future), in the style of Jean Rouch in Chronique d'un été. Both films are still very influential to Indian documentary filmmakers today. In the same vein, to celebrate twenty years of Independence, K.S. Chari and T.A. Abraham asked students, workers, and intellectuals to reflect on the notion of democracy in India in Face to Face (1967). These documentaries sought to revitalise the medium, not only in terms of content, by dealing with the deep doubts and hopes of the people, but also in terms of form, by using direct sound, fewer voice-overs, or kaleidoscope images, with the objective of breaking through the academic and rather tedious conventions used by the Films Division. Their work is particularly noteworthy, given that they had to work under the supervision of this official body. These films marked the birth of activist documentary cinema in India, but were only seen by a very limited audience. In the 1960s film exhibitors were still forced to show newsreels in their theatres, regardless of the audience's disinterest for these official versions of Indian current events, and the abandonment of this tradition in Western countries. Every foray into controversial issues was still opposed by authorities. During this period, directors who are now best-known for their feature films also joined the documentary filmmaking scene. In 1967 Shyam Benegal shot A Child of the Streets, about a young boy in need of affection who wanders around until he is institutionalized in a juvenile reform centre, with the intention of providing both a social message and an artistic experience to the audience. In 1974 Mani Kaul directed his first documentary film, The Nomad Puppeteers, chronicling the hardships of travelling puppeteers across the state of Rajasthan, as well as a disappearing art form.

With every project Kaul mixed fiction and non-fiction to document on reels aspects of Indian reality at odds with the enshrined notion of progress. Many documentarists started to break the twenty-minute duration rule imposed by the Films Division, choosing longer durations according to the needs of specific projects. In 1972 Satyajit Ray experimented with the genre and made The Inner Eye, a film dedicated to the Bengali painter Binode Bihari Mukherjee, which demonstrated the growing interest in the form among Indian filmmakers as it broke free from its formal and narrative stranglehold.

In the 1970s India went through a multi-faceted crisis that led the population to demonstrate against unemployment, inflation and political corruption. Overwhelmed by the scale of the protest, Prime Minister Indira Gandhi declared the State of Emergency in the name of national security and the media fell under her heel from 1975 to 1977. The Films Division reverted to a mere propaganda tool and broadcast films praising Indira Gandhi and her iron-fisted politics on public television—now considered the new mass medium for education and development. These restrictions provoked resistance. Other voices started making themselves heard and helped to redefine the tarnished notion of 'nation'. However, they mainly did so using the conventional aesthetics and instructional tone of earlier films.

As the 1980s began, India marked a shift away from Nehru's socialist redistributive development model to one friendlier to private businesses and foreign investors. Television sets started to spread around the country. Programmes were still driven by an official mission of information and education, yet they started to experiment with entertaining formats, such as TV serials, and became stronger competitors to the mainstream fiction films. Facing this growing interest for profitability, consumerism and entertainment, many documentarists reassessed the role of their film form and used it to question history. The 1980s saw the consolidation of political documentary filmmaking. Anand Patwardhan's work embodied this period. His immediate involvement in political, social, economic or religious events made him a role model for an entire generation of Indian filmmakers. His work helped documentaries gain respect as a medium and creative form in India. His style is rough, direct, fly on the wall. His first film, Waves of Revolution (1976), recounted the non-violent, popular and student anticorruption movement that led to the State of Emergency. Bombay: Our City (1985), produced with the help of individual and public funding, countered the government's and middle class's marginalization of slum dwellers by arguing that they fully participate to the economic life of the city (industry, construction, house staff). One of his most acclaimed films, In the Name of God (1992), investigated the motivations behind the destruction of the Babri mosque in Ayodhya by Hindu fundamentalists, and the efforts of secular Indians to fight against the rise of religious fanaticism. His work denunciated injustice and intolerance, from patriarchal and communalist violence (Father, Son and Holy War, 1994), to the Narmada dam project and the eviction of neighbouring tribal communities (Narmada Diary, 1995), and the danger of nuclear proliferation (War and Peace, 2002). His university years in Canada gave him the necessary international visual literacy, distance from his native country, and financing and distribution networks that his Indian peers often lacked.

Since the 1980s female documentarists like Bhishaka Datta, Manjira Datta, Meera Dewan, Deepa Dhanraj, Reena Mohan, Suhasini Mulay, Uma Segal, or Nilita Vachani also raise their voices. Mediastorm, a group of female filmmakers, worked on social and political problems related to women, from the right for divorce to the illegal practice of sati (immolation of widows). These committed and bold filmmakers directed uncompromising films about the living conditions of women as well as other neglected social issues, with the persistent objective of fighting against stereotypes and taboos. Shelter, by Uma Segal (1984), followed homeless people in their daily activities to condemn the eviction of the poor in favour of middle-class housing projects. By filming a woman possessed by a spirit in Eyes of Stone (1988), Nilita Vachani scrutinized female resistance options against Indian's patriarchal society without ever judging. Viewers were free to draw their own conclusions—a new development in Indian documentary filmmaking. Manjira Datta, in The Sacrifice of Babulal Bhuiyan (1988), reexamined the killing of a labourer who recycles coal waste. The film highlighted the social oppression and exploitation happening in the mining region of Bihar, explored the devastating environment of these migrant villagers, and allowed the blackness of the coal to invade the screen with a striking visual impact. The film reflects a possible analogy between these workers who tirelessly battle for solidarity and the struggle for solidarity of independent documentary makers who harvest forgotten snatches of existence and bring them back to life by turning a spotlight on them. In I Live in Behrampada (1992), Madhusree Dutta captured on the spot riots between Hindus and Muslims in Bombay, but went further than breaking news to tackle the complexity of caste and community relations in urban slums. The originality of the film lay in her decision to expound these major social issues through little details from the lives of the protagonists and offer a female point of view of the situation. In this case, history with a little 'h' took over History with a capital 'H'. In the same year, Reena Mohan shot Kamlabai, and reinvented documentary narration by letting the main character, one of the first Indian actresses, play to the camera and reveal herself on the screen, delivering a film that was both intimate and moving. Through the account of her tumultuous life throughout the twentieth century, the audience (re)discovered entire sections of Indian contemporary history. These films generally shared a common characteristic: they offered audiences a new experience (cultural, emotional, political), but did not lecture them.

This style is often labelled as activist because it unveils situations of crisis and emergency. In the 1980s, and even later in the 1990s, no training in documentary filmmaking was available in India, filmmakers were either self-trained, trained by foreign TV crews shooting in India, or went abroad to pursue film studies. They were not financed by the State, but mainly by private foreign (TV networks, the Ford Foundation) or local (non-governmental) organisations, which made the position of the Films Division obsolete, yet they still suffered from government censorship. Joining the cause of the underprivileged or marginalized led them to address darker aspects of society, from police abuse of prisoners (An Indian Story by Tapan Bose in 1981) to the multinationals' responsibility in the world's worst industrial disaster in Bhopal (Bhopal: Beyond Genocide, by Tapan Bose, Suhasini Mulay and Salim Shaikh, 1985), or the popular and non-violent protest against nuclear tests in Orissa (Voices from Baliapal, 1988). This documentary, directed by Ranjan Palit, recorded the struggle through interviews with the villagers. It was praised by the Ministry of Information and Broadcasting, but has always been banned from TV broadcasts by the same Ministry, in the name of national security. These films called sensitive official statements into question and provoked double-edged political reactions, including manipulation and censorship. More recently, Sanjay Kak took part in this alternative and confrontational form of filmmaking, with films about the struggle against the controversial construction of a dam in the Narmada Valley (Words on Water, 2003) and the impact of freedom fighting on the lives of civilians in Kashmir (Jahsn-e-Azadi: How We Celebrate Freedom, 2007). His films stood out both for their political statements and stylish camera work. Access to events and affected people influences the final form of these films, but it also reflects the independent point of view of distinctive directors without claiming to be comprehensive or totally objective.

In the 1990s the drive towards liberalization and modernization has transformed a quarter of the country into urban areas, and a growing part of the population into consumers. The satellite TV boom marked the end of public monopoly and opened new perspectives on audiovisual forms and contents. Taking this new challenge seriously, the film sector became a proper industry in 1998, allowing the main production, distribution and exhibition companies to be financed by banks, to work more closely together, to reinvent marketing and optimize profits. Documentary cinema kept standing aside from this context of liberal economy and mass entertainment. Some mature films started to have a global resonance, such as Seeds of Plenty, Seeds of Sorrow (1992), which focused on the dark side of the Indian Green Revolution and anticipated the way in which globalization would change the agrarian sector. Until the 1990s documentaries mainly addressed collective issues, adopting a didactical tone, while the last two decades refocused on individual and personal dialogues. Filmmakers followed one or several protagonists, mixed forms, recycled images, layered meanings, indulged in introspection. Political commitment no longer meant pleading a cause or looking at the underprivileged from a distance, but also getting involved in formal experiments, giving free rein to one's creativity, opening oneself to ambiguity and humour. This kind of filmmaking often followed from a genuine willingness to explore different ways of reproducing the 'real', as well as a desire to create an alternative visual culture in India. Filmmakers took advantage of up-to-date cinematic technologies, which helped them to capture the invisible, the overtones more easily. Allowing oneself to constantly break rules became the new political activism. Paromita Vohra makes films that resemble her. Unlimited Girls (2002), for instance, questioned one's individual commitment through feminism, skilfully blending nonfiction with fiction, popular or kitsch images, animation, screens of an Internet chat room, interviews, and wrapped up the final piece with a humorous and ironic tone, but one always opened to question and interpretation. More than recording aspects of Indian reality, Vohra took her audiences into unknown territory. Rejected by most film festivals, the film became a success through word of mouth. Recently, filmmaking has become easier worldwide through the introduction of video and digital technology. In India it has relieved filmmakers of the burden of reel quotas and expensive budgets. Digital technology and the Internet have allowed a wider range of people to grab a camera to shoot and circulate images of their everyday life, but also to unleash their creative instincts and flirt with intimacy. In 2005 a student couple from Mysore in South India filmed their sexual frolics. The video, Mysore Mallige, first circulated in the VHS underground circuit before being anonymously uploaded to the Internet, creating a conspicuous yet sizzling hit in the conservative country.

At the crossroads of artistic and industrial interests, documentary filmmakers are currently confronted with three major challenges: funding, censorship and distribution. In 2000 the public TV network partially took over from the Films Division and commissioned small-budget films under the banner of the Public Service Broadcasting Trust, but suggested conventional themes and aesthetics. Independent documentarians responded by taking action to emancipate themselves from government guardianship. In 2004 when the Mumbai International Film Festival (MIFF) rejected documentaries that were denied their official censorship certificate, filmmakers immediately reacted by organizing VIKALP, a counter-festival dedicated to documentaries but free from any state supervision. The Magic Lantern Foundation, founded in New Delhi in 1989, or the company Indiepix, based in New York since 2004, distributes these films in DVD format. Humanities departments in North American and British universities also offer interesting opportunities to show Indian documentaries abroad, but mainly rely on the filmmakers' networks and time. These films are thus mainly restricted to alternative distribution and exhibition networks, including film festivals at home and abroad, film societies, private screenings, and online platforms. These initiatives have shaped a niche market for independent documentaries. Over the past decade the construction of multiplexes has also sustained the showing of documentaries on the big screen. Theatres ranging from fifty to one hundred seats are open to options other than popular Bollywood productions. In 2010 Leaving Home, a mainstream documentary film recounting and praising the career of the famous rock band Indian Ocean, was shown in several multiplexes across the country. Likewise, the development of cable and satellite TV created a new market for documentaries, although these TV channels are mainly interested in filling their programme grids and require strict film formats.

A documentary film movement, defined by a specific style, recurrent characteristics and themes, does not exist as such in India, although a community has been able to unite on certain occasions. Documentary makers do not strive for any aesthetic harmony, but try to genuinely match their subject, or the mood of the moment. This position marks a new era for the Indian documentary film: the willingness to open up to a multitude of voices, to shine new light on current or past events. Freed from restrictions, be they political propaganda, collective memory, or the obsessive quest for realism, today's documentary filmmakers wish to chronicle India, little by little, to local audiences most of all. On the margins of the prolific yet manufactured Bollywood film industry, they embody the artistic and democratic vitality of India.

CAMILLE DEPREZ

Further reading

Garga, B.D., *From Raj to Swaraj, The Non-fiction Film in India*, New Delhi: Penguin Books, 2007.

Jaikumar, Priya, *Cinema at the End of Empire*, Durham, NC: Duke University Press, 2006.

Majumdar, Neepa, 'Film Fragments, Documentary History, and Colonial Indian Cinema', *Canadian Journal of Film Studies*, 2007: 63–79.

Mehrotra, Rajiv (ed.), *The Open Frame Reader: Unreeling the Documentary Film*, New Delhi: Rupa & Co., 2006.

Narwekar, Sanjit, *A History of the Indian Documentary Film*, New Delhi: Flicks Books, 1996.
Rajadhyakksha, Ashish and Willemen, Paul (eds), *Encyclopaedia of Indian Cinema*, New Delhi: Oxford University Press, 1999.

Industrial Britain

(UK, Flaherty, 1931)

Industrial Britain, a film begun by Robert Flaherty for John Grierson at the Empire Marketing Board (EMB) Film Unit, is an example of a state-sponsored documentary that emphasized people and work in an uneasy combination of the world-views of both men. Grierson brought Flaherty over from Berlin, where the American was trying to start a film project. In late 1931 the EMB Film Unit had obtained some credibility and, more important, an increased budget, enabling John Grierson and Stephen Tallents, the Unit's leaders, to employ the highest-profile documentary maker of the period (Aitken 1990: 121).

Flaherty brought with him not only a status as the crafter of great works such as Nanook of the North and Moana, but also a reputation for loose production methods, such as a high ratio of shot footage to usable material. Grierson wanted to employ Flaherty not only to make Industrial Britain but also to draw attention to Britain's documentary film movement as well as to teach upcoming filmmakers such as Basil Wright and John Taylor about filmmaking. Grierson was well aware of Flahery's methods and managed to obtain a large working budget of £2,500 (Calder-Marshall 1963: 135). Nevertheless, the production quickly ran into trouble when Flaherty ran out of money and film stock. Caught between Flaherty's comparatively extravagant production methods and the civil service constraints of government filmmaking with which Grierson had become used to dealing, the production was always going to be a difficult one. It seems that the film was edited by Grierson with Edgar Anstey's assistance. The final film was eventually put together with half a dozen two-reel documentaries to form what became known as The Imperial Six, which British Gaumont distributed theatrically. Flaherty had nothing to do with the narration, which sounds more like Grierson's words.

Nevertheless, Industrial Britain manages to reconcile the aims of on the one hand Grierson and Tallents' Film Unit—which wanted to produce socially purposive films that were not sponsored, product-based films, but publicity films with a wider market appeal—and on the other hand Flaherty's premodern romanticization of folk life. The film that Flaherty envisaged posited that the craftsmen of England were the real heroes of the Industrial Revolution; that it was the people who enabled fine products to be realized, rather than the then contemporary emphasis on machinery. At the same time, Industrial Britain straddles the strikingly composed images of large-scale industry and the close-ups of men toiling at their craft.

It is possible that Flaherty was not responsible for all of the footage that found its way into the finished film, and that Basil Wright and Arthur Elton were brought in to shoot extra footage (Calder-Marshall 1963: 139). Nonetheless, this awkward production history does not diminish the film's appeal. In what seem to be Flaherty's images of rows of chimney stacks and urban residences clouded in smoke and grime there is a classical quality that meshes with the intense close-ups of working men.

In this insistence of these images, on the personalising of the Industrial Revolution, alongside the broader industrial landscape images, Industrial Britain employs a 'poetic ambiguity', containing the 'metaphoric and associative possibilities of the montage juxtapositions' (Higson 1986: 79) in a somewhat haphazard organisation of numerous images of workers and their workplaces. In attempting to reconcile Grierson's socially purposive aesthetics with Flaherty's premodern romanticism, the film can be read as a paean to modernity. The broader images of an industrial landscape in which the British worker performs his noble work creates a filmic world that is not only about the craftsmanship that lies behind the façade of chimney stacks and production lines, it is also about how these workers are a part of a human army of craftsmen who maintain their grace and humanity in the face of the mechanisation of industry, at the same time as they become machinelike. The images of workers in Industrial Britain are not images of the automatons of capitalism but rather they are remnants of a time past, a time when craftsmanship belonged to the kinds of folk culture that Flaherty locates in Nanook of the North, Moana, and the later Man of Aran.

It is difficult to say whether Industrial Britain is a Robert Flaherty film or a John Grierson film; perhaps a more interesting proposal is that the film produces resonances representative of both worldviews, in an uneasy commingling of romantic celebration and the kind of sponsorship imperatives to which Grierson was beholden.

DEANE WILLIAMS

See also: Flaherty, Robert; Grierson, John

Industrial Britain (UK, Empire Marketing Board Film Unit, 1931, 22 mins). Distributed by the British Film Institute. Produced by John Grierson with Edgar Anstey. Directed by Robert Flaherty. Photography by Basil Wright and Arthur Elton. Edited by John Grierson, with assistance from Edgar Anstey.

Further reading

Aitken, Ian, *Film and Reform: John Grierson and the Documentary Film Movement*, London and New York: Routledge, 1990.

Calder-Marshall, Arthur, *The Innocent Eye: The Life of Robert J. Flaherty*, London: W.H. Allen, 1963.

Colls, Robert and Dodd, Philip, 'Representing the Nation: British Documentary Film, 1930–45', *Screen*, January/February 1985.

Higson, Andrew, '"Britain's Outstanding Contribution to the Film": The Documentary-Realist Tradition', in Charles Barr (ed.), *All Our Yesterdays: 90 Years of British Cinema*, London: BFI, 1986: 72–97.

Sussex, Elizabeth, *The Rise and Fall of British Documentary: The Story of the Film Movement Founded by John Grierson*, Berkeley, CA: University of California Press, 1975.

Introduction to the Enemy

(US, Wexler, 1974)

In the spring of 1974, with President Nixon besieged in the White House, the anti-war political activist Jane Fonda traveled to Hanoi (for the second time) with her husband and fellow activist, Thomas Hayden, and the cinematographer and director Haskell Wexler to make a documentary in liberated Quang Tri province. When Introduction to the Enemy had a limited release later that year, *The New York Times* praised it as a 'quiet, modest film', while Haskell called it 'a tiny jewel'. *Variety*, however, disagreed. Citing the sequence in which a crowd of locals watch Fonda and Hayden toss around a Frisbee, the scene in which Fonda argues with a North Vietnamese man who defends the US people, and the actress's 'constant use of an incongruously dippy smile to show her fondness for the peasantry', the reviewer charged Fonda with a tendency toward self-dramatization.

Introduction to the Enemy presented the 'new Vietnam' as a peasants' paradise. Fonda, Hayden, and Wexler, an avowed Communist, traveled to Vietnam when the US bombing of North Vietnam was at its peak. The trip was publicized as a tour in support of the Vietnamese people. The tour was filmed, and the footage was eventually released as Introduction to the Enemy.

Jane Fonda married Tom Hayden in 1972, and began her anti-war activities in earnest then, although she had been making appearances at rallies since 1969. She earned the moniker 'Hanoi Jane' due to her 1972 trip to Hanoi and her broadcast on Hanoi radio, in which she appealed to American pilots to end the bombing of North Vietnam. In that year, she made several anti-war skits on film. Tom Hayden was first leader of Students for a Democratic Society (SDS), which was founded at the University of Michigan in 1960. This group first protested within the Civil Rights movement, but in 1964 began to organize campus protests against the Vietnam War. By then, SDS was divided in factions, with some members embracing Communism and some joining the Weathermen. Hayden and Fonda divorced in 1989. Hayden went on to serve in the California State Assembly and Senate.

DAN STREIBLE

Introduction to the Enemy (US, IPC Films, 1974, 60 mins). Directed by Haskell Wexler, with codirection from Jane Fonda and Tom Hayden. Cinematography by Haskell Wexler. Editing by Bill Yahraus.

Iran

Mozaffareddin Shah, the fifth Shah of the Ghājar dynasty, during a visit to Europe, ordered his photographer, Mirza Ebrahim Khan, to purchase motion picture equipment and shoot a carnival (the Festival of Flowers) then taking place in Ostend, Belgium, circa 1900. This was the very first documentary shot by an Iranian. The film equipment brought to Iran soon afterwards was for royal entertainment, but then became mass entertainment similar to what occurred in Europe and the United States. According to film scholar Mohammad Tahaminezhad, the first movie theatre was opened in Iran at the same time.

The first Iranian filmmaker who pursued documentary filmmaking, Khanbaba Motazedi, brought a Gaumont camera to Iran after completing his studies in France. His earlier films, produced in the 1920s, are more like newsreels, documenting major political events and the country's development projects. Footage of his own family, the royal family, and the 1925 swearing-in ceremony of Reza Shah Pahlavi (the first Shah of the Pahlavi dynasty), are examples of his scope of activity.

After World War I a number of foreign ethnographic film crews entered Iran. In 1924 three Americans, Merian C. Cooper, Ernest B. Schoedsack and Marguerite Harrison, produced the very first ethnographic film, Grass (1925), depicting the annual migration of a nomadic tribe in Iran, the Bakhtiari. Many scholars agree that this is the first serious documentary produced by foreign nationals about Iran. The government banned the screening of the film in Iran (although it may have been shown briefly at the time), apparently interpreting it as not being in line with the country's developmental goals and objectives. Years later, after adding music and a new voice-over, the film was shown in Iran.

In 1930 a German crew produced a documentary chronicling the construction of Iran's northern railroad system. This film was also criticized for the depiction of poverty in Iranian society. In 1931 a French crew, accompanying a group of French scientists in Asia, crossed Iran on their way to Afghanistan and China and produced a film, The Yellow Caravan. This film was shown in France and apparently some Iranians living abroad wrote a letter complaining about various scenes in the film.

After these experiences with foreign filmmakers, the Iranian government adopted a censorship law to curtail what they deemed to be the negative portrayal of the country. Meanwhile the screening of documentaries and newsreels along with fiction films, which had started in 1904 with the establishment of the very first public movie theater by Mirza Ebrahim Khan Sahafbashi, continued in Iranian movie theaters.

With the beginning of World War II, screening of war newsreels became routine in Iranian movie theaters. After the arrival of American, British and Russian armies in Iran, the accompanying cameramen shot a substantial amount of footage of many political meetings as well as the armies' advances. These films were also shown in Iranian theaters. Following the tradition of the world's armies, the Iranian army also established 'the Army Studios', which produced a number of government propaganda films.

The beginning of the 1950s marked a series of political events that led to the nationalization of the Iranian oil industry. During a showdown between Mohammad Reza Shah and Mohammad Mossadegh (the popular Iranian prime minister), the Shah left Iran for a short period of time and returned to Iran following a coup-d'état backed by the United States to oust Mossadegh and reclaim his throne. Foreign media rushed to Iran to report on these events and consequently produced an unprecedented body of work. Later, the government used some of this footage to produce propaganda films.

Earlier, in 1949 a film crew from Syracuse University (aka the Syracuse Group) traveled to Iran to produce a series of informational and instructional films on a variety of subjects ranging from health and hygiene to agricultural issues. In 1953 the group was asked by the government to stay on and train Iranian filmmakers. Among the very first directors trained by the group were Hooshang Shafti (Shaghayegheh Soozan/Burning Poppy, 1963) and Mohammad Gholi Sayyar (Isfahan 1957). Films made by the Syracuse Group trainees are in simple narrative form, maintaining a chronological order along with an enhancing voice-over, a film style still present in today's Iranian documentary traditions. This is a precursor to the development of systematic documentary filmmaking in Iran.

The two decades between 1950 and 1970 encompass an important period in Iran's documentary cinema. The first group of Iranian film students returned from abroad hoping to establish a rich environment for cinema, among them Farrokh Ghafari and Hassan Shirvani. They began by educating other filmmakers, and the public, with screenings of the world's best documentaries. Other emerging filmmakers of this period who enriched Iranian documentary filmmaking with their own styles, techniques and methods were Ebrahim Golestan, perhaps the pioneer of the poetic documentary. He produced a memorable series of documentaries on the interaction of the oil industry with the environment. Among them are Az Ghatreh ta Darya/From Drop to the Sea (1957), Yek Ātash/A Fire (1957), Cheshm Andāz/Outlook (1957), and Mouj, Marjan, Va Khara/Wave, Coral, and Rock (1962). Forough Farrokhzad captivated audiences with Khāneh Siah Ast/The House is Black (1962), a sensitive, riveting work on the life of people with leprosy. Nāder Afshar Nāderi produced Baloot/Acorn (1966), the very first methodically significant anthropological documentary of this period. Manouchehr Tayyab's interest in architecture inspired him to make some of the most visually impressive documentaries about Iranian cultural heritage, among them, Masjed-e Jāme/Grand Mosque (1970) and Memari-e Safavieh/Safavid Architecture (1974). Tayyab with over ninety films and Khosrow Sinai with over seventy films in their respective portfolios are the most prolific Iranian documentary filmmakers. Sinai also studied architecture, music and cinema abroad. Upon his return to Iran in 1967, he joined the Ministry of Culture and Arts and remains one of the most prominent documentary filmmakers today. Among Sinai's most significant works is the production of the award-winning Marsye Gomshodeh/The Lost Requiem (1970–83), a documentary about Polish refugees in Iran during World War II. Later, Sinai was commissioned by the British Channel 4 to make a film about Kurdish refugees in Iran, On the Borderline (1991). He has directed also a number of narrative features including Talking with a Shadow, a docudrama on one of the most influential Iranian contemporary writers, Sadegh Hedayat. Sinai and Tayyab have made stylistic films covering a wide range of subjects, from ethnographic to Iranian cultural heritage and from arts to industrial. Among other memorable filmmakers of this period are Ahmad Faroughi (Toloo-e Fajr/Dawn), Kamran Shirdel (Oon Shab ke Baroon Oomad/The Night it Rained, 1967–74), and Hazhir Dariush (Goud-e Moghaddas/The Sacred Pit, 1964). Many documentaries of this period are either about Iranian crafts and cultural heritage or archeological discoveries. This trend may relate to a passion for rediscovering a national identity by searching through the past or, as some critics claim, gratifying the sponsoring entities of the films.

After the 1953 coup d'état and the return of the Shah, the government scrutinized all aspects of art and media production. The works of filmmakers were no exception. Critical treatment of any subject depicting the realities of Iranian life with sociological or political underpinning, or screening of any film directly or indirectly critical of the government, was subject to censorship, resulting in a self-censoring trend among film producers in order to protect their investments (a tendency still prevalent in Iran). Kamran Shirdel's Tehran Pietakht-e Iran Ast/Tehran is the Capital of Iran (1966), and Oon Shab ke Baroon Oomad/The Night it Rained (winner of the Gran Prix at the Third Tehran International Film Festival in 1974), were among the first documentaries banned by the government. The censorship caused intellectual filmmakers to turn to 'safe' subjects, reluctantly distancing themselves from relevant social and historical issues. Nevertheless, films of this period are highly stylistic and impressive to watch.

In 1966 the National Iranian Radio and Television Organization (NIRTV) was established and immediately began to attract documentary filmmakers. Television, along with the Ministry of Culture and Arts, was the main entity supporting documentary filmmaking in Iran. Feridoun Rahnema, a French-educated intellectual, was lured to Iran to establish a research center and to produce a program, Iran Zamin/The Land of Iran, showcasing documentaries on Iranian cultural heritage. Rahnema, perhaps the pioneer in methodical documentary filmmaking in Iran, began to emphasize research-oriented documentaries, something frequently ignored by many filmmakers that had led to the superficial treatment and consequently a more formalistic approach to documentary production. Rahnema's leadership attracted a number of great filmmakers to television, including established filmmakers with great portfolios: Parviz Kimiavi (Peh Mesle Pelican/P Like in Pelican, 1972), Nasser Taghvaei (Arbaein/Fortieth, 1968), Mohammadreza Asalani (Jam-e Hasanlu/Hasanlu Bowl, 1967), and a number of other well-known filmmakers. Rahnema himself directed a memorable documentary, Takht-e Jamshid/Persepolis (1962), an attempt to find historical and national identity in the ruins of Persepolis. Rahnema, a scholar and a visionary, believed that a government or private entity must support documentary cinema in Iran. He concluded that documentary filmmaking would not flourish without sustainable financial support and systematic investigation of the subject. Rahnema did not dispute the importance of documentaries on health and industrial development, but he insisted on a serious look at the roots of being an Iranian and a search for a true identity. Unfortunately, he did not live long enough to see his ideas fully implemented.

A number of early graduates from the School of Television and Cinema, a NIRTV affiliate, also made their career in making documentaries. Among them, Gholamhussein Taheridoost (Baloot/Acorn, 1973), Houshang Azadivar (Andre Malraux and Iran's Civilization, 1975) and Ebrahim Mokhtari (The Jockey, 1975). Mokhtari later established himself as one of the most successful documentary filmmakers in the postrevolutionary period with films about women's plight, including the award-winning Mokarrameh: Memories and Dreams, produced in 1999.

It is essential to acknowledge some of the remarkable anthropological films made during this period: Nasser Taghvaei's Bād-e Jen/The Wind of Jinni (1971), a startling yet informative film on a mysterious disease in the Persian Gulf region believed to be caused by evil possession of the body, and the ritual for removing it, and Parviz Kimiavi's Ya Zamen-e āhoo!/Oh, the Protector of Deer! (1970), a poetic portrayal of the pilgrims' prayers captured in the shrine of the eighth Imam of Shi'i Moslems in Iran.

After the revolution of 1979, Iranian cinema was in limbo waiting for direction to be given. A cultural reform implemented by the Islamic revolution imposed new policies on production and foreign imports. Although these changes seemed an impediment, in reality they initiated a new era in Iranian cinema. Within a few years Iranian cinema emerged with a new face and gradually captured the attention of the world by producing some of the most memorable films in the world's cinema. Some Iranian filmmakers who became staples at the world film festivals were Abbas Kiarostami, Mohsen Makhmalbaf, Majid Majidi, Jaffar Panahi, Rakhshan Bani Etemad and Tahmineh Milani, who along with others mesmerized the world with their films.

Documentary cinema, despite not having the same international exposure, has continuously progressed alongside narrative cinema. Government and government-subsidized agencies remain the main supporters of documentary filmmaking in Iran. Many documentaries now feed six television broadcast channels in Iran.

A remarkable body of work immediately before and after the revolution in Iran (late 1978 and early 1979) was produced either by amateur filmmakers using 8mm and simple 16mm cameras, Iranian television, or the Audio/Visual Unit of the Ministry of Culture and Arts. Street demonstrations, strikes, political gatherings and street clashes between the revolutionary forces and government forces were captured. Examples of films from this period are Hussein Torabi's Baray-e āzadi/For Freedom (1980) and Mohammad Ali Najafi's Lylatol Ghadr/The Night of Ghadr (1980). Immediately after the revolution, renowned Iranian filmmaker Amir Nāderi produced two documentaries about people who went missing during the revolution, Jostoju Yek/ Search 1 (1979) and Jostoju Dou/ Search 2 (1979). According to Shahaboddin Ādel (2001), the Iranian film scholar, the revolution and its immediate consequences are responsible for the appearance and expansion of two types of documentaries in Iran: the political documentary and the news documentary. He also believes that using the direct camera technique for making documentaries and collecting and archiving information for developing documentaries are the consequences of the social change.

In the period leading up to the Iran–Iraq war and immediately afterword, documentary filmmaking caught the attention of many filmmakers. A series of films seem to set a new direction and tone. Kāreez/The Canal, Continuation of Life (1985) by Mohammad Moghadasian is a study of people participating in providing for their own needs. The film documents the cooperation of people dredging a canal vital to their water supply. The other notable works are two comprehensive series, methodically researched, one on the history of Iranian calligraphy (Khat/Calligraphy), and the other on Iranian architecture (Memari-e Irani/ Iranian Architecture). These series are currently used as instructional material in schools.

The Iran–Iraq war of 1980–8 also created a new documentary style that was completely unexpected in Iranian history: war documentaries. Iranian filmmakers' experiences during the war resulted in some of the most remarkable footage from this gruesome war. Many of these films were shot in the cinéma vérité style: Pol-e Piroozi/The Victory Bridge, Karbala Panj/Karbala Five, and two series, Haghighat/The Truth and Ravayat-e Fath/ The Narrative of Victory. Some filmmakers, like Mortaza Avini (who worked on Ravayat-e Fath), lost their lives in the process of documenting the war. A number of filmmakers of this period who learnt about cinema through war documentaries, went on to become professional filmmakers in postwar cinema, including Ebrahim Hatami Kia, Ahmadreza Darvish, and Rasool Mollagholipour.

After the war, numerous films were produced documenting the rebuilding of the country and progress in the industrial and scientific sectors. Government-supported entities like Foolād-e Mobarakeh (Mobarakeh Steel Company), as well as private companies, continue to support veteran and emerging filmmakers in their efforts. Nevertheless, the filmmakers' attention was not removed from ethnographic films. Many established and emerging filmmakers continue their work in this area. Farhad Varahram (Ghatl-e Shotor/Killing of the Camel, 1991), who worked with the late Nāder Afshar Nāderi (a pioneer of ethnographic documentaries) continues his career in this genre. Farhad Mehranfar and Ali Shah Hatami have directed some of the most memorable anthropological episodes of Koodakan-e Sarzamin-e Iran/The Children of Iran, a series for Islamic Republic of Iran Broadcasting (IRIB) documenting the lives of Iranian children in various parts of Iran under unusual circumstances and extraordinary conditions.

Serious and scholarly documentary studies have emerged in postrevolutionary Iran. Mohammad Tahaminezhad, Zaven Ghookasian, Mohammad Saeed Mohasesi, Pirouz Kalantari, Robert Safarian, and other scholars, have enriched the research and analytical field with their insightful writings.

Documentary filmmaking in Iran is alive and well, and largely supported by government agencies. Many young Iranians fascinated by the power of cinema are absorbed by nonprofit organizations that provide video equipment for their experiments. No doubt, affordable and accessible video equipment is also responsible for the democratization of cinema in Iran. As Rahnema rightly observed, Iran does have many talented filmmakers who are searching for the opportunities and support needed to flourish. Currently, organizations like the Documentary & Experimental Film Center (DEFC) support production and organize an annual documentary film festival, Iran International Documentary Film—Cinéma Vérité. The Iranian Alliance of Motion Picture Guilds has two affiliate societies focusing on documentary production: the Iranian Documentary Filmmakers' Association (IRDFA) and the Association of Iranian Documentary Producers (AIDP). The Iranian Youth Cinema Society (IYCS), with offices around the country, supports young filmmakers' unquenchable desire to express themselves through film. The postrevolution generation is well educated, well read, and politically conscious. They are the ones who will chart the future course of new Iranian cinema.

New information technology has also influenced documentary filmmaking in Iran. Young filmmakers, being cyber-literate, obtain information about international film festivals and take it upon themselves to enter their films and videos into many festivals around the world. Interestingly enough, Rahnema's vision of supporting and nourishing documentary tradition in Iran is augmented by many theoretical discourses in newspapers, journals, and even in government-run television. On a television show, Mostanad-e Chahar/Documentary 4, critics and scholars discuss world documentaries and exchange ideas on film theories. In March 2011, with the beginning of a new year in the Iranian calendar, the state television inaugurated a new channel fully dedicated to showcasing documentary productions. As the filmmaker/ scholar Mohammad Tahaminezhad (*Iranian Cinema from Constitution Revolution to Sepanta*, 1970) has remarked, the third generation of Iranian documentary filmmakers is on the rise. Many of these filmmakers are women with bright careers ahead of them. Indeed, five out of the ten best documentaries produced in 2008 were made by women.

It is indeed very remarkable that with so many obstacles to producing films in Iran, spirited Iranian filmmakers somehow manage to make their films, although the audiences still have to read between the lines. Much of the criticism pointing at the lack of depth and research may be unjustified, considering that many talented Iranian filmmakers, before and after the revolution, have tried to communicate with their audiences through symbols, metaphors and allegorical expressions. Many capable filmmakers have not been mentioned in this brief history, but their efforts are noted and appreciated.

References

Ādel, Shahaboddin, *Cinema-ye Ghoumpazhoohee* (Ethnological Cinema), Tehran: Soroush Press, 2001.

Emami, Homayoon, *Cinemaye Mardomshenakhti-ye Iran* (The History of Iranian Anthropological Cinema), Tehran: Nashr–e Afkar, 2006.

Ghookasian, Zaven (ed.), *Haghighat–e Cinema va Cinema Haghighat II* (The Truth of Cinema and Cinéma Vérité II), Tehran: The Documentary & Experimental Filmmaking, 2008.

——*Haghighat–e Cinema va Cinema Haghighat*, (The Truth of Cinema and Cinéma Vérité), Tehran: The Documentary & Experimental Filmmaking, 2007.

Mehrābi, Massoud, *Tarikh-e Cinema-ye Iran: Az Āghaz Ta Sāl-e 1357*, (The History of Iranian Cinema: from Beginning to 1979), Tehran: privately published, 1992.

Omid, Jamāl, *Tarikh–e Cinema–ye Iran: 1279–1357*, (The History of Iranian Cinema: 1900–1978), Tehran: Rowzaneh Publications, Spring 1998.

Further reading (in English)

Dabashi, Hamid, *Closeup: Iranian Cinema, Past, Present, and Future*, London and New York: Verso, 2001.

——*Masters & Masterpieces of Iranian Cinema*, Washington, DC: Mage Publishers, 2004.

Issari, M. Ali, *Cinema in Iran, 1900–1979*, Metuchen, NJ: Scarecrow Press, 1989.

Maghsoudlou, Bahman, *Iranian Cinema*, New York: Hagop Kevorkian Center for Near Eastern Studies, New York University, 1987.

Naficy, Hamid, 'Iranian documentary', *Jump Cut*, no. 26, December 1981: 41–6, www.ejumpcut.org/archive/onlinessays/JC26folder/IranDocy.html (accessed 18 April 2011).

——*A Social History of Iranian Cinema, Volumes 1 & 2*, Durham, NC: Duke University Press, 2011.

Sadoul, Georges, *Dictionary of Film*, (trans. Morris Peters), Berkeley, CA: University of California Press, 1972 (published in French in 1965).

——*Dictionary of Filmmakers*, (trans. Morris Peters), Berkeley, CA: University of California Press, 1972 (published in French in 1965).

Tapper, Richard (ed.), *The New Iranian Cinema, Politics, Representation and Identity*, London and New York: I.B. Tauris Publishing, 2002.

Ireland

Cinematic documentary began in Ireland with Lumière films shot in 1896 and 1897. The cinematograph recorded an urban environment largely undifferentiated from others that it had filmed elsewhere. Dublin and Belfast were simply Victorian cities complete with horse guards, firemen, vehicles, pedestrians, buildings, and monuments; a later film even recorded Queen Victoria's own visit to the capital city. Lumière cameramen neither sought nor found either quaintness or rurality in Ireland, but a series of travelogues followed, including London to Killarney (Cooper, 1907) and Whaling Ashore and Afloat (Paul, 1908). The landscape became the defining feature of Ireland on screen, and its people little more than peasants. Such scenes, recorded in response to the demand for exotic imagery in early cinema, corresponded with popular impressions of the country in paintings and writings dating back to the seventeenth century.

Domestic practitioners, including Louis de Clerq and the Youghal-based James and Thomas Horgan, did not offer anything to detract from the impression of the country as picturesque and quaint. They recorded scenes of Irish people in largely rural environs: attending religious functions, participating at sporting events, engaging in farming activities, all of which made entertaining visuals. The ambitions of filmmakers in this period were understandably limited by predocumentary forms of nonfictional representation. Such films were intended and able to provide only the most cursory of overviews of any place and its people. As such, these travelogues and actualities did not contribute greatly to an understanding of Ireland although they certainly contributed to how people saw it.

Newsreels and newsreel cameramen registered events transpiring on the island of Ireland throughout the first decades of the twentieth century, including the growing political ferment. A specifically Irish newsreel entitled Irish Events ran between 1917 and 1920. The struggle for political independence brought with it a great deal of visual representation, but nothing comparable with the newsreel compilation work pioneered in the Soviet Union by Esfir Shub and Dziga Vertov. There was no analogous sense of the political possibilities of the medium.

By the early 1930s a relatively lively amateur filmmaking community had taken up the challenge of representing the newly independent Ireland. Individuals such as Richard Hayward, Norris Davidson, Desmond Egan, and the famous stills photographer Fr Frank Browne made several short films, but none touched on political subject matter or attempted a more comprehensive overview of issues affecting Ireland and the Irish. On the contrary, as documentary form evolved throughout the 1920s and 1930s, the majority of Irish nonfiction films still concerned themselves with agrarian and touristic subject matter. A notable proportion of these films were directed by priests or other religious leaders. Because they possessed the resources to purchase the equipment, they became the documentarians of contemporary Irish life. It is therefore unsurprising that films such as Aran of the Saints (Catholic Film Society, 1932) and Eucharistic Congress 1932 (Browne, 1932) should depict Ireland as a predominantly religious culture.

Although funded abroad, produced by an Englishman, and directed by an American, Man of Aran (Flaherty, 1934) was initially endorsed as if it were a product of an indigenous Irish cinema. The image of the islanders as rugged, self-reliant people untouched by the concerns of modernity was met with enthusiasm by government officials, who envisioned Ireland on the whole in much the same terms. This position was subsequently treated with indignation by commentators and observers who did not share this view of either the country or of its representation. Few native filmmakers possessed the skills, financial resources, or personal vision of Flaherty, however, meaning that there was little that could be shown as a rejoinder.

In 1936 The Irish Film Society was established. This body attempted to coordinate the activities of indigenous fiction and nonfiction filmmakers. The Film Society encouraged a critical engagement with the medium, which could lead to the evolution of a cinema committed to social and political change. It organised workshops, invited guest speakers from abroad, including Paul Rotha and Michael Powell, and screened European films that the society felt were being neglected in favour of Anglophone cinema. Some of their own films even aspired to political agitation, such as Aiséirghe (O'Leary, 1941), a polemical attack on the love of self-glorification in Irish politics.

State involvement in the production of documentary films began in the 1940s. The National Film Institute (NFI) was established in 1943 and became the official intermediary between filmmakers and government departments. The NFI was initially established with a grant from the department of education, but it was also financially, logistically, and morally supported by the Catholic church. Although not all films produced by the NFI bore the explicit ideological stamp of either church or state, all of them were the product of a tacit collusion between the two, which defined the range and nature of the subject matter.

The first high-profile documentary produced by the NFI was A Nation Once Again (Stafford, 1946), a celebration of the life and ideals of nineteenth-century nationalist Thomas Davis. The film informed audiences that the story of Davis's life was 'not just the story of a man, but the story of a Nation'. The generally modern and progressive portrayal of life in contemporary Ireland was undercut by its constant referral to the past as the moral and ideological centre of that life. The film explicitly linked the political ideals of nineteenth-century nationalism with the modern, industrial, and independent nation of 1946, arguing by inference that the latter owed its existence to the former.

A Nation Once Again set the tone for subsequent state-sponsored films, but it was immediately followed by a counterattack in the form of Our Country (O'Leary, 1947). Director Liam O'Leary was one of the founders of the Irish Film Society. Like Grierson, whom he referred to as 'the brilliant Scot', he was convinced that film could participate in social progress. Writing in *Invitation to the Film* (Laoghaire 1945), he argued that the cinema needed to be harnessed not to support an 'official' interpretation of Irishness, but to ask questions of it that would encourage improvement. He wrote, 'Our people need the assurance of an inner freedom which we have not yet won.'

Our Country was a direct attack on the government of the day, financed by a newly founded oppositional political party eager for publicity. O'Leary was influenced by Pudovkin and Eisenstein, and sought to shock his audience with raw imagery and juxtaposition though editing. The film featured scenes of children playing barefoot in the slums of inner-city Dublin and scenes of adults seeking passports and emigration visas to leave the country. It dramatised rising inflation using actors and spoke out on health, trade, and the lack of industrial development. Landscape scenes were used only for ironic counterpoint. The Irish countryside was portrayed as an underused resource, not a picturesque panorama.

The film confronted the Irish people with an image of themselves that they had not seen before on screen. It had such an impact that it was debated in the Irish parliament and its maker accused of being a propagandist. Unsurprisingly though, its success as a polemic further galvanised the state's support for sponsored nonfiction films. A series of public information and political propaganda films followed throughout the 1950s, including Housing Discrimination (George Fleischmann, 1953), which used inequalities in the housing policies of the Omagh Rural District Council in Northern Ireland to launch an attack on partition; and Voyage to Recovery (Healy, 1952), an influential docudrama on the treatment of tuberculosis.

Unproblematic nationalism arguably reached its apex with the historical documentary Mise Éire/I am Ireland (Morrison, 1959). Although not a state-sponsored film, it bore all the hallmarks of the rhetorical approach favoured by the majority of NFI documentaries. Director George Morrison assembled what amounted to the official history of the evolution of the Irish State to 1919, which he compiled from newsreels and newspaper clippings. Bolstered by a lush orchestral score composed by Seán O Riada and a voice-over in Gaelic, the film was a nationalist document in every sense. It was both a record and an example of the prevailing attitude to history. Mise Éire was followed by a less popular sequel, Saoirse?/Freedom? (Morrison, 1961), which partly documented the turbulent years following independence. Morrison claimed that its more critical attitude towards its subject led to its box office failure and in effect planned a trilogy that would bring history up to date and examine the failure of 'the bourgeois revolution of 1916'. This claim is not supported by the films as they stand, though, which reinforces the ideology of the 1916 generation on an epic scale.

The introduction of television in 1961 marked the next and most significant turning point. As it did elsewhere, television provided a new market for nonfiction. Although the majority of material produced for television fell within the news/journalism category, the medium provided training and opportunities for a new generation of filmmakers. It also offered a forum for new ideas about the nature of Irish society, usually articulated through chat shows and panel discussions. The early years of television were marked by an oscillation between conservativeness and radicalism. Telefís Éireann (later Radio Telefís Éireann, RTÉ) was a semi-state body answerable to a board of political appointees and was permitted to operate subject to the terms of a public service broadcasting mandate. This led to uncertainty as to exactly how much the station could challenge the status quo; most often it chose not to.

Radharc Films was an important contributor to this environment. Radharc was headed by two priests, Fr Joseph Dunne and Fr Des Forristal, and run entirely by religious personnel. The company, which was independent of RTÉ, produced a weekly series entitled Radharc, which dealt with local and international issues. It produced programmes on homelessness and poverty, shot the first film inside an Irish prison, and interviewed prostitutes when such subjects were still extremely taboo. The Radharc philosophy, drawing its inspiration from the parables of Christ, was to allow such stories to teach moral lessons without explicit commentary. The result was, among other things, a document of the changing face of modern Ireland. Inevitably though, the provocative films alternated with less challenging material on missionary work by religious orders, church openings, and pilgrimages to holy shrines.

The most groundbreaking Irish documentary of the 1960s was not made for television, nor has it ever been broadcast. In 1968 Irish-born Peter Lennon, a correspondent for *The Guardian*, based in France, directed The Rocky Road to Dublin (Lennon, 1968). The film was an angry, personal assault on the crippling effects of church and state on the minds of Irish people. It specifically targeted censorship and education, both of which demonstrated the collusion between the two institutions. Free-form in style, combining elements of cinéma vérité, rhetorical form, and personal cine-essay, the film was influenced by the experiments of the French New Wave. It used a combination of observation and direct address to point out how hypocrisy and 'bad habit' had made the people of Ireland incapable of thinking for themselves. Among its more striking images was one of a small boy so indoctrinated by religious education that he is able to recite a damning condemnation of humanity's predilection for sin. The film later poses a rhetorical question on the subject of this boy and his classmates: 'What will they grow up to be?'

The Rocky Road to Dublin was financed by freelance American producer Victor Herbert and photographed by acclaimed cinematographer Raoul Coutard. It achieved some notoriety following its screening at the Cannes Film Festival. Its defiant attack on such powerful institutions and its call for radical change made it something of a mascot for the striking students of May 1968, who screened it at the Sorbonne. The film was hailed by *Cahiers du Cinéma* as a masterpiece. Suspicious of its status as a tool of rebellion, the mainstream Irish media were largely unsupportive. Although Lennon appeared on television, where he was attacked for his attitude towards the church, the film itself ran only in one art house cinema in Dublin. It was never distributed to rural areas. Many cinema owners had either direct links or strong friendships with clergy. Without any specific words being spoken, the film was quietly banned from theatrical distribution. RTÉ chose not to broadcast it because of the 'sensitive' nature of the subject matter.

The 1970s saw a great deal of activity in Irish documentary, if little further radicalism. Filmmakers such as Bob Quinn, Louis Marcus, Kieran Hickey, and Patrick Carey directed films that won attention and awards at international film festivals. There was also a steady stream of corporate-produced and magazine-style film and television work that documented and explored much of the history, heritage, and traditions of the Irish nation. Very little of it attempted to interrogate or question. Some of those that did—such as The Family (Quinn, 1978), charting the alternative lifestyle of a hippie commune living in the west of Ireland, and the docudrama Our Boys (Black, 1981), featuring interviews with men who suffered physical abuse at Christian Brothers Schools in their childhood—were not broadcast.

In the 1980s a number of films began to find new ways of circumventing censorship and conservatism. Bob Quinn succeeded in challenging convention with his three-part documentary Atlantean (Quinn, 1984), which used humour to mask its serious concerns about the nature of representation. On the surface it covered similar ground to many of its less radical predecessors. The film purported to explore the anthropological and sociological history of the Irish people, but Quinn used his audience's familiarity with this material to confound expectation. He argued in favour of an 'Atlantean' culture that embraced roots in North Africa and Europe. He was able to use this historical investigation to question assumptions about the ethnic and cultural uniqueness of the Irish race. He used irony as a polemical tool to undermine both form and content, ultimately turning the focus on history itself and the processes of ideology that define that history.

The Road to God Knows Where (Gilsenan, 1988) took up the mantle of postmodernist fragmentation as a tool of political and aesthetic radicalism. Twenty-eight-year-old Alan Gilsenan directed the film as part of a series of Irish-themed documentaries broadcast by Channel 4(UK). The film focused on the experience of being young and Irish in the 1980s, a time of widespread unemployment and high emigration. Like Lennon and Quinn before him, Gilsenan applied a mixture of techniques to draw attention to paradoxes and contradictions. Like O'Leary, Gilsenan used shocking imagery to strip away the illusions proffered by state-run promotional authorities. Shots of dirty-faced children, rubbish-strewn fields, and abandoned factories were intercut with upbeat commentaries on the traditional values and hospitality of the Irish nation. Bizarre, surreal inserts and cutaways featuring irrelevant title cards, musicians, and a routine by a stand-up comic contributed to the atmosphere of parody and self-reflexivity. The reaction from official sources was predictably hostile. The Industrial Development Authority, charged with encouraging investment in Ireland at home and abroad, publicly criticised the film, which nonetheless received a screening on Irish television and became a focal point for discussion of the issues it raised.

The 1990s was a time of widespread change in Ireland and there was a corresponding shift in the subject matter tackled by nonfiction film. Issues such as AIDS, prostitution, abortion, homosexuality, and divorce were addressed by filmmakers, including Gilsenan, Liam McGrath, Hilary Dully, Trish McAdam, and Donald Taylor Black. Quinn and Marcus continued to produce work, whereas Belfast-born John T. Davis eschewed what he termed 'wallpaper' documentaries in favour of more personal and reflective subject matter in films like The Uncle Jack (Davis, 1996). Dear Daughter (Lentin, 1996) was arguably the most influential film of the decade because of its opening up of the issue of the abuse in state-run institutions during the early and middle decades of the twentieth century. Dear Daughter was stylistically notable for its use of reflexive reconstruction. The flashbacks were filmed with the adult women in the actual locations reenacting routines and rituals from their childhood while describing their feelings then and now. This device made explicit the links between past hurt and present trauma and won sympathy for the subject. The film marked a turning point in the debate on these issues in public and led to several others, including States of Fear (Raftery, 1999), that implicated the government as well as the religious orders.

Although documentarists consequently enjoyed unprecedented freedom to tackle contentious subject matter, they often chose uninteresting ways to do so. Stylistic innovation declined. The feminist historiography Hoodwinked (McAdam, 1997) was little more than a string of talking heads, and the much hyped five-part series The Irish Empire (Gilsenan, Walsh, Roberts, 1999) was more like a tourist documentary than a study of the neocolonial mind of the 'Celtic Tiger' Irish. Even the long-anticipated sequel to The Road to God Knows Where, Road II (Gilsenan, 2001) was conventional and unrewarding. Gilsenan's other efforts, such as Julie's Story (Gilsenan, 1999) on crime writer Julie Parsons, and Private Dancer (Gilsenan, 2001) on lap dancing in Dublin, were indistinguishable from any number of magazine-style programmes broadcast by RTÉ. The new documentary of revelation and investigation was arguably as much the product of a hyper-stimulated postmodern televisual environment as it was the result of an awareness of the potential of the medium to penetrate beneath the surface. In spite of a century of development, Irish documentary had not progressed much beyond the unproblematic relationship between the utterance and its meaning established seventy years earlier. Documentary therefore still operates on a primarily rhetorical level in contemporary Ireland, and remains part of an infrastructure of public discourse incorporating radio, television, print, and cinema. Many individual films and filmmakers are remarkable in the context of the national production environment, but only a few have embraced the medium with sufficient passion and enthusiasm to produce outstanding work on a global scale.

HARVEY O'BRIEN

See also: Lumière Brothers, The; Man of Aran

Further reading

Laoghaire, Liam, *Invitation to the film*, Tralee: Kerryman, 1945.

McIlroy, Brian, *Shooting to Kill: Filmmaking and 'the Troubles' in Northern Ireland*, Trowbridge: Flicks Books, 1998.

——*Irish Film: The Emergence of a Contemporary Cinema*, London: BFI, 2000.

McLoone, Martin, 'Ireland and Cinema', in John Hill and Pamela Church Gibson (eds), *The Oxford Guide to Film Studies*, Oxford and New York: Oxford University Press, 1998.

O'Brien, Harvey, 'Documenting Ireland', *Cineaste* 24, nos. 2–3, 1999: 64–9.

——'Historical Documentary in Ireland', *Historical Journal of Film, Radio, and Television* 20, no.3, autumn 2000: 335–50.

——'Somewhere to Come Back To: The Filmic Journeys of John T. Davis', *Irish Studies Review* 9, no. 2, autumn 2001: 167–77.

Pettitt, Lance, *Screening Ireland*, Manchester: Manchester University Press, 2000.

Quinn, Bob, *Maverick*, Mount Eagle, 2002.

Savage, Robert J., *Irish Television: The Political and Social Origins*, Cork: Cork University Press, 1996.

Isaacs, Jeremy

Sir Jeremy Isaacs has contributed to documentary film as producer, filmmaker, executive, and even film subject.

Isaacs is recognized as an accomplished documentary producer and filmmaker, having worked on the celebrated The World at War (1974–5), Ireland: A Television History (1981), and The Cold War (1998).

As Controller of Features at Thames Television until 1974, Isaacs made a lyrical programme very much in the tradition of Humphrey Jennings and John Gray. Till I End My Song celebrated the river Thames and demonstrated Isaacs's ability to combine engaging narrative and storytelling with attention to detail, accuracy, and realism.

Subsequently, he was the driving force behind The World at War, which was based on the earlier newsreel All Our Yesterdays, on which Isaacs had worked. The series offered a variety of perspectives articulated by combatants from opposing sides and used previously unseen footage. A significant number of World War II participants, witnesses, and policymakers were interviewed for the film. In its weaving together of a narrative that paid attention to the human as well as the strategic and the political, Isaacs produced a documentary series that holds our attention and holds up well.

Later, Isaacs produced The Cold War for Turner Broadcasting. Again, he sought to create a pluralist model that allowed for a diversity of voices to be heard and represented. The programme makers were able to interview an extraordinary variety of people, including former spies, heads of state, policy advisers such as Robert McNamara, and soldiers.

Isaacs was also the founding Chief Executive of the UK's Channel 4 from 1981 to 1987. During his tenure he ensured that Britain's broadcasting culture became more diverse and innovative. As Chief Executive of Channel 4, Isaacs was instrumental in allocating broadcasting slots. Although Channel 4 is not generally recognized for groundbreaking documentaries, some notable documentaries did reach the screen during Isaacs's tenure. These include Vietnam—A Television History (1983), Redbrick (1986), 11th Hour (1997), and Writing on the Wall (1996).

Isaacs went on to act as General Director of London's Royal Opera House from 1988 to 1996. However, he remained connected to the world of documentary during this time. He was a primary subject of the documentary film The Royal Opera House—Behind the Scenes (commonly referred to as The House), in which the cameras were trained on the day-to-day operations of the opera house. The resultant series exposed the dramas and melodramas behind the stage as infighting on camera exposed the political and creative tensions inherent in the running of an opera house.

In this, as in the other aspects of his career, Isaacs can be said to have contributed to and enhanced our understanding of contemporary Britain through entertaining and informative documentaries and programming.

ROBERT BEVERIDGE

Biography

Born in Glasgow in 1932. Educated at Merton College, Oxford. Went on to produce some of the most significant historical documentaries made for British television, such as The World At War (1974–5, 26 episodes), Ireland: A Television History (1981), and the Cold War (1998). After being Director of Programmes at Thames Television, appointed as the founding Chief Executive of Channel 4 (1981–7), where he established its character. Between 1988 and 1996 Isaacs was General Director of London's Royal Opera House, where he allowed filming for the documentary The Royal Opera House—Behind the Scenes.

Selected films

1973 The World at War: writer

1981 Ireland: A Television History: series producer

1998 The Cold War: writer

Further reading

Isaacs, Jeremy, *Storm over Four: A Personal Account*, London: Weidenfeld & Nicolson, 1989.

——*Cold War: For Forty-Five Years the World Held its Breath*, London: Bantam Press, 1998.

——*Cold War: An Illustrated History 1945–89*, Boston: Little, Brown, 1998.

——*Never Mind the Moon*, London: Bantam Press, 1999.

Israel

This entry follows chronologically the evolution of documentary filmmaking in Israel. Through key directors and films it pays particular attention to their various modes of address: from the early propagandistic Zionist Socialist films that dominated documentary film production until the 1950s, through the self-reflexive and politically detached artistic films of the 1960s, to the radical and critical politization found in documentaries of the 1970s and 1980s, culminating in the more recent postmodern, subversive, multicultural documentaries. It also follows the films' evolving treatment of the ongoing dominant themes of Israel's conflict with the Palestinians, of interethnic tensions among Jews, and of the figuration of the Holocaust. Finally, whenever relevant, the films are placed within their extra-textual historical context.

Israeli documentary filmmaking began well before Israel's independence in 1948. It can be traced back to the beginnings of the twentieth century with the cinematic documentation of the land of Israel/Palestine and its people from a Zionist perspective. The early documentaries, made by solitary pioneers dedicated to the Zionist cause, such as Murray Rosenberg (Ha'seret Harishon Shel Palestina/The First

Film of Palestine, 1911) or Ya'acov Ben-Dov (Eretz Israel Ha'mit'oreret/The Awakening Land of Israel, 1923), were commissioned for production or contracted for distribution by Zionist organizations, and were mostly screened in front of Jewish communities worldwide or at Zionist conventions. (The First Film of Palestine was shown to enthusiastic delegates to the 10th Zionist Congress held in Basel, Switzerland in 1911.) The thirst among Jewish communities abroad for sights of the 'Holy Land', along with the strong ideological orientation of the filmmakers and the bodies that sponsored them, led to an embellished image of the land and documentaries took the form of travelogues. The Awakening Land of Israel, for example, commissioned by the Jewish National Fund, follows a Jewish American tourist (Mr Bloomberg) and his local guide (Pnueli) as they tour the country—a tour that persuades the wealthy Bloomberg to settle in the country. This storyline serves as an excuse to show an overall sequence of documentary images that move from different Jewish historical sites such as the Wailing Wall in Jerusalem (emphasizing the historical connection of Jews to the land), through images of the general desolation of the land (presented as primeval, mostly empty and wild, generally disregarding the Arab population), and on to Jewish new towns, kibbutzim, and prominent political figures of the Yishuv ('settlement') as the growing Jewish community in Palestine called itself (emphasizing the redemption of the land of the forefathers by the Zionist movement).

The strong Zionist ideological orientation of these early documentaries was reproduced in the more prolific documentary filmmaking of the 1930s. The main divergence of these latter documentaries consists in their explicit formal and thematic framing of the Zionist project as socialist, and in their focus on Sabras (native-born Jews) or on Jews who had 'shed' their diaspora and 'nonproductive' way of life, in favor of communal life and manual, mostly agricultural, labor. This ideological reorientation resulted both from the growing predominance of Zionist socialist parties in the Yishuv, and from the fact that the major filmmakers of this period, Nathan Axelrod and Baruch Agadati, were Russian Jewish immigrants strongly influenced by the Russian revolution and by the montage experiments of Soviet filmmakers. Hence, Agadati's Zot Hi Ha'aretz/This is the Land (1933) is complexly and dynamically structured along the lines of Vertov's and Eisenstein's montage sequences. Shifting back and forth from past to future it contrasts the past aridity of a ruined and uninhabited land with images of a present filled with a vast multitude of Jews and of industrial plants working at full steam, culminating in a call to leave the cities in favor of collective agricultural work on the kibbutz. The fetishization of work recurs in other films of the period, particularly in Helmer Lerski's impressive film Avoda/Work (1933), which is dominated by close-ups of workers' shoes, legs, muscular hands, and smiling heads in dynamic cross-cuts with parts of modern machinery. Likewise, one of the dominant scenes in Axelrod's travelog Oded Hanoded/Oded the Wanderer (1933), about a Sabra boy who travels the land after having wandered away from his classmates during a school trip, shows images that emphasize the fertility of the Valley of Jezreel and offers a Soviet-styled montage sequence of collective agricultural work. The sequence contrasts other images showing the backwardness of the Bedouins and the arid terrain they inhabit. This emphasizes the social and material progress that the Zionist project will bring to the region, a theme recurring in other films of the period, such as in Alexander Ford's Tzabar/Sabra (1933). This latter film, the fictional part of which focuses on an escalating conflict between Jews and Arabs over water during a drought, a conflict resolved when water gushes from the Jews' well for the benefit of all, culminates in a documentary Soviet-styled montage epilogue showing tractors plowing the land and harvesting rows of orange trees and other images of the fertile land, overlapped by the silhouettes of agricultural workers marching up a hill toward a utopian future. This early 1930s blossoming of documentary film production sharply declined during the second part of the decade and throughout 1945. This was due to lack of funds for production, mostly brought about by the Zionist organizations' allocation of funds to secure and expand the Yishuv during the Arab riots that spread throughout the country from 1936 to 1939, followed by the economic burden on the Yishuv brought about by World War II. During these difficult years the major venue for documentary production came in the form of Axelrod's weekly newsreel Carmel (after Agadati's competing Aga Newsreel Company went bankrupt). Differing from most documentary productions, Carmel newsreels were funded through commercials and offered a constant flow of news about building projects, road construction, political events, and other aspects of life in the Yishuv. The Carmel newsreels enjoyed high popularity among moviegoers who craved local news. They continued to be produced almost uninterrupted well into the 1950s. (In 1951 Baruch Agadati's brother Yitzhak and others started a competing newsreel called Hadshot Geva/Geva News.) Newsreels were one of the most enduring and prolific documentary sources at the time. They signaled the ongoing importance of news for Israelis still evidenced today in the ever-expanding time slots allocated to television news.

Following the end of World War II and the arrival of Holocaust survivors in the Yishuv, several semi-documentaries were produced that dealt with them. Henceforward the Holocaust became one of the major themes in Israeli filmmaking. The fictional part of these early films on the subject was aimed primarily at justifying the need for a Jewish State following the Nazi atrocities, hardly mentioning the horrors of the Holocaust. There was concern with the integration of the emotionally scarred survivors into Israeli society through their transformation into Israelis by fighting in war or working the land within a collective (e.g. Helmer Lerski's film Adama/Earth, 1946, or Herbert Klein's Beit Avi/My Father's House, 1946). What stands out in these semi-documentaries is the plethora of documentary images panning an open and fertile land, literally engulfing the fictional protagonists. These images, apparently unrelated to the narrative, are presumed to infuse into the survivor a sense of liberation from the claustrophobic, terrifying past of the ghettos and death camps still resonating in his mind. The films, however, by not offering a view of the land from a survivor's point of view, maintained an image of the survivor as alien to the land, hence inadvertently countering the ideological thrust of the fictional narrative and indexing the failure of the latter's societal integration at the time.

The establishment of the State in 1948 amid war with the Arab world generated deep changes in the socioeconomic and political structure developed during the pre-State period. These changes were due to Israel's new geopolitical situation within the region and the doubling of the Jewish population within three years of independence (1949–51) following the massive immigration of Jews from Islamic lands. (Jews from Islamic lands are known as *Mizrahim* in Israel, as opposed to Jews from Eastern European or Western origin, who are called *Ashkenazim*.) Heading these drastic shifts in Israel's sociopolitical structure and undergoing a correlated political and ideological change was the Mapai (Hebrew acronym for Workers' Party of the Land of Israel) party, under the leadership of David Ben-Gurion. The Mapai shifted its pre-State hegemonic yet sectarian Zionist-socialist policy to what was termed Statism (*Mamlachtyut*). Statist policy resulted in the consolidation of Mapai's dominance over the State apparatus and allowed for the rapid industrialization of the country in the course of absorbing the massive immigration. This process, one of the major consequences of which was the correlation of ethnic origin and class, led to a reorientation of the State's dominant ideology. Hence, statist ideology, while still clinging to socialist rhetoric, shifted the image of the Sabra from being the native-born socialist revolutionary agent of Zionism to his becoming an ethno-mixed Jew who is a loyal citizen and soldier. This policy found cinematic expression in a civil servant attitude by Israeli documentaries. Gone were the embellished utopian revolutionary images. These documentaries, mostly funded by governmental agencies and Israel's leading workers' union (Ha'Histadrut) often recorded in neorealist style the hardships of the daily life of recently arrived immigrants, as in Leopold Lahola's docudrama Ir Ha'Ohalim/Tent City (1955), or in Nathan Gross's Brit Damim/Blood Covenant (1954). However, these hardships were explained away by the use of optimistic music and a patronizing voice-over narration that absolved the government of any wrongdoing by blaming the diaspora past for present hardships and ethnic strife, and by presenting through low-angled shots the government's officials and bureaucrats as detached, authoritative, and yet kind and dedicated civil servants. The films also promised a brighter future by showing through accelerating rhyming editing patterns the ethnically varied citizenry harmoniously joining hands in different projects carried out during the 1950s rapid industrialization of the country.

The expansion of the urban middle class in the early sixties—brought about by the types of trades characterizing the post-State massive immigration, along with the gradual shift in the government's econopolitical orientation toward a free market economy, and the relative geopolitical calm of the period—outdated the Statist pseudo-socialist rhetoric of the government and distanced the cultural establishment from the government. Notions of art for art's sake began to gradually exchange the politically committed and propagandistic characteristics of cultural production during the Yishuv and the first decade of the State. A new generation of filmmakers influenced by the French New Wave began to produce self-reflexive films dealing with interpersonal relations rather than large sociopolitical or geopolitical issues. This new approach also influenced the documentary films commissioned by governmental agencies, which expected effective propaganda but received instead self-reflexive and subjective films such as David Greenberg's documentary Sha'ar Ha'Gai (1965), or David Perlov's Be'Yerushalaim/In Jerusalem (1963). In Jerusalem, for example, rather than showing in an 'objective' manner the holy places with appropriate pathetic voice-over narration, showed beggars in the holy city (based on the Midrash that says the Messiah will appear from among them), documented hidden corners from oblique angles, interviewed incidental bystanders in the streets about their daily personal affairs, and offered experimental correlations of sound and image (as in a jump-cut edited sequence where a group of children smile at the camera and repeatedly ask the filmmaker to picture them). This often led to the commissioning bodies' rejection of the films produced and the further alienation of the filmmakers from the Establishment. Perlov, in particular, having experienced institutional rejection (In Jerusalem was rejected on the grounds that it showed beggars in Jerusalem), after the October War in 1973 began producing a personal low-budget diary. For over ten years he recorded his daily life, his family and friends, the streets surrounding his apartment, the television screen in his salon through which he inserted sociopolitical events, and different visual experiments dealing with the relation of film to other arts and to life. He accompanied his images with a poetic first-person narration, creating in sum a series of films called Yoman/Diary that offer a fascinating document about the relations between private and public life in Israel.

While fiction films of the 1970s continued the personal and sociopolitically detached self-reflexive experimentation that had begun in the 1960s, some of the same filmmakers began to produce documentaries in which they inscribed a growing criticism of Israeli society and politics. In films such as Igal Burstyn's Muhammad Yktzor/Muhammad Will Harvest (1972), and Judd Ne'eman's Histaklut Al Acco/Observing Acre (1975), they reacted to the drastic changes brought about by Israel's occupation of the West Bank and Gaza Strip along with its million and a half Palestinian inhabitants following the War in 1967. Even earlier, as in Tzepel Yeshurun's film Beur Ha'Ba'arut/Eradicating Ignorance (1965), they reacted to the escalating ethnic social unrest brought about by the growing resentment felt by Mizrahi Jews toward the Labor government, which they considered responsible for their low income and inferior social status. What characterizes these documentaries is their use of the formal disruption characteristic of French New Wave films to articulate a poetical and personal sense of an incumbent catastrophe awaiting a fragmented unjust society. Ne'eman's documentary Observing Acre, primarily located in a mental hospital, likens the situation of the Arab-Jewish mixed city of Acre to that of the mentally ill patients observed by the camera at the hospital. These observation sessions are intercut with two other major locations: the enclosed apartment of a bourgeois Jew comfortably disconnected from his surroundings, and the poor crowded house of a resentful Arab family whose property was confiscated by the government. The abrupt intercuts, the use of jump-cuts, and the often asynchronous combination of sound and image impart a sense of troubling disharmony and looming catastrophe.

The 1970s documentaries predicted the political overturn in the 1977 elections that brought to power for the first time the right-wing Likud party after the sixty-year hegemony of Labor parties. The main reasons for the latter's downfall were the disillusion of traditional Labor party voters by a government that had failed to predict the outbreak of the 1973 October war (which resulted in unprecedented casualties on the Israeli side), the government's undecided stand on the future of the territories occupied after the 1967 war, and the translation of the resentment felt toward the Labor party by Mizrahim into a massive vote for Likud. This overturn shocked the Labor-leaning parts of the populace and led to a radical politization of culture in general and of films in particular. The main focus of a barrage of fiction films produced during the 1980s was on criticism of the unjust ramifications of the Israeli occupation of the densely Palestinian-populated West Bank and Gaza Strip, particularly following the right-wing government's intensification of Jewish settlements in these territories and Israel's invasion of Lebanon in 1982. However, while the criticism of fiction films was confined to a narrow melodramatic moral resentment and reflected the overall paralysis of the left in their dead-end tragic conception of reality, documentary films of the period offered a complex, critical, and detailed analysis of the situation and its history using innovative documentary strategies of articulation. The most radical, comprehensive, and cinematically complex documentary production dealing with the Israeli–Palestinian conflict during the 1980s can be found in Amos Gitai's trilogy Wadi (1980), Bait/House (1980), and Yoman Sadeh/Field Diary (1982). In House, for example, which also means 'home' and even 'homeland' for Israelis, Gitai inquires into the changing ownership of a house in ruins currently in the midst of intense renovation. As it turns out, the house, recently purchased from a Jewish Mizrahi couple by an Ashkenazi economics professor, was originally the property of an Arab Palestinian family that had fled the country during the war in 1948 and was declared absentee property by the government. The house history, concisely encapsulating the main geopolitical and sociopolitical conflicts and power relations generated by the Zionist project, is articulated through a series of interviews shot on location. These are carried out with an impassive camera that records the interviewees, the house, and its surroundings in very lengthy, often recursive long shots. The camera, often leaving the interviewees in order to wander around on its own, comments, recontextualizes, and 'relativizes' the different perspectives of the house owner, the Palestinian workers who are rebuilding the house, and others, while clearly placing the camera on the side of the repressed Palestinian workers whose poor dwellings in a refugee camp are inserted into the film.

The 'surprising' outbreak of the first Palestinian intifada in 1989 also marked the end of the 1980s massive Israeli film production on the subject of the Israeli–Palestinian conflict. This may have been due to the shock of recognition on the part of Israeli filmmakers that their moralistic stand was somewhat futile, that the Palestinians had now taken matters into their own hands, and that for the Palestinians the Israeli leftist Labor positions articulated in most fiction films were part of the problem and not its solution. In any event, documentary films of the 1990s evidenced a process of introspection and historical revision, along with a postmodern-typed problematization of documentary production. These films, produced by a new generation of documentary filmmakers, are low-budget and are often personal diaries, such as Amit Goren's film about his ramified family, entitled '66 Haita Shana Tova Le'Tayarut/'66 Was a Good Year for Tourism (1992), or Dan Katsir's Yatsati Lechapes Ahava … Techef Ashuv/Out for Love … Be Back Soon (1997), which correlates his personal story with the events that led to the assassination of Prime Minister Yitzhak Rabin in 1995. Other filmmakers give voice and images to society's silenced 'others'. Hence, Michal Aviad's Jenny ve Jenny/Jenny and Jenny (1997) documents from a feminist perspective the oppressed mentality of two lower-class sisters growing up in a broken home; Tsipi Reibenbach's Ha'Bchira Ve Ha'Goral/Choice and Destiny (1993) offers disturbing and moving testimonies of Holocaust survivors focusing on the psychological traces left by the Holocaust experience; David Ben-Shitrit's Ruach Kadim/East Wind (2002) and Mi'Baad le Realat Ha'Galut/Through the Veil of Exile (1992) gives voice to militant Mizrahi Jews and Palestinian Women; July Shlez's Sanjin (1992) documents the hardships and alienation felt by recently arrived Ethiopian Jewish immigrants; and Asher Tlalim's Al Tig'u li Ba'Shoah/Don't Touch My Holocaust (1994) deals among other things with the effects of the dominant state discourse on the Holocaust upon three of society's others: an Israeli Arab and a Mizrahi Jew who had never experienced it nor had family members involved in it, and a female Holocaust survivor. One of the more original filmmakers of the past decade, whose peculiar filmmaking evidences the new postmodern trends in Israeli documentaries and which returns to cardinal societal conflicts, is Avi Mugrabi. His films Eich Hifsakti Lefached ve'Lamadeti lehitgaber al Ha'Pachad Ve'Le'ehov et Sharon/How I Learned to Overcome My Fear and Love Arik Sharon 1997) and August (2002) are radical, first-person, disjunctive narratives often telling deceitful stories about the filmmaker's personal life, political positions, and lies that nevertheless reveal some deeper truth (e.g. he deceitfully depicts how, as he documents his following of

Arik Sharon's election campaign, he slowly becomes one of his devotees, while his wife decides to leave him). In addition, through the use of various cinematic devices such as back motion or loops, he provides powerful commentaries on political aspirations or realities (e.g. using reverse motion to ironize the unfeasible, though perceived as morally justifiable Palestinian desire to cancel the Zionist project, or looping a conflictual encounter between Palestinians and Israeli soldiers in order to convey the deadlocked situation of both peoples). Mugrabi's self-conscious, self-reflexive, nomadic, deceitful, funny, ironic, and intrusive mode of filmmaking, using the home-movie format (he usually wanders alone with his camera, intruding into various forbidden places and interviewing people in a provocative way, which often leads to his being expelled or hit), depicts a disturbing clownish character of our time, offering a postmodern yet effectively subversive approach to Israeli reality.

NITZAN BEN-SHAUL

Further reading

Avisar, Ilan, 'National Fears, Personal Nightmares: The Holocaust Complex in Israeli Cinema', in Nurith Gertz, Orly Lubin and Judd Ne'eman (eds), *Fictive Looks—On Israeli Cinema*, Tel Aviv: Open University Publications, 1998 (in Hebrew).

Ben-Shaul, Nitzan, *Mythical Expressions of Siege in Israeli Films*, Lewiston, NY: The Edwin Mellen Press, 1997.

Burstyn, Igal, *Face as Battlefield*, Tel Aviv: Hakibbutz Hameuchad, 1990 (in Hebrew).

Friedman, Regine-Michal, 'Images of Destruction/ Destruction of Images', *Assaph Kolnoa, Studies in Cinema & Television*, Section D, no. 2, 2001: 247–56.

Gertz, Nurith, 'The Others in Israeli Cinema of the 1940s and 1950s: Holocaust Survivors, Arabs, Women', in Kamel Abdel Malek and David Jacobson (eds), *Israeli and Palestinian Identity*, New York: St Martin's Press, 1999.

——'Gender and Nationality in the New Israeli Cinema', *Assaph Kolnoa, Studies in Cinema & Television*, Section D, no. 2, 2001: 227–46.

Horak, Jan-Christopher, 'The Penetrative Power of Light: The Films of Helmer Lerski', in Nurith Gertz, Orly Lubin and Judd Ne'eman (eds), *Fictive Looks—On Israeli Cinema*, Tel Aviv: Open University Publications, 1998 (in Hebrew).

Klein, Irma, 'An Architectonics of Responsibility', in Paul Willemen (ed.), *The Films of Amos Gitai*, London: British Film Institute, 1993.

Ne'eman, Judd, 'Les Modernes, le manifeste inedit', in Catherine David and Lea Hermann (eds), *Cinema d'Israel*, Paris: Galerie Nationale du Jeu de Paume, 1992.

Shapiro, Owen, 'Seeing the Personal: Two Israeli Masterpieces', *Assaph Kolnoa, Studies in Cinema & Television*, Section D, no. 2, 2001: 173–92.

Shohat, Ella, *Israeli Cinema: East/West and the Politics of Representation*, Austin: University of Texas Press, 1989.

Tryster, Hillel, *Israel before Israel: Silent Cinema in the Holy Land*, Jerusalem: Spielberg Archive, 1995.

Tsimerman, Moshe, *Don't Touch My Holocaust*, Tel Aviv: Achiassaph, 2002 (in Hebrew).

——*A Hole in the Camera*, Tel Aviv: Ressling, 2003 (in Hebrew).

Italy

Italian critics have long deplored the inability of their country to offer serious, engrossing documentaries comparable to those of English-speaking nations. However, statistically, Italy is able to compete with the cinematic production of most countries. Reliable figures for the first half of the twentieth century are lacking, but it is known that after 1950 more than twenty thousand shorts were produced for the cinema only, without including those made for television.

Money was never lacking. Documentary filmmakers met with permanent support from public authorities and private sponsors. The Italian government began early to collect and circulate shorts likely to improve the country's image abroad. In 1924 various offices created l'Unione Cinematografica Educativa (Cinematic Union for Education), the acronym of which, LUCE, means Light. The Union aimed to produce and diffuse documentaries. Fascism nationalized it two years later to make LUCE its propaganda tool. The Luce Institute has often been paralleled with the General Post Office (GPO) Film Unit. Both were state institutions entrusted with informing and educating the public by way of film, but LUCE had no Grierson and its staff fluctuated according to fascism's wavering politics. Theoretically it echoed official instructions and many of its pictures were mere celebrations of Mussolini. The aim of its documentaries was to obtain mass approval for the projected deeds of the regime. Many were artistic transformations of reality. For instance, boys in uniform worked industriously to let the camaraman shoot enough material and then left.

However, the lack of a coherent management gave filmmakers relative independence. As a public institution LUCE benefited from abundant funds; the members of the GPO Film Unit could envy the technical facilities granted to the LUCE. Working there was easy and the LUCE films, even when they were basely sycophantic, were of outstanding quality. One of the prerequisites for becoming a film director was to have made a documentary, and many who would participate in the revival of Italian cinema after the war acquired their skills at LUCE.

LUCE's movies aroused spectators' interest in documentaries, and soon private production companies found it profitable to invest in shorts. In 1938 a group of journalists and technicians founded the Industria Corto Metragio (Shorts Industry, known as INCOM), which emulated LUCE. The screening of a documentary in any film show became compulsory in 1941 and five years later it was stipulated that shorts should get three percent of the takings. This meant that a short that had cost its producer two million lire could bring in ten times the initial investment. The production of documentaries boomed, reaching its peak in 1955 with one thousand one hundred and thirty-two films. INCOM made much money by leasing its pictures at bargain prices; exhibitors jumped at the offer and the three percent amply covered the cost. Sponsored by big firms, INCOM became the employers' mouthpiece. Anxious to hold the scales even between workers and employers, in 1951 the government opened the Centro di Documentazione Della Presidenza del Consiglio (Prime Minister's Documentation Centre), which produced documentaries such as Braccia e lavoro/Arms and Work (1952), Terra nova/New Land (1954), and Conquiste del Sud/Conquest of the South (1954), advertising the governmental efforts to maintain the traditions while modernizing the country. The Prime Minister had fifteen lorries traveling throughout the southern provinces and projecting shorts in villages deprived of cinema. Their screenings were said to have been attended by three million spectators in 1953. In 1956 a special office was created entrusted with making documentaries for the newly born television. Television has since been a voracious client of factual films.

Critics' pessimism about Italian documentaries can be linked to the fact that film experts have always relied on neorealism to represent Italian reality. Cesare Zavattini (1902–89), who was the main theoretician of neorealism and of documentary films, laid down strict rules. Cinema, he wrote, 'must tell reality as if it were a story', any fact 'creates its own fiction, in its own particular sense'. Take a real event, a real situation that 'lasts perhaps two minutes'; with such material you must 'make a two-hour film' so as to open 'a vast and complex world rich in importance and value, in its practical, social, economic, psychological motives'.

There were two periods in the evolution of Italian factual films, the divide occuring in about 1960. However, the most significant types of documentaries developed all along the twentieth century. Their typical features are best explained by the situation of the country when the movies were born. The political unification achieved in 1871 was purely nominal; the peninsula was split in unequally developed and often isolated provinces. In the richest regions, Piedmont and Lombardy, motor industry, chemistry, and hydroelectricity were as advanced as in Britain or Germany. In search of clients, these factories soon had to recourse to using film to advertise their goods within and without Italy's frontiers. Tourism—prosperous in the Alps, in Tuscany, and on the Riviera—did the same. The shipping industry, religious missions, and the search for employment took many Italians abroad, some of whom used films to account for their traveling.

Industrial publicity, tourism, and observation of local customs were the themes of the first documentaries and created traditions that are still in place today. Before World War I not only big companies (e.g. chemical conglomerates, department store chains, and car manufacturers) but also small firms making ceramics and furniture ordered advertisement shorts. The sponsoring of big firms resulted in the making of a series of remarkable documents. Ilva metal works subsidized Col ferro e col fuoco/With Iron and Fire (1926), which described the whole process of iron production from the mine to the manufactured article. Giorgio Ferrari's Ifigli del carbone/The Sons of Coal (1939) was a highly sophisticated film filled with technical information about coal's chemical by-products. Gianni Paolucci's La nave/The Ship (1935), developed in a diary fashion against the background of shipping docks and the building of a liner, and Umberto Barbaro's I cantieri dell'Adriatico/Adriatic Shipyards (1932) asserted the bright situation of Italian shipbuilding. The long series of movies sponsored by Fiat exemplified the quality of industrial documents. In the first (1922), two newlyweds visit the Fiat factory and follow the construction of a car; when it is finished they jump into it and leave. The film managed to show an assembly line, which was new to Europe in the early 1920s, and a vehicle built personally for Fiat's customers. In the second movie (1926), a plane flies over the test-drive platform on top of the gigantic Lingoto plant; then spectators see the new cars and rush onto the same platform before going all over the workshops. This movie was regarded as being so good that it was widely circulated in foreign countries. No other European car factory did the same at the time.

After the war the impressive takeoff of Italian industry was emphasized by a wealth of documentaries. One of the most significant operations was the order of a three-part film given to the famous Dutch filmmaker Joris Ivens by ENI, the state petroleum company. L'Italia non è un paese povero/Italy Is Not a Poor Country (1959) was a brilliant picture, an evocation of the exploitation of methane in the peninsula, told as a grand epic and likely to put Italy at the head of modern, rich countries. Ivens's work was the most conspicuous among a long series in which stood out Vittorio Gallo's Acciaio/Steel (1951), Ugo Suita's Zolfara/Sulfur mine (1949), and Virgilio Sabel's Ricerche del metano/Searching for Methane (1951). For the Edison plant in Riva Ermanno, Olmi shot Costruzioni meccaniche Riva/Mechanical Engineering Factories Riva (1956) and Venezia città moderna/Venice Modern City (1958), in which the changes affecting a laguna were illustrated by a parallel editing between San Marco and the factories. Managerial advertisement looked so important that film companies, banks, and big firms created an international festival of industrial films held in Monza since 1957. In the 1960s no fewer than twelve shorts dealing with steel were sent to Monza. Television offered factories new opportunities, especially from 1957, when Italian public television networks became partially financed by publicity. Enumerating all the programs dealing with industry, trade, and agriculture would be tedious. Suffice it to say that well-known directors participated in this endeavor, most notably Luciano Emmer with Noi e l'automobile/Us and the Car (1962) and Bernardo Bertolucci with Le vie del petrolio/The Routes of Petroleum (1966).

Tourism, which had long brought Italy great wealth, had been carefully advertised abroad since the beginning of the nineteenth century. Cinema was spontaneously used to supplement posters, leaflets, and press articles. In about 1910 shorts describing the most renowned cities and landscapes were available and were distributed in foreign countries. When Messina was destroyed by an earthquake in 1908 a film company was able to edit a picture comparing the state of the city before and after the tragedy. Taking into account visitors' prejudices, most directors, indulging in stereotypes, reduced the peninsula to the Alpine lakes and summits, the Tuscan pines and hills, and the Riviera seaside resorts. Only a few attempted to go beyond such routine. Luca Comerio's impressive views of the Alps gave birth to an important vein of mountain films. Corrado d'Errico, with Stramilano/Supermilan (1929) and Ritmi di stazione/Station's Rhythms (1933), and Mario Danicelli with La storia di ogni giorno/Everyday Story (1942) portrayed Milan as a center of frenzied activity. Conversely, Marios Costa's Fontane di Roma/Fountains of Rome (1938) and Pini di Roma/Pines of Rome (1941), disregarding Rome's historical past and religious present, disclosed the most intimate, popular aspects of the city. Luciano Emmer's Raconto da un affresco/Story Taken from a Fresco (1938) and Il paradiso terrestre/The Earthly Paradise (1941) visited old paintings as if they were telling enthralling stories. These were exceptions. Hastily shot, using typical landscapes to produce a sentimental or dramatic impression, mechanically exploring a monument or a statue, completing countless films in studios with classical music and boring explanations have been screened in cinemas and continue to this day. As a whole, they equate to two-fifths of the documentaries made in Italy.

Missionaries sent abroad, explorers or officers commissioned by the state or by a trade company to explore parts of Africa had formerly taken photographs and converted quickly to cinema. Missionaries hoped that their images would move the wealthy, politicians, and business people to persuade public opinion that it was worth building a colonial empire in the black continent. The Salesians went as far as to register a film production company that edited and circulated their pictures. Others worked with commercial studios. Numerous shorts on missions were shown in church halls during the first half of the century. Military films such as the anonymous La presa di Zuara/The Storming of Zuara (1913) or Romolo Marcellini's Legionari al secondo paralello/Legionnaires at the Second Parallel (1938) illustrated Italian presence in Africa. In the late 1930s many documentaries were shot exclusively for the domestic audience and served to reinforce its self-confidence. The impression left by such films was that Mussolini had launched a victorious colonial policy, the success of which was assured because of the technical superiority of the Italian army and economy. Beside these propaganda works, a few pictures documented local traditions and lifestyles, notably Gino Ceruti's Fiamme abissine/Abyssinian Flames (1921) and an interesting description of old customs in Eritrea and Attilio Gatti's Siliva Zulu (1928) on ritual dances in Zululand.

Exploration documentaries met with a favorable response. Anthropology had developed early in Italy—the first university chair was founded in 1870 and a museum opened a few years later in Florence. Anthropologists were photographers, making constant use of pictures in their research, giving it the same importance as the gathering of data. However, since anthropology was conceived as a study of 'primitive' countries, little was done in Italy. The only serious attempt was Giacomo Pozzi Bellini's Il pianto delle zitelle/The Spinsters' Lamentation (1939), a documentary on a yearly procession from the village of Vallepietra in Lazio to the sanctuary of the Holy Trinity in the neighboring Abruzzi. The commentary was reduced to a few introductory words, the soundtrack was filled with the cantilenas sung by women. Shooting as close as possible, the camera focused on faces, legs, arm gesticulation, and body attitudes. Such simplicity was rare at the time.

World War II put an end to the colonial dream; attention shifted from Africa to remote parts of Italy considered unexplored territories. Michelangelo Antonioni is often seen as a pioneer in the field. In 1943 he shot Gente del Po/People of the Po (only edited and released in 1947). Visiting the lower valley of the Po River, Antonioni had been struck by a muddled landscape where he could find no structure and where the few, very poor inhabitants seemed lost in dampness. Starting from the river, wandering through marshy grounds, he conjured up a cold, humid, hopeless landscape and observed a small group of fishermen, always taken from afar as if they were emerging from their hostile environment. Sober, perfectly framed, cleverly contrasting the water of the river, a pale and cloudy sky, the film was of exceptional quality. However, it was not the first. In 1942 Fernando Cerchio's Comacchio and Basilio Franchina's Gente di Chioggia/People of Chioggia dealt with small villages built on lagunas where other fishermen survived with difficulty, a long way from the urban centers that could have bought their catch. It is not by chance that in wartime three filmmakers took an interest in the life of neglected people. What critics called 'neorealism' was in part the discovery by city dwellers of forsaken communities on which they cast a benevolent but distant glance. The most famous film was Mario Lizzani's Nel Mezzogiorno qualcosa è cambiato/In the South Something Has Changed (1949), a political lampoon financed by the Communist party and aimed at denouncing the crass poverty of the southern population. In this work pictures hastily shot in a violent light gave everybody a ghostlike appearance, the editing was random, and some people were interviewed but not heard, their voices being replaced by an overwhelming, grandiose commentary. Others were less bombastic. Florestano Vancini's Delta padano/The Po Delta (1951) visited three villages where the inhabitants, attacked by typhus, often too feeble to work, spent long, idle days only looking at the skyline. The film created a strong contrast between carefully shot pictures and people's dull eyes and sickly bodies. A similar investigation was carried out by Vittorio de Seta in Sardinia and Sicily with Lu tempu di li pisci spata/The Time of Swordfish (1954), Isole di fuoco/Islands of Fire (1955), and Pastori di Orgosolo/Shepherds of Orgosolo (1958), where he emphasized the relationship between people and landscape. In Cristo non si è fermato a Eboli/Christ Did Not Stop at Eboli (1952) and Non basta soltanto l'alfabeto/The Alphabet is not Enough (1959), Michele Gandin stressed the necessity to eliminate illiteracy and to build roads to unblock the south and open it to modernity.

Italians who were witnessing a quick economic improvement (the so-called 'miracle') soon tired of films showing miserable images. Anthropologists offered them a less depressing image of their country. Italian anthropology was then led by Ernesto de Martino (1908–65), who maintained that preindustrial ways of life would look mysterious as long as researchers did not settle for a long time among the natives and did not let them talk.

The investigations were carried out in southern Italy by author de Martino. His books, which were met with an enthusiastic reception, inspired a series of directors, notably Luigi di Gianni and Gianfranco Mingozzi, whose films have been wrongly clustered under the name of 'de Martino documentaries' although they were shot independently and not by a 'school'. Luigi di Gianni illustrated southern traditions in Magia lucana/Lucanian Magic (1958), Nascita e morte nel Meridone/Birth and Death in the South (1959), and La possessione/Possession (1971). Mingozzi began with La taranta (1962), a film he remade and completed twenty years later as Sulla terra del rimorso/On the Land of Remorse (1982). The taranta, a small, inocuous, black spider was said to bite young women who then felt obliged to dance to the point of exhaustion. After a brief presentation of the land, Mingozzi filmed the rituals, offerings, and dances lit by candles and accompanied by songs and cries that surrounded the hysterical crisis and were meant to cure the sick women. Mingozzi's main work, Col cuore fermo Sicilia/Sicily in Good Heart (1965), explored the past of the island in order to explain what had made mafia possible. In the wake of Giacomo Pozzi Bellini Fernando Cerchio's Ave Maria (1947) followed a procession in a small village of Abruzzi. Antonioni's Superstizione/Superstition (1949) demonstrated how magic rites and archaic forms of religious expression had survived up to the present day. Vittorio Baldi described the festivities traditionally associated with summer works in La notte di San Giovanni and Vigilia di mezza estate/Saint John's Night, Midsummer Watching (1958). Vittorio de Seta's original project in Un giorno in Barbagia/A Day in Barbagia (1958) consisted of observing the daily lives of women in a Sardinian village where men were absent during the grazing season. The film showed them working in the fields, kneading and cooking bread, looking after the children. L'isola di Varano/Varano Island (1962), directed by Carlo di Carlo in the dry hills of Gargano, explained why the countrymen were obliged to leave their villages, deprived of water and power. Old habits and conventions vanished rapidly after television had reached the most remote parts of the south and anthropologists were anxious to record what still survived. With Liz Dantone being the only inhabitant of Vera, the highest village in the province of Trentino, Renato Morelli hurried to interview her. In his film Le stagioni di Liz: Ciclo dell'anno contadino in alta Val di Fassa/Liz's Seasons: The Cycle of the Rural Year in Upper Val di Fassa (1984) she talked about local traditions, reviewed the decline of the village from the war to the present day, and described the cycle of agricultural works. Gabriele Palmieri's Descrizione di un matrimonio/Description of a Wedding (1990) analyzed the disappearing ritual that an engaged couple had to observe in a Sardinian village from the early days of their engagement to the final ceremony.

Filmmakers were not only interested in rural communities; they also focused on urban, isolated groups that could be the object of anthropological curiosity, such as lunatic criminals discovered by Luigi Comencini in L'ospedale del delitto/Crime Hospital (1950), people obliged to stay in town during holidays filmed by Raffaele Andreassi in La città calda/The Hot City (1959), retired people visited in Ermano Olmi's I pensionati/The Pensioners (1958), and Gian Vittorio Baldi's La casa delle vedove/The Widowers' House (1960). In the postwar era many filmmakers were preoccupied by the number of orphans. The question was tackled by Comencini, whose Bambini in città/Children in Town (1946) explored the most disadvantaged sectors of Milan to show how children living in desperate plights managed to survive. Francesco Maselli's Bambini/Children (1951) and Zona pericolosa/Dangerous Area (1952) pictured the young living on the outskirts of Rome and attempted to gauge the influence that violent spectacles had on them. It is interesting to contrast these shorts with the more optimistic but more superficial Raconto del quartiere/Talking about the District (1950), in which Valerio Zurlini skimmed across the Roman Trastevere. Florestano Vancini's moving Uomini soli/Lonely Men (1959) drew spectators' attention to the Roman tramps. Beginning in a dormitory where vagrants had found a night shelter, the film recorded their evening meal; in the morning it followed their vagabondage, attended their conflicts with each other and, above all, registered their desperate idleness. In the same way, but on a more superficial level, Cesare Zavattini's I misteri di Roma/The Mysteries of Rome (1962) investigated the nocturnal life of the capital in order to disclose its most secret aspects, but indulged in trivial events such as the clandestine slaughtering of a cow or the crazy talk of a young man waiting for the arrival of flying saucers.

In the 1950s feature-length geographic or ethnographic documentaries became a specialty of Italian studios. Gian Gaspare Napolitano's Magia Verde/Green Magic (1952), a casual but pleasant ride through the United States, was a significant success. Soon came Folco Quilici's Sesto continente/Sixth Continent (1953) and Oceano/Ocean (1971), which focused on oceanic islands and maritime life; Giuliano Tomei's Eva nera/Black Eve (1954), which was a provocative survey of the conditions of females in Africa; Giulio Macchi's India favolosa/Fantastic India (1954); and Mario Craveri's Continento perduto/Lost Continent (1955) and L'impero del sole/Empire of the Sun (1955), two elegant, enthralling rides, the former throughout China and Indonesia, the latter in Peru. Most travelogs were perfectly shot. The true quality of these films—which illustrated the places visited by an imaginary traveler and related his supposed experiences—lay in their attempt to present an agreeable, undemanding story apt to please different audiences and to seduce all generations.

Documentaries about distant countries and atypical people were winning general acclaim during the early years of television. The new medium was quick to adapt to such a popular vein. Well-known directors were given exceptional facilities for long-distance investigations. Rossellini could shoot a five-hour program, L'India vista da Rossellini/India Seen by Rossellini (1959) in which he mixed beautiful landscapes and personal considerations about oriental wisdom and religious conceptions. Antonioni's Chung-Kuo Cina (1972), which was less touristic and much more critical, was violently attacked by the Chinese authorities because it went to the roots of social problems in order to reveal their causes and brought to the fore the more blatant failures in agricultural and sanitation policies. Other less famous filmmakers were obliged to stay in Italy. Mario Soldati received a lot of praise for his investigations on food and 'popular' culture throughout the peninsula, Viaggio nella valle del Po alla ricerca del cibo genuino/Trip through the Po Valley in Search of Genuine Food (1958) and Chi legge? Viaggio lungo le rive del Tireno/Who Reads? Trip along the Tirenian Shore (1960). In Viaggio nel Sud/Ride in the South (1958), Virgilio Sabel emphasized the permanence of traditions in southern Italy but two decades later Vittorio de Seta, reediting his previous pictures but completing them with new images, explained in La Sicilia revisitata/Revisiting Sicily (1979) how much Sicily had changed. Stefano Silvestrini's Il Sud Salento/South Salento (1987) confirmed such impressions by exploring an area where the economy had undergone a considerable development and where new industries had been set on the basis of traditional artisan production. In connection with the shooting of his feature films, Pasolini made a series of shorts that were simultaneously bright films and meditations on otherness. In Appunti per una orestiade africana/Notes for an African Orestia (1970) he explored the way in which age-old habits persist in the modern world and stressed the clash between different strands of civilization. In Le mura di Sana'A/The Walls of San'A (1974) he depicted San'A, capital of Yemen, as threatened to be ruined by building speculation and he denounced the brutal intervention of Western capitalism in underdeveloped countries.

Established at the very beginning of cinema, the three main types of Italian documentaries—namely industrial films, tourism pictures, and social-anthropological movies—expanded throughout the twentieth century and are still functioning. There were changes, at times unimportant and at times significant according to the way things went. For instance, ethnological films emphasized the problems of small, destitute communities in the hard times that followed World War II but returned to the depiction of domestic or foreign traditions and folklore when hardships were over. Business pictures were always numerous but boomed during the 'miracle' years. Such exceptional continuity is all the more impressive in that important transformations occurred during the 1960s. These were partially attributable to television. Public channels, which had a monopoly from the beginning of broadcasting in 1954 until 1977, created new documentary programs. Starting with the idea that Italian culture, because it gave greater priority to arts, disregarded science and technology, television directors favored scientific information. Several prime-time programs mixed interviews on set and movies. The favorite series, Quark, dealt with language, space, the brain, human behavior, energy, and other topics easily illustrated by shorts. With the expansion of commercial and local channels after 1977, the demand for factual films was so strong that all products could be sold.

However, the most important alterations took place before the television boom. The main factor was the dramatic character of political conflicts that led, in the 1970s, to terrorism. During its first decades the Italian republic had been ruled by the Christian Democrats. In the early 1960s economic prosperity, the decline of the Catholic party, and the revival of fascism brought about harsh debates on the recent past and on the responsibility of political leaders. Cinema and television began to revisit fascism and the Resistance. It must be recalled that at the time contemporary history was not taught at school. Since the young knew nothing about the first half of the century, documentaries became a substitute for inadequate instruction. Relating events from the past to situations of the present, and drawing lessons from the study of history, these works were successful but also attracted violent criticism.

The most famous and one of the first examples of this trend was Lino Del Fra, Cecilia Mangini, and Lino Micciché's All'armi siam fascisti/To Arms! We Are Fascists (1961). Going beyond the purely mechanical concatenation of events, this film related the evolution of Italy from the outset of the twentieth century through 1960. Archival images created a highly evocative visual background that did not monopolize the audience and allowed them to hear the narrator's voice. Although careful attention was paid to rhythm and the pictures created impressions, it was the commentary that offered a partial, questionable, but perfectly clear interpretation of recent history. Made at a time when neofascism was a real threat, the film tried to show a generation born after the war how Mussolini's rise to power had ended in a national disaster. After the 1968 events the debate shifted to the revolution and the end of capitalism. Ivan Palermo's Torino: la coscienza operaia/Turin: The Working-Class Consciousness (1972) attempted to explain how the memory of the resistance to Nazism could help to organize labor movements in the factories. Contrasting pictures taken during the war and contemporary interviews, the movie refused to give an ideal vision of the past. The conflicts among the members of the Resistance, between the rank-and-file and the cadres of the movement were exposed with a violence that had not been toned down by the ensuring years. Palermo's work touched on the question of historical memory but did not examine it. Using a massacre committed by the Germans as a starting point, Damiano Damiani's Piazzale Loreto/Loreto Square (1980) tried to ponder the nature of remembrance. There was a certain amount of audiovisual documentation of the slaughter but what could it show? Only victims who looked just like many other victims. Damiani based his film on the memory of the present, a lively memory capable of going forward. Confronting survivors or relatives of murdered partisans with people who had not witnessed the drama, he showed how knowledge, or the lack of knowledge, subconsciously censored the war.

Social tension grew up in the 1960s together with the political debate and culminated after 1968 in a series of often violent strikes. Previously, little had been done to observe walkouts because spectators and even workers were not used to drawing lessons from social conflicts. Carlo and Paola Gobetti's Scioperi a Torino/Strikes in Turin (1962), which documented labor unrest in the Fiat and Lancia factories, was an exception and met with a weak response. Ten years later there was a wealth of such movies shot in the heat of some event, hastily edited and circulated throughout the peninsula. Such militant documentaries were meant to distance themselves from the mainstream cinema functioning on the basis of illusionism. They often consisted of discussions with workers recorded in video and then projected to the participants who were asked to react critically. Ugo Gregoretti's Apollon, una fabbrica occupata/Apollon, A Factory Taken Over (1969) and Contratto/Agreement (1970), based on a series of interviews on location, were not content with offering a collection of talks but spoke of strikes and their favorable issues in a dramatic way, elaborating a dialectic or responsibilities between the various protagonists. Ettore Scola's Trevigo-Torino, viaggio nel Fiat-nam/Trevigo-Turin, a Trip in the Land of the Fiat (1972) accompanied an unemployed countryman who was obliged to leave his village and emigrate to Turin in search of a job. Guido Lombardi and Anna Lajola's Enua ca simu a forza du mundu/We, Who Are the Strength of the World (1971) expounded how unskilled workers employed on building sites were exposed to potentially fatal situations. After explaining how, during the second half of the nineteenth century, mining had become an alternative to the declining farming economy in Sardinia, Piero d'Onofrio and Fabio Vannini's Noistottus (1987) reconstructed the background of what has been called a 'mining culture' by moving from contemporary eyewitness accounts to shots of work in mines still operating today and to historical records, either newsreels or reconstitutions. Armando Ceste and Mimmo Calopresti's Alla Fiat era cosí/At Fiat It Was Like That (1990) brought to light the slow but irreparable exhaustion of those working at the Fiat factory.

After the 'hot' 1970s and 1980s the filmmakers who had witnessed the events and often taken part in them were able to evaluate their consequences. Interviewing communist militants at the time when the Soviet Union was collapsing, Nanni Moretti reconstituted in La cosa/The Thing (1990) the trajectory of the Italian left in the course of the past half century, while Marco Bellocchio's Sogni infranti: ragionamenti e deliri/Broken Dreams: Reasoning and Delirium (1996) expounded the hopes, mistakes, and crimes of terrorists.

Filmmakers soon turned toward ill-known, often hidden aspects of contemporary society. Their method was profoundly different from the approach that dominated the 1950s. Repudiating any aesthetic temptation, they aimed to give a right to speak to those who had never been heard. In their view what mattered was an unaffected picture of the interviewees' surroundings as well as the sound of voices likely to convey the impression made by a direct testimony. A good example of this manner was Giacomo Ferrante's Real Falchera FC (1990), a report on an amateur football team based in the Turin suburbs. Details from the life of the single players were interspersed with sequences of the collective ritual of the game, a mosaic of fragments attempted to make spectators enter into a world of human contacts and friendship, interviews were substituted by informal chats exchanged with the film crew during the moment when they were not noticeably 'a film crew'.

Such documentaries took as their premise that they were subjective visions rather than objective observations and sought actively to implicate the viewer in the process of interpretation. This new trend had been anticipated by Pier Paolo Pasolini whose Comizi d'amore/Love Meetings (1964), in spite of an eye-catching title, was a lecture and a meditation on the nature and functions of documentaries. After questioning a panel of Italians about their experience of love, Pasolini edited his interviews to show how misleading a talk can be and how difficult it is to use such material honestly, without deforming or misinterpreting its significance but also without being too long or boring. It took Pasolini's lesson ten years to be understood but its influence became obvious in the mid-1970s. Bernardo Bertolucci's La salute è malata/Health is Ill (1970), Marco Bellocchio's Matti da slegare/Raving Mad (1974), Gianni Serra's Fortezze vuote/Empty Fortresses (1975), and Silvio Soldini's Voci celate/Shut Voices (1986) denounced the pitiful situation of Italian hospitals, asylums, and health services. AIDS sufferers were interviewed in Villa Glori (1988) by Luigi Faccini and in Come prima, più di prima t'amerò/I'll Love You As Before, More Than Before (1995) by Daniele Segre, who let also transsexuals speak in Vite di ballatoio/Outside Lives (1996). The sufferings of those living on the fringe of society appeared in Giuseppe Bertolucci's Pani sporchi/Dirty Clothes (1980), Pasquale Pozzessere's Altre voci/Other Voices (1991), and Silvano Agosti's Frammenti di vite clandestine/Pieces of Hidden Lives (1992), whereas Enrico Coluso's Fine pena mai/Endless Penalty (1995) showed how prisoners serving life sentences managed to survive.

Pasolini did not merely influence what can be called social investigation documentaries; rather, his shorts opened new ways for art films. Previously filmmakers explored paintings or sculptures from without and often used a voice-over to signal the most important features of the work. Acquainting spectators with his enthusiasm, his surprise, and his hesitations, Pasolini involved himself in his films. Art films blossomed in the wake of his experiences. Making a pretext of a night ride through Rimini Pier Angellini's Bessie My Man (1985) confronted music and nocturnal images. Introducing a painter in Diario di Manarolo/Manarolo's Diary (1987), Gianni Amico composed a visual poem where canvas and landscapes mixed not because they were related to each other but because they provoked surprising sequences or contrasts. This technique was reused by Pasquale Misuraca in a 'symphonic' documentary, Progetto poesia/Poetry Project (1993), made of archival images thematically assembled. Emilio Castelli's Hodi Mlalugoma (1990) wandered among the statues that Tanzanian villagers place on tombs to communicate with the deceased. Introducing spectators to Giotto's frescos in the Paduan Scrovegni chapel, Luciano Emmer alternated his presence and voice with the painter's supposed presence and voice. The first part of his Dramma di Cristo/Christ's Drama (1994) was a dialogue between the director and the painter, whereas in the second part the characters represented in the frescos told of Christ's Passion. Stella Leonetti's Vernissage! 1607, Caravaggio/ Varnishing Day (2002) contrived a private view of Caravaggio's new works during which seventeenth-century amateurs who commented on, admired, and criticized the canvas behaved like twenty-first-century visitors.

Such examples illustrate the vitality of Italian documentaries. However, it must be acknowledged that they are exceptions, since mainstream Italian shorts have always been more factual than experimental. This is one of the reasons why critics do not generally care for them, and why spectators are not enthusiastic about them, even though television documentaries have good ratings. Italy cannot boast world-famous documentary filmmakers. Many directors started in the cinema business by making shorts but made feature-length films as soon as possible. If the country never had an avant-garde movement, Italy maintained a rare continuity in three directions—namely, business movies, art and landscape pictures, and the study of small communities. In so doing, documentaries manifested a few highly typical features of Italian life and culture.

PIERRE SORLIN

Further reading

Artoni, Ambrogio, *Documentario e film antropologico*, Rome: Bulzoni, 1992.

Bernagozzi, Gianpaolo, *Il cinema corto. Il documentario nella vita italiana dagli anni Quaranta agli anni Ottanta*, Florence: La Casa Usher, 1979.

——*Il cinema allo specchio. Appunti per una storia del documentario*, Bologna: Patron, 1985.

Boursier, Giovanna (ed.), *Aproposito del film documentario*, Rome: Archivio Audiovisivo del Movimento Operaio, 1998.

Brunetta, Gian Piero, *Storia del cinema italiano*, four vols, Rome: Editori Riuniti, 1993.

Canosa, Michele (ed.), *A nuova luce. Cinema muto italiano*, Bologna: Clueb, 2000.

Miccichè, Lino (ed.), *Studi su dodici sguardi d'autore in cortometraggio*, Turin: Lindau, 1995.

Nepoti, Roberto, *Storia del documentario*, Bologna: Patron, 1988.

Rositi, Franco, *I modelli dell'argomentazione televisiva. Analisi logica ed epistemologica dei documentari televisivi d'attualità*, Milan: Bulzoni, 1981.

Rossitti, Marco, *L'immagine dell'uomo. Le inchieste socio-antropologiche della RAI*, Pasian di Prato: Campanotto, 2001.

Zavattini, Cesare, *Polemica col mio tempo. Cinema, comunicazione, cultura, società*, Milan: Bompiani, 1995.

Ivens, Joris

Of the pioneers of documentary film, Joris Ivens can be considered as one of the most emblematic figures. His professional career spanned almost the complete documentary film history of the twentieth century. He made films on five continents and had a major influence on several national documentary film movements. His film work is very much intertwined with the sociopolitical history of the twentieth century—he was almost nineteen years old at the time of the October Revolution of 1917 and died just before the final collapse of communism, filming several of its social, political, and military battles. Furthermore, throughout his career, he continued to develop his style and techniques, and thus remained an important exponent of the documentary film world.

Ivens made his first film, De Wigwam/ Wigwam, in 1912 at the age of thirteen, but even in his early twenties he was not thinking of a career as filmmaker. He was to manage a branch of his father's chain of photo shops, and followed the appropriate education for this career: economies in Rotterdam, and photo technique and photo chemistry in Berlin. Berlin had both a cultural as well as a political influence on him. He saw the German expressionist films and the avant-garde experiments of Walter Ruttmann, and through his friends he became immersed in socialist ideas. These experiences can be found in the films Joris Ivens made throughout his life: most of his films can be characterized by their mix of artistic intentions and sociopolitical engagement, but often with a different balance between the two. Within the documentary context, Ivens's work can be considered as a perfect illustration of Kracauer's film theory, in which he distinguishes the realist from the formative tendency (Kracauer 1960). Kracauer recognized the interrelation between these tendencies that he opposed, and between which Ivens tries to find the right balance in his films.

Around 1927 Ivens started to develop his first film plans and experiments, using the equipment that was available in the Amsterdam shop he was managing. Inspired by, and having analyzed Eisenstein's Potemkin (1925) and having seen Ruttmann working on his Berlin film with an old, incomplete camera and hardly any special skills, Ivens became more serious in studying film techniques and aesthetics, which resulted in De Brug/The Bridge (1928). For him, this film was primarily a study in movement, composition, and film language. However, after its first performance, the film was received with wide acclaim and was marked as an avant-garde masterpiece, putting the Netherlands on the map of European cinema. More or less unintentionally, De Brug started Joris Ivens's professional film career. Certainly after making Regen/Rain (1929) his reputation as a filmmaker was established. These films fulfilled Ivens's artistic curiosity and aspirations, and fit in the formative tendency, defined by Kracauer, since Ivens was mainly concerned with composition, movement, and editing. These led to assignments from a workers' union (Wij Bouwen/We Are Building, 1930) and from Philips. This company wanted to promote the modern technology of its products—especially, the radio—as well as of its production line. Philips Radio (1931) became the first Dutch sound film, and Ivens's artistically most successful avant-garde film of this period. Philips Radio was also an expression of Ivens's interest in industrial progress, which may be found in some of his other works, too. Ivens also wanted to pay attention to the laborers, but Philips did not allow him to film outside the factories and to 'disturb the private life of the personnel' (Schoots 2000). Social critique, if it exists, is only implicit in this film.

However, during these same years Ivens tried to give his social and political engagement a place in his work. In 1929 he made his first socially engaged film with Leo van Lakerveld (a Communist Party member), Arm Drenthe/Poor Drenthe, which was probably (for the film is considered lost) a good illustration of Kracauer's realist tendency, and a forerunner to Misère au Borinage/The Misery of the Borinage (1934). In 1933 Henri Storck asked Ivens to join him to make a film about the misery of the miners in the Borinage region of Belgium. In style this film is quite the opposite of the Philips film. Storck and Ivens tried to avoid any aesthetic approach: 'We felt it would be insulting to people in such extreme hardship to use any style of photography that would prevent the direct honest communication of their pain to every spectator' (Ivens 1969). The realist style of Borinage led Kracauer to say that 'human suffering, it appears, is conducive to detached reporting; the artist's conscience shows in artless photography' (Kracauer 1960). Although this underlines the attempt of Storck and Ivens to avoid beauty, it remains an aesthetic choice: they had to work to get to this realist style. Despite this realist approach, Storck and Ivens didn't mind staging several scenes. Borinage can be considered one of the first social documentaries, a genre within documentary of which Joris Ivens was the pioneer, and throughout his career a major exponent.

In most of his subsequent films, but also in some of his earlier ones, the relationship between a realist and a formative approach is more in balance. Directly after the Philips film Joris Ivens got the chance to combine his fascination for industrial progress with his socialist and communist sympathies. With the film Pesn o Gerojach/Song of Heroes (1932) he was able to represent his political beliefs in the socialist utopia and at the same time to explore his artistic capacities. Cooperating with, among others, composer Hanns Eisler, who produced the soundtrack, he made a film about the building up of the socialist Soviet-state on the basis of the construction of the blast furnace town of Magnitogorsk by the Komsomol youth. 'It was exactly what I was looking for: young people and steel' (Ivens and Destanque 1982). The film sparkles with enthusiasm and propaganda for the cause of socialism and displays powerful imagery combined with strong editing. Eisler also contributed his music to Nieuwe Gronden/New Earth (1933), a film that is more a hybrid combination of a formative and a realist approach: Ivens used older footage that he had filmed for Wij Bouwen to complete it with new material of the polder works. The scene of the closing of the Zuiderzee dyke, in particular, with Eisler's stirring music, is one of the marvels of Ivens's films. However, he added a reel of a more militant character, to protest against the capitalist practice of destroying crops for market speculation instead of feeding the people who made those crops possible.

Joris Ivens left for the United States in 1936, where his films had a major impact on US film directors: his films provoked the spectator more than the films of other noted documentarists of that time, but it would be difficult to say that his films were a touchstone for them. Documentarists influenced each other, and the films of Joris Ivens matched the idea of documentary that was formed in the 1930s and further shaped in the 1940s and 1950s by 'the great documentarists' of that time, like the films of Grierson's Film Unit (e.g. Night Mail, 1936), Pare Lorentz with The River (1937), Flaherty with Louisiana Story (1948), Humphrey Jennings's Listen to Britain (1942), and, of course, the films of Joris Ivens himself, such as The Spanish Earth (1937) and Power and the Land (1941).

In the United States and after the outbreak of the Spanish Civil War, Contemporary Historians, Inc. was founded to enable the production of The Spanish Earth. Filmed at the republican front in Spain, and made to raise money for ambulances, this film is still seen as one of Ivens's most important works, characterized by powerful photography and editing, sober commentary by Ernest Hemingway, and a clear partiality against Franco's fascism. This partiality was one of the strong points of his films, but it also elicited much criticism. The Spanish Earth is also a good example of the dialectics between realist and formative tendencies: the film is a truly realist account of the events on the republican front, but Ivens uses his cinematographic skills to shape this realist account into an aesthetically strong, and therefore maybe even more convincing, film work. Such a practice defines his style, for we can discern it in many of his films, not only his political films (e.g. Le 17ème Parallèle/The 17th Parallel, 1968), but also in his poetic films (e.g. … À Valparaiso, 1963).

A year after The Spanish Earth Ivens made another antifascist film, this time on the Sino–Japanese War, The 400 Million, supported by the music of Hanns Eisler. Subsequently Joris Ivens made a number of films in the United States, alternating his antifascist convictions (Our Russian Front, 1941, and Action Stations!, 1943) with his fascination for industrial progress (Power and the Land, a New Deal propaganda film for rural electrification, 1940, and Oil for Aladdin's Lamp, a publicity film for the Shell company, 1941).

In 1945 and in spite of his communist sympathies, Joris Ivens was appointed by the Dutch government to film the liberation of Indonesia as Film Commissioner for the Dutch East Indies. However, in Ivens's opinion the Netherlands were not concerned with the liberation of Indonesia, but with its recolonization. He considered this a breach of contract on the side of the Dutch, resigned his position, and went on to make a filmic pamphlet against the Dutch policy in Indonesia. Indonesia Calling (1946) meant a breach with the Netherlands: Ivens was considered persona non grata by the Dutch government, which took his passport for a short period and gave him renewals for only three-month periods. His first official return to the Netherlands after 1936 was in 1964. He was assigned a film job in the Netherlands (not by the government) in 1965 (Rotterdam Europoort, 1966), but was only officially rehabilitated in 1985, when the Minister of Culture, referring to Indonesia Calling, stated that 'history proved you're right more than your adversaries then'. This did not hamper Ivens's film work, however. He had already filmed in various corners of the world and was now given an assignment from Eastern Europe to film the reconstruction of the countries stricken by World War II, which were now on the brink of a socialist future (The First Years, 1949). Ivens thus found himself in the center of a place where his ideals for a better society could be realized.

Until 1957 Joris Ivens continued to work in East Germany, making one of the largest productions in the history of the documentary cinema there (Das Lied der Ströme, 1954), but the films of this period were predominantly characterized by propaganda for communism and less by his artistic qualities. This occurred not only because Ivens still followed his passionate convictions and let them partly drown out his artistic aspirations as a documentary filmmaker, but also because he was given less freedom to develop them. He never was very explicit in his reactions to the events in Budapest in 1956, but it is probable that here the first cracks in his Stalinist beliefs appeared, maybe enhanced by Khrushchev's process of de-Stalinization. To his brother he wrote: 'What a long, worrying, and sometimes horrible period is necessary in order to come to a better world, to change an economic and a social system to achieve better and more humane relations between people' (Schoots 2000). He never wanted to comment on the events in Prague in 1968, but his turn toward China and Maoism probably illustrates his disillusionment with the failing Soviet ideology in which he so believed.

In 1957 Joris Ivens returned to Western Europe and made the poetic La Seine a rencontré Paris/The Seine Meets Paris, in France. This, however, did not mean that he turned away from his political and social engagement, for his films that followed were characterized by the alternation of poetry and politics, realist and formative tendencies, 'free' productions and commissioned films. In 1958 he made, apart from his work as lecturer at the Beijing Film Academy, both the poetic Before Spring and the political pamphlet 600 Million with You. After a commissioned film for the Italian state oil company, ENI (L'Italia non è un paese povero/Italy Is Not a Poor Country, 1960), once again stressing his fascination for technology, he made both the pro-revolutionary Pueblo armado/An Armed People, as well as the more poetic travel letter to Charles Chaplin, Carnet de viaje/Travel Notebook, in Cuba (both 1961).

Here he was also asked to teach at the ICAIC, and this invitation, in 1960, was a chance to dive into that fresh revolutionary climate, which promised to be the new hope and example for the socialist world, especially the Latin American world, and which closely matched Ivens's ideas and hopes for socialist progress. This was also the period in which the Cold War peaked, with Cuba as a temporary center.

Communism seemed to be in fashion in parts of Asia and Latin America. The latter was especially threatening for the United States. The possibility of socialist democracies in Latin America, as well as the American aggression in Asia, led Ivens to follow his convictions and translate them into film. In 1964 he made an election film, Le Train de la victoire/The Victory Train, for Salvador Allende to stress this hope. Allende didn't win the election, however. During the second half of the 1960s he made several militant films in Asia to demonstrate against the politics of the US, and to support the people of Vietnam: Le Ciel, la terre/The Threatening Sky (1965); Le 17ème Parallèle (1968) with Marceline Loridan; Loin de Vietnam/Far Fram Vietnam (1967), a collective work; and in Laos, Le peuple et ses fusils/The People and Their Guns (1970), also a collective work.

For Le 17ème Parallèle, Ivens used for the first time a 16mm synchronous sound camera, this being Marceline Loridan's choice, for she had already some experience with it. Initially Ivens had some reticence toward these new techniques presented by direct cinema and cinéma vérité: 'We should remain alert to the fact that with the possibility of quick observation and increased mobility comes the danger of remaining on the surface of truth, of skimming reality instead of penetrating it, of showing it without any force, daring or creative power' (Delmar 1979). Marceline Loridan and Joris Ivens show this awareness in Le 17ème Parallèle, which presents powerful photography and a skillful combination of direct sound and synchronized sound. In this way they introduced a more conscious use of the new techniques that had become so popular and easy to handle, but which also endangered professionalism. On the other hand, these new techniques were also cheaper and therefore available to more people. This had its influence on the documentaries of the 1960s, and a movement in which Joris Ivens was again an example to others (especially in France), because of his lengthy experience: militant cinema. This time his contribution was not as an innovator, but more as an agitator. With Chris Marker he became one of the exponents of political and militant cinema.

The 1960s are furthermore characterized by the two extremes in Ivens's work as a filmmaker, for before the previously mentioned militant films Ivens also made two special film poems: … À Valparaiso (1963) and Pour le Mistral/The Mistral (1965). His close collaboration with Marceline Loridan began with Rotterdam Europoort in 1965, and continued until his death in 1989. This cooperation resulted, among other things, in the monumental series lasting twelve hours, Comment Yukong deplaça les montagnes/How Yukong Moved The Mountains (1976), about the influence of the Cultural Revolution on everyday life in China. Ivens had witnessed the promise of the Great Leap Forward in 1958, without seeing the great famine of the following two years. In filming the Cultural Revolution, and especially its influence on the daily life of the Chinese people, Joris Ivens and Marceline Loridan wanted to provide answers to the questions of ignorant Westerners by letting the Chinese speak: 'It is important that in this film it isn't me or Marceline who does the talking but that 80 percent of it is the Chinese people' (Delmar 1979). Sudden changes in China's political situation made it almost impossible to film additional material, but new changes in 1976—Mao's death and a more moderate political course—made the longing for information on China greater. Yukong offered much of the information wanted, although the films were soon outdated.

Combining fictive with factual elements in his last film, Une Histoire de vent/A Tale of The Wind (1988), Joris Ivens, together with Marceline Loridan, contributed once more, but for the last time, to the documentary form. Chris Marker had already shaped this kind of personal film, especially with Sans Soleil/Sunless (1982), but Une Histoire de vent extrapolates this in extremis, being in this way not only a reflection on Ivens's own life and work and the history of changes in the world in the twentieth century, but also a reflection on documentary, truth, and the boundaries of the genre.

Toward the end of his life Joris Ivens distanced himself from the passionate convictions that largely determined his film work. His historical experience and the many changes in the world moved him to a more reflexive position. In an interview with his biographer, Hans Schoots, he stated: 'I used to say that communism was not a faith, but there is much of it in it. I stuck too long to my utopias, until I saw that History is not developing according to a book that was written at the beginning of this century.'

Ivens crossed a world that underwent many radical changes during this period. He witnessed and filmed many of those changes, giving his interpretation of reality, and always giving hope for a better world, a socialist world. His films reflect the beauty and the atrocities of this world, the poetics and the sorrow. His films are also illustrations and examples of the different tendencies in documentary film history, of which he was one of the designers and one of the main characters.

KEES BAKKER

See also: 400 Million, The

Biography

Born November 18, 1898, as George Henri Anton Ivens in Nijmegen, the Netherlands. Studied economics at Higher Commercial College in Rotterdam and photographic technique in Berlin, apprenticeship in several photographic laboratories. Started working in the Amsterdam branch of his father's CAPI photo shop in 1924. Married German photographer Germaine Krull in 1927. Cofounder of Film Liga in the same year. Worked in the Soviet Union in 1931–2 and 1934–5 before going to the United States in 1936. Married Helen van Dongen and became Film Commissioner of the Dutch East Indies in 1944. Moved to Australia to discover that the Dutch interests in Indonesia were other than the liberation of that country. Resigned his position of Film Commissioner in order to make Indonesia Calling! Persona non grata in the Netherlands, he started working in Eastern Europe, where he married the Polish poetess Ewa Fiszer in 1951. Awarded the World Peace Prize in 1955. Worked on several films for the DEFA, before returning to Western Europe in 1957, where he settled in Paris. In the following years, taught and made films in China, Mali, Cuba, and Chile. Made a campaign film for Salvador Allende in 1964. Received a Lion at the Venice Film Festival for Pour le Mistral in 1966. Started collaborating with Marceline Loridan, whom he married in 1977. Made several films against the American aggression of Vietnam in the 1960s, and worked in China in the mid-1970s to make a twelve-hour series on the Cultural Revolution. In 1984 President Mitterand made him Commander of the Légion d'Honneur. Received the Dutch Film Prize in 1985, and made his last film in 1988 with Marceline Loridan. Received in that year the Golden Lion for his complete oeuvre. Decorated with a Knighthood in the Order of the Dutch Lion. Died June 28, 1989, in Paris.

Selected films

1912 De Wigwam (aka Brandende Straal)/Wigwam (aka Shining Ray)
1927 Études des mouvements à Paris/Studies in Movement in Paris
1928 De Brug/The Bridge
1929 Arm Drenthe/Poor Drenthe
1929 Regen/Rain (with Mannus Franken)
1929 Heien/Pile Driving
1930 Wij Bouwen/We are Building
1931 Philips Radio
1932 Pesn O Gerojach (aka Komsomol)/Song of Heroes

1933 Nieuwe Gronden/New Earth
1934 Misère au Borinage/Borinage (with Henri Storck)
1937 The Spanish Earth
1939 The 400 Million
1941 Power and the Land
1941 Our Russian Front
1941 Oil for Aladdin's Lamp
1943 Action Stations!
1946 Indonesia Calling!
1949 Pierwsze Lata/The First Years
1954 Lied der Ströme/Song of the Rivers
1957 La Seine a rencontré Paris/The Seine Meets Paris
1958 Before Spring
1958 600 Million with You
1960 L'Italia non è un paese povero/Italy Is Not a Poor Country
1960 Demain à Nanguila/Nanguila Tomorrow
1961 Carnet de viaje/Travel Notebook
1961 Pueblo Armado/An Armed People
1963 … À Valparaiso
1964 Le Train de la victoire/The Victory Train
1965 Pour le Mistral/The Mistral
1965 Le Ciel, la terre/The Threatening Sky
1966 Rotterdam-Europoort/Rotterdam Europort
1967 Loin de Vietnam/Far from Vietnam (with Marceline Loridan and Jean-Luc Godard, Agnes Varda, William Klein, Alain Resnais, Claude Lelouch, and Chris Marker)
1968 Le 17ème Parallèle/The 17th Parallel (with Marceline Loridan)
1970 Le Peuple et ses fusils/The People and Their Guns (collective)
1976 Comment Yukong deplaça les montagnes/How Yukong Moved the Mountains (with Marceline Loridan)
1988 Une Histoire de vent/A Tale of the Wind (with Marceline Loridan)

Further reading

Bakker, Kees, *Inventory of the Joris Ivens Archives*, Nijmegen: European Foundation Joris Ivens, 1998.

——*Joris Ivens and the Documentary Context*, Amsterdam: Amsterdam University Press, 1999.

Delmar, Rosalind, *Joris Ivens, 50 Years of Film-making*, London: British Film Institute, 1979.

Devarrieux, Claire, *Entretiens avec Joris Ivens*, Paris: Albatros, 1979.

The Film Archive of China, *Joris Ivens and China*, Beijing: New World Press, 1983.

Grélier, Robert, *Joris Ivens*, Paris: Editeurs Français Réunis, 1965.

Ivens, Joris, *The Camera and I*, Berlin: Seven Seas Books, 1969.

Ivens, Joris, and Destanque, Robert, *Joris Ivens ou la mémoire d'un regard*, Paris: Editions BFB, 1982.

Kracauer, Siegfried, *Theory of Film. The Redemption of Physical Reality*, London: Oxford University Press, 1960.

Rotha, Paul, *Documentary Film*, London: Faber & Faber, 1936.

Schoots, Hans, Dangerous Life: A Biography of Joris Ivens, Amsterdam: Amsterdam University Press, 2000.

Waugh, Thomas, *Joris Ivens and the Evolution of the Radical Documentary 1926–46*, Ann Arbor, MI: Columbia University, 1981.

Wegner, Hans, *Joris Ivens, Dokumentarist der Wahrheit*, Berlin: Henschelverlag, 1965.

J

Jackson, Pat

Pat Jackson made an important contribution to the development of the story documentary in Britain in the late 1930s and 1940s. He had assisted Harry Watt on pioneering films such as The Saving of Bill Blewitt (1937) and North Sea (1938), which departed from the Griersonian tradition through the use of dramatically scripted scenes played by nonprofessional actors, before making his own significant mark with the seminal feature-length documentary Western Approaches in 1944.

Jackson joined the General Post Office (GPO) Film Unit on his seventeenth birthday, gaining entry through his mother's distant friendship with the postmaster general. Starting as a lowly messenger boy, he rapidly progressed to stills work and then into the cutting rooms, where he assisted Basil Wright on the celebrated The Song of Ceylon (1934). He first accompanied a shoot during the making of Night Mail (1936), once again assisted in the cutting and read the prose part of the commentary. Working with Harry Watt on this classic documentary was a major influence on Jackson. In 1937 Watt introduced the story documentary with The Saving of Bill Blewitt, adopting a characteristically novel approach to the mundane subject of Post Office savings. Jackson again worked closely with him as assistant, and gained further experience in the dramatic approach to documentary as part of Watt's team on North Sea, an account of ship-to-shore radio. As Jackson later recalled, 'Harry Watt was writing a history of England by the careful use of the non-actor'.

Jackson's directorial debut was The Horsey Mail (1937), a one-reel information film about the postal service in a small Suffolk village, although previously he had made a substantial directorial contribution to Watt's earlier Big Money (1937), which went uncredited. Of more significance was Men in Danger (1939) and in retrospect he remained particularly proud of the final sequence where the apprentice miners, who started work as young as age fourteen, were trained in the dangers of their craft. In the early war years, Jackson collaborated on numerous productions as part of the team effort at the GPO/Crown Film Unit, doing some shooting on London Can Take It (1940) and codirecting The First Days (1939) alongside Humphrey Jennings and Harry Watt. His own films were the shorts Health in War (1940), The Builders (1942), and Ferry Pilot (1941), a medium-length documentary about the transport of US planes to Britain. The uninspiring prospect of a film on the building industry actually confirmed Jackson's belief in the dramatic approach as he discovered a genuine 'vitality' in the workmen that no actor could master. In particular, a bricklayer, Charlie Fielding, and his ability to effortlessly lay bricks while conversing to camera impressed him. Jackson later commented on the scene and revealed his approach:

> Imagine asking an actor to do that! To lay bricks professionally and at the same time spiel away to the camera. Nobody could do it. Of course, you have to take trouble to test them, and cast them with great care. And we did; I tested Charlie Fielding as carefully as if I were testing a new starlet.

Jackson's greatest achievement occupied him throughout much of the later war period, and Western Approaches (1944) remains one of the finest of the wartime documentaries. The film, made on location under incredibly demanding conditions, was unusually shot in Technicolor and used a cast of real sailors who had experienced the hardships depicted on screen. As a result, Jackson realised some remarkable performances and imagery, and left a vital document of the wartime merchant service.

After a frustrating few years at MGM in Hollywood, which resulted in only a minor thriller, Shadow on the Wall (1949), Jackson returned to Britain and a modest career in commercial cinema and television. He maintained a documentary approach to his drama and encouraged a naturalistic style in performance, continuing to cast nonprofessionals for some minor roles. This was most evident in White Corridors (1951), adapted from a best-selling novel about a young female doctor in a provincial hospital and for which Googie Withers drew strong critical praise. Jackson had a less rewarding time on Virgin Island (1958), where his demand for spontaneity and naturalism in performance conflicted with method actor John Cassavetes's desire for exhaustive rehearsal. Through the 1960s Jackson directed some minor sponsored documentaries, but is better appreciated for his work in TV with Patrick McGoohan, on the cult TV action series Dangerman and The Prisoner.

Pat Jackson will be remembered for his tremendous efforts and skill in bringing the wartime feature-documentary Western Approaches to the screen. Despite often unsympathetic circumstances he retained a faith in the naturalistic performance and the marriage of documentary and drama. Although not participating himself, he was a significant influence on the celebrated renaissance in docudrama that formed in British television in the 1960s and 1970s.

ALAN BURTON

See also: Watt, Harry

Biography

Born in Eltham, London, 1916. Educated in various local schools, including Bryanston. After a brief period as an assistant cameraman at Welwyn studios, he joined the GPO Film Unit in 1934 as a messenger boy and quickly worked his way up to more senior roles. He remained with the Unit when it became the Crown Film Unit in 1940. After the war he spent an unfruitful period in Hollywood with MGM, but returned in 1950 to work in British features. From 1959, he worked on British TV series, sponsored films, and television advertisements. He died on June 3, 2011.

Further reading

Aldgate, Anthony and Richards, Jeffrey, *Britain Can Take It. The British Cinema in the Second World War*, Oxford: Blackwell, 1986.

Cardiff, Jack, *Magic Hour. The Life of a Cameraman*, London: Faber & Faber, 1996.

McFarlane, Brian, *An Autobiography of British Cinema*, London: Methuen, 1997.

n.a., *Film Dope*, 27 July 1983.

Sussex, Elizabeth, *The Rise and Fall of British Documentary*, Berkeley, CA: University of California Press, 1975.

Jacobs, Lewis

Critic, editor, filmmaker, teacher, and activist, Lewis Jacobs's place in cinema history rests primarily on his reputation as an historian. His groundbreaking text, *The Rise of the American Film*, first published in 1939, has been reprinted six times. He also edited several collections, including *The Documentary Tradition*, *The Emergence of Film Art*, *The Movies as Medium*, and *The Compound Cinema*, the last a collection of critical writings by Harry Alan Potamkin, his colleague in the Film and Photo League.

Jacobs came to film from painting, joining an amateur film club called the Cinema Crafters of Philadelphia, and his early works such as Transition (1927) and Mobile Composition No. 1 (1928) were collaborations with other members in that group. From 1930 to 1934 Jacobs was coeditor of *Experimental Cinema* with David Platt and Seymour Stern. This innovative periodical championed the cinema and theories of Eisenstein, Pudovkin, and Dovzhenko. The Film and Photo League, a collective of politically radical filmmakers and critics, exploited its pages as a forum. The period from 1931 to 1933 also marks Jacobs's involvement with that organization. Jacobs traveled through the southern USA, collecting footage that found its way into several of the League's productions, notably Western Pennsylvania and Kentucky Miners' Strike (1931), Scottsboro Trial (1932), and The Scottsboro Boys (Leo Hurwitz, 1933). He also taught at the League's Potamkin Film School during its brief existence.

While working in New York editing movie trailers and shooting footage for the Film and Photo League, Jacobs began an independent project entitled As I Walk, consisting primarily of material captured while strolling around the city during his lunch break. This work remained unfinished but yielded a fragment entitled Footnote to Fact (1934). That film's candid shots of urban poverty effectively capture the desperation of the Great Depression. Alternating with close-ups of a young woman, these brutally realistic images are presented as disturbing memories from which the woman escapes only by killing herself. Formally, the film owes a debt to the Soviet cinema Jacobs admired, particularly in the accelerating montage sequence that builds to the climax of the woman's suicide.

Jacobs's achievements as a writer and editor have tended to obscure his worth as a director. Consequently, critical commentary on his films has been largely self-penned. The two articles on experimental cinema in the United States (originally published in *Hollywood Quarterly* and reprinted in later editions of *The Rise of the American Film*) provide an excellent resource. Here, Jacobs tends to draw parallels between his personal development and that of experimental cinema. He describes himself initially as 'another devotee of French films', a tendency evident in early works such as Mobile Composition, which, he insists, was essentially realistic despite its modernist title. Nevertheless, this flirtation with abstraction would continue with Synchromy (1933), a joint effort with Mary Ellen Bute and musical composer-theorist Joseph Schillinger. Writing on the postwar situation, Jacobs distances himself from both the photographic realism of the trance film and nonobjective abstraction to ally himself with those experimental filmmakers who offer personal observations and comments on objective reality. He devotes a couple of pages to his films From Tree Trunk to Head (1939), a documentary of sculptor Chaim Gross's woodcutting technique, and Sunday Beach (1948), for which Jacobs contrived technical tricks to study people's weekend leisure activities without their knowledge.

As a writer, Jacobs tends to group individual works and broader trends into convenient totalities. For example, *The Documentary Tradition* is not simply a collection of essays organized chronologically but an attempt to render a synoptic view of documentary film that reads roughly as follows. Documentary cinema developed from modernist experiments of the 1920s into a cinema of social responsibility and political commitment in the 1930s. In the following decade, the need to battle fascism and promote the war effort eclipsed domestic issues and labor struggles. Increased professionalization in the 1950s was accompanied by bloodless content, but by the following decade new technologies such as television, portable cameras, and tape decks capable of sync sound had facilitated heightened truth, immediacy, and engagement. During the 'sober seventies' documentary kept political upheavals, civil rights struggles, and antiwar movements in front of an increasingly apathetic viewing public. For Jacobs, each period produced a cinema of fact engaged with its historical moment.

The broader survey in *The Rise of the American Film* relates a similar story: The economic crisis of the Great Depression prompted Hollywood cinema to address social, political, and economic issues. However, whereas the avant-garde turned from abstract formal experiments toward political engagement, Hollywood responded with a tepid realism diluted by romance and sentimentality. To support this claim, Jacobs contrasts Joris Ivens's The Spanish Earth (1937) with Hollywood's treatment of the Spanish Civil War as mere setting for melodrama. For Jacobs, several factors—particularly the increasing call for censorship from groups like the Legion of Decency—strangle the urge toward truth in commercial cinema. During the decade his voice often joined the chorus opposing censorship and the Production Code.

Despite his long career, Jacobs's creative heyday seems bound by the period from 1930 to 1939, yet he continued writing, teaching, and making documentaries well beyond that decade. Some films, such as The Rise of Greek Art (1960), appear uninspired and of little interest beyond their value as artifacts of educational documentary. Others, such as the 1978 film on Marcel Duchamp (Marcel Duchamp: In His Own Words) suggest an unimpaired vitality. This corpus of films awaits greater scholarly attention.

THOMAS COHEN

Biography

Born in 1905 in Philadelphia. Studied painting at the Pennsylvania Academy of Fine Art and the Art Students' League of New York. From 1930 to 1934 was coeditor of *Experimental Cinema.* During this period, became involved with the Film and Photo League. Moved to New York, landed a job as an editor of movie trailers, and taught briefly at the Potamkin Film School. In the early 1940s worked as screenwriter for MGM and Columbia. While holding teaching posts at the City College of New York, the Philadelphia College of Art, and New York University's Graduate School, continued to publish books and make documentaries, primarily on art and architecture. Died February 11, 1997.

Selected films

1934 Footnote to Fact: director
1939 From Tree Trunk to Head: director
1948 Sunday Beach: director
1950 Birth of a Building: director
1960 Rise of Greek Art: director
1978 Marcel Duchamp: In His Own Words: director

Further reading

Horak, Jan-Christopher (ed.), *Lovers of Cinema: The First American Avant-Garde 1919–45*, Madison, WI: University of Wisconsin Press, 1995.

Jacobs, Lewis (ed.), *The Compound Cinema: The Film Writings of Harry Alan Potamkin*, New York: Teachers College Press, 1977.

——*The Rise of the American Film: A Critical History*, New York: Teachers College Press, 1978.

——*The Documentary Tradition*, New York: Norton, 1979.

——'Experimental Cinema in America, 1921–47', in Eric Smoodin and Ann Martin (eds), *Hollywood Quarterly: Film Culture in Postwar America, 1945–57*, Berkeley, CA: University of California Press, 2002.

n.a., *Experimental Cinema: Complete Edition in One Volume*, New York: Arno Press, 1969.

Jacoby, Irving

Two people gave special meaning and direction to Irving Jacoby's life and career in film. The first was John Grierson, who met Jacoby in London in 1936 and inspired him to play a major part in the American documentary film movement. The second was Alberta Altman, who met Jacoby in 1948 and inspired him to play a major part in the American mental health film movement. Grierson became his lifelong friend and mentor. Alberta became his lifelong partner and wife.

Before meeting Grierson, Irving Jacoby had moved in New York's film and drama circles, working with Joseph Losey, Helen Grayson, and Jay Leyda on social-issue theater projects and writing scripts for Warner Brothers' short commercial films. On a visit to London in 1938, Jacoby was the right person in the right place at the right time, filling the writer's job that W.H. Auden had vacated at Grierson's General Post Office (GPO) Film Unit. Four decades later he told James Beveridge that it was like going to heaven. What he loved most were the camaraderie, the devotion to film as art and communication, the overriding concern with social problems, and the atmosphere of fun for all involved. It was a wonderful, exciting club, Jacoby felt, and he had become a member.

Back in New York City after his stay in London, Jacoby continued his life as an independent producer. Grierson went to Canada and set up the National Film Board (NFB) in Ottawa to make films and help train young Canadians in the art that would give Canada new visibility around the world. For the NFB, in association with the New York Zoological Society and the Office of Inter-American Affairs, Irving Jacoby produced, directed, and wrote High Over the Borders, an appealing, straightforward film about bird migration between North and South America. Tinged with the spirit of internationalism, Dutch filmmaker John Ferno gave Jacoby firsthand experience in balancing the exigencies of organizations and government agencies with his own artistic and social concerns. High Over the Borders was a major success in every way.

Back in New York, as the United States was drawn into the war, Jacoby persuaded City College officials to let him establish the Institute of Film Techniques to train students in the production and use of nonfiction films to promote the country's democratic ideals. With Joris Ivens and Jacoby as the major instructors, Grierson and Ferno, Willard Van Dyke, and Robert Flaherty were among the notable guest speakers during the Institute's first year, starting in February 1942. Jacoby hoped that the film courses would attract women students because he believed that 'girls are needed in virtually every branch of film producing'. Over one hundred and eighty students were enrolled in the program, and in one form or another the college's film program continued.

After two years at City College, Jacoby chose artist/filmmaker Hans Richter, a recent European emigré, to replace him as the Institute's director. Jacoby moved on to become Chief of the Non-Theatrical Section of the Office of War Information (OWI) Overseas Branch. In the Grierson tradition Irving Jacoby brought in the best people he could find—ace cameraman Boris Kaufman, noted pinboard animator Alexander Alexeieff (who designed the OWI's film logo), and costume designer Helen Grayson, who later became the OWI's only female director. They were additions to a staff that was a veritable who's who of documentary filmmaking: Willard Van Dyke, Alexander Hammid (formerly Hackenschmied), John Ferno, Henwar Rodakiewicz, Irving Lerner, Sidney Meyers, Heln van Dongen, Helen Levitt, Peter Glushanok, and many others. While at the OWI Jacoby wrote and produced Capital Story, a film about the US Public Health Service, informational in substance with a wraparound mystique to hold audiences' attention.

The end of World War II in 1945 gave Irving Jacoby the opportunity to make a second internationalist film that was purely documentary in form and content. The Pale Horseman starkly presented the realities of human suffering in postwar Europe and the Orient, and convincingly portrayed the role of the United Nations in providing food, clothing, shelter, and medical relief to combat famine, pestilence, and death. Although rarely shown since, it should be remembered.

To continue the advantages they had enjoyed as a group at the OWI, Van Dyke, Jacoby, Ferno, and Rodakiewicz joined together in 1946, as Affiliated Film Producers, Inc. Ferno and Rodakiewicz soon left, and Jacoby and Van Dyke remained as partners, but the group spirit still prevailed in the presence of Hammid, Glushanok, Grayson, Kaufman, and even Rodakiewicz, who continued to work with Affiliated on a freelance basis.

As an officer of Affiliated Film Producers, Jacoby functioned first as treasurer and later as president. As a working partner, he functioned mainly as producer and writer. Jacoby's first Affiliated film, Journey into Medicine, was sponsored by the US State Department, which had assumed the overseas peacetime authority that the OWI had held during the war. Affiliated Film Producers, Inc. (Van Dyke and Jacoby) received a handsome share of the State Department assignments.

Journey into Medicine followed the career of a young medical student through his years as an intern, resident, and then public health physician. With Van Dyke as director and Boris Kaufman as cinematographer, the film embarked on a new direction, having a young actor in the leading role. After all, it would not have been feasible to film a real person over a period of seven or more years. The deception was hardly noticeable. The hospital environments were real and as independent producers, Jacoby and Van Dyke had considerably more frustrations than they had had at the OWI where other people paid the bills and fought the fights.

In The Photographer, which was essentially a tribute to Edward Weston, Van Dyke's mentor and friend, self-censorship prohibited Jacoby's commentary from mentioning palsy as the reason why the aging Weston trembled visibly throughout. If they had told the State Department that Weston was ill, they felt they would not have been allowed to make the film. Films about community centers, technical aid to foreign countries, and American history were more suited to governmental regulations for overseas propaganda.

Within those limitations Affiliated Film Producers' productions were almost always above average in sensitivity and craftsmanship, although increasingly wordy. It was also a problem, Jacoby felt, that there was little audience feedback, although the films were translated into more than twenty languages.

A new format became available to Jacoby with The Marriage for Moderns series, five classroom discussion films written to accompany a McGraw-Hill textbook of that name. With nonprofessionals enacting hypothetical scenes of male/female relationships, the results were predictably uneven. However, they were taking both Jacoby and Van Dyke in new directions that would forever change their lives and their careers.

For Van Dyke, changes began with his marriage to one of the young women he had cast in the Marriage for Moderns films—and with his gradual mingling with younger filmmakers rather than those of his own generation. For Jacoby, changes began with his marriage to Alberta Altman, a mental health specialist who helped make Jacoby the virtual film guru among psychiatrists, psychologists, and social workers.

Under the aegis of the Mental Health Film Board formed in 1947, Irving Jacoby produced and wrote Angry Boy, an introduction to the then tenuous idea that children with personal and social problems could benefit, without stigma, from services available at mental health centers. Directed by Alexander Hammid, who worked with people somewhat better than Van Dyke generally, the film sold some six hundred 16mm prints in its first three years, making it a blockbuster in its time. Extensive showings of Angry Boy were credited as the major factor in gaining the public support needed to establish a child guidance center in one Wisconsin town. This was the kind of social action for which Irving Jacoby had always hoped.

Like most other documentary filmmakers, Irving Jacoby also hoped for larger audiences seeing feature-length films in real movie theaters. Already there had been several successes, among them Janice Loeb and Helen Levitt's The Quiet One, about a rejected Harlem boy, directed by Sidney Meyers with commentary by James Agee.

Jacoby's feature film The Lonely Night, which he wrote, directed, and coproduced with Van Dyke, starred actress Marian Seldes in the story of the relationship between a psychiatrist (also an actor) and a young woman driven to attempt suicide because of childhood insecurities and fears. The message of The Lonely Night was clear and useful as an introduction to the basic mental health principles. Did it succeed as art? Did it belong in movie theaters? From almost any point of view, the answers were negative.

So Jacoby and his wife Alberta resumed their film careers within the confines of standard short films designed for special audiences.

Whereas formerly the films had been produced with Irving as consultant (directors included Rodakiewicz, Francis Thompson, as well as Hammid and Van Dyke), gradually Irving took over virtually all the productions, while Alberta assured their promotion and use.

Through the years, Irving Jacoby wrote, produced, and also directed films on adolescence, old age, dropouts, home aides, father-son relationships, community health centers, public health nursing, family breakdowns, and other personal and social issues.

Irving and Alberta also had children of their own: daughter Tamar, who became a journalist/author, and son Oren, who became a filmmaker.

The clubby atmosphere that Irving Jacoby hoped to create in New York after his return from London in the 1930s had scattered in many new directions. Van Dyke became director of the Museum of Modern Art's film department. Leacock's name was synonymous with unscripted cinéma vérité. Boris Kaufman had won an Academy Award for his cinematography on Elia Kazan's On the Waterfront. Hammid and Francis Thompson were making multiscreen and IMAX productions. Aram Boyajian, the City College of New York film student Jacoby had hired at the OWI as an apprentice and at Affiliated as the house editor, was now directing and producing films on art, health, and social issues for network television.

If the Griersonian spirit was really to be found in the United States, remnants must surely have remained in Irving Jacoby. As James Beveridge had written, Irving Jacoby had had first-hand contact with the British, Canadian, and American methods and purposes of documentary filmmaking, and he remained a talented and dedicated filmmaker during all those years.

CECILE STARR

Biography

Born in New York City, May 29, 1909. Graduated from City College of New York, 1929. Studied under Max Reinhardt at the University of Vienna, 1929–30. Writer of short comedy, musical, and animated films for Warner Brothers in New York, 1931–8. Collaborated with Dr Seuss on several cartoons. Stage manager of the Fifth Avenue Playhouse; producer (with John Hammond) of several Broadway plays, including Jayhawker by Sinclair Lewis and Little Old Boy, directed by Jose Losey, 1930–6. Founder and director of Institute of Film Techniques, City College of New York, 1941–3. Chief, Non-Theatrical Film Section, Office of War Information Overseas Branch, in New York City, 1943–5. Treasurer and later president of Affiliated Film Producers, Inc. (with Willard Van Dyke and others), 1946–80. Coproducer (with Shirley Clarke and Van Dyke) of Skyscraper, Academy Award nominee in Short Documentary category, 1959. Consultant and producer-director-writer of Mental Health Film Board productions, 1948–85. Married to

Alberta Altman, 1951. American Psychiatric Association's Robert T. Morse Award, 1975. Died in New Haven, Connecticut, December 1, 1980.

Selected films

1931 Neath the Bababa Trees: cowriter (with Dr Seuss)
1942 High Over the Border: producer, director, writer
1946 The Pale Horseman: producer, director, writer
1946 Journey into Medicine: (with Van Dyke) producer, writer
1947 The Photographer: (with Van Dyke) producer, writer
1950 Marriage for Moderns series: (with Van Dyke and Hammid) producer, writer
1951 Angry Boy: (with Hammid) producer, writer
1953 The Lonely Night: producer, director, writer
1953 American History series: (with Grayson) producer, writer
1954 Man to Man: cowriter, director
1955 Tobey and the Tall Corn: (with Leacock) producer
1959 Skyscraper: (with Clarke, Van Dyke) coproducer
1961 Miracle of Spring: (for Coca Cola TV Spectacular) producer, director
1966 Community Mental Health: producer, director, writer
1968 Snow Treasure: producer, director, writer
1970 Hitch: producer, director, writer
1973 First Friends: producer, director, writer

Further reading

Beveridge, James and Grierson, John, *Film Master*, New York: Macmillan, and London: Collier Macmillan, 1978.
EFLA Service Supplement, 'Irving Jacoby', New York, Educational Film Library Association, August 1965.
Jacoby, Irving, *The Photographer*, printed text of commentary of the film, Monterey: W.T. Lee, c. 1950.
——'Interview', in *John Grierson, Film Master*, by James Beveridge, New York: Macmillan, and London: Collier Macmillan, 1978.
Starr, Cecile, 'Through the Psychiatric Looking Glass', *Saturday Review*, 12 May 1951.

Jane

(US, Leacock, 1962)

Jane was one of the last films that Drew Associates made for Time, Inc.'s Living Camera series, and one of the last films on which D.A. Pennebaker was the principal cameraman. It marks the beginning of Pennebaker's exploration of entertainers, which would reach its most acclaimed peaks with Dont Look Back and Monterey Pop, and is also most notable for its illustration of the complex relationship between subject and cameraman.

Jane records the rehearsals, preparations, and performances of a weak Broadway comedy, The Fun Couple, starring Jane Fonda in her first leading role for the theater. Pennebaker and correspondent/producer Hope Ryden worked long days following Fonda and her director/boyfriend, Andreas Voutsinas, as they rehearsed and traveled to several American cities in the time-honored tradition of taking the show to the road before presenting it in New York, the prestigious center of the American theater. The amount of footage was considerable. The film's clear structure belies the difficulties in making the film, and implicitly questions the veracity of filmmakers who must take one hundred thousand feet of film and shape a sixty-minute 'drama', which is indeed what Jane is.

One of the premises for direct cinema is its unobtrusiveness, its desire to minimize the effects of the camera's presence. What complicates matters is that many of the subjects of the most noted vérité films of the 1960s are used to the presence of the camera; this is likely the rationale for subject selection in the first place, but it nevertheless raises questions. Fonda herself was evidently aware of the difficulties, since she later admitted that the camera's presence made it impossible to tell when she was acting and when she was not (Mamber 1975). In this sense, Jane presents a 'performance' by Fonda being Jane Fonda. Despite this, it conveys the impression that Fonda, in her mid-twenties, is still trying to learn who 'Jane Fonda' is, and in the smaller details captured by the camera one can see glimpses of that struggle of a young woman becoming herself.

Fonda comes across as a nervous young girl. She registers shock as she realizes the first performance on the road is just days away by putting her fingers to her lips; she is then seen biting on her thumb as she gets berated by Voutsinas during rehearsal. The most compelling scenes take place in her dressing room, where she appears to be alone (though shots reveal her maid, whose quiet, nearly invisible presence says as much about race relations as the Drew films that made race their subject). At times, she appears to be speaking to the filmmakers (Pennebaker is briefly visible in a few shots, reflected in the many mirrors the dressing room has), trying to use the film to express her viewpoints about her career and its relation to her father's. Her dialogue has the ring of the confessional, as she explains that she has worked twice as hard and has taken more acting and dance classes than her father. Fonda seems constantly aware of the camera's presence and, not content to simply sit, she regularly find things to do: some of the most aesthetically fascinating shots feature her putting on her stage makeup and doing facial exercises. Especially interesting is a mirror shot of her drinking a tiny bottle of liquor on opening night, then turning to her left, smiling (to Ryden), and putting her finger to her lips.

Fonda's reactions to the brutal reviews form what we are to take as the climax of the film. In her reaction to Walter Kerr's *New York Herald Tribune* review, she can barely contain her tears. This, we are to presume, is the 'real' Jane Fonda—hurt, saddened, and confused, questioning her judgment. Unfortunately, because of editing decisions, we do not see the process through which her reactions become defeatist; Leacock reports that her initial reactions were dismissive, denying their relevance, and that only over time did she 'face the truth' (O'Connell 1992). Even more interesting are the final dressing room shots: having been told that the second night will be the last, Fonda is seen twirling her hair in frustration as she has to deal with failure—and do so with a camera present.

While fascinating, perhaps even revelatory, Jane is undermined by the film's editing, which imposes a 'crisis structure' in an artificial way (the 'crisis' here has considerably lowered stakes than in films such as The Chair or Crisis, or even On the Pole, where lives are literally at stake). The pressures of bringing a show to Broadway are visible in the rehearsals and performances (aided slightly by a narration that is mostly obtrusive). The fear of failure is made manifest through the representation of Kerr. He is seen briefly at the beginning of the film, is mentioned just before opening night, and is seen leaving his suburban home driving into Manhattan, talking about the theater, typing his review at his office. At a key moment in Fonda's dressing room, as she prepares to go on, the film cuts between Fonda and Kerr's trip into Manhattan, as if there were a shoot-out about to take place. 'I have a funny feeling in the pit of my stomach' is followed by a shot of Kerr talking about how few actors can carry a play. It is somewhat laudable that Kerr is given a human face, but it ultimately detracts from the overall feeling the film is trying to convey. These editing devices weaken what is a generally fascinating glimpse into the consciousness of a young entertainer.

TOM GROCHOWSKI

See also: Pennebaker, D.A.

Jane (US, Time-Life Broadcast and Drew Associates, 1962, 54 mins). Distributed by Drew Associates. Executive producer: Robert Drew. Produced by Hope Ryden. Filmmakers: D.A. Pennebaker and Hope Ryden, with Richard Leacock, Gregory Shuker, and Abbot Mills. Edited by Nell Cox, Nancy Sen, and Eileen Nosworthy. Additional photography by James Lipscomb and Alfred Wertheimer.

Further reading

Bluem, William, *Documentary in American Television*, New York: Hastings House, 1965.

Fonda, Jane, 'Jane', *Cahiers du Cinema* 25, December 1963–January 1964: 182–90.

Issari, M. Ali and Paul, Doris A., *What is Cinema Verite?* London: Scarecrow Press, 1979.

Mamber, Stephen, *Cinema Verite in America: Studies in Uncontrolled Documentary*, Cambridge, MA: MIT Press, 1975.

O'Connell, P.J., *Robert Drew and the Development of Cinema Verite in America*, Carbondale, IL: Southern Illinois University Press, 1992.

Janis

(US, Alk, 1974)

Janis has been called the most comprehensive film ever made about 1960s rock star Janis Joplin. However, in the age of the television documentary, such as VH1's Behind the Music, comprehensive seems a relative term. Critically acclaimed in its day as well as commercially successful, Janis provides ample concert footage of the rock icon and a few revealing interviews. As a compilation film, Janis portrays the public Joplin from 1967 to 1970 and consists of approximately twenty-five scenes; over half of them are devoted to performances of some of her most famous songs. More than anything, Janis is a concert film.

The most impressive aspect of Janis is the research done over a three-year period by executive producer F.R. (Budge) Crawley to secure the rights to Joplin's concert performances, rehearsals, and interviews from a variety of sources. The sources include sequences from the Monterey Pop Festival where Joplin, along with Jimi Hendrix and Otis Redding, was catapulted into international fame by D.A. Pennebaker's own critically acclaimed documentary Monterey Pop. Crawley's dedication to the project began with his own witnessing of Joplin's virtuosity during the Festival Express concert tour, which crossed Canada in 1970. Notoriously persistent, Crawley and his production company, Crawley Films Ltd, spent thousands of dollars to rescue a failing film that documented that tour, entitled Festival Express (eventually screened at the Toronto International Film Festival in 2003). Much of the Festival Express footage branched into the creation of Janis.

Although Janis was ultimately Crawley's endeavor, others contributed to its development. Howard Alk and Seaton Findlay are credited as directing and editing the film. Paul Harris worked as the production coordinator on the film, and Robert Leclair and Gary Bourgeois were responsible for sound. The film is flanked with creative touches. Mik Casey and Stephen Dennis created the psychedelic animation typical of the time period that introduces the film, and the photographic montage at the end was compiled and created by Ron Haines.

As alluded to earlier, Janis is a portrait of the public icon that Joplin created for the stage. The film never really introduces a 'backstage' Janis and never interviews anyone who might reveal that Janis to the viewer. In fact, the film never provides interviews of anyone but Joplin herself. There are three short interviews with fans about her impact, but they are negligible. A few of the Joplin interviews do hint at the despondent Joplin written about in a multitude of biographies. She is sensitive and vulnerable while being interviewed by a Texas reporter on the event of her attendance at her ten-year high school reunion in Port Arthur, Texas. The close-up shot from Joplin's side shows her eyes even as she wears her famous sunglasses for the interview. In those small windows the viewer may see a battered soul filled with hurt from never belonging. This particular interview also captures Joplin's uneven emotional state and need for approval when her sister, Laura, sitting by Joplin's side, confides that her parents describe Joplin as 'exceptional'. At this moment, Joplin's mood changes drastically, and she shrieks with delight at the discovery. There are only a few moments such as these where the viewer might get a sense of Joplin as a person. However, Joplin is always fully aware of the camera, and clearly performs for it, an act revealing in itself. Ironically, Joplin herself makes the issue of sincerity central to the film by commenting on being 'real', contrasting her identity with those women of the 1960s who wore 'cardboard eyelashes and girdles'. Janis makes this remark, about her lack of premeditation, sitting in a trademark white fur cap and coat.

Janis is an appropriate title because the film focuses on Janis exclusively and never on the members of the three bands she played with in the three short years of her celebrity. The bands, Big Brother and the Holding Company, the Kozmic Blues Band, and the Full Tilt Boogie Band, are always filmed as backup, much like their roles in her life and career. Unfortunately, documentaries function to bring relationships and their complications to life. Janis does no such thing. Bands change without notice. Only a fan or scholar of Joplin would recognize the incongruent faces throughout the film. In the compiled footage the members are given no voice. The content of the film comments on this in an early recording session of Big Brother and the Holding Company. As the producer, John Simon, stops the rehearsal to get guitarist Sam Andrew's famous introduction to 'Summertime' right, Joplin shows a lack of interest and comments that only the vocals are important. Here, the film provides another revealing moment, but these moments are few and far between.

As a concert film, Janis is impressive. The film provides footage from important historical concerts, such as Monterey Pop and Woodstock, as well as early performances by Big Brother and the Holding Company and European tour footage with the Kozmic Blues Band. As expected, much concert footage comes from the Festival

Express tour in Canada in 1970. During this tour, Joplin was with the Full Tilt Boogie Band, a band reputed to be the right fit for Joplin and a band with which she might have remained, had she not died of a heroin overdose later that same year. A majority of the film is devoted to these concert moments and Joplin's famous heartfelt monologues at the end of many of the songs. Maybe these comments are the most telling; themes of loneliness and the allusive nature of love abound, and Joplin delivers each with passion. The film ends with the number one 'Me and Bobby McGee' and Haines' chronological photographic montage. It is in this moment that the viewer gets remnants of the complicated life behind a surface that was merely skimmed.

TRACY STEPHENSON SHAFFER

Janis: A Film. (US, Crawley Films, 1974, 96 mins). Directed by Howard Alk. Written by Howard Alk and Seaton Findlay. Distributed by Universal Pictures and MCA/Universal Home Video.

Japan

Cinema arrived in Japan within a couple years of its invention, and Japanese companies were quick to exploit the possibilities of the new medium. Indeed, industries across Asia were initially begun by traveling Japanese entrepreneurs. In both contexts nonfiction was a significant part of production, especially in the early years. By the late 1930s Japan featured one of the largest industries in the world, and during World War II it expanded to cover much of the Asian continent. These films served industry, journalism, and government, but early adoption of small-gauge equipment meant that Japan also enjoyed a lively amateur scene and radical, anti-establishment documentary started as early as the 1920s. Along with this vigorous production activity, many of Japan's most important critics and philosophers have turned their attention to the documentary in rigorous essays and books about the nonfiction form. In short, Japan boasts a long tradition in documentary, the history of which is every bit as complex as better-known national cinemas such as those in Britain and the United States.

There are a number of reasons why the documentary developed so quickly and thoroughly in early twentieth-century Japan. The feature film industry was one of the largest in the world, and there was certainly some synergy with the documentary. Japan had a relatively well-educated populace, thanks to a centralized education system; these educators were well informed about the latest developments in pedagogy across the globe and were enthusiastic early adopters of 'new technology' in the form of the education film. This energized domestic production led to the importation of large film libraries from abroad, and helped to create an infrastructure for reception outside of the feature film theater. Major newspapers began producing visual supplements to their papers in 1908, showing them in public parks and temporary theaters. Finally, the government discovered the powers of film propaganda at the turn of the century with actualities of the Boxer Rebellion and the Russo-Japanese War. In coming decades they would use film to justify their colonial adventures abroad to the nation and to drum up popular support for the treasures and lives their wars would require.

In the 1910s and 1920s most documentary was produced for one of two reasons: journalism or education. Production of newsreels was sporadic in the first few decades, and covered primarily political incidents and sporting events such as boxing and sumo. Newspapers set up film units for this by 1910, and there were a number of attempts at regular production (although none went beyond ten issues or so). However, competition between newspapers *Asahi* and *Osaka Mainichi* eventually led to well-produced, regularly issued newsreels in the 1910s. Soon they were fixtures of the feature film theaters, as in the rest of the world. There was a striking proliferation of newsreels in the mid-1930s, and at the height of their popularity there were even specialized theaters just for newsreels and documentary shorts. However, the government initiated a series of consolidations during the China War as a strategy for keeping tight control over both raw film stock and content, and the number of specialized theaters was reduced to a handful by the end of the Pacific War.

The possibilities of using film for pedagogy were immediately recognized by Japanese educators. The first organization to inquire into this was formed in 1901. This was the first of many organizations that would form to debate the proper use of film for education. These groups often produced films and published books and magazines about film education. The Ministry of Education's first film was a record of the massive earthquake in Tokyo in 1923. After that it funded a wide variety of documentaries for education, created 'children's film days' across Japan, and established lending libraries. As time went on, the Ministry increasingly participated in the regulation of nonfiction film aimed at youth, from exerting influence on censorship legislation to creating a 'recognition system' that nipped problematic projects in the bud (without recognition, most theaters would not show the films in the late 1930s).

By the China War, the government had established production offices in a number of ministries, established complex censorship systems aimed at the documentary, and regularly subsidized large-scale productions by the major studios. It passed laws that required the screening of documentaries—now called 'Culture Films' after the German 'Kulturfilme'—before feature films. The studios and production companies enthusiastically rose to the occasion and there was an explosion in documentary production, including large-scale, expensive projects with military support. They also collaborated with the government in running captured film studios in the new colonies. During the Pacific War, 'Japanese documentary' would have to include studios in Taiwan, Korea, the Philippines, Java, Shanghai, and Manchuria, and a distribution system for stock, rushes, finished films, and personnel rivaled in complexity only by the Americans. As the war dragged on, the government felt the need to control scarce resources and potentially damaging content. They found that a forced consolidation of the industry was a convenient resolution to these problems. Before the 1939 Film Law there were between two hundred and three hundred documentary production companies in Japan, but by the end of the war there were only four. This new, monolithic bureaucracy could easily control the flow of chemicals and raw film stock, enforce complicated and stifling censorship laws, and regulate the workplace to a startling degree.

Amidst the gradual displacement of nonwar subjects during the China War, glimpses of subversive dissent appeared at the height of the conflict. Many of the key documentary filmmakers were leftists of one sort or another, and a number of them got their start in the Proletarian Film League of Japan, or Prokino for short. This radical collective formed in 1929, thus predating analogous movements like the Workers' Farm and Photo League and its European counterparts. At the height of their activities they had about one hundred circles across Japan, published rigorous books and journals, and produced nearly fifty films before their suppression by the government in 1934. By this time, filmmakers faced a choice between cooperation with an increasingly belligerent and militaristic government, an unrelated career, or retirement. However, those who chose to stay in the film world occasionally found subtle ways to make their frustration felt within their films.

For example, the most famous documentary filmmaker in Japan was Kamei Fumio, who never joined Prokino but did visit the Soviet Union to study painting. Upon his return to Japan, he started making documentaries, a number of which were stunningly subversive. Shanghai and Peking (both 1937) look at the continental cities under Japanese occupation; the former makes the nervousness of the Chinese palpable through clever editing, and the latter becomes something of a love song to the ancient city through creative sound montage. His Kobayashi Issa (1941) was ostensibly a tourist public relations (PR) film, but it actually noted the desperate poverty of this rural area. Kamei's greatest accomplishment, however, was Tatakau heitai (Fighting Soldiers, 1939). Toho Studios 'embedded' him with the army units invading Wuhan, and Kamei masterfully deployed all the tools of cinematography, montage, and sound editing to subvert the militaristic designs of the film's sponsors. The film was suppressed and lost for decades, and Kamei was imprisoned just before the attack of Pearl Harbor.

At the end of the Pacific War the Japanese film industry lay in ruins. However, the first two films made during the occupation are among the most important in their history. In the weeks after surrender, a group of documentary filmmakers decided that the situation in those two cities must be quickly documented, and so they embarked on a project that would result in one of the most precious films in documentary cinema. Camera crews traveled to the ravaged cities, accompanied by teams of scientists. Their intention was to document the tragedy of this attack on civilians and to send their footage to the International Red Cross. These plans were scuttled when the first US troops landed in Nagasaki and promptly arrested one of the cameramen. The footage was subsequently confiscated, and then returned on the condition that the filmmakers complete their film under the auspices of the United States Strategic Bombing Survey. It was titled Hiroshima, Nagasaki ni okeru genshibakudan no koka/The Effects of the Atomic Bomb on Hiroshima and Nagasaki (1946). This was only the first of several rounds of suppression until Eric Barnouw's efforts brought the newly declassified film to the world's attention in 1968. The film narrowly escaped the oblivion of political suppression thanks to courageous filmmakers from both countries who hid prints before handing materials over to the US government. Thanks to their efforts, we all have images of the horrifying power of atomic weaponry, as these were the only moving images collected before human death and architectural reconstruction covered up the last traces of the bombings.

The other major documentary of the immediate postwar era was Nihon no higeki/A Japanese Tragedy (1946). Directed by Kamei Fumio and produced by former Prokino member Iwasaki Akira (the only other documentary filmmaker to be imprisoned during the war), this was a collage film drawing on wartime newsreels to expose the lies perpetrated by the government since the 1931 Manchurian Incident. Rather than the subtle critique buried in Kamei's wartime films, A Japanese Tragedy bristles with anger and launches a vigorous, analytical attack on the Japanese newsreel and documentary, demonstrating through editing how documentary filmmakers collaborated with the government in waging total war. Ironically, Kamei's first film after the war was also suppressed; A Japanese Tragedy was confiscated by his liberators, the Americans, and surfaced decades later when returned by the US Library of Congress. The reason for the suppression was purely political: Kamei and Iwasaki made no secret of the fact that the source of inspiration for their critique was Marxism, and the film became the first victim of the Red Purge and the so-called Reverse Course of the Occupation.

The American Occupation did, however, play a crucial role in the reestablishment of documentary in the daily lives of the Japanese. First, they poured money into the production of films that would 'democratize' the populace and reeducate them in the fundamentals of their new political system. Second, and more importantly, they sowed the countryside with 16mm projectors. This would become the infrastructure for the independent cinema of the post-Occupation era. According to the Occupation's own figures, their films were seen by 13,017,973 Japanese spectators in 1947; 92,847,545 in 1948; 280,910,727 in 1949; 342,211,521 in 1950; and reached 472,341,919 viewers by the end of the Occupation.

In those days before the widespread use of television, PR films were one of the key tools of advertising. Thus, as the industrial might of Japan grew, so too did the documentary. As these PR films became the mainstay for independent producers, a number of filmmakers returned to political subjects in their spare time after the 1952 end of the Occupation. Once again, Kamei led the way. Collecting funds from unions and political movements, he tackled subjects as diverse as the atomic bombings, radiation poisoning, and the inevitable social problems surrounding US military bases. Among the most famous of these films is the Sunagawa Series, particularly Sunagawa no hitobito—kichi hantai toso no kiroku/The People of Sunagawa—A Record of the Anti-Base Struggle (1955). In some respects this film foreshadowed the achievements of the later Sanrizuka Series by Ogawa Productions.

It was not too long before the inevitable strictures of the PR film became restricting for filmmakers. This was occurring just as television arrived on the scene, and the money available for PR films reached its zenith. The more powerful directors were able to work within wildly large budgets, even in 35mm scope and color. They brought all their creative energies to bear on the films, subsequently leading to problems with inevitably conservative sponsors. This period coincided with both the political turbulence around the 1960 signing of the joint security treaty with the United States (which put Japan under the US nuclear umbrella) and the rhetoric of auteurism in the late 1950s and early 1960s. Before long the most talented of the young directors bolted for independence and the political and artistic freedom it promised.

The most important group of these directors came from Iwanami Productions. This is where Hani Susumu produced his Kyoshitsu no kodomotachi/Children of the Classroom (1954) and Eo kaku kodomotachi/Children Who Draw (1956), which shocked audiences with their vérité-like methods (despite predated analogous developments in Europe and America). More important, the younger members of Iwanami formed a reading and experimentation group called Blue Group (Ao no kai), where they would screen rushes and debate film theory and practice. Blue Group's membership reads like a roster of the best directors and cinematographers in postwar Japan: Ogawa Shinsuke, Tsuchimoto Noriaki, Kuroki Kazuo, Higashi Yoichi, Tamura Masaki, Suzuki Tatsuo, and a couple dozen more. Scandalized by several incidents where sponsors dictated changes in work of directors (read 'authors'), the Blue Group dissolved as its members went independent shortly after 1960.

At the very same time, the professional organizations for documentary were in turmoil. Up to this point, they had been dominated by members of the Old Left (which is ironic considering the bulk of their work was for large corporations). Around the time of the security treaty renewal in 1960, younger filmmakers, such as Matsumoto Toshio, Noda Shinkichi—along with help from others like Oshima Nagisa, Tsuchimoto Noriaki, and Kuroki Kazuo—began attacking the organization's conservatism in print and in filmmaking practice. Films such as Matsumoto's AMPO joken/Security Treaty (1960) and Kuroki's Aru marason ranaa no kiroku/Record of a Marathon Runner (1964) creatively bent rules and brought critical politics and open sexuality into the PR films. Before long the organizations split under the pressure, and the scene was set for a new era in Japanese documentary.

While somewhat arbitrary, one might mark the beginning of this era in 1965 with the production of Tsuchimoto Noriaki's Ryugakusei Chua Sui Rin/Exchange Student Chua Sui Rin (1965) and Ichikawa Kon's Tokyo Orinpikku/Tokyo Olympiad (1965). Regrettably, the latter film has come to represent Japanese documentary for many outside Japan. This is unfortunate, considering Ichikawa never showed any interest in the documentary outside of this special film; indeed, from the Japanese perspective, Tokyo Olympiad represented the ultimate sponsored film with its enormous budget from the central government and some of the largest corporations in the world. By way of contrast, Tsuchimoto worked on a shoestring to make his documentary on a Malaysian foreign student being deported at the request of the Malay government. Student activists mobilized to prevent this political deportation, and Tsuchimoto allied his film to their cause. This film stood for everything that was fresh and new in the newly stimulated documentary scene.

Tsuchimoto's film became emblematic for the new political documentary gaining footing in Japan. This approach achieved national prominence with Ogawa Shinsuke's Forest of Pressure (Assatsu no mori/The Oppressed Students, 1967). Ogawa had gathered a newsreel-like group of students from various universities for his previous film, Seinen no umi/Sea of Youth (1966), which was on the problems of distance learning. They called their group the Independent Screening Organization (Jishu Joei Soshiki no Kai), or Jieiso for short, and it quickly reached national proportions with offices staffed by young activists all over Japan. They found the subject of their next film in the noisy protests of students at a regional university. This was just as the student movement gathered steam in anticipation of the 1970 renewal of the US security treaty, and radical students began barricading themselves in the school grounds. Forest of Pressure electrified the country by showing the passion and seriousness of these students, which was particularly inspiring because it was such a minor school as opposed to one of the elite national universities.

In the coming years Tsuchimoto and Ogawa would become iconic figures of the New Left, and each made monuments of the Japanese cinema in the late 1960s and 1970s. Tsuchimoto went to southern Japan to make a series of documentaries on the victims of mercury poisoning at Minamata, and Ogawa took his collective (now named Ogawa Productions) to a rural area outside Tokyo called Sanrizuka, where the government announced it would build a new international airport. The Minamata Series and Sanrizuka Series are powerful examples of social documentary allied to political activism.

The Minamata Series and Sanrizuka Series also mark a new conception of the documentary in Japan. Up to this point, the documentary—it was argued—allied itself to the center of political power and reduced its 'subjects' to mere objects. Tsuchimoto and Ogawa demonstrated how filmmakers could center their films on the subjectivities of the people in front of the cameras. Each series is something like an extended experiment, registering the changes in their conception of documentary in the course of their filmmaking. In effect, the films become a record of the transformations in the relationships between filmmakers and the people filmed. This change is particularly pronounced in Ogawa's work, probably because he (unlike Tsuchimoto) lived in Sanrizuka with the farmers as they protested the airport construction, and also because he aspired to make films in as collective a mode as possible. The first film of the Sanrizuka Series, Sanrizuka no natsu/Summer in Sanrizuka (1968), is a roughly hewn film filled with spectacular battles between policemen and farmers. As time wore on, the farmers and their concerns come increasingly to the center of the films. By Dai-ni toride no hitobito/Peasants of the Second Fortress (1971), Ogawa was including remarkably long discussions among the farmers over issues that were probably of more interest to the farmers than his spectators. However, in this change we see the filmmaker edging increasingly closer to the subjectivity of his 'objects'. These tendencies culminate in his masterpiece, Heta buraku/Heta Village (1973).

While the Sanrizuka and Minamata Series dominate our sense of Japanese documentary history, there was a proliferation of independent documentary during the 1960s and early 1970s. Filmmakers such as Kuroki and Higashi brought documentary codes into the feature film, as feature filmmakers such as Imamura Shohei, Oshima Nagisa, and Yoshida Kiju tried their hands at documentary (often for television, which was briefly open to innovative nonfiction films). Oe Masanori, who made the first New York Newsreel film, No Game (1968), came back to Japan and attempted to start a similar movement in Japan. Adachi Masao was one of many filmmakers to start in university film club settings and move into the blurring border between the avant-garde and the documentary. He made a number of fascinating films with other authors from the journal Eiga Hihyo (Film Criticism) before his Sekigun/PFLP: Sekai senso sengen/The Red Army/PFLP: Declaration of World War (codirected with Wakamatsu Koji, 1971) led him to join the Red Army and spend several decades in Lebanon. There was explosive growth in the independent documentary in this period, and a willingness on the part of audiences to enjoy work that tampered with conventions and took up political causes of every type.

This growth started changing in the early 1970s when the student movement began winding down. People began to lose faith in social activism due to a marked increase in violence. Three policemen were killed in a skirmish at Sanrizuka, and one of the young farmers committed suicide. As for the student movement, it had always been marred by violent internal rivalry and this climaxed in 1972 when a sect of the Red Army holed up in a mountain cabin. Over the course of a winter, they 'corrected' many of their members through torture, burying several of the most unfortunate victims in the woods. The group gave up in a ten-day hostage standoff from police, which was broadcast live on national television. Aside from breaking the back of activism by alienating people from movement politics, this also heralded the new supremacy of television news.

As television came to dominate what was the domain of the PR film, and as the openness that invited the likes of Oshima to television gave way to conventionalization and an increasingly prostrate journalism world, consumer-level video came within the grasp of independent producers. That Japan was the source for much of the equipment probably contributed to its early adoption by artists. The first rumbles of this change may be traced back to the 1970 World Exposition in Osaka, which attracted independent artists of every stripe. The fair had enormous capital behind it, and sponsored many moving image media projects. This is precisely why politicized filmmakers such as Oe and Tsuchimoto agitated against it, and there was even an 'Anti-Expo' held at a nearby park, where Oe showed his six-screen Great Society (1970), which basically summed up the 1960s. However, it must have been difficult to turn down such luxurious budgets after struggling on a shoestring, and many prominent filmmakers and video artists were happy to take the money, migrate away from social engagement, and turn to personal expression in mostly apolitical avant-garde film and video art.

At precisely this moment in the early to mid-1970s, a new form of documentary called the private film reached Japanese screens. The two filmmakers most closely identified with the change are Suzuki Shiroyasu and Hara Kazuo. The latter burst onto the documentary scene in 1974 with Kyokushiteki erosu: Renka 1974/Extreme Private Eros: Love Song 1974 (1974). The film lays the filmmaker's personal relationships out for the world to see. Having left his rather abusive wife (Takeda Miyuki) and taken up with a new woman (Kobayashi Sachiko, his present wife and producer), Hara decides to make a film, as he explains in the opening voice-over, to come to terms with his ex-wife. With Kobayashi recording the sound, they follow his former wife around the country. Hara bares all: he includes the verbal abuse he takes from Takeda (some of it well-deserved), he runs his camera while making love with her, and he films her giving birth on the kitchen floor. This indulgence in the personal, this extremely public exposure of the private, proved earth-shaking in the context of a documentary world, the values of which were formed by films like the Sanrizuka Series and the Minamata Series. Hara's subsequent films, particularly Yuki yukite shingun/The Emperor's Naked Army Marches On (1989) and Zenshin shosetsuka/A Dedicated Life (1994) also focused on charismatic individuals and were no less controversial.

Hara's emergence was followed by the arrival of Suzuki, an NHK television cameraman and prominent poet. Considering this combination of vocations it should not be surprising that the contradictions between producing corporate and personal representations proved stifling. Inspired by the work of Jonas Mekas, Suzuki began producing diary films. His Nichibotsu no insho/Impressions of a Sunset (1974) and the three-hundred-and-twenty-minute Kusa no kage o karu/Harvesting Shadows of Grass (1977) recorded the mundane events of daily life, the details of the physical spaces he moved through, and his fetishistic fascination with the camera.

Thus, the early to mid-1970s seem to constitute a break, with new filmmakers rejecting the dominant conception of documentary practice in which films were produced within organizations of people, whether collectives, companies, political parties, or the military. There have been high-profile attempts to resurrect the possibilities of this collaborative mode of filmmaking, most notably Sato Makoto's Aga ni ikiru/Living on the River Agano (1982) and Hara Kazuo's Watashi no Mishima/My Mishima (1999). Both of these projects referenced Ogawa Productions' example, with Sato having his crew live with the victims of Minamata Disease in the mountains of Niigata and Hara producing his film by forming a collective of young people called Cinema Juku. These were ambitious plans that both failed and succeeded. They are interesting on their own merits, particularly Sato's film, but they also seem anachronistic, as if the age of collective production were a thing of the past. Hara's film especially indicates the transformation in Japanese youth and its relationship to the politics and activism that independent documentary tends to embrace.

In the 1990s young documentary filmmakers demonstrated no ambivalent relationship to group; rather, they probably could not see its possibilities. This is why they fell into the footsteps of Hara and Suzuki and turned the private film into something of a strong genre. However, whereas the two older directors always located their work in relation to the engaged filmmaking of the past, particularly that of Ogawa and Tsuchimoto, younger filmmakers rarely have a strong sense of historical context. Furthermore, it is probably significant that most young documentarists work in 8mm and video, and find their training in art school settings (where many of the previous generation's most progressive artists are now ensconced as teachers), which encourage self-expression and individualized work. Uninterested in or unable to take their cameras into the social world, they retreat to the safe realm of their family and friends and the comfort of the private film.

At its best, the private film looks to the social world to explore issues of loss or the desire for social connection. By far the finest director to emerge from this approach to documentary has been Kawase Naomi. After graduating from photography school, she began making personal films in 8mm. Embracing Nitsutsumarete/Embracing (1992) is a moving documentary about her search for her father, who abandoned the family in her youth. It demonstrated a striking visual sense, and managed to be profoundly moving without devolving into a simple narcissism. She followed this with a film about the aunt who raised her, Katatsumori (1994), and has since turned to documentary-inflected feature films. (Suzaku won the Camera D'Or at the Cannes Film Festival in 1997).

Outside of the private film, the movement documentary of the past continued at a smaller scale with filmmakers who would produce their work by canvasing within unions and political groups. The PR film also continued to one degree or another, although this was driven almost exclusively by filmmakers who got their start in the 1950s and 1960s. Video activism picked up after the first Gulf War with groups such as Video Act! However, since the 1980s the vast majority of documentaries are produced for television, and inevitably fit a strong set of conventions (which are particularly strict for public broadcasting in Japan). It is probably the strength of these conventions combined with the lack of alternative broadcast venues that prevented the wide variety of 1960s documentary approaches to continue to the present day.

In this regard, the Yamagata International Documentary Film Festival (and to a lesser extent, the Pia Film Festival and Image Forum Festival) has begun to open up the definition of documentary. Starting in 1989 when the image of documentary was thoroughly dominated by government television (NHK), the Yamagata festival used three main strategies for changing the documentary scene in Japan. First, it staged large-scale retrospectives of historically important documentaries, both domestic and international. Second, it created a running program of current Asian documentary, which struggled to find acceptable work at the beginning but has exploded in growth with the widespread adoption of digital video across Asia. Third, it brought the world's best filmmakers to Japan for its competition. By the turn of the century, many of the finest working documentarists had visited Japan and presented their work. These kinds of efforts have expanded the number of venues for documentary, even if television has yet to loosen its strictures, and Japanese documentary production becomes more interesting with every passing year.

ABÉ MARKUS NORNES

See also: Fumio, Kamei; Tokyo Orinpikku

Jazz on a Summer's Day

(US, Stern, 1959)

A record of one day's performances at the 1958 Newport Jazz Festival, Jazz on a Summer's Day remains surprisingly overlooked in existing explorations of documentary, music on film, or jazz. The cause for surprise lies partly in its precedent-setting influence on later concert film documentaries—Monterey Pop (1968) in particular—and partly in its singularity as a film in its own right.

Although director Bert Stern's project was in process in rough chronological parallel with the first stirrings of the direct cinema movement, the film had little in common with the movement. Stern's background was in advertising stills photography, which, in this, his first and only film, is reflected most prominently in the heavily stylized audience shots. A number of these were placed as though in response to a different performer than was actually the case, but the artfully rhythmic editing makes these instances difficult to identify. The result, however, is a highly suggestive interface of 'artifice' and 'spontaneity'.

Shot in DeLuxe Color on color-saturated Kodachrome stock, Jazz on a Summer's Day appeared at a time when the documentary remained overwhelmingly associated with gritty authenticity, social and moral purpose, and black-and-white cinematography. Color was more readily associated with spectacle in mainstream narrative cinema (Neale 1985). The frequent close-ups of the performers and the cameras often aimed directly at the stage lights seemed to utilize both cinematic modes. In sumptuous color that would not be out of place in an MGM musical, the musicians' faces appeared to offer direct access to their thought processes.

Jazz, too, existed in the popular imagination in a milieu of monochrome, metropolitan, smoky cellars. Newport Jazz Festival, an outdoor event since 1954, was, by contrast, in Rhode Island, summer haunt of the wealthy. Coinciding with the festival was the America's Cup yacht race. The opening thirty minutes of the film juxtaposed festival performances with observational detail of the harbor and the town, as well as vertiginous aerial footage of the yacht race. The resulting collisions of social setting, age, class, and race (the latter in terms of the ethnic composition of both musicians and audience) amounted to a heady mixture with immense potential for further exploration at a time when, for example, the Civil Rights movement was gaining momentum. In Jazz on a Summer's Day, however, the cameras were largely content merely to observe, against the grain of the realist aesthetic that still prevailed among large swathes of the critical establishment of the period.

Musically, the film captures a moment when jazz was in uneven transition from popular to art music, with its richly diverse cast list including Louis Armstrong, Thelonious Monk, and Gerry Mulligan. It also featured gospel (Mahalia Jackson), R&B (Big Maybelle), and rock and roll, the newly dominant popular form, which was (somewhat controversially) represented by

Figure 7 Jazz on a Summer's Day, Louis Armstrong, 1960 (Courtesy of the Everett Collection)

Chuck Berry. Overall, the film remains a fascinating snapshot of a society on the verge of a period of social and political upheaval that could barely have been suspected at the time.

JOHN YOUNG

Jazz on a Summer's Day (US, Galaxy Productions/Raven Film, 1959, 85 mins). Distributed by Galaxy Attractions. Directed by Bert Stern. Writing credits attributed to Albert D'Annibale and Arnold Perl. Cinematography by Bert Stern, Ray Phelan, and Courtney Hafela. Editing by Aram Avakian. Featuring, in order of appearance, Jimmy Giuffre, Thelonious Monk, Sonny Stitt, Anita O'Day, George Shearing, Dinah Washington, Gerry Mulligan, Big Maybelle, Chuck Berry, Chico Hamilton, Louis Armstrong, Jack Teagarden, and Mahalia Jackson. Interviews and announcements by Willis Conover. Filmed in Newport, Rhode Island.

Further reading

Arthur, Paul, 'Jargons of Authenticity (Three American Moments)', in Michael Renov (ed.), *Theorizing Documentary*, New York and London: Routledge, 1993: 108–34.

Freeman, Leonard, *Jazz and the White Americans*, Chicago: Chicago University Press, 1962.
Gabbard, Krin, *Jammin' at the Margins: Jazz and the American Cinema*, Chicago: Chicago University Press, 1996.
Hentoff, Nat, *The Jazz Life*, London: Panther, 1964: 82–95.
Neale, Steve, *Cinema and Technology: Image, Sound, Colour*, London: Macmillan Education, 1985.
Ross, Lillian, 'You Dig It, Sir?' in Ralph Gleason (ed.), *Jam Session*, London: Peter Davies, 1958: 194–210.

Jennings, Humphrey

Like many 1930s documentarists, Jennings came from a social and intellectual elite, imbued with high cultural traditions. However, these were transformed by his twin modern interests: surrealism and, from 1937, the very 'film-minded' mass observation (MO). Paul C. Ray has characterised MO as 'surrealism in reverse'. Surrealism sought to create 'a solidified dream image' by juxtaposing violently incongruous elements and, thus, to project the artist's symbolic imagination onto the objective world in order to transform it. Conversely, MO tried to recover the 'collective unconscious' that had produced the objects and images of ordinary waking reality, in effect, to psychoanalyse the social history of the imaginative drives behind it—what Jennings himself called the 'legacy of feeling'. (Indeed, in his 1936 essay, 'Surrealism', Jennings identified the quotidian as the widest, most democratic locus of the potentially significant: 'Coincidences have the infinite freedom of appearing everywhere, anytime, to anyone'.) These interrelated influences would be strongly reflected—though in a highly personal, warm, and lyrical manner—in Jennings's film work. His approach was consequently more cultural and anthropological than civic or socially purposive on the Griersonian model, and he never fully became part of the General Post Office (GPO) Film Unit. Grierson suspected Jennings of dilettantism, and only after the former became head of Canada's National Film Board did Jennings finally gain creative autonomy.

It is certainly arguable that Jennings's early filmmaking lacked definite direction or a distinctive 'auteurial' signature, although those films did show his experimental tendencies. Starting as set designer and apprentice editor under Cavalcanti (whose influence and/or collaboration was a principal creative catalyst), he quickly went on to direct Post Haste (possibly the first nonanimated film exclusively composed of prints and drawings) and Locomotives (1934). Jennings held a lifelong fascination with mechanics/industrialism and their interaction with a more 'organic' human consciousness, as well as with semi-abstract patterning. In 1936 Jennings coproduced the avant-garde puppet film, Birth of a Robot, for Shell. After returning to the GPO, Jennings sparked controversy with Spare Time (1939), the first film clearly showing his mass-observational interest in everyday pursuits and rituals of ordinary people (summed up in MO's slogan, 'Anthropology Begins at Home') and drawing, in particular, on its documentation of leisure (centred on 'Holiday Town', i.e. Blackpool). Spare Time cross-sectioned 'mass' culture, from male-voice choir, to cinema going, to wrestling, to the fairground, to a boy reading a comic at a table. Especially because of a sequence featuring a bizarre kazoo parade on a northern wasteground, around a tableau of Britannia, Jennings was charged by mainstream documentarists with a satirical tone and lack of edifying values. However, Spare Time is now generally regarded as a rare and unpatronising record of 1930s popular culture, as well as MO's methods.

World War II's extraordinary conditions restored Jennings's professional fortunes and inspired his visual lyricism. Because of newly available Ministry of Information funding, to boost civilian morale and to promote Britain's cause to undecided neutrals, Jennings found a focus for his disparate talents and influences as the GPO was reformed as the Crown Film Unit. Jennings's output is regarded as among the best records of this 'People's War' in any national cinema. His films are driven by creative tension between affection for traditions and a symbolist's eye for the telling details of a people under the stress of modern war. Initially, Jennings's Home Front documentaries were unashamedly and (given the crisis of the time) justifiably propagandist. They played a key part in mythologising the Blitz as Britain's 'finest hour' and confirming the quiet courage, calm resolve, and common decencies of its 'national character'. However, Jennings's mid-World War II work became increasingly impressionistic, backgrounding didactic messages to elliptical subtexts.

The First Days depicted war preparations in the capital in September 1939. Although

Jennings mostly contributed street footage, its overall tone points toward concerns developed more artfully in his more mature work. The film presents Britain as forced reluctantly into hostilities (opening shots show children playing on decommissioned artillery) by necessity and justice, not jingoism nor 'bogus romance'. Crucially, ordinary Londoners, waking to 'a world where everything seems strange' (epitomised by the dream-like image of a barrage balloon, half-inflated fins drooping like the tentacles of a giant cuttlefish, watched by an earthbound cat), look forward to Jennings's fuller visualising of war's forcible defamiliarisation of the texture of everyday life.

In London/Britain Can Take It (1940, approx. 8.5 mins), Jennings turned the Blitz's most celebrated image—St Paul's dome rising intact above the capital's ordeal by fire—into a metonym for defiance. Quentin Reynolds, *Collier's Magazine*'s London correspondent, was strategically coached to lower his booming tones for the commentary. The result was downbeat, intimate, and therefore more effective, but its impact is largely attributable to ingenious matches between editing and words. Jennings showed a cross-section of civilians hurrying home to change into uniforms, to transform into 'heroes by night'. The film exemplified the notion, popularised in J.B. Priestley's Radio Postscripts (the latter voiced the British version) that a 'people's army' of volunteers were 'really fighting this war'.

As Reynolds emphasised, although daytime remained peaceful enough, 'We haven't had a quiet night now for more than five weeks'. People are shown moving into cover (some of whom, Reynolds notes laconically, will die tonight), as batteries and searchlights prepare. Jennings then cuts back and forth with incongruous simultaneity, from bombardment and retaliation, to homely images of darts players and shelter sleepers. The way the film's manipulation of soundtrack and image (over dramatic reverse shots of guns and explosions) is authenticated as 'real' remains a meta-cinematic masterstroke: 'These are not Hollywood sound effects. This is the music they play every night in London, the symphony of war.' Fires are resolutely tackled until, like malevolent 'creatures of the night', the bombers pass away. Reynolds notes that the mark of a fighter is 'getting up from the ring again' as daylight reveals devastation, but also quotidian lives stubbornly continuing—exemplified by Jennings's quasi-surreal images: a commuter train negotiating a damaged bridge, and doorstep milk deliveries. As rubble is cleared, Reynolds claims he has seen no panic nor terror and, as the RAF strikes back, inevitably concludes that the Luftwaffe cannot kill people's spirit and courage: 'London can take it'. Perhaps the most famous of Home Front documentaries because Jennings seemed to capture a public mood at the right moment, this is indubitably partly an effect of the film's discursive strategies. Until then, MOI Films Division propaganda had limited success in Roosevelt's America, but Reynolds gave the appearance of an independent viewpoint ('I am a neutral reporter … ') converted by the evidence of his eyes, a process repeated vicariously for the viewer.

The British title aimed to placate other blitzed regions and avoid metropolitan bias. Although Jennings's The Heart of Britain (1941) strove to extend the same heroic solidarity treatment to the North and the Midlands, he had less success with the Distressed Areas of the 1930s. The film opens with a rock face, symbolising gritty provincial character, to Elgar accompaniment. However, footage of High Culture (Malcolm Sargent conducting Manchester's Hallé in Beethoven's Fifth) and RP voice-over (Jack Holmes, Crown's senior producer) sit uneasily with workers in a cross-section of industrial towns. Jennings was still to achieve the socially inclusive national vision for which his mid-war films became famous. Nonetheless, the film provided an important incidental record of the blitzing of Coventry. Similarly, in Words for Battle (1941), Jennings tried out the impressionistic method, which would fuse so successfully with a sense of cultural democracy in his best films, in creative partnership with editor Stewart MacAllister. Conscripting Britain's literary heritage, from Shakespeare to Kipling, Jennings tried to coordinate images of stoicism and battle-readiness with verse and prose excerpts read by Laurence Olivier, but the film's argument suffers from the strain of combining archaisms, didactic style, and visual symbolism. Nonetheless, Words for Battle is recognised as the first of Jennings's war pictures to have a completely distinctive identity.

However, in Listen to Britain (also of 1942), Jennings created a formally groundbreaking template for inclusive impressionistic montage, partly because of the return of his mass-observational interests. An almost symphonically structured cross-section of working and leisure routines of both civilians and service personnel, synchronised and/or counterpointed with natural and 'found' sound, Listen to Britain included many evocative popular songs and tunes of the period. Originally conceived as a short about Myra Hess's National Gallery concerts, Jennings and MacAllister developed a two-reel audiovisual mosaic, on a kind of 'free association' principle, without explicit narrative.

Listen to Britain sampled every level of wartime Britain's sound community, in both musical and social senses, resolving its contradictions through associations that suggested an underlying national unity. It ranged through Blackpool's Tower Ballroom; an ambulance station pianist; Canadians chorusing 'Home on the Range'; a school playground; a colliery; factory women enjoying Workers' Playtime, Flanagan and Allen's signature song; the Royal Marine's band; and finally back to Kenneth Clark and the Queen listening to Hess. The MOI distributed it widely overseas, the film's 'soft-centredness' typifying the difference from Nazi propaganda, with its hectoring belligerence, designed to terrorise neutrals.

Jennings's contribution to the mid-war convergence between factual filmmaking and topical features was the laconically titled Fires Were Started (1943), regarded as the acme of the understated emotionality of this narrative semi-documentary genre. Dramatic cinema specialised in empathic human interest, but the class-bound nature of British features retarded authentic reflection of the people's experience of the war. Like Ealing's The Bells Go Down, Fires Were Started was a retrospective on the National Auxiliary Fire Service, although the professional actors in the former perform awkwardly compared to the firefighters Jennings used to 'replay themselves'. His only feature-length picture (at just over sixty minutes), it proved that Jennings was also disciplined enough to direct sustained narrative, scripting the scenario himself. Fires Were Started represented ordinary Londoners doing extraordinary things, in response to extraordinary circumstances. Jennings combined laying claim to actuality, as 'straight' documentary does, with the psychological insight of fiction, reconstructing a typical conflagration from the last great fire raid of May 10, 1941.

Portraying a twenty-four-hour shift at substation 14Y, Fires Were Started focuses on new volunteer, Bill Barrett, as the perfect device for inducting the viewer vicariously into the crew's work and the working-class areas on the front-line in this kind of war. Bill, an advertising copywriter and pianist (played by novelist William Sansom, virtually a stand-in for Jennings himself by class and profession), is taken under the wing of cheery cabby, Johnny Daniels (Fred Griffiths), quickly defusing any social awkwardness. The disparate group of volunteers emphasises unity in a common cause. Jennings observed strict Griersonian decorum in the conscientiousness of his account of operational routine, as well as avoided sensational effects. During daylight hours, they drill, perform preparatory chores, and raise barrage balloons. The command structure is also shown by way of reports to the control centre. Following their evening meal, the crew, dubbed the 'Crazy Gang', briefly relax, becoming fully humanised through their humour, although commentators consider the sequence where Daniels sings 'One Man Went to Mow' as each fireman enters, to be suddenly cut off by the siren, Jennings's one rather contrived touch. They scramble to their task, with the added jeopardy that fire will spread to a docked munitions ship. The tense climax was re-created in an abandoned warehouse. 'Jacko' remains on the roof to steady the trapped crew's escape ladder, at the cost of plunging to his death. In deft simultaneity, Jennings cuts to Jacko's wife listening to the news—'It does not appear that casualties are likely to be heavy'—thus poignantly fleshing out personal tragedy behind the anonymity of official broadcasts.

Some have argued that because the enemy is offscreen and the firemen's work related only to their colleagues, Jennings presents the bombing not as culpable aggression but as a depoliticised force of nature. Conversely, he closes by cutting between the comrade's funeral and the munitions ship moving seawards, to further the struggle against its cause and symbolising 'the broader context of war, endurance, and victory' (Coultass 1989). Indeed, Jennings strives for methods of showing, not telling, creating what many deem a masterpiece of nondidactic information and persuasiveness. Simultaneously, Fires Were Started, unlike some other semi-documentaries, develops its characters convincingly, so they seem more than types in a social allegory.

The most unconventional product of Jennings's foray into the semi-documentary mode was The Silent Village (1943). The destruction of Lidice was an atrocity ordered by Hitler for the assassination of Reinhard Heydrich, 'Protector' of Bohemia, by Czech agents in May 1942. The Nazis even publicised it, in notorious footage of grinning soldiers, constituting a moment of international shock and prophetic insight into the workings of the *Endlösung* (final solution). Jennings transposed it onto a comparable Welsh mining village, using locals to play the victims and avoiding mere realistic reconstruction with professional actors, by imaginatively twinning Lidice and Cwmgiedd. The opening sequence of village life metonymises its innocent ordinariness. The invader then suddenly arrives at a distance, figured by a car with a loudspeaker, but virtually invisible occupants—a semi-surrealist touch characterising the film's oblique menace. Proclamations then appear, banning normal rights and activities. The miners react with a strike and sporadic sabotage, but are quelled. Jennings's narrative method is dispassionate, using minimal dialogue to advance the plot. The build-up to the massacre eschews the natural temptation to sensationalise for propaganda effect, making Jennings's tribute composed and dignified.

In 1943 Jennings picked up a story from the Mediterranean battle zone, like a surrealist objet trouvé: how a song cut across linguistic and ideological barriers to become the war's greatest international hit. Again he applied one of MO's pioneering principles, investigating cultural factors and modes of dissemination behind popular 'song consciousness' (originally conducted on the 'Lambeth Walk' craze). The True Story of Lili Marlene (1944) featured a cameo appearance by Jennings, reading the original German lyrics. The phenomenon was reconstructed: from broadcasts to Rommel's Afrika Korps; subsequent adoption by Montgomery's Eighth Army as their unofficial theme; to modification by the BBC as allied propaganda. Indeed, Jennings's mass-observation interest in modern folk rituals was pervasive in wartime. Typically, their analysis of The Pub and the People (1943) was reflected in his review of Down at the Local (1943), reminding troops in Burma about social life in Blighty. Jennings praised Richard Massingham's imaginative editing, but like his own best efforts, felt it was 'saved from cleverness by being really human'.

The influence of Jennings's audiovisual impressionism and vision of social and cultural inclusiveness is felt in other late-war documentaries, such as John Eldridge's Our Country (1945). This film follows a merchant seaman, undertaking a symbolic journey, imaging and sounding Britain's true regional, cultural, and racial diversity, on the eve of D-Day. Jennings's own Diary for Timothy (1945) was a cross-sectional record of Britain thereafter to stimulate aspirations for post-People's War social and economic reform. Some have argued that in its formal experimentation and open-endedness, Diary for Timothy is Jennings's most complex and problematic film. It combines the sound-image mosaic of Listen to Britain with the narrative drive of Fires Were Started. Beginning with the birth of Timothy James Jenkins, Jennings charts his progress, in the context of the liberation of Europe and nascence of the post-war world. The infant focuses the film's critical hopes, contrasted with the lives of a cross-section of the older generation, all intermeshing in the last year of hostilities: an engine driver, a Welsh miner, a fighter pilot, and a farmer.

Rough cut screenings provoked renewed accusations of 'artsiness' and wasting public money against MOI Films Division officials and there is undoubtedly some obscurity, or dissociation, between images. However, commentators also identify its flaws less with Jennings's audiovisual syntax than with novelist E.M. Forster's prolix commentary. Conversely, Forster himself wanted greater radicalism and objected to the choice of a child reflecting Jennings's own privileged background, rather than a representative citizen. Jennings may have done this deliberately to underscore the arbitrariness of life chances if Britain's class system continued. ('Deadly parallels', such as those between snug nursing home hearth and conditions at the face where Goronwy cuts its coal, seem to bear this out.) Perhaps uneven for both ideological and technical reasons, Diary for Timothy nonetheless includes sequences among the most celebrated in Jennings's oeuvre, for spacetime fluidity, sound-image coordination, and thematic linkage. For example, Stanley Maxted's broadcast about Arnhem cuts to the listening mother, a farmer picking it up elsewhere, then Myra Hess's hands. Jennings pans around her audience, zooms in on a girl smoothing her hair, then resumes the broadcast, telling how paratroops drank rainwater from their capes. The narrator (Michael Redgrave) then comes in, arguing the need to distinguish Germany's liberal cultural tradition from Nazism in the peace settlement. (Jennings made A Defeated People soon afterwards, a compassionate view of enemy suffering after VE Day.) Positive water images succeed, ending with the baby's baptism. The conclusive question is posed to its generation: 'Are you going to have greed for money or power ousting decency from the world as they had in the past or are you going to make the world a different place … ?' However, this incertitude is arguably indicative of Jennings's own misgivings, just as gloomy winter footage seems metaphoric for the onset of postwar pessimism.

Jennings's films record and celebrate creative tension between historical tradition and modernity, brought to crisis by the war and its adaptational challenge to Britain's national character. His best appear to effortlessly re-create the peculiar mood and circumstances of their time, although this is as much a matter of skilfully crafted documentary poetics as neutral verisimilitude. Consequently, Jennings is usually considered the screen's leading exponent of the populist, left-leaning patriotic mythology that emerged mid-war, comparable not just to Priestley but also to George Orwell's texts, such as The Lion and the Unicorn (1941) and The English People (1947). Jennings ultimately came to see his job as mediating across the dissociation between 'mass civilisation and minority culture', one of the more pernicious legacies of British capitalist industrialism, to create a truer picture of the nation's cultural and psychic identity and enable it to recognise itself. However, Jennings undoubtedly romanticises and, with rare exceptions, downplays explicit class frictions. It remains debatable how far unanimity against external threat was historically representative, when compared to alternative accounts: prejudice against evacuees, resentment at officiousness, civil disorder, looting, and so on (some, ironically, filed by MO for the Department of Home Intelligence). His sentiments evidently seemed less convincing after hostilities, during the austerity of welfare state-building and reopening of political divisions, which led to the ousting of the Attlee government in 1951. Jennings's postwar documentaries had little public impact, though Family Portrait (1950), his last, was appropriately for the Festival of Britain. Jennings's failure to recoup his distinctive touch suggests an obscure awareness that Britain's wartime experience could not be repeated. Nonetheless, Jennings was exceptional in that his products of state propaganda managed to transcend the expediencies of their making as works of art. His mature films remain virtually unique experiments, arguably never successfully imitated and carrying British documentary's capacity for poesis and cultural observation further than any other. Although Lindsay Anderson and other British Free Cinema directors of the 1960s acknowledged their debt, their own projects are formally less complex and radically different in their national vision, darker and more satiric.

KEITH WILLIAMS

See also: Cavalcanti, Alberto; Diary for Timothy, A; Family Portrait; Fires Were Started; Grierson, John; Listen to Britain; London Can Take It

Biography

Born Frank Humphrey Sinkler Jennings at Walberswick, Suffolk, in 1907. Graduated in English Literature from Pembroke College, Cambridge, in 1934. Joined the GPO Film Unit in 1934. Worked with Len Lye at Shell Films from 1936. Founded Mass Observation in 1937 with poet Charles Madge and anthropologist Tom Harrisson (Jennings led MO's southern team, based in Blackheath, with Madge). Rejoined the GPO in 1938 (reformed as Crown Film Unit in 1940), remaining with it for duration of the war. Directed for Wessex Films in 1949. Commissioned for the series, 'The Changing Face of Europe', died on location, falling from a cliff at Poros, Greece, in 1950.

Selected films

1934 Post Haste: director
1934 Locomotives: director
1934 The Story of the Wheel: editor
1936 Birth of a Robot: coproduced with Len Lye, colour decor
1938 Penny Journey: director
1939 Spare Time: director and (with Cavalcanti) writer
1939 The First Days (released in America as A City Prepares): codirected with Harry Watt and Pat Jackson

1940 Britain Can Take It (US title London Can Take It): codirected with Watt
1941 The Heart of Britain: director
1942 Words for Battle: director, writer
1942 Listen to Britain: director, coeditor
1943 Fires Were Started (US title I Was a Fireman): director, writer
1943 The Silent Village: director, writer, producer
1944 The True Story of Lili Marlene: director, writer
1944 The Eighty Days: director, producer
1945 Diary for Timothy: director, writer
1946 A Defeated People: director, writer
1947 The Cumberland Story: director, writer
1949 Dim Little Island: director, producer
1950 Family Portrait: director, writer
2000 Humphrey Jennings: The Man Who Listened to Britain: Kevin MacDonald and Fran Robertson, producer and director (Figment TV for Channel 4, 23 December)

Further reading

Aitken, Ian, *The Documentary Film Movement: An Anthology*, Edinburgh: Edinburgh University Press, 1998.
Aldgate, Anthony and Richards, Jeffrey, *Britain Can Take It: The British Cinema in the Second World War*, second edn, Edinburgh: Edinburgh University Press, 1994.
Calder, Angus, *The Myth of the Blitz*, London: Jonathan Cape, 1991.
——*The People's War: Britain 1939–45*, London: Jonathan Cape, 1969.
Colls, R. and Dodd, P., 'Representing the Nation: British Documentary Film 1930–45', *Screen* 26, no.1, January/February 1985: 21–33.
Coultass, Clive, *Images for Battle: British Film and the Second World War 1939–45*, London, Toronto and Delaware: Associated University Presses, 1989.
Grierson, John, *Humphrey Jennings: A Tribute*, London: Humphrey Jennings Memorial Fund Committee, 1951.
Harrisson, Tom, *Living Through the Blitz*, Harmondsworth: Penguin, 1990.
Harrisson, Tom and Madge, Charles (arranged and written), *Britain by Mass-Observation*, 1939; reprinted London: Cresset, 1986.
Hodgkinson, Anthony and Sheratsky, Rodney, *Humphrey Jennings: More than a Maker of Films*, Hanover, NH: University Press of New England, 1982.
Jackson, Kevin (ed.), *The Humphrey Jennings Film Reader*, Manchester: Carcanet, 1993.
Jennings, Mary-Lou and Anderson, Lindsay (eds), *Humphrey Jennings: Film-Maker/Painter/Poet*, London: British Film Institute, 1982.
Maclaine, Ian, *Ministry of Morale: Home Front Morale and the Ministry of Information in World War II*, London: Allen and Unwin, 1979.
Nowell-Smith, Geoffrey, 'Humphrey Jennings, Surrealist Observer', in Charles Barr (ed.), *All Our Yesterdays*, London: British Film Institute, 1986.
Rattigan, Neil, *British Film and the People's War, 1939–45*, London: Associated University Presses, 2001.
Ray, Paul C., *The Surrealist Movement in England*, Ithaca, NY: Cornell University Press, 1971.
Richards, Jeffrey and Sheridan, Dorothy (eds), *Mass-Observation at the Movies*, London: Routledge and Kegan Paul, 1987.
Stansky, Peter and Abrams, William, *London's Burning: Life, Death and Art in the Second World War*, London: Constable, 1994.
Tomicek, Harry, *Humphrey Jennings*, Vienna: Austrian Film Museum, 1989.
Vaughan, Dai, *Portrait of an Invisible Man: The Working Life of Stewart MacAllister, Film Editor*, London: British Film Institute, 1983.
Winston, Brian, *Fires Were Started*, London: British Film Institute, 1999.

Joli Mai, Le

(France, Marker, 1963)

Filmed in May 1963, Chris Marker and Pierre Lhomme's Le Joli Mai/The Lovely May is an investigation of the familiar—here (Paris, home) and now (this month, the historical present) as if viewed through the eyes of a stranger.

In the opening voice-over (adapted from Giraudoux, and read by Simone Signoret in the English version) Marker writes of Paris that 'one would like to see it for the first time, at dawn, without having seen it before, without memories, without habits'. It is a device that Marker has used in much of his work: both La Jetée/The Jetty and Sans Soleil/Sunless feature travelers from the future for whom our strange manner of living in the present is anything but obvious. In Le Joli Mai there is a tension between this desire to see a fresh and a more nuanced apprehension of social connections and contradictions founded on an intimate knowledge of a specific place, Paris, and its history, which is also implicated in other histories—notably in May 1962, the history of European colonialism. Combining elements of cinéma vérité, the attention to details of place of such earlier French documentaries as Lacombe's La Zone and Lotar's Aubervilliers, and Marker's own meditative, essayistic approach to filmmaking, Le Joli Mai is a kind of time capsule that refuses its viewers the comfort of nostalgia.

Credited jointly to Marker and the cinematographer Pierre Lhomme, Le Joli Mai is divided into two parts: 'Prayer from the Top of the Eiffel Tower' and 'The Return of Fantômas'. Fantômas is the criminal mastermind whose exploits were brought to the cinema by Louis Feuillade in 1914, and who functions as an emblem of the political violence that threatens to overshadow the city. Although the film's second part places somewhat more emphasis on large-scale public events, both parts combine cinéma vérité-style interviews with a very wide range of Parisians—their aspirations, their ideas of happiness, their responses to events from the Renault strike to John Glenn's orbiting the Earth—with a variety of other footage of the street life and neighborhoods of Paris. The handheld camera prowls through the narrow alleys of an Aubervilliers slum or a shanty town near Saint Ouen; looks down from the top of the Eiffel Tower on the birds and people below; catches a poet reciting couplets on the Place des Vosges; observes people dancing at a nightclub (and dances with them); sneaks into a gallery opening; and travels by car through the streets at dawn. Some of this footage is used to introduce new sequences; some is used to comment on or as counterpoint to an interview in progress; and some is worked in associatively, or linked to Marker's voice-over commentary, which itself frames and reflects on the vérité sequences. The juxtaposition of these disparate elements—the different verbal textures of commentaries and interviews, Lhomme's extraordinarily fluid and expressive cinematography, and Michel Legrand's music, itself an alternately melancholy and acerbic commentary on what's spoken and seen—produces a collective portrait of the city at a moment of both renewal and unease.

An opening title informs or reminds us that May 1962 was 'referred to by some, at the time, as "the first springtime of peace"', but the qualified phrasing invites us to question the apparent optimism of the description (and of the film's title). The Algerian war had ended the year before, but in an interview at the end of the film's first part, a young soldier, standing with his fiancée on the Pont de Neuilly, reveals that he's leaving for Algeria in a fortnight. 'I don't dare to think about anything, and I don't want to,' he says; 'Leave [political events] alone and they'll be forgotten.' However, the forgotten, the repressed of history, keeps forcing its way back into the light. Hostile to any negotiations that might lead to Algerian independence from France, Raoul Salan (the French military commander in Algeria in the late 1950s) had founded, in 1961, the OAS (Organisation de l'Armée Secrète) to conduct terror campaigns in France in an attempt to bring down the government and reassert French colonial power. Le Joli Mai includes footage of the mass anti-OAS demonstrations of February 1962, which ended with the deaths of eight demonstrators at the hands of the police, and of the memorial service in the Place de la République five days later, attended by five hundred thousand mourners. 'For the first time in the history of Paris one could hear a bird sing at noon on the Square of the Republic,' Signoret reads (and one does hear the bird on the soundtrack), but the lyrical note is unsettled by the reminder that 'thus, at the beginning of 1962, Fantômas made his return, and France had some reason to believe itself on the brink of civil war'. In May 1962 Salan was put on trial in Paris for his terrorist crimes. This trial, which ended with the commutation of his original death sentence to life in prison (he was released six years later, and pardoned in 1982—historical amnesia at work), runs as an undercurrent throughout the film, a reminder of the inescapability of history and of the consequences (including terrorism and the repression of dissent) of the attempt to forget it.

Its concern with history and politics is one of the qualities that distinguish Le Joli Mai from a film it also in some ways resembles, Jean Rouch and Edgar Morin's Chronique d'un été (1961). As in that film, the interviews in Le Joli Mai often begin by asking some version of the question, 'Are you happy?' and then probe the speaker's responses, not always gently: 'A bit limited, all that—no interest in other things?' Or, to the soldier about to go to Algeria, 'Are you only worried about your own problems?' Unlike Rouch and Morin, Marker and Lhomme do not set up confrontations among the people they interview, nor do they really aim to get at the 'truth' of the people they encounter; their approach is dialogic rather than analytic. The interviewers' manner is skeptical, but also genuinely curious and generous. In the film's final sequence, Marker writes that 'we tried to look through the eyes of a prisoner on his first day of freedom, when he, himself, tries to understand how these strange phenomena—free people—live'. The voice-over continues to reflect on the differences between free people ('those who are able to question, to refuse, to undertake, to think, or simply to love') and those who carry their prisons inside themselves. Both have been met in the film. Certainly some of those interviewed in the second part would be counted among the free: a Dahoman student who describes his encounters with the often unconscious racism of the French; a worker priest who ended up leaving the church and devoting his life to the struggle of his fellow workers; a young Algerian worker who, despite racist attacks by coworkers and police, has overcome his own impulse to hate in return, and who looks forward to a free Algeria in cooperation with France. For all the anxieties and acts of violence it registers, Le Joli Mai affirms the hopes of its most generous characters by adopting their clear-sightedness as its own method.

HAL GLADFELDER

See also: Chronique d'un été; Marker, Chris

Biography

Le Joli Mai (France, 1963, 165 mins; according to filmographies, the available English-language version is 120 mins). Directed by Chris Marker and Pierre Lhomme. Executive producer Gisèle Rebillon. Commentary read by Yves Montand (French version) and Simone Signoret (English version). Script by Cathérine Varlin. Cinematography by Pierre Lhomme. Music by Michel Legrand. Interviews conducted by Henri Belly, Henri Crespi, and Nathalie Michel. Sound by Antoine Bonfanti and Réné Levert. Camera by Etienne Becker, Denys Clerval, and Pierre Villemain. Edited by Eva Zora, Annie Meunier, and Madelaine Lecompère.

Further reading

Kustow, Michael, 'Chris Marker's Le Joli Mai', in Lewis Jacobs (ed.), *The Documentary Tradition*, second edn, New York: Norton, 1979: 395–7.

Marker, Chris *et al.*, 'excerpts from *Le Joli Mai, Le cinéma et la vérité*, issue 2 of Artsept (ed. Raymond Bellour), Lyon: La Proue, 1963: 88–92.

Tailleur, Roger, 'Parisiennes', *Le cinéma et la vérité*, issue 2 of Artsept (ed. Raymond Bellour), Lyon: La Proue, 1963: 83–7.

Thirard, P.-L., 'review of *Le Joli Mai*', *Positif* 54–5, 1963: 110–14.

Journey, The

(UK, Watkins, 1987)

Peter Watkins's monumental documentary The Journey (1987) is a unique piece in film history. A fourteen and a half-hour documentary shot during four years, from 1983 to 1986, filmed in a dozen countries, it raises fundamental worldwide questions about 'time, money, and how we spend them'. While describing the escalating nuclear arms race, we visit communities where children do not have enough money to buy shoes or to eat conveniently every day. One could say that The Journey is not just an antinuclear war film about the multiplication of arms and nuclear weapons in all parts of the world; it also offers in many ways a deep analysis of the lack of information about these issues, even when newspapers and TV news coverage refer to events related to these questions.

Director Peter Watkins often uses a comparative approach, juxtaposing scenes of some wealthy people with others, showing groups from the Third World, or sometimes matching people unaware of the consequences of the arms race with other persons who precisely work to build nuclear weapons. The film begins with the presentation of rarely seen photographs of the actual bombs falling on Hiroshima and Nagasaki in August 1945. These photographs from the Museum of Los Alamos will be shown to various groups in different countries through the film. For instance, we see a group of citizens living in Scotland who protest against the North Atlantic Treaty Organization's (NATO) presence at the Alba Aerodrome, in Stornoway, on Lewis Island. We also visit a sort of profane mausoleum built under the site where the first atomic bomb actually fell, in Hiroshima, containing countless little boxes with the ashes of some hundreds of unidentified Japanese who were killed in August 1945.

In another scene, we see another group of angry citizens living in Bangor (in Washington state) who are opposing the assembly lines during the construction of Trident missiles. Other scenes present groups that resist, and people who ignore the actual race for arms, or the victims of nuclear testing made by France in the 1970s and the 1980s—for instance on the atoll of Murarowa, near Tahiti.

Through discussions with families or groups of people in various countries, the director asked 'average citizens' if they were aware of the world arms race, and the possible effects of nuclear weapons. We also follow a US family corresponding with a Soviet family, exchanging messages on video and finally meeting for the first time in the USSR. We understand that people and families do not talk much about the consequences of a nuclear war.

The narratives used in The Journey are innovative, bringing a slower rhythm and avoiding useless editing. After some forty minutes, the narrator explains that from now on, all the cuts made in the TV clips seen in the film will be highlighted, by using a specific noise to make us aware of the increasing number of cuttings and editing in television coverage of public affairs. In fact, these cuts are made in the mainstream media to make sentences shorter. This unusual, 'underlining' method used in The Journey is explained for almost a minute, on a totally black screen; it brings a difference of tone between 'the official discourse' and the deconstructive analysis brought by Watkins.

In an important analysis of media coverage, we observe how the local Canadian reporters commented on the actual meeting between the President of the United States, Ronald Reagan, visiting the Prime Minister of Canada, Brian Mulroney, in a much mediated event (the 'Shamrock Summit') that took place in Québec City, on March 17, 1985. We follow the local reporters alongside their shooting—how they discuss the agenda, which information they selected, and how they represent the dissidents and protesters who were outside the meetings. Some local journalists filmed the protesters from the police's side and made interviews with activists, but these were not broadcast on the Canadian television network; in The Journey, we see and hear these discussions in the makings. We understand that the journalists had no interest for the protesters and did not mention their presence; they mainly referred in an anecdotal tone to the protocol and high-security measures around the city. Since the media concentrated on the funny, if not spectacular, side of the event (after a televised musical concert, the Reagan and Mulroney team went on stage at the end of the show to sing hand-in-hand a verse from an Irish song), none of the local reporters mentioned the real reason for this meeting: the replacement of the Distant Early Warning (DEW) line radar bases in northern Canada by the new North Warning System sites, which gave the United States full control of the military protection in that Canadian region. In that segment, Watkins quotes peace activist William Arkin, who protested against the meeting and highlighted the true reasons for the meeting that were not mentioned by the media.

In another scene, during a public debate made in Gaelic, Watkins will comment on his own editing process, explaining that he will insert images and faces to reduce the length of a scene. In The Journey, we see many sources: archival stock-shot, TV news broadcasts, animation, many discussion groups, and actual images of political leaders and opponents. Although a 'serious' film, The Journey is also creative: a few animated stories are included, some verses from folk songs are heard, and many children are seen.

Watkins explains that for every minute that the film lasts, $1.5 million are spent in military expenditures. Even though the East–West conflict does not exist as such anymore between the United States and communist countries, arms races still remain today in various ways, and media coverage of public affairs has not improved in the last two decades.

In sum, The Journey confirms what scholars such as Louis Althusser, Noam Chomsky, and Pierre Bourdieu have written about television: it hides even when it shows images of political issues, because the media focus only on superficial elements. A unique film, The Journey remains essential in various ways: for media studies it illustrates how TV news is constructed and biased; for those concerned with peace education, the film demonstrates how groups for peace can act and why they are rejected; if used in citizenship studies, it would show the lack of the citizens' presence in public affairs; and from an international relations perspective, it shows how political issues are related in a globalizing world. The film also brings to 'risk studies' an illustration of how people can get along with constant dangers near them; finally, the whole documentary is an eloquent example of how media literacy and media education should be made.

There were only three broadcasts of The Journey on television (WNET in New York City, and two local Canadian stations); it was presented and praised in many film festivals and retrospectives, and remains available on 16mm and video, either in English, French, or Swedish versions.

YVES LABERGE

See also: Watkins, Peter

The Journey (Sweden-Canada, Swedish Peace & Arbitration Society, with Svenska Fredsoch Skiljedomsföreningen, Films for Fred, the National Film Board of Canada, and many local support groups, 1987, 870 mins). Distributed (in the United States) by Canyon Cinema in San Francisco; on video by Facets Multimedia. Distributed (in Canada) by the National Film Board (Montréal). Produced by Peter Watkins. Directed by Peter Watkins. Production co-ordination by Catharina Bragee. Post-production by Peter Katadotis, Daniel Pinard, George Dufaux. Produced by the Swedish Peace & Arbitration Society and the National Film Board of Canada. Shooting script by Peter Watkins. Cinematography by Martin Duckworth (Canada), Aribert Wies (Germany), Kim Dok Chul (Japan), Miguel Garzon (Mexico), Jaems Grant (Tahiti and Australia), Christian Guillon (France), Odd-Geir Saether (Norway), Leif Neibon (USSR), Skip Roessel (Utica, NY, US), Eric Edwards (Portland, OR, US), Anders Nilsson (Mozambique), Jan Fester and Tom Hilton (Glasgow), and Gary Payne (Seattle, WA, US). Animation camera by Pierre Landry, Jacques Avoine, Raymond Dumas, Claude Lebrun, and Robin L. Bain. Darkroom technician: Jean-Pierre Joly. Sound by Claude Beaugrand (Canada), Uwe Cardaum (Germany), Yagone Hioraki (Japan), Fernando Camara (Mexico), Ann-Marie Chandler (Tahiti), Frédéric Ullmann (France), Magne Mikkelsen (Norway), Anatoly Stefanov (USSR), Larry Scharf (Utica, NY, US), Phillip Healy (Australia), Wayne Woods (Portland, OR, US), Gabriel Mondlane (Mozambique), Donald McLennan (Glasgow) and Jan Cyr (Seattle, WA, US). Production managing by Gwynne Basen and Christine Burt (Canada), Tillmann Scholl (Germany), Yamagami Hiromi (Japan), Roberto Lopez Marquez (Mexico), Daniel Scharf (Tahiti), Francis Fourcou (France), Jan-Eric Gammleng (Norway), Madlen Aboyan (USSR), Penny Robins (Australia), Jan Baross (Portland, OR, US), Penny Thompson (Glasgow), and David Rosen (Seattle, WA, US). Music (for titles) by André Duchesne. For Utica, New York, US: Associate producing by Scott McDonald and Don Tracy; assisted by Robert Baber and Patricia O'Connor. Project manager (in Seattle, WA, US) by Bill Wahl. In Toulouse (France): Associate producing by Guy Cavagnac and Jean-Jacques Hoquard. Edited by Peter Watkins, Petra Valier, Manfred Backer, and Peter Wintonick. Assistant editors: Michel Juliani, Anna Fudakowska, and Gerry Vansier. Sound-editing by Peter Watkins, Manfred Backer, Raymond Vermette, Vida Urbonavicius, and Tony Reed. Assistant sound editors: Nancy Hughes, Mathew Ennis, Alison McGillivray, and Ron Lee. Re-recording by Jean-Pierre Joutel. Translations by Daniel Desmarais, Tochi Honda, Patricia Nazal, Howard Scott, and Stuart Stilitz. Information systems by Mark Achbar. Graphic design by Jane Churchill and Joan Churchill. Assistant designers: Paul Rosenbaum and Heidi Quedneau. Animation by Jonathan Amitay, Hubert Den Draak, Pierre Hébert, Don McWilliams, Robert Mistysyn, and Richard Slye. Phototypesetting by Serge Gaudreau. Titles and credits by Louise Overy. Post-production by Peter Wintonick. Commentary by Peter Watkins. Narrated by Peter Watkins (for the English version). In the French version narration was by Canadian actors Jean-Louis Roux, Frédérique Colin, Jean-Pierre Cartier, and others. Filmed in numerous locations: Quebec City, Hiroshima, Leningrad, Glasgow, Scotland, Seattle (US), West Germany, Cuernavaca (Mexico), Maputo (Mozambique), Tahiti, Toulouse (France), Sweden, Norway, Utica (NY), Portland (Oregon), and Australia. Total series: 870 mins, multilingual with English subtitles, color, 16mm. Episodes 1–6: 274 mins. Episodes 7–13: 308 mins. Episodes 14–19: 288 mins.

Further reading

Laberge, Yves, 'La télévision au cinéma: exercice d'anti-propagande dans le film documentaire Le Voyage de Peter Watkins', in Catherine Saouter (ed.), *Le Documentaire: Contestation et propagande*, Montréal: Editions XYZ, Collection Documents, 1996: 85–91.

——'Le Vrai et le faux au cinéma: entre la fiction vraisemblable et le réeléquivoque', *Vice-versa*, no. 37, Avril 1992: 43–5.

Watkins, Peter, *Media Crisis*, Paris: Editions Homnisphères (Collection 'Savoirs autonomes'), 2004.

Joyce at 34

(US, Chopra and Weil, 1972)

Joyce at 34, codirected by Joyce Chopra and Claudia Weill, was one of the first important autobiographical portrait documentaries emerging from American feminist film efforts during the second-wave women's movement of the 1960s and 1970s. It was also among the first group of women's autobiographical films employing synchronous sound and the cinéma vérité style. Joyce at 34 features Chopra in her ninth month of pregnancy, the birth of her child, and how she deals with issues she must face in balancing her new role of motherhood and child-rearing while also continuing in her professional role as a filmmaker. Chopra's husband, the playwright and screenwriter Tom Cole, and other family and friends appear in the film as well. 'For the next several months she nurses the baby, travels between Boston (her home), and Brooklyn (her parents' home), directs a movie and admits that she loves the first but doesn't want a second baby' (Greenspun 1975: 20). 'We see the hassle of juggling telephone, bottles, diapers, movie reels, and having all come out in a life that somehow works together' (Nash 1974: 205).

Joyce at 34 opened on February 15, 1973, at the Whitney Museum in New York. It also aired on PBS television and received screenings at the 1973 Robert Flaherty Film Seminar at the Museum of Modern Art in New York City and the National Council on Family Relations Film Award Competition. It has also been used in screenings for study and consciousness-raising in university feminist film courses. Often categorized as a film on family and career, scenes in Joyce at 34 allow additional categorization of this film into the genre of films about filmmaking, in that it documents Chopra's efforts as she continues making films after becoming a mother.

The Chopra/Weill directing/producing team was subsequently invited to collaborate with Shirley MacLaine on the much-publicized documentary of MacLaine's visit to China entitled The Other Half of the Sky: A China Memoir (1975). The Other Half of the Sky was screened at the Cannes Film Festival and received an Academy Award nomination for Documentary Film (Feature). This film documented the visit to China of an entourage that included MacLaine and seven other women delegates, plus four women film crew members. It was a result of the Nixon administration's efforts to reopen Chinese/American relations.

Confusion involving credits on Joyce at 34 and The Other Half of the Sky has surfaced, most likely because of shared credits and the close approximation of the films to each other. Joyce at 34 was codirected by Chopra and Weill. Presumably, because of her appearance in Joyce at 34, emphasis on Chopra as the director dominated early discussions of the film. However, emphasis shifted to Weill in later years. On The Other Half of the Sky Chopra served as a producer and Weill split codirecting credits with MacLaine. Weill was also cinematographer and editor for both Joyce at 34 and The Other Half of the Sky. Joyce at 34 sound operators were Peggy Guggenheim, Anne Lewis, and Miriam Weinstein.

Joyce at 34 was well known for its 'spectacular birth scene' (Rosenberg 1983: 66), a graphic representation of Chopra's delivery of her daughter, Sara (born in 1971). It was considered an unusual film in that it documented an actual live birth outside of the medical/educational film arena. 'The film was a breakthrough feminist film in that the filmmaker documented her own experience on camera, rather than being an objectified body in another's film' (Foster 1995: 76). Cinematic devices in Joyce at 34 include the use of family photographs and home movies, voice-over, on-camera commentary about how certain individuals feel about their respective roles as parents, intercutting between on-camera commentary about the past juxtaposed against visuals of present-day activities, and a documentary structure that has been observed to more closely resemble narrative structure in that it uses seamless documentary realism, rather than self-reflexive devices that would draw attention to itself as a documentary.

Often embraced by feminist film circles, reception to Joyce at 34 was mostly positive. Discussion on the film by Jan Rosenberg reflects this positive attitude. However, Joyce at 34 did not escape negative criticism from feminists. Feminists E. Ann Kaplan and B. Ruby Rich are among critics of the film and/or the filmmakers. Kaplan scrutinized it in a 'structuralist, semiological criticism of realism' for, among other reasons, assuming a position of knowledge that forces spectators into passivity, its heavy use of techniques of realism and lack of self-reflexivity, and perpetuating a 'bourgeois illusion' (Kaplan 1983: 127). Rich described it as a 'feebly feminist signature' and criticized Chopra for 'selling out' to Hollywood when she directed Smooth Talk (1985), maintaining a conservative position on the female sexuality of young women (Rich 1998: 337). However, Chopra stated early on, 'I didn't go to make documentary films; I wanted to make movies' (cited in Rosenberg 1983: 35). Weill also directed Hollywood movies, breaking in earlier than Chopra with Girlfriends (1978) and It's My Turn (1980). Chopra and Weill have since continued as directors for numerous television projects.

Joyce at 34 was not always perceived by spectators through a feminist lens. In a positive review, *The New York Times* film critic Roger Greenspun stated, 'This is not a feminist film, though [it is] clearly aware of feminist positions' (Greenspun 1975: 20). Mental health practitioners, anthropologists, and sociologists also reviewed the film positively, albeit for different reasons than feminists. Mental health practitioners found it a valuable tool for discussion on a number of issues involved in the adjustments made when a new baby arrives concerning parental and spousal relationships and roles, as well as considering how individuals function when new feminist-oriented ideas of reversing traditional parenting roles between husband and wife are implemented. Anthropologists found the film valuable as one example of ethnographic documentation of women in modern American society. It was also recommended for inclusion in film library collections.

D. JAE ALEXANDER

Selected films

Joyce at 34 (US, New Day Films, 1972, 28 mins). Produced by Joyce Chopra and Claudia Weill. Directed by Joyce Chopra and Claudia Weill. Photography by Claudia Weill. Additional photography by Al Fiering and Eli Noyes. Production associate: Tom Cole. Editing by Claudia Weill. Sound by Polly Guggenheim, Anne Lewis, and Miriam Weinstein. VHS, color/black and white.

1975 The Other Half of the Sky: A China Memoir: directed by Claudia Weill and Shirley MacLaine; written by Shirley MacLaine (color, 74 mins).

1978 Girlfriends: directed by Claudia Weill; written by Vicki Polon (color, 86 mins).

1980 It's My Turn (aka A Perfect Circle): directed by Claudia Weill; written by Eleanor Bergstein (color, 91 mins).

1985 Smooth Talk: directed by Joyce Chopra; written by Joyce Carol Oates (story) and Tom Cole (screenplay) (color, 92 mins).

1989 The Lemon Sisters: directed by Joyce Chopra; written by Jeremy Pikser (color/black and white, 93 mins).

Further reading

Acker, Ally, 'Joyce Chopra', in *Reel Women: Pioneers of the Cinema, 1896 to the Present*, New York: Continuum, 1991: 45–6.

——'Claudia Weill', in *Reel Women: Pioneers of the Cinema, 1896 to the Present*, New York: Continuum, 1991: 32–3.

Carstens, Leone H., '1975: Seventh Annual NCFR Film Awards Competition', *The Family Coordinator* 25, no. 1, January 1976: 75–85.

Felando, Cynthia, 'CHOPRA, Joyce, American Director', in Gwendolyn Audrey Foster (ed.), *Women Filmmakers and Their Films*, Detroit, MI: St James Press, 1998: 74–6.

——'Weill, Claudia, American Director', in Gwendolyn Audrey Foster (ed.), *Women Filmmakers and Their Films*, Detroit, MI: St James Press, 1998: 448–50.

Foster, Gwendolyn Audrey, 'Chopra, Joyce (1938–)', in *Women Film Directors: An International Bio-Critical Dictionary*, Westport, CT: Greenwood Press, 1995: 75–6.

——'Weill, Claudia (1947–)', in *Women Film Directors: An International Bio-Critical Dictionary*, Westport, CT: Greenwood Press, 1995: 368–9.

Greenspun, Roger, 'A New Consciousness', in *The New York Times Film Reviews*, New York: New York Times and Arno Press, 1975, 20 (reviewed in *The New York Times* February 16, 1973, 17).

Kaplan, E. Ann, *Women & Film: Both Sides of the Camera*, New York: Methuen, 1983.

Lamphere, Louise, 'Women in Film: An Introduction', *American Anthropologist*, New Series, 79, no. 1, March 1977: 192–3.

Lieberman, Leslie and Lieberman, Leonard, 'The Family in the Tube: Potential Uses of Television', *The Family Coordinator* 26, no. 3, July 1977: 235–42.

Melton, Hollis, 'Joyce at 34', *Film Library Quarterly* 8, no. 2, 1975: 34–5.

Nash, June, 'Joyce at 34', *American Anthropologist*, New Series, 76, no. 1, March 1974: 205.

Rich, B. Ruby, *Chick Flicks: Theories and Memories of the Feminist Film Movement*, Durham, NC: Duke University Press, 1998.

Rosenberg, Jan, *Women's Reflections: The Feminist Film Movement*, Ann Arbor, MI: UMI Research Press, 1983.

Schneider, Irving, 'Film Reviews', *Community-Mental Health Journal* (ed. Edward A. Mason), 12, no. 1, spring 1976: 109–10.

Julien, Isaac

Isaac Julien is an acclaimed contemporary artist, equally accomplished in his challenging film and television work as in his inventive gallery installations. He holds a singular position in British image culture as a male, gay, black artist, whose works are a complex meditation on history, memory, and identity, seeking to articulate the diversity of black experience in Britain. His work in documentary has been unconventional and often departs radically from traditional handling of the form. He claims Derek Jarman, Antonioni, Maya Deren, and Godard as his main influences.

In the early 1980s Julien helped establish the black filmmaking collective called Sankofa, along with Nadine Marsh-Edwards, Martina Attile, and Maureen Blackwood. The black workshops, which also included the Black Audio Collective and Ceddo, developed out of funding support from the Labour-controlled Greater London Council, which aimed to support black cultural work, and the Workshop Declaration, an agreement between Channel 4 television and the trade union that sanctioned independent film and video on a nonprofit-making basis. The black workshops created a radical practice that contested both the dominant representations of race and the conventional cinematic approaches to those representations. The struggle over being black in Britain was not only seen to be material but it was also symbolic, and the most challenging of this cinema was formally innovative and questioning. Territories (1984), directed by Julien and produced at Sankofa, is a provocative documentary about the Notting Hill Carnival, the principal cultural event staged by the Caribbean community in Britain. The film is a barrage of experimental technique. Its juxtaposition of newly realised and archive footage, as well as its emphasis on the act of looking, introduces stylistics typical of the filmmaker.

The most significant films made by Sankofa and Julien in the 1980s were The Passion of Remembrance (1986) and Looking for Langston (1989). They share characteristics with other radical cinemas of the avant-garde: a self-conscious acknowledgment of the filmmaking process; a free and uncertain mixing of fiction and documentary; a stylistic eclecticism; and a rejection of spectatorial identification for a critical engagement with the text. The films go beyond the traditional 'race relations' agenda of documentary, wherein black filmmakers try to 'explain' themselves to white audiences, and attend to experiences within the black community. This is most apparent in The Passion of Remembrance, which seeks to represent the diversity among blacks in Britain and give voice to different black experiences, such as those of women and gay men. The film is highly stylised, offering two only partially related dramas, and this loose narrative flow is woven around documentary and archive material, the latter being subjected to a process of poetic translation. The film invites reflection on both the status of its historical imagery—problematising the notion of the past as merely a representation—and its own materiality, confirming cinema as complicit in this very process.

Julien is equally concerned to explore questions of sexuality and gender as well as race and class. Looking for Langston (1989), a 'meditation' on the black poet Langston Hughes and the Harlem renaissance in the 1920s, brings these concerns even further to the forefront. The effect of the stylised combination of varied archive sources, dramatic scenes, poetry, readings, and music has been described as 'a dream-like montage', and justified by Julien who aimed to:

> illuminate the necessary contestation which takes place over the memory, the legacy and the representation of an important cultural icon like Langston Hughes [...] to explore the possibility of having a sexual identity that many blacks would identify as a betrayal of their racial authenticity [...] and [...] to popularise [...] interesting debates [...] around the history of black literature and cultural expression.
>
> (Quoted in Hill 1999: 230)

His first feature, Young Soul Rebels (1991), funded by the BFI, while more accessible, further pursued Julien's interests in music, pleasure, politics, and desire, but it was not as successful, critically nor commercially, as many had hoped or expected.

Since then, Julien has mainly worked in television, music video, and gallery-based work. He has made Black and White in Colour: Television, Memory, Race (1992) for the BBC, which addresses the representations of race on British television from 1936 to 1992, and The Question of Equality (1995), a four-part series for US television. His gallery installations include Trussed (1996), The Conservator's Dream (1999), and Vagabondia (2000). A recurring motif of this later work is the interracial male couple, and Julien offers an intriguing and informed interplay of art historical references.

Julien's work in each form is concerned with the positioning of the spectator. The act of looking is central to his work, not least in his film Frantz Fanon: Black Skin, White Mask (1995), set during the Algerian war of liberation and where the meeting of looks is avoided as the consequence is likely to be violence. Furthermore, he explores the equivalences between the cultural forms; so, for example, the museum is featured within a number of films, videos, and installations.

ALAN BURTON

See also: Frantz Fanon: Black Skin, White Mask; Looking for Langston

Biography

Born in London, February 21, 1960. One of five children of parents who migrated to Britain from St Lucia. Studied fine art and film, Central St Martin's School of Art and Design, London. A founding member of Sankofa Film and Video Collective in 1983 and of Normal Films. Visiting lecturer at Harvard University and the Whitney Museum of American Art's Independent Study Program. Research Fellow, University of London, Goldsmith's College, and Oxford Brookes University. Trustee of Serpentine Gallery, London. Nominated for the Turner Prize in 2001 for his triple-screen The Long Road to Mazatlan.

Further reading

Bourne, Stephen, *Black in the British Frame: The Black Experience in British Film and Television*, London: Continuum, 2001.

Diawara, Manthia, 'Power and Territory: The Emergence of the Black British Film Collectives', in Lester Friedman (ed.), *British Cinema and Thatcherism*, London: UCL Press, 1993.

Hill, John, *British Cinema in the 1980s*, Oxford: Oxford University Press, 1999.

Julien, Isaac, 'In Two Worlds', *Sight and Sound*, July 1999: 33.

Mercer, K. and Drake, C., *Isaac Julien with Essays by Kobena Mercer and Chris Drake*, London: Ellipsis, 2001.

Junge, Winfried and Barbara

Winfried and Barbara Junge are best known for directing the longest running documentary film project in the world. Die Kinder von Golzow (1961–) follows the life stories of a class of pupils born between 1953 and 1955 in the village of Golzow in the easternmost part of the former German Democratic Republic (GDR): the Oderbruch. Starting in August 1961, when the wall between East and West Berlin had just been erected, the filmmakers chronicle the lives of the first generation brought up according to socialist ideals in the GDR. They film their protagonists' kindergarten and school days, exams, weddings, and award ceremonies. The thirteen six-to-seven-year-olds go on to become a painter and decorator, a cook and major, an electronic worker and FDJ (Free German Youth) functionary, a chemical worker, a carpenter, an engineer, an army officer, a truck driver, a locksmith, and a dairy hand. Like in the other less extensive, long-term documentary study named after a town in the GDR, Wittstock, by fellow DEFA filmmaker Volker Koepp, the filmmakers accompany the former GDR citizens into unemployment and reeducation after the collapse of the regime. The cycle of Die Kinder von Golzow manifests how under a change of political systems the same subjects changed in their response to documentary observation.

The first documentaries were short studies of the class, of between fourteen and thirty-six minutes' duration. These were screened in cinemas as supplements to the main films. Once the pupils left school, the course of their lives parted. Anmut sparet nicht noch Mühe (1979) was the last attempt to contain their life stories in a group portrait. With Lebensläufe—Die Geschichte der Kinder von Golzow in einzelnen Portraits (1980) the format changed to nine single portraits in one film. Through an extensive array of references interrelating various moments in time, Junge explains the history of the project and its subjects. With the filmmakers intentionally refusing to close an ongoing life story in spite of its perceived insignificance, the intricacies of selection and combination remain a problem. However, the project adheres to the confines of each family tree and blocks other potential narrative threads.

The availability of a vast amount of material permitted cuts between the same subject at different ages, and to a new generation who now play in the same sandpit. These children serve as reference points for the protagonists, but remain deliberately unknown. This meant that not only did the time represented become longer but also the duration of the single films stretched to over four hours; as the time narrated extended, so did the time of narration. Intertitles became necessary to bracket the diverse strands of narrative, as in Drehbuch: Die Zeiten (1992). From then the 'heroes' of the Golzow cycle—nicknamed 'Dallas East' by the DEFA studio—starred in their own spin-offs, often of over two hours' duration. In the course of time the narrative structure of the films continued to vary. On the whole, suspense was created by employing a forward-flowing chronological order, eliciting curiosity about what the subject would do next. In da habt ihr mein Leben. Marieluise—Kind von Golzow (1997) and in Jochen—ein Golzower aus Philadelphia (2001), the protagonists reflect in retrospect on episodes of their lives as they watch them on the video recorder.

From a Western perspective it may seem surprising that a continuous endeavour such as Die Kinder von Golzow is produced for film rather than television. When a similar venture subsequently began in Great Britain, the acclaimed 7Up (1964–) series, which follows the lives of a group of people at seven-year intervals, it was commissioned by Granada Television. Die Kinder von Golzow has been filmed on 35mm, nowadays combined with BETA video blown up to 35mm. In the GDR, as television became more important in the 1960s, the gaze of the censors shifted from film to television. The then premier of the GDR, Erich Honecker, ordered that Anmut sparet nicht noch Mühe (1979) be shown on television after he had personally approved it.

Lebensläufe—Die Geschichte der Kinder von Golzow in einzelnen Portraits (1980) was broadcast only on GDR television because it had already been bought by West German television. Documentary films could be made with more creative freedom at the DEFA, but were often shown only outside the country. Likewise, the only opportunity for GDR filmmakers to see Western documentaries was the international documentary film festival in Leipzig, where Junge came across the films of Joris Ivans, Robert Flaherty, the French cinéma vérité, the American direct cinema, the British free cinema, the Polish cinema of the 1960s, and Italian neorealism. He further recounts as his influences Dziga Vertov, Walter Ruttmann, Andrew and Annelie Thorndike, and Jürgen Böttcher.

Unlike the British 7Up series (Michael Apted, 1964–), the Golzow films are not ordered according to a structured schema of visits in seven-year intervals. The cycle intentionally relies on the filmmakers being invited by one of the protagonists and follows diverse strands of personal and public events, such as the anniversaries not only of the protagonists' first day in school, and therefore of the documentary series, but also of the GDR. The inclusion of political dates was sometimes motivated by the necessity of getting the films funded and approved. However, with the collapse of the GDR, the former state and its party, the Socialist Unity Party of Germany, had their life data chronicled in the film like a deceased protagonist would have: 'SED 1946–89'. In addition, the date of release of the films is irregular.

The idea for a long-term documentary series was conceived at the DEFA Studio for Documentary Film by Junge's superior, Karl Gass, eighteen years his senior, who felt it necessary to hand the project over to a younger man. Junge is twenty years older than his subjects. Barbara Junge has worked on the project since 1978 as an archivist, since 1983 as an editor, and since 1992 as a coauthor and codirector. Winfried Junge's voice carries the narration, but from Drehbuch: Die Zeiten (1992) onwards his wife interviews as well, if in a less provocative manner. The project had the same cameraman from 1962 to 1991, Hans-Eberhard Leupold, followed by Harald Klix from 1989. Leupold, who was a camera assistant on the first film, suggests that the creation of content is more dependent on the camera in documentary than in fiction film. Often the camera operator has to react quickly without directorial decisions, as the documentary film director cannot see the framing and the potential meaning it contains.

The camera does not only produce images, but content.

The more his subjects advanced in age, the more their encounters had to be planned in advance and the more they expected to be questioned after the event rather than observed in action. From 1978/9 their meetings became more stationary and verbal. However, rather than aspire to interviews with comprehensive answers, Junge is often found in an exchange where he says more than his curt counterparts. Even though he tries to provoke his subjects when he teases them about their weight or choice of marriage partner, his interventions are not confrontational. Western interviewees often react defensively to an interviewing strategy that aims at alienation—for instance that employed by Nick Broomfield. By contrast, Junge is provocative, but does not alienate. Questions that might be understood as malicious intrusions in a capitalist society were not perceived as such by his GDR subjects, who appear unperturbed. However, the positive responses of the GDR citizens were effectively constrained by a system that did not allow any criticism. Furthermore, Junge occasionally pursued opportunistic answers to preempt censorship and get his films approved. Pre-FRG, the series had a harmonising and entertaining, even sentimental, effect when passages without interviews were underlined with music. Nonetheless, the children of Golzow were deliberately by and large not socialist heroes.

In the 1950s GDR documentaries were made to illustrate a socialist realist fiction and reality had to comply with socialist planning (Zimmermann 1995). Documentaries about social and historical context were regarded as ideologically threatening and so invited censorship. While the representation of societal processes could be censored, the expressions on the faces of the individuals could not. By the time of the Golzow cycle, documentary film in the GDR had turned to the everyday and to 'the people'. For Junge, documentary should not be about a problem, but about a person. The former pedagogy student saw in film a didactic tool, so school children were ideal as subjects. As in other countries with state censorship, filming children was seen as ideologically uncontroversial. Junge would go on to make several other films about the lives of learners and teachers: Kinder lernen in aller Welt/Children Learn all over the World (1964), Vom lernenden Menschen/About the Learning Human Being (1964), Studentinnen—Eindrücke von einer technischen Hochschule/Students—Impressions from a Technical University (1965), his only fiction film Der Tapfere Schulschwänzer/The Brave Truant (1967), and Keine Pause für Löffler: Ein Lehrer und seine 6c/No Break for Löffler: A Teacher and His 6c (1974). Before the expansion of the Golzow project absorbed his time, Junge was further able to make documentaries on other topics—for instance, several films about Syria, Somalia, and Libya; another documentary series, this time about a pumping station (Sagen wird man über unsre Tage, 1974; Termin Spirale I, 1977; Markersbach—Energie des Wassers und des Menschen, 1981); and one about the pioneer organisation 'Ernst Thälmann': Ich bin ein Junger Pioneer/I Am a Young Pioneer (1973). The Junges visited northern England for the first part of a two-part comparison of the living conditions among working-class families in the Newcastle area, which Rostock coproduced with the Amber group (From Marx and Engels to Marks and Spencer, 1987/88). Winfried Junge has made over fifty documentaries altogether.

After the first film the filmmakers renounced the ostensibly 'hidden camera'. For Wenn ich erst zur Schule geh (1961) the film team looked into the class through the windows from outside, but the pupils were obviously under full 35mm lighting. This method was dismissed as it created distance and was not likely to cultivate trust. Junge has described his approach to documentary filmmaking with a phrase merging ethics and aesthetics: 'aesthetics of trust' (Zimmermann 1995). The ethics of filmmaking is affected by the temporal dimension. Due to the longevity of the cycle it could not rely on the usual 'smash-and-grab' approach of short-term filmmaking. As staging and role-playing cannot usually be sustained over a longer period of time and thus would be noticeable, performance is at odds with any long-term observation. Furthermore the director of the film and the director of the school declined official offers to supply the school with better performers in the shape of exemplary teachers. The sample had to be ordinary. As the project has spanned over forty years and more than two generations, Junge claims that it has more influence in life than in art.

The filmmaker is protective of his subjects and left out compromising rushes from the films.

In a society guided by the concept of the collective—an artificial family of sorts—the Junges and their protagonists compared their relationship to that of relatives. After all, those filmed had known their filmmakers since kindergarten. The title Die Kinder von Golzow/The Children of Golzow is thus a particularly powerful metaphor. Whereas Western documentary saw a subjective and deconstructive reaction against an overly 'objective' and impersonal observational mode, in the GDR the subject had to carry the burden of objectivity. In a Marxist society, 'history from below' meant that the working class was to lead the society. The model citizen in the workers' and peasants' state came from below, not from above. This contrasts with the notion of the marginalized populace at the bottom of a capitalist society, who eventually had their voices heard in 'minor' documentaries or through identity politics. Moreover, GDR private life was organised by the state and, like the one-party system, filming was for all: 'We all make a film about our class together with the DEFA.' After unification, the social philosophy changed from the particular as an expression of the general in the GDR to the singular as an expression of difference in the FRG. Speaking against documentary as a deductive methodology, and by implication through his actual works, Junge argues for the singularity of his subjects and allows entrusting the viewer to make of this something universal.

After the fall of the Iron Curtain and with the new rise of the 'self', the chronicle became self-reflexive. When the protagonists became Western subjects, the idea of performing a self emerged and even their names are 'privatised'. In the credits of Drehbuch: Die Zeiten (1992) they 'act' as themselves with their full names given as their 'real' identity and their first names as their character names: 'Dieter Finger as Dieter'. Persistently the protagonists are asked why they still want to continue, how the filmmaking influences them, and if they would like to ask the filmmakers questions too. We eventually see the filmmaker while we hear his dry reflections about himself and about the form and methodology of the films: 'This film has a commentary. I know this can cost him sympathy.' He reflects on the staging in the former films: 'Winfried puts his hand up exceptionally often because he has got the microphone round his neck.' He comments on the deception of appearances: 'Gudrun is not as self-confident as she wants to look.' He continues to reveal reconstructions either by showing the repeated efforts of the protagonists at getting to act as themselves or by laying bare the device through his dead-pan comments: 'We reconstruct a scene which happened like this a few minutes before.' Insight into the stagings of the GDR government are given when the film reveals how Golzow had to pretend it was a different town for a visit of the premier of North Korea at the time, Kim Il Sung.

With unification, not only did the project become self-reflexive, but its protagonists became self-conscious. After conversion from state socialism to democracy, the protagonists are uniquely reminded of their existence as GDR citizens. However, this traceability is a burden like an open Staasi file. The historical subjects of Golzow cannot deny their GDR past as so many others did, as Barbara Junge acknowledged (Kunath 1993). As GDR subjects, some of the children of Golzow were as untroubled about their careers as they were by their images on film. After unification, their fear of repercussions rose. What was rewarded under one system was punished by the next. Their affirmations under the eye of state censorship were replaced by fear that a company superior might see them. Whereas some children in the 7Up series acted as grown-ups, in the Golzow cycle what had been fully trained and employed adults under one system became learners again under the next. Their old certificates were not acknowledged and most became unemployed. Many were trained in endless reeducation programmes and taught that self-realization and motivation is everything. Reasons were individualised as well. Barbara Junge witnessed the loss of government approval that guaranteed a positive image as causing a retreat into the private; or as Winfried Junge phrased it: 'The new situation closes mouths in a different way' (Richter 1993). Thus for several reasons the reactions of the children of Golzow changed after unification of the two Germanies. The last documentary of this potentially infinite chronicle has the title Und wenn sie nicht gestorben sind … Die Kinder von Golzow—Das Ende der unendlichen Geschichte/And If they Did Not Die … The Children of Golzow—The End of Infinite History (2006).

SILKE PANSE

Biography: Winfried Junge

Born Prenzlauer Berg, Berlin, Germany, July 29, 1935. A-Levels, 1953. Pedagogic faculty of the Humboldt Universität Berlin, reading German literary studies without graduating, 1953–4. Graduate of the German Film Academy, Potsdam-Babelsberg, 1958. Film journalist for the student magazine *Forum*, 1955–61. Dramatic adviser and assistant director for Karl Gass at the DEFA Studio for Popular Science Films, 1958–61. Director at the DEFA Studio for Documentary Films, 1961–91. Director at JOURNAL Film Klaus Volkenborn KG, from 1994 with ájour film and television, 1991–. Married Barbara Becher, 1968. Deputy chairman of the documentary film and television communications section of the Association of Film and Television Workers of the GDR, 1979–90. Member of the Executive Committee of the Association of Film and Television Workers of the GDR. President of the National Documentary and Short Film Festival of the GDR for Cinema and Television, 1985–87. Vice-President of the International Documentary Film Festival Leipzig, 1990. Member of the Academy of Fine Arts Berlin-Brandenburg, 1996–. Opened a permanent exhibition about Die Kinder von Golzow, Golzow, Germany, 2000.

Biography: Barbara Junge

Born in Neunhofen, Thüringen, Germany, November 14, 1943. Graduate of the Karl-Marx-University, Leipzig, as an English and Russian translator. First in charge of foreign-language translations, later archivist, editor, co-author, and codirector at the DEFA Studio for Documentary Films, 1969–91. Married Winfried Junge, 1968. Co-director at JOURNAL Film Klaus Volkenborn KG, from 1994 with ájour film and television, 1991–. Member of the Academy of Fine Arts Berlin-Brandenburg, 1996–.

Selected films

1961 Wenn ich erst zur Schule geh (Some Day, When I Go to School/When I Finally Go to School)
1962 Nach einem Jahr (One Year Later/ Observations in a First Class)
1966 Elf Jahre alt (Eleven Years Old)
1969 Wenn man vierzehn ist/When You Are Fourteen
1971 Die Prüfung/The Exam
1975 Ich sprach mit einem Mädchen/I Talked to a Girl
1979 Anmut sparet nicht noch Mühe/Spare No Charm and Spare No Passion
1980 Lebensläufe—Die Geschichte der Kinder von Golzow in einzelnen Portraits/Biographies—The Story of the Children of Golzow
1984 Diese Golzower—Umstandsbestimmungen eines Ortes/These People of Golzow—Analysis of the Circumstances of a Place
1992 Drehbuch: Die Zeiten/Screenplay: The Times
1994 Das Leben des Jürgen von Golzow/ Jürgen of Golzow: His Life/The Life of Jürgen from Golzow
1995 Die Geschichte vom Onkel Willy aus Golzow/The Story of Uncle Willy from Golzow
1996 Was geht euch mein Leben an. Elke—Kind von Golzow/My Life is My Own Affair. Elke—Child of Golzow
1997 Da habt Ihr mein Leben. Marieluise—Kind von Golzow/I'll Show You My Life. Marieluise—Child of Golzow
1998 Brigitte und Marcel—Golzower Lebenswege/Brigitte and Marcel—Lifestyles of Golzow
1999 Ein Mensch wie Dieter—Golzower/A Guy Like Dieter—Native of Golzow
2001 Jochen—ein Golzower aus Philadelphia/ Jochen—A Golzower from Philadelphia
2003 Eigentlich wollte ich Förster werden—Bernd aus Golzow/Actually I Wanted to Be a Forrester—Bernd from Golzow
2006 Und wenn sie nicht gestorben sind … Die Kinder von Golzow—Das Ende der unendlichen Geschichte/And If They Did Not Die … The Children of Golzow—The End of Infinite History

Further reading

Alter, Nora, 'Epilogue. History in the Making: The Children of Golzow Project', in Nora Alter (ed.), *Projecting History. German Nonfiction Cinema, 1967–2000*, Ann Arbor, MI: The University of Michigan Press, 2002: 195–210.

Byg, Barton, 'GDR-Up: The Ideology of Universality in Long Term Documentary', *New German Critique*, no. 82, winter, 2001.

Eiffler, Ulrich and Halbhuber, Dietmar, 'Lebensläufe. Interview mit Winfried Junge und Hans-Eberhard Leupold', Forum, no. 21, November 1, 1981: 14.

Jordan, Günther and Schenk, Ralf (eds), *Schwarzweiss und Farbe. DEFA-Dokumentarfilme 1946–92*, Berlin: Filmmuseum Potsdam & Jovis Verlagsbüro Berlin, 2000.

Junge, Winfried, 'Papier und Realität', *Deutsche Filmkunst*, no. 11, 1962: 431–2, 441.

——'Enthüllungen des Besonderen', *Sonntag*, no. 7, February 13, 1972.

——'Drehbuch: Das Leben. Die Geschichte der Kinder von Golzow als Zeitdokument', *Film und Fernsehen*, no. 8, 1979: 4–8.

——'Der Widersprüchliche Mensch (Parts 1–3)', *Film und Fernsehen*, no. 11, 1981: 3–9 (also no. 1, 1982: 11–14; no. 2, 1982: 20–4).

——'Vom Wollen, Können, Dürfen, Müssen. Versuch einer Umstandsbestimmung des dokumentaren Films', *Film und Fernsehen*, no. 5, 1983: 11–13.

——'Besuch bei Joris Ivens', *Film und Fernsehen*, no. 12, 1986: 28–9.

——'Erfahrungen anderer Art', *Film und Fernsehen*, no. 10, 1989: 6–10.

——'Aesthetik des Vertrauens', in Peter Zimmerman (ed.), *Deutschlandbilder Ost: Dokumentarfilme der DEFA von der Nachkriegszeit bis zur Wiedervereinigung*, Konstanz: UVK-Medien/Olschläger, 1995: 133–45.

Junge, Winfried and Junge, Barbara, *Lebenslaufe—Die Kinder von Golzow. Bilder—Dokumente—Erinnerungen zur altesten Langzeitbeobachtung der Filmgeschichte*, Marburg: Schuren-Verlag, 2004.

Kunath, Sylke, 'Der längste Dokumentarfilm der Welt', *Der Tagesspiegel*, August 30, 1993.

Richter, Erika, 'Drehbuch: Die Zeiten', in *23. Internationales Forum des jungen Films Berlin*, Berlin: Internationales Forum des jungen Films/Freunde der deutschen Kinemathek, 1993.

——'Die Geschichte vom Onkel Willy aus Golzow', in *26. Internationales Forum des jungen Films Berlin*, Berlin: Internationales Forum des jungen Films/Freunde der deutschen Kinemathek, 1996.

——'Da habt Ihr mein Leben. Marieluise—Kind von Golzow', in *27. Internationales Forum des jungen Films Berlin*, Berlin: Internationales Forum des jungen Films/Freunde der deutschen Kinemathek, 1997.

Voigt, Jutta, 'Eins plus eins. Winfried Junge und Hans-Eberhard Leupold im Gespräch', *Sonntag*, no. 47, 1981: 5.

Zimmermann, Peter (ed.), *Deutschlandbilder Ost: Dokumentarfilme der DEFA von der Nachkriegszeit bis zur Wiedervereinigung*, Konstanz: UVK-Medien/Olschläger, 1995.

Junghans, Carl

Although Carl Junghans's fame rests solely on his 1929 feature So ist das Leben, on a closer look his actual significance in film history is in the field of the so-called compilation films that were abundant with leftist filmmaking during the Weimar Republic. The films Junghans made for the Communist Party were compiled from various preexisting sources, to which he rearranged and added numerous intertitles, thus giving the films a rather didactical appearance. These films served immediate purposes (elections, rallies, etc.) and usually did not have a long exhibition.

The style of Junghans's compilations changed with the advent of sound. Drawing on American newsreel material, he experimented for his Kamera Reporter rast durch New York (1930) on the textual discrepancies between images and sounds. Later on, he would do away with verbal commentaries altogether. His first attempt at a purely visual sound film, Fliehende Schatten (1932), was compromised by the addition of a fictional frame story that led to Junghans's withdrawal from the project, maintaining that he was solely responsible for the documentary footage shot in Africa.

His 1936 account of the Winter Olympiad, Jugend der Welt, for which he was in charge of the entire editing, deviates largely from a newsreel-like report, thus not covering the events chronologically, but rather grouping images in visual associations. Moreover, the film does not have any verbal or written commentary. The result is a 'symphonic poem', as he referred to it, tipping his hat to Ruttmann's Berlin: The Symphony of a Great City. Jugend der Welt, when compared to Riefenstahl's Olympia, is often seen as being less reverend to the Nazi elites. Also, Junghans showed images of defeat and failure, contradicting the notion of heroism, which would later signify Riefenstahl's film. Despite Goebbels's reservations, the film achieved worldwide distribution to great acclaim. At the Venice Film Festival it was awarded the Cup of the Luce Institute for Best Documentary.

Although he once again pulled out of Geissel der Welt, which was meant to support Franco's rebellion against the Spanish government, the final version still carried Junghans's concept: idyllic Spain, the uprising of the Popular Front, then the reinstallment of order by Franco.

Jahre der Entscheidung was to be an homage to the Nazis' rise to power. Once again, Junghans planned to make a 'symphonic film' that would appeal more to the audiences' emotions than to their reason. Delays in the finishing of the film, brought about by official interventions, plus the 'falling from grace'—his communist past kept being a burden for Junghans—caused the cancellation of his contract. The final version of the film did not mention his name in the credits.

Junghans was an exile by then, struggling to find new assignments. In the United States he turned to color photography in which he preferred documentary styles, foregoing artificial lighting, flash, and so on. His new interest in American Indian culture led him to make two documentaries: one on a healing ceremony presented by a Navajo medicine man, Sand Paintings (1947), and the other on the living conditions of southwestern Pueblo Indians, Monuments of the Past (1947). Both are, as Thomas Tode suggests, indicators of Junghans's late interest in spirituality.

ULI JUNG

Biography

Born on October 7, 1897, in Dresden, the son of a tailor. His early interest in music led him to become a pianist in a Dresden movie house when he was only ten years old. Working as an extra, film critic, and editor, he eventually made his first film, Der Cowboy im Wedding (1925), an advertising film for the trade unions. By this time he had already joined the Communist Party. Keeping up work with the accommodation of foreign films for the German market and designing advertising films for the KPD, he eventually managed to find the funding for his long-held project, So ist das Leben (1929), the film that would secure him his place in film history.

After 1933 Junghans was banned from work for some time before he was assigned to the film of the 1936 winter Olympiad, Jugend der Welt, which heralded the beginning of a long series of official assignments by the Nazi state or party. In 1938 Junghans was hired by the UFA, where he made Altes Herz geht auf Reisen (1939), an adaptation of Hans Fallada's novel of the same title. This film was banned because some parts contradicted official Nazi attitudes. Junghans left Germany for the United States, where he made only two documentary shorts on the life of the Navajos and otherwise turned to still photography. Upon his return to Germany in 1963, he supplied his So ist das Leben with a soundtrack. In the 1970s he made public appearances at festivals and the like and traveled extensively to Africa. He died on November 8, 1984, in Munich.

Selected films

1925	Der Cowboy im Wedding
1927/8	Lenin 1905–28/Der Weg zum Siege
1928	Weltwende. Zehn Jahre Republik—Zehn Jahre Sowjetunion
1928	Was wollen die Kommunisten?
1928	Rote Pfingsten/Rote Pfingsten 1928/Roter Frontkämpferbund 4. Reichstreffen in Berlin am 27. Mai 1928
1929/30	So ist das Leben (feature film)
1930	Tonfilmconference
1930	Kamera-Reporter rast durch New York/Amerika, du hast es besser
1932	Fliehende Schatten
1936	Jugend der Welt
1936	Die Geissel der Welt (Kampf in Spanien)
1938	Altes Herz geht auf die Reise (feature film)
1939	Jahre der Entscheidung
1939	Helden in Spanien/España heroica/Arriba España
1947	Sand Paintings (USA)
1947	Monuments of the Past (USA)
c.a. 1965/1971	Kärnten in vier Jahreszeiten/Die vier Jahreszeiten

Further reading

Hanisch, Michael, *Carl Junghans—Biographie eines Außenseiters*, *Prisma*, Nr. 11, Berlin/DDR: Henschel, 1980: 257–85.

Hoffman, Hilmar, 'Jugend der Welt', in *H.H. Mythos Olympia: Autonomie und Unterwerfung von Sport und Kultur*, Berlin/Weimar: Aufbau 1993: 87–92.

Tode, Thomas, entry and essay on 'Carl Junghans', in Hans Michael Bock (ed.), *CineGraph: Lexikon zum deutschsprachigen Film*, Munich: edition text + kritik, 1984.

K

Kamei, Fumio

Kamei Fumio's innovative editing and composition and bluntly political postwar documentaries changed filmmaking in Japan from the 1930s into the 1960s. Acknowledged within his own country as the central figure in the history of Japanese documentary filmmaking, Kamei is less well known outside of Japan. His ability to push the boundaries of conventional form as a film editor led to a key part for him in creating the role of director within the wartime studio system at a time when the authorship of documentaries was being contested.

The two years that Kamei spent immersed in Leningrad's film culture (1929–31) in tandem with his initiation into the Japanese film world at a time of rising cultural nationalism and brutal colonial expansion proved a difficult mix that led to a year spent in prison in 1941–2 and the subsequent curtailment of his filmmaking activities until the end of the war. His first postwar filmmaking endeavor, a compilation film made with Iwasaki Akira (a leading film critic and former head of Prokino, the Japan Proletariat Film League) called Nihon no higeki/A Japanese Tragedy (1946) was so critical of the wartime regime that American Occupation authorities, probably at the behest of Japan's then Prime Minister Yoshida Shigeru, would not allow its release. That film contains a controversial dissolve in which the Showa Emperor transforms from full military garb into a suit and tie-clad everyman. The suggestion in this sequence that the Emperor was actively behind Japan's wartime military malevolence was sacrosanct to conservative forces.

In the postwar period, Kamei has been associated with a persistent myth that casts him as Japan's only anti-war wartime filmmaker, but the truth is considerably more complex. Although Kamei's airing of discontent with the war may not make him an all-out resister, his wartime films do represent a boldly innovative negotiation with a severe if inconsistent censorship apparatus. Kamei virtually dissected wartime conventions in his 1939 film Tatakau heitai/Fighting Soldiers while simultaneously producing them. In 1938, while employed by Toho Film's Culture Film Section, Kamei agreed to edit footage of the Japanese march to Shanghai that other Toho filmmakers thought was too bleak to pass muster with the film world and military authorities. The result, Shanghai (1938), was a perfection of long-form documentary that found box office success and also met with critical acclaim. His next film, Peking (1938), made charmingly lyrical use of both synchronized and non-synchronized sound. The film, rediscovered in 1997, includes an extended traveling shot down a vibrant market street matched to a masterful montage of the exoticized sounds of local commerce.

That same year, Kamei was sent to China for four months with cinematographer Miki Shigeru and a film crew to make the army-sponsored film, Fighting Soldiers, about the Japanese advance to Wuhan. In one regard Fighting Soldiers must be understood in the context of the writing of Hino Ashihei, the popular chronicler of the daily lives of ordinary Japanese soldiers in China in the late 1930s. Hino is the lead expositor of a documentary literature whose reportage style shares definite resonances with socialist realist literature from the previous decade. However, when human-scale heroes whose toils were so captivating on the page were shown on the screen, and when the images projected were those of real fighting soldiers, it was too much for the military sponsors of the work to tolerate.

The completed work was shelved by Toho and not seen publicly until after its rediscovery in 1975.

Fighting Soldiers has no narration. It is as easy to see what is so compelling about this film as it is to understand what the Army found so objectionable. An extreme close-up of the distraught face of a Chinese peasant whose house is in flames, a cavalry pack animal lingering and then toppling, having succumbed to some battlefield hazard, Japanese infantry shown by a roadside in such a state of exhausted slumber as to look like corpses—these images are stitched together in such a way that they recall the controlled montage theories of Pudovkin and convey very plausibly the sense of how unpleasant the 'daily-ness' of war is for the people who fight it as well as those noncombatants who are victimized by it.

When he bent the framework for sponsored filmmaking in his three commissioned tourism films in 1940 and 1941, Kamei prefigured the creative interpretation of the limits of public relations filmmaking that was to take place at Iwanami Productions two and three decades later, an experience that would give rise to independent, socially engaged filmmaking in the 1960s. Fighting Soldiers was cited two years later as an example of Kamei's proclivity to inculcate dialectical materialism into his films, a charge supposedly substantiated by time that Kamei spent studying film and art in the Soviet Union and by his depictions of peasants in Kobayashi Issa (1941). That film, ostensibly a piece commissioned by local officials in Nagano Prefecture to promote tourism to the area, integrated the haiku of eighteenth-century ascetic poet Kobayashi to create an historically contextualized and compelling caricature of the people, their struggle to eke out a livelihood in farming and sericulture. In the margins of the beautifully shot 35mm film are the wealthy tourists, who enjoy the rugged beauty of the harsh landscapes, and rich pilgrims, who are patronizing a large temple complex and then vying to become, like Yasukuni Shrine in Tokyo, a repository for the souls of Japan's war dead. Critics at the time described Kobayashi Issa as a cine-poem. The Ministry of Education refused to certify the film as a *bunka eiga*, or culture film, but the studio used this refusal to tease audiences into seeing a supposedly controversial film.

Throughout his filmmaking career, Kamei's willingness to break with convention in big and small ways would repeatedly place him at the center of one controversy after another. His wartime filmmaking has consistently drawn more attention than his two and a half very active postwar decades. In fact, the political films made after 1945 have proven to be as influential on other filmmakers as his wartime films. Making Sunagawa no hitobito: kichi hantai tosô no kiroku/The People of Sunagawa: A Record of the Struggle Against the Military Base (1955), Sunagawa no hitobito: mugi shinazu/The People of Sunagawa: Wheat Will Never Die (1955), and Ryuketsu no kiroku: Sunagawa/Record of Blood: Sunagawa (1956), a trilogy of protest films about the struggle to forestall the expansion of an American air base in post-occupation Japan, led Kamei and his crew to spend a great deal of time with their filmic subjects and ultimately to depict their struggle from the insider perspective of the protestors. This lesson was absorbed by Tsuchimoto Noriaki, Ogawa Shinsuke, and Hani Susumu, who would commit themselves to their own subjects in much the same way a few years later.

Another well-regarded filmmaker (and artist), Teshigahara Hiroshi worked on two of the Sunagawa films as well as several of Kamei's films about atomic bomb blast survivors. Indeed, Kamei was the leading filmmaker of record for the nascent anti-nuclear movement in Japan in the 1950s. Beginning with Ikiteite yokkata/Still It's Good to Live (1956), he made five films that documented the aftereffects of radiation, demonstrated the limits of government support afforded those who had been exposed to radiation at Nagasaki and Hiroshima, and showed the organizing activities of victims and their supporters. He was also the first documentarian to take up the highly volatile issue of discrimination against Japan's so-called Buraku people by making a film about one such community in Osaka in 1960.

Throughout his career, Kamei showed a capacity to find inspiration in and borrow from unlikely spheres. In the late 1930s he successfully integrated montage theory into the process of making a war record film with Fighting Soldiers. In the postwar period, he was the first in Japan to attempt filmic forays into the then raging debates on *shutaisei* (subjectivity) in his Sunagawa films. These achievements earned him a claim to being among the world's least known but most accomplished documentary filmmakers.

JEFFREY ISAACS

Biography

Born on April 1, 1908 into a locally prominent Catholic family in Fukushima Prefecture, Japan. Left his studies in fine arts at Bunka Gakuin in Tokyo in 1928 to go to the Soviet Union the following year to study art. Soon began studying film as an auditor at what became in 1931 the Leningrad Institute of Cinema Engineers (LIKI), during which time he was influenced by Grigori Kozintsev, Sergei Yutkevich, and Fridrikh Ermler. Became ill with tuberculosis, prompting his sudden return to Japan in 1931. In 1933 entered Photo Chemical Laboratory (later PCL and then, in 1937, Toho.) At PCL and Toho in the Culture Film Section, distinguished himself as an editor, scenario writer, and then director of documentaries. Arrested in October 1941 and charged with inculcating Komintern ideals into films, spent just under a year in detention and was released on probation in August 1942. Was a leader in the Toho labor disputes in 1947–8. Directed or codirected five feature films from 1947 to 1953. Began producing independent documentaries in 1953 establishing Japan Document Film in 1955. Opened an antique shop in Shibuya and continued to make occasional public relations films for corporate clients during the 1980s. Returned to engaged filmmaking with two ecologically concerned films in the 1980s. Died February 27, 1987 in Itabashi, Tokyo.

Selected films

1937 Dottô o kette/Through the Angry Waves: composition and editing
1938 Shanghai: composition and editing
1938 Peking: composition and editing
1939 Tatakau Heitai/Fighting Soldiers: director
1940 Ina bushi/A Song of Ina: director
1941 Kobayashi Issa: director
1945 Seiku/Security of the Skies: story
1946 Nihonnohigeki/A Japanese Tragedy: director
1953 Kichi no kotachi/Children of the Base: director
1955 Sunagawa no hitobito: kichi hantai tosô no kiroku/The People of Sunagawa: A Record of the Struggle Against the Base: director
1955 Sunagawa no hitobito: mugi shinazu/The People of Sunagawa: Wheat Will Never Die: director
1956 Ikiteite yokkata/Still It's Good to Live: director
1956 Ryuketsu no kiroku: Sunagawa/Record of Blood: Sunagawa: director
1957 Sekai wa kyôfu suru: shi no hai no shôtai/The World Is Terrified: The True Nature of the 'Ash of Death': director
1958 Araumi ni ikiru: maguro gyomin no seitai/Living in Rough Seas: The Lives of Tuna Fishermen: director
1958 Hato wa habataku/Fluttering Pigeons: director
1959 Hiroshima no koe/Voice of Hiroshima: director
1960 Ningen mina kyodai: buraku sabetsu no kiroku/All People Are Brothers: A Record of Discrimination in the Buraku: director
1961 Gunbi naki sekai o/Toward a World Without Armaments: director
1984 Minna ikinakereba naranai: hito, mushi, tori, nôji minzoku-kan/All Must Live: People, Insects and Birds: director
1987 Seibutsu mina tomodachi: tori, mushi, sakana no komori uta/All Living Things Are Friends: Lullabies of Birds, Insects, and Fish: director

Further reading

High, Peter B., *The Imperial Screen: Japanese Film Culture in the Fifteen Years War, 1931–45*, Madison, WI: The University of Wisconsin Press, 2003.

Hirano Kyoko, *Mr Smith Goes to Tokyo: Japanese Cinema Under the American Occupation, 1945–52*, Washington, DC: Smithsonian Institution Press, 1992.

Kamei Fumio, *Tatakau eiga: dokyumentarisuto no showashi* (Fighting Films: A Documentarist's History of the Showa Era), Tokyo: Iwanami Shoten, 1989.

n.a., 'Documentarists of Japan, No. 6: Kamei Fumio', introduction by Makino Mamoru, trans. A.A. Gerow, Documentary Box No. 6, Tokyo: Yamagata International Documentary Film Festival Organizing Committee, March, 1995, www.city.yamagata.yamagata.jp/yidff/docbox/6/box6-2-e.html

Nornes, Abé Mark, *Japanese Documentary Film: The Meiji Era Through Hiroshima*, Minneapolis, MN: University of Minnesota Press, 2003.

Tsuchimoto Noriaki, 'Kamei Fumio: Shanhai kara Tatakau Heitai made' (Kamei Fumio: From Shanghai to Fighting Soldiers), in Imamura Shôhei, Satô Tadao, Shindô Kaneto, Tsurumi Shunsuke and Yamada Yôji (eds), *Kôza Nihon Eiga* no. 5, (seminar in Japanese Cinema no. 5), Tokyo: Iwanami Shoten, 1987.

Tsuzuki Masaaki, *Tori ni natta ningen: hankotsu no eiga kantoku—Kamei Fumio no shôgai* (The Human that Became a Bird: The Life of Rebellious Film Director Kamei Fumio), Tokyo: Kôdansha, 1992.

Yasui Yoshio (ed.), *Kamei Fumio Retrospective*, Tokyo and Osaka: Amagata International Documentary Film Festival Organizing Committee Tokyo Office and Planet Bibliotéque de Cinema, 2001.

Karlin, Marc

Marc Karlin was a singular figure in British documentary over the last thirty years of the twentieth century, on two counts: his political commitment and his innovative approach to documentary aesthetics, two facets of his work that he himself saw as a unity and that remained constant, even in the 1990s when these things were no longer fashionable.

Karlin's earliest work grew out of the political and aesthetic ferment of the 1960s. The child of a family of Russian-Jewish origin who grew up in Paris, he was sent to school in England and then attended the Central School of Speech and Drama in London, where he had his first taste of student militancy. He joined the Stop It Committee, formed by Americans in Britain against the war in Vietnam, and at the same time opted for film instead of theatre; his first two films were about an American deserter. For the second of them he had to go Paris, where he had just started editing when the events of May 1968 took place, and he found himself swept up in the political ferment. As a result, he met Chris Marker, who would deeply influence his aesthetics, and with whom he would later collaborate, preparing the English versions of The Train Rolls On and The Grin Without a Cat.

Returning to England, Karlin first joined Cinema Action, a London-based collective of political filmmakers, and then, seeking a different way of working, formed the Berwick Street Film Collective. The group's first major production, Nightcleaners, completed in 1975 (with a sequel, The Seven Dreams of Myrtle, a year later), began as a solidarity film for the campaign to unionise office nightcleaners but turned into a complex, exploratory, and (especially within the women's liberation movement) highly controversial essay on representation. Instead of documenting events, the film presents fragments of these events, often cut off quite arbitrarily, repeated, or interrupted by a blank screen, with similar incongruities on the soundtrack. This experimental aesthetic has the effect of emphasising what is normally suppressed in conventional styles of documentary, including the distance between the lived experience of those who are being filmed and those who are doing the filming. In this case, it also highlights the distance between the middle-class women of the women's liberation movement and the working women they were trying to organise. The intention was to challenge the viewer's normal passivity in front of the screen, but it is also a hallmark of Karlin's approach, in all his subsequent work, to question from within the doxa of the left—the pieces of conventional wisdom that are used to hide the internal contradictions of leftist thinking. Because of this combination of experimental aesthetics and political questioning from within, Karlin has been described as 'a film-maker's film-maker and a leftist's leftist' (Ellis 1999).

Given this political orientation, it is remarkable that Karlin became one of the first independent filmmakers of his generation to find a space for his work on television. For Memory, which was shot in the late 1970s as a coproduction of the British Film Institute (BFI) and BBC2 but was not screened until 1982, explored: (1) how memory is preserved and handed down in such a way that socialist history is excluded from the prevailing culture; and (2) the efforts that serve to record and hand down working-class history. The film moves from the memories of concentration camp survivors to sufferers from Alzheimer's, by way of episodes about the Levellers, the Battle of Cable Street, and the miners of Clay Cross, set against an imaginary city of the future built out of architects' models, where the past becomes ever more elusive. In two films for Channel 4, Utopias (1987) and Between Times (1993), Karlin extended this examination of the fragility of socialist dreams, attempting to understand the fundamental shifts that had occurred within the labour movement and the left in the long period of Conservative rule.

Karlin also searched out sources for alternative visions of socialism. A series of four films about the Nicaraguan revolution, shown on Channel 4 in 1985, examined the dilemmas of putting socialism into practice. Rigorously avoiding the conventions either of television reportage or of the solidarity film, these films puzzled many viewers. His omitting to portray the Sandinista leadership earned Karlin the displeasure of both the Nicaraguan authorities and the Nicaragua Solidarity Campaign. Nevertheless, he returned to make Scenes from a Revolution (Channel 4, 1990) just before the elections in which the Sandinistas were defeated.

His last two major completed films, The Outrage (1995) for BBC2, and The Serpent (1997) for Channel 4, show his aesthetic adopting a lighter touch and moving in new directions. The former is almost an anomaly in Karlin's work, an 'arts documentary', in which a thinly fictionalised offscreen voice tries to understand the puzzling work of the American painter Cy Twombly. In the latter, another thinly fictionalised character, this time on screen, becomes obsessed by Rupert Murdoch and sets out, Don Quixote-like, to resist him as much as he can. At the time of his untimely death, he was working on a typically quirky fiction film for BBC2 entitled Milton (The Man Who Read Paradise Lost Once Too Often).

Karlin played a leading role in independent film culture. He was involved in setting up the Independent Film-makers' Association (IFA) in 1974, in the independent distributor-exhibitor The Other Cinema, and in the Channel 4 Group, which helped to determine the shape of the new television channel as a public service broadcaster with a commitment to independent production. Through the film journal *Vertigo*, founded in 1993 (www.vertigomagazine.co.uk), he helped to hew out a critical space for radical films. Less visibly, he provided endless cooperative support to colleagues through advice and technical facilities.

MICHAEL CHANAN

See also: Marker, Chris

Biography

Born 1943 in Paris; studied at the Central School of Speech and Drama, London. Joined Cinema Action in 1969, and a year later formed the Berwick Street Film Collective with Richard Mordaunt, James Scott, and Humphrey Trevelyan. Active in the Independent Filmmakers' Association and The Other Cinema in the 1970s and helped to found *Vertigo* magazine in 1993. Died in London in 1999.

Selected films

1975 Nightcleaners
1982 For Memory
1984 A Voyage of Discovery
1987 Utopias
1990 Scenes from a Revolution
1993 Between Times
1995 The Outrage
1997 The Serpent

Further reading

Ellis, John, 'Conscience of Radicals', *The Guardian*, January 25, 1999.

Johnston, Claire, 'The Nightcleaners Part 1', in Margaret Dickinson (ed.), *Rogue Reels, Oppositional Film in Britain, 1945–90*, London: BFI, 1999.

Karlin, Marc, 'Making Images Explode', in Sheila Rowbotham and Huw Beynon (eds), *Looking at Class, Film, Television and the Working Class in Britain*, London: Rivers Oram Press, 2001.

——'A Passion for Images', transcript of an interview with Patrick Wright (BBC Radio 3, February 2, 1999), *Vertigo*, 1, no. 9, 1999.

Karmen, Roman

Although Roman Karmen has a good number of films to his credit as a director, his primary claim to a place in the history of cinema is as the exemplar of a particular type of cinematographer: the newsreel correspondent, Soviet style. Karmen's name is closely associated with war reportage in Spain, China, and Vietnam and is also known for his work during World War II.

The footage he shot during the year he spent in Spain was used not only for a series of newsreels for home consumption in the USSR, but also in documentaries for foreign distribution with titles such as In Defence of Madrid (1936). The same material was quickly incorporated into other films produced elsewhere in solidarity with the Republicans, including the compilations put together in Paris by Buñuel and in New York by Helen van Dongen. Many years later Karmen's images would reappear in Frédéric

Rossif's documentary To Die in Madrid (1963). Karmen is thus the author of many of the best-known icons of antifascist struggle in the 1930s.

Karmen was born in Odessa in 1906. His father was a popular writer who was killed by the White Guards during the Civil War. The income from the publication of a book of his father's writings allowed the family to move to Moscow, where the boy set about studying photography and got a job with the magazine *Ogoniok*, one of a series of illustrated journals that published the work of the new Soviet school of photography of the 1920s. Karmen's work appeared in practically all of them over the next few years, including *Tridtsat Dniei*, where he published a series of photo-documentaries on students, fashion, an automobile factory, and other topics, and which anticipated his later practice as a cinematographer in building up a sequence of shots around the subject he was filming, each shot composed on the move with an expert eye. Nor, as he puts it in his autobiography, did he escape the influence of Rodchenko, and some of his work was published in *Lef* in 1927. Two years later he entered the Moscow film school, stimulated by documentaries such as Vladimir Erofeyev's Towards a Happy Haven (1930), the cinematography of its cameraman Yuri Stillianudis, and the early films of Joris Ivens, who made his first visit to Russia at this time.

Karmen's first break was an invitation to work with Erofeyev on a film in Central Asia as second cameraman, which also gave him his first experience of sound filming. He became an early enthusiast of filming in sound—although in Spain, where he was sent in August 1936, he was to shoot without sound. Karmen's time in Spain overlapped with that of both Joris Ivens, who was filming The Spanish Earth with his cameraman John Ferno, and Ivor Montagu, who brought Norman McLaren as his cameraman to film The Defence of Madrid. However, whereas Ivens and Montagu, with their meager funds, had to come and go as quickly as possible, Karmen's role as a newsreel correspondent allowed him to stay in Spain for a year, and inevitably he conceived the idea of a long documentary of his own. In the end the project was realized by Esfir Shub under the title España; it was released in 1939, four months after the end of the Civil War. This film incorporated additional material from other sources and carried a tendentious commentary enshrining the official Soviet version of the Civil War, but the combination of Karmen's cinematography and Shub's skills as an editor gives the film enormous visual impact. Thirty years later Karmen returned to Spain to make his own retrospective documentary on Spain, Granada, My Granada (1967).

By the time España came out, Karmen had left for another tour of war duty on the other side of the world, to film the Chinese struggle against the Japanese invasion. When the Nazis finally launched their attack on the Soviet Union in 1941 Karmen already had two wars behind him, and he spent the next four years in the thick of it, filming the battles at the gates of Moscow, the siege of Leningrad, and the fighting at Stalingrad. This time Karmen had his own screen credit as director for Leningrad at War (1942), a film structured as a chronicle of the siege, from the first aid convoys, through the terrible winter without fuel, to the arrival of spring, which brings the first military victories against the invaders and the chance to bury the dead. Again, Karmen is the author of some of the key icons of the times. The end of the war saw him entering Berlin with the rank of major, together with the Russian forces. It was Karmen who filmed the Nazi Act of Capitulation in Karlshorst.

Nine years later, after various assignments within the Soviet Union—films virtually unknown in the West and probably forgotten in Russia—he went off to war again in Vietnam, following the French defeat at Dien Bien Phu. Once again he shot iconic images, this time of Ho Chi Minh in his bamboo hut in the jungle, and a remarkable interview with the captured French General De Castries calling on France to end the war. He reached Cuba, however, only after the Revolution had taken power, but still in the first flush of Soviet solidarity, a few months after Mikoyan made the first official Russian visit.

MICHAEL CHANAN

See also: Ivens, Joris; To Die in Madrid

Biography

Born 1906, Odessa. After the family moved to Moscow, began studying photography and started working for *Ogoniok* and other illustrated magazines. Entered the Moscow Film School in 1929 and soon established himself as a newsreel cameraman of exceptional sensibility. Sent to Spain in 1936 for his first foreign assignment; his work there has been compared to Robert Capa's photography. He subsequently worked as what Sadoul calls a 'film journalist' in China, Vietnam, and Cuba, as well as throughout the USSR during World War II and at the Nuremberg Trials after the war.

Much of his footage was used repeatedly, eventually becoming iconic images of the events portrayed. Also credited with directing a number of films, though sometimes these were compiled from his material by others. Died in 1978.

Selected films

1932 Moscow
1936 Salute to the Spanish Pioneers
1939 Spain (compiled by Esfir Shub)
1939 China Defends Herself
1943 The Defence of Leningrad
1947 Judgment of the People
1954 Vietnam
1960 Cuba, Island in Flames
1967 Granada, My Granada

Further reading

Barberis, Patrick and Chapuis, Dominique, *Roman Karmen: Une legende rouge*, Paris, Seuil, 2002.
Crusells, Magí, *La Guerra Civil Española: Cíne y propaganda*, Barcelona: Editorial Ariel, 2000.
Karmen, Roman, *No pasarán*, Moscow: Editorial Progreso, 1976.

Kauffmann, Stanley

As the resident film critic at *The New Republic* for more than forty years, Stanley Kauffmann established and has maintained a reputation as one of the most acute American critics of an art form that was only two decades older than himself. The author of numerous plays and of seven novels, and an active reviewer of both books and theater, Kauffmann relied, in his hundreds of weekly film reviews, on a broad cultural education and a dramatist's linguistic abilities and narrative instincts. Although he acknowledged the value of purely formal film criticism and occasionally wrote on the distinct aesthetic properties of the cinema, Kauffmann insisted in his film reviews on a plausible storyline and strong acting. His writings, and his publication of an anthology of contemporary reviews of early American films, also demonstrate a consistent interest in the history, and the future, of the medium. Film, for Kauffmann, met a singular cultural need and represented what he called the most inescapable, through its basic indexicality and its seductive immediacy, of art forms.

Working from the premise that inventions appear exactly when they do because of intense social pressures and expectations, Kauffmann assumed that film was inherently modern. Its history was related to developments in nineteenth-century photography and theater, but for Kauffmann, the appearance of moving pictures in the 1890s could be fully explained only as a response to popular will. This interest in the populist appeal of film informed, in 1966, his best-known essay, 'The Film Generation', in which he argued that current enthusiasm for film was due in part to a proprietary sense, on the part of young filmgoers, that film belonged to them because it was the art least tangled with the past. More abstractly, he suggested that the film generation could evoke the films that it wanted or needed. In a dismayed update written in 1985, however, he claimed that the appetite for film among young people had diminished, and he traced this erosion of interest to several causes, including a decline in the production of quality international films. Finally, in 1997, he stated that 'the situation is inarguably dark', although he pointed to several recent releases as evidence that quality films were still being made and could find audiences. For Kauffmann, a consistent proponent of international cinema, the heady days of 1960 were unknown to a new generation of potential cinephiles.

The vast majority of his reviews concerned fiction films, but Kauffmann did treat major documentary works—or, to use the term that he sometimes preferred, nonfiction films. He never codified his thoughts on the form, but he openly distinguished between nonfiction films in which the subjects are unaware of being photographed, and those in which the subjects are well aware of the camera's presence. For Kauffmann it was the second type that was especially provocative, or even troubling. It was not the aim of such works that was elusive; the goal of documentary films, visible even in the early work of the Lumière brothers, was related in Kauffmann's mind to a basic interest in voyeurism that was tied more to a desire for self-understanding than to any prurient interest. Seemingly uninterested in exploring the exact contours of such a desire, however, Kauffmann chose instead to emphasize what he saw as the paradox at the heart of the documentary project: the impossibility of a nominally voyeuristic cinema. Arguing that the very fact of observation altered the observed phenomenon, he concluded that the mere presence of the camera could significantly alter the behavior of a filmed subject.

This did not preclude, in Kauffmann's opinion, a successful documentary film. Even as he accented the visible influence of the lens, he also stressed the possibility and the importance of filmed subjects who might, through a rote familiarity with the camera, act or speak almost naturally. Pure naturalism was perhaps never possible in film, but moments of relative honesty could justify attempts at transparent reportage. In a 1989 review of High Fidelity, in fact, Kauffmann tried to describe the path to such a state, arguing that filmed subjects pass through an early self-consciousness and semi-forgetfulness of the lens, and then through a seeming forgetfulness still combined with performance, before emerging into nearly complete forgetfulness. Skilled makers of documentaries should thus concentrate on the last, or the last two, stages in this evolution of the subject. By extension, the most important aspect of shooting documentaries is, for Kauffmann, a simple sense of credibility, as the filmmakers must earn the trust of the subjects in order to move past the opaque intrusiveness of shot film. This credibility was never clearer for Kauffmann than in Allan King's 1967 Warrendale, but he argued that it was also the indirect product of a general cultural fluency in film and television conventions, which allowed all consumers of images (and by extension nearly all filmed subjects) a basic confidence and familiarity with the camera.

In his writings on documentary films Kauffmann also weighed the morality of aestheticized shots and nonlinear editing practices, and he generally concluded that such strategies could be condoned if they contributed to a reasonable dramatic line. In his review of Warrendale, for example, he approved of changes to the chronology of events in order to place the death of a woman nearer the end of the film. A year later, however, he objected, in a review of In the Year of the Pig, to pairings of public remarks with subsequent events, arguing that they created a misleading sense of history. Ultimately, then, for Kauffmann there could be no such thing as utterly objective reporting, but there was such a thing as objective intent, and the best documentaries acknowledged their lack of transparency, while also adhering to conventionally dramatic or artistic traditions. For this reason, as he noted, the best documentaries often chose intrinsically dramatic subjects. 'A documentary', he concluded in a 1968 review of A Face of War, 'might be defined as fact dramatized but not distorted by either prejudice or zeal.'

KERR HOUSTON

Biography

Born April 24, 1916. Published eighteen plays between 1933 and 1944; wrote eight novels between 1941 and 1960, and edited early manuscripts by Walker Percy. Began writing film criticism for *The New Republic* in 1958 after sending in an unsolicited review. Spent eight months as theater critic for *The New York Times* in 1966, before returning to *The New Republic* as associate literary editor. After writing lead book reviews for *The New Republic* from September 1966 until February 1968, returned to film criticism and was named the magazine's theater critic. Wrote regular film and theater criticism until 1979, when he reduced his involvement. Taught at the Yale University School of Drama from 1967 to 1973 and later at York College, Adelphi University, and Hunter College. Received the Outstanding Teacher Award from the Association for Theater in Higher Education in 1995 and the Telluride Film Festival Award for Criticism in 1998. Appeared as interviewee in The Tramp and the Director, 2002.

Further reading

Cardullo, Bert, *Before His Eyes: Essays in Honor of Stanley Kauffmann*, London: University Press of America, 1987.

Kauffmann, Stanley, *A World on Film: Criticism and Comment*, New York: Harper & Row, 1966.

——*Figures of Light: Film Criticism and Comment*, N York: Harper & Row, 1971.

——*American Film Criticism: From the Beginnings to Citizen Kane: Reviews of Significant Films at the Times They First Appeared*, New York: Liveright, 1972.

——*Living Images: Film Comment and Criticism*, New York: Harper & Row, 1975.

——*Persons of the Drama: Theater Criticism and Comment*, New York: Harper & Row, 1976.

——*Albums of Early Life*, New Haven: Ticknor & Fields, 1980.
——*Before My Eyes: Film Criticism and Comment*, New York: Harper & Row, 1980.
——*Theater Criticisms*, New York: Performing Arts Journal Publications, 1983.
——*Field of View: Film Criticism and Comment*, New York: PAJ Publications, 1986.
——*Distinguishing Features: Film Criticism and Comment*, Baltimore, MD: John Hopkins University Press, 1994.
——*Regarding Film: Criticism and Comment*, Baltimore, MD: Johns Hopkins University Press, 2001.

Kawase, Naomi

Although it is her fiction films that have made her Japan's most famous woman filmmaker, Kawase's documentaries have come to symbolize personal documentary in Japan since the 1980s. Her work stems in part from her unique family situation: she was adopted by her great-aunt and great-uncle at a very young age after her parents divorced. Films such as Ni tsutsumarete/Embracing (1992) and Kya Ka Ra Ba A (2001) specifically search for and approach those missing parents, particularly her father, but the general theme of absence unifies much of the rest of her work as well, including her fiction films such as Moe no suzaku/Suzaku (1996) and Shara so^ju/Shara (2002). In cinematic terms this has translated into a concern for the trace, and thus with such forms of recording as photography and audio recording. As in Ni tsutsumarete, she will present photographs on screen and seek out their origins, or, as with Mangekyo^/Manguekyo (1999) and Tsuioku no dansu/ Letter from a Yellow Cherry Blossom (2002), she will investigate the photographer and the process of tracing the image. There is an evident desire to restore that which is absent in, but indicated by, the trace, as well as to authenticate tracing itself. The sun and the shadows that it produces, the marks left by a hand on a cold window pane—such images feature prominently in her work. One can argue that Kawase seeks to fill this absence, rooted in personal history, with a system of feeling founded in what many consider the gentle gaze of her camera, epitomized by the many close-ups shot with an 8mm film camera, as well as in an interaction between filmmaker and the filmed that creates a community of emotion in works like Kaze no kioku/ Memory of the Wind (1995). The lessons she has learned from filmmakers such as Ogawa Shinsuke and Fukuda Katsuhiko about involving herself with her subject were realized in both the fictional Moe no suzaku and its documentary sequel Somaudo monogatari/The Weald (1997).

What also appears to fill this absence is an animistically viewed nature, ruled by a circular, virtually ahistorical temporality. The cycles of nature and the traditional geography and rituals of the ancient capital of Nara, her birthplace, figure prominently in such films as Katatsumori (1994) and Hotaru (2000). The citation of a transcendental, eternal time could be seen to obviate both the absences generating her cinema as well as the possibilities of political change by postulating an eternal, national culture. Kawase's voiced aversions to the political rhetoric of, for instance, feminism could lead one to link her with a tendency within personal documentary in Japan that has pursued personal subjectivity without politically theorizing it (Nornes 2002). Yet her works have consistently exhibited a tension that refuses to gloss over the absences that anchor them. This is not simply because loss and rupture continue to define her recent work, from the disappearance of a twin in Shara so^ju to a photographer facing the loss of his own life in Tsuioku no dansu, nor is it because she has elaborated on her notion of tradition in Hotaru and Shara. Rather it is because her work has always been cognizant of the limitations of representation, exhibiting both the conflicts the camera can create (for example, her quarrels with her great-aunt in Hi wa katabuki/The Setting Sun (1996)) and the general inability of this medium of traces to find the source of the trace (evinced by her refusal to fully show the father searched for in Ni tsutsumarete, even after he is found). This can reflect a profound uncertainty over the subjectivity explored in personal documentary, to the point where, even in her most narcissistic documentary Kya Ka Ra Ba A, the self itself may become merely a trace, represented by the tattoos that Kawase's body bears at the end. Although she does not exhibit the theoretical acumen of some of her American colleagues, Kawase continues to explore the absences of existence and the limitations of cinema by documenting them in her own personal way.

AARON GEROW

Biography

Born in Nara, Japan, May 30, 1969. Graduated from the Osaka School of Photography in 1989. Her independently made films Embracing (1992) and Katatsumori (1994) won the FIPRESCI Prize and New Asian Currents Jurists' Special Mention at the 1995 Yamagata International Documentary Film Festival. Her first fiction feature film, Suzaku, won the Camera d'Or at the 1997 Cannes Film Festival; her second, Hotaru, was awarded the FIPRESCI Prize at the 2001 Locarno Film Festival. She has continued her production activities in part through her own production company, Kumie.

Selected films

1988 Watashi ga tsuyoku kyo^mi o motta mono o o^kiku fix dekiritoru/I Focus on That Which Interests Me
1989 Tatta hitori no kazoku/My Sole Family
1992 Ni tsutsumarete/Embracing
1994 Katatsumori
1995 Ten, mitake/See the Heavens
1995 Kaze no kioku: 1995.12.26 Shibuya nite/ Memory of the Wind: At Shibuya on December 26, 1995
1996 Hi wa katabuki/The Setting Sun
1997 Somaudo monogatari/The Weald
1998 Tayutau ni kokyo^: hitorigurashi o hajimete, sannenme no aki ni/Wandering at Home: The Third Fall Since Starting to Live Alone
1999 Mangekyo^/Manguekyo
2001 Kya Ka Ra Ba A
2002 Tsuioku no dansu/Letter from a Yellow Cherry Blossom

Further reading

Kawase, Naomi and Gerow, Aaron, 'Documentarists of Japan, #14: Kawase Naomi', *Documentary Box*, November 16, 2000: 2–16.

Nornes, Abé Mark, 'The Postwar Documentary Trace: Groping in the Dark', *positions*, October 1, 2002: 39–78.

Novielli, Maria Roberto (ed.), *Kawase Naomi: i film i cinema*, Torino: Effata Editrice, 2002.

Yomota, Inuhiko, *Nihon eiga no rajikaruna ishi*, Tokyo: Iwanami Shoten, 1999.

Keiller, Patrick

As an architect and documentary filmmaker, Patrick Keiller is one of the most distinctive visual artists to have emerged in Britain in the 1980s and 1990s. His particular interest is in landscape and the built environment, seen as markers for the changing conditions of British life. Keiller's documentary technique involves the defamiliarization of familiar spaces and common topographical images in an attempt to make early twentieth-century critiques of modernity relevant to contemporary Britain. Inspired by the example of La Jetée (Chris Marker, 1962) and the unusual juxtapositions of the Surrealists, his first five short films shot in monochrome on 16mm (Stonebridge Park, 1981; Norwood, 1983; The End, 1986; Valtos, 1987; The Clouds, 1989) combine a montage of urban and rural images with interior monologue: a technique that Keiller developed in colour in his two major feature documentaries, London (1994) and Robinson in Space (1997).

Keiller's first full-length film, London, documents the city from the perspective of an off-screen, unnamed narrator (with the voice of actor Paul Scofield) and his sometime lover Robinson, a part-time lecturer in art and architecture at the University of Barking. Robinson's presence in the film is limited to his being featured in the narrator's travel journal, through which Keiller seeks to locate the 'problem of London' in the early 1990s. Comprising three journeys across London, the montage of (largely static) urban images is interrupted by momentous events such as the 1992 general election (the Conservative Party won against the odds, which greatly disturbs Robinson), IRA bomb attacks, and miners' demonstrations. Searching for the roots of English Romanticism, Robinson is enraptured by the French poetry of Baudelaire, Rimbaud and Apollinaire, and by the Parisian figure of the wandering *flâneur*, but he feels that this role is impossible to adopt in London with its lack of communal spaces and café culture. Keiller describes London as 'a film about a city in decline', suggesting that it is not simply the embodiment of T.S. Eliot's 'unreal city' but also 'the first metropolis to disappear'. In his attempt to 'unmask' the spaces of London, Keiller used a handheld and versatile 35mm Eclair Cameflex camera, but he has commented that the film stock actually 'flattered the subject', reducing its smog and 'sense of degradation' and lending the city an aesthetic vitality that he (and his characters) believe has been lost in the contemporary metropolis.

Robinson in Space also follows the psychogeographical exploits of Robinson through the eyes of his researcher and travelling companion, again with the voice of Paul Scofield. Modelled on Daniel Defoe's travelog and meditation on the state of the country, A Tour Through the Whole Island of Great Britain (1724–7), and preceding the release of another travel documentary, called Gallivant (Andrew Kötting, 1997), which follows the coastal route around the British mainland, Robinson in Space leaves the topography of London for a tour of the regions. Now based in Reading, Robinson has been commissioned to study 'the problem of England', and the film examines aspects of public space, culture, industry, manufacture, architecture, and housing in what Keiller calls an attempt 'to locate some of the economic activity that no longer takes place in [metropolitan] cities', exploring instead the hinterlands and outskirts of regional cities. The political subtext of the film is similar to that of London: it details the unequal distribution of wealth that occurred under the Conservative Government of the 1980s and early 1990s and regrets the UK's lack of interest in its (unexpectedly surviving) manufacturing industry. Keiller has written that he initially envisaged the film as 'a critique of English "gentlemanly" capitalism' but that instead it revealed the new landscape of an international, deregulated economy.

The narrative comprises seven picaresque trips around England: the first along the Thames to London; then to Oxford, Cambridge, and the West Country; to the Midlands; Birmingham, and Liverpool; to Manchester and Hull; to Scarborough and Whitby; and finally to Blackpool and Sellafield. The images that accompany the narrative range from the banal (shopping centers, landfill sites, and traffic signs), the iconic (the view of London from Purfleet and the Clifton Suspension Bridge in Bristol), and the industrial (particularly multinational firms such as Toyota near Derby and Samsung on Teesside), to the intriguing (a 'Brain Haulage' sign in Dagenham and a photograph of Hadrian's Wall on an English Heritage phone card). As Paul Julian Smith comments, these images mark 'the passing of the industrial era [that] is mourned and celebrated in its pathetic and curious ruins; and the narrator's earnest repetition of official statistics mirrors the modest ambitions of English life, composed as it is of continual disappointments and compromises'. The narrative resists nostalgia for a lost Britain, relying on a detached and wry tone that moves from the serious and the literary (with references to Rimbaud, Wilde, and Defoe) to the humorous and the quirky, with the voice-over and the images often juxtaposed ironically. Although Robinson remains an elusive figure, glimpses of his biography (we know he was born in Blackpool, and he claims that he has relatives in Newcastle), his aesthetic and literary interests, his health (both companions get sick after weeks of hotel food), and his sexuality (he finds a partner on the Internet) offer enough information to personalize the tour. The narrative finishes not long after the pair visit the carnivalesque Blackpool and the threatening nuclear plant at Sellafield (representing the best and worst of the northwest), ending suddenly when the two companions are told that their research 'contracts had been terminated' following the apocalyptic report of a Tornado jet crashing into the North Sea.

Keiller remains skeptical that film can capture the detail of large-format architectural photography, and he is aware of the difficulties of representing three-dimensional structures within the flat space of film (see his interview with Joe Kerr). Nevertheless, he continued to develop his documentary interests in his film The Dilapidated Dwelling (2000), which examines 'the predicament of the house in advanced economies'. A fictional researcher (with the voice of Tilda Swinton) returns from a twenty-year sojourn in the Arctic to find that, although the UK is an electronically advanced nation, the houses are among the most dilapidated in Western Europe. Keiller suggets that his subject matter was unfashionable in the late 1990s, claiming that 'the definitive experiences of modernity, or postmodernity, seemed to involve movement', whereas to stay at home was to marginalize oneself. Taking the tension between movement and stasis as its conceptual focus, the film explores whether there is a close relation or, indeed, an opposition between the state of housing and the economies of developed countries. The film contains archive footage of Buckminster Fuller, Constant, Archigram, and Walter Segal, together with interviews with

Martin Pawley, Saskia Sassen, Doreen Massey, and Cedric Price.

MARTIN HALLIWELL

Biography

Born in Blackpool in 1950. Studied at the Bartlett School of Architecture and, after working for a time as an architect in the 1970s, in the Department of Environmental Media at the Royal College of Art, London, where he began to make films and other topographic works. He released his first short films in the early 1980s, and his first audiovisual installations were exhibited at the Tate Gallery in 1982. He has also exhibited in the 1990 British Art Show, and his films are distributed in the United States and Europe. In 2002 he was an Arts and Humanities Research Board Fellow in the Creative and Performing Arts at the Royal College of Art, working on a three-year project called 'The City of the Future', which uses archive footage to explore the ways in which the city has been represented during the first century of film.

Selected films

1981 Stonebridge Park (21 mins, 16mm, black and white)
1983 Norwood (26 mins, 16mm, black and white)
1986 The End (18 mins, 16mm, black and white)
1987 Valtos (11 mins, 16mm, black and white)
1989 The Clouds (20 mins, 16mm, black and white)
1994 London (85 mins, 35mm, color)
1997 Robinson in Space (82 mins, 35mm, color)
2000 The Dilapidated Dwelling (78 mins, beta sx, color)

Further reading

Keiller, Patrick, *Robinson in Space and a Conversation with Patrick Wright*, London: Reaktion Books, 1999.

——'Port Statistics', in Iain Borden and Joe Kerr (eds), *The Unknown City*, Cambridge, MA: MIT Press, 2000: 443–57.

——'Architectural Cinematography', in Kester Rattenbury (ed.), *This is Not Architecture*, London: Routledge, 2002: 37–44.

——'Sexual Ambiguity and Automotive Engineering', in Peter Wollen and Joe Kerr (eds), *Autopia*, London: Reaktion Books, 2002.

Kerr, Joe 'To change life, however, we must first change space' (interview with Patrick Keiller), in Architecture + Film II, ed. Bob Fear, *Architectural Design* 70, no. 2, January 2000: 82–5.

Martin-Jones, David, 'Interview with Patrick Keiller', *Journal of Popular British Cinema* 5, 2002: 123–32.

Smith, Paul Julien, 'Review of Robinson in Space', *Sight and Sound* 7, no. 1, January 1997: 44.

Yates, Robert, 'Review of London', *Sight and Sound* 4, no. 6, June 1994: 54–5.

Kiarostami, Abbas

One fascinating aspect of Kiarostami's feature films is their blurring of the boundary between documentary and fiction. Nama-y Nazdik/Close-Up (1990), which perhaps ought simply to be called a documentary, is about true events, with those concerned appearing as themselves in reenactments and sometimes in what may be a filming of events as they first happen. The degree of art at play is kept constantly in question in this film. Other films, with invented stories, use nonprofessional actors in their own familiar worlds, many of them children at school or at play. Shooting is done on location, which often means on a car trip or walking trip. Kiarostami films are very much outdoors. Zendegi va digar Hich/Life and Nothing More (1992) takes in—indeed bases itself upon—the devastating earthquake in northern Iran that occurred shortly before the film was shot, and which we see in all its aftereffects. With Khaneh-ye Dust Kojast/Where is the Friend's House? (1987), Life and Nothing More, and Ta'm-e Gilas/Taste of Cherry (1996), one feels repeatedly that the film leaves, or drifts out of, the realm of imagined story and becomes just observational. The film seems to surprise itself, losing its bearings and finding itself in a new mode.

In the 1970s and 1980s Kiarostami made short experimental films using nonfictional footage for meditations on ethical, artistic, or political issues, or even using nonfiction to form a fiction. Mashq-e Shab/Homework (1990) and A.B.C. Africa (2001) are feature-length documentaries on brutalized schoolchildren in Iran and on the plight of orphans in the AIDS crisis in Uganda, respectively. In the short films and longer documentaries, as in Close-Up and the other features, crisis and even cataclysm draw Kiarostami's attention, as if this is the tenor of life now, or as if such crisis asks especially for the intervention of civilized and inventive filmmaking. Children draw this director's attention, as though defining his civilized sensibilities and giving life to his inventiveness.

In the short films, documentary images and sounds are the grains of truth around which, or out of which, a series of thoughts or a fantasy spins itself. Yet the documentation remains what it is, never giving way entirely in the dialectic with creativity. Rang-ha/Colors (1976) offers us a woman's voice-over in a cheerful lesson on color identification for children, aimed at such important understandings as how to read and obey a traffic light. However, the film we see is a series of integral images of human-made objects, fruits, goldfish, and so on, where things insist on an existence of their own. Kiarostami's editing imposes humorous juxtapositions, seeming open to the world of things in a spirit of anarchy, against the grain of the traditional teacher's sense of order. In Beh Tartib ya Bedun-e Tartib/Regular, Irregular (With or Without Order) (1981) the film's ostensible makers discuss in voice-over the virtues of doing things in an orderly way, and how best to film and edit the orderly and disorderly action: boys exiting a classroom or loading onto a school bus, or of pedestrians and traffic in a busy intersection. The words seem almost to dictate what we see. Yet what emerges in the relatively long takes is a raw energy in people and a disposition toward violating rules, attributes that ask to be accepted with good humor as a fact of life. Dandandard/Toothache (1980) is presumably a fiction about a little boy who suffers a toothache and gets treatment, but the footage at school looks real, with outdoor games, the classroom, and the boy breaking down in tears with pain. The dental clinic footage looks real, showing us a busy and bustling place with many people getting treatment. Then the documentary focus shifts as a senior dentist speaks, offering instruction on dental hygiene, aided by intercut illustrations. The cries of the boy in the dentist's chair continue in counterpoint to the instructional presentation. This film, which was made just in the wake of the Islamic Revolution, seems a metaphor for the whole idea of trauma and what is to be made of it.

Picking up on Avvali-ha/First Graders (1985), about disruptive children sent to confront the school principal, and on the feature Where is the Friend's House?, which begins and ends with seemingly real, stressful schoolroom scenes, Homework faces more fully and directly than any of Kiarostami's other work on what is done to children in the name of bringing them up to fit into society—in contemporary Iran, yes, but the film's concerns seem broader than that. Homework opens with the camera panning and moving along with boys on their way to school in snowy streets, noisy and full of high spirits. We then see them massed in their schoolyard for exercises and religious and patriotic chants. Thereafter, for more than an hour of screen time, the film is confined to a darkish room where Kiarostami questions six- to eight-year olds one by one about their problems with homework. The room has the feel of a police interrogation center, and in prolonged confinement here the viewer is made to feel a captivity like that inflicted on the children by the ideas and practices of their educational system. Kiarostami is a very gentle questioner, eliciting information about confusing assignments, unhelpful but demanding parents, beatings at home and at school. Even though he is gentle and seems progressive, however, he also aligns filmmaking with the powers that be. There are numerous cuts to an ominous close-up of a staring camera lens, what the boys are facing constantly, and the whole situation makes them nervous and fearful, so different from the way they appeared outdoors. It is as if this documentary must acknowledge and use film's violent and oppressive power in order to understand and convey an ongoing problem of violence and oppression.

There is great variety in the children's faces and in the potential for feeling that they show, and yet a sameness haunts what they say of their experience and their values, a sameness in what they seem to think they ought to think. There are glimpses of an alternative to this life during a cutaway to group religious chanting, when Kiarostami turns off the sound and the camera registers the disorderly force running through the bodies and faces of the young people. 'Let us go', these images seem to cry out. More ambiguous and disturbing is the release that comes at the end of the film, when the boy who has been most upset by the questioning begins to recite a Hymn to the Creator that he has memorized very well. Clearly the achievement of what can be learned, what the mind can be opened to, compensates in some measure for the trauma of the passage to learning. Or is what we see merely meaningless and rote recitation?

After Homework Kiarostami's films turn more to the world of adults, beginning with Close-Up. A man was arrested for impersonating the film director Mohsen Makhmalbaf and cheating a well-off family with hopes of participation in a film, and upon hearing the news, Kiarostami pursued a film project on the subject, not sleeping, he says, for forty days and nights, scurrying to interview people and do reenactments of events with them. Kiarostami's film project clearly affects the people involved, including a trial judge, and how they choose to resolve things with one another, so Close-Up becomes, among other things, a documentary on how documentary affects life. The film shows us modern Tehran high and low, the worlds of journalism (including film journalism), and the justice system. The film probes the human heart, the longing of people to escape life as it is and to become involved in a creative venture, here film, whether the impersonator's bogus film or Kiarostami's film. Close-Up is one of the crucial documentaries of recent decades; it is discussed at greater length elsewhere in this volume.

After his series of features brought increasing recognition and praise in the 1990s, Kiarostami answered the call of an international agency to make a documentary about a Ugandan organization for the aid of foster families taking in children orphaned by AIDS. A.B.C. Africa, shot in digital video, is Kiarostami's first film outside Iran, and he stresses his status as an outside observer, using voice-overs of local officials to explain things, showing himself and his crew repeatedly, keeping almost constantly in motion—touring, filming from moving cars, filming while walking about. There are beautiful long takes from a slightly high angle, the point of view of an adult looking down at children, the camera slowly exploring open market areas, little shops, and a hospital compound, finding the faces of children, all of whom engage with the camera. As always in Kiarostami, children mean life and stand as a contradiction to the way of the world that would hand them their destiny (a toddler's cheerful T-shirt reads 'ABC', a mark of what the world has in store for her to learn, but also, in the way she wears it and moves about, an expression of her energy and openness to adventure). The film becomes more and more serious as it goes along. Death becomes ever-present, as the camera discovers the seriously ill and at last a corpse. The use of freeze-frames in a hospital sequence seems almost a withdrawal from what is unbearable to contemplate in living time.

In the middle of the film all comes to a halt as the filmmakers talk at their hotel in total darkness after the routine midnight shut-off of electricity, and then fall silent. Their talk is of malaria, AIDS, and adaptation to darkness, and at last they seem at a loss for words and go to their respective rooms, the camcorder with one of them still running. It registers darkness and silence and, eventually, the sound of rain and thunder and the occasional illumination of a lightning flash. Throughout the film thunder rumbles; it seems a sign of impending doom, or relief. This night episode is a way for the film to evoke death in film's own terms, as a matter of light and dark, sound and silence, the viewer being forced to focus, for a few long-seeming moments, on nothing. Kiarostami is able to come to terms with the material about which he has been asked to make a film, because he is willing to identify film with death, here nakedly, poetically. However, throughout A.B.C. Africa the filmmakers remind us that they are an outside force, intervening, moving about freely, like the visitation of disease or the storms on the horizon. In the film's acknowledgment of its outsideness, even its negativity, it is able here, as in Homework, to meet life and give it space to define itself, provide it with something to work against and thereby to flourish.

CHARLES WARREN

See also: Close-Up

Biography

Born in Tehran on June 22, 1940. Studied fine arts and graphic design at Tehran University. Worked in advertising and made television commercials in the 1960s. Set up a filmmaking program for the Institute for the Intellectual Development of Children and Young Adults in 1969, which produced his films over the next two decades. Established himself as a well-known film director and major cultural figure in Iran with The Traveler in 1972. Became well known internationally with Where is the Friend's House? in 1987, the first of the 'Koker Trilogy'. Wrote the screenplay for Jafar Panahi's The White Balloon, released in 1995. Given a retrospective by the Film Society of Lincoln Center in 1996. Won the Palme d'Or at the Cannes Film Festival for Taste of Cherry in 1997. Published *Walking with the Wind*, a book of poems, in 1999.

Further reading

Cheshire, Godfrey, 'How to Read Kiarostami', *Cineaste* 25, no. 4, 2000: 8–15.

Dabashi, Hamid, *Close Up: Iranian Cinema, Past, Present and Future*, London and New York: Verso, 2001.

Kiarostami, Abbas, 'With Borrowed Eyes', *Film Comment* 36, no. 4, 2000: 20–5.

Lopate, Phillip, *Totally, Tenderly, Tragically: Essays and Criticism from a Lifelong Love Affair with the Movies*, New York: Anchor Books/Doubleday, 1998.

Perez, Gilberto, *The Material Ghost: Films and Their Medium*, Baltimore, MD and London: Johns Hopkins University Press, 1998.

Saeed-Vafa, Mehrnaz and Rosenbaum, Jonathan, *Abbas Kiarostami*, Urbana-Champaign, IL: University of Illinois Press, 2003.

Kieślowski, Krzysztof

Kryzstof Kieślowski, a prominent representative of Poland's 'Cinema of Moral Anxiety' in the 1970s and 1980s, started his film career directing documentary shorts for Polish state organizations. He graduated from the Lodz Film School in 1968, with a degree in direction. This prestigious institution produced the leading Polish directors of the postwar era: Andrzej Wajda, Roman Polanski, Jerzy Skolimowski, and Krzysztof Zanussi.

The experience and camaraderie of this intense four-year learning period, in the political context of 1960s communist Poland, shaped Kieślowski's view of the profession. It not only marked his approach to documentary cinema but also guided his later evolution toward fiction cinema. 'Film school taught me how to look at the world. It showed me that life exists and that people talk, laugh, worry, suffer, steal in this life, that all this can be photographed and that from all these photographs a story can be told,' he pointed out in Danusia Stok's book-length interview *Kieslowski on Kieslowski* (Stok 1993).

Working for the State Documentary Studio (WFD) and Polish television, Kieślowski made during the 1970s more than twenty-five shorts about Polish contemporary life. On the surface, these are straightforward accounts of ordinary people in everyday occurrences, but—as in the case of Marina Goldovskaya, Kieślowski's contemporary in Soviet Russia—by casting an unblinking look at reality, these portraits expose the flaws and contradictions of the socialist experiment. In *Kieslowski on Kieslowski* he commented on the unique role of Polish documentary in the 1970s:

> At that time, I was interested in everything that could be described by the documentary film camera. There was a necessity, a need—which was very exciting for us—to describe the world. The Communist world had described how it should be and not how it really was. We—there were a lot of us—tried to describe this world and it was fascinating to describe something which hadn't been described yet.
>
> (Stok 1993)

Kieślowski utilized the documentary format as a powerful tool to 'construct' the reality denied by the nomenklatura (the Polish ruling class), astutely exploiting its editing possibilities for irony and revelation. In the documentary I'm So-So (1995), directed by his collaborator Krzysztof Wierzbicki, he points out: 'Our descriptive tools had been used for propagandistic purposes[…] Outside Poland, you don't know what it means to live in a world without representation.'

Kieślowski's views on documentary were first examined in his 1968 graduation thesis. He referred to the 'dramaturgy of reality' and the possibilities that the form offers to record reality, discussing the work of French critic André Bazin and of filmmakers Robert Flaherty and Richard Leacock. In an interview, years later, he reaffirmed the training value of documentary filmmaking, 'a very good school for synthetic thinking in the cinema.'

This steadfast adherence to realism as the way to reveal the truth about people and things connects Kieślowski's documentary work to that of cinéma vérité cultivators, with their preference for fly-on-the-wall methods of observation and for avoidance of an authorial style. However, the director's vocation to record a reality outside of the official communist discourse make this corpus of shorts a powerful political and historical document to examine the bleakness of life under the Stalinist regime.

These documentaries, as well as the reality-based fiction dramas Kieślowski made for television starting in the mid-1970s, need to be seen as part of a larger political project, that of filmmakers such as Wajda, Zanussi, and Agniezka Holland who were probing the history, politics, and mores of a nation much battered by events of the twentieth century. Working doggedly within and against the constraints of the communist regime, the best postwar Polish cinema challenged the status quo in intelligent ways and spoke, beyond censors and obstacles, to a public eager to listen. Kieślowski's documentaries, then, play a double role, artistic as well as political. They constitute, as Danusia Stoks observes, a precursor of the 'Cinema of Moral Anxiety', a series of fiction films examining the social and spiritual malaise of the Polish society, from the mid-1970s to the early 1980s. The bulk of Kieślowski's documentaries were made before the emergence in 1980 of Solidarity, the workers' dissident movement, which ultimately triggered the collapse of the communist regime.

Kieślowski's shorts are deceptively simple observations of ordinary Polish citizens whose limitations, be they material, social, or ideological, define their possibilities, as noted by Annette Insdorf in Double Lives, Second Chances (1999). Many of them focus on individuals involved with State institutions. They reveal a profound compassion for the people he portrays—factory workers, doctors, tuberculosis patients, newlyweds, car racers, dancers, passengers in a train station, bureaucrats—as well as his interest in the complexities of life and politics. To some fellow countrymen at the time, several of these films seemed ambiguous toward the communist regime. To others, they were a way to survive and resist within the rules of the game. A case in point was Zyciorys/Curriculum Vitae (1975), a fictionalized account of a former secretary of the Communist Party Control Committee who appeals his expulsion. What emerges from this combination of drama and documentary is the confrontation between the reality described by the protagonist and the twisted logic of the party officials. It is also a drama about the value of the human person who faces a dehumanizing ideology.

A common thread runs through these documentary shorts. Kieślowski himself summarized it to Danusia Stok: 'All my films from the first to the most recent ones, are about individuals who can't quite find their bearings, who don't quite know how to live, who don't really know what's right or wrong and are desperately looking.' These observations about life's uncertainties and the limitations placed upon the individual are central to some of his most relevant documentaries: Murarz/The Bricklayer (1973), Pierwsza milosc/First Love (1974), Szpital/Hospital (1976), and Z punktu widzenia nocnego portiera/From a Night Porter's Point of View (1977).

In The Bricklayer, the voice-over of a forty-five-year-old Warsaw mason preparing for the May Day workers' parade reveals a poignant story of political disillusionment, party bureaucracy, and ideals betrayed, but he is proud of his work as a bricklayer, a fact that gives meaning to his life. The young unmarried couple of First Love is expecting a child. Kieślowski follows them for eight months, recording their modest wedding, the birth of their daughter, the struggle to find suitable lodging. The harsh realities of life supplant notions of romantic bliss. The irony of the title is tempered by the filmmaker's compassion in handling the difficult beginnings of family life and by the couple's realistic assessment of their possibilities. Hospital shows orthopedic surgeons at work in a Warsaw hospital during a thirty-two-hour shift. The severe limitations under which they operate become a source of black humor, especially the use of makeshift surgical instruments. The humanity of the film is restored by the sympathetic portrayal of doctors working on the edge. A more complex view of a flawed human being is displayed in From a Night Porter's Point of View, the profile of a fascistic-minded factory guard who believes that 'rules are more important than people' and whose hobby is to verify other people's fishing permits. 'The porter wasn't a bad man [...] He just happens to think that it would be a good thing to hang people publicly because that would make everybody afraid to commit crimes,' he observed to Danusia Stok.

Kieślowski gave a persuasive explanation of why he abandoned the documentary genre by the mid-1970s. He came to believe, especially after First Love, that there were boundaries that filmmakers cannot cross because 'we risk causing harm to the people we film. That's when we feel the need to make fiction features.'

Siedem dni w tygodniu/Seven Days a Week (1988) was the director's last documentary. Made as part of a Dutch collective film about cities of the world, it follows several seemingly unrelated Warsaw people from Monday through

Saturday, in a cinéma vérité style. On Sunday, when they sit at the breakfast table, we realize that they are a family.

Seen in perspective, the documentary work at the beginning of Krzysztof Kieślowski's career allowed the Polish director to hone his craft while creating a human and political record of everyday life under Communism.

MARÍA ELENA DE LAS CARRERAS-KUNTZ

See also: First Love; Goldovskaya, Marina; Poland

Biography

Born in Warsaw, Poland, June 27, 1941. Graduated from Lodz film school in 1968, with a degree in direction. Worked for Wytwornia Filmow Dokumentalnych (the State Documentary Film Studio) and Polish television, making some thirty documentaries chronicling Polish life, 1968–80. Began making fiction films with a strong documentary component in the mid-1970s. Gained international recognition with Amator/Camera Buff (1979), a fiction film about a factory worker turned documentary filmmaker, who uses the camera as an instrument to critique the shortcomings of the communist regime. His ten-part Polish television series Dekalog/The Decalogue (1988) and the French-Polish coproduction trilogy Trois Couleurs: Bleu, Blanc, Rouge/Three Colors: Blue, White, Red (1993–94) cemented his reputation as one of the leading European filmmakers of the 1980s and 90s. Died, following heart surgery, in Warsaw on March 13, 1996.

Selected films

1966 Urzad/The Office: director, writer
1968 Zdjecie/The Photograph: director
1969 Z miasta Lodzi/From the City of Lodz: director
1970 Bylem zolnierzem/I Was a Soldier: director, writer
1970 Fabryka/Factory: director
1971 Przed rajdem/Before the Rally: director
1972 Refren/Refrain: director
1972 Miedzy Wroclawiem a Zielona Gora/Between Wroclaw and Zielona Gora: director
1972 Podstawy BHP w kopalni miedzi/The Principles of Safety and Hygiene in a Copper Mine: director
1972 Robotnicy '71: nic o nas bez nas/Workers '71: Nothing About Us Without Us: director
1973 Murarz/Bricklayer: director
1974 Przeswietlenie/X-ray: director
1974 Pierwsza milosc/First Love: director
1976 Szpital/Hospital: director
1977 Z punktu widzenia nocnego portiera/From a Night Porter's Point of View: director
1977 Nie wiem/I Don't Know: director
1978 Siedem kobiet w roznym wieku/Seven Women of Differing Age: director
1980 Dworzec/Station: director
1980 Gadajace Glowy/Talking Heads: director
1988 Siedem dni w tygodniu/Seven Days a Week

Further reading

Amiel, Vincent (ed.), *Krzysztof Kieslowski: Textes réunis et présentés par Vincent Amiel*, Paris: Positif/Jean-Michel Place, 1997 (includes his graduation thesis).

Insdorf, Annette, *Double Lives, Second Chances. The Cinema of Krzysztof Kieslowski*, New York: Hyperion, 1999.

Stok, Danusia (ed. and trans.), *Kieslowski on Kieslowski*, London and Boston: Faber & Faber, 1993.

King, Allan

Allan King is among the best known of Canadian documentarians and rightly so; over his forty-five-year-long career, King has not only brought international critical attention to the nation's otherwise obscure film industry but has also repeatedly challenged his audiences with his socially conscious, thought-provoking brand of documentary filmmaking. Like many of Canada's filmmakers, King got his start through a government-sponsored organization, although in his case the organization was not the National Film Board (NFB) of Canada but the CBC. King found his opportunity when the CBC expanded to Vancouver in the 1950s. He quickly worked his way up from the entry-level position of production assistant to director, and by 1956 he had produced his first major film, Skid Row. This film, an early piece of direct cinema dealing with homeless men in Vancouver, would become emblematic of King's entire career as a documentary filmmaker.

Stylistically, Skid Row was direct cinema that predated any other film of the form in North America, including the works of the Drew Associates in America and those of the famed Unit D of the NFB. In fact, the film predated much of the sound-recording technology that marked the direct cinema revolution, resulting in a film that in parts seems to be a silent film. Nonetheless, Skid Row shows that King was becoming aware of the potential of direct cinema, and he would soon utilize the form to create some of the great observational films ever produced. His most famous films, made during the direct cinema period of his career, Warrendale (1967) and A Married Couple (1969), were to bring King international acclaim as one of the world's leading avatars of the style.

Direct cinema will always be seen as King's trademark cinematic style, but it is important to note the many variations in style that marked his career both before and after the international successes of the Allan King Associates films. Although Skid Row had established him as one of the true pioneers of direct cinema, King made documentaries that varied widely in style. In the period just preceding Warrendale, King made two notable biographical films, one of famous Canadian actor Christopher Plummer, simply titled Christopher Plummer (1964), and Bjorn's Inferno (1964), a poetic profile of a struggling anarchist poet and King's personal favorite among his films. King also showed his ability to work in the interview-driven format with Running Away Backwards (1964), an ironic interview-based profile of Canadian expatriates living on the Spanish island of Ibiza. In the films that followed A Married Couple—Come on Children (1973), Who's in Charge? (1983), and The Dragon's Egg (1999)—King employed a stylistic approach entirely different from the one he used in the films that had made him famous. Instead of continuing in the direct cinema tradition, in these films King boldly took a cinéma vérité approach by making the filmmaking the diegetic catalyst in each film. In Come on Children, the film's subjects, ten teenagers, have been invited to stay on a farm, isolated from all outside influences, and are expected to form their own community; the formation of this community is the subject of the film. Likewise, in the controversial Who's in Charge? thirty unemployed people are invited to an open-forum symposium of King's creation, which is the heart of the film. In The Dragon's Egg King stages a house-building competition, complete with cash prizes, that pits mixed teams of ethnic Estonians and Russians, traditional rivals, in Estonia against one another in a cooperation contest. These films are obviously a far cry from the fly-on-the-wall style that marked Warrendale and A Married Couple. King's foray from the world of direct cinema into cinéma vérité was one that not only presented fresh new films but also embroiled him in one ethical controversy after another.

From an ethical standpoint, the controversy that greeted Skid Row, mainly having to do with the problem of observing and exhibiting such obviously self-destructive characters, presaged the controversies that would plague his career. Most of his direct cinema films would face some sort of ethical outcry. Warrendale was criticized, and even boycotted by the CBC, for its graphic portrayal of emotionally disturbed children whose lives were too violent and whose language was too vulgar for Canadian television censors at the time. A Married Couple was likewise criticized for language and violence, but also for its frank depiction of an unhappily married couple, a depiction that was considered a possible indictment of the institution itself. Later films would raise more troubling ethical questions as the filmmaker's hand in provoking performance became more pronounced in Come on Children and Who's in Charge? Here King faced sharp criticism for isolating and manipulating his subjects for the sole purpose of filming them within situations that he himself created; this was especially the case in the latter film, which brought together thirty unemployed Canadians for a conference on their socioeconomic conditions, a conference that was arranged as more of an open forum but, in the end, was designed solely for the purpose of King's film. The outcry over the film led to King's being labeled a 'media monster' for his alleged making a spectacle of the poor and unemployed at the 'conference'.

Regardless of the controversy they aroused, King's films have always achieved their primary goal of fostering debate about their content, whether it be the social place of the willingly homeless, the treatment of the emotionally disturbed, or the institution of marriage itself. When King found his brand of filmmaking ill-suited to the institutional environment in which they were initially produced, he had the courage to go outside the CBC and form his own production company, making him, for a time,

Canada's leading independent documentarian. It would have been easy for him to continue working in the realm of direct cinema that had brought him much international acclaim, but King instead chose to continue making films that challenged not only social forces and institutions but also the discursive forces of documentary itself. Despite the ethical censure he incurred for these films, he remains Canada's greatest documentary filmmaker.

CHRISTOPHER MEIR

See also: Canada

Biography

Born in Vancouver, Canada, in 1930. Graduated with honors from the University of British Columbia with a degree in philosophy. Worked and lived in England for several years before returning to Vancouver to work as a production assistant at the CBC. Made several short films for television before the breakthrough success of Skid Row in 1956. Following this King made several films, notably Pemberton Valley (1957), Rickshaw (1960), Bjorn's Inferno (1964), and Running Away Backwards (1964). King later tired of the restraints of institutional filmmaking and formed his own production company, Allan King Associates, which independently produced his documentary films and sold broadcasting rights to television networks, usually the CBC. Achieved his greatest international successes in the late 1960s with Warrendale (1967), which shared best picture honors at the Cannes Film Festival with Antonioni's Blow-Up, and A Married Couple (1969). After these masterpieces, King's production company slowly succumbed to financial pressures and declared bankruptcy, whereupon King did freelance work and eventually moved into fiction film production, while intermittently producing documentary films such as Come on Children (1973) and Who's in Charge? (1983). His documentary The Dragon's Egg (1999) aired on the CBC to critical acclaim.

Selected films

1956 Skid Row
1957 The Pemberton Valley
1960 Rickshaw
1964 Bjorn's Inferno
1964 Christopher Plummer
1964 Running Away Backwards
1967 Warrendale
1969 A Married Couple
1973 Come on Children
1983 Who's in Charge?
1999 The Dragon's Egg

Further reading

Harcourt, Peter, 'Allan King: Filmmaker', in David Helwig (ed.), *The Human Element: Critical Essays*, Ottawa: Oberon Press, 1978.
Marsolais, Gilles, *L'Aventure du Cinéma Direct Revisitée*, Laval, Québec: 400 Coups, 1997.
Martin, Bruce, *Allan King: An Interview with Bruce Martin*, Ottawa: Canadian Film Institute, 1971.
Rosenthal, Alan, *The New Documentary in Action: A Case-book in Film Making*, Berkeley, CA: University of California Press, 1971.
——'A Married Couple: An Interview with Allan King', in Seth Feldman and Joyce Nelson (eds), *Canadian Film Reader*, Toronto: P. Martin Associates, 1977.

Kirchheimer, Manfred

Manfred (Manny) Kirchheimer was born in 1931 in Saarbrücken, Germany, and came to the United States in 1936 when his family fled the Nazis. From 1948 to 1952 he studied film production at Hans Richter's Institute of Film Techniques at the City College of New York. Subsequently he spent twenty-four years in the New York film industry as editor, director, and cameraman, while at the same time self-financing his own independent films. In 1955 he worked with Richter to complete 8X8 and The Passionate Pastime. Also in 1955 he assisted Jay Leyda in reconstituting Eisenstein's ¡Que Viva Mexico! footage into study reels for the Museum of Modern Art.

While working in New York City's film industry, he was the editor on over three hundred films, many for the documentary departments of American television networks, CBS, ABC, NBC, and National Educational Television. The subjects ranged from cultural programming, such as Leonard Bernstein in Venice for CBS, to biography for Time-Life Films, as in Krushchev Remembers. Beginning in 1963, he was the cameraman for a number of films directed by Leo Hurwitz.

In Kirchheimer's own films there is a decided tendency to explore various aspects of urban life. The subjects he chooses, be they the city's architectural environment or its graffiti or the docking of an ocean liner, not only reflect the lives of people implicated in these subjects but also create a frame for a larger understanding of city life. His films are hopeful, yet they admonish for the future. He develops a strong point of view by giving full scope to opposing arguments. Kirchheimer often presents competing claims with such appeal that audiences cannot always tell which side he is on. Often, as in the glass façades of Claw, he brings his ambivalence directly to the viewer. About this he has said, 'I trust my audience. I am eager for the audience to work, and not lose themselves while they are watching my films [… they should be] able to hold on to their own integrity and insights so they don't leave their intelligence behind. When viewers leave the theater they will be walking into the same world they just left, not one unconnected to the film they've seen.'

Kirchheimer's films adopt a somewhat poetic form that hews to an earlier filmmaking standard: iconic imagery is favored over 'live-with-sound' snatchings. Montage is worked and played out to the full, in preference to illustrative single shots. Uninterrupted on-camera talk is indulged rather than the juxtaposition of short statements and visual inserts. Tangential meanderings are cherished over 'straight-line' narratives. The complex layering of sound, to the extent of creating 'fictional' environments (sometimes with manufactured effects) is frequently used instead of the random pickup of the on-the-scene microphone. He prefers written commentary, efficient and literate, over the often discursive style of a spontaneous voice-over.

The history of Kirchheimer's films begins with Colossus on the River in 1963. This is a documentary that celebrates the docking of a large ocean liner, the United States, while at the same time it becomes an epitaph for the passing of an era of transoceanic travel. Haiku (1965), made in collaboration with Leo Hurwitz, captures a set of dances by the choreographer Jane Dudley. Leroy Douglas (1967) concerns the reaction of fellow workers in New York's garment district to the death in Vietnam of a young black colleague. Claw (1968), photographed with Walter Hess, is a fable in the guise of a documentary. The film argues that styles of contemporary urban development subordinate human values to economic ones. Claw was chosen to launch the Museum of Modern Art's landmark exhibit, 'The Machine as Seen at the End of the Mechanical Age'. It went on to theaters, museums, and public television. Short Circuit (1973), a semi-documentary made at the height of the Black Power movement, examines the reaction of a white, middle-class male with liberal politics to the encroachment into his Manhattan neighborhood of a black population and culture. Bridge High (1975) is a choreographed paean in black and white to a suspension bridge.

Stations of the Elevated (1980) and We Were So Beloved (1986) are Kirchheimer's most celebrated films. Stations is a lyrical documentary that follows elevated subway trains that are illicitly painted, by slum youths, with such messages as Crime, Hate, Slave, Pusher, Earth is Hell, Heaven is Life. Images of fire, whores, and guns are juxtaposed to what Kirchheimer calls the 'legalized vandalism' of prisons, artifacts of war, and advertising billboards. In We Were So Beloved (1986), a two and a half-hour film based on interviews, Kirchheimer probes the experiences and attitudes of Jewish refugees and survivors from Nazi Germany, who had created a community in northern Manhattan's Washington Heights. Tall: The American Skyscraper and Louis Sullivan (2004), is a lyrical documentary that tells the story of the development of the early skyscraper in Chicago and New York—and of its first great architect. The film's central conflict is the clash between adherence to principle and expedient compromise.

Kirchheimer, who is also a film teacher, has spelled out some of his filmmaking theories in a series of papers with such titles as 'Truth Without Vérité', 'The Dangers of Improvement (in oral history films and videos)', 'Beyond the Clichés of the Holocaust', 'Unadvertised Side Effects (of the new film technology)', and 'The Soul of Structure'.

WALTER HESS

Biography

Born in 1931 in Saarbrücken, Germany. His family emigrated to the United States in 1936 and settled in New York City. Educated in New York's public schools. Graduated from New York's City College (CCNY) in 1952 with a BA and a major from Hans Richter's Institute of Film Techniques at City College. His film career began with editing work for several of the city's industrial film producers. Early on, assisted Hans Richter with several of Richter's films and worked with Jay Leyda in the restoration of Eisenstein's ¡Que Viva Mexico! Associated with Leo Hurwitz for many years, primarily as cameraman. His independent films have received numerous awards in both the United States and Europe. Has taught film at CCNY, Columbia, and New York University and is today professor of film at the School of Visual Arts in New York City.

Selected films

1965 Colossus on the River: producer, director, writer, camera, editor
1967 Leroy Douglas: co-filmmaker with Peter Eliscu
1968 Claw: producer, codirector (with Walter Hess), camera (with Walter Hess), editor
1973 Short Circuit: producer, director, writer, camera (with Warren Johnson), editor
1975 Bridge High: producer, director (with Walter Hess), writer, camera (with Walter Hess), editor
1980 Stations of the Elevated: producer, director, writer, camera, editor
1986 We Were So Beloved: producer, director, writer, editor, camera (with James Calanan and Steve Juliano)
2004 Tall: The American Skyscraper and Louis Sullivan: producer, director, writer, camera, editor

Further reading

Barnouw, Eric, *Tube of Plenty: The Evolution of American Television*, New York: Oxford University Press, 1982.
Insdorf, Annette, *Indelible Shadows: Film and the Holocaust*, third edn, New York: Cambridge University Press, 2003.
Kirchheimer, Gloria de Vidas and Kirchheimer, Manfred, *We Were So Beloved: Autobiography of a German Jewish Community*, Pittsburgh, PA: University of Pittsburgh Press, 1997.
n.a., 'An Interview with Manny Kirchheimer', *Wide Angle* 6, no. 1, 1984: 42–9.
n.a., 'Rappin', Writin' and Breakin'', *Centro Spring* 1988: 34–41.

Klein, James

James Klein was a prominent producer and director in the social issue documentary movement that developed in the 1970s and early 1980s. Of particular note during that period are four documentaries that he codirected with Julia Reichert. Growing Up Female (1971), the first documentary study of the societal forces in America that mold female identities, influenced subsequent feminist documentaries through its combination of interviews, advertisements, and popular music. Methadone: An American Way of Dealing (1975) critiques the use of methadone as a method of combating drug addiction. His next two documentaries were Oscar-nominated: Union Maids (1976) blends feminist and labor history through oral interviews with three women who played roles in the unionization drives in the United States during the 1930s; and Seeing Red: Stories of American Communists (1983) records the personal oral histories of American Communist Party members from the 1930s to the 1950s. Following his work with Reichert, Klein worked as a writer, editor, and director on dramatic films and directed two documentaries that premiered on PBS. The first, Letter to the Next Generation (1989), is filmed on the campus of Kent State, where the National Guard shot and killed four students during anti-war protests on May 4, 1970. Klein uses the site to explore the ways in which today's students differ from those on campus during the shooting. The second, Taken for a Ride (1996), documents the role of General Motors in the destruction of America's public transportation system.

Like many social issue documentarians, Klein is motivated by a particular political activism. His early films with Reichert address gender and working-class life from a socialist perspective, but his activism is not limited to the choice and treatment of these subjects. Although his early films are not technically innovative, he and Reichert pioneered novel approaches to production, marketing, and distribution. In the early 1970s Klein was a founding member of New Day Films, which was originally created to promote the women's movement. New Day was the first American cooperative distribution company operated entirely by and for filmmakers.

Many of Klein's early films with Reichert were made for particular working-class audiences and distributed to them directly through a variety of political institutions and organizations, such as unions, schools, YMCAs, and health care providers. Because of this control, Klein could focus on his explicit goal of promoting discussion and social change. To that end, his films are often accompanied by discussions or meetings and often include complementary handouts and discussion questions. Methadone incorporates a midway break for discussion, and some of his work is so audience-specific that it is produced for particular working-class neighborhoods and is never distributed beyond them.

Klein also attempts to incorporate his socialist, nonhierarchical politics into the production and structure of his documentaries. His collaborative models, such as codirecting many of his films with Julia Reichert, undermine common hierarchical structures in film production. In Union Maids, for example, he and Reichert chose to work with video, despite the compromised quality, because video allowed more extended, collaborative interviews and because it enabled them to work with less experienced students. Video not only allowed more shooting but also made it possible for them to direct inexperienced cinematographers by intercom while watching on a monitor. Union Maids also exemplifies Klein's aversion to heroic figures. He and Reichert have argued in interviews that focusing on individuals and aggrandizing their actions leads the audience to believe that such people are unusually gifted and unique and that they drive history. He seeks, rather, a model of collective agency. Consequently, Union Maids mixes the testimonies of three women of different ethnicities to demonstrate the wide range of people who collaborated in the cause of unionizing American industry.

Klein's focus on agency led to an early shift in his filmmaking. His first major film, Growing Up Female, depicts the problem of gender roles in the United States but doesn't develop possible responses to the problem. His next film, Methadone, begins in a similar vein with a critique of the societal response to drug addiction, but the second half of the film explores possible solutions to the problem. In his subsequent documentaries, Klein incorporates positive role models and opportunities for agency.

Critical reception of Klein's documentary films has focused on his use of direct cinema techniques. Because Klein's early documentaries generally eschew voice-over narration and employ oral interviews extensively, they are less able to develop the broader context of the topics they explore. Further, despite Klein's aversion to portrayals of individual heroism, critics have claimed that his films aggrandize the few people interviewed. Union Maids and Seeing Red, for example, are criticized for oversimplifying social relations by giving an incomplete, uncontested story primarily through oral interviews of small numbers of like-minded people. Such an approach can be read as a legitimate form of counter-history, and recent critics have argued for the recuperation of such direct cinema techniques for the creation of counter-histories that dispute conventional representations of authority and give more heteroglossic alternatives. However, other critics have argued that Klein tends to present oral histories as independent arguments and not as primary source material in need of a broader explanatory frame. The lack of such a context, it is claimed, can make his films appear naïve—an endorsement of a partial, self-protective history rather than a metacritical response to previous histories (Nichols 1991: 252).

Klein's next documentaries, Letter to the Next Generation and Taken for a Ride, move away from most of the direct cinema techniques of his early work. Oral interviews remain prominent, but voice-over and contextual information impose an explicit explanatory frame on the material. Letter to the Next Generation is presented as Klein's subjective, personal consideration of the differences between students of the early 1970s and those of the late 1980s. There is frequent first-person voice-over narration in the form of rhetorical questions and ruminations, and Klein appears on camera periodically, commenting on the content of the film. Taken for a Ride abandons the subjective frame of Letter to the Next Generation and instead employs frequent voice-of-God narration to argue that General Motors sabotaged the public transportation system in America during the 1920s and 1930s. Oral interviews are still employed, and those interviewed are primarily like-minded in their critical view of General Motors. However, the film complements these interviews with extensive archival research, including records of antitrust court cases, corporate television promotions, and broadcast news reports.

PAUL MILLER

See also: Reichert, Julia; Seeing Red; Union Maids

Biography

Cofounded New Day Films in 1971. Graduated from Antioch College in 1972. Union Maids nominated for Academy Award for Best Documentary Feature, 1978. Won Critics Award from the French Syndicate of Cinema Critics for Union Maids, 1978. Named (with Julia Reichert) Artist of the Year by the Ohio Arts Council, 1983. Seeing Red nominated for Academy Award for Best Documentary Feature, 1984. Won Best of Festival Award at the Nashville Independent Film Festival for Taken for a Ride, 1997. Former Professor of Theatre Arts/ Motion Pictures in the Department of Theatre Arts at Wright State University.

Selected films

1970 Growing Up Female: codirector
1975 Methadone: An American Way of Dealing: codirector
1975 Men's Lives: coproducer
1976 Union Maids: codirector, editor
1983 Seeing Red: Stories of American Communists: codirector
1989 Letter to the Next Generation: director
1996 Taken for a Ride: coproducer, director

Further reading

Boruszkowski, Lilly Ann, 'An Interview with Documentary Filmmaker Jim Klein', *Journal of Film and Video* 46, no. 1, 1994: 34–42.

Georgakas, Dan, 'Seeing Red', *Cineaste* 13, no. 2, 1984: 27–8.

Kleinhaus, Chuck, 'Julia Reichert and Jim Klein', *Jump Cut* 5, 1975: 11–12.

Nichols, Bill, *Representing Reality*, Bloomington, IN: Indiana University Press, 1991.

Rosenthal, Alan, 'Union Maids', in Alan Rosenthal (ed.), *Documentary Conscience*, Berkeley, CA: University of California Press, 1980.

——(ed.), *New Challenges for Documentary*, Berkeley, CA: University of California Press, 1988.

Rubenstein, Lenny, 'Who's Who in Filmmaking: Julia Reichert and James Klein', *Sightlines* 20, no. 2, 1986–7: 22–5.

Shafransky, Renee, 'Seeing Red: An Interview with James Klein and Julia Reichert', *Cineaste* 13, no. 2, 1984: 24–6.

Waldman, Diane and Walker, Janet (ed.), *Feminism and Documentary*, Minneapolis, MN: University of Minnesota Press, 1999.

Kline, Herbert

In the late 1930s and 1940s Herbert Kline's work represented an important part of the American documentary movement's unofficial international wing. His leftist stance, similar to that of Frontier Films or Roosevelt's New Deal filmmakers, found expression in filmic essays of humanitarian crises abroad, especially in support of Popular Front antifascism. Kline hoped that these films would change Americans' perception of the world. He believed in the importance of artistic illustration and eloquent narration, leading him to consistently partner with experienced photographers and writers, but Kline maintained no set theory of documentary realism and did not even regard himself strictly as a documentarian (even though he was a member of the Association of Documentary Film Producers). For his documentaries, Kline mixed actuality footage with material he directly influenced or staged on location, a practice common among his contemporaries. However, his use of fiction increased with his production of 'story documentaries' and entirely fictional films, demonstrating his assertion that the social effect of a film was much more important than the means by which he made it.

Kline's political perspective found its most influential expression in his four films representing the broad Popular Front movement, an amalgam of liberals and leftist groups in favor of social reforms and especially opposed to fascism. These films, made between 1937 and 1940, reflected an outlook that Kline developed in travels as a young man in Depression-era America and in his association with leftist theater, including the Group Theater and playwright Clifford Odets, and editorship of the critical journal *New Theatre* (later *New Theatre & Film*). Heart of Spain (1937) and Return to Life (1938) rallied support—moral and financial—for the Loyalists fighting against the fascists in the Spanish Civil War and accused Hitler and Mussolini of cynically orchestrating the conflict for their material gain. Crisis (1939) depicted the oppressive German occupation of Czechoslovakia, earning Kline thanks from President Franklin Roosevelt for the film's visual support for the White House's grim assessment of the Nazis. Lights Out in Europe (1940) showed Nazis taking over Danzig and invading Poland and decried the inhumanity of the coming war.

As he made his Popular Front films, Kline described his position as 'foreign correspondent of the screen'. Kline felt that by making these documentaries, he and Joris Ivens, then making The Spanish Earth (1937) and The 400 Million (1939), could 'do more to damn fascist governments than all the tirades of the world'. Kline relied on what he referred to as 'candid camera' actuality shots, including some horrific and heart-wrenching scenes of warfare. On some occasions, Kline guided the subjects to better reflect the reality he observed; an example is his request to Nazi storm troopers that they stop smiling at the camera and look more serious as they ousted Czech families from their homes.

Kline also staged entire narratives in a style he referred to as 'story documentary', a term suggestive of the approach of Robert Flaherty or The Ramparts We Watch (1940). For The Forgotten Village (1941), Kline and associate Alexander Hackenschmied (later Alexander Hammid) scouted Mexican locations, cast locals, and shot from a story conceived by John Steinbeck. By some definitions, only the absence of professional actors justifies the label 'documentary'. Kline filmed My Father's House (1947), concerning the emigration of Holocaust survivors, under similar circumstances. It was shot in Palestine with nonprofessional actors in scripted roles, and advance publicity stressed the film's hybrid nature, claiming that 'fact and fiction are mingled together, as though in a single heartbeat'. Kline's planned location filming of John Gunther's Inside Africa would similarly have been a 'semi-fictional treatment'.

In addition to his fictionalized documentaries, Kline ventured into fiction films, demonstrating a documentary style and examining leftist and socially conscious subjects. These films followed the example of The Grapes of Wrath (1940), a film that *The New York Times* critic Bosley Crowther described as 'reportorial as any documentary and strictly in the spirit of the school', and anticipated similar moves by the likes of March of Time's Louis de Rochemont, producer of House on 92nd Street (1945). For Kline, a brief term at MGM ended fruitlessly, but he completed fiction films on diverse subjects, including Yugoslav resistance to the Nazis (in English and Spanish) and the Cleveland Indians' social outreach program. In 1952 Kline directed The Fighter from a Jack London story about a Mexican boxer during the 1910 revolution, a film shot by James Wong Howe and former documentarian Floyd Crosby.

Kline's partnership with Crosby and Howe reflected Kline's prioritization of photographic artistry supported by literate prose narration. In his earlier documentaries, Kline partnered with renowned still photographers Geza Karpathi, Henri Cartier (later Cartier-Bresson), and Alexander Hackenschimed (also an accomplished filmmaker) and recruited the young Douglas Slocombe in 1939. Kline felt that strong photographic content allowed greater freedom in the narration, and he augmented the images with the written words of Vincent Sheean (Crisis), James Hilton (Lights Out in Europe), John Steinbeck (The Forgotten Village), and Meyer Levin (My Father's House).

Kline's interest in the visual arts endured through his career, eventually prompting a return to documentary filmmaking after a break of over two decades. Branded a communist by the House Un-American Activities Committee in the early 1950s, Kline suffered through a series of unrealized film projects, including Inside Africa, a biography of Clarence Darrow, and 'Of Love and Terror', about Arab and Israeli conflicts. In 1971 Kline completed the documentary Walls of Fire about Mexican muralist David Alfaro Siqueiros's 'The March of Humanity in Latin America', with additional material concerning Siqueiros's political struggles and those of Diego Rivera and José Clemente Orozco. Kline followed with The Challenge … A Tribute to Modern Art (1974), featuring an array of contemporary artists (from Chagall to Pollock) and their artwork. In the 1980s Kline revisited his formative years in the leftist theater of the 1930s, directing a film about the Group Theater's Lee Strasberg, Acting: Lee Strasberg and the Actors Studio (1981), shortly before Strasberg's death and initiating a project to film great theaters of the world.

Depression-era, leftist theater and the contemporary subjective and stylistic traditions of documentary film greatly informed the work of Herbert Kline, whose most influential films extended his Popular Front's antifascism from the pages of *New Theatre* to the screen. Kline opposed fascism and war in humanitarian terms, a position not central to the didactic 'information films' that the US government would later commission to address the same events. From his Popular Front documentaries to his later films, Kline traversed and often blurred the boundary between documentary and fiction film. Regardless of the method of filmmaking, Kline always strove to express his concept of reality and, as he said in 1942, to use 'the great medium of the twentieth-century as it should be used—in the fight for a better world!'

MICHAEL D. ROBINSON

See also: Heart of Spain

Biography

Born March 13, 1909, in Davenport, Iowa. Largely self-educated on authors including Whitman, London, Dostoevsky, Dos Passos, and O'Neill. Held odd jobs in early Depression, including putting to sea from San Francisco. Followed his brother, Mark Marvin, into leftist theater, writing for *The Left* and *Left Front* and writing a one-act play, John Henry—Bad Nigger in 1933. From 1934 until January 1, 1937, edited and wrote for *New Theatre*, later *New Theatre & Film*. August through September 1935, toured European dramatic theaters, including several in USSR. Active in the New York Film and Photo League. Promoted leftist theater and Popular Front politics across the country and in Hollywood, including staging Bury the Dead in the Hollywood Bowl in 1936. Traveled to Spain in 1937 to write about the Civil War for New Masses and broadcast for EAQ Loyalist radio. Worked with Frontier Films from Spain and joined Association of Documentary Film Producers in New York. Signed with MGM in 1941 but departed while on his first project, Journey for Margaret. Independent producer, director, and writer for the rest of his career. Named a communist by the House Un-American Activities Committee in 1952, refusing to testify. Active in Los Angeles art scene from 1960s onward, associated with Bart Lytton. Walls of Fire and The Challenge … A Tribute to Modern Art received Academy Award nominations for Best Documentary. First wife: Rosa Harvan (Kline). Second wife: Josine Ianco (Kline) (Ianco-Starrels). Children: Ethan Kline and Elissa Kline Gillberg. Died February 5, 1999 in Los Angeles.

Selected films

1937 Heart of Spain: director, photographer, producer
1938 Return to Life: director, writer
1939 Crisis/Crisis: A Film of the Nazi Way: director, producer, editor
1940 Lights Out in Europe: director, producer, editor
1941 The Forgotten Village: director, producer
1947 My Father's House: director, producer
1971 Walls of Fire: director
1974 The Challenge … A Tribute to Modern Art: director, writer, producer
1981 Acting: Lee Strasberg and the Actors Studio: director, writer, producer

Further reading

Alexander, William, *Film on the Left: American Documentary Film from 1931 to 1942*, Princeton, NJ: Princeton University Press, 1981.

Campbell, Russell, *Cinema Strikes Back: Radical Filmmaking in the United States 1930–42*, Ann Arbor, MI: UMI Research Press, 1982.

Crowther, Bosley, 'Matter of Fact: Joris Ivens and Herbert Kline Focus Their Cameras on the Conflicts of Today', *The New York Times*, March 12, 1939: 154.

Hilton, James and Kline, Herbert, 'Lights Out in Europe', *Look*, May 7, 1940: 24–9.

Kline, Herbert, 'Films Without Make-Believe', *The Magazine of Art*, February 1, 1942: 58–63, 87–8. (Reprinted in Lewis Jacobs, *The Documentary Tradition*, New York: Norton, 1979: 148–57.)

——*New Theatre and Film 1934 to 1937: An Anthology*, San Diego, CA: Harcourt Brace Jovanovich, 1985.

Steinbeck, John, Harvan Kline, Rosa and Hammid, Alexander, *The Forgotten Village, with 136 Photographs from the Film of the Same Name*, New York: Viking, 1941.

Kluge, Alexander

Alexander Kluge's films mount a sustained critical assault upon the principles of cinematic realism. They dismantle the conventions of plot, character, and style that guarantee the coherence of classical narrative cinema. They discredit the credibility, veracity, and authenticity of the documentary image. Fiction and nonfiction film alike establish a system of representation that conforms to generic norms and conceals its own ideological construction. The documentary form carries a set of assumptions about its status as factual record, its value as truthful evidence, and its role as objective witness. Consequently, it certifies a particular organisation of power and knowledge. It institutes a rhetorical order of description, demonstration, exposition, argumentation, and analysis that is consonant with the dictates of instrumental reason and political economy. The documentary also screens out other possible methods for interpreting or assembling information about history, society, and culture. As a result, it naturalises the existing conditions of knowledge and belief and denies the social production of meaning by asserting the absolute identity of filmed image and real life.

For Kluge, on the other hand, human wishes and desires are the medium through which facts are perceived. The documentary method compounds the discrepancy between experience and expression because it devalues the reality of subjective fantasy or collective agency. The motive for realism, therefore, is 'never a confirmation of reality, but rather a protest'. The tasks of cinematic representation and cultural renewal are inseparable. The reconstitution of the institutional, economic, and aesthetic practices of the film and television industry is a necessary element in the project of reconstructing society. Against the official statements of cultural and legal institutions such as the media or the state, Kluge's films contribute to the creation of a *Gegen-Öffentlichkeit*, an oppositional public sphere. He has developed a range of theoretical and pragmatic strategies in order to promote institutional, conceptual, and political change through his work in film and television.

At the level of form and style Kluge's most favoured gesture for countering the 'conceptual imperialism' of the dominant mode of film production is to challenge radically the separation between documentary and fiction. He fractures narrative continuity by inserting documentary sequences into his fictional scenarios. He shatters documentary authenticity by framing real events within a fictional context. In the process, the film assumes an episodic and fragmentary structure that frustrates the spectators' attempts to impose a unified meaning on the diverse material. The coexistence of fictional and documentary imagery produces sudden shifts in perspective, interruptions, digressive or contradictory observations, and unexpected conclusions. Kluge applies the principle of montage in order to construct an alternative context (*Zusammenhang*) for understanding the relationship between history and memory, culture and politics. The capacity to differentiate, to make distinctions and associations, which Kluge marshals against the totalising logic of the 'bourgeois public sphere', is reflected in the hybrid structure of his own discursive method. Accordingly, Kluge's spectator plays an active role in making connections between the various elements of the film and providing a context for their evaluation, thereby participating in the critical project of reimagining the terms of political and social life.

Kluge collects documentary images from a wide range of sources and reassembles them in different combinations and configurations. His material includes pictures from children's books and folktales, old prints and paintings, operatic and theatrical tableaux, postcards and photographs from the nineteenth century, stills and sequences from early cinema, archival footage of historical events, World War II newsreels, maps, diagrams, architectural drawings and plans, instructional or educational films, televised recordings, interviews, vérité images of current events, and reconstructed treatments of imaginary 'case histories'. Kluge and his editor, Beate Mainka-Jellinghaus, punctuate the film with short documentary passages that, as a result of the process of juxtaposition, produce unexpected critical connections among images, ideas, and information. In addition, video technology permits a further level of manipulation and modification; in his television programme 10 to 11, Kluge will mask, insert, superimpose, colourise, or animate the image in such a way as to suggest further layers of meaning within and across the frame. More simply, he remotivates found footage by altering or adding sound; in Artists Under the Big Top: Perplexed (1967), a Nazi Party rally is accompanied by the Beatles tune 'Yesterday'. He places unusual imagery in an incongruous setting; a crudely illustrated rhyme about a resuscitated mammoth follows Anita G's imprisonment in Yesterday Girl (1966). The lives of invented characters are illustrated by still photos or archival film. Most famously, Gabi Teichert, the heroine of The Patriot (1979), observes events at the Social Democratic Party convention and interviews actual delegates about her plans to change the way that German history is taught in school. All of these examples reveal the precariousness of documentary's claim to represent the truth.

The voice of the narrator often supplies a documentary with its tone of authority. The commentary presents a series of reasonable propositions about the images on screen.

Its statements are moderate, balanced, and seemingly neutral. In this manner, the logic of the film's argument and the validity of its interpretive method appear persuasive and credible. Kluge, however, constantly undoes the obvious equating of narration to reliability and fidelity. The word does not always illustrate or explain the image. In Kluge's films the narrator's comments appear puzzling, puzzled, amusing, annoying, wry, dry, arrogant, ignorant, sympathetic, or ironic. The voice-over acts both as a point of identification for the viewer and as a means of distancing. It seems to possess an excess of knowledge and a lack of meaningful sense. For instance, in The Patriot, the knee of a soldier who died at Stalingrad reflects upon history, Germany, and the act of representation itself, as well as offering prosaic details about the visual material gathered by the film. Kluge also shows that the conventional use of narration as an instrument of verification can serve the function of falsification or fabrication. He invents facts, devises imaginary reports and records, and produces false documents. The commentary provides such a perfect imitation of bureaucratic and legal discourse in its efforts to classify, describe, analyse, and interpret the actions of characters or the significance of images and scenes that the distinctive mode of address employed in documentary film—impartial, objective, rational—assumes the characteristics of an authoritative statement of truth, a purely redundant and self-referential utterance. The voice of the narrator mediates the production of factual authenticity. Documentary, ultimately, verifies its own discursive techniques.

Even in his earliest short films, despite their more traditional style, Kluge interrogated the processes of documentary representation. Brutality in Stone (Kluge and Schamoni, 1960) confronts the repressed past by revisiting the monumental sites and symbols of the Third Reich. Kluge deploys the modernist strategies of citation, alienation, and montage, as practised by Benjamin, Brecht, and Eisenstein, in order to, in Miriam Hansen's words, '[open] up historical perspectives on the present' and to initiate the process of Trauerarbeit [Grieving]'. The film combines and contrasts the twin poles of documentary realism: the camera observes and records, and the editing interprets and analyses. Music and sound contradict the mute testimony of the visual images. Voices and film footage from the past are juxtaposed with fragments and ruins of the traumatic legacy of the Nazi times, including the now desolate set for the Nuremburg Rally featured in Triumph of the Will (Riefenstahl, 1935). In this way, according to Eric Rentschler, 'the structures of the past are recycled and worked over [umfunktioniert und aufgearbeit], ceasing to serve their original function' (n.a. 1990: 35). The film's aesthetic method, therefore, carries a political meaning.

Kluge's cinema is committed to artistic experimentation and social criticism. The creation of a counter public sphere, as previously noted, demands new forms of communication and expression if it is to interrogate the historical forces that shape contemporary reality. It will transform the system of representation, as well as establish an alternative practice of filmmaking. Since the days of the Oberhausen manifesto (1962), which proclaimed the economic, ethical, and political 'collapse of the conventional German film' industry and led to the establishment of a system of federal funding boards, filmmakers' cooperatives, and production companies, as well as an independent research facility at Ulm, Kluge has argued for a politicised form of film culture. He has advocated the filmmaker's complete autonomy in the direction and production process, as well as the development of a collective approach to film politics. Germany in Autumn (1977–8), a film that involved a number of prominent authors and directors, including Kluge, Fassbinder, Böll, Schlöndorff, and Reitz, is the most accessible attempt to implement the principle of *Gegen-Öffentlichkeit* and to intervene directly in the political discourse on the fateful events of October 1977. The authoritarian response of the state to the terrorist acts perpetrated by the Red Army Faction against the capitalist system created a climate of violence, fear, and paranoia, and provoked a crisis of legitimacy for both the left and the ruling classes. The situation reached its disastrous climax with the kidnapping and murder of Hanns-Martin Schleyer, former SS officer and head of Daimler-Benz; the alleged suicides of Andreas Baader, Gudrun Enslinn, and Jan-Carl Raspe in the maximum security prison of Stammheim; and the storming of a hijacked plane at Mogadishu by special forces and the eventual release of the hostages. As an example of Kluge's notion of a 'strategy from below', Germany in Autumn offers an initial response to the official account of events.

The film, as usual, contains a mixture of documentary and dramatised/fictional scenarios. Each director is responsible for a sequence, but Kluge's presence is evident throughout. He takes the role of narrator and, in tandem with Mainka-Jellinghaus, has structured the material in a discontinuous, elliptical fashion. The content and form of the film challenge the programmatic and sensationalist format of television, as Hansen astutely observes (Hansen 1981–2: 52–3). Indeed, the media functioned as a mechanism of censorship and control during the crisis. Kluge's footage of the funerals of Schleyer and the terrorists, on the other hand, reveals the limited scope of television reporting. He focuses on what generally escapes the frame or exceeds the allotted span of attention. He stays at the graveside after the camera crews have left. A young boy watches as a trailer full of earth is dumped into the hole in the ground. In the background, policemen mounted on horseback, like Siegfried in Fritz Lang's film, survey the scene. The spectator is free to make a judgement about the images, rather than, as with the television news, forced to accept their inevitability.

Kluge's own television output continues the project of countering the power of the media, only this time from within. Since 1986 he has been contracted to provide weekly programming for a number of privately owned channels. Kluge's alliance with the media conglomerates and state broadcasters allows him to open a 'cultural window' within commercial television, an alternative mode of address that supposedly offers a critical perspective on the production and consumption of visual images. He has not compromised his working method for a popular audience, which, despite the channel's complaints that ratings drop during his screening time, numbers around one million viewers. The twenty- to thirty-minute pieces for his series 10 to 11 are condensed versions of the essayistic style that he has developed over the years. Their heterogeneity of form and subject matter, which ranges from opera to fireworks and from the avant-garde to advertising, recall the aesthetic of early cinema and the montage of film attractions, while reproducing the look of the magazine format, complete with interviews, news readers, graphics, and assorted video clips. Kluge applies Adorno's suggestion that the structure of the revue and the circus provide cinema with a model for breaking the spell of illusion and inventing a critical practice capable of contesting the products of the culture industry. Surprisingly, the continuous flow and fractured temporality of the televisual medium provide a conducive environment for Kluge's experiment in public broadcasting. The esoteric nature of Kluge's enquiry is balanced by the intriguing and unusual manner of its presentation. High modernist art meets postmodern culture in a productive exchange. The work for television stands as a crowning achievement in an impressive and influential career.

ALAN WRIGHT

Biography

Born February 14, 1932, in Halberstadt, Germany. Attended high school in Berlin. Studied law, history, and music in Marburg and Frankfurt am Main. Awarded a doctorate (in law) in 1956. As a university student, became acquainted with Theodore Adorno. Worked as both an attorney and a university professor before turning to writing and film. Married in 1982, has two children. Has worked exclusively in television since 1988.

Selected films

1960	Brutality in Stone (Kluge and Schamoni)
1966	Yesterday Girl
1967	Artists Under the Big Top: Perplexed
1977–8	Germany in Autumn
1979	The Patriot

Further reading

Alter, Nora, 'Framing Terrorism: Beyond the Borders', in *Projecting History: German Nonfiction Cinema, 1967–2000*, Ann Arbor, MI: University of Michigan Press, 2002: 43–75.

Corrigan, Timothy, *New German Film: The Displaced Image*, Austin, University of Texas Press, 1983: 95–119.

Elsaesser, Thomas, *New German Cinema: A History*, London: BFI, 1989.

Flinn, Caryl, *The New German Cinema: Music, History and the Matter of Style*, Berkeley, CA: University of California Press, 2004: 107–69.

Hansen, Miriam, 'Cooperative Auteur Cinema and Oppositional Public Sphere', *New German Critique*, fall–winter 1981–2: 36–56.

Kaes, Anton, 'In Search of Germany: Alexander Kluge's The Patriot', in *From Hitler to Heimat*,

Cambridge, MA: Harvard University Press, 1989: 105–35.
Kluge, Alexander, 'On Film and the Public Sphere', *New German Critique*, fall–winter 1981–2: 24–5.
Liebman, Stuart (ed.), Essays by Miriam Hansen, Andreas Huyssen, Fredric Jameson, Stuart Liebman, and Heide Schlüpmann and an interview and texts by Kluge, *October* 46 (fall 1998).
Lutze, Peter C., *Alexander Kluge: The Last Modernist*, Detroit, MI: Wayne University Press, 1998.
n.a., *Special Issue on Alexander Kluge*, with essays by Miriam Hansen, Timothy Corrigan, Eric Rentschler, Helke Sander, Heide Schlüpmann and Gertrud Koch and texts by Kluge, *New German Critique* 49, winter, 1990.

Koenig, Wolf

Wolf Koenig began his forty-six-year career at the National Film Board of Canada (NFB) as a film splicer, and he ended it as a still-active producer and much-loved mentor of younger filmmakers. Along the way, he was involved in some of the key films and movements at the NFB. He was stylistically inventive and cinematically adventurous. That his contribution to the Film Board documentary is not widely known may be due in part to his retiring personality: he does not merely shun publicity; he flees it.

In 1952 Koenig photographed Norman McLaren's Oscar-winning Neighbors, an eight-minute experimental film using live actors photographed frame by frame. Although far removed generically from documentary, the film was arguably as significant in the development of the Film Board documentary as it was for Film Board animation. Its anti-war message became a recurring theme in Film Board documentaries, and its playful inventiveness informed and inspired filmmakers who worked primarily in documentary.

In 1953 a cel animation cartoon film, The Romance of Transportation, which Koenig codirected and cowrote, helped to establish another characteristic often found in NFB documentaries: self-deprecation, a willingness of the NFB to poke fun at Canada, its government, and itself. Koenig directed It's a Crime (1957), an animated film made for the Canadian Department of Labour. The film parodied with great effect and affection The Third Man, and it included a send-up of the typical NFB educational documentary of the time.

In the 1950s animation was administered by Unit B, of which Koenig was a member. Koenig's involvement in both animation and documentary facilitated the former's contribution to the latter at the Film Board. As cameraman for the lyric Corral (1954), Koenig broke two rules: a bureaucratic one stipulating that all documentaries were to be shot by members of the NFB's Camera Department, and an aesthetic one requiring that the camera be mounted on a tripod (Corral was shot in 35mm). Foreshadowing the later development of freer-form documentary, Koenig shot much of the film with the camera on his shoulder; this allowed him to mingle closely among the restless penned horses he was filming. He did the camerawork for City of Gold (1957), a film made mostly from still photographs but which, because of the camera's movement within the material, makes the viewer sometimes forget that the images are not live action.

Koenig was a director, editor, and cameraman with the team that created the NFB's watershed Candid Eye series, which lasted from 1958 through 1961. The series was made possible by the NFB's invention of a lightweight 16mm synchronized sound recording system. It was influenced aesthetically by the photographs of Henri Cartier-Bresson, whose work Koenig, especially, felt had captured the spontaneity of real life. Koenig also argued forcefully for a fluid, role-crossing production team structure that would include cameramen as fully equal members of the production team, rather than as individuals assigned to a project merely for the shooting period. Koenig was one of three credited directors for the series' prototype, The Days Before Christmas (1958), which he shot with two young French Canadian cameramen, Georges Dufaux and Michel Brault. Brault has identified Koenig's handheld tracking close-up of a Brinks guard's holstered handgun as 'a turning point in the liberation of the camera in cinema'.

Shot without a script, The Days Before Christmas is a vital mosaic of sharply observed actions and emotionally subtle edits. It catches people unawares and in unguarded moments. However, some members of the Candid Eye team felt that the film verged on the voyeuristic. Another well-known Candid Eye film, The Back-breaking Leaf (1959), directed by Terence Macartney-Filgate and produced by Koenig, was in part a rejoinder to the perceived detachment of The Days Before Christmas. Its more participatory photography employs many more close-ups of people and emphasizes the grueling character of the work of harvesting tobacco. The camera's presence is acknowledged, people speak to the audience, and off-camera questions from the director are heard. Its structure is more rhythmic and rough-hewn than the delicately nuanced The Days Before Christmas.

Although technically not a Candid Eye film, Lonely Boy (1961), which Koenig photographed and codirected, stands as a capstone for the series and a milestone in the development of scriptless documentary. A half-hour portrait of Paul Anka, the film fashions revealing direct cinema footage into a tightly structured, minimally narrated examination of Anka as an individual and as a phenomenon. The film is by turns funny, disturbing, mocking, and poignant. It incorporated reflexivity long before reflexivity became de rigueur, and it did so in a hilarious and self-deprecatory way that still contrasts with the sanctimonious, self-important tone in which reflexivity typically is introduced into films.

After the demise of Unit B in 1964 Koenig worked as a producer and executive producer in the animation department, now separated from documentary production. Among the films he produced or coproduced are: King Size (1968), an anti-smoking film aimed at children; The House That Jack Built (1967), a moral tale about the pursuit of satisfaction; Hot Stuff (1971), a cautionary film about the dangers of fire; and The Street (1976), Caroline Leaf's award-winning adaptation of a Mordecai Richler short story. In the 1980s Koenig was involved in several programs of short dramatic films directed at young people and often serving as training grounds for young filmmakers, but his last major project at the NFB was a documentary, Kanehsatake: 270 Years of Resistance (1993), an in-depth, closely observed film on a tense confrontation between native Canadians and the government over a land-use issue. The film manages to convey the anger of the protestors without demonizing the forces of order. It was directed by Alanis Obomsawin, whom Koenig had been instrumental in bringing into the Film Board years earlier.

D.B. JONES

See also: Brault, Michel; City of Gold

Biography

Born in Dresden, Germany, October 17, 1927. Emigrated with his family to Ontario, in 1937, where the family settled on a farm. Joined NFB in 1948 as a film splicer. Retired in 1994.

Selected films

1952 Neighbors (with McLaren): camera
1953 The Romance of Transportation in Canada (with Low): animation
1954 Corral (with Low): camera
1957 City of Gold: codirector, camera
1957 It's a Crime: director
1958 The Days Before Christmas: codirector, coproducer
1959 The Back-breaking Leaf (with Macartney-Filgate): coproducer
1961 Lonely Boy: codirector, camera
1967 The House That Jack Built (with Tunis): coproducer
1968 King Size (with Pindal): coproducer
1971 Hot Stuff (with Grgic): coproducer
1976 The Street (with Leaf): executive producer
1987 Wednesday's Children (with series): producer
1993 Kanehsatake: 270 Years of Resistance (with Obomsawin): coproducer

Further reading

Cartier-Bresson, Henri, *The Decisive Moment*, New York: Simon and Schuster, 1952.
Elder, Bruce, 'On the Candid Eye Movement', in Seth Feldman (ed.), *The Canadian Film Reader*, Toronto: Peter Martin, 1977.
Harcourt, Peter, 'The Innocent Eye', *Sight and Sound*, winter 1964: 19–23.
Jones, D.B., *Movies and Memoranda*, Ottawa: Deneau, 1982.
——*The Best Butler in the Business: Tom Daly of the National Film Board of Canada*, Toronto: University of Toronto Press, 1996.
Marcorelles, Louis, *Living Cinema: New Directions in Contemporary Filmmaking*, New York: Praeger, 1968.
Pâquet, André (ed.), *How to Make or Not to Make a Canadian Film*, Montréal: La Cinémathèque canadienne, 1967.

Kopple, Barbara

Barbara Kopple entered the world of documentary filmmaking as an assistant to the renowned Albert and David Maysles. The influence of their approach surely affected the evolution of Kopple's own unique style. Her first major work, Harlan County, USA (1976), was a provocative look at the coal miners' strike in Harlan County, Kentucky, against the Brookside Mine of the Eastover Mining Company. The company refused to sign a contract when the miners became members of the United Mine Workers of America. For over a year, Kopple documented the strike, living among the miners' supporters and witnessing firsthand the violence brought about by the tension between the opposing sides. The film illustrates the turmoil in the small community in a deeply personal way. The viewers are placed on the picket line with the striking workers.

They see the hatred felt both for and by the strikers and their families as the camera assumes the point of view of the viewer. The interactive nature of Kopple's approach to the subject matter makes this a strong cinematic exploration of humanity; the union here is asking for a modest increase in wages and for some improvements to ensure the safety of the workers. The film won the 1977 Academy Award for Best Documentary Feature. In 1991 the work was selected to be a part of the National Film Registry by the Library of Congress and was designated an American Film Classic.

Kopple followed the success of Harlan County, USA with some work in television as both a producer and a director. Her return to feature filmmaking led to a second Academy Award in 1991 for American Dream, a work that deals with a meatpackers' strike at the Hormel plant in Austin, Minnesota. This film investigates the struggle of Hormel employees as the company drops the pay rate by more than two dollars and then, when the packers strike, hires 'replacement workers' at the lower rate. The end of the film shows that after a settlement was reached between the company and the workers, Hormel sublet the plant to another company, this one paying workers nearly two dollars below the earlier reduced rate (four dollars under the initial pay rate). The exasperation of the packers is conveyed in such a way that the viewer's response is visceral. The personal here is made universal. American Dream also won the 1992 Director's Guild of America Award for Best Feature Documentary and captured the Grand Jury Prize, the Filmmaker's Trophy, and the Audience Award at the 1991 Sundance Film Festival. In addition, the film won the IDA Award from the International Documentary Association.

Kopple then returned to television, directing an episode of Homicide: Life on the Street in 1993. This episode won a Director's Guild of America award in 1998. In 1993 Kopple released Fallen Champ: The Untold Story of Mike Tyson, the first documentary ever featured as a Movie of the Week on NBC. The Director's Guild of America honored this film in 1994. This was followed by work as a director on a television miniseries called A Century of Women.

This continual work in television indicates that Kopple is a filmmaker interested in sharing information through all available media. While working chiefly as a documentary filmmaker, she has done directing work on various television series that feature fiction. In addition to her directorial work on such shows as Homicide, Kopple worked on the prison drama Oz in 1997, and she continues to explore the television medium.

Wild Man Blues is a 1997 work about Woody Allen's European tour with his jazz band. The film investigates the relationship between Allen and his wife (and former stepdaughter) Soon Yi Previn. The intimate nature of Kopple's approach to her subjects again places the viewer in the role of participant, a kind of non-threatening voyeur at once engaged and distant. This film was named Best Documentary by the Broadcast Critics' Association in 1998 and was honored by the National Board of Review that same year.

In 1998 Kopple released the Woodstock '94 project, documenting the 1994 Woodstock festival. This fueled the work done for My Generation, released in 2000, which investigates the legacy of Woodstock and its influences on Generation X. This work includes the 1999 Woodstock festival and relates its current cultural role to that of the 1969 and 1994 events. The film explores notions of community and the place of ritual in each of these time periods.

The Hamptons is a four-hour miniseries produced in 2002 for ABC. The work looks at the activities and thoughts of people in this affluent Long Island community from Memorial Day to Labor Day, 2001. Perhaps there is some connection here to the 'reality television' genre that is so popular in contemporary America, but the work is decidedly anthropological in its approach. The study is respectful and the representations insightful; this is genuine social investigation.

Kopple produced another television film, American Standoff, in 2002 for HBO. This work, directed by Kristi Jacobson, looks at the present-day Teamsters Union and its President, Jimmy Hoffa, Jr. Kopple's work continues to delve into areas of human experience in very personal, well-constructed films.

TAMMY A. KINSEY

See also: Maysles, Albert

Biography

Born in New York City on July 30, 1946. Assisted with projects for Maysles Brothers. Received Academy Award 1977 for Harlan County, USA. Film added to National Film Registry, 1991. Awarded Sundance Grand Jury Prize, Audience Prize, and Filmmakers Trophy for American Dreams, 1991 (the only film in history to win all three awards). Film also received Academy Award, as well as Director's Guild of America award, 1992. Won Maya Deren Film and Video Artists Award from American Film Institute, 1994. DGA Award for Fallen Champ, 1994. IDA Award, 1998, for American Dreams. DGA Award, 1998, for episode of television series Homicide. Lifetime Achievement Award, Human Rights Watch International Film Festival, 1998. Won Best Documentary, 1998, from National Board of Review and Broadcast Critics' Association, for Wild Man Blues.

Selected films

1976 Harlan County, USA
1990 American Dream
1993 Fallen Champ: The Untold Story of Mike Tyson
1994 A Century of Women
1997 Wild Man Blues
1999 A Conversation with Gregory Peck
2000 My Generation
2001 The Hamptons

Further reading

Chagolian, Steve, 'Woodstock "Generation" Floats in Limbo since '94', *Variety* 375, no. 9, July 19–25, 1999: 10.

Patterson, Troy, 'What a Beach', *Entertainment Weekly* 656, May 31, 2002: 24.

Stubbs, Liz, *Documentary Filmmakers Speak*, New York: Allworth Press, 2002.

Warren, Charles (ed.), *Beyond Document: Essays on Nonfiction Film*, Lebanon, NH: University Press of New England, 1996.

Kossakovsky, Viktor

The St Petersburg-based film director Victor Kossakovsky studied in Moscow and began his documentary work at the Leningrad Documentary Film Studio as a cameraman, editor, and director's assistant. His first documentary, Losev (1990), is an intriguing, contemplative film about the philosopher Alexes Losev. The film was awarded the prize for Best Debut, the Critic Prize, and the Silver Centaur Prize at the film festival 'Message to Man' held in St Petersburg.

Although Losev met with significant critical acclaim, Kossakovsky's real breakthrough on the international documentary scene was Belovi/ The Belovs (1993). This poetic saga on life in rural Russia during the winter, shot in black and white, has become one of the most significant and successful Russian documentaries of the post-perestroika era. This tragicomic film with little dialogue is a lyrical ode to ordinary life in rural Russia. A girl and her brothers are the main subjects. Shot in close-up, they discuss world issues, take a traditional steam bath, or hold celebrations in the countryside. Kossakovsky did the camerawork himself, as well as the editing, scriptwriting, and directing. Belovi won the Joris Ivens Award at the International Documentary Film Festival Amsterdam (IDFA) in 1993 and garnered many other main prizes at festivals around the world.

After documenting life in a rural village in Belovi, Kossakovsky turned to urban life in his next film, Sreda/Wednesday (1997). The crux of the film is that the main characters are residents of St Petersburg with the same birth date as the director. In the transition to a more democratic and capitalist form of government, some of these individuals became alcoholics or drug addicts, whereas others have started families and are struggling to lead a decent life. Through their stories, Kossakovsky dissects the postcommunist society and the mentality of people raised under the socialist doctrine. This fascinating profile of life in a post-Soviet urban environment is edited into an intriguing narrative structure that unfolds from one sequence to another. The film also depicts some private and unexpected events in the life of the filmmaker himself.

Kossakovsky worked on his next project for more than three years. His triptych I Loved You … (1998–2000) contemplates the joy, sorrow, and beauty of love. Three separate, unrelated films examine love within different generations. In Pavel and Layla/A Jerusalem Romance, the story focuses on the relationship of an elderly couple approaching separation because of the husband's fatal illness. In Sergei and Natasha/A Provincial Love Story, Kossakovsky portrays the wedding day of a young, jovial couple with conflicting families. The third member of the triptych, Sasha and Katja/First Romance, follows the love and suffering of children in kindergarten. In each of the films, the subjects face an obstacle: illness, family disputes, or an unexpected disappointment. Sasha and Katja is especially effective; it observes the behavior of children, who are uncompromisingly driven by deep emotions of love and jealousy.

Each film in I Loved You … was shot with a different technique. Pavel and Layla was shot on 35mm film, in a calm and deliberate manner, employing light and shadow as symbols. Sergei and Natasha was shot more dynamically and unpredictably on 16mm film, and Sasha and Katja was shot on digital video.

With the feature-length documentary TISHE!/Hush! (2002), Kossakovsky embraced many different elements that he had explored in his earlier works: observation-based direct cinema, a satirical note in treating the political context of the narrative, and poetical realism in approaching the story. The film has no dialogue except the title, which is spoken only at the very end of this comical documentary. TISHE! was inspired by the short story 'My Cousin's Corner Window', written by E.T.A. Hoffmann in 1822. The story features a paralyzed man who spends his time observing life through the window. Shot on video (unlike most of his earlier works, which were done on celluloid), the film focuses on a small part of a street seen through a window of the director's St Petersburg home. Focusing on this narrow view, Kossakovsky managed to make an entertaining but also politically powerful film. With the talent of a sharp observer, Kossakovsky captured the mentality during the postsocialist era in Russia, where endless repairs on the same hole in the street, done as part of the preparations for the three hundredth anniversary of St Petersburg, were taking place day and night. TISHE! is a documentary drama of the absurd but, at the same time, a lyrical ode to the city. Using different lenses and various cinema techniques, Kossakovsky filmed throughout the whole year and captured changes in both the surroundings and the inhabitants of those surroundings. The carefully shot and edited images, strengthened by an imaginative soundtrack, transport the story from realism into surrealism. At the same time, TISHE! is an expression of the author's nostalgia and attachment to the city, with all its flaws and problems. This film won the Joris Ivens Award at the International Documentary Film Festival (IDFA) in 2002.

RADA SESIC

See also: Russia/Soviet Union

Biography

Born in 1961 in St Petersburg. Studied at VGIK in Moscow. Worked as a camera assistant, editor, assistant director, and director for the Leningrad Documentary Studio. He made several films for the German producer Viola Stephan and collaborated with major European broadcasters such as BBC, ARTE, and ZDF. Later produced his own films. His films have won many awards at numerous film festivals around the world and have been sold to dozens of broadcasters worldwide.

Selected films

1990	Losev
1991	Na dnjach/The Other Day
1993	Belovy/The Belovs
1997	Sreda/Wednesday
1998–2000	Ja vas ljubil/I Loved You … Three Romances
2002	TISHE!/Hush!

Koyaanisqatsi

(US, Reggio, 1982)

The first film in Godfrey Reggio's Qatsi trilogy, Koyaanisqatsi became a surprising success when this ambitious, arty, conceptual documentary received considerable theatrical distribution (and revival), despite spurning conventions as basic as narrative, spoken word, and synchronous sound. With an acclaimed score composed by Philip Glass and a dazzling array of visual manipulations, the film was a daring return to the 'city symphony' genre of documentary popularized in the late 1920s. First-time filmmaker Reggio, however, sought to stand that tradition on its head, offering images of modernity as 'life out of balance' (as the Hopi title translates).

With its high-gloss look and high-art music, the film had an unlikely origin as an independent, spiritually based project made by an ascetic Catholic monk with no experience and little interest in film.

Shot and edited between 1975 and 1982, Reggio's documentary emerged from his work with what he called the Institute for Regional Education, a nonprofit foundation for artists and media researchers in Santa Fe, New Mexico. Raising nearly $2.5 million and working closely with cinematographer Ron Fricke, Reggio assembled an array of lustrous shots of natural landscapes and glowing cityscapes. Edited together, the contrasting images collide to create the film's transparent theme, that technocratic modernity threatens the beauty of the natural world and creates a civilization that deadens humanity.

Koyaanisqatsi is structured into some ten passages, each loosely arranged within, but demarcated by dramatic musical shifts. The film opens (and closes) with a lengthy shot of an unidentified Native American cave drawing while a deep bass voice chants the word koyaanisqatsi (which is not defined until the end titles appear). Slow-motion shots of industrial explosions and rockets are followed by aerial shots of the deserts of the American Southwest, rendered in time-lapse photography. A chorus of trumpets opens a third section, in which a visual geometry of swirling clouds and ocean waves contrasts with the earlier smoke and fire, signaling the film's apocalyptic vision. The Glass score becomes increasing frenetic and loud, full of intense repetitions. Bright, sharp cinematography captures powerful but brutal instruments of civilization transforming the Earth: electrical towers, pipelines, oil derricks, blast furnaces, acres of military hardware and, finally, the first atomic bomb mushrooming over the New Mexico desert.

People then appear amid this berserk technology. Sunbathers lie in the sand, but the camera pulls back to reveal them next to a nuclear power plant. After a montage of imploding buildings and Manhattan skylines, Reggio shows human beings as a robotic, dispirited race of city dwellers. The stuff of daily urban life—office work, assembly lines, fast food, video games, automobiles—is observed from a distant perspective and in hypernatural speed. Interspersed are slow-motion shots of sad-looking adults walking down streets and standing on corners. A pivotal moment occurs when the film suddenly provides an otherwise inconspicuous close-up of a hospital nurse holding an elderly woman's hand for comfort. This shot, incongruous within the sequence, serves as a sort of quiet climax: a human touch amid unnatural technology. Koyaanisqatsi concludes with a daring, lengthy meditation on raw footage of a NASA rocket ascending in a fiery trajectory. After several minutes a piece of burning debris peels away, and the camera tracks its fall to earth. The text of Hopi prophecies about the destruction of the Earth appear as a coda, leaving no doubt about the film's critique of modern life.

The success of Koyaanisqatsi can be measured by its having remained in circulation for more than twenty years, achieving near cult status, its appearance on the Library of Congress's National Film Registry in 2000, and its spawning of two documentaries in a similar vein. Powaqqatsi (1988), meaning 'life in negative transformation', presents disturbing, glossy footage of Third World people and places being destroyed. Teaming with Philip Glass for a third time, in 2002 Reggio released Naqoyqatsi ('civilized violence') through Miramax, with the aid of producer-director Steven Soderbergh.

DAN STREIBLE

Koyaanisqatsi (US, Institute for Regional Education, 1982, 87 mins). Distributed by Island Alive; New Cinema. Produced by Godfrey Reggio, with Francis Ford Coppola (executive producer) and associate producers Mel Lawrence, Roger McNew, T. Michael Powers, Lawrence Taub, and Anton Walpole. Directed by Godfrey Reggio. Scenario by Ron Fricke, Godfrey Reggio, Michael Hoenig, and Alton Walpole. Cinematography by Ron Fricke. Edited by Ron Fricke and Alton Walpole.

Original music composed by Philip Glass, performed by the Western Wind Vocal Ensemble and Albert de Ruiter (basso soloist), conducted by Michael Riesman. Additional music by Michael Hoenig. Filmed in New York City, Los Angeles, Las Vegas, San Francisco, Arizona, and New Mexico. Alternate title: Koyaanisqatsi: Life Out of Balance.

Further reading

Canby, Vincent, 'Koyaanisqatsi, Back to Psychedelia', *The New York Times*, 4 October 1982: C14.

Corliss, Richard, 'Koyaanisqatsi', *Time*, 17 October 1982: 90.

Dempsey, Michael, 'Qatsi Means Life: The Films of Godfrey Reggio', *Film Quarterly*, Spring 1989: 2–12.

Institute for Regional Education (IRE), www.koyaanisqatsi.org, 2001–2.

Jacobson, Harlan, 'Koyaanisqatsi', *Film Comment*, November–December 1982: 61–2.

Kramer, Robert

Throughout his career, Robert Kramer has challenged the definitions and boundaries of documentary by developing a very characteristic film style. He started as a reporter in Latin America but then in 1967 founded the Newsreel movement, which produced about sixty militant and agitational films. The films Kramer made within this collective marked him as a filmmaker of the American radical left, but his work was more than mere political pamphlets. His films were at the same time portraits of a generation opposing Western aggression against Vietnam (In the Country, The Edge, Ice, and People's War) or a reflection on oppressed or recently liberated countries. These and his subsequent films have always been portraits of people, societies, and/or communities within societies, in a very specific sociopolitical context, such as Portugal after the April Revolution (Scenes from the Class Struggle in Portugal) or independent Angola. In the first part of his career, Kramer was more political in his films, whereas later on he took a more reflective stance. His films can be considered a genre unto themselves, mixing fiction with documentary in a very specific way and always exhibiting his philosophical, essayistic approach. In a sense his films can be called 'documentaries of thought', provoking the spectator to reflect, together with Kramer, on the portraits he makes.

Kramer was recognized as a great filmmaker but could savour this relative success mainly in Europe. However, the highpoints of his work are two extraordinary un-American American films, Milestones (1975) and Route One/USA (1989). These two road movies portray Americans and American communities in a thoughtful and thought-provoking way. By mixing documentary and fiction, he invented a film form in which he could freely move, both as filmmaker and as a character in his films—sometimes through his alter ego, Doc, played by Paul McIsaac. His characteristic film style moved away from conventions of fiction and documentary, but despite the sometimes experimental character of his films (especially Notre Nazi, Berlin 10/90, and Ghosts of Electricity), they remain very accessible. This is because they combine openness to the world with personal involvement, guiding the spectator, who will always be touched by Kramer's reflections on both collective and personal experiences that make up a society or a community. In Le Manteau (1996), for instance, Kramer reflects on the sociopolitical madness of the so-called heart of darkness of Western civilization, whereas in his last, and testamentary, film Cités de la plaine (1999), he takes a much more personal and autobiographical approach but still does not omit reflection on the moral standards of Western society, in which the characters (and the spectator) move. Kramer was a nomadic filmmaker whose camera was an extension of his body and his own mind, translating his continuous dialogue with the world and his experience into film (see, for example, Ghosts of Electricity). His oeuvre is very consistent both in film style and in his approach to the world, and it is without doubt that Kramer was one of the most original filmmakers of the twentieth century.

KEES BAKKER

Biography

Born in New York in 1940. Studied philosophy and Western European history at Swarthmore College and Stanford University. He worked as a reporter in Latin America for various American publications. In 1967 he founded and organized the Newsreel movement. In the early

1980s he moved to Europe, living and working in Paris, where he died in 1999.

Selected films

1965 FALN
1966 In the Country
1967 The Edge
1969 Ice
1969 People's War
1975 Milestones
1979 Scenes from the Class Struggle in Portugal
1980 Guns
1981 Un Grand Jour en France—Naissance/A Great Day in France—Birth
1982 A toute allure/As Fast as You Can
1983 La Peur/The Fear
1984 Sarkis at Woodrow Wilson Musée d'Art Moderne
1984 Notre Nazi/Our Nazi
1985 Diesel
1986 Un Plan d'enfer/A Plan of Hell
1987 X-Country
1987 Doc's Kingdom
1989 Route One/USA
1989 Dear Doc
1990 Berlin 10/90
1990 Maquette/Scale Model
1991 Sous Le Vent/Leeward
1991 Video Letters (with Steve Dwoskin)
1991 Ecrire contre l'oubli/Writing Against Forgetting
1993 Point de départ/Starting Place
1993 La Roue/The Wheel: Greg Lemond—Andrew Hampsten
1996 Walk the Walk
1996 Le Manteau/The Mantle
1997 Ghosts of Electricity
1999 Cités de la plaine/Cities of the Plain

Krelja, Petar

Petar Krelja, Croatian film critic, scriptwriter, and director, played a crucial role in shaping the documentary scene in his country. A follower of the traditional documentary style, marked by pronounced narration and straightforward interviews, Krelja did work that is often lyrical, sometimes playful, and even humorous. From the beginning his artistic credo was based on a sincere interest in people living on the margin of society. During the communist regime he exposed the individual hidden within the statistics of social research and dealt with issues such as loneliness, delinquency, the oppression of women, and the neglect of the elderly and the ill.

In the 1960s and 1970s most directors in what was then known as Yugoslavia were making films according to the expectations of Communist Party officials. Krelja warned his colleagues about this 'unhealthy' practice of glorifying socialist rituals and the attendant celebrations of national holidays. During the movement known as Croatian Spring, a short period of liberalization in Croatia in the early 1970s, Krelja dared to express his opinion and made three documentaries that rejected the party standards. These films are quite ironic and confrontational toward the regime. Two were banned, and the third, which ridiculed the celebration of Republic Day in a small village, was destroyed.

After this short period of liberation in Croatia, President Tito reacted with a severe backlash. Artistic projects were cancelled and banned. Krelja returned to his previous interest, ordinary people, producing long and thorough studies of his characters' lives and behavioral patterns, thus achieving an enormous intimacy and mutual trust, enabling his subjects to act uninhibited and natural in front of the camera. Quite often he stayed in touch with his subjects long after the shooting of the film.

During the war in Yugoslavia and the dissolution of the nation in the 1990s, cinema was used mainly to reflect the dominant nationalistic doctrine. There was not much room for self-expression. Film directors faced a moral dilemma: whether to make propaganda films or to take a critical stance, risking not only unemployment but also their very lives. Krelja did not allow himself to conform but remained faithful to his favorite subject, marginal individuals. Unfortunately, the war supplied the Croatian community with more such people than ever before. Almost from the first day of the war, Krelja proved to be an engaged and daring filmmaker, both in terms of his preferred subjects (prisoners of war, refugees, and the displaced and forgotten) and in terms of the independent, supportive attitude he openly displayed in his films.

The quality of Krelja's war films lies in the director's profound approach. He allows his subjects to speak simply and freely about complex and difficult subjects, such as murder, rape, and the loss of family and home. Krelja always seeks in his films a spark of optimism and some wisdom about life. Even Krelja's feature fiction films are thematically consistent with the humanistic and socially engaged approach of his documentaries.

RADA SESIC

See also: Yugoslavia (former)

Biography

Born 1940. Graduated from the department of literature in the Faculty of Philosophy at Zagreb University, Croatia. Started as a film critic at Radio Zagreb in 1964; collaborated with major film magazines and newspapers. Directed thirty-one documentary films and four feature fiction films. Produced about two hundred documentary programs for Croatian television. His films have won many prizes at international film festivals. Has received numerous prestigious cultural awards in Croatia, including a lifetime achievement award.

Selected films

1968 Ponude pod broj … /Offers Under the Number …
1970 Budnica/The Reveille
1971 Coprinice/Sorceresses
1972 Recital
1972 Splendid Isolation
1986 Mariska Band
1991 Kovacica
1992 Ana i njezina braca/Ana and her Brothers
1992 Na sporednom kolosijeku/At the Railway Siding
1993 Zoran Sipos i njegova Jasna/Zoran Sipos and his Jasna
1993 Suzanin osmjeh/Suzana's Smile
1996 Americki san/American Dream

Further reading

Majcen, Vjekoslav, *Yearbook of Croatian Film and Video*, Zagreb: 1996–2000.
Sesic, Rada, 'Camera as a Magnifying Glass', *DOX* 2, 1994.
——'Ordinary People', *DOX*, 1995, Copenhagen.
Turkovic, Hrvoje, *Against the Odds—An Outline of the History of Croatian Film*, the catalogue of the Croatian Retrospective in Rotterdam, 1997.

L

Lacombe, Georges

Georges Lacombe, one of the early French documentary filmmakers, had an important but sometimes overlooked role in the development of the genre. His work was aided tremendously by the cinematic atmosphere of nonlinear, visual experimentation in France during the late 1920s. The Studio des Ursulines, a small theater and later distribution company, offered a haven for young artistic filmmakers to show their work during its sold-out subscriber series. Because of the theater's focus on the avant-garde, Lacombe's documentaries could access an audience that was less hostile than at the more conservative Ciné-Latin and Vieux-Colombier theaters. Non-narrative documentary films about Paris were in vogue during this period, and Lacombe's bold visual style created a pictorial world that was seen as transcendent and vital despite its challenging and sometimes harrowing subject matter.

Before embarking on his own Parisian documentary, Lacombe assisted René Clair with his short black-and-white subject piece about the Eiffel Tower, La Tour. Acting as both assistant director and writer of the scenario, Lacombe added his talent for recognizing compelling subjects to Clair's formidable directorial vision. Filmed in 1927 and released in 1928 at the Studio des Ursulines, this ten-minute exploration of the tower included not only intricately juxtaposed close-up and far shots of the tower itself, but intercut these visuals with long, panoramic views of Paris, notably l'Ecole Militaire, the Parc du Champ de Mars, and the Palais de Chaillot. Building on Clair's earlier portrayal of the Eiffel Tower in Paris qui dort (1923), Lacombe wrote a scenario in which La Tour Eiffel was a fantastic refuge in the sky, offering protection to whomever stood atop it. The short film was a paean to the tower from the avant-garde who saw its monolithic and infinitely reinterpretable presence as both a challenge and a comfort.

The second documentary feature with which Lacombe was involved was also the only one that he directed. The short film La Zone: au pays des chiffonniers, a twenty-eight-minute film examining the lives of rag pickers in Paris's Clignacourt district, also debuted in 1928 at the Studio des Ursulines. La Zone is Lacombe's documentary masterpiece in the truest sense of the word. In it he has absorbed and perfected the stylistic techniques of René Clair, but also imbued it with his own humanistic sentiment.

La Zone falls squarely in the footprints of two different cinematic ideologies that were dominant in the French film industry of the 1920s. The first is the realist school, the second the continually evolving avant-garde movement. Understanding the film requires locating it within these two schools of thought. French realism of the early twentieth century concentrated itself on the emerging social problems of an increasingly urban culture, with an eye toward trying to subvert and threaten the existing order that the filmmakers believed was the root of the problems. Its most important tenet was that the camera should descend into the lowest orders of the world and give a glimpse of the people dwelling there, thereby offering a commentary on this microcosm of a society in decay.

As avant-garde filmmaking, La Zone positions itself in the phalanx of what is known as the 'third avant-garde'. The first avant-garde is epitomized by the lyrical and affecting films of Abel Gance, and the second by the more blatantly surrealist Man Ray and Luis Buñuel. The third avant-garde, composed of filmmakers such as Lacombe, René Clair, Marcel Carné, and Jean Vigo, was interested primarily in documentary films and sociological study, albeit in a visual, nonquantitative way.

La Zone details the lives, their working days in particular, of the rag pickers who work in Clignancourt, one of Paris's slum areas in the eighteenth *arrondissement* at the northern edge of the city. Lacombe carries their daily struggle for existence to us through his examination of their routines: the rounding up of dustbins; the loading of paper and sundry trash onto carts; and the unloading, sorting, packing, crushing, and disposal by incineration of vast amounts of refuse. What follows is the sorting of anything recoverable into usable lots and the selling of the recovered items at the flea market in the neighborhood for little profit, but enough for the rag pickers to eke out another day. Within this larger examination of a socially invisible way of life, there are also more intimate portraits of individuals: a musician, a photographer, a gypsy, and a dancer, which detail the draconian forces that are leveled against the poor and unprivileged individuals of any city.

La Zone, then, concerns itself with the act of living, concentrating itself on lives otherwise ignored. Because it focuses on basic human struggle, it makes implicit commentary on the culture revealed by Lacombe's camera. It pulls away the façade that allows this invisible world to remain invisible and exposes it to view. It is sublime; its kaleidoscopic images of hardship and degradation do more to reveal the problems at work in French society than other longer, more explicitly condemnable films of the period.

Although Lacombe directed one of France's most important and original documentary films, he is primarily remembered as a director of feature-length dramas of the 1930s, 1940s, and 1950s, particularly the films, Jeunesse/Youth (1934), Derrière la façade/Behind the Façade (1939), Le Dernier des Six/The Last One of the Six (1941), L'Escalier sans fin/The Stairs without End (1943), and La Nuit est mon royaume/The Night is My Kingdom (1951). Although he did not film another documentary after La Zone, his break from the genre was far from clean, as many of these later films are in the realist drama and documentary fiction mode that use actual events, places, and people as their heart and embody many of the humanist ideas that Lacombe emphasized in his documentaries.

In interpreting Lacombe's documentary films, it is difficult to avoid seeing these early films through the lens of his later ones. La Zone was an early flash of brilliance from a young director whose future career was projected to be promising. Lacombe's work from the 1930s on is regarded by critics and scholars to be disciplined and efficient, but without the genius of his contemporary René Clair. Never rising above the level of an able craftsmen in his later work, Lacombe's documentaries are his most critically acclaimed achievements, and although relatively little scholarly work has been done on them, they are important to the growth of understanding of the French documentary tradition.

RYAN SMITH

See also: Zone, La

Biography

Born August 19, 1902 in Paris, France. First worked on films with René Clair as his assistant director 1924–8. Member of the 'third avant-garde' movement in Paris 1928–30. Signed on as a director with the Continental film company and distribution company Société de gestion et d'exploitation du cinéma, both collaborationist organizations 1941. Censured for his collaboration by the *épuration* committee 1945. Nominated for a Golden Lion, 1951. Died, April 14, 1990 in Cannes, France.

Selected films

1928 La Tour/The Tower: assistant director, writer

1928 La Zone: Au pays des chiffonniers/The Zone: In the Country of the Ragmen: director

Further reading

Abel, Richard, *French Cinema, the First Wave, 1915–29*, Princeton, NJ: Princeton University Press, 1984.

Armes, Roy, *French Cinema*, Oxford: Oxford University Press, 1985.

Coissac, Georges-Michel, *Histoire du cinématographe: de ses origines jusqu'a nos jours*, Paris: Editions du Cineopse, 1925.

Crisp, Colin, *Genre, Myth and Convention in the French Cinema, 1929–39*, Bloomington, IN: Indiana University Press, 2002.

Ehrlich, Evelyn, *Cinema of Paradox, Filmmaking under the German Occupation*, New York: Columbia University Press, 1985.
Hayward, Susan, *French National Cinema*, New York: Routledge, 1993.
Lanzoni, Remi Fournier, *French Cinema from its Beginnings to the Present*, New York: Continuum, 2002.
Martin, John, *The Golden Age of French Cinema, 1929–39*, Boston: Twayne Publishers, 1983.
Potamkin, Harry, 'The French Cinema', *Close-Up*, July 1929: 15–17.
Sadoul, Georges, *Le Cinéma français: 1890–1962*, Paris: Flammarion, 1981.
Slavin, David Henry, *Colonial Cinema and Imperial France, 1919–39*, Baltimore, MD: Johns Hopkins University Press, 2001.
Williams, Alan, *Republic of Images, A History of French Film-Making*, Cambridge, MA: Harvard University Press, 1992.

L'Amour existe

(France, Pialat, 1960)

Pialat's first film, with its ironic, paradoxical title, is a 'point de vue documenté' on life in the suburbs. The director, with his aloof and furious manner is, in L'Amour existe/Love Exists, up in arms.

The film's debut corresponded with the height of the nouvelle vague. Both the producer, Pierre Braunberger, and the composer, Georges Delerue, were figures in the movement, though Pialat always sought to distance himself from it. Although strictly speaking a contemporary of films such as Chronique d'un été (France) and Primary (United States), L'Amour existe seems, at first, to follow the conventions of classical documentary established in the 1930s. The film's discourse, however, clearly anticipates the philosophical trends to come. Pialat denounces the detrimental effects of advertising, the petit bourgeois mentality, and the capitalist system.

After a brief prologue showing commuter trains, subways, and traffic jams, the narration first takes up the autobiographical tone of a search for bygone days. Shortly afterward, however, 'delusions of pettiness' are scorned in a lampooning tone, and it is in the style of an indictment that damning figures are reeled off. The nostalgic tone does return, though, for the reminiscing of the elderly people, but the commentary comes to an end with a manifesto of leftist statements.

Some shots are carefully worked out to insist on absurd angles, such as that highlighting detached houses built just a few meters from an airport runway. Others are filmed in newsreel style, though with no synchronised sound: a fire in a shanty town, a child in tears alone on his bed. A few sequences, however, are clearly a result of documentary mise-en-scène: the couple at home; young louts in leather jackets fighting at night. Often the text intervenes to reformulate and clarify or extrapolate the meaning of the images: 'Urbanism conceived in terms of transport infrastructure'; 'More and more advertising prevails over reality'.

The absence of the commentary provides its own sort of eloquence. After a list of statistics is given (showing the figures for pollution, the underresourcing of cultural activity in deprived areas, and social inequality in education), no conclusion is drawn. Instead, the aforementioned night brawl between young men, with its strident jet engine background noise, presents the violence of the youths as the consequence of the statistics.

In 1961 L'Amour existe won both the Prix Lumière and a St Mark's Lion at the Venice Film Festival.

JEAN-LUC SMITH

L'Amour existe (France, Les Films de la Pleiade, 1960, 20 mins). Produced by Pierre Braunberger, production manager Roger Fleytoux. Directed by Maurice Pialat, assistant direction by Maurice Cohen. Written by Maurice Pialat. Cinematography by Gilbert Sarthre, assistant cinematographer Jean Bordes-Pages. Music by Georges Delerue. Edited by Kenout Peltier, assistant editor Liliane Korb. Commentary by Jean-Loup Reynol. Filmed in the suburbs of Paris.

Further reading

Magny, Joël and Pialat, Maurice, 'La cicatrice interieure', Paris: Cahiers du Cinema, collection 'Auteurs', 1992: 46–8.
n.a., 'La France de Pialat', in *Maurice Pialat, l'enfant sauvage*, Torino: Museo Nazionale del Cinema, France Cinema, Admiranda, Institut de l'Image, Lindau, 1992: 37–43.

Land, The

(US, Flaherty, 1941)

Robert Flaherty's essay-film, The Land (1942), made for the United States Agricultural Adjustment Agency of the Department of Agriculture, has been understood as a turning point in Flaherty's oeuvre. Originally commissioned by Pare Lorentz on the recommendation of John Grierson, the project was ill-fated from its inception. Because of Flaherty's penchant for loose production schedules and the attendant problem faced by Helen van Dongen in synthesising the material, The Land was completed only as the United States had entered World War II, and the resulting focus of the economy on the war effort diminished, in the government's eyes, the problems that Flaherty had identified.

Nanook of the North, Moana, and Man of Aran reinvented past cultures to construct exotic documents of humanity, but The Land was a representation of agricultural problems and their effect on people in contemporary 1940s America. Although almost universally dismissed, The Land signals a shift from the romantic premodernism of Nanook, Moana, and Man of Aran toward the lyrical negotiation of mechanisation and environmental wonder apparent in Louisiana Story.

Although Flaherty's earlier films used individual protagonists, around which a web of episodic accounts of the struggle to survive was spun, The Land is all-encompassing, ranging across many states and agricultural issues. Its concern is not for the land so much as for the people who depend on it. The Land uses static portraits of the people who work the land, including the opening images of a particular farm in which are imaged a farmer, his wife, and child, recalling the photography of Dorothea Lange and Walker Evans (as well as the portrait-like images in Industrial Britain) and establishing a 'farming type' similar to one that the Farm Security Administration photographers celebrated. Like these photographers' work, The Land is steeped in nostalgia, yearning for the kind of connection to the environment on which Nanook and Man of Aran were based, while perhaps clumsily proposing that the mechanisation of farming methods was the cause of erosion, dislocation, and racism.

Elliptical and episodic in structure, The Land divines its own raison d'être from the material it has to organise. Refuting the linear narratives that Lorentz used in The River and The Plow that Broke the Plains, The Land negotiates a host of agricultural, social, and economic problems, stretching the economic imperatives of the Department of Agriculture out on to the broader canvas of American life in a specific yet crucial moment in that country's history.

Based on the early work of Russell and Kate Lord, whose 1950 book *Forever the Land* contains most of the commentary, Flaherty's film wanders across vast geographical spaces that ultimately form the web of images, comments, and traces of stories that form the film. Flaherty's personal tone, accentuated by his narration, is the organising principle around which the glimpses and comments adhere. Siegfried Kracauer saw Flaherty's role in the structure as the film's strength, pointing to the naivety apparent in these 'fragments of a lost epic song' (quoted in Griffith 1972: 142).

DEANE WILLIAMS

See also: Flaherty, Robert; Lorentz, Pare

The Land (US, The Extension Service, United States Department of Agriculture, 1941, 39 mins). Directed by Robert Flaherty in collaboration with Frances Flaherty. Editorial supervision by Helen Van Dongen. Commentary by Russell Lord. Consulting by Wayne Darrow. Research and field assistance by W.H. Lamphere and Key Hart. Photography by Irving Lerner, Douglas Baker, Floyd Crosby, and Charles Herbert. Musical composition by Richard Arnell. National Youth Administration Orchestra conducted by Fritz Mahler, recorded by Robert Hufstader. Narrated by Robert Flaherty. Sound engineered by A. Dillinger and Reuben Ford.

Further reading

Calder-Marshall, Arthur, *The Innocent Eye: The Life of Robert Flaherty*, London: W.H. Allen & Co, 1963.

Griffith, Richard, 'The Land', *Documentary News Letter*, February 1942: 27.

——*The World of Robert Flaherty*, New York: Da Capo Press, 1972: 142.

Lord, Russell, 'Robert Flaherty Rediscovers America', *Land* 1, no. 1, 1941: 67–75.

Lord, Russell and Lord, Kate, *Forever the Land: A Country Chronicle and Anthology*, New York: Harper, 1950.

Winston, Brian, *Claiming the Real: The Documentary Film Revisited*, London: British Film Institute, 1995.

Land Without Bread

(Spain, Buñuel, 1932)

Filmed in a desolate mountain region in 1932, shortly after the founding of the Spanish Republic, Land Without Bread (aka Las Hurdes) was Buñuel's third film. From 1923 to 1928 Buñuel had worked in the French film industry (as Jean Epstein's assistant) and made his directorial debut in Paris with Un Chien andalou (1928) and L'Age d'or (1930). He had scripted his first films in collaboration with Dalí and had explicitly related their Freudian-inspired exploration of dreams, sexuality, and irrational impulses to the surrealist ideology. Both artists became full-fledged members of the movement at the time of the controversial release of Un Chien andalou. Buñuel broke up with the mainstream group in 1932 as a result of the political debates and purges that occurred during the mid-to-late 1920s. His work, however, continued to be informed by the iconoclastic spirit and provocative aesthetics of surrealism. In an interview recorded during the 1954 Cannes Film Festival, Buñuel acknowledged his strong affinities with the movement: 'I made Las Hurdes because I had a Surrealist vision and because I was interested in the problem of man. I saw reality in a different manner from the way I'd seen it before Surrealism' (Aranda 1976: 90–1). The idea of the documentary was inspired by Maurice Legendre's doctoral thesis on the remote Spanish region of Las Hurdes, which Buñuel had read before deciding to embark on what he described (in the opening title of the film) as 'a cinematographic essay of human geography'. The poet Pierre Unik (one of the first-generation surrealists) and the photographer Eli Lotar (who had contributed to Bataille's magazine, *Documents*, in 1929, and worked on Joris Iven's Zuiderzee, 1930) accompanied Buñuel on his two-month trip to Las Hurdes between April and May 1932. The Spanish professor Rafael Sanchez Ventura joined the small crew and acted as Buñuel's assistant alongside Unik, who also contributed to writing the commentary. The $2,000 production budget came from lottery money won by Buñuel's anarchist friend, Ramon Acin, a schoolmaster from Huesca.

Before reaching the region of Las Hurdes, the crew stopped in La Alberca, where the first sequence of the film was shot. The camera provides a panoramic view of the village, discloses one of its streets, then turns to the walls of the church, pausing for a moment on ominous skulls, which seem to preside over the destinies of the inhabitants, as the commentator's voice remarks. The deceptively reassuring presence of customary Christian inscriptions above entrance doors is shattered by the savage ceremony, which the crew witness, as they happen to arrive on a feast day. In front of the assembled villagers, recently married men on horseback have to ride at full speed and pull off the head of a cock tied by its feet and suspended on a rope across the street. Wine is served in abundance when the men have finished parading their trophies. A close-up image focuses on the gaudy decorations of a baby's dress. Though the commentator notes their apparent Christian origin, he nonetheless compares these 'sacred ornaments' to the charms of people from Africa and Oceania. The striking coupling of familiar signs and barbaric or 'exotic' rituals and beliefs sets the tone for the rest of the documentary, the objectivity of which only serves to heighten the viewer's discomfort and sense of dislocation.

Leaving La Alberca, the camera explores the mountainous landscape across which are disseminated the fifty-two hamlets of Las Hurdes, with a population of ten thousand. The ruins of a monastery in the valley of the Batuecas remind one that for centuries the Carmelite monks lived and preached the Christian religion in this region. However, the commentary adds that the Batuecas is also known for its vestiges of prehistoric life and its painted caverns, while the camera focuses on the only remaining 'inhabitants' of the abandoned ruins: toads and grass snakes (mentioned along with lizards). Buñuel's interest in entomology, which he studied as a student in Madrid in 1920, and which inspired the opening sequence of L'Age d'or (a quasi-documentary description of scorpions), points to the similar use of such images in Las Hurdes to anticipate or highlight the portrayal of terrifyingly sordid conditions of human existence. The viewer cannot fail to relate the mention of prehistoric dwellings to the image of rooftops in Martinandran (a hamlet in Las Hurdes), resembling layered crusts scattered among the trees, or, as the commentary remarks, 'the shell of a fabulous animal'. Houses have no chimneys or windows, and families live together in one room. In the first village that the crew encounters, the gutter serves for all uses: a woman washes some rags, a pig paddles in the stream, while further down the street, a little girl is giving some water to a baby that she holds on her knees. Poorly dressed children are dipping a slice of bread in the same stream before eating it. The commentary tells us that bread, which is almost unknown in the region, is given to the children by the schoolmaster, although parents usually take it away from them. The stark reality of daily life in Las Hurdes constantly overshadows every glimmer of hope or sign of progress. The village has a school, and the children are taught, like everywhere else in the world, that the sum of the angles of a triangle is equal to two right-angles, but the blatant irrelevance of this truth becomes apparent when the camera pans over the classroom filled with barefoot children, dressed in rags, some of whom have their heads shorn, and are identified by the commentary as 'pilus' (orphans from the welfare services in Ciudad Rodrigo, that the Hurdanos take into care for a meagre amount of money). The bizzare engraving depicting a marquis in a powdered wig, which decorates the wall of the classroom, seems no less ironic and out of place than the moral instruction that one of the children is seen writing on the blackboard: 'Respect the property of others'. The absurdity of this constant clash between rules of civilised society and the sheer misery and squalor of Las Hurdes is rendered unbearable by the objectivity of the camera and the dispassionate tone of the commentary read by Abel Jacquin. In Martinandran the condition of goitre sufferers is recorded and analysed with the clinical detachment of a course of entomology, just as the spread of malaria during the dry season gives rise to a scientific digression on the habits of the anopheles mosquito. Several shots of shivering men looking into the camera or lying on the ground illustrate the effects of the contamination.

A relentless accumulation of horrifying factual images of suffering and death overwhelms the viewer. A sick little girl is seen lying in the street. The camera reveals her inflamed throat, and the commentary simply informs us that 'there is nothing we can do for her', and that two days later the crew found out that the girl had died. Another instance when the passive positioning of the film crew comes sharply into view concerns the episodes devoted to the Hurdanos deficient alimentation and local industry. We are told that the staple diet consists of potatoes and beans. Occasionally, the more fortunate families raise a pig, which is killed once a year and devoured in three days. The camera then shifts our attention to a couple of mountain goats, one of which is about to leap across a ravine. Through several cuts, the image shows the goat falling to its death from the mountaintop, while the commentary remarks that goat meat becomes available when one of the animals accidentally kills itself. A similar fate awaits a mule carrying beehives, which the Hurdanos hire during the winter from La Alberca. Very often, while travelling along the arid mountain tracks, the mules stumble and spill their load of hives. The pitilessly static camera forces the viewer to watch the agony of a mule stung by thousands of bees. The animal is later shown lying dead, and a wandering dog arrives to feed off its carcass. Several other examples, however, seem to lead the powerless witness's reactions to such horrifying scenes from mere revulsion or passive empathy to revolt. Each time a positive aspect of the Hurdanos's fight for survival is mentioned, a new set of adverse natural or human factors are also made apparent, as part of a recurrent, logical progression. In *Le surrealisme au cinema*, Ado Kyrou defined the subversive mechanism of Buñuel's documentary with reference to the implicit phrase: 'Yes, but … ' The Hurdanos have few utensils, but they manage to cultivate narrow strips of land on the stony banks of the river by painstainkingly transporting sacks of soil from fertile areas; however, their gardens produce very little and are completely wiped out by floods during winter, unless the artificial soil becomes exhausted after a year (because there are no domestic animals, and therefore no manure). The peasants are bitten by vipers, but the bite is rarely lethal; however, the herbs with which they try to cure the wound provoke an infection that kills them. As Ado Kyrou eloquently concludes: 'each sequence is based […] on these three propositions, and thus the progression into horror attains limits which can only lead to revolt'.

In the last two sequences of the film the portrayal of the Hurdanos' suffering reaches a kind of absurd paroxism. The viewer is confronted with shattering images of the mentally handicapped, cripples, and dwarves, who spend their days on the outskirts of the village as goat keepers. The commentary attributes their condition to 'famine, lack of hygiene, poverty and incest'. Finally, the long journey of a funeral procession that carries the body of a dead baby in a small trough across a river, before reaching a place with enough land to bury it in, is filmed with the same unflinching lack of sentimentality. The short epilogue of the documentary intercuts scenes of the poor interior of houses at sunset and shots of the deserted streets where the eerie silhouette of an old woman passes, ringing a bell and asking for prayers for the dead. The last line of the commentary simply states: 'After a two-month stay in Las Hurdes, we left the country.'

The subversive message of the film did not pass unnoticed. A preview screening of Las Hurdes took place in 1933 in the Palace of the Press in Madrid, two months after the presentation of Buñuel's surrealist productions, Un Chien andalou and L'Age d'or. Buñuel himself read the commentary, in a tone whose detached eloquence was matched by the irrelevance of Brahms's Fourth Symphony played in the background. The audience, which gathered the capital's intellectuals, responded with angered incomprehension at the stark realism of the images. Las Hurdes was subsequently banned by the Republican government, as well as by its right-wing successor, led by General Franco. First synchronised in 1934, then officially released in Paris in 1937 at the height of the Spanish Civil War, the film was also distributed in the United States by the New York Museum of Modern Art, where Buñuel worked from 1939 until 1943, directing or supervising the dubbing and adaptation of Spanish American documentaries. At the time of its conception, Las Hurdes coincided with the sudden surge of interest in primitive cultures among French surrealists and other avant-garde artists. This phenomenon acquired particular prominence during the Dakar-Djibouti ethnographic mission, the findings of which were published in *Minotaure* (11–12, 1932). Eli Lotar, Buñuel's cameraman for Las Hurdes, had contributed a series of disturbing 'documentary' photographs taken at the Villette slaughterhouse near Paris, in Bataille's magazine, *Documents* (2, 6, June 1929). Unlike the aesthetically and ethically transgressive aspect of most avant-garde approaches to ethnographic material, however, Buñuel's ideological stance in Las Hurdes tends to emphasise the social and political dimensions of a documentary account that uncovers uncanny areas of human reality in the very midst of the familiar Western civilization: 'The pathetic thing about this country, and for this reason its psychological and human interest is very superior to that of barbaric tribes, is that, though its material civilization is rudimentary and prehistoric, its religious and moral culture and ideas are like those of any civilized country' (Buñuel, quoted in Aranda 1976: 89). Despite its declared ethnographic aim and stark objectivity, Las Hurdes expresses Buñuel's lifelong concern with social injustice, the paradoxical nature of human destiny, and the illusion of progress. It provides one of his strongest anarchistic statements against state religion and bourgeois morality, which can be seen as the underlying thematic link between his surrealist productions and his later fictional work (from Los Olvidados, 1950, winner of the Cannes award for best direction, to Viridiana, 1961, from The Discreet Charm of the Bourgeoisie, 1972, to That Obscure Object of Desire, 1977). More than a mere travelogue and objective account of daily life in a poverty-stricken area of Republican Spain, Las Hurdes compels the viewer to undertake a journey of self-discovery, which constantly challenges his or her most basic assumptions about modern civilisation, cultural tradition, and ethical values. 'Nowhere does man need to wage a more desperate fight against the hostile forces of nature', reads the opening title of the film. The optimistic conclusion, which was added to certain copies of Buñuel's documentary, and which referred to the power of human solidarity and the beneficial reforms of the short-lived Popular Front government, did not preempt recurrent critical analogies with Alain Resnais's harrowing film about concentration camps (Night and Fog, 1955). One of the first productions of its genre to question both the crew's and the spectator's passive voyeurism, along with established conventions of photographic realism, Las Hurdes retains its deeply unsettling ideological resistance to empathetic identification, and hence its socially and politically subversive potential.

RAMONA FOTIADE

Further reading

Aranda, Francisco, *Luis Buñuel: A Critical Biography*, trans. and ed. David Robinson, New York: Da Capo Press Inc., 1976: 85–99.

Buñuel, Luis, *An Unspeakable Betrayal. Selected Writings of Luis Buñuel*, with a foreword by Jean-Claude Carrière, trans. from the Spanish and French by Garrett White, Berkeley, CA and London: University of California Press, 2000.
——'Las Hurdes (Terre sans pain)', the shooting script and commentary of the film, *L'Avant-scène du cinéma*, no. 36, April 1964: 58–62.
Kyrou, Ado, *Le surrealisme au cinéma*, Paris: Editions Arcanes, 1953.
Matthews, J.H., *Surrealism and Film*, Ann Arbor, MI: University of Michigan Press, 1971: 105–13.

Langjahr, Erich

Erich Langjahr, since the beginning of the 1970s an integral part of the community of Swiss filmmakers, demonstrates in his documentaries the modern dilemma of humankind. In the course of progress and the name of order, the individual is often left behind, unsure of his or her own identity and role in the greater scheme of things. Although all of his films take place in Switzerland, particularly in Central Switzerland, this existentialist and realistic approach gives Langjahr's work universal meaning.

Having grown up in postwar Switzerland, Erich Langjahr expresses through his work the problematic relationship between individual and society in a country that has to redefine itself against the backdrop of World War II and its own projected image. The concept of Switzerland as a wholesome rural idyll began to clash drastically with the reality of an urbanized, consumerist society. In the new Switzerland, as in all of Western Europe after the war, technological advances made the traditional ways of life obsolete. With this shift in technology, a shift in ideology has occurred as well; as big farming corporations started to swallow small farmers, the individual got lost in the masses of the cities. The years of the economic boom in the 1950s and 1960s gave way to the rise of consumerism.

It is against this background of a country in transition but, even more so, of its citizens facing an existential dilemma, that Erich Langjahr formulates his philosophy of documentary movies that emphasize the individual and his or her search for identity in a new world order. Inspired by his own search for who he is and what 'home' means, Erich Langjahr's work reflects a personal conflict that reaches beyond the scope of his own personality or that of his home country and, indeed, takes on universal significance.

Resulting from his emphasis on the individual, Erich Langjahr's philosophy of documentary film entails an unobtrusive approach. Rather than commenting on what the camera sees, Langjahr believes in letting the images speak for themselves. Dialogue, if any, is provided by the people whom the camera observes. This technique enhances the realism of the movies and gives their viewers the freedom to interpret what they see in whichever way they prefer. The idea that all lies in the eyes of the beholder forms an integral part of Erich Langjahr's philosophy, for interpreting the images for the audience would propagate the same hypocrisy that his films are trying to reveal. His approach is poetic, not dogmatic. If the individual has any importance, then he or she must be guaranteed the freedom to think for himself or herself.

From the beginning of his career in the 1970s as an independent documentary filmmaker, this unequal tug-of-war between individual and society, or, more precisely, its representative the government, has been a topic essential to Erich Langjahr's work. Already his early movies, such as Justice (1973) and Sieg der Ordnung/The Victory of Order (1976), demonstrate a sense of responsibility toward his audience typical for the cinéma de nouvelle vague. All of Erich Langjahr's films are to the point; they say what there is to say without romanticizing or demonizing any particular aspect. Their realism allows for an openness that makes it possible to express discomfort with social issues and protest against them in a loud and clear manner.

At the same time, the techniques of direct cinema challenge the viewer to participate openly in a public discussion, to take a stance.

Typical of Erich Langjahr's unobtrusive way of making documentary films is that he achieves his audience's involvement without resorting to the techniques of modern TV. On the contrary, his films captivate the audience because they simply show reality without the help of racy images, quickly assembled reports, or arbitrary stories. Consequently, Erich Langjahr grants his viewers the possibility to interpret the images he shows in the way they want to even if that may not be his own way of seeing things.

According to Erich Langjahr's philosophy and his own goal of filmmaking, the search for identity and for the definition of what 'home' means remains an individual task. Thus, any indoctrination of the audience on his part would mean a betrayal of his objective as a maker of documentary films, of himself, and his viewers. One of the best examples of this attitude is probably the film Morgarten findet statt/ Morgarten is Happening (1978), in which Erich Langjahr's camera picks up images of a patriotic memorial day celebrated in central Switzerland. Whereas Erich Langjahr himself is not uncritical of the way in which this holiday is celebrated, his camera functions merely as a recording device. The people participating are shown as they are; they are in no way stigmatized or glorified as something they are not. Both the critical observer and the traditionalist are able to enjoy this film each in his or her own way. Naturally, such a goal requires an intensive study of human beings and their environment, one of the main characteristics of Erich Langjahr's films. His movies usually do not contain any comments, another fact that attests to his emphasis on creating aas realistic an impression as can be.

Although all of his movies reflect Erich Langjahr's lifelong ambition to portray the search for identity and show the struggle of individuals for survival in a society increasingly characterized by technology and globalization, it is in particular in his latest trilogy of films that he demonstrates at his best the full implications of what that change means for an entire culture. The films Sennen-Ballade/Alpine Ballad (1996), Bauernkrieg/Farmer's War (1998), and Hirtenreise ins dritte Jahrtausend/Shepherd's Journey into the Third Millennium (2002) have won Erich Langjahr international acclaim beyond Europe's boundaries. In fact, Erich Langjahr showed the final part of the trilogy, Hirtenreise ins dritte Jahrtausend, at the 2003 International Documentary Film Festival in Yamagata, Japan, The Seattle International Documentary Film Festival in 2004, and was awarded the Natasha Isaacs Cinematography Award at the Chicago International Documentary Festival in 2004 for the same movie.

In his last trilogy, Erich Langjahr's lifelong ambition comes full circle. Beginning with Sennen-Ballade, he depicts the life of a cheesemaker in the Swiss Alps. It becomes clear that not only is this way of life not as idyllic as one might think it is, but also that it is doomed to become extinct. The reasons for this become clear in the trilogy's second film, Bauernkrieg, where Langjahr shows without restraint how technology, the mass market, and consumerism continuously destroy the traditional way of farming, dehumanize this way of life, and inflict incredible damage to the environment. Finally, in Hirtenreise, Erich Langjahr's camera follows two Swiss shepherds over the stretch of seven years on their journey. Again, in this movie by the Swiss filmmaker the question of identity constitutes the focal point of his movie: how do the shepherds, who have one of the oldest professions in human history, make the transition into the third millennium?

In agreement with his philosophy, Erich Langjahr records, becoming himself a viewer behind the camera. Instead of creating a harmonic, unified experience for his audience, so that it may just sit back and enjoy, Erich Langjahr tries to fit the 'gaps and contradictions' he encounters making the film into the film itself. To him, 'bringing the piece to completion is a poetic operation dictated by a rhythm that resides deep within me' (Hiroshi 2003). For Erich Langjahr, each film constitutes a call to one's conscience because, according to his philosophy of documentary film, ethics and conscience supercede the rules of the market.

ELKE BARTEL

Biography

Born in Baar, Switzerland, 1944. Independent filmmaker since 1971. Since 1977 member of the organization Filmregie und Drehbuch Schweiz (Directing and Script Switzerland); since 1992 member of this organization's board of directors. Also since 1992 founding member of the foundation Luzern—Lebensraum für die Zukunft (Luzern—Living Space for The Future). Since 1999 member of the board of directors of the cinematic club in Zug, Switzerland. Received Innerschweizer Kulturpreis (Culture Award of Central Switzerland) in 2002 for his lifelong achievements.

Selected films

1973 Justice: director, producer, author, camera, sound, editor
1975 USA-Time: director, producer, author, camera, sound, cut
1976 Sieg der Ordnung/The Victory of Order: director, producer, camera, sound, editor

1978 Morgarten findet statt/Morgarten is Happening: director, producer, author, camera, editor
1981 Made in Switzerland: director, producer, author, camera, sound, editor
1982 Do It Yourself: director, producer, author, camera, sound, editor
1983 O.K.: director, producer, author, camera, sound, editor
1986 Ex Voto: director, producer, author, camera, sound, editor
1990 Männer im Ring/Men in the Ring: director, producer, author, camera
1992 Unter dem Boden/Beneath the Surface: director, producer, author, camera, editor
1996 Sennen-Ballade/Alpine Ballad: director, producer, author, camera, editor
1998 Bauernkrieg/Farmers' War: director, producer, author, camera, editor
2002 Hirtenreise ins dritte Jahrtausend/Shepherd's Journey into the Third Millennium: director, producer, author, camera, editor

Further reading

Breiner, Rolf, 'Partnerschaft mit Wechselwirkung', St Galler Tagblatt Online, www.tagblatt.ch, August 4, 2003.

Chicago International Documentary Festival, 'Awards', www.chicagodocfestival.org/awards.html, 2004.

Gasperi, Walter, 'Shepherds, Swiss Wrestling and Alphenhorn', FIPRESCI: The International Federation of Film Critics, www.fipresci.org/festivals/archive/2003/various_2003/Solothurn 2003_wgasperi.htm (accessed May 2003).

Hiroshi, Wada, 'Reality to the Film, the Film to You, and Then … : An Interview with Erich Langjahr', Yamagata International Documentary Film Festival Organizing Committee, 11 October 2003, www.city.yamagata.yamagata.jp/yidff/2003/interviews/039028-e.html

Kathan, Bernhard, 'Vom Untergang bäuerlicher Kultur', *Wiener Zeitung Online*, www.wienerzeitung.at, October 30, 1998.

König, Regula, 'Alpine Ballad', Yamagata International Documentary Film Festival Organizing Committee, 1997, www.city/yamagata.yamagat.jp/yidff/catalog/en/97/inter12.html

Langjahr, Erich, www.langjahr-film.ch, Langjahr Film GmbH, 2002.

Langjahr, Erich and Haselbeck, Silvia, 'Käse, Brot und Zelluloid', in *St Galler Tagblatt Online*, www.tagblatt.ch, October 31, 1997.

Macdonald, Moira, 'Seattle film festival focuses the spotlight on documentary genre', *The Seattle Times Online*, seattletimes.nwsource.com, April 11, 2004.

n.a., 'Programm Bergfilmtage Zermatt, Sennenballade', www.bergfilmfestival.ch/2002/sa.htm, July 13, 2002.

n.a., 'Swiss Films at the Chicago International Documentary Festival', *Mosaic: Midwest Outreach for Swiss Art, Innovation and Culture* 2, no. 3, 2004: 3.

Pogade, Daniela, 'Die Kuh macht Muh: Sennen-Ballade und Bauerkrieg: Erich Langjahrs Dokumentarfilme über eine fast verblichene Schweiz', *Berliner Zeitung Online*, www.berlinonline.de/berliner-zeitung/archiv, March 16, 2000.

Richter, Robert, 'Mensch und Kuh in Not', *St Galler Tagblatt Online*, www.tagblatt.ch, April 30, 1998.

Stock, Andreas, 'Unsere Bauern und der Bauer in uns: Der Dokumentarfilm Bauernkrieg von Erich Langjahr im Kino', *St Galler Tagblatt Online*, www.tagblatt.ch, September 19, 1998.

——'"Wir haben alle den Hirten in uns": Interview mit Erich Langjahr', *St Galler Tagblatt Online*, www.tagblatt.ch, October 24, 2002.

Westphal, Anke, 'Wie schnell warden Schafe müde?: Der Dokfilm Hirtenreise ins dritte Jahrtausend', *Berliner Zeitung Online*, www.berlinonline.de/berliner-zeitung/archiv, November 27, 2003.

Zimmermann, Verena, 'Zeitreisen, Kopfreisen', *St Galler Tagblatt Online*, www.tagblatt.ch, April 29, 2002.

Langlois, Henri

'First citizen of cinema', 'patron saint of cinema', 'Jules Verne of cinema', 'the dragon who watches over our treasures', are some of the many titles to honour Henri Langlois, who paid his own tribute to the seventh art: 'Movies will give us the third eye'; 'the cinema is light in darkness'.

Born on Friday, November 13, 1914 in Smyrna, in a cosmopolitan family, Henri Langlois spent his early years in that most mythical Turkish city. Caught in the explosion of nationalist violence in the aftermath of World War I, the Langlois family had to flee for France and settled in Paris in 1920.

The young Henri Langlois very early had a keen interest in cinema, in particular the silent movies of the 1920s, further enhanced by the arrival of the first talkies in 1929. He quickly became a regular spectator at the screenings organised by the numerous cine clubs that appeared in postwar Paris, creating with George Franju his own Cercle du Cinéma in 1935. A year later it became the Cinémathèque

Française, with Man Ray, Louis Lumière, George Méliès, and Jean Renoir among its founding fathers. Henri Langlois was only twenty-one years old.

The Cinémathèque was created with a view to being more than another cine club. It was soon endowed with the mission to salvage the enormous quantity of silent movies made redundant by the arrival of the talkies, and which were being systematically destroyed. Within three months of its existence, Langlois and his friends had managed to salvage one thousand films and would amass over the years a considerable collection.

Henri Langlois spent most of World War II in Paris, trying to rescue the dispersed collection of the Cinémathèque and showing the banned American, English, and even Soviet films, defying the strict German censorship. He was also there, at the Libération of Paris, making sure that cinema was part of the euphoria that greeted the end of the German occupation.

Soon the Cinémathèque acquired an international reputation, through its travelling exhibitions such as 'Images of French Cinema' in 1945, or 'The Birth of French Cinema' in 1947. It also became a valuable source of films for the newly formed Federation of Ciné-Clubs, while maintaining its independence among the politics of postwar France. On October 26, 1948 Langlois realised his lifelong dream, the opening of the Museum of Cinema, avenue de Messine, in Paris. This nineteenth-century mansion became the place of worship for a new generation of cinema buffs, who found inspiration in the retrospectives organised by Langlois.

Langlois was also secretary general of the International Federation of Film Archives (FIAF), which was based in Paris until 1960. The FIAF eventually moved to Brussels, after its break-up with the Cinémathèque. The period between 1955 and 1960 is still considered the most creative period of the Cinémathèque, during which it played a central role in the emerging New Wave, providing it with a forum for discussion and giving it access to world film production, past and present. After this time, François Truffaut, Jean-Luc Godard, Les *Cahiers du Cinéma*, to name a few, were closely involved with the Cinémathèque, and were powerful allies in times of crisis.

The Cinémathèque constantly suffered from a lack of resources. In 1955 it had to move from its premises at rue de Messine to rue d'Ulm, with its offices at rue de Spontini, then rue de Courcelles. It was not until 1964 that, under the new Gaullist administration, the Cinémathèque moved to the prestigious Palais de Chaillot, opposite the Eiffel Tower. Langlois was awarded the Légion d'Honneur, and with new premises and a strong supporter in the powerful Ministre de la Culture, André Malraux, better times seemed to lie ahead; however, this was not to be the case.

Jealous of the independence of the Cinémathèque, Langlois found himself increasingly in conflict with an administration keen to control all aspects of cultural life and that demanded a more substantial governmental representation in its management against better subsidies. Langlois resisted such state interference until February 1968, when he was suddenly sacked. He became instantly a symbol of resistance to the abuse of power of the Gaullist administration. His dismissal was met with violent protests in Paris, with the whole of the New Wave and most of the cinema industry supporting him. The numerous and violent clashes with the police were a forerunner of the general unrest in May 1968.

In April 1968 Langlois was reinstated, but the governmental change of mind was accompanied by a drastic reduction in its funding. In June 1972 the first museum of world cinema was created at the Cinémathèque, not as much a museum as a movie itself, an immersion into the world of the moving image, going much further back than the Lumière brothers, as far as Chinese shadow puppets, an initiation to the art and ambience of cinema. The museum was inaugurated three times—in 1972, 1975, and 1980—after successive closures as a result of theft, poor management, and lack of resources.

Langlois became more involved in the lecture circuit, and travelled constantly between Montreal, Harvard in Cambridge, MA, and New York, receiving an honorary Oscar in 1973 where he was introduced as 'the curator, collector and conscience of cinema'. In 1975 the Henri Langlois Foundation was created, housed in two donated buildings in the Paris suburb of Pontault-Combault. At long last it owned its premises. However, Langlois was exhausted and overworked, having had to struggle for so long to keep his lifelong commitment to the preservation of films against the odds.

Langlois died on January 13, 1977 in Paris from a heart attack, at the age of sixty-two.

France and the film industry mourned the loss of one of the most colourful and passionate advocates of cinema, but his sudden death threw the Cinémathèque into complete disarray. Three years later half of its collection of films was destroyed in a huge fire in its warehouse, followed by another fire in 1985. It would take a few more years for its future to be at last guaranteed, with its subsidy being increased fivefold under the management of its new president, the director Costa Gavras. The museum has become the Musée du Cinéma-Henri Langlois, now situated in the main entrance of the Palais de Chaillot, a last tribute to the man whose life has been a passionate dedication to cinema and who, for generations of cinemagoers in France, has been the voice and the memory of cinema.

YVAN TARDY

Biography

Born in Smyrna, Turkey, November 13, 1914. Created Le Cercle du Cinéma in 1935, which became the Cinémathèque Françaize in 1936. Secretary general of the International Federation of Film Archives. Chevalier de la Legion d'Honneur, Honorary Oscar in 1973. Died in Paris February 13, 1977.

Further reading

Bonnaud, Irène, 'La Cinemathèque dans la tourmente', *Vacarme* 83, January 2001.

Cormerais, Franck, 'Le grand demenagement de La Cinemathèque française', *Regards* 42, January 1999.

Langlois, Henri, *Trois cents ans de cinéma*, Jean Narboni—*Cahiers du Cinéma*, October 1986.

Myrent, Glenn and Langlois, Georges P., *Henri Langlois, First Citizen of Cinema*, New York: Barnes & Noble, January 1995.

Olmeta, Patrick, *La Cinémathèque Française de 1936 à nos jours*, Olmeta: CNRS Editions, 2001.

Roud, Française Richard, *A Passion for Films: Henri Langlois and the Cinémathèque Française*, Baltimore, MD: The Johns Hopkins University Press, 1999.

Lanzmann, Claude

Claude Lanzmann is primarily renowned for Shoah (1985), widely considered a landmark among documentary films and without doubt the magnum opus of a career mainly devoted to confronting the memory of the Holocaust.

With Claude Lanzmann, documentary cinema becomes a duty of remembrance and a philosophical search for truth. His films attempt to comprehend some of the most extreme deeds of the twentieth century and to give an account of them as accurately and faithfully as possible. His technique mainly consists of in-depth interviews with witnesses. Shoah, 'An Oral History of the Holocaust', is a nine-hour, thirty-minute cross-examination of the survivors and guards of the concentration camps. Conversations with Yehuda Lerner, one the few survivors of the only successful mass-revolt from one of the extermination camps, make up most of the ninety-five minutes of Sobibor, released in 2001.

The same principles underpin all his films. The intensity of war and the atrocities of the Holocaust cannot be apprehended using newsreel footage, neither through reconstruction nor fiction. It can be passed on only by the oldest method of transmission of knowledge, that of the eyewitness telling what he or she saw and did at the time of the events. The documentary film is a raw material on which the viewer has to reconstruct his or her own version based on the testimony of those interviewed. He or she is compelled to imagine what happened as recalled by witnesses to reappropriate their memory, to understand the reality as it is told, and accept it or reject it.

The result is a striking, unsettling account of the Holocaust, which also acts as a critical interrogation on humanity's encounter with its darkest side. There are few concessions to any kind of narrative or aesthetic consideration. The interviews, interceded with long shots of the concentration camps or lingering images of Poland, are essential elements designed to induce a meditation on humankind, war, life, and death.

In Tsahal, released in 1994, Claude Lanzmann goes beyond his exploration of the Holocaust, to the controversial topic of the Israeli army, applying the same technique of in-depth interviews, this time with Israeli soldiers who talk openly about their experience of the war. Tsahal was criticised for taking an ambiguous, even a partisan view of the conflict between Israel and its neighbours, an accusation that Lanzmann rejected. In a variety of interviews marking the release of his films he has become unwillingly a commentator on the conflict between the

Israelis and the Palestinians, and as such a controversial figure, a position that he has found uncomfortable.

Claude Lanzmann has always defended his role as a documentary filmmaker concerned with the authenticity of history as reported by those involved in its most extreme events and to confront humanity with its darkest sides. His relentless search for witnesses and imperious quest for truth makes him one of the most outstanding directors of documentary cinema.

YVAN TARDY

See also: Shoah

Biography

Born Paris, France, November 27, 1925. Medaille de la Resistance, Commandeur de l'Ordre National du Merite. Studied philosophy at Tübingen University in Germany. Awarded the Diplome d'Etudes Superieures de Philosophie, University of Paris. Journalist and lecturer in French literature and philosophy at the Freie Universität Berlin. Director of Les Temps Modernes and professor of documentary film at the European Graduate School in Saas-Fee, Switzerland. Director of the prestigious magazine *Les Temps Modernes*, founded by Jean-Paul Sartre and Simone de Beauvoir.

Selected films

1970 Élise ou la vraie vie/Elise, or Real Life: writer
1972 Pourquoi Israel/Israel, Why: director
1985 Shoah: director
1994 Tsahal: director
1997 Un Vivant qui passe/A Visitor from the Living: director, actor
2001 Sobibor, 14 octobre 1943, 16 heures/ Sobibor, 14 October 1943, 16 hours: director

Further reading

Brinkly, Robert and Youra, Steven, 'Tracing Shoah', *PMLA* 111/1, January 1996: 108–27.

Felman, Shoshana, 'The Return of the Voice: Claude Lanzmann's Shoah', in Shoshana Felman and Dori Laub (eds), *Testimony: Crises of Witnessing in Literature, Psychoanalysis and History*, New York and London: Routledge, 1992.

Furman, Nelly, 'The Language of Pain', in Geoffrey H. Hartman (ed.), *Holocaust Remembrance: The Shapes of Memory*, Oxford: Blackwell, 1994.

Hansen, Miriam Bratu, 'Schindler's List is Not Shoah: The Second Commandment, Popular Modernism and Herelic Memory', *Critical Inquiry* 22, winter 1996: 292–312.

Hartman, Geoffrey H., 'The Book of Destruction', in Saul Friedlander (ed.), *Probing the Limits of Representation: Nazism and the 'Final Solution'*, Cambridge, MA: Harvard University Press, 1992.

Koch, Gertrud, *The Aesthetic Transformation of the Image of the Unimaginable: Notes on Claude Landzmann's Shoah*, trans. Jamie Owen Daniel and Miriam Hansen, *October* 48, spring 1989: 15–24.

Lanzmann, Claude, *Shoah*, Grafenau: Trotzdem Verlag, 1999.

——*Un Vivant qui passe: Auschwitz 1943—Theresienstadt 1944*, Paris: Mille et une nuits, 1997.

——*Shoah: The Complete Text of the Acclaimed Holocaust Film*, Cambridge, MA: Da Capo Press, September 1995.

——*Au Sujet de Shoah: le film de Claude Lanzmann*, Paris: Editions Belin, 1990.

——*Shoah*, Paris: Editions Fayard, 1985.

——*Shoah: An Oral History of the Holocaust: The Complete Text of the Film*, New York: Pantheon Books, 1985.

Lanzmann, Claude (eds), *Les Temps Modernes 614, Revue Les Temps Modernes*, Gallimard, summer, 2001.

Lanzmann, Claude and Orenstein, Henry, *I Shall Live*, Oxford and New York: Oxford University Press, 1990.

Lanzmann, Claude and Schneider, Silke, *Formen von Erinnerung. Ein anderer Blick auf Gedenken, Erinnern und Erleben*, Marburg: Jonas-Verlag, 1998.

Rabinowitz, Paula, 'Wreckage upon Wreckage: History, Documentary, and the Ruins of Memory', in *They Must Be Represented: The Politics of Documentary*, London: Verso, 1994.

Roth, Michael S., 'Shoah as Shivah', in *The Ironist's Cage: Memory, Trauma and the Construction of History*, New York: Columbia University Press, 1995.

Weissman, Gary, 'A Fantasy of Witnessing', *Media, Culture and Society* 17, 1995: 293–307.

Young, James E., 'Holocaust Video and Cinemagraphic Testimony: Documenting the Witness', in *Writing and Rewriting the Holocaust: Narrative and the Consequences of Interpretation*, Bloomington, IN: University of Indiana Press, 1990.

Lapping, Brian

Brian Lapping, British director, producer, and author, is among those contemporary documentary filmmakers who consistently brings insightful and quality current event documentaries to the television medium. Lapping's documentaries are driven by in-depth research and remain critically appealing because of their high-profile interviews and timely topics depicted within the world's climate. Lapping's documentaries are sophisticated and nonsensational; they provide invaluable summaries and international explanations to major events. The filmmakers involved in Lapping's productions are interested in the facts leading to international decisions and achieve this by prompting those involved to articulate their choices to the camera. Lapping lets his films' stories be told by the people who were there, on the inside. His documentaries are richly time-consuming and often run as series showing on BBC1 or BBC2, The Discovery Channel, Channel 4, ITV, PBS, Devillier Donegan, and many other international broadcasters.

Lapping began his career as a journalist, a profession that has profoundly informed and influenced his approach to documentary film production. In 1970 Lapping made the transition to motion picture documentary when he joined Granada Television. From 1976 to 1979 he was executive producer of the Granada/ITV weekly current affairs production World in Action. In 1979 Lapping created a new television format based on the Harvard Law School teaching method. The outcome was the series Hypotheticals. Lapping produced thirty of these one-hour programs for Granada, and they examined a different current ethical issue through intensive case studies. Later he would go on to produce the series annually for BBC2. The format has proved highly successful as an investigative approach and has been copied extensively in the United States and other countries.

In 1988 Lapping formed his own production company, Brian Lapping Associates. Its first production (incidentally, not a documentary), Countdown to War (1989), a drama based on letters, memoirs, and official papers, was produced for ITV. Lapping quickly returned to documentary filmmaking and continued to develop his investigative style with The Second Russian Revolution (1991). The series was aired in thirty-one countries and received many awards.

Lapping's primary interests involve intense political issues, and his series are steeped in high diplomacy and complicated negotiations. Lapping believes that 'the thing that binds together all the programs […] is that the stories are very complicated, and too often the news can only handle the simple, superficial level—the level of high drama'. Lapping's series tell the story from spark to smolder, the entire history, development, and outcome. Lapping's teams visit a scenario with in-depth knowledge gained through thorough investigations of the topic's players and events.

Lapping also created the 'journalists' reconstruction'. The technique has several journalists meet and discuss a current matter with their respective countries' leaders. The journalists then pool their versions of the major international confrontation and assemble a many-sided account of how an important matter of public record came to be decided.

Lapping's trademark ability is his capacity to get the individuals at the center of an issue to tell exactly how they made the decisions that resulted in the outcome being explored. Lapping has described it as a process of flattery, wherein an individual is carefully studied and interviewed, which ultimately results in a deep impression made on the subject and prompts the interviewee to respond to that flattery by revealing more information. Lapping admits that, 'That is the process we exploit, or use, perfectly legitimately, to get people to tell their stories'. In The Second Russian Revolution, Lapping and associates were able to infiltrate and talk with members of Politburo, the traditionally tightlipped group, and again in The Death of Yugoslavia (1995) Lapping captured interviews with heads of government from Serbia, Croatia, Slovenia, and Bosnia covering issues that Western politicians would never have revealed.

Lapping describes this ability—the extraordinary access to top politicians—as a 'temporary freak'. Lapping has been able 'to get a level of access to top politicians and other decision-makers for making television programs that is denied to historians and is rarely, if ever, available to other journalists'. He cites this phenomenon as a particular effect of television. It is the power and scope of the medium that persuades those people to go before the camera and tell their story.

Another aspect of Lapping's documentaries is the depiction of actual 'events'. Lapping describes the opportunity to show an event as opposed to people talking about an event as 'The Great Toy'. In The Death of Yugoslavia, the producers' obsession with getting inside the story unearthed a boardroom film in the

Yugoslav military archive. The film depicts the Yugoslav army, Serb president, and the presidents of other states deciding on whether to go into Croatia to stop the acquisition of arms.

Although Lapping has directed in the past, he has moved exclusively into a producer role. He designs the programs and is actively involved in persuading broadcasters about programming and places the individuals involved in their production. Lapping's films are coproduced and are commissioned by multiple broadcasters because they are so expensive.

Lapping's documentaries do not achieve high ratings, but they continue to be produced largely due to the praise they receive from newspapers, historians, and broadcasters. The BBC cites Lapping and his films as 'virtually a new genre of documentary which retells momentous events from the recent past with meticulous objectivity and with most or all of the principal actors recording their version of what happened: the narratives that emerge are revelations'.

ROBERT A. EMMONS, JR

Biography

Born in London, England, September 13, 1937. Graduated from Pembroke College, Cambridge, in 1959. Journalist for the *Daily Mirror*, *Guardian*, *Financial Times*, and *New Society*. Founder of Brian Lapping Associates, eventually becoming Brook Lapping Productions in 1988. Author of several books. Awards include Gold and Silver Medals International Film and TV Festival, George Foster Peabody Award, BAFTA Best Documentary Award, Columbia University du Pont Gold Baton, and an Emmy. Chairman, Teachers' Television Department of Education, 2003–4.

Selected films

1976 Chrysler and the Cabinet: producer
1985 End of Empire: executive producer
1991 The Second Russian Revolution: executive producer
1994 Watergate: executive producer
1995 The Death of Yugoslavia: executive producer
1998 The 50 Years War: Israel and the Arabs: director, producer
1999 Finest Hour: executive producer
2001 Endgame in Ireland: executive producer
2002 Avenging Terror: executive producer
2003 The Fall of Milosevic: executive producer

Further reading

Lapping, Brian, *Apartheid: A History*, New York: G. Braziller, 1986.

——*The Bounds of Freedom*, London: Constable and Co., 1980.

——*End of Empire*, New York: St Martin's, 1985.

——*The Labour Government, 1964–70*, New York: Penguin, 1970.

Lapping, Brian and Radice, Giles (eds), *More Power to the People: Young Fabian Essays on Democracy in Britain*, London: Longman, 1968.

Latin America

The earliest manifestation of the documentary instinct in Latin America occurred in Mexico before World War I during the Revolutionary years after the uprising of 1911, when the immediate success of actualities depicting the momentous events of the day helped to stimulate the early growth of Mexican cinema. In the absence of any dominant international cinematic model for political reportage (newsreels were only in their earliest stage and hardly provided models for events like those in Mexico), these actualities developed along their own distinctive lines. According to the account of Aurelio de los Reyes (1995), filmmakers stimulated by an eager urban audience took to the battlefields, where their instinct was to pursue a positivist belief in the camera's objectivity and to eschew a political agenda of their own. A film from 1912 by the Alva brothers, for example, Revolución orozquista/The Orozco Revolution, attempts to report the events from both sides of the battle lines; the filmmakers were even caught in crossfire that damaged their equipment. It is difficult, says de los Reyes, to tell where the authors' sympathies lay; an objectivity that he adds does not survive the imposition of censorship by the Huerta regime in 1913. In this brief period Mexican filmmakers quickly developed greater skill in the construction of a documentary narrative than filmmakers north of the border, and the results are what de los Reyes calls 'a local vernacular form of representation of contemporary happenings'.

This early flowering was exceptional, the result of opportunity, initiative, and a brief absence of repressive authority. The subsequent evolution of cinema as a commercial institution under the tutelage of Hollywood, which was nowhere auspicious for documentary, was compounded in Latin America by the conditions of underdevelopment. This stunted growth and resulted only in a series of medium-to-small, sometimes tiny, local film industries, all of them plagued by structural weakness and small markets. If early documentary in Europe was succoured by the film society movement, born in Paris in 1924, and the first art houses, these did not appear in Latin America (apart from Brazil) until somewhat later (the 1940s in Uruguay and Argentina, the 1950s in countries such as Chile, Bolivia, and Cuba). Nor were there paragovernmental agencies and corporate commercial interests to develop 16mm distribution of educational documentary, as happened, for example, in Great Britain, where a strong documentary movement grew up in the 1930s as a result. It is hardly surprising, therefore, that throughout the rest of the silent period and beyond, until the rise of a new film movement in the 1950s, Latin American documentary was confined, with little exception, to minor examples of conventional subgenres like the travelogue or the scientific documentary. Nevertheless, there is evidence of a documentary instinct at work in isolated examples uncovered by scholars. Agustin Mahieu (1966) speaks of an Argentine film of 1916, El último malón/The Last Indian Uprising, shot in the province of Santa Fé by an anthropologist called Alcides Greca, which he describes as a kind of documentary reconstruction of an uprising that took place at the beginning of the century, filmed in authentic locations with the indigenous Indians as protagonists of their own story. Paulo Antonio Paranagua (1984) speaks of a documentary made for a copper company in Chile in 1919 by an Italian, Salvador Giambastiani, which places on display faces marked by the grim conditions in the mines, including a number of scenes of the men at work. More recently the same writer has chronicled the existence of a substantial number of newsreels produced in various countries from the 1920s to the 1950s, especially Argentina, Mexico, Brazil, and Cuba (Paranagua 2003). The main exception to this pattern was the work of Humberto Mauro in Brazil, subsequently claimed by Glauber Rocha as the precursor of cinema novo. Mauro produced a series of films under the general title Brasilianas between 1945 and 1956, celebrating aspects of the Brazilian countryside and popular culture, as well as a number of longer films that often contain an original mixture of fiction and documentary.

Occasionally new finds appear. A documentary of 1993 by the Venezuelan Alfredo Anzola, El misterio de los ojos escarlata/The Mystery of the Scarlet Eyes, provides a rare glimpse of unseen images of Venezuela in the 1920s and 1930s: footage shot by the filmmaker's father, who made documentaries and two silent feature films, now lost, in the 1920s, then acquired a 16mm camera and filmed mostly documentary footage throughout the 1930s and 1940s while working as the director of a radio station. A radio serial written and produced by Anzola Père provides the title of his son's film about him, a film that prompts several questions: How many others among the all but nameless Latin American filmmakers of the early years had similar careers? Might they have left undiscovered archives? How many of these aficionados have not even left their names behind? Also, Anzola, as portrayed by his son, was clearly no intellectual, but a keen cineaste, an aficionado who took his camera with him to events where he had entry as a radio producer. The point of view is uncritical and marked by his social class. However, aficionados of the same class in succeeding decades were the very people whose first filmmaking efforts represent the initial stirrings of the powerful new movement in Latin American cinema that emerged in the late 1950s.

A singular example from 1930s Mexico points in another direction. The film historian Georges Sadoul calls Redes (Nets, aka The Wave, 1934) a semidocumentary that uses nonprofessional actors in real locations, in the manner of the German film Menschen am Sonntag/People on Sunday (directed by Robert Siodmak) of 1929, to recount a story taken from everyday life, which in this case deals with the struggle of Vera Cruz fishermen against exploitation. In short, an extraordinary piece of neorealism *avant la lettre*, as well as a precursor of what will later become a major tendency of politically committed filmmaking in every corner of Latin America. A rare example, too, of collaboration as equals between North and South, the film was made at the invitation of a progressive politician, Velásquez Chávez, in charge of public education, who wrote the original script, by a team headed by the Mexican Emilio Gómez Muriel, which included two foreigners: the New York photographer Paul Strand and a young émigré from Austria, Fred Zinnemann, Siodmak's assistant director on Menschen am Sonntag. In sum, Redes is one of those films, like Kuhle Wampe by Slatan Dudow and Bertolt Brecht (1932), or Jean Renoir's Toni of 1934, which impresses themselves on the imagination as spectres of a different kind of cinema that might have been, where the simple opposition between fiction and documentary is transcended.

The emergence of Latin American documentary in the 1950s and 1960s marks the appearance of a new generation of filmmakers, who benefit from a new economic and political conjuncture. Cinema was already thoroughly dominated by Hollywood product, which easily commanded eighty percent or more of the market, while postwar modernisation extended the US presence in the expanding domains of radio and television. It also brought a drive to open up markets among the Latin American bourgeoisie for the appurtenances of the 'American way of life', which naturally included amateur cine, for which official Washington publications like the *Industrial Reference Service* (later called *World Trade in Commodities*) recorded increasing sales in several countries. The spread of film clubs and magazines, art houses, and festivals was part of the same process of cultural modernisation, but produced a sting: the new generation rejected both what they saw as the cultural imperialism of the gringos and the crass commercialism of local film industries, where they existed, which together prevented the emergence of authentic autochthonous voices. Instead they looked to new film movements in Europe for orientation. Several of the pioneers of the 1950s and 1960s had taken themselves to Italy to study cinema in Rome, bringing back with them the ideals of both neorealism and the social documentary, whatever would help them in the endeavour to discover the social, economic, and political undertow in the sight of immediate reality, whether in the form of neorealist fiction or documentary.

Documentary is a marginal form of cinema, and some of the first initiatives occurred in out-of-the-way places like Cuzco in Peru, where a film club was set up in 1955 and Manuel Chambi and others started making short documentaries on ethnographic and sociocultural themes; Sadoul called them the Cuzco School. They were not unique, but represented a new desire to be found throughout the continent for self-expression beyond the bounds that were sanctioned by the ruling Creole elites. Several such groups were linked to social movements that espoused leftist and Marxist principles, like the cultural club Nuestro Tiempo run by the Young Communists in Havana in the 1950s, which harboured several future Cuban directors. The first international meeting place for the young filmmakers was a film festival in Montevideo, set up in 1954 by the SODRE, Uruguay's national radio station and a progressive cultural promoter. Among the filmmakers attending in 1958, when John Grierson was the guest of honour, were Chambi from Peru, and Fernando Birri from Argentina. The film exhibited by Birri and his students, Tire Die/Throw Us a Dime, a collaborative social inquiry into the shanty towns around the city of Santa Fe, later came to be celebrated as the founding social documentary of the new film movement. Known simply as el nuevo cine latinoamericano (the new Latin American cinema), the designation dates from a meeting in 1967 of filmmakers from across the continent hosted by a film club in the Chilean seaside town of Viña del Mar, which had been running a festival of 8mm and 16mm with a strong documentary emphasis since 1963. Documentary, for this movement, was far from marginal, even if documentarists everywhere (except Cuba after 1959) were forced to work in the interstices of the system. In the desire to turn the cameras on the actuality of the external world, to escape the distorted imagery of the dominant cinema's imaginary, fiction was necessarily inflected by documentary and shared the documentary vocation to witness and testify to social reality. There is a long list of dramatic films, from Nelson Pereira dos Santos in Brazil in the 1950s, by way of Sanjinés in Bolivia, Peru, and Ecuador in the 1960s and after, to the recent work of Víctor Gaviria in Colombia, which represents the persistent pull that the documentary instinct and its disciplines have exercised on the Latin American fiction film.

The 1950s saw a small number of initiatives in independent documentary production, including ¡Torero! by Carlos Velo in Mexico (1956), a partly dramatised account of the career of the matador Luis Procuña, in which Procuña plays himself, and in Venezuela, an extraordinary film of poetic realism depicting everyday life in the feudal salt marshes, called Araya, by Margot Benacerraf (1959). In the next few years, new paradigms of political documentary began to appear, and a stream of films, in a variety of styles and approaches, which attested to the conditions of life from the Rio Grande to Tierra del Fuego. As one commentator has put it, 'The rise of Marxist-inflected ideologies in Latin America prescribed a dual quest: for a less stratified socioeconomic system, and for authentic, autonomous, culturally specific forms of expression' (Burton 1990). Among the films shown at Viña in 1967 were no fewer than seventeen from Brazil, where filmmakers in São Paulo were stimulated by the arrival in 1963 of Birri and several of his associates, who had been forced to flee their country. Benefiting from more up-to-date equipment, Brazilian documentary established a particularly strong line in political reportage, exemplified by films like Geraldo Sarno's Viramundo (1964) on internal migration, which constructs a montage of multiple voices that juxtaposes the aspirations of peasants from the drought-ridden northeast who migrate to São Paulo in search of work with what they find when they arrive there. A distinctive feature of these films is the dissolution of the authoritative monologue of voice-over narration in favour of a dialogical form of construction that allows the filmmaker to apply a dialectical, and hence highly politicised, interpretation of the subject matter. Other filmmakers, working without the benefit of synchronous sound recording, found imaginative solutions to the construction of the soundtrack, which also displace the voice of authority, like the Uruguayan Mario Handler's Carlos: Cineretrato de un caminante/Carlos: Cine-Portrait of a Walker (1965), which combines patiently filmed images of a vagabond's life with his edited speech, recorded afterwards, on the soundtrack. Here, through the aesthetic construction of the subjectivity of an individual discarded by society, the film exemplifies another fundamental impulse of the new documentary, that of giving voice and image to those who have been condemned to silence and invisibility. In this way, Latin American documentary shared the aim defined by the Brazilian radical Christian educationalist Paulo Freire as breaking 'the culture of silence' to which underdevelopment condemned the subaltern classes.

Among the films on show at Viña in 1967, and the following year at another international meeting in Mérida, Venezuela, were several from Cuba. If the politicisation of the 1960s received a strong fillip from the Cuban Revolution, Cuban documentary contributed powerfully to the tendency to combine explicit political content with an experimental aesthetic, above all in the work of Santiago Alvarez, who reinvented the newsreel, the compilation film, the travelogue, and every other documentary genre he laid hands on in an irrepressible frenzy of filmic bricolage licensed by that supreme act of bricolage, the Cuban Revolution. Cuba became unique in Latin America in the status it awarded to its own cinema, including documentary. Cuba was the one place in Latin America where local documentaries were widely seen in the cinemas, because distribution was controlled by a state film institute (ICAIC, the Cuban Institute of Film Art and Industry), which had been created by the Revolution within three months of taking power in 1959. ICAIC set out to supply its own documentaries and a weekly newsreel with every feature film, foreign or domestic, that it distributed. Newsreel and documentary became the requisite form of apprenticeship for new directors, a philosophy that also succoured a critical realist approach to fiction. (Although Cuban fiction films were made with professional actors, the directors quickly abandoned the studio, and even their comedies and genre films are remarkable for the documentary value of their mise-en-scène.) The euphoria of revolution imbued the institute's films with an experimentalist aesthetic, and no one was more audacious than Alvarez, who headed the newsreel unit, which he turned by his own example into a school for militant documentary. By using every kind of visual imagery, from newsreel footage to stills, archive film to cuttings from magazines, combined with animated texts and emblematic musicalisation, Alvarez amalgamated revolutionary politics and kleptomania to reinvent Soviet montage in a Caribbean setting. Best known abroad in those years were his montage films on racism and politics in the United States, Now (1965) and LBJ (1968); the lyrical Vietnam films, Hanoi Martes 13/Hanoi Tuesday 13th (1967) and 79 Primaveras/79 Springs (1969); and his eulogy for Che Guevara, Hasta la Victoria Siempre/Always Until Victory (1967).

In the 1970s researchers at ICAIC found that people sometimes went to the movies because they wanted to see the new Alvarez, and would then stay and watch whatever feature was put on after it, a complete inversion of normal cinema-going behaviour. Alvarez began making feature-length documentaries at the start of the decade, and their success prompted ICAIC to produce a whole series of feature documentaries for cinema distribution by different directors at a time when commercial cinema in the West had abandoned making documentaries for the cinema altogether. Particularly notable are two films by Jesús Díaz. 55 Hermanos/55 Brothers and Sisters (1978) follows a group of young Cuban Americans, children of émigrés returning to their country for the first time on a highly charged three-week trip that ends with a meeting with Fidel. En tierra de Sandino/In the Land of Sandino (1980) is probably the most penetrating study of the Sandinista revolution by a foreign filmmaker. ICAIC's policy produced a paradox: Cuba, where according to its enemies the public sphere had been replaced by the totalitarian control of the communists, maintained a space on the cinema screen for the documentary encounter with social reality, which was not to be found on the screens of the democracies, where commercial criteria drove them out. Nor were Cuban documentaries, or even newsreels, by any means limited to political propaganda. The newsreels were often investigative (especially compared to the conformism of broadcasting and the press), whereas many of the documentaries were broadly didactic and to that extent Griersonian. Others were poetic; many were devoted to celebrating different aspects of Cuban culture. Several are portraits of individuals who recover their memories for the collective. Notable directors include Manuel Octavio Gómez, Octavio Cortázar, Pastor Vega, Sara Gómez, Melchor Casals, and Luis Felipe Bernaza. Whenever their films were seen in Latin America, in film festivals and film clubs, they powerfully encouraged the ambitions of documentarists who had none of the access to an audience that their Cuban compadres enjoyed.

If the surge of Latin American documentary went together with social ferment in countries where political upheaval was on the agenda, this was nowhere more true than in Chile in the late 1960s, where a small tribe of young filmmakers formed a committee of support for the left-wing coalition of Popular Unity and its Marxist presidential candidate Salvador Allende. Both before and after his electoral victory in 1970 they engaged in a cinema of urgency, producing a range of highly inventive films from campaign propaganda and agitational shorts to investigations of the political process and full-scale neorealist dramatisations denouncing the ills of underdevelopment. This was the milieu in which Raúl Ruiz, who would later make his career among the French avant-garde, first discovered his talent for improvisation, the improvised fiction of Tres Tristes Tigres/Three Sad Tigers (1968) and the improvised documentary in the case of La Expropiación/Expropriation (1972). The most extraordinary film to emerge from this period, however, was Patricio Guzmán's three-part chronicle La batalla de Chile/The Battle of Chile, a record of the tumultuous months leading up to the coup of 1973 in which Allende was overthrown. A fertile mixture of direct cinema observation and investigative reportage, the footage was smuggled out immediately after Allende's fall and edited in Cuba at ICAIC, the final part appearing in 1979. The result is a work of historical testimony unique in the annals of documentary for its scope, density, and poignancy.

As with other countries that fell to the right, Chilean filmmakers were among those who were forced into exile (the latter included Guzmán's cameraman Jorge Müller). Owing to international solidarity, Chileans became the leading practitioners of a cinema of exile that grew up in the 1970s and contributed a new genre to the history of world cinema, as a number of films took the experience of exile as their subject matter, including Ruiz's semidocumentary Diálogo de exilados/Dialogue of Exiles (France, 1974), and Marilú Mallet's highly personal Journal inachevé/Unfinished Diary (Canada, 1982), an early paradigm of a new mode of feminist autobiographical documentary just then emerging in first-world filmmaking.

Dictatorship and repression also hit Brazil after the coup d'état of 1968, and Argentina after that of 1976, which brought the *guerra sucia* (dirty war) against the left in which thousands disappeared, among them Raymundo Gleyser, leading member of the militant group Cine de la Base. At the same time, authoritarian rule often had the counterintentional effect of stimulating self-activity among those it held down. Across the continent, as military regimes took power, popular organisations developed at community level to deal with the problems of inadequate housing, food, health care, water, and electricity, and became the locus for resistance to military repression, or simply the practice of popular democracy by those neglected by the state. Filmmakers seeing these organisations as the natural audience for their work created alternative exhibition circuits using portable equipment, on the rural model established in the 1960s in Bolivia by the Ukamau collective, or the urban form of independent distribution collectives like Zafra in Mexico, supplying films to groups such as film clubs and shanty town residents. In short, Latin American documentary became involved in the creation of an alternative audiovisual public sphere parallel with popular organisations within the community and sharing the same preoccupation to give voice to people normally excluded from public speech and outside the political power structures. In some cases films were made and exhibited within the orbit of particular political groups, sometimes banned ones. The most famous example is a mammoth three-part, four-hour political testimony called La hora de los hornos/The Hour of the Furnaces (1968), a product of the Peronist movement in Argentina. The film was accompanied by a manifesto, Hacia un tercer cine/Towards a Third Cinema, by two of its makers, Fernando Solanas and Octavio Getino, which offers a blueprint for militant filmmaking that was rapidly reprinted across the world.

La hora de los hornos was not only filmed clandestinely, it was also shown clandestinely. It was designed for an audience of the politically engaged, and while it might seem to be lecturing at them, it included strategically placed intertitles inviting the projectionist to pause the film to allow for debate among the audience. It thus exemplifies another essential characteristic of the movement to which it belongs, the intentional mode of address. Where independent documentary remains outside the world and discourse of television, and alternative distribution constructs a parallel public sphere for its circulation, the documentarist has the advantage of a direct relationship with small but particular sectors of the public. In Latin America this was reflected in the elaboration of a distinct vocabulary for the discussion of documentary in the journals and publications of the film movement to which they belonged: terms like cine didáctico, cine testimonio, cine denúncia, cine encuesta, cine rescate and, not least, cine militante. This list is not exhaustive or definitive and there is no single source from which it is drawn. These are only the most frequently used of a series of terms that occur across the whole range of radical Latin American film writings that express its preoccupations and objectives. They are found in film journals from several countries, with titles like *Hablemos de Cine*, *Cine al Día*, *Primer Plano*, *Octubre*, and *Cine Cubano* (from Peru, Venezuela, Chile, Mexico, and Cuba, respectively). The distinctive feature of all the terms listed is precisely their intentional character. They indicate a variety of purposes that can all be construed in political terms: cine didáctico is to teach, testimonio to offer testimony, denúncia to denounce, encuesta to investigate. Cine rescate is to bring history alive, celebrativo to celebrate revolutionary achievement. Cine ensayo is the essay film, to provide space for reflection. Cine militante or cine combate, militant cinema or cinema of combat, is the most explicit expression of the revolutionary imperative of those years.

If the politics of the movement were voluntaristic, the films generally paid scant attention to political programmes, but rather evinced an anthropological respect for their subjects combined with a sense of aesthetic search for anti-authoritarian modes of address. The filmmakers understood well enough that this required them to radicalise their own practices and develop collective working methods. It is no accident, but one of the features that justifies the designation of this variegated activity as a movement, that a strong tendency can be found from one end of Latin America to the other to work in groups, who often adopted declarative names like the two that called themselves Grupo Cine Testimonio: the first founded in Mexico in 1969 by Eduardo Maldonado, the second in Argentina in 1982. There was also a strong propensity to individual experiment, which might take several forms. The anthropological method is taken furthest in Chircales/Brickmakers (1972) by the Colombian documentarists Marta Rodríguez and Jorge Silva, who spent five years achieving a quite exceptional fusion of politics, poetry, and visual anthropology in the portrayal of workers in the brickyards on the outskirts of Bogotá. Even the most idiosyncratic experiments remain rooted in political reality, like the Mexican director Paul Leduc's ABC del Etnocidio/ABC of Ethnocide (1976), an A-to-Z of indictments against the modern Mexican state that breaks completely with the conventions of documentary exposition. Another tack is represented by Ciro Durán's Gamin (1978), a provocative and interventionist version of direct cinema that uses the technique to reveal what is under everybody's nose but is never seen: the private life of the Bogotá street urchin.

The 1980s brought a renewal of the political documentary across the continent, but in less strident forms. The forms of documentary that were cultivated in Nicaragua, where the Sandinistas took power in 1979 and immediately set up a film institute, and even El Salvador in the early 1980s, where a military junta was challenged by a guerrilla movement with its own filmmakers, gave considerable latitude for poetic expression. Elsewhere, liberalisation brought a new thematic—documenting the repression of the years of military dictatorships. One of the most thoughtful testaments of this history, its repressions and aporias, can be found in Eduardo Coutinho's Cabra Marcado para Morrer/Man Marked to Die (1984), which is not only an investigation into the assassination of a peasant leader in the northeast of Brazil twenty years earlier, but a film about its own history, recuperating the first abortive attempts to make the film more than twenty years earlier, juxtaposing actual footage from 1962, reenactment from 1964, and contemporary testimony from the early 1980s, all showing the same social actors at different ages and in different roles. As reflexive an aesthetic as anyone could want, the result was a documentary about a documentary with few to compare. In the 1990s Coutinho, now working on video, produced a number of deceptively simple but remarkable documentaries (Boca de Lixo, 1993; Babilonia 2000, 2001; Edificio Master, 2001), each presenting a cross-section of people at a particular location (scavengers on a rubbish tip, inhabitants of a *favela* (shanty town), or a middle-class apartment block), which amounts to an anatomy of the social classes of contemporary Brazil.

Another context was provided by the rise of feminism, which allowed a new generation of women filmmakers to transcend class barriers through the solidarity of gender, for which one of the first paradigms was an Argentine film memorialising the victims of military neofascism, Las Madres de la Plaza de Mayo/Mothers of the Plaza de Mayo (1985) by Lourdes Portillo and Susana Munoz. Meanwhile, women's film groups appeared in countries such as Mexico and Brazil, producing work on feminist themes like the struggle for abortion. Nevertheless, by the mid-1980s the movement as a whole found itself in a growing crisis of both confidence and identity. For a cinema founded on a political conception of itself, the transformation of the political space in which it operated as a result of the democratic turn of the decade threatened to cast it adrift. Revolutionary militancy and its rhetoric were slipping away, even before the collapse of the socialist camp shifted the balance of global power. Convictions remained, but the old prescriptions no longer served. Some Latin American documentarists were now in receipt of funding from European television stations, which also required a shift in the mode of address. Britain's new Channel 4, for example, supported a film by the exiled Argentine Jorge Denti, Malvinas, Historia de traiciones/Malvinas, Story of Betrayal (1983), which made a strength of conforming to British requirements of political balance by comparing the adventurism of Galtieri and Thatcher. A few years later they supported two films by the Chilean Ignacio Agüero: 100 niños esperando un tren/100 Children Waiting for a Train (1989), which discovers an entrancing world among children in a shanty town learning about the invention of cinema, and Sueños de hielo/Dreams of Ice (1992), a remarkable fantasy documentary about the lump of Antarctic ice that Chile sent to the World Fair in Seville.

However, there were also other developments in the shape of video, where once again Latin America would discover new forms of practice that punctured repression and the norms of representation. Indeed, video was put to such uses in Latin America with no greater delay than community video experiments in First World countries, and usually at much greater risk. In Chile, for example, the early 1980s saw clandestinely shot videos reporting on mass opposition to the rule of the junta, which would have been otherwise impossible to produce. The paradox is that video technology arrived in Chile as part of the neoliberal modernisation of the country's economy, which included investment in the advertising industry. In Argentina, the Grupo Cine-Ojo (in salute to Vertov's kino-Eye), which began working in 1982 in Super 8, made their first video documentary in 1984 (though they continued to work on 16mm as well). In Brazil, by the end of the decade video was being taken up by indigenous groups to document their traditions and organise themselves in the face of the indifference of the wider society. The indigenous video movement, which organises regional and national meetings and has spread to other countries including Bolivia, constitutes a new catalyst within both documentary and the public sphere, as it enables its participants to speak to each other, and sometimes to their Others, in a direct mode of address. This is not documentary in the old sense, but its extension into new collective spaces, where the former subjects of anthropological and political documentarists now wield the camera themselves and assert ownership of their own image. Stereotypical notions of cultural and technological backwardness are exploded by the speed with which indigenous video established itself, and even started inventing new genres and tropes of video speech.

A final example is the renaissance of documentary in Argentina in the midst of the country's nightmare of economic collapse. Once again we see the same phenomenon, the rapid adoption of the newest technologies for purposes perhaps still best described by the old-fashioned word of 'liberation' in a way that demolishes the notion that underdevelopment means backwardness in anything other than an economic sense. Thus, the same global capitalism that produces computerisation and digital telecommunication also produces the digital video cameras and computers that, during Argentina's neoliberal experiment of dollar parity, found eager buyers among a new generation of aspiring filmmakers. With the collapse of the banks, documentary was boosted by an explosive reality. Filmmakers, many of them trained in the film schools that blossomed in Argentina during the preceding decade, and often militants of one or another political association, now in full possession of the means of production, needed no funding or commissions to go out on the streets and film. Spontaneous and uncredited videos, recording popular mobilisations and *cacerolazos* (saucepan-bashing), were sold on the streets from stalls piled with copies; others rediscovered a certain Argentine documentary tradition going back to the work of Raymundo Gleyser in the 1960s. The upsurge began before the economic collapse of December 2001. Earlier that year, at Mar de Plata, an alternative festival of contemporary political documentary attracted the attention of Solanas, who withdrew from an official screening of La hora de los hornos to join the counter-event, calling the new groups the heirs of third cinema. Political opportunism? Wishful thinking? A year after the bank collapse, as many as forty groups of video filmmakers were working alongside the assemblies and *piqueteros*, the women's movement, and the workers' cooperatives who were taking control of bankrupt firms. Their work was shown at factories, community movement assemblies, and festivals, but not on television or in the cinemas. The world's eyes, or rather, the global media, may have turned away from Argentina's plight, but not the new documentarists, for whom their cameras are once again weapons in a struggle of survival that testifies to resistance in the face of adversity.

MICHAEL CHANAN

Further reading

Burton, Julianne (ed.), *The Social Documentary in Latin America*, Pittsburgh, PA: University of Pittsburgh Press, 1990.

Chanan, Michael, *The Cuban Image, Cinema and Cultural Politics in Cuba*, London: BFI, 1984.

de los Reyes, Aurelio, 'The Silent Cinema', in Paulo Antonio Paranagua (ed.), *Mexican Cinema*, London: BFI, 1995.

Mahieu, Jose Agustín, *Breve historia del cine argentino*, Buenos Aires: Editorial Universitaria, 1966.

Paranagua, Paulo Antonio, *O Cinema na América Latina*, Porto Alegre: L & P.M. Editores, 1984.

——*Cine documental en América Latina*, Madrid: Cátedra, 2003.

Law and Order

(US, Wiseman, 1969)

Law and Order shows the work of the city police force in Kansas City, Missouri, from precinct administration to routine patrol duty. Director Frederick Wiseman travels with cops in their patrol cars, and shows the police responding to different kinds of calls, ranging from domestic quarrels to armed robbery.

Stylistically, like all of Wiseman's documentaries, Law and Order offers no voice-over narration or expository titles, but presents a series of sequences that alternately depict the police as kind and cruel, as both benevolent and brutal. For every scene in which a policeman does something like find a lost purse for an elderly woman, there is another such as the one in which a detective seems inexplicably to ignore a man who wants to report someone with a gun.

In one sequence a policeman becomes a father figure to a lost little girl, bringing her to the precinct station and giving her candy. The policeman himself provides the perfect emblem of his 'parental' position by taking out a pipe and smoking it as he drives the patrol car with one arm wrapped protectively around the child, and Wiseman clearly encourages this view of him by shooting the policeman from a low angle, as if from a child's perspective. However, elsewhere in the film we see events that are likely to make us angry, such as the scene where a detective seems excessively violent to a prostitute, choking her even as he denies doing so. The event unfolds in a poorly lit basement and is the only time in the film when Wiseman uses artificial light in the form of a sun gun, tingeing the violence with a visually eerie tone.

The film thus places viewers in a conflicted position in relation to the police, their torn response analogous to the position of the police themselves. The film suggests that the sometimes inadequate or excessive responses of the police are, in turn, symptomatic of the impossible demands made on them as a result of larger social problems. Wiseman himself has said that his preconceptions about the police changed, grew more ambiguous, as a result of the experience of riding on patrol with them.

Wiseman is always interested in showing how a particular institution relates to the larger social fabric, and Law and Order suggests that American society, not unlike the police and the viewer, are torn. The police can neither solve domestic crime nor prevent it (a theme to which Wiseman returns again in Domestic Violence, 2001); often, all they can do is inform people that 'there's nothing we can do about it', the response they give in both the opening and closing sequences. The domestic emphasis of routine police work is expressed by the number of sequences in the film that refer to family and social tensions. In addition to the two domestic arguments that bracket the film, there are also, among others, a man charged with having molested a boy, a man who threatens to kill another man for molesting his niece, and a runaway boy.

Racial tensions, often present but largely submerged in Wiseman's films, loom large in Law and Order, made during a period of rising crime and racial violence in the United States. The fear of a recent race riot permeates the dialogue, and racial tension is evident throughout the film. At one point Wiseman's camera looks out the window of a moving patrol car to glimpse smoke ominously rising from a city block. A white woman who has been arrested makes a point of specifying the racial identity of the arresting officers, while the black youths arrested in the clothing store blame their fate on racial prejudice. In one sequence a young black man named Howard Gilbert is arrested for auto theft, and the camera waits with the youth and the arresting officers, who must listen to his string of racist insults for more than five minutes of screen time until the paddy wagon arrives. Richard Nixon's campaign speech near the end of Law and Order, in which he says voters are faced with a clear choice between rising crime and the reestablishment of 'respect for law and order in this country', makes explicit the social tensions that infuse the film.

In their work the police are required to enforce the law, maintain order, mediate domestic disputes, and provide a range of social services. The huge demands on the police seem almost impossible, as suggested by the film's structure. Bracketed by scenes of family arguments that the police attempt to mediate, the film structure is circular, distinguishing it from other Wiseman films such as Titicut Follies and High School, which both show beginnings and ends to their respective institutional processes. By contrast, Law and Order presents an accumulation of events, an ongoing process, more like Hospital and Welfare.

Subsequent to the scene of the arrest of Howard Gilbert, we hear two references to the fact that Gilbert has been released because he is a youthful offender. So Law and Order's structural symmetry suggests continuation rather than closure. Indeed, over the final credits, a voice from the police radio speaks of yet another dangerous suspect in a seemingly endless parade. The film's circular structure is thus apposite, given its view of police work as a ceaseless holding action against a wellspring of social discontent.

BARRY KEITH GRANT

See also: High School; Hospital; Titicut Follies; Wiseman, Fredrick

Law and Order (US, 1969, 81 mins). Distributed by Zipporah Films. Produced, edited, and directed by Frederick Wiseman. Cinematography by William Brayne. Sound recorded by Frederick Wiseman.

Further reading

Atkins, Thomas R. (ed.), *Frederick Wiseman*, New York: Monarch Press, 1976.
Benson, Thomas W. and Anderson, Caroline, *Reality Fictions: The Films of Frederick Wiseman*, Carbondale, IL: Southern Illinois University Press, 1989.
Grant, Barry Keith, *Voyages of Discovery: The Cinema of Frederick Wiseman*, Urbana, IL and Chicago: University of Illinois Press, 1992.
Mamber, Stephen, *Cinema Verite in America: Studies in Uncontrolled Documentary*, Cambridge, MA: MIT Press, 1974.
Nichols, Bill, *Ideology and the Image*, Bloomington, IN: Indiana University Press, 1981.

LBJ

(Cuba, Alvarez, 1968)

Santiago Alvarez's LBJ is a prime example, in terms of style and political focus, of the documentary work produced by the Instituto Cubano del Arte e Industria Cinematograficos (ICAIC). Founded in 1959, three months after the Cuban revolutions, the Institute (part of the Ministry of Culture) was completely funded and controlled by the government. Yet even as the Communist Revolution took hold, the Institute remained committed to artistic freedom rather than strict adherence to Socialist Realism. Alvarez was in charge of the newsreel division from the origin of the Institute into the 1980s. Fitting the title of his post, Alvarez preferred to be known as a 'news pamphleteer' rather than a documentary filmmaker. He loosely assembled films out of found materials, preferring to make films with immediate political relevancy over polished retrospectives.

LBJ presents an argument that Lyndon B. Johnson was a ruthless despot behind the murders of other prominent political leaders, both Kennedy brothers and Martin Luther King, Jr, thought to be his allies. Divided into three chapters, L for Luther, B for Bobby, and J for Jack, each section is introduced with a slot-machine animation that turns up a skull with corresponding initials to suggest that Johnson has ordered a hit on the named target.

The documentary never wavers in its assurance of Johnson's murderousness and, by implication, his targets' righteousness. Images of Johnson, his supposed victims, and the Civil Rights movement, are assembled in a way that unmistakably bears out this hypothesis. The chapter on Bobby Kennedy, for instance, opens with magazine covers that ask whether he will become the next president. This is followed by a photograph of Johnson's face imposed on a knight's suit of armor. Images of Kennedy's body and then his funeral appear shortly thereafter, chased by a photograph of an elated Johnson. The president appears as a cartoonish antagonist throughout this short feature, frequently associated with knights, and sometimes tinted in shockingly bright red and accompanied with evil cackling.

While the conspiratorial hypothesis of Alvarez's film is bluntly overdrawn, the style with which it is conveyed is much more compelling. The juxtaposition of the Kennedys and Johnson as forces of good and evil is, put simply, incorrect, but the spontaneity and inventiveness of its construction redeem the picture's didacticism. LBJ does not feature any voice-over narration. It relies, instead, on the montage of filmed photographs, and, less often, found footage. (Familiar speeches by Stokely Carmichael and Martin Luther King constitute the film's sole speaking parts.) The rhythmic and compelling flow of these images, accompanied by a range of music from Nina Simone to Carl Orff, work most effectively as a kind of swirling snapshot of America in the late 1960s. LBJ obviously features images of prominent political figures, but as often, photographs of poor, urban, and, particularly, black life. When Alvarez shows images of the Civil Rights movement, he gravitates as much to less famous pictures of demonstrations and incidents in varied city streets as to iconic events such as the March on Washington. This produces a much broader and more inclusive (if more fleeting) picture of the movement than an expository feature of equal length could portray. LBJ was not Alvarez's first study of black America. His 1965 film, Now, is a short about racial violence in the United States. Like LBJ, it valorizes the black community and its leaders with a series of filmed photographs. Unlike LBJ, Now's political argument is more focused and coherent.

Although LBJ's implication that Johnson is the evil architect of urban poverty, as well as the assassinations, is less than convincing, its commentary-via-montage works more effectively when considered as broader social criticism. LBJ is on-point in its attention to the influence of popular culture on politics. Without the need for explanatory dialogue, Alvarez suggests that the ubiquity of gunplay in popular culture plays a role in the American public's acceptance of violence perpetrated by the government as routine, and even admirable. Clips of television ads for firearms are paired with images of President Johnson joyously shooting rifles for recreation. Filming newspapers, Alvarez includes stories in the popular press about Johnson as a 'cowboy president'. This is joined with images of cowboys in TV serials riding horses like Johnson. This produces the effect of what one imagines could be a typical night of American television: Johnson on one channel, a Western on another, and perhaps a B gangster film or a gun commercial, which Alvarez also shortly excerpts, on a third. The unmistakable suggestion is that these separate genres (news, advertising, and drama), which circulate contemporaneously but are less often explicitly paired, influence the style and, more important, the reception of one another. A cowboy president on one channel is allowed, in part, by the presence of the cowboy on the Western serial on another. While Alvarez obviously has Johnson in his sights with this critique, it applies equally to presidents before and after him, who also capitalized on a rugged fighter persona.

LBJ is also effective in the way it contrasts the idealized façade of American life with the bloody facts of the country's domestic and international struggles. Alvarez does this by rapidly cutting from images of the United States romanticized through its popular culture to brutal depictions of the Civil Rights movements and interventions in Latin America. Banal images of Johnson holding babies, playing with puppies, or casually chatting with the Kennedy brothers are quickly chased by pictures of poverty, struggle, and even mutilated bodies. The film, in fact, opens with *Life* magazine's coverage of Luci Baines's marriage in 1966. It dwells slowly on the excesses of this event before moving to more sobering images. As with the cowboy president portion of the film, this aspect of the documentary is more effective when considered in general terms—as a juxtaposition of how America perceives and portrays itself, yet what it does—than in reference to Johnson himself. Such readings go against the grain of a documentary that marshals all contempt toward Johnson rather than push toward a more systemic view of social evils. Still, LBJ is prevented from becoming too rhetorical by the very nature of its form. To a certain extent, the film retains the raw quality of the found material that constitutes it. The broad variety and scope of the assembled images, outside of Johnson, leave a measure of interpretive room. LBJ and other Cuban films weren't screened in America until 1973 because of the US economic and cultural blockade.

JESSE SCHLOTTERBECK

See also: Alvarez, Santiago

LBJ (Cuba, ICAIC, 1968, 15 mins). Directed by Santiago Alvarez, additional direction by Norma Rorrado, Idalberto Galvez, Adalberto Hernandez, Pepin Rodriguez, Jorge Pucheux, Jose Martinez, Arturo Valdes, A. Fernandez Reboiro, Rosa Saavedra, and Della Quesada. Music by Miriam Makeba, Carl Orff, Nina Simone, Pablo Milanes, and Leo Brouwer.

Further reading

Chanan, Michael, *Cuban Cinema*, Minneapolis, MN: University of Minnesota Press, 2004.

——*The Cuban Image: Cinema and Cultural Politics in Cuba*, London: British Film Institute, 1985.

——(ed.), *Santiago Alvarez*, London: British Film Institute, 1980.

King, John, *Magical Reels: A History of Cinema in Latin America*, New York: Verso, 2000.

Mraz, John, 'Santiago Alvarez: From Dramatic Form to Direct Cinema', in Julianne Burton (ed.), *The Social Documentary in Latin America*, Pittsburgh, PA: University of Pittsburgh Press, 1990: 131–50.

n.a., 'Five Frames Are Five Frames, Not Six, but Five: An Interview with Santiago Alvarez', *Cineaste* 4, 1975: 16–21.

Schumann, Peter B., *Historia del cine latinoamericano*, Buenos Aires: Editorial Legasa, 1987.

Leacock, Richard

'Ricky' (as everyone called him) Leacock was first and foremost a cinematographer, but also often director, producer, and/or editor on the films he shot. He is most strongly identified with the evolution of the technology and technique that became known as direct cinema and/or cinéma vérité. Although the latter term is now used generically, an earlier distinction between the two techniques was important to Leacock, who used direct cinema for what he was doing. Cinéma vérité was the term coined by Frenchman Jean Rouch to apply to his own work beginning with Chronique d'un été/Chronicle of a Summer (1961). Rouch and Leacock had a famous debate on the differences between their methods at a conference in Lyon, France, in 1963 sponsored by the French national broadcasting system.

Leacock got into filmmaking at the age of fourteen by virtue of having made a fifteen-minute silent film entitled Canary Bananas at his home in the Canary Islands. At the time, he was attending a boarding school in England with one of Robert Flaherty's daughters. When Flaherty saw the film on a visit, he recognized the budding talent and is said to have told the young Ricky, 'Some day we'll make a film together.'

Leacock came to America in 1938 and attended Harvard University (class of 1943), majoring in physics. He was in the US Army for four years as a combat photographer in Asia, 1942–6. Sure enough, after the war Flaherty hired him as cinematographer (and associate producer) on Louisiana Story (1948). Leacock always acknowledged that his association with Flaherty and work on this film had a profound effect on him. In it there is one scene in which the father tells a story about a man who had his jaw bitten off by an alligator. According to the recollection of some of those involved, this scene occurred while the crew were setting up to shoot a scripted scene. Camera and recorder were on merely for testing, but Flaherty let them run to preserve the telling of the story. He was so taken by it that it appears in the film, though its nondirected verisimilitude is quite different from the style of the rest. It caused Leacock to wish portable synchronous sound equipment were available that would permit recording actuality in this way generally—without script, without direction, with scarcely any editing. This was truly the thing itself, for its own sake, which was what Frances Flaherty said her husband was after.

After Louisiana Story, Leacock worked on numerous documentaries with Louis de Rochemont, John Ferno, Irving Jacoby, and Willard Van Dyke among others. Through a number of films (Toby and the Tall Corn, 1954; How the F-100 Got its Tail, 1955; Bernstein in Israel, 1958; Bernstein in Moscow, 1959), he was getting closer and closer to the possibility of handheld synchronous sound shooting, through experimenting with various pieces of equipment.

During this time, Robert Drew, a *Life* magazine correspondent who was thinking along the same lines as Leacock, contacted him after seeing Toby and the Tall Corn and involved him in Robert Drew Associates once he had managed to set up that organization. Drew persuaded Time-Life Broadcasting to sponsor the development of new, lightweight, portable synchronous sound equipment that freed documentary filmmakers from the bulky, tripod-mounted, AC-powered equipment of the past. As Leacock recalled:

> After much experimenting and some wonderful failures, we managed to put together a portable, quiet sync-sound camera and recorder in 1960. Primary was the first film that our group (Bob Drew, [D.A.] Pennebaker, Al Maysles, [Terence] Macartney-Filgate and myself) made where the new equipment worked; where two people made up a whole film unit; where we could walk in and out of situations without lights, tripods, cables and all the other impedimenta which had shackled us before.
>
> (Levin 1971: 195–6)

The Drew-Leacock approach fell within the reportage tradition, coming from Drew's background in photojournalism and Leacock's experience as a documentary cinematographer. This technique assumes the possibility of an objective observer. While acknowledging that subjectivity occurs in selecting persons and situations and aspects of them, once those choices are made, the filmmakers do not direct or participate in, or even influence (they contend), the scene in any way. The presence of the camera is soon taken for granted by the subjects, it is argued—ignored mostly, sometimes forgotten altogether. In this approach, the relationship between filmmakers and subject persons must be relaxed and trusting in order for the filmmaking to fit into ongoing action without affecting it. In addition to his astonishing talent as a cinematographer, Leacock was especially adept at winning confidence from the people he was shooting; a warm and engaging person, he could be confident and unassuming with his camera and the people in front of it.

Primary and On the Pole (both 1960) were produced by Drew Associates for Time-Life Broadcasting. These undirected sync-sound records of the Wisconsin presidential Democratic primary contest between Hubert Humphrey and John F. Kennedy, and of the

Indianapolis automobile race, following driver Eddie Sachs, were shown on five stations owned by Time, Inc.

ABC-TV was sufficiently impressed by these films to hire Drew Associates to produce four one-hour documentaries for its Close-Up series (Yanki No!, X-Pilot, The Children Were Watching, and Adventures on the New Frontier), which aired in 1960–1. The first had to do with anti-Americanism in Latin America. The subject of the second is the final test flight of a new airplane and the personality of the test pilot. The third was shot in New Orleans during one week of a school integration crisis; it presents the attitudes of white segregationists and their effects on a black family whose daughter is supposed to be one of the first to attend a previously all-white school. Finally, Adventures on the New Frontier presents 'a day in the life' of President John F. Kennedy in the White House. (Leacock was heavily involved in all of these except X-Pilot, during the production of which he was working on The Children Were Watching.) Other particularly distinguished Drew productions on which Leacock played a key creative role include The Chair (1962) and Crisis: Behind a Presidential Commitment (1963).

In 1963 Leacock left Drew Associates with Pennebaker and they formed a partnership. In that year he made Happy Mother's Day, with Joyce Chopra. It was a report on the birth of quintuplets in Aberdeen, South Dakota, but during the filming the filmmakers became aware of the media and commercial exploitation occurring and made that the focus of the film. Among other important productions out of Leacock-Pennebaker were Dont Look Back (1967), which tracks Bob Dylan on a concert tour of England and deals with the singer offstage more than on. It was followed by Monterey Pop (1968), a record of a rock festival devoted almost entirely to the performances.

In 1968 Leacock left the partnership to start teaching at the Massachusetts Institute of Technology (MIT), where he developed and crusaded for the use of Super 8 sync-sound as an even lighter-weight, more flexible, and cheaper film format than 16mm for the kind of intimate nonintrusive filmmaking to which he was committed. His limited success in extending the use of this medium was cut short by the arrival and subsequent dominance of videotape, which offered even greater ease and economy. During his MIT years, Leacock continued to make various films including Community of Praise (1981) about a religious fundamentalist family, for the Middletown series on PBS-TV, and Lulu in Berlin (1984), an interview with 1920s movie star Louise Brooks.

In 1984 he retired from MIT and settled in Paris, where he met and started working with Valérie Lalonde, entirely in video. In fact, his enthusiasm and pioneering in lighter and smaller, less conspicuous and easier-to-use equipment led him to Video-8 and then to Hi8 when that format became available. Their first tape was Les oeufs à la coque de Richard Leacock/The Soft-Boiled Eggs of Richard Leacock (1991, sixty minutes), a series of short vignettes about the French people—their love of music, food, fishing, and gossip, all punctuated by the ritual of opening and eating a soft boiled egg—which aired on French and German television.

JACK C. ELLIS

See also: Chair, The; Flaherty, Robert; Happy Mother's Day, A; Louisiana Story; Monterey Pop; Pennebaker, D.A.; Primary

Biography

Born in the Canary Islands, July 18, 1921. Educated in England. Made his first film, Canary Bananas, in 1935. Moved to America in 1938. Attended Harvard University, class of 1943; majored in physics. US Army 1942–6, as combat photographer. Cinematographer and associate producer on Louisiana Story, 1948. Then worked freelance on numerous documentaries. From 1960 to 1963 was a member of Robert Drew Associates. Left to form Leacock-Pennebaker, Inc. 1963–8. Then became founder and head of Department of Film at Massachusettts Institute of Technology. In 1984 he retired from MIT and settled in Paris. Met and started working with Valérie Lalonde, entirely in video. Died March 23, 2011.

Further reading

Levin, G. Roy, *Documentary Explorations: 15 Interviews with Film-Makers*, New York: Doubleday, 1971.

MacCann, Richard Dyer (ed.), *Film: A Montage of Theories*, New York: Dutton, 1966.

Mamber, Stephen, *Cinema Verite in America: Studies in Uncontrolled Documentary*, Cambridge, MA: MIT Press, 1974.

O'Connell, P.J., *Robert Drew and the Development of Cinema Verite in America*, Carbondale, IL: Southern Illinois University Press, 1992.

Legg, Stuart

Stuart Legg, an historian by training and inclination, brought a scholarly and meticulous frame of mind to the Grierson-led documentary film movement in Britain and Canada. For most of his career he was more an aide than a commander. His strongest talent was the organization and illustration of ideas. He also contributed, like Grierson but on a much smaller scale, to the promotion and development of government and corporate sponsorship for documentary filmmaking. As a filmmaker, his most significant work was for the National Film Board of Canada during World War II.

Legg's contribution to the British documentary film movement in the 1930s lay primarily in work on projects initiated and directed by others. He edited Coalface (1935) and worked on Night Mail (1936). The Film Centre, which he cofounded with another important figure in the movement, Arthur Elton, linked government and corporate groups to filmmakers. The acclaimed Shell Film Unit grew out of this initiative.

At Grierson's suggestion, Canada's Motion Picture Bureau hired Legg in 1939 to direct two films on unemployment, The Case of Charlie Gordon and Youth is Tomorrow. While working on these unremarkable films, the National Film Board of Canada was formally established and Grierson was appointed Commissioner. Grierson immediately hired Legg as his second-in-command. With the outbreak of the war, Legg was put in charge of producing a monthly newsreel dramatizing Canada's war effort, called Canada Carries On. After about twenty films, most of them produced and edited by Legg, the series spawned the more internationally oriented The World in Action. Legg took over The World in Action; Canada Carries On was turned over to young Canadian filmmakers.

The films in both series were compilation films made from archival footage, captured enemy film, original combat footage taken by Allied cameramen, and occasional original footage. Influenced by The March of Time, which Grierson and Legg had carefully studied, the films featured extensive and often stentorian narration, and original but usually wall-to-wall music.

The films of these series embody Grierson's notion of propaganda and Legg's sense of film structure. They are hard-hitting, and they were criticized by filmmaking colleagues in Britain, who preferred the softer and more personal approach of Humphrey Jennings. Grierson, in turn, considered Jennings talented but his films effete. For Grierson, wartime propaganda should be hard-headed and rousing. However, his idea of propaganda, to which Legg subscribed, was not simplistic. The best films in the two series are well researched, strong in intellectual context, and to an extent honest; for instance, they dare to acknowledge that the enemy was formidable.

Churchill's Island (1941), one of the most successful films of the series, presents the Germans as a ferocious enemy, but the British as determined and able to repel them. The film also embodies some notions of film structure that Legg had developed. It opens and closes strongly. Sequences begin quietly, build to a crescendo, then yield to a quietly beginning new sequence that builds to a stronger crescendo. Geopolitik: Hitler's Plan for Empire (1942) also shows Germany as a formidable enemy and probably stands up even today as reliable history. The Gates of Italy (1943) expresses empathy for the Italians whose country at that time was an Axis power. The intention was to distinguish the Italian populace from the country, which was about to be invaded and, it was hoped, converted to the Allied cause. Our Northern Neighbor (1944), however, while offering a fresh perspective on the Soviet Union, glosses over unpleasantries such as the Moscow Trials. It exalts Stalin, extols the Soviet Union, and predicts a great future for the country.

Besides their sometimes overbearing tone, the main weakness in the films is that the commentary plays the dominant role. Images are used simply to illustrate the verbal argument. The images often represent deceptively what is being said in the commentary. For The Mask of Nippon, for instance, shots of Japanese swimmers in a long-distance competition are used to represent Japanese navy swimmers preparing to sabotage British ships somewhere in the Far East.

After the war, Legg returned to England and resumed his involvement with the British documentary. The most memorable of his post-NFB films is The Rival World (1955), which he produced for Shell. Directed by Bert Haanstra, this film is a gripping if technocentric account of the war between men and insects over the fruits of agriculture in Africa and the Middle East. Legg also wrote several historical books in his postwar career.

D.B. JONES

See also: Canada Carries On; Churchill's Island; Grierson, John; World in Action, The

Biography

Born in London, England, 1910. Educated at University of Cambridge. Joined the EMB Film Unit in 1932 and the General Post Office (GPO) Film Unit in 1934. Helped found the Film Centre in 1937. Joined the National Film Board of Canada in 1939 where he worked closely with Grierson in building the NFB. In 1945 joined Grierson in New York to work with The World Today. Returned to England in 1948. Produced films for Shell and other organizations. Died July 23, 1988.

Further reading

Beveridge, James, *John Grierson: Film Master*, London: Macmillan, 1979.

Ellis, Jack C., *John Grierson*, Carbondale, IL: Southern Illinois University Press, 2000.

Evans, Gary, *John Grierson and the National Film Board*, Toronto: University of Toronto Press, 1986.

Fielding, Raymond, *The March of Time, 1935–51*, New York: Oxford University Press, 1978.

Jones, *D.B., Movies and Memoranda*, Ottawa: Deneau, 1982.

——*The Best Butler in the Business: Tom Daly of the National Film Board of Canada*, Toronto, University of Toronto Press, 1996.

Nelson, Joyce, *The Colonized Eye: Rethinking the Grierson Legend*, Toronto: Between the Lines, 1988.

Sussex, Elizabeth, *The Rise and Fall of the British Documentary*, Berkeley, CA: University of California Press, 1975.

Swann, Paul, *The British Documentary Film Movement, 1926–46*, Cambridge: Cambridge University Press, 1989.

Leiser, Erwin

As a director, writer, and producer, Erwin Leiser created many interesting and provocative films over the course of a long and distinguished career. From the early 1960s most of his work was produced for movie theaters and television across Europe, Asia, and North America. He is probably best known for his films concerning the Third Reich, their propaganda movies, and Adolf Hitler's rhetoric. Primarily a documentary filmmaker, he has left an important legacy to both the cinema and society. His most famous film, Mein Kampf (1960), was rereleased in 1987, is still available, and continues to be watched and discussed by generation after generation of film spectators. The film, an international success, has been seen in hundreds of countries and is well respected by critics as a balanced but moving account.

Leiser was born on May 16, 1923 in Germany. He lived in Berlin until the age of fifteen at which time he escaped the Nazi persecution of Jews. Leiser fled to Sweden because of the 1938 anti-Semitic Nazi November Pogrom (Reichskristallnacht). Throughout his life, Leiser recounted the ways in which Jews were taken to concentration camps, synagogues were burned, and Jewish businesses were looted and seized. In Sweden, Leiser lived at a Jewish children's home in the countryside. Once he was of age Leiser attended the University of Lund in Sweden where he graduated in 1946. He became a Swedish citizen after World War II.

He became a journalist in Stockholm after college, working as the drama critic for a trade union newspaper. For eight years, beginning in 1950, he was employed by the newspaper *Morgan Tidningen*, which advocated social democratic politics. Leiser also worked as a literary translator by translating many poetry volumes and other German literary works into Swedish. In addition, he published an international theatre almanac. Leiser would continue to write throughout his life and produced several books and articles on many subjects including critical analyses of films made during the Nazi era.

Leiser was also involved in the broadcast industries, where he produced features for radio. In 1959 he started a career in the television industry. It was then that he had the idea for a documentary film on the crimes of the Third Reich and decided that he wanted to be a filmmaker.

In 1960 Leiser released his first film, a documentary about Germany under Hitler's domination. Leiser's original title for the film was Den blodiga tiden/Bloody Times, but Leiser retitled the film Mein Kampf. Mein Kampf is a compilation film made up of archival footage taken from newsreels and other sources in Germany and also retrieved from the vaults of Allied countries. The film demonstrates how Adolf Hitler became an important figure in German politics. Hitler's rejection from art school is revealed, as is his subsequent affiliation with different political groups. The film focuses on Hitler's rise to power via his divisive oratory, his hatred for the Jews, and his vilification of them for Germany's problems. His plans for their genocide are also revealed as the film depicts the aftermath of German atrocities in the concentration camps and throughout Europe. The voice-over narration explains the torture and war crimes in a moving but not over-sensationalized manner. The film includes a good deal of footage of Adolf Hitler. It also contains footage of German Chancellor Heinrich Brüning reading a statement; he later emigrated to the United States after the Nazi party won control in 1933. Weimar Republic President Friedrich Ebert is seen reviewing troops and at his state funeral. Nazi Deputy Propaganda Minister Alfred Frauenfeld is shown meeting with Franz von Papen in Vienna, Austria. Footage of the Leader of the Nazi SA (Stormtroopers), Franz Pfeffer von Salomon, and Major General Franz von Epp is also presented. The Foreign Minister, Walther Rathenau, who was hated by the Nazis and assassinated by right-wing army officers, is seen writing at his desk. A young Dutch communist working in Germany, Marinus van der Lubbe, who was found guilty of the Reichstag Fire and executed on January 10, 1934, is shown standing trial.

The two-hour documentary was an international success with screenings in many countries. Critics praised Leiser for his objective and analytical portrayal of German history, especially Hitler's cunning use of propaganda and oratory. Mein Kampf launched Leiser's career as a documentary filmmaker and remains, some forty-four years later, a testament to Leiser's work.

In 1961 Leiser permanently relocated to Zurich, Switzerland. There he released his second film, Eichmann und das dritte Reich/Eichmann and the Third Reich, in 1961. This documentary focused on the Nazi program to eliminate the Jews. Karl Adolf Eichmann was an SS leader and Gestapo chief of the Department for Jewish Affairs from 1941 to 1945. Moreover, he was in charge of the deportation of millions of Jews to extermination camps. After the war Eichmann was arrested and detained in a US internment camp, but later escaped. He traveled to Argentina where he lived for ten years as Ricardo Klement. In 1969 he was removed from Argentina by Israeli agents, who took him to Jerusalem to stand trial for his crimes. The trial was well publicized and lasted five months, ending in mid-August 1961. Eichmann was sentenced to death and executed in 1962. Leiser's movie broadly recounts the Jewish persecution orchestrated by Eichmann while using Eichmann's trial as an interwoven backdrop. The film covers the building of concentration camps, Eichmann's 'final solution' for the extermination of the Jews and certain theories concerning race that are used to justify discrimination. The motion picture includes interviews with concentration camp survivors, as well as footage of Eichmann's trial, Adolf Hitler, Hermann Göering (Commander-in-Chief of the Luftwaffe, President of the Reichstag), Heinrich Himmler (Reich SS Leader, Chief of the German police), Joseph Goebbels (Hitler's Propaganda Minister), and Reinhard Heydrich (The Butcher of Prague).

His follow-up film to Eichmann was Leiser's first color film, the fifty-five-minute documentary, Wähle das Leben/You Must Choose Life, in 1963. In 1968 Leiser's fourth documentary, Deutschland, erwache!/Wake Up Germany! was released. Wake Up Germany! was a compilation of sequences for feature films made during Hitler's reign and used as documentary evidence of the Nazis' use of the mass media for propaganda purposes. Leiser maintained that he did not present the material with any bias so as to leave the value judgments to the audience. Also that year, Leiser published a book titled *Deutschland, erwache!* (translated and released in the US as *Nazi Cinema* in 1974). Leiser wrote this book while making Wake Up Germany! as a supplement to the movie. Despite this, his text is one of the foremost analyses on German cinema of the Nazi era and is well respected and often cited by critics and scholars. Leiser explained that because he restricted himself to feature films in his movie Deutschland, erwache!, he wrote the book so that he could broadly cover all the characteristics of Nazi cinema. As Leiser describes in his book, Joseph Goebbels wanted all German films to have a political function. As a result only about one-sixth of the German productions were overtly government propaganda. Goebbels also used feature films and newsreels to great propagandistic effect. Leiser analyses almost one hundred films in *Nazi Cinema*, including Riefenstahl's Triumph of the Will, Olympia, and Lowlands. Interestingly, the book also contains documents concerning four films: Triumph of the Will, Olympia, I Accuse, and Jud Süss.

After 1968 Leiser continued to make more than fifty films, including documentaries about Nazi propaganda, the Holocaust, and portraits of artists, for film and television. Leiser made three films about Dutch/American Abstract Expressionist painter Willem de Kooning, and three films about Nobel Prize Laureate author Isaac Bashevis Singer. Leiser's works include Zum Beispiel Fritz Lang (1968), Keine Welt für Kinder (1972), and Ich lebe in der Gegenwart—Versuch über Hans Richter (1973). In addition, Leiser made two documentaries about Hiroshima and its effects.

In 1985 he released Die Mitläufer/Following the Führer, a hybrid documentary and fictionalized drama. The film takes archival footage and juxtaposes it with scripted scenes written by Oliver Storz. The film tells the story of a group of Nazis as the war comes to a close. The world they know is coming to an end as they fight for survival and realize that they can no longer cling to their belief in Hitler or his promises for the future.

Unlike Mein Kampf, the film opened to mixed reviews; some critics found the fictional sketches too melodramatic and preachy. Others thought the film might offer a too forgiving view of the everyday Germans caught up in perpetrating the Nazi terror. Yet other critics credited Leiser for contributing once again to the historical study and analysis of the Holocaust. Also during this year at a Paris festival, Eichmann and the Third Reich was shown and during the screening a bomb went off in the theater, injuring more than a dozen people.

In the later years of his career Leiser collaborated with his spouse, Vera, on several projects for television and radio. Erwin and Vera Leiser cowrote the films Die Feuerprobe—Novemberpogrom 1938/The November Pogrom 1938 (1988) and Zehn Brüder sind wir gewesen/We Are Ten Brothers (1995). Leiser and Vera codirected three films. In 1993 Leiser made the documentary Pimpf war jeder/Everyone was a 'Pimpf'. One of the people interviewed in the film states 'Everybody was a pimpf'. This remark illustrates how the young Germans were caught up in the Nazi party. If a person was not a 'pimpf' then they were not important. This idea even affected Jewish students such as Erwin Leiser. From 1932 to 1938 Leiser attended school in Germany. In his documentary he seeks out his former classmates and interviews them. The result is a view of a group of students who either fled Germany to escape the Jewish persecution or who were thrust into the war.

In 1995 Leiser made Otto John: Eine deutsche Geschichte/Otto John: A German Story. It is the story of Otto John who was involved in the conspiracy against Hitler. After the war he worked to rebuild Germany and was involved with the prosecution team at the Nuremberg War Trials. He mysteriously disappeared in 1955 from a ceremony commemorating the failed attempt to assassinate Hitler. This documentary centers on Otto John and the mysteries and controversies surrounding his disappearance to East Germany in 1954. He was suspected of defecting to the Soviet Union, but he reappeared in West Germany in 1955. He said that the KGB kidnapped him, but he was arrested and charged with treason. Otto John's trial resulted in a four-year prison sentence. Also in 1995 Leiser made his last film, Feindbider, which displayed various World War II propaganda movies and their messages to audiences regarding the enemy.

Besides being a prodigious filmmaker, Leiser was a film critic and an author. He provided critical analyses of films during the Nazi era in articles and books. In addition to *Nazi Cinema*, Leiser wrote *A Pictorial History of Nazi Germany*, *Wahle Das Leben!*, and *Leben Nach Dem Uberleben*. In 1996 the Academy of Arts in Berlin made Leiser the head of the Film and Media Arts Section. It was a fitting tribute to this creative filmmaker's life.

DANIELLE WILLIAMS

See also: Mein Kampf

Biography

Born in Berlin, Germany on May 16, 1923. Remained in Germany until 1938; forced to leave because of the anti-Semitic Nazi November Pogrom (Reichskristallnacht). Relocated to

Sweden to a Jewish children's home. Attended the University of Lund in Sweden and after graduation worked as a journalist and translator. In 1960 released his first documentary, Mein Kampf. In 1961 permanently relocated to Zurich, Switzerland. Made more than fifty documentaries for film and television through his production company, Erwin Leiser Filmproduktion. In 1995 made his last documentary but continued to work. In 1996 the Academy of Arts in Berlin made Leiser the head of the Film and Media Arts Section. On August 23, 1996, died from heart complications in Zurich, Switzerland.

Further reading

Ascheid, Antje, *Hitler's Heroines: Stardom and Womanhood in Nazi Cinema*, Philadelphia, PA: Temple University Press, 2003.

Barnouw, Eric, *Documentary: A History of the Non-Fiction Film*, second revised edn, New York: Oxford University Press, 1993.

Barsam, Richard, *Non Fiction Film: A Critical History, Revised and Expanded*, Bloomington, IN: Indiana University Press, 1992.

Craig, Gordon A., *The Germans*, New York: J.P. Putnam's Sons, 1982.

Elsaesser, Thomas, *New German Cinema: A History*, New Brunswick, NJ: Rutgers University Press, 1989.

Murray, Bruce and Wickham, Christopher J., *Framing the Past: The Historiography of German Cinema and Television*, Carbondale, IL: Southern Illinois University Press, 1992.

Sandford, John (ed.), *Encyclopedia of Contemporary German Culture*, New York: Routledge, 1999.

Leiterman, Douglas

Producer and director Douglas Leiterman is an important figure in both the history of documentary at large, but more specifically in the history of Canadian broadcasting as well. Best known as coproducer of the legendary CBC magazine program This Hour Has Seven Days, Leiterman and colleagues revolutionized current affairs programming with equal doses of satirical sketch comedy, hard-hitting interviews with prominent newsmakers, and particularly with large sections of the programme devoted to documentary films. Concurrent to this, Leiterman was also coproducer of the occasionally broadcast documentary series Document.

The CBC documentaries produced for these programs, usually exhibiting a clear point of view, as opposed to the traditional CBC practice of studied journalistic neutrality or 'objectivity', contributed to the then-emergent Canadian documentary aesthetic also associated with the National Film Board of Canada (NFB) as one at the forefront of socially committed and formally innovative documentary practice. Among the most important documentaries made for the CBC with Leiterman's significant participation (as producer, director, or executive producer) are One More River (aka Report on the Mood of the South Nine Years After the Supreme Court Ordered Integration with All Deliberate Speed, 1964), which featured an interview with Malcolm X, and the Beryl Fox-directed The Mills of the Gods: Viet Nam, an intensely moving portrait of the effects of the Vietnam War on both the American servicemen fighting there and the local peasantry. Another notable documentary from the period is The Chief, a portrait of former Canadian Prime Minister John Diefenbaker, by Leiterman and Fox (which aired on March 25, 1964 and January 31, 1965). This film, like so many of the excellent documentaries of the period, takes full advantage of the technological innovations of recently devised more portable equipment to catch images of heightened immediacy, such as in this case, fishing with Diefenbaker where his apparently more natural persona seems to emerge.

Despite the huge popularity of This Hour has Seven Days, which arguably resulted from Leiterman and his collaborators' (particularly Patrick Watson) desire to make current affairs broadcasting relevant and exciting, it was cancelled by the CBC because of the controversy that surrounded the program. Much of this controversy was attributable to the clear social agenda of the interviews and documentary reports, a condition that did not jibe with then-prevalent standards of journalistic objectivity. In one celebrated moment the program interviewed hooded members of the Ku Klux Klan. An African American Civil Rights leader was presented and the Klansmen were invited to shake hands with him. Refusing, they walked off the set.

After his dismissal by the CBC (the other creative forces behind the program were fired as well), Leiterman was hired by CBS television where his recommendations led to the creation of 60 Minutes.

Leiterman is author of a book, *Canadian Culture at the Crossroads: Film, Television and the Media in the*

1960s, from his lecture at the Wendy Michener Symposium at York University in Toronto.

PETER URQUHART

Biography

Born in South Porcupine, Ontario, Canada, in 1927. Brother of celebrated cinematographer Richard Leiterman.

Further reading

Leiterman, Douglas, *Canadian Culture at the Crossroads: Film, Television and the Media in the 1960s*, Toronto, Ontario: ECW Press, 1989.

Lelouch, Claude

A self-proclaimed 'cine-reporter' who spent much of his early career making documentary films, the prolific French filmmaker Claude Lelouch has nevertheless been most commonly associated with 'schmaltzy' melodramas and overlong epics. This reflects a critical bias that does injustice not only to the writer/director/producer/cinematographer's many forays into other genres (such as comedy, action-adventure, the biopic, literary adaptation, the western, and, above all, the heist film), but also to his intuitive knack for distilling the essence of a given situation in nonfiction shorts. True, the romantic contrivances of such films as Un homme qui me plaît/Love is a Funny Thing (1969) and La Belle histoire/The Beautiful Story (1992) weigh heavily against the subtle, self-reflexive stylings of his documentary films; and yes, Lelouch exuded a Spielberg-like sentimentality and nostalgia in his most box office-friendly films. However, one should not overlook Lelouch's contributions to the field of documentary, nor dismiss him as only a commercial filmmaker catering to mainstream tastes.

Before forming his own production company (Les Films 13) and making his feature-length film debut with Le Propre de l'homme/The Right of Man (1960) (a copy of which the director claims to have destroyed), Lelouch cut his teeth on a handful of short films—USA en vrac, Une ville pas comme les autres, Quand le rideau se lève—not to mention a series of educational documentaries for the armed services detailing everything from SOS helicopters to data-processing. Although far removed from the types of melodramatic features Lelouch would direct in the mid-to-late 1960s, these industrial films gave him a great deal of technical proficiency—something that he showed off between 1960 and 1965, when he made roughly two hundred and fifty publicity films and scopitones. Each of these petites chansons, or mini-musicals, ran for approximately two-to-three minutes and can be seen as forerunners of today's music videos.

In 1965 Unifrance Film commissioned Lelouch to make a cinematic portrait of Jean-Paul Belmondo, the Bogart-like star of A bout de souffle/Breathless (1960) and Le doulos/The Finger Man (1963). Designed to promote French cinema worldwide, this twelve-minute biopic, appropriately titled Jean-Paul Belmondo, treats its famously fickle subject as a man of sports and leisure, a kind of everyman rather than a celebrity. That same year, Lelouch also made a thirty-five-minute documentary about the Tour de France bike race entitled Pour un maillot jaune/For a Yellow Jersey (1965) (the title of the film refers to the garb worn by lead riders). As a textbook example of how to tell a story through colorful mise-en-scène, dynamic editing, and expressive sound effects, Pour un maillot jaune was widely shown in fledgling film schools throughout Europe and South America during the latter half of the 1960s.

The emphasis on human velocity and personal achievement in Pour un maillot jaune—themes accentuated through the speed and fluid movement of Lelouch's camera—set the stage for his subsequent forays into the world of sports, beginning with his documentary about the 1968 Winter Olympics, Treize jours en France/Thirteen Days in France (1968). Extensively chronicling the games held in Grenoble from February 6 to 18, Lelouch and codirector François Reichenbach intercut footage of the biathlon, bobsledding, and downhill slalom competitions with the heroic victories of ice skater Peggy Fleming and other gold medallists. This focus on Olympic winners was eventually balanced by Lelouch's interest in losers, a topic he explored in his ten-minute contribution to Visions of Eight (1973), an omnibus film about the 1972 Munich games produced by David Wolper and featuring the works of such directors as Milos Forman, John Schlesinger, and Arthur Penn.

Before making 'The Losers', Lelouch had contributed to another omnibus film, Loin du

Vietnam/Far from Vietnam (1967). Along with directors Joris Ivens, Alain Resnais, William Klein, Agnès Varda, and Jean-Luc Godard, Lelouch points up some of the ideological inconsistencies of the US government as it intervenes in yet another Asian conflict involving communism. Ironically, Lelouch's narrated sequence, which depicts American sailors loading bombs on an aircraft carrier, is reminiscent of the educational films he shot for the French military between 1957 and 1960. Forgoing politics for his next documentary, he directed the unconventional travelog Iran (1971), a film notable for its lack of dialogue and narration. He had also shot a nonfiction piece on motorcycle racing entitled Un Après-midi avec des motos (1972).

Despite being stylistically innovative, none of these shorts could have prepared audiences for Lelouch's most notorious piece of cinéma vérité. While wrapping up production on Si c'était à refaire/If I Had to Do it All Over Again (1976), the director—left with about nine minutes of unshot film and a few days remaining on his rented equipment—hatched a harebrained scheme: with just three hundred meters of celluloid at his disposal, and without the aid of special effects or optical tricks, Lelouch would film a Ferrari 365 driving through the City of Lights at breakneck speeds, from the Périphérique to the Sacré-Coeur. Clocking in at a mere eight minutes and fifty seconds, and consisting of a single, unbroken shot taken from the front bumper of the car as it careens through the streets of Paris, C'était un Rendez-vous/ Rendezvous (1976) is one of the simplest yet most elaborately staged documentaries in film history, a true cinematic curio, the production of which has become the stuff of underground legend. Shrouded in mystery for years, subject to the kind of rhapsodic hypothesizing that only Lelouch himself could settle (was he in fact behind the wheel or was it the famed Formula One driver Jacques Lafitte?), Rendezvous moves documentary filmmaking into the sphere of moral ambiguity and phenomenological uncertainty, strapping the spectator into a first-person perspective so perilously close to death that even contemporary audiences weaned on extreme sports, 'jackass'-style stunts, and racecam footage might recoil.

Several myths swirl around the production of this film, which is at once exhilarating, enthralling, shocking, and reprehensible. Allegedly arrested on the grounds that he endangered the lives of pedestrians (not to mention pets and pigeons), Lelouch was in fact given only a slap on the wrist by a sympathetic chief of police whose children, he claimed, adored the film. Although screenings were subsequently halted for fear that audiences susceptible to its visceral power might pull similar stunts, the film continued to circulate on the black market, where pirated prints and murky, third-generation videotape bootlegs could be procured at exorbitant prices. Finally, twenty-five years after the film's theatrical release, Moving Picture Company acquired a duplicate print, restored it, and helped produce a DVD of Rendezvous, giving thousands of curious cinephiles and motorcar enthusiasts the opportunity to see this miniature masterpiece and form their own opinions about its perceived political incorrectness.

What at first glance appears to be an anomaly in Lelouch's oeuvre might in fact be the summation of his career—a streamlined side-project of a self-professed speed freak that consolidates many of the persistent themes and images for which the director has become famous. Life, love, and death (to borrow the title of his 1968 film La Vie, l'amour, la mort) are obvious themes. More specifically, criminality, anarchism, and even romance (witness the titular meeting at the film's dénouement, when the female companion advances toward the vehicle from the steps of the Sacré-Coeur) are all inscribed in Rendezvous, thus situating it in various generic contexts. Although shorn of Lelouch's trademark excess (in terms of style and length), Rendezvous is, like all of his films, about a man and a woman. Un homme et une femme/A Man and a Woman (1966), Lelouch's soapy international breakthrough starring Jean-Louis Trintignant as a race car driver who teaches his son to drive his Mustang convertible and who—after having a near-fatal accident at Le Mans—participates in the Monte Carlo Motor Rally, is only the most obvious precursor—a film in which the Jacky Ickx-like protagonist says that 'the throb of the motor […] is something you can feel throughout your entire body'. Another film, La Bonne année/Happy New Year (1973), finds Lelouch's characters preparing for a jewelry heist by clocking a Mercedes Benz as it speeds through Cannes at ninety-five miles per hour. The soundtrack, like that of Rendezvous, consists of screeching tires, as well as a ticking stopwatch and voice-over keeping time as the car goes from shop to boat dock in just over one minute.

Speeding past red lights and landmarks like the Louvre, Lelouch in Rendezvous provides a kind of whiplash ethnography, a travelog tapping into the visceral thrills first unleashed at the turn of the twentieth century by documentarians such as Auguste and Louis Lumière (many of whose actualities were shot from horse-drawn and electric carriages giving viewers a street-level view of Paris). In contrast to the fly-on-the-wall approach of direct cinema filmmakers, Lelouch—who has said that he does most of his thinking in cars—gives us a fly-on-the-windshield look at a world quickly passing by. This is just one of the unique and compelling ways in which his documentaries literally move us.

DAVID SCOTT DIFFRIENT

Selected films

1957 Vol des hélicoptères en haute montagne
1958 Carte mécanographique de l'armée de l'air
1959 La guerre du silence
1960 S.O.S. hélicoptère
1963 La Femme spectacle/Night Women/Paris in the Raw
1965 Jean-Paul Belmondo
1965 Pour un maillot jaune/For a Yellow Jersey
1967 Loin du Vietnam/Far from Vietnam
1968 Treize jours en France/Thirteen Days in France
1971 Iran
1972 Un Après-midi avec des motos
1973 'The Losers' (episode in Visions of Eight)
1976 C'était un Rendez-vous/Rendezvous

Further reading

Guidez, Guylaine, *Claude Lelouch*, Paris: Saeghers, 1972.

Lelouch, Claude and Chatrier, Jean-Philippe, *Itinéraire d'un enfant très gate*, Paris: Editions Robert Laffont, 2000.

Lev, Peter, *Claude Lelouch, Film Director*, Rutherford, NJ: Fairleigh Dickinson University Press, 1983.

Lessons of Darkness

(Germany, Herzog, 1992)

Many films by contentious filmmaker Werner Herzog fluctuate between fiction and documentary, but little in his output, and perhaps in the history of film images, had suggested this film. In a prelude to its twelve sections, the opening chord of Wagner's Das Rheingold materializes from the credits, we see a landscape of swirling mist, and as a figure gestures in the distance, Herzog's voice intones: 'The first creature we encountered tried to communicate something to us.' The profilmic event is a mystery, but the accents are established from the outset: (operatically mounted) mythology shrouds a narrative that is part science fiction, and human figures are dwarfed and hermetically cut off, indicating a screen operating between subject matter and filmmakers.

It gradually emerges that we are in the clean-up phase of the Gulf War, with the prehistory of the war itself disposed of in forty seconds of CNN footage. Before that we are introduced to an eerily lit aerial view of 'A Capital City', largely empty. This is Kuwait City. The bulk of the film visually documents the attempt to extinguish oil well fires, with section headings such as 'Satan's National Parks', or 'A Dinosaur's Feast', and a passage from the biblical Book of Revelations, continuing the defiance of mainstream documentary modes.

There are concessions to the latter, with a handheld camera cataloguing implements in torture chambers, and two brief interviews with women victims of the war. Background traffic noises convey postwar life going on, punctuating the long silences of the interviewees. The first woman interviewed is unable to form words, communicating through gestures and facial grief, while the second holds her son who has been silent since being trampled on by soldiers. The norm in this film is the absence of people, and slow tracking shots of wrecks in a desert landscape, or of infernos of oil, burning with a terrible beauty. The only other close-up figures, by the end, are the firefighters, and as their fight with the elements dominates the soundtrack, any potential for analysis is bypassed.

Elements of unpredictability are also removed, with the Olympian vantage point of the camera and the (slender) narration. What we see is not even viewed as an exemplar of some kind of modern warfare. The specific historical moment, the aftermath of the Gulf War, is present in virtuosic imagery, but the 'reality' it represents is the normal domain of fiction, a staging of the Apocalypse, and of Herzog's private apocalypse. The aerial shots disorient us in what becomes a mythical landscape. Huge earthmoving equipment is viewed like a prehistoric monster. When images of the workers finally become clearer toward the end, slow-motion shots stylize them. The film confirms Baudrillard's notion that the Gulf War did not take place, but in a different sense. Dismissing the CNN images of a virtual reality, it recasts the event as an historical myth. It achieves this not least through a prominent soundtrack, many of whose musical examples function narratively as a dirge or lamentation for the West (for example, Death of Ase from Peer Gynt, the Verdi Requiem, Siegfried's Funeral Music from Wagner's Ring).

Music plays a far more prominent role than spoken commentary, absent for over half the film, and in places it yields only to the greater volume of sound effects, such as jets of water extinguishing fire. The music's national provenance seems secondary, and the prevailing sense is of spectacle, to match the slanting of the breathtaking images. The opening Rheingold Prelude is appropriate in dramatic and possibly in narrative terms, with the archetypical lust for gold conceivably matched by the contemporary greed for oil. Far less obvious is the choice of the Parsifal prelude in the section 'After the Battle'. This creates an absolute narrative discrepancy between image and sound. The camera alone is 'questing' as it tracks a static, battle-scarred landscape, which suffers the Wagnerian sound to wash over it until some sense of the non-aestheticized origin of these images is restored, as wind swirls and blends with the music toward the end.

With Lessons of Darkness, the Germanic song lines of war-tarnished Wagner have been overhauled by Wagner as world music, as harbinger of doom, but without strongly Nordic overtones. Whether consciously or not, the breadth of the original Ring-myth is reinstated after the strait-jacketing of its reception by Nazi Germany. Wagner is associated with obsequies for the West, in a war that signaled debate about unified Germany's military obligations under its return to the world stage. The rainbow bridge transporting these gods to Valhalla bears the hues of the nations of the Western alliance, and no longer just the colors of Germany.

Cultural memory is also cinematic memory, which in turn involves musical memory. Inasmuch as cultural memory can be documented, this film is a documentary beyond the subject of its visuals. The ultimate irony is that Herzog's images do not obscure the political reality for differently directed political, but for apolitical purposes. Therein lies perhaps a kinship with the self-defense of that other great, but suspect, image-maker of German cinema, Leni Riefenstahl, who in turn is overshadowed by the historically fluctuating presence of Wagner. This trio exemplify the problem of art and politics in Germany; they 'document' a nation's self-reckoning, beyond Herzog's aspirations to an ethnography of others.

ROGER HILLMAN

See also: Herzog, Werner; Riefenstahl, Leni

Lektionen in Finsternis/Lessons of Darkness (Coproduction by Premiere, BBC Television, Canal plus France, Canal plus Spain, and ITEL, 1992, 51 mins). Distributed by U/A Films. Produced by Paul Berriff and Werner Herzog. Directed by Werner Herzog. Writing credits Werner Herzog. Cinematography by Paul Berriff and Rainer Klausmann. Music by Arvo Pärt, Edvard Grieg, Gustav Mahler, Sergei Prokofiev, Franz Schubert, Giuseppe Verdi, and Richard Wagner. Edited by Rainer Standke. Filmed in Kuwait.

Further reading

Hogue, Peter, 'Genre-busting. Documentaries as Movies', *Film Comment* 32/4, July–August 1996: 56–60.

MacDonald, Scott, *The Garden in the Machine: A Field Guide to Independent Films about Place*, Berkeley, CA: University California Press, 2001: 324–8.

Pawelczak, Andy, *Films in Review 47/1–2*, January–February 1996: 63–4.

Vogel, Amos, *Film Comment*, May–June 1992: 70.

Leyda, Jay

A genuine if largely unsung renaissance man, Jay Leyda produced a vitae that gives the impression that he was a dabbler, a world traveler always moving on to new things. Such a cursory glance, however, glosses over his achievements before moving between points, and his adaptability along the way. It is no surprise that he should have gone to Moscow to study with Sergei Eisenstein for, like him, Leyda is a classic example of the artist-scholar, one whose practice flows naturally out of a wide, synthetic interest in the arts and an equally strong one in history and politics. The practice of one's art is difficult to sustain, and political art even more so. Leyda's achievements in documentary, though done over a brief period of time, span the avant-garde (A Bronx Morning), political reportage (China Strikes Back), and social protest (People of the Cumberland). He was creative in other venues as well, writing short stories, poetry, and even the libretto for an opera. In many ways, though, it was through scholarship that Leyda was able to speak with even more clarity. Having encountered and been enamored of great artists, he gravitated toward the study of them. An historian by inclination, and one who was present at a seminal happening in film history, he felt the need to document not only Eisenstein's career and that glorious early moment in Soviet film, but also the underrepresented areas of film history. Hence we have his *Dianying*, the first work on Chinese cinema in English; *Films Beget Films*, his novel approach to the documentary subgenre of the compilation film; and a number of articles on film history and criticism.

Leyda first encountered many key works in documentary and experimental photography and film via camera magazines he avidly read as a boy. Moving to New York City as the Depression began, he found work as an assistant to Ralph Steiner in the darkroom and in the making of experimental short films. Between 1931 and 1933, he began to exhibit and publish notable work in portrait photography, especially pictures of fellow artists, and it is likely that he then first became involved with the photography branch of the Film and Photo Leagues of the Workers' International Relief. He also purchased a camera and made his first film, A Bronx Morning. It received a premiere in 1932 at the noted Julian Levy gallery that had also exhibited Leyda's photography but was not widely exhibited. Leyda himself tended to dismiss his eleven-minute initial effort as too formalistic, but its stature has grown in recent years. Playful in its experiments with framing, camera movement, and shot transitions, and clearly influenced by other city symphonies and key Soviet works (even if Leyda had only seen stills of them), the film vividly portrays the suffering engendered by the Depression even while it celebrates an open-air, multiethnic, urban culture. The film also played a vital role in enabling one of the most important periods of Leyda's life: it was part of the portfolio that gained him acceptance to the Moscow Film School.

Leyda's Moscow years (1933–6) and his close studies and working relationship with Eisenstein shaped his entire life. In 1934 he met and married his wife of more than fifty years, dancer-choreographer Si-lan Chen. The production records, stills, teaching materials, writing, and firsthand working experience—especially on Eisenstein's never-completed Bezhin Meadow—provided Leyda with inspiration for his own artistic practice and the wellspring for his prodigious scholarship. After returning to the United States, Leyda worked for the Museum of Modern Art and later served as a consultant on Russia for Hollywood productions, but ties to communism would dog him for years. In fact, in his affiliation with the leftist filmmaking collective Nykino and the later Frontier Films, Leyda was compelled to use a pseudonym, Eugene Hill. The editing lessons he had learned under Eisenstein, as well as a sense of political urgency that had matured since A Bronx Morning, were applied in his work for Frontier Films co-editing China Strikes Back (1937). Harry Dunham had been the first photographer to get key footage of communists in China, and it was up to the editors to both shape the material and keep it timely, given how changes were occurring so quickly at that time. In twenty-three minutes the film effectively chronicles the war between China and Japan, the fall of Manchuria, life under occupation, and the preparation of the Chinese people for successful resistance and counterattack.

Leyda played an even more prominent role in one of Frontier's finest efforts, People of the Cumberland (1937), codirecting with Sidney Meyers (credited as 'Robert Stebbins'). Made with the aid of the founders of the famous Highlander Folk School, the film had an impressive crew: Steiner photographed it, Elia Kazan was an assistant, Erskine Caldwell helped to write the commentary, and Alex North provided the score. People chronicles the struggles of impoverished folk, some of them fifth-generation Americans, who work in the mines and mills of the Cumberland Mountains. Following the typical structure and content of Frontier's documentaries (Campbell 1978), the film establishes the lives and problems of the community; shows the hope that the school brings; includes a stylized, atypically dramatized section recreating the murder of a union organizer; then rallies strongly as the community presses on in its daily work, celebrations, and union activism. The location shoot faced technical limitations, evident in the many static shots and the attempts to get around the lack of synchronized sound, but the often splendid framing and composition, the telling details in the workers' lives, and the sympathetic and progressive urgency yield one of the warmest and most accessible political documentaries of the era.

Although late in life Leyda offered support or did interviews and voice-overs for documentaries on Eisenstein and Edwin S. Porter, his production work essentially ended with the Depression. Scholarly work, and later university teaching, fully occupied the rest of his career. He wrote biographies of Emily Dickinson and Rachmaninoff, edited volumes of Melville's fiction and a documentary 'log' of his correspondence, and translated Musorgsky. In film studies his greatest contribution would ultimately prove to be one of his earliest—compiling, translating, and editing Eisenstein's theories into the landmark twin volumes, *The Film Form* and *The Film Sense*. Invited to pursue archival research in France, Germany, Russia, and China, Leyda produced such works as Kino, still one of the standard histories of Russian and Soviet film. His championing of documentary can be found throughout his oeuvre, from the actualities and government-sponsored works described in Dianying, to the attention he brought to artists from Esfir Shub, to the German team of Andrew and Annelie Thorndike in his work on compilation documentaries. Finally, in his tenure at NYU's department of cinema studies, he offered seminars on Griffith and early cinema, Eisenstein and Soviet film, and theories of documentary and filmic fiction, inspiring a generation of scholars, doubtless in much the same way his early teachers had done for him.

DAVID M. LUGOWSKI

See also: Bronx Morning, A

Biography

Born in Detroit, Michigan February 12, 1910. Moved to New York City, worked for photographer Ralph Steiner 1930. First published and exhibited own photographs 1931–2. Helped organize the Film Society and the Film Forum 1933. Accepted for study at Moscow Film School 1933. Became assistant curator, film department, Museum of Modern Art, New York 1936. Founded quarterly magazine, *Films*, 1938. Edited, translated, and published collection of Eisenstein's essays, *Film Form*, 1941–2. Moved to California when hired by Warner Brother as consultant on Russian subjects 1941–2. Began translations of Musorgsky (later published as *The Musorgsky Reader*) 1943–4. Reconstructed Herman Melville's correspondence, co-authored biography of Rachmaninoff 1945–6. Guggenheim Fellowships for biography of Emily Dickinson 1948–9. Wrote libretto for Walter Aschaffenburg opera, Bartleby 1950–2. Invited by Cinemathèque Française to write history of Soviet film 1955. Invited to China to work in newly founded Chinese Film Archive 1959. Moved to Germany to work at Staatliches Filmarchiv der DDR 1964–9. Fellow, Ezra Stiles College, Yale University 1969–70. Professor of Fine Arts, York University 1970–3. Gottesman Professor of Cinema Studies, New York University 1974–87. Died February 15, 1988.

Selected films

1932 A Bronx Morning: director, cinematographer, editor

1935–6 Bezhin Meadow (Eisenstein): assistant director, casting assistant, still photographer, production historian

1937 China Strikes Back (no director; photography by Harry Dunham): coeditor (credited as 'Eugene Hill'), with Irving Lerner and Sidney Meyers

1937 People of the Cumberland (codirector, Sidney Meyers): codirector (credited as 'Eugene Hill')

1943 Mission to Moscow (Michael Curtiz): consultant

Further reading

The New York Times obituary February 18, 1988.

Alexander, William, *Film on the Left: American Documentary Film from 1931 to 1942*, Princeton, NJ: Princeton University Press, 1981.

Campbell, Russell, *Cinema Strikes Back: Radical Filmmaking in The United States 1930–42*, Ann Arbor, MI: UMI Research Press, 1978.

The Editors, 'Jay Leyda: A Brief Chronology' and 'Jay Leyda: A Bibliography', *October* 11, winter, 1979.

Horak, Jan-Christopher (ed.), *Lovers of Cinema: The First American Avant-Garde, 1919–45*, Madison, WI: University of Wisconsin Press, 1995.
Leyda, Jay (ed.), *The Melville Log: A Documentary Life of Herman Melville, 1819–91*, New York: Harcourt Brace, 1951 (reprinted with additions, New York: Gordian Press, 1969).
——*Kino: A History of the Russian and Soviet Film*, New York: Macmillan, 1960.
——*Films Beget Films: A Study of the Compilation Film*, New York: Hill and Wang, 1964.
——*Dianying (Electric Shadows): An Account of Films and the Film Audience in China*, Cambridge, MA: MIT Press, 1972.
Leyda, Jay, Tomlinson, Doug and Hagan, John, *Film Makers Speak: Voices of Film Experience*, New York: Da Capo Press, 1988.
Leyda, Jay and Voynow, Zina, *Eisenstein at Work*, New York: Pantheon Books/Museum of Modern Art, 1982.

Life and Death of Frida Kahlo, The

(US, Crommie, 1976)

David Crommie was working as a film director at a television station in San Francisco and his wife Karen was writing scripts for a children's program when they saw an item in a travel book about the Frida Kahlo museum and decided to visit it. Overwhelmed with the setting and her paintings, they decided upon their return to make a film about Frida Kahlo. Before this time, David had little experience with photography or cinematography, but he borrowed a camera (a Bolex wind-up with a running time for each shot of twelve seconds) from a cameraman in the newsroom of the station where he worked, a tripod from someone else, and a tape recorder from another friend. On their return to San Francisco, David and Karen rented some editing equipment and Karen assembled the film and made the first edit with a pair of rewinds and a viewer, which David admits was 'crude stuff by today's standards'. At the television station where he worked, David finished the editing, and the couple entered the film in the San Francisco Film Festival's Documentary division, where it won a top prize.

Shooting on a very tight budget, the Crommies bought rolls of film one or two at a time. Having begun filming in the museum in black and white, they realised that they could do justice to the paintings only by filming them in color. It was still beyond their budget to shoot the whole film in color film, however, so the documentary uses a combination of black and white and color footage, a pragmatic decision that makes for a stunning visual combination of life in monotones, art in colour. Even in Mexico, Kahlo was not particularly well known at that time and her paintings were not particularly valuable, so the Crommies hired an investigator to trace the paintings in private collections. The couple did not have adequate lights and so would take the paintings off the wall and put them in natural light somewhere either outside or by a window to photograph them.

The Life and Death of Frida Kahlo is a powerful example of how low-budget documentary making can nonetheless be extremely authentic. The titles are written in a Kahlo-esque style, using a script that imitates Kahlo's own hand. Interviews conducted in Spanish are left in the original language and subtitled rather than dubbed, which would remove the immediacy and emotion of the original voices. There are no shots of the speakers' faces. This is a film of and about Kahlo, and so the interviews are used as a soundtrack to the stills of Kahlo, her friends and family, and the filmed footage of her paintings and her home. For example, the story of Kahlo's miscarriage is narrated by close friend Lucienne Bloch over the visual track of the works that Frida painted in the wake of the misfortune as an expression of her grief, such as Henry Ford Hospital (Oil on Metal, 1932), which shows her bleeding in the hospital with a dead foetus, umbilical cord still attached floating above her. The result is an extremely painful and emotive sequence that privileges the autobiographical nature of Frida's art above a simple recounting of her story.

This marriage of life and art is essential to a depiction of Kahlo, whose work was extremely autobiographical. The film places Kahlo's paintings in relation to the specific events of her life: her relationship with Diego, her inability to give birth, her illness and, of course, her death. At no point is Frida Kahlo's artistic prowess sacrificed to her extraordinary life story, however. Generally speaking, the visual track focuses on the former while the soundtrack gives us the latter, so that the two aspects are resolved via the film's complementary elements. There are of course exceptions to this approach. The film incorporates numerous stills of Frida and her contemporaries, as well as filmed footage of her home, now transformed into a museum. There is also an extended discussion of Frida's artworks themselves. Her paintings are not merely illustrations, but are one of the documentary's primary subjects. Fellow artists and art critics, including Pablo O'Higgins and Raquel Tibol, comment on Kahlo's use of surrealist style and look at her use of various artistic media, stating that 'the Mexican movement could not be considered complete without Frida Kahlo'.

The Crommies' film has its flaws: it is basic, to say the least; the camera work is shaky and the film quality is poor in parts. It is somewhat polemical, making an extremely positive portrayal of Kahlo, and in compressing thirty years of Kahlo's life and work into a forty-minute film, it barely scratches the surface of her story. However, at the same time the Crommies use a number of simple camera techniques to great effect. For example, the camera constantly mimics Kahlo's method of beginning her paintings in the upper-left-hand corner of the canvas and moving to the lower left, so that most of her paintings are revealed to us as they were to her. They also use the technique of segueing from a photo to one of Frida's paintings, a device much imitated in later fictionalised accounts of Kahlo's life, such as Julie Taymor's 2002 Frida. The effect of such a technique is greatest when there is a slight disjunction between the camera's objectivity and Kahlo's subjectivity. A photo of Diego that matches his description on the soundtrack as an 'ugly big fat man' is juxtaposed with Kahlo's portrait of him, in which his eyes show us the 'gentle, tender, wise' man that his wife saw.

The Crommies succeeded in their ultimate goal: to draw the spotlight of the world's attention onto Kahlo. The film's release coincided with the time of the women's movement in the United States. Colleges and universities began to play it and then art movie houses picked it up. When Hayden Herrera saw it at a screening in New York, she contacted the couple for further information and was motivated to write her seminal autobiography of Kahlo. With the release of Herrera's book, Frida became a cult figure. Other books, theses, and films followed.

The film itself and the taped interviews conducted in preparation for the project are invaluable sources of information for any Kahlo scholar, featuring many people who knew and worked with Frida and who are no longer alive. More important, though, The Life and Death of Frida Kahlo is a potent example of the power that low-budget documentary making can have. Frida Kahlo was almost completely unknown outside of major art circles when Karen and David Crommie's The Life and Death of Frida Kahlo debuted in 1966 at the San Francisco International Film Festival. As a result of the film, the originality and power of Kahlo's paintings has been recognised, and she has become a figure of international acclaim. In 1984 the Mexican government decreed Frida's work to be national patrimony, because it has 'an unquestioned aesthetic value and has reached unanimous recognition within the artistic community'. It is doubtless due, in no small part, to David and Karen Crommie that Frida Kahlo has finally achieved such long-overdue recognition.

CATHERINE WHEATLEY

Selected films

The Life and Death of Frida Kahlo (US, 1966/1976, 40 mins). Distributed by Karen and David Crommie. Produced by Karen and David Crommie. Directed by Karen and David Crommie. All additional work by Karen and David Crommie.

1986 Frida, naturaleza viva (directed by Paul LeDuc)
1989 Diego: I Paint What I See (directed by Mary Lance)
1992 Frida Kahlo: A Ribbon Around a Bomb (directed by Ken Mandel)
2000 Frida Kahlo's Corset (dir. Liz Crow)
2002 Frida (directed by Julie Taymor)

Further reading

Herrera, Hayden, *Frida: The Biography of Frida Kahlo*, London: Bloomsbury, 1998.
——*Frida Kahlo: The Paintings*, London: HarperPerennial, 1993.
Kahlo, Frida, *The Diary of Frida Kahlo: An Intimate Self-Portrait*, ed. Sarah Lowe and Carlos Fuentes, New York: Harry N. Abrams Inc., 1998.

Life and Times of Rosie the Riveter, The

(US, Field, 1980)

Connie Field's The Life and Times of Rosie the Riveter is one of the most accomplished and well known of the exercises in popular historiography that characterised women's filmmaking in the 1970s and 1980s. The film tells the story of women workers in industry during World War II by following the personal accounts of five women, three of whom are black. The film's title comes from the popular typification of such workers, derived from a Norman Rockwell cover for the *Saturday Evening Post* in May 1943, which depicted a muscular but still 'feminine' worker at her lunch break, the word Rosie emblazoned on her lunchbox.

Using a weave of interviews and archive footage, Rosie the Riveter tells the story of how women were recruited to fill the ranks of depleted male workers in the factories and assembly lines during the war. The five women highlighted in the film have both a personal, subjective dimension and a more objective expositional function through which they become indicative of a more general process. The women's stories, illustrated by historical images, recount how women were recruited into the labour force as necessary adjuncts to the war effort, as well as the difficulties and the joys of being part of a formerly male domain. The interviewees describe how they battled dangerous working conditions, institutionalised sexism and racism, and in many cases shouldered the 'double burden' of domestic responsibility endemic to women's working lives. The story is also one of success and achievement, recounted with justified pride.

The film's strategy of interweaving the personal and the general is articulated through the introduction of the five women in the title sequence, freeze-framed and identified by caption, which opens out into a three-part structure illustrating wartime recruitment into industry, experience of wartime industrial work, and postwar return to domesticity or more traditional roles in the workforce. The interviewees are first introduced via brief prewar biographies; their stories then unfold through a series of extensive interviews that mark them as both observers and participants in the historical process they describe. Throughout the film, the women's accounts of their experiences are intercut with a range of archival footage, much of it drawn from official US propaganda footage designed first to encourage women into the labour force, and then to rationalise their displacement by men returning from the war. Newsreel sequences are also used more

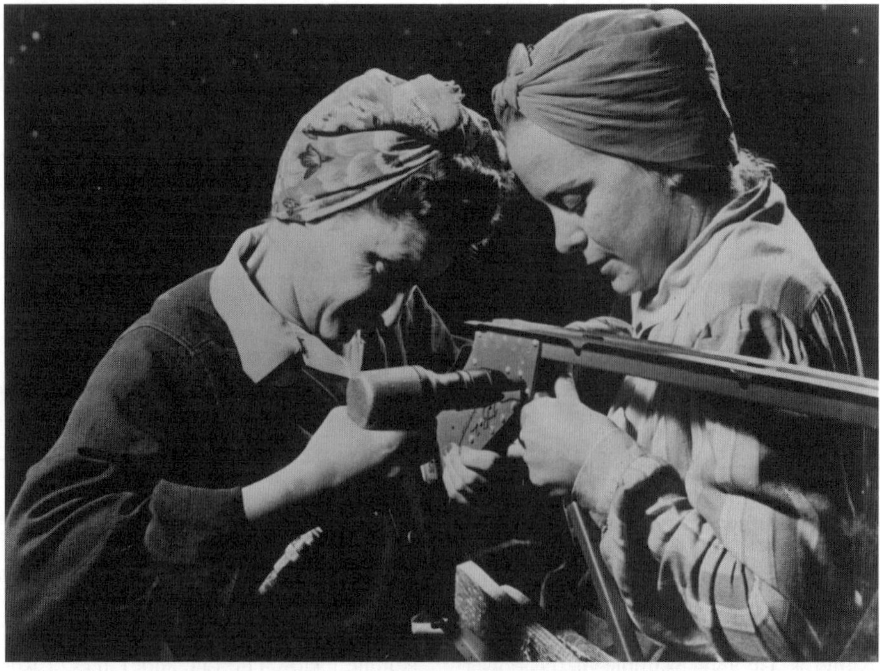

Figure 8 The Life and Times of Rosie the Riveter, 1980 (Courtesy of the British Film Institute)

descriptively and positively as a way of giving a visual realisation to many of the incidents and circumstances described by the five women.

The primary rhetorical usage of archival footage in Rosie the Riveter, however, is as a contrast to the testimony of the women. Rosie is a brilliant example of a film that uses historical film material not to confirm the truth of a situation but to demonstrate how truth claims can be made to support political goals. Connie Field's editing of propaganda footage against the grain, in an example of a politically motivated compilation technique, demonstrates the absurd contortions of logic required to facilitate differing government requirements (Nichols 2001). This critically comic dimension is aided by the retention of the propaganda footage's original soundtrack and the interviewees' remembering of a past at odds with the film's inserted historical images.

A number of similar films that rely on a string of interviews intercut with historical footage, such as Union Maids (1976) and With Babies and Banners (1977), have been accused of forfeiting an independent explanatory framework for the one provided by the participant-witnesses themselves, but the active counterpointing of the text in Rosie the Riveter reminds us that meaning is produced. The resonances set up between the interviews and the archival footage establish a perceptible sense of a textual voice that makes the film a more sophisticated, though not self-reflexive, version of the interview-based documentary (Nichols 1983).

Another way in which Rosie the Riveter avoids the dangers of the self-confirmatory role of the interview is through the degree of personal 'space' its participants occupy. John Corner argues that this space lends an integrity to the women's testimony, which renders it less appropriable by extra-textual intentions (Corner 1996).

In keeping with its project as a feminist recuperation of lost history, the film reveals an alternative history that lies beneath the national myth of women wartime workers. The ideology underlining official policy on the recruitment and postwar demobilisation of the female labour force is exposed as the workings of expediency and cynicism. Ultimately, however, although Rosie the Riveter raises a number of questions in relation to ideology and the official use of misinformation in relation to women and their role in the workforce, the film operates more as an elegy for a lost era of heroic women workers than as a cause for celebration.

MARINA BURKE

See also: Union Maids

The Life and Times of Rosie the Riveter (US, Charity Productions, 1980, 60 mins). Produced and directed by Connie Field. Associate producers Ellen Geiger, Lorraine Kahn, Jane Scantlebury, and Bonnie Bellow. Associate director Lorraine Kahn. Cinematography by Cathy Zeutlin, Bonnie Friedman, Robert Handley, and Emiko Omord. Edited by Lucia Massia Phenix and Connie Field.

Further reading

Corner, John, *The Art of Record: A Critical Introduction to Documentary*, Manchester: Manchester University Press, 1996.

Nichols, Bill, 'The Voice of Documentary', *Film Quarterly* 36, no. 6, spring 1983.

——*Representing Reality: Issues and Concepts in Documentary*, Bloomington, IN and Indianapolis, IN: Indiana University Press, 1991.

——*Introduction to Documentary*, Bloomington, IN: Indiana University Press, 2001.

Renov, Michael (ed.), *Theorising Documentary*, London: Routledge, 1993.

Waldman, Diane and Walker, Janet (eds), *Feminism and Documentary*, Minneapolis, MN: University of Minnesota Press, 1999.

Winston, Brian, *Claiming the Real: The Documentary Film Revisited*, London: British Film Institute, 1995.

Lights Out in Europe

(US, Kline, 1940)

Lights Out in Europe captures the final moments of 1939's uneasy peace and the first moments of the World War II. Director Herbert Kline, veteran of the New York Film and Photo League and an associate of Joris Ivens, intended to serve as the 'foreign correspondent' of the screen by presenting what contemporary documentarians designated 'a new genre of documentary—political film journalism'. Kline's desire to relate the effect of world events on the general population reflected the liberal social sensibilities of documentary filmmakers of the previous decade. His cinematographic collaborators brought an artistic visual touch to Lights Out in Europe, and the narration completed the effect of a film that opposed Nazi rule and decried the inhumanity of modern warfare. Criticized by some for its pacifistic tone in the face of Nazi aggression, Lights Out in Europe soon found itself appropriated (as did the documentary movement in general) by government organs seeking to illustrate their assertions of enemy barbarity and criminal guilt, and justify the war against Germany.

Herbert Kline planned to film the war as it occurred, and he did not prepare a shooting script. For his photographers, Kline again partnered with Czech filmmaker Alexander Hackenschmied (the later Alexander Hammid), his codirector for Crisis: A Film of the Nazi Way, and hired Douglas Slocombe, then a young English still photographer. Kline stationed Hackenschmied in England while he and Slocombe filmed in the free city of Danzig and in Poland. When the German military swept over the Polish border, Kline and Slocombe found themselves filming their own retreat with crowds of Polish refugees. Strafed and bombed, without proper permits from a government that no longer existed, they managed to escape to England via Riga only days before the Soviet invasion from the east. Kline returned to the continent with Hackenschmied to film in France, but encountered significant difficulties with French censors. Returning to England, Kline and Hackenschmied edited a rough cut, which they showed to an audience of documentarians assembled by John Grierson. With their colleagues' comments in mind, Kline completed the film in Los Angeles, adding James Hilton's narration, read by Fredric March, and Werner Janssen's score.

The visual style of Lights Out in Europe consists of quickly shot actuality footage augmented by some artfully composed shots. The actuality footage, visually similar to newsreels, includes tragic images of despondent villagers tossing buckets of water over their homes, now burned to ash, and Polish refugees running as German aircraft attack their train. In one shot, a woman shot through the throat slowly bleeds to death in a railway carriage. English children, bewildered and crying, struggle into gas masks; others depart the city for the countryside—tiny evacuees who might never reunite with their families. The artistic visual material demonstrated Hackenschmied's years of experience as a photographer and filmmaker, from work with Gustav Machatý to his own artistic short city film, Bezucelná procházka/Aimless Walk (1930). Traffic and pedestrians cross the fog-shrouded Thames in a sequence of careful shots using slowed motion. One shot features a layered view of the city, with passersby and advertisements in the foreground, trains moving slowly in the middle ground, and the silent form of St Paul's looming in the background. Britain's newest fighters, the graceful Spitfires, ascend and bank, and other shots of a sea of metallic interstices represent the skeletal fuselages of planes under construction.

Against this imagery, James Hilton's narration continually describes the terrible inhumanity of the coming conflagration while recalling the awful cost of World War I and associating it with the new conflict; even the title refers to a comment made in 1914. Hilton echoes the view of war and militarism expressed in his novel *Lost Horizon*, underscoring shots of blinded veterans and rows of crosses in military cemeteries, with speculation about the lost potential of those men and the apparent futility of their sacrifice. The narration decries Nazism, with its anti-Semitism and violence, but finally condemns the whole world for its willingness to fight a 'war to end all wars', but not to try a 'peace to end all wars'. Lights Out in Europe does not glorify Polish resistance, lionize British defense, or attempt to rally America's fighting spirit to intervention. In light of Kline's established reputation as an outspoken antifascist, the lack of a call to action against Germany surprised many. At least one reviewer accused Kline of mitigating his anti-Nazi stance, as some Communist sympathizers in America did as a result of the pact Germany signed with the Soviet Union.

The New York Times appreciated the moderate tone, lauding Lights Out in Europe as 'the most beautifully comprehensive report on the recent neurological prelude to war in existence'. *Time* bestowed a slightly more unusual accolade, describing the film as 'the next best thing' for 'those who cannot experience war at first hand'. However, Hollywood, having little to do with the documentary tradition from which Lights Out in Europe came, responded less warmly. In *Variety*, a short review near the back unjustly dismissed it as a mere compilation film of newsreel footage. Hollywood was not interested in 'political film journalism'.

After the attack on Pearl Harbor, however, Hollywood developed an interest in the potential for documentary film and found a use for Lights Out in Europe. The United States government charged famous studio directors—not experienced documentarians—to make high-profile documentaries about the outbreak of the war. John Ford made December 7th largely from reenactments, and Frank Capra supervised the assembly of footage from a liberal variety of sources to produce the Why We Fight series of Army 'informational films'. The rhetoric of these films matched their intention: to convince US soldiers and civilians of the justice and morality of American involvement in World War II. The Why We Fight and other information films used footage from Lights Out in Europe but took nothing of the film's humanitarian message or perspective. The National Film Board of Canada also reworked Lights Out in Europe, cutting thirty minutes of material (including all shots of military cemeteries) and inserting a new commentary over the conclusion to encourage Canadians to fight. The NFB released their film under the title Not Peace but a Sword.

The new documentaries, mobilized to support the war effort and made with Hollywood's talent, took the vanguard previously held by liberal social subjects and activist documentarians like Kline and Ivens. As originally released, Lights Out in Europe represented one of the last efforts of their school of thought. The film presents an essay, artistically illustrated, not meant to simplify war or elicit fighting spirit, but to inform audiences of the genuine tragedy of World War II.

MICHAEL D. ROBINSON

See also: Kline, Herbert

Lights Out in Europe (US, Films for Peace, Inc., 1940, 66 mins or 68 mins). A Look (magazine); Ampix Presentation, released by Mayer-Burstyn, Inc. Produced by Herbert Kline. Associate production by Peter A. Mayer. Directed by Herbert Kline. Associate direction by Alexander Hackenschmied (as Alexander Hackenschmid) and Peter A. Mayer. Production managed by Rosa Harvan Kline. Cinematography by Alexander Hackenschmied and Douglas Slocombe, assisted by J. Massey Collier. Music by Werner Janssen. Edited by Herbert Kline. Montage by Alexander Hackenschmied. Commentary by James Hilton. Narration by Fredric March. (Not Peace but a Sword: 'Epilogue' by Grattan O'Leary.) Filmed in London and surrounding areas, the Free City of Danzig, Poland, and in France. 'Sons of the Sea', music and lyrics by B. Miles and Aaron Sachs, at the Ridgeway's Late Joys; '(We'll Hang Out the Washing on) The Siegfried Line', music and lyrics by Jimmy Kennedy and Michael Carr, performed by Lupino Lane at the Victoria Palace, London.

Further reading

Alexander, William, *Film on the Left: American Documentary Film from 1931 to 1942*, Princeton, NJ: Princeton University Press, 1981.

Andel, Jaroslav, *Alexandr Hackenschmied*, Prague: Torst, 2000.

Hilton, James and Kline, Herbert, 'Lights Out in Europe', *Look*, May 7, 1940: 24–9.

Kline, Herbert, 'Documentary Films in New Theatre and in My Life', in *New Theatre and Film 1934 to 1937*, San Diego, CA: Harcourt Brace Jovanovich, 1985: 306–7.

——'Films Without Make-Believe', *The Magazine of Art* (New York), February 1, 1942: 58–63, 87–8 (reprinted in Lewis Jacobs, *The Documentary Tradition*, New York: Norton, 1979: 148–57).

Slocombe, Douglas, 'Rear-Guard Filming', *Documentary News Letter*, July, 1940: 25.

Line to Tcherva Hut

(UK, Cavalcanti, 1936)

After making Coal Face (1935), Alberto Cavalcanti directed a series of seven films set in Switzerland, one of which was Line to Tcherva Hut (1936). The seven films are Line to Tcherva Hut, We Live in Two Worlds (1937), Who Writes to Switzerland? (1937), Message from Geneva (1937), Four Barriers (1937), Alice au pays romand (1938), and Men of the Alps (1939). These films, which were commissioned by the Swiss telephone company, Pro-Telephone Zurich, were commissioned as a group, and all but Line to Tcherva Hut were made after John Grierson's departure from the General Post Office (GPO) Film Unit in 1936. Therefore, they were produced when Cavalcanti was in effective charge of the GPO Film Unit. Cavalcanti's Swiss films are quite different from the more parodic films that he produced at the GPO Film Unit between 1936 and 1939, and far more conventional in terms of their use of linear narrative structures and continuity editing. Unlike Coal Face, they also use voice-over commentary in the traditional manner to provide information and explanation for the viewer. These films have been described as technically mature models of shooting and editing and imaginative use of sound by Paul Rotha, and it is certainly the case that in these films Cavalcanti returns to a more conventional realist tradition of filmmaking. Of these seven films, Cavalcanti's favourite was also Line to Tcherva Hut, which he preferred to one of the other films in the Swiss series, the better known We Live in Two Worlds (1937).

Line to Tcherva Hut is concerned with communication systems in Switzerland and, in particular, with the building of a telephone link to an alpine refuge hut. In classic Griersonian style the film shows the process of building the telephone link in some detail, depicting all the various stages of the process of production. The film also creates dramatic development from within the process of labour activity itself, as the telephone engineers grapple with the problems posed by precipitous drops and sheer mountainsides. In fact, in its depiction of technical, labouring, and professional skills, carried out against an imposing natural background, Line to Tcherva Hut is similar to early Empire Marketing Board Film Unit films such as Arthur Elton's The Shadow on the Mountain (1931) and Basil Wright's Windmill to Barbados (1934).

Line to Tcherva Hut combines depictions of manual labour with a lyrically evocative representation of the mountainous Swiss countryside, which emphasises the natural beauty of the landscape. A kind of lyrical naturalism pervades these scenes of high glaciers and sheer chasms, and this lyrical pastoralism is reinforced by showing the workmen who lay the telephone link as tiny insignificant figures within this dramatic environment. This mood is heightened by the musical score for the film, which was composed by Benjamin Britten. Britten's music is 'very simple', but it 'augments and contributes to an imaginative film that is a model of subtle conception, shooting and editing' (Aitken 2001, p. 85).

Some of the sequences in Line to Tcherva Hut also resemble scenes from Night Mail, made in the same year, as, for example, when in the latter film the train is seen speeding through a rolling countryside of moorland and hill country. The same sense of atmosphere and imagery pervades both films, and it may be that, when Cavalcanti stated that he was particularly pleased with Line to Tcherva Hut, he was referring to the film's lyrical evocation of the natural environment.

IAN AITKEN

See also: Cavalcanti, Alberto

Line to Tcherva Hut (1936). Produced by John Grierson. Directed, photographed and edited by Alberto Cavalcanti. Music by Benjamin Britten. Produced at the GPO Film Unit.

Further reading

Aitken, Ian, *Alberto Cavalcanti, Realism, Surealism and National Cinemas*, London: Flicks Books, 2001.

——*The Documentary Film Movement, An Anthology*, Edinburgh: Edinburgh University Press, 1998.

——*Film and Reform*, London: Routledge, 1990.

Cavalcanti, Alberto, *Filme e Realidade*, Rio de Janeiro: Editora Artenova, in collaboration with Empresa Brasiliera de Filmes—Embrafilme, 1977.

Rotha, Paul, *Documentary Film*, London: Faber & Faber, 1939.

Sussex, Elizabeth, 'Cavalcanti in England', *Sight and Sound* 44, no. 4, autumn, 1975.

Lion Has Wings, The

(UK, Korda, 1940)

Produced and speedily completed in six weeks at the outbreak of World War II, The Lion Has Wings (TLHW) was a three-part hybrid documentary style (now seen as very much a period piece) that attempted to engender feelings of comfort and courage in and for the home front. It was very much a declaration of intent and a promise for the future. On its release in November 1939, and despite—or perhaps owing to—it being clearly put together in some haste but meant well, it was well received by critics and the public and went on to make a reasonable profit.

TLHW combined reconstructions, newsreel footage, fiction (excerpts from earlier Korda successes such as Fire Over England inevitably drawing parallels with and evoking the triumph over the Spanish Armada) and fact to produce a collage and montage of images and ideas to link aspects of British traditions, history, and ideology in ways that emphasised continuity, tolerance, and democracy.

Famously or infamously, King George VI leading the scouts in singing Underneath the Spreading Chestnut Tree is contrasted with a Hitler youth rally. Dalrymple (in Pronay and Spring 1982) was quite explicit in his aims, perhaps predating or alongside Balcon's wish at Ealing to 'Project Britain and the British Character': 'I opened our film with the suggestion that there was a British ideology arising from our national character; that it was valuable to the world; and that it should not be lost.' To which, even allowing for the problems inherent in defining the term British, one might well say 'amen to that'.

That apart, The Lion Has Wings was the first result of Alexander Korda's promise to Churchill amongst others that on and after the outbreak of hostilities, the British Film Industry should be supported and enabled to play a valuable part in sustaining morale and promoting propaganda. Thus were the foundations laid for future masterpieces such as 49th Parallel and The Life and Death of Colonel Blimp (Powell 1986).

Michael Powell contributed to and directed parts of TLHW, with footage of the preparations for and the return of bombers from a raid on the Kiel Canal and elements of the German High Seas fleet. Given that Powell himself was available and ready to take part in the mission the day after war was declared and would thus have been able to include real-time footage of Britain's declaration of serious intent, it remains a loss that he was not allowed to take part. Consequently, this section of the film is largely a reconstruction and, for legitimate propaganda reasons, is, in its evocation and expression of the raid, to use a much later phrase, economical with the truth.

The final section addresses fears of an aerial Armageddon, which were widespread at the time, partly arising out of earlier films such as Things to Come (1935, another Korda epic) in which the presumed ability of aircraft to bomb a city back to the stone age was articulated. According to Powell (1986), TLHW was going to show how 'an all out attack by Nazi bombers, supported by fighters, was completely wrecked by the use of radar by the fighter squadrons of the RAF'.

For good or for ill, the needs of national security meant that references to radar were not allowable and so the final section seems now to predate Mrs Miniver in its portrayal of sentimental attachment to the values of 'England's green and pleasant land' not to mention the other kingdoms that make up the United Kingdom.

Having Ralph Richardson and Merle Oberon (both in uniform, the latter as a nurse) play the lead parts and representatives of those who fight for 'Truth and beauty, and fair play and kindness' seems now, and no doubt to some then, to be somewhat incongruous and over the top. However, there is the ever-present danger of judging with the sensibilities and ideological spectacles of a future generation and changed culture, and it does not do to be too hard on a film that, whatever its faults, served some of its purpose at the time even if aesthetically or formally it did not advance the cause or culture of documentary.

ROBERT BEVERIDGE

The Lion Has Wings (UK, 1939). Producer Ian Dalrymple/Alexander Korda. Directors Adrian Brunel; Brian Hurst; Michael Powell.

Further reading

Powell, M., *A Life in Movies*, London: Heinemann, 1986.

Pronay, N. and Spring, D.W. (eds), *Propaganda, Politics & Film 1918–45*, London: Macmillan, 1982.

Listen to Britain

(UK, Jennings, 1942)

A signal work of its director, Humphrey Jennings, Listen to Britain is also an institutional product and a sterling collaboration of skilled and committed contributors. Significantly, collaboration is also its subject. It is a powerful portrait of social cohesion during difficult times, as well as being a synthesis and elaboration of existing documentary possibilities and a clear prefiguring of many of the important innovations that would change the form in years to come. However, ultimately it is not the innovativeness, but the substance, even the goodness, of Listen to Britain that most distinguishes it. These things can be ascribed to a delicate balance of complicated and potentially contradictory factors, the combination of which continues to impress the modern viewer as being deeply organic and indeed, practically perfect. This fruit of British hardship and hardihood, however, did not come about accidentally or without a long and difficult gestation.

Unlike many of his forebears and colleagues at the Empire Marketing Board and the General Post Office (GPO) Film Units, Humphrey Jennings took a long time to find his documentary bearings. He joined the GPO in 1934, and he did not thrive under Grierson. To Grierson's mind a documentarian's duty was to roll up his sleeves, to advocate and to educate, and the bookish and aesthetical Jennings was ill-equipped for the role. Pedantry and dilettantism, from a more sympathetic perspective, might also bespeak, or lead to, depth and breadth. Jennings's sensibility was subtle and indirect, qualities both native and achieved through careful cultivation. It was his bookishness, as well as the diverse investigations and involvements that fell outside of the constraints and assumptions of Griersonian production, that made him a key link in the evolution of the documentary film, and Listen to Britain was the clearest emblem of its advance.

Four things contributed to this leap and to the poetic qualities so abundantly illustrated in Listen to Britain. In the 1920s Jennings was a scholarship student at the University of Cambridge, where he effected a considerable immersion in the major movements, the signal works and authors, the main periods and issues in English literature, and of English history. His PhD work was interrupted by other impulses and involvements—in fact he never finished it—but it developed in him the ability to amass, order, and interpret sources and data, a skill that would become a major part of his method.

In addition to acquiring great knowledge, Jennings developed striking ways of seeing and organizing that knowledge. He had a sympathy for surrealism (the mid-1930s found him painting, curating, and translating under that influence). He found great resonance in the movement's incongruous juxtapositions, which advanced his scholar's knack for assimilation, helping him to find patterns and correspondences that were not obvious, or even visible to the untrained eye.

As for method of presentation, in 1937 Jennings helped to organize Mass Observation, a monumental project that was to coincide with the coronation of King George VI, and that was designed to take the principles of anthropological science and apply them not to far-flung cultures, but to the British populace itself. In contrast to the GPO's customary prescribing and proscribing, the task here was to observe, gather, and present data without compulsory means or excessive urging.

Mass Observation informs Jennings's first major film as a director, Spare Time (1939). During its production he also acquired the final key component of his mature style and sensibility. Spare Time was shot in England's industrial north, which Jennings had never before visited. The exposure was revelatory; presented for the first time with the real conditions of working-class life, Jennings found himself obliged to incorporate the emotional, to add sympathy, compassion, and regard to the cerebral, aesthetic cast of his previous efforts. The gathering clouds and the eventual declaration of war completed his sensitization and confirmed in Jennings the very documentary conviction that private impulse should be subordinated to public ends. The stage was set for Jennings's finest work.

Listen to Britain emerges out of a tangle of wartime filmmaking activity. The Crown Film Unit had changed facilities in the aftermath of the Dunkirk Blitz. The atmosphere was unsettled, and Jennings shot material for a couple of films (one on military mustering, the other on the noontime concerts at the National Gallery) that would never be finished. He was able, however, to salvage some of the footage, and the germ of an idea, from these efforts. With the destruction in May 1941 of the Queen's Hall (longtime site of the London Promenade Concerts), along with the London Philharmonic's instruments, Jennings and editor Stewart McAllister came up with a treatment called 'The Music of War'. This would become Listen to Britain. (McAllister's contribution to the eventual film was so central that he receives equal credit with the director.)

The film is difficult to summarize, in part because of its enormous cumulative effect; in the volume of its sights and sounds, it is practically encyclopedic. It is a portrait of beleaguered Britain, working and waiting, at leisure and in anxiety, abiding and, we are assured, prevailing. There is narrative and characterization, but not remotely in the ways to which we are accustomed. Rather than synopsizing, it might be more useful to enumerate the film's many satisfactions and contributions.

One of the simplest and most striking of these is its superb cinematic counterpoint of sound and image. Unlike the effects usually associated with Soviet counterpoint (for example, collision, opposition), Jennings and McAllister's counterpoint is at first glance more strictly formal. They replace the image's traditional primacy with a freer alternation of picture and sound. In doing so they oppose or at least alternate film's traditional picture/sound hierarchies and create what remains an ideal of cinematic virtuosity and expressiveness.

Jennings' previous film, Words for Battle (1941), had compiled contemporary images of wartime Britain and set them against statements and strains of music that far predated the current crisis. In doing so, Jennings conflated the epochs and, in the counterpoint of image and text, erased divisions between times and peoples and places. Listen to Britain explores this same idea synchronically, establishing a powerful present tense. It is Jennings's definitive mass observation film, with carefully chosen, intimately observed (and expertly staged) vignettes that cut across social, professional, and geographical lines, giving a vivid impression of wartime life and wartime unity, witnessed and overheard.

The manner in which Jennings observes constitutes a major shift in the role and nature of narration in the nonfiction film. The sound documentary, especially in Britain, had almost always tended towards emphatic narrative. Commentary led the way, dictating the use to which the pictures were put. This procedure was standard, and it was effective, but it also contained potential difficulties and clear contradictions. The urging, even hectoring tone of traditionally narrated documentary could betray a lack of confidence in the validity of the message, or of the ability of the audience to apprehend it. It could also betray a coercive core. If this previous approach had directed and even manipulated the viewer to particular ends, then Jennings openly invites the viewer into the process of comprehension and interpretation, not incidentally making him a more active agent in the subsequent action that documentary traditionally demanded.

In Listen to Britain commentary is not found in a narrator's explicit and manipulative proclamations—it has no narrator at all—but in the much more subtle and open juxtapositions of intellectual montage. Here are traces of Jennings's surrealist affinities. The film proceeds and makes its points by constant comparison, linking by mere proximity that which would at first seem to be completely unrelated. As with mise-en-scène style, seeming and actual realism does not mean that there is no manipulation here. Yet in the gathering and ordering of picture and sounds significance is not so underlined, meaning is left implicit, and the viewer has the responsibility and opportunity to make her own connections, her own meaning.

Work is central to the film's meaning, and it is one of its main subjects. Here it is a labour of a particular, communal kind, one that continues to come across as especially grave and moving. Documentary had always been invested in portraying work's dignity, and it was never so successful in doing so as it was here, when the most pressing labour was simply to survive and to live decently. In a time when the possibility of death or loss was constant, Jennings and McAllister discover the sufficiency of simple, careful observation, which reveals how precious plain processes and regular people can be.

Such raised stakes and heightened awareness allow for and make convincing a difficult hypothesis: that social origin and division could be effaced, that class differences could be reconciled amidst and even because of the greater conflict. Again, the detailed and affectionate rendering of mundane tasks illustrates the idea. Listen to Britain portrays a community bound by gainful employment as much as by tribulation and tragedy. The people have found themselves united in a common cause; the war has revealed the deeper affinities. The film has done so, too. Jennings and McAllister urge the case through the overlapping of sound and the juxtaposition of images. As a number of prospects and correspondences pass before us—the ballroom dancers in Blackpool, the Canadian soldiers in the transport train, the children in the schoolyard, the whistling workers in the canteen, and the concert-goers in the National Gallery—an assertion emerges that constitutes one of the central tenets of the documentary idea. Regardless of his or her role, each honest worker—including the public-minded artist—is worthy of his hire, and he is part of an interdependent community. Listen to Britain gives us, in effect, the body of Britain, where the head cannot say to the foot that it has no need of it. In fact we come to see that each member not only has its own utility, but its own beauty as well. The great Myra Hess, playing Mozart's 17th piano concerto (German music, as Barnouw has pointed out), is in some ways as skilled, and in every sense only as important, as the factory girl who sings and smiles while she wraps a package of razors.

Thus we see, or at least have proposed to us, the suggestion of a British culture utterly transformed, battered and yet full of new promise. The film brings binaries together: trades, ages, classes, farm and city, high culture and low, the present and the past. Things that have been poles apart begin to appear like they belong together.

In this a problem might arise, and a reminder that amid justifiable enthusiasm there are questions to raise. Listen to Britain was generally acclaimed on its release, but it was not received with unalloyed enthusiasm. Writing in the *Spectator*, Edgar Anstey described it as 'the rarest fiddling since the days of Nero', and 'a figment of the romantic imagination of Mass Observation'. To some blitzed Britons, the film's pacific qualities must have seemed at the least misplaced; Harry Watt's pugnacious Target for Tonight probably, and quite properly, represents a more typical representation of wartime resistance. As for its effect on the documentary community, National Film Board of Canada pioneer Tom Daly remembers that Listen to Britain was one of Grierson's locked case films, deemed to be so artistically indulgent as to constitute an actual danger to his impressionable charges.

Today a few of the film's details strike one as being less natural—the beautifully composed and patently staged 'Ash Grove' sequence—or less convincing, as in the contrived cutaway to the housewife's Highland regiment husband, than they might be. Furthermore, as was so often the case with British documentaries, there were great difficulties in the recording of the sound. Its inadequacy is most keenly felt in a film to which sound is so central.

There are other things of which modern viewers might fail to take note. Listen to Britain, for all its gentleness and subtlety, is still pointedly propagandistic. A continuous solidarity between past and present, or between class and region, was real and demonstrable. However, it was also tenuous, and the connections could be lost not only in the uncertainty of the moment, but also in the depths of real division. Furthermore, as with his earlier collaboration with Harry Watt, London Can Take It! (1940), Jennings removes fear and hostility almost completely from his account. This effacement, understandable, even justifiable, is also to some degree fictional. In these things, Jennings and McAllister effaced the joins as they fashioned their portrait, which is not without a degree of manufacture, and even manipulation.

Listen to Britain is also powerful in what it promises and proves of documentary and cinematic potential. As the cinema is in many ways a combination and a culmination of all of the arts, it is appropriate that a man of Jennings's broad background should finally have found his calling in films. His versatility, and the medium's, is superlatively manifest in this production. He was a modern painter able to see that there is more to an object, or a subject, than what presents itself to the naked eye. He was a surrealist poet who found that a direct line is not the only link between a cause and its apparent effect. He was an observer of the masses, and of the individual within, willing not only to tell, but also to hear. In the best of Jennings's work artistry and responsibility were perfectly balanced, the felicitous result being that in addressing with his own voice the specific concerns of a specific moment, Jennings was able to transcend that moment and speak for all time.

DEAN DUNCAN

See also: Jennings, Humphrey

Listen to Britain (UK, Crown Film Unit, 1942 20 mins). Produced by Ian Dalrymple. Directed and scripted and edited by Humphrey Jennings and Stewart McAllister. Photography by Chick Fowle. Sound by Ken Cameron. Music by various.

Further reading

Calder, Angus, *The People's War*, London: Cape, 1969

Calder, Angus and Sheridan, Dorothy, *Speak for Yourself: A Mass-Observation Anthology 1937–49*, London: Cape, 1984.

Ellis, Jack, *John Grierson: Life, Contributions, Influences*, Carbondale, IL: Southern Illinois University Press, 2000.

Harrisson, Tom, *Living Through the Blitz*, London: Collins, 1976.

Hodgkinson, Anthony W., Sheratsky, Rodney E. and Jennings, Humphrey, *More than a Maker of Films*, Hanover, MA: Clark University Press, 1982.

Jennings, Humphrey, *Pandaemonium: The Coming of the Machine in the Industrial Revolution*, ed. Mary-Lou Jennings and Charles Madge, New York: Free Press, 1985.

Jennings, Humphrey and Madge, Charles (eds), *May the Twelfth: Mass-Observation Day-Surveys 1937, by Over Two Hundred Observers*, London: Faber & Faber, 1937.

Jennings, Mary-Lou (ed.), *Humphrey Jennings: Film-Maker/Painter/Poet*, London: BFI, 1982.

Remy, Michel, *Surrealism in Britain*, Brookfield: Ashgate, 1999.

Sheridan, Dorothy, Street, Brian V. and Bloome, David, *Writing Ourselves: Mass-Observation and Literacy Practices*, Creskill: Hampton Press, 2000.

Winston, Brian, *Claiming the Real*, London: BFI, 1995.

——*Fires Were Started*, London: BFI, 1999.

Litvak, Anatole

The Russian-born feature film director Anatole Litvak pioneered the use of editing techniques in the pseudo-documentary. Relying on his education and expertise as a 'cutter' or film editor in both the Soviet Union and in France, Litvak juxtaposed production footage, controlled documentary footage, and newsreel footage in several feature films and, more important, in the Why We Fight series (1942–5) produced by the US Army Signal Corps during World War II. Frank Capra hired Litvak in 1942 as second-in-command of the production unit in Los Angeles. Litvak's contribution as codirector (in particular, the films The Nazis Strike, Divide and Conquer, The Battle of Russia, The Battle of China, and War Comes to America) helped to make the Why We Fight series one of the most effective examples of wartime propaganda documentaries. The psychological strength of these films proved so dynamic that more than fifty years later, after the terrorist attacks of September 11, 2001, White House officials met with top television executives in Beverly Hills to discuss how Hollywood could help support the 'war on terrorism' by means similar to the Why We Fight series. Litvak's limited use of these techniques in the Warner Bros feature film Confessions of a Nazi Spy (1939) provided a blueprint for their even more effective use in his wartime documentaries.

The style of the Why We Fight series was based on techniques first used by Esfir Shub in the Soviet Union during the 1920s. Shub is generally credited with innovating the 'compilation film'. This documentary subgenre was created through the editing of footage from numerous archival sources to construct an historical documentary film. This manipulation of preexisting footage in relation to other pieces is a key element of the compilation film. Relying for the most part on newsreel footage, Shub created a trilogy that chronicled the fall of the Romanov dynasty and the rise of the Soviet Republic. The conception of film as montage (Shub was inspired by Eisenstein's Battleship Potemkin, 1925), the fusion of film form with ideological concerns, was also an instrumental element in the compilation film's structure. In the United States during the early 1930s similar compilation films included Universal's The Fighting President (1933), compiled from Universal newsreels concerning FDR, and This is America (1933). In the late 1930s the growing concern over Hitler and the spread of fascism spawned a feature-length documentary film produced by Louis DeRochemont, Ramparts We Watch (1940), and a Warner Bros feature, Confessions of a Nazi Spy (1939). Ramparts We Watch, which used fictional reenactments combined with newsreel footage, is generally considered to be the first American wartime documentary. Confessions of a Nazi Spy, directed by Litvak, was an entirely fictive feature (though based on real events) that incorporated newsreel footage, as well as voice-over narration, into its narrative structure for added authenticity. The film was about a Nazi spy ring operating within the United States and its exposure by the FBI. Litvak purposefully wanted the film to have an authentic look associated with newsreels and incorporated them into a quasi-documentary format for the film. The intercutting of documentary footage with stage scenes often made it difficult to distinguish between the two. Louis de Rochemont's film effectively combines dramatic narrative, patriotic songs, newsreels footage, Nazi propaganda, and reenactments to trace American attitudes concerning isolationism and interventionism before World War II. The technique of both films influenced the structure and style of the Why We Fight series.

The Why We Fight series were orientation films specifically designed to instruct armed forces personnel in the reasons why they were fighting overseas. They were also shown to the general public to assuage any questioning of the war itself. The series consisted of seven films that chronologically detailed war: Prelude to War (1942), The Nazis Strike (1943), Divide and Conquer (1943), The Battle of Britain (1943), The Battle of China (1944), The Battle of Russia (1944), and War Comes to America (1945). Anatole Litvak served as codirector, along with Frank Capra, for The Nazis Strike, Divide and Conquer, and The Battle of China. He is credited as director on The Battle of Russia and War Comes to America. In The Battle of Russia, Litvak skillfully edits newsreel footage along with animation sequences, combat photography, and production sequences from Sergei Eisenstein's Alexander Nevsky to detail the numerous historical attempts to invade the nation. The film, the longest and most effective in the series, then recounts Hitler's invasion and ultimate defeat by the Russian people. Litvak's film stresses the unity of the various peoples that comprise the Union of Soviet Socialist Republics. It likewise puts an emphasis on the nation's culture and the threat to that culture by the invading Nazis. Litvak uses traditional music, as well as symphonic music as a counterpoint to the edited footage. Unity is stressed because it teaches that only a united front, in this case the Allied nations themselves, can successfully counter and defeat Nazi aggression. This particular film was originally shown in two parts.

The last film of the Why We Fight series, War Comes to America, was also originally planned to be shown in two parts, but the end of the war stopped production of part two. The film covers the events leading up to the United States involvement in World War II. Similar to De Rochemont's Ramparts We Watch, it details the shift in American attitudes from an isolationist stance to one of intervention. Litvak persuasively uses a parallel structure showing events in the spectators' lives (in this case the soldiers, for whom the series was intended) juxtaposed with world events. 'We the people' is continually stressed in the film. In one sequence the narration and images reflect the multicultural diversity that makes up America and the subsequent threat to American life caused by the war. The film itself is perhaps the most carefully constructed answer to the question proposed by the series title, Why We Fight.

RONALD WILSON

See also: Battle of Russia, The; Battle of China, The; Why We Fight

Biography

Born Mikhail Anatol Litwak in Kiev, Russia, May 10, 1902. Graduated from University of Leningrad, PhD in philosophy, in 1921. Attended State School of Theatre 1922. 1923 directed short films for Nordkino studios in Leningrad. In 1925 left the Soviet Union for Paris, then Berlin. Worked as an editor at Ufa in Berlin. 1926–30 assistant to Russian-emigré director Nicholas Alexander Volkoff, who had directed films in Czarist Russia. Moved to Paris in 1933, where he directed several feature films. The critical and box office success of Mayerling (Nero Film/ Concordia Productions, 1936) brought Litvak to the United States in 1937. 1937–41 served as a contract director at Warner Brothers studio. 1942–5 codirector for US Army Signal Corps Special Services film unit of the War Department. Died December 15, 1974, in Paris. Military honors include the Legion d'Honneur and the Croix de Guerre.

Further reading

Barsam, Richard M., *Non-Fiction Film: A Critical History*, Bloomington, IN: Indiana University Press, 1992.

Birdwell, Michael E., *Celluloid Soldiers: The Warner Bros. Campaign Against Nazism*, New York: New York University Press, 1999.

Bohn, Thomas William, *An Historical and Descriptive Analysis of the 'Why We Fight' Series*, New York: Arno Press, 1977.

Capra, Frank, *The Name Above the Title*, New York: MacMillan, 1977.

Doherty, Thomas, *Projections of War: Hollywood, American Culture, and World War II*, New York: Columbia University Press, 1993.

Eyles, Allan and Pattison, Barrie, 'Anatole Livak—A Cutter at Heart' (interview), *Films & Filming* (London), 13, no. 5, February, 1967.

Leyda, Jay, *Films Beget Films*, New York: Hill & Wang, 1964.

McBride, Joseph, *Frank Capra: The Catastrophe of Success*, New York: Simon & Schuster, 1992.

MacCann, Richard Dyer, 'World War II: Armed Forces Documentary', in Lewis Jacobs (ed.), *The Documentary Tradition*, New York: W.W. Norton, 1979.

Nolan, Jack, 'Anatole Litvak', *Films in Review* (New York), November, 1967.

Thompson, George Raynor and Harris, Dixie R., *The Signal Corps: The Test (1941–43)*, Washington, DC: Department of the Army, 1957.

Living Desert, The

(US, Algar, 1953)

The Living Desert was one of the most popular, as well as the most criticized, of Disney's True-Life Adventures series of theatrical documentaries. The film, produced by Disney's newly formed production company, Buena Vista, relied heavily on the narrative and aesthetic devices that Disney animators had used in their feature films and cartoon short subjects. Compiled from footage acquired from several freelance nature photographers, music and narration were added to create a humanization of the natural world. The resulting film was more an 'edu-tainment' than a traditional documentary.

The Living Desert was a feature-length film that was produced after the critical and commercial success of Disney's series of True-Life Adventures short subjects. The most successful of these shorts was Seal Island (1948), concerning the fur seal migration to the Pribilof Islands, off the coast of Alaska. Other films in the series included Beaver Valley (1950), Nature's Half Acre (1951), The Olympic Elk (1952), Water Birds (1952), and Bear Country (1953). The expanded feature-length films in the True-Life Adventures series, along with The Living Desert, included The Vanishing Prairie (1954), The African Lion (1955), Secrets of Life (1956), White Wilderness (1958), and Jungle Cat (1960). These films proved to be the most popular of the Disney studios productions in the 1950s.

The subject matter of The Living Desert is the flora and fauna that inhabit the dry and arid plains between the Sierra Nevada mountain range and the Rocky Mountains. After the opening credits, which feature the True-Life logo, a globe turning within a frame, an animated paintbrush paints the North American continent and shows how the desert was created by meteorological and geographic conditions. The wildlife that inhabit this region include tarantulas, scorpions, kangaroo rats, bats, rattlesnakes, and desert hawks. The final portion of the film shows a flash flood in a desert ravine and the resulting blooming of desert flowers (filmed in time-lapse photography). The sun sets on the horizon, and the narrator (Winston Hibler) explains that in the desert 'there are no endings, only new beginnings'.

The use of anthropomorphism, a chief characteristic of Disney's animated feature films, is also prevalent in the True-Life Adventures series. Musical cues, such as the square dancing of scorpions, and a tango for courting tarantulas, further the human characteristics placed on wildlife. The Living Desert presents a dichotomized natural world that stresses the duality of nature. Many of the animals in the film are either cute (the kangaroo rat, for instance) or malevolent (scorpions, rattlesnakes). Violence in the film reflects the survival-of-the-fittest ethos as a natural process. Domesticity is also a part of Disney's natural order, with scenes showing animals' parental concerns and family life. This struggle to survive in a hostile environment effectively ties into Cold War concerns of security and family.

Though Disney's humanization of nature in these films was criticized at the time, the photography is quite remarkable and set a standard for subsequent nature films. Much of the close-up camera work allows the viewer to witness the actions and events in an almost participatory effect. Likewise, these films contributed significantly to more of an ecosystem consciousness than had previous 'jungle documentaries' that stressed the hunting and capturing of animals such as Bring 'Em Back Alive (USA, Clyde Elliott, 1932) and Simba, King of the Beasts (USA, Martin and Osa Johnson, 1928). Though its faults are many, The Living Desert and subsequent films in the series created an empathy with the natural world and an awareness of humanity's role in it.

RONALD WILSON

The Living Desert (US, Walt Disney Productions, 1953, 73 mins). Distributed by Buena Vista. Produced by Walt Disney. Associate producer, Ben Sharpsteen. Directed by James Algar. Screenplay by James Algar, Winston Hibler, and Ted Sears. Cinematography by N. Paul Kenworthy, Jr, Robert H. Crandall. Additional photography by Stuart V. Jewell, Jack C. Coufer, Don Arlen, and Tad Nichols. Narrated by Winston Hibler. Animation effects by Joshua Meador, John Hench, and Art Riley. Music by Paul J. Smith. Orchestrations by Edward H. Plumb. Edited by Norman Palmer. Special processes by Ubi Iwerks. Sound direction by C.O. Slyfield. Sound recorded by Harold J. Steck.

Further reading

Gartley, Lynn and Leebron, Elizabeth, *Walt Disney: A Guide to References and Resources*, Boston: G.K. Hall, 1979.

Jackson, Kathy Merlock, *Walt Disney: A Bio-Bibliography*, Westport, CT: Greenwood Press, 1993.

King, Margaret J., 'The Audience in the Wilderness: The Disney Nature Films', *Journal of Popular Film and Television* 24, no. 2, summer 1996: 60–9.

Maltin, Leonard, *The Disney Films*, New York: Bonanza Books, 1973.

Schickel, Richard, *The Disney Version: The Life, Times, Art and Commerce of Walt Disney*, New York: Simon & Schuster, 1968.

Wasko, Janet, *Understanding Disney: The Manufacture of Fantasy*, Malden, ME: Blackwell Publishers, 2001.

Watts, Steven, *The Magic Kingdom: Walt Disney and the American Way of Life*, New York: Houghton Mifflin, 1997.

Ljubic, Vesna

Vesna Ljubic is one of the most important woman filmmakers in Bosnia and Herzegovina. Her style can be characterized as poetic realism. From the beginning of her career, she has argued for an author's approach in her cinematic work. She writes the scripts for all of her films and often works with the same crew. She tries to remain faithful to her own poetic style of expression, regardless of the dominant trends in documentary and cinema. Devoting roughly five years to each of her films, going deeply into the core of the theme, she takes a contemplative approach and adopts a personally relevant point of view. Ljubic insists on expressing authentic and genuine emotions via her treatment of her film heroes. With a unique sense of humour, in which a specific Balkan wisdom is imbedded, Ljubic touches on the lives of common people: their poverty, their endurance despite oppression, and their negotiations of the relationship between the sexes. Ljubic portrays her female characters with depth, nuance, and understanding. By applying a sophisticated, often surrealist artistic approach, the stories of ordinary people are transformed into dreamlike tales.

Ljubic began making documentaries in 1970, while studying in Rome. As a student, Ljubic assisted Frederico Fellini, who had a great influence on her development and her cinematic language. This is especially noticeable in her later feature projects Defiant Delta (1980) and The Last Switchman of the Narrow Gauge Railway (1987), the former shot in Herzegovina and the latter in Bosnia. Both of them are inspired by the difficult lives of village people during a time of political and social changes.

Ljubic does not follow the two dominant cinematic trends of the former Yugoslavia: the avant-garde movement known as Black Wave, which produces political, polemical films, and the mainstream practice of partisan or other conformist films.

Although Ljubic made a series of documentaries during the 1970s, she received sustained attention for the first time with the television film Simcha (1971), a fiction project based on the life of Jews in Bosnia. It was proclaimed Sarajevo television's Best Film of the Year and purchased by numerous Western European broadcasters, which at the time was quite rare for socialist Yugoslavia.

An especially intriguing aspect of Ljubic's films is the manner in which she combines documentary and fiction, as well as tragedy and comedy. This is especially successfully done in her half-hour semi-documentary The Illusionists (1991), made on the eve of the war in former Yugoslavia. The film tells the story of a poor man who believes that the only possible way to overcome the difficulties in his life is to perform illusions. Ljubic dramatized certain scenes according to her understanding of the man's real family lifestyle, while anticipating the upcoming downfall of Yugoslavia through the illusions of the hero.

Before the fall of Yugoslavia and the war in Bosnia, Ljubic spent a few months in India, where she made three documentary films inspired by the spirituality of the local people. Without any narrative, these films are completely driven by Ljubic's personal impressions of the people of South India. Unfortunately, all the material shot in India was destroyed during the shelling of Sarajevo.

For Ljubic, even straightforward war documentary is not meant to transmit only information. In her film Ecce homo/Behold the Man (1994), made during the siege of Sarajevo, she decided to shape her impressions of destruction in her own, cinematically poetic and uplifting style. There are no words, only fragments of different prayers (of four ethnic groups living in Sarajevo) and sounds of shelling, an approach underlining the director's conviction that image is more effective than the word. The film is shot during two years of the four-year period in which Sarajevo is completely isolated, cut off from water, food, and electricity, and suffers continuous heavy shelling. Paid only with bread and cigarettes, the whole crew takes a big risk shooting, making the first war documentary on 35mm at the time. Interpolating dramatized scenes between sensitive documentary material reporting death and murder, Ljubic expresses her own meditative state in which she concludes that death is the only way out in war-torn Sarajevo.

Ljubic's most recent film also refers to the consequences of the war. Adio Kerida (2001) is a documentary that follows the traces of the Sephardim community in Sarajevo, a community that almost completely disappeared. Structuring the work as the search for a person who died several years ago, Ljubic discovers in her own lyrical style the rich and beautiful life of the Jewish people during the twentieth century. The film ends with a marvellous scene in which a choir sings at one of the oldest Jewish cemeteries in Eastern Europe. The extinction of the Jewish people and lifestyle in Sarajevo is reflected in their ancient, now abandoned and desecrated, burial ground.

Remaining independent of any political or ethnic orientation, Ljubic's films are usually first acknowledged abroad, to be recognized at home only later. Nevertheless, Ljubic remains faithful to her own approach and specific film style, for which she has received numerous awards.

RADA SESIC

See also: Yugoslavia (former)

Biography

Born in Bosnia and Herzegovina in 1938. After obtaining the Bachelor of Arts Degree from the Department of Philosophy at Sarajevo University, studied film direction at the Centro Sperimentale in Rome, Italy. For three decades, worked for the Drama Department at Radio Sarajevo. Later became editor-in-chief, overseeing hundreds of programmes. Has served on numerous juries at film, television, and radio festivals around the world.

Selected films

1970 Putovanje/Journey
1970 Smrt se otplacuje ziveci/Death is paid off Through Living (documentary)
1971 Halil Tikvesa
1971 Simcha (fiction)
1980 Prkosna delta/Defiant Delta (fiction)
1987 Posljednji skretnicar uskotracnog kolosijeka/The Last Switchman of the Narrow Gauge Railway (fiction)
1991 Iluzionisti/The Illusionists (semi-documentary)
1994 Ecce homo-Evo covjeka/Behold the Man (documentary)
1999 Sveti prah Indije/Sacred Dust of India (documentary)
1999 Lotus/Lotus Flowers (documentary)
2001 Adio Kerida (documentary)

Further reading

Chatterjee, Vidyarthy, *Terrors of War, Yearnings for Peace*, Calcutta Festival Bulletin, 1999.

Crnkovic, Gordana P., 'Ecce Homo', review, *Film Quarterly*, summer 1999, Berkeley, CA: University of California Press.

Sesic, Rada, 'The camera as magnifying glass', *DOX Documentary Magazine*, 1994.

——'Filmer pour vivre a Sarajevo', *Cine Bulletin*, 1994.

Loach, Ken

Ken Loach is recognised widely as one of Britain's most important filmmakers. Born in 1936, by 2005 Loach had directed forty-five documentaries, television series, and feature films—about one per year since the acclaimed Z Cars (three episodes directed in 1964). His notable successes include Cathy Come Home (1966), Kes (1969), Days of Hope (1975), Riff-Raff (1990), Ladybird Ladybird (1994), Land and Freedom (1995), My Name is Joe (1998), Bread and Roses (2000), The Navigators (2001), Sweet Sixteen (2002), and the UK segment of September 11 (2002). The right-wing magazine *Economist* observed sarcastically in 2002 that in Loach the left-leaning *Le Monde* 'and indeed the rest of Europe' had discovered 'the heir to Dickens', that 'Europe's cultural elite has appointed him the supreme chronicler of contemporary Britain', and that Loach 'is also big in the Netherlands and Germany' (*Economist* 2002). However, it diminishes Loach's following in Britain as merely 'select', stating that 'his unrelenting hostility to capitalism [and]

Thatcherism […] had made his more recent work predictable' (*Economist* 2002).

Loach's films can be divided 'into two broad categories—intimate family dramas which illuminate the politics of every day life and more militant films determined to skewer both the forces of reaction and the reformist wing of the labor movement [… Families are] where most drama happens in our lives' (Ryan and Porton 1998: 5). Although many of his films are located in the north of England, Loach is concerned with issues of social class rather than locality (Ryan and Porton 1998: 5). The naturalistic treatment and subject matter of Loach's films de-differentiate Loach's documentaries from his feature films. Loach is widely acknowledged for films of revolutionary bent that confront human despair and communal and familial decline, and that portray the bureaucratic heartlessness and ineptitude of those official social and political institutions that are the agents of human misery and degradation. However, his stories demonstrate his view that it is not only the powerful external institutional forces that destroy social identity and well-being but also betrayal by one's own side, as in his 1995 documentary drama, Land and Freedom, about idealism and betrayal in the Spanish Civil War. For Loach 'the innocents become the victims of their own idealisms' (McKnight 1997: 8).

Loach's sustained criticism encompasses the inflexibility of 'state-administered social services, […] the medical and psychiatric professions, the police, the courts and […] the law, the press, the military and the various forms of state security' (McKnight 1997: 2), and the British state education system. As such, Loach is a political filmmaker. He believes that 'you shouldn't become a filmmaker unless you have something to say' (London Weekend Television 1993). Loach's Kes, about a working-class boy who is a failure at school but who catches and trains a kestrel, has been compared with Grange Hill (Jones and Davies 2001), the popular, long-running BBC TV children's drama series, which was set in a London comprehensive school and which is widely recognised and criticised for validating the culture of British working-class children (Horsfield 1982). By combining social realism and the form of the seamless classical realist text, Grange Hill, as 'macrodrama', generated a new category, 'progressive classical realism', where the characters can be read both as participants in a narrative and as voices or discourses of various social and political institutions and their controlling agencies. Many of Loach's films, such as Kes, may be theorised in the same terms as reformist or revolutionary in content, but not all can be so described: Petley warns 'against the dangers of using the label ['documentary drama' …] to obscure important formal differences between individual works […] In Diary of a Young Man […] there are echoes of the French New Wave, and especially of Godard [… We] find all sorts of diverse elements cropping up in Cathy Come Home', which is realist in a very different way to Days of Hope (Petley 1997: 51).

Loach's low-budget radical films attack the capitalist system and the reformist element of the Left and are characterised by a naturalistic aesthetic that was conceived as a departure from the 'tedious linear narrative' of the classical realist American technicolour film. Loach also acknowledges the influence of the 'street reality' of postwar Italian neorealism on his filmmaking. Tony Garnett, Loach's political and aesthetic soulmate and one-time collaborator on the BBC series The Wednesday Play, said, '[W]e used fiction to try to tell the truth [… We] wanted to make stories that got the same responses as when you saw the news, because [The Wednesday Play] came after the news and we wanted to be seen as almost part of the news' (London Weekend Television 1993). 'If Loach could shoot a film without a camera, he would' (Eaude 1995: 49).

The Thatcher-Major period of British politics, 'usually considered the most dismal epoch of the twentieth century by British radicals, engendered Loach's most productive and artistically satisfying period' (Ryan and Porton 1998: 22). Interviewed for a documentary about himself by one-time colleague Melvyn Bragg, Loach said, 'The first Thatcherite onslaught was like being knocked over by a tidal wave […] Documentary provided a quicker response to Thatcher than film. Documentary is more like a pamphlet [… and is] an appropriate form for the time to capture what was happening' (London Weekend Television 1993). Loach is highly critical of the mass media, including popular cinema, and he states that the 'majority of films have a right-wing sub-text' (Sterritt 1998: B3). Loach is concerned that the media express the ideas of our age in very concrete ways (Papadopolous 1998), but for him the media 'is about reassurance and not asking the key questions at the key times […]

It's about social control [… Their] hypocrisy says we are open to all points of view' (London Weekend Television 1993). To Loach the institutions of the press and broadcasting protect and propagate the hegemonic ideologies of the ruling and owning class and he believes that the future healthy society should have media executives who are responsible downwards and that news should be produced by democratic collectives of journalists and broadcasters (Papadopolous 1998). Loach locates many of his stories in the working class because not only is that where the raw material of drama is found, but also in the working class resides the 'progressive element. That's where the engine for change will be. It won't be brought to us as a gift from above, but by the work of people from below' (Ryan and Porton 1998: 24). Loach stated, 'The future lies in common ownership and democratic control, and a freedom from the market—not of the market—but from the exploitation of the market' (London Weekend Television 1993). His work is 'often labelled Trotskyist, but is equally amenable to positions espoused by anti-Leninist Marxists and anarcho-syndicalists' (Ryan and Porton 1998: 1). Loach's films have at times been cut or refused broadcast. Having commissioned four fifty-minute films by Loach, including The Red and the Blue (1983) and Questions of Leadership (1983), which were subtitled 'Problems of democracy in trade unions: some views from the front line', Channel 4, its charter for alternative kinds off programming notwithstanding, refused to broadcast them. Of the protracted and dispiriting process of fighting the ban, Loach expressed to *The Guardian* what he felt was the unspoken reason for the censorship:

> Working class people are allowed on television as long as they fit the stereotype that producers have of them. Workers can appear pathetic in their ignorance and poverty, apathetic to parliamentary politics, or aggressive on the picket line. But let them make a serious political analysis based on their own experiences and in their own language, then keep them off the air.
>
> (Petley 1997: 107–8)

Loach tempers the revolutionary idealism in his films with the pragmatic realities of everyday politics, and this structure provides the dramatic human elements of his narratives: 'If there is a central theme that unites Loach's work, it would be the betrayal of hope […] For, in Loach's world, the innocents become the victims of their own idealism' (McKnight 1997: 7), as, for example, in The Rank and File and Days of Hope (striking workers betrayed by their union leadership and the Trade Union Council), Hidden Agenda (workers' political aspirations lead to their own deaths or the deaths of others), The Big Flame (striking dockworkers betrayed by their leadership), and Land and Freedom (antiFascist volunteers in the Spanish Civil War) (McKnight 1997: 8).

The distinctive subgenre of Loach's work, whether in his documentaries or feature films, is 'documentary drama', which may be defined as dramatic fictions with a documentary aesthetic or 'look'. Loach's preferred creative method is to take a strong dramatic story and then to place great emphasis on casting people, including both actors and locals who are nonactors, whose social class and life experiences are directly relevant to the story and to the characters they play. Loach said, 'A kind of natural eloquence is quite important […] Again, it's a class thing. Working class men and women will often speak with a natural eloquence and rhythm' (Ryan and Porton 1998: 6). Loach invariably seeks to have the audience identify with the screen characters and can easily allocate more time to casting than to location shooting. He casts not only from actors and non-actors but from other skilled performers such as entertainers and cabaret artists. Loach regards the premeditated script, especially the spoken words, as highly malleable, and the look of social realism for which Loach has become internationally known greatly depends on his painstaking casting of people who then produce, often ad lib, the kind of reality he is seeking to portray. This method has proved highly successful in creating a succession of vivid and memorable impressions of British society, for example, in Cathy Come Home (1966), Kes (1969), and Ladybird Ladybird (1994).

However, the resulting reality effect of Loach's films has often caused alarm among the conservative about the possibility that Loach's audiences will be misled: 'The essence of the problem is that although Loach is a fiction director, he has extraordinary power to coax convincing performances from inexperienced actors, and it is hard to accept their pain is simulated. It feels like fly-on-the-wall documentary, rather than something invented' (quoted in McKnight 1997: 45–6). Such conservative concerns are common in certain kinds of media effects studies, as they assume simplistically that programme content directly determines the effect on the viewer. This fear of political influence also assumes that 'straight' documentaries are not also careful constructions, which is far from the case. Claims that Loach's films deceive the gullible and politically naïve viewing public inflect the more hostile critical literature on Loach but are yet to be supported by grass-roots empirical or ethnographic audience research.

Claims of 'undue' politicising in his films have to take into account the specificities of each film, however, for the films vary in significant ways. For example, the form and structure of Cathy Come Home mix realisms and constitute 'a series of forms of address which is actually quite disjointed and disorienting', and the film is therefore unlikely to dupe or mislead its audience (Petley 1997: 52–3). Loach noted that although questions were asked in parliament after the broadcast of Cathy Come Home on British television, nothing was really done about the problems of the homeless in Britain (London Weekend Television 1993).

Loach's films are embedded in the vigorous and continuing theoretic debate on the nature and foundations of realism in cinema and television. This debate seeks to clarify both differences and common ground between various cinematic styles or aesthetics of realism, including neorealism, cinéma vérité, classical realism, progressive classical realism, documentary, macrodrama, social realism, naturalism, and so on. McKnight (1997: 60) states that Loach's films 'are naturalist'; the aesthetic of naturalism reproduces the surface appearance of reality, whereas the classical realist text can betoken reality without the impression of verisimilitude that is the hallmark of naturalism. Petley cites John Caughie's warning about the imprecise and decontextualised formalism in writings about naturalism and the need for debate (Petley 1997: 51).

Through decades of political and social change in Britain, throughout the move to the right under Thatcher and Blair, Loach has not deviated from his left ideals and remains 'an icon of political filmmaking' (Neve 1998: 52). Loach is 'unquestionably one of Britain's most important filmmakers [...] Kes (1969), Family Life (1971), and Ladybird, Ladybird (1994) [...] are justly regarded as milestones of British social realism' (Porton 1996: 30).

BRUCE HORSFIELD

Selected films

1966 Cathy Come Home
1969 Kes
1975 Days of Hope
1983 Questions of Leadership
1983 The Red and the Blue
1990 Riff-Raff
1994 Ladybird Ladybird
1995 Land and Freedom
1998 My Name is Joe
2000 Bread and Roses
2001 The Navigators
2002 Sweet Sixteen
2002 September 11 (UK segment)

Further reading

Eaude, Michael, 'Gracias, Mr Loach', *New Statesman and Society* 8, no. 372, September 29, 1995: 48–9.

Economist, 'Ken Who?' *Economist* 362, 52–6, January 19, 2002.

Horsfield, Bruce, 'BBC TV's 'Grange Hill': Production/Audience/Ideology', unpublished PhD thesis, University of Exeter, 1982.

Jones, Ken and Davies, Hannah, 'Representing Education 1969–80: Notes on "Kes" and "Grange Hill"', *History of Education* 30, no. 2, 2001: 141–51.

London Weekend Television, *Ken Loach*, 1993.

McKnight, George (ed.), *Agent of Challenge and Defiance: The Films of Ken Loach*, Trowbridge: Flicks Books, 1997.

Neve, Brian, 'Agent of Challenge and Defiance: The Films of Ken Loach', book review, *Cineaste* 23, no. 3, April 1998: 51–2.

Papadopolous, Theodoros, 'On Media, Culture and the Prospects for a New Library Project', *December*, 1998.

Petley, Julian, 'Factual Fictions and Fictional Fallacies: Ken Loach's Documentary Dramas', in George McKnight (ed.), *Agent of Challenge and Defiance*, Trowbridge: Flicks Books, 1997.

——'Ken Loach and questions of censorship', in George McKnight (ed.), *Agent of Challenge and Defiance*, Trowbridge: Flicks Books, 1997.

Porton, Richard, 'The Revolution Betrayed: An Interview with Ken Loach', *Cineaste* 22, no. 1, April 1996: 30–1.

Ryan, Susan and Porton, Richard, 'The Politics of Everyday Life: An Interview with Ken Loach', *Cineaste* 24, no. 1, 15 December 15, 1998: 22–7.

Sterritt, David, 'Director Ken Loach: Voice for More Than Popcorn and Profits', *Christian Science Monitor* 90, no. 153, July, 3, 1998: B3.

London Can Take It

(UK, Watt, Jennings, 1940)

World War II was a remarkable period in British history and cinema. In Prime Minister Churchill's famous phrase, this was the nation's 'finest hour' and, by critical consent, it was something of a golden age for British film. At the heart of a new, mature, and socially realistic cinema was the documentary movement, which produced a number of classic studies of Britain at war. One of the most celebrated of these was London Can Take It, an account of the German blitz on the country's capital in 1940.

The film is narrated by the American war correspondent Quentin Reynolds. It begins with a series of images of London and its citizens as they prepare for the trials that the night will bring. The duties of Air Raid Precaution are carried on and queues form outside the shelters. Against images of ominous skies the drone of enemy planes begins to be heard, searchlights blink into life; anti-aircraft guns flash and bark into the darkness and fire-fighting teams tackle burning buildings. The next morning the damage is surveyed, streets are strewn with rubble, and shops have had their windows blown out, but the people struggle back to their workplaces. The emergency services set about their grim and dangerous work and the clearing-up operation commences. The King and Queen inspect the bomb damage, demonstrate their solidarity with the people, and talk reassuringly with Londoners. Reynolds concludes with an appropriate upbeat commentary about the unconquerable spirit of the city, played over an image of the statue of Richard the Lionheart with sword raised.

London Can Take It was originally conceived as a propaganda film, with the title of London Front, for exhibition in the neutral United States. The use of Reynolds, a well-known columnist for *Collier's Weekly*, helped to provide identification and objectivity for American audiences, and he worked again with director Harry Watt on a later Blitz documentary film, Christmas Under Fire (1941). The production was reassigned to the General Post Office (GPO) Film Unit from a newsreel company, Gaumont British News, which had seemingly taken an overly direct approach to its subject and would have proved too alarmist as propaganda. The official filmmakers were more attuned to the requirements of the Ministry of Information (MOI) and proved subtler in handling the sensitive material. While quietly asserting his objectivity, Reynolds, reinforced by the imagery, makes a passionate defence of civilisation and democracy as embodied in the British, while constantly exposing the cowardly, barbarous, and totalitarian nature of National Socialism. Language is crucial in this: Londoners are 'the greatest civilian army ever assembled' in 'heroic' defence of democratic freedoms; the German bombers are 'creatures of the night', a faceless and, by implication, cowardly enemy, who 'scurry away' at the coming of dawn.

The Blitz was the British name for the Luftwaffe's sustained night attacks on British cities from August 1940 to May 1941. While of some military significance, targeting docks, power stations, and important centres of communication, these largely aimed to terrorise the population and to exhaust morale. By the spring of 1941 the attacks had killed more than forty-three thousand civilians, injured a further one hundred and thirty-nine thousand, and devastated more than one million homes. London Can Take It is the outstanding documentary record of the attack against the metropolitan area and provides many seminal images of destruction and defiance that have passed into myth. A perfect example is the use of the dome of St Paul's Cathedral, which appears as a motif throughout the film. The opening credits play over its image and its placement in subsequent shots, miraculously undamaged amidst the carnage, evokes a potent symbol of defiance and the rightness of the national cause. Other shots and sequences both reinforce these values and resonate with the spirit of the People's War: householders calmly gathering their possessions into any available transport to move on to safer areas; bombed out store fronts sardonically declared as 'more open than usual'; and heavy rescue teams saving distressed cats from bombed out buildings. It is a powerful impression of the British character as stoical, courageous, civilised, self-deprecating, and indomitable.

The question of authorship is a prominent critical issue with regard to London Can Take It. There has been a tendency to attribute the achievements of the film to Humphrey Jennings, the most venerated of the wartime documentarists, with a corresponding undervaluation of the contribution of Harry Watt. It now seems clear that Watt fulfilled a supervisory role over the production, while Jennings was responsible for the remarkable imagery through leading the camera-crew out on location. For a long time, Stewart McAllister was the 'forgotten man' at the documentary film movement, but his monumental labours in editing London Can Take It and the unique care and precision he devoted to marrying sound and image have now been established beyond doubt. Perfectly in accord with the ethos of the time, London Can Take It was the product of collaborative effort, brought to realisation through the skill, effort, and dedication of a team of talented documentary filmmakers at the height of their powers.

A slightly shorter version of the film was released in Britain as part of the MOI's short film programme. It was titled Britain Can Take It, as the authorities were sensitive to criticisms of selectivity and were keen to emphasise that 'the film is representative of what is happening in every other British city and town, where resistance to intense aerial attack and powers of endurance are every bit as heroic'. According to reports prepared by Mass-Observation, the film was an overwhelming success for a short documentary and highly praised. There does seem, though, that a residue of hurt remained, as an independently produced film of the Manchester Blitz in December 1940 mischievously went under the name of Manchester Took It, Too (1941).

ALAN BURTON

See also: Jennings, Humphrey; Watt, Harry

London Can Take It (UK, GPO Film Unit, 1940). Directed by Harry Watt and Humphrey Jennings. Edited by Stewart McAllister.

Further reading

Chapman, James, *The British at War. Cinema, State and Propaganda, 1939–45*, London: I.B. Tauris, 1998.

Coultass, Clive, *Images for Battle. British Film and the Second World War, 1939–45*, London: AUP, 1989.

Sussex, Elizabeth, *The Rise and Fall of British Documentary*, Berkeley, CA: University of California Press, 1975.

Vaughan, Dai, *Portrait of an Invisible Man. The Working Life of Stewart McAllister, Film Editor*, London: BFI, 1983.

Watt, Harry, *Don't Look at the Camera*, London: Paul Elek, 1974.

Lonely Boy

(Canada, Koenig, 1961)

Wolf Koening and Roman Kroitor's raw, unscripted portrayal of twenty-year-old pop sensation Paul Anka stands as a prototypical example of the National Film Board (NFB) of Canada's style of cinéma vérité. Lonely Boy, a twenty-seven-minute, black-and-white film, made with a 16mm handheld camera and a portable sound recording system, displays all the major stylistic elements of cinéma vérité.

Some critics, notably Richard Barsam and Eric Barnouw, draw a distinction between direct cinema, which originated at the NFB, and cinéma vérité. They reserve the French term to designate the pronounced role the director plays in provoking the subject to reveal its 'true essence', whereas in direct cinema the director aims to avoid intrusion. However, this nuance, essentially a matter of degree, has been lost in general usage and the terms have coalesced to describe a rough, handheld style of filmmaking made possible by technological advances in the 1950s. The advent of lightweight, battery-powered cameras and portable sync-sound equipment extended the filmmaker's reach into more intimate quarters. Maneuverability and spontaneity promised greater authenticity.

Koening and Kroitor sought to capture Paul Anka in a medley of unscripted situations. The subject's true essence, they believed, resided in the mundane, unguarded moment. Although given the subject, the mundane in Lonely Boy is decidedly extraordinary. Anka, an Ottawa native, was the first Canadian artist to crack the American pop charts, performing his own material. Kroitor said he wanted to present Anka as a 'tragic figure'. The film takes its name from Anka's 1959 hit, 'Lonely Boy'.

Produced by Unit B, the NFB's most experimental division, Lonely Boy was the last of the short television documentaries broadcast between 1958 and 1961 under The Candid Eye program title. The aim of Candid Eye films, said Koening, was to 'show them on television to millions of people and make them see that life is true, fine, and full of meaning'. All the Candid Eye films were unscripted. This necessitated shooting more footage and spending more time on editing, where narrative structure would take shape.

The most arresting scenes in Lonely Boy involve seemingly marred footage that exposes the filmmakers' presence off camera. These 'out-takes', however, appear to be deliberate attempts to provoke the subjects into self-revelation, the defining characteristic of cinéma vérité. The first such moment occurs with Anka running late for an Atlantic City performance. Surprised by the filmmakers' presence as he bursts into his dressing room, Anka stares hard at the camera for a moment, then tells his entourage to 'just forget they're [the film crew] even there'. Koening and Kroitor thus shred the veil between camera and audience, acknowledging that the camera exerts a pull on its subjects. Anka, stripped to his underwear, hastens to dress while bantering with his drummer and manager. Does the film capture the true Paul Anka, or rather Paul Anka playing to the camera?

Lonely Boy's most telling moments occur inside New York's famed Copacabana in the interplay between Anka and the nightclub's owner, Jules Podell. The imbalance in power between Anka and Podell, a show business czar whose patronage is crucial to Anka's performing career, is the 'essence of truth' captured in mundane details. As he wends his way through the kitchen to the stage, Anka greets the well-wishing Podell with an embrace and a kiss. Noticing the older man's unlighted cigarette, Anka lights it. Unit B's Candid Eye films had rejected scripts, presumably as dishonest. Yet Koening and Kroitor unabashedly enlist Podell's help to stage a scene: 'You want the waiters to move around a little bit?' Podell asks the man behind the camera. 'OK. Bruno', he orders the maitre d', 'tell the waiters to … like move around'. The request made of Podell appears to have been a ruse used to reveal character, that is, the boss exercising power. (If the hustle and bustle of waiters Podell commanded was filmed, it was never used.) As the Podell interview progresses, the questions coming off camera, Podell asks, 'Is it alright if I light the cigar?' The filmmakers' response is audible: 'Oh, yeah. Please.'

Building on these self-referential pieces, the defining scene in Lonely Boy is the request that the directors make of Podell and Anka to reenact a kiss. Anka's manager, Irvin Feld, is seated at a booth with Podell when Anka arrives to pay homage to 'Uncle Julie' on the last night of his three-week engagement: 'Surprise, I got something for you'. Cufflinks that match Podell's ring. Anka proffers a second gift: 'I promised you something for your office. It's a picture of me'. Podell acknowledges the tribute—'that's beautiful'—leans over and kisses Anka on the cheek. 'Will you do the kiss again?' asks one of the directors. The request draws forced, prolonged laughter from Anka. Podell, hand to ear, affects not having heard the question: 'No, I think you just want us to do it [inaudible]'. 'I'll tell you what happened, the camera just moved a bit', the director entreats. Anka leans over and kisses Podell's cheek: 'Thank you, Uncle Julie.'

Lonely Boy demonstrates the power of cinéma vérité's 'truth' while exhausting its syntax. However, the film uses more than one technique and contains more than one truth. Using the traditional journalistic interview, Koening and Kroitor capture the testimony of the eyewitness by permitting subjects to shape their own stories in their own words. How does Anka explain the hordes of screaming teenage girls? 'Sex. They like to feel if I'm singing about a lonely boy, they're the girl I'm singing about.' Anka has excellent features, according to his manager: 'His eyes are great. He has a great mouth. And it's no secret last year we had a plastic surgery job on his nose.'

Ostensibly about the drive for success and the cultural phenomenon of idolatry, Lonely Boy is also a wry comment on cinematic truth. Playful and self-referential, the film is unafraid to bare and scrutinize its own assumptions. In perfectly splicing technique to subject, Koening and Kroitor created a stylistic masterpiece that endures as the lucid documentation of a key stage in the history of popular culture.

TONY OSBORNE

See also: Koenig, Wolf

Lonely Boy (Canada, Koenig, 1961, 27 mins). Distributed by the National Film Board of Canada. Produced by Tom Daly and Roman Kroiter. Directed by Wolf Koenig and Roman Kroiter. Cinematography by Wolf Koenig (uncredited). Edited by Guy L. Cote and John Spotton. Sound by Ron Alexander, Marcel Carrière, and Kathleen Shannon.

Further reading

Barnouw, Eric, *Documentary: A History of Non-Fiction Film*, New York: Oxford University Press, 1974.

Barsam, Richard, *Nonfiction Film: A Critical History*, Bloomington, IN: Indiana University Press, 1992.

Bochner, Sally, 'National Film Board of Canada: Four Decades of Documentaries and Animation', in *The Museum of Modern Art Circulating Film Library Catalog*, Ann Arbor, MI: Edwards Brothers, 1984.

Gittings, Christopher E., *Canadian National Cinema*, London: Routledge, 2002.

Jacobs, Lewis, 'Documentary Becomes Engaged and Verite', in Lewis Jacobs (ed.), *The Documentary Tradition*, New York: W.W. Norton, 1979.

Jones, D.B., 'The Canadian Film Board Unit B', in alan Rosenthal (ed.), *New Challenges for Documentary*, Berkeley, CA: University of California Press, 1988.

Leach, Jim and Sloniowski, Jeannette (eds), *Candid Eyes: Essays on Canadian Documentaries*, Toronto: University of Toronto Press, 2003.

McIntosh, David, 'Realites Incertaines: La Documentaire 1939–92', in Sylvain Garel and Andre Paquet (eds), *Les Cinemas du Canada*, Quebec: Centre Georges Pompidou, 1992.

Long Tan: The True Story

(Australia, Horsfield, 1992)

Bruce Horsfield's self-proclaimed 'revisionist' Vietnam War documentary memorialises and celebrates a brief but bloody battle in South Vietnam on August 18, 1966. Long Tan (a small village near a major Australian Army Base) gave its name to what the film calls 'a rallying point for Australia's 50,000 Vietnam veterans'. Yet it was not until almost thirty years after the event that this detailed and comprehensive expository film was made. Australian fictional films (quintessentially, The Odd Angry Shot, 1979) and later television miniseries (Sword of Honour, 1986; Vietnam: The Mini Series, 1987) had seen Australian servicemen/women and Australian society generally, as complicit victims in a pointless, degrading US Cold War adventure. Images of helicopter gunships over muddy jungles filled Australian screens in the aftermath of the US defeat in Vietnam. That Australia had lost more than five hundred soldiers in support of America made memories of the 'dirty little war' hard to celebrate in a country that had always seen itself as innocently supporting King and Empire throughout the century. 'Vietnam vets' suffered guilt and shame that were frequently portrayed by the local media as a stain on the legendary reputation of 'returned soldiers' from the World War I Gallipoli campaign or from the Pacific theatre of World War II.

Although an Academy Award had been won by Australian cameraman Damien Parer for footage of heroism and comradeship in World War II New Guinea, it was the domestic medium of Australian television news that had chronicled the seemingly unending skirmishes between 'our diggers' (soldiers) and the VC (Viet Cong), as well as the massive US presence and (occasionally) the horrors of napalm deaths among the Vietnamese villagers whom Australia was supposedly attempting to help the Americans to 'liberate'. As in the United States, mass protests against Australian involvement and against conscription ('the draft', as it became known during the Vietnam War) also counterpointed the apparently pointless suffering ritualistically broadcast in the nightly television bulletins.

Long Tan: The True Story should be seen against this background. The documentary deliberately sets out to narrate and to reflect on the military significance of a particular battle. Although formally conservative (voice-over narration, archival war footage, interviews with participants in the battle and with war historians), it showed, for perhaps the first time on national television, ordinary middle-aged Australian men reflecting not just on military tactics, but on the tragedies, mistakes, and sheer good luck that befell them as reluctant Australian fighters. Significantly, the film includes interviews with similarly aging Vietnamese soldiers and other survivors of the combat, humanising them and creating empathy as it does so. So, through celebrating both the Vietnamese people's resilience and the signal victory of what they term 'the Australian mercenaries', the film works to counteract thirty years of guilty media reporting and analysis of Australia's involvement in Vietnam.

Long Tan presents villagers and soldiers explaining that their forces outnumbered the Australians four to one, that the VC were fighting 'a people's war' because they 'wanted to liberate the people from the Saigon government and provide land'. The legitimacy of the Vietnamese struggle is never questioned, yet the ANZAC (Australian and New Zealand soldiers) victory is celebrated in tones of quiet triumphalism, in voice-over:

> The battle of Long Tan demolished forever the myth of Viet Cong invincibility, and never again did the Viet Cong seriously challenge the Australians.

As it shows the battle removed from its politically compromised history, focusing on the events and participants and presenting 'real' people's recollected stories, the film has attracted both criticism and praise. However, its achievement is that it can claim to have been significant in reinserting Australian imaginings of 'Vietnam' into the broad museum chronicle of the Australian armed services. The connotations of the guilt-laden term Vietnam shifted as a result of fact-based documentaries such as Long Tan. (It is important to remember that by the 1990s many thousands of [South] Vietnamese migrants and refugees had settled in Australia.)

The film uses words not frequently associated with Australian or New Zealand (fellow allies) recollections of the war. It speaks of a battle 'victory' in the context of the larger, humiliating American and allied defeat. Above all, it constructs the psychologically and numerically modest 'diggers' as continuing, rather than betraying, the ANZAC tradition that Australia sees as a central tenet of its national ideology.

Long Tan: The True Story was broadcast nationally by SBS TV in 1994, 1995, and 1997. It is estimated that up to two million viewers (ten percent of the Australian population) may have seen the documentary. In 1997 the film was acquired by the Australian ITS Pan-Asia Satellite and Cable Network, for broadcast in thirty-three Asia-Pacific countries.

PHILLIP BELL

Long Tan: The True Story (Australia, Communications Futures, 1993, 54 mins). Distributed by Film Australia. Produced, scripted, and directed Bruce Horsfield. Edited by Warren Hedges. New Zealand unit director: Tom Duncan. Commentary: Jim Downes; Lyndal Vozzo; Bradley White. Filmed in Australia, New Zealand, and Vietnam.

Further reading

Bell, Philip, 'Remembering Vietnam', *Current Affairs Bulletin* 65, no. 2, 1988: 16–22.

Bertrand, Ina, 'From Silence to Reconciliation: The Representation of the Vietnam War in Australian Film and Television', *Historical Journal of Film, Radio and Television* 8, no. 1, 1988: 75–89.

Moran, Albert, 'Constructing the Nation: Institutional Documentary Since 1945', in A. Moran and T. O'Regan (eds), *The Australian Screen*, Ringwood, Australia: Penguin Books, 1989: 149–71.

Longinotto, Kim

Since the early 1980s British documentarian Kim Longinotto has been making films that have enjoyed regular airings on BBC television and at film festivals in the United States and Europe. Her most recent features have brought her international acclaim and recognition as a filmmaker whose production style imbues the observational style of 'classic' cinéma vérité with a feminist commitment to social change and advocacy. Her films have won awards for their ability to communicate 'universal' insights in an effort to improve local social conditions for women and girls.

There are two significant features of a Longinotto documentary: collaborative filmmaking with an all-female crew and a focus on women's positions in sex-segregated societies. Longinotto eschews voice-overs, preferring subtitles to translate subjects' dialogue. Although she sometimes includes interview footage, the interlocutor almost always remains out of frame. Although her collaborators are not 'native' informants, they typically enjoy a greater familiarity (language, law, customs) with the local populations that the films take as their subjects. Such intimacy allows Longinotto, who always serves as director of photography, to maintain her distance: 'What I love about making documentaries is that I can disappear. It is getting involved in a situation and letting it speak for itself' (Brockes 2000).

For Longinotto, 'outsider' status is an asset because in these pervasively patriarchal societies 'outsiders [...] are merely the future come early' (Brockes 2000). An all-female crew may face certain prejudices, but they are also allowed an uncommon level of access by 'lightly breaking the rules just standing there and assuming it's all right and seeing if you can get away with it' (Teasley 2000). Through her work, Longinotto directs the viewer's attention to subjects who challenge status quo rules in a similar way: subjects often presumed by mainstream press to suffer patriarchal oppression in silence.

Longinotto finds her motivation in working for women's social progress, giving those who have been spoken for a forum to make their own voices heard. In discussing her examination of a Tehran family court in Divorce Iranian Style, she acknowledges that her personal investment shapes her documentary philosophy: 'We're proud they [critics] say we're on the side of the women, because we are. We don't want to be objective. We try to film things as they happen but our emotion is definitely on the side of the women' (Bourke 2001).

Longinotto seeks to educate her audience through the sharing of stories. In particular, she hopes to teach Western viewers about the specifics of women's experiences around the world. This is an education made more compelling in Longinotto's estimation because it is rooted in documentary film's aesthetic and ethical commitments; she explains: 'if you have a story that you can get involved hopefully what's happening is that the audience isn't being told that these people are obviously in a different culture to us, but they have the same emotions as us. A way of getting close to people is through following their stories and getting [emotionally] involved in their stories' (Bourke 2001).

JULES ODENDAHL-JAMES

Biography

Born Kimona Sally-Anne Landseer in London, February 8, 1950. Privileged child of middle-class parents. Spent formative adolescent years at Hampden House, a boarding school in Buckinghamshire, until, at the age of thirteen, she was punished by a two-year stint at Coventry, a half-way house for 'troubled' teenagers, for getting lost on a school field trip. After completing secondary education, spent some time homeless on the streets of London rather than returning to her parents' home. Uncovered an old family name, Longinotto, while making her way across Europe, and which would be the name she would adopt permanently as she entered Essex University to study English literature and writing. An internship doing 'person-on-the-street' interviews for the Lambeth council propelled her towards filmmaking. Instead of pursuing a PhD, enrolled in England's National Film School where she studied camera work and directing. Her first film, Pride of Place, was a scathing critique of her former boarding school, which was closed down in the wake of the film's run. In 1988 formed Twentieth Century Vixen Productions with Claire Hunt, which she now runs alone under the title Vixen Films.

Selected films

1979 Pride of Place: director, cinematographer, producer
1981 Cross and Passion: director (with Claire Pollak), cinematographer, producer
1982 UndeRage: director, cinematographer, producer
1989 Eat the Kimono: director (with Claire Hunt), cinematographer, producer
1990 Hidden Faces: director (with Claire Hunt), cinematographer, producer
1992 The Good Wife of Tokyo: director (with Claire Hunt), cinematographer, producer
1993 Dream Girls: director (with Jano Williams), cinematographer, producer
1995 Shinjuku Boys: director (with Jano Williams), cinematographer, producer
1998 Divorce Iranian Style: director (with Ziba Mir-Hosseini), cinematographer, producer

Further reading

Bourke, Philippa, 'Interview: With Gaea Girls, Kim Longinotto and Jano Williams Hit the Mat', *indieWIRE* 25 April 2001, www.indiewire.com.

Brockes, Emma, 'Silent Witness: Interview with Kim Longinotto', *G2: The Guardian Magazine*, February 11, 2000: 8–9.

Fowler, Catherine, 'The Day I Will Never Forget: An Interview with Kim Longinotto', *Women: A Cultural Review* 15, no. 1, March 2004: 101–7.

Holden, Stephen, 'Having Their Day, or Not, in Court', *The New York Times*, December 9, 1998: E5.

Mitchell, Elvis, 'An Unblinking Eye on a Searing Topic', *The New York Times*, March 29, 2003: D7.

Morrow, Fiona, 'Beyond the Mat', *Sight and Sound* 10, no. 9, September 2000: 38.

n.a., 'Chipping Away at Stereotypes: An Interview with Kim Longinotto and Jano Williams (Gaea Girls)', *DOX: Documentary Film Magazine*, October 31, 2000: 22–3.

Neustatter, Angela, 'Splitting Images', *G2: The Guardian Magazine*, August 23, 1999: 6–7.

Ramsey, Nancy, 'In Africa, Girls Fight a Painful Tradition', *The New York Times*, January 3, 2004: B23.

Teasley, Sarah, 'Interview with Kim Longinotto', *Documentary Box* 16, no. 1 December 2000: 17–27.

Looking for Langston

(UK, Julien, 1989)

Looking for Langston has generated more critical attention than any other work to emerge from the Black British Film movement of the 1980s. Subtitled 'a meditation on Langston Hughes (1902–67) and the Harlem Renaissance', Isaac Julien's elegiac monochrome film examines issues around black gay identity, the responsibility of the black artist, and the construction of cultural memory, by bringing together two specific historical spaces: Harlem in the 1920s and London in the 1980s. The film thus draws on and participates in what Paul Gilroy calls 'the Black Atlantic': the black diasporic culture that traverses the Atlantic in an exchange of ideas, influences, and cultural forms, challenging the category of the national through it syncretism and hybridity.

Like Marlon Riggs's video Tongues Untied (released in the same year), Looking for Langston was one of the first black productions to explicitly address the subject of black gay identity. In their sophisticated use of performance and bracketing of documentary's expository function, both exemplify what Bill Nichols calls 'performative documentary'. Less dependent than conventional documentaries on photographic indexicality and the rhetorical construction of an argument, they rely far more on the evocation of specific cultural contexts and their structures of feeling. While Tongues Untied and Looking for Langston both use a poetic structure and incorporate poetry on their soundtracks, particularly work by contemporary black gay poet Essex Hemphill, they differ considerably in their performative aspects. Whereas Riggs's video constructs a sense of immediacy through his deployment of direct address, Julien's film combines music, poetry, voice-over commentary, archival footage, and dramatic tableaux in a dreamlike montage to reconfigure the imagined space of the Harlem Renaissance within black diasporic memory.

Frequently disavowed or relegated to crude psychopathology, the question of Langston Hughes's ambiguous sexuality and its relevance to his status as a black literary icon has become a contested issue for African American studies. Yet Looking for Langston does not constitute a search to discover and document the biographical 'truth' of Hughes's life as a means to resolve this question. As its title suggests, Looking for Langston is more interested in the psychic process of historical identification, of imagining one's relation to a particular historical moment, space, or figure. Julien does not produce a biographical documentary of Hughes, but rather a 'meditation' on this black icon, opening up an imagined space, in which the significance of black gay sexuality for the Harlem Renaissance, and black culture more generally, can be explored.

Looking for Langston opens with documentary images of 1920s Harlem and a female voice-over eulogizing an unnamed black cultural icon. This eulogy provides a sound bridge to the first dramatic tableau, which presents mourners at a wake standing around an open casket. The words are those of Toni Morrison, whom Julien recorded at James Baldwin's memorial service in 1987, while the tableau image self-consciously invokes the funereal photography of James Van Der Zee's Harlem Book of the Dead. Julien himself plays the part of the dead man (Hughes) in the casket (introducing therein the theme of historical identification).

Thus begins the film's rich montage of intertextual and historical references. Whereas historical documentaries conventionally label their intertextuality to authenticate their historical referentiality, Looking for Langston moves effortlessly among its literary, visual, and archival sources, seldom labeling their historical referents. By refusing to mark such references, the film blurs the boundaries between 'fact' and fiction, 'real' and imaginary, past and present. Julien uses several aesthetic techniques to facilitate the transition between these different modes: the tonal equalization of the film's monochrome cinematography, its numerous poetic sound bridges, and the continuity of its camera movement across different spaces.

At the center of the film's imagined historical space is the character of Alex, a black gay man who bears a physical resemblance to the younger Hughes. Wearing 1920s fashion throughout the film, he first appears listening to the sound of Hughes's voice (from a 1960s television broadcast) on a gramophone. Later he arrives at a nightclub, becoming erotically interested in another black gay man, Beauty, who has a possessive white lover. This triangular encounter generates several fantasy scenes that explore the racial dynamics of the eroticized look within gay culture through the appropriation of images by two influential gay photographers, George Platt Lynes and Robert Mapplethorpe. Julien restages specific homoerotic tableaux photographed by Lynes but de-exoticizes their inscription of race, reconfiguring the image of black male sexuality, according to Bell Hooks, with an unprecedented 'softness'. His appropriation of Mapplethorpe's photographs is more explicit: the white gay man moves among these images projected onto fabric, fetishistically caressing their surface.

The act of 'looking' invoked in the film's title consequently alludes both to the eroticized look directed toward black men and to the search by a contemporary black artist for kinship with historical predecessors from a different time and space. Manthia Diawara argues that in its web of appropriations and allusions, both queer (Mapplethorpe, Lynes, Kenneth Anger, Jean Cocteau, and Jean Genet) and black (Hughes, Baldwin, Oscar Micheaux, Bruce Nugent, and Bessie Smith), Looking for Langston simultaneously confronts (queer) avant-garde cinema with its Other (that is, race) and brings to the surface that which has been repressed in the historical image of the Harlem Renaissance (that is, homosexuality).

The film was widely acclaimed in Europe, receiving the Teddy Award (given for the best gay film) at the Berlin Film Festival, but its reception in the United States was disrupted by legal interventions undertaken by the Langston Hughes estate, which objected to what it considered 'a sensationalist misuse' of Hughes as a metaphor for black gay sexuality. In its injunction against perceived copyright infringement by the film's use of Langston's name and poetry, the estate's action not only mistook the film for a straightforward biographical documentary, it also demonstrated the very cultural suppression of black gay sexuality that the film challenges. Preempting his later shift to installation-based work, Julien reworked the material of Looking for Langston in 1990 as a performance piece installed in London's Kings Cross, entitled Undressing Icons.

ROGER HALLAS

See also: Julien, Isaac

Looking for Langston (UK, Sankofa, 1989, black and white, 45 mins). Distributed by the British Film Institute (UK) and Third World Newsreel (USA). Written and directed by Isaac Julien. Produced by Nadine Marsh-Edwards. Cinematography by Nina Kellgren. Music by Blackberri and Wayson Jones. Edited by Robert Hargreaves. Art direction by Derek Brown. Sound by Martin Jackson and Ronald Bailey. Texts by James Baldwin, Essex Hemphill, Bruce Nugent and Hilton Als. Voiceovers by Erick Ray Evans, Essex Hemphill, Wayson Jones, Toni Morrison, and Stuart Hall. Cast: Ben Ellison (Alex), Matthew Baidoo (Beauty), and John Wilson (Karl). Filmed in Norfolk, London and New York City.

Further reading

Bravmann, Scott, 'Isaac Julien's Looking for Langston: Hughes, Biography and Queer(ed) History', *Cultural Studies* 7, no. 2, May 1993: 311–23.

Diawara, Manthia, 'The Absent One: The Avant-Garde and the Black Imaginary in Looking for Langston', *Wide Angle* 13, nos. 3–4, July–October 1991: 96–109.

Gates, Henry Louis, Jr, 'Looking for Modernism', in Manthia Diawara (ed.), *Black American Cinema*, New York: Routledge, 1993: 200–7.

Gilroy, Paul, *Small Acts: Thoughts on the Politics of Black Cultures*, London: Serpent's Tail, 1993.

Hemphill, Essex (ed.), *Brother to Brother: New Writings by Black Gay Men*, Boston: Alyson, 1991.

Hill, John, *British Cinema in the 1980s: Issues and Themes*, Oxford: Oxford University Press, 1999.

Hooks, Bell, *Yearning: Race, Gender and Cultural Politics*, Boston: South End Press, 1990.

Mercer, Kobena, 'Dark and Lovely Too: Black Gay Men in Independent Film', in Martha Gever, John Greyson and Pratibha Parmar (eds), *Queer Looks: Perspectives on Lesbian and Gay Film and Video*, New York: Routledge, 1993: 238–56.

Muñoz, Jose, *Disidentifications: Queers of Color and the Performance of Politics*, Minneapolis, MN: University of Minnesota Press, 1999.

Nichols, Bill, *Blurred Boundaries: Questions of Meaning in Contemporary Culture*, Bloomington, IN: Indiana University Press, 1994.

Saalfield, Catherine, 'Overstepping the Bounds of Propriety: Film Offends Langston Hughes Estate', *The Independent* (New York, NY) 13, no. 1, January–February 1990: 5–8.

Lorentz, Pare

Pare Lorentz was the first US sociopolitical documentary filmmaker. His most important films, The Plow that Broke the Plains (1936) and The River (1938), chronicled the problems and accomplishments of the New Deal, a series of initiatives by President Franklin D. Roosevelt to combat the ravages of the Depression, the Dust Bowl, and flooding in the Mississippi River Valley. Much like John Grierson in Great Britain, Lorentz saw film as a vehicle for educating and mobilizing the citizenry. Although he had never been a filmmaker, Lorentz had been a motion picture critic since 1927 when he began writing reviews for *Judge* magazine and later for the *New York Evening Journal*, *Vanity Fair*, *Town and Country*, and *McCalls*. Lorentz was well known in music circles in the United States and often wrote about the role of music in motion pictures. Following a complementary book on Roosevelt's first year as president, and an article about the Dust Bowl for *Newsweek* magazine, Lorentz was invited to make a film about the work of a New Deal relief agency, the Resettlement Administration (RA). The RA was charged with providing help for people impoverished by a long history of poor agricultural practices, the Great Depression, and a severe drought that plagued much of the mid-section of the country. Until Lorentz was hired, the RA had used only still photographs to provide a visual portrayal of the misery of the people in the region. Lorentz's goal was to make a government film that would be entertaining and commercially successful.

The Plow that Broke the Plains chronicled the settlement of the Midwestern portions of the United States and the farming and grazing practices that contributed to its degradation. Moving pictures of a dangerous dust storm provided much of the drama in the film, and a brief message at the end heralded the work of the RA in relocating displaced persons. In many ways, The Plow was the visual equivalent of John Steinbeck's famous novel, The Grapes of Wrath. In fact, in gathering material for the novel, Steinbeck traveled with Lorentz and 'listened to him expound his theory of the documentary film [and …] unconsciously absorbed many of the Lorentz principles'. Lorentz combined images of the country's rugged individualism and entrepreneurship with American folk songs and a lyrical commentary never before seen in US documentaries. He used an unusual editing style, scoring the film and using the music to guide the editing. The music was composed by Virgil Thomson, who understood the need to blend hymns and folk songs with traditional orchestral and symphonic music. From the start, Lorentz saw music as an integral part of the film. 'From the beginning of my moviemaking years, even though I had never set foot in the cutting room or been behind a camera, I wished to keep control of the three elements of my film—pictures, music, and words—and to emphasize the elements in that order'. Lorentz's commentary, influenced by the style of French author Antoine de Saint-Exubery and by F.W. Murnau's Sunrise, and delivered by a former opera singer, Thomas Chalmers, was written in free verse. Its rhythm was achieved through alliteration, particularly the repetition of words and phrases, reminiscent of the style of American poet Walt Whitman. 'High winds and sun … High winds and sun', the narrator warned, as settlers recklessly plowed the fragile ground. After the devastation caused by years of over-plowing, overgrazing, a severe drought and dust storms, the narrator intoned of the farmers, 'Baked out—blown out—and broke!' Another Lorentz technique was the use of counterpoint, particularly ironic comment. In one scene, as the camera surveys an abandoned home and surrounding landscape choked by the fallout from dust storms, organ music from The Doxology ('Praise God, from whom all blessings flow … ') playing in the background provides an ironic contrast to the images on the screen. Despite resistance from Hollywood to distribute a government film, and the complaint that The Plow was too long for a short feature and too short for a long feature, the film opened at a major theater in New York City, The Rialto, on May 28, 1936. Other bookings soon followed. Critics were generally favorable in their reviews, but some politicians, particularly those from areas featured in the film, believed that Lorentz had distorted the facts. A more ominous response was the belief by some in private industry and in Congress that the government had no business competing with Hollywood.

Pare Lorentz's other major film of merit was The River, produced in 1938. Its focus was on the Mississippi River Valley, a large section of the eastern and middle United States, the rivers and streams of which flowed into the Mississippi River, causing considerable flooding in springtime, often displacing people and washing away topsoil. The theme was the relationship among water, land, and people. At one point the narrator states: 'But you cannot plan for water and land unless you plan for people.' *The New York Times* critic Bosley Crowther wrote that with the possible exception of Robert Flaherty's Nanook of the North, The River was the most famous American documentary film before World War II. While acknowledging its propaganda value in promoting the New Deal policies of President Franklin D. Roosevelt, Crowther said 'It turned out to be so finely written, so beautifully executed, and it had such an apt and original musical score that it gained a worldwide reputation as a great work of screen poetry.' The organizational structure of The River follows a chronological order much like that of The Plow. The film begins with a roll call of rivers that identifies the geographical area and sets the stage for their commercial use—particularly the transportation of cotton grown in the River Valley and lumber from adjacent mountains and hills. Next, it shows an impoverished South, reeling from the effects of a four-year civil war (1861–5) and the erosion of its farmland. The situation is made worse by lumbering practices in the North that leave the Valley vulnerable to flooding. 'We cut the top off Minnesota and sent it down the river. We cut the top off Wisconsin and sent it down the river. We left the mountains and the hills slashed and burned, and moved on.' The climax of the film is the flood sequence, dramatized by Lorentz's filming of the devastating flood of 1937 that killed people and livestock and left thousands homeless. The solution to the problem, given greater attention in The River than in The Plow, is a series of dams to control flooding, a forest and soil conservation plan, low-cost loans to build homes, and hydroelectric power, all provided by the government.

Lorentz again chose Thomas Chalmers to narrate the documentary and Virgil Thomson to score it. As in The Plow, Thompson used a combination of folk tunes, hymns, and original music inspired by the pictures. Lorentz wrote the narration. James Joyce described it as 'the most beautiful prose I have heard in ten years'. The key to Lorentz's writing was his poetic style and skillful use of alliteration, particularly repetition. 'The water comes downhill, spring and fall; Down from the cut-over mountains, Down from the plowed-off slopes, Down every brook and rill, rivulet and creek, Carrying every drop of water that flows down two-thirds the continent.'

Lorentz used an editing technique that biographer Robert Snyder called parallel structure. The three main sequences in the film, an opening sequence featuring a roll call of rivers, a lumbering sequence with a roll call of trees, and a flood sequence that repeats the names of rivers, are cut in a somewhat similar manner. According to Snyder, they 'reveal two of the most striking qualities of The River—its unity, and the artistic relationship between the visual and aural elements of the film'. The River was shown initially in cities in the Mississippi River Valley where it was greeted with much enthusiasm. It was first shown publicly in New York City on February 4, 1938. Paramount Pictures agreed to distribute the film. The River won first prize in the 1938 Venice Film Festival (over Leni Riefenstahl's Olympia) and made such a favorable impression on President Roosevelt that he offered to establish the United States Film Service, with Lorentz as its director.

The US Film Service, the purpose of which was somewhat similar to that of Great Britain's General Post Office (GPO) Film Unit, lasted from 1938 until 1941, although as early as 1939 Lorentz saw that the war in Europe would preclude any possibility of continuing support from President Roosevelt, as the nation's attention changed from domestic to international issues. During its brief existence, Lorentz began a film project on unemployment called Ecce Homo, which was never finished, and produced and directed a feature-length film, The Fight for Life, about the dangers encountered in childbirth. For the first time, Lorentz used professional actors and a detailed script. Some of the film was shot on location at the Chicago Maternity Center, located in Chicago's slums, and the rest on a sound stage in Hollywood. Controversy arose over the maternity death-rate figures cited by Lorentz. Nevertheless, the film garnered much praise from the medical profession for its realistic portrayal of the problems that obstetricians face, particularly when compounded by the poor health habits of people from poverty-stricken areas. The Fight for Life premiered in

New York City in March 1940 and was distributed by Columbia Pictures. Ironically, the police department in Chicago, offended by shots of Chicago slums, banned the film from being shown there. The US Film Service attracted two well-known documentary filmmakers, Joris Ivens and Robert Flaherty. Ivens produced Power and the Land (1940), a film showing what government-provided electricity meant to a typical farm family. The sponsor was the Rural Electrification Agency (REA), a New Deal agency that provided farms with inexpensive electric lighting and power. Lorentz hired Flaherty to direct The Land (1941), a film about the problems of farm families, including migrant farmers, and the government's role in promoting better use of the land. The Land was never shown commercially and in fact was not completed until Lorentz had resigned from the Film Service. Also, in 1940 the US Film Service lost its production authority and transferred responsibility for completion to the Agricultural Adjustment Administration.

Throughout its existence, the US Film Service had never received a permanent budget or congressional approval. Its budget had come from funds designated for various relief agencies. Despite the quality of films produced under his direction, Lorentz failed to convince Congress that a permanent government filmmaking body was in the best interest of the country. Unlike John Grierson, Lorentz was not a skilled politician. Powerful congressmen, suspicious that Lorentz and his colleagues were too far left-of-center, wary of Roosevelt's New Deal programs, and doubtful of the legality of a government motion picture production service, opposed the establishment of the Film Service. So did the public, who along with some congressmen were concerned about a domestic propaganda organization, and so did Hollywood, whose executives resented government intrusion into the entertainment business. These obstacles, coupled with President Roosevelt's preoccupation with events in Europe and the Far East, brought about the demise of the US Film Service.

During World War II Lorentz served in the Air Force and produced overseas flight crew briefing films. In 1946 he became Chief of Motion Pictures, Music and Theater for the Civil Affairs Division of the US Department of War. In that capacity he collaborated with Stuart Schulberg on Nuremberg (1946), an unimaginative but absorbing account of the Nuremberg Trials. Much of the footage shown by prosecutors was of Nazi atrocities.

CHURCHILL ROBERTS

See also: Plow that Broke the Plains, The; River, The

Biography

Born in Clarksburg, West Virginia, December 11, 1905. Attended Wesleyan College 1922, and West Virginia University 1923–5. Motion picture critic for various magazines beginning in 1926 and co-author of *Censored: The Private Life of the Movies* (1930). Wrote *The Roosevelt Year: 1933* (1934). Went to work for the Resettlement Agency in 1935 and directed his first film, The Plow that Broke the Plains (1936). Resettlement Administration transferred to the Department of Agriculture in 1937 and renamed the Farm Security Administration where Lorentz directed his second film, The River (1938). Director of United States Film Service 1938–40. Air Force Major and Lt. Col. in World War II. Died in Armonk, New York, March 4, 1995.

Selected films

1936 The Plow that Broke the Plains: writer, director
1938 The River: writer, director
1940 The Fight for Life: writer, director
1948 Nuremberg: archival researcher

Further reading

Alexander, William, *Film on the Left: American Documentary Film From 1931 to 1942*, Princeton, NJ: Princeton University Press, 1981.

Bergman, Andrew, *We're in the Money: Depression America and its Films*, New York: New York University Press, 1971.

Crowther, Bosley, *Vintage Films: 50 Enduring Motion Pictures*, New York: Putnam, 1977.

Lorentz, Pare, *FDR's Moviemaker: Memoirs and Scripts*, Reno, NV: University of Nevada Press, 1992

——*Lorentz on Film*, New York: Hopkinson and Blake, 1975

——*The River*, New York: Stackpole Sons, 1938.

Snyder, Robert L., *Pare Lorentz and the Documentary Film*, Norman, OK: University of Oklahoma Press, 1968.

Stott, William, *Documentary Expression and Thirties America*, reprinted edn, Chicago: University of Chicago Press, 1986.

Louisiana Story

(US, Flaherty, 1948)

Often considered Robert Flaherty's masterwork, Louisiana Story is the culmination of Flaherty's poetic method, formally and thematically drawing together the promise that can be seen in Nanook of the North, Man of Aran, and The Land, with a mediation between modernity and regionalism. Whereas The Land marks a shift from the premodern nostalgia of the early film to an engagement with modernity, Louisiana Story directly addresses the issue of the environmental impact of mechanisation on the pristine environment of the bayous of Louisiana in a film sponsored by Standard Oil, albeit with the approval of the sponsor.

Louisiana Story tells the tale of the disruption that mechanisation, in particular the speculative oil drilling performed by an oil company in the hitherto untouched, pristine environment of a Louisiana bayou can bring to the environment. The film focuses on the Cajun Latour family, in particular Alexander Napoleon Ulysses Latour whose youth and innocence personifies the virgin wetlands, recalling the figures of Nanook and Moana from the earlier films. As Louisiana Story is a sponsored documentary, evidence of the sponsor must appear. Thus, although the presence of the oil derrick initially disrupts the environment, normality is returned when the mobile oil drilling mechanism moves on.

Like many of the classic documentaries of this era, Louisiana Story used some of the foremost practitioners of the era. Helen Van Dongen was an experienced editor who had worked with Joris Ivens on films such as Rain, Borinage, The New Earth, and The Spanish Earth and had worked on The Land with Flaherty; therefore she was used to his more speculative approach to narrative construction. Richard Leacock was a young camera operator who, of course, was to forge his own notable career. Frances Flaherty, Leacock, and Van Dongen also provided production and editorial assistance. Another member to join the production was composer Virgil Thomson, who had provided the scores for Pare Lorentz's The Plow that Broke the Plains and The River. Thomson's role was crucial in incorporating the multitude of natural sounds with a variety of themes associated with the different characters. Thomson achieved this remarkable feat mainly through his early association with the production. He viewed early rushes and versions of the film and became an integral part of the working-up of the final film, rather than being presented with images and dialogue on which to layer music (Calder-Marshall 1963: 223).

Of all these people it is probably van Dongen who especially warrants further mention. She had the unenviable task of working without a shooting script, with Flaherty insisting on obtaining a vast amount of material that contained particular symbols or tones, with little regard for their effectiveness in the overall script. Van Dongen's concern for continuity and narrative combined well with Flaherty's search for tonal images; not one aspect forsaken for the other but a dilution of narrative imperatives to accommodate the naivety of Flaherty's vision for the world seen through the eyes of the Cajun boy.

Louisiana Story recalls Grierson's enthusiasm for Flaherty's use of 'the found story'. It is reported that in their research trip through the southern states of the United States, Frances and Robert Flaherty stumbled across an oil derrick being relocated, and that this provided the initial images and commencement point for the production. In Louisiana Story it is possible to see a convergence of the found story and the 'slight narrative' that Kracauer derives from Paul Rotha (Kracauer 1997: 247). Flaherty's notion that the documentary narrative should 'come out of the life of a people, not from the actions of individuals' as part of the daily routine of his native people (Rotha 1968), is used in the rendering of a life lived on the bayou. The slight narrative is affected through the ripples created by the appearance of the oil derrick, making for a tendentious narrative device that recalls Flaherty's earlier films such as the hunting of the walrus in Nanook and of the basking shark in Man of Aran. Yet in Louisiana Story the episodic nature of Flaherty's oeuvre is restrained, less melodramatic, and more concomitant with an appeal to the fragility of the world initially under threat from the industrial world of oil production.

Unlike Flaherty's earlier films, Louisiana Story marks a reconciliation of industrial modernity, initially dealt with in The Land, with an endemic regionalism apparent in the likes of Nanook and Moana. In this reconciliation it is possible to understand Kracauer's enthusiasm for the film whereby the alienation from the modern world is directly addressed through its filmic representation. The response to modernity imposing itself on the environmental and psychic realms of postwar capitalism is countered through Flaherty's insistence on a naive vision that promotes a sense of wonder at not only the natural world but at how that natural world can be understood in the face of the industrialisation of this Eden. For Flaherty and Kracauer, the poetic rendering of the world makes it possible to reengage the spectator who feels that they have been alienated from things such as the 'the ripple of leaves stirred by the wind' (Kracauer 1997: 31) or, in the case of Louisiana Story, the ripples on the water stirred by the passing of a canoe.

DEANE WILLIAMS

See also: Flaherty, Robert

Louisiana Story (US, The Standard Oil Company of New Jersey, 1948, 77 mins). Produced and directed by Robert Flaherty. Story by Frances and Robert Flaherty. Associate producers: Richard Leacock and Helen Van Dongen. Photography by Richard Leacock. Edited by Helen van Dongen. Music by Virgil Thomson. Sound recording by Benjamin Doniger, with assistance from Leonard Stark.

Further reading

Barsam, Richard Meran, *The Vision of Robert Flaherty: The Artist as Myth and Filmmaker*, Bloomington, IN: Indiana University Press, 1988.

Calder-Marshall, Arthur, *The Innocent Eye: The Life of Robert Flaherty*, London: W.H. Allen, 1963.

Grierson, John, 'First Principles of Documentary', in Forsyth Hardy (ed.), *Grierson on Documentary*, London: Faber & Faber 1966: 199–211.

Kracauer, Siegfried, *Theory of Film: The Redemption of Physical Reality*, second edn, Introduction by Miriam Bratu Hansen, Princeton, NJ: Princeton University Press, 1997.

Rotha, Paul, *Documentary Film, With Contributions from Sinclair Road and Richard Griffith*, Glasgow: The University Press, 1968.

Winston, Brian, 'The White Man's Burden', *Sight and Sound*, LIV: 1, winter 1984–5: 58–60.

Low, Colin

The National Film Board (NFB) of Canada's Colin Low stands as one of the finest examples of the multitalented filmmakers employed by the institution during its history. Over a span of fifty-five years at the NFB, the director/producer/animator/cinematographer was involved with nearly two hundred films. With interests ranging from animation shorts to technology-intensive nonfiction features to socially relevant projects, Low is responsible for some of the most successful films in the NFB's history in terms of sales and circulation, and is recognized as one of the single most influential figures in Canadian documentary.

As a member of the prolific group of filmmakers in the NFB of Canada's Unit B of the 1950s and early 1960s, Low was one of several figures who helped to refine both documentary film language and the collaborative working method that epitomized Canadian nonfiction filmmaking. Low's earliest documentary work was clearly rooted in his experience as an animator. Low felt that the 'patient, detailed single-frame work [required of animation] generated a working discipline quite different from the [contemporary] live-action documentary school' (Jones 1981). His first documentary with Unit B, Corral (1954), was part of the Faces of Canada project designed to find the 'Canadian character' in Canadian towns. A lyrical short capturing the lonely life of a western Canadian rancher, the documentary won critical acclaim and first prize at the 1954 Venice International Film Festival and is now considered one of the NFB's first 'auteur films'. Released without voice-over commentary at the request of the filmmaker, Corral illustrated Low's deft ability to anticipate the pattern and poeticism of the images before they had been confirmed in the editing room. His follow-up, City of Gold (codirected by Roman Kroitor, 1957), featured a poetic commentary from Pierre Berton and, with its groundbreaking use of still photography, asserted Low's interest in technology's role in filmmaking, leading to a series of projects that would each result in major filmmaking innovations.

As part of the Challenge for Change program implemented in 1967, Low moved into socially conscious filmmaking. Low's indelible print on the program was made with the Fogo Island series, consisting of twenty-eight films focusing on the residents of a small, increasingly unsustainable fishing community north of Newfoundland. Low's focus was to give a voice to his subjects and a vehicle for its delivery to local and federal government. 'I thought it was a lot better to examine a situation', said Low, 'the outcome of which was not yet determined, rather than look at another melancholy social mistake' (Jones 1981).

Throughout his career, Low was a leader at the NFB with a number of important roles including tenure as the director of Regional Production beginning in 1976, a period that confirmed his status as an icon and mentor to a new generation of documentary filmmakers. With his final film at the NFB, Moving Pictures (2000), Low glanced back on his career by tracing his own awareness of war with a dissection of technology's increasing ability to create and distribute still and moving images more efficiently.

MICHAEL B. BAKER

See also: Canada; Challenge for Change/ Société Nouvelle

Biography

Born in Cardston, Alberta on July 24, 1926. Attended the Banff School of Fine Arts and the Calgary Institute of Technology before joining the National Film Board of Canada as an animator in 1945. Appointed Head of the Animation Unit at the NFB 1950. Directed first documentary short, Corral, 1954. Pioneered large-format filmmaking with In the Labyrinth (codirected by Roman Kroitor), 1967. Established Memorial University Film Unit in Newfoundland while working on the Fogo Island series 1967. Appointed executive producer of Studio C 1972. Appointed director of Regional Production 1976. Introduced OMNIMAX technology with Atmos 1979. Appointed to the Royal Order of Canada 1996. First Anglophone awarded Prix Albert Tessier/Prix du Québec 1997. Retired from NFB following final film Moving Pictures, 2000. Member of the Royal Canadian Academy.

Selected films

1953 The Romance of Transportation: director
1954 Corral: director, writer
1957 City of Gold: codirector
1960 Circle of the Sun: director, cowriter
1967 Billy Crane Moves Away (part of the twenty-eight-film Fogo Island series): director
1967 In the Labyrinth: codirector
1974 Cree Hunters of Mistassini (Ianzelo, Richardson): producer
1982 Standing Alone: director
2000 Moving Pictures: director, writer, narrator

Further reading

Evans, Gary, *In the National Interest: A Chronicle of the National Film Board of Canada from 1949 to 1989*, Toronto: University of Toronto Press, 1991.

Glassman, Marc and Wise, Wyndham, 'A Filmmaker of Vision: Take One's Interview with Colin Low' *Take One* 23, spring 1999.

Jones, D.B., *The Best Butler in the Business: Tom Daly of the National Film Board*, Toronto: University of Toronto Press, 1996.

——*Movies and Memorandum: An Interpretative History of the National Film Board of Canada*, Ottawa: Canadian Film Institute, 1981.

Tibbetts, John C., 'All That Glitters', *Film Comment* 2, March–April, 1995.

Villeneuve, Rene, 'Interview with Colin Low, Tony Ianzelo, Ernie McNabb', *Perforations* 2, April 1992.

Lozinski, Marcel

Polish documentaries have frequently served to depict the often volatile societal developments in that nation. Marcel Lozinski, however, dominated Polish documentary film in the 1990s not by the direct representation of extraordinary political events, but by the indirect representation of such events through the stories of individuals in everyday situations.

Although Lozinski does not avoid inspiring events, his is a quest to present viewers with the opportunity to explore the mystery, the innocence, and the tragedy of the everyday. His expertise in taking a documentary subject and presenting to the viewer not only a glimpse into an individual life, but a glimpse into the societal struggles of a village or city, the biases between the genders or age groups, or the political injustices of his country, exemplifies his contribution to documentary film. Lozinski's films convey the universality of life, exposing the depths of human struggle and hardship waiting beneath the surface of our every action.

In the short subject field, Lozinski demonstrates his mastery of indirect sociopolitical revelation. His 1993 film, 89mm From Europe, focuses on one trivial event, the hardly perceptible relations between European passengers traveling on a train, and the railwaymen who change the wheel track of all trains entering their country. Lozinski presents the demarcation line between Western and Eastern civilizations, between the rich and the poor, between those who aspire to achieve success but fail and those who have succeeded in making a name for themselves. Even the title—89 millimeters—reveals Lozinski's probing style, as it represents the measured difference between the rail widths of the rails in Europe and the rails of the former Soviet Union.

Lozinski's next project, Everything Can Happen (1995), again takes on the sublimity of humanity, by focusing on a sequence of conversations between a young boy and elderly people lingering on a park bench, and transforming the encounter into a philosophical treatise. Lozinski contrasts the naive sincerity of six-year-old Tomaszek with the dignity of elderly people engaged in the polite activity of adapting themselves to the child's comprehension level. The universal topics of loneliness, life, and fear of death find a direct voice through the indirect convergence of individuals, young and old, engaged in the simple activity of conversation. Here, Lozinski presents to his viewers questions often avoided or feared, by exploring the concept of death through the innocence of the young.

Lozinski conceives of the documentary film as a medium through which the viewer feels, through contact with real subjects, the essence of life and the irreversibility of the passage of time. In a Visit (1974) and So It Doesn't Hurt (1998), Lozinski enters the lives of two women who have succeeded in their chosen professions—one as a city journalist and the other as a rural farm manager. Lozinski chronicles the contrasting views of two women experiencing different definitions for the concept of ambition that spans more than two decades and in the process opens a window into the complexities of the competitive nature of society that views one person's accomplishment as another person's laxity.

Lozinski played an active role in the rise of Production Unit X. Created under the supervision of Andrzej Wajda, a leading figure of Polish cinema, this group of filmmakers became known as the representatives of the cinema of moral anxiety. Lozinski brought to this collection of filmmakers an ability to pursue the moral dilemmas of contemporary Polish society from an indirect perspective. His interest in seeking conciliatory answers to difficult situations of human existence and presenting them through the medium of film imparted his work with a timeless character.

CHRISTINE MARIE HILGER

See also: Poland

Biography

Born in Paris, France in 1940. Earned a degree in documentary film from the State Academy of Film, Television, and Theatre of Lodz in 1971. In 1973 began career as a director for the Warsaw Documentary Studio. Awards for documentary film include the FIPRESCI award (1981), an Oscar nomination (1994), and the Golden Pigeon award (1998). In 2001 participated in the Shoah Foundation by codirecting I Remember with Polish director Andrzej Wajda.

Selected films

1973 Happy End: producer, director
1981 Microphome Test: producer, director
1991 Katyn Forest: director
1994 89mm From Europe: director
1994 Everything Can Happen: producer, director
1998 So It Doesn't Hurt: director
2001 I Remember: codirector

Further reading

Ackerman, Peter and DuVall, Jack, *A Force More Powerful: A Century of Nonviolent Conflict (Polish Documentary)*, New York: St Martin's Press, 2000.

Aitken, Ian, *European Film Theory and Cinema: A Critical Introduction*, Edinburgh: Edinburgh University Press, 2001.

Corner, John, *Documentary and the Mass Media*, London: Arnold, 1986.

Orvell, Miles, *After the Machine: Visual Arts and the Erasing of Cultural Boundaries*, Jackson, MS: University Press of Mississippi, 1995.

Rotha, Paul, *Documentary Diary*, New York: Hill and Wang, 1973.

Lumière Brothers, The

In the history of cinema, the significance of Louis and Auguste Lumière cannot be overstated. The device they invented, the cinematographe, was a major contribution to the institution we today refer to as cinema. The special qualities of this device were critical in the development of documentary film practice. Although it is a bit of an oversimplification to accept the divide between the Lumières and George Méliès as the founders of the two major strands of film, documentary and fiction, it is nevertheless the case that the Lumières' films represent the origins of a method of filming that attempts to show life as it is lived. All documentary filmmakers, from Flaherty to Grierson, Drew Associates to Ken Burns, Michael Moore to Errol Morris, owe some debt to the practice of the Lumières and their cameramen. Louis Lumière in particular is considered by many scholars to be the father of documentary film (Barnouw 1993).

The Lumières had substantial access to capital that financed their efforts. They were the sons of a successful painter and photographic equipment manufacturer, as evidenced by the first motion picture film they shot, Workers Leaving the Lumière Factory (1895). The Lumière family had a substantial business that employed three hundred people in a single factory in Lyon, France. They were encouraged by their father, Antoine, to improve on Edison's kinetoscope, which debuted in France in 1894.

The brothers—in particular Louis—developed the cinematographe in early 1895. The camera had several advantages over Edison's device (and those of other competitors). A hand-crank operated the machine (as opposed to the battery-powered electricity of the kinetograph), thus making the device portable. It was also a three-in-one device: camera, printer, and projector, allowing the operator to record the events happening around him and project such recorded films with great speed.

The first known films by Louis Lumière were of his employees leaving the factory. The event was clearly carefully staged, and indeed at least two other films of Workers Leaving the Lumière Factory are known to exist, suggesting Lumière's interest in careful composition. In the first film, dated March 1895, the doors to the factory are already open and workers are pouring out. By the time Lumière filmed them months later, a degree of narrative has been developed: the doors open, workers leave, and the doors close (almost—one person sneaks back inside at the last minute).

Lumière also filmed his family. He filmed his brother Auguste and sister-in-law feeding their baby, and his father and two associates drinking beer, for example.

Louis Lumière next took the cinematographe to the streets of Lyon, filming what would be called actualities: the streetcars and horse-drawn carriages and, in a famous film, a train arriving at La Ciotat station. The latter film suggests some degree of cinematic composition. For example, the diagonal perspective of the train moving from the upper right background to the lower left foreground becomes a common set-up for the camera, which provided remarkable depth of focus.

In terms of the birth of the cinema, the screening for a paying audience of a program of ten short films in the Salon Indien, in the basement of the Grande Café in Paris on December 28, 1895 is commonly accepted as the first time motion pictures were so presented. The program, modestly advertised, was an immediate success; soon after the debut, the Grand Café was running twenty half-hour shows daily, bringing in 2,500 francs (Barnouw 1993). The famous story of viewers ducking to get out of the way of the moving train is probably apocryphal, though Barsam (1992) suggests that this reaction should be considered in the context of a widely reported railroad accident at the Gare Montparnasse two months earlier (the first train film was not filmed at the time of the first screening; see later). Nevertheless, much was made of the power of the device to capture life. The projection of the film for an audience contributed to this reception, for it contrasted with the single-view, peep-show format of the kinetoscope. At the Grand Café, and soon other theaters around the world, the cinematographe presented large, well-photographed moving images that suggested fragments of life. Viewers noted the way in which the leaves moved in the background of several of the films, which added to the feel of authenticity to the presentations. As Andre Gaudreault (in Elsaesser 1993) observes, it was the sense of spontaneity of the nonhuman movement of the leaves and of the waves in a film such as Boat Leaving the Port that astonished audiences.

By the time of the cinematographe's debut, Louis Lumière had already established his economic strategy for exploiting the device. He had contracted an engineer to manufacture several hundred cameras and was training operators to take the device around the world. The company also delayed accepting purchase orders for the device so that it would ensure itself profits from the device's first appearances abroad. Shortly after the Grand Café opening, scores of cinematographe premieres began: London, New York, Brussels, Rome, Moscow, Copenhagen, Tokyo, Melbourne, and Delhi. A special feature of the programs was that the operator could film a scene in the daytime and show it to that audience in the evening, thus ensuring the audience's confidence that the program was not a trick-show. People got to see themselves projected onto the screens of local theaters and music halls. Within two years of Lumière's first films, the catalogue numbered more than seven hundred and fifty films, which began to be sold to individuals willing to purchase the equipment to project them. At this time Lumière announced a shift in its policy. Their demonstration tours, which had brought such fame to the device and began cinema as an institution in at least dozens of countries, would cease, and the company would concentrate on the sale of equipment, including raw film stock and the catalogue of films (by 1900 this catalogue numbered almost one thousand three hundred). No more would the company be involved in filmmaking, although several of their camera operators would remain active in teaching cinematography and working with other organizations.

Given the cinematographe's portability, Lumière cameramen traveled the world, filming daily activities. Some films were street scenes of hustling city dwellers; others created motion by placing the camera on a moving object such as a boat or train. Yet these were not wholly improvised slices of life. As mentioned previously, camera framing was crucial, but more important, individuals were in some cases prodded into various kinds of actions. The servant in the beer-drinking film is clearly exaggerating his interest in his master's card game. In Water Toboggan, a film of a flume ride, one person, having left the frame, returns and beckons his companions to do the same, pretending to look at something in the water, in an effort to 'kill time' until the film runs out. Most famously is the case of the so-called first comic film L'Arroseur arrosé (translated as The Waterer Watered, but other titles include The Gardener's Trick, A Trick on the Gardener, Watering the Gardener, and others). There are two known versions of this film. In one the framing is flat, almost two-dimensional; the other film, presumably shot later, suggests a greater understanding of composition in depth.

If we credit Lumière with being the father of documentary, we must also acknowledge that the 'problems' posed by documentary films also began with Lumière. The selection of events to film reflects particular subjective positions. In France it was probably easy enough to film the middle and working classes in public places and create fascinating composition (see, for example, Washerwomen on the River, with at least four planes of activity in clear focus: the women washing, their reflections in the water, men above them watching, and trucks traveling along the road above). However, in many places abroad, the device became used primarily to photograph royalty. Events such as the coronation of Czar Nicholas II of Russia and the funeral of Queen Victoria of England became common. They became testaments to imperial authority. The films also were testaments to colonialist thinking: films of natives dancing in ceremonies, such as African Knife Dance, arguably the first ethnographic films, appeal to Western audiences' presumptions about indigenous peoples. A particularly disturbing film is Children Gathering Rice Scattered by Western Women, filmed in Vietnam, then the French colony Indochina. The women, dressed in fine clothes, toss rice to poorly dressed Vietnamese children, as if they were feeding animals at a zoo.

It is difficult to fully express how these films were received; the motion picture camera represented a new mode of perception, and indeed the Lumières tended to believe in the camera's scientific importance rather than its artistic aspect. The Lumière brothers stated their belief that the camera, after its novelty phase, would largely serve a scientific function. They did not foresee all the possibilities their device would unleash, including a massive entertainment industry. The Lumières' legacy is enormous, in part for the very device they developed, but also for a mode of recording life in a new manner.

To coincide with the one hundredth anniversary of their achievements, the Lumière Trust invited sixty filmmakers to work on a project titled Lumière and Company. Each director was given an opportunity to work with a refurbished cinematographe to produce a single fifty-second film, working as close to within the confines of the original cameramen as possible (sound was permitted). Some created fictional formats; others, such as Spike Lee's footage of his young son, recall the home-movie styles of films like Feeding the Baby. It was an interesting tribute, but more a testament to what the Lumières' device had wrought than to the aesthetic they pioneered.

TOM GROCHOWSKI

See also: Workers Leaving the Lumière Factory and Other Lumière Shorts

Selected films

Note: the Lumière catalogue is too large to list here; all titles mentioned in this article are available on video and DVD in the United States on Kino International's The Lumière Brothers: The First Films. The following is a list of the ten films first presented at the Grand Café:

Workers Leaving the Lumière Factory
Horseback Jumping
Fishing for Goldfish
Debarkation of the Photographic Congress Members at Lyon
The Blacksmiths
A Little Trick on the Gardener
Feeding the Baby
Blanket Toss
The Place des Cordeliers at Lyon La Mer

Further reading

Barnouw, Erik, *Documentary: A History of the Non-fiction Film*, New York: Oxford University Press, 1993.

Barsam Richard M., *Nonfiction Film: A Critical History*, Bloomington, IN: Indiana University Press, 1992.

Elsaesser, Thomas (ed.), *Early Cinema: Space, Frame, Narrative*, Bloomington, IN: Indiana University Press, 1993.

Musser, Charles, *The Emergence of Cinema*, Berkeley, CA, University of California Press, 1990.

Lye, Len

The New Zealand-born filmmaker, painter, kinetic sculptor, writer, and theorist Len Lye became a leading avant-garde artist in London and New York, bridging pre- and post-World War II movements and trends. Associated with many important art groups, beginning with London's Seven and Five Society in the 1920s, the International Surrealist Movement in the 1930s, and the Kinetic Art Movement in the 1960s, Lye is best remembered for his contributions to the development of international abstract cinema. In the early 1930s he experimented with color printing processes such as Dufaycolor and Gasparcolor while pioneering 'direct animation', a method of painting, scratching, and stenciling directly onto motion picture celluloid. Aided by commissions from the British General Post Office (GPO), the Imperial Tobacco Company, Shell Motor Oil, and Imperial Airways, his whimsical animated films of the mid-to-late 1930s included original 'camera-less' techniques, advertising slogans, and dynamic musical rhythms. A fierce individualist and anarchistic thinker, Lye claimed that: 'There has never been a great film unless it was created in the spirit of the experimental filmmaker.' When applied to his seldom seen but formally inventive war effort films, this statement illuminates Lye's underrecognized contribution to the British documentary movement.

Commissioned by John Grierson in 1934 to produce promotional films for the GPO Film Unit, Lye did not share Grierson's social-democratic corporatist ideology; nor did Lye's early handmade films display the didactic, institutional form of the GPO's more widely circulated productions during this formative period. Conversely, Grierson's notion of documentary as the 'creative treatment of reality', coupled with his strong sense of social responsibility, may have focused Lye's thinking when he began directing instructional films for Britain's Ministry of Information during World War II. His theory 'Individual Happiness Now', developed in 1941 and refined throughout the war years, provides an important context for these films. Stressing spontaneity, individuality, and artistic experience, Individual Happiness Now was conceived 'as an alternative to the usual wartime appeals to nationalism or religion' (Horrocks 2001). Though Lye's information films were the product of their wartime context, these documentaries contain distinct auteur traces, experimental techniques, and technological innovations that run counter to their training and propaganda objectives.

Lye's Work Party (1942), a slice-of-life film about women working in a munitions factory, was criticized at the time of its release for not having enough 'propaganda value' (Horrocks 2001). Anticipating cinéma vérité, Work Party featured handheld camerawork and an unobtrusive, observational style. When The Pie Was Opened (1941), a film about coping with food rations, included surrealist diversions, an imaginative, playful storyline, and visual and aural puns. Newspaper Train (1941), about the importance of keeping people informed and countering Nazi propaganda, mixed live-action and animation and used an unusual, disjunctive editing style. It was also the first film to print two separate soundtracks side-by-side, one for dialogue and one for sound effects. Kill or Be Killed (1942), a taut psychological thriller pitting German and British soldiers against one another in a test of skill and dexterity, is considered one of the best war effort films. Inserting dramatic elements into a standard training film, Kill or Be Killed demonstrates Lye's ability to formulate new genres or genre hybrids while expanding documentary parameters. Cameramen at War (1943), a compilation of footage taken by World War I and II newsreel cameramen, was Lye's last assignment for Britain's Ministry of Information. Constructed on the editing bench from archival material, the film highlights his decisive editing technique, specialized ability, and professional approach. At the same time Lye must have felt some personal kinship with his subjects, who were likewise pressed into documentary film out of wartime circumstances.

Lye's contribution to the history of documentary film continued with his work for Louis de Rouchemont's international newsreel program, The March of Time. From 1944 to 1951, Lye worked as a field director for the series, directing short documentaries and newsreel sequences and gathering footage for the monthly news magazines. After relocating from London to New York to direct a March of Time assignment on Basic English with the literary critic I. A. Richards, Lye suddenly found himself in the new centre of modern art. Galvanized by the creative energy of New York's art scene, Lye spent most of the 1950s writing and developing commercial and noncommercial film projects. Synthesizing his work in experimental and documentary film, Rhythm (1957) combines amateur and professional modes of production. Made using documentary outtakes of the Chrysler assembly line, which were reedited, hole-punched, and scratched on, the kinetic Rhythm pioneered TV commercial jump cutting. After a long struggle to find employment on Madison Avenue from the late 1950s to the late 1960s, however, Lye ceased making films, devoting most of his artistic energies to kinetic sculpture.

Although Lye's documentaries often belied his anarchistic spirit and leftist values, it is important to recognize that these films were collaborative productions financed by a government information ministry at a time of war. Working within a compartmentalized production system where every staff member was paid the same and given equal credit, it may be inaccurate to claim that Lye 'authored' these films. His work in documentary film was short-lived and ephemeral, but its traces can still be located in the cinéma vérité movements of the following decades. Throughout his career Lye tested the limits of experimental and documentary cinema. An outsider with the determination, intuition, and insight to move within several artistic and industrial circles simultaneously, Lye's films opened up space for an art of documentary.

BRETT KASHMERE

See also: Grierson, John; March of Time, The

Biography

Born in Christchurch, New Zealand, July 5, 1901. Studied briefly at Wellington Technical Institute 1915, and at Canterbury Art College, New Zealand 1919. Lived for a year in the Polynesian islands of Samoa, 1923, before being deported to Sydney, Australia. Arrived in London, England 1926. Exhibited with London's Seven and Five Society 1927. Pioneered direct animation techniques 1933. Received first commission from British GPO Film Unit 1934. Won prize at the Brussels Film Festival 1935. Participated in International Surrealist Exhibition in London 1936. Directed war effort documentaries for the British Ministry of Information 1941–3. Hired by The March of Time film series 1943. Moved to New York's

Greenwich Village 1944 and continued working on The March of Time until 1951. Won second prize at the Belgian International Experimental Film Competition 1958. Became a leading figure in the kinetic art movement during the 1950s and 1960s. First kinetic sculpture, Fountain, exhibited at Leo Castelli Gallery 1961. Tangible Motion Sculptures exhibited at the New York Museum of Modern Art 1961. Died in New York City, May 15, 1980.

Selected films

1941	Newspaper Train
1941	When The Pie Was Opened
1942	Work Party (aka Factory Family)
1942	Kill or Be Killed
1943	Cameramen at War
1944–51	The March of Time: contributing director and cameraman
1957	Rhythm

Further reading

Curnow, Wystan and Horrocks, Roger, *Figures of Motion: Len Lye, Selected Writings*, Auckland: Auckland University Press, 1984.

Davy, Sarah, 'Len Lye: The Film Artist in Wartime', in *Len Lye: A Personal Mythology*, Auckland: Auckland City Art Gallery, 1980.

Fielding, Raymond, *The March of Time, 1935–51*, New York: Oxford University Press, 1978.

Horrocks, Roger, *Len Lye: A Biography*, Auckland: Auckland University Press, 2001.

Sussex, Elizabeth, *The Rise and Fall of British Documentary*, Berkeley, CA: University of California Press, 1975.

Swann, Paul, *The British Documentary Film Movement*, Cambridge: Cambridge University Press, 1989.

Macartney-Filgate, Terence

Terence Macartney-Filgate—scriptwriter, cinematographer, director, producer, and iconoclast—is best known for his pioneering work on Candid Eye, the landmark series of documentary films made by the National Film Board (NFB) of Canada for CBC Television in 1958–9. These films, which combined a reportage style with handheld camera, sync-sound, natural lighting, and noncontinuity editing, represented an important challenge to the authoritative, didactic documentary tradition entrenched by the NFB's founder and first commissioner, John Grierson.

Macartney-Filgate's interest in this new approach to documentary filmmaking was sparked by the films of the British 'Free Cinema' movement of the 1950s, which demonstrated to him the possibility of taking people in situ, rather than forming them to a pre-structured story. He was further inspired by the work of French photographer Henri Cartier-Bresson, whose book, *The Decisive Moment*, became the Candid Eye team's 'bible'. Along with Wolf Koenig and Roman Kroitor, two of his chief 'Candid Eye' collaborators, Macartney-Filgate attempted to do in film what Cartier-Bresson was doing with stills, allowing the films' structure to arise organically out of everyday activities in the lives of ordinary people, which were candidly recorded by the camera.

We may regard Macartney-Filgate as one of the most important influences on the development of direct cinema, primarily because of his observational style and detached point of view, which, when allied with the formal aspects of his work (objectivity, mobile camera, on-location sound, contrapuntal editing), characterized this new documentary movement as a whole. His approach also bears significance specifically for Canadian national cinema. The underlying sense of irony that permeates Macartney-Filgate's films has been interpreted as an expression of colonialist attitudes and dialectical tensions inherent within Canadian cinema during this period: on the one hand, committed to the national culture constructed and institutionalized by the NFB, while on the other hand, turning on that same culture the critical, distant gaze of the disenfranchized and rebellious young filmmakers who chafed against its limitations.

Over time, Macartney-Filgate's frustration with his fellow filmmakers' increasing inclination toward more structured, dramatic films with a predetermined philosophical 'hook', led him to depart from the Candid Eye team and the National Film Board in 1960, to pursue his ideal of 'film before essence'. During the next decade he was involved in numerous award-winning projects throughout the world, yet he remains unwilling to sell his work, or promote himself as a pioneering filmmaker. 'Sometimes I think I'm merely a hewer of raw material, that I have an ability to just go out and pan for gold and get enough and then it's up to the refinery and the people who make the ingots and shape it, and sell it [and] wrap it.'

GILLIAN HELFIELD

See also: Canada; Primary

Biography

Born in England in 1924. Came to the NFB in 1954, to work as a scriptwriter for military training films. Moved to the famed UnitB, and directed seven of the thirteen landmark Candid Eye films 1958–9. Left the NFB in 1960 to work with Leacock, Drew *et al.* on Primary. Worked around the world on several award-winning projects. Returned to Canada permanently in 1969. Worked for the NFB, and for the CBC as a producer 1970–89. Taught film production at York University and broadcast journalism at Ryerson Polytechnic University. 1959 Canadian Film Award; 1960 Grand Prix Eurovision Award, Cannes; 1961 American Film Festival Award; 1964 Academy Award, Best Theatrical Documentary; 1979 and 1980 Gemini Award for Best Direction; 1980 Prix Anik, Cannes; 1981 Silver Screen Award; 1991 Gemini Award for Best Documentary. Currently lives in Toronto.

Selected films

Candid Eye Series: director
1958 Blood and Fire
1958 The Days Before Christmas
1958 Police
1958 Pilgrimage
1959 One Third Down and 24 Months to Pay/ The Cars in Your Life
1959 End of the Line
1959 The Back-Breaking Leaf
1960 Primary
1964 Robert Frost: A Lover's Quarrel
1978 The Hottest Show on Earth
1979 Dieppe 1942—Part 1 The Battle Begins, Part 2 Echoes of Disaster (CBC)
1980 This is an Emergency
1991 Timothy Findley—Anatomy of a Writer

Further reading

Almenay-Galway, Mary, *A Postmodern Cinema: The Voice of the Other in Canadian Film*, Lanham, MD and London: Scarecrow Press, 2002.

Cartier-Bresson, Henri, *The Decisive Moment*, New York: Simon & Schuster, 1952.

Clandfield, David, *Canadian Film*, Toronto: Oxford University Press, 1987.

Elder, R. Bruce, *Image and Identity: Reflections on Canadian Film and Culture*, Waterloo: Wilfred Laurier Press, 1989.

——'On the Candid Eye Movement', *Canadian Film Reader* n.d.: 86–94.

Evans, Gary, *In the National Interest: A Chronicle of the National Film Board of Canada from 1949 to 1989*, Toronto, Buffalo and London: University of Toronto Press, 1991.

Feldman, Seth, 'The Days Before Christmas and the Days Before That', in Jim Leach and Jeannette Sloniowski (eds), *Candid Eyes: Essays on Canadian Documentaries*, Toronto, Buffalo and London: University of Toronto Press, 2003: 31–47.

——(ed.), *Take Two: A Tribute to Film in Canada*, Toronto: Irwin Publishing, 1984.

Gobeil, Charlotte, *Terence Macartney-Filgate: The Candid Eye*, Ottawa: Canadian Film Institute, 1966.

Helfield, Gillian, *Il etait une fois au cinema quebecois: The Persistence of Myth and Folklore in Early Cinema Direct Documentaries 1958–64*, PhD Dissertation, University of Warwick, 1999.

Jennings, Sarah, 'An Interview with Terence Macartney-Filgate', in Seth Feldman and Joyce Nelson (eds), *Canadian Film Reader*, Toronto: Peter Martin and Associates, 1977: 77–85.

Jones, D.B., *The Best Butler in the Business: Tom Daly of the National Film Board of Canada*, Toronto, Buffalo and London: University of Toronto Press, 1996.

Kubecek, Linda, 'Shoot Alberta', *Cinema Canada* 80, 1981–2: 19.

Morris, Peter, *The Film Companion*, Toronto: Irwin Publishing, 1984.

n.a., *Movies and Memoranda: An Interpretative History of The National Film Board of Canada*, Ottawa: Canadian Film Institute, 1981.

Nelson, Joyce (ed.), *Canadian Film Reader*, Toronto: Peter Martin Associates, 1977.

Veronneau, Pierre and Handling, Piers (eds), *Self Portrait: Essays on the Canadian and Quebec Cinemas*, Ottawa: Canadian Film Institute, 1980.

MacDonald, Kevin

Kevin MacDonald is known for his arts documentaries about filmmakers, artists, and musicians, and for *Imagining Reality: The Faber Book of Documentary*, a practical, accessible, non-theoretical book written for readers interested in documentary at all levels.

MacDonald started his career-making profile documentaries including Howard Hawks: American Artist (1997), and Chaplin's Goliath (1996). He directed Witness: The Making of an Englishman (1995), a film about his grandfather, Emeric Pressburger, alongside *Emeric Pressburger: The Life and Death of a Screenwriter*, his publication on the same subject. Wanting to make films that were more than profiles he started to research, write, and edit *Imagining Reality* with cowriter Mark Cousins, in an attempt to further understand styles and opportunities in documentary filmmaking, and the learning process became the book. MacDonald became interested in the idea of productions for cinema release for a smaller but dedicated audience. Both One Day in

September (2000) and Touching the Void (2003) were planned with a pace, visual scale, and use of sound and music intended for a big screen.

MacDonald felt that television's tight control often resulted in a prescriptive style of documentary structure, formulaic in narrative style and type of subject, and that concentrating on cinematic release would mean he could make films outside of this genre. He was commissioned by the BBC to make a fifty-minute documentary about Scottish artist and filmmaker Donald Cammell, and when Scottish Arts doubled his budget he was able to make a seventy-five-minute feature, Donald Cammell: The Ultimate Performance (1998), codirected with Chris Rodley.

MacDonald uses visual effects as storytelling tools, some archive-based, some more experimental, influenced by collaborating editor Justine Wright, who came from a commercials and pop-promo background. He is not a purist about what is used as long as it is used well as an appropriate tool of communication: if used for dramatic and cinematic effect, it is appropriate whether archive-based or animated. Touching the Void is an example of his use of reconstructions, where he uses actors and climbing doubles.

MacDonald is unique in having made two documentaries about documentary filmmakers, A Brief History of Errol Morris (2000) and Humphrey Jennings: The Man Who Listened to Britain (2000), for British television. The former has affected the way in which he approaches the documentary. He has intellectual ideas about structure, storytelling, and character, and is interested in how people portray themselves through language in an interview situation, feeling that certain interview techniques will uncover hidden depths, and the way his subjects act and speak in an interview is as valid a form of portraying human nature as other forms of documentary. He found that long periods of shooting contingency footage often revealed the most important elements and that the heart of a documentary is the spontaneity captured within planned, structured, preshaped shoots, and the friction between what is considered and composed and what is spontaneous, unplanned, or accidental.

ALISTAIR WARDILL

Biography

Born in Glasgow, Scotland, October 28, 1967. Grandson of Emeric Pressburger and brother of producer Andrew MacDonald. Graduated from Oxford, reading English Literature, in 1989. Lived in Spain, teaching English. Has taught at the National Film and Television School, The Swedish Film Institute, Salford University, and the Cuba International School of Film and Television. Has worked for the Edinburgh Film Festival programming documentary and as a judge at the Latin American Film Festival, Brazil. Has been an associate editor at Faber & Faber since 1995. Wrote *Emeric Pressburger: The Life and Death of a Screenwriter* (winner of BFI film book of the year and shortlisted for the NCR nonfiction prize), and co-edited *Imagining Reality: The Faber Book of Documentary*. His journalism has appeared in numerous publications in the United Kingdom including the *Guardian*, *Observer* and *Telegraph*. Recipient of the following awards, for Touching the Void: Banff Festival, Canada, Best Film, 2003; Evening Standard Film Awards, Best Film, 2004; Kendal Mountain Film Festival, Grand Prize, 2003; Autrans Festival of Mountain and Adventure Films, France, 2003; for One Day in September: Academy Award, United States, 2000; British Independent Film Awards, Douglas Hickox Award, 2000; International Emmy, 2000; European Film Awards, Best Documentary Award, 2000; International Documentary Association, IDA Award, 2000.

Selected films

1995 Witness: The Making of an Englishman (TV, Figment Films/PCP/Channel 4): director, writer
1996 Chaplin's Goliath (Figment Films/STV): director, writer
1997 The Moving World of George Ricky (BBC): director
1997 Howard Hawks: American Artist (TV, BFI/BBC/Bravo/Canal+/Star): director
1998 Donald Cammell: The Ultimate Performance (BBC/Total Performance Ltd): director, producer
2000 One Day in September (Arthur Cohn/BBC/British Screen): director

2000 Humphrey Jennings: The Man Who Listened to Britain (TV, Figment Films/Channel 4): director
2000 A Brief History of Errol Morris: director
2001 Being Mick (TV, Jagged Films/Channel 4): director, cinematographer
2003 Touching the Void (BDarlow Smithson/Film Council/Film 4/Pathé, US distribution: IFC Films): director

Further reading

Collins, David, 'What's Up Doc?' interview, *Creation*, November 2000: 10–12.
Falcon, Richard, 'White Ladder', review, *Sight and Sound*, January 2004.
MacDonald, Kevin, *Emeric Pressburger: The Life and Death of a Screenwriter*, London: Faber & Faber, 1994.
MacDonald, Kevin and Cousins, Mark, *Imagining Reality: The Faber Book of Documentary*, London: Faber & Faber, 1996.
Mottram, James, 'Oscar H. One Day in September', *Film Review* 594, 2000: 81.
n.a., 'Patriot Games', interview, *Film Ireland* 76, June/July 2000: 22–3.
Wylie, Liam, 'One Day in September', *Film West* 40, 2000: 28–31.

McElwee, Ross

Ross McElwee was part of a small group of Massachusetts Institute of Technology (MIT) film students in the 1970s who, under the aegis of then faculty members Ed Pincus and Richard Leacock, sought to move away from what was perceived as an inherent lack of humanity in the traditional cinéma vérité style. As a result he became a major contributor to a movement toward a more personal and intimate form of documentary filmmaking sometimes referred to as the autobiographical or memoir film. In this enterprise, McElwee was the benefactor of a group of filmmakers such as Pincus, Martha Coolidge, and Amalie Rothschild who, in turning the camera on themselves and their own domestic settings, not only broke with the traditional premise of recording reality without the intrusion of the filmmaker, but foregrounded the author's presence to such an extent that the filmmaker became a central subject of the work.

The work of McElwee and his contemporaries, sometimes referred to as 'the second generation of cinéma vérité', is distinguishable from its predecessor primarily in its move toward a more skeptical self-interrogation, which often problematized documentary's ability to uncover truth. Appearing on the heels of 1960s cinéma vérité, which maintained a much more overt relationship to political and social causes, this tendency led some to deem the work passive and self-obsessed, but in hindsight it can be understood as reflective of a general trend at work across the arts whereby a central concern of the work becomes an interrogation of its own means of representation.

Despite his apparent dissatisfaction with vérité, McElwee nonetheless preserves many of its fundamental practices in his approach. Throughout his career, he has remained adamant in his mistrust of 'directed' sequences, artificial lighting, and preproduction of any kind and has instead chosen to shoot without notice and without extensive preparation.

Although occasionally experimenting on collaborations, McElwee tends to work singularly during shooting, as both camera operator and sound recordist, a style that bears the influence of Leacock's 'integrated process'. Because of the unassuming front it poses to those in front of the camera, the technique allows McElwee to garner more natural, unembellished on-screen performances. This, added to the fact that the majority of his subjects are either family members or close acquaintances, creates a convincing representation of the everyday, an aesthetic that in earlier films, such as Charleen and Backyard, often borders on the home movie.

A central point of departure from traditional vérité, however, is McElwee's highly subjective narration, the lyricism and humor of which is often cited as the product of the filmmaker's enthusiasm for literature. Beyond their narrative function, these tangential voice-overs create a dialectic between narration and image that serves the works' broader enterprise of calling into question the objectivity of filmic images. This technique came to full fruition in his most commercially successful film, Sherman's March: A Meditation on the Possibility of Romantic Love in the South During an Era of Nuclear Weapons Proliferation, where the filmmaker, as if acutely aware of his inability to fill the role of male protagonist in a narrative based on romantic relationships, perfected his now signature deadpan, antihero persona.

A crucial component of this persona is often McElwee's displaced status as a Southerner living in the North. This vantage point seems to render him an outsider in both contexts, but it is often called on to uncover insights not available to those within the milieu itself. It is in these subtle observations regarding issues such as race relations in Backyard or southern femininity in Sherman's March that McElwee continues the tradition of politically charged documentary film.

The addition of narration in postproduction also opens a temporal disjunction within the world of McElwee's films, which reflect a phenomenon that the filmmaker has referred to as 'retrophenia', whereby one experiences the images recorded at an earlier date as if they were in the present. This layering of time, as well as the filmmaker's multiple roles of cameraman, on-screen performer, and narrator, often leaves McElwee oscillating between observer and participant. This dialectic continually bleeds into a dialogue on filmic representation as in the case of Six O'Clock News where McElwee constantly negotiates reality against both the reality that his film is presenting and that which television presents of the same event.

These continual efforts to undercut the tradition of the invisible camera led McElwee to foreground its presence to such an extent that it not only catalyzes action as Jean Rouch prescribed, but participates in the on-screen action as an entity in itself. Thus, technical malfunctions such a camera jams or dwindling batteries are transformed in the hands of McElwee into evidence of metaphysical currents that selectively disrupt the action, often prompting extended narration that attempts to supply the missing images to a blank screen.

Not only do participants continually refer to the presence of the camera, but in trying times even request that it be turned off, a request that McElwee often obliges. The result is again blank or obstructed images that mark rare instances where life is privileged over art. These moments range from the disturbing, as for instance when Charleen, a high school poetry teacher, friend, and recurring player in McElwee's films, comes home from the hospital after a fit of hysteria, to the sacred as when his fiancée, Marilyn Levine, demands that he turn off the camera in the moments before the couple's wedding in Time Indefinite.

With the autobiographical format, McElwee's filmography composes a diary of sorts, with the filmmaker's own narrative providing the continuum between films. The audience meets McElwee as a shiftless bachelor, uncertain of his career path and eager for companionship, and follows him through his marriage, the death of his father, and the birth of his son. These events are not merely subjects of inquiry for McElwee, but are formative of the filmmaking process itself. In Time Indefinite, we find McElwee trying to balance the responsibilities of filmmaking and fatherhood and as certain requirements, such as going on the road for months, are no longer as tenable as they once were, an accompanying stylistic shift occurs in his work. This shift is best illustrated later in the same film when, after the screen has gone blank during the birth of his son, the action starts again with a rare shot of McElwee himself, who, having his hands full as a new father, has entrusted his cousin Mary to shoot the scene with her video camera.

THOMAS STUBBLEFIELD

See also: Leacock, Richard; Pincus, Edward

Biography

Born in 1947 in Charlotte, North Carolina. Received BA from Brown University in 1971, and an MS in filmmaking from MIT in 1977. Upon graduation worked as studio cameraman for evening news, househelper show, and gospel hour for local television station in North Carolina. Also worked as freelance cameraman for D.A. Pennebaker's Energy War (1977) and John Marshall's N!ai, the Story of a !Kung Woman (1980). In 2000 Sherman's March was chosen for preservation by the National Film Registry. Visiting Professor of Visual and Environmental Studies at Harvard University since 1986.

Selected films

1978 Charleen
1979 Space Coast (in collaboration with Michel Negroponte)
1982 Backyard
1986 Sherman's March: A Meditation on the Possibility of Romantic Love in the South During an Era of Nuclear Weapons Proliferation
1990 Something to Do with the Wall (in collaboration with Marilyn Levine)
1993 Time Indefinite

1996 Six O'Clock News
1997 Kosuth (in collaboration with Marilyn Levine, digital video)
2003 Bright Leaves

Further reading

Lucia, Cynthia, 'When the Personal Becomes Political: An Interview with Ross McElwee', *Cineaste* 20, no. 2, December 1993: 32–8.

MacDonald, Scott, 'Ross McElwee', in *A Critical Cinema 2: Interviews with Independent Filmmakers*, Berkeley, CA: University of California Press, 1992: 265–82.

Stubbs, Liz, 'Ross McElwee: Personal Journeyman', in *Documentary Filmmakers Speak*, New York: Allworth Press, 2002: 93–108.

McLean, Ross

Television producer Ross McLean first came to prominence with the evening public affairs program Tabloid. While at the CLBT in Toronto, he developed the daily half-hour show to highlight information and news, rather than variety and dramatic programming. Although civically minded, Tabloid served audiences as a light-hearted approach to information. To that end Tabloid was sued after a 1956 stunt that has become television folklore in Canada. A Montreal physician wrote a terse letter of complaint to the show that was read on-air by host Dick MacDougal. Viewers were encouraged to write or call the doctor at the address and number provided on screen. Dr E.E. Robbins found himself inundated with phone calls, hate mail, and even taxis at his front door. McLean was promptly suspended until an apology was made. McLean begrudgingly returned to Tabloid three weeks later.

McLean left Tabloid to begin a late evening sister show called Close-Up. As a result of dedicated support from the CBC, Close-Up was able to send correspondents into the field for commentary, documentary, and investigative reports. This expanding format led to the thirty-minute show's expansion to an hour-long public affairs program. The format of multiple eight- to ten-minute segments set a programming precedent that is present in news coverage today. Described as 'the Daddy of all the information shows like 60 Minutes, The Journal, or The Fifth Estate', by Pierre Berton, Close-Up was McLean's attempt to mask information as entertainment. Interestingly, McLean modeled the tone of the show after interviews he'd seen with Mike Wallace, of 60 Minutes. The controversial storylines of the day, Paul Robeson, homosexuality, drug addiction, and euthanasia, also created a news-programming paradigm present today.

McLean's production work with Q is for Quest marked a move from news and information to documenting new and emerging performance. Q is for Quest focused on the fine and performing arts. During McLean's leadership, the program adapted and produced plays, recorded recitals, conducted interviews with painters, and produced one-person performances by Bertolt Brecht and others. This inclination toward the artist led MeLean to in-depth personality programming.

As a producer for the inaugural year of Telescope, McLean helped to create yet another industry standard, documentary entertainment programming. Telescope, a half-hour documentary series, presented single-subject features on notable figures in the arts, politics, and Canadian society. This mini-documentary allowed subjects to garner wider audience recognition. Christopher Plummer, featured at the beginning of the series, saw his fame skyrocket while filming The Sound of Music, due in large part to Telescope. One of the series' most notable interviews came in 1964 with Alfred Hitchcock, in A Talk with Alfred Hitchcock.

Ross McLean returned to his Close-Up roots as producer for The Way It Is, Close-Up's successor, in 1967. The Way It Is marked a change in McLean's production style and programming trends. Whereas McLean's renowned innovative vibrancy proved successful for many years, CTV's W5 was proving that solid research was equally satisfying to audiences and safer in terms of production. McLean's The Way It Is became less whimsical and safer. News returned to being information, rather than entertainment.

Ross McLean died June 1, 1987.

AMY L. DARNELL

Selected films

1953–60 Tabloid
1957–63 Close-Up
1961–4 Q is for Quest
1963–4 Telescope
1964 A Talk with Alfred Hitchcock
1967–9 The Way It Is

Further reading

Collins, Richard, *Culture, Communication, and National Identity: The Case of Canadian Television*, Toronto: University of Toronto Press, 1990.

Kesterton, Wilfred H., *The Law and the Press in Canada*, Toronto: McClelland and Stewart, 1976.

Peers, Frank W., *The Public Eye: Television and the Politics of Canadian Broadcasting*, Toronto: University of Toronto Press, 1979.

Makavejev, Dusan

Makavejev's most important contribution to documentary is the innovative technique of associative montage, which he developed mostly in feature films made from 1967 to 1975. His visual commentary on the world's political and historical process, straight out of the countercultural zeal of the 1960s, was a profoundly subversive one, aiming at anxieties at the intersection of libidinal and ideological indoctrination. He had a taste for combining Soviet and Nazi propaganda with counterculture material from beatnik America. His unique style of political collage, rich in historical references, impacted radical filmmaking worldwide.

The director started his career as an amateur cineaste for a Belgrade club, where he directed several documentaries in the 1950s and collaborated on many others. These early films are a crossbreed between feature and documentary, often with topics at the intersection of sexuality and revolutionary politics, as seen in the 1958 short Spomencina ne treba verovati/Don't Trust Monuments, where a woman is seen trying to seduce a monument, overwhelmed by the silent self-adoring superiority of the marble figure. While cinema club Beograd produced most of 1950s documentaries, those from the early 1960s were put out by a variety of key production organisations across Yugoslavia—Avala, Sutjeska, Dunav, Zagreb. On some of the Croatian-made films, Makavejev collaborated with celebrated poet Vasko Popa and cinematographer Octavian Miletic; he regularly worked with editor Marko Babac. By the mid-1960s Makavejev had to his credit about twenty experimental shorts and documentaries, adding to the impressive record of Yugoslav documentary of this period.

Nevertheless, Makavejev's main contribution remains the innovative way in which he brought together the documentary and feature genres. The features he made in the late 1960s and early 1970s are marked by an 'extensive, heterogeneous usage of found footage' (Arthur 2001: 12). Documentary footage is usually incorporated into feature film by adding the documentary as an extension to the fictional narrative, normally to contextualize the fictional part. Makavejev, however, ventured into the realm of associative montage by bringing into the fictional narrative familiar visual documents for reexamination and placing them in nonconventional combinations for the purposes of creating new context. Here, a widely accepted reading of given documentary footage was subjected to questioning from the individual perspective of the filmmaker, who uses the footage to create a personalized and sometimes subversive vision of 'truth' about a given historical period or social order. In such a highly personal context, 'objective' historical record is replaced by associative collage (Iordanova 2001a). (Variations of this approach have been used by Andrzej Munk in Poland and by Andrei Tarkovsky in Russia.)

The first time Makavejev ventured into intersecting feature and documentary clips was in his second feature film, Ljubavni slučaj ili tragedija sluzbenice PTT/Love Affair or the Case of the Missing Switchboard Operator (1967). In a scene that was supposed to be the prelude to a first sexual intercourse, Makavejev had his Yugoslav protagonists watch TV footage of revolutionary Russians pushing down church crosses (from Esfir Shub's The Fall or the Romanov Dynasty). By using this seemingly unrelated documentary footage, Makavejev was not only setting up a sociopolitical context for the love story but was also creating a complex allegory. The challenge to the previously erect but now falling symbols of the religious establishment was a visual equivalent to the vulnerability of phallic power that the film examined.

These techniques were perfected in the 1968 Nevinost bez zaštite/Innocence Unprotected (1968), in which he used parts of a prewar Yugoslav melodrama cross-edited with newsreel material and current interviews. Since its release in 1968, the film has become a classical example of nonlinear narrative.

Makavejev's innovative approach culminated in WR: Misterije organisma/WR: Mysteries of Organism (1971), a film about American bigotry, counterculture, Yugoslav communism, world revolution, and sexual liberation. The film opens with a twenty-minute documentary on the American period in the life of Frankfurt school's Wilhelm Reich; it combines feature and documentary to make a nonconformist statement on social and sexual liberation, totalitarianism and imperialism, communism and free love. Among overlapping subplots that can qualify as fly-on-the-wall documentaries by themselves, WR included a more or less straightforward fictional narrative featuring a tense love affair between a Yugoslav female communist activist and a Soviet ice skater (named Vladimir Ilich, after Lenin), the protagonists symbolizing two communist powers at odds with each other. Standing in for both Wilhelm Reich and World Revolution, WR was a work of an avant-garde quality, unconventionally structured around a wide array of cinematic techniques, mostly musical collages and associative montages of documentary and feature film (from documentary footage of crowds cheering Mao to feature excerpts from a 1948 Soviet glorification of Stalin, to 'shock corridor'-style scenes from an American mental institution). In his next film, the controversial Western-made Sweet Movie (1975), the director continued this type of referencing by using background documentary footage of the 1941 exhumations of the Khatyn forest massacre (committed by Soviets against Polish army officers but blamed on the Germans).

The director has said on many occasions that to him cinema is 'a guerrilla operation' that is meant to undermine everything 'that is fixed, defined, established, dogmatic, eternal' (Arthur 2001). The Yugoslav Marxist-humanist group Praxis and its aesthetics have particularly influenced Makavejev's political views, by American avant-garde filmmaking and the 1960s counterculture (he has identified Kenneth Anger as a major influence), as well as early Soviet montage. Having been exposed to the works of early Soviet cinema, Makavejev developed a technique that is influenced by the principles of Soviet montage, which he adapts for his idiosyncratic use. According to Arthur (2001: 12), by extending the principles of shot-to-shot montage ('to encompass clashes of material and elements or stylistic properties—fiction/documentary, interviews/newsreels, black and white/colour, colour stock/hand tinting, rapid editing/long takes, classical/folk music'). Makavejev, in fact, 'radicalized Eisenstein's categories of "tonal" and "intellectual" montage in a manner that layers intense visceral sensations over historically resonant particulars'.

Makavejev also perfected the art of using stereotypes and humour. Most of his protagonists are stereotypical representatives of a category such as a Serbian simpleton-strongman, an indoctrinated stiff Russian lover, a hygiene-obsessed Texas oil tycoon, a sensually glamorous Latino singer, or a sexually inhibited Swedish housewife. However, he defies all stereotyping by placing his protagonists amidst nontraditional associative sequences of cultural signifiers, thus challenging commonplace imagination and conducting an act of antirepression.

As a proponent of radical artistic and political views, Makavejev suffered a range of censorship acts throughout his career, both in Yugoslavia and the West. His work enjoyed such a strong reputation for controversy that only a few of his numerous projects were completed, mostly because of difficulties with financing.

Compelled to work, Makavejev made three features in the 1980s that did not make use of his trademark associative referencing of sexuality and politics that troubled the censors so much (and which, no wonder, were not particularly successful). He returned to using associative political referencing and collages of feature and documentary footage in Gorilla Bathes at Noon (1993), dealing with the end of the Cold War. In the 1990s he completed an autobiographical documentary Hole in the Soul (1994), produced by BBC Scotland, but failed to secure funding for a documentary project about Yugoslavia's break up. In 2000 he said that he wished to make a one-minute animation that would evolve around the endlessly changing Balkan maps.

Film specialists consider Makavejev's work a major contribution to the development of nonlinear narrative and associative montage. Concerned predominantly with issues of sexuality and politics, his oeuvre remains intricately linked to the countercultural spirit of the 1960s. However, he is also something of a social prophet: in a subplot meant to expose the commodification of people in consumer society, Makavejev's Sweet Movie (1975) opened with a mock live TV show in which a Texas millionaire was shown selecting a bride among an eager group of contestants. A quarter of a century later, an almost identical setup played out for real. In February 2000 the Fox network broadcast live a programme, 'Who Wants to Marry a

Millionaire?', in which property developer Rick Rockwell was seen choosing a bride among a number of finalists and proposing on the spot. The fictional stereotype of American kitsch that Makavejev had proposed twenty-five years before had now become a feature of real life.

DINA OIRDANOVA

See also: Yugoslavia (former)

Biography

Born October 13, 1932 in Belgrade. Attended secondary school in Novi Sad and graduated in psychology from the University of Belgrade in 1955. Enrolled in the Academy of Theatrical Arts in the class of Professor Hugo Klain. First worked on amateur shorts in a Belgrade club in 1953 and has been actively involved with documentaries since 1958. Worked also as a TV film editor, a journalist, edited a collection of fairy tales, and cowrote a comedy. By the time he made the controversial WR: Mysteries of Organism (1971), he had become an internationally acclaimed Yugoslav filmmaker (awards at Berlin, Cannes, Chicago, Sao Paulo). WR was deemed outrageous by the Yugoslav Ministry of Culture and shelved. Further projects did not receive production approval. As travel abroad for Yugoslav citizens was not restricted at the time, the director and his wife, Bojana Marian (musical editor of all his films), chose to leave the country. They live in Paris, but have also spent extensive periods working in the United States, Canada, Sweden, the Netherlands, Germany, Australia, and Israel. Spent most of the 1990s teaching at various Universities in the United States, from Harvard to Berkeley.

Selected films

1953 Jatagan mala/Yatagan Mala (Yugoslavia): director
1956 Pečat/The Seal: director, writer
1957 Antonijevo razbijeno ogledalo/Anthony's Broken Mirror (Yugoslavia): director, writer
1957 Spomenicima ne treba verovati/Don't Trust Monuments (Yugoslavia): director, writer
1957 Boje sanjaju/Colours are Dreaming (Yugoslavia): director
1957 Šta je to radnički savet/What is a Worker's Council (Yugoslavia): director, writer
1957 Eci pec pec/One Potato, Two Potato ... (Yugoslavia): director, writer
1957 Pedagoška bajka/Educational Fairy Tale (Yugoslavia): director
1957 Film o knjizi A.B.C./The Film About the Book A.B.C. (Yugoslavia): director, writer
1962 Parada/Parade (Yugoslavia): director, writer
1962 Ljepotica 62/Miss Yugoslavia 62 (Yugoslavia): director, writer
1962 Nova domaća zivotninja/New Domestic Animal (Yugoslavia): director
1962 Ljubavni slučaj ili tragedija sluzbenice PTT/Love Affair of the Case of the Missing Switchboard Operator (Yugoslavia): writer, director
1968 Nevinost bez zaštite/Innocence Unprotected (Yugoslavia): writer, director
1971 WR: Misterija organizma/WR: Mysteries of the Organism (Yugoslavia): writer, director
1975 Sweet Movie (France/Canada/Germany): writer, director
1993 Gorilla Bathes at Noon (Germany): writer, director
1994 Hole in the Soul (UK): writer, director

Further reading

Arthur, Paul, 'Escape from Freedom: The Films of Dusan Makavejev', *Cineaste*, Winter 2001: 11–18.

Blazevski, Vladimir (ed.), *Dusan Makavejev: 300 Cuda*, Belgrade: Studenski kulturni centar, 1988.

Eagle, Herbert, 'Yugoslav Marxist Humanism and the Films of Dusan Makavejev', in David Paul (ed.), *Politics, Art and Commitment in the East European Cinema*, New York: St Martin's Press, 1983: 131–49.

——'The Films of Dusan Makavejev', in Graham Petrie and Ruth Dwyer (eds), *Before the Wall Came Down: Soviet and Eastern European Filmmakers Working in the West*, New York: University Press of America, 1990.

Goulding, Daniel, 'Makavejev', in D. Goulding (ed.), *Five Filmmakers*, Bloomington, IN: Indiana University Press, 1995.

Horton, A, 'The Mouse That Wanted to F–k a Cow', in Andrew Horton (ed.), *Comedy/Cinema/Theory*, Berkeley, CA: University of California Press, 1991: 222–39.

Iordanova, Dina, *Cinema of Flames: Balkan Film, Culture and the Media*, London: BFI, 2001a.

——'Dusan Makavejev', in Derek Jones (ed.), *Censorship: A World Encyclopedia*, London and Chicago: Fitzroy Dearborn, 2001b: 3, 1505–6.

Makavejev, Dusan, 'Film Censorship in Yugoslavia', *Film and the Public*, Spring 1995.

O'Grady, Gerald (ed.), *Makavejev Fictionary. The Films of Dusan Makavejev*, Boston and New York: Harvard Film Archive/American Museum of the Moving Picture/Film Comment, July–August, 1975.

Malle, Louis

In a special issue devoted to the documentary films of Louis Malle, *Film Library Quarterly* calls him 'one of the most important documentary directors to emerge since WW II', and explains that his work in this area has tended to be overlooked because of 'the wide recognition [...] given to his narrative films'.

Louis Malle was born in Thumeries, France on October 30, 1932. In 1952, while still a student at IDHEC (Institut des Hautes Etudes Cinématographiques), Malle was hired as a cameraman by the undersea explorer Jacques-Yves Cousteau and four years later began his career as a filmmaker with Le Monde du silence/The Silent World, a classic documentary codirected with Cousteau. He also worked as the assistant of Robert Bresson on his 1956 film Un condamné à mort s'est échappé/A Man Escaped. Malle later recalled that his experience in documentaries was the reason Bresson hired him to work on this fiction film based on the real experiences of a World War II Resistance fighter in occupied France.

Malle rose to prominence with the French New Wave and his first fiction film, the award-winning Ascenseur pour l'échafaud/Frantic, made in 1957 and starring Jeanne Moreau. He made several other fiction films, as well as several short documentaries, before turning to his major documentaries shot during a trip to India in 1967–8. He was to continue this pattern of alternating documentaries and fiction films throughout his career in France and in the United States. His documentaries varied in subject matter but were generally shot as direct cinema simultaneously recording sound and image on location without the intervention of actors, written dialogue, and preestablished programs (Gauthier 2003). His last film, Vanya on 42nd Street, made in 1994, is a semi-documentary rendition of a rehearsal of the Chekhov play directed by André Gregory in an old New York theater.

Le Monde du silence, the 1956 documentary codirected by Malle and Cousteau, covers two years of undersea exploration in the Mediterranean, the Red Sea, the Persian Gulf, and the Indian Ocean on the ship *Calypso*. The film won the Palme d'Or at Cannes and the Academy Award for the best documentary that year.

In this film, divers using experimental equipment are seen swimming with schools of fish, examining coral reefs and sunken vessels. The *Calypso* braves a monsoon and takes part in a bloody battle with sharks and a school of whales. The film critic and cofounder of *Cahiers du Cinéma*, André Bazin, speaks of the poetry and intelligence of the Cousteau/Malle documentary and underscores the importance of the work of Louis Malle. What Bazin finds most admirable in the film is 'the a posteriori organization of unforeseen events by giving them a clear presentation and logic without diminishing their authenticity'. From this perspective, the greatest moment in the film is, according to Bazin, the whale sequence and most particularly the death of the baby whale, wounded by the ship's motor and then devoured by sharks.

In 1956 Malle made a fourteen-minute, black-and-white documentary entitled Station 307, describing a voyage of the *Calypso* in the Persian Gulf to experiment in applying the methods of underwater diving in the search for oil deposits. This film was written, directed, shot, and edited by Malle, who proudly commented that he was the entire crew of his first short film. That year he also made another fourteen-minute, black-and-white film, La Fontaine du Vaucluse/The Fountain of the Vaucluse, documenting underwater exploration of this famous geological site in the south of France.

After the success of his first feature film, Ascenseur pour l'échafaud, Malle made a number of feature films including Zazie dans le métro/Zazie in the Metro (1960) and Le Feu follet/The Fire Within (1963), as well as several short documentaries including Vive le Tour! a film on the Tour de France, the arduous bicycle race run in France every summer, and Bons baisers de Bangkok/Love and Kisses from Bangkok, a documentary for French television on daily life in the capital of Thailand, shot during a 1964 trip to Asia.

The most impressive and best-known of Malle's documentaries are the films made from footage shot during a six-month stay in India in 1967–8. This material was edited into a one-hundred-and-seven-minute documentary on Calcutta, the second largest city and the capital of western Bengal, and a series of seven fifty-minute films prepared for French and later British television on other aspects of Indian life.

Malle said that it was in India that he really discovered his approach to documentary or direct cinema. He said that he wanted to immerse himself in India, the real, not the Westernized India, to see what would happen, and to do it with a camera. 'It was a very subjective approach—I tried to describe my reaction to India. It was very personal. I feel these films made in India, these supposed documentaries, are probably the most intimate work that I've done so far' (Rollet 1976b). His very direct and affecting image did not please official India and in the same late-1970s interview Malle says that he had been refused a visa and felt that he had become 'one of the public enemies of the Indian government'.

Calcutta (1969) is a film that is both beautiful and shocking. Malle focuses intently on the life of the city—the religious rituals and celebrations, the animals and the people who live on the streets, the disfigured faces and bodies of the leper beggars, the student demonstrations, the acrobats, wrestlers, and public storytellers. Though we get some views of the life of the Anglicized upper classes at the Royal Calcutta Golf Club and the horse races, the focus of the film is on poverty, crowded conditions in the rat-infested slums, sickness, and death. In one memorable sequence the camera looks closely at the cremation of a woman and follows her husband as he lights the fire and then slowly, in accordance with the religious ritual, walks around the pyre sprinkling water and incense as we see the flames consume the body. The voice-over, spoken by Malle in a calm, unsensational tone, informs and gives statistics without commenting or judging. The final sequence of the film shows the dark-skinned immigrants from Madras, who live isolated and shunned by the other slum dwellers of Calcutta. The last words of the voice-over refer to them in a language that seems to have wider application for the spectator of this deeply moving film. 'They are astonished to be filmed. They are astonished to be pitied and to be a source of indignation.'

L'Inde fantôme/Phantom India is the general title of the series of seven fifty-minute films prepared for French television from footage from the same journey. In these films Malle's focus is on specific aspects of Indian culture such as the caste system or Indian religion, as well as life in cities such as Madras and Bombay. An English-language version was shown in Great Britain and Louis Malle was the voice-over commentator in both. 'In the commentary, I always returned to the fact that I had understood nothing about India,' Louis Malle said. 'Every time I thought that I had understood something, I discovered that I had been wrong [...] We thought that we had filmed a reality and, behind this reality, there was another. Truth is always more complicated, more tortuous.' Throughout his career, Malle believed in the virtues of the camera rather than the virtues of didacticism, and allowed himself always to be guided by his own gaze rather than ideology (Prédal 1989).

Humain, trop humain/Human, Too Human (1972) is a seventy-five-minute documentary on the manufacture of cars at the Citroën factory in Rennes (Brittany). In the first part of the film teams of workers are shown, often in close-up, working together on the assembly line. On the soundtrack the factory noises are occasionally accompanied by Gregorian-like chants to underscore the ritualistic aspect of the work. The second part begins with a long, high angle over the Paris Auto Show and then moves down to observe camera salesmen and customers, 'adoring and worshipping these cars' as Malle himself told an interviewer (Rollet 1976b). In the last section of the film, a final return to the factory emphasizes the boredom, discomfort, noise, and difficulty of the work. The faces of the workers are seen through the holes and gaps of the metal stamping machines they operate. Humain, trop humain is Malle's only documentary in which there is no commentary. 'I tried to keep away from any kind of easy stereotyped political statement' (Rollet 1976b). The spectator himself has to do the work of drawing conclusions.

In 1978 Malle made Pretty Baby, his first American film, and the following year began working on an English-language documentary, God's Country, shot and produced in the United States for the PBS with a grant from the National Endowment for the Humanities. Louis Malle wrote, directed, and shot this documentary on Glencoe, a city of five thousand inhabitants about fifty miles from Minneapolis. Malle and his crew first went to Glencoe in 1979 to interview and film the inhabitants as they lived their daily lives: farmers, bankers, police chiefs, members of an all-women baseball team. Because of a lack of funding and the pressures of other projects (including the making of Atlantic City in 1980 and My Dinner with André in 1982), Malle put off editing the rushes for several years. He returned to Glencoe in 1985 to film the same people, now showing the effects of the passage of time and changes in economic conditions. Malle spoke of making this film as an extremely interesting and agreeable experience, which brought him back to the basics of life. 'I found the same pleasure of total improvisation while filming this small city in Minnesota that I had experienced in India.'

To make his next American documentary, And the Pursuit of Happiness, produced and financed by HBO and shown on the cable network and later public television in 1986, Malle traveled across the United States interviewing recent immigrants. These include the West Indian poet Derek Walcott, a Russian actor teaching the Stanislavsky method, a Vietnamese doctor practicing in Nebraska, Egyptians in Los Angeles, Cubans in Florida, and others. The desire to obtain a certain cross-section of backgrounds and ethnicities required more planning and less improvisation than was usual in Malle's documentaries. It was a somewhat more traditional approach to filmmaking, Malle admitted, yet he insisted that, in this film as in his other documentaries, he was 'neither didactic nor systematic in his approach' (Prédal 1989).

In 1987 he returned to France to make one of his best-known and most admired fiction films Au revoir les enfants/Goodbye Children. This film, like the earlier Lacombe, Lucien (1974), reflects his lifelong moral concern with the behavior of the French people during the Occupation in World War II. He always saw a close relationship between his documentaries and his fiction films, many of which reflect his thinking about moral issues, and the historical and cultural context of societal values. A documentary entitled The Passions of Louis Malle, made by Don Boyd in 2003, celebrates the filmmaker's great body of work and includes interviews with his wife Candice Bergen, Brigitte Bardot, David Hare, and Philip French.

EVA MARIA STADLER

See also: Human, Too Human; Phantom India; Silent World, The

Biography

Born in Thumeries, France on October 30, 1932. Studied at the Institut des Hautes Etudes Cinematographiques (IDHEC). Died in Beverly Hills, California on November 23, 1995.

Selected films

1956 Le Monde du silence/The Silent World (86 mins, Technicolor)
1962 Vive le Tour! (17 mins, color)
1964 Bons baisers de Bangkok (15 mins, black and white)
1968 Calcutta (107 mins, color)
1969 L'Inde fantôme/Phantom India (350 mins, color)
1972 Humain, trop humain/Human, Too Human (75 mins, color)
1985 God's Country (95 mins, color)
1986 And the Pursuit of Happiness (80 mins, color)

Further reading

Bazin, Andre, 'Le Monde du silence', in *Qu'est-ce que le cinema*, Paris: Cerf, 1975.
Billard, Pierre, *Louis Malle—Le Rebelle Solitaire*, Paris: Plon, 2003.
French, Philip, *Conversations avec Louis Malle*, Paris: Denoël, 1993.
——(ed.), *Malle on Malle*, London: Faber & Faber, 1996.
Gauthier, Guy, *Le Documentaire: un autre Cinéma*, Paris: Nathan, 2003.
Jankowski, Paul, 'In Defense of Fiction: Resistance, Collaboration, and Lacombe, Lucien', *Journal of Modern History* 63, September 1991: 457–82.
Mallecot, Jacques, *Louis Malle par Louis Malle*, Paris: Althanor, 1978.
Prédal, Rene, *Louis Malle*, Paris: Edilig, 1989.
Rollet, Ronald, 'The Documentary Films of Louis Malle', *Film Library Quarterly* 9, no. 4, 1976a: 7–44, 54–8.
——'An Interview with Louis Malle', *Film Library Quarterly* 9, no. 4, 1976b: 45–7, 61–4.

Malraux, André

Before his appointments as the civil steward of French culture for the post-Liberation Gaullist Fourth and Fifth Republic, André Malraux first achieved renown through his writing, attracting both high praise (his novel, *La Condition humaine* earned the Prix Goncourt for 1933) and criticism (Leon Trotsky had found Malraux's portrayal of Chinese revolutionaries in *Les Conquerants*, 1928, problematic). In his fiction writing, Malraux experimented with a narrative aesthetic that can be characterized as aligning with those of the social realist school (in the pejorative sense, Malraux's work had been indicted as 'inspired reportage' by his critics), basing many of his novels on his own experiences with leftist political action, and demonstrating a particular agreement with antifascist movements. French critic André Bazin noted, in 1945, that Malraux's fictional work shared a resemblance to certain narrative techniques found in the cinema and praised him specifically for his use of ellipsis and metaphor. Outside of his fiction, Malraux wrote numerous essays on art and art appreciation outlining a program of ideals that forwarded a conceptual model of universal cultural heritage that claimed a continuity between the art of antiquity and modern artistic praxis, and declared cultural production as a direct means for the 'interrogation of the universe'.

After his service with the España Squadron fighting for the Republicans in Spain against Franco in 1937, Malraux embarked on a fund-raising tour of North America for the Spanish Medical Bureau. During this period Malraux began to collect his notes on his experiences in the civil war, which would become the basis for his novel *L'Espoir* (1937) and a film scenario based on his tour of duty in the Republican air force. The film project was developed after Malraux had witnessed that Joris Ivens's documentary, The Spanish Earth (commissioned by the Contemporary Historians, Inc., a group of writers that included Lillian Hellman and Ernest Hemingway who were sympathetic to the Republican cause) failed to prompt formal American intervention in the Spanish civil war on the side of the Republicans. The production of Sierra de Teruel (aka L'Espoir/Man's Hope) was meant to rectify Ivens's failure and would expose Malraux to the complexities of feature film finance and the physical demands of location-based production under extreme duress. The film began production in Spain with an up-front budget supplied by Spanish loyalists and was to feature a degree of verisimilitude similar to that of Ivens's documentary. The source of the film's realism was to be reinforced by the use of location-based sets in Spain (documenting the actual physical transformation of the Spanish republic as it 'bled' through its civil war) and nonprofessional performers, placing Malraux's film aesthetic within the same cultural-political milieu to that of British documentary pioneer John Grierson, who argued that documentary film (or, more appropriately for Malraux, propaganda film) must not only record a fact but also take a point of view. Unfortunately for Malraux, fighting in Spain escalated, forcing him to complete the film in France with a new financier. A final version of the film was completed for commercial distribution in 1939; however, the film's premiere was delayed by the start of World War II. Following the Liberation, Edouard Corniglion-Molinier sold the rights to Sierra de Teruel to a distributor who retitled the film L'Espoir and made subsequent edits to the film's footage and altered its title cards before its commercial release in 1945. L'Espoir failed to stimulate the political effects that Malraux had so consciously designed the film to produce and would go on to enjoy only limited critical praise from predominately leftist-oriented film journalists and critics.

During the German occupation of France through World War II American films were banned from the commercial circuit, and the scale of French film production accelerated under the patronage of organizations such as the German-owned Continental Films. Malraux during this time was active in the Resistance and had temporarily suspended his cultural activities. Liberation after the war freed French culture industries from external control; however, the signing of the Blum-Byrnes agreement between France and the United States in 1946 exposed the French film industry to American competitors through a system of quotas in return for economic aid for the reconstruction of France. The influence of Blum-Byrnes would play a significant role in determining the structural design of the French film industry and spreading the principle of cultural protectionism that would later dominate much of the discourse regarding French cultural policy and the policy frameworks constructed to preserve the concept of national French culture. In his role as Minister of Culture for the Fifth Republic under the stewardship of its President, Charles de Gaulle, Malraux was given authority to manage the Centre National de la Cinematographie (CNC). The CNC was founded in 1946 and had previously been placed under the supervision of the Ministry of Industry and Commerce to provide assistance, through subsidies, to the indigenous French film industry. In 1953 the CNC had been responsible for administrating a selective support system for *films d'art et essai*, aiding the early work of noted documentary filmmakers Jean Rouch, Chris Marker, Agnes Varda, and Alain Resnais through a *fonds de developpement*. During his tenure as Minister Malraux oversaw the establishment of an *avance sur recettes* loan system at the CNC that allowed producers to acquire partial financing from a support fund (*fonds de soutien*) based on a film's future profit. This subsidy and the relative strength of the French domestic box office (centered primarily in urban markets with its major market centered in Paris) helped to sustain the work of many practitioners of fictional film and documentary including several of the filmmakers associated with the nouvelle vague, who had adopted many of the precepts of documentary realism that Malraux had attempted to explore in Sierra de Teruel.

Malraux stepped down from his post as Minister of Culture in 1969, after de Gaulle's resignation as President. His departure was not unproblematic and he left the ministry amidst a scandal involving the attempted removal of Henri Langlois from his post as the director of the Cinemathèque Française, alienating him from many of the filmmakers his ministry had aided. In a rare return to private life after his civil service, Malraux would continue to write and maintain his lifelong interest in both art and politics.

JOSHUA AMBERG

See also: Man's Hope

Biography

Born in Paris November 3, 1901. Attended the Rue de Turbigot school in Paris 1915–17. 1921 publication of *Lunes en papier*. 1923–4 in Cambodia, arrested and convicted for theft. Political activity in Indo-China 1925–6. 1926 publication of *La Tentation de l'Occident*. 1928 publication of *Les Conquerant*. 1933 publication of *La Condition humaine*, awarded the Prix Goncourt. Political activity in Spain 1936–7. 1937 publication of *L'Espoir*. Production of Sierra de Teruel (aka L'Espoir/Man's Hope) 1938–9. 1939–40 served in the French army. Captured by the Germans 1940. 1941–4 activity with the French Resistance. Served as Minister of Information for Fourth Republic 1945–6. Publication of *Le Musee imaginaire* 1947. Served as Minister of Culture for Fifth Republic 1959–69. Died November 23, 1976 in Paris.

Selected film

1945 L'Espoir/Man's Hope: director, writer

Further reading

Cate, Curtis, *André Malraux: A Biography*, London: Hutchinson, 1995.

Cate, Curtis and Ahearne, Jeremy (eds), *French Cultural Policy Debates: A Reader*, London: Routledge, 2002.

de Courcel, Martine (ed.), *Malraux: Life and Work*, London: Weidenfeld & Nicolson, 1974.

Lewis, R.W.B. (ed.), *Malraux: A Collection of Critical Essays*, Englewood Cliffs, NJ: Prentice-Hall, 1964.

Michalczyk, John J., *André Malraux's Espoir: The Propaganda/Art Film and the Spanish Civil War*, University: Romance Monographs, Inc., 1977.

Romeiser, John B., *André Malraux: A Reference Guide 1940–1990*, New York: G.K. Hall & Co., 1994.

Man of Aran

(UK, Flaherty, 1934)

Man of Aran is Robert Flaherty at his most poetic and most removed from reality. In making the film, he took extreme measures to evade questions of the social and political context of the events and circumstances he portrayed while also shooting some of the most dramatic and beautiful images of the sea ever committed to film. The action takes place on the Aran Islands, off the coast of Ireland. A small fishing family face the perils of the sea when the son spots a basking shark and the local men go off in pursuit. Though their boat is lost in a storm, the men swim safely to shore. The film ends with the family making their way home in exhausted defiance of the sea that both nurtures and challenges them.

Man of Aran reconstructed an historical world that no longer (or perhaps never) existed, altering the profilmic until it fit the director's vision of what it should be like to live on an island. To obtain the desired rugged heroism in his characters, Flaherty cast three unrelated individuals as his mythical family. The two most important factual documentary sequences in the film, the farming and the shark hunt, were both reconstructed from practices that had long ceased; shark hunting had not taken place on the islands in more than two hundred years. Flaherty also violated ethnographic and ethical standards by significantly altering the rhythms of his subjects' lives and putting them in unnecessary physical danger. The fishermen's unfamiliarity with shark-hunting techniques meant that there was a genuine risk of their boat being capsized, and during the dramatic rescue of the boat from the sea in the opening scenes, Maggie Dirrane was almost swept out to sea while Flaherty filmed from a quarter of a mile away.

The idea for the film came from John Grierson, for whom Flaherty had just completed work on Industrial Britain (Flaherty, 1931). While Grierson shaped Flaherty's footage into something more closely resembling Grierson's conception of social documentary, he suggested that Flaherty might find the kind of isolated, agrarian community that fascinated him on the Aran Islands. After preliminary research, including reading the dramatic and documentary writings of J.M. Synge, Flaherty agreed. The film was produced by Michael Balcon, then head of Gaumont-British, for Gainsborough Pictures. In spite of Flaherty's poor reputation for working within industrial/studio conditions, Balcon gave him a budget of £30,000 and prepared to market the new epic documentary from the maker of Nanook of the North (Flaherty, 1922).

Like Flaherty's previous films, Man of Aran operates by alternating images of the faces and the environments of people. Significantly, the director's conception of the environment inhabited by these people was not of the land, but of the sea. Rather than a story of man and Aran, it is a story of man and the Atlantic. This had important effects on how he conceived of, or rather chose to omit, the social, cultural, and political aspects of life on the islands. By concentrating on fishing and the drama of a storm, Flaherty was able to sidestep a study of the islands as a community within the newly independent Irish state. The film became instead a romantic evocation of a people at the edge of civilisation, isolated and besieged by the intractable Atlantic.

The film was shot using a lightweight, spring-loaded camera and with a variety of long lenses of which Flaherty wrote appreciatively in 1934. Shooting up to half a mile away from his subjects, he claimed, gave the director the ability to eliminate self-consciousness and capture scenes that would have been impossible to film any other way. The photography of both human beings and the natural world was certainly more vivid and more monumental than ever before. The film used a greater amount of painstakingly arranged establishing shots and used the familiar fictional arrangement of shot-reverse shot to enhance and clarify the characters' reactions to events and circumstances. The overall visual rhythm was more conventional than in his previous films, a fact perhaps as much the result of his working with editors John Goldman and John Monck as a fundamental change in Flaherty's approach. The film established artful visual relationships among characters and between those characters and the environment in ways more closely resembling the conventions of epic drama than documentary. The final scenes, for example, frame the man against the skyline in a classic heroic pose, followed by an image of his son emulating it. The meaning of the sequence is clear; the son will battle the sea like his father in an endless and unchanging 'natural' cycle.

Though shot silently, the film was released with a soundtrack to correspond with the expectations of cinemagoers. Flaherty himself had little interest in or knowledge of sound. The musical score by John Greenwood seemed separate from the film and heightened the sense of romantic escapism. A largely random selection of wild-track sounds was also recorded, some of which were used effectively for atmosphere. The cast also recorded some vocalisations in a studio after the completion of principal photography.

The film was released as an authentic documentary record of life on the Aran islands amid a blaze of publicity and was a commercial success. It was only in later years that it was criticised, alongside most of the director's other films, for its romantic indulgences. Grierson had already written glowingly but cautiously of Flaherty 'I hope the neo-Rousseauianism implicit in Flaherty's work dies with his own exceptional self'. Paul Rotha would later be even more critical in his pronouncement that 'the Flaherty method is an evasion of the issues that matter most in the modern world'. Man of Aran was probably the most Rousseauian of all of the director's films and was proof of his continuing distance from those whose work he had inspired, including Grierson. It is more valuable as a documentary of Flaherty's vision of life than of life itself.

HARVEY O'BRIEN

See also: Flaherty, Robert

Man of Aran (UK, Gainsborough Pictures, 1934, 75 mins). Distributed by Gaumont-British Pictures. Produced by Michael Balcon. Directed by Robert Flaherty, with the collaboration of Frances Flaherty and John Goldman. Written by John Goldman. Edited by John Goldman and John Monck. Assistant direction by Pat Mullen. Field Laboratory by John Taylor. Music by John Greenwood. Musical Direction by Louis Levy. Sound by Harry Hand. Filmed in Inismore Island, Ireland.

Further reading

Barsam, Richard, *The Vision of Robert Flaherty*, Bloomington, IN and Indianapolis, IN: Indiana University Press, 1988.

Flaherty, Robert, 'Account of Making the Film—Man of Aran', Box 31, Flaherty Papers, New York: Columbia University, n.d.

——'Filming Real People', in Lewis Jacobs (ed.), *The Documentary Tradition*, second edn, New York and London: Norton, 1979.

Man with the Movie Camera

(USSR, Vertov, 1929)

Man with the Movie Camera is a film that has been claimed, justifiably, by historians of both documentary and avant-garde cinema (see, for example, Barnouw 1983; Sitney 1975). It is indeed a prime example of the considerable overlap between these two traditions in the 1920s and early 1930s, and serves as a reminder for contemporary viewers of just how audaciously experimental documentary can be (Nichols 2001). The crucial point, however, is that Man with the Movie Camera is an audio-visual manifesto demonstrating how cinema could be reinvented. Its director, Dziga Vertov, issued many written manifestos during the 1920s and 1930s, arguing for the need to film 'life as it is' and to organise filmed material according to a 'higher mathematics of facts' (Michelson 1984). Man with the Movie Camera elaborates these arguments on film.

Structurally, Man with the Movie Camera relates to the 1920s cycle of 'city symphony' films exemplified by Berlin: The Symphony of a Great City (Walter Ruttmann, Germany, 1927). These follow a 'day in the life' of the city. Man with the Movie Camera extends this basic idea in several ways. It combines material shot in Moscow, Kiev, and Odessa. It emphasises the interpenetration between rest, work, and productive leisure in the lives of good Soviet citizens. It loosely follows the adventures of a cameraman (Mikhail Kaufman) filming in diverse locations. Moreover, it represents its own making as a form of productive labour and undertakes a reflexive examination and celebration of cinematic vision (Michelson 1972). Bearing this in mind, Man with the Movie Camera's structure can also be seen in terms of charting its own construction and exhibition, from shooting and editing through to a triumphant final screening. On a more abstract level it is possible to argue that certain visual motifs recurring across the film give it another layer of structural coherence (Petric 1987).

Stylistically, Man with the Movie Camera exploits a gamut of devices to illustrate how the cinematic apparatus can augment human perception. The cinematography uses shots from every conceivable location, angle, and distance, including trick shots that play perceptual games with the viewer. Slow motion, freeze-frame, superimposition, and split screen effects are also deployed. Some shots are cut so rapidly that the viewer barely registers their content yet receives a dynamic impression of movement and energy. More generally, the film's complex and unusual editing matches and contrasts graphic elements and movements across similar and disparate shots. It utilises some of the conventions of features editing such as eye-line matching and matching on action, but often turns them to its own ends. Faced with this barrage of cinematic virtuosity, it is quite possible that first-time viewers of Man with the Movie Camera will simply be overwhelmed by the film. Particularly with repeat viewings, however, it is possible to discern some of the patterns and concepts articulated within its overall design.

Vertov and his 'kinoks' collaborators (cinematographer Kaufman and editor Elizaveta Svilova) were militant exponents in 1920s post-Revolutionary Soviet cinema of the avant-garde insistence on the need for a complete break with the culture of the past. In Man with the Movie

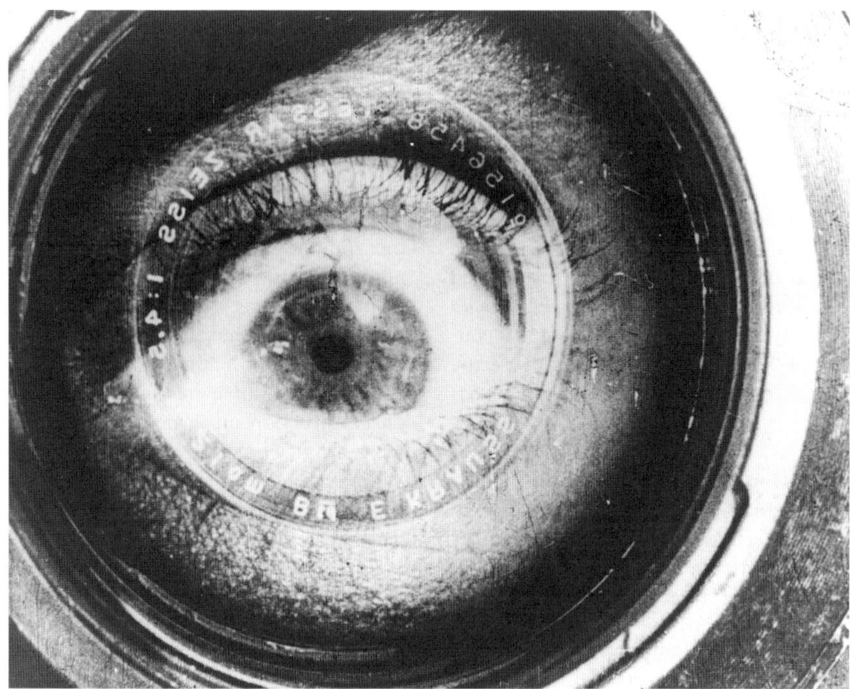

Figure 9 Man with the Movie Camera, 1929 (Courtesy of the British Film Institute)

Camera this is provocatively visualised near the end of the film. In a split screen shot, the Bolshoi Theatre, home of traditional art, breaks apart and collapses. Similarly, mainstream cinema had to be rejected because it hindered realisation of the medium's true social and technological potential and prevented audiences from engaging with reality. This is summarised near the beginning of Man with the Movie Camera. The eponymous cameraman walks past a poster for an entertainment film. A high-angle shot of a bustling city square, a low-angle shot of an industrial chimney, and a shot of a miner working underground follow. In four shots the film moves away from mainstream cinema into 'life as it is'. The combination of these shots into a 'higher mathematics of facts' reveals one of the power sources fuelling city life (Tsivian 1998).

Fundamentally, Man with the Movie Camera envisages cinema as the cultural electricity powering revolutionary progress. It operates like an alternating current, channelling energy between different aspects of an integrated Soviet society. Pleasure is linked to social production and productive work is joyful rather than alienating. The individual intersects with technology and collective activity. Shots of working hands, healthy torsos, and smiling faces are joined with aestheticised shots of machines. Industrial workers enjoy their work as well as athletics, music, and most of all cinema, within an accelerating cinematic rhythm. This rhythm feeds back into work practices and, within the utopian virtual city that the film constructs, speeds up the pace of progressive social development. The lives of good Soviet citizens represented in Man with the Movie Camera, and by implication the lives of its audience, are enhanced through synthesis with technology in the same way that human perception is expanded by watching the film (Turvey 1999).

Beyond its immediate Soviet, avant-garde context, the cultural 'year zero' premise and utopian dimension of Man with the Movie Camera connects with some long-established Russian cultural traditions. Cultural historians have highlighted the prominence of two parallel streams within nineteenth- and early twentieth-century Russian culture (Billington 1970; Stites 1989). One is a violent, morally outraged rejection of previous and current culture, a desire to wipe the slate clean that often borders on the nihilistic. The other is an explicitly or quasi-theological belief in the power of art and the artist to redeem or reconstruct society. Both streams feed into Man with the Movie Camera and partially account for the visionary extremism it shares with the work of other Soviet avant-garde figures such as the poet Vladimir Mayakovsky.

Man with the Movie Camera's formal innovations and uncompromising cultural politics did not lend it to easy assimilation either in the Soviet Union or abroad. At home it attracted accusations of formalism, and subsequent Soviet debates about the role of documentary contributed to the further marginalisation of Vertov and the kinoks' approach to filmmaking (Roberts 1999). Abroad, Man with the Movie Camera was noticed by influential commentators. For example, the German film and cultural theorist Siegfried Kracauer wrote a positive review to accompany its Berlin screening. Exhibited at the Eighth Street Playhouse in New York in 1930, it was the first Soviet film seen by Jay Leyda, future Eisenstein scholar and author of the classic *Kino: A History of the Russian and Soviet Film.* Nonetheless, British documentary filmmakers John Grierson and Paul Rotha typified the predominant foreign response to Man with the Movie Camera by praising its undeniable technical and experimental accomplishments but failing to see its point.

It is tempting to describe Man with the Movie Camera as a film defiantly ahead of its time. Several decades passed before it received sustained attention from film scholars and filmmakers. There was some revival of interest in Vertov and the kinoks in the Soviet Union during the post-Stalin 'thaw' of the later 1950s and early 1960s, when the Soviet avant-garde suppressed under Stalinism was cautiously reappraised. In France around the same time, Jean Rouch developed his notion of cinéma vérité, pursued in Chronique d'un été/Chronicle of a Summer (Jean Rouch and Edgar Morin, 1961), with reference to the occasional practice of filming 'life caught unawares' in Man with the Movie Camera. 'Life caught unawares' was Vertov's term for experiments with recording the reactions of subjects unexpectedly confronted with the camera. An example in Man with the Movie Camera occurs when Kaufman, using a car-mounted camera, films two expensively dressed, wealthy women in a horse-drawn cab. Unlike the beaming workers seen elsewhere in the film, one of them reacts rather self-consciously to being observed.

At the end of the 1960s Jean-Luc Godard and his collaborators in the radical Dziga Vertov Group seized on another aspect of Man with the Movie Camera. The film insistently compares the work of the filmmakers to the work of productive Soviet labourers. Svilova is shown at her editing table working on shots from the film. The French Dziga Vertov Group sought to incorporate a similarly reflexive explicitness about the process of film construction into their own productions. A widespread feeling among radical filmmakers at this time was that documentaries and other forms of filmmaking should reveal rather than conceal their processes of construction in order to encourage more active and critical responses from audiences. Where the Dziga Vertov Group films differ from Man with the Movie Camera is in their lack of utopianism about the contemporary political situation. Simultaneous with this more politicised appropriation, Man with the Movie Camera, because of its experimental aspect, also began to be screened alongside the work of Stan Brakhage, Malcolm LeGrice, and others within avant-garde circles.

Man with the Movie Camera's revival and its influence on later generations of filmmakers have been accompanied by a considerable and still growing body of scholarly work devoted to its exegesis. Annette Michelson's pioneering essay on the film highlighted its reflexive dimension and its makers' ambition to use all the resources of the cinematic apparatus for enlightenment rather than illusionism (Michelson 1972). Subsequent commentators offered more detailed analyses of, for example, how particular sequences in Man with the Movie Camera critique the social and economic inequalities perpetuated by the New Economic Policy (NEP), which was drawing to a close in the late 1920s (Crofts and Rose 1977). Given the film's complexity, most of this scholarly effort has concentrated on elucidating its makers' intentions. However, some more recent work has raised questions about how Man with the Movie Camera constructs gender within its utopian world and about how it deals with issues of ethnicity (Mayne 1989; Stollery 2000).

Initially, the appropriation of Man with the Movie Camera by the Dziga Vertov Group and some radical scholars generated an aura of political irreproachability around the film. Prompted by the demise of the Soviet Union, some more recent commentators have argued that although Vertov himself was dismissed as a formalist and increasingly marginalised during the Stalinist 1930s and 1940s, Man with the Movie Camera nevertheless shares some basic political assumptions with Stalinism. Its radiant workers and harmonious synthesis of humanity and technology mystify the actual historical conditions of labour in the Soviet Union during the 1920s (Tsivian 1998). Its unqualified endorsement of rapid industrialisation and, more tenuously, its metaphorical references to cleansing society of unproductive elements can be seen as an anticipation of Stalinist practice during and after the First Five-Year Plan (1928–33) (Roberts 2000).

Defenders of Man with the Movie Camera's cultural politics might argue that there is a significant difference between its genuine, zestful, possibly naive utopianism and the cynically conformist utopianism of later Stalinist Socialist Realism. The success of the alternative, emancipatory social role for cinema that Man with the Movie Camera agitates for was crucially dependent on its makers' optimism about underlying progressive tendencies within Soviet society being vindicated. Their gamble on the direction history would take did not pay off. Rather than intervening significantly into its immediate context, Man with the Movie Camera lay dormant for many years before reemerging as an important reference point for a diverse range of later documentary and avant-garde filmmakers and scholars. One of the many reasons why the film remains so compelling is because even though people may now no longer believe they are ever realisable, it affords a nostalgic glimpse into cinematic and social possibilities that might have been.

MARTIN STOLLERY

See also: Vertov, Dziga

Man with the Movie Camera/Chelovek s Kinoapparatom (USSR, VUFKU, 1929). Direction and scenario by Dziga Vertov. Edited by Elizaveta Svilova. Cinematography by Mikhail Kaufman, possibly assisted by Peter Zotov. Filmed in Moscow, Kiev and Odessa.

Further reading

Barnouw, Erik, *Documentary: A History of the Non-fiction Film*, New York: Oxford University Press, 1983.

Billington, James, *The Icon and the Axe: An Interpretive History of Russian Culture*, New York: Random House, 1970.

Crofts, Stephen and Rose, Olivia, 'An Essay Towards Man With a Movie Camera', *Screen* 18, no. 1, 1977: 9–58.

Mayne, Judith, *Kino and the Woman Question*, Columbus, OH: Ohio State University Press, 1989: 837.

Michelson, Annette, 'The Man With the Movie Camera: From Magician to Epistemologist', *Art Forum* 10, no. 7, March 1972: 60–72.

——(ed.), *Kino-Eye: The Writings of Dziga Vertov*, London: Pluto Press, 1984.

Nichols, Bill, 'Documentary Film and the Modernist Avant-Garde', *Critical Inquiry* 27, no. 4, summer 2001: 580–610.

Petric, Vlada, *Constructivism in Film. The Man with the Movie Camera. A Cinematic Analysis*, Cambridge: Cambridge University Press, 1987.

Roberts, Graham, *Forward Soviet! History and Non-fiction Film in the USSR*, London: I.B. Tauris, 1999.

——*The Man with the Movie Camera*, London: I. B. Tauris, 2000.

Sitney, P. Adams (ed.), *The Essential Cinema*, New York: New York University Press, 1975.

Stites, Richard, *Revolutionary Dreams*, Oxford: Oxford University Press, 1989.

Stollery, Martin, *Alternative Empires: European Modernist Cinemas and Cultures of Imperialism*, Exeter: University of Exeter Press, 2000.

Tsivian, Yuri, *commentary to The Man with the Movie Camera Video*, London: BFI/Connoisseur, 1998.

Turvey, Malcolm, 'Can the Camera See? Mimesis in Man with a Movie Camera', *October* 89, summer 1999: 25–50.

Manhatta

(US, Sheeler and Strand, 1921)

The emergence of the 'city symphony' as a film form in the 1920s arose from the intense interest among filmmakers to document the dynamism of the modern city. Films such as Berlin: Die Sinfonie einer Großstadt/Berlin: The Symphony of a Great City (Walter Ruttmann, 1926), Rain/Regan (Joris Ivens, 1929), and Man with the Movie Camera/Chelovek s Kinoapparatom (Dziga Vertov, 1929) focused on Berlin, Rotterdam, and Moscow, respectively, with the filmmakers using a variety of modernist techniques, including cutting, tracking, abstraction and perspectival shots, to convey the multiple points of view that were a central feature of urban modernity. Preceding all these films, the visual artists Paul Strand and Charles Sheeler had collaborated to make an American city symphony,

Manhatta, that became influential on both sides of the Atlantic for testing the cinematic possibilities of city films. Strand and Sheeler began collaborating on the film in early 1920 and worked on it for most of that year. Manhatta has been the accepted title since 1927, but Strand periodically referred to it as Mannahatta; at its premiere in July 1921 at the Rialto Theater on Broadway it was called New York the Magnificent; and in 1922 in Paris it had the title Fumée de New York.

Strand and Sheeler were trained in painting and photography but were drawn to moving images to represent the rhythms of the city. They shared the belief that film should develop its own cinematic language, but they were novice filmmakers (particularly Strand) and relied on photographic forms in composing urban scenes. A contemporary review by Robert Allen Parker makes this clear: they 'sought to apply the technical knowledge gained from their experiments and achievements in still photography to the more complex problems of the motion picture'.

Manhatta is generally accepted as one of the first avant-garde films in America, with its emphasis on modernist experimentation. The seven-minute film interposes shots of Manhattan with lyrics taken from two of Walt Whitman's city poems, 'Crossing Brooklyn Ferry' (1881) and 'Mannahatta' (1888), which are used as inter-titles and superimposed over a mythical image of the Manhattan skyline. This fusion of literary and cinematic idioms supports the view that Strand and Sheeler saw film as a hybrid form. The lyrics can be seen either to reinforce the image of New York as 'the city of ambition' (as Alfred Stieglitz dubbed it in his 1910 photograph), or offer an ironic juxtaposition to the moving images of a city full of smoke and industry, facilitating working life at the expense of community and leisure. The close match between poetry and visual images substantiates Jan-Christopher Horak's claim that the lyrics were intended as an integral part of the film (reflecting the interest in Whitman among other modernist artists like Joseph Stella), but Scott Hammen asserts that the Rialto Theater managers added the lines after completion. Whatever their provenance, as Miles Orvell argues, the lyrics serve to 'soften the effect of the actual modern city, a city that as pictured is far beyond what even Whitman might have imagined'.

In terms of exhibition, Horak notes that Manhatta 'was released commercially as a "scenic", a quasi-travelogue, shown in cinemas [to piano accompaniment] as a short before a feature presentation', in the same vein as Robert Flaherty's later homage to New York City, Twenty-Four Dollar Island (1927). However, Strand and Sheeler's artistic ambitions for the film were much stronger than its early exhibition record attest. In a 1921 press release, Strand commented that they had restricted themselves 'to the towering geometry of lower Manhattan' and 'tried to register directly the living forms in front of them and to reduce through the most rigid selection, volumes, lines and masses, to their intensest terms of expressiveness'. In this drive to abstraction, Strand compares Manhatta to one of the most distinctive examples of silent German avant-garde film, The Cabinet of Dr Caligari/Das Kabinett des Dr Caligari (Robert Wiene, 1919), suggesting that he and Sheeler were attempting 'to do in a scenic with natural objects what in The Cabinet of Dr Caligari was attempted with painted sets'.

Although Manhatta is a non-narrative film, it retains the structure of a day in the life of New Yorkers in downtown Manhattan, focusing on the area around Battery Park, the Staten Island Docks, and Wall Street. The island topography of the city is emphasised, from the opening images of the arrival of workers to the closing scenes of boats in the harbour at dusk (suggesting a closure or cyclical return). In the middle sections the camera continually shifts its perspective from street-level shots to high angles from the top of skyscrapers (some of which are in the process of construction), in an attempt to render the extreme and multiple viewpoints that the modern city engenders. One of the most interesting features is the inclusion of some of the most iconic images of American modernism such as Strand's Wall Street (1915), which portrays indistinct figures dwarfed by the huge dark windows of the Morgan & Company Bank, and Stieglitz's The Ferry Boat (1910), depicting the transportation of a crowd of workers to the city island (as well as other images published in Stieglitz's photographic journal, *Camera Work*). Many of these images depict New Yorkers as silhouettes or distant figures lacking individuality. Although the film depicts the drive of urban forces and portrays crowds as 'swarms of ants' when viewed from above, however, Strand and Sheeler stop short of representing an entirely dehumanised city or what Karen Lucic calls the 'disturbing sense of anonymity and conformity' of metropolitan life. By developing Stieglitz's aesthetic interest in the interplay between nature and modernity in his photographs from the 1910s, they balance the geometrical harshness of new buildings with shots softened by mist, sky, and sea. This more balanced view of the city falls in line with Horak's claim that despite Strand and Sheeler's interest in the abstractions of the city, their inclusion of natural imagery (together with Whitman's lyrics) reveals 'a romantic longing for a universe in which man remains in harmony with nature'.

MARTIN HALLIWELL

Manhatta (US, 1921, 7 mins). Direction, editing, and photography by Paul Strand and Charles Sheeler. Verse by Walt Whitman. Filmed in lower Manhattan, 1920.

Further reading

Hammen, Scott, 'Sheeler and Strand's "Manhatta": A Neglected Masterpiece', *Afterimage* 6, no. 6, January 1979: 6–7.

Horak, Jan-Christopher, 'Modernist Perspectives and Romantic Desire: Manhatta', *Afterimage* 15, no. 4, November 1987: 8–15 (a longer version in Paul Strand: Essays on his Life and Work, ed. Maren Stange, New York: Aperture, 1990: 55–71).

——'The First American Film Avant-Garde, 1919–1945' and 'Paul Strand and Charles Sheeler's Manhatta', in Jan-Christopher Horak (ed.), *Lovers of Cinema: The First American Film Avant-Garde, 1919–45*, Madison, WI: University of Wisconsin Press, 1995: 14–66, 267–86.

Jacobs, Lewis, 'Avant-Garde Film Production in America', in Roger Manvell (ed.), *Experiment in the Film*, London: Grey Walls Press, 1949 (New York: Arno Press, 1970).

Lucic, Karen, *Charles Sheeler and the Cult of the Machine*, London: Reaktion, 1991.

Orvell, Miles, 'The Artist Looks at the Machine: Whitman, Sheeler and American Modernism', in *After the Machine: Visual Arts and the Erasing of Cultural Boundaries*, Jackson, MS: University Press of Mississippi, 1995: 3–27.

Parker, Robert Allen, 'The Art of the Camera', *Arts & Decoration* 15, no. 6, October 1921: 396.

Stebbins, Theodore E., Jr, and Keyes, Norman, Jr, *Charles Sheeler: The Photographs*, Boston: Museum of Fine Art, 1987: 17–21.

Tashjian, Dickran, *Skyscraper Primitives: Dada and the American Avant-Garde*, Middletown, CT: Wesleyan University Press, 1975.

Man's Hope

(France, Malraux, 1939)

André Malraux made only one film in the course of a life crowded with major (and heroic) achievements of art and action and, after death, a burial in the Panthéon as a Hero of France. Among other things, he was a great novelist, antifascist political activist, leader in the French resistance against the Nazi invaders, author of influential and beautifully written meditations on the visual arts and, as Minister of Culture under President Charles de Gaulle, the man who ordered the buildings of Paris to be cleansed of their centuries of grime so as to visually renew the City of Lights.

The film he entitled Sierra de Teruel, later renamed Espoir/Man's Hope, was made with few resources under difficult conditions during the Spanish civil war. Malraux had performed a vital role for the Spanish Republic by organizing an international air force to counter the uprising of the Nationalists, which was supported by most of the Spanish military and was soon to be heavily aided by men and equipment from Nazi Germany and Fascist Italy. His novel, *L'Espoir* (1937), is a fictionalized panorama of the war at a time when victory for the forces of the Republic still seemed a possible outcome. Through characters based on Republican leaders and ordinary fighters, Spaniards and international volunteers, the novel presents a combination of vividly realized history, richly varied characters at war, and a modern yet classically resonant prose poetry of the battlefields, of human beings in passionate action under the all-darkening shadow of death. Among the events are those experienced by Malraux himself (Magnin in the novel) in his role as commander of an aerial squadron of international and Spanish volunteers. The film Sierra de Teruel deals with one sequence of that squadron's experience (though the events are expanded and some dramatic moments are added). The major action takes place in the hill country of Teruel in the province of Aragon, the key moment being a raid on a Nationalist airfield and the destruction of a bridge by two Republican bomber planes.

Malraux and his collaborators, all of them combatants on the side of the Republic or supporters of the Republican cause and untrained as actors, began filming in 1938 in Barcelona and the surrounding hills of Catalonia, but the advance of the Nationalist troops forced them to move to southern France, where the film was completed in 1939. After being shown three times to limited audiences, it was banned in September 1939 by the French government, and all the prints but one were reportedly destroyed by the Nazi occupiers during World War II. In 1945, with Germany defeated, the film (renamed Espoir to clearly connect it with the novel) was shown to a large public and awarded the prestigious Prix Luis Delluc for best French film of the year.

Stylistically, Espoir the film reflects the major characteristics of the novel, sometimes transmuting them into impressive cinema, but sometimes falling far short of a successful translation into the new medium. Especially at the beginning, there are awkward scenes of novelistic dialogue and brief moments of political declamation. The limited budget is reflected in battle scenes that consist only of the sounds of gunfire accompanying otherwise peaceful footage or the conclusion of an episode with dark screen and mere sound when a car full of combatants destroyed or a plane crashes, to avoid the necessity of simulating explosions. Yet, as in Malraux's novels, powerful moments of visual poetry advance or punctuate the action. The off-screen sounds of bombing are echoed by the trembling of water within a large flask. Panicking sheep filling a meadow become an analogy for civilians fleeing before the advance of General Franco's crack Moorish mercenaries.

The documentary aspects of the film include the use of actual combat footage, and the influence of Robert Flaherty in the sculpturesque treatment of the faces and forms of common people, as well as in the recreation of community events, here a community of struggle. The early films of Sergei Eisenstein also are reflected in some of the dramatic mass shots and heroic close-ups. (Malraux, who was always very interested in cinema, had begun but then abandoned a project to film his novel *L'Espoir* with Eisenstein.) However, at a point nearly two-thirds of the way into the film, the action literally and figuratively takes off into its finest and most original moments.

Two bombers, with Spanish and international crews, begin a mission. One bomber is to locate and raid a Nationalist airfield and hold their planes on the ground long enough for the other bomber to destroy a bridge. They must take off at night, and there is no working generator for normal airstrip lights. Cars have been volunteered from a series of small towns, and we see the headlights turn on, car by car, across a dark distance that the planes, in turn, traverse and rise above. This image of solidarity is followed by the raids and the destruction of the bridge, done with a cross-cutting of the crews and aerial combat footage, impressive for its time. One plane returns safely but the other crashes in the mountains of Teruel. The crew of the fallen plane is then transported down the mountains, the dying and those who will survive on improvised stretchers, one dead airman in a bouncing white coffin strapped to a mule. Long, ever-growing lines of peasants, seen close up and in long shot against the rugged mountains, accompany the descent to honor the airmen who are given silent, solemn respect by crowds in the villages they cross. While the novel *L'Espoir* ends with a major character filled with hope (*espoir*) for victory, the film concludes with this magnificently realized vision of solidarity but also of elegy and mourning, whether intended or not, for the lost cause of the Spanish Republic.

MIRA BINFORD

See also: Malraux, André

Espoir/Man's Hope (aka Sierra de Teruel) (France, 1939, 75 mins, black and white). In Spanish, available with French and English subtitles. Directed by Andre Malraux assisted by Boris Peskin and Max Aub. Script: Andre Malraux assisted by Denis Marion. Cinematography: Louis Page and Andre Thomas. Music: Darius Milhaud. Produced by Corniglion-Molinier. Filmed in Spain and France.

Further reading

Lyotard, Jean-Francois, *Signed, Malraux*, trans. Robert Harvey, Minneapohs, MN: University of Minnesota Press, 1999.

Malraux, Andre, *L'espoir, a novel, Gallimard (1937)*, trans. Stuart Gilbert and Alistair MacDonald as *Man's Hope*, Random House, 1938.

——*Esquisse d'une psychologie du cinéma*, Paris: Editions Nouveau Monde, 2003.

Marion, Denis, *Le Cinéma selon André Malraux*, Paris: Petite bibliothèque de Cahiers du Cinema, 1970.

Michalczyk, John J., *Andre Malraux's Espoir: The Propaganda/Art Film and the Spanish Civil War*,

Romance Monographs no. 27, Jackson, MS: University of Mississippi, 1977.
n.a., *Screenplay with commentary, L'Espoir—Sierra de Teruel*, Paris: Gallimard Folio, 1937.

Manufacturing Consent: Noam Chomsky and the Media

(Canada, Achbar and Wintonick, 1992)

Noam Chomsky, the noted linguist and famed scholar, acts as the protagonist in Mark Achbar and Peter Wintonick's loose narrative, Manufacturing Consent: Noam Chomsky and the Media. The film chronologically charts the rise of the socialist activist Chomsky, who holds himself outside the mainstream media so as to retain the ability to critique it. This feature-length documentary is an epic and engaging examination of Noam Chomsky's critique of corporate news-gathering and the vested interests that lie behind media coverage.

Divided into two large segments composed of smaller informational units, each addressing a specific element of Chomsky's theses concerning the media, Manufacturing Consent is swiftly paced considering its nearly three-hour running time. Part one, 'Thought Control in a Democratic Society', focuses on Chomsky's background and his rise to prominence among the Western world's foremost scholars before establishing his leading role in the world of political activism. Achbar and Wintonick are careful to divide the intellectual's academic pursuits from his activism. Time and again the case is made that Chomsky's political position is a simple matter of 'being able to look at yourself in the mirror each day' and the scholar's contemporary critiques of power politics are removed from the 'Chomskyan Revolution of Linguistics' that established him in academia during the 1960s. Part two offers a far more detailed examination of Chomsky's role in contemporary activism and outlines several of his targets. Chomsky's application of the propaganda model to American news reportage of events in Cambodia and East Timor from 1975 to 1979 is presented as an example of how corporate and government concerns shape the news. During this documentary, within the documentary, the filmmakers skilfully combine file footage, interview material, and original illustrations to offer Manufacturing Consent's most dramatic example of the behaviour of the corporate press.

Throughout Manufacturing Consent, quotes from Chomsky's literature and documentary footage from separate segments of Achbar and Wintonick's film appear on billboards during brief transition shots featuring public spaces such as airports, shopping malls, and baseball stadiums. This 'recontextualization' of both Chomsky's politics and the filmmakers' imagery points up the absence of such oppositional viewpoints in mass media outlets. In fact, this device goes so far to strengthen the filmmakers' thesis concerning the importance of Chomsky's message as the activist's own words do. Other self-reflexive moments involve regular appearances of the filmmakers on-screen, often as illustrators of Chomsky's theories and arguments.

More than five years in the making, Manufacturing Consent aims to assist in the 'development of courses of intellectual self-defence', or independent thought, that led Chomsky to his self-professed stance as a 'rationalist-libertarian-socialist'. Lacking the conventional voice-over narration that generally orders such compilation films, Manufacturing Consent allows viewers to come to their own decisions concerning the material presented.

MICHAEL B. BAKER

Manufacturing Consent: Noam Chomsky and the Media (Canada, Necessary Illusions/ National Film Board of Canada, 1992, 168 mins). Distributed by Zeitgeist Films. Co-directed by Mark Achbar and Peter Wintonick. Produced by Dennis Murphy, Colin Neale, Adam Symansky, Peter Wintonick, Francis Miquet, and Mark Achbar. Cinematography by Mark Achbar, Norbert Bunge, Antonin Lhotsky, Francis Miquet, and Barry Perles, Ken Reeves, Kirk Tongas, Peter Wintonick. Videography by Mark Achbar, Eddie Becker, Dan Garson, Michael Goldberg, William Turnley, Peter Walker, and Peter Wintonick. Edited by Peter Wintonick. Music by Carl Schultz.

Further reading

Achbar, Mark and Wintonick, Peter, 'Manufacturing Dissent', *Cineaste* 3, 1993.
Chomsky, Noam and Herman, Edward S., *Manufacturing Consent: The Political Economy of the Mass Media*, New York: Pantheon Books, 1988.

Glassman, Marc, 'Mediating Noam Chomsky. Manufacturing Consent: Noam Chomsky and the Media', *Take One* 2, winter 1993.
Kubey, Robert, 'In Praise of Chomsky', *Intermedia* 4, August–September 1994.
Mattick, P., Jr, 'Manufacturing Consent: Noam Chomsky and the Media', *Cineaste* 1, 1993.
Peck, James (ed.), *The Chomsky Reader*, New York: Pantheon Books, 1987.

March of Time, The

(US, 1935–51)

The March of Time (MOT) had the most substantial and sustained success of any documentary-like film series before the advent of television. It offered a new and distinctive form of screen journalism, a cross between newsreel and documentary. At its peak in the late 1930s and during World War II, it was seen in the United States alone by more than twenty million people a month, in nine thousand theaters. It was distributed internationally as well.

MOT was sponsored by the Time-Life-Fortune organization headed by Henry Luce. The monthly film series was preceded by a weekly radio series of the same title. Roy E. Larson of *Time* was responsible for the initiation of both series; Louis de Rochemont became the principal creative and operational head of the film series. The films and magazine functioned as promotion for each other.

Although sponsored by a politically conservative organization, MOT was identified with a liberal stance, more so than *Time* magazine. This was particularly true in foreign affairs; the films tended to be more conservative or erratic on domestic issues. Still, although feature films in the 1930s ignored or dealt only covertly with the Depression, MOT acknowledged unemployment, bread lines, and political demagoguery.

Internationally, newsreels avoided controversial political and military developments, but MOT tackled the machinations of Hitler, Stalin, Mussolini, and Tojo. One of the most politically controversial films in the history of American cinema was MOT's 'Inside Nazi Germany' (1938). It examined in some detail (sixteen minutes) the regimentation of the German people, the control and consolidation of nationalistic allegiances, and the preparations being made for future military and economic expansion. This was at a time when the majority of the American public was still strongly isolationist and the government maintained a careful impartiality.

The success of The March of Time—fueled by the controversy it aroused, as well as its energetic innovations—encouraged imitations, especially after World War II began. Created along the same lines were the National Film Board (NFB) of Canada's monthly Canada Carries On (1939–50) and World in Action (1940–5). When the distribution of The March of Time moved from RKO to Twentieth Century Fox in 1942, RKO replaced it with its own series, This is America (1942–51). The influence of MOT extended into American government documentaries of World War II as well, the most important being the Why We Fight series. Immediately after the war, in the UK, the J. Arthur Rank organization produced and distributed This Modern Age (1946–50). MOT was the principal model for the historical compilation documentary that became so prevalent on American television after the impressive success of Victory at Sea (1952–3).

A standard format for The March of Time was established early and varied little, regardless of subject. The fixed form may have been necessitated by the pressures of monthly production with modest resources; it must also have come to seem desirable given the considerable popularity of the series in the form in which it was offered. One of the most important ingredients was the voice and delivery style of its commentator, Westbrook Van Voorhis. His 'Voice of Time' (sometimes irreverently referred to as the 'Voice of God') was deep and commanding, ominous and reassuring at the same time. Spoken words carried the weight of the communication; the footage (largely stock), music (obvious and clichéd), and sound effects (sparse and highly selective) were cut to them. Often the pictures were given their meaning by the words, as part of 'the dramatization of the news' that MOT practiced. An extreme close-up of a face and mouth at a telephone becomes 'An angry refusal'; a long shot of a city street at night with a few electric signs becomes 'That evening Shanghai is tense' (War in China, 1937). Editing was the key. The pace is fast, with a hard rhythmic impact; a great deal of information is presented dramatically to capture the attention of the popcorn-chewing, Friday-night audience.

Structurally, each issue has four parts, with titles announcing each part. The first establishes the magnitude and urgency of the problem being dealt with. The second offers an historical survey of its origins and causes. Part three presents the immediate complications, confirming its newsworthiness. The concluding part looks to the future, stressing that the problem is a matter for continuing and serious concern.

By 1951 the losses of The March of Time had become too heavy for even the Luce organization to sustain. It was suffering from the competition of television news and public affairs programs, which could do the same thing as MOT films in theaters, with much greater immediacy. It was suffering even more from rising costs and inadequate rentals paid for shorts by the theaters, geared largely to the selling of feature films. Finally, it was no doubt suffering from its own fixed style and approach, which, through repetition of two hundred and five issues over sixteen years, had lost much of the freshness and excitement of its earlier days.

The March of Time must be acknowledged, however, as a memorable phenomenon in the history of popular American culture. Its influence has extended down to much of the documentary and public affairs programming on television today.

JACK C. ELLIS

See also: Rochemont, Louis de

The March of Time (US, Time, Inc., monthly, 1935–51, about 20 mins per issue). Distributed its first year by First Division Exchanges, then by RKO/Radio, and later Twentieth Century Fox. Produced by Louis de Rochemont and Roy Larson, but in 1943 Louis was replaced by his brother Richard de Rochemont. Edited by Louis de Rochemont and Roy Larson; Louis replaced by brother Richard during World War II. Technical management by Jack Bradford and Lothar Wolff. Commentary read by Westbrook Van Voorhis.

Marker, Chris

The French-based writer, photographer, filmmaker, and multimedia artist Chris Marker is a major—if elusive—figure in the development of documentary since World War II. Best known as a pioneer and accomplished exponent of the essay-film, in Marker's case the term is a catch-all for an extraordinarily diverse body of work that encompasses travelog, portraiture, political argument, and philosophical enquiry (often all in the course of a single film), and draws its impetus as much from shifts in the political and aesthetic climate as from his own enthusiasms and preoccupations.

Marker is credited with rephrasing cinéma vérité as 'cine, ma vérité' (cinema, my truth), a gesture that conveys not only the humour and intelligence that distinguish his films, but the essence of Marker's achievement in placing the subjectivity of the maker at the heart of the documentary enterprise, and linking this to an understanding that truth is not an objective quality to be discovered in the world, but the outcome of human creation, interpretation, and contestation. Long before the concept of reflexivity gained currency in documentary debates, Marker made films that play commentary and images off against each other to question and open up the processes by which documentary realities are arrived at. The identity of their maker is similarly treated as a fluid projection ('Chris Marker' is a long-standing pseudonym). The disembodied commentators of Marker's films are fictional characters who may share certain familiar and recurring traits with the author (a love of travel, a passion for cats and owls, an ingrained mistrust of received ideas), but can never simply be equated with him.

Marker emerged as a filmmaker in the 1950s, nourished by the wider contemporary flourishing in France of a distinctly personal approach to nonfiction subject-matter. He sustained close friendships and working collaborations with several of its key directors, including Mario Ruspoli, François Reichenbach, Agnès Varda, and Alain Resnais, with whom he codirected his first film, Les Statues meurent aussi (1950–3). Marker established his reputation through four films released in the later 1950s and early 1960s. All are based on journeys to countries and regions in transition: China in Dimanche à Pékin (1956), Siberia in Lettre de Sibérie (1958), Israel in Description d'un combat (1960), and Cuba in Cuba Sí! (1961). The intimate, engaging commentaries of these films, which recount the experiences and observations of an unseen visitor, disregard conventional hierarchies of documentary content to combine political exposition with lighthearted humour, poetic reverie with historical insight, and philosophical erudition with delighted interest in the banalities of everyday life. This playful mixing of registers is most developed in Lettre de Sibérie, which extends it to the image track by using animation and an invented commercial for reindeer products alongside more conventional observational footage. Its purpose is most clearly manifested in the celebrated sequence of a street scene, road menders, and squinting passer-by in the city of Yakoutsk. The sequence is repeated four times: first without commentary, then in turn with a pro-Soviet paean, an anti-communist critique, and an account of the visitor's own observations. Each of these representations is understood to have a bearing on the reality of Siberia, but none is granted the privilege of being the truth.

In the early 1960s Marker turned to the new lightweight equipment that was revolutionising documentary practice in France and the United States. Le Joli Mai (1962) was a departure for Marker in several respects. Far longer than his previous films, it is based around interviews with a cross-section of Parisians recorded in the spring of 1962, immediately after the end of the Algerian War. Le Joli Mai extends the subjective premise of Marker's earlier work to ordinary Parisians, who recount their hopes, opinions, experiences, and dreams at this moment of historical transition. In contrast to Rouch and Morin's Chronique d'un été, which used the camera as a catalyst to bring Parisians together, the interviewees of Le Joli Mai remain isolated in their own worlds and value systems. This may lead the film to a melancholy conclusion, but it does allow Le Joli Mai to preserve the texture of individual experiences while effectively mapping how they help to create and reinforce the social, racial, and political fault lines of French society.

In 1967 Marker organised and edited the collective film Loin de Vietnam, which marked the beginning of a decade of involvement with the left political film culture that flourished after 1968. This period culminated in Le Fond de l'air est rouge (1977), an epic compilation work that tracks the changing political fortunes of the international revolutionary Left after 1967. Composed of off-cuts and outtakes from hundreds of militant films, on the principle that with hindsight these abandoned fragments might possess greater historical significance than the finished works from which they were originally excluded, Le Fond attempts nothing less than to give cinematic form to the chaotic and contradictory movement of world history during this tumultuous decade. Marker harnesses the affective, aesthetic principles of montage to convey the rapid momentum of revolutionary uprising, shifting patterns of allegiance, gathering forces of reaction and repression, and developments that went unremarked at the time, but in retrospect assume decisive historical importance. That Marker's choices and interpretations have been hotly contested by participants in this history, and that Marker himself has 're-actualized' the film on several occasions (1988, 1993, 1997, and 1998), to take account of subsequent developments, only extend the film's relevance as an exemplary work of documentary historiography.

Sans Soleil (1982), widely regarded as Marker's masterpiece, returns to the personal register and the compulsive globetrotting of his earlier film-essays, but filtered now through the political experience of the intervening decades. Touching down in Japan, Africa, Iceland, the United States, and Île-de-France, and narrated as a series of letters sent by a fictional cameraman to an anonymous woman who reads and comments on them, Sans Soleil eloquently distills Marker's trademark concerns and fascinations into two major themes that would set the tone for much of his subsequent output: the function of memory and the potential of new media technologies for reworking images of the past in a critical and original way. Sans Soleil ponders the function of remembering on both a personal and a collective level, recognising that individuals and societies have memories only because they cast much of the past into oblivion. The film includes sequences where film footage is processed by an image synthesiser, transformed into shifting fields of vivid pixellated colour, which makes the images bear physical signs that approximate the deforming mental processes of memory and historical representation.

Marker's enthusiastic willingness to embrace new media as vehicles for lucid and responsible documentary enquiry offers a salutary alternative to the sense of crisis in documentary representation brought about by the digital revolution. His most recent feature film, Level Five (1996), explores the historical oblivion of the catastrophic Battle of Okinawa, by reimagining the battle as an unfinished computer game that carries the moral prerogative of refusing to allow a human protagonist, Laura, to rewrite history. It offers an audacious vision of cyberspace and the Internet as the memory banks of the human race, balancing the allure and advantages of instant access with a sobering, necessary reminder that limits still remain to our capacity for fully understanding and representing the historical past.

CATHERINE LUPTON

See also: Cuba Sí!; Joli Mai, Le; Sans Soleil

Biography

Born 1921, Neuilly-sur-Seine, France. Animator for the organisation Travail et Culture 1946–9. From 1947 wrote poetry, articles, and reviews for *Esprit* and other journals. Published a novel, *Le Cœur net* (1949) and a critical study of the playwright Giraudoux, *Giraudoux par lui-même* (1952). Editor at Editions du Seuil, Paris 1954–57. Published the photo-text book *Coréennes* (1959). Significant works other than documentaries include La Jetée (1962), Si j'avais quatre dromedaires/If I Had Four Camels (1966), the multimedia installations Zapping Zone (1990) and Silent Movie (1995), and the CD-ROM Immemory (1997). Lives in Paris.

Selected films

1950–3 Les Statues meurent aussi/Statues Also Die (with Alain Resnais)
1956 Dimanche à Pekin/A Sunday in Peking
1958 Lettre de Sibérie/Letter from Siberia
1960 Description d'un combat/Description of a Struggle
1961 Cuba Sí!
1962 Le Joli Mai/The Lovely May
1965 Le Mystère Koumiko/The Koumiko Mystery
1967 Loin de Vietnam/Far from Vietnam: organiser, editor
1968 La Sixième face du Pentagone/The Sixth Face of the Pentagon (with François Reichenbach)
1968 A bientôt j'espère/Hope To See You Soon (with Mario Marret)
1970 La Bataille des dix millions/The Battle of the Ten Million
1971 Le Train en marche/The Train Rolls On
1974 La Solitude du chanteur de fond/The Loneliness of the Long-Distance Singer
1977 Le Fond de l'air est rouge/A Grin Without a Cat
1982 Sans Soleil/Sunless
1985 A.K.
1989 L'Héritage de la chouette/The Owl's Legacy (thirteen-part television series)
1993 Le Tombeau d'Alexandre/The Last Bolshevik
1993 Le 20 Heures dans les camps/Prime Time in the Camps
1995 Casque bleu/Blue Helmet
1996 Level Five
2000 Un Journée d'Andrei Arsenevich/One Day in the Life of Andrey Arsenevich

Further reading

Kämper, Birgit and Tode, Thomas, *Chris Marker: Filmessayist*, Munich: CICIM 45/46/47, September 1997.

Gauthier, Guy, *Chris Marker, écrivain multimédia*, Paris: L'Harmattan, 2001.

Kear, Jon, *Sans Soleil*, Trowbridge: Flicks Books, 1999.

n.a., 'Chris Marker', *Images Documentaires* 15, 1993.

n.a., *Chris Marker, catalogue of the XXXII Pesaro Film Festival*, ed. Bernard Eisenschitz, Rome: Dino Audino Editore, 1996.

n.a., 'Dossier Chris Marker', *Positif* 433, March 1997: 76–104.

Predal, Rene, 'Un cinema direct à la première personne: Chris Marker', *CinémAction* 76, 1995: 18–24.

Rafferty, Terence, 'Chris Marker', in *The Thing Happens*, New York: Grove Press, 1993.

Van Wert, William F., 'Chris Marker: the SLON Films', *Film Quarterly* 32, no. 3, 1979: 38–46.

Marshall, John

John Marshall's career trajectory as a filmmaker anticipated and paralleled major shifts in documentary film, ethnography, and anthropology in the second half of the twentieth century. Soon abandoning his early mythic narrative style, Marshall embraced the observational possibilities of direct cinema, recording social interactions in Africa and the United States. His short 'event films' were followed by a reflexive turn in which the interventions of filming were made explicit. Then Marshall concentrated on what David MacDougall has labeled 'participatory cinema': collaborative productions driven by the economic and political needs of subjects.

John Marshall was only seventeen when his father took him to Africa, gave him a 16mm camera, and assigned him a task that shaped his life. In 1950 Laurence Marshall had resigned as president of Raytheon, which he had cofounded. Trained as a civil engineer, the elder Marshall believed that objective methods were possible in any field. He urged his son to make 'a record, not a movie' of the Ju/'hoansi (Marshall 1993). While Laurence Marshall financed and led seven trips of family members and various scientists to Southwest Africa over three decades, John developed his fluency in Ju/'hoansi and his abilities as a cinematographer, shooting massive amounts of color film. Co-edited with Robert Gardner, Marshall's first film, The Hunters (1957), was immediately embraced by anthropologists and remains an ethnographic classic. Often compared to the work of Robert Flaherty by admirers and detractors alike, The Hunters tells a thrilling story of a giraffe hunt, with footage assembled from various hunting occasions. Later Marshall would dismiss The Hunters as a 'romantic film by an American kid [that] revealed more about [the director] than about Ju/'hoansi' (Marshall 1993; see Gonzales 1993, who offers a counterargument).

Despite the success of The Hunters, Marshall shifted his filming style. Now having access to a synchronous sound system developed in 1955 by Danny Blitz, Marshall concentrated on long takes, without directorial or editorial intervention. Far removed from similar experiments in Europe and North America, Marshall was inventing direct cinema on his own as he filmed interactions played out in real time to document the nuances of spontaneous social life. A Joking Relationship (1962) follows the contours of a playful exchange between a young married Ju/'hoansi girl and her great-uncle. Marshall edited his first sync-sound footage into Bitter Melons (1971), another revelatory exploration of the negotiation of social rules. According to Marshall, his filmmaking has been shaped by the intensely interactive and egalitarian Ju/'hoansi people, whose transactions are characterized by intimacy. His Ju/'honasi mentor and namesake taught him how to use social space and to value specificity and truth-telling (Marshall 1993).

Forced to leave Southwest Africa in 1958 (and prevented from returning for twenty years), Marshall returned to the United States, where he studied anthropology and formed associations with Richard Leacock and D.A. Pennebaker, pioneers in the then-nascent direct cinema movement. Marshall joined another emerging central figure in documentary, Frederick Wiseman, to make a film at a prison hospital for the criminally insane. The result of this collaboration, Titicut Follies (1967), is an unforgettable record of institutional neglect and mistreatment, characterized by intense camera work by Marshall, whose self-described, career-long determination 'to get close to people' pulls the viewer into the horrors of the Massachusetts prison.

To make ethnographic film materials available, Marshall founded Documentary Educational Resources (DER), which soon became a major distributor with an unrivaled international collection. Continuing his concerns with pedagogy and direct cinema experimentation, Marshall filmed the activities of the Pittsburgh police, then cut the footage into short, 'thick event' films, further developing a theory of shooting and construction dictated by the actions of the participants and shaped by real time and space (Marshall and de Brigard 1995). The police films are striking in the intimacy and fluidity of Marshall's cinematography as he attempted to film as if a participant, rather than an observer. Use of these sequence-based films—often of interventions in family disputes—by the police deepened Marshall's belief in the utility of documentary to understand social interactions.

In 1978 Marshall returned to Africa and filmed N!ai, the Story of a !Kung Woman (1980). The ahistorical limitations of direct cinema required moving to another form to construct the autoethnographic N!ai, in which N!ai recalls her own life and also tells the wrenching story of her people over three decades. Structured around N!ai's direct address interviews and archival footage from the 1950s, N!ai was broadcast in the American public television series Odyssey and positioned Marshall's work in a popular venue. The film anticipates a major turn in contemporary documentary with N!ai's recognition of Marshall's camera and her reflections on the consequences of filming on her life.

In the 1980s Marshall intensified his advocacy work in Africa and co-created a development foundation. With colleague Claire Ritchie he produced short films shown to the press, funding agencies and groups whose knowledge and opinions could influence policy and help Ju/'hoansi establish farms and water resources. Marshall successfully lobbied to include local governments and cooperative land ownership in the 1989 Namibian Constitution. To Hold Our Ground (1991) reached a nationwide audience when broadcast on Namibian television during a debate on communal lands policy. Because of his deep and obvious commitment to the Ju/'hoansi, Marshall was relatively insulated from criticism directed against many First World image-makers whose depictions of 'the Other' were questioned, as a crisis of representation enveloped visual anthropology in the 1980s and 1990s.

A five-part series (2002) summarizes and concludes Marshall's record of the Ju/'hoansi over decades. A Kalahari Family begins with first contact between the Marshalls and the Ju/'hoansi in the 1950s, documents the move to communal farming and local governments, tracks the search for dispossessed relatives, and finally argues that representations of Ju/'hoansi as hunter-gatherers hinder their ability to adapt to the exigencies of a mixed economy. The series incorporates material from the Ju/'hoan Bushmen archive, which contains nearly two million feet of 16mm film and forty hours of videotape, a collection unequaled by any other body of ethnographic footage. Also unequaled have been John Marshall's commitment to the Ju/'hoansi and his place within documentary as he merged the goals of ethnographic filmmaking and development anthropology for half a century.

CAROLYN ANDERSON

See also: Hunters, The; Titicut Follies

Biography

Born in Boston, Massachusetts, November 12, 1932. Joined family expeditions to Southwest Africa 1950–8. Graduated from Harvard University, BA and MA, Anthropology. Photographed and directed The Hunters, released 1958. Associate director, Film Study Center, Harvard University 1958–60. Directed the Bushman Film Unit, Harvard University 1960–3. News photographer, National Broadcasting Company (US), Cyprus and Athens 1964–5. Photographed and codirected Titicut Follies with Frederick Wiseman 1967. Photographed and directed eighteen short films, Pittsburgh Police Series 1968–70. Founded and directed Documentary Educational Resources 1968. Advisory Committee Member, Cultural Survival, Inc., Cambridge, MA 1975–90. Directed Ju/'hoan (!Kung) Demographic Project, Namibia 1980–2. Cofounded and codirected Ju/'hoan Bushman Development Foundation, Namibia 1982. Awarded Rockefeller Foundation Fellowship 1989. Presented Honorary PhD of Fine Arts, Rhode Island School of Design 1995.

Selected films

1957 The Hunters: director, photographer, editor (with Robert Gardner)
1962 A Joking Relationship: director, photographer, editor
1967 Titicut Follies (with Frederick Wiseman): photographer, codirector
1969 An Argument about a Marriage: director, photographer
1970 Inside/Outside Station 9: director, photographer, producer (with Lemberg Center for the Study of Violence, DER)
1971 Three Domestics: director, photographer, producer (with Lemberg Center for the Study of Violence, DER)
1971 Bitter Melons: director, photographer
1973 Men Bathing: director, photographer
1978 If It Fits: director, photographer
1980 N!ai, the Story of a !Kung Woman: director, photographer (with Ross McElwee and Mark Erder), editor (with Adrienne Miesmer), producer (with Sue Marshall Cabezas and Michael Ambrosino)
1985 Pull Ourselves Up or Die Out: director, photographer (with Cliff Bestall)
1990 To Hold Our Ground: director, photographer, editor (with John Terry)
2002 A Kalahari Family (five-part series: A Far Country, End of the Road, The Real Water, Standing Tall, Death by Myth): producer, codirector (with Claire Ritchie), photographer (with others), coeditor

Further reading

Anderson, Carolyn and Benson, Thomas W., *Documentary Dilemmas: Frederick Wiseman's Titicut Follies*,

Carbondale, IL: Southern Illinois University Press, 1991.

——'Put Down the Camera and Pick Up the Shovel: An Interview with John Marshall', in Jay Ruby (ed.), *The Cinema of John Marshall*, Philadelphia, PA: Harwood, 1993.

Barbash, Ilisa and Taylor, Lucien, *Cross-Cultural Filmmaking: A Handbook for Making Documentary and Ethnographic Films and Videos*, Berkeley, CA: University of California Press, 1997.

Biesle, Megan, 'Reclaiming a Cultural Legacy: The Ju/'hoansi of Namibia', *Aperture* 119, 1990: 50–7.

Devereaux, Leslie and Hillman, Roger (eds), *Fields of Vision: Essays in Film Studies, Visual Anthropology, and Photography*, Berkeley, CA: University of California Press, 1995.

Gonzales, Nancie L., 'An Argument about Film', in Jay Ruby (ed.), *The Cinema of John Marshall*, Philadelphia, PA: Harwood, 1993.

Heider, Karl G., *Ethnographic Film*, Austin, TX: University of Texas Press, 1976.

Hocking, Paul (ed.), *Principles of Visual Anthropology*, second edn, Berlin and New York: Mouton de Gruyter, 1995.

Marshall, John, 'Filming and Learning', in Jay Ruby (ed.), *The Cinema of John Marshall*, Philadelphia, PA: Harwood, 1993.

Marshall, John and de Brigard, Emilie, 'Idea and Event in Urban Film', in Paul Hocking (ed.), *Principles of Visual Anthropology*, second edn, Berlin and New York: Mouton de Gruyter, 1995.

Ruby, Jay, *Picturing Culture: Explorations in Film & Anthropology*, Chicago: University of Chicago Press, 2000.

Mauro, Humberto

From the arrival of sound until the late 1950s, Brazilian documentary developed basically around INCE, the National Institute of Educational Cinema. In the early 1930s Humberto Mauro was a famous movie director (having already directed six fiction feature films) and a central personality in Rio de Janeiro society. The sound crisis, however, radically changed Brazilian cinema and forced Mauro to look for different opportunities in film production. In 1936 Roquette-Pinto (a well-known Brazilian intellectual) invited Mauro to direct the newly founded INCE. In his first writings and lectures about his work at INCE Mauro mentioned the influence of the French Institute of Scientific Cinematography and the work of Jean Painlevé. Contacts also were made with the Mussolini-inspired Luce Institute in Italy and the German Educational Film Institute, a government agency within National Socialist Germany. The exchange with Grierson and the British documentary tradition seemed to be absent. Humberto Mauro was the head of the Institut for thirty years (from 1936 to 1966), making only nonfiction films during that time. As the principal filmmaker of INCE, he directed three hundred and fifty-four short and medium-length nonfiction films. During this period he also directed, outside INCE, two fiction feature films and the docudrama O Descobrimento do Brasil/The Discovery of Brazil (1937), about the arrival of the Portuguese in Brazil in 1500, one of the biggest productions of the 1930s.

His documentary production at INCE can be largely divided into two periods. The scientific film takes its part in the first period, with a strong educational tone, having nationalism as its major proposal. The influence of positivism on the presentation of different fields of knowledge, such as medicine, biology, physics, chemistry, and history, is evident. In Mauro's first years at INCE he produced short scientific films with names such as Practical Lesson in Taxidermy, Superficial Muscles of the Human Being, Struggles against Ophidianism, and Stomach Extirpation. Scientific films seem to have been emphasized until the end of the 1930s, along with an increasing emphasis on nationalistic narration in films such as Brazil's Sky (1936), Vitória Régia (1937), Nation's Day of 1937. Bandeirantes (colonial explorers, 1940), and Invocação dos Aimorés/Praise to the 'Aimorés' Indians (1942).

In the 1940s and 1950s Mauro's documentaries exhibited a culturalist emphasis. In this second period of his career in INCE, there is a stronger focus on Brazilian folklore and culture, interacting with the 'classificatory' bias. The function of documentary appears to be related to the preservation of a disappearing rural culture and its traditions. Films such as Ceramics of Marajó (1939), Musical Culture (1951), Rural Hygiene—Dry Cesspool (1954), Hard Brown Sugar (1958), Rural Wells (1958), and Ox Cart (1945 and 1974) are examples of this period. Here the rationality of scientific knowledge is confronted with the universe of rural culture as a form of retrieving it. A melancholic/nostalgic tone is more and more evident. The director, who lived in Rio until he retired, draws on his poetic sensitivity when he represents his distant rural world of Minas Gerais. In 1945 Mauro began a series of short films named Brasilianas, a highlight of his documentary career. In Brasilianas we find a condensation of Mauro's most fertile work in documentary and fiction. The concern about traditions and customs is approached in a melancholy way, and the testimony of songs takes centre place. The dryness of the forms comes up naturally, as the simplicity of the culture he depicts.

FERNÃO PESSOA RAMOS

Biography

Born in the city of Volta Grande, in Minas Gerais state, in 1887. Began his work as a filmmaker in the small city of Cataguases, Minas Gerais, where he directed his first feature-length fiction film, Na Primavera da Vida/Spring of Life, in 1926. While still in Cataguases, directed three more feature-length films that affirmed his importance to Brazilian cinema (Tesouro Perdido/The Lost Treasure, 1927, Brasa Dormida/Reposing Ember, 1928, and Sangue Mineiro/Blood of Minas, 1929). Moved to Rio de Janeiro after receiving an invitation from Adhemar Gonzaga, the most important Brazilian producer at the time. Directed Lábios Sem Beijos/Lips without Kisses, as well as his most important fiction film, Ganga Bruta/Rough Gangue, for Gonzaga's new studio, Cinedia. During the early 1930s also made A Voz do Carnaval/The Voice of Carnival (1933), and Favela dos Meus Amores/Slum of My Loves (1935). In 1936 entered INCE (Instituto Nacional do Cinema Educativo), where he remained until 1966, specializing in documentaries, a genre in which he did some of the most important work of his career. Directed three hundred and fifty-four short and medium-length nonfiction films. O Descobrimento do Brasil/The Discovery of Brazil, a feature-length film made in 1937, was a large-scale historical production that depicted the arrival of the Portuguese in Brazil in 1500. The film was not well received at the time. Argila, a psychological drama, was directed in 1940 and met with a similarly disappointing response. Ended his fiction career with O Canto da Saudade/The Longing Corner (1950). Continued to film and to be active in the filmmaking community until his death in 1983.

Selected films

1936 Práticade Taxidermia I e II/Practical Lesson in Taxidermy I and II
1936 Mùsculo Superciais do Homem/Superficial Muscles of the Human Being
1936 Um Parafuso/A Screw
1936 Os Inconfidentes/The Independence Struggle
1936 Dia da Pátria/Patriotic Day
1936 O Céu do Brasil I e II/Brazil's Sky I and II
1937 Luta Contra o Ofidismo/Struggles against Ophidianism
1937 Circulação de Sangue na Cauda do Girino/Blood Circulation in the Tadpole Tail
1937 Vitória Regia
1937 O Descobrimento do Brasil/The Discovery of Brazil
1939 Leishmaniose Visceral Americana/American Visceral Leishmaniasis
1939 O Puraquê/Electric Fish
1939 Um Apólogo/Machado de Assis
1939 Tipos de Cerâmica de Marajó/Ceramics of Marajo
1940 Bandeirantes/Colonial Conqueror
1942 Lagoa Santo
1942 Carlos Gomes, o Guarani
1942 Invocação dos Aimorés/Praise to the Aimorés Indians
1942 O Despertar da Redentora/The Waking of the Slave Liberator
1942 O Dragãozinho Manso/Easy Little Dragon
1943 Indios de Mato Grosso/Indians of Mato Grosso
1945 Carro de Bois 1/Ox Cart 1
1945–56 Brasilianas, including: 1945 Canções Populares: Chuá, Chuá e Casinha Pequenina/Popular Songs: Chuá, Chuá and Small House; 1948 Canções Populares: Azulão e Pinhal/Popular Songs: Bird and Tree; 1954 Aboios e Cantigas/Cattle Chants and Songs; 1955 Engenhos e Usinas/Engines and Mills; 1955 Cantos de Trabalho/Working Songs I; 1956 Manhã na Roça—Carro de Bois/Morning on the Farm—Ox Cart; 1958 Cantos de Trabalho 2/Working Songs II
1950 Alberto Nepomuceno
1954–6 Série Educação e Higiene Rural/Education and Rural Hygiene Series: 1954 Fossa Seca/Dry Cesspool; 1954 A Captaçãoda Agua/Water Intake;

	1955 Higiene Doméstica/Domestic Hygiene; 1955 Silo Trincheira/Trench Silo; 1955 Preparo e Conservação de Alimentos/Food Preparation and Conservation; 1956 Construções Rurais/Rural Buildings
1956	Meus Oito Anos/When I was Eight
1956–9	Historical Cities of Minas Gerais Series: 1956 Sabará—Museu do Ouro/Sabará—Gold Museum; 1957 Cidade de Belo Horizonte/City of Belo Horizonte; 1957 Congonhas do Campo—Capelas dos Passos, Profetas e Basilíca do Senhor Bom Jesus/Congonhas do Campo—Chapel of Steps, Prophets, and Basilica of Our Lord Jesus; 1958 Cidade de Caeté/City of Caeté; 1958 São João del Rei
1958	Fabricação de Rapadura/Hard Brown Sugar Fabrication
1958	O Café—história e penetração no Brasil/Coffee History in Brazil
1959	Poços Rurais/Rural Wells
1959	Cidade de Mariana/City of Mariana
1964	A Velha a Fiar/Old Woman Spinning
1974	Carro de Bois 2/Ox Cart 2

Further reading

Aguiar, Claudio Almeida, *O Cinema como 'Agitador de Almas'—Argila, uma cena do Estado Novo*, São Paulo: Annablume/FAPESP, 1999.

Cesar, Ana Cristina, *Literatura nãoé documento*, Rio de Janeiro: MEC/FUNARTE, 1980.

Gomes, Paulo Emilio Salles, *Humberto Mauro, Cataguases, Cinearte*, São Paulo: Perspectiva, 1974.

Perdigão, Paulo, *Trajetória de Humberto Mauro, Filme Cultura* 3, January/February 1967: 4–23.

Ramos, Fernão Pessoa, 'Mauro, Documentarista (Humberto Mauro)', in Paulo Antonio Paranagua (ed.), *Cine documental en América Latina*, Madrid: Cátedra, 2003.

Roquete-Pinto, E., *Ensaios Brasilianos*, São Paulo: Companhia Editora Nacional, n.d.

Schvarzman, Sheila, *Humberto Mauro e as imagens do Brasil*, São Paulo: Ed. Unesp, 2004.

Souza, Carlos Roberto, 'Humberto Mauro', in Paulo Antonio Paranagua (ed.), *Le Cinema Brésilien*, Paris: Centre Georges Pompidou, 1987.

——*Catálogo de Filmes Produzido pelo INCE*, Rio de Janeiro: Fundacão do Cinema Brasileiro/MINC, 1990.

Souza, Jose Inacio de Melo, *O Estado Contra os Meios de Comunicação (1889–1945)*, São Paulo: Annablume, 2003.

Viany, Alex (ed.), *Humberto Mauro, sua vida, sua trajetória no cinema*, Rio de Janeiro: Artenova/Embrafilme, 1977.

Maysles, Albert

No documentary cinematographer has had a more long-lasting, influential career than Albert Maysles, a pioneer of direct cinema who has shot scores of documentaries, many of them American documentary classics.

After studying psychology, Maysles plunged into documentary filmmaking on a trip to the Soviet Union, during which he photographed patients at mental hospitals. Psychiatry in Russia (1955) is prescient of all his later work in its compassionate fascination with human behavior. While hitchhiking across the United States and traveling by motorcycle from Munich to Moscow, Maysles and his younger brother David developed their curiosity about life stories and forged a close artistic partnership.

Their first joint production, Youth in Poland, was broadcast on NBC in the United States in 1957 and opened the way for the brothers to join a group of young, innovative journalists who were making experimental documentaries in the Living Camera series for Time, Inc., under the leadership of Robert Drew. Using lightweight, mobile cameras, portable recorders, directional microphones, and high-speed film, Drew and his colleagues pioneered a North American version of cinéma vérité: direct cinema. This style reflected a 1960s urge to explore the real world through media, eschewing voice-over narration, interviews, and staged action, instead forming an allegiance with the possibilities and demands of an essentially observational documentary style.

Albert Maysles, along with two other exceptional cameramen, Richard Leacock and D.A. Pennebaker, photographed Primary (1960), which defined a burgeoning film movement and documented an important political moment in American history as John Kennedy moved toward the presidency. It was Maysles who filmed (arguably) the best-known and -remembered single shot of early American direct cinema: the one minute twenty second wide-angle follow shot of Kennedy entering a Milwaukee political rally, moving through a crowd of outstretched hands to the hall stage in Primary. It was Maysles who put a human face on the Cuban revolution in the Drew production Yanki No! (1960) (O'Connell 1992).

When Drew Associates officially formed the Maysles brothers declined to join; instead, they formed their own production company, Maysles Film, Inc. in 1962. The brothers operated as a filmmaking team, with consistent work tasks. David recorded sound and supervised the editing, while Al was the cameraman and the technician behind camera innovations (Reynolds 1979). They shared business responsibilities and routinely financed their more personal projects by producing corporate promotional films and reality-based commercials. In contrast to the issue-oriented Drew films or Frederick Wiseman's documentary series on social institutions, Maysles's documentaries track the vagrancies of personal interactions. Colleague Ellen Hovde describes a continuing goal of the Maysles brothers: 'pushing in film terms toward a novel of sensibility more than a novel of plot' (Hovde 1980). Their documentaries have often focused on the experiences of celebrated individuals—movie producer Joseph E. Levine; rock musicians, the Beatles and the Rolling Stones; classical musicians, Leonard Bernstein, Vladimir Horowitz, Jessye Norman, and Seiji Ozawa; actor Marlon Brando; writer Truman Capote; conceptual artist Christo; boxers, Muhammed Ali and Larry Holmes; and, consequently, on an American infatuation with fame. Three of their most esteemed films, Salesman (1968), The Burk Family of Georgia (1976), and Grey Gardens (1976), however, move from the spotlights to the dark corners of American lives. In Salesman the Maysles brothers returned to the Irish Boston of their boyhood and to memories of working their ways through college as door-to-door salesmen themselves, when they followed four Bible salesmen on their rounds. The result, later included in the (US) National Film Registry, was one of the first direct cinema films screened theatrically. Salesman remains a classic observation of the centrality of selling—and religion—in American life. The Burk Family, set in rural poverty, was part of a six-part television series on the American family. Without shying from documenting the harsh realities of the Burkes's lives, the Maysles documentary presents the family with a respect and warmth absent in typical profiles of poor Southerners. Grey Gardens examines an intensely competitive relationship between Edith Bouvier Beale and her middle-aged daughter, Edie, two witty eccentrics secluded in their disintegrating estate. The frank intimacy of Grey Gardens struck an emotional chord with audiences. Some found its level of self-disclosure discomforting; more commonly the documentary was considered important, revelatory nonfiction. Grey Gardens stands as one of the most complex examinations of obsessive family relations on film.

After David's unexpected death in 1987, Al Maysles continued and intensified his collaboration with a group of skilled documentary editors and coproducers, including Charlotte Zwerin, Ellen Hovde, Muffie Meyer, and Susan Froemke. Despite the rhetoric of 'uncontrolled cinema', cinéma vérité has always depended on subtle, intricate editing (Hall 1991; Benson and Anderson 2002). Indeed, 'the camera work and editing are directing in cinema verite' (Hovde 1980) and the strength of the Maysles' work partially flows from the imaginative cutting of the films by their colleagues. In the 1990s Maysles shot documentaries for cable television on topics ranging from abortion, care for the terminally ill, and the economic legacies of slavery to a series of profiles of film directors; however, each film is characterized by its frank, but deeply sympathetic, attention to individual experience. Along with other direct cinema practitioners, Maysles has encountered criticisms commonly lodged against observational documentaries: voyeurism, and a failure to meet a supposed promise of objectivity. To Maysles, mutual respect and solid relationships with documentary subjects are the central means of avoiding voyeurism. One of his documentary 'commandments' is 'to distance yourself from a point of view', while simultaneously recognizing that one will always have a frame of reference toward a subject (Maysles 2002). The veteran cinematographer considers personal integrity the necessary foundation for credible documentary production and urges documentarians to try to understand their subjects.

Although never active contributors to documentary theory, the Maysles brothers, through their best work, anticipated and influenced two important contemporary documentary trends: a recognition of power dimensions within family life (Grey Gardens) and a reflexive acknowledgment of the filmmaking process within the documentary text (Gimme Shelter). After filming for nearly half a century, Al Maysles retains his fascination with the complexity and ambiguity of human personality, his willingness to embrace new (most recently digital) technology, and his belief in the possibilities of direct cinema for documenting the intricacies of personal experience.

CAROLYN ANDERSON

See also: Drew, Robert; Gimme Shelter; Leacock, Richard; Pennebaker, D.A.; Primary; Salesman; Wiseman, Frederick

Biography

Born in Boston, Massachusetts, November 26, 1926. Graduated from Syracuse University (BA) and Boston University (MA) in Psychology. Served in the Tank Corps during World War II. Taught Psychology briefly; began filmmaking in 1955. Worked as a cinematographer on Primary (1960) and Yanki No! (1960). With brother David, formed Maysles Films, Inc. in 1962. Made a Guggenheim Fellow 1965. Received Academy Award nominations 1974, 2001; Emmy Awards 1985, 1991, 1992; the International Documentary Association's Career Achievement Award 1994; SMPTE John Grierson Award for Documentary 1997; the American Society of Cinematographers' President's Award 1998; the Boston Film and Video Foundation's Vision Award 1998; the Flaherty Award 1999; and the Sundance Film Festival Award for Documentary Cinematography 1991, 2001. Named one of the world's one hundred finest cinematographers by Eastman Kodak 1999.

Selected films

1960 Primary: (Robert Drew) photographer (with Richard Leacock, D.A. Pennebaker, and Terence Macartney-Filgate)
1960 Yanki No!: (Robert Drew) photographer (with Richard Leacock)
1963 Showman: photographer, coproducer and codirector (with David Maysles)
1968 Salesman: photographer, codirector (with David Maysles and Charlotte Zwerin)
1970 Gimme Shelter: photographer, codirector (with David Maysles and Charlotte Zwerin)
1974 Christo's Valley Curtain: photographer, coproducer (with David Maysles)
1976 Grey Gardens: photographer, coproducer (with David Maysles and Susan Froemke), codirector (with David Maysles, Ellen Hovde and Muffie Meyer)
1976 The Burk Family of Georgia: photographer, codirector (with David Maysles)
1980 Muhammed and Larry: photographer, coproducer (with David Maysles)
1990 Christo in Paris: photographer, codirector (with David Maysles, Susan Froemke, and Deborah Dickson)
1992 Abortion: Desperate Choices: photographer, codirector (with Susan Froemke and Deborah Dickson)
1996 Letting Go: A Hospice Journey: photographer, codirector (with Susan Froemke and Deborah Dickson)
2001 LaLee's Kin: The Legacy of Cotton: photographer, codirector (with Susan Froemke and Deborah Dickson)
2001 With the Filmmakers: Portraits by Albert Maysles: photographer, codirector (with Antonio Ferrera and Larry Kamerman) (four-part series with Martin Scorsese, Robert Duvall, Jane Campion, and Wes Anderson)

Further reading

Anderson, Carolyn, 'David Carl Maysles', in *American National Biography*, volume 14, Cary, NC: Oxford University Press, 1999.

Benson, Thomas W. and Anderson, Carolyn, *Reality Fictions: The Films of Frederick Wiseman*, second edn, Carbondale, IL: Southern Illinois University Press, 2002.

Davidson, David, 'Direct Cinema and Modernism: The Long Journey to Grey Gardens', *Journal of the University Film Association* 33, no. 1, winter 1981: 3–13.

Hall, Jeanne, 'Realism as a Style in Cinema Verite: A Critical Analysis of Primary', *Cinema Journal* 30, no. 4, 1991: 24–50.

Hovde, Ellen, 'Grey Gardens', in Alan Rosenthal (ed.), *The Documentary Conscience: A Casebook in Film Making*, Berkeley, CA: University of California Press, 1980.

Levin, G. Roy, 'Albert and David Maysles', in *Documentary Explorations: 15 Interviews with Film-Makers*, Garden City, NY: Doubleday, 1971.

Mamber, Stephen, *Cinema Verite in America: Studies in Uncontrolled Documentary*, Cambridge, MA: MIT Press, 1974.

Maysles, Albert, 'Digital Verite: Albert Maysles on DV Filmmaking', *RES (Resolution Independent)* 5, no. 3, 2002: 30.

O'Connell, P.J., *Robert Drew and the Development of Cinema Verite in America*, Carbondale, IL: Southern Illinois University Press, 1992.

Pryluck, Calvin, 'Seeking to Take the Longest Journey: A Conversation with Albert Maysles', *Journal of the University Film Association* 28, spring 1976: 9–16.

Reynolds, Charles, 'Focus on Al Maysles', in Lewis Jacobs (ed.), *The Documentary Tradition*, second edn, New York: W.W. Norton, 1979.

Rosenthal, Alan, 'Salesman: Interviews with Albert Maysles and Charlotte Zwerin', in The New Documentary in Action: A Casebook in Film Making, Berkeley, CA: University of California Press, 1971.

Winston, Brian, *Claiming the Real: The Documentary Film Revisited*, London: British Film Institute, 1995.

Meat

(US, Wiseman, 1976)

Frederick Wiseman's Meat shows the entire process of meat-packing—what Ken Monfort, the owner of Monfort Meat Packing in Greeley, Colorado, where the film was shot, calls 'animal fabrication'—from the animals grazing in apparent freedom to the shipping to market of meat products. Wrapped in plastic, stamped by government inspection, and sealed in boxes, the final product bears little resemblance to the animals at the beginning. Power saws slice easily through the carcasses in seconds, flaying is done by giant machines that effortlessly peel away the animals' skin, and hooves are clipped off by powerful, ominous-looking scissor machines. Every part of the animals, from hide to intestines, is accounted for in the process, which is nothing if not efficient.

Meat is one of Wiseman's bleakest, most pessimistic views of American institutional life. As Wiseman documents the process, the animals unknowingly move from the fields and feedlots increasingly closer to the computerized packing plant, which looms on the horizon like an Orwellian ministry. Near the beginning of Meat we see several extreme long shots of cattle from high angles, visually reducing the animals to such an extent that they look like mere specks in the image, a graphic suggestion of their helplessness. Sure enough, at the entrance to the plant waits the inevitable butcher with a cattle prod and stun gun. The animals' movement toward their fate is consistently regulated and constrained by fences, gates, aisles, highway lanes, and entrance ways, and a variety of pens, corrals, cages, and boxes. Ultimately the animals themselves are transformed into boxed objects, consumer goods to be shipped across America.

Everywhere in Meat, life is quantified, a matter of weight and cost. Statistics and dollar figures make up the content of most of the dialogue in the film, including the auctioneer's patter, the exchange between the feed-truck drivers and the computer operators, the tour of the plant given to the Japanese businessmen, and the salesmen's telephone chatter. Even the weather is quantified as the feedlot supervisor reports to Monfort the relevant data on the climate at the two feedlots.

The work of animal fabrication, like the animals themselves, has been sliced into little pieces, each worker repeatedly performing the same one task on the disassembly line. The minimal camera movement in the film is primarily functional, serving to contain the flow of animals through pens and on ramps or to keep within the frame the various tasks performed by the workers. Most shots are stationary, and they accumulate with a rhythmic regularity that reflects the stultifying, repetitious tasks of the workers. The film's style thus matches perfectly the alienated, desensitized world shown inside the Monfort Plant.

Unlike most of Wiseman's films, Meat tends to avoid long takes and to rely instead on editing within sequences. Several lengthy sequences in the film are built out of numerous brief shots. These sequences have little or no dialogue, the soundtrack is dense only with the ambient sounds of machines at work. The 'beefkill' sequence, depicting the cattle being unloaded, killed, disemboweled, inspected, and placed in cold storage, contains no dialogue at all (the workers shout and make noise, but use no words), and is composed of ninety-two shots taking twenty minutes of screen time.

The film compares the alienated labor of the plant workers with the animals in several ways. In the cafeteria, for example, the workers, looking bored and alienated, eat in rows, arranged on either side of the long tables like the sides of beef in cold storage. Their faces, as they stare into the distance, doze, and glance at their watches, seem as expressionless as those of the dead animals. The workers also are shown punching out their time cards, their time slotted and calculated by company management, analogous to the treatment of the animals. In the meeting of union representatives, a worker named Bill voices his fear that the company is 'gonna start chopping our heads'.

Meat's structure brilliantly conveys this sense of alienated labor. The film is divided into two parts, each showing the slaughtering and packing process from beginning to end. The first part, which lasts about an hour, or roughly half the film, shows the process applied to cattle. As it nears completion, one cannot help but wonder what else the film can show. The answer, as many viewers are probably dismayed to discover, is that it chronicles the process once again, from the beginning. However, the second time around, the process, this time involving the smaller sheep, seems not only repetitious but decidedly anticlimactic. While the cowhides must be removed by big machines, the sheepskins are peeled away merely by a firm tug of the hand; and while the jaws of the cattle must be pried open by placing them in special metal receptacles, the sheep skulls are unceremoniously squashed like nutshells by giant stamping machines. If Primate (1974) is structured by a sense of mounting horror, as the animal experiments seem to become increasingly grotesque and violent, Meat works oppositely, draining what it shows of drama, just as the animals themselves are drained of blood. In short, Wiseman strategically places the slaughter of the smaller animal second, to make it seem even less 'interesting'. For some viewers the film quickly induces disinterest, even boredom. Indeed, how very quickly the film moves from the potential frisson of the abattoir to the dull banality of routine. See how quickly and easily, the film 'prods' us to realize, we too may be processed.

At the end of Meat, the meatpacking plant is suddenly thrust into a moral perspective when Monfort is asked by a local news reporter about his and the consumer's (that is, the viewer's) moral responsibility. The mounds of ground beef Wiseman shows after Ken Monfort's discussion of morality in meat packing inevitably speak to the ethics of conspicuous consumption that characterize the American way of life.

BARRY KEITH GRANT

See also: Wiseman, Frederick

Meat (US, 1976, 113 mins). Distributed by Zipporah Films. Produced, edited, and directed by Frederick Wiseman. Cinematography by William Brayne. Sound recorded by Frederick Wiseman.

Further reading

Atkins, Thomas R. (ed.), *Frederick Wiseman*, New York: Monarch Press, 1976.

Benson, Thomas W. and Anderson, Caroline, *Reality Fictions: The Films of Frederick Wiseman*, Carbondale, IL: Southern Illinois University Press, 1989.

Grant, Barry Keith, *Voyages of Discovery: The Cinema of Frederick Wiseman*, Urbana, IL and Chicago: University of Illinois Press, 1992.

Mamber, Stephen, *Cinema Verite in America: Studies in Uncontrolled Documentary*, Cambridge, MA: MIT Press, 1974.

Nichols, Bill, *Ideology and the Image*, Bloomington, IN: Indiana University Press, 1981.

Mechanics of the Brain, The

(Russia, Pudovkin, 1925–6)

Vsevolod Pudovkin directed The Mechanics of the Brain: The Behavior of Animals and Man/ Mekhanika golovnogo mozga: Povedenie zhivotnykh i cheloveka for the studio Mezhrabpom-Rus. It was Pudovkin's first film as a director and followed his final apprentice work for Lev Kuhleshov on The Death Ray (1925), where he served as actor, screenwriter, and designer. The assignment is only a seemingly incongruous beginning for the director of such accomplished narrative feature films as Mother (1926), The End of St Petersburg (1927), and Storm over Asia (1928). Pudovkin, who had been trained in the natural sciences, embraced the assignment to make a popularization of Ivan Pavlov's theories of conditioned reflexes. Pavlov's theories about the mechanical quality of learning fit in well with the Bolshevik doctrine of education as a mechanical, perfectible, and egalitarian process (although Pavlov would later change his view that everything came down to training). Pudovkin's stated aim for the film was to reveal that the conditioned reflex lay at the basis of the soul.

Mechanics, which has been largely neglected in studies of Pudovkin's career, typifies the Soviet enthusiasm for experimentation, and it differs significantly from Pudovkin's later hagiographies of military leaders and scientists that were carried out during Stalinism's preference for monumental biographies. In Mechanics, instead of focusing on details of Pavlov's life, Pudovkin explains Pavlov's scientific work in a reflexive manner, transposing his theories of conditioned reflexes into the realm of film form. The film's remarkably frequent use of the iris and circular mask is the most salient example of this reflexivity. These devices were a prominent stylistic feature of the popular science film in the 1910s, emblematizing the genre's tendency to isolate significant details, usually by magnification. Pudovkin uses these devices in an attempt to approximate Pavlovian methods of training the spectator's attention, the circular framing simultaneously cuing the spectator's attention and calling attention to the film's strategies of manipulation. As Pudovkin wrote in a press release for the film, 'It depends on the director whether the spectator becomes a good or bad observer'. The contemporary nonfictional form on which these experimental strategies are overlaid is that of the *Kulturfilm* as it was developed in Germany (and, as Jay Leyda has noted, Mechanics bears comparison to Secrets of a Soul (G.W. Pabst, 1925–6), which also was conceived of as an instructional film). Mechanics was one of the few Soviet *Kulturfilms* to make a profit.

The original and longest version of Mechanics was approximately an hour long, probably corresponding to six reels. The opening sequence consists of numerous shots of animals being fed at the Leningrad zoo, illustrating the concept of stimulus-response. The film then shows a number of demonstrations of the effects of electricity on frog cadavers, replicating experiments that were conducted by Pavlov's predecessor Ivan Sechenov. This section contains remarkable animated sequences, the second venture of a specialized unit of Mezhrabpom-Rus. These sequences schematically depict the functioning of the nervous systems and demonstrate what happens when certain parts of the brain are removed. The next sequence contains demonstrations of experiments on the cerebral localization of sensory and motor functions that had been performed by Eduard Hitzig and Gustav Fritsch, David Ferrier and Hermann Munk. These experiments either stimulated the cerebral cortex with electricity to make certain limbs move or involved removing parts of the brain, which resulted in specific disturbances (blindness, loss of motor function). A final sequence in the animal laboratory depicts recreations of some of Pavlov's famous experiments on dogs that show the formation of conditioned reflexes—salivation that has been conditioned to respond to the sound of a bell and a motor reflex (the movement of a leg) that has been conditioned by the application of an electric shock.

The following sequences illustrate the applicability of these observations to humans. After shots of a baby being born, the film shows how the newborn quickly learns to locate and feed at its mother's breast. There follow scenes that compare the eating and grooming behavior of children from the ages of one to six. The sequence culminates with a scene where a group of children collectively solves a problem: a quoit has been hung on a nail out of their reach. One child leads the others to a solution that involves stacking chairs on top of a table to reach the desired object, demonstrating what the culminating intertitle calls 'the intentional reflex', that is, the ability to pursue a goal. The next sequences depict Pavlov's conditioned-response experiment previously performed on the dogs with a human subject, a child with a cheek fistula (which, an intertitle informs us, was the result of a previously existing condition). This sequence was filmed at a laboratory for child reflexology run by Professor Krasnogorski, a former assistant of Pavlov's. A final sequence compares a mentally retarded adult with a one-year-old child. Extant prints differ in the number of sequences they include and the order in which they are presented. The final two sequences are missing from the officially censored version of the film at Gosfilmofond and from other versions as well.

The film's cameraman, Anatoli Golovnia, who became Pudovkin's collaborator on subsequent narrative features, complained about the difficulties involved with filming 'mad men, idiots, paralytics, a woman in childbirth, new-born infants and not new-born [...] ordinary dogs and dogs without a brain, dissected frogs and undissected, frogs, monkeys, lions, bears, eagles, cows, horses, hippopotami, crocodiles'. Pudovkin and Golovnia had to resort to a number of special techniques, such as building a blind in the children's laboratory. This need to rely on a hidden camera links Mechanics not only with strategies familiar from wildlife filmmaking but also with some of Dziga Vertov's techniques for capturing candid footage in the service of his documentary project. During the filming of Mechanics Pudovkin made Chess Fever, a comedy that used footage his camera crew took under the pretenses of shooting a newsreel at the International Chess Tournament held in Moscow. Pudovkin's easy transition between these two projects as well as his subsequent move into feature narratives point toward the fluid boundaries between documentary and fiction film in this period.

OLIVER GAYCKEN

Further reading

Leyda, Jay, *Kino: A History of the Russian and Soviet Film*, third edn, Princeton, NJ: Princeton University Press, 1983.

Pudovkin, Vsevolod, *Film Technique and Film Acting*, trans. and ed. Ivor Montagu, New York: Grove Press, 1976.

——*Die Zeit in Großaufnahme: Erinnerungen/Aufsätze/Werkstattnotizen*, Berlin: Henschel, 1983.

Sargeant, Amy and Pudovkin, Vsevolod, *Classic Films of the Soviet Avant-Garde*, New York: I.B. Tauris, 2000.

Sarkisova, Oksana, '"Life as it Should Be?": Early Non-fiction Cinema in Russia: From Kulturfilm to Documentary', *Medien & Zeit* 18, no. 1, 2003: 41–61.

Vöhringer, Margarete and Hagner, Michael, 'Vsevolod Pudovkins Mechanik des Gehirns. Film als psychophysiologisches Experiment', in *Bildweltendes Wissens. Kunsthistorisches Jahrbuch für Bildkritik* 2, no. 1, Berlin, n.d.: 82–92.

Mein Kampf

(Sweden, Leiser, 1960)

Erwin Leiser's film Mein Kampf is a compilation documentary. That is, it uses only authentic documents taken from film materials of the Russians, Americans, British, French, and the National Socialists. Among the visual documents are photos, newsreel footage, propaganda footage, and material from other documentaries. A text scrolling upward across the screen as the film opens assures viewers that 'every scene is authentic' and that, although the ensuing film focuses on Poland, the Nazi atrocities were not limited to that country. The text continues that twenty-five million lives had been consumed in 'Hitler's Hell' by the end of the war, and dedicates the film 'in guilt to his victims'. Finally, the text admonishes viewers that 'we are responsible for what he did, for he was one of us and we permitted this to happen', and against a background of drums, just before the first visuals begin, the scroll cautions viewers 'may we be wise enough and strong enough to prevent this from ever happening again'. In spite of this promising beginning and although Leiser presents a compelling document of an historical crime, Mein Kampf remains problematic both as a film of warning about the mistakes of the past and one that helps viewers come to terms with the legacy of the Third Reich.

Erwin Leiser's documentary on the rise and fall of the Third Reich, Mein Kampf (1960), was one of the first postwar films to ask how the tragedy of the Holocaust could happen. Unlike Alain Resnais, who in Nuit et Brouillard/Night and Fog (1955) suggests that we (the viewers) are responsible, regardless of our actual complicity, Leiser, in spite of credits telling viewers otherwise, implicates mostly politics, historical figures, history itself, but not the viewer. In that regard, he follows the lead of several German narrative features that preceded Mein Kampf by only a few years, among them Karl May's 08/15 trilogy (1955), Frank Wisbar's Hunde, wollt ihr ewig leben?/Dogs, Do You Want to Live Forever? (1958), and especially Kurt Hoffman's Wir Wunderkinder/Aren't We Wonderful? (1959). Leiser's admonition that 'it must never ever happen again', which intones over a scene of crosses as the movie ends, reflects similar warnings in the three feature films. Mein Kampf seems reminiscent of Hoffmann's comedy, in particular, the episodic scenes of which seek to explain Hitler's rise to power, the destruction of the war, and its aftermath, and are introduced with documentary-style newsreel footage. However, if May, Wisbar, and Hoffmann spare viewers from being complicit in the crimes of the Third Reich, they nonetheless locate guilt in the general population's cowardice, opportunism, and uncritical acceptance of the government—my country right or wrong. Leiser's documentary, in contrast, might chastise viewers for their guilt, but his visuals spare the viewer and locate guilt for what occurred between 1933 and 1945 in mishandled treaties (Versailles), misinformed leaders (Chamberlain), and madmen (Hitler and the Nazis). Thus the admonition with which Leiser ends his film warns against an evil that lies outside our sphere of control.

In spite of its ultimate failure to serve as a useful warning against repeating history, Mein Kampf is nonetheless a powerful indictment of the Nazis and of the Western Powers for allowing the tragedy to transpire. Leiser divides his material into three major parts: 1914–33, 1933–9, and 1939–45. Each has its own tone, reflecting the period being depicted, the source of the material, and the closeness to the actual tragedy. The pre-Nazi years are the most objective in visual and aural material. The years 1918 to 1929 are narrated using well-known iconography of postwar Europe and the

Weimar Republic: among these are the Russian Revolution, Lenin, Karl Liebknecht, the signing of the Versailles Treaty, the Freikorps, turmoil in the cities, and a photo montage of Hitler's childhood and early manhood, including his introduction to anti-Semitism and eventually to Germany's right-wing militarists. The material comes from newsreels, newspapers, and family photo albums and is neutral in tone. The background narration is matter-of-fact and the music also befits the visuals, militaristic during war scenes, classical at other times. The most overtly subjective element comes in a visual pun as the screen shows a newsreel of a listing, sinking German ship just before the war ends.

Leiser introduces a more urgent tone into his film to highlight the years 1929–33 as the Nazis exploit the world economic crisis and eventually come to power with the elections of 1933. Neutral visuals here give way to an election poster of the Nazi opposition that warningly asks 'who will save us from the Nazis?' The urgent tone continues as the film shows events from 1933–8, as the Germans tighten their hold on the government and the people. Leiser uses a dialectical style during this middle sequence as he juxtaposes scenes of torchlight parades of the Nazis and Hitler at an open window savoring the adulation of crowds with scenes of citizens being taken and loaded into police transports. Meanwhile, the narration also adopts a subjective tone by commenting that people are being 'dragged from homes and beaten up'. Finally, scenes of the Nazi leaders speaking to crowds and proclaiming their victory for a new Germany effect gooseflesh in the viewer. Much of the material for this section that depicts Hitler and his leaders is taken from Leni Riefenstahl's Triumpf des Willens/Triumph of the Will (1935), adding to the ominous feeling that the section produces in viewers.

Any pretense to neutrality of visuals or objectivity of narration disappears as the film enters the third phase of its story. Again using newsreel footage and clips from films shot by the Nazis for propaganda purposes, as well as end-of-war documents filmed by the Allies, Leiser uses the invasion and destruction of Poland, the deportation of Polish Jews, and the uprising in the Warsaw Ghetto, to represent the misery throughout Europe. Shots of young children starving, corpses being collected from the streets and dumped into mass graves, and Polish civilians being hanged reflect events going on

Figure 10 Mein Kampf (aka Den blodiga tiden) documentary, 1960 (Courtesy of the Everett Collection)

outside Poland: invasion and destruction of Eastern and Western Europe, attack on Stalingrad, and deportation and killing of almost three-fourths of Europe's Jews. The soundtrack, too, adds to the desperation of the situations in this last third of the film. As scenes of the Warsaw Ghetto cross the screen, the narrator intones that Jews 'must live and die like rats'. As the corpses are being dumped into mass graves, a cantor singing Kaddish is heard on the soundtrack. Finally, as German captives march through a frozen Russian landscape, Leiser reprises a scene from Triumph des Willens, in which young Germans proudly call out where they are from, indicating that all of Germany is represented in the country's adulation of the Führer.

As the film closes, Leiser overwhelms viewers with the enormity of the tragedy by citing statistics of death and destruction read as the visuals show the suitcases, clothes, shoes, toys, hair, glasses, teeth, and skeletons of the Nazis' victims. In the scene that directly precedes this one, Nazi leader after Nazi leader at the Nuremberg trials pleads not guilty as charges are read, and the narrator asks, 'Did Hitler do everything himself?' The visuals cannot lie; they indict everyone, everyone involved with the Nazi government, that is. For taken as a whole, the film condemns the Nazis alone. It suggests that they were helped into power because governments and citizens looked the other way, but never expresses others' complicity beyond the mere fact that they were passive and/or too trusting. Thus the film fails as a warning against repeating the mistakes of the past, but it also fails to help viewers come to terms with the past, for there is nothing to come to terms with on a personal level. On another level, however, the film succeeds. As documentation of what occurred, the film is a chilling example of how far to destruction the insanity of ideology can lead a country. In this regard, Leiser achieved one of his stated goals, which was to reach a generation of Germans and other Western youth who were growing up ignorant of history and were thus susceptible to messages from the right, misappropriating Nazi symbols to shock their parents, and even sometimes just for fun.

ROBERT C. REIMER

See also: Leiser, Erwin; Riefenstahl, Leni; Triumph of the Will

Mein Kampf (original title: Den blodiga tiden, Sweden, Minerva Film AB, 1960, 111 mins). Distributed by Columbia Pictures and Vci Home Video. Produced by Tore Sjöberg. Directed by Erwin Leiser. Written by Erwin Leiser. Edited by Ingemar Ejve. Commentary for English-language version by Claude Stephenson. Compilation film composed of news and documentary footage.

Further reading

Bishop, Christopher, 'Mein Kampf', review, *Film Quarterly* 14, no. 56, winter 1960: 56.

Leiser, Erwin, *Auf der Suche nach Wirklichkeit: Meine Filme 1960–96*, Stuttgart: Europäisches Medienforum, 1996.

Quigly, Isabel, 'Rewards of Atrocity', review, *Spectator*, April 14, 1961: 516–17.

Whitebait, William, 'Eichmann and All', review, *New Statesman*, April 14, 1961: 600.

Memorandum

(Canada, Brittain, 1965)

Memorandum, made ten years after Night and Fog (1955) and well before the spate of Holocaust documentaries and dramatic films of recent decades, is notable for its richly complex structure and its little-known status among Holocaust films.

The film follows the pilgrimage by a group of North American Jews to Bergen Belsen, the site of their internment during World War II. The documentary uses as its structural spine one member of the group, Bernard Laufer, a glazier now living in Toronto. Interwoven with Laufer's journey, which is filmed in vérité style, is an impressively varied amount of other documentary material: contemporary scenes of Germany and Poland; on-site interviews with other survivors; archival footage of the camps; and certain original scenes filmed before the trip that function as flashbacks. The film's disparate material is connected to Laufer and made into a coherent whole through inventive editing and a sweeping commentary.

Thematically the film is influenced by Hannah Arendt's characterization of the Holocaust as 'the banality of evil'. The film's title functions not only as an admonition to remember the Holocaust but also as a metaphor for the bureaucratic manner in which the Nazis implemented it. The film emphasizes the apparent ordinariness of some of the worst culprits. A montage of suited men carrying briefcases and other quotidian contemporary scenes reinforce the sense of potential evil still lurking behind everyday respectability.

The film's greatest achievement is its establishment of a link between an individual victim of the Holocaust and the almost incomprehensible vast enormity of it. Bernard Laufer is a severely private man who projects little energy or emotion. He is on the screen for only a few minutes of the total running time, but the film's structure creates a sense that everything we are shown somehow reflects the essence of Laufer's memories and thoughts.

An element in Memorandum's complexity is its melange of film styles. The almost pure vérité style of most of the film's original footage forms an unusual match with the extensive and impersonal commentary delivered with professional polish by Alexander Scourby. This odd mixture makes the film hard to categorize stylistically and might help to account for its relative obscurity, but it also constitutes a tour de force and arguably makes Memorandum the apotheosis of director Donald Brittain's distinctive documentary editing and writing skills.

D.B. JONES

See also: Canada; Night and Fog; Shoah

Memorandum (Canada, National Film Board, 1965, 58 mins). Distributed by the National Film Board of Canada. Produced by John Kemeny. Directed by Donald Brittain. Cinematography and editing by John Spotton. Sound recorded by Roger Hart. Narration written by Donald Brittain, spoken by Alexander Scourby.

Further reading

Blumer, Ron and Schouten, Susan, 'Donald Brittain: Green Stripe and Common Sense', *Cinema Canada* 15, August–September, 1974: 36–40.

Breitrose, Henry, 'Memorandum', *Film Quarterly* xx, no. 2, n.d.: 57–9.

Denby, David, 'Who's the Best Canadian Director?' *New York Magazine*, October 1977.

Harper, Ray, *Brittain on Brittain: Program 6: Memorandum*, Ottawa: National Film Board of Canada, 1989.

Jones, D.B., *Movies and Memoranda*, Ottawa: Deneau, 1982.

——*The Best Butler in the Business: Tom Daly of the National Film Board of Canada*, Toronto, University of Toronto Press, 1996.

Kolomeychuk, Terry (ed.), *Donald Brittain: Never the Ordinary Way*, Winnipeg: National Film Board of Canada, n.d.

Martin, Kent (director), *Donald Brittain: Filmmaker*, (film), Ottawa: National Film Board of Canada, 1992.

Memphis Belle

(US, Wyler, 1944)

The following summary of Memphis Belle is provided by Thorpe and Pronay:

> A daylight bombing expedition over the Continent of Europe by American Flying Fortresses from a base in England. The film shows preparations, briefing, the flight out, the general plan of attack (by diagrams), defence against enemy fighters and flak, bombing of targets, the return home, attention to wounded, and visits to the bomber base by distinguished personages. The combat scenes were shot in action over enemy territory.
>
> (Thorpe and Pronay 1980: 156)

William Wyler was one of three top Hollywood directors to make significant wartime documentaries of lasting value. John Ford made The Battle of Midway (1942) and December 7th (1943), and John Huston made The Battle of San Pietro (1945) and Let There Be Light (1946). ([Col.] Wyler's other documentary was Thunderbolt, 1945, about the work of P47 fighter-bombers in Italy.) All three seemed surprisingly at ease in the nonfiction mode. Memphis Belle is, in a way, an answer to the British Target for Tonight (1941). It is interesting that Wyler, whose most valued fiction features had been adaptations of literary and dramatic works, used candid color footage of a real raid (one of the cameramen was killed while filming) with voice-over narration, while documentarian Harry Watt used recreated action (some of it shot in a studio), scripted dialogue, and directed performances.

The *Memphis Belle* is a Boeing B17 on its twenty-fifth and final bombing mission over Germany before its veteran crew is sent home. The world we see and hear is that of the airmen—refracted images of sky and enemy fighter planes seen through Plexiglas, the drone of engines, and excited voices over the intercom. The film seems to come very close to the reality of their experience. Or, as James Agee put it in a review at the time (*The Nation*, April 15, 1944), 'Everything is seen, done, and experienced as if from inside one or another of the men in the plane'. Agee goes on to say that, 'The man in over-all charge of making this good film was William Wyler, whose talent I respected in Wuthering Heights and even in Mrs. Miniver, without caring for the pictures. Postwar planners should work out a better fate for him than going back to Hollywood.' That did not happen, of course, but the *Memphis Belle* rests on the court house lawn in Memphis, Tennessee.

JACK C. ELLIS

See also: Target for Tonight

Memphis Belle (US, War Department in cooperation with the Army Air Force First Motion Picture Unit, 1944, 40 mins). Distributed by the War Activities Committee through Paramount Pictures. Directed by William Wyler. Cinematography by 8th Air Force cameramen and combat crew members.

Further reading

Thorpe, Frances and Pronay, Nicholas, *British Official Films in the Second World War*, Oxford: Clio Press, 1980.

Mexico

Mexican documentaries tended to be historical during the 1950s and 1960s, political during the 1960s and 1970s, and social and ethnographic during the 1970s and 1980s. In the 1970s some documentaries were taken back to the communities where they had been shot and used to facilitate discussion of the social problems affecting the communities. During the 1990s and 2000s documentaries revealed familial histories as they intersect with Mexican history and the rest of the world.

The history of documentary-making in Mexico has been strongly marked by the institutions, such as film schools or centers for documentary-making, which provided documentarians with the most opportunities to do their work. Until the late 1990s the state-educated artists and audiences funded artists' works and sponsored exhibitions. Funding was scarce and very competitive, which limited the length and quantity of the documentaries. Documentaries were shown only on a particular exhibition circuit, consisting mostly of film clubs or other cultural institutions. With the introduction of video in the 1980s, the opportunities for making documentaries, especially for public television, grew. During the 1990s documentaries continued to be shown at film clubs or in documentary cycles at the Cinetecas, but they also began to be exhibited at commercial theaters and even won prizes typically awarded to 'fiction' films at festivals.

The first feature-length documentaries, compilation films about the Mexican Revolution, were made during the 1950s and 1960s. During the early 1910s, cameramen from the United States and Mexico (Jesús Abitia, Salvador Toscano, the Alva brothers) documented the Revolution by following the generals in their campaigns. Their footage was shown in Mexican cities, where spectators flooded the theaters to see the war in moving images. As the Revolution went from its military (1910s–20s) to its political phase (1920s–40s), however, newsreels became increasingly propagandistic and didactic.

In the 1950s–60s Carmen Toscano, in Memorias de un mexicano/Memories of a Mexican (1950), and Gustavo Carrero in Epopeyas de la Revolución/Epics from the Revolution (1961) compiled newsreel footage from earlier periods. Both films represent the Revolution as the foundation of modern Mexico, although they use diverse cinematic strategies. Toscano uses a fictional firsthand observer's voice-over narration in the first person to present footage, most of which her father had shot during the Revolution. Using Jesús H. Abitia's footage and a melodramatic omniscient narrator, Carrero tells a simplistic story in which heroes (Madero, Carranza and Obregón) defeat villains (Porfirio Díaz and Victoriano Huerta).

Carlos Velo also used archival material (newsreels depicting bullfights) to make Torero/Bullfighter (1956), a film about the well-known Mexican bullfighter Luis Procuna. Torero neorealistically represents Procuna's youth in the slums using images of broken shoes, and of groups of bullfighters smoking to avoid feeling hungry, while a voice-over narration claims that

Procuna began bullfighting to escape poverty. Having fled his impoverished beginnings, however, Procuna (played by the bullfighter himself) remains haunted by the fear of an audience insatiably thirsty for spectacle. As an established master of the documentary, Velo set up the Centro de Producción de Cortometraje (CPC) in the 1970s, under the sponsorship of the Secretary of Education; in 1975 he also founded Mexico's second film school, Centro de Capacitación Cinematográfica (CCC).

Indeed, film schools and state-subsidized public institutions supporting filmmaking education proliferated during the 1960s–80s. At the beginning of the period students from Mexico City's first film school, CUEC (Centro Universitario de Estudios Cinematográficos, 1963), made politically oriented documentaries. Using a direct cinema style, intertitles and voice-over narration, CUEC students shot and edited El grito/The Scream (Leobardo López, 1968). This political documentary recounts events leading up to the political turmoil of 1968 and gives testimony of the police attack that caused the massacre in Tlatelolco Square in Mexico City. Because of its testimonial images and soundtrack (some of which comes from an independent radio program run by students), El grito accurately represents the ideologies and popular cultures of the late 1960s. CUEC's critique of status quo politics continued in the 1980s to 2000 as Carlos Mendoza, a CUEC graduate and professor, created canal6dejulio/channel6ofjuly (1989) to produce muckraking videos that uncovered government corruption and were sold at newspaper stands.

Velo had established CPC to provide film-school graduates, who were not allowed to participate in the film industry, an opportunity to make documentaries, albeit at the margins of the industry. Through CPC Eduardo Maldonado coproduced (with Canada's National Film Board) Jornaleros/Salary Workers (1976), an ethnography and a political commentary on the lives of Mexican migrant cotton workers. Jornaleros has an observational ethnographic tone that changes to a politically expository tone as the film proceeds. In the second half of the film, a suddenly introduced voice-over narration explores alternatives to migration. Jornaleros was exceptionally well received; in the first year more than one hundred and fifty thousand viewers, many of them *jornaleros*, watched the film. Maldonado's film is representative of the many 1970s–80s documentaries committed to social change.

Graduates of CCC and CUEC also made documentaries about social justice issues during the 1980s. CUEC graduate Mari Carmen de Lara filmed No les pedimos un viaje a la luna/We Are Not Asking for a Trip to the Moon (1986), which denounces the government for failing to aid the seamstresses who lost their jobs after the 1985 Mexico City earthquake, and shows the seamstresses organizing themselves into a cooperative. No les pedimos was watched by more than three thousand seamstresses and won important international awards. One of Maldonado's students at CCC, Dana Rotberg (joined later by Ana Díez), made Elvira Luz Cruz, pena máxima/Elvira Luz Cruz, Maximum Punishment (1986) about an illiterate indigenous woman who had been accused of murdering her four children. In Elvira, an interview with Cruz's defense lawyer shows that Cruz was condemned without a fair trial. The judge believed the account given by Cruz's husband, a policemen and major suspect.

Film school students and graduates were committed to social change and to documenting the lives of indigenous people. They also seriously engaged the questions of national heritage and identity circulating in the 1970s and 1980s. During the 1980s public television, another venue for graduates, produced two thousand half-hour programs on topics of national heritage. The unit for cultural television, UTEC (Unidad de Televisión Educativa y Cultural), sponsored by the Secretary of Education, made television documentary series on various topics, such as Mexican ethnic groups or Mexican artists. UTEC, where many of the female graduates worked, produced an innovative television documentary series on women's issues that used gender as a category to construct national identity.

Notable among the documentaries that help to construct national identity was Nicolás Echavarría's Niño Fidencio, taumaturgo de Espinazo/Fidencio, the Healer from Espinazo (1980), about pilgrims who pay homage to a deceased popular *mestizo* healer in northern Mexico. Stylistically innovative, Niño, produced at CPC, uses long takes and few interviews. Echavarría ingeniously allows the voices of pilgrims to narrate the healer's deeds and the songs of an ambulant singer (the saint's 'brother') to tell the saint's life-story.

CPC and the National Indigenous Institute (Instituto Nacional Indigenista, INI) produced in the 1980s anthropological documentaries that contributed to the construction of indigenous identities. At CPC Echevarría made María Sabina, mujer espíritu/María Sabina, Spiritual Woman (1978), which celebrates internationally acclaimed Mazatec healer María Sabina. Echevarría's film romanticizes the healer's connection to 'nature'. Likewise, Roberto Rochín's Ulama: El juego de la vida y la muerte/Ulama: The Game of Life and Death (1987), a thorough study of the Mayan ball game in classical and contemporary times, reinscribes myths about Mayans as gifted in the supernatural. Some such ethnographic work tended to exoticize indigenous groups; however, some filmmakers begin to defy romanticized content as well as traditional documentary-making techniques in ethnographic film.

Challenging the common distancing of indigenous history from Mexican identity, Enrique Escalona independently made the animated documentary Tlacuilo, el que escribe pintando/Tlacuilo, He Who Writes While Painting (1987). Referencing Joaquín Galarza's research, Tlacuilo reads the Mendocino codices as a sophisticated, logical, and systematic writing system, which is both an indigenous and Mexican historical cultural artifact. Thus, the Aztecs themselves are constructed as simultaneously indigenous and Mexican. Through the INI film unit, Sonia Fritz made De bandas, vidas y otros sones/Of Bands, Lives and Other Musics (1985). Fritz's documentary follows a band of musicians from the mountains to the town where some of the musicians have already emigrated. Within the alienating town, music helps the musicians and their audiences to build a sense of trust and to maintain cultural identity. The film also includes scenes in which indigenous women refer to the presence of the camera and react to it; thus De bandas innovatively makes the traditionally invisible cinematic apparatus visible. Some documentarians later became interested in cross-cultural (mis)interpretation. In Mercedes Moncada's La pasión de María Elena/María Elena's Passion (2003), a white woman kills the son of a Raramuri Indian (María Elena) but fails to accept full responsibility for the child's death. The white woman seems unaware that her refusal to accept responsibility ostracizes María Elena from her community. Increasingly, indigenous groups took control over their representation; indeed, beginning in the 1990s, the binational (US–Mexico) group Chiapas Media Project provided video cameras and trained indigenous people from Chiapas in video-making and editing. The project has so far produced several videos.

In the 1990s many documentarians began to explore the intersections of familial and Mexican history. Marisa Sistach and José Buil's La línea paterna/The Paternal Line (1995) exhibits footage from 1925 to the 1940s shot by Buil's father, who used a Pathé Baby camera to document the history of the family. By the 1990s some filmmakers emphasized the partial, subjective narrative points of view that constitute even deeply familial history. In El abuelo Cheno/Grandfather Cheno (1995), CCC graduate Juan Carlos Rulfo, for example, begins his interviews by attempting to obtain an objective account of his grandfather's death. The campesinos, however, give different accounts, which are edited in short takes that cut across interviews. As the film proceeds, the attempt to clarify the past becomes unfeasible. Instead, the interviews, intersected with poetic images and the director's metacommentary, open up historical narrative as a vital and dynamic process. For the campesinos, remembering revivifies both stories and their tellers. El abuelo was shown at multiple festivals and won many awards.

Quite a few of the documentaries made in the 2000s voice an internationalist perspective. In Gregorio Rocha's Los rollos perdidos de Pancho Villa/Pancho Villa's Lost Reels (2003), for instance, the director appears on screen as he is searching for a film in which the famous revolutionary general acted. As Rocha walks the environs of numerous international libraries, he examines General Villa's story from an international perspective, thus simultaneously integrating Mexico into the wider world, while challenging Mexico's nationalist interpretations of itself. Giving a complex view of the Mexican hero, Los rollos shows that Villa made a deal with a US production company to restage some of his battles for a profit. Another example of a documentary expressing a global perspective is Juan Carlos Martín's Gabriel Orozco: un proyecto filmico documental/Gabriel Orozco: A Documentary Film Project (2002), produced by CCC. Using diverse media and MTV editing speed, Gabriel Orozco approaches the artist from the perspective of curators from internationally renowned museums. Orozco suggests that in the year 2000 the international community associates Mexico with Orozco's conceptualism, rather than with figurative art, as most Mexicans do. Marcela Arteaga's Recuerdos/Remembrances (2003), produced by CCC, situates Mexico within the international context of World War I, World War II, and the Spanish civil war by reconstructing the travels and exile of Lithuanian emigrant, Luis Frank. Arteaga, a CCC graduate, introduces objects to prompt emotions; an image of a chair burning on an empty beach, for example, can be connected to the nostalgia of exile and the emotional wounds caused by war.

Mexico's long tradition of documentary filmmaking began in the 1910s, grew as filmmakers trained in the film schools during the 1960s–90s, and gained extraordinary vitality by the beginning of the twenty-first century.

ISABEL ARREDONDO

Further reading

Aviña, Rafael, *México íntimo y profundo: cine documental mexicano contemporáneo*, Huesca: Festival de Cine de Huesca, con la colaboración de la Filmoteca Española, 1999.

Burton, Julianne, *The Social Documentary in Latin America*, Pittsburgh, PA: University of Pittsburgh Press, 1990.

Davalos Orozco, Federico, *Albores del cine mexicano*, Mexico, DF: Clío, 1996.

De Orellana, Margarita, 'The Voice of the Present over Images of the Past: Historical Narration in Memories of a Mexican', in *The Social documentary in Latin America*, Pittsburgh, PA: University of Pittsburgh Press, 1990: 211–13.

García Riera, Emilio, *Historia documental del cine mexicano*, Guadalajara, Jalisco, Mexico: Universidad de Guadalajara, 1992.

Muñoz, Eva Pichardo, 'El cine documental en Mexico (1963–67)', Dissertation. Universidad Nacional Autonoma de Mexico, 1985.

Paranagua, Paulo Antonio and Avellar, Jose Carlos, *Cine documental en América Latina*, Madrid: Cátedra, 2003.

Rovirosa, Jose, *Miradas a la realidad: ocho entrevistas a documentalistas mexicanos*, Mexico, DF: Coordinacion de Difusion Cultural, Centro Universitario de Estudios Cinematograficos, Universidad Nacional Autonoma de Mexico, 1990.

——*Miradas a la realidad: entrevistas a documentalistas mexicanos II. Vol. II*, Mexico, DF: Centro Universitario de Estudios Cinematograficos, UNAM, 1992.

Meyers, Sidney

In all the films that Sidney Meyers directed, there appears, somewhere, a brief shot of a blind man (played by Meyers himself). This persistent figure honors the blind man who befriended Meyers as a young boy aged twelve or thirteen. The man was a socialist, the neighborhood radical. Meyers would help his friend negotiate the neighborhood and then in evenings he would attend meetings with him. The day after a meeting he would come to school and repeat what he had heard and call the children in his class 'comrades'. It was the beginning of his political education.

From an early age Meyers displayed a keen interest in music. At the age of twenty-one Fritz Reiner invited him to join the Cincinnati Symphony. He remained with them for several years. He subsequently played with an orchestra subsidized by the local and federal government.

In addition to politics and music, Meyers was interested in photography. By 1932 he had become involved with the Workers' Film and Photo League. The league was interested, among other things, in using the camera to document social conditions for a working-class audience, as well as providing a space where workers might learn about the making of both films and photographs. Since Meyers was still working as a musician, he could not go out with film crews on his rehearsal days, so more and more his film work concentrated on the editing table and the soundtrack.

In early 1935 his writing career began. He became a film critic and editor for *New Theatre* and other periodicals, choosing 'Robert Stebbins' as a pseudonym to protect his other jobs. In 1936 he permanently left the orchestra for filmmaking. Through the Film and Photo League, his literary ventures, and the contacts he made through his wife's friends, Meyers became acquainted with a large number of talented people who were to become major contributors to both the American documentary movement and to theatrical film, including Leo Hurwitz, Irving Lerner, Ralph Steiner, and Ben Maddow.

By 1937 a new organization had come into existence: Frontier Films. Frontier was staffed by many people who had also worked at the Workers' Film and Photo League. The organization's task was to present the United States in a fresh way; in a way not shown by the commercial film industry. In the words of

Leo Hurwitz, it was to present a vivid sense that 'When you put your hand in your pocket and you can touch your total savings, your life is revealed as not the private thing it seemed before. It becomes connected with others who share your problem' (Alexander 1981: 17).

Frontier, while still on the left in its political orientation, was independent of outside influences in that its staff raised their own funds for their own projects. Their ideal was to work cooperatively on each project. The writer, director, editor, and camera were all to collaborate at each stage of the undertaking. China Strikes Back (1937) was composed out of raw newsreel footage that detailed the life of the Eighth Route Army. The footage was smuggled out of China and was one of Frontier's early productions. The editing room is usually the place where such footage is shaped into a film. The credits for China Strikes Back, in order, read: Sidney Meyers, Ralph Lerner, Ben Maddow, and Jay Leyda.

People of the Cumberland (1937) was a combination of reenacted drama and documentary footage that details how a poverty-stricken and uneducated community struggles to become an efficient, productive society through education and the labor movement. Direction is credited to Meyers and Jay Leyda.

For the Chrysler company's exhibit at the 1939 World's Fair, Frontier made a six-minute film, The History and Romance of Transportation. It was fashioned entirely out stock material. Participating in its making were Berman, Maddow, and Meyers. White Flood, completed in 1940, is another Frontier film that had to be made in the cutting room. The footage came principally from William Osgood Field, who had made a number of films on scientific and cultural topics. White Flood was pieced together from his own Alaskan 16mm shooting, alpine footage shot by Sherman Pratt, and from snowstorm scenes that were shot by Frontier cameras. Lionel Berman, Ben Maddow, and Meyers scripted and edited the film. The film is now remembered for its beautiful footage and original music score by Hanns Eisler.

With the approach of World War II many of the participants in Frontier drifted away. After Pearl Harbor, the British Ministry of Information gave Meyers the responsibility of preparing their films for American audiences, and eventually the Office of War Information employed his talents to plan and supervise their films. In the postwar years much of his livelihood was derived from directing and/or editing films for the American television networks, as well as directing a series of highly regarded films for Monsanto, the Girl Scouts, and the Ford Motor Company.

The two major films for which Meyers had a significant share of responsibility, and on which much of his reputation rests, were The Quiet One, released in 1949, and The Savage Eye, released in 1960. Both were independently made, outside the Hollywood studio system. Both The Quiet One and The Savage Eye were made in the communal and collaborative manner that was the practice at Frontier Films. For The Quiet One Meyers directed and edited, and Richard Bagley provided camera work. Janice Loeb and the photographer Helen Levitt produced. When the film was nominated for an Oscar, all four names were recorded as authors of best original screenplay; when, as a result of the film, Hollywood beckoned Myers, his acceptance depended on the inclusion of the whole group. Hollywood declined. The film was in production for a year and a half. Shot in 16mm, it cost $28,000 of their pooled resources.

The Quiet One was the first major American film to use a black youth as its protagonist and one of the first nonfiction films to deal with issues of racism and black poverty in the United States. Donald Thompson is about ten years old and born and raised in Harlem. It is just one of Meyer's achievements that the audience thoroughly identifies with the boy, as we see how an oppressive slum environment robs him of his childhood. The boy has never known his father, never known the meaning of emotional security. His mother remarries when he is an infant, and he is forced to live with his grandmother, a tired, beaten woman, incapable of supplying Donald with the love of which he is starved. Desperately in need of affection and human warmth, Donald roams the streets of Harlem searching for someone to befriend. Donald is one of the lucky ones. His descent into delinquency is stopped when he is accepted into the Wiltwyk School for Disturbed Children, where through friendship and therapy he begins to understand himself and his world.

The Savage Eye began with Meyer and Maddow's notion of trying to see corrupt 1950s Los Angeles as the seventeenth-century artist William Hogarth might see it. A film was started that would be nine years and nine scripts in the making. The collaborators worked in any spare time they found and, inevitably, the ideas of the film changed. The idea of integrating Hogarth into the film was abandoned; what remained was the attempt to find modern parallels of Hogarth's vision. As for writing, direction, production, and editing, the film was signed for all these functions by Maddow, Meyers, and Joe Strick.

WALTER HESS

Biography

Born in the Bronx, New York, March 9, 1906. Attended New York public schools and New York's City College. Studied the violin. At the age of twenty-one, invited by Fritz Reiner to join the Cincinnati Symphony. Interest in photography brought him to the Film and Photo League, Nykino, and Frontier Films. During World War II worked for the British Ministry of Information, as well as for the American Office of War Information. Made a number of highly regarded industrial films for sponsors as varied as the Ford Motor Company and the Girl Scouts. During the 1950s and 1960s worked as an editor on numerous features, including Martin Ritt's Edge of the City, and several films directed by Joseph Strick. Died in 1969.

Selected films

1937 China Strikes Back: director, writer, editor (as 'Robert Stebbins', in collaboration with Jay Leyda as 'Eugene Hill', Irving Lerner as 'Peter Ellis', Ben Maddow as 'David Wolf')
1937 People of the Cumberland: codirector, coeditor (as 'Robert Stebbins', with Jay Leyda as 'Eugene Hill')
1940 White Flood: director, writer, editor (in collaboration with Lionel Berman, Ben Maddow as 'David Wolf')
1948 The Quiet One: director, editor
1951 Steps of Age: director (in collaboration with Ben Maddow, Joseph Strick), editor
1953 Decision for Chemistry: director, editor
1954 The American Farmer: director, editor
1957 Adventuring in the Arts: director, editor
1959 The Savage Eye: director and writer (in collaboration with Ben Maddow and Joseph Strick), editor

Further reading

Alexander, William, *Film on the Left: American Documentary Film from 1931 to 1942*, Princeton, NJ: Princeton University Press, 1981.
Jacobs, Lewis, *The Documentary Tradition: From Nanook to Woodstock*, New York: Hopkinson and Blake, 1971.
Meyers, Sidney (as 'Robert Stebbins'), 'The Screen: Frontier', *New Masses* 7, January 1936: 29–30.
——'Redes', *New Theater*, November 1936: 20–2.
——'Film: To the Editor', *TAC*, October 1938.
——'One Man's Contribution', *TAC*, November 1938: 6.
——'Movies', *TAC*, April 1939: 14–15, 22.
Rosenblum, Walter, 'The Quiet One: A Milestone', *Photo-Notes*, spring 1949 (also in *The Documentary Tradition*, above).

Miller Adato, Perry

The documentaries of Perry Miller Adato are, according to the director herself, aimed at '"education" in the broadest sense, that is, in broadening the area of people's understanding, knowledge or enjoyment'. Inspired by documentaries such as, notably, the Why We Fight series that she saw on US television just after the Vietnam War, Miller Adato became very interested in 16mm distribution as a way of reaching people directly, in their own environments, whether through schools, public libraries, churches, unions, clubs, or film societies. She learned everything she could about 16mm distribution and started working gratis with different organisations, trying to get them interested in using films. Later, when she took a job as a researcher for CBS, she was employed to find films around which the network could build programs. It was while working at CBS that Miller Adato came across a short film directed by Rollie McKenna on Bob Dylan and, using this as the basis for her research, made her first film: Dylan Thomas: The World I Breathe.

Miller Adato's biographies resemble filmic scrapbooks, collating professional works and personal memories. They draw on a wealth of memorabilia from every conceivable source and are composed of intimate letters, rare stills, art work, home movies, radio broadcasts, vintage news clips and film footage, as well as numerous talking heads. As one article states, 'If there's something or somebody relevant to her subject's story, Miller's got it on film' (Trojan 1978).

Such a thorough approach undoubtedly springs from her background in research: during her time at CBS Miller Adato was known as one of the most effective researchers in the field. Her production method consists of collating as much material as possible and then cutting it down to the required length. This approach means that before she begins a documentary, and as she is working on it, she has little idea of what the finished product will be composed. Beginning from the briefest of outlines, the final script comes out of the interviews conducted, existing materials, letters, and quotes. At the editing stage Miller Adato types up transcripts and edits these into a script working alongside a script editor, before working with a film editor to bring the film together visually. She states that her films are 'made or lost in the cutting room'. Unusually for the genre, Miller Adato's film's are fast-paced, most likely the result of the vast amount of material that she aims to incorporate, never using one picture 'when we thought two of three or ten would be better' (Schutzer 1972).

Perry Miller Adato's films have, more often than not, focused directly or indirectly on the creative person who remains vital in age as well as youth. They recount the contributions of the artist to their field, as well as conveying a sense of the emotional and personal side of the subject. Although she has stated that she is anxious not to canonize her subjects, her films generally make positive portrayals and aim to imitate the style of the subject's work. When making a documentary about an artist, Miller Adato tends to incorporate a wide selection of their own work into the film, often in the order in which individual pieces were created, so that the changes in the subject's life can be seen in parallel to the developments in their art. She appears to have a great respect for her subjects and their work, and it is a rule in each of her films that if pictures, sculptures, or photographs are shown in details or cuts, they must at some point be shown in their entirety, out of respect for the artwork. When making films about other filmmakers, as in the case of Charles and Ray Eames, or writers, such as Gertrude Stein, such an ethos becomes more complicated to put into practice. However, Miller Adato remains focused on respecting the integrity of the subject's work while making it work for the larger program, incorporating discrete sequences or passages with no cuts.

Adato's films hover between biography and artistic homage. The longer films, such as Gertrude Stein: When This You See, Remember Me, and Carl Sandburg: Echoes and Silences, tend to work more effectively from this point of view than the one- or half-hour documentaries, as the greater length of time allows the director to more thoroughly resolve the personal and professional portraits of her subjects. Shorter films, such as Mary Cassat: Impressionist from Philadelphia, are less successful in this regard. Miller Adato's thoroughness seems to be the problem, for in attempting to cover an entire life, its context, and an artist's work all in thirty minutes, Miller Adato can condense too much into too small a space with the result that the viewer is left feeling that he or she has only scratched the surface.

A filmmaker with an obvious passion for her subjects, Miller Adato's strength, and her weakness, is her desire to know everything about them. Her works have a very personal touch. The director feels it is important to develop some kind of personal relationship with each person she interviews. This can be seen to its greatest advantage in the films of length, and, to this end, her best works are arguably the pair of films she made about Georgia O'Keefe and Alfred Stieglitz. Both are admirable films in their discrete forms and were made with no intention that they be viewed together, but taken together they allow Miller Adato to create an interesting diptych in which each portrait reflects back on the other, and Miller Adato can dedicate an appropriate length of space to each subject. In contrast to the shorter films, neither documentary seems rushed; each takes its time to thoroughly reveal its subject's life and art. Had they been made as one, shorter film, one suspects that much would have been lost.

Her work is also notable for its preoccupation with female artists. The films on Cassatt, O'Keefe, and Betye Saar are amongst some of Miller Adato's films made as part of a WNET series on women artists entitled The Originals: Women in Art. Portrait of an Artist: Anonymous Was a Woman, another film in the series, contends that the originator of the many works, especially as with regard to folk arts, that are frequently attributed to a mysterious 'Anonymous' was most often a woman, and a skilled and highly creative one at that. This program argues that although never singled out for fame or lauded for their endeavours, these silent women nevertheless achieved remarkable designs and imminently useful items for use in and around the home, and is by far the closest to a feminist film that Miller's works come. Even her film on the Eames can be read in a feminist light, however: Miller Adato acknowledges that if the film had not been made with a woman director and two women editors, Ray Eames would not have received as much attention as her more celebrated husband Charles.

Miller Adato, while not seeing herself as a feminist filmmaker, acknowledges that her gender has a strong influence on the films that she makes: 'it's just fascinating how much you have in common with every other woman artist or even every other working woman'. It is because she and her female subjects know 'exactly what each other has been through', Miller claims, that she can 'tell you all about their lives'. On the subject of Cassatt, Stein, and O'Keefe, and their inherent feminism, Miller Adato has stated that 'they were not conscious in the sense that a lot of women are today', but that 'they were just interested in living their lives and doing their work'. In many ways this is perhaps the best description of Miller Adato's own attitude to her filmmaking.

HELEN WHEATLEY

See also: Gertrude Stein: When This You See, Remember Me

Biography

Spent ten years as a film consultant to CBS-TV, where she worked on Adventure, Odyssey, Seven Lively Arts, Conquest, Calender, and Roots of Freedom, and coproduced The Best is Yet to Be. In 1964 joined WNET, where she was associate producer for a film in the History of Negro People Series and Georges Braques in the Creative Person series. Produced eight one-hour programs for The Film Generation and Dance, which was shown at the Robert Flaherty seminar. Produced her first documentary in 1967: Dylan Thomas: The World I Breathe, which won an Emmy Award for Best Cultural Documentary.

Selected films

1968 Dylan Thomas: The World I Breathe: producer, director
1969 The Film Generation: coproducer
1969 The Film Generation and Dance: director, coproducer
1970 Gertrude Stein: When This You See, Remember Me: producer, director
1972 The Great Radio Comedians: producer, director
1974 An Eames Celebration: producer, director
1975 Mary Cassatt: Impressionist from Philadelphia: producer, director
1977 Georgia O'Keeffe: producer, director, writer
1977 Spirit Catcher: The Art of Betye Saar: producer
1977 Anonymous was a Woman: producer
1982 Carl Sandburg: Echoes and Silences: director
2001 Alfred Stieglitz: The Eloquent Eye: producer, director, writer

Further reading

Nordstrom, Kristina, 'Who's Who in Filmmaking: Perry Miller Adato', *Sightlines* 8, no. 2, winter 1974–5: 15–16.

Schutzer, Anne, 'Interview with Perry Miller Adato', *Filmmakers' Newsletter* 5, no. 5, March 1972: 20–5.

Trojan, Judith, 'The Documentaries of Perry Miller Adato', *Film Library Quarterly* 11, no. 1, 1978: 28–35.

Mills of the Gods: Viet Nam, The

(Canada, Fox, 1965)

Although this film has maintained a relatively high profile since its production in the mid-1960s, certainly among films made during and about the Vietnam War, it is currently enjoying something of a resurgence in interest and popularity. This renewed interest is perhaps a result of its restoration in 2000 and subsequent release on DVD by the Masterworks Program of the Canadian Audio-Visual Preservation Trust, a body charged with maintaining Canada's media past. So significant is the film to the history of the media in Canada, that The Mills of the Gods: Viet Nam was selected in the very first batch of masterworks for restoration by the organization, which selects twelve worthy texts from radio television and film annually.

Directed and produced by Beryl Fox, executive produced by Douglas Leiterman, and edited by Don Haig, this film benefited from participation from three very significant figures in film and television in Canada. Produced for the CBC's Document series, an irregularly scheduled programme, loosely affiliated with the incendiary This Hour Has Seven Days, which broadcast documentaries by several important Canadian filmmakers, the film was first broadcast on December 5, 1965, and it went on to win many awards including the Film of the Year at the Canadian Film Awards.

Composed of images of both a wide variety of American service personnel and of Vietnamese peasants, the film provides a sobering, provocative, sad, and ultimately extremely poignant examination of the effects of the war on both the American servicemen and the Vietnamese peasants. Among images of napalm, bombs, and death, Fox intersperses moments of quotidian reality for the local residents, of working, shopping in the market, and so on. It is the juxtaposition of the graphic images of horrendous warfare with these everyday goings-on that lends the film its lasting poignancy.

The film was shot entirely in Vietnam and contains no archival footage or presenter commentary, relying on the words of those Fox encountered and interviewed and the images of events their camera encountered. Some of these images remain shocking to this day, including the strafing of a Viet Cong bunker and the torture of a prisoner.

The Mills of the Gods: Viet Nam was one of a series of socially committed documentaries produced by the CBC in the early 1960s in a cycle that produced moving early films by many important Canadian documentarians. In addition to those by Fox, which include One More River (aka Report on the Mood of the South Nine Years After the Supreme Court Ordered Integration with All Deliberate Speed, 1964, codirected by Douglas Leiterman, and featuring an interview with Malcolm X), Donald Brittain and Allan King also worked under this moment of ferment at the CBC.

Haunting, arresting, and universal in its consideration of the relationship of individuals to ideology, Mills of the Gods: Viet Nam appeared on television early enough in the war, and in a moment of emergent politically committed practitioners of broadcasting, to be seen today as an important example of the social potential of documentary as a film practice.

PETER URQUHART

The Mills of the Gods: Viet Nam (Canada, 1965, 56 mins). Produced and directed by Beryl Fox.

Mita, Merata

Merata Mita's role as a Maori filmmaker has been crucial for the documentary and feature film traditions of Aotearoa/New Zealand and for indigenous filmmaking internationally. The first indigenous woman to have made a feature film—Mauri/Life Force (1987)—Mita was also the first woman to have directed a feature-length film in Aotearoa, the documentary Patu!/A Club: To Assault (1983). Mita's work is informed by the roles that *whakapapa* (genealogy) and *whai koorero* (oratory) play in Maori tradition. This is manifest most clearly through the approaches to camera work, editing, narrative structure, and treatment of subjects within each film. Generally, her work is characterised by a style that eschews an easy distinction between conventions of documentary and those of fiction. Through techniques of juxtaposition, slow motion, and the insertion of still photographs, these documentaries speak of her concern to evoke a sense of life beyond what is immediately apparent on screen. Similarly Mauri, although a fictional work, cast untrained actors in lead roles, a technique that effectively drew from the aura of these real-life social actors (Zac Wallace and Eva Rickard were recognised spokespeople for Maori, trade union, and land rights issues).

Films made between 1979 and 1990 represent the first stage of Mita's practice. Here, a movement can be traced from a period of internship on documentary films about community and struggle within *Maaoritanga* (Maori culture) and trade union movements to work that integrates these perspectives of cultural resistance within the forms of feature and archival film (Mauri, and Mana Waka/Power of the Canoe, 1990). This period was informed by an environment of Maori cultural and political renaissance growing through the 1970s and 1980s, during which Mita became involved with an activist group, Nga Tamatoa (young warriors), a Maori organisation of urban, often university-educated *rangatahi* (modern youth), who had an agenda for social change through legislative, educational, cultural, and protest strategies.

Gerd Pohlmann, Mita's then partner, made a significant contribution to New Zealand documentary film through his body of work about trade union politics and industrial disputes, documentaries on which Mita also worked in various capacities from codirector to researcher. The Mer-Ger Productions films were made alongside work that was an extension of Mita's involvement with Nga Tamatoa. These films focused on Maori land rights, in Bastion Point: Day 507 (1980); oppositional movements against local and international racism, in Patu!; and Maori communities, in Karanga Hokianga/A Welcome to the Hokianga (1979), and Keskidee-Aroha/Universal Love (1981, the name of a theatre troupe).

Nga Tamatoa's dialogue between modern change and tradition is manifest in those documentaries that take articulations of protest as their subjects, and those works where tradition comes to a fore, such as Mauri and Mana Waka. Mita has referred to film's power to make the present eternal and, accordingly, editing choices facilitate the way in which a Maori understanding of historical time as 'the past being the present being the future' is built into the narrative structure of her films.

Women are central to the narratives of Mita's documentaries; they are often portrayed as strong community leaders. These representations invoke historical role models, inferring a line of connection between the women leaders of yesterday and those of today. As with other contemporary Maori women, Mita affirms *mana waahine Maaori* (the power of Maori women) as a means of understanding the strength of women within *Maaoritanga*, as well as asserting cultural difference from *paakehaa* (non-Maori) feminism, a difference that is largely predicated on race.

Although Mita has been based in Hawaii since completing Mana Waka, Aotearoa has remained *tuurangawaewae* (a place to stand). She returns often for documentary projects and teaching commitments. The last decade has seen her documentary work maintain an exploration of ways in which tradition operates within contemporary contexts. Dread (1996) is the study of a Maori Rastafarian community within the Bay of Plenty. Te Paho (1997) is a quest drawing from ethnomusicology in search of a Maori drum. Hotere (2000), moves back to a manipulation of editing, cinematography, and sound to both animate and hold in contemplation the work of a renowned artist who prefers not to speak for the camera. It can be said that in the spirit of *whai koorero*, *whakapapa*, and *mauri*, Mita's work has taken on a life of its own.

GERALDENE PETERS

Biography

Born in Maketu, Bay of Plenty, Aotearoa/New Zealand, June 1942. Affiliations are with the *hapu* (sub-tribe) Ngati Pikiao, and the *iwi* (principal tribe), Te Arawa. Trained as a secondary school teacher, introducing Maori students to film as a medium through which to tell their stories. Involvement with Nga Tamatoa from 1970. Liaison work between overseas film crews and Maori communities 1977–9. Directed first film Karanga Hokianga 1979. Continued making documentaries, alongside acting in television dramas and feature films; working as a Maori current affairs presenter; and directing her first feature film 1980–90. Resident of Hawaii since 1990, teaching documentary film production at the University of Hawaii-Manoa. Worked alongside partner, New Zealand director Geoff Murphy, in assistant director roles for two Hollywood feature films and a television pilot. Continued to produce documentaries within the Pacific and Aotearoa. Awarded the Flaherty Seminar's Leo Dratfield Award for Commitment and Excellence in Documentary 1996. Winner of the Mountain Award for excellence, commitment, and innovation, Taos Film Festival 1999. Screenwriting tutor, documentary juror, adviser to Native Programming with the Sundance Film Institute, 2000 to the present.

Selected films

1979 Karanga Hokianga: director, coeditor
1980 Bastion Point Day 507: codirector, coeditor
1980 The Hammer and the Anvil: codirector, coproducer
1981 Kinleith '80: community liaison
1981 Keskidee-Aroha: codirector, coproducer
1982 The Bridge: A Story of Men in Dispute: codirector
1983 Patu!: director, producer

1990 Mana Waka: director, sound designer
1996 Dread: director, writer
1997 Te Paho: director, writer
2001 Hotere: director, writer, producer

Further reading

Horrocks, Roger, 'Merata Mita', *New Zealand Film Makers at the Auckland City Art Gallery* 2, August 1984: 1–4.

Horrocks, Roger and Mita, Merata, 'Patu!', *Alternative Cinema* 11, nos. 2–3, winter/spring 1983: 11–21.

Jesson, Bruce and Mita, Merata, 'Film and the Making of Politics', *The Republican*, February 1983: 8–15.

Lamche, Pascale, 'Interview with Merata Mita', *Framework* 25, 1984: 2–11.

Mita, Merata, 'The Soul and the Image', in Jan Bieringa and Jonathan Dennis (eds), *Film in Aotearoa New Zealand*, Wellington: Victoria University Press, 1992.

Parekowhai, Cushla, 'Puea o te Ao: Rise to the Surface of the World. Merata Mita and Mana Waka', in Christina Barton and Deborah Lawler Dormer (eds), *Alter/Image: Feminism and Representation in New Zealand Art 1973–93*, Auckland: Auckland City Art Gallery and Wellington: City Gallery, 1993.

Peters, Geraldene, 'Lives of Their Own: Films by Merata Mita', in Ian Conrich and Stuart Murray (eds), *New Zealand Film Makers*, Michigan: Wayne State University Press, 2007.

Mitchell, Denis

A central figure in television documentary in the late 1950s and 1960s, Denis Mitchell established himself as one of the first television auteurs through a highly personal body of work. Unlike many documentaries in the late 1950s, usually marked by an 'objective', journalistic approach, Mitchell's work had more in common with cinematic precedents. Two of the most notable predecessors Mitchell can be linked to are the more poetic filmmakers who worked for the British documentary film movement and filmmakers associated with Free Cinema in the 1950s.

Cinematic links are important, but it should also be stressed that Mitchell's background was actually in radio, a medium that also significantly influenced his approach to television documentary. In radio he started to experiment with a portable tape recorder, making 'wild track' recordings of a variety of 'ordinary', mostly working-class people. Using these raw, direct recordings in his radio programmes was innovative because at the time the routine manner by which the working classes were represented was subject to heavy mediation. First they were interviewed, then their speech was 'tidied up', and eventually an actor would voice this 'common speech'.

Mitchell eventually secured work for television when he was asked to make a short film on teenagers for Special Enquiry, a current affairs series consisting of a number of diverse items. Mitchell again made heavy use of his portable tape recorder, creating a fragmented montage of teenage voices accompanying nonsynchronised images of teenage life. Using a nonsynchronous image track meant that the camera was lighter and easier to move around. This allowed a number of images from different positions to be shot and edited together. While the film featured narration, it was noted for its aesthetic character, the way in which it conveyed an impressionistic portrait of teenage life.

The film on teenagers met with wide acclaim; both Mitchell's technical accomplishments and his ability to 'get closer' to everyday life were praised. This led him to make his first television feature for the BBC in 1957. In Prison was the first attempt to explore prison life on television.

Mitchell researched the programme in depth and even spent time in a cell in Strangeways prison, where the programme was filmed. The film again used a mixture of wild track recordings, narration, and aesthetically framed observations of prison life. These were mixed, however, with some dramatic reconstructions plus some expressive sound effects and music.

Mitchell then began to adopt the even lighter 16mm camera, which enabled him to film location footage with more ease and with greater mobility. In 1959 he made one of his most critically acclaimed programmes for the BBC, Morning in the Streets. The film, which won an award at the Prix Italia, was shot in Salford and Liverpool and was a poetic evocation of life in working-class neighbourhoods. With the extra mobility afforded by the 16mm cameras, the film contains a greater sense of movement and fluidity than Mitchell's previous work; it also dispenses with narration, thus adding to its aesthetic, poetic qualities. The artistic rendering of working class life is reminiscent of some films from both the documentary film movement and the Free Cinema films. Yet Mitchell's films tended to focus, almost fetishistically, on 'down-and-out' characters, and his films are thus filled with a greater sense of despair. Also, by using 16mm and portable tape, his films can also be connected to the direct cinema movement that emerged in the early 1960s in the United States. It is true that Mitchell did not at this time use synchronised portable film and tape equipment, and that he was concerned with personal expression in a way that direct cinema proponents disavowed. His shots are often carefully framed and thus avoid the shaky camera movements often found in early direct cinema films. Yet his tape experiments and his freer use of cameras can be related to direct cinema in that they seemed more immediate than many other documentaries that were being made on British television at the time.

After making a number of films for the BBC in a similar vein, including House on the Beach (1960), Chicago (1961), and the series The Wind of Change (1960), which included Dennis Potter's documentary Between Two Rivers, Mitchell joined Granada in 1964. Here, working with Norman Swallow, he began to diverge from his previous methods by using videotape, which was still in its infancy in this period and was extremely difficult to edit. He made two films with Swallow in 1964 on videotape: Wedding on Saturday and The Entertainers. While the former was still a familiar anthropological dissection of working-class life in an industrial region (but which featured a lot more synch-sound than before), The Entertainers was a change in direction. The film straddled the borders of documentary and fictional filmmaking in that it was an observation of six different entertainers residing in the same lodging house for a period of time. In an early precursor of Big Brother (2000–), ordinary people were placed in an artificial situation and their interactions were dissected (the single location was convenient in that video cameras were cumbersome and difficult to move from place to place). Yet spontaneous interaction was mixed with more expressive, staged sequences, which added a dramatic impetus to the interpersonal dynamics.

Mitchell and Swallow then set up a freelance television company, Denis Mitchell Films, which was based in Hampstead. They negotiated a contract with Granada for which they produced the series This England. The series, which documented various aspects of the country, ran from 1965 until 1967 and gave new directors such as Dick Fontaine and Mike Grigsby a chance to make programmes. (Mitchell also directed a few programmes himself, as did Swallow.) The series reappeared on the television schedules for a slightly longer run between 1977 and 1980.

After This England Mitchell's star began to fade a little and his reputation for innovation waned. Yet, while the late 1950s to the late 1960s may have been his golden period, he continued to make documentary films on themes that interested him for most of his life. Unlike other figures he refused to delve into television drama (though he did sometimes use 'dramatic' elements for expressive purposes), believing that real lives and real people were of far more interest. He relentlessly pursued his personal interests, returning again and again to making films of those who were on the margins of society. He made some films for World in Action in the late 1960s and early 1970s. He then went on to make a series of character documentaries in Seven Men (1971), which included his famous film on Quentin Crisp. In 1977 he continued his analyses of marginal figures by making Never and Always, which portrayed the lives of three 'ordinary' people struggling to make a living in Norfolk.

JAMIE SEXTON

Biography

Born in Cheshire, 1911. Attended drama school and became an actor. Emigrated to South Africa after the war and began to work in a number of jobs including broadcasting. Returned to Britain in the 1940s and worked in Manchester as a radio talks producer. Set up Denis Mitchell Films in 1963. Died in 1990.

Selected films

1957 In Prison (BBC): director, producer
1959 Morning in the Streets (BBC): director
1959 Soho Story (BBC): director, producer
1960 House on the Beach (Redifussion): director
1960 The Wind of Change (BBC, series): director, producer
1961 Chicago (BBC): director, producer
1964 Wedding on Saturday (Granada): director

1964	The Entertainers (Granada): director, producer
1965–7	This England (coproduced with Norman Swallow, series): director, coproducer
1970	World in Action: St Mungo's People (Granada): director
1970	World in Action: Ian Paisley (Granada): director
1971	Seven Men (Granada, series): director, producer
1972–3	A European Journey (Granada, series): director, producer
1977	Never and Always (Granada): director
1977–80	This England (Granada, series): director
1986	Don of the Dais (Channel 4): director, producer
1986	Changing Times (Channel 4, series): director

Further reading

Bell, Elaine, 'The Origins of British Television Documentary: the BBC 1946–55', in John Corner (ed.), *Documentary and the Mass Media*, London: Edward Arnold, 1986.

Corner, John, 'Documentary Voices', in John Corner (ed.), *Popular Television in Britain: Studies in Cultural History*, London: BFI, 1991.

Orbanz, Eva (ed.), *Journey to a Legend and Back: The British Realistic Film*, trans. Stuart Hood, Berlin: Edition Volker Spiess, 1977.

Purser, Philip, 'Think-Tape: A Profile of Denis Mitchell', *Contrast* 1, no. 2, winter, 1961.

Robinson, David, 'Shooting on Tape', *Contrast* 3, no. 1, autumn 1963.

Scannell, Paddy, 'The Social Eye of Television 1946–55', *Media, Culture and Society* 1, no. 1, 1979.

——'The Stuff of Radio', in John Corner (ed.), *Documentary and the Mass Media*, London: Edward Arnold, 1986.

Swallow, Norman, *Factual Television*, London: Focal Press, 1966.

Mitry, Jean

Jean Mitry was an author, teacher, film historian and theoretician, and occasional actor and director. He was the most prolific film historian in Europe in the twentieth century; he was active from 1924 until his death in 1988. Few people are aware today that Mitry was one of the co-founders of the famous Cinémathèque Française, on September 9, 1936, with Henri Langlois, Georges Franju, and Paul-Auguste Harlé.

In his early twenties Jean Mitry was already fascinated by movies. He organized a Ciné-Club, wrote about films for many French journals, worked as an assistant for various film directors (such as Pierre Chenal), and appeared in minor roles in short films, as well as in Jean Renoir's La Nuit du carrefour (1932). Mitry also worked as a film editor for Alexandre Astruc's baroquedrama, Le Rideau cramoisi (1952).

Mitry directed approximately twenty short films, most of them experimental films or documentaries. Many depicted how moving images could illustrate pieces of classical music in a rhythmic synchronism. Mitry won a prize for best editing (in the short film category) at the Cannes Film Festival in 1949 for his first film as director and editor, originally entitled Pacific 231 (1949). In this short film influenced by Abel Gance's La Roue (1922), Mitry tried to create synchronicity between moving images of wheels and locomotives and a soundtrack by Swiss composer Arthur Honegger. Mitry later explained that Honegger and he wanted to explore 'the definition of the various relationships between acoustic and visual rhythm' (quoted in Mitry 1997: 260).

Among Jean Mitry's most important films are En bateau (1951), Images pour Debussy (1951), and Rêverie de Claude Debussy (1952), a cycle of three essays inspired by the music of Claude Debussy, for which Mitry tried to find a visual counterpoint, with pastoral and natural images. Mitry teamed up with French composer Pierre Boulez to find a visual equivalent to a more abstract, contemporary music, with a thirteen-minute film titled Symphonie mécanique (1955), which was initially planned to be on a multiscreen.

One of Mitry's last short films is a technical documentary about how a film is produced, titled Derrière le décor/Behind the Set (1969), a didactic work that presents the duties of every member of the film crew. Oddly, Mitry's only feature film made as a director was a weak adaptation of a novel by Léo Malet, Énigme aux Folies-Bergères (1959). Today, Mitry's films can only be found at the Cinémathèque Française and in a few other film archives.

In the 1960s Jean Mitry published his three most ambitious works that confirmed his respected position in French film studies. First, he released a theoretical synthesis on film studies in two volumes, *Esthétique et psychologie du cinéma* (The Aesthetics and Psychology of the Cinema, 1963 and 1965), which was for many generations the fundamental reference in film theory. The same year, Mitry published the first general dictionary dedicated to cinema, simply titled *Dictionnaire du cinéma* (Mitry 1963), which contained entries for major directors, actors, movies, followed (in appendices) by two valuable filmographies on selected short films (documentary and fiction) (on pp. 310–25) and another selection of classic documentaries of more than an hour produced between 1911 and 1959 (pp. 326–7). Just four years later Mitry released another monument: his multi-volume world film history, titled *Histoire du cinéma* (1967), which was acclaimed for its exhaustive spectrum and neutral tone, although it was sometimes overly criticized for minor errors (see Collet *et al.* 1980). A much celebrated book, *The Aesthetics and Psychology of the Cinema* contained several remarks about Mitry's conception of the documentary film: 'Conversely, when documentary presents an original and personal vision of the world and its objects, that is, when it becomes an eye, it also becomes a "poem". And as a poem it is organized, dialectically composed; in other words, it becomes language' (Mitry 1997: 59).

A film expert without an academic degree, Jean Mitry was nevertheless an extraordinary communicator, with an incomparable knowledge of film history and a vast memory of the thousands of films he had watched in various countries (Passek 1998). He was never a tenured *professeur d'université*, but he often taught as a lecturer, first at the Institut des hautes études cinématographiques (IDHEC) in Paris, sometimes at the Université de Paris 1, and later in Québec at the Université de Montréal (in the early 1970s).

During the 1980s, when semiotics became a popular field of academic inquiry, and for many professors the only way to apprehend film studies, Mitry published a courageous and accurate critique of the current French semiotic obsession, entitled *La sémiologie en question* (1987). That polemical book, one of Mitry's most important, demonstrated how futile and limited were Christian Metz's theories on film semiotics, in terms of film theory and film history. In that debate, Mitry also questioned the 'Marxist trend' and leftist doctrine that emerged in some French film studies, as seen in some authors of *Cahiers du cinéma* and *Cinéthique* in the early 1970s, such as Jean-Louis Comolli, Jean Narboni, Jean-Patrick Lebel, and Pascal Bonitzer. Mitry was the first to question that tendency and therefore courted controversy. It was attacked or ignored by many Parisian academics and contributed to the rejection of Mitry's incomparable contribution as a film historian and theoretician in some academic circles.

A prolific and generous author, Mitry also edited a *Bibliographie internationale du cinéma et de la télévision* in seven volumes, and edited a thirty-volume *Filmographie universelle*. Mitry also wrote monographs on film directors (John Ford, 1954; Eisenstein, 1961), and poetry (his last book, *L'Ange Vénus*). Today, Jean Mitry is remembered in France by an Association Jean-Mitry and a prize, the Prix Jean-Mitry.

YVES LABERGE

Biography

Born in Soissons, France, 1904, with the full name Jean Rene Pierre Goetgheluck le Rouge Tillard des Acres de Presfontaines. Chose his shorter pseudonym, Mitry, from the name of a little town near Paris. Died in La Garenne-Colombes, France, 1988.

Selected films

1949	Pacific 231: director, writer
c. 1950	Écrire en images/Writing with Images: director, writer, editor
1951	Images pour Debussy/Images for Debussy: director, writer
1951	En bateau/On a Boat: director, writer
1952	Rêverie de Claude Debussy/Claude Debussy's Dreaming: director, writer
1955	Symphonie mécanique/Mechanical Symphony: director, writer
1969	Derrière le décor/Behind the Set: director

Further reading

Andrew, J. Dudley (ed.), *The Major Film Theories: An Introduction*, New York: Oxford University Press, 1976.

Collet, Jean, with Marie, Michel, Percheron, Daniel, Simon, Jean-Paul and Vernet, Marc, *Lectures du film*, third edn, Paris: Albatros, 1980.

Lewis, Brian, *Jean Mitry and the Aesthetics of the Cinema*, Ann Arbor, MI: UMI Research Press, 1984 (from a thesis on Jean Mitry, defended at the University of Iowa, 1980).

Lowry, Edward, *The Filmology Movement and Film Study in France*, Ann Arbor, MI: UMI Research Press, 1985.
Mitry, Jean, *The Aesthetics and Psychology of the Cinema* (translated from the abridged 1900 edition of *Esthétique et psychologie du cinéma*), Bloomington, IN and Indianapolis, IN: Indiana University Press, 1997.
——*Semiotics and the Analysis of Film*, London: British Film Institute, 2000 (translated from *La sémiologie en question*, Paris: Cerf, 1987).
——*Dictionnaire du cinéma*, Paris: Larousse, 1963.
——*Histoire du cinéma (Art et industrie)*, five volumes, Paris: Editions universitaires, 1967 (also 1969 and 1973).
——(ed.), *Le cinéma expérimental: histoire et perspectives*, Paris: Seghers, 1974.
——(ed.), *Bibliographie internationale du cinéma et de la télévision*, seven volumes, Paris: IDHEC, 1966.
——*Filmographie universelle*, thirty volumes, Bois d'Arcy (France): Editions du Service des Archives du Film, 1963–72.
——*L'Ange Vénus*, Longueuil: Le Preambule, 1979 (poetry book published in Canada, with some verses in English).
Passek, Jean-Loup (ed.), *Dictionnaire du cinéma*, Paris: Larousse, 1998.

Moana

(US, Flaherty, 1926)

After the very considerable success of Nanook of the North (1922), Robert Flaherty, its creator, was approached by Jesse L. Lasky of Famous Players-Lasky (which became Paramount Pictures), the first firm to have turned down distribution of Nanook. Lasky offered Flaherty what amounted to a blank check. He was to go anywhere in the world and bring back 'another Nanook'.

Flaherty had become interested in the South Seas through the eloquent descriptions of a friend, Frederick O'Brien, who had written a popular book on the subject: *White Shadows in the South Seas*. O'Brien urged Flaherty to go to Samoa to record the lovely culture of its gentle people before it was further eroded by the incursions of foreigners and disappeared altogether. With his wife Frances, three small daughters, their nursemaid, and his brother David, he set sail for the Southwest Pacific.

Flaherty was aware of what Hollywood expected from him—another box office success—and wondered what he would find in Samoa that could provide the drama of human survival that Nanook contained. (Two years after the film was released Nanook died of starvation, as many of his people had.) On the way to Samoa, Flaherty learned that a giant octopus had been sighted from another ship. Maybe enormous sea creatures threatened human life in Samoa.

Once there he found no sea monsters. On the contrary, Samoan existence seemed to provide no drama at all. For weeks a dejected Flaherty sat on the veranda drinking apple beer, gloomily contemplating what form he might give to a film about Samoans.

Through his informal investigations into the culture, he had learned of a practice no longer carried out that interested him. Formerly, young Samoan men had been initiated into manhood by undergoing elaborate and intricate tattooing over much of their bodies (the knees being particularly painful), which took several weeks. Flaherty concluded that because there were few physical threats to their existence, the Samoans had invented a test of endurance involving considerable pain. He revived this custom for the purposes of his film, and organized it around the initiation of one Samoan youth named Moana. Preceding and paralleling the scenes of tattooing are scenes of the gathering of food (in the jungle, from the sea, and along the shore), the making of clothing and ornaments, the preparing and cooking of a feast, and the dancing of the Siva by Moana and his intended bride. When the tattooing is completed, there is a ceremonial drinking of kava (an alcoholic beverage made from the crushed root of a shrubby pepper) by the chiefs and a celebratory dance by the men of the village in honor of Moana's courage.

If Flaherty in his first two films became a special kind of storyteller, he was also a subtle and engaging teacher. His visual exposition is generally exemplary in its simplicity and clarity. Also, his pedagogy uses mystery and suspense to arouse our curiosity, to make us want to learn about the subjects that fascinated him. One of many similar instances of this method occurs early in Moana when Moana's younger brother, Pe'a, climbs a palm tree. First we see him mid-frame, on a section of the trunk. He is allowed to climb up out of frame; then the camera tilts up to re-center him. Pe'a again climbs out of frame and is again pursued by the camera. On the third climb/tilt, the top of this majestic tree is revealed. By that time we are not only craving to see the top, we are prepared to accept this as the tallest palm in the world. In another scene we see Pe'a looking at something, and a title tells us he has come upon 'a telltale bit of evidence—an empty coconut shell'. We do not learn what it is evidence of, however, and the mystery builds as Pe'a scrambles about the rocks, peers in the crevices between them, tries to move one, and starts a small fire accompanied by smoke until a creature emerges. Only then does a title say, 'Ah, Mr. Robber Crab, you won't climb my father's coconut trees any more'.

Though Flaherty tended to profess ignorance of technological matters, he seems to have been a natural and perhaps superb technician. For Moana he was the first to use the new panchromatic film. Though black and white (before color was available), panchromatic film is sensitive to all colors of the spectrum, unlike the orthochromatic film then in standard use. Although orthochromatic did not respond to red and was prone to harsh contrasts, Moana offers a Samoa rich in varied tones of gray. It was also on this production that Flaherty first began to make extensive use of long (telephoto) lenses. Almost all of it was shot with lenses of six inches focal length and upward (two inches being standard for 35mm). Their use had the obvious advantage of permitting the filming of distant and inaccessible subjects, the outrigger in the surf, for example. Also, Flaherty found that his people were less self-conscious and behaved more naturally if the camera was some distance from them. He also thought certain special photographic qualities resulted through the use of long lenses: 'The figures had a roundness, a stereoscopic quality that gave to the picture a startling reality and beauty [...] alive and real, the shadows softer, and the breadfruit trees seemed like living things rather than a flat background.'

Moana prompted John Grierson, then a young Scot visiting the United States, to devise a new use for the word documentary. He introduced it casually, as an adjective, in the first sentence of the second paragraph of his review of Moana for *The New York Sun*: 'Of course, Moana being a visual account of events in the daily life of a Polynesian youth and his family, has documentary value.' Grierson carried the word and his developing aesthetic theory and sense of social purpose back to Great Britain where he began and then led what would become a documentary film movement.

JACK C. ELLIS

See also: Flaherty, Robert; Nanook of the North

Moana (US, Famous Players-Lasky, 1926, 95 mins). Distributed by Paramount Pictures. Produced, directed, photographed, and edited by Robert J. Flaherty. Filmed in British Samoa.

Moffatt, Tracey

Tracey Moffatt is an indigenous Australian visual artist and filmmaker whose films speculatively document the 'real' via humour, narrative implication, and by challenging generic conventions. She began her film work with a ten-minute health promotion for the Aboriginal Medical Service (Redfern, Australia). Spread the Word (1988) was 'experimental and avant-garde at the time, with distinctive artificial sets, comedic characterisation, computer-generated art and rap music' (Langton 1993: 16). In 1988 she made Moodeitj Yorgas. Solid Women for the Western Australian Women's Advisory Council to the Premier. This lyric, twenty-two-minute video features interviews with prominent Aboriginal women: their voices are heard (but not synchronised) over silent videotaped portraits that are linked using dramatic segments of women in black silhouette who enact brief vignettes over stories told in two Aboriginal languages. Of her four independent films, only one has been marketed (by Ronin Films) as 'documentary': the twenty-eight-minute video Heaven (1997). Two of her 'fiction' films, however, the feature length BeDevil (1993) and the seventeen-minute Nice Coloured Girls (1987), are also significant for documentary film discourse.

First, her stylistic references to documentary in these films critique documentary filmmaking's 'necessary fiction' (in Herbert Blau's sense) that there is a vast difference between narrative fiction film's and documentary's choice and treatment of subject matter. They suggest that the combined devices of both 'fiction' and 'nonfiction' film might indeed be needed for 'documenting' the particular social issue that all Moffatt's films address: race relations between indigenous and nonindigenous Australians. This issue involves the telling and keeping of many 'secrets', recalling Michel Foucault's sense of a secrecy that simultaneously protects people's privacy and reinforces institutionalised abuse. Performances of 'secrets' by both professional and social actors in Moffatt's films glide constantly between fictional and nonfictional conjunctions of space and time. Second, when she uses or refers to documentary modes of filmmaking, Moffatt does so primarily through manipulating the cinematic gaze. Her films specifically critique the 'documentary gaze', which is 'constitutively multiform, embroiled with conscious motives and unconscious desires, driven by curiosity no more than by terror and fascination' (Renov 1999: 321). Third, while commenting on various modes of documentary filmmaking, Moffatt's films themselves can be understood in the context of documentary's fifth mode: the performative (Nichols 1994).

In the second ghost story of BeDevil, 'Choo Choo Choo Choo', Moffatt performs the role of her own mother, Ruby. Using a style suggestive of cinéma vérité, 'documentary characters' tell a story from the time when Ruby lived by a railway siding in outback Queensland. They invite their audience into a parody of the idyllic 'bush picnic'—at a rubbish dump in the desert, beside a derelict house. The camera zooms onto a middle-aged Aboriginal woman reclining and sipping a glass of cold Chardonnay who says directly to camera: 'Shoo! Don't do that!' This 'documentary' sequence explicitly critiques the documentary filmmaking devices of the 'intrusive' camera and the frequently stereotyping narratives of ethnographic film. The first ghost story also comments on documentary filmmaking, although less humorously. During the telling of 'Mr Chuck', the audience experiences the ravaged face of a middle-aged Aboriginal man (actor Jack Charles) who describes his childhood as he sits talking, not to camera, but past the camera, toward the unidentified person who is 'interviewing' him. The setting with its glass wall strongly evokes a prison interview room. This look 'past the camera' can be understood as a specific critique of documentary interview situations that rely on unequal power relations between those who interview and those whom they interview. In Patricia Mellencamp's words, 'Moffatt reacts against ethnography, the realist tradition of representing black Australia' (Mellencamp 1993–4: 136). Moffatt's films communicate the experience of Australian race relations; within their texts 'the 'unsaid and unseen' can be experienced, felt. Aboriginal characters don't simply see or look as much as they witness or evade. They don't speak as much as they testify or parody' (Mellencamp 1995: 60). BeDevil's 'documentary' sequences resonate strongly with performative documentary: 'overarching conceptual categories such as exile, racism, sexism, or homophobia [...] are seldom named and never described or explained in any detail' (Nichols 1994: 104).

Nice Coloured Girls (seventeen minutes) is again a fictional narrative with explicitly documentary overtones. Three young Aboriginal girls 'pick up' a middle-aged white Australian man at a bar in Sydney's infamous 'red light' area, Kings Cross. They lure him into buying them dinner; he gets drunk and they steal his wallet, giggling and disappearing into a taxi in the half-light of dawn over Sydney Harbour. We do not hear the actors speak. The soundtrack is full of ambient city noise and a male voice-over that intones British officials' early accounts of meetings with aboriginal women at the time of Sydney's early settlement in the late eighteenth century. Scenes of the girls' 'night out' are interrupted periodically by images of anonymous white hands pulling at black hands and legs, black legs climbing up rope ladders, old photographs, and smashing glass. The contemporary story is filmed in a style that suggests 'observational' documentary: the images are grainy, badly lit, and sometimes awkwardly framed. The 'flashes' of historical comment are explicitly staged and sharply framed. A dark woman's face is blown by a gentle wind; her expression is of quiet curiosity as we see her face looking at us, and we are caught into an experience of looking at someone whom we never thought to see and who is looking back at us. This film violently unsettles looking relations that conventionally exist between those who have access to power and those who do not. The story is drawn from Moffatt's childhood, she says: 'I used to do it, I used to do it with my sisters [...] we're not little angels' (in Mellencamp 1993–4: 152). Through this film we are given 'a glimpse into some young Aborigines' ways of seeing their world' (Kaplan 2000: 68). Both in this sense, and in the sense that the film combines historical documents with a narrative that 'reenacts' the filmmaker's own experience, Nice Coloured Girls can be understood as a performative documentary which 'clearly embodies a paradox: it generates a distinct tension between performance and document, between the personal and the typical, the embodied and disembodied' (Nichols 1994: 97).

Heaven, although marketed by Ronin Films as documentary, was produced in the context of video art for Moffatt's 1997 exhibition at the Dia Center, New York. It features staged and unstaged footage of 'good-looking' male surfers removing wet suits and otherwise 'changing' their clothes, and combines surveillance-styled footage of unaware surfers with interactions between surfers and the various anonymous (handheld) camera operators who were commissioned by Moffatt. Not one surfer is identified in the film. We never hear the spoken voice; we hear instead waves washing on a beach (as in Nice Coloured Girls) and intermittent, unidentified 'tribal' drumming and chanting. Once again, the documentary gaze is under review: for its dialectic of power and subversion, for its humour, and for its manifestation of our desire to 'watch' other people. Through Heaven, with its closing images of a dark female hand pulling away a blue towel from a white naked male body, Moffatt again challenges and explores the conventions of documentary film.

CATHERINE SUMMERHAYES

Biography

Born in 1960 in Brisbane, Australia. Graduated in 1982 from the Queensland College of the Arts in Brisbane, where she studied film and video. Principally known for her visual art that has been widely exhibited internationally: photoseries including Something More (1989), Scarred for Life (1994), Guapa—Good-looking (1995), Up in the Sky (1997), Laudanum (1999), and Invocations (2000). Lives and works in Sydney and New York.

Selected films

1987 Nice Coloured Girls: director, writer
1988 Moodeitj Yorgas. Solid Women: director, writer
1989 Night Cries: A Rural Tragedy: director, writer
1993 BeDevil: director, writer
1997 Heaven: director

Further reading

Jennings, Karen, *Sites of Difference: Cinematic Representations of Aboriginality and Gender*, South Melbourne: Australian Film Institute Research and Information Centre, 1993.

Kaplan, E. Ann, 'Aborigines, Film, and Moffatt's "Night Cries: A Rural Tragedy": An Outsider's Perspectives', in Julie Marcus (ed.), *Picturing the 'Primitif': Images of Race in Daily Life*, Canada Bay, Australia: LhR Press, 2000.

Langton, Marcia, *'Well, I heard it on the radio and I saw it on the television': an essay for the Australian Film Commission on the politics and aesthetics of filmmaking by and about Aboriginal people and things*, North Sydney: Australian Film Commission, 1993.

Mellencamp, Patricia, 'Haunted History: Tracey Moffatt and Julie Dash', *Discourse* 16, no. 2, winter 1993–4: 127–63.

——*A Fine Romance: Five Ages of Film Feminism*, Philadelphia, PA: Temple University Press, 1995.

Morris, Meaghan, 'Beyond Assimilation: Aboriginality, Media History and Public Memory', *Aedon* 4, no. 1, November 1996: 12–26.

Nichols, Bill, *Blurred Boundaries. Questions of Meaning in Contemporary Culture*, Bloomington, IN and Indianapolis, IN: Indiana University Press, 1994.

Renov, Michael, 'Documentary Horizons: An Afterword', in Jane M. Gaines and Michael Renov (eds), *Collecting Visible Evidence*, Minneapolis, MN and London: University of Minnesota Press, 1999.

Summerhayes, Catherine, 'Moving Images: The Films of Tracey Moffatt—so far … ', in Lisa French (ed.), *Women Vision: Women and the Moving Image in Australia*, Melbourne: Damned Publishing, 2002.

Momma Don't Allow

(UK, Reisz, 1956)

One of the emblematic films of the Free Cinema group, Momma Don't Allow is a portrait of a jazz club in North London, with music provided by the Chris Barber Band. Jointly directed by two of the group's leading figures, Karel Reisz and Tony Richardson, and made with support from the British Film Institute's (BFI) Experimental Film Fund, it was included in the first Free Cinema programme in 1956.

Lindsay Anderson, the group's leading light, was always ready to admit that the term Free Cinema was a label of convenience, but as one of their handouts declared, these films were free 'in the sense that their statements are entirely personal' and 'produced outside the framework of the film industry […] without obligation to subscribe to the technical or social conventions imposed on work under commercial conditions' (Lovell and Hillier 1972: 136). As the film critic

Alexander Walker concluded, they represented themselves as a challenge to orthodoxy, but as long as their films remained closer to essays rather than revolutionary pamphlets, they were not considered a political danger (Walker 1974: 33).

Momma Don't Allow exemplifies the characteristics of the group in several respects, including its 'personal' treatment of unfamiliar subject matter representing the candid portrayal of the contemporary world, here without the mediation of a commentary. On this occasion, however, the segment of the world portrayed is not one to which the filmmakers were social outsiders, but one in which, as young members of the artistic community of the capital city, they might expectedly participate. The Chris Barber Band was at the centre of the traditional jazz revival of the 1950s, which was one of the defining features of taste for a generation. A few years later Richardson included Barber's trumpet playing in his first feature film, Look Back in Anger.

The filmmakers adopt a sociological approach reminiscent of the work of Humphrey Jennings, beginning with introductions to a range of characters who finish their day's work and set out for the club: a female railway cleaner, a butcher's boy, a dentist's nurse—all cross-cut with the band setting up in the room at the pub that serves as the club's venue. The shooting is agile (though not as daring as Richard Leacock filming a similar subject in New York a year or two earlier), and the editing expertly disguises the fact that the film is shot without synchronous sound. It is all beautifully done, including a delicate moment when a couple who have had a tiff make up in a corridor. It is here that the film betrays its transitional status between the old style of constructed documentary and a new free form to which the group aspired, but that was not yet quite within their grasp. However, this can also be read another way: if these episodes are necessarily set up for the camera, they also hint at ambitions towards a new tone for realist fiction that both directors went on to realise in their early feature films.

MICHAEL CHANAN

See also: Reisz, Karel

Momma Don't Allow (UK, British Film Institute Experimental Film Fund, 1956, 22 mins). Directed by Karel Reisz and Tony Richardson. Photographed by Walter Lassally. Sound and editing by John Fletcher.

Further reading

Durgnat, Raymond, 'Loved One', *Films and Filming* 12, no. 5, February 1966: 19–23.

Ellis, John (ed.), *1951–76: British Film Institute Productions*, London: British Film Institute, 1977.

Lovell, Alan and Hillier, Jim, *Studies in Documentary*, London: Secker and Warburg/BFI, 1972.

Walker, Alexander, *Hollywood, England, The British Film Industry in the Sixties*, London: Michael Joseph, 1974.

Welsh, James M. and Tibbetts, John C. (eds), *The Cinema of Tony Richardson: Essays and Interviews*, New York: State University of New York, 1999.

Mondo Cane

(Italy, Jacopetti, 1962)

An immensely popular and influential compilation documentary that problematises, and effectively collapses, the boundaries separating fiction from nonfiction filmmaking practices, Mondo Cane/A Dog's Life initiated its own subgenre of 'Mondo Films' (or 'Shockumentaries', as they were affectionately referred to by fans), begat a wave of imitators, and has proven formative for such diverse pop- and pseudo-documentary traditions as the 'snuff' film, the mockumentary, hardcore pornography, execution videos, and even reality television. Purporting to subscribe to the adage that 'truth can be stranger than fiction', all the while betraying its own principles by presenting often misleading voice-over commentary and manipulated (if not wholly faked) footage, Gualtiero Jacopetti's sensationalist travelogue-cum-nature film set out to 'shock the audience with its exposé of bizarre cultural behaviour, fluctuating from the exotic to the erotic to the undeniably repellant' (Kerekes and Slater 1998). Although fairly dated and only intermittently outrageous by today's far more cynical and raunchy viewing standards, Mondo Cane (pronounced car-nay) was an international box office hit at its initial release and resulted in a veritable cottage industry of derivative (though increasingly graphic) sequels and series that continue to attract audiences to this day, particularly in the home video market.

A one-time journalist and war correspondent who later provided acerbic commentary for an Italian newsreel corporation, Jacopetti found himself distressed with the saccharine voice-over narration he was hired to write for Luigi Vanzi's Il Mondo di notte/World By Night (1959) and Alessandro Blasetti's Europa di notte/European Nights (1959). These celebratory compilation films of popular nightclub acts gave Jacopetti the initial idea for Mondo Cane; only his documentary would showcase, and exploit, whenever possible, all that was lurid and sensational by contemporary Western standards. Persuading producer Angelo Rizzoli to fund his undertaking, Jacopetti travelled across Europe, Asia, North America, and Africa, with associates Paolo Cavara and Franco Prosperi, collecting assorted footage of tribal ceremonies (replete with topless African women, their heads and legs often cropped in order to focus attention on the breast area), extreme cruelty to animals, religious rituals involving cross-dressing and self-flagellation, and environmental catastrophes (notably a long and languorous look at the deleterious effects of atomic radiation on the wildlife of Bikini atoll). This random material, its common denominator nothing more—although nothing less—than Jacopetti's conviction that seeing it would shock and titillate viewers, was then assembled into a one hundred and five-minute episodic whole, the various segments connected by the thinnest of associative links. (One cut takes the viewer from a dog cemetery in Pasadena, California to a restaurant in Taiwan that specialises in fresh dog meat; another cut takes us from a religious sect in Rome that periodically honours the bones of victims of the Black Plague, to a Hamburg beer-house in which the spectacle of drunken men and women flailing around, getting into fights, and falling asleep on the street supposedly demonstrates how 'a rather desperate concentration on the cult of life distracts the Germans from the memory of the cult of death'.)

Along with its bloated orchestral score (the theme song, 'More', actually became something of a hit on the pop charts, winning a Grammy Award for Best Instrumental Theme and garnering an Oscar nomination for Best Song), the film's pretentious and heavily ironic voice-over commentary became key ingredients of the Mondo film cycle to follow. The opening words of Mondo Cane are privileged by appearing as text on the screen in addition to being spoken by narrator Stefano Sibaldi: 'All the scenes you will see in this film are true and are taken only from life. If often they are shocking, it is because there are many shocking things in this world. Besides, the duty of the chronicler is not to sweeten the truth but to report it objectively.' Even if it were the case that the scenes then presented were 'true' in the sense of being detached and unbiased recordings of actual events—which they clearly are not (the only question concerns precisely which footage is real, which is reconstructed, which is completely staged, and which is otherwise manipulated)—Mondo Cane can still be charged with breaking its promise, as its reportage is anything but 'objective'. Besides dishing out the occasional piece of gross misinformation (for example, the male members of a mountain-dwelling clan in Papua New Guinea are called 'the last cavemen'), Sibaldi's voice-over narration, co-authored by Jacopetti and Cavara, is haughty and condescending in both content and tone. This narration sometimes takes on racist dimensions, as native peoples are regularly referred to as 'barbarians' and 'savages', and a Catholic mission fifty miles north of Geroka in the South Pacific is identified as 'the last outpost of civilization' to distinguish it from the tribal communities located nearby.

Complicating any straightforwardly xenophobic reading of the film, however, are its segments ridiculing various Western cultural practices. So we enter a gourmet restaurant in New York that serves an assortment of fried insects to its wealthy clientele, and tour with a gaggle of American senior citizens who seem eager to waste their retirement savings on a hokey Hawaiian vacation package. In this respect, and despite the sometimes objectionable narration, the creators of Mondo Cane finally come across as equal opportunity exploiters. By the end, and as the film's alternative title declares, it does indeed seem like we are watching 'a dog's life' ('Mondo Cane' translates literally as 'World of Dogs').

The Mondo Film can be credited, and criticised, for being the first documentary-style genre to cater specifically to the most voyeuristic and puerile, even sadistic, desires of modern viewers. In a 1964 essay for *The Atlantic Monthly*, Pauline Kael lamented the apparent fact that contemporary 'audiences [...] enjoy the shocks and falsifications, the brutal series of titillations of a Mondo Cane, one thrill after another, don't care any longer about the conventions of the past, and are too restless and apathetic to pay attention to motivations and complications, cause and effect. They want less effort, more sensations, more knobs to turn'. While the promise of showcasing increasingly bizarre and graphic sexual behaviour in the Mondo Film went by the wayside after the 1972 release of Deep Throat and the subsequent rise of hardcore porn, Mondo Cane's legacy is apparent today in the seemingly endless parade of filmic and televisual material that claims (often with tongue held firmly in cheek) to be presenting 'true' footage of real-life cruelty, violence, disaster, death, and perversity.

STEVEN JAY SCHNEIDER

Selected films

1959 Europa di notte/European Nights (director Alessandro Blasetti)
1959 Il Mondo di notte/World By Night (director Luigi Vanzi)
1962 Mondo Cane/A Dog's Life (director Gualtiero Jacopetti; associate director Paolo Cavara and Franco Prosperi)
1963 La Donna nel mondo/Women of the World (directors Paolo Cavara and Gualtiero Jacopetti)
1964 Mondo Cane 2/Mondo Pazzo (directors Gualtiero Jacopetti and Franco Prosperi)
1966 Africa Addio/Farewell Africa (UK video title), or Africa Blood and Guts (USA cut version) (directors Gualtiero Jacopetti and Franco Prosperi)
1975 Ultime grida dalla savana: la grande caccia/Savage Man … Savage Beast (directors Antonio Climati and Mario Morra)
1978 Faces of Death (director Conan le Cilaire)
1995 Executions (directors David Herman, Arun Kumar, and David Monaghan)

Further reading

Black, Joel, 'Real(ist) Horror: From Execution Videos to Snuff Films', in Xavier Mendik and Steven Jay Schneider (eds), *Underground USA: Filmmaking Beyond the Hollywood Canon*, London: Wallflower Press, 2003.

Duggan, E.J.M., 'Review of Killing for Culture: An Illustrated History of Death Film from Mondo to Snuff', *Scope: An Online Journal of Film Studies*, May 2000, www.nottingham.ac.uk/film/journal/bookrev/killing_for_culture.htm

Hight, Craig and Roscoe, Jane, *Faking It: Mock-documentary and the Subversion of Reality*, Manchester: Manchester University Press, 2001.

Jackson, Neil, 'Cannibal Holocaust, Realist Horror, and Reflexivity', *Post Script: Essays in Film and the Humanities* 21, no. 3, 2002.

Kael, Pauline, 'Are Movies Going to Pieces?' *Atlantic Monthly*, December 1964, www.theatlantic.com/unbound/aandc/movies/movies2.htm

Kerekes, David and Slater, David, *Killing for Culture: An Illustrated History of Death Film from Mondo to Snuff*, London: Creation Books, 1998.

Tombs, Pete, *Mondo Macabro: Weird & Wonderful Cinema Around the World*, New York: St Martins/Griffin, 1998.

Montagu, Ivor

Although he is better remembered for his collaboration with feature filmmakers like Alfred Hitchcock and Sergei Eisenstein, Ivor Montagu has left his mark on the documentary too, as on so many areas of culture, science, and sports in which he was actively involved. Born into a wealthy Jewish banking family as the youngest son of Lord and Lady Swaythling, Montagu studied zoology at Cambridge. Here he moved in left-wing circles and published his first film reviews. Although he would never lose interest in zoology, he chose to enter the world of the cinema as a journalist after obtaining his degree. Returning from a visit to the Berlin film studios for *The Times* newspaper in 1924, Montagu met film actor Hugh Miller on the train. This meeting led to the establishment of the Film Society in London, based on the model of the already existing Stage Society. Its purpose was to present to members only films that for some reason or other did not get a commercial release. Among the founding members of the Film Society were film critic Iris Barry (later film archivist at the Museum of Modern Art) and film exhibitor Sidney Bernstein (later founder of Granada Television), and thanks to his personal network, Montagu was able to recruit George Bernard Shaw, H.G. Wells, Julian Huxley, J.B.S. Haldane, J.M. Keynes, and Anthony Asquith as 'shareholders'. Despite the animosity of the film trade and the occasional interference by the authorities, the Film Society became a huge success, not in the least because of the Soviet films, banned by the censor, that it managed to show from time to time. Montagu's lengthy visit to the new workers' and peasants' state in 1925, taking him from Leningrad to Tiflis, opened his eyes to the virtues of Communism, but he did not join the Communist Party of Great Britain (CPGB) until the early 1930s.

After his return to the United Kingdom, Montagu teamed up with filmmaker Adrian Brunel. The two earned a living by adapting foreign films for exhibition in British cinemas. In 1926 Montagu was asked to help out Alfred Hitchcock, then at the start of his career, with the titles for his film The Lodger. This successful collaboration would be continued in the 1930s, when Montagu acted as associate producer on such well-known Hitchcock thrillers as The Man Who Knew Too Much (1934) and The 39 Steps (1935). In 1927 Montagu joined the Gainsborough Studios, where Michael Balcon was in charge as producer. The next year he decided to set up his own company, Angle Pictures, and produce and direct three short comedies, based on stories by novelist H.G. Wells. Adapted by his son Frank Wells and featuring actress Elsa Lanchester, Blue Bottles, Day-Dreams, and The Tonic presented a mixture of avant-garde film idiom and old-fashioned slapstick, reflecting the taste of Film Society audiences. Commercially, however, they were flops.

In September 1929 Montagu was sent as a delegate of the Film Society to the International Congress of Independent Cinema in La Sarraz, Switzerland. There he befriended Soviet filmmaker Sergei Eisenstein, who was touring Western Europe with his companions Grigory Alexandrov and Eduard Tisse to study the sound film. The three Russians were invited to the United Kingdom by the Film Society, which managed to present an uncensored version of Battleship Potemkin for the occasion. Next Montagu and his wife Eileen Hellstern (commonly known as 'Hell') accompanied Eisenstein and company on their trip to the United States, following an offer by the Paramount Studios. When the Hollywood company turned down the scripts of Sutter's Gold and An American Tragedy, which he had cowritten with Eisenstein and Alexandrov, Montagu returned home instead of following the Russians to Mexico.

Back in the United Kingdom Montagu tried his hand at various translations, including two collections of writings of Soviet filmmaker Vsevolod Pudovkin, *Film Technique and Film Acting*, which were highly influential among young filmmakers. He formed part of the team that organised, on behalf of the mastermind of Communist propaganda Willy Münzenberg, the 'Counter Trial' in London in September 1933 to prove Nazi culpability regarding the Reichstag fire. In that same year he returned to the film industry, to work with producer Michael Balcon at Gaumont-British—and not, as was fashionable among left-wing artists and intellectuals, with John Grierson's documentary film unit at the Empire Marketing Board. In fact, Montagu was highly critical of the work of the documentary movement, and of its 'godfather' Robert Flaherty in particular. At Gaumont-British Montagu did script and edit, together with Geoffrey Barkas, the Academy Award-winning documentary Wings over Everest, based on footage shot by an RAF crew while flying over the heights of the Himalayas. He was also among the founding members of the Association of Cine-Technicians (ACT). An active member, he served for many years on the council of this film technicians' trade union, which was to play such an important role in the British film industry.

Montagu's expertise on film censorship, much of it laid down in his pamphlet *The Political Censorship of Films* (1929), was highly appreciated by the nascent workers' film movement. A central role was played by Kino, which had started in 1933 as a Film Section of the Workers' Theatre Movement but was soon to develop into a proper distribution company for 16mm (substandard), left-wing films. It ran into trouble over the exhibition of Eisenstein's Battleship Potemkin, which had been banned by the British Board of Film Censors, in Jarrow, a 'distressed' Tyneside town notorious for its high unemployment. Montagu enlisted the services of the National Council of Civil Liberties (NCCL) to help out Kino and the Boldon Colliery Miners' Hall. As he had pointed out in his pamphlet, the 1909 Cinematograph Act applied only to films on inflammable stock. Therefore a print of Battleship Potemkin on 16mm non-inflammable stock could be screened on any premises as long as these were not licensed under the 1909 Act. The NCCL lawyers had no problem proving this in court, and consequently the charges against both Kino and the Boldon Colliery Hall were dismissed. This result was an enormous boost to the distribution of left-wing films on 16mm in the United Kingdom. Typically, Montagu decided instead to concentrate on the distribution of the few left-wing films available on 35mm. For this purpose he set up the Progressive Film Institute (PFI, a pun on the recently founded British Film Institute), with his wife Hell manning the office. Among the PFI's customers were some miners' cinemas in South Wales and art house theatres in London and Glasgow.

In support of the work of the Relief Committee for the Victims of German Fascism, the PFI adapted an American documentary on the German Communist leader Ernst Thaelmann. Under the title Free Thaelmann (1935), this eighteen-minute film was distributed on 35mm by the PFI and on 16mm by Kino. In November 1936 Montagu left for Madrid, where it seemed that the Republican forces would be overrun at any moment by the Nationalist insurgents led by General Franco. He was accompanied by Norman McLaren, a young graduate from the Glasgow School of Arts, who earlier that year had made Hell Unltd, an impressive antiwar film. Kodak had made available two 16mm cameras and even some new colour stock, with which the two filmed the havoc caused by Italian airplanes, the activities of the Republican army and the International Brigade, and the relief work undertaken in Great Britain. Being partisan, silent, and lasting only half an hour turned out to be no problem for Defence of Madrid. All over the United Kingdom audiences flocked to see the film, which was distributed by Kino. Thus Defence of Madrid raised £6,000 for Spanish aid.

Through its connections with the Republican government, the PFI had access to other film material from Spain. English-language versions were made by either sticking to the original (for example, Non-Intervention, on the proof of Italian intervention found after the battle of Guadalajara) or using the material to compile a totally new film (for example, News from Spain, with a commentary spoken by Isabel Brown, whose fame for emptying people's purses for Spain was legendary). After a while it was thought that it might be more effective from a propaganda point of view for the PFI to go to Spain and make some films there. Montagu was given £3,000 in cash to do so by the end of 1937. He recruited six members of the ACT, who were paid expenses only, to join him. On arrival in Barcelona in mid-January 1938, the crew was immediately treated to a series of air raids. In fact, the deteriorating military situation made the realisation of the films as planned impossible. Back in London after two months of filming in Spain, two twenty-minute campaign films could be edited from the footage: Spanish ABC (director, Thorold Dickinson), presenting the Republican Government's literacy campaign, which was being pursued under the most difficult circumstances, and Behind the Spanish Lines (director Sidney Cole), showing how democracy worked in Spain and how Italy and Germany were making a farce of 'Non-Intervention'. In Barcelona Montagu had been given the opportunity to film with a hidden microphone (in those days observers did not automatically associate filming with the recording of sound) German and Italian prisoners of war being interrogated about their presence in Spain. Their confessions offered conclusive proof that their native countries were knowingly violating the Non-Intervention agreement. Montagu edited this footage into a four-minute, 35mm newsreel film, Prisoners Prove Intervention in Spain, which he persuaded some fifty cinemas all over the United Kingdom to show. Under the sarcastic title Testimony of Non-Intervention, a thirty-minute version was also released. However, Montagu's efforts to present the film at government level as irrefutable evidence of the violation by Germany and Italy of the Non-Intervention agreement failed.

From 1936 onwards Montagu was working as a journalist on the *Daily Worker*, the CPGB's newspaper. Inevitably, the Party decided to make use of his qualities as a filmmaker. With a camera crew he covered the XVth Congress of the CPGB in Birmingham. Held in September 1938, it was overshadowed by the Munich Crisis. The ten-minute sound film XVth Congress was clearly destined for a Communist audience, but a subsequent PFI production, Britain Expects, was aimed at the broadest possible audience. This film set out to show how the lives of British seamen were endangered as a consequence of the government's policy on Spain. The theatrical version was censored of the vital fact about the intervention of Germany and Italy. Britain Expects served on the unsuccessful election campaign of the Duchess of Atholl, a staunch supporter of Republican Spain. In January 1939 Montagu got together an ACT crew to film the homecoming of the British members of the International Brigade at the Empress Hall in London, but the footage was never edited into a proper film.

Late in 1938 Montagu was approached by the CPGB to make a thirty-minute film to be used during the forthcoming General Election. Its central theme was the defeat of the Chamberlain government. Entitled Peace and Plenty, it was an audiovisual adaptation of General Secretary Harry Pollitt's report at the XVth Congress of the CPGB, bearing similarities to Jean Renoir's French Communist election film La Vie est à nous (1936). It made effective use of stills and stock footage to ridicule members of the Chamberlain government. The mother of actress Elsa Lanchester made a puppet of Chamberlain especially for the film, while well-known bandleader Van Phillips wrote the music free of charge. It was Montagu's idea to end Peace and Plenty with a sequence in colour, to startle the spectators so that they would listen to what Communist leader Harry Pollitt had to say. Unfortunately, it turned out to be too expensive to have the colour sequence included in the distribution prints. A powerful indictment of the Chamberlain government, breaking completely with the realist conventions that dominated British documentary in the 1930s, Peace and Plenty was shown from March 1939 onwards in Communist circles and much appreciated. Because of the outbreak of World War II, however, the elections for which it was meant were postponed until 1945. By then the film's message had inevitably become obsolete.

Apart from journalistic work, Montagu was occupied during the war with the release of Russians films in the United Kingdom. After the German invasion of the Soviet Union in 1941, he set up the Soviet Film Agency for this purpose. Later Michael Balcon offered him work at the Ealing Studios, of which he had been in charge since 1939. Using stills, diagrams, and cartoons (not unlike Peace and Plenty) and a commentary spoken by Julian Huxley, Montagu refuted Nazi race theories in a short, government-sponsored documentary Man, One Family (1945). Also at Ealing he worked as a scriptwriter on Scott of the Antarctic (1948) and associate producer on Another Shore (1949). The Cold War forced him to wind up the Soviet Film Agency and the PFI. A part of the latter's film library and some modest financial benefits were bequeathed to Plato Films, a company founded in 1951 by Montagu's protégé Stanley Forman to distribute films from the socialist world. A similar outfit, Contemporary Films, established around the same time by Charles Cooper, could also count on Montagu's support. During the heyday of the Cold War his contacts (as a member of the World Peace Council or chairman of the International Table Federation) across the Iron Curtain were highly appreciated by his ACT colleagues, even by those who did not share his political views.

Plans for a new CPGB election film in 1960–1, scripted by Montagu along the lines of Peace and Plenty, failed to materialise because of the costs. The Pelican publication *Film World* (1964) offered Montagu the opportunity to present his personal views on the cinema, rather than those of Pudovkin or Eisenstein, whose writings he had so loyally translated to a large audience. Stating that 'documentary is not per se truer or nobler than "story" film', he distanced himself from the prevalent Griersonian discourse. Montagu's contacts with the SED leadership in East Germany led to a British-GDR coproduction on the occasion of the fiftieth anniversary of *Labour Monthly*. Entitled Fifty Fighting Years (1972), this forty-five minute documentary was scripted by Montagu, Forman, and Roger Woddis and directed by Forman and Roland Bischoff. It featured the recollections of veteran Communists Rajani Palme Dutt and Robin Page Arnot, illustrated with rare archive footage. Although this was the last film production in which he was actively involved, Montagu continued to write on film (he was a regular contributor to *Sight and Sound*) and give his support to the reemerging left-wing film culture until his death in 1984.

BERT HOGENKAMP

Biography

Born in London, April 23, 1904. Educated at Westminster School, the Royal College of Science, London, and King's College, Cambridge. Founding member and first president of the Film Society 1925. Founding member of the International Table Tennis Federation in 1926 and its first president until 1967. Companion to Eisenstein during his visit to the United States 1930–1. Founding member of the Association of Cine-Technicians 1933. Founder of the Progressive Film Institute 1934. Journalist at the *Daily Worker* 1936–41. Visits to Spain, November–December 1936 and January–March 1938. Founder of the Soviet Film Agency

1941. Awarded the Lenin Peace Prize 1959. Died in London, November 5, 1984.

Selected films

1934 Wings over Everest: director (with Geoffrey Barkas)
1936 Defence of Madrid: director, cameraman
1938 Spanish ABC: producer
1938 Behind the Spanish Lines: producer
1938 Prisoners Prove Intervention in Spain: producer, editor
1938 Testimony on Non-Intervention: producer, editor
1938 Britain Expects: producer, editor
1939 Peace and Plenty: director
1945 Man, One Family: director
1973 Fifty Fighting Years: scriptwriter

Further reading

Hogenkamp, Bert, *Deadly Parallels: Film and the Left in Britain 1929–39*, London: Lawrence & Wishart, 1986.
——*Film, Television and the Left in Britain, 1950–70*, London: Lawrence & Wishart, 2000.
n.a., 'Interview: Ivor Montagu', *Screen* 13, no. 3, autumn 1972: 71–113.
Montagu, Ivor, *Film World: A Guide to Cinema*, Harmondsworth: Pelican Books, 1964.
——*The Youngest Son: Autobiographical Sketches*, London: Lawrence & Wishart, 1970.
——*With Eisenstein in Hollywood*, Berlin-GDR: Seven Seas Publishers, 1968.

Monterey Pop

(US, Leacock, Pennebaker, 1968)

In capturing the events of the three-day 1967 Monterey Pop Music Festival, filmmaker D.A. (Donn Alan) Pennebaker (1925–) pioneered the 'rockumentary' genre later exemplified by films such as Woodstock (Michael Wadleigh, 1970), Gimme Shelter (David and Albert Maysles and Charlotte Zwerin, 1970), and The Last Waltz (Martin Scorsese, 1979). Pennebaker's work is often associated with the American incarnation of cinéma vérité, the direct cinema movement of the 1960s, in which light, handheld cameras were used to capture action directly (and often in intimate close-up), without narration or apparent intrusion or participation on the part of the filmmaker. Following Primary (1960), a direct cinema documentary about John F. Kennedy and Hubert Humphrey locked in the struggle for votes in the 1960 Wisconsin presidential primary election, Pennebaker made his first foray into music documentaries with Dont Look Back (1967), a film about Bob Dylan's 1965 tour of Great Britain.

As he had done in Dont Look Back, Pennebaker attempted to make Monterey Pop more than just a filmed record of the concert's musical performances from the perspective of the audience. The film does not have the strong sociological focus of Wadleigh's later Woodstock, but an effort is made at capturing the entirety of the concert atmosphere and, more broadly, the emerging youth counterculture of 1960s California. Thus, the film's musical sequences are sometimes intertwined with footage that seems to have little to do with music: local police voicing concerns about the Hell's Angels and Black Panthers attending the concert, frolicking flower children with painted faces and day-glow buses, festival goers camping out on the football field of a nearby high school. In most cases, however, such as the opening sequence that depicts the hectic preparations for the event beneath a soundtrack featuring Scott McKenzie's peaceful ballad '[If You're Going to] San Francisco', even the nonperformance footage is presented with a soundtrack consisting of music from the festival. The overall effect links the visual record of the festival's activities and its music almost seamlessly.

It is the performances themselves and Pennebaker's rendering of them that make Monterey Pop truly memorable. Although Bob Dylan's irreverent backstage demeanor had provided much of the interest a few years earlier in Dont Look Back, the filmmaker was quick to realize that by the end of the 1960s, rock music was becoming more and more visual, and that a psychedelic era rock documentary should explore the spectacle, as well as the sound of the performance. Thus, film viewers are treated to the full gamut of the concert performance not accessible to a listening audience: the surreal, acid-tinged stage countenance of Country Joe and the Fish, and the psychedelic light shows accompanying Jefferson Airplane, Hugh Masekela, and The Animals. Other, more shocking, visual images include Pete Townshend smashing his guitar at the end of The Who's 'My Generation', only to be outdone by Jimi Hendrix ritualistically setting fire to his guitar before smashing it at the end of 'Wild Thing'.

Pennebaker's handheld cameras seldom settle on the performers in a standard, straightforward fashion. Often, the camera drifts away from stars and focuses instead on backup musicians—drummers, keyboard players, and background vocalists. Just as often, close-ups of individual members of the festival's audience fill the screen. In several instances the camera captures the reactions of the musicians themselves as audience members, such as Mama Cass Elliot's expression of awe as she takes in Janis Joplin's performance of 'Ball and Chain', and Jimi Hendrix's reverent attention to the Indian sitar master Ravi Shankar.

Such expressions of mutual admiration among the musicians, in which the traditional barriers between East and West, pop and rock, audience and the performer are broken down, underscore the key theme emerging from Pennebaker's film—love and community among the youth counterculture of the 1960s. Although cinéma vérité and direct cinema generally place a high value on objectivity and look with distain on artificially shaping film footage to produce a desired impression by the audience, in the final analysis 'reality' must always be shaded by the filmmaker. Throughout Monterey Pop, Pennebaker subtly but insistently introduces the theme of love and community. From the opening statements of audience members, in which one young woman predicts that the event would be 'a big love-in', to the serene shots of California hippies dancing, embracing, and camping in communal teepees, to performers like Otis Redding referring to the audience as 'the love crowd', Pennebaker idyllically captures the 1960s zeitgeist of peace, love, and brotherhood. It would be a theme that would be picked up and further embellished in Woodstock, turned on its head in Gimme Shelter, treated with nostalgia in The Last Waltz, and affectionately mocked in This is Spinal Tap. More important, Pennebaker's Monterey Pop provided a lively stylistic model for these and many other concert documentaries that would follow.

ROD PHILLIPS

See also: Dont Look Back; Gimme Shelter; Leacock, Richard; Pennebaker, D.A.; Woodstock: Three Days of Peace and Music

Monterey Pop (US, Leacock Pennebaker, Inc., 1968, 79 mins). Produced by John Phillips and Lou Adler. Directed by D.A. Pennebaker. Cinematography by James Desmond, Barry Feinstein, Richard Leacock, Albert Maysles, Roger Murphy, D.A. Pennebaker, and Nick Proferes. Sound recorded by Wally Heider. Music by Scott McKenzie, Mamas and Papas, Canned Heat, Simon and Garfunkel, Hugh Masekela, Jefferson Airplane, Big Brother and the Holding Company, Janis Joplin, Eric Burdon and the Animals, The Who, Country Joe and the Fish, Otis Redding, Jimi Hendrix, and Ravi Shankar. Editing by Nina Schulman. Filmed in Monterey, California.

Further reading

Hall, Jeanne, '"Don't You Ever Just Watch?": American Cinema Verité and Dont Look Back', in Barry Keith Grant and Jeannette Slonowski (eds), *Documenting the Documentary: Close Readings of Documentary Film and Video*, Detroit, MI: Wayne State University Press, 1998: 223–37.

Mamber, Stephen, *Cinema Verité in America: Studies in Uncontrolled Documentary*, Cambridge, MA: MIT Press, 1974.

Pennebaker, D.A., 'Interview with Donn Alan Pennebaker', in G. Roy Levin (ed.), *Documentary Explorations: 15 Interviews with Filmmakers*, New York: Doubleday, 1971: 221–70.

Rosenthal, Alan, *The New Documentary in Action: A Case-book in Film Making*, Berkeley, CA: University of California Press, 1971.

Seldes, Hal, 'D.A. Pennebaker: The Truth at 24 Frames per Second', *Avant-Garde*, March 7, 1969: 46–9.

Moore, Michael

Michael Moore's Fahrenheit 9/11 (2004) became the most successful (and arguably most controversial) nonfiction film in history, earning more than $100 million in its first two months on release and turning its creator into a celebrity recognized as a one-man muckraking industry whose films, books, and public appearances were suggested by some to even be a factor in the 2004 election. Moore's films have frequently come under attack, especially by those he targets (General Motors tried to counter the charges in Roger & Me by distributing copies of negative reviews outside theatres), but with Fahrenheit 9/11 Moore's unique brand of populist agitprop became headline news.

Fahrenheit 9/11 ridicules the ineptness and incompetence of an American president by turning his own news footage and photo opportunities against him. Moore presents George W. Bush as a ideological puppet, so bored by the demands of his job that even delivering an anti-terrorism sound bite is considered a nuisance interrupting his golf game, and so unfit to lead that he reacts to the news of the World Trade Center attacks by sticking to the script of a packaged photo-op reading of a children's book called *My Pet Goat* to a group of Florida schoolchildren.

Following in the footsteps of such filmmakers as Nick Broomfield and Ross McElwee, whose on-screen presence personalize their efforts to reveal a story, as well as archivists and collagists like Kevin and Pierce Rafferty, Moore's methods involve guerilla interview techniques, ironic use of stock footage and music, and, most significantly, the creation of an on-screen persona: a naive man with a baseball cap and a microphone who watches innocently while his interview subjects make fools of themselves. Moore's on-screen role is that of the average guy, a dumbstruck citizen who cannot believe that anybody would ever stop him from wandering into the office of the head of General Motors or the home of actor Charlton Heston. Acting more dumbfounded than outraged, he suggests that he is only asking the corporate heads (or more frequently their publicists and handlers) questions that any average American would put to them.

Moore's first film, Roger & Me, explored an economic crisis in his hometown of Flint, Michigan, after General Motors (GM) closed an auto production plant there. Rather than present a dry economic analysis, Moore presented a wide-ranging and free-wheeling portrait of a community where the wealthy spend their time in a dream world of country clubs and parties, the political forces mask their ineffectuality through frivolous public relations campaigns, and the middle and working classes are driven to selling blood or raising rabbits in their backyards to survive. The Roger of the title is GM executive Roger Smith, who dodges Moore's attempts to interview him throughout the film. As part of the promotional campaign for the film, Warner Brothers asked that every theatre playing it leave one vacant seat, just in case Smith wanted to drop in.

Roger & Me introduced Moore as a filmmaker provocateur, using methods that he would refine and polish on two television series, TV Nation and The Awful Truth. It also sparked attacks that would challenge each of his subsequent films. Moore's critics claim that his films are distorted and loose with facts, charges that he has answered on his website and elsewhere. He is also frequently criticized for using interviews as a form of attack, making his subjects look ridiculous. His defense is that most of the people in front of his camera are professional publicists or media figures and therefore fair game. This rationale does not entirely defend his methods, but it does point out the irony that those who have squealed most loudly about Moore's characterization have been those with the most media experience. However, if someone like Bob Eubanks, a television host with forty years of experience, chooses to tell a witless and anti-Semitic joke while a camera is running (in Roger & Me), it can hardly be blamed solely on Moore's interviewing technique.

The 2002 film Bowling for Columbine showed a willingness on Moore's part to move from the activist/populist stance of his television work to a larger and more extended critique of domestic issues. Sparked by the 1999 massacre at a Colorado high school, Moore's film uses that and other violent crimes to indict both the US obsession with guns and a political system that promotes paranoia and fear in its citizens. Predictably, the film's critics were more concerned with charging that the filmmaker had ambushed celebrity interviewees like NRA president Charlton Heston and TV producer Dick Clark, and that some of the more provocative segments, like a visit to a bank where guns are given away to anyone opening an account, were staged on Moore's behalf.

The success of Columbine and the resulting controversy (Moore was booed for making political remarks when he accepted an Academy Award) were little more than a prelude to the reception of Moore's follow-up, Fahrenheit 9/11, a relentless and scathing investigation of the Bush administration and the war in Iraq. Even after winning the grand prize at the Cannes Film Festival (the first documentary ever to do so), the producers, Miramax Films, were forbidden by their parent company, Disney, from releasing the film. By the time it hit theatres in the summer of an election year, 2004 (released by a consortium that bought out Miramax's interest), Moore's film had become as big a political story as the presidential race itself, dissected by news analysts, attacked from the stage of the Republican National Convention and even accused of violating election laws. The now-routine criticism of Moore's satirical approach and documentary ethics had become a subject of national interest.

Controversy aside, Fahrenheit 9/11 is Moore's most polemical film, a cry of outrage over the war and the deceptive policies that led to it. Though it remains, through the director's narration, a deeply personal statement, Moore diminishes his usual role as on-screen surrogate to rely instead on television feeds and news footage showing the Bush administration in unflattering situations. As in Roger & Me, Moore views the war from a middle-class perspective, with the most emotional segments coming through the presence of Lila Lipscomb, a Flint, Michigan woman who had gone from supporting the war to protesting it after her own son was killed in Iraq. Moore remains a satirist, but humor takes a back seat to indignation at the things that his targets of ridicule have perpetrated.

ROBERT HUNT

See also: Roger & Me

Biography

Born in Flint, Michigan, April 23, 1954. Elected to local school board aged eighteen. Founded newspaper, *The Flint Voice*, in 1976. Edited *Mother Jones* magazine 1986–7. Produced his first film, Roger & Me, with money raised by bingo games and from his settlement with *Mother Jones*. After success of Roger & Me, directed a fictional comedy, Canadian Bacon, in 1994. Produced TV series TV Nation 1994–5, and The Awful Truth 1999–2000. Author of *Downsize This*, *Adventures in a TV Nation*, *Stupid White Men* and *Dude, Where's My Country?* 2002 Academy Award-winner for Best Documentary, and a special jury prize at the 2002 Cannes Film Festival.

Moretti, Nanni

Nanni Moretti's cinema stands out in the panorama of contemporary art house filmmaking for its combination of fiction, autobiography, and sociopolitical documentary. Along with his fictional production, Moretti has to date authored one 'classical' documentary, La cosa/The Thing (1990), as well as four docufictions: the shorts L'unico paese al mondo-9/The Only Country in the World-9 (1994), and Il giorno della prima di Close-Up/Opening Day of Close-Up (1996), and two full-length films adopting a diary structure, Caro diario/Dear Diary (1994), and Aprile/April (1998).

On November 12, 1989, two days after the fall of the Berlin Wall, Achille Occhetto, leader of the Italian Communist Party (PCI), announced that the party would change its name, and the sobriquet *la cosa*, 'the thing', was adopted for the nameless party. This event was the apex of a long, difficult phase for Italian, as well as European Communism, deriving from the sociopolitical changes that in the course of the 1980s led to the dissolution of the Soviet bloc, and to the questioning of the basic ideological beliefs of the Left. Occhetto's contentious proposal brought PCI's grassroots members back to the cells to engage in a discussion that released repressed rage and disconcertion, but also passion and enthusiasm. Moretti, who had just finished a fiction film about the crisis of PCI, Palombella rossa/Red Wood Pigeon (1989), decided to shoot these animated discussions. The result is La cosa, a traditional documentary of montage, devoid of voice-over and captions bar those indicating the film's locations. Ideologically, La cosa is consistent with Palombella rossa, the emphasis being on the problem of redescribing seventy years in the political life of a community that had identified with ideals that were by now severely challenged, if not fading.

By ceding the entire screen time to the voters' words, Moretti shows that language is the nub of the problem: if the old metaphors are no longer able to describe the community, it is necessary to coin new, better-suited ones to give the community new life.

Whereas La cosa does not overtly investigate the thorny question of the filmic documenting of reality, Caro diario and Aprile carry the filmmaker's reflection on the relationship between fiction and nonfiction to high levels of sophistication. In all of his films Moretti plays the protagonist, but in Caro diario he uses his real name instead of the habitual pseudonym Michele Apicella. In the first of three episodes, Nanni rides his Vespa through the deserted streets of summertime Rome while listing the things he likes to do best; in the second he visits the Eolie Islands with a friend; in the third we are shown his struggle against Hodgkin's disease. In interviews, Moretti repeated that in this film he plays himself, or even that he is himself. Most critics took him at his word and talked of autobiography. The insertion in the third episode of Moretti's real-life chemotherapy treatment prompted critics to extend the statutes of documentary to the whole film: 'Having presented his brief documentary sequence, Moretti tells the rest of the story in flashback, simulating the rounds of medical visits and providing narrative continuity in voice-over. But the fact that we witnessed the chemotherapy session in newsreel form confers authority and gravity on the subsequent performance, for the body we see on screen is the same body that went through the ordeal to which we bore documentary witness' (Marcus 1996: 244).

Only a minority of critics questioned the authenticity of Moretti's self-portrait in Caro diario (Villa 1999), in spite of the fact that fiction in this film is amply prevalent, and that autobiography is itself a problematic genre for its ambiguous mix of memory and imagination, of document and personal reflection. Caro diario is best seen as the culmination of Moretti's previous work on the creation of a 'fictional autobiography', or even of a fiction that looks like a documentary on the life of citizen Nanni Moretti. In the previous films spectators were encouraged to think that Michele Apicella was the alter ego of the filmmaker through the reappearance of the same biographical details and personality traits in each film and the use of Moretti's family and friends as actors. With Caro diario it seemed as if Nanni went a step further and straightforwardly filmed himself and his life, although this film only intensified the effect of autobiography and documentary already achieved by his previous work. This view is confirmed by Aprile, the diary of Moretti's life, as well as of Italy at large, from the general election of March 1994, won by Silvio Berlusconi, to the next election two years later that saw the victory of the Left. In terms of autobiography, the film covers the pregnancy of Nanni's partner and the birth and first months of his child Pietro, as well as Nanni's reluctance to work on two films: a musical with a political slant, and a documentary about contemporary Italy. Aprile includes many scenes shot in Moretti's own house and office, with members of his family, friends, and collaborators, as well as documentary takes of the electioneering and other sociopolitical events. The autobiographical/documentary effect is challenged by the irony pervading the film, by the exaggeration and self-mockery of Moretti's behaviour, as well as by discrepancies between what Moretti says and what he shows. For instance, he announces that he will never allow his son to become an actor, but then 'casts' him in one of the film's main roles. The greatest discrepancy, though, is between Nanni's declared impotence in making a documentary about Italy, and the fact that Aprile is ultimately the documentary he claimed to be unable to make.

L'unico paese al mondo-9 and Il giorno della prima di Close-Up can also be described as short diaries. The first is the ninth episode of a collective film critical of Berlusconi's entry into the political arena. Nanni rides his Vespa through Paris, observing that Berlusconi tried in vain to make it in France, and commenting on the differences between the Italian and French bourgeoisie. In the second short, Moretti appears in his role as director of his cinema in Rome, the Nuovo Sacher. He meticulously prepares for the premiere of Abbas Kiarostami's Close-Up, advertising the film in the press, checking which sandwiches are sold in the cinema, coaching his staff to answer the spectators' questions, and discussing the volume of the sound with the projectionist. Both shorts present the same ambiguous mix of fiction, autobiographical effect, and documentary as the major diary films.

LAURA RASCAROLI

Biography

Born in Brunico (Bolzano, Italy), August 19, 1953. Joined the Italian water polo junior team 1970, and played in the Italian first division. Active in the extra-parliamentary Left 1970s. Founded with Angelo Barbagallo the production house Sacher Film 1987. Andre Labarthe dedicated to him an episode of Cinéma de notre temps (La Sept and Channel 4), 1990. Opened a cinema in Rome, the Nuovo Sacher, 1991. The Toronto Film Festival dedicated a retrospective to him 1993. Founded the Sacher Film Festival for shorts 1996. With Angelo Barbagallo, Roberto Cicutto, and Luigi Musini, founded the distribution company Tandem 1997. Lives in Rome.

Selected films

1990 La cosa/The Thing: director, producer, writer
1994 Caro diario/Dear Diary: director, producer, writer, actor
1994 L'unico paese al mondo-9/The Only Country in the World-9: director, producer, writer
1996 Il giorno della prima di Close-Up/Opening Day of Close-Up: director, producer, writer, actor
1998 Aprile/April: director, producer, writer, actor

Further reading

Aspden, Peter, 'Caro diario (Dear Diary)', *Sight and Sound*, December 1994: 42–3.
De Bernardinis, Flavio, *Nanni Moretti*, Milan: Il Castoro, 2001.
Marcus, Millicent, 'Caro diario and the Cinematic Body of Nanni Moretti', *Italica* 73, 1996: 233–47.
Porton, Richard and Ellickson, Lee, 'Comedy, Communism, and Pastry. An interview with Nanni Moretti', *Cineaste* 1–2, 1995: 11–15.
Samueli, Anna, 'L'unique pays au monde', *Cahiers du Cinéma* 479, no. 80, 1994: 66–7.
Valens, Gregory, 'La cosa and La première de Close-Up', *Positif* 464, 1999: 174–5.
Villa, Federica, 'Oggi farò delle belle riprese, sí, anche se mi vergogno un pò. Percorso nel raccontar leggero', in *Nanni Moretti*, Turin: Paravia Scriptorium, 1999.
Wagstaff, Chris, 'Aprile', *Sight and Sound*, April 1999, 36.

Morin, Edgar

Edgar Morin, a French philosopher, sociologist, ecologist, and documentary film director, played a leading role in the cinéma vérité movement (based on the Russian movement Kino-Pravda led by Dziga Vertov) during the 1960s. Morin's theory of documentary film was developed in collaboration with the ethnographic filmmaker Jean Rouch.

Morin produced with Rouch the documentary Chronique d'un été/Chronicle of a Summer (1961), a significant and unique work. Chronique d'un été is set in Paris after the Algerian war. The film displayed a new documentary aesthetic, marked by a nonlinear structure, uninterrupted takes, and non-manipulated locations. The documentary focuses on the city of Paris and communicates the opinions of the directors regarding 1960s French society and culture. The new methods of documentary filmmaking displayed in Chronique d'un été exemplified cinéma vérité.

Several technical advancements and developments made it possible for documentary filmmakers to use their chosen medium to study societal developments and mores in great depth. These include the development of compact 16mm cameras, less dependence on artificial lighting, the use of real and synchronized sound, and an acceptance of filmmakers appearing in their own documentaries.

Chronique d'un été is a perfect example of a documentary film that incorporates nontraditional documentary filmmaking techniques to allow the film to better address the primary questions of the directors: How can I identify the differences between reality and fiction, objectivity, and subjectivity? Do those differences truly exist? How can I, as a director, transmit my vision to others? Morin and Rouch appear in front of the camera during the film, talking, explaining their thesis as scientists and artists, making evident their own point of view as directors, and at the same time learning new things about the French society throughout the entire production and interviews. This is a masterpiece and a door for discussion between reality and fiction and the way to produce documentaries.

Cinéma vérité practitioners focused their efforts to renew the documentary language with more realistic characters, locations, and histories, without the use of make-up and trying to give to this style the most pure representation. The language, technique, structure, mounting, photography, characters, sound, and background all constructed this reality giving surprises and knowledge to the entire audience.

Morin's thinking was affected by the state of the world around him. He said:

> History tells us that we have to reckon with the improbable. Historically speaking, I have twice lived through the victory of the improbable. First, with the defeat of Nazism in 1945, even though Germany's victory was probable in Europe in 1941; then, with the collapse of the Communist

> system in 1989–90. The worst is never certain; in the words of Hölderlin, 'wherever danger grows, salvation grows too', reminding us that danger will help us perhaps to find a way out, providing we become aware of it.
>
> (Rapin 1977)

Morin did not produce any documentaries other than Chronique d'un été, but this accomplished film has a place in the history of documentary film.

CATALINA CERON

See also: Chronique d'un été; Rouch, Jean; Vertov, Dziga

Biography

Born in Paris, France July 8, 1921. Studied history, geography, and law. Served during World War II 1942–4. Received honorary degrees from the University of Perugia, the University of Palermo, the University of Geneva, and the University of Brussels. Investigator for the CNRS (National Center for Scientific Research) 1950–89. Director of the magazine *Arguments* 1956–62. Director of the magazine *Communications*. President of the United Nations Educational, Scientific and Cultural Organization's (UNESCO) European Agency of Culture. His books include: *L'Homme et la mort*, 1951; Le *Cinéma ou l'homme imaginaire*, 1956; *L'Esprit du temps*, 1962–76; *Introduction à une politique de l'homme*, 1965; *Le Paradigme perdu: la nature humaine*, 1973; *Pour sortir du XXe siècle*, 1981; *Penser l'Europe*, 1987; *Terre-Patrie*, 1993; *Mes démons*, 1994; *La Complexité humaine*, 1994; *Amor poésie sagesse*, 1997; *Une politique de civilisation*, 1997; *La tête bien faite*, 1999; *Relier les connaissances*, 2000; *Les sept savoirs nécessaire à l'éducation du futur* (Seven Complex Lessons in Education for the Future) 2001; *Journal de Plozevet*, 2001; *Methode, l'humanité de l'humanité*, 2001; *Pour une politique de civilisation*, 2002.

Selected film

1961 Chronique d'un été: codirector (with Jean Rouch)

Further reading

Barnouw, Eric, *A History of the Non-fiction Film*, Oxford: Oxford University Press, 1992.

Freyer, Ellen, 'Chronicle of a Summer—Ten Years Later', in Lewis Jacobs (ed.), *The Documentary Tradition: From Nanook to Woodstock*, New York: Hopkinson and Blake, 1971.

Kofman, Miron and Reader, Keith, *Edgar Morin*, London: Pluto Press, 1996.

Morin, Edgar, *The Film or the Imaginary Man*, Paidos, 2001.

Rapin, Anne, *Interview with Edgar Morin, Label France Magazine Humanities* no. 28, 1977.

Reader, Keith and Powrie, Philip, *French Cinema: A Student's Guide*, Oxford: Oxford University, 2003.

Sadoul, George, *Dictionary of Films*, Berkeley, CA: University of California Press, 1972.

——*Historia del Cine Mundial—Desde los Orígenes*, Siglo XXI, 1992.

Morris, Errol

Errol Morris is an American documentarist who represents the subjectivity of perception through a combination of interview and dramatic illustration. Morris is more interested in the psychological and perceptual grounds for human behaviour than the procedural details. He focuses on unusual people in particular circumstances or environs that he examines not for observational or expositional purposes, but because of his interviewees' distinctive worldviews. He is concerned with mortality and motivation and is therefore interested in individuals whose unique perspectives on life and death (and often their lack of perspective on themselves) inform his exploration of the schism between personal truth and socially determined reality. His aim in these films is to deconstruct notions of absolute truth and infallible knowledge by emphasising the relativity of people's experiences of human existence.

Morris's distinctive use of the interview was developed in his two first films, Gates of Heaven (1978) and Vernon, Florida (1981), in which monologues of up to several minutes were presented without interruption. He did not change camera angles and only rarely used cutaways to illustrate points of information while people were speaking, allowing his subjects to reveal more of themselves than was necessary for narrative alone. By refusing to provide visual distraction, Morris compelled viewers to listen more carefully and to study the face, body language, and immediate environment of the interviewee. As there was often no narrative function in their utterances, hearing the flow of their language and observing how their thoughts unfolded was just as important as knowing what they said. Consequently, a rich sense of the people and their environment emerged. The resultant assemblage of personal perspectives gave greater depth to stories that might otherwise have seemed trivial, namely in the first case the lives of those affected by two Californian pet cemeteries, and in the second the peculiar lives and views of the residents of an enclosed community in rural Florida.

The Thin Blue Line (1988) seems, on the face of it, to be Morris's most atypical film, an investigative documentary that successfully challenged the case against a man convicted of the murder of a police officer in 1976. In spite of its generic familiarity and its incorporation of the stylistic and structural conventions of the thriller, it is yet another exploration of subjective perspective. The use of dramatic reconstruction to stage and restage the murder based on the testimony of different individuals was merely another tool that allowed the director to problematise notions of an absolute truth. 'Truth isn't guaranteed by style or expression', he argues, 'It isn't guaranteed by anything' (Bruzzi 2000).

Morris' approach to the adaptation of Stephen Hawking's *A Brief History of Time* (1992) was equally representative of lateral thinking. Seeing the book as 'a thinly disguised romance novel' about Professor Hawking's relationship with the universe, Morris made the film as a combination of biography and science lesson. It sought to explain how this unique individual came to have such a singular perspective on reality and how that perspective informed his work. Morris's rejection of the stylistic conventions of documentary went even further in this film than in The Thin Blue Line. Surreal, often absurdist imagery was used to illustrate Hawking's theories, while studio sets were built to accommodate the friends and family who related stories from the professor's life. The physical environment itself had become relative in a film that embodied and represented how the conceptual can and does exceed the constraints of the physical.

In Fast, Cheap, and Out of Control (1997) Morris began to develop what he would later term 'first person cinema', an attempt to allow remarkable individuals to tell their own stories free from the necessity to provide context in social, political, economic, or religious discourse. The film was a multilayered exploration of the lives of four people: a lion tamer, a topiary gardener, a robot builder, and a breeder of mole-rats. It mixed observation and speculation, interviews and abstract imagery, and even incorporated different film and video formats. Morris was drawn to these people because of their immersion in their own private universes, and he celebrated their common concern with primal themes of human existence: life, death, reproduction, and self-expression.

In Mr Death: The Rise and Fall of Fred A. Leuchter, Jr (1999), the director was compelled to take a different attitude toward his subject's exclusion of a sense of external context. The film told the story of an eccentric designer of execution equipment whose belief in his own expertise had led him to the conclusion that the Nazis could not have carried out mass executions at Auschwitz. The first version of the film, shown to students at Harvard, presented Leuchter's worldview without explicit commentary. Morris felt that Leuchter's basic oddness was evidence enough that his perspective was subjective and his conclusions of questionable veracity. Many of those who saw the film at first did not agree; it was too easy to be immersed in Leuchter's world and lose touch with an 'objective' perspective. Morris subsequently reshot substantial portions of the film. He included interviews with people who disagreed with Leuchter and presented evidence to prove his theories were very much his own.

Morris's subsequent work includes a series of shorts compiled under the title First Person (2000) for broadcast on the UK's Channel 4. The films use the director's trademark interviewing machine, christened 'the interrotron', to represent and embody his attitude to documentary as a process of human communication. The interrotron is a live recording and feedback system derived from a standard teleprompter. Interviewees look directly into the camera and see an image of Morris looking directly back at them, which is filmed by another camera located elsewhere. This device allows his subjects to retain direct eye contact with the audience when the footage is broadcast, which increases the sense of connection between human beings. For Morris, this is the cornerstone of a truly first-person cinema, which will contribute to a broader understanding of the subjective experience of shared external reality.

In 2003 Morris presented The Fog of War: Eleven Lessons from the Life of Robert S.

McNamara. McNamara, who served as Secretary of Defense under Presidents John F. Kennedy and Lyndon B. Johnson, looks back on his career and the major political events of his tenure and the twentieth century. Morris won the 2004 Academy Award for Best Documentary Feature for The Fog of War.

HARVEY O'BRIEN

Biography

Born Hewlett, Long Island, New York, February 5, 1948. Studied and played cello at the Putney School, Vermont. Graduated from University of Wisconsin, Madison, reading history, in 1969. Undertook graduate studies at Princeton and University of California at Berkeley but did not submit a doctoral thesis. Undertook an independent research project interviewing and studying mass murderers and became involved with the Pacific Film Archive as an assistant programmer. Recipient of three fellowships from the National Endowment for the Arts, a Guggenheim Fellowship, and a MacArthur Fellowship. Currently lives in Cambridge, Massachusetts with wife, Julia Sheehan, an art historian, and son, Hamilton.

Selected films

1978 Gates of Heaven
1981 Vernon, Florida
1988 The Thin Blue Line
1992 A Brief History of Time
1997 Fast, Cheap, and Out of Control
1999 Mr Death: The Rise and Fall of Fred A. Leuchter, Jr
2000 First Person
2003 The Fog of War: Eleven Lessons from the Life of Robert S. McNamara

Further reading

Details and reprints of interviews with Errol Morris can be found at: www.errolmorris.com

Arthur, Paul, 'Jargons of Authenticity', in Michael Renov (ed.), *Theorizing Documentary*, London and New York: Routledge, 1993.

Bruzzi, S., *New Documentary. A Critical Introduction*, London: Routledge, 2000: 6.

Gordon, Ian E., *Theories of Visual Perception*, Chichester, New York, Brisbane, Toronto, and Singapore: Wiley & Sons, 1989.

Paget, Derek, *No Other Way to Tell It: Dramadoc/Docudrama on Television*, Manchester and New York: Manchester University Press, 1998.

Rabiger, Michael, *Directing the Documentary*, Boston and London: Focal Press, 1992.

Williams, Linda, 'Mirrors without Memories: Truth, History, and The Thin Blue Line', in Barry Keith Grant and Jeannette Sloniowski (eds), *Documenting the Documentary: Close Readings of Documentary Film and Video*, Detroit, MI: Wayne State University Press, 1998.

Moullet, Luc

Luc Moullet was only nineteen years old when he was offered the opportunity to write reviews for *Cahiers du cinéma*, a fashionable film magazine, then right-wing but nonconformist and hostile to cinematic establishment. Moullet's humorous papers were much appreciated, and his review of Godard's Breathless helped to give the French New Wave its theoretical framework. The films Moullet directed from 1961 through 1968 were fictions verging into parody, with odd characters mixed up in muddled, uncanny situations. The events of May 1968 brought about significant change in the editorial board of *Cahiers*, which adopted a more political, doctrinaire stance, leading Moullet to distance himself from the review and to collaborate with more conventional cinema magazines.

Considering that he was only one among millions like him and that his views and deeds offered an insight into the problems and concerns of contemporary society, Moullet decided that he and his companion, Antonietta Pizzorno, would play their own part in his films: 'my presence', he noted, 'indicates the documentary character of my films'. At the same time he came to the conclusion that sophisticated shots and an elaborate editing process were uselessly expensive. With a more casual treatment, a fixed camera, and no ornamental musical score, films would attract fewer people, but, being cheaper, they would be profitable. Some criticised Moullet for his 'amateurism' and the poor quality of his images; others thought that by contriving an original style combining actual scenes with reenacted ones he had reinvigorated the documentary tradition, which, they contended, had become rather humdrum. The classical distinction between shorts and feature-length films does not apply to Moullet who was totally indifferent to the duration of his works. The best division we can adopt is between amusing, often satirical movies and serious, analytical ones. Among the former we can single out Ma première brasse/ My First Stroke (1981), an autobiographical sketch originating from his first experience in a swimming-pool; Barres/Bars (1984), a fantasy about the barriers installed in the métro and the ways of avoiding them; L'empire de Médor/ Médor's Empire (1986), a lampoon against dog owners who, under the pretext of loving their pets, in fact martyr them; La comédie du travail/The Comedy of Work (1987), which told the adventures of three unemployed men who hopelessly look for a job; La valse des médias/ Waltz of the Media (1987), a look at readers' behaviour in French and Moroccan libraries; and Imphy capitale de la France/Imphy, Capital of France (1995), or why it would be better to transfer the capital from Paris, where unnecessarily complicated ways of doing things officially poison life, to a small, quiet town in the centre of France. Les sièges de l'Alcazar/The Seats of the Alcazar (1989) deserves special mention. The title is a pun, the siege (in French the same word means seat and siege) of the Alcazar was a famous episode of the Spanish civil war. In the late 1980s many films lamented the closure of old picture houses. Recreating the life of a cinema in a suburban district, Moullet indulged in the same vein but with more detachment and no nostalgia.

Anatomie d'un rapport/Anatomy of a Relationship (1976) was Moullet's first committed film, a view over the sexual problems of a couple through an observation of his relationship with Antonietta Pizzorno. The latter complains that she is not sexually satisfied; both try to improve their intercourse; a pregnancy and an abortion do not help the situation. Genèse d'un repas/ Genesis of a Meal (1978) opens with the same couple eating an omelette, tuna fish, and bananas. Where do these products come from? Moullet investigates at his grocer, in Normandy, where they breed hens, in Antilles to track the origin of bananas, and in Africa for the fishery of tuna fish. By interviewing workers in foreign countries as well as in packaging plants in France, he understands that these people do not realise that they are mere pawns in a system that exploits them for the benefit of others. The film ends with the filmmaker pondering over his own function, as a consumer, in the circuit of capitalism. Despite the considerable lapse of time between the two films, Toujours plus/ Always More (1994) was a sequel to Genèse. Moullet settled in a supermarket where he followed the customers, noting what they bought and how much they paid; then he interviewed the employees. Without making any commentary, only by juxtaposing piles of consumer goods and the complaints of check-out assistants, Moullet blames the profit motive for the unlimited development of consumption. The same criticism surfaced in Le ventre de l'Amérique/ The Belly of America (1995). Assuming that big cities are a small part of the United States and that they conceal its real face, Moullet attempted to reach the heart of America. Des Moines, Iowa, was chosen because it is in the centre, the 'belly' of the country, but the film was merely a hasty, superficial and at times unfair satire of the free enterprise economy, with an emphasis on fatness; the inhabitants of Des Moines are shown to be wandering bellies. The method had not changed since the late 1960s. Moullet himself was still a perceptive observer of his time, but the point of view had become more and more pessimistic.

After 1995 the director returned to fiction films, but his works met with a reserved response because viewers thought of him as a documentarian. Moullet has often been labelled an iconoclast or a rebel individualist. Owing to his personal involvement in his films he has carved out a special place in the history of documentaries. Many works shot for television have adopted his approach. It seems banal, nowadays, to see the filmmaker play a part in his film or to watch a combination of authentic and contrived shots. Moullet's works feature prominently in documentary film festivals, often as a counterpart to more elaborate movies. Spectators are usually fond of their jocular mood, of their bizarre way of touching serious problems and, above all, of their critical perspective.

PIERRE SORLIN

Biography

Born in Paris in 1937. After studying in a Parisian secondary school, became a journalist. Worked successively for *Cahiers du cinéma*, *Télérama*, *Arts*. Founded a small production company specilialising in documentaries and directed eleven feature films and twenty-four shorts, which established his reputation as an independent filmmaker.

Selected films

1976 Anatomie d'un rapport/Anatomy of a Relationship: writer, director
1978 Genèse d'un repas/Genesis of a Meal: writer, director
1981 Ma première brasse/My First Stroke: writer, director, producer
1984 Barres/ Bars: writer, director, producer
1986 L'empire de Médor/Médor's Empire: writer, director, producer
1987 La comédie du travail/The Comedy of Work: writer, director
1987 La valse des médias/Waltz of Media: writer, director
1989 Les sièges de l'Alcazar/The Seats of the Alcazar: writer, director
1994 Toujours plus/Always More: writer, director
1995 Imphy capitale de la France/Imphy, Capital of France: writer, director
1994 Le ventre de l'Amérique/The Belly of America: writer, director

Murrow, Edward R.

During the 1951–2 television season, Edward R. Murrow and Fred W. Friendly's See It Now (out of their radio series Hear It Now) appeared on CBS-TV. It was the first regular documentary series on American television. (Also in 1951 The March of Time series, produced for the movie theaters, ended.) See It Now was a sort of news magazine of feature stories in The March of Time tradition, though it had a much quieter and more intimate tone suitable for the living room. Murrow and Friendly produced it; Murrow was the on-screen host and commentator.

At first, See It Now, like March of Time and the present-day 60 Minutes, presented several different stories in each half-hour program. In 1953 the format changed to only one story a week. Among the memorable See It Now programs are Christmas in Korea (1953), made during the Korean War; several programs dealing with McCarthyism, including one in 1954 in which Senator Joseph McCarthy was afforded the right to reply (consistent with an American broadcasting dictum called 'the fairness doctrine'); and a visit with nuclear physicist J. Robert Oppenheimer (1955). Details of two other programs may give some sense of the series' subjects and of its distinctive style.

Argument in Indianapolis (1953) presented opposing factions in that city when the American Civil Liberties Union, attempting to form a local chapter, was opposed by the American Legion post. One of the extraordinary things about that program was its balance in handling a controversial subject, necessary, no doubt, for it to be telecast at all. Depending on your sympathies, the American Legion members become fascist monsters or upholders of true Americanism; the ACLU group pleasant, sensitive intellectuals or dangerous radicals and subversives. At any rate, the faces, speech, and manner of the protagonists are caught more or less candidly. A remarkable study is offered of diverse ideologies and personalities that exist in uneasy relationship to each other within this republic.

Segregation in Schools (1954) was made the week after the United States Supreme Court decision that declared separate education for blacks and whites to be neither equal nor constitutional. It reported on reactions to the decision in two Southern towns: Natchitoches, Louisiana, and Gastonia, North Carolina. What seems a curious stiffness and formality on the part of both black and white interviewees, with stand-up microphones visible and some statements read or clearly rehearsed, may have to do with extremely strong feelings being controlled, as well as a less flexible technology than is available today. When emotion does break through—actual expressed emotion of an elderly black woman, a black high school youth, an elderly white woman, and a black teacher—it is moving and becomes real in a way that helps us to understand more fully what is involved than do the prepared statements.

In 1955 Alcoa withdrew its sponsorship from See It Now. It then changed from regularly scheduled weekly half-hours to hour-long programs appearing at intervals, 'specials' in effect. Media critic Gilbert Seldes quipped that it had become See It Now and Then. In 1958 See It Now was terminated, to be followed by CBS Reports. Murrow appeared on the latter series occasionally. His last program was Harvest of Shame (1960), about the exploitation and hardships of migrant agricultural workers. Aired on Thanksgiving Day, it created noteworthy furor. Murrow left CBS to become director of the

United States Information Agency and died shortly thereafter of lung cancer. Cigarettes were invariably a part of his image.

JACK C. ELLIS

Biography

Born April 25, 1908 in Greensboro, North Carolina. 1913–21 lived in Blanchard, Washington. 1926–30 attended Washington State College, Pullman. 1930–5 lived in New York City; worked for National Student Federation of America and then for Institute of International Education. 1935–7 Director of Talks for Columbia Broadcasting System. 1937–45 in London as European Director for CBS; broadcast from London to the United States throughout World War II. 1946–7 Vice-President and Director of Public Affairs for CBS. 1947–50 newscaster for CBS. 1950–1 Hear It Now weekly radio series on CBS. 1951–5 See It Now weekly television series on CBS-TV. 1961–3 Director, United States Information Agency. Died April 27, 1965, in Pawling, New York.

Further reading

Bluem, A. William, *Documentary in American Television*, New York: Hastings House, 1965.

Curtin, Michael, *Redeeming the Wasteland: Television Documentary and Cold War Politics*, New Brunswick, NJ: Rutgers University Press, 1995.

Friendly, Fred W., *Due to Circumstances Beyond Our Control* … , New York: Random House, 1967.

Kendrick, Alexander, *Prime Time: The Life of Edward R. Murrow*, Boston: Brown, Little, 1969.

Murrow, Edward R. and Friendly, Fred W., *See It Now*, New York: Simon and Schuster, 1955.

Sperber, A.M., *Murrow: His Life and Times*, New York: Freundlich Books, 1986.

Nana, Mom and Me

(US, Rothschild, 1975)

Nana, Mom and Me is a self-reflexive biographical documentary and a powerful account of three generations of women. The film explores issues of femininity, family memory, mother-daughter dynamics, and the challenges of documenting one's own kin.

With the intent of documenting her grandmother, with whom Rothschild feels a special affinity, the filmmaker instead confronts a matriarch who refuses to take the camera seriously or to talk in any detail about her own past. Frustrated, Rothschild turns her probing camera to her own mother, with whom she does not feel as connected, and a rich portrait of family issues and the act of filmmaking emerges. Old photographs and home movies are intercut with present-day interviews and observational footage in a way that truly sets the stage for future autobiographical documentaries. Nana, Mom and Me incorporates elements of journals, diaries, self-interviews, poetry, and alternative formal devices.

Rothschild's mother becomes the primary object of the camera's attention. As such, she offers a narrative of deeply personal growth and self-definition, as well as a comment on society's changing ideal for women.

C. MELINDA LEVIN

Nana, Mom and Me (US, New Day Films, 1975, 47 mins). Distributed by New Day Films. Produced and directed by Amalie Rothschild. Cinematography by Daniel Drasin and Amalie Rothschild. Original music by Randolph S. Rothschild. Edited by Amalie Rothschild and Bronwen Sennish.

Nanook of the North

(US, Flaherty, 1922)

Nanook of the North by Robert Flaherty is a seminal work in the field of documentary film. The film was hailed upon its 1922 release as an aesthetic (and anthropological) triumph, and it performed well at the box office. Its success opened up a whole range of new cinematic possibilities. Since then the film has continued to be a touchstone and an inspiration for film pioneers and practitioners.

Nanook's importance is undeniable, but its influence is not universally appreciated. As time has passed and the film's stature and influence have increased, so too have the controversies attached to it. Concerns about its nonfiction status, doubts regarding Flaherty's method, questions about its sensitivity to indigenous realities—all are subjects of debate.

During Flaherty's youth his family lived a nomadic existence, much of it in Canada, where they passed from mining camp to mining camp. Flaherty frequently went on lengthy prospecting expeditions, learning by example the outdoor arts and observing the conditions of northern life. Much of Flaherty's practical education was received from native teachers, expeditionary guides whose wisdom and facility he admired. He also came to realize that this cultural wisdom was being encroached upon and endangered by incursions of European culture and capitalism. As Flaherty grew up and became a mining engineer in his own right, he became more and more aware of his paradoxical position. As an explorer in the north he represented a vanguard, bringing advantages of trade and technology to needy and isolated communities. Simultaneously, he was also the agent for irreversible change, as pressures of integration

Figure 11 Nanook of the North, Nanook, 1922, harpoon (Courtesy of the Everett Collection)

and modernization forced out old ways that were, for all the disregard of white sensibility, frequently artful and abundant.

In 1910 Flaherty was hired by Sir William Mackenzie to prospect the vast area east of the Hudson Bay for its railway and mineral potential. Over the course of several years and through four lengthy expeditions, Flaherty had frequent contact with the region's Inuit people. As before, Flaherty found himself to be an appreciative beneficiary of native craft. He was taken by the Inuit's survival skills. Flaherty recognized that such traditional practices were threatened by modernization. Therefore, on one of his next expeditions, he brought a motion picture camera.

In tracing his transition from engineer to ethnographer, it has proved easy to exaggerate the uniqueness of Flaherty's aims and accomplishments, as well as the seriousness of his shortcomings. Flaherty inherited the sensibilities and interests of his age, and his work is a key point in the cultural continuum tracing the interaction of Europeans and natives of colour. In this context, the exalted reputation of Nanook of the North, much disputed and denied in more recent years, is complex but indubitably justified.

Nanook was not intended as a documentary; the genre had not even been defined at the time of the film's production. The film was made with an eye to commercial distribution and exhibition, and it was made for audiences that were accustomed to narrative fiction films. Flaherty was not an ethnographer, but he built his story out of the materials of real life. In this he was innovative and accomplished, especially given that the tenets of anthropological filmmaking were far from established at the time.

Flaherty had spent a good part of the previous ten years with the Inuit. However, he did not depend on his own experience alone. Flaherty screened his footage for the film's participants, who were encouraged to make suggestions. Many of these suggestions were incorporated into the film. This practice would later become fundamental to ethnographic filmmaking.

Consistent with this substantial artistic and cultural collaboration, and contrary to a narrative and stylistic impulse that would prevail elsewhere for many more years, Flaherty does not intrude on his subject. He is not the star of his film, and even though his effaced presence causes a few unsightly wrinkles (unfortunate contrivances—such as Nanook's biting of the phonograph record—are perceived as actual and natural), for the most part it means that the credit for the film's feats of courage and grace go precisely where they belong: to the Inuit. If Nanook is Flaherty's film, then it is his in collaboration with its subjects, who emerge as almost wholly admirable.

In ethnographic matters, Nanook began a trend that has affected documentary ever since. Its progress is seen in the Griersonian documentary, in the National Film Board of Canada's Faces of Canada series, in films like Jean Rouch's Moi, un noir, in the NFB's Challenge for Change series, and in the work of ethnic filmmakers such as Trinh T. Minh-ha. That trend would eventually enable the indigenous individual to tell his or her own story, to that individual's own community as well as to the outsider, leading to a greater hope for mutual comprehension, cinematically and in unmediated social interaction.

Commentary has focused on the film's place in a trajectory of ethnic relations and representations, but Nanook of the North is also important for a contribution that crosses borders and reduces divisions. In its earliest years (1895–1902), film production was dominated by actualities—short pictures of actual people in actual places. These films favoured a largely unmediated view of the world over arranged spectacle, and although they gave place in popularity to the narrative fictions of the likes of Georges Méliès and Edwin Porter, they continued to be produced in great number.

However, there was a reason for their commercial eclipse. The early actuality basically evolved into two types of film production, both valuable and yet both somewhat lacking. The first category, the travelogue, took the viewer to faraway places with strange-sounding names. There was an inherent appeal in the journey, but the spectator's visit seldom provided more than a superficial glimpse of the picturesque.

A second type of actuality film flourished, for the most part in Britain (primarily but not exclusively during the reign of Edward VII). These films were more substantial portraits of industrial processes—also valuable for the way they revealed the rhythms of workers' lives, the conditions of their labour, and the superb skill that in some ways shone through the difficult conditions—but given the escapist impulses that already held audiences in thrall, their commercial appeal was limited.

Robert Flaherty's great innovation, perhaps most clearly and successfully articulated in Nanook of the North, was simply to combine the two forms of actuality, infusing the exotic journey with the details of indigenous work and play and life. By so doing Flaherty transcended the travelogue, as now the picturesque became a real and respectful portrait.

That portrait contained two things that remain, even today, at the very core of the documentary idea. These are process and duration, or the detailed representation of how our everyday things are done (burning moss for fuel, covering a kayak, negotiating ice floes, hunting, caring for our children, etc.) and how long the doing takes. In Nanook this combination leads to a number of lovely moments, most particularly in its stunning igloo sequence. Here labour is not only revealed in its (romanticized) social context but also emerges, through Nanook's skill and Flaherty's cinematic revelation, as an ideal of beauty and even spirituality. First there is shelter, then warmth, and finally light (the window!). Here and elsewhere, by giving real processes a human dimension, craftsmanship and artistry, life and enactment and representation, become one.

Nanook is a film of great accomplishment, but it has also provoked controversy and protest. Flaherty's film is not a pure documentary. For example, the family at the film's centre was not really a family. These were photogenic Inuit, simultaneously presenting themselves and enacting a dramatic role. The characters' authentic clothes were actually a nostalgic hybrid; the Inuit had started to integrate Western wear with their own traditional garb some time before. This integration was in fact quite general: igloos were giving way to southern building materials, many harpoons had been replaced by rifles, many kayak paddles by motors.

Given that all this was true, observers (starting with John Grierson) would come to accuse Flaherty of ignoring contemporary realities and real crises (cultural integration, unemployment, various modern social ills), in favour of romances that were, for all their prettiness and partial anthropological interest, socially irrelevant. (This complaint would be applied even more vigorously to some of Flaherty's later films, such as Moana, 1926, and Man of Aran, 1934.)

Other fabrications have caused more serious concern on social and even ethical grounds. The seal that appears to be engaging Nanook in a delightful tug of war is actually dead; Nanook is in fact being pulled around by some friends who are at the other end of the rope, standing just off camera. During the famous walrus hunt, the hunters desperately asked Flaherty to stop shooting the camera and start shooting the rifle. Flaherty pretended not to hear, and kept filming until the prey was taken in the old way. A failed bear hunt (not appearing in the film, but related in Flaherty's northern memoir, *My Eskimo Friends*) left its participants, Flaherty included, stranded and nearly starving for weeks.

Flaherty's shortcomings, as well as those of his films, are certain, and they should be acknowledged. However, it is fair to point out that with regard to endangerments for the film's sake, Flaherty exposed the Inuit to difficulties that were not only within the realm of traditional, historical experience, but that were to some degree still current. As for stereotyping, if Nanook is not quite the perfect ideal of cultural comprehension, it still stands as a remarkable plateau, especially given the surrounding contemporary landscape.

Despite its contradictions and controversies, Nanook of the North holds a central place in the history of documentary film. Its strong documentary elements are set in a fine romantic story, and its romance is made profound by the loving detail that decorates and humanizes it.

DEAN DUNCAN

See also: Challenge for Change/Société Nouvelle; Flaherty, Robert; Grierson, John; Man of Aran; Moana; Trinh T. Minh-ha

Nanook of the North (US, Revillon Frères, 1922, 75–80 mins). Distributed in the United States by Pathé, in the UK by Jury. Scenario, direction, and photography by Robert Flaherty. Assisted by Captain Thierry Mallet. Titles written by Carl Stearns Clancy and Robert Flaherty. Edited by Robert Flaherty and Frances Flaherty. Featuring Allariallak as 'Nanook'. Also featuring 'Nyla', 'Cunayou', 'Allee', and 'Allegoo'. Filmed near Inukjuaq, in the Nunavik region of northern Québec, Canada.

Further reading

Barnouw, Erik, *Documentary: A History of the Non-Fiction Film*, New York and Oxford: Oxford University Press, 1974 (revised 1983, 1993).

Barsam, Richard, *The Vision of Robert Flaherty: The Artist as Myth and Filmmaker*, Bloomington, IN: Indiana University Press, 1988.

Berton, Pierre, *The Mysterious North: Encounters with the Canadian Frontier, 1947–54*, Toronto: McClelland and Stewart, 1989 (revised).

Brownlow, Kevin, *The War, the West and the Wilderness*, New York: Knopf, 1979.

Calder-Marshall, Arthur, *The Innocent Eye: The Life of Robert J. Flaherty*, London, W.H. Allen, 1963.

Carpenter, Edmund, *Eskimo*, Toronto: University of Toronto, 1959.

Danzker, Jo-Anne Birnie (ed.), *Robert Flaherty, Photographer/Filmmaker: The Inuit, 1910–22*, Vancouver: Vancouver Art Gallery, 1979.

Flaherty, Frances Hubbard, *The Odyssey of a Film-Maker: Robert Flaherty's Story*, Putney, VT: Threshold Books, 1984.

Flaherty, Robert, *My Eskimo Friends*, Garden City, NY: Doubleday, 1924.

Griffith, Richard, *The World of Robert Flaherty*, New York: Duell, Sloan and Pearce, 1953.

Houston, James A., *Confessions of an Igloo Dweller*, Boston: Houghton Mifflin, 1995.

Rotha, Paul, *Robert J. Flaherty: A Biography*, edited by Jay Ruby, Philadelphia, PA: University of Pennsylvania Press, 1983.

Native Land

(US, Strand, 1942)

Native Land was the culminating project of Frontier Films, a nonprofit filmmaking company aligned with Labor-left groups in the United States between 1937 and 1942. Drawing on testimony presented to the LaFollette Civil Liberties subcommittee of the US Senate Committee on Education and Labor in the late 1930s, the film dramatizes acts of anti-union espionage and violence and argues for the right of workers to organize as a traditional American civil liberty in modern dress. Frontier previously had limited production to short subjects, and the scale of this documentary feature strained the organization's resources, contributing to Frontier's dissolution the year of the film's release. However, Native Land, with its inventive design and professional polish, also attracted greater critical attention than earlier Frontier projects and, in retrospect, can be viewed as a capstone to a decade of experimentation in American documentary filmmaking on the political left.

The driving forces behind Native Land were Paul Strand and Leo Hurwitz, Frontier's president and vice-president, respectively, who assumed control of the project in April 1938 when they found preliminary work by other members of the group wanting. A feature-length script was hammered out collaboratively, with poet Ben Maddow (under the pseudonym of David Wolff) writing the commentary. In addition to sharing directing credit, Strand was responsible for the cinematography and Hurwitz for the editing. Over the next three years, production progressed intermittently, given available funds; at various times footage was screened in New York, Washington, and Los Angeles in an effort to gain additional backing.

Strand estimated that as many as fifteen thousand people saw parts of Native Land this way, and he likened the process to 'making a film in a fish bowl'. Upon completion of an answer print on December 8, 1941, Frontier recruited actor-singer Paul Robeson to read the commentary and composer Marc Blitzstein to write the score; their reputations added further luster to the project.

Central to Strand and Hurwitz's approach to Native Land was a Popular Front politics that recast the conflict between socialism and capitalism as a struggle between democracy and fascism and staked a claim for patriotic symbols on behalf of Labor's cause. Equally important was the filmmakers' ambition to stretch documentary forms to accommodate the psychological dimension of dramatic fiction. In this regard, Native Land would bring to fruition ideas that had been advanced by Hurwitz and former colleague Ralph Steiner when they founded the experimental filmmaking collective, Nykino, in association with the Group Theater, in 1934. Given the latent drama in the LaFollette Committee testimony, Hurwitz, Strand, and Maddow devised a hybrid format for Native Land that combined expressive acting and character-centered editing with documentary montages, vocal commentary, musical scoring, and song. Actors from the Group Theater were recruited for key roles, and theater veterans William Watts and Alfred Saxe assisted with the direction of the performers.

In its finished form, Native Land interweaves historical events on three levels. The middle sections are dominated by a series of discrete, dramatized acts of violence: the murder of a Michigan farmer, of a Cleveland Labor organizer, and of two Arkansas sharecroppers; the flogging and tar-and-feathering of a progressive political leader by the Ku Klux Klan in Tampa, Florida; and a longer, fictional scenario featuring actors Art Smith and Howard de Silva and involving internal espionage and personal betrayal within a local union. Over the course of the film these isolated incidents then are stitched together to reveal a pattern of corporate conspiracy, the details of which constitute Native Land's central mystery plot. The antidote to this conspiracy, Native Land suggests, is union solidarity and democratic processes at the national as well as local level, political forces given graphic power in documentary montages of workers waking, laboring, meeting, protesting, and relaxing, and of the congressional investigators in Washington patiently reconstructing anti-Labor crimes.

Framing these contemporary events in Native Land is a long-range, mythic history. A seven-minute prologue recounts the settlement of the New England wilderness by ancestral European citizenry, as founding figures fight and die to vouchsafe civil liberties, an inheritance out of which the modern era of industry and labor emerges. The language and imagery of this prologue is recapitulated at the close as a way of offering comfort and inspiration to the families and colleagues of the victims of the Chicago Republican Steel Massacre on Memorial Day 1937. Invoked at both the beginning and the end of Native Land, then, is an epic national struggle, the true dimensions of which can be appreciated only on a time scale that exceeds the purview of a single generation. The commentary delivered forcefully by Robeson gives voice to that legacy, and in the end Native Land invites the audience, along with the working-class figures on screen, to set their sights on this longer view.

Topical events, however, would have an impact on the film's reception. Native Land played at a World Theatre in New York City for three months in the spring of 1942 and was widely and well reviewed in the mainstream press, with the photography, music, and performances especially receiving high marks. In light of the US entry into world war the previous December, questions were raised about the Native Land's timeliness, a problem the filmmakers sought to finesse by attaching an epilogue in which Robeson acknowledged that the struggle to defeat the Axis powers abroad now took precedence. Much to the disappointment of Hurwitz and Strand, no national distributor elected to pick up their unconventional feature, not even the left-based Garrison Films, which had previously handled Frontier's releases. Except for sporadic showings in a few other cities, Native Land quickly dropped from sight without earning back its initial costs. Following a brief rerelease in 1946, under the pressure of Cold War politics the film disappeared even from the nontheatrical market, not resurfacing until Hurwitz and Strand gained control of the film in the early 1970s.

Since that time, Native Land has entered into the standard repertory of political documentary filmmaking. As some contemporary critics have noted, the agrarian and industrial iconography of the film seems far removed from the contemporary media landscape, and its romanticizing of the origins of American democracy and its generalized critique of corporate conspirators at home seem at times curiously evasive. However, Native Land provides evidence of the expressive power of a left-wing American patriotism, passionately articulated at an historical moment when the meaning of national symbols was in flux, and of a tradition of creative thinking about the plasticity of documentary cinema as a poetic form.

CHARLES C. WOLFE

Further reading

Alexander, William, 'Frontier Films, 1936–41: The Aesthetics of Impact', *Cinema Journal* 15, no. 1, fall 1975: 16–28.

——*Film on the Left: American Documentary Film from 1931 to 1942*, Princeton, NJ: Princeton University Press, 1981.

Campbell, Russell, *Cinema Strikes Back: Radical Filmmaking in the United States, 1930–42*, Ann Arbor, MI: UMI Research Press, 1992.

Hurwitz, Leo, 'One Man's Journey: Ideas and Films in the 1930s', *Cinema Journal* 15, no. 1, fall 1975: 1–15.

Klein, Michael, 'Native Land: Praised Then Forgotten', *Velvet Light Trap* 14, winter 1975: 12–16.

Klein, Michael and Klein, Jill, 'Native Land: An Interview with Leo Hurwitz', *Cinéaste* 6, no. 3, 1974: 2–7.

Strauss, Theodore, 'Homesteading Our "Native Land"', *The New York Times*, May 3, 1942: X3.

Wolfe, Charles, 'Modes of Discourse in Thirties Social Documentary: The Shifting "I" of Native Land', *Journal of Film and Video* 36, fall 1984: 13–20, 61.

——'The Poetics and Politics of Nonfiction: Documentary Film', in Tino Balio (ed.), *Grand Design: Hollywood as a Modern Business*, New York: Charles Scribner's Sons, 1993.

Nazis: A Warning from History, The

(UK, Wood/BBC, 1997)

A television documentary in six episodes, The Nazis: A Warning from History is particularly interesting for its focus on two aspects of Nazism: the horror perpetrated by the Nazis in Eastern Europe; and the extensive popularity that the Nazis enjoyed in Germany. Written and produced by Laurence Rees, The Nazis: A Warning from History was broadcast for the first time on the BBC from September 10, 1997, to October 15, 1997, for a total running time of almost two hundred and ninety minutes. The six episodes, which unfold in chronological order, offer a broad view of the historical, cultural, and political events that produced Hitler and his politics of expansion. They focus predominantly on the occurrences linked to the rise and fall of Nazism from a German perspective. World War II itself receives little coverage. Little or no attention is devoted to military tactics; there is no trace of the invasion of France, of D-Day, or of the battles against Britain. The documentary concentrates instead on the human aspects and motivations of Nazism.

By showing contemporary images of the historical settings, documents from the Gestapo archives, and official acts signed by Hitler, The Nazis: A Warning from History reconstructs step by step the political and legislative acts that led to dictatorship in Germany. It analyzes the conflicts internal to the Nazi Party, the enthusiastic support of the pro-Nazi masses, and the gradual elimination of anti-Nazi political antagonists through the official endorsement of the racial laws and their consequences. The first two episodes, entitled Helped into Power and Chaos and Consent, offer an analysis of the long- and short-term causes that gave rise to Nazism and focus on the illusion of order offered by Hitler and on the life of the German population under the dictatorship.

Without drawing from the better-known Nazi propaganda films, The Nazis presents numerous sources and documents of the time, intertwined with contemporary images and interviews. The interviews are not dubbed but subtitled, and an old photograph of each interviewer is shown. The authors privilege testimonies of ordinary people who adhered to Nazism and who show some signs of nostalgia; the interviewer often seems to seek a confession, an admission of guilt. The documentary as a whole highlights the popular consent to Nazism; we watch Austrians and German-speaking inhabitants of Eastern European countries cheering at the arrival of the Nazi troops and note the support of the German population for the anti-Semitic laws. There is a particular focus on the civilians who collaborated with the Gestapo; we see letters written by ordinary citizens to denounce neighbors or friends, and in a dramatic sequence we even witness an interviewee, an elderly German lady, being confronted with the letter that she handwrote fifty years before, betraying a neighborhood girl.

The authors employ as many images and sequences as possible in color. From a purely cinematic perspective, the high-quality color film of the 'Night of the Amazons' in Munich is of particular interest, with its dancers and female riders who parade almost naked through the centre of the Bavarian capital at night, a testimony to the cult for the body and the superiority of the Aryan race. The sequence is followed by an interview with one of the women who participated in the parade and who stresses the positive sides of Hitler and of life in Nazi Germany.

The image of Hitler that the authors construct is, perhaps surprisingly, that of an indolent man, intent on maintaining competition among his close collaborators. We are shown the sites of Nazi power as they were then and as they are today, the pastimes of the party officials, and their holiday destinations. Hitler's politics of expansion are associated by the authors with his passion for England and for films set in the British countryside or in India; his dream of an alliance with Britain against Russia is explored. The episode The Wrong War elucidates his project to make Germany great once again by bringing back to the fatherland the German-speaking populations from bordering countries. It documents the advance of the German troops and the greeting they received in Austria and Poland; it illustrates the Nazi policy of expropriating goods, shops, and houses and redistributing them to German speakers coming back to Germany after the wave of emigration that followed World War I. It shows how, in the regions where Germans and the Polish both lived, the former became, virtually overnight, the persecutors of their neighbors. The invasion of Poland is observed with particular attention in the episode The Wild West, which is entirely dedicated to the partition of Poland and to the treatment of the Polish population.

One of the most interesting aspects of The Nazis is its attention to Nazi crimes in Lithuania—in particular, the ramifications of the order to eliminate, without delay, communist and Jewish women and children. The central piece is an interview with a Lithuanian, then a voluntary member of the SS. After twenty years in prison for war crimes, he offers a cold and lucid testimony, despite the repeated attempts of the interviewer to break his aloofness.

The episode The Road to Treblinka investigates the concentration camps. Rather than showing horrific images of the Holocaust, it focuses on the development of the Polish Treblinka camp, from the planning phase to its construction, between July 1942 and August 1943, thus investigating the Nazi will driving the extermination effort and the efficiency of their 'killing factories'.

The Nazis: A Warning from History closes on images of the defeat of an entire people, not only of the party officials. One of the last sequences is an interview with a woman shot on one of the rivers that surround the city of Berlin. She claims to have seen entire families committing mass suicide in the river in the wake of the German defeat. The film closes with images of the Holocaust and with the words of the German philosopher Karl Jasper, which are also the documentary's title, warning that the horror that has happened could happen again, any day, anywhere in the world.

STEFANO BASCHIERA

The Nazis: A Warning from History (UK, BBC, 1997, 290 mins). Written and produced by Laurence Rees. Narrated by Samuel West. Series historical consultant: Prof. Ian Kershaw.

Further reading

Rees, Laurence, *The Nazis: A Warning from History*, London: BBC Consumer Publishing, 1997.

Near/Middle East

The Middle East, or, alternatively, the Near East, is a rough-hewn area situated between Mauritania and Mali in West Africa and Iran and Afghanistan in Central Asia. The region is often associated with the Arab and Islamic worlds, but both of these parameters insufficiently describe the diversity of ethnic and cultural backgrounds present. Various empires have controlled vast sections of land that stretch from Africa's Atlantic coast to the Himalayan ranges. These empires have left their influence not only on the landscape, but also on the various cultures living in this region. Most recently France and Britain governed much of this area until the widespread push for national independence after World War II. Yet, international and regional political ambitions have continued to define much of the Middle East in the postcolonial era. It follows that the cinematic traditions in many of the nations have been tied to these political prerogatives. In fact, colonialism, conflict, state oppression and, ultimately, exile have influenced the development of documentary film in the region more than any other factors.

Documentary film in the Middle East, like narrative film, was introduced as part of Western modernization. Europeans and Americans intent on discovering images of the Orient pioneered film production in the region. The lure of the 'Holy Land' attracted both the Lumière company and Thomas Edison to shoot footage in what was then called Palestine. Also on behalf of the Lumière brothers, the French Algerian cinematographer Felix Mesguich began filming actualités in Algeria in 1905 and a year later in Egypt, and then in 1907 he captured on film the French invasion of Morocco.

Many of the earliest documentaries from the region were produced under colonial rule and presented little more than official propaganda. The deployment of propaganda films during the colonial period and the emergence of resistance films during the postcolonial period present some of the most salient examples of early documentary in the region. Following these early endeavors, documentary film in the Middle East has continued to be influenced by various forms of political domination, if not delineated in opposition to them. In fact, the bulk of Middle Eastern documentaries present a tenacious social critique of political power, but severe censorship by both colonial and national governments has limited the reception of many of these films.

The French and British domination of the region, especially after the Sykes-Picot agreement in 1916, effectively stifled the development of national cinemas in the Middle East. Under French authority the development of national cinemas was discouraged in favor of colonial assimilation. Thousands of informational and documentary films were made in the French colonies in order to disseminate pedagogic advice and political propaganda. There was almost no opportunity for indigenous filmmaking to take shape prior to independence from Europe. Only after the French realized the popularity of Egyptian cinema in the 1940s did they begin to endorse films made with Arabic dialogue in Morocco, though still under the auspices of the French Protectorate.

Indeed, only Egypt was able to develop a national film industry during the colonial period. Initially, Egyptian cinema took root in the production of news films that depicted, among other things, the funeral of head of state Mustafa Kamil. Muhammad Bayumi is most notable for his regular Amun newsreels. Yet, these documentary endeavors quickly gave way to the production of Egyptian narrative films more concerned with entertaining the masses than with informing them. After the founding of Studio Misr (Studio Egypt) in the 1930s, Cairo established itself as the capital of popular Arab cinema and proved a minor player in documentary film production until the founding of the National Documentary Film Center in the 1970s.

In North Africa, indigenous filmmaking lagged until the late 1950s when Morocco and Tunisia gained national independence. The film industries in these two countries have developed in fits and starts, producing sporadic but significant film traditions. However, documentary film has been largely overshadowed by the production of narrative features. One notable exception, Ahmed el Maanouni's Alyam! Alyam!/The Days, the Days (1978), blurs the distinction between fiction and documentary film to blast the effects of modern development and neo-colonial power in Morocco.

In Algeria, where the French encountered a persistent rebellion through the same decade, Ahmed Rachedi, Mohamed Guenez, Djamal Chanderli, and Frenchman René Vautier formed Groupe Farid as a resistance film unit of the FLN (Front de la Libération Nationale), in order to film the struggle for independence. Rachedi's L'aube des damnés/The Dawn of the Damned (1965) is the most notable film to emerge from this collective. Though not a documentary per se, it presents a history of anti-imperialism across Africa with many documentary elements.

The Battle of Algiers (1965), an Algerian-Italian production, helps to illustrate the documentary threads of these projects. While imprisoned in France, FLN rebel leader Saadi Yacef wrote a film script based on his experiences fighting French colonial rule. After his release he approached a number of Italian directors working in the neorealist tradition. Despite the film's explicit anti-imperialist underpinnings and financial backing by the new Algerian government, director Gillo Pontecorvo offers a surprisingly balanced depiction of escalating violence (terror and torture) by both the French and the Algerians. The astute portrayal of guerilla tactics against the colonizers significantly bolstered the popularity of this film with the Black Panthers in the United States in the 1960s and, more recently, with the US government for use as a counterterrorism training tool. Simulating documentary footage and utilizing locals as well as former FLN members for cast and crew made it possible to replicate the hostilities and chaos so effectively that the film's distributors issued a notice stating, 'Not one foot of newsreel has been used in this reconstruction of "The Battle of Algiers"'. The newsreel, whether recycled or recreated, continues to be an important stylistic element of both narrative and documentary film in the region.

For several years Algerian cinema remained obsessed with its colonial past and the battles waged for national independence, continuing to celebrate the heroes and martyrs of the war. By the 1970s, however, Algerians were rejecting this obsession with the war, and their popular films became more concerned with agrarian reform.

Since national independence, film industries throughout the region have struggled to achieve their own autonomy. Lacking the infrastructure, audience base, and funding necessary to become entirely self-reliant, many filmmakers have depended on foreign sources. France and other Western countries have offered many Arab filmmakers education, funding, and distribution opportunities, and the large Moroccan and Algerian populations in France have ensured transnational audiences for these films. Thus the former French colonies in the Levant or Mashreq (principally Lebanon, Syria, and Palestine) and the Maghreb (Morocco, Algeria, and Tunisia) continue to benefit from the francophone cultural mission. Yet, the cumulative effect of these factors challenges the notion of a national cinema.

Several recent documentaries from North Africa reveal the postcolonial dimension of film production, while also offering a commentary on transnational existence. Yasmine Qassari's heartbreaking film Indama Yabki al-Rigal/When Men Cry (1999) reveals the harsh reality for Moroccans trying to emigrate to Spain illegally. French director Yamina Benguigi's two documentaries Mémoires d'immigrés/Immigrants' Memories (1998), and The Perfumed Garden (2000) portray the experience of North African immigrants in France, and Hakim Belabbes's Boujad: A Nest in the Heat (1992) offers a perspective on separation, independence, and return as he chronicles his journey from the United States to visit his family in Morocco. In Fitouri Belhiba's whimsical Mirror Effect (1999), he tells the story of a Belgian ice-cream vendor in Tunisia, while deconstructing common notions of identity. Each of these films is, to some extent, a multinational production.

For some filmmakers this dependence on Europe is a mixed blessing that carries its own set of concerns about neocolonialism and Orientalism. Although support and funding may be generous resources for these filmmakers, there may be demands to use mostly French dialogue or to adhere to lucrative themes, such as violence. This is particularly the case for the countries in the eastern Mediterranean, which have experienced tremendously more civil strife in recent years than most others in the region. After the unyoking from centuries of Ottoman authority, the slicing up of the Middle East after World War I, and the eventual placement of Israel in Palestinian land, the violence of this region has spawned some of the most provocative documentary films being made in the Middle East today. Largely in reaction to the chronic violence in these locales, Lebanese and Palestinian filmmakers have produced some of the most innovative work in Arab documentary.

Following World War I, Britain favored the creation of a Zionist homeland in an effort to keep the French out of Palestine. This raised the ire of the Arabs, who had hoped for independence after helping to defeat Turkey during the war. Zionist filmmaking, which began before the founding of Israel, employed propaganda approaches in much the same way as the French and British, depicting Arabs in general, and Palestinians specifically, as barbaric, if they were depicted at all. The tribulations of World War II exacerbated the conflict. Largely prompted by the atrocities of the Holocaust, the United Nations passed a resolution in 1947 to create separate Jewish and Arab states in Palestine. Fighting erupted almost immediately and led to the 1948 War, when over seven hundred thousand Palestinian Arabs fled to neighboring Arab countries or further abroad. Distrust between Isreal and its neighbors continued to escalate for the next two decades. Fearing an Arab invasion during the summer of 1967, Israel launched a preemptive strike against Egypt, Jordan, and Syria and subsequently captured the Sinai Peninsula, the Gaza Strip, the Golan Heights, and the West Bank, including the eastern sector of Jerusalem.

Like the resistance efforts against European colonialism, the creation of Israel as a Zionist state and the ongoing warring effectively spawned Palestinian documentary filmmaking. After the 1967 War cinematographic activism developed in connection with the armed struggle. A Palestinian film unit began operating in Jordan and was eventually annexed by Yassir Arafat's resistance organization Al-Fatah. After the 1970 Black September massacre of Palestinian resistance members in Jordan, the film unit relocated to Beirut, where several other Palestinian organizations were actively documenting military actions and life in the refugee camps. The infusion of Palestinians into Lebanon disrupted the balance of power and is partly blamed for the outbreak of war in Lebanon.

Under the banner of the Dziga Vertov Group, Jean-Luc Godard and Jean-Pierre Gorin had documented Al-Fatah's training program prior to Black September, as an ideal model of revolutionary preparedness, in Jusqu'a La Victoire (Until Victory—or—Palestine Will Win, 1970). However, the devastating defeat in Jordan forced the filmmakers to reevaluate the validity and promise of their project; they abandoned the film and it was never completed. After being ousted by Jordan, the Palestinian Liberation Organization (PLO) had relocated to Lebanon, where it launched attacks on Israel. This eventually prompted the brutal Israeli invasion of Lebanon in 1982, which halted the production of films and destroyed much of the archived materials. The PLO film unit transferred to Tunis and began coproduction with Western filmmakers, but in Lebanon Hezbollah (the Party of God) emerged as a Shiite resistance group poised to resist Israel along the southern border of Lebanon. Hezbollah has adopted the documentary filming of their martyrs in action.

The First Intifada (1987–94) marked the emergence of a strong Palestinian resistance within the occupied territories until the Oslo Accords brought a temporary end to the fighting. By 2000 the peace process broke down again, and the Second Intifada has persisted despite intense Israeli efforts to sequester the Palestinian resistance. These momentous historical events set the scene for documentary film to flourish.

Many of the most prolific and talented narrative filmmakers began their careers documenting this conflict. Indeed, the Lebanese documentary tradition cannot be adequately understood without also discussing the development of Palestinian documentary filmmaking. In 1974 Lebanese filmmaker Borhan Alawiya filmed Kafr Kassem, about a massacre of Palestinians by Israeli troops, before going on to become an enduring voice in Lebanese cinema. Michel Khleifi emerged as a prominent filmmaker after his first feature-length documentary, Al-dhakira al-khasba/Fertile Memory (1980), in which he employs narrative elements to examine the lives of Palestinian women living under occupation. His later work veers more toward fiction, but he continues to use documentary aesthetics. One of the few filmmakers to remain prolific during the Lebanese civil war(s), Mohamed Soueid uses documentary and fictional elements in his video essays. In his recent Nightfall (2000), he draws from his diaries to recount his participation in 'The Student Squad' of Al-Fatah during the Lebanese wars. His stories tell of old friends, some of whom have died while others live with their memories and solitude. In the tradition of documenting history in the making, Mohamed Bakri's Jenin, Jenin (2002) offers very little hope for the future for the Palestinians. After the Israeli army has flattened Jenin, grief and sorrow overwhelm the residents' testimonies in this film.

Jean Chamoun and Mai Masri, a Lebanese-Palestinian husband and wife team, are two of the more prolific documentary filmmakers from the region. Churning out film after film about the continued conflict and violence in Palestine and Lebanon, they convey the human element behind these devastating events. Though often depicting the lives of women and children immersed in struggle or families attempting to rebuild their lives in the wake of war and exile, their documentaries maintain a resilient element of hope that other filmmakers have long since abandoned. Some of their most notable documentaries are Under the Rubble (1983), about Israel's invasion of Lebanon; Suspended Dreams (1992), chronicling the rebuilding of lives and relationships after the Lebanese civil wars; Children of Fire (1990), revealing the place of children in the Palestinian uprising; and Children of Shatila (1998), a film about life within a refugee camp from the perspective of children that utilizes footage recorded by the children themselves. Chamoun revisited the Lebanese wars recently in his narrative debut, In the Shadows of the City (2000). The return to the war in narrative films has been the trend among many Lebanese documentarians working during the war, revealing the difficulty of moving beyond the traumatic events for many of these individuals.

It is worth highlighting the role that female filmmakers played from early in the development of these traditions, because they have had a pronounced presence in Palestinian and Lebanese documentary film. Heiny Srour's Saat al-tahrir Dakkat Barra Ya Isti'mar/The Hour of Liberation has Sounded—The Struggle in Oman (1974) documents the struggle against imperialist oil interests in Oman, paying particular attention to the role that women play. Her next film, Leila wal-dhiab/Leila and the Wolves (1984), about women in the Palestinian resistance, earned an unprecedented broadcast in England of an Arab film. Her recent film on women during the Vietnam conflict, Rising Above—Women of Vietnam (1996), continues her look at female resistance movements. Like many Arab filmmakers residing abroad, Srour uses a Western locale (London) as her base, while continuing to film in non-Western locations.

Trained as a journalist, Jocelyne Saab covered conflicts in the Middle East for European television in the early 1970s. She produced dozens of short reportage documentaries for television before turning to a more personal approach in Lettre de Beyrouth/Letter from Beirut (1979), and Beyrouth ma ville/Beirut My City (1982). Her innovative feature Once Upon a Time, Beirut (1994) is structured around a fascinating montage of over three hundred Arab, French, and American film clips—depicted as Beirut's memory.

Maysoon Pachachi and Noura Sakkaf have made several documentaries in the region. Their most recent film, Bitter Sweet (2003), offers a sad portrait of Bourj al Barajneh refugee camp in Lebanon and the continued restrictions that Palestinians face in their Arab host countries, where citizenship (among other things) is not granted. Other women documentarians have challenged the gendered stereotypes of the Middle East. In Egypt, Attiat al-Abnoudi's Ahlam Mumkina/Permissible Dreams (1989) brings women together to discuss female agency and their struggles with patriarchy in Egypt. Yousry Nasrallah has also contributed to this debate, most recently with Sibyan wa banat/ Regarding Boys and Girls and the Veil (1995). Owing to increased financing by local and international development organizations, al-Abnoudi's and Nasrallah's works have emerged within a trend in Egyptian documentary that has refocused its attention on development and gender issues. The American filmmaker Elizabeth Fernea has also collaborated with women on these issues. For instance, The Veiled Revolution (1982) shows Egyptian women redefining not only the meaning of the veil but also the nature of their own sexuality.

Sexuality is also central to Mona Hatoum's deeply personal video Measures of Distance (1988), which marks the distance from 'home' through a dense layering of visual and audio media. While residing in London, her mother sends letters from Beirut during the war, where her family has been living since their displacement from Palestine. The narrative consists of her mother's letters, whose constant references to the distance in communication (sporadic letters and unreliable telephone connections) help punctuate the layers of displacement. In effect, Hatoum articulates an aesthetic of exile recurrent in Arab video art today.

Among the countries in the Mashreq (Arab East), Lebanon has had one of the richest film histories, emcompassing decadent popular cinema, conflict-based social documentary, and most recently the emergence of experimental video essays. In fact, during the nationalist period in Egypt under Gamal Abdel Nasser,

Lebanon dominated the region's popular market, albeit using many exiled Egyptian actors and maintaining the preference for the Egyptian dialect. The major role that Lebanese financiers and distributors played in Arab cinema and the large audience of filmgoers made Lebanon an ideal surrogate for Egyptian cinema during the 1960s and early 1970s.

Lebanon, popularly described as the meeting point between the Occident and Orient, attracted the decadence of jet-set oil sheikhs, European chic, and Hollywood's rich and famous. In addition to hosting this cosmopolitan population, Lebanon was known as a playground for international intrigue and espionage. The outbreak of intense violence in Lebanon during the mid-1970s brought an end to this 'Golden Age' and to popular Lebanese cinema. Yet, the Lebanese civil war(s) (1976–91), partially precipitated by the heightened conflict between Israel and its other contiguous Arab neighbors, initiated a turn to social documentary.

Since the Lebanese civil war(s) ended in 1990, Beirut has become the preeminent capital of Arab visual media. Many artists and intellectuals who returned during the postwar 1990s have helped to create a vibrant environment for politics, theory, and art to converge. Furthermore, the increased accessibility of digital video has fostered the production of independent documentaries, both artistic and journalistic. Many of these videos have an autobiographical foundation but blur the boundaries between personal and communal narratives, as well as between documentary and fiction approaches.

For many, the return to a 'home' violently altered—and known, perhaps, only from the distance of Western news reportage—has prompted innovative introspection on identity and representation. The exiled or diasporic location has also fostered a documentary genre critical of ethnocentrism abroad. In both documentary and video art, artists often appropriate and rework archival news footage in creative and critical ways. Applying the cut-up tradition to hundreds of news and movie clips, Palestinian filmmaker Elia Suleiman and Lebanese Canadian video artist Jayce Salloum create a dense montage of Orientalist discourse in their Introduction to the End of an Argument (1990). They show in no uncertain terms that the American media are ardently racist in their depiction of Arabs.

The rise in popularity of satellite television throughout the region has also played a role in the development of documentary in the Middle East. The competing broadcast centers in Lebanon, the United Arab Emirates, and Qatar have all shown interest in documentary film, sponsoring either productions or film festivals. Under the auspices of Qatar's satellite news station Al-Jazeera, Omar al-Issawi directed an impressive ten-hour chronicle of the Lebanese civil wars. The War of Lebanon (1996) combines interviews with a variety of players from different factions and newsreel footage in an effort to provide a better understanding of these events and their international influences—a rather sensitive topic regarded as taboo in Lebanon itself. The focus of Jehane Noujaim's Control Room (2003) was Al-Jazeera's news coverage of the American and British invasion of Iraq. Because of its political commentary, this film has been one of the few Arab documentaries to get a relatively broad theatrical release in the United States. At first polemically focusing on differences in attitude between the Arab journalists and the American communications officer in charge of the US military's Centcom, Noujaim deftly brings them into closer dialogue and greater understanding.

Even though numerous efforts have been made to 'objectively' document the violent conflicts and their effects, many film- and video-makers have realized the futility of any attempt to present an objective account of these 'unreal' events. Furthermore, by acknowledging the impossibility of making sense of the senseless violence, many filmmakers have delved into an intensely personal perspective on violence and the accompanying rupture of self. This is especially the case for filmmakers who have experienced these harrowing realities personally; however, many of the recent documentaries emerging throughout the Middle East have also had to account for the distance of exile.

Armenian filmmaker Nigol Bezjian, who lived in the United States during the war, appropriated news footage to create an intimate essay about his relationship with Beirut in A Road Full of Apricots (2001). Juxtaposing newsreels with personal places and memories, he draws attention to the way in which the city is popularly mediated, but he also reinscribes lived experience where it has seemed absent. Jayce Salloum undertook a similar project shortly after the war in his This Is Not Beirut (1994). Culling from found footage and video shot during 1992 in Lebanon, Salloum examines the popular misrepresentations of Lebanon and Beirut, chronicling his own assumptions, which he inherited during his upbringing in the West. Among many others making documentary-informed videos, Jalal Toufic, Akraam Zaatari, and Mahmoud Hojeij deserve acknowledgement. They are among the most active and influential video artists in Beirut today, and each offers an important documentary commentary on culture and politics in Lebanon. Although he is based in New York, the work of Walid Raad provides one of the most acute and humorous perspectives on the history of Lebanon. His videos advance subtle but ingenious critiques by cloaking fabulous stories about the war under the guise of documentary filmmaking. His short, Hostage: The Bachar Tapes (2001), regarding the narratives that come to dominate a place, inserts an Arab perspective within the hostage narratives that emerged from Beirut's terrorism in the 1980s.

Work in documentary film has been more limited elsewhere in the Arab Middle East, but notable filmmakers have emerged throughout the region. In the late 1960s many filmmakers adopted the political framework of Third Cinema. For those participating in this project, the potential for inciting state censorship prevented many from making documentaries. Yet they adapted a documentary aesthetic within fictive settings in order to advance resolute political and social critiques. Somewhat in contrast to this situation, Shadi Abdes-Salam was prevented from making a second feature film after his debut, Al-momia/The Night of Counting the Years (1969), thoroughly blasted the social divisions in Egypt. Despite the authorities' indignation, he went on to become a prolific documentarian. Similarly, the prolific Syrian filmmaker Omar Amiralay was censored in Syria for his critique of the government in al-Hayat al-Yawmiyya fi Qaria Suriyya/Daily Life in a Syrian Village (1974). He is now based in Beirut, where he continues his critique of political power, as in his documentary on Lebanese Prime Minister Rafiq Hirari, L'Homme aux semelles d'or/The Man with the Golden Soles (2000). Amiralay's unprecedented access to Hirari reveals the sway and charm of this powerful and wealthy leader.

In Kuwait, the Indian-trained Khalid Siddik made a number of television and government-endorsed documentaries before moving on to fictional features. In these films he borrows from folklore and traditions to present a counterpoint to the stereotype of oil-rich Kuwaitis. In similar fashion Iraqi cinema lagged until the emergence, in the 1960s, of a governmental agency that produced dozens of documentaries before the feature film industry blossomed in the late 1970s. Muhammad Shukri Jamil's early work on documentary exemplifies this trend. Khadija al-Salami, in Ard Al-Saba/Land of Saba (1997), places the modern history of Yemen in relation to the national archaeological heritage, partly to help Western audiences better understand his country.

On the periphery of the African Middle East, Mauritania's famed filmmaker Med Hondo, more often identified as an African cineaste than as part of the Middle East's tradition, has made all of his films in exile in France. In places such as Sudan, ethnographic film has traditionally been much more prolific than indigenous productions. Documentaries by Westerners still dominate the cinematic landscape of Sudan, but they provide important perspectives on the state of affairs for those affected by the continued conflict between the Islamic-oriented government and the indigenous southern population. Arthur Howe's continued interest in Sudan is exemplified in Kafi's Story and Nuba Conversations (both 2001). Indigenous examples of filmmaking are scarce, but Ibrahim Shaddad provides a poignant example of experimental Arab cinema emerging from the Sudan. Shot without dialogue, Insan (1994), meaning 'human' or 'person' in Arabic, creatively deploys sound to present an unsettling account of urban alienation for a shepherd from southern Sudan.

With what is often a more amusing approach, some filmmakers have begun to ask introspective questions about identity and authenticity. Omar al-Qattan's film Going Home (1995) chronicles the return of a British army officer to the 1948 battlefields and how he remembers those final days of the mandate. Al-Sheikh Inglizi Wal-gentlman al-Yamani/The English Sheikh and the Yemeni Gentleman (2000) by Bader Bin Hirsi offers an interesting reversal of traditional roles, as the British resident of Yemen introduces the Western-raised Yemeni to Arab culture. Hamid Rahmanian's Sir Alfred of Charles de

Gaulle Airport, about an Iranian national residing in the Paris airport, offers a unique perspective on transnational movement and the instability of identity. The liner notes describe the video as 'the story of a human being whose only aspiration is to be somebody else'. No matter how much Rahmanian tries to make this man stand for larger issues about exile, the self-named Sir Alfred repeatedly spurns these efforts and eventually refuses to speak with him. Sir Alfred's residence at the Charles de Gaulle Airport and his schizophrenic becoming-other steadfastly resist extrapolation into grand narratives. Yet, the desire to fix these identities is renewed in Steven Spielberg's latest film, The Terminal (2004), starring Tom Hanks, which clearly draws on this true story. Ultimately, however, it seems more interested in Rahmanian's determination to impose meaning than in Sir Alfred's subjective experience.

In terms of international acclaim and popularity, Iranian cinema easily surpasses all other national cinemas in the region. Numerous international festivals have highlighted the work of Abbas Kiarostami, Mohsen Makhmalbaf, and other Iranian filmmakers. Similar in many ways to Italian neorealism, Iranian cinema presents the beauty and struggle of everyday living by using documentary footage, nonactors, and self-reflexivity to achieve a quotidian aesthetic. Early in Kiarostami's career he launched the film division of the government-sponsored Center of the Intellectual Development of Children and Young Adults (Kanoon). Here Kiarostami made many educational and documentary films, developed his artistic impulses largely independent of commercial and political pressure, and established Iranian cinema's long-standing tradition of making films about children for all audiences.

The recycling of documentary scenes in Kiarostami's narrative films and the centrality of child characters is well demonstrated in his outstanding trilogy Khaneye doust kodjast?/Where is the Friend's Home? (1987), which recounts the efforts of a small boy to return his classmate's notebook. Zendegi va digar hich/Life Goes On—or—Life, and Nothing More (1991) is about the director of the first film (played by Farhad Kheradmand) and his young son trying to locate the first film's actors after a massive earthquake in a remote part of Iran. Many documentary images of the devastated landscape, shot out of the car window, serve as the backdrop for this father-and-son journey. The hope and perseverance demonstrated by the people encountered en route serve as inspiration for the final film, Zire darakhatan zeyton/ Through the Olive Trees (1994). The three films become increasingly self-reflexive of the film-making process. In the third film, the production of a film actually serves as the plot structure for the narrative subtext to emerge. Here another director (played by Mohamad Ali Keshavarz) comes to film an event from the second film, but this enables Kiarostami to present an endearing love story taking place behind the scenes.

Despite this monumental cinematic tradition, new trends in Iranian documentary (and narrative) utilize the 'small media' format of digital video. Not unlike the dissemination of cassette tape sermons, which helped prompt the Iranian Revolution, most documentaries in Iran rely on a more underground existence. Many documentaries are now being made without the censors' permission, a trend emerging throughout the Middle East.

There has been a significant blurring of genre distinctions in Middle Eastern cinema. From the neorealist approaches popular in Iranian cinema to the extradiagetic insertion of behind-the-scenes footage in new Lebanese cinema, the cinematic avant-garde has increasingly pulled documentary elements into their narratives. Conversely, the presentation of 'actuality' nowadays often self-consciously challenges the notion of reality, thus blurring the distinction among documentary, docudrama, and video essay. This trend marks one of the most dynamic developments in Middle Eastern filmmaking. Yet, more often than not, the current development of Middle Eastern documentary depends greatly on a transnational web of festival spectatorship and on the tenacity of independent filmmakers.

MARK WESTMORELAND

See also: Kiarostami, Abbas

Selected films

Abdes-Salam, Shadi, The Night of Counting the Years/Al-momia (1969)

al-Abnoudi, Attiat, Permissible Dreams/Ahlam Mumkina (1989); Days of Democracy/Ayam al-dimuqratiyya (1996)

Alawiya, Borhan, Kafr Kassem (1974)

al-Issawi, Omar, The War of Lebanon (1996)
al-Joundi, Dima, Between You and Me, Beirut/Bayni wa baynik Bayrut (1992)
al-Qattan, Omar, Going Home (1995)
al-Salami, Khadija, Land of Saba/Ard al-Saba (1997)
Amiralay, Omar, Daily Life in a Syrian Village/al-Hayat al-Yawmiyya fi Qaria Suriyya (1974); The Man with the Golden Soles/L'Homme aux semelles d'or (2000)
Babai, Brahim, And Tomorrow/Wa ghadan (1972)
Bakri, Mohamed, Jenin, Jenin (2002)
Belabbes, Hakim, Boujad: A Nest in the Heat (1992)
Belhiba, Fitouri, Mirror Effect (1999)
Benguigi, Yamina, Immigrants' Memories/Mémoires d'immigrés (1998); The Perfumed Garden (2000)
Bezjian, Nigol, A Road Full of Apricots (2001)
Bin Hirsi, Bader, The English Sheikh and the Yemeni Gentleman/Al-Sheikh Inglizi wal-gentlman al-Yamani (2000)
Chamoun, Jean, In the Shadows of the City (2000)
el-Maanouni, Ahmed, The Days, the Days/Alyam! Alyam! (1978)
Farrokhzad, Forugh, The House is Black (1962)
Fernea, Elizabeth, The Veiled Revolution (1982)
Godard, Jean-Luc and Gorin, Jean-Pierre, Until Victory, or Palestine Will Win/Jusqu'a la Victoire (1970)
Hadjadj, Belkcem, A Woman Taxi Driver in Sidi Bel-Abbes (2000)
Hatoum, Mona, Measures of Distance (1988)
Hojeij, Mahmoud, Palermo, Beirut, Palermo (1998)
Hondo, Med, The Black Wogs Your Neighbours/Les Bicots-nègres vos voisins (1974)
Howe, Arthur, Kafi's Story (2001); Nuba Conversations (2001)
Jamil, Muhammad Shukri, The Thirsty/al-Zami'un (1972)
Khamis, Mona, The Cleaner (2001)
Khan, Hassan, Six Questions for the Lebanese (2001)
Khleifi, Michel, Fertile Memory/Al-dhakira al-khasba (1980)
Kiarostami, Abbas, Jahan Nama Palace/Kakh-e Jahan Nama (1976); Tribute to the Teachers/Bozorgdasht-e Mo allem (1977); Where is the Friend's Home?/Khane-ye doust kodjast? (1987); Life Goes On, or Life, and Nothing More/Zendegi va digar hich (1991); Through the Olive Trees/Zire dar-akhatan zeyton (1994)
Lakhdar-Hamina, Mohamed, Chronicle of the Years of Embers/Chroniques des années de braise (1975)
Longinotto, Kim and Mir-Hosseini, Ziba, Divorce Iranian Style (1998)
Makhmalbaf, Mohsen, A Moment of Innocence/Nun va Goldoon (1999); Kandahar/Safar e Ghandehar (2001)
Masri, Mai and Chamoun, Jean, Under the Rubble (1983); Suspended Dreams (1992); Children of Fire (1990); Children of Shatila (1998)
Mesguich, Felix, Algeria (1905); Egypt (1906); French Invasion of Morocco (1907)
Nasrallah, Yousry, Regarding Boys and Girls and the Veil/Sibyan wa banat (1995)
Noujaim, Jehane, Control Room (2003)
Pachachi, Maysoon and Sakkaf, Noura, Bitter Sweet (2003)
Pontecorvo, Gillo, The Battle of Algiers (1965)
Qassari, Yasmine, When Men Cry/Indama Yabki al-Rigal (1999)
Ra'ad, Walid, The Dead Weight of a Quarrel Hangs (1996–9); Hostage: The Bachar Tapes (2001)
Rachedi, Ahmed, The Dawn of the Damned/L'aube des damnés (1965)
Rahmanian, Hamid, Sir Alfred of Charles de Gaulle Airport (2000)
Reggb, Mohamed, The Barber of the Poor Neighborhood/Halaq darb al-fuqara' (1982)
Saab, Jocelyne, Letter from Beirut/Lettre de Beyrouth (1979); Beirut My City/Beyrouth ma ville (1982); Once Upon a Time, Beirut (1994)
Salloum, Jayce, This Is Not Beirut/Hadha laysat Bayrut (1994)
Shaddad, Ibrahim, Insan (1994)
Siddik, Khalid, The Cruel Sea/Bass ya bahr (1971)
Soueid, Mohamed, Tango of Yearning (1998); Nightfall (2000)
Spielberg, Steven, The Terminal (2004)
Srour, Heiny, The Hour of Liberation Has Sounded—The Struggle in Oman/Saat al-tahrir Dakkat Barra ya Isti'mar (1974); Leila and the Wolves/Leila wal-dhiab (1984); Rising Above—Women of Vietnam (1996)
Suleiman, Elia and Salloum, Jayce, Introduction to the End of an Argument (1990)
Toufic, Jalal, Credits Included: A Video in Red and Green (1995)

Zaatari, Akraam, All is Well on the Border Front (1997); Crazy for You/Majnounak (1997)

Further reading

Armbrust, Walter, *Mass Culture and Modernism in Egypt*, Cambridge: Cambridge University Press, 1996.

Armes, Roy, *Third World Film Making and the West*, Berkeley, CA and London: University of California Press, 1987.

Asfour, Nana, 'The Politics of Arab Cinema: Middle Eastern Filmmakers Face up to Their Reality', *Cineaste* 1, no. 26, 2000: 46–8.

Diawara, Manthia, *African Cinema: Politics & Culture*, Bloomington, IN: Indiana University Press, 1992.

Fawal, Ibrahim, 'Three Perspectives on Arab Cinema', *Edebiyat: The Journal of Middle Eastern Literatures* 2, no. 11, 2000: 275–82.

Ghareeb, Shirin, 'An Overview of Arab Cinema', *Critique Journal for Critical Studies of the Middle East* 11, fall 1997: 119–27.

Ghazoul, Ferial J., 'Arab Cinematics: Toward the New and the Alternative', *Alif: Journal of Comparative Poetics* 15, 1995.

Malkmus, Lizbeth and Armes, Roy, *Arab and African Film Making*, London and New York: Zed Books, 1991.

n.a., 'Toward a Revolutionary Arab Cinema: An Interview with the Palestinian Cinema Association', *Cinéaste* 2, no. 6, 1974: 32.

Naaman, Dorit, 'Middle Eastern Media Arts: An Introduction', *Framework* 2, no. 43, 2002: 5–13.

Sadoul, Georges, *The Cinema in the Arab Countries*, Beirut: Interarab Centre of Cinema and Television, 1966.

Shafik, Viola, *Arab Cinema: History and Cultural Identity*, Cairo: The American University in Cairo Press, 1998.

——'Class Difference, Nation and Subjectivity: Two Egyptian Documentaries', *Framework* 2, no. 43, 2002: 104–16.

Sherzer, Dina (ed.), *Cinema, Colonialism, Postcolonialism: Perspectives from the French and Francophone Worlds*, Austin, TX: University of Texas Press, 1996.

Negro Soldier, The

(US, Heisler, 1944)

To depict The Negro Soldier as the dawn of African American consciousness-raising cinema may be something of an exaggeration, but the film is certainly a milestone in the treatment of blacks on screen. America's entry into World War II raised several race-related issues in acute form. The US Army was officially committed to racial segregation, a policy that was not to end until 1948—and then only by presidential decree. In the higher echelons of the military there was more than a little hostility to the idea of African Americans in combat roles; not least, there was their long-standing portrayal in the media as deferential servants or slow-moving, shiftless buffoons, but in every instance markedly inferior to whites.

The genesis of the project to rectify this situation emanated from Frank Capra and the Bureau of Motion Pictures, a branch of the Office of War Information (OWI). The idea was that a morale-boosting picture for and about the contributions of blacks in the armed forces would be ideal as an instrument of social engineering. It might enhance the image of the eight hundred and fifty thousand then in uniform and perhaps help undermine conventional stereotypical attitudes toward African Americans in general. Nevertheless, the project was undertaken with much bureaucratic trepidation. An OWI memorandum of 1942 cautioned against racial profiling, suggesting, for example, that the casting of black soldiers most Negroid in appearance be 'played down' and that reference to the race's supposed affinity for watermelon and fried pork be avoided. It was thought best to omit all mention of contentious issues such as slavery, emancipation, post-Reconstructionism, and black radical movements. After two false starts, a script by Carlton Moss, a black writer who had worked for the Federal Theater Project, was approved. Capra chose Stuart Heisler as director mostly on the strength of his film The Biscuit Eater, which he had made in Georgia with an interracial cast.

In their social construction of the milieu of The Negro Soldier, the filmmakers reflected dominant ideological attitudes and liberal values of the period, even if, from today's standpoint, these seem painfully tentative. The bulk of the first part is set in a church of improbable grandeur, all carved stone and soaring spires. The preacher, played by Moss himself, is clean-cut and mellow-voiced, and the attentive, all-black congregation is, without exception, well-dressed, with military uniforms, two-piece suits, and fur stoles much in evidence. In short, these are the kinds of African Americans whom most white audiences would find nonthreatening (neat and restrained). The intention of the film, in this segment, is to undermine the conventional portrait of uninhibited exuberance in blacks' practice of religion. The narrative is contained within the pastor's sermon as he guides his congregation through a condensed account of black participation in the nation's history from the American Revolution to the present, although mention of the Civil War is pointedly limited to a travelling shot of Lincoln's statue with a voice-over declaiming his definition of democracy from the Gettysburg Address. Stock footage from, among other fictional works, D.W. Griffith's America and John Ford's The Iron Horse have inserts of black actors in situ. Newsreel excerpts provide visuals for the story from the turn of the century to the present, ending with a staged version of black steward Dorie Miller's seizing a gun from the hands of a dying comrade and aiming it at Japanese planes during the raid, December 7, 1941, on Pearl Harbor, thus making him the first black in World War II to fire at the enemy. An epilogue to this catalogue of virtuous deeds is provided by a female parishioner reading from her son's letter. He relates how he has smoothly mastered basic training, encountered the work of black poet Langston Hughes, and won his Army commission. A gifted choir brings matters to a conclusion with spirited renditions of 'Onward, Christian Soldiers' and 'Joshua Fit' de Battle ob Jericho' as musical counterpoint to scenes of marching soldiers.

Apprehensions that some portions of The Negro Soldier might offend led to excisions in the prerelease print. No white men were to be seen under the command of black officers; the amount of combat footage involving African Americans was scaled back; and a brief shot of a black man receiving a massage from a white physiotherapist was removed. Contemporary reviewers tended to deplore the homogenised blandness of the outcome, a depoliticised discourse that studiously avoided racial issues then endemic in all branches of the US military.

Following the premiere of The Negro Soldier in April 1944 as Official Film 51, tepid exhibitor enthusiasm meant it received very limited theatrical exposure, playing in fewer than one cinema out of five in the United States, a ratio that was significantly lower in the Deep South. In this respect it performed more poorly than any other short subject released under government auspices during the war. However, its subsequent track record in the noncommercial market was considerably brighter. Several African American groups campaigned for a wider audience by way of distribution in 16mm format to public libraries and educational institutions overseas as well as at home. Those efforts were successful to the extent that the film was in constant demand even beyond the war's end.

It must be acknowledged that in The Negro Soldier there is the implicit assumption that to succeed, the race must accept and assimilate white, middle-class norms of social behaviour and attitude. This was, to be sure, a simplistic solution that ignored or consigned to irrelevancy the more deeply rooted issues of political and economic inequality. It was a legacy that vitiated the thrust of much of Hollywood's postwar 'race problem' films. Yet it is ironic that the officially segregated Army sanctioned a work, the thrust of which, however tentative, was toward racial integration; also, that the race's contribution to the war effort had been recognised was a source of pride for a segment of the population that had hitherto been ill-served by the motion picture.

JAMES M. SKINNER

The Negro Soldier (US, 1944). Produced by Frank Capra. Directed by Stuart Heisler. Script by Carlton Moss. Music score by Dimitri Tiomkin (choral items by Jester Hairston).

Further reading

Cripps, Thomas, *Slow Fade to Black: The Negro in American Film, 1900–942*, London: Oxford University Press, 1977.

Koppes, Clayton R. and Black, Gregory D., *Hollywood Goes to War: How Politics, Profits and Propaganda Shaped World War II Movies*, New York: The Free Press, 1987.

Leab, Daniel, *From Sambo to Superspade: The Black Experience in Motion Pictures*, Boston: Houghton Mifflin, 1975.

MacCann, Richard Dyer, *The People's Films: A Political History of U.S. Government Motion Pictures*, New York: Hastings House, 1973.

Rollins, Peter C. (ed.), *Hollywood as Historian: American Film in a Cultural Context*, Lexington, KY: University of Kentucky Press, 1983.

Short, K.R.M. (ed.), *Film and Radio Propaganda in World War II*, London: Croom Helm, 1983.

Winkler, Allan M., *The Politics of Propaganda: The Office of War Information, 1942–45*, New Haven, CT: Yale University Press, 1978.

Nestler, Peter

> Since I started to shoot films, I only tried to analyze the topics, which I had chosen from the bottom. I tried to find the shortest way for me and to show the most important aspects: to perceive, to recognize and to decide with others, this should be changed or that should be preserved or not be overlooked.
>
> (Nestler 1974)

This fundamental statement seems to summarize the approach of Peter Nestler's films perfectly. He was always interested in people's daily lives, their situation, and the changes in society reflected in their existence. His very personal films show us people who are oppressed by the capitalist entrepreneur or the fascist politician or who have had to fight against changes in their living conditions. These people resist, and this is an important aspect of his films, which are often very political. However, these stories do not seek to create a sensation, even though some of them are sensational. Instead he concentrates on everyday life, which is portrayed in strong images that stick in our minds. In his sometimes sparing use of images and sounds, we feel the concentration of arguments, which are investigated thoroughly. In his portraits of people, the concrete and the typical are tightly linked. The French filmmaker Jean-Marie Straub, who discovered him at a very early stage, is convinced that Peter Nestler is the most important filmmaker in Germany after 1945 because he is perhaps the only one 'who just shoots what is there and does not attempt to provoke the people' (Philipp 2001). His images often speak for themselves and are not explained in the commentary, which he frequently delivers himself.

With his debut film Am Siel/At the Sluice (1962), which he made in cooperation with the photographer Kurt Ulrich, he portrays a small village on the North Sea in a very poetic and essayistic way from the perspective of the sluice. Thus a confrontation between nature and civilization appears from the very beginning. The sluice comments on changes in the village and in traditions but also offers a much broader perspective, speaking as a voice of natural history. Aufsätze/Compositions (1963) portrays a small school in the Swiss mountains, where the pupils have to write a paper in class and tell about their weekday. The viewer can concentrate on this closed world in long shots, which fit perfectly with the voice of the child who is telling his story. This work is quite similar to his first film for the SDR, the Stuttgart public TV station. In Ödenwaldstetten (1964) he depicts changes in a small village in the Swabian mountains, which is on the one hand very traditional, with collective bread-baking and handling of farm animals; however, industrialization has also come to this small place, and most of the inhabitants work in the brewery or the cloth factory. Nestler's collage of statements, commentary, and images corresponds to that place. 'Rough is the landscape, rough are the people and rough is the voice of the commentator. The program does not tell anything new, but it tells it a new way. It was not a standard reportage, but the attempt to adapt the report totally to the object' (Hoffmann 1996: 206), as a film critic wrote in 1964. Nestler lived in Ödenwaldstetten for four weeks to observe the community before shooting for two weeks, mostly without sound. The montage concentrates on detailed shots, and long shots are very rare. The inhabitants tell their stories in their dialects, which are sometimes summarized in the commentary. The film generated considerable controversy, and its critical approach was attacked, especially from official quarters.

The next film for the SDR was Ein Arbeiterclub in Sheffield/A Working-Men's Club in Sheffield (1965), which is often discussed as one of his strongest films of that period, because it reflects the history and the current situation of the workers' movement so precisely. At the TV station it was seen critically and was broadcast only under the new title Menschen in Sheffield/People in Sheffield. 'Nestler['s work contrasts markedly with] everything made in documentaries during the last 25 years. His aesthetic not only stands in opposition to the classical cultural film [...] but also retreats from the new cinéma vérité of the '60s (with original sound and light, moveable cameras). His works have nothing in common with journalistic reports or features in television. Because of the economic chances of the documentary film, they could be produced for television, but only for public TV, because a commercial station never would take such a risk' (Roth 1990). This quality and individuality came at a price. Nestler had to finance his next film, Von Griechenland/From Greece

(1965), by himself, and it was not broadcast because some critics viewed it as communist propaganda.

Peter Nestler emigrated to Sweden, where after a year holding down different jobs, he was able to work on the youth and children's programme for Swedish public TV. Besides this he made films independently, which often were broadcast on Swedish or German television. They were frequently very political, but even in Sweden his films on neo-fascist tendencies in West Germany and on Chile were not broadcast. Besides making political films on Vietnam, Spain, and fascism in 1969, he and his wife Zsóka started a cycle on traditional craftsmanship, which tells the social history of work and production techniques and explores the relationship of the workers toward their craft. 'Interrelations are also typical for his films in the '70s, in which Nestler follows the history of specific products and production techniques like glass or paper, book printing or ore mines. His profound examinations in this multipart series are not free from stylistic adaptations from the classical cultural film, but are always told from the perspective of the craftsman and worker and not from [that of] the factory owner' (Roth 1982: 66). It is very typical of his films is that time periods mingle to build a bridge between historical events and the present. 'The films are working, so that no injustice is forgotten, they are a search for a direct way to make clear specific conditions of class and property; the dynamics of social contradictions are analysed by the visible and the dependence of politics on the economy is illustrated' (Becker 1984: E4). This is what gives the films of Peter Nestler such currency and timelessness.

KAY HOFFMANN

Biography

Born June 1, 1937, in Freiburg (Breisgau), Germany. After school he worked two years as a sailor and travelled around the world. Study of painting at the art academy in Munich; work as an extra in various German movies. 1961/2 debut film Am Siel/At the Sluice, which was followed by seven other films in Germany. Emigrated to Sweden in December 1966. 1968 commissioning editor at SVT2, mainly working on the children and youth programme. Besides that, he continuously produced independ films, often with his wife Zsóka. His filmography includes more than fifty shorts and documentaries, and he won many prizes at international film festivals.

Selected films

1962 Am Siel/At the Sluice: director, script, camera, editing (all with Kurt Ulrich), producer

1963 Aufsätze/Compositions: director, script (both in colloboration with Kurt Ulrich and Marianne Beutler), camera (with Kurt Ulrich), editor, producer

1964 Mühlheim (Ruhr): director, script (both with Reinald Schnell), camera, editing, producer

1964 Ödenwaldstetten: director, script, camera (all with Kurt Ulrich), editing

1965 Ein Arbeiterclub in Sheffield/A Working-Men's Club in Sheffield: director, script, camera (with Kurt Alvermann), editing

1965 Von Griechenland/About Greece: director, script (both with Reinald Schnell), editor, sound, speaker, producer

1967 I Ruhromradet/In the Ruhr Area: director, script (both in colloboration with Zsóka Nestler and Reinald Schnell), camera, editor (with Bengt G. Erikson)

1968 Greker i Sverige/Greeks in Sweden: director, script, editing

1969 Hur bygger man en orgel?/How Does One Build an Organ?: director, script (both in colloboration with Zsóka Nestler), camera, editing

1970 Varförär det krig?/Why War?: director, script (both in colloboration with Zsóka Nestler), camera, editing

1970 Att vara zigenare/Being a Gypsy: director, script (both in colloboration with Zsóka Nestler), camera, editing

1971 Får de komma igen? Om nyfascistiska tendenseri Västtyskland/Are They Allowed to Return? About Neo-fascist Tendencies in West Germany: director, script (both in colloboration with Zsóka Nestler), camera, editing

1972 Bilder från Vietnam/Pictures from Vietnam: director, script (both in colloboration with Zsóka Nestler), camera, editing

1973 Spanien!/Spain!: director, script (both in colloboration with Taisto Jalamo), camera, editing

1978 Något om USAs indianer/Something About the Indians in the USA: director, script, camera, editing
1982 Det är krig i Centralamerica/A War is Going on in Central America: director, script, editor
1988 Die Judengasse/The Jewish Lane: director, script, editing, sound, speaker
1991 Die Nordkalotte/The Northkalotte: director, script, editing
1997 Pachama—Unsere Erde/Pachama—Our Earth: director, script, speaker
2000 Flucht/Escape: director, script, sound
2002 Die Verwandlung des guten Nachbarn/The Metamorphosis of the Good Neighbour: director, script, DV-camera, sound
2003 Mit der Musik gross werden/Growing Up with Music: director, script (both in colloboration with Zsóka Nestler), DV-camera, sound (with Ferenc Gerendai), editor

Further reading

Becker, Jörg, 'Peter Nestler', in Hans Michael Bock (ed.), *CineGraph. Lexikon zum deutschsprachigen Film*, München, 1984.

Belz, Corinna, 'Die Filme Peter Nestlers im Kontext der zeitgenössischen Dokumentarfilmdiskussion', unpublished Master's degree work, Free University West Berlin, 1981.

Hoffmann, Kay, *Zeichen der Zeit. Zur Geschichte der Stuttgarter Schule*, Munich, 1996: 97–9, 206–13.

Huber, Jörg, 'Mit vielen sagen: Dieses gehört geändert', in *Cinema*, Zürich, Basel, Frankfurt: Territorien, 1986: 96–117.

——'Zur Filmarbeit von Peter Nestler', *Filmpodium* (Zeitschrift des Kommunalen Kino Zürich), March 1988.

Koch, Gertrud, 'Den Alltag sichtbar machen', *Frankfurter Rundschau*, January 15, 1974.

Nestler, Peter, 'Zusammenhänge', *Filmkritik* May 19, 1974: 228–35.

——'Arbeiten beim Fernsehen in Westdeutschland und Schweden. Ein Gespräch mit Gisela Tuchtenhagen, Klaus Wildenhahn und Angela Wittlich', *Filmkritik*, August 1975: 341–53.

——'Die gedehnte Demokratie', *Konkret*, June 1976: 30.

Netenjakop, Egon, 'Kunstvoller Dokumentarbericht', *Funk-Korrespondenz* 36, March 9, 1964.

Peters, Elke, '"Eine Art, dokumentarisch zu arbeiten'. Eine Annäherung an drei Filme von Peter Nestler. Mühlheim/Ruhr, Ein Arbeiterclub in Sheffield, Spanien!", unpublished Master's thesis, University Osnabrück, 1979.

Philipp, Claus, '"Ästhetik der Armut" und des Widerstands. Eine Höhepunkt: Tribute für Peter Nestler', *Der Standard*, October 10, 2001.

Pirschtat, Jutta (ed.), *Zeit für Mitteilungen. Peter Nestler*, Essen: Dokumentarist, 1991.

Roth, Wilhelm, *Der Dokumentarfilm seit 1960*, Munich, Lucerne, 1982: 63–6.

——'Peter Nestler. Scheitern und sich durchsetzen', in Cornelia Bolesch (ed.), *Dokumentarisches Fernsehen*, Munich, Leipzig, 1990: 128.

Scurla, Frank, 'Analytiker ohne Kompromisse', *Medium*, November 1973: 14–17.

New Earth

(The Netherlands, Ivens, 1933–4)

In 1929 Joris Ivens was commissioned to make a film by the Dutch Construction Workers' Union to celebrate their twenty-fifth anniversary. This became the film Wij Bouwen/We are Building (1929), on the different construction works in the Netherlands. One of its parts, 'Zuiderzee Works', dealt with the reclamation of land and the construction of polders. Joris Ivens extended this part and gave it a separate release in 1930 as Zuiderzee. This film was reworked several times during the following years as the reclamation and cultivation of the land progressed.

Nieuwe Gronden/New Earth can be regarded as the final version of Zuiderzee. The first two parts of the film are taken from earlier versions of Zuiderzee, whereas the last part consists of new material taken mainly from newsreels. Joris Ivens himself compared the continuity of the film with the structure of a joke: the first three quarters of the film works to a specific, expected climax, but then the story takes an unexpected turn (Ivens 1969).

In Nieuwe Gronden the first part shows the construction of the dykes and sluices and the reclamation of land. The second part shows the subsequent cultivation of the land to make it habitable. We see endless fields of grain, and the spectator would expect a happy ending, but suddenly this idyll is disrupted: the lush corn fields are intercut with hunger marches, riots, images of stock markets, and the destruction of crops in order to drive up the prices at those markets.

This is a sudden change not only in tone (even in literal tone, because Ivens's commentary voice changes radically) but also in style. The first two parts are taken from the earlier versions of Zuiderzee, which are all marked by a formalist style: well-composed images, aesthetic photography, informative commentary, and an elaborate editing. The last part, however, is mainly taken from different newsreels, which explains the variation in aesthetic and technical quality of these images. Furthermore, the excited and angry voice of Ivens—Nieuwe Gronden is one of the two films in which Ivens himself speaks the commentary text—is in stark contrast with the quiet and educational tone of the earlier parts of the film.

Nieuwe Gronden is known for its montage sequence of the closing of the dyke. Although Ivens did most of the filming in 1929 for the film Wij Bouwen, in the following years it was mainly his collaborators who continued filming: Joop Huisken, John Fernhout (later better known as John Ferno), and Helen van Dongen. Joris Ivens himself was usually working on other projects abroad, among them a film in the Soviet Union on the Komsomol: Pesn o Gerojach/Song of Heroes (1932). For the closing sequence he gave each of the camera operators a specific role. The land camera followed the struggle of the land against the sea. The sea camera identified itself with the waves and the strong currents that take away the clay that was dumped by men and their machines, who were followed by the third camera. The best qualities of Joris Ivens, Helen van Dongen, who did the editing, and Hanns Eisler, who composed the music, are combined, resulting in a haunting montage sequence of powerful images accompanied by stirring music.

Again, this high point of documentary aesthetics is in stark contrast with the conclusion of the film. The aesthetic and educational approach is abandoned and overtaken by the militant anticapitalist ending of the film: the work on the reclamation of the land is done, and while the abundant corn fields are waving to the camera, the workers who made this possible are unemployed and starving. Instead of feeding hungry people, the crops are used for speculation: they are dumped into the sea to make the prices go up. Ivens does not limit himself to the Dutch polders anymore but, rather, uses the images of the worldwide economic crisis to dismiss the global capitalist attitude of giving priority to stock markets instead of considering the poor and starving people around the world. The film ends with the ironic 'ballad of the sack dumpers', which is accompanied by images of men dumping sacks of grain into the sea. That it was actually a couple of Ivens's assistants who were dumping sacks of flour into the Seine river doesn't change the message. It does, however, illustrate Ivens's approach to documentary filmmaking amid his determination to be subjective and persuasive.

Given the changes in style and tone, Nieuwe Gronden can be considered a hybrid film. At the same time, it is emblematic of Ivens's work. This film marks a shift toward a more politically committed way of filmmaking, but Ivens always combined this with the aesthetic approach he applied from the beginning. His next film, Borinage, would lean more toward the militant approach, but subsequent films are much more balanced in their aesthetics and their political stance.

KEES BAKKER

See also: Ivens, Joris

Nieuwe Gronden/New Earth (The Netherlands, CAPI Amsterdam, 1933, 30 mins). Produced and directed by Joris Ivens. Script by Joris Ivens. Cinematography by Joris Ivens, Joop Huisken, Helen van Dongen, Eli Lotar, and John Fernhout. Edited by Joris Ivens and Helen van Dongen. Sound edited by Helen van Dongen. Music by Hanns Eisler. Commentary written and spoken by Joris Ivens. Ballad written by Iulian Arendt, sung by Jan van den Broek.

Further reading

Bakker, Kees (ed.), *Joris Ivens and the Documentary Context*, Amsterdam: Amsterdam University Press, 1999.

Delmar, Rosalind, *Joris Ivens, 50 Years of Film-making*, London: British Film Institute, 1979.

Ivens, Joris, *The Camera and I*, Berlin: Seven Seas Books, 1969.

Ivens, Joris and Destanque, Robert, *Joris Ivens ou la mémoire d'un regard*, Paris: Editions BFB, 1982.

Schoots, Hans, *Living Dangerously: A Biography of Joris Ivens*, Amsterdam: Amsterdam University Press, 2000.

Waugh, Thomas, *Joris Ivens and the Evolution of the Radical Documentary 1926–46*, PhD dissertation, Columbia University, 1981.

Night and Fog

(France, Resnais, 1955)

One of the earliest films on the subject, Alain Resnais's Night and Fog (Nuit et brouillard) is considered to be among the most powerful films about the concentration camps of Nazi Germany. As a documentary, it treads on novel ground, and its unusual use of structure, music, and imagery is as original today as it was in 1955.

The establishing shot of Nuit et brouillard presents a green field under a dark, heavy sky. The camera then moves slowly down to reveal barbed wire. This movement is repeated twice more, always with a camera that presents the scenic view first and then pulls back in order to reveal the fencing around a camp. In the last movement, the camera moves directly into the camp. These scenes are accompanied by a subtle, rhythmic drum and the light-hearted melody of a flute, along with a voice-over informing the audience that 'Even a quiet country scene … even a field with crops harvested and crows flying … even a road with cars and people passing … even a village fair may lead directly to a concentration camp'.

In this first sequence, the film introduces some of its key concerns: first, the reality of the concentration camps existed side by side with the reality of beautiful, tranquil landscapes and that—no matter how unimaginable—they belong to the same universe. Second, anything—including serene villages and fields—might not be what it seems at first glance. Third, the past is contained in the present, and it can be and must be uncovered in order to keep the memory alive, even if all that remains are scattered and fragile traces—the brick walls, the crematoria, the photographs, the imagination. Fourth, the film itself fails to describe the full dimension of the events. Finally, what happened in the concentration camps is not an isolated event of only one time and one place.

The Comité d'Histoire de la Déportation de la Seconde Guerre Mondiale commissioned Nuit et brouillard in 1955 to mark the tenth anniversary of the liberation of the concentration camps by Allied forces and to make the history of the concentration camps of World War II more broadly accessible. Alan Resnais, whose work displays a preoccupation with war, with time, and with memory and forgetting, and who was already a well-known filmmaker, at first declined to make the film. His concern was that only a survivor and someone who had been to the camps could possibly create a film that would be able to represent the 'univers concentrationnaire' authentically. The solution was found in Resnais's collaboration with Jean Cayrol, a poet and novelist and a survivor of the Mauthausen concentration camp, who would write the commentary of the film. The third collaborator was Hanns Eisler, a composer and collaborator of Bertolt Brecht and himself a refugee from Nazi Germany. The collaboration of Resnais, Cayrol, and Eisner resulted in a rich documentary with innovative uses of imagery, text, and music.

The imagery in Nuit et brouillard—the title evokes both Hitler's 'Night and Fog Decree' (Nacht-und-Nebel-Erlass) and a collection of poems by Jean Cayrol—comprises both new recordings and historical footage. These two types of film material are used alternately and signify two different time lines, which become more and more intertwined as the film proceeds. Although the first cuts from historical to contemporary footage might still take the audience by surprise, Resnais's montage often matches images with similar structures and angles in order to create a careful interweaving of the two types of images. For example, a camera travels past rows and rows of barbed wire fences and cuts to a camera traveling past rows of marching soldiers. Or a train full of people leaves the station, followed by a cut to the camera traveling along train tracks overgrown with grass.

The first set of images consists entirely of black-and-white archival film and photo footage (taken by both the Nazis and the Allies) and includes a minor scene from Leni Riefenstahl's 1934 propaganda documentary Triumph des Willens/Triumph of the Will about the Nazi Party rally in Nuremberg. It covers chronologically the rise of Nazism, the emergence of the concentration and extermination camps, the trains and deportations and the suffering in the camps, right until after the war when the perpetrators declare their innocence. The ordering of the material is not only chronological in the larger historical sense but also reconstructs the hypothetical journey of a deported person. The close-up photograph of the terror-widened eyes of a man upon his arrival at a camp reinforces this effect, as does the fact that once inside the camp, the camera never leaves it again. The result for the audience is a subtle identification with a deported person.

The second set of images used in Nuit et brouillard consists of contemporary footage from 1955, only ten years later than the black-and-white footage. These images of the decayed concentration camps of Auschwitz and Madjanek in Poland are shot entirely in color. The mixing of black-and-white and color in a single film was a formal innovation for documentary at the time, and its effect has lost none of its power since.

Whereas the black-and-white footage of the past chronicles historical events and includes photographic and filmic images of the victims as well as of the perpetrators, the color images of the present are produced by an investigative, subjective, and perpetually moving camera: 'No footstep is heard but our own.' The tracking camera follows closely the train tracks to the camp and then continues to scrutinize the remaining buildings, inside and outside, of the former campsite, as if the camera is looking for something. 'Today there is sunlight on those lines. We follow them slowly, seeing what? Traces of bodies that fell out when the cars were opened?' The restless camera strives to discover traces of the monumental. The assumption is that the violent death of millions of people must have left traces other than a few badly maintained buildings: 'The only traces now, if you know what they are, are on the ceiling,' the commentary informs the viewer when the camera glides through the fake shower rooms, the gas chambers. The camera's movement through the camps becomes a journey back in time, and architectural details of the campsite—a brick wall, a window, a room—trigger images of the past. It is in that gap between contemporary imagery and a voice-over imagining the past that the imagination of the audience is most active in searching for their own images of what it might have been like. When we look at contemporary images of the camps—a row of bunk beds or latrines—while at the same time listening to descriptions of the past, the past is pulled closer into the present and, by extension, closer to the viewer.

In its concern with what can and what cannot be represented, Nuit et brouillard touches on a key dilemma of art that treats 'the unimaginable'. The paradox of the impossibility of adequately representing the bureaucratic preparation and execution of millions of people in gas chambers on the one hand, and the need to bear witness on the other, also leaves its marks in this documentary. The narration faces this dilemma pointedly and on various levels. There is, for example, the use that the film makes of footage produced by the Nazis. Because there are few images of life inside the camps other than Nazi material, the perpetrators' material has a privileged position in the narration of the events. Where images are missing, contemporary images and the commentary strive to fill the gap. Additionally, there is the voice of the narrator, which at times breaks off or pauses and at other times does not finish a sentence at all, unable to find language to articulate the horror: 'With the bodies … but words fail … with the bodies, they tried to make soap. As for the skin … ' And finally, there is the commentary itself, which admits that 'no image, no description can capture their true dimension of constant fear'.

A novelist and poet and a survivor of the Mauthausen concentration camp, Jean Cayrol, wrote the text for Nuit et brouillard. Cayrol, who was to collaborate with Resnais again for Muriel (1963) a few years later, created a text that is precise, pragmatic, and poetic. The text, read by actor Michel Bouquet, at times sounds so laconic and so emotionally restrained as to almost appear comical. In one scene, for example, different concentration camp styles are described as though they were pieces in a design show. The effect of a voice and a text that does not sentimentalize the tragedy of the events, however, is to distance the viewer, forcing more of an intellectual than an emotional response. The more poetic parts of the text emerge when Cayrol uses metaphors and metonyms: 'death makes his first pick … the second one is made on arrival in the night and fog'. Strikingly, Resnais and Cayrol avoid assigning specific guilt to a nation, referring instead to Nazi Germany as 'the machine'. Even more remarkable is the fact that the film makes no specific reference to the Holocaust—in the sense of the extermination of Jewish people—and makes few references to the Jews as specific victims. Once we see the Star of David sewed onto a camp inmate's jacket, but the four victims that the film names are chosen to illustrate the diversity of the victims: 'Burger, a German workman, Stern, a Jewish student in Amsterdam, Schmulski, a shopkeeper in Krakow, Annette, a schoolgirl in Bordeaux'. In addition, the commentary twice mentions the number of nine million dead, which, because it includes the non-Jewish people who died in the camps, exceeds the commonly accepted number of Holocaust victims by three million.

One reason for this may be that Jean Cayrol chose not to focus on the Jewish victims of the camps exclusively because he himself, a camp survivor whose brother had died in Oranienburg, was a Catholic. However, Cayrol and Resnais seem to be interested in yet another point: that what happened is a tragedy of unimaginable dimensions, and that the tragedy does not depend on who was killed but only on the fact that they were killed and how they were killed. The camps did not happen outside of history. They could happen again, in another place and another time: 'who watches to warn of new executioners? Do they really look that different from us?'

The third component of the film is Eisler's musical score. Eisler, one of the inventors of twelve-tone music, had been a close collaborator of Bertolt Brecht and had already composed the music for Jacques Feyder's Le grand jeu (France, 1933) and Fritz Lang's Hangmen Also Die (USA, 1942).

Eisler's musical score for Nuit et brouillard consists of two main themes played alternately. First, there is an almost sentimental melody, played by soft violins and flutes and, at times, trumpets. Then there is a more piercing, tense melody, carried by a violin's pizzicati and staccati strokes and, at times, a trumpet and a dissonant-sounding piano. One of the characteristics of Eisler's score is its constant shifting from one theme to the next and its constant changes in rhythm and pace. Often, the effect is jarring. In one scene the images show the books in which the names of the dead, as the commentary tells us, have been crossed out, while the music plays a lighthearted, almost cheerful tune. It might in fact be such variations in the music, as well as its driving pace, that carry the audience through the film and particularly through the last third, which presents the film's most brutal images. As with the voice-over, the use of music (especially its more cheerful parts) generates an alienating effect, which ultimately serves to force the audience to engage intellectually with the horror of the concentration camps.

JACOBIA DAHM

See also: Resnais, Alain

Nuit et brouillard/Night and Fog (France, 1955, 31 mins). Directed by Alain Resnais. Assistant director: André Heinrich, Jean-Charles Lauthe, and Chris Marker. Production by Philippe Lifchitz and Anatole Dauman of Argos, and Samy Halfon of Como Films. Production director: Edouard Muszaka. Cinematography by Ghislain Cloquet and Sacha Vierny (assistant). Editing: Henri Colpi and Jasmine Chasney. Editing assistant: Anne Sarraute. Special Effects: Henry Ferraud. Musical director: Georges Delerue. Music: Hanns Eisler. Commentary by Jean Cayrol. Voice by Michel Bouquet (English version: Alesander Allan, German version: Paul Celan). Historical advisors: Henri Michel and Olga Wormser. Filmed in Auschwitz and Madjanek, Poland.

Further reading

Armes, Roy, *The Cinema of Alain Resnais*, London: A. Zwemmer Ltd, and New York: A.S. Barnes & Co., 1968.

Avisar, Ilan, *Screening the Holocaust: Cinema's Images of the Unimaginable*, Bloomington, IN and Indianapolis, IN: Indiana University Press, 1988.

Barnouw, Erik, *Documentary: A History of the Non-Fiction Film*, New York: Oxford University Press, 1993.

Colombat, André Pierre, *The Holocaust in French Film*, Filmmakers No. 33, London and Metuchen, NJ: The Scarecrow Press, 1993.

Insdorf, Annette, *Indelible Shadows: Film and the Holocaust*, Cambridge Studies in Film, with a foreword by Elie Wiesel, third edn, Cambridge: Cambridge University Press, [1983] 1989.

Jacobsen, Wolfgang, *et al.*, *Alain Resnais*, Munich: Hanser Verlag, 1990.

LaCapra, Dominick, *Representing the Holocaust: History, Theory, Trauma*, Ithaca, NY: Cornell University Press, 1994.

Monaco, James, *Alain Resnais: The Role of Imagination*, London: Secker and Warburg, and New York: Oxford University Press, 1978.

Raskin, Richard, *Nuit et Brouillard: On the Making, Reception and Functions of a Major Documentary Film*, Aarhus: Aarhus University Press, 1987.

Rothman, William, 'Night and Fog', in *Documentary Film Classics*, Cambridge: Cambridge University Press, 1997.

Ward, John, *Alain Resnais or The Theme of Time*, London: Secker and Warburg, in association with the British Film Institute, 1968.

Warren, Charles (ed.), *Beyond Document: Essays on Nonfiction Film*, Hanover, NH and London: Wesleyan University Press, 1996.

Night Mail

(UK, Watt, Wright, 1936)

Night Mail was one of the most critically acclaimed films to be produced within the British documentary film movement of the 1930s. It was also one of the most commercially successful, and it remains, even today, the film most commonly identified with the movement. By 1936, when Night Mail appeared, film output at the General Post Office (GPO) Film Unit was divided between the production of relatively routine films that promoted post office services and procedures and the production of more important films that experimented with the use of sound, visual style, narrative, and editing technique. Night Mail falls into the latter of these two categories.

Night Mail was the product of collaborative, rather than individual, authorship. Although it was primarily directed by Harry Watt, Basil Wright developed the script and had overall production responsibility for the project. The resulting film was also edited by Wright and Alberto Cavalcanti. John Grierson and Stuart Legg were involved in its production. The music score was arranged by Benjamin Britten and Cavalcanti, and the rhyming verse used in the film, which was spoken by Grierson, was written by W.H. Auden. Auden was also appointed assistant director for the film. This model of team authorship was promoted at the time by Grierson as a means of developing a variety of filmmaking skills throughout his young team. However, it proved to be a source of later friction as various individuals involved in the making of Night Mail put forward competing claims for the character and quality of their contribution to the film. Cavalcanti, in particular, felt that his own crucial contribution to Night Mail had been seriously undervalued.

Night Mail is an account of the operation, over the course of a single day and night, of the Royal Mail train delivery service. It shows the various stages and procedures of that operation and interactions between workers and management. The film begins with a voice-over commentary describing how the mail is made ready and collected for transit. Then, as the train proceeds along the course of its journey, we are shown the various regional railway stations at which it collects and deposits mail. Inside the train the process of sorting goes on, and we see procedures such as the pick-up of mailbags at high speed. As the train nears its destination there is a sequence—the best-known in the film—in which the spoken verse of W.H. Auden and the music of Benjamin Britten are superimposed over montage images of racing train wheels. Finally, an emotive voice-over by Grierson emphasizes the importance of the mail to national communication.

Although the narrative architecture of Night Mail is concerned with issues of national communication and integration, the thematic centre of the film is more closely linked to representations of the regional environment. For example, the railway and mail service are represented as a set of institutional practices closely associated with traditional, provincial, and regional milieux. This elevation of the regional and indigenous above the national is further reinforced by the portrayal of the railway as separate from the metropolitan environment, and little attempt is made to link the railway and its workers with the city. Night Mail also channels representations of modern technology and institutional practice away from an account of the industry and organization of postal delivery, and into an imagistic study of the train as a powerful symbol of modernity, in its natural element speeding freely into the countryside, away from the dark city stations.

Night Mail also illustrates the existence of an underlying contradiction within Grierson's theory of documentary film. Grierson had argued that documentary should both provide substantial information about social practices, and use innovative, thematic, and stylistic technique to achieve that end. However, in a film such as Night Mail, this double imperative leads, on the one hand, to the inclusion of some relatively pedestrian descriptive sequences, and, on the other, to sequences that are far more aesthetically significant. Furthermore, although a concern with the relationship among the rural, technology, and nature lies at the heart of Night Mail, this relatively abstract, symbolic thematic concern fits uneasily with the need to describe the operation and function of routine institutional practices. As a consequence, although Night Mail contains some strikingly lyrical shots of the train traversing open moorland, and one particularly celebrated modernist montage sequence, the main body of the narrative, and much of the photography, is handled in a fairly prosaic and unoriginal manner.

In fact, Night Mail is probably most renowned for the sequence referred to above, in which the poetry of Auden and the music of Britten are superimposed over a montage of images of speeding train wheels. The origin of this sequence lies, ultimately, in Cavalcanti's interest in the creative conjunction of sound and image. Cavalcanti had been experimenting with the relationship between sound and image since the early 1930s, and his influence in this respect can be seen in films such as Pett and Pott (1934), The Song of Ceylon (1934), and Coal Face (1935), all of which were made within the documentary film movement. Coal Face, in particular, on which Cavalcanti also worked alongside Auden and Britten, contains a number of modernist stylistic techniques that were later to be more fully developed in Night Mail.

Night Mail is, ultimately, an uneven film that lacks the stylistic and symbolic potency of earlier films made within the documentary film movement, such as Drifters and The Song of Ceylon. In these films, the ambitious attempt to combine a depiction of provincial, indigenous regionalism, and national-institutional subject matter, with symbolic, 'imagist' technique, is achieved successfully. However, this is not the case with Night Mail, which remains a film of interesting sequences, rather than a fully realized and unified work. Despite this, Night Mail is one of the best-known films to emerge from the British documentary film movement, and it continues to play a role in introducing scholars to the ideas and work of the movement.

IAN AITKEN

See also: Cavalcanti, Alberto; Coal Face; Grierson, John; Jennings, Humphrey; Legg, Stuart; Watt, Harry; Wright, Basil

Night Mail (UK, GPO Film Unit, 1936, 24 mins). Distributed by Associated British Film Producers. Produced by John Grierson, Alberto Cavalcanti, and Basil Wright. Directed by Harry Watt, additional direction by Basil Wright. Shooting script by Basil Wright. Cinematography by Chick Fowle, Pat Jackson, and Jonah Jones. Assistant direction and verse by W.H. Auden. Music by Benjamin Britten. Edited by Alberto Cavalcanti, Humphrey Jennings, and Basil Wright. Sound directed by Cavalcanti. Commentary by Stuart Legg and John Grierson. Filmed in London, Crewe, Glasgow, Edinburgh, and Dumfries.

Further reading

Aitken, Ian, *Film and Reform*, London: Routledge, 1990.

——*The Documentary Film Movement: An Anthology*, Edinburgh: Edinburgh University Press, 1998.

——*Alberto Cavalcanti: Realism, Surrealism and National Cinemas*, London: Flicks Books, 2000.

Ellis, Jack C., *John Grierson*, Carbondale, IL: Southern Illinois University Press, 2000.

Hardy, Forsyth, *John Grierson: A Documentary Biography*, London: Faber, 1979.

Sussex, Elizabeth, *The Rise and Fall of British Documentary*, Berkeley, CA: University of California Press, 1975.

Now

(Cuba, Alvarez, 1965)

Now is a film to a song; it consists of seven minutes of photographs and archive footage of racism and civil rights protests in the United States, a kind of political music video *avant la lettre*. Using for the soundtrack a protest song by Lena Horne that had been banned in the United States, Santiago Alvarez constructs a powerful collage on racial discrimination in the United States, which he had observed during a visit many years before, on a trip from Florida, through the Deep South, and up to New York. The pre-title sequence establishes the film's ironic tone by juxtaposing shots of racist incidents in California in August 1965 and a photograph of President Johnson meeting with a group of blacks under the leadership of Martin Luther King (whom Alvarez was to eulogise on film three years later, after his assassination, in LBJ).

This short film essay is impressive not only for the resourcefulness with which it uses its found materials, including pirated newsreel, but also for the syncopation of the editing, which intensifies the insistence of the song and leads up to its militant ending more effectively than slavishly

Figure 12 Now, 1965 (Courtesy of the British Film Institute)

following the music's surface beat. The rousing tune of the song is the well-known Hebrew dance 'Hava Nagila', which is associated with the pioneering period of Zionism and thus carried antifascist connotations that Lena Horne and Alvarez are both mobilising. The film quickly acquired the reputation of being a work of great and forceful originality and made Alvarez a director to be watched.

MICHAEL CHANAN

Now (Cuba, 1965, 7 mins black and white). Directed by Santiago Alvarez.

Obomsawin, Alanis

Alanis Obomsawin's films have documented the historical and contemporary struggles of the Inuit, Métis, Cree, Mohawk, Ojibway, and Mi'gmaq peoples. Her films, all made at the National Film Board, grew out of a first career as a songwriter, storyteller, and educator, and from her lifelong commitment to political activism on behalf of Canadian first nations peoples. At their most fundamental level, Obomsawin's films have given native peoples an opportunity to be heard in a number of poignant recordings of their experience. Christmas at Moose Factory (1971) used children's drawings to evoke life in an isolated northern community. Mother of Many Children (1977) is composed of interviews with women from many groups to paint a composite portrait of native matriarchy. The text of Richard Cardinal: Cry from the Diary of a Métis Child (1986) was taken from the words of a seventeen-year-old boy who committed suicide after a short lifetime in institutions and foster homes.

In many of her films, Obomsawin (also known as Kolilawato) herself is a major presence, adopting the style of the storyteller, to present not simply the immediate subject before her but also the broader contexts of native experience that have shaped it. She speaks calmly and often with great sadness. As Pick writes, 'Her work demystifies notions of disinterested observation in cinema direct by inscribing her presence in the film, as narrator and subject. In her hands, documentary practice becomes a rhetorical intervention that places the enabling subject at the centre of discourse' (Pick 1999: 77). It is in this mode that Obomsawin's film Poundmaker's Lodge: A Healing Place (1987) documents life inside a native-run treatment centre for drug and alcohol abuse, while arguing that the problem itself is the inevitable product of a long history of cultural dispossession. She uses a similar approach in No Address (1988), a film focusing on the Montréal Native Friendship Centre, as a means of exploring the larger issue of displaced natives in urban centers.

If Obomsawin's work, as Jerry White suggests, has been to create an imagined native community (White 2002: 371), that work came to fruition after the 1990 Oka Crisis. Native attempts to prevent the appropriation of an ancient burial ground near Montréal ended in a shoot-out with Québec Police, followed by a seventy-eight-day standoff between armed natives and the Canadian Army, while other natives blocked a commuter bridge to Montréal. Obomsawin's response was four films. The first of these, Kanehsatake: 270 Years of Resistance (1993) interspersed Obomsawin's footage from behind the native lines with an historical essay tracing the crisis to the first treaties between the Oka natives and French settlers. My Name is Kahentiiosta (1995) is a portrait of an Oka protester held by authorities for refusing to identify herself by anything other than her native name, and Spudwrench—Kahnawake Man (1997) depicts a steelworker who found himself a warrior behind the barricades. Obomsawin's fourth Oka film, Rocks at Whisky Trench (2000), provides historical and social context for an incident in which angry Montréal suburbanites stoned a convoy of native women and children leaving the blockade.

In her 2002 film, Is the Crown at War with Us?, Obomsawin treats a 2000 dispute between Mi'gmaq fishermen in New Brunswick and

Canadian fishery officials attempting to abrogate their treaty rights.

SETH FELDMAN

Biography

Born August 31, 1932, in New Hampshire. Spent part of her childhood on the Abenaki first nations reserve near Sorel, Québec. She is a widely known native singer, songwriter, storyteller, and activist for native rights whose work was documented in Ron Kelly's film Alanis (1965). In 1967 hired as a consultant by the National Film Board (NFB), where, after preparing multimedia educational kits on native language and customs, began her career as a filmmaker with Christmas at Moose Factory in 1971. Her films are distributed widely by the NFB in Canada and abroad and have received more than thirty international awards. Has provided narration and music for other NFB work. Serves as an advisor for films on natives and women of color at the NFB and Canada Council. Inducted into the Order of Canada in 1983, and has received honorary degrees from Concordia University (1993), Carleton University (1994), and York University (1994).

Selected films

1971 Christmas at Moose Factory: director
1977 Amisk: director
1977 Mother of Many Children: director
1986 Richard Cardinal: Cry from the Diary of a Métis Child: director
1987 Poundmaker's Lodge: A Healing Place: director
1988 No Address: director
1993 Kanehsatake: 270 Years of Resistance: director
1995 My Name is Kahentiiosta: director
1997 Spudwrench—Kahnawake Man: director
2000 Rocks at Whisky Trench: director
2002 Is the Crown at War with Us?: director

Further reading

Alioff, Maurie and Schouten Levine, Susan, 'The Long Walk of Alanis Obomsawin', *Cinema Canada* 142, 1987: 10–15.

Doxtater, Mike, 'Alanis Obomsawin', *Native People* 12, 1979: 13.

Gittings, Christopher E., *Canadian National Cinema*, London: Routledge, 2002, pp.217–25.

Pick, Zuzana, 'Storytelling and Resistance: The Documentary Practice of Alanis Obomsawin', in Kay Armatage, Kass Banning and Brenda Longfellow (eds), *Gendering the Nation*, Toronto: University of Toronto Press, 1999: 76–93.

White, Jerry, 'Alanis Obomsawin, Documentary Form and the Canadian Nation(s)', in William Beard and Jerry White (eds), *North of Everything: English-Canadian Cinema Since 1980*, Edmonton: University of Alberta Press, 2002: 364–75.

Olympia

(Germany, Riefenstahl, 1938)

Olympia, Leni Riefenstahl's documentary on the Olympic Games held in Berlin, Germany, in 1936 creates a fusion of art film and sports documentary that no director since has achieved. The film has been hailed by some critics and film historians as a masterpiece. Others have condemned it as National Socialist propaganda. Both positions have validity, depending on one's point of departure when analyzing the film. Divorced from its Nazi context, the director's bravura style is equaled in few documentaries and could support any ideology in which physical strength plays an important role, but embedded in the political, historical context of the Third Reich, Riefenstahl's camera work, editing, lighting, and settings evoke images of power and sacrifice that are the hallmarks of a fascist aesthetic.

Riefenstahl herself was the most active champion of separating her films from the political, historical context of the Third Reich. The director never tired of insisting that her documentary Triumph des Willens/Triumph of the Will (1935) is not political in nature, except in the sense that it is a document of a National Socialist rally. In similar fashion, in interviews and print, she repeatedly argued that Olympia is not a documentation of Hitler's or the Nazi's Olympic Games, but a film about the Olympics, which happened to take place in Berlin that year. In a lengthy defense of her film before the Filmbewertungsstelle (Committee of Film Review) in 1958, in an attempt to get her film released for public showing in West Germany, Riefenstahl argued that 'until its premiere, no National Socialist official had seen any of the film', and that, moreover, 'the Olympic film had no scenes that glorified the National Socialist regime' (in Graham 1986: 280). Her supporters have echoed this defense, citing the film's emphasis on the victories of Jesse Owens, the African American athlete from the United States; the surprisingly few shots of Hitler, the Nazi flag, or other references to the Third Reich; and most of all the way in which the film elevates human effort, not German effort, through excellence in sport.

Detractors, of whom Susan Sontag is perhaps the most well known, use these same points to discredit the film. For example, the emphasis on physical beauty and performance sport suggests allegiance to the aesthetics of fascism, which she defines as 'situations of control, submissive behavior and extravagant effort'. The film's critics also emphasize that Olympia, as well as being an excellent sports film, was also a great public relations vehicle for the Third Reich at a time when the world was beginning to question internal politics in the country.

On the one hand, the politics of those who criticize or praise the film, as well as the politics of the film itself, influences their positions on Riefenstahl's Olympia. The harshest critics have been Americans, both those writing at the time of the film's release and postwar American critics. However, West German critics have also been disapproving, Ulrich Gregor and Karsten Witte being two of the most critical. Witte challenges Riefenstahl's claims that the film is politically neutral by pointing out the militaristic tone of the commentary as well as the chauvinistic tone of the film (Witte 1993: 131). Yet all commentators, regardless of their political leanings, tend to use phrases drawn from the lexicon of combat to announce sporting contests, and the English commentator is no less biased in his reporting of the English athletes than the German commentator is in his remarks about the Germans. The most favorable reviews came from contemporary critics in Germany, France, and Sweden. Finally, postwar film critics who focus on the film as film, not as historical

Figure 13 Olympiad (aka Olympia 1. Teil-Fest der Volker), 1938 (Courtesy of the Everett Collection)

document, tend to support Riefenstahl's claims of neutrality.

On the other hand, ambiguity originates in the nature of Olympia itself, for the film documents both the games and the setting for those games. Moreover, in both instances, Riefenstahl has shaped the raw material through placement of images and inclusion or exclusion of information.

Consisting of two parts, Fest der Völker/Festival of the People, and Fest der Schönheit/ Festival of Beauty, Riefenstahl's Olympia has three major themes: individual accomplishment in sports, the unifying power of athletic events, and Germany's place in the seemingly harmonious world of athletes. Through the artistry of her directing—camera work, editing, mise-en-scène, lighting, and music—she interprets sports competitions (whether contests of strength, skill, or endurance) as celebrations of physical beauty. Furthermore, she champions the accomplishments of the individual within the collective of high-performance athletics. Finally, she locates Berlin, Germany, within a community of nations tracing their origins back to ancient Greece. Thus, through the formal means already on display in Triumph des Willens, Riefenstahl transforms the expected content of a sports document (athletic events, athletes, crowds, victory and defeat) into a paean to sacrifice for an abstract ideal.

In its presentation of individual competitions, Olympia eschews political favoritism and avoids fascist aesthetics. Part 1, Fest der Völker, devotes over half of its nearly two hours to individual accomplishments from discus throwing to relay racing. Part 2, Fest der Schönheit, also devotes over half of its one-and-a-third hours to competition, from yacht racing to team sports events. In all of these events Riefenstahl focuses on the top athletes in the field, who more often than not come from nations other than Germany.

To ensure that events would be as exciting for viewers after the fact as for spectators at the games, Riefenstahl films from odd angles, from high above the event or trenches below the event, from under the water, and from cameras specifically constructed to race along on tracks beside the runners. To obtain optimal viewing position for events such as yacht racing, skulls, and diving, the director included footage from practice sessions, when cameras were allowed to intrude more on the space of the competition. In addition, she had some contests reenacted after the event to be sure that the winners are highlighted in the finished film.

In spite of her resorting to such cinematic tricks and deception, however, the sports information presented is free of ideology. At no time does Riefenstahl emphasize German athletes over the athletes of any other nation, except when they are the winners of an event. Furthermore, she showcases the individual events in which Jesse Owens excelled, thus ensuring the African American athlete a high profile in the finished documentary. The ten-minute section on the decathlon creates suspense by emphasizing the changing rankings of the top three participants, all Americans. For the victory ceremony in this contest, the film focuses on the US flag and America's anthem. In similar fashion, she showcases many of the winners of individual games, always highlighting the anthem and flag of the appropriate country, be it Great Britain, France, Finland, or Germany. Finally, Riefenstahl focuses attention on individual effort or team effort, whichever is relevant to the sport, without relegating the athlete and his or her accomplishment to a secondary position behind his or her nation. That is, the individual athlete wins, not the country that the athlete represents.

Besides documenting athletic ability and endurance, Olympia celebrates physical beauty through lighting, camera placement, and choice of faces and bodies. Moreover, it often places these beautiful images within a greater community of athletes. This is particularly evident in the nonathletic events and in those that are presented outside of a competitive narrative. Thus the opening of each of the individual films dwells on the perfect human form. Fest der Völker showcases the ideal beauty found in Greek sculptures of the human body, shots of individual statues dissolving into live human forms. In similar fashion, the first sequence of Fest der Schönheit devotes over five minutes—longer than the time allocated to some of the sporting events—to naked male athletes running through the woods, emerging from a lake, playing in a sauna, and relaxing on a deck of their Olympic village. Riefenstahl also focuses on physical form, rather than on the athletic event, in some of the sports competitions. In the javelin throw the camera stays on an individual athlete's form as he runs and releases the javelin, rather than following the object to see how far it has been thrown. She edits the five-hour pole vaulting event into ten minutes, filming the athletes from below against an ominous sky and from above, then finally filming the human forms in shadow. In both of these events, the individual contestants recede into the totality of the communal event. These sequences lend Olympia its undeniable beauty, but they also suggest Riefenstahl's acquiescence to her and the Nazis' cult of physical perfection as desirable for the community. Moreover, they support the claims of her detractors that the film glorifies physical strength and beauty to the exclusion of other human values and attributes.

Olympia's competitive and non-competitive footage when viewed within the film's historical context does indeed suggest an ideological purpose behind the documentary. The Nuremberg laws denying Jews their rightful citizenship in Germany were passed in 1935, turning official international public opinion against the country.

There was an unsuccessful attempt to withdraw the games from Berlin, which had been chosen to host the games before the Nazis assumed power. America threatened to boycott the Berlin Games because of Germany's racial policies. Seen from this historical perspective, even the neutral, non-objectionable elements of Olympia seem orchestrated to present a Germany that did not exist—one that did not practice anti-Semitism, welcomed black athletes, and believed in peace and harmony. In short, Olympia offers a picture of Germany quite different from that found in Triumph des Willens. Although both films present Germany as a peace-loving nation, Triumph des Willens situates the Third Reich within the country's Pan-German borders and emphasizes the country's link to its past. Moreover, it portrays the nation's growing nationalism as a source of power and pride. Olympia, on the other hand, locates Germany within the world of nations. Power and pride accrue to the community through the accomplishments of individuals.

The opening sequence of Fest der Völker suggests how much Riefenstahl intended the film to present Nazi Germany as heir to antiquity and guarantor of peace in central Europe. As the film begins, the camera lingers on the ruins of ancient Greece, panning slowly as stones give way to columns that give way to an entire structure, which dissolves into the Berlin stadium. Then, for the lighting of the torch, the film begins with an athlete in Greece who runs and passes the torch on to the next runner, and so on and on, in a sequence that takes viewers through all of Greece and Middle Europe until the flame reaches Berlin. The sequence, which takes twenty minutes, places Germany in an honored position, as heir to the ideals of ancient Greece, as a nation in the middle of Europe that desires to uphold those ideals.

Olympia closes with a three-minute ceremony of bells ringing, focusing until the end on the Olympic flame, whose rays form a sun that radiates over the screen as the last shot of the documentary. This close is preceded by perhaps the most famous sequence of the movie: a diving sequence almost five minutes long that supports both an apolitical and an ideological reading of the film. As the sequence begins, Riefenstahl chooses shots that focus on individual divers as they spring from the board, glide through the air, and enter the water. As it continues, the tempo increases so that the time between dives is reduced; simultaneously, less and less emphasis is placed on divers entering the water. Eventually the shots focus only on the start of the dive, as the athletes spring from the board and glide—even fly—through the air. In one instance, a reverse shot carries a diver first into the air then backwards so that he soars like a bird. Increasingly the divers are filmed from below, silhouetting their bodies against clouds in the sky. Finally, divers are filmed falling off the high platform singly and in twos, their arms outstretched as if falling on faith that they will be caught, as indeed the angle that highlights their silhouettes sailing through the sky suggests. In this sequence, as Riefenstahl's supporters might note, the individual event has been transformed into a display of abstract beauty, devoid of political or ideological intentions. Detractors, on the other hand, might say that the divers have been transfigured into objects or film props for illustrating the idea of sacrifice.

ROBERT C. REIMER

See also: Riefenstahl, Leni

Olympia (Germany, 1938, 201 mins). Distributed by Belle & Blade Studios. Produced by the International Olympic Committee, Olympia Film, and Tobis Filmkunst. Directed, written, produced, and edited by Leni Riefenstahl. Original music by Herbert Windt. Nonoriginal music by Richard Strauss.

Further reading

Berg-Pan, Renata, *Leni Riefenstahl*, Boston: Twayne Publishers, 1980.
Graham, Cooper C., *Leni Riefenstahl and Olympia*, Metuchen, NJ, and London: Scarecrow Press, 1986.
Hinton, David B., *The Films of Leni Riefenstahl*, Metuchen, NJ, and London: Scarecrow Press, 1978.
Hull, David Stewart, *Film in the Third Reich: A Study of the German Cinema 1933–45*, Berkeley, CA: University of California Press, 1969.
Infield, Glenn B., *Leni Riefenstahl: The Fallen Film Goddess*, New York: Thomas Y Crowell, 1976.
Kracauer, Siegfried, *From Caligari to Hitler: A Psychological Study of the German Film*, Princeton, NJ: Princeton University Press, 1947.
Mueller, Ray, *Die Macht der Bilder Leni Riefenstahls*, New York: Kino Video, 1993.
Schwartzman, Roy J., 'Racial Theory and Propaganda in Triumph of the Will', in Bonnie Braendlin and Hans Braendlin (eds), *Authority and Transgression in Literature and Film*, Gainesville, FL: University Press of Florida, 1996: 136–51.
Sontag, Susan, 'Fascinating Fascism', *New York Review of Books*, February 6, 1975: 23–5.
Witte, Karsten, 'Film im Nationalsozialismus: Blendung und Überblendung', in Wolfgang Jacobsen, Anton Kaes and Hans Helmut Prinzler (eds), *Geschichte des deutschen Films*, Stuttgart and Weimar: J.B. Metzler, 1993.

On the Bowery

(US, Rogosin, 1957)

On the Bowery followed the models and demonstrated the viability of a narrative documentary approach made evident in Robert Flaherty's Lousiana Story and Sidney Meyers's The Quiet One (both 1948). It was Lionel Rogosin's first film, financed with his own money (his father was a wealthy industrialist). The other crew members had had considerable experience: Richard Bagley was cinematographer on The Quiet One. Rogosin conceived of the idea for his film over several years of research on New York City's infamous skid row.

On the Bowery was an extraordinary breakthrough in a number of ways. Its subject matter—the ravages of alcohol on human life, the degradation of a derelict existence—had been used often enough in conventional fiction features. What was unusual here was the taking of the camera (mostly a 35mm Arriflex with a four-hundred-foot magazine) and tape recorder into the actual jungle of metropolitan life, which enabled a much closer look at this particular reality than audiences were used to.

This film was also different from conventional documentaries, especially in that it had a slight storyline and developed, to a limited degree, characters who interact with each other. Three men who play the main roles are followed; one of them in particular, an ex-lawyer who had been unable to cope with the pressures of his previous life, becomes the basis of the narrative structure.

The problems of making this kind of film, from a production standpoint, are, of course, enormous—human problems as well as technical problems. Not only are the filmmakers working in a situation that demands maximum tact and care, innumerable clearances, and cooperation that may or may not be volunteered, but they must also lead nonactors through performances, get them to deliver lines, and teach them to behave as though the camera were not there. The film was made just before the availability of the technology that would make possible what would become cinéma vérité and/or direct cinema. At the time, it seemed to many filmmakers and critics to open up a whole new production method and range of subject matter.

Veteran British documentarian Basil Wright wrote of it, 'On the Bowery is neither a propaganda film nor a piece of reportage. It is a film made from the inside, in the way Flaherty made Nanook and Moana[…] In the bars and on the sidewalks, the camera leans sympathetically across table or grating towards these men and women who have passed the point of no return, and have reached a hideous sort of happiness achieved at best by gin and whisky, and at worst (when purchasing power has gone) by a shared squeeze from a can of metal-polish' (*Sight and Sound*, Autumn 1956). On the Bowery received first prizes at the Venice International Film Festival and from the British Film Academy.

JACK C. ELLIS

See also: Rogosin, Lionel

On the Bowery (US, Lionel Rogosin in association with the other crew members credited, 1957, 65 mins). Distributed by Contemporary Films. Produced and directed by Lionel Rogosin. Written by Mark Sufrin. Cinematography by Richard Bagley. Edited by Carl Lerner. Filmed in New York City.

Ophüls, Marcel

Ophüls's style of documentary filmmaking represents in many ways a synthesis of two forms: the compilation film and cinéma vérité. The historical perspective of the compilation film, constructed through editing to form a type of nonfiction narrative, is combined with interview techniques in an effort to come to terms with a past event. This style is most evident in two of Ophüls's most famous works, The Sorrow and the Pity (1971) and Hotel Terminus: The Life and Times of Klaus Barbie (1988). Ophüls's style was influenced by the work of Emile de Antonio, as well as by the historical compilation films of television and the films of Jean Rouch. The documentarist also relied heavily on advances in technology that enabled him to go into the field to conduct interviews and use small film crews. Ophüls is very much representative of the documentary approach known as participatory or interactive, whereby the filmmaker is a presence in his or her work. This type of approach relies on the interview process to help reveal a kind of truth. When it is combined with archival historical film footage, it presents a selection and arrangement of material that often, in Ophüls's case, is juxtaposed to create an effect on the spectator. According to Bill Nichols, 'The filmmaker's felt presence as a center of attention for the social actors as well as the viewer leads to an emphasis on the act of gathering information or building knowledge, the process of social and historical interpretation, and the effect of the encounter between people and filmmakers when that experience may directly alter the lives of all involved' (Nichols 1991). This style was unique for its time and has influenced other documentary filmmakers, such as Peter Davis and Michael Moore.

Ophüls's worldview was shaped by several factors, including the political turmoil of the 1960s both in America and Europe, the culture shock of being a European émigré in Hollywood, and his father's filmmaking style and sensibilities. The chaotic events of the 1960s—political assassinations, the Vietnam War, and the student protest movement—set the tone for a questioning of authority, as well as the historical record of the past. The culture shock of being a European (German-French) in America allowed for a questioning of both cultural and familial values. The classic style of narrative filmmaking of both European and American cinema invited a questioning of those as well. His father's fluid camera technique and deliberate composition enabled viewers to become a part of the narrative, determining for themselves the 'truth' within a pseudo-realistic mise-en-scène. What Ophüls is able to do is to synthesize these influences into his own unique approach to documentary film.

The compilation film had become a mainstay of documentary filmmaking since the pioneering work of Soviet documentarist Esfir Shub. The use of archival footage to provide an historical account of events was a tool in such works as Louis de Rochemont's The March of Time and Frank Capra's Why We Fight series. It wasn't until the 1960s and the films of Emil de Antonio that the compilation film was used to critique the past rather than valorize it. De Antonio's Point of Order (1963) used archival television footage of the McCarthy-Army hearings as social and historical critique of the communist witch hunts of the 1950s. Although de Antonio does not use contemporary interviews in this film, he does use them in his subsequent work, providing, as Randolph Lewis has suggested, a 'dialectic between past and present' (Lewis 2000). This 'dialectic' is very much a part of the documentary approach of Marcel Ophüls.

The primary themes that underlie Ophüls's films are history and memory. In films such as The Sorrow and the Pity, Memory of Justice, Hotel Terminus: The Life and Times of Klaus Barbie, and Munich, or Peace in Our Time, the filmmaker concentrates on events of the past and how people remember them. Ophüls is concerned with perception and truth, and he focuses on historical events and people's perception of them. Ophüls often moves back and forth from the past (using newsreel footage) to the present (with contemporary interviews) in order to situate the perception of events being described. It is here that the influence not only of cinéma vérité (in the use of interviews) but also of broadcast journalism reportage is most apparent. The appearance of cinéma vérité in the 1960s with films such as Jean Rouch's Chronique d'un été/Chronicle of a Summer (1961) and the use of lightweight, portable equipment, allowed the filmmaker a more intimate access to subjects. Ophüls utilizes these innovations to enhance his ability to edit his found footage, complementing it with interviews to recollect the past, and in his juxtaposition of images come to terms with that past. Ophüls uses an interview technique that often catches his subjects off guard, but only after they have relaxed in the interview process. In this regard, Ophüls is very much a provocateur, who has an agenda all along but simply waits for the right moment to announce it. It is very much a controlled form of documentary in its reliance on editing. Ophüls's documentaries also concern national identity and question the perception of a single collective viewpoint.

The primary characteristics of Ophüls's style include the lack of voice-over narration, the use of archival footage juxtaposed with contemporary interviews, the use of nondiegetic music juxtaposed with both archival footage and interviews, an epic length, the presence of the filmmaker himself (within the interviews, or seen reflected in a mirror, or simply heard), and an often ironic tone that becomes noticeable during the course of the film. Although the compilation film itself used a voice-over narrator, Ophüls eschews this approach in favor of a journalistic interview technique that is revelatory. The director allows time for revelations to emerge and, during the editing process, juxtaposes archival footage with the interviews to create certain effects. Sometimes these effects are achieved by the use of feature film footage as well as music or songs to effect irony. Recordings of Maurice Chevalier, for instance, are used in certain parts of The Sorrow and the Pity to create not only nostalgia for the past, but also the devil-may-care attitude that Ophüls's film associates with Occupied France during World War II. Form follows function in Ophüls's films. Because Ophüls's primary interest is in the subjects of memory and history, historical recollection is part of the interview process. This historical memory is coupled with newsreel footage pertaining to the event itself. Any historical event is never merely one-sided, so the interview process must include a number of subjects. Ophüls could simply have made a compilation film from the archival footage itself, but instead, through interviews and their juxtaposition with filmic images of the past, he offers the viewer a perception of truth—or at least suggests a questioning of the historical record. The filmmaker's presence (more noticeable in Ophüls's later films, beginning with Hotel Terminus) provides additional insight into the recollection of events. The filmmaker essentially becomes not only a catalyst, but also a character, in the film's narrative: a searcher, as well as a researcher, for historical truth. Ophüls incorporates dozens of interviews in order to show the wide range of choices and recollections of a particular event. According to one critic, 'The brilliance of Ophuls's editing lies in its capacity to pose uncomfortable questions for the viewer—or, to put it another way, [in] its capacity to force the viewer into uncomfortable subject-positions in relation to the material […] Ophuls's editing obliges the viewer to ask, Whom do I believe and who do I think is lying? Whose ideas do I share? Whom do I identify with? Where are my loyalties?' (Suleiman 2002).

RONALD WILSON

See also: Sorrow and the Pity, The

Biography

Born in Frankfurt-am-Main on November 1, 1927. The only son of film director Max Ophüls and actress Hilde Wall. Became a French citizen in 1938, then an American citizen in 1950. He attended Hollywood High School and graduated in 1945. In 1946 he was in service with a theatrical unit of the US occupation forces in Japan. He furthered his education at Occidental College and then the University of California at Berkeley. Returning with his family to France in 1950, he attended the Sorbonne, where he studied philosophy. In 1951 he began to work in the French film industry as a third assistant director using the name Marcel Wall. He worked as an assistant to such directors as Julien Duvivier, John Huston, Anatole Litvak, and his own father, Max Ophüls. Between 1956 and 1959 he served as radio and TV story editor for Sudwestfunk, Baden-Baden, West Germany. He eventually debuted as a radio and stage director and also directed four productions for German television. Ophüls returned in 1960 to Paris, where he began to write and direct filmscripts, also contributing articles to *Cahiers du Cinéma*. In 1966 he worked for ORTF (French TV monopoly) as a reporter and director for news magazine features, and during this period Ophüls developed his interview technique. In 1967 he directed his first major historical documentary feature film, Munich, or Peace in Our Time, for ORTF: it was broadcast over two evenings. In the wake of the May 1968 uprisings he moved to Hamburg, where he became the senior story editor at NDR (German TV). In 1971 he directed The Sorrow and the Pity for German and Swiss TV. Between 1973 and 1974 he was the Senior Visting Fellow, Council of the Humanities, at Princeton University. From 1975 to 1978 Ophüls served as the staff producer at CBS News and then at ABC News. In 1979 he returned to Europe and resumed making television documentaries. Between 1980 and 1983 he contributed articles to various journals, including *American Film*, *Positif*, and *Les Nouvelles Littéraires*. Since 1995 he has lived in retirement in the south of France.

Selected films

1967 Munich, ou la paix pour cent ans/Munich, or Peace in Our Time: director

1969–71 Le Chagrin et la pitié/The Sorrow and the Pity: director, writer

1976 The Memory of Justice: director

1988 Hotel Terminus: The Life and Times of Klaus Barbie: director, writer

1992 Jours en Novembre—Voix et chemins/November Days: director

1994 Veillées d'armes/The Troubles We've Seen: A History of Journalism in Wartime: director

Further reading

Ciment, Michel, 'Joy to the World! An Interview with Marcel Ophuls', *American Film* XIII, 10, September, 1988.

Ellickson, Lee, 'The Troubles He's Seen: An Interview with Marcel Ophuls', *Cinéaste* 21, no. 3, summer 1995.

Greene, Naomi, 'La Vie en Rose: Images of the Occupation in French Cinema', in Lawrence D. Kristman (ed.), *Auschwitz and After: Race, Culture and the Jewish Question in France*, New York: Routledge, 1995.

Hoffman, Stanley, *Introduction to The Sorrow and the Pity: A Film by Marcel Ophuls*, New York: Outerbridge & Lazard, 1972.

Jacobsen, Kurt, 'Memories of Injustice: Marcel Ophuls' "Cinema of Conscience"', *Film Comment*, July–August, 1996.

James, Carol Plyley, 'Documentary & Allegory: History Moralized in Le Chagrin et la Pitié', *The French Review* LIX, no. 1, October 1985.

Lewis, Randolph, *Emile de Antonio: Radical Filmmaker in Cold War America*, Madison, WI: University of Wisconsin Press, 2000.

Nichols, Bill, *Representing Reality: Issues and Concepts in Documentary Film*, Bloomington, IN: Indiana University Press, 1991.

Suleiman, Susan Rubin, 'History, Memory, and Moral Judgement in Documentary Film: On Marcel Ophuls' Hotel Terminus', *Critical Inquiry* 28, winter 2002.

O'Rourke, Dennis

Dennis O'Rourke, a noted Australian documentary filmmaker with an established international reputation in Australia, Europe, and North America, has focused mainly on the dissonances between European and traditional cultures. His films are located in various Southwest Pacific cultures, including Australia, Papua New Guinea, and Micronesia. O'Rourke typically expresses his subject matter through his own strong ideological frames. In Yap … How Did You Know We'd Like TV? (1980), O'Rourke films the cultural impact of the United States' gratuitous introduction of television on the life ways of the Yapese people when Yap ceased to be a US trust territory. O'Rourke infuses local suspicion of the United States into Yap, hinting that the unasked-for television service, replete with commercials for Western-style processed foods and goods, was an act of US cultural imperialism designed to keep Yap within the American sphere of strategic influence.

O'Rourke theorises his reflexive documentary practice. For example, in making Cannibal Tours (1988), O'Rourke rejected 'the sanctimonious position of the documentary filmmaker as culture hero', because his project is 'to subvert the normal narrative expectations so that the documentary form can address the unquantifiable and the metaphysical' (O'Rourke 1989). The Western tourists of Cannibal Tours are 'representative of a particular development in Western culture—a high bourgeois value oriented system which has an ignorant relationship to the other cultures, especially black ones' (O'Rourke 1989). O'Rourke states that the tourists' cameras are an icon of preferring technical to cultural values, and by presenting the tourists' images of the Papua New Guineans, he forces the viewer to shift focus. By asking questions but offering no answers, Cannibal Tours 'is trying to make a window into the unfathomable'.

O'Rourke avoids the term documentary, preferring the term nonfiction film: 'the so-called documentary is dry, it's about facts, it's about Truth with a capital T. And I've always been interested in Emotion with a capital E' (Hawker 2001). After the making of the highly controversial The Good Woman of Bangkok (1991), for which O'Rourke lived with a Thai prostitute, Aoi, O'Rourke wrote:

> Always, for it to work, the filming process must be an ordeal of contact with perceived reality—I must place myself within the flux of what I am attempting to film in order to discover the authenticity of peoples and places, and to fix my emotional perspective within a social and political process, which is not academic. The process is empirical, emotional and instinctive. I always try not to be rational but instead to trust my intuition and my feelings. In fact, I think you have to be irrational, because when you try to be rational the true meaning and beauty of any moment or idea will escape you.
>
> (O'Rourke 2002: 1)

O'Rourke vehemently rejects as fantasy any idea that the documentary film can be some kind of pure and unproblematic representation of reality (O'Rourke 2002: 2). He derides documentary filmmakers whose approach to truth makes them implicitly the 'heroic protagonists' of their own films and the 'moral shield of the spectator'. He attacks the notion of the documentary as offering 'palatable truth' designed to make the audience feel good as 'part of an enlightened elite' (ibid). He attacks moralising critics whose frame of reference is journalistic news and current affairs programmes, which O'Rourke regards as 'the most crude form of storytelling that exists' (O'Rourke 2002: 5). His heresy, O'Rourke says, is his belief that truth is 'ultimate and undefinable' and 'messy and upsetting' (ibid). The Good Woman of Bangkok was meant to be 'a critique of prevailing notions of "higher claims to truth" in the documentary film genre' embedded in the term (O'Rourke 2002: 2).

O'Rourke contests the definition of documentary, describing the term as misleading and more acceptably used as an adjective. The documentary, he says, is an artefact, so he prefers the category documentary fiction film, which uses 'some of the techniques of the traditional documentary, but ignores and then subverts the naturally accepted implication of truth and meaning that these techniques foster' 'The authenticity of the film—its "truth"—is entirely subjective' (O'Rourke 2002: 4). This results in the challenge of representation, which is 'how to articulate the relationship of the subject to the author to the audience [...] In all my films, the observed reality—the subjective experience of observation—is coated with "re-description", which becomes another narrative and [...] more complex experience' (ibid). Re-description is a voyeuristic process that puts the viewer both inside and outside the frame simultaneously and introduces self-recognition and embarrassment, which O'Rourke sees as the true subject of the film (O'Rourke 2002: 5). For example, O'Rourke states that in The Good Woman of Bangkok, 'we can recognise the imperfections of the "film maker" character in his naïve, imperialistic and morally impossible stances—and we can recognise something about ourselves' (ibid). This self-recognition is painful for the professional critics who, in a 'post-religious world' of dogma and the drive 'to judge before we understand', recall Goddard's comment that 'critics are like soldiers who fire on their own men' (ibid). O'Rourke observes, 'I don't make the film, but the film makes me' (Sheffield International Documentary Festival 2001: 1). In The Good Woman O'Rourke hoped that, 'as with Brecht, the work would confront members of the audience with a vision of themselves, thus forcing the consideration of how personal sexuality affects our political and philosophical beliefs. We are all implicated in some way' (ibid).

For Cunnamulla (2000), which was his first film set in Australia and which resulted in legal action against O'Rourke in 2002 for deceptive and misleading conduct by two underage girls who appeared in the documentary, O'Rourke lived in the western Queensland rural town of Cunnamulla for nine months, establishing relationships with local people and then filming them. This was typically his 'intimate contract' with the people he wished to film that would demonstrate the fallacy of the subject/object dichotomy of the documentarist. O'Rourke was attracted to an Australian rural town as an expression of his disgust at what he saw as the marginalisation and neglect of country people by politicians and the elite metropolitan media. He said that he chose a Queensland town deliberately: 'I do believe there's something about Queensland [...] I can't pin it down, but as you cross the border, things turn gothic [...] something happens' (n.a. 2002).

BRUCE HORSFIELD

See also: Good Woman of Bangkok, The

Biography

Born in Brisbane in 1945. After travelling in the Outback, the Pacific Islands, and South-East Asia, taught himself photography and was a photojournalist before becoming a cinematographer for the Australian Broadcasting Commission. Lived for five years in the decolonising Papua New Guinea, working for the new government teaching documentary filmmaking to Papua New Guineans. Has won the American Film Festival Blue Ribbon Award, the Jury Prize at the Berlin Film Festival, the Eastman Kodak Award for Best Cinematography, the Director's Prize for Extraordinary Achievement at the Sundance Film Festival, and the Australian Film Institute's Byron Kennedy Award.

Selected films

1976 Yumi Yet—Independence for Papua New Guinea
1976 Ileksen—Politics in Papua New Guinea
1980 Yap ... How Did You Know We'd Like TV?
1982 The Shark Callers of Kontu
1984 Couldn't Be Fairer
1985 Half Life—A Parable for the Nuclear Age
1988 Cannibal Tours
1991 The Good Woman of Bangkok
1993 The Pagoda da Tia Beth
2000 Cunnamulla

Further reading

Hawker, Philippa, 'Inciting Indignation with a Capital I', www.theage.com.au, 2001.

n.a., 'Dennis O'Rourke: Australian Contemporary Filmmaker', (film), The Australian Film, Television and Radio School, Sydney, 1989.

n.a., 'O'Rourke, Dennis: Cunnamulla', *Urban Cinephile*, www.urbancinephile.com.au, May 25, 2002.

O'Rourke, Dennis, 'Documenting a Life—Documentary Fictions: Bibliography, Truth and Moral Lies', National Library of Australia, May 2002.

Sheffield International Documentary Festival, 'Dennis O'Rourke Masterclass: "I Don't Make the Film, But the Film Makes Me"', *Programme Schedule*, October 22–8, 2001, www.sidf.co.uk/festival01/programme/sessions/dennis_orourke.htm (accessed 24 May 2002).

Ottinger, Ulrike

For much of her career, Ulrike Ottinger focused on making fictional, feature-length films, the only notable exception being Berlin-Fieber, Happening für Ada (1973), a short documentary about the German artist Wolf Vostell. Although she is a major German filmmaker, Ottinger's documentaries are generally overlooked in contemporary documentary film studies.

The subject of her first lengthy documentary, China, der Alltag, die Künste (1985), is daily life in China. It was shot in the tradition of the travelog, as interpreted by Michelangelo Antonioni in the 1970s, while scouting locations for Johanna d'Arc of Mongolia (1988). Ottinger's conception of documentary film becomes apparent in the chronological structure of her itinerary, indicating her conviction that the camera should play the role of a central instrument of perception able to record the visible life of public spaces. The observing function of the camera is its primary function. The structure of Ottinger's documentary is based on following the traveller's route in long sequences, with linear editing.

Ottinger eschewed commentary, in keeping with her belief that the camera will record reality and that the documentary cannot presume to interpret or gloss that reality. Her approach to documentary filmmaking is to depict the world without embracing or suggesting any sort of personal or political context. The primary intrusions into an unmediated recording experience are the simple captions that Ottinger employs. However, in an attempt to maintain an unmediated experience, she does not use any interviews or footage external to the events at hand.

In keeping with Ottinger's method of radical empiricism, production is carried out cautiously and conservatively. Her films are shot by small crews. Ottinger herself frequently did the 16mm camera work.

In Taiga (1991–2), her documentary about the life of nomads in Mongolia, Ottinger's film-making aesthetic is consistently maintained over the course of five hundred and one minutes. She did the same in Countdown (1990), a three-hour documentary about the ten days in Berlin preceding the reunification of East and West Germany. Exil Shanghai (1997), two hundred and seventy-five minutes long and based on interviews, traces the lives of six Jewish emigrants who escaped from Hitler's Germany and Stalinist Russia to Shanghai. In this film Ottinger modified her style by editing a montage of historical print documents and photographs, combining this with what her travelling camera recorded in the contemporary Chinese city, and filming long takes in which she searches for the lost places of emigrant history. With Southeast Passage: A Journey to New Blank Spots on the European Map (2002), Ottinger returned to her concept of cross-country chronicle. In this examination of residents of Berlin, Istanbul, and Odessa—those on the edge of Europe, who had not benefited from the end of the Cold War—she used a digital camera for the first time.

ANNETTE DEEKEN

Biography

Born in Konstanz, Germany, on June 6, 1942. Studied art in Munich from 1959 to 1961, worked as artist (painting and photography) in Paris. Since 1973 living in Berlin, Germany. First film in 1972 Laokoon & Söhne. Founded her own film production company. Since 1978 photo exhibitions, radio plays, theater productions, and feature films, such as Madame X, Eine absolute Herrscherin (1977), and Freak Orlando (1981). 2002 Invitation to the world art exhibition Documenta 11, Kassel, Germany.

Selected films

1973 Berlin-Fieber, Happening für Ada
1985 China, der Alltag, die Künste
1990 Countdown
1991–2 Taiga
1997 Exil Shanghai
2002 Southeast Passage: A Journey to New Blank Spots on the European Map

Further reading

Deeken, Annette, *Ästhetik des Reisefilms*, Remscheid: Gardez-Verlag, 2004.

Freunde der Deutschen, Kinemathek e.V., *Ulrike Ottinger*, Berlin: Kinemathek, no. 86, 2001.

Ottinger, Ulrike, *Taiga. Eine Reise ins nördliche Land der Mongolen*, Berlin: Verlag Dirk Nishen, 1993.

Schöning, Jörg, 'Ulrike Ottinger: Filmemacherin', *Cinegraph: Lexikon zum deutschsprachigen Film, Lieferung*, no. 11, München, 1988.

P

Parer, Damien

Damien Parer is Australia's most respected war photographer. His 'moment' was World War II, when he filmed the experiences of the ordinary soldier close to or in contact with the enemy in North Africa, New Guinea, and the Southwest Pacific. He won Australia's first Academy Award for his Kokoda Front Line, documenting the grim jungle war against the Japanese in Papua New Guinea. Parer grew up during the Great Depression in the milieu of Australian Irish Catholic anti-British feeling and the ideological struggles in 1930s Europe, becoming a committed Catholic, political liberal, and social egalitarian. Both by temperament and as a keen member of the Catholic Campion Society, Parer was staunchly anticommunist, anti-Nazi, and antifascist, intensely patriotic, and, until he visited what was then Palestine in World War II, anti-Semitic (McDonald 1994: 42).

He was self-taught as a stills photographer, moving into cinematography as camera operator on the feature films of Australian director Charles Chauvel. Parer not only taught himself professional camera skills such as lighting, aperture setting, and selecting and framing the shot, but—unusual for an Australian professional photographer—he also evolved informed ideas about European film theory. Parer was a serious intellectual in his approach to film, and he studied foreign films such as Eisenstein's Battleship Potemkin and October. Parer also engaged critically with film theory debates of this period. For example, he disagreed with Pudovkin that the single shot and the single word are equivalent, and his main theoretic influence was Vladimir Nilsen's *The Cinema as Graphic Art*, which arose from the montage controversies in 1920s revolutionary Russia (McDonald 1994: 13–14). Parer agreed with Nilsen that technique without purpose was vacuous, and he shared Ruskin's conviction that 'art is the definition of an idea through a form', a dictum where form and idea coalesce (Brennan 1994: 47). Parer read avant-garde film journals addressing European and Russian film theory, and he was influenced by John Grierson, whose definition of documentary, 'the creative treatment of actuality', was displayed in Parer's workroom (McDonald 1994: 14). He became convinced of the central importance of narrative structuring in film, even in newsreels and stills news photographs.

Appointed as an official stills and movie war photographer in January 1940, Parer had already identified his mission: to apply his skills and theories to recording truths of the Australian soldier at war and to explain the war and its contexts to the Australian public and the world. At his best when applying the style of the pictorial and still photographers to film, he moved resolutely from one theater of war to another, always looking for opportunities to express truth as he saw it with artistry, freshness, and vitality. His training and commitment gave him a sense of compositional discipline and artistic orientation, even during the frequent unnerving moments when he was with troops under fire. He invariably sought a profound honesty and penetration below mere appearances, eschewing wherever possible simulations and reenactments and seeking pictures expressive of an Australian identity and self-definition that would enhance the national culture and self-reliance of what was then a minor British colony. Although there was clearly powerful war propaganda potential in his striking frontline material, Parer scorned what he regarded as the mere surface realities of propaganda footage, insisting on the transcendent value of the truthful pictorial statement. He was adept at filming soldiers—unnoticed by them—at their most intense moments of perception or reaction, but would not press them if they were reluctant to be filmed. Filming the soldier's spontaneous personal responses to his war experiences became an ideal that often drove Parer to position himself out in front of advancing soldiers to capture faces, eyes, and gestures. This insistence on a rear-facing camera position in 'no-man's-land' led directly to his death in 1944.

Although he was a noncombatant, Parer's stamina, professionalism, and empathy earned him the respect of fighting soldiers wherever he worked. He carried his cumbersome camera gear across the debilitating Kokoda Track in New Guinea, a gruelling system of high ridges, braving knee-deep mud, rain, cold, malaria, tropical ulcer, dysentery, and a host of diseases that drastically reduced in numbers whole fighting battalions. The gloomy jungle was useless for filming, and action shots were restricted to the jungle clearings. With film stock always in short supply, Parer carefully filmed the fighting and suffering around him, editing in camera and selecting his shots sparingly. He was technically proficient enough to maintain his cameras and to improvise when they broke down.

Parer's Papua New Guinea films were also driven by his deep concern that although the Japanese Army was on Australia's doorstep, the Australian people seemed to lack a sense of urgency about the war and were ignorant of the hardship their soldiers were undergoing in Papua New Guinea.

This concern gave his documentary aesthetic a further significance, and he sent back unsettling, disturbing footage of the chaos, confusion, mismanagement, official neglect, and exhausted soldiers during the Australian retreat from the Japanese along the Kokoda Track. However, despite the appalling conditions along Kokoda, and Parer's increasing fatigue, he kept firmly to his production ethic.

Parer's nationalism caused him to react against the public relations media material emanating from General Douglas McArthur's headquarters in Australia. Although Australian forces in New Guinea inflicted on the Japanese their first defeat of the war, McArthur continued to minimise Australian successes in his press releases, while inflating the achievements of American troops. Parer hoped that his coverage of Australians would correct this slight by giving the Australians their fair share of public recognition.

Parer's best-known war films include Sons of the Anzac (documentary), Assault on Salamaua, Bismarck Convoy Smashed, Kokoda Front Line, Men of Timor, Salamaua Frontline, and War on the Roof of New Guinea (newsreels).

BRUCE HORSFIELD

Biography

Born Melbourne, Australia, August 1, 1912, into a staunch Catholic family of Spanish ancestry. After school, became a highly skilled photographer before joining Charles Chauvel's movie production of Heritage as a camera assistant. Filmed several features before joining the Department of Commerce as a camera operator and stills photographer. With the outbreak of World War II in 1939, his department was absorbed by the Department of Information, and Parer became a war photographer of the Australian forces. From 1940 until late 1943 filmed Australian troops, often in fierce battles, in Palestine, North Africa, Greece, the Middle East, and Papua New Guinea. In 1943 Kokoda Front Line won an Academy Award for Parer and Ken Hall jointly. After a series of disagreements with management, resigned from the Department of Information and joined US Paramount News covering the American thrust through the Southwest Pacific in Tarawa, New Britain, the Admiralty Islands, Hollandia, and Guam. In September 1944 was killed by Japanese machine gun fire on Peleliu Island in the Palau Group.

Further reading

Brennan, Niall, *Damien Parer, Cameraman*, Melbourne: Melbourne University Press, 1994.

Brune, Peter and McDonald, Neil, *200 Shots: Damien Parer and George Silk with the Australians at War in New Guinea*, Sydney: Allen and Unwin, 1998.

The Chester Wilmot Files, Australian Archives (SP 300/4).

The Department of Information Files, Australian Archives (SP 109/1).

Legg, Frank, *The Eyes of Damien Parer*, Adelaide: Rigby Ltd, 1963.

McDonald, Neil, 'Damien Parer and Chester Wilmot at Tobruk', *Quadrant* 44, nos 7–8, July–August, 1986.

——*War Cameraman: The Story of Damien Parer*, The Parer Papers, Mitchell Library, Sydney (MLMSS 197/Melbourne: Lothian, 1994, 1–4).

Routt, William D., 'Review of Damien Parer: Cameraman by Niall Brennan and My Friend Parer by Maslyn Williams', *Metro* 101, 1995: 85–6.

Paris 1900

(France, Nicole Védrès, 1948)

Although rarely given more than a passing mention in surveys of French cinema and documentary film, Paris 1900 was in its time a much-loved popular success and a significant landmark in the development of the compilation film. Composed of footage drawn from over seven hundred actualités, newsreels, and fiction films from the 1900–14 period, the film offers a panorama of the events, pastimes, and personalities of Belle Epoque France. It is unashamedly rose-tinted in its nostalgic evocation of this lost epoch, and it is not difficult to imagine its appeal to French audiences still reeling from the impact of war and occupation. Yet it conveys, too, the potent and unexpected freshness of discovering a forgotten past preserved in celluloid. Much of the continuing fascination of Paris 1900 lies in seeing such legendary figures as Sarah Bernhardt, Auguste Renoir, and a young Maurice Chevalier captured on film (and on records), but the film also catches and reflects on the poignancy of contemporary celebrities who were not so well remembered by posterity.

Paris 1900 was the product of a collaborative effort. Its producer, Pierre Braunberger, had the original idea for the film before World War II. He wrote a complete treatment with Marc Allégret in 1941, while staying with Allégret in Cannes. Braunberger had originally approached Henri Langlois to plan Paris 1900, but he found that despite the latter's prodigious memory of films and their content, Langlois did not possess the necessary creative skills to shape the project. Upon returning to Paris after the war, Braunberger pursued his plans for Paris 1900, hiring Nicole Védrès to write the commentary and direct the film, and a young Alain Resnais as her assistant.

Braunberger claims that he and the editor Myriam Borsoutzky were the true directors of the film, creating together its overall shape and its key innovations in montage. Other commentators have given more weight to Védrès's input. Jay Leyda emphasises the importance of her rediscovery of early French cinema through Langlois's screenings at the Cinémathèque Française, and the extraordinary montage book of photographs, *Images du cinéma français* (1946), which she compiled in the wake of this experience—a work that anticipates the achievement of Paris 1900 in creating a persuasive formal and thematic cohesion out of radically disparate source materials.

Paris 1900 opens with actualité street scenes of Paris as a background to key events and icons heralding the new century: the Exposition Universelle, the Eiffel Tower, and the first métro. It ends in 1914 with the first mobilization and the affecting image of a troop train pulling away from the camera, packed with conscripts waving goodbye to the viewers. Between these two historical turning points, the film is organized into loose thematic clusters that compress and rearrange chronological events but are composed overall to convey a sense of change and historical momentum. One early sequence begins with a lighthearted survey of women's fashions in the 1900s, and then considers how the handicap of long skirts impeding women's participation in sport led to the 'scandal' of women wearing trousers. Symbolically empowered by the new garments, if not actually shown wearing them, women appear doing traditionally male jobs such as driving a tram. This leads to accounts of the later women's suffrage campaigns, then back on a lighter note to examine the tyrannies of the corset.

Such effective blending of topical novelty with larger social and historical transformations is typical of the way Paris 1900 handles its different themes, integrating a concern for the minutiae of everyday life and the ephemeral forms of popular culture into a wider narrative of the flowering and fading of the Belle Epoque.

Paris 1900 carries echoes of the city symphony films of the 1920s. It loosely follows their 'day in the life' pattern of beginning at dawn—with footage of the market traders in Les Halles—and closing with night falling and a new dawn, as a symbolic shot of an electric street light going out is linked to the declaration of war. It also adopts the city symphony films' presentation of social microcosms by ranging thematically through urban rituals, fashion, leisure, popular entertainment, theatre, art, politics, sports, and topical events. The vision of France that dominates much of Paris 1900 is of an eternal summer holiday of social contentment, leisure, and relaxation. It is only in the last quarter of the film, heralded by a visit to the squalor and poverty of the Zone, that the tone and emphasis shift to examine political unrest and the negative consequences of modernization for the labour force. This move in turn opens up a widening geographical and political focus as the film rapidly traces the international events leading to the outbreak of World War I.

As Jay Leyda notes, the successful compilation film relies on sensitivity to the formal qualities of its archival sources and on the ability to use montage to create graphic associations between disparate pieces of film that will shape and carry the meanings of the compilation work. Paris 1900 is exemplary in this respect, because it is able to achieve a smooth integration even between actualité and fiction footage, by capitalizing on similarities of composition and content. Discussing her working methods (in Leyda 1964: 79), Védrès also emphasises the importance of what she calls the second meanings of filmed images, dominant moods or feelings that may have little connection to their manifest content. Such feelings are often precisely the product of historical distance from the original sources, or, more specifically, the benefit of hindsight. Thus the brief shot of a 'sinister' bearded man used to create a disquieting mood, appropriate to the growing shadow of war, works effectively by making emotions appear to come from the original material itself, as well as by evoking the distance between past and present knowledge.

The sense of historical distance also inflects the seemingly random associations made by the commentary, as one theme or idea triggers another in a deceptively effortless flow, creating a movement akin to the digressive processes of human memory. As the film images appear in response or in parallel to the commentary, the effect is of their being spontaneously remembered. André Bazin registers this effect in finding the achievement of Paris 1900 to be its forging of a collective memory that, although it does not belong to individual spectators, is experienced as powerfully as if it did.

Ultimately, if unconsciously, Paris 1900 attests to the role of film itself as a specific medium through which the past reaches us. It offers a compendium of the techniques and developing conventions of early cinema, from the spontaneous charm of people glancing and smiling at the camera in the earliest actualités, through the sets and performance conventions of early narrative melodramas and filmed plays, to the inventory of newsreel parades and political meetings that close the film. It even holds a mirror up to its own medium, with a fantasy short shown as a film-within-a-film and preceded by a delightfully ironic reminder of those days when, some thought, cinema was an invention without a future.

CATHERINE LUPTON

Paris 1900 (France, 1948, 79 mins). Pantheon Productions. Produced by Pierre Braunberger. Directed and researched by Nicole Védrès. Scenario and commentary by Nicole Védrès. Production supervision by Claude Hauser. Assistant supervision and research by Alain Resnais. Edited by Myriam Borsoutzky, assisted by Yannick Bellon. Music by Guy Bernard. Sound engineered by Claude Carrère.

Further reading

Bazin, Andre, 'Nicole Védrès', in *Le Cinéma français de la Libération à la nouvelle vague, 1945–58*, Paris: Cahiers du Cinema/Editions de l'Etoile, 1983: 166–9.

Braunberger, Pierre, *Cinéma mémoire*, Paris: Centre Georges Pompidou/Centre nationale de la cinematographie, 1987.

Leyda, Jay, *Films Beget Films*, London: Allen & Unwin, 1964.

Pelechian, Artavazd

Armenian filmmaker Artavazd Pelechian remains shamefully neglected among the world's great documentary filmmakers. Creator of an astounding series of montage-based short films that were for many years shelved by the Soviet authorities, he has done little work in recent years, despite support in the West, as a consequence of the challenging nature of his experimental work. His latest completed films are the companion pieces Konec/End (1992) and Zizn'/Life (1993), which run for eight and seven minutes, respectively.

It is impossible to ignore the legacy of Eisenstein's thinking in the work of the Armenian. Since the late 1960s Pelechian, an important theorist as well as practitioner, has situated his work within the problematic of 1920s Soviet Montage theory and practice.

His main aim has been to extend montage theory—in particular the more radical aspects of Eisensteinian thought—to capture the movement of life on a cosmic scale. In line with recent developments in both science and the arts (for example, musical aesthetics), Pelechian's 'montage at a distance' concentrates on the material reality of the work, seeking to emphasise and exploit the shot's nonrepresentational features. It is a concept of abstraction and a use of the medium that presuppose in the filmic material the persistence of connections that exceed its sense and signification from a spectatorial viewpoint. Pelechian writes,

> The fundamental elements, the principal detonator of contrapuntal montage, exercise a reciprocal action on all the other elements according to a law and fulfill a function that one can qualify as nuclear. This involves a double contrapuntal link with every or any other point of the film according to vectorial lines. They provoke a bilateral chain reaction amongst all the subordinate links, first descending, then ascending.

Pelechian's position is as much influenced by the post-1968 Godardian version of montage theory (and in turn his Natchalo, Nacalo or Skisb/In the Beginning, 1967, will be a model for Godard's masterpiece Histoire(s) du cinéma, 1988–98), and as much by the radical formal innovations of American underground artists such as Brakhage and Conner, as it is by Eisenstein.

Pelechian's relation to Eisenstein can be summarised in the following terms. Through inflecting Eisensteinian montage theory in the direction of more broadly cosmic concerns, Pelechian can relativise the historical/historicist perspective of Eisenstein. Pelechian pits the David of little Armenia against the Goliath of Eisenstein's Soviet Union. Menk or My/Us (1969), his most overtly political film, uses material from the Central State Archives and the Documentary archives of Yerevan studios to remember this lost people of history, its culture, and its landscape. Tarva Yeghanaknere or Vremena goda/The Seasons (1972) presents images of the human fully immersed in nature, carried along on its waves, no longer its master as in the Western, Cartesian tradition, but forming one energetic element in the grand turbulent system of life. Whether he uses images of crowds or of flocks of birds (as he did in Obitateli or Bnakitchnere/The Inhabitants, 1970), historical footage or material staged in the present, his cinema constitutes a kind of rhythm-analysis whereby Pelechian seeks to express all of the forms of movement and all of the dimensions of reality. In forcing the cinema to 'acquire other dimensions', the Armenian invents a contrapuntal method emphasizing what he calls the 'pitches of expressivity' whereby, as in the philosophical notion of univocity, the world sings of itself. This univocal tendency (the work's ontological facet that on occasion can allow the mood to veer unproblematically, with a mere shift in intensity, from tragedy to burlesque) is in line with Pelechian's immanent methodology, a criteria of selection and placement of shots whereby no external necessity dictates the logic of cutting and assembly, lending each work a unique rhythm and temporality. There is no belief in transcendence; religion is merely a social fact and progress a ruse (see Pelechian's answer to Kubrick's 2001 A Space Odyssey, Nas vek or Mer dare/Our Century or Cosmos, 1982). His fascination with the science of complexity, in particular the physics of clouds, has led to the effect on the viewer of his unique method of selecting and ordering shots being compared to the butterfly effect; that is, the 'fluttering' of a single shot can produce turbulence in all the other shots.

Whereas Eisenstein's dialectical thinking rests on a sensorimotor unity of man and nature, and, therefore, in Deleuzian terms (and it has largely been within this conceptual frame of reference that the Armenian's work has been considered by critics), remains a cinema of movement-images, Pelechian's univocal philosophy has led him to produce genuine time-images, and in The Seasons the complete lack of spatiotemporal coordinates and sociocultural landmarks has given rise to an abstract and cosmic vision of life as aberrant movement (in which the human is merely one rhythmic force among others) in fusion with the enveloping 'chaosmosis' of torrential nature.

Following from this, I would suggest that there is a new logic of thought in Pelechian, one that perhaps moves him furthest away from Eisenstein's position. If there is a certain sense of impenetrability (but one that accounts for the films' incredible intensity) about Pelechian's montages, it is an essential element of this new thought; we can no longer sanction the all-powerful thought of dialectics and the grand narratives to which it gave rise. To think of the cosmos is to recognise the void at the heart of thought that no logical succession or associative chain (and no *Aufhebung*) can fill. Montage at a distance can express what is unthought of in our manner of being, seeing, and doing. Against the Eisensteinian organic totality wherein all oppositions are overcome according to the laws of dialectics, the whole for Pelechian is a non-totalizing Becoming governed by a dissociative force—the force of time, an interstitial universe ceaselessly emitting incommensurable series.

In line with Deleuze's account of the neo-Baroque times in which we live, there are no harmonic resolutions in Pelechian, only dissonant tunings. In manipulating found or staged footage through acceleration, slow-motion photography, repetition, inversion, or running images backwards, Pelechian rejects what he calls, in his influential text *Contrapuntal Editing*, 'the classical rules of montage: exposition, development, resolution', in favour of an ever-increasing turbulence, without beginning or end.

FERGUS DALY

Biography

Born in Leninakan, Armenia, in 1938. In the 1960s studied cinema at the VGIK (Cinematic Institute of Moscow). Made his first film in 1964. Although his films were suppressed under Soviet rule, he has since achieved a measure of acclaim worldwide and received the Scam Prize for Television in 2000.

Selected films

1964 Gornyj patrul/Mountain Patrol
1967 Natchalo, Nacalo or Skisb/In the Beginning
1969 Menk or My/Us
1970 Obitateli or Bnakitchnere/The Inhabitants
1972 Tarva Yeghanaknere or Vremena goda/The Seasons
1982 Nas vek or Mer dare/Our Century
1992 Konec/End
1993 Zizn'/Life

Further reading

Cazals, Patrick and Danielou, Laurent, 'The Galaxy Pelechian: Interview with Pelechiam', *Discourse*, January 22, 2001.
Godard, Jean-Luc, 'Un Language d'avant Babel, conversation entre Arthur Pelechian et J-L Godard', *Le Monde*, April 2, 1992.
Niney, Francois, 'Montage with Images That Don't Exist: Against Time', *Discourse*, January 22, 2001.
Pelechian, Artavazd, 'Le montage à contrepoint, ou la theorie de la distance', *Trafic* 2, spring 1992.
——'Time Against Me, My Cinema Interview with A. Pelechian', *Discourse*, January 22, 2001.
Pigoullie, Jean-Francois, 'Pelechian: Le montage-mouvement', *Cahiers du Cinéma* 454, April 1992.

Pennebaker, D.A.

A pioneer in the cinéma vérité movement in the United States, D.A. Pennebaker has brought his observational style to music and politics since the 1960s and continues his practice today.

After completing several short works, he traveled to Moscow and made Opening in Moscow (1959) with the help of Albert Maysles, though the sponsors refused to pay for the film. That same year he joined Drew Associates, where he helped develop the first portable, synchronized 16mm camera and sound system.

With Drew Associates, Pennebaker worked on a variety of landmark films that helped define the cinéma vérité movement in America, including Primary (1960), On the Pole (1960), David (1961), Jane (1962), and Crisis: Behind a Presidential Commitment (1963). A new style emerged in the making of these films, noted primarily for their eschewing of traditional documentary conventions, such as reenactments and voice-over narration, in favor of seemingly pure observation. The mobility of the newly developed equipment facilitated unprecedented access to private situations, creating the illusion of the camera operator acting like a 'fly on the wall'. It is this style that Pennebaker continued in his own films after leaving Drew Associates in 1963 and starting his own company with Richard Leacock.

Pennebaker first made a name for himself with Dont Look Back [sic] (1967), a prototypical concert film that set the standard for others to follow, and that incorporated many of the cinéma vérité traditions started in the Time-Drew Associates films. Begun on just a handshake and without funding, the film followed

Bob Dylan on his 1965 British concert tour and became a classic document of the counterculture movement. Dont Look Back refuses to paint a realistic portrait of the enigmatic Dylan, instead opting for as much irreverence toward its subject as its subject had for the world. Pennebaker captures Dylan's duality in his personality through the musician's disrespect for the press on the one hand and through his charisma with his fawning fans on the other. Numerous concert film conventions (some of them derivatives of cinéma vérité conventions) begin in this film, including the informal backstage jams with Donovan and other artists, interaction with British fans, travel time, press conferences and interviews, and, of course, onstage performances before enraptured audiences.

In this film Pennebaker also celebrates his level of access into private spaces and moments. He highlights the behind-the-scenes planning performed by manager Albert Grossman through his extensive telephone negotiations. He follows Dylan down a long hallway to the stage (a convention often featured in other concert films and even spoofed in This is Spinal Tap, 1984). During one of Dylan's concerts the sound system fails and Pennebaker keeps us backstage with the crew members as they frantically scramble to get the correct cables plugged in and the sound working again. All of these work to provide a greater sense of intimacy with the subject, a key characteristic of many of Pennebaker's works.

After his success with Dont Look Back, Pennebaker continued to make documentaries in cinéma vérité style about music, musicians, and music festivals. Monterey Pop (1968) and Sweet Toronto (Keep on Rockin') (1972) chronicle two rock festivals. Both films favor the long take and attempt to maintain a fidelity to the festivals' happenings. In some ways this fidelity creates complications in Ziggy Stardust and the Spiders from Mars, a 1973 film of David Bowie's final performance as Ziggy Stardust. This work focuses primarily on onstage events, although critics of the camera work complain about the lack of framing on Bowie himself. Critics also complain about the poor sound quality and lack of backstage access, something flaunted in Dont Look Back. Another music-subject film from this time by Pennebaker is Company—The Original Cast Album (1970).

In 1977 Pennebaker met and began working with Chris Hegedus. Their first films together took on political subjects such as the proposal to deregulate natural gas in Energy War (1978). The pair's best-known collaboration is probably The War Room (1993). In keeping with the cinéma vérité tradition, the film follows Bill Clinton's 1992 campaign staff, including the fiery James Carville and the staid George Stephanopoulos. From the New Hampshire primary to the election night victory, it chronicles the pitfalls that mired the campaign, including Gennifer Flower's allegations of sexual misconduct, draft-dodging accusations, and other mud-slinging. The film earned an Oscar nomination for Best Documentary Feature and won the D.W. Griffith Award for Best Documentary of the Year.

The War Room (which refers to the Clinton campaign headquarters in Little Rock, Arkansas) also demonstrates the risk involved in this type of documentary filmmaking. In pursuing real life in real-life contexts with as little interference as possible, there is little guarantee of the outcome. If Clinton had lost the election, there would not have been much in terms of a sellable film.

Music remains the primary passion for these collaborators, and their titles cover a wide variety of music genres. Depeche Mode 101 (1989) features the 1980s pop group's massive concert at the Rose Bowl Stadium in Pasadena, California, and a group of fans who travel cross-country to witness it. The Music Tells You (1992) is a portrait of jazz saxophonist Branford Marsalis. Down from the Mountain (2001) returns Pennebaker to his concert film origins, though this time in bluegrass music, not rock; Only the Strong Survive (2002) is a who's who of soul, including Wilson Pickett, Carla Thomas, Mary Wilson, and the Chi-Lights.

Their 2004 film was the Emmy Award-winning Elaine Stritch at Liberty, a portrait of the Tony-winning Broadway legend.

Pennebaker and Hegedus married in 1982 and run Pennebaker Hegedus Films, based in New York City.

HEATHER MCINTOSH

See also: Dont Look Back; Hegedus, Chris; Leacock, Richard; Primary

Biography

Born in 1925 in Evanston, Illinois. Earned a degree in mechanical engineering from Yale in

1947 and spent a year studying naval architecture at the Massachusetts Institute of Technology before joining the Navy for two years. Then held a variety of odd jobs in New York City, and during this time began experimenting with and making films. Joined Drew Associates in 1959. Left Drew Associates in 1963 to start his own company with Richard Leacock. In 1977 met and began working with Chris Hegedus. Married Hegedus in 1982. Currently runs Pennebaker Hegedus Films, based in New York City.

Selected films

1959 Opening in Moscow
1960 Primary: cinematographer, editor
1963 Crisis: Behind a Presidential Commitment: cinematographer
1967 Dont Look Back
1968 Monterey Pop
1970 Company—The Original Cast Album
1970 Sweet Toronto (Keep on Rockin')
1973 Ziggy Stardust and the Spiders from Mars
1978 Energy War (with Chris Hegedus)
1989 Depeche Mode 101 (with Chris Hegedus and David Dawkins)
1992 Branford Marsalis: The Music Tells You (with Chris Hegedus)
1993 The War Room (with Chris Hegedus)
2001 Down from the Mountain (with Nick Doob and Chris Hegedus)
2002 Only the Strong Survive (with Chris Hegedus)
2004 Elaine Stritch at Liberty (with Nick Doob and Chris Hegedus)

Further reading

Levin, G. Roy, 'Donn Alan Pennebaker', in *Documentary Explorations: 15 Interviews with Film-makers*, Garden City, NY: Doubleday and Company, 1971: 223–70.

Mamber, Stephen, *Cinéma vérité in America: Studies in Uncontrolled Documentary*, Cambridge, MA: MIT Press, 1974.

Pennebaker Hegedus Films, www.phfilms.com

Rosenthal, Alan, 'Dont Look Back and Monterey Pop: Don Alan Pennebaker', in *The New Documentary in Action: A Casebook in Filmmaking*, Berkeley, CA: University of California Press, 1971: 189–98.

Stubbs, Liz, 'D.A. Pennebaker and Chris Hegedus: Engineering Nonfiction Cinema', in *Documentary Filmmakers Speak*, New York: Allworth, 2002: 41–68.

Swift, Lauren Lowenthal, 'Pennebaker: D.A. Makes' 'em Dance', *Film Comment* 24, no. 6, November 1988: 44–9.

Peries, Lester James

Lester James Peries, founder of indigenous Sinhala cinema, laid the foundations for a serious national cinema in Sri Lanka and played a pivotal role in shaping a vigorous film culture in the island from the mid-1950s to the present.

Influenced by his early training as a documentary filmmaker, Peries was the first to take the camera outside the confines of the cardboard houses built in South Indian film studios and shoot on location in natural light, with amateur actors. His first feature film, Rekawa/Line of Destiny (1956), was the first Sinhalese movie to portray people, their environment, and their culture in a realistic way.

From 1939 to 1952 Peries led a bohemian existence in London. Although he had gone there to start his career as a writer, that period in Britain was crucial to his formation in a different way. London was then the centre of a vigorous documentary film tradition associated with the British General Post Office (GPO) Film Unit formed by Grierson, Cavalcanti, and Wright, among others. One of the most popular of these films was Night Mail (Wright, Watt, Cavalcanti, and others, 1936), a film about the functioning of the mail trains that transported the post all over Britain.

It was this vigorous tradition of the documentary cinema that Peries inherited when, in 1952, he returned to Colombo to work for the Government Film Unit (GFU) as assistant to the British chief producer Ralph Keene and began churning out several documentaries on several subjects, including malaria and vehicle traffic.

The GFU was established in 1948 to produce newsreels and documentaries to educate people about their newly won independence. Noted for its 'creative treatment of actuality' and high filmmaking standards, it became the nursery from which many of Sri Lanka's future eminent filmmakers emerged. One of them was Lester James Peries (Varma 1997).

In the beginning the GFU was headed by Guido Petroni and Federico Serra, two Italian filmmakers influenced by the neorealism movement who brought elements of it into their Sri Lankan films, though Serra's film Royal Mail, about the country's postal service, showed that the British influence was also in the air.

However, it was under the stewardship of Ralph Keene that the GFU—with films such as Kandy Perahera (George Wickramasinghe), Rhythms of the People (Pragnasoma Hetiaracchchi), Makers, Motifs and Materials (Pragnasoma Hettiaracchchi), and Conquest of the Dry Zone (Lester James Peries, 1954), a fourteen-minute film on the eradication of malaria from the North Central Province of Ceylon that was awarded a diploma of honour at the Venice Film festival in 1954—radically changed the style of documentary filmmaking in Ceylon (Dissanayake and Ratnavibhushana 2000).

In those years, Peries and his colleagues were being trained in the finest traditions of British documentary (Peries 2001). At that time he also assisted Keene with Heritage of Lanka (1953) and the prizewinning film Nelugama (1953), depicting the life of a fishing community, and made many documentaries for numerous private-sector firms and organizations. For the Ceylon Tobacco Company (CTC) he shot at least two. One was on Navajeevana, CTC's five-hundred-acre farm in Mahiyangana where the company settled sixty farmer families and opened a new chapter in farming, introducing new crops such as soya and maize. The other was on another of CTC's diversified projects: the sugarcane cultivation and manufacture of jaggery at a time when sugar was a scarce commodity due to foreign exchange shortage.

In 1955, when he had just finished a film on road safety, Be Safe or Be Sorry (1955), and had been asked to make a film on venereal diseases, Peries's second cousin suggested starting a company to produce Sinhala films. Bored with the subject matter of the GFU films, and more interested in fiction, characters, and human beings, Peries resigned from the GFU and embarked on the shooting of his first feature film, Rekawa/Line of Destiny and his subsequent film career.

Peries developed a personal film style, the twin hallmarks of which were the stylistic construction of narrative and his ability to capture and project actualities in a realistic manner. It was his documentary experience and his literary background that made this possible. Peries succeeded in portraying the existential realities and nuances of rural Sri Lanka and its ontological veneer (Jeyaraj 2000).

Even after resigning from the GFU and enjoying international success with his feature films, Peries continued to make documentaries, including Too Many Too Soon (1961), a documentary for the Family Planning Association; Home from the Sea (1962), on the lives of fishermen and their faith in St Anthony; and Steel (1969), a documentary record of the construction and working of a steel-rolling mill at Oruwela, for the National Steel Corporation.

VERÓNICA JORDANA

See also: Grierson, John; Night Mail; Wright, Basil

Biography

Born on April 5, 1919 in Dehiwela, a suburb of Colombo, Sri Lanka. Studied at St Peter's College in Colombo. At the age of seventeen left school to pursue a career as a journalist and to escape from his teachers' intention that he become a priest. Wrote for the *Kesari*, a cultural newspaper, and worked as a broadcaster for Radio Ceylon reviewing books 1939. Left for London, where he led a bohemian life and worked as a correspondent for the *Times of Ceylon* 1940–54. Shot and finished Soliloquy, his first short film, which won an award for artistic and technical merit from the Institute of Amateur and Research filmmakers of Great Britain in 1951. Returned to Sri Lanka and joined the Government Film Unit (GFU), where he shot several documentaries 1952–7. Resigned from the GFU and, with cameraman Willie Blake and Titus Thotawatte, made Rekawa/Line of Destiny, his first feature film. A member of the Légion d'Honneur (France), he received the Lifetime Achievement Award at the International Film Festival of India in January 2000. Received UNESCO's Fellini Gold Medal at the Cannes Festival, 2003.

Selected films

1952 Nelugama: assistant director
1953 Heritage of Lanka: assistant director
1954 Conquest of the Dry Zone: director, writer
1955 Be Safe or Be Sorry: director, writer

1956 Rekawa/Line of Destiny: director, writer
1961 Too Many Too Soon: director, writer
1962 Home from the Sea: director, writer
1969 Steel: director, writer

Further reading

Ariyadasa, Edwin, 'The History of Sinhala Cinema', *Framework: The Journal of Cinema and Media* 37, 1989.
Asian Film Center, *A Brief History of Sri Lanka Cinema*, Sri Lanka, 1999.
Dissanayake, Wimal and Ratnavibhushana, Ashley, *Profiling Sri Lankan Cinema*, Sri Lanka: Asian Film Centre, 2000.
Jeyaraj, D.B.S., 'Sinhala Film's Line of Destiny', *The Sunday Leader*, March 12, 2000.
Peries, Lester James, 'Pragnasoma Hettiarachchi: A Personal Tribute', *Sunday Observer*, October 7, 2001.
Varma, Mitu, 'Historical Perspective: Films in Search of a Movement', in *Himal Magazine*, December 1997.

Perrault, Pierre

Pierre Perrault practiced law for two years in Montreal before he found a job with the Canadian Broadcasting Corporation (CBC), producing programs on the rural areas of Québec, in 1956.

He was hired by the National Film Board of Canada (NFB) in 1962 to work with Michel Brault on a project on the people of Île-aux-Coudres, an island in the St Lawrence River. The resulting film was Pour la suite du monde/The Moontrap (1963), the first Canadian feature documentary shown at the Cannes Film Festival and generally recognized as marking the high point of the direct cinema movement in Québec. At the core of the film are a group of middle-aged men who try to resuscitate the traditional beluga whale hunt that their fathers practiced forty years earlier. The revival of the whale hunt was in fact initiated by the filmmakers themselves, as means both to recapture a disappearing way of life and to provide a unique opportunity to record the voices and faces of the men and women of Île-aux-Coudres as they came together to reanimate their past. While Brault was primarily responsible for the splendid images of the film, Perrault focused on collecting the words of these people by spending extended periods of time with them to establish a genuine dialogue. Perrault directed two other films on Île-aux-Coudres: Le régne du jour/The Reign of the Day (1966) and Les voitures d'eau/The Water Cars (1968); both are imbued with the rustic poetry of his subjects.

Some of his films are explicitly political, such as Un pays sans bon sens!/Wake Up, Mes Bons Amis (1970) and L'Acadie, l'Acadie!?!/Acadia, Acadia?!? (1971), but most are concerned less with politics per se than with the people who make up the nation of Québec. In the 1970s Perrault concentrated his energy on two ambitious series or cycles of films, one on the Abitibi region of northwest Québec (four films), and the other on the native peoples of Northern Québec (three films). In the 1980s Perrault abandoned his cycles to direct a few seemingly heterogeneous films, all of which, however, reflect his fascination with the land. La bête lumineuse/The Shimmering Beast (1982) follows a group of men on a moose-hunting trip. Les voiles bas et en travers/Lower the Sails (1984) and La grande allure/Sailing at Great Speed (1985) examine the life of French explorer Jacques Cartier and his role as the forefather of Québec culture. His last two films, L'oumigmag ou l'objectif documentaire/Oumigmag or the Documentary Objective (1993) and Cournouailles/Icewarrior (1994) were shot in Québec's far north and are at once visual poems on the musk ox and evocative reflections on the very act of filming wilderness.

Pierre Perrault holds a unique place in the history of Québec cinema. One of the very few filmmakers of his generation who never made mainstream fiction films, he is also one of the few who have found a place within the highbrow discourse of French film theory, especially in the work of Gilles Deleuze. Deleuze, in Cinéma2 (1985), is especially interested in how Perrault creates temporal shifts among past, present, and future with individuals and groups who generate 'la suite du monde' (the future of the world) through a present-tense narrative of their past. Perrault was also a prolific writer, publishing commentaries on his films, poems, and other creative works. Jean-Daniel Lafond's film Les traces du rêve (1986) documents Perrault's life.

ANDRÉ LOISELLE

See also: Brault, Michel

Biography

Born June 29, 1927, into an upper-class family. Studied law in Montreal, Toronto, and Paris. Practiced law for two years in Montreal. Hired by the Canadian Broadcasting Corporation (CBC) in 1956. Hired by the National Film Board of Canada (NFB) in 1962 to work with Michel Brault on a project on the people of Île-aux-Coudres. Died June 24, 1999.

Selected films

1963 Pour la suite du monde/The Moontrap
1967 Le Règne du jour/Reign of the Day
1968 Le Beau Plaisir/Beluga Days
1968 Les Voitures d'eau/The Water Cars
1970 Un pays sans bon sens!/Wake Up, Mes Bons Amis
1971 L'Acadie, l'Acadie?!?/Acadia, Acadia?!?
1975 Un royaume vous attend/A Kingdom is Waiting for You
1976 Le Retour à la terre/Back to the Land
1977 C'était un Québécois en Bretagne, Madame!/He was a Québecker in Brittany, Lady!
1977 Le Goût de la farine/The Taste of Flour
1980 Gens d'Abitibi/People of Abitibi
1980 Le Pays de la Terre sans arbre ou le Mouchouânipi/The Land Without Trees or Mouchouanipi
1982 La Bête lumineuse/The Shimmering Beast
1983 Les Voiles bas et en travers/Lower the Sails
1985 La Grande Allure (1re partie)/Sailing at Great Speed I
1985 La Grande Allure (2e partie)/Sailing at Great Speed II
1993 L'Oumigmag ou l'Objectif documentaire/Oumigmag or the Documentary Objective
1994 Cornouailles/Icewarrior

Further reading

Brûle, Michel *Pierre Perrault ou un cinéma national*, Montreal: Presses de l'Universite de Montreal, 1974.

Deleuze, Gilles, *Cinéma 2, L'Image-Temps*, Paris: Les Editions de Minuit, 1985.

Perrault, Pierre, *Écriture de Pierre Perrault*, Montreal: Cinemathèque quebecoise, 1983.

Warren, Paul, *Cinéaste de la parole*, Montreal: Hexagone, 1996.

Waugh, Tom, *To Wake the Heart and the Will: Pierre Perrault and Cinéma-Direct in Québec, 1956–71*, PhD dissertation, Columbia University, 1974.

Phantom India

(France, Malle, 1969)

By the mid-1960s the prominent French director Louis Malle was profoundly bored with working in the mainstream film industry. Partly to make a break with France, he accepted a cultural mission to India to promote New Wave cinema in film clubs and other Indian cultural centres. On his arrival in India, Malle was immediately fascinated by the nation. Symbolism and spiritualism seemed to infuse every aspect of Indian social life. Accompanied by his sound man Jean-Claude Laureux and his photographer Etienne Becker, Malle returned to shoot documentary material. It was out of this quasi-instantaneous set of encounters that Malle would edit together two substantial pieces, the film Calcutta (1969) and the better-known seven-part television series Phantom India (1969).

Malle's decision to focus so intently on India marked a significant turning point in his career. The films were the first substantial documentaries that he had made since working as an assistant director to Jacques Cousteau in the mid-1950s on The Silent World (1956). Therefore, the Indian films reignited the director's interest in a form that would prove vital to his career. With the benefit of historical hindsight, one can also interpret Malle's Indian experience as a quintessentially 1960s episode. Rejecting Western European sociopolitical values, Malle, like many members of his generation, was attracted to the alternative model perceived to have been provided by India.

Phantom India is a free-flowing travelog. It is a self-reflexive work in which Malle is frequently seen on screen and heard via voice-over. Appropriately, everything that Malle shows through his camera is offered as exclusively his own vision. It is for this reason that the films can be interpreted as a treatise on a Westerner's awestruck encounter with India, rather than as a dissection of that nation per se. Many passages from the series of films are moving and visually impressive. At its best, Phantom India demonstrates both its director's passion for India and that country's rich cultural variety.

Figure 14 Phantom India, 1969 (Courtesy of the British Film Institute)

Malle identified his films as an exercise in the free-flowing direct cinema form that he would hone further in Place de la République (1974). However, as American critic Todd Gitlin noted as early as 1974, parts of the films are very troubling. Malle's enthusiasm for the people and groups that he encountered tends to lack any moral or ethical centre. Thus, when Malle visits a tribe in which women are indoctrinated to worship men, to literally kiss their feet, the director describes this group as a Utopian society. Such comments are unnerving. In part, they are indicative of Malle's increased fascination with the politics and provocation of sexual freedom, later also played out in fictional exercises such as Le Souffle au coeur (1971) and Pretty Baby (1978). Nevertheless, in light of such statements, the viewer is left suspicious of Malle's numerous tracking shots of beautiful young Indian women, his camera endlessly exploring their social space, seemingly without much regard to their viewpoint or concern with their consent.

Other aspects of the films are also unsettling, not least Malle's commentary on the Indian Jewish community, which he describes as decadent. However, it was neither because of these remarks nor because of explicit and implicit sexism that the films proved controversial upon their initial release. Purchased by the BBC, the films were shown on British and French television. The reaction to the series was especially intense in Britain and India. The British Indian community felt that Malle had shown an exclusively one-sided picture that concentrated on an impoverished and backward India, rather than on a modernizing nation. The Indian government felt similarly insulted, and a diplomatic incident quickly ensued. The Indian authorities were so irritated by Malle's work that they challenged the BBC to cease broadcasting it or face severe penalties. The BBC stood by Malle and was indeed briefly ordered to leave its New Delhi bureau. This telling postcolonial incident has long since been forgotten. It deserves renewed historical research.

HUGO FREY

Phantom India/L'Inde fantôme (France, 1969). Produced by Nouvelles Editions de Films (Paris). Directed by Louis Malle. Photography by Etienne Becker and Louis Malle. Sound by

Jean-Claude Laureux. Edited by Suzanne Baron. Narration by Louis Malle.

Further reading

Billard, Pierre, *Louis Malle: le rebelle solitaire*, Paris: Plon, 2003.
French, Philip (ed.), *Malle on Malle*, London: Faber, 1993.
Frey, Hugo, *Louis Malle*, Manchester: Manchester University Press, 2004.
Gitlin, Todd, 'Phantom India', *Film Quarterly* 27, no. 4, 1974: 57–60.
Malle, Louis, *Malle sur Malle*, Paris: Editions de l'Athanor, 1978 (includes published extracts from Malle's India diaries).
——'Louis Malle', in C. Devarrieux and M.-C. de Navacelle (eds), *Cinéma du réel*, Paris: Autrement, 1988: 22–31.

Pictures of the Old World

(Slovakia, Hanák, 1972)

Dušan Hanák's Obrazy Star ho Sveta/Pictures of the Old World was not widely seen when it was completed in 1972, but more than fifteen years after it was suppressed by communist censors, this Slovakian film won awards at film festivals around the world and made a name for its director. Even though Hanák made mostly feature films, his only documentaries, Pictures of the Old World and Paper Heads (1995), have earned him the most attention.

As indicated by the title, Pictures of the Old World is about people who live in the modern world yet adhere to more traditional, modest means of subsistence. Filming the inhabitants of rural communities in the remote Tatra Mountains, Hanák captures the everyday facts of their existence while the subjects provide free-form commentary. The men he profiles often comment on their inclusion in the project. One subject informs the director that his profile had better be funny, because 'one is interested in what is funny'. In a unique move, Hanák includes a series of still and filmed photographs for each subject, who often comment on the pictures in synch with their appearance on the film. Inverting the more conventional documentary style, where a carefully composed script is read over the filmed material, Hanák allows the subjects' commentary to overlay the images whenever simultaneously recorded sound is not present. Although the director is virtually absent from the sight and sound of the film, his hand is evident in the structure of the work.

Pictures of the Old World features a series of nine self-contained portraits, all of poor, rural people living alone. With few exceptions—two women and one younger man—Hanák profiles only elderly men. (A sequence where numerous respondents take on 'what is most important in life' shows that Hanák probably conducted extensive interviews with a broader range of subjects before deciding to focus almost exclusively on older men.) One could be critical of Hanák for so limiting his subjects, but even though the men featured in the film are from the same generation, they express a wide range of views. The range of experiences accounted for is, perhaps, made all the more remarkable by the similarity of the sampled demographic. Each subject appears free to comment on his life however he sees fit, and accordingly, the final cut includes contrasting responses. While leading similar lives as poor, agricultural workers, these men view their experiences in fundamentally different ways. Some find gratification in their labor; others find solace only in the promise of an afterlife. Some find simplicity and satisfaction in their modest way of life. (One man says, 'You city people will get hard and dried on asphalt. Your heart is made of cement. I live on a proud bunk'. Another remarks that 'Whoever's got some wants more, whoever's got nothing, got a grand time'.) A third, however, finds similar conditions inhumane. He says, 'A man puts up with more than an animal'. (The ubiquity of alcohol is the only absolutely consistent element through every profile.) Still, the film is most intriguing when the profiled subject possesses a singular interest. One old man is still consumed by memories of his stint in the army, and another spends his time making elaborate mobiles. The sixth man featured stands out as the most exceptional. He speaks a few sentences in passing of his work (for another farmer) and his partner's (selling newspapers) but is otherwise monomaniacally obsessed with space exploration. His face lit with glee, this man lists one astronomical fact after another as Hanák, in a rare move, splices appropriate footage of space exploration alongside his commentary.

Although the title of the film, Pictures of the Old World, and the quote that opens it ('These are the stories of people rooted in the soil they came from. Replanted they would perish') imply the possibility of sentimentalizing or romanticizing the lives of these elderly villagers, the film proceeds to work conscientiously against this tendency. The range of statements both in opposition to and in endorsement of this style of life show a filmmaker more interested in exploring the ambiguity of his subjects than motivated to produce a piece with a particular argument. It is clear from the material on display in this cut that Hanák, had he wanted, could have crafted a piece about the bucolic simplicity of village life or, conversely, about the forbidding harshness of it. He chose, instead, to include both sides.

The style of Pictures of the Old World is similarly two-sided, as Alojz Hanúsek and Martin Martincek shift between unselfconscious, straightforward means of filming with a single, handheld camera and more stylized sequences. In one instance, the camera focuses on a subject's feet and then moves up his body at a horizontal angle before turning upright at the man's face. The filmmakers also appear fond of the extreme close-up, although it is not clear whether this was a conscious decision or they simply chose to indulge subjects who wanted to be inordinately close to the camera. Still, in accordance with conventional documentary style, the film tends more toward straightforward shooting than toward stylized sequences. In the context of a primarily observational documentary, it is notable that the stylized sequences are present at all.

The use of a single handheld camera, black-and-white film, and the usually unadorned style of Hanák's picture could lead to comparisons with the direct cinema approach, but the director deliberately breaks the transparency of the film on numerous occasions. He includes shots that emphasize the making of the picture. In one sequence, a bashful elderly couple awkwardly pass a microphone back and forth, uncertain what to say. Hanák also shows a woman who shouts her answers into the mike, evidently unsure how well such devices work. Although the director could have coached his subjects into being more conventional interviewees, he chose, instead, to include their tentative early encounters with the filmmaking process. These scenes effectively portray the villagers' lack of familiarity with modern technology, in addition to emphasizing the construction of the picture. Using another hallmark technique of self-reflexive documentaries, Hanák sometimes includes sound clips of himself asking the interviewees questions. More often, documentarians erase their questions from the final cut to create the illusion of a single, coherent monologue from the subject's point of view.

The use of music in Pictures of the Old World is also notable. It ranges from naturalistic, sometimes simulated, on-location sounds and folk songs sung by the subjects to an expressive but minimal classical score and strange, high-frequency synthetic noises.

Following Pictures of the Old World's release in 1988, Hanák earned a Special Mention at the European Film Awards in 1989 and was given an award for a lifetime's achievement in cinema at the first National Free Festival of Czech and Slovak films the following year.

JESSE SCHLOTTERBECK

Pictures of the Old World/Obrazy starého sveta (Slovakia, Slovak Film Institute, 1972, 64 mins). Written and directed by Dusan Hanák. Original music by Vaclav Halek and Jozef Malovec. Nonoriginal music by Georg Friedrich Händel. Cinematography by Alojz Hanúsek and Martin Martincek. Film edited by Alfred Bencic. Sound by Andrej Polomsky.

Pilger, John

Australian-born television documentary maker John Pilger is first and foremost a journalist. He made his first television documentary in 1970 (The Quiet Mutiny), which revealed the rejection of the Vietnam War by large numbers of US conscripts. Pilger's print journalism output is prolific (it includes a regular column in the *New Statesman*), and he has published numerous books and a play, as well as more than fifty television documentaries, always on controversial political issues. He is an accredited war correspondent and has reported from conflicts in Vietnam, Cambodia, Bangladesh, Biafra, and the Middle East.

Pilger's film style is direct, and some have called it 'polemical', whereby he confronts the objects of his criticism in a direct and uncompromising manner. He is said to have a knack for getting people in authority to make statements on camera that they would not normally make. He has said that he 'grew up in Sydney in a very political household, where we were all for the underdog' (Barsamian 2002). However, although they critique the wrongs of society and present the voice of the powerless, his films stop short of offering the viewer any alternatives. He says, 'I am not going to offer anything in its place. I am saying that people should be aware of it and identify it and then they have the power of that knowledge to do something about it if they want to' (*Sydney Morning Herald*, April 11, 1998).

One of his best-known documentaries is In Search of Truth in Wartime, which critically scrutinizes the role of the war correspondent in conflicts ranging from Crimea to Vietnam. Impressively structured, the film begins with the famous black-and-white footage of the little Vietnamese girl running terrified from the flames of napalm during the Vietnam War, to illustrate immediately where Pilger's strongest sympathies lie in any conflict—with its innocent victims. In reflecting on the role of the journalist in war, he suggests that many reporters wittingly or unwittingly serve the state in sanitizing and rationalizing war, exemplified by the images they send to their media organizations back home, such as those of the soldiers' coffins draped respectfully in flags as they are met at airports by dignitaries and family. It is unusual for journalists to criticize their own profession, but to Pilger nobody is exempt from his critical gaze if it means an opportunity to bring to light unjust practices or institutions.

Pilger calmly informs us (direct to camera from a domestic interior) of the press collusion in the British government's conspiracy to hide the futility and extent of the carnage of World War I. The complicity of the journalists having been established, we are shown newsreel after newsreel, revealed by Pilger to the contemporary viewer as clear propaganda, but not seen as such at the time. With more recent wars, we move to Pilger's interviews with some of the journalists who covered the conflicts. In these interviews, more cases of collusion between government and the press are revealed, including stories fabricated by the US government of barbaric 'official' North Korean press releases and the CIA's staging of the filmed 'invasion' of South Vietnam by the North, needed to justify the commencement of US aerial bombing of North Vietnam.

Controversial as always, Pilger refutes the myth that the media affected the outcome of the Vietnam War, either positively or negatively, except that free media access during this conflict prompted the subsequent decision by the British Ministry of Defence never to give cameras the same freedom in any future war. This fact is then illustrated by news footage of the Falklands War (1982), in which a former correspondent from that war states that the British government allowed only a few handpicked British journalists to cover the conflict.

Pilger made two documentaries entitled Palestine is Still the Issue (1974 and 2002), the first of which was one of his most widely viewed films. These documentaries comment on the irony that the Palestinians have become for the Israelis the displaced people that the Jews were for the Europeans before the creation of the state of Israel. Interviews take place with people on both sides of the conflict, most of whom express a strong desire for peace and cannot see war as the solution. In the sequel Pilger addresses the camera: 'If we're to speak of the great injustice here, nothing has changed. What has changed is that the Palestinians have fought back'.

In some films, Pilger is not afraid to implicate himself among those he attacks. In The Secret Country (1985), about the systematic but officially unacknowledged mistreatment by white Australian settlers of Aboriginal people (made during the period leading up to the Bicentenary of European settlement in that country), Pilger locates a cottage built by his own father on the site of a one hundred-year struggle between Aboriginals and settlers. He also talks of the sanitization of the 'encounters' between Europeans and Aboriginals 'when I learned history at school' in his native Sydney. Pilger is not a 'holier-than-thou' journalist, morally separated from the objects of his critique; rather, his is the concerned, serious voice of someone deeply troubled by what his career has led him to witness and what his astute mind, impeccable training, and political consciousness have driven him to expose.

Pilger's films are didactic and ideologically motivated. Numerous accusations of bias have been leveled at him by the establishment, because his films confront power cliques and hegemonic interests, including governments and the media. He lives in an era when few documentary makers consistently critique such interests, and his films have frequently been refused screenings in the United States. He has been described by the right as 'a left-wing polemicist' ('Editor Falls Victim to Iraq "Scoop"', *Sunday Mirror*, May 16, 2004) and a 'professional conspiracy theorist' ('Truth is Pilgered', *The Australian*, Features, February 17, 2003: 10). His documentary on the Israel–Palestine conflict was even denounced as 'one-sided [...] factually incorrect, historically incorrect' by his own producer at Carlton Television ('Pilger Biased, Says TV Boss', *The Times*, Overseas News, September 20, 2002: 15). Auberon Waugh, right-wing journalist and staunch critic of Pilger, joked that 'Pilger' was a verb that meant 'to seek to arouse indignation by inflated or absurd propositions', and that to 'Pilgerise' meant 'to distort in a tendentious way'.

On the other hand, Phillip Knightly, a journalist supporter of Pilger, provided his own definition of the 'verb' to Pilger as 'to regard with insight, compassion and sympathy, coined as a tribute to the work of one John Pilger, a well-known humanitarian journalist who wrote about the world's underprivileged'.

Pilger continues to be a prolific writer and documentary film producer, with productions including Breaking the Silence: Truth and Lies in the War on Terror (2003), about the US and British prosecution of their 'war on terror' in Iraq. Here Pilger uses his trademark archival footage accompanied by interviews with human rights activists, members of the White House staff, and former intelligence analysts to make his case that Bush used the September 11 terrorism as an excuse to activate plans to assert control over Iraq's oil. Pilger again juxtaposes benign footage of Bush and Blair arguing that the war in Iraq is moral and just with interviews and images which that suggest the opposite. Conservative criticism of his journalistic stance has clearly not diminished the volume of his documentary output, nor has it softened his confronting style. Pilger has received numerous awards for his journalism in Britain, in the United States, and from the United Nations.

JULIANNE STEWART

Further reading

Arnove, Anthony, 'Cautionary Tales: Documentaries on the UN Sanctions and War with Iraq', *Cinéaste* 28, no. 2, spring 2003.

Barsamian, David, 'The Progressive Interview: John Pilger', *The Progressive* 66, no. 11, November 2002, www.progressive.org/nov02/intv1102.html (accessed May 23, 2004).

Hayward, Anthony, *In the Name of Justice: The Television Reporting of John Pilger*, London: Bloomsbury, 2001.

Sweeney, Brian, 'Siding with the Enemy', *The Weekend Australian*, Features, July 5, 2003: 26.

Pincus, Edward

With Diaries (1971–6) (1980), Ed Pincus made an extraordinary breakthrough in the realm of the film about one's own life, shot as it is happening. This film, along with Pincus's teaching at the Massachusetts Institute of Technology Film/Video Section in the 1970s, helped to shape the work of a generation of autobiographical filmmakers—Joel DeMott, Ross McElwee, Rob Moss, Mark Rance, Ann Schaetzel, and others. Pincus's work is not as well known or as much discussed as it deserves to be, because he retired young from filmmaking, and his films have not been promoted or widely distributed (one must contact him personally to obtain a print, and nothing is available on videotape or DVD).

Pincus became active in the American Civil Rights movement of the early 1960s and began making films at that time in the cinéma vérité or direct cinema mode established by Robert Drew, Richard Leacock, Albert and David Maysles, D.A. Pennebaker, and others. Pincus's Black Natchez (1966) is an exemplary film of this kind, a sixty-minute, strictly observational account of the Mississippi city and its black population's struggles to organize political protest in the face of white violence. Pincus, working with David Neuman, shoots here with handheld camera and synchronous sound recording. He has clearly won the confidence of people and made himself inconspicuous enough so that he gets remarkable footage of everyday life, political meetings, a secret society, and infighting. The film is a complex portrait of political debate and movement toward decisive action at a time of great tension.

Shot at the same time in Natchez, but completed only later, Panola (1970) is a different kind of film. Here the thirty-five-year-old black man named in the title addresses the camera, talks about his hard life and his aspirations, engages the filmmakers in interplay, invites them into his house in the black slums, appears drunk at one point, behaves histrionically. However truthful a report on black life in the South and on the state of mind of one charismatic, disturbed, ordinary man, the film is nevertheless a performance, a display of speech and action offered with full consciousness of the camera, a display made for the camera by one who can command it.

Diaries (1971–6) comes to rest after its three hours and twenty minutes, on a hilltop in Vermont on the holy day of Yom Kippur. Indeed, this film is a work of atonement, bringing together what is in conflict, working toward peace in a process of moral growth. The film centers on Pincus, his wife Jane, and their small children, as the couple come to deepen their commitment to each other, ultimately deciding to move to a new home in a new place. The world of the film takes in the Cambridge, Massachusetts, filmmaking scene, Pincus's and Jane's extramarital affairs, anti-Vietnam War politics, the Women's Movement of the 1970s, rural Vermont, and trips to New York, the American Southwest, and California. Pincus's lovers, friends, and professional associates become major characters. Pincus films life as it evolves, not knowing where it will go, often turning the camera on himself. He gets remarkably intimate—even painful—encounters on film, and of course he also elicits self-consciousness, performance, even melodramatics, all of which has its way of being revealing. The film is alive with the possibilities of sex and of political and social change. The shaping of the material into the finished work is at one with Ed and Jane's process of coming to understand themselves better and to make decisions about their family life and future.

Diaries has a curious double quality. On the one hand it seems raw, as if abundant life is caught awkwardly on film and assembled into a simple chronology. This in itself is fascinating. However, the film is artistically masterful. Every shot and the structuring seem deeply well judged. The camera is always in the right place. In the many conversations in cars, the interior lines of the vehicle, and what passes in the window, slowly, quickly, or in a blur, seem to define the state of mind of the speaker. The images of a trip to the Grand Canyon, Las Vegas, and elsewhere seem mental, indicating an expansion of spirit, an irresponsible lark that is a contribution to growth. The film moves more quickly, changing places and acknowledging diverse actions, when Ed and Jane are in creative turmoil, thinking, forming a new plan for life. Diaries draws on and realizes that basic power of documentary film, and of film in general, to capture to some extent what is vital and uncontrollable, and to transfigure life into an art shape or art structure that amounts to understanding.

CHARLES WARREN

Biography

Born in Brooklyn, New York, July, 6, 1939. Graduated from Brown University in 1960. Studied philosophy at the graduate level at Harvard University 1961–3. Established the Film/Video Section at the Massachusetts Institute of Technology 1969, brought in Richard Leacock, Steven Ascher, and others to teach, and taught there himself until 1980. Taught filmmaking at Harvard 1980–3. Coauthored *The Filmmaker's Handbook* with Steven Ascher, 1984. At that time, gave up filmmaking to work as a cut-flower farmer in Vermont.

Further reading

Lane, Jim, 'The Career and Influence of Ed Pincus', *The Journal of Film and Video* 49, no. 4, 1997: 3–17.

——*The Autobiographical Documentary in America*, Madison, WI: University of Wisconsin Press, 2002.

Levin, G. Roy, *Documentary Explorations: 15 Interviews with Filmmakers*, Garden City, NY: Doubleday, 1971.

Pincus, Ed, 'New Possibilities in Film and the University', *Quarterly Review of Film Studies*, 2, no. 2, 1977: 159–78.

Rothman, William, 'Looking Back and Turning Inward: American Documentary Films of the Seventies', in David Cook (ed.), *Lost Illusions: American Cinema in the Age of Watergate and Vietnam, 1970–80*, vol. 9 of *Scribner's History of the American Cinema*, New York: Scribner's, 1999.

Plow that Broke the Plains, The

(US, Lorentz, 1936)

Pare Lorentz's first film, The Plow that Broke the Plains, marked a significant point in the history of documentary film in the United States. It was the most widely publicized peacetime attempt by the federal government to communicate to its entire citizenry through a motion picture, and its elaborately synchronized soundtrack was groundbreaking. It was the first film to be placed in congressional archives, and President Franklin Roosevelt wanted it to be shown before a joint session of Congress, which would have happened had the Capitol chambers been equipped to present a sound film. The film had been produced under the sponsorship of the Resettlement Administration (RA), a New Deal agency directed by Rexford Tugwell (one of Roosevelt's 'brain trusters'). The RA's mission was to find relief for the chronic rural poverty in the central part of the United States then known as the Dust Bowl, and its recuperative strategies included providing housing, financial, medical, and educational aid to the displaced families, as well as finding ways to restore and conserve the environment. Property interests among the middle and upper classes feared the loss of cheap labor and the undermining of rental rates that could occur as a result of government assistance.

Several factors, not the least being the perceived 'socialist' bent of the RA, conspired to hinder the film's distribution. For one, its length (around half an hour) was deemed awkward—too short to fill a feature-length slot, but too long to be a newsreel. The timing of the film's release (May 1936) coincided with a particularly sensitive moment in US partisan politics, as Roosevelt and the reforms of the Democratic Party's New Deal were facing a major reelection campaign in November of 1936.

For that reason, Republicans widely criticized the film, although a number of Democratic elected officials, especially those from the states depicted in a negative light, also took issue with The Plow's images of devastation and poverty (an Oklahoma Democrat publicly threatened to punch Tugwell in the nose over the film). Real estate interests from the Plains states bemoaned the negative representations. Finally, the distribution of a government-produced film through the established commercial channels was perceived by the film industry as a competitive threat, so the film was denied bookings through the major theater chains. Despite that opposition, and because of the efforts of RA staff to promote the film through the Midwest in the summer of 1936, The Plow was shown through independent theater chains, at an estimated three thousand of the approximately fourteen thousand commercial theaters in the United States at that time. The experiment of the state-produced film of persuasion could probably not be declared an unqualified success as an effective new mode of disseminating information, although it did lead to a handful of further films produced by the US government (The River, The Fight for Life, and the uncompleted Ecce

Figure 15 The Plow that Broke the Plains, 1936 (Courtesy of the British Film Institute)

Homo!) and to a short-lived United States Film Service run by Lorentz (1938–40).

Sometimes compared to Grierson, Lorentz is one of the great pioneers in US documentary film history. His blending of the visual (shot composition, mise-en-scène, editing), the musical (with noted composers Virgil Thomson and Louis Gruenberg), and the poetic (his narration for The River was praised by James Joyce as the 'most beautiful prose' he had heard in ten years) created a kind of cinematic *Gesamtkunstwerke*, or 'total work of art', intended here not for an elite Aryan audience but rather for mainstream media consumption in the United States. Lorentz was purported not to have liked the term documentary, preferring instead the somewhat immodest term film of merit; he used the terms documentary musical picture and melodrama of nature to describe The Plow that Broke the Plains in his own review of his film. Lorentz began working with the RA in the summer of 1935, not long before the Information Division of the RA started documenting its activities and the state of rural living by assembling a team of still photographers that included Dorothea Lange and Arthur Rothstein, both of whom would have connections to The Plow: Lange, skilled at posing subjects, assisted Lorentz in filming the California migration sequence, and Rothstein's famous steer skull photos were probably influenced by Lorentz's imagery in Plow. In addition to still photographs, radio programs, and pamphlets, the RA in 1935 decided to add motion pictures as a way of dramatizing the violence of dust storms.

With experience only as a film critic, Lorentz was a novice filmmaker when he began work on The Plow that Broke the Plains. He hired a group of experienced cameramen (Leo Hurwitz, Ralph Steiner, and Paul Strand) who were involved with the left-wing Film and Photo League and later the filmmaking collectives known as Nykino and Frontier Films. Some of the greatest drama associated with Plow would take place off camera, as the photographers found their ideological and professional differences with Lorentz increasingly intolerable. Lorentz envisioned a fantasy sequence where presumably wealthy men in top hats would walk across a field, mount tractors, and plow up the land—just one example from a flimsy script that Strand found unfilmable. The three cameramen went 'on strike', as reported in *Variety*, and offered Lorentz an alternative script that infuriated him. After they filmed what he needed—Lorentz sent Hurwitz and Strand off to film dust storms while he and Steiner teamed up to shoot, among other things, the top hat sequence—Lorentz released his crew (the fact that he did not hold all the cameramen in equal esteem is reflected in their nonalphabetical listing in the credits). Lorentz then went to California to purchase stock footage and to film the final sequence at a roadside migrant camp on US Highway 99. He was able to purchase stock footage only through the insider assistance of his Hollywood friend King Vidor (whose 1934 film Our Daily Bread may have provided some visual inspiration for Plow). Filming of the final sequence was facilitated by a fourth cameraman, Paul Ivano, and Dorothea Lange, on loan from Roy Stryker's Historical Section of the RA.

The film follows a chronological arc that attempts to explain how the Plains became the Dust Bowl, ostensibly tracing a history of the place and people, yet as an historical document the narrative is incomplete, and as a piece of rhetoric the argument is perhaps too subtle, because Lorentz tends to focus more on elemental forces at the expense of political and economic ones. The excised epilogue contains the only direct narrational references to the government programs offering relief. A similar historical narrative and several key phrases appeared earlier in a 1935 *Fortune* story by Archibald MacLeish called 'Grasslands', which may have provided a framework for Lorentz. In place of dialogue and identified characters, Lorentz wrote a script for Thomas Chalmer's godlike narration. Beginning with an animated map of the entire United States, the affected regions called 'the Plains' are traced out and exaggerated with dotted lines; the words '625,000 sq miles' and '400 million acres' appear before an image of waving grasslands fills the area within the dotted lines, and then the region's borderlines wipe outward so that the landscape fills the entire frame. If nothing else, the film works powerfully to create a national issue out of a regional problem. Sweeping panoramic shots of lush grasslands are next followed by the introduction of cattle grazing and by the massive homesteading and settlement of the region. After a sequence depicting early drought problems, a montage showing the necessity of wheat during World War I suggests that overproduction led to further misuse of the soil, culminating in dust storms and families fleeing the devastation.

One of the most vexing issues surrounding this famous documentary is the fact that two versions exist: a three-minute epilogue explaining the RA's role was screened for some audiences in 1936 (most initial reviews refer to it) but was then, for reasons still only speculative, removed. The Museum of Modern Art preserved the copy with the epilogue, but the version that was shown through the summer of 1936, as well as the version rereleased by the Department of Agriculture in 1962, lacked the epilogue. The epilogue's narration overtly stated what had only been implied up to that point: irresponsible and shortsighted use of the soil led to the creation of a disaster area, and government intervention was now required. Images of 'model farms in Nebraska' may have borne too close a similarity to Soviet communal farms, particularly given the Republican cries of 'New Deal propaganda' that preceded the 1936 fall elections.

The film's musical accompaniment, written by Thomson (famous at that time for Four Saints in Three Acts), was called 'the finest musical score of any American film' in a 1936 review, and it accounts for much of the film's power. Partly borrowed—including, for example, cowboy songs and a Protestant hymn ('Old Hundred')—and partly original material, Thomson's underscoring employs considerably more dissonance than was allowed in Hollywood's music at that time, although it did rely on certain stock musical conventions, such as pounding tom-toms supporting melodies in parallel fourths as a code for 'Indians' (although 'Indians' are mentioned only once in Lorentz's narration, the music provides multiple invocations of those earlier inhabitants who managed to live on the land for centuries without driving it into dust). Once hoping to work as a music critic, Lorentz provided several articulate and detailed sets of instructions for Thomson. He interviewed eleven other composers before settling on Thomson. Lorentz showed his rough edit to Thomson, who composed a score that Lorentz then used to re-edit his final cut. Thomson converted the entire score into a suite for concert performance, where it has become a recognized part of the twentieth-century musical canon, and parts of its style (such as its fondness for open intervals) were quickly absorbed into Hollywood's musical codes for 'Americana'.

Throughout The Plow that Broke the Plains, music and images rely on repetition and dialectic. Lorentz calculatedly contrasted scenes of fecundity with drought. Pan shots of lush grasslands are matched later in the film with a succession of still images showing cow skulls and abandoned farm equipment resting on cracked, baked-out soil; Thomson underscored the pastoral idyll with a theme in a major key that returns for the drought scenes in a minor key, reorchestrated for saxophone. In sequences meant to depict the overproduction of wheat during World War I, Lorentz's images alternate rapidly between tractors and tanks, bayonets and plow blades, cannon and grain chutes. Their rapid juxtaposition, together with the narration ('Wheat will win the war!'), suggests that wheat became a weapon for the allies. Thomson matches the visual cross-cutting by alternating the famous World War I melody 'Mademoiselle from Armentières' between major and minor keys. The 1920s are set up as a period of economic, ecological, and social excesses through Thomson's jazz-inflected score and images of an African American jazz musician, all culminating in the stock market crash, which is metonymically signaled by a stock ticker breaking on the ground. Moments of the score, such as the cattle sequences accompanied by cowboy songs, are genuinely ebullient, but Thomson occasionally slips in ironic commentary. In one scene showing a home overpowered by a dust storm, we see the dust swirling through the living room as we hear a harmonium play 'Old Hundred', a hymn the words of which refer to a divine bounty that is notably absent. The most puzzling musical-visual juxtaposition occurs with the shots of migrant workers driving into California camps, as Thomson transforms a melody from earlier in the film into a haunting tango the associations of which with upper-class leisure are asynchronous with the images of impoverished domestic life and ecological disruption. Both score and film indulge in melodramatic excesses: the narrative cueing is overstated, and its emotional ranges are limited to extremes. Particularly without the epilogue, The Plow that Broke the Plains is 'agit' without the 'prop': its images and sounds are powerfully affecting, but they only hint at the larger structural causes of the Dust Bowl and make no explicit mention of the federal relief programs in existence.

NEIL LERNER

See also: Lorentz, Pare

The Plow that Broke the Plains (US, 35mm, black and white, monosound, Resettlement Administration, 1936, 25 mins; a three-minute epilogue was shown to some audiences in 1936). Written and directed by Pare Lorentz. Photographed by Leo T. Hurwitz, Paul Ivano, Ralph Steiner, and Paul Strand. Music composed by Virgil Thomson, orchestrated by Henry Brant, and conducted by Alexander Smallens. Narrator, Thomas Chalmers. Research editor, John Franklin Carter, Jr. Editor, Leo Zochling. Sound technician, Joseph Kane. Filmed in Montana, Wyoming, Colorado, Kansas, Texas, and California. Starring Bam White (others unnamed). Budget of $6,000 grew to $19,260.

Further reading

Alexander, William, *Film on the Left: American Documentary Film from 1931 to 1942*, Princeton, NJ: Princeton University Press, 1981.

Allan, Blaine, 'Canada's Heritage (1939) and America's The Plow that Broke the Plains (1936)', *Historical Journal of Film, Radio and Television*, April 19, 1999: 439–72.

Curtis, James, *Mind's Eye, Mind's Truth: FSA Photography Reconsidered*, Philadelphia, PA: Temple University Press, 1989.

Lorentz, Pare, *Movies 1927 to 1941: Lorentz on Film*, New York: Hopkinson and Blake, 1975.

MacCann, Richard D., *The People's Films: A Political History of U.S. Government Motion Pictures*, New York: Hastings House, 1973.

O'Connor, John E., 'Case Study: The Plow that Broke the Plains', in John E. O'Connor (ed.), *Images as Artifact: The Historical Analysis of Film and Television*, Malabar, FL: Robert E. Krieger Publishing Company, 1990.

Rabinowitz, Paula, *They Must Be Represented: The Politics of Documentary*, London and New York: Verso, 1994.

Snyder, Robert L., *Pare Lorentz and the Documentary Film*, Norman, OK: University of Oklahoma Press, 1968.

Thomson, Virgil, *Virgil Thomson*, New York: Dutton, 1966.

Van Dyke, Willard, 'Letters from The River', *Film Comment*, 1965: 38–56.

Podnieks, Juris

Juris Podnieks, best known as a chronicler of the decline of the Soviet Union, was part of a new wave of documentary filmmaking that emerged in the wake of Mikhail Gorbachev's perestroika and corresponding attempts at glasnost, begun in 1985. As these forces began to take hold in the film industry, the first reaction to the new situation came from the documentary cinema. The renaissance of documentary was evident across the Soviet Union, in the studios of the Ukraine, Belarus, the Urals, and Siberia, as well as Juris Podnieks's native Latvia. The documentary emerged as one of the most active expressions of glasnost, as documentarists addressed a series of formerly taboo subjects linked to social and political problems in the Soviet Union.

Podnieks's Is it Easy to Be Young? (1986) was one of the first and most distinguished of these hard-hitting documentaries. The film opens with a rock concert in Riga, in July 1985—images that in themselves are an important statement about the increasing significance of pop music in Soviet youth culture—and follows its young subjects (not all of whom were present at the concert) over a period of almost two years. The film addresses juvenile delinquency, teenage suicide, and drugs, topics that were to assume a vital role in a number of subsequent documentaries. From a portrayal of youth lost in crime, suicide, and drugs, the documentary turns, for the first time on a Soviet screen, to the war in Afghanistan, adding to the picture of a lost generation new political and moral dimensions. Podnieks depicts a widespread sense of confusion, disappointment, and antisocial feeling with startling honesty, in a characteristically rhythmic and startling juxtaposition of images punctuated by increasingly disturbing interviews and held together by an edgy electronic soundtrack. Not surprisingly, the film broke box office records in the Soviet Union and later enjoyed a wide international distribution.

As the Soviet Union crumbled, Podnieks's collaborations with Central Television and Channel 4 added up to a haunting collective portrait of a society disintegrating morally, physically, and socially. The five-part series transmitted as Hello, Do You Hear Us? (1990) ranges over diverse topics and portrays a wide variety of individuals all over the Soviet Union, in a kaleidoscope of rapidly edited images drawn from personal interviews, newsreel, and found film footage, and amateur videotape. As in Is It Easy to Be Young?, there is a question mark at the end of the series's title, suggesting a tentative investigation rather than any ready or easy answers.

Homeland (1991), also made for Central Television, is a powerfully lyrical portrait of the emergent Baltic republics, structured around the 20th Latvian Song Festival. The songs and music provide an evocative soundtrack for Podnieks's highly accomplished cinematography and more muted polemics, and make this one of his most coherent and powerful films.

His final film, (A Portrait of an) Unfinished Business (1993), was completed by his crew after his untimely death. It depicts the slow and painful rebirth of three former Soviet republics through the central linking device of a Trans-Siberian train journey. Uncharacteristically, the film adds an intermittent voice-over to the scenes from daily life, based on Podnieks's filming notebook. The speculative tone of the commentary, together with testimonies from various crew members, leaves us with a sense of a man firmly in the tradition of 'spiritual' cinema in the Soviet sense of a preoccupation with serious matters of the human mind and spirit.

Formally, Podnieks's documentaries are distinguished by their powerful images and rhythmic editing, and by a detached narrative style that eschews voice-over and relies on a mixture of interviews, music, and archive footage—a style described by Horton as 'expressionistic cinema verité' (Horton 1992: 75). In all of his films, it is the faces and voices of ordinary people caught in the fallout from the disintegration of the Soviet empire that give them their haunting poetic density. Encouraged by the unobtrusive off-camera questioning, people reveal themselves with extraordinary openness. At times, however, as Julia Neuberger points out, Podnieks's passionate empathy can result in a loss of the ambivalence that is so revealing throughout his films and slip into a 'heroic one-sideness', favouring some ethic groups over others. (Neuberger 1994: 297).

MARINA BURKE

See also: Russia/Soviet Union

Biography

Born in Riga, Latvia, in 1950. Graduated from the cinematography faculty of VGIK, the State Film Institute in Moscow, in 1975. Went to work at the Riga Film Studio, first as assistant cameraman, then as cameraman, before finally becoming a director in 1979. His first production, The Cradle, won a prize at the Leipzig Festival, and The Kokar Brothers took first prize at the Kiev Youth Festival in 1981. In the same year, won widespread recognition both inside and outside the Soviet Union for his film Constellation of Rifleman, which won honours at the 17th All State Festival in Leningrad and also the Latvia Komsomol prize. The film that first won international recognition was Is It Easy to Be Young? (1986), which exploded many popular myths about Soviet youth. Subsequently commissioned by Central Television to make the series of documentaries about the Soviet Union at the end of the 1980s that were transmitted on Channel 4 in 1990 as Hello, Do You Hear Us? While filming the follow-up to Homeland (1991), two members of Podnieks's film crew were killed after coming under sniper fire during the Soviet coup in Riga. Podniek himself died in a freak diving accident on June 23, 1992.

Selected films

1982 Constellation of Rifleman/Strelnieku Zvaigznajs
1985 The Stone of Sisyphus/Vel Sizifs Akmen
1986 Is It Easy to Be Young?/Legko li byt' molodym?
1990 Hello, Do You Hear Us?
1991 Homeland/Krestyni put'
1991 End of Empire
1993 Unfinished Business

Further reading

Graffy, Julian, 'Juris Podnieks', *Sight and Sound* 3, no. 2, February 1993: 30–1.
Horton, Andrew, 'Nothing Worth Living For: Soviet Youth and the Documentary Movement', *Wide Angle* 12, no. 4, October 1990: 38–47.
Horton, Andrew and Brashinsky, Michael, The Zero Hour: Glasnost and Soviet Cinema in Transition, Princeton, NJ: Princeton University Press, 1992.
Neuberger, Julia, 'Soviets', *Russian Review* 53, no. 2, April 1994: 296–7.
Plakhov, Andrei, 'Soviet Cinema into the 90s', *Sight and Sound* 58, spring 1989: 53–7.

Poirier, Anne Claire

Anne Claire Poirier, who joined the National Film Board of Canada (NFB) in 1960, spent a few years working as assistant editor and assistant director in the shadow of her male colleagues, who included Claude Jutra, Michel Brault, and Gilles Groulx. In 1963 she was commissioned to direct a documentary on the actor Christopher Plummer (30 Minutes, Mister Plummer), and the following year wrote and directed her first fiction short, La Fin des étés/ The End of Summers (1964), starring Geneviève Bujold. Poirier is credited with initiating feminist filmmaking in Québec in 1967 with her landmark feature-length documentary De mère en fille/Mother-to-Be. A personal as well as political reflection on pregnancy and maternity, De mère en fille was the first feature film ever directed by a French Canadian woman.

A few years later, as part of her proposal to the NFB for the establishment of a production program coordinated by women, Poirier, along with Jeanne Morazain Boucher, published the text *En tant que Femmes: Rapport de recherches* (As Women: Research Report) (1971). This veritable manifesto for the creation of an interventionist feminist cinema in Québec would break the isolation of women and educate men on the female condition. It led to the production of the En tant que femmes film series, the first significant wave of activist documentaries and docudramas created by women at the NFB. While head of the En tant que femmes program, from 1972 to 1974 Poirier produced four films by female directors, as well as directing two films of her own: Les Filles du Roy/They Called Us 'Les Filles du Roy' (1974), a history of Québec women's traditional roles as servants, mothers, and wives, which employed an effective mixture of historical reconstruction and personal commentary to paint a vibrant picture of a subject systematically ignored by male cinéastes; and Le Temps de l'avant/Before the Time Comes (1975), a straightforward dramatic feature aimed primarily at sensitizing men to the issue of abortion.

In 1979 Poirier achieved full recognition as a major filmmaker with the release of her strikingly innovative and daring docudrama on rape, Mourir à tue-tête/A Scream from Silence. In this uncompromising look at the individual and collective brutalization of women's bodies, Poirier adopts a radical feminist perspective that blends documentary and fiction to criticize society and institutions for failing to provide victims with the support to which they are entitled. The film's graphic depiction of rape and its putative suggestion that all men are potential rapists raised a storm of debate seldom seen in the history of Canadian film.

A cry of rage that still echoes today, Mourir à tue-tête is certainly the most controversial production of Poirier's career. In contrast, her fiction films, La Quarantaine/Forty Something (1982), and Salut Victor!/Hi Victor! (1988) are accessible, traditional dramas on how friendship can transcend time and differences. Her most recent documentary film, Tu as crié Let Me Go!/You Screamed, Let Me Go! (1997), returns to the violent theme of Mourir à tue-tête. However, the explicit political agenda of the 1979 production is replaced here by a highly personal outlook on the corruption of contemporary society, as Poirier reflects, with a mixture of pain and serenity, on the murder of her own daughter in October 1992 in a drug-related dispute. In 1989, for the fiftieth anniversary of the NFB, she made a documentary on the representation of women in dozens of NFB films: Il y a longtemps que je t'aime/I've Loved You for a Long Time.

ANDRÉ LOISELLE

Biography

Born June 6, 1932 in Montreal. Studied law before switching to drama. Worked at the Société Radio-Canada. Joined the National Film Board of Canada (NFB) in 1960. Made her first feature-length film, De mère en fille/Mother-to-Be, in 1967.

Selected films

1963 Mister Plummer: director, script, editing
1965 Les Ludions/Players: director
1967 De mère en fille/Mother-to-Be: director, script
1974 Les Filles du Roy/They Called Us 'Les Filles du Roy': producer, director, script
1979 Mourir à tue-tête/A Scream from Silence: producer, director, script
1989 Il y a longtemps que je t'aime/I've Loved You for a Long Time: director
1997 Tu as crié Let Me Go!/You Screamed, Let Me Go!: director, script

Further reading

Special issue on Anne Claire Poirier, *Copie Zéro* 23, Montreal: Cinemathèque quebecoise, 1985.

Loiselle, Andre, *Mourir à tue-tête/Scream from Silence*, Trowbridge: Flicks Books, 2000.

Poirier, Léon

Although Léon Poirier has been largely forgotten by contemporary cinema scholars, he was among the most popular and technically ambitious French filmmakers of the 1920s and 1930s. A versatile director, writer, and producer, he set new quality standards for on-location shooting in standard documentary and historical reconstruction, or docudrama. The success of La Croisière noire/The Black Journey (1926), Verdun, visions d'histoire/Verdun, Visions of History (1928), L'Appel du silence/The Call (1936), and Brazza, ou l'épopée du Congo/ Brazza, or the Saga of the Congo (1940) helped to integrate both genres into the commercial mainstream and had a lasting impact on the form and practice of documentary cinema. In his films, Poirier critiqued the decadence and materialism of modern Western civilization, positing spirituality, patriotic self-sacrifice, and contact with 'primitive' cultures as antidotes to the identity crisis that Europe confronted in the wake of World War I.

Poirier began his career as a theatre manager, producer, and owner in Paris. He came to cinema after suffering serious burns in an automobile fire that led to his bankruptcy and a temporary job making short entertainment films for Gaumont just before World War I. After his demobilization in 1919, Poirier returned to the profession full-time, directing several critically acclaimed literary adaptations (Jocelyn, 1922; Geneviève, 1923; La Brière/The Salt Marsh, 1924), the outdoor shooting in rugged rural environments of which created a unique painterly depth, pictorial realism, and documentary feel.

In 1924 automobile manufacturer André Citroën hired Poirier and assistant Georges Specht to film a twenty-thousand-kilometre, seven-month expedition across Africa. Simultaneously a grandiose marketing tool and a suspense-filled adventure story that dramatized man and machine conquering some of the harshest terrain on Earth (including the Sahara desert, dense rainforests, raging rivers, and vast savannahs), La Croisière noire was also an unabashed tribute to colonialism that symbolically unified French possessions in North, West, and Central Africa. In the spirit of newly instituted associationist colonial policy that encouraged respect for rather than erasure of native cultures, Poirier crafted a well-intentioned, though methodologically naive ethnographic study in the picturesque and the exotic. His footage of collective rituals and distinctive physical characteristics is consistently charged with an unselfconscious voyeurism that betrays a European fear of decadence and desire for renewal by appropriating the uncorrupted vitality of 'primitive' African cultures.

Released in late 1926, La Croisière noire was a critical and commercial mega-hit that elevated documentary to the level of feature film. More important, it paved the way for subsequent ethnographic documentaries (including Marc Allégret's Voyage au Congo, 1927) and established representational conventions that would inform colonial cinema and popular perceptions of Africa throughout the interwar period. For Poirier, the experience was a personal revelation that decisively influenced his conception of documentary. As he wrote in the July 1926 issue of *Ciné-Miroir*:

> An exotic film is not a script that one carries in one's luggage; it is a work of art that one shapes along the way with the landscapes that one encounters, the human characteristics that one analyzes, and the incidents that one records. By virtue of his sensitivity, the cinematographer must extract the poetry, joy, and pain directly from the lives he discovers, then fashion a work of art capable of making others feel what he himself felt.

Verdun, visions d'histoire applied this approach to reconstructing the bloody 1916 battle in which Poirier had fought. Shot on location in France and Germany with actual veterans playing all but a few roles, the film echoed Abel Gance's classic J'accuse/I Accuse (1919) in its pacifist denunciation of war and internationalist plea for reconciliation among the belligerent nations. Stylistically Verdun was a striking mix of expressionist allegory and documentary realism that integrated universal-type characters such as the Mother, the Son, the Husband, the Wife, the Peasant, and the Intellectual with graphic reenactments of combat, death, and the soldiers' psychological agony. Poirier further amplified this realism by editing several segments of authentic newsreel footage into the military scenes—the first time such a technique had been used in a film about the Great War. Like La Croisière noire, Verdun drew international acclaim and performed well at the box office, thereby solidifying the director's reputation in the French film industry.

Yet like many directors of his generation Poirier found the transition to sound cinema difficult. After releasing two mediocre fiction films set in eastern Africa (Caïn, aventures des mers exotiques/Cain, 1930; La Voie sans disque/The Unmarked Track, 1933) and an overblown remake entitled Verdun: Memories of History (1931), he undertook a cinematic biography of Charles de Foucauld, an obscure soldier-turned-Catholic missionary who had been killed in 1916 during an anti-French uprising. L'Appel du silence, which brought together the themes of Western decadence, spiritual regeneration, pacifism, and patriotic martyrdom present in Poirier's previous work, marked the crowning achievement of his career and made Foucauld an instant national hero.

Financed by Poirier himself and small public donations collected during a two-year fundraising tour, the film was shot primarily on location at Foucauld's isolated retreat in the Algerian Sahara. In addition to winning the 1936 Grand Prize of French Cinema, it was the top box-office draw of the year, selling nearly a million tickets in Paris and ranking among the five biggest successes of the entire decade. French conservatives seized on L'Appel du silence to validate their agenda and discredit the socialist-led Popular Front government that had recently taken power, but the film contains no clear endorsement of any party, instead portraying all politics as corrupt. As for moral regeneration and colonialism, at the time both were broadly pan-ideological values—hence the film's extraordinary popularity. Nevertheless, cinema historians have often retrospectively cast Poirier as an apologist for the Right.

Poirier's next project, Brazza, ou l'épopée du Congo, focused on the late nineteenth-century exploration of Equatorial Africa by Pierre Savorgnan de Brazza, who, like Foucauld, is presented as a visionary Christ figure seeking to revitalize France spiritually and culturally through benevolent colonialism. Shooting in the rainforests of Gabon and the Belgian Congo was an enormous logistical challenge that required specially modified film and sound equipment, as well as a production team of two hundred native labourers, half-a-dozen French engineers, and a small fleet of boats. Though its technical quality and thematic appeal equalled that of L'Appel du silence, Brazza was overshadowed by World War II, its run cut short by the German invasion.

Poirier remained in France during war, but maintained a low profile to preserve his independence in an industry that was tightly regulated by Vichy French and German authorities. He made only one film during the Occupation, a melodrama titled Jeannou, the proruralist message of which led to postwar suspicions of Pétainism but no formal indictment or sanctions like those levied against so many of his peers. In 1947 Poirier made his final film, La Route inconnue/The Unknown Road, about Charles de Foucauld's early-life adventures in Morocco and spiritual awakening. Its failure to resonate with postwar audiences pushed him into retirement, bringing an otherwise distinguished career to an abrupt and anticlimactic end.

BRETT BOWLES

Biography

Born in Paris, 25 August 1884, nephew of Impressionist painter Berthe Morisot. Successful theatre manager, producer, and owner 1906–13. Served in artillery unit during the Great War 1914–18. Fiction film director and producer at Gaumont 1919–24. Transition to documentary with hits The Black Journey and Verdun: Visions of History 1924–8. Brief return to fiction film and experimentation with sound cinema 1929–33. Made The Call and Brazza, or the Saga of the Congo 1935–9. Virtual inactivity during World War II 1940–5. Researched and shot The Unknown Road 1946–8. Retired to Urval-le-Buisson, France, became mayor, and published memoirs 1949–53. Died in Urval, June 26, 1968.

Selected films

1926 La Croisière noire/The Black Journey: director

1928 Verdun, visions d'histoire/Verdun, Visions of History: director, writer, producer

1931 Verdun, souvenirs d'histoire/Verdun, Memories of History: director, writer, producer
1934 La Croisière jaune/The Yellow Journey (Andre Sauvage): editor
1936 L'Appel du silence/The Call: director, writer, producer
1940 Brazza, ou l'épopée du Congo/Brazza, or the Saga of the Congo: director, writer, producer
1948 La Route inconnue: Charles de Foucauld au Maroc/The Unknown Road: Charles de Foucauld in Morocco: director, writer, producer

Further reading

Abel, Richard, *French Cinema: The First Wave, 1915–29*, Princeton, NJ: Princeton University Press, 1984.

Boulanger, Pierre, *Le Cinéma colonial de 'L'Atlantide' à' 'Lawrence d'Arabie'*, Paris: Seghers, 1975.

Haardt, Georges-Marie and Audouin-Dubreuil, Louis, *La Croisière noire: expédition Citroën Centre-Afrique*, Paris: Plon, 1927.

Leprohon, Pierre, *L'Exotisme et le cinema: les chasseurs d'images à la conquête du monde*, Paris: J. Susse, 1945.

Levine, Alison J., 'Film and Colonial Memory: La Croisière Noire, 1924–2004', in Alec Hargreaves (ed.), *Memory, Empire, and Post-colonialism: Legacies of French Colonialism*, Lexington, KY: Lexington Books, 2005.

Piault, Marc Henri, 'L'exotisme et le cinema ethnographique: la rupture de La Croisière noire', *Journal of Film Preservation* 63, 2001: 6–16.

Poirier, Leon, *Vingt-quatre images à la seconde: du studio au désert*, Tours: Maison Mame, 1953.

——*A la recherche d'autre chose*, Bruges: Descleede Brouwer, 1968.

Slavin, David, *Colonial Cinema and Imperial France, 1919–39*, Baltimore, MD: Johns Hopkins University Press, 2001.

Ungar, Steven, 'Leon Poirier's L'Appel du silence and the Cult of Imperial France', *Journal of Film Preservation* 63, 2001: 41–6.

Poland

Short documentary films first appeared in Poland in the years before World War II. They were a means by which ideas that would otherwise have remained suppressed in the communist nation could be discreetly presented for interpretation by viewers. At the time, Polish documentaries either focused mainly on social themes or were 'avant-garde and experimental films created by artists closely connected with avant-garde circles in painting and poetry' (Fuksiewicz 1973: 58). Studios and films were subsidized by the state (Kornatowska 1992: 47). Shorts had to be produced in such a way that the government would approve of them and see them as being of educational value to the nation. The subject matter covered by documentaries was limited.

It was after World War II that a reorganization of Polish cinematography occurred, as the young generation began taking over and working with shorts. This new generation turned to documentaries as a means to explore their creativity and their new ideas. During the war photographs and other materials were collected and later used to produce documentaries on the Polish contribution to the victory over Nazism (Fuksiewicz 1973: 58). This led to a sense of nationalism among the Polish people and helped to unite them during war. The first short films to be made in Poland after liberation were Jerzy Bossak's Bitwa O Kolobrzeg/The Battle for Kolobrzeg (1945) and Zaglada Berlina/The Annihilation of Berlin (1945). 'Antoni Bohdziewicz's Ostatni Parteitag w Norymberdze[/The Last Parteitag in Nuremburg (1946)] was an attempt at a complete settlement of accounts with Nazi war crimes' (Fuksiewicz 1973: 59).

During and after the war, the devastation and rebuilding of Poland were a central theme of documentary. One of the most popular works on this theme remains Tadeusz Makarczynski's Suite Varsovienne/Warsaw Suite (1946).

Throughout the postwar period Polish cinematography began developing at a much faster pace. An increase in films led to an increase in the range of subjects being depicted and accepted by the public. As the film industry expanded, the number of filmmakers in Poland grew.

In the 1950s four main influences led to the increasing number of documentaries and short films in Poland. The first was the expansion of the film industry, which led to an expansion of production studios, greater willingness to take risks, enhanced creativity, and the exploration of a variety of new ideas. The second factor to play an important role in the increased production of documentaries in Poland was the emergence of young directors newly graduated from the Higher State Film School. The third major influence was the change in the political and social climate that took place in the mid-1950s. Finally, there was the founding of The Warsaw

Documentary Film Studio, the principal location where documentaries began to be made.

In 1955, with the introduction of so-called Black documentaries, a new atmosphere emerged in Poland. 'The term "Black series" bracketed those films which attacked problems that were not supposed to exist' (Bren 1986: 48). W.I. Borowik's film Paragraf Zero/Paragraph Zero (1957) is one such film; it depicts the life of prostitutes. Another such film is Jerzy Hoffman and Edward Skorzewski's Uwaga Chuligani/ Watch Out! Thugs! (1955), which dealt with the growing problem of juvenile delinquency in Poland. At this point, filmmakers started to intertwine fiction with reality in order to produce documentaries. The documentaries were grounded in fact, but the filmmakers used fictional means to create their characters. It was these 'Black' films that made the public more aware of the documentary genre.

As their atmosphere and surroundings changed, directors relied on documentaries to illustrate the economic and social changes taking place in Poland. Changes such as the growth and expansion of industry, the variety of career paths becoming available to the younger generation, and the everyday working life of the nation were themes that dominated the documentaries. Following the theme of transformations emerging in Polish life, Witold Lesiewicz's Wesola II/Vesola II (1952) traces the opening of a coal mine.

In the late 1950s two key elements transformed documentaries yet further: the intimate way of perceiving work and the remarkable way in which individuals were being portrayed. Between 1956 and 1957 documentaries began to report the various kinds of negligence and social ills that accompanied rapid industrial development. Films such as Hoffman and Skorzewski's Dzieci Oskarzaja/The Children Accuse (1955) revolve around themes such as alcoholism invading lives and the backwardness of regions untouched by new development. Films helped to remind Polish audiences of difficult, complex social problems, while giving them glimpses of positive changes within the community. Documentaries mimicked reality, which forced individuals to face issues directly. As documentaries continued developing and evolving, direct sound recording soon became a basic element in their production. While realist documentaries gained in popularity, there also began to emerge 'philosophic shorts', which were polar opposites of realist documentaries in that they gave filmmakers freer rein to creativity and personal interpretation of new ideas. Films such as these often exposed the disturbances in our modern world, such as human ruthlessness, cruelty, and egotism. Roman Polanski's Dwaj Ludzie z Szafa/ Two Men and a Wardrobe (1958) is one of the better-known of these films.

In the following years, filmmakers began to focus less on immediate problems and more on the individual. Interest in social themes remained, but producers stopped singling out specific Polish affairs and instead adopted a wider, calmer perspective. Issues of national crisis and war became less prevalent, as social issues such as gambling, alcoholism, childhood, and the intimacy of human life took over. This trend continued and developed in the years that followed, as more experienced documentary film producers moved on to making feature films and the younger generation continued to explore the world of shorts (Fuksiewicz 1973: 65). One of the more popular shorts produced at this time was Jerzy Hoffman and Edward Skorzewski's film Gangsterzy i Filantropi/Gangsters and Philanthropists (1962).

In 1961 the Short Film Festival took place in Krakow. It was the first Polish film festival to be held in the country. By 1964 it had evolved into an international festival, and the majority of the productions shown were documentaries. The grand prize of the first Krakow Festival was awarded to Muzykanci/Musicians (1960), a classic documentary made by Kazimierz Karabasz. It was Karabasz, along with another film producer, Jerzy Bossak, who gave rise to the documentary approach of marrying ethics with aesthetics in the course of production.

By the second half of the 1960s, World War II was being examined by documentary filmmakers. A great deal of historical material became newly available to filmmakers: material that depicted Nazi crimes and Poland's struggle throughout the war.

By the late 1970s and early 1980s many changes being made in Polish society affected the documentary film industry. For instance, in 1978 the Film and Television School at Katowice was founded. This film school taught students a documentary-oriented style of production and was seen as a direct competitor to the National Film School at Lodz (one of the first film schools to be founded in Poland). Up until the 1980s Polish documentary films were seen merely as 'additions' that would precede feature films. In the late 1980s it became obvious that the additions were competing with the feature films in terms of aesthetics. It did not take long for documentaries to be viewed independently of any other type of film. Clearly, they were a means by which views that would otherwise be suppressed by communist authorities could be 'smuggled in'.

The year 1989 brought great changes to the film industry in Poland, because it was during this year that Polish society made the transition from a communist regime to a democracy. Following the 1989 'Freedom Shock', the state-controlled and state-owned industry was transformed into independent studios and companies, which were free to make their own financial and production decisions. 'The relationship between the state and the artist, as well as between the artist and its audience had been modified dramatically […] The idea was to create a new system in which state patronage co-exists with private initiatives' (Haltof 1995: 137, 139).

One year later, in 1990, there was yet another drastic alteration to the Polish film industry: censorship was abolished. Film producers and directors suddenly were responsible for both the successes and the failures of their products. 'As a consequence of these recent political transformations, hidden archives and victimized dissidents no longer constituted the Polish film landscape' (Haltof 1995: 15). Filmmaking quickly shifted from a national and social mission to a strictly professional endeavor. Now filmmakers were held accountable for their own productions. They had their films as a defense, rather than the state as well. It was now up to the producer to decide what was to be censored and what was to be portrayed to the audiences. This movement granted film producers greater liberty, but it also led some to feel an immense, sometimes unbearable sense of responsibility. During this post-communist period filmmakers attempted to deviate from issues of politics and history, because the Polish audiences had grown tired of these central themes.

In the late twentieth century, many social, economic, and political problems arose as a result of Poland's transition to a market economy. In order to keep film production numbers up and steady, three government funding bodies were introduced in 1991: the Script Agency, the Film Production Agency, and the Film Distribution Agency. The Script Agency (Agencja Scenariuszowa) was established in order to ensure the existence of a prominent market for film scripts in Poland. The funds available through the Script Agency are used to support script development and pre-production work. The Film Production Agency (Agencja Produkcji Filmowej) was founded as a means of collecting funds used mostly for the production of projects that are seen as having 'cultural value', such as documentaries and educational films. Finally, the Film Distribution Agency (Agencja Dystrybucji Filmowej) was initiated to ensure the distribution of important cultural and national films.

The future of Polish cinema is uncertain. Today, there are many foreign and international filmmakers entering Poland. Polish filmmakers are worried that their national cinema runs the risk of undergoing commercialization by Western distributors entering the Polish market. In 1992, for example, 'more than seventy percent of the Polish repertoire consisted of American films; Polish films made up only thirteen percent' (Haltof 1995: 141). Although movie directors such as Steven Spielberg are traveling to Polish soil to film productions such as Schindler's List (1993), the demand for Polish productions is waning. It is important to support coproductions, but it is equally important that Polish theaters do not become filled with American movies. Needless to say, Polish critics are insisting that the influx of films needs to be controlled in order to preserve the Polish film industry.

Despite the turbulence and uncertainty that the Polish film industry has faced since the 1989 'Freedom Shock', Polish documentary film continues to thrive. Today, between one hundred and fifty and two hundred documentary films are produced each year in Poland. The majority of these are broadcast on television and have attracted the attention of worldwide audiences. One of the most popular documentary series that airs on television in Poland is Czas Na Dokument/Time for a Documentary. Other documentaries, such as Maciej Drygas's Uslyszcie Moj Krzyk/Hear My Cry (1991), Marcel Lozinski's 89mm Od Europy/89mm from Europe (1993), Dariusz Jablonski's FotoAmateur/Amateur Photographer (1998), and Wojciech Staron's Syberyjska Lekcja/Siberian Lesson (1998) have all earned great critical acclaim and have received awards at international film festivals.

Present-day Polish documentaries, and those of the 1990s, can be divided into four main categories. The first two categories are named in honor of two famous Polish documentary makers, Marcel Lozinski and Andrzej Fidyk. The last two categories consist of historical and biographical documentaries. The four different types of shorts are more thoroughly summarized below.

Lozinski documentaries are documentaries in which the producer's main interest lies in the everyday life of the everyday individual. Locating the absolute essence of the ordinary life lived by the ordinary person is a mysterious process. The producer feels a great sense of responsibility in depicting the life of the individual, and the individual himself or herself, as accurately as possible. Films such as Lozinski's Wizyta/A Visit (1974) and Marcin Latalla's Slad/Trace (1996) are world-renowned documentaries that fall in this category.

Fidyk documentaries are similar to Lozinski documentaries, but they are less interested in everyday life and more committed to making contemporary issues as attractive as issues depicted in Hollywood productions. The Fidyk documentary deals with contemporary problems and present-day changes in customs and morals. However, it is produced in such an ingenious way that rather than getting bored, contemporary audiences are naturally drawn in. Included in this genre are Fidyks's Defilada/Parade (1989), Sladkowski's Szwedzkie Tango/Swedish Tango (1999), and Piotr Morawski's Tata, I Love You/Daddy, I Love You (1998). Such films are known for 'attracting the most interest but, at the same time, arousing the most controversy and disputes' (Lubelski 2004: 10).

The third type of documentary prevalent today consists of historical documentaries. A great majority of them were produced in the early 1990s, right after the communist regime collapsed in Poland. Historical documentaries were produced more as a duty to the country than anything else. Filmmakers believed that they owed it not only to their nation, but also to the community to produce films that continued to document Polish history. This was critical then, because with the abolition of censorship, filmmakers had an opportunity to retell history accurately, without interference. Thanks to unlimited access to historical archives, Marek Drazkiewicz's documentary Zdrada/Treason (1991) is one such film in which 'there is a new approach presented to the history of Polish foreign policy in the period between the two world wars' (Lubelski 2004: 12). Historical documentaries aim to discover the truth behind history and to uncover all the distortion that characterized postwar 'history'.

The final group of short films consists of biographies. These films trace the lives of politicians, scientists, and artists, offering educational value to the nation. Films such as Jadwiga Zajicek's Zycie Jak Film/A Life Like a Film (1994) and Andrzej Wajda's Idac, Spotykajac/Going, Meeting (1999) not only educate audiences but also show how famous individuals, including leading filmmakers, got to where they are today.

In the past, Polish producers had to face the challenge of producing documentaries that accurately represented reality but at the same time appealed to both the Polish audience and the communist authorities. As the years progressed and Poland entered a postwar era that transformed the economy into a democracy, the major challenge for film producers was to uncover the truths that remained hidden. Although today the state has no say in what type of film an artist decides to produce, the filmmaker has just as big a challenge to face as ever before. The challenge is no longer to please a state, a government, or a body of authorities but, rather, to attract an audience that has disintegrated into numerous entities. With democracy comes freedom, and with freedom comes the liberty to voice countless opinions on countless subjects. The challenge facing the present-day filmmaker in Poland is significant: to produce documentaries that will be accepted and praised by audience members of varying tastes both at home and around the globe.

SAPNA GUPTA

See also: Bossak, Jerzy; Lozinski, Marcel

Further reading

Bren, Frank, *World Cinema 1: Poland*, London: Flicks Books, 1986.

Dowell, Pat, 'The Man Who Put Poland on the Post-War Map of Cinema: An Interview with Andrzej Wajda', *Cineaste* 19, fall 1992: 51–4.

Fuksiewicz, Jacek, *Polish Cinema*, Poland: Interpress Publishers, 1973.

Haltof, Marek, 'A Fistful of Dollars: Polish Cinema after the 1989 Freedom Shock', *Film Quarterly* 48, spring 1995: 15–25.

——'Everything for Sale: Polish National Cinema After 1989', *Canadian Slavonic Papers* 39, March–June 1997: 137–53.

Kornatowska, Maria, 'Polish Cinema', *Cineaste* 19, fall 1992: 47–51.

Lubelski, Tadeusz, 'Polish Contemporary Documentary Film: Essays on Polish Culture', *Culture.pl*, August 25, 2004, www.culture.pl/en/culture/artykuly/es_film_dokumentalny

Michalek, Boleslaw and Turaj, Frank, *The Modern Cinema of Poland*, Bloomington, IN: Indiana University Press, 1988.

Rogerson, Edward, 'Polish Cinema: An Internal Exile?' *Sight and Sound* 55, summer 1986: 195–7.

Sosnowski, Alexandra, 'Cinema in Transition: The Polish Film Today', *Journal of Popular Film and Television* 24, spring 1996: 10–16.

Warchol, Tomasz, 'Polish Cinema: The End of a Beginning', *Sight and Sound* 55, summer 1986: 190–4.

Portillo, Lourdes

Lourdes Portillo is a Mexican-born, Chicana-identified documentary filmmaker. Her work has centered primarily on gendered Latin American and Chicano/Latino themes. She was part of a Marxist film collective in the 1970s called Cine-Manifest, and later founded the oldest Latino film organization, Cine Acción, which operates to this day in San Francisco. After receiving her MFA at the San Francisco Art Institute, she began working on her first documentary, After the Earthquake/Después del terremoto (1979), a piece about a Nicaraguan immigrant who flees his native country and settles in the Bay Area.

Her 1985 film, Las Madres: The Mothers of the Plaza de Mayo, which she codirected with Susana Muñoz, was nominated for an Academy Award for Best Documentary. It describes the heroic efforts made by the mothers of the *desaparecidos* or 'disappeared' children who were kidnapped and killed during Argentina's Dirty War, a dictatorship which lasted from 1976–83.

Portillo has focused her work on documenting the role of women within the Chicano/Latino/Latin American community and related issues of identity, politics, and culture in a contemporary setting. Her documentaries have ranged from Argentine 'maternal' activists, Mexican practices of the 'Day of the Dead' ritual celebration, a portrait of the Tejana singer Selena and her fan base in Corpus Christi, Texas, her familial probe into the death of her favorite uncle Oscar in Mexico, to the unresolved case of over two hundred young women murdered in the maquiladora town of Juárez, Mexico.

Rosa Linda Fregoso, Portillo's foremost biographer and critic, sums up Portillo's aesthetic sensibility in the following manner: 'While her work conforms to the realist aesthetics of cinema, Portillo has created a genuinely hybrid style of filmmaking insofar as she crosses the border of multiple styles and playfully blends aesthetic traditions' (Fregoso 2001: 100). In films such as The Devil Never Sleeps, for instance, she mixes the traditional documentary mode of interviews with beautiful and stylized shots of images such as tomatoes, toy tractors, and family photographs suspended on rippling water.

In her documentary, La Ofrenda: Days of the Dead, Portillo connects common themes between the Mexican and Mexican-American experiences of the Day of the Dead ceremony. She examines the traditional ritual in small Mexican villages, but then shifts to a more modern rendition in the gay Latino community of San Francisco. Her idea is to trace parallels between the Mexican religious ritual and the altars made in the United States to honor the deaths caused by AIDS. By making these connections, Portillo is making radical claims about the Latino diaspora and the collective identity of Latinos that is ultimately deterritorialized, but remains unified by cultural and religious ritual. By bridging the gap between Latin Americans, Chicanos/as and US Latino/as, she is acting in political ways to stress commonalities and linkages between these geographically separated groups.

Portillo's strengths in her documentaries have been the uses of unorthodox or 'non-legitimate' sources of knowledge, such as rumor, folktales, telenovela clips, dichos (proverbs) and other forms of popular culture (they are often 'feminized' practices such as gossip) to examine how knowledge is constructed in Mexico and in the United States. Her films often share themes of border crossing, the nature of truth, and the filmmaker's self-reflexivity in story-telling. Fregoso states that The Devil Never Sleeps also 'sketches the permeable borders between nations, genres, and the political/familial identities' (Fregoso 2001: 90). Portillo has deemed this film a melodocumystery due to its form of crossing genres, borders, and styles of filmmaking. Her aim was to infuse the traditional US documentary form with some elements of melodrama, a narrative device often utilized in Latin

America, but frequently disliked by Americans. In an interview she states that 'in traditional documentaries, there's a sense of objectivity in documentary where you are not supposed to feel strong feelings. And that's what melodrama is about, the exaggeration of drama' (Portillo in Fregoso 1999: 324).

Humor is also an important device used in Portillo's films. In 1993, to commemorate and contest Columbus's 'discovery' of America, Portillo teamed up with the Chicano comedy troupe, Culture Clash, to create the eighteen-minute piece Columbus on Trial whereby the main character, a Native American named Stormcloud (Richard Montoya) charges Columbus with genocide in a comedic parody of courtroom dramas. This piece utilizes an inventive use of blue screen, whereby you can see Portillo's hand in placing 'exotic backdrops' to illustrate the various voyages that Columbus made. While it appeals to the viewer's sense of humor, it simultaneously engages the audience to critically rethink Columbus's legacy from the point of view of oppressed citizens.

Señorita Extraviada/Missing Young Woman tells the haunting story of the more than two hundred kidnapped, raped, and murdered young women of Cuidad Juárez, Mexico since 1993. The majority have come to the border city from the rural villages to work in the maquiladoras. Portillo spent three years in Juárez, meeting with human rights groups and speaking with the family members of the victims, who became the protagonists of the film. This documentary could be considered part of the Latin American literary/film genre the testimonio, whereby silenced or marginalized people are given a space to speak of their traumatic experiences. These stories, in the words of Portillo, 'spoke to me and became the heart of my film. These voices were the most important because they rang true and demanded justice' (Portillo 2003: 230).

The film tries to outline some of the possible murder suspects by describing a tangled web involving police complicity, government corruption, and a powerful group of drug traffickers in Juárez. Portillo's film worked as a consciousness-raising tool and a call to action. Portillo, along with Mexican filmmaker María Nováro organized both indoor and outdoor film screenings in Mexico to educate the public about this group of unsolved murders. The film helped to galvanize discussion, and soon various human rights and women's groups visibly organized around this issue (Portillo 2003: 232).

Although Portillo tackles difficult and sometimes taboo subjects in her native Mexico (e.g. questions of homosexuality, adultery, rape, and political corruption), she is able to gain entré into this society due to her Northern Mexican roots, but also because of her special status as an outside observer coming from the United States. Her dual subject positions as a Mexicana and Chicana allows her to straddle two worlds: she takes the critical distance needed to see the problems of Mexican society from an outsider's point of view, while intimately understanding the nuances of the people and the culture she has such an interest in comprehending.

TAMARA L. FALICOV

Biography

Born in Chihuahua, Mexico, Portillo was raised in Los Angeles from the age of thirteen. In 1978, after graduating from the San Francisco Art Institute, Portillo was awarded the American Film Institute (AFI) Independent Filmmaker Award to create an internationally acclaimed narrative film, After the Earthquake/Después del terremoto, about a Nicaraguan refugee living in San Francisco. In 1985 Portillo won an Academy Award nomination in the Best Documentary category for Las Madres: The Mothers of the Plaza de Mayo. This film won twenty awards and positioned her to obtain PBS funding to complete her next film, La Ofrenda: The Days of the Dead, in 1989. In 1992, in connection with commemoration of Columbus's 'discovery' of America, Portillo won an NEA Inter-Arts grant to produce a performance piece called 'Columbus on Trial', featuring the Chicago comedy troupe Culture Clash. It screened at the London and Sundance film festivals. This film was selected for the 1993 Whitney Biennial. In 1994 she was awarded a Guggenheim fellowship in recognition of her achievements in filmmaking. Continuing with Mexican and Mexican American themes, she next created a film about border crossing and family secrets in Mexico called The Devil Never Sleeps/El diablo nunca duerme. In 1999 she directed the documentary Corpus: A Home Movie for Selena about the impact that the Tejana singer Selena Quintanilla had on young Chicanas in Texas. Her most recent film, Señorita Extraviada, is a grim story of the two hundred murdered young women of Juárez, Mexico. The filmmaker poetically investigates the circumstances of the murders and the horror, fear, and courage of the families whose children have been taken.

Selected films

1979 After the Earthquake/Después del terremoto
1986 Las Madres: The Mothers of the Plaza de Mayo
1988 La Ofrenda: The Days of the Dead
1992 Columbus on Trial
1994 The Devil Never Sleeps/El diablo nunca duerme
1999 Corpus: A Home Movie for Selena
2001 Señorita Extraviada/Missing Young Woman

Further reading

Fregoso, Rosa Linda, *Lourdes Portillo: The Devil Never Sleeps and Other Films*, Austin, TX: University of Texas Press, 2001.

——'Sacando los trapos al sol (airing dirty laundry) in Lourdes Portillo's Melodocumystery, The Devil Never Sleeps', in Duana Robin and Ira Jaffe (eds), *Redirecting the Gaze: Gender, Theory and Cinema in the Third World*, New York: SUNY Press, 1999: 307–29.

Fusco, Coco, 'Las Madres de la Plaza de Mayo: An Interview with Susana Muñoz and Lourdes Portillo', *Cineaste* 15, no. 1, 1986: 22–5.

Gonzalez, Rita, 'The Said and the Unsaid: Lourdes Portillo Tracks Down Ghosts in Señorita Extraviada', *Aztlan: A Journal of Chicano Studies* 28, no. 2, fall 2003: 235–40.

Portillo, Lourdes, 'Filming Señorita Extraviada', *Aztlan: A Journal of Chicano Studies* 28, no. 2, fall 2003: 229–35.

Portugal

The first Portuguese documentaries were a series of short films produced in 1896 by the film pioneer Aurélio da Paz dos Reis (1852–1931). Obviously influenced by the Lumière brothers, the films depicted scenes of daily life in Portugal—cattle markets, firemen at work, arrival of trains, and a very typical Saída do Pessoal Operario da Fabrica Confiança/Workers' Exit from the Confiança Shirt Factory. Although Paz dos Reis can be considered the first filmmaker of the Iberian peninsula, his career was extremely brief. When a screening of his films in Brazil in 1897 failed, he lost all interest in filmmaking.

During the first twenty-five years of cinema in Portugal, the documentary was reduced to the filming of newsreel scenes, which led to the curious fact that all films of more or less 'documentary' condition were generically defined as actualidades, or newsreels. It was not until the end of the silent cinema that the influence of foreign filmmakers, and the critical commercial success of works by Flaherty, Ruttmann, and Vertov, marked a turning point in Portuguese documentary filmmaking. This turning point was marked by the release of three important films: Nazaré, Praia de Pescadores/The Fishers of Nazaré (1929), Alfama, Velha Lisboa/Alfama, the Oldest Lisbon (1929), and Douro, Faina Fluvial/Working at the Douro (1931).

Filmed in 1928, Nazaré was photographed and produced by Artur Costa de Macedo (the only name in the credits when it was first released) and directed by José Leitão de Barros. According to its title, it shows daily life in that fishermen's village, with great attention to atmospheric detail. The critics hailed the superb photography and handsome editing, and soon it was classified as a milestone in Portuguese cinema. Unfortunately, the prints preserved are fragmentary. In the two following decades, Leitão de Barros (1896–1967) became one of the major Portuguese filmmakers, although not in the documentary genre. He directed such epics as the first 'talkie', A Severa (1931, filmed in Paris), Bocage (1936), and Camões (1946).

Alfama, Velha Lisboa is forgotten today, but in 1929 it was warmly received. Because its credited director was an amateur, a medical student named João de Almeida e Sá, the merits of the film are usually attributed to its cinematographer, again Artur Costa de Macedo.

Douro Faina Fluvial is the most accomplished of these three films, in part because of the name of its director, the now nonagenarian and still active Manoel de Oliveira (born 1908), but also because of its modern, avant-garde cinematic language that was probably one of the reasons for its weak critical and commercial reception. In 1934 the film was rereleased in a new version, which had been slightly reedited by Oliveira and had an added soundtrack, as a companion to the successful feature Gado Bravo/Brave Bulls, directed by Oliveira's former assistant António Lopes Ribeiro. Douro Faina Fluvial was reevaluated by critics and is now considered a classic.

Between 1933 and 1974 and after the military coup of 1926, Portugal lived under an authoritarian regime called Estado Novo. António de Oliveira Salazar, professor of economics at the University of Coimbra, was the leader of this dictatorship, which was based on the political clichés of religion, family, and authority, with the addition of light fascist elements and a solid friendship with one democratic power, Great Britain, which actually was the main supporter of Salazar's regime until its very last years. Cinema was not one of the priorities of the new regime's politics; in fact, the Portuguese film industry was practically nonexistent, and theatres only showed foreign films, but Salazar knew that control of every medium was necessary.

Because the number of fiction films being produced was minimal, all efforts were concentrated on documentaries. In 1933 a propaganda office called the Secretariado da Propaganda Nacional, Alfama, Velha Lisboa (SPN) was created to oversee the ideological messages circulated by newspapers, radio, and cinema (in 1944 the name was subtly changed to Secretariado Nacional da Informação, Cultura Populare Turismo: SNI). The main collaborator among cinema people was António Lopes Ribeiro (1908–95), who was responsible for the most important cinematic projects of Salazarism. One of them was related to the colonies: during nine months of 1938, the SPN organized an expedition to Portuguese Africa ('Missão Cinegráfica às Colónias de África'), led by Ribeiro, to shoot enough material to edit a series of films of variable length. The results led to an eighty-minute documentary, Viagem de Sua Exa. O Presidente da República a Angola/Journey of His Excellency the President to Angola (1939), some short subjects like Guiné, Berço do Império/Guinea, Birth of Empire (1940, twenty minutes), Aspectos de Moçambique/Vistas of Mozambique (1941, twelve minutes), or Angola, a Nova Lusitánia/Angola, a New Lusitania (1944, thirty minutes), and a feature film with actors, Feitiço do Império/The Enchantment of Empire (1940). Ribeiro continued his service to Salazar until 1974.

In 1956 Manoel de Oliveira, retired from filmmaking since 1942, presented a thirty-minute documentary entitled O Pintor e A Cidade/The Painter and the City, a tribute to his native city, Porto (like the earlier Douro Faina Fluvial) as well as to the painter António Ruiz. The release of this film acted as the prelude to the most productive period of Portuguese documentary—paradoxically the result of a negative factor.

In the mid-1950s film production in Portugal collapsed as a result of several factors. The weak domestic market contributed to the problem, while the lack of markets for export reduced the production of newsreels and documentaries, most of them shot inexpensively using 16mm equipment and black-and-white photography. This was not the case for Rapsódia Portuguesa/ Portuguese Rhapsody (1958, directed by João Mendes), a 35mm, colour, handsomely mounted travelog produced by the SNI for strictly touristic purposes; however, it does characterize A Almadraba Atuneira/The Tunny-Fishery (1961), the film debut of the best documentarist filmmaker of Portugal, António Campos (1922–99). Campos's innovative and courageous work is largely unknown, even in Portugal, and merits attention. He generally writes and shoots his own films, and receives production support from cultural institutions, mainly the Gulbenkian Foundation, where he was a civil servant for years. His films are little masterpieces of ethnographic cinema. To name only a few from a filmography of almost fifty titles, we can select two medium-length works, Vilarinho das Furnas (1971) and Falamos de Rio de Onor/Talking About Rio de Onor (1974), both clever studies of primitive rural societies.

Apart from the films of Campos, marked by their ethnographic approach, the documentaries produced during the 1960s can be classified by subject. The less interesting are those made to promote tourism, some of them edited only in English versions, like José Fonseca e Costa's (later a noted feature director) The Pearl of the Atlantic (about Madeira, 1969) and Golf in the Algarve (1972).

Another subject was figures of Portuguese culture, living or dead. Among the writers profiled, the best examples are the tributes to poet Sophia de Mello Breyner Andresen (1968, released 1972) by João César Santos (later known as Monteiro), and to novelist Fernando Namora (1969) by Manuel Guimarães. Both films were produced by Ricardo Malheiro, who, along with Francisco de Castro, was one of the most enterprising producers of those years. Malheiro was also the sponsor of 27 Minutos con Fernando Lopes-Graça/27 Minutes with

Fernando Lopes-Graça (shot 1968–9, released 1971), directed without credit with another future great filmmaker, António Pedro Vasconcelos (Lopes Graça was a musician), and Castro produced Almada Negreiros Vivo, Hoje/Almada Negreiros Live, Today (1969), homage to this painter by Antonio de Macedo, which was one of the most celebrated titles of this series. Manuel Guimarães produced and directed Carta a Mestre Dórdio Gomes/A Letter for Mr Dórdio Gomes (1971, about a painter) and Areia, Mar—Mar, Areia/Sand, Sea—Sea, Sand (1973, about sculptor Martins Correia). Distinguished documentary specialist Faria de Almeida (born in Mozambique in 1934) provided one of the most ambitious 'biographic' films about a living writer: Vida e Obra de Ferreira de Castro/Life and Works of Ferreira de Castro (1971, released 1974), which included scenes of the character's childhood, testimonies of colleagues like Jorge Amado, and excerpts from amateur films. It was produced by Telecine-Moro, a company specializing in commercial filmlets that contributed to the production of documentaries and newsreels. A more conservative approach was given by veteran Lopes Ribeiro in his Gil Vicente e o Seu Teatro/Gil Vicente and his Theatre (1965), an official SNI production for the fifth centennial of the famed playwright.

The most accomplished film about a living character was Belarmino (1964), directed by Fernando Lopes (born 1935) and produced by António da Cunha Telles, based on the remembrances of Belarmino Fragoso, a former boxing champion. An incisive portrait of a man and a city (Lisbon), this testimonial documentary is justly remembered today as one of the landmarks of the 'New Portuguese Cinema' and one of the few films of this period with a real social concern, only comparable to another Lopes title, Nacionalidade: Português/Nationality: Portuguese (1972, released 1974), a slightly softened exposé of the hard conditions of the life of Portuguese workers in Paris.

Indicative of the strange situation of the film industry during this period is a series of documentary shorts with diverse sponsors. For example, Francisco de Castro produced for the National Tobacco Factory the politically incorrect (by the standards of the time) Nicotiana (1963). This film marked the beginning of a ten-year collaboration with the director António de Macedo (born 1931), probably the main specialist of 'industrial' films, among them, História Breve da Madeira Aglomerada/A Short History of Agglomerate Wood (1970), a surprisingly good treatment of the subject. The other great director in this field was Faria de Almeida, who, with Faça Segundo a Arte/Make it as You Know (1965), produced by the Indústria Portuguesa de Especialidades Farmacêuticas, succeeded in making the process of manufacturing medical drugs entertaining.

Glorification of empire persisted, despite the increasing unrest in colonial territories. Some films with propaganda goals were sufficiently ambiguous to arouse censorship suspicions. The most flagrant case was that of Faria de Almeida's Catembe (1965), about daily life in Mozambique, which, after a semi-clandestine preview, was cut from eighty-seven to forty-five minutes. The most impressive effort in colonialist propaganda was Angola na Guerra e no Progresso/Angola: War and Progress (1971), a widescreen, colour blockbuster produced by the Serviço de Informação Pública das Forças Armadas (SIPFA) and directed by Quirino Simões, an Air Force officer who was also an accomplished filmmaker. Simões (born 1931) is the author of another accomplished work of propaganda, Guiné, A Caminho do Futuro/Guinea, the Road to the Future (1971), a tribute to Gen. António de Spinola, then Governor of Guinea, as well as two fiction films (shot in 1967 and 1991).

The Carnation Revolution of April 25, 1974 changed Portugal's political landscape, which was reflected by film. Cinema and television documentaries were conceived as propaganda weapons. The first report of the Revolution (and an impressive depiction of its time) was As Armas e o Povo/Arms and the People (shot in 1974, edited in 1975), which, as with many of the titles produced during this period, was presented without directorial credit, as a production of a group calling themselves 'Trabalhadores da Actividade Cinematográfica'/'workers of the activist cinema'. Among these 'workers' were such noted filmmakers as Luis Galvão Teles (one of the main animators of this militant cinema), Fernando Lopes, Alberto Seixas Santos, António de Macedo, António de Cunha Telles, António Pedro Vasconcelos, José Fonseca e Costa, and Brazilian talent Glauber Rocha. The other important piece of militant cinema was Deus, Patria, Autoridade/God, Country, Authority (1975) by Rui Simões. If the earlier film was the first cinematic portrait of revolutionary days, the second was the first critical approach to the forty years of Salazar's dictatorship. Coproduced by the newly formed Instituto Português de Cinema (IPC) and the RTP (Portuguese Television), its message sounds today a little partisan, but it was a phenomenal success.

One of the most active filmmaker cooperatives of this period was the Grupo Zero, responsible for two documentaries on agrarian reform made in 1976: A Lei da Terra/The Law of the Earth, also know as Alentejo 76, mainly directed by Alberto Seixas Santos; and A Luta do Povo/ The People in Arms, which according to the most credible sources was directed by Swedish-born Solveig Nordlund. Nordlund was the editor of Alberto Seixas Santos's curious experiment on Estado Novo, Brandos Costumes/ Sweet Habits, 1975, a mix of documentary and fiction elements filmed in part before April 25, 1974 and later completed with archive material. Another important purveyor of militant films was Cinequanon, a company founded by Luis Galvão Teles. Among its titles were O Outro Teatro/The Other Theatre (1976) by António de Macedo, about the staging of politically non-conformist plays, and Colonia e Vilões/Colonies and Villages (1977) by Leonel Brito, about political and religious repression on the island of Madeira. The most elaborate and widely known piece on agrarian reform was a coproduction with West Germany about a people's cooperative, Torre Bela (1977), directed by Thomas Harlan, son of Veit Harlan, famous (or infamous) for his cinematic contributions to Nazi propaganda. The independence of African territories was another political subject for documentaries, Fernando Matos Silva's Acto dos Feitos da Guiné/History of the Events of Guinea (1980) being one of the most accurate. The cycle of political documentaries ended in the late 1970s, with Rui Simões' Bom Povo Português/Good Portuguese People (1981) standing as a sort of summary of the illusions and disappointments of the revolutionary period.

Despite the increasing presence of political messages in documentaries, some of them managed to follow the lines established before 1974. In the ethnographic category, we have a masterpiece by António Campos, Gente da Praia da Vieira/People from Praia da Vieira (1975), a tribute to this fishermen's village where he directed one of his first amateur films, Um Tesouro/A Treasury (1958). The impoverished villages of the northeast of Portugal were the subject of Máscaras/Masks (1975) by Noémia Delgado and the superb Trás-os-Montes (1976) by António Reis and Margarida Martins Cordeiro. The daily life of women in the village of Lanheses was beautifully portrayed by Manuela Serra in O Movimento das Coisas/Things in Motion (1985).

Among biographical films, one of the best is Ma Femme Chamada Bicho/My wife, Bicho (1976), produced by the Gulbenkian Foundation and directed by José Álvaro Morais, about the artist couple Maria Helena Vieira da Silva and Arpád Szenes. An original approach was that of Lauro António's Prefácio a Vergílio Ferreira (1975), which was a sort of preface to a later adaptation by António of one of the most celebrated novels by Ferreira, Manhã Submersa/ Hidden Dawn (1979). A little disappointing were Herculano, filmed in 1978 by João Matos Silva for the centennial of one of the great Portuguese writers, and Maranos (1978) by Dórdio Guimarães, about poet Teixeira de Pascoaes, produced by IPC and the Ministry of Culture. However, the most original work of this category appeared some years later: A Ilha de Moraes (1984) by Paul Rocha, a study of Wenceslaus de Moraes, a nineteenth-century writer enchanted by Japanese culture. De Moraes had previously been the hero of Rocha's time-consuming feature film, A Ilha dos Amores, which was shot with great difficulty in Japan between 1979 and 1982.

The mid-1980s marked the collapse of documentary production, or, to be exact, of those films intended to be shown in a theatre. An audience who turned increasingly toward television and away from the cinema, an increase in costs, and a decrease in state sponsorship were the main causes of the decline in film production.

In the early 1990s, however, a slight revival took place because of two factors. One was exclusively technical: the increased use of video stock, which was less expensive and easy to edit, decreased costs. The increased participation of national institutions like the ICAM (Instituto de Cinematografia, Audiovisuais e Multimédia, known as IPACA until 1999) and, especially, Portuguese Television (RTP) in filmmaking also helped.

The points of view covered were, curiously, generally the same as in earlier years. For example, the ethnographic approach was apparent in the depiction of the rural areas of Portugal in Fernando Matos Silva's Alentejo—As Quatro Estações/Alentejo—The Four Seasons (1994) and A Luz Submersa/The Obscured Light (2001), as well as Rabo de Pexe/Isinglass Island (2000) by Joaquim Pinto and Nuno Leonel; the African and Asian immigrants to Portugal in Afro Lisboa/Afro Lisbon (1996) by Ariel de Bigault, Kulandakilu (1998) by Margarida Leitão, or Swagatam/Bemvindos (Swagatam/Welcome (1998) by Catarina Alves Costa. Current life in the former colonies was portrayed in O Homem da Bicicleta/The Bicycle Man (1997) by Ivo M. Ferreira and António Pedro, Céu Aberto/Open Sky (1998) by Graça Castanheira, A Dama de Chandor/The Lady from Chandor (1998) by Catarina Mourao, Com Quase Nada, Brincar em Cabo Verde/With Near Nothing, or How Children Play in Cabo Verde (2000) by Carlos Barroco and Margarida Correia. The team Pinto-Leonel produced some titles about Brazil such as Surfavela/Poor Man's Surf (1996) and Moleque da Rua/Children of the Streets (1998).

Another important approach of previous decades, the biographical portrayal, was typified by Aurélio da Paz dos Reis (1995) by veteran Faria de Almeida; Táxi Lisboa (1996) by the Bavarian Wolf Gaudlitz, about and made with the writer Vergílio Ferreira; Vencer a Sombra/Fighting with Shadows (1996) by Paulo Ares and Pedro Madeira, about an aged boxer, a sort of sequel to Fernando Lopes's Belarmino; As Escolhidas/The Elected Women (1997) by Margarida Gil, about painter Graça Morais; Joaquim Bravo (1999) by Jorge Silva Melo, about this painter; No Quarto da Vanda/In Vanda's Room (2000) by Pedro Costa, a one hundred and sixty-minute mix of reality and fiction on the daily life of Vanda Duarte, former actress of Costa's Ossos/Bones (1997), in Fountainhas, the caboverdians' quarter of Lisbon; Ilusíada—A Minha Vida Dava Um Filme/The Illusitans or My Life Would Be a Movie (2001) by Leonor Areal, about four unknown characters whose modest lives reflected fifty years of Portuguese history, which was presented theatrically as a one-hundred-and-thirty-five-minute film and in three fifty-eight-minute chapters for television; and Agostinho Neto (2001) by Orlando de Fortunato, about the Angolese leader. Bruno de Almeida's A Arte de Amália/The Art of Amália (2000) was a tribute to legendary fado singer Amália Rodrigues, which used footage from the 1920s until her death in 1999, including live clips from her concerts.

The designation of Lisbon and Portugal as European Cultural Capitals in 1994 and 2001 encouraged the production of the following documentaries by prestigious filmmakers: Joaquim Leitão's A Cidade Qualquer/Just Another City (1994) opted for an experimental, pseudo-impressionistic approach, and Manoel de Oliveira's Porto da Minha Infância/Port of My Childhood (2001) used Fellini-like fictionalized sequences for a nostalgic trip to a city that he had depicted cinematically on other occasions, for example in his early masterpiece Douro, Faina Fluvial.

RAFAEL DE ESPAÑA

Further reading

de España, Rafael, *Directory of Spanish and Portuguese Filmmakers and Films*, Westport, CT: Greenwood Press, 1994.

de Matos-Cruz, José, *Anos de Abril (Cinema Português 1974–82)*, Lisbon: Instituto Português do Cinema, 1982.

——*Cinema Novo Português, 1960–74*, Lisbon: Cinemateca Portuguesa, 1985.

——*Prontuario do Cinema Português 1896–1988*, Lisbon: Cinemateca Portuguesa, 1989.

——*O Cais do Olhar. O Cinema Português de Lungametragem e a Ficção Muda*, Lisbon: Cinemateca Portuguesa, 1999.

de Pina, Luís, *Documentarismo Português*, Lisbon: Instituto Português do Cinema, 1977.

Passek, Jean Loup, Ribeiro, M. Felix, de Pina, Luís and de Matos Cruz, José, *Le cinéma portugais*, Paris: Centre Georges Pompidou, 1982.

Paulo, Heloísa, 'Documentarismo e Propaganda. As Imagense os Sons do Regime', in Luís Reis Torgal (ed.), *O Cinema Sob o Olhar de Salazar*, Lisbon: Temas e Debates, 2001.

Ramos, Jorge Leitão, *Dicionário do Cinema Português 1962–88*, Lisbon: Caminho, 1989.

Prayer

(Cuba, Trujillo, 1983)

Prayer, directed by Cuban filmmaker Marisol Trujillo, is a short documentary film in the tradition of the aesthetic and political experimental work associated with Third Cinema practitioners. The film embodies a Third Cinema aesthetic in its commitment to 'an imperfect cinema' that challenges First Cinema practices and seeks to address audiences at a political level (Chanan 1985: 251). Trujillo's hard-hitting film harks back to an exceptional period of experimentation in radical political film in the 1960s and 1970s associated with the Cuban Institute of Cinematographic Art and Industry (ICIAC). Representative works include Santiago Alvarez's Now (1965), which offers a powerful exposition of institutionalised racism in America, and LBJ (1968), which delivers a stinging critique of American political life through a montage of found images that associatively link Lyndon B. Johnston with political corruption.

Throughout Prayer, Trujillo draws on the traditions of Soviet montage filmmaking and employs montage editing techniques to juxtapose still and film footage of found images, with music, and poetic dialogue. These elements function cumulatively to mount a powerful Marxist critique of the ideological structures and institutions of Western capitalism, in a visual style similar to that of her fellow Cuban filmmaker Alvarez.

Trujillo was one of several female Cuban filmmakers who worked under the auspices of ICAIC. Prayer embodies a strong Marxist-feminist aesthetic in the way images of Marilyn Monroe's life are juxtaposed with political events of the time. For much of the film, the spoken verse of Ernesto Cardenal's poem Oración por Marilyn Monroe (Prayer for Marilyn Monroe) is superimposed over the visuals, presenting a catalogue of abuse associated with Marilyn Monroe, from child rape, through her time as a product of the 'Hollywood Dream Factory', to her early suicide.

Trujillo's selection of found images of Marilyn Monroe emphasizes the way in which the female body is objectified by mainstream media conventions and would seem to directly reference the work of film theorist Laura Mulvey (1975) on 'the male gaze'. The film includes many promotional 'glamour shots' of Marilyn Monroe as media celebrity and film footage of her in her many roles as screen goddess, posed suggestively in revealing costume, while the camera, by lingering on parts of her body, fragments and dehumanises the woman into 'body parts': breasts, legs, or open yielding mouth. These striking visual sequences represent Marilyn as the object of the male gaze and illustrate the way in which the female body is exploited as a mere spectacle for male pleasure.

Marilyn's 'glamour shots' and other images of fetishised female 'body parts' are juxtaposed with conflicting images from the latter part of Marilyn's troubled career, clearly interpreting her as a hunted victim of media intrusion. Archive photographic material from Marilyn's childhood and youth are also included with a spoken dialogue, which refers to her longstanding history of abuse and domination prior to her celebrity status and entrance into the Hollywood Studio system. Throughout Prayer, Marilyn's image functions as a cinematic metaphor for patriarchal oppression.

Through the use of associative montage, the film's thematic concern with Marilyn's exploitation within a patriarchal system shifts to a more direct critique of political regimes and the ideological structures that oppress their people. There are many startling and repetitive motifs throughout the film that link Marilyn's exploitation and death with that of 'innocents' throughout the world. The overriding thematic concern with Marilyn is interspersed with stills and film footage from around the world (hunger marches, political rallies, children living on the street, child prostitutes) and juxtaposed with images of state violence, police beatings, and military hardware. In one sequence, images of Marilyn's softly yielding mouth are juxtaposed with startling images of an open-mouthed starving child from the Third World: in another, pictures of the headless bodies and the decapitated heads of political victims echo the 'body parts' imagery of earlier visuals of Marilyn. The film constructs strong links between global capitalism and Third World oppression.

Throughout the film, in spoken dialogue and imagery, the ideological practices of Western media are critiqued. Twentieth Century Fox in particular is singled out as representative of the exploitive practices of global capitalism and is associatively linked to the oppression, violence, and poverty experienced by many people living in the Third World. Prayer offers its audience a harrowing visual catalogue of brutality and exploitation, which is reinforced by Cardenal's poetic dialogue.

Nevertheless, the film ends on a note of optimism. As it reaches its climax, Cardenal's dialogue is overlaid with Blake's 'Jerusalem', which rises to a crescendo as, in a rapid montage sequence, edited images of 'people empowerment' flash across the screen. The pace picks up as the film shifts from cataloguing injustice throughout the world to images of revolutionary militancy. Transcultural motifs of arms raised in power salutes are interspersed with iconic images of Che Guevara and of heavily armed young revolutionaries, male and female 'brothers' in arms, who are represented as having literally taken up arms in their determination to protect 'the innocent'. There would seem to be no place for patriarchal oppression within the revolution (an optimistic if conflicting statement on female empowerment within Cuban society, given that *machismo* remained a powerful influence in Cuban society after the revolution). The film ends with a long take on the static image of a small child of indeterminate sex, smiling with arms outstretched in exuberance, happy and at peace. The screen fades to black as the audience is left to contemplate this lasting image of carefree childhood, a powerful visual statement on moral obligation.

In addition to Prayer, Trujillo made several other documentaries under the auspices of ICIAC, focusing on Cuban culture and famous Cuban artists. Motivations (1988) profiled the Cuban painter and sculptor Manuel Mendive and explored the sources for his art. Encounter (1981) documented the meeting between the Cuban prima ballerina Alicia Alonso and the Soviet dancer Vladimir Vasiliev when they met in preparation for their duet in *Giselle*. Woman Before the Mirror (1983) profiled the Cuban dancer Rosario Suarez.

PAT A. COOK

See also: Alvarez, Santiago; LBJ; Now

Further reading

Chanan, Michael, *The Cuban Image*, London: BFI, 1985.

Mulvey, Laura, 'Visual Pleasure and Narrative Cinema', *Screen* 16, no. 3, 1975: 6–18.

Pines, Jim and Willemen, Paul, *Questions of Third Cinema*, London: BFI, 1989.

Wayne, Michael, *Political Film: The Dialectics of Third Cinema*, London: Pluto Press, 2001.

Prelorán, Jorge

Jorge Prelorán, a native of Argentina, is the most widely recognized and prolific ethnographic filmmaker of Latin America. His films generally focus on the folkways of individual subjects within a rural or natural environment. The majority of his work explores the various indigenous tribes throughout the provinces of Argentina, but it includes portraits of indigenous people and communities in countries such as Venezuela and Ecuador. He has also worked as the codirector and coproducer on a film that one of his former University of California, Los Angeles (UCLA) students made about a poet, philosopher, and cabin builder in Oregon, USA, entitled Luther Metke at 94 (1979). This film was nominated for an Academy Award the following year.

Preferring the term ethnobiographer to ethnographer, Prelorán tends to focus on one man's life experiences and perspectives, which become emblematic of a tribe or people typically living on the margins. To achieve a strong rapport with his subject, he would spend long stretches of time with his subject before turning on a film camera. After a comfort level was achieved, Prelorán would record an audio track with his subject and would later intertwine the subject's voice with silent camera footage recorded later. Prelorán has produced over seventy films, in which he has worked as the director, cameraman, soundman, and editor. Many times he will complete a film, only to go back months later to recut the film into a different version. Over a span of years, a work may have multiple incarnations. Just as culture is constantly in flux, so too are Prelorán's films.

His style has been compared to Flaherty's depictions of the harmony between man and nature. However, in an interview, Jorge Prelorán has stated that although he identifies with Flaherty's humanism, he has been influenced the most by the Italian neorealists of the 1950s. His interest focuses primarily on documenting indigenous culture in Latin America as a way to preserve the folk traditions and rituals, while simultaneously elevating the importance of these cultures, which are too often marginalized and threatened with extinction in the Americas. Despite the fact that Prelorán's work is widely recognized and studied by visual anthropology scholars, he prefers to categorize his films as simply 'human documents'. Because his interviews are in Spanish, a language he can understand, Prelorán labels his films as folkloric, rather than ethnographic. In this way, he believes that 'the magic of his human documents is the sensitivity with which many of the things shot were achieved' (Sherman 1985).

His best-known film, Hermógenes Cayo (Imaginero) (1969), features Cayo, a deeply spiritual and religious icon carver in the province of Santiago del Estero. As Sharon Sherman (one of Prelorán's former students), explains, 'his early films look at single events which place the protagonists in their environments, but the rituals themselves, rather than the participants, are the central focus' (Sherman 1985). Prelorán, while interviewing subjects such as Hermógenes and others, excises his questions out of the voice-over narration to avoid calling attention to himself as a main narrative framing agent for the film. With the exception of the film on the Warao, a Venezuelan tribe, all of Prelorán's films since 1967 have used the subjects' voices to describe their own lives. In this way, according to Sherman, he has chosen a group of characters who represent a culture. Documenting their quotidian activities alongside their religious and cultural traditions, Prelorán tries to be an invisible filmmaker, much in the style of traditional documentarians. However, this does not rule out what he calls the 'subjective' or 'artistic' focus in which filmmaking can be an art—that is, whereby the language of cinema and the dramatic structure of fictional film are used (Prelorán 1995). According to filmmaker Ron Norman, Prelorán's films 'have the humanism of Jean Renoir and Akira Kurosawa, the inner or personal life of Ingmar Bergman, and the revelations of Robert Flaherty and Satyajit Ray' (Taquini 1994).

Politically, he is committed to eliminating any trace of his own ideology from his films: 'I do not want to impose my own ideas. This means that my films are not political or ideological. I have no intention to use my film as a vehicle for my ideas rather than [those of] the protagonists. I try to listen to people and convert this into a film.' Although he may not be overtly adopting a political agenda, it is clear that he aims to empower these communities that are often excluded from Latin American public sphere by making them visible. He has shared some of the money made in film screenings and sales with his films' protagonists. It is clear that Prelorán's self-described 'apolitical' work has been aimed at bettering the life of rural people in Argentina, and this could have had dangerous consequences after a military junta seized power in 1976. Fleeing in exile to the United States, Prelorán and his wife Mabel, also a filmmaker, left their country definitively in search of better working conditions.

Prelorán then lived in Los Angeles, where he was professor emeritus of ethnographic film at UCLA's School of Film and Television. His work has been recognized widely in ethnographic film festivals, but otherwise, it is not readily accessible. Always working outside of the studio system in Argentina and the United States, he has generally worked solo or with his wife to produce and promote his films. Only one film, Mi Tia Nora, filmed in Ecuador, was a fictional film based on a true story and was produced as a feature-length commercial release.

TAMARA L. FALICOV

Biography

Born May 28, 1933, in Buenos Aires, Argentina. Studied architecture at the Universidad Nacional de Buenos Aires but left to attend the University of California, Los Angeles, where he finished film school in 1961. Awarded a Tinker Foundation Grant to direct four films on Argentine *gauchos* in 1963. Funded by the National University of Tucuman (an Argentine provincial city) in 1967 to document various folkloric traditions in Argentina. In 1976 he fled Argentina and began living in exile in the United States, where he became professor emeritus in the Ethnographic Film program in the School of Film and Television at the University of California, Los Angeles. He produced more than seventy films over a period of twenty years. Died 28 March 2009 in Culver City.

Selected films

1963 The Argentine Gaucho Today/El gaucho argentino, hoy: director

1966–71 Araucanos of the Ruca Choroy/Araucanos de Ruca Choroy: director

1967 The Image Maker/Hermógenes Cayo (Imaginero): director

1973 Ona People/Los ona: Vida y muerte en Tierra del Fuego: director

1975 Cochengo Miranda: director

1978 Zerda's Children/Los hijos de Zerda: director

1980 Luther Metke at 94: codirector (with Steve Raymen), coproducer (with Richard Hawkins)

1982 Zulay Confronts the Twentieth Century/Zulay frente al siglo XX: director
1983 My Aunt Nora/Mi Tia Nora: director

Further reading

Ardevol, Elisenda and Perez Tolon, Luis (eds), *Imagen y cultura: perspectivas del cine ethnográfico*, Biblioteca de etnología 3, Granada, Spain: Publicaciones del diputacion provincial de Granada, 1995.
Barnard, Timothy, 'Hermógenes Cayo (Imaginero)', in Timothy Barnard and Peter Rist (eds), *South American Cinema: A Critical Filmography, 1915–94*, Austin, TX: University of Texas Press, 1996: 50–2.
Chicello, Ruben D., 'Jorge Prelorán: The Documentary as Poetry', *Américas* 34, no. 6, November–December 1982: 55.
Devereaux, Leslie and Hillman, Roger (eds), *Fields of Vision: Essays in Film Studies, Visual Anthropology, and Anthropology*, Berkeley, CA: University of California Press, 1995.
Kriger, Clara and Sendros, Parana, 'Jorge Preloran', in Clara Kriger and Alejandra Portela (eds), *Diccionario de realizadores*, Buenos Aires: Ediciones del jilguero, 1997: 128–9.
MacDougall, David, *Transcultural Cinema*, Princeton, NJ: Princeton University Press, 1998.
Mathieu, Agustin, *Breve historia del cine nacional*, Buenos Aires: Alzamor Editores, 1974.
Prelorán, Jorge, 'Conceptos eticos y esteticos en el cine etnografico', in Elisenda Ardevol and Luis Perez Tolon (eds), *Imagen y cultura: perspectivas del cine ethnográfico*, Biblioteca de etnología 3, Granada, Spain: Publicaciones del diputacion provincial de Granada, 1995: 123–60.
Sherman, Sharon, 'Human Documents: Folklore and the Films of Jorge Preloran', *Southwest Folklore* 6, 1985: 17–61.
——*Documenting Ourselves: Film, Video, and Culture*, Lexington: University of Kentucky Press, 1998.
Taquini, Graciela, *Jorge Prelorán*, Buenos Aires: Centro Editor de America Latina, 1994.

Preston, Gaylene

Gaylene Preston, director and producer of both documentaries and fiction films, is one of Aotearoa's (New Zealand) senior filmmakers, a status earned through the quality of her own productions and her efforts at all levels—from education to funding—to help other local filmmakers with their work. Preston's interest in telling local stories for local audiences has tied her to Aotearoa (New Zealand), although she has often wished for bigger budgets and more consistent funding for her projects (the advantage of accepting local budgetary restraints has been total control of all her projects). In keeping with her understanding of film as an important part of its local community, she acknowledges film's collaborative nature and refers to her 'creative team'. She has played, and continues to play, an important role in developing creative talent and practical skills among a large and varied group of protégées, through hiring them to assist her, producing their early efforts, mentoring via Women in Film and Television, the New Zealand Film Commission, and the Film School, and through her efforts to attract local and national government support for the New Zealand film and television industries. An active filmmaker who made the second feature-length fiction film directed by a woman in Aotearoa (New Zealand) (a gender-bender thriller entitled Mr Wrong, 1984), she was honored as film laureate for the country.

Although Preston has made several successful fiction films (including a comic satire, Ruby and Rata, 1990, that deals with ethnic, gender, and class stereotypes, and Bread and Roses, 1994, a television miniseries/feature film docudrama based on the autobiography of nurse, social activist, and eventually MP Sonja Davies), the bulk of her work has taken the form of documentaries about extraordinary individuals as seen through Preston's eyes. Her favorite film, she says, is one of her earliest, Learning Fast (1981), about a group of small-town teenagers whom she and her camera track over approximately a year of their lives as they make the transition from school to unemployment. The teenagers start with high hopes and confidence, but the town's lack of employment opportunities wears them down. Typically, this film sympathizes with the individual's point of view at the same time that it situates the individual's dilemma within an acute analysis of the social context.

The best example of Preston's ability to draw attention to systemic frameworks for individual dissatisfactions comes at the close of Married (1993), Preston's contribution to a series of TV dramas made by women in honor of the centenary of women's suffrage in Aotearoa (New Zealand). Having established that the married couple in question have their own joys and troubles, Preston ends her film with the frustrated wife sitting on the back steps; the camera pulls away to show a long row of similar houses in the dawn light, each with its own, presumably similar story to tell of husbands and wives boxed in by economic limitations. According to Preston, Married is her 'most unpopular film' because it is done 'in doco-realism', a style that doesn't let audiences 'off the hook'.

If a group of unemployed teenagers might not seem particularly extraordinary, Preston's first documentary subject was more obviously unusual. Bruce Burgess, incapacitated by cerebral palsy, wanted to get to the top of Mount Ruapehu, one of Aotearoa's (New Zealand) active volcanoes. All the Way Up There (1978), which documents his successful ascent (accomplished with the aid of committed expert climbers), was a financial success for Preston (Encyclopaedia Britannica bought it) as well as a *succès d'estime* that won Preston international prizes and some local recognition. Her next film, Hold-Up (1981), is a docudrama in the sense that it combines a dramatized scene of a hold-up witnessed by three disabled bystanders with interview material about the players' own responses as disabled persons to the idea that their testimony would have no credibility because of their disabilities.

Although Making Utu (1982) is about Geoff Murphy's second complete feature film, it is not a 'making of' movie, partly because of Preston's experience dealing with similar issues while contributing extensively to Merata Mita's Patu! (1983), a politicized documentary about the 1981 Springbok rugby tour. Like later Preston documentaries, Making Utu is more evocative than denotative. During the 1980s, while working on projects expressive of her political convictions, Preston also worked in advertising and in music videos.

The success of All the Way Up There meant that Preston attended the Cannes market, one result of which was that she and Robin Laing formed a professional partnership as director and producer that has lasted nearly twenty years. In 1995 they produced War Stories Our Mothers Never Told Us, a feature-length opportunity for seven women (including Preston's own mother) to talk about their experiences during World War II—the embodiment of Preston's desire to get her subjects 'to relive the moment of past experience'. A mix of simple presentation and engrossing storytelling, War Stories has achieved international recognition and has played to record domestic audiences for a feature-length documentary.

Preston calls Kai Purakau (1987) and No Other Lips (1997) her 'bookends', because they are television documentaries about New Zealand writers: Booker Prize winner Keri Hulme and poet Hone Tuwhare. The former was made for Thames Television to be broadcast in Britain, the latter for Greenstone Pictures and New Zealand television. Preston comes from the same part of the country as Hulme, which has figured in responses to criticism that a Maori should have made the film about Hulme, who identifies as Maori. Despite similar criticism a decade later, Hone Tuwhare himself invited her to direct the film about him, and the warm feeling between subject and documentarist, as well as Preston's characteristic appreciation of humor, pervades the film.

Working increasingly as a producer, Preston also codirected Getting to Our Place (1999), a 'fly-on-the-wall documentary' about meetings—specifically, the meetings involved in constructing Te Papa, the country's new national museum that has become internationally influential. Simultaneously, Preston produced Punitive Damage (1999), a documentary focusing on a New Zealand mother's grief over the loss of her son in civil unrest involving the East Timorese and Indonesians.

Finally, in Titless Wonders (2001), Preston presents stories of breast cancer survivors and of friends who have succumbed to the disease. It is her most specifically local film, despite the universality of its topic. Her ability once again to bring a joyous humor to a painful subject—her ability to celebrate life—is the hallmark of a Preston film.

HARRIET MARGOLIS

Biography

Born in 1947 in Greymouth, on the West Coast of the South Island, Aotearoa (New Zealand). Attended boarding school in Nelson and art school in Christchurch. Received Dip Art Therapy, St Albans School of Fine Arts, England, 1974. While using art therapy to help psychiatric patients, made first short films. Returned to Aotearoa (New Zealand) 1976, and worked for six months at John O'Shea's Pacific Films. Served on New Zealand Film Commission 1979–85. With Robin Laing, formed Preston

Laing Productions, 1984. One child, a daughter, born in 1987. Board member of New Zealand On Air and of Creative Film Fund. Turned down Centenary of Suffrage medal (1993) because of political disagreements with the then prime minister. Named a Laureate of New Zealand 2001. Received a Media Peace Award 2001, for Titless Wonders. Honored as an officer of the New Zealand Order of Merit for services to the New Zealand film industry 2001.

Further reading

Ahuriri, Monika, 'Stubborn Bloody Mindedness', *Newsreel* (The New Zealand Film Archive) 48, November 2001: 3.

Beattie, Keith, 'First Say and Last Cut', *Media Studies Journal* (Massey University), 1996: 4–16.

Benjamin, Julie and Maclean, Alison, 'Revolving Clotheslines and Morris Minors: A Discussion of New Zealand Film Making with Gaylene Preston', *Alternative Cinema* 11, no. 4, summer 1983–4: 21–4.

Dennis, Jonathan, 'Reflecting on Reality: An Interview with Gaylene Preston', in Jonathan Dennis and Jan Bieringa (eds), *Film in Aotearoa New Zealand*, Wellington: Victoria University Press, 1992: 161–72.

Hardy, Ann, 'Gaylene Preston', in Annette Kuhn and Susannah Radstone (eds), *The Women's Companion to International Film*, London: Virago, 1990: 325–6.

Horrocks, Roger, 'Gaylene Preston', *New Zealand Film Makers at the Auckland City Art Gallery*, part 5, November 1984.

Johnson, Stephanie, 'Through Women's Eyes', *Quote Unquote*, June 1995: 14–17.

n.a., 'The Benefits Outweigh the Compromise', *The Business of Film* (New Zealand Special Issue), May 2001: 85.

Shepard, Deborah, 'Gaylene Preston', in Christina Barton and Deborah Lawler-Dormer (eds), *alter/image: Feminism and Representation in Recent New Zealand Art*, Wellington: City Gallery, 1993: 99, 115–16.

——*Reframing Women: A History of New Zealand Film*, Auckland: HarperCollins, 2000.

Primary

(US, Drew, 1960)

Primary is a landmark in the development of direct cinema as an aesthetic and journalistic movement, both because it exemplifies the work done by the seminal television documentary team of Drew Associates and because it provides access to aspects of the political campaign process inaccessible before and since. As a hybrid of traditional and direct cinema styles, Primary bears traces of a struggle between pre-television documentary's reliance on voice-over narration and classic Hollywood conventions and an emerging style of mobile reportage further developed by Drew Associates alumni Richard Leacock, Donn Alan Pennebaker, and Albert and David Maysles. Primary's own reliance on editing and sound-image matching to mold reality into dramatic form belies its claim of objectivity, but its success in stripping away accumulated conventions through direct cinema techniques was rightfully hailed as a leap forward in documentary filmmaking's quest to capture 'truth'.

Primary's style of detached observation is strikingly different from Jean Rouch's Chronicle of a Summer (1961), a cinéma vérité documentary released one year later that continually reminds both the on-camera participants and the audience watching it that a film is being made. Like Chronicle, however, Primary pursues a subject ripe with social, cultural, and political insights waiting to divulge itself: the 1960 Wisconsin presidential primary between senators John F. Kennedy and Hubert Humphrey. As narrator Joseph Julian intones in a low-key voice-over heavy-handed by today's standards, 'Now, traveling along with them, hot on the heels of two fast-moving presidential hopefuls, you are about to see a candidate's view of this frantic process, and an intimate view of the candidates themselves.'

The film's delivery on this promise proved groundbreaking in its capture of intimate details of candidate behavior. Humphrey, for example, flips to The Red Skelton Show as he seeks diversion from disappointing voter returns, and an atypically nervous Kennedy paces the floor of his hotel suite while anxiously dragging on a cigarette. Primary also delights in exposing through this backstage form of reportage the subjective limitations of newspapers, photography, and radio in their interpretations of the candidates as people and politicians.

During a sitting for a campaign poster, for example, Kennedy sits in a small portrait studio encircled by spotlights opposite a photographer and his camera. Catching himself after offering up a glad-handing grin for the camera, Kennedy acknowledges to the photographer (who has just tinkered with his equipment and adjusted the candidate's shirt sleeve cuffs), 'It's not time to smile yet, Wally'. A cut that juxtaposes the perfectly coiffed and stiff-backed Kennedy posing for the portrait with a campaign poster of a smiling Humphrey on the back of a bus overlays the image of Kennedy's rival with the photographer's request to 'swing your body a little bit more to the camera'. Recalling Robert Drew's observation that the studio portrait session was a 'ritual in many small towns', the juxtaposition of the photographer's instructions with the paper image of a smiling Humphrey implies that the campaign posters that pervade Primary are a painstakingly staged construction of personhood that cannot compete with the raw veracity of direct cinema's handheld shots, synchronous sound, and (often) poorly lit passages of footage.

In a reversal of the cut from the photo session to Humphrey's campaign poster, Primary juxtaposes Humphrey's behind-the-scenes preparation for a television call-in show with a video image of Kennedy on a television screen. Staking out a position in the television studio behind a TV camera, Humphrey supplies the show's host with the first question to be asked of him, instructs the camera operator where to focus, and informs his wife Muriel that she has thirty seconds of air time to summarize for viewers how she has spent the day. The cut from Humphrey to Kennedy reminds the audience that the latter's erudite television image is also the product of technical preparation and planning.

The filmmakers arrange these scenes in symmetrical bookend fashion in order to suggest that they have taken great pains to remain value-neutral in their presentation of the candidates. Furthermore, both scenes remind us that the Drew team avoids both directing the subjects (as the photographer directs Kennedy in the studio) and being directed by them (as Humphrey directs the camera operator in the television studio).

Conversely, Primary fails to acknowledge the visual and aural sleights of hand that characterize its own reportage. In one of the most celebrated sequences of the film, Albert Maysles's camera follows Kennedy's arrival at a rally in Milwaukee, snaking down a long corridor, up a stairway, through a doorway, and out onto a stage where a cheering crowd greets both camera and candidate. The claustrophobia of the narrow path, the anticipation of the crowd, and the burst of blinding light and applause that accompanies Kennedy's arrival on stage deliver a riveting example of narrator Julian's opening promise. Subsequent shots of the rally, however, subjectively frame the panoply of events by carefully isolating details, overlapping sound and image, and using matches-on-action to establish cause-and-effect relationships between discrete bits of footage.

As the ever-poised Jacqueline Kennedy addresses the crowd, for example, a close-up reveals her white-gloved hands fidgeting nervously behind her back. Students of direct cinema objected to the use of a cut (rather than a zoom) to the close-up, arguing that the filmmakers juxtapose the steady and confident sound of Mrs Kennedy's voice with the image of her hands in a way that achieves verisimilitude without being real. Other instances of this imposition of form on raw footage appear throughout the film, revealing the subjectivity inherent in direct cinema's claim of ostensible objectivity.

The rising cost of television network air time during the 1970s led Drew to lament the replacement of single-subject documentaries such as Primary by multi-subject television news magazines such as 60 Minutes, which he derided as 'entrapment journalism' because of their reliance on hidden cameras and ambush interview techniques (Drew 1988: 401). Even though Primary also fell short in its effort to capture filmic truth, its pursuit of this goal proved an invaluable contribution to documentary filmmaking.

CHRIS JORDAN

See also: Leacock, Richard; Maysles, Albert; Pennebaker, D.A.

Primary (US, 1960, 53 mins). Distributed by Direct Cinema. Produced by Robert Drew. Photographed by Richard Leacock, Donn Alan Pennebaker, Terence Macartney-Filgate, and Albert Maysles. Written by Robert Drew. Edited by Robert Drew, Richard Leacock, Donn Alan Pennebaker, and Terence Macartney-Filgate.

Further reading

Bluem, A. William, *Documentary in American Television*, New York: Hastings House Publishers,1965.

Bruzzi, Stella, *New Documentary: A Critical Introduction*, New York: Routledge, 2000.

Drew, Robert, 'An Independent with the Networks', in Alan Rosenthal (ed.), *New Challenges for Documentary*, Berkeley, CA: University of California Press, 1988.

Hall, Jeanne, 'Realism as a Style in Cinema Verite: A Critical Analysis of Primary', *Cinema Journal* 39, no. 4, summer 1991: 38–45.
Hammond, Charles Montgomery, *The Image Decade: Television Documentary 1965–75*, New York: Hastings University Press, 1992.
Nicols, Bill, *Representing Reality: Issues and Concepts in Documentary*, Bloomington, IN: Indiana University Press, 1991.
O'Connell, P.J., *Robert Drew and the Development of Cinema Verité in America*, Carbondale, IL: Southern Illinois House, 1981.

Pull My Daisy

(US, Frank and Leslie, 1959)

Part documentary, part Dada-esque farce, Robert Frank and Alfred Leslie's short film Pull My Daisy stands, along with films such as John Cassavetes's Shadows (1959), as one of the most important cinematic statements of the postwar Beat Movement. Based loosely on the third act of Jack Kerouac's unproduced stage play The Beat Generation, the film provides a brief glimpse into the lives of bohemian artists and writers of 1950s New York City.

The play was adapted for the screen by Frank and Leslie, who changed the title to Pull My Daisy after learning that MGM was planning to produce a Beat exploitation film titled The Beat Generation. The new title came from a whimsical 1949 poem by Kerouac and Allen Ginsberg—a poem that, when set to music by David Amram, provided the film's theme song and set the tone for the film's eccentric action.

Both Robert Frank (1924–) and his codirector, contemporary realist painter Alfred Leslie (1927–), were members of The Group, a small collective of American independent filmmakers formed in 1960 with loose ties to Free Cinema in England and to the nouvelle vague in France. Frank had been best known as a still photographer prior to the release of Pull My Daisy in 1959. His still photographs, such as those published in The Americans (1959), a collection of more than eighty photos bluntly chronicling life in postwar America, pioneered the 'snapshot aesthetic' in which the documentary image is rendered starkly with a minimum of conscious artistry. It was a visual aesthetic well matched to the Beat Movement's embrace of literary spontaneity to capture experience, once described briefly by poet Allen Ginsberg as 'First thought, best thought'. Not surprisingly, Frank's first motion picture shares the same stark imagery and spontaneous feel of both his earlier photographs and much of the poetry and prose produced by writers of the Beat Movement.

Filmed silently in black and white, with an overdubbed narration, Pull My Daisy documents a single day in the lives of a small circle of bohemian poets and artists in a dingy loft apartment on New York's Lower East Side. The cast is made up of some of the Beat Movement's most important artists. Poets Allen Ginsberg, Peter Orlovsky, and Gregory Corso appear as themselves. Composer/musician David Amram plays the role of jazz musician Mezz McGillicuddy, and painter Larry Rivers appears as Milo, the working-class poet at the center of the film's storyline (a character whose life bears a strong resemblance to Kerouac's friend Neal Cassady). Although Kerouac does not make an appearance in the film, he acts as the narrator and supplies all of the voices for the film's characters (the only exception is the voice of a small boy, probably provided by Robert Franks's son Pablo).

Much of the film is concerned with the tension between the routine life of work, family, and home and the less constrained and more spontaneous life offered by the Beat Movement. The film begins with a peaceful domestic scene typical of the period: a young woman (identified in the credits only as 'Milo's wife') readies her son for school while she awaits the return of her husband Milo from his job as a railroad brakeman. The morning's calm is broken, however, as poets Ginsberg and Corso arrive, quickly making themselves at home with wine, marijuana, and an animated discussion of poetics. When Milo arrives home from work a few hours later, accompanied by Peter Orlovsky, he tells the assembled poets that a bishop will be paying the household a visit that evening and warns them to be on their best behavior. As the bishop arrives for what Milo's wife hopes will be a pleasant visit, accompanied by his sister and his very proper mother, the scene quickly turns into an uncomfortable evening of increasingly bizarre and intoxicated antics, as the poets ask the cleric strange yet pointed questions about the spiritual realm. Despite Milo's wife's best efforts to control the tone of the event, the evening further disintegrates with the arrival of jazz musician Mezz McGillicuddy, who turns the apartment into the scene of a jam session, as the bishop and his family look on in quiet shock. The film ends with Milo's wife in tears, as the bishop and his party leave abruptly, and Milo is jubilantly led out of the apartment by his bohemian friends for an adventurous night on the town.

Pull My Daisy documents a moment of interaction between two worlds: the mundane, proper, and feminized life of the mainstream (exemplified by Milo's wife, the bishop, and his mother and sister), and the wild, joyous, and very masculine life of 'kicks' to be found among the bohemian artists of the Bowery (exemplified by Milo, Ginsberg, Orlovsky, and McGillicuddy). Contemporary viewers will no doubt be troubled by the irresponsible and, at times, seemingly sexist actions presented by the film's subjects and may find themselves in agreement with Beat scholar Joyce Johnson, who has suggested that the film is 'about the right to remain children'. Nonetheless, the work provides a striking visual representation of the Beat Movement and its struggle with the stifling conformity of the 1950s.

ROD PHILLIPS

Pull My Daisy (US, G-String Productions, 1959, 20 mins). Produced and directed by Robert Frank and Alfred Leslie. Cinematography by Robert Frank and Alfred Leslie. Written and narrated by Jack Kerouac. Featuring David Amram, Beltiane (Delphine Serig), Gregory Corso, Pablo Frank, Allen Ginsberg, Sally Gross, Alice Neal, Denise Parker, Mooney Peebles (Richard Bellamy), Peter Orlovsky, and Larry Rivers. Edited by Leon Prochnik, Robert Frank, and Alfred Leslie. Music by David Amram. Filmed in New York City.

Further reading

Allen, Blaine, 'The Making (and Unmaking) of Pull My Daisy', *Film History* 2, 1988: 185–205.

Frank, Robert, *The Americans*, Millerton: Aperture, 1959.

Sargeant, Jack, *Naked Lens: Beat Cinema (Creation Cinema Collection #7)*, London: Creation Books, 2002.

Sterritt, David, *Mad to Be Saved: The Beats, the '50s, and Film*, Carbondale, IL: Southern Illinois University Press, 1998.

Tyler, Parker, 'For Shadows, Against Pull My Daisy', *Film Culture* 24, 1962: 28–33.

Pumping Iron

(US, Fiore and Butler, 1976)

Pumping Iron generated intense public interest in bodybuilding, an activity that theretofore lacked credibility as a legitimate sport or art form. It also started Arnold Schwarzenegger on his rise to superstardom, catapulting him into public consciousness in a way that his previous films, The Long Goodbye (1973) and Stay Hungry (1976), had failed to do. At almost every level, the film was a collaborative effort. Based on the book of the same name, written by Charles Gaines and George Butler, Pumping Iron as a film project was carried from conception to completion by the efforts of Butler. Butler coproduced the film with Jerome Gary and codirected with Robert Fiore. Larry Silk and Geof Bartz handled editing. Michael Small oversaw music throughout and wrote the title song for the film.

From the opening credits, featuring quaint clips of old-time muscle men and backed by Small's engaging, humorous score, the film never takes itself too seriously. When the viewer is then faced with a compelling human drama, it comes as unexpected delight. Filmed across the United States and culminating in South Africa, Pumping Iron follows the workouts and preliminary competitions through which the world's top bodybuilders must pass to become 'Mister Olympia', the ultimate glory for the bodybuilding community. Success, each contestant understands, involves more than approximating bodily perfection. To become Mister Olympia ultimately requires besting the dominating international presence in the sport—Schwarzenegger.

Unlike its sequel, Pumping Iron II: The Women (1985), this low-budget, intimate film foregoes contrived dramatic elements and lets contestants speak for themselves through word and deed. With minimal narration and only occasional interviews to 'flesh out' main characters, Butler and Fiore gently offer the viewer the chance to love or hate each of the Mister Olympia hopefuls, though there is little doubt that only 'Arnold! Arnold!' (as his mesmerized fans chant) will win the title. In a film replete with people literally larger than life, Schwarzenegger stands head and shoulders above his peers physically and mentally, while demonstrating a depth of personality and psyche that few in Hollywood can match on camera. A smash box office success, and available on the shelves of film rental stores ever since because of Schwarzenegger's popularity, Pumping Iron remains one of the most financially successful American documentaries.

MICHAEL S. CASEY

Pumping Iron (US, White Mountain Films, 1976, 85 mins, color). Distributed by Cinema 5 Distributing. Produced by George Butler and Jerome Gary. Directed by George Butler and Robert Fiore. Cinematography by Robert Fiore. Music by Michael Small. Edited by Larry Silk and Geof Bartz. Sound by Harry Lapham. Lighting by Michael Lesser. Titles by Martin S. Moskof. Narrated by Charles Gaines. Peter Davis and Charles Gaines served as consultants. Filmed in NewYork, Los Angeles, San Francisco, Holyoke, Massachusetts, and South Africa.

Further reading

Butler, George, *Arnold Schwarzenegger: A Portrait*, New York: Simon & Schuster, 1990.

Gaines, Charles, *Pumping Iron: The Art and Sport of Bodybuilding*, New York: Simon & Schuster, 1982.

Nowell-Smith, Geoffrey, *The Oxford History of World Cinema*, London: Oxford University Press, 1996.

Schwarzenegger, Arnold and Hall, Douglas Kent (contributor), *Arnold: The Education of a Bodybuilder*, reprint, New York: Fireside, 1983.

R

Rain

(Holland, Ivens, 1929)

With the premier of Rain at the Filmliga (Film League) in Amsterdam in 1929, Joris Ivens established his reputation as a serious director. His previous film, The Bridge (1928), had been well received, particularly among followers of the avant-garde, but Rain was hailed as a ciné-poem by French critics (Ivens 1969), an ideal synthesis of thematic and formal elements communicated through moving images.

As Bill Nichols suggests, Rain could be seen as operating within the modernist 'poetic mode' of documentary: a style that goes against the standards of continuity editing to explore associations and patterns that arise out of 'temporal rhythms and spatial juxtapositions' (Nichols 2001). Indeed at this point in his career, Ivens was closely aligned with the ideological and aesthetic aims of Amsterdam's Film League, a group founded in 1927 to promote the screening of avant-garde films and that associated mainstream cinema with the masses, with 'the commercial regime, America, kitsch' (Stufkens 1999). Ivens served as the Film League's technical advisor and agreed that films should offer an alternative to the monolithic cinema industry that produced low entertainment and seduced the public 'by adapting to the public's bad taste' (Stufkens 1999). Rain does go against many of the common practices of silent continuity editing, but does not go so far as to dispense with narrative entirely. Instead, a narrative unfolds that dramatizes the rhythms of a natural event, a single rain shower, which in turn gestures toward larger existential and aesthetic concerns. In Rain, the built urban environment is utterly transformed not only by the natural event but also, perhaps more important, by the steady gaze of the camera, which can capture those fleeting visual patterns produced by everyday movements that might be missed by the naked eye.

In his autobiography, Ivens recalls that he and an assistant, Chang Fai, shot Rain over several months in 1928, using two 35mm amateur hand cameras. In all, however, the twelve-minute film took almost two years to complete. The story, based on a scenario by Mannus Franken, is straightforward: a bright day in the city gives way to a darkening sky, wind, the first drops of a rain shower, and then a deluge that increases in force until it finally ebbs away, the weakened daylight returning to a drenched landscape. Within this slight narrative frame, other more abstract impressions are communicated through the camera's meditation on movements, patterns, and forms. Changing light effects are highlighted through the interplay of sun and shadow in the early scenes; reflections produced in pools, puddles, and rain-slicked streets are emphasized in later scenes. The film rarely focuses on human actions, which are subordinate to those of the primary player, the rain. With the exception of an obviously staged shot of a man holding out his hand to feel for raindrops, then turning up his collar and rushing for cover, people are primarily shot from behind or overhead. Human figures, although integral to the mise-en-scène, remain wholly anonymous. Still, these shots are not deployed to produce sterile, carefully composed scenes surveyed from a safe distance; instead they work with other moments in the film that align the spectator's eye more closely with the camera's lens. Rain conspires to make viewers' experience the rainstorm firsthand. Ivens wanted audiences to feel 'damp' after watching his 'super-wet' images (Ivens 1969).

Many critics have noted the influence of Walter Ruttmann's Berlin: The Symphony of a Great City, which Ivens saw when he met the director in 1927, though years later Ivens would distance himself from that film, suggesting that 'a city film with human interest and content could be done without Ruttmann's virtuosity and superficial effects' (Ivens 1969). Rain's emphasis on the formal composition of shots and on the juxtaposition of different movements, shot scales, and camera angles also suggests an affinity with the contemporary montage experiments of Sergei Eisenstein and Dziga Vertov, whom Ivens met while working with the Film League. What sets Ivens's film apart, however, is its sustained focus on a single event, its formal unity and coherence, and its ability to capture kinetic images that are imbued with the singularity and compositional intensity of still photographs. Patterns produced by juxtaposing movement and stasis are revealed in images such as a boat traveling under a bridge, while the steady shadow of the bridge's iron railing cuts across the movement of the boat beneath it. The recurring motif of raindrops falling into water further suggests a dialectic of motion and stillness: a seemingly stable aesthetic form both produces, and is produced out of, the force of multiple, fragmented movements and events.

One of the film's most striking sequences begins with a street scene framed by the arch of an umbrella, which cuts to a traveling shot of a man under an umbrella. Further images of groups of people holding umbrellas cut to raindrops falling into a puddle, and then several arresting overhead shots of a street scene appear in succession, in which groups of umbrellas form a recognizable, yet somewhat surreal, shuddering mass. The sequence is tied up when the final shot fades to black, a technique used only sparingly in the film. Although the images might appear simply to indulge in aesthetically pleasing forms, they also indirectly articulate the relationship between the modern city dweller and the anonymous masses, suggesting the constant interplay between the individual and the social organism, the whole and its innumerable parts.

Rain preceded Ivens's more openly political phase, generally considered to have begun after 1929. He would later see his early films as failed attempts to fight bourgeois ideology through formalist revolutionary strategies, labeling his late-1920s work as fundamentally apolitical and 'parochial' (Stufkens 1999). However, Rain was clearly a foundational film for Ivens and a defining moment in the modernist avant-garde. The subtleties of Rain's camera work—capturing images both banal and arresting, like the street filmed through the streaming windows of a moving tram—are typical of an attention to documentary aesthetics that would persist throughout Ivens's long career.

JEFFREY GEIGER

See also: Ivens, Joris

Rain (the Netherlands, 1929, 12 mins, silent). Produced, directed, and written by Joris Ivens and Mannus Franken. Photographed and edited by Joris Ivens. Music composed by Lou Lichtveld (1932) and Hanns Eisler (1941). Production company, CAPI Amsterdam. Filmed in Amsterdam.

Further reading

Heller, Berndt, 'The Reconstruction of Eisler's Film Music: Opus III, Regen, and The Circus', *Historical Journal of Film, Radio, and Television* 18, October 1998: 541–60.

Ivens, Joris, *The Camera and I*, Berlin: Seven Seas Publishers, 1969.

Leyda, Jay and Meyers, Sidney, 'Joris Ivens: Artist in Documentary', in Lewis Jacobs (ed.), *The Documentary Tradition*, New York: Norton, 1979.

Nichols, Bill, *Introduction to Documentary*, Bloomington, IN: Indiana University Press, 2001.

Stufkens, André, 'The Song of Movement: Joris Ivens's First Films and the Cycle of the Avant-garde', in Kees Bakker (ed.), *Joris Ivens and the Documentary Context*, Amsterdam: Amsterdam University Press, 1999.

Reichert, Julia

Julia Reichert was a prominent producer and director in the social issue documentary movement the 1970s and early 1980s. Of particular note are four documentaries she codirected with James Klein. Growing Up Female (1971), the first documentary study of the American societal forces that mold female identities, influenced subsequent feminist documentaries through its combination of interviews, advertisements, and popular music. Methadone: An American Way of Dealing (1975) critiques the use of methadone as a method of combating drug addiction. Her next two documentaries were Oscar-nominated: Union Maids (1976) blends feminist and labor history through oral interviews of three women who played roles in the unionization drives in the United States during the 1930s; Seeing Red: Stories of American Communists (1983) records the personal oral histories of American Communist Party members from the 1930s to the 1950s.

After 1983 Reichert began working on dramatic films, although the subject of one of those films, Emma and Elvis (1992), is a middle-aged, countercultural documentary filmmaker. She has recently returned to documentary filmmaking. She worked as a creative consultant on Welcome to Warren (2003), which examines the relationship of inmates and guards at the Warren Correctional Institution in Warren, Ohio, and she was a collaborator on A People's History: Dayton's People's History, Twenty Years Later (2003). In 1997 Reichert began work on A Lion in the House, which marks her return to directing. The film, scheduled to air on PBS in 2005, uses the subject of adolescent cancer patients as a context to discuss larger social issues such as health care, race, and poverty.

Like many social issue documentarians, Reichert is motivated by a particular political activism. Her primary interests are gender and working-class life, and she approaches them from a socialist perspective, but her activism is not limited to the choice and treatment of these subjects. Though her early films are not technically innovative, she pioneered novel approaches to production, marketing, and distribution. In the early 1970s Reichert was a founding member of New Day Films, which was originally created to promote the Women's Movement. New Day was the first American cooperative distribution company operated entirely by and for filmmakers (the company is still active today, and distributes the work of over fifty filmmakers: see www.newday.com).

Many of her films are made for particular working-class audiences, and are distributed to them directly through a variety of political institutions and organizations such as unions, schools, YMCAs, and health care providers. Because of this control, Reichert can focus on her explicit goal of promoting discussion and social change. To that end her films are often accompanied by discussions or meetings and include complementary handouts and discussion questions. Methadone incorporates a midway break for discussion, and some of her work is so audience-specific that it is produced for particular working-class neighborhoods and never distributed beyond them. She has written a book on film distribution, *Doing It Yourself*, devoted to the dissemination of this model.

Reichert also attempts to incorporate her socialist, nonhierarchical politics into the production and structure of her documentaries. Her collaborative models, such as codirecting many of her films with James Klein, undermine common hierarchical structures in film production. In Union Maids, for example, she and Klein chose to work with video, despite the compromised quality, because video allowed more extended, collaborative interviews, and because it allowed them to work with less experienced students. Video not only allowed more shooting, but also allowed them to direct inexperienced cinematographers by intercom while watching on a monitor. Union Maids also exemplifies Reichert's aversion to heroic figures. Reichert has argued in interviews that focusing on individuals and aggrandizing their actions leads the audience to believe that such people are unusually gifted and unique, and that they drive history. She wishes, rather, to forward a model of collective agency. Consequently, Union Maids mixes the testimonies of three women of different ethnicities to demonstrate the wide range of people who collaborated in the cause of unionizing American industry.

Reichert's focus on agency led to an early shift in her filmmaking. Her first major film, Growing Up Female, depicts the problem of gender roles in the United States, but does not develop possible responses to the problem. Her next film, Methadone, begins in a similar vein with a critique of the societal response to drug addiction, but the second half of the film explores possible solutions to the problem. In her subsequent documentaries, Reichert incorporates positive role models and opportunities for agency.

Critical reception of Reichert's documentary films has focused on her use of direct cinema techniques. Because Reichert's documentaries generally eschew voice-over narration and use oral interviews extensively, they are less able to develop the broader context of the topics they explore. Further, despite Reichert's aversion to portrayals of individual heroism, critics have claimed that her films aggrandize the few people interviewed. Union Maids and Seeing Red, for example, are criticized for oversimplifying social relations by giving an incomplete, uncontested story primarily through oral interviews of small numbers of like-minded people. Such an approach can be read as a legitimate form of counterhistory, and recent critics have argued for the recuperation of such direct cinema techniques for the creation of counterhistories that dispute conventional representations of authority and give more heteroglossic alternatives (see entry on Union Maids). Other critics, however, have argued that Reichert tends to present oral histories as independent arguments and not as primary source material in need of a broader explanatory frame. The lack of such a frame, it is claimed, can make her films appear naive—an endorsement of a partial, self-protective history rather than a meta-critical response to previous histories (Nichols 1991: 252).

DEREK LOH AND PAUL MILLER

See also: Klein, James; Union Maids

Biography

Graduated from Antioch College in 1970 with a degree in documentary arts. Cofounded New Day Films 1971. Cofounded the Film Fund, a foundation to promote social issue films, 1977. Published *Doing It Yourself: A Handbook of Independent Film Distribution*, 1977. Union Maids nominated for Academy Award for Best Documentary Feature 1978. Named Artist of the Year by the Ohio Arts Council (with James Klein) 1983. Seeing Red nominated for Academy Award for Best Documentary Feature 1984. Named by the American Film Institute as one of nineteen artists who influenced the decade in film 1985. Appointed to the Ohio Humanities Council by Governor Celeste 1986. Vice-President of Ohio Valley Regional Media Arts Coalition and Professor in the Department of Theater Arts and the School of Medicine at Wright State University.

Selected films

1970 Growing Up Female: codirector
1975 Methadone: An American Way of Dealing: codirector
1975 Men's Lives: coproducer
1976 Union Maids: codirector, editor
1983 Seeing Red: Stories of American Communists: codirector
1992 Emma and Elvis: director, cowriter, coproducer
2003 Welcome to Warren: creative consultant
2003 A People's History: Dayton's People's History, Twenty Years Later: cowriter, coproducer

Further reading

Kleinhaus, Chuck, 'Julia Reichert and Jim Klein', *Jump Cut* 5, 1975: 11–12.

Nichols, Bill, *Representing Reality*, Bloomington, IN: Indian University Press, 1991.

Reichert, Julia, *Doing It Yourself: A Handbook on Independent Film Distribution*, New York: Association of Independent Film and Video Makers, 1977.

——'Feminist Film Comes of Age', in Patricia A. Johnson and Janet Kalven (eds), *With Both Eyes Open: Seeing Beyond Gender*, New York: Pilgrim Press, 1988.

Rosenthal, Alan, 'Union Maids', in Alan Rosenthal (ed.), *Documentary Conscience*, Berkeley, CA: University of California Press, 1980.

——(ed.), *New Challenges for Documentary*, Berkeley, CA: University of California Press, 1988.

Rubenstein, Lenny, 'Who's Who in Filmmaking: Julia Reichert and James Klein', *Sightlines* 20, no. 2, 1986–7: 22–5.

Waldman, Diane and Walker, Janet (eds), *Feminism and Documentary*, Minneapolis, MN: University of Minnesota Press, 1999.

Reisz, Karel

The film director and producer Karel Reisz was a prominent member of the Free Cinema movement (1956–9), an informal group of young artists that also included Lindsay Anderson, Tony Richardson, and the cameraman Walter Lassally. Free Cinema was concerned with the relationship between art and society, and the need for the film auteur to be free from the commercial constraints of mainstream cinema, so that committed artists might make films that offered significant commentary on contemporary society.

Reisz chose initially to work in documentary film, but was outspoken about his antipathy to what he considered the legacy of the 1930s British Documentary Film Movement, and a tendency to make documentaries about, 'the Lake District, Stirling Moss, old trams and the beauties of spring' (Lovell 1977: 138). He did acknowledge, however, the strong influence of Humphrey Jennings's poetic realism on the Free Cinema practitioners and referred to Jennings's film Fires Were Started (1943) as 'the source film for Free Cinema' (Orbanz 1977: 57).

The Free Cinema movement was essentially six programmes of films presented at the National Film Theatre between 1956 and 1959, and a series of critical articles in journals such as *Sequence*, which Reisz cofounded in 1947 with Lindsay Anderson, and *Sight and Sound*, in which they set out the broad themes of the group. Reisz's short documentary film, Momma Don't Allow (1955), codirected with Tony Richardson and funded by the British Film Institute (BFI) Experimental Film Fund, was screened at the first Free Cinema programme in September 1956.

We Are the Lambeth Boys (1959) directed by Reisz, was part of the Last Free Cinema programme in 1959. Both films embody the low-budget production style and the attitude of Free Cinema in capturing the mood of the late 1950s by focusing on the working class and an emerging youth culture in a sympathetic manner.

Reisz, along with Anderson and Richardson, went on to achieve critical acclaim in mainstream cinema and all three became prominent figures in the British New Wave of socially concerned realist films, popular between 1959 and 1963. Focusing on working class experience, their work included Saturday Night and Sunday Morning (Karel Reisz, 1960), A Taste of Honey (Tony Richardson, 1962), and This Sporting Life (Lyndsey Anderson, 1963). Given their Oxbridge background, however, their representations of working-class life have been called into question (Armes 1978: 2–5).

PAT A. COOK

See also: Anderson, Lindsay; Fires Were Started; Jennings, Humphrey; Momma Don't Allow; We Are the Lambeth Boys

Biography

Born in Ostrava, Czechoslovakia in 1926. Emigrated to Britain as a young man and joined the Royal Air Force towards the end of World War II. After the war, studied Natural Sciences at Emmanuel College, Cambridge. Worked for three years as the Programmes Officer at the National Film Theatre. In 1956 became head of the Ford Motor Company's TV and Film Programme. Coauthored, with Gavin Miller, *Techniques of Film Editing* (1953). Died in London in 2002.

Selected films

1955 Momma Don't Allow (UK): director
1958 We Are the Lambeth Boys (UK): director
1960 Saturday Night and Sunday Morning (UK): director
1964 Night Must Fall (UK): director
1966 Morgan: A Suitable Case for Treatment (UK): director
1968 Isadora (UK): director
1974 The Gambler (US): director
1978 Who'll Stop the Rain (UK): director
1981 The French Lieutenant's Woman (UK): director
1985 Sweet Dreams (US): director
1990 Everybody Wins (US): director
2000 Act Without Words 1 (UK, BBC Television): director

Further reading

Armes, Roy, *A Critical History of British Cinema*, London, 1978: 2–5.
Barsam, Richard, *Non Fiction Film: A Critical History*, Indianapolis, IN: Indiana University Press, 1992: 249–54.
Lovell, Alan and Hillier, Jim, *Studies in Documentary*, London: Secker and Warburg, 1977: 133–72.
Murphy, Robert, *Sixties British Cinema*, London: British Film Institute, 1972: 18–21, 73–4, 271–2.
n.a., *Films and Filming* 25, no. 4, January 1979: 12–17.
n.a., *Stills* 1, no. 4, winter 1982: 7–15.
Orbanz, Eva, *Journey to a Legend and Back: The British Realistic Film*, Berlin: Volker Speiss, 1977: 53–63.

Resnais, Alain

'If the short film had not existed, Resnais would surely have invented it', Jean-Luc Godard wrote in praise of Resnais's documentaries in 1959, the miraculous year when the French New Wave was born and Resnais had just made his first feature, Hiroshima mon amour/Hiroshima, My Love. Godard added that without Resnais's work, 'the new young French cinema would not exist'.

Between 1946 and 1948 Resnais made a number of 16mm films including a series of 'Visits' to contemporary artists. These films were not released, but prints are in the archives of the Centre Pompidou in Paris. From 1947 to 1958 Resnais worked as editor on six films made by others. His own career as a professional documentary filmmaker, which lasted for ten years, also began in 1948 with his 35mm Van Gogh.

Resnais's eight short documentaries, generally commissioned works, focus not on people but on things and places. Three are art films; three, including Nuit et brouillard/Night and Fog, are works that focus on places charged with memories; and the last two are explorations of issues surrounding contemporary industrialization. They constitute an important body of work in the history of short film and also served as a testing ground for techniques and themes that have contributed to making Resnais's feature films among the most important works of twentieth-century cinema.

In the documentaries, Resnais shows his lack of interest in the so-called realist cinema and his commitment to raising formal questions and confronting difficult, enigmatic contemporary philosophical and social issues. 'I want to make films that are experiments. All experiments are interesting,' he told an interviewer in 1961 (cited by Armes 1968).

Resnais's training and work as a film editor have had a marked impact on all his films. Except for Nuit et brouillard and Le Mystère de l'Atelier Quinze/The Mystery of Workshop Fifteen, Resnais was both director and editor of all his documentary films. For him the crucial stage in the making of a film is the editing, not only the montage of the images but also sound editing and mixing. The musical score establishes rhythms, punctuates patterns of montage, and plays a central role in the films.

Ghislain Cloquet, who was cinematographer for Les Statues meurent aussi/Statues Also Die, Nuit et brouillard, and Toute la mémoire du monde/All the Memory of the World, comments on the impact of this focus on sound and rhythm on the cameraman. Cloquet sees a development from what he calls 'normal' camera movements or pans in the first documentaries to dolly shots in Night and Fog, and shots that allow a fuller exploration of three dimensions in Toute la mémoire du monde. He writes that Resnais opened his eyes through his patient and careful observation of objects (Pingaud and Samson 1990). The resulting long tracking shots are characteristic of Resnais's style. The camera moves into the subject, whether it is a painting by Picasso, the camp at Auschwitz, or the French National Library, to find traces of the past, to learn, to explore.

Memory and closed worlds are recurrent themes. It has been suggested that by editing his tracking shots, Resnais has created a form that allows one to see and to feel the strange and disturbing resemblance between many seemingly disparate sites of modern life. 'Resnais's short films show the vast imprisonment which controls our lives and our fear of death in a world from which we are separated', Neyrat has noted. He goes on to underscore, however, that 'against this imprisonment the films also bring a power of liberation—the aesthetic power of the cinema, its power of redeeming the contingent through form and beauty'.

In Van Gogh (1948), which won the Academy Award for Best Foreign Short Subject in 1950, Resnais takes the camera on a 'voyage into painting'. We are shown only images from the paintings; there are no photographs of real landscapes. Resnais treats 'the whole of the artist's output as one large painting over which the camera has wandered as freely as in any ordinary documentary' (Bazin 1967). The camera tracks into the paintings, selects and fuses. The material selected serves neither art criticism nor biography but allows the filmmaker to find out, as Resnais stated after finishing the film in 1948, 'whether painted trees, painted people, painted houses could, thanks to the editing, fulfill the role of real objects and whether, in this case, it was possible to substitute for the spectator and almost without his knowing it, the interior world of the artist in place of the world as it is revealed by photography' (Armes 1968). The film is shot in black and white and this reveals hidden potentialities of the paintings and allows the filmmaker more freedom to explore space and create links between the canvases. The musical score by Jacques Besse plays a predominant role in structuring the shots. 'It is no longer there "to accompany the images" but to create the very backbone of the film,' Resnais wrote in 1948 (Armes 1968).

Gauguin (1950) is a much shorter film tracing the journey of the painter, Paul Gauguin, from his native Brittany to Tahiti. It is told in much the same way as Van Gogh, using the paintings and, this time, a musical score by Darius

Milhaud and commentary drawn from the writings of Gauguin. Economic circumstances rather than aesthetic choice forced Resnais to shoot this film in black and white; however, the paintings of the great colorist were not suited for this approach and Resnais, in a 1960 interview, spoke of this film as a failure.

Resnais's third art film, Guernica, also made in 1950, takes Picasso's fresco as subject for another black-and-white documentary. Picasso's 'Guernica', painted in black, white, and tones of gray, is well suited for this approach. The filmmaker dismantles the spatial arrangement of the painting and rearranges the pieces along with other Picasso paintings and sculptures, as well as photographs of the ruined Spanish town, newspaper headlines, and graffiti in a new pattern focusing on the destruction and suffering caused by war. Over images of death and desolation the voice of the actress Maria Casarès recites a text written by the poet Paul Eluard. 'Stylistically [...] Guernica represents for the director the first totally successful fusion of all the elements on which his mature style is based. Fragments of photographs, painting and sculpture are welded into a visual rhythm and set against an aural rhythm of music and verbal poetry bound together in a tone that combines documentary realism with pure lyricism,' Armes has written. 'I was very moved by the massacre at Guernica because it seemed to me like the prelude to all the massacres which were to follow,' Resnais recalled in 1983 (Fleischer 1998).

Les Statues meurent aussi (1950–3), codirected with Chris Marker, is a tribute to African art and a rebuke of the colonizer who negated its value, took it out of its context, treated it as folklore, and thus contributed to its decline. The documentary also serves to recall the European efforts to shape Africa in its own image: 'All this is dominated by the White Man who sees everything from his position and raises himself above the contradictions of reality,' the voice of Marker's commentary reminds the viewer (cited by Gauthier 1995). The film, which was awarded the Prix Jean-Vigo in 1954, was banned by the French government for more than ten years.

Nuit et brouillard, shot in 1955 in a mix of black and white and color, is no doubt Resnais's finest and best-known documentary. In this thirty-one-minute film dealing with the Holocaust the filmmaker undertook the challenge of presenting a reality that seems impossible to document. The film is narrated from the perspective of ten years after the end of World War II and opens on a long take of a seemingly peaceful countryside shot in muted color. Then the camera tilts up, moves through torn barbed wire, and tracks slowly through the remains of what was the camp at Auschwitz—the empty buildings, the factories, the latrines, the gas chambers. Intercut with this probing inquisition by the camera, archival footage, in black and white, alternates to show the past and the horror of the camps: the construction of the sites, the rounding up of people all over Europe, the cattle trains, the naked and emaciated prisoners, the massed bodies of the dead. Photographs of piles of eyeglasses, combs, shoes, shorn hair, and endless lists of names bear silent witness to the enormity of the carnage. The camera searches to understand. 'We can only show the surface', the voice-over comments in a low-key, almost neutral tone, which itself seems to question our ability to grasp what is being described. Language seems paralyzed before the moral outrage. Jean Cayrol, the author of the commentary who had himself been deported during the Holocaust, wrote that he and Resnais wanted the film to reach a wide audience not only to have people remember but also to sound a warning against all future nights and fogs (Raskin 1987). The magnificent musical score by Hanns Eisler adds to the profound meaning of the film. In an essay accompanying the DVD release of the film, Philip Lopate has noted that this didactic work against war and violence, this very personal examination of the meaning of memory and forgetfulness, anticipates the modern documentary genre of the essay-film.

In Toute la mémoire du monde, a film about the French National Library made in 1956, Resnais invites the viewer to penetrate the memories that reside in books. Treasures from the past are presented by the camera's eye along with present-day works: the Maya Codex alongside the comic strip of Mandrake the Magician. Who knows, the commentary asks, which will bear more authentic witness of our civilization? The film is technically striking as the camera tracks back and forth through corridors and passageways. Cloquet recalls that 'Resnais wanted us to move through the National Library as if in a rocket, like a fish through water' (cited by Pingaud and Samson 1990).

Resnais and Remo Forlani, who wrote the script for Toute la mémoire du monde, projected a series of forty short films centered on the subject of 'The Organization of Work'. This project was unrealized, although a 35mm documentary, Le Mystère de l'atelier quinze, related to the project, was made in 1957 and codirected by Resnais. It is the least known of Resnais's documentaries and focuses on the case of a workman who falls ill for no apparent reason. The commentary was written by Chris Marker and the film, though entirely planned by Resnais, was actually directed by his former assistant, André Heinrich.

Resnais's last documentary, Le Chant du Styrène/The Song of Styrene, was commissioned by Péchiney Industries in 1958 to show the complex transformation of materials in the manufacture of polystyrene plastic, an entirely manufactured product. Resnais handled the assignment in a surprising manner and in a 1962 interview explained that this film is 'far less an industrial documentary than a synthesis of verbal abstraction and lyricism' (cited by Kreidl 1977). The commentary, written by the novelist and poet Raymond Queneau in alexandrine verse, serves as a humorous and informative accompaniment to the patterns created by widescreen shots of pipes and machines in brilliant, often unrealistic color. In its use of musical rhythms, Le Chant du Styrène can be seen to prefigure Resnais's later 'musical' films (Fleischer 1998).

Jean-Luc Godard called Le Chant du Styrène 'an Olympian film, a serious film without equal'. Just a few months later Resnais released his first feature, Hiroshima mon amour, a film that won the International Critics' Prize at Cannes in 1959 and worldwide acclaim for the director.

Hiroshima mon amour grew out of a commission to make a documentary on the effects of the atomic bomb. Marguerite Duras, author of the script, calls Resnais's first feature 'a false documentary', and, indeed, one of the themes of this structurally complex love story revolves around memory and the impossibility of documenting the events that had occurred at Hiroshima.

A number of critics writing about Alain Resnais's feature films since 1959 have underscored the importance of the short documentaries in developing the formal and thematic issues central to his work as a whole. Bounoure, Armes, and Monaco have drawn actual parallels between individual documentaries and later feature films. The importance of the work of Alain Resnais as a documentarist cannot be overestimated either in its impact on the filmmaker's later work or, as Neyrat (2002) has observed, 'as an extended meditation on modernity, on the changes of man and art in the age of technology and aesthetics'.

EVA MARIA STADLER

See also: Night and Fog

Biography

Born in Brittany on June 3, 1922. A few years older than Godard and the other young filmmakers associated with the *Cahiers du cinéma* and the New Wave. As a boy, showed great interest in comics and movies, asked for the gift of an 8mm camera, and began a number of film projects. In 1940 went to Paris, first to study acting and two years later filmmaking/editing.

Selected films

1948	Van Gogh (20 mins, black and white)
1950	Gauguin (11 mins, black and white)
1950	Guernica (12 mins, black and white)
1950–3	Les Statues meurent aussi (30 mins, black and white)
1955	Nuit et brouillard (32 mins, black and white and Eastmancolor)
1956	Toute la mémoire du monde (21 mins, black and white)
1957	Le Mystère de l'atelier quinze (18 mins, black and white)
1958	Le Chant du Styrène (14 mins, CinemaScope/Eastmancolor)

Further reading

Armes, Roy, *The Cinema of Alain Resnais*, London: A. Zwemmer Ltd and New York: A.S. Barnes & Noble, 1968.

Bazin, André, 'Painting and Cinema', in *What is Cinema?* Translated by Hugh Gray, Berkeley, CA: University of California, 1967.

Bounoure, Gaston, *Alain Resnais*, Paris: Seghers, 1962.

Burch, Noel, 'A Conversation with Alain Resnais', *Film Quarterly*, spring 1960.

——'Four Documentaries', *Film Quarterly*, fall 1959.

Fleischer, Alain, *L'Art d'Alain Resnais*, Paris: Centre Pompidou, 1998.

Gauthier, Guy, *Le Documentaire—un autre cinéma*, Paris: Nathan, 1995.

Godard, Jean-Luc, 'Chacun son tour', *Cahiers du Cinéma* 92, February 1959.
Kreidl, John Francis, *Alain Resnais*, Boston: Twayne, 1977.
Marcorelles, Louis, 'Rebel with a Camera', *Sight and Sound*, winter 1960.
Monaco, James, *Alain Resnais: The Role of Imagination*, New York: Oxford University Press, 1979.
Neyrat, Cyril, 'Horreur/bonheur: métamorphose', in Stéphane Goudet (ed.), *Alain Resnais—Anthologie*, Paris: Gallimard, 2002: 47–54.
Pingaud, Bernard and Samson, Pierre, *Alain Resnais ou la créations au cinéma*, 'L'Arc', Paris: Duponchelle, 1990.
Raskin, Richard, *Nuit et brouillard by Alain Resnais*, Denmark: Aarhus University Press, 1987.

Retour, Le

(France, Cartier-Bresson and Banks, 1946)

Le Retour is a thirty-two-minute documentary film depicting the return home of prisoners of war, deportees, and refugees from camps in Germany and former German-occupied territories at the end of World War II. The film was produced by the Office of War Information (US), at the request of the French Ministère des Prisonniers, Déportés et Rapatriés, and it premiered in Paris in January 1946. As its scriptwriter, editor, and technical consultant, French photographer and filmmaker Henri Cartier-Bresson worked with two officers from the US Army Signal Corps.

During World War II the Signal Corps had documented every major military campaign (film and photographs) and gathered visual evidence of the Nazi atrocities on the European Theater of Operations. This material was used in films presenting war crimes, such as Nazi Concentration camps (George Stevens, United States, 1945) or reeducation films such as Die Todesmühlen/Death Mills (Hanuš Burger, United States/Germany, 1945). Le Retour also made use of this material, and it added segments about displaced persons and prisoners returning home in 1945.

World War II resulted in destruction and human suffering on an unprecedented scale. Le Retour documents a singular moment in the war, when the arms fall silent and the gigantic task of repatriating millions of displaced persons across the continent began: Allied soldiers liberated from prisoner of war camps; civilian deportees who survived detention in concentration camps; millions of others brought to Germany as slave labor. All wanted to go home. Their immediate needs were enormous—clothing, medicine, transportation—and the chaotic return demanded military organization and Soviet-American cooperation. On the last leg of the journey, the camera witnesses the emotional minutes when former French prisoners get off the train in Paris and look at anxious awaiting relatives and friends. On both sides there was apprehension, hope, and restrained joy.

Henri Cartier-Bresson (1908–2004) was internationally known as a photographer and a reporter. On the Left of French politics, he became interested in film during a visit to the United States in 1935. Afterwards, he became assistant filmmaker to Jean Renoir and a film director in his own right, in the polarized political context of the Spanish civil war (Victoire de la vie, 1937, and L'Espagne vivra, 1938). Having been a prisoner of war from 1940 until his escape in February 1943, he brings sensibility to this film. As with his documentaries on Spain, he envisioned Le Retour as a testimony to human resilience in time of war. Cartier-Bresson mastered composition and always tried to capture the 'decisive moment' defined by a person or an event. As a way of life, he strove 'to place head, heart and eye along the same line of sight'.

The thematic filmography on deportation developed slowly and did not initially identify the specificities of persecutions against particular groups. Films were made in different countries and languages. Le Retour is one of the most well-known documentary films; it focuses on repatriation and the moment of reunion with loved ones. Its time frame is the present and its theme opens the future.

Le Retour presented prisoners of war and deportees in the same breath without differentiating them; this problematic interpretation was supported by the French authorities of 1945, who emphasized national unity. Soldiers became prisoners because of the defeat of the French army in 1940; other prisoners were civilians, arrested and deported for political or racial reasons. The first group were combatants, the latter victims. They were not in the same camps, they were not treated the same way, but the film blurs this distinction by mixing together images from the military camps and the concentration camps. As the title indicates, Le Retour was all about the return and causes were minimally addressed.

People had been taken away by the war; victory allowed their return. At the time, it was not possible to ask the painful question: why were these civilians (resisters, political militants, Jews) deported from France? The Vichy government had collaborated with the German occupation forces and therefore shared responsibility for the criminal internment of deportees from France.

The very name of the Ministry responsible for prisoners and deportees only aggravated the confusion. It was an ambiguous subject for filmmakers. The defeated soldiers of 1940 and racial deportees were not heroes. Apart from Le Retour, this theme was absent from French cinematography until the end of the 1940s. In Retour à la vie/Return to Life (1949), four of five short stories are about prisoners of war. Only Le retour d'Emma, by André Cayatte, was about the return of a deportee. Both Le Retour and Retour à la vie focus on the return as the central event, without venturing into the causes.

It was several years before the necessary distinctions were made and the difficult questions asked. Even then, censorship was watching, as demonstrated by the controversy about the documentary film Nuit et brouillard/Night and Fog (Alain Resnais, France, 1955–6). The film had been commissioned to commemorate the tenth anniversary of the liberation of the camps. Nonetheless, state collaboration was still taboo in French films and Resnais had to camouflage the képi of a French gendarme guarding an internment camp in France in order to break the visual link between the French authorities and deportation.

Before they were screened, films were examined by a Commission de contrôle des films cinématographiques (the film censorship board) and filtered through a system of mandatory visas for internal and export markets. National interest was one of the principal concerns of the state. The military struggle took precedence over the ideological conflicts of World War II. This less contentious interpretation of the war was favored by the government and included in Le Retour. In film, just as in official commemorations, the fate and the wartime experience of racial and political deportees were ignored.

SUZANNE LANGLOIS

Le Retour (France/US, Services américains d'information/Office of War Information, 35mm, black & white, 1944–6, 32 mins). Produced by the Office of War Information; producer Noma Ratner. Directed by Henri Cartier-Bresson; codirectors Richard Banks and Jerrold Krimsky from the US Army Signal Corps. Scriptwriter and technical consultant: Henri Cartier-Bresson. On-screen commentary: Claude Roy. Cinematography by US Army Signal Corps, Henri Cartier-Bresson and Claude Renoir. Edited by Henri Cartier-Bresson and Richard Banks. Music by Robert Lannoy. Archival material from the last months of the war, American troops in Germany, Dachau concentration camp, Elbe river, aerial views of Paris, Gare d'Orsay. A nineteen-minute version, Reunion (1946), was adapted from Le Retour by the US Army Pictorial Service.

Further reading

Butler, Margaret, *Film and Community in Britain and France: From La Règle du jeu to Room at the Top*, London: I.B. Tauris, 2004.

Cartier-Bresson, Henri, *Henri Cartier-Bresson: Photographer*, Boston: Little, Brown and Co., 1992.

Langlois, Suzanne, *La Résistance dans le cinéma français 1944–94, de la Libération de Paris à Liberame*, Paris: L'Harmattan, 2001.

Lindeperg, Sylvie, *Les Écrans de l'ombre. La Seconde Guerre mondiale dans le cinéma français (1944–69)*, Paris: CNRS Editions, 1997.

n.a., *De qui s'agit-il? Henri Cartier-Bresson*, Paris: Fondation Henri Cartier-Bresson/Gallimard and Bibliothèque nationale de France, 2003.

Namer, Gérard, *Batailles pour la mémoire. La commémoration en France de 1945 à nos jours*, Paris: Papyrus, 1983.

Rousso, Henry, *The Vichy Syndrome: History and Memory in France since 1944*, Cambridge, MA: Harvard University Press, 1994.

Thompson, George Raynor, *The Signal Corps: The Outcome (mid-1943 through 1945)*, Washington, DC: Office of the Chief of Military History, US Army, 1966.

Riefenstahl, Leni

Leni Riefenstahl is generally regarded as one of the most brilliant and controversial filmmakers in the history of cinema. Though she preferred fiction, in which she excelled as an actress, writer, and director, she will be forever linked to nonfiction on the strength of two classic documentaries—Triumph des Willens/Triumph of the Will (1935), and Olympia (1938).

Trained in classical ballet, Leni Riefenstahl displayed an early interest in and talent for the visual arts and music. She often choreographed her own dance routines, selected the music, and designed her costumes. An injury forced her to suspend dancing, and during recovery she happened to see a film that changed her life. Berg des Schicksals/Mountain of Destiny (1924), a film by Dr Arnold Fanck, was shot in the Dolomite Mountains in northern Italy. The realistic setting, with images of angular rocks and clouds and alpine slopes, made such an impression that she boldly set out to meet the star of the film, Luis Tenker, and the director, Franck, and to offer her services as an actress. The ploy worked, and soon Leni Riefenstahl was starring in mountain films herself. In the first such film, Der heilige Berg/The Holy Mountain (1926), Leni played the role of a dancer, Diotima, caught in a love triangle. She went on to star in other mountain films such as Der grosse Sprung/The Great Leap (1927), Die weißse Hölle vom Piz Palü/The White Hell of Pitz Palu (1929), and Stürme über dem Montblanc/Storm over Mont Blanc (1930), her first film with sound. The films required Riefenstahl to master mountain climbing and barefoot rock climbing, and to endure the hardships of freezing temperatures and blizzard-like conditions. All the while she was performing as an actress, Riefenstahl was studying and mastering the techniques of cinema.

By the time she directed her first film, the fairy tale Das blaue Licht/The Blue Light (1932), Riefenstahl was already one of Germany's best-known actresses. With her directing debut she became world famous. The Blue Light, which she produced, collaborated on the screenplay, starred in, directed, and edited, tells the story of Junta, a young mountain girl accused by nearby villagers of being a witch and causing the deaths of young men who perished in their attempts to climb Monte Cristallo on nights when a full moon casts a shimmering blue light over the mountain. Junta inadvertently allows her lover to discover the source of the blue light, a crystal grotto that villagers find out about and loot. Junta, believing she has been betrayed, leaps to her death. The Blue Light was filmed on location in the village of Ticino and the Dolomites. With a perfectionist's eye, Riefenstahl calculated every lens setting and focal length before shooting, and even ordered a special lens and more sensitive film stock to achieve a nightlike effect.

In 1932 Riefenstahl met Adolf Hitler, soon to be named Chancellor of Germany. The leader of the National Socialist German Workers' Party, or Nazis, Hitler was a spellbinding orator whose message of German nationalism and strength resonated with a population beset by unemployment and the still lingering humiliation of defeat in World War I. Like many other Germans, Riefenstahl was attracted to the worldview that Hitler promoted. Hitler in turn admired Riefenstahl's films, particularly The Holy Mountain and The Blue Light. In her autobiography she quotes Hitler as saying, 'Once we come to power, you must make my films.' Despite an apolitical nature, Riefenstahl agreed to make a film about the annual party rally in Nuremberg. Hastily put together, the short film Sieg des Glaubens/ Victory of Faith (1933), contained only seeds of what would become the next year the most famous propaganda film of all time, Triumph des Willens/ Triumph of the Will (1935).

The timing of Triumph of the Will could not have been more important. Hitler had come to power in January 1933 and had begun immediately to suspend civil liberties and issue anti-Jewish decrees. In August of the next year, the president of Germany, the revered World War I leader Field Marshall Paul von Hindenburg, died, enabling Hitler to combine the office of chancellor and president. A few months before, to appease the military, Hitler had ordered a purge of his own party, assassinating the leader of the SA (*Stürmabteilung* or 'Brownshirts'), Ernst Röhm.

With the world press raising questions about Germany's direction, and party stalwarts uneasy about their own fates, a film promoting party solidarity and German unity would be a public relations coup. On this score, Riefenstahl delivered a masterpiece of propaganda, a one-hundred-and-fourteen-minute film that would solidify Hitler's role as Führer and forever brand Leni Riefenstahl as a Nazi sympathizer. Ostensibly, Triumph of the Will is an account of the Sixth National Socialist Party Rally held in Nuremberg in September of 1934. Financed and distributed by the German film studio UFA, whose largest shareholder, Alfred Hugenberg, was a supporter of Hitler, Triumph of the Will had a crew of eighteen camerapersons. The documentary is chock-full of speeches, rallies, ceremonies, parades, and ritual, but it is made with such artistry and such an understanding of German values and needs that it rises above the typical propaganda film. Triumph begins with Hitler's arrival in Nuremberg as his plane descends from the clouds and glides above the spires of the ancient city. The mystical quality of the arrival is enhanced by the anticipation of the crowd, straining on tiptoes to catch a glimpse of the Führer. After a motorcade into the city and a welcome rally, Riefenstahl changes the pace of the film, which she likens to the changes in the rhythm of a musical composition. The viewer sees Nuremberg at daybreak, still asleep, the absence of people a prelude to the activity that follows. The pace quickens as the camera captures a tent city of young soldiers and workers—shaving, cooking, playing games, and always smiling and laughing. Next, the viewer is treated to a folk parade in honor of the Führer. After inspecting a group of flag bearers, Hitler boards his open Mercedes limousine and, surrounded by other party leaders, disappears. Riefenstahl allows the camera to lose focus, thereby adding to the mysticism of the moment. For the opening of the Party Congress, Riefenstahl features short clips of speeches by Party leaders. Perhaps the most important of Hitler's speeches is his address to the SA, the only time Hitler refers to the purge several months before: 'Men of the SA and the SS. A few months ago, a black shadow spread over the movement. Neither the SA, nor any other institution of the party, had anything to do with this shadow.'

Ever mindful of the importance of symbols, Riefenstahl makes full use of them and the many symbolic acts carried out—a solemn wreath-laying ceremony, a flag consecration, parades of swastika flags, jack-booted SS troops marching in unison, and always, endless salutes and tributes to the Führer. Nuremberg itself was filled with historic symbolism, its Imperial Castle and medieval walls a reminder of the first so-called Reich, The Holy Roman Empire. Music in Triumph was likewise symbolic. Scored by Herbert Windt, it made liberal use of the Party anthem, the Horst Wessel song, composed by an early martyr of the Nazi Party. Windt also included German folk music and German marches as well as music of Hitler's favorite composer, Richard Wagner.

The film premiered in Berlin in March 1935. After complaints by the German army that it had been slighted in Triumph, Riefenstahl agreed to make a short film of the next Party Conference, focusing on military maneuvers. The result was a twenty-eight-minute film, Tag Der Freiheit!—Unsere Wehrmacht!/Day of Freedom!—Our Armed Forces! (1935).

Riefenstahl claimed that one of the most difficult aspects of making the Party films was working with the propaganda minister Joseph Goebbels. A notorious womanizer who worshipped Hitler and saw Riefenstahl as a rival for the Führer's affections, Goebbels controlled the film industry during the Third Reich and resented competition from Riefenstahl, who at one point earned the unofficial title of 'Film Expert to the National Socialist Party'. Throughout her life Riefenstahl maintained that her relationship with Goebbels was anything but cordial, a result of Goebbels's failure to interest her romantically. Nevertheless, in a 1993 documentary, The Wonderful, Horrible Life of Leni Riefenstahl, director Ray Müller confronted Riefenstahl with excerpts from Goebbels's 1933 diary suggesting that he and Riefenstahl visited one another socially.

Some critics question whether Triumph was really a documentary. Siegfried Kracauer believed the rally was staged for the camera, though, in fact, Nazi Party rallies had been held in Nuremberg since 1927. David Hinton argued that editing Triumph in the chronological order in which events occurred was of little importance to Riefenstahl—that the guiding principle was a 'deliberately conceived sense of rhythm'. Lotte Eisner and Susan Sontag condemned Riefenstahl as a pawn of Hitler. Despite the many criticisms of Triumph as pure propaganda—an ode to fascism or paean to Hitler—Richard Barsam (1975) said it fused art and politics and was 'a masterful blend of the four basic elements of cinema—light, darkness, sound, and silence—but it is not just an achievement in cinematic form, for it has other essential elements—thematic, psychological, mythological, narrative, and visual interest—and it is in the working of these elements that Riefenstahl transcends the limitations of the documentary film and the propaganda film genres'.

Leni Riefenstahl's other major contribution to documentary film was Olympia: Fest der Völker/Olympia: Festival of the People, and Olympia: Fest der Shönheit/Olympia: Festival of Beauty (1938), and a two-part film of the 1936 Berlin Olympics hosted by Germany. The first great sports film ever made, it featured staged prologues, innovative camera techniques, and a fluid editing style that elevated it far above the typical sporting events film. Sanctioned by the International Olympics Committee as the official film of the 1936 Olympics, and financed and distributed by the German film company TOBIS, Olympia begins with a reverential tribute to the origin of the games—Ancient Greece. The camera tracks through smoky, silhouetted statues and ruins of ancient temples. Suddenly one of the statues is transformed into a human being—a discus thrower. A dance scene that includes Riefenstahl herself precedes the lighting of the Olympic torch and a symbolic journey from Ancient Greece to modern Berlin. The first part of Olympia features the many track and field events. Riefenstahl always thought in terms of the most artistically composed shot, so for the pole-vaulting sequence, she had pits dug to capture the athletes catapulted across the sky. In slow motion, their graceful bodies seem to defy gravity. Throughout both parts of the film, Riefenstahl used balloons, dollies, catapults, telescopic lenses, any means she could use to convey the pain and ecstasy of competition. For the diving competition, Riefenstahl used underwater cameras to follow the divers below, as well as above the surface of the water. Perhaps the most famous sequence is the high-diving competition in part two of Olympia. The sequence begins with a series of fast-paced dives that gradually become more silhouetted as the sky darkens. Projected in slow motion, the ballet-like acrobatics of the divers framed against a cloud-laced sky appear almost superhuman. In fact, one of the criticisms of Olympia is that Riefenstahl's seemingly cult-like obsession with beauty, particularly the beauty of the human body, reflected a fascist aesthetic consistent with the ideals of the Nazi Party. This argument is undermined, however, by the fact that the star of the 1936 Olympics was an African American athlete, Jesse Owens, who received prominent attention in the film and contradicted Nazi notions of a superior Aryan race. Olympia premiered in 1938 at the UFA-Palast am Zoo in Berlin and was later shown throughout Europe. It won numerous awards, including the Grand Prize at the International Film Festival in Venice. In 1956 American directors designated it one of the ten best films of all time.

In 1938 Riefenstahl traveled to the United States to promote Olympia, but her visit was marred by anti-Nazi sentiment that followed Germany's Crystal Night, a night of terror in which Jewish synagogues, homes, and businesses were wrecked, burned, and looted, and more than thirty thousand Jews were arrested. Hitler biographer John Toland noted: 'The reaction from abroad was immediate and the acts of brutality were given an unforgettable name—inspired by the multitude of smashed windows—Crystal Night. On all sides Germany was assailed as a barbarous nation.' Despite a friendly visit in Chicago with automobile tycoon Henry Ford, the film world by and large shunned her. Gary Cooper cancelled an invitation to meet her, and Walt Disney declined an offer to screen Olympia. Later, he told the press he really didn't know who Leni Riefenstahl was.

During World War II Riefenstahl served for a brief time as a war photographer and worked whenever possible on a feature film she directed and starred in, Tiefland/Lowlands (1954), begun in 1934 but not completed until after the war. At the close of World War II she was arrested by US authorities and then released. The US Army concluded that she may not have been aware of what went on in Nazi Germany and that her sin was one of omission, 'which appears all the more serious due to the fact that she, more than any person, had the opportunity to get to the truth. She is a product of the moral corruption which characterizes the regime. But it would be false to picture her as an ambitious female who wanted to attain fame and wealth on the NSDAP bandwagon. She is certainly no fanatical National Socialist who had sold her soul to the regime. Admiration for Hitler had closed her eyes to all that his regime meant for Germany. His protecting hand insured her artistic activities—contrary to those of so many others. His hand offered protection from the political clutches, and built a dream-world for her in which she could live with "her art" [...] If her statements are sincere, she has never grasped, and still does not grasp, the fact that she, by dedicating her life to art, has given expression to a gruesome regime and contributed to its glorification.'

The French military was less forgiving. Shortly after being released by the US Army, Riefenstahl was arrested by French police and remained in custody until 1947. In 1949 she was officially de-Nazified by a French tribunal. The Baden State Commisariat classified her as a 'fellow traveler'.

Eventually, most of the films that had been confiscated from her were returned, either by government or court action. Though she attempted to resume her career as a filmmaker, press coverage of her activities made financing impossible to obtain. Riefenstahl claimed that Jewish organizations and not the German government were to blame. In the 1950s and 1960s Riefenstahl began traveling to Africa, at first to make a film, but later to take still photographs of tribes in the southern Sudan. The result was her first book of still photographs, published in English as *The Last of the Nuba* (1974). About the same time, Riefenstahl learned to dive and became an accomplished underwater photographer, using both still and motion picture cameras. With her companion, Horst Kettner, she organized diving expeditions to the Red Sea, Honduras, the Caribbean, the Indian Ocean, and elsewhere to capture the undersea world. In 1976 a second book of Africa photographs was published, *The People of Kao*, followed two years later by a book of underwater photographs, *Coral Garden* (1978). She wrote the text and composed the layout for a fourth book, *Leni Riefenstahl's Africa* (1982). Her autobiography, *Leni Riefenstahl: A Memoir*, was published in 1987 and another book of still photographs, *Wonders under Water*, in 1991. The last of her publications, *Leni Riefenstahl: Five Lives*, appeared in 2000. The 'five lives' refers to her many careers—as a dancer, actress, director, photographer, and diver.

CHURCHILL ROBERTS

See also: Olympia; Triumph of the Will

Biography

Born in Berlin, August 22, 1902. Showed an early interest in gymnastics, music, poetry, and dance. Finished schooling at the Kollmorgen Lyceum in Berlin in 1918, then attended the Grimm-Reiter Dance School and later the Jutta Klamt School and the dance school of Dresden. In 1923 gave first solo dance performance. In 1924 met actor Luis Trenker and director Arnold Fanck and soon starred in her first film, The Holy Mountain. In 1932 directed The Blue Light, followed by Triumph of the Will (1935) and Olympia (1938). War photographer in 1939, worked intermittently on a feature film, Tiefland, completed in 1954. Arrested in 1945 and released in 1947. Made the first of many trips to Africa in 1956 and in 1973 passed a diving test. First of five books of still photographs published in 1973. Photographed the 1972 Olympics for the *Sunday Times Magazine* and was guest of honor at the summer Olympics in Montreal in 1976. In 1982 awarded a gold cup by the International Olympics Committee for Olympia. Died in 2003 at the age of 101.

Selected films

1926 The Holy Mountain: actress
1929 The White Hell of Pitz Palu: actress
1930 Storm over Mont Blanc: actress
1932 The Blue Light: actress, director, editor
1933 Victory of Faith: director, editor
1933 SOS Iceberg: actress
1935 Triumph of the Will: director, editor
1935 Day of Freedom!—Our Armed Forces!: director, editor
1938 Olympia Part I: Festival of the People: director, editor
1938 Olympia Part II: Festival of Beauty: director, editor
1954 Tiefland: director, actress, editor

Further reading

Barsam, Richard M., *Film Guide to Triumph of the Will*, Bloomington, IN: Indiana University Press, 1975.
Berg-Pan, Renata, *Leni Riefenstahl*, Boston: Twayne Publishers, 1980.
Fanck, Arnold, *Erführte Regie mit Gletschern, Stürem, Lawinen*, Munich: Nymphenburger Verlagshandlung, 1973.
Ford, Charles, *Leni Riefenstahl*, Paris: La Table Ronde, 1978.
Hinton, David B., *The Films of Leni Riefenstahl*, third edn, Lanhan, MD: Scarecrow Press, 2000.
Hull, David Stewart, *Film in the Third Reich*, New York: Simon and Schuster, 1973.
Infield, Glen B., *Leni Riefenstahl: The Fallen Film Goddess*, New York: Thomas Y. Crowell Company, 1976.
Riefenstahl, Leni, *Leni Riefenstahl: A Memoir*, New York: Picador USA, 1995.
——*Leni Riefenstahl: Five Lives*, Cologne: Taschen, 2000.
Rother, Rainer, *Leni Riefenstahl: The Seduction of Genius*, London: Continuum, 2002.
Salkeld, Audrey, *A Portrait of Leni Riefenstahl*, London: Pimlico, 1997.

Rien que les heures

(France, Cavalcanti, 1926)

Rien que les heures/Nothing but the Hours was Alberto Cavalcanti's first directed film. The film was produced by Pierre Braunberger, an enlightened entrepreneur, committed to the enhancement of French independent film culture, who also produced films for other independent filmmakers during the 1920s.

Rien que les heures opens with an intertitle stating that 'this film does not need a story, it is no more than a series of impressions on time passing'. Nevertheless, the film does contain a story, concerning a day in the life of the city of Paris, although, unlike other 'city symphony' films of the period, such as Joris Ivens's Regen/Rain (1929), chronology is neither linear nor logical in the film. No explanation is given, either, for these odd discrepancies. The primary function of the characters in the film is also to reinforce the central thesis of Rien que les heures, which is that underlying the apparent civilised façade of bourgeois society there exists a darker reality marked by violence, inequality, and brutality. This thesis, which is represented metaphorically in various sections of the film, is given particular substance in the film's subplot of criminality, violence, and victimisation.

One of the characters in the film is an old woman. Unconnected to the narrative causality of the film's story, she seems to function as a symbol, and metaphorical victim, of the degenerate urban world around her. Although a sense of irony pervades much of Rien que les heures, particularly in the way in which playful juxtapositions and modernist special effects are used, the sequences involving the old woman appear strikingly harsh and harrowing, and the last time she is seen, sitting down in an abandoned rubbish yard, could be interpreted as signifying her impending death.

At a retrospective of his work mounted at the National Film Theatre in 1977, Cavalcanti chose, rather surprisingly, to select a number of light Parisian songs to accompany a screening of Rien que les heures. This apparently had the effect of making the film appear largely ironic and even comic in parts, and of making the figure of the old woman appear paradoxic rather than tragic. The reasons for Cavalcanti's decision to use popular songs to accompany the film are unclear, but it is difficult to imagine how the old lame woman in the film could have been rendered comic by such treatment. Whatever Cavalcanti's motives were in 1977, a careful viewing of the film suggests that this character is to be read realistically, rather than paradoxically.

The use of modernist devices in Rien que les heures, such as wipes, dissolves, and superimpositions, also serves to emphasise the authorial source of the critique of bourgeois norms mounted within the film, and the vision of the filmmaker is foregrounded here through the application of these explicitly modernist devices. Rien que les heures does not use these modernist devices for merely experimental purposes, but to demystify conventional forms of representation in order to critique bourgeois society. The film, therefore, can be said to possess a subversive intent.

Underlying Rien que les heures is also a notion of reality as masked, and the film uses juxtapositions to render the impression that a gradual unmasking process is taking place as the film unfolds. The film also uses a binary oppositional structure as part of this unmasking process, as conventional images based on clichéd perceptions of Parisian life repeatedly give way to others that subvert or contradict them. One example of this is a scene in which shots of food in a marketplace are followed by glimpses of rubbish in a bin. Again, the underlying idea is that, beneath the civilised façade, something far more primal and animalistic lurks.

Rien que les heures undoubtedly cemented Cavalcanti's reputation as an important avant-garde director. It is difficult, however, to compare the film with others of the period. Although Siegfried Kracauer has compared the film to Ivens's Regen, the two films are not really comparable. The anarchistic modernism of Rien que les heures also means that the film cannot really be compared with French cinematic impressionism, or the cinema pur. The use of melodramatic characterisation in the film also means that it cannot be compared easily to the 'city symphony' genre. Perhaps the easiest association is with René Clair's Entr'acte (1924), although Cavlcanti's film still lacks the overtly Dadaist aspirations of Clair's film. Cavalcanti drew on many influences in making Rien que les heures, and the film is best regarded as a distillation of these influences, rather than a film that can be closely associated with others of the period. Rien que les heures was also the first, and almost the last high-modernist film made by Cavalcanti, and he was only to return to this type of filmmaking once more during the course of his career, with the collaborative project of Coal Face in 1935.

IAN AITKEN

See also: Cavalcanti, Alberto

Rien que les heures (France, 1926). Directed and edited by Alberto Cavalcanti. Produced by Pierre Braunberger and Neo-Films.

Further reading

Aitken, Ian, *Alberto Cavalcanti, Realism, Surealism and National Cinemas*, London: Flicks Books, 2001.
——*Film and Reform*, London: Routledge, 1990.
——*The Documentary Film Movement, An Anthology*, Edinburgh: Edinburgh University Press, 1998.
Cavalcanti, Alberto, *Filme e Realidade*, Rio de Janeiro: Editora Artenova, in collaboration with Empresa Brasiliera de Filmes—Embrafilme, 1977.
Ghali, Noureddine, *L'Avant-Garde Cinématographique en France dans les Anées Vingt*, Paris: Editions Paris Experimental, 1995.
Pellizari, Lorenzo and Valentinetti, Claudio M. (eds), *Alberto Cavalcanti*, Locarno: Editions du Festival international du films de Locarno, 1988.
Sussex, Elizabeth, 'Cavalcanti in England', *Sight and Sound* 44, no. 4, autumn, 1975.

Riggs, Marlon

The filmmaker Marlon T. Riggs used film as a means to inform mainstream America of the complexities of African American gay life, and to deconstruct black visual representation. In terms of focus, Riggs followed in the tradition of documentarians such as William Greaves and alongside filmmakers such as Henry Hampton, both of whom believed in the power and viability of the media to convey important social concerns regarding African Americans. Riggs worked throughout the 1980s and early 1990s, during the presidencies of Ronald Reagan and George H.W. Bush. At that time, the United States enjoyed tremendous financial gains, while simultaneously undermining and eliminating social services for the poor and people of color. The much-touted 'cultural wars' shaped the artistic landscape. The culmination of enhanced commerce and communication advances led to an explosion of visual opportunities, especially via cable.

In his work, Riggs emphasized both commonalities and differences between the black gay community and black communities at large. He calls into question black spirituality, African heritage, black duality, and black humanity. He distinguishes a radical black aesthetic while pushing the boundaries of black aesthetics in general. Riggs's works addressing black gay life include Tongues Untied (1989), Affirmations (1990), Anthem (1991), and Non, Je Ne Regrette Rien/No, I Regret Nothing (1992).

The self-reflexive stance in Riggs's works offers an important commentary on African Americans specifically and others more generally. His confrontational approach of examining black homosexuality locates dialogue discrepancies within black communities. Because his work advocates change, his productions incited critical and popular debate.

Tongues Untied became Riggs's most controversial and celebrated work. Appearing on the national public television series P.O.V. in 1989, the documentary received the Best Documentary Award at the Berlin Film Festival and awards at other film festivals. It later became the center of a heated debate involving funding for the National Endowment for the Arts (NEA) and the Corporation for Public Broadcasting. Criticizing the film as vulgar and amoral, the Christian Coalition edited a sensationalized clip of the film and distributed it to every member of Congress. Republican Patrick Buchanan reedited a twenty-second clip from the film to use in an attack on the NEA during the 1992 presidential primary. Riggs responded with an op-ed piece in *The New York Times* entitled 'Meet the New Willie Horton'.

Tongues Untied centers on the realties of black, male homosexual love. This was the first televised frank discussion of black homosexuality. In interviews Riggs said that he drew on his own personal experience in creating the documentary. He wanted to speak loudly about the painful experiences of being gay and black. Tongues Untied contemplates the nuances of self-definition, and the pressures and demands of an attempt to define oneself via multiple identities.

In Tongues Untied the audience is directly addressed through the multilayering of both sounds and images. Alone and in concert with other voices, Riggs juxtaposes words, music, and sound to accost his audience. This cacophonous musical tradition plays very much into African-American sensibilities. Black music and oral traditions unify because they confront individuals with the truth of black existence. This same usage of music occurs in his film short Anthem. For example, Blackberri's rendition of the song 'America' is positioned subversively to illuminate its irony for blacks and gays. Riggs uses rhythmic African drumbeats throughout Tongues Untied and Anthem to draw a line of continuity between the present and the past. Through Riggs's positioning of music in the background, as well as in the narrative of his films, he addresses gay and heterosexual African Americans in ways that transcend sexuality and race.

Not all of his projects take this combative, highly personal approach. Ethnic Notions (1987), his first major project, traced the evolution of racial stereotypes. It received an Emmy Award and has become a core text in college courses across the United States. Color Adjustment (1991) takes on television representations of blacks. For its insightfulness and creativity, it received one of television's highest accolades, the George Foster Peabody Award. These documentaries offer more traditional approaches to African American representation in the commodified world of television and film. They use 'voice-of-God' narration, scholarly experts, and multilayered images of blacks depicted over the span of seventy years in film and television. While in some ways Riggs's use of the prevailing techniques of majority aesthetics seems to give credence to them, it serves more usefully to undermine those same techniques by presenting subject matter rarely seen.

In his final work, Black Is ... Black Ain't (1995), Riggs tackled the complex inner workings of black identity. Through his creative production methods, use of black aesthetics, and inclusion of his dying body as a template, Riggs's art functions as a foundation for critical examinations of African American relations as a whole. Overall, Marlon Riggs's documentaries provide a road map for collective introspection and progress.

BERETTA E. SMITH-SHOMADE

Biography

Born in Fort Worth, Texas, February 3, 1957. Graduated magna cum laude from Harvard University and received Master's degree from the University of California, Berkeley. Appointed a professor in Berkeley's Graduate School of Journalism. At the age of thirty-seven died of AIDS, on April 5, 1994. His final film, Black Is ... Black Ain't, was completed by his coproducer Nicole Atkinson and editor/codirector Christiane Badgely from the footage shot previously and notes left by Riggs.

Selected films

1987 Ethnic Notions
1989 Tongues Untied
1990 Affirmations
1991 Anthem
1991 Color Adjustment
1992 Non, Je Ne Regrette Rien/No, I Regret Nothing
1995 Black Is ... Black Ain't

Further reading

Becquer, Marcos, 'Snap!thology and Other Discursive Practices in Tongues Untied', *Wide Angle* 13, no. 2, April 1991: 6–17.

Datcher, Michael, 'Pride and Prejudice: Groundbreaking Filmmaker Marlon Riggs Explores Two of Today's Most Controversial Issues: Race and Sexuality', *San Francisco Focus*, February 1994: 38–43.

Grundmann, Roy, 'New Agendas in Black Filmmaking: An Interview with Marlon Riggs', *Cineaste* 19, nos 2–3, 1992: 52–4.

Riggs, Marlon, 'Black Macho Revisited: Reflections of a Snap! Queen', *The Independent*, April 1991: 32–4.

River, The

(US, Lorentz, 1937)

Pare Lorentz's follow-up film to The Plow that Broke the Plains (1936), The River, tells a story of the economic and ecological changes experienced along the Mississippi River and its tributaries. Its goal was to inform US citizens about the problems posed by the rivers and their abuse, as well as to promote the solutions offered by a number of President Franklin Roosevelt's New Deal agencies, chiefly the Tennessee Valley Authority but also the Farm Security Administration (FSA) and the Civilian Conservation Corps (the Resettlement Administration, the agency behind Plow and The River, ceased to exist and many of its missions were absorbed within the FSA). Although it was first screened only to southern US audiences, The River was intended for national distribution, which it eventually got through the assistance of Paramount Pictures. Considered to be Lorentz's greatest achievement, it beat seventy other films (including Leni Riefenstahl's Olympia) when it became the first US film honored as the best documentary film at the Venice International Film Festival.

The film uses a documentary paradigm familiar in the 1930s: an initial situation is described (the Mississippi region was beautiful and held economic value), a problem is revealed (misuse of the land has led to soil erosion and flooding), and finally a solution is recommended (a variety of government agencies can restore the region to its original state). 'Conservation', as suggested in The River, only implied the TVA's policies of flooding vast valleys to create dams and cheap hydroelectric power. Surrounding these federally funded dams were controversial issues including the government creation of electrical power, afforestation, reforestation, and the relocation of farmers from flooded lands to less productive areas in the hills. It was a project that would have massive political, economic, and ecological repercussions for the entire region. A film explaining this project would be representing and advocating many New Deal policies and agencies, and thus Roosevelt was willing to provide a much larger budget for The River than Plow, which was filmed in five states while The River was filmed in fourteen.

Lorentz filmed along the Mississippi River and its tributaries in late 1936, thinking he would use stock footage of floods and flooding as he finished his initial shooting in January 1937. Photographer Willard Van Dyke, whose letters written during the filming provide an important source of information on Lorentz's shooting process, estimated that Lorentz took one hundred thousand feet of film for a final product that would only total three thousand feet. The devastating floods of early 1937 allowed him the rare chance to capture shots of the flooded Mississippi and Ohio Rivers; the fresh memories of that natural disaster must have played a powerful role in the film's critical and popular reception. Furthermore, in contrast to the bleak ending in Plow, which ended, in the more widely shown version without its epilogue, with dust storms and displaced families heading off to an uncertain future, The River has a far more hopeful conclusion, showing images of ecological and economic regrowth: majestic shots of hydroelectric dams and power cables, of workers restoring fields. Its remarkably optimistic tone was popular among politicians, critics, and especially audiences, many of whom were reported to have cheered and applauded at the screenings. The initial four-reel version was shortened to a three-reel version where it enjoyed widespread distribution for many years among schools.

The collaboration between Lorentz and composer Virgil Thomson rivals that of Eisenstein and Prokofiev in their tight coordination between the visual and audible parts of the film. Dialectical gestures involving image and music, such as the alternating major-minor mode contrasts showing fertile and barren soil in Plow, return in The River, where Thomson instead contrasts diatonic and chromatic versions of a trumpet melody to underscore the distinction between lush and abused nature scenes. In addition to recycling parts of his earlier Symphony on a Hymn Tune (1928), Thomson wrote original cues based on a study of southern Protestant hymns and regional folk songs. Thomson's music for the log sequences includes quick-paced arrangements of popular songs like 'Hot Time in the Old Town Tonight' as we see log after log shoot off the sluices into the water. The music accompanying the flood sequence is based on the hymn named 'Mississippi' whose (unheard) lyrics describe an apocalyptic scene, and Thomson's treatment of this musical material builds synergistically with the imagery. As the flood on the image track builds up from dripping icicles to an overpowering deluge, the music grows from a single line stating the hymn melody into a thick fugue, finally culminating in the original harmonization of the hymn as found in the shape-note books. Visuals—long aerial shots of the bloated river and submerged houses—and music climax at this moment. Parts of The River's score were reused in Nicholas Meyer's ABC-TV movie about nuclear bombings, The Day After (1983).

The River has been widely praised for its careful and effective blending of image, word, and music. Lorentz's narration, which has been compared to the poetry of Walt Whitman, and which James Joyce reportedly called the most beautiful prose he had heard in ten years, was not written until after the score had been composed and the film edited into its final form. Epic catalogues of river names and towns are repeated, as are key phrases. Parts of Lorentz's argument in The River have been criticized for being overly subtle, hyperbolic, and obtuse. He perhaps overemphasizes the connection between deforestation and flooding. As in Plow, Lorentz sought to encourage national identification with a regional problem and he again exaggerates the amount of territory in question; the rivers on Lorentz's maps take on Brobdagnigian proportions, although without any Swiftian irony. His focus on larger natural and national forces tends to diminish the individuals and their reactions to adversity, although The River contains memorable images of intense human suffering, such as the shots of the faces of flood victims and migrant farmers.

NEIL LERNER

See also: Lorentz, Pare; Plow that Broke the Plains, The

The River (US, black and white; Western Electric Mirrophonic Recording; Farm Security Administration; 1937, 35mm, 36 mins; 16mm, 27 mins). Released October 29, 1937, premiering in New Orleans, Louisiana; Memphis, TN, November 1, 1937; St Louis, November 10; Washington, DC, December 7. Distributed by Paramount Pictures. Written and directed by Pare Lorentz. Photographed by Floyd Crosby, Stacy Woodard, Horace Woodard, and Willard Van Dyke. Music composed by Virgil Thomson, orchestrated by Henry Brant, and conducted by Alexander Smallens. Narrator: Thomas Chalmers. Editors: Lloyd Nosler; Leo Zochling. Research editor: A.A. Mercey. Sound: Al Dillinger. Filmed along the Mississippi River Valley from October 1936 through March 1, 1937. Cost: c. $50,000.

Further reading

Alexander, William, *Film on the Left: American Documentary Film from 1931 to 1942*, Princeton, NJ: Princeton University Press, 1981.

Barsam, Richard M., *Non-Fiction Film: A Critical History*, revised and expanded edition, Bloomington, IN and Indianapolis, IN: Indiana University Press, 1992.

Lerner, Neil, 'Damming Virgil Thomson's Music for The River', in Jane M. Gaines and Michael Renov (eds), *Collecting Visible Evidence*, Minneapolis, MN and London: University of Minnesota Press, 1999.

MacCann, Richard D., *The People's Films: A Political History of U.S. Government Motion Pictures*, New York: Hastings House, 1973.

Rabinowitz, Paula, *They Must Be Represented: The Politics of Documentary*, London and New York: Verso, 1994.

Rollins, Peter C., 'Ideology and Film Rhetoric: Three Documentaries of the New Deal Era', *The Journal of Popular Film* 5, no. 2, 1976: 126–45.

Snyder, Robert L., *Pare Lorentz and the Documentary Film*, Norman, OK: University of Oklahoma Press, 1968.

Thomson, Virgil, *Virgil Thomson*, New York: Dutton, 1966.

Tommasini, Anthony, *Virgil Thomson: Composer on the Aisle*, New York and London, Norton, 1997.

Van Dyke, Willard, 'Letters from The River', *Film Comment*, 1965: 38–56.

Widgery, Claudia Joan, *The Kinetic and Temporal Interaction of Music and Film: Three Documentaries of 1930s America*, PhD dissertation, University of Maryland, 1990.

Rochemont, Louis de

Best known and remembered as the creative head of The March of Time series, Louis de Rochemont was an innovator in other types of filmmaking that were also influential and imitated, all of which featured a certain emphasis on realist technique and style. His early (begun in adolescence) and extensive background was as a newsreel cameraman and director.

In 1934 he created The March of Time (MOT) with Roy Larson of *Time* magazine (its first issue was February 1935) and remained its head until 1943. The MOT was a twenty-minute monthly news magazine of one to three stories. De Rochemont called it 'pictorial journalism', and it made use of interviews, newsreel footage, and recreations of actual events. In 1940 MOT released a feature-length compilation entitled The Ramparts We Watch, which summarized the European situation after the outbreak of World War II.

From 1943 to 1946 de Rochemont was a producer at Twentieth Century Fox (which was distributing The March of Time). His work included the feature-length Technicolor documentary The Fighting Lady (1944), about the final phase of the war in the Pacific (the title refers to an aircraft carrier, the Yorktown in this case). It was directed by famed still photographer Edward Steichen and narrated by movie star Robert Taylor, both then in the Navy (de Rochemont had himself been a naval officer from 1917 to 1923).

At Fox he began production of semi-documentary features based on actuality: The House on 92nd Street (1945) was about the FBI exposure of a German espionage ring; 13 Rue Madeleine (1947) focused on the training and a mission of Office of Strategic Services (OSS)

agents during the war; and Boomerang! (1947) was based on events in the life of Homer Cummings, who became Attorney General under Franklin Roosevelt. Although these films do not otherwise seem to have much in common with the British wartime semi-documentaries, they share the same characteristic documentary concentration on how things are done. Most pointedly, they use a voice of time-style narration over their openings and subsequently to provide explanations and transitions, and to imply their authenticity.

After leaving Fox in 1948, he established Louis de Rochemont Associates. This firm continued to make occasional semi-documentary theatrical features (Lost Boundaries, 1949; The Whistle at Eaton Falls, 1951), sponsored films for advertising and public relations use, and classroom films. His major educational project was The Earth and its Peoples series of thirty-six films, each about twenty minutes long, containing such titles as Eskimo Hunters, Highlands of the Andes, Horsemen of the Pampas, Farmers of India, and On Mediterranean Shores.

As far as documentary film is concerned, de Rochemont remains a peripheral, if highly influential, producer. The March of Time set off a succession of similar series. John Grierson and members of his group were involved with it in England and New York, and Grierson carried its conception with him to Canada as the model for the National Film Board's The World in Action series. In the United States there were several imitative competing series including Pathé News and Paramount News. The influence of The March of Time, and perhaps most especially the compilation feature coming out of it, The Ramparts We Watch, is very evident in the US Armed Forces Why We Fight series supervised by Frank Capra. MOT influence even carried over recognizably into television in the Murrow/Friendly See It Now (1951–8), and 60 Minutes (1968–). De Rochemont's semi-documentaries established precedents for subsequent theatrical features based on fact, including The China Syndrome (1979), about the possible meltdown of a nuclear reactor, and Missing (1982), about the disappearance and death of an American writer in Chile.

However, de Rochemont, while never exactly part of the Hollywood filmmaking community, was not at home among the documentarians working in New York City and Washington, DC. He is best categorized as on the edge of the theatrical film industry, with his early experience in newsreels a central influence.

JACK C. ELLIS

See also: March of Time, The

Biography

Born in Chelsea, Massachusetts, January 13, 1899. Attended Massachusetts Institute of Technology; Naval Aviation School; Harvard Naval Cadet School. Served in British Military Intelligence 1916–17. Officer in United States Navy 1917–23. Cameraman for International, and for Pathé News; director of short film program, Twentieth Century Fox (Adventures of a Newsreel Cameraman and Magic Carpets of Movietone series) 1923–9. Created, with Roy E. Larson, The March of Time series 1934. Creative head of The March of Time 1935–51. Producer, Twentieth Century Fox 1943–6. Founded Louis de Rochemont Associates 1948. Produced The Earth and its Peoples educational series, and films in Cinerama and other widescreen processes. Received Special Academy Award for The March of Time 1936. Died December 23, 1978.

Further reading

Fielding, Raymond, *The March of Time: 1935–51*, New York: Oxford University Press, 1978.

Lafferty, William, 'de Rochemont, Louis', in *International Dictionary of Films and Filmmakers*, Detroit: St James Press, 1993: vol. 4, 211–13.

Rodríguez, Marta and Jorge Silva

The Colombian team of Marta Rodríguez and Jorge Silva began to make their mark with their first film together, the remarkable Chircales/Brickworkers, a portrait of a family of workers in the brickyards on the outskirts of Bogotá. The film was completed in 1972 after five years of work. It was immediately recognised internationally for its originality and beauty as a quite exceptional fusion of politics, visual poetry, and ethnographic documentary.

Marta Rodríguez came to documentary through sociology and anthropology; Jorge Silva, the cinematographer of the pair, through journalism, photography, and the film club movement. Their collaboration, which ended in 1987 with Silva's early death, was a harmonious union in which the two were entirely complementary. It also conjoined the lyricism of Silva's camerawork with the new radical sociology associated with Camilo Torres, and the new thinking about visual anthropology of Jean Rouch, with both of whom Rodríguez studied in Bogotá and Paris, respectively. As she explained in a 1974 interview, 'When you combine the social sciences with a mass medium like film, you are challenging the uses to which both are put by the privileged class while simultaneously putting them at the service of the working class. In contrast to the kind of hermetic treatise that only five initiates can read, this is a way to use anthropology or sociology so that the working class can put it to use analyzing their particular situation.'

This approach explains the time they took to make Chircales and subsequent films. The methodology required extensive periods of field work, using stills photography and tape recordings, then the elaboration of a script, followed by filming and then editing, all the while allowing time for the subjects of the film to participate in the process at each stage. The result is to draw the discourse of documentary into the subjects' own subjectivity without losing a sociopolitical perspective. In thus uncovering the whys and wherefores of everyday life among the most marginalised victims of social 'progress' in the Third World, their work also exemplified the aims of the new documentary then emerging across Latin America.

Planas, testimonio de un etnocidio/Planas: Testimony About Ethnocide (1970) was made rather more rapidly, while Chircales was still being completed. This is a denunciatory film that documents the genocide of the Guajibo people of the Amazon region and explores the economic and social causes of the slaughter. Then in 1976 they completed Campesinos/Peasants, which turns to questions of popular memory, reconstructing the peasant struggles for land of the 1930s through the recollection of the older generation. For the next five years they worked with an indigenous group in the region of Cauca on Nuestra Voz de Tierra, Memoria y Futuro/Our Voice of Land, Memory and Future (1981), which takes the discourse of documentary further into the interior spaces of social identity and ideology. In telling the story of the creation of the Regional Indigenous Council of Cauca (CRIC), the film uses enactment to visualise an old legend about a landowner who makes a pact with the devil to rob the peasants of their land and labour. However, this is a long way from the docudrama conventions of British or American television, both in style and intent. Here, the social subjectivity of myth and legend is seen as a living metaphor of exploitation, the symbolic expression of the process of extraction of surplus value.

Before Nuestra Voz ... was completed, they again interrupted their work to make another film of denunciation, La voz de los sobrevivientes/The Voice of the Survivors (1980), made at the request of the CRIC to condemn the assassination of a number of peasant leaders. Then followed Amor, Mujeres y Flores/Love, Women and Flowers (completed 1989 by Rodríguez after Silva's death), an investigation of the Colombian flower industry—the country's second largest export industry at the time—and its use of pesticides, made by companies like Bayer, which are banned at home but freely exported to the Third World. There they are used, as in this case, to produce perishable consumer goods that are whisked back to Europe to be sold, leaving the women who sort the flowers with damaged health, and their children born with genetic defects. A multilayered film told from the point of view of the men and particularly women who work within it, the film unfolds a graceful metaphor that brings women and flowers together, intertwining the process of production with the cycle of life and death—the life and death of the flowers against the life and death of the workers. The film refrains from explicit denunciation of responsibility, but critics at home, when it was shown on television, worried that it would damage Colombian flower sales abroad, while one of its foreign funders, the US Interamerican Foundation, was so upset that they took their name off the credits.

After Silva's death, Rodríguez made one more documentary on film, Nacer de nuevo/Born Again (1987), a reflection on death, solitude, and love told by two aged survivors of the eruption of the Nevado del Ruiz, before she turned to video, working with indigenous groups in workshops she helped to set up in 1992, which have joined the indigenous video movement that began in Brazil and has subsequently spread through the countries of the Andes.

MICHAEL CHANAN

Biography

Marta Rodríguez. Born 1938 in Bogotá, Colombia.

Jorge Silva. Born 1941. Died 1988.

Selected films

1971 Planas: testimonio de un etnocidio: codirectors
1972 Chircales: codirectors
1975 Campesinos: codirectors
1980 La voz de los sobrevivientes: codirectors
1981 Nuestra voz de tierra: memoria y futuro: codirectors
1987 Nacer de Nuevo: Marta Rodríguez, director
1988 Amor, mujeres y flores: codirectors
1992 Memoria vida: Marta Rodríguez, director

Further reading

Burton, Julianne (ed.), *Cinema and Social Change in Latin America: Conversations with Filmmakers*, Austin, TX: University of Texas Press, 1986.

Paranagua, Paulo Antonio (ed.), *Cine Documental en America Latina*, Madrid: Editorial Cátedra, 2003 (also *Jump Cut* No.38).

Roger & Me

(US, Moore, 1989)

Roger & Me was the debut film of radical journalist Michael Moore and an immediate critical and, rare for a nonfiction film, commercial success. It has attracted endless criticism for its formal inventiveness and complex rhetoric, and an equal measure of controversy regarding the filmmaker's supposed violation of the documentary code of ethics. The result, according to one critic, is 'an extraordinary film which is likely to be regarded as a major landmark in contemporary documentary' (Corner 1996: 156).

The film traces the industrial decline of Flint, Michigan, the 'company town' of General Motors (GM) and home to Michael Moore. The filmmaker sets off in search of Roger Smith, GM chairman, to confront him about the factory closures and the plight of the town in the 1980s. Moore draws on a panoply of interactive and reflexive techniques to construct his film: home movies, promotional videos, news sources and interviews combine to produce a hilarious but telling critique of the postindustrial corporate system and the shallowness of public discourses in dealing with the consequences of industrial change.

The production cost of about $160,000 was paid for by Moore, donations, product placement, and various fundraising events. It played to enthusiastic screenings at film festivals and, in one of the saga's many ironies, was acquired for distribution for an unprecedented $3 million by the world's then largest media corporation, Time-Warner. Initially, influential critics like Roger Ebert and Vincent Canby praised the film highly, but accusations of bad practice surfaced in a published interview with Moore in *Film Comment*, which doubted the validity of the film's depicted chronology; Pauline Kael endorsed this view at the *New Yorker* and furthermore questioned the derogatory treatment of some of the respondents in the film and its presumed moral superiority. Some radicals were put off by the film's whimsicality. Many were quick to defend the filmmaker, however, and a wide-ranging debate now surrounds Roger & Me, Moore's populism, and his unconventional style and legacy.

Juxtaposition and contrast are the principal characteristics of the film. These are evident in the fundamental opposition of Moore's personal, biographical and hence subjective placement in the text, and his objective responsibility as an investigative journalist in exposing the 'truth' about economic and social conditions in Flint. Moore brilliantly extends this approach to his film style. The local officials' pathetic attempts to talk up the virtues of the town and develop its tourism are stood against a seemingly endless series of evictions of families from their homes. While the wealthy and secure, at their garden parties and golf clubs, harp on about opportunities that await those with the right positive attitude, we meet laid-off workers queuing to sell their blood for a few dollars or forlornly shooting hoop at the local mental health clinic. The callousness of the 'better classes' is further exposed in their thoughtless enjoyment of an opening-night party at a newly commissioned jail, which Moore revisits when it is full of disillusioned and criminalized former car-workers, presided over by former colleagues now forced to work for a much lower hourly rate. The film culminates in a masterly intercut sequence between Roger

Figure 16 Roger & Me, Michael Moore, with Rhonda Britton (Flints Bunny Lady) and Fred Ross (Repo Man) in front of a Buick ad, 1989 (Courtesy of the Everett Collection)

Smith delivering his annual Christmas message to GM workers and stockholders, and the eviction in the snow of a poor black family. While Smith mouths his platitudes, a little child looks on in dismay as the sheriff's men dump Christmas presents on the sidewalk. Throughout, Moore retains a keen eye for the quirky and bizarre: the self-styled Captain Dada, come to rescue Flint in its hour of need, is summarily shot by a nervous police force; the inability of U-Haul to keep any trucks in Flint due to the exodus of people out of the luckless town; and the sudden blackening of a Nightline broadcast on the factory closures following the theft of the OB truck by a disgruntled local citizen.

It is widely assumed that the backlash of negative criticism cost Roger & Me the Oscar for Best Documentary. GM was quick to circulate copies of Kael's scathing review. Moore's manipulations of chronological sequence to heighten thematic and narrative effect seriously undermined the integrity of the film for some, but for supporters these are mere trifles when compared to the larger issues of unemployment, poverty and the abuse of corporate responsibility. After all, no one can dispute the fact of the plant closures and their effects. Adopting this line, Miles Orvell argues that Moore sacrifices historical accuracy for satiric fiction and 'what Moore delivers is not the "straight" truth of documentary but the oblique truth of satire' (Orvell 1994–5). From such a position, the film's radical credentials are not undermined.

The film grossed $7 million on its initial North American run, and was followed up in 1992 with the short Pets or Meat, which updated the story of the earlier film's leading characters, Deputy Fred and the Bunny Lady. Moore has continued to produce popular, commercial, and controversial documentaries, notably with Bowling for Columbine (2002) and Fahrenheit 9/11 (2004); the latter is likely to become the most successful documentary film of all time.

ALAN BURTON

See also: Moore, Michael

Further reading

Corner, John, *The Art of Record. A Critical Introduction to Documentary*, Manchester: Manchester University Press, 1996.

Jacobson, Harlan, 'Michael and Me', *Film Comment*, November–December, 1989: 16–26.

Orvell, Miles, 'Documentary Film and the Power of Interrogation. American Dream & Roger and Me', *Film Quarterly*, winter, 1994–5: 10–18.

Pierson, John, Spike, Mike, *Slackers and Dykes. A Guided Tour across a Decade of Independent American Cinema*, London: Faber & Faber, 1996.

Rogosin, Lionel

Lionel Rogosin, the controversial director initially recognized by the free cinema movement in the mid-1950s, rejected traditional documentary style and technique. Rogosin emphasized a focused and personal approach toward storytelling. With postwar optimism competing against Cold War paranoia, Rogosin directed his attention to the individual problems that existed against such a politicocultural backdrop.

By the time Rogosin had entered the film world, the development of lightweight equipment, coupled with the advent of magnetic sound tape, allowed the cameraman and film director more freedom of mobility. Suddenly filmmakers were able to easily venture forth, into a variety of environments. Rogosin used this new technology on his first film, On the Bowery (1957), which focused on the inhabitants of New York's skid row. Rogosin took his camera to the streets where the homeless congregated, capturing the uninterrupted daily exchanges of those living the life of the downtrodden. The images captured in these shots are not only indicative of his work in general, but more often prove to be the key aspect of his work's influence on subsequent filmmakers and critics.

In his work, the long take is valued for its expansive and atmospheric qualities, rather than as an instrument of pure voyeurism. The direct cinema movement argued that such emphasis on capturing life from a 'fly-on-the-wall' perspective was key to the entire documentary enterprise. Many, however, considered this a controversial stance, and questioned whether the camera was picking up life uninterrupted, or was inherently interpreting what was recorded, from the perspective of the director's point of view.

Rogosin often presented his documentary films as the temporal progression of a loosely scripted narrative. Rather than writing a lengthy script and then contracting actors to portray the characters, however, Rogosin and his crew found real individuals who embodied the characters of his vision.

There are elements of compassion in the mise-en-scène of Rogosin's work, which at times elevate his films beyond others of the time. Part of this can be attributed to Rogosin's ability to never fully align himself with just one theoretical approach—he was influenced by Robert Flaherty, as well as John Grierson and others. On the Bowery was recognized for its honest portrayal of the gritty underside of human existence, while maintaining an aversion to melodrama. As significant as his films are, however, they were also criticized for the elements of staging that occurred, a controversial aesthetic that would follow throughout Rogosin's career, but one that Rogosin himself defended as necessary.

Rogosin's next film, Come Back, Africa (1960), was received with mixed reviews. It was as if to review the film one had to acknowledge it as two separate films in one. Many seemed to recognize the emotional power of the documentary segments, especially given the difficulty Rogosin faced in obtaining the footage.

At the time of filming, government control forbade depictions of apartheid, and Rogosin's crew obtained visas to film in South Africa only under the false guise of an innocuous musical about mine workers. As bogus dailies of the musical were given to the government for approval, the real documentary footage of widespread repression and poverty was smuggled out of the country in suitcase lining.

As important a feat as it was for Rogosin to make Come Back, Africa, and as powerful as the clandestine footage was, those are only some aspects of the film, not the complete work. As with many of his films, the dialogue sequences proved confusing and left many to ponder the value of their inclusion in the film, and to question Rogosin's decision to include such staged material in what was otherwise a well-constructed documentary. In one particular sequence there is a fifteen-minute roundtable discussion, half improvisational, half scripted, that is broken up only by a musical number from Miriam Makeba. A dialogue sequence of this length would seem somewhat excessive in most pictures, and to many reviewers it appeared especially so with such amateur actors. Rogosin always stuck by the merits of his nonactors and continued to use them in similar socially conscious films for the next two decades.

Rogosin's theories on the documentary were often as controversial as his films. He seemed to support the use of nonfiction almost as a scientific base to help project his interpretations into the mind of the viewer, to create an alternate reality for that viewer. When one takes into account his background in chemical engineering it seems to make sense, if one considers the friction he created by juxtaposing raw realist footage diegetic narratives, for example.

DINO EVERETT

See also: On the Bowery

Biography

Born the son of a wealthy industrialist in New York City, January 22, 1924. Studied chemistry at Yale University before leaving to serve as an engineer during World War II on a US Navy minesweeper. After the war, returned to school and graduated from Yale with a degree in chemical engineering before turning his focus toward film in his early thirties. Hired by the United Nations to direct a public information film in 1956. In 1958 won the grand prize for a documentary from the Venice Film Festival, a British Film Academy award, and was nominated for an Oscar for his first independently produced feature, On the Bowery (1957). In 1960–74 was owner of the Bleeker Street Cinema in Greenwich Village, an important venue for independent films. In 1966, along with Shirley Clarke and Jonas Mekas, was one of the founding partners in the Film-Maker's Distribution Center, a nonprofit releasing venture that sought to spread the films of the avant-garde. Continued to make socially conscious films throughout the late 1960s and 1970s while lecturing on college campuses. Father of producer/director Daniel Rogosin. Died of a heart attack on December 8, 2000, in Los Angeles.

Selected films

1956 Out: cinematographer
1957 On the Bowery (Sufrin): producer, codirector, cinematographer, cowriter
1960 Come Back, Africa (aka An African Story): director, cowriter
1966 Good Times, Wonderful Times: director
1972 Black Fantasy: director
1973 Woodcutters of the Deep South: director

Further reading

Davis, Peter, 'Rogosin and Documentary', *Film Culture* 24, spring 1962: 25–8.

Dickinson, Thorold, 'A Note on Out', *Sight and Sound*, spring 1957: 174.

Hey, Kenneth R., 'Come Back Africa (1959): Another Look', *Film & History* X, no. 3, September 1980: 61–6.

James, David E., *To Free the Cinema*, Princeton, NJ: Princeton University Press, 1992.

Rogosin, Lionel, 'Interpreting Reality (Notes on the Esthetics and Practices of Improvisational Acting)', *Film Culture* 21, summer 1960: 20–8.

Sufrin, Mark, 'Filming A Skid Row', *Sight and Sound*, winter 1955–6: 133–9.

Romania

Only five months after its world premiere in Paris, the cinematograph arrived in Bucharest (Romania), on May 27, 1896, brought along by a team of the Lumière Company, led by Edwin Schurmann. The first projections took place inside the building of the French-language newspaper, *L'Indépendance roumaine,* which had been printed in Bucharest since 1876. Schurmann's team showed a number of early cinéma vérité productions including: A Dinner-Party, Cycling Lessons, The Conservatory, Parishioners Leaving the Church, Breakfast Picnic, Place de l'Opéra, The Buffet, as well as the legendary Arrival of a Train in the Ciotat Station.

The first film made in Romania was a newsreel recording of the Royal Parade in Bucharest on May 10, 1897, shot by the Lumière cameraman Paul Menu (1876–1973). Within two months, sixteen other similar newsreels on various topics followed: The Moshilor Fair, The Hippodrome and the Races at Baneasa, The Terrace of the Capşa Café, The Flood in Galatzi, The Training of Terrestrial Marines, The Ships of the Danube Fleet, and others. Paul Menu became known as a Romanian filmmaker during his stay in the country. His camera was later bought by Dr Gheorghe Marinescu (1863–1938), who used it for his research in neurology, and who eventually completed the first scientific film in the world (Walking Disturbances of the Physical Paresis, 1898), together with the Romanian cameraman, Constantin M. Popescu. The same year, Professor M. Benko introduced audiences from Transylvania to the cinematograph, at a time when the region was still part of the Austro-Hungarian Empire. This accounts for the independent manner in which the cinematographic industry developed across the Romanian territory during the first two decades of its existence (that is, before Transylvania joined the other two provinces, Moldavia and Valachia, in 1918). One of the important figures of this early period was the Hungarian-born filmmaker Eugen (Jeno) Janovics, who made several documentaries about Romania (for production companies based in Cluj), before contributing to some of the first Hungarian fiction films (such as A sarga csiko, 1913), as coproducer alongside Pathé.

The first photographers (turned filmmakers) born in the Balkan region, however, were the Romanian-Macedonian brothers Ienake Manaki (1878–1954) and Miltiade Manaki (1882–1964), who captured still images of a popular uprising in 1903 for the Romanian newspaper *Universul.* Before them, the Romanian painter Carol Popp de Szathmary (1812–88), became the world's first war correspondent, taking photographs of the Crimean War in the 1850s. The Manaki brothers successfully exhibited their work at the 1906 International Exhibition in Bucharest, where they saw the cinematographic camera for the first time. The two bought a Bioscope 300 camera from the Charles Urban & Co. firm during a trip that took them from Paris to London, owing to a grant from King Karol I. During the same year they made a documentary film, Household Traditions of the Romanian-Macedonian Women from Pind, soon followed by several other productions showing popular dances, religious rituals, weddings, and funerals of the same region, which can be considered among the first, if not the first ever, ethnographic films in the world. The Manaki brothers also pioneered the longer newsreel film by recording the visits of Sultan Mehmed Rashid V to Salonika and Bitola in 1911. Less than two decades later, in 1928, Professor Dimitrie Gusti and his team of trained sociologists started making the first sociological documentaries: Romanian Folkloric Traditions (1928, directed by Mihail Vulpescu), Draguş—Life in a Romanian Village (1929, directed by Paul Sterian, Nicolae Argintescu-Amza), A Village in Bessarabia—Cornova (1931, directed by Henri Stahl, Anton Golopenţia), and Traditions from Bucovina (1937, directed by Henri Stahl, Constantin Brailoiu).

As in most other countries, the documentary as a genre predated fiction films in Romania. The earliest Romanian feature production (Amor Fatal) dates from 1911, shortly followed by the first historical production, The Independence of Romania, in 1912. During World War I the Romanian government was relocated to Iaşi (in Northern Moldavia), where the Cinematographic Service of the Romanian Army came into existence in December 1916. It was one of the earliest state-run production companies in the world that specialised in documentary films. A number of cameramen, such as Constantin Ivanovici, Tudor Posmantir, Georges Ercole, and Nicolae Barbelian, started their careers in this company, making newsreel films during the war. The Cinematographic Service was endowed with its own studio in 1937, a year before the company became independent. A constant production of newsreels on Romanian and foreign current affairs marked the activity of the newly founded National Office for Cinematography during the 1930s. Other topics dealt with in existing newsreels of the period include cultural and sports events, natural disasters, religious services, demonstrations, as well as installments of the serialised documentary, Get to Know Your Country (which presented picturesque places in Romania).

During World War II several Romanian documentaries were awarded prizes at the Venice Film Festival: The Motzilor County (1939, directed by Paul Calinescu, with a commentary by the novelist Mihail Sadoveanu), which disclosed the survival of traditions dating back to the Middle Ages in a remote mountainous community; Romania and the Fight against Bolshevism (1941, directed by Paul Calinescu), a film based on newsreel recordings from the Eastern Front; and We (1942, directed by Ion Cantacuzino), which presented an outline of Romanian history.

The first dedicated studio for documentary films, Sahia, was founded in 1949. At its height the studio reached a maximum turnaround of one hundred films per year. As in the case of other Eastern Europe communist countries, a proportion of these productions represented commissioned propaganda, touristic, or scientific films, but a significant number of documentaries have maintained their interest despite the passage of time. The wave of postwar documentary filmmakers in Romania gained international recognition during the 1960s and 1970s, when an important corpus of films was produced. Mirel Ilieşu won the Palme d'Or at Cannes in 1969 with The Renaissance Songs, a film about the Romanian choir, Madrigal. In 1962 Dumitru Done and Sergiu Nicolaescu codirected Ordinary Spring, which was awarded the First Prize at the International Documentary Film Festival in Prague. The following year Sergiu Nicolaescu completed The Memory of the Rose, a short film that used spectacular slow-motion photography and soundtrack as part of a metaphorical reflection on the transitory nature of beauty, confronted with the violence of barbed wire and machine guns. After winning the Grand Prize at Edinburgh and getting into the official selection at Cannes in 1963, The Memory of the Rose was awarded the Silver Medal at Trieste (1965). The same year, Eric Nussbaum's art documentary Ciucurencu won a prize at the Film Festival in Venice. Dona Barta's Ephemerae (1968), which provided a refined visual meditation on the short-lived existence of insects, won a medal at the Buenos Aires Film Festival. The evolution of the scientific documentary genre in Romania, starting with Dr Gheorghe Marinescu's early experiments with Marey's chronophotographic camera at the Salpêtrière Hospital in 1889, was marked by the activity of a number of exceptional filmmakers during the 1960s and 1970s, such as Dona Barta (The Quiet Swamp, 1967; The Silk Moth, 1975; Diatoms, the Jewels of Nature, 1976), Mircea Popescu (The 14th Element, Silicon, 1969), and Ion Bostan (Under the Eagle's Wing, 1964; The Flooded Forest, 1973; Impressions from the Delta, 1978). One of the founding fathers of the Romanian documentary and the author of an impressive filmography, Ion Bostan remains associated with an exceptional series of documentaries on the Danube Delta, The Sanctuary of Nature, which collected thirteen episodes, spanning several years of shooting and totalling one hundred and sixty-nine minutes of screening time. His outstanding achievement was matched only by Titus Meszaros's Reeds (1966), a memorable feature-length documentary on the harsh life of manual workers in the Danube Delta. It is significant that Ion Bostan's earlier productions included equally compelling explorations of the art world: The Painter Nicolae Grigorescu (1955), The Slaying of the Infants (1957), and Bach—El Greco (1970).

Many filmmakers turned to ethnographic and natural life documentaries during the 1960s and 1970s in an attempt to escape censorship and the increasing ideological pressure of the Communist government. Slavomir Popovici, who started off as a remarkable analyst of social phenomena (The Factory, 1964; Harsh Romances, 1966), later adopted less controversial topics, relating either to artistic creation or ethnography (The Black Sun, 1968; The Chronicle of Hrib, 1974). Among those who chose to pursue their career in exile, Paul Barbaneagra, came to prominence in the early 1960s, with films such as The Conductor (1964), and then settled in Paris, where his visual essays on art achieved wider recognition (for example, Sacred Architecture and Geography, Mircea Eliade and the Re-discovery of the Sacred), earning him a mention in Georges Sadoul's *History of World Cinema from its Origins to the Present*. Conversely, Nina Behar's outstanding art documentaries were quickly forgotten after the author left Romania for Israel, then France, in the 1970s. Two decades passed before her work was rediscovered and celebrated alongside that of major filmmakers such as Alain Resnais, at the

Biennale internationnale du film d'art in Paris, in 1996. Nina Behar's early experiments, such as Luchian, 1958; An Artist Accuses the World, 1964; Monumental Art, 1966; The Painter's Hands, 1967; Looking at a Painting, 1972; and Patraşcu, 1973, can still be said to provide some of the finest examples of the rapidly evolving montage and mise-en-scène techniques during the 1960s and 1970s.

The ethnographic documentary genre was given a new impetus at the time by directors who either endeavoured to perfect the art of the cinematographic poem (such as in Paula Popescu Doreanu's work: Head Ornaments, 1967; Caluşarii, 1968; The Nieces' Celebration, 1973), or strove to emphasise the scientific aspect of the commentary (for example, Ion Bostan's productions of the 1950s, such as The Song of the Olt River, which foreshadowed his landmark series of films on the Danube Delta, The Sanctuary of Nature). In a slightly different vein, Iancu Moscu's The Eternal Feminine (1970) won a prestigious prize at the Film Festival in Melbourne, although the author was mostly known in his own country for propaganda works commissioned by the Communist government (for example, Romania, a Country without Arms, and Romania—Songs of Praise). The output of several other talented documentary filmmakers displayed a similar tension between their aesthetic explorations (for example, Ioniţa Octav's Rhythms, 1972), and their commissioned works (for example, Octav's Romania, My Country, 1972; Romania Today, 1974; and Sweet Romania, 1975).

In the area of the cinéma vérité productions, Florica Holban, the first camerawoman at Sahia, directed a number of compelling 'cinematic reports' or newsreel documentaries on daily life: Whose Fault Is It? (1965), which dealt with the situation in Romanian orphanages, and included children's testimonies; Children, Yet Again (1966); Where Can We Play? (1968), and others. Along the same lines, Alexandru Boiangiu's films captured social and psychological aspects of the interaction between individuals and the communities in which they live: Our Beautiful House (1963), which disclosed the contradictions between a GP's professional discourse on hygiene and her lifestyle, and Mr D's Case (1966), an analysis of the situation of old people in residential care.

At the beginning of the 1970s one film in particular seemed destined to become the manifesto of a new generation of documentary filmmakers. Water Like a Black Buffalo (1971) recounted the devastating effects of large-scale flooding in Romania, as well as the fight for survival and rescue operations that took place in remote areas of the country. Seven young directors took part in the filming and contributed to its unique blend of poetic images and objective presentation of events: Dan Piţa, Mircea Veroiu, Petre Bokor, Iosif Demian, Stere Gulea, Dinu Tanase, and Andrei Catalin Baleanu. Even if none of the major documentary authors who emerged later in the 1970s (that is, Constantin Vaeni, Nicolae Cabel, Ada Pistiner, and Felicia Cernaianu) were involved in this film, Water Like a Black Buffalo had an undeniable impact on the work of celebrated fiction filmmakers such as Dan Piţa (Philip the Good, 1974), or Stere Gulea (The Green Grass from Home, 1977), while continuing to inform the stylistic and thematic concerns of the documentary directors during the 1980s. Ada Pistiner's films (for example, And One … , 1978; A Team of Young People and the Others, 1976; A Community Arts Centre, 1977) can be said to represent the pinnacle of documentary production during the 1970s. Nevertheless, a number of Constantin Vaeni's social studies, in particular And Then the City was Born (1972), which displays strong similarities with Water Like a Black Buffalo, also marked a decisive departure from the restrictive ideological framework of the time and managed to provide, alongside Nicoale Cabel's similar explorations into a poetics of visual language (The Earth Like a Beautiful Gift, 1979; George Bacovia, Tomorrow's Poem, 1983; and The Morning Horses, 1986), the trademark for the most recent stylistic experimentation at the borderline between documentary and fiction films.

During the 1980s a more introspective approach came to the fore, although many young directors also started to privilege the narrative and dramatic potential of the social reality they observed. A significant number of documentaries focused on their protagonists' feelings, or on their reactions to an idea or to a given situation: the wish-fulfilment reasoning of children in Tereza Barta's witty and lighthearted If I Were a Fairy (1980); the feeling of solitude of an international competition athlete in Ovidiu Bose Paştina's And as for Emotion: A Crystal (1987); the unhappiness of construction workers in Sabina Pop's What's a Builder's

Life Like, Ion? (1983); the isolation of displaced workers from rural communities in Adrian Sârbu's I'm in Good Health and Doing Well (1982); the anxieties of waiting and the nature of hope in Ioana Holban's If There Was No Love (1983), and Copel Moscu's Evening Classes (1982). Among the more recent productions of the same generation, Sabina Pop's prize-winning Panc (1990), which won important distinctions in Oberhausen, Bordeaux, Zlatibor, Uppsala, and Kaliningrad, followed the tribulations of an amateur theatre group from a deprived, remote village in Romania where the passion for artistic expression manages to transform people's lives.

The popular uprising that toppled the communist government in December 1989 inspired a number of documentaries, starting with the well-known Free Diary/The Romanian Revolution of 1989 (1990), to which a great number of filmmakers contributed: Adrian Sârbu, Sabina Pop, Horia Bolboceanu, Tiberiu Lazar, Ovidiu Miculescu, Cornel Mihalache, Catalina Fernoaga, Anita Gârbea, Doru Spataru, and others. The same intention of capturing the overwhelming emotional charge of the moment, while nevertheless providing an accurate account of events, guided Ovidiu Bose Paştina's directorial vision in Timişoara—December 1989 (1991). The stylistic unity of this film, and its perceptive comments on individual and collective responses to an unprecedented violent upheaval, earned the author a prize at Neubrandenburg and placed him among the twenty best documentary filmmakers to be included in the official selection at Tokyo in 1992. Two other documentary productions made intelligent use of reel-footage (captured on amateur or professional cameras) to reflect on the significance of recent political events: The Shortest Day, by Ştefan Gladin, retraced the presidential couple's movements during the last day before their capture in December 1989, while On Christmas Day We Had Our Share of Freedom (scripted and directed by two students in cinematography, Catalina Fernoaga and Cornel Mihalache) described the euphoria of the early postrevolution days. The film that had the greatest impact in Romania, however, was Stere Gulea's The University Square—Romania (1991), which at times adopted the style of a news report or live commentary of events.

A number of dedicated production companies and studios for documentary films opened after the demise of the communist regime in Romania: Editura Video, FAV (The Visual Arts Foundation), Astra Film Studio, and Video Dialog. This enabled young filmmakers, such as Sorin Ilieşiu, to complete an impressive number of political documentaries in the early 1990s (for example, The Monarchy Saves Romania, 1992; We'll Die and We'll Be Free, 1992; and Liberation, 1993). Another strand in recent years can be said to gather those who, like Viorel Branea, have a background in television and have started to investigate the long-term effects of social and economic neglect on certain categories of the population during the Communist era. As early as 1990, Viorel Branea's shattering documentaries, Apocalypse '90 and Our Working Class Goes to Heaven, disclosed the poverty, humiliation and large-scale ecological disaster in Copşa Mica and Valea Jiului, two of the most deprived mining regions of Romania. The director of the Astra Film Studio, based in Sibiu, Dumitru Budrala, authored, scripted, or produced an impressive number of documentaries, which renewed the tradition of ethnographic films in Romania: Transylvanian Winter (1996); On the Road (1998), which won the Silver Medal at the Kalamata International Festival in 2000, and was a finalist in the Cinéma du Réel competition in Paris, in 1999; Village of the Watermills (2001); Traditions in Festival (2002); and Zina, the Story of a Village in the Carpathians (2004).

Other filmmakers, such as Alexandru Solomon and Radu Igaszag, successfully pursued more formal explorations in the art documentary genre (for example, Duet for Paoloncello and Petronome, 1994; Via Regis, 1995). In recent years Alexandru Solomon also directed a feature-length political documentary, The Great Communist Train Robbery (2004), which aired on BBC4. He had previously been awarded twice the prize for the best documentary in the Dakino Film Festival for The Man with a Thousand Eyes (2001) and A Dog's Life (1999). In 1993 he won the prize for the best experimental film at the 'Mediawave' Festival in Hungary for Shriek into the Ear-Drum (1993). The same year, Cornel Mihalache directed an equally memorable docudrama, entitled The Sculptor (1993), inspired by the life and work of the Romanian artist Constantin Brancusi.

The Visual Anthropology Foundation, which was set up in 1995 as a production company and nonprofit, nongovernmental organisation, runs a biennial documentary film festival (the Astra

Film Festival). At its seventh festival, in 2004, it had already attracted large numbers of film-makers, students, and scholars in visual anthropology from across Europe. Another noteworthy initiative concerns the activity of the Visual Arts Foundation, which teamed up with the Swiss Foundation for Culture, Pro-Helvetica, in 1999, and launched The Centre for Audiovisual Memory, with the aim of creating a multimedia archive based on ethnographic and cultural research into the Romanian rural civilisation. A CD-ROM encyclopedia of Romanian traditions is being developed as part of this collaborative project.

RAMONA FOTIADE

Further reading

Cernat, Manuela, *A Concise History of the Romanian Film*, Bucharest: Editura Enciclopedica, 1983.

Damian, Laurent, *iu Damian, Filmul documentar. Despre documentar … înca ceva în plus*, Bucureşti: Editura Tehnica, 2003.

Sadoul, Georges, *Histoire du cinéma mondial des origines à nos jours*, Paris: Flammarion, 1998.

Romm, Mikhail

After gaining prominence with his much-praised directorial debut, Boule de Suif (1934), Mikhail Romm continued to make films that were both narratively engaging and politically tendentious. His transposing of John Ford's The Lost Patrol to the Russian Civil War as The Thirteen (1936) is typical. These qualities are also present in Romm's first attempts to use nonfiction material: the historical dramas Lenin in October (1937) and Lenin in 1918 (1939). These are gross distortions of the historical facts of the Revolution and Civil War years whereby Trotsky is excised and Bukharin vilified. Lenin becomes an incarnation of perfect justice who all but appoints Stalin his successor.

Romm's first use of documentary film, Vladimir Il'ich Lenin (1949), articulates the same vision of history by combining documentary footage and genuine photographs with paintings incorrectly showing Stalin to have been Lenin's closest confidante from 1905 onwards and to have played a pivotal role in the Revolution. Moreover, despite the film's title, this chronologically constructed narrative reaches 1924, the year of Lenin's death, five reels from the end. As a result, over one-third of the film stresses Stalin's continuation of his cause through industrialisation, World War II, and postwar reconstruction.

Romm's next documentary project, Living Lenin (1958), was made after the death of Stalin had precipitated something of a conversion to a humanistic vision of socialism and seems to be an attempt to atone for the excesses of Vladimir Il'ich Lenin, in that it is entirely composed of authentic newsreel footage of Lenin shot during his lifetime. Yet where the voice-over in the earlier film at times possessed a polemical bite, Romm's concern in this film is solely to corroborate the authenticity of the material and consequently it lacks dynamism.

His next documentary project, Ordinary Fascism (1965), effectively combines a highly expressive voice-over spoken by Romm himself, with a concern for authenticity. It is his most celebrated work and along with his factional film about Soviet nuclear scientists, Nine Days of a Year (1961), one of the Russian films of the period that had the greatest impact. Romm's final documentary project, Yet I Still Believe (1975), about young people, was completed posthumously.

JEREMY HICKS

Biography

Born January 24, 1901 in Butyriatiia, Siberia. Served in the Red Army during Russian Civil War 1918–21. Completed Moscow Higher Institute of Art and Crafts in sculpture 1925. Worked as a screenwriter and assistant director from 1931. Directorial debut Boule de Suif (1934) won a prize at the Venice Film Festival after which made a series of highly commended films. Member of Communist Party from 1939, decorated with the People's Artist of the USSR 1950. From 1949 onwards taught at State Film Institute (VGIK), becoming a professor in 1958, where he taught Andrei Tarkovskii and numerous others. Became a liberal figurehead after his denunciation of Soviet anti-Semitism in 1962, for which he was publicly rebuked by Khrushchev in 1963. Died November 1, 1971.

Selected films

1949 Vladimir Il'ich Lenin: codirector
1958 Zhivoi Lenin/Living Lenin: codirector
1965 Obyknovennyi fashizm/Ordinary Fascism: co-author, director, voice-over
1975 I vse-taki ia veriu/Yet I Still Believe: co-author and director

Further reading

Romm, Mikhail, *Izbrannye proizvedeniia*, 3 vols, Moscow: Iskusstvo, 1980–2.

Woll, Josephine, *Real Images: Soviet Cinema and the Thaw*, London: I.B. Tauris, 2000.

Zak, Mark, *Mikhail Rommiego fil'my*, Moscow: Iskusstvo, 1988.

Roos, Jørgen

Jørgen Roos, one of the most important Danish documentary filmmakers of the postwar period, combined work for different government agencies with experimental avant-garde films. His work is in some ways typical of the independent filmmakers in Scandinavia. Roos made many films, around one hundred documentaries, both films of information and more artistic films, and one of the characteristic features of his work is that he handles a broad spectrum of themes and genres.

Jørgen Roos started as a camera assistant in the Danish company Minerva Film in Copenhagen in 1939, and his first assignment was photographing the documentary filmmaker Theodor Christensen leaving for England to visit John Grierson. Roos has been categorized as a documentary filmmaker in the Griersonian tradition of social critique, information, and public enlightenment. His first films as a director, however, were the first experimental films in Denmark. Flugten/The Escape (1942), with the artist Albert Merz, and Spiste Horisonter/Eaten Horizons (1950) were among his early experimental films.

Roos worked as a photographer and editor for Theodor Christensen, and his first documentaries were influenced by Christensen and his work. Roos made many short films about cultural history and specialized in portraits of places, cities, and people. His En by ved navn København/A City Called Copenhagen (1960) was disliked by the municipal experts who commisioned the film and was shelved for two years, but was finally released to great acclaim. The success of this beautiful portrait of Denmark's capital resulted in assignments in other countries, but after Jørgen Roos zeigt Hamburg/Jørgen Roos Shows Hamburg (1962) and Oslo/Oslo (1963), he turned down all other offers to make films about cities.

Roos has made his mark on the genre of the portrait. Often he made portraits of artists, like Johannes V. Jensen—Grundtanken i mit forfatterskap/Johannes V. Jensen—The Core of My Authorship (1947), or Carl Th. Dreyer (1966), but he has also made portraits of inventors or explorers. His award-winning portrait of the Danish expert on Greenland, Knud Rasmussen, Knud (1966), is one of his best portraits, and with this film he also started a series of films on Greenland. He made travelogs and portraits of people from Greenland, as well as educational films on language and history. Mostly Roos has depicted modern life in Greenland, and often he has been critical of Denmark's treatment of the Greenlanders, but he has also shown national pride in Denmark's presence in Greenland. His many films about life in Greenland, like 17 minutter Grønland/17 Minutes on Greenland (1967), or Kaláliuvit? (Er du Grønlænder?)/Kaláliuvit? (Are You from Greenland?) (1970), have been shown extensively in schools in Denmark, so Roos has heavily influenced several generations of Danes and contributed to their vision of Greenland.

Among his most famous films are his film-essays about bacon production, Den strømlinede Gris/The Streamlined Pig (1952), and noise, Støj/Noise (1965). In films like these Roos is a committed social critic, examining the dysfunctional aspects of modern society. These films inspired a new generation of Danish filmmakers in the late 1960s and early 1970s.

In addition to directing nearly one hundred documentaries, Roos worked as a photographer or editor on many films by other directors. He covered all sorts of issues and themes, from films about cultural history (Historien om et slot/History of a Castle, 1951), to depictions of an urban slum (Slum, 1952); from a film about the photographs made of the writer H.C. Andersen (Andersen hos fotografen/Andersen Visiting the Photographer, 1975), to a three-part film about the history of documentary filmmaking in Denmark (Den levende virkelighed/The Living Reality, 1989). He even made a feature fiction film, Seksdagesløpe/The Six-Day Race (1958).

Roos was regarded as one of the most important European documentary filmmakers, especially in the 1960s, and several of his films received awards at international film festivals. A City Called Copenhagen received second prize in Cannes in 1960, and was nominated for an Academy Award. His portrait of the explorer and expert on Greenland, Knud, received the Golden Bear at the Berlin Film Festival in 1966.

The documentaries made by Roos are characterized by a combination of warmth and sober detachment. His often ironic editing, with great emphasis on details and rhythm, marks him as a personal and committed filmmaker. He is perhaps the most important Danish documentary filmmaker, and his work has influenced many Scandinavian documentary filmmakers.

GUNNAR IVERSEN

See also: Scandinavia

Biography

Born in Gilleleje, Denmark, in 1922. Worked as camera assistant, and later cameraman and director for the company Minerva Film from 1939. Freelance photographer, editor, writer, and director. One of the founders of the Association Internationale des Documentaristes in 1964. Became a Fellow of the Royal Society of Arts in Denmark in 1965. Died in 1998 at the age of seventy-six.

Selected films

1942 Flugten/The Escape
1947 Johannes V. Jensen—Grundtanken i mit forfatterskap/Johannes V. Jensen—The Core of My Authorship
1950 Spiste Horisonter/Eaten Horizons
1951 Historien om et slot/History of a Castle
1952 Den strømlinede Gris/The Streamlined Pig
1952 Slum
1958 Seksdagesløpet/The Six-Day Race
1960 En by ved navn København/A City Called Copenhagen
1962 Jørgen Roos zeigt Hamburg/Jørgen Roos Shows Hamburg
1963 Oslo
1965 Støj/Noise
1966 Carl Th. Dreyer
1966 Knud
1967 17 minutter Grønland/17 Minutes on Greenland
1970 Kaláliuvit? (Er du Grønlænder?)/Kaláliuvit? (Are You from Greenland?)
1975 Andersen hos fotografen/Andersen Visiting the Photographer
1989 Den levende virkelighed/The Living Reality

Further reading

Bang, Hans V. (ed.), *Jørgen Roos—et liv som dokumentarist*, Haderslev: Dok Film Akademiet & Det Danske Filminstitut/Videoværkstedet, 1998.
Birkvad, Søren and Diesen, Jan Anders, *Autentiske Inntrykk*, Oslo: Samlaget, 1994.

Rossif, Frédéric

Frédéric Rossif, the French director who began his career in the 1950s, was known primarily for his television work on such varied subjects as wildlife, luminaries of the entertainment world, and historical events. Rossif was responsible for several successful French television series, and his historical and political documentary films also met with acclaim. His compilation films were considered both creative and controversial. The combination of his World War II experiences (being of Jewish ancestry, he fled his home in Yugoslavia) with his residence in a postwar country gave his political films a strong, sometimes unsettling presence.

Rossif's documentary work generally displays a realist aesthetic and an observational approach. In television programs on wildlife, Rossif presented his subjects in natural environments, but often adjusted the temporal aspects to heighten the meaning. At times the speed and strength of an animal would be conveyed through quick editing, slow motion, or collision montage, similar to that used by Eisenstein. By using such techniques, Rossif developed a relationship that takes the viewer beyond the observational into a more psychological meditation on humankind's relation to animals.

Rossif's work was generally praised, but at times he was criticized for his extensive use of editing. At a time when the genre was moving away from the influential aesthetic of Vertov, Rossif rarely used the long take, which was gaining favor. In the case of a film such as Brel

(1982), his homage to the Belgian-born singer, this contributed to the criticism. Throughout the film, which is rooted in Brel's live performances, Rossif is careful never to let the viewer become too absorbed in the performance of a song. Brel's song performances are broken up, and intercut with elements such as newsreel footage, historical events, and landscape scenes. Rossif collides the various images, runs the clips backwards, and toys with the composition to make some scenes almost unrecognizable. Thus the director plays with the passivity of the documentary viewer.

When focusing on historical topics, Rossif made compilation films similar to those of Vertov by assembling found footage from national archives; however, he enhanced the films through aesthetic manipulations, such as sound editing. In these films, he often addressed painful historical topics, forcing the viewer to confront difficult and unsettling events. These films met with praise and critical acclaim, most notably Mourir a Madrid/To Die in Madrid (1963). As a result, in 1967 Rossif's crew was the first Western film unit allowed to film extensively in the Soviet Union. Rossif was also given access to the Soviet film archives, with permission to reproduce any footage he wished. The resulting film, Revolution d'Octobre/October Revolution (1967), was composed from original footage shot by Rossif, as well as a great amount of archival footage, including segments from Vertov's Chelovek s Kinoapparatom/Man with the Movie Camera (1929).

Rossif was recognized primarily for his overtly political films; however, the bulk of his work was made for television. Ultimately, he contributed to more than three hundred programs. He made one fiction film, Aussi loin que l'amour/As Far as Love Can Go (1971), but it was unsuccessful, and he returned to the documentary genre.

Rossif's film career ended on the same subject it began: World War II. That conflict brought Rossif to France to begin his film career, so it seemed appropriate that his career conclude with an exposé of the atrocities of war criminals—the types of crimes that forced him to flee his homeland. Released posthumously, De Nuremberg à Nuremberg/From Nuremberg to Nuremberg (1989) uses a more traditional approach than much of his work. Nevertheless, it remains shocking and effective.

DINO EVERETT

See also: Man with the Movie Camera; To Die in Madrid; Vertov, Dziga

Biography

Born in Centinje, Montenegro, Yugoslavia, August 14, 1922. Being of Jewish ancestry, fled Yugoslavia in 1941, stopping for a time in Athens, Greece, and then Katerni, avoiding the Germans, until finally arriving in France. Served in the French Foreign Legion until the end of World War II. After the war worked for many years as a draftsman for Renault and Citroën. Worked for the Cinémathèque Française in the 1950s. Directed his first programs for French TV, including Cinepanorama in 1956 and the news program Cinq Colonnes à la Une in 1959. Awarded the Prix Jean Vigo in 1963. Nominated for an Oscar in 1966. Won both the British Academy of Film and Television Arts (BAFTA) Flaherty Documentary Award and the Berlin International Film Festival Golden Bear in 1968. Began a twenty-year collaboration with the composer Vangelis in 1972. Continued to alternate between film and television work and appeared as an actor in a cameo role in Etienne Chatieliez's 1990 feature Tatie Danielle. Died April 18, 1990 of a heart attack in Paris. His final film, the two-part De Nuremberg à Nuremberg, was released posthumously.

Selected films

1956 Cinepanorama (TV): director, producer
1959 Cinq Colonnes à la Une/Five Columns on the Front Page (TV): director
1961 Le Temps du Ghetto/The Witnesses: director, cowriter
1963 Mourir à Madrid/To Die in Madrid: director, writer
1963 Les Animaux/The Animals: director
1967 Revolution d'Octobre/October Revolution: director, writer
1970 Un mur à Jerusalem/A Wall in Jerusalem: director
1976 La Fête Sauvage/The Wilderness Party: director
1982 Brel: director, writer
1989 De Nuremberg à Nuremberg/From Nuremberg to Nuremberg: director

Further reading

Chapsel, Madeleine, *Mourir a Madrid, Film de Frederic Rossif*, Paris: Seghers, 1963.
Colombat, Andre, *The Holocaust in French Film*, Metuchen, NJ: Scarecrow Press, 1993.
Landy, Marcia (ed.), *The Historical Film: History and Memory in Media*, New Brunswick, NJ: Rutgers University Press, 2001.
Payne, Stanley G., *The Spanish Civil War, the Soviet Union and Communism*, New Haven, CT: Yale University Press, 2004.
Rossif, Frédéric, *Revolution d'octobre*, Paris: Hachette, 1967.
Rubenstein, Leonard, 'Facism Revisted', *Film Society Review*, February 6, 1971: 41–6.
——'Facism Revisted', *Film Society Review*, December 4, 1970: 43–7.
Vertov, Dziga, *Kino-Eye: The Writings of Dziga Vertov*, Berkeley, CA: University of California Press, 1995.

Rouch, Jean

Jean Rouch is a significant figure in ethnographic film, the stylistic development of cinéma vérité, and he inspired the young filmmakers of the nouvelle vague. His career spans more than fifty years and more than one hundred and twenty films. He is best known for his earlier documentary works, but he continued to make films until 2003. More than a documentary filmmaker, Rouch was an ethnographer and cinematic innovator and is often referred to as the Father of African Cinema. He is credited for coining the term cinéma vérité and for developing it with sociologist Edgar Morin. Rouch is responsible for elevating the use of the handheld camera style and natural lighting to a respectable position in the art of cinema. Proponents of the style and techniques of cinéma vérité argue that his stylistic developments allow filmmakers to capture reality.

Cinéma vérité is both a philosophy and a style of filmmaking. The fundamental concept of 'cinema truth' is explored, developed, and demonstrated in Rouch's many ethnographic films. His best-known documentary films are focused on the Songhay people and traditions of the West African state of Niger. Having first gone to Africa as a civil engineer in the early 1940s, Rouch was struck by African culture and belief. His drive to document and understand what he saw inspired him to film this region and its people over the course of many years. This pursuit to capture what he experienced on celluloid has become know as 'visual anthropology'. Yet in doing so, Rouch was careful not to oversimplify, dismiss, or evaluate in his films. His goal was to document and in that pursuit he invited his subjects to participate in the filmmaking process, thus making important strides in developing participatory ethnography. His techniques and cinematic experiments were not universally accepted, and he was criticized by some traditional ethnographers and academics. His movies are thematically centered on racism, cultural interaction, colonialism, the poor, migration of young Africans from traditional homelands to populated coastal cities, and materialism.

During the Nazi occupation of France, Rouch was active in the Resistance. In 1941, however, he left France for Niger where he could work as a civil engineer. He began his civil service career building a road in the isolated town of Niamey. During construction, Rouch became friends with Damoré Zike, a Nigerian road foreman. Zike introduced Rouch to the mysterious spirituality of the Songhay people and would aid him in the making of several films. Damoré's grandmother was a high priestess of the Naimey and initiated Rouch into the world of Songhay magic and possession. Rouch became fascinated by the surreal ceremonies that he attended. As ethnographer Paul Stoller (1992: 31) explains, 'Rouch had entered a truly surreal world … At that moment Rouch may have realized that film was the best way to capture the dream he was living.' Rouch began documenting the ceremonies in ethnographic writing and photos that he sent to Marcel Griaule in Paris. Griaule introduced Rouch's work to the Institute Française d'Afrique Noire, which took an interest in Rouch. In the early 1940s Rouch presented his first paper on Africa via an IFAN seminar. In 1943 Rouch joined the Free French Army Corps of Engineers and was able to go back to Paris after it was liberated. There he once again returned to his studies with Griaule and held an entry-level position at the Institute Française d'Afrique Noire.

In 1946 Rouch returned to Africa with two French colleagues to travel the length of the Niger River in a dugout canoe. The trip was financed by stories the three wrote for Agence France Press (AFP) before and during the trip and by a financial gift from AFP once they were in Niger and in need of money. Rouch took a war surplus 16mm camera on the expedition and for nine months they traversed the river. Thus Rouch began his filmmaking career in 1947 with Au pays des mages noirs/In the Land of the Black Seers. The film recounts Rouch's trip down the Niger to the ocean. During the trip Rouch was asked to photograph a hippopotamus hunt by the local people. Because of an accident, Rouch was unable to use a tripod and decided to shoot the footage by holding the camera in his hand. Thus he adopted one of his most cherished techniques, the handheld camera. Most of the footage of the trip was stolen along with the bulk of the troupe's possessions, but the hippopotamus hunt and some of the other footage survived and comprises the documentary with the addition of added stock footage. In 1949 Rouch received the Grand Prix du Documentaire at the Biarritz Film Festival organized by Henri Langlois, the founder of the Cinémathèque Française. Rouch was awarded the top prize for his films La Circoncision/The Circumcision (1948–9), and Initiation a la danse des possesedes/Initiation to the Dance of the Possessed (1948–9). Both these films and Les magiciens de Wanzerbe/The Magician's of Wanzerbe were shot from 1947–8, when Rouch returned to Niger to complete his ethnographic field work for his thesis. As Stoller (1992: 6) explains, 'the bulk of Rouch's work [...] concentrates on Songhay possession. There are cinematic interviews with possession priests [...] and a score of short films on Songhay yenaandi ceremonies, the possession rites during which spirits are asked to bring rain.'

Les magiciens de Wanzerbe is one of Rouch's less-seen works. It is a portrait of the priests' incantations, medicinal plants, and magician's dance, and this short film introduces the audience to the wizards of Wanzerbe and their rituals. Perhaps the most important aspect of the film is the magician's dance during a purification ceremony. The magician dances for hours and is joined by his son. Both seem to be in trances. At one point he jolts and vomits a magic chain, which hangs from the end of his tongue and is then swallowed again and he will continue to carry the enchanted power chain until he dies. The film also contains footage of the annual ceremony in which a cow is sacrificed and butchered to ensure a healthy and bountiful year. The film provoked critics to accuse Rouch of African exoticism, and Stoller (1992) reported that even the people of Wanzerbe complained of misrepresentation; however, the documentary stands as an important ethnographic recording of these riveting ceremonies.

In the mid-1950s Rouch released Les Maîtres fous/The Mad Masters. The film is a cinematic study of the possession rituals of a group of Songhay known as the Hauka. The ritual is reportedly a means by which the Hauka contact the spirits of their former colonial 'masters'. In the ritual entranced participants behave as the members of the colonial military and then act out a violent ceremony in which a dog is sacrificed, boiled, and eaten. They also cut a chicken's throat and spill the blood on an already bloodstained alter. In their trances they act out military marches and conferences. Afterward, the Hauka people are shown carrying on with their normal daily routines. The Hauka sect became very popular in the region and despite the attempts of government officials, the group grew in numbers. Rouch described the popularity of the group as a way for the people to show defiance toward colonial oppression. He punctuates this belief cinematically by adding scenes of the British colonial military with the scenes of the Hauka ritual. Rouch filmed the ceremony at the request of the leaders of the Hauka sect. The film was controversial and was banned in the region. Some African and French intellectuals rejected the film as reinforcing black stereotypes and for lacking objectivity; others objected to Africans presenting such violent representations of Europeans. Yet the film was awarded the Grand Prix at the Venice Film Festival in 1957 and remains a fascinating view of this ritual that combines elements of traditional spiritual trance and possession ceremonies with modernized spirits in the form of colonial military personnel. In this way the film symbolically represents the clash of traditional African cultures with the enforced modernization brought on by colonialism. This cinematic ideological comment was probably the reason for the film's popularity throughout Europe.

Rouch's La chasse au lion à l'arc/The Lion Hunters (1957–64) follows Songhay hunters as they track and kill a group of dangerous lions with only bows and arrows. The movie presents the viewer with the African bush, a wild and seemingly dangerous place for humans. Then the film juxtaposes the bush with the cultivated land of the hunters, known as the Gow, a subgroup of the Songhay. The hunters must track and kill a lion that is attacking and killing domestic animals of the Fulan people. The lion is not eating its victims, so the hunters know that it is the same lion making all the kills. The film presents many details of the hunt, but its focus is on the rituals that are performed in the course of the expedition. It took Rouch seven years to complete the film, beginning in 1957 and concluding in 1964. Because of delays with the hunt, Rouch had to make several trips to Africa during this time period to film different aspects of the hunt and the related ceremonies such as the making of the poison for the arrows, and the killing of the lions trapped in the Gow hunters' iron leg traps. The hunters first trap and kill a young lion and kill it with their poison arrows. Next they trap a lioness, but she is able to free herself and attack one of the herdsmen before she is killed by the hunters. Interestingly, Rouch was unable to film the complete attack, but his sound person captured the frightening incident and so the entire episode is presented in the film. The film was a critical success and was awarded the Golden Lion at the Venice Film Festival. Critics praised this film as Rouch's masterpiece and suggested that it elevated him to the elite group of French filmmakers. Stoller (1992) argued that the film successfully demonstrates the inseparable union of the Songhay people's mundane and sacred lives. Further, Stoller explains that Rouch has dialectically linked film and ethnography but suggests that Rouch crosses the boundary between reality and fictional narrative many times.

Rouch's first feature film, Moi, un noir/I, a Black (1957), combines documentary and fiction. The film was shot fairly objectively in Côte d'Ivoire, in a slum of Abidjan. It follows the daily life of a stevedore, Oumarou Ganda (who calls himself Edward G. Robinson) and two friends. Ganda then records the voice-over narration of the film, filling in his hopes and aspirations as a backdrop to the 16mm cinematography. Later Ganda became a leading figure in African filmmaking as a director in Niger. The film was banned by the Côte d'Ivoire government. Critics of cinéma vérité argue that the move into fictionalized cinema demonstrates that cinéma vérité is no more than a style of filmmaking, where handheld 16mm cameras and natural lighting are the accepted conventions, much like high production values and beautiful cinematic shots are conventions of classic narrative cinema. Rouch followed in 1959 with La Pyramide humaine/The Human Pyramid, which used a fictional story to explore the interaction of black and white teenage students at an Abidjan school, the Lycée d'Abidjan. The film was shot silently and Rouch attempted to have the students revoice the commentary in voice-over, but this did not work out well, as the students were unable to relive their spontaneous conversations after the fact. Proponents of the film argue that it is an important text that seeks to explore racism and segregation in an innovative and stylistically interesting manner.

Before the early 1960s, most documentary film was shot silently, with music, narration, and other sound effects added in after production. This condition resulted from the lack of sound equipment that was portable enough to use effectively and efficiently in the field. The advent of lightweight and reliable portable tape recording equipment with 16mm camera synchronization became widely available in the late 1950s. The availability of the equipment revolutionized the making of documentary film. This was especially true in France, where Rouch led the revolution by using the new technology in the cinéma vérité movement. Rouch was central in the development of cinéma vérité and used it in the style and form of his films in controversial ways. In his Chronique d'un été/Chronicle of Summer (1960), Rouch and Edgar Morin explored French culture just after the Algerian War from the streets of Paris. Rouch uses the same approach that he used in his African documentaries. The film is partly an answer to critics who accused him of only filming in exotic locales and the first film to be self-consciously cinéma vérité. The film is unique in that it incorporates some of the responses of the people interviewed to their own footage, thus undermining some of the 'objective distance' of the documentary. The use of handheld cameras and diegetic sound and a denunciation of the objective narrator were indicative of Rouch's larger rejection of earlier documentary filmmaking style and classic narrative film conventions. Reliance on a classic cinematic style that emphasized beautiful shots and compelling stories was cast aside as an obstacle to filmic truth. From this initial interest in transforming documentary, cinéma vérité moved to a focus on developing innovative narrative film styles. Chronique d'un été was not a commercial success, but Rouch followed it up with La Punition/The Punishment. Although the film was shot very quickly and in the innovative style of cinéma vérité, the unrehearsed actors and improvised scenes about a girl who is sent home from school and spends the day looking for something to do, preferably with a male, is criticized for being too aimless. Although the cinéma vérité movement was influential to the directors of the French New Wave, these two Rouch films are most significant for what they suggest about the relationship of film to reality rather than as testaments to the success of the style.

Jaguar (1967) is a further development of Rouch's hybrid between documentary and fiction. Some scholars use the term ethnofiction to describe this type of filmmaking. Unlike the docudrama, ethnofiction relies on the basic tenets of ethnographic filmmaking. The film follows the lives of three young Songhay men who migrate from their tribal homes to the Gold Coast of West Africa in a quest of discovery and experience, and who return changed men. Rouch's ethnographic writings on this theme explore the history of this migration and its cultural significance. The film marks a movement away from Rouch's earlier focus on the mystical Songhay world of magic and ritual, by concentrating on the social, or mundane, aspects of these men's lives and their reasons for taking part in the migration. Thus the title of film is not about the animal; for these men being a jaguar means that they are successful and that they look and behave in a 'cool' fashion. Eventually, the men return home with stories and material goods before the seasonal rains begin. The idea for Jaguar was conceived in 1954. The film was shot silently, primarily in 1957. Later, Rouch had the principals do the voice-over commentary as they watched the film. Thus their improvisation is driven by the images locked in the celluloid. The entire commentary was completed in a single day in a sound studio in Ghana. The film was shown at different times before its final release in 1967. In the film we see the men make the long journey to the Gold Coast on foot through the grasslands and mountains. There they meet the Somba, 'primitive others', whose male members wear only penis sheaths. Once they arrive at the coast they split up, and the film crosscuts from one to another as they establish their daily lives and work. The men are able to achieve jaguar status, the condition of being 'with it' and 'cool', but eventually decide that it is time to return to their homes and their old lives. Once they return, they give away all the material possessions that they bring with them and settle back into their former lives and roles. Stoller (1992) suggested that this ethnofiction film exemplifies Rouch's *pourquoi pas?* (why not?) method of research and filmmaking, and this lends the film a sense of play. Some critics feel that the film stands as Rouch's anticolonial testament and brings to light several problems brought on by modernization facing West Africans at the time.

Rouch wrote many ethnographic books and articles with a wealth of thick description and photographs of the Songhay people and their spiritual artifacts. His written works are more detailed and ethnographically informative than his films. Rouch's 'why not?' method of filmmaking does little to answer the questions that his movies ask. The films themselves are often visually exotic, provocative, and challenging, thus leaving his viewers shocked and interested but confused as to context and explanation.

Rouch was killed in an automobile crash in Niger on February 18, 2004. He had returned once more to Africa to attend a film festival.

J. EMMETT WINN

See also: Chronique d'un été

Biography

Born May 31, 1917 in Paris. His father was a naval scientist and meteorologist who instilled a scientific interest in Jean as the family traveled extensively. In the late 1920s they lived in Morocco, where his father was the Director of the Oceanographic Museum. There Rouch first experienced Africa and its peoples. At school in Paris, in the 1930s, became very interested in surrealism. Also developed into an avid film enthusiast, often attending the programs at the Cinémathèque Française. Studied civil engineering at L'Ecole des Ponts et Chausseés. Active in the Resistance during the Nazi occupation of France. In 1941 left France for Niger to work as a civil engineer. Served as the Director of Research at the Centre National de la Recherche Scientifique 1966–86, and was the General Secretary of the Cinémathèque Française 1985–6, after which he was its Director 1987–91. Rouch was married twice, first to Jane George in 1952, and then to Jocelyne Lamothe in 2002. Killed in an automobile crash in Niger on February 18, 2004.

Selected films

1946–7 Au pays des mages noirs: director
1948–9 Les Magiciens de Wanzerbe/The Magicians of Wanzerbe: director, cinematographer, producer
1948–9 Initiation à la danse des possédés/ Invitation to the Dance of the Possessed: director, cinematographer, producer
1948–9 La Circoncision/The Circumcision: director, cinematographer, producer
1953–4 Les Maîtres fous/The Crazy Masters: director, cinematographer
1954–67 Jaguar: director
1957 Moi, un noir/Myself as a blackman: director, writer
1957–64 La Chasse au lion à l'arc: director, cinematographer
1958–9 La Pyramide humaine/The Human Pyramid: director, writer
1960 Chronique d'un été/Chronicle of a Summer: director (with Edgar Morin)
1960 La Punition/The Punishment: director, writer
2003 Le Rêve plus fort que la mort/ The Dream Stronger than Death: director

Further reading

Adams, John W. and Marshall, John, 'John Rouch Talks About his Films to John Marshall and John W. Adams', *American Anthropologist* 80, 1978: 1005–22.

Armes, Roy, *French Cinema*, New York: Oxford University Press, 1985.

DeBouzek, J., 'The Ethnographic Surrealism of Jean Rouch', *Visual Anthropology* 2, 1989: 301–17.

Eatons, Mick (ed.), *Anthropology—Reality—Cinema: The Films of Jean Rouch*, London: British Film Institute, 1979.

Feld, Steven, 'Themes in the Cinema of Jean Rouch', *Visual Anthropology* 2, 1989: 223–49.

Lanzoni, Rémi Fournier, *French Cinema: From its Beginnings to the Present*, New York: Continuum, 2002.

Ruby, Jay (ed.), *The Cinema of Jean Rouch*, London: Harwood Academic Publishers, 1989.

Stoller, Paul, *The Cinematic Griot: The Ethnography of Jean Rouch*, Chicago: Chicago University Press, 1992.

Williams, Alan, *Republic of Images: A History of French Filmmaking*, Cambridge, MA: Harvard University Press, 1992.

Rouquier, Georges

As a teenager, Georges Rouquier already admired the great directors of his time. Having obtained his *certificat d'études*, he took a job as an apprentice typographer in Montpellier. He gradually learned how to operate the linotype and, at the age of sixteen, he left for Paris and found employment as a skilled linotypist. He dedicated his spare time to the cinema, frequenting such film societies as l'Etoile's and the famous Studio 28 movie theatre.

It was on account of these visits that he met director Eugen Deslaw, who had just completed La Marche des Machines/The Operation of the Machines (1928) with relatively little money. Following Deslaw's advice, he bought a second-hand Debrie Sept 35mm camera and learned how to operate it, even taking it apart for better understanding and mastery. He devoted his next holiday to making his first motion picture, Vendanges/Grapeharvest (1929), about the grape harvest near Lunel. The film was later destroyed. Rouquier then completed his military service before going back to work as a linotypist.

At this point Rouquier was little more than a cultivated, film-loving linotypist. Thirteen years after Vendanges, however, he met the producer Etienne Lallier, who agreed to back the making of a short, Le Tonnelier/The Cooper (1942). The resulting composition focuses on the two-day labour process required for the production of one barrel (a demi-muid) by an elderly artisan and his apprentice, under the supervision of the master cooper. The film was once again shot in Lunel and displays great maturity and harmony. Though derived of ambient sound, it magnifies handicraft, dexterity, and know-how, depicting the craftsmen's traditional techniques in a way that would inspire many other films, including some of Rouquier's own. The next year it was awarded a Grand Prix at the Premier Congrès du Film Documentaire in Paris alongside Marcel Ichac's A l'Assaut des Aiguilles du Diable/ Climbing the Peak of the Devil, and René Lucot's Rodin.

Now determined to become a filmmaker, Rouquier directed three commissioned films in 1943. Le Charron could in some ways be compared with Le Tonnelier, while La Part de l'enfant/The Child's share and L'Economie des métaux/The Economy of Metals are much less personal.

Lallier subsequently suggested that Rouquier direct a feature film about peasant life. This came to be Farrebique, often compared with Storck's Symphonie Paysanne/Peasant Symphony, which follows a similar outline. Farrebique succeeds owing to its feeling of authenticity, which the documentary mise-en-scène method respects. Although rewarded several times, this once controversial film, the filmmaker's most famous opus, did not guarantee the director's success.

Rouquier continued to make shorts on commission, addressing diverse subjects. L'Oeuvre scientifique de Pasteur/The Scientific Work of Pasteur (1947) was codirected by Jean Painlevé. Le Chaudronnier/The Boilermaker (1949), a 'handicraft film' again depicts how the artisan technique of the coppersmith had to adapt itself to industrial times. Le Sel de la terre/The Salt of the Earth (1950), 'a documentary western' (Auzel 2002), is an apology for the fertilization plan to the area of the Camargue, albeit an original, lyrical, and aesthetic one.

In 1955 Rouquier produced his young assistant Jacques Demy's first film, Le Sabotier du Val de Loire/The Clogmaker of the Val de Loire. In the mid-1950s he also tried his hand at fiction, with two feature films. Sang et lumière/Blood and Light was the first French film to use the Eastmancolor process. A Spanish version was made concurrently. The results are far from convincing. SOS Noronha (1957), inspired by reality, drew a parallel between the uprising of political prisoners in Brazil and an accident involving the pilot Mermoz, both events perceived from a radio guiding station. This Franco-German-Italian production is no achievement either. More convincing were Rouquier's various performances in a dozen French feature films, among which was Costa-Gavras's Z (1969).

As a filmmaker, Rouquier showed a preference for documentary. His curious Lourdes et ses miracles/Lourdes and its Miracles (1955) was produced by a Catholic corporation, a religious adviser appearing in its credits. The subject matter is that of the allegedly miraculous recoveries of pilgrims. Rouquier endeavoured to present an objective standpoint, maintaining that 'it is up to the spectator to conclude'. Having no facility to record direct synchronous sound outdoors, he nonetheless used authentic (ambient) sound material to full advantage. The way in which Rouquier appears on-screen to introduce and conclude the film prefigures to some extent the 'performative' documentary mode to come.

Rouquier's career came to a close with two films that echoed his first two. Le Maréchal ferrant/The Blacksmith Farrier (1979) is the portrait of a craftsman, which inevitably recalls Le Tonnelier; however, it situates the main character and his trade in a rural world altered by modernisation, and questions the issue of transmitting artisan know-how. Biquefarre (1983) is the sequel to Farrebique that the filmmaker had wished to make for nearly forty years.

The enthusiasm of American scholars and a subsidy from the National Endowment for the Humanities enabled Rouquier to elaborate the script. Two French producers then managed to convince the Crédit Agricole de l'Aveyron to get involved in the project. Rouquier was to depict what his family's farm—and subsistence farming in general—had become. He essentially used the same method as in 1946 (real characters, documentary mise-en-scène). The story, however, displays a finer type of coherence. It intertwines sociopolitical (and ecological) issues with the individual's destiny to demonstrate in a bittersweet mood how a whole world is coming to its end. It remains the testimony of a man who constantly paid tribute to the humble.

JEAN-LUC LIOULT

Biography

Born 1909. Descended from peasants on his father's side. Worked on the family farm as a youth. Having obtained his *certificat d'études*, returned to the farm for a short while before beginning his job as an apprentice typographer in Montpellier. Left for Paris aged sixteen and found employment as a linotypist. Worked nights, learned the new sound techniques in filmmaking during the day. Called up to military service in 1939 and served as an artilleryman until the end of World War II. Died in 1989.

Selected films

1942 Le Tonnelier/The Cooper: director, writer, narrator
1946 Farrebique: director, writer, narrator
1949 Le Chaudronnier/The Boilermaker: director
1955 Lourdes et ses miracles/Lourdes and its Miracles: director, narrator

1979 Le Maréchal ferrant/The Blacksmith Farrier: director, writer, narrator
1983 Biquefarre: director, writer, narrator

Further reading

Auzel, Dominique, *Georges Rouquier, de Farrebique à Biquefarre*, Paris: Petite Bibliothèque des Cahiers du Cinéma, 2002.
Gauthier, Guy, *Le Documentaire, un autre cinéma*, Paris: Nathan Université, 1995.
Piault, Marc-Henri, 'Changer sans changements: résister à l'histoire avec Georges Rouquier', in *Anthropologie et cinéma*, Paris: Nathan Cinéma, 2000.

Rubbo, Michael

Michael Rubbo is an Australian filmmaker who first made his mark at the National Film Board (NFB) of Canada, where he wrote and directed some of its most memorable documentaries—Sad Song of Yellow Skin (1969), Wet Earth and Warm People (1971), Waiting for Fidel (1973), Solzhenitsyn's Children … Are Making a Lot of Noise in Paris (1978), Daisy: Story of a Facelift (1984), and many more. Rubbo is known for a very personal style of filmmaking that takes the viewer on a journey or exploration and allows the person to experience the subject matter through the thoughts, observations, and feelings of the filmmaker. His on-screen interventions make his films as much about him as about his subjects. Author and filmmaker Alan Rosenthal cites other distinctive aspects of Rubbo's films—a diary form of storytelling and an avoidance of the expected.

These characteristics are especially apparent in Waiting for Fidel (1973) in which Rubbo is one of the major characters. The other two are former Newfoundland premier Joey Smallwood and radio and television tycoon Geoff Stirling. The supposed purpose of the film is to follow Smallwood and Stirling as they visit Cuba and talk to Fidel Castro about socialism, admired by Smallwood but disparaged by Stirling. As they await the meeting with Castro, the camera records their discussions at a protocol house where they are staying and at schools and hospitals they visit. Instead of being a background figure, Rubbo is very much in the foreground, posing questions, getting into arguments, particularly with Stirling, the film's underwriter, and through narration giving the audience a diary-like impression of what he is witnessing. The title of the film is taken from Samuel Beckett's play, Waiting for Godot, and as in the play, Fidel (Godot) never shows up, so the film turns out to be about Rubbo's encounters with Smallwood and Stirling.

In a number of films Rubbo comes across as a curious, sensitive outsider/amateur observer trying to understand or unravel a foreign culture or a complex personality or an unresolved mystery. Film professor Joan Nicks (1998) says 'Rubbo's on-screen persona foregrounds the inexpert "self", the out-of-place NFB filmmaker acting and improvising his way through the shooting […] The impulse that propelled Rubbo to "dig in" culturally as an inexpert persona, in the guise of a footloose documentary filmmaker displaced from the Board and Canada (and his native Australia), ultimately mocks the imperialist bias of most Western documentaries about exotic others.'

A good example of Rubbo's tendency to 'dig in' culturally is Sad Song of Yellow Skin (1970), a look at how the Vietnam War and the American presence in Vietnam affected the lives of Vietnamese in Saigon. The film is seen through the eyes of three journalists/peace activists from the United States who, along with Rubbo, are outsiders trying to understand the people and their culture. One journalist lives on a monk's island of peace in the Mekong River. Another seeks to befriend people in a seedy, isolated part of town called the cemetery. A third provides a home, or semblance of a home, for street kids—shoe-shine boys who pimp and steal on the side. Rubbo is along to observe and to tell the viewer what he is observing: street-smart kids who use and are used by American soldiers, young girls turned prostitutes, children laughing and playing in the midst of filth and poverty, the burial arrangements for an old, opium-addicted cabaret performer and mistress whose heyday was during the French occupation. Throughout the film, Rubbo intersperses sounds and images of the United States: popular music, Richard Nixon on television, GIs looking for a good time, and an American Forces weathercast featuring a dancing weather woman billed as a 'bubbling bundle of barometric brilliance'. These sounds and images, along with Rubbo's quiet but pointed commentary about Americans (they believe all Vietnamese are gooks—some good gooks, some bad gooks, but all gooks), about what the Vietnamese think of Americans (Americans either kill or give), and about what he sees as

American influence (GIs came looking for girls and marijuana, now all that remains are the babies they left behind), paint a picture of a culture being corrupted by American dollars and American values.

In Wet Earth and Warm People (1971) Rubbo is again the outsider trying to understand another culture, this time Indonesia. 'Watching Indonesia', Rubbo observes, 'is like watching a snake shed skins'. The skins refer to past influences, particularly Dutch influence. In this film Rubbo tries to understand Indonesia's struggle to modernize. He follows Jakarta's chief of police (who is also a singer with his own television program) and also the driver of a Pedi-cab or becak (Indonesia's traditional means of transportation, often regarded as a symbol of its backwardness), and travels to a small village to experience the true Indonesia, with its puppet plays and agrarian practices. The reflexive nature of Rubbo's documentaries is most apparent in Wet Earth and Warm People (1971). In diary-like form, Rubbo accounts for some of the problems and possible resentment that the crew has encountered: the cameraman looks like a colonialist, the sound man (making his first trip outside North America) appears to be on a tropical trip, and Rubbo's own correspondent's suit is mistaken for military. These revelations take the viewer backstage, as well as on stage, and make the process of filmmaking an integral part of the story.

Rubbo's interventionist style is also at the forefront of Daisy: The Story of a Facelift. In part the story of a feisty middle-aged woman (and fellow employee of the NFB) determined to turn back time, it is also the story of a twentieth-century cultural phenomenon—society's preoccupation with physical appearance. Rubbo explores the underlying motives for cosmetic surgery (breast enlargements, tummy tucks, nose jobs, and the like), and follows Daisy on her personal odyssey as she discusses her youth, marriages, growing old, and fears and expectations. The close, personal relationship between filmmaker and subject is apparent in the banter between Rubbo and Daisy and in Rubbo's provocations of Daisy, at one point pushing Daisy to ask a total stranger (in a patient waiting room) what he is doing there. Nicks (1998) believes that the film 'assumes the character of a parody of male voyeurism in Rubbo's obsession with what drives Daisy's pursuit of a more youthful face to recapture a romantic past'.

In Much Ado about Something (2002), commissioned by the Australian Broadcasting Corporation, Rubbo tries to unravel the authorship of William Shakespeare's plays and sonnets. Following some colorful characters known as Marlovians, all of whom are convinced that Christopher Marlowe was the hidden hand behind Shakespeare, Rubbo tests their ideas against what is known—or not known—about Shakespeare and Marlowe. Presented as a kind of tongue-in-cheek, 'whodunit' murder mystery (literally in the case of Marlowe's death), Much Ado about Something (2002) features Rubbo as chief detective and provocateur, a role he has played in previous films. What is different about Much Ado is that Rubbo also does most of the camera work, using an inexpensive, lightweight, digital camera.

CHURCHILL ROBERTS

See also: Canada; Sad Song of Yellow Skin; Waiting for Fidel

Biography

Born in Melbourne, Australia. Studied anthropology at Sydney University and completed a master's degree in film at Stanford University. In 1965 went to work for the National Film Board of Canada, where he wrote and directed more than thirty-five films. 1980–90 wrote and directed feature films for children, among them The Peanut Butter Solution (1984), Tommy Tricker and the Stamp Traveler (1986), and Vincent and Me (1990). Returned to his native Australia in 1995 and headed the documentary division and special projects of ABC TV. At ABC developed the series Race Around the World and produced and directed Little Box that Sings (1999) and The Man Who is Still Going (1999), an update of a 1973 NFB film. Has lectured widely on documentary and has taught at the Australian Film Television and Radio School and at Harvard University. Independent filmmaker and painter residing in Avoca Beach, Australia.

Selected films

1970 Sad Song of Yellow Skin: writer, director
1971 Wet Earth and Warm People: writer, director
1974 Waiting for Fidel: director, editor

1978 Solzhenitsyn's Children … Are Making a Lot of Noise in Paris: writer, director
1982 Daisy: The Story of a Facelift: director, editor
1984 Margaret Atwood: Once in August: writer, director
1984 The Peanut Butter Solution: writer, director
1988 Tommy Tricker and the Stamp Traveler: writer, director
1991 Vincent and Me: writer, director
1998 The Little Box that Sings: writer, director
2002 Much Ado about Something: writer, director

Further reading

Ellis, Jack, *The Documentary Idea: A Critical History of English-Language Documentary Film and Video*, Englewood Cliffs, NJ: Prentice Hall, 1989.

Nichols, Bill, *Introduction to Documentary*, Bloomington, IN: Indiana University Press, 2001.

Nicks, Joan, 'The Documentary of Displaced Persona: Michael Rubbo's Daisy: Portrait of a Facelift', in Barry Keith Grant and Jeannette Sloniowski (eds), *Documenting the Documentary: Close Readings of Documentary Film and Video*, Detroit, MI: Wayne State University Press, 1998: 302–17.

Rosenthal, Alan, '"Sad Song of the Yellow Skin" and "Waiting for Fidel": Michael Rubbo', in *The Documentary Conscience: A Casebook in Film Making*, Berkeley, CA: University of California Press, 1980: 232–44.

——*Writing, Directing, and Producing Documentary Films and Video*, revised edition, Carbondale, IL: Southern Illinois University Press, 1996.

Russia/Soviet Union

Russia has been extremely influential in the development of documentary film. From early newsreels to avant-garde experimentations to multi-part television series, Russian filmmakers have captivated the world for nearly a century. Supported by a government who not only saw film as an effective tool for reaching the masses but also went so far as to open a state-supported film school, Russian filmmakers have, from the beginning, remained in the forefront of technology and technique.

Shortly after the revolution of 1917 the Union of Soviet Socialist Republics (USSR) began to recognize the power of cinema. According to the head of the People's Commissariat of Education, Anatoli Lunacharsky, Lenin considered cinema to be the most important of all the arts for the newly formed republic. During this time, Denis Arkadievich Kaufman (1896–1954), the son of a librarian, was in Petrograd (St Petersburg) studying medicine and psychology. Influenced by the futurist poet Vladimir Mayakovsky, Kaufman began writing his own poetry, rejecting traditional syntax in favor of word montages. Like most futurists, he reveled in the clamor and rhythm of machines in a world quickly becoming industrialized. He created an audio laboratory where he would create sound montages and changed his name to Dziga Vertov, a name that denotes turning or revolving, signaling that he would become a driving force in the new cinematic movement.

In October 1917 Vertov volunteered to serve on the Cinema Committee in Moscow and was appointed editor of its newsreel Kino-nedeyia/Cinema Week. For three years Vertov's job was to take all incoming bits of film, which included fragments of struggle, crisis, disaster, and victory, and assemble them into a meaningful structure before sending them out again for viewing by the public. His mission was to unite the people by keeping them informed of the ups and downs of the struggle. While compiling the newsreels Vertov began to reuse footage, stringing it together to create features that provided a much broader context than was possible in the newsreels. Three of the most important of these early full-length features are Godovchina revoljutsii/Anniversary of the Revolution (1919), La Bataille de Tsaritsyne/The Battle of Tsaritsyne (1920), and Istoriya grazhdanskoj vojny/History of the Civil War (1922). Vertov felt that these films played an increasingly important role in the struggles of the new Soviet Republic.

Soon after the struggle ended, film stock was scarce and new projects sat waiting to be produced. Fiction films returned to theaters and Vertov found himself editing footage supplied by other filmmakers. In 1920–2 he began to write manifestos that attacked the current state of film in the Soviet Union, which he saw as 'movie dramas garbed in splendid technological dressing', and called for a new breed of filmmakers to rise to the challenge of creating a new Soviet Cinema by 'experiment[ing] with this dying organism'. Vertov saw fiction film as 'opium for the people' and wanted the new Soviet Cinema to document socialist reality (Barnouw 1993: 54).

With his wife, Yelizaveta Svilova, as editor and his brother, Mikhail Kaufman, as cameraman, Vertov formed the Council of the Three and began to produce a series of monthly newsreels entitled Kino-Pravda/Cinema Truth (1922–5). During its three-year run, twenty-three issues of the series appeared. Running approximately twenty minutes and generally covering three separate topics, each issue focused on everyday experiences in the marketplace, bars, and schools. Vertov rarely asked permission to film and usually used a hidden camera to capture the hidden truth of socialist reality. The cinematography is simple, functional, and minimalist. The issues included non-narrative vignettes and exposés: the renovation of a trolley system, the organization of farmers into communes, and starvation in the emerging Marxist state. Although the issues of Kino-pravda rarely included reenactments or stagings, one notable exception is a segment about the trial of the Social Revolutionaries in which Vertov staged several scenes, including newspapers being sold on the streets and read in the trolley. Vertov's tendency toward propaganda is also present. One issue runs the subtitle: 'Tanks on the labor front', as the former Tsar's tanks help to prepare the foundation for a new airport. Although the series continued to run, it had become so experimental after half its issues that critics began to dismiss Vertov's work as 'insane'. This did not deter Vertov who, at the end of the final episode, encouraged his audience to contact him with interesting stories for future projects.

While producing Kino-Pravda, Vertov continued his practice of providing context by expanding shorter pieces into features. The result was Kinoglaz/Kino-Eye: Life Caught Unawares (1924), a documentary that examines the joys of life in a small Soviet village. Some of its various segments are interesting; some are not. One segment focuses on the activities of the 'Young Pioneers', children who spend their days pasting propaganda posters on walls, passing out pamphlets, and encouraging everyone to buy from the cooperative. Other segments highlight a Chinese magician who performs tricks for bread, a cocaine addict, and a murdered factory worker. The three most interesting and experimental portions of the film focus on the slaughter of a bull, the baking of bread, and a series of dives. Each of these segments begins with the final frame and then reverses, showing respectively the entrails moving back into the bull, the skin closing, the bull standing up, walking backwards onto a train car, and rejoining the herd; the bread coming out of the oven, reversing from dough to batter, and eventually from batter to its original ingredients; and divers going into and then coming back out of the water. Kinoglaz also includes one animated segment. The film ends in a mental health hospital. Although there is no structured narrative of any sort—all the images are simply ones captured unaware by the camera eye—Kinoglaz is interesting for its cinematography and techniques. The reverse segments are the first of their kind and are only now beginning to be used in contemporary documentary and fiction films.

Drastic ninety-degree angles capture views of the countryside, city, and people in interesting ways. Ultimately the film is important as a document of a way of life that no longer exists, and for Vertov's experimental techniques.

Five years later, Vertov completed his masterpiece, Chelovek s kinoapparatom/Man with the Movie Camera (1929). Like Kinoglaz, this film is experimental, but is much more cohesive. It is a silent documentary film about filmmaking. Vertov follows a cameraman, his brother Mikhail Kaufman, around various cities. The film intercuts Kaufman's footage with Vertov's footage of Kaufman filming and footage of Yelizaveta Svilova editing. The film introduces a number of innovative cinematic techniques: double exposure, fast and slow motion, freeze-frame, jump cuts, split screens, Dutch angles, extreme close-ups, and tracking shots. The self-reflexive storyline is also the first example of a meta-documentary. Vertov superimposes a shot of Kaufman setting up his camera atop a second camera and later inside a glass. Although at the time cameras were large and noisy, Vertov was sending a message about the prevalence and unobtrusiveness of film and again encouraging Soviet filmmakers to capture life unawares. Claiming that 'we cannot improve our eyes but we can always improve the camera', Vertov ends his film by animating the camera and letting it walk away from Kaufman, no longer reliant on human control. Again critics attacked Vertov and his film for a few obvious stagings and its drastic experimentation, but the film has since become a classic of the genre and was released on DVD in 1996 with a new soundtrack performed by the Alloy Orchestra. Based on notes left by Vertov, the soundtrack incorporates sound effects including sirens, babies crying, and crowd noise.

Over the years Vertov frequently debated film theory and philosophy with his colleague, Sergei Mikhailovich Eisenstein (1898–1948), known mainly for his fact-based historical dramas. Vertov championed the unobtrusive kino-eye, but Eisenstein argued that the Soviet Republic needed a kino-fist to impress on people the message of socialism. Although they differed in their ideas of film construction, they both agreed on the importance of editing to the finished product and the illusion of reality. Although Eisenstein's films were scripted fictions based on historical fact, they often took the form of newsreels and documentaries. In fact, the single most important technique pioneered by Eisenstein that is still used by documentary filmmakers today is montage. Montage stresses the fragmentation of events by rearranging them and juxtaposing shots that do not 'naturally' go together. By using montage techniques, the filmmaker constructs new impressions and insights, creating a visual metaphor that comments on the camera's subject. Eisenstein believed that through cinema, filmmakers were not simply documenting reality, but creating a new reality:

> Is this not exactly what we of the cinema do [...] when we cause a monstrous disproportion of the parts of a normally flowing event, and suddenly dismember the event into 'close-up of clutching hands', 'medium shot of the struggle', and 'extreme close-up of bulging eyes', in making a montage disintegration of the event in various planes? In making an eye twice as large as a man's full figure! By combining these monstrous incongruities, we newly collect the disintegrated event into one whole, but in our aspect. According to the treatment of our relation to the event.
>
> (Donald *et al.* 1999: 34)

Bronenosets Potyomkin/Battleship Potemkin (1925) glorifies the 1905 mutiny against oppressive officers on a battleship. Using the form of a newsreel, Eisenstein carefully crafts his propaganda film by painstakingly editing it in a way that would manipulate the audience and produce the strongest emotional response possible. This subtely crafted montage encourages the viewer to sympathize with the rebellious sailors and despise the cruel officers. The most famous scene from the movie is the Odessa Steps Massacre in which ruthless soldiers of the Tsar, like machines, march rhythmically down an endless flight of stairs and slaughter a crowd of innocents who are attempting to flee. The scene has been imitated and parodied over the years and still has an emotional impact on audiences who travel to the country to see the Odessa Steps. Interestingly enough, the entire scene is fictitious and scripted, a testament to the power of filmed 'reality'.

Two years later, Eisenstein created the first mockumentary with Oktyabr/October: Ten Days that Shook the World (1927). Commissioned by the Soviet government to honor the tenth anniversary of the 1917 October Revolution, Eisenstein used the film to advance what he saw as the further development of his theories of montage, using a concept he described as 'intellectual montage'. The film was not as successful or influential as Bronenosets Potyomkin, and Eisenstein's metaphorical experiments met with official disapproval. Eisenstein was ordered to reedit the work to expurgate negative references to Trotsky and to make it more accessible to the masses. In recent years, however, the film has come to be considered an historical epic and powerful representation of Eisenstein's genius and artistry. Eisenstein's theories and techniques continue to influence documentary filmmakers, both in Russia and internationally, as montage laid the groundwork for the pioneering compilation documentaries of Esfir Shub and the didactic emphasis that John Grierson gave to documentary in Great Britain of the 1930s.

While Eisenstein and Vertov argued and debated, Esfir Shub (1894–1959), a young female filmmaker, diligently worked on her own documentaries. Although she is not as well known as either of her colleagues, her methods and techniques have proven to be more influential to Soviet cinema than either of the other two directors. Born into a family of landowners, Shub studied literature in Moscow before attending classes at the Institute for Women's Higher Education. She joined the State Commissariat of Education and was appointed as Theatre Officer, a job that allowed her to work closely with Vsevolod Meyerhold, a famous avant-garde theatre director. After leaving the Commissariat, Shub joined the Goskino film company where she met Vertov. Although they maintained a lifelong professional friendship, it was often stormy because of their theoretical disagreements. Shub shared Vertov's belief in the intrinsic power of film to reveal the hidden aspects of reality, but she differed from Vertov in that she believed that film could be used in the representation and interpretation of history, not simply as a document of the contemporary world.

She learned the art of editing by recutting 'approved' versions of imported films such as D.W. Griffith's Intolerance (1916) and Fritz Lang's Dr Mabuse, der Spieler/Dr Mabuse, King of Crime (1922). When the film stock shortage slowed down the production of new projects, Shub did not wait for stock to become available or recoat existing stock. Rather, she sifted through archival footage in search of material that could be edited and interpreted for the masses. She was so diligent in her work that she was given access to the Tsar's personal film library. The footage she found and compiled enabled her to produce a trilogy of documentary films: Padeniye dinastij Romanovykh/The Fall of the Romanov Dynasty (1927), Velikij put/ The Great Way [Road] (1927), and Rossiya Nikolaya II i Lev Tolstoy/Leo Tolstoy and the Russia of Nicholas II (1928). While making the trilogy Shub was faced with two major problems: finding the 'right' footage and compensating for damaged or missing footage. Once she had collected the most valuable existing footage, she 'replaced' any relevant damaged footage with new footage. By doing so, she provided a contemporary context for the archival footage. Padeniye dinastij Romanovykh, the first part of the trilogy, has had the most lasting resonance. It follows the sequence of events in Russia from the first Russian revolution in 1905 to the second revolution in October 1917. Shub introduces leaders of the Duma (the lower house of the Russian parliament), gentry and peasants, soldiers and sailors, the bourgeoisie, and the Tsar. In May 1913 Europe's crowned heads came to Petrograd to celebrate three hundred years of Romanov rule, even as most of them prepared for war. With great skill and care Shub produced a dramatic account of events as they were actually happening. The result is a film that still has an emotional impact when viewed today.

Unknowingly, Shub created a completely new genre: the historical compilation film. She later claimed that she simply wanted to create newsreels with an editorial slant. Both critics and colleagues admired Shub's work. She had successfully found a balance between narrative and documentary forms. Although she remained quiet and out of the spotlight, working sporadically, she did return to the documentary form with a collaboration with Vsevolod Pudovkin (1893–1953) entitled Kino za XX let/Twenty Years of Soviet Cinema (1940). After this successful film Shub left Goskino to become chief editor for Moscow's central studio for documentary film, where she spent her final years confined to editing duties. Although Vertov and Eisenstein helped to define avant-garde filmmaking and theory, Esfir Shub's style and technique have survived as the most prominent form in modern documentary filmmaking. In addition, her scholarly achievement in researching and locating valuable archival footage helped to encourage the development and maintenance of film archives.

The year 1928 brought about yet another change in Soviet cinema, with the publication of Alexei Gan's essay 'Constructivism in the Cinema'. Like Vertov before him, Gan called for a new type of cinema that, though rooted in reality, was poetic and expressed the mark of the filmmaker:

> It is not enough to link, by means of montage, individual moments of episodic phenomena of life, united under a more or less successful title. The most unexpected accidents, occurrences, and events are always linked organically with the fundamental root of social reality. While apprehending them with the shell of their outer manifestations, one should be able to expose their inner essence by a series of other scenes. Only on such a basis can one build a vivid film of concrete, active reality, gradually departing from the newsreel, from whose material this new ciné form is developing.
>
> (Gan 1974: 130)

This essay addresses the issue of film form, specifically the assembly of shots into a pattern that affirms the voice of the filmmaker, by calling for a new style that moves beyond simply showing 'attractions' or making unobtrusive scientific observations. Gan, like Eisenstein, was calling on filmmakers not only to document but also to comment on their subjects. Two filmmakers who quickly answered the call were Victor Turin (1895–1945) and Mikheil Kalatozishvili, more commonly known as Mikhail Kalatozov (1903–73).

Victor Turin's Turksib (1929) documented the construction of a railroad linking Turkestan and Siberia through the harshest region of the central Asian desert. The end of the film, showing a locomotive looming on the horizon under a blast of thick black smoke, signals the triumph of modern technology. Turin's organization of his huge project, and his success in giving it innovative dramatic impact, won wide admiration and influenced documentary filmmakers throughout the world. A memorable sequence, introduced with the simple title 'Strangers … ', shows people in a remote Turkestan desert village watching the arrival of surveyors. This scene sets the stage for a later climactic sequence in which an engine arrives on the new track for the first time. Some men on horseback ride up and cautiously inspect the new contraption as it stands at rest, puffing quietly. As the engine starts up, the terror of the horses and men and their temporary retreat provide fascinatingly authentic moments. Later we see them joyfully racing the engine across vast plains. One major innovation of Turin's film is the incorporation of lengthy subtitles that seem to anticipate spoken commentary.

Born Mikhail Kalatozishvili in Tiflis, Kalatozov originally studied to be an economist. In 1925, however, he began working as an actor in the Georgian studios. Shortly after this he began to learn the art of shooting and editing film, which led him to create his first short documentary, Mati samepo/Their Empire, in 1928. Two years later he created an amazingly beautiful, stark, and blunt chronicle of life in post-Revolutionary Russia with Jim Shvante (marili svanets)/Salt for Svanetia (1930). The film focuses on a starkly isolated mountain community between the Black and Caspian Seas, which has been deprived of an essential mineral: salt. The villagers and animals all suffer and go to any lengths necessary to find the precious commodity. Kalatozov shows the viewer a farmer lying down in his field to rest from his labor. As he does so, a cow comes to lick the sweat from his brow. After the farmer urinates, the cattle lick his urine. Whenever a baby is born, dogs lick the placental fluid from its body. Kalatozov's film sends out the message that the people are not only suffering from a lack of salt, but also from their cultural isolation from the progress of the new Republic. The villagers retain their primitive beliefs by adhering to their religion and giving what little money they have to the Church, which is powerless to help. The climax of the film comes as a Soviet-built road is constructed, and thanks to Soviet progress, Svanetia is saved by a shipment of salt.

The Stalin regime felt that the film was unbalanced and unfair to Svanetia and that Kalatozov was far too fascinated by the backwardness and superstition of Svanetia, and too overtly pushed the socialist solution. Kalatozov had allowed his voice to sound too loudly in the film as opposed to simply documenting the reality. Kalatozov followed Jim Shvante with Lursmani cheqmashi/Nail in the Boot (1931), a film that received more of the same criticism and was ultimately banned. Kalatozov was then assigned to strictly administrative duties within the film industry. During World War II he was appointed to the office of Chief Administrator of Soviet Feature Film Production. During this time he sometimes worked in Los Angeles as the Soviet cultural representative. After the war Kalatozov received an appointment as Deputy Minister of Film Production and was allowed to resume his directing career. Twenty-seven years after making Jim Shvante, Kalatozov received the Palme d'Or at the Cannes Film Festival for Letjat zhuravli/The Cranes are Flying (1957), a wartime romantic drama. Unfortunately, he left no other documentaries in his short but impressive catalogue.

The Soviet films of this early period helped to develop modern documentary filmmaking style and techniques. Their focus on the modern world, politics, and historical contexts sought to agitate viewers and move audiences to action. Unfortunately, the artistic peak of this early phase of Soviet cinema was short-lived. As Stalin's regime grew stronger and more paranoid in the 1930s, more and more documentaries were censored or banned outright and the voices of their creators silenced. Still, their influence survives in worldwide documentary filmmaking today, even as new voices in Russia are emerging.

Having written, directed, and starred in more than thirty films, Eldar Ryazanov (1927–) has established himself as one of Russia's most formidable filmmakers. His films are distinctly Russian in nature, as he himself says that he can inhabit no other country than his own and embraces his native climate, culture, and language. Ryazanov tends to work in the area of comedic fiction, but he still attempts to capture the reality of Russian life by focusing on stories about ordinary people and unforgettable situations. He believes the most important element of the film director's profession is a carefully balanced combination of tenderness and toughness. He tries to capture the raw reality of life in the most cinematically beautiful way possible. It is this combination that he brings to his four-part documentary series on the Russian bard Vladimir Vysotsky, Chetyre vechera s Vladimirom Vysotskim/Four Meetings with Vladimir Vysotsky (1987). In the documentary, Ryazanov acts as director, writer, and commentator as he explores the life of Vysotsky through four stages. The first part deals with Vysotsky's early life, the second with his career as an actor in the theater, the third with his career as a film actor, and the final installment with his career as Russia's preeminent poet, singer, and musician.

Using archival footage and providing his own modern commentary, Ryazanov beautifully captures the hard-living, hard-drinking actor who was admired by virtually all circles of Soviet society. Through his music Vysotsky was a voice of dissent who was often banned, but through his films he was a simple entertainer. Although he was 'discovered' while playing Hamlet on stage, his most memorable role was captured on Russian television as he took on the role of tough homicide detective Gleb Zheglov in the series Mesto vstrechi imenit nelzya/Can't Change the Meeting Place (1979). With this documentary, Ryazanov in many ways returns to Vertov by making a film about film and its power. Unlike Vertov, however, Ryazanov is not promoting the government through propaganda. Rather he is criticizing it by creating a testament to one of Russia's greatest critics. Although Vysotsky held no office, he did play an important political role by condemning the system under which he was born. Throughout his lifetime the government was able to silence and control his criticism, but through Ryazanov's film Vysotsky's voice has been captured. This marks a major departure from the Stalinist regime that all but destroyed the documentary tradition in Russia.

In the 1990s Stanislav Govorukhin (1936–) emerged as the dominant documentary filmmaker of Russia. A member of the Duma, Govorukhin is not only one of the favorite directors, but also a politician whose opinions are listened to and respected. He is known for making emotionally charged speeches that motivate some listeners and enrage others. With many reforms beginning to take place in his country in the early 1990s, Govorukhin created documentaries with a definitive political slant. His films lash out at emerging criminal elements including corruption and white-collar crime. When criticized for mixing his politics with his art, he replied, 'This is a creative process [...] I don't see much difference between politics and directing.' His films are as up-front and daring as his speeches and the titles make no attempt to sanitize the director's opinions. Tak zhit nelzya/You Can't Live Like That (1990), Rossiya, kotoruyu my poteryali/Russia that We've Lost (1992), and Velikaya kriminal'naya revolyutsiya/Great Criminal Revolution (1994) make up a trilogy that provides Govorukhin's view of historical and contemporary events in Russia, tracing its context and consequences from the final years before the 1917 October Revolution, its public and economic life, the Bolshevik rule that turned out fatal for the people, to the fate of Russia, complete with its historical role and prospects for the future. According to Govorukhin in the films, 'A pessimist is a well-informed optimist [...] What I know suggests that things are pretty bad. Nevertheless, I do hope that life in Russia will gradually improve.' Govorukhin is reluctant to discuss the future, but he often talks nostalgically of the past, stating that his time is the nineteenth century and that it is a pity that he was not born a century earlier. Although he has turned to narrative fiction, another documentary project was a filmed interview with the famous writer Alexander Solzhenitsyn. The film includes narration about Solzhenitsyn's life and work in America, his family, his dreams, and intentions. In 2003 Govorukhin released Blagoslovite zhenshchinu/Bless the Woman, another narrative drama that focuses on a tiny Soviet village in the years before World War II.

Beginning in 1993, the Krupny Plan Motion Picture and Video Association teamed with Castle Communications and Eastern Light Productions to produce documentaries that would reflect the lost footage and films of the Stalin era. By using the talents of a number of directors, including Aizenberg, M.K. Kaufman, and Zolotukhin, Rossiya: zabytie gody/Russia: The Forgotten Years covers such diverse historical topics as the Revolution and the final years of Romanov rule, as well as cultural topics including the Russian ballet and histories of the naval fleet, aviation squadron, and the space race. Istoriya grazhdanskoi voiny/The History of the Civil War (1993) covers the period 1918–22 and informs the viewer of the most significant events on the eve of the civil war through its opening stages. There is a considerable amount of archival footage and newsreels that has been made available for the first time. One of the most interesting segments documents the creation of the Red Army and its vital role in maintaining central Russia and achieving crucial victories on all fronts despite desperate resistance from the White forces. The beautiful cinematography and clever editing capture the suppression of the Kronstadt uprising in 1921 and the final expulsion of Japanese forces from Vladivostok in late 1922, marking the end of five years of conflict and establishing the Soviet Union as a major power.

Velikaya otechestvennaya voina/The Eastern Front (aka The Great Patriotic War) (1993) makes up three films in the series as the filmmakers use various newsreels to recreate a grandiose picture of the 1941–5 battle, with its magnificent victories and enormous losses. The trilogy begins with Hitler's invasion of the Soviet Union in June 1941, possibly the most dramatic campaign of World War II, and follows the war through the anticipated Blitzkrieg on the Eastern Front, and the Wermacht's first major defeat at Moscow. The film then dramatically captures the battle at Stalingrad, where the Russian troops fiercely held their ground against overwhelming forces and the momentous tank battle at Kursk. This segment, documenting the epic actions that turned the tide of World War II, could take their place alongside the great war films of history. The trilogy concludes with Operation Bagration, the destruction of the Wermacht in Byelorussia. The filmmakers do not hide the fact that the Red Army's thrust to Germany's border turned into a fierce and costly campaign, but show both the horrors and triumphs as Zhukov's two-million man force crushes Hitler's last defenses in Berlin.

Istoriya krasnoi armii/The History of the Red Army (1994) further explores one of the world's most powerful fighting forces. Emerging in 1918 under the control of Lev Trotsky, the Red Army was initially made up of three hundred thousand soldiers, but within two years had grown to more than five million. This documentary traces the first twenty years of its history from the civil war through its battles in World War II. The film strongly criticizes Stalin, who had purged the forces, leaving them decimated as they entered the most important war of their history. Although the footage of the army's victory over the Nazi forces is impressive, the most impressive segments deal with the campaigns against the Japanese in Manchuria, the Finnish, and of the army's later involvement in Hungary, Czechoslovakia, and Afghanistan. Editing together unique and unseen archival footage, the documentary reaches high drama at many points.

One final important film of the Forgotten Years series is Chekisty/The Story of the KGB (1994). The film is divided into two parts, with part one covering the period 1917–33, the beginnings of the KGB, and part two focusing on the professional police force active from 1934–53. Having perfected the art of espionage, political assassinations, and rigged trials under the guidance of Feliks Dzerzhinsky, under Stalin the KGB became the ultimate tool for maintaining control over the country. During the 1930s and 1940s the secret police force orchestrated mass purges and consolidated immense resources and political power and permeated every aspect of Soviet reality. This film in the series again uses archival footage mixed with contemporary commentary to create a great dramatic thriller while representing the reality of the Soviet people.

All of the films in the Forgotten Years series hark back to the style created by Esfir Shub, taking existing footage and arranging it in a way to provide an interpretation for a new audience. Since Vertov, Russian cinema has pushed the boundaries of possibility with film. Ever striving for new styles and techniques, Russian filmmakers all seem to share one bond: the voice of the filmmaker must be heard. Although many critics argue that documentary filmmakers should not be explicit in their views and, like Vertov, should simply attempt to capture 'life unawares', the modern Russian filmmaker is more in line with Eisenstein's kino-fist. The events should not be staged, they should be natural, but in the editing process they should be arranged in a way to achieve the proper response from the audience. After many silent years, Russian cinema is back in the forefront, searching the archives of the past to move forward into the future.

CHARLES BANE

See also: Fall of the Romanov Dynasty, The; Man with the Movie Camera; Shub, Esfir; Turin, Viktor; Turksib; Vertov, Dziga

Further reading

Barnouw, Erik, *Documentary: A History of the Non-Fiction Film*, second revised edn, Oxford: Oxford University Press, 1993.

Bordwell, David and Thompson, Kristin, *Film Art: An Introduction*, sixth edn, New York: McGraw-Hill, 2001.

Donald, James *et al.* (eds), *Close Up 1927–33: Cinema and Modernism*, Princeton, NJ: Princeton University Press, 1999.

Gan, Alexi, 'Constructivism and the Cinema', in Stephen Bann (ed.), *The Tradition of Constructivism*, New York: Viking, 1974.

Grant, Barry Keith and Sloniowski, Jeannette (eds), *Documenting the Documentary: Close Readings of Documentary Film and Video*, Detroit, MI: Wayne State University Press, 1998.

Jacobs, Lewis, *The Documentary Tradition*, second edn, New York: Norton, 1979.

Mouratov, Sergei, 'The Unknown Cinema: Documentary Screen, Glasnost Era', *Journal of Film and Video* 44, nos 1–2, 1992: 9–18.

Nichols, Bill, *Introduction to Documentary*, Bloomington, IN: Indiana University Press, 2001.

Roberts, Graham, *Forward Soviet!: History and Non-Fiction Film in the USSR*, New York: I.B. Tauris, 1999.

——*The Man with the Movie Camera*, New York: I.B. Tauris, 2001.

Vertov, Dziga. *Kino-Eye: The Writings of Dziga Vertov*, trans. Kevin O'Brien, Berkeley, CA: University of California Press, 1995.

Zimmermann, P.R., 'Reconstructing Vertov: Soviet Film Theory and American Radical Documentary', *Journal of Film and Video* 44, nos 1–2, 1992: 80–90.

S

Sad Song of Yellow Skin

(Canada, Rubbo, 1970)

Sad Song of Yellow Skin, directed by Michael Rubbo, is one of the most enduring films to emerge from the Vietnam War. The film is representative of the then-recent ascendancy of the director's role at the National Film Board (NFB) of Canada and marks a significant development toward what would become Rubbo's signature style. It also stands apart from more conventional documentary treatments of the war.

In the early 1960s the NFB was organized into production units headed by executive producers. The units functioned in varying degrees autocratically, and filmmakers generally were subordinate to producers. In 1964–5 rebellious filmmakers forced a dismantling of the unit system and the adoption of a 'pool' system that gave directors the power often to propose subjects, initiate projects, and choose producers. As a result, a spate of films representing the personal or political interests of the filmmakers emerged in the latter part of the 1960s and continued into subsequent decades.

Rubbo entered the NFB in 1966 and for several years made sponsored films as well as children's films. As the Vietnam War dragged on, he proposed making a film about the war. An overtly antiwar film would not have been permitted at that time, and the NFB had a policy that each of its films had to have 'Canadian content'. Rubbo's proposed film would be centered on the work of a Canadian-sponsored foster parents program in Vietnam. Once in Vietnam, however, he discovered that the program offered meager filmic possibilities. He wired the NFB and got permission from his producer, Tom Daly, to focus on three idealistic young Americans in Saigon who were working against the war and its effects.

Rubbo's change of focus proved pivotal in several ways. Sad Song of Yellow Skin became the NFB's first significant documentary without any Canadian content (with the exception of some NFB films sponsored by the United Nations). By using the three likeable Americans as his guide, Rubbo avoided simplistic anti-Americanism. Most important, the opportunity enabled Rubbo to make a film that did not pretend to project the knowledge he did not have.

Rubbo, who narrates the film off camera, explores Saigon through the three Americans and their work, and the audience discovers Saigon through his search. The film is structured such that Rubbo's initial disorientation in a hectic foreign city is represented in a fast-moving series of images of exotic bustle; our gradual if ultimately limited familiarity with Saigon follows Rubbo's own.

Except for details, the knowledge we ultimately gain is essentially the knowledge of mystery. One of the most moving scenes in the film is the funeral of an opium addict Rubbo had met through one of the Americans. The woman had been a highly admired dancer; she died in wretched destitution. Her tearful older daughter holds the baby sister she must now care for alone while neighbors arrange her mother's corpse in a primitive wooden coffin lined with sawdust. The film ends on the 'Island of Peace', a serene Buddhist colony headed by a withered old priest on an island in the Mekong River. The priest, educated in Europe as an engineer, hopes to bring peace to Vietnam by symbolic means: his daily trek from Hanoi to Saigon on a wooden platform shaped and painted to resemble a map of Vietnam. The film's conclusion in death and spiritual quest is at once strange and familiar. As if Rubbo is aware that he has strayed far from the subject of war, the last sounds we hear are bursts of machine-gun fire laid in over the final credits.

Sad Song of Yellow Skin was dismissed by some for its apparent lack of political analysis. The film is devoid of the anger of such Vietnam-era films as Hearts and Minds (1974) and Interviews with My Lai Veterans (1971) or the battle content of The Anderson Platoon (1967). Its only direct representation of military presence is the occasional shot of a US soldier in Saigon and those bursts of machine-gun fire; the latter seem like less a reminder than an afterthought. Some critics sensed a patronizing tone to the film. When it was shown to a group of Cuban film-makers, for instance, Rubbo was asked why the camera seemed to always be looking down at the Vietnamese—which it does, but largely because the American subjects were tall and the cameraman was six feet four inches tall. Rubbo's reliance on US guides has also been questioned, but there is an honesty in the way it shows the film's sources on screen. Some people were put off by Rubbo's first-person narration, which he delivers in an almost matter-of-fact, sometimes hesitant, groping style. The Canadian Broadcasting Corporation refused to air the film because of its personal, nonobjective point of view.

Although they were perceived by some as shortcomings, Rubbo developed these aspects of Sad Song of Yellow Skin into a distinctive style. Beginning with his next film, Wet Earth and Warm People (1971), Rubbo didn't just personally narrate; he stepped in front of the camera to engage with the material as another character. He would often use intermediaries as guides to the subject of his inquiries, as in Solzhenitsyn's Children … Are Making a Lot of Noise in Paris (1978). He would treat his villains gently, as in Persistent and Finagling (1971). The quintessential Rubbo film, where the various components of his approach mesh together most effectively, is Waiting for Fidel (1974).

D.B. JONES

See also: Canada; Grierson, John; Hearts and Minds; Rubbo, Michael; Waiting for Fidel

Sad Song of Yellow Skin (Canada, National Film Board, 1970, 58 mins). Distributed by the National Film Board of Canada. Produced by Tom Daly. Directed by Michael Rubbo. Cinematography by Martin Duckworth and Pierre Letarte. Sound by George Croll, Michel Descombes, Les Halman, and Pierre Letarte. Edited by Torben Schioler and Michael Rubbo. Narration written and spoken by Michael Rubbo.

Further reading

Dobi, Steve, 'Michael Rubbo' (interview), *Sightlines*, fall 1975: 17–20.

Handling, Piers, 'The Diary Films of Mike Rubbo', in Seth Feldman (ed.), *Take Two*, Toronto: Irwin Publishing, 1984.

Hughes, John, 'Michael Rubbo: Hiding behind the "I"', (interview), *Cinema Papers*, January/February 1981: 41–5, 89.

Jones, D.B., *Movies and Memoranda*, Ottawa: Deneau, 1982.

——*The Best Butler in the Business: Tom Daly of the National Film Board of Canada*, Toronto: University of Toronto Press, 1996.

Rosenthal, Alan, 'Sad Song of Yellow Skin and Waiting for Fidel', (interview with Michael Rubbo), in *The Documentary Conscience: A Casebook in Film Making*, Berkeley, CA: University of California Press, 1980.

Sadness: A Monologue by William Yang

(Australia, Ayres, 1999)

Sadness: A Monologue by William Yang is one of the most innovative documentaries to be produced in Australia in the late 1990s. Sadness existed as a highly acclaimed performance piece by Australian photographer and performance artist, William Yang, before it was adapted for the screen by writer and director Tony Ayres in 1999. It is the combination of performance, documentary, and Yang's evocative monologue that marks Sadness as a unique Australian documentary.

Funded by SBS Independent and Film Australia's National Interest Program initiative, Sadness weaves together a number of different narratives in such a way as to construct a commentary on identity, community, and nationhood. These many narratives represent aspects of Yang's experience that function, for him, as sites of mourning. Following the death of his mother, Yang travels through Australia's north-eastern state, Queensland, in order to discover the truth about the murder of his uncle, William Fang Yuen, which occurred in the 1920s. He visits family and other witnesses, and while the accounts he collects are conflicting, everyone agrees that the misconducted murder trial represented the authorities' lack of regard for the Chinese Australian community.

These scenes concerning family, past and present, are interspersed with sequences devoted to a number of friends Yang lost to AIDS in Sydney's gay community. Yang describes his relationship with Scotty, David, Nicholas, and others, as their physical decline becomes apparent on screen. Through juxtaposing the two discourses of family and gay identity, Sadness problematises the way they are often considered mutually exclusive. As a documentary, Sadness can be understood within a tradition of essayist filmmaking in the sense that the self-consciously subjective and performed nature of the narrative allows for the productive juxtaposition of seemingly divergent discourses.

This bricolage across the different aspects of Yang's experience works to displace the construction of a centre and a margin, or the 'Australian' identity and the 'ethnic' identity, while also denying the possibility of a singular notion of identity.

In Sadness, Yang himself presents his monologue in a type of stage-set environment and his photography is either projected in this space or shown in cutaways. It is through this still photography that the audience is given access to the different characters that inhabit the stories. The differing versions of the murder and Yang's journey are portrayed through reenactments and employ the technique of back-projection, lending a highly stylised aspect to these sequences. The trace of the earlier staged performance piece is present in the documentary in ways that extend and render visible the authored and performative aspect of all documentary. As is the case with many examples of reflexive documentary, in Sadness, realism and documentary truth are rethought in order to privilege a more subjective approach that questions the production of meaning and the relationship between history and experience and identity and cultural stereotypes. Through a personal engagement with narratives of mourning, Sadness works to explore the complexity of a gay Chinese Australian subjectivity. These political and thematic concerns can also be found in Ayres's earlier documentary, China Dolls (1997).

BELINDA SMAILL

Sadness: A Monologue by William Yang (Australia, Film Australia, 1999, 52 mins). Distributed by Film Australia. Produced by Michael McMahaon and Megan McMurchy. Directed by Tony Ayres. Based on the original work Sadness by William Yang. Script by Tony Ayres. Script consultant William Yang. Cinematography by Tristan Milani. Edited by Riva Childs. Sound by Pat Fiske, Livia Ruzic and Peter Walker.

Further reading

Chan, Dean, 'The Dim Sum vs. the Meat Pie: On the Rhetoric of Becoming an In-Between Asian Australian Artist', in Ien Ang, Lisa Law and Mandy Thomas, *Alter/Asians: Asian-Australian Identities in Art, Media and Popular Culture*, Sydney: Pluto Press, 2000: 141–51.

Khoo, Tseen, 'Re-siting Australian Identity: Configuring the Chinese Citizen in Diana Giese's Astronauts, Lost Souls and Dragons and William Yang's Sadness', in Wenche Ommundsen (ed.), *Bastard Moon: Essays on Chinese Australian Writing*, Melbourne: Otherland Journal, 2001: 95–109.

Smaill, Belinda, 'Disorientations: Sadness, Mourning and the Unhomely', *The Journal of Australian Studies* 73, 2002: 161–9.

Yang, William, *Sadness*, Sydney: Allen & Unwin, 1996.

Salesman

(US, Maysles, 1969)

Salesman is a landmark film of the American direct cinema movement of the 1960s and 1970s. In the documentary, the camera accompanies four Bible salesmen over the course of six weeks as they advance from door to door, trying to sell Bibles for the Mid-American Bible Company, first in the greater Boson area and later in the suburbs of Miami. The film is striking for its mixture of humor and melancholia. It is equally striking for its form: filmed and packaged as a documentary, yet generating drama and tension as it documents the decline of a profession.

Salesman, as is the case for many direct cinema films, is shot in black and white, reflecting the origins of new style in photojournalism. The film is one of many collaborations between director and cameraman Albert Maysles and his brother David, his long-standing editor and sound engineer. Until 1961 both had been part of Drew Associates, a group of innovative young filmmakers developing a new documentary film style with journalist and filmmaker Robert Drew.

The technological innovations of the decade before Salesman—faster and more light-sensitive 16mm film stock, portable (and hence less intrusive) wireless cameras, and synchronous sound—had made unobtrusive filmmaking possible. It was henceforth feasible for the camera, as illustrated by Salesman, to follow people into their private spaces, without involving complex planning or, supposedly, resulting in the loss of spontaneity of the subjects. The camera was able to catch people as they were, directly.

It has been argued that, despite their various claims of filming authentic experience, and unlike their French contemporaries participating in cinéma vérité, the practitioners of direct cinema did not always observe life at its most ordinary.

Earlier direct cinema films revolved around celebrities such as John F. Kennedy (Robert Drew, Crisis, 1963) and Jane Fonda (D.A. Pennebaker, Jane, 1962). These films were able to rely on the 'natural' attraction of their subjects to keep audiences engaged (Rosenthal 1988: 127–8). Salesman stands out because it concerns itself with ordinary people.

Salesman portrays four real-life, middle-aged Bible salesmen, their frustrations, and the hardship that accompanies a life on the road and a job where competition is tough, where few get rich, and where many fall by the wayside. The settings alternate between sparse motel rooms, often poor and small homes and constrained lifestyles, and the cars in which the salesmen drive to prospective customers.

The film starts out with the main protagonist, fifty-six-year-old Paul Brennan, confidently explaining (over a screenshot of the Bible with 'Holy Bible' in lavish print across the cover): 'The best seller in the world is the Bible. For one reason. It's the greatest piece of literature of all time.' Paul will never again sound so reassured, as the audience watches him move from one failed sales pitch to another. His colleagues—Raymond 'The Bull' Martos, Charlie 'The Gipper' McDevitt, and James 'The Rabbit' Baker (all nicknamed after their sales strategies)—are both pals and rivals, and as time goes by, Paul's decline, and his resulting anger and frustration, leave him increasingly isolated from these friends. Slowly it becomes clear that Paul is not going to catch up on his subscriptions and will likely lose his job.

Although one of direct cinema's self-declared approaches to documentary was observing, rather than narrating, it is clear from early on that Salesman is a carefully edited film. In fact, the film follows a suspense dramaturgy. The tension is set up just a few minutes into the film, when the manager announces that the company has to 'eliminate a few men'. The audience has already witnessed that Paul is having difficulties meeting the sales requirements, and now they know what is at stake. Paul's situation singles him out among his three colleagues and serves as the structuring point of the narrative.

While 'unscripted and unrehearsed' (Barsam 1973: 302), Salesman uses a range of techniques to maintain the flow of the narrative. When Paul is on a train to the Chicago sales meeting and quietly looks out the window, the off-voice of manager Ken fades in, giving one of his bullying speeches. This technique is more specific to fiction than to documentary storytelling. In blending the image of Paul and the voice of Ken, the filmmakers move beyond what can be known through direct observation alone. Salesman also uses nondiegetic sound, as can be seen later in the film, as the Beatles song 'Yesterday' accompanies Raymond 'The Bull' Martos as he leaves another successful sale. Even more striking is how the protagonist Paul is at one point given control over the narrative. While driving in Miami, he describes his pals and their different sales approaches. Laughing and talking, he looks directly into the camera and his words trigger a string of sequences, illustrating his stories about the sales styles of the Gipper, the Rabbit, and the Bull.

Ultimately, the film's drama is anchored in the sales pitches themselves. The sales pitches provide the moments of tension, with the success of the salesmen depending on their skill in manipulating the prospective buyers—however impoverished—into enough guilt so that they end up buying. Moreover, the absurdity of many of the sales pitches provide comical scenes that are interspersed through the film, as the men try to reconcile the materialistic with the religious aspects of their enterprise, and the desperation of their economic conditions.

JACOBIA DAHM

See also: Drew, Robert; Maysles, Albert

Salesman (US, 1968, 91 mins, black and white). Directed by Albert and David Maysles and Charlotte Zwerin. Produced by Albert and David Maysles. Cinematography by Albert Maysles. Edited by David Maysles and Charlotte Zwerin. Contributing film editor: Ellen Giffard. Assistant editor: Barbara Jarvis. Sound mixer: Dick Vorisek. Filmed in Boston, Chicago, and Miami.

Further reading

Allen, Robert C. and Gomery, Douglas, *Film History. Theory and Practice*, New York and London: McGraw-Hill, 1985.

Barnouw, Erik, *Documentary: A History of the Non-fiction Film*, Oxford, New York: Oxford University Press, 1993.

Barsam, Richard M., *Nonfiction Film. A Critical History*, Bloomington, IN: Indiana University Press, 1973.

Breitrose, Henry, 'On the Search for the Real Nitty-Gritty: Problems & Possibilities in Cinéma Vérité', *Film Quarterly*, 17, no. 4 (summer 1964): 36–40.

Bruzzi, Stella, *New Documentary: A Critical Introduction*, London and New York: Routledge, 2000.

Kolker, Robert Philip, 'Circumstantial Evidence: An Interview with David and Albert Maysles', *Sight and Sound* 40, no. 4, autumn 1971: 183–6.

Levin, G. Roy, *Documentary Explorations. 15 Interviews with Film-Makers*, New York: Anchor Press, 1971.

Macdonald, Kevin and Cousins, Mark, *Imagining Reality. The Faber Book of the Documentary*, London and Boston: Faber & Faber, 1996.

Mamber, Stephen, *Cinema Verité in America*, Cambridge, MA: MIT Press, 1974.

Nichols, Bill, *Representing Reality. Issues and Concepts in Documentary*, Bloomington, IN: Indiana University Press, 1991.

Rosenthal, Allan (ed.), *New Challenges for Documentary*, Berkeley, CA and London: University of California Press, 1988.

Stubbs, Liz, *Documentary Filmmakers Speak*, New York: Allworth Press, 2002.

Warren, Charles (ed.), *Beyond Document. Essays on Nonfiction Film*, Hanover, NH and London: Wesleyan University Press, 1996.

Young, Colin, 'Cinema of Common Sense', *Film Quarterly* 17, no. 4, summer 1964: 26–9.

Salt of the Earth

(US, Biberman, 1954)

Salt of the Earth is often recognized as one of the only blacklisted US films from the McCarthyism days of the early 1950s. Although other labor-referent films dating back to the 1920s dealt with their share of opposition, that which surrounded Herbert Biberman's film and its participants stands out in some ways due to the fact the film was made in the face of political and industry opposition. The film continues to find an audience in spite of its original exhibitive difficulties. In many ways it is the film's reliance on telling the story as a bio-fictional fantasy-type narrative, rather than that of a realist documentary, that gives the film its strength and applicable longevity.

Salt of the Earth was made not only at a time of great political upheaval in the Hollywood film industry but also from those with firsthand experience. The idea for the film originated with blacklisted screenwriters Paul Jarrico and Academy Award-winner Michael Wilson, who developed the story from a labor dispute unfolding in Grant County, New Mexico, and presented it to their partner, director Herbert Biberman. Biberman had recently spent time in jail as one of the infamous 'Hollywood Ten' for refusing to discuss his political affiliations after being named as a Communist by Budd Schulberg in one of the House Un-American Activities Committee (HUAC) hearings. The trio had been looking for a film project to develop of exactly this sort, and set about making the film in direct collaboration with the subjects they would be portraying.

The story in Salt of the Earth focuses on a fair wages and conditions strike between the Mexican American members of the International Union of Mine, Mill and Smelters Workers Local #890, and Empire Zinc. For legitimacy, many of the miners portrayed in the film were members of the Local #890, including one of the main characters, Ramon Quintero, portrayed by Juan Chacon, on whom the character was based. As the strike wears on unsuccessfully, the story unfolds with many of the wives of the strikers (spearheaded by Esperanza Quintero (Rosaura Revueltas), a character based on Chacon's wife Virginia) overcoming their initial sociopatriarchal positioning to join the fight on the front lines, while the men stay at home with the families. Such social reversals took the narrative beyond the labor-capitalist models developed in the silent era and allowed the film enough ambiguity to stand in for oppression of all sorts. This approach, coupled with some early suggested changes in the script from union members, allowed the film to avoid the typical racial and sexual stereotyping of the times. In tandem, this provided the film with fewer polemics to date the fight than bits of optimism, allowing future viewers to apply the struggle to multiple social and political interpretations.

The entire production and exhibition process of Salt of the Earth was met with resistance because the film was made by individuals blacklisted in the industry and was being labeled as narratively relative to certain Communist ideology. This obstacle manifested itself not only in the reluctance of Hollywood unions to allow production workers be hired on the film but also in postproduction, as labs and editing houses were threatened with repercussions of their own, should they participate. Opponents as influential as RKO's Howard Hughes and Californian Congressman Donald Jackson labeled the film as anti-American propaganda and broadened the call to stop its production. The fact that a crew was assembled and even did so by breaking with certain industry Jim Crowisms only added to the importance that the film has garnered over the years. Lead actress Revueltas even had a run-in with immigration and was deported and blacklisted from the United States. Her remaining scenes and emotional narration had to be completed in Mexico, away from Biberman and the principal production, with film being smuggled back and forth across the border. Revueltas, who was one of the few trained actors in the film, and a successful one, eventually found her career somewhat stifled because of the film, finding only occasional work after Salt of the Earth, such as a short stint in Berlin as part of Bertolt Brecht's company.

Completed in 1954, Salt of the Earth became an enigma of sorts, as initial exhibition was, at best, sparse. The film did manage to run in a few metropolitan areas, such as Los Angeles and New York, but even those were cut short due to continued pressure on the theaters, this time including projectionist unions. In some regard the conservatives appeared to have won: although they were unable to stop the film entirely, they were certainly able to suppress the film from the majority of the 1950s audience. It wasn't until many years later, when politically active students rediscovered the film and recognized the ongoing relevance of not only the struggle depicted onscreen but the one that occurred in bringing the story to the screen, that the film finally received the widespread exhibition it had always deserved. In 1969 the film began regular showings on university campuses around the United States, at times even accompanied by lectures from Biberman. The dissention resulting from the students' protests resembled all too closely that which was experienced by Biberman, and diegetically by the Quintero characters.

Aesthetically speaking, Salt of the Earth is a decent film, and one that requires no real concessions for any of its shortcomings. The majority of actors who worked on the film were not professionals, which Biberman acknowledges in the closing credits. Although the performances may come across as rudimentary, perhaps they compensate for the overtly picturesque cinematography, keeping the film somewhat grounded in realism, while the visuals maintain an aura of fantasy. Biberman's style is more that of classical Hollywood than a utilization of documentary conventions, providing more ambiguity in the film's message than the iconoclastic subversiveness of which the film was accused. As with many controversial entities, Salt of the Earth fails to deliver in the way of sensationalism, but its political and social relevance will continue to be recognized for generations to come.

DINO EVERETT

Salt of the Earth (US, Independent Productions Corporation, 1954, 94 mins). Distributed by Independent Productions Corporation. Produced by Paul Jarrico, Adolfo Barela, and Sonja Dahl Biberman. Directed by Herbert J. Biberman. Written by Michael Wilson, additional writing by Michael Biberman. Cinematography by Stanley Meredith and Leonard Stark. Music by Sol Kaplan. Edited by Joan Laird and Ed Spiegel. Filmed in Grant County, New Mexico, and parts of Mexico.

Further reading

Kael, Pauline, 'Morality Plays Right and Left', *Sight and Sound* 24, no. 2, October/December 1954: 67–73.

Lorence, James J., *The Suppression of Salt of the Earth*, Albuquerque: The University of New Mexico Press, 1999.
Miller, Tom, 'Salt of the Earth Revisited', *Cineaste* XIII, no. 3, 1984: 31–6.
Ross, Steven J., *Working Class Hollywood*, Princeton, NJ: Princeton University Press, 1998.
Trumbo, Dalton, *The Time of the Toad: A Study of Inquisition in America*, New York: Harper & Row, 1972.
Wilson, Michael and Silverton Rosenfelt, Deborah, *Salt of the Earth*, Old Westbury, NY: The Feminist Press, 1978.

Sander, Helke

Helke Sander belongs to the first generation of political filmmakers who emerged from the leftist milieu of the 1960s in Germany. Widely labeled as the 'The New German Film', this movement had ultimately withdrawn from the misguided development of postwar German cinema with the conception of the *Oberhausener Manifest*, a pamphlet published in 1962 by a collective of twenty-six filmmakers (among them Alexander Kluge and Edgar Reitz). The declaration constituted a clear breach with the commodities and conventions of the films produced within the German industry after World War II, a quixotic mixture of kitschy *Heimatfilms* and artless comedies.

As a matter of principle, Helke Sander—as well as her contemporaries Ulrike Öttinger, Helma Sanders-Brahms, and Margarethe von Trotta—must be seen in the context of this so-called German New Wave, although Sander soon opposed the authoritative position of her male colleagues, criticizing that their manifesto had not accounted for one single female opinion. Her own films were a radical move away from the predominantly paternalistic practice of political filmmaking in the 1960s and 1970s, which culpably dismissed women as an active political subject. Returning from Finland in 1965 where she had directed a number of television and theater productions, Sander became one of the first female students who graduated from the newly founded Deutsche Film- und Fernsehakademie Berlin (DFFB).

Sander's notion of filmmaking as a political practice shaped not only the first generation of female filmmakers and media workers in Germany but also resonated in the steadily growing women's liberation movement of the early 1970s. Her claim for a radical shift of the social paradigm within German society corresponded with current debates about equal rights, abortion laws, and the economical status of women within the domestic work sphere. Films such as Brecht die Macht der Manipulateure/Break the Power of the Manipulators (1967/8), Eine Prämie für Irene/A Bonus for Irene (1971), and Die allseitig reduzierte Persönlichkeit—Redupers/The All-Sided Reduced Personality (1977) addressed a variety of social and political issues that directly affected women's everyday lives.

By the early 1970s Sander had realized that women's emancipation as societal subjects was likely to fail as long as the means of production remained distributed disproportionately. In November 1973 her conception of a collectively political practice culminated in the Internationale Frauenfilmseminar in Berlin, which established a network of female filmmakers from all over the world and entailed the foundation of the self-published journal *Frauen und Film*. However, Sander did not succeed in elaborating on a coherent practical framework of feminist filmmaking; rather, she provided a fundamental critique of the patriarchal control mechanisms in Western societies. Considering her inadequate labour conditions, it is no surprise that Sander never accomplished such a practical foundation of her work. Throughout her career many projects had collapsed due to resentments and a lack of funding, which left considerable gaps in her body of work.

Whether Helke Sander's complete work is divided into two categories—the fiction, or rather fictitious, film with biographical and historiographical elements and the classical documentary—one characteristic distinguishes all of her films: her treatment of content over form. Aesthetical issues were never a concern for her. Far from being ideological, Sander's films struggle with the disavowal of female subjectivity in a broader cultural sense and the difficulty of political articulation with a predominantly male terminology. Her 'fictitious' films of the 1960s and 1970s featured playful and ironic approaches to these structural problems and made her a key figure among feminist filmmakers in Germany. However, it was primarily the documentary, Befreier und Befreite (1991/2), a critical account of the war crimes of Russian soldiers towards German women during World War II, that finally put her name on the map of internationally acclaimed documentary filmmakers.

ANDREAS BUSCHE

Biography

Born in Berlin, Germany, January 31, 1937. Studied German Language/Literature and Psychology at the University of Helsinki, Finland 1960–2. Directed productions for Finnish Television 1964–5. Returned to Berlin 1965. Student at the Deutsche Film und Fernsehakademie Berlin 1966–9. Foundation of the women's collective 'Brot und Rosen' 1972. Coorganized the Internationale Frauenfilmseminar in Berlin 1973. One year later founded the journal *Frauen und Film*, published and edited by Sander until 1982. Teaching position at the School for Plastic Arts in Hamburg 1975. In 1992 her documentary film, Befreier und Befreite, caused controversy in the United States. Professorship at the School for Plastic Arts in Hamburg 1981–2001. 1989–93 codirector of the Bremer Institut Film/Fernsehen.

Selected films

1967–8 Brecht die Macht der Manipulateure: director, writer
1971 Eine Prämie für Irene: director, writer
1977 Die allseitig reduzierte Persönlichkeit: director, writer
1981 Der subjektive Faktor: producer, director, writer
1983 Der Beginn aller Schrecken ist Liebe: coproducer, director, writer
1989 Die Deutschen und ihre Männer: producer, director, writer
1992 Befreier und Befreite: coproducer, director, writer

Further reading

Elsaesser, Thomas, *New German Cinema—A History*, Basingstoke and New Brunswick, NJ: Macmillan/ Rutgers University Press, 1989.

Hansen, Miriam, 'Frauen und Film and Feminist Film Culture in West Germany', in Sandra Frieden, Richard W. McCormick, Vibeke R. Petersen, and Laurie Melissa Vegelsang (eds), *Gender and German Cinema: Feminist Interventions, Vol. 2*, Oxford: Providence, 1993.

Knight, Julia, *Women and the New German Cinema*, London and New York: Verso Books, 1992.

Mohrmann, Renate, *Die Frau mit der Kamera*, Munchen and Wien: Hanser Verlag, 1980.

Silverman, Kaja, *Helke Sander and the Will to Change*, *Discourse* 6, 1983.

Sang des bêtes, Le

(France, Franju, 1949)

Le Sang des bêtes/The Blood of the Beasts, the first of Georges Franju's documentaries, is among the most beautiful and upsetting of films: for Franju, the two attributes were inseparable. In interviews he observed that 'in my short films, when I could choose the subject, I was always drawn to themes that I didn't want to touch because they frightened me', and that he had chosen to make a film about slaughterhouses 'because I love animals' (Milne 1975). No film before or after Le Sang des bêtes has administered such concentrated doses of pity and terror; yet in defiance of Aristotle's canons of tragedy, Franju offers the viewer no catharsis. Shifting abruptly from surrealist disorientation to misty lyricism to matter-of-fact horrors so extreme as to elicit laughter, Le Sang des bêtes is both indelible and utterly resistant to interpretation. Franju's most famous short film, it is also, at moments, almost unwatchable: a contradiction emblematic of its director's conflicted relationship to documentary.

According to Franju, the subject came first: 'I never wanted to be a filmmaker at all [...] I wanted to investigate a particular subject' (Levin 1971). Thirty-seven years old when Le Sang des bêtes was made, he had been involved with film for more than a decade as an archivist and administrator when the slaughterhouse idea came to him. For a first film, Le Sang des bêtes is extraordinarily accomplished, due in large part to Franju's astute choice of collaborators: the cinematographer Marcel Fradetal (who had worked on Dreyer's Vampyr), the composer Joseph Kosma (who had worked regularly with Renoir and Carné on such films as La Régle du jeu and Les Enfants du paradis), and Franju's colleague at the Institut de Cinématographie Scientifique, Jean Painlevé, maker of documentaries on vampire bats and sea urchins, among other creatures, and author of the voice-over commentary to Le Sang des bêtes.

With the exception of Painlevé, Franju's collaborators did not come from a documentary background, and this accounts (in part) for the film's disconcertingly elegant visual and aural textures, its likeness to the work of such directors as Lang and Murnau. For Franju, in documentary 'you endow what's natural with an aspect of the artificial [...] some of the skies that I waited for in Le Sang des bêtes seem almost to be studio skies' (Levin 1971). As with all his subsequent documentaries, Franju had scripted and planned the editing of Le Sang des bêtes before he began shooting. Yet far from allowing us to feel a comfortable aesthetic distance from the violence that the film depicts, Franju's careful deployment of artifice only brings the reality of the slaughterhouse more painfully, because more deliberately, to light—to light, that is, in a literal as well as a metaphorical sense. Franju later explained that 'the choice of the month of November for shooting the interiors was dictated by the fact that at this season of the year the animals are slaughtered by electric light, and the blood steaming in the glacial cold of the scalding bays allowed us, despite all the technical problems, to compose our images' (Durgnat 1967). The animals' blood becomes, perhaps cruelly, an aesthetic means, but a means for revealing, precisely, the horror of bloodshed.

One could describe Le Sang des bêtes as a work composed of a prologue and four movements or episodes, followed by a coda. In the prologue, which Gabriel Vialle has called a 'surrealist overture' (Vialle 1968), we are shown a series of views, from panoramic shots to extreme close-ups, of a wasteland on the outskirts of Paris with scattered high-rises, a bare tree and, incongruously, bits of a flea market: a chandelier hanging from a branch, a man sitting alone at a huge Louis XV table, and, juxtaposed in one shot, a nude armless female mannequin, a phonograph horn, and the line of a train in the distance cutting across the screen. A young woman's voice describes the scene in a lyrical voice-over; a young couple kiss; and Franju cuts to an off-kilter medium shot of a train and a slagheap. The voice-over resumes: at the Porte of Vanves, there are also the abattoirs of Vaugirard; these specialize in the slaughter of horses. A man's voice now takes over, enumerating the different tools of the abattoir as we see a close-up of a hand picking up each in turn: poleaxes, spikes, stun guns. A white horse is led up to the slaughterhouse door. The first movement, then, shows the slaughter of horses; the second, of cattle (another white beast); the third, of calves for veal (whiteness again: 'for the white meat of veal, total blood drainage by decapitation is necessary'); the fourth, of sheep.

The voice-over names each new location, introduces some of the men who work there, and describes the procedures in a scrupulously neutral tone. No outrage is voiced. It is the film's aesthetic composure, in fact, that imprints the horror it reveals so indelibly. Franju does not overwhelm us with gore or use cinematic shock tactics (amplified animal cries, fast cutting, extreme close-ups, weird angles) to augment the violence. Rather, the film's visual style—the diffuse light registered in carefully modulated greys, the use of mainly medium and long shots at eye level, the lucid but unemphatic mise-en-scène—is designed not to hector but to let us see. This is why all the reassuring interpretative claims made for Le Sang des bêtes—the idea, for example, that as we watch, 'a sense of reconciliation floods the screen' (Milne 1980); the idea that the film condemns animal slaughter; the idea that it doesn't condemn animal slaughter; the idea that slaughter stands allegorically for the Holocaust—ring so false. Simply by looking, Franju uncovers the insolite, the strange, in the everyday. A long shot of twelve headless sheep lying on a conveyor belt, their legs still kicking, looks like a dance number out of Busby Berkeley; another shot of six pure white, flayed veal carcasses laid out on six workstands, a mist rising off them, evokes nineteenth-century spirit photographs. Such moments of violence are, in Franju's phrase, 'lyrical explosions' that shock us into seeing, but Le Sang des bêtes does not make our judgments for us.

HAL GLADFELDER

See also: Franju, Georges

Le Sang des bêtes/The Blood of the Beasts (France, 1949, 22 mins). Directed by Georges Franju. Assistant directed by André Joseph and Julien Bonardier. Script by Georges Franju. Commentary by Jean Painlevé, spoken by Nicole Ladmiral and Georges Hubert. Cinematography by Marcel Fradetal, assisted by Henri Champion. Edited by André Joseph. Music by Joseph Kosma. Sound by Raymond Verchére. Produced by Forces et Voix de France.

Further reading

Durgnat, Raymond, *Franju*, London: Studio Vista, 1967.

Franju, Georges, 'Le Sang des bêtes', shooting script, *L'Avant-Scéne du Cinéma* 41, 1964: 46–50.

Levin, G. Roy, 'Georges Franju', in *Documentary Explorations: 15 Interviews with Film-makers*, Garden City, NY: Anchor Press, 1971: 117–29.

Milne, Tom, 'Georges Franju: The Haunted Void', interview, *Sight and Sound* 44, no. 2, 1975: 68–71.

——'Georges Franju', in Richard Roud (ed.), *Cinema: A Critical Dictionary*, New York: Viking, 1980: 387–93.

Sloniowski, Jeannette, '"It Was an Atrocious Film": Georges Franju's Blood of the Beasts', in Barry Keith Grant and Jeannette Sloniowski (eds), *Documenting the Documentary: Close Readings of Documentary Film and Video*, Detroit, MI: Wayne State University Press, 1998.

Vialle, Gabriel, *Georges Franju*, Paris: Editions Seghers, 1968.

Sans Soleil

(France, Marker, 1982)

Like many of his other films, Chris Marker's Sans Soleil/Sunless might be described as an imaginary documentary made of real documents—or is it, as the voice that narrates the film repeatedly asks, the other way around? As a work that continually calls into question the status and significance of its own representations, Sans Soleil has been classified as 'an instance of postmodernism' (Branigan 1992), but its closest affinity may rather be with a work like Laurence Sterne's *Tristram Shandy*, written over two hundred years earlier. Like Sterne's novel, Marker's film is an invented autobiography of often breathtaking digressiveness, complexity, poignancy, and wit, which unfolds not according to a linear chronology or argument but across a network of associations, echoes, and resemblances—both a meditation on history and memory and a disenchanted interrogation of its own form.

Marker has described the 'story' of Sans Soleil in these terms:

> An unknown woman reads and comments upon the letters she receives from a friend—a freelance cameraman who travels around the world and is particularly attached to those 'two extreme poles of survival'—Japan and Africa, represented here by two of its poorest and most forgotten countries, even though they played an historical role: Guinea-Bissau and the Cape Verde Islands. The cameraman wonders (as cameramen do, at least those you see in movies) about the meaning of this representation of the world in which he is the instrument, and about the role of memory he helps to create. A Japanese pal of his, who clearly has some bats in the belfry (Japanese bats, in the form of electrons) gives his answer by attacking the images of memory, by breaking them up on the synthesizer. A filmmaker grabs hold of this situation and makes a fiction of it, but rather than present the characters and show their relationships, real or supposed, he prefers to put forward the elements of the dossier in the fashion of a musical composition, with recurrent themes, counterpoints, and mirror-like fugues: the letters, the comments, the images gathered, the images created, together with some images borrowed. In this way, out of these juxtaposed memories is born a fictional memory.
>
> (Marker 1983)

The narrative structure that Marker outlines here is like that of another film he made twenty-five years before, Letter from Siberia (1957), the opening voice-over of which—'Je vous écris d'un pays lointain' ('I'm writing to you from a far-away country')—could stand as the epigraph to his whole career as a filmmaker. As with others of Marker's works, it is unclear where collaboration ends and mythomania begins. According to an end credit, 'Sandor Krasna's letters were read by Alexandra Stewart' (Florence Delay in the French version), but Sandor Krasna, the cameraman, seems to be a fictional surrogate for Marker himself, notwithstanding the straight-faced biography included in the film's publicity material; certainly his letters are unmistakably Markerian in their language, their obsessions, their speculative improvisations on the themes of memory and time. In which case Sandor's brother, Michel Krasna, credited with the film's electronic sound, is presumably yet another of the filmmaker's fictional personae. The 'Japanese pal', Hayao Yamaneko, credited with the synthesized manipulation of the cameraman's images—a key element in the film's provocatively antirealistic visual texture—is perhaps real, but in fact the very uncertainty that Marker creates by listing elusive, untraceable collaborators as coauthors of this intensely personal film is precisely the point: personal identity is rooted in memory narratives that are unstable, impersonal, and endlessly vulnerable to manipulation and decay.

Sans Soleil is typical of Marker's work in the prominence—indeed, the shaping role—of its voice-over commentary. Although there are certainly visual continuities created through the recurrence and transformation of certain motifs (cats, emus, dreaming passengers on ferries and trains, neighborhood festivals, political demonstrations, video games, women in a marketplace), it is the commentary that links the disparate elements of the film together and articulates its principal themes. In part, this could be seen as a response to the practical problem of assembling a single coherent film out of footage accumulated over fifteen or more years from extremely far-flung locales: Iceland, Japan, Guinea-Bissau and Cape Verde, Île-de-France, the Netherlands, Okinawa, San Francisco, the island of Sal, and perhaps others. Of course, this 'problem' was of Marker's own invention. There was no outward necessity to bring these particular materials together, so the decision to do so through the device of a (partly) fictional commentary suggests that the film's real subject is disparateness itself, the myriad forms of temporal, geographical, historical, and social distance that travel and all the varieties of information technology (not least, film itself), far from repairing, only multiply.

The juxtaposition of commentary, documentary image (much of the footage filmed vérité-style with handheld cameras), and electronic manipulations of both sound and image allows Marker to comment in passing on an extraordinary range of philosophical, political, and aesthetic issues. Those most directly relevant to the subject of documentary film involve the fraught relationship between images and different sorts of truth, the image as a repository of cultural and historical memory. Late in the film, half a world away from Japan, the speaker reads these words: 'I remember that month of January in Tokyo. Or rather I remember the images I filmed of the month of January in Tokyo. They have substituted themselves for my memory—they are my memory. I wonder how people remember things who don't film, don't photograph, don't tape'. In this passage, the writer both affirms the efficacy of the mechanically reproduced image in making memory possible and registers a sense of loss: he no longer has the capacity to remember within himself, independent of technological mediation. Perhaps he never had that capacity. If Marker seems sometimes to lament his and our dependence on mechanical forms of memory, at other moments—such as during his account of the revolutionary struggles in Guinea-Bissau that led to the overthrow of the Portuguese dictatorship—the documentary image enables memory to outlast or circumvent historical oblivion. By isolating and reflecting on the images out of which it is made, Sunless places itself in the same relation to documentary as *Tristram Shandy* occupies in relation to the novel: at once the most singular and, as Viktor Shklovsky contended, 'the most typical' of its kind.

HAL GLADFELDER

See also: Marker, Chris

Sans Soleil/Sunless (France, 1982, 100 mins). Distributed by Argos Films. Conception and editing by Chris Marker. Assistant direction by Pierre Camus. Editorial assistance by Anne-Marie L'Hôte and Catherine Adda. Commentary read by Alexandra Stewart (English version) and Florence Delay (French version). Electronic sound by Michel Krasna and Isao Tomita. Music by M. Moussorgski, J. Sibelius (treated by Isao Tomita); song by Arielle Dombasle. Sound mix by Antoine Bonfanti and Paul Bertault. Special effects by Hayao Yamaneko. Film extracts from Sana na N'hada (Carnival in Bissau), Jean-Michel Humeau (Ranks ceremony), Mario Marret and Eugenio Bentivoglio (Guerilla in Bissau), Danié le Tessier (Death of a Giraffe), and Haroun Tazieff (Iceland 1970). Still photography by Martin Boschet and Roger Grange.

Further reading

Branigan, Edward, *Narrative Comprehension and Film*, London: Routledge, 1992.

Casebier, Allan, 'A Deconstructive Documentary', *Journal of Film and Video* 40, no. 1, 1988: 34–9.

Howe, Susan, 'Sorting Facts; or, Nineteen Ways of Looking at Marker', in Charles Warren (ed.), *Beyond Document: Essays on Nonfiction Film*, Hanover, NH: Wesleyan University Press, 1996: 295–343.

Lopate, Philip, 'In Search of the Centaur: The Essay Film', in Charles Warren (ed.), *Beyond Document: Essays on Nonfiction Film*, Hanover, NH: Wesleyan University Press, 1996: 243–70.
Marchessault, Janine, 'Sans Soleil', *CineAction!* 5, 1986: 2–6.
Marker, Chris, unpublished publicity material for *New Yorker Films* press kit for the American release of Sunless/Sans Soleil, 1983, from Pacific Film Archives (Berkeley, CA) CineFiles website, www.mip.Berkeley.edu/cinefiles
——'Sunless', *Semiotext(e)* 4, no. 3, 1984: 33–40.
Rafferty, Terrence, 'Marker Changes Trains', *Sight and Sound* 53, no. 4, 1984: 284–8.
Russell, Catherine, *Experimental Ethnography: The Work of Film in the Age of Video*, Durham, NC: Duke University Press, 1999.
Walsh, Michael, 'Around the World, Across All Frontiers: Sans Soleil as Dépays', *CineAction!* 18, 1989: 29–36.

Sauvage, André

André Sauvage (1891–1975) was one of the most talented filmmakers to emerge in Paris during the 1920s. He figures among the small group of avant-garde cinematographers who were passionate about this new form of expression and who actively explored the medium's formal and social potential. Film historians qualify the short period of European cinema between 1927 and 1933 as the 'nouvelle vague documentaire' (the documentary New Wave of 1928), which ensured the transition between silent and sound film. That brief period was the most important time for André Sauvage's 'poetic modernist documentary films' (Aitken 2001).

The 1920s were years of exciting developments in documentary film. The camera, ever more mobile, was a part of the renewed discovery the world, near or far. The profound human quality of Nanook of the North (Robert Flaherty, 1923), the Swedish avant-garde interest in nature as an autonomous film subject, and the dynamism of the formal experimentation of the Soviet montage techniques captured the imagination of a generation. Human adventure, the perpetual motion of people in time and space and the technological challenges of his time became André Sauvage's major cinematographic themes. The loose narrative structure of his films, combined with his mastery of film technique and careful imagery, transformed his work into visual poetry. This is especially true of his films on Paris and Greece. He often worked alone (shooting and editing) with limited funding and equipment, or with very small crews. He created his own production company, Les Films André Sauvage, more to suit his independent personality than as a venue for his commercial abilities.

André Sauvage turned his camera on mountain climbers (La Traversée du Grépon, 1923); on the urban environment as the ideal microcosm of modernity and on ordinary Parisians working and strolling in their city (Études sur Paris, 1927); on Greece past and present, deftly depicting the archeological sites, the fishing villages, country roads, and peasants (Portrait de la Gréce, 1927); on his own children playing in the garden of his house (Rue du Pré-aux-Clercs (les Sauvages), 1930); and on the trying but extraordinary car expedition across Central Asia between Beirut and Peking (La croisière jaune/ The Yellow Cruise, 1934). André Sauvage did not like to categorize film in genres. Ghali wrote that Sauvage may have been afraid of marginalizing documentary films, whereas his artistic aims were to couple truth and reality without excluding imagination. This is what is implied in the expression 'creative documentary' (Jeancolas 1989).

His best-known films are the series of five short cinematographic studies on Paris, Études sur Paris (1928), an evocative urban journey through the diverse activities of the city, quietly observed using subdued lighting: Nord-Sud; Paris-Port; Petite Ceinture; Les Îles de Paris; and De la Tour Saint-Jacques à la Montagne Sainte-Geneviéve. They reflect his intimate knowledge of the city's rhythms and his fascination with movement. He introduced impressionist and sometimes mysterious images of the less well-known parts of Paris, such as the barges slowly passing through the underground section of the Canal Saint-Martin. Some shots take the viewer out to the city's limits, along the old line of fortification, where the rag-pickers in La Zone: Au pays des chiffonniers/The Zone: In the Country of the Ragmen lived and toiled (Georges Lacombe, 1928), or recall sequences of other city films such as Walther Ruttmann's Berlin: Die Sinfonie der Großstadt/Berlin: The Symphony of a Great City (1927).

The 1931–2 film work for La croisière jaune confirmed his talent. This feature-length documentary film was financed by the French car manufacturer André Citroën to display Sauvage's versatile half-tracks. André Sauvage disavowed the film that premiered in March 1934, much delayed by serious postproduction problems and the sponsor's decision to seize the film stock and hire another filmmaker, Léon Poirier, to do the final cut. Sauvage believed that the editing, the music score, and the commentary had destroyed his film beyond recognition; however, enough of the extraordinary images remain of men and machines progressing through magnificent scenery, combined with his mastery of light, his empathy towards ordinary people—local guides and carriers recruited along the way between Persia and China—who made the adventure possible. There are also segments of direct sound—traditional music or brief conversations and messages—recorded by pioneering sound technician Robert William Sivel.

André Sauvage had a keen eye, a sensitive approach to his subjects, and a wonderful sense of humor. In what is left of his films, his empathy is expressed in his choice of characters and how he discreetly captured the social contrasts of his time, whether he was filming workers in Paris or servants in British India. During the Citroën expedition he did not shy away from filming the political violence inflicted on the Chinese people by warlords, as their country moved toward disintegration. In his cinematography he combined the eye of the painter with the eye of the social observer. At the age of forty-three, disgusted by the takeover of his film material of the Central Asia expedition—which, according to Philippe Esnault, amounted to one hundred and fifty thousand metres of negatives, positives, images, and sounds—André Sauvage abandoned filmmaking altogether.

SUZANNE LANGLOIS

Biography

Born July 1891 to a middle-class merchant family from the Bordeaux region in southwestern France. Upon his father's death, he quit his graduate studies and in 1917 went to Paris. There, he met a group of young writers and poets and was attracted to artistic work. He began to write, but soon became more interested in painting, before being seduced by film. Sauvage started a career in filmmaking in the early 1920s, but ended it abruptly in 1934, following the sad ending of the croisière jaune expedition. Although he lived to eighty-four years of age, he never returned to filmmaking, preferring farming and painting.

Selected films

1923 La Traversée du Grépon: director
1927 Portrait de la Gréce: director, producer
1928 Études sur Paris: Nord-Sud; Paris-Port; Petite Ceinture; Les Îles de Paris; De la Tour Saint-Jacques à la Montagne Sainte-Geneviéve: director, editor, producer
1930 Rue du Pré-aux-Clercs (les Sauvages): director, producer
1934 La croisière jaune: cinematographer

Further reading

Abel, Richard, *French Cinema: The First Wave 1915–29*, Princeton, NJ: Princeton University Press, 1984.

Aitken, Ian, *European Film Theory and Cinema. A Critical Introduction*, Bloomington, IN: Indiana University Press, 2001.

Albera, François and Gili, Jean A. (eds), 'Dictionnaire du cinéma français des années vingt', *1895 Revue de l'Association française de recherche sur l'histoire du cinéma* 33, June 2001.

De Comes, Philippe and Marmin, Michel (eds), *Le cinéma français 1930–60*, Paris: Editions Atlas, 1984.

Esnault, Philippe, 'André Sauvage, cinéaste maudit', *La Revue du cinéma* 394, May 1984: 92–4.

Gauthier, Guy, *Le Documentaire. Un autre cinéma*, Paris: Nathan/VUEF, 2003.

Ghali, Noureddine, *L'Avant-garde cinématographique en France dans les années vingt*, Paris: Editions Paris Expérimental, 1995.

Jeancolas, Jean-Pierre, 'N.V.D. 28, appel à témoins', in *100 Années Lumière*, Paris: AFAA Intermedia, 1989: 20–7.

Scandinavia

In Scandinavia, the documentary film is highly respected, and documentaries are popular on television and at the cinemas. They play an important role in public debates, and state funding supports the production of shorts and feature-length documentaries. Recently there have been two documentaries with successful commercial releases in the theatres: Heftig og begeistret/Cool and Crazy (2001), about a male choir in a small fishing village in the northern part of the country, and Alt om min far/All about My Father (2002), about a family dealing with a father who is a transvestite. In Sweden and Denmark, important directors such as Stefan Jarl, Eric M. Nilsson, Peå Holmquist, Lennart Nilsson, Jørgen Leth, Jon Bang Carlsen, Sami Saif, and Anne Wivel produce groundbreaking films.

Local actualities were produced in Scandinavia by the late 1890s, and out of the most popular types two documentary genres evolved in the 1920s: the travelogue and the 'nation-film'. The most popular early documentary genre in Scandinavia was the travelogue, and especially the expedition film. In Sweden, directors such as Prince Wilhelm and Oscar Olsson traveled to Africa, and the exotic Bland vildar och vilda djur/Among Savages and Wild Animals (1921) became a huge success. In Denmark and Norway, the camera expeditions looked mostly to colder territories. Knud Rasmussen and Roald Amundsen always made films as a part of their expeditions. The four feature-length documentaries Amundsen's cameramen made in the 1920s were very popular in Scandinavia, and even made an international impact. Unlike a film such as Nanook of the North, the documentaries produced by Amundsen employed a more 'primitive' view and aesthetic quality, resembling a series of magnificent slides, but always looking at the foreign cultures from outside. These expedition films were often marked by a nationalistic pathos, especially when exploring unknown territories.

Scandinavian filmmakers also explored their own countries, in a genre called 'nation-films'. In Sweden, the director Ragnar Ring produced different types of documentaries for the industry or for tourist promotion. In 1924 he made a feature-length film about Sweden, Sverige, vårt vackra land/Sweden, Our Beautiful Country. With this film a new genre was born, and after Ring's poetic homage to his country, several long documentaries were made that explored both countryside and cities. These films were very popular, since most people did not have the means or opportunities to travel, even in their own country. Some of these films from Norway and Sweden were also intended for the population of Scandinavians in the United States—for example, Se Norge/Norway Today by Gustav Lund in 1924. This genre remained popular in the early 1930s, and Norge, vårt Norge—i toner og billeder/Our Norway, in Music and Pictures by Lyder Selvig also became a success in Sweden in 1930.

While the Swedish and Norwegian 'nation-films' were tourist-like and idyllic in their images of their countries, some of the Danish films were more critical, and employed a degree of social commentary. The film Danmark/Denmark (1935), made by the Danish architect and writer Poul Henningsen, was heavily criticized in Denmark. This film has a more poetic form, and marks the beginning of a more ambitious documentary tradition in Scandinavia, both in terms of style and social criticism.

Documentaries in Scandinavia both before and after World War II were seldom concerned with social issues. Another important genre that was popular especially in Sweden and Norway was the nature and wildlife film. The Swedish director Bengt Berg's films about wild birds were popular in the early 1920s, and in Norway the director Per Høst made his first long documentaries in the late 1930s.

In Sweden, Stig Wesslén and Arne Sucksdorff are the most important names in documentary film. Wesslén's wildlife films often use the annual cycle as a way in which to organize his filmic observations of wildlife. A film such as I lapplandsbjörnens rike/The Realm of the Lapp-Bear (1940) depicts a wealth of animal life, but also makes points about the importance of defending the country. Arne Sucksdorff is one of the biggest names in Scandinavian documentary history, and his wildlife films were international hits. He started out making shorts, depicting nature and animals in the films En Sommarsaga/A Summer Saga (1940) and Trut!/Seagull! (1944), but also the city symphony, as in Människor i Stad/City People (1947). Sucksdorff often criticized civilization, but he was himself often criticized for using tame animals and having an anthropomorphic perspective on animals. This is clear in his first feature-length documentary, Det stora Åventyret/The Big Adventure (1953), in which animals sometimes seemingly think and act like people.

Like many other wildlife filmmakers, Sucksdorff turned to a more ethnographic perspective in the late 1950s. His next feature, En Djungelsaga/A Jungle Saga (1957), was a portrait of the Muria tribe in India. In his last features, Pojkeni trädet/The Boy in the Tree (1961) and Mitt hem är Copacabana/My Home is Copacabana (1965), he presents fully realized portraits of young people who are alienated by society. His social consciousness is important, and in the 1960s he became the mentor of Stefan Jarl, the most important modern documentarist in Sweden.

Other documentarists in the 1950s turned from wildlife to ethnography. In Norway, the most popular documentary filmmaker was Per Høst. He was a zoologist, but turned to filmmaking, and produced a wealth of short films from the 1940s throughout the 1960s. His most famous film, Same Jakki/The Laplanders (1957), was an ethnographic study of the Lapps in northern Norway and their relationship to nature.

The most famous Scandinavian documentary film in the 1950s was Kon-Tiki, which won an Oscar in 1952. The film was a joint Swedish-Norwegian venture, produced by the Swedish company Artfilm and directed by Olle Nordemar, but based on the 16mm material that the archaeologist and adventurer Thor Heyerdahl filmed when he traveled from Peru to the Polynesian islands on a balsa raft in 1947. This expedition film gave the audience a new and sensuous feeling. The low quality of the filmic material helped convey a sensation of actually being on the raft, due to the fluid and trembling images. This was a new aspect of expedition or wildlife films in the 1950s. Films no longer merely presented the world, but tried to recreate the experience of being in the represented moment with the filmmaker.

The 1950s was a golden age for documentary film in Scandinavia. Short films accompanied most features, and a large number of feature-length documentaries were produced. The introduction of television to Denmark in 1954, Sweden in 1956, and Norway in 1960 brought this golden age of short films to a close. The newsreels disappeared and were replaced by television news. Both short films and full-length documentaries nearly disappeared from the screens during the 1960s. Many filmmakers got jobs in the national television organizations, making programs in the same genres as before—biographies, travelogues, portraits, and so on—but it became harder to produce documentaries outside of the television organizations, and even harder to produce documentaries not intended for television.

Some documentary filmmakers managed to produce short films. In Denmark, Theodor Christensen and Jørgen Roos are among the most important. Theodor Christensen met John Grierson in 1939. During and after the World War II he made several outstanding shorts, including Skoven/The Wood (1941) and Det gælder din frihed/It's about Your Freedom (1946), with Karl Roos. Like most other independent directors, Christensen made shorts for different government agencies, but he managed to turn out films that not only informed the citizens about issues, but he commented on these issues as well, often in an ironic way. Christensen also made important contributions to the documentary film in Denmark when he worked at the new State Film School in the 1960s.

In Norway, the director Erik Løchen had an equal position. He started the production company ABC-Film with friends, and this company produced over one hundred shorts over the course of twenty years. They made films for different government and municipal agencies, but were also pioneers in creating the 'free artistic short film'. Erik Løchen, and friends and colleagues Erik Borge and Carsten Munch, were tired of making purely informative films. They wanted most of all to make documentaries without voice-over, and succeeded in getting the government to support the production of more artistic and poetic meditations, the first being Nedfall/Fallout (1963) by Erik Borge. This film was a poetic impression of village life, but emphasized its vulnerability in the event of atomic fallout. Løchen made several influential modernist documentary shorts, the most famous being Søring Nordover/Southerner Going North (1976), on the differences between south and north Norway.

Many documentaries produced in Denmark after World War II were journalistic or informative in character, but there were also strong connections between the documentary filmmakers and the avant-garde movement. These connections were stronger than in Norway, and the director Jørgen Roos made some of the earliest experimental films in Denmark with Flugten/Flugten (1942), with Albert Mertz, and Spiste Horisonter/Eaten Horizons (1950). Jørgen Roos is one of the most important Danish documentary filmmakers, and his work is in some ways typical of the independent filmmakers in Scandinavia. Roos made many films—informative films as well as more artistic films—and one of the characteristic features of his work is the fact that he handles a broad spectrum of themes and genres. He has made portraits of famous people and cities, travelogues, and even a three-part film about documentary filmmaking in Denmark, Den levende virkelighed/The

Living Reality (1989). At the same time, he has made film-essays about bacon production, Den strømlinjede gris/The Streamlined Pig (1952), and noise, Støj/Noise (1965).

Few Scandinavian documentaries made before the late 1960s were overtly political or discussed social issues, but later in the decade this changed. Suddenly a new generation of filmmakers turned to the political documentary, using filmmaking as a weapon in the fight for radical societal changes. In Sweden, the novelist and painter Peter Weiss, another avant-garde artist turning to filmmaking, made the first controversial social documentaries with Ansikteni skugga/Faces in the Shadows (1956) and Enligt Lag/By Law (1957). These portraits of outcasts in the welfare society, made without the use of voice-over, marked the beginning of a new type of social documentary in Scandinavia, focused on attacking the wrongs perpetuated in and by the welfare society.

In the late 1960s and the early 1970s a wave of political radicalism swept through the arts in Scandinavia, leaving its mark on documentary film production. A new, angry generation of filmmakers emerged. Most important of these new filmmakers was the Swedish director Stefan Jarl. He helped to establish the organization Film-Centrum in 1968, which was an important base for the new radical filmmakers, but he is best known for his 'Mods Trilogy'—three full-length films that follow two members of Sweden's underclass, and their children, over several decades. The first two films, Dom kallar oss Mods/They Call Us Misfits (1968) and Ett Anständigt Liv/A Decent Life (1979), made an enormous impact on Scandinavian documentary film and society. The second film was shown in all schools in Sweden and Norway as part of a project to inform schoolchildren about the dangers of narcotics. Jarl's films are frightening, showing how the youngsters Kenta and Stoffe change from happy-go-lucky boys in opposition to bourgeois society, to drug addicts. Although often criticized for his methods, Jarl shows absolute solidarity with the boys. The death of Stoffe gives Ett Anständigt Liv a tragic dimension. In his third film, Det Sociala Arvet/The Social Heritage (1993), Jarl follows the children of Kenta and Stoffe, who, surprisingly, are relatively prosperous and successful. In this film Jarl includes himself to a larger degree, making a reflexive, even performative, auto-critique of his own film practice.

Stefan Jarl is mostly known for his angry social documentaries, which inspired many Scandinavian filmmakers, but also for his nature documentaries, particularly those dealing with Lapps. His film Hotet/The Threat (1987) dealt with Chernobyl's effect on the Lapps, and the short Jåvna, Renskötare år 2000/Jåvna: Reindeer Herdsman in the Year 2000 (1991) is a portrait of a young boy with a difficult future, squeezed between two cultures. He also made the angry ecological film Naturens Hämnd/The Revenge of Nature (1983) about the havoc wreaked by chemical fertilizers on agricultural cycles. Jarl's attention to detail, interest in regional cultures, and careful integration of the landscape makes him a cinematic poet, a true heir to Arne Sucksdorff.

The nature poet Sucksdorff has also been Jan Troell's inspiration. He switches successfully between documentary and fiction film, like many Scandinavian directors, and has made many short poetic documentaries. Troell is kinder and milder in his artistic temperament. His major documentary is the three-hour Sagolandet/Land of Dreams (1988), which is an essayistic reflection on life in a welfare society, where the state takes care of its citizens from birth to death.

In Denmark some radical films were made in the 1970s, attacking the smug bourgeoisie, but the most important director, Jørgen Leth, was an experimental modernist that kept a distance from any specific trend. He started out making stylistic and ironic commentaries on life and people in Denmark, with films such as Det Perfekte Menneske/The Perfect Man (1967) and Livet i Danmark/Life in Denmark (1971), but turned to making sport films and personal portraits or travelogues. Among his essayistic travel films are the highly original 66 scener fra Amerika/66 Scenes from America (1981) and Haiti—uden Titel/Haiti—Without Title (1996). His most famous films are his cycling documentaries, his full-length film about Giro d'Italia, Stjernerne og Vandbæreren/The Stars and the Water-Carriers (1973), and En Forårsdag i Helvede/Springtime in Hell (1976).

Norwegian documentary changed drastically in 1972, when the young filmmaker Oddvar Einarson first used documentary film to attack the government, focusing on the close connections between the Norwegian government and US businesses in Kampen om Mardøla/The Fight for Mardøla (1972). The film depicted the clash between environmentalists and the police, and Einarson used every means available to criticize or ridicule the government, resulting in a fierce debate in society.

The most important modern Norwegian documentary filmmaker, Sigve Endresen, is a typical representative of the generation of radical documentarists after Kampen om Mardøla, and he started working as a member of a student film collective making the short Aldri Mer!/Never Again! (1977)—a film about neo-Nazism. Like many other Scandinavian filmmakers, he was inspired by Stefan Jarl's films about youth and drugs, and his feature-length For Harde Livet/ For Your Life (1989) became a huge success. It depicted a treatment program for young drug addicts. Endresen and his team followed a group of young drug addicts for one-and-a-half years. The film has an open ending, and thus offers no traditional narrative closure. Endresen made a follow-up with Store gutter gråter ikke/Big Boys Don't Cry (1995), concentrating on a treatment program for young drug addicts in jail. Endresen's direct cinema-inspired approach has also been fruitful in his more recent works; Leve blant løver/Living among Lions (1998), a portrayal of a group of youths suffering from (and dying of) cancer, and Vektløs/Weightless (2002), about a female artist with an eating disorder.

The main representative of the socially concerned documentary in Norway today, besides Endresen, is Margreth Olin. Whether documenting daily life in a senior citizen's home in Dei mjuke hendene/In the House of Angels (1998) or discussing how Western society encourages women to develop negative body images in Kroppen min/My Body (2002), she makes courageous, personal, and important documentaries.

The personal approach is also an important feature in modern Danish and Swedish documentary. In Denmark, veteran master Jørgen Leth still makes personal portraits of artists, while another veteran, Jon Bang Carlsen, makes provocative self-reflexive documentaries. Sometimes he makes meta-films, such as How to Invent Reality (1996), or portraits, such as Addicted to Solitude (1999), a portrait of two white women living in an undeveloped and sparsely populated part of South Africa. Carlsen's approach has been criticized, since normally he first observes and then stages the entire film, even writing the lines for the characters who play themselves, but like the earlier Før gæsterne kommer/Before the Guests Arrive (1986), his sense of detail and ability to find beauty in any person makes him an important director. Among the younger directors, Sami Saif is one of the most important Danish talents. His Family (2001), about the director's search for his father, is a heart-warming and vulnerable, but still analytical, documentary.

In Sweden, Jarl and Troell still make important documentaries, and among the pioneers working with television documentaries one finds Lennart Nilsson, with his fabulous journeys through the human body, or the highly original essayist Eric M. Nilsson, who makes films about communication (or the lack thereof). Younger directors Kristian Petri, Peå Holmquist, and Susanna Edwards have also made important contributions to the genre.

Documentary filmmaking is important in Scandinavia. The public subsidizing of documentaries, both from film institutes and the 'cassette tax funds', as well as via public service television, guarantees high quality and independence. Factual entertainment and soap documentaries reach increasingly wider audiences on television in Scandinavia, but independently produced documentaries can still be controversial and angry, or essayistic and personal.

GUNNAR IVERSEN

See also: Bang Carlsen, Jon; Roos, Jørgen

Further reading

Birkvad, Søren, *Verden er Leth*, Odense: Odense Universitetsforlag, 1992.

Birkvad, Søren and Diesen, Jan Anders, *Autentiske Inntrykk*, Oslo: Samlaget, 1994.

Brinch, Sara and Iversen, Gunnar, *Virkelighetsbilder*, Oslo: Universitetsforlaget, 2001.

Edström, Mauritz, *Sucksdorff-främlingen i hemmaskogen*, Stockholm: Norstedts 1968.

Furhammar, Leif, *Filmen i Sverige*, Stockholm: Wiken,1991.

——*Med TV i verkligheten*, Stockholm: Etermedierna i Sverige, 1995.

Nilsson, Mats, *Rebell i verkligheten—Stefan Jarl och hans filmer*, Göteborg: Filmkonst, 1991.

Schadt, Thomas

Coming from a photography background, Thomas Schadt became one of the most active and respected German documentary filmmakers of his generation. He generally develops his projects, produces them with his own company, Odysee-Film, in Berlin, and then acts as cameraman, shooting the footage himself. However, Schadt also values the input of his team. He discusses his concepts and strategies in his courses at film schools and universities, and published two books in 2002 on these topics.

The structure of an image has tremendous importance for Schadt, and his goal is to capture the right moment, even if only by coincidence. He also favors strong personalities, displaying people with this characteristic prominently in his work. The camera and sound equipment, whether film or video, is determined based on the topic and the conditions of the production.

One of Schadt's first films was Das Gefühl des Augenblicks/Sensibility of the Moment (1989), in which he traced the career of the American photographer Robert Frank. An interview conducted with Frank, which did not go smoothly, communicated the value of authenticity and its importance for documentary. The same aesthetic is evident in Die vergessene Stadt/The Forgotten Town (1992), about the town Butte, Montana, which Schadt shot on 35mm film, for theatrical release.

Schadt gained recognition for his television works, such as Der Autobahnkrieg/War on the Highway (1991), about reckless driving on German highways, and Eiserne Engel/Iron Angels (1995), about medical rescue teams that use helicopters. He followed Gerhard Schröder on his campaign in 1998 and portrayed him again in 2001, and even Schadt got the impression that it was impossible to get close to the Chancellor of Germany. He also faced difficulties while filming Wall Street (1997) because it was difficult to gain access to some locations.

One of his most ambitious projects was Berlin: Sinfonie einer Großstadt/Berlin: Symphony of a City (2002), in which he built on Walter Ruttmann's classic Berlin: Die Sinfonie der Großstadt/Berlin: The Symphony of a Great City (1927) to shoot an actual portrayal of Berlin. He did not want to shoot a remake of the montage film, in which Ruttmann presented a futuristic vision of the metropolis, but rather chose to provide a new interpretation. Schadt appropriated the symphonic concept, the aesthetic of black-and-white photography in 35mm, and the narrative structure in his portrayal of the city from early morning to midnight. His images are supported by modern music composed by Helmut Oehring and Iris ter Schiphorst. Over the course of one year, Schadt and his assistant, Thomas Keller, filmed throughout Berlin, capturing typical moments that reflect Berlin today and its history over the last seventy-five years, since the premiere of Ruttmann's film. They developed a highly abstract concept for the camera movements, which depend on the time of day being filmed. Stills from the film prove the photographic talents of Thomas Schadt.

KAY HOFFMANN

Biography

Born 1957 in Nuremberg, Germany. After a high school apprenticeship as a photographer, worked as projectionist, camera assistant, and theater photographer. From 1980 to 1983 studied at the Film and TV Academy (DFFB) in Berlin. Founded his own production company, Odysse-Film, in 1983. Since 1991 has taught at film schools and universities. Professor of documentary film at the film academy Baden-Wuerttemberg in Ludwigsburg since 2000. Cofounded the documentary initiative Der Zweite Blick (The Second View) in 2001.

Selected films

1982 Was hab I in Hawaii verloren: director, camera, producer
1983 Für die Ewigkeit: director, camera, producer
1986 Unterwegs nach immer und überall: director, camera, producer
1989 Das Gefühl des Augenblicks: director, camera, producer
1989 Trash-Altenessen: director, camera, producer
1990 Das Magazin der Bilder: director, camera, producer
1991 Der Autobahnkrieg: director, camera, producer
1992 Die vergessene Stadt: director, camera, producer
1993 Elf Freunde müst ihr sein: director, camera, producer
1994 Mordkommission M I/4: director, camera, producer
1995 Eiserne Engel: director, camera, producer
1996 Herr W und Herr W: director, camera, producer (together with Gerd Hoffmeister)

1997 Wall Street: director, camera, producer
1997 Manhattan Stories: director, camera, producer
1998 Augenzeugen: director, camera, producer (together with Reiner Holzemer)
1998 Leben ohne Arbeit: director, camera, producer (together with Peter Schmidt)
1998 Der Kandidat: director, camera, producer
1999 Haupstadtzeitung: director, camera, producer
2000 Demokratie im Schloss: director, camera, producer (together with Peter Schmidt)
2001 My Way—James Last: director, camera, producer
2001 Kanzlerbilder: director, camera, producer
2001 Straße des ewigen Friedens: director, camera, producer
2002 Berlin: Sinfonie einer Großstadt: director, writer, camera, coproducer
2002 Doppelleben: director, camera, coproducer

Further reading

Fuhr, Eckhard, 'Berlin zum Kuscheln', *Die Welt* 12, no. 4, 2002.

Gottstein, Björn, 'Die Stadt ohne Eigenschaft', *Die Tageszeitung* 12, no. 4, 2002.

Menden, Alexander, 'Leistungssport. Haupstadt-Filmmusik live: "Berlin: Sinfonie einer Großstadt"', *Süddeutsche Zeitung* 12, no. 4, 2002.

Schadt, Thomas, *Das Gefühl des Augenblicks—Zur Dramaturgie des Dokumentarfilms*, Bergisch-Gladbach: Bastei-Lübbe, 2002.

——*Berlin: Sinfonie einer Großstadt*, Berlin: Nicolai, 2002.

Schlesinger, John

John Richard Schlesinger attended Balliol College, Oxford, where he first became seriously involved with acting and filmmaking. During his student days he acted with the Oxford University Dramatic Society, served as president of the local Experimental Theatre Club, and produced his first short film, Black Legend (1948).

In 1957 he joined BBC TV as a second unit director and piloted several episodes of The Valiant Years about Winston Churchill and short topical and arts features for Tonight and Monitor under Huw Wheldon, winning an Edinburgh Festival prize for The Innocent Eye (1959). Although recent BBC administrations have usually sought to buy in programmes from freelance production companies, in the 1950s current affairs shows such as Monitor were known for nurturing a diverse range of filmmakers. Subsequently, Schlesinger directed pieces on the Cannes Film Festival, Italian opera, and comparative studies of painters.

Out of this experience, which served as a sound technical foundation for his later work, Schlesinger was offered a thirty-minute piece by the veteran documentary maker Edgar Anstey. The British Transport Films-sponsored documentary Terminus (1961) became the celebrated culmination of his series of BBC TV documentaries. Set at Waterloo station, in Schlesinger's hands it became far more than a mere observation piece: substories formed, vanished, and reappeared displaying elements of social realism that foreshadowed his subsequent work. Utilising many different perspectives—close-ups, long shots, and high and low angles—Schlesinger chose on-location sound over narration to show how democratising train travel was. A poignant story of a little boy lost, handcuffed convicts being taken to Dartmoor, discarded flowers meant for an arrival who did not show—these were just some of the many vignettes of everyday life that made up Schlesinger's cinéma vérité portrait of a London railway station. His Terminus won Schlesinger a Golden Lion award at the Venice Film Festival and a British Academy award for Best Short Film.

Schlesinger directed some two dozen documentaries on a vast range of subjects, but he was perhaps best known for his fiction movies, such as Midnight Cowboy (1969), for which he won an Academy Award for Best Director, despite the film having an X rating. Schlesinger's oeuvre was characterised by a lifelong preoccupation with gender relations, particularly homosexuality; an interest in analysing and representing subcultures, minorities, and other discriminated social groups; a relatively intellectual, middle-class outlook; and a commitment to filmmaking as entertainment rather than politics. Schlesinger also directed theatre and opera and in 1970 he was made CBE (Commander of the British Empire).

D. BRUNO STARRS

Biography

Born February 16, 1926, in London. Attended Balliol College, Oxford. After serving in the army in World War II in England and the Far East, studied English Literature and graduated from Oxford in 1950. Produced his first short film, Black Legend, as a student in 1948. Suffered a stroke in 2000 from which he never fully recovered, and died on July 25, 2003, with his companion of many years, the photographer Michael Childers, at his side.

Selected films

1948 Black Legend
1959 The Innocent Eye
1961 Terminus
1969 Midnight Cowboy

Further reading

BBC Education, *Face to Face: John Schlesinger in Conversation with Jeremy Isaacs*, broadcast February 3, 1993, www.bbc.co.ulc/education/lzone/movie/schles.htm (accessed May17, 2004).

BBC News, *BAFTA to Honour Schlesinger*, broadcast April 26, 2002, news.bbc.co.uk/1/hi/entertainment/film/1953423.stm (accessed 17 May 2004).

——*Your Tributes to John Schlesinger*, broadcast July 29, 2003, news.bbc.co.uk/1/hi/talking_point/3095415.stm (accessed 17 May 2004).

Brooker, Nancy J., *John Schlesinger: A Guide to References and Resources*, Boston: G.K. Hall, 1978.

Davidson, Ewan, 'Terminus (1961)', *Screenonline*, British Film Institute, 2003, www.screenonline.org.uk/film.id.520921 (accessed 17 May 2004).

Phillips, Gene D., *John Schlesinger*, Boston: Twayne, 1981.

Schoedsack, Ernest B.

Ernest Beaumont Schoedsack is best known for bringing a touch of the grand spectacle to the documentary form in the wake of Robert Flaherty's Nanook of the North (1922), but his films Grass: A Nation's Battle for Life (1925) and Chang: A Drama of the Wilderness (1927) did more than merely capitalize on Nanook's unprecedented success. Made in collaboration with his partner, Merian C. Cooper, Schoedsack's travel adventures marked the height of the expeditionary genre. Curiously, neither film is mentioned in André Bazin's famous essay, 'Cinema and Exploration', although when Bazin discusses the emergence after World War I of what he calls 'travel-films-in-the-grand-manner'—such as Léon Poirier's colonial epic, La croisière noire (1926)—he is describing a genre that Cooper and Schoedsack helped to define (Bazin 1967). Just as John Ford was credited with the coming of the 'sur-western', Cooper and Schoedsack brought an added dimension to the documentary travelogue, imbuing the form with a heightened sense of scale and depth; Cooper himself would go on to produce some of Ford's best-known westerns.

Schoedsack's autobiographical accounts of his adventures leading up to the making of Grass border on the fantastic. He ran away from home aged fourteen, working with engineering road gangs and as a surveyor before starting work as a cameraman at the Mack Sennett Keystone Studios. During World War I he flew combat missions and acted as a photographer for the Army Signal Corps, specializing in images captured while under heavy fire. He sought action even after the Armistice, working as a Red Cross photographer and assisting Polish refugees during the Polish–Russian conflict. Schoedsack drove ambulances, rescued refugees from Russian oil fields, and filmed the destruction of the Dnieper Bridge as the Polish retreated from Kiev. In the midst of this period, in 1918, he first encountered Cooper—a recent prisoner of war—in a Viennese railroad station. In the ensuing years Schoedsack continued to eke out a living doing newsreel camerawork in Europe; in the meantime Cooper was shot down while flying missions for the Polish Army and spent time in a Moscow prison, from which he made a dramatic escape (Schoedsack 1983).

In 1923 Cooper contacted Schoedsack to join a photographic expedition ship in Djibouti and they traveled throughout the Middle East, spending a brief period with Haile Selassie in Addis Ababa. The two men's symbiotic relationship was defined from the start: Schoedsack was primarily an action photographer, whereas Cooper was an enthusiastic promoter and showman. They became determined to make a film about nomadic migrations in Iran and Iraq (then known as Persia and British-occupied Mesopotamia, respectively) because it promised the possibility of witnessing skirmishes between Kurds and their neighbors, a prospect they found 'alluring' (Schoedsack 1983). Cooper went to the United States to secure funds, returning with a budget of $10,000 and accompanied by the journalist Marguerite Harrison, who had assisted him in his escape from a Soviet prison. Attempting to economize with their limited film stock, they began in Turkey, shooting travelogue and newsreel footage.

Cooper and Harrison began filming the migration of Bakhtiari tribespeople in Persia in April of 1924. The three intended first to follow the tribe's journey from winter to summer grazing grounds, then to capture some intimate scenes of daily life between outward and return migrations, and finally to accompany the group on its journey back. Due to financial constraints, however, the film ended up chronicling a one-way journey, and would ultimately lack the personal details that the filmmakers intended. Barnouw criticizes the film for precisely this, noting that, unlike Flaherty's films, the tribespeople in Grass remain strangers, and 'no individual portrait emerges from them' (Barnouw 1983). In place of ethnographic detail, Grass sets up the theme of the documentary filmmaker as an adventurer/explorer, a figure who would reappear later in the barely disguised fictional character of Carl Denham, the showman-hero at the center of King Kong (1933). Like Denham, Cooper is referred to early on in Grass as the impresario behind the spectacle: the 'engineer who conceived the idea of recording the migration'.

Although for Schoedsack Grass would always remain a 'great lost opportunity', fragmented and rushed into completion for economic reasons, the film was successful enough to convince Jesse Lasky to fund a second expedition to Siam (now Thailand) to film Chang (Schoedsack 1983). Chang follows a more carefully scripted narrative than Grass, leading most critics to label it a 'semidocumentary'. It attempts to focus on the personal and domestic details that were absent in Grass, telling the story of a family living on the edge of the jungle and of their constant encounters with wild animals. It is the animals, and the photographers' heroic efforts to capture them on film, that quickly take center stage, and the film culminates with a dramatic elephant ('chang') stampede.

While the epic scale of Cooper and Schoedsack's early films set them apart from most documentary and travelogue work of the day, their talents were quickly (and, apparently, without their resistance) appropriated by Hollywood's increasing demand for fictional adventure films grounded in authentic locations. The Four Feathers (1929) was typical of this hybrid approach, with scenes shot in the Sudan interspersed with principal work done in a Hollywood studio. At the same time, directors such as W.S. Van Dyke were standardizing the practice of the exotic on-location shoot with films such as White Shadows in the South Seas (1928) and Trader Horn (1931).

Rango (1931), which takes place in Sumatra, saw Schoedsack's return to the wild animal adventure drama, but his live-action work was now primarily lending authenticity and immediacy to the mise-en-scène of fictional productions. In many ways King Kong was the next logical step in this migration from fact to fantasy, and is itself a kind of hybrid film: a fascinating and disturbing allegory of the will of the photographer-adventurer to capture spectacular ethnographic images, and of the public's insatiable demand for them. Cooper and Schoedsack would part ways in the 1930s, Cooper to concentrate on producing, while Schoedsack would continue directing, though he was partially blinded in an aviation accident in the 1940s. They joined forces once more for Mighty Joe Young (1949) and another spectacular experiment in actuality filmmaking, This is Cinerama (1952).

JEFFREY GEIGER

See also: Chang; Cooper, Merian C.; Grass

Biography

Born in Council Bluffs, Iowa, June 8, 1893. Worked on road gangs and as a surveyor, then as cameraman for the Mack Sennett Studios, early 1910s. Aviator and picture correspondent in US Signal Corps during World War I. Red Cross photographic unit and freelance cameraman in Europe 1918–22. Joined Merian C. Cooper on photographic correspondence tour 1923. Produced and directed Grass with Cooper and Marguerite Harrison 1924–5, distributed by Paramount. Made Chang with Cooper in Thailand, funded and released by Paramount in 1927. Married Ruth Rose, screenwriter 1926. Made a number of features with Cooper and/or Rose 1928–35, including King Kong. Thereafter worked as feature director in Hollywood. Received permanent eye injury while testing photographic equipment during World War II. Died December 23, 1979, in Los Angeles, California.

Selected films

1925 Grass (Grass: A Nation's Battle for Life/ Grass: The Epic of a Lost Tribe): codirector, coproducer, cophotographer
1927 Chang: codirector, coproducer
1929 The Four Feathers: coproducer, codirector
1931 Rango: director, producer
1932 The Most Dangerous Game (The Hounds of Zaroff): codirector, coproducer
1933 King Kong: codirector, coproducer
1952 This is Cinerama: codirector, prologue only

Further reading

Barnouw, Eric, *Documentary: A History of the Non-Fiction Film*, Oxford: Oxford University Press, 1983.
Bazin, André, *What is Cinema? volume 1*, ed. Hugh Gray, Berkeley, CA: University of California Press, 1967.
Brownlow, Kevin, *The War, The West and the Wilderness*, New York: Albert A. Knopf, 1979.
Griffith, Richard, 'Grass and Chang', in Lewis Jacobs (ed.), *The Documentary Tradition*, New York: W.W. Norton, 1979: 22–4.
Mould, David H. and Veeder, Gerry, 'The Photographer-Adventurers: Forgotten Heroes of the Silent Screen', *Journal of Popular Film and Television* 16, autumn, 1988: 118–29.
Rony, Fatimah Tobing, *The Third Eye: Race, Cinema, and Ethnographic Spectacle*, Durham, NC: Duke University Press, 1996.
Schoedsack, Ernest B., 'Grass: The Making of an Epic', *American Cinematographer* 64, February 1983: 40–4, 109–14.

Scotland

Scotland has made a substantial and distinctive contribution to documentary tradition, culture, theory, and practice. The contribution of Scotland to documentary film is multifaceted, and a subject of dispute. The debate extends beyond questions of form, aesthetics, and subject matter to issues of theory and the conditions and constraints of cultural production.

There are a number of different Scotlands, each discernible to other Scots by a set of signifiers. The Highlands and the islands are overlapping but distinct, and the Hebrides differ from the Orkneys and Shetlands. What some term the Central Belt contains both Edinburgh and Glasgow, two cities with strongly contrasting cultures. There are three languages spoken in Scotland: English, Scots, and Gaelic. Given these differences, it is inevitable that there are a number of tensions and ambiguities present in the creation, construction, and reception of media texts.

One might expect documentary to reject 'tartanry', and to develop a discourse that moves beyond sentimental, stereotypical depictions of Scotland and Scottish life. However, the enduring strengths of the images, meanings, and iconography of tartan, and the romantic nostalgia for a rural elegiac arcadia were and are such that documentary filmmakers have had to operate within the dominant hegemonic ideology that contained strong (albeit not unchallenged) versions of history and national identities.

The problem for critics and radicals, such as Colin McArthur, is that the image and echoes of tartanry were and remain popular with the populace, and that even when a film attempts modernism, as does Seawards the Great Ships (Harris, 1961), this is at the very time when what is being recorded is about to disappear into the past and comprise a part of an alternative urban and nostalgic mythology of Clydeside. Nonetheless, documentaries as different as Children of the City and Culloden ensure that humane, humanist, and socialist values are made available—in the case of these two films, quite explicitly.

A consideration of Scotland and documentary can reasonably begin with John Grierson, often considered the founding father of the British Documentary Movement. The then somewhat austere, Presbyterian, and patriarchal nature of Scottish society and culture likely informed Grierson's ideology, and thus played a distinct role in the shaping of modern documentary film.

First shown at the London Film Society in November 1929, Drifters (Grierson, 1929) is perhaps one of the most famous documentaries. Filmed in part in the Shetlands, some scenes were filmed in the North Sea on vessels the home ports of which were in England. The film faced technical and logistical difficulties, some of which were impossible to overcome with the cameras and equipment available at that time. The shoals of herring featured in the film, therefore, were filmed in the tank of a marine biological station—and the fish were apparently roach rather than herring. Despite these caveats, this silent film uses montage and a simple storyline to give the viewer an insight into the industrial processes and the human experiences and lives that are required to enable the cook and the shopkeeper to provide a simple and nutritious meal on the family table.

Partly filmed in the fishing village of Footdee in Aberdeen, Drifters gives an impressionistic sense of a community; it has its own rituals and rhythms, its own values and truths. It successfully combines a romanticized vision of masculine labor with the articulation of the economic and industrial context. In so doing, and in common with many documentaries of this type, it never quite succeeds in resolving the tensions that are integral to such an endeavor.

Born in Edinburgh, Harry Watt (1906–87) worked for both the General Post Office (GPO) Film Unit and the Crown Unit, and codirected Night Mail (with Basil Wright, 1936) and London Can Take It (with Humphrey Jennings, 1940). He directed North Sea (1938) and Target for Tonight (1941) and later joined Ealing Studios. A competent rather than a brilliant director, his contribution can be exemplified and his inclusion justified not only because of these films but also because of their ethos, best described by Watt himself when speaking of Target for Tonight as being 'an understated and unemotional account of an average air raid'. No better epitaph for the Watt tradition and contribution to documentary can be articulated.

North Sea (1938) is an account of a trawler facing difficulty. It had narrative tension and a happy ending, and can perhaps be criticized on those grounds alone, but there are always dangers in post hoc analysis and in applying and projecting the cultural and ideological ideas from one era onto another or into the past. North Sea, like other documentaries, can also be judged by the art of the possible, and by this criterion, it was and remains a significant achievement.

Seawards the Great Ships (1960) was directed by Hilary Harris and made for Films of Scotland. It won the 1961 Oscar for best live action short film, and was the first Scottish-made film to win an Oscar. Based on a treatment by John Grierson, the film celebrates the work of shipbuilders and shipbuilding on the River Clyde at a time when that industry was about to disappear forever. The film is aesthetically distinctive in that it contains a number of abstract and almost surreal shots that use angles and shadows to develop a montage of images and icons that turn machinery and metals into a kind of art in themselves.

Waverley Steps (1947), directed by John Eldridge, presents glimpses of life in Edinburgh, and the activities of individuals visiting or living there over the course of a weekend. Waverley Steps was a commercial and critical success. It avoided tartanry and Scottish stereotypes, and realistically conveyed the thoughts and emotions of the citizens of Edinburgh regarding their city. It also managed to capture something of the contemporary reality of the city for a tourist but also for some natives at a time when it had just launched what was to become the biggest arts festival in the world. The film celebrates Edinburgh as a European city—and as an international, as opposed to merely 'British', city.

Jenny Gilbertson (née Brown) is included not because of a prolific output but rather because she is almost unique in being a woman director of documentary during the period in which she worked. Her 1934 film The Rugged Island—A Shetland Lyric is an example of a kind of drama documentary and can be said to foreshadow Michael Powell's much better known The Edge of the World (1978), which was also filmed in the Shetlands. The Rugged Island is an anthropological study of the tension between choosing to stay in poverty or opting for exile. The documentary aspects lie in the photography and the evocation of land, lifestyle, community, and place.

John Gray (born 1918) worked with the GPO Film Unit and on films such as North Sea. He later moved on to a successful career with the BBC in which he was influential in news and radio. He helped to establish and/or organize the Edinburgh Film Festival and later the Television Festivals, and he thus helped to ensure a continuing and vibrant debate and discourse around film as well as media policies and texts. His own work as a filmmaker includes the somewhat elegiac and impressionistic.

West Highland (1960) was one of the last films imbued with the lyrical documentary style dominant in the 1930s. This BBC Scotland documentary was produced and directed by John Gray, who worked in collaboration with Grierson and the GPO Film Unit. West Highland follows a day in the life of the railway line from Glasgow Queen Street to Mallaig. It clearly demonstrates the linkages between city and country; urban and rural, and traces a society and lifestyle that has now largely vanished. The story is objective and elegiac and the camerawork benefits from the stunning scenery. The context is Scottish, but the message is universal.

Despite his 1967 Academy Award for The War Game (Best Documentary Feature), Peter Watkins remains best known in Scotland for Culloden (1964), a documentary that can be said to have deconstructed, with savagery and accuracy, the romantic and sentimental mythologising of tartanry and Bonnie Prince Charlie.

Based on the historical book of the same name by John Prebble, Watkins elected to film Culloden in newsreel style, with the Battle of Culloden (1746), the last battle to occur on the British mainland, taking place as though cameras were there at the time and reporters were able to ask questions of the combatants. The battle saw the end of the attempts by the exiled Prince to regain power and the throne. It was also the beginning of the end of the clan or tribal lifestyles of the Gaelic ethnic and highland rural minority. Their destruction allowed their culture and symbols to be safely sentimentalised around eighty years later and subsequently through Victorian and early twentieth-century tartanry. Many of the extras and actors in the film were local and native descendants of those who had fought in the battle some two hundred years before, and this added to the authenticity and realism of the sometimes shocking scenes.

The residual folk memory of the ruthlessness of the victors of Culloden, the Hanoverians and the Duke of Cumberland, were well shown in the film, but more moving and powerful was the articulation of the hopelessness of the situation of the common man. The inevitability of the defeat due to the incompetence of the Jacobite leaders, and the pain of a civil war in which family members were on opposite sides are powerfully conveyed in the film, as is the horrifying nature of a mid-eighteenth-century battle. Throughout, the narrative is interspersed with interviews with participants; generals and foot soldiers were each allowed their say directly to the camera and the interviewer.

The Edinburgh Film Guild can lay claim to being one of the oldest continuous film societies in the world, as it was founded in 1930. The Guild continues to meet on Sundays in the Filmhouse in Edinburgh and provides opportunities for the viewing of a range of classic and international films that include documentaries. The journal *Cinema Quarterly* (founded in 1932) grew out of the Guild.

The Edinburgh International Festival of Documentary Films was founded in August 1947 with a program of approximately seventy-five films submitted. Although it eventually became the Edinburgh Film Festival, and during the 1950s moved beyond its original focus on documentary, the importance of the festival as a cultural and intellectual event for filmmakers, filmgoers, and film theorists cannot be understated and the stated intention to provide a stage for the documentary idea and practice was achieved.

The Films of Scotland Committee was set up by the Scottish Development Council in the late 1930s in order to ensure that there would be films on modern Scotland for the 1938 Glasgow Empire Exhibition. These films, like many Griersonian documentaries, were a blend of promotion and social comment; of corporate communication and constrained radicalism; of romanticism and modernism. What is significant, however, in the context of the ideological balance of power at the time and since is the fact that as Grierson put it, the committee was a deliberate attempt to use the film for national purposes.

The committee's life began with the need to have available films on contemporary Scotland for the 1938 Glasgow Empire exhibition. The result was four documentaries: The Face of Scotland; They Made the Land; The Children's Story; and Wealth of a Nation. Inevitably, these films present an optimistic view of the policies of development. Despite this, and their clear subservience to and operation within a contemporary unionist and deferential discourse, the films were excluded by the British Council from the 1939 New York-based World Fair on the grounds that they were not complementary to the heritage and royal version of England that was on display.

The Second Films of Scotland Committee operated from 1954 until 1982, and continued some of the traditions of its prewar predecessor. Many of its films were of the travelogue tourism variety, with highland and island landscapes omnipresent. A number were also about Edinburgh's culture, history, and arts, Glasgow's urban redevelopment, and new towns such as East Kilbride and Cumbernauld. Some films about Scottish artists and writers were produced.

The committee acted as a catalyst to persuade other bodies to invest in films and filming. Toward the end of its existence, it became increasingly apparent that although it might be possible to produce, the question of exhibition was becoming ever more problematic given the decline of going to the cinema and the move toward single-feature showings. Television thus became the route and the destination for documentary makers in Scotland and beyond.

ROBERT BEVERIDGE

See also: Drifters; Grierson, John; Target for Tonight; War Game, The; Watkins, Peter; Watt, Harry

Secrets of Nature

(UK, Woolfe, 1922–33)

Secrets of Nature is the name of a series of popular science films produced by British Instructional Films that began in 1922 and continued until 1933. H. Bruce Woolfe founded British Instructional shortly after World War I, with a view toward attracting intellectuals to work in the cinema. The company specialized in nonfiction films; in addition to the Secrets series, British Instructional focused on documentary reconstructions of episodes from World War I, such as Zeebrugge (1924). In the preface to The Secrets of Nature (1939), Woolfe recounts how an encounter with Gilbert White's Natural History of Selborne (1788/9) led him to conceive of a series of nature films. White, a curate in Selborne, made detailed studies of the flora and fauna that surrounded his residence. His reliance on field observations makes him a precursor of the field of ethology, which proceeds from the observation of animals in their natural habitats instead of in laboratory settings. Other practitioners of ethology, such as the French entomologist Jean-Henri Fabre, influenced the popular scientific film of the 1910s in France. Secrets of Nature continued this tradition of utilizing the cinema in a manner consistent with ethological principles of observation, although without any explicit claims to the methods of professional science. Indeed, one of the typical approaches used by the films was to anthropomorphize its plant and animal subjects, and this recourse to analogy is something that professional science would reject. The Secrets series was consciously and expertly produced for a mass audience, providing an excellent example of how 'to administer the powder of instruction in the jam of entertainment'.

Renowned for their high-production values and clever, humorous commentary, the films found favor with audiences not only in England but abroad as well, especially in Europe and America. During the series' twelve-year run, one hundred and forty-four one-reel films appeared; some years saw the release of as many as thirty films whereas in other years none were released. This erratic production schedule may have resulted from the occasional changes in leadership and institutional circumstances, and it may also have been due to the unpredictable nature of the subjects being filmed (some films were said to have taken as long as four years to complete).

Stoll Picture Productions took over British Instructional in 1924, but Woolfe remained the head of the company. His increasing involvement in producing other projects for Stoll, including Anthony Asquith's early films, led him to cede oversight of the Secrets of Nature production unit to Mary Field, who began working for British Instructional as a technical advisor on the subject of seventeenth-century fishing in the West Atlantic before she worked her way up through the ranks. One of the only women in the British film industry to figure prominently in the field of production, Field was the main editor of Secrets of Nature and was responsible for directing the majority of zoo films.

Field's principal collaborator was Percy Smith, whose name has become synonymous with the series. Smith's career as a popular scientific filmmaker began in 1907 when Charles Urban, who was impressed by Smith's photomicrographs of the tongue of a bluebottle fly, employed the young Board of Education clerk. Smith's many films for Urban included Kinemacolour time-lapse studies of blooming flowers (The Birth of a Flower, 1910) and studies of insect behavior (The Balancing Blue-Bottle, 1908, and The Strength and Agility of Insects, 1911). These subjects received extensive and enthusiastic press coverage, and the remarkable ingenuity and humor they displayed would carry over into Smith's work on the Secrets of Nature. His work for British Instructional consisted of films about insects, plants, underwater creatures, and microscopic subjects. Smith filmed many of his subjects in the laboratory/studio that he established in his house in Southgate. An inveterate tinkerer, he engineered sophisticated devices for time-lapse films.

Although Smith's quirky charm perhaps best characterizes the Secrets of Nature, he was by no means the only individual to make films for the series. In addition to Field's contributions, no less than half a dozen other naturalists provided their expertise to Secrets. Charles Head shared the insect film duties with Smith, making one of the series' first films, The Lair of the Spider (1922). He also made films about bird life and small mammals. Other prominent contributors included Edgar Chance, who was responsible for The Cuckoo's Secret (1922). The first film of the series, The Cuckoo's Secret detailed the life cycle of the cuckoos of Worcestershire and was the product of many years of field observation. H.A. Gilbert and Walter Higham also provided films about birds and small mammals, as did Oliver Pike, who had contributed films about birds to Pathé's popular science catalogue as early as 1912. The bird films underline the affinity that the Secrets series had with such vernacular scientific activities as bird-watching; in general, the series appealed to a fascination with how scientific observation could transform the everyday world into a fantastic and wonderful place.

The first five years of the series (1922–6) were characterized by various cameramen and editors, but Woolfe's supervision enabled the finished product to maintain a consistent tone. In 1927, when the company went public, the core staff became more stable, with Field and Smith taking over the primary duties and Head, Pike, Gilbert, and Higham providing additional material.

The series made the switch to sound production in 1930. In 1933 British Instructional was acquired by British International Pictures, which was then in turn taken over by Associated British Picture Corporation. The head of the latter company was against what he saw as British Instructional's production of 'films for the intelligentsia'. Woolfe resigned his position shortly after the takeover and founded a similar unit, Gaumont British Instructional (GBI), at the Gaumont British Picture Corporation, where Mary Field and Percy Smith also found employment. Secrets of Nature was retitled Secrets of Life in 1934, and it continued to produce educational short films until the death of Percy Smith in March 1945. Many of the Secrets films are currently held by British Pathé.

OLIVER GAYCKEN

Further reading

Field, Mary and Smith, Percy, *The Secrets of Nature*, London: The Scientific Book Club, 1939.

Gaycken, Oliver, 'The Sources of the "Secrets of Nature": The Popular Science Film at Urban, 1903–11', in Alan Burton and Laraine Porter (eds), *Scene-Stealing: Sources for British Cinema before 1930*, Trowbridge: Flicks Books, 2003: 36–42.

Low, Rachel, *A History of the British Film 1906–14*, London: Allen & Unwin, 1949.

McKernan, Luke, '"Something More than a Mere Picture Show": Charles Urban and the Early Non-Fiction Film in Great Britain and America, 1897–1925', University of London, PhD thesis, 2004.

Seeing Red

(US, Reichert and Klein, 1983)

Seeing Red (1983) is the last of a series of documentaries codirected by James Klein and Julia Reichert that address feminist and working-class topics from a socialist perspective using contemporary interviews, archival footage, and popular music. Klein and Reichert's first film together, Growing Up Female (1971), is considered the first sustained documentary study of the societal forces in the United States that mold female identities. Methadone: An American Way of Dealing (1975) critiques the use of methadone to combat drug addiction. The Oscar-nominated Union Maids (1976) collects the oral histories of three women who played roles in the unionization drives in the United States during the 1930s.

In Seeing Red, which was nominated for an Oscar, the directors incorporate the direct cinema techniques of their previous films, but they expand the scope of their research and oral interviews. In the early 1980s Reichert and Klein interviewed four hundred of the one million people who had been members of the American Communist Party from the 1930s to the 1950s. Of the four hundred people interviewed, sixteen appear in Seeing Red. The codirectors note that people who were angry and dissatisfied with their involvement in the

Communist Party declined interviews, so the sixteen who appear in the film are generally positive about their experiences in the Communist Party (Shafransky 1984: 25). The sixteen were chosen to give a balanced representation of regions, gender, and race in the United States, although the focus of the film is on the rank and file members of the Communist Party.

Critics have noted that the directors' attempts to address controversial issues, such as the undemocratic structure of the Communist Party, are largely unsuccessful, and that those interviewed often have incomplete or dubious historical interpretations. In interviews, Klein and Reichert defend their approach as an emphasis on personal storytelling rather than history and analysis. Cultivating a sympathetic relationship with the people who will elicit their stories, they claim, precludes a separate, analytic voice (Georgakas 1984: 27; Shafransky 1984: 26).

This concern over analytic distance is related to a broader, theoretical controversy over the direct cinema techniques employed in the film. Seeing Red, it should be noted, is by no means a pure form of direct cinema: it employs nondiegetic music, there is no immediate drama (it is concerned with past events recalled by those who lived them), it sometimes shows an onscreen questioner during interviews, and it includes archival footage. Seeing Red is firmly in a tradition of critical political documentary, pioneered by De Antonio's In the Year of the Pig (1969), which draws on direct cinema techniques. In this tradition there are extensive interviews, archival footage, nondiegetic music, and little voice-over narration. Instead of limiting the scope of a film to the immediate representation of a single event in the manner of purer forms of direct cinema, critical political documentary traces broader issues and trends. Films in this subgenre include With Babies in Banners (1978), Word is Out (1979), The Wobblies (1979), The Day After Trinity (1980), and Lodz Ghetto (1989). Often such films would include shots of demonstrations or other current political events, but these are precluded by Seeing Red's focus on the past (archival footage can represent some of these past events, but such footage isn't direct cinema in the strict sense).

Because Seeing Red employs oral interviews extensively and generally eschews voice-over narration and other modes of objective commentary, the directors are less able to analyze their material or develop the broader context of the topics they explore. Indeed, as noted earlier, instead of attempting to maintain any objective distance from the interviewees during the making of the film, the directors were sympathetic both with them and their politics, and they attempted to edit the film in ways that preserved the narrative, and the convictions, of those interviewed. In this sense, Seeing Red can also be categorized as a late example of engaged cinema, not only because of its openly militant stance but also because of its production and distribution. Engaged cinema, which flourished during the 1960s and early 1970s, avoided mainstream media and sought to build alternative collectives to finance and market films. Both Reichert and Klein are founding—and current—members of one such engaged cinema collective, New Day Films, and Union Maids is often cited as a prototypical engaged cinema film (Thompson and Bordwell 1994: 644).

A controversy arose over films in the tradition of critical political cinema and engaged cinema centers on the limited perspective allowed by the direct cinema techniques. Union Maids and Seeing Red, for example, are criticized for oversimplifying social relations by giving an incomplete, uncontested story primarily through oral interviews of small numbers of like-minded people.

Such an approach can be read as a legitimate form of counterhistory, and recent critics have argued for the recuperation of such direct cinema techniques for the creation of counterhistories that dispute conventional representations of authority and give more heteroglossic alternatives (see the entry on Union Maids). However, other critics have argued that Reichert and Klein tend to present oral histories as independent arguments and not as primary source material in need of a broader explanatory frame—a frame that at the very least would make clear the distinction between conveying the recollection of others and the meta-critical, reflexive attempt to question conventional representations of authority and history. The lack of such a frame, it is claimed, can make films such as Seeing Red appear naïve—an endorsement of a partial, self-protective history rather than a meta-critical response to previous histories (Nichols 1991: 252).

PAUL MILLER

See also: Klein, James; Reichert, Julia; Union Maids

Seeing Red (US, Heartland Productions, 1983, 100 mins). Directed by Julia Reichert and James Klein.

Further reading

Arthur, Paul, 'Jargons of Authenticity (Three American Moments)', in Michael Renov (ed.), *Theorizing Documentary*, New York: Routledge, 1993.

Aufderheide, Pat, 'The Good Fight', in Alan Rosenthal (ed.), *New Challenges for Documentary*, Berkeley, CA: University of California Press, 1988.

Boruszkowski, Lilly Ann, 'An Interview with Documentary Filmmaker Jim Klein', *Journal of Film and Video* 46, no. 1, 1994: 34–42.

Georgakas, Dan, 'Seeing Red', *Cineaste* 13, no. 2, 1984: 27–8.

Kleinhaus, Chuck, 'Julia Reichert and Jim Klein', *Jump Cut* 5, 1975: 11–12.

Nichols, Bill, *Representing Reality*, Bloomington, IN: Indiana University Press, 1991.

Rosenthal, Alan, 'Union Maids', in Alan Rosenthal (ed.), *Documentary Conscience*, Berkeley, CA: University of California Press, 1980.

——(ed.), *New Challenges for Documentary*, Berkeley, CA: University of California Press, 1988.

Rubenstein, Lenny, 'Who's Who in Filmmaking: Julia Reichert and James Klein', *Sightlines* 20, no. 2, 1986–7: 22–5.

Shafransky, Renee, 'Seeing Red: An Interview with James Klein and Julia Reichert', *Cineaste* 13, no. 2, 1984: 24–6.

Thompson, Kristin and Bordwell, David, *Film History*, New York: McGraw-Hill, 1994.

Waldman, Diane and Walker, Janet (eds), *Feminism and Documentary*, Minneapolis, MN: University of Minnesota Press, 1999.

Seidl, Ulrich

Stretching the definition of the term documentary film to an extreme, Austrian filmmaker Ulrich Seidl has developed a controversial method of documentary realism and the visual imagery of the 'authentic' since the late 1980s. Seidl's films are by no means documentaries, although the documentary quality of his oeuvre is indisputable. His style is rather a complex blend of various modus operandi: exploiting core values of cinéma vérité, such as intimacy and immediacy, Seidl's work blurs the boundaries between documentation and fiction, the factual and the poetic, the grotesque and the poignant beyond recognition.

With this unapologetic approach Seidl can confidently be seen as an anticipator of a new generation of documentary filmmakers which has become increasingly popular—not to mention populist—since the late 1990s. The convergence of the documentary toward feature film aesthetics and narrative forms was a widely observed phenomenon during these years, not least due to the international popularity of figures as Errol Morris and Michael Moore. Ulrich Seidl could be fairly credited to this group of filmmakers even if his aesthetics differ from the aforementioned to a considerable extent.

The fashionable hybrid term docudrama captures the idea behind Seidl's method best. Seidl himself, rejecting the categorization 'documentary' for his work, characterizes the nature of his films as 'calculated arrangements'. His films are not so much concerned with authentic depictions of social milieux, but rather with condensed, dramatic reenactments of a social climate, constantly exploring the relation and tensions between public and private spheres in society. This artistic license enables Seidl to create an austere imagery of social milieux that highlights a harsh criticism of contemporary Austrian existential orientations.

As a matter of consequence, his work inevitably touches issues of national identity as Seidl's 'semidocumentaries' are engaged in the typology of 'the Austrian' as such to a great deal. The remaining influence of Catholicism in society, the slow transformation (and deformation) of the vast middle class, its underlying xenophobia, and the connection with the legacy of National Socialism resonate throughout his films. The consideration of this cultural environment is a key to the understanding of Seidl's stylistic and aesthetical choices.

Since his work is not influenced by a certain school or 'limited' by documentary ethics, Seidl can use his films as demonstrations of subjective 'truths'. Dramatization of the largely fact-based material is crucial to his notion of the purposiveness of documentary film: the ability to involve the viewer emotionally by juxtaposing different societal milieux. This decision results in a highly stylized visual conception: rather vérité-like observations of often redundant actions in long and alienated shots are contrasted with concisely framed tableaux vivants that give his images an almost photographic quality.

Seidl's work, largely discussed in the context of the documentary film, is particular interesting for its laissez-faire attitude toward ethical considerations. It should be noted that Seidl's appreciation for the documentary format was initially a matter of convenience. In the 1980s in Austria documentaries were easier to finance through the public funding system. However, Seidl held fundamental resentments against the 'aesthetical double-standard of the form'. His notion of the traditional canon of ethical values as obsolete ran parallel with a reconsideration of the documentary codices in other European countries during the 1990s. The acknowledgment of new strategic practices and the increasingly casual exposure to far less 'purist' documentary ethics coincided with the rise of the Danish 'Dogma' manifesto that aesthetically bore resemblance to Seidl's method.

The growing popularity of the 'dogma' aesthetics during the mid-1990s was clearly an indicator for the necessity for a repositioning of the documentary film as such. 'Authenticity' was becoming a quality characteristic to which the fiction film laid claim. The significance of Seidl's work must be understood in the context of this shift of paradigm. His films accompanied, partially even anticipated, this continuous development; at the same time it certainly had a sustainable effect on the reception of his work in terms of its 'documentary virtues'. Seidl's work exemplifies a new understanding of the documentary film that has abandoned the paths of traditional thinking. In Seidl's documentary style 'subjectivity' is no longer a discursive address but simply an assumption.

ANDREAS BUSCHE

Biography

Born in Vienna, Austria, in 1952. Studied publishing, theater studies, and art history. In 1978 he attended the Vienna Film Academy and directed his first short films, Einsvierzig (1980) and Der Ball (1982). Dropped Film Academy in 1982. In 1989 Seidl finished the feature-length documentary Krieg in Wien, codirected with his regular cinematographer Michael Glowegger. His 1990 film, Good News. Von Kolporteuren, toten Hunden und anderen Wienern, is widely regarded as Seidl's debut. Since 1984 Seidl has also worked as a freelance filmmaker for Austrian television. In 2001 directed Hundstage (Dog Days), which is generally considered as Seidl's first fiction film, although his method hasn't changed in comparison to his previous films.

Selected films

1990 Good News. Von Kolporteuren, toten Hunden und anderen Wienern: director, writer
1993 Mit Verlust ist zu rechnen: director, writer
1995 Tierische Liebe: director, writer
1997 Der Busenfreund: director, writer
1999 Models: director, writer
2001 Hundstage: director, writer
2003 Jesus, Du weißt: director, writer

Further reading

Dox: Documentary Film Quarterly 10, winter 1996: 34–7.
Film Comment 6, November/December 2001: 16–17.
Illetschko, Peter (ed.), *Gegenschuss—16 Regisseure aus Österreich*, Wespennest: Wien, 1995.
Positif 500, October 2002: 192–201.

Seleckis, Ivars

Ivars Seleckis's documentary films present realistic representations of human society. His documentaries have been noted for their detailed and sophisticated analysis of the social processes. His is a mission to capture the daily struggle for survival in the world, the continuous battle to raise and educate children, to live a decent life in this difficult day and age. Seleckis sees his role of documentary filmmaker as one of rudimentary importance. Through his films the smallest countries and the most insignificant individuals floundering in an ocean of globalization can explore their growing sense of apparent nothingness. In The Crossroad Street (1988), Seleckis presents the contemporary people of Riga, a town destined to become the capital of the independent Republic of Latvia. The people will face not only a political crisis but also the more cataclysmic threat of losing their connection to their culture, their language, their people, and ultimately themselves.

Seleckis follows this project with an examination of peasant life in the film Come Down Pale Moon. Shot in the Vidzeme region of Latvia in 1993, Seleckis follows the cycle of peasant life from spring through autumn during a critical time in Latvian political history. These men and women spent the last fifty years living, working, and dying under Soviet rule and Seleckis is there to reveal the jubilation, the fear, and the uncertainty of peasants regaining their land after so many years. His use of documentary as chronicler of political and economic transition creates a biography of the peasant, the unexpected victor over the great Soviet military machine.

Seleckis revisits Riga in New Times at Crossroad Street (1998) ten years later. With the Soviet Union in collapse and the creation of the new Latvian Republic, Seleckis chronicles the challenge the people face in preventing themselves from dissolving into a single common primitive mass. The viewer visits inside the evolving world of what by Western standards constitutes the insignificant and discovers the universality of human struggle and achievement.

CHRISTINE MARIE HILGER

Biography

Born in 1934 in Riga, Latvia, and graduated from the Academy of Agriculture and the Faculty of Food Technology in Jelgava in 1957, then from the State Institute of Cinematography in 1966. Began work in a Riga film studio in 1958 as an assistant cameraman. In 1968 directed his first film and went on to receive numerous distinctions, including Merited Master of Arts (1975) and the Three Stars Order, which is the highest reward of the State of Latvia.

Selected films

1980 The Widening of the World: director
1988 The Crossroad Street: director
1994 Come Down, Pale Moon: director
1998 New Times at Crossroad Street: director

Further reading

Ackerman, Peter and DuVall, Jack, *A Force More Powerful: A Century of Nonviolent Conflict*, New York: St Martin's Press, 2000.

Aitken, Ian, *European Film Theory and Cinema: A Critical Introduction*, Edinburgh: Edinburgh University Press, 2001.

Corner, John, *Documentary and the Mass Media*, London: Arnold, 1986.

Rotha, Paul, *Documentary Diary*, New York: Hill and Wang, 1973.

Selling of the Pentagon, The

(US, Davis, 1971)

The CBS Reports documentary The Selling of the Pentagon aired on February 7, 1971. Writer and director Peter Davis and correspondent Roger Mudd based much of their investigation of the Department of Defense's domestic public relations apparatus on Senator J. William Fulbright's book *The Pentagon Propaganda Machine.* The Selling of the Pentagon told an estimated nine million viewers that the Pentagon engaged in a pervasive, persuasive, improper, and expensive propaganda campaign to convince the American people that the United States military and its war in Southeast Asia represented essential and effective checks to the spread of international communism. Instantly controversial, the film drew condemnation and accusations of distortion from government sources, but ultimately won a congressional confrontation by successfully invoking the applicability of First Amendment protection to broadcast journalism.

In The Selling of the Pentagon, director Davis interviews 'major taxpayers' impressed with their elaborate tour of military facilities, shows Pentagon speakers extolling military confrontation to international communism, and juxtaposes a segment featuring Green Berets displaying hand-to-hand combat at an Armed Forces day with shots of nearby children mimicking their combat moves. Davis investigates the Pentagon film program, finding a marketing effort crowded with celebrities and expressing an outdated 'obsession with monolithic communism'. A montage of title cards illustrates the point: 'A Day in Vietnam', 'The Big Picture', 'Why Viet-Nam', 'Freedom and You', and 'Red Chinese Battle Plan'. Davis excerpts segments featuring Robert Stack cleaning a rifle, Chet Huntly standing atop an aircraft carrier, John Wayne discussing revolutionaries with a well-posed group of Marines, and CBS's Walter Cronkite authoritatively intoning that America 'must build forces at home' to confront communism. Davis examines several scenes from Red Nightmare, the Pentagon's imaginative fictional narrative produced with Warner Brothers to illustrate the dangers of a communist takeover in small-town America.

The Pentagon exalts the virtues of free thought and debate in Red Nightmare, but The Selling of the Pentagon accuses the Pentagon of stifling the free thought and commentary of America's media. Correspondent Roger Mudd describes military sources bombarding local news outlets with thousands of TV and radio tapes and millions of press releases about the military and the war in which 'The only news [...] is good news'. *The New York Times*'s George Wilson adds that reporters assigned to the Pentagon have no alternative but to 'trust big daddy', and shots of daily briefings in Vietnam illustrate their moniker, 'Five O'Clock Follies'. Meanwhile, the Pentagon maintains five teams in Vietnam filming or staging material for television news in what a former Air Force photographer describes as 'propagandizing'.

The Selling of the Pentagon represented a landmark in the confrontation of US journalists with the Pentagon, reinforcing the schism visually with techniques borrowed from direct cinema. By 1971 most journalists reporting on the Pentagon and the war filed stories adversarial to the Pentagon's positive perspective, and even CBS's staid Cronkite openly broke with the administration in 1968 to advocate a negotiated peace and to warn Americans to no longer place any faith 'in the silver linings [American leaders] find in the darkest clouds'. Davis illustrated the dichotomy of perspective in The Selling of the Pentagon by contrasting CBS's handheld camera shots, tight close-ups, focus racking, and occasional whip pans with the slick images emanating from the Pentagon. Davis augmented this direct cinema camerawork with editing in the same tradition, using juxtaposition, jump cuts, and sequential arrangement to serve as an overt tool of commentary.

Responding to The Selling of the Pentagon, *The New York Times* spoke of 'integrity' while Vice President Spiro Agnew accused CBS of airing 'alleged facts which are untrue'. F. Edward Hébert, chairman of the House Armed Service Committee, called the report a 'hatchet job' and declared it 'un-American'. CBS followed a March 23, 1971, rebroadcast with fifteen minutes of edited critical comments from Agnew, Hébert, and Secretary of Defense Melvin R. Laird, and a rebuttal by CBS News President Richard S. Salant. An estimated fourteen million Americans watched the program, hearing Salant argue that no specific claims had been made against the essential accuracy of the program, only the editing of interviews and one speech within the film. However, the allegations of misleading and misrepresentative editing provided the grounds for another vocal critic, Representative Harley O. Staggers, to mount a congressional investigation.

Staggers, chairman of the House Committee on Interstate and Foreign Commerce, subpoenaed CBS and its president, Frank Stanton, for all materials relating to the production of The Selling of the Pentagon. Stanton testified but refused to turn over outtakes and production notes. CBS admitted that it had violated its own operating standards guidelines relating to attributing answers to questions in taped interviews, but Stanton claimed that congressional oversight of broadcast journalism would have a 'chilling effect', and was in violation of the First Amendment's protection of the press.

Staggers countered that 'the press' does not include broadcast journalism, and added that as a licensee of public airways, CBS was answerable to Congress. In open debate, representatives widely condemned CBS, but recognized the courts' previous decision that 'no rational distinction can be made' between broadcast journalism and print media in terms of First Amendment protection. The House did not act against Stanton and CBS, and it never voted on the 'Truth in News Broadcasting Bill', introduced during the floor debates. The bill demanded any 'factual reporting', including edited events or interviews, to be 'explicitly labeled throughout [the] entire showing'.

The congressional battle over First Amendment protection remains the lasting legacy of The Selling of the Pentagon, especially in connection with the nearly concurrent Supreme Court case over the Pentagon Papers. CBS continued to defy administration intimidation in 1972, when Walter Cronkite broadcast a two-part investigation of the Watergate scandal on the CBS Evening News, becoming the first major media center to support *The Washington Post*'s story. Peter Davis embarked on an independent project that would become the controversial 1974 Vietnam War documentary Hearts and Minds. Taking even more from direct cinema, Davis eliminated a narrator and constructed his argument with carefully edited and assembled interviews, location filming, and historical footage. Cronkite's broadcast and Davis's documentary follow the example of The Selling of the Pentagon, itself following a decade of increasing conflict between journalism and government in the United States. The Selling of the Pentagon represented a major public victory for broadcast journalism both in terms of securing First Amendment protection and demonstrating the potential ability of determined media to inform on political wrongdoing, even in the face of determined official intimidation.

MICHAEL D. ROBINSON

See also: Hearts and Minds

The Selling of the Pentagon (US, CBS, 1971, 60 mins). Produced, written, and directed by Peter Davis, with correspondent Roger Mudd. Executive produced by Perry Wolff. Photographed by William Wagner *et al.* Edited by Dena Levitt.

Further reading

Dunham, Corydon B., *Fighting for the First Amendment: Stanton of CBS vs. Congress and the Nixon White House*, Westport, CT: Praeger, 1997.

Fulbright, J. William, *The Pentagon Propaganda Machine*, New York: Liveright, 1970.

Gould, Jack, 'The Unselling of the Pentagon', *The New York Times*, March 7, 1971: D17.

Jowett, Garth S., '"The Selling of the Pentagon": Television Confronts the First Amendment', in John E. O'Connor (ed.), *American History, American Television: Interpreting the Video Past*, New York: Ungar, 1983.

Reeb, Richard H., *Taking Journalism Seriously: 'Objectivity' as a Partisan Cause*, Lanham, MD: University Press of America, 1999.

Rogers, Jimmie N. and Clevenger, Theodore, Jr, '"The Selling of the Pentagon": Was CBS the Fulbright Propaganda Machine?' *Quarterly Journal of Speech* 57, no. 3, 1971: 266–74.

Salant, Richard S., *Salant, CBS, and the Battle for the Soul of Broadcast Journalism: The Memoirs of Richard S. Salant*, Susan and Bill Buzenberg (eds), Boulder CO: Westview Press, 1999.

Sense of Loss, A

(France, Ophüls, 1972)

Released between The Sorrow and the Pity (Ophüls, 1969) and The Memory of Justice (Ophüls, 1976), A Sense of Loss is one of Marcel Ophüls's least discussed films. When written about, usually in reviews rather than scholarly texts, the film is often damned with faint praise. Ephraim Katz was able to call it 'sensitive'; Leonard Maltin has dubbed it 'thoughtful'. Peter Biskind was somewhat closer to the mark with his observation that 'compassion without commitment leads to the confused, paralysed humanism of Ophüls' A Sense of Loss', and he was using the film only as a point of comparison in a review of Hearts and Minds. The most detailed analysis to date has come from Brian McIlroy (1998), who speaks of it as a 'lightning-rod' on which debate may be focused rather than as a fully realised documentary treatment of its subject.

A Sense of Loss was an attempt to explore the 'Troubles' in Northern Ireland through a series of interviews. The interviews were illustrated with footage shot on location between December 1971 and February 1972. Supplementary scenes and interviews were also filmed in London, Dublin, and New York. Ophüls spoke with people representing nationalist and loyalist traditions, with Protestants and Catholics, with politicians, paramilitaries, and private citizens. An emphasis was given to the experiences of those who had lost relatives during the violence, sometimes by accident, sometimes as a direct result of military or paramilitary activities. Within this framework, Ophüls attempted to provide an overview of the political and social issues at stake in Northern Ireland as seen by those who lived there. By designating it 'A film report by Marcel Ophüls', he presumably hoped to sidestep the social and political issues raised by embarking on a more comprehensive 'chronicle' such as The Sorrow and the Pity.

The film was thematically organised around the idea of human loss, which allowed Ophüls to avoid engaging in active discourse and eliminated the need to come to specific political conclusions. The director's sympathy with the nationalist community was evident, nonetheless, in his selection and juxtaposition of segments, although this partisanship was presented in terms of a liberal-humanist empathy with human tragedy rather than as a political perspective. The film's stated thematic preoccupation with loss raised larger questions about the 'loss' of Northern Ireland itself in broader historical terms, which the film did not fully vocalise. Although he presented the stated views of nationalists and loyalists of varying degrees of extremity, Ophüls's questions led his interviewees to use religious designations rather than political ones. This semantic distinction had the effect of portraying the conflict in Northern Ireland as a relatively clear-cut sectarian antagonism that had been instigated by colonial and imperialist Britain imposing its religious values on the native Irish. This provided safe grounds for an empathetic response to the losses represented in the film: loss of family, loss of peace, and loss of innocence.

The film begins and ends with references to the death of children. Its longest and least interrupted interview is with the parents of a baby who was killed in a bomb blast. As the film begins, Ophüls is heard speaking to his mother. The interview in full is not shown until later, but it is used in the opening as part of a montage sequence to sound a note of human tragedy that will inform the film on the whole. The film's conclusion actually intercuts two deaths, one of an IRA volunteer (whose mother also features in the opening montage), the other of a schoolgirl killed in a road accident involving an army patrol vehicle. Although there is a political subtext, emotion once again centres on the tragic randomness of the latter death and on the familial context of the former. The loss of the future is at issue here; the death of a child represents the end of a life not yet lived. It is in this symbolism that we find the film's controlling metaphor. A Sense of Loss is not concerned with the reasons for loss or the context in which loss has occurred, but rather the effect that loss has on people and their hopes for the future.

The film remains reticent about what shape the future might take. It does represent political viewpoints, but Ophüls chooses to do so through his interviewees, which often prompts a response to his presentation of people's personalities rather than of their arguments. The stiff, smug manner of Sir Harry Tuzo, commander of British army forces in Northern Ireland, the fussy, dismissive attitude of anti-Catholic publisher John McKeague, and the characteristic bombast of Reverend Ian Paisley screaming from his pulpit do little to represent a moderate voice for loyalism. Meanwhile, images of nationalist politician Bernadette Devlin walking by the sea, of left-wing activist Gerry O'Hare making breakfast for his children, and of the grieving family of IRA volunteer Gerald McDade give good reason for sympathy for their cause, especially when the film on the whole lacks a representation of the historical context of the struggle itself.

Stylistically, Ophüls confessed, the film was challenged by its subject. He said, 'The idea is that you rush around to thirty or forty people in different towns, trying to create epic frescoes on the basis of straight interviewing' (quoted in McIlroy 1998). Ophüls's devotion to the interview may have provided The Sorrow and the Pity with a powerful centre, but the director's understanding of, and engagement with, his subject was so much more profound in that case that interviews were merely another tool with which he probed the delicate threads of past and present. In the absence of a true understanding of Northern Ireland and its history, Ophüls was ultimately only barely more enlightening on this subject than the dozens of film and TV crews who had, as Marilyn Hyndman put it, 'parachuted in for a couple of weeks' and left with footage to be used and reused in news and magazine programmes throughout the world. A Sense of Loss was nonetheless banned from broadcast by the BBC, fearful that the film would contribute to the climate of sectarian bitterness, which it sought to envision in terms of its human costs.

HARVEY O'BRIEN

See also: Ophüls, Marcel; Sorrow and the Pity, The

A Sense of Loss (US/Swiss, Cinema X/Sociéte Suisse de Television, 1972, 135 mins). Produced and directed by Marcel Ophüls. Edited by Marion Kraft. Director of photography: Simon Edelstein. Second unit direction by Edouard Fenwick. Assistant director: Ana Carrigan. Additional photography by Elliott Erwitt. Production manager: William Stitt. Assistant editor: Anne Lewis. Assistant cameraman: Claude Paccaud. Sound engineer: Claude Pellot. Chief electrician: Alain Borga. Chaffeur. Social guide: Robert Moon. Research Assistant: Kathy Keville. Rerecording: Richard Vorisek. Contributing journalist: John Whale of *The Sunday Times*. Executive Producer: Max Palevsky.

Further reading

Baker, Keith, 'Reporting the Conflict', in Martin McLoone (ed.), *Broadcasting in a Divided Community: Seventy Years of the BBC in Northern Ireland*, Belfast: Institute of Irish Studies, The Queen's University of Belfast, 1996.

Buruma, Ian, 'Marcel Ophuls', in Kevin Macdonald and Mark Cousins (eds), *Imagining Reality: The Faber Book of Documentary*, London and Boston: Faber, 1996.
Butler, David, *The Trouble with Reporting Northern Ireland*, Aldershot: Avebury, 1995.
Hyndman, Marilyn, 'Resisting Cultural Arrest', *Film Ireland*, November/December 1992: 16–17.
McIlroy, Brian, *Shooting to Kill: Filmmaking and the Troubles in Northern Ireland*, Trowbridge: Flicks Books, 1998.
Pryluck, Calvin, 'Ultimately We Are All Outsiders: The Ethics of Documentary Filming', in Alan Rosenthal (ed.), *New Challenges for Documentary*, Berkeley, CA and London: University of California Press, 1988.

Septemberweizen

(Germany, Krieg, 1980)

Septemberweizen/September Wheat is an especially notable film made by the director Peter Krieg. It brought him an international reputation as well as the Adolf-Grimme-Preis, the prestigious German TV award. The film analyses problems of American agriculture, where many farmers have to give up their small farms and even the large farming corporations do not earn enough money and are in an economic crisis. In the United States around forty thousand farmers gave up in 1978, eight hundred each week. The film shows that farming is closely connected to the capitalist system and is dependent on the agriculture industry, which is continually attempting to create products to streamline farming processes, such as hybrid wheat or a revolutionary fertilizer. The film remains relevant, given its complex and sustained analysis, and the fact that industrial farming remains a controversial issue.

'September wheat' refers to contracts with the wheat exchange in Chicago (harvests are sold in September). The entire American harvest is sold there, fifty percent of it intended for export. Peter Krieg follows the wheat from planning and growth through its sale to the consumer, narrating the tale in seven chapters (the number seven is a reference to the biblical story of Joseph, who saw seven fruitful years and seven years of drought). Krieg's essayistic style avoids an educational commentary, instead concentrating on interviews with people involved, while creating an intriguing montage of images, sounds, and music, which are sometimes used in an ironic way. For example, the crisis of the farmers is accompanied by the song 'America, the Beautiful'; a montage will contrast expensive homes in the United States with photos of hungry children around the world. Many details and facts are conveyed by short radio reports offscreen, which is an original device.

Krieg succeeds in investigating many of the secrets of this business and analyzing the worldwide food problems and political crises, which are strongly related to wheat production. Only six companies controlled the US market in 1980. They set the prices and decided who received wheat. Producers of seed corn developed new hybrid forms and the farmers became dependent on them. The farmers are then forced to pay high prices, and have to invest in efficient new machinery and fertilizer to obtain the most returns from their investment. However, they receive lower prices at the wheat exchange, because of overproduction. The surplus is exported to so-called Third World countries, influencing the agriculture there and manipulated by the US government as a political tool.

Septemberweizen was released at the time when the environmental movement and Third World groups became influential in Germany. Although the system of industrial production has changed and become even more efficient, Septemberweizen is still an interesting case study, an in-depth political analysis free of ideological clichés, which tries to use film as a medium of enlightenment.

KAY HOFFMANN

Septemberweizen/September Wheat (Germany, Teldoc und ZDF/Kleines Fernsehspiel, 1980, 96 mins). Directed by Peter Krieg. Edited by Peter Krieg. Script by Peter Krieg. Sound by Peter Krieg. Mixing by Thomas Buser. Music by Rolf Riehm. Narrated by Ilse Böttcher, Elenor Holder, Rolf Klein, Klaus Krauleidies, Berthold Korner, Peter Loth, and Ullo von Peinen.

Further reading

Krieg, Peter, *Der Mensch stirbt nicht am Brot allein*, Frankfurt: Vom Weizen zum Brot zum Hunger, 1984.

Seta, Vittorio de

Sicilian director Vittorio de Seta has been active in the field of documentary film since the 1950s. De Seta's cinema, which may be thought of as poetic anthropology, owes much to Grierson's educational conception of the director's role, and bears a resemblance to Flaherty's work in its attention to nature and the reality of human life, as well as in its ethical ambition of discovering the human story. Even so, De Seta's cinema is utterly original for the creative and narrative function that it assigns to the editing of images and, particularly, of sound, the latter always having a leading role in the construction of rhythm and meaning in his films. De Seta's understanding of southern popular culture is diametrically opposite to mainstream ideological discourse wherein the South is depicted as an irredeemably backward land of poverty, crime, and illiteracy, a burden to the industrialized and progressive North. Following in the footsteps of realist writers such as Giovanni Verga (*I Malavoglia*) and of filmmakers such as Luchino Visconti (La terra trema/The Earth Trembles, 1948), De Seta polemically portrays the southern condition as a complex, millennial culture that has died a violent death.

De Seta's work can be roughly divided into four periods: the self-produced 35mm short documentaries made between 1954 and 1959, set in Sicily, Sardinia, and Calabria, a phase concluded by the docufiction Banditi a Orgosolo/Bandits at Orgosolo (1961); the fiction, including the highly successful film for television Diario di un maestro/A Schoolmaster's Diary (1973); the 16mm documentaries for television, mostly produced by RAI, the Italian public broadcasting service, from 1978 to 1983; and the return to the cinema after ten years of silence with the documentary In Calabria (1993).

The 1950s in Italy saw the production of hundreds of documentaries every year, owing to a law that encouraged vast production but did not set up criteria for discrimination or quality control. In this context, De Seta's early shorts stand out as innovative and eccentric in their poetic and technical characteristics. Their combination of techniques were widely perceived as conflicting—the 'realism' of the subject matter and of the sound, and the 'unrealism' of colour and cinemascope—which was very unusual compared with traditional Italian documentaries. Their subject matter consisted of:

> the catching of swordfish in the Strait of Messina, the tuna processing station, the sulphur mine, the sacred representation at Easter, the fishing boats in the Sicilian Channel, the Barbagia shepherds, the peasants harvesting and threshing grain, the 'forgotten people' of a little village in Calabria, are taken away from historical immediacy, from social phenomenology, from political dialectics, and restored to the long, unforgettable time in which those gestures, those rites, that culture were formed and took on a precise identity.
>
> (Consolo 1995: 37)

Real voices, songs, and sounds were recorded on the set and then mixed in studio—a highly unusual practice at a time when the majority of Italian documentaries adopted the mix of voice-over and studio-recorded music. De Seta's early documentaries, bar the last one of the series, I dimenticati/The Forgotten Ones (1959), were instead completely devoid of voice-over, in an attempt to let reality speak for itself. Another way in which De Seta went against mainstream conventions was by using colour at a time when this was seen as an unnecessary luxury for documentaries, and also as an unrealistic device; and by adopting the cinemascope: 'It was my impression that the wide screen, together with the colour, helped me in presenting those "landscapes". This wideness, this 180-degree look, exalted the realism of the representation, even if it was daring to go and light up the mines and then film them in cinemascope' (De Seta quoted in Fofi and Volpi 1999: 14, my translation). It must be said that this innovatory attitude is not accompanied by a revolutionary ideological stance. An 'aristocratic' author akin to Visconti, De Seta does not share the latter's articulation of a Marxist viewpoint in film, and instead frees the narration of any ideological superimposed reading in an attempt to reach the truth that emerges 'naturally' from faces, actions, and sounds.

Whereas the early ten- and eleven-minute shorts were typically constructed around the twelve hours of daylight, from dawn to sunset, Banditi a Orgosolo is a black-and-white, ninety-eight-minute feature with a story that spans a few days. Shot with a troupe consisting only of himself, his wife and collaborator Vera Gherarducci, cameraman Luciano Tovoli, and casting true Sardinian shepherds, the film is a lucid analysis of the phenomenon of the Sardinian bandits, and of their clash with the alien logic of the State. As in the shorts, it is the silences, the sounds, the gestures, and the environment that take centre stage, making this film a docufiction that impressed the jury and audience of the 1961 Venice Film Festival. Banditi a Orgosolo won the prize for the best debut film, and the critic of *Cahiers du cinéma* described it as the only revelation of the festival (Douchet 1961). Notable among the documentaries for television produced by RAI is La Sicilia rivisitata/Sicily Revisited (1980), which returns to the settings of the early documentaries only to find that the ancient traditions, rites, and work practices have disappeared, leaving behind an incommensurable void.

After ten years of silence due to the death of his wife and main collaborator, two operations on his eyes, and to a deep discontent for the direction taken by the Western world, he returned to the cinema with In Calabria, a documentary that programmatically highlights the contrast between the sparse surviving areas of an ancient, peaceful culture that functioned in tune with nature, and the questionable 'modernization without progress' of this region, with the monsters that it produced—loss of roots and traditions, emigration, environmental degradation, organized crime, and unemployment.

LAURA RASCAROLI

Biography

Born in Palermo (Sicily), October 15, 1923. Studied architecture in Rome 1941. Joined the Navy 1943. Arrested by the German Army after September 8, sent to a camp near Salzburg, from which he attempted to escape three times. Returned to Rome after the liberation 1945. Joined the Italian Communist Party 1947. Made his debut in the cinema as assistant director of Jean-Paul Le Chanois 1953. His wife and main collaborator, Vera Gherarducci, died in 1979. Had two eye operations in the 1980s. Moved to a family residence in Sellia Marina, Calabria.

Selected films

1954 Pasqua in Sicilia/Easter in Sicily: director, photographer, editor, producer
1954 Lu tempu di li pisci spata/The Swordfish Season: director, photographer, editor, producer
1955 Isole di fuoco/Islands of Fire: director, photographer, editor, producer
1955 Surfarara/Sulphur Mines: director, photographer, editor, producer
1959 I dimenticati/The Forgotten Ones: director, photographer, editor, producer
1961 Banditi a Orgosolo/Bandits at Orgosolo: director, photographer, editor, producer
1980 La Sicilia rivisitata/Sicily Revisited: director, photographer, editor
1993 In Calabria: director, photographer, editor

Further reading

Consolo, Vincenzo, 'De Seta's Use of the Verga Method', in Alessandro Rais (ed.), *Il cinema di Vittorio de Seta* (The Films of Vittorio de Seta), Palermo: Giuseppe Maimone Editore, 1995.

Douchet, Jean, 'Le bandit d'Orgosolo', *Cahiers du cinéma*, October 1961.

Farassino, Alberto, 'De Seta: The "grand form" of the documentary', in Alessandro Rais (ed.), *Il cinema di Vittorio de Seta* (The Films of Vittorio de Seta), Palermo: Giuseppe Maimone Editore, 1995.

Fofi, Goffredo and Volpi, Gianni, *Vittorio de Seta. Il mondo perduto*, Turin: Lindau, 1999.

Maffettone, Alberto and Soci, Enrico (eds), *Vittorio de Seta. Una vita d'autore*, Bassano del Grappa: Istituto Paolo Valmarana, 1989.

79 Springtimes of Ho Chi Minh

(Cuba, Alvarez, 1967)

79 Primaveras/79 Springtimes of Ho Chi Minh is one of a number of films by Alvarez from the 1960s in which the leading documentarist of the Cuban Revolution seems to reinvent the agitprop of Soviet cinema in the 1920s. An incomparably poetic tribute to the Vietnamese leader Ho Chi Minh, the title refers to his age at the time of his death. The film takes the form of a biographical resumé of the principal dates in Ho Chi Minh's political life; decorative titles announce the passing years interspersed among archive footage and other intertitles inscribed with lines of Ho Chi Minh's poetry.

The opening is beautifully constructed: first come slow-motion shots of flowers opening, then a shot of bombs dropping almost gracefully through the sky. The screen goes blank and we hear the human cry of a singer. After the first credit, a negative image of the young Ho Chi Minh appears, which transforms itself into a positive image and then dissolves into close-ups. These close-ups are refilmed on an optical camera to become somewhat grainy, which at the same time serves to emphasize their material nature and intensify the plasticity of the image. We see Ho Chi Minh aging, the image returns to the negative, the screen turns a brilliant white, and the titles resume. At the end of the credits, we see a close-up of Ho sitting in the open air at his typewriter. A title, 'They tied my legs with a rope', is followed by a shot of him washing his feet; another title, 'And they tied my arms', is followed by a close-up of his hands rolling a cigarette—a man, the montage says, like any other.

When the biographical resumé reaches the victory of Dien Bien Phu, the film begins to shift gear. The 'Internationale' is heard and we see the faces of international Communist leaders at the funeral. We cut to a popular Cuban performer singing, 'The era is giving birth to a heart, it is dying of pain and can stand no more … ' and her audience of cheerful Vietnamese children. The scene is violently interrupted by bombs and the devastation of napalm. Over horrific images of children's burned faces and bodies the music becomes violent and discordant. A title declares: 'They began to kill in order to win'. Then, in slow motion, one of the most infamous images of the Vietnam War, a couple of North American soldiers beating a Vietnamese who has collapsed on the ground: we see feet and hands and the rifle butts of his attackers, but not their faces. Then: 'And now they kill because they cannot win'. No one has ever commented on the Vietnam War with greater economy or dignity.

From here the film moves to shots of anti-war demonstrators in the United States holding placards that unequivocally establish a universal message: 'Vietnam, Watts, it's the same struggle', 'Avenge Che', and 'Fuck the draft'. Then another of the most notorious media images of Vietnam—a pair of GIs taking souvenir snapshots of their victims on the battlefield, to which Alvarez attaches another piece of poetry by Ho Chi Minh—and in these lines the film knits its imagery together:

> Without the glacial winter, without grief and death, Who can appreciate your glory, Spring? The pains which temper my spirit are a crucible And they forge my heart in pure steel.

At this point, many a filmmaker would have been content to conclude—but not Alvarez, who has the nerve, or the chutzpah, to proceed with more scenes of the funeral, set to the music of Iron Butterfly. This is not simply a grand aesthetic gesture. Since the film was made in a period when sectarians were vocal and Western pop music was banned from Cuban airwaves, Alvarez is making pointed solidarity with popular US protest music.

Then comes the coup de grâce. A new title appears: 'Don't let disunity in the Socialist camp darken the future'. Using animation, the title is torn apart into little pieces that slide off the edges of the frame to leave the screen blank. The music disappears. A gunshot announces a split-screen, multi-image sequence of war footage, freeze frames, scratches, sprocket holes, flashes, guns, planes, bombs, sounds of battle with electric keyboard noises on the soundtrack, in which brutal reality bursts through the limits of its portrayal on celluloid in an unrelenting and terrifying assault that ends in the annihilation of a freeze frame, which burns up before our eyes, again leaving a blank white screen. Then the torn pieces of the title reappear and join up again. The picture cuts to rockets firing, to the accompaniment of energizing music by Bach; bursts of gunfire flash across the screen, the flowers reappear, and a final title appears: 'The Yanquis defeated we will construct a Fatherland ten times more beautiful'.

If 79 Primaveras is a testimonial of the solidarity that the Cubans felt with the Vietnamese in their struggle against the same enemy, it is also a paradigm of Alvarez's revolutionary aesthetics. Politically an orthodox Marxist-Leninist-Fidelista, artistically Alvarez had a strong anarchistic streak that made him distrustful of conventions, schools, and aesthetic orthodoxy. Instead, he reinvented the newsreel, the compilation film, the travelog, and every other documentary genre he laid hands on in an irrepressible frenzy of filmic bricolage licensed by that supreme act of bricolage—the Cuban Revolution. He learned to raid the archives and incorporate what he found into a pithy, intelligent, didactic montage, in which, abandoning the all-knowing voice of the commentary, he replaced it with something much more playful and open, something that mobilized the cultural gains of the Revolution's literacy campaign: the animation of words on the screen. The result was a dynamic style where deconstruction meets anti-imperialism in a fusion of politics and poetry.

MICHAEL CHANAN

79 Primaveras/79 Springtimes of Ho Chi Minh (Cuba, ICAIC, 1967, 21 mins). Directed by Santiago Alvarez. Photography by Iván Nápoles. Special effects by Jorge Pucheux, Pedro Luis Hernández, Pepín Rodríguez, and Santiago Penate. Location recording by Raúl Pérez Ureta. Edited by Norma Torrado. Sound and music edited by Isalberto Gálvez. Sound engineer: Carlos Fernández. Archive material: Hanoi Film Studios, Texts y Ho Chi Minh and Jose Martí.

Further reading

Chanan, Michael (ed.), *Santiago Alvarez, BFI Dossier No. 2*, London: BFI, 1980.

——*Cuban Cinema*, Minneapolis, MN: University of Minnesota Press, 2004.

Hess, John, 'Santiago Alvarez: Cine-Agitator for the Cuban Revolution and the Third World', in Thomas Waugh (ed.), *"Show Us Life", Toward a History and Aesthetics of the Committed Documentary*, Metuchen, NJ and London: Scarecrow Press, 1984.

Mraz, John, 'Santiago Alvarez: From Dramatic Form to Direct Cinema', in Julianne Burton (ed.), *The Social Documentary in Latin America*, Pittsburgh, PA: University of Pittsburgh Press, 1990.

Seybold, Katrin

Katrin Seybold is one of Germany's most politically engaged documentarists. To date she has made over fifty films that champion the cause of the political outsider, including children, dissidents, Gypsies, and Jews. Her most celebrated cause is the historical persecution of the Roma and Sinti (Gypsies) by the Nazis and the continuing discrimination against this minority. Seybold and Melanie Spitta, a Sinteza who serves as Seybold's consultant and codirector, have produced four films on the Sinti and Roma. The first and second, Schimpft uns nicht Ziguener/Don't Call us Gypsies (1980) and Wir sind Sinti Kinder und keine Zigeuner/We are Sinti Children and not Gypsies (1981), focus on contemporary Gypsy life and negative attitudes of the general populace toward Gypsy culture. The third and fourth, Es ging Tag und Nacht, liebes Kind: Zigeuner (Sinti) in Auschwitz/It Went on Day and Night, Dear Child: Gypsies (Sinti) in Auschwitz (1982), and Das falsche Wort/Calumny (1987), focus on the nature of Nazi persecution and its echo in official policies that deny reparations to the Gypsies.

Seybold's films make clear that historical and contemporary attitudes toward Gypsies have two major origins: general ignorance about Gypsy culture and received perceptions that distort their culture. Accordingly, her films inform viewers who may know little or nothing about Gypsies. She includes vignettes of home life to correct the cultural and historical stereotypes that have resulted from centuries of cultural and historical misinformation. Thus her films show Gypsies working, studying, and celebrating family life. Absent are the negative images, first encountered in sixteenth-century literature, of the Gypsy as lazy, sneaky, dirty, and promiscuous. Also absent is the nineteenth-century romantic image of the Gypsy as musically inclined and sensual. Seybold's Gypsies are the same as the German viewer, except that they desire to be left alone. That is, they ask that society accept them but not assimilate them.

Seybold's engagement with individuals and groups she feels are left out of the political power structure are the strength and weakness of her style, which is especially apparent in her films on the Sinti and Roma. The rhetoric of the titles reveals from the start that Seybold does not pretend to project objectivity. The films confront viewers with accusations that they turned away from racial genocide, condone the continued use of racial slur, and support government lies. On the one hand, the sympathy she brings to her subjects gives her work an impassioned voice and urgency often missing from the documentary form. On the other hand, her commitment to her subjects has also led to accusations that she 'lacks distance'. Indeed, her films play like broadsides rather than documented reality. Of equal concern is that the lack of objectivity creates its own stereotype—a monolithic, homogeneous world of Gypsies. It is a world that ignores crime, ignores drugs, and for the most part ignores internal dissent. The depiction of Gypsies comes perilously close to the romantic era's noble savage, in particular as it has been manifested in the modern liberal's view of the American Indian or other patronized minorities.

Other Seybold films include Seit ich weiß, daß ich nicht mehr lange lebe, bin ich Stark. Aidskranke berichten/Since I Found Out That I Won't Live Much Longer, I Am Strong. Reports from AIDS Patients (1987), a television documentary in the series Kontakte (Contacts); Deutsch ist meine Muttersprache. Deutsche Juden errinnern sich an ihre christliche Mitbürger/German Is My Native Language. German Jews Remember Their Christian Neighbors (1990), a television documentary; Alle Juden raus! Judenverfolgung in einer deutschen Kleinstadt 1933–45/All Jews Out! The Persecution of the Jews in a Small German Town 1933–45 (1990); and Nein! Zeugen des Widerstandes in München 1933–45/No! Witnesses of the Resistance in Munich 1933–45 (1998).

ROBERT C. REIMER

Biography

Born in 1943. Learned filmmaking with Edgar Reitz, among others. Founded her own production company in 1979. Makes television programs on various social issues. Recognized for her documentary films on the persecution of the Roma and Sinti by the Nazi regime, and the continuing discrimination suffered by this minority.

Selected films

1980 Schimpft uns nicht Ziguener/Don't Call us Gypsies
1981 Wir sind Sinti Kinder und keine Zigeuner/We are Sinti Children and not Gypsies
1982 Es ging Tag und Nacht, liebes Kind: Zigeuner (Sinti) in Auschwitz/It Went on Day and Night, Dear Child: Gypsies (Sinti) in Auschwitz
1987 Das falsche Wort/Calumny
1987 Seit ich weiß, daß ich nicht mehr lange lebe, bin ich Stark. Aidskranke berichten/Since I Found Out That I Won't Live Much Longer, I Am Strong. Reports from AIDS Patients
1990 Deutsch ist meine Muttersprache. Deutsche Juden errinnern sich an ihre christliche Mitbürger/German Is My Native Language. German Jews Remember Their Christian Neighbors
1990 Alle Juden raus! Judenverfolgung in einer deutschen Kleinstadt 1933–45/All Jews Out! The Persecution of the Jews in a Small German Town 1933–45
1998 Nein! Zeugen des Widerstandes in München 1933–45/No! Witnesses of the Resistance in Munich 1933–45

Further reading

Bock, Hans-Michael (ed.), 'Katrin Seybold—Dokumentarfilm Regisseurin', in *Cine-Graph: Lexikon zum deutschsprachigen Film*, Munich, 1984.

Reimer, Robert C. and Reimer, Carol J., *Nazi-retro Film: How German Narrative Cinema Remembers the Past*, Boston: Twayne Publishers, 1992: 165–6.

Shannon, Kathleen

From its inception in 1939, Canada's National Film Board (NFB) had regularly produced documentaries on women's topics. Well into the 1960s these tended to reflect a patriarchal de haut en bas approach. However, the burgeoning feminist movement occasioned deep attitudinal changes throughout North American society, and the NFB was not immune. If any one figure came to symbolize a new articulation of the female condition on film, it was producer/director Kathleen Shannon.

Shannon was dismissive of the NFB's professed policy of detached objectivity, regarding it as institutional, fence-sitting blandness. Her attitude toward the director's role was diametrically opposed to that of the increasingly fashionable cult of the auteur. She was adamant that her position as producer be perceived as one of team coordinator, appreciative of the sensitivities of subjects before the camera. She was insistent on personal involvement in the promotion of the finished product through traditional outlets. In this last regard, her thinking ran contrary to that of her superiors. By the mid-1970s NFB films were finding a larger audience on television than in the time-honoured method of viewing in classrooms and community centres. Her series of ten documentaries on the social and economic demands faced by women reentering the workforce,

Working Mothers (1974), was not telecast at her insistence. She felt their impact would be dulled by the ambiance of television spectatorship, with its commercial interruptions, focus on ratings, and instant competition from other channels. Attitudes were more likely to be formed, changed, or concentrated when a targeted audience was exposed to the topic in a communal setting without distraction.

The critical and popular success of Working Mothers and the Canadian government's decision to give special recognition to International Women's Year, 1975, prompted Shannon to lobby for a production unit devoted almost exclusively to women's and family issues, again with output intended primarily for nontheatrical venues. The idea came to fruition with Studio D. An overwhelmingly female staff, coupled with a self-proclaimed mandate to explore 'decades, centuries, millennia of repressed or forgotten history and meanings' gave rise to criticism that the NFB had created a feminist cultural enclave where even sympathetic male filmmakers were less than welcome. Nevertheless, under Shannon's tutelage, it rapidly became the most widely recognized and controversial arm of the NFB. Not a Love Story (1981), a scathing condemnation of pornography, gained notoriety by being banned in two provinces. It became, perhaps not coincidentally, the highest grossing film in NFB history. If You Love This Planet (1982), a graphically illustrated, pro-nuclear disarmament lecture by activist Dr Helen Caldicott, elicited government protest in both Canada and the United States for its perceived special pleading.

While Kathleen Shannon raised the profile of female filmmakers in Canada, her mission to create a truly feminist 'counter-cinema' faltered. With contemporary subjects, there tended to be an easy progression in the flow of events that suggested containment and completion, although reality was often far less ordered or coherent. A more theoretically informed approach, especially to historical themes, such as The Burning Times (on the persecution of witches), might have placed as much emphasis on the structural and deep-rooted causes of women's oppression as on their effects.

JAMES M. SKINNER

See also: Canada

Biography

Born in Vancouver, Canada, 1935. Music cataloguer for Crawley Films 1952. Joined the National Film Board of Canada 1956, as sound and music editor. Directed her first film, Goldwood, in 1970. Founded Studio D 1974. Acted as executive producer of Studio D 1974–86. Retired from the NFB 1992. Died 1998.

Further reading

Evans, Gary, *In The National Interest: A Chronicle of the National Film Board of Canada from 1949 to 1989*, Toronto: University of Toronto Press, 1991.

Gwyn, Richard and Gwyn, Sandra, 'The Politics of Peace', *Saturday Night*, May 1984.

Hartt, L., 'Working Mothers Series', *Cinema Canada* III, no. 15, August–September, 1974.

Macerola, Francois, *Five Year Operational Plan*, Montreal: National Film Board, 1984.

Shinjuku Boys

(Japan, Longinotto, 1995)

Filmed in Shinjuku, Tokyo's queer commercial district, Shinjuku Boys focuses on the lives of three *onnabes*, women who live as men and who work as 'hosts' for female clients at the New Marilyn Club. The film marks the continued investigation of gender and sexuality in contemporary Japan by the documentary filmmaking team of Kim Longinotto and Jano Williams. Their films are explicitly concerned with women whose lives challenge prevalent assumptions about sex and gender in Japan.

Longinotto and Williams have collaborated on documentaries about Japanese women since Eat the Kimono, their 1989 documentary portrait of outspoken feminist and anti-imperial performer Hanayagi Genshu. Shinjuku Boys is the second of three films that the duo made in the 1990s about female gender transgression in Japan. Dream Girls (1993) explores the world of the Takarazuka Revue, an enormously popular musical theater in which young women play the roles of both sexes. Gaea Girls (1999) documents the grueling training regime of aspiring female wrestlers in a camp outside Tokyo.

In all three films Longinotto and Williams employ a mix of interactive and observational documentary modes, combining interviews with closely observed pro-filmic action. Shot by a low-impact, three-woman crew, Longinotto and Williams's films frequently produce a sense of relaxed intimacy and trust between the filmmakers and their subjects. While Dream Girls and Gaea Girls furnish their depiction of particular institutions (the Takarazuka theater school and the Gaea training camp) with representative individual portraits of women within them, Shinjuku Boys is explicitly presented as a documentary about three particular women, Gaish, Tatsu, and Kazuki. The film's pre-credit sequence introduces its 'characters' individually: Gaish is dressing up in front of a mirror, Kazuki is binding his breasts, and Tatsu is at the barber's. At the end of each of these shots, the frame freezes and the subject's name appears across the image.

In a group interview early in the film, the three *onnabes* are asked to characterize each other. They agree that Gaish is the 'tough guy', Kazuku, the 'cuddly type', and Tatsu, the 'good-time guy'. While this scene performs a conventional documentary shortcut in distinguishing individual subjects as 'character types', Shinjuku Boys does not use them for their common documentary function: to facilitate an overarching narrative plot for the film. Rather, these self-characterizations provide the basis on which the film develops its portrayal of the genuine diversity among *onnabes* in terms of their sexual and gender identities. Although Shinjuku Boys does use a disembodied female voice-over narration (read in English by Shuko Noguchi), the film restricts it to providing only the most basic expository information. Most of the knowledge the viewer receives about these 'Shinjuku boys' comes either from direct address interviews or observed conversations, including one particularly powerful scene in which Kazuki calls up and reconnects with his estranged mother.

Gaish relishes his womanizing role, maintaining several ongoing relationships with clients outside the club. Yet he declares in an interview that he neither wishes to undergo hormone treatment nor identify as a lesbian. His relationship to his clients relies on maintaining the illusion of maleness, which necessitates keeping his clothes on during sex and never letting the client touch him sexually. Both Kazuki and Tatsu are in long-term relationships sustained outside the culture of the New Marilyn Club. Kazuki lives with Kumi, a male-to-female postoperative transsexual, who is a well-known dancer at a local drag bar (one scene is devoted to Kumi's stage performance with Kazuki proudly watching from the bar). Interviewed together in an intimate medium shot, they frankly describe the relationship's blurring of gender roles and its nongenital sexuality. Tatsu has taken male hormones for several years and lives with Tomoe, a nineteen-year-old female student, whom he met at the club. Their interview together is framed in an even more intimate manner by Longinotto's camerawork, which frames only the subject currently speaking, panning whenever the other subject interjects. Tatsu speaks of his desire to know what it feels like to live and have sex as a biological male, while Tomoe adds that if it could happen even for just one day, they would be able to conceive a child together and start a family.

Shinjuku Boys compellingly demonstrates the performativity of gender. The frequent scenes showing the three *onnabes* grooming, dressing up, and generally getting ready for their job emphasize such an understanding of gender as performance. Moreover, the film lends credence to Judith Butler's influential argument that women and queer subjects may achieve agency only through the appropriation and resignification of existing gender norms. The queer reconfiguration of norms performed by *onnabes* consequently generates a proliferation of genders that challenge the hegemony of gendered binaries. Similar to the obsession of teenage girls and housewives with the top 'male' Takarazuka stars seen in Dream Girls, the heterosexual women who make up the majority of the clients at the New Marilyn Club are attracted to *onnabes* because they see them as 'ideal men'. Their allure resides in a masculinity 'softened' by its female performance. Although both films imply that these institutions (the *onnabe* club and the Takarazuka Revue) provide women (as performers, hosts, spectators, and clients) with vital opportunities to resist the patriarchal hegemony of Japanese society, Dream Girls qualifies the suggestion of such resistance by emphasizing how the authoritarian discipline of the Takarazuka school in fact produces 'ideal wives' in its performers who are generally pressured to leave the revue in their mid-twenties in order to get married. In its focus on the personal and professional lives of its three principal subjects, Shinjuku Boys largely elides questions about the New Marilyn Club, the institution that brings together *onnabes* and their clients.

Consequently, the film's remarkable exploration of gender and sexuality overshadows a consideration of class issues within the onnabe scene. Internationally popular at documentary and lesbian and gay film festivals, Shinjuku Boys exemplifies the recent surge of documentaries, including Paris is Burning (1990), Transexual Menace (1996), and Gendernauts (1999), which have been concerned with transgender issues.

ROGER HALLAS

See also: Longinotto, Kim

Shinjuku Boys (UK, Twentieth Century Vixen, 1995, color, Japanese with English subtitles, 53 mins). Distributed by Women Make Movies (USA). Written and directed by Kim Longinotto and Jano Williams. Produced by Kim Longinotto. Cinematography by Kim Longinotto. Music by Nigel Hawks. Edited by John Mister. Sound by Simmy Claire and Rosie Straker. Narrated by Shuko Noguchi. Filmed in Tokyo, Japan.

Further reading

Brockes, Emma, 'Silent Witness', *The Guardian*, February 11, 2000: 8.

Butler, Judith, *Bodies That Matter: On the Discursive Limits of 'Sex'*, New York: Routledge, 1993.

Elley, Derek, 'Shinjuku Boys', *Variety*, November 20, 1995: 48–9.

Lunsing, Wim, *Beyond Common Sense: Sexuality and Gender in Contemporary Japan*, London: Kegan Paul, 2001.

Teasley, Sarah, 'Interview with Kim Longinotto', *Documentary Box*, no. 16, December 1, 2000, www.city.yamagata.yamagata.jp/yidff/docbox/16/box16-2-1-e.html

Shoah

(France, Lanzmann, 1985)

Claude Lanzmann's epic film Shoah ('wasteland' or 'destruction' in Hebrew) is often considered to be one of the most important documentaries ever made. The film's subject is the Holocaust. Yet, the film's scope and its impact on many different disciplines and fields, from Jewish studies to theories of postmodernism, underscores not only the need for viewers to reflect on the incongruous horror that was and is the Holocaust but also to examine ways in which Lanzmann and his film address issues of historical representation. Over a ten-year period Lanzmann and his camera crew filmed over three hundred and fifty hours of interviews from eyewitnesses to the Holocaust: from death camp survivors, Polish farmers, and Nazi guards now in hiding—all gave their testimonies to Lanzmann who, with his editors, Ziva Postec and Anna Ruiz, distilled the film to its running time of nine hours and thirty minutes. While this long running time may be seen by some as pretentious, it is not; the detailed discussions with the witnesses along with the stark, unsettling nature of many of Lanzmann's exterior shots (such as those from Treblinka) arrest the viewer with their documentation of history.

For the field of documentaries what Lanzmann chooses to show the viewer is of particular importance. For Lanzmann, the decision whether to include archival footage of the Holocaust was an ethical one. Unlike other films the subject of which is the Holocaust, such as Nuit et brouillard/Night and Fog (1955) or more recent works such as The Long Way Home (1997), Shoah contains no trace of archival material. The footage in Shoah concerns present-day accounts detailing the events that took place, as told by eyewitnesses. Lanzmann himself has stated that if he did come across a piece of archival footage showing the gassing of Jews, he would destroy it. There is also no reconstruction seen in Shoah, a device used by documentary as well as other filmmakers of historical subject matter who desire to re-create the past though fabrication. Lanzmann has been critical of such filmmakers who attempt to reconstruct the past through such figurative devices of emplotment, characterization, and external nondiegetic sound, saying that such cinematic techniques by filmmakers trivialize the unique nature of the Holocaust through the directors' transgressions of trying to fictively represent its indescribable horror. In creating a new form, one devoid of archival materials and reconstruction, Lanzmann presents a work of art that, through its content and form, bears witness to what occurred.

As mentioned, the witnesses—the victims, the tormentors, the townspeople who turned a blind eye to the atrocities—all present their unique testimony and commentary on the events. This is where we see the intense human side of the Holocaust, of the people trying to put into words what it was they saw, and at times failing. Simon Srebnik, one of two survivors of the four hundred thousand men, women, and children killed at Chelmno, tells Lanzmann as they walk through the green field that was the crematorium, 'It was terrible. No one can describe it. No one can recreate what happened here. Impossible? No one can understand it. Even I, here, now … I can't believe I'm here.' Most of the eyewitness accounts, such as Srebnik's, are spread throughout the film. Each interview then acts as if it were its own small narrative within a much larger narrative framework on which it is commenting. In Shoah there is no grand narrative, no overreaching single story that encapsulates the experiences of all those who died in the Holocaust and those who survived. Instead, Shoah can be seen as a series of meta-narratives that, through the accounts told, presents a collection of histories that seek to speak for those unable to.

Lanzmann is very good at getting people to speak, particularly former SS officers who are in 'hiding'. One such person is Franz Suchomel, a former Nazi guard at Treblinka. Through the use of a hidden camera, Lanzmann is able to get Suchomel to sing a disturbing work song from Treblinka ('No Jew knows that today!' Suchomel exclaims) and to describe, in a very matter-of-fact tone, the detailed process of unloading the trains of Jews and then sending them to the gas chambers. Hannah Arendt's concept of the 'banality of evil' is, when viewing the testimonies of the Nazi guards and of the villagers at Chelmno or Treblinka, so very apt; the guards were ordinary men, and those who were in hiding at the time of filming continue to lead very ordinary lives, yet they were responsible for the machinations of the Holocaust.

Shoah is also a film that, through its directness and repetition, steers the viewers into confronting their own perceptions of and feelings toward the genocide that took place. So often in Shoah Lanzmann repeats certain images and locations. The stones at Treblinka, the forests around Sobibor, and the trains that led through the countryside to the death camps are some images that are all repeated, and in doing so a great weight is placed on the viewer in witnessing the somber, yet meticulous, method in which Lanzmann has framed each shot. It is no wonder, then, why Shoah has become such a touchstone in the field of trauma, for the film presents the testimonies of those who have lived through this traumatic reality and are now, in a sense, confronting it; and the viewers who, through their engagement with the film and its testimonies, may go through a traumatic experience of their own.

The power of Shoah is that it disturbs those who watch it. It should: after all, Shoah is a film about death. Lanzmann would return to the subject of the Holocaust with his films Hotel Terminus: The Life and Times of Klaus Barbie (1988) and Sobibor, Oct. 14, 1943, 4 P.M. (2001), yet Shoah remains the film for which he is best known. The final shot of Shoah—that of a train rolling on into infinity—means that the Holocaust has no end.

ALEXANDER L. KAUFMAN

See also: Lanzmann, Claude

Shoah (France, Les Films Aleph, 1985, 570 mins). Distributor: New Yorker Films Video. Directed by Claude Lanzmann. A coproduction by Les Films Aleph and Historia Films with the assistance of the French Ministry of Culture. Production managers: Stella Gregorz-Quef and Séverine Oliver-Lacamp. Production administrator: Raymonde Badé-Mauffroy. Research assistants: Corrina Coulmas, Iréne Steinfeldt-Levi, and Shaimi Bar Mor. Assistants to the director: Corrina Coulmas and Iréne Steinfeldt-Levi. Interpreters: Barbara Janica (Polish), Francine Kaufmann (Hebrew), and Mrs Apfelbaum (Yiddish). Cameramen: Dominique Chapuis, Jimmy Glasberg, and William Lubchansky. Camera assistants: Caroline Champetier de Ribes, Jean-Yves Escoffier, Slavek Olczyk, and Andrés Silvart. Gaffer: Daniel Bernard. Sound engineers: Bernard Aubouy and Michel Vionnet (in Israel). Editors: Ziva Postec and Anna Ruiz (Treblinka sequence). Assistant editors: Geneviève de Gouvion Saint-Cyr, Bénédicte Mallet, Yael Perlov, and Christine Simonot. Sound editor: Danielle Fillios, Anne-Marie L'Hôte, and Sabine Mamou. Sound editing assistants: Catherine Sabba and Catherine Trouillet. Mixing: Bernard Aubouy. Subtitles: A. Whitelaw and W. Byron. Filmed in Chelmno, Berlin, Munich, Frankfurt, Wannsee, Warsaw, Treblinka, Sobibor, Grabow, Vilna, Wlodawa, Malkinia, Kolo, Auschwitz, Tel Aviv, Ben Shemen, Corfu, Cincinnati, New York City, Washington, DC, and Burlington, Vermont. Awarded the Best Documentary by the

New York Film Critics Circle (1985); the Special Award by the Los Angeles Film Critics Association (1985); the Caligari Film Award, the FIPRESCI Prize, and OCIC Award—Honorable Mention by the Berlin International Film Festival (1986); the BSFC Award for Best Documentary by the Boston Society of Film Critics (1986); the IDA Award by the International Documentary Association (1986); the Rotterdam Award for Best Documentary by the Rotterdam International Film Festival (1986); and the Flaherty Documentary Award by the British Academy of Film and Television Arts (1987).

Shoot to Kill

(UK, Kosminsky, 1990)

In May 1984 John Stalker was appointed to head the inquiry into the deaths of six republican men shot dead by the Royal Ulster Constabulary's (RUC) antiterrorist unit, E4A, in Northern Ireland in 1982. The docudrama Shoot to Kill was based on the 'Stalker Inquiry' and followed the RUC and the 'shoot to kill' incidents of November and December 1982. The program was broadcast by Yorkshire Television in the UK in May 1990.

On November 11, 1982, three Irish Republican Army (IRA) volunteers were shot a total of one hundred and nine times at an RUC roadblock near Lurgan, County Armagh. On November 24 another IRA member was shot dead by RUC members at a hay shed in Lurgan, and on December 12 two more were shot dead by the RUC at Mullacreevie estate, Armagh. The program follows Stalker as he apparently gets closer to the truth and his subsequent dismissal.

Director Peter Kosminsky had planned to make a documentary about the Stalker inquiry, but this proved untenable, given that the majority of those he wished to interview were either dead, unavailable, or could not speak because of the Official Secrets Act. Although Kosminsky recognized the advantage of using drama to reach a wider audience, the focus was that the documentary aspect should have primacy over the dramatic elements: 'We strove very hard to not sacrifice reality to the demands of good television'.

Kosminsky saw the docudrama as an unproblematic vehicle for the telling of 'one of the great untold stories'. Others, however, used the label to diminish any claims made by the film. The full committee of the IBA watched the film before it was broadcast, because of the sensitive nature of the subject matter, and agreed to allow the broadcast on the basis that the film would be clearly marked as a docudrama. This was presumably to safeguard viewers who may have been misled into thinking of it as a 'true' document of the events. The labeling of the film as a docudrama provided a safeguard for the government, in that any material considered as potentially damaging could be dismissed as fictional.

Shoot to Kill does not mimic or utilize documentary aesthetics, or a 'documentary look', in any systematic way. Instead, its referentiality is developed through its use of specific names, places, and dates. The broadcast itself was framed through its use of a voice-over at the beginning, which states that it is based on real events and that actors are used to portray real people. This serves to reinforce the notion that the film uses drama merely to fill in the gaps, and encourages viewers to evaluate it as documentary.

Although the film does not employ documentary codes and conventions systematically, there are instances in which documentary aesthetics are referenced. For example, there is an early scene in which members of the RUC are seen running toward an old farmhouse that has been under surveillance. This is shot from the point of view of the RUC and uses a shaky camcorder style. This serves to suggest the authenticity of the action and heightens the dramatic tension. In another scene, a 'fly-on-the-wall' style is used. Members of the RUC are again on surveillance after being given information regarding 'suspected' members of the IRA. As the suspects are spotted leaving by car, the surveillance team follows them. A car chase ensues and when the suspects refuse to stop, there is a shooting sequence that ends with the killing of the suspects. The car chase takes place from the RUC point of view. Shoot to Kill has a narrative structure that broadly resembles the expositional documentary. The problem has been set up, and the narrative is driven by the desire to collect the facts, analyse them, and present a final solution to the initial question or problem. For example, a key aspect of the investigation is to clarify and confirm the accuracy of RUC officers' accounts of events surrounding the killing of unarmed civilians suspected of terrorist activities. In doing so, Stalker compares officer accounts with the accounts provided by the forensic team in order to establish the truth. However, a final result was never achieved by the Stalker team because as they delved more deeply into the matter, the inquiry was aborted.

After the screening of the film, a televised studio discussion took place. In Shoot to Kill: The Issues, Kosminsky, along with representatives from the Conservative party, the Social Democratic Labour party, the Ulster Unionists, and Amnesty International, were invited to discuss the issues raised by the film. Kosminsky was challenged on the basis that the film was misleading and that it had served to encourage the IRA and to discourage the RUC. David Trimble of the Ulster Unionists stated that 'film has not told the truth, it has told a lie'. He argued that it was misleading because people would be left with the impression that there was a 'shoot to kill' policy. He pointed out that neither the Stalker nor the Sampson inquiries had found any evidence of a shoot to kill policy. However, neither inquiry had been published and so it was difficult to use them as evidence. Although there is little chance of ever reaching a definitive account of the events and issues, Shoot to Kill aligns itself with the discourses of documentary and factuality, thus making claims to truthfulness and accuracy.

JANE ROSCOE

Shoot to Kill. (UK, Zenith Productions, for Yorkshire Television, 1990, 222 mins). Produced by Yorkshire Television. Directed by Peter Kosminsky. Written by Michael Eaton. Starring Jack Shepherd as John Stalker.

Shub, Esfir

Along with Ol'ga Preobrazhanskaya, who worked in conventional narrative film, Esfir (or Esther) Shub was one of the most prominent female filmmakers of her generation. Along with Dziga Vertov, the filmmaker with whom she had a close (and frequently stormy) professional relationship, Shub is credited with the creation of the compilation film, a type of documentary constructed almost exclusively of retrieved archival film. While Vertov worked with more contemporary material, Shub recontextualized old newsreel footage to create new films, most notably the trilogy comprising The Fall of the Romanov Dynasty, The Great Way, and The Russia of Nicholas II and Lev Tolstoi. Produced under the auspices of Sovkino, in cooperation with the Museum of the Revolution, the trilogy represents a formidable amount of research; it is estimated that Shub viewed close to three million feet of newsreel footage. This was material shot by multiple, often anonymous, cameramen who had filmed both prerevolutionary and contemporary events. These films are in effect a visual history of Russia from the end of the nineteenth century, through the October Revolution, and up to the tenth anniversary of the Revolution.

Shub applied to nonfiction film the 'montage of attractions' most commonly associated with Sergei Eisenstein (Bruzzi 2000: 22), but unlike Eisenstein's startling collisions, Shub's films use a subtle method of montage that brings a great deal of ironic play to bear on her material, a technique that radically distinguished her work. The concept she developed for selecting and juxtaposing shots was not schematic but more intuitive and associational. Her ultimate goal was to comment on events by this selection and juxtaposition, while preserving the ontological authenticity of the shots themselves.

This quality was noted with approval by contemporary critics, most notably the Constructivist theorists grouped around the magazine Novy Lef. Shub's strength lay in what was considered her mastery of 'long sequence' montage, which recreated events while preserving their integral characteristics, and their temporal and spatial reality. At the same time, Shub had a refined and sophisticated conception of the implications and limitations of what she called *podlinnii material* (authentic material). She wrote:

> To assemble a documentary film you only have to think clearly. The spectator has to manage to not only see people and events properly, but to memorise them. Let the lovers of cheap montage effects remember, that to edit simply and with a clear sense is not at all easy, but very difficult.
>
> (Shub 1971: 18)

Today (1929, released 1930), in which she set up a number of bold oppositions between what she saw as the spiritual as well as economic crisis in the United States and the development of the Soviet Union, was her last compilation film, except for one further venture in 1939. Like a number of her contemporaries, most notably Vertov, Shub had difficulty entering the Stalinist era. She was the victim of Party philistines and ideological prejudice against formal experimentation. Her style changed; she stayed in documentary mode, but as she was dealing with contemporary themes, she began shooting material herself rather than using archive material. Her only exercise in compilation filmmaking thereafter was Spain (1939), using film shot by Roman Karmen and Boris Makaseev. Her legacy remains in that form of political documentary cinema where archive material is used dialectically or against the grain as part of a historical argument or debate.

MARINA BURKE

See also: Fall of the Romano Dynasty, The; Vertov, Dziga

Biography

Born in 1894 in the Ukraine into a family of landowners. Studied literature in Moscow a few years before the October Revolution. After the revolution, initially worked for the theatrical department of Narkompros (the Commisariat of Education), but then in 1922 entered the film profession through the auspices of the newly formed Goskino, where she worked as a re-editor of foreign and prerevolutionary films for Soviet audiences. Between 1922 and 1925 re-edited and made new intertitles for about two hundred foreign films and ten domestic feature films, most famously Fritz Lang's two-part Dr Mabuse der Spieler (1922), on which Eisenstein worked as her assistant. In 1927 and 1928 made her famous film trilogy, which traces the birth of the USSR through to the tenth anniversary of the October Revolution. Between 1933 and 1935 supervised the montage class in Eisenstein's workshop in VGIK. In 1935 awarded the title of Most Honoured Artist of the Republic. During the war, edited newsreels and continued to teach montage in VGIK, then transferred to Alma Ata. In 1942 became chief editor of Novosti Dnya (News of the Day) in the Central Studio for Documentary Film in Moscow. Wrote *Krupnym planom* (In Close-Up) in 1959, reissued with additional material as *Zhizn moya-kinematograf* (Cinema is My Life) in 1971. Died in Moscow in September 1959.

Selected films

1927 The Fall of the Romanov Dynasty/Padenie dinastii romanovykh
1927 The Great Road/Velikii put'
1928 The Russia of Nicholas II and Lev Tolstoi/Rossiya Nikolya II i Lev Tolstoi
1930 Today/Segodnya
1932 Komsomol—Leader of Electrification/K-Sh-E
1939 Spain/Ispaniya
1942 The Native Country/Strana rodnaya
1946 On the Other Side of the Araks/Po tu storonu Araksa

Further reading

Bruzzi, Stella, *New Documentary: A Critical Introduction*, London: Routledge, 2000.

Leyda, Jay, *Films Beget Films: A Study of the Compilation Film*, London: Allen & Unwin, 1964.

Petric, Vlada, 'Esfir Shub: Cinema is My Life', *Quarterly Review of Film Studies*, Fall 1978: 429–47.

——'Esfir Shub's Unrealised Project', *Quarterly Review of Film Studies*, fall 1978: 448–56.

——'Esther Shub: Film as a Historical Discourse', in Thomas Waugh (ed.), *'Show Us Life!': Towards a History and an Aesthetic of the Committed Documentary*, Metuchen, NJ: Scarecrow Press, 1984.

Roberts, Graham, *Forward, Soviet! History and Non-fiction Film in the USSR*, London: I.B. Tauris, 1999.

Shub, Esfir, *Zhizn moya-kinematograf* (Cinema is My Life), Moscow: Isskustvo, 1971.

Yampolsky, Mikhail, 'Reality at Second Hand', *Historical Journal of Film, Radio and Television* 2, no. 2, 1991: 161–71.

Shuker, Gregory

Gregory B. Shuker was a journalist, filmmaker, and producer, as well as a core member of Drew Associates, a group of journalists and filmmakers, founded in 1959 and commonly regarded as the originators of the pioneering American Direct Cinema Movement.

Born in Charleston in West Virginia, Shuker studied at Northwestern University. As editor-in-chief of the student newspaper he visited Russia in 1954 and on his return had six of his 35mm color slide pictures published by *Life* magazine. Shuker was later hired as a reporter by *Life*, where he worked on last-minute foreign and domestic news. There he met Robert Drew, who had been working as a correspondent for *Life* since 1946. In 1959 Shuker became one of the first members of Drew Associates, an independent production team founded by Robert Drew that was to play a pivotal role in the 1960s renaissance of American documentary film. The idea behind Drew Associates was to make films that would transport the photojournalism as developed at *Life* magazine into documentary films, in order to move away from the staged, more instructive and illustrative style of documentary filmmaking, and to better represent social realities as they unfold in front of the camera. The most prominent trademark of Drew Associates was the handheld, lightweight 16mm camera and the newly developed synchronous, portable sound, which shaped the style of direct cinema and allowed for a radical rethinking of documentary aesthetics. Other members of Drew Associates alongside Gregory Shuker were Tom Bywaters, Anne Drew, Mike Jackson, Richard Leacock, James Lipscomb, Albert and Davis Maysles, D.A. Pennebaker, and Hope Ryden.

It is often difficult to identify which members of Drew Associates were responsible for which aspects of the work. Since none of these young journalists and filmmakers considered their stories made by them, they generally avoided the use of the term 'director'. Moreover, since many regularly performed multiple tasks in pre-production, shooting, and postproduction, they simply called themselves 'correspondents'. By and large, however, Shuker's role was that of a producer. Shuker's central tasks were to 'find' stories—stories that did not need narrating, that already contained enough dramatic elements to be able to tell themselves. According to Robert Drew, Shuker's success lay in his ability to operate in ways that did not attract attention—crucially important in a genre that is trying to film people as unselfconsciously as possible.

The first documentaries that Shuker produced for Drew Associates were The Children Were Watching, a documentary about racism and desegregation in New Orleans and Kenya: Land of the White Ghost (I) and Kenya: Land of the Black Ghost (II), which in two thirty-minute episodes documented the outcome of the first election after independence in Kenya, all shot in 1961. These films, with cinematography by Richard Leacock, were produced for the Close Up series of the American Broadcasting Company (ABC).

In the years 1961 to 1962 Drew Associates produced a number of television documentaries for The Living Camera, a series of ten direct cinema films later distributed by Time-Life. These films generally focused on one individual, often public figures such as Jane Fonda and John F. Kennedy. Among the films that Shuker produced for the series are Nehru, a fifty-five-minute documentary about the first Indian Prime Minister's last election campaign (in which Shuker breaks the direct cinema 'rules' by asking Nehru a question), Susan Starr, about a nineteen-year-old concert pianist performing at an important international competition, and Eddie (aka On the Pole), about the race driver Eddie Sachs's unpredicted defeat in the Indianapolis 500 race.

Two of Drew Associates' most celebrated films were also produced by Shuker. The first, The Chair (1962), a fifty-five-minute film focused on twenty-two-year-old Paul Crump who had been sentenced to death by electric chair. Crump had befriended a prison warden and asked the warden to be the man to pull the switch. Shuker 'found' this story and entered the prison to film these extraordinary moments. The film was the second-to-last film of the Living Camera Series and won the Special Jury Prize at the Cannes Film Festival.

The second celebrated film was Crisis: Behind a Presidential Commitment, a dramatic documentary shot in 1963, which follows the growing crisis between Alabama Governor George Wallace and President John F. Kennedy over Wallace's refusal in 1963 to allow the enrollment of the first black students (after Autherine Lucy in 1956) at the University of Alabama. Shuker was instrumental in persuading Robert Kennedy to allow the camera into the White House. The film moves between John and Robert Kennedy in the Oval Office, Governor Wallace, the students Vivian Malone and James A. Hood and the Deputy Attorney General Nicholas Katzenbach. As Kennedy federalized the National Guards and each party involved weighs the possibilities, the suspense heightens until, finally, Governor Wallace concedes on June 11. When the film was broadcast on ABC four months later it caused a storm of protest over the admission of cameras into the White House and also received harsh criticism by *The New York Times*, which called the access given by the President's office 'ill advised' and the film 'a peep-show'.

Another film produced by Shuker—and the last one of the Kennedy series—is Faces in November, made in 1964. The camera quietly observes the funeral of John F. Kennedy by focusing almost exclusively on the faces of the mourners. The film was well received at the Venice Film Festival in the following year.

In 1965 Shuker produced the fifty-minute documentary Letters from Vietnam, the first film to use synchronous sound in the depiction of combat. Shuker and cameraman Abbot Mills flew with over sixty missions with a helicopter squadron in Vietnam, and the film was later broadcast by ABC.

In the mid-1960s—long after Pennebaker, Leacock, and the Maysles brothers had left to start their own companies—Gregory Shuker left Drew Associates and went on to produce films of his own. He continued making films of a highly political nature. An important example is the fifty-two-minute documentary Free at Last: His Final Days, which consists of footage of Martin Luther King, Jr, taken between January and April 1968 during his 'Poor People's Campaign' and breaking off with King's death. The film won the Grand Prize at the Venice Film Festival and an Emmy Award.

In the following years Shuker worked increasingly on industrial projects and made a range of commercial films, alongside films such as Life in Outer Space, sponsored by NASA, and various mini-documentaries for IBM. In 1972 Shuker cofounded Playback Associates, which produced industrial training videos and instructional tapes.

Shuker died in New York on March 29, 2000. His career in filmmaking—as a producer, a cameraman, and a finder of stories—was shaped by a commitment to political concerns and a belief in the educational and the history-shaping power of the medium.

JACOBIA DAHM

See also: Drew, Robert

Biography

Born in Charleston, West Virginia. Studied at Northwestern University. Hired as a reporter by *Life* magazine. Met Robert Drew and in 1959 became one of the first members of Drew Associates. Died in New York on March 29, 2000.

Further reading

Barnouw, Erik, *Documentary: A History of the Non-fiction Film*, Oxford and New York: Oxford University Press, 1993.

Barsam, Richard M., *Nonfiction Film. A Critical History*, Bloomington, IN: Indiana University Press, 1973.

Bluem, A. William, *Documentary in American Television*, New York: Hastings House, 1965.

Breitrose, Henry, 'On the Search for the Real Nitty-Gritty: Problems & Possibilities in Cinéma Vérité', *Film Quarterly* 17, no. 4, summer 1964: 36–40.

Gould, Jack, 'TV: Too Many Cameras; Documentary on the Segregation Crisis Termed Just a Peep Show', *The New York Times*, October 22, 1963: 75.

Lipscomb, James C., 'Cinema-verite', *Film Quarterly* 18, no. 2, winter 1964: 62–3.

Macdonald, Kevin and Cousins, Mark, *Imagining Reality. The Faber Book of the Documentary*, London and Boston: Faber & Faber, 1996.

n.a., *Cinema vérité. Defining the Moment* (videorecording, 102 mins), directed by Peter Wintonick, National Film Board of Canada, 1999.

O'Connell, P.J., *Robert Drew and the Development of Cinema Verité in America*, Carbondale, IL and Edwardsville, IL: Southern Illinois University Press, 1992.

Rosenthal, Allan (ed.), *New Challenges for Documentary*, Berkeley, CA and London: University of California Press, 1988.

Watson, Mary Ann, *The Expanding Vista: American Television in the Kennedy Years*, New York: Oxford University Press, 1990 (also Durham, NC: Duke University Press, 1994).

Young, Colin, 'Cinema of Common Sense', *Film Quarterly* 17, no. 4, summer 1964: 26–9, 40.

Silent World, The

(France, Cousteau, 1956)

Jacques Cousteau's The Silent World/Le Monde du silence is a landmark in wildlife documentary filmmaking. Co-directed with the help of the young Louis Malle, the picture follows the trials and tribulations of the crew of the *Calypso* as they voyage through the Red Sea, the Persian Gulf, and the Indian Ocean. The completed documentary was some two years in the making and is reported to have been founded on more than one thousand dives. Although sharing its title with an earlier Cousteau publication, The Silent World is an original work that served to popularize the previously marginal form of the underwater documentary. Until that film, Cousteau's work had been limited to short reportage-style essays, commercial projects for companies such as British Petroleum, and photographic expeditions associated with publications such as *National Geographic*. After The Silent World Cousteau was able to develop any number of projects in his own right.

The Silent World premiered in Paris on February 7, 1956, at a formal conservative soirée attended by the then President of the Republic, René Coty. Subsequently it was a commercial success that was also garlanded with many glittering prizes. Thus, in April 1956 it was awarded the Palme d'Or at Cannes and just one year later was presented with an Academy Award for Best Documentary. The victory at Cannes was especially impressive since the film was in competition against Henri-Georges Clouzot's Mystére Picasso and Ingmar Bergman's Smiles of a Summer Night. Remarkably, until the famous victory of Michael Moore's Fahrenheit 9/11 in 2004, The Silent World continued to be the only documentary film to have been awarded the Palme d'Or. Furthermore, it is a fascinating historical coincidence that at the same festival that heralded the arrival of The Silent World, the

Figure 17 The Silent World, Jacques Cousteau, 1956 (Courtesy of the Everett Collection)

organizers were unprepared to support Alain Resnais's lyrical work devoted to the Holocaust, Nuit et brouillard/Night and Fog. In contrast to the triumph of The Silent World, Resnais's moving piece was expelled to the fringes of the event, and only shown 'outside competition'. In this context it is important to note that the same Cannes jury included the disgraced actress, Arletty. Like Cousteau, she had worked during the Vichy period (1940–4). Her prominent role at Cannes 1956 therefore marked something of an official return to the mainstream postwar industry. It is in this wider sociopolitical context of the collective rewriting of the war and France's role in the Holocaust that The Silent World proved triumphant and Night and Fog was unjustly marginalised. Clearly, Cousteau's work was far more palatable for audiences who preferred light entertainment over challenging moral or historical reflection.

Cousteau and Malle's treatment of undersea wildlife represented a radical advance in cinematography. Genuinely revolutionary underwater photography was developed in the making of the documentary. New cameras and diving equipment filmed sea life at previously unseen depths of the ocean floor. The Silent World created bold iconic underwater images that have been repeated and modified around the world in numerous films and television series. Thus, it is not an exaggeration to suggest that The Silent World almost single-handedly instigated a minor but entertaining subgenre. More generally speaking, Cousteau and Malle's work launched the global fashion for amateur diving and photography. The fundamental aesthetic 'look' of the film has probably also influenced fictional work ranging from Stephen Spielberg's Jaws (1975) to James Cameron's The Abyss (1989). Rather more amusingly, Cousteau is also referred to extensively throughout Wes Anderson's comedy Rushmore (1998). Such postmodern irony is indicative of the genuine artistic significance of Cousteau's original work.

In retrospect, significant elements of The Silent World appear to be horribly dated. For example, the crew's mode of encounter with sea life is predominantly cast through a quasi-Conradian ethic of man's struggle against the untamed force of the natural world. Such implicit philosophical underpinnings are closer to the social value system of the 1890s than to the undercurrents of reform that were already preparing the way for New Wave cinema and the freedoms of the 1960s. Similarly, the film also predates Cousteau's famous turn to support the ecological movement. For example, The Silent World contains several passages that would make today's environmentalists wince with discomfort. Thus, Cousteau shows his sailors' uncontrollable massacre of a shoal of sharks. Later, the same crew casually hurls dynamite into a coral reef to identify the range of dead crustaceans and fish that gradually float to the surface. Any sense of ecologism or environmentalism is limited and it was not until 1960 that Cousteau began to commit himself to that now more fashionable cause.

The production history of The Silent World remains clouded in mystery. Speaking to Philip French in the early 1990s, Louis Malle implied that Cousteau had simply plucked him from the Institut des Hautes Etudes Cinématographiques (IDHEC, the Parisian film academy) to work as an intern on the *Calypso*. However, Pierre Billard has suggested that the background to the making of the picture was a more complex commercial affair. For instance, Billard alludes to the fact that Malle not only acted as an assistant director on the film but was also probably influential in obtaining a loan to support part of its production costs. Any investment on the part of the Malle family, who owned the Béghin sugar empire, was richly rewarded, if never explicitly credited. Moreover, the success of the film ensured that the young Malle gained an important profile in the industry. Shortly afterwards, Malle briefly assisted his hero Robert Bresson on Un condamné à mort s'est échappée/A Man Escaped (1956) and then produced his own first solo feature, L'Ascenseur pour l'échafaud/Lift to the Scaffold (1957). Cousteau's future career was also secured by the triumph. It was on the basis of the global success of The Silent World that the Commander resigned his post from the French navy and was appointed to Monaco's oceanographic institute, quickly becoming an international celebrity.

HUGO FREY

See also: Cousteau, Jacques-Yves; Malle, Louis; Night and Fog; Resnais, Alain

The Silent World/Le Monde du silence (France, Requins Associés, 1956, 86 mins). Directed by Jacques Cousteau and Louis Malle.

Cinematography: Edmond Séchan (Technicolor). Photography: J. Cousteau, L. Malle, Frédéric Duma, and Alberto Falco. Music: Yves Baudrier. Editing: Georges Alépée. Special effects: Noël Robert. Commentary: James Dugan (English-language edition).

Further reading

Billard, Pierre, *Louis Malle: le Rebelle solitaire*, Paris: Plon, 2003.

Cousteau, Jacques, and Dumas, Frédéric, *The Silent World*, London: Hamish Hamilton, 1953.

French, Philip (ed.), *Malle on Malle*, London: Faber, 1993.

Frey, Hugo, *Louis Malle*, Manchester: Manchester University Press, 2004.

Madsen, Axel, *Cousteau*, London: Robson Books, 1989.

Violet, Bernard, *Cousteau*, Paris: Plon, 1993.

Silva, Jorge

See entry: Rodríguez, Marta and Jorge Silva

Sinclair, Upton

Writer and political activist Upton Sinclair was a peripheral figure in film history, but he played a vital role in a misadventure involving a far more significant writer/activist—Sergei Eisenstein. Together they embarked on the debacle that was Que Viva Mexico!

By the time Sinclair met Eisenstein he had established a reputation as a leading socialist and the prolific author of muckraking novels. Sinclair's involvement with Que Viva Mexico! was not his first contact with the film world. He had long been keen to break into it so that he could extend the message of his books to a new audience, and make enough money to allow himself the freedom to pursue his political activities.

He had appeared as an agitator in the 1914 adaptation of his 1906 novel, *The Jungle*, exposing conditions in the Chicago stockyards, the first pro-labor feature in the United States. Another adaptation, The Money Changers (1920), intended as a critical examination of financier J.P. Morgan, became, in Sinclair's view, a melodrama on the Chinatown drug trade. The Wet Parade (on Prohibition) was filmed in 1932. Also, Charlie Chaplin's short The Adventurer (1917) had been based on a Sinclair story. None of these had been as financially successful as Sinclair had hoped. More lucrative was his 1933 book, *Upton Sinclair Presents William Fox*, charting the rise and fall of a movie mogul. After Que Viva Mexico! Sinclair adapted the anti-VD propaganda film Damaged Goods (1937).

Eisenstein, together with his assistant Grigori Alexandrov and cinematographer Edouard Tissé, had been invited to the United States in 1930 by Paramount, who wanted to capitalize on his reputation. After failure to agree on a project, and with vocal hostility to his presence in the United States from the right-wing press, Eisenstein's contract was terminated in October. Rather than return to the Soviet Union, he approached Sinclair, through Chaplin, for help in financing his dream to make an independent film in Mexico. Eisenstein had met Robert Flaherty in Hollywood and had discussed an ethnographic approach using amateur actors within the framework of a fictional film.

Sinclair had mixed motives in agreeing: he wanted to participate in a financially successful project but he also felt that Eisenstein had been treated badly in the United States, and wanted him to be able to make at least one film before returning to Moscow. Sinclair and his wife, Craig, raised $25,000 and Eisenstein signed a contract on November 24, 1930, with Craig to make a nonpolitical film in three to four months. The contract was heavily weighted in favor of Craig: there was no reference to Eisenstein editing the film, and crucially everything produced by the Mexican team was to be her property. By signing, Eisenstein showed himself to be naive in business matters, trusting that the Sinclairs' political leaning would render the terms a formality. Eisenstien's party left for Mexico the following month.

Geduld and Gottesman (1970) provide a chronology of the project by means of the principals' letters, although as it is based on Sinclair's archives it is weighted toward him, with Eisenstein underrepresented. Eisenstein clearly considered the contract to be elastic, and conceived a scheme, involving six separate episodes, that could never be completed within the time-scale and budget specified (Eisenstein later claimed that had they adhered to the original agreement his efforts 'would have merely resulted in a pitiful travelogue').

The modest budget and time scale were quickly abandoned as Eisenstein's demands increased in line with his ambition. Unable to compromise his artistic vision, he stayed in Mexico for fourteen months and more than doubled the budget. Eventually, Sinclair, who was spending a huge amount of time raising funds and acting as producer, to the detriment of his writing and health, came to feel that he was being blackmailed by Eisenstein, who indicated that unless he received additional funds and film stock there would be no film and the investment would be lost.

Added to the financial difficulties that Eisenstein's prolonged stay in Mexico were causing Sinclair, political developments in the Soviet Union were creating a climate inimical to the sense of aesthetic adventure that had prevailed when Eisenstein left in August 1929, and the Mexican film's lyricism ran counter to the emerging doctrine of Socialist Realism. Additionally, Eisenstein had originally been granted permission to travel for only one year and had so far exceeded this period that Sinclair received a telegram from Stalin himself in November 1931 warning that Eisenstein was in danger of being perceived as a deserter at home.

Sinclair, under pressure from his wife, finally called a halt in February 1932, leaving shooting unfinished. He had concluded that Eisenstein had no intention of finishing the project, using it as a pretext to avoid returning to Moscow. Having stopped the filming, Sinclair initially still hoped that Eisenstein would be able to edit the footage but ultimately felt he could not trust him or the Soviet authorities. Instead, producer Sol Lesser was engaged to carve a commercial film from it after Eisenstein had returned home. Sinclair needed a return on the investment—thereby endorsing critics who charged that he was a capitalist at heart.

A campaign against Sinclair was mounted by Eisenstein's supporters, notably Seymour Stern, editor of *Experimental Cinema*, and Sinclair's left-wing credentials were damaged both at home and in the Soviet Union. Given his aspirations, and the problems they had caused, it is ironic that he should have spent such an enormous amount of time and energy struggling to facilitate Eisenstein's relatively nonpolitical film, when shortly afterwards King Vidor wrote and directed the socially aware Our Daily Bread (1934), with its vision of working-class solidarity, the dispossessed organizing to create a collective farm.

In order to recoup some of the costs, in addition to the films that Lesser produced, footage was sold to Marie Seton, an early biographer of Eisenstein, and more to Bell and Howell to make six educational documentaries. Sinclair presented the remaining material to New York's Museum of Modern Art (MoMA) in 1954, where Jay Leyda assembled a six-hour compilation. In 1973 much of MoMA's holding was sent to Gosfilmofond, where Alexandrov also tried to re-create the spirit of Eisenstein's intentions.

TOM RUFFLES

Biography

Born in Baltimore, Maryland, on September 20, 1878. Attended New York City College, funded by writing for newspapers and magazines. Published first novel in 1901, followed by a steady stream of books and articles on social issues. Achieved fame with *The Jungle* (1906), after which he became known as a muckraking journalist and novelist, exposing institutional corruption. Moved to California in 1915. Active in politics from the age of twenty-four, initially for the Socialist Party, for which he stood for Congress and Senate and for governorship of California. Switched to the Democrats in 1933. Again ran unsuccessfully for governorship of California on platform 'End Poverty in California' (EPIC) in 1934. Wrote over ninety books, fiction and nonfiction. Won the Pulitzer Prize in 1943 for novel *Dragon's Teeth*. Moved to Buckeye, Arizona in 1953. Died in Bound Brook, New Jersey on November 25, 1968.

Films produced from Eisenstein's Mexican footage

1933 Thunder Over Mexico (Sol Lesser)
1933 Death Day (Sol Lesser)
1933 S.M. Eisenstein in Mexico (Sol Lesser)
1939 Time in the Sun (Marie Seton)
1942 Mexican Symphony: Mexico Marches; Conquering Cross; Idol of Hope; Land and Freedom; Spaniard and Indian; Zapotec Village (Bell and Howell)
1957 Eisenstein's Mexican Project (Jay Leyda)
1979 Que Viva Mexico! (Grigori Alexandrov)

Further reading

Amengual, Barthélemy, *Que Viva Eisenstein!* Lausanne: Editions L'age d'homme, 1981.
Eisenstein, Sergei, *Que Viva Mexico!*, revised edn, London: Vision, 1972.
Foner, Philip S., 'Upton Sinclair's "The Jungle: The Movie"', in Dieter Herms (ed.), *Upton Sinclair: Literature and Social Reform*, Frankfurt: Peter Lang, 1990.
Geduld, Harry M. and Gottesman, Ronald (eds), *Sergei Eisenstein and Upton Sinclair: The Making and Unmaking of Que Viva Mexico!* London: Thames and Hudson, 1970.
Harris, Leon, *Upton Sinclair: American Rebel*, New York: Thomas Y. Crowell, 1975.
Scott, Ivan, *Upton Sinclair, The Forgotten Socialist*, Lewiston, New York: The Edwin Mellen Press, 1997.
Seton, Marie, *Sergei Eisenstein—A Biography*, revised edn, London: Dennis Dobson, 1978.
Sinclair, Upton, *The Autobiography of Upton Sinclair*, revised edn, London: W.H. Allen, 1963.

Siodmak, Robert

Robert Siodmak is best known as one of the most talented and prolific directors of film noir from the 1940s. One recalls the masturbatory frenzy of a jazz drummer lusting after a B-girl surrounded by expressionistic shadows in Phantom Lady (1944); the placement of killer, potential victim, and avenging angel at different levels on the eponymous structure of The Spiral Staircase (1946); and the hushed resignation of the 'Swede' to his own death in The Killers (1946). Like other notables making noir (Billy Wilder, Max Ophüls), Siodmak was a Jew who began in Germany, fled after 1933 to France, and emigrated to the United States during World War II. Siodmak's importance to documentary is twofold: (1) his work on the semi-documentary Menschen am Sontag/People on Sunday (1930); and (2) his use in noir of documentary stylistics after World War II.

Siodmak and others raised the funds needed to shoot the late silent Menschen am Sontag, which he codirected with Edgar Ulmer. As if teaming these notables were not enough, Fred Zinnemann assisted them; the screenplay was by Wilder, based on reporting by Curt Siodmak (Robert's brother): and Eugene Schufftan did the cinematography. Billed as a 'film without actors', featuring people 'before the camera for the first time in their lives', the film connects with the city symphonies of Ruttmann, Cavalcanti, and Vertov, even if it is less avant-garde in focusing on specific characters and featuring a straightforward narrative. The film sketches a Berlin summer day as five performers, charmingly unselfconscious, essentially play themselves. Taxi driver Erwin and his ladies' man friend Wolfgang enjoy their day off with record seller Brigitte and film extra Christl. Hurt feelings ensue when Wolfgang flirts with both women, and Erwin returns home to find that his wife, Annie, has slept the day away.

Menschen's freshness surely resulted from the talented neophytes behind the scenes. An early tracking shot of motorcycles and trains links people with the rhythms of the city. The film overflows with documentary moments: shots of street cleaners, field hockey, naked babies, a man dripping water on a caterpillar, and the like. The 'story' scenes also feature extraneous moments (e.g. a disorienting shot of a man playing cards). Lengthy plotless scenes commence even before the picnic, as Erwin and Annie deal with an uncooperative door, read the paper, and have a fight. Reflexive in-jokes appear when they discuss Greta Garbo or angrily destroy film postcards. One later finds playfully vertiginous camera angles, with use of natural shadows, as if the future noirs of Siodmak and Ulmer were present in early form. Nonetheless, it is the reportage aspects that proved most influential. Documentary style is foregrounded in a delightful sequence where photographs are taken and the frame freezes for each, while a montage of statues seems more indebted to Soviet editing and the 'real' city symphonies. Associative editing keeps the story within persuasive documentary contexts, much as neorealism would later do. The film's open-air quality and use of nonprofessionals made it a classic, possibly influenced neorealism and genuine documentary, and proved a poignant record of a Germany soon to vanish.

Siodmak's French and early Hollywood films reprise little of Menschen's documentary qualities. Nonetheless, for all his Germanic stylizations, documentary creeps into his noir in the deglamorized studio streets, the clinical detailing of crime scenes, and a growing penchant for long takes and deep focus. Overtly documentarian noir really emerges after films like Jules Dassin's Naked City (1948). Siodmak's most stunning venture into this realm is the underrated Cry of the City (1948), set in New York's Little Italy. Siodmak was reportedly unhappy with the location work and preferred the control possible within the studio, but the final product belies his mastery of combining documentary and expressionistic modes within noir. Before returning to Europe, Siodmak helmed a lesser but even more documentary-style film, The Whistle at Eaton Falls (1951), a Capraesque drama about a unionized worker who is named president of a plastics factory. Based on an actual case history, the film strongly bears the mark of March of Time producer Louis de Rochemont. Still, de Rochemont had already produced seminal documentary-style noirs like The House on 92nd Street (1945) and Boomerang! (1947), and the teaming with Siodmak is often successful, as lengthy sequences document mill life in rural New Hampshire.

DAVID M. LUGOWSKI

Biography

Born in Dresden, Saxony, Germany (some sources say Memphis, Tennessee, while his father was on a business trip) August 8, 1900. Attended Marburg University, 1917–20. Got a job writing subtitles for US films shown in Germany 1925. Joined UFA, working as a writing scout, film cutter, assistant director 1927. Left Germany for Paris after the Nazi takeover 1933. Left for the United States the day before Hitler's army marched into Paris; with brother's aid was signed by Paramount 1940. Began working for Universal; signed seven-year contract 1943–4. Returned to Europe, first to France, then Germany 1952. Died March 10, 1973.

Selected films

1930 Menschen am Sontag/People on Sunday: codirector (with Edgar Ulmer)
1934 La Crise est finie/The Crisis is Over, or The Depression is Over: director
1939 Piéges/Snares, or Personal Column: director
1942 Fly by Night: director
1944 Phantom Lady: director
1944 Christmas Holiday: director
1945 The Strange Affair of Uncle Harry: director
1946 The Killers: director
1946 The Spiral Staircase: director
1948 Cry of the City: director
1949 Criss Cross: director
1951 The Whistle at Eaton Falls: director
1952 The Crimson Pirate: director
1957 Nachts, wenn der Teufel kam/The Devil Strikes at Night: director, producer
1958 Dorothea Angermann: director
1967 Custer of the West: director

Further reading

Alpi, Deborah Lazaroff, *Robert Siodmak*, Jefferson, NC: MacFarland, 1998.

Greco, Joseph, *The File on Robert Siodmak in Hollywood, 1941–51*, Dissertation.com, 1999.

Hirschhorn, Clive, *The Universal Story*, New York: Crown, 1983.

Naremore, James, *More Than Night: Film Noir in its Contexts*, Berkeley, CA: University of California Press, 1998.

Silver, Alain and Ward, Elizabeth, *Film Noir*, Woodstock, NY: Overlook Press, 1979.

Sokurov, Aleksandr

The Russian director Aleksandr Nikolajevich Sokurov has made about twice as many documentaries as fiction films. One reason for this might be that under the Soviet regime Sokurov's masterly graduate fiction film Odinoky Golos Cheloveka/The Lonely Voice of a Man (1978) for the State Film School (VGIK), was rejected on grounds of what was called 'formalism' in state socialism: it was more interested in aesthetics than in ideology, which in itself was regarded as anti-Soviet. Already in this first film, Sokurov rejected aiming at (changing) an outside social or socialist reality in favor of an adaptation of realist literature to initiate a process that starts from an internal perspective—in his documentaries sometimes the literary form of a diary provides the internal voice in response to a filmed reality. Sokurov's insightful critic Mikhail Yampolsky observed: 'The mentality of Sokurov's heroes is always limited; they can never comprehend reality as a whole' (Yampolsky 1994: 114).

The reproach of Sokurov's films being regarded as prerevolutionary was thus predictable. The filmmaker did not make things easy for himself. Consequently, Sokurov graduated one year earlier, but was denied the professional qualification for directing feature films—'feature' generally meaning 'fiction' film—and only given official permission to direct documentaries.

Supported alone by Andrej Tarkovsky, who, although in exile and regarded as subversive by the Soviet officials, nevertheless got him work at Lenfilm Studios. Sokurov went on to make feature films with Lenfilm, and the Leningrad Studio for Documentary Films continued to fund his documentaries. However, until 1987 all his films remained unscreened. Sokurov frequently had to hide the film rolls to protect his films from being destroyed by the Soviet censors. His films were only approved by the April 1985 Plenary Meeting of the CPDSU Central Committee in the wake of the democratic reforms of perestroika (Stishova 1995: 260). In 1986 the Soviet Filmmmakers' Union appointed a new First Secretary, Elem Klimov, who himself had had several of his films banned and was keen to help other filmmakers who had been subjected to censorship. From 1987 onward, Sokurov's films could be screened publicly at home and abroad.

Like his most successful fiction film, Russkij kovcheg (2002), Sokurov's documentary Elegiya iz Rossii (1992) opens with a black screen. For the first four minutes we hear only the sound of breathing and voices, which seem to indicate that this is the breath of a dying person. After the breathing has stopped, an image emerges from the darkness: only after death, we can finally see. For Sokurov, film is another life (Galetski 2001: 4). His continuous and original explorations of death have specific implications for documentary. Death cannot be documented; it is a fiction for film as well as for the living. 'Documenting' death is a paradox that exceeds comprehension. This is where Sokurov's documentaries go beyond the terrain of conventional subjective documentary about (lived) experience. In many of his documentary elegies (a poetic lament for the dead), as well as in several fiction films, Sokurov explores the subject of death also in terms of movement. His images are often static with barely any motion. Sometimes only the falling of snow, the flying of seagulls, or the moving of light indicate that we are looking at a film and not a photo or a painting. Sokurov's films frequently show people who are only a few movements away from eternal stillness and darkness. In Elegiya iz Rossii an old man is lying immobile on a bed. First we cannot discern whether we see a photo or if he is dead, but then he moves. Sokurov's images evoke uncertainty as to whether their subjects are alive or dead: is the motionlessness of the image or in the image?

Sokurov has taken Tarkovski's rejection of montage and the embrace of the long take even further. As his films emerge with the seemingly least possible movement, they make the already slow pans of his mentor seem like action films. Sokurov's patience with the long take frequently evokes comparisons to André Bazin.

This neorealist critic sought the long take with a deep focus for a truer, spiritual understanding of reality manifested in the documentary quality of the images. In contrast to interpretations of Sokurov's long takes as Bazinan (French 2003), however, this spiritual filmmaker rejects documentary realism and depth-of-field in favor of a flat and opaque painterly look. Unlike the promotion of surface through the long take in Andy Warhol's Sleep—or Sam Taylor Wood's video of the sleeping celebrity David Beckham—when Sokurov films a person with his or her eyes closed or sleeping, it suggests a blocking of externality as superficial in favour of an internal reality. Since external reality is usually that which features in documentaries and is in some quarters regarded as the only reality it is possible to document, his subjective documentaries are frequently classified as 'semidocumentaries' or not as documentaries at all. Recently, critics have linked Sokurov's deliberate, textual exploration of 'blind images' in his work since the late 1970s with the deterioration of Sokurov's own eyesight since the late 1990s (Macnab 2003).

The rejection of reality as external for Sokurov goes together with a heightened importance of often ambient sound. He thus suggested that the visual film and the sound film 'ought to be able to exist apart from one another. If you listen to the sound on the film, it should be enough on its own' (Sokurov in Christie 1999: 16). The stillness in Sokurov's images is equivalent to the silence on the voice tracks. In many of his documentaries—for example Mariya (1978/1988), Dukhovnyje golosa (1995), Hubert Robert. Schastlivaya zhizn (1996), Povinnost (1998), Elegiya dorogi (2001)—and also in his fiction film Russkij kovcheg (2002), the filmmaker narrates in a whisper directly into the microphone as though he were speaking silently to himself. Sometimes his narration describes what we see in the images—often sensual, immediate impressions. In Dukhovnyje golosa (1990), for example, we see a landscape clouded in dust to which his voice repeats 'Everything is clouded with dust'.

However, the repetition of what we see in his narration does not heighten the immediacy; instead, it manifests the distance between the voice of the documentary subject and what it talks about, which is often what is shown. Thus, paradoxically, the closeness of the filmmaker's voice enhances the distance to its object; intimacy here brings isolation. The reality of the narrator is distinct from the external documentary reality—it is not an objective commentary that uses images illustratively as evidence. Apart from the fact that his father was a professional soldier, Sokurov's frequent observation of soldiers is perhaps also motivated by the fact that they—like their documentary observer—are already in an alien environment. Sokurov even assumes a position of distance with respect to his own past thoughts, by using them like quotes from a literary source rather than as direct expressions. In Dukhovnyje golosa, for instance, he narrates: 'Here's another entry from my diary: "I feel calm and unafraid walking along these paths, following these people. I don't feel excluded by them". But maybe I'm wrong. Maybe I'm wrong in thinking that I've become one of them.' Sokurov's documentaries originally have turned observation into a literary, poetic form. They seldom give their subjects a voice in direct speech and they are not informative. For example, Dukhovnyje golosa, depicting Russian soldiers at a border post between Afghanistan and Tajikistan, does not provide any substantial context. Sokurov observes the traces of their existence, not their tasks or their goals. When we finally 'see' a soldier shoot, we do not see what he shoots at. We hear the sound and see the ground on which used ammunition casings fall. A pan upwards then shows a soldier from behind. His aim can only be deduced indirectly.

Sokurov's documentaries often manifest disorientation and question understanding. In Elegiya dorogi the off-screen narrating filmmaker is uncertain about what he sees and where he is. In his fiction film Russkij kovcheg the filmmaker, too, provides the voice of an invisible commentator who wonders where he is. However, whereas in the fiction film the effect of this uncertainty is merely theatrical, in the documentary Elegiya dorogi the purported lack of agency of the filmmaker in and over his video has consequences with regard to referentiality. Sokurov's passive narrator's stance pushes the observational attitude of documentary filmmaking to its impossible limits: he denies knowledge and responsibility as a filmmaker and as his own protagonist. The disorientation is not only with respect to his narrative journey in the video but also with regard to the materiality of the medium and the referentiality of the images he sees: he addresses eighteenth-century paintings as though they depicted his recent past, and his own documentary reality as though it were a distant event, directed by someone else. In Elegiya dorogi Sokurov's exaggeration of the notion of documentary filmmaking as a passive following of events reverts the orders of before and after, of creation and documentation. Sokurov blocks the viewers' comprehension not only of content but also of the very visual image itself. His images are blurred, soft, dark, and contorted or they take an exceptionally long time to focus. It is often hard to make out what they actually depict. Superimpositions haunt his images like ghosts. The viewer is disorientated by long cross-fades with indiscernible transitions. One does not know what one looks at—or in which medium one looks at it: a photo or a moving image, a painting or reality. As with Wittgenstein's duck-rabbit, one can either switch between the two options or see an altogether new image that does not make sense. Sokurov's images keep us from being able to fully comprehend what we see by making themselves hard to read.

SILKE PANSE

Biography

Born July 14, 1951, in Podorvikha, near Irkutsk, Russia. Tenure as director's assistant for Gorki television and MA in history at Gorky University 1968–74. Studied film production in the class of Alexander Zguridi at the State Film School (VGIK) in Moscow with an Eisenstein Scholarship 1975–9. Employed by Lenfilm, Leningrad 1980. Still lives and works in St Petersburg.

Selected films

1957–90 Leningradskaya retrospektiva (1957–90)/ Leningrad Retrospective (1957–90) Parts 1–16
1978/88 Mariya/Krestyanskaya elegiya/Maria/ Peasant Elegy
1979/89 Sonata dlya Gitlera/Sonata for Hitler

1981 Altovaya sonata: Dmitrii Shostakovich/Sonata for Viola. Dmitri Shostakovitch: codirector (with Semyon Aranovitj)
1982/7 I nichego bolshe/And Nothing More
1984/7 Zhertva vechernyaya/Evening Sacrifice
1985/7 Terpenie trud/Patient Labour
1986 Elegiya/Elegy
1986/8 Moskovskaya elegiya/Moscow Elegy
1989 Sovetskaya elegiya/Soviet Elegy
1990 Petersburgskaya elegiya/Petersburg Elegy
1990 Leningradskaya kinochronika No. 5 'K Sobytiyam v Zakavkazye'/Leningrad Film Chronicle Newsreel No. 5, Special Issue 'On the Events in the Transcaucasian Region'
1990 Prostaya elegiya/Simple Elegy
1991 Primer intonatsii/An Example of Intonation
1992 Elegiya iz Rossii/Russian Elegy, or Sketches for Sleep
1995 Soldatski Son/Soldier's Dream
1995 Dukhovnyje golosa/Spiritual Voices Parts 1–5
1996 Vostochnaya elegiya/Oriental Elegy
1996 Robert. Schastlivaya zhizn/Hubert Robert: A Fortunate Life
1997 Smirennaya zhizn/A Humble Life
1997 Petersburgski dnevnik. Otkrytie pamjatnika Dostoevskomu/The St Petersburg Diary. Inauguration of a Monument to Dostoevsky
1998 Petersburgski dnevnik. Kvartira Kozintseva/The St Petersburg Diary. Kozintsev's Flat Povinnost/Confession Parts 1–5
1998 Besedy s Solzhenitsynym/The Dialogues with Solzhenitsyn
1999 Dolce … /Tenderly …
2001 Elegiya dorogi/Elegy of a Voyage
2004 Peterburgski dnevnik. Motsart Rekviem/The St Petersburg Diary. Mozart's Requiem

Further reading

Christie, Ian (ed.), 'Dossier: Aleksandr Sokurov, The Russian Idea', *Film Studies: An International Review*, no. 1, spring 1999: 63–77.

——'The Civilising Russian', *Sight and Sound* 13, no. 4, April 2003: 10–11.

French, Phillip, 'Take a Chance on a Long Shot', *The Observer* 6, no. 4, 2003.

Galetski, Kirill, 'The Foundations of Film Art: An Interview with Alexander Sokurov', *Cineaste* 26, no. 3, 2001: 4–9.

Halligan, Benjamin, 'The Remaining Second World: Sokurov and Russian Ark', *Senses of Cinema: An Online Film Journal Devoted to the Serious and Eclectic Discussion of Cinema*, no. 25, March–April 2003.

Jameson, Frederick, 'On Soviet Magic Realism', in Frederick Jameson (ed.), *The Geopolitical Aesthetic: Cinema and Space in the World System*, Bloomington, IN: Indiana University Press, 1992: 87–113.

Macnab, Geoffrey, 'Eyeless in Turin', *The Guardian* 19, no. 11, 2003.

Schrader, Paul, 'The History of an Artist's Soul is a Very Sad History', *Film Comment* 33, no. 6, 21.11, 1997: 20.

Sokurov, Alexandr, 'Sokurov on Sound', Ian Christie (ed.), and 'Returning to Zero', *Sight and Sound* 8, no.4, April 1998: 4, 14–17.

——'Death, the Banal Leveller (on Tarkovsky)', *Film Studies: An International Review*, no. 1, spring 1999: 64.

Stishova, Elena, 'Look Who's Here! A New Trend in Soviet Cinema!' in Elle E. Berry and Anesa Miller-Pogacar (eds), *Re-entering the Sign: Articulating New Russian Culture*, Ann Arbor, MI: University of Michigan Press, 1995: 259–69.

Tuchinskaja, Alexandra, 'The Creation', *The Island of Sokurov*, 2001, sokurov.spb.ru/island_en/crt.html

Yampolsky, Mikhail, 'The World as a Mirror for the Other World', in Michael Brashinsky and Andres Horton (eds), *Russian Critics on the Cinema of Glasnost*, Cambridge: Cambridge University Press, 1994: 114–15.

Song of Ceylon, The

(UK, Wright, 1934–5)

The Song of Ceylon, a relatively lengthy, intricate, lyrical film directed by Basil Wright, is acclaimed as the crowning achievement of the first phase of the British documentary movement. It clearly displays the shaping influence of modernist aesthetics on early British documentary practice, as well as the more specific influence of documentary pioneer Robert Flaherty. The Song of Ceylon won the Prix du Gouvernement Belge at the 1935 Brussels film festival and has long enjoyed a reputation as one of the key texts in the documentary film canon. In recent years critical interest has extended from analysis of the film's aesthetics to interrogation of its relationship to colonial discourse and acknowledgment of its homoerotic representation of Ceylonese bodies.

The Song of Ceylon's genesis lay in the decision by Gervas Huxley at the Ceylon Tea Marketing Board to sponsor a series of public relations films. In doing so he emulated the policy promoted by Stephen Tallents, his former boss at the Empire Marketing Board (EMB). The initial conception was to produce a series of four short films on topics such as Ceylonese agriculture and fisheries. Production began during a period of transition as John Grierson's documentary film unit moved from the EMB to the General Post Office (GPO). Despite these uncertain circumstances Grierson remained fully committed to Wright's project. As the quality of the material became apparent he encouraged Wright to integrate it into a single, more substantial film. Wright's shorts prior to The Song of Ceylon had attracted positive critical attention, with some commentators even proclaiming him the first British documentary film 'poet'. Although Grierson was resistant to any kind of 'art for art's sake' stance, having one of his film-makers regarded in this way enhanced the movement's standing within highbrow British film culture.

Wright always considered The Song of Ceylon to be his best film, partly because he became so immersed in the process of directing it. The contemplative aspects of Buddhism impressed him deeply and he sought to incorporate this feeling into the film. Wright, assisted by John Taylor, was responsible for cinematography as well as direction, and his images represent Ceylon as a domain of calm and beauty, ease and grace. Finely judged camera pans made possible by a tripod with a fluid gyrohead contribute to this impression. Wright had worked with Flaherty earlier in his career and his influence can be detected in camera pans that anticipate subjects' movements. This technique is used to particularly good effect in the sequence featuring marvellously adorned male dancers near to the end of the film.

Several British documentary films of this period, for example Night Mail (1936), were influenced by modernist aesthetics. Night Mail, however, inaugurated more narrativised forms of British documentary, whereas The Song of Ceylon's structure is indebted to an earlier tradition. It resembles the modernist 'city symphony', exemplified by films such as Rien que les heures (Alberto Cavalcanti, France, 1926) and Berlin, The Symphony of a Great City (Walter Ruttmann, Germany, 1927) insofar as it is structured in terms of a geographical demarcation and thematic linkages between shots and sequences (Guyn 1998). The Song of Ceylon is subdivided into four sections, each with its own title: '1. The Buddha', concerned with religious observances; '2. The Virgin Island', on traditional handicrafts, house building, harvesting, fishing and the training of dancers; '3. The Voices of Commerce', which represents imperial trade and industrialisation; and '4. The Apparel of a God', which returns to the religious emphasis of the first section.

One important difference between The Song of Ceylon and the city symphonies set in Western metropolises is that they often concentrate on diversity and change, whereas Wright's film privileges uniformity and continuity. The Song of Ceylon implies that the religious and traditional practices it represents constitute the essence of an entire culture rather than a selective record primarily of its rural areas. Urban space and industrial, administrative, and professional work is only briefly represented toward the end of 'The Voices of Commerce', and there is no explicit reference to the existence of different ethnic groups, religions other than Buddhism, or secular lifestyles. By referring to the country as a whole rather than just a particular area or aspect of the culture, the title promises comprehensiveness, but this is something The Song of Ceylon does not actually deliver.

Ceylon also stands largely outside history in this film. As its opening titles explain, the bulk of the voice-over narration consists of extracts drawn from an account of Ceylon written in 1680 by the Scot Robert Knox. Visual images illustrating this account seem to confirm that little has changed in the intervening time. In conventional narrative, film editing dissolves, usually between sequences, denote the passing of a brief period of time, but in The Song of Ceylon they are used so frequently within as well as between sequences that time becomes indeterminate. This is particularly the case in 'The Buddha', when pilgrims ascend the holy mountain known to Europeans as Adam's Peak. This is as much a spiritual journey as a temporal one. Through such devices the film constructs a representation of the eternal spirit of Ceylon.

Contemporary film historians have argued that early British documentaries adapted modernist techniques to represent unified and harmonious rather than conflictual and contradictory social relationships (Higson 1986; Nichols 2001). The Song of Ceylon bears this out. Its editing derives from the modernist European montage tradition but generally emphasises correlation rather than radical juxtaposition. One example at the end of the 'The Buddha' is a series of exquisite shots of a bird perched on a branch and in flight silhouetted against a lake and sky. These alternate with shots of Buddhist monuments. The abruptness of these transitions and the contrast between static monument and moving bird is tempered by careful matching across shots of the bird's flight, the water's flow, and rapid camera pans along the monument. The cumulative effect of this subtle cross-cutting is to conjure into existence a harmonious realm where Buddhism is part of the natural order rather than an historical or cultural phenomenon that changes and develops over time.

The Song of Ceylon's voice-over narration, spoken by Lionel Wendt, does not conform to the stereotype of a reductive, didactic commentary bludgeoning the listener into submission. It is intermittent and does not attempt to explain everything on the image track. Its quietly meditative tone and unusual accent differentiates it from the confidently authoritative southern English, white, middle-class, male voice heard, for example, in Housing Problems (Edgar Anstey and Arthur Elton, 1935). Wendt was a Burgher, an English-speaking descendant of native Ceylonese and early European colonists. His voice-over narration conveys empathy, even reverence, toward the subject matter, rather than a detached assessment or contextualisation of it. This emphasis on feeling and experience as well as explanation includes the recitation of passages from Buddhist religious texts, the delivery of which sometimes approximates a mantra. The Song of Ceylon's unconventional voice-over is comprehensible to white Western listeners but does not provide complete access, except perhaps intuitively, to the alluring non-Western world the film represents.

Tantalising inaccessibility is also rendered visually in Wright's film. Graham Greene, in a perceptive review, noted that The Song of Ceylon begins and ends with dark shots of fans of foliage that stand as a natural barrier between the onlooker and the beautiful existence glimpsed in the film. The Song of Ceylon constructs Ceylon as a desirable space, different to and separate from the world inhabited by its implied white Western viewers. Wendt's voice-over narration tails off toward the end of 'The Apparel of a God'; words are ultimately incapable of providing access to all the sacred mysteries of Ceylonese culture. For this film the essence of Ceylon is something felt rather than something that can be fully explained through rational exposition. The Song of Ceylon's culminating dance sequence eschews voice-over narration and instead utilises anticipatory camera movements to incorporate the viewer into the rhythms of the dancer's movements.

Experimentation with sound was made possible by the British Visatone system newly acquired for the GPO film unit's premises at Blackheath in London. All of The Song of Ceylon's sound was recorded during post-production. Wright, Alberto Cavalcanti, and composer Walter Leigh were the main collaborators at this stage. Cavalcanti was the only member of this trio with significant experience of sound film and, like Flaherty earlier in his career, Wright found him a congenial mentor who encouraged him to innovate. While working on the soundtrack, Wright co-authored a manifesto in the highbrow journal *Film Art* endorsing the idea of sound-image counterpoint pioneered in particular by Soviet film maker Sergei Eisenstein in the late 1920s (Macpherson 1980).

'The Voices of Commerce' is the only one of The Song of Ceylon's sections where a discordant note is struck. An assortment of voices, including those of Wright, Cavalcanti, Grierson, and Stuart Legg, conduct business and state commodity prices over images of traditional Ceylonese manual labour (Barnouw 1983). These voices sound coldly impersonal and indifferent to the spiritual and human dimensions of Ceylonese culture referred to in Wendt's narration and valorised on the image track. Some commentators familiar with the ideas expounded in Wright's manifesto interpreted sound-image counterpoint in 'The Voices of Commerce' as a concealed critique of imperialist exploitation (Stollery 2000).

'The Voices of Commerce' section obliquely hints at possible criticisms of Empire without openly subverting the sponsor's brief. More pervasive in The Song of Ceylon is a Romantic conception of non-Western otherness. 'The Buddha' opens the film with religious representations and the concluding section 'The

Apparel of a God' returns to this theme. The film's overarching structure emphasises the timelessness of Ceylon's profoundly traditional culture and the visual style lends beauty to its representation. The extracts from Robert Knox's text narrated by Wendt accentuate Ceylon's otherness for the white Western viewer. The full text of Knox's 'An Historical Relation of Ceylon' discusses early Portuguese and Dutch colonisation, but there is no acknowledgment of the long record of Western domination and Ceylonese-European interaction in the quotations used in The Song of Ceylon. Apart from what might be gleaned from 'The Voices of Commerce', this history is largely absent from the film. Fundamentally, it posits Ceylon as essentially other, a partially accessible space offering a seductive alternative to Western modernity (Stollery 2000).

One of The Song of Ceylon's most seductive aspects is its focus on Ceylonese male bodies, which seem in tune with nature and at ease with their physicality (Waugh 1996). The British documentary film movement was committed to the cinematic representation of men at work; The Song of Ceylon aestheticises and eroticises this commitment. The buttocks, torsos, and supple limbs of semi-naked men feature prominently in the film. Particularly impressive in this respect is the sequence of a fisherman stripped to the waist standing in water casting his nets in 'The Virgin Island'. Typically, this eroticisation takes place in the context of documenting traditional labour practices, but more languorous moments, such as a semi-naked lone male worshipper praying in 'The Apparel of a God', also carry a similar charge. The experience, which cannot be adequately explained in words, of the dance performed by beautifully adorned men at the end of the film is also a sexual one. Wright's Ceylon is in part the locus for the celebration of a desire that could not be overtly expressed in either fictional or documentary filmmaking at that time.

A Song of Ceylon (Laleen Jayamanne, Australia, 1985) is a nonnarrative film directed by a Sri Lankan-born filmmaker. Like The Song of Ceylon, it experiments with sound, image, and a voice-over narration quoting extracts from a preexistent anthropological text. Unlike its predecessor, A Song of Ceylon does not intimate an essential, timeless Ceylon, elusively located outside Western modernity but perhaps fleetingly accessible through intuition and emotion. Its concern is not to record or represent Ceylon/ Sri Lanka as such but rather to challenge some of the abiding preoccupations and assumptions of Western colonial discourse (Vigneswaran 2000).

The crucial difference between the two films is that A Song of Ceylon rejects the categorical distinction between the Western and non-Western world on which The Song of Ceylon ultimately rests. Instead, it contains utopian moments where unorthodox framing, colour processing, and editing collapse visible differences between Western, non-Western, male, and female bodies. For all its aesthetic sophistication, coded critique of imperialism, and genuine admiration for aspects of Ceylonese culture, The Song of Ceylon still belongs to a tradition of representing inhabitants of the non-Western world as essentially more vital, primitive, and sexual than the white, Western viewers the film is designed to address.

MARTIN STOLLERY

See also: Wright, Basil

The Song of Ceylon (UK, GPO/New Era, 1934–5). Produced by John Grierson. Direction by Basil Wright. Cinematography by Basil Wright. Edited by Basil Wright. Assistant John Taylor. Script by John Grierson, Basil Wright, and others. Commentary by Lionel Wendt. Sound recorded by E.A. Pawley. Sound supervision by Alberto Cavalcanti. Music by Walter Leigh. Filmed in Ceylon (now Sri Lanka) and London.

Further reading

Aitken, Ian, *The Documentary Film Movement: An Anthology*, Edinburgh: Edinburgh University Press, 1998.

Barnouw, Erik, *Documentary: A History of the Non-fiction Film*, New York: Oxford University Press, 1983.

Guyn, William, 'The Art of National Projection: Basil Wright's The Song of Ceylon', in Barry Keith Grant and Jeannette Sloniowski (eds), *Documenting the Documentary*, Detroit, MI: Wayne State University Press, 1998: 83–98.

Higson, Andrew, '"Britain's Outstanding Contribution to the Film": The Documentary-Realist Tradition', in Charles Barr (ed.), *All Our Yesterdays*, London: BFI, 1986: 72–97.

Macpherson, Don (ed.), *Traditions of Independence*, London: BFI, 1980.

Nichols, Bill, 'Documentary Film and the Modernist Avant-Garde', *Critical Inquiry* 27, no. 4, summer 2001: 580–610.

Starr, Cecile, 'The Song of Ceylon: An Interview with Basil Wright', in Kevin Macdonald and Mark Cousins (eds), *Imagining Reality: The Faber Book of Documentary*, London: Faber, 1996: 102–11.

Stollery, Martin, *Alternative Empires: European Modernist Cinemas and Cultures of Imperialism*, Exeter: University of Exeter Press, 2000.

Sussex, Elizabeth, *The Rise and Fall of British Documentary*, Berkeley, CA: University of California Press, 1975.

Swann, Paul, *The British Documentary Film Movement 1926–46*, Cambridge: Cambridge University Press, 1989.

Vigneswaran, Priyadarshini, 'Hysteria and the Hybrid Body in Laleen Jayamanne's A Song of Ceylon', *Journal of Australian Studies*, June 2000: 173–80.

Waugh, Thomas, *Hard to Imagine: Gay Male Eroticism in Photography and Film from Their Beginnings to Stonewall*, New York: Columbia University Press, 1996.

Sorrow and the Pity, The

(France, Ophüls, 1969)

The Sorrow and the Pity is not only the most famous of Marcel Ophüls's films; it is also one of the most controversial documentary films in the history of French cinema. Both its subject and the conditions of its release explain its considerable success in France and abroad. It deals with one of the most contentious periods of contemporary French history—the occupation of France by German troops during World War II. The film also raises the issue of artistic independence from the pressures of politics.

The Sorrow and the Pity is an account of life in Clermont-Ferrand during the German occupation, and mainly consists of interviews. As the full title indicates, it is a 'Chronicle of a French City under the Occupation'. Most of the interviews are with local people from this midsize town in the Auvergne region of France. The choice of Clermont-Ferrand as the setting is significant, given its proximity to Vichy, where the collaborationist government of Maréchal Pétain and Pierre Laval retreated from Paris. It is also in the Auvergne region that the armed Resistance, known as the Maquis, originated in 1943. In its geographical isolation and long history dating back to the Gauls, it is a perfect example of a provincial and insular France, often referred to as 'La France profonde'. The title of the film is taken from the comment made by one of the town residents when asked what she felt about the occupation: 'Sorrow and pity', she replied.

Conducted by Marcel Ophüls and André Harris, the interviews feature several inhabitants of Clermont-Ferrand. Going beyond the local dimension, and avoiding a purely anecdotal version of events, the film also includes interviews with political personalities, among them Pierre Mendés-France the ex-French Prime Minister, Sir Anthony Eden, and Jacques Duclos, a prominent figure in the French Communist Party.

The Sorrow and the Pity portrays a town divided, uncertain how to cope and which side to take. The interviews are interweaved with newsreels dating back to World War II. The film carefully avoids being judgmental or even formulating a specific opinion about these events, giving instead a more balanced view of living conditions during these years. It nevertheless aims to challenge the version of life under German occupation promoted by various regimes since the War, in particular the Gaullist idea of a France united against the occupant, and the glamorization of the Resistance. While the public and most commentators have welcomed this openness about an era largely suppressed until the early 1970s, others criticized its prejudices.

The Sorrow and the Pity is considered a landmark among French documentary films. One of the striking features of the film is the manner of openness with which the interviews are conducted. Marcel Ophüls, who, as a Jew, had to flee France to escape persecution, is often credited with having adopted a humanistic approach to these interviews. He allows for collaborationists as well as resistance fighters, German soldiers, and ordinary French people to talk freely about their experience of the war and their role in it. The result is a strikingly blunt account of life during the occupation.

Wartime newsreels are presented in montage, and emphasize that much of the information made available to the French people at the time was propaganda put forth by the Germans or the Vichy regime. The Sorrow and the Pity also includes film footage from the BBC, in which de Gaulle is given a low profile. Here again, the public is not provided with any particular interpretation of facts, but a mere account of what it was like to live under German occupation.

As such, the newsreels add more depth to the film, giving another dimension to the interviews, and acting as a complement to them.

Marcel Ophüls has frequently explained how he perceives his role as an historian. As a documentary filmmaker, he is not concerned with a history made of great narratives, based on theories and generalisations (a Hegelian vision). He prefers instead to collect stories as told by those who were witnesses, which he then places in the context of the period he is exploring, a pragmatic approach that he developed while working in the United States. The result can be anecdotal, and he has been criticized for a kind of downgrading of events to individual experience, but the use of footage allows him to recreate a wider historical perspective. The Sorrow and the Pity is a perfect example of his method, which broke new ground in documentary film at the time of its release, and offered new ways to analyse and present an historical subject.

In The Sorrow and the Pity, the subject is not just an account of the everyday struggle of the average person. The film is about how memory of a painful time, like the German occupation, can be easily altered, in favour of that of a glorious nation united against the enemy—a version of events that General de Gaulle and the Resistance were all too keen to promote. The film therefore made very uncomfortable viewing for the generation that experienced the wartime events firsthand, and its emphasis on the collaborationists shattered the official version of events that had been passed on to the next generation.

The conditions of the release of The Sorrow and the Pity are highly significant, reflecting the unease of French leaders with the Occupation. Ophüls, who never made a secret of his left-leaning political inclination, belongs to a generation of filmmakers who found themselves in conflict with the Gaullist regime. In the late 1960s he was working for the ORTF, the French state-owned television company, where he was a segment director of Zoom, one of its most popular current affairs programmes. In 1967 he made Munich, or Peace in Our Time, produced by André Harris and Alain de Sédouy, which became a television success. The Sorrow and the Pity would have followed, if it had not been for the unrest of May 1968.

Ophüls was among those who openly criticized the attempts of the government to censure the reporting of the unrest that shook France in May 1968. Having left the ORTF, he found funding with Swiss and German television, and after months of filming and editing over sixty hours of interviews, The Sorrow and the Pity was released in 1969. It became a huge commercial success abroad, and was nominated for Best Documentary at the Academy Awards. It won the National Society of Film Critics Special Award.

In France, The Sorrow and the Pity was first screened on April 5, 1971, in a small left-bank cinema in Paris, the Studio Saint Séverin. Due to the enthusiastic response of the public, it was then screened at the Paramount-Elysées, where it remained a feature for a record eighty-seven weeks. Nevertheless, Ophüls had to wait another ten weeks before his film was shown on French television, for which it was originally intended. Although not censored, as is commonly thought, it was simply either turned down or ignored by French television until 1981, when a leftist administration came into power. The television premiere on FR3 attracted fifteen million viewers, confirming the success it had already had in theatres, and providing vindication for Ophüls.

The film is two hundred and sixty minutes long, divided into two parts. The first part, 'The Collapse', lasts one hundred and twenty-seven minutes, and the second part, 'The Choice', runs over one hundred and thirty-three minutes. It was shot in black and white using a 16mm Éclair Coutant (NPR) and a Nagra with a budget of 500,000 Deutsche Marks. The editing of sixty hours into four and a half is one of the features that made the film so famous, not only to the aficionados of the documentary film but also to the wider public. While Ophüls or André Harris conducted the interviews, the camera operators were trusted with a large degree of flexibility regarding which techniques to use, the result providing an additional layer of texture to these interviews. The cross-cutting technique used in the editing gives a dynamic to the interviews that sustains the attention of the audience over four and a half hours. The depth of the research into the archives for the footage contributes to the richness of the film.

Ophüls directed Nuremberg and Vietnam: An American Tragedy (1976) as a sort of sequel to The Sorrow and the Pity. Apart from working for the radio and making a variety of documentaries in France, Germany, and the United States, his three adopted countries, Ophüls's other major work related to the war years is

Hotel Terminus: The Life and Times of Klaus Barbie (1988).

The Sorrow and the Pity played a key role in the reassessment of the French during the German occupation. Ophüls is often credited as the director who inaugurated what are known as the 'retro years' of French cinema. While markedly different as a work of fiction, Lacombe Lucien, directed by Louis Malle in 1974, is a similar attempt to demystify these years. Claude Lanzmann's 1985 Shoah also attempts to determine the truth of a dark and turbulent time in history.

YVAN TARDY

See also: Ophüls, Marcel; Shoah

The Sorrow and the Pity: Chronicle of a French City under the Occupation/Le Chagrin et la pitié: Chronique d'une ville française sous l'Occupation (1969, distributed by Milestone Film and Video Release, Harrington Park, NJ, USA, 260 mins). Directed by Marcel Ophüls. Produced by André Harris and Alain de Sedouy (Productions Télévision Rencontres SA, 1969). Production director: Wolfgang Theile, assisted by Claude Vajda. Script and interviews by Marcel Ophüls and André Harris. Photography by André Gazut and Jurgen Thieme. Edited by Claude Vajda assisted by Heidi Endruweit and Wiebke Vogler. Mixing by Wolfgang Schroter. Sound by Bernard Migy. Music by Maurice Chevalier ('Notre Espoir', 1941) and Jean Boyer ('ça fait d'excellent français', 1939). Publications: Francis Day SA ('ça sent si bon la France', 1942) and Sam Coslow ('Sweeping the Clouds Away', 1930).

Further reading

Avisar, Llan, *Screening the Holocaust: Cinema's Images of the Unimaginable*', Bloomington, IN: University of Indiana Press, 1988.

Canby, Vincent, 'A Look Back in "Sorrow and Pity"', *The New York Times*, March 26, 1972.

Cantor, Jay, 'Death and the Image', *TriQuarterly* 79, fall 1990: 173–98.

Demby, B.J., 'The Sorrow and the Pity, A Sense of Loss. A Discussion with Marcel Ophuls', *Filmmakers' Newsletter*, Ward Hill, MA: December 1972.

Greene, Naomi, 'La Vie en Rose: Images of the Occupation in French Cinema', in Lawrence D. Kritzman (ed.), *Auschwitz and After: Race, Culture, and 'the Jewish Question' in France*, New York: Routledge, 1995: 283–98.

James, Carol Plyley, 'Documentary and Allegory: History Moralized in Le Chagrin et la Pitié', *The French Review* 59, no. 1, October 1985: 84–9.

Kazin, Alfred, 'Don't Believe They Didn't Know about Hitler', *The New York Times*, November 28, 1971.

Knight, Arthur, 'Marcel Ophul: "The Sorrow and the Pity"', in Lewis Jacobs (ed.), *The Documentary Tradition*, second edn, New York: W.W. Norton, 1979: 521–3.

Lyon, Christopher, *The International Dictionary of Films and Filmmakers*, Volume II, New York: Pedigree Books, 1984.

Porton, Richard, 'The Troubles He's Seen: An Interview with Marcel Ophuls', *Cineaste* 21, no. 3, 1995: 8–13.

Reilly, C.P., 'The Sorrow and the Pity', film review, *Films in Review*, XXIII, no. 4, April 1972: 248.

Reynolds, Sian, 'The Sorrow and the Pity Revisited: Or, Be Careful, One Train Can Hide Another', *French Cultural Studies* 1, no. 2, June 1990: 149–59.

Rubenstein, L., 'The Sorrow and the Pity', film review, *Cineaste* V, no. 1, winter 1971–2: 15–18.

Silverman, Michael, 'The Sorrow and the Pity', film review, *Film Quarterly* XXV, no. 4, summer 1972: 56–9.

Wakeman, John (ed.), *World Film Directors: Volume Two, 1945–85*, New York: H.W. Wilson Company, 1988.

Wilhelm, Elliot, *VideoHound's World Cinema*, Detroit, MI: Visible Ink Press, 1999.

South

(UK, Hurley, 1919)

South is the best known and most widely shown version of the feature documentary compiled from footage taken by the photographer and filmmaker Frank Hurley (1885–1962) during the 1914–16 attempt to cross Antarctica undertaken by a team of polar explorers led by the former merchant seaman, Sir Ernest Shackleton (1874–1922). Its restoration by the UK's National Film and Television Archive (NFTVA), completed in 1998, stimulated renewed interest and research in British polar exploration in general and Shackleton in particular.

The first decade of the twentieth century saw intense interest in polar exploration, focused primarily on the race to reach the South Pole on foot between Shackleton's former colleague Robert Falcon Scott and the Norwegian explorer Roald Amundsen in 1910–11. The Scott expedition set a precedent that

Figure 18 South, 1919 (Courtesy of the British Film Institute)

Shackleton's team would follow, in that a celebrity photographer (Herbert Ponting) was hired to accompany the expedition and produce still and moving images for subsequent commercial exploitation. As the opening scenes of the Ealing dramatisation of the Scott expedition, Scott of the Antarctic (UK 1948, directed by Charles Frend), point out, fundraising was always a major problem for the Edwardian polar explorers. Advance sales of exploitation rights for photographs and film had proved to be an important source of revenue for Scott.

Although initially reluctant to do likewise, Shackleton was eventually persuaded to hire the Australian photographer Frank Hurley on the strength of his photographs and film (released in Australia as Home of the Blizzard) taken on the 1910–14 Douglas Mawson expedition. The Imperial Trans-Arctic Film Company was filmed to manage the exploitation rights, and the expedition eventually set off in July 1914.

In terms of its stated objective, the Shackleton expedition was, like Scott's, a complete failure. Their ship, the *Endurance*, became trapped in pack ice some eighty miles from the Antarctic ice shelf, from where it was carried north by tidal currents for nine months before being abandoned on October 27, 1915, and crushed by the pack ice on November 21. The events that then unfolded, however, provided Hurley with some spectacular material that formed the basis of the film as it was eventually released four years later. Footage of the *Endurance*'s gradual destruction by the ice is one such example, and interest in the film was stimulated when details of Shackleton's spectacular rescue operation began to emerge. After abandoning the ship, a group of six crew members sailed a small wooden dinghy for seventeen days and eight hundred miles across the storm-ridden Southern Ocean, eventually reaching the island of South Georgia on May 10, 1916. There then followed a two-day forced march across the island in order to reach its only inhabitants. With help from the Uruguayan and Argentine navies, Shackleton then organised a fresh expedition to rescue his remaining colleagues, including Hurley.

South is the edited version of Hurley's film as released in 1919, two years after the survivors' return to Britain. It performed moderately well at the box office, but suffered to a certain extent from the fundamental change in political climate that had resulted from the events of World War I. This is clearly demonstrated in the opening intertitles to the film as released, which state that the expedition had set off 'one month after Shackleton had offered his ship, stores and all personnel to the cause of the country, only to be told that the authorities desired that the Expedition, which had the full support of the Government, should proceed'. Although the rescue operation was universally acknowledged to be an astonishing achievement and a vastly preferable outcome to that of the Scott expedition (which had resulted in several deaths), there was a school of thought that held that Shackleton's abilities might have been more usefully deployed fighting the Kaiser than on yet another polar exploration venture that had failed in all its key objectives. On the back of the release of Ponting's sound version of the Scott footage, 90° South, a subsequent version of Hurley's footage was shown in 1933 with a synchronised commentary and music. The title says it all—Endurance: The Story of a Glorious Failure.

South remained out of circulation for almost eighty years after its initial release until it was restored from a wide range of surviving elements by the NFTVA. The archivists who worked on the project took several years to establish the correct running order of each shot and select the best quality extant elements from which to construct the version used to produce the new preservation master. The NFTVA finally released the film in new tinted and toned 35mm prints and a DVD with extensive contextualising material. The marketing of Caroline Alexander's book on the expedition, published in the same year, was coordinated with that of Hurley's film.

This raises the issue of the role that moving image archives play in mediating our access to moving image heritage, especially in the area of nonfiction film where exposure through other means (e.g. broadcasts and retail video/DVD sales) is significantly lower. South was an obvious candidate for a major restoration, both from a technical standpoint (i.e. the techniques were available to enable high-quality photochemical duplication from surviving elements, which themselves enabled the complete film to be reconstructed) and a cultural one. The preexisting, almost mythological status of Captain Scott as established by Ponting's footage and Scott of the Antarctic created a public interest in and a market for the polar exploration genre. The details of Shackleton's spectacular rescue mission also ensured the newsworthiness of the restoration of the film, not to mention a revival of interest in Hurley's career as a photographer. However, it also illustrates the increasing tendency of national moving image archives to prioritise major projects around a restricted range of films, which some would argue is to the detriment of other titles that are of equal cultural importance but a less attractive marketing proposition.

LEO ENTICKNAP

See also: Great White Silence, The

Further reading

Alexander, Caroline, *The Endurance: Shackleton's Legendary Antarctic Expedition*, New York: Alfred A. Knopf, 1998.

Bickel, Leonard, *In Search of Frank Hurley*, London: Macmillan, 1980.

Shackleton, Sir Ernest, *South: The Story of Shackleton's 1914–17 Expedition*, London: Heinemann, 1919.

Worsley, Frank, *Endurance*, London: George Allen & Unwin, 1931.

Southeast Asia

Geographically speaking, Southeast Asia is made up of Brunei, Cambodia, Indonesia, Laos, Malaysia, Myanmar (Burma), the Philippines, Singapore, Thailand, and Vietnam. It is an area covering over forty-three thousand miles and contains a diverse region of countries, dialects, and religions. It is a region that has experienced war, political upheaval, and economic and social instability. These themes are dominant within the documentary films originating from, and being made within, these Southeast Asian nations. A common thread that ties all of these countries together is strong government intervention and censorship, thus documentaries produced and exhibited by citizens of the respective nations are considered to be quite important.

Some countries are yet to rediscover their past through the restoration and rediscovery of documentaries and archives—Laos and Cambodia are prime examples. Decades of war and struggle have resulted in less than favorable conditions for local filmmakers and lack of governmental or private funding in these countries means that most documentaries are produced and distributed overseas, or in neighboring countries. Due to the lack of local education, facilities and services, such as equipment, costs, and bureaucratic red tape, it is quite the norm to have foreign filmmakers shoot documentaries within the region. Traditionally, 'wealthier' countries such as Singapore, Indonesia, the Philippines, and Thailand already had an existing documentary film history (and thus professionally maintained and funded archives) that contributed to being able to produce and sustain local documentary film, whereas poorer countries, such as Laos and Cambodia, required more funding and local facilities and education. This status quo has continued to the present day, although it is hoped that as countries such as Laos and Cambodia open up to commerce and tourists this may gradually change. Greater economic power should mean increased funding and facilities to promote documentary film.

In Indochina, it was historically the French who brought cinema and thus documentary film and various cinematic techniques to Southeast Asia. The French colonial government had extended influence (as French protectorates) in present-day Myanmar, Cambodia, Laos, Thailand, and Vietnam, and as such were able to bring in new technology. Myanmar, Malaysia, and Singapore had access to Indian film markets and technology, whereas the Philippines had both Spanish/European and United States influence and money, thus it also maintains a high level of involvement in all matters of film. It is assumed that documentary filmmaking was introduced into the countries by foreign persons, not by the evolution of an internal film industry, and it appears that the trend in foreign filmmaking has continued to the present day.

The majority of contemporary documentaries on Southeast Asia, whether political, economic, socioanthropological, or entertainment, are created and produced either with a fully funded foreign crew or a partially funded local and foreign crew. Singapore, Thailand, Indonesia, Vietnam, and the Philippines are arguably the exceptions, as they have a rich cinematic culture and internal production facilities. However, state censorship is almost always at the forefront of documentary production by domestic producers—especially when dealing with politically sensitive issues.

The Kingdom of Brunei's independent film industry is virtually nonexistent: most locally produced content is passed by government censors as the privately owned press falls under the Sultan's jurisdiction (all are family-owned with the exception of satellite television). However, the country has made four historically important documentaries under the auspices of the Brunei Information Service (now Information Department). The 1954 documentaries were of the ear-piercing ceremony of the Princess, the birthday of the King, the birthday celebrations of the prophet Mohammad, and the first landing of aircraft at the local airport. They are important as they map a local history of the Sultan and the introduction of technology to this nation; however, they are difficult to purchase and view.

Myanmar (Burma) had a lively film history and was receptive to Indian cinema from across the border. The most famous of Myanmar producers are U Nyi Pu and U Ohn Maung, who are believed to be the country's first documentary film directors. At the behest of the Myanmar government, they exhibited their commissioned film in London for the 1919 Empire Exhibition—a documentary on the silk, rice, and teak trade in Myanmar. It was the first Myanmar documentary to be exhibited overseas. U Ohn Maung also shot a documentary on the death of a delegate, U Htoon Shein, his funeral procession shown in the Cinéma de Paris in Yangon. This was the first documentary shown in Myanmar made by a national.

Unfortunately, with the indigenous tribes technically at war, it is virtually impossible to film documentaries within the country any longer without significant risk. Political documentaries do exist in relation to the Junta party, in particular the political struggles of humanitarian Aung San Suu Kyi. Aung San Suu Kyi: The Prisoner of Rangoon (Claude Schauli, 2003) is an example. Major television stations such as the BBC and CNN show documentaries commissioned by themselves, but most are mainly interviews with additional footage of protests dispersed throughout, and are usually dependent on informants within Myanmar for information or permission to film a specified event for a specified amount of time. With the use of hidden cameras, documentaries have increasingly dealt with the indigenous tribes within Myanmar and the problems associated with one-party rule. The Forgotten War (Frank Smith, 2002) is one such example.

King Norodom Sihanouk has arguably been one of the few Cambodian documentary filmmakers to successfully produce and exhibit his own films. Creating documentaries from the early 1960s to the 1990s, King Sihanouk created a Cambodia in his image, the films usually obscuring or avoiding references to poverty, war, and other hardship that the country has suffered at the hands of Pol Pot and the Khmer Rouge. The most well-known documentaries include Cambodia 1965 (1965), The Visit of General de Gaulle to the Kingdom of Cambodia (1966), and The Pagoda of the Emerald Buddha at Phnom Penh (1995).

The majority of available Cambodian documentaries are mainly on Pol Pot and the Khmer Rouge. Most documentaries and their producers are not living in Cambodia, as facilities are lacking. The most famous Cambodian documentary producer is Rithy Panh, who is based in France. Panh produced four well-known documentaries that are considered to be Cambodia's finest attempt at addressing the issue of genocide at the hands of the Pol Pot Regime. Panh shot Around the Borders (1989), semi-documentary Bophana, a Cambodian Tragedy (1996), The Land of Wandering Souls (1999), and S21 The Khmer Rouge Killing Machine (2003). S21 was awarded the International Human Rights Film Award.

Indonesia has an extensive documentary history. It has a state-run center that produces sanctioned and approved documentaries for television. Documentaries and films must be approved by the Directorate of Film of the Department of Information in Jakarta.

Indonesia covers a vast area and many different religions, thus the range of documentary film on offer is quite astounding. Sociological and anthropological documentaries are common, most focusing on cultural aspects of Indonesian society. The Three Worlds of Bali (Ira Abrams, 1979) is especially well known. The Suharto and Sukarno regimes are popular topics, and Chris Hilton's Shadowplay (2002) is perhaps one of the most famous examples of a film on this topic.

Laos, now a Communist nation, once had a promising cinema and documentary film industry. In 1975 the Communist insurgents overthrew the ruling monarchy and, as a result, few official cinematic representations of the country exist. What did exist had been withheld, or kept in Vietnam at the Vietnam Film Institute until 1998, when it was repatriated to the new Lao National Film Archive and Video Center. It was estimated that around one thousand one hundred and ninety-two Lao films were returned; however, it is unknown whether politically sensitive documentaries and footage of the former royal family were retained in Vietnam or destroyed. The Lao National Film Archive and Video Center now consists of over two thousand titles and is seen as the official government body in charge of Lao film and video.

The oldest known independently produced documentary film in Laos was shot and produced around 1956 and featured glimpses of the royal family. The majority of documentaries that exist today are shot by either the Communist Lao Patriotic Front Documentary Film Service, which filmed various documentaries about their activities (post- and pre-wartime), or Lao and Vietnamese soldiers filming incursions into Laos, including Xayxana Ladulaeng/Dry Season Victory (1970) and Xaopi Haeng Karnpathiwath/Twenty Years of the Revolution (1965). As both Laos and Vietnam are still considered Communist nations, it remains difficult to gain comprehensive and correct information on documentaries produced within the country, especially when dealing with restoration and 'preservation' of important historical records. It is hoped that as the new archive center becomes more autonomous, the Lao will have greater control over visual historical material. Audiovisual material within Laos is also heavily censored.

Documentaries made by non-Lao persons are far more common, however, and receive the most exposure outside of Laos' national boundaries. Some interesting Lao-themed documentaries include The Mekong, A Turbulent River: Laos and Thailand (1989), Moving Mountains (Elaine Velasquez, 1990), and Blue Collar and Buddha (Taggart Siegel, 1987). The latter are documentaries that attest to cultural, social, and political upheaval of Lao to the United States, a theme readily explored in the majority of films shot outside of Laos.

In Vietnam the main topic of documentary interest is the Vietnam War and the postwar era. American involvement in the region and the global consequences of the war have resulted in a higher awareness of the country, and an increased interest in making and showing documentaries. Previously, most readily available (outside of Vietnamese borders) documentary footage shot in Vietnam was shot during the war, with the exception of Vietnamese agents shooting films in neighboring Laos. American GIs and persons stationed in the region to report on the war were avid filmmakers—indeed, quite a lot of documentaries shot in Vietnam are joint productions between US and Vietnamese filmmakers. Domestically, however, Vietnam produces more documentaries than feature films and has had a local history of documentary production. The Electric Line to the Song Da Construction Site (Le Manh Thich, 1981) and Nguyen Ai Quoc-Ho Chi Minh (Pham Ky Nam) are famous documentaries.

The Vietnam Central Documentary Film Unit has been established in contemporary Vietnam, and one of its employees is Vietnam's best-known contemporary documentary producer. Tran Van Thuy's 1998 documentary, The Sound of the Violin in My Lai/Tieng Vi Cam O My Lai, won the 2000 Best Documentary Prize at the Asia Pacific Film Festival. The documentary also won the Golden Dove Prize and the Silver Dove Prize at the Leipzig International Film Festival.

The first set of documentaries thought to have originated in Malaysia were produced by American Frank Buck in the late 1920s to mid-1930s. The relative success of these meant that a series of wildlife documentaries called Bring 'Em Back Alive (Clyde Elliott, 1932), Wild Cargo (1934), and Fang and Claw (1935) were also shot in Malaysia.

Malaysia has had a solid National Archive since 1957. However, the storing and preserving of film media started to occur only in the late 1970s to early 1980s. The Archives have a standing arrangement with the Malaysian National Film Department and Radio Television section to deposit and store such items. Malaysia also purchased quite a number of documentaries from the United Kingdom and Japan to build on the collection. The Japanese occupation of Malaya also saw documentary newsreels and mini-documentary films produced as propaganda tools. It is believed that the Bunka Eiga Gekijio (Government Propaganda Unit) produced and screened over two hundred such documentaries, although this was also spread throughout the countries that it occupied.

The Philippines has had a tumultuous film culture, possibly due to the intervention of the Spanish, American, and Filipino interests at particular periods in history. Documentary film is thought that have been introduced to the Philippines by two Swiss businessmen in 1987. They presented a captive audience with a documentary of events and natural disasters taking place in Europe. The first locally produced series of documentaries are thought to have been shot by a local filmmaker Albert Yearsley. A documentary of the Rizal day celebrations was filmed in 1909 and the ensuing enthusiasm that surrounded it enabled him to film The Manila Carnival (1910), The Eruption of Taal Volcano (1911), The Tondo, Paco and Pandacan Fires (1911), Igorots to Barcelona (1912), and The Cebu Typhoon (1912). The first Filipino filmmaker was Jose Nepomuceno, who shot a documentary on the funeral of Dona Estefania Velasco Vda. De Osmena (wife to the former president). He went on to produce documentaries on the growing Filipino industrial sector and social commentary documentaries on US presidential elections.

The first color lab in the Philippines created the first color documentaries and newsreels in 1934 and later evolved into feature films. Filipino cinema is one of the top producers of feature films in the world and thus supports the production of a greater number of documentary films. eKsperimEnto, the Festival of Film, Video and New Media in Manila showcases new local documentaries and has gained quite a global following. Various documentaries are shown that might not otherwise have an audience.

The nation of Singapore has a thriving documentary community and supports documentary filmmakers more adequately than most Southeast Asian nations. The annual Singapore International Documentary Film Festival aims to bring international documentary films and their directors to the nation as well as exposing Singaporean and Southeast Asian documentaries to the international community. Sixteen international broadcasting channels have made Singapore their regional base, thus documentaries are readily available and are screened regularly on air. National Geographic Channels International coupled with Singapore Economic Development Board donate from US $8–$10 million for funding documentaries produced in Singapore. This is considered to be the most allocated funding available within Southeast Asia for documentary film production.

Contemporary Singapore has a strong tertiary emphasis on media, thus despite its totalitarian attitude, it appears to be quite free to make documentaries with the minimal amount of intervention. Arguably the most well-known contemporary Singaporean documentary producer is Royston Tan. His cutting-edge documentary 15 (2003) was produced with a grant from the Singapore Film Commission and won the NETPAC/FIPRESCI Award at the Singapore International Film Festival and also represented Singapore at the first Paris Asian Film Festival in 2004.

Thailand is often viewed as the entrance to mainland Southeast Asia and has an extensive cinematic history. Thailand, Vietnam, Indonesia, and the Philippines are often seen as the four countries that produce more documentaries than their neighbors. Thailand has a strong filmic culture, and as such has both the funding and facilities to continue its strong presence. Thailand's National Film Archive is said to have over four thousand documentary films in storage. Most are not considered to fall within the strict confines of 'documentary', as they depict everything from celebrations of the Kingdom to simple visual records of areas, and are not filmed with a narrative. They are regarded as such because they provide a visual documentary history of events that may or may not have been publicized outside of the Kingdom. Historically Thai documentary film (film shot within Thailand by Thai nationals) has been somewhat censored, with authorities and various official departments controlling content, distribution, and exhibition. The United States Information Service played a part in producing anti-Communist-themed documentaries within Thailand during the Vietnam War and the showing of such films (and trading of skills and equipment) saw Thailand become accustomed to the dispensation of information visually.

Thailand remains, as most of Southeast Asia, a censored society, and documentaries that depict political and socioeconomical struggles are rare. Two of Thailand's bloodiest demonstrations calling for constitutional reforms occurred on October 14, 1973, and during May 17–20, 1992. People from different levels in society attended great public rallies. The brutal government crackdown on the protesters in 1973 resulted in an unknown number of deaths, while in 1992 over fifty-two deaths were recorded. For both incidents all nonofficial visual footage of the event was supposedly censored or confiscated. Thus the independent release of October 14 (Anuthin 14 Tula) by Bu Shin Klaipan (1973) is considered to be a very important documentary. Another uncensored, independently produced documentary was handed out on the streets of Bangkok. It is called Bloody May/Phrutsapha Mahawippayok, featured actual scenes of the fighting in 1992, and is an unofficial record of events. It, too, is considered to be of high importance to independent documentary film in Thailand.

An equally important and more well-known political documentary is Hara Factory Workers Struggle/Karn Torsu Kong Kammakorn Rongngan Hara by Jon Ungpakorn (1975). The documentary deals with the fight to keep factory jobs by garment workers in Nakhon Pathom, to the west of Bangkok. Workers were arrested and subject to harassment, and the poor working conditions were caught on film. This documentary, and its sequel in 1976, are rare, as they illustrate Thailand as a military dictatorship where people could not even approach police or welfare agencies for fear of reprisal.

As the region grows and borders open, documentary film will provide both a visual history of change as well as a connection to the past that feature films often fail to capture.

SAMARA L. ALLSOP

Selected films: Myanmar

In the Shadows of the Pagodas—The Other Burma (Irene Marty, Switzerland)
2001 Saved (David Saunders, USA)

Selected films: Cambodia

1989 Samsara: Death and Rebirth in Cambodia (Ellen Bruno, Department of Communications, Stanford University, USA)
1995 Sos Kem (King Sihanouk and Marcel Talabot)
Cambodge: Le pays du sourire/Cambodia: Land of Smiles
Guardians of Angkor (Dean Love, National Geographic Television, Singapore and USA)

Selected films: Indonesia

1946 L'Indonésie appelle (Joris Ivens)
1999 Indonesia in Revolt—Democracy or Death (Jill Hickson, Australia)

Selected films: Laos

1988 Keeping our Culture Alive (Kmhmu Apprenticeship Program, Boston, USA)
1991 From Mulberry Leaves to Silk Textiles (Bouyavong, Douang, Deuane, Vientiane Video Center for the Ministry of Culture, Laos)
2001 Laos: Closed to Prying Eyes (ABC Australia)

Selected films: Malaysia

1995 Bakun or the Dam (Bernice Chauly, Malaysia)

Selected films: Thailand

1993 October 14, 1973 (Ben Anderson and Kritsadarat Watthanasuwan, Thailand)
1993 Threads of Life (Susan Morgan, Thailand)

Selected films: Vietnam

1991 La Memoire et l'oubli (Ada and Yves Remy, France 3 TV, France)
1994 Tolerance for the Dead/Mot Coi Tam Linh (Tran Van Thuy, Channel 4 Productions, Vietnam)
2003 The Friendship Village (Michelle Mason, Cypress Park Productions, USA)

Further reading

Alexander, William, 'Vietnam: An Appropriate Pedagogy', *Jump Cut*, March 31, 1986: 59–62.

Bayer, William, 'Films in Vietnam', *Film Comment* 5, no. 2, spring 1969: 46–80.

Biran, Misbach Yusa, 'The History of Indonesian Cinema at a Glance', in David Hanan (ed.), *Film in Southeast Asia: Views from the Region*, Vietnam: SEAPAVAA in Association with the Vietnam Film Institute and the National Screen and Sound Archive of Australia, 2001.

Blum-Reid, *East-West Encounters—Franco-Asian Cinema and Literature*, London: Wallflower Press, 2003.

Boonyaketmala, Boonrak, 'The Rise and Fall of the Film Industry in Thailand', *East-West Film Journal* 6, no. 2, 1992: 62–98.

Charlot, John, 'Vietnamese Cinema: First Views', in Wimal Dissanayake (ed.), *Colonialism and Nationalism in Asian Cinema*, Bloomington, IN: Indiana University Press, 1994.

Debrett, Mary, 'Reclaiming the Personal as Political: Three Documentaries on East Timor', *Metro Magazine*, fall 2003.

Hanan, David (ed.), *Film in Southeast Asia: Views from the Region*, Vietnam: SEAPAVAA in Association with the Vietnam Film Institute and the National Screen and Sound Archive of Australia, 2001.

Latif, Baharudin, 'A Brief History of Malaysian Film', in David Hanan (ed.), *Film in Southeast Asia: Views from the Region*, Vietnam: SEAPAVAA in Association with the Vietnam Film Institute and the National Screen and Sound Archive of Australia, 2001.

Morgan, Jennyn, *The Film Researcher's Handbook: A Guide to Sources in North America*, South America, Asia, Australasia and Africa, New York: Routledge, 1996.

Phichit, Bounchao, 'Lao Cinema', in David Hanan (ed.), *Film in Southeast Asia: Views from the Region*, Vietnam, SEAPAVAA in Association with the Vietnam Film Institute and the National Screen and Sound Archive of Australia, 2001.

Romey, Eliza, 'King, Artist, Film-Maker: The Films of Norodom Sihanouk', in David Hanan (ed.), *Film in Southeast Asia: Views from the Region*, Vietnam: SEAPAVAA in Association with the Vietnam Film Institute and the National Screen and Sound Archive of Australia, 2001.

Salumbides, Vicente, *Motion Pictures in the Philippines*, Manila: Vicente Salumbides, 1952.

Sotto, Agustin, 'A Brief History of Philippine Cinema', in David Hanan (ed.), *Film in Southeast Asia: Views from the Region*, Vietnam: SEAPAVAA

in Association with the Vietnam Film Institute and the National Screen and Sound Archive of Australia, 2001.
Uhde, Jan and Uhde, Yvonne Ng, *Latent Images: Film in Singapore*, Oxford: Oxford University Press, 2000.

Spain

Spanish documentary film developed at a relatively late stage. In the early days of cinema, Spanish screens were filled with French films and then, from the 1920s, with American films. The political, social, and economic situation influenced filmmaking in Spain. Spain was a constitutional monarchy, with a powerful king and a universal male vote controlled by important landlords, a phenomenon known as *caciquismo*, or authoritarianism of local bosses. Some fifty percent of the population were illiterate and sixty-eight percent of the population were rural. Society, dominated by the Catholic church and the military, was preoccupied with colonial ventures in Africa. Employers were continuously confronted with workers' unrest and hired gunmen, and industrial investment depended on foreign capital. In addition, General Primo de Rivera imposed a dictatorship with fascist features in 1923.

The first Spanish images were taken when the Lumière brothers started selling their equipment. Topical reportage was the most developed genre, since it was cheap and brought relatively easy profit. It became a source of industrial funding for companies (Pérez Perucha 1995).

At first, Barcelona dominated the film industry. However, Madrid eventually imposed itself as a national filmmaking centre by the 1920s. As of 1925 the banking industry started to invest in the sector—for ideological reasons, however, and not because of economic considerations. The production diversified but without a great take-off: censorship, foreign competition, and limited exports hindered its expansion. The difficulties caused by the new sound film and the need to invest in new equipment created many problems.

Despite this irregular development, film extended as a popular entertainment. The first cameramen came from different fields, such as photography, optics, theatre, and even cabinetmaking. Some of them studied or worked with large French companies, for example José Gaspar Serra, Ricardo de Baños, and Segundo de Chomón Ruiz, one of the most creative cameramen. In those days only small companies existed, which could not survive due to the lack of capital and industrial organization.

Filmed reports were common topics that ensured success. Images of Alfonso XIII were plentiful; the Spanish audience liked them and they could easily be exported. Reports were also produced about current events, such as Semana Trágica de Barcelona/Tragic Week in Barcelona (José Gaspar Serra, 1909) and La Guerra del Rif/The War of the Rif (Hispano Films, 1909). Some were reconstructions, such as El asesinato de Canalejas/The Assassination of Canalejas, created by the journalist and theatre director Adelardo Fernández Arias in 1912, in which actors interpreted the moment of the assassination. The film also included real images from the funeral of Canalejas, the former Prime Minister of the Spanish government. These films alternated in cinemas with other, everyday life-types of films. The most interesting Spanish films were set around bullfighting.

World War I marked the heyday of Spanish filmmaking. The conflict allowed the Spanish film industry to develop, because the distribution of European films at the time was limited. Twenty-eight production companies produced two hundred and forty-two films, of which seventy-seven were documentaries. When the war was over, however, the foreign production companies returned.

The need for information about World War I led to the creation of the first newsreel in Spain: Revista Española (Spanish Magazine) and Revista Estudio (Studio Magazine, 1915–20), produced by Studio Films under the direction of Solá-Mestres and Fontanals, who edited the first fifty instalments. Shortly before closing its studios in 1921, Studio Films shot España en el Rif/Spain in the Rif, a report about the African issue that did not address any unpleasant aspects of the colonial ventures.

After World War I most nonfiction films covered sports and bullfighting. Some had a strong impact on the audience, but this was owing to the topic, not the quality, as was the case with Trágica muerte de Joselito/The Tragic Death of Joselito (1919). Educational films made by Regia Art Film, whose manager was the expert José Gaspar Serra, also gained a high profile. Many of these films were made in Catalonia and Valencia. They dealt with the small industries typical of these regions, such as bobbin lace-making. Their quaint character led to their presentation in US cinemas.

One of the most important reports was Las Hurdes, País de Leyenda. Viaje de SM el Rey Alfonso XIII/Las Hurdes, Land of Legend: Journey of HM the King Alfonso XIII (1922), created by Armando Pou, a specialist in colonial film and film advertising. It focused on three basic elements: the land, responsible for social misery; its inhabitants as the victims of the situation; and the royal delegation as their saviours. The king represented hope and change: 'His Majesty enters the Alberca being proclaimed redeemer of Las Hurdes'. Ten years later the famous Spanish director Buñuel went on the same trip and, in Las Hurdes, tierra sin pan/Las Hurdes, Land without Bread, proved that nothing had changed.

The Spanish avant-garde did not greatly contribute to the film industry, but a notable avant-garde documentary was Esencia de verbena/ The Essence of Feasts (1930) by the writer and politician Ernesto Giménez Caballero. Through popular feasts, it reflected on the character and the typical customs of the people of Madrid. It has a remarkable montage based on associating visual ideas, close-ups, and sophisticated techniques.

When the monarchy fell, the Spanish Second Republic was proclaimed. In these times of political agitation and the establishment of a regime that defended civil rights, social conditions of the working class improved and the growth of the entertainment industry was encouraged. The contribution of film clubs, which created film audiences, were important. However, the various republican governments showed little interest in film: censorship was regulated, national production was protected, and taxes were introduced.

Filmmakers and distributors increasingly responded to informational needs. The Casanova family founded Cifesa (Valencia, 1932), one of the most important production companies of the day. Its political orientation was conservative, Catholic, and anti-Marxist. Spanish newsreels appeared (Spanish Film Information and Spanish Sound News) and, between 1931 and 1936, approximately ninety-five documentaries were produced. They dealt with a variety of topics—for example, travel and cultural issues that have a strong tradition in Spain. Enrique Guerner, a Jewish refugee, produced the following documentaries for Cifesa in 1935: Costa Brava, Granada, and Valencia. They stand out because of the camera technique and lighting used. Un río bien aprovechado/A River Well Used (1935) by the Catalan Ramón Biadiu had an original theme: it followed the river Llobregat from its source to its estuary, describing the industries that were lined up alongside it.

Documentaries that focused on formal expression were produced as well, dealing with literary and artistic themes. They were meant for entertainment purposes, and did not attempt to reflect the social reality. A notable example is Canto a la emigración/A Hymn to Emigration (Antonio Román, 1934).

The most important documentary references of these years are Carlos Velo and Fernando García Mantilla. Velo was a biologist and a university professor. Collaborating with Fernando García Mantilla, a radio and film critic, he produced many documentaries for Cifesa in 1935, such as Felipe II y El Escorial/Philip II and El Escorial, Castillos en Castilla/Castles in Castile, Tarraco Augusta, Galicia y Compostela/Galicia and Compostela, and La ciudad y el campo/The Town and the Country. Infinitos/The Infinite, based on an idea by the writer Mauricio Maeterlinck, stands out. It is a scientific and poetic film that, with imagination and artistic ability, recreates the world of microbes. However, his most important piece was Almadrabas/Trap-Nets, about fishing for tuna on the coast of Cadiz. It initiated the tradition of social documentaries in Spain, which was interrupted in 1939. The nets full of tuna caught by the fishermen with harpoons and hauled into the boat, as well as the quartering and preparation of the cans, make for expressive scenes. The main storyline focuses on the nature of the human labour, analysed by the camera with an extraordinary functionality, without succumbing to the picturesque.

In 1933 Luis Buñuel produced Las Hurdes, tierra sin pan. This anthropological film showed the causes of the ailments suffered in a region of Extremadura, and served to denounce the political, social, educational, and religious circumstances of the time. The film team included Eli Lotar, Pierre Unik, and Sánchez Ventura. The means and funds for the shoot were limited. Some scenes were constructed for the camera, such as the shot in which a goat is to be thrown off a cliff. The documentary contains many surrealistic elements. It was drawn up using a dramatic architecture: a problem is presented, hope is raised, and then hope is destroyed.

During the Spanish Civil War (1936–9), film acquired new momentum: it was used as an instrument of propaganda by both sides. On the Republican side the initiatives were taken by the central and regional governments, as well as by political parties and trade unions. High-quality newsreels, such as España al día (Spain Today), were given great importance.

The anarchists used film for indoctrination and social revolutionary purposes. Their production concentrated on the campaigns of the anarchist leader Durruti: Aguiluchos de la FAI por tierras de Aragón/Eaglets of the FAI in the Lands of Aragon (1936), Bajo el signo libertario/ Under the Libertarian Sign (1936), and En la brecha/In the Division (1937).

The Communists regularly produced films, as a result of the creation of the production company Film Popular. They distributed Soviet films and produced documentaries and reports. They cooperated with the Catalan newsreel España al día, of which they later created their own version. Their goal was to defend the 'single command' (Mando único, 1937) and to show the educated character of the Republic (Tesoro artístico nacional/National Artistic Treasure, 1937).

The Republican government in Madrid used film to project a favourable image of the country abroad. España 1936/Spain 1936, created by Buñuel and Le Chanois, is an example of this strategy. Film also served the specific needs of the country, such as mobilization (Movilización del campo/Mobilization in the Country, and Cuando el soldado es campesino/When Peasants Become Soldiers, both from 1937), or instructing popular militia how to handle weapons (El manejo de la ametralladora/Handling a Machine Gun, 1937).

The regional government of Catalonia (the Generalitat) created large film campaigns with its production company Laya Films. This company edited the newsreel España al día between March and June 1939 together with Film Popular. It produced numerous documentaries about the war (Jornadas de victoria: Teruel/Days of Victory, Teruel, 1938) and the brutality of the enemy, in order to discredit them (Catalunya mártir/Martyr Catalonia, 1938), and about government actions, culture, and work (Danzas catalanas y aragonesas/Dances from Catalonia and Aragon, 1936–7) to portray Catalonia abroad as an educated and hardworking region.

The film production of the Basque government was more limited. It focused on showing the Catholicism of the government (Semana Santa en Bilbao/Easter in Bilbao, 1937), because the Basques were worried about the anticlericalism attributed to the Republic.

In the Nationalist (Franco's) camp, film was treated in a different way. Initially, only military operations were shown, without any propaganda. From October 1936, the Falange (a party with its own organization of propaganda) and private production companies (Cifesa) produced documentaries about military successes, such as the series Para España/For Spain. Film was also used to spread awareness of political messages and platforms. When the government of Burgos was created in February 1938, the Francoist Film Services gained power. The entente with Nazi Germany was decisive. Documentaries were created to spread the principles of the new state (Juventudes de España/Youth of Spain, 1938) and to respond to Republican attacks (Prisioneros de guerra/Prisoners of War, 1938). Similarly, the Noticiario Español (Spanish newsreel) was created, which edited news items to reflect the propagandistic needs of the state.

When the conflict ended, a fascist and Catholic dictatorship was established in Spain, with General Franco as the *caudillo*, or leader. His objective was to obtain ideological unity—many different groups had participated in the rebellion—and to justify his actions. Propaganda was therefore essential. Filmmaking was marked by this political situation, the postwar economic crisis, and the situation of isolation.

During Franco's rule, professional competition barely existed as a consequence of the exile of many technicians who left the country after the war. Documentary films were considered a subgenre. Distribution mechanisms were lacking, as well as governmental policies to protect and aid this type of film. The film protection norms were established in 1941 and 1944, and showing documentaries became obligatory. In practice, this requirement was met by showing foreign newsreels (by Fox, UFA, and Luce) and, from 1943, NO-DO, the official Spanish newsreel.

In the 1950s the dictatorship tried to create a more positive image for itself, in the wake of the Allied victory in World War II. Spain became a member of various international organizations and signed, in addition to the Concordat with the Vatican, a bilateral agreement with the United States. Institutions were reorganized and the Ministry of Information and Tourism (July 1951) was put in charge of film production. García Escudero, a man with liberal ideas, was named film director, but lasted only one month in this position.

In 1952 a new Classification and Censorship Board was created to evaluate the moral, political, and social content of films. Financial aid increased; however, it was given based on national interest'. Films with certain social or political commitment did not receive any subsidies. Nevertheless, the law favoured 'Spanish feature films distributed together with Spanish short films'. The following prizes and festivals were founded: National Prizes for Short Films; the International Film Festival in San Sebastián (1953), which included prizes for documentaries; and the International Latin American and Philippine Documentary Film Contest (1958), later called the Documentary Film Festival of Bilbao. These festivals were designed to promote Spanish documentaries and to present foreign documentary films in Spain. Financial protection and film rates (quotas of screen time) improved, but the main problem remained: the organizers showed little interest in documentaries.

The Spanish newsreel NO-DO (1943–81) was created as a joint stock company, but with a state subsidy. It enjoyed a monopoly over film-related information. It also controlled documentary production and means of distribution (Tranche and Sánchez-Biosca 2001). Its main activity was the creation of the newsreel. To make use of news items, the film magazine *Imágenes* (Images) was organized in 1945, offering reports.

Documentary film production developed sporadically until the 1960s. The usual topics were towns, customs, museums, and geography. The films showed false popular reality, with a timeless appearance. Technically, they were mediocre. Official film, however, gathered great momentum throughout the 1940s and 1950s. Official bodies such as the Ministry of Agriculture, the Ministry of Industry, the National Trade Union Office, and the National Train Network organized their own services to produce documentaries promoting their activities.

Several production companies specializing in documentary film were founded (Hermic, Studio Film, and Filmarte). They encountered many obstacles: a limited range of topics, difficulty in obtaining the licence for filming (which was managed by NO-DO), and censorship. Their financial profits were marginal. Art documentaries made the most interesting contribution. They did not cause political problems and made use of the newly added colour feature. A remarkable documentary series was shot about the black paintings by Goya (Desastres de la guerra/Disasters of War, La tauromaquia/The Art of Bullfighting, and Los Caprichos/The Caprices). With great precision, they reflected the violence and power that Goya applied in his paintings—thanks to a perfect symbiosis between the camera movement and the painting (López Clemente 1960).

José Val del Omar was an exception in the filmmaking industry of those years. He was an original author who was not understood by his contemporaries. He tried to build a new audiovisual architecture—the so-called pulsating lighting that consisted of changing rhythm, intensity, color, and light location—in order to achieve a more complete vision. He also created the panoramic overlap technique, based on a double projection of the same still, and the diaphonic sound technique, which contrasted two sound sources.

Val del Omar produced two documentaries. The first one was Aguaespejo granadino/Watermirror of Granada, shot between 1952 and 1955, which garnered attention at the Berlin Film Festival in 1956. The second documentary was Fuego en Castilla/Fire in Castile, which was awarded a prize at the Cannes Film Festival in 1961 for its technical innovations.

In the 1960s Spanish film was given a new lease of life. The so-called Conversations of Salamanca (1955) were an important starting point. This meeting was organized by the film club of the University of Salamanca and directed by Basilio Martín Patino. The participants, film professionals and critics, published a manifesto with the following conclusions: 'Our documentary film must acquire a national character by creating films that fulfill a social function and reflect the life of the Spanish people, their conflicts, and their reality in our time.' They defended realism against the fascist aesthetics of the regime. Similarly, they demanded the end of the monopoly of NO-DO.

By the end of the 1950s young filmmakers were making films that were close to the proposals of the Conversations of Salamanca. Cuenca (1958) by Carlos Saura is an example. This documentary continued the tradition set by Buñuel in Tierra sin pan. It was funded by the city. It is divided into three parts. The first shows the inhabitants of the place, peasants, shepherds, and woodcutters. The camera focuses on their faces and sweat, caused by their labour. The second part deals with the history of kings and castles. In the last part, everyday life is the centrepiece displayed through popular feasts: 'Cuenca: different, yet always the same'.

España 1800/Spain 1800 (Jesús Fernández Santos, 1958) is also part of this renewal. It recreated eighteenth-century Spain through Goya's paintings. Hombres y toros/Men and Bulls (José Luis Font, 1958) about the feasts of San Fermín, is another exponent of the renewal.

Definitive societal change came in the 1960s. The decade witnessed rapid economic growth due to the Development Plans launched by the government. Tourism and Spanish emigration favoured openness towards the outside world. In 1966 Franco organized a referendum, which maintained his position as the head of state, and in 1970 he appointed the then Prince Juan Carlos as his successor.

The administration dedicated itself to celebrating the 'twenty-five years of peace'. The campaign was designed by the Ministry of Information and Tourism. It did not focus on commemorating the end of the Civil War, but rather on emphasizing the 'successes' of the regime. Two documentaries supported this endeavour: Franco, ese hombre/Franco, That Man (Sáenz de Heredia, 1964), a hagiography of the dictator, and Morir en España/To Die in Spain (Mariano Ozores, 1965), which was conceived as a reaction to the French documentary Mourir à Madrid/To Die in Madrid (Frédérix Rossif, 1963). No political film existed that would challenge the official line. Owing to the political changes since 1973, militant filmmaking developed under the auspices of trade unions and community and student associations.

In 1963 a new Censorship Code was approved and García Escudero was again named head of Film Direction (1962–9). The Code prevented arbitrariness and was valid until February 1975 (Franco died in November of that year). Work techniques improved with the use of lighter and more portable cameras, direct sound, and more sensitive unexposed film. Production costs were lower. New companies, such as Eurofilms, appeared, encouraged by the governmental financial aid programmes of 1964. Exhibition space was increased: festivals became stronger, film clubs expanded and, in 1964, the alternative Art and Performance Halls appeared, in which films were shown in their original versions and subtitled. The number of spectators increased, as well as that of spectators who participated in cultural discussions and read specialized magazines, such as *Nuestro Cinema* (Our Film) and *Film Ideal* (Ideal Film). Regional filmmaking developed in Catalonia, the Basque Country, and Galicia, due to the recovery of cultural autonomy.

A group of anti-establishment filmmakers, calling themselves New Spanish Film, was set up in Madrid, and the New School of Barcelona in Barcelona. They came from the Film Research and Experience Institute (1947–62) and the Official Film School (1962–76). Their documentaries dealt with the typical Francoist topics (towns, geography, travels, art), but employed a vision that differed from the official perspective.

Juguetes rotos/Broken Toys (Manuel Summers, 1966) presents the world of boxing, football, and entertainment through pathetic losers who in other times were praised and admired by the great audience. Spectators are presented with a critical version of the 'national myths.' Censorship forced the producers to add a commentary, which was ironic and sharp, with a moralist content repeating that all Spanish people were responsible for forgetting the old national glories. Even without listening to the voice-over, the images speak for themselves with an overwhelming force through stereotypes, prejudices, and images of black Spain. It was not commercially successful. Torerillos 61/Little Bullfighters 61 (Basilio Martín Patino, 1962) won the top prize at the Documentary Film Festival in Bilbao. It is a chronicle of a Spain that is hungry and lives in poverty. Its reality is shown through the characters of three boys who want to become bullfighters, who wish to escape their world and become famous.

In the 1960s NO-DO started a new era as a company producing documentaries on travel, art, and sports as a result of competition with television. In 1956 Spanish Television (TVE) started to broadcast. Its monopoly lasted until 1983, when the first regional television broadcasters were founded. Private channels were authorized in 1990.

Initially, TVE received its news, technical means, and staff from NO-DO. It also produced documentary films. Biographies, travelogues, art, and industry were broadcast for educational purposes. Series were created with screenplays written by specialized authors. They were produced by the staff of TVE. Some examples are Figuras en su mundo/Figures in Their World (1966), Lo que va de siglo/The Century until Now (1968), and La noche de los tiempos/The Night of the Times (1971).

Other documentaries responded to the requirements of informative production, such as the series A toda plana/A Full Page (1964), dedicated to important international reports. Nature documentaries by Dr Félix Rodríguez de la Fuente were very successful: Fauna (1968), Mi amigo el océano/My Friend the Ocean (1970), and the different series of El Hombre y la Tierra/Man and the Earth.

Several years before Franco died, the dictatorial regime had started to break down. These years of disintegration until the proclamation of the Spanish democratic Constitution in 1978 are known as the Transition. Measures were taken to free up the process of film production. From 1975 NO-DO lost its monopoly status, and in 1981 it disappeared altogether. In 1977 the Ministry of Information and Tourism was renamed the Ministry of Culture and Welfare (later only Culture). The National Entertainment Trades Unions and the practice of censorship disappeared as well. A new system of subsidies came into place that favoured artistic and cultural values, cinema ratings, and film distribution. However, the reforms were not able to ward off the effects of the world economic crisis. The number of filmgoers diminished, and the production costs of filmmaking increased.

Two emblematic films of those years were El desencanto/Disenchantment (Jaime Chavarri) and Canciones para después de una guerra/Songs for after a War (Basilio Martín Patino). The first documentary was made in 1971 and the second in 1975; both were shown for the first time in 1976. They represented two different documentary forms. El desencanto dealt with the present through interviews in the style of cinéma vérité. Canciones para después de una guerra is a montage that recreates the past. Forty songs—hits of those years—summarize life in Spain in the ten years after the Civil War. The images follow each other in a collage. However, each shot is carefully selected. Music is related to the image in order to achieve specific meanings. The documentary is very powerful and creative. As in El desencanto, the lack of objectivity is not disguised.

The change in the political climate allowed filmmakers to tackle delicate topics from the past, such as the Civil War and the dictatorship. Documentary film was used to present viewpoints that differed from the official one. ¿Por qué perdimos la guerra?/Why Did We Lose the War? (Diego Santillán and Luis Galindo, 1977), for example, delivers an anarchist version of events.

Film also lent a voice to those who had actively participated in the Civil War, and whose voices could not be heard in Franco's Spain. La vieja memoria/The Old Memory (Jaime Camino, 1977) offers interviews with left-wing politicians, intercut with archival material. Opinions are compared and organized into dialogues that never existed in reality, such as the statements of Dolores Ibarruri and Federica Montseny about the disagreement between the Communists and the anarchists.

The figure of Franco inspired several documentaries, such as Caudillo/The Leader (Basilio Martín Patino, 1975). Patino gathered diverse material, some of it unpublished. There is no chronological order; themes follow each other in a dynamic montage, full of contrasts. The music, the way of using image and colours (warm tones for the Republican camp and cold ones for the Francoists), without commentary, creates a specific analysis of the Civil War, close to the anarchist view. Franco is portrayed as a grotesque dictator who caused devastation and death.

Raza, el espíritu de Franco/Race, Franco's Spirit (Gonzalo Herralde, 1977) mixes fragments of the film Raza/Race (1942), the screenplay of which was written by Franco himself, with interviews with the main character, the actor Alfredo Mayo, and the General's sister, Pilar Franco. Documentary films that treat the dictatorship period leniently were also produced—for example, España debe saber/Spain Must Know (Eduardo Manzanos, 1976).

The political openness allowed newsreels and documentaries to become tools of nationalism. In Catalonia, the newsreel Noticiari de Barcelona (Newsreel of Barcelona, 1977–80) was created. It was directed by Joseph María Forn and financed by the city government of Barcelona. In 1981 it was replaced by Noticiari de Catalunya (Newsreel of Catalonia), which was less critical and protected by the regional government. In the Basque Country, reports focused on nationalist issues, appeared. Documentaries were made with the same objective. One of the most controversial documentaries of those years was El proceso de Burgos/The Process of Burgos (Imanol Uribe, 1979), which recalls the trial of several ETA militants during the dictatorship. It takes the side of the terrorist organization.

Documentary film was able to shed light on topics previously prohibited by censorship. They began to publicize the plight of the mentally ill, homosexuals, and others perceived as living outside mainstream society. Examples include El asesino de Pedralbes/The Murderer of Pedralbes (Gonzalo Herralde, 1978) and Vestida de azul/Dressed in Blue (Jiménez Rico, 1983).

The most significant progress was made in television, which gained a large audience. Documentaries about nature topics, successfully developed by Rodríguez de la Fuente, were consolidated. Notable reports, in which the figure of the reporter became very important, also achieved great success (Otros pueblos/ Other Countries, Los marginados/The Down-and-Outs, and La ruta de los conquistadores/ The Route of the Conquerors). Together with these reports, documentaries about folklore and popular traditions (the series Flamenco, Fiesta/ Feast, directed by Pío Caro Baroja, and Raíces/ Roots), and travel were successful.

When the political enthusiasm of the Transition years waned, the documentary film greatly diminished in importance. During the socialist era (1982–96), with Pilar Miró as General Director of Film, public subsidies were very high, but the effect of this policy was negative: nothing was produced without a subsidy. In 1989 Jorge Semprún, the then Minister of Culture, adjusted the aid to the European model and full control was given to autonomous regional administrations to create protection policies for their own films. This legislation was mainly favourable to fiction films. Even the Goya Prizes, awarded by the Academy of Arts and Film Science, neglected the documentary genre; the prize for the best short film was abolished in 2001.

Nevertheless, the documentary has gained in strength in contemporary Spain, in parallel with developments in Europe. Its main source is television. Public channels, especially TV2, broadcast the largest number of documentaries between 1998 and 1999, supported by their own production. Among the private channels, Canal Plus offers the most documentaries; Spanish documentary films represent the minority, but the number of coproductions with Spanish private companies has grown recently. Among the regional channels, those in the Basque Country offer a reasonable number of documentaries. Canal 33 in Catalonia does so as well, favouring European productions.

Despite this progress, the old problems remain. A solid industry dedicated to this type of production is missing, as are specific public subsidies (until 1999 documentaries were not included in the agreements between RTVE, or Spanish Radio and Television, and producers). The same applies to exclusive distributors of documentary films as they exist in other European countries (Català, Cerdán and Torreiro 2001). Television channels buy documentary films from international markets because it is less expensive.

However, the Spanish audience increasingly demands Spanish-made films about specifically Spanish topics. Documentary films are increasingly screened in cinemas, as the artistic possibilities of the genre have become more widely recognized.

El sol del membrillo/The Sun of the Quince Tree (Víctor Erice, 1992) is a documentary film following the work of the painter Antonio López in a very natural manner, depicting the way the artist creates the painting, as well as his moral strength and search for beauty. The camera is involved in the figurative universe of the painter and his memories, as the quince tree he paints is part of his childhood memories. The camera also captures the environment, including the artist's wife, friends, a house that is being built, the surroundings of the town, and the sky. It is a continuous dialogue between film and painting, two artistic forms of visual representation.

In Sevillas (1992) and Flamenco (1995) Carlos Saura merges film with music, showing different varieties of these genres. In Sevillas, which was shot in a studio, dance, dimension, and sense of space, as well as colours and movement, prevail. In Flamenco the best artists in each style act on different stages. In this case, the singing, the gestures, and the characters are stressed. The camera gets into the heart of the melody in a magical way. These films are not musical catalogues, but rather documentaries that show the history of the art of a nation.

Historical documentaries have become more successful. Asaltar los cielos/Attach the Skies (Javier Rioyo and López Linares, 1996) reconstructs the life of Ramón Mercader, the assassin of Leon Trotsky. It explains the context and conditions in which Mercader lived, the influence of his mother, and his obsession with the Soviet Union. It involves great research work, including archive images, photographs, documents, and evidence. The range of testimonies of politicians, relatives, friends, and artists is quite varied.

Francisco Boix, un fotógrafo en el infierno/ Francisco Boix, a Photographer in Hell (Lorenzo Soler, 2000) narrates the story of the Spanish photographer Francisco Boix, a Republican who, when the Civil War was over, left to fight in France. Taken prisoner, he was interned in the Mauthausen concentration camp, where he worked in a photographic laboratory, hiding the pictures that were proof of the Nazi regime's murders. His evidence was decisive at the Nuremberg trials. As with the previous documentary, it does not just describe the heroic deeds of this Spaniard, but deals with many other topics, such as the agreement between Franco's and the Nazi governments to exterminate the Spanish Republicans.

The Civil War is again the primary inspirational theme for documentaries. They are not about claiming political positions—although all of them are anti-Franco—but rather about preserving the testimonies of the victims of the conflict: members of the International Brigades and the Spanish Division who fought against the Russians in World War II (Extranjeros de sí mismos/Foreigners to Themselves (Javier Rioyo and López Linares, 2000); children sent to the Soviet Union to save their lives during the conflict (Los niños de Rusia/The Children of Russia (Jaime Camino, 2001); and those who continued fighting against Franco clandestinely—los maquis—(La guerrilla de la memoria/Guerrilla of the Memory (Javier Corcuera, 2001).

Social documentaries are important as well. Their goal is to move the spectators' consciences. One of the most striking films is La espalda del mundo/The Back of the World (Javier Corcuera, 2000), in which three stories are intertwined, stressing the extreme situations of the characters: a Peruvian eleven-year-old child who works in a quarry; a Turk exiled in Stockholm who lives alone; and a prisoner sentenced to death.

Monos como Becky/Monkeys Like Becky (Joaquín Jordá and Nuria Villazán) investigates the life of Egas Moniz, a Nobel Prize winner for medicine in 1949 for his work in neurosurgery. The monkey, Becky, was the patient on which he performed surgery to eliminate aggressiveness of the mentally ill. It is a complex mixture of archive images, theatrical representation of the ill in a mental hospital, and camera movements that are typical of horror films. The film is a metaphor of the many strategies used by the forces in power to control any kind of behaviour considered antisocial.

En construcción/Under Construction (José Luis Guerin, 2001) found great success at the Festival of San Sebastián. The theme is rather simple: a block of flats being built in a popular neighbourhood in Barcelona. The camera captures all of the events that happen during the construction and the characters that are, in different ways, related to it, such as emigrants, pensioners, children, drug addicts, and prostitutes. It shows how the changing urban landscape also implies a change in the human landscape.

MARÍA ANTONIA PAZ REBOLLO

See also: Land Without Bread

Further reading

Bonet, Eugeni and Palacio, Manuel, *Práctica fílmica vanguardia artística en 1925–81* (Film Practice and Artistic Avant-Garde 1925–81), Madrid: Universidad Complutense de Madrid, 1983.

Català, Joseph María, Cerdán, Josetxo and Torreiro, Casimiro (eds), *Imagen, memoria y fascinación. Notas sobre el documental en España* (Image, Memory, and Fascination. Notes about the Documentary Film in Spain), Madrid: Ochoy Medio, 2001.

De la Madrid, Juan Carlos, *Primeros tiempos del cinematógrafo en España* (The Early Days of Film in Spain), Oviedo: Universidad de Oviedo, 1996.

Del Amo, A. and Ibáñez Ferradas, M.L., *Catálogo general del cine de la Guerra Civil* (General Catalogue: Film of the Spanish Civil War), Madrid: Cátedra, 1996.

González Ballesteros, Teodoro, *Aspectos jurídicos de la censura cinematográfica en España* (Legal Aspects of the Film Censorship in Spain), Madrid: Universidad Complutense, 1981.

López Clemente, José, *Cine documental español* (Spanish Documentary Film), Madrid: Rialp, 1960.
Medina, Pedro, Mariano y Velásquez González, Luis and Martín, José (eds), *Historia del cortometraje español* (History of the Spanish Short Film), Madrid: Film Festival in Alcalá de Henares, 1996.
Pérez Perucha, Julio, 'Narración de un anciago destino (1896–1930)', in Roman Gubern, José Enrique Monterde, Julio Pérez Perucha, Esteve Riambau and Casimiro Torreiro (eds), *Historia del Cine Español* (History of Spanish Film), Madrid: Cátedra, 1995: 19–121.
Sáenz de Buruaga, Gonzalo (ed.), *Insula Val del Omar: visiones en su tiempo, descubrimientos actuales* (The Isle Called Val del Omar: Visions in his Days, Current Discoveries), Madrid: Consejo Superior de Investigaciones Científicas, 1995.
Tranche, Rafael R. and Sánchez-Biosca, Vicente, *Nodo. El tiempo y la memoria* (Nodo. Time and Memory), Madrid: Cátedra, 2001.
Vallés Copeiro del Villar, Antonio, *Historia de la política de fomento del cine español* (History of the Policies Supporting the Spanish Film), Valencia: Filmoteca de la Generalitat Valenciana, 1992.

Špáta, Jan

Jan Špáta is among the most prolific and well-known filmmakers in the history of Czech documentary. He is a cameraman-director whose career spanned the series of ideological and political shifts that gripped the Czech nation in the second half of the twentieth century. With his sensitive portraits of individuals and cultures, his interest in philosophical questions of life and death, Špáta pioneered a style of documentary filmmaking that is markedly his own, and that has become a trademark of the Czech documentary tradition.

Špáta graduated from the camera department at FAMU, the Film Faculty of the Academy of Music and Performing Arts in Prague, in 1957, preceding by a few years the filmmakers of the Czech New Wave. At the end of the 1950s documentary in Czechoslovakia had begun a fundamental shift, moving away from the socialist notion of film as the propagator of an idealized image of society—'smiling socialism', as Czech film critic Antonín Navrátil (2002) has called it—to an interest in authenticity and facts.

This process of change resulted from a combination of internal and external forces in the early 1960s in Czechoslovakia. Internally, as economic and social inequalities in the socialist state became increasingly evident, the notion of reality put forth by the Communist party began to seem false. As politicians began to grapple with new realities, a vanguard of journalists adopted a rational, scientific attitude toward the events they reported, relying on facts rather than ideology to describe events. Simultaneously, international film culture was shifting toward an interest in authenticity. Cinéma vérité and direct cinema, aided by technological developments such as portable sound equipment and lighter, handheld film cameras, such as the Éclair, allowed filmmakers to represent the world as they encountered it. Students at FAMU (if not the general public) were exposed to films by John Cassavetes, Shirley Clarke, Richard Leacock, Robert Drew, and others, and graduates in the late 1950s and early 1960s started to integrate cinéma vérité techniques into their filmmaking.

It was amidst this trend of rational investigation and renewed interest in authenticity that Špáta began his career. After working as a cameraman for a series of documentary directors (among them Jiří Papoušek, Jaroslav Šikl, and Václav Táborský), in 1962 Špáta met director Evald Schorm, with whom he would have a long collaborative relationship, both as cameraman and codirector. In 1963 the two men codirected Proč?/Why? (1963), an exploration of the declining birth rate in Czechoslovakia. Why? was the first Czechoslovak film to use the man-on-the-street interview, combining methods of sociological investigation with cinéma vérité techniques. Špáta revisited this method in later films, including his directorial debut (and the film for which he is best known), 1964's Nevětší přání/The Greatest Wish, in which he asked young people to describe their greatest wish.

Beyond their interest in people's lives and work, Špáta and Schorm shared a philosophical concern with human attitudes towards life and death, and explored these questions in successive films. Their 1965 vérité film Zrcadlení/Reflections, shot in a hospital, examined the border between life and death, ultimately asking the unanswerable: What is the meaning of life? Reflections' combination of poetic vérité images and philosophical voice-over became a trademark of Špáta's style in films such as Respice finem/Hospice, which he directed after Schorm began to work in fiction filmmaking. In this 1967 film he showed viewers the lives of solitary elderly women in the country—women for whom death is a constant presence. The film ends in a shot taken from within a grave—an existential, poetic vision that is striking in a film the style of which is so fundamentally based in objectivity.

Špáta's interest in humanity extended to the lives of people in foreign countries. Between the 1960s and 1990s he made films in locations as far flung as Cuba, Ireland, and Greece, documenting cultures, livelihoods, and customs. Among the most well-known of his travel films is Zeměsvatého Patricka/The Land of St Patrick, shot in Ireland in 1967. It is notable that after August 1968, when the Soviet invasion put an end to the Czechoslovak political thaw and implemented the twenty-year period of so-called normalization, Špáta was able to continue making films; it is especially remarkable that he was allowed to travel out of the country. It is perhaps precisely his humanism that allowed Špáta to keep working. His films, especially after 1968, focused on 'small' human stories such as that of a doctor whose hobby and passion is the family tradition of making and playing violins, in Terapie Es dur/Therapy in E-minor (1974). These films were politically innocuous, as were films like Šumavské Pastorale/Sumava Pastoral (1975) and Molto Cantabile (1989), practically wordless symphonies of poetic images and music.

Some writers have criticized Špáta as being a prisoner of his own style (Brdečková and Hádková 1990) and have written that his post-1960s films tended toward sentimentality. Regardless, several of the many films Špáta shot or directed between 1968 and 1989 are noteworthy. Music is a great theme in Špáta's work, and several of his films from those years figured musical personalities. Particularly significant is Etuda o zkoušce/Study of a Rehearsal (1976), Špáta's last collaboration with Schorm, this time as a cameraman. The film, a portrait of conductor Václav Neumann preparing Beethoven's Fifth Symphony, highlights Špáta's mastery of the camera as an expressive medium, particularly in one unbroken ten-minute shot of Neumann conducting.

After the collapse of the Soviet regime in Czechoslovakia in 1989, Špáta revisited an old theme in Nevětší přání II/The Greatest Wish II, which he combined with 1968's Nevětší Přání to make a feature-length documentary that demonstrates the continuity in human desires and values between moments of social upheaval twenty years apart. In 2001, after completing his final films, Laská, kterou opouštím I & II/ The Love I am Leaving I & II, and when he could no longer operate a camera with ease and grace, Špáta decided to end his career in filmmaking.

ALICE LOVEJOY

Biography

Born October 25, 1932, in Náchod, Czechoslovakia. Graduated from the camera department at FAMU, the Film Faculty of the Academy of Music and Performing Arts in Prague, in 1957. Taught at the Hochschule für Gestaltung in Ulm (NSR) in 1967. From 1992 taught in FAMU's documentary department, where he was named professor in 2002. Špáta's films have been honored at numerous festivals. He died in August 2006.

Selected films

1963 Proč?/Why? (with Evald Schorm)
1963 Žít svůj život/To Live One's Life: cameraman (directed by Schorm)
1964 Nevětší přání/The Greatest Wish
1965 Zrcadlení/Reflections (with Schorm)
1967 Respice finem and Zeměsvatého Patricka/The Land of St Patrick
1974 Terapie Es-dur/Therapy in E-minor
1975 Šumavské pastorale/Sumava Pastoral
1976 Etuda o zkoušce/Study of a Rehearsal: cameraman (directed by Schorm)
1980 Variace na téma Gustava Mahlera/Variations on the Theme of Gustav Mahler
1989 Molto Cantabile
1990 Nevětší přání II/The Greatest Wish II
1998 Laská, kterou opouštím I & II/The Love I Am Leaving I & II

Further reading

Brdečková, Tereza and Hádková, Jana, *Jan Špáta Dívej se dolů* (Jan Spata: Look Down), Prague: Czech Film Institute, 1990 (in Czech).

Buchar, Robert, *Czech New Wave Filmmakers in Interviews*, Jefferson, NC: McFarland, 2004.

Hames, Peter, *The Czechoslovak New Wave*, Berkeley, CA: University of California Press, 1985.

Liehm, Antonín J. and Liehm, Mira, *The Most Important Art: Eastern European Film After 1945*, Berkeley, CA: University of California Press, 1977.

Navrátil, Antonín, *Cestykpravděčilži: 70 letčeskoslovenského dokumentarního filmu* (The Path to Truth or Lies: 70 Years of Czechoslovak Documentary Film), Prague: FAMU, 2002 (in Czech).
Slater, Thomas J., 'Czechoslovakia', in Thomas J. Slater (ed.), *Handbook of Soviet and East European Films and Filmmakers*, New York: Greenwood Press, 1992.
Stoll, Martin, *Hundred Years of Czech Documentary Film (1898–1998)*, Prague: Malá Skála, 2000.
——*Okamžiky radosti: Rozhovor Martina Štolla s Janem Špátou* (Moments of Joy: Jan Spata Interviewed by Martin Stoll), Prague: Malá Skála, 2002 (in Czech).

Spellbound

(US, Blitz, 2003)

Producer/director Jeff Blitz's Academy Award-nominated debut documentary Spellbound examines regional spelling bee competitions and the 1999 Scripps Howard National Spelling Bee in which they culminate. The film begins by introducing eight of two hundred and fifty National Spelling Bee contestants: Angela, a second-generation Mexican immigrant in rural Texas; Nupur, a middle-class girl of Indian descent in Miami; Ted, an aloof loner in a lower-class Missouri town; Emily, an upper-class daughter of academic parents in Connecticut; Ashley, an African American teen living with her mother and sister in a Washington, DC apartment; Neil, an affluent Indian American living in a beach house in California; Amber, a working-class daughter of a bartender in a small, industrial hub of Pennsylvania; and Harry, the son of an office worker in New Jersey. The action intensifies when the eight converge in Washington, DC for the actual spelling bee and the film climaxes in a duel between the last two spellers.

Blitz masterfully constructs a narrative arc that is at once comedic, dramatic, and suspenseful. The children, at times overzealous in their desire to succeed, and the parents, supportive, indulgent, and proud, provide comic relief. The personal narratives of each family make the film enthralling and socially relevant, and ongoing competition at the regional and culminating spelling bees builds an uneasy sense of competition and conflict that propels the film out of its steady state.

Blitz provides no narration of his own, but sews together interviews from the spelling bee participants, their family members and mentors, and former spelling bee contestants. This technique adds to the authentic, intimate, and seemingly objective nature of the film, yet it does not remove Blitz from the film; instead, his presence is often detectable and never far from the lens of the camera. Blitz uses interstitial slates and consistent music to orient the viewer, introduce the participants, and buttress the narrative.

Although the narrative is structured around the children's preparation for and participation in spelling bees, Blitz uses the spelling bee as an exemplar for the value of education and the opportunity that it holds for Americans. By selecting children from various ethnic and socioeconomic groups, Blitz shows a plurality of children working diligently to better themselves through America's educational system.

Blitz emphasizes the distinctively American roots of spelling bees, and, by extension, education in general, by engaging images, sounds, and commentary that provoke a sense of Americana and patriotism. A former spelling bee champion comments, 'It's just a great American tradition that has filtered out to the world.' Blitz peppers the film with shots of the American flag, Washington Monument, and a parade, as well as Harry strumming the American Anthem on his guitar. Spellbound suggests that despite one's race or social class, anyone can advance economically in America, given enough fortitude. Ashley is shown ascending an escalator much as she hopes to rise in the world, with the frame freezing as she is about to step off at the top. In another sequence, while Ashley comments 'as I go higher my goals go higher, too […] I just keep on reaching', images of the Washington Monument are shown, reminiscent of both American ideals and the March on Washington.

This message is articulated more directly by the spelling bee announcer, who says, 'In America back in the eighteenth century, people had this sense of opportunity, you could leap out of one social class, you could move up, and I think they understood education was a basic part of that.' Other interviews serve to reinforce the assertion. An Indian mother remarks, 'You don't get second chances in India the way you do in America.' Another Indian émigré, the father of Neil, comments, 'There's no way you can fail in this country […] if you work hard you will make it […] that's nonexistent in other parts of the world'.

On the surface, the subtext in Spellbound is valid: education is a fundamental means of advancing one's economic class in America regardless of one's racial background or economic status; however, the finer nuances of this assertion go unexamined. Using primarily pathos, Spellbound puts little substantial evidence, by way of sociologists, historians, and statistics, behind its assertions. Spellbound implies that through hard work and perseverance members of any race or class can achieve success in America. Unfortunately, this optimistic portrait of American life fails to impart the burdens that racism, prejudice, and poverty truly place on American minorities, immigrants, and lower classes.

Rather, the film's emphasis on diversity within such a small sample, and with a necessarily superficial treatment of its eight subjects, runs the risk of perpetuating race- and class-based stereotypes. For instance, Ashley, the only African American individual in the film, has two uncles who are incarcerated; Ted and his brother, who live in rural Missouri, like to 'shoot guns'; Emily, an only child whose parents have a large colonial home in New Haven, speaks of the 'au pair' as though they are her possession; and Angela, the only Mexican American, is the daughter of parents who tried to cross the border illegally. By attempting to achieve diversity with such a small group of students, Blitz ultimately may have presented his subjects as little more than stereotypical caricatures. Moreover, although the children are from disparate backgrounds, they may not be as dissimilar as they seem. In fact, they share some critical commonalities that transcend race and class. They all have supportive, involved parents; teachers or tutors who provide sustained mentorship; and determination, self-motivation, and high cognitive skills.

Ultimately, Spellbound is entertainment, and the characters are perhaps more entertaining than widely representative. On her uphill walk home from school, Ashley hints that this might be the case; she says, 'My life is like a movie […] I go through different trials and tribulations and then I finally overcome'. In Spellbound, we see the trials and tribulations, but we do not quite see any of them overcome. Herein lies the false promise of Spellbound: in America, just like elsewhere, there is no guarantee of who will get the last word.

JEFF BERGIN

Spellbound (US, THINKFilms, 2003, 97 mins). Distributed by HBO/Cinemax. Produced by Jeffrey Blitz and Sean Welch. Directed by Jeffrey Blitz. Edited by Yama Gorskaya. Musical score composed by Daniel Hulsizer. Graphics by Adam Byrne. Additional Producer: Ronnie Eisen. Rerecording Mixer: Peter Brown. Sound FX Editor: Joe Dzuban.

Further reading

Bruzzi, Stella, *New Documentary: A Critical Introduction*, New York: Routledge, 2000.

Howard, Maureen, 'You Are There', in Charles Warren (ed.), *Beyond Document: Essays on Nonfiction Film*, Hanover, NH: University Press of New England, 1996.

Nichols, Bill, *Introduction to Documentary*, Bloomington, IN: Indiana University Press, 2001.

Plantinga, Carl R., *Rhetoric and Representation in Nonfiction Film*, Cambridge: Cambridge University Press, 1997.

Shapiro, Arnold, 'Ten Golden Rules', in Michael Tobias (ed.), *The Search for Reality: The Art of Documentary Filmmaking*, Studio City: Michael Wiese Productions, 1998.

Sherman, Sharon R., *Documenting Ourselves: Film, Video, and Culture*, Lexington, KY: University Press of Kentucky, 1998.

Spottiswoode, Raymond

As a student at Oxford University, Raymond Spottiswoode had written *A Grammar of the Film: An Analysis of Film Technique*, published in 1935. Though in it his approach is resolutely aesthetic and mainly devoted to the fictional feature film, he gives what must have been considered an inordinate amount of attention to the early documentary film, beginning with the statement that: 'England's only solid contribution to the cinema lies in her documentary groups, and in particular the G.P.O. Film Unit'.

He proceeds to offer one of the most adequate definitions of documentary, as it was being made in the 1930s, at any rate: 'The documentary film is in subject and approach a dramatized presentation of man's relation to his institutional life, whether industrial, social or political; and in technique a subordination of form to content.' However, Spottiswoode does not acknowledge as part of documentary the filmmakers' social purposes or their concern with the effects of their films on audiences.

Spottiswoode was subsequently hired at the General Post Office (GPO) Film Unit by John Grierson, who had read that important book of theory and classification (had reviewed it severely, in fact) and ordained, as a result, that Spottiswoode should begin his training as a tea boy. After six months, Grierson thought Spottiswoode still was not humble enough, according to a popular anecdote, anyway. Grierson regarded the purposes and effects of films of ultimate importance.

After Grierson became founding head of the National Film Board (NFB) of Canada in 1939, he brought Spottiswoode, then at Metro-Goldwyn-Mayer in Hollywood, to Canada, along with other veterans of British documentary. By this time a trained technician and producer, Spottiswoode was made coproducer with Stuart Legg on a Film Board production about the Commonwealth Air Training Plan, entitled Wings of Youth. After producing some other films, along with teaching NFB apprentices, he became supervisor of technical services for the Board, writing a valuable summary of 'Developments at the National Film Board of Canada, 1939–44', published in the *Journal of the Society of Motion Picture Engineers* (of which he was a Fellow).

When Grierson left the Film Board after the war to set up the short-lived The World Today in New York City, Spottiswoode went with him. He produced the most successful by far of its few films, Round Trip: U.S.A. in World Trade (1947). Directed by Roger Barlow (who had also directed Wings of Youth), it was sponsored by the Twentieth-Century Fund, a foundation that sought to promote liberal economic policy, including lowering or total removal of tariff barriers. Spottiswoode also produced a film for the Motion Picture Association of America on new techniques for teaching classroom subjects. Subsequently he became particularly interested in stereoscopic film, returned to England during the Festival of Britain in 1951, and was technical director of the stereoscopic film program at the Telekinema in London.

Spottiswoode also became a writer on film of considerable distinction, particularly regarding technical subjects. In 1950 the University of California Press republished his *A Grammar of the Film*, and in 1951 his *Film and its Techniques*. In the 1950s he was engaged in thorough research into the potential development of 3-D systems of cinematography, and co-authored the book, *Theory of Stereoscopic Transmission* (1953). Among other publications was his general editorship of *The Focal Encyclopedia of Film & Television Techniques*, a monumental work begun in 1964 and published in 1969.

JACK C. ELLIS

Biography

Born 1913 in London. Oxford University, MA c. 1933. General Post Office (GPO) Film Unit c. 1935–7. Metro-Goldwyn-Mayer c. 1937–9. National Film Board of Canada, producer and then technical supervisor c. 1940–5. The World Today, New York City 1946–8. Technical director of the stereoscopic film programs shown at the Telekinema during the Festival of Britain 1951. His principal books are *A Grammar of the Film*, 1935; *Film and its Techniques*, 1951; and *The Theory of Stereoscopic Transmission* (with Nigel Spottiswoode), 1953. Died 1970.

Further reading

Ellis, Jack C., *John Grierson: Life, Contributions, Influence*, Carbondale, IL: Southern Illinois University Press, 2000.

Hardy, Forsyth, *John Grierson: A Documentary Biography*, London: Faber & Faber, 1979.

Stern, Bert

Bert Stern stands as an unusual case in documentary history, for he entered and left in a whirlwind that closely resembles his career as a photographer. Stern has made only one film, Jazz on a Summer's Day (1960), but it exists as perhaps one of the greatest concert films ever made, and certainly the most well-known film about the jazz experience.

Stern began his career as an art director, but his ambition and skill quickly made him a preferred artist in freelance photography. His sharpness and artistry vaulted him into high commodity status with his work on various advertisement campaigns, and eventually his unique style brought him world fame through fashion photography and the images he created of Marilyn Monroe. Stern's photographs have appeared in *Vogue*, *Esquire*, *Life*, *Glamour*, and many other magazines. It is apparent that his career as a photographer and designer prepared him well for his single cinematic effort. Stern's desire to find new angles on his subjects makes Jazz on a Summer's Day a celebratory experience and less a traditional documentary, once again putting him outside the mainstream, while at the same time making his work highly distinct.

Stern's first experiences with filmmaking and photography came as part of the US Army's Motion Picture Division from 1951 to 1953. Self-taught, he advanced quickly from mailroom clerk to art director of *Mayfair Magazine*. From there he went on as a freelance photographer in the mid-1950s. His unique vision, often brash and irreverent, proved to be a success in Stern's commercial work. This led to clients as diverse as IBM, Pepsi, Volkswagen, Smirnoff, US Steel, DuPont, and others. Stern was able to break away from the standard photographic experience because he was able to recognize and capture both artistry and effectiveness in his commercial photography, and later, in his fashion and profile work. He was capable of selling ideas, products, people, lifestyles, and visions without commercial crassness. Stern's style has strictly adhered to the 'less is more' concept, and his use of lighting and composition replaced the cluttered and contrived photographs that inundated the commercial market before his arrival.

Perhaps Stern's greatest breakthrough and legacy is his photographic essay on Marilyn Monroe titled 'The Last Sitting'. Stern's two-day shoot of Monroe was her last before her death, and the photographs are as passionate as they are revealing, both externally and internally of the movie star.

Much of his passionate technique and irreverence transferred to his only attempt at filmmaking as well in 1958 at The Newport Jazz Festival. Jazz on a Summer's Day remains an engaging and elegant film, though its place in the history of documentary is murky. The reason lies somewhere between its experimental format and singularity. Jazz on a Summer's Day is shot as Stern would have photographed one of his beautiful models or objects. It is highly stylized and dramatically executed. Stern designed the festival's stage lighting and chose all the film's camera movements and placements. Stern fashioned still photographic long lenses to his film cameras so that he could invade spaces unnoticed. In technique and film mechanics, he was an innovator.

He was not afraid to get in his subject's face. He often used extreme close-ups, where performers would be-bop in and out of frame. He manages to use extremely static shots but still convey the passion and urgency of the performance. Stern, filming within an audience of hundreds, was able to provide a separate and unique intimate experience for his film audience. It is the result of the relationship that is obtained between artist and subject and artist and audience.

Jazz on a Summer's Day flows gracefully. Stern's editing is a stream of fluid crosscuts between the festival and the concurrent World's Cup Race. He uses images of water, boats, and birds as matching visuals to the festival's swaying beats.

Stern is as interested in the audience as much as in the performing artists. The woman in the red sweater, the man in the little hat, the dancing, drinking coed, the interracial couple all become as important to the film as the musicians. The film celebrates a musical form and a cultural movement.

Jazz on a Summer's Day began as a single passion for Stern. A life goal of the artist was to make a film by the time he was thirty. The project was almost abandoned on several occasions, but Stern credits his final decision to a conversation he had with another passenger on a plane. On returning from a scouting trip of the grounds, Stern wrote off the location as uninteresting and unmanageable. The gentleman he was sitting next to on the plane, after hearing about the reason for Stern's trip, insisted that Stern must make the film. Coming out of that experience Stern was finally convinced that the film should be made.

At the start of production the film went through many trials and changes. It began as a hybrid documentary/fictionalized narrative. Stern and his team devised scripts, and even shot rehearsals for an improvisational love story. The idea felt stale and unbelievable when it came time for actual filming and Stern dropped the contrived storylines. In an interview in 1999, included on the DVD release, Stern discussed the film's development: 'We tried to devise a story, but I wasn't equipped to produce a story […] so I stuck to the festival and to the music, and interpreted that with my camera.'

Some controversy hovers over the making of the film. Stern's producing partners still claim more stake in the film's creation than Stern has given them. While others claim directorial credit, Stern writes it off as his vision created entirely by himself. He sums the argument up in the 1999 interview by saying, 'I don't know if you want to call the movie directed. It's more of a happening […] Jazz on a Summer's Day is not directed. It was produced and filmed.'

Jazz on a Summer's Day does not adhere to traditional investigative or exploratory documentary formulas. The film exists as a celebratory film documenting a people, place, and event. Stern brings glamour to an open field in Rhode Island and brings 'jazz into the sun', as he describes it. Stern achieves what most concert films hope to with the experimentalism and newness of the form it documents: a lasting image of a singular moment in musical history.

ROBERT A. EMMONS, JR

See also: Jazz on a Summer's Day

Biography

Born in Brooklyn, New York, October 3, 1929. US Army 1951–3. Freelance photographer with L.C. Gumbiner Agency, New York, NY 1953–71; freelance commercial and magazine photographer 1959–. Founder and president of Libra Productions, a television commercial production company, New York, NY 1961–71. Has exhibited his photographs around the world from New York to France, Germany, and Switzerland. Author of several books, publishing his own library of work as well as texts on photographic process and technique. Received the Documentary Film Award, Venice Film Festival for his only film, Jazz on a Summer's Day, 1960, as well as several Art Directors Club Awards 1964–71.

Selected film

1960 Jazz on a Summer's Day: producer, writer, director, editor

Further reading

Silverman, Harold, *Gilbert Simon, Bert Stern, and Milton Glaser, The Pill Book*, New York: Bantam Books, 1980.

Stern, Bert, *The Photo Illustration*, New York: Crowell, 1974.

——*The Last Sitting*, New York: William Morrow & Co., 1982.

Stern, Bert and Sobieszek, Robert A., *Bert Stern: Adventures*, Boston: Bantam Books, 1998.

Stern, Horst

In the 1970s the television series Sterns Stunde (Stern's Hour) broke new ground in exposing and examining the relation of society to nature and animals. Horst Stern eschewed traditional filmmaking in his approach to his chosen topic. To Stern, an examination of our relationship to nature is important because it teaches us about ourselves and our society.

Twenty-six episodes of Sterns Stunde were produced between 1969 and 1979. The topics covered included animals as a food source, animals as pets, and animals in scientific experiments. He also devoted episodes to single species and creatures, such as spiders, butterflies, and hedgehogs. He always spoke the commentary with his hoarse and rough voice. His style was sharp, provocative, ironic, sometimes even polemic. His approach was marked by a scientific and educational, as opposed to entertaining, tone. His programs were always meticulously researched.

Stern did not refrain from airing his opinions. On Christmas Day in 1971, his program Bemerkungen über den Rothirsch/Remarks on the Red Deer was broadcast, in which he criticized German hunters for not hunting and killing enough deer. Other episodes attacked industrialized agriculture, which submits chickens and cows to miserable, mass production conditions. Other episodes discussed the use of animals in sports and the circus. The 1978 three-part program on animal experimentation in the pharmaceutical industry generated much discussion and controversy.

Besides these political statements, he and his cameramen, especially Kurt Hirschel, produced cinematographic masterpieces, for which they developed new techniques to shoot animals such as spiders and bees. One of his theses was that the best way to respect animals in nature is to simply leave them alone.

Horst Stern was under the impression that all his efforts to change society were not as successful as he had hoped, thus he stopped shooting films and started a print magazine in 1980. In the mid-1980s he resigned and started to write literature. In his novel *Klint*, he describes a journalist who despairs over his love for unblemished nature and his sorrow about the destruction of the environment.

KAY HOFFMANN

Biography

Born in Stettin, Germany, October 24, 1922. Did an apprenticeship at a bank. Served in World War II. Worked as a court reporter for a Stuttgart newspaper in 1947. Worked as a consultant for the publisher Delius Claasing in Bielefeld. Became Editor-in-Chief for various leisure magazines. In the 1960s wrote more than fifty radio programs on animals for the school program of Süddeutscher Rundfunk (SDR), the public broadcaster for southwest Germany. From 1969 on, directed the ecological television series Sterns Stunde for SDR. In 1972 founded the Gruppe Ökölogie (Ecology Group) with Konrad Lorenz, Irenäus Eibl-Eibesfeldt, Bernhard Grzimek, and Heinz Sielmann. In 1974 awarded an honorary doctorate from the University of Stuttgart-Hohenheim. In 1980 started the magazine *Natur*. Publisher and Editor-in-Chief until 1984. Published three novels, which were quite successful in Germany.

Selected films

1970 Bemerkungen über das Pferd/Remarks on the Horse: director, writer
1970 Bemerkungen über die Biene/Remarks on the Bee: director, writer
1970 Bemerkungen über das Rind/Remarks on the Cow: director, writer
1971 Bemerkungen über das Huhn/Remarks on the Dog: director, writer
1971 Bemerkungen über den Rothirsch/Remarks on the Red Deer: director, writer
1973 Bemerkungen über das Tier im Handel/Remarks on the Animal in Handel: director, writer
1973 Bemerkungen über den Storch/Remarks on the Stork: director, writer
1975 Bemerkungen über die Spinne/Remarks on the Spider: director, writer
1976 Bemerkungen über den Hund als Ware/Remarks on the dog as a commodity: director, writer
1978 Die Stellvertreter—Tiere in der Pharmaforschung: director, writer
1979 Bemerkungen über Gemse: director, writer
1997 Sterns Bemerkungen über einen sterbenden Wald: director, writer

Further reading

Grefe, Christiane, 'Horst Stern—Das Vertrauen ins Fernsehen ist verloren', in Cornelia Bolesch (ed.), *Dokumentarisches Fernsehen*, Munich: List, 1990: 76–80.
n.a., 'Horst Stern', in catalogue 16, Internationales Dokumentarfilmfestival München, Munich, 2001.
Stern, Horst, *Sterns Bemerkungen über das Pferd … die Biene … die Hunde*, Munich: Kindler, 1971.
——*Tierversuche in der Pharmaforschung*, Munich: Kindler, 1979.
——*Jagdnovelle*, Munich: Kindler, 1989.
——*Klint. Stationen einer Verwirrung*, Munich: Knaus, 1993.

Stewart, Charles

Although not a household name, cameraman and director Charles Stewart has played a crucial part in the development of television documentary from the 1960s to the present day. He is probably best known for his work with Roger Graef, for whom he has shot a number of programmes. He also codirected Police (BBC, 1980–81) with him. He thus played a central role in the dissemination of direct cinema techniques within British television during the 1960s and, most prominently, the 1970s (when the 'fly-on-the-wall' documentary began to become an established part of British television). He has also worked in other forms, such as television drama, feature films, and anthropological documentaries.

Stewart became an early innovator in the use of handheld, sync-sound camera work. He quickly became adept at using the Éclair NPR and, as lightweight cameras became increasingly taken up within television, his services were in more and more demand. Using the NPR, he could handhold the camera and thus capture a large range of different events in many different spaces. Free from the restrictions of lighting set-ups and camera repositioning, Stewart could work faster and create a fluid sense of action, breaking down the distance between action and camera.

It was unsurprising that Stewart began to work for Alan King Associates (AKA), which became a kind of centre for young, innovative filmmakers working with new, lightweight equipment. Stewart first worked with Graef when making a film under the aegis of AKA: The Life and Times of John Huston Esq. (BBC, 1967) was a Graef-directed documentary on the film director that mixed vérité techniques with some dramatic, symbolic sequences. This programme led to the creation of a twelve-part series on artists that mixed vérité techniques with occasional experimental sequences: Who Is? (BBC, 1968) was an attempt to break new ground in arts documentaries and was the first series to be coproduced by four different television companies from around the world (the BBC, the Canadian Broadcasting Corporation, National EducationTelevision, United States, and Bayerischer Rundfunk, Germany). In between the Huston programme and the Who Is? series, Stewart had worked on the Mike Hodges-produced series New Tempo (ABC, 1967), an extremely experimental, montage-based arts series.

Towards the end of the 1960s, in line with the growing confluence of documentary and drama in many areas, Stewart shot many documentary-influenced television dramas and feature films. These included work with directors such as Ken Loach and Jean-Luc Godard, who represented the 'realistic' and 'experimental' sides of lightweight camera use, with both of which Stewart was associated. Perhaps the most controversial documentary-influenced drama that Stewart shot in this period was Roy Battersby's Some Women (BBC, 1968), a film covering interviews with women who had been in prison. Based on extensive research, the film used actresses to reenact original interviews and was not transmitted until 1969 because of the manner in which it was seen to confuse the boundaries between fact and fiction. Stewart shot the film in an intimate, still manner, diverting from the more roving manner associated with lightweight equipment.

In the 1970s Stewart undertook work with Graef on a number of fly-on-the-wall documentaries, most often documenting a number of decision-making processes. The first of these was The Space Between Words (BBC, 1972), a five-part series that filmed a series of incidents that reflected communication problems within different environments (such as in a family, at work, and at school). This documentary marked a new stage of vérité within Britain, a much more austere and painstaking detailing of words, movements, and gestures. This called for Stewart to observe a whole set of details at quick speed, so that he could shift his focus appropriately. The series was shot on a relatively high ratio of 30:1, which allowed the crew to amass a wealth of film and thus select what they thought were the most interesting sequences for transmission. Graef continued this style for a number of documentaries made for Granada, including State of the Nation: A Law in the Making (Granada, 1973) and Decision (Granada, 1976). In 1981 Graef and Stewart made the now famous Police (transmitted 1982) for the BBC, a thirteen-part, minutely focused portrait of the Thames Valley police force, which attracted more than ten million viewers, an enormous number for a documentary.

Stewart is most famous for his work with Graef, but he has also worked in many other fields, and has often worked as sole director. His first directorial assignment was an ATV documentary on a road-widening scheme, Could Your Street Be Next? (ATV, 1972). In the late 1970s he made two television dramas, both of which evidence a realistic tone: Speech Day (Thames, 1977) and Billy (BBC, 1979). In the 1980s Stewart began to work on programmes that documented environmental and political aspects of Ethiopia in Seeds of Despair (Central, 1984) and Seeds of Hope (Central, 1985). These programmes (the second of which was a six-part series) evidenced influences of both vérité and anthropological television that had developed in the 1970s and with which Stewart was involved. Stewart shot some episodes of Granada's popular anthropological series Disappearing World (Granada, 1970–91), as well as Adrian Cowell's well-received, experimentally tinged anthropology programme The Tribe That Hides from Man (ATV, 1970).

Although Stewart's work was varied, it was also marked by certain thematic and stylistic preoccupations: capturing 'authentic', minimally mediated action; detailing events often 'hidden' or ignored by the media; plus a sensitivity to detail and an ability to capture the minutiae of human interaction, such as facial expressions or significant body gestures. He was, along with Dick Fontaine, among the most innovative camera stylists working with lightweight equipment in British television during the 1960s, helping to break down the boundaries between drama and documentary in the late 1960s and early 1970s, and was involved in the new wave of politically sensitive anthropological documentaries in the 1970s and 1980s.

JAMIE SEXTON

See also: Graef, Roger

Biography

Born in Newcastle-upon-Tyne, 1937. Two years national service in the navy from 1956. In 1958 went to Regent Street Polytechnic to study photography. Moved to London in 1961 and started to work as a fashion photographer. Started documentary film production in 1964. In 1965 began working with AKA, and first met Roger Graef.

Selected films

1967 New Tempo: photographer (ABC, series, various directors)
1968 The Life and Times of John Huston Esq.: photographer (BBC, Graef)
1968 Who Is?: photographer (BBC, series, various directors)
1969 Some Women: photographer (BBC, Battersby)
1970 The Tribe that Hides from Man: photographer (ATV, Cowell)
1970 The Important Thing is Love: photographer (ATV, Kitts)
1971 Rank and File: photographer (BBC, Loach)
1972 The Space Between Words: photographer (BBC, series, Graef)
1972 Could Your Street Be Next: director (ATV)
1973 The State of the Nation—A Law in the Making: photographer (Granada, Graef)
1974 Disappearing World: Masai Women: photographer (Granada, Curling)
1974 Disappearing World: Masai Manhood: photographer (Granada, Curling)
1974 Retirement: End or Beginning?: director (ATV)
1975 The State of the Nation: Inside Brussels HQ: photographer (Granada, Graef)
1976 Decision: photographer (Granada, series, Graef)
1977 Disappearing World: The Rendille: photographer (Granada, Curling)
1978 Decision: British Communism: photographer (Granada, Graef)
1979 Billy: director (BBC)
1982 Police: director, producer (BBC, series co-directed and produced with Roger Graef)
1984 Seeds of Despair: director (Central)
1985 Seeds of Hope: director (Central)
1991 Cutting Edge: Plague in Your Own Home: director (Channel 4)
1992 Town Hall: director, producer (BBC, series)
1995 Witness: Mecca on the Thames: director (Channel 4)
1996 True Stories: Inside Sellafield: director, producer (Channel 4)
1996 Red Base One Four: director, producer (Channel 4)

Further reading

Orbanz, Eva (ed.), *Journey to a Legend and Back: The British Realistic Film*, trans. Stuart Hood, Berlin: Edition Volker Spiess, 1977.
Petley, Julian, ‘The Good Stewart’, *Broadcast*, July, 19, 1985.
Swallow, Norman, ‘Television, the Integrity of Fact and Fiction’, *Sight and Sound* 45, no. 3, summer 1976.
Winston, Brian, *Claiming the Real: The Griersonian Documentary and its Legitimations*, London: BFI, 1995.
Wyver, John (ed.), *Nothing but the Truth: Cinéma Vérité and the Films of the Roger Graef Team*, London: ICA/BFI, 1982.
——‘Police Taped’, *Framework* 18, 1982.

Stoney, George

George Stoney is a leading figure in the American documentary film movement, having made more than fifty documentaries and founded a movement of community-based media producers in the 1960s and 1970s in North America. He has played a major agenda setting role in debates about documentary, its forms, its ethics, and its social function. Stoney began his career working in 16mm as a socially aware documentary filmmaker using aspects of direct cinema, and later switched to video format in the 1970s as it was ideal for the mobility and ease needed for the informal community-based media he produced or over which he saw production. In addition to using video as a means of making media more democratically available to nonprofessionals, he also was responsible for leading the creation of public access cable, a designated community 'free speech' zone negotiated with cable operators. Stoney also provided the pedagogy and philosophy to underpin the production of this new genre of video documentary. As the cofounder of the influential Alternative Media Center in 1970, which became a training ground for the first generation of producers, Stoney played a major role in influencing the content of this programming. Besides working in television, Stoney has collaborated on numerous films around the world, including those by his many former students, which share a common commitment to social change media in their production, content, and distribution.

From his first documentary, All My Babies in 1953—a training film for the Georgia Department of Public Health of a dramatic reenactment of a black midwife's work from her perspective—he has been committed to producing films and videos that show life from the perspective of people who have been disenfranchised or excluded from mainstream media. He uses narrative as a strategy, preferring to tell a story or cover an event than letting the camera be a 'fly on the wall'. This extends to letting participants in the film take the microphone, use direct address and other surprising rule-breaking moments in the films, and video productions that have, as their goal, social change and education rather than aesthetic purity.

Stoney's filmmaking practice and philosophy challenges the auteurship that defined direct cinema. A former student of Basil Wright and an educator for the FSA using Pare Lorentz's films, his filmmaking practice comes with an awareness of the history and practices that inform his work. His interest in the history of documentary film culminated in his intensive study of documentary pioneer Robert Flaherty in How the Myth Was Made (1978). This acclaimed film critically explored the early roots of documentary practice. Indeed, despite his critical approach, all of Stoney's films are informed by fundamental attributes of cinéma vérité such as direct address, natural lighting, and ambient sound, but always with a question of the morality of filmmaking, an issue that some direct cinema directors eschewed. Thus, Stoney's interest in who and how the story is being told—its fidelity to truth—is more than an aesthetic but an ethical working out of the filmmaker-subject relationship, a debate that shaped the direct cinema movement.

His respect for the subject's perspective extends to letting them shape the final cut, a process that few directors would ever allow. This active engagement with the subjects allows them to retain authorial control. He established this practice early on, and it has stayed with him throughout his career. It was his concern with retaining the subjectivity of the participants in documentary that led him to take a job as an executive producer of an experimental project at the Canadian Nation Film Board (NFB) in 1968. One of his first films, You are on Indian Land, involved an Indian film crew that was trained by the NFB and covered a border dispute from an Indian perspective, countering the view of the television news. It was used also as a tool of understanding and shown to Royal Canadian Mounted Police and the local police.

It was while at Challenge for Change that Stoney recognized the importance of the newly developed lightweight video portapak in community production. It enabled filmmakers to make documentary films in the field, cheaply and without expert training, making it an ideal medium for social activists who could now gain the authority of media producers without the cost or technical expertise of film. A documentary of the use of this early video tool was *VTR St. Jacques*. Shot on 16mm, it chronicles the first use of half-inch, consumer grade black-and-white video as a tool for community building and people empowerment. In 1970, when he returned from the Challenge for Change program, he took the next step toward creating a democratized distribution to match the style and content of the video's community-based productions when he cofounded the Alternative Media Center at New York University. In this effort, he is fundamentally concerned with the documentaries-audience relationship, which owes its concern to political activism and the pedagogical strategies of Paulo Frerie. Stoney uses media in situations that would encourage dialogue and understanding and lead to political change. This meant creating other groundbreaking forums for viewing in and out of the public sphere, as in public access's carving out of a space for community media in a medium surrounded by mainstream productions, and also in other ways, such as in the screenings of films in unusual places or to facilitate dialogue among groups.

DANIELLE SCHWARTZ

See also: Wright, Basil

Biography

Born in 1916, studied journalism at the University of North Carolina and at New York University. Worked as freelance journalist, an information officer for the Farm Security Administration and a photo intelligence officer in World War II. Joined the Southern Educational Film Service as a writer and a director in 1946. In 1948 he received a Rosenwald Fellowship. Appointed the first executive director of the Canadian Film Board's Challenge for Change Program 1968. In 1972, with Red Burns, he cofounded the Alternate Media Center at New York University. In 1976 he was founder of the National Federation of Local Cable Programmers. Stoney is currently Paulette Goddard Professor in Film, Tisch School of the Arts, Department of Film and Television.

Selected films

1953 All My Babies
1965 The Mask
1972 First Transmissions of ACTV
1978 Shepherd of the Night Flock (with James Brown)
1978 How the Myth Was Made
1978 VTR St. Jacques
1989 We Shall Overcome
1995 The Uprising of '34: codirected with Judith Helfand

Further reading

Barnouw, Eric, *Documentary: A History of the Non-Fiction Film*, New York: Oxford University Press, 1993.
Mertes, Cara, 'Toasts and Tributes', *Wide Angle* 21, no. 2, March 1999: 137–65.
n.a., special issue devoted to George Stoney, *Wide Angle* 21, no. 2, 1999.
Rapport, Leonard, 'George Stoney, Writer: The Early Years', *Wide Angle* 21, no. 2, March 1999: 19–25.
Stoney, George, 'The Mirror Machine', *Sight and Sound* 41, no. 1, winter 1971–2: 9–11.
——'The Future of Documentary', *Sightlines*, fall–winter, 1983–4.
Sturken, Marita, 'An Interview with George Stoney', *Afterimage*, January 1984.
Watson, Patricia, 'Challenge for Change', *Art Canada* 1970: 142–3.
Winston, Brian, 'Documentary: How the Myth Was Deconstructed', *Wide Angle* 21, no. 2, March 1999: 71–86.

Storck, Henri

Having made more than seventy films, comprising for the most part documentaries and shorts combined with a few medium- and feature-length films, Henri Storck is undoubtedly the leading figure of Belgian cinema. Throughout his varied career he dealt to a greater or lesser degree with such practices as formalism, impressionism, social and political concerns, and ethnography. He generally worked in an ordered fashion, gained a certain reputation with art critique films, but never fulfilled his Hollywood dreams. He fought relentlessly for a national cinema, sometimes displayed ideological flexibility, never abandoned his life's passions and remained a genuinely modest individual.

His first attempts at film, shot on 9.5mm and subsequently on 35mm, focused on his immediate surroundings, and combined formal research, an acute study of social behaviour and a surrealist sense of rebellion. Films d'amateur sur Ostende/Amateur Films over Ostende (1928) and Images d'Ostende/Images of Ostende (1929), with their poetic mood and rhythmic feeling, recall the early works of Joris Ivens. In 1930 Trains de plaisir/Trains of Pleasure, Les Fêtes du centenaire/Feasts of the Centenary, Ostende, reine des plages/Ostende, Queen of the Beaches all display an aptitude for observing rituals and feasts. Storck had in fact been declared 'the official cinematographer of the city of Ostende'.

Images d'Ostende, Trains de plaisir, and Une pêche aux harengs/Herring Fishing (1930) were shown at the 2nd International Congress of Independent Cinema, held in Brussels between November 27 and December 1, 1930. Storck's work met with acclaim. During the congress Storck met Joris Ivens, with whom he would later collaborate on Borinage, Boris Kaufman, Jean Painlevé, and Jean Vigo, who was to become his close friend. In 1931 he moved to Paris and became involved with Zéro de conduite, in which he had a small role, that of a priest. By the end of 1933, however, Storck had moved back to Brussels.

In 1932 Storck directed two films: Sur les bords de la caméra/On the Edge of the Camera and Histoire du soldat inconnu/History of the Unknown Soldier. These two short films, made on commission (Storck had to edit sequences of athletics taken from news images), exploit a surrealist and often satirical vein reminiscent of René Clair's Entr'acte (1924) or Vigo's A propos de Nice (1930). Histoire du soldat inconnu is, in addition, a pacifist manifesto denouncing the illusions of the Briand-Kellog Pact (1928), the rise of fascism, and the impotence of the League of Nations.

In 1933, at the behest of the Screen Club of Brussels (Club de l'Ecran de Bruxelles), Storck began the Borinage project (Misère au Borinage). Contacted by the leaders of this leftist cine club, known for its projection of avant-garde and political films, Storck took on the project and requested the collaboration of Joris Ivens, who accepted immediately. The film, largely based on a study into the wretched living conditions of the mining community, written by a doctor and published by Workers Aid International (Secours Ouvrier International), depicts the strike movement and the confrontations with law enforcement. It is a testimony to the consciousness of filmmakers and left-wing intellectuals with regard to the subject. The film ends with a direct call for the dictatorship of the proletariat. The film was made with little money: there is no soundtrack and it is filmed largely with lightweight cameras that are, above all, hidden from the authorities.

To depict the episodes concerning the strikers' conflict, however, the two directors were faced with the problem of reconstruction. They needed to show, for example, the tactic implemented by the community to avoid eviction (other miners would arrive and strategically sit on the furniture to prevent the bailiff from seizing it). The directors had no other choice than to 'produce an honest and direct imitation' (Ivens), and for this they needed to hire two police uniforms and find two miners willing to act the part of policemen. The other important scene that had to be reconstructed was that of the demonstration that appears at the end of the film and that had taken place to commemorate the fiftieth anniversary of the death of Karl Marx. The directors asked the miners to proceed as normal. The portrait of Marx, held by two men, leads the march, followed by small groups of men, each group separated by about ten paces from the next, thus rendering them an impossible target and facilitating escape in the event of police intervention. According to Ivens, the miners forgot that they were participating in the making of a film, and the scene became a genuine demonstration, hence the arrival and intervention of the police and the urgent need to hide the camera.

In 1934 Henri Storck, along with René-Ghislain Levaux, created the organisation Cinéma-Edition-Production (CEP), which would later fulfil numerous commissions. Les Maisons de la Misère/Houses of Poverty (1937), made for The National Society for Low Cost Housing (Société Nationale des Habitations à Bon Marché), is reminiscent of both Housing Problems (Anstey and Elton, 1935), which Storck had viewed, and certain scenes of Borinage. One of the two cameramen was Eli Lotar, who worked for Buñuel on Las Hurdes and would subsequently direct Aubervilliers. Whereas Borinage used the real protagonists and adhered to a documentary structure, the production of Les Maisons de la Misère opted for professional stage actors.

La Belgique nouvelle/New Belgium (1937) is essentially a film of election propaganda for the Prime Minister Van Zeeland, and it is entirely a product of its context, that of the front against fascism. Le Patron est mort/The Boss is Dead (1938) retraces the funeral procession of socialist leader Emile Vandervelde (nicknamed *le patron*, the boss). The particular attention paid to the behaviour of the largely working-class crowds during this ritual prefigures the ethnographic approach of his later works.

In the period leading up to World War II Storck devoted much energy to an historical production about the colonisation of the Congo, Bula Matari. His associate, Le Vaux, from the CEP, spent a long period between 1939 and 1940 in Hollywood, trying to secure the interest of the majors. He seemed to be on the verge of success when the war broke out. The project was relaunched in 1950 with Alexander Korda, only to fall through once again.

In the middle of World War II, from 1942 to 1944, Storck devoted himself to Symphonie paysanne/Peasant Symphony, a feature-length documentary in five parts (the four seasons plus a rural wedding celebration, which serves as a conclusion). Aesthetically speaking, this film is probably Storck's chef-d'oeuvre; however, from an ideological and symbolic perspective, the film is somewhat surprising. This chronicle of rural farm life in Brabant, which omits any reference to the current world conflict, seems to glorify the values of 'a return to the land', 'back to nature', and 'national cohesion', values greatly extolled by the occupying forces. The semi-ethnographic approach is also completely ahistorical, and the continual insistence on the timeless rural rituals and the cyclical concept of time immemorial are in total opposition to any progressive vision.

After the war Storck mainly focused on films about art. In 1945 the innovative short film Le Monde de Paul Delvaux/The World of Paul Delvaux broke new ground in its seeming ability to penetrate the interior of the art works. Storck would later return to this subject in 1970 with Paul Delvaux ou les femmes défendues/Paul Delvaux or Forbidden Women. Rubens (1948), made in collaboration with the critic Paul Haesaerts, anticipated an analytical approach that would become widespread many years later. The use of split screen, crosscutting, extreme close-ups, and the superimposition of geometric lines on the artwork, all produced on 35mm black-and-white film, prefigured the video effects which made the French series Palettes (Alain Jaubert) so successful in the 1990s.

In this postwar period, Storck also worked on one of his rare fiction films, Le Banquet des fraudeurs/The Smuggler's Banquet (1951), which deals with the creation of Bénélux in the context of the Marshall Plan. This humorous chronicle of a village with three borders, two of which are going to disappear, paradoxically goes to great lengths to appeal to a wide European audience.

Without interrupting his numerous and diverse commissions such as Au Carrefour de la vie/At the Crossroad of Life (1949), commissioned by the United Nations on the subject of the rehabilitation of young offenders, Storck increasingly turned to films about Belgian society, history, and traditions. Fêtes de Belgique ou l'effusion collective/Feasts of Belgium or Collective Effusion (1970–1), a series of ten short films on 35mm, provided a perfect ethnographic example of the country's folk traditions.

Storck's career drew to a close in 1985 with a feature-length biopic on the painter Permeke. Toward the end of his life, Storck, anxious to pass on his experiences and documents, agreed to participate in various interviews by filmmakers and researchers. Such examples include Henri Storck, Cinéaste/Henri Storck Filmmaker (1986) by Robbe de Hert and Mes entretiens filmés/My Conversations on Film (1998) by Boris Lehman.

Storck was always motivated by his love of the cinema. He initiated many projects. He was cofounder of the Cinématheque Royale de Belgique (1938), he created the Audiovisual Centre in Brussels (Centre de l'Audiovisuel, CBA), and the Centre for Films on Art (Centre du Film sur l'Art). In 1950 he carried out a study for the United Nations Educational, Scientific and Cultural Organization (UNESCO) into the recreational film for the child spectator. In 1959 he produced Les Seigneurs de la forêt/Masters of the Congo Jungle (Heinz Sielmann and Henri Brandt), and in 1967 Luc de Heusch's Jeudi on chantera comme dimanche/Thursday We Shall Sing Like Sunday. In 1975 he appeared in Chantal Ackerman's film Jeanne Dielman.

In terms of Storck's ideas, he was not devoid of certain surprising contradictions: a poetic filmmaker who admired John Ford, a modest director who dreamed of making Hollywood blockbusters, a staunch socialist who sometimes accepted astonishing political concessions, a quiet man who was also a determined rebel. In the famous May 1968 revolt in Paris, despite being a teacher at the renowned National School of Cinema (IAD, Ecole Nationale de Cinéma), he took the side of the students, a decision that cost him his teaching post.

Storck was acquainted with many highly esteemed directors and lived through the leading cinematic trends of the twentieth century. The imprints left by this father figure of Belgian cinema are still visible today. A formal invention, an openness to international subjects, and a commitment to social concerns—which today epitomise the Belgian documentary movement—are all inherent in Storck's varied work.

JEAN-LUC LIOULT

See also: Ivens, Joris

Biography

Born September 5, 1907 to shoe shop owners. Graduated with a degree in physics from the Université Libre de Bruxelles. Died September 23, 1999.

Selected films

1928 Films d'amateur sur Ostende/Amateur Films over Ostende: cinematographer, director
1929 Images d'Ostende/Images of Ostende: cinematographer, director
1930 Une pêche au hareng/Herring Fishing: cinematographer, director
1932 Histoire du soldat inconnu/History of the Unknown Soldier: cinematographer, director, editor
1933 Borinage: co-cinematographer, codirector, writer
1936 Les Maisons de la misère/Houses of Poverty: director
1944 Symphonie paysanne/Peasant Symphony: cinematographer, director, writer, editor, producer
1949 Rubens: director, writer, editor, producer
1971 Paul Delvaux ou les femmes défendues/Paul Delvaux or Forbidden Women: director
1973 Les Fêtes de Belgique/Feasts of Belgium: director
1998 Mes entretiens filmés/My Conversations on Film (Lehman): actor

Further reading

Aubenas, Jacqueline (ed.), *Dic Doc, Le Dictionnaire du Documentaire—191 réalisateurs*, Bruxelles: Communauté Française de Belgique Wallonie-Bruxelles, 1999.

Geens, Vincent, *Bula Matari: Un rêve d'Henri Storck*, Crisnée: Fonds Henri Storck/Yellow Now Côté cinéma, 2000.

Lioult, Jean-Luc, 'Autour du Rubens de Storck et du Van Gogh de Resnais: quels films sur l'art?' in *Le Film sur l'Art et ses Frontières*, Aix-en-Provence: Publications de l'Université de Provence & Institut de l'Image, 1998: 45–60.

n.a., 'Le Borinage: "la gréve des mineurs de 1932 et le film de Joris Ivens et Henri Storck"', *Revue belge du Cinéma* 6–7, 1983–4, Bruxelles: APEC.

Vichi, Laura, *Henri Storck—De l'avant-garde au documentaire social*, Crisnée: Yellow Now Côté cinéma, 2002.

Strand, Paul

Paul Strand is one of the most important figures in the development of modern American photography, as well as contributing to a series of groundbreaking documentary films between the 1920s and early 1940s. A pioneer of photographic abstraction in the 1910s, Strand dealt with subject matter that ranged from urban scenes and landscapes to found objects and intensely personal close-ups. He was particularly interested in the purity of simple images and geometric patterns and composed his photographs to capture what in 1917 he called 'a formal conception born of the emotions, the intellect, or of both'. He was a modernist in his belief that the camera gives access to the truth of objects, and the photograph brings to life a hidden potentiality often overlooked in daily life. Alan Trachtenberg has argued that although Strand was interested in documenting the factual world, he developed a romantic version of modernism in searching for organic properties within hard forms, heightening perceptions and illuminating hidden depths.

Born into a Jewish family on the Upper West Side of New York City, Strand was educated at the Ethical Culture School in New York in 1904–9. His teacher, the social reformer Lewis W. Hime, taught Strand how to use a camera to document working-class life and introduced him to art exhibitions in 1907. After graduation and a short trip to Europe, Strand joined the Camera Club of New York and worked briefly as a commercial portrait photographer. He began working in pictorialist and impressionist modes, but in the mid-1910s became very interested in 'straight photographs', in which he achieved a high measure of objectivity by reverting to a sharp-focus lens and refusing to tamper with the negative. The purity of Strand's work caught the interest of the photographic innovator and art exhibitor Alfred Stieglitz in 1915. Stieglitz held Strand in high esteem; he was the only photographer Stieglitz would exhibit in the late 1910s, and in a June 1917 issue of *Camera Work*, Stieglitz praised him for his 'brutal directness' and for resisting trickery for his visual effect.

Towards the end of his career, in 1971, Strand spoke about three roads that opened for him after he saw Stieglitz's Armory Show of 1913: first, 'to understand the new developments in painting'; second, 'a desire to express certain feelings I had about New York'; and, third, a desire to 'photograph people without their being aware of the camera'. Strand followed Stieglitz's preference for a handheld camera to take instantaneous pictures, which enabled events to come together by chance, rather than viewing composition in a fixed, unmoving way. He discussed ideas with artists that Stieglitz exhibited in his 291 Gallery on Fifth Avenue, including Morgan Russell, Marcel Duchamp, and Francis Picabia. However, where Duchamp and Picabia's art explored the chaos of modernity, Strand sought a heightened objectivity that was epitomized by the modernity of Manhattan. Sometimes he appeared to celebrate urban designs through his sharply focused images and his interest in light, line, and volume, whereas at others (such as a 1922 essay in Broom), he set his work against the destructive force of mechanization. Just as Stieglitz was interested in the relationship between industry and nature, so Strand was keen to rescue a sense of organicism from inanimate forms.

In the mid-1910s and early 1920s (on either side of serving in the US Army Medical Corps as an X-ray technician), Strand spent most of his energy putting into effect his 'brutal directness' to document New York City life. His photograph of 'Wall Street' (1915), for example, on one level portrays just another day in the life of the financial district; however, the photograph depicts a group of figures reduced to little more than silhouettes: no facial features are discernible, and they walk mechanically and in isolation from each other. Long shadows are cast by a restricted light source located outside the frame, and the sombre mood of the photograph is exacerbated by a sequence of gigantic dark windows of Wall Street that loom over the figures. Other photographs from this time are more conventional and lighter in tone, replicating Stieglitz's interest in the interaction between urban and natural forces (such as 'City Hall Park', 1915), but with much closer attention to the abstract shapes conjured up by the developing city. Although Strand photographed nonurban images (such as 'Abstraction, Porch Shadows' and the almost cubist 'Still Life, Pear and Bowls' in a 1916 trip to Twin Lakes, Connecticut), he was deeply engaged with the variety of city life, where European impulses fused with native experiences. Although he spent time photographing working Manhattan, he was also interested in the poor immigrants living in areas such as the Bowery. One of his most haunting images is 'Blind Woman' (1916), depicting an ageing woman with a 'blind' placard around her neck who stares away from the camera without recognition. In a different context, this could be seen as an exploitative image, but Strand had deep respect for his subjects and he spoke of the blind woman's 'absolutely unforgettable and noble face'.

Many of the still images of New York, including 'Wall Street' and 'City Hall Park', were reused in Strand's seven-minute documentary collaboration, Manhatta, with the painter Charles Sheeler (1921). Manhatta pioneered the vogue for city symphonies, leading to documentaries on Berlin, Amsterdam, and Moscow in the 1920s. Strand and Sheeler used Walt Whitman's poetry as a lyrical contrast to the multiple perspectives they deployed to depict a working day in downtown Manhattan. Just as Strand's written statements shift between fascination with the modern city and a critique of new forms of alienation created by urban development, so Manhatta can be read either as a paean to, or a critique of, city life. The plumes of smoke pumped out by boats in the Hudson Bay contrast ironically with the still image of the celestial city that frames Whitman's celebratory lyrics (see Manhatta entry). This interest in textuality resurfaced later in Strand's mid-1940s collaboration with Nancy Newhall, Time in New England (1950), in which written texts were juxtaposed with ninety-four images of New England to create 'a portrait more dynamic than either medium could present alone' (although Strand was not altogether pleased with the result).

From the mid-1920s Strand moved away from New York City as his primary location, taking his 'brutal directness' to other North American scenes, particularly New England, Canada, and the Southwest. He shared an interest with Mexico and the Southwest with Stieglitz's partner Georgia O'Keeffe, but Strand offered a different perspective from O'Keeffe's painterly exuberance. He visited the Southwest regularly between 1930 and 1932, developing location and portrait photographs that retain a directness born out of his urban sensibility, together with a respect for the peoples of the region. Strand also became more radical in the early 1930s, advising the Group Theatre, visiting the Soviet Union (where he met Sergei Eisenstein), and collaborating on the documentary The Plow that Broke the Plains (1935), the first publicly shown federal government documentary that focused on the creation of the Dust Bowl as a result of over-ploughing and the drought of 1929. He shared the photographic credits for the film with Ralph Steiner and Leo Hurwitz under Pare Lorentz's direction. Lorentz had been inspired by Dorothea Lange's photographs of the effects of the Depression and had been commissioned by the Resettlement Administration to document the plight of workers in the Great Plains region. Strand and Hurwitz favoured a script that would cast blame on greedy capitalists, but Lorentz was more moderate in his politics and argued that this would undermine the emphasis on the drought and the 'melodrama of nature'. Strand and Hurwitz spent much of their time taking location shots of dust-storms, with Lorentz working closely with Ralph Steiner on the narrative sections. Although Strand thought that 'the guts had been taken out' of the film, his influence can be seen in the montage of still images (skull, disused machinery, cracked earth, desolate landscape) that heighten the impact of the disaster.

Strand's work on The Plow that Broke the Plains had been preceded by his work on The Wave/Redes, sponsored by the Mexican government, completed in 1934 but not shown in the United States until 1936. The Wave explored the economic problems faced by a fishing village near Vera Cruz, developing Strand's interest in working Mexican life, emphasizing the meagre wage that fishermen receive for a long day's work and the united action of workers. Strand was the chief architect of the film, even though it was directed by Fred Zinnemann. William Alexander argues that one of Strand's photographic signatures is used to great effect in The Wave: a technique in which shots 'begin with a single, posed figure in close-up or medium close-up; movement in the shot then consists of a single movement of the head'. This aesthetic mode was developed in Heart of Spain in 1937, co-edited by Leo Hurwitz, which dealt with the Loyalist fight against Franco. The central focus of Heart of Spain is on the relationship between Spanish peasants and the land, which creates a romantic-poetic drama rather than a narrative-based documentary.

Strand's most important film project was the prolabor film Native Land in 1942. Once again Strand collaborated with Hurwitz, this time as codirectors, under the label of Frontier Films, which had been formed in 1936 as a development of the Group Theatre project. Frontier Films was 'an independent, nonprofit motion picture organization devoted to the production of realistic depictions of American life' set against Hollywood's emphasis on individualism and sentimentality. The influence of Eisenstein and Dovzhenko is apparent in Native Land, which is filmed in a Soviet documentary style to expose pernicious right-wing forces in America. It was scripted by Ben Maddow and uses Paul Robeson's narrative voice against a panoply of stark images to highlight the perversion of American ideals, the deep-rooted corruption of exploitative capitalists, and the fascism of the Ku Klux Klan. The film is deeply prolabor and anti-fascist, as emphasized at the end of Robeson's spoken epilogue: 'With the united power of field and factory and arms, we will deliver the blows to crush fascism. For only absolute victory over Hitler and Japan can safeguard our democratic gains and preserve the independence of America.'

Through his film projects, Strand retained his interest in photographic montage, but Native Land is much more impressionistic than Strand's 'straight photography' of the 1910s and 1920s. This shifting style demonstrated that he did not wish to be pigeonholed as an artist who could only work within a single aesthetic mode. His work was much more politicized in the 1930s and 1940s; his involvement in the left-wing film projects of Frontier Films actually led to un-American accusations being levelled against him and the blacklisting of the Photo League in 1947. Strand stood firmly along with photographers, such as Ansel Adams, against the blacklisting, and when the Photo League called a special meeting in December 1947 to discuss what action should be taken, Strand commented defiantly: 'although artists have not in the past wanted to mix art with politics the politicians have already mixed politics in art. So we are now in politics, very much so.' Strand was active in the late 1940s in defending the blacklisted Hollywood Ten, and he joined with the playwright Clifford Odets in June 1949 in calling for a Bill of Rights conference to protest 'the police state methods of certain Army and FBI officials'. The charges against him and the blacklisting of Leo Hurwitz were the main reason why Strand moved to France at the beginning of the 1950s, but these statements on the intermingling of art and politics are a gauge of how far his art had progressed since the 1910s.

Strand turned away from filmmaking after World War II (partly for financial reasons), settling in Orgeval near Paris in 1951 and spending time travelling and photographing in Europe and Africa. The first full Paul Strand exhibition was held in the Museum of Modern Art, New York City in 1945, which was followed by a Strand retrospective at the Philadelphia Museum of Art in 1971, and exhibitions at the New York Metropolitan Museum of Art and the Los Angles Country Museum in 1973.

MARTIN HALLIWELL

See also: Heart of Spain; Manhatta; Native Land; Plow that Broke the Plains, The

Biography

Born in New York City, October 16, 1890 to middle-class Jewish parents. Attended the private Ethical Culture School from 1904–9, where he was introduced to photography by Lewis W. Hime. First photographs published in 1911. Began correspondence with Alfred Stieglitz in the 1910s; started to visit the 291 Gallery in Manhattan. Began abstract phase of photography in 1916 and was published in Stieglitz's *Camera Work*. From September 1918 to July 1919 served in the US Army Medical Corps as X-ray technician. Experimented with a movie camera owned by Charles Sheeler and released Manhatta as New York the Magnificent in 1921. Married Rebecca Salsbury in 1922; worked on news and sports coverage and experimented with machine photographs. Freelance work dried up when film industry moved to California and first marriage broke down in 1931; spent time in the Southwest and Mexico 1930–4; visited the Soviet Union in 1935. Worked on documentary films and photography through the 1930s and early 1940s. Married Virginia Stevens in 1935–48 and then Hazel Kingsbury in 1951. Settled in Orgeval, near Paris, in 1951. Frequently exhibited in Europe and America and travelled to Africa in 1960s. Stopped working due to cataracts in 1970s; died at home in Orgeval in 1976.

Selected films

1921 Manhatta: codirector and photographer (with Charles Sheeler)
1935 The Plow that Broke the Plains: photographer (with Ralph Steiner and Leo Hurwitz)
1936 The Wave/Redes: director, producer and photographer (with Augustine V. Chávez, Henwar Rodakiewicz and Fred Zinnemann)
1937 Heart of Spain (edited by Paul Strand and Leo Hurwitz)
1942 Native Land: codirector and photographer (with Leo Hurwitz)
1944 Tomorrow We Fly: photographer

Further reading

Alexander, William, *Film on the Left: American Documentary Film from 1931 to 1942*, Princeton, NJ: Princeton University Press, 1981.
Busselle, Rebecca and Stack, Trudy Wilmer (eds), *Paul Strand Southwest*, New York: Aperture, 2004.
Crowther, Bosley, 'Native Land, Impassioned and Dramatic Documentary Film on American Civil Liberties', *The New York Times*, May 12, 1942: 16.
Hammen, Scott, 'Sheeler and Strand's "Manhatta": A Neglected Masterpiece', *Afterimage* 6, no. 6, January 1979: 6–7.
Homer, William Innes, *Alfred Stieglitz and the American Avant-Garde*, Boston: New York Graphic Society, 1977.
Horak, Jan-Christopher (ed.), *Lovers of Cinema: The First American Film Avant-Garde, 1919–45*, Madison, WI: University of Wisconsin Press, 1995.
MacCann, Richard Dyer, *The People's Films: A Political History of U. S. Government Motion Pictures*, New York: Hastings House, 1973.
Newhall, Nancy, *Strand: Photographs 1915–45*, New York: The Museum of Modern Art, 1945.
Rosenblum, Naomi, *Paul Strand: The Stieglitz Years at 291 (1915–17)*, New York: Zabriskie Gallery, 1983.
Strand, Paul, 'Photography', *Seven Arts* 2, August 1917: 524–25 (reprinted in *Camera Work* 49–50, June 1917: 3–4; and in *Classic Essays on Photography*, ed. Alan Trachtenberg, New Haven: Leete's Island Books, 1980: 141–4).
——*Time in New England*, ed. Nancy Newhall, New York: Oxford University Press, 1950 (reprinted New York: Aperture, 1980).
——*Paul Strand: Sixty Years of Photographs*, New York: Aperture, 1976.
——*Essays on his Life and Work*, ed. Maren Stange, New York: Aperture, 1990.
Whelan, Richard (ed.), *Stieglitz on Photography: His Selected Essays and Notes*, New York: Aperture, 2000.

Strick, Joseph

During World War II, Strick was a cameraman with the US Army Air Force. After the war he worked with Irving Lerner, jack-of-all-film-crafts, to learn how to make movies, while serving as copyboy at the *Los Angeles Times*. Together they created the short Muscle Beach (1948), candid impressions of muscle-builders beside the Pacific Ocean in Venice, California. Later Strick became a wealthy businessman, owning a controlling interest in several large electronic corporations, and was able to form a new collaboration that led to The Savage Eye (1959), which he initiated. It was worked on part-time for four or five years, mostly on weekends. Strick's first feature, the most important of his few documentaries, it was an anomaly in many ways.

Made mostly by people who had been on the political left, The Savage Eye attempted to combine a scathing view of current social ills and disorders with the new emphasis on American documentaries on individuals, narrative, and characterization. The film is credited as being 'by' Ben Maddow, Sidney Meyers, and Joseph Strick. Cinematographers are listed as Jack Couffer, Helen Levitt, and Haskell Wexler. The last of these would subsequently become a highly valued Hollywood cameraman (with Academy Awards for Who's Afraid of Virginia Woolf?, 1966, and Bound for Glory, 1976), and also sometime director (Medium Cool, 1969). Two others are listed as 'contributing photographers', but it was said that Strick was responsible for about half the camera work, though he took no cinematography credit. Music is by Leonard Rosenman. Irving Lerner is credited as technical consultant.

The visuals are made up largely of unstaged scenes of the seamier side of Los Angeles: sleazy bars, beauty and massage parlors, wrestling matches, traffic jams, animal cemeteries, addicts and transvestites, strippers and faith healers. All this is seen through the eyes of a recently divorced, alienated, and angry woman (played by Barbara Baxley); hers is 'the savage eye'. As she wanders through these urban settings, she carries on a dialogue with a subjective interlocutor, 'the poet' (voice of Gary Merrill), who introduces himself to her as her 'vile dreamer, conscience, ghost'.

Initially The Savage Eye received a great deal of attention, including several international festival awards. At the Edinburgh International Film Festival, instead of being shown once, as scheduled, it had to be shown eight times to accommodate all those who wanted to see it. Reviewing it in the *New York Post* (June 7, 1960), Archer Winston concluded: 'The Savage Eye is all of one piece, masterfully, artfully wrought by its three makers, a work that must be recognized as great no matter how unlikable, a film that will be seen for many a year no matter who rejects it now.'

The contrary proved to be the case. It soon fell into virtual obscurity, remembered chiefly as a precursor of cinéma vérité, which was about to begin. Today we are more likely to agree with another critical reaction at the time: 'The fragments of documentary film in themselves are bitterly sure-footed. They show us clearly the irresolute and pernicious side of modern American life. Personally, I would like very much to see this footage combined into another form, without the contrived story and dialogue' (Jackson 1960).

In the 1960s Strick turned away from documentary to a succession of literary adaptations including his controversial version of James Joyces's Ulysses (1967). The only noteworthy exception was Interviews with My Lai Veterans (1970), which he wrote, produced, and directed. It received an Oscar for Best Documentary Short.

JACK C. ELLIS

Biography

Born 1923, in Pittsburgh. Attended University of California at Los Angeles c. 1941–3, until military service as cameraman in the US Army Air Force c. 1943–5. Worked on the *Los Angeles Times* and then television.

Selected films

1948 Muscle Beach
1949 Jour de Fête
1953 The Big Break
1959 The Savage Eye
1970 Interviews with My Lai Veterans

Further reading

Jackson, Benjamin T., 'The Savage Eye', review, *Film Quarterly* 13, no. 4, summer 1960: 53–7.

Swallow, Norman

Norman Swallow was a pioneer of British documentary television and a leading producer at both the BBC and independent companies. He helped to determine a specific identity for documentary television, which initially was in the thrall of the critically praised traditions in film and radio, developing a more journalistic approach while maintaining the reformist character of the earlier forms. This was evident in his first great achievement, the current affairs series Special Enquiry (1952–6), which each month addressed national problems such as immigration, illiteracy, and slum housing. Swallow was determined to make the programme accessible, 'to be doing the programme from the point of view of the audience, not from the top down, but from the bottom up. We were not the Establishment. We were not the BBC telling the people what they should think' (quoted in Bell 1986: 78).

His contribution to current affairs programming continued at the BBC, where he served as assistant editor on the acclaimed Panorama series. In 1963 he joined the thrusting commercial channel Granada, based in Manchester, where he produced the influential A Wedding on Saturday (1964). The film was an observational treatment of this family occasion occurring in a Yorkshire mining village. It used the minimum of intervening narration or commentary and won the Prix Italia for its pioneering use of video to record unobtrusively a natural and ordinary event.

Norman Swallow made significant contributions to arts television in Britain, being editor of the celebrated Omnibus series at the BBC in the late 1960s, and acting as head of arts programmes for BBC TV between 1971 and 1974. His status in television documentary was evident in his participation in international coproductions like Ten Days that Shook the World (1967), made with Grigori Alexandrov to mark the fiftieth anniversary of the Soviet Revolution, Lorna Pegram's and Robert Hughes's acclaimed Shock of the New (1980), and ambitious series like Television, a detailed history of the medium made for Granada in 1985. He was awarded BAFTA's Desmond Davis Award for his 'outstanding creative contribution to television'.

ALAN BURTON

Biography

The son of a headmaster born in Eccles, Lancashire in 1921, educated at the Manchester Grammar School, and awarded a scholarship to Oxford where he read History and Moral Philosophy. Served in the Duke of Cornwall's Light Infantry during the war and later in Palestine as an intelligence officer. Joined the BBC in Manchester in 1946 as a radio features producer, transferred to the BBC TV Service at Alexandria Palace in 1950 and was Assistant Head of Films 1957–60. In 1963 moved to Granada TV, but later in the 1960s was back at the BBC working primarily in arts programming. Produced several prestigious series for Granada in the 1970s and 1980s. Died in London on December 5, 2000.

Further reading

Bell, Elaine, 'The Origins of British Television Documentary: The BBC 1946–55', in John Corner (ed.), *Documentary and the Mass Media*, London: Edward Arnold, 1986.

Swallow, Norman, 'Documentary TV Journalism', in Paul Rotha (ed.), *Television in the Making*, London: Focal Press, 1956.

——*Factual Television*, London: Focal Press, 1966.

Switzerland

Switzerland is one of the few countries in the world where documentary feature films are regularly released in theaters and find an audience. A cinephile country where almost one-third of a total of roughly six hundred screens are located in art house theaters, Switzerland has also been a fertile ground for documentary production for several decades, with theatrical films being shown on television after their initial release and television production of documentaries feeding back into the theatrical market in important ways. Because of the constraints of a domestic market of only seven million divided into three language groups and the reluctance of the country's famous, and sometimes infamous, financial service industries to invest in a business as unsafe as film production, fiction film production in Switzerland has always been relatively weak, despite occasional peak periods in the war and postwar years, when a domestic popular cinema with its own set of stars and patriotic themes flourished briefly, and in the 1970s and 1980s, when directors such as Alain Tanner, Claude Goretta, and Fredi M. Murer put the Swiss auteur film on the map of the art cinema world.

By contrast, documentary production has been characterized by an impressive continuity both in terms of the quantity and the quality of output. Nonfiction films account for the majority of films produced before the 1960s, and nonfiction film production has served as both the economic backbone of film production in general and as a fertile training ground for both fiction and documentary filmmakers and technicians throughout the decades. Until fairly recently, critics considered documentary as the domain of Swiss German filmmakers, and the fiction film was considered to be the domain of their Swiss French colleagues—a notion, however, that was always rather dubious. Culturally, the strength of the Swiss documentary may also be rooted in the country's strong tradition in pedagogy (Johann Heinrich Pestalozzi, one of the founders of modern pedagogy, was a Swiss school teacher) and in Switzerland's predominantly protestant urban culture, which tends to favor art forms with pedagogical and other useful side effects over those that merely aim to please and entertain.

Although many of the directors working in nonfiction film before the 1960s remain virtually unknown even inside the country—their work has been researched only in recent years—avant-garde filmmakers such as Hans Richter found work in Switzerland directing public service films for state authorities and private companies in the 1930s and 1940s. In the early 1960s the federal government started funding for film production, joining a trend toward similar programs in other European countries. State funding was initially limited to documentary films, a restriction that proved to be productive in the sense that it contributed to the emergence of an auteurist documentary cinema, a tradition of documentaire de création, to cite the French term generally used in the French part of Switzerland that has continued to this day. In fact, conventional film histories suggest that the New Swiss cinema of the 1960s and 1970s began with a series of documentary films produced by such notable figures as Henry Brandt in connection with the Swiss national exhibition in Lausanne in 1964, and with the work of documentarists Walter Marti and Reni Mertens who, after a number of short films, attracted particular notice with Ursula oder das unwerte Leben (1966), a portrait of a handicapped woman.

The year 1964, the same time as the Swiss national exhibition, also saw the production of Siamo Italiani/We are Italians, directed by Alexander J. Seiler, June Kovach, and Rob Gnant, the first feature-length auteur documentary in Swiss cinema. Siamo Italiani focused on the daily lives of Italian immigrant workers in Switzerland and awakened the Swiss public to the presence and the plight of an important migrant workforce in their midst, a migrant workforce that had remained mostly invisible despite its substantial contribution to the country's postwar economic boom. Financed in part with money from the Swiss government, Siamo Italiani was a social documentary in a kind of direct cinema style that signaled a departure for, as well as a departure from, a commercial film production in crisis. If state funding laid part of the groundwork for documentary feature production in Switzerland and the emergence of the New Swiss film, television also played an important role. The contribution of television is particularly evident in the early work of Swiss French filmmakers such as Alain Tanner and Claude Goretta. Formed in the creative climate of 1950s British cinema, where they attracted critical attention with their experimental short Nice Time in 1957, Tanner and Goretta joined Swiss French television TSR on their return to Switzerland in the 1960s to work as documentary filmmakers. In the late 1960s Tanner, Goretta, and a number of their television-trained colleagues, such as Michel Soutter, moved into fiction films and emerged among the figureheads of the New Swiss cinema in the 1970s. The respective careers of Alexander J. Seiler and Alain Tanner are quite typical for the trajectories of Swiss directors in and through the field of documentary. Seiler devoted his entire career to the documentary genre, but Tanner used the documentary as a stepping stone to the feature film and only once returned to the genre after his move into fiction in 1969 with Charles mort ou vif, with Les hommes du port, a documentary about port workers in Genoa harbor from 1995. Like Tanner, other important fiction film directors, such as Fredi M. Murer and Daniel Schmid, made a passage through documentary cinema at one point in their careers. The country's most important experimental filmmaker in the 1960s, Fredi M. Murer, shot Wir Bergler in den Bergen … , a documentary about three small alpine valleys in his native canton of Uri in 1974. He later developed the material into his fiction film Alpine Fire from 1985, a story of an incestuous relationship between a mute peasant's son and his sister and arguably the most artistically accomplished film ever to come out of Switzerland. Daniel Schmid, a friend and sometime collaborator of German director Rainer Werner Fassbinder in the 1970s, went back and forth between fiction and documentary throughout his career. After a series of fiction films, Schmid turned to documentary in 1984 with Il Bacio di Tosca, a film about a retirement home for opera singers in Milan, and in 1995 he traveled to Japan for the production of The Written Face, a documentary portrait of a male Kabuki actor who specializes in female roles. Both Il Bacio di Tosca and The Written Face count among Schmid's strongest works.

Although Schmid has remained an occasional documentarist, his two films about artists are quite representative of one of the four main strands of documentary filmmaking in Switzerland, the artist documentary. Apart from films about art and artists, the four major strands include a strong tradition of ethnographic documentaries, a continuous output of political documentaries, particularly of films focusing on state authorities and institutions and their procedures, and a more recent, but very strong tradition of filmmaking about migration and the blurring of ethnic and geographical boundaries.

The two major representatives of ethnographic filmmaking in Switzerland are Jacqueline Veuve, a documentary auteur of the first generation and a creator of an important body of work on rural handicraft, and Erich Langjahr, whose films and particularly his peasant trilogy, Sennenballade (1996), Bauernkrieg (1998), and Hirtenreise ins dritte Jahrtausend (2002), chronicle the rapid transformation of rural life in Switzerland over the last twenty-five years. If ethnographic filmmaking in Switzerland focuses on the country's alpine interior rather than on more traditionally 'exotic' (foreign) subjects, this may be read as an indication of the important symbolic charge that rural life carries in Swiss society, despite the fact that farmers now make up only two percent of the working population. Not least under the influence of Jean-Jacques Rousseau, a Swiss native, modern Switzerland has defined itself as a democracy historically rooted in rural self-governance, even at a time when it was the most industrialized country on the continent. According to this somewhat delusional self-definition, what happens to the peasant happens to the country. In addition, in the 1970s, and again in the spirit of Rousseau, critical documentary filmmakers chose rural life as one of the privileged sites in which to locate alternatives to the rampant capitalism of the urban and industrialized parts of the country. Thus many filmmakers sought the remedy to capitalist alienation on the green pastures of the Alps, only to find there more evidence of the destructive forces of capitalism at work. Apart from the films of Jacqueline Veuve and Erich Langjahr, this logic informs, in varying degrees of consciousness, Fredi M. Murer's Wir Bergler in den Bergen … and another one of the key works of the filmed ethnography of rural life in Switzerland, Beatrice Michel and Hans Stuerm's Gossliwil (1985), a monumental long-term study of one peasant village in the Swiss Mittelland.

Whereas Jacqueline Veuve and Erich Langjahr have stayed true to the ethnographic documentary throughout their careers, few filmmakers have limited themselves to the field of documentaries about artists and art with such consistency. The major example is perhaps Felix Kappeler, whose portraits of artists such as the popular singer-songwriter Mani Matter (2002) have sometimes reached audiences as large as those of Hollywood mainstream films. A number of filmmakers have been active in both documentaries about artists and the political documentary. Hans-Ulrich Schlumpf started out with a portrait of Armand Schulthess (Armand Schulthess—j'ai le téléphone, 1974), a key figure of 'art brut' in the 1970s, and later went on to make Kongress der Pinguine in 1993, an ecologist manifesto about the life of penguins in the Arctic that was one of the major box office successes for Swiss cinema in the 1990s. Richard Dindo, perhaps the best-known documentary filmmaker of his generation outside of Switzerland, has combined political issues with an interest in art and particularly the literary genre of the autobiography in his films, often using literature and painting as a means to approach political topics such as the Holocaust (Charlotte—vie ou theater, 1992, a film about a French Jewish painter who disappeared in the Nazi concentration camps), the Middle East conflict (Genet à Chatila, 1999), or the violent police crackdown on rebellious youths in Switzerland in the 1980s (Dani, Michi, Renato und Max, 1987). Feminist filmmakers have made an important, albeit critically somewhat neglected contribution to the political documentary in Switzerland, with key works such as Gertrud Pinkus Il valore della donna è il suo silenzio (1980) often blurring the boundaries between fiction and nonfiction filmmaking. Working at the crossroads of ethnographic and political documentary, one of the most interesting filmmakers of the 1990s, Thomas Imbach, explored the professional world of bank employees in Well Done in 1994, and the private lives of suburban youths in Ghetto in 1997. Using a distinctly innovative style of serial montage of dialogue and action fragments, the films of Imbach, who has moved on to experimental fiction films since, broke new ground both in terms of documentary aesthetics and subject matter in Swiss documentary and beyond.

Although political documentaries have always formed an important part of documentary production in Switzerland, a number of strongly political films have been among the most important films released in theaters in recent years. Although reflecting a worldwide surge in interest in nonfiction formats and critical documentary films, as witnessed in the global successes of Michael Moore, this trend can also be explained by the emergence of a new generation of documentary filmmakers who replace the dour didacticism of much earlier work in political documentary with a new kind of critical stance that is both penetrating and humorous. Key figures are Sabine Gisiger and Marcel Zwingli, who chronicle the adventures of a group of Swiss would-be terrorists from the 1970s in Do It (2000), and Jean-Stéphane Bron, who casts an ironic look at the Swiss secret service in Connu de nos services (1997), and paints a highly engaging and dramatic portrait of a parliamentary commission at work on a new law on genetic engineering in Le génie helvétique (2003). Continuing a long tradition of documentaries dealing with state authorities and institutions at work, Bron's films found a wide audience, and Le génie helvétique was even picked up by the Swiss foreign ministry to explain the Swiss political system to audiences in emerging democracies (a backhanded compliment of sorts).

Finally, films about migration and the crossing and blurring of ethnic, as well as other boundaries, have formed a major part of Swiss documentary filmmaking in the 1990s. Swiss-Canadian filmmaker Peter Mettler insistently and inspiringly explores geographically and socially marginal spaces in such films such as Picture of Light (1994), and Gambling, Gods and LSD (2002); Andrea Staka, a Swiss-born filmmaker of Bosnian origin, reflects on her condition as an artist in exile in Yugodivas (2000), a group portrait of female artists from the former Yugoslavia living in New York; Samir Jamal Aldin, a Zurich film director and producer, traces his Iraqi family origins in Forget Bagdad (2002); and finally, Gabrielle Baur ventures into world of drag kings in Venus Boyz (2002), a documentary exploration of the boundaries of gender and geography that covers the nightclub scenes of London, New York, and other cities.

If there is anything distinctly Swiss about these films and filmmakers, it is perhaps their shared sensibility for the lives of cultural differences, a sensibility that is easily gained and lost in a society that is in itself composed of a multitude of language groups and cultures.

VINZENZ HEDIGER AND ALEXANDRA SCHNEIDER

Further reading

For further information and documentation see also www.swissfilms.ch

Blöchlinger, Brigitte, von Niederhäusern, Claudine, Ganz-Blättler, Ursula and Keil, Erika (eds), *Cut: Film- und Videomacherinnen Schweiz von den Anfängen bis 1994: eine Bestandesaufnahme*, Basel: Stroemfeld, 1995, Nexus, 11.

Buache, Freddy, *Trente ans de cinéma suisse: 1965–95*, Paris: Centre Georges Pompidou, 1995.

Giger, Bernhard *et al.*, *Film in der Schweiz*, München: Hanser, 1978.

Giger, Bernhard and Scherer, Theres (eds), *1957–76—von Nice Time bis Früchte der Arbeit: Materialien zur Entwicklung des Dokumentarfilms in der Schweiz*, Bern: Kellerkino, 1977.

Roth, Wilhelm, *Der Dokumentarfilm seit 1960*, München: Bucher, 1982.

Schlappner, Martin and Schaub, Martin, *Vergangenheit und Gegenwart des Schweizer Films (1896 bis 1987): eine kritische Wertung*, Zürich: Schweizerisches Filmzentrum, 1987.

T

Target for Tonight

(UK, Watt, 1941)

In Target for Tonight, documentary approach and technique was applied for the first time to a feature-length war film. The result was the most commercially successful documentary film of the time.

Unlike Britain Can Take It, Target for Tonight is, in Watt's words, a 'hitting back film'. Unlike the Why We Fight series, it is primarily concerned with people, not battles, and focuses on small groups in operation rather than a vast struggle between right and wrong. Like other British war films, it exalts the sense of mission, not destiny. Undeniably aimed to propagandize, its approach in human terms is congruent with Humphrey Jennings's notion of 'propaganda for the human race'.

An account of a night bombing raid on Germany, Target for Tonight describes the operation as an apparently easy, if carefully planned, procedure. Out of real individuals it creates an anonymous collective hero of unshakeable optimism.

Harry Watt had been previously assigned to direct another Royal Air Force (RAF) film, Squadron 992 (1939), about the work of a balloon squadron, which he found boring. For Target for Tonight, he went through two or three thousand reports of bombing raids. He came to an agreement with the RAF Bomber Command on a script he considered 'utterly straightforward, just the choice of a new small target, the selection of a squadron to bomb it, and the adventures of one bomber, 'F for Freddie', during the raid'. The Mildenhall RAF bomber station (renamed 'Millerton' in the film) had been chosen as the operations base.

Watt greatly valued the use of nonprofessional actors, and he insisted on using the airmen themselves, casting every single one in his own role, from gunners to pilots to officers, up to the Commander-in-Chief. These amateurs proved to be so good that *Variety* could not believe that they were not actors. Watt also carefully struck a balance of the men's origins: one half of F for Freddie's crew appears to be English; the other three men can be identified as one Scot, one Australian, and one Canadian. Conversely, only two women—of the Women's Auxiliary Air Force (WAAF)—come into view.

The script reproduces the airmen's idiomatic language, with a good amount of humour. The pilot suggests that they should 'go down and smell the breath' of a little German city 'famous for its breweries', or asserts 'the natives appear hostile' as flak bursts around the aircraft.

Shooting on location at Mildenhall started on the second week in April, and the film delivery deadline was mid-summer. Watt and his crew were able to gather documentary footage of the N 149 Squadron and its two-engined Vickers Armstrong Wellington aircraft, but procuring good images of bombing turned out almost impossible because of the lack of film stock sensibility; however, some dramatic shots of F for Freddie flying against the clouds were obtained.

Every interior sequence was made in the studio. The airmen's changing room was reconstructed at Elstree Studios. A sound stage at Denham Studios was converted into a replica of the Operations Room. To convey a sense of action on board the aircraft, the camera and lights had to be placed in a split-up Wellington fuselage. The shots of anti-aircraft guns operated by men in German helmets were provided by the Army Film Unit. Twelve feet of German newsreel material appear in reel four.

Target for Tonight had its premiere in London on July 24 at the Empire Theatre. As early as August 18, two councillors of the Ministry of Information in film distribution, Sidney Bernstein and Arthur Jarratt, left for the United States, carrying a copy of the film. Bernstein came to an agreement with Warner Brothers for its commercial distribution, which turned out to be an enormous success. Fifty million people overall viewed Target for Tonight in the United States. The film made a profit of over £73,000 for the Ministry during the war.

JEAN-LUC LIOULT

See also: Watt, Harry

Target for Tonight (UK, Watt, 1941, 48 mins). Distributed by Warner Bros. Produced by Crown Film Unit and Ministry of Information. Directed by Harry Watt (uncredited). Written by Harry Watt (uncredited). Cinematography by Teddy Catford and Jonah Jones. Edited by Alfred Hitchcock and Stewart McAllister.

Further reading

Aitken, Ian, 'The Crown Film Unit, 1941–52', in *The Documentary Film Movement, An Anthology*, Edinburgh: Edinburgh University Press, 1998.

Barsam, Richard M., 'British Films for World War II', in *Non-Fiction Film, A Critical History* (revised and expanded), Bloomington, IN and Indianapolis, IN: Indiana University Press, 1992.

Lioult, Jean-Luc, 'Autour de Passage to Marseille : figures du héros de la 2ème guerre mondiale, du mythique au politique, et retour', in Trudy Bolter (ed.), *Cinéma anglophone et politique: vers un renouveau du sens*, Paris: L'Harmattan, 2007.

Short, K.R.M, 'RAF Bomber Command's *Target for Tonight* (1941)', *Historical Journal of Film, Radio and Television* 17, no. 2, 1997: 181–218.

Swann, Paul, 'The Documentary Movement during the War, 1939–45', in *The British Documentary Film Movement, 1926–46*, Cambridge: Cambridge University Press, 1989.

Taylor, John

John Taylor's work in documentary was firmly tied to that of John Grierson, leader of the British documentary movement. To begin with, he was Grierson's brother-in-law, younger brother of Grierson's wife, Margaret. He joined the Empire Marketing Board Film Unit in 1930, shortly after it was formed, at the age of sixteen. His first noteworthy assignment was in 1931, accompanying and assisting Robert Flaherty in the production of Industrial Britain. After that he was loaned to Flaherty in 1932 to assist on Man of Aran; it was said (by Harry Watt, who was also assisting) that Taylor shot more than a little of the footage. After that, in 1933, he went with Basil Wright to serve as his assistant on The Song of Ceylon. While with the General Post Office (GPO) Film Unit Taylor served as cameraman on Housing Problems (1935), made for the British Commercial Gas Association, and on four films that Alberto Cavalcanti made in Switzerland for the GPO and Pro Telephon, Zürich.

When Grierson left the GPO in 1937 Wright also left to form the Realist Film Unit and Taylor joined it shortly thereafter. For Realist he directed The Smoke Menace (1937). The next year Wright left Realist to join Film Centre, a promotional body that Grierson had helped to set up, and Taylor ran Realist from that time on through the war. Realist's most ambitious prewar production was The Londoners (1939), which Taylor wrote and directed.

During the war the government was the sole sponsor of documentary films in Britain, and the Ministry of Information assigned hundreds of nonfiction films on all sorts of subjects to the independent documentary units. For example, Cameramen at War (1943), Atlantic Trawler (1944), and Plastic Surgery in Wartime (1944) were among the forty-seven films assigned to Realist, one of the busiest of the units. Taylor seems to have been credited as producer on all of these. Though he directed a few films of value, his real strengths appear to have been as cinematographer in the early part of his career and producer in the latter part; a steady contributor rather than a star.

After the war Taylor became producer in charge at the Crown Film Unit (in January 1947) and remained in that position until 1949. After Grierson's return to Britain to become head of the Films Division of the Central Office of Information (peacetime equivalent of the Ministry of Information), under which Crown Film Unit came, Taylor was moved to the Colonial Film Unit. After a year he returned to private documentary production. This included involvement with Countryman Films and its biggest success, The Conquest of Everest (1953), most of the profits of which, curiously, went to the government-funded Group 3, which Grierson by then coheaded.

Although these postwar events strained their relationship, Taylor remained close to Grierson. Taylor and his wife, Barbara Mullen, a popular actress (and daughter of Flaherty's cicerone on Aran, Pat Mullen), were the only persons other than his wife Margaret whom Grierson would see in his last days before he died.

JACK C. ELLIS

See also: Flaherty, Robert; Grierson, John; Housing Problems; Industrial Britain; Man of Aran; Song of Ceylon, The; Wright, Basil

Biography

Born 1914, London. Employed: Empire Marketing Board Film Unit, 1930–3; General Post Office (GPO) Film Unit, 1933–7; Realist Film Unit, 1937–47; Crown Film Unit and Colonial Film Unit, 1947–9; private documentary production units from 1949. Most significant productions: assistant on Industrial Britain, Man of Aran, The Song of Ceylon; cinematographer on Pett and Pott, Housing Problems; director on Smoke Menace, The Londoners. Died September 15, 1992 in London.

Further reading

Ellis, Jack C., *John Grierson: Life, Contributions, Influence*, Carbondale, IL: Southern Illinois University Press, 2000.

Hardy, Forsyth, *John Grierson: A Documentary Biography*, London: Faber & Faber, 1979.

Rotha, Paul, *Documentary Diary: An Informal History of the British Documentary Film, 1928–39*, New York: Hill and Wang, 1973.

——*Robert J. Flaherty: A Biography*, Philadelphia, PA: University of Pennsylvania Press, 1983.

Testimony on Non-Intervention

(UK/Spain, Montagu, 1938)

Testimony on Non-Intervention is one of several films produced by the British Left in response to the Spanish civil war, urging their fellows to protest against it and to support the Popular Front, Spain's democratically elected government, as a buttress against fascism. Though the subject was covered by filmmakers from several countries, in Britain this flurry of films was in large part driven by the communist aristocrat Ivor Montagu. Montagu had been involved with several left-wing film organisations and in March 1935 helped set up the Progressive Film Institute (PFI), which began as a distribution company before moving into production, making several films on the Spanish civil war. The best known of these is The Defence of Madrid (1936), which Montagu directed, but there were also social documentaries such as Spanish ABC, directed by Sidney Cole and Thorold Dickinson (1938) and dealing with the literacy campaign. Other countries also joined in, and Joris Ivens's The Spanish Earth (1937) is particularly famous, perhaps for the participation of Ernest Hemingway. Testimony on Non-Intervention's severe aesthetic, however, has prevented it from becoming popular or even relatively well known, and it fell under the shadow of these other films.

In January 1938 producer/director Montagu arrived in Barcelona with his small PFI crew: cameramen Arthur Graham and Alan Lawson, assistants Philip Leacock and Ray Pitt, and editors Sidney Cole and Thorold Dickinson. They intended to make three films on a range of subjects, but conditions were such that they completed only Spanish ABC, though they did shoot material towards several other projects.

Germany and Italy were among the countries that had agreed not to become involved in the Spanish civil war, but it was clear that troops from both nations were supporting Franco. To show this participation to a wider public, Montagu filmed Italian and German prisoners of war relating their experiences, and back in London used these to make the short Prisoners Prove Intervention in Spain. At the time, and to make the same point, they made Behind the Spanish Lines. Despite its dryness, Prisoners Prove Intervention in Spain was popular and useful in raising funds for Spanish relief, and Montagu returned to the footage almost immediately, drawing on it much more extensively, and within three months released the seven-times longer Testimony on Non-Intervention.

The content of the forty-minute Testimony on Non-Intervention can be easily described: four soldiers (three Italians and a German) are interviewed about their involvement in the Spanish civil war. Questions include how they came to take part and the degree of their nations' involvement. The static camera looks over the questioner's shoulder and edits within the interviews are minimal. Each interview begins with the soldier giving his name and rank, before going on to explain how he came to go to Spain.

The interviews show that rank and file soldiers entered the conflict unwillingly if not in ignorance. One was told that he would be a trainer in an unspecified foreign country, while another reports having volunteered. When the interviewer expresses surprise at this, the prisoner says that 'nonvolunteers' would have been punished. Some Italians were diverted from Africa implying that intervention in Spain was seen as more important than their own conflict in Abyssinia. They continued to think of themselves as Italian and not Spanish soldiers despite being paid by both Italy and Spain, showing the home country's collaboration and underlining the soldiers' uncertain position, as they did not know when they were to be sent home. While Spain is made complicit, Spaniards themselves were used only in menial, non-fighting positions.

Both Germany and Italy provided and exclusively used their own weaponry and transport, though the German prisoner exposes the underhand measures by revealing that the markings on armaments were removed to conceal their provenance. He further says that both 'armies', composed exclusively of men from their respective countries, were kept completely apart, knowing nothing of each others' activities but then, as he notes, 'I'm a nobody'. Despite this, the German thinks that his compatriots are clearly the better fliers.

Testimony of Non-Intervention's antifascist message is particularly pointed by its use of soldiers from Germany and Italy, the other two centres of European fascism, and Franco's natural allies. Unfortunately in doing this it massively simplifies the situation, ignoring splits within 'right' and 'left' and the role of the Catholic Church.

The film clearly attempts to persuade the viewer of its objectivity, with its unblinking camera and catechism of questions; however, even before that, the title, with its echoes of legal process, implies that this is a cinematic court, investigating all the circumstances, a proposal strengthened by the lack of any credits that could remind the viewer of the makers' presence. Yet the title's 'Non-Intervention' is obviously an ironic comment, the film's only moment of lightness, counterbalancing Testimony's 'objectivity'. The format had worked well for Prisoners Prove Intervention, but Testimony's attempts to persuade the viewer of its objectivity quickly becomes boring: the shorter, first film had made the point more concisely. For the monoglot English viewer, the film is rendered even more difficult by the number of exchanges that are completely untranslated, and this must have affected its popularity and effectiveness, if not making people suspect that only those sequences that were politically acceptable were translated.

In 1939 Britain recognised Franco's government and as the wider world situation darkened, British left-wing film circles turned to the wider threat and the home front. Having thoroughly documented the civil war, the PFI moved on, though quickly fell into abeyance.

JOHN RILEY

See also: Montagu, Ivor

Testimony on Non-Intervention (Progressive Film Institute, 1938, 40 mins). Director Ivor Montagu.

Further reading

Dickinson, Thorold, 'Experiences in the Spanish Civil War', *Historical Journal of Film Radio and Television* 4, no. 2, 1984: 189–94.

Hogenkamp, Bert, *Deadly Parallels: Film and the Left in Britain 1929–39*, London: Lawrence and Wishart, 1986.

Jones, Stephen G., *The British Labour Movement and Film, 1918–39*, London: Routledge and Kegan Paul, 1987.

Thin Blue Line, The

(US, Morris, 1988)

The title of Errol Morris's third film is taken from Doug Mulder's closing arguments in the 1977 capital murder trial of Randall Adams, a 'drifter' accused of shooting Dallas police officer Robert Wood. Mulder referred to law enforcement personnel as the 'thin blue line' protecting law-abiding citizens and ordered society from chaos and crime. This compelling metaphor also serves as the thesis of Morris's self-described 'nonfiction Twilight Zone episode', a piece that marked a simultaneously emerging investment and investigation into reflexivity and performativity within documentary film (and photography) in the late 1980s.

The Thin Blue Line opens with the story of how a chance meeting between two men—twenty-eight-year-old Ohio native Randall Adams and sixteen-year-old Texas teenager David Harris—on November 27, 1976, resulted in both the death of a police officer and the conviction of an innocent man. Morris spends the majority of the film dissecting the multiple players in this crime drama, directing the viewer's attention to they ways in which individuals construct events according to their beliefs and obligations. In an effort to enhance both the contradictory and fragmentary nature of testimony, Morris focuses on three surprise witnesses from the original trial who, under the camera lights, reveal personal stakes in the case that significantly undermine their credibility. It is here that Morris's investment as 'director-detective' appears most clearly on screen, even as his physical presence does not. There is no attempt to disguise the theatrical nature of the interview; the subjects are staged for the camera by the director. 'That unblinking eye in some strange way makes people willing to talk', Morris asserts. It is this staging and its artificiality, argues Morris, that lures the informants into revealing themselves with a kind of complicated honesty that is too often lost in documentary's use of 'natural' surroundings: 'What I do has absolutely nothing to do with cinéma vérité[…] We go in with a lot of equipment, the camera is on a tripod, and the person who speaks to the camera is perfectly aware of what is going on. In some sense, he is performing for the camera' (Dieckmann 1988).

Each eyewitness account is accompanied by a dramatic reenactment. These staples of fictional storytelling appear in this documentary, however, to undermine the veracity of the witnesses without conceding the factuality of the investigation. The original score by Philip Glass pulses underneath the film with an unrelenting theme, punctuated by slight but significant variations in tone or pitch to match the film noir elements (lighting and camera angle specifically) of the reenactments without forfeiting their surrealist qualities to melodramatic emotionalism. Tight close-ups on the neon clock and popcorn popper at a drive-in concession stand, the slow-motion catapult of a chocolate milkshake to the ground, a partial view of the words of a police report, iconic images of the tools of the crime—these details do not culminate, at least not on screen, into a climatic reversal of fortune for the story's hero, Adams. Instead, they are parts of a puzzle whose final image changes depending on who selects and connects them. Slowly, inexorably, the drama that unfolds in The Thin Blue Line exposes how many of the puzzle pieces were reformed during Adams's investigation and trial and forced fit into a predetermined portrait, one created and controlled by the police and prosecutors in their rush to justice for a heinous crime.

The Thin Blue Line straddles multiple narrative categories, a hybridity not lost on critics who struggled with genre-specific language available to them on the film's debut. Morris engages an uncanny mix of styles, because, as the filmmaker himself asserts, the film is not just an investigation of a murder mystery, it is a murder investigation. In light of the evidence he uncovers, Morris himself describes the film as a 'nonfiction feature' in the tradition of Truman Capote's In Cold Blood. For Morris, this documentary pushes the envelope, with its generic expectation of objectivity, focusing instead on the possible rhetorical and aesthetic value of the form. He argues: 'There's no reason why documentaries can't be as personal as fiction filmmaking and bear the imprint of those who made them. Truth isn't guaranteed by style or expression. It isn't guaranteed by anything' (Bates 1989).

Perhaps in response to definitions of the 'postmodern' emerging in cultural theory in the late 1980s as nihilist, anarchist, and apolitical, Morris maintains that his intention, unlike Akira Kirosawa's in Rashamon, a film to which The Thin Blue Line is often compared, was to expose the 'fact of what happened […] We have access to the world out there. We aren't just prisoners of our own fantasies and dreams. I wanted to make a movie about how truth is difficult to know, not how it's impossible to know' (O'Connor 1989). Morris's very personal and political document engages and embraces the idea that subjectivity, historicity, and cultural predispositions imbue our perception without ceding that this particular form of investigation could uncover a truth capable of 'combating the pernicious scapegoating fictions that can put the wrong man on death row' (Williams 1998).

Many critics assumed that Morris's highly praised film would garner the 1988 Academy Award for Best Documentary, but the film was not even nominated. Writers have speculated that this exclusion was due to any number of factors, including the employment of Morris's footage in Adams's appeals process, his own assessment of the piece as a 'non-fiction feature', the use of stylized reenactments, and subsequent charges of manipulation by informants. Nonetheless, this omission would serve to fuel subsequent debates over documentary film's form, focus, and function. In the year surrounding the release of The Thin Blue Line, other films that extended the boundaries of foundational documentary film principles would appear (for example, Roger and Me, Who Killed Vincent Chin, Tongues Untied, and Surname Viet Given Name Nam), some even gaining both mainstream box office success and Academy Award nominations, reflecting the growing incursion of postmodernist perspectives, politics, and innovations on the 'real' and its documentation.

JULES ODENDAHL-JAMES

See also: Morris, Errol

The Thin Blue Line (US, Third Floor Productions, 1988, 101 mins). Distributed by Miramax Films. Produced by Mark Lipson, Lindsay Law, and Brad Fuller in association with Channel 4 (UK), The Program Development Company and American Playhouse. Directed by Errol Morris. Original score by Philip Glass. Cinematography by Robert Chappell and Stefan Czapsky. Edited by Paul Barnes. Production design by Ted Bafoloukos. Interviews filmed in Dallas, Huntsville, and Vidor, Texas. Reenactments filmed in locations in New York City and New Jersey with Randall Adams played by Adam Goldfine, David Harris played by Derek Horton, Officer Robert Wood played by Ron Thornhill, Officer Teresa Turko played by Marianne Leone. Received following awards: Best Movie of 1988, Washington Post Film Critics Survey; Best Documentary, New York Film Critics Circle, 1988; Best Documentary, National Board of Review, 1988; Best Documentary, International Documentary Association, 1988; Best Documentary, National Society of Film Critics, 1988; Best Documentary, Kansas City Film Critics, 1988; Best Foreign Film, Taiwan International Film Festival, 1988; Best Motion Picture, Edgar Allan Poe Award, 1989; #95 on Premiere magazine's list of '100 Most Daring Films Ever Made', 1998; selected for National Film Registry by National Film Preservation Foundation, 2001.

Further reading

Barnouw, Dagmar, 'Seeing and Believing: The Thin Blue Line of Documentary Objectivity', *Common Knowledge* 4, no. 1, 1995: 129–43.

Bates, Peter, 'Truth Not Guaranteed: An Interview with Errol Morris', *Cineaste* 17, no. 1, 1989: 16–17.

Dieckmann, Katherine, 'Private Eye', *American Film* 8, no. 4, January/February 1988: 32–8.

McIllroy, Brian, 'Observing and Walking the Thinnest of Lines: Phenomenology, Documentary Film and Errol Morris', *Recherches-Semiotiques/Semiotic-Inquiry* 13, nos 1–2, 1993: 285–99.

Michaels, Lloyd, 'The Thin Blue Line and the Limits of Documentary', *Post Script: Essays in Film and the Humanities* 13, no. 2, 1994: 44–50.

Nichols, Bill, '"Getting to Know You … ": Knowledge, Power, and the Body', in Michael Renov (ed.), *Theorizing Documentary*, New York: Routledge, 1993: 174–92.

O'Connor, John, 'The Film That Challenged "Dr. Death"', *The New York Times*, May 24, 1989: C22

Plantinga, Carl R., *Rhetoric and Representation in Nonfiction Film*, Cambridge: Cambridge University Press, 1997.

Sherwin, Richard K., 'Law Frames: Historical Truth and Narrative Necessity in a Criminal Case', *Stanford Law Review* 47, 1994: 39–83.

Williams, Linda, 'Mirrors without Memories: Truth, History, and the New Documentary', in Barry Keith Grant and Jeannette Sloniowski (eds), *Documenting the Documentary: Close Readings of Documentary Film and Video*, Detroit, MI: Wayne State University Press, 1998: 379–96.

Thomas, Antony

Antony (sometimes Anthony) Thomas's documentary films have made a significant contribution to British and American public television broadcasting since the late 1970s. His documentaries are predominantly news-style films produced for television. In the style of public television and investigative documentary filmmaking, his documentaries are characterized by in-depth research, numerous interviews, and a narrator. His films have a Rashomon-esque quality, presenting varying subjective perspectives; he juxtaposes interviews, paces sequences, and includes voice-over narration to create a cohesive argument that reveals his own perspectives through cinematic and editorial techniques. Although his films address a range of topics over several decades, they share one commonality; they deal exclusively with social or political topics contentious at the time of their release. His views on certain issues have changed over time, particularly those on apartheid and South African politics as expressed in The Anatomy of Apartheid (1964), The South African Experience (1977), and the feature film Rhodes: The Life & Legend of Cecil Rhodes (1997). His biases, particularly in his later films, are intentionally transparent, making them best understood within the cultural context of their production. His contribution to documentary film, particularly in the realm of public television, has been to challenge public opinion on controversial topics through his own occasionally contentious stances.

Not shy of debate, his films espouse positions on issues as diverse as celibacy in the Catholic Church, animal rights, issues of genetic predisposition in biology and psychology, and the role of fundamentalism in politics, whether American or Saudi. His 2002–4 film Celibacy presents celibacy as a late Medieval amendment to Catholic doctrine that assures priestly wealth revert to the Church on death, and the film explores the potential relationship of repressed sexuality to the contemporary abuse scandals of the Catholic Church. Fat (1997–8) explores cultural and medical views on obesity that submit to cultural aesthetics and disregard genetic diversity when diagnosing clinical obesity. Twins: The Divided Self (1997), which won eight international awards, probes genetic predispositions for character and intelligence. Winning six prestigious awards, To Love or Kill: Man vs. Animal (1995) reveals human-animal relationships as both loving and gory. Thy Kingdom Come, Thy Will Be Done (1987) links the Christian Right and American politics. Thomas won the US Emmy for Frank Terpil: Portrait of a Dangerous Man (1982), for which he interviewed the ex-CIA agent, who was living in hiding at the time. David Fanning produced this film; he also co-wrote and produced the docudrama Death of a Princess (1979–80), which aired to one of the highest ratings in PBS broadcast history, won The Gold Award at the New York International Festival, and disrupted British-Saudi diplomatic relations. The film reenacts Thomas's investigation of the public execution of a Saudi princess and her lover. The subject matter and docudrama style both provoked debate and criticism; however, the genre choice made it feasible to present explosive subject matter without compromising the safety of Thomas's sources by revealing their identities.

By 1980 Antony Thomas had already demonstrated his affinity for politically transgressive topics. The South African Experience (1977) had exposed the apartheid regime, and earned him both the British Academy Award and prohibition from his home-country, South Africa. The publicity scandal surrounding Death of a Princess, however, irrevocably established both Antony Thomas and co-writer/producer David Fanning as provocative documentary filmmakers. It also established a long-term relationship between Antony Thomas and Frontline, for which Fanning is the cofounder and executive producer. In the vein of public television, the framework within which the majority of his films have been created, Antony Thomas's documentaries are story-driven and pointedly controversial, stimulating debate on and adding liberal nuance to mainstream media representations.

SHEENA WILSON

See also: Death of a Princess

Biography

Born Calcutta, India in 1940. Lived in South Africa between 1946 and 1967. Aged twenty-seven, moved to England. Later banned from South Africa because of political views expressed in The South African Apartheid Experience (1977, trilogy). Continues to reside in Britain. Has won prestigious awards including the George Foster Peabody Award for Twins: The Divided Self (1997), the Grierson Award for Best British Documentary for Man and Animal (1995), an Emmy for Frank Terpil—Portrait of a Dangerous Man (1982), and the British Academy Award for his trilogy The South African Experience (1977). Since the 1994 fall of apartheid has been able to return to South Africa, which provided a rich backdrop for the six part historical feature film Rhodes: The Life & Legend of Cecil Rhodes (1997), and the two-part documentary The Real Olympics (2002–4). Continues to write, direct, and produce TV documentaries that are aired internationally on PBS, HBO (United States), ITV, BBC, CBC (Britain & Canada), Televisio Valencia (Spain),

Odeseia (Spain & Portugal), Yes TV (Israel), ATV (Hong Kong), and SABC (South Africa). His portfolio also includes non-documentary films and he is the author of *Rhodes* (1996) and co-author of *The Arab Experience* (1975).

Selected films

1964	The Anatomy of Apartheid: director
1970	A Touch of Churchill, A Touch of Hitler (The Life of Cecil Rhodes); director
1977	The South African Experience (trilogy): director, producer
1979–80	Death of a Princess: writer, director
1982	Frank Terpil: Portrait of a Dangerous Man
1987	Thy Kingdom Come, Thy Will be Done (two parts): director
1990	Never Say Die: The Pursuit of Eternal Youth (UK title: Heaven Must Wait)
1994	By Satan Possessed: The Search for the Devil (UK title: In Satan's Name)
1995	To Love or Kill: Man vs. Animal (UK title: Man & Animal)
1996	Between Life and Death
1997	Twins: The Divided Self
1997–8	Fat (six-part series)
1999–2000	A Question of Miracles (UK title: Miracles): writer
2002–4	The Real Olympics (UK title: The Ancient Greek Olympics) (two parts)
2004	Celibacy (UK title: Flesh and the Devil): director

Further reading

Bullert, B.J., *Public Television Politics and the Battle Over Documentary Film*, New Brunswick, NJ: Rutgers University Press, 1997.

Burns, James, 'Biopics and Politics: The Making and the Unmaking of the Rhodes Movies', *Biography* 23, no. 1, 2000: 108–26.

Hees, Edwin, '"Truly, the Ways of the White Man Are Strange": Tribal Utopianism in Two South African Propaganda Films', *South African Theatre Journal: SATJ* 5, no. 1, 1991: 74–97.

Pfaff, Francoise, *Focus on African Films*, Bloomington, IN: Indiana University Press, 2004.

Rosenthal, Alan (ed.), *Why Docudrama? Fact-Fiction on Film and TV*, Carbondale, IL: Southern Illinois University Press, 1999.

Thomson, Margaret

Margaret Thomson's prolific instructional filmmaking career, like many of her female contemporaries in the nonfiction sector, has been neglected in most histories of documentary film. Thomson worked more or less continuously in instructional filmmaking for more than forty years. Arriving in Britain from New Zealand in 1934 with a degree in zoology, she started her film career at Bruce Woolfe's Gaumont-British Instructional. After a year in the library shot listing films, she was offered a series of her own, and in 1936–7 she directed six educational films examining different ecosystems in Britain. These films were in the tradition of the Secrets of Nature series using animation, diagrams, and macro-photography as well as actuality footage and proved an excellent training ground for Thomson; however, the film industry slump in 1938 found Thomson out of work. For the next three years she did a variety of jobs both in and out of the film industry including editing for various documentary units, making travelogues with Marion Grierson for the Trade and Industrial Development Association, teaching English in Spain, and beginning to retrain as an electrician.

In 1941 Thomson found regular work at the Realist Film Unit making instructional films as part of the wartime Home Front propaganda campaign, mainly for nontheatrical distribution. Her first six films, made for the Dig for Victory campaign, illustrate the basic skills required to work an allotment, and store, produce, and maintain gardening tools. Later films were made for specialised audiences such as the farming community and introduced new farming methods, showcased traditional crafts, and exemplified ways of increasing yields. Thomson also made four films about anaesthesia for medical undergraduates. Considering the diversity of the subject matter, all of the films are characterised by their visual simplicity, clear instruction, and ability to relay complex information to the audience in a clear, nonpatronising way.

After the war, Thomson produced two children's hygiene films, but she returned to directing to make two recruitment films for the Ministry of Education, Children Learning by Experience (1946) and Children Growing Up with Other People (1947). She filmed children playing on London's bomb sites and in parks and said that she tried not to intrude on the children's environment, allowing shots to run longer than normal to consider the significance of the children's behaviour. She believed this to be an early example of the cinéma vérité style. In 1948 she returned to New Zealand where she directed several cinemagazines for the New Zealand Film Unit before coming back to work for the Crown Film Unit in Britain in 1950. In 1953 she made a fiction film for children, Child's Play, which was funded by the government-backed feature unit Group 3. After several years as a children's acting coach at Pinewood Studios, she returned to nonfiction filmmaking, directing industrial and government-sponsored medical films, including several for the Coal Board, until she retired in 1977.

SARAH EASEN

Biography

Born Australia, 1910 and educated in New Zealand. Emigrated to Britain in 1934. Film librarian, Gaumont-British Instructional 1938. Director, Gaumont-British Instructional 1936–37. Freelance cutter, 1938. Director, editor, and producer, Travel and Industrial Development Association; New Zealand Trade and Industrial Development Association 1939. Director, Realist Film Unit, 1941–7. Director, New Zealand Film Unit, 1948–9. Director, Crown Film Unit, 1950–1. Director, Group 3, 1954. Children's acting coach, Pinewood Studios, 1954. Director, various production companies, 1955–77. Died December 30, 2005.

Selected films

1936–7 Chalk Downlands, Meadowlands, Moorlands, Oakwoods, Salt Marshes, Healthlands
1941 Cultivation, Storing Vegetables Indoors, Storing Vegetables Outdoors
1942 Clamping Potatoes, Hedging, Ditching, Making a Compost Heap, Garden Tools
1943 Clean Milk, Making Good Hay, Making Grass Silage, Re-seeding for Better Grass, Save Your Own Seeds
1944 The Technique of Anaesthesia (series): director of four of the eleven films in the series
1945 Your Children's Ears, Your Children's Eyes, Your Children's Teeth: producer
1946–7 Children Learning by Experience, Children Growing Up with Other People
1948–9 Cinemagazines for the New Zealand Film Unit
1950–1 A Family Affair, Cross-infection in Children's Wards No. 1 and No. 2
1954 Friend of the Family
1955–6 Continuous Observation of a Depressed Patient, Understanding Agression
1957 Yorkshire Imperial on Thames, Yorkshire Imperial Way With Water
1960s Medical training films for the nursing profession
1967–77 Coal Board filmstrips, TB: The Forgotten Disease, Margin of Safety

Three Songs About Lenin

(USSR, Vertov, 1934)

Contemporary Western film scholars typically consider Soviet director Dziga Vertov's Tri pesni o Lenine/Three Songs about Lenin less important than his reflexive masterpiece Chelovek s kinoapparatom/Man with the Movie Camera (1929). In the Soviet Union, however, Three Songs about Lenin represented the more acceptable face of Vertov's work, even though the director himself continued to be regarded with suspicion by the cinema authorities because of his modernist leanings. Although hampered by considerable difficulties during its production and initial distribution, Three Songs about Lenin earned Vertov the Order of the Red Star and was endorsed by film industry chief Boris Shumyatksy as an improvement on his earlier work. The film was reedited in 1938 to include additional material favouring Stalin. The hundredth anniversary of Lenin's birth in 1970 saw a version closer to the original print restored by Vertov's editor, Elizaveta Svilova. Whatever its aesthetic value, Three Songs about Lenin was more central to Soviet cultural history than Man with the Movie Camera.

Three Songs about Lenin, produced to mark the tenth anniversary of Lenin's death, documents his funeral and includes shots of him working, meeting people, and giving speeches.

In an attempt to document how Leninism has enabled the country to progress in the intervening ten years, the film represents the liberation of Soviet Asian women and industrial achievements of the First Five-Year Plan in diverse parts of the Soviet Union. There is, of course, no indication of the scale of coercion and sacrifice involved. Footage from the civil war is also included to remind viewers of the momentous struggle to secure the revolution.

Like Shestaya chast' mira/One Sixth of the Earth (Dziga Vertov, 1926), Three Songs about Lenin was an ambitious undertaking, combining library footage with new material shot across a vast geographical area. Three Songs about Lenin's cinematography is less distinguished than Man with the Movie Camera's; the earlier film's outstanding cameraman Mikhail Kaufman had left Vertov's group to direct his own documentaries. Svilova painstakingly trawled through archives and collated fragments of newsreel film of Lenin to construct a fuller cinematic record of the revered leader's public activities than had previously been possible. Similarly, sound engineer Shtro reconstructed part of a Lenin speech for the film. According to Vertov's diaries, this arduous work was constantly disrupted by a lack of support and resources during production and attacks from opponents critical of his conception of documentary film. Finally, there were difficulties getting the completed film distributed.

Contemporary Western film scholars tend to dismiss Three Songs about Lenin not only on aesthetic grounds but also because they see it as a wholesale capitulation to Stalinism and the pseudo-religious Lenin cult (Michelson 1992). These retrospective judgements need to be carefully contextualised. From a Stalinist perspective, one of the film's shortcomings was the initial lack of prominence it gave to Stalin. Also problematic is the stridency of the Lenin speech heard midway through the film and reiterated on revolving intertitles near the end. 'The landowners and capitalists, destroyed in Russia, will be defeated throughout the world' was inconsistent with mid-1930s Soviet foreign policy as it moved toward its more conciliatory Popular Front phase (Roberts 1999). Three Songs about Lenin highlights how there was some scope within the Lenin cult for emphasising different aspects of his political legacy. Equally, a limited range of different perspectives on Lenin himself was possible. This film stresses Lenin's exemplary humanity, industriousness, and unpretentiousness—his status as a role model for good Soviet citizens—rather than just his deification.

Vertov saw Three Songs about Lenin as a continuation of his ongoing kino-eye and, after the coming of sound, radio-eye experiment to develop an international film language. It can be seen and listened to as one of the last examples of early European film modernism. Vertov wanted to develop a film practice that would facilitate communication between workers in geographically disparate locations. Three Songs about Lenin represents their unity and, according to Vertov, the film's combination of sounds and images achieved a 'crystalline' purity of universal accessibility (Michelson 1984). Thus, even if the spoken language of the industrial and collective farm workers and engineer who address the camera directly towards the end of the film is not translated, their gestures and facial expressions enable them to be understood within its overall context.

As the film's title suggests, it is primarily structured around various types of music rather than interviews or voice-over narration. Folk songs sung by Soviet Asian women subdivide the film, moving gradually from lamenting their oppression in the first song, to sorrow at Lenin's death in the second, to optimism in the third. Two other types of music also feature significantly; nineteenth-century classical at Lenin's funeral, and Yuri Shaporin's modern Soviet 'The March of the Shock Workers,' written specially for the film. Shaporin's composition dominates the soundtrack whenever intense productive activity is represented, particularly the final section's images of coal transportation, steel works, and newly constructed factories, canals, and dams. Ultimately, Shaporin's music is the sound of the future in Three Songs about Lenin.

Three Songs about Lenin was quite well received by Soviet and Western audiences in the 1930s, gaining plaudits from luminaries as diverse as Walter Benjamin and Cecil B. de Mille. The documentary Turksib (Viktor Turin, USSR, 1929) had scored a similar success several years earlier. What the two films share is a basic ideological contrast between progressive modernity and the backward East that cuts across Soviet–Western differences. In its representation of primitive, stagnant Islamic cultures and veiled women, Three Songs about Lenin taps into a fund of imagery familiar to other European imperial cultures (Stollery 2000). Revealingly, the film's most blatant transgressions of Vertov's commitment to filming 'life caught unawares' occur in shots underwriting the notion that Soviet power in Central Asia constitutes liberation and not domination. Early in the film women unveil and smile at the camera. Later on close-ups of their eyes signify sadness at Lenin's death and the new Leninist vision they have attained. These are carefully lit, manifestly staged images rather than any kind of documentary record of reality.

MARTIN STOLLERY

See also: Vertov, Dziga

Three Songs about Lenin (USSR, Mezhrabpomfilm, 1934). Direction and scenario by Dziga Vertov. Edited by Elizaveta Svilova. Assisted by Ilya Kopalin, Semiramida Pumpyanskaya. Cinematography by Mark Magidson, Bentsion Monastyrsky, Dmitri Surensky. Sound by Pyotr Shtro. Music by Yuri Shaporin. Filmed in Turkmenistan, Uzbekistan, Azerbaijan, and elsewhere in the Soviet Union.

Further reading

Leyda, Jay, *Kino: A History of the Russian and Soviet Film*, London: George Allen and Unwin, 1983.

Michelson, Annette, 'The Kinetic Icon in the Work of Mourning', in Anna Lawton (ed.), *The Red Screen*, London: Routledge, 1992: 113–31.

——(ed.), *Kino-Eye: The Writings of Dziga Vertov*, London: Pluto Press, 1984.

n.a., 'Intertitles to Three Songs of Lenin', *October* 52, 1990: 40–51.

Petric, Vlada, 'Vertov, Lenin and Perestroika: The Cinematic Transposition of Reality', in Charles Warrent (ed.), *Beyond Documents: Essays on the Non-fiction Film*, Hanour, NH: University Press of New England, 1996: 271–94.

Roberts, Graham, *Forward Soviet! History and Non-fiction Film in the USSR*, London: I.B. Tauris, 1999.

Stollery, Martin, *Alternative Empires: European Modernist Cinemas and Cultures of Imperialism*, Exeter: University of Exeter Press, 2000.

Taylor, Richard, *Film Propaganda: Soviet Russia and Nazi Germany*, London: I.B. Tauris, 1998.

Taylor, Richard and Christie, Ian (eds), *The Film Factory: Russian and Soviet Cinema in Documents 1896–1939*, London: Routledge, 1988.

Tumarkin, Nina, *Lenin Lives!: The Cult of Lenin in Soviet Russia*, Cambridge, MA: Harvard University Press, 1997.

Youngblood, Denise, *Soviet Cinema in the Silent Era, 1918–35*, Austin, TX: University of Texas Press, 1991.

Times of Harvey Milk, The

(US, Epstein, 1984)

On November 27, 1978, Dan White climbed through a window into San Francisco City Hall and shot to death Supervisor Harvey Milk and Mayor George Moscone. White fired eight times at Moscone, reloaded his gun, and then went down a hallway and emptied it again into Harvey Milk. The deaths shocked the city and its gay community. With the killing, Milk had become the modern gay movement's first martyr (Benson 1984: 1).

Dan White was an embittered ex-supervisor who had resigned and then wanted his job back. Moscone, backed by Milk, refused to have him reinstated. The rejection precipitated the murders. White had resigned because of the defeat of Proposition 6, an amendment that barred gays and lesbians from employment in California public schools.

The planned documentary was originally to focus on White. However, director and coproducer Robert Epstein found White uninteresting. 'The more we got into the story', Epstein said, 'the more rich it became as to what it represented—which was trying to better humanity. Harvey Milk was really trying to do something positive' (Smith 1985: 1). This shift in focus resulted in The Times of Harvey Milk, a ninety-minute portrait of San Francisco's first openly gay elected official. Shot in 16mm, the documentary took six years and cost $300,000 to make.

Narrated by Harvey Fierstein, the documentary opens with news footage. Included are the gurneys carrying the bodies of Milk and Moscone, the attempt to capture Dan White, and the tearful press announcement by supervisor (now senator) Diane Feinstein of the murders. The footage was on-the-scene coverage, as the story unfolded, adding to its drama.

The film then turns to the years leading up to the murders. While some of Milk's youth is disclosed, the filmmakers focus on his emergence as a political leader. The viewer sees Milk transformed from a quirky ex-hippy into a savvy, polished politician who advocated for gay and minority rights, senior citizen rights, and rent control. One of his first political challenges came after California State Senator John Briggs introduced Proposition 6 onto the State ballot. It was intended to ban all openly gay people from working in the public school system, playing on parents' fears that their children might hold up gay people as role models or be molested by them. Milk debated Briggs and is credited with helping to defeat the measure, which for a time seemed certain to pass. Milk's stature and reputation grew.

The film's closing scenes are powerful. The filmmakers recorded a silent candlelight walk by forty thousand people held on the evening of Milk and Moscone's deaths. The film then moves ahead six months when White is found guilty, not of murder, but of the lesser charge of involuntary manslaughter. His defense attorney argued that White had become deranged by eating too much junk food, which became known as the 'Twinkie defense'. The verdict caused a riot in San Francisco. City Hall was stormed, and six police cars were burned.

White served five and a half years of his seven-year sentence. He received no psychiatric treatment. In October 1985, nearly two years after his release, White committed suicide.

The film's structure includes segments focusing on eight San Francisco men and women, both heterosexual and homosexual, who each talk about how Harvey Milk affected their lives. One of the more poignant remarks of the eight is spoken by Jim Elliot, a machinist and secretary of a local union. When he first met Milk, and heard he was gay, Elliot wondered how he was 'gonna go back to these guys at the union and tell them that we're supporting a fruit?' Then Elliot goes on to say, 'But as I listened to him, you realized that he wasn't only for gay rights. He was for anything that affected little people'.

The film does not examine Dan White's character or trial in any depth. Some critics considered this one of the film's few weaknesses. Other than this, the film's critics were nearly unanimous in their praise for this 'extraordinarily wise and sensitive' film (Mathews 1984).

Although eloquently partisan, the film is much more than a 'gay' film. It is a positive story about one man who made a difference in the lives of others. The film is a triumph of democratic hope. As many have said, the story is not about gay rights, but human rights.

LOU BUTTINO

The Times of Harvey Milk (US, Black Sand Productions/Pacific Arts, 1984, 90 mins). Distributed by New Yorker Films and TC Films International. Directed by Rob Epstein. Written by Judith Coburn and Carter Wilson. Academy Award Winner: Best Feature. New York Film Critics Circle Award: Best Documentary. Three National Emmy Awards.

Further reading

Benson, Shiela, 'The Times of Harvey Milk', *Los Angeles Times*, November 2, 1984: 1.

Galbraith, Stuart, IV, 'The Times of Harvey Milk', www.dvdtalk.com/reviews/read, 2, n.d.

Mathews, Jack, 'Hollywood', *USA Today*, October 16, 1984.

n.a., 'The Times of Harvey Milk', *The New York Times*, October 28, 1984.

Smith, Lynn, 'Harvey Milk Film—Pride, Sorrow: UCI Presentation of Honored Picture Triggers Emotions' (Orange County Edition), *Los Angeles Times*, October 31, 1985: 1.

Tire Dié

(Argentina, Birri, 1956, 1959)

Tire dié/Throw Me a Dime is considered to be the most important documentary short from Latin America. It was made collaboratively between Argentine filmmaker Fernando Birri and his students at the Documentary School of Santa Fé at the University of Litoral (Santa Fé, Argentina), the first school of its kind in Latin America. Tire dié is a thirty-three-minute document of poor children in Santa Fé, (a city in a northern province of Argentina) where a mode of survival is for the children to await passing trains, balance precariously on the elevated tracks, and to run alongside the trains, begging for small change by shouting 'Tire dié! Tire dié!' (throw me a dime).

On its release in 1958, the film marked the entrance of an Italian neorealist-inspired political filmmaking that was to indelibly mark the landscape of Latin American film production from the late 1950s to the 1970s. Dubbed the New Latin American Cinema movement, these films documented and exposed the economic, social, and political disparities in Latin America, often made absent in the studio-made films from the 1940s and 1950s. Fernando Birri was trained at the prestigious film school, the Centro Sperimentale in Rome, where he worked as an

Figure 19 Tire Dié, 1956, 1959 (Courtesy of the British Film Institute)

assistant to Zavattini and De Sica. There he was inspired by neorealism, or what he described as 'the tenderness of the Italian films that in a simple manner document the everyday' (Sendros 1994). On returning to Argentina and seeing the lack of infrastructure for filmmaking, coupled with the harsh reality of poverty, Birri resolved to make what he dubbed a 'cinema of underdevelopment'. He condemned apolitical cinema in a manifesto by stating that 'one must place oneself face to face with the reality with a camera and document it, document underdevelopment [...] Cinema which makes itself an accomplice of that underdevelopment is subcinema' (Birri 1987).

Tire dié is a landmark film because of the direct, honest, and gritty portrayal of its subject matter, but it was also important in terms of the production process. Birri worked with two borrowed film cameras and nonprofessional sound recording devices. Birri's aim was to make films despite the lack of infrastructure and financing, because he felt that social problems were important to make visible vis-à-vis the cinema. His philosophy of making films under difficult circumstances and not for commercial profit would not be labeled until the late 1960s with the term an imperfect cinema (un cine imperfecto), coined by Cuban filmmaker Julio García Espinosa.

Birri's class of eighty students was split up into various groups to spend time with the subjects in a riverside squatters' community. Birri described the making of the film:

> Tire dié was the product of constant, ongoing discussion. During that two-year period [that the film took to complete], we went almost every afternoon to the river flats to film. We went to observe and understand and exchange ideas with the people who lived there, but we ended up sharing their lives. The film became secondary to the interpersonal relationships that developed between us.
>
> (Burton 1986: 6)

The film opens with an aerial shot of Santa Fé. The voice-over narration that accompanies these shots of the city describes in a matter-of-fact manner the typical information one would ascribe to a traditional documentary (for example, geographic location, population). As Julianne Burton observes:

> As conventional descriptive data give way to the less conventional (statistics concerning the number of streetlamps and hairdressers) the parodistic becomes clear. As the houses give way to shanties, the narrator declares, 'Upon reaching the edge of the city proper, statistics become uncertain. This is where, between four and five in the afternoon during 1956, 1957, and 1958, the following social survey film was shot.'
>
> (Burton 2000)

Birri and his students first spent time documenting the children and their families with a still camera and a tape recorder and then later transformed the photo documentary into a film. The film project was first cut as a sixty-minute version. During the premiere of the film in Santa Fé, a cross-section of the population numbering four thousand in total filled the university theatre. Present were the subjects of the film along with the filmmakers, the children of the slums and their parents, along with the student filmmakers. In addition, university and city officials and film critics were in attendance. The film met with an enthusiastic crowd and was replayed three times that evening for the same audience. After the screening, hundreds of questionnaires were given out, and consultations were done with the film subjects about which parts were effective, and why. Through this collaboration to some extent the film advocated for the problems of the poor in Santa Fé. Moreover, it served as a model of collaborative filmmaking, one in which subjects determined, to some extent, how they were being represented.

The result was a more concise, thirty-three-minute version replete with a new voice track. Two revered film actors of the time, Francisco Petrone and Maria Rosa Gallo were asked to speak over the voices in the film that were poorly recorded. According to Birri and his student filmmakers, the point was not to dub over what people were saying, but rather to have the actors' additional vocal support for the subjects. Some critics have charged that this voice-over approach ultimately undermined the original intent of the film's democratic agenda. Although this may have altered the objective of having a marginalized community speak for itself, it worked on a practical level to vastly improve the sound quality of the original film. Inadvertently, it provided increased opportunities for the film to be screened outside of local settings.

The film was shown at film festivals in Argentina and Uruguay, and it circulated throughout the provinces of Argentina via a rudimentary mobile cinema van that provided a no-cost viewing opportunity for poor residents. This was especially important in areas with an absence of movie theatres.

Tire dié is a groundbreaking film and has significant historical importance in the annals of Latin American film scholarship. Despite its great influence, however, the film is practically impossible to see, in Latin America included. As Julianne Burton points out, 'most viewers know only the fragment presented in Fernando Solanas and Octavio Getino's three-part documentary on Argentine politics, The Hour of the

Furnaces (La hora de los hornos) (1969)' (Burton 2000). Nonetheless, Tire dié epitomized and served as a template for the continent-wide movement of political filmmaking in Latin America through the late 1970s.

TAMARA L. FALICOV

See also: Hour of the Furnaces, The

Tire dié (first version) (Argentina, 1956, 60 mins). Produced by the Institute of Cinema of the National University of the Litoral. Directed by Fernando Birri and students Hugo Abad, Blanca C. de Brasco, Eduardo Ates, Elena de Azcuenaga, Cesar Caprio, Manuel Horacio Gimenez, Rodolfo Neder, Juan Oliva, Carlos Pais, Ninfa Pajon, Eduardo Pallero, Jose M. Paolantonio, Jorge Planas, Viader y Enrique Urteaga. Script, Birri and above-mentioned students. Narrator, Alfredo Daniel Carrio; Editor, Antonio Ripoll; Sound, Leopoldo Orlazi; Film stock, black and white, 16mm film, developed at Alex Laboratories. Shot in Santa Fé, Argentina.

Tire dié (second, more widely released version) (Argentina, 1959, 33 mins). Distributed by Argentina Sono Film. Produced by the Institute of Cinema of the National University of the Litoral. Produced, scripted and directed by the above-mentioned people. Voices, Francisco Petrone, Maria Rosa Gallo. Narrator, Guillermo Cervantes Luro. Assistant Director, Manuel Horacio Gimenez; Sound, Mario Fezia; Rerecording, Argentina Sono Film; Film stock, transferred to black and white, 35mm. Shot in Santa Fé, Argentina. Awarded the following: Grand Prize for the Best Short Film, SODRE festival, Montevideo, Uruguay (1956); Grand Prize for the Special Jury Selection, 4th International Documentary and Experimental Film Festival of Montevideo, Uruguay (1956); Special Prize at the Educational Film Festival in the Province of Buenos Aires (1962).

Further reading

Birri, Fernando, *La escuela documental de Santa Fe*, Santa Fe: Editorial Documento del Instituto de Cinematografia de la UNL, 1964.

——*Pionero y peregrino*, Buenos Aires: Editorial Contrapunto, 1987.

Burton, Julianne, *Cinema and Social Change: Conversations with Filmmakers*, Austin, TX: University of Texas Press, 1986.

——*The Social Documentary in Latin America*, Pittsburgh: University of Pittsburgh Press, 1990.

——'Tire dié', in Sara Pendergast and Tom Pendergast (eds), *International Dictionary of Films and Filmmakers, Vol. 1*, Detroit, MI: St James Press, 2000: 215–17.

Pick, Zuzana, *The New Latin American Cinema: A Continental Project*, Austin, TX: University of Texas Press, 1993.

Sendros, Parana, *Fernando Birri*, Buenos Aires: Centro Editor de America Latina con el Instituto Nacional de Cinematografia, 1994.

Titicut Follies

(US, Wiseman, 1967)

Filmed from April to June 1966, over twenty-nine days, and culled from forty hours of material, Titicut Follies would lay the foundation for Frederick Wiseman's vision of documentary film, with its observational shooting style and exclusion of voice-over narration. Wiseman and codirector James Marshall captured the day-to-day routine of the patients, guards, and care staff at the Massachusetts Correctional Institution at Bridgewater. The facility, designed to hold both criminal offenders and nonthreatening psychiatric patients admitted for observation, was selected by Wiseman because of his familiarity with Bridgewater and its superintendent, Charles Gaughan, after visits made by the filmmaker as part of summer seminars during his time as a law instructor at Boston University during the late 1950s. An indictment of the practices captured on film at Bridgewater is never explicitly stated, but it is clear that the filmmakers take issue with the treatment of the patients.

Titicut Follies will likely be remembered as much for its content as for the stories surrounding both its production and its troubled release. With his portrait of the patients at the MCI Bridgewater, first-time filmmaker Wiseman presented audiences with a controversial glimpse inside the state-funded facility and was met with both harsh criticism and praise. The film was banned in the Commonwealth of Massachusetts for twenty-four years for reasons pertaining to the issue of informed consent with regard to the patients and their appearance in the film and, secondarily, the right of the state to approve of the finished film. Commercial screenings did occur outside of the Commonwealth after several other state Supreme Courts refused to ban the film: Titicut Follies' first public showing occurred at the 1967 New York Film Festival. All screenings within Massachusetts during that period, however, were required to meet strict regulations related to the nature of the viewing audiences. Only students and professionals in fields related to the concerns of the film were permitted to view Titicut Follies, and the screenings were not open to the general public. Its first national television broadcast did not occur until 1993. As the only film ever censored in the United States for reasons other than national security or obscenity, the legacy of Titicut Follies and its status as a canonical nonfiction film is tied to these issues of censorship and documentary ethics.

From daily cell inspections that reveal the startling conditions of the facility, to conversations between guards and patients that reveal the human side of Bridgewater (particularly senior correction guard Edward Pacheco who figures prominently throughout the film), the lives of the men at the institution are observed with a cool detachment rarely inflected by a humanist concern. That is not to suggest that Titicut Follies should be considered an attempt to objectively present life at the institution; the creative rendering of events at Bridgewater through Wiseman's editing confirms the constructed nature of the film's central narrative, thus fracturing any notion of a strictly observational positioning. Sequences spotlighting specific patients seem designed to promote sympathy and identification with the men, a viewer position presumably shared by Wiseman.

The sequence for which Titicut Follies is best remembered is the most stylized of the film and illustrates Wiseman's subjective construction of the text. It involves the tubefeeding of an aged and starving patient and offers one of Wiseman's most direct attacks on the senior staff at Bridgewater. Repeated scans of the patient's body as the chief medical officer inserts a rubber tube into his nostril are cross-cut with images of a mortician prepping a corpse for embalming. The intensity of these inserts increases during the feeding until the corpse, dressed and placed behind the steel door of a morgue storage compartment, is positively identified as the force-fed man. Throughout Titicut Follies, Wiseman casts particular members of Bridgewater's senior staff in a suspect light while patients appear as victims; in this case, it is with the inclusion of footage clearly detailing the doctor's disregard for the patient as he carelessly inserts the feeding tube well beyond the safety threshold indicated by a white marker. The doctor, smoking a cigarette with its ash dangling over the patient's head, notices his error only after an assisting guard points it out to him. It is this type of parallel editing system that would be further developed in Wiseman's subsequent work and operates as a virtual commentary guiding the viewer through the narrative, absent in its conventional documentary form of voice-over commentary.

That James Marshall acted as director of photography while Wiseman handled the sync-sound recording equipment not only indicates the magnitude of the role Marshall played in the production, but also suggests the importance of sound in Wiseman's representation of life at Bridgewater. All through Titicut Follies, Wiseman bridges distinct segments of the film with a lapse in the synchronous soundtrack. The result not only suggests a temporal and spatial linearity of the presentation, but comments on the manic sonic environment of the facility. This privileging of the sonic space of the profilmic location greatly informs Wiseman's representation of reality.

Described by some as a film that created one set of social problems as it sought to alleviate another, the production of Titicut Follies, its exhibition, and its trials raise crucial issues about the relation of social documentary to its subjects and audiences (Anderson and Benson 1991). As is the case with all of his films, Wiseman is the sole distributor of the film through his own company, Zipporah Films. In spite of the legal issues that marred the original release of Titicut Follies and restricted its audience for decades, the film remains a critical text with regards to issues of consent, participation, and representation within nonfiction film.

MICHAEL B. BAKER

See also: Wiseman, Frederick

Titicut Follies (US, Bridgewater Film Company, Inc., 1967, 84 mins). Distributed by Zipporah Films. Directed and produced by Frederick Wiseman. Co-directed and photographed by James Marshall. Edited by Frederick Wiseman. Associate editor, Alyne Model. Associate producer, David Eames.

Further reading

Anderson, Carolyn and Benson, Thomas W., *Documentary Dilemmas: Frederick Wiseman's Titicut Follies*, Carbondale, IL: Southern Illinois University Press, 1991.

Armstrong, Dan, 'Wiseman's Realm of Transgression: Titicut Follies, the Symbolic Father, and the Spectacle of Confinement', *Cinema Journal* 29, 1989.

Atkins, Thomas R. (ed.), *Frederick Wiseman*, New York: Monarch Press, 1976.

Ellsworth, Liz, *Frederick Wiseman: A Guide to References and Resources*, Boston: G.K. Hall, 1979.

Grant, Barry K., 'Ethnography in the First Person: Frederick Wiseman's Titicut Follies', in Barry Keith Grant and Jeannette Sloniowski (eds), *Documenting the Documentary: Close Readings of Documentary Film and Video*, Detroit, MI: Wayne State University Press, 1998.

——*Voyages of Discovery: The Cinema of Frederick Wiseman*, Urbana, IL: University of Illinois Press, 1992.

Levin, G. Roy, *Documentary Explorations: 15 Interviews with Filmmakers*, New York: Doubleday, 1971.

Stevenson, Jack, 'Interview with Frederick Wiseman', *Pandemonium* 3, 1989.

To Die in Madrid

(France, Rossif, 1962)

On March 26, 1962, French producer Nicole Stéphane asked the Spanish government for permission to shoot in Spain some scenes needed for a TV documentary entitled Espagne éternelle/Eternal Spain, to be directed by the prestigious filmmaker Frédéric Rossif. The Francoist officials were uncertain and surprised, because the proposed script dealt with the most crude clichés about Spain: gypsies, flamenco music, bullfights, and Catholicism, for example. The production was supported by Marcelin Defourneaux, then cultural attaché to the French Embassy in Madrid and representative of Unifrance Film, who assured the administration that the image of contemporary Spain presented in the film would be absolutely positive. Subsequently permission to film was granted, as was the unconditional cooperation of the local authorities involved in the five weeks of shooting.

Some months later, in an interview to the weekly magazine *Candide*, Rossif discussed the Espagne éternelle affair, stating that his intention was not to make a film on contemporary Spain, but only to find images to complement the archive footage that he had selected for a full-length documentary on the Spanish civil war to be titled Mourir à Madrid/ To Die in Madrid. Since the approach was to be anti-Franco, the images captured in 1962 Spain were clearly appointed to give the audience the impression that Franco's victory had been disastrous for Spain.

The film premiered in Cannes during the Festival—but not in the Festival, due to its documentary condition—and received unanimous critical acclaim, mainly for its proloyalist, anti-Franco bias, but also for its technical skill in the editing of the great amount of old footage taken from various film archives around the world. The contemporary shots defined Rossif's message: the foggy, somber Castilian landscape, inhabited by long-suffering, impoverished peasants, was a symbol of Franco's victory and his subsequent reign of terror.

Nevertheless, some objections to the film were raised. Conservative Roman Catholics reacted angrily against the film for its attack on the right-wing side of the Spanish civil war. According to the traditionalist interpretation, the Alzamiento was a crusade against the enemies of Spain and the religion. However, there was also criticism from the Left. The prominent Catalan anarchist and former minister in the days of the Popular Front, Frederica Montseny, accused Rossif's film of being communist propaganda that deliberately ignored the contribution of the Libertarian movement to the Revolution in Spain. In fact, this was partly true. Rossif centers its interpretation in the defense of Madrid, defining very well the enemy, that is, the 'evil ones'—the Army, the Church, the Falange, the Italians, and the Germans—but is somewhat imprecise in the depiction of the 'good' Republicans. The viewer learns little about the Republican ideology. One curious example is that the gigantic posters with the faces of Lenin and Stalin, which decorated the streets and squares of Madrid during all the war years, are never shown on screen. Spanish Republicans are seen only as innocent victims of savage bombardments and sadistic repression, through such events as the Guernica massacre, or the murder of Federico García Lorca. On the other hand, the role of the International Brigades is overemphasized. Another objection was addressed to the 'aestheticist' treatment of some episodes, heavily supported by a solemn (especially in the French soundtrack) spoken commentary. It is curious to note that Rossif's

Figure 20 To Die in Madrid, 1962 (Courtesy of the British Film Institute)

only concession to 'impartiality' is his approbation of one of the classic myths of Francoist propaganda: the siege of the Toledo Alcázar.

The reaction of Spanish authorities to the critical and commercial success of Mourir à Madrid was a blend of impotence and anger. They were unable to forbid its release abroad, but did try, via diplomacy, to curb its reception in 'friendly' countries, with some degree of success. The Spanish government also sponsored two full-length documentaries intended to refute Rossif's thesis. Morir en España/To Die in Spain (1965, Mariano Ozores) made relatively imaginative use of some interesting archive shots, but ¿Por qué morir en Madrid?/Why to Die in Madrid? (1966, Eduardo Manzanos) was considered ineffective, and the film was never released. The original Mourir à Madrid premiered in Spain in May 1978.

RAFAEL DE ESPAÑA

See also: Rossif, Frédéric

Mourir à Madrid/To Die in Madrid (France, Rossif, 1962, 83 mins). An Ancinex production. Written and directed by Frédéric Rossif. Narrated by Madeleine Chapsal. Voices: Suzanne Flon, Germaine Montero, Roger Mollion, Pierre Vaneck, and Jean Vilar. English adaptation: Helen Scott, with the voices of John Gielgud, Irene Worth, William Hutt, and George Gonneau.

Further reading

Crusells, Magí, *La Guerra Civil española: cine y propaganda*, Barcelona: Ariel, 2003: 107–32.

Cuenca, Carlos Fernandez, *La Guerra de España y el cine*, Madrid: Editora Nacional, vol I, 1972: 427–41.

de España, Rafael, 'Images of the Spanish Civil War in Spanish Feature Films, 1939–85', *Historical Journal of Film, Radio and Television* 6, no. 2, 1986: 223–36.

del Amo, Alfonso (ed.), *Catálogo general del cine de la Guerra Civil*, Madrid: Catedra/Filmoteca Española, 1996: 637–9, 765–6.

Furhammar, Leif and Isaksson, Folke, *Politics and Film*, London: Studio Vista, 1971: 54–5.

Gubern, Roman, *1936–39. La Guerra de España en la pantalla*, Madrid: Filmoteca Española, 1986: 132–4.
Rossif, Frédéric and Chapsal, Madeleine, *Mourir à Madrid*, Paris: Seghers, 1963.

Tokyo Orinpikku (Tokyo Olympiad)

(Japan, Ichikawa, 1965)

Tokyo Olympiad is generally recognized, along with Leni Reifenstahl's Olympia (1938), as one of the finest documentaries on the Olympics. The film was originally to be directed by Kurosawa Akira. In the course of preproduction, however, it became evident that Kurosawa desired an unprecedented degree of creative control that spilled out into the events themselves. He demanded, for example, the right to design and choreograph the Opening Ceremony himself in order to lend the event to cinematography. Kurosawa was summarily replaced by Ichikawa Kon, who was known both for his cinematic craftsmanship and also for reliably rescuing troubled films in mid-production. Ichikawa was also famous for his adaptations of previous texts, which also may have been a factor in his selection; unlike Kurosawa, he was not interested in tampering with the original text of the Olympics.

The year 1964 was a crucial time in Japanese history. The government was intent on using the Olympics to signal Japan's reemergence on the world stage after its devastating defeat in World War II. They had renewed their security relationship with the United States, and their economy was entering a phase of high growth. Tokyo, which had been leveled to dust during the war, was transformed into a bustling modern landscape of paved roads and a newly modernized environment, something to which Ichikawa gestures at the beginning with images of prewar buildings being torn down with a wrecking ball. He also seems to inject the film with the faint stench of Japanese nationalism with stylized images of the rising sun, stunningly shot by the renowned documentary cameraman Hayashida Shigeo.

The finished film, however, was roundly criticized by both the conservative government and the Communist Party, which we can probably take as a measure of Ichikawa's achievement. Before the film was even finished, it ran into severe problems with the government ministry that was overseeing the production. A preview was staged for Hirohito, and rumors flew in the popular media that the emperor was displeased. Numerous government officials publicly attacked Ichikawa, baffled by his aestheticization of the games and calling for a new version that was 'record centric' (*kirokuchushin*) and not 'artistic' (*geijutsuteki*). Ironically, a similar debate over the nature of documentary aesthetics took place in 1930s Japan and was resolved in favor of artfulness by the immensely popular reception of Reifenstahl's Olympia. Ichikawa basically prevailed and completed a one-hundred-and-fifty-four-minute film that became the highest grossing film in Japanese history in 1965. The film has recently been restored to Ichikawa's original one hundred and sixty-nine-minute cut. There are countless regionalized versions, however, as local distributors typically cut out what they felt was unimportant: for example, the initial US version was thirty minutes of gold medal victories by American athletes.

It seems that one cannot discuss the film without mentioning a slew of statistics that indicate its unusual scale: one hundred and sixty-four cameramen, one hundred cameras, two hundred and fifty lenses, fifty-seven sound recordists, one hundred and sixty-five thousand feet of audio tape, and seventy hours of film exposed. The film was made 'under the sign of gigantism', as Jacques Demeure so aptly put it (Cazdyn *et al.* 2001: 315). Seen in today's era, when the Olympics are an exclusively televisual event, the film is truly a wonder to behold. Ichikawa shot in CinemaScope and stereo sound, with enough access and control to set his cameras where he wished and light scenes with the polish of his feature films. The director's eye for abstract pattern and spectacular splashes of color found ample material in the pageantry of the Olympics. Although he certainly knew he was expected to produce a document of national pride, Ichikawa managed to undercut the political nature of the games with his patent irony, a wry attention paid to the banal margins adjacent to the spectacle of Olympian feats of bodily strength, and an unusual emphasis on the athletes' pain and suffering in their quest for gold. For every predictable, if unforgettable, image of Olympic spectacle, there is a sequence so ambiguous or perplexing that it infuses the film with contradiction that simultaneously invites and frustrates interpretation. The film is often singled out to represent the best of Japanese documentary, but it is really quite anomalous (other Tokyo Olympics films by Noda Shinkichi and Kuroki Kazuo are far more typical, especially in their political charge). Ichikawa's film is best seen as a great Olympics film, perhaps the last great one now that we have entered the age of global live television, to which it stands in such striking and admirable contrast.

ABÉ MARK NORNES

Tokyo orinpikku (Tokyo Olympiad) (Japan, 1965). Produced by Taguchi Suketaru. Directed by Ichikawa Kon. Written by Ichikawa Kon, Shirasaka Yoshio, Tanikawa Shuntaro, Wada Natto. Cinematography by Miyagawa Kazuo, Murata Shigeo, Nagano Shigeichi, Nakamura Kenji, Tanaka Tadashi. Music by Mayuzumi Toshiro. Sound recorded by Inoue Toshihiko. Edited by Ehara Yoshio, Nakashizu Tatsuji. Art direction by Kamekura Yusaku. Narration (Japanese version) by Mikuni Ichiro.

Further reading

Cazdyn, Eric, Nornes, A.M., Quant, James, Russell, Catherine and Yoshimoto, Mitsuhiro, 'Tokyo Olympiad: A Symposium', in James Quant (ed.), *Ichikawa Kon*, Toronto: Cinemateque Ontario, 2001: 315–6 (reprinted as liner notes for Criterion Collection's DVD of Tokyo Olympiad, 2002).

Vaughn, Dai, 'Tokyo versus Berlin', in *Documentary: Twelve Essays*, Berkeley, CA: University of California Press, 1999: 90–110.

Toscano, Salvador

Toscano's career began at the end of nineteenth century, shortly after Lumière's representatives brought the cinematograph to Mexico, and ended around 1920, when Hollywood fiction films practically put an end to the commercial exhibition of documentaries. Unfortunately, most of Toscano's works have not survived as they were originally edited—silent and with titles—but many fragments were reedited in Memorias de un mexicano (Carmen Toscano, 1950), a fiction film made by his daughter.

In his first years as a filmmaker, Toscano shot city monuments, landscapes, theater numbers, popular festivals, parades, bullfights, and the results of catastrophic events such as floods and earthquakes. Thematically similar to their French models, most of these documentaries were only a few minutes long and composed of conservative shots, with no camera movement or outstanding emplacements. They simply recorded, from a fixed point of view, selected events from reality. Toscano, like other filmmakers and the Mexican public in general at that time, shared the assumption that documentaries had an informative or recreational purpose similar to that of the press. In any case, they satisfied communicative needs in an almost totally illiterate country.

By 1906 the development of film narrative allowed Toscano to make longer and more complex films, such as Fiestas presidenciales en Mérida (1906), Inauguración del tráfico internacional en el istmo de Tehuantepec (1907), and his first feature, Fiestas del centenario de la Independencia (1910). Their character was again journalistic, but at the same time they were in a sense propaganda films, because they invariably presented a fairly positive image of dictator Porfirio Díaz and the material achievements of his administration. As far as we can see in the surviving fragments, the style of these films was still based on a very discreet use of the camera, although there is some innovation in shots.

Fiestas del centenario de la Independencia, which registered the one-month celebrations held to commemorate the centenary of the beginning of the war of independence against Spain, was a popular film, but its success was far surpassed by the 1911 documentaries, which showed episodes related to Francisco I Madero's military rebellion against President Díaz. Toscano's main work about that event was La toma de Ciudad Juárez y el viaje del héroe de la revolución don Francisco I Madero (1911), a long film that combined information and propaganda. Until then, the image of Porfirio Díaz had been emphasized in documentaries about his trips and the high points of his government. Now, there was also a trip, but in this case it was enhanced by a much more important element for the construction of a charismatic image—that of military victory.

Madero defeated Díaz and became the new president of the country, but was attacked and put to death by his own army. After that there was another revolution, which lasted for about five years. Many documentary makers of this period showed Pancho Villa, Álvaro Obregón, Venustiano Carranza, Emiliano Zapata, or some other *caudillo* defeating their enemies in battles or cities under siege. These films almost always presented the perspective of the winner and ended with the victory of one group, as in Toscano's Historia completa de la revolución de 1910 a 1915 (1915). They were propaganda films intentionally covered up with the objective aura of informative reportage: partial victories were presented as definite, local processes as national, and so on. The effect produced by their sensational contents guaranteed their success, although their form was still conservative. They were structured in chronological order, their 'clear' shots aimed basically at fulfilling the minimum requirements needed to make the events represented intelligible for any public. In a sense, this lack of aesthetic or narrative risks is what characterizes Toscano's style and that of most Mexican revolution documentary makers. Another central characteristic is that almost none of them resorted to using recreated scenes, studio shots, or other inauthentic documentary material.

Toscano went beyond combining information and propaganda, however. In his long career as a filmmaker, he collected scenes of different political regimes, and this in turn became the source of a panoramic historical film first entitled Historia de la revolución de 1910 a 1920 (1920), and finally, with the addition of excerpts filmed by other documentary makers, Historia completa de la revolución mexicana, 1900–1927 (1927). In this last thirty-five-reel film, there were no value judgments about the actions of the protagonists or about the traumatic social process that occurred during that period. That is, the film gave equal legitimacy to all its main characters, both on the side of the government and of the rebels. Other Mexican documentary makers, like Jesús H. Abitia, also intended to give an encompassing, historical overview of the same period, but their pictures inevitably revealed their sympathies for one *caudillo* or another. Only Toscano, who never fully embraced a political cause, managed to give a detached version of that turbulent episode.

The Mexican revolution ended in 1917. That same year, a crucial transformation of documentaries occurred when war films came to an end. Filmmakers became involved with the new government and redirected their production. Toscano was commissioned to film Las riquezas de Quintana Roo (1917) so as to promote inversion in, and migration to, that abandoned region; a few years later he was again contacted to make the official film of the festivals held to commemorate the centenary of the consummation of independence: Las fiestas del centenario (1921). Although this was in fact his last documentary, he never stopped adding scenes, filmed by others, to his great work in progress, Historia de la revolución mexicana.

ÁNGEL MIQUEL

See also: Mexico

Biography

Born in Guadalajara, Jalisco, Mexico, March 24, 1872. Graduated as an engineer from Universidad Nacional de Mexico, 1897. Up to 1921, combined his career with filmmaking and exhibition; afterwards, worked mainly in highway construction. Collected films, stereographic photographs, and early film posters which now form part of one of Mexico's main private historical archives. Died April 14, 1947 in Mexico City.

Selected films

1906 Fiestas presidenciales en Mérida
1907 Inauguración del tráfico internacional en el istmo de Tehuantepe
1910 Fiestas del centenario de la Independencia
1911 La toma de Ciudad Juárez y el viaje del héroe de la revolución don Francisco I Madero
1915 Historia completa de la revolución de 1910 a 1915
1920 Historia de la revolución de 1910 a 1920
1921 Las fiestas del centenario
1927 Historia completa de la revolución mexicana, 1900 a 1927

Further reading

de los Reyes, Aurelio, *Vivir de sueños, vol. I of Cine y sociedad en México 1896–1930*, Mexico City: UNAM, 1983.

Miquel, Angel, *Salvador Toscano*, Mexico City: Filmoteca de la UNAM, Universidad de Guadalajara, Universidad Veracruzana, Secretaría de Cultura del Estado de Puebla, 1997.

Ramírez, Gabriel, *Crónica del cine mudo mexicano*, Mexico City: Cineteca Nacional, 1989.
Toscano, Carmen, *Memorias de un mexicano*, Mexico City: Fundación Carmen Toscano, 1996.
Vaidovits, Guillermo, *El cine mudo en Guadalajara*, Guadalajara: Universidad de Guadalajara, 1989.

Trinh T. Minh-ha

The filmmaker, writer, composer, and cultural critic Trinh T. Minh-ha radically redefines cinematic conventions through films that attempt to challenge the structures of oppression and domination in commercial cinema and in Western society as a whole. A key figure among contemporary postcolonialist feminists, Trinh uses innovative forms such as poetic language, disruptions of linear time, negative space and silences, multiple voices, repetition and recontextuality, and cultural repositioning in her films and writing to critique patriarchal fixed meanings and notions of Otherness.

Trinh has been influenced by the work of influential postmodern thinkers including Jacques Derrida, Michel Foucault, Roland Barthes, Jean-François Lyotard, and Hélène Cixous. Like them, Trinh questions the viability of scientific objectivity and linguistic certainty. Trinh's work also shares the commitment to reclaiming marginalized subjectivities with feminists such as Gloria Anzaldua and Audre Lorde. A filmmaker of the Asian diaspora, Trinh is part of an intellectual movement of women of color whose work has been particularly affected by the shift from colonialism to a global capitalist economy, which has fostered migrations, the dominance of Western mass media, and the commodification of 'native' cultures. Trinh has written extensively about cinematic theory, and her films serve to put those theories into practice. She has also gone to great lengths to share her own 'readings' of her films through numerous interviews and essays.

Trinh's films aim to deliberately blur the boundaries of genre. Her documentaries such as Reassemblage (1982) on Senegal, Naked Spaces—Living is Round (1985) on rural West Africa, Surname Viet Given Name Nam (1989) on Vietnamese female subjectivity, Shoot for the Contents (1991) on culture and politics in China, and The Fourth Dimension (2001), a digital video on Japanese culture, all incorporate narrative and poetic language, carefully manipulated visuals, and experimental sounds and music. Moreover, her films use nonlinear structure, silences, abrupt jump cuts, repetition of images and sounds, and unsynched rhythms. She also uses almost random panning to, in her words, avoid moving from one captured object to another, and to expose the limits of a camera eye that purports to present the viewer with a unified, 'objective' package. In all her films, Trinh repeats diverse images and sounds with slight changes in an effort to displace viewers and to avoid the certainty and closure of traditional documentaries.

Trinh questions the motives and methods of commercial filmmaking through her own departures from mainstream conventions, which serve to foreground and interrogate these practices. For example, instead of speaking for or speaking about her subjects, Trinh describes her position as 'speaking nearby'. None of her works use a traditional, objective, male voice-over concerned with informing spectators about 'other' cultures. An example of her method is provided by Reassemblage, a montage of images and sounds of the everyday life of women and children in Senegal. This film features Trinh's own voice, which, according to interviewer Berenice Reynaud, proves 'unsettling', since the narrative is 'unmistakably feminine, unmistakably foreign, hesitant yet resolute, ironical yet poetic' (Trinh 1999). Naked Spaces, on life in Senegal, Mauritania, Mali, Burkina Faso, Benin, and Togo, also departs from the omniscient voice-over with three female narrators from different yet nonconflicting stances.

Trinh's departure from traditional documentary practice is most evident in Surname Viet Given Name Nam. The film includes staged reenactments of interviews with Vietnamese women, although the viewer is never informed that the interviews are inauthentic. Surname also confronts viewers with a barrage of voices, in the form of simultaneous voice-overs, written text, and speech in both English and Vietnamese. Shoot for the Contents, Trinh's film about Chinese culture, features narration by two Chinese American women, a series of interviews, and Trinh's own voice. Again, not all of the language is translated, drawing attention to the notion, as Trinh has pointed out, that documentaries constitute a form of translation on both the part of the filmmaker or speaker, and the spectator.

Trinh's films feature both difference and similarity within differences. The appearance of a different albino child in her two films about Africa, the use of Vietnamese Americans in the staged interviews of women in Surname, and the appearance of an African American interviewee speaking on Chinese culture in Shoot all function as subtle reminders of the unfixed boundaries of subjectivity. As Trinh has noted, most documentaries use scholars or other 'experts' on a culture to push the filmmaker's message. Her practice of featuring nonexperts or unexpected voices of authority calls that into question and asserts the mobility of marginalized peoples across boundaries. Trinh's own relationship to Africa, Vietnam, China, and Japan in her documentaries underscores the shifting quality of insider/outsider status. Although she is an outsider filming these peoples, as a Vietnamese American she shares their marginalization by Western culture.

In recent years, Trinh has incorporated more narrative into her work. The Fourth Dimension (1991) is a visual essay on time and ritual. A Tale of Love (1995), a story about a Vietnamese American model who investigates a traditional Vietnamese love poem, and Night Passage (2004), on a spiritual journey undertaken by two Asian women and a little boy, are both feature-length narratives.

SHARON SHELTON-COLANGELO

Biography

Born in Hanoi, Viet Nam, in 1952. Graduated from Wilmington College in Ohio in 1972 with a BA in French literature and music. Received MA in French literature in 1973, MFA in music composition in 1976, and PhD in French literature in 1977 from the University of Illinois. Taught at the National Conservatory of Music in Dakar, Senegal, and in US universities including San Francisco State, Cornell, and Harvard. Currently teaches in the Departments of Women's Studies and Rhetoric at the University of California at Berkeley. Winner of numerous awards including the 1991 AFI National Independent Filmmaker Maya Deren Award, the 1992 Sundance Film Festival Jury's Best Cinematography Award, the 1992 Athens International Film Festival Best Experimental Feature Documentary, the 1990 American Film and Video Festival's first-prize Blue Ribbon Award for Best Film as Art Feature, the 1990 Society for the Encouragement of Contemporary Art's first prize Film as Art Award, the 1990 Bombay International Film Festival's Merit Award, the 1987 American Film and Video Festival's first prize Blue Ribbon Award for Best Experimental Feature, the 1986 Athens International Film Festival's Golden Athena Award for Best Feature Documentary, the 1984 Hong Kong International Film Festival's Certificate of Recognition, and the 1982 Humboldt State Film Festival's Honorable Mention Award.

Selected films

1982 Reassemblage
1985 Naked Spaces—Living is Round
1989 Surname Viet Given Name Nam
1991 Shoot for the Contents
2001 The Fourth Dimension

Further reading

Feng, Peter X, *Identities in Motion: Asian American Film and Video*, Durham, NC: Duke University Press, 2002.

Foster, Gwendolyn Audrey, *Women Filmmakers of the African and Asian Diaspora: Decolonizing the Gaze, Locating Subjectivity*, Carbondale, IL: Southern Illinois Press, 1977.

MacDonald, Scott, *Avant-Garde Film: Motion Studies*, New York: Cambridge University Press, 1993.

Meskimmon, Marsha, *Women Making Art: History, Subjectivity, Aesthetics*, New York: Routledge, 2003.

Peckham, Linda, 'Surname Viet Given Name Nam: Spreading Rumors & Ex/Changing Histories', in Peter X. Feng (ed.), *Screening Asian-Americans*, New Brunswick, NJ: Rutgers University Press, 2002.

Trinh T. Minh-ha, *Women, Native, Other: Writing Postcoloniality and Feminism*, Bloomington, IN: Indiana University Press, 1989.

——*When the Moon Waxes Red: Representation, Gender and Cultural Politics*, New York: Routledge, 1991.

——*Framer Framed*, New York: Routledge, 1992.

——*Cinema Interval*, New York: Routledge, 1999.

Triumph of the Will

(Germany, Riefenstahl, 1935)

Triumph of the Will/Triumph des Willens is a documentary—some have even called it a staged documentary—of the Nationalist Socialist Party rally held in Nuremberg in 1934. One of the best-known documentaries ever made and certainly the best-known German documentary, Triumph des Willens brought its director Leni

Riefenstahl both fame and infamy that continued to follow her throughout her life. The controversy surrounding the filmmaker and her film focused on three major issues: the extent to which the Ministry of Propaganda, under the control of Joseph Goebbels, was involved in the project; the degree to which the film is an authentic document of history; and the genuineness of Riefenstahl's claim that she did not make the film because of any belief in or support for the ideology of National Socialism.

The genesis of the making of a documentary film of the 1934 National Socialist Party Congress in Nuremberg contributes to doubts that Riefenstahl worked independently of National Socialist control on Triumph des Willens. One year earlier the director had completed a film on the 1933 Party Congress, Sieg des Glaubens/Victory of Faith (1933). The film was short, according to accounts, either because Riefenstahl had not been informed by Joseph Goebbels that she was to make the film and thus, with only three cameramen to assist her, hurried it into production only a few days before the Congress was to begin (Hinton 1978: 28) or because Goebbels placed so many obstacles in her path during production that she could not get enough footage. Her difficulties with Goebbels, whether preproduction or during production, reportedly moved Hitler to offer her a chance to direct a film of the 1934 Nuremberg Congress, which she at first declined (Infield 1976: 62).

Riefenstahl initially turned down directorial duties for Triumph des Willens to work on a narrative feature film Tiefland/Lowlands (1940–53). She turned the project over to Walther Ruttmann, director of Berlin: Die Synfonie der Großstadt/Berlin: The Symphony of a Great City (1927), who completed the opening credit sequence before Riefenstahl, at Hitler's insistence, took over directorial duties. Perhaps because Hitler was intent on having Riefenstahl make the movie (Berg-Pan 1980: 98), the director insisted on three conditions: the film had to be made by her production company, neither Hitler nor Goebbels could see the film before completion, and Hitler would never ask her to make another film (Hinton 1978: 30). Yet even if her production company made the movie, evidence indicates that the main source of financing came from the Nazi Party. Moreover the Party's cooperation before and during filming suggests that even if Riefenstahl had artistic control, the film nonetheless suggests outside involvement.

Persistent allegations that Triumph des Willens is not a genuine documentary, but that the events of the party congress were staged for the film, can be traced back to Siegfried Kracauer's comments in his book *From Caligari to Hitler*. Kracauer insists that 'the Convention was planned not only as a spectacular mass meeting, but also as spectacular film propaganda' (Kracauer 1947: 301). Susan Sontag, in her essay 'Fascinating Fascism', likewise claims that Riefenstahl's film 'was from the beginning, conceived as the set of a film spectacle' (Sontag 1975: 24), backing up her accusation with a quote from a book that Riefenstahl published in 1935 in which the director wrote that 'the ceremonies and precise plans of the parades, marches, processions, the architecture of the halls and stadium were designed for the convenience of the cameras' (Sontag 1975: 25). On the other hand, that the rally accommodated Riefenstahl's crews does not prove that the film rally was staged for the documentary. David Hinton asks: 'is it really logical to presume that the Rally, and the architecture designed for it, would have been any different without the presence of Riefenstahl and her camera crews?' (Hinton 1978: 55).

Riefenstahl's commitment to Nazi ideology, as related to Triumph des Willens, is unambiguous for most critics. Berg-Pan summarizes the film's reception in her book on Riefenstahl, concluding herself that 'there is little doubt, however, that no director or producer could have made a film such as Triumph of the Will without having an avid interest in the subject: Hitler and the Nazi Party'. Riefenstahl herself, however, maintained that the film was simply the result of accepting a commission to document history: 'A commission was proposed to me. Good. I accepted. Good. I agreed, like so many others, to make a film [...] It is history. A pure historical film [...] It reflects the truth as it was then' (quoted in Berg-Pan 1980: 127). As late as 1997, when Riefenstahl was interviewed by Ray Mueller for a documentary on the filmmaker, Riefenstahl maintained that she was not political and neither was her film.

Critics may disagree about the extent of Nazi participation in the planning and producing of the film, the integrity of the film as a document of a genuinely historical rally, and Riefenstahl's commitment to the Nazi cause. Yet, they are unanimous in their belief that the film is a powerful work of Nazi propaganda, owing to Leni Riefenstahl's insistence on artistic perfection.

The director's skill for creating emotional response in viewers through editing, image content, and soundtrack is indeed astonishing, although the incessant marching scenes and speechifying might lessen the impact on nonsympathetic viewers. That is, removed from the historical context, audiences, whether German or non-German, could easily find the film tedious.

That contemporary audiences were moved by the film testifies to Riefenstahl's love of movement. The film differs from the newsreels or documentaries of the time in that the film is never static, and because of the flow of images, the film can eschew conventional narration. Riefenstahl attributed the movie's power as follows: 'It's a feeling for links between images, a connection between one picture and the next [...] or from one visual colour-range, say from grey tones, to another. It's like a musical composition. It's very important to put a climax at the right point in a film [...] so that there's a continuous build-up.'

A close analysis of any of the twelve to sixteen sequences (depending on how one divides the segments) reveals that Riefenstahl did indeed score the film's images like a musical composition, beginning with quiet images, for example, a plane flying through the clouds (opening sequence showing Hitler's arrival in Nuremberg), a glimpse of church towers in the morning dawn (third sequence introducing labor's role in Nazi Germany), and a roll call of workers (fifth sequence, relating labor's role to the military). She intensified the scenes, building excitement through faster and faster editing (opening sequence), a series of segments displaying an escalating degree of fun among the camp participants (third sequence), and increasing emotional content (fifth sequence). She ended each of these sequences with a crescendo, crowds along a parade route shouting 'Heil Hitler' (first sequence), participants being tossed high in the air in a blanket (third sequence), and flags that had been lowered being suddenly lifted into the air (fifth sequence). Scenes of dramatic intensity are interspersed with ones of tranquility. Thus sequence two shows a crowd outside Hitler's window at night. The screen reveals points of light in an otherwise dark landscape. The camera slowly glides over underlit images finding rest on the words 'Heil Hitler', which are flanked by Nazi flags. Sequence four presents the Nazi leadership, each speaker iterating the theme of Hitler's contribution of work and peace to the nation. In these sequences and throughout the film, the motion and rest seem paramount, as Riefenstahl emphasized what she viewed as the movie's main themes, employment and peace, and underscores the idea that Germany was improving because of Hitler.

If Triumph des Willens emphasizes the themes of work and peace, it does so, as many film historians and critics have pointed out, to present, or even sell, Hitler and the Nazis first to the German people and then to the rest of the world. Although the Party had been in existence since the early 1920s, and Adolf Hitler had gained notoriety through the Munich Putsch (1924) and was known to Germans as the head of the National Socialist Party and as a member of parliament, he and his party had been in power only nineteen months, as the film proclaims in its prologue. The footage of Victory of Faith, Riefenstahl's attempt at filming the Nazi Rally of 1933, shows a more chaotic meeting. More important, the footage suggests a less central role for its leader, who appears as part of the Nazi leadership, rather than above and apart from it. For example, during one speech, *Sturmabteilung* (SA, Storm Section) leader Ernst Röhm appears next to and on the same level as Hitler. By the time of the 1934 Rally, Hitler's clique in the Party was beginning to solidify its power, having assassinated Ernst Röhm and other SA members a few months early in a violent purge known as the 'Night of the Long Knives'.

Viewed from this historical context, Triumph des Willens becomes more than a movie to sell Hitler and the Nazis to the public. It becomes one of the first films of the Nazi era to legitimize him and the Party, to place National Socialism into German history, indeed into world history. The opening credits, for example, imprinted in Gothic script and styled like woodcarvings, create a link to Nuremberg, the city of emperors and also the city of the great artist Albrecht Dürer. The text further relates Nazi Germany to the Germany of Kaiser Wilhelm, lamenting Germany's defeat in World War I and proclaiming its rebirth, thus jumping over and essentially discounting the intervening years of the Weimar Republic. The opening scene of Hitler's arrival continues the fusion of past and present, as Hitler deplanes to cheering crowds as a returning Roman leader might have marched triumphant in earlier times. The soundtrack in this scene intones Herbert Windt's score, which here approaches the grandeur of Wagnerian opera, followed by the strains of the Nazi anthem, 'Die Fahne hoch'. In sequence four Windt's soundtrack continues, weaving a thread between past and present, as a melody from Wagner's *Meistersinger von Nürnberg* underscores a visual of Nuremberg's cathedral towers in the dawn. The subsequent sequence varies the theme, showing how universally German the Nazi movement is, presenting workers individually and in unison from every part of Germany, united under Hitler. However, even a connection is made to the past, as the workers take part in a ceremony honoring the fallen heroes of World War I. The scene is meant to once again connect pre-1918 Germany to Nazi Germany and remind viewers at the same time of the ignominy forced on the country by the intervening and now past years of the Weimar Republic, whose books had been burned in a sequence preceding this one. Throughout the film Riefenstahl makes connections between Germany past (pre-1918) to Germany present, German regionalism to Germany united, German youth to German leadership.

Triumph des Willens is much more than Riefenstahl's interpretation of a simple documentation of Hitler and what he meant to the German populace. It is also more than a propaganda document meant to introduce Hitler and more than a love feast meant to impress and scare with its scenes of unity and militaristic power. Feature films of the Third Reich were generally not political in theme, but their content was certainly political in that they were concerned with German classics, historical leaders, and great men of letters, hoping the viewer would make the association between Nazi Germany and past German greatness. In similar fashion, Riefenstahl's film is also not political, or not just political. It is a narrative playing to the emotions of a public wanting answers to problems but also wanting to connect to a more heroic German past.

Although we cannot answer definitively whether the Nuremberg Rally was genuine, whether the Nazis or Riefenstahl produced the movie, and whether Riefenstahl supported Nazi ideology, it is clear that the overly controlled nature of the film's style produces the effect of something that was staged. Furthermore, there is no doubt that the Nazis benefited from the film, whether or not they were involved in its making. Finally, whether or not Riefenstahl supported Nazi ideology, her film clearly does. The movie is an undeniably powerful piece of propaganda filmmaking, glorifying the political and military power of the Nazis. Riefenstahl uses the human form as architectural building blocks, elevates military marching into a religious ritual, and encloses and opens space with banners, flags, and columns.

Whether one sees the film as serving the art of documentary filmmaking or the evils of National Socialism, however, there is no denying its effect as propaganda and its influence on filmmakers. Erwin Leiser uses several scenes from the film, including the well-known sequence of the Nazi labor corps (earlier discussed as sequence five) in his documentary Mein Kampf (1960). Directors of entertainment films have also referenced Riefenstahl, including George Lucas in Star Wars (1977), Lewis Teague in Jewel of the Nile (1985), Jim Sharman in The Rocky Horror Picture Show (1975), and Paul Verhoeven in Starship Troopers (1997).

ROBERT C. REIMER

See also: Mein Kampf; Riefenstahl, Leni

Triumph of the Will/Triumph des Willens (Germany, Riefenstahl, 1935, 114 mins). Produced by Leni Riefenstahl-Produktion and NSDAP Reichsleitung. Directed by Leni Riefenstahl. Written by Leni Riefenstahl and Walter Ruttmann.

Further reading

Berg-Pan, Renata, *Leni Riefenstahl*, Boston: Twayne Publishers, 1980.

Hinton, David B., *The Films of Leni Riefenstahl*, Metuchen, NJ: Scarecrow Press, 1978.

Hull, David Stewart, *Film in the Third Reich: A Study of the German Cinema 1933–45*, Berkeley, CA: University of California Press, 1969.

Infield, Glenn B., *Leni Riefenstahl: The Fallen Film Goddess*, New York: Thomas Y. Crowell, 1976.

Kracauer, Siegfried, *From Caligari to Hitler: A Psychological Study of the German Film*, Princeton, NJ: Princeton University Press, 1947.

n.a., 'Leni Riefenstahl—Regisseurin, Schauspielerin', in Hans-Michael Bock (ed.), *Cinegraph: Lexikon zum deutschsprachigen Film*, Munich, 1984.

Schwartzman, Roy J., 'Racial Theory and Propaganda in Triumph of the Will', in Bonnie Braendlin and Hans Braendlin (eds), *Authority and*

Transgression in Literature and Film, Gainesville, FL: University Press of Florida, 1996: 136–51.
Sontag, Susan, 'Fascinating Fascism', *The New York Review of Books*, February 6, 1975: 23–5.

Troubles We've Seen, The

(France, Ophüls, 1994)

Although the primary topic of the film is the war in Bosnia and its journalistic coverage, Veillees d'armes: le journalisme en temps de guerre, 1er et 2ème voyages/The Troubles We've Seen: A History of Journalism in Wartime, 1st and 2nd Journeys, Marcel Ophüls's postmodern documentary collage, is dedicated to a wider investigation into Western reporting on conflict and its underlying motives. To Ophüls, concern for others is only an extension of a self-centered interest, hence the variety of inherent ethical tensions found in international news production.

Troubles was produced by the director's friend Bertrand Tavernier, who secured most of the financing (Jacobsen 1996). Contributions to the budget were made by the BBC (quoted at £80,000) and by the French subsidy system. The plan was to make a three-part documentary, but by 1994 only two parts were completed and shown. Ophüls has said on various occasions that Troubles should be regarded as a work in progress. There were indications that in the late 1990s he was still thinking of completing it, but no third part had been released as of 2011.

The first two parts of what was supposed to be a trilogy, First Journey (92 mins) and Second Journey (139 mins) were screened at the closing day of Cannes Film Festival in 1994, with little preliminary information released. Later, the film was screened at the festivals in Toronto and New York and was broadcast by the BBC in September 1995.

Ophüls's central concern is the effect of the media's instant and continuous live reporting on Western perceptions and reactions to conflicts abroad. He looks into a wide spectrum of journalistic behaviour by placing it into the framework of morality in war reporting. Even though the focus is on Bosnia, there are numerous references to media coverage and construction of past conflicts, mostly the Gulf War, but also the Vietnam War, World War II, and the Spanish civil war. In an interview, Ophüls hinted that it was the distinction between legitimate show business and 'perverted show business' that sustained his interest in news production and international conflict coverage (Jacobsen 1996).

The two parts of the film are structured loosely around two journeys to Bosnia, with the first part concentrated mostly on the logistics and the morals of reporting from the war zone and the second on war reporting at the recipient end and its function within the Western (mainly French) public discourse. Even though the filmed interviews are cut and presented in a mosaic fashion, one can distinguish two main spheres of investigation. In Bosnia, Ophüls talks to numerous Western journalists based in Sarajevo (*The New York Times*' John F. Burns, the BBC's John Simpson, France Presse's Remi Oudran, TF1's Isabelle Ballancourt), uses footage of reporters such as Christiane Amanpour (CNN) and Martin Bell (BBC), and enters street dialogues with some ordinary inhabitants of the city and visiting Westerners (such as film director Romain Goupil). The investigation in this part looks mostly into the inherent ethical tensions of the trade and the journalist's special attitudes to danger, courage, and moral responsibility.

The second part explores the coverage of conflict as seen at the recipient's end, in Western Europe, and mostly in France. Ophüls uses his friend Philippe Noiret to deliver some biting commentary on the indifference of French politicians and their evasive PR strategy over Bosnia. He features interviews with intellectual critic Alain Finkielkraut and with self-proclaimed humanitarian Bernard Kouchner. No one is spared, from General Philippe Morillon to Simone Veil and François Mitterand; all are shown making compromising statements. Ophüls also challenges the superficial approach of French TV star anchor Patrick Poivre d'Arvoir, dispatched into Sarajevo on a twenty-four-hour parachute-style visit.

In this film Ophüls is particularly sensitive to the 'rhetorical potency of Eisensteinian montage' (Lopate 1994). He cuts back and forth between seemingly unconnected footage, to impose his own political associations on the viewer and build the argument. From a Serb priest blessing a house, he cuts to an archival newsreel of a Nazi cleric blessing the troops. He exposes the evasiveness of the United Nations (UN) by featuring embarrassing press conference moments of officials such as José María Mendiluce and Boutros Boutros-Ghali. He adds scenes of

President Clinton's jogging routine, President Mitterand's interview with the wife of one of his own ministers, and footage of public statements made by Chancellor Kohl and Prime Minister John Major. In addition, the film cross-references a range of well-known Hollywood pictures—from the Marx brothers' Duck Soup (1933) and Max Ophüls's De Mayerling à Sarajevo (1940), to Mark Sandrich's Holiday Inn (1942) and Fellini's 8½ (1963)—to sharpen the contrast between a self-obsessed West and a forsaken Bosnia. A frequently used ironic device, for example, is Bing Crosby's song from the film Holiday Inn, hummed by the war correspondents stationed at the infamous 'Holiday Inn' hotel in Sarajevo. Another sequence of the film shows a woman and child running through a snowy square in Sarajevo to escape sniper fire. The background music is the song 'White Christmas', again from Holiday Inn.

Yet another line of referencing is the inclusion of staged episodes from everyday life routines in the West, once again asserting the indifferent attitude of ordinary Westerners to conflict between faraway peoples. These include footage from Venice; for example, like Sarajevo, it is a dying city, yet one that is absorbed by its self-importance. Ophüls does not spare himself either, and extends the sarcasm by including a set-up scene showing him in a Viennese hotel room, shortly after he has left Sarajevo, discussing the Bosnian project on the phone, while in the background a naked woman sips champagne, waiting for him in bed. It is a clear statement of self-criticism: as a Westerner he is, by default, complicit in the attitudes he exposes.

As far as the Bosnian dimension of the film is concerned, Ophüls never becomes too involved, even though he has declared his official commitment to the plight of Bosnian Muslims. During his Northern Ireland investigation in Sense of Loss (1972) he talked extensively to the ordinary victims of terror, but in Sarajevo his discussions with local people are restricted to occasional street interviews. Although present throughout the film, the experiences of ordinary Bosnians remain outside the main narrative and do not integrate into the investigation, which remains preoccupied with Western journalists' coverage of the conflict.

As a legendary filmmaker, Ophüls enjoys privileged treatment and is granted exclusive interviews with some of the main players in the conflict, including Nikola Koljević, Radovan Karadzić, and Slobodan Milošević. Because his investigative focus lies elsewhere, however, he does not make much use of this rare material and only includes occasional sound bites from these conversations. Pursuing his own line of inquiry, he takes this particular conflict as a backdrop for the moral investigation that evolves around Western coverage.

Ophüls neglects important statements made by the Yugoslav and Bosnian players and fails to analyse the rhetoric of blaming Western media coverage, widely practised by these politicians. Many of the issues discussed in The Troubles We've Seen make sense only in the wider context of themes such as history, remembrance, and morality, which have been the focus of Ophüls's work throughout his career. It is a context in which Bosnia's function is of a case study, a background against which he develops his views.

The main line of inquiry in Marcel Ophüls's work has always been a moralistic one, from dissecting the reasons why ordinary people turn a blind eye to historical horrors such as the deportation of Jews in occupied France (The Sorrow and the Pity, 1971; The Memory of Justice, 1976; Hotel Terminus, 1988), through exposing the tragic consequences of the mismanaged dialogue in Northern Ireland (A Sense of Loss, 1972), to dealing with the side effects of the German reunification (November Days, 1992). Ophüls's mature brand of investigative sarcasm sets the tone also in Troubles, where he once again looks into the question of why knowledge of injustice and atrocities does not change the outcome of conflicts and why Western politics are once again inoperative when confronted with abundant evidence of ethnic cleansing and terror. Opening with evidence of uninformed shallowness in war reporting, he explores whether the superficiality in reporting is due to intrinsic media patterns or to the deeply ingrained smugness of institutionalised consumer culture. He remains sceptical about the possibility of adequately conveying information across borders and cultures. Some critics read his pessimism as a general 'radical scepticism about the moral decency of any image-making' (Lopate 1994: 74), whereas others found that the turns of his investigation were taking 'rambling, frequently surprising ways' and were excessively subjective (Maslin 1994). Yet, given the fact that officially sanctioned injustice was Ophüls's life-long topic and that the métier of the director was exposing complicity in all its subtle forms, according to others, Troubles was to be seen as a logical continuation in his earlier investigations (Jacobsen 1996).

As with most of Ophüls's other films, the reception of Troubles was a mixture of admiration and reservation over the ponderous and long-winded format that causes 'bafflement and irritation' (Dunkley 1995). Once again, critics noted, it was a profoundly subjective piece of work, which never pretends otherwise. Even though the film was seen as 'too elliptical' (Dunkley 1995), critics noted with satisfaction that Ophüls had managed to once again successfully sustain his obstinate role as a 'thorn in the side of all authorities' (Jacobsen 1996) and that it was 'tremendously valuable to have one person ignoring the perpetual straining after balance and objectivity to go instead for ultra subjectivity' (Dunkley 1995). Many critics questioned the associative choices made by the director, but all were unanimous that if one is ready to trust Ophüls and follow his investigation, many answers become clear at the end.

In an international political climate marked by a continuous range of armed conflicts and civil wars, the theme of The Troubles We Have Seen remains persistently important. The film became topical, once again, with the 2002 resignation of the Dutch government over revelations of the 1995 inaction of its soldiers in the Bosnian safe heaven in Srebrenitza, which resulted in the deaths of more than seven thousand Bosnian men. Alongside academic investigations on the workings of media in covering armed clashes (by authors such as Daniel Hallin, Philip Taylor, Tim Allen, Jean Seaton, Susan Carruthers, and others), Troubles could be considered a classical work on issues of media and international coverage. Even in its unfinished format, the film should be made available to wider audiences.

DINA IORDANOVA

See also: Ophüls, Marcel; Sorrow and the Pity, The

The Troubles We Have Seen: A History of Journalism in Wartime (1st and 2nd Journeys)/ Veillees d'armes: le journalisme en temps de guerre (1er et 2ème voyages) (France/UK/ Germany, Little Bear Productions (Paris); premiere (Germany), with the participation of Canal+, BBC, 1994, 231 mins). Produced by Bertrand Tavernier and Frederic Bourboulon. Directed and written by Marcel Ophüls. Cinematography by Pierre Boffrey, Pierre Milon. Assistant direction by Dominiki Moll, Laurent Cantet. Edited by Sophie Brunet. Sound by Michel Faure and Eric Devulder. Sound edited by Ariane Doublet. Filmed in Sarajevo, Zagreb, Vienna, Paris. Dialogue in English, French, German, Serbian and Croatian.

Further reading

Dunkley, Christopher, 'War from a Different Perspective', *Financial Times*, September 2, 1995: xii.

Iordanova, Dina, *Cinema of Flames: Balkan Film, Culture and the Media*, London: BFI, 2001: 153–5.

Jacobsen, Kurt, 'Memories of Injustice: Marcel Ophuls's Cinema of Conscience', *Film Comment* 32, no. 4, July 1996: 61–71 (includes an interview with Ophüls).

Johnson, William, 'A Short Take on Long Films, Very Long Films', *Film Comment* 31, no. 5, September 1995: 78.

Lopate, Phillip, 'New York Film Festival', *Film Comment* 30, no. 6, November 1994: 72–7.

Maslin, Janet, 'A Report on Reporters in the World's Hot Spots', *The New York Times*, October 6, 1994: C-17.

Nesselson, Lisa, 'The Troubles We Have Seen', *Variety*, June 19, 1994.

True Glory, The

(UK, Carol Reed, 1945)

The last film in the victory series—which included Desert Victory (1943), Tunisian Victory (1944), and Burma Victory (1945)—The True Glory covers the period from the preparations for the D-Day landings in Normandy through the fall of Berlin to the establishing of contact between the Western Allies and Soviet troops at the Elbe River. Made from five and a half million feet of combat footage shot by five hundred American, British, and other Allied cameramen, it is a vast panorama, yet intensely human, even intimate at moments.

Emotional involvement is gained largely through the experimental use of commentary. Alternating with blank verse choruses are multiple voices representing soldiers involved with the particular action being shown. The words are complementary to the images, sometimes in humorous or ironic counterpoint to them. The general's version, spoken by Dwight D. Eisenhower himself, supreme commander of Allied forces in Europe, is irreverently interrupted by enlisted men who were there: New York cab driver, cockney Londoner, member of the French Maquis, and others. One marvelous moment occurs when a black American MP directing military traffic at a crossroads explains that the situation is tough, that the invasion forces are bottled up in the Caen Pennisula. 'Then we heard that the Third Army was taking off', he says. 'They'd pulled a rabbit out of a hat—and what a rabbit! A rabbit with pearl-handled revolvers'. As he says this a tank bearing an erect General George S. Patton roars by.

The True Glory was the triumphant record and hymn to Allied victory in Europe. The occasion permitted a kind of boasting and self-congratulation without it appearing to be so. Pride is expressed in the massiveness and efficiency of the military machine and in its democratic nature. The participation of many nations is indirectly reiterated without explicit statement being required. The Allied attitude toward war is presented as being purposeful and matter-of-fact, its violence accepted as part of a job to be done, as in the British semi-documentaries (Target for Tonight, 1941; Fires Were Started, 1943; Western Approaches, 1944). Unlike the semi-documentaries, however, dislike and distrust of the German enemy are strongly stated. The horrors of what the advancing forces found at the Belsen concentration camp are included. An American GI, talking about guarding German prisoners of war, says: 'I just kept 'em covered […] It wasn't my job to figure 'em out […] But, brother, I never gave 'em more than the Geneva convention, and that was all'. Finally, though, it is the positive corollary of the GI's attitude that receives the strongest emphasis. What The True Glory is saying mostly is that this was a just and necessary war and that those on the Allied side can all feel proud of their part in winning it. Like Desert Victory before it, it was awarded an Oscar by the Academy of Motion Picture Arts and Sciences as 'the most Outstanding Documentary Feature of 1945'.

JACK C. ELLIS

See also: Burma Victory; Desert Victory; Tunisian Victory

The True Glory (US/UK, British Army Film and Photographic Unit and American and Allied Film Services, 1945, 87 mins). Distributed by Office of War Information and Ministry of Information. Produced and directed by Carol Reed and Garson Kanin. Screenplay by Eric Maschwitz, Arthur Macrae, Jenny Nicholson, Gerald Kersh, Guy Trosper. Music by William Alwyn. Cinematography by British Army Film Unit and American Army Pictorial Service. Editing supervision by Robert Verrell; edited by Leiberwitz, Bob Farrell, Jerry Cowen, Bob Carrick, Bob Clarke. Commentary read by Robert Harris.

True Story of Lili Marlene, The

(UK, Jennings, 1943)

The True Story of Lili Marlene raises important questions relating not only to the films of Humphrey Jennings but to the entire British documentary film movement, and indeed to any canonical hierarchy selected from a more general range of expression and discussion. The films that we write about and remember contribute much to our critical attitudes and our historical understanding. A closer look at the films that we have not remembered reminds us of how arbitrary the processes of selection and validation can be.

Discussions about the work of Humphrey Jennings have often proceeded in terms of masterpieces and also-rans, with the latter quickly disappearing from view. Contemporary reports suggest that this division is rooted in the initial reactions to the various films. The acknowledged masterpieces Listen to Britain, I Was a Fireman/ Fires Were Started, and A Diary for Timothy were much remarked upon and generally, though not universally, appreciated from the start. Some of the other films, less effective, or perhaps more elusive, also elicited immediate responses, which seem for the most part to have been quite a bit cooler.

The hardening of this division into a kind of received wisdom probably begins with Lindsay Anderson's celebrated appreciation of Jennings's work, which first appeared in *Sight and Sound* in 1954. This critical eulogy, entitled 'Only Connect', is a superb piece of sympathetic criticism that is largely evaluative. This is to say that Anderson is speaking of good films and bad films, and that his judgments are based on criteria that are more personal than they are textual or historical. The result is a critical position that is quite defensible without being quite comprehensive.

The Humphrey Jennings in Anderson's portrait is an intellectual and a propagandist, who in his finest work avoids by his great humanity the pitfalls of these parts, the elitist inaccessibility and the hectoring coercion to which intellectuals and propagandists are prone. This is certainly a true likeness, or at least part of one, and through its continued inclusion (Jacobs 1975; MacDonald and Cousins 1996) or reflection (by Barnouw, Ellis, Barsam) in the most popular documentary anthologies and histories, it has become a matter of record.

In a survey sense this is as it should be, but connected to all this enthusiasm there has emerged a consistent and connected idea that appears even in the more specialized studies of Jennings's work. This idea is that the other, more complicated elements of Jennings's personal and aesthetic makeup—the scholarly complexity, the intellectual's irony, the surrealist's awareness of the indeterminate—are not as easy to contain or to comprehend. It is suggested that the films that are reflective of these less tractable qualities are less coherent, less representative, and, finally, less useful.

The True Story of Lili Marlene is one of these films, and if its almost universal dismissal needs reconsidering, then its undoubted difficulties also need to be accounted for. Both its subject and treatment are unlikely. It traces the permutations of a sentimental German song, 'Lili Marlene', from its first appearance in the 1920s, through its appropriation as part of the Nazi propaganda machine, to its final 'capture' and recouping by the victorious Allies. Its careful juxtapositions and its telling use of music are typical of Jennings's work, but the lack of a real protagonist, single or collective, and the lack of a clearly unifying mood or message or even through line separate it from the best known and, most would say, the best of his films.

The record suggests that Jennings himself was frustrated during the film's production and not fully satisfied with the final result. It is not coincidental that this frustration, the mixed feelings and lack of focus, would become the explicit subject of Jennings's next film and last unequivocal success, A Diary for Timothy. With regard to finding a place for Lili Marlene, it could at the very least be argued that its production provided a refining space in which Jennings confronted and came to terms with his own confusions, the better to counsel with and console his countrymen in their own.

However, Lili Marlene has merit beyond its contribution to more acclaimed works. As with Jennings's similarly underconsidered Eighty Days and The Silent Village (both 1943), in this film we see the intellectual emerging from beneath his propagandist's banner. If the results are uncertain then it is at least partly because Jennings is exploring new ground, both in representing the war and in critically questioning the documentary film's place in that representation.

Lili Marlene reveals much about the conflict during late 1943 and early 1944, as well as the state of the nation and its citizens. With the tide having turned and victory becoming a real possibility, the need for unambiguously reassuring propaganda gave way and made room for admissions of doubt and vulnerability, for searching and questioning. If Eighty Days hints at how bewildered and broken the victims of German bombings must have been, even in the days when London was proclaiming how well it could take it, then Lili Marlene reaffirms the common ground—humanity, sentimentality and sentiment, susceptibility to suggestion—that all of the combatants shared.

It is particularly in exploring that susceptibility, in turning its gaze on its own workings, that Lili Marlene marks an advance, however tentative, in the history and maturing of the documentary film, most particularly in Britain. The elusiveness of its story suggests that story is only the ostensible subject, a means to investigate the rhetorical and ideological underpinnings of our unquestioned communications. Its formal and narrative strategies and its much criticized unconventionality and artificiality all inhibit conventional illusion and identification, allowing for and even demanding a deeper intellectual engagement. This is not a propaganda film, so much as it is a film about propaganda.

The True Story of Lili Marlene raises the possibility that there is a substantial neutrality in the songs, stories, ideas, and representations that we take to heart and take for granted. It is no wonder, then, that a wartime film about propaganda's neutral nature, and its susceptibility to tone and context, a film that exposes the workings of narrativity by tracing the history of a not-so-Nazi air, did not quite motivate the masses like the standard words for battle. These many years later such notions are familiar and just as disconcerting. Jennings's neglected film deserves credit and attention for its contribution to this current and always relevant discussion.

DEAN DUNCAN

See also: Diary for Timothy, A; Fires Were Started; Jennings, Humphrey; Listen to Britain

The True Story of Lili Marlene (UK, Crown Film Unit, 1943, 30 mins). Produced by J.B. Holmes. Direction and script by Humphrey Jennings. Narrated by Marius Goring. Cinematography by Henry 'Chick' Fowle. Music by Dennis Blood, directed by Muir Mathieson. Edited by Sid Stone. Sound by Ken Cameron.

Further reading

Brecht, Bertolt, 'The Modern Theatre is the Epic Theatre', in John Willett (ed. and trans.), *Brecht on Theatre*, New York: Hill and Wang, 1957.

Hodgkinson, Anthony W. and Sheratsky, Rodney E., *Humphrey Jennings: More than a Maker of Films*, Hanover, NH: University Press of New England, 1982.

Jackson, Kevin (ed.), *The Humphrey Jennings Film Reader*, Manchester: Carcanet Press, 1993.

Jacobs, Lewis (ed.), *The Documentary Tradition*, New York: Hopkinson and Blake, 1979.

Jennings, Mary-Lou (ed.), *Humphrey Jennings: Film-Maker, Painter, Poet*, London: British Film Institute, 1982.

MacDonald, Kevin and Cousins, Mark, *Imagining Reality: The Faber Book of Documentary*, London: Faber, 1996.

Sussex, Elizabeth, *The Rise and Fall of British Documentary*, Berkeley, CA: University of California Press, 1975.

Swann, Paul, *The British Documentary Film Movement*, Cambridge: Cambridge University Press, 1989.

Winston, Brian, *Claiming the Real*, London: British Film Institute, 1995.

Tsuchimoto Noriaki

One of the most important directors of his generation, Tsuchimoto Noriaki was among the first Japanese documentary filmmakers to chart a genuinely independent course. In the process he became one of the most important directors of Japanese 'art' documentaries. His highly politicized, self-reflexive, predominantly 16mm films were distributed not by major studios but through a variety of independent routes. Along with his friend and colleague Ogawa Shinsuke, Tsuchimoto established a paradigm of steadfastly independent Japanese documentary filmmaking that remains influential to this day. Tsuchimoto's influence, however, extends not only to the construction and distribution of documentary films, but also to the social function and cultural status of documentary filmmaking. Between the 1960 rebellion against the Japanese-American security treaty and the even more violent protests against the renewal of that treaty in 1969 (protests that Tsuchimoto eloquently documented in Paruchizan zenshi/ Prehistory of the Partisans, 1969), a major shift in the meaning of documentary filmmaking occurred. At the start of the decade, the word documentary referred almost exclusively to purportedly objective public relations and social problem films; by its end, documentaries had become part of a vast spectrum of cinematic 'image arts' embraced, dissected, and internalized by a highly dynamic film culture. Tsuchimoto played a crucial part in effecting this transformation by pioneering a participatory, 'continual' mode of activist documentary that spilled over into reality, a mode exemplified by films such as Paruchizan zenshi and Ryugakusei Chua Sui Rin/Exchange Student Chua Swee Lin (1965).

Although he made his directorial debut with Aru kikanjoshi/An Engineer's Assistant (1962), Tsuchimoto's career proper began one year earlier when he became a founding member of 'Ao no Kai' (The Blue Group), a film research group that called for creative and financial independence. Ao no Kai was the documentary equivalent of the Shochiku nouvelle vague (made up of filmmakers such as Oshima Nagisa and Imamura Shohei and formed a year earlier), and the highly collaborative, experimental spirit of the group would remain a powerful influence on Tsuchimoto for the remainder of his career. In early PR films such as Aru kikanjoshi and Dokyumento rojo/Document: On the Road (1963), Tsuchimoto created highly evocative, lyrical portraits of ordinary Japanese workers notable for the precision of their montage and their acute sense of the rhythm of daily life. With Ryugakusei Chua Sui Rin, however, Tsuchimoto, a member of the newly formed 'Image Arts Society', became truly independent and broke new ground by partially dissolving the barrier between film and spectator. The film, about a Malaysian exchange student expelled from Chiba University for participating in the Malayan independence movement, reflected some of the major social issues of the day while also treating its protagonist as a multifaceted individual, not simply as fuel for an ideological argument. Indeed, as passionate and engaged as it is, Tsuchimoto's film never devolves into reductive propaganda. In yet another break with Japanese documentary tradition, rather than simply recording protests from a distance, it actually launched a movement in support of Chua Swee Lin.

Tsuchimoto extended his participatory approach in Paruchizan zenshi, a collaborative film documenting student preparations for the final phases of the 1969 protests against the renewal of the security treaty. The title of Tsuchimoto's most important theoretical book, *Film is the Work of a Living Thing*, is a cogent epigram for his methodology in this period, which focused on dynamic, starkly individual protagonists like Chua Swee Lin or Takita Osamu (the 'star' of Paruchizan zenshi) and called for audience activism. Tsuchimoto didn't want to simply overwhelm his audience with blind fervor, however, and made an effort to encourage reflection by creating a crucial distance from the action on screen at the moments of greatest emotional pitch. In the midst of a particularly tense scene in Paruchizan zenshi, for example, Tsuchimoto cuts from the increasingly virulent student protesters to a long shot of Kyoto University from the perspective of nearby Mt Hiei. This carefully modulated tension between distance and identification, with neither pole dominating the form of the film for too long, is the essence of Tsuchimoto's art, and it is one of the reasons why his works of the 1960s became, and remain, so influential.

Two years after he made Paruchizan zenshi for Ogawa Productions, Tsuchimoto launched the epic Minamata series of films that became his most iconic works. Minamata is a village in Kyushu where the deadly effects of mercury poisoning, caused by the pollution spewed by nearby chemical companies, first came to light; the disease, which can result in severe physical handicaps and death, is now known as Minamata disease, and Tsuchimoto's three-hour film Minamata: kanjo-san to sono sekai/Minamata: The Victims and Their World (1971) made the disease public. As the title suggests, Tsuchimoto's goal here is to represent the worldview of the victims by abandoning the constructivist editing of his early films and extending the dialectical tension of Paruchizan zenshi to a less individualized, more epic scale.

A member of the Communist Party and former leader of the student movement Zengakuren, Tsuchimoto, in his films, has always privileged the political over the aesthetic, but in the Minamata films this tendency became an overriding operating principle. According to his former assistant director Koike Masato, when presenting his films before an audience unfamiliar with the disease, Tsuchimoto would stop the film at a critical juncture to reiterate key points with a slide show. The Minamata films are progressive in spirit and have proved highly influential. Some audience members who have seen the film have even taken decisive action to help curb the mercury poisoning. That said, the Minamata films are hampered by a didacticism and an overt political heaviness that many would argue mar most of Tsuchimoto's work from 1971 on (Genpatsu kirinukicho/A Scrapbook About Nuclear Power Plants, 1982, is a notable exception).

Regardless of the issues that they are tackling and the mode of address they adopt, however, Tsuchimoto's films are always acutely, often penetratingly, intelligent. What they sometimes lack in poetry they make up for in the careful selection of their images, the cogent lucidity of their arguments, and the urgency with which they present their causes. In addition, Tsuchimoto has left a powerful legacy that may, in the end, prove even more important than the films themselves. His influence can be felt in the work of filmmakers as diverse as Hirokazu Koreeda and Koike Masato, and his extensive body of work continues to stand, for many, as a paragon of documentary 'image art' and a model of cinematic independence.

RICHARD SUCHENSKI

Bibliography

Born in Gifu Prefecture December 11, 1928. In 1946 he joined Waseda University and became an active member of the Communist Party. He was later expelled from Waseda for participation in sometimes violent student revolts, and he spent much of the 1950s working with leftist political organizations such as the Japan/China Friendship Society. In 1956 he became a contract director for Iwanami Productions, then the dominant force in Japanese documentary production. In 1961 he became a founding member of the 'Ao No Kai' film group, and he made his directorial debut the next year with Aru kikan joshi. After directing the highly regarded Document rojo, he directed his most influential film, Ryugakusei Chua Sui Rin. After directing Paruchizan zenshi for Ogawa Productions, he launched the epic Minamata series of documentaries with Minamata: Kanjasan to sono sekai in 1971. In the following years he directed a series of films such as Yomigaeru karezu/Afghan Spring (1989) and Genpatsu kirinukicho/A Scrapbook About Nuclear Power Plants (1989), which protested against social injustice, state oppression, and ecological destruction. He died June 24, 2008.

Selected films

1962 Arukikanjoshi/An Engineer's Assistant: director, writer
1963 Dokyumento rojo/Document: On the Road: director, writer
1965 Ryugakusei Chua Sui Rin/Exchange Student Chua Swee Lin: director
1968 Shiberiajin no sekai/The World of a Siberian: director
1969 Paruchizan zenshi/History of the Partisans: director
1971 Minamata: Kanjasan to sono sekai/ Minamata: The Victims and Their World: director
1973 Minamata ikki-issho o tou hitobito/ Minamata Revolt—A People's Quest for Life: director
1974 Igaku toshite no Minamatabyo-daiichi bu: shiryo-shogen hen; Daini bu: byori-byozo hen/Minamata Disease: A Trilogy: director
1975 Shiranui kai/Shiranui Sea: director
1976 Minamata: Sono 20 nen/Minamata: Those 20 Years: director
1982 Genpatsu kirinukicho/A Scrapbook About Nuclear Power Plants: director
1984 Umitori—shimokita hanto hamasekine/ Sea Thief: director
1987 Minamata: Sono 30 nen/Minamata: Those 30 Years: director
1989 Yomigare karezu/Afghan Wind: director
2003 Mo hitotsu no Afuganisutan—Kabul nikki 1985 nen/Another Afghanistan— Kabul Diary 1985: writer, director
2003 Arishihi no Kabul hakubutsukan—1988 nen/Traces: The Kabul Museum 1988: writer, director

Further reading

Burch, Noël, *To the Distant Observer: Form and Meaning in the Japanese Cinema*, Berkeley, CA: University of California Press, 1979 (also Ann Arbor Center for Japanese Studies, *Electronic Reprint Series*, 2004).

Gerow, Aaron, 'Documentarists of Japan, No. 7: Tsuchimoto Noriaki', *Documentary Box* 8, 1995.

n.a., *Tsuchimoto Noriaki Filmography 2004*, Tokyo: Tsuchimoto Noriaki Firumogurafii ten 2004 Jikkoiinkai, 2004.

Yoshio, Yasui (ed.), *Japanese Documentaries of the 1960s*, Tokyo: Yamagata International Documentary Film Festival, 1993.

——(ed.), *Japanese Documentaries of the 1970s*, Tokyo: Yamagata International Documentary Film Festival, 1995.

Tunisian Victory

(US and UK, Capra and Stewart, 1944)

Jointly produced by the British and US army film units during 1943–4, Tunisian Victory was designed to provide domestic audiences in both countries with a vivid pictorial account of the Allied victory in North Africa and put a positive face on Anglo-American cooperation in the conduct of the war. The making of the film, however, also revealed the challenges and limitations of coordinating international efforts in the production of wartime propaganda in light of national divisions that the rhetoric of Allied unity inevitably masked.

Work on Tunisian Victory originated in separate British and American projects: Africa Freed, a follow-up to Desert Victory (1943), the British army and air force film units' acclaimed account of the expulsion of Rommel's African Korps from Libya and Egypt; and Operation Torch, undertaken by Frank Capra's newly formed US Signal Corps Special Coverage Unit (with John Huston, Anthony Veiller, and George Stevens) in an effort to give greater visibility to the participation of US forces in the North African campaign. Under pressure to promote the trans-Atlantic partnership, and hoping to reap the benefits of pooled combat footage, officials at the British Ministry of Information and the Office of War Information decided to merge the projects in the summer of 1943. Capra joined Hugh Stewart in London as coproducer/ director, and writing duties were divided between Veiller and H. Hodson, the latter the author of Desert Victory's spoken commentary. By all accounts collaboration was tense and work proceeded slowly, in part because of what Capra later described as 'sticky high policy decisions involving dual command and national pride and prejudices' (Capra 1971: 352). Capra and Stewart oversaw postproduction in Los Angeles in the winter of 1943–4, with Stewart using the opportunity to encourage stronger ties between the British and American film industries. At its commercial release in March 1944 the completed documentary received high praise from the Hollywood trade press but mixed reviews from US critics and still less favorable ones in Great Britain.

Like Desert Victory, Tunisian Victory outlines military strategy in North Africa, links battle preparation to events at home, and uses voiceover commentary to provide an overarching narrative of the unfolding campaign. During combat passages, camera jolts, rapid montages, and percussive sound effects register the impact of explosions and artillery fire. Even Tunisian Victory's controversial fabrication of two night battles—the British crossing of Wadi Zig-Zauo (shot at Pinewood studios) and the American assault on Tunisia's Hill 609 (staged by Capra and Huston in the Mojave Desert for Operation Torch)—have precedent in combat scenes reconstructed at Pinewood for Desert Victory.

However, Tunisian Victory's strenuous evenhandedness—evident in the patterned alternation between US and British convoys, camps, and combat sites—makes for a knottier story, as does its tentative effort to incorporate French forces into the drama. The complicated logistics are clarified in part through the use of slick animated diagrams and extensive commentary by Veiller and his British vocal counterpart, Leo Glenn. In a bid to personalize the drama, Tunisian Victory also adds into the mix the voices of a fictional British Tommy (Bernard Miles) and a fictional American GI (Burgess Meredith), who convey the thoughts of soldiers in their respective camps, then enter into a colloquy at the close. Both praised and criticized at the time, this last device provides the occasion for the film to consider the prospects for postwar renewal, as an array of Germans prisoners of war (POWs), North African refugees, and Allied soldiers from many nations appear on screen. Here Tunisian Victory trades the immediacy of a combat record—victory in Tunis, after all, was by now a full year past—for a longer view in which the fate of postwar international alliances must be considered.

CHARLES C. WOLFE

Further reading

Aldgate, Anthony, 'Creative Tension: Desert Victory, the Army Film Unit and Anglo-American Rivalry, 1943–45', in Philip M. Taylor (ed.), *Britain and the Cinema in the Second World War*, London: Macmillan, 1988.

——'Mr Capra Goes to War: Frank Capra, the British Army Film Unit, and Anglo-American Travails in the Production of "Tunisian Victory"', *Historical Journal of Film, Radio and Television* 11, no. 1, 1991: 21–39 (reprinted as 'National Pride and Prejudices: Tunisian Victory', in Anthony Aldgate and Jeffrey Richards (eds), *Britain Can Take It: The British Cinema in the Second World War*, second edn, Edinburgh: Edinburgh University Press, 1994).

Capra, Frank, *The Name above the Title: An Autobiography*, New York: Macmillan, 1971.

Chapman, James, *The British at War: Cinema, State and Propaganda, 1939–45*, London and New York: I.B. Tauris, 1998.

Coultass, Clive, 'Tunisian Victory—a film too late?', *Imperial War Museum Review* 1, 1986: 64–73.

——*Images for Battle: British Film and the Second World War, 1939–45*, Newark, NJ: University of Delaware Press, 1989.

Huston, John, *An Open Book*, New York: Alfred A. Knopf, 1980.

Krome, Frederic, '"Tunisian Victory" and Anglo-American Film Propaganda in World War II', *The Historian* 58, no. 3, spring 1996: 517–30.

McBride, Joseph, *Frank Capra: The Catastrophe of Success*, New York: Simon and Schuster, 1992.

Turin, Viktor

Viktor A. Turin was a Russian director who lived in America and trained in Hollywood before the Russian Revolution. His best-known film, Turksib (1929), is a documentary on the construction of the Turkestano–Siberian railroad, one of Stalin's projects for industrializing the Soviet Union. An argument for efficient transportation and trade between regions of the country, the film best illustrates Turin's ideas about what the documentary should accomplish. Although it makes a dry economic argument comprehensible, it also tells a story and rouses an emotional response. Soviet cinema made a distinction between 'played' (or fiction) and 'unplayed' (or documentary) films, but Turin was willing to blur that distinction to make the film's message more effective. This included staging scenes to make a point that was valuable in the film's larger argument. Turin's philosophy of the documentary, then, is at the intersection of communism and Hollywood: a film should appeal to the masses, but it should also teach them something.

Turin began working on Turksib at a time when the Soviet culture-film (a didactic documentary) had fallen out of favor. Most of the films were so poorly or cheaply done that bad filmmaking turned the audiences away from ideologically good ideas. Turin felt that documentary films could present complex ideas to mass audiences, but only if they were presented in an exciting (and often staged) narrative that made the ideas worthy of attention. His ideas about the making of documentary film differed dramatically from those of Dziga Vertov, the most important Soviet documentarian of the era. Vertov was opposed to fiction films and staged scenes, arguing instead for films that showed 'life caught unawares' and presented unfiltered reality. In contrast, Viktor Turin used his Hollywood training to plan for and construct Turksib in a way that was remarkably similar to a fiction film. Viktor Shlovkii wrote a scenario for the film (though much of it was abandoned in production), and Turin expressed regret at several 'good shots' that he missed. This position resulted in many elements of the film that seem more allegorical or stereotypical than realistic. The characters are very broadly drawn and easily understood 'types' like the noble savage and the heroic engineer, for example, and the film's economic argument is thematized in anecdotal scenes like the race between native horse and modern automobile.

Turin adhered to a more constructed version of the documentary because he felt that structure and story was necessary to make complex ideas palatable to the average viewer. He spoke to a worker's club on the obligation of filmmakers to come into contact with and speak to the working classes; the culture-film's lack of recent success was, he felt, a result of its inability to connect with the masses through a clear and compelling story. In this respect, Turin believed a film's successful communication of an argument can be judged only by its reception:

> The greatest defect in most of the culture-films produced up to now seems to be the absence of a precisely articulated theme[...] The usual result is a tiresome hodgepodge of shots spliced together with merely mechanical links [...] This makes even the sharpest facts grow dull on the screen and leaves the spectator unmoved.
>
> (Leyda 1960)

The director and editor have the responsibility to plan the story and shape the shots' relationship to one another so that the film presents not mere reality but a precisely articulated argument that can change the spectators' minds, both through facts and through emotions. The first section of Turksib, for example, tells spectators the facts about Turkish production of cotton; it also affects spectators by cutting from worried faces to wilting fields to a panting dog, links that are emotional rather than merely mechanical. Also, the film's editing begins at a leisurely pace when it lays out the background information for its argument, but it speeds up at the end to create excitement in the audience as the film concludes. Most critics feels that the film's success was due to the clarity of its argument and the simplicity of its structure, one that combined the comprehensibility of the fiction film and the articulacy of the culture-film.

The need for both emotional impact and a clear argument leads to a disjunction between two important elements of Turin's style. Although his characterizations and anecdotes within the film are often stereotypical, the film is consistently shot in a style that was much more direct, similar to a newsreel in its graininess and focus. Jay Leyda, for example, marvels at the fact that a Hollywood-trained director would make such an 'anti-pretty' film, particularly because he made Turksib at a time when even documentaries had a more glossy style and used a cameraman accustomed to shooting fiction films (Leyda 1960). This choice of style may have been Turin's way of maintaining a visual authenticity that gave credence to his argument—another way of creating an emotional connection with the audience by giving them the sense that this problem was an immediate and real one.

Turin's gritty style shared important characteristics with those of other filmmakers working in the same era. The newsreel was one of the most important documentary forms during and after the Russian Revolution, and other filmmakers used newsreel footage in larger documentary work (like Esfir Shub) or imitated its style (like Sergei Eisenstein) to communicate immediacy and realism. Like these other filmmakers, Turin used 'newsreel' realism as a style with a specific and intentional emotional result, an aesthetic choice rather than a direct or unproblematic way of representing the real world.

This combination of fiction and reality is one of Turin's most important contributions to the theory of the documentary in Soviet Russia. In addition, his emphasis on the residents of Turkestan as exotic and Eastern led to an interest in orientalism in films such as Vertov's Tri pesni o Lenine/Three Songs About Lenin (1934). Critics disagree about the effects of Turksib on Turin's career, but all agree that his union of Hollywood and communism—the live and the staged, the East and the West—was unique and influential in Soviet documentary history.

SUNNY STALTER

See also: Turksib

Biography

Born *c.* 1895 in Leningrad, Russia. Died 1945.

Selected films

1929 Turksib
1938 Bakintsy

Further reading

Leyda, Jay, *Kino: A History of the Russian and Soviet Film*, New York: Macmillan, 1960.

Payne, Matthew, 'Viktor Turin's Turksib (1929) and Soviet Orientalism', *Historical Journal of Film, Radio, and Television* 21, no. 1, 2001: 37–62.

Roberts, Graham, *Forward Soviet!: History and Non-fiction Film in the USSR*, London and New York: I.B. Tauris, 1999.

Shlapentokh, Dmitry and Shlapentokh, Vladimir, *Soviet Cinematography 1918–91: Ideological Conflict and Social Reality*, New York: Aldine de Gruyter, 1993.

Taylor, Richard and Christie, Ian (eds), *The Film Factory: Russian and Soviet Cinema in Documents 1896–1939*, London and New York: Routledge, 1988.

Youngblood, Denise, *Soviet Cinema in the Silent Era, 1918–35*, Ann Arbor, MI: UMI Research Press, 1985.

Turksib

(USSR, Turin, 1929)

Turksib is a Soviet culture-film (a didactic documentary) about the Turkestano–Siberian railway. The film was directed by Viktor A. Turin and released by Vostok-Kino, a studio mandated to make films for the eastern areas of the Soviet Union. Acclaimed at home for its comprehensible argument and compelling story, it was also critically lauded in Europe and America for its modernist techniques and exotic subject. In spite of its initial critical and popular reception, Turksib was banned in the mid-1930s. The film was thought not to give enough credit to Stalin for the railway plan, it did not deal with communist ideals like class-consciousness, and some Russian critics found fault in the film's combination of documentary and fiction film techniques. Today, the film is best understood both in the tradition of Soviet orientalism and the communist belief in technology's power to conquer nature, as well as in the wider context of modernist meditations on the primitive and the machine.

Documentary film had an important role as propaganda in the Soviet Union from the time of the Russian Revolution. The Soviet film industry in the 1920s, however, moved away from overtly didactic films. One of the key reasons for this shift was that documentaries were often so poorly made that they alienated their audiences and worked against their own ideological purposes. Turin believed the failure of the culture-film in the 1920s was based on its failure to articulate its theme, something he tried to accomplish through a combination of logical structure and exciting storytelling (Payne 2001).

The interest in storytelling was what led to later suspicion and criticism of the film. The background of those involved and Turin's intentions in making the film place Turksib squarely in opposition to the philosophy of documentary film espoused by Dziga Vertov. The most important Soviet documentarian of the 1920s, Vertov harshly criticized all fiction film and even staged documentaries, famously stating that film should display 'life caught unawares'. Turin had spent ten years working in Hollywood, and the rest of his crew had similar experience in the world of fiction. The scenario was written by Viktor Shlovskii, a noted literary critic, and his cameraman, Evgeni Slavinksky, had worked on fiction films since before the Revolution.

Turksib is perhaps closest to the films of Sergei Eisenstein in its combination of staged scenes and gritty visual aesthetic. Turin's film uses the techniques of fiction film to tell what would otherwise be a dry economic argument about the need for efficient transportation and trade between different regions of the Soviet Union. The first section, called 'Cotton', shows Turkestani farmers laboring in hot fields. Because of their limited supply of water, they are forced to choose between irrigating the cotton they could trade with the rest of the Soviet states and the wheat they need to survive. These problems are all presented rapidly, in an abbreviated and impressionistic style. The heat is suggested by panting dogs, concern over the crops by cuts between close-ups of worried faces and wilting fields.

The film's second section, called 'The Way of the Road', deals with movement as the underlying cause of the economic impediments in regions like Turkistan and Siberia. Transportation's inefficient progress is subject to the whims of the natural world. In the best-known sequence illustrating this conflict, the Turks' camel caravan, while attempting to trade the cotton and wool, is halted in the desert by a sandstorm. This scene has a surreal quality, reveling in the sculptural beauty of the sand dunes but juxtaposing this with an intertitle describing the scene as 'a burial ground for travelers and their cargoes'.

This chaos contrasts dramatically with the abilities of the planners introduced in the third section, 'Here Come the Engineer-Surveyors'. Not only can they move efficiently through and above the Kazakh steppes in their car and airplane, but they can also rationalize movement through this area with their maps and plans for railroad construction. This section moves from a direct illustration of the region's problems to an imagined solution. In a scene indebted to avant-garde art styles such as constructivism and Russian futurism, stop-motion, animated blueprints, charts, and numbers dance around the screen; an animated train draws its path across a map, showing the distance between the regions it will be connecting.

This section of the film has the most obviously staged sequences, including a race between the engineers' car and a Kazakh nomad on a horse. This scene makes clear the film's intentions in equating the Eastern with the primitive and the Western with the technologically advanced or modern. Some critics think that Turksib avoided conventional communist issues of this era, such as class conflict, to emphasize the clear distinction between East and West, a distinction that may have led to the film's popularity elsewhere (Payne 2001).

Primitivism places the film within the modernist colonialist tradition. The audience is meant to be fascinated by and desire to subjugate cultural others. In addition, the film's belief in the conquering power of the machine over nature is both part of Marxist theories of collectivization and the American theories of Taylorist efficiency. The railroad workers' labor is naturalized through crosscutting with the work of reapers, but the construction of the railroad is meant to rationalize nature by taming it. The cutting speeds up as the film moves back and forth between the mechanized movements of workers and the humanized movements of machines. The film ends with the exhortation to finish the railway line by 1936, but Turin's combination of logic and emotional appeal make the construction seem inevitable.

Western film critics have dismissed the film in the recent past, characterizing it as unsuccessful or not truly documentary; however, even more recent assessments of Turksib ignore genre arguments to address its historical and cultural complexity. The film's stylistic and ideological impurity both lead to unevenness in technique between different sections of the film, but it has an overall emotional and intellectual coherence that is quite powerful. Turksib is an underrated Soviet documentary, one that uses modernist film techniques in a powerfully populist way.

SUNNY STALTER

See also: Russia/Soviet Union; Turin, Viktor; Vertov, Dziga

Turksib (USSR, Vostokkino, 1929, 57 mins). Distributed by Amkino Corporation and Kino International Corp. Directed by Viktor A. Turin. Written by Yakov Aron and Viktor Shklovsky. Cinematography by Boris Frantsisson and Yevgeni Slavinsky.

Further reading

Leyda, Jay, *Kino: A History of the Russian and Soviet Film*, New York: Macmillan, 1960.

Payne, Matthew, 'Viktor Turin's Turksib (1929) and Soviet Orientalism', *Historical Journal of Film, Radio, and Television* 21, no. 1, 2001: 37–62.

Roberts, Graham, *Forward Soviet!: History and Non-fiction Film in the USSR*, London and New York: I.B. Tauris, 1999.

Shlapentokh, Dmitry and Shlapentokh, Vladimir, *Soviet Cinematography 1918–91: Ideological Conflict and Social Reality*, New York: Aldine de Gruyter, 1993.

Taylor, Richard and Christie, Ian (eds), *The Film Factory: Russian and Soviet Cinema in Documents 1896–1939*, London and New York: Routledge, 1988.

Youngblood, Denise, *Soviet Cinema in the Silent Era, 1918–35*, Ann Arbor, MI: UMI Research Press, 1985.

Tyneside Story

(UK, Gunn, 1944)

Tyneside Story was one of the wartime films of social purpose that has led some critics to believe that British documentary cinema contributed to the radicalisation of the public during the 'People's War' and ushered in the postwar Labour government with the mandate to win the 'People's Peace'. Numerous shorts and documentaries distributed by the Ministry of Information, films like Dawn Guard (1941), New Towns for Old (1942), World of Plenty (1943), and The Plan and the People (1945), articulated a set of peace aims about reconstruction and postwar planning. These helped to determine an outlook that firmly rejected the bankrupt prewar social and political framework and raised expectations about a planned and managed economy predicated on state welfare.

The film commences with a documentary sequence concerning the history and tradition of shipbuilding in Newcastle, which had declined as a result of depression. The great Eldon Yard is now closed, but we are reminded of its proud tradition. It built the first oil tanker, and it once launched three iron steamships in a single day. In the wartime emergency the yard is being made good again, brought back to life through orders from the Admiralty. The Ministry of Labour tackles the problem of a shortage of skilled workers and seeks out former employees to re-recruit them. Some are keen to return and reignite their skills, but Fred is less sure. He now works on a building site and does not want to uproot only to get thrown out again at some future date. Within a short time British craftsmen are active again building ships and a vessel is launched. Skilled men are in short supply, however, and to confront the problem women are being instructed at a government training centre where they are told that there are 'hundreds of jobs in the yards that can be done by women as well, or better than, men'. There are carefully presented scenes of women being trained as welders and other essential skills of shipbuilding, and viewers are informed that one operative, Betty, 'is as good as any man in the yard'.

The wartime policy is a success and the resurrected industry on Tyneside now builds cargo ships, tankers, submarines, and aircraft carriers. As the narrator patriotically declares: 'As long as Britain calls for ships, the call will be answered by the ring of steel on steel in the shipyards of the Tyne.' Finally, Fred returns as the voice of scepticism and declares direct to camera: 'Aye, but wait a minute. Tyneside's busy enough today, old uns and young uns hard at work makin' good ships, but just remember what the yards looked like five years ago: idle, empty, some of 'em derelict, and the skilled men that worked in them scattered and forgotten. Will it be the same again five years from now? That's what we on Tyneside want to know.'

The presentation of peace aims was officially avoided during the war, and attention was concentrated on the difficult job of winning the conflict. It has been argued, however, that 'by the close of World War II, significant sections of the British people had been treated to visions of a grandiose post-war Utopia which exceeded anything promised during World War I' (Pronay 1983). Paradoxically, this propaganda emanated from the Films Division of the Ministry of Information (MOI), which commissioned huge numbers of documentary films during the war and distributed them nontheatrically to vast audiences. The progressive nature of some of these films derived from the left-leaning members of the documentary film movement who contributed seventy-four percent of the titles produced or commissioned by the MOI. Basil Wright and Paul Rotha were perhaps the most outspoken advocates of the 'world revolution', but New Jerusalem ideals found their way into significant numbers of documentaries. Gilbert Gunn and Michael Hankinson at Spectator Films preceded Tyneside Story with Birth of a Tank (1942) and Women Away from Home (1942), two people's war titles documenting wartime social changes and the home front's contribution to the war effort. Gunn followed it with Housing in Scotland (1945), a significant example of the later wartime emphasis on planning and reconstruction. Taken together these films were typical presentations of the loosely articulated peace aims that circulated through wartime documentary cinema.

Tyneside Story was a classic example of this wartime progressive documentary cinema. The cast was drawn from the local socialist drama collective, the People's Theatre Company, and its message conformed to the characteristic 'never again' idealism of the time and its rejection of the boom and bust polarities of unregulated private enterprise and the newly acknowledged potential of the fully planned economy. The wartime emergency had produced the will to resurrect the idle yards; the will now had to be carried forward into the peace and the commitment to maintain jobs and to draw on workers' skills.

ALAN BURTON

See also: Wright, Basil

Tyneside Story (UK, 1944, 14 mins). Produced by Spectator Films for the Ministry of Information. Directed by Gilbert Gunn and produced by Michael Hankinson. Story by Jack Common. Photography by A.H. Luff. Edited by Ralph Kemplen. Sound by W.S. Bland. Music by Ken Hughes. Featuring Alf Simpson, Alan Thompson, W. Crabtree, John Bell, G.G. Whitingham, Sal Sturgeon and F.R. Gibson.

Further reading

Addison, Paul, *The Road to 1945*, London: Jonathan Cape, 1975.

The Arts Enquiry, *The Factual Film*, London: PEP, 1947.

Burton, Alan, 'Projecting the New Jerusalem: The Workers' Film Association, 1938–46', in Pat Kirkham and David Thoms (eds), *War Culture. Social Change and Changing Experience in World War Two*, London: Lawrence and Wishart, 1995.

Forman, Helen, 'The Non-theatrical Distribution of Films by the Ministry of Information', in N. Pronay and D.W. Spring (eds), *Propaganda, Politics and Film, 1918–45*, London: Macmillan, 1982.

Pronay, Nicholas, '"The Land of Promise": The Projection of Peace Aims in Britain', in K.R.M. Short (ed.), *Film and Radio Propaganda in World War II*, London and Canberra: Croom Helm, 1983.

Swann, Paul, *The British Documentary Film Movement, 1926–46*, Cambridge: Cambridge University Press, 1989.

Thorpe, Frances and Pronay, Nicholas, *British Official Films in the Second World War*, Oxford: Clio Press, 1980.

U

Union Maids

(US, Reichert and others, 1976)

Union Maids is one of a number of films that emerged out of the growth of the women's movement in the United States at the end of the 1960s. As women began to move into documentary filmmaking in increasing numbers, a number of films in which women and their environments were made visible in a new way appeared. This was frequently done through the use of archival film material and contemporary interviews, an aesthetic derived in many cases from Emile de Antonio's prototype In the Year of the Pig (1969). Union Maids, made by the team of Julia Reichert, James Klein, and Miles Mogulescu in 1976, was one such project of historical excavation.

The film is a collective portrait of three women labour organisers in the late 1920s and 1930s, who were part of a community of working-class Chicago socialists. Using a compilation structure that mixed archive footage and direct interview, the filmmakers attempt to reconstruct a history of women's involvement in labour organising. The women, Kate Hyndman, Stella Nowicki, and Sylvia Woods, tell their stories in the course of three separate interviews, which are intercut with each other and with period newsreel footage. In a partial retreat from direct cinema aesthetics, these interviews are conducted by audible and sometimes visible interviewers, a technique that adds to the personal and strongly narrative thrust of the documentary. The interviewees recount their experiences of organising to counteract exploitation in the workforce from a strongly radical perspective. They also tell a tale of sexism on the job, as well as within the unions and among leftist men. The one black woman, Sylvia, speaks of racial discrimination and her own conversion to interracial class unity by evidence of white class solidarity.

Union Maids works best as a tale of three working-class heroines in a period of great working-class power. The film is full of stirring stories of the women's militancy and bravery. Sylvia Woods describes how in the laundry where she first worked the women conducted what she believes may have been the first sit-down strike of the 1930s. Stella Nowicki recounts how often the packing house workers would stop the line, shutting down production. Kate Hyndman, the most obviously radical of the women, was laid off after writing an article for the *Daily Worker*. The use of three exceptional women, however, means that the film denies the larger reality of women's working lives, which were concentrated in mainly nonunionised clerical and service work. The film also skirts somewhat coyly around the question of the women's likely affiliations with the Communist Party, a strategy that ultimately serves to weaken both the film's documentary stance and radical underpinnings.

On a formal level, critical reception of Union Maids was initially informed by the 1970s critique of realism that affected both nonfiction and fiction film studies. A number of feminist film critics objected to the use of direct cinema techniques in the presentation of history. It was felt that the privileged film subjects of the interview format could become problematic if a film relied on them as the primary informants. The accounts of oral history subjects could be partial, fragmentary, idiosyncratic, and possibly misleading. In the context of a perceived need to construct a cinema that could both present individuals within the context of a complex social structure and simultaneously critique the film process itself, Union Maids was viewed as a flawed text.

The film was seen by several contemporary critics as deriving its central importance as an organising tool for women's and worker's organisations. Its importance as a potential catalyst was thus considered to render it immune from ideological analysis (McCormick 1977; Nichols 1991). The problem is one of unaccustomed 'against the grain' readings of leftist texts, texts that may contain a number of ideological contradictions. In the case of Union Maids, these devices could be said to be the interview format itself and the intersection of discourses of biography, autobiography, and popular narrative history. For Noel King, these discourses coalesce to present a problematic humanist-historicist, populist mode, particularly evident in the interview format used in the film. In this reading Union Maids tells its story of past events through an uncontested representation of the memories of the three women, suppressing any awkward questions on the social construction of these women themselves. Bill Nichols has also drawn attention to the epistemological problems presented by the use of archival footage as a confirmation for commentary, which normalises the footage as authentic (Renov 1993).

More recently, a critical recuperation of the realistic strategies used in Union Maids and similar historical documentaries has underlined its status as a feminist counterhistory. While recognising the dangers of an uncritical acceptance of documentary's realist illusions, several writers have pointed out that the same formal attributes of interviews, photographs, or voice-over narration can serve different functions in different films (Waldman and Walker 1999). Recognition of past struggles of working-class women, such as those depicted in Union Maids, can illuminate the extent to which individual volition and equal opportunity can be illusory or at least conditional.

MARINA BURKE

See also: In the Year of the Pig; Reichert, Julia

Union Maids (US, New Day Films, 1976, 54 mins). Produced and directed by James Klein, Miles Mogulesco, and Julia Reichert. Edited by James Klein and Julia Reichert. Cinematography by Sherry Novick and Tony Heriza. Archival Film and Photographic Research by Julia Reichert with Barbara Tuss and Sherry Novick.

Further reading

Erens, Patricia, 'Women's Documentary Filmmaking: The Personal is Political', in Alan Rosenthal (ed.), *New Challenges for Documentary*, Berkeley, CA: University of California Press, 1988.

Gordon, Lynda, 'Union Maids: Working Class Heroines', in Peter Steven (ed.), *Jump Cut: Hollywood, Politics and Counter-Cinema*, Toronto: Between the Lines, 1985.

Kaplan, E. Ann, 'Theories and Strategies of the Feminist Documentary', in Alan Rosenthal (ed.), *New Challenges for Documentary*, Berkeley, CA: University of California Press, 1988.

King, Noel, 'Notes on "Union Maids" and "Harlan County USA"', *Screen* 22, no. 2, 1981: 7–18.

Lesage, Julia, 'The Political Aesthetics of the Feminist Documentary Film', *Quarterly Review of Film Studies*, fall 1978: 506–23.

McCormick, Ruth, 'Union Maids', *Cineaste* 8, no. 1, summer 1977.

Nichols, Bill, *Representing Reality*, Bloomington, IN: Indiana University Press, 1991.

Renov, Michael (ed.), *Theorising Documentary*, London: Routledge, 1993.

Waldman, Diane and Walker, Janet (eds), *Feminism and Documentary*, Minneapolis, MN: University of Minnesota Press, 1999.

Winston, Brian, *Claiming the Real*, London: British Film Institute, 1995.

United Kingdom

The emergence of documentary filmmaking in Britain may be traced back to footage shot by amateur and professional cameramen who chronicled various expeditions during the early years of the twentieth century. Although such footage hardly resembles documentaries in the sense in which the term is commonly used today, these films used the cinematic medium to document 'realistic' elements that later would be exhibited for public audiences. Such visual records include the wildlife films of Cherry Kearton (which began production as far back as 1908) and the long-running Secrets of Nature series (1919–33), produced by Harry Bruce Woolfe and Percy Smith. After World War I, filmmakers such as Woolfe, Walter Summers, and Geoffrey Barkas produced films (including Armageddon (Woolfe, 1923), The Battle of the Falkland and Coronel Islands (Summers, 1927), and Q Ships (Barkas, 1928)), which combined authentic combat footage with reconstructed sequences. Although Britain was not the first to document elements outside the realm of fiction, such works were foundational in using film for educational and instructional purposes. Films such as these may be considered logical predecessors to what would become the British documentary film movement of the 1930s, arguably Britain's greatest contribution to the development of cinema.

After World War I, the outlook of domestic politics changed in Britain. The nature of the British government began to transform from the limited hierarchical undertakings of the nineteenth century to one that embraced a more active public interaction. The state began to feel an obligation to become involved in how its citizens were informed about various policies via publicity. The Empire Marketing Board (EMB) was set up in May 1926 by a Conservative government to administer the newly created Empire Marketing Fund to improve trade. Although the majority of the EMB's budget was spent on research, the Board became most recognized for its publicity activities.

The EMB's approach toward publicity was greatly influenced by public relations policies practiced in the United States. Such policies stressed the importance of education as the foundation for public relations initiated by government departments. Developments in media such as the use of film for publicity had effectively been used in the United States during World War I, and it soon became clear to the EMB that any official department would logically use film as a means to instruct and educate citizens. The secretary of the EMB was Stephen Tallents (1884–1958), an instrumental figure in the formation of the British documentary film movement. It was Tallents who would meet and collaborate with John Grierson and, in the process, initiate the assemblage of filmmakers who would compose the movement.

John Grierson (1898–1972) was born in Scotland and graduated from Glasgow University with an MA degree in English and moral philosophy in 1923. The next year he traveled to the United States on a Rockefeller research fellowship in social science. It was while studying in America that he became interested with how mass media (the popular press and eventually the cinema) could be used to propagandistic ends. During the late 1920s Grierson became influenced by the work of American author Walter Lippmann, whose views on education made quite an impression on him. Lippmann's *Public Opinion* (1922) is widely credited for inspiring Grierson to consider American propaganda expertise to develop films that would serve as educational tools. Grierson believed 'that because the citizen, under modern conditions, could not know everything about everything all the time, democratic citizenship was therefore impossible' (Grierson, in Forsyth Hardy, H (ed.) Grierson on Documentary (London: Faber & Faber, 1946), p. 207). Considering that motion pictures are a form of expression that target a mass audience, Grierson became dedicated to developing films that would inform citizens of social concerns with which they perhaps weren't familiar, ideally contributing to the formation of citizens who could make informed decisions based on democratic ideals.

Grierson believed that documentary films (or all films constructed from natural material, as he describes) were better suited to portray the reality of social issues in Britain than the dramatic conventions of fiction. Hollywood's motivation was purely commercial by his assessment, completely devoid of qualities he believed to be moral or artistic. Early cinematic influences on Grierson were the films of Robert Flaherty (1884–1951) and Soviet cinema of the 1920s; both provided an alternative to Hollywood through their tendency to dramatize fiction. Grierson himself familiarized the term documentary when he used it in a review of Flaherty's Moana (1926), describing it as 'a poetic record of Polynesian tribal life which had "documentary value"'. Grierson's insistence that documentary film was the most effective means to educate the public is reiterated in his three principles of 'documentary proper'. First, 'Documentary would photograph the living scene and the living story' (Grierson, in Forsyth Hardy, H (ed.) Grierson on Documentary (London: Faber & Faber, 1946), p. 147). Grierson believed that studio films largely ignored the potential for film to open up the screen to reality and instead relied on artificiality to communicate to an audience. Second is '(the belief) that the original (or native) actor, and the original (or native) scene, are better guides to a screen interpretation of the modern world' (ibid.). Finally, Grierson subscribed to '(the belief) that the materials and the stories thus taken from the raw can be finer (more real in the philosophic sense) than the acted article' (ibid.).

Grierson returned to Britain from the United States in 1927 and met Stephen Tallents, who at the time was developing a feature film suggested by Rudyard Kipling for the EMB entitled One Family. Tallents had appointed Walter Creighton, a man who knew little of filmmaking, as director of the project at the suggestion of Kipling. On meeting Grierson, Tallents was impressed with his ideas but had already appointed Creighton as the EMB's first Film Officer. Unwilling to lose Grierson as a collaborator, Tallents asked him to write a series of reports on film production for the EMB Film Committee. The first report (which dealt with the two issues most valuable to the Committee—how to use film as propaganda and how to compete with the American film industry) was titled 'Notes for English Producers'. In it, Grierson stated his interest in establishing a permanent film unit within the EMB. Grierson's second report dealt with the topic of film distribution and explained the possibilities of non-theatrical distribution as a means to circulate the films he envisioned the EMB producing. He also began to organize a series of screenings at the Imperial Institute where he screened various films such as British Instructional's Secrets of Nature series and various Russian films from the early 1920s.

In early 1928 Grierson proposed the production of two films to the Film Committee, to be made from newly shot footage. One of the films was to concern the herring industry, a topic that interested Financial Secretary to the Treasury Arthur Samuel (who contributed in approving the decision to begin film work) because of his position as Britain's authority on herring. On approval, Grierson set out to direct his first film, Drifters, in the summer of 1928.

The EMB entered into a contract with New Era Films in order to finance and distribute Drifters, as production of Creighton's feature film One Family had secured a generous amount of the Board's funding without any tangible results. The film was shot quickly and for the sum of nearly £3,000. Running for fifty minutes, the film depicts fishermen as they pursue herring shoals along the east coast of Britain. Shot by professional cameraman Basil Emmott, Drifters is obviously influenced by the silent Soviet filmic style, which Grierson was familiar with and admired. The film is among the first attempts at national cinema to stray from the Hollywood style of illusionism and to make use of montage to locate melodramatic effects in realistic material. It also portrays the working class in a romantic manner, a thematic development to which Grierson's productions would repeatedly return.

Drifters was finished in the summer of 1929. It premiered in a noncommercial setting on a bill with Eisenstein's Battleship Potemkin in front of the London Film Society, where it was well received. The film enjoyed commercial success as well, practically recouping its production costs after one year of distribution. The major triumph of Drifters was that it suggested that an alternative method of obtaining finance for filmmaking was possible, which existed largely (although not entirely) outside commercial concerns. Its success aided Grierson in convincing the EMB to set up its own film unit in January 1930.

After officially being appointed Assistant Film Officer of the EMB Film Unit in 1930, John Grierson began to assemble a crew of collaborators who would produce many of Britain's most important early documentary works. Among Grierson's first recruits for the EMB Film Unit was Basil Wright (1907–87), who began work in December 1929. Under Grierson, Wright assembled Conquest in 1930, a compilation film designed for schools about the wilderness of North America and the effects of technology, which pulls a portion its source material from footage of American westerns such as The Covered Wagon (James Cruze, 1923). In addition to Wright, those filmmakers who would become the first generation of the documentary film movement in Britain included Arthur Elton, Edgar Anstey, Stuart Legg, J.N.G. Davidson, John Taylor, Paul Rotha, Donald Taylor, Grierson's sisters, Marion and Ruby, Evelyn Spice, and Margaret Taylor, who would become Grierson's wife. The EMB Film Unit was also among the few units that would employ women behind the camera during this period. The majority of the recruits were middle class and had had a public school and university (Oxbridge) education. Of these new recruits, only Davidson, Elton, and Rotha had previous significant filmmaking experience.

Nearly all of Grierson's collaborators spent the early part of their time with the unit assembling films out of existing footage, as budget limitations prevented excessive shooting of new footage. These films found their source material from large stocks of film available from various parts of the Empire, primarily Canada, where a large number of travel films were available. The unit also produced 'poster' films, which were loops of film intended for use on projectors at EMB exhibitions and in shop windows. These early predecessors to the television commercial typically involved promoting Empire products such as Scottish tomatoes, Empire timber, wool, and butter.

By the 1920s American film industries had managed to dominate ninety-five percent of the film market in Britain, which led to the establishment of the Cinematograph Films Act in 1927. The purpose of the Act was to introduce a system of quotas that would increase the number of British films shown in the country, but in reality it had little effect. Although the British film industry did recover somewhat in the 1930s, American films still made up for more than seventy percent of films shown in Britain after the drafting of the Act. In addition, many of the films that were produced to meet the quota were made cheaply and shown to empty cinemas. Documentary films typically did not count in meeting the demands of the quota. It was not until the Cinematograph Films Act of 1938, when a separate standard of quotas were introduced for short films, that documentary films became eligible. The failure of documentary films to be incredibly successful in commercial release would lead Grierson and his collaborators to look toward nontheatrical distribution for the films that they were producing.

In January 1931 Grierson wanted to expand the production of the unit by producing a series of films that would be intended purely for nontheatrical distribution, including distribution to schools. He and the unit began to produce films that were slightly more advanced than previous efforts. Arthur Elton (1906–73) produced An Experiment in the Welsh Hills (1931), which documents a professor's experiments to obtain grasses and increase the suitability of sheep rearing in the Welsh mountain region. Elton also made Upstream (1931), which concerns salmon fishing in Scotland and makes use of impressive visuals, including a sequence of salmon leaping from waterfalls. Basil Wright made a one-reel film called Lumber (1931), which compiles footage from Canada about lumberjacking, and also shot The Country Comes to Town (1931), which draws connections between the countryside and the food industry. Wright also made his first truly personal film in 1932 with O'er Hill and Dale, a film about a Border shepherd in the lambing season. Documentary pioneer Robert Flaherty collaborated with Wright on The Country Comes to Town and became loosely associated with the unit in 1931. Grierson decided to spend nearly £2,500 to allow Flaherty to produce a film for the unit on craftsmanship in industry. Flaherty set out to film the steel bridge at Saltash, but the result was footage that began to come back to London without a concrete script. The EMB could not afford to continue the project, so the collaboration ended. Industrial Britain was later produced, however, combining the Flaherty footage with footage of waterways shot by Basil Wright and footage of coal mining shot by Arthur Elton. The film was released in 1933 under a combined production credit of Grierson and Flaherty. The necessity to maintain films for use in schools and other nontheatrical venues led to the creation of the Empire Film Library in October 1931. By 1936 the Empire Film Library was the largest film distributor to schools in Britain.

The incorporation of sound into motion pictures made it more difficult for the EMB Film Unit to get their films commercially released. The unit possessed no resources for recording sound, and all of the films made by the unit were silent, with some manner of musical accompaniment produced during exhibition. By 1932 it was difficult for silent films to obtain commercial distribution at all. Grierson, realizing the potential for the unit's films to obtain commercial distribution if sound were to be incorporated, asked the Film Committee in December 1931 for additional funds to create a sound studio. Although the Committee denied his request, both Tallents and Grierson began to negotiate with Gaumont-British Distributors in 1932 for the sale of six EMB films for commercial release. The films that were purchased—Shadow on the Mountain (Elton, 1933), King Log (Wright, 1932), The Country Comes to Town, Industrial Britain, Upstream, and O'er Hill and Dale—were given commentaries and musical scores by Andrew Buchanan (a leading short film director and producer) and packaged as the Imperial Six in 1933. Shadow on the Mountain and King Log were actually Elton's An Experiment in the Welsh Hills and Wright's Lumber, but were retitled and slightly edited when synchronized sound was added to them. Unfortunately, the films of the Imperial Six compromised

Grierson's original vision. The commentaries and musical scores proved to be quite contradictory to the films themselves, and the Imperial Six proved to be the only films the EMB Film Unit would get into commercial release.

Grierson soon realized that industrial sponsorship could provide additional resources to finance films. Individual members of the unit were successful in obtaining sponsorship from industry and Arthur Elton made Voice of the World for His Master's Voice Gramophone Company in 1932, the first film to be made for an outside body by the unit. By this time Grierson's abilities as a producer were known outside of the confines of the unit, and he advised government agencies such as the Travel and Industrial Association and the Ministry of Labour on the unit's film activity. Such films produced as a result included Donald Taylor's Lancashire at Work and Play (1933) and Spring Comes to England (1934), as well as travel films such as So This is London (1933) and For All Eternity (1934) by Marion Grierson. Edgar Anstey (1907–87) emerged with his first two solo efforts, Eskimo Village and Uncharted Waters in 1932, while Aero Engine established Arthur Elton as a skilled filmmaker in 1934. Another film financed outside the central government was Stuart Legg's The New Generation, completed for the Chesterfield Education Authority in 1932.

By 1932 an earlier decision by the Select Committee on Estimates to abolish the EMB had begun to reveal its consequences. It had become increasingly difficult for Grierson to maintain funding for the unit, and he had begun to keep Tallents and many of his collaborators in the dark about financial and production concerns. Around this period, Tallents had been appointed the first public relations officer of the Post Office and ensured that the film unit would be among those organizations saved from the dissolvement of the Board. Tallents believed in Grierson's vision that film had the potential to play perhaps the most important role in public information services and, in September 1933, he and the unit moved under the authority of the Post Office.

The commercial film trade industry began to become hostile toward the newly christened General Post Office (GPO) Film Unit after its transition from the EMB. The Gaumont-British group of film companies entered into the field of educational films in late 1933 and believed that the unit's intention to produce films for agencies outside the GPO would provide unfair competition. Even the Accountant-General's Department within the GPO felt that the unit's current home perhaps was not the best agency for a film unit to take on work for other departments and semipublic bodies. Despite the protests, the Treasury authorized the transfer of the unit to the Post Office for a trial period of six months.

The unit's transfer to the GPO provided the acquisition of sound recording equipment, although what was provided was not competitive with the equipment used by the Hollywood studios of the era. Nevertheless, the ability to record sound allowed the unit to become potentially more competitive in securing regular commercial distribution for their films. Grierson and his collaborators continued to operate much in the same manner that they did when the unit was part of the EMB. Grierson ensured that only himself and his office manager Stanley Fletcher were on the GPO's official payroll. The others members of the unit were employed by New Era Films, which by then no longer operated as a commercial company and largely participated solely in carrying out work for the GPO. Grierson used the employment of his unit by New Era to deter any accusations by the commercial film trade of using public resources to enter into competition with private enterprise. Grierson claimed that the unit was actually employing a commercial contractor in hiring New Era, and thereby satisfied requests by the film trade for the unit to exclusively hire outside contractors for their film work. The Treasury eventually realized what the unit was up to and ruled that the unit had to directly employ its staff and would not be allowed to produce work for other governmental departments and outside bodies.

Grierson then reorganized the unit according to the Treasury's requirements while largely ignoring the other restrictions it implemented. He continued production as he saw fit by maintaining that staff members not on the official payroll would continue to produce films for outside bodies, but those films already in production could be completed by staff members on the payroll. One of the most interesting films begun while the unit was still under the EMB was Granton Trawler (1934), a companion piece to Drifters that chronicles dragnet fishing off the Scottish Coast. Although John Grierson has claimed that he produced the film himself, various records list J.D. Davidson as cameraman and Edgar Anstey as editor. Other significant films beginning their production while the unit was still under the EMB included The Song of Ceylon (Basil Wright, 1934), BBC: The Voice of Britain (Stuart Legg, 1934), and Workers and Jobs (Arthur Elton, 1935).

The Empire Tea Marketing Expansion Board had requested four one-reel films of Ceylon in 1933 and Basil Wright traveled there to shoot them after completing footage for Cargo from Jamaica, Liner Cruising South, and Windmill in Barbados shortly beforehand the same year. He returned to cut The Song of Ceylon in 1934 and a soundtrack was subsequently added. The film, a combination of the four one-reelers, juxtaposes its soundtrack (including a seventeenth-century description of Ceylon and the modern echoes of radio broadcasts and phone conversations) with a beautiful visual depiction of the practices and rituals of Ceylon's inhabitants. The result draws attention to a contrast between the effect that the soundtrack provides and the stability of traditional practices in Ceylon. The Song of Ceylon is widely considered to be one of the most important documentaries to be produced by the movement and received first prize in the documentary class at the International Film Festival in Brussels. The film signified a renewed level of artistic achievement for the films of the British documentary movement.

The GPO Film Unit received £7,500 from the BBC in 1932 to produce BBC: The Voice of Britain. Like The Song of Ceylon, the film is a collaborative effort under the primary guidance of one filmmaker, in this case Stuart Legg. The film was the longest and most expensive venture the movement had undertaken up to that point, and even Grierson expressed some doubt that it would be completed efficiently. BBC: The Voice of Britain chronicles one day of broadcasting in Britain, which served to assist the BBC in showing the public a glimpse behind the scenes of its operations and a view of its new building. The film was widely shown in cinemas and was regarded as a triumph by the public and the film trade. While working for the GPO Film Unit, Arthur Elton produced Workers and Jobs for the Ministry of Labour in 1935. Elton wasn't officially on the payroll and thus was able to complete the work in accordance with the Treasury's requests. The film is about the work of Labour Exchanges and is revolutionary in its pioneering use of direct speech recording on location. The film resembles a newsreel and predates technically similar television reports by several years.

A major addition to the GPO Film Unit to come from the commercial film industry was Brazilian filmmaker Alberto Cavalcanti (1897–1983) in 1933. Cavalcanti had previously been a director in France and perhaps saw the GPO Film Unit as a way to break into the British feature film industry. He initially contributed to The Song of Ceylon by suggesting various experiments to Basil Wright, and he directed the films The Glorious Sixth of June and Pett and Pott for the GPO Film Unit in 1934. Cavalcanti's contribution to the film Coal Face (1935) is particularly notable. Although there is some dispute about the screen credits for Coal Face, it generally is regarded as Cavalcanti's film. It portrays an informative account of Britain's coal industry and emphasizes the tragedies of mining labor. The film features the collaboration of W.H. Auden and Benjamin Britten on the film's script and musical score, respectively, and '(foregrounds) the use of music and sound in a non-naturalistic way, so that natural sounds, dialogue, speech, music, and choral singing (are) integrated into a dramatic unity' (Aitken 1990). Although the film was not widely praised on its release, it received a medal of honor at Brussels. Grierson labeled the film 'Empo', a term he used to label films he thought were experimental.

The British Commercial Gas Association and the Gas Light and Coke Company commissioned Arthur Elton and Edgar Anstey early in 1935 to produce a number of films, two of which would prove to be significant: Housing Problems (1935) and Enough to Eat? (1936). Elton and Anstey had begun to allow subjects they were filming to speak directly for themselves on the soundtrack while filming. Housing Problems was significant in that it was among the first films to make use of interviews in this manner (predating the March of Time style of interviewing, which was typically manipulated in the studio) and to be sponsored by an industry that has no direct promotion in the film. The film introduces slum dwellers who in their own words explain their living conditions. For the first time, underprivileged people spoke freely about the condition of their lives, a radically different portrayal of citizens compared to the romantic image of the working class in many other films produced by Grierson. In 1936 Anstey wrote and directed Enough to Eat?, a film based on the work of Sir John Boyd Orr, which draws parallels between malnutrition and social class in Britain.

The direct interviews in the film were of 'experts' commenting on the film's subject, an innovation that would set the standard for thousands of informative documentary films.

Also in 1936 came Night Mail, directed by Basil Wright and Harry Watt (1906–87). Watt began working for Grierson in 1931 as a general assistant at the EMB. The film portrays a postal express train traveling from Euston to Glasgow, collecting and distributing mail. It contains little commentary and sound for the film was shot on location. One scene depicting letters being sorted in a railway carriage was actually recreated in a studio. Films such as Night Mail 'were not, significantly, of the straightforward pedagogical type of film, but were much more humanistic, and most important perhaps, employed narrative devices such as scripted dialogue, studio sets, and conventional dramatic development and resolution, which engaged viewers like regular commercial motion pictures' (Swann 1989). Paul Rotha mildly criticized Grierson for the use of overt romanticism toward the end of Night Mail, speculating that its inclusion may have been prompted by an attempt for box-office appeal (Rotha 1973). Regardless, the film proved to be one of the most popular documentaries turned out by the movement, achieving wide critical success and enjoying a modest theatrical run in commercial cinemas.

Paul Rotha (1907–84) was among the first of Grierson's collaborators to venture away permanently from the unit. Rotha wanted to make what he believed to be more personal films, an ambition that was not possible while working with Grierson's unit. Having previously made short trailers for the unit, Rotha produced Contact in 1933, a film that was financed by Shell-Mex and British Petroleum for £2,500. The film demonstrates how air routes and planes are assembled and concludes with a journey by air. Rotha would receive commercial backing from British Instructional over the next several years and would produce films such as Roadwards (1933), Rising Tide (1934), and Great Cargoes (1935). For Vickers Armstrong and the Orient Shipping Line, Rotha made Shipyard,a project shot over a period of months in 1934–5. The film documents the building of an Orient liner called the Orion and communicates the notion that, on completion of the ship, thousands of workers will face unemployment. Another significant film directed by Rotha is The Face of Britain (1935), which was sponsored by Hugh Quigley of the Central Electricity Board and deals with the use of electricity to organize a more efficient Britain. In 1935 Rotha would join an independent company called the Strand Film Unit as Director of Productions, producing sponsored documentary films to be shown in commercial cinemas.

Eventually, the restrictions placed on the GPO Film Unit and the desire to work elsewhere led to a number of significant departures. Arthur Elton left to make films for the Ministry of Labour and later would create the Shell Film Unit. Edgar Anstey departed to work for Shell and then ran the American March of Time series British film unit. Stuart Legg left to work for the Strand Film Company and Basil Wright parted ways to establish the Realist Film Unit. Finally, John Grierson left the unit in June 1937 to create Film Centre, an organization with the intent to take over the functions of Associated Realist Film Producers, which included the organization of sponsors and filmmakers.

Grierson's departure from the GPO Film Unit was met with the promotion of A.G. Highet to the position of Controller of Publicity and J.B. Holms to the post of Production Supervisor. Alberto Cavalcanti and Harry Watt both stayed on with the unit and brought a significant change to the kind of films the unit would produce. Cavalcanti and Watt led the GPO Film Unit away from the type of filmmaking for which the unit was previously known and toward films that used narrative techniques commonly associated with commercial cinema. Harry Watt made one of the first of these types of films while Grierson was still at the GPO Film Unit, called The Saving of Bill Blewitt (1936). The film makes use of scripted dialogue and studio sets and is based around a fictitious story. The film also is largely shot on location and uses nonprofessional actors. It proposes that the Post Office Savings Bank is the solution to the small businessman's problems. Harry Watt was to continue to produce these types of story documentaries on a much larger scale with North Sea (1938), a film he made for presentation at the Empire Exhibition in Glasgow. Based on true events, the film dramatizes a series of reports that Watt read involving ships caught in winter storms. The film was the most widely distributed film of all films produced by the GPO Film Unit, even receiving commercial distribution overseas.

The GPO Film Unit also produced a series of films dealing with international communications, including We Live in Two Worlds (1937) and Line to Tcherva Hut (1937), both directed by Alberto Cavalcanti. In addition to North Sea, other films produced for the Empire Exhibition included Mony a Pickle (1938) and The Tocher (1938). Another film the unit produced for the Ministry of Health was Health for the Nation (John Monck, 1939), which was a social documentary film directly about its sponsor. The unit also produced a series of films for display in the British Pavilion at the 1939 New York World's Fair dealing with British workers, including Men in Danger (Pat Jackson, 1939), British Made (George Pearson, 1939), and Spare Time (1939) directed by Humphrey Jennings (1907–50), one of the most significant directors of the British documentary movement. Spare Time is based on Jennings's connection with Mass Observation, a movement that attempted to apply ethnography to British society. The film shifts among portrayals of a brass band in the steel industry, the marching of a carnival band in the cotton industry, and the singing of a coal miners' choir. It contains hardly any commentary and tends to place its emphasis on the individuals in the various industries. The film paints a sympathetic, yet hardly romanticized, depiction of working-class leisure activities, later leading John Grierson to criticize the film. It would be the beginning of an artistically impressive output of production from Jennings during World War II.

The GPO Film Unit became the Crown Film Unit early in 1941, after the relocation of the unit's activity to the newly created Ministry of Information. The Crown Film Unit continued to produce documentaries that possessed a style similar to commercial films, a trend that had been occurring more frequently toward the end of the 1930s. The result was a steady output of films that were readily embraced by commercial audiences. Harry Watt's Target for Tonight (1941), which portrays a day in the life of a bomber squadron, became the most commercially successful documentary produced during World War II. Pat Jackson's Western Approaches (1944) was cast entirely from merchant seamen and depicts the aftermath of a torpedo attack on a convoy. Desert Victory (Roy Boulting, 1943) won the Academy Award for best feature-length documentary. By this point the unit had access to increased budgets and elaborate studio sets, factors that would distinctly separate their films from other documentaries of the time. The films they produced were also now regularly rented commercially.

The films of Humphrey Jennings during this period have been especially praised for their contribution to film art. His short film, Listen to Britain (1942), depicts a day in the life of Britain during wartime, presenting such imagery as factory workers juxtaposed with leisure activities taking place in a dance hall. Jennings's Fires Were Started (1943) documents a unit of the Auxiliary Fire Service and uses actual firemen as performers, and A Diary for Timothy (1944–5) combines the four stories of a farmer, an RAF pilot, a miner, and a railway engineer with the tale of a baby named Timothy. The contribution of Jennings's poetic marriage of sound and visual image remains a focus of critical attention on the documentaries produced by the Crown Film Unit.

The development of documentaries for television in Britain had begun as early as 1934, when the Selsdon Committee was formed to consider the medium's development. The BBC had established itself as a major sound broadcasting organization and was reluctant initially to invest its attention in television. By 1939 television in Britain had become a modest success, although during World War II the BBC would close down its operations and not reinstate them until 1946. By 1953 the BBC had begun to prioritize television's development and appointed former Grierson collaborator Paul Rotha as Head of Documentaries. Rotha saw the potential for television documentary and was committed to developing the new medium to socially inform Britain's citizens.

The television unit at the BBC during these early years was characterized by members who came from a multitude of backgrounds including Steve McCormack (theatre), Robert Barr and Norman Swallow (journalism), Caryl Doncaster (education), and Denis Mitchell (radio features). Three categories of programs that fell under the identification of 'documentary' were the dramatized documentary, the actuality documentary, and the magazine documentary (Bell 1986).

The dramatized documentary was a scripted, live production that featured professional actors. Locations were typically reproduced in the studio if possible, and the content of the stories for these films was taken from true life situations. Various subjects these films engaged included 'hooliganism, borstal, drugs, working women, children in care, problems of youth, marriage and old age, prostitution, industrial relations, declining industries' (Bell 1986). These programs were met with immediate popularity, but the cost of their production was significant. These dramatized documentaries re-created situations that caused controversy among those purists who were used to the documentation of real life events or 'actualities' in documentary film. Rotha defended these dramatized films through his assessment that realism within subject material was the true nature of documentary, regardless of how films are constructed.

Both the magazine and the actuality documentaries possessed content that was more journalistic than the dramatized documentary. Both used 'actualities' rather than scripted acting and interviews. One such notable actuality documentary production was the monthly series Special Enquiry (1952–7), which involved such national dilemmas as racial discrimination, illiteracy, slums, and international problems such as refugees, malaria, and soil erosion (Bell 1986). Special Enquiry was the first television program to speak from the point of view of the audience. It began to invite a consideration of documentary as a form of reporting (Corner 1991). Each episode was forty-five minutes long, consisting of an introduction from a studio presenter and concluding with a discussion with a studio guest following a filmed location report. The series was influential to the structure of British television journalism through its presentation of nonofficial speakers and presented a documentary type that moved beyond the sole portrayal of filmed or photojournalistic depiction.

The magazine documentary was far less serious in its intentions. Among the most popular television documentaries to be developed at the time, the magazine documentary resembled 'highly skillful travelogues with less scenery and more people' (Bell 1986). Within this form, represented by series such as London Town and About Britain, the first unscripted interviews in television documentary were used. The Documentary Department at the BBC was dissolved with the arrival of commercial television in 1955, with Rotha and its staff moving on to other projects.

Beginning in 1956, screenings at the National Film Theatre were organized in London. The films screened were organized by a group of young filmmakers and exhibited under the banner of Free Cinema. Those organizing the screenings (including Lindsay Anderson, best known as a critic at the time, and Karel Reisz, who had been program planner of the National Film Theatre) exhibited a variety of films, including documentary films they had produced. 'In the broadest terms, Free Cinema had two objectives: to show what it valued in the cinema, with the emphasis on the work of young contemporary filmmakers; and (to show) films to encourage other films to be made' (Hillier and Lovell 1972). The Free Cinema programs were committed to demonstrating the relationship between society and art, and the documentaries screened were assumed by the young organizers to portray this notion.

The films shown in the Free Cinema programs were generally free from the formal constraints placed on many commercial documentaries of the era. Their subject material, including a candid study of a jazz club in Momma Don't Allow (Karel Reisz and Tony Richardson, 1956), and an examination of popular culture through the people and exhibits of an amusement park in O Dreamland (Lindsay Anderson, 1953), were far different than many conventional documentary topics. Lindsay Anderson's Every Day Except Christmas (1957) offers a celebratory portrayal of British working-class people and owes much of its formal technique to the wartime films of Humphrey Jennings. Such films made use of new, lightweight equipment, which brought a renewed level of intimacy to documentary. The films were more ambiguous than previous documentary efforts and brought the viewer into places that were previously restricted. Lorenza Mazzetti's Together (1953) stands apart from other Free Cinema offerings because of its unique composition. The film uses long takes and slow editing rhythms to portray two oppositional communities, one of deaf mutes and the other of traditional working-class people. Although most all of the documentaries screened at the Free Cinema programmes may be described simply as portrayals of British society in the 1950s, they approached their representations from a contemporary perspective that had not been experienced before. The Free Cinema showings lasted for nearly three years and included a total of six programs. Its organizers would shortly thereafter venture into the realm of feature filmmaking, producing films that would make use of many of the techniques of the Free Cinema documentaries. Such notable examples include Look Back in Anger (Tony Richardson, 1959), The Entertainer (Tony Richardson, 1960), A Taste of Honey (Tony Richardson, 1961), and Saturday Night and Sunday Morning (Karel Reisz, 1960).

In the early 1960s, the nature of programming at the BBC began to change. New possibilities were offered through technological advances (such as the use of videotape), allowing broadcasts to depart from transmitting live dramatic performances. The boundary between fiction and documentary subsequently began to blur in broadcasts known as documentary dramas, programs that took advantage of the opportunities offered by the advances such as editing and the incorporation of nonprofessional actors into productions. Among the most influential directors of such works is Ken Loach (1936–), who along with socialist playwright Jim Allen (1926–99), would produce some of the most important documentary dramas of the era

Loach's career at the BBC began as director of three episodes of Z Cars (1962–78) in 1964 and soon led him to direct three episodes of the six-part series Diary of a Young Man in late 1964. These early works, however, were not representative of the stylistic blurring of documentary and drama that Loach would use in his later films. In 1965 he began to direct the first of ten plays he would produce for The Wednesday Play series. Three of these plays, Up the Junction (1965), Cathy Come Home (1966), and In Two Minds (1967), would establish Loach as a politically minded visionary whose films combine social and political dilemmas as a commentary on the contemporary climate of Britain.

Up the Junction's realistic depiction of abortion was viewed by more than ten million people during its first transmission. More than four hundred complaints were expressed to the BBC after its broadcast, most concerning the film's use of language and portrayal of abortion. The film uses documentary elements including an interview with a doctor who suggests the revision of laws preventing legalized abortions. Many viewers were confused as to whether they were watching a news broadcast or a fictionalized drama when the film originally aired, as it was shown directly after the evening news. Loach claimed that '(he) was very anxious for (his) plays (to) not be considered dramas but as continuations of the news'. Up the Junction makes use of 1960s pop music and uses a fragmentary narrative structure similar to its source novel, written by Nell Dunn.

Cathy Come Home's portrayal of homelessness and poverty has reached iconic status in Britain since its original broadcast in 1966. The film's blending of documentary elements with fiction realistically portrays the tragedies that befall a working-class family after an accident, eventually resulting in the family's destruction. In one particularly memorable scene, Social Services removes Cathy's (Carol White) children from her after her separation from husband Reg (Ray Brooks). The film favors location shooting, and its formal techniques owe much to the stylistic influence of the Free Cinema documentaries. Cathy Come Home also prompted political outrage from its audience after its original broadcast, so much so that its re-airing a few months later revealed several omissions from the version originally broadcast. The reaction from the film's audience eventually led to the establishment of Shelter, a homelessness charity.

In Two Minds involves the story of Kate Winter (Anna Cropper), a young woman who eventually is driven to madness by her familial environment. Loach would remake the film in 1971 as Family Life, but not before controversy would surround the original. In Two Minds prompted concern from critics such as James Thomas in the *Daily Express*, who believed that its intense style was too realistic not to carry announcements before and after broadcasts explaining the film's fictional nature. The film also received criticism from the psychiatric community, who judged its portrayal of schizophrenia and of medical workers who assist Kate as inaccurate.

Loach's collaborations with Jim Allen are arguably his most politically important works produced for television. Having previously written scripts for the British soap opera Coronation Street in 1964, Allen was commissioned to write The Lump for Wednesday Play in 1967. His first collaboration with Loach, The Big Flame (1969), recounts the story of the occupation of a port in Liverpool by dock workers. Widely considered to be among Loach's most political films, The Big Flame 'dealt head-on with fundamental questions of ownership, class conflict, the role of the state, and political organization and mobilization' (Petley 1997). The dock workers form a port workers' council and attempt to run the dock themselves. Eventually they are defeated by forces that include the trade union movement and the Labour Party. 'Here appears the key theme which will dominate much of Loach's subsequent work, whether in dramas such as The Rank and File (1971) and Days of Hope (1975), or ill-fated documentaries, such as Questions of Leadership (1983): namely, that Labour politicians and trade union leaders are terrified of mass action by the militant working class, since it threatens the very structures on which their own power and position are based' (Petley 1997).

Loach and Allen would again work together on the film The Rank and File, based on the Pilkington's glass workers' strike of 1970. The film was followed by yet another collaboration, the ambitious four-part Days of Hope in 1975, a film that traces the upheavals of the British Labour movement from 1916 to the General Strike in 1926. The film (Loach's first historical piece) unveils its narrative through the lives of three characters. It is strongly influenced by the politics of 1970s Britain and was condemned by Conservative politicians for its harsh portrayal of the government. The film's style continues Loach's naturalistic visual approach and breaks the conventional expectations of television drama through the use of a technique with spoken dialogue that seems improvisational and disorganized. Ultimately, Allen was accused of mixing fact and fiction and of distorting the facts of history to deliver a political message, and some critics began to suspect that the BBC was adopting a left-wing philosophy. Loach would move toward directing feature films in the years after working for the BBC including Poor Cow (1967), Land and Freedom (1995), Carla's Song (1996), My Name is Joe (1998), and The Navigators (2001).

Another important figure who produced groundbreaking documentary dramas for the BBC is Peter Watkins (1935–). After receiving his education at Cambridge, Watkins became an amateur documentary filmmaker, producing short works such as The Diary of an Unknown Soldier (1959), in which a World War I soldier narrates his last days of being alive, and The Forgotten Faces (1961), a film concerning a revolt in Hungary. In 1964 Watkins was hired by the BBC and produced his first notable work, Culloden. The film showcases Watkins's trademark style, which combines drama with handheld camerawork and faux 'newsreel' interview footage of nonprofessional actors who were instructed to acknowledge the camera. Culloden follows a television crew as they cover the 1746 Battle of Culloden and contains realistic battle footage as Watkins places the viewer 'on location' with the news crew, complete with jarring camerawork and a soundtrack that allows the viewer to hear the horrors of war without actually viewing them. The film not only challenges the notion of how history has traditionally been recorded but also makes evident the fallacies of historical fiction.

Watkins's next film was The War Game (1965), which again uses his distinctive style to portray the atrocities of nuclear war. The film features interviews with 'survivors' of a nuclear strike on Britain and is convincing through its use of documents, scientific studies, charts, and face-to-face interviews. The BBC originally banned the film from being broadcast in 1966 because of its intensely graphic nature and the chance that it could convince its viewers into believing its authenticity. The film was eventually transmitted on television nearly twenty years later in 1985. The War Game did receive a small theatrical run shortly after its completion, winning the Oscar for Best Documentary Feature in 1967. Watkins later would direct his only feature film, the science fiction failure Privilege, with funding from Universal in 1966 and subsequently worked primarily in Scandinavia after leaving the United Kingdom. Punishment Park (1971), a pseudo-documentary that follows a group of soldiers as they escort liberals across a desert, and Edvard Munch (1974), a biography of the Norwegian artist, later followed.

In 1964 Britain's Granada Television began what would become the longest running documentary series in visual history with the production of 7Up (Paul Almond), a film that interviews a group of British children from various backgrounds about a variety of subjects, including their outlook on life and prospects for the future. Michael Apted (who was an assistant on the film) revisited the same children seven years later and directed 7 Plus Seven in 1970. Apted would revisit the children in seven-year intervals after 7 Plus Seven, resulting in the films 21 Up (1977), 28 Up (1984), 35 Up (1992), and 42 Up (1999). The films provide an interesting chronology of the social progression of Britain and contemporary culture at large, as various participants become poverty stricken while others appear to find fulfillment in their lives.

One of Britain's most recognizable documentary filmmakers, Nick Broomfield (1948–), is also one of documentary film's most innovative. His insistence on placing himself within the context and frame of those subjects and situations he documents has become characteristic of what Stella Bruzzi calls 'performative' documentary filmmaking. Broomfield's presence within his films draws attention to the construction of nonfiction filmmaking as one type of representation, as opposed to a portrayal of unmediated reality (Bruzzi 2000).

Broomfield was born in London and made his first film, Who Cares? (1971), a study of a working-class community in Liverpool, with financial assistance from the British Film Institute. After studying law at Essex University, he joined the National Film School at Beaconsfield and produced Proud to Be British in 1973. The film is a series of opportunities for various citizens to explain what it means to them to be British. Behind the Rent Strike was completed in 1974 and features people from Who Cares? as a companion piece to the earlier film. Beginning in 1976, Broomfield made the first of several films with American filmmaker Joan Churchhill and began to apply a style more aligned with the observational cinema of Fredrick Wiseman. Juvenile Liaison (1976) follows two police officers and their dealings with youth. The film documents the incredibly harsh treatment of youth at the hands of the police and was later withdrawn from distribution after pressure from the authorities. Broomfield would later revisit the subject in 1990 with Juvenile Liaison 2 (1990).

After temporarily dissolving his partnership with Churchill, Broomfield began to more readily exhibit the confrontational, participatory documentary style that has characterized his career, with 1988's Driving Me Crazy. The film, about the making of a film of a black stage musical, begins to take an unfortunate turn, and Broomfield soon places himself within the film's frame. The result is what Broomfield believes to be a more honest approach to filmmaking, allowing the viewer to make decisions based on the interaction between interviewer and interviewee instead of the former hiding behind the scenes.

Broomfield uses the same stylistic approach in his film The Leader, His Driver and the Driver's Wife (1991), a documentation of Eugene Terreblanche, the leader of the neo-Nazi Afrikaner Resistance Movement (the AWB) in South Africa. Tracking Down Maggie (1994) continues to use the same participatory approach through its attempt to document Margaret Thatcher, with little success, as do many of Broomfield's more recent and financially successful documentaries, including Aileen Wuornos: The Selling of a Serial Killer (1992), Heidi Fleiss: Hollywood Madam (1995), Kurt and Courtney (1998), and Biggie and Tupac (2002).

Filmmaker Molly Dineen similarly uses herself as an active participant in her films. Instead of becoming actively visible like the stylistic approach of Broomfield, however, Dineen uses her voice behind the camera not only to communicate with on-screen interviewees but also to constantly remind the viewer of the constructedness of documentary. Her earlier work includes Home from the Hill (1985), a film made while she was attending the National Film and Television School that documents a retired soldier and safari operator returning from Kenya to England, and My African Farm (1988), a portrait of Colonel Sylvia Richardson and her servants on a farm in Kenya over Christmas. A documentary about people working at the Angel Underground Station, 1989's Heart of the Angel, characterizes Dineen's early style in that it refuses explanatory voice-over narration in an exchange for Dineen's personal encounters with her subjects. 'As with many 1960s direct cinema films such as Salesman, Heart of the Angel is reliant upon the subjects' performances for and to the camera' (Bruzzi 2000).

Dineen's 1993 BBC effort, The Ark, is a series of four one-hour films about London Zoo during six months of crisis. Facing financial ruin, the zoo exports more than 1,300 animals (about one-third of the entire zoo's collection) and 26 keepers. The film clearly continues the observational style of Dineen's previous efforts, with scenes extending for minutes without any commentary from the director. Critics drew parallels between the situation presented in the film and growing turmoil within official bodies such as the Labour Party, The Church of England, and the BBC itself. The film never really sentimentalizes the subject material and instead offers the observation of stunning visuals to communicate to its audience. Dineen's later work includes: In the Company of Men (1995), a series of three one-hour films with The Prince of Wales company of the Welsh Guards on a tour of duty in Northern Ireland; Tony Blair (1997), a ten-minute portrait of Tony Blair broadcast before the 1997 election campaign; and Geri (1999), a ninety-minute documentary that follows Geri Halliwell (also known as Ginger Spice) in the three months after her departure from the pop group The Spice Girls. In 2002 Molly Dineen produced The Lord's Tale, a film for Channel 4 about the reform of the House of Lords.

Another notable filmmaker hailing from Britain who helped to destroy the conventions associated with documentary is Nicholas Barker. Barker's television series, Signs of the Times (BBC, 1992) consists of a series of interviews with individuals about good and bad taste. The approach to the series 'is minimalist, stylized and possesses a stylistic uniformity that gives it a clear identity and lends it a fetishistic intensity, mesmerized by superficialities, appearance and detail' (Bruzzi 2000). Stella Bruzzi argues that because Signs of the Times is self-conscious in its style, it reflects its subjectivity and authorship and thereby becomes performative by challenging notions of fixed identity and truth. The characters on the show 'are performative on two counts: they are performing their words by being the embodiments of their identified tastes and attitudes, and they perform their interviews in such a way as to raise questions about spontaneity and documentary authenticity' (Bruzzi 2000).

Barker's film Unmade Beds (1997) expands on this notion through setting up a premise that calls attention to the authenticating procedures of documentary. Barker, deciding to make a film about the personals scene in New York City, began interviewing more than 400 candidates before eventually deciding on the four individuals used in the film. Working from the actors' own versions of their life stories, Barker produced a script that the actors followed while shooting the film. The result is a fictional documentation based on real life events and acted out by the people on whom those events are based. Questions of authenticity are problematic in the film and in the process raise important questions about the possibility of truthful representation. Unmade Beds demonstrates that perhaps all representations contain elements of both fiction and nonfiction, and that the attempt to capture 'reality' in visual media is indeed an impossible pursuit.

KEVIN SHERMAN

See also: Anderson, Lindsay; Anstey, Edgar; BBC: The Voice of Britain; Cavalcanti, Alberto; Coal Face; Desert Victory; Drifters; Elton, Arthur; Enough to Eat?; Every Day Except Christmas; Granton Trawler; Grierson, John; Housing Problems; Industrial Britain; Legg, Stuart; Line to Tcherva Hut; Loach, Ken; Momma Don't Allow; Night Mail; Reisz, Karel; Song of Ceylon, The; Target for Tonight; War Game, The; Watkins, Peter; Watt, Harry; We Live in Two Worlds; Wright, Basil

Further reading

Aitken, Ian, *Film and Reform: John Grierson and the Documentary Film Movement*, London and New York: Routledge, 1990.

Bell, Elaine, 'The Origins of British Television Documentary: The BBC 1946–55', in John Corner (ed.), *Documentary and the Mass Media*, London: Edward Arnold, 1986.

Bruzzi, Stella, *New Documentary: A Critical Introduction*, London and New York: Routledge, 2000.

Corner, John, 'Documentary Voices', in John Corner (ed.), *Popular Television in Britain: Studies in Cultural History*, London: British Film Institute, 1991.

Grierson, John, *Grierson on Documentary*, London: Fabor & Fabor, 1946.

Hillier, Jim and Lovell, Alan, *Studies in Documentary*, London: Secker & Warburg, 1972.

Izod, John, Kilborn, Richard and Hibberd, Matthew (eds), *From Grierson to the Docu-Soap: Breaking the Boundaries*, Luton: University of Luton Press, 2000.

Laing, Stuart, 'Ken Loach: Histories and Contexts', in George McKnight (ed.), *Agent of Challenge and Defiance: The Films of Ken Loach*, Westport, CT: Praeger Publishers, 1997.

Low, Rachael, *Documentary and Educational Films of the 1930s*, London: Allen & Unwin, 1979.

Orbanz, Eva, *Journey to a Legend and Back: The British Realistic Film*, trans. by Stuart Hood, Berlin: Volker Speiss, 1977.

Petley, Julian, 'Factual Fictions and Fictional Fallacies: Ken Loach's Documentary Dramas', in George McKnight (ed.), *Agent of Challenge and Defiance: The Films of Ken Loach*, Westport, CT: Praeger Publishers, 1997.

Rotha, Paul, *Documentary Diary*, New York: Hill & Wang, 1973.

Sussex, Elizabeth, *The Rise and Fall of British Documentary*, Berkeley, CA: University of California Press, 1975.

Swann, Paul, *The British Documentary Film Movement 1926–46*, Cambridge: Cambridge University Press, 1989.

Urban, Charles

Charles Urban is arguably the leading pioneer of the nonfiction film. Others, such as the Lumières, Léon Gaumont, Charles Pathé, and George Kleine, may have worked in similar fields, but none spoke as loudly or covered so wide a range as Urban. His ambitions were laid out in his 1907 booklet, *The Cinematograph in Science, Education and Matters of State*, which expounded his belief in the instructional role that film had to take in society (as well as having what is probably the first use in English of the word documentary in a filmic sense). Urban's career is distinctive not only for its idealistic espousal of nonfiction film, but because he tried to marry this mission with the fields of salesmanship and showmanship in which his career was grounded. His career demonstrates both the exciting range of options for the producer that the early cinema period seemed to promise and the narrowing of those options in reality as the cinema programme became established along specific lines.

Urban's rise and fall can be traced through five distinctive phases, each illustrative of the options open to the producer of nonfiction film in the first years of cinema. The first phase, to 1903, was that of the American salesman galvanising the complacent early British film business. Urban's first thirty years were spent in America, where he started out as a high-class book salesman, moving through the systems of automation and production found in office stores to market phonographs, Kinetoscopes, Vitascopes, and finally his own film projector, the Bioscope. It was with this practical device that he came to Britain in 1897, turning an American off-shoot company into the dynamic Warwick Trading Company. As producer, distributor, and equipment supplier, Urban made an indelible stamp on the British film business and laid the groundwork for what seemed like a native aptitude for film of reality.

The second phase saw Urban as owner of his own company, the Charles Urban Trading Company (founded 1903). Here Urban opened up the range of nonfiction films as fiction films themselves began to grow in length and range of forms. For Urban, his films of science, travel, sport, exploration, and medicine were every bit as entertaining as the fiction film, with the added value of social usefulness. 'To amuse and entertain is good', ran one of his slogans, 'to do both and instruct is better'. Urban employed skilful scientific filmmakers with a populist bent, such as F. Martin Duncan and Percy Smith, French surgeon Eugène-Louis Doyen, mountaineer F. Ormiston-Smith, and war cameraman Joseph Rosenthal, all of whom could contribute to Urban's proudest slogan, 'We put the world before you'. At a time when fifty percent of all British film production was nonfiction, at least fifty percent of all British nonfiction film was produced by Urban. He established Britain's national cinematic picture of itself.

In 1908 Urban launched Kinemacolor (first named in 1909), a natural colour process using red and green filters, which seemed to promise cinema's greatest fidelity to real life yet. Urban's Kinemacolor productions caused a sensation in the period 1909–13, for the dazzling nature of the colour (inadequate as it now seems to modern eyes), for its theatrical presentation and consequent high prices, for the unprecedented length of its programmes, and particularly for its emphasis on royal spectacle. Urban's greatest Kinemacolor triumph came with With Our King and Queen Through India (1912), which ran for two and a half hours and featured the spectacular Delhi Durbar ceremonies.

Kinemacolor fiction films were made as well, but Urban had little aptitude for drama, and the results were notably poor. Urban sold exclusive Kinemacolor licences to international territories and seemed to have made his fortune, but a court case from a rival colour system in 1913 led to the invalidation of the patent.

World War I saw Urban faced with the reality of putting his motion pictures at the service of the state. What Urban had advocated urgently, in practice proved far more problematic. He produced a documentary feature for the covert War Propaganda Bureau, Britain Prepared, and was directed to take it to America in 1916. Urban battled equally against hostile American exhibitors and British propagandists unsympathetic toward his showman's sensibilities. Urban edited the outstanding documentary feature, The Battle of the Somme, but found this no easier to get onto American scenes, blundering badly when he tried to get a distribution deal with the anti-British Hearst's International Film Service. America's entry into the war made Urban's task suddenly much easier, and he proved an effective editor and distributor of British official films in America for the remainder of the war.

The British film business now in ruins, Urban decided to settle once more in America and, in the final phase of his career, to establish himself as an educational filmmaker. Urban had always viewed himself in this light, producing the world's first educational film catalogue in 1908, even if the specific educational utility of his films was never made clear. In postwar America, the Visual Education movement was encouraging greater use of moving pictures in the classroom, and Urban was one among many producers fighting for this new market. Urban became over-ambitious, creating the grandiose Urban Institute building in Irvington, NY, and pouring thousands into a filmless disk viewer called the Spirograph; however, all that Urban had to support this activity were two minor cinemagazines and some imaginative documentary features made with the naturalist Raymond Ditmars. His business collapsed in 1924. Ironically, 16mm film and a fully fledged nontheatrical film circuit now emerged, just as Urban—who had so long advocated for film to reach out to where specific audiences needed it—was forced to bow out of the scene.

Urban was the preeminent advocate of the full function of cinema at just that time when the options for exhibiting films were at their narrowest. As the cinema programme evolved, the nonfiction film came to occupy an increasingly small portion of what was shown on the screen. Exasperated by the inexorable rise of the fiction film, Urban was ultimately a prophet for the nontheatrical film who never himself made it to the promised land.

LUKE MCKERNAN

See also: Battle of the Somme

Biography

Born Cincinnati, Ohio, April 15, 1867. Settled in Detroit in 1889, opening Phonograph parlour, 1893. Expanded business to include Kinetoscopes, 1895. Obtained Michigan agency for Vitascope projector, before developing own projector, the Bioscope, 1896. Moved to Britain as manager of London branch of Maguire & Baucus, 1897, which became Warwick Trading Company, 1898. Formed own film business, Charles Urban Trading Company, 1903. Launched two-colour natural colour film system, later called Kinemacolor, 1908. Natural Color Kinematograph Company forced into liquidation, 1914. Produced documentary feature Britain Prepared for War Propaganda Bureau, 1915. Marketed British official war films in America, 1916–18. Formed Urban Motion Picture Industries, based in Irvington, NY, 1920. Urban Motion Picture Industries bankrupt, 1924. Returned to Britain by end of 1920s and retired from film business. Died in Brighton, August 29, 1942.

Selected films

1902 Le Sacre d'Edouard (Méliès): producer
1907 Torpedo Attack on HMS Dreadnought: producer
1908 The Balancing Bluebottle: producer
1910 A Day in the Life of a Coal Miner: producer
1910 S.S. Olympic: producer
1911 The Coronation of King George V and Queen Mary: producer
1912 With Our King and Queen Through India: producer.
1915 Britain Prepared: producer
1916 The Battle of the Somme (McDowell, Malins): editor
1921 The Four Seasons (Ditmars): producer
1921 Permanent Peace: producer
1923 Evolution (Ditmars): producer

Further reading

McKernan, Luke, 'Putting the World Before You: The Charles Urban Story', in Andrew Higson (ed.), *Young and Innocent? The Cinema in Britain, 1896–1930*, Exeter: University of Exeter Press, 2002.

Urban, Charles, *A Yank in Britain: The Lost Memoirs of Charles Urban, Film Pioneer*, Luke McKernan (ed.), Hastings: The Projection Box, 1999.

V

Vachek, Karel

From his cinéma vérité films of the 1960s through his 'film novels' of the 1990s, maverick Czech filmmaker Karel Vachek has been known for his outspoken refusal to conform to aesthetic or political trends and for pioneering a new visual and narrative style for social documentary. A 1963 graduate of FAMU, the Film Faculty of the Academy of Music and Performing Arts in Prague, Vachek has been called the enfant terrible of the Czechoslovak New Wave (Navrátil 1992), a group of artists whose formal and conceptual experimentation gained international recognition in the 1960s. This reputation was born with his FAMU thesis film, Moravská Hellas/Moravian Hellas (1963). The thirty-three-minute documentary, filmed at the Strážnice folk festival, satirized communist perversion of folk culture, using a hybrid style that combined elements of cinéma vérité with staged interviews. The film was so controversial that after its release Vachek was banned from filmmaking until 1968, when the reforms of Alexander Dubček's 'socialism with a human face' eliminated censorship and lessened restrictions on personal and creative expression. That year, Vachek produced the cinéma vérité film Spřižnění volbou/Elective Affinities (1968).

Shot on a handheld 16mm Éclair camera, the film chronicles the events and climate surrounding Antonín Novotný's fall from power and the beginning of Ludvík Svobodá's presidency. Less than six months later, Warsaw Pact armies invaded Czechoslovakia, marking the end of the Prague Spring and heralding the beginning of more than twenty years of Soviet rule. With censorship and restrictions on artists more stringent than ever, Vachek, like many other intellectuals and artists, was unable to make films. After a five-year period of exile in France and the United States, and a number of years working outside of the film industry in Czechoslovakia, Vachek returned to his profession in 1989.

Vachek's films of the 1990s mark a shift in his style and approach, although his new work retains characteristics of his cinéma vérité heritage. The four parts of the Little Capitalist Tetralogy, each between three and four hours long, are Nový Hyperion aneb Rovnost volnost bratrsví/New Hyperion or Equality Liberty Brotherhood (1992), which traces the presidential elections of 1990 in Czechoslovakia; Co Dělat? Cesta z Prahy do Českého Krumlova aneb Jak jsem sestavoval novou vladu/What Is to be Done? A Journey from Prague to Cesky Krumlov or How I Formed a New Government (1996), which follows a group of artists and intellectuals on a bus trip between the two cities, capturing their debates and arguments alongside the mystical history of Cesky Krumlov; Bohemia Docta aneb Labyrint světa a lusthauz srdce (Božská Komedie)/Bohemia Docta or Labyrinth of the World and Paradise of the Heart (Divine Comedy) (2000), a commentary on the state of the intellectual in the Czech Republic; and Dalibor: Kdo bude hlídat hlídače aneb Klíčk chaloupce strýčka Toma/Dalibor: Who's Gonna Watch the Watchman? or The Key to Uncle Tom's Cabin (2003), a probing of the state of the nation at the end of the millennium, set during a piano rehearsal of Bedřich Smetana's opera *Dalibor*. Taken collectively, the films comprise a dialogic history of the political and social changes that gripped the Czech lands between 1990 and the end of the millennium.

The films of the Tetralogy develop their narratives with a mixture of vérité moments, staged sections, and long on-screen conversations between the director and a series of subjects, set in aesthetically interesting or connotative locations. Most of the men and women who populate the films, many of them recurring figures, were generally dissidents or outsiders under the Soviet regime and remain on the fringes of post-1989 society. They are artists and professors, writers and political activists. Vachek guides these subjects through philosophical or political debates in circuitous, frequently comical paths toward a poetic vision of the state and the individual in the modern world. Although politics are central to these films, Vachek is primarily concerned with the philosophical aspects of politics. His perspective is that of an exile, guided by a conviction that social and political change can originate only on the periphery of society.

Although the Tetralogy draw its characters and themes from the era in which it was created, the films resist strict categorization as documentary, moving instead between reportage and fictionalization, performance and poetic reflection. The director, in fact, objects to his films' classification as documentaries, preferring to call them 'film novels'. Their titles, indeed, are derived from literature—New Hyperion, for example, from Holderlein, and What Is to be Done? from Chernishevsky. Further distinguishing his work from traditional documentary, Vachek uses aesthetics borrowed from fiction films. He shoots with cumbersome, expensive 35mm film instead of video or 16mm film; his sequences and shots are highly planned; and, alongside documentary moments, Vachek inserts staged scenes. Although Vachek's films have been criticized as hermetic or provocative, his work has nonetheless proved a central influence on a successive generation of documentary filmmakers in the Czech Republic, among them Jan Gogola Jr and Vít Janeček, and has found a pedagogical home in the documentary department of FAMU, where Vachek has taught since 1993.

ALICE LOVEJOY

Biography

Born August 4, 1940 in Tišnově, Czechoslovakia. Atttended FAMU, the Film Faculty of the Academy of Music and Performing Arts in Prague, from 1958–63, where he studied directing under Elmar Klos. Banned from filmmaking after the release of Moravian Hellas in 1963, and again after the release of Elective Affinities in 1968. Emigrated in 1979, first to France, and then to the United States. Returned to Czechoslovakia in 1984. Awarded the Berlinale Camera award in 1990. Since 1993, has taught documentary at FAMU; since 2002, chair of FAMU's documentary department.

Selected films

1963 Moravská Hellas/Moravian Hellas
1968 Spřižnění volbou/Elective Affinities
1992 New Hyperion or Equality Liberty Brotherhood
1996 Co Dělat? Cesta z Prahy do Českého Krumlova aneb Jak jsem sestavoval novou vladu/What Is to be Done? A Journey from Prague to Cesky Krumlov or How I Formed a New Government
2000 Bohemia Docta aneb Labyrint Světa a Lusthauz Srdce (Božská Komedie)/ Bohemia Docta or Labyrinth of the World and Paradise of the Heart (Divine Comedy)
2003 Dalibor: Kdo bude hlídat hlídače aneb Klíčk chaloupce strýčka Toma/Dalibor: Who's Gonna Watch the Watchman or The Key to Uncle Tom's Cabin

Further reading

Buchar, Robert, *Czech New Wave Filmmakers in Interviews*, Jefferson, NC: McFarland, 2004.
Camhi, Leslie, 'Spring Forward', *The Village Voice*, February 13–19, 2002.
Hames, Peter, *The Czechoslovak New Wave*, Berkeley, CA: University of California Press, 1985.
Liehm, Antonín J. and Liehm, Mira, *The Most Important Art: Eastern European Film After 1945*, Berkeley, CA: University of California Press, 1977.
Navrátil, Antonín, 'Nejdelsí Cesky Film', in *Lidové*, Noviny, April 16, 1992 (in Czech).
Slater, Thomas J., 'Czechoslovakia', in Thomas J. Slater (ed.), *Handbook of Soviet and East European Films and Filmmakers*, New York: Greenwood Press, 1992.
Stoll, Martin, *Hundred Years of Czech Documentary Film (1898–1998)*, Prague: Malá Skála, 2000.

Varda, Agnès

Agnès Varda is often referred to as the 'grandmother' of the French New Wave. Varda is the only woman strongly connected to this avant garde film movement of the 1950s and 1960s, and her work is both technically innovative and politically motivated as she uses the camera as a tool for social investigation. Varda's interest in the construction of gender and the inherent codification of gender via popular representation is seen throughout her body of work. Her La Pointe Courte (1956) is often cited as the first New Wave feature. Sandy Flitterman-Lewis argues for this association as she describes the aesthetics of the film, noting its 'concern with temporality, the interfacing of subjective realities, the articulation of discursive modes, the pervasive "sense of place", the aspect of research, both sociological and linguistic, the interest in permutations of the narrative form, the techniques of distancing and cultural critique, the redefinition of spectatorship, the self-reflexivity about cinematic meaning, and the challenge to establish forms of cinematic storytelling' (Flitterman-Lewis 1990: 260). The film explores the struggles of people in a small Mediterranean fishing village. Her L'Opéra-Mouffe (1958) displays her evolving documentary technique, as it shows scenes from a market without the intervention of reportage or other narration.

As her work continued, Varda made both documentary and fictional narratives, using each to engage in social commentary. Her films deal with personal expression, the differences between people and the way they behave, and the social and cultural contexts that shape us. After a few well-received feature narratives, Varda made two documentaries in the United States in the late 1960s. Her Uncle Yanco (1967) deals with the 'discovery' of Varda's uncle living in San Francisco, California. This was followed by her 1968 documentary, Black Panthers, a piece that showed this politically active group as an integral part of the shifting culture in the United States. The work shows the experience of a rally to free Panther Huey Newton from jail. Panthers Stokely Carmichel, Bobby Seale, and H. Rap Brown are also shown.

Daguerreotypes (1975) looks at the use of the still image within a motion picture. There are close-ups of objects and shopkeepers in Rue Daguerre. As the film continues, objects are shown in different contexts, and the ways in which this causes the image to change is paramount. At the end of the film, the human subjects shown each turn to face the camera for several seconds, a live, in-motion, still moment. The interplay between the filmed image and the photographed still is contemplated as the piece ends. Varda's documentary works began to look at the idea of memory and the passage of time as an element of our culture in the late 1970s and into the 1980s.

Jacquot de Nantes (1990), Varda's tribute to the life and work of her late husband, uses black-and-white images for tales from Demy's childhood in the 1930s and 1940s and color images of Demy in the 1980s. These are edited into this charming work along with clips from Demy's films to show the ways in which his work reflected his life and interests.

Varda's The Gleaners and I/Les Glaneurs et la Glaneuse (2000) was shot entirely on digital video. The work looks at people who harvest the castoff belongings of others and survive from their 'hunting' in gutters, trash bins, and other such places where useful but unwanted things are found. This is a vision of recycling and reusing in a grand sense. Varda's film explores this notion in an art-making context as well; she sees herself as a collector of images, a gleaner in both the gathering of material and the assemblage of it. Varda spoke of her approach to this work: 'I think that documentary means "real", that you have to meet these real people, and let them express what they feel about the subject. The more I met them, the more I could see I had nothing to make as a statement. They make the statement; they explain the subject better than anybody. So it's not like having an idea about a subject and "let's illustrate it". It's meeting real people and discovering with them what they express about the subject, building the subject through real people. So it is a documentary, but the shape that I gave to it—including the original score and the editing—is really for me a narrative film. Not that documentary is "not good" and narrative is "good". But I really work as a filmmaker, I would say, to give a specific shape to that subject. And so far, it's worked, because whether people are cinephiles or not, they like the film. They like the people they meet in the film' (Anderson 2001: 25–6).

When Varda received the 2003 Inaugural Eisenstein Award from University of Southern California's School of Cinema-Television, University Provost Lloyd Armstrong described Varda as an artist 'whose work challenges the artificial constructs that separate people and ideas' (*In Motion* 2004: 10). The award honors filmmakers with international stature for their visionary work and distinguished contributions to the cinematic arts. Varda continues to work in documentary film and to explore cultural diversity in ways that delve into the experience of being human.

TAMMY A. KINSEY

Biography

Born May 1928, Brussels, Belgium. Trained in art history and photography. Worked as official photographer for Jean Vilar's Theatre National Populaire. Married to filmmaker Jacques Demy from 1962 until his death in 1990. Commissioned to make two short films for French National Tourist Office, late 1950s. Won César Award for Best Documentary Short for Ulysse, 1982. Museum of Modern Art Retrospective show, 1997. Awarded Méliès Prize for Best French Film of 2000 by French Union of Film Critics for The Gleaners and I.

Selected films

1958 L'Opéra-Mouffe
1958 Du côté de la Côte
1959 La Cocette d'Azur
1960 Champagne France
1960 Italy
1963 Salut les Cubains/Salute to Cuba
1964 Les Enfants du musee/Episode of television series Chroniques de France
1967 Loin du Vietnam
1968 The Black Panthers
1975 Daguerreotypes
1980 Murs Murs/Murals, Murals
1984 Les Dites Caryatides
1993 Les Demoiselles ont eu 25 ans/The Young Girls Turn 25
1995 L'Univers de Jacques Demy/The World of Jacques Demy

Further reading

Anderson, Melissa, 'The Modest Gesture of the Filmmaker: An Interview with Agnès Varda', *Cineaste* 26, no. 4, fall 2001: 24–7.

Anthony, Elizabeth, 'From Fauna to Flora in Agnès Varda's Cleo de 5 a 7', *Film Quarterly* 26, 1998: 88–96.

Darke, Chris, 'Refuseniks', *Sight and Sound* 11, no. 1, January 2001: 30–3.

Flitterman-Lewis, Sandy, *To Desire Differently: Feminism and the French Cinema*, Urbana, IL: Illinois University Press, 1990.

In Motion, winter 2004, USC School of Cinema-Television.

Vas, Robert

Hungarian exile Robert Vas went from being a marginal figure on the periphery of Free Cinema to one of the most highly regarded documentary film directors working at the BBC in the 1960s and 1970s. During those years he made thirty films before his tragically early death at the age of forty-seven. Essentially an autodidact strongly influenced by the work of Humphrey Jennings, Vas was less concerned with political ideology than with liberal humanist consciousness.

The personal sensibility that marks Vas's best work cannot be grasped without reference to his experiences as a refugee living in exile. Although his family survived the Holocaust in the Budapest ghetto by acquiring Swedish passports, his mother committed suicide after the war and his father abandoned the family, emigrating to Australia. Military service as an army projectionist was terminated by a nervous breakdown and a spell in a psychiatric hospital. Unable to acquire a formal education, Vas did, however, attend lectures at the Academy of Dramatic Arts and later worked as a trainee script editor at the National Theatre in Budapest. The failure of the 1956 Hungarian Uprising led him to leave the country, crossing the border into Austria with his wife and child and making his way to London shortly afterward.

Initially working in menial cleaning jobs, he soon found a niche in the Information Department at the British Film Institute (BFI), where he gained an encyclopaedic knowledge of world cinema as well as a passion for the films of Humphrey Jennings. Contact with Lindsay Anderson and Karel Reisz led to his first film, funded by the newly formed BFI Experimental Film Fund. Refuge England combined documentary observation with acted scenes to tell the story of a refugee's first day in London. This was screened in the final Free Cinema programme in March 1959 alongside Reisz's We Are the Lambeth Boys. Vas's next project, The Vanishing Street (1962), about a Jewish community in the East End was followed by his first film for the BBC, the autobiographical The Frontier shot on the Austro-Hungarian border.

During the next fourteen years, Vas consolidated his work as a freelancer, straddling different departments at the Corporation and making films for strands such as Omnibus and Horizon. Subjects included popular culture in The Golden Years of Alexander Korda (1968) and Cuckoo—A Celebration of Laurel and Hardy (1974); science and society in films on Arthur Koestler (Koestler on Creativity, 1967) and Claude Lévi-Strauss (The Savage Mind, 1970); portraits of artists (Miklos Radnoti, 1969) and directors Miklos Janscó (The Quiet Hungarian, 1967) and Humphrey Jennings (Heart of Britain, 1970); and the world of music in Bartók (1970) and the Austrian conductor Bruno Walter (1972).

It was in a series of historical films that Vas made his mark, in some cases even causing political controversy. The Issue Should Be Avoided (1971), an investigation into the 1941 Katyn Forest massacre where more than four thousand captive Polish officers were murdered by the Soviet NKVD, was later to be complemented by the magisterial two-and-a-half-hour Stalin in 1973. Nine Days in '26 (1974), exploring untold accounts of the 1926 General Strike from the miners' point of view, was deemed to be sufficiently sensitive to be unofficially shelved by the BBC for several months, much to Vas's dismay. To Die—To Live (1975) dealt with the legacy of Hiroshima; Orders from Above (1975) examined the forcible repatriation of Russian prisoners of war by Allied troops between 1945–7. Based on The Last Secret by Nicholas Bethell, the film triggered extensive debate.

Vas's filmmaking methods were eclectic and varied. He used actors to portray historical figures on location and in the studio and combined eyewitness reports with archive, poetry, and commentary to create work that, although not overly marked by formal experiment, was multilayered and complex in its range. My Homeland (1976) arguably his finest film, was both an elegy on the twentieth anniversary of the Hungarian Revolution and a deeply subjective meditation on memory and loss in the poetic tradition he so admired in Jennings. Very much an authored essay, the film stands out in its use of counterpoint, juxtaposing banal colour travel films of the 1970s with starkly contrasting black-and-white stills of the uprising. Often taking over at the editing table himself, Vas could be single-minded to the point of obstinacy, but his visionary passion also engendered fierce loyalty amongst his collaborators.

Robert Vas saw his artistic mission as being to remind and warn, primarily of the abuses of power. Regarding himself as a victim of both totalitarian ideologies of the twentieth century, he avoided making explicit political judgments other than putting forward a broad liberal humanism, but he defined his task according to a strict moral imperative, untrammelled by relativism. Likewise, although his Judaism was secular rather than religious, he could never forget that ninety percent of Budapest's Jews did not survive the Holocaust.

Vas's death in 1978 came as a shock to friends and colleagues, who held him in highest regard. Ironically, after a lifetime's insecurity, he had only just signed a staff contract at the BBC. Years later the circumstances and cause of his death still raise strong and contradictory passions. The drug overdose and weeks of ensuing coma and death on April 10, 1978 are regarded by some as suicide and by others as a tragic accident. Perhaps also lost with him was the tradition of the subjective, poetic vision that he had made his signature as a filmmaker.

JOHN BURGAN

See also: Anderson, Lindsay; Jennings, Humphrey; Reisz, Karel

Biography

Born in Budapest, Hungary, March 3, 1931. Survived the Holocaust in the ghetto. Military service interrupted by a spell in psychiatric hospital. Fled to the West after the failure of the 1956 Hungarian uprising, arriving in London as a refugee. Worked in the Information Department of the British Film Institute and wrote criticism for *Sight and Sound* and *Monthly Film Bulletin*. First film made in 1959 for the British Film Institute's newly formed Experimental Film Fund. Worked as a film editor in the early 1960s, then as producer/director for the BBC 1964–78. Died in London on April 10, 1978 after a drug overdose and lengthy coma.

Selected films

1959 Refuge England: writer, director
1964 The Frontier: director

1968 The Golden Years of Alexander Korda: writer, producer
1970 Heart of Britain: writer, director
1971 The Issue Should Be Avoided: writer, director
1973 Stalin: writer, producer
1974 Nine Days in '26: producer
1975 Orders from Above: producer
1976 My Homeland: writer, director

Further reading

Lovell, Alan and Hillier, Jim, *Studies in Documentary*, London: Secker and Warburg, 1972.

Rosenthal, Ian, *The Documentary Conscience: A Casebook in Film Making*, Berkeley, CA: University of California Press, 1980.

Vertov, Dziga

The Soviet Russian director Dziga Vertov was instrumental in transforming actuality and newsreel filmmaking into what became known as documentary. Extending Russian and communist traditions of interpretive political journalism to cinema, Vertov's films used the inherent evidential power of documentary footage rhetorically, not simply to illustrate and record, but overwhelmingly for political persuasion, revealing film's immense capacity for the visual presentation of an argument. At the same time, Vertov's enduring commitment to formal experimentation meant that his greatest films combined this rhetorical force with poetry's heightened expressive freedom and associative combination of images. This example exerted a powerful influence not only on documentary filmmaking from Grierson to Marker and beyond, but also on the style of 1920s Soviet Montage films, particularly those of Sergei Eisenstein. His expansive style of filmmaking jarred with the tight control of cinema in 1930s Soviet Union and led to his marginalisation for unacceptably formalist tendencies.

Although Vertov's theoretical writings bear the heavy imprint of an age of iconoclastic modernist manifestos, he nevertheless makes a seminal attempt to defend and define what was dubbed documentary film. Vertov drew a fundamental distinction between unstaged (*neigrovye*) films such as his and staged, acted films. Not content simply to dispense with the use of actors, he advocated the method of 'life caught unawares' (*zhizn' vrasplokh*) aimed at ensuring that the subjects photographed are not posing. He attempt to achieve this by a wide variety of means including telephoto lenses, as well as hidden and decoy cameras. Yet probably the most characteristic aspect of Vertov's concept of filmmaking is the stress on the 'organisation' of this ontologically authentic material through editing so as to show 'life as it is' (*zhizn' kak ona est'*). This misleading notion does not imply a striving to be impartial or objective. On the contrary, the material is to be analysed and arranged so as to persuade the spectator of the communist perspective. Characteristic of this method was his groundbreaking newsreel series, Kino-Pravda (film truth), named by analogy with the Soviet Communist Party daily newspaper, *Pravda* (meaning truth). In place of the long takes recording official visits, portraits of dignitaries, sports events, and train crashes that were the staple of newsreels of the time, Kino-Pravda strove to use editing to combine images in a dynamic and highly tendentious manner, as, for example his coverage of the famine on the Volga in Kino-Pravda no.1 (1922), which begins with the slogan 'Save the starving children' as an intertitle. Shots of children starving are then intercut with pictures of the destruction of icons for their valuables. The sequence ends with an image of children being fed soup accompanied by the intertitle 'Every pearl saves a starving child'.

Vertov called his approach to filmmaking kino-eye, and dubbed his collaborators and followers *kinoki*, a neologism combining the Russian words for cinema and for eye. The *kinoki* were conceived as a grassroots international organisation of filmmakers and would-be filmmakers, dedicated to rescuing cinema from entertainment and commerce and turning it to the rational political analysis of everyday life. Films were to develop from observation, rather than from an already written screenplay. The term *kinok* also symbolizes Vertov's determination that the technology of film should be used to enable a step change in perception and thought. The camera for Vertov was associated with the enhanced power of scientific optical tools such as the microscope and the telescope. Whereas the microscope enabled the human eye to see natural phenomena invisible to the naked eye, Vertov thought that by means of techniques such as superimposition, reverse motion, and editing the camera could enable people to see the meaning underlying the misleading chaos of the world as it appears to unassisted human vision. A typical example of this approach is his treatment of Lenin's death in Kino-Pravda nos 21 and 22 (1925), whereby the slogan 'Lenin is dead but his cause lives on' is illustrated by superimposition of the image of Lenin on the mausoleum in Red Square. Similarly, Kino-Eye (1924) uses reverse motion to resurrect grazing cattle from the butcher's slab so as to prove that meat bought in a cooperative comes directly from the countryside. This kind of sequence attracted criticism as unwarranted stylistic exuberance in a film, the main purpose of which should be to inform. This commitment to formal experiment grew stronger in films such as Forward, Soviet! and One Sixth of the World. In the latter the organisation of much of the film has been shown to resemble that of the poetry of Walt Whitman (Singer 1987). The culmination of this drive to innovate was the film for which he is most celebrated outside Russia, The Man with the Movie Camera (1929), a silent film made without intertitles, 'directed toward the creation of a genuine, international purely cinematic language' (Feldman 1979). Variously described as celebration of the city (Roberts 2000), meta-cinema (Mayne 1975), and the first database film (Monovich 1999), this dazzling display of cinema's expressive power is at the same time demythification of that power and an extended enquiry into the nature of film and the place of cinema in society.

In his lifelong hostility to films made with actors, Vertov was articulating a view influential in the 1920s Soviet avant-garde. In particular productivists and constructivists argued that art, and especially fiction, was conceived by bourgeois societies to distract people from their essential dissatisfaction with the capitalist world. Art under communism should not divert people from real life, but rather be a reworking of real material, a remaking of life, using tools and techniques derived from art. It is this perspective that informs Vertov's striving not only to use documentary footage for the purposes of political persuasion, but also to seek to experiment formally, to expand the borders of cinematic expression. Vertov's practice, however, was not always as rigorous as his programmatic statements might lead us to believe. Even his most experimental films, Kino-Eye and The Man with the Movie Camera included obviously staged footage, notably in the latter of a man holding a camera.

Although, like many other Soviet Montage filmmakers, he found it increasingly difficult to work in the 1930s, unlike them, Vertov immediately welcomed the coming of sound cinema as affording new opportunities. Indeed, Vertov had anticipated sound cinema as early as 1925 with his theory of radio-eye, an audio concept of documentary equivalent to kino-eye. Indeed Enthusiam (1930) was the name of his first sound film, a celebration of the industrial transformation of the first five-year plan, which incorporated a wide variety of source sound, recorded on location in the Donbass region. This is a bold experiment in which the sounds of heavy industry, church bells, and military bands interact symbolically, not simply illustrating the image with which they are combined. Vertov's other major film of the talking era was Three Songs about Lenin (1934). This film revisited a theme treated with much success by Vertov in the 1920s, but this time he drew on popular conceptions of Lenin in the folk songs of Azerbaijan, Turkmenistan, and Uzbekistan. Made in physically demanding circumstances in a critical climate increasingly hostile to Vertov's approach to documentary film, this film nevertheless retains much of the engaging visual style, creative use of sound, and poetic qualities of his earlier films. After considerable delays and wrangles it eventually reached the public and won Vertov critical and official recognition, but all was not as it seemed. Three Songs about Lenin broke the unwritten laws of the Lenin cult film of the time by failing to show Stalin to have been his right-hand man and faithful disciple. It was withdrawn soon after its release and later reedited so as to foreground the role of the Soviet leader (Feldman 1979). The point was not lost on Vertov. When next given an opportunity to make a feature-length documentary, Lullaby (1937), he made sure it included the requisite lengthy standing ovation to Stalin. Yet, in this film little remains of the stylistic élan of his earlier works, and it is barely distinguishable from the run-of-the-mill products of the Soviet Newsreel Studio. The years of administrative obstruction and hostility began to take a toll on his creative powers as well as his health, and by the end of World War II, Vertov gradually ceased even to produce new projects. The last decade of his life was spent editing newsreels of the kind he had long abhorred.

JEREMY HICKS

See also: Man with the Movie Camera; Three Songs About Lenin

Biography

Born David Abelovich (later Denis Arkadievich) Kaufman in Bialystok, then Russia, now Poland, on January 2, 1896. Mobilised by Russian Imperial army during World War I and sent to Military-Musical College in Chuguev, Ukraine, before being decommissioned on grounds of ill health. Enrolled in St Petersburg Psycho-neurological Institute. After February revolution of 1917 came to Moscow, where in early 1918 he became secretary of the newsreel department of Moscow Cinema Committee (later the All-Russian Photo-Cinema Department or VFKO). Changing his name to Dziga Vertov (meaning something like 'spinning gypsy'), directed group of newsreel filmmakers 1918–19 making Kinonedelia/Cine Weekly, ran cinema section of agittrains and ships, 1920, and made propaganda shorts about Russian Civil War (1918–21). From 1922 initiated Kino-Pravda newsreel series, as well as making Goskino's newsreel series Goskinokalendar from 1923 to 1925. Also employed from 1924 by Kultkino, a educational or documentary films department of Goskino (later Sovkino) until sacked in 1926. Worked for the rival Ukrainian Film Directorate (VUFKU) from 1927 to 1932. Visited Western Europe in 1929 and 1931 to promote his films and views of film. Made Three Songs About Lenin at Mezhrabpom Films from 1932, for which he was awarded The Order of the Red Star in 1935. Taken on by Soviet Newsreel Films (Soiuzkinokhronika) in 1935. Here, with the exception of a short spell at the Soviet Children's Film Studio (Soiuzdetfilm) between 1939 and 1941, he continued to work editing Novosti dnia/News of the Day newsreel compilations until his death, in Moscow, February 12, 1954.

Selected films

1922–5 Kino-Pravda/Film-Truth (23 editions): writer, director
1924 Kino-Glaz/Kino-Eye: writer, director
1926 Shagai, Sovet!/Forward, Soviet!: writer, director
1926 Shestaia chast' mira/One Sixth of the World: writer, director
1928 Odinnadtsatyi/The Eleventh Year: writer, director
1929 Chelovek s kinoapparatom/The Man with the Movie Camera: writer, director
1930 Simfoniia Donbassa (Entuziazm)/Enthusiasm, Or the Symphony of the Donbass: writer, director
1934 Tri pesni o Lenine/Three Songs About Lenin: writer, director
1937 Kolybel'naia/Lullaby: writer, director

Further reading

Feldman, Seth, *Evolution of Style in the Early Work of Dziga Vertov*, New York: Arno Press, 1975.
——*Dziga Vertov: A Guide to References and Resources*, Boston: G.K. Hall, 1979.
Mayne, Judith, 'Ideologies of Metacinema', unpublished PhD thesis, State University of New York at Buffalo, 1975.
Monovich, Lev, 'Database as Symbolic Form', *Millennium Film Journal* 34, fall 1999: 24–43.
Petric, Vlada, *Constructivism in Film: The Man with the Movie Camera: A Cinematic Analysis*, Cambridge: Cambridge University Press, 1993.
——'Vertov's Cinematic Transposition of Reality', in Charles Warren (ed.), *Beyond Document: Essays in Nonfiction Film*, Hanover, NH and London: Wesleyan University Press, 1996.
Roberts, Graham, *Forward Soviet!*, London and New York: I.B. Tauris, 1999.
——*The Man with a Movie Camera*, London and New York: I.B. Tauris, 2000.
Roshal, Lev, *Dziga Vertov*, Moscow: Iskusstvo, 1982.
Singer, Ben, 'Conoisseurs of Chaos: Whitman, Vertov and the "Poetic Survey"', *Literature/Film Quarterly* 15, no. 4, 1987: 247–58.
Stollery, Martin, *Alternative Empires: European Modernist Cinemas and Cultures of Imperialism*, Exeter: Exeter University Press, 2000.
Vertov, Dziga, *Dziga Vertov: stat'i, dnevniki, zamysly*, edited by Sergei Drobashenko, Moscow: Iskusstvo, 1966.
——*Kino-Eye: The Writings of Dziga Vertov*, ed. Annette Michelson, trans. Kevin O'Brian, Berkeley, CA: University of California Press, 1984.

Victory at Sea

(US, Salomon and Kleinerman, 1952–3)

This epic-length television documentary concerning naval operations during World War II combined wartime footage with narration and music to present an emotional view of combat history. Produced during the Korean conflict of the Cold War, the compilation film series, as its title implies, focused on the strength and ultimate triumph of Allied forces (particularly American forces) during wartime. One of the most ambitious documentaries produced by network television, the twenty-six-episode series originally aired on NBC from October 1952 to April 1953 on Sunday afternoons from 3:00pm to 3:30pm. Critically acclaimed during its time, the series won more than thirteen industry awards, including a George Peabody Award and a special Emmy for Best Public Affairs Program. The series demonstrated that an historical compilation documentary was a viable television format and led to the production of several others in the genre, particularly The Twentieth Century (CBS, 1957–69).

Victory at Sea was the brainchild of World War II veteran and naval historian Henry Salomon and his former college classmate, Robert Sarnoff, the son of RCA/NBC patriarch David Sarnoff. Robert Sarnoff was then an executive at NBC-Television. In the early days of television, film projects had distinct practical advantages over live television shows, particularly the idea for residual incomes through syndication. The half-hour series relied on archival footage obtained from many sources including the US Signal Corps, the US Navy and newsreels, and European and Japanese archives. The archival footage obtained amounted to approximately eleven thousand miles of film, which was then reduced to sixty-two thousand feet. The editor for the series, Isaac Kleinerman, relied on an indexing system of sixty thousand note cards so as to organize the quantity of film for the compilation series. The addition of composer Richard Rodgers's name to the credits added further prestige to the project. It also allowed NBC to gain additional revenues through the marketing of LP recordings of the series' musical score. The Richard Rodgers score was sold in several record versions by RCA-Victor. By 1963 the album had grossed US $4 million, and one tune from the score, 'No Other Love', earned additional sales as a single.

Unlike many wartime propaganda films, Victory at Sea presented a narrative of more historical sweep encompassing as it did both the Eastern and Western hemispheres. The series, however, was not without bias toward the victors. Produced at a time when the world was in the depths of the Cold War struggle between the United States and the Soviet Union, the series had an organizing theme—the triumph of democracy and freedom over totalitarianism. The active role of the United States in international affairs is constantly invoked, as is the determination to bring 'freedom' to those parts of the world under the yoke of military despotism. Its ethnocentric viewpoint was constantly expressed using the rhetoric of liberation and military strength by reinforcing the historical conflict as a lesson of history, a rhetoric that continued to grow into the polarity of Cold War era politics and diplomacy.

RONALD WILSON

Victory at Sea (US, NBC Television, 1952–3, 26 episodes). Produced by Henry Salomon. Written by Henry Salomon with Richard Hanser, based on the multivolume *History of the United States Naval Operations in World War II* by Samuel Eliot Morison. Directed by M. Clay Adams. Music by Richard Rodgers. Musical arrangement by Robert Russell Bennett conducting the NBC Symphony Orchestra. Narrated by Leonard Graves. Edited by Isaac Kleinerman. Technical Advisor Captain Walter Karig, USN Film research by Daniel Jones and Douglas Wood. Television coordinator Robert M. Sarnoff.

Further reading

Bartone, Richard C., 'Victory at Sea: A Case Study in Official Telehistory', *Film and History* XXI, no. 4, December 1991.

Kepley, Vance, Jr, 'The Origins of NBC's Project XX in Compilation Documentaries', *Journalism Quarterly* 61, 1984: 1–2.

——'Victory at Sea', in Horace Newcomb (ed.), *Encyclopedia of Television*, Chicago: Fitzroy Dearborn Publications, 1997.

Leyda, Jay, *Films Beget Films*, New York: Hill and Wang, 1964.

Morison, Samuel Eliot, *History of United States Naval Operations in World War II*, 15 vols, Boston: Little, Brown and Co., 1947–62.

Rollins, Peter C., 'Victory at Sea: Cold War Epic', *Journal of Popular Culture* VI, spring, 1973.

Video Diaries

(UK, BBC, 1990–2001)

The Video Diaries series was a product of the BBC's Community Programme Unit (CPU), developed by unit head Jeremy Gibson and series producer Bob Long. First broadcast on Saturday evenings on BBC2 in the summer of 1990, the series proved an immediate success with audiences and critics. Exceptionally for BBC access programming, it regularly received up to 1.5 million viewers and won a number of awards for both the series and individual programmes.

Video Diaries was a radical extension of the CPU's remit to provide members of the public with access to television broadcasting. It built on the department's previous access programming strands Open Door and Open Space, where selected individuals and groups who approached the Unit worked alongside professional crews to produce programmes on specific topics of concern. The innovative approach taken by Video Diaries involved training chosen applicants in the use of domestic video camcorders, enabling them to record their own material themselves. This experiment was both an attempt by the CPU to engage with the newly emerging camcorder culture, and a genuine attempt to redefine the parameters of access television. Allowing individual subjects to control their own representation was directly aimed at circumventing the mediating influence of professional filmmakers, with their often highly developed personal or institutional methodologies.

Selected Video Diaries applicants received training in the basics of film grammar and use of S-VHS or Hi-8 camcorders. Diarists gathered their own footage and later edited this in collaboration with the CPU postproduction team. Throughout the process there was both support and monitoring from CPU staff who oversaw the development of the project. Although the aim was to give the individual as much control as possible, the Unit always exerted a corrective influence, steering the project through in an attempt to ensure that the structure of the programme was both intelligible to audiences and communicated the diarists' intentions in the most efficient way. The early series of Video Diaries were also notable for having programmes of variable length. Within a range that spanned between one and two hours, programme-makers were allowed to find the duration that best suited the requirements of the project. In 1993 the CPU introduced Teenage Diaries, which followed a similar approach but were produced by diarists under 18 years of age.

The degree of control exerted by the CPU over the outcome has been an area of critical debate. Although the CPU has been seen as providing a constraining influence on the diarists' intuitive approach to their subject, it could equally be said that they often challenged diarists to step outside the normative approaches to documentary practice as absorbed via their own television viewing. It was this dynamic between the diarists, who underwent a demanding developmental experience as they sought to tell their stories, and the guiding hand of the experienced CPU staff that produced a blend of formally inventive programmes, which, if sometimes demanding of their audience, were nonetheless coherent. The diarist, as well as offering insights into their specific areas of concern, also provided, via piece-to-camera or voice-over, a diary of the production process. Thus, elements usually excluded in mainstream documentary filmmaking were often a central part of the diary's developing narrative, as the diarists sought to find their own voice, while negotiating the video technology and developing a working methodology. The often crude technique and undisguised subjectivity of the diarist seem to give Video Diaries an honesty and an emotional impact that was regarded by many as a welcome revitalization of the television documentary form. If technical naivety in itself is no guarantee of 'authenticity', the particular production context of the CPU did provide an ethical framework that mitigated against the 'amateurish' technique becoming just a stylistic device (Keighron 1993).

Video Diaries covered a wide range of subjects, from light-hearted offerings such as Steve Feltham's monster-quest Desperately Seeking Nessie (1990), to the Bafta Award-winning The Man Who Loved Gary Lineker (1992), Ylli Hasani's account of his life as an Albanian doctor and refugee. One of the most challenging programmes in the first series was Willa Woolston's My Demons (1990). In this programme the diarist returned to her hometown to confront the personal legacy of systematic abuse she had suffered from her stepmother as a child. This high level of introspection was regarded by some as an uncomfortable precedent, pushing television documentary into the realms of personal therapy. It could be debated that the relative success of this series encouraged the shift toward a more populist, character-centred documentary programming, a widely observed trend in the more competitive multichannel environment of contemporary British television. However, My Demons provoked a significant response from viewers who had also suffered abusive family situations, and led to the establishment of a support network for sufferers. By often dealing with significant situations and issues, the diaries, although based on intensely personal stories and subjective viewpoints, could also be seen as a continuation of the more overtly social campaigning work of the CPU.

Video Diaries was undoubtedly important institutionally for challenging barriers to broadcast television access that had been long-maintained through rigid standards of professional practice and an insistence on the use of expensive video or film formats as guarantors of image quality. Although these distinctions have, to a certain extent, been rendered obsolete by the high-quality images now afforded by digital camcorders, Video Diaries was influential in opening up British television screens to a much wider range of video material from nonprofessional sources.

The video diary form has become an integral part of many other documentary and television genres such as travel programmes and 'reality' television. Despite the ubiquity of the approach and the less serious ends to which it is now often used, the series' innovative force should not be underestimated. Video Diaries represented a significant widening of the BBC's Public Service remit and extended democratization of the broadcast documentary. It also encouraged many more people outside television to realize the potential of domestic camcorders for personal exploration and social activism.

DAVID CHAPMAN

Video Diaries (UK, BBC Community Programme Unit, 11 series between 1990 and 2001). CPU Head, Jeremy Gibson. Series producer/CPU Head Bob Long. Producers/Series Producers, Rachel Foster and Steve Sklair.

Further reading

Barker, Paul, 'The Rise of Camcorder Culture', *The Times*, July 27, 1992. (Reprinted in MacDonald, Kevin and Cousins, Mark, *Imagining Reality*, London, Faber & Faber 1998.)

Dovey, Jon, 'Old Dogs and New Tricks: Access Television in the UK', in Tony Downent (ed.), *Channels of Resistance*, London: BFI 1993.

Humm, Peter, 'Real TV: Camcorders, Access and Authenticity', in Christine Geraghty and David Lusted (eds), *The Television Studies Book*, London: Arnold, 1998.

Keighron, Peter, 'Video Diaries: What's Up Doc?', *Sight and Sound* 3, 10, 1993: 24–25.

Keighron, Peter and Wayne, Mike, 'Video Diaries', *Independent Media* 101–2, July–August 1990: 8–9.

Kilborn, Richard and Izod, John, *An Introduction to Television Documentary*, Manchester: Manchester University Press, 1997.

Visions of Eight

(US/West Germany, various directors, 1973)

Leni Riefenstahl's poetic record of the 1936 Berlin Games, Olympische Spiele/Olympia (1938), is often singled out as a sensual celebration of the human form in flight and—despite its links to the Nazi Party—is generally thought to be 'the definitive cinematic treatment of the Games'. Nevertheless, it falls short of the pyrotechnics on display in what is perhaps the most unusual of Olympic documentaries, Visions of Eight/München 1972–78 berühmte Regisseure sehen die Spiele der XX Olympiade.

On the surface, this multi-director episode film produced by legendary documentarian David L. Wolper and Stan Margulies (then vice-president of Wolper Productions) appears curiously 'empty' insofar as it captures only fleeting, impressionistic glimpses of the festival held in Munich (from August 26 to September 11, 1972) and furthermore only begrudgingly alludes to the deadly act of terrorism that capped the Olympics that year. Nevertheless, as an omnibus film composed of eight discrete yet connected sections, each averaging ten minutes, Visions of Eight is in fact a very 'full' evocation of the Olympic experience, for it manages to convey both the personal and collective aspirations of the participants involved (athletes as well as filmmakers) through a narrative form naturally amenable to political allegory and the theme of competition.

Ironically, it was Wolper's interest in the ostensibly apolitical world of sports-based entertainment (he had already made October Madness: The World Series (1965) and Pro Football: Mayhem on a Sunday Afternoon (1965)) that gave him a decided advantage in the race to make the official film about the 1972 Summer Olympics. This event would become mired in political debate when, on September 5, eight Palestinian guerrilla fighters known as 'Black September' climbed the cyclone fence surrounding the Olympic Village and took eleven members of the Israeli wrestling team hostage before killing them. Dedicated to the memory of the martyred athletes, Visions of Eight actually makes only passing reference to the actions of the terrorists, who easily circumvented the minimum-security measures that fateful day in Munich and put all of Germany—a nation eager to dissociate itself from Hitler's Berlin Games—on high alert. That the film at first appears so uncommitted in its political aspirations, that it seems so disinterested in the ideological implications of the Olympics, can be partly attributed to the fact that ninety percent of its principal photography had been completed by the time the terrorists took their hostages. Wolper, who had no intention of extending the schedule to include footage of an event that would already be telecast around the world before the film's theatrical debut the next year, left the task of footnoting the tragic occurrence to the one filmmaker who had not yet completed his contribution to Visions of Eight, John Schlesinger.

Although the making of any documentary is rife with potential problems, filming the Olympics proves to be particularly challenging, even for those producers like Wolper who are experienced in the fine art of on-location shooting, crowd control, juggling simultaneous events, deploying large numbers of crew members, and maintaining a balance between proximity and distance. Given the vast nature of the event, just choosing what to shoot can be a vexing and time-consuming endeavor. Fortunately, Wolper had hit on the novel idea of apportioning those choices to a handful of the world's top directors—Juri Ozerov, Mai Zetterling, Arthur Penn, Michael Pfleghar, Kon Ichikawa, Claude Lelouch, Milos Forman, and John Schlesinger.

Fittingly, the film kicks off with The Beginning, Ozerov's tension-filled depiction of athletic preparation. Through powerful yet whimsically juxtaposed images that foreshadow the yawning judge in Forman's Decathlon episode, Ozerov captures the preperformance jitters and boredom faced by the world's greatest athletes—men and women fluttering between patience and nerve-jangling anticipation. A Soviet filmmaker who would later direct the feature-length account of the Olympic Games held in Moscow, O Sport, Ty-Mir (1980), Ozerov—an outspoken communist—draws on the theories of dialectical and poetic montage launched by his cinematic predecessors (Eisenstein, Vertov, Pudovkin) and turns the clash between individuality and community, between secular and spiritual comforts into a profound (if all-too-brief) meditation on the underlying ideals of Western culture.

Following Ozerov's episode is Mai Zetterling's contribution to Visions of Eight, a look at the men's weightlifting competition entitled The Strongest. Although initially attracted to the idea of filming the women athletes in Munich, Zetterling instead set her sights on what she described as the most 'sensual' and 'obsessive' of Olympic events. As a result, this pioneering feminist filmmaker (who admits in the episode's introduction to not being interested in sports) expanded her already diverse repertoire of key themes—sexual awakening, personal isolation, and the various forms of violence perpetrated against women—to accommodate these mutually impacting images of masculine hegemony and physical prowess. The Highest, Arthur Penn's contribution, comes next—a decidedly apolitical and poetic vision of pole-vaulters reaching for the heavens.

With little-to-no sound to accompany the balletic movements of the vaulters' bodies rising and falling in midair, this sequence is the most abstract and impressionistic of the film, capturing in slow motion (96 to 600 frames/second) and soft-focus shots the sense of transcendence and freedom that only a select few experience in their struggle against gravity to clear the fragile bar.

After witnessing these men plant their poles in the ground and push themselves upward, the viewer—perhaps struck by the conflation of sexual and spiritual aims implicit in such imagery—can be excused for feeling disappointed when literally brought back to earth in the fourth episode. Entitled The Women, this episode finds German filmmaker Michael Pfleghar casting a decidedly male gaze at female athletes. Among the cinematically fetishized bodies are fifteen-year-old Australian swimmer Shane Gould, Russian gymnast Ludmilla Tourischeva, and West German pentathlete Heidi Rosendahl (world record-holder in the long jump), whose accomplishments in Munich and capacity for liberating mobility and agency are undercut by Pfleghar's leering close-ups and fragmented editing. Putting as much emphasis on their hairdressers as on the finish lines, this episode nevertheless says less about women than men—its reliance on film's traditional visual paradigm (masculine viewing subject and feminine object of desire) unwittingly underscoring an engrained facet of Western culture, which continues to perpetuate gender stereotypes through ocularcentric fictions.

Thankfully, this low point in the film is followed by one of its most effective and self-reflexive sequences: Kon Ichikawa's The Fastest. Armed with a battalion of thirty-four over-cranked cameras, Ichikawa and his cinematographers filmed the men's 100-meter dash as it had never been filmed, effectively transforming this most accelerated of sports into a decelerated evocation of the dedication and training that goes into the Olympics. By stretching a ten-second race into a grueling, eleven-minute mini-marathon of facial contortions and wobbling muscles, Ichikawa not only conveys a Muybridge-like fascination with human physiognomy and locomotion, but also taps into the very technological preconditions behind their cinematic recording (the medium's ontological grounding in photographic realism plus the various apparati that confer the illusion of movement onto still images). This reflexive gesture is compounded by the director's decision to show all eight sprinters in a line, head-on, their individual yet contiguous lanes connoting the eight separate yet linked episodes of the film. A voice-over draws the spectator's attention to the runners' expressions, their eyes focused and full of yearning. After the gunshot is fired, one of the runners falls behind and gives up. These small details, in addition to Ichikawa's decision to show with 600mm telephoto lens each runner individually before capturing the entirety of the event in wide-shot, evokes the sense of humanity that comes, ironically, from selfhood—a theme for which the filmmaker has become famous.

Like Ichikawa, who had earlier made Tokyo Olympiad (1965), Claude Lelouch was no stranger to the Olympics. Four years before Visions of Eight, the French director had teamed up with François Reichenbach to chronicle the 1968 Winter Olympics held in Grenoble. Titled Treize jours en France/Thirteen Days in France (1968), this documentary gave international audiences a taste of the joy of victory, juxtaposing images of such heroic gold-medallists as skater Peggy Fleming and skier Jean-Claude Killy with political figures like President Charles de Gaulle. In Munich, however, Lelouch was drawn not to the Flemings and Killys of the world, not to the record-setting swimmer Mark Spitz (the famous Californian who in 1972 took home seven gold medals), but rather to the nearly seven thousand 'nameless' men and women who—like the runner who gives up mid-race in Ichikawa's episode—know the bitter taste of defeat and sudden loneliness. These imbricated themes inform The Losers, which segues from a boxer throwing a 'hissy-fit', to an injured bicyclist, to weeping women athletes, to equestrian collisions, to dejected swimmers, to injured yet persistent wrestlers.

Of interest, The Losers comes in sixth, not last, among the eight episodes, immediately preceding Milos Forman's humorous interlude The Decathlon. Ostensibly concerned with the most demanding and drawn-out of the disciplines (ten different events performed over two days), Forman's episode opts for a satiric critique of Olympic officialdom and spectatorship itself, a mode of dispassionate engagement personified by a green-suited judge who struggles to stay awake in the stands during the decathlon. Departing periodically from the Games to explore the city's various manifestations of local color (yodeling, bell-ringing, Bavarian folk-dancing, and the Munich Symphony Orchestra's performance of 'Ode to Joy' from Beethoven's Ninth), Forman manages to convey yet another aspect of Olympic spectatorship, which is pulled in several directions by cultural and sporting events and therefore dispersed or discursive in a way that resonates with both the multi-event decathlon and episodic film spectatorship (a mode of engagement that can be literally wrenching insofar as viewers are habitually yanked from one story, setting, or group of characters to a completely different one).

If Forman's comic juxtapositions undercut the grandeur of the Olympics, this irreverence seems downright irrelevant in light of the tragedy that befell the 'Games of Peace and Joy'.

As mentioned earlier, the only episode that references the act of terrorism is the final one, John Schlesinger's The Longest. Like runners with tunnel vision, the first seven contributing directors focus exclusively on the nonpolitical aspects of the Olympics. Ironically, the concept of tunnel vision is personified by British runner Ron Hill, the ostensible subject of Schlesinger's episode whose utter refusal to see beyond his personal goal and whose outward indifference toward the incident disquieted the politically committed filmmaker. Although Schlesinger was as unprepared for the shocking news at Munich as the rest of Wolper's crew, he was the most prepared insofar as he had done extensive filming back in England. Having set up camp in the Lancashire countryside where Hill did his rigorous training (running approximately 130 miles a week outside his Manchester home), the director was able to interview his subject about the upcoming marathon, a twenty-six-mile race that he and his forty-five camera units would eventually cover with sixty-five cameras. In a sense, Schlesinger had been preparing for this moment his entire career, which stretches back to the mid-1950s, when he was first drawn to the documentary form during his prep school days at Uppingham. (There he shot Sunday in the Park (1956), eventually cutting his teeth making dozens of short nonfiction films for Tonight and Monitor, two BBC series enjoying popularity during the 1950s.)

Images of the last runner finally trickling into the stadium in the rain are intercut with a shot of Olympic official Avery Brundage declaring the Games officially ended. The flame is extinguished, and shots of the Olympic flag at half-mast and the Israeli flag provide sobering reminders that, behind the joyful façade, several lives have been wasted. A sign reading 'Montreal 1976' is visible in these final images, which bring closure to Visions of Eight and gesture toward the next Olympics.

DAVID SCOTT DIFFRIENT

See also: Ichikawa, Kon; Lelouch, Claude; Schlesinger, John; Zetterling, Mai

Visions of Eight (München 1972–78 berühmte Regisseure sehen die Spiele der XX Olympiade) (US and West Germany, Wolper Productions, 1973, 109 mins). Distributed by Cinema 5 Distributing and EuroVideo. Directed by Juri Ozerov, Mai Zetterling, Arthur Penn, Michael Pfleghar, Kon Ichikawa, Claude Lelouch, Milos Forman, and John Schlesinger.

Further reading

Guttmann, Allen, *The Erotic in Sports*, New York: Columbia University Press, 1996.

——*The Olympics: A History of Modern Games*, Urbana, IL: University of Illinois Press, 2002.

Phillips, Gene D., *John Schlesinger*, Boston: Twayne Publishers, 1981.

Plimpton, George, 'Olympic "Visions of Eight"', *Sports Illustrated* 39, August 27, 1973: 30–5.

Quand, James (ed.), *Kon Ichikawa*, Bloomington, IN: Indiana University Press, 2001.

Wolper, David L., *Producer: A Memoir*, New York: Scribner, 2003.

Young, David C., *The Modern Olympics: A Struggle for Revival*, Baltimore, MD: Johns Hopkins University Press, 2003.

Voigt, Andreas

Voigt's participation in Leipzig im Herbst/ Leipzig in Autumn, the documentation of the protests in Leipzig in October and November 1989, established his international reputation. He became one of the most important younger directors to document the political changes in East Germany after unification. Particularly his five films on the city of Leipzig function as a sensitive seismograph of the feelings of the people. Voigt started his career as director quite late. His diploma film Alfred (1987), in which he portrayed a worker who was expelled from the party, had already gotten him into political trouble with the Communist Party. The film could be seen only at restricted screenings, because it indirectly criticized the economic system of the German Democratic Republic (GDR), when a group of workers sit together to complain about their working conditions. 'The fact that Voigt was given a contract as a director of the DEFA-Studios für Dokumentarfilme is categorical proof that times were changing. During the early and mid-eighties barely any filmmakers had been given full contracts' (Hughes 1999: 288).

The protests against the GDR government began on October 7, 1989, but the documentary studio did not begin shooting until October 16, after the filmmakers met at the film festival in Brandenburg and realized that they could sit together and discuss the issues, but the real changes were taking place on the streets. Therefore, they decided to document these events in different towns. The DEFA team, with its heavy 35mm camera and additional lighting, was welcomed warmly by the protesters, a sequence that opens the film Leipzig im Herbst. In the interviews, they openly demand more freedom, free elections and travel, and the right to express their political opinions. In contrast, the state officials were thinking only of how best to control the situation. The aesthetic style is typical for the DEFA, with an interesting *cadrage* in black and white, long takes, and patient interviews with the protesters to get the essence of what was happening. The camera actively participates in getting an impression of the atmosphere at this demonstration. There are also ironic situations, as for example when the street cleaners remove protest banners from the streets, but at the same time agree that their demands are totally correct. The film, collectively made by Andreas Voigt, Gerd Kroske, and cameraman Sebastian Richter, was shown at the Leipzig Documentary Festival, the most important documentary festival in the GDR, and won the Jury Prize there in 1989.

His next film, Letztes Jahr Titanic/Last Year Titanic (1991) follows a journalist, a worker, a left-wing skinhead, a teenager, and a pub owner between December 1989 and 1990, the last year of the GDR and the first one in reunified Germany. This film centers not on political opinions but on actual situations, developments, and personal feelings. Of course, at the beginning of the shoot reunification could not have been predicted, so the film is an important document about the time of change, the social and economic insecurity, but it also has some ironic and even absurd moments and uses the metaphor of the last dance. Voigt's fourth Leipzig film, Glaube Liebe Hoffnung/Faith, Love, Hope (1994), portrays a group of skinheads, some politically left wing, others extremely right wing. One feels the cold atmosphere of the society. The film was controversial. It was praised by some for its insight into the skinhead scene, but attacked by others for giving these radicals a platform for their arguments. Even more confusing were the images in its brilliant black-and-white cinematography. The last film in his Leipzig cycle is Großse Weite Welt/Big Wide World (1997). It addresses the statements of the protagonists of his other Leipzig films by showing their development and how their lives have changed. His most recent film, Invisible—Illegal in Europe (2004) follows five people, who are either illegal refugees or trying to enter Europe, over a one-year period. It is a film about hopes and dreams, about the search for luck, and the despair of a system that did not allow existence under humane conditions. The wall has fallen, but Europe is still protecting its borders.

KAY HOFFMANN

Biography

Born August 25, 1953 in Eisleben, Germany. Grew up in Dessau. Studied physics for one year in Kraków, then political economy and economic history in Berlin from 1973 to 1978. From 1978 on, Voigt worked as a dramaturgist at the DEFA documentary studio and shot children's programs as a director. 1984–7 external study at the film school in Potsdam Babelsberg. 1987–90 director and author at the DEFA documentary studio. 1988–90 member of directory of the Federation of Film and TV Creators of the GDR. After 1991 independent documentary filmmaker, author and producer for cinema and television, Voigt won many prices at national and international film festivals (for example, Adolf-Grimme-Preis, Silver Wolf Amsterdam, Taube Leipzig Festival, Grand Prix Strasbourg).

Selected films

1987 Alfred: director
1988 Leute mit Landschaft/People with Landscape: director
1989 Leipzig im Herbst/Leipzig in Autumn: director with Gerd Kroske, co-script
1991 Letztes Jahr Titanic/Last Year Titanic: director, co-script
1992 Grenzland eine Reise/Frontierland, a Journey: director, script
1994 Glaube Liebe Hoffnung/Faith, Love, Hope: director, script
1995 Ostpreussenland/Land of East Prussia: director, script
1995 Mr Behrmann Leben Traum Tod/Mr Behrmann Life Dream Death: director, script
1995 Begegnung mit Krystof Kieslowski/Meeting with Krystof Kieslowski: director, script
1996 Neues Leben/New Life: director, script

1997 Großse Weite Welt/Big Wide World: director
1999 Trouble Spots: director
2001 David@New York: director, script
2004 Invisible—Illegal in Europe: director, script

Further reading

Hauke, Lutz, 'Deutschland, Deutschland. Wertewandel im Prozeß der Wiedervereinigung im Blickfeld Berliner Dokumentarfilmer (1988–91)', in Peter Zimmermann (ed.), *Deutschlandbilder Ost. Dokumentarfilme der DEFA von der Nachkriegszeit bis zur Wiedervereinigung*, Konstanz, 1995: 201–15.

Hecht, Heidemarie, *Der letzte Akt. 1989 bis 1992, in Schwarzweiß und Farbe. DEFA-Dokumentarfilme 1946–92*, Günter Jordan and Ralf Schenk (eds), Berlin, 1996: 235–67.

Hughes, Helen, 'Documenting the Wende: The Films of Andreas Voigt', in Séan Allan and John Sanford (eds), *DEFA. East German Cinema, 1946–92*, New York and Oxford, 1999: 283–301.

Voyage au Congo

(France, Allégret and Gide, 1927)

Voyage au Congo at first appears to be a simple travelog of Marc Allégret's journey with his uncle, André Gide, through what was then known as French Equatorial Africa. Gide, sensing his age and seeking renewed inspiration for his writing, sold his collection of presentation copies in 1925 and set sail with Allégret for the Congo, hoping to retrace the steps of Joseph Conrad's *Heart of Darkness*. Working from an itinerary determined by Allégret, the pair wound their way up the Congo River and beyond, passing through what is now the Congo, Central African Republic, Chad, and Cameroon. The trip would yield the twenty-five year old Allégret's first motion picture, initiating an illustrious career in the French film industry. Gide himself remained largely detached from the filming process, absorbed in writing the journals that would later be published successively as *Voyage au Congo* (1927) and *Le retour du Tchad* (1928).

In spite of opening titles that proclaim, 'rapportées par André Gide et Marc Allégret', the film is almost wholly Allégret's, with participation from Gide that mainly extended to the intertitles. Allégret performed the essential geographical, ethnographic, and medical research for the journey, and it was Allégret's idea, in the summer of 1924, to further validate his role by including still photography and, soon after, a motion picture camera (Allégret 1987). What resulted was neither a simple travelog, nor an ethnographic study, nor a documentary, but an experimental mixture of approaches loosely organized around the theme of the journey. It includes images of travel; staged reenactments of indigenous daily life; actuality scenes of local performances, games, and customs; as well as brief shots of landscapes and exotic flora and fauna. At times the film's episodic structure seems to follow the example of Robert Flaherty, whose Nanook of the North (1922) was much admired in France. Daniel Durosay, however, argues that Allégret consciously went against these tendencies, deliberately suppressing in the film any visual impression of effort, risk, or adventure (Allégret 1987). In this sense, the principles behind Voyage au Congo could be seen as more closely aligned to Flaherty's second film, Moana (1926). Subtitled 'a romance of the Golden Age', Moana focused more on domestic daily activities, physical sensuality, and bodily movement. A little more than a month after returning from his African trip, Gide wrote of seeing the 'voluptuous' Moana in Paris, though it is unknown whether the film had an influence on Allégret's final cut (Geiger 2000).

Allégret's fantasy of the primitive shares with Flaherty a tendency towards romantic idealism and fails to acknowledge the colonial framework within which it operates and the effects of that colonial system. Allégret was hardly shielded from the fact of colonialism; on the contrary, as Gide's journals attest, French commercial interests and the exploitation of African labour were everywhere in evidence, and even prevented the pair from finding the ideal, unspoiled Africa they were seeking. Yet the film also suggests contemporary trends in ethnographic surrealism as practiced by Paul Rivet, Lucien Lévy-Bruhl, and Marcel Mauss, who were establishing the Institut d'Ethnologie in Paris during the same year as Allégret and Gide's travels. The primitivist fantastic would take on other forms in Allégret's later work, particularly in such projects as the Josephine Baker film Zou Zou (1934), which portrayed Baker as a bird in a golden cage.

The content and style of Voyage au Congo gesture to various modes of documentary practice, but as a whole it does not comfortably fit into any single category. Opening with scenes on the deck of the *Asie* off the coast of the Canary Islands, the film sets itself up as a spectacular travel narrative seen through Western eyes. The viewer is at first positioned with the traveller, as the camera shows a woman playfully taking a pair of binoculars and looking through them in the direction of the camera. Soon afterward the viewer follows the route of the Matadi-Kinshasa colonial railroad, with the camera perched on a moving train. Assisted by maps marking the route, the traveler is encouraged to identify with the camera as a journeying eye. One of the first glimpses of a native, near Bangui, takes on overtones of romanticized first contact, as out on the river a young man standing in a canoe glides across the water toward the camera, arriving like a guide who embodies primitive life harmoniously at one with nature.

Allégret includes some visually powerful images, such as the falls at M'Bali and a dance presented by the Dakpas near Bambari. These fragments lead to the core of the film, which is made up of episodes structured around five indigenous groups. Each sequence incorporates a distinct style and theme, always with an emphasis on display and performance. The Bayas are shown at work, as men hunt and women dig for tubers, suggesting a self-sustaining world at harmony with nature. The film then moves to the Saras where Allégret, in perhaps the film's most striking episode, inserts an intricately staged tale of a marriage negotiation between two young lovers, Kaddé and Djimta. The film's underlying voyeurism and primitivism is suggested in the shot introducing Kaddé, which tightly pans along her torso to her breasts, then moves across her body to reveal her face, where a small disc is fixed to her upper lip. The image recalls an earlier shot of Sara's girls: their bodies are examined in a slow left-to-right pan while the intertitles explain that they 'in turn prove their value'.

The Kaddé and Djimta interlude is followed by further travelogue sequences. The Massas are featured for their striking architecture, and the scenes among the Moundangs are almost wholly given over to an extravagant dance. The final episode shows a ceremony filmed at Rei-Bouba, offering a glimpse of local hierarchies, games, and the equestrian displays that Gide also describes with admiration in his journals. Though the film rarely achieves the sort of sensitivity to the colonial setting found in Gide's writings, or in Conrad's novel, it is a remarkable feature-length work, full of the rich aesthetic sensibilities also on display in Allégret's still photographs. Though it resists argument or instruction, its final moments do begin to incorporate a sense of ambiguity. After scenes at Rei-Bouba, images of 'la civilisation' flash across the screen: a protestant mission school, schoolchildren playing in uncomfortable-looking Western clothing, the endless transit of boats arriving and leaving at the port of Douala, and finally the sky over the sea, fading to black.

JEFFREY GEIGER

See also: Allégret, Marc; France

Voyage au Congo (France, 1927, 100 mins approx.). Produced, directed, written, photographed and edited by Marc Allégret. Titles by Allégret and André Gide. Filmed in Congo, Central African Republic, Chad, and Cameroon.

Further reading

Allégret, Marc, *Carnets du Congo: Voyage avec Gide*, Introduction and notes by Daniel Durosay, Paris: Presses du C.N.R.S., 1987.

Durosay, Daniel, 'Analyse synoptique du Voyage au Congo de Marc Allégret avec l'intégralité des inter-titres', *Bulletin des Amis d'André Gide*, January 22, 1994 : 71–85.

——'Les "cartons" retrouvé s du Voyage au Congo', *Bulletin des Amis d'André Gide*, January, 22, 1994: 65–70.

Geiger, Jeffrey, 'Sightseeing: Voyage au Congo and the Ethnographic Spectacle', in Tom Conner (ed.), *André Gide's Politics*, New York: Palgrave Macmillan, 2000: 111–30.

Gide, André, *Travels in the Congo* [Voyage au Congo/ Le retour du Tchad], trans. Dorothy Bussy, Hopewell, NJ: Ecco Press, 1994.

Waiting for Fidel

(Canada, Rubbo, 1974)

Waiting for Fidel is the film in which Australian-born National Film Board (NFB) of Canada director Michael Rubbo consolidated his inimitable style of personal filmmaking. The film meshes three elements tentatively present in his earlier documentary, Sad Song of Yellow Skin (1970), and that here, in full-bodied combination, make Rubbo's style distinctive to him. These elements are his participation in the on-screen action, his generosity toward his subjects, and a recognition of the superficiality and unreliability of documentary truth.

The film begins with three men in an airplane on their way to Cuba to film a promised interview with Fidel Castro. Geoff Stirling, a hip, capitalist media mogul, is making the film in coproduction with the NFB. Rubbo is the director. Joining them is the former Prime Minister of Newfoundland and the man who brought the province into confederation with Canada, the socialist Joey Smallwood. Different as their personalities are, at a certain level of generality the three share the hope that the interview with Castro will promote understanding between Cuba and the capitalist West.

As hinted in the film's title, the interview never happens. The film team bides its time in comparative luxury, waiting and hoping for the phone call summoning them to meet Castro. The focus of the film becomes the interaction among the three characters and their responses to Cuba. It is through this interplay among characters and between them and Cuba that the film rewards the audience with entertainment and insight.

The most famous scene in the film occurs late, when the three men have become frustrated at the stonewalling their quest for a promised interview has met. Rubbo has been filming their dinners, their recreations, and their controlled visits that their Cuban liaison man set up for them at such sites as a housing project, two schools, a chicken farm, and the Bay of Pigs. Stirling, who has put up the outside money for the project, gets into a heated argument with Rubbo over his shooting ratio. Rubbo has been filming at roughly a 25:1 clip. Stirling insists that a 3:1 clip would be more than sufficient. He berates Rubbo for his profligacy and calls him incompetent. Rubbo defends his way, and the NFB's way, of making documentaries. During their argument, they curse a lot, their cuss words bleeped out on the soundtrack. It is funny and revealing, but its charm also lies in Rubbo's involvement as an actor, not just an observer, and his willingness to allow his own foolishness to remain on screen. Few directors who appear in their films are as willing to be as harsh on themselves as they are on others.

Rubbo's generosity toward his characters is remarkable. Stirling could have been made to look merely ridiculous and unsavory. He seems incapable of acknowledging anything positive in the Cuban system, railing against the fact that schoolchildren have to spend part of their day working in a factory and complaining that a broadcaster like him would not be allowed on the air in Cuba. Smallwood, who is in his seventies, could have been portrayed as tiresome and dotty, but he comes off as admirable in his low-key but stubborn determination to think the best of Cuba and to do his best to ensure that the film contributes positively to international understanding. Interspersed throughout the film are brief scenes of Smallwood preparing his questions for Castro. The film's Cuban liaison comes off as a likeable, unofficious human being, somewhat bemused by the antics of his Canadian charges. Rubbo's willingness to see himself as one of the characters, with foibles and blind spots of his own, saves the film from the kind of condescension or sanctimony that so often detracts from films featuring the filmmaker as the documentary protagonist.

Ostensibly the film may appear to offer a vision of Cuba in lieu of the hoped-for scoop with Castro. In the state-sponsored location scenes, we get some interesting, off-the-cuff interaction with Cubans speaking without script. A pair of university students set the visitors straight on finer points of Marxism. An inmate of a mental hospital suggests that Rubbo, not her, may be the crazy one. A lyrically shot scene of a pick-up baseball game seems to capture a certain innocence in the Cuban personality. However, these encounters are superficial, and Rubbo knows it. What matters is not what they reveal about Cuba, because they reveal very little. Far more interesting is what they reveal about Stirling, Smallwood, and Rubbo. They interpret the encounters so that they fit in with their existing ideological concerns. For Stirling, nothing he sees is good; only the restoration of capitalism can save Cuba. Smallwood is impressed by the progress Cuba has made and thinks it is headed in the right direction. Rubbo is ambivalent, wanting to be impressed. What the film finally demonstrates has little to do with Cuba and everything to do with how our mindsets shape the way we perceive and interpret new experiences.

It is now quite common for documentary filmmakers to assume an on-screen role of provocateur. What remains rare, however, is the willingness to keep one's on-screen role roughly equal in dramatic force to other characters. Rubbo's awareness of the limitations of documentary, while widely shared, is rarely expressed in such a natural way, organic to the story, but instead is typically announced or stated in a way external to the narrative.

D.B. JONES

See also: Rubbo, Michael; Sad Song of Yellow Skin

Waiting for Fidel (Canada, National Film Board, 1974, 58 mins). Distributed by the National Film Board of Canada. Produced by Tom Daly and Michael Rubbo. Directed and edited by Michael Rubbo. Cinematography by Douglas Kiefer. Sound by Jacques Chevigny.

Further reading

Denby, David, 'How to Make a Castro Movie Without Castro', *The New York Times*, November 16, 1975.

Dobi, Steve, 'Michael Rubbo' (interview), *Sightlines*, fall, 1975: 17–20.

Handling, Piers, 'The Diary Films of Mike Rubbo', in Seth Feldman (ed.), *Take Two*, Toronto: Irwin Publishing, 1984.

Hughes, John, 'Michael Rubbo: Hiding Behind the "I"', (interview), *Cinema Papers*, January–February 1981: 41–5, 89.

Jones, D.B., *Movies and Memoranda*, Ottawa: Deneau, 1982.

——*The Best Butler in the Business: Tom Daly of the National Film Board of Canada*, Toronto: University of Toronto Press, 1996.

Knelman, Martin, 'Waiting for Fidel', *Toronto Globe & Mail*, July 24, 1976.

Rosenthal, Alan, 'Sad Song of Yellow Skin and Waiting for Fidel' (interview with Michael Rubbo), in *The Documentary Conscience: A Casebook in Film Making*, Berkeley, CA: University of California Press, 1980.

Sloniowski, Jeannette, 'Questioning the Master Narratives: Michael Rubbo's Waiting for Fidel', in James Leach and Jeannette Sloniowski (eds), *Candid Eyes: A Canadian Documentary Reader*, Toronto: University of Toronto Press, 2003.

War Game, The

(UK, Watkins, 1965)

Peter Watkins's meticulously researched vision of a 'limited' nuclear attack on England, The War Game, was officially banned from television screens worldwide for twenty years. It was produced for BBC Television in 1965, released for cinema in 1967, but not shown on television until 1985. The extent of its suppression and the political controversy that hounded it are perhaps unparalleled in UK television history. Watkins believed that there was a conspiracy of silence on the subject of nuclear warfare. Certainly this film touched such a raw nerve that the BBC, the government, and the right-wing press (which dubbed it propaganda for the Campaign for Nuclear Disarmament) all conspired to suppress it. However, it had its champions as well as denigrators, and the debate about whether to shelve it raged for over a year.

Watkins's film is a tour de force of cinematic techniques, using a fluid, handheld camera style that he had developed since his amateur days. He subverts the forms of documentary and newsreel to deliberately disorientate the viewer, engaging them emotionally, intellectually, and actively. In this way the film has been compared somewhat to Orson Welles's radio broadcast of *The War of the Worlds* (1938). The War Game is a drama shot to look like a documentary, a film with an inner logic that immediately suspends disbelief and invites the viewer to question the morality of nuclear weapons and the state's civil defence policy. As its narrative unfolds, the consequences of nuclear war at a very human level are explored, creating a reaction that is overpowering in its intensity.

Brechtian detachment techniques are deployed at times to create emotional distancing, such as the cameos to camera of some of the 'experts' attempting to reassure us of the 'wisdom' of nuclear weapons, but the effect is one of ironic counterpoint to the dramatic newsreel-like action on the screen. The contrast between these scenes is like attending a lecture on thermonuclear weapons and being there when one explodes. Occasionally Watkins breaks the narrative to question the cast directly about their knowledge of nuclear weapons, civil defence, and the Cold War. The War Game was shot on 16mm black and white to add to its illusory documentary/newsreel feel. This effect was further enhanced by a deliberate increase in tonal contrast at the processing stage to give the scenes after the bomb had dropped a stark, nightmare quality. The War Game used an amateur cast, as is Watkins's preference. He has been criticised for the occasional 'stiffness' of their performances, but feels that new faces and actors free from the traditional conventions of film acting are important additions to his conception of film realism. The stunning special effects of The War Games (such as the battlefield combat scene using 'tactical' nuclear weapons in Europe and the hellish firestorm depicted in England) all owe much to the crew's inventiveness rather than a big budget.

The film achieved notoriety even before it was screened. The cofounder of the 'Clean-up Television' campaign, Mary Whitehouse, wrote on September 5, 1965 to Hugh Carleton Greene, the Director-General of the BBC, and Prime Minister Harold Wilson that nuclear war was not a subject for 'entertainment'. She added, ominously, that 'the Home Office, not the BBC' should decide whether or not to show it. The letter was quoted in *The Guardian* (1965) and other sources. The decision to ban The War Game was raised at 10 Downing Street, discussed in the Cabinet, and debated in Parliament. A salvo of communication passed between the Home Office (the government department responsible for broadcasting and civil defence) and the BBC. It should not be forgotten that The War Game exposed, for the first time on film, the rudimentary 'protect and survive' methods that were promoted by the government against nuclear attack.

The Guardian (1999) reported that Prime Minister Churchill personally intervened in 1955 when the BBC proposed to make a film about the newly developed hydrogen bomb. These new weapons were thousands of times more deadly than the atomic bombs used on Japan in 1945. Churchill's edict to the BBC declared that any plans for a film on the H-bomb should be discussed in advance. The BBC 'at once accepted—very willingly' his order. Cold War tension was the underlining factor here, but also the curious relationship between the BBC and the British government, which only grants the BBC a licence to broadcast for a period of usually up to ten years at any one time. In 1965 the protocol was that the Home Office could instruct the BBC via the Postmaster General to ban any programme it considered 'not in the National interest'. The BBC Chair of Governors in 1965 was Lord Normanbrook, whose previous posts included Secretary to the Cabinet and Head of the Civil Service, and was reputedly one of Churchill's most trusted advisers (Colville 1985). In 1954 he headed a top-secret committee to advise on civil defence and war strategy in the event of a nuclear attack, a role well documented in Hennessy (2002).

Retired Member of Parliament and ex-Cabinet Minister Tony Benn was the Postmaster General in 1965. He told me personally and in writing (2003) that he was instructed by the Home Office to officially ban The War Game: 'My recollection is that the Home Secretary—[Frank] Soskice—decided to ban The War Game and, as PMG [Post Master General] and Minister for the BBC, I was told to transmit the instruction to them.'

The film was eventually granted a licence for cinema release but only after public protest, led by Watkins himself. It was shown in church halls, municipal buildings, and independent cinemas and immediately galvanised support. Cultural icons, such as John Lennon and Yoko Ono, Paul McCartney, and the Beatles' manager, Brian Epstein, all supported Watkins's film. The respected theatre and film critic, Kenneth Tynan (1966), wrote in the *Observer*: 'It may be the most important film ever made. We are always being told that works of art cannot change the course of history. Given wide enough dissemination, I believe this one can.' Lennon, in *Rolling Stone* (1970), said that seeing the film and corresponding with Watkins 'was like getting your call up papers for peace'. This impact on Lennon and Ono's 'give peace a chance' activities is elaborated in Coleman (1995).

The War Game further embarrassed the BBC by winning the Academy Award in 1967 for the Best Documentary Feature of 1966. Typically, Watkins declined to attend. Kenneth Adam, the Director of BBC Television, was sent to represent him, although one of the BBC's explanations for its decision not to show the film was that it was 'less than a masterpiece' and a failed 'experiment' (Gomez 1979). However, Watkins sent a telegram insisting that Adam was not to accept the Oscar if he won and the BBC was denied this opportunistic moment of reflected glory.

As a child Watkins lived in London and experienced the Blitz, the V-1 flying bomb, and the even more terrifying V-2 rocket. After the war he was conscripted for military service, and his abhorrence of war found expression in most of his subsequent work.

Tynan (1966) wrote that Watkins is 'the finest auteur we have', responsible for 'three masterpieces, more than any other living English director' (Culloden, 1964; The War Game, 1965; and Edvard Munch, 1973).

PATRICK MURPHY AND JOHN COOK

See also: Watkins, Peter

The War Game (UK, BBC Television, 1965, 47 mins). Distributed by the British Film Institute, London, on VHS or DVD with voice-over commentary and audio essay by Patrick Murphy. Written, produced and directed by Peter Watkins. Photography Peter Bartlett. Editor Mike Bradsell. Art direction Tony Cornell and Anne Davey. Action sequences Derek Ware. Sound Derek Williams, Lou Hanks, and Stanley Morcom. Costumes Vanessa Clarke. Make-up Lilias Munro. Production assistant Peter Norton. Commentaries Dick Graham and Michael Aspel. Filmed in Kent, England.

Further reading

n.a., 'Letter to PM on TV Film', *The Guardian*, UK, September 7, 1965: 5.

n.a., *Rolling Stone*, US/UK, February 7, 1970.

BBC, *The BBC Handbook*, London, published annually.

Coleman, R., 'Peace', in *Lennon: The Definitive Biography*, London: Pan Books, 1995, revised edn.

Colville, J., *The Fringes of Power*, London: Hodder & Stoughton, 1985.

Cook, J. and Murphy, P., 'After the Bomb Dropped: The Cinema Half-Life of the War Game', *The Journal of Popular British Cinema* 3, 2000: 129–32.

Ferris, P., 'The War Game', in *Sir Huge: the Life of Huw Wheldon*, London: Michael Joseph, 1990.

Gomez, J., *Peter Watkins*, Boston: Twayne Publishers, 1979.

Hennessy, P., *The Secret State*, London: Allen Lane, The Penguin Press, 2002.

Murphy, P., 'Let Them Watch Strindberg', *The Times Higher Education Supplement*, London, February 7, 1997.

——'The Film the BBC Tried to Bury', *The New Statesman*, London, August 24, 1997: 22–4.

——'The War Game—The Controversy, Sweden', *Film International* 3, 2003: 25–8.

Rosenthal, A., 'The War Game', in *The New Documentary in Action*, Berkeley, CA: University of California Press, 1971.

Travis, A., 'Churchill Gagged BBC on H-bomb', *The Guardian*, August 20, 1999: 6.

Tynan, K., 'A Warning Masterpiece', *Observer*, London, February 13, 1966.

Watkins, P., *The War Game*, London: Sphere Books/ Andre Deutsch, 1967.

Welsh, J.M., *Peter Watkins—A Guide to References and Resources*, Boston: G.K. Hall, 1986.

War Room, The

(US, Pennebaker and Hegedus, 1993)

The War Room follows two documentary traditions pioneered with Primary (1960): cinéma vérité and the insider's view on US presidential election campaigns. Like Primary, The War Room observes events on the campaign trail, but instead of limiting itself to one state, the film follows Bill Clinton's 1992 odyssey through the New Hampshire primary, the Democratic Party nomination and bus tour, the debates, and the election night victory. The film also addresses the monkey wrenches thrown into the works, including Gennifer Flowers's allegations, draft-dodging accusations, and other mud-slinging on platform issues. In all, filmmakers D.A. Pennebaker (who worked on Primary) and Chris Hegedus spent almost thirty-five hours inside the war room, Clinton's moniker for his campaign headquarters in Little Rock, Arkansas.

The film does show some moments with Clinton (one features him wearing a baseball cap, an Arkansas Razorbacks T-shirt, a digital watch, and running shoes as he talks to a reporter on the phone), but The War Room is more about his image and his image-makers than Clinton himself. As such, the focus is more on campaign manager James Carville and communications director George Stephanopoulos. The two are polar opposites, yet both are dedicated to seeing their candidate win. With his Southern affectations, quick mind, and dazzling one-liners, 'Ragin' Cajun' Carville brings his passionate spirit to meetings, press conferences, and even radio talk shows. George Stephanopoulos plays the straight man to Carville's one-man act, though he brings no less dedication to the efforts.

Pennebaker and Hegedus also incorporate television clips and shots of newspaper headlines to fill in some gaps in their timeline. In doing so, they provide an additional perspective on events, that of the mass media. Television footage reveals the dents in the candidate's reputation. One early segment juxtaposes Flowers's press conference ('Did Governor Clinton use a condom?' asks one reporter) and her revelation of their affair with shots of reporters asking Clinton for comments on the accusations. Newspaper headlines chart Clinton's rise and fall at both primary and public opinion polls.

The filmmakers played the cinéma vérité waiting game in making The War Room, but Carville delivers an emotional climax. During a staff meeting, Stephanopoulos calmly introduces Carville with a thank you. Carville gets up to give a final rally cry for the troops, but a close-up reveals his chin quivering as he speaks. A tear emerges and he wipes it away, fighting the wash of tears coming on.

The filmmakers also risked Clinton losing the election. If he had lost, according to Hegedus, 'the value of a film about a losing campaign staff wasn't going to be too salable for us. There is a risk in any story where you're following real life and you don't know what's going to happen' (Stubbs 2002: 46). Voters elected Clinton by a 'landslide', in Stephanopoulos's word.

The film shows how an unconventional candidate needs an unconventional team. By mixing observed footage with television clips and newspaper headlines, Hegedus and Pennebaker create a forum in which to showcase Carville, Stephanopoulos, and the rest of Clinton's staff.

HEATHER MCINTOSH

The War Room (US, Pennebaker Associates, 1993, 96 mins). Distributed by October Films. Directed by Chris Hegedus and D.A. Pennebaker. Produced by R.J. Cutler, Wendy Ettinger, and Frazer Pennebaker. Cinematography by Nick Doob, D.A. Pennebaker, and Kevin Rafferty. Film Edited by Chris Hegedus, Erez Laufer, and D.A. Pennebaker.

Further reading

Pennebaker Hegedus Films, www.phfilms.com

Stubbs, Liz, 'D.A. Pennebaker and Chris Hegedus: Engineering Nonfiction Cinema', in *Documentary Filmmakers Speak*, New York: Allworth, 2002: 41–68.

Warhol, Andy

Pop artist Andy Warhol made many films in the 1960s in his New York studio, the well-known 'Factory'. Warhol began working with 16mm film around 1963 and continued to produce great numbers of cinematic works for several years. These films are among the most noted of the 1960s avant-garde and are counted among the canon of experimental film, as they challenged narrative convention and explored daily life in exciting new ways. This movement into filmmaking was a natural progression for Warhol, whose work as a painter and illustrator was already revered. The pop icon was always interested in new ways to replicate the events and people of the world around him, and the film camera provided a direct and seemingly truthful means of capturing this. As Warhol evolved as a filmmaker, his works became less clearly documentary and more fictional in their content. So, too, the formal aspects seen in Warhol's early films changed as the decade continued, an apparently organic aesthetic response to the times.

The first Warhol films recall the simple constructions of the Lumières' actualities from the 1890s. These works are far more complex, however, and may be seen as a perfect representation of the prevailing attitudes and concerns of their time. Sleep (1963), the first Warhol film shown publicly, is a record of John Giorno in bed sleeping. The film is in real time, so it lasts more than five hours and is a complete document of a man sleeping. The impact of showing such an event in real time cannot be underestimated. Viewers are often disturbed by this technique, and they may become agitated or angry, perhaps even verbally abusive to the screen itself. Warhol continued his investigation of real time with such works as the trio of Haircut films (1963), Empire (1964), and Eat (1964). Each of these titles refers rather directly to the content of the film. In the Haircut works, numbered consecutively in order of creation, we witness various men having haircuts. In Eat, we watch painter Robert Indiana slowly consume a mushroom, an experience that lasts nearly forty minutes. Warhol's notorious Empire is an eight-hour study of the Empire State Building. The camera is unmoving, and only a full viewing of the film can show that there is much movement indeed, as sunlight shifts and falls, clouds drift by, and electrical lights are switched on and off in the building.

This cinematic experimentation evolved in several different ways. These very early films investigated time in a meditative way, but other 'real time' works moved less slowly in the same period. Kiss (1963–4) is a series of short works that cleverly defies the viewer-viewed comfort zone. Warhol was interested in voyeurism and sought to play with this concept in his film work. Kiss also exploits the single-spool (reel) of home movies and independent filmmaking. Each set of people seen in the Kiss works engages in kissing for nearly three minutes, the length of one reel of 16mm film. The couples are diverse (same sex, opposite sex, questionable gender, etc.), as are the styles of kissing seen (from very passionate to softly tender). What is undeniable here is the atypical experience of watching anyone kiss for more than the usual thirty seconds or less seen in typical movies. Blow Job (1964) is of the same time period, and it also strongly deals with the nature of voyeurism and the viewer's experience. In this film, a man leans against a brick wall as fellatio is performed on him. The framing of this scene is paramount, as the shot shows the man's head, shoulders, and torso, but nothing below his midsection. The viewer is left to ponder the unseen person kneeling in front of the subject, and as the film lasts more than thirty minutes, the act of watching the subject's face is clearly the point of the exercise.

One of the most fascinating projects seen in the Warhol film archive is that of the Screen Tests (1964–6), which also exploited the 100' reel of 16mm film as a time element. There are more than five hundred known Screen Tests (The Andy Warhol Museum is in the process of identifying and cataloging all of the works that have surfaced in Warhol's belongings), each a three-minute study of a person's face. With the camera mounted on a tripod, turned on, and left to create a record, each subject reacted differently. Facing a camera is a difficult task for some, a chance to perform for others, but each Screen Test shows a change in the subject's face as the minutes of this confrontation pass. These works are beautiful in their formal simplicity and extremely intriguing as complex explorations of individuals.

These types of investigations continued throughout the 1960s and into the early 1970s, as Warhol turned his camera onto the people who hung around the Factory. Documentary studies were still the bulk of the films made, but they became more elaborate studies of the artists, musicians, junkies, and superstars who were a part of the Warhol scene. Chelsea Girls (1967) is a double-projected film (two reels shown side-by-side and simultaneously) that is more than three hours long. It moves from room to room in the Chelsea Hotel, pausing for various periods of time to reveal these people in various scenarios in largely unscripted scenes. The 'actors' play themselves here, and the film is a document of these people in this time doing the strange things they did. Other works were made with this same kind of curiosity and honesty as these lives were memorialized in hundreds of films.

TAMMY A. KINSEY

Biography

Born near Pittsburgh, PA, 1928. Attended Carnegie Institute of Technology (now Carnegie Mellon University). Moved to New York City 1949. Began working in commercial art as an illustrator. First exhibition, Ferus Gallery 1962. Included in group show at the Guggenheim Museum 1963. Received Independent Film Award from Film Culture 1964. Film installation exhibited in New York Film Festival 1964. Produced Exploding Plastic Inevitable, multimedia events that included performances by the Velvet Underground 1966. Produced first rock and roll album by Velvet Underground and Nico 1966. Shot and seriously wounded by Valerie Solanas, former Factory dweller 1968. First retrospective show, Europe 1968. First issue of *Interview* magazine published 1969. Major retrospective show, United States and Europe 1970. Produced short segments, 'Andy Warhol's TV' for use on Saturday Night Live 1981. Directed music video for the Cars 1984. Hosted Andy Warhol's Fifteen Minutes, regular program on MTV 1985–87. Died from complications following routine gallbladder surgery 1987.

Selected films

1964 Couch
1965 Horse
1966 Suicide
1968 Blue Movie

Further reading

Koch, Stephen, *Stargazer*, New York: Marion Boyars, 1973.

O'Pray, Michael (ed.), *Andy Warhol: Film Factory*, London: British Film Institute, 1989.

Warhol, Andy and Hackett, Pat, *POPism: The Warhol 60s*, New York: Harper & Row, 1980.

Wolf, Reva, *Andy Warhol, Poetry, and Gossip in the 1960s*, Chicago and London: University of Chicago Press, 1997.

Watkins, Peter

In 2000 Peter Watkins completed a three hundred and forty-five-minute documentary commissioned by La Sept ARTE, the French-German TV network. La Commune de Paris 1871 was produced with a cast of more than two hundred, recruited from newspaper adverts, who researched and improvised together the story of the uprising. Told through the eyes of two fictional TV stations, the actors, in and out of character and in and out of period, debate the issues of the Commune, but also the role of the media in 1871 and at the end of the millennium. La Sept ARTE first tried to reedit, then scheduled the programme for the graveyard shift. Distributed on video by supporters, the film has done the round of festivals to considerable acclaim and some controversy. It has also been effectively kept off the television screens for which it was designed and on which it comments so directly. It is, as far as there is such a thing, a typical Watkins project.

In his online account of the film, Watkins's comments of TV that 'The medium has become a thoroughly mean-spirited profession, ruthlessly resisting all dialogue for change, completely devoid of respect, and allied without reservation to the development of globalization in its most centralizing and brutal forms.' The bitter tone is all too familiar and only too understandable. A prizewinning amateur filmmaker, Watkins clearly relished the inventive, improvisational character of nonprofessional documentary and continues to draw on it in his most recent work. With Culloden (1964), he achieved star status, bringing his vérité camera, direct address, voice-over, and volunteer cast aesthetic to the network public and critical esteem. His follow-up, The War Game (1965), despite its Best Documentary Oscar, was banned from British broadcasting for twenty years. Characterized by the same gritty montage of dramatization, recitations of fact, and precise naming of protagonists that characterised his earliest films, The War Game's depiction of the likely effects of a nuclear strike on Kent, England, made the fatal error of tying its horrors not just to Vietnam, as he had done in Culloden, but to the fire-bombing of Dresden, subject of at least two other documentaries banned on British television.

Forays into speculation as a mode of political commentary followed—1966's Privilege, 1969's The Gladiators (The Peace Game), 1971's Punishment Park—beginning Watkins's peripatetic career outside a United Kingdom that remained closed to him and largely closed to his films. In 1974 he completed Edvard Munch for Norwegian television, a vivid historical reconstruction of the decaying society and personal tragedies of the celebrated painter. Far removed from the norms of costume drama, this docudrama uses a cold palette dominated by greens and blues to communicate the tubercular world of its protagonist, and in what seems a deeply personal statement, covers the artist's family and professional life as a series of Brechtian 'gestus', marked by incomprehension, refusal, and despair.

There followed a series of low-budget experiments, mainly with Scandinavian companies, exploring with increasing fascination the powers of the long take and mobile camerawork to reveal with increasing intensity the emotional life of his characters. In 1987 the various strands of Watkins's career came together in an extraordinary project, released as The Journey. More than fourteen hours long, shot in more than a dozen countries, always with scraps of money, short-ends, volunteer craft and cast, The Journey documents not so much the international effects of nuclear war, its ostensible subject, as its own process. Actors move in and out of character to debate the rights and wrongs of their actions, and Watkins's theatrical investment in revealing his sets as sets moves toward making explicit the produced nature of the documentary, while at the same time assaulting the network wisdom that an hour is forty-three minutes punctuated by adverts. The duration of the piece derives from its internal logic, not that of broadcast sales, two reasons for its lack of distribution.

The Freethinker (1994) returns to the territory of Munch in its dramatization of the life of Strindberg. Shot on video with cast and crew derived from a film school where Watkins was working, the film also resembles Munch in its portrait of a reviled creator. Like The Journey, The Freethinker expends much of its energy investigating the conditions of its making, a self-conscious essay on the potential of documentary to inform drama; to engage its performers' knowledge, opinions, and passion into the script; to foreground the medium by intrusive anachronisms, especially direct 'TV' interviews of characters; and the willingness to allow viewers time to watch, listen, and decide about the actions presented. The Freethinker is also characterised by a complex spiral structure interweaving five distinct times in Strindberg's life, not just contesting chronological biography, but allowing complex rhymes and analogies between phases of a life to emerge into the light.

The bulk of critical writing on Watkins concentrates on earlier work, largely because The War Game and Culloden remain the easiest of his films to find. The disastrous relationship with La Sept ARTE means that his most significant achievement to date, La Commune, is scarcely beginning to have the impact it deserves. The film draws together previous technical developments in his oeuvre but also develops a powerful use of wide-angle lenses and handheld mobile camera takes of up to ten minutes to assert the complexity of understanding a history made by crowds rather than by individuals or even types. As the amateur cast debate the action and its relation to contemporary events in France, Watkins draws racism, gender, and colonialism into the history of the Commune. All the while, the stories are conveyed by two contrasting TV stations, using, as in The War Game, intertitles to add information and draw parallels. Characters and actors alike disagree with the film's thesis, apologizing for the massacre of the communards, appealing for the past to be forgotten. None of this is excluded, though the direction frequently allows an expression of opinion to be interrupted by new narrative action, and vice versa. Still committed to a pedagogical documentary form, still at war with the 'monoform' standards of broadcast media, Watkins can easily be portrayed as a dinosaur. His work, however, is increasingly relevant to any claim that documentary has a public role in a postmodern mediascape.

SEAN CUBITT

See also: War Game, The

Watson, Patrick

Patrick Watson's influence on Canadian television is profound. Affected by Marshall McLuhan's ideas of electronic media producing a global village, Watson has stridently challenged the medium of television as a tool for mass communication and thought-provoking work.

To develop these ideas, Watson initially delved into the political realm of Parliament Hill, producing and presenting news and current affairs programs such as Close-Up (1959) and Inquiry (1960). Dissatisfied, Watson wanted to produce a cutting-edge current affairs programme that could combine McLuhan's philosophy, approach controversial topics, and have entertainment value. The satirical This Hour Has Seven Days (1964–6) fulfilled his ideas for merging political and current affairs to the general television public. It was the most watched programme in Canada and caused a furore of complaints and compliments—exactly what Watson had wanted.

After the cancellation of This Hour, Watson, with his newly formed independent production company, started to produce and direct a wider range of television programming, including such examples as Steeltown (1966), The Undersea World of Jacques Cousteau (1968), Witness to Yesterday (1970), 51st State (1970), and Question of Television Violence (1972). Most of these documentaries try to understand the world in which we live, and with this information, encourage the public to ask questions about that world.

The 1970s and 1980s saw more of Watson's penchant for Canadian history and politics with an array of programs such as The Watson Report (1975–81) and The Canadian Establishment (1980). Reaching viewers beyond Canada, he wrote, produced, and presented the highly acclaimed series The Chinese (1983) and The Struggle for Democracy (1989).

The Struggle for Democracy would become his crowning achievement. To explore the idea of democracy, this series would be five years in the making and take him to thirty countries. It was an ideal project that brought together all of Watson's talents as a presenter, researcher, philosopher, and historian. It was the first documentary series to be transmitted simultaneously in French and English on the CBC in January 1989. This series cemented Watson's status as an auteur.

Watson's thirty-year career with the CBC came to a climax in 1989, when he became chairman, with the mandate to strengthen the CBC and help turn it into a world-class broadcasting organization. Watson soon found this challenge frustrating, as the board of directors was rife with Conservative patronage appointments, which in turn fuelled the on-going debate over privatization. Most frustrating of all was the public's high and unrealistic expectations of Watson, in an ineffectual role, as saviour of the CBC. Watson resigned in 1991, four months before his tenure expired.

Patrick Watson saw the potential of television as a limitless device for communicating and provoking discussion. He made Canadians aware of social and political issues, as well as their global environment. Long before his 1989 mandate to strengthen the CBC as a world broadcaster, Watson wanted the Corporation to be at the forefront of this media revolution, constantly pushing them to have more ingenuity with programming ideas. He saw the general television public as people with a thirst for knowledge, which is why as a documentarian, Watson is so successful and popular: he connects high ideals with popular communication.

MELISSA BROMLEY

Biography

Born Toronto, Ontario, Canada, December 23, 1929. Graduated from University of Toronto, MA, DLitt. Companion in the Order of Canada 2002. Radio actor 1943, producer, writer at the CBC 1955–66. Became an independent producer, director, and presenter founder of Patrick Watson Enterprises 1966. Cofounder of Immedia 1967. Chair of the CBC 1989–94; first North American filmmaker to film in the People's Republic of China; recipient of ACTRA Outstanding Achievement to Canadian Broadcasting; creative director of the CRB Foundation's Heritage Project and commissioning editor, documentaries, for History Television.

Further reading

Barber, Benjamin and Watson, Patrick, *The Struggle for Democracy*, Toronto: Key Porter Books, revised edn, 2002.

Lee, Rohama, 'The Struggle for Democracy', *Sightlines* 4, 1989: 32–3.

Manera, Tony, *A Dream Betrayed: The Battle for the CBC*, Toronto: Stoddart Publishing Co. Ltd, 1996.

McLuhan, Marshall, *Understanding Media*, London: Routledge Classics edn, 2001.

McLuhan, Marshall and Fiore, Quentin, *The Medium is the Message*, Corte Madera, CA: Gingko Press, 2001.

Nash, Knowlton, *The Microphone Wars: A History of Triumph and Betrayal at the CBC*, Toronto: McClelland & Stewart Inc, 1994.

Watson, Patrick, *The Canadians: Biographies of a Nation, Volume III*, Toronto: McArthur and Co., 2002.

Watt, Harry

Harry Watt was a key figure in the rapprochement between British documentary and realist feature film production during World War II. In a career spanning the documentary movement of the 1930s and early 1940s, and Michael Balcon's regime at Ealing studios in the 1940s and 1950s, he successfully directed both types of film. He came into his own as a filmmaker in the latter part of the 1930s at the General Post Office (GPO) Film Unit, having joined its previous incarnation, the Empire Marketing Board (EMB) Film Unit, after studying at Edinburgh University and working at various jobs including sailor and shop worker. In this respect he differed from other recruits to the British documentary movement, for example Basil Wright, who joined immediately after university. Watt shared a middle-class background with his colleagues, but his down-to-earth manner and personal experience of some of the occupations represented in the movement's films partly account for his ability to coax credible performances from nonactors in documentaries such as North Sea (1938) and Target for Tonight (1941).

BBC-Droitwich (1935), one of the earliest documentaries that Watt directed, benefited from a concluding experimental sound montage of radio transmissions devised by Alberto Cavalcanti. Temperamentally, Watt found Cavalcanti's professional yet Catholic approach to filmmaking more congenial than John Grierson's. Watt's career as a director with an emerging style of his own flourished after Cavalcanti succeeded Grierson as head of the GPO Film Unit in 1937. Subsequent developments in Watt's filmmaking emphasised previously neglected or subordinate aspects of the documentary project. One ambition Watt and Cavalcanti shared, which Grierson gave less emphasis to in the later 1930s, was to get documentaries screened in mainstream theatrical circuit cinemas. North Sea, a narrative documentary reconstructing an actual incident in which a fishing trawler caught in a storm was guided home by a radio station, was specifically designed with this in mind.

Rudimentary narrative structures and reconstruction of events that had happened or would typically happen existed within British documentary before Watt's work (Winston 1995). Drifters (John Grierson, 1929), like North Sea, used the basic journey structure of a trawler's fishing expedition and incorporated footage shot on a specially constructed set to represent the interior of the trawler's cabin. From the outset rudimentary narrative structures and reconstructions were taken for granted as a standard part of documentary practice, but what generated support from critics and endowed the documentary movement with cultural legitimacy during its earlier phase was modernist experimentation in, for example, Drifters, The Song of Ceylon (Basil Wright, 1934–5), and even BBC-Droitwich (Stollery 2000). Watt's innovation in documentaries such as North Sea was to explicitly prioritise narrative and characterisation and attract attention and praise for doing so.

Night Mail (1936) is Watt's transitional film. It uses a multifunctional voice-over, and its cinematography and editing are indebted to the modernist experimentation of the documentary movement's earlier phase (Guynn 1990; Aitken 1998). At the same time, the sync-sound equipment, which had been available only to the GPO Film Unit for a couple of years, enabled Watt to direct sequences featuring actual postal workers conversing in a set built to resemble the interior of a sorting carriage. The scripted dialogue they speak nominally individualises their characters, advances the narrative, and conveys information about the mail sorting process. Combined with the narrative momentum of the train's journey and the use of diegetic sound, this gives a particular sense of realism to the actions represented. These broad similarities to feature film technique partly account for Night Mail's relative success in mainstream cinema exhibition.

In The Saving of Bill Blewitt (1937), a robust Cornish fisherman saves money with the Post Office and in the latter part of the narrative works to a deadline to achieve his goal of buying a new boat. The film largely eschews voice-over commentary and uses an attenuated version of continuity editing favouring long and medium shots to draw the spectator into its narrative while locating its protagonist within a social context. North Sea (1938) is more sophisticated. Its narrative structure and editing strategies are similar to, yet more complex than, Watt's previous film (Higson 1986). Suspense is engendered by alternating between a worried community and radio operators on land, and endangered men at sea. The storm provides modestly spectacular action recorded in overexposed footage, giving the film a compellingly raw texture. Editing links the actions of different crew members and radio operators to construct a visceral impression of integrated team work. Voice-over commentary is used briefly at the end to generalise the incident by referring to the numerous Post Office radio stations guarding Britain's ships.

North Sea was a commercial success, heralded as a minor breakthrough by reviewers and the trade press. Nonetheless certain British documentary filmmakers closer to Grierson felt Watt's approach to narrative made the film less informative about work processes than it should have been (Aitken 1998). Unlike some of his colleagues, Watt was not inclined to theoretical debate, but in an article written to accompany North Sea's release, he argued that what gave the film credibility was its narrative restraint. For him the absence of the dramatic embellishment that a fictionalised treatment would have brought to the narrative guaranteed its documentary authenticity (Vaughan 1983). Watt further refined the template he established in North Sea in Target for Tonight, a classic wartime documentary about an RAF bombing raid (Short 1997).

The influence of North Sea and Target for Tonight is evident in prestigious Crown Film Unit documentary productions for the Ministry of Information (MOI), such as Western Approaches (1944), directed towards the end of the war by Watt's former assistant Pat Jackson (Jackson 1999). Watt's activities during World War II included recording and reconstructing some of the earliest iconic documentary images associated with this period in The First Days (Watt, Humphrey Jennings, Pat Jackson, 1939). Subsequent films, London Can Take It (Watt, Jennings, 1940), and Christmas Under Fire (1941), narrated by American journalist Quentin Reynolds, were designed to build American support for Britain's war effort.

In 1942 Watt followed Cavalcanti to Ealing Studios to direct his first feature, Nine Men (1943) (Barr 1999). This was a logical extension of the direction his documentaries had taken. Other Ealing films such as The Foreman Went to France (Charles Frend, 1942) and certain British wartime features beyond Ealing registered the influence of what critic Dilys Powell described as Watt's 'semi-fictional documentaries' (Short 1997). In retrospect, the films in this category directed by Watt have been criticised, along with other strands of 1930s and 1940s British documentary, for ignoring controversial social, political, and economic issues because of institutional constraints. Watt himself concedes this criticism in his candid memoirs (Watt 1974). Yet his most notable documentaries played an historically significant role, contributing to an emerging tendency within wartime and postwar British cinema towards a new type of realist representation.

MARTIN STOLLERY

See also: Night Mail; Target for Tonight

Biography

Born in Glasgow, Scotland, October 18, 1906. Attended Edinburgh University. Joined Empire Marketing Board (EMB) Film Unit 1931–2. Assisted Robert Flaherty during the production of Man of Aran (1934). Codirected his first film, Six-Thirty Collection, with Edgar Anstey 1934. Moved with the film unit to the General Post Office (GPO) in 1934, stayed on when it became the Crown Film Unit 1939, and also worked for the Army Film Unit between 1939 and 1942. Contributed items to The March of Time 1936–37. Directed second unit on Jamaica Inn (Alfred Hitchcock, 1939). Directed numerous documentaries including North Sea (1938) and Target for Tonight (1941). Joined Ealing Studios in 1942 and directed seven features there including The Overlanders (1946), on location in Australia, and Where No Vultures Fly (1951), in Africa. Worked as a producer at Granada Television 1955. Published his memoirs *Don't Look at the Camera* in 1974. Died April 2, 1987.

Selected films

1935 BBC-Droitwich: director
1936 Night Mail: director
1937 The Saving of Bill Blewitt: director
1938 North Sea: director
1939 The First Days: codirector (with Humphrey Jennings and Pat Jackson)
1940 London Can Take It: codirector (with Humphrey Jennings, both uncredited)
1941 Christmas Under Fire: codirector (with Charles Hasse)
1941 Target for Tonight: director and writer (uncredited)
1943 Nine Men: director

Further reading

Aitken, Ian, *The Documentary Film Movement: An Anthology*, Edinburgh: Edinburgh University Press, 1998.
Barr, Charles, *Ealing Studios*, third edn, Moffat: Cameron and Hollis, 1999.
Guynn, William, *A Cinema of Nonfiction*, London: Associated University Press, 1990.
Higson, Andrew, 'Britain's Outstanding Contribution to the Film: The Documentary-Realist Tradition', in Charles Barr (ed.), *All Our Yesterdays*, London: BFI, 1986: 72–97.
Jackson, Pat, *A Retake Please! Night Mail to Western Approaches*, Liverpool: Liverpool University Press, 1999.
Short, K.R.M., 'RAF Bomber Command's Target for Tonight (1941)', *Historical Journal of Film, Radio and Television* 17, no. 2, June 1997: 181–218.
Stollery, Martin, *Alternative Empires: European Modernist Cinemas and Cultures of Imperialism*, Exeter: University of Exeter Press, 2000.
Vaughan, Dai, *Portrait of an Invisible Man*, London: BFI, 1983.
Watt, Harry, *Don't Look at the Camera*, London: Elek, 1974.
Winston, Brian, *Claiming the Real*, London: BFI, 1995.

We Are the Lambeth Boys

(UK, Reisz, 1959)

We Are the Lambeth Boys was the main film in The Last Free Cinema programme shown at the National Film Theatre in March 1959, and was the second (and last) in the Ford-sponsored Look at Britain series (of which Lindsay Anderson's Every Day Except Christmas was the first). The film is linked in several ways with Every Day Except Christmas: both were part of the Free Cinema movement, and Reisz was coproducer of Anderson's film. At least one of the youths in We Are the Lambeth Boys worked in Covent Garden market, where Anderson's film was shot; Every Day Except Christmas looked at work, while We Are the Lambeth Boys looks at leisure time, documenting the activities of the Alford House youth club in Lambeth. That the film was explicitly about working-class young people links it strongly to the so-called British New Wave of fictional features, of which Reisz's Saturday Night and Sunday Morning (1960) was a key film.

Like Every Day Except Christmas, We Are the Lambeth Boys was photographed by Walter Lassally and recorded and edited by the often overlooked John Fletcher, but the years between the two films were marked by important changes in technology. Whereas Every Day Except Christmas appears to have little or no direct sound—though efforts are made to fake it from time to time—some major sequences in We Are the Lambeth Boys make important use of it (as well as of more mobile cameras). The discussion about murder and the death penalty, for example, and the late-night chip shop sequence—both relatively controlled situations—rely on it. Indeed, near the start of the film, when the boys are in the cricket nets and the girls are chatting in groups, and they begin to tease each other, the film seems to celebrate its ability to use direct sound recorded on location.

Elsewhere, however, sound is used in the same 'creative' way that it was used in Every Day Except Christmas, and the same way it was used in most 1930s and wartime British documentary films. Having shown us the end of a club evening, and larking about in the chip shop and street, the film fades to black then fades in on: morning, deserted block of council flats, one boy leaves on his own on his bicycle, sound of a train (atmospheric, though no train is visible); voice-over: 'Being young in the morning is different from being young at night … ' This is followed by a sequence of two younger boys arriving at school and singing a hymn ('The King of Love My Shepherd Is') in school assembly, which is continued over a sequence of shots of other young people at work—seamstress, office worker, post office boy, butcher's apprentice, assembly line pie-maker, all later put into context—learning a trade, waiting to get married, and so on—by the voice-over.

Although it is undoubtedly true that Free Cinema films, and perhaps We Are the Lambeth Boys in particular, offered relatively new, fresh images (and sounds) of British society and especially of youth culture—images in which we could at last, however partially, recognise ourselves—such a sequence raises large questions about the way the film uses voice-over commentary and music, and about the film's use of 'we' in its title. Though the subjects of the film—aside from those (barely glimpsed) who run the club and the Mill Hill School boys (who seem really only a foil for the Lambeth boys)—are working class, the filmmakers are conscious that they are not. The heated club discussion about capital punishment, for example, is both introduced by the middle-class voice-over and crucially framed by it.

It is less likely that the filmmakers were conscious of the implications of their choice of music—orchestrated jazz composed by Johnny Dankworth. The music is generally effective at setting the tone of the film (and for punctuating it at certain points), but why jazz? Remembering Momma Don't Allow (one of the first Free Cinema films, directed by Tony Richardson and Reisz, 1955), about a traditional jazz club, and even the Happy Wanderers street jazz band in Every Day Except Christmas, jazz seems to be one of the popular culture credentials of the middle-class filmmakers, whereas, as the film makes clear, what the young people themselves like is rock 'n' roll and 'skiffle'. The jazzy score, then, functions as another, unspoken judgment or commentary, implying that jazz is a superior popular form, just as the voice-over implies that the boys' political or moral judgements are defective or underdeveloped (though it could be argued that the film's critique is directed at the education system).

Overall, the class aspects of the film are quite difficult to discern, partly because the film sometimes suggests a critique but then withdraws from elaboration into easier conclusions. Having raised questions about the adequacy of the boys' judgements in the capital punishment discussion, for example, the voice-over retreats with: 'Not that they're worried. They're good at making the most of everyday, and just talking about things, like this, is a beginning. And it's good for a giggle.'

The extended sequence that follows, of the boys' trip to Mill Hill School for the annual cricket match, and an occasion allowing the overt juxtaposition of the working-class boys and the public school class, is more difficult to read. The boys' initial exuberance is replaced by what may be sullen passivity or jealousy, or just reflection, as they see the sumptuous facilities of the school. The return to Lambeth is marked by the boys' apparently wanting to leave their noisy mark on Central London as they pass through, but the film wants us to believe that, on crossing Westminster Bridge, the boys fall silent and, again, reflective or even morose. Why? Are we to feel that the boys are conscious of their class disadvantages, of their more limited opportunities? This is not made at all clear or explicit, and the film ends on a less uncomfortable note: Saturday night dancing at the club and the commentary's conclusion that 'a good evening for young people is much as it has always been, it's for being together with friends, and shouting when you feel like it—things we'd all like to do' (although the close of the film, with its nocturnal views of council flats, perhaps strikes a darker note).

JIM HILLIER

See also: Every Day Except Christmas; Reisz, Karel

We Are the Lambeth Boys (UK, Graphic Films for the Ford Motor Company Ltd, 1959, 52 mins, the second film in Look at Britain series). Distributed by the British Film Institute. Produced by Leon Clore. Directed by Karel Reisz. Cinematography by Walter Lassally. Music composed by Johnny Dankworth, played by members of the Johnny Dankworth Orchestra. Edited by John Fletcher. Commentary spoken by Jon Rollason. Assistants Louis Wolfers and Raoul Sobel. Filmed in London.

Further reading

Anderson, Lindsay, 'Free Cinema', *Universities and Left Review* 2, summer 1957 (reprinted in Barsam, Richard Meran (ed.), *Nonfiction Film Theory and Criticism*, New York: E.P. Dutton, 1976).

Ellis, Jack, *The Documentary Idea*, Englewood Cliffs, NJ and London: Prentice-Hall, 1989.

Gaston, Georg, *Karel Reisz*, Boston: Twayne Publishers, 1980.

Hoggart, Richard, 'We Are the Lambeth Boys', *Sight and Sound* 28, summer–autumn, 1959.

Lambert, Gavin, 'Free Cinema', *Sight and Sound* 25, spring 1956.

Lovell, Alan and Hillier, Jim, *Studies in Documentary*, London: Secker & Warburg; New York: Viking, 1972.

Reisz, Karel, 'A Use for Documentary', *Universities and Left Review* 3, winter 1957.

Sussex, Elizabeth, *The Rise and Fall of British Documentary*, Berkeley, CA and London: University of California Press, 1975.

We Live in Two Worlds

(UK, Cavalcanti, 1937)

We Live in Two Worlds (1937) was the second of the seven films that Alberto Cavalcanti directed for the Swiss telephone company Pro-Telephone Zurich between 1936 and 1939. The seven films are Line to Tcherva Hut, We Live in Two Worlds (1937), Who Writes to

Switzerland? (1937), Message from Geneva (1937), Four Barriers (1937), Alice au pays romand (1938), and Men of the Alps (1939). We Live in Two Worlds is also the best known of these films, principally because of the involvement of the novelist and public figure, J.B. Priestley. Paul Rotha thought the film to be the best General Post Office (GPO) Film Unit film, alongside Harry Watt's The Saving of Bill Blewitt, to emerge in 1937. Forsyth Hardy, John Grierson's biographer, also thought We Live in Two Worlds to be particularly successful. However, Cavalcanti himself believed that another of the Swiss films, the less well-known Line to Tcherva Hut (1936) was a better film than We Live in Two Worlds.

The origins of We Live in Two Worlds lay in John Grierson's wish to utilise the footage left over from the making of Line to Tcherva Hut. Such a practice of reusing stock footage to make new films was common within the documentary film movement. To achieve this goal in this particular film, Grierson asked J.B. Priestley to compose an appropriate 'film talk', which could then be illustrated by the leftover footage. Priestley then constructed the narrative around the footage. Priestley called this process of 'turning a series of photographs into a narrative', 'creating a film backwards', and he went on to 'concoct a little talk about nationalism and the new internationalism of transport and communication' (Aitken 2001: 86–7).

Priestley had been associated with the documentary film movement for a few years before the making of We Live in Two Worlds. His book *English Journey* (1934) had directly inspired Paul Rotha's The Face of Britain (1935), and he had also published several articles in *World Film News*, one of the house journals of the documentary film movement. In books such as *Angel Pavement* (1930) and *English Journey*, Priestley focused on problems of corruption, unemployment, and poverty in Britain, and he was also active in the antifascist movement of the late 1930s. All this made him sympathetic to the general aims of the documentary film movement and eager to participate in the making of We Live in Two Worlds.

In We Live in Two Worlds, a distinction is made between the two worlds that characterise modern society: the world of separate nation states, and the 'growing international world'. The film begins by depicting traditional Swiss folk and labour practices. Then the film shifts to the theme of the modernisation of Switzerland and, in particular, to the role played by mass communication in creating links with Switzerland's neighbours. In contrast, the growth of nationalism and militarism in neighbouring Germany is explicitly criticised and contrasted with Swiss internationalism.

We Live in Two Worlds could be regarded as a Griersonian documentary because of its emphasis on international communications and the relationship between labour and institutional structures, and this, in turn, may explain why Griersonians, such as Paul Rotha and Forsyth Hardy, thought so highly of it. The truth is, however, that We Live in Two Worlds is a rather mediocre film, whilst Priestley's commentary, which is full of pompous, vernacular Yorkshire gravitas, is often predictable and rudimentary.

Cavalcanti's influence on We Live in Two Worlds can be found mainly in the film's use of sound and in the music track, which was composed by Cavalcanti's old acquaintance, Maurice Jaubert. That influence can also be seen most clearly in the final sequences of the film, in which Priestley's pedestrian didacticism gives way to an idealistic proclamation concerning the way in which the natural world transcends artificial nationalistic demarcations. These final sequences are almost abstract in quality as, for example, when superimposed images of ships at sea fade into a shot of the earth against Priestley's rhetorical claim that 'rain and sea and air serve all men'. The final shots of the film recreate abstract patterns of rain drops, and this leads on to the end titles of the film.

These final sequences, with their innovative and impressionistic use of sound and image, are reminiscent of other Cavalcanti films from the mid-1920s to the late 1950s. They can be clearly associated with Cavalcanti in We Live in Two Worlds, and it is this aspect of the film, rather than Priestley's commentary, that makes the film still worth watching today.

IAN AITKEN

See also: Cavalcanti, Alberto

We Live in Two Worlds (UK, 1937). Directed and edited by Alberto Cavalcanti. Music by Maurice Jaubert. Produced by John Grierson and Alberto Cavalcanti. Commentary by J. B. Priestley.

Further reading

Aitken, Ian, *Film and Reform*, London: Routledge, 1990.
——*The Documentary Film Movement, An Anthology*, Edinburgh: Edinburgh University Press, 1998.
——*Alberto Cavalcanti, Realism, Surealism and National Cinemas*, London: Flicks Books, 2001.
Cavalcanti, Alberto, *Filme e Realidade*, Rio de Janeiro: Editora Artenova, in collaboration with Empresa Brasiliera de Filmes—Embrafilme, 1977.
Rotha, Paul, *Documentary Film*, London: Faber & Faber, 1939.
Sussex, Elizabeth, 'Cavalcanti in England', *Sight and Sound* 44, no. 4, autumn, 1975.

Weiss, Andrea

Independent documentary filmmaker Andrea Weiss engages a complex terrain of simultaneous roles. Weiss is a director, author, educator, archival researcher, producer, and historian. In 1984 Weiss and her partner Greta Schiller cofounded the nonprofit film company Jezebel Productions. Weiss's successful negotiation of her numerous roles has resulted in a rich array of projects that bespeak her commitment to pedagogy, representational ethics, and creative ingenuity.

Weiss has made or participated in making films about a range of provocative subjects, including: the US election process (Recall Florida); the lives of Thomas Mann's oldest children during Hitler's ascendancy (Escape to Life); a Hungarian girl's life during the Holocaust (Seed of Sarah); the stereotyping of gay characters by the mainstream British film industry since World War II (A Bit of Scarlet); the role of women in the literary and art world of the Parisian Left Bank during the early twentieth century (Paris Was a Woman); a multiracial all-women jazz and swing band of the 1940s (International Sweethearts of Rhythm); the long-term relationship of African American lesbian jazz musicians Tiny Davis and Ruby Lucas (Tiny & Ruby: Hell Divin' Women); and the history of the gay and lesbian community in the United States before the onset of the modern LGBT liberation movement (Before Stonewall).

During the introductory voice-over to Paris Was a Woman, the audience is told, 'Neither mistress nor muse, Paris became a haven for a new kind of woman'. This 'new kind of woman' not only indexes the independently minded (and often bourgeois) intellectual women who moved from the United States to Paris at the beginning of the twentieth century to make a 'new life', but implicitly refers to the largely open orientation toward lesbianism and other homosocial alliances between women in Paris at that time.

In Paris, Janet Flanner describes cubism as 'what you cannot see rendered visible'. This remark could also be made regarding the film's treatment of lesbian relationships in early twentieth-century Paris.

Flanner's statement likewise announces the film's stance and Weiss's perspective as a filmmaker: there is value in uncovering 'silenced' voices and 'missing' texts, and it is crucial to critique oversimplified and often romanticized revisionist histories by presenting the crucial contributions of multidimensional people who speak on their own behalf in the films and books that represent and describe them. By speaking with and through her films' images and by sensitively promoting her narrators' voices, Weiss points out that, as African American lesbian musician 'Ruby' puts it, '[the past] wasn't quite as open as it is now' (Tiny & Ruby). Weiss's work teaches viewers about racism, homophobia, classism, and sexism, and promotes social justice.

In her discussion of minority-produced feminist documentaries, Alexandra Juhasz notes that '"realist" footage ends up recording people reflexively discussing the meaning, reinterpretation, and importance of their own identity' (Juhasz 1999: 208). Juhasz asserts that this is especially important '[b]ecause so much of feminist and other "identity" video movements are specifically about constructing our own identities in a society that has usually done this for minorities' (ibid., original emphasis). Thus, the formal elements of 'realism' in these kinds of films may be used to forward a specialized feminist cultural critique, a visualizable social constructionism.

According to Juhasz, feminist documentaries have the potential to engage anti-essentialist notions of identity for political ends, because they can '[provide] a space in culture where political women with limited access to cultural production can partake in "radical postmodernism"' (Juhasz 1999: 212). Explaining 'radical postmodernism' (as borrowed from bell hooks), Juhasz states, 'the political instance of access to media production allows us to speak our needs, define our agenda, counter irresponsible depictions of our lives, and recognize our similarities and differences' (ibid.). As vehicles for marginalized narrators, both living and as depicted posthumously, Weiss's films are instances of 'radical postmodernism'.

Escape to Life is described on the Jezebel Productions website as a 'remarkable pairing between fiction and nonfiction'. Using a 'postmodernist' orientation to blur the boundaries between reality/fantasy and truth/fiction, Escape frames the relationship between Erika and Klaus Mann. In its meta-narrative form and content, the film may be read as doubly postmodern, because Erika and Klaus Mann enacted their own fusion of fiction and nonfiction in order to survive. Using an approach that today might be called 'passing', they pretended to be identical twins when they were different genders and more than a year apart in age.

Weiss's films consistently show how those who have social dominance wield power and how disempowered individuals strategically engage their subject positions. During a portion of Tiny & Ruby, the narrators discuss the racially segregated lesbian house parties of the 1940s through 1960s. Feminist scholars Kennedy and Davis (1994) argue that these parties played a crucial part in setting a tone for the American lesbian and gay liberation movement in the decades preceding Stonewall. At one point Tiny looks directly at the camera and asserts that if one wants to 'do something' and 'has the power', then one can 'do it'. Tiny's advice, a note of appreciation for having the opportunity to tell her story on film and a commentary on her identity, relays to both the audience members and the filmmakers her awareness of her power as compared with the power of the filmmakers who re-present her story.

As part of a supplement on film and history, Weiss was recently asked by the editors of *Cineaste* magazine to respond to a documentary filmmaker questionnaire. She remarks, 'I'm searching for something too through these women's lives and through the stories of all the people in my entire collection of films—I'm searching for clues for how to live my own life, a life lived by my own wits, in several different countries, a life without conventional forms or models to follow' (n.a. 2004: 60). Weiss, an out Jewish lesbian who lives in the UK and the United States, is a role model for those who negotiate a variety of complicated borders and boundaries in order to function within and critique late capitalism.

DIANE R. WIENER

Biography

Born in New York City, 1956. PhD Cultural History, Rutgers University 1991. Won a 1987 Emmy Award for Best Historical Research for her work on Before Stonewall, which also won an Emmy for Best Historical and Cultural Program. Won a 1989 Teddy Award for Best Documentary Film for Tiny & Ruby at the Berlin International Film Festival. Won 'Best of the Fest' award for A Bit of Scarlet at Edinburgh Film Festival in 1996, and also won Best Documentary at the Creteil women's film festival, Festival de Films de Femmes. Artist-in-residence at the Banff Centre for the Arts in Canada 1998, where she produced the short experimental video Seed of Sarah (a revisiting of the longer film made three years earlier), which premiered in the Marseilles Documentary Festival, Vue sur les Docs. Escape to Life, which premiered at the 2001 Rotterdam International Film Festival and was a special festival program at Berlin, was chosen as the closing night event of the New German Film Series at the Museum of Modern Art in New York and won the 'Award for Excellence' for Best Documentary at the 2001 Seattle Lesbian and Gay Film Festival. Co-author (with Greta Schiller) of *Before Stonewall: The Making of a Gay and Lesbian Community* (1988). Author of *Vampires and Violets* (originally published 1992), *Paris Was a Woman: Portraits from the Left Bank* (published 1995, won a Lambda Literary Award in 1996), and *Flucht ins Leben: Die Erika und Klaus Mann Story* (2000, published in English as *Escape to Life: The Erika and Klaus Mann Story*). Resides in London with partner and collaborator Greta Schiller.

Selected films

1985 Before Stonewall: The Making of a Gay and Lesbian Community: archive research director
1986 International Sweethearts of Rhythm: codirector and coproducer
1988 Tiny & Ruby: Hell Divin' Women: codirector and coproducer
1995 Paris Was a Woman: writer, researcher, coproducer

1995 Seed of Sarah: director, editor, coproducer
1997 A Bit of Scarlet: director and editor
2000 Die Erika und Klaus Mann Story (aka Escape to Life: The Erika and Klaus Mann Story): cowriter and codirector
2003 Recall Florida: writer, editor, coproducer

Further reading

Jezebel Productions website, www.jezebel.org
Edelman, Rob, 'Greta Schiller', in Amy L. Unterburger (ed.), *The St James Women Filmmakers Encyclopedia: Women on the Other Side of the Camera*, Detroit: Visible Ink Press, 1999: 370–72.
Gross, Larry, *Up From Invisibility: Lesbians, Gay Men, and the Media in America*, New York: Columbia University Press, 2001.
Holmlund, Chris and Fuchs, Cynthia (eds), *Between the Sheets, in the Streets: Queer, Lesbian, Gay Documentary*, Minneapolis, MN: University of Minnesota Press, 1997.
Hooks, Bell, *Yearning: Race, Gender, and Cultural Politics*, Boston: South End Press, 1990.
Hunn, Deborah, 'Andrea Weiss', in *GLBTQ: An Encyclopedia of Gay, Lesbian, Bisexual, Transgender, and Queer Culture*, n.d., www.glbtq.com/arts/weiss_a.html
Juhasz, Alexandra, 'They Said We Were Trying to Show Reality—All I Want to Show is My Video: The Politics of the Realist Feminist Documentary', in Jane M. Gaines and Michael Renov (eds), *Collecting Visible Evidence*, Minneapolis, MN and London: University of Minnesota Press, 1999: 190–215.
Kennedy, Elizabeth Lapovsky and Davis, Madeline D., *Boots of Leather, Slippers of Gold: The History of a Lesbian Community*, New York: Penguin Books, 1994.
Murray, Raymond, 'Greta Schiller', in *Images in the Dark: An Encyclopedia of Gay and Lesbian Film and Video*, New York: Plume (Penguin Books), 1996: 118–19.
n.a., 'Film and History: Questions to Filmmakers and Historians', *Cineaste* 29, no. 2, spring 2004: 55–68.
Weiss, Andrea, *In the Shadow of the Magic Mountain*, Chicago: University of Chicago Press, 2008.
——*Paris Was a Woman: Portraits from the Left Bank*, San Francisco: Harper San Francisco, 1995.
——*Vampires and Violets: Lesbians in Film*, New York: Penguin Books, 1993.
Weiss, Andrea and Schiller, Greta, *Before Stonewall: The Making of a Gay and Lesbian Community*, Tallahassee: Naiad Press, 1988.

Welfare

(US, Wiseman, 1975)

In Welfare, by American filmmaker Frederick Wiseman whose films tend to focus on institutions and their operations, a New York City Welfare Office where the film was shot is presented as the closed system par excellence, a nightmare vision of institutional bureaucracy out of control. It is no accident that, chronologically, Welfare comes between Primate (1974) and Meat (1976), for the titles of these two films express how far, for Wiseman, living has become objectified and commodified.

The film, like the welfare center itself, is swamped with various kinds of forms. We see or hear about application forms; referral slips; notarized, registered, and certified letters; verifications of pregnancy; marriage licenses and driver's licenses; bills and receipts; change of address forms and prenatal forms; written budgets and pay stubs; food stamps; Medicaid cards and social security cards; housing deeds, disability checks and pro-ration checks; carbon copies and photocopies; time clock cards; computers; and printouts. One client complains that she has to 'get a notarized letter for this, a notarized letter for that'. Another client, standing aimlessly against a post, launches into a monologue about the 'rigamarole of forms' he must fill out; 'Papers, papers, papers', he says, finally dropping them on the floor and leaving in frustration.

In the film, the camera leaves the building just once—at the beginning. After this we remain confined within, unlike most of Wiseman's films, which at least offer periodic exterior shots as rhythmic punctuation. Here, though, our physical point of view remains claustrophobically confined within the harsh walls of this one welfare office, an absurd *huis clos* where we as spectators must dwell along with the system's needy clients. The first thing we hear in the film, a receptionist's 'Please have a seat', is not only a self-reflexive acknowledgment to the viewer that the film is now beginning, but also an ironic invitation to sit through a long ordeal, as the applicants themselves must. Welfare's lengthy running time of just under three hours is itself an expression of the labyrinthine and involved system of procedures and paperwork through which welfare applicants must navigate.

Consistent with the film's sense of enclosure and entrapment, Wiseman structures the film through a motif of circles. Clients are frequently trapped in a variety of Catch-22 situations, the victims of circular logic. One client, for example, wants to move but cannot, because there is no record of housing violations, but she is unable to get a buildings inspector to come and formally record the necessary violations; another client becomes ineligible for benefits because he missed his appointment at the welfare office while attending his hearing required by welfare procedures. Toward the beginning of the film, a man seeking immediate help says that he is getting a 'run around'. The phrase is echoed periodically by several other clients, and yet again toward the end by the woman who, speaking for her mother, angrily complains that she is caught in a never-ending 'vicious cycle'. The first couple interviewed in the film are shown again at the end, waiting, suggesting that they have hardly progressed in their application.

In Welfare, social and economic relations are reduced to a seemingly interminable series of exchanges between welfare workers and clients, the clients seeking the money that the workers have the power to dispense. Welfare foregrounds the economic disparity shown in some of Wiseman's other films, as everyone seeking help from the welfare system is penniless, many seeming on the verge of starvation, and they must prove their poverty. As Mr Hirsch, the final client shown in the film, says, 'There's no middle class any more. There's just the rich and the poor'.

Like a pressure cooker, this enclosed world of Welfare inevitably reaches the boiling point. So after watching a parade of clients being frustrated in every possible way for two hours, we are not surprised when two of them are unable to restrain themselves any longer and tempers flare. The welfare worker Elaine also loses her temper in turn: 'Get a job', she snaps unhelpfully at one of the clients. The evident anger and frustration of both worker and clients in this climactic scene are the understandable result of everything that has come before. The institutional workers at the welfare center, as in many other Wiseman films, have become inured to the pain and misfortune of the clients in order to cope with the burdens of administering an overloaded public system. In one problematic case, the supervisor instructs the worker to reject or accept the client, 'either one', not wanting to become involved any further.

The institution's regulations and procedures have overwhelmed the human element in the welfare office. The welfare workers speak of 're-entertaining applications' and 'financial servicing' for the clients, their language like the euphemistic discourse of military indoctrination in Basic Training and of nuclear holocaust in Missile. 'Void this 913', says one worker, using a kind of newspeak to avoid the harsh reality of the client's fate. Like the split between morality and technology in High School, one client complains that in the welfare office 'You give me technicality. I'm telling you about a condition.'

In keeping with its depressing depiction of the welfare system, the film ends on a bleak and ironic note. One of the clients, Mr Hirsch, who has been made to sit and wait alone on a bench, looks up and addresses the neon firmament and an absent God, saying he will wait as long as He deems it necessary.

BARRY KEITH GRANT

See also: High School; Meat; Wiseman, Frederick

Welfare (US, 1975, 167 mins). Distributed by Zipporah Films. Produced, edited, and directed by Frederick Wiseman. Cinematography by William Brayne. Sound recorded by Frederick Wiseman.

Further reading

Atkins, Thomas R. (ed.), *Frederick Wiseman*, New York: Monarch Press, 1976.

Benson, Thomas W. and Anderson, Caroline, *Reality Fictions: The Films of Frederick Wiseman*, Carbondale, IL: Southern Illinois University Press, 1989.

Grant, Barry Keith, *Voyages of Discovery: The Cinema of Frederick Wiseman*, Urbana, IL and Chicago: University of Illinois Press, 1992.

Mamber, Stephen, *Cinema Verite in America: Studies in Uncontrolled Documentary*, Cambridge, MA: MIT Press, 1974.

Nichols, Bill, *Ideology and the Image*, Bloomington, IN: Indiana University Press, 1981.

West Indies and the Caribbean

Historically, documentary films in the Caribbean, like films in the Caribbean generally, make up a broad array of productions, the diversity of which on one level is defined by language (including the work of Anglophone Caribbean, Francophone Caribbean, Hispanic Caribbean, and Dutch Caribbean producers) (Cham 1992). Consideration of some key documentary productions from the Caribbean region, however, reveals common themes, styles of production, and similar experiences shared by the documentary filmmakers of this ethnically, historically, culturally, and linguistically diverse region. Documentary films of the Caribbean are a heterogeneous body of work representing a culturally complex region, but there are many Caribbean productions that deserve to be included in the broader canon of documentary film. This article provides introductions to key producers of Caribbean documentary film, the cultural significance of Caribbean documentary, and the economic and political issues dealt with by Caribbean documentary filmmakers.

The local development of film industries and documentary film production has been a concern for both independent producers and Caribbean governments alike to varying degrees for more than fifty years. State-authored manifestations of these concerns include Jamaica's 1948 Motion Picture Industry (Encouragement) Law (Lent 1977), Martinique's 1977 Service Municipal d'Action Culturelle (Cham 1992) and Trinidad and Tobago's 2003 Master Plan for the Strategic Development of the Trinidad and Tobago Film Industry (Tourism and Industrial Development Company of Trinidad and Tobago, 2003). Documentaries from and about this region reflect the significant social and political struggles of the constituent countries as they emerged from colonial domination, through social revolution to cultural revitalization. Christian Lara's definition of Caribbean or Antillean film provides a basis on which Caribbean documentary film can be defined. Caribbean documentary is used here to include productions whose directors are from the Caribbean, with subject matter focusing on the Caribbean, featuring Caribbean lead actors, using Creole, and produced by a Caribbean production unit (Cham 1992). Although these criteria provide useful guidelines for attempting to represent a canon of Caribbean documentary film, there are also films whose place in such a canon is significant even though they may not fulfill one or two of the outlined criteria.

In the Caribbean from the 1970s to the early 2000s, nongovernmental documentaries were produced as a result of Caribbean filmmakers' struggles for recognition within local media cultures in which prepackaged, imported programs were readily received and broadcast for economic reasons (Lent 1977; Brown 1987). During this period, television stations across the Caribbean justified the high percentages of imported (usually North American or European) programs, including documentaries, by citing the lower costs associated with importing programs against the higher costs of producing local programs. Station-originated television documentaries were thus a low priority in the management of television stations across the Caribbean (Lent 1977). Further, after the advent of television in the 1960s and color in the 1970s, television stations placed emphasis on investigative reports on contemporary issues, while local documentary film production was ignored (St Juste 2004).

In the preindependent Caribbean, documentaries were also produced by colonial governments, tracing the stories of peoples of the then-colonies and the development of the Caribbean from colonial rule to independence (Warner 2000). Spanning the 1950s and 1960s, these colonial documentaries provided valuable insights into colonial rule. In the pre-independence era, the Colonial Office in England sent documentaries to the colonies for viewing. In later colonial times, however, the Colonial Film Unit was closed down, as it became more cost effective to train people in the colonies in documentary filmmaking. These documentaries were produced in black-and-white, 35mm film and usually dealt with population and health issues (St Juste 1992).

This archive of preindependence Caribbean documentaries included: a film intended to motivate Jamaican teachers in the face of adversity (Builders of the Nation) (Warner 2000); coverage of prerevolutionary Cuba (Cuba Collection, 1950s); Marketing What We Grow (1963), a documentary about farming practices in Jamaica; This is Ska (1964), a two-part production on the origins of Ska music by the Jamaican Film Unit; The Lion of Judah (1966), a documentary account of the state visit of Ethiopian Emperor Haile Selassie to Jamaica; The Royal Tour of the Caribbean (1966), a film produced by the Colonial Office about the Queen's 1966 visit to British Guiana, Trinidad and Tobago, Grenada, St Vincent, Barbados, St Lucia, Dominica, Montserrat, Antigua, St Kitts-Nevis, Tortola, Grand Turk, the Caicos, the Bahamas, and Jamaica. Outside the realm of colonial pasts, historically there has been significant interest by international producers, researchers, and scholars to use film to document different aspects of culture, geography, and history of the Caribbean region (Found 2003–4).

After Caribbean nations gained their independence, documentary film, like other media, became an outlet for the expression of emerging national identities and a medium for the exploration of regional development. Documentary film, against the broader backdrop of the visual mass media, became sensitive to building and maintaining cultural sovereignty within the Caribbean (Brown 1987). In the Caribbean in the 1970s significant social and cultural development included the rise in popularity of Caribbean music, struggles for political or economic independence, and the increasing empowerment of the previously disempowered. Further along this path of evolution, in the 1980s, 1990s, and early twenty-first century, Caribbean filmmakers (and documentary filmmakers) placed emphasis on and explored themes of postcolonial nationalism and concerns for cultural imperialism resulting from foreign investment and ownership (Brown 1987; Cham 1992; Warner 2000).

Several significant documentary films exemplify this Caribbean focus on themes of postcolonialism, national identity, and the effects of globalization and tourism in the countries that make up this geographical region. Three such films are And the Dish Ran Away with the Spoon (1992), Los Hijos de Baragua/My Footsteps in Baragua (1996), and Life and Debt (2001). And the Dish Ran Away with the Spoon, originally produced to address regional environmental problems, took the unique approach of exploring the dominance of North American programming in the Caribbean region as an environmental issue (Laird 2004). Los Hijos de Baragua explores the cultural history of Anglophone West Indians in Cuba and the sociopolitical reasons for their migration. In Life and Debt documentary filmmaker Stephanie Black explored aspects of Jamaican everyday existence that are affected by economic agendas of such entities as the World Bank, the Inter-American Development Bank (IADB), and the International Monetary Fund (IMF). This documentary reveals the contradictions of Jamaican life most often not seen by visiting tourists (Black 2001–2). These three Caribbean documentaries explore identity and culture, the Caribbean diaspora, postcolonialism, and the search for cultural and political sovereignty.

One series of documentaries, Caribbean Eye, was produced in 1992 by Banyan, a video production house based in Trinidad and Tobago, whose contributions across the Caribbean included coproductions and the training of video units throughout the region (Banyan 2004). Key players in the founding and development of Banyan included Bruce Paddington, Christopher Laird, and Anthony Hall. Thirteen one-hour episodes made up the full series of Caribbean Eye, with each episode focused on a different aspect of Caribbean culture, including dance, theatre, festivals, indigenous peoples, music, oral traditions, women, leaders, games, and film. The Caribbean Eye series was recognized for excellence in documentary production and won numerous awards including the Caribbean Publishers and Broadcasters Association award for 'Best Caribbean Television Series' and the Caribbean Community (CARICOM) Prize 'for fostering regional integration' (Banyan 2004). One episode of Caribbean Eye, titled Film Caribbean, explored factors influencing regional production, featuring the works of filmmakers from the Dutch-, French-, Spanish-, and English-speaking Caribbean, noting that Cuba is the only Caribbean territory in which there had been significant production up to the date of production for that episode (Banyan 2004).

Banyan produced And the Dish Ran Away With the Spoon in 1992, the same year as the Caribbean Eye series. This documentary, which was part of the BBC/TVE Developing World series, focused on the domination in the Caribbean of television programs from the North, primarily the United States. And the Dish Ran Away With the Spoon illustrates the wider project of Banyan and its producers, 'to produce a uniquely Caribbean approach' to television and documentary production. This unique Caribbean approach positions this documentary as both reflexive and performative (Hight and Roscoe 2001). Through juxtaposition of interviews, poetry, music, performance, and excerpts of imported and indigenous television programs, the producers explored the question, 'What happens when people have to dream other people's dreams?' And the Dish Ran Way with the Spoon was not simply an account of a trend in Caribbean media, it was also an indictment of the North American practice of jamming signals from Cuban broadcasting houses, in response to Cuba's policy to restrict programming to local, or at least regional (and non-North American), content. 'Dish' and the Caribbean Eye series crystallized the talents of Caribbean documentary producers and showcased the wealth of documentary material in the Caribbean, and the ability of local filmmakers to produce high-quality, regionally significant films using local production resources and talent.

The documentaries of Cuban filmmaker Gloria Rolando provide important windows into Afrocuban culture and serve the strategy of Rolando's desire to 'rescue and preserve afrocuban [sic] cultural expressions' (Rolando 2004). Themes of transcending borders take on multiple forms in Rolando's documentaries, including Nosotros y el Jazz/Us and Jazz, which spotlights the common cultural history of Afro-cubans and African Americans, and El Acaran/The Scorpion, which celebrates the music and dance styles of Congo origin that are popular in Cuban carnivals (Rolando 2004). Los Hijos de Baragua (1996) is a feature documentary by Rolando, about the presence of English-speaking West Indians settled in Cuba. Rolando's documentaries have advanced themes of diaspora, exploring cultural artifacts and texts that survived through migration. In Los Hijos de Baragua Rolando revealed the stories of Caribbean men and women who traveled throughout the Caribbean seeking work and opportunity in the early twentieth century. Like And the Dish Ran Away with the Spoon and Life and Debt, Los Hijos explored themes of imperialism, colonialism, exploitation, identity, and culture. In Los Hijos de Baragua these themes are traced by following the stories of West Indians in Cuba, who preserved their traditions and cultural pride through music and dance, despite their existence in segregated towns culturally dominated by North American companies.

From the mid-twentieth century to the early twenty-first century, documentary filmmaking in the Caribbean required resourcefulness and dedication on the part of producers and directors. Financial collaboration and other support frequently came from institutions both within and outside the Caribbean (UNESCO, TVE, and the BBC in the case of Banyan; PBS in the case of Stephanie Black's Life and Debt; and ICAIC, the Cuban national film institute, in earlier Rolando productions). In her later productions (including those documentaries produced under her own organization, 'Images del Caribe' or Images of the Caribbean), Gloria Rolando relied on the unpaid work of friends and family. Like many independent documentary filmmakers in the Caribbean, Rolando often began her documentary projects without the means to finish them, but with a desire to share the documented stories of Caribbean people and Caribbean life through film (Morris 1998).

North American documentary filmmaker Stephanie Black produced Life and Debt in 2001. Black had previously produced H-2 Worker, a documentary about the abuses of Caribbean farm workers in the sugarcane fields of Florida (Black 2001–2). According to Lara's definition of Caribbean film, Black's films could be excluded from the canon of Caribbean documentary films because she is not a Caribbean filmmaker. However, Life and Debt becomes a significant inclusion, as the film spent many weeks in Jamaican cinemas, playing to audiences eager to see Jamaica represented on screen (Popplewell 2003), demonstrating the film's significance to the local audience. Life and Debt also underscored issues that are key to the Caribbean experience, including economic and political subjugation by external forces. This documentary was successful in achieving acclaim and exhibition success both in Jamaica and internationally, which to many Caribbean critics became further indicative of cultural imperialism at work and raised the question of why documentaries by native Jamaicans or Caribbean filmmakers were not received with equal local and international interest.

Life and Debt received international critical acclaim (winning the Paris Human Rights Film Festival Special Jury Prize and the 2002 One World Prague Human Rights Film Festival Audience Award for Best Film of the Festival), but it also became the focus of debate regarding Jamaican emphasis on tourism and development and the severe costs that were paid in the struggle toward development as tradition and modernity collided (Black 2001–2). Discourse in the Jamaican context surrounding the release of Life and Debt was divided along the lines of prodevelopment versus pronationalism, the former represented by Jamaicans who argued the importance of tourism and foreign investment in Jamaica's economy, and the latter asserted by those who believed that Jamaican everyday life was negatively affected by the mounting billion-dollar debt under which Jamaica, according to Black's film, had become enslaved to the IMF, the IADB, and the World Bank.

The style of Life and Debt was similar in significant ways to that of And the Dish Ran Away with the Spoon. Life and Debt mixed interviews, poetry, music, and narration in its exploration. The genesis of this documentary was, in fact, the nonfiction text A Small Place by Antiguan writer Jamaica Kincaid, whose voice provides narrative bridges throughout the film (Black 2001–2). Using this hybrid style, director Stephanie Black delved into the complexity of Jamaican sovereignty against the backdrop forces of globalization, tourism, and industrial development. Life and Debt thus represented the voices of the Jamaican government, the workers whose lives were changed by the coming and going of multinational corporations, the Jamaican farmers whose crops went unsold, the executives within the IMF and the World Bank, and the American tourists. The result of this approach was a documentary that manifests as a polyvocal ethnography, consisting of partial truths and fragments of discourse that provide the viewer with a handle for entering the world of others through the stories of ethnographers (Clifford 1986; Tyler 1986) and, in this case, the stories told by the documentary filmmaker.

Life and Debt captured the widespread recognition in Jamaican society of the implications of Jamaica's ties to the IMF and the World Bank. Black interviewed farmers who asserted their views on the role that these institutions play in Jamaican policy-making and in everyday life. Jamaican audience reception of this documentary also illustrated the widespread relevance and concern that these issues held in Jamaican society at the time of this film's release. When Life and Debt was shown in Jamaican cinemas, audiences filled the cinemas, a fact that confirmed the dual significance of this film (Popplewell 2003–4). The first significance was that Jamaican (and wider Caribbean) audiences were drawn to images and representations of themselves on large and small screens. The second significance of audience reception of Life and Debt was that a documentary dealing with sober sociopolitical issues had significant appeal to a broad cross-section of Jamaican society.

In the English-speaking Caribbean, the University of the West Indies has played an important role in the training of emerging visual artists, filmmakers, and documentary producers (Brown 1987). At the Mona campus in Jamaica, the Caribbean Institute of Mass Communication (CARIMAC) offers an undergraduate program in Broadcast Journalism, with an emphasis on television. This program provides students with 'a variety of creative experiences in the conceptualization [sic], development and production phases of film and television' (UWI Mona 2004). In Trinidad and Tobago, at the St Augustine Campus, the Centre for Creative and Festival Arts offered a Bachelor of Arts degree in Visual Arts, including courses in Film and Video production (UWI St Augustine 2002). By 2004 students of this Visual Arts program had produced more than sixty short films, including documentaries. One such film, shown at the 2004 end-of-year exhibition, looked at basic infrastructure in a developing country and explored the problems with pipe-borne water in Trinidad and Tobago (Holder 2004). Modules in the St Augustine program were taught by scholar/producer/director and one of the original founders of Banyan, Bruce Paddington, and by Yao Ramesar, a prominent contemporary Caribbean filmmaker who refers to his production aesthetic as 'Caribbeing' (UWI 2003). The focus in this program at St Augustine was helping filmmakers to develop a unique Caribbean and local aesthetic, and an understanding of local, small-budget filmmaking (Gibbons 2004). The philosophical emphases of Paddington and Ramesar, as well as of Rawle Gibbons (the Head of the Centre for Creative and Festival Arts) have been geared notably toward the development of local voices and local visual aesthetics (Gibbons 2004).

Caribbean documentary films also feature narratives that focus on musicians and dancers of the region or that use music and dance in their telling. Chutney in Yuh Soca (1996) is one such film, which explored the fusion of Afro-Caribbean and Indo-Caribbean culture. Calypso Dreams (2002) explored the stories and music of key calypsonians from Trinidad and Tobago, celebrating the history and evolution of calypso as an art form. Horace Ové's Reggae (1970) also built on the centrality of music to Caribbean culture and documented the significance of the 1970 London Reggae Festival at

Wembley through interviews, songs, and the narration of Caribbean author Andrew Salkey. In 1988 Christopher Laird produced a musical documentary titled Crossing Over, the narrative of which follows a Trinidadian calypso musician to Ghana to explore Ghanaian highlife music and then follows a Ghanaian musician to Trinidad where Trinidadian musicians and practitioners of West African Orisha embrace him (Banyan 2004). As outlined earlier, the work of Cuban filmmaker Gloria Rolando also uses music to trace Caribbean migrations and cultural influences.

Caribbean filmmakers have produced documentaries despite the often-lacking incentives to produce local features. The focus on the importance of localizing visual culture through television and cinema continued to increase through the early twenty-first century. In Trinidad and Tobago a new community-based television station was born of the production house Banyan. Launched in 2004, Gayelle the Channel promised ninety percent local content, and used its archive of shorts, series, features, and documentaries, as a source of programming. With such changes taking place in the first few years of the new millennium, scholars, filmmakers, and other media practitioners were optimistic that the media landscape would change toward increasing localization, including increases in the numbers of Caribbean documentary films produced. With the popularization of digital technologies, productions budgets for documentaries decreased, as did the training required, thereby increasing access of a wider cross-section of producers and directors to the equipment used for documentary production. In the late 1990s and early 2000s digital video technology became significant to increased activity in and the localization of production (Laird 2004) and specifically to increased activity in the production of Caribbean documentary films.

SUSAN MCFARLANE-ALVAREZ

Selected films

1992 And the Dish Ran Away with the Spoon (Banyan Ltd/BBC, 49 mins; dirs Christopher Laird and Anthony Hall)

1996 Los Hijos de Baragua/My Footsteps in Baragua (Images Caribes, 53 mins; dir. Gloria Rolando)

2001 Life and Debt (Tuff Gong Pictures, 80 mins; prod. and dir. Stephanie Black)

Further reading

Banyan, 'Inside the People TV', 2004, www.pan-caribbean.com/banyan/banyan.htm

Black, Stephanie, *Life and Debt: A Film by Stephanie Black*, www.lifeanddebt.org, Kingston: Tuff Gong Productions, 2001–2.

Brown, Aggrey and Sanatan, Roderick, *Talking with Whom? A Report on the State of the Media in the Caribbean*, Mona: CARIMAC, University of the West Indies Printery, 1987.

Caribbean Studies Black Asian History (CASBAH), www.casbah.a.uk/cats/print/224/OFTP00001.htm

Cham, Mbye, 'Introduction: Shape and Shaping of Caribbean Cinema' in Mbye Cham (ed.), *Ex-iles: Essays on Caribbean Cinema*, Trenton, NJ: Africa World Press, 1992.

Clifford, J., 'Introduction: Partial Truths', in J. Clifford and G. Marcus (eds), *Writing Culture: the Poetics and Politics of Ethnography*, Berkeley, CA: University of California Press, 1986.

Found, William, 'Documentary Films on Caribbean Islands', York University, www.arts.yorku.ca/geog/wfound/video, 2003–4.

Gibbons, Rawle (Head/Theatre Arts Coordinator, Centre for Creative and Festival Arts, The University of the West Indies), Personal interview, January 2004.

Hight, Craig and Roscoe, Jane, *Faking It: Mock Documentary and the Subversion of Factuality*, Manchester: Manchester University Press, 2001.

Holder, Zia, 'Films with Local Flavour: UWI Students Exhibit 12 Pieces', *Trinidad Express*, May 13, 2004: 27.

Laird, Christopher, *Personal Interview*, Trinidad and Tobago, January 2004.

Lent, John, *Third World Mass Media and Their Search for Modernity: The Case of the Commonwealth Caribbean 1917–76*, Lewisburg, PA: Bucknell University Press, 1977.

Morris, Holly, 'Winging It on Lots of Dream', www.abcnews.com, 1998.

n.a., 'Overseas Film and Television Centre Collection Description', London: Institute of Commonwealth Studies, 2002.

Popplewell, Georgia, 'Picture This', *Business Trinidad and Tobago*, 2003–4 edn.

Rolando, Gloria, www.gloriarolando.com, Havana, Cuba (accessed June 2, 2004).

St Juste, Franklyn, 'Interview', in Mbye Cham (ed.), *Ex-iles: Essays on Caribbean Cinema*, Trenton, NJ: Africa World Press, 1992.

——Telephone and e-mail interviews, *Jamaica-Atlanta*, May to June 2004.

Tourism and Industrial Development Company of Trinidad and Tobago, *A Master Plan for the Strategic Development of The Trinidad and Tobago Film Industry*, 2003.

Tyler, S., 'Post-modern Ethnography: From Document of the Occult to Occult Document', in J. Clifford and G. Marcus (eds), *Writing Culture*, Berkeley, CA: University of California Press, 1986.
UWI, 'Second Festival of African and Caribbean Film', humanities.uwichill.edu.bb/filmfestival/2003, Cave Hill, Barbados: University of the West Indies, 2003.
UWI St Augustine, 'Centre for Festival and Creative Arts', www.festival.uwi.tt/courses5.htm, University of the West Indies St Augustine, 2002.
UWI Mona, 'CARIMAC', www.mona.uwi.edu/carimac/Pubjt.html, University of the West Indies at Mona, 2004.
Warner, Keith, *On Location: Cinema and Film in the Anglophone Caribbean*, London and Oxford: Macmillan Education, 2000.

When the Dog Bites

(UK, Woolcock, 1988)

Throughout the 1970s the loosely affiliated independent film sector in Britain maintained a difficult relationship with the industry trade union, the Association of Cinematograph and Television Technicians. One particular contention concerned the status of independent film-makers working unpaid or supported by small grants, an important framework for radical cinema practice. A degree of rapprochement was achieved at the end of the decade with the Workshop Agreement, 'an extraordinary innovation which gave formal recognition to the principles of workshop practice and opened up the possibility of extending them as a basis for fully professional participation in the industry' (Dickinson 1999: 58–9). This new policy endorsed a number of workshops around the country managed by the workers and operating on a nonprofit basis. Trade Films in Gateshead was established on this format and immediately set about the task of documenting the stark economic and social prospects of the North-East in the Thatcher period.

When the Dog Bites (WTDB, 1988) is an unconventional documentary that deals with the town of Consett in County Durham in the years after the closure of the principal industry, the steel works. It draws on a plethora of documentary techniques to assess the impact of economic restructuring on the town, the resulting frustration and nostalgia engendered in the community, and efforts to establish alternative forms of employment. By using juxtaposing interviews (sometimes in strikingly unexpected settings), observational techniques, stylistic allusions to canonical fictional films, dramatic enactments, and a degree of self-parody, the film displaces the conventional evidential foundation of vérité and traditional journalistic modes with a more associational and playful approach. Director Penny Woolcock, recently having worked on Trade Films' Northern Newsreels, had felt constrained thematically and formally by the predictable framework of current affairs programming and purposely set out to create 'an element of fantasy and desire, a more dreamy quality' (Corner 1996: 151).

The formal inventiveness of WTDB arguably undermined the film's accessibility, and, although acceptable in a radical independent work, was untypical of a film destined for national television broadcast. Aired on Channel 4 Eleventh Hour slot, a showcase for new approaches and experimentation, WTDB proved controversial in Consett, where the film was deemed too arty and audiences were unready for self-conscious directorial stylisation. In addition, local officials and representatives thought the film was irresponsible and had portrayed the area negatively; some of the people in the film thought they had been treated dishonestly. The film now stands as a fascinating imaginative response to acute social change and once again raises the time-honoured problem of balance between form and purpose, so central to the documentary project.

ALAN BURTON

When the Dog Bites (UK, Trade Films, 1988). Directed by Penny Woolcock. Produced by Belinda Williams and Ingrid Sinclair. Cast includes Lisa Sanderson and Art Davies.

Further reading

Corner, John, *The Art of Record. A Critical Introduction to Documentary*, Manchester: Manchester University Press, 1996.
Dickinson, Margaret, *Rogue Reels. Oppositional Film in Britain, 1945–90*, London: BFI Publishing, 1999.

When We Were Kings

(US, Gast, 1996)

When We Were Kings portrays the 1974 match between heavyweight boxing champion George

Foreman and underdog Muhammad Ali, which promoter Don King staged in Zaire (now the Democratic Republic of Congo). The film highlights Ali's mix of boxing prowess, black politics, and comic bravado, all of which strives to link African Americans and their ancestral home. A chronicle of press conferences, training, travel, and especially a black music festival precedes the fight and builds the expectation that Foreman, a heavy favorite, will annihilate Ali. The audience is well prepared for the stirring upset and the aftermath pays homage to Ali's courage and determination.

The film is a hybrid of documentary trends, blending sports, biography, music, and cultural history into a heroic political anthem. When We Were Kings combines observational filming of the 1974 events, compilation materials that develop historical perspective, and contemporary interviews reflecting on Ali's mix of self-promotion, physical ability, and social concern. Its extraordinary emotional impact arises from its graceful design and harmonious synthesis of elements.

The subject evolves out of the history of its production. When We Were Kings was initially planned as a concert film. Leon Gast, a New York filmmaker and still photographer, was commissioned to shoot the three-day music festival that was to precede the 1974 bout and produce an African American Woodstock in the direct cinema style. Gast had already made Hell's Angels Forever and two music films, The Dead, on the San Francisco rock band The Grateful Dead, and Salsa, featuring the Panamanian singer Rubén Blades. Four days before the title fight, however, George Foreman received a cut over his eye that required the bout to be delayed for six weeks.

The concert went ahead as scheduled, but the tie-in with the fight was aborted and the audience inconsequential. Nonetheless, Gast remained in Zaire after the concert, filming the scene as everyone lingered. More than three hundred thousand feet of film was shot, but financing for the movie dried up. Gast nursed plans to complete the project for twenty-two years. In 1989 David Sonenberg, a talent manager in the music business, raised money and over the next six years he and Gast put together eight different versions. Eventually they decided to shift the focus onto Muhammad Ali and acquired additional fight footage and archival material to frame the story around the boxing champion. In addition to the nine concert numbers, Sonenberg added two new songs at the close of the film, 'When We Were Kings' and 'Rumble in the Jungle'. The music track functions as a rhythmic foundation thoroughly integrated into the unfolding montage of events and underlining the film's politics.

In 1995 Taylor Hackford joined the team and convinced them to include contemporary interviews. The commentators included Norman Mailer, George Plimpton, and Malik Bowens, each of whom witnessed the bout more than twenty years before and remembered it vividly. A screening at the Sundance Film Festival drew seventeen offers to distribute the motion picture. Its successful theatrical run culminated in its winning the Academy Award for Best Documentary Feature in 1997. Over the years, When We Were Kings evolved from a concert film into an homage to a boxing legend. In doing so, it had taken on an historical perspective that turned out to be essential to its impact.

Leon Gast constructs his documentary like a heroic legend that unfolds in four movements. The first movement focuses on Ali's background as a fighter and the announcement of the forthcoming title bout in Zaire. Episodes from Ali's early career are associated with the Civil Rights struggle and further matched with images from the anticolonial rebellion in the Democratic Republic of Congo. The film treats Ali as a political leader working to reunite black America and black Africa. The film's second movement follows the Americans to Africa, and, as they prepare for the bout, Ali meets his brethren in Zaire, serenaded by songs from the black music festival such as 'Say It Loud, I'm Black and I'm Proud'. The former champion ties himself so closely to the destiny of the black community that the Africans express surprise when the champion arrives and they discover that he is black, too. George Foreman, meanwhile, displays an underdeveloped social consciousness. Ali ties his quest to awakening black America from the political apathy personified by Foreman. The third movement begins with the injury to Foreman, which delays the fight and allows the alliance between Ali and the Africans to grow. The movement culminates in the bout and Ali's victory, which becomes a triumph for a renewed American African brotherhood. The closing act meditates on the meaning of Ali as an historical hero and suggests a reunification of black and white America in their mutual recognition of, and admiration for, the heroic boxer. The film embraces Ali as a crusader whose courage and determination evokes a time 'when we were kings', when heroism raised common men and women to majesty.

When We Were Kings attempts to revive African American solidarity in the 1990s through a quest for racial identity. The film highlights the connection between blacks in America and Africa, but finally the quest focuses on the black athlete as a community hero. History and memory link the racial politics of 1974 to the need for revival in 1996. The crossing between continents parallels the crossing back through time to embrace the heritage embodied in Muhammad Ali.

In addition to promoting the Ali legend, When We Were Kings celebrates the optimism, fortitude, and determination necessary to command one's destiny. The hero in When We Were Kings emerges as a crusader for social justice whose identity is drawn from his racial community. The closing 'When We Were Kings' montage does not simply valorize Ali, but inspires the audience to acknowledge the prospects for heroic action that combines physical excellence with social leadership, fervent conviction, self-sacrifice, and a commitment to others. When We Were Kings imparts a feeling of renewed possibility and the suggestion of the potential for heroism in everyday life.

LEGER GRINDON

When We Were Kings (US, 1996, 87 mins). A Gramercy Pictures release, a DAS Films presentation. Directed by Leon Gast. Produced by David Sonenberg, Leon Gast, and Taylor Hackford. Edited by Leon Gast, Taylor Hackford, Jeffrey Levy-Hinte, and Keith Robinson. Cinematography by Maryse Alberti, Paul Goldsmith, Kevin Keating, Albert Maysles, and Roderick Young. Cast features: Muhammad Ali, George Foreman, Don King, James Brown, B.B. King, Mobutu Sese Seko, Spike Lee, Norman Mailer, George Plimpton, Thomas Hauser, Malik Bowens, Lloyd Price, The Spinners, the Crusaders, and Miriam Makeba. Music Credits: 'Am Am Pondo' (written by Miriam Makeba, performed by Miriam Makeba), 'Say It Loud, I'm Black and I'm Proud (written by James Brown and Alfred James Ellis, performed by James Brown), 'Young Rabbits' (written by Wayne Henderson, performed by The Crusaders), 'Musical Interlude' (written by Tabu Ley Rochereau and Seigneur Rochereau, performed by L'Orchestre Afrisa International), 'I'm Coming Home' (written by Thom Bell and Linda Creed, performed by The Spinners), 'Sweet Sixteen' (written by B.B. King and Joe Josea, performed by B.B. King), 'In a Cold Sweat' (written by James Brown and Alfred James Ellis, performed by James Brown), 'Gonna Have a Funky Good Time' (written by James Brown, performed by James Brown), 'African Chant' (written by Franco Luongo, performed by OK Jazz), 'When We Were Kings' (written by Andy Marvel, Amy Powers, and Arnie Roman, performed by Brian McKnight and Diana King), 'Rumble in the Jungle' (written by Wyclef Jean, Prakazrel Michel, Lauryn Hill, Benny Anderson, Bjorn Ulvaes, Stig Anderson, Chip Taylor, Kamaal Fareed, Malik Taylor, Trevor Smith, and John Forte, performed by The Fugees).

Further reading

Corliss, Richard, 'When We Were Kings', *Time* 49, no. 7, February 17, 1997: 83.

Denby, David, 'When We Were Kings', *New York* 47, no. 7, February 24, 1997: 123.

Early, Gerald, 'Ali's rumble', *Sight and Sound* 7, no. 5, May 1997: 10–12.

Gelder, Lawrence Van, 'In Africa with Ali and the Rope-a-Dope', *The New York Times*, Friday, October 25, 1996: C26–7.

McCarthy, Todd, 'When We Were Kings', *Variety* 362, no. 2, February 12, 1996: 82–3.

Macdonald, Kevin, 'When We Were Kings', *Sight and Sound* 7, no. 5, May 1997: 56.

Mailer, Norman, *The Fight*, Boston: Little, Brown, 1975.

O'Brien, Richard, 'When We Were Kings', *Sports Illustrated* 85, no. 19, November 4, 1996: 20.

Ryan, Susan, 'When We Were Kings', *Cineaste* 22, no. 4, fall 1996: 54–5.

Whitehead, Peter

Peter Whitehead is renowned as the consummate documentarist of the 1960s counterculture. In a series of films made between 1965 and 1969 he not only captured the events, places, people, and attitudes that defined the decade, but succeeded in tapping deep into its shifting zeitgeist. Whitehead's knack for being in the right place at the right time (and switching the camera on at the right moment) has certainly contributed amply to the compulsive mythography of the 'swinging sixties', but his films also offer a sophisticated analysis and critique of the procedures by which such legends are created. They register and extend the wider preoccupations of an era when the role of media representations in shaping, controlling, and potentially transforming human experience was at the forefront of radical artistic, intellectual, and political concerns.

Whitehead's early films show his fascination with the immediacy and involvement of American cinéma vérité. In later works vérité shooting methods are fused with the visual lexicon of underground cinema and the self-reflexive, Brechtian strategies developed by Jean-Luc Godard. This stylistic amalgam points to Whitehead's distinctive authorship of his work, a fact materially underlined by his artisanal working methods as director, producer, editor, and cameraman of his own films. From the outset Whitehead approached vérité filming as a subjective process, openly acknowledging that his works register personal choices, opinions, and reactions to circumstances, and refusing the shibboleth of objectivity that has tended (unjustly) to dominate responses to American vérité work.

The film that first made Whitehead's reputation was Wholly Communion (1965), a record of the International Poetry Incarnation that took place at the Royal Albert Hall on June 11, 1965. Whitehead borrowed an NPR Éclair 16mm camera to film the proceedings with minimal disturbance and took in forty-five minutes' worth of film stock. For an event scheduled to last more than three hours, this meant that he was compelled from the outset to be highly selective in what he chose to shoot. The resulting thirty-three-minute film clearly registers Whitehead's personal interpretations and reactions to the occasion, as the trademark zooms, pans, and sweeps of vérité filming are used to shift focus between performers and audience, and to frame the poets differently according to the tone, delivery, and reception of their readings (Sargeant 1997). Gregory Corso's introspection is conveyed by initially framing the seated poet between two chatting spectators, and then holding his face in a tight close-up. In contrast, the public gravitas of Adrian Mitchell reading his cathartic Vietnam poem 'To Whom It May Concern' is carried by using a medium close-up of the poet and cutaways to rapt faces in the audience. Whitehead's focus on the collective experience of the event in the interaction of performers and listeners anticipates the subsequent view of the Royal Albert Hall reading as less about individual performers and their work than as a defining moment in the self-awareness and public visibility of the counterculture.

On the strength of Wholly Communion, Whitehead was approached by The Rolling Stones' manager, Andrew Oldham, and invited to film the band. Charlie Is My Darling (1965), a film diary of the Stones' 1965 tour of Ireland, predates better-known rock documentaries like D.A. Pennebaker's Dont Look Back (1967) in minting the trademark vérité iconography of the mundane routines of touring, and probing the enigmatic contrast between on-stage and off-stage performance. Unlike Pennebaker's film, which follows many vérité documentaries in avoiding direct interaction with its subject by filming press interviews, Charlie Is My Darling includes sequences in which Whitehead interviews the band members, his articulate voice on the soundtrack probing and questioning them in a manner that occasionally—notably when targeting a diffident Charlie Watts—ruptures the vérité protocol of invisible observation and feels painfully intrusive. Whitehead's use of the same technique when pressing a group of fans about why exactly they like the band and getting only vague and unconvincing replies has the disquieting effect of making the Stones' undeniable talent and power as performers seem suddenly fragile and insubstantial, which perhaps explains the frequent assessment of the film as melancholy and elegaic.

For Benefit of the Doubt (1966), Whitehead filmed a performance of Peter Brook's Royal Shakespeare Company production of the anti-Vietnam War play, U.S., and conducted a series of interviews with Brook and his cast members including Glenda Jackson. The treatment of the performance recalls Wholly Communion in attending as much to the audience as to the actors, but the film also anticipates Whitehead's later film, The Fall, in its ultimate scepticism toward the political efficacy of radical theatre.

Whitehead's involvement with The Rolling Stones led him into filming other bands and making pop promos for Top of the Pops. His position at the centre of the London counterculture led him to undertake a wider exploration of the scene, galvanized by the media spectre of 'Swinging London' launched by *Time* magazine in 1966. Tonite Let's All Make Love in London (1967), billed by Whitehead as 'a Pop concerto for Film', remains an unparalleled celebration and dissection of the mystique of the 1960s. It features stage and studio footage of rock bands, including the Animals and The Rolling Stones (material reused from Charlie Is My Darling), and impressionistic sequences shot in London's streets and nightclubs, some processed in slow motion or edited to create lyrical stop-motion effects. Interviews, both relatively formal encounters with celebrities like Michael Caine, Julie Christie, Mick Jagger, and David Hockney, and spontaneous vox-pops with anonymous 'dolly birds' sound out the moral temper of the times. Whitehead again proves willing to press his subjects hard from behind the camera about their opinions and values, situating himself as a detached observer as much as a participant and bringing out both conviction and flimsiness in contemporary attitudes. The critical stance toward the poses and values of 'Swinging London' is enhanced by the Brechtian (Godardian) division of the film into chapters, and the ambitious early montage of the media images and articles that spawned the phenomenon, which is reminiscent of the ironic all-out visual assaults found in the underground films of Bruce Conner.

The Fall (1969), Whitehead's most searching and accomplished film and his final contemporary meditation on the iconic images and realities of the 1960s, may have started out as 'Tonite Let's All Make Love in New York', but quickly mutated under subjective and external pressures into something very different. The film is divided into three sections: 'Image', 'Word', and 'Word + Image'. The first two explore shooting and editing as stages in the production of filmed images, and all three together reconstruct Whitehead's attempt to document political and underground activity in New York (while conducting an affair with a fashion model), his increasing loss of faith in the ability of media images to have any significant impact in a revolutionary situation, and finally his discovery of a solution in direct political action, when he joins and films the student occupation of Columbia University and its eventual violent liquidation by police in the spring of 1968. The Fall is a landmark of counter-cinema in its reflexive interrogation of personal commitment, media imagery, and the possibility of direct political intervention, but it also retains tremendous documentary significance as a work that captured and gave form to the rapidly shifting temper and fortunes of the counterculture as the 1960s drew to a close, when protest was abandoned in favour of direct action, and the response of the authorities escalated to the use of extreme violence.

Although The Fall was not Whitehead's last film, the journey out from under the weight of media representations that it records was to prove prophetic. In 1973 Whitehead abandoned filmmaking for falconry, judging that the vérité camera that he had believed connected him to the world was in fact keeping him apart from it.

CATHERINE LUPTON

Biography

Born 1937, Liverpool. Degree in Philosophy of Science and Crystallography from Cambridge 1961. Scholarship to Slade School of Art 1963. News cameraman for Italian television in London 1964. Made scientific documentary, Perception of Life, for the Nuffield Foundation 1964. Wholly Communion won the Gold Medal at the Mannheim Documentary Film Festival 1965. Published English translations of thirty-two classic film scripts under the Lorrimer imprint 1966–71. Took up falconry 1972. Directed two further films, Daddy (1974, with Niki de St Phalle), and Fire in the Water (1977). Ran falcon-breeding centre for Prince Khalid al-Faisal in Saudi Arabia 1982–90. From 1990 published novels: *Nora and …* (1990), *The Risen: A Holographic Novel* (1994), *Pulp Election: The Booker Prize Fix* (1996, under the pseudonym Carmen St Keeldare), *Brontëgate* (1997), *Girl on the Train* (1998), *Tonite Let's All Make Love in London* (1999); interactive novel *Nohzone* (2000).

Selected films

1965 Wholly Communion
1965 Charlie Is My Darling
1966 Benefit of the Doubt
1967 Tonite Let's All Make Love in London
1969 The Fall
1994 Pink Floyd, London: 1966–7

Further reading

Crofts, Stephen, 'Peter Whitehead Talks About His New Film—The Fall', *Cinema*, December 1968: 18–21.

Drummond, Phillip, 'Peter Whitehead and The Fall', *Isis* 21, May 1969.

Durgnat, Raymond, 'Tonite Let's All Make Love in London', *Films and Filming* 14, no. 5, February 1968: 22–3.

——'The Falconer: Three Lives of Peter Whitehead', *Entropy* 1, no. 1, 1997: 10–21.

Paul, R.F., 'The Inadvertent Agent', *Mondo*, 2000: 46–59.

Sargeant, Jack, 'A Few Poets Trying to Be Natural', in *Naked Lens: Beat Cinema*, London: Creation Books, 1997.

Whitehead, Peter (ed.), *Wholly Communion*, London: Lorrimer Films, 1965.

Who Bombed Birmingham?

(UK, Granada, 1990)

During the 1990s there were a number of drama documentaries produced in the United Kingdom based on the Troubles in Northern Ireland, and 1990 stands out as a particularly fruitful year with the production of Shoot to Kill (Yorkshire TV), The Treaty (Thames/RTE), and the controversial Who Bombed Birmingham? (Granada), also known in the United States as Investigation: Inside a Terrorist Bombing.

Drama-documentary has been produced with relative frequency on British television and is a hybrid genre based on journalistic research and evidence, in a similar mode as the traditional documentary, but that also uses the aesthetic codes of drama to mediate the real world. There have been a number of docudrams produced in the United Kingdom that have dealt with the cases of innocent people charged by the state and wrongly convicted for crimes they did not commit.

One of the most eminent in the genre is Who Bombed Birmingham?, which recounts the British Labour MP Chris Mullen's campaign to free the Birmingham Six and which also led to public pressure to free the men wrongfully convicted of the IRA terror attack on a pub in Guildford fifteen years earlier.

The programme recounts how Mullen challenged the convictions and eventually ascertained that the Six were never members of the IRA, that their confessions emerged after suffering assaults by the police, that the forensic evidence was seriously flawed, and that the police were aware of the identity of the actual bombers. The programme is based on Mullen's journey to establish who planted the bombs and on the reconstruction of the night of November 21, 1974, when five Irish immigrants with families in Birmingham were arrested as they prepared to return to Northern Ireland. The five men were travelling back to Belfast for the funeral of an IRA man, James McDaid, killed by his own bomb in the West Midlands city of Coventry.

The programme recounts the journey as the group made their way to catch the ferry back to Belfast, and as the IRA detonated two bombs in two pubs, The Mulberry Bush and The Tavern, killing twenty-one people and injuring more than one hundred and sixty in Birmingham city centre. All five were arrested and later a sixth man was also arrested. Confessions were extracted from some members of the group by West Midlands Police after their arrests.

Indeed, there was widespread revulsion at the attack and the men received heavy sentences despite withdrawing their confessions and claiming police brutality at their trial. After a campaign by the men's families, investigative journalists, human rights activists and politicians, however, many began to believe that the Six were in fact innocent. What the programme also uncovered was a police file that detailed the interrogation of an alleged IRA informer in December 1975. The programme-makers claimed that this exonerated the Six and identified the perpetrators.

Questions were subsequently raised about the tactics deployed by the West Midlands Police to gain the confessions, with widespread allegations of police brutality and dubious forensic evidence. The case also had particularly sensitive aftereffects for the British legal system after an unsuccessful appeal and allegations that the judiciary did not want to admit to a miscarriage of justice.

The imminent broadcasting of Who Bombed Birmingham? provoked widespread discussion within the various authorities involved, and the British Home Office, the Chief Constable of Birmingham Police, and the British Prime Minister were in complete agreement in their claim that no new evidence would emerge and therefore nothing would change. Indeed, Who Bombed Birmingham? undeniably brought the appeal cases of the Birmingham Six to the attention of huge television audiences, with a pre-broadcast furore in Parliament seeing Conservative ministers having to answer difficult questions and Prime Minister Margaret Thatcher claiming that no television programme would alter any decisions concerning the case.

Programme makers Granada Television's current affairs programme World in Action had declared that they were about to reveal the identities of the people they believed to be responsible for the Birmingham bombs. The programme was by now highly controversial and the ethics of this decision were widely discussed in the British press in the days before the broadcast, which ensured a massive build-up in publicity and virtually guaranteed large viewing figures. The programme was finally broadcast on various ITV channels and also on RTE on a Wednesday evening in March 1990.

Despite the staunch position in Parliament, the programme did indeed reveal evidence to suggest that the Six were wrongly imprisoned, and the police and government were forced to investigate the case once more. A year later the sentences of the Birmingham Six were quashed.

The programme was undeniably powerful in its aims and managed successfully to portray realistic depictions of an investigative reporting programme, as the team interviews various people and tries to disprove the tests through the use of flashbacks, and follows the current affairs team's attempts to prove the men's innocence by querying the reliability of the forensic evidence.

The three lead actors, John Hurt as Mullen, Roger Allam as World in Action journalist Charles Tremayne, and Martin Shaw as his producer, Ian McBride, give commanding performances, and the Six, played by Ciaran Hinds, Niall Tobin, Brendan Laird, Niall O'Brien, Vincent Murphy, and Brendan Cauldwell, in turn offer heartbreaking performances with the occasional poignant comic interplay. Bob Peck, Terence Rigby, and John Woodvine provide fascinating portrayals of different faces of the law and, most notably, John Kavanagh's depiction of the IRA gang's bomb-maker, Donal McCann's indignant republican, and Sean McGinley's tormented terrorist.

Despite the eventual triumph of Who Bombed Birmingham?, the programme raises a number of critical concerns about the hybrid nature of docudrama as a form. The method of casting well-known charismatic actors such as John Hurt in the roles that the programme makers endorse and often unknown performers to portray the opposition, which, coupled with the visual grammar of television journalism designed to portray the truth, makes a potent combination that more than any other genre leaves the viewer hopelessly dependent on the good faith of the director.

Yet Who Bombed Birmingham? is without doubt a powerful television programme that has since set the standard for British TV docudramas based on real events, including Jimmy McGovern's Hillsborough, Paul Greengrass's Bloody Sunday, and the more recent Omagh.

KIRSTY FAIRCLOUGH

Who Bombed Birmingham? (UK, Granada Television, 1990, 105 mins). Directed by Mike Beckham. Written by Rob Ritchie. Produced by Mike Beckham. Original music by Shaun Davey. Cinematography by Ken Morgan. Sound by Nick Steer. Cast: Roger Allam, Andy Bradford, Brendan Cauldwell, Ciarán Hinds, John Hurt, John Kavanagh, Brendan Laird, Robert Lang, Patrick Malahide, Donal McCann, Gerard McSorley, Vincent Murphy, Niall O'Brien, Bob Peck, Terence Rigby, David Ryall Martin Shaw, Niall Toibin, and John Woodvine.

Further reading

Paget, D., *No Other Way to Tell It: Dramadoc/Docudrama on Television*, Manchester: Manchester University Press, 1998.

Pettitt, L., *Screening Ireland: Film and Television Representation*, Manchester: Manchester University Press, 2000.

Rosenthal, Alan (ed.), *Why Docudrama? Fact-fiction on Film and TV*, Carbondale, IL: Southern Illinois University Press, 1998.

Why We Fight

(US, Capra, 1942–5)

Why We Fight was the most widely circulating North American propaganda documentary series about World War II, both inside and outside the United States. The producer, Frank Capra, made this series between 1942 and 1945, directing a large team of Hollywood volunteers—script writers, editors, directors,

Figure 21 Why We Fight (part five, Battle of Russia), documentary by Frank Capra and Anatole Litvak, 1943 (Courtesy of the Everett Collection)

music composers, commentators, and so on—among whom were, most noticeably, Anthony Veiller, Anatole Litvak, Walter Huston, William Hornbeck, Carl Foreman, Lloyd Nolan, Dimitri Tiomkim and Eric Knight. Although Ivens and Flaherty participated in the project on a temporary basis, their contributions were not significant to the final result. What was significant was the collaboration of the Disney studios in producing the geographical animations. The series consists of seven episodes: Prelude to War (1942), The Nazis Strike (1942), Divide and Conquer (1943), The Battle of Britain (1943), The Battle of Russia (1943), The Battle of China (1944), and War Comes to America (1945).

Why We Fight was produced to motivate North American recruits who were mobilized for the war. Before the attack on Pearl Harbor, the majority of North Americans viewed the war in Europe as something remote and rather strange. Pearl Harbor marked a radical change in this perception and mobilized the entire country. The production was subject to strict control measures. The initial content of the series was defined by the Army's Bureau of Public Relations in fifteen texts, slightly before Pearl Harbor. A team of script writers made the first adaptation, and Capra started to screen any type of filmed material, including Nazi, Italian, and Soviet material such as documentaries and newsreels. In May 1942 the final setup of the chapters and their basic features were determined. September 1942 already saw the first rough-cut editing of the first parts. In November 1942 the first film of the series, Prelude to War, was released. Each phase of the production process was meticulously revised by the military.

In Why We Fight, Capra opted for persuasive arguments and emotive techniques. His messages were simple, clear, and repetitive. First of all, the war was necessary; survival so dictated it. Refraining from engaging in it was equivalent to choosing slavery under the Japanese, German, and Italian enemies. The enemy was represented as cruel and treacherous; the message was to beat them first and then talk. The Allied countries were defended, especially Great Britain and the Soviet Union. The corresponding explanations did not leave the audience with any doubts either: France had fallen into German hands through inside treason, as had Danmark, Sweden, and Norway; Great Britain and the

Soviet Union had resisted surrender by their own efforts and had fought until the end like heroes. There were no sociological analyses or ideological explanations. The one-front policy that the state propaganda proclaimed required straightforward explanations that were easy to understand. Capra and his team converted the series into the concise and all-understanding history that the recruits needed to be able to face their enemies.

For the editing of Why We Fight, Capra used a large variety of filmed material. This obviously included newsreels and documentaries from both the Allied Forces and the enemy, blended, however, with footage from feature films. The series reminded one of The March of Time; however, the typical hints of humor, sentiment, human feeling, decision, and determination were Capra's, who followed the final cuts from a close distance.

In Why We Fight everything was subjected to efficiency in terms of propaganda. It is impossible to prove the persuasive argument of the series; however, the results of the questionnaires completed by soldiers gave the semblance of a major success. Not all of the chapters were equally successful. The first four chapters were appreciated the most. Their impact surpassed any expectations. In the United States the series won an Oscar, which facilitated its way to commercial cinemas, apart from being obligatory material in the military training for North American recruits. It was also released in Allied and neutral countries, as copies were distributed in various languages. For obvious reasons, The Battle of Britain was shown in Great Britain, on direct instruction by Churchill, and The Battle of Russia was released in the Soviet Union, ordered expressly by Stalin. No real information is available, however, about the audience at the time. In 2000 the National Film Preservation Board decided to include Why We Fight into the National Film Registry.

JULIO MONTERO

See also: Capra, Frank

Why We Fight series:

Prelude to War (US Army Special Service Division; US War Department. Animation: Walt Disney Productions; Research Aid: Academy of Motion Picture Arts and Sciences; Photography: Consolidated Film Industries, CFI, 1942). Distributed by Twentieth Century Fox Film Corporation; LS Video; Office of War Information, Bureau of Motion Pictures; War Activities Committee; Questar Video Inc. Produced by Frank Capra (uncredited) and Anatole Litvak (uncredited). Writing credits: Julius J. Epstein, Phillip G. Epstein, Robert Heller (uncredited), Eric Knight (uncredited) and Anthony Veiller (uncredited). Original music by Hugo Friedhofer (uncredited), Leigh Harline (uncredited), Arthur Lange (uncredited), Cyril J. Mockridge (uncredited), and David Raksin (uncredited). Cinematography by Robert Flaherty (uncredited). Film edited by William Hornbeck (uncredited). Narrators (uncredited): Walter Huston and Anthony Veiller.

The Nazis Strike (US Army Special Service Division; US War Department Distributed by Office of War Information, Bureau of Motion Pictures; War Activities Committee; Questar Video Inc., 1942). Produced by Frank Capra. Directed by Frank Capra and Anatole Litvak. Writing credits: Julius J. Epstein and Phillip G. Epstein. Original music by Anthony Collins (uncredited), Louis Gruenberg (uncredited), Leigh Harline (uncredited), Dimitri Tiomkim (uncredited), and Roy Webb (uncredited). Film edited by William Hornbeck (uncredited). Narrator: Walter Huston (uncredited).

Divide and Conquer (US Army Special Service Division; US War Department. Animation: Walt Disney Productions. Distributed by Office of War Information, Bureau of Motion Pictures; War Activities Committee; Questar Video Inc., 1943). Produced by Frank Capra (uncredited). Directed by Frank Capra and Anatole Litvak (uncredited). Writing credits: Julius J. Epstein and Phillip G. Epstein. Original music by Dimitri Tiomkim. Film edited by William Hornbeck (uncredited). Narrators: Walter Huston and Anthony Veiller (uncredited).

The Battle of Britain (US Army Special Service Division; US War Departament. Animation: Walt Disney Productions. Distributed by Office of War Information, Bureau of Motion Pictures; War Activities Committee; Questar Video Inc., 1943). Produced by Frank Capra (uncredited). Directed by Frank Capra and Anthony Veiller (uncredited). Writing credits: Julius J. Epstein and Phillip G. Epstein. Original music by Dimitri Tiomkim (uncredited), Howard Jackson (uncredited), William Lava (uncredited), and Max Steiner (uncredited). Film edited by William Hornbeck (uncredited). Narrators: Walter Huston and Anthony Veiller (uncredited).

The Battle of Russia (US Army Special Service Division; US War Department, 1943. Distributed by Twentieth Century Fox Film Corporation; Office of War Information, Bureau of Motion Pictures; War Activities Committee; Questar Video Inc.). Produced by Frank Capra (uncredited). Directed by Frank Capra and Anatole Litvak. Writing credits: Julius J. Epstein, Phillip G. Epstein, Anatole Litvak, Anthony Veiller, and Robert Heller. Original music by Dimitri Tiomkim. Film edited by William Hornbeck (uncredited). Narrators: Walter Huston and Anthony Veiller (uncredited).

The Battle of China (US Army Special Service Division; War Departament, 1944. Distributed by Office of War Information, Bureau of Motion Pictures; War Activities Committee; Questar Video Inc. and MPI Home Video). Produced by Anatole Litvak (uncredited). Directed by Frank Capra and Anatole Litvak (uncredited). Writing credits: Julius J. Epstein and Phillip Epstein. Original music by Dimitri Tiomkim (uncredited). Film edited by William Hornbeck (uncredited). Narrators: Walter Huston and Anthony Veiller (uncredited).

War Comes to America (US Army Pictorial Services, 1945. Distributed by MPI Home Video; Questar Video Inc.; RKO; War Activities Committee of the Motion Pictures Industry). Produced by Frank Capra. Directed by Frank Capra and Anatole Litvak. Writing credits: Julius J. Epstein, Phillip G. Epstein, Anatole Litvak, and Anthony Veiller. Original music by Dimitri Tiomkim (uncredited). Film edited by William Hornbeck. Narrators: Lloyd Nolan and Walter Huston (uncredited).

Further reading

Bohn, Thomas W., *An Historical and Descriptive Analysis of the 'Why We Fight' Series*, with a new Introduction, New York: Arno Press, 1977.

Capra, Frank, *The Name above the Title: An Autobiography*, New York: Da Capo Press, 1997.

Culbert, David, '"Why We Fight": Social Engineering for a Democratic Society at War', in K.R.M. Short (ed.), *Film & Radio Propaganda in World War II*, London and Canberra: Croom Helm, 1983.

Murphy, William, 'The Method of Why We Fight', *Journal of Popular Film* I, 1972: 185–96.

Wild, Nettie

A former actor and radio journalist, Wild is known for four feature-length documentaries made since 1988. The films, direct cinema studies of complex political and social confrontations, are driven by what Wild refers to as her 'sense of cinematic drama'.

Her first feature, A Rustling of Leaves: Inside the Philippine Revolution, placed her and her crew within a guerrilla war waged against the government of Corazon Aquino and right-wing paramilitary squads. Throughout the documentary, the filmmakers negotiate their vulnerability, first with members of the heavy-handed Filipino army and death squads and later, when traveling with the guerrilla New People's Army, against the hazards of the war itself. The film's most shocking moment is a firefight between the rebels and government forces in which Wild's soundman is shot and killed.

Wild's second film, Blockade, focuses on the struggle between the Gitksan first nation in British Columbia and nonnative logging families to determine who controls the forests around them. The Gitksan block the Canadian Pacific Railway tracks, leading to a confrontation with the Royal Canadian Mounted Police. Wild, although sympathetic to the Gitksan, recognizes that the nonnative loggers, many of whom have worked in the woods for generations, are being placed in an equally precarious situation.

In her ambitious film A Place Called Chiapas, Wild studies the aftermath of the 1994 Zapatista revolution. The film is not only a study of the peasant rebellion itself but also of the role of an outside observer. In one sequence the enigmatic Subcommandante Marcos invites sympathizers from North America and Europe to visit his 'postmodern revolution'. Wild films the political tourists with various degrees of bemusement but also with a growing realization that she herself is just another visitor. When she finally is granted her interview with Marcos, the resulting footage says as much about the awkwardness of the encounter as it does about the nature of the revolution.

It is with this same sense of nondetached irony that Wild filmed a small revolution in her own city. Fix: The Story of an Addicted City documents the personalities around efforts to build North America's first legal safe drug-injection site in Vancouver's notorious Downtown Eastside. For two years Wild followed the charismatic Dean Wilson, a heroin addict and president of the Vancouver Area Network of Drug Users and his equally dedicated partner, Ann Livingston, a faith-based organizer and nonuser. Opening the injection site in the face of opposition from the nearby community, Dean and Livingston also work with Vancouver's conservative mayor, Phillip Owen, in an effort to establish a humane and realistic policy toward the city's addicts (an effort that would later cost Owen his own party's support for reelection).

As was the case with her other films, Wild and her company, Canada Wild Productions, used Fix as an organizing tool. The film has played mainstream cinemas in more than forty Canadian cities. Each screening has been followed by a community forum with local drug users, health care professionals, activists, politicians, and police.

SETH FELDMAN

Biography

Born in New York City in 1952 and educated at the University of British Columbia. Beginning her career as an actor, she cofounded and performed with Touchstone Theatre and Headlines Theatre (where she produced, wrote, as well as acted in various productions). Wild worked as a broadcast journalist for the Canadian Broadcasting Corporation, producing documentaries for several radio programs as well CBC's national news. Wild's first independent documentary was a video based on the Headlines Theatre production of Buy, Buy, Vancouver. The documentary, about the disappearance of affordable housing, was the first video invited to the Grierson Documentary Seminar, where it attracted the attention and support of Santiago Alvarez. Her subsequent films have been widely recognized. A Rustling of Leaves won the People's Choice Award at the 1989 Berlin Film Festival (Forum of New Cinema), the Prix du Public at the National Film Board's Salute to the Documentary, and the Grand Prize at the Houston Film Festival. In 1993 Blockade shared honors as Most Popular Canadian Feature at the Vancouver International Film Festival, won the Red Ribbon at the American Film and Video Festival, and the Silver Award at the Houston International Film Festival. In 1998 A Place Called Chiapas won the Audience Award for Best Documentary at the AFI-Los Angeles Film Festival, Best Feature Documentary from the International Documentary Association, and a Genie Award for best Canadian Feature Documentary. In 2003 Fix won Wild's second Genie for Best Canadian Documentary. That same year, her work was the subject of a retrospective at the Hot Docs documentary film festival in Toronto.

Selected films

1988 A Rustling of Leaves: Inside the Philippine Revolution: director, producer, writer

1993 Blockade: director, producer, second camera

1999 A Place Called Chiapas: director, producer, writer, cocamera

2002 Fix: The Story of an Addicted City: director, producer, cocamera

Further reading

Hoover, Travis, 'Nettie Wild: The Documentarian Becomes the Documented', *Film Freak Central*, www.filmfreakcentral.net/hotdocs/hotdocsnettiewild.htm, n.d.

Posner, Michael, 'Hanging onto the Horses: A Rustling of Leaves: Inside the Philippine Revolution', in *Canadian Dreams: The Making and Marketing of Independent Films*, Vancouver: Donglas & McIntyre, 1993: 51–78.

Wild, Nettie, 'Just Some Lady with a Camera: Canadian National Railroad versus Filmmaker Nettie Wild', *Point of View*, fall, 1993: 6–8.

——'In Search of Light', *Brick* 63, fall, 1999: 8–17.

——'Nettie Wild', *Point of View* 39, 2000: 11.

——'Interview', *University of Calgary Gauntlet*, March 25, 2004, gauntlet.ucalgary.ca/story/3746

Wintonick, Peter, 'Time, Trust and Money', *Cinema Canada* 160, 1989: 13–16.

Wildenhahn, Klaus

Klaus Wildenhahn's career ran parallel to the development of television documentary in postwar Germany. Wildenhahn came to television two years after the six regional stations in Western Germany had been merged into the federal umbrella organization ARD (Arbeitsgemeinschaft der öffentlich-rechtlichen Rundfunkanstalten). His first assignment, to the political magazine programme Panorama in 1961, occurred when the administrative structure of public service television was still a work in progress. Wildenhahn profited from the fact that in these formative years editorial responsibilities and limits had yet to be established. This freedom enabled him to experiment with new journalistic formats.

The political situation at that time provided an important background for Wildenhahn's professional career, as well as for his ideas on the ethics of documentary filmmaking. During the 1950s Germany had experienced a radical turn toward political and cultural conservatism as a result of the decade-long governance of the Christian-Democratic Party (CDU) under chancellor Konrad Adenauer. Wildenhahn's early setting must be understood in this context. Against the historical backdrop of the Third Reich, the first German postwar government had established a rigorous political agenda based on the denial of moral guilt for the Holocaust and the subordination of civic needs to the state's requirements in favour of public welfare. By the mid-1950s the 'Wirtschaftswunder' (economic miracle) had led to a social climate of exclusion and economic sedation. The rise of the television medium became strongly interwoven with the idea of national identity, not least owing to the victory of the German soccer team at the World Championship in 1954, the first major televised event of postwar Germany.

Wildenhahn's ideas of the purposiveness of documentary films were shaped in these particular years of rapid social change. Claiming the necessity of an ethical bias toward misrepresented milieux and social groups in documentary film, Wildenhahn considered television to be an important mouthpiece for the 'unheard voices' (Wildenhahn 1992) in society. In retrospect it can be said that the urgency of his demand was underlined by the fact that throughout the 1960s, in which Wildenhahn realized two documentaries a year, the Adenauer government was succeeded by two other conservative governments. Wildenhahn's description of his style as an 'aesthetic of resistance', in reference to the German culture critic Peter Weiss, must be seen in this political context.

Wildenhahn's work was almost exclusively concerned with subjects of social justice and public life. In his second documentary for Panorama, Der Tod kam wie bestellt (1962), Wildenhahn examined the murder of Patrice Lumumba and the involvement of the UNO. His leftist biography earned him the reputation of a controversial figure, and typically this judgement did not change when the Social-Democratic Party came into power in 1969. By the mid-1960s the seeming liberalism during the first years of public service television had turned out to be nothing more than an early misconception that was corrected with a few personnel changes. That Wildenhahn was able to work within the structure of the ARD until his retirement in 1995, however, underlines his pivotal role in the development of the documentary film and television journalism in Western Germany.

Wildenhahn repeatedly criticized the authoritative top-down configuration of public service journalism. In opposition to this intellectual elitism cultivated by the political class, he claimed that the documentary content itself should determine its form. For Wildenhahn, the virtues of documentary film were not defined aesthetically, but solely by ethical and political nature: through the intimacy between the filmmaker and the filmed person, thorough, long-term observations, long shots, and the renunciation of external comments or 'synthetic' inserts. This documentary altruism affected a whole generation of German filmmakers and became the main characteristic of Wildenhahn's distinctive style.

In the late 1970s, this influence led to the controversy between Wildenhahn and the media critic Klaus Kreimeier about partiality in the documentary film and the filmmaker's deliberate subordination under the reality of the camera. Their disagreement provoked an influential debate about the political and social responsibility of the documentary film as a part of the media public. In his 1980 essay 'Industrielandschaft mit Einzelhändlern' (Industrial Landscape with Retailers), Wildenhahn responded to Kreimeier's criticism with the argument that 'the documented' themselves should take over the author's role, as the filmmaker only provides the technical framework for their story.

Wildenhahn was not so naive to believe that his documentary method would automatically reveal an absolute truth or an accurate representation of social reality. He had become familiar with the work of D.A. Pennebaker, Albert Maysles, and Richard Leacock in 1963 while working on a TV feature about the beginnings of direct cinema. The impact of their work was already noticeable in Wildenhahn's first 'on location' documentary, Parteitag '64 (1964) about the national convention of the Social-Democratic Party. Wildenhahn was the first German filmmaker to adopt the methods of the direct cinema movement, but he remained sceptical about its effect on filmic realism, the new immediacy of the documentary experience, as a sheer consequence of smaller and therefore more mobile film equipment. He considered an ideological discourse primarily based on a technological premise as equally problematic as the hierarchical practice he tried to overcome. Wildenhahn evaded this dilemma by turning toward a highly political position. Because the documentary filmmaker can never achieve absolute objectivity, he or she has no other choice but to endorse this partiality.

Wildenhahn's output of 'worker films' remained the strongest indication of this ethical bias. According to Wildenhahn the working-class milieu was the scene where the slow transformation of the government's social paradigm became most evident. He continuously returned to close observations of workplaces and documentations of worker strikes until the early 1990s. The strong position films, such as Emden goes to the USA (1975–6), or Rheinhausen. Herbst '88 (1988), adopted between the factions of workers and the union emphasized the social-democratic values maintained in the body of Wildenhahn's work. His conviction that only a unified position would help to defy the forces of free market made his films a rare example of social- and class-conscious documentary filmmaking in German television.

Constancy characterizes Wildenhahn's oeuvre. He consistently articulated his social policy, even in his late films. His final documentary for the ARD in 1995 was the only one not shot on 16mm film.

ANDREAS BUSCHE

See also: Leacock, Richard; Maysles, Albert; Pennebaker, D.A.

Biography

Born in Bonn, Germany, June 19, 1930. Studied sociology, publishing and political science at the Free University Hamburg. Left the university 1953 and moved to London, where he worked in a psychiatric hospital. Returned to Hamburg 1959. Produced commercials on 35mm for the National Lottery. 1960–64 'visual realizer' for journalistic television programmes at the ARD. 1964–75 editor in 'teleplay' department at the NDR/ARD. 1968–72 scholar at the German Film- und Fernsehakademie (Film and Television Academy), Berlin. 1969 first documentary, 'Institutssommer', with the newly founded filmmaker collective 'Gruppe Wochenschau'. In 1975 laid off at the NDR/ARD for his controversial documentary 'Emden geht nach USA'. 1976 'Emden geht nach USA' wins Golden Grimme Award. 1975 freelance editor at the radio of the WDR/ARD. 1977/1979/1980 jury member of the documentary film festival Duisburger Filmwoche. 1975–95 freelance editor for the 'education', 'philosophy, history, education', 'religion and history', 'feature, documentary, history', and 'society and education' departments at the NDR/ARD, and freelance contributor for the WDR/ARD. Retired in 1995.

Selected films

1964 Parteitag 1964: director, concept, writer
1967 In der Fremde: director, writer
1971 Der Hamburger Aufstand Oktober 1923: director, concept, cowriter
1975–6 Emden geht nach USA: director, concept, cowriter
1988 Rheinhausen. Herbst '88: director, narrator,
1992 Freier Fall: Johanna K.: director, concept
1994–5 Reise nach Mostar: director, concept

Further reading

Berg, Jan, 'Die Fiktion des Nichtfiktionalen. Zur Abbildtheorie von Klaus Wildenhahn', *Filme* 4, August 1980.

Biedermann, Werner and Haardt, Angela (eds), *Beiträge aus der Wirklichkeit*, Duisburg: Filmforum der Volkshochschule, 1981.

Kluge, Alexander, 'Debatte über den Dokumentarfilm', in Klaus Eder and Alexander Kluge

(eds), *Ulmer Dramaturgien. Reibungsverluste*, München: Carl Hanser Verlag, 1980.
Schröder, Nicolaus (ed.), *Klaus Wildenhahn, Dokumentarist*, Berlin: Freunde der Deutschen Kinemathek, 2000.
Wildenhahn, Klaus, *Teilstücke in Fernsehdokumentarismus. Bilanz und Perspektiven*, Peter Zimmermann (ed.), Stuttgart: Europäisches Medienforum, 1992.

Wintonick, Peter

With roots in fiction filmmaking during a period of the late 1970s and early 1980s, Canadian Peter Wintonick turned his interests to documentaries after honing his skills as an editor on a series of feature-length productions. The New Cinema (1984), a feature video documentary about independent film, marked Wintonick's directorial debut and hinted at his future as a filmmaker interested in the social ramifications of the form and its ties with fiction. The use of both fiction and nonfiction film language and techniques under the rubric of documentary filmmaking is a recurrent feature of Wintonick's highly constructed work, resulting in texts that touch but do not quite blur the line between the two practices.

Wintonick's films are pragmatic in nature, his exploration of subject matter satisfying both his personal search for knowledge and his desire to share that information with an audience. Much of his body of work could be classified as committed filmmaking insofar as his socio-ideological position behind the camera is rarely concealed. Although Wintonick's personal politics are not necessarily on display, his perspective is echoed in the particular discourse presented onscreen.

Wintonick is best known for Manufacturing Consent: Noam Chomsky and the Media (1992), an epic feature-length documentary detailing activist-academic Noam Chomsky's critique of corporate news-gathering and the vested interests that lie behind media coverage. Co-directed with Mark Achbar, the film is a complex system of compilation footage, interviews, and staged elements. According to the National Film Board of Canada, it is the most successful documentary in Canadian history. It has played theatrically in two hundred cities around the world, won twenty-two awards, appeared in more than fifty international film festivals, has been broadcast in thirty markets, and has been translated into a dozen languages. It marked the first production from Necessary Illusions, a company founded by Wintonick, Achbar, and Francis Miquet devoted to the development, production, and distribution of media on sociocultural issues. Preceded by a number of smaller productions prepared for television broadcast, Cinéma Vérité: Defining the Moment (1999), was Wintonick's next major achievement. It continued his examination of media, filmmaking, and journalism through his own filmmaking while attempting to delineate the major currents that spawned the vérité movement and established its profile within the documentary world. A hybrid of documentary styles, the film is notable for its first-person interviews with the luminaries of the movement, including Robert Drew, Richard Leacock, Jean Rouch, and Michel Brault.

Wintonick's interest in the virtual forum of information exchange offered by the Internet led to his development of the Virtual Film Festival. Founded in 1996, the site functioned as a point of convergence for documentary filmmakers to showcase their independently produced digital works and exchange ideas with other documentarians from around the world. Issues related to funding ultimately saw the closing of the site, but Wintonick's interest in multimedia as a vital link between both filmmakers and audiences alike continues to inform his ongoing role as a postproduction consultant and executive producer for independent productions.

MICHAEL B. BAKER

See also: Manufacturing Consent: Noam Chomsky and the Media

Biography

Born in Trenton, Ontario, June 10, 1953. Attended Carleton University in Ottawa with an interest in journalism, theatre, film, photography 1972. Graduated from the Algonquin College Film Production Centre in Ottawa 1973. Editor at the International Cinemedia Centre Ltd 1972–7. Editor and associate producer for Ron Mann's Poetry in Motion, a theatrical documentary about the history and art of performance poetry. Produced and directed first documentary, The New Cinema, winner of the Blue Ribbon Award at the American Film Festival 1984. Formed Necessary Illusions with Mark Achbar and Francis Miquet 1988.

Associate Professor at Concordia University in the Department of Film Studies 1988–9. Completed Manufacturing Consent: Noam Chomsky and the Media, a coproduction of Necessary Illusions and the National Film Board of Canada 1992. Coproducer and codirector of web-based Virtual Film Festival (now archived on CD-ROM) 1994–6. Cofounder/ Chair of the Banff New Media Institute's Digidocs programme 1995. Programmer for Canadian International Documentary Festival (Toronto), Visions on the Real (Adelaide), and Amsterdam International Documentary Festival.

Selected films

1982 Poetry in Motion (Mann): associate producer, editor
1984 The New Cinema: director, producer, editor
1985 The Journey (Watkins): coproducer, coeditor (Canadian unit)
1987 A Rustling of Leaves: Inside the Philippine Revolution (Wild): editor, associate producer
1992 Manufacturing Consent: Noam Chomsky and the Media (Achbar): codirector, coproducer, editor
1999 Cinéma Vérité: Defining the Moment: director, coeditor
2002 Seeing is Believing: Handicams, Human Rights and the News (Cizek): codirector, coproducer

Further reading

Achbar, Mark and Wintonick, Peter, 'Manufacturing Dissent', *Cineaste* 3, 1993.
Enright, Robert, 'Vérité, Vérité, All is Vérité', *Border Crossings* 3, 2000.
Glassman, Marc, 'Mediating Noam Chomsky. Manufacturing Consent: Noam Chomsky and the Media', *Take One* 2, winter 1993.

Wiseman, Frederick

Frederick Wiseman is a vérité documentary filmmaker with a long record of achievement. He chose a 'fly-on-the-wall' approach to filmmaking and continued with this method throughout his career. Wiseman lets the camera roll for long periods and does not use interviews, music, titles, or narration.

Editing is where the film's structure is born. He has been called a 'pioneer' of vérité, along with D.A. Pennebaker and the Maysles brothers (Poppy 2002), and is considered 'one of the most influential and prolific figures in documentary filmmaking' (Aftab and Weltz n.d.: 1).

Trained in law, Wiseman was teaching at Boston University's Institute of Law and Medicine when he turned his attention to the conditions at a nearby Massachusetts mental hospital. He was an amateur filmmaker and uninterested in the abstractions of the law. The result, in 1967, was his eighty-four-minute film Titicut Follies. It is considered by many to be a documentary classic. Because of its importance to Wiseman's career and documentary filmmaking, it is worth focusing on.

The story takes its name from a musical revue put on by the guards and mental patients at the Bridgewater State Hospital for the Criminally Insane. The black-and-white footage heightens the drama and terror; the unfolding story blurs the lines between sanity and insanity. So controversial was the film that the Massachusetts Supreme Court banned it from being shown. It ruled that the film was both obscene and exploitive, and had invaded inmate privacy. However, supporters of the film argued that the public's right to know what happens at public institutions outweighs privacy issues. Wiseman himself has argued that if an institution receives public tax support, citizens are entitled to observe its operation.

Though a masterpiece to many, Titicut Follies was not without its critics. A *Time* magazine reviewer said that the film was 'a raw poorly edited report', that offered no solutions (n.a. 1967a). A critic maintained that the privacy issue was bogus and that the real question was whether the film was an 'objective documentary' or a 'propaganda stunt' (ibid.). Accused of filming with hidden cameras, Wiseman denied the charge. Additionally, the film raised questions as to whether or not it was art. In 1993, twenty-four years later, the film aired on public television.

Titicut Follies helped to launch a career that included more than thirty documentaries. PBS nationally broadcast Wiseman's Law and Order, Hospital, Juvenile Court, Essene, Basic Training, Primate, Welfare, Meat, Canal Zone, and Sinai Field Mission, among others.

Wiseman's films have won numerous awards, including at the New York Film Festival, San

Francisco International Film Festival, Spoleto Film Festival, London Film Festival, Athens International Film Festival, American Film Festival, and the Melbourne and Sydney Festivals. He has earned Emmy Awards, Dupont Awards, and the Personal Achievement Gabriel Award, presented by the Catholic Broadcasters' Association. Retrospective screenings of his work have taken place at the Chicago Film Festival, London Film Festival, and Paris Film Cinemathèque, among other venues.

Wiseman has remained steadfast in his convictions regarding documentary filmmaking. To the annoyance of some, he refuses to comment about what his films are about and what should be done in terms of what he has exposed. He believes this information is in the film and viewers have to make up their own mind. His films have also been criticized for being overly long.

Though often considered the 'dean' of 'cinéma vérité', Wiseman himself says that it is, 'just a pompous French term that has absolutely no meaning as far as I'm concerned. The effort is to be selective about your observations and organize them into a dramatic structure' (Aftab and Weltz n.d.: 2).

Wiseman's long and somewhat controversial career has provided the United States and the world with some of the most poignant examinations of institutions and life in America. He continues to see America as a largely unexplored country cinematically. Although primarily a documentary filmmaker, he has made two fiction films (The Stunt Man, 1980, and Seraphita's Diary, 1982).

LOU BUTTINO

See also: Basic Training; High School; Hospital; Law and Order; Meat; Titicut Follies; Welfare

Biography

Born in Boston, Massachusetts, January 1, 1930. BA, Williams College, Williamstown, MA, 1951. LLB, Yale University. Initially practiced and taught law before taking up documentary filmmaking in 1967.

Films

1967 Titicut Follies
1969 High School
1969 Law and Order
1970 Hospital
1971 Basic Training
1972 Essene
1973 Juvenile Court
1974 Primate
1975 Welfare
1976 Meat
1977 Canal Zone
1978 Sinai Field Mission
1980 Model
1983 The Store
1985 Racetrack
1986 Multi-handicapped
1986 Adjustment & Work
1987 Deaf
1987 Missile
1989 Near Death
1991 Aspen
1993 Zoo
1994 High School II
1995 Ballet
1996 La Comédie Française
1997 Public Housing
1999 Belfast, Maine
2001 Domáestic Violence I
2002 Domestic Violence II

Further reading

Aftab, Kaleem and Weltz, Alexandra, 'Fred Wiseman', www.iol.ie/galfilm/filmwest, n.d.

Arlen, Michael J., *The Camera Age: Essays on Television*, New York: Penguin, 1982.

Barnouw, Erik, *Documentary: A History of Non-fiction Film*, New York: Oxford University Press, 1974.

Benson, Thomas W., *Documentary Dilemmas: Frederick Wiseman's 'Titicut Follies'*, Carboridale, IL Southern Illinois Press, 1991.

Eames, David, 'Watching Wiseman Watch', *The New York Times Magazine*, October 2, 1977: 96–102, 108.

Edelstein, David, 'Frederick Wiseman', *The New York Times*, March 16, 2003.

Ellsworth, Liz, *Frederick Wiseman: A Guide to References and Resources*, Boston: G.K. Hall & Co., 1979.

Fenton, John H., 'Film Stirs Furor in Mass., Legislators See Follies Made at Memorial Hospital', *The New York Times*, October 18, 1967: 40.

Gill, Brendan, 'The Current Cinema', *The New Yorker* 43, October 28, 1967: 166–7.

Houston, Bobby, 'Titicut Follies', *Documentary*, December 2003.

n.a., 'The Talk of the Town: New Producer', *The New Yorker* 39, September 14, 1963: 33–5.
n.a., 'Cinema: Festival Action, Side Show Action, Titicut Follies', *Time* 90, no. 13, September 29, 1967a.
n.a., 'Tempest in a Snake Pit', *Newsweek* 70, November 11, 1967b: 539.
Nichols, Bill, 'Fred Wiseman's Documentaries: Theory and Structure', *Film Quarterly* 31, no. 3, spring 1978: 15–28.
O'Connor, John, 'Wiseman's Latest Film is Another "Reality Fiction"', *The New York Times*, November 7, 1976: 27.
Poppy, Nick, 'Frederick Wiseman', Salon.com.2002/01/30, 2002.
Rosenthal, Alan (ed.), *New Challenges in Documentary*, Berkeley, CA: University of California Press, 1988.
Schickel, Richard, 'Sorriest Spectacle: The Titicut Follies', *Life* 63, December 1, 1967: 12.
Walker, Jess, 'The Cool World', *Film Comment* 2, 1964: 51–2.

Woodstock: Three Days of Peace and Music

(US, Wadleigh, 1970)

Michael Wadleigh's epic documentary of the three-day Woodstock Music and Art Fair, which took place on August 15–17, 1969 at Max Yasgur's farm outside Woodstock, in upstate New York, represents one of the most vivid accounts of the 1960s American counterculture. The Woodstock Festival built on the success of the International Pop Festival at Monterey, California in June 1967 and the free concert in Hyde Park, London (Stones in the Park) in June 1969, attracting an audience of four hundred thousand over the three days. Filmed by D.A. Pennebaker as Monterey Pop (1968), the Monterey Festival was the first to bill a plethora of West Coast rock bands such as Country Joe & The Fish, Canned Heat, Jefferson Airplane, and Big Brother & The Holding Company, with The Who and Jimi Hendrix headlining. The Woodstock Festival also concentrated on folk, blues, and rock, featuring many of the bands that played at Monterey, together with Joan Baez, Joe Cocker, Crosby, Stills & Nash, Arlo Guthrie, and Richie Havens, all of whom feature in the film, as well as Ravi Shankar, The Grateful Dead, and The Band, who were not included. The original director's cut of two hundred and twenty-five minutes was made from more than one hundred and twenty hours of footage of the Festival, but edited to one hundred and eighty-five minutes for the film's release in 1970. The director's cut has been available since 1994, with eight further segments on the widescreen DVD released by Warner in 2000.

Wadleigh's film won Best Documentary Feature at the Academy Awards in 1971 (as well as being nominated for Editing and Sound awards), and it is regarded by many as the best concert film ever made. Shot on 16mm film, Woodstock combines a vivid account of many of the artists and bands that played over the three days, with attention given to the audience (listening, dancing, talking, tripping on drugs, bathing, getting soaked), as well as interviews with the organisers and the reaction of locals. Wadleigh intended to depict the Festival as a contemporary version of The Canterbury Tales: a pilgrimage for hippies seeking communal expression of music and love. The film begins with images of the bucolic setting, symbolic of the ideal lifestyle that the Festival attempted to embody. In the early scenes the camera cuts between pastoral images and the building of the enormous concert stage, switching from ground-level angles to helicopter-eye views of events. The visual style derives from the editing work of Thelma Schoonmaker and a young Martin Scorsese (whose music documentary of The Band, The Last Waltz, 1978, shows the influence of Woodstock), particularly the liberal use of split screens that are deployed partly to incorporate extra footage, partly to emphasise the massive scale of the event, and partly to juxtapose images of the crowd, the musicians, and the construction of the stage.

Although individual performances stand out in the film—notably, those of Joan Baez, The Who, and Jimi Hendrix—the gathering of so many people suggests, as Sheila Whiteley argues, that the triumph of the Festival was to engender 'participation rather than passivity' in the audience. Given that there was not enough stock to film all the acts, Wadleigh was more interested in documenting antiwar and political songs than ballads. This political edge is most evident when Joan Baez calls for the release of the labor union organiser Joe Hill, with Country Joe McDonald singing the quintessential anti-Vietnam anthem 'I-Feel-Like-I'm-Fixin'-to-Die-Rag'. Three tracks from Jimi Hendrix's set ('Voodoo Chile', 'The Star Spangled Banner', and 'Purple Haze'), played at 6:30am on the Monday, close the film in electrifying fashion.

Although Woodstock is commonly seen as the apotheosis of the counterculture and peace movement, Wadleigh's film also hints at the commercial side of the Festival, as it provided a forum for the promoters and organisers to target the crowds as consumers. The Festival promoters, Joel Rosenman and John Roberts, make a case for the commercial integrity of the event in Young Men with Unlimited Capital, but the fact that the audience was vastly greater than expected meant that it was impossible to control tickets and many avoided paying. Wadleigh's film and the album were part of the $1,500,000 package that offset the $3,400,000 spent on or after the Festival (leaving only a loss of $100,000 a year on). Wadleigh's film does not detail these figures, but it does provide glimpses of the tensions between the free festival that Woodstock became and the economics of running the event. This commercial undercurrent affected many of the rock festivals in the late 1960s and early 1970s, particularly the three Isle of Wight Festivals held in August 1968, 1969, and 1970. The documentary Message to Love: The Isle of White Festival (Murray Lerner, 1995) conveys the almost complete organisational breakdown of the third Festival in 1970, revealing a discontented audience, many of whom refused to pay the entrance fee. Both documentaries offset the musical exuberance of the bands by exposing some of the logistical problems of running such massive-scale events, with muddy roads, congested campsites, lack of adequate facilities, and electrical problems hampering filming. Problems also surfaced in the production of Woodstock, most notably when the music producer David Geffen exerted control over the film, arguing that Wadleigh could not use the concert footage of Crosby, Stills & Nash unless he included their version of Joni Mitchell's 'Woodstock' as the closing song (a track inspired by the Festival).

MARTIN HALLIWELL

See also: Monterey Pop

Woodstock (US, Warner Bros, 1970, 216 mins). Distributed by Warner Bros. Produced by Bob Maurice. Directed by Michael Wadleigh. Cinematography by Michael Wadleigh, David Myers, Richard Pearce, Don Lenzer, and Al Wertheimer. Music by Joan Baez, Canned Heat, Joe Cocker & The Grease Band, Country Joe McDonald, Country Joe & The Fish, Crosby, Stills & Nash, Arlo Guthrie, Richie Havens, Jimi Hendrix, Jefferson Airplane, Janis Joplin, Santana, John Sebastian, Shanana, Sly & The Family Stone, Ten Years After, and The Who. Edited by Thelma Shoonmaker and Martin Scorsese. Sound directed by Larry Johnson. Filmed at White Lake, Bethel, New York, August 1969.

Further reading

Hinton, Brian, *Message to Love: The Isle of Wight Festival 1968–69–1970*, Chessington: Castle Communications, 1995.

Makower, Joel, *Woodstock: The Oral History*, New York: Doubleday, 1989.

Palmer, Robert, *Rock & Roll: An Unruly History*, New York: Harmony Books, 1995.

Rosenman, Joel, *Young Men with Unlimited Capital: The Story of Woodstock*, New York: Harcourt Brace Jovanovich, 1974 (reprinted Houston, TX: Scriveny Press, 1999).

Santelli, Robert, *Aquarius Rising: The Rock Festival Years*, New York: Dell, 1980.

Spitz, Robert Stephen, *Barefoot in Babylon: The Creation of the Woodstock Music Festival 1969*, New York: Viking, 1979.

Whiteley, Sheila, *Women and Popular Music: Sexuality, Identity and Subjectivity*, London: Routledge, 2000.

Young, Jean, *Woodstock Festival Remembered*, New York: Ballatine Books, 1979.

Workers Leaving the Lumière Factory and Other Lumière Shorts

(France, Lumière, 1895)

The technical contributions of the Lumière brothers, Auguste and Louis, to the development of the motion picture have received much-deserved recognition in most histories of the cinema. The reputation of the films they produced between 1895 and the turn of the century has fared less well. More than one commentator has dubbed them 'primitive cinema' in the most pejorative sense, devoid of any form, artistry, or purpose beyond that of recording movement. Their approach has been likened to that of today's rank amateur with a video camera, eager to record scenery, family life, and action but sadly deficient in terms of cinematic literacy, resulting in fifty-foot home movies running for a minute or less. Theirs, it is charged, was simply the recording of an unadjusted, unmodified reality. Thus it happened that these Frenchmen, with their images of daily life (*actualités*, or unbiased records of observation), unwittingly established that nonfictional genre of the cinema, the documentary, which may be some compensation for the alleged lack of structure in their considerable output.

This unflattering depiction of two artless, naïve pioneers requires revision. A useful starting point is their extraordinarily successful careers as owners of a photographic plate manufacturing business in Lyons, already well established by the time they encountered motion pictures. Like Thomas Alva Edison, they viewed their invention, the cinématographe, as a potentially profitable expansion of an existing enterprise. It is surely not accidental that two of their earliest public screenings, in June 1895, of Disembarcation of Congress Members at Neuville-sur-Saône/Arrivée des Congressistes à Neuville-sur-Saône, and of the eminent physicist, Pierre-Jules-César Janssen in Conversation, were presented within twenty-four hours of their creation, to the subjects of the film. This group was a technically knowledgeable audience of scientists and photographers whose interest, presumably, would be in the practical and financial possibilities of the new medium rather than in the entertainment value of the vaudeville turns of their competitor, Edison's Kinetoscope. In a sense, these *actualités* were publicity projects designed to flatter and impress potential customers with the capabilities of their camera-printer-projector. It is illuminating to note that this movie demonstration, in Lyons, and subsequently at the Brussels Exposition that same summer, was only part of the programme. The remainder was devoted to another of their commercial ventures, Autochromie, a colour photographic process, also designed to reproduce life more realistically. Obeying one of the most important tenets of business, they waited until they had shot a sufficient number of movie items to satisfy demand before staging their much-publicized exhibition in Paris on December 28. Significantly, it opened with what can be regarded as an industrial 'commercial' for their centre of production, Workers Leaving the Lumière Factory/Sortie d'usine. So many prints had to be made that the original negative wore out, necessitating the shooting of an identically staged version in 1896, the movie industry's first remake! The same business acumen is observable in their initial foray into Russia in May of that same year. The subject, Coronation of Tsar Nicholas II, was carefully chosen for its potential appeal to the tens of millions throughout his empire. Its success was not lost on the tsar himself, who ordered the appointment of two movie photographers to film future state occasions. Naturally they used equipment rented from the Lumières.

Of course entrepreneurial skill is not necessarily synonymous with artistic ability. It must be admitted that the sheer volume of titles produced in the first two years—in the many hundreds—include numerous examples of the 'unmediated representation of reality' charge levelled at them by critics. This was, perhaps, inevitable given that the Lumières had limited control over their scores of cameramen operating on four continents. Trains enter and leave stations with much of a sameness; what could be interchangeable crowds promenade around race courses from Melbourne to Madrid; and there are multiple episodes of cavalry galloping to and from the camera. That said, we may discern a definite pattern in those items that were the work of the brothers themselves. First, they conform to fundamental narrative conventions, with beginnings, middles, and conclusions. Second, their expertise as still photographers is diligently transferred to the new medium with due attention paid to compositional framing, balance, and perspective. Consider, again, Workers Leaving the Lumière Factory. The audience sits, as if in a live theatre facing a proscenium arch, the screen. As the film begins, the two factory doors are closed. Then, continuing the theatrical analogy, they swing open for the camera as if the curtain is being raised. Men and women stream out into the street. Unlike the conventioneers disembarking at Neuville sur Saône, who acknowledge Louis Lumière by smiling or doffing their hats to the camera, these workers are totally oblivious to its objectivity as they move out of range to the left and right, at the same time giving the scene its symmetry. Once all have exited, the left-hand door begins to swing shut. After all movement has stopped, the camera ceases operation signifying the end of the episode. Because it is rooted to the spot throughout, the opening and closing images are virtually identical to the extent that they could be spliced together and the entire incident shown in a never-ending loop.

This concern with beginnings and ends, features usually associated with the narrative mode, is observable in many of their very early works. Destruction of a Wall/Démolition d'un mur opens with a group of workmen contemplating the task at hand, after which one of them applies a winch to the free-standing edifice. While a second labourer delivers a series of blows to weaken the foundation, a third looks on, ready to assist him. The supervisor orders more pressure to be applied by the winch at which point the wall falls over. In a cloud of dust all three labourers begin to smash the debris into smaller pieces. There is a comprehensiveness in this 'how to' film that is surely at odds with its categorization as a formless vignette. Similarly, Carmaux: Bringing Out the Coke/Carmaux: défournage du coke is a step-by-step account of dealing with one component of iron production. A long slab of red-hot coke emerges from its oven and is set on by a worker wielding a hose of cold water. Others join him with long metal rods and proceed to prod at the mass to reduce it to useable chunks.

On the negative side, it must be admitted that the Lumières, at least in the earliest years, were prisoners of their own limited technique and technology. A camera that remained rigidly anchored, moving neither to the left nor right, and a magazine's capacity to hold, effectively, no more than one minute's running time of film, were singly or in combination responsible for certain shortcomings, not the least of which are inconclusive endings to a number of their films. Arrival of a Train at the Station/L'Arrivée d'un train en gare de La Ciotat, one of the works included in the Paris exhibition, opens with an angle shot of the platform and waiting passengers. An engine, pulling eleven carriages, steams into the foreground and comes to a stop as the doors open and a few people disembark. Those waiting prepare to board at which point the film comes to an end. Though we have been privileged to see one step in the process of passenger movement, it would have made for more satisfactory viewing had the process of embarkation been complete, but that would have entailed a running time at least half as long again. The limitation imposed by the amount of film in the camera is more dramatically illustrated in Boat Leaving the Harbour/Barque sortant du port. Two men row an open boat towards the open sea while a third sits in the stern. Their actions are observed from the edge of a breakwater by two women with small children. As the craft passes the jetty, one of the women acknowledges them. Both females then prepare for departure. At this point, a large wave hits the craft, turning it at right angles to its intended direction, and forces it dangerously near the breakwater. Filming ceases at this juncture, and so we are denied what might well have been a dramatic reaction by those spectators to the rowers' plight.

The lack of fluidity imposed by the Lumières' immobile camera is illustrated in what is probably their most famous work from this early period, The Gardener and the Bad Boy/L'Arroseur arrosé. A humorous anecdote, it contains the seeds of what was to become a staple of the silent screen for the next three decades: slapstick comedy. Again, careful symmetrical construction of the scene is observable in the opening frames where, left of centre, a gardener is busily watering a flowerbed. A boy enters from the right and steps on the hose located centre. The flow of water stops and the gardener, puzzled at what has happened, turns the nozzle towards his face to investigate. The boy then releases his foot and the water gushes out with so much force that it knocks the gardener's cap from his head. Enraged, he drops the hose and runs after the perpetrator. At this juncture both individuals disappear left of frame, and one wishes the camera would make a slight pan in their direction. Instead, the victim of the prank has to drag the boy into view before administering a spanking, after which the youngster exits right. The story ends as it had begun with the gardener returning to his watering chore. Despite the technical shortcoming, this film lends itself to reflection on at least two levels. It may be regarded as a simple morality tale: interfere with the work of a diligent labourer and one must pay the consequence, although the spectator can find enjoyment both in the naughty deed and in the miscreant's punishment. As a precursor of silent screen comedy, it embodies a number of classic elements. The participants are mere moving objects, lacking any character trait that might detract from enjoyment of the joke. The gardener is an innocent victim; the spanking he administers is a mild one, otherwise the audience would be uneasy; and, in the end, after comic disruption has upset the status quo, moral equilibrium is restored.

The films of the Lumière brothers constitute a milestone in the representation of the real. In the innumerable scenes of life on city streets that predominate in their catalogue listings, we are witnessing a mode of representation first made available in the picture postcard. That, in turn, was made possible with the appearance of high-speed emulsion, as distinct from the collodion wet-plate process. The latter had permitted the reproduction of static rural vistas, but the newer one enabled filmmakers to capture the fin-de-siècle urban landscape in all its unscripted, unpredictable hustle and bustle. The Lumières and their cameramen chose a framing to catch moments of reality, known in outline only, and filmed them without attempting to manipulate the subjects before their lens. The results, for all their shortcomings, fascinated audiences of the day, and have continued to do so for more than a century.

JAMES M. SKINNER

See also: Lumière Brothers, The

The Lumière catalogue lists more than two thousand entries made by the company between 1895 and 1904, when production ceased. These are accessible to the public only in compilation form. The most complete of these is The Lumière Brothers' First Films (1895–7), 1996, made in collaboration with the Institut and containing eighty-three titles, with narration by Bernard Tavernier. The Movies Begin: Volume II, The European Pioneers, produced by Kino Video and utilizing British Film Institute archival material contains examples personally directed by Louis Lumière. These include, La Sortie des usines/Exiting the Factory (1895), Démolition d'un mur/Demolition of a wall (1895), Querelle enfantine/Childish Quarrel (1895), Carmaux, défournage du coke/Carmaux: Drawing out the Coke (1896), and several examples of assistants' work in the US in 1896. Granada Television's Early Photography: Camera & Moving Pictures, Vol. 8, includes L'Arroseur arrosé/The Gardener and the Bad Boy (1895), Partie d'écarte/Card Game (1895), Barque sortant du port/Boat Leaving the Harbour (1895), Arrivée d'un train en gare de La Ciotat/Arrival of a Train at La Ciotat Station (1895), and films made abroad, including examples from Russia (Couronnement du Tsar/Crowning of Tsar Nicholas II, 1895), Switzerland (Cortège arabe/Arab Cortege, 1896), Australia and Egypt.

Further reading

Barsam, Richard M., *Non-Fiction Film: A Critical History*, Bloomington, IN: Indiana University Press, 1963.

Burch, Noel, *Life to these Shadows*, London: BFI, 1990.

Elsaesser, Thomas (ed.), *Early Cinema: Space-Frame-Narrative*, London: BFI, 1990.

Fell, John L. (ed.), *Film Before Griffith*, Berkeley, CA: University of California Press, 1983.

——*Film and the Narrative Tradition*, Berkeley, CA: University of California Press, 1986.

Mitry, Jean, *Histoire du cinema, art et industrie, 1895–1914*, T.1, Paris: Editions Universitaires, 1967.

North, Joseph H., *The Early Development of the Motion Picture, 1887–1900*, New York: Arno, 1973.

Pinèl, Vincent, 'Lumière: Anthologie du cinéma no. 78', Supplement to *L'avant-scène cinéma*, no. 147, May, 1974.

Sadoul, Georges, *Louis Lumière*, Paris: Seghers, 1964.

World at War, The

(UK, Thames Television, 1974–5)

The World at War is one of the most ambitious and comprehensive documentaries on World War II. It consists of a series of twenty-six episodes, each lasting almost one hour, produced by Jeremy Isaacs for Thames Television. The first episode, A New Germany, was broadcast on the BBC on October 31, 1973. Three years later six new episodes were added, for a total running time of almost thirty-two hours. Broadcast in many countries around the world, The World at War won several awards, including an International Emmy and the George Polk Memorial Award. It is regularly used as an educational aid in British secondary schools.

The team that produced the programme included fourteen writers and ten producers, with Dr Noble Frankland DFC as Chief Historical Adviser. The voice of the popular Sir Laurence Olivier provided continuity to the first twenty-six episodes. Work on the documentary began in 1971, with research carried out in the archives of many countries. The World at War presents excerpts from an array of original audiovisual materials, including newsreels, original raw rushes from war cameramen, filmed testimonies and interviews, propaganda films, photographs taken by soldiers on the battlefront, and fragments of radio transmissions, documentaries, songs, and music from the war years. The final result is a montage of thousands of images and clips, which convey the chronological progression of the events, as well as give an account of a multiplicity of points of view. Despite this sweeping kaleidoscope of materials, the documentary presents a strong narrative continuity, being divided into episodes that are coherent both in spatial and chronological terms. The World at War, which is clearly aimed at eliciting the empathy of the spectator, includes many testimonies that intertwine with and comment on the original documents. There is no academic commentary; much space is given instead to interviews, including with ordinary people, veterans, and survivors. Among the better-known interviewees are Karl Wolff (Himmler's adjutant); Traudi Junge (Hitler's secretary); John Colville (Parliamentary Private Secretary to Winston Churchill); and actor James Stewart, former USAAF bomber pilot.

The original twenty-six-episode series opens with A New Germany, dedicated to Hitler's rise to power in Germany; this is followed by twenty-four episodes that give an account of the involvement of the various countries in the war and analyse the most important battles. The last episode, Remember, is entirely devoted to the testimonies of survivors and to official celebrations and yearly gatherings of veterans. The structure of the programme is partly reminiscent of Frank Capra's series of films, Why We Fight.

The organization of each episode is similar: an analysis of the domestic political situation and of the foreign agenda of each country is followed by a study of the military tactics and of the reality of the war front. Attention is always devoted to the preparations for war, both in terms of the protection of civilians (construction of bunkers, distribution of gas masks) and in terms of the race to arms and to technological innovations in weaponry. The breaking of the war into the daily life of the various cities targeted by air raids is documented, as well as the international reactions to the bombings.

The various episodes are connected through the use of animation maps and of contemporary images of the sites of the great battles. Images of the two fronts alternate, in the attempt to recreate the battle step-by-step; the involvement of the spectator is encouraged by a series of questions and answers: What will be the right move? Why did the Maginot Line not hold? The advancements of the troops are recreated by a forward movement of the camera, conveying a subjective vision. Spectators are invited to be entirely involved in the flow of images and music; rarely are they informed about their sources. Olivier's persuasive voice is simultaneously the strong and the weak point of the documentary. Because it is easily recognizable, it functions as a real bond between the different episodes; on the other hand, the actor's at times subdued, at times emphatic tones seek to elicit the audience's emotional response, almost undervaluing the force of the images.

After the first few episodes, which follow a predominately chronological development ending with the entrance of the United States in the war, The World at War presents a series of episodes devoted to the great battles and to the crucial moments of the war. We travel to Africa with Desert—The War in North Africa; to Russia with Stalingrad and Red Star—The Soviet Union; to Italy for the march of the Allies with Tough Old Gut; and to Asia for the British defeat with It's a Lovely Day Tomorrow. Special episodes are devoted to the atomic catastrophe (The Bomb) and to the Holocaust (Genocide). Britain Alone is devoted to the situation in Great Britain after the capitulation of France and before the American intervention, to the heroic resistance to the Nazi air raids, to the preparation of the cities and coastal lines against the feared German landing. In line with documentary films such as Listen to Britain (Jennings, 1942), Britain Alone places emphasis on the characteristic British understatement and reserve: we see the population carrying out the normal working activities in a London destroyed by the bombs. Many of the episodes devoted to Britain, in fact, look like the products of the Crown Film Unit. The most spectacular and dramatic episode is doubtlessly Morning, devoted to the D-Day invasion. It presents a succession of sequences from the two fronts, in which the preparations of the German defence alternate with those for the American landing. We are shown the training of the American soldiers, the generals' speeches, the long preparations, and the departure for Normandy. The landing is shot with a subjective camera, and we are not spared the most gruesome images of the dead and injured on Omaha beach.

The six episodes added in 1976 (Secretary to Hitler, Who Won World War II?, Warrior, Hitler's Germany, The Two Deaths of Adolf Hitler, and The Final Solution—Auschwitz), are a sort of appendix to the documentary. They further examine some of the topics of the previous series, and in particular Nazism, the concentration camps, and the figure of Hitler. Hitler's Germany investigates the German history before the material covered by the first series, including the Weimar Republic and the ascent of Hitler to power. The last six episodes are no longer narrated by Sir Laurence Olivier, but by Eric Porter. Among the new episodes, Warrior is an examination of the memories of veterans of all factions focusing on their traumas and problems, somehow suggesting the communal destiny of all the fighters of World War II.

STEFANO BASCHIERA

The World at War (UK, Thames Television, 1973–6, almost 32 hours). Distributed by Thames Television. Series Producer: Jeremy Isaacs. Unit Production Manager: Liz Sutherland. Writers: Laurence Thompson, Peter Batty, Jerome Kuehl, J.P.W. Mallalieu, Neal Ascherson, Charles Douglas-Home, David Wheeler, John Williams, Angus Calder, Charles Bloomberg, Stuart Hood, Courtney Browne, David Elstein, and Jeremy Isaacs. Producers: David Elstein, Peter Batty, Ted Childs, Martin Smith, Ben Shephard, John Pett, Phillip Whitehead, Michael Darlow, Hugh Raggett, and Jermome Kuehl. Chief Historical Adviser: Dr Noble Frankland DFC. Music: Carl Davis. Narrated by Sir Laurence Olivier and Eric Porter.

World in Action, The

(Canada, National Film Board, 1942–6)

Shortly after it was founded, and with the outbreak of World War II, the National Film Board (NFB) of Canada began two monthly theatrical series of twenty-minute news magazines modeled on the highly successful American The March of Time. The first was Canada Carries On, intended to depict Canada's part in the war to its own people and to others. It was produced by Stuart Legg, veteran British documentarian whom John Grierson, head of the NFB, had brought over to assist in the work of the new institution. Once the first series was underway (the first issue was in April 1940), Legg began to develop the second, The World in Action (WIA), which became his project. With some exceptions he wrote and directed every issue. United Artists distributed the series.

This is Blitz (January 1942) was the first of the WIA. It used captured newsreel footage to reveal the devastation that German aggression had caused. The second part dealt with Allied counter-strategy. Many of the issues concerned noncombative but important wartime topics. Its treatment of economic/social/political issues became one of its special distinctions. Food—Weapon of Conquest (March 1942) was the second WIA release. *Time* magazine called it 'a blueprint of how to make an involved, dull, major aspect of World War II understandable and acceptable to moviegoers'. Inside Fighting Russia (April 1942) was composed mostly of footage obtained from the Soviets. As the Russians tended to be secretive, this represented quite a coup. War for Men's Minds (June 1943) concerned psychological warfare. The most ambitious and intellectual of the WIA films, it was also the first of the Canadian films to look ahead to peace.

The two series were noteworthy for their departures from usual wartime propaganda strategy: they contain little hatred or violence. There are two recurrent emphases: one is that we Canadians are doing our part (in a distinctive Canadian way); the other is that Canada is an important part of the world. These themes would seem to follow from Canada's uncertainty about its national character and its sense of geographical isolation, from its newness as a nation and lack of recognition as a world power. The divisive issue of differences between French-speaking Canada (which did not fully support the war) and English-speaking Canada (which did) was avoided.

The World in Action emphasis shifted from matters of immediate wartime concerns to those that would concern the postwar world. The international view and steady look ahead to peace were quite exceptional during wartime. Examples of internationalism would be Labour Front (October 1943) and especially Global Air Routes (April 1944). Grierson took satisfaction in turning the globe upside down, as he put it, in the NFB films: putting Canada at the center rather than the periphery of the world. When Asia Speaks (June 1944) was so accurate and farseeing in its analysis that it was still in active nontheatrical distribution long after the war. Now—The Peace (May 1945) dealt with the new United Nations organization.

If Canada Carries On paid The March of Time the compliment of imitation, The World in Action began to compete with it in the world market, including the United States. By the end of the war WIA was reaching a monthly audience of thirty million in twenty-one countries. Although Canada Carries On lasted until April 1951 (the same year The March of Time ended), however, The World in Action appeared only irregularly after 1946. One can assume that at least part of the reason for this was because Grierson and Legg had left Canada. It remains a memorable achievement in the history of the National Film Board.

JACK C. ELLIS

See also: Grierson, John; Legg, Stuart; Canada

The World in Action (Canada, National Film Board, 1942–46, 20 mins each monthly issue). Distributed by United Artists. Written, produced, and directed by Stuart Legg. Usual collaborators: assistant editor Tom Daly; music composed by Lucio Agostini; commentary read by Lorne Greene; animated maps by Evelyn Lambart.

Further reading

Ellis, Jack C., *John Grierson: Life, Contributions, Influence*, Carbondale, IL: Southern Illinois University Press, 2000.

Evans, Gary, *John Grierson and the National Film Board: The Politics of Wartime Propaganda*, Toronto: University of Toronto Press, 1984.

The John Grierson Project, McGill University, *John Grierson and the NFB*, Toronto: ECW Press, 1984.

Hardy, Forsyth, *John Grierson: A Documentary Biography*, London: Faber & Faber, 1979.

Jones, D.B., *Movies and Memoranda: An Interpretive History of the National Film Board of Canada*, Ottawa: Canadian Film Institute and Deneau Publishers, 1981.

McKay, Marjorie, *History of the National Film Board of Canada*, Montreal: National Film Board, 1964.

Nelson, Joyce, *The Colonized Eye: Rethinking the Grierson Legend*, Toronto: Between the Lines, 1988.

Wright, Basil

Basil Wright developed an interest in film aesthetics and made some student films at Cambridge. He became the first young filmmaker inducted into the British documentary film movement by its founder, his lifelong mentor, John Grierson. Wright joined the movement shortly after being hugely impressed by the famous November 1929 London Film Society double bill of Drifters (John Grierson, 1929), and Battleship Potemkin (Sergei Eisenstein, USSR, 1926). Wright's landmark achievement, The Song of Ceylon (1934), demonstrated that the movement was capable of producing outstanding work. It established Wright as a noted documentary filmmaker but has somewhat overshadowed his other films and his contributions as a producer, writer, and conscientious documentary activist.

Wright was the first British documentary movement filmmaker to have the adjective 'poetic' applied to his work. He was accompanied during the shooting of his first full-fledged directorial assignment, The Country Comes to Town (1931), by Robert Flaherty, renowned director of Nanook of the North (1922). Wright credited Flaherty with showing him how to immerse himself in the environment being filmed, and with making him aware of the value of recording serendipitous events. Flaherty also demonstrated how to frame shots with sensitivity and, through careful observation, anticipate subjects' movements. Wright returned the favour by contributing strong material to Industrial Britain (Robert Flaherty, 1931), an important early documentary produced in the collaborative manner typical of the movement during this period (Calder-Marshall 1963). Later, Wright played a key role in the similarly collaborative Night Mail (1936).

Wright consolidated his personal style and attracted serious critical attention with the direction of Liner Cruising South (1933), Cargo from Jamaica (1933), and Windmill in Barbados (1933–4), filmed en route to and in the Caribbean. Far removed from the other documentary movement filmmakers, he exercised considerable autonomy shooting these films. Grierson encouraged the maturation of Wright's individual poetic talent, offering creative input and imposing control during postproduction. Wright's modest trilogy, characterized by graceful camera pans, an eye for human and natural beauty, and a slightly elliptical tone, was praised by modernist critics writing for the influential journals *Close-Up* and *Film Art*, as well as by Grierson (Stollery 2000). The consequences for film art of the coming of sound was a live issue at this time. Alberto Cavalcanti's collaboration with Wright as Windmill in Barbados' 'sound supervisor' presaged their more extensive experimental work on The Song of Ceylon.

After Wright's early years at the Empire Marketing Board (EMB) and the General Post Office (GPO) Film Unit the documentary movement diversified. He moved into more senior roles as an organizer and producer, founding the Realist Film Unit and working with Grierson at Film Centre to supply documentaries for a range of sponsors. Wright directed Children at School (1937), on good and bad practices and conditions in state education. This was part of the series of documentaries, including Housing Problems (Edgar Anstey and Arthur Elton, 1935), commissioned to promote the gas industry while simultaneously addressing social problems. The Face of Scotland (1938) reunited Wright with The Song of Ceylon's composer, Walter Leigh, and displayed some similarities to their earlier collaboration.

Wright's wartime commissions for the Ministry of Information (MOI) provided less scope for innovation. Harry Watt continued experimenting with narrativised forms of documentary in films such as Target for Tonight (1941), before directing features at Ealing, but Wright remained faithful to a more purist conception of the aesthetic and social role of documentary. However, it was Humphrey Jennings and Stewart McAllister, for example in Listen to Britain (1942), who advanced the development of poetic documentary during World War II. As a senior figure, Wright's major contribution was advisory and supervisory. He worked intermittently with Grierson in Canada, then in 1945 briefly took over as producer in charge of the Crown Film Unit.

An underexplored dimension of Wright's work is its representations of the world beyond Britain. Internationalism was a central preoccupation of Grierson's that Wright revisited in a number of different contexts. Some of Wright's earliest published writing criticized conventional travelogues, a genre he sought to elevate through modernist aesthetics in his Caribbean films and in The Song of Ceylon (Low 1979). Wright's films differed from other British documentary movement Empire films, such as Contact (Paul Rotha, 1933), which tended to celebrate modernisation, Western technology, and progress. Wright's early Empire films take a more individualistic approach. They romanticize non-Western cultures as appealing yet tantalisingly inaccessible repositories of sensuality and traditional wisdom (Stollery 2000).

In the 1930s liberal internationalism overlapped with enlightened imperialism; different emphases arose from different combinations of collaborators and sponsors. Modern Orphans of the Storm (Basil Wright and Ian Dalrymple, 1937), was a campaign film responding immediately to the plight of child refugees displaced by the Spanish civil war. Men of Africa (Alex Shaw, 1940), written and produced by Wright for the Colonial Office, can be seen as a hybrid between orthodox British documentary perspectives on Empire and Wright's more Romantic view of native cultures. It lauds the benevolence of British rule in East Africa, representing apparently progressive developments in various fields of endeavour, but also celebrates the vibrant sights and sounds of African cultures.

After the war an optimistic, progressive internationalism prevailed within the documentary movement, and Wright began working with Grierson for the United Nations Educational, Scientific and Cultural Organization (UNESCO). Along with others in the movement, Wright argued, for example in his 1947 essay 'Documentary Today', that documentary production must arrive at a new equilibrium between national and international concerns (Aitken 1998). World Without End (Basil Wright, Paul Rotha, 1953) integrates Wright's delicately poetic approach with the urgent internationalism of The World is Rich (1947), Rotha's earlier film about world food. In World Without End material shot by Wright in Thailand is intercut with material shot by Rotha in Mexico, outlining the need for global solutions to global problems.

Grierson's status as British documentary's leading proponent, with Rotha a close second, has led to Wright's publications being overlooked. Yet in a quieter way he, too, was constantly active as a proselytizer for the movement, writing for all the documentary movement journals and becoming *The Spectator*'s film critic in 1938. In 1936, when the movement's diversification required a new London-based publication to keep its various constituents and sponsors in touch with each other, Wright's family's money helped to establish *World Film News* (Low 1997). Later in his career he wrote books and began teaching. Wright's most illuminating reflections occur in articles or interviews where he discusses his individual creative processes, his collaborations, and specific technicalities of filmmaking. In this respect he is the most intimate of the early British documentary theorist-practitioners. He lived in an era and belonged to a tradition, however, that precluded any public recognition of the gay sensibility informing some of his more poetic, personal work.

MARTIN STOLLERY

See also: Night Mail; Song of Ceylon, The

Biography

Born London, June 12, 1907. Graduated Corpus Christi College, Cambridge, reading classics and economics in 1929. Met John Grierson and joined Empire Marketing Board (EMB) Film Unit in 1930, directed first film 1931. Directed his most acclaimed film, The Song of Ceylon, 1934–5. Moved with the film unit to the General Post Office (GPO) in 1934. Moved into producing, cofounded the Realist Film Unit and joined Grierson at Film Centre 1937. Made films for the Ministry of Information during World War II and advised Grierson on National Film Board policy in Canada. Appointed producer in charge of the Crown Film Unit 1945. Worked at UNESCO with Grierson and Julian Huxley in the immediate postwar period. Lectured on filmmaking at the University of California in the 1960s. Published a critical history of film, *The Long View*, 1974. Died October 14, 1987, in London.

Further reading

Aitken, Ian, *The Documentary Film Movement: An Anthology*, Edinburgh: Edinburgh University Press, 1998.

Calder-Marshall, Arthur, *The Innocent Eye: The Life of Robert J. Flaherty*, London: W.H. Allen, 1963.

Hardy, Forsyth H. (ed.), *Grierson on Documentary*, London: Faber, 1946.

——*John Grierson: A Documentary Biography*, London: Faber, 1979.

Low, Rachael, *Films of Comment and Persuasion of the 1930s*, London: George Allen & Unwin, 1979.

——*Documentary and Educational Films of the 1930s*, London: Routledge, 1997.

Stollery, Martin, *Alternative Empires: European Modernist Cinemas and Cultures of Imperialism*, Exeter: University of Exeter Press, 2000.

Sussex, Elizabeth, *The Rise and Fall of British Documentary*, Berkeley, CA: University of California Press, 1975.

Swann, Paul, *The British Documentary Film Movement 1926–46*, Cambridge: Cambridge University Press, 1989.

Wright, Basil, *Use of the Film*, London: Bodley Head, 1948.

——*The Long View*, London: Secker & Warburg, 1974.

Y

Yugoslavia (former)

The first documentary films in the territory of the former Yugoslavia were made by Dr Karel Grossman in Slovenia (1903), and by Milton Manaki who was filming local rituals and folk dances of Macedonia (1905). The Arrival of the Sultan Reshad the Fifth in Solun and Bitolj was one of the first important documentaries by Manaki, an amazing film enthusiast after whom, during the 1990s, the Camera Film Festival in Bitola was named. Another man holding a special place in history is the Croat Josip Karaman for using film media to express his patriotic feelings, employing the Croatian language instead of Italian, which was predominant at that time in Dalmatia (1910).

During the time of the Kingdom of Yugoslavia, between the two World Wars, documentary production was very lively. In Croatia the School of National Health made popular and scientific films, and The State Film Centre in Belgrade managed production and distribution for the whole country. World War II made the country unable to indulge in film activities, except for Croatia, where under the occupation of Nazi Germany, the puppet nationalistic regime NDH (Independent State of Croatia) erected the Film Company Hrvatski Slikopis. Besides the militant propaganda films, NDH produced romantic, patriotic documentaries that emphasised 'national values'. At the same time a partisan resistance movement, led by the Communist Party, became aware of the importance and power of moving images. The committee decided to register on-camera some of the important war battles and, in 1943 the first film team was formed.

More importance was accorded to film the next year, when Marshall Tito, the leader of the Communist resistance, ordained the founding of The Film Association as a part of the National Liberation Struggle. Two years later, when the war was over, the Federal Republic of Yugoslavia started its first National Film Committee. Cinema was considered to be a powerful means of mass propaganda. Film became a 'must' in a new society that was enthusiastically creating 'people's culture' and had also to deal with illiteracy. The very first films were documentaries that reflected on the tragedy of the war that had just ended. Films like Jasenovac by Gustav Gavrin and Kosta Hlavaty, on the horror of the biggest concentration camp in Yugoslavia, or Belgrade by Nikola Popovic, Steps of Freedom by Rados Novakovic, and Istra by Branko Marjanovic, were all made in 1945, the year of the liberation.

The first two postwar years were a period of documentary making that acted as film education, which officially did not exist at the time. A huge number of filmmakers entered the business either by order or by recommendation of the Communist Party; they schooled themselves through practice. Later, many of them went into feature fiction production (Marjanovic, Popovic, Novakovic).

The newsreel monthlies Filmski Mjesecnik were the first regular documentaries produced by the state in socialist Yugoslavia. They captured the relevant issues regarding spreading Communist political doctrine, enthusiasm for rebuilding the country, agrarian reforms, and important political and cultural events. They were screened on a regular basis in cinemas before feature films were shows. At first, after World War II, cinema production and distribution from Slovenia to Macedonia were managed by The State Film Company of Yugoslavia (Drzavno Filmsko Poduzece Jugoslavije), but soon thereafter, according to the governments' intentions to decentralise film production, new companies came into being in each republic and autonomous territory. Some of them specialised in producing documentaries and shorts (Dunav film, Zastava, Bosna, Duga, Kinoteka 16, Zagreb, Studio film).

Because films were produced, distributed, and owned by the state, censorship was an obligatory aspect of the film business. Nevertheless, it was far less rigid than in other countries of Eastern Europe. A certain degree of freedom regarding the choice of the film theme, and especially regarding the style, was always present. The authors were exposed to cinema from the West, and some of them followed new trends such as cinéma vérité and direct film styles. The filmmakers travelled with their works to Western and Eastern European festivals and were in touch with new cultural movements.

After making 'politically correct' films in the 1950s that glorified the revolutionary struggle and the working class and denouncing the bourgeoisie, most of the filmmakers switched in the 1960s to visually strong and poetic documentary miniatures or analytical essays that were critical of society. Most of these short pieces were visually powerful and verbally ascetic, fitting perfectly in regular screenings as a prefilm in the theatres. No wonder Yugoslavian spectators held the documentary genre in high esteem.

A remarkable opus was created by filmmakers Rudolf Sremec, Krsto Skanata, Stjepan Zaninovic, and Zika Ristic. The cinematic approach of Croatian director Sremec was characterised by a 'friendly' camera style. With his almost one hundred films, he showed an enormous ability to penetrate invisibly into the lives of the people he filmed. His moving documentary Time of Silence/Vrijeme sutnje (1971) unveiled the shocking custom in a Slavonian village of 'storing' old people in houses on the edge of the forest and leaving them alone to die. This devoted documentary maker was known abroad for his People on Wheels/Ljudi na tockovima (1963), in which he vividly portrayed people who travel every day from the rural area to the cities for work. Krsto Skanata and Stjepan Zaninovic marked the early documentary production in Serbia and became known by challenging the themes that concerned the consequences of World War II. Krsto Skanata approached his subjects in the style of direct cinema. He tried to follow the path of the truth and make films that would reveal the essence of the problem. At the same time, he was smart enough to nuance his approach in such a way that censors would accept and approve the film. One of his first films, In the Shadow of Magic/U senci magije (1955), uncovers the deep backwardness in socialist Yugoslavia. His film First Case—a Man/Prvi padez—covek (1964) addresses the human dignity of a miner who loses his arm and has to struggle on his own. Soldier, At Ease!/Ratnice, voljno! (1966) focuses on the tragedy of a soldier who fought in the war and believed in a certain ideology that he later realised was false. Skanata's style was straightforward and analytical. Stylistically, the films were often made in a traditional manner. His reputation allowed him to challenge all sort of subjects, those that were pro-regime as well as those that questioned the justice of it. The films Terrorists/Teroristi (1970) and 12 Months of Winter/12 Meseci zime (released 1983, shot 1971) were banned from public screening in certain parts of Yugoslavia and only released later on.

Another author who dealt with revolution and the indebtedness of those who survived toward those who fell for freedom is Sjepan Zaninovic. His first big success was the film Messages/Poruke (1960), which revived the ideals of people who inscribed graffiti on the walls of the war prisons during World War II. His film The Dialogue of Comrades on a War Photo/Dijalog drugova sa ratnog fotosa (1968) portrayed the destinies of freedom fighters and of those who disappeared after the war in the post-revolutionary madness. Zika Ristic from Bosnia and Herzegovina produced remarkable documentaries both in quantity and quality. The best ones are The Barge-Steerers of the Drina/Splavari na Drini (1951), an exciting ode to humanity's struggle against nature; Yet—a City/Ipak jedan grad (1966), a satirical commentary on bureaucracy; and Helmets/Sljemovi (1967), an engaged essay on war and peace. In the embrace of Bosna Film, later on Sutjeska, many documentary enthusiasts gathered in Sarajevo and created dozens of inspiring films.

In Croatia, a director who introduced a new approach in treating small, everyday subjects was Kreso Golik. His film From 3 to 22/Od 3 do 22 (1966) follows a working mother through her exhausting daily activities. Through the destiny of an individual, Golik portrays the socialist society in many of its dark shades. This sharp and visually strong documentary is even today one of the most powerful ever made in Yugoslavia.

A director from the younger generation, Krsto Papic mastered portraying the mentality of the tough people from the robust area of Herzegovina. When My Knife Strikes You/Kad te moja cakija ubode (1968) deals powerfully with murderers who confess their crimes which were often triggered for trivial reasons. Following the cinéma vérité style, Papic treats every issue quite critically, giving a profound analysis of the social milieu. Special Trains/Specijalni vlakovi (1972) is a socially and politically engaged film that observes the consequences of the huge workers' emigration that took place in Yugoslavia during the 1960s and 1970s, when hundreds of thousands of people went to work in West Germany.

One of the most profound documentary makers in Croatia is Petar Krelja, who devoted his whole opus to people on the margins of society, uncovering the daily lives of those who seem to be merely a statistic in social research (see the entry for Petar Krelja).

During the movement in the early 1970s known as the Croatian Spring, a short period of liberalisation, Krelja dared to make some documentaries that went beyond the Communist Party norms, and three of his films were banned. This was the time of national 'awakening', with attempts to political and cultural decentralisation toward the different Republics of Yugoslavia. It was the struggle for a more liberal socialism—'socialism with a human face'.

As a reaction to these tendencies, the existing political establishment forbade many filmmakers from continuing with their projects. President Tito reacted severely, and many film authors had a hard time returning to their previous positions.

The Serbian director Želimir Žilnik suffered a similar fate. His June Turmoil/Lipanjaska gibanja (1969), which depicted student demonstrations, was banned. Žilnik, who took an active part in a cultural movement in fiction film called Black Wave, was considered by the authorities as a dangerous, provocative political rebel, and many of his films were banned; however, he was highly appreciated for his directness and visually expressive film language by the film critics at home and abroad. The film The Unemployed/Nezaposleni ljudi (1968) received the Grand Prix at the Oberhausen Festival but was criticised at home on ideological grounds, along with Freedom or Cartoons/Sloboda ili strip (1972), which was banned.

At the same time, a younger generation of filmmakers became influenced by film trends in the West and became more intrigued by film aesthetics than political issues. Zoran Tadic made sophisticated documentaries about human solitude. His films Last Post Station Donji Dolac/Zadnja posta Donji Dolac (1971), Friends/Druge (1972), Plaits/Pletenice (1974), and Festivity/Dernek (1975) were made with an ascetic constraint and minimalism, but emphasised the intimacy of the human stories. His profoundly composed visual miniatures were odes to the values of a simple lifestyle.

Nikola Babic became known for his visually powerful analysis of human nature. His films Sije (1970), Vox Populi (1970), Bino, Seagull's Eye/Bino, oko galebovo (1973) were cinematically intriguing studies of people's mentalities.

Meanwhile, in Serbia, apart from Skanata, Zaninovic, J. Zivanovic, and M. Strbac, a group of film enthusiasts gathered around Dunav Film and started to make more exciting and fresher documentaries. Italian film critics in 1966 named the style of the new authors Sarajevo's Documentary Film School. Most of these directors later went into fiction film, but at that time Aleksandar Petrovic, Purisa Djordjevic, Dusan Makavajev, and later Petar Lalovic and Aleksandar Ilic introduced a contemplative, philosophical, and cinematically thrilling approach in treating reality. Filmmakers tried to avoid the traditional narrative structure and followed an unconventional way of storytelling, characterised by poetic, rather surrealist inputs. Some of them, such as Makavejev, were able to perform intriguing twists in treating politically and socially sensitive issues. The Parade/Parada (1962) portrays one of the socialist-populist marches with humour and hidden sarcasm.

Two directors who gained a special place in the documentary scene are Vlatko Gilic and Zivko Nikolic. Both were born in Montenegro, lived in Belgrade and were often concerned with aspects of life in their home country such as rigid traditionalism, suppression of women, and the tough life in the hilly, deserted areas. What made their work special was a strong personal imprint in crossing borders of film genres and mixing the real and surreal. Their contemplative films, characterised by specific moods and atmospheres, were transforming the documentary starting point at a metaphorical level.

In Gilic's film In continuo (1971), the focus is on a slaughterhouse, transmitting the metaphor of human destiny toward killing and bloodshed. In his Love/Ljubav (1973), there is an ordinary meeting of a wife and husband during a lunch break that gets elevated to an ode to pure love. During the 1980s Zivko Nikolic was even more radical in breaking the conventions of fiction and documentary. He would recreate a whole mysterious world out of a small documentary element. With few words and a minimalist soundtrack, Nikolic's visuals, carefully created in many layers, invoke a philosophical discourse on life. Ane (1980) portrays the world of a woman who is patiently waiting for her husband, a sailor. The Builder/Graditelj (1980) speaks of a man who builds houses for others but does not have one himself. Marko Perov (1975) creates the world of an old dying man who observes life around him. A Stamp/Biljeg (1981) is a powerful, ironic work on the society in which a hydrocentre is erected in an area where there is no water.

In Macedonia the most remarkable documentary maker was Stole Popov, whose films Australia, Australia (1976) and Dae (1979) spoke eloquently about the pain and nostalgia of Macedonians abroad and of the Gypsy minority at home, respectively. In Slovenia, the most intriguing author was Dusan Povh, whose film Three Monuments/Trije spomeniki (1958) evokes poetical memories of World War II. Milan Ljubic, Filip Robar Dorin, and Frantisek Cap also made films that merged political and social ideas.

The years after the death of President Tito (1980) brought a certain degree of disobedience and rebellion. Some political issues were more directly addressed; others, not being previously touched at all, were now courageously depicted. Zaninovic stirred the public with the documentary The Case of Dr Milos Zanko/Slucaj dr Milosa Zanka (1987), in which he anticipated the decay of Yugoslavia. Some politically radical directors appeared again on the documentary scene, such as Želimir Žilnik, Lordan Zafranovic, Joca Jovanovic, Petar Ljubojev, and, from the younger generation, Nikola Lorencin, Nenad Puhovski, Selamu Taraku, Mirjana Zoranovic, Želimir Gvardiol, Miroslav Mandic, Vuk Janic, Vladimir Perovic, Momir Matovic, and Milan Knezevic. Their films dealt with social and political changes, emigration, injustice, and people's dissatisfaction.

In 1991 and 1992 peaking conflicts led to war and the final split of Yugoslavia into five independent states. Although the cinema industry was heavily hit both by the transitional structural socioeconomic processes and by poverty caused by war, documentary filmmaking was still alive and very vivid. Each of the new states focused on making documentaries in favour of their national policy, justifying the deeds of military and political authorities. Alongside more or less hidden propaganda films made during the period of war (1991–5) and the time of transitional crises (1991–9), some valuable documentary pieces were also created.

Because with the fall of the country only Serbia and Montenegro retained the name Yugoslavia, the following sections do not concern the independent states of Croatia, Slovenia, Bosnia and Herzegovina, and Macedonia, but only documentary production in the new Yugoslavia.

In Serbia, production was mostly television-orientated, with many attempts by small producers to create relevant works. Dozens of new companies appeared, but only a few made an impact and survived. One of the most ambitious is Film Focus, led by Miroslav Bata Petrovic, who made interesting, often humorous comments on the turbulent reality, as well as giving others a chance to make these kinds of films. The independent media group B 92, besides radio and television production, indulged itself in the production of meaningful documentaries. Belgrade Follies (1997), directed by feature film director Goran Markovic, is a shocking and disturbing documentary about people's anger towards Milošević's regime. His next feature-length autobiographical documentary, Serbia, Year Zero/Srbija, godine nulte (2001) is a rather moving self-analysis of the responsibility of those who witnessed the tragedy of Yugoslavia, made in a personal and quite humorous style. Goran Radovanovic is one of the Belgrade-based authors who found support abroad and managed to make several daring and intriguing films. Both My Country—For Internal Use Only/Moja domovina—za unutrasnju upotrebu (2000) and Otpor! The Fight to Save Serbia/Otpor! Borba za opstanak Srbije (2001) were critical of the regime of that time. His last feature-length documentary, Casting! (2003), speaks of the devaluation of moral values among youngsters in today's Serbia.

In Montenegro, one of the rare directors who continued from the 1980s onwards is Momir Matovic. He stayed faithful to his personal, special style of nonnarrative, nonverbal documentary impressions of life. The Last Cinema Screening/Posljednja bioskopska predstava (1993) portrays a cinema freak who walks dozens of kilometres every day to go to the cinema. The String of Life/Zica zivota (1996) depicts the sober, ascetic lifestyle of villagers far from civilisation. Similar in approach is another Montenegro-born director working in Serbia, Vladimir Perovic, who often, like Matovic, expresses political criticism in a hidden way. His films The Guard/Cuvar (2002) and Vanishing/Nestajanje (2003) are made without words. They focus on people who lead lonely lives in an absurd society, guarding a factory that does not work or going to a school that has only one student.

After the fall of the former Yugoslavia, the five new states that used to logistically depend upon each other before the war had to learn how to survive on their own in the film world. The political conflict created an atmosphere of noncollaboration and hostility which only started to diminish in around 2000. Economical crises in all of the new states caused a lack of money for independent productions, and the possible solution lies in cooperation with Western European funds, as well as in the reconstruction of the previous cultural liaisons between the different states of the former Yugoslavia.

RADA SESIC

Yugoslavia: Death of a Nation

(UK, MacQueen and Mitchell, 1995)

More than 200 documentaries have been made on the topic of Yugoslavia's break-up in the 1990s. Among those, Yugoslavia: Death of a Nation (1995) remains probably the best known, commonly perceived as a film in which 'the facts are allowed to speak for themselves, and responsibilities are made clear' (Cohen 1995).

The international television coproduction was realised by the London-based Brian Lapping Associates, a production company specialising in current affairs, including documentaries on the Falklands War, the Gulf War, South Africa, as well as the acclaimed series on the end of the Soviet Union, The Second Russian Revolution (1992). Producer Norma Percy has to her credit a number of documentaries dealing with controversy and conflict, ranging from the US Watergate scandal to the Israeli–Arab troubles, and including works on Algeria, China, and Northern Ireland.

Death of a Nation was completed in 1995 and broadcast in the United Kingdom and Europe in the autumn (after the Srebrenica massacre had taken place) and in the United States (Discovery Channel) during Christmas week. It also played in the former Yugoslav republics. An accompanying book, by journalists Laura Silber (who had acted as a consultant) and Allan Little, was also published, to make for a complete study pack. Lesson plans, containing clips from the film and excerpts from the book, are available on study websites supported by *The Guardian* newspaper and the Discovery Channel.

The film tells the story through well-selected footage and features numerous interviews with various parties in the conflict. It follows a chronological approach, tackling the crisis by beginning with the early Kosovo troubles, and structuring the story around the 1987 rise of Milošević to political leadership. From this narrative point of view, it then gives accounts on the break-up of Slovenia, Croatia, and Bosnia. In five hour-long segments (The Cracks Appear, Descent into War, The Collapse of Unity, The Gates of Hell and No Escape), it attempts to present a systematic account of the reasons and responsibilities for the country's violent break-up. It makes use of a large variety of documentary sources and features interviews with most of the main Yugoslav players. Even though issues of Western involvement in the conflict are not addressed explicitly, a number of Western diplomats are also interviewed. The result is a convincing account of the claims, misunderstandings, and reactions of the main actors, presented within an absorbing narrative revealing how the recent tensions mounted. Although historians questioned some of the choices, the overall recognition was that the book and the documentary had granted to all sides the opportunity to speak, thus making the bias negligible and remaining an 'accessible guide to the immediate causes and the detailed course of the wars' (Stokes, Lampe and Rusinow 1996: 147).

Norma Percy has stated that, above all, she is interested in 'how big decisions are made'.

A leading principle in her approach is to stress the role that individuals play in the story by securing interviews with key players, aiming to have them experience a 'catharsis on camera'. 'Things are generally dictated by a few people or one man', she said, '[s]o we try to speak to everyone involved, which is a very good research technique, in that you check statements against each other' (quoted in Cohen 1995). During the preproduction period, a series of informal interviews were carried out, allowing identification of the major themes that were also to be researched. Later, the filmmakers returned for filmed interviews, during which the same question was often put to the interviewees, particularly to those who were known to have been involved in a key situation. For example, both Milošević and Tudjman were questioned about their alleged 1991 meeting over the division of Bosnia between Serbia and Croatia, both presenting twisted and evasive accounts.

Background researchers looked through hundreds of hours of archival material. Michael Simkin's discovery of a forgotten reportage showing Milošević's notorious visit to Kosovo in 1987 became one of the best-known images related to Yugoslavia's break-up. A wealth of videotaped events was made available to the filmmakers in all republics (for example, unused footage of atrocities in the town of Zvornik by Arkan's paramilitary Tigers, was found in Reuters' Belgrade office). According to director Paul Mitchell, the warring parties filmed most events 'because they believed they would thus be able to show who had allowed Yugoslavia to be destroyed' (quoted in Cohen 1995).

The film enjoyed wide international acclaim. However, it also became the subject of criticism, raising questions of a wider theoretical nature regarding the function of documentary film as historical record.

Talking of the film, political scientist Susan Woodward (1997) identified three problematic consequences of what she described as 'journalistic dominance' and its 'insidious influence for historical scholarship': first, the leading 'role of narrative in shaping perceptions of the war'; second, 'the ahistorical character of these narratives that, ironically, seem almost obsessed with identifying these conflicts as historical'; and third, the use of a 'personalized "source" as primary evidence'. In Death of a Nation, she noted, facts that did not fit the narrative had been frequently ignored, and similar events had been recorded with different sympathies in different parts of the country. These seemingly minor inaccuracies, Woodward argued, were accountable for the most serious troubles. She criticized the film for taking nationalism out of its concrete politicoeconomic context, for misunderstanding and misreporting the blank-labelled 'Titoist period' and its immediate aftermath, and for selectively paying attention to nationalist tendencies and outcomes. The causes of nationalism, she claimed, could never be correctly identified if they were only explained by referencing incidents of 'rising nationalism' (as seen in the use of Milošević's visit to Kosovo as a key historical event taken out of socioeconomic context). While putting together an absorbing narrative, the filmmakers had failed to trace the roots of nationalism in the changes of domestic economic powers of the republics, in the controversial policies of the International Monetary Fund, and in the adverse impact that economic reforms had on employment and redistribution during the 1980s. Leaving those issues out meant that the film failed to identify the real factors behind the rise of nationalism, Woodward insisted.

As a current affairs documentary, Death of a Nation inevitably catered to the explanatory needs of the day. It explained the violence by referencing to select events and thus asserting certain causal links that brought most elements together in a plausible narrative. Deciding which images and events to use and which ones to lay to rest depended on the preferred narrative on Yugoslavia's break-up adopted by the filmmakers. The approach was premised on a belief that there is a direct causal link between the present-day state of things and concrete past events. However, which events precisely? In their interpretative endeavors, the filmmakers were compelled to highlight events that fell in line with the chosen explanatory framework, thus walking a dangerous tightrope between reconstruction and manipulation. While claiming that 'social sweep and history are not really our focus' (Percy quoted in Cohen 1995), the authors of the film extensively adjusted the complex picture of the past to fit the prevailing media interpretation of current events (Iordanova 2001).

The credibility of Death of a Nation was seriously questioned on at least one occasion. During the first trial at the International Tribunal for War Crimes in Yugoslavia at the

Hague in 1996, British political scientist James Gow, who had acted as one of the film's consultants, was called in by the prosecution as an expert witness. In his testimony, Gow used excerpts from the film. In cross-examination, defense attorney Fons Orie questioned examples of incorrect translation of statements made during interviews (some by Milošević), and asked Gow to elaborate on his views of the difference between translation and interpretation. In response, Gow explained that the translations were a matter 'of the choice of a particular word which in this case, I think, made no substantive difference to the sense [...] it is important for the translator to interpret the sense which is intended to be conveyed by the speaker' (Gow in Tadic-Transcripts 2004: 577–8).

Using Death of a Nation as evidence set a precedent that was continued in The Hague with the use of other documentaries. In 2002, during opening statements at his trial, Slobodan Milošević screened excerpts of the BBC documentary Moral Combat (Alan Little, 2000) and the entire German film Es began mit einer Lüge/It Began with a Lie (Jo Angerer and Mathias Werth, 2002). This use of documentaries (as works that inevitably contain significant interpretative element) as evidence raises a range of further questions.

The troubles in Yugoslavia continued beyond 1995 and the country was in the news headlines on a continual basis. The well-known visuals of the Bosnian war and of Milošević's visit to Kosovo were continuously recycled by broadcasters. At the time of the Kosovo war in 1999, Death of a Nation was edited and played in a shorter version on the BBC, the narrative adjusted to stress the Kosovo aspects, creating a suitable background introduction to the continuing hostilities. The book and the film remain the most popular background material on the Yugoslav wars, thus making the chosen narrative line shape all further perceptions about the region.

DINA IORDANOVA

See also: Krelja, Petar

Yugoslavia: Death of a Nation (US/UK/France, BBC (UK), Canal+ (France), Discovery USA, ORF (Austria), VRPO (The Netherlands), RTBF (Belgium), SVT2 (Sweden), NRK (Norway), Danmarks Radio (Denmark), and ABC (Australia), 1995, 250 mins). Produced by Brian Lapping Associates (Norma Percy), London. Directed by Angus McQueen and Paul Mitchell. Narrated by Robin Ellis. Consultant Laura Silber.

Further reading

Cohen, Roger, 'Covering All Sides in the Balkan War', in *The New York Times*, 24 December 1995, Section 2: 37.

Gow, James, 'Testimony at Dusko Tadic Trial', Tadic-Transcripts, International Criminal Tribunal for the Former Yugoslavia, 2004: 534–78, available at www.un.org/icty/inde.htm (accessed 13 May 1996).

Gow, James, Paterson, Richard and Preston, Alison (eds), *Bosnia by Television*, London: British Film Institute, 1996.

Iordanova, Dina, *Cinema of Flames: Balkan Film, Culture and the Media*, London: BFI, 2001: 71–89.

Silber, Laura and Little, Allan, *The Death of Yugoslavia*, London: Penguin Books/BBC Books, and New York: Penguin Books, 1995.

Stokes, Gale, Lampe, John and Rusinow, Dennison, with Julie Mostov, 'Instant History: Understanding the Wars of Yugoslav Succession', in *Slavic Review* 55, no. 1, spring, 1996: 147.

Woodward, Susan L., 'It Depends on When You Start the Story: Narratives as Camouflage and the Political Use of Scholarship on the Yugoslav Wars, 1991–96', paper presented at the workshop on 'Doing History in the Shadow of the Balkan Wars' Working Group on Southeast European Studies, University of Michigan, Ann Arbor, January 17–18, 1997.

Z

Zahn, Peter von

Having made more than one thousand films for television, Peter von Zahn is one of the legends of German TV history. He was one of the pioneers of the first trial operations of radio and television in Hamburg (NWDR), and he became the head of the text department as early as July 1945. His characteristic reportage style was very much influenced by Anglo-American journalism. He was sent to the United States by the NWDR as a result of conflicts with Chancellor Konrad Adenauer about his independent radio commentaries. There he started his TV reports, Berichte aus der neuen Welt/Reports from the New World in 1955. He reported with his typical, high-pressured voice about daily life and his family's experiences in this modern society. These stories set standards for reportage and documentary in early German television. His style was a mixture of the features that he had made for radio and the American style of reporting represented by Edward R. Murrow, Fred Friendly, and others. This style was primarily oriented to text and content and then looked for the images needed to illustrate it. It stands in sharp contrast to the newsreels and the cultural films of the Third Reich period, which concentrated strongly on the image and dynamic editing. His personal features, which were broadcast once a month, shaped the image of the United States in postwar Germany.

Beside the series Berichte aus der neuen Welt, von Zahn also created a series called Bilder aus der farbigen Welt/Images from the Colourful World, where he presented political topics from Africa, South America, and Asia and showed the clash between modern industrialization and traditional cultures. He built a worldwide network of journalists working for his own Washington-based company, Documentary Programs Inc. The idea was to report on the same topic from different countries and thus provide a deeper perspective. In October 1961 he started the weekly series Reporter der Windrose/ Reporter of the Wind Rose and reported from different regions in the world to bring them into German homes. The idea was for audiences to learn about and see something of the countries and cultures outside of Europe. It was the first attempt at a regular broadcast on foreign affairs subjects. The goal was to analyze the structure of the societies in the modern world and to compare developments. The first program was titled People on the Move and presented case studies of people moving to the huge cities and political emigrants, as well as economic migration and holidays in sunny places. After one hundred and four programs and two years of intensive work, the stations decided to terminate the series and begin using their own foreign correspondents in different countries. Peter von Zahn also produced portraits of important statesmen like Ben Gurion, which brought him the Grimme Prize in 1964.

Besides shaping the documentary work of the SDR (Stuttgarter Schule), Peter von Zahn successfully established another journalistic style in German television, which was influenced by the radio essays and Anglo-American school of reporting. He produced many more films until 1993, when at 80 years of age, he decided to withdraw from active filmmaking but still published columns as a journalist and wrote his memoirs. He is seen as one of the pioneers and legends of German television.

KAY HOFFMANN

Biography

Born January 29, 1913, in Chemnitz; grew up in Dresden. After working as a voluntary worker in a publishing house, began to study jurisprudence, history, and philosophy in Vienna, Jena, and Freiburg in 1931. 1939–45 soldier in World War II. After the war, worked for the British military station 'Radio Hamburg' and became one of the pioneers of the Northwest German Radio (NWDR). 1948–51 head of the Düsseldorf studio of NWDR. 1951–60 American correspondent for the NWDR, first only in radio, then from 1955 onward for TV as well. Founded own company, Documentary Programs Inc., in Washington. Back in Germany, founded own production company, Windrose Film- und Fernsehproduktion GmbH in 1960 and Anatol AV und Filmproduktion GmbH in 1976; worked as director, author, and producer until 1996. Died July 26, 2001 in Hamburg.

Selected films

1955 Bilder aus der Neuen Welt/Images from the New World: director, script
1961 Bericht aus der farbigen Welt/Images from the Colourful World: director
1961 Reporter der Windrose/Reporter of the Wind Rose: producer, director
1963 Windrose der Zeit/Wind Rose of Time: director
1970 Die Kuba-Krise 1962/The Cuba Crisis 1962: director
1974 Die geheimen Papiere des Pentagon/The Secret Papers of Pentagon: director
1976 Fünf Prüfungen des Oberbürgermeisters—Konrad Adenauer/Five Examinations of the Mayor—Konrad Adenauer: script
1993 Shalom Dresden: director
1996 Beobachtungen im Ruhrgebiet I & II/Observations on the Ruhr Area I & II: script, director

Further reading

Zahn, Peter von, *Stimme der ersten Stunde. Erinnerungen 1913–51*, Stuttgart, 1991.

——*Reporter der Windrose. Erinnerungen 1951–64*, Stuttgart, 1994.

——'Reporter der Windrose', in Heinz B. Heller and Peter Zimmermann (eds), *Blicke in die Welt. Reportagen und Magazine des nordwestdeutschen Fernsehens in den 50er und 60er Jahren*, Konstanz, 1995: 117–25.

——*Bilder aus der farbigen Welt, in Strategie der Blicke. Zur Modellierung von Wirklichkeit in Dokumentarfilm und Reportage*, Dieter Ertel and Peter Zimmermann (eds), Konstanz, 1996: 177–82.

Zimmermann, Peter, 'Beruf Reporter. Ein Interview mit Peter von Zahn', in Heinz B. Heller and Peter Zimmermann (eds), *Blicke in die Welt, Reportagen und Magazine des nordwestdeutschen Fernsehens in den 50er und 60er Jahren*, Konstanz, 1995: 127–40.

Zetterling, Mai

A pioneering feminist filmmaker noted for her social consciousness, Mai Zetterling made psychologically complex films in the latter half of her career that challenge various orthodoxies (religious, sexual, ideological) and exhibit a pessimistic, sometimes bleak, worldview familiar to fans of her more famous compatriot, Ingmar Bergman. Although a product of the same industrial/artistic complex in which Bergman and earlier luminaries of Swedish cinema (such as Victor Sjöström, Mauritz Stiller, and Gösta Werner) came into being, Zetterling evinces in her work a more modern take on heterosexual relationships and institutionalized forms of injustice.

This can be partly attributed to her exposure, both direct and indirect, to a wide variety of cultures and lifestyles throughout the world before the actress's mid-career makeover as a writer-director. Indeed, it was during her years spent abroad as an actress working primarily in British and American film that she first came to inhabit the worlds of spiritually dispossessed and emotionally estranged women—roles that would prove substantive for her own controversial forays into Freudian-Marxist territory. Any attempt to sort through the major themes of Zetterling's work behind the camera should therefore take into account her many onscreen appearances across a range of internationally diverse productions, from her countrymen's angst-ridden social dramas of the 1940s to the English-language potboilers in which she starred during the 1950s. While critics often remarked on the actress's charm and beauty (her blue eyes and blonde hair were apparently made for Technicolor), these stereotypically Swedish traits were matched by a rigorous intelligence and devotion to philosophical inquiry, key elements of her stark black-and-white films.

After training at Stockholm's Royal Dramatic Theater and starring in such plays as Ella Wilcke's En sommar på egen hand/A Summer of One's Own (1941), the sixteen-year-old Swede made her screen debut in the swashbuckler Lasse-Maja (1942). Her most famous early starring role was Bertha, the teenage girlfriend of a school pupil in Alf Sjöberg's Hets/Torment (1944). With a plot that sounds reminiscent of those peppering Zetterling's own oeuvre, the film explores Bertha and Jan-Erick's titular feelings of anguish, which spring from the latter's sadistic teacher (whose own torment drives him to rape and murder the young girl).

After winning international acclaim for her role in Hets, which gave the nineteen-year-old actress the opportunity to betray a mature understanding of the cruelties that people inflict on others, Zetterling continued acting in Swedish films (including Gustaf Molander's domestically successful Nu Borjar Livet/We Live Now (1948) and Ingmar Bergman's Musik i mörker/Night is My Future (1948)), making the occasional trip to London to appear in such films as Basil Dearden's Frieda (1947). This latter film, which concerns an immigrant woman residing in England during the postwar period, contains autobiographical elements impossible to ignore, for by this time in her career Zetterling was oscillating not only between stage and screen but also between two countries, with England becoming her temporary residence after she signed on with the Rank Organisation. This British film company was intent on molding her into an international star, although the spate of melodramas and crime thrillers in which she appeared did little to further this goal. Throughout the 1950s, a period of economic uncertainty and upheaval for the British film industry, many of Zetterling's star-vehicles were box office failures; however, in tackling a multitude of roles in low-budget films, and by eventually gravitating away from Rank, she was able to expand her acting repertoire to accommodate different ethnicities and cultural backgrounds (playing everything from a French exchange student in Edmond T. Greville's The Romantic Age (1949) and an exploited prima ballerina in Val Guest's Dance Little Lady (1954), to a murder suspect in Marc Allégret's Blackmailed (1951)). Significantly, she played numerous German roles throughout this period, from the frowned-upon war bride of a British RAF officer in Frieda, to Hildegarde, the amnesiac object of a German professor's fatherly desire, in Portrait from Life (1948). Whether in these British films or in such Hollywood fare as A Prize of Gold (1955), a drama about a war refugee dedicated to saving a group of German orphans, Teutonic themes and iconography frequently congealed around the Swedish actress as cross-cultural signifiers of her uncanny 'otherness'.

By the early 1960s Zetterling had become increasingly dissatisfied with her acting career and was seeking opportunities to step behind the cameras. Given the green light by Roger Moorfoot of the BBC, she directed numerous shorts for television, including The Polite Invasion (1960), concerning Swedish immigration; Lords of Little Egypt (1961), about the Gypsies at St Maries-de-la-Mer; The Prosperity Race (1962), which delves into the emerging sense of affluence and entitlement among the Swedish middle class; and Do-It-Yourself Democracy (1963), her look at social and political concerns unique to Iceland. Among this BBC batch, her antiwar short, The War Game (1961), stands out not only because it garnered the Golden Lion award at the 1963 Venice Film Festival, but, more importantly, because of its satirical take on the way violence (here represented by a toy gun) snakes surreptitiously into childhood.

Five years after her divorce from dance choreographer Tutte Lemkow, Zetterling wed director and screenwriter David Hughes. Their marriage, which lasted from 1958 to 1979, was mutually nourishing as a source of cinematic inspiration and collaboration. The two codirected a half-dozen films, beginning with the flashback-laden literary adaptation Älskande par/Loving Couples (1964) and ending with a ten-minute episode for the omnibus feature Visions of Eight (1972–3), entitled The Strongest. These two films bookend an extremely fertile period in Zetterling's career, one that witnessed not only a stylistic maturation but also a developing sense of the struggles historically faced by women from various social and cultural backgrounds. Fed into her introspective narratives are images of loneliness and obsession—themes that, as biographer Louise Heck-Rabi argues, permeate her filmography and filter into the director's vested interests in feminism. Although these motifs are primarily reserved for her nondocumentary work—most notably Doktor Glas (1968), the pessimistic story of a physician driven to murder by his insatiable desire for a pastor's nonreciprocating wife, and Nattlek/Night Games (1966), a notoriously provocative examination of what polite society deems sexually perverse (incest, orgies, masturbation) and corporeally abject (vomiting, childbirth)—one can detect analogous themes percolating throughout her nonfiction films as well. For instance, Vincent the Dutchman, her 1971 color documentary about Vincent Van Gogh, pivots on isolation and obsession, customary states of mind for the notoriously tormented and introspective painter.

After making Vincent the Dutchman for British television, Zetterling was approached by producer David Wolper and asked to contribute an episode to the multi-director documentary Visions of Eight. Appropriately entitled The Strongest, this segment—which playfully deconstructs the men's weightlifting competition at the 1972 Olympic Games in Munich and provides yet another glimpse of the filmmaker's interest in man's peculiar fixations—finds her tapping into her own strengths as a satirist, as well as a technical virtuoso attuned to the short-film format. In the wake of Visions of Eight came even more documentary shorts. These run the gamut from a tour of the city of Stockholm to a hagiographic piece on tennis legend Stan Smith. Zetterling's frequent forays into nonfiction filmmaking throughout the 1970s suggest that she, like the narrator of her 1976 novel *Bird of Passage*, was becoming 'a creature of habit', sensitive not only to each day's 'particular rhythm' (Zetterling 1976: 102), but also to the guiding spirit of documentary investigation—its purported pursuit of truth and ontological grounding in reality.

With the publication of *Bird of Passage*, Zetterling had already begun making a name for herself as an accomplished novelist and essayist, pursuits she had begun a decade earlier when her book, *Night Games*, was unleashed on an unsuspecting public. A passage from that 1966 novel—'One concentrates on one's perversions to get rid of that greasy film of boredom that has begun to form on everything and everyone one knows' (Zetterling 1966: 30)—might just as well have been included in her 1985 autobiography, *All Those Tomorrows*, so indicative is it of Zetterling's own modus operandi. That she became even more focused on the 'perversions' of modern life during the 1980s that she continued to zero in on the tormented psyches of women in such films as Scrubbers (1982), a reform school/prison drama, and Amorosa (1986), a documentary-like biopic concerning the short, scandal-ridden life of Swedish novelist Agnes von Krusenstjana (the author on whose work Zetterling's first feature, Älskande par, was based), is a testament of her lifelong dedication to feminist concerns. By the time she succumbed to cancer in London on March 17, 1994, Zetterling had amassed a staggering body of work, the legacy and longevity of which secure her a pivotal place in film history.

DAVID SCOTT DIFFRIENT

See also: Visions of Eight

Biography

Born Mai Elizabeth Zetterling in Västerås, Sweden on May 24, 1925. Lived with her mother and stepfather in Australia from 1929 to 1932 before returning home and beginning a career in stage acting. After training at Stockholm's Royal Dramatic Theater and starring in such plays as Ella Wilcke's En sommar på egen hand (1941), made her screen debut in Lasse-Maja (1942). Continued acting in Swedish films throughout the 1940s and 1950s. Began directing shorts for television in the early 1960s. Married and divorced the dance choreographer Tutte Lemkow. Married director and screenwriter David Hughes in 1958. Divorced from Hughes in 1979. Died in London March 17, 1994.

Selected films

1960 The Polite Invasion: director
1961 Lords of Little Egypt: director
1961 The War Game: director, producer
1962 The Prosperity Race: director
1963 Do-It-Yourself Democracy: director
1971 Vincent the Dutchman: codirector (with David Hughes), producer
1973 The Strongest (episode in Visions of Eight): codirector (with David Hughes)
1978 The Rain's Hat: director, editor

Further reading

de Beauvoir, Simone, *The Second Sex*, New York: Vintage, 1989 reissue.

Gilbert, Harriet (ed.), *The Sexual Imagination: A Feminist Companion*, London: Jonathan Cape, 1993.

Heck-Rabi, Louise, 'Zetterling, Mai', in Amy L. Unterburdger (ed.), *The St James Encyclopedia of Women Filmmakers*, Farmington Hills, MI: Visible Ink Press, 1999.
Kaplan, E. Ann (ed.), *Feminism and Film*, Oxford: Oxford University Press, 2000.
McGregor, C., 'Mai is Behind the Camera Now', *The New York Times*, April 30, 1972.
Meyer, Donald B., *Sex and Power: The Rise of Women in America*, Russia, Sweden and Italy, Middletown, CT: Wesleyan University Press, 1987.
Waldman, Diane and Janet Walker (eds), *Feminism and Documentary*, Minneapolis, MN: University of Minnesota Press, 1999.
Zetterling, Mai, *Night Games*, New York: Coward-McCann, Inc., 1966.
——*Shadow of the Sun*, New York: Vintage, 1975.
——*Bird of Passage*, New York: Vintage, 1976.
——*All Those Tomorrows*, Grove Press, 1985.

Zielke, Willy

Willy Zielke is one of few German filmmakers notable for having done avant-garde work during the National Socialist, or Nazi, era in Germany. His work is exemplary for many. After a visionary start in the 1920s, his career stagnated under National Socialism, and he enjoyed only modest success in the new Federal Republic.

Zielke originally worked as a photographer. In 1929 he presented a series of studies at the pioneering film and photography exhibition (FiFo) in Stuttgart, which established photography as a serious art form worthy of respect and brought attention to Zielke's concern with objectivity.

In 1931 Zielke experimented with film. Critics praised the original camera tricks and the unusual settings of his unfortunately forgotten first silent films: Bubi träumt (1931), München. Willy Zielke zeigt eine Stadt (1931), and Anton Nicklas, ein Münchner Original (1932).

In 1932 Zielke shot his first contracted work (without pay), a socially engaged short film with the title Arbeitslos—Das Schicksal von Millionen/Unemployed—The Destiny of Millions. Most of the actors were found at an unemployment office, and production costs were covered by donations from Munich factories. The film, which was influenced by the aesthetics of Brecht's proletarian theater, denounced unemployment as a hopeless, demoralized state of being. Assembled images and symbolic characters showed the influence of Zielke's photographic work, as well as the Constructivists, known for their cutting technique. After its debut performance on April 3, 1933, in the Atlantic Cinema in Munich, the film disappeared from public view.

In 1943 Zielke agreed to direct a longer, funded version of Arbeitslos—Das Schicksal von Millionen, changing the name of the film to Die Wahrheit/The Truth. The dominant figure in the newer version of the film is the idealized worker, who replaces the realistic portrait of the unemployed found in the first Arbeitslos. The workers enter empty factory halls in marching formation to the song 'Deutschland erwache' (Germany Awake). The passage from the Weimar Republic to the National Socialist regime is presented as the solution to the world economic crisis.

Until 1934 Zielke taught at the Bayerischen Staatslehranstalt. He left his academic position to devote himself entirely to filmmaking. He married Elfriede Weissberger and lived in Munich.

In July 1934 Zielke was asked to create a film with sound to mark the one hundredth anniversary of the German railway system. He wrote, directed, and did camera work for Das Stahltier/The Steel Animal, a title he chose himself. He did not follow the conventional pattern of such films by enumerating the steps of development. Rather, he mixed elements from feature films, documentaries, and experimental films to present his theme from multiple perspectives. Das Stahltier defies established aesthetic and generic conventions. This film is also influenced by the Russian Constructivist, as well as Brechtian theater.

Technical modernization is presented in the film as the superior means of modern social development. In the plot, a prospective engineer overcomes the initial suspicion and distrust of the workers, gaining their respect and trust. Zilke used railway workers, rather than actors, to play the roles of the workers. Close-ups of their expressive faces and gestures are reminders of Zielke's photographic background. Some scenes, which show the men working half-naked or wrestling, suggest a homoerotic element, at least when viewed today.

The financial backers of Das Stahltier were not pleased with the results, as the film was intended to promote train travel and use the opportunity of the one hundredth anniversary as an occasion for propaganda and advertisement. Das Stahltier was not approved for public screening. The film was shown at Walter Frentz's seminar for cinematic film at the Lessing faculty, the only public screening during the National Socialist regime.

Leni Riefenstahl attended the seminar and was impressed by Das Stahltier. She hired Zielke as a cameraman for her production company. Their first project together was made in 1935, and was called Tag der Freiheit! Unsere Wehrmacht!/Freedom Day! Our Army!, a film that was supposed to document Germany's military power on the occasion of the reintroduction of the armed forces.

Riefenstahl's Olympia Film GmbH asked Zielke to make the prologue to a film on the 1936 Olympic Games. Riefenstahl used the material shot by Zielke, but she cut a new prologue to the film, which he rejected. Their cooperative relationship ended in a quarrel.

In February 1937, Zielke was admitted into the University Hospital in Munich, with a diagnosis of schizophrenia. He spent the next five years in several psychiatric institutions and in the labor camp Herzogsägmühle in Bavaria. His diagnosis had drastic consequences, as his disease and prognosis were classified as 'genetically transmitted with no recovery' and, on the basis of this judgment, he was sterilized. Zielke suffered harsh treatment in numerous mental hospitals under the Nazi regime.

In 1942, Leni Riefenstahl arranged for Zielke's release. From 1944 until the end of the war in 1945, Zielke shot for Riefenstahl's Tiefland in Kitzbühel (Bavaria) and later in Prague. Riefenstahl, however, claimed she was unable to use the footage. She stated that she could not find any use for Zielke's material. During this period, Zielke married his second wife, Ilse.

Zielke suffered though a long period of sickness on his release from the mental hospitals, as a result of his treatment there. After working for Riefenstahl on Tiefland, he stopped working until 1952. He made a fresh start, under the name Viktor Valet, with a short film about the landscapes of Niederrhein, Verzauberter Niederrhein/Magic Niederhein. The expressionist, structured imagery is highly reminiscent of the German silent film tradition.

Despite several small contracts with the innovative production company Gesellschaft für bildende Filme (GbF) in Munich, Zielke could barely support himself. He was consigned to do some takes for Schöpfung ohne Ende/Neverending Creation, a film by GbF produced for the Bavarian factories. He ignored schedules and production specifications, and was considered difficult and uncooperative by his colleagues and assistants on the film.

Das Stahltier, long considered lost, resurfaced in France in 1953. The legal owner of the film, the now-called Deutsche Bahn AG, agreed to a public presentation after some of the more experimental scenes were edited out. Zielke saw this as a destructive infringement of his rights as a filmmaker. Nevertheless, in February 1954 the edited version was shown in Frankfurt am Main.

In 1956 Zielke made Verlorene Freiheit/Lost Freedom. The plot, which centers on a little blind girl's failed attempts to set a bird free, suggests a parallel with Zielke's situation and his sense of frustration at the restrictions placed on his creativity. Aluminium—Porträt eines Metalles/Aluminum—Portrait of a Metal, which appeared in 1957, was the last Zielke film to receive a public screening. The picture, produced by the GfB, traced the development of aluminum. The filmmaker's innovative use of color, light, and montage illustrate that, even at this late stage in his career, Zilke remained a creative artist.

In the 1960s Zielke accepted sporadic German/Russian translation projects, mostly under the name Viktor Valet. In 1962 he patented one of his technical shooting processes, the jalousie system (sun drape system).

During the last ten years of his life, Zielke enjoyed a renewed interest in his photography. He had an exhibition of his photography in Arles, France in 1982.

THOMAS TODE

See also: Riefenstahl, Leni

Biography

Born in Lodz, Poland, September 18, 1902. Relocated to Munich, 1921. Student at the Bayrischen Staatslehranstalt für Fotografie in Munich until 1926. Assistant in the portrait studio of Franz Grainer, Munich and Minya Dietz-Dührkoop, Hamburg, 1927. Member between 1928 and 1934 of the Gesellschaft Deutscher Lichtbildner (GDL). Assistant Professor at the Bayrischen Staatslehranstalt für Fotografie. Admitted to the Schwabing hospital because of a nervous breakdown, February 1937. Two months later, transferred to the psychiatric hospital Eglfing Haar (München), with a diagnosis of schizophrenia. In October, sent to the Wanderhof Herzogsägmühle work camp. Initiated a hunger strike and was committed to the Eglfing Haar psychiatric hospital from 1939 to 1942. Upon release, moved in with mother and uncle, and met Ilse, whom he later married. Resided in Berlin from 1961. Moved to Lichtenberg 1969. Died September 16, 1989, Hannover, Lower Saxony, West Germany.

Selected films

1931 Bubi träumt
1931 München. Willy Zielke zeigt eine Stadt
1932 Anton Nicklas, ein Münchner Original
1933 Arbeitslos—Das Schicksal von Millionen
1934 Die Wahrheit
1935 Das Stahltier
1953 Verzauberter Niederrhein
1956 Verlorene Freiheit
1957 Aluminium—Porträt eines Metalles

Further reading

Cozarinsky, Edgardo (ed.), *Resistance des images, tilages, sauregarde et restaurations dans la collection films de la Cinemateque francaise*, Paris: Cinemateque française, 1996.
Elsaesser, Thomas, *Das Weimarer Kino—aufgeklärt und doppelbödig*, Berlin, 1999.
Graham, Cooper C., *Leni Riefenstahl and Olympia*, New York, 1986.
Riefenstahl, Leni, *Memoiren*, Frankfurt/Main: Ullstein Verlag, 1996.
Rother, Rainer, *Leni Riefenstahl—Die Verführung des Talents*, Berlin, 2000.
Schöppe, Wilhelm Sch (Hg), *Meister der Kamera erzählen*, Halle/Saale, 1935.
Wetzel, Kraft and Hagemann, Peter, *Zensur: Verbotene deutsche Filme 1933–45*, Berlin, 1978.
Zielke, Willy, *Technik des Bromöl-Umdruckes, Enzyklopädie der Photographie und Kinematographie*, Heft 116, Halle Saale, 1931.
——*(n)akt-Einführung in die Aktfotografie*, n.d..

Zone, La

(France, Lacombe, 1927)

La Zone: au pays des chiffonniers/The Zone: The Rag-pickers' Country is a twenty-eight-minute documentary film about the rag-pickers and secondhand dealers of Paris. This historic trade allowed poor people to earn a meager living in the urban wasteland on the outskirts of the capital. La Zone belongs to the cluster of poetic documentaries with a social awareness made during the late 1920s, a dynamic period of filmmaking just before the arrival of sound film. It blends together different strands of French avant-garde, modernism, naturalism, and impressionism.

The film opens with chain mixes that set the scene and atmosphere about the 'unknown places' in our midst that the viewer is about to discover. An animated map of Paris demarcates the old fortifications surrounding the city. Beyond that point is a no-man's land, a material and psychological frontier between the city and its suburbs, an uncertain zone between two worlds that is as alien to the ordinary inner-city Parisian as a foreign land with unusual inhabitants. Its narrowness is visually conveyed by the opening's long shots of alleyways. What there is to discover here is the appalling living conditions of the poor in a shantytown only a stone's throw away from the last stop on the Métro.

The narrative structure of La Zone uses the time frame of one day in the city, which is also found in other films of the period, including Rien que les heures (Alberto Cavalcanti, 1926) and Berlin: Die Sinfonie der Großstadt/Berlin: The Symphony of a Great City (Walther Ruttmann, 1927). The final fade-out signals the end of the day, not the end of the story. The people who live in La Zone create a familiar social structure in their particular urban environment: working families, children playing, dogs and cats in alleyways, a lunch break on the job, neighbors chatting, street musicians and vendors, and the flea market, the 'commercial center' of La Zone. What underpins this recognizable setting is a realization of how some of them make a precarious living; they recycle what richer people throw away.

The film story follows the work day of a team, a woman and two men, as they begin their collection route in the early hours of morning before the garbage trucks pick up what still has some value: glass, paper, clothes, bread. It is an efficient working team, moving rapidly along the streets, foraging in the rubbish with their bare hands, and taking away what they find in a wheeled cart. They sell what can be recycled. There is also a 'lower caste' in the world of the chiffonniers—those who work the huge garbage piles and try to salvage what may have been missed once the trucks reach the city incinerator.

Georges Lacombe depicted a harsh reality of urban society that many would prefer to ignore altogether. He did so with empathy: the chiffonniers do useful work. There are also other people living in this parallel city, people who have lost everything. One is the former music hall singer, La Goulue, who has only memories to share, but who found shelter in La Zone.

The 1920s were a time of profound turmoil in European life and social conditions that were a consequence of years of war and revolution. It was also a time when new technologies were becoming facts of everyday life for the increasing urban masses—the radio, the automobile, the refrigerator. Despite this new way of life, old social problems and barriers persisted, aggravated by economic uncertainties and postwar migration. Poor immigrants, fleeing devastated Eastern Europe, arrived in Western Europe. Some were skilled workers, like the Polish miners who restarted the coal mines of northeastern France; however, many were unskilled, and some ended up joining the small army of social outcasts living and working, surviving at the geographical and social periphery of rich Parisian arrondissements.

Film audiences of the 1920s were increasingly attracted to exploration and ethnographic films. The camera could renew the discovery of the world and its peoples. These films were diverse; they could introduce traditional societies, as did Nanook of the North (Robert Flaherty, 1922), or present some technological challenge and travel adventure such as La Croisière noire (Léon Poirier, 1926), the Citroën expedition across Africa. Some films praised the colonial empire; others introduced a documentary point of view—Voyage au Congo (Marc Allégret, 1927)—at a time when reporter Albert Londres published his powerful indictment of colonialism. The subtitle of La Zone: Au pays des chiffonniers, introduces some 'foreign' locale, another 'country' subtly playing on words and depicting a disquieting world of its own.

Georges Lacombe (1902–90) was assistant director to René Clair. Like several filmmakers of his generation, he started with a short film, using basic equipment and taking advantage of his immediate urban surroundings. He looked at it with a curious and open mind. La Zone was his first and most accomplished essay in short documentary film, and it caught the attention of the cinematographic avant-garde of the 1920s.

Other films would later explore this universe on the margins of society and often include a subtext defending those who have been abandoned or humiliated (Aubervilliers, Eli Lotar, 1945). La Zone was not a militant film but a statement of fact revealing social implications, and Lacombe benefited from the specialized infrastructure—theaters, periodicals, and ciné-clubs—put in place during the 1920s to support avant-garde films.

La Zone: Au pays des chiffonniers has become a classic of the era and continues to be regularly scheduled in film retrospectives around the world. Its topic, its critical and social perspective, and its formal quality beautifully blending its realist content and impressionist images all contribute to its relevance in documentary film history, as well as in social history.

SUZANNE LANGLOIS

See also: Lacombe, Georges

La Zone: Au pays des chiffonniers (France, 1928, 35mm, 28 mins). Produced by La Société des films Charles Dullin. Directed by Georges Lacombe. Photography: Georges Périnal and D. Pierson. Filmed in Paris and its surroundings, along the city limits of the old fortifications, the municipal incinerator at Ivry, and the flea market at the Porte de Clignancourt.

Further reading

n.a., *100 Années Lumière*, Paris: AFAA Intermedia, 1989.

n.a., 'Dictionnaire du cinéma français des années vingt', in François Albera and Jean A. Gili (eds), *1895 Revue de l'Association française de recherche sur l'histoire du cinéma* 33, June 2001.

Abel, Richard, *French Cinema: The First Wave 1915–29*, Princeton, NJ: Princeton University Press, 1984.

Aitken, Ian, *European Film Theory and Cinema. A Critical Introduction*, Bloomington, IN: Indiana University Press, 2001.

Bordwell, David, *French Impressionist Cinema: Film Culture, Film Theory and Film Style*, New York: Arno Press, 1980.

Ghali, Noureddine, *L'Avant-Garde cinématographique en France dans les années vingt*, Paris: Editions Paris Expérimental, 1995.

Index

Film titles in *italics* have an entry in the text.

B

C

D

F

G

H

I

J

N

O

Q

R

T

W

X

Y

Z